Western Europe

Loretta Chilcoat, Reuben Acciano, Fiona Adams, Sarah Andrews, Becca Blond, Terry Carter, Geert Cole, Michael Grosberg, Sarah Johnstone, Amy Karafin, John Lee, Alex Leviton, Leanne Logan, Amy Marr, Craig McLachlan, Tom Parkinson, Josephine Quintero, Miles Roddis, Simon Sellars, Lisa Steer-Guérard, Andrew Stone

D1445997

Contents

Destination Western Europe

How does one define a region so diverse as Western Europe? You can't really. There are simply too many once-in-a-lifetime destinations to discover, and only you can decide how to experience them. What this guide aims to do is give an honest, down-to-earth review of our favourite places and invite you to create your own memories along the way.

Think of Western Europe as an enigmatic theme park that never closes. Whether your goal is to throw back creamy dark pints and listen to old yarns in Irish pubs, swoosh down the legendary slopes of the Alps, flit from island to island in Greece or experience a seductive flamenco performance in Spain, your passport is an all-access pass to these adventures.

Though border controls are looser and currencies unified, there is still a feeling of crossing into different worlds when travelling between countries. Admission prices and souvenirs vary, of course, and there's bound to be queues for some adventures: opening day for an English footy team, a ticket to the Vienna Boys' Choir, or entrance to Oktoberfest, one of the wildest festivals in Western Europe. Certain sections of this grand theme park may still be under construction, while others are ever-expanding their attractions: new museums in the Netherlands, the former Olympic stadium in Athens, a new beach in Barcelona. There's always a section where you can try something totally foreign: skiing in Liechtenstein, mud-flat walking in the Netherlands or soaking in Andorra's thermal lagoons. And the food! Spicy paella in Spain, melt-in-your-mouth French crepes, Germany's Wiener schnitzel and, for the adventurous, haggis in Scotland.

ARAN ISLANDS (p657)
Go island-hopping among the craggy Aran Islands for a true taste of Irish isolation

LONDON (p134)
Catch an awesome view of the capital on a double-decker Routemaster before they're retired forever

D-DAY BEACHES (p304)
A solemn stroll along the D-day beaches is a poignant reminder of the toll of war

SINTRA (p868)
Saunter around the fabulous palaces, villas and sumptuous gardens of this wooded hilltop retreat

BARCELONA (p927)
Discover the strangely beautiful architecture of Barcelona's famous artist, Gaudí

0 ___ 500 km
0 ___ 300 miles

Shetland Islands

Orkney Islands

Inverness

Scotland   Aberdeen

Oban   Dundee

Outer Hebrides

Glasgow   Edinburgh

Derry   Newcastle-upon-Tyne

Northern Ireland   Belfast   Isle of Man

Galway   Middlesborough

IRELAND   Irish Sea   York

Dublin   Liverpool   Manchester

Killarney   Cork

Rosslare   Wales   BRITAIN

St George's Channel   Birmingham

Swansea   England

Cardiff   Oxford

Bristol   London

Plymouth   Portsmouth

ATLANTIC OCEAN   English Channel

Channel Islands   Brussels

BELGIU...

Le Havre

Brest   Caen   Rouen

Quimper   St Malo   Rheims

Paris   Seine

Rennes

St Nazaire   Nantes   Blois

Tours   Dijon

La Rochelle   FRANCE

Bay of Biscay   Limoges   Geneva

La Coruña   Bordeaux   Clermont-Ferrand   Lyon

Santiago de Compostela

Vigo   Gijón   Santander   ALP...

León   Bilbao   Bayonne   Toulouse   Nîmes

Porto   San Sebastián   PYRENEES   Avignon   Marseille

Pamplona   Golfe de Lion

Coimbra   Douro   Salamanca   Andorra la Vella   ANDORRA

Sintra   Zaragoza   Tarragona   Barcelona

PORTUGAL   Tajo   Madrid

Lisbon   Toledo   SPAIN

Évora   Badajoz   Valencia   Mallorca   Menorca

Guadiana   Palma

Faro   Córdoba   Ibiza   Balearic Islands

Guadalquivir   Seville   Alicante

Cádiz   Granada   Murcia

Málaga   Almería   MEDITERRANEAN SEA

Strait of Gibraltar   Gibraltar Br

Tangier   Ceuta Sp

Tetouan   Melilla Sp   Oran   Algiers

Rabat   ALGERIA   Annaba

Casablanca   Meknès   Fès   Oujda   Constantine

Marrakesh   MOROCCO

Agadir   ATLAS

AMSTERDAM (p817)
Hash bars, a sex museum
and a fantastic brewery tour –
it's all in Amsterdam

THURINGIA (p434)
Put on your hiking boots for a
scenic stroll through ancient
foliage in Thuringian Forest

LIECHTENSTEIN (p789)
Forget the Alps – tell the folks
back home you hit the
ski slopes in Liechtenstein

SCHLOSS MIRABELL (p63)
Live out your 'Sound of Music'
fantasies in the gardens
of this famous Austrian castle

UFFIZI GALLERY (p743)
Italy's awe-inspiring
art museum is a must-see

ATHENS (p544)
Take a walk through
sporting history at the site
of the first Olympic games

NORWAY
Bergen
Stavanger
Kristiansand
NORTH SEA
Frisian Islands
THE NETHERLANDS
Hague
Amsterdam
Rotterdam
Düsseldorf
Cologne
LUXEMBOURG
Luxembourg
Nancy
Strasbourg
Freiburg
Bern
Lausanne
Basel
SWITZERLAND
LIECHTENSTEIN
Vaduz
Mt Blanc 4807m
ALPS
Turin
Milan
Genoa
Bologna
MONACO
Ligurian Sea
Pisa
Florence
ITALY
APPENINES
Corsica
Elba
Ajaccio
Sardinia
Sassari
Cagliari
TYRRHENIAN SEA
Naples
Salerno
Palermo
Bizerte
Tunis
TUNISIA
Sousse
Isole Pelagie
Pantelleria
Sicily
Catania
Reggio di Calabria
IONIAN SEA
Valletta
MALTA
Aeolian Islands
Bari
Taranto
Golfo di Taranto
ADRIATIC SEA
Venice
Trieste
SLOVENIA
Ljubljana
Zagreb
CROATIA
Zadar
Split
Dubrovnik
BOSNIA & HERCEGOVINA
Sarajevo
Podgorica
SERBIA & MONTENEGRO
Pristina
Tirana
ALBANIA
Vlore
Corfu
GREECE
Larisa
Lesvos
AEGEAN SEA
Evia
Patra
Athens
Piraeus
Kalamata
Cyclades Islands
Crete
Hania
Iraklio
Sea of Crete
Rhodes
Dodecanese Islands
Kaş
TURKEY
İzmir
Kuşadası
İstanbul
Sea of Marmara
Bursa
BLACK SEA
Varna
Burgas
Constanta
BULGARIA
Sofia
Plovdiv
Skopje
MACEDONIA
Thessaloniki
Belgrade
ROMANIA
Craiova
Bucharest
Timişoara
Cluj-Napoca
CARPATHIAN MOUNTAINS
MOLDOVA
Chişinău
Odesa
Danube
HUNGARY
Budapest
Szeged
Győr
Bratislava
Vienna
AUSTRIA
Salzburg
Linz
Munich
Stuttgart
GERMANY
Frankfurt-am-Main
Leipzig
Dresden
Berlin
Hanover
Hamburg
Schwerin
Lübeck
Stralsund
Szczecin
POLAND
Poznań
Wrocław
Katowice
Kraków
Ostrava
Brno
SLOVAKIA
Prague
CZECH REPUBLIC
Plzeň
Rhine
Danube
Vistula
Warsaw
Łódź
Białystok
Lublin
Brest
Lviv
UKRAINE
Kiev
Zhytomyr
Dnipro
Dnister
Kraków
DENMARK
Aalborg
Århus
Odense
Zealand
Copenhagen
Helsingborg
Malmö
Bornholm
BALTIC SEA
Öland
Gotland
Ventspils
Liepāja
Klaipėda
Kaliningrad
Russia
Gdańsk
Hrodna
BELARUS
Minsk
Mahileu
Homel
Pripet
LITHUANIA
Kaunas
Vilnius
LATVIA
Riga
Daugavpils
Vitsebsk
Smolensk
ESTONIA
Tallinn
Tartu
Pskov
Novgorod
RUSSIA
St Petersburg
Vyborg
Lake Ladoga
Gulf of Finland
FINLAND
Helsinki
Turku
Åland
Saaremaa
Gulf of Riga
Tampere
Jyväskylä
Gulf of Bothnia
SWEDEN
Stockholm
Uppsala
Örebro
Norrköping
Linköping
Vänern
Vättern
Bollnäs
Oslo
Lillehammer
Skagerrak
16°E
24°E
42°N

From the ancient cities of Athens and Rome to the Celtic ruins of Ireland, Western Europe is punctuated with poignant reminders of events and empires that changed the course of history. Revisit the sites of world and national wars, such as Normandy and Berlin; explore the alpine castles of Bavaria and the wacky Gaudí architecture of Spain; or relax in a serene Swiss hamlet. Enjoy the vistas from a walled mountaintop villa in Provence, cycle through the countryside of Tuscany or bird-watch along the rugged cliffs of Ireland's Aran Islands. Alternatively, whet your appetite with the indoor treasures of Western Europe's world-famous galleries and museums.

View the spectacular jagged teeth of the Dolomites (p738), towering over the Italian countryside

Discover the secret artist within at Museo del Prado (p906), Madrid, Spain

Wander the extravagant gardens and grand halls of Château de Versailles (p287), France

MANFRED GOTTSCHALK

Soak up the mystical atmosphere of Stonehenge (p173) at sunrise, Britain

JOHN ELK III

Pay a poignant tribute to soldiers killed in the Battle of Normandy in the American Military Cemetery (p305), Normandy, France

View the streets of Paris from the grand heights of the Eiffel Tower (p272), France

RICHARD I'ANSON

DENNIS JOHNSON

Get lost Hansel-and-Gretel style in the Black Forest (p480), Germany

Sip a latté and soak up the medieval atmosphere of the Markt (p110), Bruges, Belgium

Take your breath away tip-toeing the sheer Cliffs of Moher (p654), Ireland

Gaze out over Florence's skyline and the breathtaking tiered façade of the Duomo (p741), Italy

Marvel at the Acropolis (p546), perched above Athens, Greece, with the marble Parthenon as its jewel

Getting Started

So you've decided you want to see Western Europe – now what do you do? A good plan, whether your trip is by the seat-of-your-pants or once-in-a-lifetime, is essential to a successful and happy journey. Who wants to spend half the trip making and rearranging plans? We've outlined the basics to get you going and to help you make the most of your time in your destination, including insider tips on when to go, what to bring, and how much it's going to cost.

Western Europe is such a varied region, but it's accessible for travellers of all budgets. From funky hostels to posh resorts, from ramshackle food stands to Michelin-rated restaurants, we'll give you the lowdown on where to find the best match for your wallet.

WHEN TO GO

Any time can be the best time to visit Western Europe, depending on what you want to see and do. Summer lasts roughly from June to September and offers the best weather for outdoor pursuits in the northern half of Europe. In the southern half (Mediterranean coast, Iberian Peninsula, southern Italy and Greece), where the summers tend to be hotter, you can extend that period by one or even two months either way, when temperatures may also be more agreeable.

See Climate Charts (p1054) for more information.

You won't be the only tourist in Western Europe during the summer months – all of France and Italy, for instance, goes on holiday in August. Prices can be high, accommodation fully booked and the sights packed. You'll find much better deals – and far fewer crowds – in the shoulder seasons on either side of summer; in April and May, for instance, flowers are in bloom and the weather can be surprisingly mild, and Indian summers are common in September and October.

DON'T LEAVE HOME WITHOUT...

Since you'll probably buy things as you go along, it's better to start with too little rather than too much. A few basics to consider are a backpack or travel pack (combo backpack/shoulder bag), or a suitcase with wheels; a smaller zip bag for souvenirs; and clothing that is easily layered. You should also consider the following packing list:

- skirt or pair of trousers/pants for a night on the town
- a solid pair of closed-toe walking shoes and/or summer walking sandals
- sandals or thongs (flip-flops) for showers
- raincoat, waterproof jacket or umbrella
- medical kit and sewing kit
- padlock
- Swiss Army knife
- ISIC card
- phrasebook

There are also a few musts for certain countries, eg high UV-protection sunscreen for Greece (it's expensive and hard to find there) and Sterling travellers cheques for Britain (for exchange purposes).

On the other hand, if you're keen on winter sports, resorts in the Alps and the Pyrenees begin operating in late November and move into full swing after the New Year, closing down when the snows begin to melt in March or even April.

The Climate and When to Go sections in individual country chapters explain what to expect and when to expect it, and the climate charts (p1054) will help you compare the weather in different destinations. As a rule, spring and autumn tend to be wetter and windier than summer and winter. The temperate maritime climate along the Atlantic is relatively wet all year, with moderate extremes in temperature. The Mediterranean coast is hotter and drier, with most rainfall occurring during the mild winter. The continental climate in eastern Germany and the Alps tends to have much stronger extremes in weather between summer and winter.

When summer and winter are mentioned throughout this book we generally mean high and low tourist seasons, ie for summer read roughly May to September and for winter read October to April.

You might want to time your trip with a major local festival or celebration. Use the boxed text (p12) as a guideline, and see also the individual country chapters for details.

Lonely Planet's *Read This First: Europe* is an excellent source of important preliminary information.

COSTS & MONEY

One of the big questions when travelling is 'how much money will I need?' Luckily, in this day of the euro (€), travellers won't have to fiddle with changing money at every border crossing. However, this doesn't necessarily mean prices are even throughout Western Europe, and it will depend on what currency travellers are starting out with. Expect your money to be stretched in non-euro countries like Switzerland and the UK, and in capital cities. Backpackers eating street meals and sleeping in hostels can expect to pay per day from about €30. Mid-range travellers eating in cafés and sleeping in hotels can expect a daily budget starting from €90. Travellers opting for full-course restaurant meals and resort-style accommodation, expect to pay from €200.

Tips on stretching your money include picking up local magazines and newspapers, and looking for coupons and discounts on attractions and dining out (most museums have a 'free' day once a week/month; many restaurants have 'fixed-price menus' which are half the price). You can also use websites like **Travelocity** (www.travelocity.com) to book packages well in advance, which works best for families and groups travelling together.

For Irish flavour, if you can't make it through James Joyce's *Ulysses*, try Roddy Doyle's *Paddy Clark Ha Ha*.

A combination of credit or cash card and travellers cheques is recommended so you have something to fall back on if an ATM swallows your card or the banks in the area are closed. Credit cards are widely accepted in metropolitan areas throughout Western Europe, and travellers will find ATMs plentiful throughout the cities. Travellers cheques and Eurocheques (see Money p1060) are also easily exchangeable in major cities at banks and *bureaux de change*. In more rural areas, ATMs are sparse or nonexistent, and shops may or may not take travellers cheques. It's a good idea to travel with some local currency in cash; the equivalent of, say, US$100 should usually be enough.

READING UP

There are so many books out there to spur on the travel dream factor, it's hard to know where to begin. First check out the travel selection at

---

CONDUCT IN EUROPE

Although dress standards are fairly informal in northern Europe, your clothes may well have some bearing on how you're treated in southern Europe.

Dress casually, but keep your clothes clean, and ensure sufficient body cover (eg shoulders covered and wear trousers or a knee-length dress) if your sightseeing includes churches, monasteries, synagogues or mosques. Wearing shorts away from the beach or camping ground is not very common among men in Europe.

Some nightclubs and fancy restaurants may refuse entry to people wearing jeans, a tracksuit or sneakers (trainers); men might consider packing a tie as well, just in case.

While nude bathing is usually restricted to certain beaches, topless bathing is very common in many parts of Europe. Nevertheless, women should be wary of taking their tops off as a matter of course. The basic rule is that if nobody else seems to be doing it, then you shouldn't either – and stick to this rule.

You'll soon notice that Europeans are heavily into shaking hands and even kissing when they greet one another. Don't worry about the latter with those you don't know well, but get into the habit of shaking hands with virtually everyone you meet. In many parts of Europe, it's also customary to greet the proprietor when entering a shop, café or a quiet bar, and also to say goodbye when you leave.

---

www.lonelyplanet.com to try and narrow down your destination(s). Travelogue classics include the *Provence* series by Peter Mayle, the selected travels of Paul Theroux in *To the Ends of the Earth*, and the mouthwatering combo of food and travel in Frances Mayes' *Under the Tuscan Sun*.

More modern yarns include anything by travel humorist Tim Cahill and his wacky adventures on the road, including *Road Fever* and *A Wolverine Is Eating My Leg*; the amusing travel journals of fellow humorist, Bill Bryson; and Susan Allan Toth's romantic observations of England in *England As You Like It*. For Irish flavour, if you can't make it through James Joyce's *Ulysses*, try novels such as Joseph O'Connor's *The Secret World of the Irish Male*, Patrick McCabe's *The Butcher Boy*, and Roddy Doyle's *Paddy Clark Ha Ha*. James Michener's epic, *Iberia*, details the essence of Spain with its vivid people and places. What better book to highlight Italy than a cookbook? Try *Eating Up Italy: Voyages on a Vespa* by Matthew Fort and *Al Dente* by William Black for a culinary kick. *The Bells in Their Silence: Travels Through Germany*, by Michael Gorra, is an excellent insight into this country's dark past and triumphant present.

Books

Following is a list of titles recommended by the authors of this book which will make great companions on any trip.

- *Disturbia* (Christopher Fowler) A mysterious and history-packed scavenger hunt of London's favourite haunts.
- *The Great Beers of Belgium* (Michael Jackson) One of the world's best beer writers details all that Belgium has to offer.
- *Helden Wie Wir* (*Heroes Like Us*; Thomas Brussig) A humorous tale of how a man's penis brought on the collapse of the Berlin Wall.
- *How to Remain What You Are* (George Müller) A Luxembourg psychologist's humorous look at local ways.
- *The New Spaniards* (John Hooper) An in-depth look at the real Spain and her culture since the death of Franco.
- *Notes From a Small Island* (Bill Bryson) Yet another big laugh from this best-selling author's pithy observations of the UK's whimsical, and sometimes odd, culture.

The Red Lion is the most popular pub name in Britain.

- *The Vanishing* (Tim Krabbe) A sinister tale about what not to do at a petrol station when travelling through the Netherlands.
- *Zorba the Greek* (Nikos Kazantzakis) This classic story of the region's culture and politics has a message that rings true in modern times.

Websites

The Internet is a rich resource for travellers. You can research your trip, hunt down bargain air fares, book hotels, check weather conditions or chat with locals and other travellers about the best places to visit. For a list of country-specific websites, see Tourist Information (p1063).

Airline Information (www.travelocity.com) What airlines fly where, when and for how much.

Airline Tickets (www.priceline.com) Name your price – if an airline has an empty seat for which it would rather get something than nothing, then this US-based website lets you know.

Currency Conversions (www.xe.net/ucc) Exchange rates for hundreds of currencies worldwide.

Lonely Planet (www.lonelyplanet.com) Here you'll find succinct summaries on travelling to most places on earth, postcards from other travellers, and the Thorn Tree bulletin board, where you can ask questions before you go or dispense advice when you get back. The subwwway section links you to the most useful travel resources elsewhere on the Web.

Tourist Offices (www.towd.com) Lists tourist offices around the world.

Train Information (www.raileurope.com) Train fares and schedules on the most popular routes in Europe, including information on discount rail and youth passes.

MUST-SEE MOVIES

- *A Lisbon Story* Directed by Wim Wenders, this is a fascinating quasi-documentary about a day in the life of a movie soundman wandering the streets, trying to salvage a film that has been abandoned by the director. He falls in love, has a close call with gangsters and is pursued by school children.
- *All About My Mother* (p900) From the unconventional mind of Pedro Almodovar, this is a heart-warming film about life, love and transvestites, as a woman searches for the secret to her past.
- *An Eternity and One Day* (p542) What do you do when you know you're going to die? This film, by Theo Angelopoulos, explores that very question in his native country.
- *Everybody Famous* (p93) Dominique Deruddere's film about a factory worker who dreams of celebrity status for his overweight daughter – a Madonna wannabe.
- *Turks Fruit* (p814) This is one of the Netherlands' most famous flicks, directed by Paul Verhoeven who's better known outside the Netherlands for films such as *Robocop* and *Starship Troopers*.

FAVOURITE FESTIVALS & EVENTS

- **Amsterdam Fantastic Film Festival** (p848) The Netherlands
- **Cannes Film Festival** (p388) France
- **Hellenic Festival** (p606) Greece
- **Notting Hill Carnival** (p252) Britain
- **Oktoberfest** (p460) Germany
- **San Fermíne** (aka 'Running of the Bulls'; p948) Spain
- **Schueberfouer** (p807) Luxembourg
- **Semana Santa** (p970) Spain
- **Venice International Film Festival** (p727) Italy

RESPONSIBLE TRAVEL

As a visitor, you have a responsibility to the local people and to the environment. When it comes to the environment, the key rules are to preserve natural resources and to leave the countryside as you find it. Those Alpine flowers look much better on the mountainside than squashed in your pocket (and many species are protected anyway).

- Wherever you are, littering is irresponsible and offensive. Mountain areas have fragile ecosystems, so stick to prepared paths whenever possible, and always carry your rubbish away with you.
- Do not use detergents or toothpaste (even if they are listed as biodegradable) in or close to any watercourses.
- If you just gotta go when you're out in the wilderness somewhere, bury human waste in holes at least 15cm deep and at least 100m from any watercourse.
- It's always good to know a few handy phrases, such as 'please', 'thank you' and 'where is...?' in the local language (p1085) – you'll be addressed more cordially and the locals really do appreciate your efforts.
- Recycling is an important issue, especially in Austria, Germany and Switzerland, and you will be encouraged to follow suit.
- Traffic congestion on the roads is a major problem, and visitors will do themselves and residents a favour if they forgo driving and use public transport.

Itineraries
CLASSIC ROUTES

THE ULTIMATE EUROPEAN VACATION
One to Two Months

This huge 7955km trek hits all the hot spots, providing a technicolour postcard selection to write home about. You could do it in one month – but if you want to fully experience the uniqueness of each country take the full two.

Have limited time, but want to see a little bit of everything? Start in **Dublin** (p624) and spend a few days sampling the vibrant pubs and traditional Irish craic. From Ireland, take either take a ferry to **Liverpool** (p213) or a direct flight to **London** (p134), catching a musical at the **Royal National Theatre** (p158). From London, take a bus to the **Cliffs of Dover** (p164) where you can hop on a ferry to **Calais** (p299) and head for **Paris** (p268). Alternatively, board a train at London's Waterloo Station and take the **Channel Tunnel** (p255) directly to Paris.

Now that you're on 'the Continent' you can use the Eurail pass, the buses or car hire to explore the wonders of the rest of Western Europe.

From Paris head north to **Brussels** (p95) for some exquisite chocolates, and further north to **Amsterdam** (p817), not forgetting to hit the Van Gogh Museum. Head east and spend a few days exploring **Berlin** (p406) and its biergartens. Next, **Vienna** (p38) beckons with its classical music riches. From there, head east to **Zürich** (p1026) and **Liechtenstein** (p789) for their awe-inspiring ski slopes.

Now head south to **Rome** (p689) for spectacular Roman architecture. Board a bus at Brindisi for a long (but panoramic) ferry ride to Greece to see the 2004 Olympic complex in **Athens** (p544) and explore a few ancient ruins. Back on the mainland, try your luck at gambling in the casino at **Monte Carlo** (p372) on your way to **Madrid** (p903) and spend a few days there discovering the fantastic public parks and world-class museums. End your whirlwind trip in laid-back **Lisbon** (p858), and enjoy a glass of local port wine to celebrate completing your grand journey!

BRITAIN AND BEYOND

Three to Five Weeks

London (p134) is arguably one of Western Europe's major transport spring-boards, and this itinerary is a bit of a choose-your-own-adventure.

For the UK version, head north to **Cambridge** (p194) for a punt on the River Cam and a stroll through the various colleges of one of the world's most esteemed universities. Next is **York** (p199) with its Roman fortifications and imposing cathedral, then the vibrant Scottish city, **Edinburgh** (p221) and a pint along the **'Royal Mile'** (p223). Move north to **Inverness** (p238), and birthplace of the legendary 'Loch Ness Monster' myth. Take the Skye Bridge to the **Isle of Skye** (p241) and try your hand (and feet) at 'Munro bagging' before checking in to one of the most scenic youth hostels in the resort town, **Oban** (p237).

On to **Glasgow** (p226), which is undergoing a cultural restoration and has a kickin' nightlife scene. Discover the breathtaking beauty of the **Lake District** (p215), where serious walkers set up camp. Soak up some R&R down south in **Bath** (p179), where you can tour a fully operational thermal spa. Then its time for more prestigious academia in **Oxford** (p186), before finishing back in London.

For an Ireland detour, take a Norse Merchant ferry from **Liverpool** (p213) to **Belfast** (p662) to explore the city's raucous nightlife and lovely **Botanic Gardens** (p663). Then journey through the heart of Ireland to **County Galway** (p654) and explore the craggy landscape of the **Burren** (p653). Head southeast, passing through **Kilkenny** (p638) to admire the 12th-century castle, and on to Dublin for a quick flight to London, or move south to **Rosslare Harbour** (p636) for a ferry to Pembroke in Wales and spend a day exploring the **Pembrokeshire Coast National Park** (p246).

For a taste of the Continent, take a high-speed ferry from Dover to **Ostend** (p123), then travel to the medieval city of **Bruges** (p110) for a lovely canal ride. Pop over to **Antwerp** (p102) for a tour of its Gothic **cathedral** (p104) before circling back to **Ypres** (p113) and its evocative WWI battlefields. Take a tram from Belgium into the sparkling Flemish town of **Lille** (p297) before heading to **Paris** (p268) and, via the Channel Tunnel, back to London.

> England is this itinerary's springboard for jumping straight into remote Scottish splendour (1938km), the best Irish craic (1413km), and choccies and other sinful pleasures on the Continent (909km); allow three to five weeks to complete the dive.

MEDITERRANEAN JOURNEY – BY LAND & SEA   Two Months

Start in southern Spain with a hint of British flavour in **Gibraltar** (p984), where you can view the only wild primates in Europe. Slowly make your way up the eastern coast past the Moorish town of **Málaga** (p979) and on to Valencia, where you can take a ferry to the party-hearty **Balearic Islands** (p959).

Back on the mainland, **Barcelona** (p927) is a beautiful Basque town, filled with the whimsical architecture of **Gaudí** (p930). From here head into France's **Provence region** (p355) and the picture-postcard town of **Marseille** (p355), where you can see the fortress that was inspiration for the novel *The Count of Monte Cristo*. On to the **Côte d'Azur** (p363) and the perpetually sunny playground for the rich and famous, **St Tropez** (p371). A quick stop in the capital of the French Riviera, **Nice** (p363), makes a good jumping-off point for other Riviera hotspots like **Cannes** (p368).

Take a ferry to **Corsica** (p378) where you'll experience the traditional Mediterranean lifestyle of quiet fishing villages. Hit the snowy peaks at **Calvi** (p379) and the fragrant eucalyptus groves of **Porto** (p380), before hopping down to the Mediterranean's second-largest island, **Sardinia** (p775). From Sardinia, take a long ferry ride or a quick flight to **Sicily** (p768) to visit its colossal Greek temples and the famous volcano, **Mt Etna** (p773).

Catch a ferry to **Naples** (p756) on the Italian mainland and take a side trip to see the ruins of **Pompeii** (p762). Move east to **Brindisi** (p766) for a ferry to Greece, landing in its third-largest city, **Patra** (p559). Before training it to Athens, take a thrilling trip on the **Diakof-Kalavryta Railway** (p561) for mind-blowing views. Head to **Athens** (p544) to wonder at its ancient archaeological treasures, then take a plane, or retrace your steps to the ferry, back to Italy. Head north to **Rome** (p689), allowing time to wander amid its gracious ruins, churches and piazzas. Continue through **Tuscany** (p740), stopping off at **Pisa** (p748) to see the famous 'leaning tower'. Finish your trip along the Ligurian coast in the port city of **Genoa** (p712) via the delightful coastal towns that make up the **Cinque Terre** (p714), where you can stroll along the **Via Dell'Amore** (p714).

Pack the sunscreen and your best shades for the sun and fun of the Mediterranean. Best to take this one slow, enjoying breezy ferry crossings and a hair-raising railway journey straight up a mountain.

TAILORED TRIPS

RHYTHM NATIONS

You'll still find oompah bands at **Oktoberfest** (p460), sensual cabarets in **Paris** (p283), flamboyant Spanish **flamenco** (p971), and lilting Irish **trad music** (p654), but Western Europe also offers a less-stereotypical musical assortment. From crowded British weekend **music festivals** (p144) to the world's largest **jazz festival** (p831) in Den Haag, and the soulful ballads of Greece's **rembetika music** (p554), there's a beat for every traveller.

Rock to the rhythm of London's vibrant **club scene** (p157) or take a **Magical Mystery Tour** (p214) in Liverpool, the Beatles' birthplace. Listen to the lyrical compositions of Germany's three Bs – Bach, Beethoven and Brahms – at a performance by the **Berlin Philharmonic** (p420). Catch a concert by the 'original' boy band, the **Vienna Boys' Choir** (p51). Experience opera at the renowned **Staatsoper** (p50) or at Venice's **Teatro La Fenice** (p733). Chill to cool jazz at a former torture chamber in **Paris** (p283) or at a smoky café in **Brussels** (p100), birthplace of the saxophone. Experience Ibiza's almost unrivalled **nightclub scene** (p964), where many a dance craze originated; you can hear anything from Andalucian to zarzuela.

ARCHITECTURAL WONDERS

Western Europe's World Heritage (Unesco) sites, both manmade and natural, often evoke an audible gasp from awestruck travellers. In Ireland, marvel at **Neolithic tombs** (p635) that predate Egypt's pyramids by more than six centuries. Step lightly over the geometric patterns of the **Giant's Causeway** (p669) in Northern Ireland. See how far the Roman Empire stretched in Britain at **Hadrian's Wall** (p208). Spend a day at the magnificent 13th-century **cathedral** (p287) at Chartres and admire one of the world's largest ensembles of medieval stained glass. Climb 366 steps for the breathtaking view from Bruges' famous **belfry** (p110) or check out the Netherlands' Kinderdijk region in summer to see all 19 **windmills** (p839) twirl simultaneously. Roam the ramparts in Switzerland's beautiful castle city, **Bellinzona** (p1023), or spend an afternoon wandering through the old town's **fortifications** (p798) in Luxembourg City. In Germany explore the **Roman ruins** (p490) in Trier. In Italy don't miss **Pompeii** (p762) and **Paestum** (p765). Stroll through lavish gardens and the 1440-room Hapsburg palace of Schönbrunn, near Vienna (p43). In Greece the ancient city of **Delphi** (p565) is a must-see. Finally, gape at the towering aqueducts in **Segovia** (p920) and **Tomar** (p878).

The Authors

LORETTA CHILCOAT
Coordinating Author & Destination, Getting Started, Itineraries, Snapshots, Directory, Transport

Loretta is the Coordinating Author for *Western Europe 7*. She's lived and worked in England and Spain, and despite a few hairy situations like a tube fire in London and a train robbery in Pamplona, she thoroughly enjoyed her time trekking across Western Europe, especially in the Hartz Mountains of Germany, the chocolate shops of Belgium and the remote splendour of Ireland's Aran Islands.

My Favourite Trip

Ah, so many places in Western Europe, it's hard to narrow down a favourite. I'd have to say mine was driving a car from Dublin to Galway – the long way. After negotiating about seven roundabouts just to get out of Dublin, I headed south through Kilkenny, taking a car mirror or two out along its narrow streets. Further south through the Knockmealdown Mountains, where several roads were washed out, I got into a staring match with some very bold sheep. Moving across to County Cork and the beautiful seaside town of Kinsale, I stuffed myself silly in gourmet restaurants and then drove north along deserted highways to County Galway, ending at an oyster festival in Clarenbridge.

ATLANTIC
OCEAN

GALWAY
○ Clarenbridge
IRELAND
○ Dublin
○ Kilkenny
▲ Knockmealdown
CORK   Mountains
○ Kinsale

REUBEN ACCIANO
Italy

Trekking around Europe taught Reuben many truths: chemical memory *isn't* a myth and you *can* thrive solely on pistachios, fruit, cheese and red wine. When bussing through Italy he was gobsmacked; Italians really do 'Do It Better'. Well, most things. Reuben loves northern Italian pride; a quiet self-belief that's a subtler counterpoint to their southern cousins' explosive flamboyance. Reuben has authored a number of Lonely Planet guides.

FIONA ADAMS
Spain

In love with all things latina, Fiona worked as a journalist in South America for three years – some of her more memorable adventures include piranha fishing in the Amazon. Fiona has a masters in Latin American Studies and has worked on a number of Lonely Planet titles, including *Spain*. Fiona and her husband live in the Scottish Highlands, but are considering swapping cock-a-leekie broth for gazpacho and upping sticks to Andalucía.

SARAH ANDREWS
Spain

Sarah has lived in Barcelona since 2000, where she writes articles and guidebooks about her adopted country. She's also the Barcelona stringer for the Associated Press. For this guide, Sarah spent three months travelling across northern Spain, re-visiting old haunts and falling in love with one city after another. She won't pick a favourite spot, but Barcelona's gothic quarter, Santiago de Compostela's buzzing street scene and the elegant city of San Sebastián all rank high on her best-of-Spain list.

BECCA BLOND Switzerland & Liechtenstein

Becca and Switzerland became acquainted at an early age – she was born in Geneva. Although she moved to the States at a young age, her American parents didn't let her forget the country. She has embarrassing childhood memories of wearing traditional Swiss alpine dresses to functions, and fonder ones of family vacations in the Swiss Alps. These early holidays inspired her to travel and she swapped newspaper reporting on homocides and rock stars for wandering the world for Lonely Planet.

TERRY CARTER Greece

Terry's first visit to Greece was with a Greek-Australian friend returning to his local village in Rhodes for their annual festival. He quickly learnt that even the coolest Greek guys only need a couple of ouzos for the inner *zeïmbekiko* dancer to surface. While still preferring to play the Turkish *saz* than the bouzouki, he now has a clear understanding on how making Greek coffee differs from brewing Turkish coffee. Terry is a freelance writer and designer based in Dubai.

GEERT COLE Belgium & Luxembourg

Though now living in Australia, Geert regularly follows the calling back to his native Belgium and hometown Antwerp. For the last decade or so, he has covered the length and breadth of Belgium and Luxembourg for various Lonely Planet titles, scouring small villages for new things to see, combing large cities for the best B&Bs, and forever on the lookout for a fab new pub. Every trip reaffirms his essential belief – Belgium is bigger than ever, but most people have yet to discover it.

MICHAEL GROSBERG Germany

Michael's interest in Germany began in earnest while pursuing graduate work in New York City, focusing on German literature and philosophy. Wanting to combine his knowledge gleaned from books with actual experience, and having established a network of friends in Germany, he made several trips to the country. Post academia, he has since taken many random jobs and currently teaches at university in between trips abroad.

SARAH JOHNSTONE Austria

Sarah is a freelance journalist based in London. Her writing has appeared in the *Times*, the *Independent on Sunday* and the *Face*. She thinks that studying German at university in Queensland a long time ago is responsible for the trouble she's now in. Sarah has worked on *Germany*, *Switzerland* and several other guidebooks for Lonely Planet, and has also been exploring Austria as a journalist for many years.

AMY KARAFIN Ireland

Amy Karafin grew up on the USA's Jersey shore with a keen curiosity about the horizon that eventually developed into a phobia of staying too long in one place. She spent many years behind desks in publishing houses in New York, leaving every job as soon as she had enough money for a trip, and finally relinquished her MetroCard and her black skirts altogether to make a living on the road. She now lives in Dakar, Senegal, where she works as a freelance writer and translator in a studio by the sea.

JOHN LEE   Britain

Born and raised in St Albans, Hertfordshire, John moved to Canada's West Coast in 1993, becoming a full-time freelance travel writer soon after. His work has appeared in more than 60 publications around the world. He specialises in stories on the UK and Canada and regularly returns to Britain to stock up on Marmite, strong tea and TV comedy videos.

ALEX LEVITON   Britain

Most of Alex's life was spent either in California (getting a master's degree in journalism) or travelling (studying Roman history, belly dancing on a boat in Turkiye etc). She's now a freelance writer living in a tobacco warehouse in Durham, North Carolina. After developing an addiction to scenic train journeys and scones and cream in 1994, she's visited Britain many times and her aim is to hike the South West Coast Path next. Or at least stroll it. Between tea shops.

LEANNE LOGAN   Belgium & Luxembourg

After more than a decade of working with Lonely Planet, Leanne is as connected to Belgium as she is to her homeland, Australia. She has lived in Belgium for several years and now has a half-Flemish toddler daughter, Eleonor, who can already sling that guttural Flemish 'g'. Leanne's curiosity compels her to get under the skin of a country she's touring; she's biked around Bruges, delved into the avant-garde in Antwerp, pub-crawled around Brussels and chilled out in the Ardennes.

AMY MARR   Italy

Boston-bred Amy's love affair with Italy began with an early addiction to Sicilian-style pizza from the North End. She studied Art History and Italian at Williams College and in Florence, and led and researched bike and hiking trips throughout Italy. Now a writer for magazines and a publisher of food and entertaining books, Amy tempers restlessness with morning bike rides on Mt Tam, cooking Italian feasts for friends, and regular trips to Italy. Amy has co-authored numerous Lonely Planet titles.

CRAIG MCLACHLAN   Greece

A Kiwi with an adventurous streak and a bad case of wanderlust, Craig markets himself as a 'freelance anything'. His jobs titles have included author (three titles in English and Japanese), pilot, hiking guide, interpreter and karate instructor and he has worked on LP's *Japan* and *Hiking in Japan*. Craig presently runs Wilderness Adventures in Queenstown, New Zealand. Craig is still wondering what to do when he grows up.

TOM PARKINSON   Germany

Tom first visited Germany at the age of three. He started learning the language in school and has been coming back ever since, eventually completing a German degree before striking out as a dictionary editor, freelance journalist and Lonely Planet author. Having spent a year living and working in Berlin, written on Germany and co-authored Lonely Planet's latest *Berlin* guide, Tom was more than happy to re-explore his favourite capital and the rest of the former East Germany for this book.

JOSEPHINE QUINTERO   Portugal
Josephine started travelling with a backpack and guitar in the late '60s. Further travels took her to Kuwait where she was held hostage during the Iraq invasion. Josephine moved to the relaxed shores of Andalucía, Spain, shortly thereafter, from where she has enjoyed exploring neighbouring Portugal. Josephine has contributed to more than 20 travel guidebooks and writes regularly for in-flight magazines and travel websites.

MILES RODDIS   Andorra
Living in Valencia, on Spain's Mediterranean coast, Miles has lost count of the times he's nipped up to Andorra for a ski break – though never, ever to shop. Andorra is also the starting point for the 23-day Pyrenean Traverse, a route he's twice trekked with enormous satisfaction. Miles has contributed to over 25 Lonely Planet titles, including guides – both general and walking – about Spain and France, Andorra's immediate neighbours.

SIMON SELLARS   The Netherlands
Simon has travelled to the Netherlands on a number of occasions, each time becoming ever more fascinated with Dutch innovations in art, sport and film. He worked as an in-house editor at Lonely Planet before leaving to write fulltime. Now based in Melbourne, Simon is the founder of the respected online magazine *Sleepy Brain* and writes for major Australian newspapers. This is his first title as a Lonely Planet author.

LISA STEER-GUÉRARD   Britain
Born in the Southeast and bred in South London, Lisa now lives in Paris and regularly comes back to see what's new in her favourite English cities – London and Brighton. Lisa has updated two guides on England, as well as writing articles and guidebooks on France and Southeast Asia. Favourite London things: park culture on a sunny day and the view of London from Jubilee bridge.

ANDREW STONE   France
Andrew's first experience of Southern France was as a schoolboy barely out of short trousers. A large extended French family (10 cousins) scattered around the countryside and an addiction to the country's wine and food ensure he remains a regular visitor.

Snapshots

Western Europe is no doubt a good place to be right now. Thanks to the strength of the euro, the region's spending power dominates other world currencies such as the Japanese Yen and US Dollar. The financial status has improved dramatically in countries that were never really seen as economic players in pre-euro times (eg Italy and Ireland). Examples of boom-time include Portugal's €450 million facelift, and Athens' dramatic makeover for the 2004 Olympic Games, which created a much-needed infrastructure. Even though there is ongoing squabbling between the UK and other EU (European Union) countries over dissolving the British pound and incorporating the euro, economically, the EU is firmly in the black.

Culturally, Western European countries still retain their individual identities and beliefs, despite some countries undergoing radical changes. While France enacted a law banning religious symbols such as Muslim headscarves in schools, the relationship between cigarettes and alcohol took a major hit in Ireland when smoking was banned in all workplaces…including pubs. Contrary to the belief that locals would be left crying in their Guinesses, the ban has been hailed a success, pulling more pints and non-smokers to the locals, and there have been murmurings in Britain about following suit. Ireland also made headlines on the hotly contested topic of immigration in 2004, banning automatic citizenship granted to babies born in the country – the only EU nation to have had that birthright – in an attempt to prevent women from flocking to Ireland to give birth.

Tourism throughout Western Europe is also thriving: many residents are travelling themselves, taking advantage of their strong currencies and enjoying the freedom of borderless journeys in the EU. With 10 new countries entering the EU (the last induction was 1 May 2004), it remains to be seen how their entry will affect visitors' travel trends.

Though tourism is thriving, travellers are naturally concerned about anti-terrorism measures in foreign countries. Western Europe is certainly not immune to threats. Most of them come in the form of subway delays in cities like London, Paris and Germany. In the aftermath of September 11, European governments are struggling to organise reinforcement of anti-terrorism measures. Travellers in general will find heightened security in all transport terminals throughout Western Europe. But hey, a little extra security for extra piece of mind doesn't seem to ruffle too many travellers' feathers.

Politics are always the source of hot debate in the EU, and no more so than at the 2004 meeting of EU political leaders to decide on a unifying EU constitution. It still needs to be ratified by each of its 25 member states before confirmation in October 2005, but some members have voiced concerns: France about its European influence and diminishing importance of the French language; Italy about the lack of Christianity mentioned in the constitution; the Netherlands over the cost of the EU; and others including Portugal, Spain, and the UK, that the EU could potentially become a 'superstate', paying less attention to smaller countries.

As for Western Europe's religious beliefs? Easy – it's the one passion these countries all share. Football. What better way to draw thousands of people together, engaging in weekly pilgrimages to the pubs for 'spirit'ual guidance and ecclesiastical exclamations as minutes tick down?

Yes, now is indeed a good time to be in Western Europe.

The submarine, helicopter and mop were all invented in Spain.

Parmigiano reggiano is so revered in Italy, its wheels were once used as a form of currency.

Andorra

FAST FACTS

- **Area** 464 sq km
- **Capital** Andorra la Vella
- **Currency** euro (€); A$1 = €0.58; ¥100 = €0.76; NZ$1 = €0.54; UK£1 = €1.50; US$1 = €0.83
- **Famous for** skiing, shopping, smuggling
- **Key Phrases** *hola* (hello); *adéu* (goodbye); *si us plau* (please); *gràcies* (thanks)
- **Official Language** Catalan
- **Population** 67,100
- **Telephone Codes** country code ☎ 376; international access code ☎ 00
- **Visas** not necessary

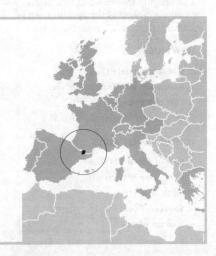

Slip the principality of Andorra into the conversation, and people will tell you, with either horror or joy, that it's all skiing and shopping. They'll probably add that it's a one-road, one-town ministate. And that its only highway, which links Spain and France, cuts a swathe through its only town, Andorra la Vella – which in turn is little more than one vast traffic jam bordered by cut-price temples to human greed.

They're a bit right but mostly wrong. Shake yourself free of Andorra la Vella's tawdry embrace, head along one of the state's three secondary roads and you'll find villages as unspoilt as any in the Pyrenees. Although Andorra absorbs over 11 million visitors each year (most of whom just pop in to shop), there are still areas where you can be completely alone.

Tucked into the Pyrenees between Spain's Catalonia region and France, this tiny political anomaly, rucked and buckled, with scarcely a flat square metre to its name, has some of the most dramatic scenery and by far the best – and cheapest – skiing in all the Pyrenees. And once the snows have melted, there's plenty of great walking, from hands-in-pockets strolling to challenging day hikes.

HIGHLIGHTS

- Go trekking just about anywhere in the principality, especially around **Ordino** (p29) and **Soldeu** (p28).
- Check out **Casa de la Vall** (p26), the quaint parliament building of one of the world's smallest nations.
- Rejuvenate yourself at the space-age spa complex, **Caldea** (p26).
- Ski the snowfields of **Grandvalira** (p31), by far the most extensive in all the Pyrenees.

HISTORY

From the Middle Ages until 1993, Andorra's sovereignty was vested in two 'princes': the Catholic bishop of the Spanish town of La Seu d'Urgell and the French president (who inherited the job from France's pre-Revolutionary kings). Nowadays, democratic Andorra is a 'parliamentary co-princedom', the bishop and president remaining joint but largely nominal heads of state. Andorra is a member of the UN and the Council of Europe, but not a full member of the EU.

PEOPLE

Andorrans form less than 40% of Andorra's total population, and are outnumbered by the Spaniards. Reflective of this percentage is the fact that the official language is Catalan, which is related to both Spanish and French. Most people speak a couple of these languages, sometimes all three, and the younger people, especially in the capital and in the ski resorts, can manage more than a smattering of English as well.

HOW MUCH?

- **Mid-range hotel** €15-20
- **Restaurant meal** from €12
- **Loaf of bread** €0.45
- **One-day ski lift pass** €23.50-33.50

LONELY PLANET INDEX

- **Litre of petrol** €0.75-0.80
- **Litre of water** €0.60-0.70
- **Small beer** €1
- **Souvenir T-shirt** €10-15
- **Medium pizza** €6-8

ANDORRA LA VELLA

pop 25,500 / elevation 1030m

Andorra la Vella (Vella, pronounced 'vey-yah', means 'old'), capital and sole town of the tiny principality, is squeezed into the Riu Gran Valira Valley and is mainly engaged in retailing electronic and luxury goods. With the constant din of jackhammers and the shopping-mall architecture, you might be in Hong Kong – but for the snowcapped peaks and a distinct absence of noodle shops!

ANDORRA

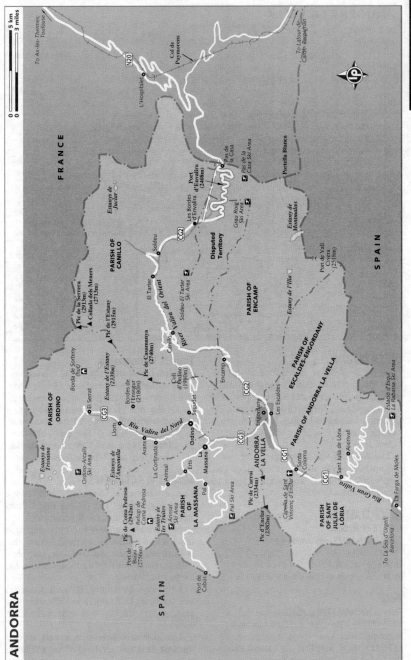

ANDORRA

ANDORRA LA VELLA

INFORMATION
E-Café.....................................1 C1
French Consulate..................2 D1
French Embassy.....................3 D1
French Post Office................4 E2
Future@point.......................5 E2
Hospital Nostra Senyora de
  Meritxell............................6 G1
Municipal Tourist Office........7 E2
National Tourist Office..........8 C2
Police Station.........................9 D2
Spanish Embassy..................10 D2
Spanish Post Office..............11 E2
Telephones..........................12 F2

SIGHTS & ACTIVITIES   (pp26–7)
Caldea Spa Complex.............13 H1
Casa de la Vall.....................14 B2
Public Lift to Plaça del Poble...15 C2

SLEEPING   (p27)
Hostal del Sol......................16 C1
Hotel Costa..........................17 D2
Hotel Florida........................18 C1
Hotel Pyrénées....................19 B2
Pensió La Rosa.....................20 B2

EATING   (pp27–8)
Can Gourmet.......................21 D3
Pa Torrart...........................22 B2
Pans y Company..................23 C2
Pans y Company..................24 F2
Papanico.............................25 C2
Pyrénées Department Store...26 D2
Restaurant Ca La Conxita....27 B2

DRINKING   (p28)
Cerveseria l'Albadia............28 C2
La Borsa.............................29 D3

TRANSPORT   (p28)
Bus Station.........................30 D3
Buses for Pal, Ordino, La Massana,
  Arinsal, Canillo, Soldeu, El Tartar
  & Pas de la Casa...............31 C2
Buses for Santa Coloma & Seu d'Urgell...32 C2

ORIENTATION

Andorra la Vella is strung out along the main drag, whose name changes confusingly from Avinguda del Príncep Benlloch to Avinguda de Meritxell to Avinguda de Carlemany along its length. The town's tiny historic quarter is split by this heavily trafficked artery.

The edges of the town now merge with the once-separate villages of Escaldes and Engordany to the east and Santa Coloma to the southwest.

INFORMATION
Internet Access
E-Café (☎ 865 677; Carrer l'Alziranet 5; per hr €3; ☾ 9am-midnight Mon-Fri, 10am-midnight Sat)
Future@point (☎ 828 202; Carrer de la Sardana 6; per hr €2.80; ☾ 10am-11pm Mon-Sat, to 10pm Sun)

Post
Correus (Correos) i Telègrafs (Carrer Joan Maragall 10; ☾ 8.30am-2.30pm Mon-Fri, 9.30am-1pm Sat) The Spanish post office.
La Poste (Carrer de Pere d'Urg 1; ☾ 8.30am-2.30pm Mon-Fri, 9am-noon Sat) The French post office.

Tourist Information
Municipal tourist office (☎ 827 117; turisme@ comuandorra.ad; Plaça de la Rotonda; ☾ 9am-9pm daily Jul & Aug, 9am-1pm & 3.30-7pm Mon-Sat, to 1pm Sun Sep-Jun) Also carries information for the entire country.
National tourist office (☎ 820 214; www.turisme.ad; Carrer Doctor Villanova s/n; ☾ 9am-1pm & 3-7pm Mon-Sat, to 1pm Sun Jul-Sep, 10am-1.30pm & 3-7pm Mon-Sat, to 1pm Sun Oct-Jun) Just off Plaça de Rebés.

SIGHTS & ACTIVITIES

Pamper yourself at **Caldea** (☎ 800 995; Parc de la Mola 10; adult/child €26/19.60; ☾ 10am-11pm, last entry 9pm) in Escaldes, just a 10-minute walk upstream from Plaça de la Rotonda. Enclosed in what looks like a futuristic cathedral, this is Europe's largest spa complex, complete with lagoons, hot tubs and saunas, and fed by thermal springs.

The small **Barri Antic** (Historic Quarter) was the heart of Andorra la Vella when the principality's capital was little more than a village.

The narrow cobblestone streets around the **Casa de la Vall** are flanked by attractive stone houses.

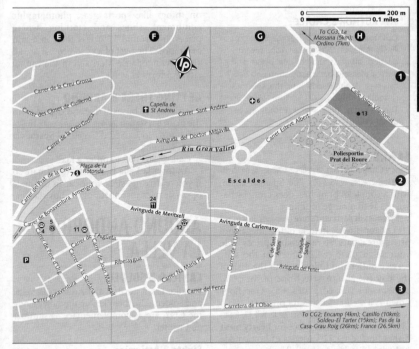

Built in 1580 as a private home, the Casa de la Vall (House of the Valley) has served as Andorra's parliament building since 1702. Downstairs is **El Tribunal de Corts**, the country's only courtroom. The **Sala del Consell**, upstairs, is one of the cosiest parliament chambers in the world. There are **guided tours** (☎ 829 129; admission free; ⏰ 9.15am-1pm & 3-7pm Mon-Sat year-round, 10am-2pm Sun Jun-Nov) in several languages, including English. Book at least a week ahead in summer to ensure a place – though individuals can be squeezed in last-minute.

The **Plaça del Poble** occupies the roof of a modern government office building. Giving good views, it's a popular local gathering place, especially in the evening.

SLEEPING

Camping Valira (☎ /fax 722 384; Avinguda de Salou; per person/tent/car €4.50/4.50/4.50; 🏊) Just west of town, Valira has a small indoor swimming pool.

Hostal del Sol (☎ 823 701; fax 822 363; Plaça Guillemó 3; s/d €13.50/27) This friendly, family-run place has 12 spruce, excellent-value rooms, and there are several cheap eateries just below.

Pensió La Rosa (☎ 821 810; Antic Carrer Major 18; s/d with shared bathroom €13/24) At the heart of the Barri Antic, La Rosa offers simple accommodation with washbasin, including a couple of dorms that sleep six (€72).

Hotel Costa (☎ 821 439; fax 824 867; 3rd fl, Avinguda de Meritxell 44; s/d with shared bathroom €15/26) Hotel Costa has clean, no-frills rooms. Badly indicated at street level – you need to crane your neck to see the sign way up high – its entrance is in the shopping arcade.

Hotel Florida (☎ 820 105; www.hotelflorida.ad; Carrer la Llacuna 15; s/d from €36.50/44) This delightful, modern hotel sits on a quiet side street. Relax in the sauna and hammam (free to guests), or tone yourself up in their mini-gym. All rooms, attractively furnished in blue, have mock-parquet flooring.

Hotel Pyrénées (☎ 860 006; www.hotelpyrenees .com; Avinguda Príncep Benlloch 20; s/d €35/56) Constructed in 1940 and exuding style, Hotel Pyrénées ranks among the most venerable buildings in the principality. The attractively furnished rooms have plenty of appealing dark woodwork. In high season, half-board (€50 per person) is compulsory.

THE AUTHOR'S CHOICE

Can Gourmet (☎ 808 861; Avinguda Tarragona 46-48; mains €11-20) This stylish, recently opened, all-glass-and-chrome place is at once a pleasant bar, pastry shop and deli-catessen. Light floods into the spacious restaurant through tall picture windows. The weekday lunch *menú* (€10) is exceptional value.

EATING

Pans y Company (Plaça de Rebés 2 & Avinguda de Meritxell 91; baguettes €2.75-3.60) The Spanish chain, with a couple of branches, does crunchy ba-guettes with a range of fillings.

Pyrénées department store (Avinguda de Meritxell 21) The top-floor caféteria of this megastore offers great fare at reasonable prices. Pile your salad plate (€4.20) high at the self-service buffet and follow it with the dish of the day (€4.25), or select one of the *plato combinados* (mixed plates; €6). One floor down is a well-stocked supermarket.

Pa Torrat (☎ 865 065; Carrer de la Vall 18; mains €8-17) Here's a splendid place for hearty meat dishes, including 11 varieties of homemade *butifarra* (Catalan sausage). The menu's only in Catalan, but the friendly staff are happy to provide a gloss.

Papanico (☎ 867 333; Avinguda Príncep Benlloch 4) This cheery place does tasty tapas from €2.45, and a range of sandwiches, *platos combinados* (from €6.40) and mains (€8 to €18).

Restaurant Ca La Conxita (☎ 829 948; Placeta Monjó 3; mains €16-20; ⏱ Mon-Sat) This bustling family business, where you can see the staff preparing your hearty meal, is another tempting choice where you're sure to come away satisfied.

DRINKING

La Borsa (Stock Exchange; ☎ 827 657; Avinguda de Tarragona 36) The price of each drink varies according to the night's consumption here, so keep a weather eye on that electronic, computer-controlled screen.

Cervesería l'Albadia (☎ 820 825; Cap del Carrer 2) For serious beer drinkers, with over eight classics on tap and many more bottled.

SHOPPING

If you've still got enough left in the kitty for some shopping, you can make big savings on things like sports gear, photographic equipment, shoes and clothing, where prices are around 25% less than in Spain or France. The best places to browse are all along Avinguda de Meritxell in the capital city, Andorra la Vella.

GETTING THERE & AROUND

Long-distance buses arrive and depart from the main **bus station** (Avinguda de Tarragona). Buses run hourly to La Seu d'Urgell, in Spain, via Santa Coloma.

Call ☎ 863 000 to order a taxi.

Andorra la Vella is a traffic nightmare so if you're driving, stick your car in the huge open-air park just north of the bus station.

AROUND ANDORRA LA VELLA

CANILLO & SOLDEU

Canillo, 11km northeast of Andorra la Vella, and Soldeu, a further 7km up the valley along the CG2, are as complementary as summer and winter.

Sights & Activities

In summer, Canillo (1500m) offers canyon clambering, a *via ferrata* ('iron way') climb-ing gully and climbing wall. There is also the year-round Palau de Gel with ice rink and swimming pool, guided walks, and endless possibilities for hiking (including La Ruta del Gallo, an easy 6.5km, signed nature walk that follows the valley downstream from Soldeu). The helpful **tourist office** (☎ 751 090; www.vdc.ad; ⏱ 8am-8pm Mon-Sat, to 4pm Sun) is on the main road at the east end of the village.

In winter, Soldeu and its smaller neigh-bour **El Tarter** come into their own.

The slopes of Soldeu-El Tarter, wooded in their lower reaches, are often warmer than Andorra's other more exposed ski areas and offer the Pyrenees' finest skiing and snowboarding.

You'll find a week's worth of walks around Canillo and Soldeu in Lonely Planet's *Walk-ing in Spain*.

Sleeping & Eating

Camping Santa Creu (☎ 851 462; per person/tent/car €3.10/3.10/3.10; ⏱ mid-Jun–Sep) The greenest and quietest of Canillo's five camping grounds.

Aina (☎ 851 434; colonies.aina@andorra.ad; dm €12, half-board €18; ⚅ Sep–mid-Jun) Just east of Canillo, Aina functions as a youth hostel outside high summer. Dormitories sleep six, and you need your own sleeping bag.

Hotel Roc de Sant Miquel (☎ 851 079; www.hotel -roc.com; s/d winter incl breakfast €39/58, summer incl breakfast €21/32) This relaxed, laid-back Soldeu hotel – the owner also plays lead guitar in a local band – hires out mountain bikes to guests.

Hotel Bruxelles (sandwiches €3-3.75, menú €9.90) A cheerful restaurant on Soldeu's main drag with a small terrace, well-filled sandwiches, whopping burgers and a tasty menú.

El Mosquit (☎ 851 030) Off the main highway and in the village of El Tarter, 'The Mosquito' is at once an intimate bar, a restaurant and, below, a heaving pub.

Entertainment

The music pounds on winter nights in Soldeu. Pussy Cat and its neighbour Fat Albert rock until far too late for impressive skiing next day, while **Avalanche** (☎ 852 282) and **Aspen** (☎ 851 974) feature daily music and a live band at least twice a week.

Getting There & Around

Hourly buses run from Andorra la Vella to Soldeu via Canillo and El Tarter till 8pm. In winter there are free shuttle buses (for skiers) between Canillo and the two upper villages.

ORDINO & AROUND

Despite recent development, Ordino, on highway CG3 8km north of Andorra la Vella, is a charming little village, with most buildings still in local stone. At 1000m, it's a good starting point for summer activity holidays. The **tourist office** (☎ 737 080; www .vallordino.com; ⚅ 8am-7pm Mon-Sat, 9am-5pm Sun Jul-Sep, 9am-1pm & 3-7pm Mon-Sat, 9am-1pm Sun Oct-Jun) is beside the CG3.

Sights & Activities

Museu d'Areny i Plandolit (☎ 836 908; adult/child €2.40/1.20; ⚅ 9.30am-1.30pm & 3-6.30pm Tue-Sat, 10am-2pm Sun), in a 17th-century manor house, offers half-hour guided visits, in Spanish or Catalan, of its richly furnished interior.

In the same grounds is the far from nerdy **Museo Postal de Andorra** (☎ 836 908; adult/child €2.40/1.20; ⚅ 9.30am-1.30pm & 3-6.30pm Tue-Sat,

10am-2pm Sun). It has a 15-minute audiovisual presentation (available in English), and set upon set of stamps issued by France and Spain specifically for Andorra.

The **Centre d'Interpretació de la Natura** (Nature Interpretation Centre; ☎ 837 939; adult/student/child €3.70/1.85/free; ⚅ 9.30am-1pm & 3.30-6pm Tue-Sat, to 1.30pm Sun) is a good multimedia introduction to Andorra's flora and fauna. A guided visit follows a 10-minute slide-video presentation (both with English option).

There are several excellent walking trails around Ordino. Pick up *Thirtysix Interesting Itineraries on the Paths of the Vall d'Ordino & the Parish of La Massana* (€2) from the tourist office.

Sleeping & Eating

Camping Borda d'Ansalonga (☎ 850 374; www.camp ingansalonga.com; per person/tent/car €4/4/4; ⚅ mid-Jun–Sep & Nov-Apr; ⚇) This enjoys an attractive valley site just outside the village.

Hotel Santa Bàrbara de la Vall d'Ordino (☎ 738 100; santabarbara@andorra.ad; plaça d'Ordino; s/d €45/60; Ⓟ) Above the main square and facing the church, this family-run hotel with its small, attractive bar is excellent value.

Restaurant Armengol (☎ 835 977; ⚅ Jun-Apr) Offers menús for €10.50 and €15, and also does a wide range of generously-portioned à la carte meat and fish dishes (€9 to €17).

MIND HOW YOU GO

A law passed in 1999 makes Catalan obligatory for all signage, publicity, restaurant menus, public announcements and the like. However, since massive tourism is Andorra's lifeblood, most notices are also in Spanish and English, and sometimes in French.

But not always: even though Catalan is opaque to the vast majority of visitors, we came across the following monolingual signs, to which, for your safety, we append the English translation!

- *Perill: Zona Voladures* = beware of falling stones
- *Caiguda de Neu* = watch out for snow sliding from roofs
- *Risc Allaus* = risk of avalanche

Alternatively, just jump when the locals jump.

ANDORRA

Bar Restaurant Quim (🕙 Jun-Apr) Next door to Restaurant Armengol, Quim is friendly and more snacky; it has a great range of tapas and does a filling lunch *menú*.

Getting There & Away
Buses to/from Andorra la Vella run every half-hour from 7am to 9pm.

ARINSAL
In winter, Arinsal, 10km northwest of Andorra la Vella, has good skiing and snowboarding and a lively après-ski scene. It's linked with the smaller ski station of Pal. The combined stations, which share a website (www.palarinsal.com), have 63km of pistes with a vertical drop of 1010m. A one-day lift pass costs €23.50 (€28 in high season).

In summer, Arinsal is a good departure point for mountain walks. From Aparthotel Crest, at Arinsal's northern extremity, a trail leads northwest, then west to **Estany de les Truites** (2260m), a natural lake. The steepish walk up takes around 1½ hours. From here, it's another 1½ to two hours to **Pic de Coma Pedrosa** (2964m), Andorra's highest point.

Sleeping & Eating
Camping Xixerella (☎ 836 613; www.campingxixerella.com; per person/tent/car €4.20/4.20/4.20; 🕙 Nov-Sep; 🏊) Between Pal and Arinsal, this large, well-equipped site has an outdoor pool.

Hotel Coma Pedrosa (☎ 737 950; fax 737 951; d €44, half-board per person €38; closed 4 weeks Jun or Jul) With its cosy bar, this is another welcoming place, popular with both skiers and summer walkers.

Refugi de la Fondue (☎ 839 599) As a change from the plentiful snack and sandwich joints, it does cheese or meat fondue dishes (€13.50) and, in summer, outdoor barbeques.

THE AUTHOR'S CHOICE

Hostal Pobladó (☎ 835 122; hospoblado@ andornet.ad; B&B per person €25, with shared bathroom €20; 🕙 Dec-Oct) Hostal Pobladó sits right beside the cabin lift, handy for skiing in winter and for taking off on summer day walks. It's friendliness itself and a great place to make contact with other skiers or walkers. It has a lively bar and an Internet point (€3.60 per hour), and rents out skis.

Restaurant el Moli (mains €5.50-12) Bills itself as Italian – and indeed offers the usual staple pastas and pizzas (both €7 to €9.40) – but also has more exotic fare such as Thai green coconut chicken curry (€12). Both restaurants are on the main drag.

Entertainment
In winter, Arinsal fairly throbs after sunset. In summer, it can be almost mournful. When the snow's around, call into Surf, near the base of the cabin lift. A pub, dance venue and restaurant, it specialises in juicy Argentinian grilled meat dishes (€7 to €13.20).

Seeking somewhere congenial and quieter? **El Café Gourmet d'Arinsal** (🕙 mid-Jun–mid-May), on the main street, does delightful snacks and also has an **Internet point** (per hr €4).

Getting There & Away
Five buses daily leave Andorra la Vella for Arinsal via La Massana. There are also about 15 local buses daily between La Massana and Arinsal. In winter, a special ski bus runs six times daily from La Massana to Arinsal.

ANDORRA DIRECTORY

ACCOMMODATION
Tourist offices stock a free booklet, *Guia d'Allotjaments Turístics*, but it's far from a comprehensive listing, and while the rest of the information is reliable, the prices it quotes are merely indicative.

Outside Andorra la Vella there are few budget options for independent travellers. To compensate, there are plenty of camping grounds, many of which are beautifully situated. In high season (December to March and July/August), some hotels put prices up substantially and don't take independent travellers.

For walking enthusiasts, Andorra has 26 off-the-beaten-track *refugis* (mountain refuges), all except one unstaffed and free. If you're trekking, ask at tourist offices for the free *Mapa de Refugis i Grans Recorreguts*, which pinpoints and describes them all.

ACTIVITIES
Above the main valleys, you'll find attractive lake-dotted mountain country, good for skiing in winter and walking in summer. The largest and best ski stations are the inter-

SNOW MATES

In the winter of 2003, the ski resorts of Soldeu-El Tarter and Pas de la Casa-Grau Roig (on the French border) put paid to decades of jealously eyeing each other's slopes and fortunes, agreed to install a short, umbilical lift, and joined forces. The result is the combined snowfields of **Grandvalira** (☎ 808 900; www.grandvalira.com), far and away the most extensive in all the Pyrenees, with 192km of runs and a combined lift system that can shift 90,000 skiers per hour. Lift passes, valid for the combined area, cost €33.50/87 (€35/90.75 high season) for one/three days.

connecting resorts of Soldeu-El Tarter and Pas de la Casa-Grau Roig. Others – Ordino-Arcalís, Arinsal and Pal – are a bit cheaper but often colder and windier. Ski passes cost €23.50 to €27.50 per day, depending on location and season; downhill ski gear is €8 to €11 per day, and snowboards €17 to €20. In summer, you can rent mountain bikes in some resorts for around €18 a day.

BUSINESS HOURS

Shops in Andorra la Vella are generally open 9.30am to 1pm and 3.30pm to 8pm daily, except (usually) Sunday afternoon.

EMBASSIES & CONSULATES

Andorra has embassies in France and Spain:
France (☎ 01 40 06 03 30; 30 Rue d'Astorg, 75008 Paris)
Spain (☎ 91 431 74 53; Calle Alcalá 73, 28001 Madrid)

France and Spain maintain reciprocal missions in Andorra la Vella:
France (☎ 869 396; Carrer les Canals 38-40)
Spain (☎ 800 030; Carrer del Prat de la Creu 34)

POST

Andorra has no postal system of its own; France and Spain each operate separate systems with their own Andorran stamps, which you stick on only for international mail (letters within Andorra are delivered free). You can't use regular French or Spanish stamps.

EMERGENCY NUMBERS

Police, fire, ambulance ☎ 112

It's swifter to route international mail (except letters to Spain) through the French postal system. Tourist offices sell stamps.

TELEPHONE

The cheapest way to make an international call is to buy a *teletarja* (phonecard; sold at tourist offices and kiosks for €3 and €6) and ring off-peak (9pm to 8am and all day Sunday). A three-minute off-peak call within the EU costs €0.60 (€0.92 to Australia or the US). You can't make a reverse-charge (collect) call from Andorra.

TRANSPORT IN ANDORRA

GETTING THERE & AWAY

The only way to reach Andorra, unless you trek across the mountains, is by road from the bordering countries of Spain or France.

France

Autocars Nadal has two buses (€21, 3½ to four hours) on Wednesday, Friday and Sunday between Andorra la Vella and Toulouse's bus station. Novatel Autocars runs two minibuses daily (€28, 3½ hours) between Andorra la Vella and Toulouse airport.

By rail, take a train from Toulouse to L'Hospitalet (2¼ hours, three to eight daily). From L'Hospitalet, buses leave for Andorra la Vella at 7.35am and 7.45pm daily (€6.80).

In the reverse direction, they leave the Andorran capital at the unholy hour of 5.45am and 5pm. On Saturday, up to five buses run from L'Hospitalet to Pas de la Casa, just inside Andorra.

You can also drop to the Mediterranean. From Latour-de-Carol, trains go to Perpignan (€20.30, four hours, two to four daily).

Spain

Autocars Nadal (☎ 805 151; www.autocarsnadal.com) runs four to six buses daily between Andorra la Vella and Barcelona's airport (€25, three to 3¾ hours), via the Sants train station (€20, 3¼ hours).

Alsina Graells (☎ 827 379) has five buses daily (€19.50, 3½ hours) between Barcelona's Estació del Nord and Andorra la Vella's **bus station** (Avinguda de Tarragona 42). Three are nonstop.

Minibuses of **Novatel Autocars** (☎ 803 789; www.andorrabybus.com) make four runs daily between Andorra la Vella's bus station and Barcelona airport (€25).

Viatges Montmantell (☎ 807 444; www.mont mantell.com, in Spanish) runs three buses daily between Andorra la Vella and Lleida (€15, 2¾ hours) to connect with Madrid-bound high-speed trains. From Barcelona, five trains daily climb to the frontier terminus of Latour-de-Carol, where buses leave for Andorra at 10.45am and 1.15pm daily.

Hispano Andorrana (☎ 821 372) runs hourly buses between La Seu d'Urgell, just across the border, and Andorra la Vella (€2.40, 40 minutes).

GETTING AROUND

There are buses running regularly along the principality's three main roads. All the bus services are run by **Cooperativa Inter- urbana** (☎ 806 555). Ask at any tourist office for the free current timetables for the eight bus routes that radiate out from Andorra la Vella.

The speed limit is 40km/h in populated areas and 90km/h elsewhere. Two problems with driving in Andorra are the reckless- ness of local drivers and Andorra la Vella's horrendous traffic jams – bypass the latter by taking the ring road around the south side of town. Petrol is about 25% cheaper than in Spain or France.

Austria

CONTENTS

AUSTRIA

Although it likes to consider itself virtually twinned with California these days, Austria (Österreich) really couldn't be more different – and it's not just that Arnold Schwarzenegger's homeland offers mountains and snow instead of sun and surf. As a cultural bastion of 'old Europe', Austria is still clinging to its very un-Californian traditions of caffeine (coffee houses), cigarettes (everywhere) and calorific cuisine (schnitzel and apple strudel).

Indeed, it's the country's seeming refusal to bow to the diktats of the modern world that attracts so many visitors, wooed by the historic treasures of the former Habsburg empire, by the sounds of Mozart and Strauss, or by the Alps, which offer summer hiking and winter skiing.

However, if baroque palaces, sparkling mountain vistas and Danube cruises don't do it for you, Austria *does* have a forward-looking side: the modern-art Museums Quarter in Vienna, the architecturally adventurous Kunsthaus (arts centre) in Graz and the Bergisel tower in Innsbruck are just a few exciting developments in recent years.

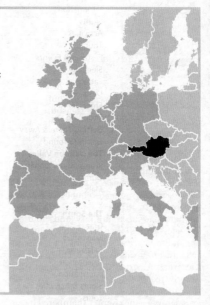

FAST FACTS

- **Area** 83,855 sq km
- **Capital** Vienna
- **Currency** euro (€); A$1 = €0.58; ¥100 = €0.76; NZ$1 = €0.54; UK£1 = €1.50; US$1 = €0.83
- **Famous for** apple strudel, Wiener schnitzel, Adolf Hitler, Arnold Schwarzenegger and Freudian pschyoanalysis
- **Key Phrases** *Grüss Gott* (hello); *Servus!* (hello and goodbye); *Ba Ba* (bye bye)
- **Official Language** German (Slovene, Croat and Hungarian are also official languages in some southern states)
- **Population** 8.2 million
- **Telephone Codes** country code ☎ 43; international access code ☎ 00
- **Visa** EU nationals don't need a visa; most other nationalities can stay for up to 90 days in any half-year without a visa

HIGHLIGHTS

- Soak up the impressive museums, Habsburg treasures and Gustav Klimt artwork in **Vienna** (p38).
- Sing along on a fabulously kitsch *Sound of Music* tour in the picture-postcard city of **Salzburg** (p61).
- Choose between skiing, snowboarding or hiking in the spectacular mountain-scape of **Innsbruck** (p72).
- Wend through the Hohe Tauern National Park along the **Grossglockner Hochalpenstrasse** (p79), one of the world's most scenic highways.
- Admire one of contemporary architecture's gems: the quirky, bubble-shaped **Kunsthaus** (arts centre; p57) in Graz.

ITINERARIES

- **Two days** Fill this entire time up in Vienna. Visit the Habsburg palaces and a few museums, and relax in the coffee houses.

One week Spend three days in Vienna, a day in Salzburg, two days visiting the Salzkammergut lakes and a day exploring Innsbruck.

CLIMATE & WHEN TO GO

Austria has a typical central European climate, with Vienna enjoying an average maximum of 2°C in January and 25°C in July. Some people find the *Föhn* – a hot, dry wind that sweeps down from the mountains in early spring and autumn – rather uncomfortable. See also Climate Charts, p1055.

Austria hangs out its *Zimmer frei* (rooms vacant) signs year-round, but its peak seasons are from July to August and Christmas to New Year. Christmas to late February is the peak skiing time. Alpine resorts can be pretty dead between seasons, ie May, June and November.

HISTORY

Austria is a little nation with a big past. From 1278 it was the epicentre of the mighty Habsburg empire and, in the 20th century, a pivotal player in the outbreak of WWI. For centuries the Habsburgs used strategic marriages to maintain their hold over a territory now encompassing parts of today's Bosnia-Hercogovina, Croatia, Czech Republic, Hungary, Poland, Romania, Slovakia, Slovenia and, for a period, even Germany. But defeat in WWI brought that to an end, when the small republic of Austria was formed in 1918.

There had been military and political struggles before. Twice the neighbouring Ottoman Empire reached Vienna, in 1529 and 1683. In 1805 Napoleon defeated Austria at Austerlitz. Austrian Chancellor Metternich cleverly reconsolidated Austria's power in 1815 after Waterloo, but in the 1866 Austro-Prussian War, the country (hampered by an internal workers' revolution in 1848) lost control of the German Confederation. At this point, the empire's Hungarian politicians asserted themselves and forced the formation of Austria-Hungary.

However these setbacks pale beside Archduke Franz Ferdinand's assassination by Slavic separatists in Sarajevo on 28 June 1914. When his uncle, the Austro-Hungarian emperor Franz Josef, declared war on Serbia in response, the ensuing 'Great War' (WWI) would prove the Habsburg's downfall.

HOW MUCH?

- **Litre of milk** €0.85
- **Loaf of bread** from €1.15
- **Bottle of house white** from €9
- **Newspaper** €0.80-1.20
- **Short taxi ride** €5

LONELY PLANET INDEX

- **Litre of petrol** €0.90
- **Litre of water** €0.40-2.10
- **Half-litre of beer** from €3
- **Souvenir T-shirt** €15
- **Street snack (wurst)** €2.80

During the 1930s Nazis from neighbouring Germany assassinated Austrian Chancellor Dolfuss, installing a puppet regime. With Hitler, a native Austrian, also as German chancellor, the German troops met little resistance when they invaded recession-hit Austria in 1938. A national referendum supported the *Anschluss* (union).

Heavily bombed during WWII, Austria has since worked hard to be a good global citizen, maintaining its neutrality and in 1995 joining the EU. However, echoes of its fascist history regularly come back to haunt it. In the 1980s rumours surfaced that President Kurt Waldheim had been involved in war crimes in WWII. In the late 1990s other European nations briefly imposed sanctions when the far-right Freedom Party (FPÖ) and its controversial leader, Jörg Haider, joined the national government.

Haider remains on the scene but is no longer personally in the government (although at the time of writing Chancellor Wolfgang Schüssel of the People's Party, or ÖVP, maintained a coalition with the FPÖ). In fact, in 2004 there was a tiny swing to the left when socialist Heinz Fischer was narrowly elected the country's President.

PEOPLE

Austrians don't enjoy the best reputation in Europe. Firstly, 20th-century politicians like Jörg Haider only added to a history of anti-Semitism, reinforcing the notion that their country is extremely right-wing.

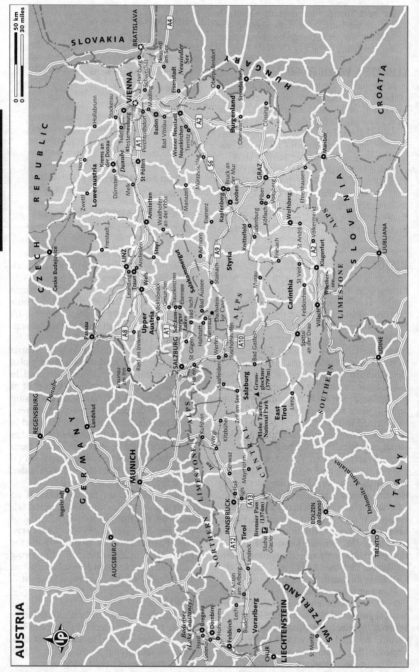

Secondly, the people themselves are allegedly a grumpy lot. However, Austria has loosened up a lot since the collapse of the Iron Curtain along its border more than 15 years ago. That last stereotype, in particular, is starting to lose its grip.

Within the country, Vienna has always been a special case, mixing Austrian conservatism with a large dollop of decadence. The scene you might get at Viennese balls of grand old society dames flirting with drag queens aptly reflects this. The capital's pervading humour, *Wiener Schmäh,* is quite ironic and cutting, but is also meant to be charming. In essence, it's quite camp.

Nearly one fifth of the population lives in Vienna, but other cities are small, so more than two-thirds live in small towns or in rural areas.

RELIGION

Although Vienna once had a sizeable Jewish population, Austria today is a largely Christian nation. Some 80% of the population is Catholic. The rest is Protestant, concentrated in Burgenland and Carinthia.

ARTS

Austria's musical heritage tends to elbow most of its other artistic achievements off the page. European composers were drawn to the country by the Habsburgs' generous patronage during the 18th and 19th centuries: Beethoven, Brahms, Haydn, Mozart and Schubert all made Vienna their home during this period. The waltz originated in the city, perfected by Johann Strauss junior (1825–99).

However, Vienna at the end of the 19th century was also a city of design and painting. The Austrian Secessionist movement, the local equivalent of Art Nouveau *(Jugendstil),* turned out such talents as the painter Gustav Klimt and architect Otto Wagner. These were followed by the Expressionist painters Egon Schiele and Oskar Kokoschka, and modernist architect Adolf Loos.

While Austrian literature is not well-known in the outside world, Arthur Schnitzler's *Dream Story (Traumnovelle)* did inspire the Stanley Kubrick film *Eyes Wide Shut.* Football fans should be familiar with one famous work by Carinthian novelist Peter Handke, *The Goalie's Fear of the Penalty Kick (Der Angst des Tormanns beim Elfmeter).*

Today, Austria's fine musical tradition has moved in the entirely different direction of chilled, eclectic electronica and dub lounge. Celebrity DJs Kruder & Dorfmeister have had the greatest global success, but the scene is loaded with other talent, including Pulsinger & Tunakan, the Vienna Scientists and the Sofa Surfers.

Meanwhile, expat film director Michael Haneke has also been creating a splash with suburban hostage-taking in the controversial *Funny Games* (1997) and the twisted romance of the much-lauded *The Piano Teacher* (2001). The country's most famous TV export is the detective series *Inspector Rex (Kommisar Rex).* As well as being big in Germany and Australia, Rex, a German shepherd dog who regularly proves invaluable to his police owners, apparently has a cult following in some 93 countries.

ENVIRONMENT

More than half of Austria's 83,855 sq km is mountainous. Three chains run west to east: the Northern Limestone Alps, the Central (or High) Alps, which have the tallest peaks in Austria, including the 3797m Grossglockner, and the Southern Limestone Alps. They are banded around the middle and the south of the country, occupying most of its western half, and leaving flats around the Danube Valley and Vienna in the northeast and Graz to the southeast.

Meadows and forests cover much of the country. Although Austria is home to Europe's largest national park, Hohe Tauern, only 3% of its landmass is national park. These protected wilderness areas are good places to spot wildlife such as marmots. Hohe Tauern itself has many species of alpine wild flower, and the bearded vulture and lyre-horned ibex were reintroduced in recent years.

Austria is highly environmentally conscious and no-one wants to spoil the pristine landscape by littering.

FOOD & DRINK
Staples & Specialities

There's more to Austrian cuisine than Wiener schnitzel (a veal or pork cutlet coated in breadcrumbs). Traces of the country's wider historical reach endure in the Hungarian paprika used to flavour several dishes, including *Gulasch* (beef stew), and in the Styrian

WHAT'S ON A COFFEE DRINKER'S MIND?

Watching your fellow customers lingering over their cappuccino, *Grosser Brauner* or *Melange* in a Viennese *Kaffeehaus*, it's easy to believe that Austrians have always been born with a coffee spoon in their mouth. But those great tea-drinkers, the English, opened their first coffee house before the Austrians ever did, so how did the tradition take such a hold here?

Local schoolchildren are taught that the beverage entered their country after the Ottoman Empire's siege of Vienna in 1683. Polish merchant Georg Kolschitzky smuggled a message out of his adopted city to the Polish king, who eventually came to Vienna's rescue; and Kolschitzky asked to be rewarded with the sacks of coffee beans abandoned by Kara Mustafa's retreating army. As historian Simon Schama put it, Austria managed to 'resist the Turkish siege but (was) defenceless against the coffee bean'.

Only much later, from the 18th century, did the tradition of spending long hours in coffee houses really become entrenched. To escape Vienna's mostly unheated apartments, impoverished artists and intellectuals would set up shop at their coffee-house tables, writing, and holding meetings and debates. Sigmund Freud was a regular at the **Café Landtmann** (Map pp44-5; 01, Dr Karl Lueger Ring 4) and Leon Trotsky spent hours at Café Central (p49), plotting, playing chess and running up a tab for hot drinks. When the Russian revolution started, he left Vienna – much to the chagrin of the head waiter – without paying his bill.

Today, coffee drinking remains a central plank of Viennese, and to a lesser extent Austrian, life. It goes beyond a simple Starbucks culture (but surprisingly that chain now exists here, too). The true coffee house is still a place for music, exhibitions and cultural events; see what's on at www.wiener-kaffeehaus.at. Above all, in the birthplace of psychoanalysis, it's somewhere to offset the stresses of the everyday. As the owner of Café Diglas (see p49) once theorised to the *Guardian* newspaper: 'The coffee is the medicine, the waiters, the therapists.'

polenta and pumpkinseed oil popular in Italian and Slovenian cuisine respectively. Some staples like wurst (sausage) and regional dishes such as *Tiroler Bauernschmaus* – a selection of meats served with sauerkraut, potatoes and dumplings – can be very fatty and stodgy. However, hearty soups often include *Knödel* (dumplings) or pasta.

Besides *Strudel* (filo pastry filled with a variety of fruits, poppyseeds or cheese), *Salzburger Nockerl* (a fluffy soufflé) is a popular Austrian dessert.

Known for its lager beer – from brands like Gösser, Schwechater, Stiegl and Zipfer to *Weizenbier* (wheat beer) – Austria also produces some white wines in its east. Heuriger wine is the year's new vintage, and is avidly consumed, even in autumn while still semi-fermented (called *Sturm*).

Where to Eat

A traditional Austrian inn is called a *Beissl* or *Stüberl*. A *Beissl* (from the Hebrew word for 'house') tends to be more about meeting friends and having a drink, with food a necessary but ancillary pastime, whereas the emphasis is usually more on the food itself in a *Stüberl* (from the word *Stube*, meaning

'cosy living room'). Not all *Beissl* or *Stüberl* will be 100% traditional, however only a few of them in the middle of Vienna are touristy enough to be wary of.

Of course, lots of Asian restaurants and pizzerias dot the countryside. These, in addition to the dumplings in local cuisine, mean that vegetarians shouldn't have any trouble.

For cheap food, try university canteens (*Mensens*). The main meal is at midday, when many restaurants provide a good-value set meal (*Tagesteller* or *Tagesmenu*).

VIENNA

☎ 01 / pop 1.6 million

If New York is the big apple, Vienna (Wien) is the big wedding cake – a wonderfully rich indulgence packed with galleries and museums. Marzipan-like buildings decorate the city's inner circular road, the Ringstrasse, but they're only the tiara in a cultural treasure trove. The history of the Habsburg dynasty can be traced through the rooms of the Hofburg palace or Schloss Schönbrunn, while the legacy of Art Nouveau artists

Gustav Klimt and Egon Schiele is on show at the Secession Building, Schloss Belvedere and the Leopold Museum.

At the crossroads of eastern and western Europe, Vienna has always brimmed with creative energy. It was here that Johann Strauss invented the waltz and Sigmund Freud developed his psychoanalytic theories. But if the city's diet of music, art and philosophy starts to feel a bit stodgy, it can be easily washed down in an atmospheric coffee house, or forgotten atop the *Riesenrad*, the Ferris wheel featured in the *Third Man* movie.

ORIENTATION

Many historic sights are in the old city, the Innere Stadt. This is encircled by the Danube Canal (Donaukanal) to the northeast and a series of broad boulevards called the Ring or Ringstrasse. Most attractions in the centre are within walking distance of each other. Stephansdom (St Stephen's Cathedral), in the heart of the city, is the principal landmark.

In addresses, the number of a building within a street *follows* the street name. Any number *before* the street name denotes the district, of which there are 23. District 1 (the Innere Stadt) is the central region, mostly within the Ring. Generally, the higher the district number, the further it is from the city centre. The middle two digits of postcodes refer to the district, hence places with a postcode 1010 are in district 1, and 1230 means district 23.

The main train stations are Franz Josefs Bahnhof to the north, Westbahnhof to the west and Südbahnhof to the south; transferring between them is easy. Most hotels and *pensions* are in the centre and to the west.

INFORMATION
Bookshops

British Bookshop (Map pp44-5; ☎ 512 1945; 01, Weihburggasse 24-6) English-language titles.
Freytag & Berndt (Map pp44-5; ☎ 533 8685; 01, Kohlmarkt 9) Maps and guidebooks.
Reisebuchladen (Map pp44-5; ☎ 317 3384; 09, Kolingasse 6) Specialises in guidebooks.
Shakespeare & Co Booksellers (Map pp44-5; ☎ 535 5053; 01, Sterngasse 2) New and second-hand books.

Internet Access

Bignet (Map pp44-5; ☎ 503 9844; Kärntner Strasse 61; per 10/30min €1.45/3.90)

VIENNA IN TWO DAYS

Starting at the **Stephansdom** (p41), head via Graben and the Kohlmarkt to the **Hofburg** (p41). Wander around outside and maybe take a tour of the **Kaiserappartments** (p42). Drop by the **Kaisergruft** (p42), and if you have the time and inclination explore the **Albertina** (p42). Find yourself a coffee house to settle down in for a long break. After lunch, hop on a tram No 1 around the Ringstrasse. Do one circuit and a half, just taking in the sights, before alighting near the **Museums Quartier** (p42). Visit the **Leopold Museum** (p42) and anything else that takes your fancy. Try to get tickets to the **opera** (p50) for the evening or head for a club like **Flex** (p50), down on the Danube Canal.

On your second morning, choose a favourite gallery or museum. Klimt fans should head to the **Schloss Belvedere** (p42) or **Secession** (p42), and Hundertwasser enthusiasts to the **KunstHausWien** (p42). If it's a summer's afternoon, spend it lazing in the gardens at **Schloss Schönnbrunn** (p43). If it's chilly or raining, explore another coffee house or museum. For your final evening, venture into the suburbs for some wine in Vienna's *Heurigen* (wine taverns; p50).

Surfland Internetcafé (Map pp44-5; ☎ 512 77 01; Krugerstrasse 10; initial charge €1.40, €0.08 per min thereafter)

Medical Services

Allgemeines Krankenhaus (general hospital; Map pp40-1; ☎ 40 400; 09, Währinger Gürtel 18-20)
Dental Treatment (☎ 512 2078; ✆ 24hr)

Money

Banks are open from 8am or 9am to 3pm Monday to Wednesday and Friday, and to 5.30pm on Thursday; smaller branches close from 12.30pm to 1.30pm. Numerous *Bankomats* (ATMs) allow cash withdrawals. Train stations have extended hours for exchanging money.

Post

Main post office (Map pp44-5; 01, Fleischmarkt 19; ✆ 24hr) Post offices open long hours are at Südbahnhof, Franz Josefs Bahnhof and Westbahnhof.

AUSTRIA

AUSTRIA

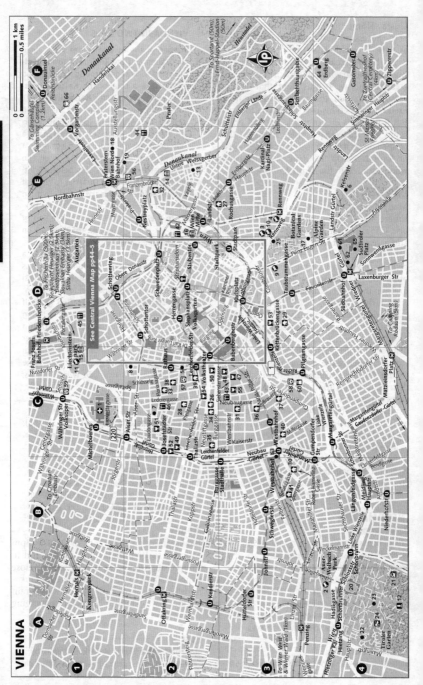

VIENNA

See Central Vienna Map pp44-5

AUSTRIA

Tourist Information

Tourist offices and hotels in Vienna sell the Vienna Card (€16.90), which provides admission discounts and a free 72-hour travel pass.

Information & Hotel Reservation Counters Westbahnhof (8.30am-9pm); Airport arrivals hall (8.30am-9pm)
Jugend-Info Wien (Vienna Youth Information; Map pp44-5; ☎ 17 99; 01, Babenbergerstrasse 1; noon-7pm Mon-Sat) Offers various reduced-price tickets for 14- to 26-year-olds.
Tourist-Info Zentrum (Map pp44-5; ☎ 245 55; www .wien.info; 01, Am Albertinaplatz; 9am-7pm)

Travel Agencies

American Express (Map pp40-1; ☎ 51 540; 01, Kärntner Strasse 21-23; 9am-5.30pm Mon-Fri, to noon Sat)
STA Travel Vienna (Map pp44-5; ☎ 401 48-0; 09, 09, Garnisongasse 7; 9am-5.30pm); Central Vienna (Map pp44-5; ☎ 40 148-7000; 09, Türkenstrasse 6B; 9am-6pm); Central Vienna (Map pp44-5; ☎ 50 243-0; 04, Karlsgasse 3; 9am-6pm)

SIGHTS

Vienna's ostentatious buildings and beautifully tended parks make it a lovely city just to stroll through. If you catch tram No 1 or 2 around the Ringstrasse (the road circling the centre) you'll experience the flavour of the city, passing the neo-Gothic **Rathaus** (city hall), the Greek Revival–style **Parlament**, and the 19th-century **Burgtheater**, among others. You can even glimpse the baroque **Karlskirche** (St Charles' Church) from the tram.

Wandering along the pedestrian-only tree-lined **Kärntner Strasse** will take you past plush shops, cafés and street entertainers. The main point of interest in Graben is the knobbly **Petsäule** (Plague Column), designed by Fischer von Erlach and built to commemorate the end of the Plague. There's also a concrete **Holocaust memorial** by Rachel Whiteread in Judenplatz, Austria's first Holocaust memorial.

Interesting buildings in the centre include **Loos House**, now a Raiffeisen bank, across from the Hofburg. The Art Nouveau **Postsparkasse** (Savings Bank; Georg Coch Platz) and **Stadtbahn Pavilions** (train station pavilions; Karlsplatz) are all by architect Otto Wagner.

Stephansdom

The tall, latticework spire of St Stephen's Cathedral makes this 13th-century Gothic masterpiece one of the city's prime points of orientation, and the geometric pattern of its roof tiles is also striking.

Inside, you can take the lift up the north tower (€4) or the stairs up the higher south tower (€3) – but travellers are sometimes disappointed by the fairly ordinary views. Some of the internal organs of the Habsburgs reside in urns in the church's **Katakomben** (catacombs; admission €3).

Hofburg

The Hofburg (Imperial Palace) was the Habsburg's city-centre base. It has been added to many times since the 13th century, resulting in a mix of architectural styles. Wander around a bit and admire the exterior before venturing inside. While not as ornate as Schönbrunn's rooms, the **Kaiserappartements & 'Sissi' Museum** (Map pp44-5; ☎ 535 7575; Hofburg; U-Bahn Herrengasse; adult/concession €7.50/5.90; ✹ 9am-5pm) are worthwhile seeing because they relate the unusual life story of Empress Elisabeth (Sissi). You don't particularly have to be a fan to enjoy the experience: the empress' 19th-century gym and her obsession with her looks are attention-grabbing enough. Plus, the museum helps explain why Sissi's face still adorns shop windows in Vienna today. A ticket to the Kaiserappartements includes entry to the **Silberkammer** (silver chamber).

Among several other points of interest within the Hofburg you'll find the Burgkapelle (Royal Chapel) where the Vienna Boys' Choir performs, and the Spanish Riding School; see Entertainment, p51.

Kaisergruft

Also known as the Kapuzinergruft, the **Imperial Vault** (Map pp44-5; 01, Tegetthofstrasse/Neuer Markt; U-Bahn Stephansplatz; adult/concession €4/1.50) offers another weirdly compelling take on the cult of 'Sissi'. Stabbed by an Italian anarchist on the waterfront in Geneva in 1898, Empress Elisabeth was brought back here as her final resting place. Her coffin, still strewn with flowers by fans, lies alongside that of her husband, the penultimate emperor Franz Josef, and other Habsburgs. It's as bizarre as anything on TV's *Six Feet Under*.

Museums Quartier

Small guidebooks have been written on the popular **Museums Quartier** (Map pp44-5; ☎ 523 0431; 07, Museumsplatz 1; U-Bahn Museumsquartier), so only a taster can be given here. The highpoint is undoubtedly the **Leopold Museum** (☎ 52 570-0; adult/senior/student €9/7/5.50; ✹ 10am-7pm Wed-Mon, to 9pm Fri), which houses the world's largest collection of Egon Schiele paintings, with some minor Klimts and Kokoschas thrown in. However, in a complex that shows Vienna can be cutting-edge contemporary (an all-in-one ticket can be bought for €25) there is also:

Museum Moderner Kunst, Stiftung Ludwig Wien (Museum of Modern Art; ☎ 52 500; adult/concession €8/6.50; ✹ 10am-6pm Tue-Sun, to 9pm Thu)

Kunsthalle (City Art Gallery; ☎ 52 189-33; adult/concession Hall 1 €6.50/5, Hall 2 €5/3.50; ✹ 10am-7pm, to 10pm Thu)

Architekturzentrum Wien (Architecture Centre; ☎ 522 3115; adult/concession €6.50/5; ✹ 10am-7pm)

Zoom Kindermuseum (Children's Museum; ☎ 524 7908; adult/child €4.50/3.50; ✹ 9am-4pm Mon-Fri, 11am-5pm Sat & Sun)

Schloss Belvedere

This **palace** (Map pp40-1; ☎ 79 557-134; www.belvedere.com; combined admission adult/concession €7.50/5; ✹ 10am-6pm Tue-Sun, to 5pm Nov-Mar) consists of two main buildings. One is the **Oberes Belvedere & Österreichische Galerie** (Upper Belvedere & Austrian Gallery; 03, Prinz Eugen Strasse 37; adult/concession €6/3), where you'll find instantly recognisable works, such as Gustav Klimt's *The Kiss*, accompanied by other late-19th to early-20th-century Austrian works. The other is the **Unteres Belvedere** (Lower Belvedere; 03, Rennweg 6A; tram D to Schloss Belvedere; adult/concession €6/3), which contains a baroque museum. The buildings sit at opposite ends of a manicured garden.

Secession Building

This popular Art Nouveau 'temple of art' **building** (Map pp44-5; ☎ 587 5307; 01, Friedrichstrasse 12; U-Bahn Karlsplatz; adult/student €5.50/3; ✹ 10am-6pm Tue-Sun, to 8pm Thu) was built in 1898 and bears an intricately woven gilt dome that the Viennese say looks like a 'golden cabbage' – and it does. The highlight inside is the 34m-long *Beethoven Frieze* by Gustav Klimt.

KunstHausWien

Hey, where did the floor go? This fairytale **art gallery** (Map pp40-1; ☎ 712 0491-0; 03, Untere Weissgerberstrasse 13; tram N or O to Radetzkyplatz; adult/concession €9/7, temporary exhibitions €15/12, half-price Mon; ✹ 10am-7pm) certainly sweeps you off your feet with its uneven surfaces, irregular corners, coloured ceramics and mirrored tiles. Designed by Friedensreich Hundertwasser as a repository for his art, it's vaguely reminiscent of Anton Gaudi's buildings in Barcelona. Down the road there's a block of residential flats by Hundertwasser, on the corner of Löwengasse and Kegelgasse.

Albertina

Simply reading the highlights among its enormous rotating collection – several Michelangelos, some Raphaels and Albrecht Dürer's *Hare* – might give a misleading impression of this reopened **gallery** (Map pp44-5; ☎ 53 483-540; www.albertina.at; 01, Albertinaplatz 1A; U-Bahn Karlsplatz or Stephansplatz; adult/senior/student €9/7.50/6.50; ☺ 10am-6pm, to 9pm Wed). When we visited, the exhibitions ranged from Pop Art to Rembrandt and included two fascinating photography displays, making it feel quite modern. The curators do a superb job; so keep an eye out for what's on here.

In addition to the mostly temporary exhibitions, a series of Habsburg staterooms are always open.

Schloss Schönbrunn

The single attraction most readily associated with Vienna is the Habsburgs' **summer palace** (Map pp40-1; ☎ 81 113-0; 13, Schönbrunner Schlossstrasse 47; U-Bahn Schönbrunn; self-guided 22-/40-room tour €8/10.50, students €6.90/7.99; ☺ 8.30am-5pm Apr-Oct, to 4.30pm Nov-Mar). However, the sumptuous 1440-room palace is so vast, crowded and out of the way that you'll need to put aside at least half a day to see it, and it won't be to everyone's taste.

Inside this mini-Versailles you'll traipse through progressively more luxurious apartments. The most impressive, the **Audience Rooms**, are only included in the 40-room grand tour.

The grounds are more enjoyable. Highlights here include the formal gardens and fountains, the **maze** (adult/concession €2.10/1.45), the **Palmenhaus** (greenhouse; adult/concession €3.30/2.40) and the **Gloriette Monument** (adult/concession €2.10/1.45), whose roof offers a wonderful view over the palace grounds and beyond. There is even a **Tiergarten** (zoo; adult/concession €9/6).

Two combined tickets in the summer (€14/17.20) provide good value if you're interested in several features, and there are public, albeit expensive, swimming baths (see Watersports, p45).

Liechtenstein Museum

The collection of Duke Hans-Adam II of Liechtenstein is now on show at Vienna's new **museum** (Map pp40-1; ☎ 319 5767-0; 09, Fürstengasse 1; U-Bahn Friedensbrücke or Franz Josefs Bahnhof; adult/senior/student €10/8/5; ☺ 9am-8pm Wed-Mon), located in a refurbished, frescoed, baroque palace. There are classical paintings, including some by Rubens, and it's quite impressive.

Kunsthistorisches Museum

A huge range of art amassed by the Habsburgs is showcased at the **Museum of Fine Arts**

(Map pp44-5; ☎ 52 524-0; www.khm.at; 01, Maria Theresien-Platz; U-Bahn Volkstheater or Museumsquartier; adult/concession €10/7.50; ☺ 10am-6pm Tue-Sun, to 10pm Thu). Included are works by Rubens, van Dyck, Holbein and Caravaggio. Paintings by Peter Brueghel the Elder, including *Hunters in the Snow*, also feature. There is an entire wing of ornaments, clocks and glassware, and Greek, Roman and Egyptian antiquities.

Other Museums

Vienna has so many museums you might overlook the superlative **Haus der Musik** (House of Music; Map pp44-5; ☎ 51 648-51; www.haus-der-musik-wien.at; Seilerstätte 30; U-Bahn Karlsplatz or Stephansplatz; adult/concession €10/8.50; ☺ 10am-10pm). Try not to. Interactive electronic displays allow you to create different forms of music through movement and touch, and to connect with something a lot deeper than just your inner child.

The **Museum für Angewandte Kunst** (MAK; Map pp40-1; ☎ 71 136-0; 01, Stubenring 5; U-Bahn Stubentor or tram No 1 or 2; adult/concession permanent exhibition €2.20/1.10, temporary exhibition €6.60/3.30, free Sat; ☺ Tue-Sun) displays Art Deco objects from the Wiener Werkstatte and also 20th-century architectural models.

Some former homes of the great composers, including one of Mozart's, are open to the public; ask at the tourist office. There is also the fairly low-key **Sigmund Freud Museum** (☎ 319 1596; 09, Bergasse 19; U-Bahn Rossauer or Schottentor; admission €5; ☺ 9am-6pm Jul-Sep, to 5pm Oct-Jun).

Cemeteries

Beethoven, Schubert, Brahms and Schönberg have memorial tombs in the **Zentralfriedhof** (Central Cemetery; 11, Simmeringer Hauptstrasse 232-244), about 4km southeast of the centre. Mozart also has a monument here, but he is actually buried in the **St Marxer Friedhof** (Cemetery of St Mark; 03, Leberstrasse 6-8).

Naschmarkt

Saturday is the best day to visit this **market** (Map pp44-5; 06, Linke Wienzeile; U-Bahn Karlsplatz or Kettenbrückengasse; ☺ 6am-6pm Mon-Sat) when the usual food stalls and occasional tatty clothes stall are joined by a proper flea market. Curios and trinkets sit beside delicious produce from Austrian farms, plus there are cafés for an alfresco breakfast, lunch or refuelling stop.

AUSTRIA

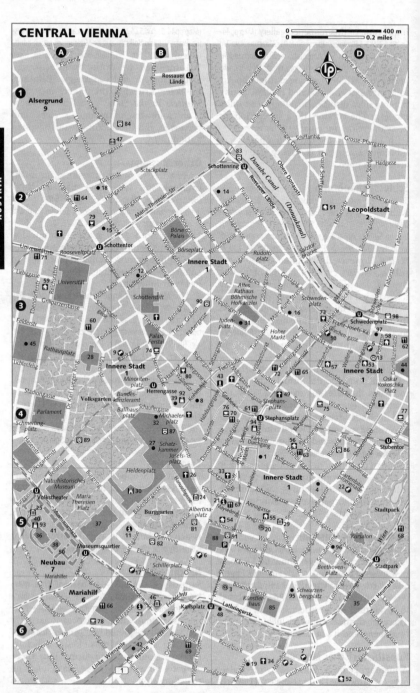

CENTRAL VIENNA

ACTIVITIES

Riesenrad

In theory, riding the **Riesenrad** (giant wheel; Map pp40-1; U-Bahn Praterstern; admission €7.50) in the Prater amusement park allows you to relive a classic film moment: when Orson Welles ad-libbed his immortal speech about peace, Switzerland and cuckoo clocks in *The Third Man*. In practice, you'll be too distracted by other passengers and by the views as the Ferris wheel languidly takes you 65m aloft. It's fun, but not quite the London Eye.

Watersports

You can swim, sailboard, boat and windsurf in the stretches of water known as the Old Danube, northeast of the Donaustadt island and the New Donau, which runs parallel to and just north of the Donaukanal (Danube Canal). There are stretches of river bank with unrestricted access. Alternatively, visit the **Schönbrunn baths** (Map pp40-1; U-Bahn Schönbrunn; full day/afternoon incl locker €9.50/6.50; May-Sep).

TOURS

The tourist office publishes a monthly list of guided walks, called *Wiener Spaziergänge*.

Vienna Walks (774 8901; www.viennawalks.tix.at) organises **Third Man tours** (adult/concession €16/13.50; 4pm Mon & Fri), including through the city's sewers, and a tour of **Jewish Vienna** (adult/concession €11/10; 1.30pm Mon). **Pedal Power** (Map pp44-5; 729 7234; 02, Ausstellungsstrasse 3) organises guided bicycle tours.

The operators listed in The Danube Valley section (p53) also conduct tours along the Danube in Vienna, or ask the tourist office for more options.

FESTIVALS & EVENTS

The **Vienna Festival**, from mid-May to mid-June, has a wide-ranging arts programme. Contact the **Wiener Festwochen** (Map pp44-5; 58 922-22; www.festwochen.or.at; Lehárgasse 11; U-Bahn Karlsplatz; Jan–mid-Jun) for details.

The extremely popular **Vienna Spring Marathon** is held April/May and Vienna's **Summer of Music** runs from mid-July to mid-September; contact **KlangBoden** (Map pp40-1; 40 00-8410; 01, Stadiongasse 9; U-Bahn Rathaus). Reduced student tickets go on sale at the venue 10 minutes before the performance.

Look out for free rock, jazz and folk concerts in the **Donauinselfest**, held at the end of June. The free open-air **Opera Film Festival** on Rathausplatz runs throughout July and August.

Each year Vienna's traditional **Christmas market** *(Christkindlmarkt)* takes place in front of the city hall between mid-November and 24 December. For other Vienna events, including its gala balls (January and February), see p83.

SLEEPING
Budget
Vienna is difficult for budget travellers, so take care to book ahead, particularly in summer. Tourist offices list private rooms and offer a useful *Camping* pamphlet. They will also book rooms (for €2.90 to €4.50 commission).

CAMPING
Camping Rodaun (☎ /fax 888 4154; 23 An der Au 2; site per adult/tent €5.50/4.50; ☺ Apr-Nov) There's a slightly more rural feel, and a lake, at this camp site on a distant edge of the Wienerwald. Take S1, 2 or 3 to Liesing, then bus No 253, 254 or 255.

Wien West (☎ 914 2314; www.wiencamping.at; Hüttelbergstrasse 80; site per adult/tent Sep-Jun €5/3.50, Jul-Aug €6/3.50, 2-/4-person cabin Apr-Oct €27/37; ☺ closed Feb) On the edges of the Wiener Wald (Vienna Woods), but just 20 minutes from town, this well-equipped site has modern facilities, and even a wireless Internet hot spot. Take U4 or the S-Bahn to Hütteldorf, then bus No 148 or 152.

HOSTELS
For those who prefer small, intimate hostels and don't mind being a little cramped, options include **Believe It or Not** (Map pp40-1; ☎ 526 4658; 07, Apt 14, Myrthengasse 10; dm €12.50) and **Panda Hostel** (Map pp40-1; ☎ 522 5353; 3rd fl, 07, Kaiserstrasse 77; dm with shared bathroom €12.50).

Hostel Ruthensteiner (Map pp40-1; ☎ 893 4202; www.hostelruthensteiner.com; 15, Robert Hamerling Gasse 24; dm with shared bathroom €11.50-14, d with shared bathroom from €38; 🖳) This is a free and easy place. With American college boys trying to chat up the English-speaking reception staff and the 'Outback' summer dorm (€11), there's a low-key party atmosphere. There are four- to 10-bed dorms, a nice courtyard garden and a small kitchenette.

Jugendherberge Myrthengasse (Map pp40-1; ☎ 523 6316; hostel@chello.at; 07, Myrthengasse 7; dm/d with shared bathroom €15/34; ☺ check-in 11am-4pm) Provides a similar level of accommodation to Myrthengasse, but with four- to six-bed dorms only and less of the frat house feel.

Westend City Hostel (Map pp40-1; ☎ 597 6729; www.westendhostel.at; 6, Fügergasse 3; dm €16.80-19, s/d €40.50/49; 🖳 ☒) The weirdest thing behind the pale purple façade isn't the knowledge that this was once a *bordello*. It's the particleboard-encased en-suite bathrooms in some of the mixed dorms; these bathrooms have extra mattresses on their mezzanine roof. Still, the place is well located and friendly.

Brigittenau (☎ 332 8294; jgh1200wien@chello.at; 20, Friedrich Engels Platz 24; dm from €15) This large Hostelling International (HI) hostel is popular with school groups. To get here take the U6 to Handelskai and then bus 11A one stop to Friedrich Engels Platz.

Hütteldorf-Hacking (☎ 877 0263; jgh@wigast.com; 13, Schlossberggasse 8; dm €16) Another large HI hostel in the suburbs; take the U4 to Hütteldorf and leave the station by the Habikgasse exit.

Wombat's (Map pp40-1; ☎ 897 2336; www.wombats.at; 15, Grangasse 6; dm/d incl breakfast €19.50/49; 🖳 ☒) Top-flight comfort and cleanliness combine with a packed party bar to make Wombat's hugely popular. The mixed-gender dorms have industrial-strength flooring, wooden bunk beds and modern bathrooms. It's where the cool kids stay – if they remember to do something as terminally uncool as book.

HOTELS & PENSIONS
Lauria (☎ 522 2555; www.lauria-vienna.at; 3rd fl, 07, Kaiserstrasse 77; d/tr/q from €60/75/92, with shared bathroom €46/63/80, apt €115, 1st night surcharge €5) A good place for young couples or small groups of travellers staying a couple of nights. You get your own homy room, your own keys and access to a kitchen.

Pension Lehrerhaus (Map pp40-1; ☎ 404 2358-100; www.lhv.at; 08, Lange Gasse 20; s/d with shower from €27/49, with shower & toilet from €41/70) Designed as digs for visiting teachers, this pension offers a variety of different rooms – some with shower only, some with shower and toilet. All are very modest, but also clean.

Pension Hargita (Map pp40-1; ☎ 526 1928; www.hargita.at; 07, Andreasgasse 1; s/d €50/62, with shared bathroom from €33/46) One of the cleanest and most charming budget pensions in Vienna, even if it doesn't serve breakfast and doesn't have a lift. Rooms have aqua blue or sunny yellow features and the friendly Hungarian owner keeps things spotless.

Pension Kraml (Map pp40-1; ☎ 587 8588; www .pension.kraml.at; 06, Brauergasse 5; d €68, s/d with shared bathroom from €28/48) Family-run and traditionally decorated, this is another reasonable choice. The breakfast here is generous.

Hotel Kugel (Map pp40-1; ☎ 523 3355; www.hotel kugel.at; 07, Siebensterngasse 43; s/d from €50/66, with shared bathroom €33/45, no credit cards; closed mid-Jan– mid-Feb; P) While the four-poster beds are appealing to some travellers, Kugel's simpler rooms – without four-posters or ensuite bathrooms – also offer great value.

STUDENT RESIDENCES

These are available to tourists from 1 July to 30 September during the summer holidays. Central booking is available through two agencies: **Academia** (☎ 40 176-55; www.academia -hotels.co.at), whose best of three options is **Gästehaus Pfeilgasse & Hotel Avis** (Map pp40-1; 08, Pfeilgasse 4-6; s/d/tr €46/62/81, with shared bathroom €23/40/54).

Among its accommodation options, **Albertina Hotels** (☎ 512 7493; www.albertina-hotels.at) has two new, central establishments: **Accordia** (Map pp44-5; 02, Grosse Schiffgasse 12; s/d €45/75) and **Haus Technik** (Map pp40-1; 04, Schäffergasse 2; s/d €45/75).

Mid-Range

Pension Wild (Map pp40-1; ☎ 406 5174; www.pen ion-wild.com; 08, Langegasse 10; s/d €65/90, with shared bathroom from €37/45) Most of the rooms at gay-friendly Pension Wild have been renovated in recent years, but some cheaper accommodation remains, with showers and toilets outside the rooms. All guests can prepare snacks in the small kitchenette on each floor.

Pension Dr Geissler (Map pp44-5; ☎ 533 2803; www.hotelpension.at; 01, Postgasse 14; s/d from €65/88, with shared bathroom from €39/50; P) Don't be deterred by the slow lift. Rooms are an eclectic mix of faux baroque and 1950s retro, and the airport bus to Schwedenplatz almost brings you to the door.

Hotel Post (Map pp44-5; ☎ 51 583-0; www.hotel -post-wien.at; 01, Fleischmarkt 24; s/d €75/115, with shared bathroom €44/70; P) The strongest point about this hotel is its location, right in the heart of things. With its parquet flooring in the rooms, long, carpeted hallways and decorative cast-iron lift, it feels like a grand, if somewhat faded, 19th-century boarding house.

Hotel Urania (Map pp40-1; ☎ 713 1711; www.hotel -urania.at; 03, Obere Weissgerberstrasse 7; s/d/tr/q from

€55/70/95/115) This hotel is tacky, but fun. Episodes of various Austrian TV series (eg *Inspector Rex)* have been filmed here, and as a guest you'll feel you're in one too. Not all of the eclectic rooms will be to everyone's taste (a knight's boudoir with animals skins on the floor, anyone?). Others, as in the Hundertwasser and Japanese rooms, are actually quite chic. The hotel is quiet, but central.

Pension Residenz (Map pp44-5; ☎ 406 4786-0; www.pension-residenz.co.at; 01, Ebendorferstrasse 10; s/d €60/90; P) This pension is a model of restraint. Traditionally decorated, with white, light-coloured fittings, it has a pleasant, if not overly personal feel. Its location near the university is also handy.

Hotel-Pension Zipser (Map pp40-1; ☎ 40 454-0; www.zipser.at; 08, Lange Gasse 49; s/d from €69/109; P) This place has elegant contemporary furnishings and some rooms have balconies facing a garden.

Kärtnerhof (Map pp44-5; ☎ 519 1923; www .kartnerhof.com; 01, Grashofgasse 4; s/d from €80/105; P) Tucked away in a cul-de-sac in the centre, Kärtnerhof is a terrific find, with quietly elegant rooms, many of them with bathtubs. It has a policy of not accepting tour groups.

Hotel zur Wiener Staatsoper (Map pp44-5; ☎ 513 1274; www.zurwienerstaatsoper.at; 01, Krugerstrasse 11; s/d from €85/126; P) Famous for its appealing façade, its rooms are small, but its prices great value for such a central location.

Top End

If anything, Vienna has a glut of four- and five-star hotels. Every major chain is here and even the city's most recognisable names now belong to one of these groups.

Kaiserin Elisabeth (Map pp44-5; ☎ 51 526-0; www.kaiserinelisabeth.at; 01, Weihburggasse 13; s/d from €75/200; 🍽 🗶 P) Try the central Kaiserin with its mix of chandeliers, red velvet, wooden floors, and rugs.

Dorint Biedermeier Wien (Map pp40-1; ☎ 71 671-0; www.dorint.com/wien; Landstrasser Hauptstrasse 28; s/d from €150/180; 🍽 🗶 P) The delightful Dorint is another sound choice. It's memorably located in a mews.

Also recommended:

Hotel Sacher (Map pp44-5; ☎ 51 456-0; www.sacher .com; 01, Philharmoniker Strasse 4; s/d from €215/315; 🍽 P)

Hotel im Palais Schwarzenberg (Map pp44-5; ☎ 798 4515; www.palais-schwarzenberg.com; 03, Schwarzenbergplatz 9; s/d from €255/330; 🍽 P)

AUSTRIA

EATING

The city's signature dish, Wiener schnitzel, is widely available and Vienna is renowned for its excellent pastries. You can buy groceries outside normal shopping hours at Franz Josefs Bahnhof and Westbahnhof.

Budget

Cheap student cafeterias include the **Technical University Mensa** (Map pp44-5; 04, Resselgasse 7-9; mains €3.20-4.80; 11am-2pm Mon-Fri) and **University Mensa** (7th floor, 01, Universitätsstrasse 7, mains €4.20-4.80; 11am-2pm Mon-Fri). Though the latter is closed in July and August, its adjoining **café** (8am-3pm Mon-Fri) remains open year-round.

Tunnel (Map pp40-1; 08, Florianigasse 39; mains €5-11, lunch specials €4) This student haunt has cheap, satisfying meals (and cheap, unsatisfying service).

Trzesniewski (Map pp44-5; ☎ 512 3291; 01, Dorotheergasse 1; sandwiches €0.80; Mon-Sat) You can really feel like one of the Austrian emperor's minions on the way home from the factory at this stand-up café. It sells tiny open sandwiches, usually featuring egg or fish of some description, which you wash down with a tiny *Pfiff* (125mL) beer.

Schnitzelwirt Schmidt (Map pp40-1; 07, Neubaugasse 52; schnitzel from €5.10; Mon-Sat) With fabulously grumpy waiters – who'll shout at you if you get in their way – and huge Wiener schnitzels, this buzzing place lets you experience the authentic Vienna of today.

OH Pot, OH Pot (Map pp44-5; ☎ 319 4259; 09, Währinger Strasse 22; hotpots lunch/dinner €6.20/8.20) Painted in warm Mediterranean colours, this sweet boho restaurant has decent ethnic stews (or hotpots) on the menu. Whether African Asian, central European or South American, they all come with either soup or salad. The best deal is from 3pm to 6pm, when prices drop to €4.90.

Ra'an (Map pp44-5; ☎ 319 3563; 09, Währinger Strasse 6-8; lunch €5.80, dinner €6.40-11.60) Ra'an looks like a cool noodle bar and has what listings magazine *Falter* has decreed the 'cutest cardboard lunch boxes in town'. The menu ranges from sushi and rice dishes at lunch to more elaborate Thai and Vietnamese in the evening.

Ra'mien (Map pp44-5; ☎ 585 4798; 06, Gumpendorfer Strasse 9; mains €6.80-15.50; Tue-Sun). Located across town, this is Ra'an's more straightforward noodle-bar sister.

Expedit (Map pp44-5; ☎ 512 3313-0; 01, cnr Wiesingerstrasse & Biberstrasse; mains €5.50-11; lunch & dinner Mon-Fri, dinner Sat) This is a cross between a bistro and an upmarket English gastro pub, with its bare floorboards and an open-plan dining space. The food is 'Ligurian' (ie Italian – mainly pasta and salads) and there are a few long communal tables.

Schweizerhaus (Map pp40-1; ☎ 319 3563; 02, Strasse des Ersten Mai 116; mains €5.40-17; Mon-Sat Mar-Oct) In the Prater park, this place serves up *Hintere Schweinsstelze* (roasted pork hocks) and the like to a rowdy crowd of international travellers, who wash it all down with huge mugs of beer.

Also recommended:

Pizza Bizi (Map pp44-5; 01, Rotenturmstrasse 4; pizza & pasta €5.40-5.80; lunch & dinner) Italian for those in a hurry.

Rosenberger Markt (Map pp44-5; 01, Maysedergasse 2; mains €6.20-7.80; lunch & dinner) Charmless but convenient motorway-style restaurant with a real value-for-money buffet.

Mid-Range & Top-End

Immervoll (Map pp44-5; ☎ 5135 2288; 01 Weihburggasse 17; mains €9-14.50) Run by a famous Austrian actor, Immervoll (literally, 'always full') attracts an arty crowd to its uncluttered small room. The menu changes daily, but the delicious food often has Hungarian and Italian influences.

Wrenkh (Map pp44-5; ☎ 533 1526; 01, Bauernmarkt 10; lunch €11) Quiche, mung beans and nut roast are *not* on the menu at this vegetarian restaurant. Instead, this is an upmarket affair, with sleek customers and lip-smacking Mediterranean, Austrian and Asian fare – from risotto to tofu.

Stomach (Map pp40-1; ☎ 310 2099; 09, Seegasse 26; mains €10-17; dinner Wed-Sat, lunch & dinner Sun) Many vegetarian dishes have dropped off the menu at Styrian-style Stomach, but some remain, and the quaint, ramshackle rooms and their courtyard remain a rustic outpost in the big city.

DO & CO (Map pp44-5; ☎ 535 3969; 01, Haas Haus, Stephansplatz 12; mains €14.50-23; lunch & dinner) The food and the views over Stephansplatz keep this elegant restaurant in business. Seasonal dishes like asparagus are highlighted, but it also serves Austrian classics, Uruguayan beef and Thai cuisine.

Indochine 21 (Map pp40-1; ☎ 513 7660; 01 Stubenring 18; mains €17-30; lunch & dinner) This is one of Vienna's hotter, newer restaurants, having been named the best Asian restaurant in the city in 2004. The food is upmarket French/Vietnamese, while red-lacquered umbrellas hang on the walls like circles and exotic potted plants evoke a vaguely colonial ambience.

Steirereck (Map pp44-5; ☎ 713 3168; 08, Heumarkt 3; mains €24-28; ☺ Mon-Fri) This long-standing gourmet temple was still getting ready to move to this Heumarkt address in the Stadtpark at the time of writing. So if you fancy some Austrian classics done to perfection, but the phone number no longer works, ask at the tourist office.

DRINKING
Bars
The area around Ruprechtsplatz, Seitenstettengasse and Rabensteig near Schwedenplatz is dubbed the **Bermudadreieck** (Bermuda Triangle; Map pp44-5) for the way drinkers disappear into its numerous pubs and clubs, but you'd have to seriously overindulge to become lost here. Venues are lively and inexpensive, but not particularly atmospheric.

Fischerbräu (☎ 369 5941; 19, Billrothstrasse 17) For more convivial, Austrian-style drinking, try the beers and the shady garden here.

7Sternbräu (Map pp40-1; ☎ 523 6157; 07, Siebensterngasse 17) A Styrian brewery with an interesting range that covers hemp beer to Prager Dunkel (dark Prague beer).

Centimeter (Map pp40-1; ☎ 524 3329; www.centimeter.at; 07, Stiftgasse 4) Look out for this chain which has rollicking establishments selling Austrian food and a wide range of beer (sold by the centimetre). There are other branches listed on the website.

Shebeen (Map pp40-1; ☎ 524 7900; 07, Lerchenfelder Strasse 45-47) This remains a popular evening spot for English-speaking travellers and expats alike. Major football matches are screened here.

Schultz (Map pp40-1; ☎ 522 9120; 07, Siebensterngasse 31) On the same street as 7Stern, this designer bar serves cocktails to a young, trendy but relaxed crowd.

Das Möbel (Map pp40-1; ☎ 524 9497; 07, Burggasse 10) Also near the Museums Quartier there's Das Möbel, which is remarkable for its furniture. This ranges from cube stools to a circular ping-pong table, various moulded lamps and decorations – copies of which are on sale there.

THE AUTHOR'S CHOICE
A bit like Goldilocks testing her porridge, we find some Viennese coffee houses too ornate and sterile, others too shabby and undistinguished. **Café Sperl** (Map pp44-5; ☎ 586 4158; 06, Gumpendorfer Strasse 11; ☺ closed Sun until 3pm & all day Sun Jul & Aug), however, is *just right*. With its scuffed, but original, 19th-century fittings and cast of slacker patrons playing chess and reading the newspapers, it's exactly how you want a coffee house to be. Under the high ceiling and old-fashioned lights, wooden panelling reaches up to meet mustard-coloured wallpaper, battered wooden legs hold up red-patterned chairs and a few billiard tables add a modern twist. We know it's had some horrible customers in the past, but even that can't ruin Sperl's charm.

Café Stein (Map pp44-5; ☎ 3197 2419; 09, Währinger Strasse 6-8) This trendy, student café/bar-cum-diner has been an institution on the scene for several years and if you're willing to pay a premium you can surf the Internet while enjoying a drink.

Schikanader (Map pp40-1; ☎ 585 5888; 04; Margaretenstrasse 22-4), in the foyer of a cinema, and **Die Wäscherei** (☎ 409 2375-11; 08, Albertgasse 49), which has lots of draught beers, are also cool places to drink. Further out from the centre, the U-Bahn arches near the Gürtel have long offered a good choice of bars such as **Rhiz** (Map pp40-1; ☎ 409 2505; Lechenfelder Gürtel 37-38), a mecca of Vienna's electronic music scene, and **Chelsea** (Map pp40-1; ☎ 407 9309; Lechenfelder Gürtel 29-31), which is more underground with frequent indie bands and DJs.

Coffee Houses
Vienna's famous *Kaffeehäuser* (coffee houses) are like economic forecasts; ask two people for a recommendation and you'll get four answers. Following are a couple of local favourites – a full-sized coffee costs roughly €3 to €3.50, but you can take as long as you like to drink it without being moved on.

Café Central (Map pp44-5; ☎ 533 3763; 01, Herrengasse 14; ☺ closed Sun) A lot more commercialised than when Herr Trotksy drank here, we dare say, but still with appealing vaulted ceilings, and palms.

Café Diglas (Map pp44-5; ☎ 512 5765; 01, Wollzeile 10) Striking good balance with ornate surroundings and a relaxed vibe.

Café Hawelka (Map pp44-5; ☎ 512 8230; 01, Dorotheergasse 6; ☽ closed Sun) Smoky, crowded, noisy, with nicotine-stained walls and arty regulars.

Café Prückel (Map pp44-5; ☎ 512 6115; 01, Stubenring 24) A 1950s-style café that's the epitome of shabby chic.

Heurigen (Wine Taverns)

Vienna's wine taverns or *Heurigen* are a good way to see another side of the city. Selling 'new' wine produced on the premises, they have a lively atmosphere, especially as the evening progresses. Outside tables and picnic benches are common. There's usually buffet food, and often strolling piano-accordian musicians entertaining with folk songs.

Because *Heurigen* tend to be clustered together, it's best just to head for the wine-growing suburbs to the north, south and west of the city and look for the green wreath or branch hanging over the door that identifies a *Heuriger*. Opening times are approximately 4pm to 11pm, and wine costs less than €2.50 a *Viertel* (250mL).

The *Heurigen* areas of Nussdorf and Heiligenstadt are near each other at the terminus of tram D, north of the city centre. In 1817 Beethoven lived in the **Beethoven-haus** (19, Pfarrplatz 3, Heiligenstadt). Down the road (bus No 38A from Heiligenstadt or tram No 38 from the Ring) is Grinzing, an area favoured by tour groups. There are several *Heurigen* in a row where Cobenzlgasse and Sandgasse meet, of which **Reinprecht** (☎ 320 1471; 19, Coblenzgasse 22) is the best. It's housed in a former monastery, with a larged paved courtyard and a lively, if somewhat touristy, atmosphere. Alternatively, catch bus No 38A east to the final stop at Kahlenberg and walk 15 minutes to **Sirbu** (☎ 320 5928; 19, Kahlenberger Strasse 210; ☽ Mon-Sat Apr-Oct), which has great views of the Danube.

If you don't have time to venture out into the suburbs, you can get an approximate taste of the *Heuriger* experience at **Esterházykeller** (Map pp44-5; ☎ 533 3482; Haarhof 1; ☽ from 11am, closed Sat & Sun evening).

ENTERTAINMENT

Check listings magazine *Falter* (€2.05) for weekly updates. The tourist office has cop-ies of *Vienna Scene* and produces monthly events listings.

Cinema & Theatre

The **Burgkino** (Map pp44-5; ☎ 587 8406; 01, Opernring 19) screens *The Third Man* every Friday evening and Sunday afternoon, if you want to revisit this classic movie while in Vienna. Otherwise, check local papers for listings. Seats cost €5.50 to €8 and are cheapest on Monday.

There are performances in English at the **English Theatre** (Map pp40-1; ☎ 402 8284; www .englishtheatre.at; 08, Josefsgasse 12) and the **International Theatre** (Map pp44-5; ☎ 319 6272; 09, Porzellangasse 8).

Classical Music

Performances at the **Staatsoper** (State Opera; Map pp44-5; ☎ 51 444-2960; 01, Opernring 2; seats €5.50-220, standing room €3.70) are lavish, formal affairs, where people dress up. The **Volksoper** (People's Opera; Map pp40-1; ☎ 514 44-3670; 09 Währinger Strasse 78; seats €17-75, standing €1.50-24) puts on more modern performances and the atmosphere is a little more relaxed.

The state ticket office, **Bundestheaterkassen** (Map pp44-5; ☎ 51 444-7880; www.bundestheater.at; 01, Goethegasse 1), sells tickets without commission for both. In the hut by the Stadtsoper, **Wien Ticket** (Map pp44-5; ☎ 58 885) also charges little or no commission for cash sales.

The cheapest deals are the standing-room tickets that go on sale at each venue an hour before the performance. However, you may need to queue three hours before that for major productions. An hour before the curtain goes up, unsold tickets also go on sale at cheap prices to students under 27 (from €3.70; home university ID plus international student card necessary).

The **Musikverein** (Map pp44-5; ☎ 505 1890; www.musikverein.at; 01, Bösendorferstrasse 12; seats €16-110, standing €5-7) is the opulent and acoustically perfect (unofficial) home of the Vienna Philharmonic Orchestra. You can buy standing tickets three weeks in advance at the box office to hear this world-class orchestra .

There are no performances in July and August. Ask at the tourist office for details of free concerts at the Rathaus or in churches.

Nightclubs

Flex (Map pp44-5; ☎ 533 7525; Donaukanal, via Augartenbrücke) is Vienna's leading club, having developed an international reputation and attracting top DJs (including Kruder & Dorfmeister occasionally). The fact that it's along a fairly urban-looking stretch of the Danube Canal doesn't stop people hanging out on the waterfront. It's open every night.

In the middle of the park of the same name, **Volksgarten** (Map pp44-5; ☎ 533 0518; 01, Burgring 1) is also very popular. There's modern dance and an atmospheric 1950s-style salon that was once a former *Walzer Dancing* place. Friday and Saturdays are the big nights, although it's open other evenings.

Other slightly more underground clubs to try include **Club Fluc** (Map pp40-1; ☎ 0669-1925 5637; 02, Praterstern, near the bicycle tunnel), which plays electro music daily. **Club U** (Map pp44-5; ☎ 505 9904; 04, Karlsplatz; ☺ Tue-Sun) is in the ornate Otto Wagner Stadtbahn Pavilions café. It's a bit like a squat party and plays indie/alternative music. If you're into jazz, don't miss **Porgy n Bess** (Map pp40-1; ☎ 512 8811; 01, Riemergasse 11).

Why Not? (Map pp44-5; ☎ 535 1158; 01, Tiefer Graben 22; ☺ Wed-Sun) is a popular gay and lesbian bar/disco, although Wedneday nights are men only. Gays and lesbians might also like to drop by the pink-and-purple **Rosa Lila Villa** (Map pp40-1; ☎ 586 8150; 06, Linke Wienziele 102). Besides being an information centre, it has a bar and restaurant.

Spanish Riding School

The famous Lipizzaner stallions strut their stuff in the **Spanish Riding School** (Map pp44-5; fax 535 0186; tickets@srs.at; seats €45-145, standing room €24-25) behind the Hofburg. Performances are sold out months in advance, so write to the Spanische Reitschule, Michaelerplatz 1, A-1010 Wien, or ask in the office about cancellations (unclaimed tickets are sold 45 minutes before performances); there's no phone. Travel agents usually charge commission on top of the listed prices.

You need to be pretty keen on horses to pay so much, although a few tricks, such as a stallion bounding along on its hind legs like a demented kangaroo, do stick in the mind. Same-day **tickets** (€11.50, or with entry to the Lippizaner Museum €14.50; ☺ 10am-noon Tue-Sat Feb-Jun & Sep-Dec) can be bought to watch the horses train. The best riders go first and queues disappear by 11am. Watching the weekly final **rehearsal** (€20; Fri & Sat) is also an option.

Vienna Boys' Choir

Never mind bands like Take That and Nsync; the Vienna Boys' Choir *(Wiener Sängerknaben)* is *the* original boy band. The original troupe was put together in 1498 and the latest bunch of cherubic angels in sailor suits still holds a fond place in Austrian hearts.

The choir performs weekly at the **Burgkapelle** (Music Chapel; Map pp44-5; ☎ 533 9927; hofmusikkapelle@asn-wien.ac.at; Hofburg, Rennweg 1; seats €5.50-30, standing free, tickets Fri & 8.15am Sun; ☺ performances 9.15am Sun, except Jul–mid-Sep). Concerts are routinely sold out and there's often a crush of fans to meet the choir afterwards. The group also performs regularly in the **Konzerthaus** (Map pp44-5; ☎ 242 002; 03, Lotheringerstrasse 20; 3.30pm Fri May, Jun, Sep & Oct).

SHOPPING

Österreiche Werkstätten (Map pp44-5; Kärntner Strasse 6) Good for Art Deco–type jewellery and household objects in the Viennese tradition. Other local specialities include lamps, handmade dolls, and wrought-iron and leather goods.

Café Demel (Map pp44-5; ☎ 535 1717-0; 01, Kohlmarkt 14; ☺ daily) Lavish Café Demel has the old-world atmosphere that makes a great coffee house, but it's usually too crowded. Instead, pop in to buy some fantastic cake, chocolates or biscuits here.

HAPPY SNAPS

Want to give your holiday photos extra pizzazz? Want to be able to put on a slide show back home that won't send friends and family to sleep? Well, as Vienna is the home of Lomo – inventor of the ActionSampler – it's a perfect place to rediscover your love of photography.

Of course, Lomo cameras – plastic compacts that, for example, put nine identical images in one frame or that capture a sequence of four actions in one picture – are a worldwide cult. Although originally a Russian brand, they are now designed in Vienna, which also hosts the Lomographic World Archive at www.lomography.com. The **Lomo Shop** (Map pp44-5; ☎ 521 890; MuseumsQuartier; U-Bahn Volkstheater; ☺ 10am-7pm), next to the Kunsthalle, is eminently browsable, as you can just admire the artistic photos on its walls.

Rave Up (Map pp40-1; ☎ 596 9650; 06, Hofmühlgasse 1) A good record shop to head to if you want to catch up with Vienna's electronic scene.

GETTING THERE & AWAY
Air
Regular scheduled flights link Vienna to Linz, Salzburg, Innsbruck, Klagenfurt and Graz. Check with **Austrian Airlines** (Map pp44-5; ☎ 17 89; 01, Kärntner Ring 18, Vienna). There are also daily nonstop flights to all major European destinations; see p86 for further details.

Boat
Between April and November, fast hydrofoils travel eastwards to Bratislava (one way/return €22/33.50, bike extra €6, daily Wednesday to Sunday June to September, 1½ hours) and Budapest (one way/return €75/99, bike extra €18, at least daily, 5½ hours). Bookings can be made through **DDSG Blue Danube** (Map pp44-5; ☎ 58 880-0; www.ddsg-blue-danube.at; 01, Friedrichstrasse 7) or **G Glaser** (Map pp40-1; ☎ 726 0820; www.members.aon.at/danube; 02, Handelskai 265).

Heading west, a series of boats ply the Danube between Krems and Passau (in Germany), with a handful of services originating in Vienna. Operators are listed on p53.

Bus
Bus operator **Eurolines** (www.eurolines.at) has two locations. Most buses leave from its terminal at **Südbahnhof** (Map pp40-1; ☎ 796 8552; 03, Arsenalstrasse; ☯ 7am-7pm), including those to Belgrade (one way/return €40/60, nine hours), Budapest (one way/return €25.20/39, 3½ hours), Ljubljana (one way/return €36/60, 15 hours 20 minutes), Warsaw (one way/return €34/62, 13½ hours) and Zagreb (one way/return €26/42, 4¾ hours).

However, services to Bratislava (one way/return €3.90/7.80, 1½ hours) leave from outside Eurolines' **city office** (Map pp40-1; ☎ 798 2900; 03, Erdbergstrasse 202; ☯ 7am-7pm).

Euroline's services to Prague depart from 01, Rathausplatz 5 (one way/return €20/34, five hours). Call ☎ 93 000-34305 for details.

Car & Motorcycle
The Gürtel is an outer ring road which joins up with the A22 on the north bank of the Danube and the A23 southeast of town. All the main road routes intersect with this system, including the A1 from Linz and Salzburg, and the A2 from Graz.

Train
International trains leave from Westbahnhof or Südbahnhof. Westbahnhof has trains to western and northern Europe and western Austria. Services to Salzburg leave roughly every hour; some go on to Munich and terminate in Paris (14½ hours total). To Zürich, there are two trains during the day (€77.70, nine hours) and one night train (same fare, plus charge for fold-down seat/couchette). Eight trains a day go to Budapest (€37.60, 3½ hours).

Südbahnhof has trains to Italy (eg Rome, via Venice and Florence), Slovakia, the Czech Republic, Hungary and Poland, and southern Austria. Five trains a day go to Bratislava (€15.40, 1½ hours) and four to Prague (€40.70, five hours), with two of those continuing to Berlin (10 hours in total).

Wien-Mitte Bahnhof handles local trains only and Franz Josefs Bahnhof has local and regional trains.

For train information, call ☎ 05-1717.

GETTING AROUND
To/From the Airport
It's 19km from the city centre to **Wien Schwechat airport** (☎ 70 07-0; www.viennaairport.com). The **City Airport Train** (☎ 25 250; www.cityairporttrain.com; one way €9) takes 15 minutes between Schwechat and Wien Mitte. The S-Bahn (S7) does the same journey (single €2.90, 25 minutes).

Buses (single €6) run every 20 or 30 minutes, 24 hours, from the airport. Services include one to Südtiroler Platz, Südbahnhof and Westbahnhof and another direct to Schwedenplatz in the centre.

Taxis cost about €32. **C&K Airport Service** (☎ 444 44) does the trip for a €22 fixed fare one way.

Bicycle
There's a system of **Vienna city bikes** (☎ 0810 500 500; www.citybikewein.at/; €2 deposit, 1st hr free, 2hr €2, 4hr €2/8, per hr thereafter €2). They are well-priced, but you need a Maestro debit card to be able to use the payment machines. Check the website for locations.

The rather steeply priced **Pedal Power** (☎ 729 7234; 02, Ausstellungsstrasse 3; rental per half/full day €17/27) is the city's dominant operator, but the tourist office should be able to point to others near your hostel or hotel. *Tips für Radfahrer* is available from the tourist office and shows circular bike tours.

Car & Motorcycle

Parking is difficult in the city centre and the Viennese are impatient drivers. Blue parking zones allow a maximum stop of 1½ or two hours from 9am to 8pm (to 7pm in the Innere Stadt) on weekdays.

Parking vouchers (€0.40 per 30 minutes) for these times can be purchased in *Tabak* shops and banks. The cheapest parking garage in the centre is at Museumsplatz.

Fiacres

Before hiring one of these horse-drawn carriages *(Fiakers)* by the Stephansdom for a ride around town, it's worth asking yourself whether these are pony traps or tourist traps. Sure, they're kind of cute, but at €65/95 for a 30-/60-minute ride…well, you do the maths.

Public Transport

Vienna has a unified public transport network, encompassing trains, trams, buses, the underground (U-Bahn) and suburban (S-Bahn) trains. Routes are outlined in the free tourist office map.

Before use, all advance-purchase tickets must be slotted into the validation machines at the entrance to U-Bahn stations or on trams and buses. Tickets are cheaper to buy from ticket machines in U-Bahn stations or from *Tabak* shops, where single tickets cost €1.50. On board, they cost €2. Singles are valid for an hour, and you may change lines on the same trip.

Daily passes *(Stunden-Netzkarte)* cost €4/5 (8am to 8pm/valid 24 hours from first use); a three-day pass costs €12 (valid 72 hours); and an eight-day multiple-user pass *(8-Tage-Karte)* costs €24 (validate the ticket once per day per person). Weekly tickets, (valid Monday to Sunday) cost €12.50.

Children under six always travel free; those under 16 travel free on Sunday, public holidays and during Vienna school holidays (photo ID necessary). Senior citizens should ask about discounts.

Ticket inspections are not very frequent, but fare dodgers pay an on-the-spot fine of €62. No excuses will be accepted. Austrian and European rail passes (see p1079) are valid on the S-Bahn only. Public transport finishes around midnight, but there's also a comprehensive night bus service, for which all rail tickets are valid.

Taxi

Taxis are metered for city journeys: €2 or €2.10 flag fall, plus €1.09 or €1.38 per kilometre – the higher rate is on Sunday and at night. There is a €2 surcharge (€2.10 at night) for phoning a radio taxi.

THE DANUBE VALLEY

Terraced vineyards, ruined castles and medieval towns line the most picturesque stretch of the Danube River, between Krems an der Donau and Melk. The best way to appreciate the river here is to take a cruise or cycle along its banks, following one of Austria's most famous bike routes.

Getting Around

Boats generally operate from early April to late October. For example, **DDSG Blue Danube** (Map pp44-5; ☎ 01-58 880-0; www.ddsg-blue-danube .at; 01, Friedrichstrasse 7, Vienna) has three departures daily (one daily in October) passing through the Wachau region. From Melk to Krems (1¾ hours, downstream) or from Krems to Melk (three hours, upstream) costs €15.80/20.50 one way/return; shorter journeys between Melk and Spitz cost €9.20/12.20 one way/return. **Brandner** (☎ 07433-259 021; www.brandner.at) offers the same trips at the same prices.

Ardagger (☎ 07479-64 64-0; dsa@pgv.at) connects Linz and Krems three times a week in each direction during summer. **Wurm & Köck** (☎ 070-783 607; www.donauschiffahrt.com; Untere Donaulände 1, Linz) has services once a day (Tuesday to Sunday, six hours) between Linz and Passau in Germany, which stop in the Wachau region.

G Glaser (☎ 01-726 0820; www.members.aon.at/dan ube; 02, Handelskai 265, Vienna) sails between Passau and Budapest, stopping at Krems and Melk.

Most operators carry bicycles free of charge along these routes.

You might not want to tackle the entire 305km **Danube Cycle Path**, which actually goes all the way from Vienna to Passau. However, the Wachau stretch is idyllic. For more information, ask the tourist offices in this section, or go to www.radtouren.at/ english.

The route by road is also scenic. Hwy 3 links Vienna and Linz and stays close to the north bank of the Danube much of the way.

AUSTRIA

KREMS AN DER DONAU
☎ 02732 / pop 23,000

Quaint as it is, Krems is unlikely to be more than a stopover on a boat or bike trip through the Danube Valley. There's riverside camping at **ÖAMTC Camping Krems** (☎ 84 455; Wiedengasse 7; site per person/car €4.50/3.65, per tent €2.20-4.50) and an HI **Jugendherberge** (☎ 83 452; Ringstrasse 77; dm €12.20, €2.20 surcharge for stays under 3 nights), both are which are open April to October. Otherwise try the atmospheric **Gästehaus Einzinger** (☎ 82 316; fax 82 316-6; Steiner Landstrasse 82, Krems-Stein; s/d €36/52), which has individually designed rooms around a leafy sunken courtyard (but rather precarious stairs).

The **tourist office** (☎ 82 676; www.tiscover.com /krems; Kloster Und, Undstrasse 6; ☺ 9am-6pm Mon-Fri, 10am-noon & 1-5pm Sat, 10am-noon & 1-4pm Sun Apr-Oct) can provide further accommodation details.

The boat station *(Schiffsstation)* is a 20-minute walk west from the train station along Donaulände. Between three and five buses leave daily from outside the train station to Melk (€8.20, one hour five minutes). Trains to Vienna (€10.50, one hour) arrive at Franz Josefs Bahnhof.

DÜRNSTEIN
☎ 02711 / pop 1000

Dürnstein, west by road or rail from Krems, is where English king Richard I (the Lionheart) was imprisoned in 1192. His unscheduled stopover on the way home from the Crusades came courtesy of Austrian archduke Leopold V, whom he had insulted. A trip today to the ruins of the **Künringerburg castle** hints that the kidnapped English monarch, at least potentially, had wonderful views of the Danube.

For more about Dürnstein, contact the **Rathaus** (☎ 219; www.duernstein.at; Hauptstrasse) or the makeshift **tourist office** (☎ 200; Nah & Frisch grocery store; ☺ Apr-Oct).

MELK
☎ 02752 / pop 6500

Featured in the epic medieval German poem *Nibelungenlied* and Umberto Eco's best-selling novel *The Name of the Rose*, Melk's impressive Benedictine monastery endures as a major Wachau landmark.

Orientation
The train station is 300m from the town centre. Walk straight ahead from the train station along Bahnhofstrasse, turning right into Abt Karl Strasse if you're going to the hostel or continuing ahead for the town. The quickest way to the central Rathausplatz is through the small Bahngasse path (to the right of the cow's-head mural at the bottom of the hill), rather than veering left into Hauptplatz.

Turn right from Bahngasse into Rathausplatz and right again at the end, following the signs to the tourist office.

Information
Post office (Wiener Strasse 85; ☺ 9am-7pm Mon-Fri, 9am-5pm Sat)
Tourist office (☎ 52 307-410; melk@smaragd.at; Babenbergerstrasse 1; ☺ 9am-noon & 2-6pm Mon-Fri, 10am-2pm Sat Apr-Jun & Sep-Oct, 9am-7pm Mon-Sat & 10am-2pm Sun Jul & Aug, closed Nov-Mar)

Sights & Activities
On a hill overlooking the town is the ornate golden abbey **Stift Melk** (☎ 555-232; www .stiftmelk.at; adult/senior/student under 27 €6.90/5/4.10, guided tours extra €1.60; ☺ 9am-6pm May-Sep, 9am-5pm Oct-Apr, guided tours only Nov-Mar). Once a noble abode, then home to monks since the 11th century, the current building was erected in the 18th century after a devastating fire. Consequently, it's an elaborate example of baroque architecture, most often lauded for its imposing marble hall and beautiful library, but just as unforgettable for the curved terrace connecting these two rooms. You can easily imagine past abbots pausing to take in the views of the Danube and feeling like lord of all they surveyed. (The film *The Name of the Rose* was shot elsewhere.) There's also a new **Abbey Museum** outlining the history of the building and the church in Austria generally.

Useful explanatory booklets (€3.50) for the whole building are available in various languages, or phone ahead if you want a tour in English, which works out cheaper.

Sleeping & Eating
Camping Melk (site per adult/tent/car €2.60/2.60/1.90; ☺ Mar-Oct) On the west bank of the canal that joins the Danube. Reception is in restaurant **Melker Fährhaus** (☎ 53 291; Kolomaniau 3; dishes from €5.75; ☺ Mar-Oct).

Jugendherberge (☎ 52 681; fax 54 257; Karl Strasse 42; dm under/over 19 years €12.20/15.70, surcharge for stays under 3 nights €2; ☺ Mar-Oct, check-in 5-9pm) This HI hostel is modern and comfy, although it often plays host to groups.

Gasthof Goldener Stern (☎ 52 214; fax 52 214-4; Sterngasse 17; s/d from €30/60, with shared bathroom €22/44) When the friendly owners renovated recently, they decided to keep some cheaper 'student' rooms for budget travellers. At the other end are the so-called 'romantic' rooms (€34 per person), all individually decorated. The place has a welcoming feel and two dogs.

Restaurant **Pasta e Pizza** (☎ 53 686; Jakob Prandtauerstrasse 4; pizza €6-8) is tucked away from the main tourist trail, while there is a **Spar supermarket** (Rathausplatz 9) for self-caterers.

Getting There & Away

Boats leave from the canal by Pionierstrasse, 400m behind the monastery. Trains to Vienna Westbahnhof (€12, 75 to 90 minutes) are direct or via St Pölten.

LINZ

☎ 070 / pop 208,000

Poor Linz. Essentially industrial by nature, it discovered years ago that its small, old-town centre couldn't compete with Vienna or Salzburg. Its biggest claims to 'fame' were being Adolf Hitler's favourite town and having a type of cake – Linzer torte – named after it. So the city decided to carve a niche for itself by building a world-beating cyber-centre, a stunning contemporary art gallery and appealing attractions for kids.

Orientation

Most of the city is on the south bank of the Danube. The main square (Hauptplatz) is reached from the train station on tram No 3. To walk here, turn right (northeast) out of the station forecourt, Bahnhofplatz, then continue straight ahead until you come to a park on the left. Turn left here into Landstrasse and continue for 10 minutes to get to Hauptplatz.

Information

Ars Electronica Center (☎ 72 720; www.aec.at; Hauptstrasse 2; Internet access free; ☺ 9am-5pm Wed & Thu, 9am-9pm Fri, 10am-6pm Sat & Sun)

Bignet (☎ 7968 2010; Graben 17; Internet per 30min €3.70; ☺ 10am-midnight)

Main post office (Bahnhofplatz 11-13; ☺ 7am-9pm Mon-Fri, 7am-6pm Sat, 7am-1pm Sun)

Tourist office (☎ 707 017-77; www.linz.at;

Hauptplatz 1; ☺ 8am-7pm Mon-Fri, 10am-7pm Sat & Sun May-Oct, 10am-6pm Nov-Apr) Has the Linz City Ticket (€20), which offers free public transport, sightseeing discounts and a free €10 meal.

Sights & Activities

Architecturally eye-catching and artistically impressive, the riverside **Lentos Kunstmuseum Linz** (☎ 7070 3600; www.lentos.at; Ernst Koref Promenade 1; adult/concession €6.50/4.50; ☺ 10am-6pm Wed-Mon, to 8pm Thu) is an important new addition to the Linz scene. It's built a little like an asymmetric tray table, with legs on either side. Behind its partially reflective glass façade lie works by Klimt, Schiele, Picasso, Kokoscha, Matisse, Haring, Warhol and more. Lit up at night, the building looks spectacular.

Across the Danube lies an older art and technology centre that will help you indulge your childhood superhero fantasies, without having to jump off the garage roof and graze your knee. At the **Ars Electronica Center** (☎ 72 72-0; www.aec.at; Hauptstrasse 2; adult/student €6/3; ☺ 9am-5pm Wed & Thu, 9am-9pm Fri, 10am-6pm Sat & Sun), you'll be given a virtual-reality headset, then strapped to the ceiling and sent 'flying' over Linz and into the future. If you like this, you'll also love the world's only public 'cave', a virtual environment where you can travel through space and time.

A ride on the **Pöstlingbergbahn** (funicular railway; ☎ 7801 7002; one way/return €2/3.20, children half-price; ☺ 5.20am-8pm Mon-Sat, 11.40am-8pm Sun) offers great views and is bound to keep kids of all ages happy. It looks like a quaint street trolley from a movie and climbs slowly to the ornate twin-spired church and **children's grotto railway** (☎ 3400 7506; www.linzag.at; adult/child €4/2; ☺ 10am-5pm, to 6pm May-Sep) atop the Pöst-lingberg hill. To reach the Pöstling-bergbahn take tram No 3 to Bergbahnof Urfahr .

If you still have time, head to the **Schlossmuseum** (castle museum; ☎ 774 419; Tummelplatz 10; adult/concession €4/2.20; ☺ 9am-6pm Tue-Fri, 10am-5pm Sat & Sun), which has one of Beethoven's pianos. Otherwise, explore the old city around the Hauptplatz and the street called Altstadt.

Festivals & Events

The **Ars Electronica Festival** (☎ 72 72-0; www .aec.at) in early September showcases cyber-art, computer music and other marriages of technology and art. This leads into the **Brucknerfest** (Bruckner Festival; ☎ 775 230; www .brucknerhaus.at; Brucknerhaus Kasse, Untere Donaulände, A-4010 Linz), which pays homage to native son Anton Bruckner with a month of classical music between mid-September and mid-October. For this, you should book early.

In July there's the **Pflasterspektakel street performers' festival**.

Sleeping

Decent, reasonably priced accommodation is scarce in Linz, so book ahead.

Pichlinger See (☎ 305 314; Wiener Bundesstrasse 937; per adult/tent & car €4/9; ☷ Apr-Oct) Some way out of town, 10km southeast, this lakeside camping site is particularly popular with caravan-owners.

Jugendgästehaus (☎ 664 434; fax 664 434-75; Stanglhofweg 3; dm/s/d €15.60/19.60/26) Modern and comfortable, even if it's a little way from the centre of town; take bus No 17, 19 or 27.

Jugendherberge (☎ 782 720; zentral@jutel.at; Kapuzinerstrasse 14; dm under/over 19 years €12/15; closed around Nov-Mar) Dorms are rather cramped. Each hostel closes its reception at intermittent times, so phone ahead.

Wilder Mann (☎ 656 078; wilder-mann@aon.at; Goethestrasse 14; s/d €35/55, with shared bathroom €28/48) Despite first impressions at this boarding house-style place, the rooms are reasonably comfy and the bathrooms clean. Try to avoid the top floor, where frosted-glass door panels let in hall light.

Goldener Anker (☎ /fax 771 088; Hofgasse 5; s/d from €42/70) The mid-priced rooms are quite comfortable and convenient.

Hotel Wolfinger (☎ 773 291-0; www.austria-classic -hotels.at/wolfinger; Hauptplatz 19; s/d €81/114, with shared bathroom from €42/64; ☒) This central hotel is a wonderful former cloister renovated in baroque style. It has a very limited number of cheaper rooms.

Eating

Etagen Biesel (Domgasse 8; mains €6.70-12) A lively, friendly place with homy Austrian lunches and dinners; post-it notes of thanks from previous customers line the walls.

Stiegelbräu zum Klosterhof (Landstrasse 30; mains €11-17.50) A huge beer garden and a fine gastronomic reputation. It seems popular for business lunches and tourist outings alike.

Café Traximayr (☎ 773 353; Promenadestrasse 16; ☷ closed Sun) An elegant coffee house, with only a few snooker tables breaking up the formal environment of white walls, marble, mirrors and chandeliers. Try the Linzer torte. This heavy, nutty-tasting sponge filled with strawberry jam isn't on the menu but it is in the cake trolley, so just ask.

Sky Loft Media Bar (Ars Electronica Center, Hauptstrasse 2; ☷ 9am-5pm Wed & Thu, 9-2am Fri & Sat) This glassed-in bar is a great place for a beer or cocktail overlooking the Danube and the Lentos Museum.

Mangolds (Hauptplatz 3; salads from €1.13 per 100g; ☷ closed Sun) offers self-serve veggie food, while **Gelbes Krokodil** (Dametzstrasse 30; mains €6-8; ☷ lunch & dinner Mon-Fri, dinner Sat & Sun) also attracts midday diners.

Getting There & Around

Low-cost **Ryanair** (www.ryanair.com) flies in daily from London Stansted to **Linz airport** (www .flughafen-linz.at), providing a shuttle bus (€2.20, 20 minutes) to the main train station.

Linz is halfway between Salzburg and Vienna on the main road and rail routes. Trains to Salzburg (€17.70) and Vienna (€23.50) take between 1¼ and two hours. Trains leave approximately every hour.

City transport tickets are bought before you board: €0.70 per journey or €3 for a day card. Some of the bus services stop early in the evening. The suburban **Lilo train station** (☎ 654 376; Coulinstrasse 30) has bike rental (€7 a day).

THE SOUTH

Austria's two main southern states, Styria (Steiermark) and Carinthia (Kärnten), retain elements of Italian, Slovenian and Hungarian culture – unsurprising as they have historical connections with each of those countries.

GRAZ

☎ 0316 / pop 225,000

You have to love a city whose emblematic clock tower has its hands on back-to-front. Graz's jaunty medieval *Uhrturm* perches on the hill above town, with a long hand marking the hours and a shorter minute hand. The mix-up rightly suggests that time isn't of the essence here.

But alongside its laid-back provincial and university charm, the Styrian capital increasingly has a funky side. That's best demonstrated by its striking, blob-like Kunsthaus (arts centre) and artificial river island, both built during the city's reign as European Capital of Culture in 2003.

Orientation

Austria's second-largest city is dominated by its *Schlossberg*, or castle hill, above the town centre. The River Mur runs in a north-south path in front (west) of the hill, separating the centre from the main train station (Hauptbahnhof). Tram Nos 3, 6 and 14 run from the station to the central Hauptplatz. Several streets radiate from this square, including café-lined Sporgasse and the main pedestrian thoroughfare, Herrengasse, which leads to Jakominiplatz, a major transport hub.

Information

INTERNET ACCESS

Sit 'n Surf (Hans Sachs Gasse; per 30min €2.60; ☺ 8am-midnight)
Speednet-café (Train station; per 10/30min €1.30/3.30; ☺ 8am-10pm Mon-Sat, 10am-10pm Sun)

MONEY

Die Steiermärkische (☎ 8033 2909; Hauptplatz 16; ☺ 5am-midnight) Has an ATM.

POST

Main post office (Neutorgasse 46; ☺ 7.30am-8pm Mon-Fri, 8am-noon Sat)

TOURIST INFORMATION

Graz Tourismus (☎ 80 75-0; www.graztourismus.at; Herrengasse 16; ☺ 9am-6pm Mon-Sat, 10am-6pm Sun)
Tourist information counter (☎ 80 75-21; Train station; ☺ 8.30am-1pm & 2-5.30pm Mon-Wed & Fri, to 6.30pm Thu)

Sights & Activities

Most visitors head first for the **Schlossberg** to get an overview of the city and explore the remnants of its fortress. These include the medieval **clock tower**, which looks to all intents and purposes as if it's wearing a wooden hat, plus a **bell tower**, **bastion** and **garrison museum** (☎ 827 348; adult/concession €1.45/0.65; ☺ 10am-5pm Tue-Sun Apr-Oct). There are three main ways to ascend: the glass **Schlossberglift**, hewn through the hill; the **Schlossbergbahn** funicular railway (both requiring a Zone 1 transport ticket, €1.60) and the 260 steps near the lift (free).

From this vantage point, you can't help but notice the bubble-shaped **Kunsthaus Graz** (☎ 8017 9200; www.kunsthausgraz.at; Lendkai 1; adult/senior/student €6/4.50/2.50; ☺ 10am-6pm Tue, Wed & Fri-Sun, to 8pm Thu), an acrylic-coated creation by UK architects Colin Fournier and Peter Cook. Locals like to call it a 'friendly alien'. It's also been compared to a mutant bladder, a liver and a whale, but there's general agreement that it's one of Europe's leading modern buildings. Whatever the temporary exhibitions – and these are often very good – it's the structure that's the star.

AUSTRIA

THE ARNIE EFFECT

Given that another of the world's top tourist destinations has a similar name, it's unsurprising that Austria has suffered from an identity crisis, with jokey T-shirts proclaiming, 'No Kangaroos in Austria'. Now the Alpine nation believes help has arrived in the bulky shape of a Styrian body-builder-turned-movie-star-turned-politician.

Arnold Schwarzenegger, locals hope optimistically, will help even the most geographically ignorant American schoolchild locate their tiny country on a map.

When the Terminator became the Californian 'Gubernator' in late 2003, even left-wing Austrians put aside their reservations for the evening. Bar-goers in Graz, just a few miles from Schwarzenegger's boyhood home of Thal, erupted in cheers.

'Mozart is no longer the world's most famous Austrian', Dieter Hardt-Stremayr of the Graz tourist office told AFP.

While Californians have since been welcomed in Austria like long-lost members of the family, there's little Arnie memorabilia for them, or anyone else, to see. Two Russian artists have been trying to erect a huge Terminator statue in Graz's Stadtpark. However, they've met with resistance because, ultimately, Arnie is a controversial figure in Austria. Even he suggested that the millions to be spent on a sculpture would be better going to charity. Currently, all that marks his presence in Graz is the Arnold Schwarzenegger Sports Stadium and its paltry (at least when we visited) Schwarzenegger 'museum'. The stadium is to the southwest of the city centre; take tram No 4.

AUSTRIA

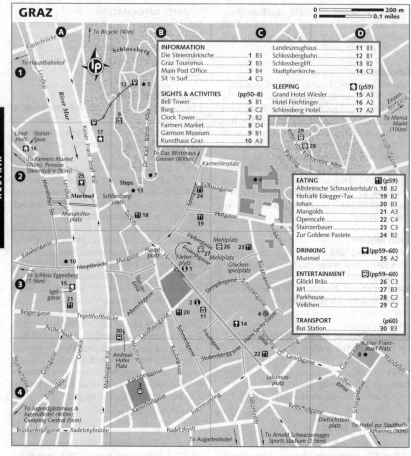

GRAZ

0 ———— 200 m
0 ———— 0.1 miles

INFORMATION	
Die Steiermärkische..............1	B3
Graz Tourismus....................2	B3
Main Post Office..................3	B4
Sit 'n Surf........................4	C3

SIGHTS & ACTIVITIES	(pp50–8)
Bell Tower.........................5	B1
Burg................................6	C2
Clock Tower........................7	B2
Farmers Market....................8	D4
Garrison Museum...................9	B1
Kunsthaus Graz....................10	A3

Landeszeughaus....................11	B3
Schlossbergbahn...................12	B1
Schlossberglift...................13	B2
Stadtpfarrkirche..................14	C3

SLEEPING	(p59)
Grand Hotel Wiesler...............15	A3
Hotel Feichtinger.................16	A2
Schlossberg Hotel.................17	A2

EATING	(p59)
Altsteirische Schmankerlstub'n..18	B2
Hofcafé Edegger-Tax...............19	B2
Iohan.............................20	B3
Mangolds..........................21	A3
Operncafé.........................22	C4
Stainzerbauer.....................23	C3
Zur Goldene Pastete...............24	B2

DRINKING	(pp59–60)
Murinsel..........................25	A2

ENTERTAINMENT	(pp59–60)
Glöckl Bräu.......................26	C3
M1................................27	B3
Parkhouse.........................28	C2
Veilchen..........................29	C2

TRANSPORT	(p60)
Bus Station.......................30	B3

Likewise, the **Murinsel** (⏱24hr), an artificial island in the River Mur that's connected to both banks, north of the Kunsthaus and Hauptbrücke (main bridge). Designed in the form of an open seashell, the glass, concrete and steel construction, by New York artist Vito Acconic, is an oft-photographed fixture. The outer swirl of the 'shell' is an amphitheatre; the inner part, a trendy café/bar (p59) in aqua blue.

Graz's two morning **farmers markets** (Kaiser-Franz-Josef Platz & Lendplatz; ⏱Mon-Sat) offer an enticing array of produce such as apples, fresh fruit juices, pussy willow and schnapps – depending on the season.

After visiting one of these, check out the old town centre, which has several highlights.

One is the **Burg** (Hofgasse) complex of the Styrian parliament; to the left of the door marked 'Stiege III' there's a double-winding staircase as good as any perspective-defying drawing by MC Escher. The **Stadtpfarrkirche** (Herrengasse 23) is (in)famous for the stained-glass window behind the altar that depicts Hitler and Mussolini looking on as Jesus is tortured.

Military buffs will appreciate the extensive **Landeszeughaus** (armoury; ☎ 8017 9810; Herrengasse 16; adult/senior/student €4.50/3/1.50, guided tour in English extra €1.50; ⏱9am-5pm Tue-Sun Mar-Oct, 10am-3pm Tue-Sun Nov & Dec), while fans of the baroque style will enjoy the opulent **Schloss Eggenberg** (☎ 583 264-0; Eggenberger Allee 90; tram No 1; adult €5.45, senior or student €4.30; ⏱Tue-Sun Apr-Oct), outside town.

The tourist office organises **guided walks** of Graz (from €7.50), daily in summer and on Saturday in winter.

Sleeping

Camping Central (☎ 378 5102; fax 697 824; Martinhofstrasse 3; camp site for 1/2 people €13/20; ☺ Apr-Nov) Beside the tree-shaded, trimmed lawn here there's a huge outdoor swimming pool (with a separate nudists' area). About 6km southwest of the centre, the site also has excellent shower and laundry facilities.

Jugendgästehaus & Jugendhotel (☎ 708 350; jgh.graz@jgh.at; Idlhofgasse 74; dm/d in hostel €17/40, d/f in hotel €47/80, 1st night surcharge €3; ☺ reception 7am-10pm Mon-Fri, 7-10am & 5-10pm Sat & Sun; P). Ten minutes on foot from the train station, this was named the best Austrian hostel in 2003. It's ultra-modern and comfortable, with en suite rooms, spacious reception/restaurant areas in cheery Mediterranean colours, and full wheelchair access. Individual travellers are accommodated in the hostel wing, groups and families in the hotel section.

Pension Steierstub'n (☎ 716 855; www.pension-graz.at; Lendplatz 8; s/d/tr from €37/66/99; P) Unquestionably our favourite budget hotel in Graz. The young, friendly owners put fresh flowers and fruit in the simple, modern rooms – and place local pumpkinseeds, rather than chocolates, on your pillow. The relaxed Styrian restaurant below serves tasty food and there's free loan of bicycles.

Das Wirtshaus Greiner (☎ 685 090; www.wirtshaus-greiner.at; Grabenstrasse 64; s/d from €46/72; P) Immaculate, albeit slightly more starchy, with its white walls and dark polished floorboards. The restaurant/reception closes at weekends, so phone ahead then.

Hotel zur Stadthalle Johannes (☎ 837 766; www.stadthalle.co.at; Münzgrabenstrasse 48 & 87; s/d from €46/68) Rooms at this older, well-kept hotel have wooden floors and beds. The breakfast room goes for a more Italianate style.

Hotel Feichtinger (☎ 724 100; www.hotel-feichtinger.at; Lendplatz 1A; s/d from €49/92; ✗) Graz's newest hotel isn't especially full of character, but its rooms offer a high level of comfort for the price. It is on the outer boundary of Graz's tiny and largely inoffensive red-light strip, but when it's this close to town few will mind.

Graz has three particularly notable top-end hotels. The best is the Art Deco **Grand Hotel Wiesler** (☎ 70 66-0; www.hotelwiesler.com; Grieskai 4; s/d from €170/230; P ✗), but the modern designer-style **Augartenhotel** (☎ 20 800-0; www.augartenhotel.at; Schönaugasse 53; s/d from €120/160) and old-world **Schlossberg Hotel** (☎ 80 70-0; www.schlossberg-hotel.at; Kaiser Franz Josef Kai 30; s/d from €140/170; P ✗) also score big points.

Eating

With green, leafy salads dressed in delicious pumpkinseed oil, lots of polenta, fish specialities and *Pfand'l* (pan-grilled) dishes, Styrian cuisine feels lighter and healthier than most regional Austrian cooking.

Altsteirische Schmankerlstub'n (☎ 823 211; Sackstrasse 10; mains €7.50-16.50) Hidden in a passageway off Sackstrasse, this rustic restaurant serves Styrian staples such as *Bauernschmaus* (roast pork with blood sausage, sauerkraut and dumplings), *Ochsenfetzen* (beef strips with sour cream and roast potatoes) and *Vogerlsalat* (green salad) with roast potatoes, egg, tomatoes and pumpkinseed oil.

Iohan (☎ 821 312; Landhausgasse 1; mains from €18; ☺ dinner Tue-Sat) Where locals come for a treat. In the former cold-storage room of the city hall, it has formal white tablecloths, draped white canvas chairs and a cool, somewhat more relaxed bar. The select menu might include saddle of lamb with black lentils or veal with polenta and mushrooms.

Its sculptured wood façade makes **Hofcafé Edegger-Tax** (Hofgasse 8; ☺ Mon-Fri & Sat morning) the most tempting of the city's coffee houses from outside, but the interior of the **Operncafé** (Opernring 22; ☺ daily) is more atmospheric.

Other places to sample the local cuisine include the pinky-red **Zur Goldene Pastete** (☎ 823 416; Sporrgasse 28; mains €9-12), which is Graz's oldest inn, and the elegant **Stainzerbauer** (☎ 821 066; Bürgergasse 4; mains €13.80-23.50; ☺ closed Sun), where white linen-and-lace tablecloths and curtains decorate a dark-timbered room. At the latter, try the fillet of pork in chanterelle sauce with polenta slices and pumpkin. (There's an English menu.)

Cheap eats are available all around the university, especially at the **Mensa Markt** (Schubertstrasse 2-4; menus €3.70-4.30). For an ultra-healthy and reasonably cheap vegetarian buffet, head to **Mangolds** (Griesgasse 11; salad from €1.05 per 100g; ☺ 11am-8pm Mon-Fri, to 4pm Sat).

Drinking & Entertainment

Murinsel (☎ 818 669; ☺ café/bar 9am-11pm Sun-Wed, to 2am Thu-Sat) You'll never again drink anywhere quite like the Murinsel, so at least start the evening in this shimmering, fluorescent-lit platform in the middle of the river. There are DJs some evenings.

Parkhouse (☎ 827 434; Stadtpark 2) For a less self-conscious vibe, join the crowd at this atmospheric and friendly place in the city park.

Veilchen (☎ 8277 3416; Stadtpark 1) Near the Parkhouse is this new art gallery and community centre that usually has DJs every Saturday.

Graz, like Vienna, has a 'bar zone' known as the Bermudadreieck. It's located between Sporgasse, Färbergasse and Stempfergasse, where you'll find venues ranging from the humble **Glöckl Bräu** (☎ 814 781; Glockenspielplatz 2-3) to the 3rd-floor **M1** (☎ 811 233; Färbergasse 1), favoured by the beautiful people. There are other clusters of hip bars at the top of Sporgasse and behind the Kunsthaus.

Getting There & Away

Ryanair (www.ryanair.com) flies daily from London Stansted to **Graz airport** (☎ 29 020; www .flughafen-graz.at). Direct Intercity (IC) trains to Vienna's Südbahnhof depart every two hours (€26.90, 2¾ hours). Trains depart every two hours to Salzburg (€36.50, 4¼ hours), either direct or changing at Bischofshofen. Two daily, direct trains depart for Ljubljana (€34.30, four hours), and every hour or two to Budapest (€55.20, 6½ hours) via Szentgotthard and Szombathely. Trains to Klagenfurt (€27.70, three hours) go via Bruck an der Mur, roughly every two hours. The A2 autobahn from Vienna to Klagenfurt passes a few kilometres south of the city.

Getting Around

Public transport tickets cover trams, buses, the Schlossbergbahn and the Schlossberglift. Tickets cost €1.60 each. The 24-hour/weekly passes cost €3.20/7.50. Bus Nos 600, 630 and 631 connect the airport with the train station, Hauptplatz or Jakominiplatz (€1.60); the same journey by taxi costs about €15.

Bicycle (☎ 821 357-0; Körösistrasse 5) can rent you a set of two wheels (from €7.50/42 a day/week).

Around Graz

The **stud farm** (adult/senior/student €10/8/5; ☼ Easter-end Oct) that produces the Lipizzaner stallions that perform in Vienna is 40km west of Graz

at Piber. Get directions from the Graz tourist office or take its English tour on Saturday at 2pm (adult/child €24/9). It's also possible to make a day trip from Graz to **Bärnbach**, where there's a remarkable parish church created by Hundertwasser and other artists.

KLAGENFURT

☎ 0463 / pop 87,000

Klagenfurt's charms lie not so much in the city itself – which is pretty dull, really – as in its location near the Wörthersee (lake) and the surrounding 'Austrian Riviera'. The capital of Carinthia is known for another reason, too: it was the seat of power of regional governor Jörg Haider, one of Austria's most controversial politicians in recent years.

Orientation

The heart of the city is Neuer Platz, which is 1km north of the main train station. Walk straight down Bahnhofstrasse and turn left into Paradiesergasse to get there, or take bus No 40, 41 or 42 to Heiligengeistplatz, just around the corner from Neuer Platz.

Information

Gates Cafebar (Waagplatz 7; Internet access per 10min €1; ☼ 9-1am Mon-Fri, 7pm-1am Sat & Sun)

Main post office (Dr Hermann Gasse 4; ☼ 7.30am-6pm Mon-Fri, 8-11am Sat)

Tourist office (☎ 537-2223; www.info.klagenfurt.at; Rathaus, Neuer Platz; ☼ 8am-8pm Mon-Fri, 10am-5pm Sat & Sun May-Sep, 8am-6.30pm Mon-Fri, 10am-3pm Sat & Sun Oct-Apr)

Sights & Activities

The **Wörthersee**, 4km west of the centre, is one of the region's warmer lakes, thanks to subterranean thermal springs. In winter it's used as an ice-skating rink. In summer you can swim or go boating. Steamers embark on circular tours; get details from **STW** (☎ 21 155; schifffahrt@stw.at). The **cycle path** around the lake is one of Austria's top 10. Ask the tourist office or check www.austria-tourism.at for details.

Also near the lake, Europa Park has various attractions, including the theme park **Minimundus** (☎ 211 94-0; Villacher Strasse 241; adult €10, senior & student €8.50/4.50; ☼ Apr-Oct), which displays more than 150 models of famous international buildings on a 1:25 scale.

The Neuer Platz is dominated by the town emblem, the **Dragon Fountain**. At the western end of the pedestrianised Alter Platz is the 16th-century **Landhaus**, with a **Hall of Arms** (Wappensaal; adult/student €2/1; ☺ Sat & Sun Apr-Sep). Paintings of 655 coats of arms cover the walls, while a trompe l'oeil creates the illusion of a balcony.

Sleeping
Camping Strandbad (☎ 21 169; fax 21 169-93; adult €7, tent & car €4) Near the lake in Europa Park, Camping Strandbad is comfortable, with its own grocery store and mini-golf, but it gets very packed with Austrian and German families in summer.

Jugendherberge (☎ 230 020; jgh.klagenfurt@oejhv.or.at; Neckheimgasse 6; dm €17.50, dm as d €42; ☺ reception 7am-11am & 5-10pm; ℗ 🖳) Modern and clean, this HI hostel is located near the university and Europa Park. Take Bus No 12 to get there.

Hotel Geyer (☎ 57 886; www.hotelgeyer.com; Priesterhausgasse; s/d €55/95; ℗) Though hotels in town are fairly pricey, this is the one everyone always recommends (including us). It has compact but modern rooms, helpful staff and serves a generous breakfast buffet.

Eating
Zum Augustin (☎ 513 992; Pfarrhofgasse 2; mains €6.20-17.10) A smoky brewery, popular with the after-work crowd. It serves a decent range of regional food.

The **University Mensa** (Universitätsstrasse 90; mains from €4.20; ☺ 11am-2.30pm Mon-Fri) is by Europa Park, while back in the centre, the stalls in the **Benediktinerplatz market** serve hot meals for only about €4.

Getting There & Around
Ryanair (www.ryanair.com) flies from London daily, and runs a shuttle bus to the centre. Trains to Graz (€27.70, five hours) go via Bruck an der Mur and depart roughly every two hours. Trains to western Austria, Italy and Germany go via Villach, 40 minutes away.

Bus drivers sell single tickets (€1.50), while a strip of 10 costs €12 from ticket machines. Daily/weekly passes cost €3.30/13. For the Europa Park vicinity, take bus No 10, 11, 12, 20, 21 or 22 from Heiligengeistplatz in the centre. To the airport, take bus No 42 or a taxi (about €16). Bikes can be hired from **Zweirad Impulse** (☎ 516 310).

SALZBURG
☎ 0662 / pop 145,000
The joke 'if it's baroque, don't fix it' would make a perfect motto for Salzburg; the picturesque old town nestled below steep hills looks much as it did when Mozart was born here. Ornate 17th-century buildings still line the narrow, cobbled streets, while attractive manicured gardens surround the baroque Schloss Mirabell.

By night, the medieval Hohensalzburg fortress hovers in an arc of lights above the city. By day, the warren of courtyards, plazas, fountains and churches below is fully revealed.

The year 2006 marks the 250th anniversary of Mozart's birth. However, even then the great composer will be sharing the stage with *The Sound of Music*, as visitors still tour the movie's locations in and around Salzburg, Austria's charming capital of kitsch.

ORIENTATION
The pedestrianised old town is on the south bank of the River Salzach, tightly wedged between the river and Mönchsberg behind it. Many sightseeing attractions and the fashionable shopping street of Getreidegasse are located here. On the north bank is Mozart's Wohnhaus and Schloss Mirabell, as well as the new town centre, with most of the cheaper hotels. Bus Nos 1, 6, 51 and 55 will take you from the train station to the centre. To walk, turn left out of the station into Rainerstrasse and follow it (taking the second, not the first tunnel under the railway) to Mirabellplatz.

INFORMATION
Internet Access
Prices are €1.50 to €1.80 for 10 minutes.
Bignet (☎ 841 470; Judengasse 5-7; ☺ 9am-11pm, to midnight in summer)
Cybar (☎ 844 822; Mozartplatz 5; ☺ 9am-10pm)
Piterfun (Ferdinand-Porsche-Strasse 7; ☺ 10am-10pm)

Laundry
Bubble Point Waschsalon (☎ 471 1484; Karl Wurmb Strasse 2; ☺ 7am-11pm)

Medical Services
St Johanns-Spital (☎ 44 82-0; Müllner Hauptstrasse 48)

AUSTRIA

AUSTRIA

SALZBURG

0 — 300 m
0 — 0.2 miles

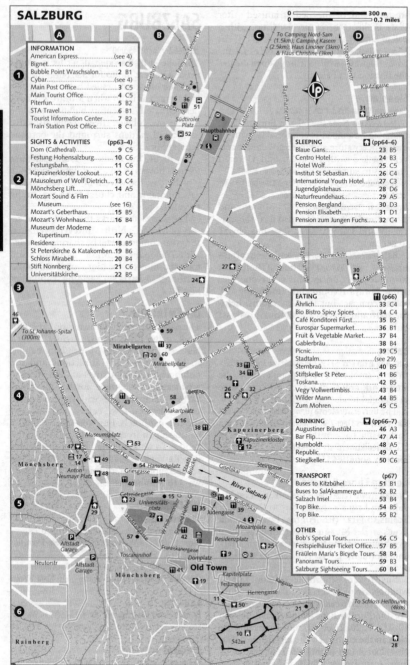

To Camping Nord-Sam
(1.5km); Camping Kasern
(2.5km); Haus Lindner (3km)
& Haus Christine (3km)

INFORMATION
American Express.................(see 4)
Bignet..1 C5
Bubble Point Waschsalon........2 B1
Cybar.................................(see 4)
Main Post Office..........................3 B5
Main Tourist Office.....................4 C5
Piterfun...5 B2
STA Travel......................................6 B1
Tourist Information Center........7 B2
Train Station Post Office............8 C1

SIGHTS & ACTIVITIES (pp63–4)
Dom (Cathedral)..........................9 C5
Festung Hohensalzburg............10 C6
Festungsbahn.............................11 C6
Kapuzinerkloster Lookout.......12 C4
Mausoleum of Wolf Dietrich...13 C4
Mönchsberg Lift........................14 A5
Mozart Sound & Film
Museum...................................(see 16)
Mozart's Geburtshaus..............15 B5
Mozart's Wohnhaus..................16 B4
Museum der Moderne
Rupertinum............................17 A5
Residenz......................................18 B5
St Peterskirche & Katakomben.19 B6
Schloss Mirabell........................20 B4
Stift Nonnberg...........................21 C6
Universitätskirche......................22 B5

SLEEPING ▢ (pp64–6)
Blaue Gans..................................23 B5
Centro Hotel...............................24 B3
Hotel Wolf...................................25 C5
Institut St Sebastian..................26 C4
International Youth Hotel..........27 C3
Jugendgästehaus.......................28 D6
Naturfreundehaus......................29 A5
Pension Bergland.......................30 D3
Pension Elisabeth......................31 D1
Pension zum Jungen Fuchs......32 C4

EATING ▯ (p66)
Ährlich...33 C4
Bio Bistro Spicy Spices.............34 C4
Café Konditorei Fürst................35 B5
Eurospar Supermarket..............36 B1
Fruit & Vegetable Market.........37 B4
Gablerbräu..................................38 B4
Picnic...39 C5
Stadtalm...................................(see 29)
Sternbräu....................................40 B5
Stiftskeller St Peter....................41 B6
Toskana.......................................42 B5
Vegy Vollwertimbiss.................43 B4
Wilder Mann...............................44 B5
Zum Mohren...............................45 C5

DRINKING ▢ (pp66–7)
Augustiner Bräustübl................46 A3
Bar Flip..47 A4
Humboldt....................................48 A5
Republic.......................................49 A5
Stieglkeller..................................50 C6

TRANSPORT (p67)
Buses to Kitzbühel.....................51 B1
Buses to SalÄkammergut..........52 B2
Salzach Insel...............................53 B4
Top Bike......................................54 B5
Top Bike......................................55 B2

OTHER
Bob's Special Tours....................56 C5
Festspielhäuser Ticket Office....57 B5
Fräulein Maria's Bicycle Tours..58 B4
Panorama Tours.........................59 B3
Salzburg Sightseeing Tours......60 B4

Money

At the airport, money can be exchanged between 8am and 8pm, plus there's an ATM. There are plenty of exchange offices in the centre, but beware of high commission rates.

Currency-exchange counter (Main train station; ✆ 8.30am-7pm Mon-Fri, 8.30am-2.30pm Sat, ATM 6am-10pm)

Post

Main post office (Residenzplatz 9; ✆ 7am-7pm Mon-Fri, 8-10am Sat)
Train station post office (✆ 7am-8.30pm Mon-Fri, 8am-2pm Sat, 1-6pm Sun)

Tourist information

Tourist offices and hotels sell the Salzburg Card (€21/28/34 for 24/48/72 hours), which provides free museum entry and public transport, and offers various reductions. Students get a 10% discount. The tourist office's commission for hotel reservations is €2.20, or €4 for three or more people.

Main tourist office (info ✆ 88 987-330, hotel reservations ✆ 88 987-314; www.salzburg.info; Mozartplatz 5; ✆ 9am-6pm May-Jun & Sep-Oct, 9am-7pm Dec, Jul & Aug, 9am-6pm Mon-Sat Nov & Jan-Apr)
Tourist information counter (Platform 2A, main train station; ✆ 9.15am-8pm) Opening hours vary.

Travel Agencies

American Express (✆ 80 80; Mozartplatz 5; ✆ 9am-5.30pm Mon-Fri, to noon Sat)
STA Travel (✆ 458 733; Fanny-von-Lehnert Strasse 1; ✆ Mon-Fri)

SIGHTS & ACTIVITIES

A Unesco World Heritage site, Salzburg's old town centre is equally entrancing whether viewed from ground level or from the hills above.

Residenzplatz, with its horse fountain and views of the Festung Hohensalzburg, is a good starting point for a wander. Head south to the **Dom** (cathedral), with its three bronze doors symbolising faith, hope and charity. From here, head west along Franziskanergasse, and turn left into a courtyard for **St Peterskirche**, an abbey dating from AD 847. Among lovingly tended graves in the abbey's grounds you'll find the entrance to the **Katakomben** (catacombs; adult/student €1/0.70; ✆ 10.30am-5pm summer, to 3.30pm winter). The western end of Franziskanergasse opens out into

Max Reinhardt Platz, where you'll see the back of Fisher von Erlach's **Universitätskirche** (Universitätsplatz), an outstanding example of baroque architecture. The **Stift Nonnberg** (Nonnberg Abbey), where *The Sound of Music* first encounters Maria, is back in the other direction, to the east of the Festung Hohensalzburg.

Another way to appreciate Salzburg's beauty is from on high. You get great views from the Festung Hohensalzburg (below), but you can also walk between the new Museum der Moderne and the Festspielhäuser (Festival Halls, p64). Take the Mönchsberg lift (€1.30/2.60 one way/return) from Anton Neumayr Platz or the stairs from Toscaninihof, behind the Festival Halls. Alternatively, follow the stairs up from Linzer Gasse 14 to the lookout at **Kapuzinerkloster** (Capuchin Monastery).

Festung Hohensalzburg

Towering above Salzburg is its **fortress** (✆ 842 430-11; www.salzburg-burgen.at; Mönchsberg 34; adult/concession for grounds only €3.60/3, for interior & audio guide €7.20/6; ✆ 9am-6pm 15 Mar-14 Jun, 9am-7pm 15 Jun-14 Sep, 9am-5pm 15 Sep-14 Mar). Built in 1077, the castle was home to the many archbishop-princes (who ruled Salzburg from 798). Inside are the impressively ornate staterooms, torture chambers and two museums.

It takes 15 minutes to walk up the hill to the fortress, or you can catch the funicular **Festungsbahn** (✆ 849 750; Festungsgasse 4; adult/concession one way incl admission to fortress grounds €5.60/5; ✆ 9am-9pm May-Sep, to 5pm Oct-Apr).

Schloss Mirabell

The formal gardens of **Schloss Mirabell** (✆ dawn-dusk; parts of the garden are off-limits in winter), with their tulips, crocuses and Greek statues, are the main attraction at this palace which was built by the archbishop-prince Wolf Dietrich for his mistress in 1606. From their western end (looking east toward the fortress) is one of Salzburg's most attractive vistas. Having featured in *The Sound of Music*, the gardens are now popular with wedding parties. 'Musical Spring' concerts (among others) are held in the palace, and there are sometimes open-air performances in the garden.

Museums

Although Mozart is now a major tourist drawcard, the man himself found Salzburg stifling and couldn't wait to leave. Consequently, Mozart's **Geburtshaus** (birthplace; ☎ 844 313; Getreidegasse 9; adult/concession €5.50/4.50; ☺ 9am-6pm Sep-Jun, to 7pm Jul & Aug, last entry 30min before closing) and his **Wohnhaus** (residence; ☎ 874 227-40; Makartplatz 8; adult/concession €5.50/4.50; ☺ 9am-6pm Sep-Jun, to 7pm Jul & Aug, last entry 30min before closing) cover only his early years as a prodigy and young adult, until he left town in 1780 at 24 years of age. A combined ticket to both houses is €9 (students and seniors €7). The Wohnhaus is more extensive, and houses the **Mozart Sound and Film Museum** (admission free).

In the **Residenz** (☎ 80 42-2690; www.salzburg-burgen.at; Residenzplatz 1; adult/student €7.30/5.50; ☺ 10am-5pm, gallery closed Wed Oct-Mar) you can visit the archbishops' baroque staterooms and a gallery housing good 16th- and 17th-century Dutch and Flemish paintings.

The **Museum der Moderne Rupertinum** (☎ 8042 2541; www.museumdermoderne.at; Mönchsberg; prices vary; ☺ 10am-6pm Tue-Sun, to 9pm Wed) adds a contemporary touch to historic Salzburg. Ask the tourist office about other museums.

Mausoleum of Wolf Dietrich
In the **graveyard** (Linzer Gasse; ☺ 9am-7pm Apr-Oct, 9am-4pm Nov-Mar) of the 16th-century St Sebastian's Church sits Wolf Dietrich's not-so-humble **memorial** to himself. Both Mozart's father and his widow are buried in the graveyard.

TOURS
Sound of Music Tours
Although these are the tours that interest the greatest number of visitors, how much fun you have depends on whether your fellow passengers enter into the kitsch, tongue-in-cheek attitude necessary. If you can, try to get together your own little posse. Otherwise, hope to find yourself among manic Julie Andrews impersonators flouncing in the fields, screeching 'the hills are alive', or some such thing.

Tours take three to four hours and mostly spend most time in neighbouring Salzkammergut, rather than Salzburg itself. Operators include:

Bob's Special Tours (☎ 849 5110; Rudolfskai 38; adult/concession €35/31; ☺ 9am & 2pm, 10am only in winter)
Fraülein Maria's Bicycle Tours (☎ 0646-342 6297; Makartplatz; adult €16; ☺ 9.30am mid-May–Sep) At the entrance to Mirabellgarten, behind Hotel Bristol.

Panorama Tours (☎ 874 029; Mirabellplatz; adult/child €33/17; ☺ 9.30am & 2pm)
Salzburg Sightseeing Tours (☎ 881 616; Mirabellplatz; adult/child €33/17; ☺ 9.30am & 2pm)

River Tours
Boats operated by **Salzburg Schiffahrt** (☎ 825 769-12) cruise along the Salzach (adult/child €11/7, 40 to 50 minutes) leaving half-hourly to hourly from 10am to 6pm May to September. Others go to Schloss Hellbrunn (adult/child €14/10), departing at 12.45pm September to June, 9.30am and 12.45pm July to August. The company also has atmospheric tours by night in late July and August.

Ships leave from the Salzach Insel, on the city side of the Makart bridge.

Other Tours
One-hour walking tours (€8) of the old city leave from the main tourist office. A pony-and-trap (*Fiaker*) ride for up to four passengers costs €33 for 20 to 25 minutes.

FESTIVALS & EVENTS
Austria's most renowned classical music festival, the **Salzburg Festival** (www.salzburgfestival.at), attracts international stars from late July to the end of August. Book on the website before January. Alternatively, ask about cancellations during the festival at **Festspielhäuser ticket office** (☎ 80 45; Herbert von Karajan Platz 11; ☺ 9.30am-6.30pm during the festival, 9.30am-3pm for the few weeks before).

In 2006 Salzburg is planning to celebrate the **250th anniversary of Mozart's birth** with performances of all of his 22 operas. The smaller of the two Festival Halls will be totally refurbished.

SLEEPING
Ask for the tourist office's hotel brochure, which gives prices for hotels, pensions, hostels and camping grounds. Accommodation is at a premium during festivals.

Budget
CAMPING
Just north of the A1 Nord exit is **Camping Kasern** (☎ /fax 450 576; campingkasern@aon.at; Carl Zuckmayer Strasse 4; site per adult/car/tent €4.50/3/3; ☺ Apr-Oct), while **Camping Nord-Sam** (☎ 660 494; www.camping-nord-sam.com; Samstrasse 22A; adult/car & tent €5.50/8; ☺ Easter & May-Sep) is slightly closer to town.

HOSTELS

Naturfreundehaus (☎ /fax 841 729; Mönchsberg 19; dm €13.50; 🕑 mid-Apr–mid-Oct) The rooms are little more than glorified cupboards, but the hostel is atop the Mönchsberg hill and you forget the cramped conditions when you wake up to such amazing views. There is a 1am curfew. To get here, take the Mönchsberg lift (€2.60 return) from Anton Neumayr Platz or the stairs from Toscaninihof, behind the Festival Halls. There's also a café called Stadtalm (p66).

International Youth Hotel (YoHo; ☎ 879 649; www .yoho.at; Paracelsusstrasse 9; dm with shared bathroom from €15, s/d/tr with shared bathroom & 1x10min shower per day €27/40/54, prices decrease slightly after 1st night; 🕑 all day; P) If you're after a bar with cheap beer, friendly staff and regular events, including daily screenings of *The Sound of Music*, this sociable hostel is for you. It charges separately for just about every extra – eg an additional 10 minutes in the shower (€0.50), so try to arrive with freshly washed hair! At least the women's showers on the 3rd floor are new. Phone reservations are accepted only one day in advance for its fairly spartan rooms, although you can book ahead on the Internet. Lockers cost €0.50 to €1, breakfast is €1 and there's a €5 deposit for sheets.

Jugendgästehaus (☎ 842 670-0; jgh.salzburg@jgh .at; Josef Preis Allee 18; dm from €18, d with shared bathroom from €13.90, d €36, 1st night surcharge €2.50; 🕑 check-in from 11am, access to rooms from 1pm; P) Lots of Austrians and families stay at this comfy HI hostel. However, many overseas travellers check in, too. The eight-bed dorms without private facilities feel a bit like boarding school, but the en suite four-bed dorms and twins on the floors above could belong to a nice budget hotel. Services include free lockers, a bar and meals (€6). Discounted *Sound of Music* tours (€29) are available for anybody who shows up by 8.45am or 1.30pm.

Institut St Sebastian (☎ 871 386; www.st-sebastian -salzburg.at; Linzer Gasse 41; dm/s/d €17/33/54, s/d with shared bathroom €29/48) Minutes from the city bridge, through the gate marked 'Feuerwache Bruderhof', on Linzer Gasse, Institut St Sebastian is closer to the action than any other Salzburg hostel-style accommodation. In fact, when the church bells ring next door, you'll find this student abode is too close to the action. Once again, dorms are ordinary, while singles and doubles are pleasant. There's a roof terrace and kitchen.

HOTELS & PENSIONS

Pension Elisabeth (☎ 871 664; Vogelweiderstrasse 52; s/d from €44/66, with shared bathroom from €35/42; P) A small, friendly budget hotel; bright rooms come with white duvets, coloured upholstered chairs and wooden floors. The pension is near the Breitenfelderstrasse stop of bus No 15, which heads for town every 15 minutes. In July and August, there's a whopping 20% premium for single-night stays.

Pension zum Jungen Fuchs (☎ 875 496; Linzer Gasse 54; s/d/tr €25.50/33.50/44) Centrally located and a solid, if unremarkable, budget choice. Its cramped stairwell opens out into reasonably sized rooms with wooden floorboards.

PRIVATE ROOMS

The tourist office's list of private rooms and apartments doesn't stretch to the Kasern area, but this area, up the hill from the Salzburg-Maria Plain main-line train station (warning – not to be confused with the Maria-Plain station on the local train network), has the best bargains.

Haus Lindner (☎ 456681; info@haus-lindner.at; Panoramaweg 5; d/tr €30/45) The largest and one of the most popular private-room options, with comfortable rooms and a homy atmosphere. Breakfast is provided, but there are kitchen facilities, too.

Haus Christine (☎ 456 773; Panoramaweg 3; s/d/tr €15/30/45) This is a neighbour to Haus Lindner and another good option among the forest of *Zimmer frei* (rooms vacant) signs.

Mid-Range & Top End
HOTELS & PENSIONS

Pension Bergland (☎ 872 318; www.berglandhotel.at; Rupertgasse 15; s/d/tr/f €56/86/102/120; P ✕) Austrian rustic meets '70s retro in the folksy rooms of this friendly, family-run pension, about a 15-minute walk from the old town.

Hotel Wolf (☎ 843 453-0; www.hotelwolf.com; Kaigasse 7; s/d from €68/98) With its neat living room set off from the main entrance hall, this family-owned hotel immediately feels like a real home. Austrian country-style bedrooms have been reconstructed in this 500-year-old abode, which has none of the mustiness of most buildings its age.

Centro Hotel (☎ 882 221; www.centro-hotel.com; Auerspergstrasse 24; s/d €68/104; P ✕) Veering slightly towards the minimalist, the well-proportioned rooms here have wooden furniture offset with touches of green; many

AUSTRIA

come with their own balcony. The hotel is especially popular with Italian tourists and sometimes caters to groups.

Blaue Gans (☎ 842 491-0; www.blauegans.at; Getreidegasse 41-43; s/d from €115/165) One of Salzburg's oldest inns converted into a trendy 'art hotel', this hotel combines modern luxury with its historic setting.

EATING
Budget
If you wish to eat cheaply in Salzburg, it's worth following the Austrian tradition of making lunch your main meal, because some cheaper restaurants open only during daylight hours on weekdays.

Bio Bistro Spicy Spices (☎ 870 712; Wolf-Dietrich-Strasse 1; mains €5.50) Serves 'holistic' Indian meals and salads.

Picnic (Judengasse 15; meals €4.90-9.50; ☽ closed Tue Oct-Apr) A charming grotto lined with vintage advertising signs and plastic flowers, Picnic is great for sandwiches and pizzas. Our experience of the gratins, however, would suggest giving them a miss.

Wilder Mann (mains €5.20-12; ☽ Mon-Fri) Traditional Austrian food in a friendly, bustling environment, in the passageway off Getreidegasse 20. Tables, both inside and out, are often so packed it's almost impossible not to get chatting with fellow diners.

Stadtalm (☎ 841 729; Mönchsberg 19C; mains €5.50-9.90; ☽ 10am-5pm Tue-Sun Apr-Oct) The meals are standard Germanic fare – wurst, Wiener schnitzel and *Züricher Geschnetzeltes* (veal in cream sauce). You won't care, though, with such fantastic views.

Café Konditorei Fürst (Alter Markt) Salzburg's coffee houses are all pretty touristy, but Café Konditorei Fürst boasts that its *Mozartkugeln* chocolates – wrapped in blue and silver paper instead of the usual red and gold – are the originals.

Reasonably priced, delicious meals can also be found at Humboldt (p67). Food is also served at Republic (p67).

Among the restaurants that open only during the day are the university mensa **Toskana** (Sigmund Haffner Gasse 11; mains €3.50-4.20; ☽ 8.30am-5pm Mon-Thu, 8.30am-3pm Fri) and wholefood veggie outlet **Vegy Vollwertimbiss** (Schwarzstrasse 21; salads from €3.20, lunch menu €7.20; ☽ 11am-5pm Mon-Fri).

Salzburg has no shortage of markets, with a **fruit and vegetable market** (Mirabellplatz) on Thursday morning, and market stalls and fast-food stands on Universitätsplatz and Kapitelplatz. There's a **Eurospar supermarket** (☽ Mon-Sat) opposite the train station.

Mid-Range & Top End
Gablerbräu (☎ 88 965; Linzer Gasse 9; mains €7.80-10.80) Low-key and pleasant. Home-made pasta and lip-smacking Styrian specialities are served in four atmospheric rooms, with a stained-glass arch, tiled oven and other rustic features.

Ährlich (☎ 871 275-60; Wolf-Dietrich-Strasse 7; mains €10.80-16.30; ☽ dinner Tue-Sat, lunch Jul & Aug, closed Feb & Mar) If you've had enough of wurst and *Tafelspitz*, this organic restaurant provides relief, with a brief, seasonal menu of international veggie and meat mains. It does sometimes have a bit of a weird health-farm vibe, but the food is tasty.

Zum Mohren (☎ 484 2387; Judengasse 9; mains €7.90-15.60; ☽ Mon-Sat) A cellar restaurant, offering traditional food in a cosy environment. Dishes include roast pork, Hungarian goulash and Tirolian calf's liver with bacon.

Be prepared to play the tourist if you visit the much-advertised Austrian specialists **Sternbräu** (☎ 826 617; btwn Getreidegasse 36 & Griesgasse 23; mains €6.40-14.90) or **Stiftskeller St Peter** (☎ 841 268-34; St Peter Bezirk I/4; mains €12.50-20). The latter is the less tacky of these two huge dining complexes, and its baroque main salon is worth a peek, even if you don't stay for the food.

DRINKING
Salzburg's most famous stretch of bars, clubs and discos remains Rudolfskai, but it is largely patronised by teenagers. Those who've already hit their 20s (or beyond) will probably prefer the scene around Anton Neumayr Platz, where things keep going until 4am on weekends.

Augustiner Bräustübl (☎ 431 246; Augustinergasse 4-6; ☽ 3-11pm Mon-Fri, 2.30-11pm Sat & Sun) It's Oktoberfest all year round at this cavernous place. Well, perhaps it's not *quite* so boisterous, but this hill-side complex of beer halls and gardens is not to be missed. The local monks' brew – served in litre or half-litre ceramic mugs – keeps the huge crowd of up to 2800 humming.

Stieglkeller (Festungsgasse 10; ☽ 10am-10pm Apr-Oct) A slightly smaller beer hall, below the fortress and with a terrace overlooking the town.

Bar Flip (☎ 843 643; Gstättengasse 17) A dark, low-ceilinged student bar serving cocktails and cheap beer.

Humboldt (☎ 843 171; Gstättengasse 4-6) Slightly more upmarket, with jellybean dispensers, a video projection of the Mirabellgarten on one wall and a pair of traditional antelope's horns…painted purple.

Republic (☎ 841 613; Anton Neumayr Platz 2) A hip, American bar/brasserie, which is liable to have MTV DJs in for its regular club nights.

GETTING THERE & AWAY
Air
The **airport** (☎ 85 80-0; www.salzburg-airport.at) handles regular scheduled flights to Amsterdam, Brussels, Frankfurt, London, Paris and Zurich, and charter flights to the Mediterranean. Contact **Austrian Airlines** (☎ 854 511-0) or go online to no-frills **Ryanair** (www.ryanair .com), which has two flights a day (three on Saturday) from London.

Bus
Services to the Salzkammergut region leave from just to the left of the main train-station exit. Destinations include Bad Ischl (€7.60, 1¾ hours), Mondsee (€4.60, 50 minutes) and St Wolfgang (€6.90, 1½ hours).

Buses to Kitzbühel (€12.40, 2¼ hours, at least three daily) go via Lofer; they depart from Südtiroler Platz, across from the train station post office.

There are timetable boards at each departure point and a bus information office in the train station. Alternatively, call ☎ 46 60-333 for information.

Car & Motorcycle
Three autobahns converge on Salzburg and form a loop round the city: the A1 from Linz, Vienna and the east; the A8/E52 from Munich and the west; and the A10/E55 from Villach and the south. Heading south to Carinthia on the A10, there are two tunnels through the mountains; the combined toll is €10 (€7 for motorcycles).

Train
Fast trains leave for Vienna (€36.50, 3¼ hours) via Linz every hour. The express service to Klagenfurt (€27.70, three hours) goes via Villach. The quickest way to Innsbruck (€29.50, two hours) is by the 'corridor'

train through Germany via Kufstein; trains depart at least every two hours. There are trains every hour or so to Munich (€25.80, two hours), and hourly trains to Salzburg (€7.40) via St Gilgen.

GETTING AROUND
To/From the Airport
Salzburg airport is 4km west of the city centre. Bus No 2 goes there from the main train station (€1.70). A taxi costs about €12.50.

Bus
Bus drivers sell single bus tickets for €1.70. Other tickets must be bought from the automatic machines at major stops, *Tabak* shops or tourist offices. Day passes are €3.20 and weeklies cost €10. Children aged six to 15 years travel half-price; those under six travel free.

Car & Motorcycle
Most of the old town is pedestrianised. The nearest central parking area is the Altstadt Garage under the Mönchsberg. Attended car parks cost €1.40 to €2.40 an hour. On streets with automatic ticket machines (blue zones), a three-hour maximum applies (€0.50 for 30 minutes) during specified times – usually shopping hours.

Other Transport
Bicycle hire is available from **Top Bike** (☎ 0676 476 7259; www.topbike.at), which has two locations: the Intertreff Café just outside the train station and on the main city bridge.

For a taxi, call ☎ 81 11 or go to the ranks at Hanuschplatz, Residenzplatz or the train stations.

AROUND SALZBURG
Schloss Hellbrunn
Four kilometres south of Salzburg's old town centre is the popular **Schloss Hellbrunn** (☎ 820 372-0; www.hellbrunn.at; Fürstenweg 37; adult/ student €7.50/5.50; ⏰ 9am-4.30pm Apr & Oct, 9am-5.30pm May, Jun & Sep, 9am-10pm Jul & Aug). Built by bishop Markus Sittikus, this 17th-century castle is known for its ingenious trick fountains and water-powered figures. When the tour guides set them off, expect to get wet! Admission includes a tour of the **baroque palace**. Other parts of the garden (without fountains) are open year-round and free to visit.

City bus No 55 runs to the palace every 30 minutes from Salzburg main train station, via Rudolfskai in the old town. Salzburg tickets are valid.

Werfen

☎ 06468 / pop 3000

The world's largest accessible ice caves are in the mountains near Salzburg. These **Eisriesenwelt Höhle** (giant ice caves; ☎ 56 46; www.eisriesenwelt .at; adult/concession with cable car up €17/15, without cable car €8/7; ⓨ 1 May-26 Oct) house elaborate and beautiful ice formations. Take warm clothes because it gets cold inside and the tour lasts 1¼ hours – you need to be reasonably fit.

The **Hohenwerfen Fortress** (adult/student €9/7.50; ⓨ Apr-Nov) stands on the hill above the village. Originally built in 1077, the present building dates from the 16th century. Admission includes an exhibition, a guided tour of the interior and a dramatic falconry show, in which birds of prey swoop low over the heads of the crowd. The walk up from the village takes 20 minutes.

Both attractions can be visited in one day if you start early (tour the caves first, and be at the castle by 3pm for the falconry show). The **tourist office** (☎ 53 88; www.werfen.at; Markt 24; ⓨ 9am-5pm Mon-Fri mid-Aug–mid-July, 9am-7pm Mon-Fri, 5-7pm Sat mid-Jul–mid-Aug) is in the village main street.

Werfen can be reached from Salzburg along the A10. By train (€7.40) it takes 50 minutes. The village is a five-minute walk from Werfen station. Getting to the caves is more complicated, though scenic. A minibus service (€6.50 return) from the station operates along the steep, 6km road to the car park, which is as far as cars can go. A 15-minute walk then brings you to the cable car (adult/concession €9/8 return), from which it is a further 15-minute walk to the caves. Allow four hours return from the station, or three hours from the car park (peak-season queues may add an hour). The whole route can be hiked, but it's a very hard four-hour ascent, rising 1100m above the village.

SALZKAMMERGUT

The Salzkammergut is Austria's Lakes District. Not only does this picturesque region of mountains and more than 80 lakes east of Salzburg make an idyllic spot for hiking, water sports or relaxation, it also boasts salt mines (after which it's named) and ice caves.

The Salzkammergut offers some wintertime skiing, with the general Salzkammergut Lammertal ski pass costing from €51 for a minimum of two days. The main season, however, is summer, when nature lovers and families invade. Its good transport links make Bad Ischl the most obvious base, but Hallstatt is the region's true jewel.

Throughout the year, resorts have a holiday/guest card *(Gästekarte)* offering region-wide discounts; ask your hotel, hostel or camping ground for this. Alternatively, buy the Salzkammergut Card (€4.90; available May to October), which provides a 25% discount on sights, ferries, cable cars and some buses.

Bad Ischl is at the geographical centre of Salzkammergut. Hallstatt and the Dachstein ice caves lie to its south on the Hallstätter See (lake). West of Bad Ischl is the Wolfgangsee, while the Attersee and popular Mondsee lie to its northeast.

Getting There & Around

The major rail routes bypass the heart of Salzkammergut, but regional trains cross the area north to south. You get on this route from Attnang-Puchheim on the Salzburg–Linz line. The track from here connects to Bad Ischl, Hallstatt and Obertraun in one direction, as well as to Gmunden in another. When you're travelling from a small, unstaffed station *(unbesetzter Bahnhof)*, you buy your ticket on the train; no surcharge applies.

After Obertraun, the railway continues eastwards via Bad Aussee before connecting with the main Bischofshofen–Graz line at Stainach-Irdning.

Attersee can also be reached via Vócklamarkt, the next stop on the Salzburg–Linz line before Attnang-Puchheim.

Regular buses connect the region's towns and villages, though less frequently on weekends. Timetables are displayed at stops, and tickets can be bought from the driver.

Passenger boats ply the waters of the Attersee, Traunsee, Mondsee, Hallstätter See and Wolfgangsee.

To reach Salzkammergut from Salzburg by car or motorcycle, take the A1 or Hwy 158.

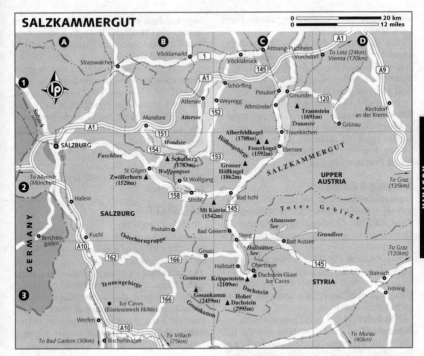

SALZKAMMERGUT

BAD ISCHL

☎ 06132 / pop 13,000

WWI – or what became WWI – was declared in Bad Ischl. It's an unlikely birthplace for such brutality, given that it's a spa resort devoted to rather more relaxing and healthier pursuits, and now a genteel retirees' paradise to boot. However, in the 19th and early 20th centuries, it was fashionable for Austria's powerbrokers to 'take the cure' in the town's salty waters. Emperor Franz Josef was enjoying his annual summer holiday here in 1914 when difficulties with Serbia demanded his urgent attention.

Orientation

The town centre rests within a bend of the Traun River. To head into town, turn left into the main road as you come out of the train station; you'll pass the tourist office and post office.

Information

Post office (Aübockplatz 4; ⏰ 8am-6pm Mon-Fri, 9am-noon Sat)

Salzkammergut Touristik (☎ 240 00-0; www .salzkammergut.co.at; Götzstrasse 12; ⏰ 9am-8pm) Has Internet access.

Tourist office (Kurdirektion; ☎ 27 757-0; www.badischl .at, in German; Bahnhofstrasse 6; ⏰ 8am-6pm Mon-Fri, 9am-3pm Sat, 10am-1pm Sun Jul-Sep, 8am-5pm Mon-Fri, 8am-noon Sat Oct-Jun)

Sights & Activities

The **Kaiservilla** (☎ 23 241; www.kaiservilla.at; Kaiserpark; tours €9.50; ⏰ May–mid-Oct) was Franz Josef's summer residence and shows he loved huntin', shootin' and fishin' – it's decorated with an obscene number of animal trophies. The villa can be visited only by guided tour (in German but with written English translations), during which you'll pick up little gems like the fact that Franz Josef was conceived in Bad Ischl after his mother, Princess Sophie, took a treatment to cure her infertility in 1828. There are several 40-minute tours daily during the main season and only three on Wednesday (noon, 2pm and 3pm) from January to April.

The teahouse of Franz Josef's wife, Elisabeth, is now a **photo museum** (admission €1.50).

Admission to the grounds alone costs adult/child €3.20/2.50.

Free *Kurkonzerte* (spa concerts) are held regularly during summer; the tourist office has venues and times. An operetta festival takes place in July and August; for details and advance reservations call ☎ 23 839.

Bad Ischl has downhill skiing from **Mt Katrin** (winter day-pass €19.50) and various cross-country skiing routes. In summer, the Mt Katrin cable car costs €12.50 return.

The tourist office has information on **health treatments** in Bad Ischl.

Sleeping & Eating

Jugendgästehaus (☎ 26 577; fax 26 577-75; Am Rechensteg 5; dm €12.50, s/d €25.50/36.50; ⏰ reception 8am-1pm & 5-7pm) Overlooking the Kaiservilla, this HI hostel is in the town centre behind Kreuzplatz.

Haus Rothauer (☎ 23 628; Kaltenbachstrasse 12; s/d €20/48) The family-run Haus Rothauer is immaculately clean and feels like staying with friends of the family. It's also one of Bad Ischl's cheapest deals.

Villa Dachstein (☎ 23 151; www.villadachstein.at; Rettenbachweg; s/d from €32/64) High on the hill above the river, this turreted villa looks like something from a Victorian Gothic novel; the rooms are spacious and salubrious.

Umeko (☎ 28 063; Rettenbachweg 1; mains €6.90-10.90) Umeko is near the villa and offers a delightful fusion of tasty Asian cuisine and Austrian farmhouse décor. At lunch time (except Sunday) you can eat your fill from the €5.80 buffet. The only thing that doesn't always live up to expectations is the dim sum (€3.60 a piece).

Blauen Enzian (☎ 28 992; Salinenplatz; dishes €8-14; ⏰ Mon-Sat) The laid-back Enzian offers a variety of pastas, salads, and regional and seasonal dishes.

Café Zauner (Pfarrgasse 7) This café is a traditional Café Konditorei almost unchanged since imperial times. Its summer pavilion on the Esplanade by the river is equally as atmospheric.

Getting There & Around

As a regional transport hub, Bad Ischl provides a good base for exploring the Salzkammergut region.

Trains from Salzburg (€15.50, two hours) arrive via Attnang-Puchheim. Trains on to Hallstatt depart roughly hourly between 6am and 6pm (€2.90, 50 minutes); however beware that you need to catch a ferry from this station to the actual village (see Getting There and Away p71).

Buses to and from Bad Ischl stop in front of the train station. They run hourly to Salzburg (€7.40, 1¾ hours) via St Gilgen between 5am and 8pm. To St Wolfgang (€3.10), you generally need to change at Strobl (although you can buy one ticket straight through). Buses depart for Hallstatt every couple of hours (€3.60, 50 minutes), arriving in the village itself.

Salzkammergut Touristik (see p69) offers bikes for rent.

HALLSTATT

☎ 06134 / pop 1150

There's evidence of human settlement at Hallstatt as long as 4500 years ago. The village, now a Unesco World Heritage site, is in a breathtaking location – clinging to a steep mountainside beside a placid lake. Mining salt in the peak above the village was the main activity for thousands of years. Today, tourism is the major money-spinner. Fortunately, the crowds of summer day-trippers only stay a few hours, then calm returns.

Orientation & Information

Seestrasse is the main street. Turn left from the ferry to reach the **tourist office** (☎ 82 08; hallstatt@inneres-salzkammergut.at; Seestrasse 169; ⏰ 9am-noon & 1-5pm Mon-Fri year-round, 10am-5pm Sat May-Oct, to 2pm Sun Jul-Aug). The **post office** (Seestrasse 160) is around a bend in the road, and changes money.

Sights & Activities

Hallstatt is rich with archaeological interest. Near the mine, 2000 graves were discovered, dating from 1000 BC to 500 BC. Don't miss the macabre **Beinhaus** (Bone House; admission €1) near the village parish church; it contains rows of decorated skulls from the 15th century and later.

Around the lake at Obertraun are the **Dachstein Rieseneishöhle** (Giant Ice Caves; admission €8, with Mammoth Cave €12.30; open early May–mid-Oct). These include a giant stone (rather than ice) cave with sheer walls meeting in an arched ceiling called the Mammoth Cave. A cable car provides easy access.

Above the village are the **Salzbergwerk** (Saltworks; ☎ 84 00; admission €14; ⏰ 9am-4pm late Apr-26

Oct, to 3.30pm from mid-Oct). Riding the funicular up adds €5.50 to the salt mine ticket, or costs €7.50 return if you just want to get up the mountain. Ask the tourist office about the two scenic hiking trails you could take to get there.

Sleeping & Eating

Some private rooms are available during the busiest months of July and August only; others require a minimum three-night stay. The tourist office will telephone around for you without charge.

For camping there's **Campingplatz Krausner-Höll** (☎ 83 22; Lahn 201; adult/tent/car €5.80/3.70/2.90; ☺ Apr-Oct). Tax is extra. There are two hostels: **Gasthaus zur Muhle** (☎ /fax 83 18; Kirchenweg 36; dm €15) is on the Hallstatt hillside and overlooks the lake. Lots of independent travellers stay here, but with its large dorms it is quite basic. The HI **Jugendherberge** (☎ 82 12; Salzbergstrasse 50; dm €15; ☺ May-Oct, check-in 5-6pm), near the Lamm bus station is more expansive, but is also usually full with groups in July and August.

The friendly and charming **Pension Hallberg** (☎ 87 09; www.pension-hallberg.at.tf; Seestrasse 113; per person €35-60; ☐) is near the tourist office, and is the hub of the lake's scuba-diving community.

Hallstatt's steep pavements certainly help you work up an appetite. Good restaurants include **Bräu Gasthof** (☎ 20 012; Seestrasse 120; dishes €7.40-16; ☺ May-Nov), for typical Austrian food in an old-fashioned atmosphere; **Gasthof Weisses Lamm** (☎ 83 11; Mortonweg 166; mains €7.50-14.50), which has some healthier options; and the friendly, spacious **Grüner Anger** (☎ 83 97; Lahn 10; mains €7-11.50) near the Jugendherberge.

Getting There & Away

There are six buses a day to/from Bad Ischl. You alight at 'Lahn', just south of the road tunnel. Beware, as services finish very early and the last guaranteed departure from Bad Ischl is 4.10pm. There are at least nine train services a day from Bad Ischl (€2.90, 50 minutes). The station is across the lake from the village, but the ferry captain waits for trains to arrive before making the short crossing (€1.90). Though trains run later, the last ferry departs the train station at 6.30pm (leaving Hallstatt at just after 6pm). Parking in the village is free if you're staying the night and therefore have a guest card.

WOLFGANGSEE

You can swim or go boating on this lake, climb the mountain above it, or just sit on the shore, gazing at the scenery. However, its proximity to Salzburg means the Wolfgangsee can become crowded in summer.

Orientation

The lake is dominated by the Schafberg peak on the northern shore. Next to it is the resort of St Wolfgang. St Gilgen, on the western shore, provides easy access to Salzburg, 29km away.

Information

St Gilgen tourist office (☎ 06227-23 48; info@stgilgen .co.at; Rathaus, Mozartplatz 1; ☺ 9am-noon Mon-Fri & 2-5pm Mon, Tue, Thu & Fri Sep-Jun, 8.30am-7pm Mon-Sat, 9am-noon Sun Jul & Aug)

St Wolfgang tourist office (☎ 06138-22 39-0; info@ stwolfgang.at; ☺ 9am-noon Mon-Sat & 2-5pm Mon, Tue, Thu & Fri Sep-Jun, 8am-8pm Mon-Sat, noon-6pm Sun Jul & Aug)

Sights & Activities

Some people like to climb mountains because they're there; others prefer the less strenuous train ride to the top. The former will love the four-hour hike to the peak of the **Schafberg** (1783m). The rest need to get there between early May and the end of October, when the Schafberg cog-wheel railway operates. It runs approximately hourly during the day and costs €12.70 to the top or €20.90 return. There is also a stop halfway up.

Hot-air ballooning and paragliding are also popular (ask at the tourist office).

The village of St Wolfgang's 14th-century **Pilgrimage Church** (☺ 9am-6pm) still attracts pilgrims interested in viewing this highly ornate church.

Sleeping

Camping Appesbach (☎ 06138-22 06; Au 99; adult/ tent & car €5/6; ☺ Easter-Oct) is on the lakefront, 1km from St Wolfgang heading south toward Strobl.

The local HI **Jugendgästehaus** (☎ 06227-23 65; Mondseestrasse 7; dm/tw/d €12.50/15/18.50; ☺ check-in 5-7pm) is in St Gilgen. Some of the rooms have lake views.

Both St Wolfgang and St Gilgen have numerous *pensions*, starting from about €20. Ask the local tourist offices for details and bookings.

Getting There & Away

A ferry operates from Strobl to St Gilgen, stopping at various points en route, including St Wolfgang. Services are from late April to 26 October, but are more frequent from early July to early September. The ferry journey from St Wolfgang to St Gilgen takes 45 to 50 minutes (€4.50), with boats sailing during the high season approximately twice an hour between 8am and 8pm.

Buses from St Wolfgang to St Gilgen and Salzburg go via Strobl on the east side of the lake. From St Gilgen the bus to Salzburg (€4.80, 50 minutes) departs hourly until at least 8.30pm.

NORTHERN SALZKAMMERGUT

West of Attersee is **Mondsee**, a lake whose warm water makes it a favourite swimming spot. Mondsee village has an attractive church that was used in the wedding scenes of *The Sound of Music*.

East of Attersee is another lake, **Traunsee** and its three main resorts: Gmunden, Traunkirchen and Ebensee. **Gmunden** is famous for its twin castles, linked by a causeway on the lake, and its ceramic manufacturing.

TIROL

When picture-postcard companies want to capture quintessential Alpine scenery, they could do a lot worse than Tirol (also spelled Tyrol), where several of Austria's mountain ranges converge. In the northeast and southwest are superb ski resorts. In the southeast, separated somewhat from the main state since part of South Tirol was ceded to Italy at the end of WWI, lies the protected natural landscape of the Hohe Tauern National Park, and the country's highest peak, the Grossglockner (3797m). Back further west, in the middle of the main state, sits Innsbruck, the baroque jewel in a mountainous crown.

INNSBRUCK

☎ 0512 / pop 111,000

Nearly everywhere you move in Innsbruck, majestic snowcapped mountains dominate your view. True, when you're in the narrow, covered streets of the medieval town they may disappear from sight. However, once you've seen the famous Golden Roof and re-emerge, there they are still. It's hard to resist the urge to get up high – to the reopened winter Olympics stadium and the new Bergisel ski-jump tower, or on an all-day hike.

As a two-time host to the winter Olympics – in 1964 and 1976 – it's unsurprising that the region around Innsbruck remains a skiing mecca. In fact, on the Stubai Glacier 40km to the south, you can ski or snowboard at any time of the year.

Orientation

Innsbruck, in the valley of the River Inn, is scenically squeezed between the northern chain of the Alps and the Tuxer mountains to the south. The town centre is compact, the main train station (Hauptbahnhof) only a 10-minute walk from the pedestrian-only old town centre (Altstadt). The main street in the Altstadt is Herzog Friedrich Strasse.

Information

INTERNET ACCESS

Bubble Point Waschsalon (☎ 565 007; www.bubble point.com; Brixner Strasse 1; per 30min €1.50) Internet café and laundrette combined.

Internetcafé Moderne (☎ 58 48 48; Maria Theresien Strasse 16)

MEDICAL SERVICES

Landeskrankenhaus (University Clinic; ☎ 504-0; Anichstrasse 35)

MONEY

There are various *bureaux de change* around town, as well as *Bankomats*. The tourist office also exchanges money, but it charges a hefty commission.

POST

Main post office (Maximilianstrasse 2; ⏰ 7am-9pm Mon-Fri, to 3pm Sat, 8am-7.30pm Sun)

Post office (Main train station, lower concourse; ⏰ 7am-7.30pm)

TOURIST INFORMATION

Main tourist office (general info ☎ 59 850, tickets & packages ☎ 53 56, hotel reservations ☎ 562 000-0; www.innsbruck.info; Burggraben 3; ⏰ 9am-6pm) There is a €3 booking fee for hotel reservations. The Innsbruck Card, sold here, gives free entry to museums and free use of public transport. It costs €21/26/31 for 24/48/72 hours. The tourist office's free newspaper *Innsbruck Hallo!* has a map and lots of useful information.

Tourist counter (Main train station, lower concourse; ⏰ 7am-7pm)

INNSBRUCK

0 _____ 500 m
0 _____ 0.3 miles

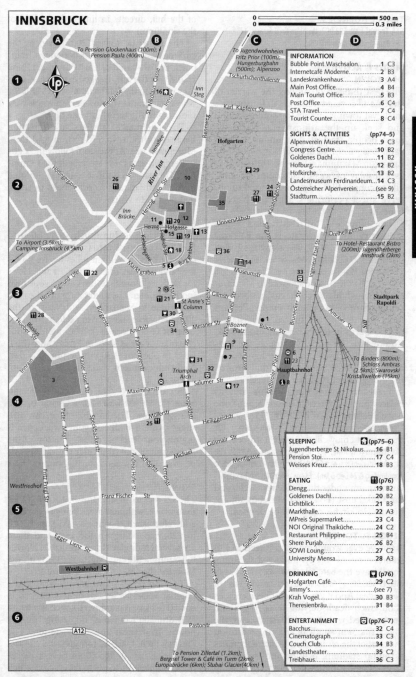

INFORMATION

Bubble Point Waschsalon	**1** C3
Internetcafé Moderne	**2** B3
Landeskrankenhaus	**3** A4
Main Post Office	**4** B4
Main Tourist Office	**5** B3
Post Office	**6** C4
STA Travel	**7** C4
Tourist Counter	**8** C4

SIGHTS & ACTIVITIES (pp74–5)

Alpenverein Museum	**9** C3
Congress Centre	**10** B2
Goldenes Dachl	**11** B2
Hofburg	**12** B2
Hofkirche	**13** B2
Landesmuseum Ferdinandeum	**14** C3
Österreicher Alpenverein	(see 9)
Stadtturm	**15** B2

SLEEPING (pp75–6)

Jugendherberge St Nikolaus	**16** B1
Pension Stoi	**17** C4
Weisses Kreuz	**18** B3

EATING (p76)

Dengg	**19** B2
Goldenes Dachl	**20** B2
Lichtblick	**21** B3
Markthalle	**22** A3
MPreis Supermarket	**23** C4
NOI Original Thaiküche	**24** C2
Restaurant Philippine	**25** B4
Shere Purjab	**26** B2
SOWI Loung	**27** C2
University Mensa	**28** A3

DRINKING (p76)

Hofgarten Café	**29** C2
Jimmy's	(see 7)
Krah Vogel	**30** B3
Theresienbräu	**31** B4

ENTERTAINMENT (pp76–7)

Bacchus	**32** C4
Cinematograph	**33** C3
Couch Club	**34** B3
Landestheater	**35** C2
Treibhaus	**36** C3

AUSTRIA

TRAVEL AGENCIES
STA Travel (☎ 588 997; Wilhelm Greil Strasse 17; ⓨ 9am-5.30pm Mon-Fri)

Sights & Activities
OLD TOWN
The best thing to do among the warren of streets and covered walkways in Innsbruck's medieval town is simply to wander around and soak up the atmosphere. Naturally, most people start at the famous **Goldenes Dachl** (Golden Roof; Friedrich Herzog Strasse). Built by Emperor Maximilian I in the 16th century as a display of wealth, it comprises 2657 gilded copper tiles. Maximilian used to observe street performers from the balcony beneath.

The other old town attraction where crowds rightly congregate is the **Hofkirche** (Imperial Church; ☎ 584 302; Universitätsstrasse 2; adult/student under 27 €2.20/1.45, admission free Sun & holidays; ⓨ 9am-5pm Mon-Sat, before 8am, noon-3pm & after 5pm Sun), which contains a memorial to Maximilian. Although his 'sarcophagus' has been recently restored, it's actually empty. Perhaps more memorable are the 28 giant statues of Habsburgs lining either side of the cask. You're now forbidden to touch the statues, but numerous inquisitive hands have already polished parts of the dull bronze, including Kaiser Rudolf's codpiece!

Travellers not visiting Vienna and its palaces might appreciate a tour around the ornate **Hofburg** (Imperial Palace; ☎ 587 186; Rennweg 1; adult/senior/student €5.50/4/3.60; ⓨ 9am-4.30pm). Or they might enjoy climbing the 14th-century **Stadtturm** (City Tower; ☎ 561 500; Herzog Friedrich Strasse 21; adult/student & senior €2.50/2; ⓨ 10am-5pm Apr-Oct, to 6pm Jul-Aug & 24 Dec-6 Jan). However, the Maximilian museum under the Goldenes Dachl, and the Volkskunst (Folk Art) Museum adjoining the Hofkirche, can easily be skipped.

BERGISEL TOWER
If you've ever wondered what it feels like to stand on top of an Olympic-sized ski jump, you'll leave the **Bergisel tower** (☎ 589 259; adult/child €7.90/3.90; ⓨ 9am-5pm, to 6pm Jun-Nov) with a better idea. And if you've never been curious about such death-defying feats, you'll still be rewarded with truly fantastic views; the tower sits 3km south of the city centre on the crest of the refurbished Winter Olympics ski-jump stadium, overlooking Innsbruck. (Some wag has built a cemetery over the lip of the hill, directly in line with the end of the ski jump.)

The futuristic tower (2003) evinces the curving design typical of its designer – Iraqi-born, British-based celebrity architect Zaha Hadid. For the fully fledged experience, stop for a coffee in the **Café im Turm** (meals €8.50-16.60), whose panorama windows give a whole new meaning to the term 'caffeine high'.

To get here, take tram/bus No 1 (direction Bergisel) or tram No 6 (direction Igls) from Museumstrasse. At the stop, follow the signs to Bergisel, up a fairly steep path for 15 minutes. The stadium is still used for ski-jumping in June and January, so ring ahead to check that it's OK to visit.

HIKING
Those staying in Innsbruck are entitled to the Club Innsbruck card (see p75), which includes guided mountain hikes for free. This is a fantastic deal, offering remarkable views for nothing more than the cost of your own food and water. The hiking programme runs from June to September, with most of the 40-odd diverse hikes leaving at 9am from the **Congress Centre** (Rennweg 3). The popular sunrise hikes leave at 4.45am Friday and you'll need to book by 4.30pm the previous day. Night-time lantern walks depart at 7.45pm Tuesday.

For details, contact the **AlpinSchule Innsbruck** (☎ 546 000; www.asi.at, in German) or the tourist office. The tourist office can also suggest where to hike on your own, depending on your level of fitness. The top of the Hungerburgbahn (funicular railway; see Alpenzoo p75) is a good starting point.

SKIING
The ski region around Innsbruck continues to improve, with new areas being opened up and refurbished. A one-day ski pass is €20 to €26, depending on the area, and there are several multiday tickets available. Downhill equipment rental starts at €15. With the Club Innsbruck card, ski buses are free.

You can ski or snowboard all year at the popular **Stubai Glacier**. A one-day pass costs €34.50 (€24.10 in summer). Catch the white IVB Stubaltalbahn bus, departing roughly hourly from near the train station. The journey there takes 80 minutes and the last bus back is usually at 5.30pm. Several places offer complete packages to the glacier, which compare favourably with going it alone. The **tourist office** (☎ 53 56) has a package for €49 including transport, passes and equipment rental. This works out to be a good deal in summer. In winter, however, there's a free ski bus leaving from various hotels, so compare going it alone with taking a tourist office package before making a decision.

ALPENZOO
The **Alpine Zoo** (☎ 292 323; www.alpenzoo.at, in German; Weiherburggasse 37; adult/student/child €7/5/3.50; ☽ 9am-6pm, to 5pm winter) houses a comprehensive collection of alpine animals, including ibexes, bears, an eagle and a bearded vulture. Walk up the hill to get there or take the Hungerburgbahn, which is free if you buy your zoo ticket at the Hungerburgbahn station.

SWAROVSKI KRISTALLWELTEN
The recently expanded **Crystal Worlds** (☎ 05224-51080; www.swarovski.com/kristallwelten; Kristallwelten-strasse 1; adult/child €8/free; ☽ 9am-6pm) is a glitzy showcase for all things Swarovski. Subterranean caves feature crystal artworks from the likes of Salvador Dali, Andy Warhol and Keith Haring, and explanations of the crystallising process, mosaics and projections. The centre in Wattens is best reached by bus (€6.20 return, 30 minutes).

OTHER SIGHTS & ACTIVITIES
The **Landesmuseum Ferdinandeum** (☎ 59 489; Museumstrasse 15) has a massive collection of Gothic statues and altarpieces. The **Alpenverein Museum** (Alpine Club Museum; ☎ 59 547-19; Wilhelm Greil Strasse 15; adult/child €2.20/1.10; ☽ 10am-5pm Mon, Tue, Thu & Fri, noon-7pm Wed, 10am-1pm Sat May-Oct) has a collection of Alpine art and relief maps. **Schloss Ambras** (☎ 01-52 524-745; www.khm.at/ambras; Schlossstrasse 20; adult/concession €4.50/3, Apr-Oct €8/6; ☽ 10am-5pm, to 6pm Aug, closed Nov), 2.5km east of town, features a Renaissance Spanish Hall and more; you can get there by tram No 3 or 6, or bus K. Ask at the tourist office for details.

A new 'hop on, hop off' **Sightseer bus** (adult/concession day ticket €8/5.60; ☽ services half-hourly 9am-5pm, from 10am Nov-Apr) does make getting to some of the more remote sights a little easier. Pick up a brochure at the tourist office.

Sleeping
The tourist office has lists of private rooms in Innsbruck and Igls from €20 per person.

If you're staying at a hostel or hotel, ask for the complimentary Club Innsbruck card. It provides various discounts and benefits, such as guided mountain hikes between June and September (see p74).

BUDGET
Camping Innsbruck Kranebitten (☎ 284 180; www.campinginnsbruck.com; Kranebitter Allee 214; adult/tent/car €5.35/3/3) In an idyllic location west of town under the mountains, this camping ground is open year-round and has a restaurant, bike rental and shuttle service into town.

Jugendherberge St Nikolaus (☎ 286 515; www.hostelnikolaus.at; Innstrasse 95; dm/d/tr per person with shared bathroom €15.80/20.20/17.50; ☽ check-in 5-10pm; ▣) None of Innsbruck's hostels are particularly convenient, but this is probably the best located. It has a bar and restaurant and is a sociable place, although the rooms are a little cramped.

Pension Glockenhaus (Weiherburggasse 3; www.hostelnikolaus.at; s/d per person €31/23.80; ▣) There's more privacy, but more of a draught too, in St Nikolaus' sister hostel up the hill.

Jugendherberge Innsbruck (☎ 346 179; www.jugendherberge-innsbruck.at; Reichenauerstrasse 147; dm with shared bathroom €11.50-14.50, d with shared bathroom €46; ☽ closed 10am-3pm summer, 10am-5pm rest of year, curfew 11pm; ▣) This hostel still seems stuck in the Soviet era, even though Austria never had one. Seen from afar, it's a huge, concrete and pebble-dash monstrosity, but its dorms are quite modestly sized. Prices include breakfast. To get here, take bus O (direction Olympisches Dorf/Josef Kerschbaumer Strasse) from Museumstrasse.

Jugendwohnheim Fritz Prior (☎ 585 814, 585 814-4; Rennweg 17B; s €14-18, d/tr/f €36/52/56; ☽ Jul, Aug & New Year, check-in from 5pm) This is another hostel option to try in summer, located just north of the centre.

Pension Paula (☎ 292 262; www.pensionpaula.at; Weiherburggasse 15; s/d €34/56, with shared bathroom €27/47; Ⓟ) This hilltop *pension* looks out over the city, with views from the front rooms and the outdoor seating next to the buffet breakfast room. Rooms are fairly humble, but most bathrooms are quite new.

Pension Stoi (☎ 585 434; fax 87 282; Salurner Strasse 7; s/d €37/58, with shared bathroom €32/51) Offers simple rooms with wooden floors in a central location, but doesn't serve breakfast. It's in the little alley behind the Flamingo tourist agency.

AUSTRIA

MID-RANGE

Weisses Kreuz (☎ 59 479; www.weisseskreuz.at; Herzog Friedrich Strasse 31; s/d €70/88, with shared bathroom €35/66; ✗ P) Creaky, atmospheric but comfortable nevertheless, this hotel once played host to Mozart.

Binders (☎ 33 436-0; www.binders.at; Dr Glatz Strasse 20; s/d €43/64, with shared bathroom €40/54; P) East of the main train station, Binders is a rare thing: a designer hotel for those on a budget. Brightly coloured lampshades, pillows or armchairs create a splash against a neutral, modern background. Just east of town, this is excellent value for money.

Pension Zillertal (☎ 582 129; www.pensionzillertal.com; Fritz Konzert Strasse 7; s/d/tr from €54/85/128; ✗ P) A family-run bed and breakfast establishment in a converted apartment building, south of town and close to the Bergisel tower. The recently renovated rooms are spotless and have TVs and phones.

Hotel-Restaurant Bistro (☎ 346 319; www.tiscover.at/hotel-bistro; Pradlerstrasse 2; s/d €42/84; P) This small family-run hotel won't win any interior-design awards; it's plain, business-like and unassuming. However, rooms are comfortable and offer good value for money, and the staff are welcoming and friendly.

Eating

BUDGET

University Mensa (Herzog Siegmund Ufer 15; mains €3.90-5; ✆ 11am-2pm Mon-Thu, to 1.30pm Fri) Enjoy great views of the Alps while lunching here.

SOWI Lounge (Universitätsstrasse 15; mains €3.20-5; ✆ 8am-5pm Mon-Thu, 10am-3pm Fri) Less scenic, but with more appetising-looking food.

Restaurant Philippine (☎ 589 157; Müllerstrasse 9; menu €6.80-7.80; ✆ 11.30am-2pm & 6.30-8pm Mon-Sat) Touts itself as a veggie outlet, but as it also serves fish, it's probably better described as a health-conscious option.

Shere Purjab (☎ 282 755; Innstrasse 19; mains €5.45-8.50) Innstrasse is lined with cheap eats, including this cut-price Indian restaurant, which has a daily menu and, naturally, lots of veggie food.

NOI Original Thaiküche (☎ 589 777; Kaiserjäger-strasse 1; mains €4-11; ✆ lunch & dinner Mon-Fri, dinner Sat) Serves delicious Thai staples, such as soups, noodle dishes and curries. It's small, but in summer has lots of outdoor tables with brightly coloured chairs.

There is an **MPreis Supermarket** (✆ 6am-9pm) in the train station and a large indoor food market by the river in **Markthalle** (Herzog Siegmund Ufer; ✆ Mon-Fri & Sat morning).

MID-RANGE

Dengg (☎ 582 347; Riesengasse 11-13; mains €13-18) A more upmarket eatery, serving everything from Thai coconut curry soup to international fish and meat dishes.

Goldenes Dachl (☎ 589 370; Hofgasse 1; mains €9.90-14.80) Offers Tirolean specialities such as *Bauerngröstl*, a pork, bacon, potato and egg concoction served with salad (€9.90). Other dishes include Schnitzel and various types of *Braten* (roasts).

TOP END

Lichtblick (☎ 566 550; 7th fl, Maria Theresien Strasse 18; daytime snacks €6.10-8.90, evening menu €30-40; ✆ closed Sun) This is the city's hot ticket, and little wonder, given both the views and the delicious modern international food. The Alps rise up along one side of this small, glassed-in restaurant, while in the other direction you can see the Bergisel tower. It's a romantic spot at night, and worth dropping by for a daytime coffee just to experience it.

Drinking

Jimmy's (☎ 570 473; Wilhelm Greil Strasse 17) Very cool, very industrial looking, the hub of Innsbruck's hip nightlife is here. It features lots of metal and exposed stone, and a Buddha on the wall that oversees the proceedings.

Hofgarten Café (☎ 58 88 71; Rennweg 6A) This remains another favourite. In the middle of the palace gardens (despite the misleading address), it's convivial, atmospheric and has reasonably cheap beer.

Krah Vogel (☎ 5801 4971; Anichstrasse 12) The red-walled Krah Vogel is a favourite student haunt.

Theresienbräu (☎ 587 580; Maria Theresien Strasse 53) Overseas travellers will be more interested in the home-brewed beer here than anything else.

Entertainment

The tourist office sells tickets for 'Tirolean evenings' (€32 for alpine music, folk dancing, yodelling and one drink), classical concerts, and performances in the **Landestheater** (Rennweg 2).

For clubbing, there's the hip **Couch Club** (Anichstrasse 7; ✆ Thu-Sat) and the arty, community-minded **Treibhaus** (☎ 586 874; Angerzellgasse

8), which hosts live music, short-film festivals and the like. On Sunday, there's a 'jazz breakfast' from 10.30am and 'five o'clock tea'.

Bacchus (☎ 940 210; Salurnerstrasse 14) is a mixed/gay club that attracts what German speakers succinctly call *ein gemischtes Publikum* (all ages, all tastes and all looks).

Cinematograph (☎ 578 500; Museumstrasse 31) screens independent films in their original language.

For further details, try to pick up a copy of *Innsider,* found in cafés across town.

Getting There & Away
AIR
Austrian Airlines has three flights a week from London Gatwick to **Innsbruck airport** (☎ 22 525). Tyrolean Airways flies daily to Amsterdam, Frankfurt, Paris, Vienna and Zürich.

BUS
Long-distance bus departures were in a state of flux at the time of research. Check the board outside the front door of the main train station, or ask at the tourist counter inside the station for directions.

CAR & MOTORCYCLE
The A12 and the parallel Hwy 171 are the main roads to the east and west respectively. Hwy 177, heads north to Germany and Munich. The A13 motorway is a toll road (€7.99) southwards through the Brenner Pass to Italy; it includes the impressive Europabrücke (Europe Bridge), several kilometres south of the city. Toll-free Hwy 182 follows the same route, passing under the bridge.

TRAIN
Fast trains depart seven times a day for Bregenz (€25.10, 2¾ hours) and every two hours to Salzburg (€29.50, two hours). Regular express trains head north to Munich (via Kufstein; two hours) and south to Verona (3½ hours). Connections are hourly to Kitzbühel (€12.20, 1¼ hours). On many trains to Lienz, people travelling on Austrian rail passes must pay a surcharge for travelling through Italy. Ask before boarding or call ☎ 05-17 17, available 24 hours.

Getting Around
The airport is 4km west of the centre. To get there, take bus F, which departs from opposite the main train station half-hourly (hourly on Saturday afternoon and Sunday) and passes through Maria Theresien Strasse.

A taxi from the train station to the airport costs around €10.

Single bus tickets, including to the airport, cost €1.60. A 24-hour pass is €3.20 and a weekly €10.10.

Street parking is very limited in the centre. Parking garages (eg under the Altstadt) cost €10 and upwards per day.

KITZBÜHEL
☎ 05356 / pop 8200
Kitzbühel is a fashionable and prosperous winter resort, offering excellent skiing. It's renowned for the daring Hahnenkamm downhill ski race in January.

Orientation & Information
From the main train station to the town centre is 1km. You emerge from the train station onto Bahnhofstrasse and walk straight ahead, then turn left onto Josef Pirchl Strasse; take the right fork (no entry for cars), which is still Josef Pirchl Strasse, and continue past the post office. Following this road will eventually take you to the **tourist office** (☎ 62 155-0; www.kitzbuehel.com; Hinterstadt 18; ☽ daily high season, Mon-Fri & Sat morning low season).

Activities
SKIING
In winter there is good intermediate skiing on Kitzbüheler Horn to the north and Hahnenkamm to the south. A one-day general ski pass costs €35, though some pensions/hotels can offer 'Ski Hit' reductions before mid-December or after mid-March.

HIKING
Dozens of summer hiking trails surround the town; the tourist office gives free maps and free guided hikes. Get a head start to the heights with a one- or three-day cable-car pass for €14.50/35.

There is an alpine flower garden (free) on the slopes of the Kitzbüheler Horn (a toll road for drivers). The scenic Schwarzsee is a fine location for summer swimming.

Sleeping
Campingplatz Schwarzsee (☎ 62 806; Reither Strasse 24; ☽ year-round) You can pitch your tent here by the lake, but Kitzbühel's hostel (Hotel Kai-

ser) now prefers only to take school groups. Prices quoted for pensions and hotels are for the winter high season.

Pension Hörl (☎ /fax 63 144; Josef Pirchl Strasse 60; s/d €20/40, with shared bathroom €18/36) This is the closest place to stay to the train station. It's cheap, friendly and more comfortable than its jumble-sale décor first suggests.

Pension Schmidinger (☎ 63 134; Ehrenbachgasse 3; s/d from €35/70) The spotless rooms are decorated in a pleasant country style and have new bathrooms.

Pension Mühlbergerhof (☎ 62 835; fax 64 488; Schwarzseestrasse 6; s/d from €35/70) The colour scheme in the public areas of this pension are somewhat darker than Schmidinger, but the rooms are light and airy. The owners here serve breakfast featuring fresh produce from their farm.

Eating

Huberbräu Stüberl (☎ 65 677; Vorderstadt 18; mains €6.20-12.50) This is a Kitzbühel 'must', although so many diners come for the Austrian food and beer that the service is sometimes rather offhand.

La Fonda (☎ 65 677; Hinterstadt 13; mains €6-7; ☯ dinner) The kitschy Tex-Mex décor here seems to make this place a hit.

Zinnkrug (☎ 62 613; Untere Gänsbachgasse 12) This is another typically Austrian inn. It's known for its pork spare ribs (€15.60).

On Bichlstrasse (corner of Ehrenbachgasse) there's a **Spar supermarket** (☯ Mon-Sat), while grocery store **Asia Markt** (Josef Pirchl Strasse 16; meals €4.50-6.50; ☯ Mon-Sat) serves light weekday lunches and early evening meals.

Getting There & Away

Direct trains to Innsbruck (€12.20, one to two hours, depending on the service) only leave Kitzbühel every two hours or so, but there are hourly services to Wörgl, where you can change for Innsbruck. Trains to Salzburg (€20.80, two hours) leave roughly hourly. Slower trains stop at Kitzbühel-Hahnenkamm, which is closer to the centre than the main Kitzbühel stop.

Getting to Lienz by public transport is awkward. The train is slow and the bus is infrequent (€12.50, two hours). There are four bus departures Monday to Friday and two each on Saturday and Sunday.

Heading south to Lienz, you pass through some marvellous scenery. Hwy 108 (the Fel-

ber Tauern Tunnel) and Hwy 107 (the Grossglockner mountain road, closed in winter) both have toll sections.

LIENZ
☎ 04852 / pop 13,000

Thanks to the jagged Dolomite mountain range, which crowds its southern skyline, the capital of East Tirol makes a scenic starting point for travelling through the Hohe Tauern National Park (see p79).

Orientation & Information

The town centre is within the junction of the Isel and Drau Rivers. To reach Hauptplatz from the train station, cross the road (or take the 'Zur Stadt' exit) and follow the street past the post office. The **tourist office** (☎ 65 265; www .lienz-tourismus.at; Europaplatz 1; ☯ 8am-6pm Mon-Fri, 9am-noon Sat, 9am-noon Sun in summer & winter high season) will find rooms free of charge, or you can use the hotel board (free telephone) outside.

Sights & Activities

There is downhill skiing on the nearby **Zettersfeld** and **Hochstein** peaks. A one-day ski pass covering both is €29.50. However, the area around Lienz is more renowned for its cross-country skiing; the town fills up for the annual **Dolomitenlauf** cross-country skiing race in mid-January.

In summer, there's good hiking in the mountains. The cable cars are closed during the off season (April, May, October and November).

Sleeping & Eating

Just south of the town, **Comfort-Camping Falken** (☎ 64 022; Eichholz 7; camp site without/with electricity €8/10.50, adult €6; ☯ mid-Dec–Oct) has good washing facilities, a restaurant and marvellous mountain views.

Few other accommodation establishments have quite the same close-up of the Dolomite range, but there are some good bargains to be had. Some allow a single night's stay, like the **Haus Egger** (☎ 72 098; Alleestrasse 33; s/d €14/28) or the **Gästehaus Masnata** (☎ 65 536; Drahtzuggasse 4; apt per person €19-20).

The atmospheric, spacious **Altstadthotel Eck** (☎ 64 785; altstadthotel.eck@utanet.at; Hauptplatz 20; s/d from €55/110) provides all the comfort you'd expect from one of the town's leading hotels.

There are ADEG supermarkets on Hauptplatz and Tiroler Platz. **Pick Nick Ossi** (☎ 71 091;

Europaplatz 2; snacks €3-7) has salads, pizzas and other fast food. There are lots of places to try regional dishes, such as **Adlerstüberl** (☎ 62 550; Andrä Kranz Gasse 5; meals from €7.80), which has daily specials. **Goldener Fisch** (☎ 62 132; Kärntner Strasse 9; menus €8.10-10.80) is also good.

Getting There & Away

Except for the 'corridor' route through Italy to Innsbruck, trains to the rest of Austria connect via Spittal Millstättersee to the east. Trains to Salzburg (€26.90) take at least three hours. Villach, between Spittal and Klagenfurt, is a main junction for rail routes to the south. To head south by car, you must first divert west or east along Hwy 100.

HOHE TAUERN NATIONAL PARK

Despite its size, little Austria contains the largest national park in the Alps. The Hohe Tauern National Park stretches over 1786 sq km, straddling Tirol, Salzburg and Carinthia. At the heart of this protected oasis of flora and fauna (including marmots and some rare ibexes) lies the **Grossglockner** (3797m), Austria's highest mountain. The Grossglockner towers over the 10km-long Pasterze Glacier, which is best seen from the outlook at **Franz Josef's Höhe**.

Although camping is not allowed in the park, there are mountain huts and hiking trails. Ask the tourist office in Lienz (p78) for details. If you're on foot, the most direct public transport into the park from Lienz is by bus to Franz Josef's Höhe. This goes via Heiligenblut, where there's an HI **Jugendherberge** (☎ 04824-22 59; Hof 36; ☼ mid-Dec–mid-Oct) and other accommodation. Buses run from mid-June to late September, but infrequently on a very complicated and confusing schedule, so ask the Lienz tourist office *and* your bus driver before boarding in front of the train station. The return fare is covered by a zonal day pass for Carinthia (available in Lienz; €10.20), plus a €2.70 toll for the park.

The highway through the park is considered one of the world's most scenic. The **Grossglockner Hochalpenstrasse** (Hwy 107; www.grossglockner.at, in German) winds upwards 2000m past waterfalls, glaciers and Alpine meadows.

The highway runs between Lienz and Zell am See, and if you catch a bus from Lienz to Franz Josef's Höhe, you'll be traversing the southern part of this route. If you want to travel further north, ask your driver, or the **Kärntnen tourist office** (☎ 04824-200 121) just up the road from the bus stop in Heiligenblut, about current bus schedules.

If you have your own vehicle, you'll have more flexibility. However, beware that the road is open only between May and mid-September, and you must pay tolls (of at least €26/17 for a car/motorcycle, but more if you take a circular route).

At the northern end of the park, turn west along Hwy 168 (which becomes Hwy 165) to reach the spectacular, triple-level **Krimml Falls**.

VORARLBERG

Vorarlberg is Austria's western panhandle. Trickling down from the Alps to the shores of Lake Constance (Bodensee), it's a destination in its own right for everyone from classical music buffs to skiers. It's also a gateway, by rail or across the lake, to Germany, Liechtenstein or Switzerland.

BREGENZ
☎ 05574 / pop 27,500

With its face to the waters of Lake Constance and its disproportionate number of expensive clothes stores, Bregenz feels more like a posh seaside village than the provincial capital it is. The town is busiest during its annual music festival in summer.

Orientation

Bregenz is on Lake Constance's eastern shore. Turn left at the main train station exit and take Bahnhofstrasse to the centre (five minutes). Buses for the city leave from outside the train station.

Information

Cockpit Café (Seegalerie, Bahnhofstrasse 10; Internet per 15min €1.20; ☼ 5pm-midnight)

Post office (Seestrasse 5; ☼ 7am-7pm Mon-Fri, 8am-noon Sat)

Tourist office (☎ 4959-0; www.bregenz.at, in German; Bahnhofstrasse 14; free Internet access; ☼ 9am-noon & 1-5pm Mon-Fri, to noon only Sat, to 7pm Mon-Sat during Bregenz Festival)

Sights & Activities

A feature that makes the **Bregenzer Festspiele** (Bregenz Festival) in July and August so remarkable is its setting. During the four-week programme, operas and classical works are performed from a floating stage on the lake's edge. For tickets, contact the **Kartenbüro** (☎ 407-6; www.bregenzerfestspiele.com; Postfach 311, A-6901) about nine months beforehand, or ask about cancellations on the day. It's also worth keeping an eye out for rock concerts on the floating stage, major artists like Pink and Peter Gabriel have performed here.

Music aside, Bregenz offers spectacular views from its **Pfänder** mountain; a **cable car** (☎ 421 600; www.pfaenderbahn.at, in German; adult/ senior return €9.80/8.80; ☼ 9am-7pm, closed 2 wks in Nov) carries you up and back. There are hiking trails at the top.

Bregenz is also of interest to architecture fans. Its most notable modern building is the shimmering art gallery block, the **Kunsthaus**, by award-winning Swiss architect Peter Zumthor.

Sleeping & Eating

Private singles/doubles start at €20/24; ask at the tourist office, which has a room-booking service (€3).

Camping Lamm (☎ 71 701; Mehrerauerstrasse 51; adult/tent/car €3.50/3.30/2.60; ☼ May–mid-Oct) This small, slightly ramshackle camping ground is 1.5km west of the station and has its own stables and ponies.

Jugendgästehaus Bregenz (☎ 42 867; jgh.breg enz@jgh.at; Mehrerauerstrasse 5; dm summer/winter from €19/17, s/d in winter €24/48, s/d not available in summer) This HI hostel is near the skateboard park; take the 'Zum See' exit from the train station and pass the casino. Rooms are modern and comfortable, most with five or six beds and their own bathrooms.

Pension Gunz (☎ /fax 43 657; Anton Schneider Strasse 38; s/d from €31/56, d with shared bathroom from €54; ☼ reception Wed-Mon) A humble, but comfortable abode, with an attached restaurant.

Pension Sonne (☎ 42 572; Kaiserstrasse 8; s/d €40/78, with shared bathroom €35/66; ☼ closed winter) This pension has basic rooms with wooden floors.

Gästehaus am Tannenbauch (☎ 44 174; Im Ge-hren 1; s/d €40/80; ☼ May-Oct; ℗) Travellers with a taste for something different might prefer this quirky guesthouse. From the outside it looks like a normal house; inside it explodes into an ornate display of baroque kitsch. The highlight is the regal breakfast room.

Leutbühel (Römerstrasse 2; lunches from €6.50; ☼ Mon-Sat) Trek through the 1st-floor clothes department in the GWL centre on Römerstrasse for salads and sausage dishes.

Gösserbräu (Anton Schneider Strasse 1; dishes €7-11; ☼ Tue-Sun) Serves up local cuisine that's hearty rather than stodgy; its vegetarian mushroom goulash with dumplings is divine.

Goldener Hirschen (☎ 42 815; Kirchstrasse 8; dishes €7.40-17.80; ☼ Wed-Mon) This is another popular choice for Austrian food.

Getting There & Away

Trains to Munich (€34.20, 2½ hours) go via Lindau. There are also regular departures to St Gallen and Zürich. Trains to Innsbruck (€25.10, 2¾ hours) depart every two hours.

Boat services operate from late May to late October, with a reduced schedule from early March. For information, call ☎ 42 868. Bregenz to Lake Constance (Bodensee) by boat via Friedrichshafen takes about 3½ hours and there are about seven departures a day. Special boat passes offer discounts.

ARLBERG REGION

The Arlberg region, shared by Vorarlberg and neighbouring Tirol, has some of the best skiing in Austria. Summer is less busy, when many bars are closed.

St Anton am Arlberg is the largest resort, where you're as likely to hear a cheery antipodean 'G'day' or Scandinavian *God dag* as you are to hear an Austrian *Grüss' Di*. There are good medium-to-advanced runs here, as well as nursery slopes on Gampen and Kapall. The **tourist office** (☎ 05446-22 690; www.stantonamarlberg.com), on the main street, has details. Head diagonally left from the train station to find it.

A ski pass valid for 83 ski lifts in St Anton and neighbouring St Christoph Lech, Zürs and Stuben costs €37 for one day and €171 for six (reductions for children and seniors).

Sleeping & Eating

Accommodation is mainly in a bewildering number of small B&Bs. The tourist office has brochures or try the accommodation board with free telephones outside the office. Many budget places (prices from €29 per person in winter high season) are booked months, or even years, in advance.

Central **Haus Wannali** (☎ 05446-23 50; Arlberg Strasse 509; s/d €38/76) has a friendly atmosphere and entertaining regulars. Some of the best views in town are enjoyed from the relatively spick-and-span **Pension Strolz Christian** (☎ 05446-30 119; fax 05446-30 119-4; Ing Gomperz Strasse 606; s/d €40/80).

When the hunger pangs hit, there is a Spar supermarket on the main street and good pizzas at Pomodoro. At night there is certainly a whiff of testosterone in the St Anton air. Piccadilly is loud, bawdy and English. Things are more relaxed in the subterranean Indian restaurant-cum-club Kandahar. Krazy Kanguruh is a popular bar on the slopes.

Getting There & Away

St Anton is on the main railway route between Bregenz (€14.30) and Innsbruck (€13.10), less than 1½ hours from both. St Anton is close to the eastern entrance of the Arlberg Tunnel, the toll road connecting Vorarlberg and Tirol. The tunnel toll is €9.45/7.25 for cars/motorcycles. You can avoid the toll by taking the B197, but no vehicles with trailers are allowed on this winding road.

AUSTRIA DIRECTORY

ACCOMMODATION

Reservations are recommended at Christmas, Easter and during summer. They are binding on both parties, so if you don't take a reserved room, the price could still be deducted from your credit card. Hostels tend to be more flexible, however small groups booking into hostels might find their reservation for a four-bed room translated into four separate beds on arrival.

Tourist offices can supply lists of all types of accommodation and will generally make reservations – sometimes for a small fee.

Many resort towns hand out a *Gästekarte* (guest card) to people staying overnight. This card is funded by a resort tax of around €1 to €2 per night, added to the accommodation tariff, and it offers useful discounts on transport, sporting facilities and museums. Check with the tourist office if you're not offered one at your resort accommodation. In smaller towns, the first night's accommodation can cost slightly more than subsequent nights.

There are more than 500 camping grounds in Austria, but most close in winter. If you pitch a tent outside an established camping site you need the property owner's approval; on public land it's illegal. Outside Vienna, Tirol and protected areas, free camping is allowed in a campervan, but only if you don't set up equipment outside the van. The **Austrian Camping Club** (Österreichischer Camping Club; ☎ 01-71 199-1272; Schubertring 1-3, A-1010 Vienna) has information.

In the mountains, hikers can take a break from camping by spending the night in an alpine hut. See Activities following for further details.

Two HI-affiliated hostelling associations operating within the country are **Österreichischer Jugendherbergsverband** (Map pp44-5; ☎ 01-533 5353; www.oejhv.or.at; 01, Schottenring 28, A-1010 Vienna) and **Junge Hostels Austria** (Map pp44-5; ☎ 01-533 1833; www.jungehotels.at; 01, Helferstorferstrasse 4, Vienna). Prices are generally €13 to €20 per night.

It's quite common for houseowners to rent out rooms in their home (€15 to €30 per person). Look out for the ubiquitous *Zimmer frei* (room vacant) signs.

The cheapest budget hotels start at around €25/40 singles/doubles for rooms with a shared bathroom, and €35/60 for those with private facilities. Most mid-range hotels start at around €50/80 for rooms with private facilities.

Accomodation prices quoted in this chapter are for the high summer season (or winter in ski resorts) and include all taxes. Unless otherwise stated, all rooms have private facilities and breakfast is included.

ACTIVITIES
Skiing & Snowboarding

Austria has some of the world's best skiing and snowboarding. The most popular regions are Vorarlberg and Tirol, but Salzburg province and Carinthia offer cheaper possibilities. Unusually, skiing is possible year-round at the famous Stubai Glacier near Innsbruck.

The skiing season starts in December and lasts well into April at higher altitude resorts. Count on spending €20 to €38 for a daily ski pass (to ride the ski lifts). Rental generally starts at €15 for downhill equipment or €13 for cross-country skis; rates drop for multiple days.

AUSTRIA

Hiking & Mountaineering

Walking and climbing are popular with visitors and Austrians alike, and most tourist offices sell maps of hiking routes. Mountain paths have direction indicators and often markers indicating their level of difficulty. Those with a red-white-red marker mean you need sturdy hiking boots and a pole; a blue-white-blue marker indicates the need for mountaineering equipment. There are 10 long-distance national hiking routes, while three European routes pass through Austria. Options include the northern alpine route from Lake Constance to Vienna, via Dachstein, or the central route from Feldkirch to Hainburger Pforte, via Hohe Tauern National Park.

Don't try mountaineering without the proper equipment or experience. The **Österreichischer Alpenverein** (ÖAV; Austrian Alpine Club; Map p73 ☎ 0512-587 828; office@alpenverein-ibk .at; Wilhelm Greil Strasse 15, A-6010 Innsbruck) has touring programmes and also maintains a list of alpine huts in hill-walking regions. These provide inexpensive accommodation and often have meals or cooking facilities. Members of the club take priority but anyone can stay. It's a good idea to book huts. Listing your next intended destination in the hut book on departure provides you with an extra measure of safety, as search-and-rescue teams will be alerted should a problem arise.

Spa Resorts

There are spa resorts throughout the country, identifiable by the prefix *Bad* (bath), eg Bad Ischl. While perfect for the self-indulgent pampering which stressed-out city-dwellers nowadays so often crave, they also promise more traditional healing cures for respiratory, circulatory and other ailments. The **Austrian National Tourist Office** (www.austria-tourism.at) can provide details, as can the **Österreichischer Heilbäder & Kurortverband** (Austrian Thermal Baths & Spa Association; ☎ 01-512 1904; oehkv@newsclub.at).

BOOKS

Lonely Planet has guides to both *Austria* and *Vienna*, and has Western/Central Europe phrasebooks.

Graham Greene's evocative spy story *The Third Man* is set in Vienna, as is John Irving's *Setting Free the Bears*. Numerous travel writers, from the masterful Patrick Leigh Fermor (*A Time of Gifts*) to the amusing Bill Bryson (*Neither Here Nor There*), have passed through the city.

BUSINESS HOURS

Shops usually open 9am to 6pm Monday to Friday, and 9am to 1pm or 5pm on Saturday. However, grocery stores might open as early as 6am, and other shops don't close their doors until 7.30pm. In smaller cities, there's sometimes a two-hour closure over lunch.

Banks keep remarkably short hours, usually 9am to 12.30pm and 1.30pm to 3pm Monday to Friday, with 'late' (5.30pm) closing on Thursday.

CUSTOMS

There are no set limits on goods purchased within the EU for personal use (see the Regional Directory, p1055). People aged 17 or over can bring in to Austria 200 cigarettes (or 50 cigars or 250g of tobacco), 2L of wine and 1L of spirits from non-EU countries.

DANGERS & ANNOYANCES

Handbag theft is so rife in Vienna that the tourist authorities print brochures advising you how to avoid it. Pickpockets particularly work in Vienna's two main train stations and pedestrian centre.

Take care in the mountains; helicopter rescue is expensive unless you are covered by insurance (assuming they find you in the first place).

DISABLED TRAVELLERS

People with disabilities will find their needs are well catered for. The Vienna Tourist Info Zentrum (p41) has a booklet on wheelchair-accessible hotels and museums, as well a general guide to the city for disabled visitors. You can dowload this from the **website** (www .wien.info/wtv/handicap.rtf).

EMBASSIES & CONSULATES
Austrian Embassies & Consulates

Following is a list of Austrian dipomatic missions abroad. For futher details visit www .auslandsoesterreicher.at, and click on 'Österreichische Botschaften und Konsulate' under 'Kontakte'.

Australia (☎ 02-6295 1533; www.austriaemb.org.au; 12 Talbot St, Forrest, Canberra, ACT 2603)
Canada (☎ 613-789 1444; www.austro.org; 445 Wilbrod St, Ottawa, ON K1N 6M7)

France Embassy (☎ 01-40 63 30 63; www.aussenminist erium.at/paris; 6, rue Fabert-75007 Paris); Consulate (☎ 01- 40 63 30 90; 17, avenue de Villars-75007 Paris) Visas only at the consulate.
Germany (☎ 30-202 87-0; www.oesterreichische -botschaft.de; Stauffenbergstrasse 1, D-10785 Berlin)
Ireland (☎ 01-269 45 77; dublin-ob@bmaa.gv.at; 93 Ailesbury Rd, Dublin 4)
The Netherlands (☎ 70-324 54 70; den-haag-ob@bmaa .gv.at; van Alkemadelaan 342, 2597 AS Den Haag)
New Zealand (☎ 04-499 6393; diessl@ihug.co.nz, Level 2, Willbank House, 587 Willis St, Wellington)
UK (☎ 020-7235 3731; www.austria.org.uk; 18 Belgrave Mews West, London SW1X 8HU)
USA (☎ 202-895 6700; www.austria.org; 3524 International Court NW, Washington, DC 20008)

Embassies & Consulates in Austria

Only embassies *(Botschaften)* and consulates *(Konsulate)* in Vienna issue visas. In an emergency, you might be redirected to a limited-hours consulate in a nearer city. The following diplomatic missions are located in Vienna unless otherwise stated:
Australia (Map pp44-5; ☎ 01-50 674-0; www.australian-embassy.at; 04, Mattiellistrasse 2-4)
Canada (Map pp44-5; ☎ 01-53 138-3000; www.kanada.at; 01, Laurenzerberg 2)
Croatia (☎ 01-48 487 83-0; 17, Heubergg 10)
Czech Republic (Map pp40-1; ☎ 01-89 437 41; 14, Penzingerstrasse 11-13)
France (Map pp44-5; ☎ 01-50 275-0; www.ambafrance-at.org; 04, Technikerstrasse 2)
Germany (Map pp40-1; ☎ 01-71 154-0; 03, Metternichgasse 3)
Hungary (Map pp44-5; ☎ 01-53 780-300; 01, Bankgasse 4-6)
Italy (Map pp40-1; ☎ 01-712 5121-0; 03, Rennweg 27)
Ireland (Map pp44-5; ☎ 01-715 4246-0; 01, Rotenturmstrasse16-18)
The Netherlands (Map pp44-5; ☎ 01-58 939; 01, Opernring 5)
New Zealand (☎ 01-318 8505)
Slovakia (☎ 01-318 9055-200; 19, Armbrustergasse 24)
Slovenia (Map pp44-5; ☎ 01-586 1309; 01, Niebelungengasse 13)
Switzerland (Map pp40-1; ☎ 01-79 505-0; 03, Prinz-Eugen-Strasse 7)
UK (Map pp40-1; ☎ 01-71 613-0; www.britishembassy .at; 03, Jaurèsgasse 12)
USA Embassy (Map pp40-1; ☎ 01-31 339-0; www .usembassy.at; 09, Boltzmanngasse 16); Consulate (Map pp44-5; ☎ 512 5835; 01, Gartenbaupromenade 2) Visas at the consulate only.

FESTIVALS & EVENTS

The **ANTO** (www.austria-tourism.at) has a list of annual and one-off events on its website; just click on 'Events'. Following is a list of major festivals.

February

Fasching This Shrovetide carnival before Lent involves parties, waltzes and a parade; celebrated country-wide.

May/June

Festwochen (Vienna) The Vienna Festival focuses on classical musical, theatre and other performing arts.
Lifeball (Vienna) One of the final balls of the season, this is a huge gay/straight AIDS fundraising gala attracting celebrity guests (www.lifeball.org).

July

Bregenzer Festspiele (Bregenz) Opera with a difference – performed on a floating stage on Lake Constance.
Salzburger Festspiele (Salzburg) Austria's leading classical musical festival attracts major stars like Simon Rattle and Placido Domingo.
Love Parade (Vienna) Austria hosts its own version of the popular techno street parade.

September

Ars Electronica Festival (Linz) This is a celebration of weird and wonderful technological art and computer music.
Bruckner Fest (Linz) This highbrow classical musical festival pays homage to native Linz son, Bruckner.

November

Christmas Markets (particularly Vienna and Salzburg) Quaint stalls selling traditional decorations, foodstuffs, mulled wine and all manner of presents heralding the arrival of the festive season.

December

Krampus (Innsbruck and elsewhere) St Nicholas, his friend Krampus (Black Peter) and an array of masked creatures cause merriment and mischief in a parade that harks back to pagan celebrations.
Kaiserball (Vienna) The Imperial Ball kicks off Vienna's three-month season of balls, combining glamour and high society with camp decadence.

GAY & LESBIAN TRAVELLERS

Public attitudes to homosexuality are less tolerant than in most other Western European countries, except perhaps in Vienna. A good information centre/meeting point in Vienna is **Rosa Lila Villa** (Map pp44-5; ☎ 01-586 8150; 06, Linke Wienzeile 102). The age of consent for gay men

AUSTRIA

is 18; for everyone else it's 14. Vienna has a Pride march, the Rainbow Parade, on the last Saturday in June.

HOLIDAYS

New Year's Day 1 January
Epiphany 6 January
Easter Monday March/April
May Day 1 May
Ascension Five and a half weeks after Easter
Whit Monday Seven weeks after Easter
Corpus Christi 10 days after Whit Monday
Assumption of the Virgin Mary 15 August
National Day 26 October
All Saints' Day 1 November
Immaculate Conception 8 December
Christmas Day 25 December
Boxing Day 26 December

INTERNET ACCESS

There are 'surf points' in many post offices (buy a prepaid card from the counter). **Bignet** (www.bignet.at) is the country's leading chain, with reliable, well-equipped outlets in Vienna, Salzburg and Linz.

INTERNET RESOURCES

The **Austrian National Tourist Office** (ANTO; www.austria-tourism.at) is a comprehensive starting point, with general information and details on different attractions and types of holidays.

Train times and fares are available from **Österreiche Bundesbahnen** (ÖBB; Austrian Railways; www.oebb.at).

Herold (www.herold.at) maintains an online telephone book. Budget travellers might also find quite useful the *Mensa* (university canteen) listing at www.mensen.at (in German).

LANGUAGE

Although they understand Hochdeutsch ('high' or received German), Austrians use different words and some even speak a dialect. Apart from using the expressions *Grüss Gott, Servus!* and *Ba Ba* (see the Fast Facts box p34), they join their Bavarian cousins in forming the diminuitive with 'erl' instead of the northern German 'chen'. Therefore when Austrians say *ein Bisserl*, they mean *ein Bisschen* (a little), and they use the word *Mäderl* (girl) instead of *Mädchen*. Some expressions of time are also unique. *Heuer* means 'this year' and Aus-

trians talk not of the German *Januar*, but of *Jänner* (January).

English is widely understood, particularly in cities, but see the Language chapter (p1088) for German pronunciation guidelines and useful words and phrases.

MAPS

Freytag & Berndt (see p39) and Krummerley + Frey both publish good maps in varying scales, including hiking and cycling routes.

MEDIA

Austria has four national daily newspapers. The mid-market tabloid *Kronen Zeitung* is the most popular and populist; *Kurier* is similar, but slightly less reactionary. *Die Presse* is a conservative, fairly business-oriented affair, akin to the *Financial Times*. *Der Standard* is the liberal, intellectual heavyweight.

English-language newspapers and magazines such as The *Times, International Herald Tribune* and *Newsweek* are available for €2.50 to €4.75.

FM4 is a news and music station, mostly in English, with hourly news until 7pm. It's on 103.4FM in Vienna. Austria has only two (terrestrial) national TV channels (ORF 1 and 2), and a commercial channel (ATV). Vienna has one cable TV provider, Telekabel.

MONEY

The currency is the euro, although you'll still hear some references to its Austrian predecessor, the Schilling. Straight conversion of prices from Schilling to euro is the reason for occasionally strange prices – eg €3.63 for a phone card, €2.91 for a coffee.

Major train stations have currency offices and there are plenty of banks, *bureaux de change* and *Bankomats* (ATMs) across the country.

Costs

Expenses in Austria are average for Western Europe, with prices highest in big cities and ski resorts. Budget travellers can possibly scrape by on €40 a day, after rail-card costs; double this amount if you intend to avoid self-catering or staying in hostels. The minimum you can expect to pay per person is €13/25 for a hostel/hotel and €5/10 for a lunch/dinner.

Taxes & Refunds

Value-added tax (*Mehrwertsteuer* or MwSt), is charged at either 10% (eg travel, food and museum entry) or 20% (drinks and luxury goods). Prices always include taxes. For purchases over €75, non-EU residents can reclaim the MwSt either upon leaving the EU or afterwards. (Note that one-third of your refund will be absorbed in charges.) Ensure the shop has the forms to be filled out at the time of purchase, and present the documentation to customs on departure for checking and stamping. The airports at Vienna, Salzburg, Innsbruck, Linz and Graz have counters for instant refunds, as do some land crossings to non-EU countries. You can also reclaim by post.

Tipping & Bargaining

Austrian waiters aren't renowned for friendly or speedy service, but it's still rude not to round off the bill so that it includes a 10% tip. Pay it directly to the server; don't leave it on the table. Taxi drivers will also expect tips of 10%. Bargaining is unheard of.

POST

Post office hours vary: typical hours in smaller towns are 8am to noon and 2pm to 6pm Monday to Friday (money exchange to 5pm), and 8am to 11am Saturday, but a few main post offices in big cities are open daily till late, or even 24 hours. Stamps are also available in *Tabak* (tobacco) shops.

Postcards and standard letters (up to 20g) cost €0.55 both within Austria and to Europe. Standard letters to other destinations cost €1.25. Heavier letters, up to 50g, can be sent either economy or priority, costing €1 or €1.10 to Europe and €1.25 or €1.75 to other destinations.

SENIOR TRAVELLERS

Women over 60 years of age and men over 65 qualify for senior discounts. Some sightseeing attractions offer discounts for those 62 years and over. Vienna-based **Seniorenbüro der Stadt Wien** (Map pp40-1; ☎ 01-40 00-8580; 08, Schlesingerplatz 2; ☺ 8am-3.30pm Mon-Fri) can give advice.

TELEPHONE

Don't worry if a telephone number you're given has only four digits, as many as nine digits, or some odd number in between.

> **EMERGENCY NUMBERS**
>
> ■ Alpine Rescue ☎ 140
> ■ Ambulance ☎ 144
> ■ Police ☎ 133
> ■ Fire ☎ 122

The Austrian system often adds direct-dial (DW) extensions to the main number after a hyphen. Thus, say ☎ 12 345 is a main number, ☎ 12 345-67 will be an extension, which could be a phone or fax. Mostly, a -0 gives you the switchboard operator.

From a public phone, it costs €0.12 per minute to call anywhere in Austria, be it next door or across the country.

Mobile Phones

Mobile phones in Austria operate on GSM 900/1800, which is compatible with other European countries and Australia, but not with the North American GSM 1900 system or the system used in Japan.

If you're staying for a while, it's possible to get a prepaid phone in Austria or strike a deal where you pay for calls and line rental but get your handset free. Try **Max.Mobil** (Map pp40-1; ☎ 0676 2000; 03, Kelsenstrasse 5-7) or **Mobilkom** (☎ 0800 664 300).

Phonecards

The minimum tariff in phone boxes is €0.20. Some boxes only accept phonecards (Telefon-Wertkarte), which can be bought from post offices in two denominations – €3.60 and €6.90.

TIME

Austria operates on Central European Time (see the Regional Directory p1063). Clocks go forward one hour on the last Saturday night in March and back again on the last Saturday night in October.

TOILETS

There is no shortage of public toilets; some may charge about €0.20.

TOURIST INFORMATION

Tourist offices (usually called *Kurverein*, *Verkehrsamt* or *Tourismusverband*) tend to adjust their hours from one year to the next, so hours listed in this chapter are a guide only and may have changed slightly by the time you arrive.

The **Austrian National Tourist Office** (ANTO; www.austria-tourism.at) has a number of overseas offices, including those in the following list. Some offices aren't open to personal callers, so phone first. There is a comprehensive listing on the ANTO website.

Australia (☎ 02-9299 3621; info@antosyd.org.au; 1st fl, 36 Carrington St, Sydney, NSW 2000)
UK (☎ 020-7629 0461; info@anto.co.uk; 14 Cork St, London W1S 3NS)
USA (☎ 212-944 6880; info@oewnyc.com; PO Box 1142, New York, NY 10108-1142)

VISAS

Visas are not required for EU, US, Canadian, Australian or New Zealand citizens. Visitors may stay a maximum of three months (six months for Japanese citizens). There are no time limits for EU and Swiss nationals, but they should register with the police before taking up residency. Most African and Arab nationals require a visa.

WOMEN TRAVELLERS

Women are unlikely to suffer any harassment. In the event of an attack, call the **Rape Crisis Hotline** (☎ 01-71 719) in Vienna.

WORK

EU nationals can work in Austria without a permit. For employers to take on non-EU nationals, they must apply for a work permit for their employee.

Seasonal work in ski resorts is the most obvious and readily available option. Non-EU nationals who accept anything more permanent need a residency permit, as well as their work permit.

TRANSPORT IN AUSTRIA

GETTING THERE & AWAY
Air

The national carrier, Austrian Airlines, has an excellent safety record and specialises in linking numerous Eastern European cities to the West via Vienna.

Low-cost airlines also serve Austria. Ryanair flies from London to Graz, Klagenfurt, Linz and Salzburg; Air Berlin flies to Vienna from Germany; and German Wings has limited services from Düsseldorf and Stutt-

gart. Central European low-cost carrier Sky Europe flies to Croatia, France, Hungary, Italy, Poland and more. Be warned, though, that its 'Vienna' airport is far from the city – in Slovakia, actually.

See Getting There & Away in the relevant city sections for details of the international airports in Vienna (p52), Graz (p60), Innsbruck (p77), Klagenfurt (p61) and Salzburg (p67).

Major international airlines, reputable regional carriers and low-cost airlines flying to and from Austria include:

Air Berlin (code AB; ☎ 0820 400 011; www.airberlin.com)
Air France (code AF; ☎ 01-50 222-2400; www.airfrance.com)
Alitalia (code AZ; ☎ 01-505 1707; www.alitalia.com)
Austrian Airways (code OS; ☎ 05-17 66; www.aua.com)
British Airways (code BA; ☎ 01-79 567-567; www.ba.com)
Croatia Airlines (code OU; ☎ 01-70 07-36163; www.croatiaairlines.com)
CSA (code OK; ☎ 01-512 3805-0; www.czechairlines.com)
German Wings (code 4U; ☎ 01-50 291-0070; www.germanwings.com)
Iberia (code IB; ☎ 01-795 6761-2; www.iberia.com)
KLM (code KL; ☎ 0900-359556; www.klm.com)
LOT Polish Airlines (code LO; ☎ 01-961 0885; www.lot.com)
Lufthansa (code LH; ☎ 0810-1025 8080; www.lufthansa.com)
Ryanair (code FR; ☎ 0900-210 240; www.ryanair.com)
SAS Scandinavian Airlines (code SK; ☎ 01-68 055-4466; www.scandinavian.net)
SkyEurope Airlines (code NE; ☎ 01-9985 5555; www.skyeurope.com)
Swiss International Air Lines (code LX; ☎ 0810-810 840; www.swiss.com)

Land
BORDER CROSSINGS

There are many entry points from the Czech Republic, Hungary, Slovakia, Slovenia and Switzerland; main border crossings are open 24 hours. There are usually no border controls to/from Germany and Italy.

BUS

Buses leave Austria for as far afield as England, the Baltic countries, the Netherlands, Germany and Switzerland. But most significantly, they provide access to Eastern European cities small and large – from the likes of Belgrade, Sofia, Warsaw, to Banja Luka, Mostar and Sarajevo.

Services operated by **Eurolines** (www.eurolines
.at) leave from Vienna (see p52) and from
several regional cities; check the Eurolines
website under 'Adressen' for more details.

CAR & MOTORCYCLE
Austria levies fees for its entire motorway
network. Therefore tourists need to choose
between a 10-day pass (motorcycle/car
€4.30/7.60), a two-month pass (€10.90/21.80)
or a yearly pass (€29/72.60) and then clearly
display the chosen toll label (*Vignette*) on
their vehicle. Passes are available at borders,
on freeways or from service stations. Without one, you will face an on-the-spot fine
of up to €220 or, if you don't pay up immediately, a €2180 fine. For details see www
.oesag.at (in German).

HITCHING
Lonely Planet doesn't recommend hitching,
as it is never entirely safe. If you must, however, stay clear of the route from Salzburg
to Munich, one of Europe's most difficult
spots to get a lift.

TRAIN
The main rail services in and out of the
country include the route from Vienna's
Westbahnhof to Munich, via Salzburg and
Bregenz. Trains to the Czech Republic leave
from Südbahnhof in Vienna. Express services to Italy go via Innsbruck or Villach;
trains to Slovenia are routed through Graz.

For Austrian rail passes that extend into
other countries, see Train, p88.

River & Lake
Hydrofoils run to Bratislava and Budapest
from Vienna (see p52). Other boats go from
Linz to Passau in Germany (see p53). Ger-
many and Switzerland can be reached from
Bregenz (see p80).

GETTING AROUND
Air
Austrian Airlines and its subsidiary, Tyrolean
Airlines, operate regular internal flights, but
train, bus and car travel usually suffices in
such a small country.

Bicycle
Private operators and hostels rent bikes; ex-
pect to pay anything from €7 to €10 a day.
Vienna has cut-price city bikes.

You can pay separately to take your bike
on slow trains (€2.90/7.50/22.50 for a daily/
weekly/monthly ticket); on fast trains it
costs €6.80 a day, if space allows. Booking is
advisable, because if there's no space in the
passenger carriages, you will have to send
your bike as registered luggage (€21.40). If
a group of you are travelling with bikes, ask
about the '1-Plus Freizeitticket' (passenger
plus bike).

Boat
Services along the Danube (see p53) are
mainly scenic pleasure cruises, but provide
a leisurely way of getting from A to B.

Bus
Both *Postbuses* and *Bahnbuses* are now operated by the railways, ÖBB. Bus services
are generally limited to less accessible regions, such as the Salzkammergut or Hohe
Tauern National Park. Between major cities
in environmentally friendly Austria, only
train services exist.

Buses are single-class, clean, efficient and
run on time. Generally you can only buy
tickets from the drivers. Call ☎ 01-71 101
for inquiries.

Car & Motorcycle
AUTOMOBILE ASSOCIATIONS
The **Austrian Automobile Club** (Map pp44-5; Österreichischer Automobil, Motorrad und Touring Club; ÖAMTC;
☎ 01-71 199-0; Schubertring 1-3, A-1010 Vienna) provides emergency breakdown assistance via
its **24-hour phone line** (☎ 120). It charges non-
members an initial call-out fee of €95/135
day/night, on top of other service charges.

BRINGING YOUR OWN VEHICLE
Cars can be transported by train; Vienna is
linked by a daily motorail service to Innsbruck, Salzburg and Villach.

DRIVING LICENCE
Visitors from the EU can drive on their own
licence, those from elsewhere require an international driver's licence.

FUEL & SPARE PARTS
Motorway service stations are found at regular intervals. Basic spare parts are widely
available. Ordering more specialised parts,
especially for non-European models, takes
time and can be costly.

AUSTRIA

HIRE

Multinational car-hire firms **Avis** (www.avis.at), **Budget** (www.budget.at) **Europcar** (www.europcar.co.at) and **Hertz** (www.hertz.at) all have offices in major cities. At the time of research, Budget and Avis (in that order) offered the best deals, but local rental agencies may be cheaper; ask at tourist offices for details. The minimum age for renting small cars is 19 years, or 25 for larger, 'prestige' cars. Customers must have held a licence for at least a year. Many contracts forbid customers to take cars outside Austria, particularly into Eastern Europe.

ROAD CONDITIONS

Roads are generally good, but care is needed on difficult mountain routes. Snow chains are highly recommended in winter. There are tolls (usually between €2.50 and €10) for some mountain tunnels.

ROAD RULES

Traffic drives on the right, and you must give way to vehicles on the right. On mountain roads, buses always have priority; otherwise, priority lies with uphill traffic. The usual speed limits are 50km/h in towns, 130km/h on motorways and 100km/h on other roads. There's a steep on-the-spot fine for drink-driving (over 0.05% blood alcohol content) and your licence may be confiscated. If you plan to drive on motorways, you must pay a tax and affix a *Vignette* to your windscreen (see Car & Motorcycle p87).

Many city streets have restricted parking (called 'blue zones') during shopping hours. Parking is unrestricted on unmarked streets.

Motorcyclists must have their headlights on during the day and crash helmets are compulsory for riders and passengers.

Hitching

It's illegal to hitchhike on Austrian motorways (and for minors under 16 years of age to hitch anywhere in Burgenland, Upper Austria, Styria and Vorarlberg).

Train

The efficient state network, ÖBB, is supplemented by a few private lines. Eurail and Inter-Rail passes (see p1070) are valid on the former, but only sometimes on the latter. There is no supplement on Eurail and Inter-Rail passes for national travel on faster EC (Eurocity) and IC (Intercity) trains. Tickets purchased on the train cost about €3 extra. Fares quoted in this chapter are for 2nd-class tickets.

Before arriving in Austria, EU residents can buy a Eurodomino Pass (see p1080) for Austria for €104 for three days and €10 for each extra day for up to eight days in total.

Available to non-EU residents are the Austrian rail pass (US$109 for three days; US$20 each extra day up to eight days in total) and the European Eastpass (US$160 for five days; US$23 for each extra day up to 10 days in total), for travel within Austria, the Czech Republic, Hungary, Poland and Slovakia. Both are valid for a month. The Austria & Switzerland Pass (US$256/210 over/under 26 years for four days, and $30/27 for each extra day up to 10 days in total) is valid for two months.

Within Austria, anyone can buy a Vorteilscard (adult/under 26 years/senior €99.90/19.90/26.90) which reduces fares by 45% and is valid for a year.

Nationwide train information can be obtained by dialling ☎ 05-17 17 (local rate).

Belgium

BELGIUM

Belgium is a bizarre little place. Called 'Europe's most eccentric country' in one breath, and 'boring' in the next, if you want something a bit offbeat, this is it.

Ruled for centuries by ever-changing European powers, België to the Dutch speakers and La Belgique to the nation's French speakers only came into being in 1830. These days it's a bit like a teenager – world-weary, unruly and avant-garde all rolled in one.

The country boasts one of Europe's richest art histories. From the passions of the Flemish Primitives to Gothic masterpieces, Art Nouveau jewels and strokes of surrealism, all are fabulously displayed.

To top it off, Belgians have a keen sense of the good things in life – they know how to eat well, they make some of the world's best beers and there's no need to introduce their chocolate.

FAST FACTS

- **Area** 30,000 sq km
- **Capital** Brussels
- **Currency** euro (€); A$1 = €0.58; ¥100 = €0.76; NZ$1 = €0.54; UK£1 = €1.50; US$1 = €0.83
- **Famous for** chocolate, beer
- **Key Phrases** *goeiendag/bonjour* (hello; Dutch/French); *tot ziens/au revoir* (goodbye; Dutch/French); *bedankt/merci* (thanks; Dutch/French); *ja/oui* (yes; Dutch/French); *ness/non* (no; Dutch/French)
- **Official Languages** Dutch, French, German
- **Population** 10.2 million
- **Telephone Codes** country code ☎ 32; international access code ☎ 00; reverse-charge code ☎ 1224
- **Visas** no entry requirements or restrictions on EU nationals; citizens of Australia, Canada, Israel, Japan, New Zealand and the USA do not need visas to visit the country as tourists for up to three months

HIGHLIGHTS

- Explore the crowded but must-see sights of the medieval city of **Bruges** (p110).
- Be seduced by the capital, **Brussels** (p95), with its Art Nouveau architecture, surrealist art, and chocolate shops galore.
- Surrender yourself to dynamic **Antwerp** (p102), a city with attitude that lures fashionistas, foodies and party queens.
- Immerse yourself in the poignant landscape of the **Ypres Salient** (p113), with its reminders of some of WWI's most devastating battles.
- Cycle around the Ardennes town of **Rochefort** (p118), and visit its ancient caves filled with nature's wonders.

ITINERARIES

- **Three days** Brussels, Bruges and Antwerp: three cities in as many days. It *can* be comfortably done thanks to proximity and human scale. In Brussels, start with the Grand Place, followed by the Musée Horta. In Bruges, don't miss a canal ride and the Groeningemuseum. Antwerp essentials include Onze Lieve Vrouwkathedraal and Oud Arsenaal.

- **One week** Follow the three-day itinerary, but add an extra night in both Brussels and Bruges. A day-trip to Ypres is also a must. For a taste of Belgium's French-speaking region, burrow down at Namur and/or Rochefort.

CLIMATE & WHEN TO GO

Belgium's weather is fickle. To avoid major dampness, visit between May and September. 'Wretched' best describes the winter months from November to March – the days are grey and wet with occasional light snow.

HISTORY

Bruges, Ghent and Ypres were Belgium's first major cities, booming in the 13th and 14th centuries on the manufacturing and trading of cloth. Their craftspeople established powerful guilds (organisations to stringently control arts and crafts), whose elaborate guildhalls you'll see in many cities – the most famous are those on Brussels' Grand Place (p98).

When Protestantism swept Europe in the 16th century, the Low Countries (present-day Belgium, the Netherlands and Luxembourg, often referred to as the Benelux) embraced it, much to the chagrin of their ruler, the fanatically Catholic Philip II of Spain. He ordered the Inquisition to enforce Catholicism, a move that led to the Iconoclastic Fury, in which Protestants ran riot, ransacking churches, including Antwerp's Onze Lieve Vrouwkathedraal, Belgium's finest Gothic cathedral. Inevitably, in 1568, war broke out. It lasted 80 years and, in the end, roughly laid the region's present-day borders. Holland and its allied provinces victoriously expelled the Spaniards, while Belgium and Luxembourg stayed under their rule.

For the next 200 years Belgium remained a battlefield for successive foreign powers. After the Spaniards came the Austrians, and in turn the French. Napoleon was trounced in 1815 at Waterloo (p102), near Brussels. In 1830 the Catholic Belgians won

independence from the Netherlands and finally formed their own kingdom.

The ensuing years saw the start of Flemish nationalism, with tension growing between Flemish (Dutch) and French speakers that has continued to this day.

Then, from 1885, came Belgium's most shadowy period – King Léopold II's rule of the Congo. For details, see the boxed text on p102.

Despite Belgium's neutrality, the Germans invaded in 1914 and the town of Ypres was destroyed. Tours of the Ypres Salient (p114) offer poignant WWI reminders.

During WWII the whole country was taken over within three weeks of a surprise German attack in May 1940. Controversy over the questionable early capitulation by King Léopold III led to his abdication in 1950 in favour of his son, King Baudouin, whose popular reign ended with his death in 1993. Childless, Baudouin was succeeded by his brother, the present King Albert II.

Although the headquarters of the EU and the North Atlantic Treaty Organization (NATO), Belgium kept a low profile on the international arena right up until the end of the 20th century, when it became best known for poisoned chickens and paedophiles. Sick of mismanagement and neglect, the nation turned to radical political reform and, in 1999, booted out the Christian Democrat party after 40 years in power.

The new Liberal prime minister, Guy Verhofstadt, quickly sought to raise public

BELGIUM

BELGIUM

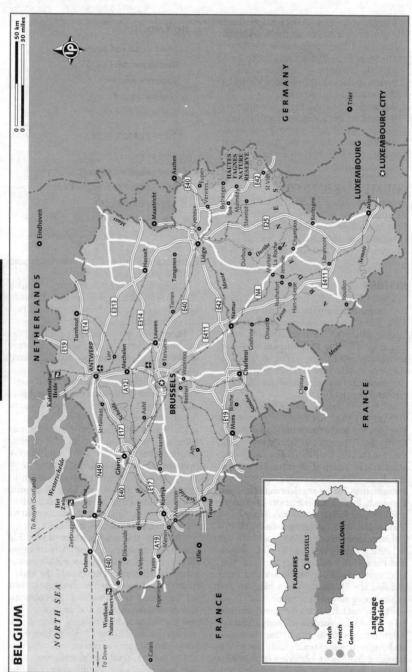

morale by reinventing Belgium with robust foreign policies and new moral freedoms. Belgium is the second country (following the Netherlands) to legalise gay marriage and euthanasia. In 2003, the country vocally sided with France and Germany against the US-led war in Iraq. The same year, a failed attempt was made to prosecute former US president George Bush in the Belgian courts for war crimes.

In 2004, the trial of murderer and paedophile Marc Dutroux once again brought Belgium into the international spotlight.

And in world tennis, Belgium shines (see p93).

PEOPLE

Belgium's population is basically split in two: the Flemish (Dutch) and the Walloons. Language is the dividing factor, made official in 1962 when a linguistic divide was drawn across the country, cutting it almost equally in half. To the north of the divide lies Flanders (Vlaanderen), whose Flemish speakers make up 60% of Belgium's 10.2 million population. South of the divide is Wallonia (La Wallonie), where French-speaking Walloons make up most of the population. The remainder is a German-speaking enclave in the far east, in an area known as the Eastern Cantons.

SPORT

If it wasn't for Kim Clijsters and Justine Henin-Hardenne, there'd be almost nothing to say here. But, in 2003, Belgium's tennis aces became the world's top two female tennis players – a feat that no other country, except the USA, has managed.

Cycling is the only other sport to have sprouted an international hero. Grocer's son Eddy Merckx is revered as the greatest natural cyclist ever, winning the Tour de France five times in the 1960s and '70s.

RELIGION

Christianity was established early and today Catholicism reigns supreme – roughly 75% of the population is Roman Catholic. While church attendance has dropped dramatically in recent decades, religious traditions remain strong and influence many aspects of daily life, including politics and education. Belgium also has sizeable Protestant, Jewish and Muslim communities.

ARTS
Literature

Any Inspector Maigret fan would know that Belgium celebrated the 100th anniversary of the birth of Liège novelist Georges Simenon in 2003.

Comic strips are a Belgian forte. A literary milestone in 2004 was the 75th anniversary of the birth of Tintin by Georges Remi, aka Hergé.

Hugo Claus' *The Sorrow of Belgium* weaves a story based on Nazi collaboration during WWII.

Amélie Nothomb is a contemporary author whose book *The Stranger Next Door* goes into strange events in the Belgian countryside.

Cinema

Belgian cinema devotes itself to black humour and down-to-earth realism, best exemplified by the 1999 Cannes winner, *Rosetta*, by brothers Luc and Jean-Pierre Dardenne.

Anyway the Wind Blows (2003), by Tom Barman, looks at 32 hours in the lives of eight characters, set against the backdrop of Barman's home-town Antwerp.

Everybody Famous (2000), Dominique Deruddere's twisted comedy about a factory worker who dreams of celebrity status for his overweight daughter, a Madonna wannabe, was nominated for a best foreign-language Oscar.

Belgium's biggest export to Hollywood is the 'Muscles from Brussels', actor Jean-Claude Van Damme. He debuted in *Bloodsport* (1987) and, off screen, finds time to provide fodder for the British tabloids.

Music

Jazz is at home in Belgium. Adople Sax invented the saxophone and octogenarian Toots Thielemans still enthrals audiences with his legendary harmonica playing. To get right among the jazz scene don't miss Brussels' **Jazz Marathon** (www.brusselsjazzmarathon .be) on the last weekend in May.

In the 1950s Jacques Brel took the French-speaking world by storm and is still much loved in his homeland. Also from this era is Johnny Haliday.

Arno Hintjens is the godfather of Belgian rock. Love or loathe him, Helmut Lotti is also Belgian (not German), and pumps out the classics.

K's Choice, Axelle Red and Hooverphonic are among contemporary names to look out for.

The country's most prestigious classical-music event is the **Concours Musical International Reine Élisabeth de Belgique** (Queen Elisabeth International Musical Competition; www.concours-reine-elisabeth.be). The best place to catch opera or classical music is La Monnaie/De Munt (p100).

Architecture

Many of Belgium's earliest buildings are on Unesco's World Heritage list. These include mighty belfries such as that in Bruges (p110), many Flemish *begijnhoven* (see Bruges' begijnhof, p112) and, of course, Brussels' famous Grand Place (p98).

On the flip side, there's little in the way of exciting modern architecture. Swathes of Brussels have gone under the demolition ball to make way for the boring glass buildings that typify the EU quarter. But in other old art cities, designers have realised that modern can sit harmoniously alongside ancient, as seen in Bruges' new Concertgebouw (p113) and bOb Van Reeth's Zuiderterras café (p106) in Antwerp.

Not to be missed is Belgium's Art Nouveau architecture, best seen at Brussels' Musée Horta (p98) and the Old England building (p98). Art Nouveau swept across Europe at the end of the 19th century and blended architecture with daily aspects of life. Check out guided tours by the Atelier de Recherche et d'Action Urbaine (p98).

Visual Arts

Belgium's rich art heritage began in Bruges in the late Middle Ages with painters known as the Flemish Primitives. Their works greatly influenced the course of European art and, centuries later, still astonish viewers. Key players included Jan Van Eyck and Hans Memling; their paintings are best viewed at Bruges' Groeningemuseum (p110) and Memlingmuseum (p110), and also at Ghent's St Baafskathedraal (p107).

The greatest 16th-century Flemish painter was Pieter Breugel the Elder, who lived and worked in Brussels. The capital's Musées Royaux des Beaux-Arts (p98) exhibits an excellent range of his works.

Antwerp held the cultural high ground during the 17th century, mainly due to

Flemish baroque painter Pieter Paul Rubens. Some of his famous altarpieces can still be seen in the city's Onze Lieve Vrouwkathedraal (p104).

The 19th century's James Ensor was a pioneer of expressionism. See his work at Antwerp's Koninklijk Museum voor Schone Kunsten (p104).

Surrealism, a movement that developed in Paris in the 1920s, found fertile ground here. Works by René Magritte and Paul Delvaux are displayed at Brussels' Musées Royaux des Beaux-Arts (p98).

Belgium's best-known contemporary artist is the avant-garde Panamarenko. His bizarre sculptures fuse authentic and imaginary flying contraptions and can be seen at Ghent's Stedelijk Museum voor Actuele Kunst (p107).

Theatre & Dance

Belgium's dynamic contemporary dance scene centres on two companies – **Rosas** (www .rosas.be) in Brussels and Charleroi/Danses and **Plan K** (www.charleroi-danses.be), based in Charleroi. For classical ballet, see the Koninklijk Ballet van Vlaanderen (p106). To combine theatre and dance, investigate Brussels' **KunstenFestivaldesArts** (www.kunstenfestivaldesarts .be), held in the last two weeks of May.

ENVIRONMENT

Belgium's environmental picture is ugly and the scene is not getting rosier – in the 2003 national elections the country's two green parties were catapulted out of government. The only nationally protected reserve is the Hautes Fagnes Nature Reserve (p116). Water and noise pollution, urbanisation and waste management are the most pressing environmental issues.

FOOD & DRINK

Belgians love food. They are reputed to dine out, on average, more than any other people in the world.

Staples & Specialities

Meat and seafood are abundantly consumed and although there are traditional regional dishes – such as Ghent's famous *waterzooi* (a cream-based chicken stew) – the most popular dishes have crossed local boundaries. Italian, Greek, Turkish, Portuguese and Asian cuisines thrive, too. In Brussels there are a few African eateries, reflecting Belgium's colonial past.

Belgium's national dish is *mosselen/moules* – mussels cooked in white wine and served in steaming cauldrons with a mountain of chips. Offal is big on menus, and you'll also come across *paardefilet/steack de cheval* (horse steak) and *filet américain*. Don't be deceived, the latter is not a succulent American steak but a blob of minced beef served raw.

Belgians swear they invented *frieten/frites* – chips or fries – and, judging by the availability, it's a claim few would contest. Every village has at least one *frituur/friture* where *frites* are served smothered until unrecognisable with thick mayonnaise.

A *belegd broodje/sandwich garni* is half a baguette with a prepared filling – an immensely popular snack food.

And then there's chocolate. The Belgians have been quietly making some of the world's finest chocolate for well over a century. Filled chocolates, or pralines (pronounced 'prah-leens'), are the nation's forte.

On the drinking scene, beer rules. No country in the world boasts a brewing tradition as rich and diverse as Belgium. And nowhere will you find the quantity of quality beers offered by this little nation. Somewhere between 400 and 800 beers exist. Try a dark Trappist beer made by monks, golden nectars such as Duvel (named after the devil himself), a thirst-quenching white beer such as Hoegaarden or the acquired taste of tangy, fruity *lambics*. For the latter, don't miss Brussels' Musée Bruxellois de la Gueuze (p98).

Where to Eat & Drink

Any place, any time, you'll find honest food being served at much-loved eateries. At lunch time, many restaurants offer a *dagschotel/plat du jour* (dish of the day), which often represents excellent value. Also watch for a 'menu of the day' (*dagmenu/menu du jour*). These menus comprise three courses, and work out cheaper than selecting individual courses à la carte.

Those here to drink will be spoiled for choice. All cafés serve alcohol and most stay open until the last person leaves. True beer lovers should head to specialist cafés, such as Het Biercircus (p100) or 't Brugs Beertje (p113).

Vegetarians & Vegans

Fear not! Belgium may be carnivore kingdom but vegetarians are catered for, albeit reluctantly at times. Vegans, on the other hand, will go hungry almost everywhere except at Antwerp's zany Lombardia (p105).

BRUSSELS

pop 992,000

It's hard to fathom how Brussels (Brussel in Dutch, Bruxelles in French) got labelled 'boring'. In a city where fine food is mandatory, café culture common, Art Nouveau architecture prolific and the bizarre and surreal comfortably at home, how did anyone find it dull? It's true that for a long time Brussels didn't go out of its way to impress – it was, and still is, a secretive city.

HISTORY

Legend has it that St Géry, Bishop of Cambrai and Arras, built a chapel on an island in the swampy Senne (Zenne) River in AD 695, though the name Bruocsella (from *bruoc,* marsh or swamp, and *sella,* dwelling) wasn't recorded until 966.

In 1695 Louis XVI's French army bombarded Brussels for two days in retaliation for Dutch and English attacks on French Channel ports. They destroyed 4000 houses and much of the city's magnificent central square, Grand Place, although this was restored to its full glory within five years.

An opera performance at Brussels' La Monnaie theatre (p100) in August 1830 sparked the revolution that brought about Belgian independence. During the next century, the city grew enormously in both population and stature, due largely to the wealth pouring in from the Congo and the expansionist policy of King Léopold II (see p102).

At the end of the 19th century, Art Nouveau swept through Europe, leaving Brussels with a bevy of gorgeous buildings such as the Musée Horta (p98).

After WWII, the capital developed unchecked, first becoming the headquarters of NATO and later the EU. In 2004, the EU welcomed 10 new members and talk in Brussels these days often centres on the impact this ever-increasing union will have on the city.

BELGIUM

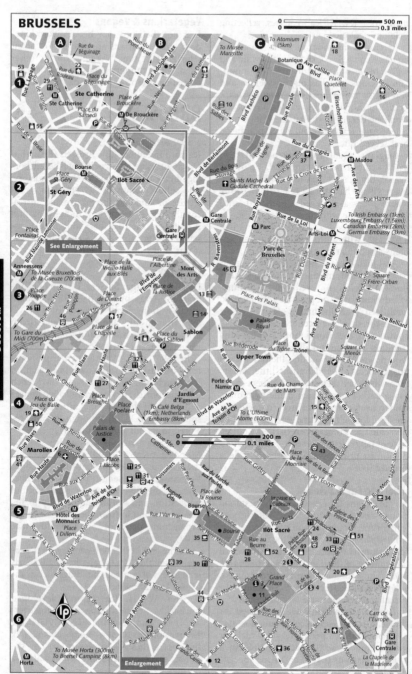

BELGIUM

INFORMATION				
ATM	(see 4)	Breugel	17 B3	Le Greenwich	38 B5
Australian Embassy	1 D3	Centre Vincent Van Gogh	18 D1		
Belgian Tourist Information Centre	2 C5	Hôtel Galia	19 A4	ENTERTAINMENT	(pp100–1)
Brussels International	3 C6	Hôtel La Madeleine	20 D6	AB	39 B5
Fortis Banque	4 D6	Hôtel Le Dixseptiéme	21 D6	Arenberg-Galeries	40 D5
French Embassy	5 D2	Résidence Les Écrins	22 A1	Fuse ĝ Food	41 A5
Hôpital St Pierre	6 A4	Sleep Well	23 B1	L'Archiduc	42 B5
Main Post Office	7 B1			La Monnaie/De Munt	43 D4
New Zealand Embassy	8 D4	EATING	(pp99–100)	Le Belgica	44 B6
US Embassy	9 D3	Aux Armes de Bruxelles	24 D5	Musée du Cinéma	45 C3
		Bonsoir Clara	25 B5	Recyclart	46 A3
SIGHTS & ACTIVITIES	(p98)	Comme Chez Soi	26 A3	Tels Quels	47 B6
Centre Belge de la Bande Dessinée	10 C1	Easy Tempo	27 A4	Théâtre Royal de Toone	48 D5
Hôtel de Ville	11 C6	GB Express	28 C5		
Manneken Pis	12 C6	Jacques	29 A1	SHOPPING	(p101)
Musée des Instruments de		La Galletierre	30 B5	De Biertempel	49 C5
Musique	13 B3	Le Pain Quotidien	31 B5	Fleamarket	50 A4
Musées Royaux des Beaux-Arts de		Le Perroquet	32 B4	Galeries St Hubert	51 D5
Belgique	14 B3	Taverne du Passage	33 D5	Galler	52 C5
Old England Building	(see 13)			Martin Margiela	53 A1
		DRINKING	(p100)	Pierre Marcolini	54 B3
SLEEPING	(pp98–9)	À la Mort Subite	34 D5	Stijl	55 A1
B&B Guilmin	15 D4	Falstaff	35 B5		
B&B Phileas Fogg	16 D1	Goupil le Fol	36 C6	OTHER	
		Het Biercircus	37 C2	ARAU	56 B1

ORIENTATION

The Grand Place, Brussels' imposing 15th-century market square, sits dead centre in the Petit Ring, a pentagon of boulevards enclosing central Brussels. The centre is divided into the Lower Town, comprising the medieval core and atmospheric quarters such as Ste Catherine, St Géry and the Marolles, and the Upper Town, home to major museums and chic shopping precincts based around the Sablon and Ave Louise.

East of the Petit Ring is the real-life Gotham City of the EU.

Gare Centrale, Brussels' most central train station, is about five minutes' walk from the Grand Place; Gare du Midi, where international trains arrive, is 2.5km from the famous square.

Unlike anywhere else in Belgium, Brussels is officially bilingual. Everything – from the names of streets to train stations – is written in both Dutch and French. We have used the French versions.

BRUSSELS IN TWO DAYS

Grand Place (p98) is the essential start; **Galeries St Hubert** (p98) comes second. Head to the Upper Town for the **Musées Royaux des Beaux-Arts** (p98). Stock up on pralines at **Pierre Marcolini** (p101) before tramming it to **Musée Horta** (p98). By night, trawl **Rue des Bouchers** (p98) and then hit the **pubs/cafés** (p100).

On day two, visit the **Koninklijk Museum voor Midden-Afrika** (p102).

Maps

Lonely Planet's Brussels City Map contains five maps including Greater Brussels and comes in a handy plastic-coated (waterproof) format. Many hotels and hostels provide free city maps.

INFORMATION
Internet Access
Concepts Telecom (Gare du Midi; ⏲ 9am-8.30pm Mon-Fri, 10am-7.30pm Sat)

Medical Services
Helpline (☎ 02 648 40 14; ⏲ 24hr) Assistance line run by Community Help Service.
Hôpital St Pierre (☎ 02 535 31 11, emergency 02 535 40 51; cnr Rue Haute & Rue de l'Abricotier; ⏲ 24hr) Central hospital offering emergency assistance.

Money
Fortis Banque (☎ 02 289 05 70; Rue de la Colline 12; ⏲ 9am-12.30pm & 1.30-4pm Mon-Fri) Bank near the Grand Place; has a handy ATM.

Post
Main post office (1st fl, Centre Monnaie, Blvd Anspach; ⏲ 8am-6pm Mon-Fri, 9.30am-3pm Sat)

Tourist Information
Belgian Tourist Information Centre (☎ 02 504 03 90; www.visitflanders.com or www.belgique-tourisme.net; Rue du Marché aux Herbes 63; ⏲ 9am-6pm or 7pm Mon-Fri, 9am-1pm & 2-7pm Sat & Sun May-Oct, 9am-6pm Mon-Fri, 9am-1pm & 2-6pm Sat, 9am-1pm Sun Nov-Apr) Supplies national tourist information.
Brussels International (☎ 02 513 89 40; www .brusselsinternational.be; Grand Place; ⏲ 9am-6pm

BELGIUM

Easter-Oct, 9am-6pm Mon-Sat, 10am-2pm Sun Nov-Dec, 9am-6pm Mon-Sat Jan-Easter) The City of Brussels tourist office, located inside the town hall and usually crammed. **Tourisme Bruxelles** (Gare du Midi; ☺ 8am-8pm Sat-Thu, to 9pm Fri May-Sep, 8am-5pm Mon-Thu, to 8pm Fri, 9am-8pm Sat, 9am-2pm Sun Oct-Apr) For visitors arriving by Eurostar or Thalys.

SIGHTS

Brussels' magnificent central square, **Grand Place**, tops every newcomer's itinerary. Here you'll find the splendid Gothic-style **Hôtel de Ville**, the only building to escape the 1695 French bombardment – ironic considering that it was the target. The square's splendour is due largely to its antique frame of **guildhalls**, erected by merchant guilds and adorned with gilded statues and elaborate symbols.

Galeries St Hubert, one block northeast of Grand Place, is a European first and a must-visit. Opened in 1847, this *grande dame* of Brussels' shopping arcades contains an eclectic mix of shops, as well as a cinema, restaurant and cafés. Coming off one of the galleries is **Rue des Bouchers**, the capital's famous dining street and well worth a wander.

The **Musées Royaux des Beaux-Arts** (☎ 02 508 32 11; www.fine-arts-museum.be; Rue de la Régence 3; metro Parc; adult/concession €5/3.50; ☺ 10am-5pm Tue-Sun) houses Belgium's premier collections of ancient and modern art and is particularly well endowed with works by Pieter Breugel the Elder, Rubens and the Belgian surrealists. To get there, walk up from the Lower Town or use the metro or tram Nos 92, 93 or 94.

A superb introduction to the Art Nouveau movement is the **Musée Horta** (☎ 02 543 04 90; www.hortamuseum.be; Rue Américaine 25; admission €5; ☺ 2-5.30pm Tue-Sun). It occupies two adjoining houses in St Gilles that Horta designed in 1898. To get there, take tram No 91 or 92 from Pl Louise.

The **Musée des Instruments de Musique** (☎ 02 545 01 53; www.mim.fgov.be; Montagne de la Cour 2; metro Gare Centrale; adult/concession €5/3.50; ☺ 9.30am-5pm Tue, Wed & Fri, to 8pm Thu, 10am-5pm Sat & Sun) boasts one of the world's biggest collections of instruments. It's located in the **Old England building**, a former department store and Art Nouveau showpiece built in 1899 by Paul Saintenoy.

Anyone with even a vague interest in Belgian beers must not miss the excellent **Musée Bruxellois de la Gueuze** (☎ 02 521 49 28; www.cantillon.be; Rue Gheude 56; adult/concession €3.50/3; ☺ 9am-5pm Mon-Fri, 10am-5pm Sat). This working brewery is a 10- to 15-minute walk from Lemonnier premetro station or Gare du Midi.

An absolutely anonymous, suburban yellow-brick house – that's the façade of the **Musée Magritte** (☎ 02 428 26 26; www.magritte museum.be; Rue Esseghem 135; adult/concession €6/5; ☺ 10am-6pm Wed-Sun), where Belgium's most famous surrealist artist lived from 1930 to 1954. To get there, take the metro to Simonis and then tram No 19.

The **Centre Belge de la Bande Dessinée** (☎ 02 219 19 80; www.cbbd.be, in Dutch & French; Rue des Sables 20; adult/concession €6.20/5; ☺ 10am-6pm Tue-Sun) is a tour through the country's vibrant comic-strip culture. It's housed in an Art Nouveau building designed by Horta, and is a 10-minute walk from Grand Place.

Despite being a national symbol and known throughout the world, the **Manneken Pis** (cnr Rue de l'Étuve & Rue du Chêne) fountain – a little boy cheerfully taking a leak into a pool – never fails to disappoint visitors due to its diminutive size. It's three blocks from the Grand Place.

The **Atomium** (☎ 02 475 47 77; www.atomium .be; Blvd du Centenaire; metro Heysel; adult/concession €6/4.50; ☺ 9am-7pm Jul & Aug, 10am-5pm Sep-Jun) is a space-age leftover from the 1958 World Fair – a model of an iron molecule enlarged 165 billion times. Take the metro or, more scenically, tram No 81.

TOURS

For specialised tours contact **Atelier de Recherche et d'Action Urbaine** (ARAU; ☎ 02 219 33 45; www.arau.org; Blvd Adolphe Max 55; metro De Brouckère). This heritage conservation group runs tours that offer entry into some of the private Art Nouveau showpieces.

SLEEPING
Budget

Beersel Camping (☎ 02 331 05 61; campingbeersel@ pandora.be; Steenweg op Ukkel 75; adult/child/tent/car €3/2/2/1.35; ☺ year-round) Small ground in Beersel, south of Brussels. Tram No 55 (direction Uccle) stops 3km away, from where you take bus UB (direction Halle).

Centre Vincent Van Gogh (☎ 02 217 01 58; chab@ ping.be; Rue Traversière 8; metro Botanique; dm/s/tr €12/ 26.50/40, bed sheets €3.75; ✄ ▣) This is Brussels' most groovy hostel. The rooms are clean but basic; some doubles have private bathrooms for no extra cost. It's strictly 17 to 35ers only. Located 1.2km uphill from Gare Centrale.

Sleep Well (☎ 02 218 50 50; www.sleepwell.be; Rue du Damier 23; metro Rogier; dm/s/d/tr €15.75/26.50/48/64; ✗ ☐) Bright, modern hostel-cum-hotel close to brash Rue Neuve, Brussels' main shopping thoroughfare. It's all very polished.

Résidence Les Écrins (☎ 02 219 36 57; www.lesecrins.com; Rue du Rouleau 15; metro Ste Catherine; s/d from €50/60) Gay-friendly hotel well located in the Ste Catherine quarter. It's discreet and sweet, with 11 simple, bright, modern rooms.

Also recommended:

Hôtel Galia (☎ 02 502 42 43; www.hotelgalia.com; Pl du Jeu-de-Balle 15; metro Gare du Midi or Lemonnier; s/d/ tr €60/65/70; ✗) No-frills hotel located on this famous bric-a-brac market square.

Breugel (☎ 02 511 04 36; www.vjh.be; Rue du St Esprit 2; metro Gare Centrale; dm/s/d €16.75/25/40; ✗ ☐) Most central of Brussels' three HI hostels.

Mid-Range & Top End

Most of Brussels' B&B accommodation is organised by **Bed & Brussels** (☎ 02 646 07 37; www .bnb-brussels.be).

B&B Guilmin (☎ 02 512 92 90; www.chez.com /chambreenville, in French; Rue de Londres 19; metro Trône; s/d €60/80, one-night supplement per room €15) Revolting façade on a poky backstreet just metres away from the EU's gleaming quarter – arrive here and you'll wonder what you're in for. Once inside, it's obvious. In a word: lovely.

B&B Phileas Fogg (☎ 02 217 83 38; www.phileasfogg.be; Rue Van Bemmel 6, St Josse; metro Madou; s/d/ tr/f €75/85/100/120; ✗) Exotic B&B run by an exuberant young mother and avid traveller. All the rooms have private bathrooms, though two share a toilet. The Blue Room is a favourite.

Hôtel La Madeleine (☎ 02 513 29 73; www.hotel-la-madeleine.be; Rue de la Montagne 20-22; metro Gare Centrale; €55-95, d €105) This simple hotel has an excellent location.

Hôtel Le Dixseptième (☎ 02 502 57 44; www .ledixseptieme.be; Rue de la Madeleine 25; metro Gare Centrale; s/d €120/200, ste €250-390; ✗ ☐) Discreet doesn't begin to describe this exclusive hotel just a steeple's fall from the Grand Place. The 24 rooms are sumptuously decorated and all unique. The Breugel and Jordaens rooms are the most opulent.

EATING
Budget

La Galletierre (☎ 02 512 84 80; Rue des Pierres 53; metro Bourse; mains €6-9; ☺ lunch & dinner Mon-Sat) Intimate creperie close to the Grand Place that does excellent buckwheat pancakes, either sweet or savoury, beast or veggie. There are just six tables, so reservations are wise.

Easy Tempo (☎ 02 513 54 40; Rue Haute 146; metro Porte de Namur; pizza €7-10; ☺ lunch Tue-Sun, dinner Tue-Sat) Marolles pizza joint where an ultra-friendly crew skim along the counter topping pizzas with marinated aubergine, sun-dried tomatoes and artichokes. The tiled wall is a protected monument.

Le Perroquet (☎ 02 512 99 22; Rue Watteeu 31; metro Porte de Namur; light meals €8-10; ☺ noon-1am) Art Nouveau café in the affluent Sablon. Salads and stuffed pitas, including vegetarian options, are the mainstay.

Taverne du Passage (☎ 02 512 37 31; www.tavernedupassage.com; Galerie de la Reine 30; metro Gare Centrale; mains €12-20; ☺ noon-midnight, closed Wed & Thu Jun & Jul) Consistently keen service and faithful Belgian meals are the pivotal points of this Brussels institution. Located in Galeries St Hubert, stepping through the draped doorway is like zapping away a century. The aproned blokes are unfailingly friendly and kids are genuinely welcomed.

Also recommended:

Le Pain Quotidien/Het Dagelijks Brood (☎ 02 502 23 61; Rue Antoine Dansaert 16; metro Bourse; sandwiches €4-7; ☺ 7.30am-5pm; ✗) Smoke-free tearoom offering pies and sandwiches.

GB Express (Rue au Beurre 25; metro Bourse; ☺ 8am-10pm) Essentials sold at this little supermarket near the Grand Place.

Mid-Range & Top End

L'Ultime Atome (☎ 02 513 48 84; Rue St Boniface 14; mains €9-16; ☺ noon-midnight) Just one of many great eateries in this Ixelles backstreet. An eclectic crowd keep this brasserie buzzing day and night and there's a wide range on offer, including vegetarian fare.

Bonsoir Clara (☎ 02 502 09 90; Rue Antoine Dansaert 18; metro Bourse; dishes €15-22; ☺ lunch Mon-Fri, dinner daily) One of the capital's enduring success stories. The twin salons boast bold colours, subtle lighting and lots of metal and geometry. Generous portions of modern European food, particularly Mediterranean flavours.

Aux Armes de Bruxelles (☎ 02 511 55 98; Rue des Bouchers 13; metro Bourse; mains €20-28, 3-course menu lunch/dinner €25/45; ☺ noon-11pm Tue-Sun) The hordes of restaurants lining Rue des Bouchers are largely tourist strongholds but this is the exception. A battalion of elderly, starched waiters march around serving ample portions of Belgian classics.

Jacques (☎ 02 513 27 62; Quai aux Briques 44; metro Ste Catherine; dishes €14-23, mussels €18; ☺ lunch & dinner, closed Sun) Down-to-earth seafood restaurant that has been around for over 60 years.

Comme Chez Soi (☎ 02 512 29 21; Pl Rouppe 23; metro Anneessens; mains €38-55, 4-course menu from €65; ☺ lunch & dinner Tue-Sat; ✂ ☺) Ask any Bruxellois to name the city's finest restaurant and the answer is invariably CCS. Chef Pierre Wynants' innovative cuisine will bite a good chunk out of your weekly wage. Reservations needed.

DRINKING

Café culture is ingrained in Brussels. Hardly a street in the city centre doesn't have at least one pub, café or bar.

À la Mort Subite (☎ 02 513 13 18; Rue Montagne aux Herbes Potagères 7; metro Gare Centrale; ✂) Long café with wood panelling, mirrored walls and brusque service. A must.

Falstaff (☎ 02 511 87 89; Rue Henri Maus 17; metro Bourse) Art Nouveau *grand café*, designed by Horta disciple Houbion. Exotic world of mirrors, glass and fluidity.

Goupil le Fol (☎ 02 511 13 96; Rue de la Violette 22; metro Gare Centrale) Bastion of French chanteuse…you'll only hear the likes of Barbara, Édith Piaf and Brussels' own Jacques Brel in this kooky little café. Couples love the discreet nooks and crannies.

Café Belga (☎ 02 640 35 08; Pl Flagey 18; ☺ from 9.30am) Hippest-of-hip brasserie in Ixelles. Spacious, split-level, Art Deco–style interior and ample outdoor tables. Take tram No 81.

Le Greenwich (☎ 02 511 41 67; Rue des Chartreux 7; metro Bourse) Big, ancient café that has been attracting chess players for decades. The atmosphere's thick with smoke and concentration, and the beers are cheap.

Het Biercircus (☎ 02 218 00 34; Rue de l'Enseignement 89; metro Madou; ☺ noon-2.30pm & 6-midnight Mon-Fri) For serious beer buffs.

ENTERTAINMENT

The English-language magazine *Bulletin* has a 'What's On' guide with excellent entertainment coverage.

Cinema

Arenberg Galeries (☎ 02 512 80 63 from 2pm; Galerie de la Reine 26; metro Gare Centrale) Remodelled Art Deco cinema located inside Galeries St Hubert. Foreign and art-house films are the staples.

Musée du Cinéma (☎ 02 507 83 70; Rue Baron Horta 9; metro Gare Centrale; admission €2.50; ☺ from 5pm) One to make cinema buffs swoon. Two auditoriums: silent movies with live piano accompaniment are screened in one every night of the year; the other is devoted to classic talkies.

Gay & Lesbian Venues

Tels Quels (☎ 02 512 32 34; www.telsquels.be, in French; Rue du Marché au Charbon 81; metro Anneessens; ☺ from 5pm daily, from 2pm Wed & Sat) The group's headquarters is home to a popular café-cum-information centre, the only meeting place in town specifically aimed at both lesbians and gay men.

Le Belgica (www.lebelgica.be; Rue du Marché au Charbon 32; metro Bourse; ☺ 10pm-3am Thu-Sun) Despite the unassuming façade, this is one of the city's oldest and best gay pubs.

Live Music, Dance & Theatre

AB (☎ 02 548 24 00; www.abconcerts.be; Blvd Anspach 110; metro Bourse) Great venue smack in the heart of town. AB, or Ancienne Belgique, has two auditoriums accommodating international and home-grown bands.

L'Archiduc (☎ 02 512 06 52; Rue Antoine Dansaert 6; metro Bourse; ☺ 4pm till late) Exclusive Art Deco bar built in the 1930s and located on one of the city's hippest streets. Jazz concerts every weekend.

La Monnaie/De Munt (☎ 02 227 12 00; www .demunt.be; Pl de la Monnaie; metro De Brouckère) Brussels' premier venue for opera and theatre and also the place to catch contemporary dance by Anne Teresa De Keersmaeker's innovative company, Rosas.

Théâtre Royal de Toone (☎ 02 511 71 37; Petite Rue des Bouchers 21; metro Gare Centrale; €10) Famous marionette theatre.

Nightclubs

Fuse + Food (☎ 02 511 97 89; www.fuse.be; Rue Blaes 208; metro Porte de Hal; admission free before 11pm, €5-12 depending on DJs; ☺ 10pm-7am Fri & Sat) The Marolles techno club that put Brussels on the international circuit; recently merged with house club Food.

Recyclart (☎ 02 502 57 34; www.recyclart.be; Gare de la Chapelle, Rue des Ursulines 25; metro Anneessens) Located in a disused train station in the Marolles and run by a nonprofit organisation bent on recycling. Club nights are listed on the website.

SHOPPING

Pierre Marcolini (☎ 02 514 12 06; Pl du Grand Sablon 39; metro Porte de Namur) For Belgium's most expensive pralines.

Galler (☎ 02 502 02 66; Rue au Beurre 44; metro Bourse) A step up from the average chocolate chain shop.

De Biertempel (☎ 02 502 19 06; Rue du Marché aux Herbes 56; metro Bourse) Stocks 400 Belgian brews plus matching glasses.

Stijl (☎ 02 512 03 13; Rue Antoine Dansaert 74; metro Ste Catherine) Home to top Antwerp fashion designers, including members of the Antwerp Six (p106).

Martin Margiela (☎ 02 223 75 20; Rue de Flandre 114; metro Ste Catherine) New shop by the unofficial seventh member of the Antwerp Six.

Place du Jeu-de-Balle fleamarket (Pl du Jeu-de-Balle; metro Hotel des Monnaies; ☽ 7am-2pm) The Marolles' famous *brocante* (second-hand) market.

Gare du Midi market (☽ 6am-1pm Sun; metro Gare du Midi) Brussels' biggest general market sprawls next to the railway lines and has a distinctly Mediterranean feel.

GETTING THERE & AWAY
Air
Brussels National Airport (☎ 02 753 42 21; ☎ flight information 0900 70 000; www.brusselsairport.be) is 14km northeast of Brussels. For airlines servicing Brussels, see the list on p122.

Bus
Eurolines (☎ 02 274 13 50; www.eurolines.be, in Dutch & French; Rue du Progrès 80) buses pick up and set down from this office at Gare du Nord. For information on services, see p123.

Car & Motorcycle
For details on car-rental companies, see p123.

Train
Brussels three main train stations are Gare du Midi (South Station), Gare Centrale (Central Station) and Gare du Nord (North Station).

Gare du Midi is the main station for international connections: the Eurostar and Thalys fast trains stop here only. For any international and national enquiries call ☎ 02 528 28 28.

For further information on international train services, including Eurostar and Thalys trains, see p123. For information on getting to other towns or cities in Belgium, see the Getting There & Away section for individual towns.

GETTING AROUND
To/From the Airport
The **Airport City Express** (one way €3; ☽ 5.30am-11.30pm) train runs between the airport and the city's three main train stations – Gare du Nord, Gare Centrale and Gare du Midi. The service runs every 15 minutes and the trip takes 15 to 25 minutes (depending on the station).

A taxi between the airport and central Brussels costs €27.

For details on shuttle buses between Brussels and Brussels-Charleroi airport, see p116.

Public Transport
Brussels' efficient public-transport system is operated by **Société des Transports Intercommunaux de Bruxelles** (☎ 02 515 20 00; Rue l'Evêque 31); buses, trams and the metro run from about 5.30am to midnight.

Taxi
Call **Taxis Bleus** (☎ 02 268 00 00) or **Taxis Verts** (☎ 02 349 49 49). Taxes are officially included in the meter price, so ignore requests for extra service charges.

AROUND BRUSSELS
Leuven
pop 90,400
About 25km east of Brussels is Leuven (Louvain in French), Flanders' premier university town. The town's main tourist attraction is its flamboyant 15th-century **Stadhuis** (town hall; ☎ 016 21 15 40; Grote Markt; admission €2).

Leuven is also famed for **Rock Werchter** (www.rockwerchter.be), held for three days over the first weekend of July. Together with Glastonbury (England) and Roskilde (Denmark), this is one of Europe's biggest 'field' rock festivals.

BELGIUM

LÉOPOLD II & THE CONGO

In 1885, Belgium's King Léopold II personally acquired the Congo in Africa, an area almost 100 times the size of his homeland. Between then and 1908, when the Belgian state stripped the king of his possession, it is estimated up to 10 million Africans died due to starvation, overwork or murder carried out in Léopold's quest for rubber, ivory and other commodities.

A BBC TV documentary, aired in Belgium in 2004, shone this period of history squarely into Belgian faces – and some didn't like what they saw. Outspoken foreign minister Louis Michel retaliated, saying it was biased and didn't take into account the social context of that time.

It will be impossible to know for sure the number of people who died. On Léopold's orders, the Congo archives were all burnt. According to Adam Hochschild in his book *King Léopold's Ghost*, the furnaces in the Congo offices in Brussels burnt for over a week. But what is sure is that the booty from this barbarity was enormous. Brussels' landmarks – such as the Arcade du Cinquantenaire – were built on these proceeds. So too was the **Koninklijk Museum voor Midden-Afrika** (Royal Museum of Central Africa; ☎ 02 769 52 11; www.africamuseum.be; Leuvensesteenweg 13, Tervuren; adult/concession/child €4/3/1.50; ☉ 10am-5pm Tue-Fri, to 6pm Sat & Sun). This museum makes for an easy half-day excursion that won't be readily forgotten.

Located at Tervuren, a Dutch-speaking town 14km east of the capital, this museum houses the world's most impressive array of artefacts from Africa. But in all the vast galleries there's no mention of the millions of Congolese who died, though the Belgians who never returned are remembered in the Memorial Hall. Since 2001, the museum has been undergoing renovation and modernisation – a process due for completion by its centennial in 2010. It will be interesting to see then whether the Belgian state acknowledges its darkest period in history.

To get to the museum, take the metro to Montgoméry then tram No 44 (20 minutes).

Waterloo
pop 28,900

Waterloo, the battleground where Napoleon was defeated in 1815 and European history changed its course, is 18km south of Brussels. Unless you're a war or history buff, it's fairly staid. What's more, the most important sites are spread out over several kilometres, making it tedious to get around with public transport. You will need to catch a TEC bus W from Ave Fosny at Brussels' Gare du Midi train station; ask the driver for a €5.50 day card.

The best place to start is at the **Office du Tourisme** (☎ 02 354 99 10; www.waterloo-tourisme.be, in Dutch & French; Chaussée de Bruxelles 218, Waterloo; ☉ 9.30am-6.30pm Apr-Sep, 10.30am-5pm Oct-Mar). Bus W stops at the tourist office and staff will assist with timetables for getting around.

FLANDERS

Belgium's northern region is flat ol' Dutch-speaking Flanders. Visitors don't come here for the geography – it's the historic and contemporary social scenes that make Flanders so attractive.

ANTWERP
pop 452,500

Cosmopolitan, confident and full of contrasts, Antwerp (Antwerpen in Dutch, Anvers in French) is an essential stop. Appreciated by art and architecture lovers, mode moguls, club queens and diamond dealers, Belgium's second biggest city once again revels in fame and fortune.

Orientation

Antwerp flanks the Scheldt River. The historic centre, based around the Grote Markt, is 1km from the impressive Centraal Station. The two are linked by the pedestrianised Meir (pronounced 'mare'), a bustling shopping thoroughfare.

Not far from the Grote Markt is St Andries, the fashionista hub. Het Zuid (The South), commonly abbreviated as 't Zuid, is one of the nightlife zones.

North of the Grote Markt is the old sailors' quarter, 't Schipperskwartier, together with a regenerated docklands district known as 't Eilandje (Little Island).

Just south of Centraal Station is the diamond district and adjoining Jewish neighbourhood. Further southeast is Zurenborg, famed for its *belle époque* architecture.

ANTWERP

Information

INTERNET ACCESS
Influence (☎ 03 293 97 38; Melkmarkt 11; ☻ 11am-midnight) Spacious Internet centre located on the 1st floor of a popular music shop.

MEDICAL SERVICES
St Elisabethgasthuis (☎ 03 234 41 11; Leopoldstraat 26; ☻ 24hr) Central hospital.

MONEY
ATMs Main post office (Groenplaats 43); KBC Bank (Eiermarkt); Post office (Pelikaanstraat); Fortis Bank (Wapper)
Goffin (☎ 03 232 20 56; Suikerrui 36; ☻ 9.30am-6.30pm) Exchange bureau close to the Grote Markt.

POST
Main post office (Groenplaats 43)
Post office (Pelikaanstraat)

TOURIST INFORMATION
Main tourist office (☎ 03 232 01 03; www.visit antwerpen.be; Grote Markt 13; ☻ 9am-5.45pm Mon-Sat, 9am-4.45pm Sun)
Tourist office (Koningin Astridplein 26; ☻ 9am-5.45pm Mon-Sat, 9am-4.45pm Sun)

Sights

The heart of Antwerp is the **Grote Markt**, a vast, pedestrianised market square presided over by the impressive Renaissance-style **Stadhuis** (town hall; ☎ 03 220 80 20; 40min guided tours €0.75; ☻ 2pm Mon-Thu). Entrance to the Stadhuis is via Suikerrui. The Grote Markt is lined on two sides by Renaissance-style **guildhalls**, most of which were reconstructed in the 19th century. Rising from a rough pile of rocks in the centre of the Grote Markt is the voluptuous, baroque **Brabo Fountain**.

Antwerp's **Onze Lieve Vrouwkathedraal** (☎ 03 213 99 40; Handschoenmarkt; adult/concession €2/1.50; ☻ 10am-5pm Mon-Fri, 10am-3pm Sat, 1-4pm Sun) is Belgium's largest and finest Gothic cathedral (1352–1521). It houses four early canvases by Rubens – the most celebrated is *The Descent from the Cross* (1612).

The prestigious **Rubenshuis** (☎ 03 201 15 55; Wapper 9-11; adult/concession €5/2.50, free on Fri; ☻ 10am-5pm Tue-Sun) was the home and studio of Pieter Paul Rubens, northern Europe's greatest baroque artist. Little more than a ruin when acquired by the city in 1937, it has been superbly restored along original lines. Unfortunately, only a handful of Rubens' lesser works are displayed.

The **Koninklijk Museum voor Schone Kunsten** (☎ 03 238 78 09; www.antwerpen.be/cultuur/kmska; Leopold De Waelplaats 1-9, 't Zuid; adult/concession €5/4; ☻ 10am-5pm Tue-Sat, to 6pm Sun) houses an impressive collection of paintings dating from the Flemish Primitives to contemporary times. The best sections are the 17th-century Flemish Baroque masters, including Rubens, and the section devoted to Ensor. Take tram No 8 from Groenplaats or bus No 23 (direction Zuid) from Franklin Rooseveltplaats.

In 2002 Antwerp's much-celebrated **Modenatie** (www.modenatie.com; Nationalestraat 28) fashion complex opened. It's home to the Flanders Fashion Institute as well as the **Modemuseum** (MoMu; ☎ 03 470 27 70; www.momu.be; adult/concession €7/4; ☻ 10am-6pm Tue-Sun). Keeping firmly with avant-garde, MoMu changes its exhibits every six months.

The **Nationaal Scheepvaartmuseum** (☎ 03 201 93 40; Steenplein 1; adult/concession €4/2; ☻ 10am-5pm Tue-Sun) occupies the remainder of Antwerp's medieval riverside fortress. An engaging collection of model ships, instruments and maps tells the city's maritime history.

Zurenborg, about 2km southeast of Centraal Station, is famed for the eclectic architecture found in a handful of streets. The showcase is **Cogels-Osylei**, where affluent citizens went wild a century ago, creating competing and highly contrasting homes. Tram No 11 (direction Eksterlaar) runs along Cogels-Osylei.

A block from the Grote Markt, next to the river, is a raised promenade known as **Zuiderterras**. Built decades ago alongside the city's main dock, it offers a great skyline view plus an essential pit stop (see p106).

Wander the length of Zuiderterras to arrive at **St Jansvliet**, a small tree-lined square and entry to **St Annatunnel**, a 572m-long pedestrian tunnel, built in the 1930s under the Scheldt, that links the city centre with the **Linkeroever**, or Left Bank, from where there's a fab city panorama.

Sleeping

BUDGET
Camping De Molen (☎ 03 219 81 79; Thonetlaan; adult/car/tent €1.60/0.90/2.10; ☻ Apr-Sep) The pick of Antwerp's two camping grounds, located on the Linkeroever; take bus No 81 or 82 (direction Linkeroever).

Scoutel (☎ 03 226 46 06; www.scoutel.be; Stoomstraat 3; dm €17, s/d 25 yrs & under €25/40, 26 yrs &

over €27/45; P ⊠) Modern scouts' residence that welcomes travellers. Friendly staff and excellent location close to Centraal Station. The spartan modern rooms all have private bathrooms.

Hostel Op Sinjoorke (☎ 03 238 02 73; www.vjh.be; Eric Sasselaan 2; dm/s/d €13.75/24/38; ☒ closed Dec; ⊠) Run-of-the-mill HI-affiliated hostel nearly 3km south of the centre. To get there, take tram No 2 (direction Hoboken).

MID-RANGE

B&B Ribbens (☎ 03 248 15 39; www.bbantwerp.com; Justitiestraat 43; s/d/f €42/50/75, Fri-Sun €50/60/85) Wooden floors and old-fashioned furniture are the salient features of this spacious and charming B&B. It's a 25-minute walk from the Grote Markt, or take bus No 290 (direction Hoboken) from Franklin Rooseveltplaats and get off at the Gerechtshof stop.

B&B Enich Anders (☎ 03 231 37 92; enich.anders@antwerpen.be; Leeuwenstraat 12; s/d/tr/f €45/50/65/80; ⊠) A stone-sculptor's home, superbly located and popular with independent types – if you don't mind things being a bit rough around the edges, this is your place. The rooms have small refrigerators and kitchenettes. Babies and kids most welcome (cot €5).

Rubenshof (☎ 03 237 07 89; www.rubenshof.be; Amerikalei 115; s/d/tr €50/65/80, with shared bathroom €25/40/55; ▢) Small hotel occupying a townhouse on a boulevard near 't Zuid. No two rooms are alike. Take tram No 24 (direction Zuidstation) from Franklin Rooseveltplaats as far as the Brederodestraat stop.

TOP END

B&B Charles Rogier XI (☎ 04752 999 89; www.charlesrogierxl.be; Karel Rogierstraat 11, 't Zuid; d €160; ⊠ 😂) A world away from reality; that's the only way to describe this B&B. The three rooms are loaded with antiques, heavy fabrics and floral designs. And should you happen to fall in love with that deer-hoof stool – or anything else in your room – it's up for grabs. Take tram No 8 from Groenplaats.

De Witte Lelie (☎ 03 226 19 66; www.dewittelelie.be; Keizerstraat 16-18; s/d €180/240, ste from €250; P €15; ⊠ 😂 ▢) Gorgeous hotel with just 10 rooms.

Eating

BUDGET

Lombardia (☎ 03 233 68 19; Lombaardvest 78; light meals €4-8; ☒ 7.45am-6pm Mon-Sat) Legendary

health-food shop-cum-café that has been around for three decades. The food's all bio (organic) and the décor's bizarre. Milkshakes, either beastie or vegan, go for €6, fresh juices are €4 and there's a range of salads, vegetable pies and sandwiches.

Soep & Soup (☎ 03 707 28 05; Kammenstraat 89; small/large bowl €4.25/5.50; ☒ 11am-6.30pm Mon-Sat) Buzzy soup bar in trendy St Andries. Five pots of soup, with fresh ingredients, simmer away. Vegetarians can ask to hold the meatballs.

Berlin (☎ 03 227 11 01; Kleine Markt 1-3; dagschotel €8.50, mains €11-14; ☒ 7.30am-1am Mon-Thu, 9.30-3am Fri-Sun) Spacious new brasserie beneath the police tower in St Andries. Attracts an eclectic crowd from jeans-minded teens to the old lady next door.

Façade (☎ 03 233 59 31; Hendrik Conscienceplein 18; mains €11-19; ☒ lunch Sat & Sun, dinner Thu-Tue) Unpretentious restaurant that occupies a quaint pair of houses on one of the most delightful public squares in Antwerp. The French/Belgian cuisine is beautifully presented and prices are a snip.

Super GB (Groenplaats; ☒ 8.30am-8pm) Supermarket in the Grand Bazar shopping centre.

MID-RANGE & TOP END

Coco C. (☎ 03 216 96 43; Volkstraat 58; mains €18-20; ☒ lunch Mon-Fri, dinner daily) One of many restaurants in this part of 't Zuid. The décor and the food – Asian meets French – are the hippest of hip.

De Kleine Zavel (☎ 03 231 96 91; Stoofstraat 2; mains €20-30; ☒ lunch Sun-Fri, dinner daily) Bistro-style décor and an informal atmosphere belie this restaurant's standing as one of the most sought-after and reliable eateries in Antwerp. Inventive fusion cooking, accenting fish and Mediterranean flavours.

Gin Fish (☎ 03 231 32 07; Haarstraat 9; 4-course menu incl wine €75; ☒ dinner Tue-Sat; 😂) New frontier for former Michelin chef Didier Garnich. Just 13 diners sit side-by-side along a black marble counter watching the team devotedly transforming fish into feast. There are three sittings – 6pm, 8.30pm and 10pm – and bookings are essential.

Drinking

The only thing better in Antwerp than eating is drinking. Small convivial pubs, converted warehouses and *grand cafés* abound.

Oud Arsenaal (☎ 03 232 97 54; Pijpelincxstraat 4; ☒ closed Thu) Catch the city's most congenial brown café while it lasts. Beers are among the cheapest in town (just €2.25 for a Duvel) and it's one of the few everyday pubs in Belgium to stock Westvleteren Trappist beer.

Zuiderterras (☎ 03 234 12 75; Ernest van Dijckkaai 37; ☺ 9am-midnight) Modern landmark café/restaurant located at the southern end of the riverside promenade and designed by the city's eminent contemporary architect, bOb Van Reeth. Super spot to while away an hour or two.

Bierhuis Kulminator (☎ 03 232 45 38; Vleminckveld 32; ☺ from 8pm Mon, from 11am Tue-Fri, from 5pm Sat) Boasts more than 600 types of beer.

Entertainment
CINEMAS
Cartoons (☎ 03 232 96 32; Kaasstraat 4-6) Arthouse movies and quality foreign films are screened in three auditoriums.

GAY & LESBIAN ANTWERP
Den Draak (☎ 03 288 00 84; www.hetrozehuis.be, in Dutch; Draakplaats 1; ☺ 3pm-midnight Mon-Fri, noon-midnight Sat & Sun) Café and community centre for Antwerp's gay and lesbian community. Located in the Zurenborg – take tram No 11, direction Eksterlaar.

Atthis (☎ 03 216 37 37; Geuzenstraat 27; ☺ from 8.30pm Fri & Sat) Meeting place–cum-bar for Belgium's longest-running lesbian group. Celebrated 25 years in 2003.

Red & Blue (☎ 03 213 05 55; www.redandblue.be; Lange Schipperskapelstraat 11; ☺ 11pm-7am Sat) The biggest (and awarded best) gay nightclub in this corner of Europe, drawing a mixed crowd to house, techno, rap and soul.

The Boots (☎ 03 231 34 83; Van Aerdtstraat 22; ☺ 10.30pm-late Fri & Sat) Has the distinction of being the country's most disreputable nightclub, with rooms devoted to fulfilling almost every imaginable sexual fantasy.

LIVE MUSIC, THEATRE & DANCE
Café Hopper (☎ 03 248 49 33; Leopold De Waelstraat 2) Cosy café in 't Zuid that doubles as the city's best jazz venue; performances Sunday to Wednesday.

deSingel (☎ 03 248 28 28; www.desingel.be, in Dutch; Desguinlei 25) Antwerp's chief venue for classical music, international theatre and modern dance.

Koninklijk Ballet van Vlaanderen (☎ 03 234 34 38; Westkaai 16, 't Eilandje) The Royal Flanders Ballet is the nation's only classical-dance

company. See performances here at its impressive theatre, a purpose-built palatial grey building.

NIGHTCLUBS
Antwerp runs on party time. One of the biggest parties is **Antwerp is Burning** (www.antwerpisburning.be), held towards the end of summer on open fields on the Linkeroever.

Café d'Anvers (☎ 03 226 38 70; www.café-d-anvers.com; Verversrui 15; ☺ 11pm-7.30am Fri & Sat) This legendary club does funk and house, disco and soul in a refurbished church in the city's red-light district in the old sailors' quarter. Many of Belgium's top DJs started here.

Café Local (www.cafélocal.be; Waalsekaai 25, 't Zuid; ☺ from 10pm Fri-Sun) Another long-time favourite, previously known for its techno parties but these days preferring salsa and global grooves.

Shopping
Antwerp's role as a celebrated fashion hub means it's a magnet for shoppers. For a city its size, it boasts an astonishing number of world-acclaimed avant-garde fashion designers, the best known of which are the 'Antwerp Six' – Ann Demeulemeester, Dries Van Noten, Walter Van Beirendonck, Dirk Van Saene, Dirk Bikkembergs and Marina Yee.

Some recommended shops:

Louis (☎ 03 232 98 72; Lombaardstraat 4) Great introduction to various Belgian players, including newer designers such as Jurgi Persoons, Véronique Branquinho and Raf Simons.

Walter (☎ 03 213 26 44; St Antoniusstraat 12) Van Beirendonck's outlet looks more like an ultramodern art gallery than somewhere to buy clothes.

Het Modepaleis (☎ 03 233 94 37; Nationalestraat 16) Headquarters and shop of Dries Van Noten.

Ann Demeulemeester (☎ 03 216 01 33; Verlatstraat 38) Stocks her complete line of men's and women's clothing.

Getting There & Away
BUS
Eurolines (☎ 03 233 86 62; Van Straelenstraat 8) buses pick up and set down from this office near Franklin Rooseveltplaats. For information on services, see p123.

TRAIN
Antwerp's beautiful **Centraal Station** (☎ 02 528 28 28) is about 1.5km from the historic

centre. National connections include IC trains every half-hour to Brussels (€5.60, 35 minutes) and Ghent (€7.20, 45 minutes), and hourly trains to Bruges (€11.40, one hour 10 minutes).

Getting Around

De Lijn Antwerpen (☎ 07 022 02 00; Centraal Station; ☎ 8am-4pm Mon-Fri) runs a good network of buses, trams and a premetro (a tram that runs underground for part of its journey). The main bus hubs are Franklin Roosevelt-plaats and Koningin Astridplein.

In summer, bikes can be hired from **De Windroos** (☎ 03 480 93 88; Steenplein 1a; per 1hr/day €2.50/12.50).

GHENT

pop 228,000

Likeable Ghent (known as Gent in Dutch and Gand in French) is often overlooked on the art-town hop between Brussels, Bruges and Antwerp. Compact and unpretentious, this lively university city has all the things that make Flemish towns famous – great architecture, restaurants and cafés – as well as excellent B&Bs.

Time a visit for **De Gentse Feesten** (www .gentsefeesten.be, in Dutch), an annual 10-day festival in mid-July that transforms the city into a party of music and theatre. The festival includes **10 Days Off…** (www.10daysoff.be), one of Europe's biggest techno parties.

Orientation

Ghent's medieval core contains three central squares separated by two imposing churches and a belfry. This trio has long been the skyline's trademark, and is best viewed from St Michielsbrug, the nearby bridge over the Leie River.

Halfway between the city centre and the train station is the university quarter, spread along St Pietersnieuwstraat.

Information

ATM (post office, Maria Hendrikaplein) Opposite the train station.

Coffeelounge (☎ 09 329 39 11; Botermarkt 6; ☼ 10am-7pm Mon, Wed, Thu & Sun, to 11pm Fri & Sat) For Internet access.

Europabank (☎ 09 221 00 31; St Pietersstation; ☼ 10am-12.30pm & 2-6.30pm) Exchange agency located inside the train station.

Main post office (Lange Kruisstraat 55)

Tourist office (☎ 09 266 52 32; www.visitgent.be; Botermarkt 17; ☼ 9.30am-6.30pm Apr-Oct, to 4.30pm Nov-Mar)

Sights

Though **St Baafskathedraal** (☎ 09 269 20 45; St Baafsplein; ☼ 8.30am-6pm) is unimpressive from the outside, formidable queues form to see the **Adoration of the Mystic Lamb** (adult/concession €3/2.50; ☼ 9.30am-5pm Mon-Sat & 1-5pm Sun Apr-Oct, 10.30am-4pm Mon-Sat & 1-4pm Sun Nov-Mar). This lavish representation of medieval religious thinking is one of the earliest-known oil paintings, executed in 1432 by Flemish Primitive artist Jan Van Eyck. It's not to be missed.

The 14th-century **Belfort** (Botermarkt; adult/child €2/1; ☼ 10am-12.30pm & 2-5.30pm Easter–mid-Nov) affords spectacular views of the city and can be climbed either by a lift or, if you're so inclined, stairs.

The **Gravensteen** (☎ 09 225 93 06; St Veerle-plein; adult/child €6/free; ☼ 9am-6pm Apr-Sep, to 5pm Oct-Mar), located smack in the heart of the city, belonged to the 12th-century counts of Flanders and is the quintessential castle.

Ghent's highly regarded **Stedelijk Museum voor Actuele Kunst** (☎ 09 221 17 03; www.smak.be; Citadelpark; admission €5; ☼ 10am-6pm Tue-Sun), better known as SMAK, contains works by Karel Appel, Pierre Alechinsky and Pan-amarenko – three of Belgium's best-known contemporary artists – as well as works by international celebrities.

The **Museum voor Vormgeving** (Design Museum; ☎ 09 267 99 99; www.design.museum.gent.be; Jan Brey-delstraat 5; adult/child €2.50/free; ☼ 10am-6pm Tue-Sun) is one of Ghent's little-known gems, with a mix of furnishings from the Renaissance through to contemporary.

Formerly a Middle Ages meat market, the **Groot Vleeshuis** (☎ 09 267 86 07; Groentenmarkt 7; ☼ 10am-6pm Tue-Sun) is now a tasting hall for local products.

Ghent's **Museum voor Schone Kunsten** (☎ 09 222 17 03; www.mskgent.be; Citadelpark) is expected to reopen following renovation in 2006. In the meantime, some of its collection is exhibited in St Baafskathedraal (p107) and at SMAK (p107).

Sleeping

BUDGET

Camping Blaarmeersen (☎ 09 266 81 60; Zuiderlaan 12; adult/child/tent/car €4/2/4/2.25) A long way west

BELGIUM

BELGIUM

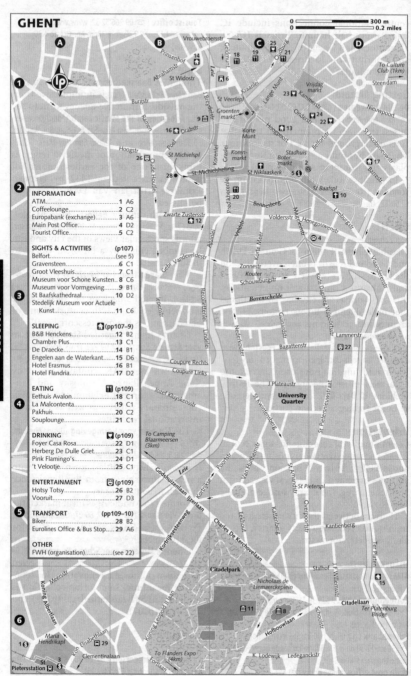

GHENT

0		300 m
0		0.2 miles

INFORMATION
ATM..**1** A6
Coffeelounge....................................**2** C2
Europabank (exchange)...................**3** A6
Main Post Office..............................**4** D2
Tourist Office...................................**5** C2

SIGHTS & ACTIVITIES (p107)
Belfort..(see 5)
Gravensteen......................................**6** C1
Groot Vleeshuis................................**7** C1
Museum voor Schone Kunsten..**8** C6
Museum voor Vormgeving............**9** B1
St Baafskathedraal.........................**10** D2
Stedelijk Museum voor Actuele
Kunst...**11** C6

SLEEPING (pp107–9)
B&B Henckens..................................**12** B2
Chambre Plus....................................**13** C1
De Draecke..**14** B1
Engelen aan de Waterkant...........**15** D6
Hotel Erasmus...................................**16** B1
Hotel Flandria...................................**17** D2

EATING (p109)
Eethuis Avalon.................................**18** C1
La Malcontenta.................................**19** C1
Pakhuis..**20** C1
Souplounge.......................................**21** C1

DRINKING (p109)
Foyer Casa Rosa...............................**22** D1
Herberg De Dulle Griet....................**23** C1
Pink Flamingo's................................**24** D1
't Velootje...**25** C1

ENTERTAINMENT (p109)
Hotsy Totsy..**26** B2
Vooruit...**27** D3

TRANSPORT (pp109–10)
Biker..**28** B2
Eurolines Office & Bus Stop.....**29** A6

OTHER
FWH (organisation)...................(see 22)

of the city. Take bus No 9 (direction Mari-akerke) from St Pietersstation to the Europa-brug stop, then bus No 38 or 39, which stops out front.

De Draecke (☎ 09 233 70 50; www.vjh.be; St Widos-traat 11; dm/tw €15.75/38; ☒) One of Belgium's best HI-affiliated hostels, occupying a reno-vated warehouse smack in the heart of town. From the train station, take tram No 1, 10 or 11 to St Veerleplein.

Hotel Flandria (☎ 09 223 06 26; www.flandriacentrum .be; Barrestraat 3; s/d from €33/38) A rabbit warren of cheap, decent rooms tucked away on a quiet backstreet. Avoid the rooms on the top floor in summer as they're stifling.

B&B Henckens (☎ 09 224 34 05; www.bedandbreak fast-gent.be; Zwartezustersstraat 3; s/d/tr from €30/45/60; ☒) Homy B&B that was once part of an old cloister. The three guestrooms are done in rich colours and share one bathroom. Children welcome.

MID-RANGE & TOP END

Ghent's thriving B&B scene is organised by the **Gilde der Gentse Gastenkamers** (☎ 09 233 30 99; www.bedandbreakfast-gent.be).

Chambre Plus (☎ 09 225 37 75; www.chambreplus .be; Hoogpoort 31; s/d/ste €65/80/140; ☒) Gorgeous B&B with a fab location on a pedestrian-ised street in the heart of the city. The ex-otic rooms are complemented by convivial hosts and a gastronomic breakfast.

Hotel Erasmus (☎ 09 224 21 95; www.proximedia .com/web/hotel-erasmus.html; Poel 25; s/d/f €79/99/150, luxury s/d €85/110) Renovated 16th-century townhouse with creaking floorboards and a medieval ambience.

B&B Engelen aan de Waterkant (☎ 09 223 08 83; www.engelenaandewaterkant.be; Ter Platen 30; s/d/tr €80/100/135) You'll be hard pressed to find a more angelic or romantic B&B in Belgium – in a word, stunning. It's 1.5km from the city centre.

Eating

Souplounge (☎ 09 223 62 03; Zuivelbrugstraat 6; small/ large soup €3/4.50; ☼ 10am-7pm) One of the new breed of modern soup kitchens and great for a light, fast meal.

Eethuis Avalon (☎ 09 224 37 24; Geldmunt 32; dagschotel €8, 3-course menu €10.50; ☼ lunch Mon-Sat) Spacious vegetarian restaurant close to the Gravensteen. Inside it's a warren of little rooms, or you can dine outside on a small terrace.

Pakhuis (☎ 09 223 55 55; Schuurkenstraat 4; mains €14-25; ☼ noon-midnight Mon-Sat) Huge brasserie-cum-restaurant occupying a restored textile warehouse on a dog-eared backstreet; draws young and old alike.

La Malcontenta (☎ 09 224 18 01; Haringsteeg 7; mains €12.50-16; ☼ dinner Wed-Sat) One of many restaurants located in the intimate Patershol quarter.

Drinking

't Velootje (☎ 09 223 28 34; Kalversteeg 2; ☼ from 9pm but variable) Extraordinary pub in the Patershol quarter crammed from floor to ceiling with all manner of junk and riches.

Herberg De Dulle Griet (☎ 09 224 24 55; Vrijdag-markt 50; ☼ noon-1am) Ghent's best-known beer pub. Local brews include Guillotine (9.3%), Delirium Tremens (9.5%) and the city's strongest beer, Piraat (10.5%).

Pink Flamingo's (☎ 09 233 47 18; Onderstraat 55; ☼ noon-midnight Sun-Thu, 2pm-3am Fri & Sat) Off-the-planet café where the authentic kitsch décor changes every three months.

Entertainment

Culture Club (☎ 09 267 64 41; www.cultureclub.be; Afrikalaan 174) According to one British mag-azine, this is the 'world's hippest club' – some recommendation. It's northeast of the centre – take a taxi.

Hotsy Totsy (☎ 09 224 20 12; Hoogstraat 1; ☼ from 8pm Tue-Sat) The unassuming façade of this bar belies its local standing as one of the city's most popular spots for everything from jazz to poets.

Vooruit (☎ 09 267 28 28; St Pietersnieuwstraat 23) Ghent's main venue for dance and theatre. This impressive building, built in 1912 as a cultural centre for the Socialist Party, is worth a look in itself.

Foyer Casa Rosa (☎ 09 269 28 16; Belfortstraat 39; ☼ 3pm-1am Sun-Thu, to 2am Fri & Sat) Gay and lesbian café run by **Federatie Werkgroepen Ho-moseksualiteit** (FWH; www.fwh.be, in French & Dutch; Kammerstraat 22), Flanders' biggest gay and lesbian organisation.

Getting There & Around

The **Eurolines** (☎ 09 220 90 24; Koningin Elisabethlaan 73) office is 100m from St Pietersstation. For details on bus services see p123.

Ghent's main train station is **St Pieterssta-tion** (☎ 02 528 28 28), 2km south of the city centre. There are trains every half-hour to Antwerp (€7.20, 45 minutes), Bruges (€5, 20 minutes) and Brussels (€6.80, 45 minutes), as well as hourly connections to Ypres (€8.80, one hour).

The city's public transport network is operated by **De Lijn** (☎ 09 210 93 11). Trams to the city centre (Nos 1, 10, 11, 12 and 13) depart from the tram station in the tunnel to the right as you exit the train station.

Bikes can be rented from the **train station** (☎ 02 528 28 28; €9 per day plus a €12.50 deposit) or from **Biker** (☎ 09 224 29 03; St Michielsstraat 3; half /full day €6.50/9).

BRUGES
pop 117,000

Touristy, overcrowded and a tad fake. Describe any other city in these terms and it would be left for dead. But not Bruges (Brugge in Dutch, Bruges in French). This Flemish city is Belgium's most popular destination and, despite the crowds, it's not to be missed.

Suspended in time centuries ago due to misfortune that drove the townsfolk away, Bruges is one of Western Europe's most-visited medieval cities and dreamily evokes a world long since gone. But its reputation as one of the most perfectly preserved cities is in part fabrication. While what you see reflects that of centuries ago, much of the architecture dates only to the 19th and 20th centuries.

Orientation

Central Bruges fits neatly into an oval-shaped series of canals. At its heart are two squares, the Markt and the Burg, where the tourist office is located. The city is an ambler's ultimate dream, its sights sprinkled within leisurely walking distance of its compact centre. The train station is about 1.5km south of the Markt; buses shuttle regularly between the two.

Information
INTERNET ACCESS
Coffee Link (☎ 050 34 99 73; www.thecoffeelink.com; Mariastraat 38; 🕒 10am-7pm) Atmospheric café with coffee, cakes and a bank of terminals.

MONEY
ATM (Markt 5) Attached to the main post office.
ING Bank (☎ 050 44 45 40; Markt 19; 🕒 9am-12.30pm & 1.30-4.15pm Mon-Fri, 9am-noon Sat)

POST
Main post office (Markt 5)

TOURIST INFORMATION
Toerisme Brugge (☎ 050 44 86 86; www.brugge.be; Burg 11; 🕒 9.30am-5pm Mon-Fri, 9.30am-noon & 2-5pm Sat & Sun)
Train station branch office (🕒 9.30am-12.30pm & 1.15-5pm Tue-Sat)

Sights

Exploration of Bruges always starts at the historic **Markt**, a large open square from which rises Belgium's most famous **Belfort** (belfry; Markt; adult/concession/child €5/3/free; 🕒 9.30am-5pm Tue-Sun, last tickets sold 4.15pm). The 366 steps to the top are usually a crowded climb but well worth it.

Smaller but arguably more impressive than the Markt is the adjoining **Burg.** This square is home to the **Heilig-Bloedbasiliek** (Basilica of the Holy Blood; Burg; 🕒 9.30-11.50am & 2-5.50pm Apr-Sep, 10-11.50am & 2-3.50pm Oct-Mar), where a few coagulated drops of Christ's blood is kept and cherished. This phial is paraded through the city every year in the elaborate Heilig-Bloedprocessie (Holy Blood Procession) on Ascension Day (5 May in 2005 and 25 May in 2006).

Belgium's oldest and arguably most beautiful **stadhuis** (town hall) also rises from the Burg.

Bruges' prized collection of art dating from the 14th to 20th centuries is housed in the small **Groeningemuseum** (Dijver 12; adult/ concession €8/5; 🕒 9.30am-5pm Tue-Sun). If viewing things chronologically is your thing, start in Room 2 – which presents the Flemish Primitives – then backtrack to Room 1 and from there proceed through the rest of the museum.

The prestigious **Memlingmuseum** (Mariastraat 38; adult/concession €8/5; 🕒 9.30am-5pm Tue-Sun) is home to a handful of masterpieces by Hans Memling plus many works by less-well-known painters of his time. Don't miss Memling's reliquary of St Ursula – the attention to detail is stunning.

The **Onze Lieve Vrouwkerk** (Church of Our Lady; Mariastraat; adult/concession €2.50/1.50; 🕒 9.30am-12.30pm & 1.30-5pm Tue-Sat, 1.30-5pm Sun) has one remarkable art treasure – Michelangelo's *Madonna and Child* (1504). This small marble statue was the only work of art by Michelangelo to leave Italy in his lifetime.

BRUGES

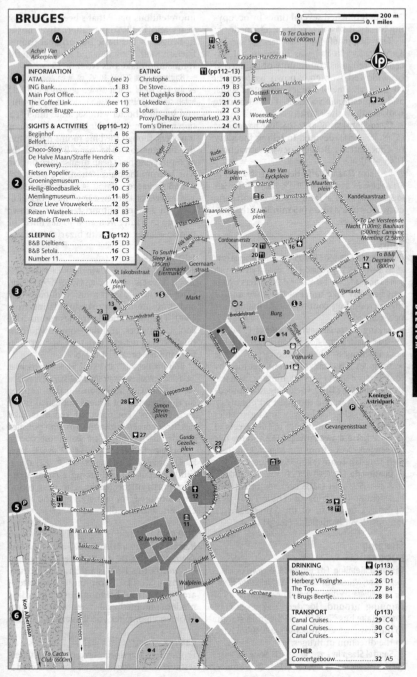

0   200 m
0   0.1 miles

INFORMATION
ATM...(see 2)
ING Bank...1 B3
Main Post Office...........................2 C3
The Coffee Link..........................(see 11)
Toerisme Brugge..........................3 C3

SIGHTS & ACTIVITIES (pp110–12)
Begijnhof.......................................4 B6
Belfort..5 C3
Choco-Story...................................6 C2
De Halve Maan/Straffe Hendrik
  (brewery)...................................7 B6
Fietsen Popelier............................8 B5
Groeningemuseum........................9 C5
Heilig-Bloedbasiliek...................10 C3
Memlingmuseum........................11 B5
Onze Lieve Vrouwekerk...........12 B5
Reizen Wasteels.........................13 B3
Stadhuis (Town Hall).................14 C3

SLEEPING (p112)
B&B Dieltiens..............................15 D3
B&B Setola..................................16 C3
Number 11..................................17 D3

EATING (pp112–13)
Christophe....................................18 D5
De Stove.......................................19 B3
Het Dagelijks Brood...................20 C3
Lokkedize....................................21 A5
Lotus..22 C3
Proxy/Delhaize (supermarket)...23 A3
Tom's Diner................................24 C1

DRINKING (p113)
Bolero..25 D5
Herberg Vlissinghe.....................26 D1
The Top.......................................27 B4
't Brugs Beertje.........................28 B4

TRANSPORT (p113)
Canal Cruises..............................29 C4
Canal Cruises..............................30 C4
Canal Cruises..............................31 C4

OTHER
Concertgebouw...........................32 A5

BELGIUM

To Ter Duinen
Hotel (400m)

To De Versteende
Nacht (100m); Bauhaus
(500m); Camping
Memling (2.5km)

To B&B
Degraeve
(800m)

To Snuffel
Sleep In
(350m)

Koningin
Astridpark

To Cactus
Club (600m)

Although pinched several times by occupying forces, it has always been returned.

The **begijnhof** (admission free; 🕑 9am-7pm Apr-Sep, to 6pm Oct-Mar) was home to a 13th-century religious community of unmarried or widowed women, known as *begijnen* (Beguines). One of Bruges' quaintest spots, and unquestionably a must, it's a 10-minute walk south of the Markt.

Choco-Story (☎ 050 61 22 37; St Jansplein; admission €5; 🕑 10am-5pm), devoted to telling the story of chocolate, is Bruges' newest attraction. It's well done.

De Halve Maan/Straffe Hendrik (☎ 050 33 26 97; Walplein 26; admission €3.70; 🕑 11am-4pm Apr-Sep, to 3pm Oct-Mar) is a family brewery offering crowded guided tours (45 minutes) that finish with a beer.

Tours

Quasimundo (☎ 050 37 07 75; www.quasimundo.com; 26 yrs & over €18, 25 yrs & under €16, under 8 yrs free, with your own bike €12; 🕑 mid-Mar–mid-Oct) offers excellent half-day bike tours of the town and/or the surrounding countryside. Bookings are necessary.

Taking a **canal tour** (adult/child €5.20/2.60; 🕑 10am-6pm Mar–mid-Nov) is touristy, but what isn't in Bruges? Viewing the city from the water gives it a totally different feel than by foot. Boats depart every 20 minutes from jetties south of the Burg, including Rozenhoedkaai and Dijver, and tours last 30 minutes.

The clip-clop of hooves hitting cobblestones resounds constantly in the streets of Bruges. **Horse-drawn carriages** (€27.50 for five passengers) leave from the Markt, and their well-trodden route takes 35 minutes.

Quasimodo (☎ 0800 975 25; www.quasimodo.be; 26 & over/25 & under €48/38 incl lunch) offers two excellent bus day trips – a 'Triple Treat' tour of Bruges or a tour of the Ypres Salient's famous WWI battlefields (see p113).

Sleeping

BUDGET

Camping Memling (☎ 050 35 58 45; www.camping-memling.be; Veltemweg 109, St Kruis; adult/child/tent/car €4/2.80/4/4; 🕑 year-round) The quietest local camping ground, located 2.5km east of town. Take bus No 11 from the train station to the Vossensteert stop and walk 400m back in the direction of Bruges.

Snuffel Sleep In (☎ 050 33 31 33; www.snuffel.be; Ezelstraat 47-49; dm/d per person €11/15; ✗) Funky,

unpretentious place that's been around for years and is the most 'alternative' hostel in Bruges. It has basic but original rooms, friendly staff, a kitchen and a bar. From the train station take bus No 3 or 13.

Bauhaus (☎ 050 34 10 93; www.bauhaus.be; Langestraat 135; hostel section dm/d/tr per person €11/15/13, hotel section s/d/tr €24/36/51, breakfast €3) Big and bustling hostel with separate hotel section next door. A popular hang-out for young travellers, though the blue rooms hardly fuel the imagination. The bar's lively and the adjoining café has cheap meals. Take bus No 6 or 16 from the train station.

B&B Degraeve (☎ 050 34 57 11; www.stardekk.com/bedbreakfast; Kazernevest 32; s/d/tr €33/45/58) Located in a quiet, untouristed part of town and run by a zany woman who has filled the two spacious rooms with bizarre décor.

MID-RANGE

B&B Setola (☎ 050 33 49 77; www.bedandbreakfast-bruges.com; St Walburgastraat 12; s/d/tr/f €50/55/75/95, €10 extra for one-night stay; ✗) Get away from old world and brocante in this mansion dating from 1740. The three 2nd-floor guestrooms have cool, clean vibes, and the woman who runs this B&B is a delight. Can't get a better location and the breakfast is fab.

B&B Dieltiens (☎ 050 33 42 94; www.users.skynet.be/dieltiens; Waalsestraat 40; s/d/tr €50/55/75, €10 extra for one-night stay) Classical mansion that featured on the first map of Bruges published in the 16th century. Lovingly restored, this B&B has three gorgeous guestrooms with polished wooden floors and subtle warm tones.

Ter Duinen Hotel (☎ 050 33 04 37; www.terduinenhotel.be; Langerei 52; s/d from €89/98; P ✗) Beautifully executed hotel facing a canal about 1km north of the Markt. The neat rooms have a refined, romantic air and the staff is efficient and friendly.

TOP END

Number 11 (☎ 050 33 06 75; www.number11.be; Peerdenstraat 11; d €115-140, ste €215) There's no mincing words: this B&B is a stunner. The three rooms – 'Vanilla', 'Grey' and 'Chocolate' – are charming, harmoniously blending modern and medieval styles. Ask about the kookiest chandelier you'll ever see.

Eating

From cosy *estaminets* (taverns) to first-class restaurants – Bruges has all bases covered.

Het Dagelijks Brood (☎ 050 33 60 50; Philipstockstraat 21; snacks €5-11; ☺ 7am-6pm, closed Tue; ☒)
Part of a national bakery/tearoom chain, with just one big table where you can eat salads or *boterhammen* (sandwiches).

Lokkedize (☎ 050 33 44 50; Korte Vuldersstraat 33; dishes €8-10; ☺ from 7pm Wed & Thu, from 6pm Fri-Sun)
One of the city's most convivial *eetcafés* and a great spot for a late-night bite (kitchen open till midnight).

Tom's Diner (☎ 050 33 33 82; West Gistelhof 23; mains €10-15; ☺ 6.30pm-1am, closed Tue) To the north of town, a little way out of the tourist centre and all the better for it. Stylish food at very affordable prices. Locals love it.

De Stove (☎ 050 33 78 35; Kleine St Amandsstraat 4; mains €18-28; ☺ closed Wed & Thu) Charming restaurant tucked away on a pedestrian lane. The eight tables are arranged around an old stove, the service is intimate and the food – fish specialities – is excellent.

Also recommended:

Lotus (☎ 050 33 10 78; Wapenmakerstraat 5; meals €9.20; ☺ 11.45am-2pm Mon-Sat) Excellent lunch-time vegetarian restaurant.

Christophe (☎ 050 34 48 92; Garenmarkt 34; mains €24; ☺ 7pm-1am Thu-Mon) Coolest bistro in town and an excellent late-nighter.

Proxy/Delhaize (Geldmuntstraat) Supermarket.

Drinking

Herberg Vlissinghe (☎ 050 34 37 37; Blekersstraat 2; ☺ from 11am, closed Tue) Someone has been pouring beer at Bruges' oldest café since 1515 – mind-blowing really.

The Top (St Salvatorskerkhof 5; ☺ from 9pm Tue-Sat, from 10pm Sun) Coolest bar in town. Opens late and moves until morning.

't Brugs Beertje (☎ 050 33 96 16; Kemelstraat 5; ☺ 4pm-1am, closed Wed) Belgium's most famous beer pub. It's a tiny place situated on a poky backstreet and offers around 250 national brews, listed by brewery. The staff, unfortunately, seem to be over tourists.

Bolero (☎ 050 33 81 11; Garenmarkt 32; ☺ 9pm-4am, closed Tue) The only gay and lesbian bar in town.

Entertainment

Concertgebouw (☎ 050 47 69 99; www.concertge bouw.be; 't Zand 34) Contemporary comes to Bruges in the form of this concert hall, the newest building on the city's skyline. Opened in 2002 to celebrate Bruges' stint as the European City of Culture, its minimal design incorporates the city's three famous towers.

Cactus Club (☎ 050 33 20 14; www.cactusmusic.be; Magdalenastraat 27) The city's premier venue for contemporary and world music – either live or DJ.

De Versteende Nacht (☎ 050 34 32 93; Langestraat 11; ☺ from 6pm Tue-Sat) Atmospheric pub given over to live jazz sessions most Wednesdays from 9pm.

Getting There & Away

BUS

Eurolines buses to/from the UK pick up passengers at the train station. Tickets can be bought from **Reizen Wasteels** (☎ 050 33 65 31; Geldmuntstraat 30a). For details on services see p123.

TRAIN

Bruges' **train station** (☎ 02 528 28 28) is about 1.5km south of the city centre. There are trains every half-hour to Brussels (€10.80, one hour) and Ghent (€5, 20 minutes), and hourly trains to Antwerp (€11.40, one hour 10 minutes). For Ypres (Ieper in Dutch; €9.30, two hours), take the train to Kortrijk, from where there are hourly connections.

Getting Around

A small network of buses operated by **De Lijn** (☎ 059 56 53 53) covers destinations in and around Bruges. To get from the train station to the Markt, take any bus marked 'Centrum'.

Bruges is great for cyclists. Rent a bike from **Fietsen Popelier** (☎ 050 34 32 62; Mariastraat 26; per hr/half-day/day €3/6/9, tandem €7/13/20; ☺ 10am-6.30pm, until 8pm Jul & Aug).

YPRES

pop 35,100

In the country's southwest corner, Ypres (Ieper in Dutch) and the surrounding area was the last bastion of Belgian territory unoccupied by the Germans in WWI. As such, the region was a barrier to a German advance towards the French coastal ports around Calais. More than 300,000 Allied soldiers were killed here during four years of fighting that left the medieval town flattened. Convincingly rebuilt, the town and its surrounds, known as the Ypres Salient, are dotted with cemeteries and memorials. Unless you've got a car, the best way to visit is by guided tour (p114).

BELGIUM

Information

Post office (Diksmuidsestraat 33)

Ypres Visitors Centre (☎ 057 23 92 20; www.ieper.be; Lakenhalle, Grote Markt; 9am-6pm Mon-Fri, 10am-6pm Sat & Sun Apr-Sep, until 5pm Oct-Mar)

Sights

The town's hub, the **Grote Markt**, is dominated by the enormous **Lakenhalle** (cloth hall) with its 70m-high belfry. This hall is evidence of Ypres importance, alongside Bruges and Ghent, as a medieval cloth town. Attached to the eastern end of the Lakenhalle is the Renaissance-style **Stadhuis**, noted for its lovely arcade gallery.

On the 1st floor of the Lakenhalle is **In Flanders Fields Museum** (☎ 057 23 92 20; www.inflandersfields.be; Grote Markt 34; adult/child/family €7.50/3.50/18; 10am-6pm Apr-Sep, 10am-5pm Tue-Sun Oct-Mar). This museum, devoted to the promotion of peace as much as the remembrance of war, is a moving testament to the wartime horrors experienced by ordinary people.

The **Menin Gate** (Meensestraat) is perhaps the saddest reminder of the town's past. The huge white gate is inscribed with the names of 54,896 British and Commonwealth troops who were lost in the quagmire of the trenches and who have no graves. Every evening at 8pm, traffic is halted while buglers sound the last post.

For details on **Tyne Cot Cemetery**, see Around Ypres, later.

Tours

Two companies offer good bus tours of the Ypres Salient. Book at least a day or two in advance.

Quasimodo (See p112.)

Salient Tours (☎ 057 21 46 57; tours@battlefields.freeserve.co.uk; 2½/4hr tour €15/21; Thu-Tue Mar-Nov) Run by an Englishman based in Ypres.

Sleeping & Eating

Jeugdstadion (☎ 057 21 72 82; info@jeugdstadion.be; Leopoldlaan 16; adult/tent/car €3/1.50/4.50; mid-Mar–Oct) Basic camping ground attached to a youth centre, 900m southeast of Grote Markt.

B&B Hortensia (☎ 057 21 24 06; www.guesthouse-ypres.be; Rijselsestraat 196; s/d €46/56) In the heart of town with modern, sober rooms. No fuss or bother.

Hotel Regina (☎ 057 21 88 88; www.hotelregina.be; Grote Markt 45; s €65-90, d €75-100) Smack on the Markt and overlooking the Lakenhalle, this is Ypres' most atmospheric hotel. The cheaper rooms are old and ordinary; the most expensive ones are large and rustic.

In het Klein Stadhuis (☎ 057 21 55 42; Grote Markt 32; mains €10-15; closed Sun Oct-May) Smooth, split-level café tucked away in a quaint guildhall next to the Stadhuis. Offers good-value meals day and night.

Getting There & Around

From Ypres **train station** (☎ 02 528 28 28) there are hourly trains direct to Kortrijk (€4, 30 minutes) and Ghent (€8.80, one hour). For Brussels (€13.50, 1½ hours), Bruges (€9.30, 1¼ hours) and Antwerp (€15.10, two hours), change in Kortrijk.

Regional buses leave from the bus station to the left outside the train station.

Rent bikes from **Jeugdstadion** (see Sleeping & Eating, earlier) for €5 per day.

AROUND YPRES

Tyne Cot Cemetery

The largest British Commonwealth war cemetery in the world, **Tyne Cot** sits on a plateau about 8km northeast of Ypres. The Northumberland infantrymen who tried to take this ridge in WWI named the cemetery. They fancied the German bunkers positioned on the hillside looked like Tyneside cottages. As cemeteries go, this one is hugely moving; in all, 11,956 soldiers are buried here. The cemetery is best visited by guided tour (see opposite).

Bellewaerde Park

This **amusement park** (☎ 057 46 86 86; Meenseweg 497; adult/child €25/19; 10am-6pm Jun-Aug, to 5pm Easter holidays & Wed-Sun May) is one of Belgium's biggest. It's 5km from Ypres along the road to Menen (or take the bus marked 'Menen' from the train station).

WALLONIA

Wallonia, Belgium's French-speaking southern half, is a world away from the affluent Flemish art cities to the north. From intimate villages to industrial decay, forests to furnaces, this region offers both Belgium's most scenic and septic landscapes. For the former, burrow down deep in Wallonia's southeastern corner, an area known as the Ardennes. Here, tranquil stone villages and ancient castles nestle in river valleys below high plateaus – all very beguiling.

LIÈGE

pop 184,300

Visitors love or loathe Liège (Luik in Dutch). Sprawled along the Meuse River, about 90km east of Brussels, Liège is the Ardennes' largest city – a gritty place that takes time to know. For Simenon fans, this is George's birthplace and his primary place of homage (though there's little to see).

Orientation & Information

The central district runs along the western bank of the Meuse River, which splits in two, creating the island of Outremeuse. The main train station, Gare Guillemins, is 2km south of Place St Lambert, the city's heart and main bus hub.

Maison du Tourisme (☎ 04 237 92 92; www.liege.be; Pl St Lambert 32; ☯ 9am-6pm Jun-Sep, 9.30am-5.30pm Oct-Mar) City tourist office.

Office du Tourisme (☎ 04 221 92 21; www.liege.be; Féronstrée 92; ☯ 9am-5pm Mon-Fri) City tourist office.

Sights

A good starting place is **Montagne de Bueren** (Hors Château). The flight of 373 stairs leads up to a former citadel (now a hospital) and an excellent city panorama.

The excellent **Musée d'Art Réligieux et d'Art Mosan** (Museum of Religious Art & Art from the Meuse Valley; ☎ 04 221 42 25; Rue Mère Dieu; adult/child €3.80/2.50; ☯ 11am-6pm Tue-Sat, to 4pm Sun) is chock-full of well-preserved regional religious relics.

Life as it was for some in the 18th century is depicted in the beautiful **Musée d'Ansembourg** (☎ 04 221 94 02; Féronstrée 114; adult/child €3.80/2.50; ☯ 1-6pm Tue-Sun). If you've just come from the previous museum, you'll find this rich, Regency-styled mansion wonderfully uncluttered.

The **Musée de l'Art Wallon** (☎ 04 221 92 31; Féronstrée 86; adult/child €3.80/2.50; ☯ 1-6pm Tue-Sat, 11am-4.30pm Sun) accommodates art by French-speaking Belgians, including surrealists René Magritte and Paul Delvaux.

Sleeping & Eating

Auberge de Jeunesse (☎ 04 344 56 89; liege@laj.be; Rue Georges Simenon 2; dm/s/d €15.75/24/38; ☒ ▯) Modern HI-affiliated hostel on Outremeuse; take bus No 4 from Gare Guillemins to Pl St Lambert and change to bus No 18.

Hôtel Les Acteurs (☎ 04 223 00 80; www.lesacteurs .be, in French; Rue des Urbanistes 10; s/d €50/60, breakfast €5; P €10) Comfy modern hotel which tries hard to be artistic. It's well located and bus Nos 1 and 4 stop about 200m away.

As Ouhès (☎ 04 223 32 25; Pl du Marché 21; mains €17-32) Liège institution that specialises in rich Walloon cuisine. Note the restaurant's apt logo – a gluttonous man sitting on a mound of hams, waffles and sausages.

Getting There & Away

Eurolines (☎ 04 222 36 18; Rue des Guillemins 94) buses leave from Rue du Plan-Incliné, next to the train station.

The principal train station is **Gare Guillemins** (☎ 02 528 28 28), from where there are connections to Brussels (€11.40, one hour), Namur (€6.80, 50 minutes), Spa (€4, 50 minutes), Tongeren (€3.50, 30 minutes) and Luxembourg City (€26, 2½ hours).

AROUND LIÈGE
Tongeren

pop 29,700

Tongeren, 20km north of Liège in Flanders, is Belgium's oldest city. The original locals put up considerable resistance under the leadership of Ambiorix when the area was besieged by Roman troops in 15 BC. The **Gallo-Roman Museum** (☎ 012 67 03 30; www.limburg .be/gallo, in French & Dutch; Kielenstraat 15; adult/concession €5/4; ☯ noon-5pm Mon, 9am-5pm Tue-Fri, 10am-6pm Sat & Sun) has findings from these times.

Tongeren is also well known for its Sunday **antique market** (Veemarkt) and the elegant **Onze Lieve Vrouwbasiliek** (Basilica of Our Lady; Grote Markt; ☯ 8am-noon & 1.30-5pm), currently undergoing archaeological excavation but still worth a visit.

For more information, head to the **tourist office** (☎ 012 39 02 55; www.tongeren.be, in Dutch; Stadhuisplein 9; ☯ 8.30am-noon & 1-4.30pm Mon-Fri, 10am-4pm Sat & Sun).

Spa

pop 10,500

There's no bursting its bubble. Spa, Europe's oldest health resort, has for centuries embraced royalty and the wealthy who came to drink, bathe and cure themselves in the mineral-rich waters that bubble forth here.

In 2004, the town opened its spanking new **Thermes de Spa** (☎ 087 77 25 60; www.thermes despa.com, in French & Dutch), a palatial hill-top

BELGIUM

complex reached by rack rail that takes off near the tourist office.

Spa is 40km southeast of Liège and connected by regular trains (€3.90, 50 minutes). The **Office du Tourisme** (☎ 087 79 53 53; www.spa-info.be, in French & Dutch; Pl Royale 41; ☿ 9am-6pm Mon-Fri, 10am-6pm Sat & Sun) can help with inquiries.

Hautes Fagnes Nature Reserve

The Hautes Fagnes, or High Fens, is a plateau of swampy heath, woods and windswept moors that sweeps over to Germany's Eifel hills. The area is popular with walkers and cyclists.

Start a visit at the **Botrange Nature Centre** (☎ 080 44 03 00; www.ful.ac.be/hotes/cnatbotrange, in French; Route de Botrange 131; ☿ 10am-6pm), located 2.5km from the sturdy stone **Signal de Botrange** that marks Belgium's highest point (694m).

It takes at least 1¼ hours to arrive here on public transport from Liège – take the train to Verviers (€3.20, 20 minutes, hourly) and then bus No 390 (30 minutes, five daily) to Rocherath.

CHARLEROI
pop 200,500

A city on the edge – Charleroi, born of coal, iron and glass, flanks the formerly coal-rich Sambre Valley and was the powerhouse of the steel industry up until the 1970s. These days it's surrounded by a blackened industrial landscape with belching chimneys and old slag heaps – hardly fuel for tourists.

The city's **airport** (www.charleroi-airport.com), called Brussels-Charleroi or Brussels' South, is 6km north of the city and is serviced by Ryanair flights from Ireland, Britain and several European destinations. Frequent shuttle buses connect the airport with Brussels' main train station, Gare du Midi (buses pick up and set down at the corner of Rue de France and Rue de l'Instruction near Gare du Midi; €10 one way).

In the unlikely event you should want to explore Charleroi, bus A and No 68 runs from the airport to Charleroi train station.

TOURNAI
pop 67,400

Tournai (Doornik in Dutch) is, together with Tongeren in Flanders, the oldest city in Belgium. It started life as a Roman trading settlement known as Tornacum but, unlike Tongeren, it has little to hark back to these times.

Just 10km from the French border and 80km from Brussels, Tournai enjoys a pleasant position on the Scheldt River (known as the Escaut in French) and has one of the country's finest cathedrals plus a cache of enjoyable museums.

Information

Internaute (☎ 069 84 67 43; info@internaute.be; Rue du Château 63; ☿ 10am-midnight) Funky Internet bar.
Office du Tourisme (☎ 069 22 20 45; www.tournai.be; Vieux Marché aux Poteries 14; ☿ 8.30am-6pm Mon-Fri, 9.30am-noon & 2-5pm Sat, 10am-noon & 2.30-6pm Sun)
Post office (Rue des Chapeliers)

Sights

The five towers of the striking but sober **Cathédrale Notre Dame** (Grand Place; admission free; ☿ 9.30am-noon & 2-6pm) have long been the trademark of Tournai's skyline. Pummelled by a freak tornado in 1999, major works to realign the towers are still underway, leaving much of the World Heritage–listed cathedral off limits to tourists.

Tournai's 72m-high **belfry** (☎ 069 22 20 45; Grand Place; admission €2; ☿ 10am-1pm & 2-5.30pm Tue-Sat, 11am-1pm & 2-6.30pm Sun) is Belgium's oldest, dating from 1188. Climb the 256 steps.

The **Musée des Beaux-Arts** (☎ 069 22 20 43; Enclos St Martin; admission €3; ☿ 9.30am-12.30pm & 2-5.30pm, closed Tue) is the city's little gem. Housed in a building designed by Victor Horta, it contains an enjoyable collection of paintings and sculptures by local, national and international artists.

Tapestry lovers should not miss the **Musée de la Tapisserie** (☎ 069 84 20 73; Pl Reine Astrid; admission €2.50; ☿ 10am-noon & 2-5.30pm, closed Tue).

Sleeping & Eating

Auberge de Jeunesse (☎ 069 21 61 36; www.laj.be; Rue St Martin 64; dm/s/d €13.75/24/38) Modern and pleasant hostel around the corner from the Musée des Beaux-Arts. It's a 20-minute walk from the train station – take bus No 4 (direction Baisieux).

Hôtel d'Alcantara (☎ 069 21 26 48; hotelalcantara@ hotmail.com; Rue des Bouchers St Jacques 2; s/d from €75/85; P €7.50) Not the most expensive hotel in town but certainly the most charming. Attentive service and 15 well-priced, modern rooms set behind a discreet courtyard.

La Tartine Quotidienne (☎ 069 23 35 88; Rue de Paris 7; light meals €6.20-8; ☿ lunch Mon-Fri, dinner Fri) Café doing salads, quiches and sandwiches, with toddlers watching from the walls.

Le Giverny (☎ 069 22 44 64; Quai du Marché au Poisson 6; mains €20, menus €35-60; ☿ lunch Tue-Fri & Sun, dinner Tue-Sat) Occupies an old bakery and is a lovely eating space with great classic French food.

Getting There & Away

Tournai's **train station** (☎ 02 528 28 28) is about 900m from the heart of town, the Grand Place. There are regular trains to Brussels (€9.90, one hour) and Ypres (€7.20, one hour).

NAMUR
pop 105,700

Namur (Namen in Dutch) is an excellent jumping-off point for exploring the forested Ardennes corner of Wallonia. Some 60km southeast of Brussels, it's a picturesque town, built at the confluence of the Meuse and Sambre Rivers and presided over by a citadel that, in times gone by, ranked as one of Europe's mightiest.

Information

Office du Tourisme (☎ 081 24 64 49; www.pays-de -namur.be; Sq de l'Europe Unie; ☿ 9.30am-6pm) Main tourist office, located near the train station.

Tourist office kiosk (☎ 081 24 64 48; Pl du Grognon; ☿ 9.30am-6pm Apr-Sep) At the base of the citadel.

Sights

Don't miss the **Trésor du Prieuré d'Oignies** (☎ 081 23 03 42; Rue Julie Billiart 17; adult/child €1.50/0.75; ☿ 10am-noon & 2-5pm, closed morning Sun & Mon), a one-room hoard of exquisite Gothic treasures housed in a modern convent. Ring the bell to be taken on a guided tour by one of the nuns.

The **Musée Félicien Rops** (☎ 081 22 01 10; www .ciger.be/rops; Rue Fumal 12; adult/child €3/1.50; ☿ 10am-6pm Tue-Sun, daily Jul & Aug) is devoted to works by the 19th-century Namur-born artist Félicien Rops (1833–98), who fondly illustrated erotic lifestyles and macabre scenes.

What remains of Namur's once-mighty **citadel** is slung high above the town on a rocky outcrop. It covers a huge area, though only towers, tunnels and much of the outer walls still exist. It's most easily accessed by a **tourist train** (☎ 081 24 64 49; €1; ☿ 10am-5pm

Jun–mid-Sep, Sat & Sun Apr & May), which departs hourly from the tourist office. Alternatively, you can walk up.

Sleeping & Eating

Camping Les 4 Fils Aymon (☎ 081 58 02 94; Chaussée de Liège; tent/caravan €6.50/12; ☿ Apr-Sep) Pleasant ground located about 8km east of Namur; bus No 12 (hourly) from the bus station.

Auberge de Jeunesse (☎ 081 22 36 88; www.laj .be; Rue F Rops 8; dm/s/d €15.75/24/38; ☿ mid-Feb–Dec; ☒ ▣) Attractive hostel on the riverfront, about 3km southwest of the train station. Bus Nos 3 and 4, which both depart hourly from Pl de la Station, stop nearby.

Hôtel Les Tanneurs (☎ 081 24 00 24; www.tanneurs .com; Rue des Tanneries 13; s €50-197, d €55-205, breakfast €8; P ☒ ▣) Unique hotel, situated on a shabby street in the heart of town, which unites modern comfort with 17th-century charm. Book well ahead.

Brasserie Henry (☎ 081 22 02 04; Pl St Aubain 3; mains €12-18; ☿ noon-midnight Mon-Thu, until 1am Fri & Sat) Sociable brasserie and an institution among Namur's late-night diners.

La Bonne Fourchette (☎ 081 23 15 36; Rue Notre Dame 112; mains €12-20, menu €20; ☿ dinner daily, lunch Sat & Sun) Intimate Belgian/French restaurant, just out of the central hub, with plum décor and hovering angels.

Getting There & Away

BUS

Local and regional buses are operated by **TEC** (☎ 081 25 35 55; Pl de la Station; ☿ 7am-7pm). Regional buses leave from either the bus station near the C&A department store or from Pl de la Station. Details of bus services to regional destinations are given in the Getting There & Away section in each of the following towns.

TRAIN

Namur is a major rail hub in this part of Belgium and boasts a gleaming new **train station** (☎ 02 528 28 28). Regional connections include Brussels (€6.80, one hour), Dinant (€3.60, 30 minutes), Jemelle (€6.80, 40 minutes), Liége (€6.80, one hour) and Marloie (€6.20, 35 minutes).

DINANT
pop 12,800

This heavy, distinctive town, 28km south of Namur, is one of the Ardennes' tourist hot spots. Pressed between rock and river, its bulbous cathedral, **Église Notre Dame** (Pl Reine Astrid; admission free), competes for attention with the cliff-front **citadel** (☎ 082 22 36 70; Pl Reine Astrid 3; adult/child €5.50/4; ◷ 10am-4pm Sat-Thu Oct-Mar, to 6pm Jul & Aug, closed Mon-Fri Jan). In summer the main thoroughfares through town are choked with traffic and the place feels hot and claustrophobic – it's good for a pit stop but there are better places deeper in the Ardennes to kick back.

The **tourist office** (☎ 082 22 28 70; www.dinant -tourisme.be, in French & Dutch; Ave Cadoux 8; ◷ 8.30am-7pm Mon-Fri, 9.30am-7pm Sat, 10am-6pm Sun) is on the opposite side of the river from the cathedral.

ROCHEFORT & HAN-SUR-LESSE
pop 23,000
As a base in this part of the Ardennes, Rochefort's hard to beat. Together with its neighbour Han-sur-Lesse, Rochefort is famed for the millennia-old underground limestone grottoes that attract visitors from all over Belgium. The caves at Han are the more spectacular of the two but Han itself is a tourist trap; stay in Rochefort and commute between towns.

Rochefort is also well known for the Trappist beer brewed by local monks, and there's no shortage of watering holes where you can sample these brews.

The Rochefort **tourist office** (☎ 084 34 51 72; www.valdelesse.be; Rue de Behogne 5; ◷ 8am-6pm Mon-Fri, 9.30am-5pm Sat & Sun Jul & Aug, 8am-5pm Mon-Fri, 10am-5pm Sat, 10am-5pm Sun Sep-Jun) is in the centre of town.

Sights & Activities
The impressive **Grottes de Han** (☎ 084 37 72 13; Rue Lamotte 2; adult/child €11/6.50; ◷ 10am-noon & 1.30-5.30pm Apr-Oct, 11.30am-4pm Nov, Dec & Mar) is a series of caves situated a little way out of Han – a toy train chugs to the entrance and a barge brings you back. Rochefort's cave, **Grotte de Lorette** (☎ 084 21 20 80; Drève de Lorette; adult/child €7/4.50; ◷ 10.30am-4.30pm Apr-Oct), is smaller but well worth seeing.

The area is a great base for **walking** and **cycling**. The tourist office sells a map covering numerous walking trails and cycling routes. One trail for cyclists is **Le Ravel**, an 18km stretch of disused railway line linking Rochefort and the village of Houyet. Bikes can be rented in Rochefort from **Cycle**

Sport (☎ 084 21 32 55; Rue de Behogne 59; half-/full-day €15/20; ◷ 9.30am-noon & 1.30-7pm Mon-Sat, 9.30am-noon Sun).

Sleeping & Eating
The following options are all in Rochefort.

Camping Communal (☎ 084 21 19 00; Rue du Hableau; adult/child €2/1, car & tent €3; ◷ Easter-Oct) Next to the Lomme River, immediately below the main part of town.

Le Vieux Moulin (☎ 084 21 46 04; www.giteroche -fort.be; Rue du Hableau 25; demi pension 25 yrs & under/26 yrs & over €18/21; ◷ year-round) Pleasant *gîte d'étape* hostel in the heart of town. The overnight price includes breakfast and one meal.

Hôtel La Fayette (☎ 084 21 42 73; www.hotel -lafayette.net, in French; Rue Jacquet 87; s/d/tr/f €45/50/70/80, with shared bathroom €37/42/60/70, breakfast €4.90, mains €10-20) Whitewashed hotel/restaurant that's yet to emerge from the '70s.

Hôtel Le Luxembourg (☎ 084 21 31 68; leluxem -bourg@proximedia.be; Pl Albert Ier 2; s/d €50/72, mains €15-20; ◷ closed Mon Sep-Jun) This hotel's restaurant and reception are located 100m from the tourist office; the rooms are in a modern townhouse further down the road.

La Bella Italia (☎ 084 22 15 20; Rue de Behogne 50; pizzas €7.50-10) Enjoy excellent pizzas at this busy Italian restaurant in the heart of town.

Getting There & Away
Rochefort is linked by bus to Han-sur-Lesse and the train stations of Jemelle and Houyet. To get here from Namur, take the train to Jemelle (40 minutes, hourly) and from there, bus No 29 to Rochefort (seven minutes, hourly), which continues on to Han (seven minutes).

LA ROCHE-EN-ARDENNE
pop 4100
La Roche is a vibrant little town, hidden in a deep valley, crowned by a ruined castle and surrounded by verdant hills. One of the Ardennes' most popular summer resorts, it hums with Belgian holiday-makers buying up big on smoked hams and getting into outdoor pursuits.

The **tourist office** (☎ 084 35 77 36; www.coeurde -lardenne.be, in French; Pl du Marché 15; ◷ 9am-5pm) is on the main street.

Sights & Activities
From the main street, steps head up to the ruins of La Roche's picture-postcard medi-

eval **castle** (adult/child €3/2; ⏲ 10am-noon & 2-5pm Apr-Oct, 1.30-4.30pm Mon-Fri, 10am-noon & 1.30-4.30pm Sat & Sun Nov-Mar). Perched on the crag above town, there's not actually much to see – a small museum with a few archaeological relics is the focal point.

The most popular kayaking excursion involves a 25km paddle along the Ourthe River (€20, four to six hours). The main operator is **Ardennes-Aventures** (☎ 084 41 19 00; Rue du Hadja 1), next to the bridge at the northern end of town. It also hires mountain bikes (€17/22 half-/full day) for exploring the many marked hiking/biking trails that crisscross the surrounding hills.

Sleeping & Eating

Camping Le Vieux Moulin (☎ 084 41 13 80; www .strument.com; Petite Strument 62; adult/child/site €2.50/ 2.50/8; ⏲ Easter–mid-Nov) Draped for what seems an eternity along a stream next to the Hôtel Moulin de la Strument. Great site.

Domaine des Olivettes (☎ 084 41 16 52; www .lesolivettes.be; Chemin de Soeret 12; dm €12, s/d from €28/56) Hotel-cum-auberge-cum-equestrian centre, perched on a hill above town. The hotel rooms are pleasant; alternatively there's a separate auberge with dormitory-style accommodation.

Hôtel Moulin de la Strument (☎ 084 41 15 07; www.strument.com; Petite Strument 62; s/d €64/71; ⏲ closed Jan; **P**) La Roche's most agreeable hotel is nestled in a secluded wooded valley next to a babbling stream and is part of an old mill.

Maison Bouillon et Fils (☎ 084 41 18 80; Pl du Marché 9) Where but the Belgian Ardennes would a butcher's shop have its own café? Dine in with an *assiette ardennaise* (plate of mixed local charcuterie, €9) or takeaway from this must-see *boucherie*.

Le Clos René (☎ 084 41 26 17; Rue Châmont 30; snacks €5-8; ⏲ 11am-11pm Jul & Aug, closed Thu Sep-Jun) When you can't stand the sight of another sausage or smoked ham, escape to this tasteful creperie.

Getting There & Away

Buses are the only form of public transport reaching La Roche. If you're coming from the direction of Namur, the nearest rail junction is Marloie from where bus No 15 goes to La Roche (35 minutes, six per day). From Liège, get a train to Melreux and then a bus to La Roche (30 minutes, seven a day).

BASTOGNE
pop 14,000

It was in Bastogne, close to the Luxembourg border, that thousands of soldiers and civilians died during WWII's Battle of the Bulge. Today this little town is full of wartime reminders. The main square – a parking lot adorned with a tank – has been renamed Pl McAuliffe after the famous American general whose reply to the German call to surrender was 'Nuts!'.

The **Maison du Tourisme** (☎ 061 21 27 11; www .bastogne-tourisme.be, in French; Pl McAuliffe; ⏲ 9am-6pm mid-Jun–mid-Sep, to 5.30pm mid-Sep–mid-Jun) is in a conspicuous building in the heart of town.

Sights

The main attraction is the star-shaped **American Memorial** to the battle that stands on a hill a little outside town. Next to the memorial is the **Bastogne Historical Centre** (☎ 061 21 14 13; Colline du Mardasson; adult/child €7.50/5; ⏲ 10am-4.30pm Feb-Apr & Oct-Dec, 9.30am-5pm May-Sep). Here the battle is recounted with a 30-minute film using actual war footage and period displays.

Sleeping & Eating

Camping de Renval (☎ 061 21 29 85; Route de Marché 148; adult/child/site €5/2.50/15) Closest camping ground to town, located about 1km from the tourist office.

Hôtel Le Caprice (☎ 061 21 81 40; www.horest.be; Pl McAuliffe 25; s/d €55/67, breakfast €5; **P**) Handy location and saccharine-sweet pink rooms.

Restaurant Léo (☎ 061 21 14 41; Rue du Vivier 4; mains €12-20; ⏲ lunch & dinner Tue-Sun) Just off Pl McAuliffe, this restaurant occupies a renovated train carriage and does an excellent *assiette ardennaise* (11 types of charcuterie) for €13.

Getting There & Away

The closest rail junction is Libramont, from where bus No 163b departs every two hours for Bastogne (45 minutes).

BELGIUM DIRECTORY

ACCOMMODATION

Accommodation in this chapter is ordered from budget to mid-range then followed by top end.

BELGIUM

Camping and caravanning facilities are plentiful and at their best in the Ardennes. Rates vary widely – expect to pay €9 to €18 for two adults, a tent and vehicle.

Belgium has many hostels (*jeugdherberg* in Dutch or *auberge de jeunesse* in French) affiliated with Hostelling International (HI) as well as a small number of private hostels offering slightly cheaper accommodation. HI hostels charge €14 to €16 per night in a dorm, including breakfast and sheets, or €24/38 in a single/double room. Contact **Vlaamse Jeugdherbergcentrale** (☎ 03 232 72 18; www.jeugdherbergen.be; Van Stralenstraat 40, B-2060 Antwerp) for hostels in Flanders and **Les Auberges de Jeunesse** (☎ 02 219 56 76; www.laj.be; Rue de la Sablonnière 28, B-1000 Brussels) for Wallonia.

In Wallonia's rural areas you'll occasionally come across *gîtes d'étapes*, basic hostel-style places mostly set up for large groups, though individual travellers are welcome.

B&Bs (*gastenkamers/chambres d'hôtes*) usually represent excellent value. Spacious rooms, private bathroom facilities, breakfast feasts and vibrant hosts are the salient features. Prices start at single/double €30/45, rising to €50/65 for mid-range options and levelling out at €100 to €160 at the top end.

The cheapest hotels charge between €30 and €40 for a single room and from €45 to €55 for doubles. Cheap rooms usually have shared bathroom facilities. Mid-range hotel prices average €65 to €90 for singles and €75 to €100 for doubles. Top-end establishments start at €120. Many hotels in Brussels, and some other cities, offer weekend discounts due to the influx of Eurocrats and businesspeople on weekdays, and their mass exodus at weekends.

ACTIVITIES
Cycling
Cycling is one of Belgium's national passions. There are two cycling genres: in flat Flanders, bikes are a popular means of everyday travel and relaxation and many roads have dedicated cycle lanes; in Wallonia, the hilly terrain is favoured by mountain bike (VTT, or *vélo tout-terrain* in French) enthusiasts.

Bikes are not allowed on motorways but can be taken on trains (one way/return €4.20/7.20). Hire them from private operators or from most train stations for around €6/9 per half-/full day or €50 per week. You may be required to pay a deposit (€12 to €20) and show your passport. For more on cycling, see p123.

Walking
Walkers have the choice of easy, flat terrain in Flanders or the more inspiring hills of the Ardennes in Wallonia. Local tourist offices have copious information about paths and they sell regional hiking maps.

Canoeing & Kayaking
The Ardennes is the place to ride rivers. Canoes and kayaks can be hired at La Roche-en-Ardenne (p119), but don't expect rapids of any magnitude.

Rock Climbing
The most popular area for rock climbers is along the Meuse River near Namur and Dinant. It was here, near Marche-les-Dames, that King Albert I died after a climbing fall in 1934. Belgium's escarpments are mostly high-quality limestone. Pick up *Selected Rock Climbs in Belgium & Luxembourg* by Chris Craggs from bookshops in Brussels.

BOOKS
Some suggested reads are: *Belgium & Luxembourg*, Lonely Planet's comprehensive guide; *The Great Beers of Belgium* by one of the world's best beer writers, Michael Jackson, details all that Belgium has to offer; *King Léopold's Ghost* by Adam Hochschild investigates the atrocities committed in the Congo during Léopold II's reign and chronicles the small band of activists who fought his rule; Belgium warrants two fun-filled chapters in Bill Bryson's European sojourn *Neither Here Nor There*; Harry Pearson's tale of family travel in Belgium, *A Tall Man in a Low Land*, spotlights the country's many idiosyncrasies; *Tintin & the World of Hergé: An Illustrated History* by Benoit Peeters traces Tintin's development.

BUSINESS HOURS
Restaurants open from 11.30am to 2pm or 3pm and again from 6.30pm to 11pm. Brasseries usually stay open until 1am.

Bars and cafés open when they want and close when the last customer leaves (or when the bar staff calls it quits). Most cafés open by 10am and many will still be going at dawn.

Shops open from 9am to 12.30pm, then again from 2pm to 6pm Monday to Saturday. Many shops in major cities remain open at lunch time, and many also open on Sunday.

Banks open from 8.30am or 9am and close between 3.30pm and 5pm Monday to Friday. Some close for an hour at lunch and many also open Saturday mornings.

EMBASSIES & CONSULATES
Belgian Embassies & Consulates
Australia (☎ 02-6273 2501; fax 6273 3392; 19 Arkana St, Yarralumla, ACT 2600)

Canada (☎ 613-236 7267; fax 236 7882; Constitution Sq, 360 Albert St, ste 820, Ottawa ON K1R 7X7)

France (☎ 01 44 09 39 39; fax 01 47 54 07 64; rue de Tilsitt 9, Paris F-75840 Cedex 17)

Germany (☎ 49-3020 6420; fax 3020 642 200; Jäger-strasse 52-53, Berlin D-10117)

Ireland (☎ 01-205 7100; fax 283 8488; 2 Shrewsbury Rd, Ballsbridge, Dublin 4)

Luxembourg (☎ 25 43 251; fax 45 42 82; Résidence Champagne, rue des Girondins 4, Luxembourg City L-1626)

The Netherlands (☎ 070-312 34 56; fax 364 55 79; Alexanderveld 97, The Hague NL-2585 DB)

New Zealand (☎ 09-915 9150; fax 915 9151; Level 2, Orica House, cnr Kingdon & Carlton Gore Sts, Auckland)

UK (☎ 020-7470 3700; fax 7259 6213; 103-105 Eaton Sq SW1W 9AB)

USA (☎ 202-333 6900; fax 333 3079; 3330 Garfield St, NW, Washington DC, 2000)

Embassies & Consulates in Belgium
The following diplomatic missions are all embassies and are located in or around Brussels (Map pp96-7):

Australia (☎ 02 286 05 00; fax 02 230 68 02; Rue Guimard 6, B-1040)

Canada (☎ 02 741 06 11; fax 02 741 06 43; Ave de Tervuren 2, B-1040)

France (☎ 02 548 87 11; fax 02 513 68 71; Rue Ducale 65, B-1000)

Germany (☎ 02 774 19 11; fax 02 772 36 92; Ave de Tervuren 190, B-1150)

Ireland (☎ 02 235 66 76; fax 02 235 66 71; Rue Wiertz 50, B-1050)

Luxembourg (☎ 02 735 57 00; fax 02 737 57 10; Ave de Cortenbergh 75, B-1000)

The Netherlands (☎ 02 679 17 11; fax 02 679 17 75; Ave Herrmann-Debroux 48, B-1160)

New Zealand (☎ 02 512 10 40; fax 02 513 48 56; 7th fl, Sq de Meeus 1, B-1000)

UK (☎ 02 287 62 11; fax 02 287 63 55; Rue d'Arlon 85, B-1040)

USA (☎ 02 508 21 11; fax 02 511 27 25; Blvd du Régent 27, B-1000)

HOLIDAYS
New Year's Day 1 January
Easter Monday March/April
Labour Day 1 May
Ascension Day 40th day after Easter
Whit Monday 7th Monday after Easter
Festival of the Flemish Community 11 July (Flanders only)
National Day 21 July
Assumption 15 August
Walloon Community 27 September (Wallonia only)
All Saints' Day 1 November
Armistice Day 11 November
Christmas Day 25 December

LANGUAGE
Belgium has three official languages – Dutch, French and German. For details on the country's linguistic make up, see People (p93).

MONEY
Banks are the best place to exchange money. Outside banking hours, exchange bureaux (*wisselkantoren* in Dutch, *bureau d'échange* in French) operate at Brussels National airport and at main train stations, however they mostly have lower rates and higher fees than banks. Automated teller machines (ATMs) are widespread.

Tipping is optional as service and VAT are included in hotel and restaurant prices.

POST
Mail can be sent either *prioritaire* (priority) or *nonprioritaire* (nonpriority) but, given the delays experienced with priority mail, don't even consider sending things nonpriority. Letters under 50g to EU countries cost €0.60 and to non-EU countries, €0.85.

Poste restante attracts a €0.35 fee and you may need to show your passport. Some useful poste restante addresses include:
Poste Restante Hoofdpostkantoor, Groenplaats, B-2000 Antwerp
Poste Restante Hoofdpostkantoor, Markt 5, B-8000 Bruges
Poste Restante Bureau de Poste Central, Centre Monnaie, B-1000 Brussels

TELEPHONE
Belgium's international country code is ☎ 32. To telephone abroad, the international access code is ☎ 00. For an international operator, call ☎ 1224.

BELGIUM

EMERGENCY NUMBERS

■ Ambulance ☎ 100

■ Fire ☎ 100

■ Police ☎ 101

Local phone calls are metered and cost a minimum of €0.25. Telephone numbers prefixed with 0900 or 070 are pay-per-minute numbers (€0.17 to €0.45 per minute). Numbers prefixed with 0800 are toll-free calls. Those prefixed with 075, 0476 to 0479, 0486 and 0496 are mobile numbers. Note also that a call to the national and international directory assistance (☎ 1405) costs an arm and a leg (€2.20).

TIME
Belgium runs on Central European Time. See the World Time Zones map (p1084) for time zones.

TOURIST INFORMATION
For details on the Belgian Tourist Information Centre, see p97.

VISAS
There are no entry requirements or restrictions on EU nationals visiting Belgium. Citizens of Australia, Canada, Israel, Japan, New Zealand and the USA do not need visas to visit the country as tourists for up to three months. Except for people from a few other European countries (such as Switzerland and Norway), everyone else must have a visa issued by a Belgian embassy or consulate.

For up-to-date visa information, check Belgium's Ministry of Foreign Affairs website at www.diplomatie.be.

TRANSPORT IN BELGIUM

GETTING THERE & AWAY
Departure Tax
Departure tax for airline passengers is included in the plane ticket. There's no departure tax when leaving by sea.

Air
Belgium's national airline, Sabena, went bankrupt in 2001. The only Belgian airlines now operating are SN Brussels Airlines,

which has flights from Brussels National airport to European and African destinations, and VLM Airlines from Deurne airport near Antwerp to London City.

Belgium's main international airports:
Brussels National Airport (www.brusselsairport.be; ☎ 0900 70 000)
Brussels-Charleroi (www.charleroi-airport.com)
Luchthaven Deurne (☎ 03 285 65 00; www.antwerp airport.be) Near Antwerp.

Airlines flying into Belgium include:
Aer Lingus (code EI; ☎ 02 548 98 48; www.airlingus.com)
Air France (code AF; ☎ 02 541 42 11; www.airfrance.com)
British Airways (code BA; ☎ 02 717 32 17; www.britishairways.com)
KLM (code KL; ☎ 070 22 27 47; www.klm.be)
Lufthansa (code LH; ☎ 02 745 22 26; www.lufthansa.be)
Ryanair (code FR; ☎ 0902 88 007; www.ryanair.com)
SN Brussels Airlines (☎ 070 35 11 11; www.flysn.com)
Virgin Express (code TV; ☎ 070 35 36 37; www.virgin-express.com)
VLM Airlines (☎ 03 287 80 80; www.vlmairlines.com)

Land
BUS
Eurolines (☎ 02 274 13 50; www.eurolines.com) operates international bus services to and from Belgium. It has regular buses to many European destinations, as well as North Africa. There is no service to Luxembourg.

Depending on the destination and the time of year, Eurolines buses stop in Brussels, Antwerp, Bruges, Ghent and Liège. Tickets can be bought from its offices in these cities or from travel agencies – for details see the relevant city's Getting There & Away section.

Services from Brussels include Amsterdam (€15, 3¾ hours, six daily), Frankfurt (€33, 5¼ hours, one daily), London (€42, 8½ hours, six daily) and Paris (€15, 3¾ hours, nine daily).

Some Busabout services also pass through Belgium – for details see p1074.

CAR & MOTORCYCLE
The main motorways into Belgium are the E19 from the Netherlands, the E40 from Germany, the E411 from Luxembourg and the E17 and E19 from France. There are no controls at border crossings on these routes.

TaxiStop (☎ 070 22 22 92; www.taxistop.be; Rue du Fossé aux Loups 28, Brussels) is an agency that matches long-distance travellers and drivers headed for the same destination for a reasonable fee.

TRAIN

Eurostar (☎ 02 400 67 31; www.eurostar.com) operates trains between Brussels' Gare du Midi station and London's Waterloo station (two hours 20 minutes, nine trains daily) through the Eurotunnel. Standard 2nd-class fares are €223/330 one way/return, though cheaper weekend fares are available (conditions apply).

For details on **Eurotunnel** (☎ 070 22 32 10; www.eurotunnel.com) services between France and the UK, see Train in the Britain (p255) and France (p391) chapters.

Thalys (☎ 070 66 77 88; www.thalys.com) fast trains link various cities in Belgium with destinations in France, the Netherlands and Germany. In Brussels, Thalys trains depart only from Gare du Midi. Fully flexible fares, known as Librys tickets, include Brussels to Paris (€68.50, 1½ hours, hourly), Cologne (€37, 2½ hours, six daily) and Amsterdam (€41, 2½ hours, 10 daily). Cheaper Thalys fares are available on weekends and for trips booked well in advance. People aged 12 to 26 get a 50% discount and seniors a 30% reduction.

Sea

Hoverspeed (www.hoverspeed.com) has stopped operating fast ferries between Belgium and the UK. However, it runs a bus twice daily between Ostend in Belgium and Calais in France (€16, 1¼ hours) to connect with its ferry services out of Calais.

Two overnight car ferry services exist. The operators are:

P&O (Belgium ☎ 02 710 64 44; UK ☎ 0870-520 2020; www.poferries.com) Sails overnight from Zeebrugge in Belgium to Hull in the UK (14 hours) and charges from €125/205 one way/return for a car. Adult passengers pay from €60 one way.

Superfast Ferries (Belgium ☎ 050 25 22 52; UK ☎ 0870-234 08 70; www.superfast.com) Ultramodern ferry sails nightly between Zeebrugge in Belgium and Rosyth in Scotland (17½ hours). Fares start at €111/202 one way/return for a car. Adult passengers pay from €68 one way.

GETTING AROUND
Bicycle

Cycling is a great way to get around in Flanders. The Flemish countryside is riddled with well-marked cycling routes and if you hire a bike, or buy a cheap second-hander, it's easy to cycle from destination to destination, or to go from city to city by train, using the bike to explore once you're there.

Those serious on a cycling holiday should get the new multilingual *Topogids Vlaanderen Fietsroute*. This book details the 800km Flanders Cycle Route, plus shorter circuits. It's available from the Belgian Tourist Information Centre (p97).

For more on cycling, see p120.

Bus

Buses are a secondary means of getting around as the rail network is so widespread. The exception is the Ardennes region in Wallonia. Here, train lines run to bigger settlements but many smaller places are connected only by bus. Without a vehicle, you'll find relatively short distances can involve long waits as bus routes are often sparsely serviced.

Car & Motorcycle

The **Touring Club de Belgique** (☎ 02 233 22 11; www.touring.be, in French & Dutch; Rue de la Loi 44, B-1040 Brussels), Belgium's biggest motoring club, offers a 24-hour breakdown service (☎ 07 034 47 77) that's free for members and foreign visitors who are members of their own country's automobile club; nonmembers must pay €90.

Road rules are generally easy to understand, although the peculiar give-way-to-the-right law takes a lot of getting used to. Standard international signs are used and motorways are toll-free. The speed limit is 50km/h in towns, 90km/h outside towns and 120km/h on motorways. The blood alcohol limit is 0.05%. Fuel prices per litre are €1/1.05 for lead-free/super and €0.75 for diesel.

Major car-rental companies have offices in central Brussels as well as offices at Brussels National airport and Gare du Midi, the city's main train station. Rentals from either the airport or Gare du Midi cost considerably more due to additional taxes.

Car rental companies include:

Avis (☎ 02 537 12 80; www.avis.be, in Dutch; Rue Américaine 145, Brussels)

Budget (☎ 02 646 51 30; www.budget.com; Ave Louise 327b, Brussels)

Hertz (☎ 02 513 28 86; www.hertz.com; Blvd Maurice Lemonnier 8, Brussels)

Hitching

It's illegal to hitch on Belgian motorways.

Local Transport

Buses and trams (and small metro systems in Brussels and Antwerp) are efficient and reliable. Single tickets cost €1.40, a book of 10 tickets is €9.80 and a one-day card costs €3.80. Services generally run until about midnight.

Taxis are metered and generally wait outside train stations and close to major city hubs.

Train

Train is the best way to get around. Belgium built continental Europe's first railway line (between Brussels and Mechelen) in the 1830s and has since developed an extremely dense network. Trains are run by the **Belgische Spoorwegen/Société National des Chemins de Fer Belges** (Belgian Railways; ☎ 02 528 28 28; www.nmbs.be, in Dutch). Major train stations have information offices, open until about 7pm (later in large cities).

There are four levels of service: Inter-City (IC) trains (the fastest), InterRegional (IR), local (L) and peak-hour (P) commuter trains. Depending on the line, there will be an IC and IR train every half-hour or hour.

Trains have 1st- and 2nd-class compartments; both are completely nonsmoking.

COSTS

Second-class tickets are 50% cheaper than 1st-class tickets. At weekends, return tickets to anywhere within Belgium are 50% cheaper than on weekdays. Children under 12 travel for free when accompanied by an adult, provided the journey starts after 9am. Seniors over 65 (including visitors) pay only €3 for a return 2nd-class trip anywhere in Belgium.

If you intend doing day excursions, investigate discounted packages known as B-Excursions. They're always good value.

TRAIN PASSES

Benelux Tourrail Allows five days' travel in one month in Belgium, Luxembourg and the Netherlands, and costs €160/120 in 1st/2nd class (under 26 €90, 2nd class only). It can be purchased in Belgium or Luxembourg but not in the Netherlands (though it's valid for use there).

Go Pass Provides 10 one-way trips anywhere in Belgium for people under 26 (€41.50, 2nd class only).

Multi Pass Valid for one journey anywhere in Belgium for a small group. Costs €37/43/47 for three/four/five people (one person must be over 26 years).

Rail Pass Gives 10 one-way trips anywhere in Belgium. Valid for one year and costs €96/62 in 1st/2nd class.

Britain

BRITAIN

The world's 78th largest nation has traditionally exerted way more than its fair share of global influence: Britain once ruled 20% of the planet, sparked the Industrial Revolution and has produced enough cultural icons – including Shakespeare, Charles Dickens, the Beatles and Monty Python – to be forgiven for dumping Posh Spice and hubby David Beckham on an unsuspecting world.

For visitors, it's a nation dripping with obvious history that's nevertheless still vibrant. Locals drink nonchalantly in pubs that are hundreds of years old while arguing noisily over whether Brit Art *enfant terrible* Damien Hirst should be strung-up for his latest creation.

And while London remains the first stop for most visitors, Britain is so full of cultural, historic and philosophical differences that travelling just a few miles outside the capital can produce its own eye-opening rewards. Manchester, Newcastle and Glasgow are keen rivals for Britain's most happening cities, while Northumbria, Wales and the Scottish Highlands are forged from heartbreakingly beautiful vistas. For history, York, Edinburgh and Oxford can keep most travellers happy for days, while those seeking spiritual succour will check out some of the world's finest cathedrals, some standing as dramatic skeletal ruins on windswept hilltops.

Whatever corner of the British Isles you indulge in, there's one 'tradition' about the English, Scots and Welsh you'll quickly realise is false. Overturning stereotypes of formality and aloofness, the British are usually delighted to share their insider knowledge and reveal a few gossipy stories that may never make the official history books.

FAST FACTS

- **Area** 240,000 sq km (149,130 sq miles)
- **Capital** London
- **Currency** pound sterling (£); A$1 = £0.39; €1 = £0.66; ¥100 = £0.49; NZ$1 = £0.35; US$1 = £0.56
- **Famous for** historic cities, castles, cathedrals, rolling countryside, royal family, Shakespeare, haggis, kilts, football
- **Official Language** English, Gaelic (Scotland), Welsh (Wales)
- **Telephone Codes** country code ☎ 44; international access code ☎ 00; international operator (for overseas reverse-charge calls) ☎ 155
- **Visas** None required for citizens of the USA, EU and several Commonwealth countries; visas for all other nationalities must be obtained in advance of arrival

HOW MUCH?

- **Hostel bed** £11
- **Restaurant main** £8
- **Loaf of bread** 65p
- **Local phone call** 20p
- **Cappucino** £1.80

LONELY PLANET INDEX

- **Litre of petrol** 80p
- **Litre of bottled water** 50p
- **Half-pint of beer** £1.20
- **Souvenir T-shirt** £10
- **Takeaway kebab** £2.50

HIGHLIGHTS

- Take in the contemporary art and stunning industrial architecture at London's **Tate Modern** (p140), and enjoy its river views from the upper floors.
- Soak up the cool bohemian vibe of Brighton in the **Lanes** and **North Laine** (p166).
- Bask in the lofty academic atmosphere of **Cambridge** (p194) then have a go at punting on the river.
- Walk six or all 630 miles (1104km) of the **Southwest Coast Path** (p171) through coastal villages, ocean mist and ancient lands, or tramp the craggy peaks, rolling hills or ragged coastline of the **Lake District** (p215), **Exmoor National Park** (p178) or **Scotland's West Coast** (p232).
- Dress up to the nines or get down with the indie crowd out on the town in **Manchester** (p211).
- Challenge your preconceptions at Newcastle's **Baltic** (p206) centre and Glasgow's **St Mungo's Museum of Religious Life & Art** (p228).

ITINERARIES

Depending on the duration of your stay, consider the following itineraries:

- **One week** Start east from London to Canterbury, the ancient centre of the Church of England, before heading west to Bath, a former Roman settlement and World Heritage city. Next stop is northeast to Oxford, with its dreamy college spires and cosy pubs. Continue on to Cambridge, for a punt along the Cam River.
- **Two weeks** Drive to Britain's best national parks and enjoy several varied day hikes in each. Recommended parks include Exmoor, the Lake District, the Peak District and North York Moors in England; Snowdonia and the Brecon Beacons in Wales; and the Cairngorms in Scotland.

CLIMATE & WHEN TO GO

Although Britain's climate is mild and its annual rainfall unspectacular (912mm), grey, overcast skies can make for depressing days any time of year. The average July temperature in London is 17.6°C (64°F), and the average January temperature is 4°C (39°F). Further north it's generally cooler; see Climate Charts p1054.

July and August are the busiest months, and should be avoided if possible, especially in tourist magnet cities like London and Edinburgh, where you can easily blow your budget just calling around to find a room. You are just as likely to enjoy fine weather in spring and autumn, so May to June and September to mid-October are the best times to visit.

HISTORY

See the individual England, Scotland and Wales sections later in this chapter for in-depth historical information.

PEOPLE

With a population of 58 million, Britain is one of the world's most densely populated nations. Despite sprawling mega-cities like London, Birmingham and Manchester – with their cosmopolitan communities drawn from around the world – there are thousands of tiny villages and many regions where trees, sheep and hills easily outnumber people.

Surprisingly, there are myriad diverse regional identities in Britain: it's common to travel less than 50 miles (80km) and find a completely different accent with its own distinctive vocabulary. Southerners will tell you they don't understand a word uttered by the Geordies, while northerners will happily tease the Welsh over the way they speak. For the most part, this regional rivalry is fairly friendly – although it's wise to avoid calling someone 'English' if they come from Scotland or Wales.

BRITAIN

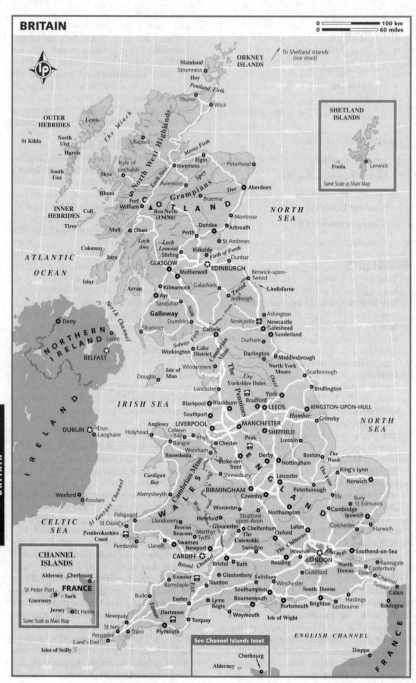

BRITAIN

0 —————— 100 km
0 —————— 60 miles

RELIGION

In the nation's most recent census, 72% of Brits identified themselves as Christians, with Muslims being the second biggest group at 3%. The remaining largest faiths were Hindus, Sikhs, Jews and Buddhists. Around 16% said they had no religion – a category that included agnostics, atheists, heathens and those who claimed a spiritual affiliation with the Jedis of *Star Wars* fame.

The main Christian religion, the Church of England (C of E), became independent from Roman Catholicism in the 16th-century. It's led by the Archbishop of Canterbury, with Queen Elizabeth as its figurehead. While in recent years it has undergone a crisis of relevance, the church's presence is still felt across the nation: most holiday periods are Christian in origin. Aiming to keep up with the times, the church recently accepted the ordination of women priests and is struggling mightily with the question of gay ordination. North of the border, the Church of Scotland is independent from the Church of England, although its services are similar.

While the C of E still dominates the statistics, the nation has dozens of other Christian religions, including Baptists, Methodists and Catholics – one in 10 Brits claim Catholicism as their faith. Whatever the role of Britain's Christian faiths in today's society, they maintain some of the most exquisite cathedrals and churches in the world, almost all built centuries ago.

ARTS

Britain has a colourful history of contributions to the world of culture that stretches back for centuries. While theatre and literature are at the forefront of these historic achievements – there have been few world-renowned British painters and composers – the UK's latter-day popular culture and conceptual art movements currently resonate throughout the world.

Literature

Travelling in the footsteps of legendary English, Scottish or Welsh writers can be the highlight of any visit to Britain. Walking through the cobbled streets of Canterbury today can be a reminder of Chaucer's ribald comedy, while strolling in the Scottish glens should easily invoke the spirit of Robbie Burns. Spirits of a different variety should be sampled in a visit to the pubs of Wales, some of which inspired the evocative poetry of Dylan Thomas.

For most lit-lovers, a visit to Stratford-Upon-Avon (p190) is a must. Not only is this the historic hometown of perhaps the greatest playwright in history, it's also the world centre of Shakespeare performance and the home of the renowned Royal Shakespeare Company.

Shakespeare is also a big part of London life, with frequent performances of the Bard's work at venues including the Globe Theatre (p158), an authentic recreation of an Elizabethan theatre-in-the-round. Look out for the blue plaques (www.blueplaque .com) on buildings throughout the city; they show where legendary authors, including Charles Dickens, Jane Austen and Lewis Carroll, once lived.

Among the most telling of recent Scottish novels are the works of Irvine Welsh, whose *Trainspotting* and *The Acid House* explore the dark underbelly of life north of the border. Contemporary English authors, by comparison, often produce more whimsical fare, with the works of Nick Hornby (*High Fidelity* and *About a Boy*) and Helen Fielding (*Bridget Jones's Diary*) speaking to the humorous side of everyday life.

Brits are voracious readers, which explains the wealth of high street bookshops in even the smallest towns. It's worth picking up a couple of paperbacks by authors you've never heard of to gain a valuable insight into the way those who reside here view their lives.

Cinema & Television

While the BBC is continually threatened by funding cuts and tabloid suggestions about how it should be run, it remains the finest public service broadcaster in the world. While many complain about its bureaucracy, there's no denying its astonishing level of innovation and creativity in TV and radio broadcasting. In TV comedy alone, its legendary gems have ranged from *Monty Python's Flying Circus* to recent Golden Globe cult hit *The Office*.

Britain's home-grown movie industry has undergone a box office boom in recent years, although most hits depict a whimsical version of the nation that can be as grating as it is entertaining to many Brits. *Notting Hill, Billy Elliot* and *Love Actually* are undeniably heart-warming confections but not as edgy as less Hollywood-friendly but more rewarding films like *Shallow Grave* and *Trainspotting*.

Music
British artists continue to enjoy huge record sales around the world, with the Rolling Stones, Elton John and Paul McCartney routinely topping the lists of highest-grossing concert tours. In recent years, the Britpop surge of the mid-1990s has fallen by the wayside with bands like Blur and Oasis losing their iconic status. They've been replaced by a host of singer-songwriters – including Dido, Moby, Coldplay and David Gray – who enjoy broad, almost ubiquitous popularity. There's also a great depth of classical music performance in Britain, with several major cities hosting their own world-renowned symphony orchestras.

Visual Arts
Britain's contribution to modern art has undergone a transformation in recent years, with new galleries and public art spaces creating broad debates throughout the nation. While cities like Glasgow, Manchester and London feature some of the finest national and regional galleries in Europe, new developments like the capital's Tate Modern (p140) and Newcastle's Baltic (p206) have become dramatic and highly popular showcases for the latest artistic movements at home and abroad.

Public art has also taken on a new role, with the Angel of the North (p206) – a giant metal sculpture in Gateshead – becoming a symbol of northern pride, while arguments over what should occupy an empty Trafalgar Square plinth preoccupied the national newspapers for several weeks in early 2004. Britain's contemporary artists can always make the front pages of the outraged tabloids, with *agents provocateurs* Damien Hirst and Tracey Emin taking it in turns to cause controversy with their latest 'offensive' works.

ENVIRONMENT
The Land
At less than 600 miles (966km) from north to south and under 300 miles (483km) at its

widest point, Britain is roughly the same size as New Zealand or half the size of France. There is a huge variety of landscapes, including the Snowdonia mountains in northwest Wales, the Yorkshire Dales in England and the barren islands off western Scotland.

Wildlife
Mostly famous in Britain for being run over on roads, hedgehogs are commonly seen throughout the nation, even in urban settings where they scavenge for food at night. Another night-time scavenger, though a rarer sight for most, is the fox. While deer occupy large estates, particularly in the north, you're more likely to see grey squirrels, which will often eat from your hand.

Environmental Issues
House prices are white hot in some parts of Britain as the number of houses – fewer and fewer homes have been built over the years – fails to meet demand. The government's belated response to this overcrowding issue has been to announce a massive house-building programme on 'brown land' that has been farmed for centuries.

FOOD & DRINK
The words 'British' and 'cuisine' never used to be uttered in the same sentence without a nervous laugh or gagging reflex. Those days are long gone and there's a rich variety of local dishes alongside an impressive array of more cosmopolitan options, reflecting the nation's ethnic diversity.

Staples & Specialities
Travellers are often introduced to British cuisine via the uniform cooked breakfasts dished up at B&Bs. A rib-sticking fry-up of eggs, bacon, sausages, beans and tomato, it's changed little over the years. In contrast, many of the nation's other traditional dishes have enjoyed a recent renaissance, reinvented for serious foodies at some of Britain's finest restaurants. These newly revered dishes – which are still available in less gourmet fashion at pubs across the land – include fish and chips, bangers and mash, steak and kidney pie, Sunday roast and ploughman's lunch: a salad heavily reliant on pickles, cheese and cold pies rather than fresh vegetables.

Most Brits have also embraced a huge variety of ethnic cuisines imported by immigrants. It's hard to find a town that doesn't have Italian, Indian and Chinese restaurants – indeed curry from the Indian sub-continent is the most popular food in Britain, with cities like Glasgow, London, Birmingham and Manchester each claiming to be the nation's curry capital.

Where to Eat & Drink

While not every pub serves food, most provide an inexpensive, filling meal. It's also the perfect opportunity to try the local beers, which can vary enormously from region to region. If you've been raised on lager, a traditional bitter or ale is a bit of a shock – not as cold or as effervescent. Ale is similar to bitter – it's more a regional name difference than anything else. Stout is a dark, rich, foamy drink; Guinness is the most famous brand. Do your homework before you go, check out the website of **Campaign for Real Ale** (www .camra.org.uk).

If you're not ready for a big pub meal, crisps are the snack of choice for most beer drinkers, who may also indulge in the dubious pleasures of a greasy kebab on their way home. Remember that most pubs still close at 11pm, with some charging for entry after that. Few pubs have good wine cellars and most restaurants do not allow you to bring your own bottle, which is a shame because supermarkets sell some great bargains around the £5 mark.

ENGLAND

With Scotland and Wales gaining increasing powers to run their own affairs, to the obvious delight of nationalists in those countries, the idea of what it means to be English – as opposed to British – is being re-examined. For centuries, the English have buried their identity in that of greater Britain but English iconography is now more proudly displayed across the country than at any time since WWII. Fashionable T-shirts with the heraldic three lions or the red cross of St George are commonly displayed in high street shops and bought by night-clubbing 20-somethings.

Following a crisis of confidence linked to its economic malaise in the 1970s and 1980s, many of England's cities and regions are more vibrant now than ever before, with several formerly depressed cities enjoying a cultural and economic renaissance. While London and Manchester are obviously buzzing, others like Newcastle, Liverpool, Birmingham, Nottingham and Bristol are hot on their heels.

HISTORY
Celts & Romans

Occupied by nomadic bands of fur-wearing hunter-gatherers for centuries, England was shaken up around 4000 BC when cosmopolitan Europeans with their new-fangled stone tools arrived. While some English still claim to be the result of superior, unfettered breeding, the arrival of the Europeans was just the start of thousands of years of imported genes.

The only evidence today of this obscure period are the impressive ceremonial stone columns at Stonehenge (p173) and Avebury, (p173), along with hundreds of smaller near-forgotten rock circles dotted throughout the countryside. Historians remain divided over what exactly went on at these sites, although claims that they were early football stadiums have been largely discredited.

The next important influx into the English gene pool came from the Celts of Central Europe, whose bronze and iron smelting skills launched a mini-cultural revolution. London's British Museum (p138) and many town and city museums across the country display artefacts from this period, and metal detector enthusiasts regularly unearth exciting finds.

Even more numerous are the excavated discoveries from England's colourful Roman era. In AD 43, the modern storm troopers of the Empire arrived on England's shores, overcoming fierce resistance to establish dominion over much of the land for the next 350 years. They were a major civilising influence, creating buildings, fortifications and roads that can still be seen in areas including Chester (p212) and York (p199), and at Hadrian's Wall (p208).

Dark Ages

With its empire crumbling, the Romans abandoned England in around 410, launching a period of near-forgotten history in the region that is still poorly understood. This is also the time when the idea of England began to shape itself. With tribes gradually carving larger territories across the land and entering uneasy pacts to protect their regions, the Saxons, Angles and Jutes began to rule the roost, while Christianity became the religion of choice.

With such a fragile network of power, England was ripe for invasion and by the end of the first millennium, both the Danes and the Norwegian Vikings occupied large swathes of land across northern and eastern England. York was the capital of the Danish region and the sights, sounds and smells of the settlement are colourfully evoked today at the city's Jorvik Centre (p199).

By 1016 the Danes had taken tenuous control of the country, but a period of turmoil ensued involving rival claims to the barely unified crown. The chaos continued until the Battle of Hastings in 1066, when the Norman, William the Conqueror, acquired his name by defeating his main rival Harold on the English south coast. The Normans had as much impact on England as the Romans had, importing French aristocrats to take charge and building an imposing network of hulking castles and astonishing cathedrals. Many of these architectural treasures can be visited today, although they're often now romantic ruins. Among the most remarkable intact Norman structures are Windsor Castle (p162), Westminster Abbey (p138) and Durham Cathedral (p205).

Middle Ages

The ensuing centuries saw England racked by intrigue and conspiracy as aristocratic families squared off against each other and sought to influence the succession. Costly wars with France, itself as disunified as England, eventually brought English defeat. But the period's main victor was Parliament, which consolidated its power against the monarchy, sowing the seeds for future strife. By 1485, King Henry VII had been crowned, launching a period of rule that's much in evidence today in the timber-framed Tudor streets and buildings of many English towns.

A brewing power struggle with the Catholic church came to a head in 1536 during the reign of Henry VIII, when Papal power in England was renounced and the monarch became head of a new Church of England. Many splendid abbeys and cathedrals were sacked or destroyed, some forever. The ruins

of some of these – including Whitby Abbey (p204) and Glastonbury Abbey (p183) – can still be visited and they appear like skeletal reminders of the past. Others were eventually rebuilt, although often altered in the process. The religious strife was not over, however, and the conflict dissolved into a bitter civil war in 1642, with Parliament rising to the full extent of its power, ultimately leading to the execution of Charles I. When the war's instigator Oliver Cromwell died in 1658, the monarchy was restored.

Victorian Age

The monarchy and Parliament were never the same again. By the 18th century, the new position of prime minister began to assume greater power while the monarchy, soon represented by Queen Victoria, sank into a largely ceremonial role.

By the 19th century, England had built a formidable global empire, using its territories to fuel immense commercial expansion. The country was perfectly placed to launch an Industrial Revolution, which tied machine innovation to population explosion. The cultural impact of the Victorian era is evident throughout England, where giant glass-domed train stations and imposing commercial buildings – like temples to enormous wealth – can be found in most cities.

The New Millennium

England's 20th century was a period of war and end-of-empire followed by cultural and economic resurgence. Two world wars brought the nation almost to its knees, although many people still recall the 1940 Battle of Britain, when the nation resisted a three-month air attack from Germany, as its finest hour. Many former British dominions were restored to independence after WWII and the nation's manufacturing industries entered a period of slow,painful decline.

By the 1990s, though, England had bounced back and entered the new millennium with one of the world's largest and strongest economies; its role on the world stage exemplified by its relationship with the USA and participation in military campaigns in Afghanistan and Iraq. Echoing a history of protest and political argument, millions took to the streets of London and other major English cities to protest the nation's involvement.

ENGLAND

0 ———— 75 km
0 ———→ 45 miles

BRITAIN

Firth of Lorn

Dundee
Stirling
Earn
Kirkcaldy
Glasgow
Edinburgh
Berwick upon Tweed
River Tweed
Lindisfarne
Campbeltown
Kilmarnock
Ayr
Hawick
Kale Water
A1
Alnwick
North Channel
Stranraer
SCOTLAND
Dumfries
Nith
Morpeth
NORTH SEA
Belfast
NORTHERN IRELAND
Northumberland National Park
Newcastle
Gateshead
South Shields
Sunderland
Carlisle
Solway Firth
Workington
Durham
Hartlepool
ISLE OF MAN
Penrith
Bishop Auckland
Middlesbrough
Lake District National Park
Darlington
Danby
Whitby
Windermere
North York Moors National Park
Grosmont
Douglas
Kendal
Scarborough
IRELAND
IRISH SEA
Barrow-in-Furness
Settle
Yorkshire Dales National Park
Helmsley
Pickering
Harrogate
ENGLAND
York
Bray
M6
Leeds
North Channel
M6
Blackpool
Bradford
Halifax
Kingston-upon-Hull
Holyhead
Preston
Rothdale
M62
Bangor
Southport
Wigan
Huddersfield
Grimsby
Caernarfon
St Helens
Bury
Oldham
M1
Liverpool
Manchester
Stockport
M18
Scunthorpe
Warrington
Sheffield
Wrexham
Chester
Peak District National Park
Chesterfield
Lincoln
Stoke-on-Trent
M1
A1
Derby
Shrewsbury
Nottingham
King's Lynn
M6
Loughborough
Cardigan Bay
Walsall
Leicester
Peterborough
Great Yarmouth
Aberystwyth
Wolverhampton
Norwich
St George's Channel
Dudley
Birmingham
Lowestoft
Kidderminster
Coventry
M1
WALES
Northampton
A1
Bury St Edmunds
Worcester
Stratford-upon-Avon
Bedford
Cambridge
Carmarthen
Hereford
Milton Keynes
M11
Ipswich
Cheltenham
Luton
Colchester
Aylesbury
St Albans
Harlow
Swansea
Newport
Gloucester
Oxford
Chelmsford
Port Talbot
M5
High Wycombe
Cardiff
Swindon
River Thames
Southend-on-Sea
To Cork
Barry
M4
Reading
London
Rochester
Margate
Bristol Channel
Bristol
Bath
Newbury
M3
M2
Canterbury
Basingstoke
Maidstone
Wells
Guildford
Dover
Barnstaple
Exmoor National Park
Glastonbury
Salisbury
Crawley
Folkestone
Taunton
Winchester
Brighton
Hastings
Yeovil
Chichester
M5
Southampton
Eastbourne
Boulogne-sur-Mer
Dartmoor National Park
Bournemouth
Portsmouth
Strait of Dover
Newquay
Exeter
Weymouth
St Ives
Torquay
English Channel
Penzance
Falmouth
Plymouth
Dartmoor
Land's End
Dieppe
ATLANTIC OCEAN
Cherbourg
FRANCE
Saint Peter Port
le Havre
Yvetot
Deauville
Rouen
Elbeuf
Louviers
Vernon
Saint Helier
Bayeux
Caen
Saint-Lô
Lisieux
Evreux
Coutances

LIGHTS, CAMERA, ACTION...

While Hollywood relies on clever set construction to make its movies, in England most film-makers simply step outside. From untouched rolling vistas and dark London streets to castles, cathedrals and villages that have remained unchanged for centuries, England is a giant outdoor movie set waiting to happen. For visitors, this means the fun of identifying familiar or not-so-familiar backdrops from favourite movies.

The *Harry Potter* movie series is the most prominent current user of English locations. From train stations to suburban streets and even London Zoo, the movies stretch across England, with the magical Hogwarts School of Witchcraft and Wizardry being comprised from interiors and exteriors at Gloucester Cathedral, Wiltshire's Lacock Abbey, Northumberland's Alnwick Castle and Oxford's Bodleian Library (p186) and Christ Church College (p186). The most popular site for visitors, though, is Hogsmead Station. Played in the movie by the charming Goathland Station (p203) in the North Yorks Moors, it's barely changed since opening in 1865.

While some movie locations are instantly recognisable, many historic sites often substitute for someplace else. Hertfordshire's St Albans Cathedral has stood for more than 1000 years but its movie appearances have almost all been anonymous. It played a Camelot church in Sean Connery's *First Knight* and doubled as Westminster Abbey for the abandoned coronation of a usurping monarch in Rowan Atkinson's comedy *Johnny English*.

Other sites are even less obvious. Holywell Bay near Cornwall's Newquay (p177) doubled as a North Korean battlefield in James Bond's *Die Another Day*, while the opening battle scenes in *Gladiator*, supposedly set in Germany during Roman times, were shot near Farnham in Surrey.

Not surprisingly, London (below) is England's movie location capital with hundreds of films having been shot in and around the capital since the first director yelled 'action' more than a century ago. Recent movies include *Elizabeth* (Tower of London), *Notting Hill* (have a guess), *Lock Stock and Two Smoking Barrels* (Staples Market and Borough Market), *The Madness of King George* (St Paul's Cathedral and Royal Naval College, Greenwich), and *Shakespeare in Love* (Marble Hill House and the Thames River near Barnes). Check out *28 Days Later*, for some incredibly eerie scenes of the city's empty streets.

PEOPLE

With 49 million residents, England dominates the numbers when it comes to Britain's population. There is great cultural diversity throughout the regions, though, with many areas retaining a distinct identity that often includes specific accents and vocabulary. Many major English cities – particularly London, Birmingham and Manchester – have large and vibrant Asian communities.

LONDON

☎ 020 / pop 7.2 million

From familiar landmarks like Big Ben, the Tower of London and St Paul's Cathedral to its world-famous museums and galleries, London has always seduced visitors with its rich history, architectural treasures and royal pomp. But it has never relied on its bygone charms. London has often been the barometer of what's cool in music, fashion and the arts, and in recent years its confidence has grown with the reinvention of parts of the city and many of its sights. The most evident are the South Bank and Bankside, once-forgotten backwaters, now vibrant neighbourhoods, thanks to millennium project favourites like the Tate Modern, the British Airways London Eye and the Millennium Bridge. These forward-thinking changes have enhanced the *frisson* between the traditional and the modern, making London an even more exciting place to visit.

The special atmosphere and dynamism of London comes from its multicultural nature. Propelled by the energy, vitality and aspirations of a population comprising some 40 different ethnic groups, the city fizzes with a creative energy that produces cutting-edge designers, a bristling music scene, a hard-core club culture, and an arts scene that's admired the world over. With over 5000 pubs and bars to choose from, serious retail therapy, and an endless choice of entertainment options, you're limited only by your staying and spending power.

The trouble is, London can be a massive tug on the purse strings. Save some money by heading for the major museums and galleries, most of which are free. Also, if you're lucky enough to get a sunny day, do as the locals do; buy some beer, park yourself in one of the many verdant gardens, and lounge your day away watching everyone get burnt with blissful abandon.

HISTORY

Although a Celtic community established itself around a ford across the River Thames, it's the Romans who are credited with the founding of Londinium in AD 43. Despite this first development collapsing – with avenging Britons led by Queen Boadicea burning it to the ground in AD 60 – the Romans returned to the site in AD 200. With proper walled fortifications, a bridge and a population of some 30,000, the 'square mile' finally took on a defined structure, and the City of London was born.

Although little trace of the Dark Ages remains, during the Viking raids of the 9th century London became a prime target for attack. Focus moved from the then capital, Winchester, to London, and London took on the capital status it retains today. Fifty years before the Normans arrived, Edward the Confessor built his abbey and palace at Westminster.

William the Conqueror found a city that was, without doubt, the richest and largest in the kingdom. He raised the White Tower (part of the Tower of London) and confirmed the city's independence and right to self-government. Medieval Tudor and Jacobean London was virtually destroyed, first by the Plague of 1665 and then by the Great Fire of 1666. The devastation gave Christopher Wren the opportunity to redesign great chunks of London and to rebuild his famous churches.

By 1720 there were 750,000 inhabitants, and London, as the seat of parliament and focal point for a growing empire, was becoming ever more important. Georgian architects and then Victorian architects set to work building some of London's great landmarks and museums.

The bombing of WWII destroyed many of the gains achieved in the previous century, and these were replaced with ugly housing and low-cost developments. Some economic prosperity returned in the late 1950s, leading to the 'Swinging '60s' when London became the epicentre of all that was hip. In the '70s there was an economic downturn and the '80s saw Thatcher's policies create a canyon between rich and poor. Since then, even though the mid-1990s notion of 'Cool Britannia' felt more like a New Labour marketing ploy, and the cost of living is continually soaring, London has again become a place to watch.

In 2003, the mayor of London, Ken Livingston, brought in controversial measures that improved the city's traffic problems. He also pushed for the revamping of Trafalgar Square, which is now an occasional events venue and a gathering point for many a street protest. This, and the changing modern skyline propelled by the celebrated architect Norman Foster (Millennium Bridge, the 'Gherkin' building, etc), as well as the 2012 Olympic bid, reflects London's newfound confidence and forward-looking attitude.

ORIENTATION

The city's main geographical feature is the Thames, a river that was sufficiently deep (for anchorage) and narrow (for bridging) to first draw the Romans here in AD 43. It divides the city roughly into north and south.

Despite all the flak it receives, the London Underground system (known as 'the tube') makes this enormous city relatively accessible. The underground map is easy to use although geographically misleading. Most important sights, theatres, restaurants, and even affordable places to stay, lie within a reasonably compact rectangle formed by the tube's Circle Line (colour-coded yellow), which encircles central London just north of the river.

Get your bearings in the chaotic and colourful West End; at its centre are the neighbourhoods of Soho and Covent Garden. Propelled by a torrent of locals and visitors searching for a good time, this area is packed with pubs, restaurants, clubs, cinemas and some of the best shopping in the world. The West End also includes Trafalgar Square and its national galleries, intellectual Bloomsbury with the British Museum and University of London, as well as the fading grandeur of the Strand.

Southwest of this patch are Westminster and St James – the traditional seats of parliamentary and royal power where you'll find No 10 Downing St, the Houses of Parliament, Big Ben, Westminster Abbey and Buckingham Palace, behind which is the transport hub of Victoria. Added to the regal and political is the exclusive mix of glitzy Mayfair, chichi Chelsea, haughty Hyde Park and the museumlands of Kensington. Just west of here is Earl's Court, a backpacker's haven of inexpensive hotels; and heading north on the Circle Line is hip Notting Hill, home to the famous Notting Hill Carnival and the Portobello markets.

East of the West End is The City, the commercial heart of London; St Paul's Cathedral is the main attraction for visitors here. Further east is the multicultural East End, traditional home of the cockney, consisting of terminally cool Clerkenwell, Hoxton and Shoreditch. North of this area is bourgeois-Bohemian Islington and grungy Camden.

Across the Thames is the South Bank and Bankside, home to some of London's top attractions, including the London Eye, Tate Modern, and Shakespeare's Globe theatre. The neighbourhoods just south of here (such as Borough and Bermondsey) are becoming another trendy hub.

Head east downriver to witness the dramatic revival of the Docklands and the fascinating history of Greenwich. Heading west upriver you'll come to the green havens of Richmond Park, Kew Gardens and Hampton Court Palace.

Maps

A decent London map is vital. A single-sheet map like Lonely Planet's *London City Map* will orientate you easily and discreetly. The *London A–Z* is the definitive street guide and comes in a mini version. Alternatively, pick up free maps at any Tourist Information Centre (TIC; see p137).

INFORMATION
Discount Cards

If you plan to do a lot of sightseeing, the **London Pass** (☎ 0870 242 9988, 01664 500 107; www .londonpass.com) is worth buying as it means free entry and queue-jumping for over 50 attractions. It starts at £12 per day (if you buy six days), with an option to include the use of public transport for a bit extra. The pass can be bought at Visitor Information Centres, on the London Pass website or by phone.

Emergency

In an emergency dial ☎ 999 (free) to call the police, fire brigade or ambulance.

Internet Access

If you have your own laptop and cables you can go online from your hotel room. If not, drop into any Internet café in the capital.

easyInternetcafé (www.easyInternetcafé.com; per hr £1; ☏ 8am-midnight); Kensington (Map pp146-7; 160-166 Kensington High St W8; tube High St Kensington); Oxford St (Map pp142-4; 358 Oxford St W1; tube Bond St); Tottenham Ct Rd (Map pp142-4; 9-16 Tottenham Ct Rd W1; tube Tottenham Ct Rd); Trafalgar Square (Map pp142-4; 7 Strand WC2; tube Charing Cross); Victoria (Map pp142-4; 9-13 Wilton Rd SW1; tube Victoria) This huge franchise is an inexpensive bet.

Left Luggage

Eurostar Left Luggage (☎ 08701 600 052; Arrivals area, Eurostar Terminal, Waterloo International; per item per 24hr £5; ☏ 6am-11pm)

Excess Baggage (☎ 0800 783 1085; www.excess -baggage.co.uk; per item per 24hr £5; ☏ 6am-11pm) Has branches at all the main train stations and Heathrow and Gatwick airports.

Media

Useful London-focused magazines and newspapers:

Evening Standard (40p, daily) Focuses on London news.

Metro (free, daily) Easy reading for fuzzy morning heads, this newspaper can be found at tube and train stations.

Time Out (£2.35, Wed) This is *the* London listings guide, covering and reviewing everything going on in the capital.

TNT Magazine; Southern Cross; SA Times (free, weekly) Found in boxes at tube stations; have classifieds on cheap tickets, shipping services, accommodation and jobs.

Medical Services

Charing Cross Hospital (☎ 8846 1234; Fulham Palace Rd W6; tube Hammersmith) Has a 24-hour accident and emergency department.

Dental Emergency Care Service (☎ 7955 2186; fl 23 Guy's Tower, Guy's Hospital, St Thomas St SE1; tube London Bridge; ☏ 8.30am-3.30pm Mon-Fri) Has a walk-in service, but get there early.

MediCentre (☎ 0870 600 0870) A drop-in health service at Victoria and Waterloo train stations.

NHS Direct (☎ 0845 4647; ☏ 24hr) Gives help with diagnosis, and information such as the locations of the nearest pharmacies.

University College Hospital (Map pp142-4; ☎ 7387 9300; Grafton Way WC1; tube Euston Sq) Has a 24-hour accident and emergency department.

Money

Banks and ATMs abound across central London. If you must use bureaux de change, check the commission rates carefully first. All the airports have 24-hour bureaux de change, as well as ATMs. Reliable places to change money in town include:

American Express (Map pp142-4; ☎ 7484 9600; 30-31 Haymarket SW1; tube Piccadilly Circus; ☉ 9am-6pm Mon-Sat, 10am-5pm Sun)

Thomas Cook (Map pp142-4; ☎ 7853 6400; 30 St James's St SW1; tube Green Park; ☉ 8.30am-6pm Mon-Fri) Has many branches scattered around central London.

Post

Trafalgar Square Post Office (Map pp142-4; ☎ 7484 9307; 24 William IV St WC2; tube Charing Cross; ☉ 8am-8pm Mon-Fri, 9am-8pm Sat). Unless you (or the person writing to you) specify otherwise, poste restante mail sent to London ends up here. Mail will be held for four weeks and ID is required.

Tourist Information

Britain & London Visitor Centre (Map pp142-4; www.visitbritain.com; 1 Regent St SW1; tube Piccadilly Circus; ☉ 9.30am-6.30pm Mon, 9am-6.30pm Tue-Fri, 10am-4pm Sat & Sun) There are information desks here for London, England, Wales, Scotland and Ireland, as well as a map and guidebook shop; independent agents who arrange accommodation and tours as well as train, air, coach and car travel; and a theatre ticket agency. International telephones and a bureau de change are also available. This is a walk-in only service, so if you are not in the area visit their website: www.visitbritain.com.

London Tourist Information Centres (☎ 0906 866 3344, calls per min 60p; www.visitlondon.com) London Visitor Centre (Arrivals Hall, Waterloo International Terminal SE1; ☉ 8.30am-10.30pm); Southwark TIC (☎ 7357 9168; Vinopolis, 1 Bank End SE1; tube London Bridge; ☉ 10am-6pm Tue-Sun); Greenwich TIC (☎ 0870 608 2000; Pepys House, 2 Cutty Sark Gdns SE10; DLR Cutty Sark; ☉ 10am-5pm) For comprehensive information on London check out the website or phone the recorded tourist information service.

Travel Agencies

London has always been a centre for inexpensive air travel. Long-standing and reliable firms with branches around the city are listed here:

Flight Centre (Map pp142-4; ☎ 7916 0600; www.flightcentre.co.uk; 64 Goodge St W1; tube Goodge St; ☉ 9.30am-6pm Mon-Fri, 11am-5pm Sat)

STA Travel (Map pp146-7; ☎ 7581 4132; www.statravel.com; 86 Old Brompton Rd SW7; tube South Kensington; ☉ 10am-6pm Mon-Fri, 11am-5pm Sat)

Trailfinders (Map pp146-7; ☎ 7938 3939; www.trailfinders.com; 194 & 215 Kensington High St W8; tube High St Kensington; ☉ 9am-7pm Mon-Fri, to 6pm Sat, 10am-6pm Sun)

Following are some of the best online resources for buying good-value plane tickets:
www.cheapflights.co.uk
www.ebookers.com Travel agents in Heathrow, Terminal 3 and Gatwick, South Terminal.
www.lastminute.com
www.opodo.com

DANGERS & ANNOYANCES

London has considerable anti-terrorist measures in place. As a visitor *never* leave your bag unattended – you may trigger a security alert. If you do see an unattended package, don't touch it and alert the authorities.

While an empty wallet is more likely to be a result of hiked prices than something more sinister, crime in London shouldn't be downplayed. Your main hazard will be pickpockets, whose haunts include Oxford St and Leicester Sq tube. Women should take particular care if alone after dark, especially on the tube (choose a carriage with lots of people); a walk down Brixton's Coldharbour Lane late at night is not for the faint-hearted! Always take a licensed taxi.

Scams

Due care and attention should also be taken when using ATMs, as 'shoulder surfing' (someone watches you type in your pin and later pickpockets you to get your card) is becoming more common. So too is the scam of con artist one distracting you when your cash is about to be delivered, while con artist two swipes it from the machine.

SIGHTS

London is brimming with fascinating ancient treasures, cutting edge projects and quirky gems. Here we review a selection of sights, including the major museums, galleries, palaces and parks.

The West End
NATIONAL GALLERY

The **National Gallery** (Map pp142-4; ☎ 7747 2885; www.nationalgallery.org.uk; Trafalgar Square WC2; tube Charing Cross; admission free; ☉ 10am-6pm Mon-Tue & Thu-Sun, to 9pm Wed, guided tours 11.30am & 2.30pm) is one of the largest galleries in the world, with

BRITAIN

more than 2000 Western European paintings spanning the 13th to 20th centuries. Seminal paintings from every important epoch in the history of art are here, including works by Giotto, Leonardo da Vinci, Michelangelo, Titian, Velazquez, Van Gogh and Renoir.

NATIONAL PORTRAIT GALLERY

Around the corner from the National Gallery, the **National Portrait Gallery** (Map pp142-4; ☎ 7306 0055; www.npg.org.uk; St Martin's Pl WC2; tube Charing Cross; admission free; 🕑 10am-6pm Mon-Wed, Sat & Sun, to 9pm Thu & Fri) is the place to put faces to the famous and infamous names of Britain's past and present. The ground floor is the most fun, focusing on contemporary figures from British popular culture.

BRITISH MUSEUM

Founded in 1753, the **British Museum** (Map pp142-4; ☎ 7323 8000; www.thebritishmuseum.ac.uk; Great Russell St WC1; tube Russell Sq/Tottenham Ct Rd; admission free, variety of free tours available; 🕑 10am-5.30pm Sat-Wed, to 8.30pm Thu & Fri) is one of the world's oldest and finest museums. The collection has some seven million items, augmented by judicious acquisition and the controversial plundering of empire. Its anthropological wonders and the Egyptian, Mesopotamian, Greek and Roman antiquities are unparalleled. Marvel at the spectacular architecture of the Great Court, the largest covered public square in Europe.

SOMERSET HOUSE

The courtyard of **Somerset House** (Map pp142-4; ☎ 7845 4600; www.somerset-house.org.uk; Strand WC2; tube Temple/Covent Garden) is a lively ice rink in winter and a concert venue in summer. Home to the **Courtauld Institute Gallery** (Map pp142-4; ☎ 7848 2526; www.courtauld.ac.uk; adult/concession £5/4, admission free 10am-2pm Mon; 🕑 10am-5.15pm), famous for its Impressionists paintings; the **Gilbert Collection** (Map pp142-4; ☎ 7420 9410; www.gilbert-collection.org.uk; adult/concession/child £5/4/free; 🕑 10am-5.15pm) and its collection of decorative arts; and the **Hermitage Rooms** (Map pp142-4; ☎ 7845 4630; www.hermitagerooms.com; adult/concession/child £5/4/free; 🕑 10am-5.15pm), with its treasures from the State Hermitage Museum, St Petersburg.

ROYAL ACADEMY OF ARTS

Established in 1768, the **Royal Academy of Arts** (Map pp142-4; ☎ 7300 8000; www.royalacademy.org.uk; Burlington House, Piccadilly W1; tube Green Park/Piccadilly Circus; adult/concession/child £7.50/5.50/3, child under 8 yrs admission free; 🕑 temporary exhibitions 10am-5.30pm Mon-Thu, Sat & Sun, to 9.30pm Fri, permanent exhibition 1-4.30pm Tue-Fri, 10am-6pm Sat & Sun) was Britain's first art school. Although it has a permanent collection of British art from the 18th century, the Academy is renowned for its popular temporary shows, particularly the Summer Exhibition (early June to mid-August), which showcases the work of contemporary artists.

PHOTOGRAPHERS' GALLERY

The thought-provoking **Photographers' Gallery** (Map pp142-4; ☎ 7831 1772; www.photonet.org.uk; 5 & 8 Great Newport St WC2; tube Leicester Sq; admission free; 🕑 11am-6pm Mon-Sat, noon-6pm Sun) is always good for an impromptu visit on the way to Covent Garden. The contemporary photographs in its three galleries and café won't disappoint.

St James's, Westminster & Pimlico

WESTMINSTER ABBEY

The rich history of **Westminster Abbey** (Map pp142-4; ☎ 7222 5152; www.westminster-abbey.org; Parliament Sq SW1; tube Westminster; adult/concession/ child under 11/family £7.50/5/free/15; 🕑 9.30am-4.45pm Mon-Tue & Thu-Fri, to 8pm Wed, to 2.45pm Sat, worship only Sun) started with Edward the Confessor building a church here in the 11th century. The coronation chair, where all but two monarchs since 1066 have been crowned, is behind the altar, and many greats – from Darwin to Chaucer – are buried here. Soak up the atmosphere at the Choral Evensong (5pm Monday to Friday, 3pm Saturday and Sunday).

TATE BRITAIN

Built in 1897, the venerable **Tate Britain** (Map pp142-4; ☎ 7887 8000; www.tate.org.uk; Millbank SW1; tube Pimlico; admission free; 🕑 10am-5.50pm) has the definitive collection of British art from the 16th to the late 20th centuries. Look for works by William Blake, Constable, Gainsborough, Hogarth, Hockney, Bacon and Moore, to name but a few. There is a boat service to Tate Modern from here, which also stops at the London Eye; see p160.

BUCKINGHAM PALACE

Built in 1705 as Buckingham House for the duke of the same name, **Buckingham**

Palace (Map pp142-4; ☎ 7766 7300; www.royal.gov
.uk; Buckingham Palace Rd SW1; tube Victoria/Green
Park; adult/concession/child/family £12.95/11/6.50/32.50;
♥ 9.30am-4.15pm 31 Jul-26 Sep, changing of the guard
11.30am Apr-Jun, alternate days Jul-Mar) has been the
royal family's London lodgings since 1837.
Nineteen lavishly furnished State Rooms are
open to visitors in the summer, as well as
the Picture Gallery, and the Throne Room,
which features kitschy his-and-hers pink
chairs initialled 'ER' and 'P'. Walks can be
taken in the garden.

CABINET WAR ROOMS
The magnificently evocative **Cabinet War Rooms**
(Map pp142-4; ☎ 7930 6961; www.iwm.org.uk; Clive
Steps, King Charles St SW1; tube Westminster; adult/
concession/child £7.50/6/free; ♥ 9.30am-6pm Apr-Sep,
10am-6pm Oct-Mar) occupies the bunkers where
Churchill, with his cabinet and generals, met
during WWII and governed the country.
Within the Cabinet War Rooms, the **Churchill
Museum** is a new museum dedicated to all
things Churchillian and commemorating
the 40th anniversary of Churchill's death.

HOUSES OF PARLIAMENT
During the Parliamentary summer holidays,
Houses of Parliament (Map pp142-4; ☎ 7219 3003,
tour bookings 0870 906 3773; www.parliament.uk; Westminster SW1; tube Westminster; adult/concession/child/
family guided tours £7/5/3.50/20 must pre-book; ♥ Jul-
Sep) are open for 75-minute guided tours.
They include the House of Commons and
the House of Lords main chambers.

ST JAMES'S PARK
Bordering The Mall as it heads towards
Buckingham Palace, **St James's Park** (Map pp142-
4; ☎ 7930 1793; www.royalparks.gov.uk; The Mall SW1;
tube St James's Park; ♥ 5am-dusk) has great vistas,
including Buckingham Palace, and Whitehall to the south. The plentiful flowerbeds,
large lake and waterfowl make this a lovely
place to relax.

Kensington & Knightsbridge
VICTORIA & ALBERT MUSEUM
Dating from 3000 BC to the present day the
Victoria & Albert Museum (Map pp142-4; ☎ 7942
2000; www.vam.ac.uk; Cromwell Rd SW7; tube South
Kensington; admission free; ♥ 10am-5.45pm Mon-Tue &
Thu-Sun, to 10pm Wed) has the world's greatest
collection of decorative arts. Spreading over
nearly 150 galleries, the rooms are filled

with everything from furniture to fashion
and ceramics to sculpture. The regular temporary exhibitions, like the recent Vivienne
Westwood retrospective, are also very compelling and worth seeing.

NATURAL HISTORY MUSEUM
Lots of fascinating interactive exhibitions
make the **Natural History Museum** (Map pp142-
4; ☎ 7942 5000; www.nhm.ac.uk; Cromwell Rd SW7; tube
South Kensington; admission free; ♥ 10am-5.30pm Mon-
Sat, 11am-5.30pm Sun) a favourite for kids and
adults alike. Highlights include the Darwin
Centre, with plant and animal specimens
collected by Captain Cook, the dramatic
earthquake experience, and the impressive
dinosaur skeletons.

SCIENCE MUSEUM
The **Science Museum** (Map pp142-4; ☎ 0870 870
4868; www.sciencemuseum.org.uk; Exhibition Rd SW7; tube
South Kensington; admission free; ♥ 10am-6pm) does
a terrific job of bringing to lustrous life a
subject that is often dull and impenetrable.
Exhibits on the first steam train or the landing on the moon, demonstrate the world's
science, technology, industry and medicine,
and the new Wellcome Wing shows how
contemporary science and technology work
in everyday life.

KENSINGTON PALACE
A royal home since William III, birthplace
of Queen Victoria, and home to the late
Princess Diana, **Kensington Palace** (Map pp142-
4; ☎ 0870 751 5170; www.hrp.org.uk; Kensington Gdns
W8; tube High St Kensington/Notting Hill Gate; adult/
concession/child/family £10.80/8.20/7/32; ♥ 10am-
5pm Mar-Oct, to 4pm Nov-Feb) has a wealth of royal
history. The State Apartments and the Royal
Dress Collection are open to the public and
there are regular temporary exhibitions. The
Palace and gardens have become something
of a shrine to Princess Diana with the Memorial Fountain and the Diana, Princess of
Wales Memorial Playground.

HYDE PARK
With neatly manicured gardens and wild,
deserted expanses of overgrown grass **Hyde
Park** (Map pp142-4; ☎ 7298 2000; www.royalparks.gov
.uk; tube Hyde Park Corner; ♥ 5am-dusk) is central
London's largest park. Just south of its lake,
visit the splendid contemporary art space of
the **Serpentine Gallery** (Map pp142-4; ☎ 7402 6075;

BRITAIN

www.serpentinegallery.org; Kensington Gdns W8; tube Knightsbridge/South Kensington; admission free; ☉ 10am-6pm). You could also row a boat on the Serpentine, go **horse riding** (☎ 7298 2100), take a dip in the outdoor **swimming pool** (☎ 7706 3422), or heckle the soapbox orators at **Speakers' Corner** (Map pp142-4; 22 Park Lane; tube Marble Arch; ☉ Sun).

The City
ST PAUL'S CATHEDRAL
Sir Christopher Wren's masterpiece, **St Paul's Cathedral** (Map pp142-4; ☎ 7246 8348; www.st pauls.co.uk; The Chapter House, St Paul's Churchyard EC4; tube St Paul's; adult/concession/child/family £7/6/3/17; ☉ 8.30am-4pm Mon-Sat, services only Sun) is the proud bearer of the capital's largest church dome. Attractions include the Whispering Gallery, so called because if you talk close to the wall it carries your words around to the opposite side, 32m away; and the upper galleries, for a breathtaking view of London.

TOWER OF LONDON
Home to the dazzling Crown Jewels, Beefeaters and ravens, the **Tower of London** (Map p150; ☎ 0870 756 6060; www.hrp.org.uk; Tower Hill EC3; tube Tower Hill; adult/concession/child/family £13.50/10.50/9/37.50; ☉ 9am-5pm Tue-Sat, 10am-5pm Sun-Mon Mar-Oct, closes 4pm Nov-Feb) has been a fortress, royal residence, prison and place of execution. To avoid the admission queues, buy your tickets in advance at any tube station.

TOWER BRIDGE
With its neo-Gothic towers and blue suspension struts, **Tower Bridge** (Map p150; tube London Bridge/Tower Hill) is an iconic symbol of London. There are excellent views from the bridge's walkways. **Tower Bridge Exhibition** (Map p150; ☎ 7403 3761; www.towerbridge.org.uk; Tower Bridge SE1; tube London Bridge/Tower Hill; adult/concession/child £5.50/4.25/3; ☉ 10am-5.30pm Apr-Sep, 9.30-5pm Oct-Mar) explains the nuts and bolts of it all.

Along the South Bank
TATE MODERN
Already an iconic image of London, the hugely popular **Tate Modern** (Map pp142-4; ☎ 7887 8008; www.tate.org.uk; Bankside SE1; tube Blackfriars/Southwark; admission free; ☉ 10am-6pm Sun-Thu, to 10pm Fri & Sat) houses 20th-century art in what was once an empty Bankside power station. The permanent collection, with artists

ranging from Rothko to Lichtenstein, is arranged according to themes, like Still Life, Object, Real Life. The cafés on levels 2 and 7 (☉ 10am-5.30pm Sun-Thu, to 9.30pm Fri & Sat) are renowned for their fabulous views over the Thames. There is a boat service to Tate Britain from here, which also stops at the London Eye; see p160.

BRITISH AIRWAYS LONDON EYE
On a clear day from the **British Airways London Eye** (Map pp142-4; ☎ 0870 500 0600; www.ba-london eye.com; Jubilee Gdns, South Bank SE1; tube Waterloo; adult/concession/child £11.50/9/5.75; ☉ 10.30am-7pm Feb, Mar & Oct-Dec; to 8pm Apr, May & Sep; 10am-10pm Jun-Aug) you can see for 25 miles (40km) in every direction. The 32 glass-enclosed gondolas of the world's largest Ferris wheel take 30 minutes to rotate completely, so passengers (up to 25 in each capsule) really get time to take in the experience. You buy tickets from the office behind the wheel, or better still, book ahead.

SAATCHI GALLERY
The **Saatchi Gallery** (Map pp142-4; ☎ 7823 2363; www.saatchi-gallery.co.uk; County Hall SE1; tube Waterloo/Westminster; adult/concession/family £8.75/6.75/26; ☉ 10am-7.15pm Sun-Thu, to 9.15pm Fri & Sat) is a roll call of the greatest hits of the so-called Young British Art (YBA) movement, where the works of Damien Hirst, Tracey Emin, Sarah Lucas and the like are on permanent display. Bought by the adman and collector Charles Saatchi, his approval and their in-yer-face oeuvres often led to artistic super stardom, a new phenomenon in the 90s.

IMPERIAL WAR MUSEUM
Although there are lots of military hardware and interactive exhibits dealing with all aspects of the major wars (from spying to trench living), a large percentage of the **Imperial War Museum** (Map pp142-4; ☎ 7416 5339; www .iwm.org.uk; Lambeth Rd SE1; tube Lambeth North; admission free; ☉ 10am-6pm) deals with the human and social cost of conflict. The Holocaust Exhibition (not recommended for under 16s) and a gallery devoted to crimes against humanity, are outstanding. There is a Tibetan Peace Garden to head to afterwards.

MILLENNIUM BRIDGE
Opened in 2000, the **Millennium Bridge** (Map pp142-4; tube St Paul's/Blackfriars) was closed after

just three days, when it began to sway alarmingly under the weight and movement of pedestrian traffic. Re-opened 18 months later, the elegant, 'blade of light' design now carries millions of people from St Paul's Cathedral on the north side of the river to Tate Modern on the south.

DESIGN MUSEUM

Aesthetic and ascetic in appearance, the 1930s-style white cube that is the **Design Museum** (Map p150; ☎ 0870 833 9955; www.design museum.org; Shad Thames SE1; tube London Bridge/Tower Hill; adult/concession/family £6/4/16; 🕙 10am-5.15pm Mon-Thu, Sat & Sun, to 8.30pm Fri) covers all aspects of contemporary product design. Recent exhibitions on Manolo Blahnik shoes, the best of European design, and chair design in the past 100 years give a flavour of what the museum does.

FASHION & TEXTILE MUSEUM

Dedicated to fashion from 1950 to the present day, the **Fashion & Textile Museum** (Map p150; ☎ 7403 0222; www.ftmlondon.org; 83 Bermondsey St SE1; tube London Bridge; adult/concession/family £6/4/16; 🕙 10am-4.15pm Tue-Sat, noon-4.15pm Sun) is clad in the signature colours – orange and pink – of its creator, the eccentric British designer Zandra Rhodes. The split-level interior holds brilliant temporary exhibitions, as well as a permanent collection of dresses by the likes of Christian Dior, Chanel, Ossie Clark and Mary Quant.

DALÍ UNIVERSE

Home to Europe's largest collection of Dalí, the **Dalí Universe** (Map pp142-4; ☎ 7620 2720; www .daliuniverse.com; County Hall, Riverside Bldg, London SE1; tube Waterloo/Westminster; adult/concession/child/family £8.50/7/5.50/23; 🕙 10am-5.30pm) is arranged in three themed areas: Sensuality & Femininity, Religion & Mythology, and Dreams & Fantasy. There are more than 500 works displayed, including his famous Mae West Lips Sofa and one of his Lobster Telephones.

JUBILEE BRIDGE

Reaching from the Embankment tube station to the Royal Festival Hall and London Eye, the pedestrian **Jubilee Bridge** (Map pp142-4; Embankment/Waterloo tube) has wonderful Thames views. Especially pretty at night, the white pylons look like they are floating in the air.

HAYWARD GALLERY

Part of the concrete hulk of the South Bank Centre, the world-renowned **Hayward Gallery** (Map pp142-4; ☎ 7960 4242; www.hayward.org.uk; Belvedere Rd, South Bank SE1; tube Waterloo/Embankment; adult/concession/child £8/6/free; 🕙 10am-6pm Mon & Thu-Sun, to 8pm Tue-Wed) shows four major contemporary art exhibitions annually.

South London
GREENWICH

Greenwich can absorb the best part of a day and needs time to be fully explored. Start with the stunning **Cutty Sark** (☎ 8858 3445; www.cuttysark.org.uk; King William Walk SE10; DLR Cutty Sark/train Greenwich; adult/concession/child/family £4.25/3.25/2.95/10.50; 🕙 10am-5pm), the only surviving tea-and-wool clipper. Wander around the excellent **Greenwich market** (Greenwich High Rd, Stockwell St & Thames St; 🕙 9.30am-5.30pm Thu-Sun), and then visit the **Queen's House** (☎ 8858 4422; www.nmm.ac.uk; Romney Rd SE10; admission free; 🕙 10am-6pm Jul-Aug, to 5pm Sep-Jun) designed in 1616 by Inigo Jones as a retreat for the wife of James I, Queen Anne of Denmark. Britain's famous naval traditions are covered in fascinating fashion at the **National Maritime Museum** (8858 4422; www.nmm.ac.uk; Romney Rd SE10; admission free; 🕙 10am-6pm; Jul-Aug, to 5pm Sep-Jun). Beside the river, the elegant **Old Royal Naval College** (☎ 8269 4747; www.greenwichfoundation.org .uk; King William Walk SE10; admission free; 🕙 10am-5pm) was designed by Wren, its Painted Hall and Chapel are stunning.

Climb the hill behind the museum to the **Royal Observatory** (☎ 8858 4422; www.nmm.ac.uk; Romney Rd SE10; admission free; 🕙 10am-6pm; Jul-Aug to 5pm Sep-Jun). A brass strip in the courtyard marks the Prime Meridian that divides the world into eastern and western hemispheres. The displays show famous timepieces, including those first used to accurately calculate longitude. There are great views over the Docklands.

An alternative to the train is a boat from Westminster Pier to Greenwich, see p160.

West of London
KEW GARDENS

The Royal Botanic **Kew Gardens** (☎ 8332 5648; www.kew.org; Richmond TW9; tube Kew Gardens; adult/ concession/child £8.50/6/free; 🕙 9.30am-6pm Mon-Fri, to 7pm Sat & Sun 28 Mar-5 Sep, to 5.30pm 6 Sep-30 Oct, to 3.45pm 31 Oct-27 Mar) covers 300 acres and grows more species than any other garden in the

BRITAIN

CENTRAL LONDON

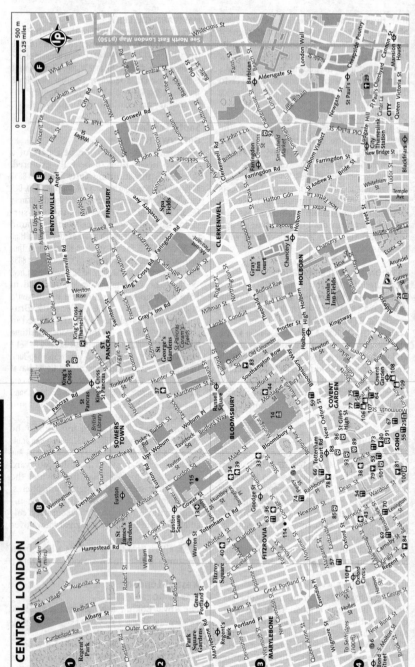

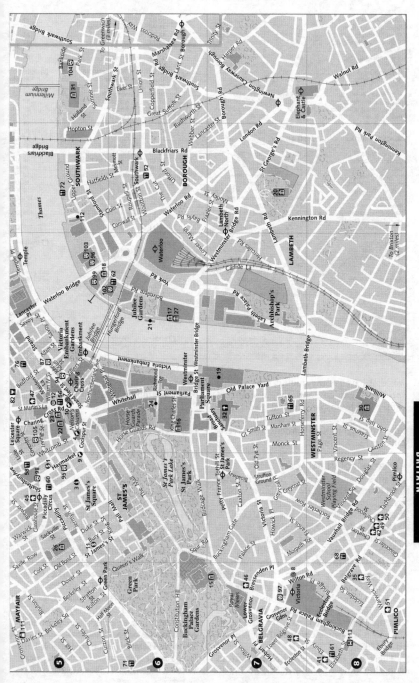

world. A haven of tranquillity, the stunning variety of gardens and the magnificent conservatories display tropical plants from around the globe. As an alternative to the tube, boats go to Kew Gardens from Westminster Pier, see p160.

HAMPTON COURT PALACE

Britain's grandest Tudor house, **Hampton Court Palace** (☎ 0870 752 7777; www.hrp.org .uk; palace & grounds adult/concession/child/family £11.80/8.70/7.70/35, gardens only £4/3/2.50/12, maze only adult/child £3.50/2.50; ⏰ 10.15am-5.15pm Mon, 9.30am-5.15pm Tue-Sun Apr-Oct, closes 3.45pm Nov-Mar) has a beautiful mix of architectural styles, from Henry VIII's splendid Great Hall to the State Apartments built by Wren for King William III and Queen Mary II. There are 60 acres of immaculate gardens, including the world-famous maze, the Great Vine – the oldest vine in the world – and the Privy Garden, recently restored to the way it was when completed for William III in 1702.

There are trains every half-hour from Waterloo (one way/return £4.50/5.10, 30 minutes) to Hampton Court station. For a boat to Hampton Court from Westminster Pier see p160.

FESTIVALS & EVENTS

Popular festivals and events held annually in London include:

London Marathon (April; www.london-marathon.co.uk) Some 35,000 masochists cross London from Greenwich Park to the Mall in the world's biggest road race.

Chelsea Flower Show (May; www.rhs.org.uk; Royal Hospital Chelsea) The world's most renowned horticultural show attracts green-fingers from near and far.

Trooping of the Colour (June; Horse Guards Parade, Whitehall) The Queen's birthday is celebrated with much flag-waving, parades, pageantry and noisy flyovers.

Wimbledon Lawn Tennis Championships (June; www.wimbledon.com) The world's most splendid tennis event in (hopefully) summery June is as much about strawberries, cream and tradition as smashing balls.

Pride Parade (July; www.pridelondon.org) Gays and lesbians paint the town pink in this annual parade.

Notting Hill Carnival (August; www.thecarnival.tv) Europe's biggest outdoor carnival over the bank holiday weekend is a celebration of Caribbean London.

London Film Festival (October; www.lff.org.uk; National Film Theatre) See the best of British and international films before their cinema release.

New Year's Eve Celebration Join the crowds and count down to midnight in Trafalgar Square.

SLEEPING

Staying in London is an expensive business whatever your budget. It's always best to book ahead, especially in summer. Visit London's **Accommodation Line** (☎ 7932 2020; www.visitlondonoffers.com), which offers some very good deals and doesn't charge a booking fee. Alternatively, contact hotels directly using the information provided below.

For a full list of hostels in London contact the **Youth Hostels Association** (☎ 0870 770 6113; www.yha.org.uk) or the **YMCA** (☎ 8520 5599; www.ymca.org.uk), most of which are covered here. A little pricier is the student accommodation or university halls of residence let to non-students during the summer; ontact **London School of Economics** (☎ 7995 7575 or 7107 5750; www.lse.ac.uk/collections/vacations) for information.

Unsurprisingly, renting is also expensive. To get abreast of current prices, consult the classifieds such as *Loot, TNT, Time Out* and the *Evening Standard*'s Wednesday supplement *Homes & Property*.

Pimlico & Victoria

Victoria may not be the most attractive part of London, but the budget hotels are better value than those in Earl's Court. Pimlico is more residential but convenient for the Tate Britain gallery at Millbank.

BUDGET

Victoria Hotel (Map pp142-4; ☎ 7834 3077; www.astorhostels.com; 71 Belgrave Rd SW1; tube Pimlico; dm £15-18; ☑) This recently and funkily refurbished hostel has 60 beds so it's busy without being too impersonal. It's staffed by pausing travellers, has 24-hour reception, and is within easy walking distance of the Tate Britain and Westminster Abbey.

Brindle House Hotel (Map pp142-4; ☎ 7828 0057; www.brindlehousehotel.co.uk; 1 Warwick Pl North SW1; tube Victoria; B&B s/d/tr/q £45/60/75/89, s/d with shared bathroom £35/48) Recently refurbished, the rooms are pristine but the en-suite showers and toilets are rather squashed. Staff are helpful and friendly.

Luna & Simone Hotel (Map pp142-4; ☎ 7834 5897; www.lunasimonehotel.com; 47/49 Belgrave Rd SW1; tube

Victoria; s £40, s/d/tr with shower £50/60/80; ☑ ▢) In a road stuffed full of varying quality B&Bs, this is a shining example of good value simply done. The rooms have satellite TV, are bright, airy and spotlessly clean.

A good, if pricier alternative is **Victor Hotel** (Map pp142-4; ☎ 7592 9853; www.victorhotel.co.uk; 51 Belgrave Rd SW1; tube Victoria; B&B s/d/tr £70/90/135).

MID-RANGE & TOP END

James House & Cartref House (Map pp142-4; ☎ 7730 7338; www.jamesandcartref.co.uk; 108 & 129 Ebury St SW1; tube Victoria; s/d/tr/q £62/85/110/135; ☑ ▢) The best in the street for the budget, these two B&Bs are situated across the street from each other. They are run by a very friendly couple with a good knowledge of Victoria, and have freshly decorated and clean rooms.

Windermere Hotel (Map pp142-4; ☎ 7834 5163; www.windermere-hotel.co.uk; 142-144 Warwick Way SW1; tube Victoria; B&B s/d/ste from £89/104/145, s/d with shared bathroom £69/89; ☑) The award-winning Windermere has 22 small, singularly designed and spotless rooms in a sparkling, white mid-Victorian town house that offers character and warmth in an area not exactly renowned for such. There is a well-regarded British restaurant on site and the rooms have modem points.

Tophams (Map pp142-4; ☎ 7730 8147; www.tophams.co.uk; 28 Ebury St SW1; tube Victoria; B&B s/d/tr/f £115/130/170/260; ▢) Consisting of five small, inter-connected houses, Tophams is calm and cosy and has a delightfully higgledy-piggledy feel. Run by the same family since 1937, the pretty furnishings evoke a sense of yesteryear but some of the fixtures and fittings are looking a bit shabby. The rooms have modem points.

Rubens at the Palace (Map pp142-4; ☎ 7834 6600; www.rubenshotel.com; 39 Buckingham Palace Rd SW1; tube Victoria; s/d/ste from £120/150/190; ☑ ☒ ▢) Overlooking the walls of the Royal Mews and Buckingham Palace, this hotel is for those who are into a romantic idea of Olde England. With a slightly faded grandeur, it has royal emblems throughout, paintings of hunting scenes and Earls, grand chandeliers and high tea.

The West End & Covent Garden

Here you're in the centre of the action, but you pay for the convenience.

Oxford St YHA (Map pp142-4; ☎ 7734 1618; oxfordst@yha.org.uk; 14 Noel St W1; tube Oxford Circus/Tottenham

CENTRAL WEST LONDON

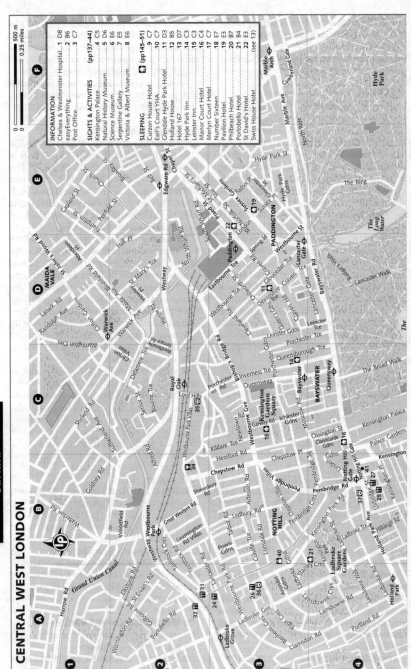

BRITAIN

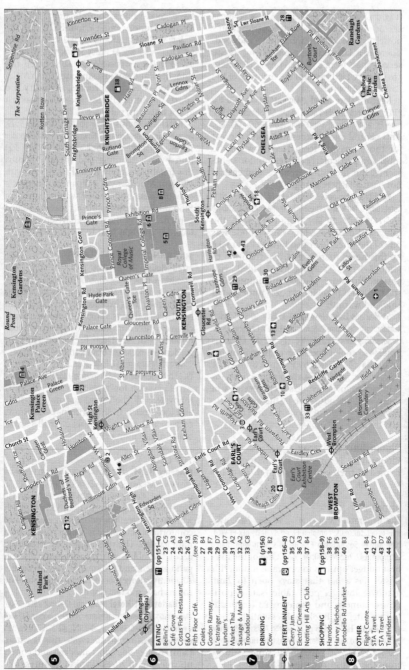

EATING	📶 (pp151–6)
Bellini's	23 C5
Café Grove	24 A3
Costas Fish Restaurant	25 B4
E&O	26 A3
Fifth Floor Café	(see 39)
Geales	27 B4
Gordon Ramsay	28 F7
L'estranger	29 D7
Lundum's	30 D7
Market Thai	31 A2
Sausage & Mash Café	32 A2
Troubadour	33 C8

DRINKING	🍷 (p156)
Cow	34 B2

ENTERTAINMENT	🎭 (pp156–8)
Cherry Jam	35 C2
Electric Cinema	36 A3
Notting Hill Arts Club	37 B4

SHOPPING	🛍 (pp158–9)
Harrods	38 F6
Harvey Nichols	39 F5
Portobello Rd Market	40 B3

OTHER	
Flight Centre	41 B4
STA Travel	42 D7
STA Travel	43 D7
Trailfinders	44 B6

Ct Rd; dm adult/YHA member £22.60/18.20, tw per person £26; ✕ ▢) The most central of London's hostels is basic, clean, welcoming and loud. There is a large kitchen but no meals are served apart from a packed breakfast. There are laundry facilities and the majority of the 75 beds are twins.

Regent Palace Hotel (Map pp142-4; ☎ 0870 400 8703; www.regentpalacehotel.co.uk; Glasshouse St W1; tube Piccadilly Circus; s/d/tr from £64/89/99; ✕ ▢) This central and inexpensive hotel is great for those arriving from Heathrow on the tube, and particularly convenient for sight-seeing. But the rather frenetic ambience is not particularly relaxing.

Hazlitt's (Map pp142-4; ☎ 7434 1771; www.hazlitts hotel.com; 6 Frith St W1; tube Tottenham Ct Rd; s/d/ste £205/240/352; ✕ ✕ ▢) Beginning with the essayist William Hazlitt, whose abode was one of the three Georgian houses that make up this hotel, there is a strong tradition of famous writers staying here. Filled with antique furniture placed with impeccable style, this boutique hotel oozes understated chic and warmth.

St Martins Lane (Map pp142-4; ☎ 7300 5555; www .ianschragerhotels.com; 45 St Martin's Lane WC2; tube Leicester Sq; s/d/ste from £235/275/400; ℗ ✕ ✕ ▢) This hotel is so cool it doesn't even have its name on display. Designed by Philippe Starck, the chic, white, minimalist rooms have floor-to-ceiling windows giving sweeping views of the West End, but some of the doubles are very small. Beautiful people fill the Light Bar and the Asia de Cuba restaurant.

Bloomsbury & Fitzrovia

Bloomsbury is an altogether more sedate, refined district with prices half those of the West End.

BUDGET

The Generator (Map pp142-4; ☎ 7388 7666; www .the-generator.co.uk; Compton Pl, off 37 Tavistock Pl WC1; tube Russell Sq; B&B dm £12.50-17, s/tw/tr with shared bathroom £42/26.50/22.50; ✕ ▢) One of the liveliest budget options in central London, this hostel has a bar that stays open to 2am, a movie lounge, pool table, safe-deposit boxes, laundry and canteen (£3 for pizza) but no kitchen. Booking is essential.

Pickwick Hall (Map pp142-4; ☎ 7323 4958; www .pickwickhall.co.uk; 7 Bedford Pl WC1; tube Holborn; dm/d £20/44; ✕ ▢) A convenient stone's throw from the British Museum, this hostel offers basic, good-value accommodation. There's a kitchen, laundry and TV lounge.

Indian Student YMCA (Map pp142-4; ☎ 7387 0411; www.indianymca.org; 41 Fitzroy Sq W1; tube Warren St; dm/s/d £20/34/40, d from £55; ✕ ▢) For all nationalities and not just students, this YMCA has good-sized, clean rooms, a laundry and sports facilities. Prices include breakfast and a tasty curry dinner.

Hotel Cavendish (Map pp142-4; ☎ 7636 9079; www.hotelcavendish.com; 75 Gower St WC1; tube Goodge St; B&B s/d/tr/q with shared bathroom £40/50/75/90; ✕) Run by a welcoming and friendly family, this hotel has simply furnished rooms with William Morris-style wallpapers. There is a cosy breakfast room filled with paintings of Bloomsbury writers and a pleasant walled garden. None of the rooms have en suite but facilities are right next to the rooms.

MID-RANGE

Arran House Hotel (Map pp142-4; ☎ 7636 2186; arran@dircon.co.uk; 77-79 Gower St WC1; tube Goodge St; dm £16-21, B&B s/d/tr £55/85/103, with shared bathroom £45/62/80; ▢) This excellent-value, family-run hotel has lodgings ranging from spotlessly clean and airy dormitories to stylish and cosy doubles with Art-Deco fireplaces. The rose garden is a pleasant bonus in the summer.

Arosfa (Map pp142-4; ☎ 7636 2115; 83 Gower St WC1; tube Goodge St; B&B s/d/tr/q £45/66/79/92; ✕) Arosfa (Welsh for 'a place to stay') recently renovated; all the rooms are now en-suite and look much fresher with new furniture, carpets and paint. There is a small garden open in the summer.

TOP END

Academy Hotel (Map pp142-4; ☎ 7631 4115; www .etontownhouse.com; 21 Gower St WC1; tube Goodge St; B&B s/d/ste from £140/163/215; ✕ ✕) This town-house hotel has managed to do traditional English without the twee. The doubles are elegant and comfortable, and there is a suite with its own mini garden. The plush but not overbearing décor, the rabbit-warren cosiness, the discreet patio garden, and the small library, make the Academy altogether *orrrfully* English. The rooms have modem points.

Charlotte St Hotel (Map pp142-4; ☎ 7806 2000; www.firmdale.com; 15 Charlotte St W1; Goodge St; s/d/ ste from £229/270/388; ℗ ✕ ✕ ▢) A favourite with visiting media types, this is where Laura Ashley goes post-modern and comes up smelling of roses. Typical gestures, like placing paintings by the Bloomsbury posse alongside abstract art, give this superficially traditional English-looking hotel an edge.

South Kensington & Earl's Court

South Kensington is close to the museums and has some top-notch accommodation. Earl's Court offers the inexpensive options but some of it can be appalling – you can usually tell instantly by the hallway and the general atmosphere.

BUDGET

Earl's Court YHA (Map pp146-7; ☎ 7373 7083; earls court@yha.org.uk; 38 Bolton Gdns SW5; tube Earl's Ct; dm adult/under 18 yrs £19.50/17.20; ✖ 🖳) Set in a recently refurbished Victorian townhouse, this immaculate and spacious hostel has mainly four-bed dorms and very helpful staff. There is a well-equipped self-catering kitchen, large lounge and satellite TV, as well as a large courtyard garden.

Curzon House Hotel (Map pp146-7; ☎ 7581 2116; www.curzonhousehotel.co.uk; 58 Courtfield Gdns SW5; tube Gloucester Rd; B&B dm £15-17, s/d/tr with shared bathroom £30/44/63) In a quiet square overlooking a pretty church this hotel offers basic rooms, a kitchen and a cable-TV room. The staff are some of the friendliest you'll meet.

Merlyn Court Hotel (Map pp146-7; ☎ 7370 1640; www.merlyncourthotel.com; 2 Barkston Gdns SW5; tube Earl's Ct; B&B s/d/tr/q £40/65/70/75, with shared bathroom from £30/45/60/65; ✖) Near the tube, this hotel set in an Edwardian square has recently been freshened up. The décor is simple but the rooms are especially convenient for families with its mainly three-or four-bed options.

MID-RANGE & TOP END

Philbeach Hotel (Map pp146-7; ☎ 7373 1244; www.philbeachhotel.freeserve.co.uk; 30-31 Philbeach Gdns SW5; tube Earl's Ct; B&B s/d £59/81, with shared bathroom £50/63; 🖳) The Philbeach is one of London's few gay hotels. Set in the middle of a sweeping crescent, its 40 rooms are stylish and pristine. The onsite bar and Thai restaurant are both popular with the local gay crowd.

Swiss House Hotel (Map pp146-7; ☎ 7373 2769; www.swiss-hh.demon.co.uk; 171 Old Brompton Rd SW5; tube Gloucester Rd; B&B s/d/tr/q from £56/97/132/147) This relaxed, uncluttered and modern hotel is a breath of fresh air on this strip full of rather average accommodation. The large, light-filled rooms have laminated floors and a simple, contemporary décor.

Hotel 167 (Map pp146-7; ☎ 7373 0672; www.hotel167.com; 167 Old Brompton Rd SW5; tube Gloucester Rd; B&B s/d from £72/90) Although a bit frayed around the edges, this stylish hotel is full of quirky surprises. The rooms are flowery with painted photographs, old desks, fridges, modem points and large bathrooms.

Number Sixteen (Map pp146-7; ☎ 7589 5232; www.numbersixteenhotel.co.uk; 16 Sumner Pl SW7; tube South Kensington; s/d from £95/170; ✖ 😣) With cool grey, muted colours, tasteful clarity and choice art throughout, this is a stunning place to repose. Additionally, the idyllic back garden set around a fishpond, the lovely conservatory, and a sumptuous drawing room complete with cosy fire, make it blissfully idyllic.

Bayswater, Paddington & Notting Hill

This area has a good selection of inexpensive hostels and hotels, with some funky options at the higher price range.

BUDGET

Hyde Park Inn (Map pp146-7; ☎ 7229 0000; www.hydeparkinn.com; 48-50 Inverness Terrace W2; tube Queensway; B&B 10-bed dm/s £10/28; ✖ 🖳) Situated in what seems to be hostel central, this place has a variety of different-sized dorms. The staff are friendly, the place is relaxed and there's a games and pool room, laundry and recently refitted kitchen.

Holland House YHA (Map pp146-7; ☎ 7937 0748; hollandhouse@yha.org.uk; Holland Walk, Kensington W8; tube High St Kensington; B&B dm adult/under 18 yrs £21.60/19.30; ✖ 🖳) Built into the Jacobean wing of Holland House in the middle of Holland Park, this hostel's location is gorgeous. Care is needed however after dark when the park gates shut and access is via a poorly lit side path. There is a café, kitchen and laundry facilities.

Leinster Inn (Map pp146-7; ☎ 7229 9641; www.astorhostels.com; 7-12 Leinster Sq W2; tube Bayswater; B&B dm £13.50-18, s/d from £26/40; ✖ 🖳) In a large, old house northwest of Bayswater tube station and close to Portobello Rd Market, this 372-bed hostel has a café, a laundry, and a bar with a 4am licence and monthly theme parties.

Manor Court Hotel (Map pp146-7; ☎ 7727 5407; 7 Clanricarde Gdns W2; tube Notting Hill Gate; s/d £40/50, with shared bathroom £25/40) Due for a nip and tuck, this hotel nonetheless still provides decent accommodation at a reasonable price, and

BRITAIN

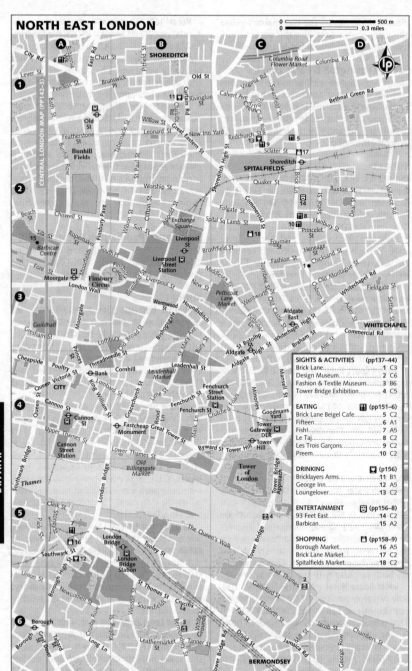

NORTH EAST LONDON

SIGHTS & ACTIVITIES		**(pp137–44)**
Brick Lane		1 C3
Design Museum		2 C6
Fashion & Textile Museum		3 B6
Tower Bridge Exhibition		4 C5
EATING	🍽	**(pp151–6)**
Brick Lane Beigel Cafe		5 C2
Fifteen		6 A1
Fish!		7 A5
Le Taj		8 C2
Les Trois Garçons		9 C2
Preem		10 C2
DRINKING	🍷	**(p156)**
Bricklayers Arms		11 B1
George Inn		12 A5
Loungelover		13 C2
ENTERTAINMENT	🎭	**(pp156–8)**
93 Feet East		14 C2
Barbican		15 A2
SHOPPING	🛍	**(pp158–9)**
Borough Market		16 A5
Brick Lane Market		17 C2
Spitalfields Market		18 C2

BRITAIN

it's not far from the lights and life of Notting Hill.

MID-RANGE

Glendale Hyde Park Hotel (Map pp146-7; ☎ 7706 4441; www.ghphotel.com; 8 Devonshire Terrace W2; tube Paddington; s/d £45/55; ✗ ▣) Despite rather too much pastel, all 20 rooms have en-suite bathrooms and a TV, phone and fridge.

St David's Hotel (Map pp146-7; ☎ 7723 4963; www .stdavidshotels.com; 16-20 Norfolk Sq W2; tube Paddington; s/d £49/69, with shared bathroom £39/59) A warm welcome and huge, tasty breakfasts make this hotel stand out. The rooms have satellite TV, modem points and phones, and are clean and comfortable with calming creamy colours and dark wood furniture.

TOP END

Pavilion Hotel (Map pp146-7; ☎ 7262 0905; www .pavilionhoteluk.com; 34-36 Sussex Gdns W2; tube Paddington; s/d/tr from £60/100/120; ℗) 'Fashion, Glam & Rock'n'Roll' is the motto of this place, so if you'd like to cap off your holiday by throwing a TV set out the window, the Pavilion could be for you. With sumptuous décor and interesting details throughout, there are 30 individually themed rooms, including the 70s themed 'Honky Tonky Afro'.

Portobello Hotel (Map pp146-7; ☎ 7727 2777; www.portobello-hotel.co.uk; 22 Stanley Gdns W11; tube Notting Hill Gate; s/d from £120/160; ✗ ✗ ▣) From the Sex Pistols to Johnny Depp and Kate Moss, this famous hotel has been a firm favourite of rock and movie stars for years. There's a 24-hour bar to fuel guests on their merry way and the individually decorated rooms (with themes like Morocco and Japan) are elegantly plush, loosely colonial and achingly cool.

EATING

British food has long surpassed its dire reputation; there is now a host of imaginative chefs giving innovative twists to traditional British staples, as well as the bewildering array of cuisines from all corners of the globe. It all amounts to a feasting opportunity of gastronomic proportions that even the smallest budget will be able to take advantage of.

The listings here are in order of price. If you're self-catering, supermarkets and grocery stores are everywhere.

Westminster & Pimlico

Heavy on hotels, light on restaurants – this part of town is for recliners rather than diners.

Kazan (Map pp142-4; ☎ 7233 7100; 93-94 Wilton Rd SW1; tube Victoria; starters £3-5, mains £8-13; ✆ noon-11pm; ✗) This minimalist-style Turkish restaurant is cosied up with candles and leather chairs. There is a good selection of tasty grills and seafood, as well as hot and cold mezze starters, a few of which could make a substantial main. The lunch-time flatbread 'sandwiches' are a good deal at £3.55 each.

Footstool (Map pp142-4; ☎ 7222 2779; St John's, Smith Sq SW1; tube Westminster; lunch mains £10-13, buffet £7, 2-course dinner £13.50; ✆ 11am-2.45pm Mon-Fri, 5.30-10.30pm) Set in the crypt of an 18th-century baroque church (now a concert hall) this atmospheric, brick-vaulted space is a favoured lunch-time retreat of MPs. It offers a buffet (good for a quick eat before or after a concert upstairs) as well as having a more formal restaurant serving Mediterranean dishes.

Ebury Wine Bar & Restaurant (Map pp142-4; ☎ 7730 5447; 139 Ebury St SW1; tube Victoria; mains £10-20, 2-course lunch/pre-theatre menu £12.50; ✆ 11am-11pm Mon-Sat, noon-3pm & 6-10.30pm Sun; ✗) The unpretentious 'traditional pub'-style environment and the equally unfussy food make this a popular place with Pimlico locals and tourists alike. Dishes like beef and ale sausages with Pye lentils are accompanied by a superb selection of wines.

Piccadilly, Soho & Chinatown

These days Soho is London's gastronomic centralis. You'll find plenty of choice along Old Compton and Dean Sts. Gerrard and Lisle Sts form London's Chinatown and offer set-menu bargains.

Pollo (Map pp142-4; ☎ 7734 5917; 20 Old Compton St W1; tube Leicester Sq; mains under £5; ✆ noon-midnight; ✗) With a massive selection of generous and filling pasta dishes, risottos and pizzas, Pollo is noisy and usually crowded but great value for money.

Stockpot (Map pp142-4; ☎ 7287 1066; 18 Old Compton St W1; tube Leicester Sq; mains £4-6; ✆ 11.30am-midnight; ✗) Like Pollo next door, Stockpot is a London institution and one of the few places where you can get a three-course meal for under a tenner. Sturdy staples include the likes of spaghetti bolognese, beef stroganoff and steak.

Café de Hong Kong (Map pp142-4; ☎ 7534 9898; 47-49 Charing Cross Rd WC2; tube Leicester Sq; mains £4.20-6.50; ☺ noon-11pm) If the traditional-style Cantonese restaurants with ducks hanging in the window put you off, then Café de HK is probably more up your street. It has brought Hong Kong café culture to London with its sleek and modern minimalist design and street hawker-style dishes.

Mildred's (Map pp142-4; ☎ 7494 1634; 45 Lexington St W1; tube Tottenham Ct Rd; mains £5.50-7.50; ☺ noon-11pm Mon-Sat; ✕) This superb vegetarian/vegan restaurant serves generously portioned dishes like the virtuous organic energising detox salad and the more indulgent mushroom, tofu and ale pie. There are also naughty puddings and an impressive selection of organic wines. Takeaway available.

Masala Zone (Map pp142-4; ☎ 7287 9966; 9 Marshall St W1; tube Oxford Circus; mains £5.50-11.50; ☺ noon-3pm, 5.30-11pm; ✕) The industrial, canteen-like design, juxtaposed against terracotta walls and tribal Indian art, fits perfectly with the modern Indian cuisine. Dishes range from street food, sandwiches and salads to *thalis*, noodle bowls and curries.

Carluccio's (Map pp142-4; ☎ 7636 2228; 8 Market Pl W1; tube Oxford Circus; mains £5.95-10.75; ☺ 7.30am-11pm Mon-Sat, 10am-10pm Sun) Just behind the hubbub of Oxford St is the relatively quiet Market Pl where you can eat well-priced pasta dishes or more meaty mains. Good for coffee and cakes too, there is a delicatessen, pavement tables and a bar (handy for when there is a wait).

Chuen Cheng Ku (Map pp142-4; ☎ 7437 1398; 17 Wardour St W1; tube Leicester Sq; mains £6.50-9; ☺ 11am-11.30pm) This massive Cantonese restaurant has dishes such as dumplings, noodles and paper-wrapped prawns trundled around on trolleys so you can just point out what you want.

Busaba Eathai (Map pp142-4; ☎ 7255 8686; 106-110 Wardour St W1; tube Tottenham Ct Rd; mains £5-11; ☺ noon-11pm Mon-Sat, to 10pm Sun; ✕ ✕) This buzzing, modern Thai restaurant with large wooden communal tables and low-lit lanterns serves fast food without any of the bad associations. Innovative dishes like butternut pumpkin curry and rose apple stir-fry arrive at the table within five minutes. You can't book, so expect to queue.

Criterion (Map pp142-4; ☎ 7930 0488; 224 Piccadilly W1; tube Piccadilly Circus; mains £10.50-22.50, 2-/3-course lunch & pre-theatre menu £15/18; ☺ noon-2.30pm, 5.30-11pm Mon-Sat; ✕) This beautiful Marco Pierre White restaurant is all chandeliers, mirrors, marble and sparkling mosaics but its most spectacular feature is the modern French food, which ranges from the delicate mussel and saffron soup to duck confit with béarnaise sauce.

Covent Garden & the Strand

There is a huge choice of eateries around here. These are our favourites:

Food for Thought (Map pp142-4; ☎ 7836 0239; 31 Neal St WC2; tube Covent Garden; mains £3-6.50; ☺ noon-8.15pm Mon-Sat, to 4.45pm Sun; ✕ ✕) This cherished and tiny vegetarian institution serves huge portions of imaginative salads, crispy stir-fries, smooth curries and thick quiches. The menus change every day and food can be taken away.

Café in the Crypt (Map pp142-4; ☎ 7839 4342; St Martin-in-the-Fields, Duncannon St WC2; tube Charing Cross; mains £3.95-7.50; ☺ 11.30am-3pm Mon-Sat, noon-3pm Sun, 5-7.30pm Mon-Wed & Sun, to 10.30pm Thu-Sat) Right next to Trafalgar Square, this caféteria-style eatery set in the arched crypt of the St Martin-in-the-Fields church is the perfect place to rest weary bones and enjoy wholesome food. Expect a good choice of salads, British mains, proper puddings and teas and scones.

World Food Café (Map pp142-4; ☎ 7379 0298; 1st fl, 14 Neal's Yard WC2; Covent Garden tube; mains £6-8; ☺ 11.30am-4.30pm Mon-Fri, to 5pm Sat; ✕) Decorated with rich colours and travel photos taken by the owners, this vegetarian restaurant overlooking the greenery and alternative lifestyle shops of Neals Yard serves piled-high Mexican dishes, Thai curries, Turkish meze and Indian *thalis*, as well as thick *lassis* and healthy juices.

Rock & Sole Plaice (Map pp142-4; ☎ 7836 3785; 47 Endell St WC2; tube Covent Garden; mains £8-9; ☺ 11.30am-10pm Mon-Sat, noon-9pm Sun) Established in 1871, this landmark sit-down and takeaway chippy does fantastic cod, Dover sole, scotch salmon or tuna steak in perfectly crisp batter along with tasty thick chips.

Rules (Map pp142-4; ☎ 7379 0258; 35 Maiden Lane WC2; tube Covent Garden; mains £16-21; ☺ noon-11.30pm Mon-Sat, to 10.30pm Sun; ✕ ✕) Quintessentially British, Rules achieves kudos as London's oldest restaurant (1798) and specialises in game from its Pennine estate. Despite the history, it's not a museum piece and its succulent dishes and sustained vitality attract locals as well as tourists.

The Ivy (Map pp142-4; ☎ 7836 4751; 1 West St WC2; tube Leicester Sq; mains £10-25; ☺ noon-3pm & 5.30-midnight) With its liveried doorman and celebrity clientele, just managing to snag a table here is a showbizzy event in itself. The service is courteous and unpretentious, and the fare consists of glorious versions of mainly British staples such as shepherd's pie and kedgeree.

Bloomsbury

Due to the student contingent, Bloomsbury has some reasonably priced places to eat, as well as some more exclusive pockets.

Coffee Gallery (Map pp142-4; ☎ 7436 0455; 23 Museum St WC1; tube Tottenham Ct Rd; mains £3-4; ☺ 9am-6pm Mon-Fri, to 7pm Sat, 11am-7pm Sun; ☒) After the British Museum drop in here and choose from the mainly organic and vegetarian, pasta, salads and sandwiches.

Fitzrovia (Map pp142-4; ☎ 7636 2744; 29 Tottenham St W1; tube Goodge St; mains £3.60-9.20; ☺ noon-3pm, 6-11pm) Just off Charlotte St, this hidden gem looks like it's been pulled out of an Italian village, and has a slightly faded charm. Great value, no-frills Italian dishes are served here, and it's filled with a mixture of older Bloomsbury locals and students.

Rasa Samudra (Map pp142-4; ☎ 7637 0222; 5 Charlotte St W1; tube Goodge St; mains £9-16, 4-course menu veg/seafood £22.50/30; ☺ noon-3pm Mon-Sat, 6-11pm Mon-Sun; ☒) You can't miss the Barbie-pink exterior of this South Indian restaurant, but don't be put off, the interior is tastefully decorated and there's a great choice of truly delectably Keralan seafood and vegetarian dishes.

Hakkasan (Map pp142-4; ☎ 7907 1888; 8 Hanway Pl W1; tube Tottenham Ct Rd; mains £4-35; ☺ noon-3pm, 6-11pm Sun-Tue, noon-midnight Wed-Sat) This fashionable haunt is the first Chinese restaurant in London to get a Michelin star. The stylish restaurant serves sophisticated and innovative Chinese cuisine, and the adjoining bar has extremely persuasive cocktails.

South Bank & Bankside

Reflecting the development of the area itself, this part of town offers down-to-earth cafés and 'gastropubs', as well as upmarket refinement.

Festival Square (Map pp142-4; ☎ 7928 2228; ground fl, Royal Festival Hall, South Bank SE1; tube Waterloo;

mains £5-10; ☺ 8.30am-11pm Mon-Fri, 10am-11pm Sat, 10am-10pm Sun) With fresh and inventive modern European meals this contemporary café and bar is a handy pick-me-up point along the South Bank sightseeing strip.

Anchor & Hope (Map pp142-4; ☎ 7928 9898; 36 The Cut SE1; tube Southwark/Waterloo; mains £10-15; ☺ noon-2.30pm Tue-Sat, 6-10.30pm Mon-Sat) With mainly British fare, such as stuffed duck or Lancashire hotpot, the food here has received accolades galore, including the *Evening Standard's* 2004 'gastropub of the year' award. There's a simple oak décor, relaxed atmosphere, and a good selection of cask ales and wines.

fish! (Map p150; ☎ 7407 3803; Cathedral St SE1; tube London Bridge; mains £9-17; ☺ 11.30am-11pm) Situated in an all-glass Victorian pavilion overlooking Borough Market and Southwark Cathedral, fish! serves a good choice of super-fresh seafood prepared simply: steamed or grilled, and served with one of five sauces.

Oxo Tower Restaurant & Brasserie (Map pp142-4; ☎ 7803 3888; 8th fl, Barge House St SE1; tube Blackfriars/Waterloo; mains £16-26, 2-/3-course lunch £24/29; ☺ noon-3pm, 6-11pm Mon-Sat, 6-10.15pm Sun; ☒) Magnificent views over the Thames guarantee a night to remember in this elegant blue and white restaurant, but the menu of French cuisine with a spice of oriental is less uniformly reliable. For a more casual atmosphere with cheaper options, book at the brasserie.

Chelsea, South Kensington & Earl's Court

From cheap eats to three Michelin stars, all budgets are well catered for in these areas.

Troubadour (Map pp146-7; ☎ 7370 1434; www .troubadour.co.uk; 265 Old Brompton Rd SW5; tube Earl's Ct; mains £3.25-11; ☺ 9am-11pm) Bob Dylan and John Lennon have both performed here, and Troubadour remains a wonderfully relaxed bohemian hangout decades later – great for just coffee, a reasonably priced, home-cooked meal or the live music that still plays most nights. They also have a deli next door.

Lundum's (Map pp146-7; ☎ 7373 7774; 117-119 Old Brompton Rd SW7; tube Gloucester Rd/South Kensington; lunch mains £4.50-9.75, dinner mains £13.75-18.50; ☺ 9am-5pm, 6-11pm Mon-Sat, noon-4pm Sun; ☒) Set in a beautiful Edwardian building with a fresh white and yellow décor and lots of light, this welcoming family-run Danish restaurant serves traditional fare at lunch (marinated herrings and open sandwiches) with a more modern take at dinner (Danish ingredients with a French twist).

Gordon Ramsay (Map pp146-7; ☎ 7352 4441; 68-69 Royal Hospital Rd SW3; tube Sloane Sq; 3-course lunch £35, 3-course dinner £65-80; ◷ noon-2.50pm, 6.30-11pm Mon-Fri) The only restaurant in the capital with three Michelin stars, this creation of celebrity chef, Gordon Ramsay, is hallowed turf. A blissful treat right through from the taster to the truffles, the only quibble is that due to the specific eat-it-and-beat-it slots you don't get time to savour this luxurious modern European cuisine. He also has restaurants in **Claridge's** (☎ 7499 0099) and **Berkeley Hotel** (☎ 7235 1010).

Kensington & Knightsbridge

Cheap eats are few and far between around here, as these cosmopolitan 'villages' still cater mainly for their chic and moneyed clients.

Bellini's (Map pp146-7; ☎ 7937 5520; 47 Kensington Ct W8; tube High St Kensington; mains £8-16, 2-/3-course lunch £7.65/9.15; ◷ noon-11pm) This Italian restaurant with great pizza, pasta and meaty mains, has a few pavement tables and views of a flower-bedecked alley.

Fifth Floor Café (Map pp146-7; ☎ 7823 1839; Harvey Nichols, 109-125 Knightsbridge SW1; tube Knightsbridge; mains £9.50-14.50; ◷ 10am-10.30pm Mon-Sat, 11am-6pm Sun) On the same floor as the glitzy designer restaurant, this café is the perfect place to drop after a shop. You can enjoy light and innovative Mediterranean meals beneath a stunning metal and glass ceiling canopy or go out on the terrace if the weather is fine.

L'estranger (Map pp146-7; ☎ 7584 1118; 36 Gloucester Rd SW7; tube Gloucester Rd; mains £15.50-21, 2-/3-course lunch £14.50/16.50; ◷ noon-3pm & 6-11pm; ✖) This smart and contemporary styled restaurant has a menu based on French cuisine, with an Indochinese twist. A favourite is steamed fillet of sea bass with ginger and coriander. Globally sourced wine is on the menu, and if something takes your fancy, there is the associated wine shop next door.

Nobu (Map pp142-4; ☎ 7447 4747; Metropolitan Hotel, 19 Old Park Lane W1; tube Hyde Park Corner; mains £5-30; ◷ noon-2pm Mon-Fri, 6-10.15pm Mon-Thu, to 11pm Fri & Sat, 6.30-9.30pm Sun) Overlooking Hyde Park, this strong contender for the best Asian food in town has a comfortably

minimalist décor, anonymously efficient service, and is out of this world when it comes to the exquisitely prepared and presented sushi and sashimi.

Notting Hill

Notting Hill is yet another good eat-out option, with everything from cheap takeaways to trendy restaurants, some quite quirky.

Costas Fish Restaurant (Map pp146-7; ☎ 7727 4310; 18 Hillgate St W8; tube Notting Hill Gate; mains £6.90; ◷ noon-2.30pm, 5.30-10.30pm Tue-Sat) This fondly regarded local puts a Cypriot spin on the traditional chippy and has a huge array of fish dishes at market prices.

Geales (Map pp146-7; ☎ 7727 7528; 2 Farmer St W8; tube Notting Hill Gate; mains £7.25-11.50; ◷ noon-3pm, 6-11pm Mon-Sat, 6-10.30pm Sun) Decorated in a maritime blue and white, this is a slightly more upmarket chippy to the nearby Costas and offers good kedgeree and fish pie as well as classic fish and chips.

Sausage & Mash Café (Map pp146-7; ☎ 8968 8898; 268 Portobello Rd W10; tube Ladbroke Grove; mains £6-7; ◷ 11am-11pm) Entertainingly known as 'S&M', this place does an upmarket version of an English favourite. There are 20 types of sausage to choose from (including vegetarian options), and variations of mash and gravy.

Market Thai (Map pp146-7; ☎ 7460 8320; The Market Bar, 240 Portobello Rd W11; tube Ladbroke Grove; mains £5-8; ◷ noon-3pm, 6-10.30pm Mon-Fri & Sun, noon-10.30pm Sat) Set on the first floor of the Market Bar, with drippy white candles, carved arches and wrought-iron chairs that make it feel way beyond the market crowds. Hospitable staff and fresh, delicately spiced Thai cuisine make it a delightful spot.

Café Grove (Map pp146-7; ☎ 7243 1094; 253A Portobello Rd W11; tube Ladbroke Grove; mains £5.50-9.50; ◷ 9.30am-6.30pm Mon-Sat, 10.30am-5pm Sun) Known for its gigantic and imaginative breakfasts (as well as dishes like risotto and pasta), this café has a large balcony overlooking the market – an ideal spot for watching the hustle and bustle on a weekend morning.

E&O (Map pp146-7; ☎ 7229 5454; 14 Blenheim Cres W11; tube Notting Hill Gate/Ladbroke Grove; mains £3-22; ◷ 12.15-3pm, 6.15-10.30pm Mon-Sat, 1-4pm, 6.15-10pm Sun) Trendy Eastern & Oriental presents fusion fare, which usually starts with an Asian base, and then pirouettes into something resembling Pacific Rim, like red pumpkin, aubergine and lychee curry. The décor is stark and minimalist and there is dim sum at the bar.

Camden

Camden is better for its bars, clubs and eclectic nightlife than its eateries, but has a few tantalising options. Those selected can all be reached from Camden Town tube.

Fresh and Wild (☎ 7428 7575; 49 Parkway NW1; mains £1.20-8; ☺ 11am-7pm; ☒) This strictly organic health-food chain sells a good line of light bites by weight (£1.20 for 100gms). Sit among the homeopathy books and enjoy shepherd's pie or the more plentiful vegetarian options.

Bar Gansa (☎ 7267 8909; 2 Inverness St NW1; mains £3-12; ☺ 10am-midnight Mon-Wed, to 1am Thu-Sat, to 11pm Sun) Like a traditional Spanish tapas joint this place is smoky, loud, cramped and run by Spanish staff. Whether you feel like picking or porking out, the menu ranges from tasty titbits to manly mains. It has a late licence and is howlingly popular.

Lemongrass (☎ 7284 1116; 243 Royal College St; mains £5-8; ☺ 6-10.30pm; ☒) At this cute and calming little place you can tuck into a solid and inexpensive line of fresh and tasty authentic Thai classics (with Cambodian twists).

Mango Rooms (☎ 7482 5065; 10 Kentish Town Rd NW1; mains £9-12; noon-3pm Tue-Sat, 6pm-midnight Mon-Sat, noon-11pm Sun) Considered by many to offer the best in Caribbean cooking, this chilled-out place is kind of de-caff Caribbean, although there's no holding back with the food. Dishes like snapper with mango and hot peppercorn sauce and the jerk chicken were great. The early ska/Jamaican jazz soundtrack is wicked.

Islington

Islington is stuffed full of eateries, especially on Upper St. Most of the restaurants chosen here are just off the main Upper St strip and the tube station for all of them is Angel.

Afghan Kitchen (☎ 7359 8019; 35 Islington Green N1; mains £4.50-6; ☺ noon-3.30pm, 5.30-11pm Tue-Sat) This tiny gem is known for its vegetarian concoctions (such as the scrumptious kidney bean, chickpea and potatoes cooked in yogurt, mint and lime) but the fish and meat dishes are equally as good. The décor is a calming pale green and light wood.

The Elk in the Woods (☎ 7226 3535; 39 Camden Passage N1; mains £4.80-8.80; ☺ 10am-11pm) Set in

the charming cobbled Camden passage, this cosy restaurant/bar with its standard lamps and flowered wallpaper almost feels like you are going round to granny's for tea. But the jovial bohemian Islington crowd and the fantastic, inexpensive modern European food is soon indicative that this isn't a place just for tea and cakes.

Almeida (☎ 7354 4777; 30 Almeida St N1 mains £12.50-19.50, 2-/3-course menu £14.50/17.50; ☺ noon-3pm, 6-11pm; ☷) Set in a muted-coloured dining room, this Terence Conran restaurant serves classic French mains that are reliably good. The bar serves tapas influenced by the southwest of France and Spain.

East End

Brick Lane is lined with Indian and Bangladeshi restaurants. Those with a more cosmopolitan palate might do better to stick to Hoxton as there's more variety.

Brick Lane Beigel Bake (Map p150; ☎ 7729 0616; 159 Brick Lane E2; tube Shoreditch; filled bagels 70p-£1.30; ☺ 24hr) This café/deli provides the ultimate cure for late-night munchies. You won't find cheaper or fresher bagels anywhere else.

Preem (Map p150; ☎ 7247 0397; 120 Brick Lane E1; mains £4-5; ☺ noon-2am) A Bengali favourite, this is one of the better restaurants found on the strip.

Les Trois Garçons (Map p150; ☎ 7613 1924; 1 Club Row E1; tube Liverpool St; mains £15-26; ☺ 7-11pm Mon-Sat) The latest place for fashionable types, this camp and eccentric French restaurant has surprising treasures in every nook and cranny. The food – largely French but with a modern twist – is very good, although a tad overpriced.

Fifteen (Map p150; ☎ 0871 330 1515; 15 Westland Pl N1; tube Old St) Restaurant (lunch mains £11-28, 8-course tasting dinner menu £65; ☺ noon-2.15pm, 6.30-10pm) Trattoria (mains £12-15; ☺ 9am-11pm Mon-Sat, to 5pm Sun) Jamie Oliver's successful not-for-profit venture to train and employ 15 young underprivileged people as chefs, has had a recent revamp of its mainly Mediterranean-inspired restaurant and trattoria menus. You can just walk into the trattoria but it will take about three months to get into the retro-style restaurant.

Another recommended place is the modestly dressed **Le Taj** (Map p150; ☎ 7247 4210; 134 Brick Lane E1; tube Liverpool St; mains £5-10; ☺ 11.30am-midnight).

BRITAIN

Greenwich

Greenwich's eateries are packed into a triangle formed by the Market, Greenwich Church St and Nelson Rd. The Cutty Sark DLR is the convenient station.

Bar du Musée (☎ 8858 4710; 17 Nelson Rd; mains £10.50-13; ☺ noon-midnight Mon-Thu, to 1am Fri-Sun) More café than bar, this relaxed place serves well-executed French staples, as well as having a fantastic patisserie. Indulge in coffee and cakes on comfy sofas in the new conservatory.

Pistachios (☎ 8853 0602; 15 Nelson Rd; mains £6-7; ☺ 8am-6pm) An ideal place for a hearty English breakfast, there is also a good range of traditional British dishes like bangers and mash, and roasts.

DRINKING

From ancient, atmospheric taverns to slick DJ bars, London is awash with drinking holes, all of which close at a puritanical 11pm (10.30pm Sunday). Some of our favourites are listed.

Bars

Bar Italia (Map pp142-4; 22 Frith St W1; tube Leicester Sq; paninis £3.50-5; ☺ 7-4.30am) Pep yourself up at any time with coffees, juices, pastries and paninis. Perch on the stools or on the small terrace lined with lambrettas.

Bradley's Spanish Bar (Map pp142-4; 44 Hanway St W1; tube Tottenham Ct Rd) One of the most shabbily small, charming bars in London – downstairs is dimly lit with alcoves, red velvet seats and a bar; upstairs is similarly decorated with Spanish trinkets; there's a wicked jukebox.

Two Floors (Map pp142-4; 3 Kingly St W1; tube Oxford Circus/Piccadilly Circus) Attracting a mix of bohemian and trendy types, Two Floors always seems to play the music that you've just got into. Drinks are bottled beers and cocktails.

Loungelover (Map p150; 1 Whitby St E1; tube Liverpool St) Totally over the top and addictive with its chandeliers, quirky antiques and comfy lounge chairs.

Pubs

Lamb & Flag (Map pp142-4; Rose St WC2; tube Covent Garden) Manic just after office hours, it is loved by all for its family-like quality. Interesting, then, that it used to be called 'The Bucket of Blood'.

Coach & Horses (Map pp142-4; 29 Greek St W1; tube Leicester Sq) This busy boozer retains the ambience of old Soho bohemia with a regular clientele of soaks, writers, hacks and tourists.

Queen's Larder (Map pp142-4; 1 Queen Sq WC1; tube Russell Sq) Used by Queen Charlotte to store delicacies for George III, this place now offers a handy retreat set in a lovely square, with outside benches and pub grub.

George Inn (Map p150; Talbot Yard, 77 Borough High St SE1; tube London Bridge/Borough) Dating from 1676, London's last surviving galleried coaching inn, with its low-ceilings and dark-panelled rooms, is mentioned in Charles Dickens' *Little Dorrit*.

Bricklayers Arms (Map p150; 63 Charlotte Rd EC2; tube Old St) A determinedly down-to-earth stalwart of the Hoxton scene, it attracts an unpretentious but cool-looking, mid-to-late 20-something crowd.

Cow (Map pp146-7; 89 Westbourne Park Rd W2; tube Westbourne Park/Royal Oak) Tom Conran, the son of renowned restaurateur Sir Terence, made this old side-street boozer into a jovial gastropub. Apparently, it's Madonna's favourite place to sip a pint when she graces these shores.

ENTERTAINMENT

By day and by night, London plays host to a lively, vibrant mix of welcome distractions. It's rich in contemporary and classical music, film, theatre and nightclubs.

Cinema

The choice of movies to watch in London is dazzling. For Hollywood blockbusters head to Leicester Sq, for a more eclectic choice try the cinemas listed here.

Curzon Soho (Map pp142-4; ☎ 7439 4805/7734 2255; www.curzoncinemas.com; 93-107 Shaftesbury Ave W1; tube Leicester Sq) With its art-house repertory and cool bar downstairs, this is the lounge lizard of cinemas.

Electric Cinema (Map pp146-7; ☎ 7908 9696/7229 8688; www.electriccinema.co.uk; 191 Portobello Rd W1; tube Ladbroke Grove/Notting Hill Gate) The UK's oldest purpose-built cinema has an auditorium with luxurious armchairs, sofas and footstools.

National Film Theatre (Map pp142-4; ☎ 7928 3232; www.bfi.org.uk/showing/nft/; South Bank Centre SE1; tube Waterloo) Screens an impressive range of classic, unusual, experimental and foreign films. Directors and actors often do talks. The London Film Festival is held here in October (see p145).

POPULAR MUSICALS

Tickets for musicals cost between £15 and £50. All the theatres listed here can be found on Map pp142-4. Check the website www.officiallondontheatre.co.uk for further details.

- **Chicago** (☎ 0870 030 303; Adelphi, Strand WC2; tube Charing Cross)
- **Mamma Mia!** (☎ 7839 5987; Prince of Wales, 31 Coventry St W1; tube Piccadilly)
- **Les Miserables** (☎ 7494 5040; Queen's, Shaftesbury Ave W1; tube Piccadilly Circus)
- **The Phantom of the Opera** (☎ 7494 5400; Her Majesty's, Haymarket SW1; tube Piccadilly Circus)

Gay & Lesbian Venues

Soho is the heart of gay London – head for the main strip of Old Compton St where there are plenty of bars and cafés, and pick up free listings like *Boyz* and *QX*. More serious papers and magazines include *Pink Paper*, *Diva*, *Gay Times* and *Attitude*. Useful websites are www.rainbownetwork.com and www.uk.gay.com. Pride Parade is in July (see Festivals & Events p144). Popular clubs and bars include those following.

BARS & PUBS

Candy Bar (Map pp142-4; ☎ 7437 1977; 23-24 Bateman St W1; tube Tottenham Ct Rd; 5pm-1am Mon-Tue, to 3am Thu-Sat, to midnight Sun) is London's best lesbian bar; it has a cruisey vibe with DJ's and late nights. **Compton's of Soho** (Map pp142-4; ☎ 7479 7961; 51-53 Old Compton St W1; tube Leicester Sq) is a good cruising place for the boys. Over, the road, **Admiral Duncan** (Map pp142-4; ☎ 7437 5300; 54 Old Compton St) is more mixed and down-to-earth.

NIGHTCLUBS

Ghetto (Map pp142-4; ☎ 7287 3726; 5-6 Falconberg Ct W1; tube Tottenham Ct Rd; 10-3pm Mon-Thu, from 10.30pm Wed, 10.30pm-4.30am Fri & Sat) attracts the fashionable glitterati. **Astoria** (Map pp142-4; ☎ 7434 0044; 157 Charing Cross Rd WC2; tube Tottenham Ct Rd; 10.30pm-4am, Mon & Thu, 11pm-4am Fri, 10.30am-5am Sat) plays mainly commercial beats.

Heaven (Map pp142-4; ☎ 7930 2020; Villiers St WC2; tube Charing Cross; 10.30pm-3am Mon & Wed, 10pm-3am Fri, 10pm-5am Sat) is ever popular and

has some mixed nights. **DTPM** (9.30pm-5am Sun) at the superclub **Fabric** (Map pp142-4; ☎ 7336 8898; 77a Charterhouse St EC1; tube Farringdon) and **Fiction** (10.30pm-5am Fri) at **The Cross** (Map pp142-4; ☎ 7837 0828, Goods Way Depot, York Way N1; tube King's Cross) are good gay nights.

Live Music

London's live rock and pop music scene with its hundreds of venues simply can't be beaten. Some of the major venues for live contemporary music include the **Brixton Academy** (☎ 7771 3000; 211 Stockwell Rd SW9; tube Brixton) and **Shepherds Bush Empire** (☎ 8354 3300; Shepherds Bush Green W12; tube Shepherds Bush). Smaller places with more club-like atmospheres that are worth checking out include: **12 Bar Club** (Map pp142-4; ☎ 7916 6989; 22 Denmark Pl WC2; tube Tottenham Ct Rd); **Borderline** (Map pp142-4; ☎ 7434 9592; Orange Yard, WC2; tube Tottenham Ct Rd), off Manette St; **Garage** (☎ 7607 1818; 20-22 Highbury Corner N5; tube Highbury & Islington); **Notting Hill Arts Club** (Map pp146-7; ☎ 7460 4459; 21 Notting Hill Gate W11); and the **Union Chapel** (☎ 7226 1686; Compton Tce N1; tube Highbury & Islington). Ring ahead to find out which bands are playing.

If you're a jazz fan, keep your eye on **Ronnie Scott's** (Map pp142-4; ☎ 7439 0747; 47 Frith St W1; tube Leicester Sq), the **Jazz Café** (☎ 7916 6060; 5 Parkway NW1; tube Camden Town), and **100 Club** (Map pp142-4; ☎ 7636 0933; 100 Oxford St W1; tube Oxford Circus).

Major classical music venues include the **Barbican** (Map p150; ☎ 7638 8891; Silk St EC2; tube Moorgate/Barbican), home to the London Symphony Orchestra; and the **South Bank Centre** (Map pp142-4; ☎ 7960 4242; Belvedere Rd SE1; tube Waterloo) with its Royal Festival Hall, Queen Elizabeth Hall and Purcell Room.

Nightclubs

Keep an eye on *Time Out* magazine to see what's hot and what's not on the club scene. Admission prices vary from £3 to £10 between Sunday and Thursday, and £14 and £20 on Friday and Saturday. A selection of the best clubs include: **Fabric** (Map pp142-4; ☎ 7336 8898; 77a Charterhouse St EC1; tube Farringdon; 9.30pm-5am Fri & Sun, 10pm-7am Sat) with its kidney-shaking 'sonic boom' dance floor; **93 Feet East** (Map p150; ☎ 7247 3293; 150 Brick Lane E2; tube Liverpool St; 8pm-2am Thu-Sat) with its typically cool Hoxton crowd. **Pacha** (Map pp142-4; ☎ 7834 4440; Terminus Pl SW1; tube Victoria; 10pm-6am Fri & Sat) for Balearic beats. **The Cross** (Map

BRITAIN

pp142-4; ☎ 7837 0828, Goods Way Depot, York Way N1; tube King's Cross; ⊙ 10.30pm-5am Fri & Sat, to 4pm Sun) for soulful funk and garage, and **Cherry Jam** (Map pp146-7; ☎ 7727 9950; 58 Porchester Rd W2; tube Royal Oak; ⊙ 7pm-1.30am Thu-Sat) with its club nights ranging from Latin to deep-house, as well as live bands and readings.

Theatre

With the likes of Nicole Kidman and Dame Judi Dench treading its boards, London's theatreland is an innovative and exciting place. Rip-roaring musicals are ever popular. Visit www.officiallondontheatre.co.uk to find out what's on and where.

Book in advance through the theatre's box office or agencies like: **Ticketmaster** (☎ 7344 4444; www.ticketmaster.co.uk) or **First Call** (☎ 7420 0000; www.firstcalltickets.co.uk). On the day of performance only, you can queue outside the **Tkts** (Map pp142-4; ⊙ 10am-7pm Mon-Sat, noon-3pm Sun) in Leicester Sq to get discounted West End show tickets.

Royal National Theatre (Map pp142-4; ☎ 7452 3000; www.nationaltheatre.org.uk; South Bank SE1; tube Waterloo; £7-35), Britain's flagship theatre, showcases a mix of classic and contemporary plays performed by excellent casts.

Shakespeare's Globe (Map pp142-4; ☎ 7401 9919; www.shakespeares-globe.org; 21 New Globe Walk SE1; tube London Bridge; seated £13-29, standing £5; ⊙ May-Sep) is the home of authentic Shakespearean theatre, not only in the sense that it's a near-perfect replica of the building Shakespeare himself worked in from 1598 to 1611, but because it also largely follows Elizabethan staging practices. The building is open to the elements and most people buy the standing tickets (for the mainly Shakespearean works) so they can emulate the 17th-century 'groundlings', who shouted and cajoled as they wished.

Sport

The new 80,000-capacity, state-of-the-art Wembley Stadium in northwest London will become the premier venue for football, rugby league and athletics competitions when it's completed in early 2006. Football is at the very heart of English culture; adopt a team and join the cheering throngs in their local clubs. Premier League football teams include **Arsenal** (☎ 7413 3366; www.arsenal .com, Avenell Rd N5; tube Arsenal; admission £25-45) and **Chelsea** (☎ 7385 5545/7386 7799; www.chelseafc.co.uk;

Stamford Bridge Stadium, Fulham Rd SW6; tube Fulham Broadway; admission £11-40).

The shrine English rugby is **Twickenham** (☎ 8892 2000; www.rfu.com; Rugby Rd, Twickenham; tube Hounslow East then bus 281, or rail Twickenham; admission £26-53). The two major venues for cricket are **Lord's** (☎ 7616 8500; www.lords.org; St John's Wood Rd NW8; tube St John's Wood; admission £20-40) and **The Oval** (☎ 7582 7764; www.surreycricket.com; Kennington Oval SE11; tube Oval; admission £20-40). **Crystal Palace** (☎ 8778 0131; www.crystalpalace.co.uk; Ledrington Rd SE19; rail Crystal Palace; admission from £10) is the venue for important athletics events.

Watch tennis and eat strawberries and cream at **Wimbledon** (☎ 8944 1066, 8946 2244; www.wimbledon.org; Church Rd SW19; tube Southfields/ Wimbledon Park; admission £12-50) – see p144.

SHOPPING

The manically busy Oxford St is full of high street chains like the flagship store of **Top Shop** (Map pp142-4; tube Oxford St) – great for designer copies at bargain prices. The streets around nearby Bond St are more upmarket, with the likes of **Burberry** (Map pp142-4; 21 New Bond St W1; tube Bond St) and **Vivienne Westwood** (Map pp142-4; 6 Davies St W1; tube Bond St), as well as the classy one-stop shop, **Selfridges** (cnr Oxford & Orchard Sts; tube Bond St). For a whole street of bookshops such as Blackwell's (academic/general titles), Al-Hoda (Muslim and Arab bookshop), Borders (general) and Shipley (fine art), go to the stretch of **Charing Cross Rd** (Map pp142-4; tube Tottenham Crt Rd), between Tottenham Court Rd and Leicester Sq. Apart from the touristy old market hall, Covent Garden has more individual boutiques – head to Monmouth St for the high fashion at **Koh Samui** (Map pp142-4; tube Covent Garden) and the gorgeous shoes of **Poste Mistress** (Map pp142-4; tube Covent Garden), Floral St for **Paul Smith** (Map pp142-4; tube Covent Garden) and **Ted Baker** (Map pp142-4; tube Covent Garden), or otherwise **Neals Yard** (Map pp142-4; tube Covent Garden) for hippy trinkets. Knightsbridge is home to the department stores **Harvey Nichols** (Map pp146-7; 109-25 Knightsbridge SW1; tube Knightsbridge) a mecca for fashionistas, and **Harrods** (Map pp146-7; 87 Brompton Rd SW1; tube Knightsbridge) for fans of all things traditionally British.

Markets

London's many markets represent London at its most diverse and cosmopolitan; a must-see for any self-respecting visitor.

Borough Market (Map p150; Borough High St/Stoney St SE1; tube London Bridge; 🕙 noon-6pm Fri, 9am-4pm Sat) 'London's Larder' attracts the cream of the farming crop from around the country. Find products ranging from home-made pork pies to Somerset cider.

Brick Lane (Map p150; Brick Lane E2; tube Aldgate East; 🕙 8am-1pm Sun) This lively East End pearl is a real hotchpotch of treasures and trash.

Brixton (Electric Lane & Electric Ave SW9; tube Brixton; 🕙 8am-6pm Mon-Sat, to 3pm Wed) Find barrows piled high with Caribbean fruit and veg, miscellany like incense and wigs, and plenty of characters around.

Camden (Camden Lock; tube Camden Town; 🕙 10am-6pm Sat & Sun) Camden is full of tourists and Goth teenagers rummaging through mainly tack. The best bit is Stables Market (beyond the railway arches) with its antiques and vintage clothes stalls.

Portobello Rd (Map pp146-7; tube Notting Hill Gate/Ladbroke Grove; 🕙 7am-7pm Fri & Sat, 9am-4pm Sun) On Saturday, find the antiques market at the Notting Hill end of the road, and vintage and new designer clothes (best days are Friday and Saturday) further down.

Spitalfields (Map p150; Commercial St, btwn Brushfield & Lamb Sts, E1; tube Liverpool St; 🕙 9.30am-5.30pm Sun) A favourite among Londoners, you'll find cool stuff like funky new fashions and retro furniture.

GETTING THERE & AWAY

As London is Britain's major gateway, most of the Getting There & Away information has been covered in the Transport section (p254).

Bus

Bus travellers will arrive at **Victoria Coach Station** (Map pp142-4), Buckingham Palace Rd, about 10 minutes' walk south of Victoria station. See Transport p255 for booking and information lines.

Train

Eurostar passengers arrive at Waterloo International (Map1), which is in the same station as Waterloo train and tube station. Each of the 10 main-line stations serves various parts of Britain, so the station you arrive at might not be the one you'll leave from. For more information see Transport in Britain (p255) or contact the **National Rail Enquiry Service** (☎ 0845 748 4950; www.nationalrail.co.uk).

GETTING AROUND
To/From the Airports
HEATHROW

Fifteen miles (24km) west of central London, Heathrow (☎ 0870 000 0123, www.baa.co.uk/heathrow) has four terminals, with a fifth one on its way. It's accessible by main-line train, tube (underground train) and bus.

Going to and from Paddington station and all four Heathrow Terminals is the **Heathrow Express** (☎ 0845 600 1515; www.heathrowexpress.co.uk; one way/return £13/25), which leaves every 15 minutes between 5.10am and 11.40pm, and takes 15 minutes to Terminals 1, 2 or 3, and 23 minutes to Terminal 4. British Airways (BA) and United Airlines have check-in facilities at Paddington.

Two Piccadilly-line **Underground** (☎ 7222 1234; www.thetube.com; one way £3.80) stations are directly linked to the airport terminals (every two to eight minutes, 5.30am to 11.30pm, one hour from central London).

The **National Express Airport** (☎ 0870 580 8080; www.nxairport.com; one way/return £10/15) connects London Victoria coach station, and other bus stops throughout town, with Heathrow central bus station (every 30 minutes, 7.15am to 11.30pm, 45 minutes).

A metered trip to/from central London (Oxford St) with **London black cabs** (☎ 7272 0272; www.londonblackcabs.co.uk) will cost about £53.

GATWICK

Some 30 miles (48km) south of central London, Gatwick (☎ 0870 000 2468, www.baa.co.uk/gatwick) is accessible by main-line train and bus. The North and South terminals are linked by an efficient monorail service; journey time is about two minutes.

Trains of the **Gatwick Express** (☎ 0870 530 1530; www.gatwickexpress.co.uk; one way/return £11/21.50) link Victoria station with the South Terminal (every 15 minutes, 24 hours a day, 30 minutes). BA and American Airlines passengers can check in at Victoria station. **South Central trains** (☎ 08457 48 49 50; www.flybytrain.co.uk; one way/return £8/16) This less comfortable service also runs from Victoria station (every 15 minutes, 35 minutes).

The **National Express Airport** (☎ 0870 580 8080; www.nxairport.com; single/return £6/11) connects London Victoria coach station, and other bus stops throughout town, with the South and North Terminal (every hour, 7am to 11.30pm, one hour 20 minutes).

A metered trip to/from central London (Oxford St) with **London black cabs** (☎ 7272 0272; www.londonblackcabs.co.uk) will cost about £74.

STANSTED

About 35 miles (56km) northeast of central London, Stansted (☎ 0870 000 0303, www.baa .co.uk/stansted) is London's third busiest international gateway. It's accessible by mainline train, bus and taxi.

The **Stansted Express** (☎ 0845 748 4950; www .standstedexpress.com; one way/return £13/21) links Liverpool St station to the airport (every 15 to 30 minutes, 5.30am to 11pm, 45 minutes).

Connecting London Victoria coach station, and other bus stops throughout town, to Stansted Airport coach station is **National Express Airport** (☎ 0870 580 8080, www.nxairport .com; one way/return £10/15) (every 15 minutes, 24 hours a day, one hour 40 minutes).

A metered trip to/from central London (Oxford St) with **London black cabs** (☎ 7272 0272; www.londonblackcabs.co.uk) will cost about £87.

LONDON CITY

Six miles east of central London, **London City Airport** (☎ 7646 0000; www.londoncityairport.com) is in the Docklands by the Thames. The easiest way to get to the airport is by shuttle bus.

The **Blue airport Shuttlebus** (☎ 7646 0088, www.londoncityairport.com/shuttlebus; one way/return £6/12) links Liverpool St station with the airport (every 10 minutes, 6am to 9.30pm, 25 minutes). **Green airport Shuttlebus** (one way/return £3/6) Goes to and fro Canning Town station (Jubilee line) and the airport (every 10 minutes, 6am to 9.30pm, five to 10 minutes).

A metered trip to/from central London (Oxford St) with **London black cabs** (☎ 7272 0272; www.londonblackcabs.co.uk) will cost about £26.

LUTON

Luton (☎ 01582-405100, www.london-luton.co.uk) is a small-ish airport some 35 miles (56km) north of London. **Thameslink** (☎ 0845 748 4950; www.thameslink.co.uk; one way/return £10.40/20.80) runs trains from King's Cross Thameslink station to Luton Airport Parkway station (every five to 15 minutes, 7am to 10pm, 30 to 40 minutes), from where a shuttle bus will take you to the airport in eight minutes.

A metered trip to/from central London (Oxford St) with **London black cabs** (☎ 7272 0272; www.londonblackcabs.co.uk) will cost about £90.

Bicycle

Hire a bike at the **London Bicycle Tour Company** (Map pp142-4; ☎ 7928 6838; www.londonbicycle. com; 1a Gabriel's Wharf SE1; tube Waterloo; ⏰ 10am-6pm) for £2.50 per hour or £14 for 24 hours (£7 for subsequent days); a large deposit is required. They also offer three-hour bike tours (2pm Saturday and Sunday) for £15, including bike hire.

Boat

New boat services are popping up all the time, call ☎ 7222 1234 for general information. If you have a Travelcard (see p161) you'll get one-third off all fares listed below. Most useful for visitors are:

Tate-to-Tate (☎ 7887 8888; www.tate.org.uk; one way/day ticket £3.40/5) ferries operates between Bankside Pier at Tate Modern and the new Millennium Pier at sister museum Tate Britain, stopping en route at the London Eye (every 40 minutes, 10am to 5pm, 18 minutes). One of the ferries is a Damien Hirst dot painting, so you can't miss it.

Catamaran Cruisers (☎ 7987 1185/7925 2215; www.bateauxlondon.com; Hopper Pass: adult/child/family £8.50/4.25/21; Greenwich: adult/child one way £6.60/3.30, return £8/4) Links Embankment, Bankside, Tower and Greenwich Piers (every 40 minutes, departing 10am to 4.20pm returning 12.20pm to 6.40pm, one hour 10 minutes). The Hopper Pass allows unlimited use of the service for one day.

Westminster Passenger Service Association (☎ 7930 2062, www.wpsa.co.uk; adult/child one way to Kew £9/4.50, return £15/7.50, one way to Hampton Ct £12/6, return £18/9; ⏰ depart 10.30am-2pm, return noon-6.30pm Apr-Sep) goes to Kew Gardens (one hour 30 minutes) and Hampton Court (three hours 30 minutes) from Westminster Pier.

Car & Motorcycle

We do not advise driving in London: traffic jams are common, parking space is at a premium, there are extortionate parking charges, and annoyingly dutiful traffic wardens. The **congestion charge** (☎ 0845 900 1234; www.cclondon.com; £5 btwn 7am-6.30pm Mon-Fri) adds to the expense of driving but on the upside, the reduced number of cars has made bus and taxi journeys shorter. Currently, the congestion zone is south of the Euston Rd, west of Commercial St, north of Kennington Lane and east of Park Lane. There is a proposed plan to extend the zone to most of Kensington, Chelsea and Westminster in 2006. You know you are entering the chargeable zone when you see a large letter 'C' in a red circle.

Public Transport

For information regarding the London bus, tube (Underground), Docklands Light Railway (DLR) or train networks contact **Transport for London** (☎ 7222 1234; www.tfl.gov.uk) or go the TfL centres at Victoria, Piccadilly Circus, Euston, Liverpool St stations and Heathrow airport.

BUS & TUBE

Although traffic may make your journey substantially longer than by tube, buses have recently become a much cheaper transport option. Single tickets or one-day bus passes to anywhere in London cost £1 and £2.50 respectively. These prices include the comprehensive network of night buses that runs from or through Trafalgar Square (routes are denoted by the letter 'N'). There are machines next to all bus stops where you have to buy your ticket before you board. Pick up a free bus map at a TfL centre. The top decks of routes like the No 11 offer great DIY sightseeing tours.

Travelcards are the easiest option if you'll be using all public transport – they can be used on London trains, the DLR, buses and the tube. A Zones 1 and 2 card costs £5.30 before 9.30am, £4.30 after. If you're in London for only the weekend, opt for the Weekend Travelcard (£6.40) as it's cheaper than buying two separate Off-Peak Day Travelcards. A carnet of Zone 1 tube tickets costs £15 for 10 rides. If you are staying for a week or longer get an Oyster Card (an electronic card that you swipe over a yellow 'reader' each time you go through the ticket machine (Zones 1 & 2, 1 week £20.20).

Times of the last tube trains vary from 11.30pm to 12.30am, depending on the station and line.

DLR & TRAIN

The monorail-like, driverless Docklands Light Railway (DLR) links the City at Bank and Tower Gateway with Canary Wharf, Stratford, Beckton, Greenwich and Lewisham. Fares operate the same way as on the tube.

Trains are the primary means of transport to much of London's suburbia. All main-line stations interchange with the tube and you can use your Travelcard for any parts of the journey within London.

Taxi

The famous **London black cabs** (☎ 7272 0272; www.londonblackcabs.co.uk) can be hailed when the yellow 'for hire' sign is lit. They can carry five people but are not cheap. All fares are metered and the meter starts running the moment you get in. Surcharges are added for extra passengers, luggage or if it's late at night. You can tip taxi drivers up to 10% but most people round up to the nearest pound.

Minicabs can carry four people and tend to be cheaper than the black cabs. Although they are only supposed to be hired by phone and need a license to operate, hawkers abound in popular spots at night. Women, particularly if alone, are advised to steer clear. They're also unmetered, so make sure you barter hard on a price before you get in.

Small minicab companies are based in particular areas – ask a local for the name of a reputable company, or phone one of the large **24-hour minicab operations** (☎ 7387 8888, 7272 2222, 7272 3322, 8888 4444). Women could phone **Ladycabs** (☎ 7254 3501). Gays and lesbians can choose **Freedom Cars** (☎ 7734 1313).

PEDICABS

Found mainly in Soho, these three-wheeled cycle rickshaws that seat two or three people are a fun and environmentally sound way to take short trips around town (around £3 per person within Soho). The best-known company is the non-profit **Bugbugs** (☎ 7620 0500; www.bugbugs.co.uk; 🕒 7pm-2am Mon-Fri, to 5am Sat & Sun). Daytime trips can be booked in advance.

AROUND LONDON

When the hubbub of the city gets too much, there are plenty of nearby respites to escape to. Whether you want to wind down in a cosy country pub or go for a city with a different vibe, places like Brighton, Bath, Cambridge and Oxford are within daytripping distance. Closer to the city are the more royal options of Windsor, Eton and Hatfield House.

BRITAIN

Windsor & Eton

☎ 01753 / population 31,000

One of three official residences of the Queen, **Windsor Castle** (☎ 020 7766 7304; www.royalresidences.com; adult/concession/child/family £12/10/6/30, half-price when State Apartments are closed; ⌚ 9.45am-4pm Mar-Oct, to 3pm Nov-Feb, changing of the guard alternate days 11am Mon-Sat Apr-Jun) has been home to English sovereigns for over 900 years. Attractions include the 14th-century St George's Chapel, which is the burial place of 10 monarchs (closed to visitors on Sunday), the amazing Queen Mary's Doll's House and the opulent State Apartments. The latter are closed when the royal family are in residence; phone to check. The Queen's at home when the Royal Standard is flying.

A short walk along Thames St and across the river brings you to **Eton College** (☎ 671177; www.etoncollege.com; adult/child £3.80/3, 1hr tours £4.90/4; ⌚ 10am-4.30pm 27 Mar-20 Apr & 3 Jul-7 Sep, 2-4.30pm 21 Apr-2 Jul & 8 Sep-3 Oct, tours 2.15pm & 3.15pm), the famous public school that has educated 18 prime ministers and a number of royals, the most recent being Princes William and Harry. Several buildings date from when Henry VI founded the school in the mid-15th century.

Trains go directly and twice hourly from London Waterloo to Windsor & Eton Riverside station (one way/return £6.40/6.70, one hour).

Hatfield House

Home to the Marquess of Salisbury, **Hatfield** (☎ 01707-287010; www.hatfield-house.co.uk; house, park & gardens adult/child £7.50/4, park & gardens £4.50/3.50, park only £2/1; ⌚ house noon-4pm Easter Sun-Sep, park & gardens 11am-5.30pm Easter Sun-Sep) is England's most celebrated Jacobean house – a graceful red-brick and stone mansion full of treasures amid 42 acres of gardens. In the grounds is the remaining part of the Royal Palace of Hatfield, where Elizabeth I spent much of her childhood.

There are trains from King's Cross Station to Hatfield (one way/return £6.90/7.30, 20 minutes) every 15 minutes.

SOUTHEAST ENGLAND

The Southeast is a region exceptionally rich in beauty and history, and it caters to those unshakeable traditional images of England – picturesque villages with welcoming old pubs, spectacular coastlines, impressive castles and magnificent cathedrals. There are also a number of excellent walks along the South and North Downs.

Yet the Southeast is not just about recapturing an England past and pastoral. Nowadays, you will find Michelin-starred cuisine under the Tudor beams in Winchester while the trendiest boutique hotels in the land are in Brighton.

Due to their proximity to London, the counties of Kent, East and West Sussex and Hampshire are home to a large chunk of the capital's workforce. There are thus plenty of fast, regular rail and bus services, making it possible to see the main sights on day trips.

Orientation & Information

Chalk country runs through the region along two hilly east–west ridges, or 'downs'. The North Downs curve across the Kent farmland to Dover and the white cliffs. The South Downs run from near Portsmouth and end spectacularly at Beachy Head, near Eastbourne. Contact the **South East England Tourist Board** (☎ 01892 540766; www.southeastengland.uk.com) for information on walks along the Downs.

Getting Around

For information on all public transport options in the region, contact **Traveline** (☎ 0870 608 2608; www.traveline.org.uk).

BUS

An Explorer ticket gives unlimited travel for one day (adult/concession/family £5.95/4.25/7.99); buy them from bus drivers or bus stations. **Stagecoach Coastline** (☎ 0845 1210170; www.stagecoachbus.com) offers Goldrider tickets (£15) that allow one week's unlimited travel in the region.

TRAIN

There is an interesting rail loop from London via Canterbury East, Dover, Ashford, Rye, Hastings, Battle (via Hastings), Brighton, Arundel, Portsmouth and Winchester, which can be cheaper using a BritRail SouthEast pass (see p258) if you are from overseas.

CANTERBURY

☎ 01227 / pop 46,000

Canterbury, with its charming medieval centre of cobbled streets and characterful buildings, is reigned over by the Gothic spires of its magnificent and historically important cathedral.

When St Augustine arrived in England in 597 to carry the Christian message to the pagan hordes, he chose Canterbury as his primary see, and built an abbey on the outskirts of town. Canterbury cathedral became its successor, and it was here in 1170 that Archbishop Thomas à Becket was murdered by four of Henry II's knights as a result of a dispute over the church's independence. An enormous cult grew up around the martyred Becket, and Canterbury became the centre of one of the most important medieval pilgrimages in Europe, immortalised by Geoffrey Chaucer in the *Canterbury Tales*.

Orientation & Information

The centre of Canterbury is enclosed by a medieval city wall and a modern ring road. It's easily covered on foot: the two train stations are both a short walk from the centre; the bus station is just within the city walls at the eastern end of High St. The **Visitor Information Centre** (☎ 378100; www .canterbury.co.uk; 12-13 Sun St; ☀ 10am-4pm) is near the entrance to the cathedral. Free Internet access is available at the **Library** (☎ 463608; High St) but bookings are required. Alternatively, **Café Venue** (☎ 825460; Debenhams, Guild Hall St; per 30min £1.50 ☀ 9am-5.30pm) is opposite the Cathedral Gate.

Sights

Due to fires, the first church on the site of **Canterbury Cathedral** (☎ 762862; www.canterbury -cathedral.org; adult/concession/family £4.50/3.50/11, tours £3.50/2.50/1.50; ☀ 9am-6.30pm Mon-Sat Easter-Sep, to 4.30pm Mon-Sat Oct-Easter, to 2.30pm Sun year-round, tours 10.30am, noon & 2.30pm Mon-Fri, 10.30am, noon & 1.30pm Sat) was rebuilt in 1070 by the Normans, and again in 1174 in an Early English Gothic style. A tour is recommended, as the cathedral is a treasure trove of associated stories. The one that has drawn pilgrims for centuries, and later tourists, was the brutal martyrdom of Archbishop Thomas à Becket. Stay for the beautiful choral singing just before dusk.

The **Roman Museum** (☎ 785575; www.canter bury-museums.co.uk; Butchery Lane; adult/concession/ family £2.80/1.75/7.20; ☀ 10am-4pm Mon-Sat, 1.30-4pm Sun) is built underground around the remains of a Roman townhouse. You can visit the reconstructed Roman marketplace, smell the odours of a Roman kitchen, handle artefacts and see the extensive remains of a mosaic floor.

Most fun in the **Museum of Canterbury** (☎ 475202; www.canterbury-museums.co.uk; Stour St; adult/concession/family £3.10/2.10/8.20; ☀ 10.30am-4pm Mon-Sat all year, 1.30-4pm Sun Jun-end Sep) is the medieval discovery gallery, as well as the children's museum featuring characters associated with Canterbury, like Bagpuss and Rupert Bear.

This entertaining introduction to Chaucer's classic story of 14th-century pilgrims, **Canterbury Tales** (☎ 479227; www.canterburytales .org.uk; St Margaret's St; adult/concession/child/family £6.95/5.95/5.25/22.50; ☀ 10.30am-4.30pm), is told with rather jerky hydraulic puppets.

Founded by St Augustine in AD 597, the ruins of **St Augustine's Abbey** (☎ 767345; Longport; adult/concession/child £3.50/2.60/1.80; ☀ 10am-5pm Apr–end Sep, to 3.30pm Wed-Sun Oct–end Mar) offer an audio tour and a museum housing original artefacts.

Sleeping

Kipps (☎ 786121; www.kipps-hostel.com; 40 Nunnery Fields; dm/s/d £13/18.50/32, f £40-60; P ☒ ▯) This clean and friendly hostel south of the centre has a games room, tuck-shop, kitchen, laundry facilities and garden.

Acacia Lodge & Tanglewood (☎ 769955; www .acacialodge.com; 39/40 London Rd; s £30-40, d £42-55; P ☒) Located north of the centre, two 19th-century farm cottages have been converted into one welcoming and cosy B&B.

Tudor House (☎ 765650; 6 Best Lane; s £22-25, d £45-50; P) This lovely B&B in a 450-year-old cottage is great value for its central location. The rooms have a traditional, flowery style and one of the doubles opens onto the garden, which backs onto the Stour River.

Cathedral Gate Hotel (☎ 464381; www.cathgate .co.uk; 36 Burgate; B&B s £46-60, d £68-90, f £110-120, with shared bathroom s £26-35, d £50-60) This hotel has unparalleled views overlooking the cathedral. The staff are very friendly and the rooms are comfortable but the hotel is looking shabby and could do with a makeover.

Falstaff (☎ 462138; www.corushotels.com/the falstaff; 8-10 St Dunstan's St; B&B s/d/ste from £90/100/122; P ☒) Housed in a 600-year old coaching inn, this atmospheric hotel is full of low beams, wonky corridors and old squires. The quintessential English feel follows through to the style of the rooms. There is a pretty courtyard, British restaurant and cosy bar. Rooms have modem points.

Eating

BUDGET

Café St Pierre (☎ 456791; 41 St Peter's St; baguettes £3.50; ☺ 8am-6pm Mon-Sat, 9am-5.30pm Sun) This friendly French café with seating out the back has pastries, baguettes and quiches that come from France every day.

Olive Grove (☎ 764388; 12 Best Lane; mains £5.15-13.95; ☺ noon-10.30pm) For an informal Italian meal this restaurant serves well-priced pizza, pasta and meat dishes. It also has a salad bar and does filled ciabatta for lunch.

There's a **Safeway** supermarket on the St George's Place before New Dover Rd.

MID-RANGE

The Old Weaver's House (☎ 464660; 1 St Peter's St; mains £6.25-13.95; ☺ 11am-10.30pm) Built around 1500, this rustic restaurant serves good, hearty British fare like beef and Guinness pie. There is an outdoor terrace overlooking the Stour River.

Café des Amis du Mexique (☎ 464390; 95 St Dunstan's St; lunch £4.95-7.50, dinner £7.25-12.95; ☺ noon-10.30 Mon-Sat, to 9.30pm Sun) This popular and colourful Mexican restaurant serves fantastic burritos, enchiladas and *fajitas*. In the daytime it's great for kids, and in the evening, with its Latin music and list of tequilas, it's fun for adults.

TOP END

The Goods Shed (☎ 459153; Station Rd; mains £8.50-22; ☺ market 10am-7pm Mon-Sat, restaurant noon-2.30pm, 6-9pm Mon-Sat) Just left of Canterbury West station, this former Victorian warehouse is now home to the local farmers market, and on a raised platform, a restaurant that uses market produce.

Augustine's (☎ 453063; 1 Longport; mains £11.50-16.50; ☺ noon-1.30pm, 6.30-9pm Tue-Sat, noon-1.45pm Sun) This intimate restaurant faces St Augustine's Abbey. Although the pine and salmon décor could do with updating, dishes like rack of lamb with basil compote are sublime.

Drinking & Entertainment

There's not much of a nightlife in Canterbury but there are some lovely pubs. For events information, go to www.canterbury.co.uk and click on the 'What's On?' tab.

Two cosy, traditional pubs are **The Miller's Arms** (☎ 456057; Mill Lane) and **Thomas Becket** (☎ 464384; 21 Best Lane) The former is by the old locks and the latter is in the centre of town. **Bar 11** (☎ 478707; 11 Burgate) and **Ha Ha!** (☎ 379800; 7 St Margaret's St) have minimalist style décor and a cool ambience with a good range of beers, wines and cocktails. **Marlowe Theatre** (☎ 787777; www.marlowetheatre .com; The Friars; ☺ box office 10am-9pm Mon-Sat) puts on a variety of plays, dances and concerts year-round.

Getting There & Away

There are **National Express** coaches leaving every half-hour from London's Victoria station to Canterbury (one way/return £10/16, one hour 50 minutes). **Stagecoach East Kent's** (☎ 0870 243 3711) No 115 bus runs hourly (less frequently on Sunday) from Canterbury to Dover (one way/return £2.90/4.80, 30 minutes).

There are two train stations: Canterbury West, accessible from London's Charing Cross and Waterloo stations; and Canterbury East (for the YHA hostel) accessible from London's Victoria station. In both cases trains run every half-hour (one way/return £17.30/19.60, 90 minutes). There are hourly trains operating between Canterbury East and Dover Priory (one way £4.80, 30 minutes).

DOVER

☎ 01304 / pop 32,600

Dover is England's 'Gateway to Europe' and has two things going for it: the famous white cliffs and its spectacular medieval hill-top castle. The foreshore of Dover is basically an enormous, complicated (though well signposted) and unattractive vehicle ramp for the ferries.

Orientation & Information

Dover runs back from the sea along a valley formed by the Dour River. Ferry departures are from the Eastern Docks (accessible by bus) below the castle. Dover Priory train station is off Folkestone Rd, a short walk to the west of the town centre. The bus station is on Pencester Rd, north of the Market Sq.

In the town centre, **Dover Visitor Centre** (☎ 205108; www.whitecliffscountry.org.uk; Old Town Gaol, Biggin St; ☺ 9am-5.30pm) has an accommodation and ferry-booking service. **Café on**

Route 66 (☎ 206633; Bench St; per hr £3.50; ☺ 9am-9pm), not far from the Market Sq, offers Internet access.

Sights

The main attraction of **Dover Castle** (☎ 211067; www.english-heritage.org.uk; adult/concession/child/family incl tunnels £8.50/6.40/4.30/21.30; ☺ 10am-6pm Apr-Sep, to 4pm Oct-Mar), a well-preserved medieval fortress, is its spectacular views. The excellent 50-minute tour of the **secret wartime tunnels** covers the castle's history during WWII and takes you through the tunnels that burrow beneath the castle.

With great interactive exhibitions, the **Dover Museum & Bronze Age Boat Gallery** (☎ 20 1066; www.dovermuseum.co.uk; Market Sq; adult/concession £2/1.25; ☺ 10am-5.30pm Mon-Sat) covers Dover's history from the prehistoric past to the present day and displays the Bronze Age Boat – the world's oldest boat (3600 years), discovered off the Dover coast in 1992.

Sleeping

Dover Youth Hostel (☎ 202236; dover@yha.org.uk; 306 London Rd; B&B dm adult/under 18 yrs £14.90/11.60; ☐) In a restored Georgian townhouse five minutes' walk from Market Sq, this hostel has a kitchen, café and garden.

East Lee Guest House (☎ 210176; www.eastlee .co.uk; 108 Maison Dieu Rd; s/d from £35/58; ☒) This pretty Victorian townhouse has opulent burgundy and gold furnishings and a friendly atmosphere.

Churchill Hotel (☎ 203633; www.bw-churchillhotel .co.uk; Waterfront; s/d from £64/84; ℗ ☒) Set in a curve of Regency townhouses, the pristine rooms have great sea views and modem points, and there is a lovely terrace.

Eating

Jermain's (☎ 205956; 18 Beaconsfield Rd; mains £4.50; ☺ 11.30am-2pm; ☒) Near the hostel, this restaurant has a range of traditional British lunches like roast beef with all the trimmings, and steak and kidney pie.

Cullin's Yard (☎ 211666; 11 Cambridge Rd; mains £6.50-19.80; ☺ noon-11pm) This rustic bistro specialises in seafood ranging from kippers to lobster. It also serves British dishes like beef and ale casserole. A lively, friendly place.

The Cabin (☎ 206118; 91 High St; mains £9.20-12.90; ☺ 6.30-10pm Tue-Sat) The best restaurant in Dover, this intimate place of seven tables specialises in traditional English and game

dishes and uses locally sourced produce. A total gem.

Getting There & Away

See the Transport section (p256) for details of ferries to mainland Europe.

To Dover, National Express coaches leave hourly from London's Victoria station (one way/return £9.50/£10.50, 2¼ hours). Dover to Canterbury (30 minutes) costs one way/return £2.90/4.80. There's an hourly bus to Brighton but you'll need to change at Hastings (No 710) and Eastbourne (No 712).

Every 30 minutes trains leave from London's Victoria and Charing Cross stations to Dover Priory (one way/return £20.70/23.40, one hour 50 minutes).

Getting Around

The ferry companies run complimentary buses every 20 minutes between the docks and the train station. **Central Taxis** (☎ 240441) and **Heritage** (☎ 204420) have 24-hour services. A one way taxi trip to Folkestone or Deal costs about £11 to £13.

HEVER CASTLE

Idyllic **Hever Castle** (☎ 01732-865224; www.hever castle.co.uk; near Edenbridge, Kent; adult/concession/child/family castle & garden £8.60/7.40/4.50/22.40, garden only £7/6/4.60/18.60; ☺ garden 11-dusk, castle noon-dusk Mar–late Nov) was the childhood home of Anne Boleyn, mistress to Henry VIII and then his doomed queen. Restored by the Astor family, it has a 'Tudor' village, double moat with a water maze and one of the finest Italian gardens in Britain.

Hourly trains from London's Victoria station (one way/return £7/7.90, 50 minutes, change at Oxted) go to the nearest train station, Hever, which is one mile from the castle itself.

KNOLE HOUSE

In a country that is full of extraordinary country houses, **Knole House** (☎ 01732-450608; www.nationaltrust.org.uk/places/knole; Sevenoaks, Kent; adult/child/family £6/3/15; ☺ 11am-3.30pm Wed-Sun Apr-Oct), with its surrounding deer park, is outstanding. It seems as if nothing substantial has changed since the early 17th century. Virginia Woolf based the novel *Orlando* on the history of the house and family.

Take a twice-hourly train from London's Charing Cross to Sevenoaks (one way/return

£6.90/7, 35 minutes), Knole House is 1½ miles to the south of Sevenoaks.

LEEDS CASTLE

One of the world's most famous castles, **Leeds Castle** (☎ 01622-765400; www.leeds-castle.com; near Maidstone, Kent; adult/concession/child/family castle & gardens £12.50/11/9/39, gardens only £10/8.50/6.50/33; ☾ 10am-5pm Apr-Oct, to 3pm Nov-Mar) stands on two small islands in a lake, and is surrounded by woodlands, an aviary, and a hedge maze that has a grotto of mythical beasts in the centre. Inside is filled with medieval furnishings, and there's a strange collection of antique dog collars.

National Express (adult/child Monday to Friday £16/11, Saturday, Sunday, and bank holidays £18.50/13, 90 minutes) does a combined admission and travel ticket that leaves from Victoria coach station (it must be pre-booked). The coach leaves at 9am and returns at 3.05pm.

South Eastern trains also has a combined ticket service that includes the train from London Victoria to Bearsted station, a bus service and castle admission (adult/child £22.50/10.80, hourly 9.18am to 12.18pm, returns hourly 2pm to 5pm; 70 minutes).

BRIGHTON & HOVE

☎ 01273 / pop 250,000

Brighton is a tantalising mix of the country's most popular seaside resort and one of its most innovative cities. Once a fishing village called Brighthelmstone and now a city named Brighton & Hove, its seven-mile coastline and liberal persuasion has attracted an eclectic mix to its pebbly shores.

A favourite playground of Londoners since the 1750s, when they came to 'take the waters', things really got going when the Prince Regent and his entourage came to frolic in his fantastical abode, the Pavilion. Since the 1960s, Brighton has had a reputation as the club and party capital of the south, later enshrined in the cult movie *Quadrophenia*.

Nowadays, you'll find bohemians into environmental living and artistic pursuits, a large student population, a vivacious gay community and urban hipsters escaping the rat race. All have put their stamp throughout the city with its hedonistic nightlife, vibrant art scene, unusual shopping, and countless restaurants and cafés.

Orientation

To the west of Old Steine (a major road) is The Lanes; cross North St to come to North Laine (see Sights following). Hove lies further to the west. East of the Old Steine is Kemp Town, and further east is the Marina. Brighton train station is a 15-minute walk north of the beach. The bus station is in Poole Valley, south of the Lanes.

Information

The **Visitor Information Centre** (☎ 0906 7112255, per min 50p; www.visitbrighton.com; 10 Bartholomew Sq; ☾ 9.30am-5pm) has maps and free listings magazines. **Curve Internet** (☎ 603031; 45 Gardner St; per hr £1.50; ☾ 10am-10pm Mon-Sat, 11am-8.30pm Sun) is above Curve brasserie. Brighton & Hove is a great place to study English with a choice of 32 schools and a good student support network. Visit www.visitbrighton .com and click on 'Learning English' for more details.

Sights

The original fishing village of Brighton is known as **The Lanes**, and its maze of 17th-century narrow alleyways are crammed with a menagerie of shops, restaurants and bars. In the **North Laine** area, just above The Lanes, the atmosphere is more hip and bohemian with alternative therapy centres, cooperative cafés, vintage clothes shops and designer boutiques.

Built between 1815 and 1822 for the Prince Regent (later George IV), the **Royal Pavilion** (☎ 290900; www.royalpavilion.org.uk; adult/concession/child £5.95/4.20/3.50, guided tours £1.25; ☾ 9.30am-5pm Apr-Sep, 10am-4.30pm Oct-Mar, guided tours 11.30am & 2.30pm) palace is a fantasy of Asian exoticism mixed with English eccentricity. Not to be missed.

Brighton Museum & Art Gallery (☎ 290900; Royal Pavilion gardens; www.brighton.virtualmuseum.info; admission free; ☾ 10am-7pm Tue, to 5pm Wed-Sat, 2-5pm Sun) has fascinating interactive displays and exhibitions devoted to subjects like fashion and style, 20th-century art and design, and Brighton's history.

Brighton's most distinctive landmark is the **Brighton Pier** (☎ 609361; Madeira Drive; www .brightonpier.co.uk; admission free; ☾ 9-2am), the epitome of the British seaside. Fast food, flashing lights, amusement arcades and two new white-knuckle rides – it's tacky but lots of fun.

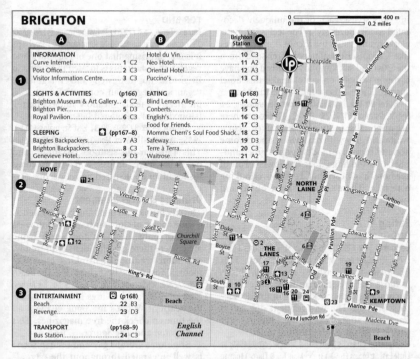

BRIGHTON

INFORMATION	
Curve Internet	1 C2
Post Office	2 C3
Visitor Information Centre	3 C3

SIGHTS & ACTIVITIES	(p166)
Brighton Museum & Art Gallery..	4 C2
Brighton Pier	5 D3
Royal Pavilion	6 C3

SLEEPING	(pp167–8)
Baggies Backpackers	7 A3
Brighton Backpackers	8 C3
Genevieve Hotel	9 D3

Hotel du Vin	10 C3
Neo Hotel	11 A2
Oriental Hotel	12 A3
Puccino's	13 C3

EATING	(p168)
Blind Lemon Alley	14 C2
Conberts	15 C1
English's	16 C3
Food for Friends	17 C3
Momma Cherri's Soul Food Shack..	18 C3
Safeway	19 D3
Terre à Terra	20 C3
Waitrose	21 A2

ENTERTAINMENT	(p168)
Beach	22 B3
Revenge	23 D3

TRANSPORT	(pp168–9)
Bus Station	24 C3

Festivals

For the first three weeks in May, Brighton hosts the **Brighton Festival** (☎ 292961; www .brighton-festival.org.uk), the largest arts festival outside Edinburgh. Much is free and in public spaces.

Every August thousands of revellers dress to the nines and celebrate their sexual orientation in **Brighton Pride** (☎ 775939; www .brightonpride.org), a flamboyant street festival.

Sleeping
BUDGET
Baggies Backpackers (☎ 733740; 33 Oriental Place; dm/d £12/30, key deposit £5; ✕) By far the best hostel in Brighton, it has a laid-back and cosy feel. The owner encourages a communal spirit and keeps the dorms spick and span.

Brighton Backpackers (☎ 777717; www.bright onbackpackers.com; 75-76 Middle St; dm/dm seafront annexe/d £11/12/30) Although this hostel has a cramped feel with its small dorms and narrow stairways, the funky murals painted by travellers and its good location almost make up for it.

MID-RANGE
Genevieve Hotel (☎ 681653; www.genevievehotel .co.uk; 18 Madeira Place; s £45, d £54-95; P ✕) Of the cluster of B&Bs in this area, this cosy, pristine establishment with a very friendly proprietor is the best. The large, airy rooms are great value and some have four-poster beds and sea or pier views.

Puccino's (☎ 204656; 1 Bartholomewmews; per person £30; ✕) Above this café the owner runs two B&B doubles. The rooms are cosy with wooden floors, pine furniture and ethnic rugs, as well as fold up single futons.

Oriental Hotel (☎ 205050; www.orientalhotel.co.uk; 9 Oriental Place; B&B s with shared bathroom Sun-Thu £30, Fri & Sat £35-40, d Sun-Thu £60-85, Fri & Sat £80-105; ☐) A great mix of Brighton bohemia and cool design, this hotel is run by the welcoming owners and their friends. It has chic minimalist style rooms punctuated with Asian treasures gathered on their travels.

TOP END
Neo Hotel (☎ 711104; www.neohotel.com; 19 Oriental Place; B&B s/d £50/125, with shared bathroom £40/85; P ☐) Owned and refurbished by a former

BRITAIN

interiors stylist, each of the uniquely decorated rooms oozes style. The feel is intimate, elegant, and ultra ultra cool. Luxe touches like Chinoiserie wallpapers (reissued from the '30s) and silk kimonos (handy if you have a room without en suite) make this hotel special. There's also a funky cocktail bar.

Hotel du Vin (☎ 718588; www.hotelduvin.com; 2-6 Ship St; d/ste from £119/225; P X) The rooms here are minimalist in style but luxe in content – white and grey with dark wood and chrome accents, they have modem points, freestanding baths and huge walk-in showers. Part of the hotel has 'beach hut' rooms overlooking a terrace. There's also a smart bistro and two bars.

Eating
BUDGET
Conberts (☎ 625222; 16 Sydney St; sandwiches £1.95-3.75; ☽ 10am-6pm Mon-Sat, noon-4pm Sun) This bijou two-level teashop serves such things as loose-leaf teas in beautiful vintage china, cucumber sandwiches and handmade Victoria sponge. The tiny resident dog called Pascale is adored, as is the Queen – her shrine is in the golden throne toilet.

Momma Cherri's Soul Food Shack (☎ 774545; 11 Little East St; mains £6.50-13; ☽ Mon-Tue & Thu 6-11pm, to midnight Fri, 11am-midnight Sat, 10.30am-8pm Sun) With a soundtrack of funky soul, and a décor festooned with colour, this small American soul food restaurant is about eating well and having fun. Pile-high dishes like the New Orleans speciality 'Jambalaya' (a spicy rice dish) are hugely popular.

For self-catering Brighton & Hove has a **Safeway** (St James's St) and **Waitrose** (Western Rd).

MID-RANGE
Food for Friends (☎ 202310; 17/18 Prince Albert St, The Lanes; mains £7.95-9.95; ☽ 11.30am-9.45pm Mon-Fri, to 10.15pm Sat & Sun) This light and airy café-style vegetarian restaurant serves delicious British, Mediterranean, Mexican and Indian dishes.

Blind Lemon Alley (☎ 205151; 41 Middle St; mains £8-14, 2-course lunch/3-course dinner £5.95/10.95; ☽ 12.30am-11pm) Tuck into American favourites such as burgers, steaks and ribs in this intimate restaurant with wooden benches, lots of cushions and dimmed lighting. The staff are friendly, the atmosphere is laid back and there is live blues and jazz on Sunday nights.

TOP END
Terre à Terre (☎ 729051; 71 East St; mains £11.50-12.50; ☽ noon-10.30pm Tue-Sun, 6-10.30pm Mon; X) Perhaps it is not surprising that one of England's best vegetarian restaurants is located in bohemian Brighton. Sophisticated and imaginative vegan and vegetarian concoctions, such as the hearty 'meady meadow mulled barrel' (stuffed leeks) are offered here.

English's (☎ 327980; 29-31 East St; mains £14.95-19.95; ☽ noon-10.15pm Mon-Sat, 12.30-9.30pm Sun) This 150-year-old seafood restaurant and oyster bar serves unfussy and well-executed dishes in an opulent red velvet décor.

Drinking & Entertainment
The city brims with pubs and bars, as well as a wide choice of clubs with world renowned DJs. For pubs, head for the North Laine area where there is a high density of trendy, and more traditional, drinking establishments. Most of the best clubs, like **The Beach** (☎ 722272; www.cside.co.uk; 171-181 Kings Rd Arches; admission £5-10), are in Kings Road Arches on the seafront. What's in vogue changes all the time so check the free magazines, *This Is Brighton* and *The Source*.

Brighton's vibrant gay and lesbian scene is well integrated throughout the city, although a concentration of bars and clubs are in Kemp Town (east of the Old Steine). A classic club is **Revenge** (☎ 606064; www .revenge.co.uk; 32-43 Old Steine; £3-9). To find out what's hot and what's not pick up the free *G Scene* and *3Sixty* magazines.

Getting There & Away
If you book online, www.megabus.com offers one-way/return tickets from London to Brighton for £1.50/3; there are two departures daily. National Express coaches leave hourly from London Victoria to Brighton (one way/return £9/15, two hours). **Stagecoach East Kent** (☎ 0870 243 3711) bus No 712 runs to Eastbourne, which connects with the No 710 to Hastings and the No 711 to Dover.

The **National Express Airport** (☎ 0870 575 7747) runs buses to all London airports: Stansted (one way/return £26/31, three hours 50 minutes), Luton (£16/27, four hours), Heathrow (£19.50/24.50, two hours) and Gatwick (£6/9, 45 minutes).

The quickest way to Brighton is by the twice-hourly train service from London's Victoria station (one way/return £15.90/21,

50 minutes). There are two trains hourly from Brighton to Portsmouth (one way/return £12.80/17.60, 90 minutes), and frequent services to Canterbury and Dover.

PORTSMOUTH
☎ 023 92 / pop 190,000

Portsmouth is the traditional home of the Royal Navy, whose ships once exported the empire to far-flung corners of the world. Portsmouth is still a busy naval base and unfortunately, it's not a particularly attractive city, largely due to WWII bombing. The main attractions are the historic ships and museums of the Naval Heritage Area.

Orientation & Information

The train and bus stations and ferry terminal for Isle of Wight are a stone's throw from the Heritage Dockyard and the **Visitor Information Centre** (☎ 826722; www.visitportsmouth .co.uk; The Hard; ⏰ 9.30am-5.15pm Oct-end Mar), which provides an accommodation service. The shopping, eating and entertainment complex of Gunwharf Quays is just south of the Historic Dockyard. Further south is the atmospheric Old Portsmouth. Southsea, where the beaches are, as well as accommodation, restaurants and bars, is about 2 miles south of Portsmouth Harbour.

Free Internet access is available at the **Library** (☎ 819311; Civic Offices, Guildhall Sq; ⏰ 9.30am-7pm Mon-Fri, to 5pm Sat, 12.30-4pm Sun). It's necessary to pre-book in person.

Sights

Portsmouth's centrepiece is the **Historic Dockyard**, which has four main attractions: the HMS *Victory*, HMS *Warrior*, *Mary Rose*, and the Royal Navy Museum. For all Historic Dockyard attractions there is one inclusive ticket (☎ 861512; www.historicdockyard.co.uk; adult/child/family £14.85/11.90/47.55; ⏰ 10am-4.30pm). Exploring **HMS Victory**, Lord Nelson's flagship at the Battle of Trafalgar, is about as close as you can get to time travel. **HMS Warrior** was the first all-iron warship but doesn't have the same magic as the *Victory*. After 437 years underwater, the remains of Henry VIII's favourite ship, the **Mary Rose** can be seen. Its time-capsule contents are displayed in the **Mary Rose Museum**. The **Royal Navy Museum** covers the Navy's history and the nearby **Action Stations!** is a showcase for the modern navy with rescue mission films and interactive games.

The new **Spinnaker Tower** (www.portsmouthand .co.uk/tower) at Gunwharf Quays can be scaled with a high-speed internal lift or a slower glass one for fantastic sea views.

Sleeping

Southsea Backpackers Lodge (☎ 832495; www.ports mouthbackpackers.co.uk; 4 Florence Rd, Southsea; dm £10, d £26-29; ⊠ 🖳) This hostel is comfortable and friendly with a satellite TV lounge and laundry facilities.

Sailmaker's Loft (☎ 823045; 5 Bath Sq; r per person £25; ⊠ 🖳) This recently renovated B&B is run by a retired merchant seaman who can tell you a lot about Portsmouth. There are great views across the harbour.

Queen's Hotel (☎ 822466; www.queenshotel-south sea.co.uk; Clarence Parade, Southsea; s/d £45/89, d/ste with sea view £99/130; P ⊠ 🖳) A large, Edwardian-style hotel with old-world charm. Some rooms have balconies and there are modem points and great sea views.

Eating

Twigs (☎ 828316; 39 High St; sandwiches £1.50-3.75; ⏰ 10am-5pm) With its wooden tables and large windows overlooking a pretty church, this is a pleasant place to have a sandwich or coffee stop.

Sur la Mer (☎ 876678; 69 Palmerston Rd; mains £10-15, 2-course menu £6.50, 3-courses £7.50-15; ⏰ noon-3pm, 6.30-10pm Mon-Sat) Popular with locals, this is an intimate but informal French restaurant.

Still & West (☎ 821567; 2 Bath Sq; mains £8-18; ⏰ noon-2.30pm, 6-9pm) This pub and (mainly) fish restaurant overlooks part of Portsmouth harbour. Perch on the terrace for an outdoor drink or settle in the restaurant to take your pick from the fresh fish counter.

Getting There & Away
BOAT

A passenger ferry operated by **Wightlink** (☎ 0870 582 7744; www.wightlink.co.uk) goes from The Hard to Ryde pier (£9.80 day return, 15 minutes). It also runs a car-and-passenger ferry to Fishbourne every half-hour (£9.30 day return, car £44.40 day return, 35 minutes). **Hovertravel** (☎ 01983-811000; www.hover travel.co.uk) runs a passenger Hovercraft from Southsea to Ryde (£9.80 day return, 10 minutes).

See p256 for details of ferries to France and Spain. The Continental Ferryport is north of Flagship Portsmouth.

BRITAIN

BUS

If you book online, www.megabus.com offers one-way/return tickets to Portsmouth for £1.50/3, with two departures daily. National Express has an hourly bus service from London Victoria to Portsmouth (one way/return £12/17, 2½ hours). **Stagecoach Coastline** (☎ 0845-1210170) bus No 700 runs between Brighton and Portsmouth every 30 minutes (one way/return £3.10/6, 3½ hours) and bus No 69 runs to/from Winchester hourly from Monday to Saturday.

TRAIN

There are over 40 trains a day from London's Victoria and Waterloo stations (one way/return £21/25.70, two hours). Two trains hourly go to/from Brighton (one way/return 12.80/17.60, 90 minutes) and Winchester (one way/return £7.30/7.60, 55 minutes).

WINCHESTER

☎ 01962 / pop 38,000

Winchester is a beautiful cathedral city on the Itchen River, interspersed with water meadows. It has played an important role in the history of England, being both the capital of Saxon England and the seat of the powerful Bishops of Winchester from AD 670. Much of the present-day city dates from the 18th century, with its rich history in evidence throughout, none more so than its main attraction, the stunning cathedral.

Orientation & Information

The city centre is compact and easily negotiated on foot. The train station is a 10-minute walk to the west of the centre, and the bus and coach station is on Broadway, directly opposite the Guildhall and **Visitor Information Centre** (☎ 840500; www.visitwinchester.co.uk; Guildhall, Broadway; ☒ 9.30am-5.30pm Mon-Sat, 11am-4pm Sun), which has regular guided walking tours throughout the year (adult/child £3/free, 90 minutes). **The Byte** (☎ 863235; 10 Parchment St; per hr £3.50; ☒ 9am-5pm Mon-Fri) has Internet access.

Sights

One of the most beautiful cathedrals in the country, **Winchester Cathedral** (☎ 853224; www.winchester-cathedral.org.uk; The Close; adult/concession/child £3.50/3/50p; ☒ 8.30am-5.30pm) is a mixture of Norman, Early English and Gothic Perpendicular styles. There are fascinating 20th-century paintings and sculptures dotted

around the place. Jane Austen's grave is in the northern aisle. There are one-hour **free tours** (☒ hourly 10am-3pm Mon-Sat).

Winchester College (☎ 621209; www.winchester college.org; College St; tours adult/concession £3.50/3; ☒ 10.45am, noon, 2.15pm & 3.30pm), founded in 1382, was the first of Britain's exclusive public schools. Explore the college by guided tours that concentrate on its medieval heart.

Begun by William the Conquer, Winchester Castle was where Sir Walter Raleigh was tried in 1603. The only part of the castle that Oliver Cromwell did not destroy was the **Great Hall** (☎ 846476; www.hants.gov .uk/discover/places/great-hall.html; Castle Ave; admission free; ☒ 10am-5pm), which houses **King Arthur's Round Table**, now known to be a fake at 'only' 600 years of age.

Sleeping & Eating

Youth Hostel (☎ 0870 770 6092; winchester@yha.org .uk; 1 Water Lane; dm adults/under 18 yrs £10.60/7.20) Set in a beautiful 18th-century water mill that spans the Itchen River, this hostel is in the heart of town.

Wykeham Arms (☎ 853834; 75 Kingsgate St; s/ste £55/120, d £90-98; mains £11-16; ☒ noon-2.30pm, 6.30-9pm Mon-Sat) An inn since the mid-18th century, this hotel and gastropub has oodles of character and some rooms overlooking the college. The popular restaurant serves Mediterranean food.

Hotel du Vin & Bistro (☎ 841414; www.hotel duvin.com; Southgate St; d/ste from £109/185; mains £14-16; ☒ bistro 12.30-2pm & 7-10pm; ☒) Set in a Georgian townhouse, this smart boutique hotel has stylish rooms with luxe touches like monsoon showers and Egyptian linen, as well as modem points. The elegant bistro serves English and French cuisine.

Loch Fyne (☎ 872930; www.lochfyne.com; 18 Jewry St; mains £9-35; ☒ 10am-10.30pm; ☒) This seafood restaurant's specialities are oysters fresh from Scotland and sublime shellfish platters. There is a pretty courtyard for use in the summer.

The Chesil Rectory (☎ 851555; 1 Chesil St; 4-course menu £45; ☒ noon-2pm Sat, 7-10pm Tue-Sat) This Michelin-starred restaurant is housed in the city's oldest secular building (1450) and serves delectable Modern European dishes.

Getting There & Away

National Express coaches go directly to Winchester every two hours from London's

Victoria station (one way/return £11.50/16, two hours). **Stagecoach Hampshire Bus** (☎ 0845 121 0180) has a good network of services linking Salisbury, Southampton, Portsmouth and Brighton.

Trains depart twice hourly from London's Waterloo station (one way/return £19.90/23.30, 1¼ hours), Southampton (one way £4, 30 minutes) and Portsmouth (one way £7.30, 55 minutes).

CHANNEL ISLANDS

Across the Channel from Dorset and just off the coast of France lie the small islands of Jersey, Guernsey, Alderney, Sark and Herm. Although there are pleasant beaches, good walks and cycle rides on some islands, and there's the famous **Jersey Zoo** (☎ 01534-860000; www.durrell.org; Les Augres Manor, Trinity; ⏰ 9.30am-5pm) started by Gerald Durrell, compared to mainland Britain or the Scottish islands there's really not a lot to see and do. Jersey is the biggest and busiest of the islands, Alderney the most peaceful. For more information on the numerous B&Bs, contact **Jersey Tourism** (☎ 01534-500777; www.jersey.com; Liberation Sq, St Helier; ⏰ 8.30am-6pm) and, for all the other islands, **Guernsey Tourism** (☎ 01481-723552; www .guernseytouristboard.com; St Peter Port; ⏰ 9am-4pm).

Getting There & Away

There are daily flights to the Channel Islands from a few UK airports on several airlines including **British European** (☎ 0870 567 6676; www.flybe.com) and **Aurigny Air Services** (☎ 01481-822886; www.aurigny.com). It costs approximately £140 for a return ticket.

Condor (☎ 01305-761551; www.condorferries.co.uk) runs passenger ferries and high-speed catamarans from Portsmouth, Weymouth and Poole to the Channel Islands.

SOUTHWEST ENGLAND

The Southwest of England overflows with some of the most beautiful countryside in all of Europe. Cornwall's sweeping coastal landscapes – dotted with thatched-roof cottages, ancient architecture, sheep and surfers – will inspire awe. Until the 18th century there were still Cornish speakers in Cornwall, and the people retain an independent spirit, often differentiating themselves from their eastern neighbour, that country, England.

From Bristol to Dorset and Salisbury to Land's End, there is nary an ugly spot in the region. In the east, the story of English civilisation is signposted by some of its greatest monuments: the Stone Age left Stonehenge and spellbinding Avebury; hikers in Dartmoor can check out Iron Age hill forts; between them, the Romans and the Georgians created Bath; the legendary King Arthur is said to be buried at Glastonbury; and the Middle Ages left the great cathedrals at Exeter, Salisbury and Wells.

Exeter is an immensely liveable university town with a great city scene. Watch out as Bristol becomes one of the up-and-coming great English cities. The sites and 'meanderability' of Bath make it one of the most beloved tourist destinations in England. Dorset and the Moors allow ample space for hiking and exploring in relative peace.

National Parks

The Southwest of England is home to Dartmoor (p175) and Exmoor (p178). Both areas offer spectacular and often isolated scenery and plenty of outdoor activities. Dartmoor has a more barren, open wilderness, and Exmoor covers some of the most beautiful countryside in England – the coastal stretch from Ilfracombe to Minehead is particularly spectacular.

Activities

HIKING

The Southwest Coast Path is Britain's longest national trail, following the coastline round the peninsula for 630 miles (1014km) from Poole Harbour near Bournemouth to Minehead in Somerset, giving spectacular access to the best and most untouched sections of Cornwall and Dorset. While you'll often have the stunning ocean scenery and fields of wildflowers to yourself (especially in the shoulder season), B&Bs or hostels are never more than half a day's journey from one another. See www.swcp.org.uk for details.

Many other well-known walking areas offer short strolls from a car park or week-long treks. The 40-mile Ridgeway near Avebury passes through ancient fortifications and religious monuments. Dartmoor offers dozens of marked trails sprinkled with prehistoric remains, burial grounds (known as cairns), rocky tors (high hills), medieval stone crosses and lush boglands.

SURFING

The capital of British surfing is Newquay on the west Cornish coast, and it's complete with surf shops, bleached hair and Kombi vans. The surfable coast runs from Porthleven (near Helston) in Cornwall, west around Land's End and north to Ilfracombe in Devon. The most famous reef breaks are at Porthleven, Lynmouth (populated almost exclusively by locals) and Millbrook; although good, they are inconsistent.

CYCLING

Bikes can be hired in most major regional centres, and the infrequent bus connections make cycling even more sensible than usual. There's no shortage of hills, but the mild weather and quiet back roads make this excellent cycling country.

Getting There & Around

Although train and coach services make travelling around the Southwest very accessible by public transport during summer, getting around the more remote spots of Cornwall, Devon and the Moors can be nigh on impossible even during peak season. Call **Traveline** (☎ 0870 6082608) to plan ahead.

If you're considering renting a car, you might want to do so in some of the more remote spots such as Exmoor or Dartmoor, or to experience the coast around Tintagel and Land's End.

For Glastonbury, Tintagel, Wells, Dartmoor, Exmoor, Stonehenge and Avebury, you'll need to catch coaches or local buses. Contact the national **Traveline** (☎ 0870 6082608, per min 60p) for information on all regional bus and coach information.

Trains congregate in Bristol, Bath, Salisbury and Exeter, and also reach Weymouth, Bournemouth, Plymouth, St Ives, Newquay and Penzance. Several regional rail passes are available, including the Freedom of the Southwest Rover (£61 for eight days of travel in 15 consecutive days) which covers Salisbury, Bath, Bristol, Cornwall and Weymouth. Phone ☎ 0845 7484950 for rail information.

SALISBURY

☎ 01722 / pop 40,000

Salisbury is justly famous for its cathedral and its close, but its appeal also lies in the fact that it is still a bustling market town. Markets have been held in the town centre every Tuesday and Saturday since 1361, and the jumble of stalls still draws a large, cheerful crowd.

The town's architecture is a blend of every style since the Middle Ages, including some beautiful, half-timbered black-and-white buildings. It's a good base for visiting the Wiltshire Downs, Stonehenge and Avebury. Portsmouth and Winchester are also easy day trips if you're travelling by rail.

Orientation & Information

The town centre is a 10-minute walk from the train station – walk down the hill onto Fisherton St, directly into town. The bus station is just northeast of the TIC, along not-so Endless St.

The **TIC** (☎ 334956; www.visitsalisburyuk.com; Fish Row) is behind the impressive 18th-century Guildhall, on the southeastern corner of Market Sq.

Sights

Beautiful **St Mary's Cathedral** (suggested donation £3.80) is built in a uniform style known as Early English (or Early Pointed). This period is characterised by the first pointed arches and flying buttresses, and has a rather austere feel. The cathedral owes its uniformity to the speed with which it was built. Between 1220 and 1258, over 70,000 tons of stone were piled up. The spire, at 123m, is the highest in Britain.

The adjacent **chapter house** is one of the most perfect achievements of Gothic architecture. There is plenty more to see in the **cathedral close**, including two houses that have been restored and two museums.

Out of town but well worth the trek is **Old Sarum** (☎ 335398; adult/concession/child £2.80/ 2.10/1.40; ⏰ 10am-5pm Apr-Jun & Sep, to 4pm Oct & Mar; Ⓟ), the site of the original Salisbury Cathedral, with vestiges left of prehistoric settlements and the Norman cathedral. It's easy to get to by bus: take Nos 3, 5, 6, 8, 9 or almost anything that heads to Amesbury.

Sleeping & Eating

Salisbury Youth Hostel (☎ 327572; Milford Hill; salisbury@yha.org.uk; dm adult/under 18 yrs £14.90/11.60, d £33.80; Ⓟ ✗ 💻) An attractive old building among grassy surroundings, a five-minute walk from the city centre.

Griffin Cottage (☎ 328259; www.smoothhound .co.uk/hotels/griffinc.html; 10 St Edmunds Church St; d £45) is a central and peaceful B&B where breakfast can cater to those on special diets.

Red Lion Hotel (☎ 323334; Milford St; www.the -redlion.co.uk; s/d £94/122; **P**) England's oldest purpose-built hotel dates back to the 13th century and is decorated with almost museum-quality furnishings. The enjoyable hotel also has a restaurant that is extremely popular with locals.

Fisherton St, running from the centre to the train station, has Chinese, Thai, Indian and other restaurants. For outdoor dining from April to October, head to **The Market Inn** (☎ 327923; Butcher Row; mains £2-6), a casual pub that serves light meals. Dine olde worlde at the **Haunch of Venison** (☎ 322024; 1-5 Minster St; bar menu from £2.50, mains £8; ☻ noon-2.30pm, 6-9.30pm, shorter hrs in winter), amid cask ales, oak beams and a pewter bar.

Getting There & Away

National Express has three buses a day from London via Heathrow to Salisbury (£12, three hours).

Try **Wilts & Dorset** (☎ 336855; www.wdbus.co.uk) for bus information through the region. Its Explorer ticket (adult/child £6/3) is great value within the area. There are daily buses to Avebury and Stonehenge. If you're going through to Bristol or Bath, via Somerset (Wells, Glastonbury) or Gloucestershire (Cotswolds), get the First Bus Day Explorer ticket (£6). Wilts & Dorset run an hourly bus No X4 to Bath (£4, 2¼ hours).

Salisbury is linked by rail to London Waterloo station (£4.40, 1½ hours, at least every hour), Portsmouth (£11.60, 1¾ hours, hourly), Bath (£10.40, 50 minutes, at least hourly) and Exeter (£21.70, 1¾ hours, 11 per day).

Getting Around

Local buses are reasonably well organised and link Salisbury with Stonehenge (£6 return); phone ☎ 336855 for details. Bikes can be hired from **Hayball Cycle Centre** (☎ 411378; The Black Horse, Winchester St; £10 per day).

STONEHENGE

Stonehenge is the most famous prehistoric site in Europe – a ring of enormous stones (some of which were brought from the mystical Preseli mountains in Wales), built in stages beginning 5000 years ago. Although Stonehenge is one of the most visited sites

in Britain, be emotionally prepared; while it's historically fascinating, it's a bit visually underwhelming, as hordes of tourists crowd around a roped-off corridor, shuffling out through the gift shop and the 'Stonehenge Kitchen'. Avebury, 18 miles (29km) north, is much more impressive in scale and recommended for those who would like to commune with the ley lines in relative peace.

Two miles west of Amesbury at the junction of the A303 and A344/A360, and 9 miles from Salisbury (the nearest station) is **Stonehenge** (☎ 01980 624715; adult/concession/child/ under 6 yrs £5.20/3.90/2.60/free). Some feel that it's unnecessary to pay the entry fee, because you can get a good view from the road. Tour companies visit Stonehenge from as far off as London or Bath, but the easiest way to get there using public transport is from Salisbury (bus No 3, £6 return, every 15 minutes, guided double-decker buses in summer) or, better yet, buy an Explorer ticket in Salisbury (£6) and visit Avebury as well.

AVEBURY
☎ 01672 / pop 250

Avebury (between Calne and Marlborough, just off the A4) stands at the hub of a prehistoric complex of ceremonial sites, ancient avenues and burial chambers dating from 3500 BC. In scale the remains are more impressive than Stonehenge, and it's quite possible to escape crowds if you visit outside summer weekends.

In addition to an enormous stone circle, there's Silbury Hill (the largest constructed mound in Europe), West Kennet Long Barrow (a burial chamber) and a pretty village with an ancient church.

The **Avebury TIC** (☎ 01380 729408; Green St; alltic@kennet.gov.uk; ☻ 9am-5pm Wed-Sun) can help with accommodation. Within the circle itself is **Manor Farm** (☎ 539294; s/d £50/70) or nearby, **The Red Lion** (☎ 539266; redlion.avebury@laurel.net; d £80), an atmospheric country pub.

Avebury is most easily reached from Salisbury (Wilts & Dorset bus No 5, £4, 1½ hours, at least hourly) or by bus Nos 5, 6 or 49 from Swindon.

DORSET

The greater part of Dorset is designated as an area of outstanding natural beauty but, with the exceptions of Poole and Weymouth, it avoids inundation by tourists.

The coast varies from sandy beaches to shingle banks and towering cliffs. Lyme Regis is a particularly attractive spot, made famous as the setting for John Fowles' book *The French Lieutenant's Woman,* and the subsequent film.

For those who've read Thomas Hardy, however, Dorset is inextricably linked with his novels. You can visit his birthplace at Higher Bockhampton, or Dorchester (Casterbridge), the unspoilt market town where he lived. Maiden Castle, the largest Iron Age fort in England, is nearby.

There is no YHA hostel in Dorchester or Weymouth but there are hostels in Swanage, Lulworth Cove, Portland and Litton Cheney, all convenient for walkers on the Dorset Coast Path. Dorchester and Lyme Regis have some B&Bs while Weymouth is positively packed with them.

There are hourly trains from London's Waterloo station to Dorchester (£35, 2½ hours, 16 direct per day) and from Dorchester to Weymouth (£2.70, 10 minutes, at least hourly), Bath (£10.50, 1¾ hours, eight per day) and Bristol (£11.40, 2¼ hours, eight per day).

There are also buses on these routes but, although cheaper, they tend to be prohibitively slower.

Getting Around

There are regular buses between Dorchester and Weymouth, Salisbury, Bournemouth and Bridport. Contact **Traveline** (☎ 0870 6082608) for more information.

EXETER

☎ 01392 / pop 102,000

Exeter is the heart of the West Country with a lively university scene, stunning cathedral, eminently walkable centre and a thriving nightlife. It's also a good starting point for Dartmoor and Cornwall.

Orientation & Information

There are two train stations, but most intercity trains use St David's, which is a 20-minute walk west of the city centre, and Central station. From St David's, cross the station forecourt and Bonhay Rd, climb some steps to St David's Hill and then turn right up the hill for the centre, 0.75 miles to High St.

The **TIC** (☎ 265700; www.exeter.gov.uk/visiting; Civic Centre, Paris St; ⊙ 9am-5pm Mon-Sat year-round &

Sun in summer) is just across the road from the bus station, a short walk northeast of the cathedral. The website is extremely helpful for pre-planning. Internet access is available at the **central library** (Castle St; 30min free).

Sights

The **cathedral** is one of the most attractive in England, with two huge Norman towers surviving from the 11th century. From AD 50, when the city was established by the Romans, until the 19th century, Exeter was a very important port, and the waterfront (including a large boat museum) is gradually being restored.

Exeter has an incredible collection of **walking tours**, many free. Check at the TIC.

Sleeping

Exeter YHA (☎ 0870 7705826; exeter@yha.org.uk; 47 Countess Wear Rd; dm/d £13.40/30.80; ⊙ closed Christmas; ▯ ℗ ✕) Welcoming and with knowledgeable staff, the comfortable hostel is 2.5 miles southeast of the city towards Topsham. From High St, catch minibus K or T (10 minutes) and ask for the Countess Wear post office. Camp sites available.

Exeter Globe Backpackers (☎ 215521; www.exeter backpackers.co.uk; 71 Holloway St; dm/d £12/30; ▯) In an 18th-century Georgian building, this one has fabulously hot showers.

There are several comparable B&Bs on St David's Hill, including No 75 **Telstar** (☎ 272466; www.telstar-hotel.co.uk; s/d £26/45; ℗ ✕), and No 81 **Kellsmoor** (☎ 211128; kellsmoor@exeter81.fsnet .co.uk; d £44-50). There's another batch of option on Blackall Rd, including **Raffles** (☎ 270200; raffleshtl@btinternet.com; 11 Blackall Rd; s/d from £36/48; ℗), which serves an organic breakfast.

Eating & Drinking

Café Phoenix & Bar (☎ 667062; Gandy St; mains £8, sandwiches £6) You could eat here for a month before trying anything twice (see also Entertainment following). The delicious sandwiches are a step up (try the spicy lamb with guacamole), and the mains (stuffed portabellas; roasted butternut squash with an orange, sage and nutmeg cream sauce) are positively incredible. A wide selection of international wines is available here until 11pm.

Coolings (☎ 434184; 11 Gandy St; mains £6.95) A busy brasserie on a medieval, pedestrianised street; it's signposted off High St.

Self caterers will find a **Tesco** (☎ 440025; Castle St; 🕑 7am-10pm Mon-Sat, 11am-5pm Sun) in town.

Entertainment

A one-stop entertainment venue is the **Exeter Phoenix Arts and Media Centre** (☎ 667080; Gandy St; www.exeterphoenix.org.uk) which showcases the best the area has to offer: visual arts, theatre, music, comedy, even puppetry, cohabited by contemporary, traditional and fringe artists. The place for live music is **Cavern Club** (☎ 425309; 83-84 Queen St at Gandy), where you can check out underground bands before they make it big.

Getting There & Away

Nine buses per day run between London, Heathrow airport and Exeter (£20, four hours, eight daily). From Exeter there are frequent services to Plymouth (£6, 1¼ hours, every 90 minutes) and Penzance (£20.50, 4½ hours, three daily). For bus information phone **Traveline** (☎ 0870 6082608) or **Stagecoach Devon** (☎ 01392 427711).

Exeter is at the hub of lines running from London's Waterloo and Paddington stations (£42, 3¼ hours, hourly), Bristol (£16.20, 1¾ hours, hourly), Salisbury (£21.70, 1¾ hours, 12 per day) and Penzance (£26.10, 3½ hours, approximately hourly). The 39-mile branch line to Barnstaple (£10.10, 1¼ hours, nine per day) gives good views of traditional Devon countryside.

For rail information, phone ☎ 0845 7484950.

PLYMOUTH

☎ 01752 / pop 249,000

Plymouth's renown as a maritime centre was established long before Sir Francis Drake's famous game of bowls on Plymouth Hoe in 1588. Devastated by WWII bombing raids, much of the city is modern but the Old Quarter by the harbour, from where the Pilgrim Fathers set sail for the New World in 1620, has been preserved.

Orientation & Information

The **TIC** (☎ 304849; www.visitplymouth.co.uk; 9 The Barbican; 🕑 9am-5pm Mon-Sat, 9am-5pm Sun summer) is a five-minute walk south of the bus station and about ten from the train station. To the west is Plymouth Hoe, a grassy park with wide views over the sea.

Many ferries head from Plymouth to France, Spain and Ireland. Brittany Ferries offers a two-day cruise to Santander, Spain, starting at £79 per person off-season. Check www.brittanyferries.com or ask at the TIC for schedules.

Sleeping

Globe Backpackers Plymouth (☎ 225158; www.backpackers.co.uk/plymouth; 172 Citadel Rd, The Hoe; dm £10) The city's only hostel is welcoming and central; it's a five-minute walk from the ferry port.

B&Bs cluster round the northwestern corner of the Hoe and are generally good value, from £18 per person.

Kynance Hotel (☎ 266821; www.kynancehotel.co.uk; 107-113 Citadel Rd West; s/d/£28/44, f £52-68; **P**) Ask for a room with a view at this comfortable place, which offers an early breakfast for ferry-goers.

Duke of Cornwall (☎ 275850; www.thedukeofcornwallhotel.com; Millbay Rd; s/d/f/ste from £94/104/120/160; **P**) For top-end budgets, this Victorian hotel has a stunning entrance, individually designed rooms and suites that offer champagne upon arrival and flowers, fruit and big fluffy robes.

Getting There & Away

There are frequent buses to and from Exeter with **Stagecoach Devon** (☎ 01392 427711). National Express has direct connections to numerous cities, including London (£25, five hours, six a day) and Bristol (£23.50, around 2¾ hours, four daily).

Trains are faster to London's Paddington station (£74.50, 3½ hours, at least hourly) and Penzance (£10.70, 1½ hours, every hour or so) but more expensive.

DARTMOOR NATIONAL PARK

Although the park is only about 25 miles (40km) from north to south and east to west, it encloses some of the wildest, bleakest country in England – a suitable terrain for the hound of the Baskervilles (one of Sherlock Holmes' most notorious foes). Manicured fields give way to windswept barren tableland, with jutting tors and scrubby gorse. To make it even more haunting, hundreds of semi-wild ponies roam free.

There are several small market towns surrounding the tableland, but the only village of any size on the moor is the ho-hum

Princetown. The countryside in the southeast is more conventionally beautiful, with wooded valleys and thatched villages. This is hiking country par excellence.

Orientation & Information

The National Park Authority (NPA; www .dartmoor-npa.gov.uk) has eight information centres in and around the park, or visit the TICs at Exeter and Plymouth before setting off. The **High Moorland Visitor Centre** (☎ 01822 890414; Princetown; ☻ 10am-5pm, to 4pm in winter) can help with accommodation and activities. The **Ministry of Defence** (☎ 0800 458468) has three live firing ranges in the northwestern section (Merrivale, Willsworthy and Okehampton); phone for an update on firing schedules.

Sleeping

Most of Dartmoor is privately owned, but the owners of unenclosed moorland don't usually object to campers who keep to a simple code: don't camp on moorland enclosed by walls, within sight of roads or houses or near heavily trafficked areas; don't stay on one site for more than two nights; and leave the site as you found it. Dial ☎ 01200 420102 for camping barn locations.

The **Bellever Youth Hostel** (☎ 0870 7705692; bellever@yha.org.uk; dm £11.80; P ✗) is across from the Postbridge TIC. From here, you can take a literary stroll through the setting of the *Hound of the Baskervilles*. **Steps Bridge Youth Hostel** (☎ 0870 7706048; adult/child £9.30/6.70; P), near Dunsford between Moretonhampstead and Exeter, is set amid countless trees. Be warned: the driveway is extremely steep. Both hostels encourage public transport users by offering a £1 discount (take bus No 98 from Tavistock or No 82 going between Plymouth and Exeter).

B&Bs are plentiful in the larger towns on the edge of the park (like Buckfastleigh, Okehampton and Tavistock). The delightful **Lydgate House** (☎ 01822 880209; www.lydgatehouse .com; Postbridge; s/d £50/45-65) is smack in the park set far off the main road, and has wellappointed rooms, luxurious bedding and offers meals and delectable cream teas. The convivial **Plume of Feathers** (☎ 01822 890240; www.plumeoffeathers-dartmoor.co.uk; Princetown; s/d £17.50/35, bunkhouse dm £5.50-7, camp sites £2.50-4) has clean facilities for campers, comfortable guesthouse rooms, plus a cheery pub and restaurant.

Getting There & Away

Exeter and Plymouth are the best starting points for the park. Public transport offseason is spotty at best so consider hiring a bicycle from **Flash Gordon** (☎ 01392 213141; 1 Polsloe Rd, Exeter; £10 per day).

National No 82 (the Transmoor Link, £4 to £5), running between Exeter and Plymouth via Moretonhampstead, Postbridge and Princetown, runs daily (three buses each way) from late May to late September; the rest of the year there are weekend services only. From Exeter, take No 359.

A one-day Rover ticket (£6) allows you to get on and off whenever you like. Outside summer, their are infrequent services and changing schedules. Contact the **Devon County Public Transport Help Line** (☎ 01392 382800), **Traveline** (☎ 0870 6082608) or any TIC.

SOUTH CORNWALL COAST
Penzance
☎ 01736 / pop 20,000
At the end of the railway line from London, Penzance is a sweet little seaside resort town. A bit worn around the edges, it makes a good base for walking the Coastal Path from Land's End to St Ives, a dramatic 25-mile section with many inexpensive B&Bs along the way, plus you can take public tranportation to the spectacular outdoor Minack Theatre (see Land's End p177). Penzance is the place to catch ferries to the Isle of Scilly, actually a rather serious nature preserve.

The **TIC** (☎ 362207; pztic@penwith.gov.uk; ☻ 9am-5.30pm Mon-Fri, to 5pm Sat, 10am-1pm Sun May-Aug, 9am-5pm Mon-Sat, 10am-1pm Sun Sep, 9am-5pm Mon-Fri, 10am-1pm Sat Oct-Apr) is just outside the train station. Bikes can be hired at **Pedals Bike Hire** (☎ 251671; 17 Wharfside Shopping Centre; per day/week £10/50).

Situated on the outskirts of town is the **Castle Horneck YHA** (☎ 362666; penzance@yha.org.uk; Castle Horneck, Alverton). Take bus No 5B or 6B from the train station to the Pirate Inn from where it's a half-mile walk. More central is the friendly **Penzance Backpackers** (☎ 363836; www.pzbackpack.com; Alexandra Rd; dm £10, d £24; ☐).

Alexandra Rd is lined with mid-range options and here you'll find the pleasant **Dunedin Hotel** (☎ 362652; www.dunedinhotel.co.uk; per person £22-28). For old-fashioned comfort and a sea view head to the **Queens Hotel** (☎ 362371; www .queens-hotel.com; The Promenade; r from £55; P), with a lovely restaurant that serves cream teas.

The **National Express** (☎ 08705 808080) runs buses from Penzance to Newquay (£4.75, 1¾ hours, two daily) and to Plymouth, Exeter and London. Local bus No 8a goes to Zennor (where there's a basic but beautifully situated hostel) and St Ives every 40 minutes.

The train station is behind the TIC. Trains go to London's Paddington station (£59, 5¼ hours, seven or eight direct services daily), St Ives (£2.90, 20 minutes direct or 40 minutes, 14 daily), Exeter (£19.90, three hours, 11 daily), Plymouth (£10.70, 1¾ hours, at least hourly).

Land's End
☎ 01736

The scenery around Land's End – miles of sea-battered coastline, granite cliffs and white-capped ocean straight to Newfoundland – create a vista unparalleled in all of Britain. Drivers will have to pay to park at tacky **Land's End Complex** (☎ 871501; parking £3; ⌚ 10am-5pm), full of campy snack bars and 'Last … in Britain!' shops. Alternatively, there's a great walking trail. Start at Sennen Cove just below Whitesand's Lodge and follow the coastal path.

The adventurous can continue on (or drive the 4 miles) to Porthcurno, where you'll find the dramatically incomparable **Minack Theatre** (☎ 810181; www.minack.com; Porthcurno; tours adult/child £3.20/1.20; ⌚ 9.30am-5.30pm Apr-Sep, 10am-4pm Oct-Mar; **P**), a Roman-style amphitheatre carved out of granite and stone in the cliff, one woman's 50-year mission, but call as sometimes it's closed during the week. If you're here during summer, don't even consider leaving without seeing a **theatre performance** (tickets £4-7.50; ⌚ 8pm Mon-Fri, 2pm Wed & Fri). First Bus runs a post-performance bus back to Penzance. Dress warmly.

Colourful **Whitesand's Lodge** (☎ 871776; www .whitesandslodge.co.uk; Sennen village; dm £12.50, d in guesthouse £50; **P** 🖳) is on the main road 2 miles before Land's End. It's the ultimate in a relaxed holiday setting – surf instruction, cosy log fires, a bar and restaurant, tent space and this being Cornwall, yoga classes and spiritual workshops. Take bus No 1 or 1a from Penzance to get to the lodge or complex.

The coastal hills between St Just and St Ives, with their dry stone walling, form one of the oldest, most fascinating agricultural landscapes in Britain that still follow an Iron Age pattern. There are numerous prehistoric remains and the abandoned engine houses of old tin and copper mines.

WEST CORNWALL COAST
St Ives
☎ 01736 / pop 9500

St Ives is the ideal to which other seaside towns can only aspire. The omnipresent sea, the harbour, the beaches, the narrow alleyways, steep slopes and hidden corners are captivating, but it gets mighty busy in summer. Artists have long been attracted to St Ives, and in 1993 a branch of London's **Tate Gallery** (☎ 796226; Barnoon Hill; adult/child £4.75/2.50; ⌚ 10am-5.30pm, closes 4pm winter, closed Mon) was opened here, featuring mostly modern and many local artists.

The **TIC** (☎ 796297; www.stives-cornwall.co.uk; the Guildhall, St-an-Pol; ⌚ 9am-6pm Mon-Fri, to 5.30pm Sat, 10am-4pm Sun Jun-Sep, 9am-5pm Mon-Fri, 10am-1pm Sat, closed Sun May-Oct) is a short walk from the train station. There are several surf shops on the Wharf (the street edging the harbour) where it's possible to rent boards.

The busy **St Ives Backpackers** (☎ 799444; www .backpackers.co.uk/st-ives; Lower Stennack; dm £10.95-15.95) occupies a converted chapel and still has sensational stained glass; prices vary depending on the season. A free shuttle bus goes to the Newquay hostel. Right in town is **Sunrise B&B** (☎ 795407; 22 The Warren; s £22-30, d £48-54; closed for a month after Easter, Oct & Nov; **P**), featuring a fabulous breakfast (vegetarian available), patios and ocean views. Ask for the red balloon room. Also available is the **Kynance Guest House** (☎ 796636; enquiries@kynance 24.co.uk; The Warren; per person £23; **P**) next door.

Near the Tate, relax after a hectic day sunning on the beach at the **Porthmeor** (☎ 796712; www.porthmeor.com; Godrevy Terrace; d per person £27.50-42.50; **P** ❌), watching movies in the guest lounge or enjoying the awesome ocean views.

To enjoy the scenery, stop in for a drink or a bite at **Hub** (☎ 799099; 4 The Wharf; dishes £2-7), the social centre of St Ives.

Trains head to London's Paddington station (£60, 5½ hours, five daily) and Penzance (£2.90, 20 minutes direct or 40 minutes, 14 daily).

Newquay
☎ 01637 / pop 14,000

The surfing capital of Britain, Newquay teems with everything you'd expect from a mildly tacky English seaside resort – souvenir shops, chain restaurants and fairy floss. But hey, it's all enclosed in a rather harmless pedestrianised zone, and you're here to soak up the sun and surf and leave that culture stuff for another day. Soft sandy beaches dot the area, several right in town (including Fistral Beach for board riders). This is a great place to learn how to surf (see below).

The **TIC** (☎ 854020; info@newquay.co.uk; Marcus Hill; ◷ 9.30am-5.30pm Mon-Sat, to 1pm Sun, hrs vary in winter) is near the bus station in town. Several surf shops on Fore St hire fibreglass boards and wetsuits, each around £6 per day.

Newquay has many independent hostels geared up for surfers. **The Original Backpackers** (☎ 874668; 16 Beachfield Ave; dm from £10) is in an excellent central position overlooking Towan Beach, and is a great place to make new friends over a pint (or seven). Exuding laidback hipness is the new **Endless Summer Surf Lodge** (☎ 851522; www.endlesssummersurflodge.com; 15-16 Mount Wise; per person £25; P □ ☎), with a sand-covered first floor, tiki bar decorated with Warhol paintings where DJs spin almost every night, 107 old-school hotel rooms, and its very own dive and surf school; this is a destination in and of itself.

There are four trains a day between Newquay and Par (£4.70, 45 minutes), which is on the London–Penzance line, and numerous buses to Truro.

Tintagel
☎ 01840 / pop 1750

Even tacky Arthurian souvenirs and summer crowds don't diminish the surf-battered grandeur of **Tintagel Castle** (☎ 770328; Tintagel Head; adult/concession/child £3.70/2.80/1.90). According to legend, this is the castle that saw the birth of King Arthur and the magic of Merlin. There's a slight problem, however: if there was a King Arthur or Merlin, they lived 800 years before the castle was built. Nevertheless, it's a spectacular site with a climb a StairMaster would envy.

It's also worth visiting the picturesque 14th century **Old Post Office** (admission £2.30). You'll find one of the most spectacularly beautiful and isolated hostel settings in the world at the **Tintagel YHA** (☎ 0870 7706068, reservations@yha.org.uk; Dunderhole Point; lockout 10am-5pm; P ☒), which is worth the slog (even in a car) to reach it. In the village, the **Old Borough House** (☎ 770475; theoldboroughhouse@

hotmail.com; Bossiney; d/tr £70/120; ☒) is an AA five-diamond charmer. No children under 12. For information on bus services, phone **Traveline** (☎ 0870 6082608).

Just north of Tintagel is the eminently quaint village of **Boscastle**, situated on a quaint harbour. Next door to a fabulous **YHA** (☎ 0870 7705710) is the **Witchcraft Museum** (☎ 01840 250111; www.museumofwitchcraft.com; The Harbour, Boscastle; ◷ 10.30am-6pm Mon-Sat, 11.30am-6pm Sun Apr-Hallowe'en; adult/concession £2.50/1.50), the pre-eminent museum of its kind anywhere in the world. Read the story behind broomsticks, pierced dog hearts and crystal balls. It sometimes stays open late.

NORTH DEVON

North Devon is one of the most beautiful regions in England, with a spectacular, largely unspoilt coastline and the superb Exmoor National Park, which protects the best of it.

Exmoor National Park

Exmoor is one of the UK's 13 national parks. Small in size, with only 265 sq miles (426 sq km), the northern area and along the coast have particularly breathtaking scenery, with dramatic humpbacked headlands giving superb views across the Bristol Channel.

A high plateau rises steeply behind the coast, but is cut by steep, fast-flowing streams. On the southern side the two main rivers, the Exe and Barle, wind their way south along the wooded coombs. Pony herds, descended from ancient hill stock, still roam the commons, as do England's last herds of wild red deer.

There are a number of particularly attractive villages: Lynton/Lynmouth, twin villages joined by a water-operated railway; Porlock, at the edge of the moor in a beautiful valley; Dunster, which is dominated by a castle, a survivor from the Middle Ages; and Selworthy, a National Trust village with many classic thatch-roofed cottages.

For walkers, arguably the best and easiest section of the Southwest Coast Path is between Minehead and Padstow. This is excellent countryside for riding horses; contact any of the visitors centres or TICs for a list of stables.

Exmoor is accessible from Barnstaple (train from Exeter) and Taunton.

There are five NPA visitor centres in and around the park including **Dulverton**

(☎ 01398 323841; Fore St) and **Lynmouth** (☎ 01598 752509; The Esplanade; ☺ late Mar-Oct), but it's also possible to get information from the TICs at Ilfracombe, Lynton and Minehead.

There are YHA hostels at **Ilfracombe** (☎ 08707705878), **Minehead** (☎ 08707705968), **Lynton** (☎ 0870 7705942) and **Exford** (☎ 0870 7705828) in the centre of the park. All these hostels close part of the winter – either on Sunday or Monday or in January and February – so phone ahead. **Ocean Backpackers** (☎ 01271 867835; www.oceanbackpackers.co.uk; 29 St James Place, Ilfracombe; dm/d £11/31) is central and popular with surfers.

B&Bs are scattered throughout the park but the main swarm is around Lynton/Lynmouth. Try the **Victoria Fernery** (☎ 01598 752440; enquiries@thefernery.co.uk; Lydiate Lane, Lynton; s/d £22/40) or contact the **Lynton TIC** (☎ 01598 752225) for more suggestions.

Barnstaple is at the western end of the Tarka Line railway from Exeter and connects with a number of bus services around the coast.

To get to Exmoor, change from either the train or a coach in Taunton. The local North Devon bus No 300 runs every hour Monday to Saturday (less frequent on Sunday) connecting Taunton to Minehead and a few smaller villages, including Porlock, Exford, Lynmouth (£6 for a one-day Explorer Pass). Contact National Traveline for details. A timetable covering local public transport is available from TICs, or you can phone **Taunton Coach Station** (☎ 01823 272033). Mountain bikes are available from **Tarka Trail** (☎ 324202; per day £10) in the train station.

BATH
☎ 01225 / pop 86,000

Bath is historically, geographically and architecturally the quintessential English tourist destination. Combining Roman history and Georgian buildings dressed in the honey-coloured Bath stone, the town is practically a theme park of public space, attractions, museums, charming accommodation, shops and park.

History

Bath has been a spa destination ever since Emperor Claudius held office. The local Celtic Dobunni tribe worshipped Sulis – the goddess of rivers and possibly curative powers – through offerings (including some rather unlucky human ones) from the Druids at the hot springs. When the Romans invaded via the military outpost Fosse Way, instead of wiping out all Celtic culture, they created Aquae Sulis, an enormous complex of baths and temples dedicated to Sulis-Minerva.

Thousands flocked to the baths for relaxation and healing until the barbarians trashed the place, about AD 367. The complex fell into ruin, and Bath became a monastic centre during the Middle Ages, starting to regain its fame as a place to take the waters only in the late 16th century.

Throughout the 18th century, Bath was the most fashionable haunt of English society. Aristocrats flocked here to gossip, gamble and flirt, and Jane Austen was a familiar face.

Orientation

Bath's train and bus stations are both just south of town near the Avon River. Most of the main sites and accommodation listed are within walking distance of each other, contained in the boomerang-shaped Avon.

Information

Internet access is available at **Click** (☎ 481008; 13a Manvers St; per 20min £1; ☺ 10am-10pm), and there's a **TIC** (accommodation ☎ 0870 4201278, per min 50p, ☎ 0906 7112000; www.visitbath.co.uk; Abbey Chambers, Abbey Churchyard; ☺ 9am-7pm Mon-Sat, to 6pm Sun mid-Jun–mid-Sep, 9am-5pm Mon-Sat, to 4pm Sun late Sep-early Jun). Advance booking of accommodation is essential over Easter, during the Bath International Festival (late May), over summer weekends and throughout July and August.

Sights & Activities

When in Rome...er Bath, do as the Romans did 2000 years ago at the **Thermae Bath Spa** (☎ 331234; www.thermaebathspa.com; Hot Bath St; 2hr/4hr/full day £19/29/45, treatments from £14; ☺ 9am-10pm). Your ticket buys you a day of bliss swimming in the open-air rooftop thermal pool, taking a t'ai chi class or enjoying the aromatherapy-infused steam rooms. Reservations advised, especially for treatments. Watsu – water shiatsu massage – is as deliciously relaxing as it sounds. Swimwear is obligatory. Towels and robes for rent. If you want a quick soak, try the **Cross Baths** (per 90min £12) across the street.

BRITAIN

The **Roman Baths Museum** (☎ 477785; adult/child £9/5, with Museum of Costume £12/7; �), 9am-5pm, to 9pm Jul & Aug) is a series of excavated passages and chambers beneath street level, taking in the sulphurous mineral springs (still flowing after all these years), the ancient central-heating system and the bath itself, which retains its Roman paving and lead base. Many of the treasures found here are on display in the museum.

A worthwhile 20-minute walk uphill are the **Assembly Rooms & Museum of Costume** (☎ 477785; www.museumofcostume.co.uk; Bennett St; adult/child £5.50/3.75, with Roman Baths £12/7; ☒ 11am-4pm Nov-Feb, to 5pm Mar-Oct). Fashions from the last four centuries reflect the reigning culture of the time.

Bath was designed for wandering around and you'll need at least a full day. There is a **covered market** next to the Guildhall, and don't miss the maze of **passageways** just north of Abbey Churchyard. Free walking **tours** (☒ 10.30am & 2pm Mon-Fri, 10.30am Sat, also 7pm Tue, Fri & Sat May-Sep) leave from outside the Pump Room; contact the TIC for information.

Try to see a play at Bath's sumptuous **Theatre Royal Bath** (☎ 448844; Sawclose Rd; www .theatreroyal.org.uk; tickets £16.50-24.50, matinees £11), which often features shows before their London run.

The **Bath Abbey**, built between 1499 and 1616, boasts 56 stunning stained-glass windows depicting stages in the life of Christ.

Across the street from **Abbey Churchyard** (an open square) is the **Pump Room** (see p181), an opulent restaurant that exemplifies the elegant style that once drew the aristocrats.

The **Circus** is an architectural masterpiece by John Wood the Elder, designed so that a true crescent faces each of its three approaches. It opens onto the **Royal Crescent**, designed by John Wood the Younger and even more highly regarded than his father's effort. **No 1** (☎ 428126; adult/concession £4/3.50; ☒ 10.30am-5pm, to 4pm winter; closed Mon) has been superbly restored to its 1770 glory, down to the minutest detail.

Sleeping

B&BS & HOTELS

Bath's B&Bs are expensive. In summer most charge at least £35/55 for a single/double. The main areas are along Newbridge Rd to the west, Wells Rd to the south and around Pulteney Rd in the east.

> **BABA**
>
> The YHA has a service called BABA – Book a Bed Ahead. Any YHA can accept payment to book future stays at other hostels, saving valuable time and money, as well as giving peace of mind.

Ashgrove Guesthouse (☎ 421911; 39 Bathwick St; s/d £30/50; **P** ☒) Recently refurbished, this is a charming and lovingly cared-for home away from home.

Ashley House (☎ 425027; ashleybath@waitrose .com; 8 Pulteney Gardens; s/d/f 35/62/72; ☒) Popular and wisteria-clad this place has seven comfortable rooms and offers discounts in the off-season.

Royal Crescent Hotel (☎ 823333; www.royalcrescent .co.uk; 16 Royal Crescent; d from £330) For the splurge of a lifetime, try this Georgian delight with its own river-boat launch, spa (featuring Georgian architecture and a specially built watsu pool) and hot air balloon. Check for good discounts mid-week in January and February or just visit the gardens for tea.

Also recommended: **Toad Hall Guest House** (☎ /fax 423254; 6 Lime St; from s/d/f £22/40/50; ☒), a stone's throw from the train station; the historic and centrally located **Kennard Hotel** (☎ 310472; 11 Henrietta St; s without toilet £48-58, s/d/f 79/98/160; **P** ☐); and **Cheriton House** (☎ 429862; www.cheritonhouse.co.uk; 9 Upper Oldfield Park; s/d from £48/66, 2-night min; **P**), which has a lovely garden. Also **Belvedere Wine Vaults** (☎ 330264; www .belvederewinevaults.co.uk; 25 Belvedere; r £40-80) has a few sleekly furnished guest rooms.

HOSTELS

YMCA International House (☎ 325900; www.bath ymca.co.uk; Broad St Place; weekends dm £11-13, s/d/tr/q incl breakfast £24/38/48/60; ☐) Almost a hotel and comfortable enough for all ages. Rates are lower during the week, there's a gym at reduced rates and £2 daily luggage storage.

Bath Backpackers Hostel (☎ 446787; bath@hostels .co.uk; 13 Pierrepont St; dm/tw £12/30; ☐) It's not pretty nor all that clean, but it's lively, a fabulous place to meet new friends, and a five-minute walk from the bus and train stations.

Bath Youth Hostel (☎ 465674; bath@yha.org.uk; Bathwick Hill; Badgerline bus No 18 or 418; adult/under 18 yrs dm £11.80/8.50; **P** ☐) A good 25-minute walk from town, but worth it for the views and the building's fine Italianate architecture.

BRITAIN

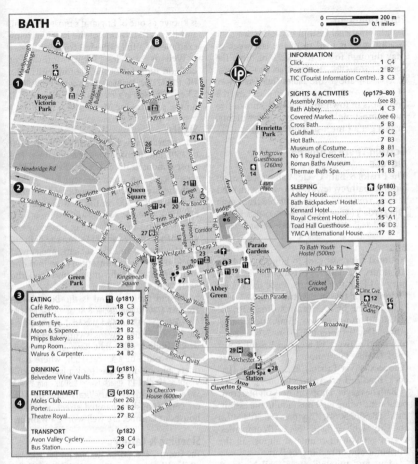

BATH

0 — 200 m
0 — 0.1 miles

Eating

Pump Room (☎ 444477; cream teas £9.75; ☼ 9.30am-last orders 4pm) Perfect your pinkie-extending muscles while sipping tea and heap your scones with jam and clotted – as in clotted arteries – cream while being serenaded by the Pump Room Trio.

Eastern Eye (☎ 422323; 8a Quiet St; mains £7-15) One of England's most popular upscale Indian restaurants; serves excellent tandoori.

Demuth's (☎ 446059; 2 North Parade Passage; mains £5-12; ☼ 10am-10pm Sun-Fri, 9am-11pm Sat; ✗) This place will please vegetarian gourmets, sweets lovers and adventurous children alike.

Try **Café Retro** (☎ 339347; 18 York St; Aberdeen beef burgers £8, sandwiches £6) for a little 40s flair. A funky eatery is the **Walrus & Carpenter** (☎ 314864; 28 Barton St; ☼ noon-2.30pm & 6-11pm; mains £10, sandwiches £6). **Phipps Bakery** (☎ 462483; Kingsmead Square; light lunches £4) has excellent filled rolls, vegetable curries and spinach turnovers. There are several fast-food places in this area.

The **Moon & Sixpence** (☎ 460962; 6a Broad St; 2-course lunch £5) is a pleasant pub. Pubs are good bets for cheap evening meals, too.

Drinking

Belvedere Wine Vaults (☎ 330264; www.belvedere winevaults.co.uk; 25 Belvedere; tapas £2.50-5; ☼ dinner served 6-9.30pm or so Mon-Sat, lunch Sun) offers it all: a large selection of wine and flavoured vodkas, a tapas menu, non-smoking bar and accommodation (see p180).

Entertainment

Bath International Festival (☎ 463362; www.bath musicfest.org.uk) is held from the last week of May through to the first week of June. **The Porter** (☎ 424104; ◷ 11am-11pm Mon-Sat, noon-10.30pm Sun) above the **Moles Club** (☎ 404445; 14 George St; ◷ 9pm-2am, to 4am Fri & Sat) are the best spots in town to catch well-known live bands most nights, comedy Sunday nights, or just get a pint just about any time.

Getting There & Around

BICYCLE

The Bristol & Bath Cycle Walkway, an excel lent footpath/cycleway, follows the disused railway route. Bikes are available from **Avon Valley Cyclery** (☎ 442442; Bath Railway Station; half-day £10, full-day £15, deposit required; Mon-Sat 9am-5.30pm).

BUS

National Express heads to London (£14.50, 3¼ hours, 11 daily), Portsmouth via Salisbury (£14,50, three hours, once daily) and Oxford (£12, two hours, two daily).

Badgerline bus X39 runs to/from Bristol (£3.60, 50 minutes, every 15 minutes). Badgerline's Day Explorer (£5.70) gives you access to a good network of buses in Bristol, Somerset (Wells, Glastonbury), Gloucestershire (Gloucester via Bristol) and Wiltshire (Lacock, Bradford-on-Avon, Salisbury).

Bath has several hop-on, hop-off bus companies, including First Bus (adult/concession/child £8.50/6.50/4), Citytour (£6.50/4.50/2) and City Sightseeing (£8/6/4). All companies' tickets get you discounts at almost all the museums and attractions of Bath.

Maps and timetables are available from the bus station. Call **Traveline** (☎ 0870 6082608) for inquiries.

TRAIN

From Bath, it's faster but more expensive to London's Paddington station (£33 to £45, 1½ hours, at least hourly) and slower, cheaper and more scenic to or from Waterloo (£21.90, 2½ hours, 10 daily), changing in Salisbury (£10.40, 50 minutes). It's an easy connection to Cardiff (£11.90, 1¼ hours, hourly) and Bristol (£4.80, 15 minutes, every half-hour).

WELLS

☎ 01749 / pop 9500
Wells is a small cathedral city that has kept much of its medieval character; its cathedral

is known as one of England's most beautiful, and it is certainly one of the best surviving examples of a full cathedral complex.

Wells is 21 miles (34km) southwest of Bath on the edge of the Mendip Hills. The **TIC** (☎ 672552; touristinfo@wells.gov.uk; ◷ 9.30am-5.30pm, 10am-4pm in winter) is in the town hall on the picturesque Market Pl.

Sights

The **cathedral** was built in stages from 1180 to 1508 and incorporates several styles. The most famous features are the extraordinary west façade, an immense sculpture gallery with the largest gallery of medieval sculptures in the world – 300 on the west façade. The elaborate interior scissor arches are a brilliant solution to the problem posed by the subsidence of the central tower; the delicate chapter house; and the ancient mechanical clock in the north transept. Try to join one of the free tours during summer (on the hour from 10am to 3pm).

Beyond the cathedral is the **Bishop's Palace** (☎ 678691; adult/senior & student/disabled/child 4/3/1.50/1; ◷ 10.30am-6pm Mon-Fri, 1-6pm Sun, some Sats Apr-Oct), where swans swim in moats in which boiling oil might have once flowed, and the ruins of a Great Hall, where banquets and bloody trials took place, are still visible. **Market Pl** (markets ◷ 8.30am-4pm Wed & Sat) and the 14th-century **Vicars' Close**, the oldest continuously inhabited street of private houses in Europe, are well worth a wander.

Sleeping & Eating

The Crown (☎ 673457; www.crownatwells.co.uk; Market Pl; s/d/4-poster room with spa £50/80/95) is Wells' oldest hotel, dating back to the 1450s. Commanding an almost perfect location, **Canon Grange B&B** (☎ 671800; www.canongrange.co.uk; Cathedral Green; s/d/f per person from £22.50) is a 15th-century home with impeccable views of the Cathedral's West Front.

The **City Arms** (☎ 673916; 69 High St; mains around £5) used to be the city jail but now serves good pub grub. Near the bus station the **Good Earth Restaurant** (☎ 678600; 4 Priory Rd; mains £4-7) produces excellent home-made soup, pizzas and puddings at reasonable prices.

Getting There & Away

The bus station is just south of the centre on Princess St. Local buses go to Glastonbury (£2.10, about 20 minutes, every 30 minutes), coaches go to Bristol (£3.90, one hour, at least every hour), Bath (£3.90, 1¼ hours, 11 daily), Taunton (£4, 1½ hours, every two hours). To get around the area, buy a First Bus Day Southwest ticket for £6 (£5 after 9am), which allows you travel in Cornwall and Somerset on First Group coaches.

GLASTONBURY

☎ 01458 / pop 7000

Legend and history combine at Glastonbury to produce an irresistible attraction for romantics and eccentrics of every description. It's a small market town with the ruins of a 14th-century **abbey** (☎ 832267; adult/concession/child £3.50/3/1.50; ☽ 9.30am-6pm or dusk if earlier), and a nearby tor with superb views.

According to various legends, Jesus travelled to Cornwall as a young man on family business. In AD 63, Joseph of Arimathea brought the Holy Grail, buried at Chalice Well. Joseph's staff that he thrust into the ground was said to have sprouted overnight into a blossoming tree. Off-shoots of the tree, that blooms at Christmas, are still said to exist at the Glastonbury Abbey. It's also the burial place of the legendary King Arthur and Queen Guinevere, and the tor is either the Isle of Avalon or a gateway to the underworld. Whatever you choose to believe, a climb to the top of the tor is well worthwhile. Turn right at the top of High St (the far end from the TIC) onto Chilkwell St and then left onto Dod Lane; there's a footpath to the tor from the end of the lane.

The **Glastonbury Festival** (☎ 832020; www.glastonburyfestivals.co.uk), a three-day extravaganza of music, theatre, circus, mime, natural healing etc, is a massive affair with over 1000 acts. It takes place over three days in late June at Pilton, eight miles from Glastonbury; admission is by advance ticket only (£119 for all three days).

The **TIC** (☎ 832954; 9 High St, The Tribunal; www.glastonburytic.co.uk; ☽ 10am-5pm Sun-Thu, to 5.30pm Fri & Sat Apr-Sep, closes one hour earlier in winter) can supply maps and accommodation information; there are plenty of B&Bs for around £25 per person. The **Glastonbury Backpackers Hostel** (☎ 833353; backpackers@glastonbury/online.com; Crown Hotel, 4 Market Pl; dm £10, d £30) is perfectly central but has a rather dodgy bar downstairs. Experience B&B perfection at the **AppleTree House** (☎ 830803; www.appletreehouse.org.uk; s/d £30/60) – borrow movies for your VCR, relax

in the stone circle garden, eat the homemade bread or chocolate and biscuits left in your room. Another possibility is the **Street Youth Hostel** (☎ 0870 7706056; fax 0870 7706057), 4 miles south.

There are Badgerline buses from Bristol to Wells, Glastonbury and Street. Bus No 163 leaves every 15 minutes or so from Wells and continues to Bridgwater, from where there are buses to Minehead (for Exmoor).

BRISTOL

☎ 0117 / pop 406,000

Bristol is by far and away the region's largest and coolest city, home to Massive Attack, Tricky, and Wallace and Gromit. Approaching through the unlovely southern suburbs, you might wonder what you're getting into, but the centre has some magnificent architecture, docks and warehouses that are being rescued from ruin, and a plethora of bars, pubs and restaurants. Bristol is divided into neighbourhoods, each with its own distinct feel, so visitors can spend two or three days exploring the tourist-friendly Harbour, upscale Clifton and trendy Park St.

Bristol is most famous as a port, and it grew rich on the 17th-century trade with the North American colonies and the West Indies (rum, slaves, sugar and tobacco).

Orientation & Information

The city centre lies north of the Floating Harbour – a system of locks, canals and docks fed by the tidal Avon River. The central area is compact and easy to get around on foot, if rather hilly.

The main train station is Bristol Temple Meads, about 1 mile to the southeast of the centre, although some trains use Bristol Parkway 5 miles to the north. The coach station is to the north of the city centre. Bristol is connected to virtually everywhere in England by train and coach, but especially the Southwest.

The **TIC** (☎ 0906 7112191, per min 50p; www.visitbristol.co.uk; Wildscreen Walk, Harbourside; ☽ 10am-6pm, to 5pm Nov-Feb) is at Bristol's newly transformed waterfront.

Sights & Activities

The spectacular **Clifton Suspension Bridge** (☎ 9744664), designed by Isambard Brunel and completed in 1864, crosses the equally spectacular Avon Gorge. The suspension bridge is quite a walk from the centre of town – catch bus No 8 or 8a from bus stop 'Cu' on Colston Ave, or from Temple Meads station.

Check out the **Clifton Observatory and Camera Obscura** on top of the hill next to the bridge while you're there, and take in the view from Giant's Cave.

People have been shopping at **St Nicholas Market** (cnr St Nicholas St & Exchange Ave) for over 250 years, and now find funky clothes, fashionable antiques and deliciously affordable takeaway.

The **British Empire and Commonwealth Museum** (☎ 9254980; Clock Tower Yards, Temple Meads; adult/concession/child £6.50/5.50/3.95; ☯ 10am-5pm) details the building (1450–1800), rise (1800–1900) and decline (1900–today) of the British Empire through photographs, sound recordings, plundered objects and various travelling exhibits.

Close to the TIC is College Green, flanked by impressive council offices and the imposing **Bristol Cathedral**. Up the hill (Park St) there are numerous restaurants, the university and, 1.5 miles beyond, the genteel suburb of Clifton, which is dominated by fine Georgian architecture.

Bristol and its harbour are inextricably linked, the latter responsible for the wealth and prestige of the former. At the harbour, you'll find the **Maritime Heritage Centre** (☎ 9291843; centre admission free, ships adult/pensioner/child £6.25/5.25/3.75; ☯ 10am-5.30pm, to 4.30pm Nov-Mar) with Brunel's SS *Great Britain*, the first modern ship, and the *Matthew*, a replica of the ship John Cabot sailed from Bristol to Newfoundland; and the **Industrial Museum** (☎ 9251470; admission free; ☯ 10am-5pm Sat-Wed; boat trips & train rides available during the summer).

Near the harbour, take a stroll around King St, with its old buildings, now used as restaurants and clubs, and the **Llandoger Trow**, a 17th-century pub reputed to be the Admiral Benbow in Robert Louis Stevenson's *Treasure Island*.

Sleeping

The best place for low-priced B&Bs is along Coronation Rd in Southville.

Bristol Youth Hostel (☎ 0870 7705726; bristol@yha.org.uk; 14 Narrow Quay; dm £16.40, d £26-30) Occupying a converted warehouse right at the waterfront this excellent hostel features a café and thankfully small rooms.

Bristol Backpackers (☎ 9257900; www.bristol backpackers.co.uk; 17 St Stephen's St; dm/r £14/35; ☐) Central, clean and charming.

The Hawthorns (☎ 9545555; www.bris.ac.uk; Woodland Rd, Clifton; from s/d £20/32) The university lets out rooms at this Georgian establishment in an area well-populated with bars and restaurants. Available July to September; rates include breakfast.

Arches (☎ 9247398; www.archest-hotel.co.uk; 132 Cotham; s/d/f £38.50/53.50/66.50; ✗) Go green at this modern hotel committed to recycling, fair trade and no genetically modified foods. Vegetarian-only breakfast.

Hotel du Vin (☎ 9255577; www.hotelduvin.co.uk; The Sugar House, Narrow Lewins Mead; r £125-190) Exuding individuality and modern grandeur, it occupies a cluster of stylishly renovated warehouses and has been known to host a few rock stars.

Eating

Bristol is well endowed with restaurants, and most are reasonably priced. The trendy cafés in the Watershed and Arnolfini arts centres on either side of the Floating Harbour have some delicious dishes for under £4. The grand old bank buildings along Corn St now house pubs, café/bars and restaurants.

Mud Dock (☎ 9349734; 40 The Grove; mains £6-8) Housed in an old warehouse with an industrially maritime bar, the Mud Dock serves salmon salad, sandwiches, and a good selection of beer.

Aqua (☎ 9156060; Welshback; ☯ 11am-7pm) This riverfront place has a mouth-watering menu and a not-to-be-missed £10.79 two-course meal, with choices like liver parfait and Thai green vegetable curry.

Belgo (☎ 9058000; Queen Charlotte St; mains from £8) Provides the mussels to accompany over 100 beers in the basement bar.

Self-caterers will find a Tesco supermarket at Broadmead Shopping Centre.

Drinking

Get a copy of *Venue* (£2), Bristol's and Bath's answer to *Time Out*.

Across from Temple Mead station is the **Reckless Engineer** (no phone, Temple Gates), former hangout of Isambard Brunel. The legendary **Bierkeller** (☎ 9268514; All Saints St), is unpretentious, popular with students (read: cheap) and has live music on Wednesday and Saturday.

Entertainment

One-stop entertaining shopping can be found at the arts complex **Arnolfini** (☎ 9299 191; 16 Narrow Quay), including cinemas, visual arts galleries, performance art etc.

For a different dancing experience, patrons at **Thekla** (☎ 9293301), on a boat at The Grove, are dressed fairly casually and dance to funk and garage.

There are several entertainment options on King St, ranging from new jazz at the traditional **Old Duke pub** (☎ 9277137; 45 King St) to one of three theatres in the **New Vic** (☎ 9877877; King St).

Getting There & Away
BUS

Chances are you'll end up in Bristol if you're taking coaches through the Southwest. National Express coaches head to London's Victoria station, usually at 45 minutes past the hour (£14.50, three hours, hourly), Heathrow (£28.50, 2¼ to three hours, three daily), Gatwick (£30, 3¾ hours, three daily), Cardiff (£6, 1¼ hours, three daily), Exeter (£10.75, two hours, four daily), Penzance (£34.50, 6¾ hours, two daily) and Oxford (£14.50, 2½ hours, once daily at 3.55pm).

Badgerline has numerous services each day to/from Bath (£4). There are also services to Salisbury and north to Gloucester. A First Bus & Rail costs £6 and allows travel between Bath, Bristol and Weston-Super-Mare. For all bus information including city services, phone **Traveline** (☎ 0870 6082608).

TRAIN

Bristol is an important rail hub with two main stations: Temple Meads and Parkway. Regular connections run to London's Paddington station (£34 to £44.50, 1¾ hours, every half-hour), Bath (£4.80, 15 minutes, every half-hour), Cardiff (£7.40, one hour, hourly), Exeter (£16.20, one hour, hourly) and Oxford (£12.40, 1¾ hours, change at Didcot Parkway, every half-hour). Trains head to Fishguard (£22.40; 4½ hours) at 6.57am and 7.10pm to correspond with ferry departures. Phone ☎ 0845 7484950 for timetable information.

Getting Around

The nicest way to get around is on the ferry which, from April to September, plies the Floating Harbour. There are a number of stops including Bristol Bridge, the Industrial Museum, the SS *Great Britain* and Hotwells. The **ferry** (☎ 9273416) runs every 20 minutes; a single fare is £1.20, a return ticket £5. Day tickets on the bus are £2.60.

There's a good **local bus system** (☎ 9412525).

CENTRAL ENGLAND

The English heartland covers a vast swathe of territory that includes some of England's highs and lows. What it lacks in prettiness, it makes up for in personality, and there is a real feel to the East Midlands that isn't always found in the tourist meccas of the Cotswolds and the Peak District.

Some of Britain's most popular tourist sites are in the southern part of the Midlands, among them Blenheim Palace, Stratford-upon-Avon and Oxford.

To the west, however, it's a different story. The southwest sections of the Chilterns remain largely unspoilt and are accessible to walkers of the Ridgeway.

The Cotswolds embody the popular image of English countryside. The combination of golden stone, flower-draped cottages, church spires, towering chestnuts and oaks and rolling hills can make the Cotswolds villages look more like postcards than actual towns.

To the north, Shrewsbury is an attractive town that's well worth a visit, and the Peak District National Park is one of England's most beautiful regions.

Hiking

The Cotswolds Way, with easy accessibility to accommodation, winds 100 miles (161km) from Chipping Campden south to Bath, but it is quite feasible to tackle a smaller section. Bath is obviously easily accessible, but you'll have to contact the **Gloucestershire inquiry line** (☎ 01452-425543) for information about the infrequent buses that run between Chipping Campden and Stratford or Moreton-in-Marsh.

The main walking area in the north of this region is the stunning Peak District National Park.

Getting Around

Bus transport around the region is fairly efficient, and particularly good in the Peak

BRITAIN

District and to and from Oxford. Trains run regularly through Birmingham, Shrewsbury, Oxford and to the start of the Cotswolds, but Stratford requires some pre-planning.

OXFORD
☎ 01865 / pop 134,000

It's impossible to pick up any tourist literature about Oxford without reading about its dreaming spires, which is surprisingly apt. Looking across the meadows or rooftops to Oxford's golden spires is certainly an experience to inspire purple prose.

Tourists and students create an international feeling rivalled by few other towns its size, and the plethora of performances, lectures, drinking spots, and historical sights make for an intellectually and visually stimulating holiday. Overwhelming numbers stream through, especially in summer and on holidays, so be prepared for a lightning storm of camera flashes in what sometimes feels like a tourist trap for the learned.

History

Oxford University is the oldest university in Britain. While there's no exact starting date, people began learning here around 1069, with University, Balliol and Merton Colleges established between 1249 and 1264. Oxford has seen the education of many esteemed people – 24 prime ministers, Lewis Carroll, Christopher Wren and Mr Bean.

There is no single central university; instead, about 16,800 students attend 39 autonomous colleges. All colleges teach the same 17 subjects but each has their own personalitxy.

Orientation

The city centre is surrounded by rivers and streams on the eastern, southern and western sides, and can easily be covered on foot. Drivers will do best to leave cars at one of the Park & Ride areas and take a bus into town.

The train station is to the west of the city, with frequent buses to Carfax Tower. Alternatively, turn left off the station concourse onto Park End St and it's a 15-minute walk. The bus and coach station is nearer the centre, on Gloucester Green (there's no green).

Information

A visit to the hectic **TIC** (☎ 726871; 15-16 Broad St; www.visitoxford.org; ⏱ 9.30am-6pm Mon-Sat, closes earlier winter, 10am-3.30pm Sun summer & bank hols) is essential. Book walking tours here. Information about the university is available at Oxford University's website, www.ox.ac.uk. Internet access is available at **Mic@s.com** (118 High St ☎ 726364; per 30min £1; ⏱ 9am-11pm; 91 Gloucester Green ☎ 726009; per 30min £1; ⏱ 9am-11pm).

Sights & Activities
COLLEGES

Starting at the Carfax Tower, cross Cornmarket St and walk down the hill, along St Aldate's, to **Christ Church** (☎ 286573; admission £4), perhaps the most famous college in Oxford, and the only university college in the world with a cathedral, albeit the smallest in England, on its grounds. It dates back to Norman times (1140s). The main entrance is beneath Tom Tower, which was built by Christopher Wren in 1680. Most of the world will recognise its Great Hall as Harry Potter's Hogwarts School.

Magdalen College (☎ 276000; adult/concession & child £3/2), one of the richest Oxford colleges, has extensive and beautiful grounds, with a deer park, river walk, three quadrangles and superb lawns. This was CS Lewis' college and the setting for the film *Shadowlands*.

Merton College (☎ 276310) is one of the three oldest colleges, dating to 1264. The present buildings mostly date from the 15th to 17th centuries. The stained glass window in the chapel is particularly remarkable. There are four tours daily April to October and two daily November to March.

Check out the fabulous view of those dreaming spires from the **University Church of St Mary the Virgin tower** (adult/child £1.60/0.80). Turn right up Catte St to the distinctive, circular **Radcliffe Camera** (admission £1.50), a reading room for the **Bodleian Library** (☎ 277224). You're looking at a tiny fraction of the library; much of its 100 miles (161km) of storage space is underground, and it could take up to 24 hours to check a book out.

On New College Lane is the **Bridge of Sighs**, modelled after the eponymous Venetian *Ponte de Sospiri* and connecting the two sides of Hertford College. Wren's **Sheldonian Theatre** (☎ 277299; Broad St; ⏱ 10am-12.30pm & 2-4.30pm, to 3.30pm in winter, closed Sun) hosts Oxford graduations.

MUSEUMS

Established in 1683, one of Britain's best (and its oldest) museums is the **Ashmolean**

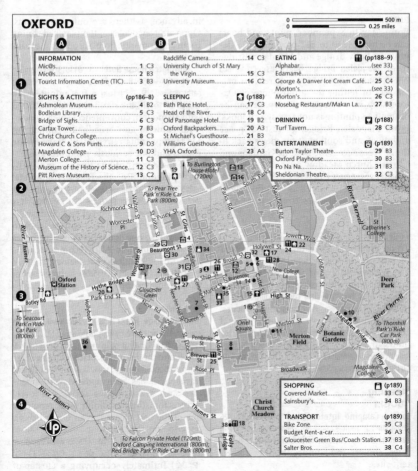

OXFORD

0 — 500 m
0 — 0.25 miles

INFORMATION	
Mic@s	1 C3
Mic@s	2 B3
Tourist Information Centre (TIC)	3 B3

SIGHTS & ACTIVITIES	(pp186–8)
Ashmolean Museum	4 B2
Bodleian Library	5 C3
Bridge of Sighs	6 C3
Carfax Tower	7 B3
Christ Church College	8 C3
Howard C & Sons Punts	9 D3
Magdalen College	10 D3
Merton College	11 C3
Museum of the History of Science	12 C3
Pitt Rivers Museum	13 C2

Radcliffe Camera	14 C3
University Church of St Mary the Virgin	15 C3
University Museum	16 C2

SLEEPING	(p188)
Bath Place Hotel	17 C3
Head of the River	18 C4
Old Parsonage Hotel	19 B2
Oxford Backpackers	20 A3
St Michael's Guesthouse	21 B3
Williams Guesthouse	22 A3
YHA Oxford	23 A3

EATING	(pp188–9)
Alphabar	(see 33)
Edamamé	24 C3
George & Danver Ice Cream Café	25 C4
Morton's	(see 33)
Morton's	26 C3
Nosebag Restaurant/Makan La	27 B3

DRINKING	(p188)
Turf Tavern	28 C3

ENTERTAINMENT	(p189)
Burton Taylor Theatre	29 B3
Oxford Playhouse	30 B3
Po Na Na	31 B3
Sheldonian Theatre	32 C3

SHOPPING	(p189)
Covered Market	33 C3
Sainsbury's	34 B3

TRANSPORT	(p189)
Bike Zone	35 C3
Budget Rent-a-car	36 A3
Gloucester Green Bus/Coach Station	37 B3
Salter Bros	38 C4

(☎ 278000; www.ashmol.ox.ac.uk; Beaumont St; admission free; ☼ 10am-5pm Tue-Sat, 2-5pm Sun), housing extensive displays of European art (including works by Raphael and Michelangelo) and Middle Eastern and Egyptian antiquities.

In a superb Victorian Gothic building, the **University Museum** (☎ 272950; Parks Rd; admission free; ☼ noon-5pm) displays the natural sciences – palaeontology, mineralogy, etc – in stunning surroundings. Continue through to the **Pitt Rivers Museum** (☎ 270927; admission free; ☼ noon-4.30pm Mon-Sat, 2-4.30pm Sun). The glass cases here are crammed to overflowing with everything from a sailing boat to a gory collection of shrunken South American heads.

Near the TIC is the **Museum of the History of Science** (☎ 277280; Broad St; admission free; ☼ noon-

4pm Tue-Sat, 2-5pm Sun), with a multitude of early and modern scientific instruments (including some of Einstein's blackboard lecture notes on the theory of relativity), all housed in the world's oldest purpose-built museum.

AIRPORT CONNECTIONS

Oxford has easy connections to both Gatwick and Heathrow. If you want a less hectic (and cheaper) alternative than staying in London, try staying in Oxford and catching a comfortable and direct half-hourly (Heathrow) or hourly (Gatwick) bus; see Getting There & Away, p254. Plan ahead, as a return ticket is only slighter higher than a single.

PUNTS

From May to September, punts and boats can be hired (£10 to £12 per hour, £25 deposit) at Folly Bridge and Magdalen Bridge from **Magdalen Bridge Boathouse** (☎ 01865 202643; 10am-dusk late Mar-Oct). There's no better way of letting the atmosphere of Oxford seep in, however the seepage can be dramatic – punting is not as easy as it looks. From Magdalen Bridge, go east for peace and quiet, and southwest for views back to the colleges across the Botanic Gardens and Christ Church Meadow.

Salter's Steamers (☎ 243421; Folly Bridge) hires out punts for £10 as well as scheduled boat trips along the Thames from late May to late September.

Tours

To do the town justice, take a walking tour or buy one of many detailed guidebooks. The *Welcome to Oxford* brochure (£1.50) has a walking tour with college opening times.

The TIC has **walking tours** (adult/concession £6.50/3; ⏲ 11am & 2pm) of the minor colleges, lasting two hours. Several hop-on, hop-off companies offer tours year-round (shorter hours in winter), including **City Sightseeing** (adult/concession/child £9/7/3) and **The Oxford Full Circle** (adult/concession/child £8/6/3).

Sleeping

BUDGET

Oxford Camping International (☎ 244088; 426 Abingdon Rd; adult £2.90-5.80, child £1.80-free; P) Near the city centre, this camping ground offers shower and laundry facilities and 85 tent sites.

YHA Oxford (☎ 0870 7705970; oxford@yha.org.uk; 2a Botley Rd; adult/under 18 yrs dm £19.50/14.40, tw £46; 🖳 ✖) Well located in a new building directly behind the train station. Book in advance, as this impeccably run hostel is deservedly popular, especially during holidays and summer.

Much less spick-and-span is **Oxford Backpackers** (☎ 721761; 9A Hythe Bridge St; dm £12-13; 🖳), closer to town with larger rooms. Prices vary depending on the size of the dorm (four to 18 beds).

MID-RANGE

Williams Guesthouse (☎ 721880: 14 Holywell St; s/d £35/50; P ✖) Unless you're lucky enough to happen upon a rare cancellation, book far in advance, as there are only four rooms. Opposite New College, the panelled dining room and romantic fireplace add to the tranquil feel.

Burlington House Hotel (☎ 513513; www.burlington-house.co.uk; 374 Banbury Rd; s/d £58/80, s with shared bathroom £40; P ✖) Just a five-minute walk north of town, the rooms here are outfitted with all modern conveniences, such as powerful showers and broadband connection for laptops, plus refreshment trays in the rooms and one seriously good breakfast.

Of the dozens of guesthouses and B&Bs on Abingdon Rd, the **Falcon Private Hotel** (☎ 511122; 88/90 Abingdon Rd; www.oxfordcity.co.uk/hotels/falcon; s/d/tr/q £38/72/80/88; P ✖) has a lovely vegetarian breakfast and well-equipped rooms. It's fifteen minutes' walk to town, or take one of dozens of passing buses towards Abingdon. Also recommended is the no-frills **St Michael's Guesthouse** (☎ 242101; 26 St Michael's St; s/d/f £35/55/66) a block from Gloucester Green.

TOP END

Old Parsonage Hotel (☎ 310210; www.oldparsonage-hotel.co.uk; 1 Banbury Rd; s/d/ste from £125/135/195; P ✖ ✖) For a bit of immunised time travel, check into this luxurious place. Once a refuge for persecuted clergy, now a refuge for weary travellers, it has been updated with amenities such as babysitting services, a lovely terrace for summer dining and reputedly one of the best cream teas in Oxford (both open to non-residents).

Bath Place Hotel (☎ 243235; www.bathplace.co.uk; 4-5 Bath Pl; s/d £95/100, ste & cottages £125-165; P ✖) Intimately occupying a cluster of 17th-century cottages, once used as housing for some very lucky students, now with 21st-century comforts. The neighbouring Turf Tavern can be noisy at night.

Eating

Edamamé (☎ 246916; 15 Holywell St; sushi from £2.50, mains from £4; ⏲ lunch Tue-Sun, dinner Thu-Sat) The city's student hotspot is a hopping Japanese restaurant with communal tables, excellent prices and beautiful presentation.

Nosebag Restaurant/Makan La (☎ 203222; 6 St Michael's St; soups £2.75, mains £6.25) Filling soups and a good range of vegetarian choices; the Asian-inspired downstairs restaurant serves up noodle and vegetable specialities, including a spicy *mee goreng* (£5).

Turf Tavern (☎ 243235; 4 Bath Pl; snacks & mains from £4) There's excellent pub grub at this recommended watering hole, dating from the 16th century and hidden away down an alley.

Head of the River (☎ 721600; Folly Bridge; mains from £4) Named for the victor in the annual inter-collegiate rowing regatta, this pub has an ideal location with a heated outdoor patio, and is very popular.

George & Danver Ice Cream Café (☎ 516652; 55 Little Clarendon St; ☯ to midnight; ice cream, light meals from £2) Serves pizzas and bagels as well as delicious home-made ice cream.

For self-caterers, there's a **Sainsbury's super-market** (☯ Mon-Sat 7am-11pm, 11am-5pm Sun) in the centre. **Morton's** (☎ 200860; 22 Broad St; sandwiches £2) can't be faulted for its tasty baguettes and attractive garden. The **covered market** (☯ 8am-5pm Mon-Sat) has a dozen places for sweets and takeaway, including another **Morton's** (☎ 200867), and the organic **Alphabar** (☎ 250499).

Entertainment

One need not look any further than signposts, walls or entryways for the best entertainment in Oxford. Leaflets and posters line Oxford and announce all sorts of events throughout all 39 colleges. **Po Na Na** (☎ 249171; 13 Magdalen St) is a late-night bar-cum-club. Sir John Gielgud and Dame Judi Dench have both graced the stage at the **Oxford Playhouse** (☎ 305305; Beaumont St), which has a mixed bag of theatre, dance and music. **Burton Taylor Theatre** (☎ 305305; Gloucester St) has more offbeat student productions.

Shopping

Check out the **covered market** (off Cornmarket & High Sts) with aisles of groovy clothing, funky antiques, butchers, fresh produce and cake shops.

Getting There & Away

BUS

Oxford is easily and quickly reached from London, and there are a number of competitive bus lines on the route. A return ticket from London on the **Oxford Tube** (☎ 772250) costs £9 and is valid two days; the trip to Oxford takes 1¾ hours. It starts at London's Victoria coach station but also stops at Marble Arch, Notting Hill Gate and Shepherd's Bush. The service operates 24 hours.

National Express heads to Bristol (£12.40, 1¾ hours, hourly). From Bristol there are connections to Wales, Devon and Cornwall. Buses to Shrewsbury, North Wales, York and Durham go via frequent connections to Birmingham.

The Oxford Bus Company (☎ 785400) operates three services: the Oxford Express, with 24-hour departures to London's Victoria station (£9 single, £13 three-month return, 1½ hours, every 15 to 30 minutes); the Airline, a half-hourly bus from Gloucester Green to Heathrow (one way adult/child or senior £14/7); and an hourly bus to Gatwick (one way adult/child £21/10.50). Pay on board with sterling, euro, or US dollars. Phone for the variety of fare details.

CAR

If you wish to drive, **Budget** (☎ 724884; budgetoxford@yahoo.co.uk; Osney Lane) is behind the train station.

TRAIN

Trains head to London's Paddington station (£14.90, one hour) about every 15 minutes. Oxford is a good connection option for the Cotswolds, including Gloucester, Cheltenham and Moreton-in-Marsh (£8.20, 35 minutes, 12 daily), for Stow. Trains also go to Bath (£16.20, 1¼ hours, at least hourly), Bristol Temple Meads (£12.40, 1¾ hours with a change at Didcot Parkway, every half-hour) and into Cornwall via Penzance (£58, 5½ hours with a change at Reading, nearly hourly). For train inquiries, phone ☎ 0845 7484950.

Getting Around

Local buses and minibuses leave from all over Oxford, including around Carfax Tower. For information on Stagecoach services phone ☎ 772250.

There are a number of places where you can hire bicycles. **Bike Zone** (☎ 728877; 6 Market St) is central and charges £10 a day or £20 a week.

Park'n'Ride links 4000 parking spaces with the city centre.

BLENHEIM PALACE

One of the largest palaces in Europe, **Blenheim Palace** (☎ 0870 602080; Woodstock; www.blenheimpalace.com; adult/concession £11/8.50; ☯ house 10.30am-5.30pm mid-Feb–mid-Dec, closed Mon-Tue Nov-

Dec, park 9am-4.45pm year-round) was a gift to John Churchill from Queen Anne and Parliament as a reward for his role in defeating Louis XIV. Sir Winston Churchill, the cousin of the 9th Duke of Marlborough, was born here several weeks early.

Designed and built by John Vanbrugh and Nicholas Hawksmoor between 1705 and 1722, with gardens by Capability Brown, Blenheim is an enormous baroque fantasy, and is definitely worth visiting. Blenheim is just south of the village of Woodstock. Catch a Stagecoach bus (Nos 20a–c) from Oxford's Gloucester Green or train station to the palace's entrance (£3.70 return, at five or 35 minutes past the hour). Check ahead, as the grounds host flower shows, craft fairs and the like, especially on summer weekends.

STRATFORD-UPON-AVON
☎ 01789 / pop 24,000

Stratford is a pleasant Midlands market town that just happened to be William Shakespeare's birthplace. It's now one of Britain's biggest tourist draws, and not just for those interested in the plays and sonnets of Shakespeare.

The Royal Shakespeare Company has three theatres here, in addition to its London venues, and there's nearly always something on. Warwick, with its wonderful castle, is just to the north.

Orientation & Information

Stratford is easy to explore on foot. The main street changes names several times as it extends from the river to the train station.

The **TIC** (☎ 293127; www.shakespeare-country.co.uk; Bridgefoot; ☯ 9am-6pm Mon-Sat, 10.30am-4.30pm Sun) has plenty of information about the sights and the numerous B&Bs. For Internet access, head to the **library** (☎ 292209; Henley St; ☯ 9.30am-5pm Mon-Sat, noon-4pm Sun).

Sights & Activities

Five museums filled with recreations and the history behind William Shakespeare make up **Shakespeare Houses** (☎ 204016; adult/concession/child £13/12/6.50), including Shakespeare's Birthplace, Nash's House & New Place, Hall's Croft, Anne Hathaway's Cottage and Mary Arden's House. Ring for opening hours.

Seeing a production by the **Royal Shakespeare Company** (☎ 0870 6091110; www.rsc.org.uk; tickets £10-50; ☯ box office 9.30am-8pm) should not

be missed. Tickets are often available on the day of performance, but get in early. Stand-by tickets (£12) are available to students immediately before performances and there are almost always standing-room tickets (£5). If you can't get in for a performance, you can also take a **tour** (adult/concession £5/4) of the RSC, including backstage and the legendary Swan Theatre.

Sleeping

Youth Hostel (☎ 0870 7706052, fax stratford@yha.org.uk; Hemmingford House, Alveston; adult/under 18 yrs incl breakfast £17/12.30; P ☐) Nearly a half-hour walk (2 miles) from town up B4086 (or a quick jaunt on bus Nos 18 or 77), this well-maintained, fully serviced and restored Georgian mansion is nestled amidst a sleepy village and garden setting.

White Swan (☎ 297022; www.thewhiteswanstratford.co.uk; Rother St; s/d/f £60/80/130; P ✗) The best mid-range bet in town, where you can enjoy soundproofed windows, 24-hour room service, and well-appointed furnishings. Check in the off-season for substantial discounts.

B&Bs are plentiful just west of the centre on Evesham Place, Grove Rd and Broad Walk. From the train station, turn right at the first traffic light and you'll find dozens of places, all fairly similar. Try the **Dylan** (☎ 204819; thedylan@lineone.net; 10 Evesham Pl; per person £25), the delightful **Twelfth Night** (☎ 414 595; 13 Evesham Pl; d from £55), **Carlton** (☎ 293548; 22 Evesham Pl; s/d from £22/45) or **Woodstock** (☎ 299 881; www.woodstock-house.co.uk; 30 Grove Rd; per person £25-30; ✗).

Also in town is the **Payton** (☎ 266442; www.payton.co.uk; 6 John St; d from £50; P ✗), a lovely and extremely pink guesthouse.

Eating

Sheep St offers a fine selection of dining possibilities.

The Vintner (☎ 297259; 4-5 Sheep St; afternoon tea £4-7, mains £9-16) This is a wine bar that serves Eastern-inspired dishes during the day.

Bulrush Dining Rooms (☎ 297022; Rother St; dishes £4.50-12.25) Well-liked by locals, the Bulrush is in the White Swan Hotel. Here you can have dinner or a cream tea in a low-beamed restaurant that pre-dates Shakespeare by 100 years.

Thespians (☎ 267187; 27 Sheep St; mains £5-12) Serves up delicious South Indian fare, with especially tasty vegetarian mains.

Dirty Duck (☎ 297312; Waterside) Serves ales and light meals to theatregoers and actors.

Getting There & Away
National Express buses link Stratford with many towns, including London, Birmingham, Oxford and Heathrow.

Phone ☎ 01788-535555 for local bus information. The X20 operates regularly to Birmingham (£3.40, 1¼ hours), the X16 to Warwick (£2.55, 20 minutes) and Coventry (£3.20, 1½ hours), and No 50 to Oxford (change bus at Chipping Norton, £5.25, 2½ hours).

Stratford has spotty train service. Some trains from Bath, for instance, require three changes. Direct service goes to London's Paddington station (£22.90, two hours, four to five daily) stopping in Oxford (£9, 1¼ hours). For further information phone ☎ 0845 7484950.

COTSWOLDS
The Cotswolds are a range of beautiful limestone hills rising gently from the Thames and its tributaries in the east, but forming a steep escarpment overlooking the Bristol Channel in the west. The hills are characterised by honey-coloured stone villages and a gently rolling landscape. The villages were built on the wealth of the medieval wool trade and are these days extremely popular with tourists.

Orientation & Information
The hills run north from Bath for 100 miles (161km) to Chipping Campden. The most attractive countryside is bounded in the west by the M5 and Chipping Sodbury, and in the east by Stow-on-the-Wold, Burford, Bibury, Cirencester and Chippenham.

There are train stations at Cheltenham, Kemble (serving Cirencester), Moreton-in-Marsh (serving Stow-on-the-Wold) and Stroud.

Bath, Cheltenham, Stratford-upon-Avon and Oxford are the best starting points for the Cotswolds. Cirencester is the region's capital. Trains from London's Paddington station reach Moreton-in-Marsh (£21.20, 1½ hours, 10 to 11 daily).

The TICs in surrounding towns all stock information on the Cotswolds, but those dealing specifically with the region are **Cirencester TIC** (☎ 01285 654180; Market Pl) and

Stow-on-the-Wold TIC (☎ 01451 831082; The Square; closed Sun off-season).

The Cotswolds area is not particularly well served by YHA hostels, but there are countless B&Bs and hotels, most fairly pricey.

For Internet access, check the Stow **library** (☎ 01451 831633; The Square; 🕑 10am-12.30pm, 2-7pm Tue & Fri, to 12.30pm Wed, 9.30am-12.30pm Sat); the first half-hour is free; £1.50 per half-hour after that.

Getting Around
Getting around the Cotswolds by public transport isn't easy. If you're trying anything ambitious, contact **Traveline** (☎ 0870 6082608). Bikes can be hired in Bath, Oxford and Cheltenham. **Compass Holidays** (☎ 01242 250642) has bicycles for hire (£12 per day) at Cheltenham station.

Stow-on-the-Wold
☎ 01451 / pop 2000
Stow, as it is known, is one of the most impressive (and visited) towns in the Cotswolds. It's a terrific base if you don't have a vehicle, because several particularly beautiful villages, including the famous Upper and Lower Slaughters, are within a day's walk or cycle ride.

The **Youth Hostel** (☎ 0870 7706050; stow@yha .org.uk; The Square; adult/under 18 yrs £13.40/9.30; 🖳) is extremely popular with families and has top-notch facilities. At the top end there's the historic **Stow Lodge Hotel** (☎ 830485; www .stowlodge.com; The Square; s/d from £79/101; P ✗) in a lovely setting with all the amenities and a very popular restaurant.

Number 9 (☎ 870333; 9 Park St; rooms £70) is a stylish B&B or try the **Limes Guest House** (☎ 830034; thelimes@zoom.co.uk; Evesham Rd; s/d £25/46; P), just outside the town's centre.

You can reach Stow by bus from Moreton-in-Marsh, which is on the main line between Worcester and Oxford. Contact **Pulhams' Coaches** (☎ 820369) for a timetable.

Cheltenham
☎ 01242 / pop 93,000
Cheltenham is a large and elegant spa town easily accessible by bus and train. The **TIC** (☎ 522878; 77 Promenade) is helpful. Cheltenham is on the main Bristol–Birmingham train line, and can be reached by train from South Wales, Bath and Southwest England, and Oxford (changing at Didcot and Swindon).

BIRMINGHAM

☎ 0121 / pop 969,000

Although Birmingham is England's second largest city, it's not often thought of as a tourist destination. That's because it isn't. However, it's a transport hub, and the city centre is slowly revitalising itself into a place you wouldn't mind spending half a day or so. Recently, however, things have looked up, with a vibrant cultural scene and the restoration of the old canal network, and the opening of innumerable restaurants and bars in the Brindleyplace area.

Most of Birmingham's sites are within five to 10 minutes of the New St and Moor St train stations.

The **TIC** (☎ 6936300; Victoria Sq) can help with visitor information.

Fans of Frodo, Gandalf and Middle-Earth: head thee to **The Tolkien Trail** (www.tolkiensociety .org). JRR Tolkien grew up in the hamlet of Sarehole, which you can visit with a brochure, using public transport (DaySaver adult/child £2.50/1.70) or by car. See Tolkien's boyhood haunts, as well as the inspirations for the Two Towers of Gondor and the Shire.

Museum & Art Gallery (☎ 3032834; ☒ 10am-5pm Mon-Thu & Sat, from 10.30am Fri, 12.30-5pm Sun) has a fine collection of Pre-Raphaelite paintings and overlooks **Victoria** and **Chamberlain Squares**, both of them full of interesting statuary. The old **Jewellery Quarter**, where – surprise – jewellery was made, is looking much smarter than formerly; it also houses a couple of interesting small museums.

Try a balti restaurant for Birmingham's own version of Indian cooking. The original is **Royal Alfaisel** (☎ 4495695; 136 Stoney Lane; buffet £5.95; ☒ noon-midnight), but balti zones are cropping up around Ladypool St and in the Sparkhill area.

ALTHORP

The cult continues at the memorial, museum and ancestral home of the late Diana, Princess of Wales at **Althorp** (☎ 01604 770107; Althorp, Northampton; adult/pensioner/child £11.50/9.50/5.50, upstairs extra £2.50; ☒ 11am-5pm Jul & Aug; ℗). Six rooms devoted to Diana's life and charities will assuage the most fervent Diana fans, but lay people will enjoy the stately manor that's been the Spencer home for 500 years.

SHREWSBURY & AROUND

☎ 01743 / pop 67,400

Shrewsbury's main attraction is that it has no main attraction, making it a wonderful destination in which to wander among its many half-timbered black and white 'magpie' buildings, or to use as a base for many nearby sites – Ironbridge Gorge Museums, Stokesay Castle, Shropshire's walking country, plus connections to North Wales. Two famous railways into Wales terminate here and it's possible to do a fascinating circuit of North Wales from here.

Orientation & Information

The town is strategically sited within a loop of the Severn River. Across the narrow land bridge formed by the loop is the train station, a five-minute walk north of the town centre. The bus station, Smithfield Rd, is central. The **TIC** (☎ 281200; www .visitshrewsbur.com; The Square; ☒ 9.30-5.30 in summer, 10am-5pm in winter Mon-Sat, to 4pm Sun year-round) is in the Music Hall. The TIC offers walking tours (adult/child £3/1.50) every Saturday at 2.30pm. Online resources are available at www.shropshiretourism.info.

Sights & Activities

Wandering the **medieval streets** whose names – Butcher Row, Fish St and Milk St – hark back to the days when these trades were conducted here. The **Abbot's House** on Butcher Row is a fine example of the distinctive timber-framed architecture of that time. The TIC organises daily **walking tours** (adult/concession £2.50/1) of the town at 2.30pm from May to October.

The town's main museum is **Rowley's House** (☎ 361196; Barker St; admission free; ☒ 10am-5pm), which features Roman and medieval finds.

Comprising 10 museum sites strung along the gorge are the **Ironbridge Gorge Museums** (☎ 884391; adult/student & child £13.25/8.75; ☒ 10am-5pm). There's Blists Hill Victorian Town, which re-creates an entire community; the Coalport China Museum, with more than you ever wanted to know about porcelain; the Museum of Iron; the Museum of the Gorge; and, among other sites, the beautiful iron bridge – the world's first. The bridge is close to the TIC and is the best place to start.

From Shrewsbury, bus No 96 runs every two hours to Telford via Ironbridge (35 minutes). There are also regular buses from Telford's town centre. Unless you're into walking, you'll need your own transport to get around the sites – it's 3 miles from Blists Hill to the Museum of Iron.

Sleeping & Eating

Lucroft Hotel (☎ 362421; Castle Gates; www.lucroft hotel.co.uk; s/d £20/35) The youth hostel has closed, so the Lucroft, just steps from the train station has taken over the role. It's inviting if a bit worn; ask for a back room if you mind street or post-pub noise.

Tudor House (☎ 351735; www.tudorhouseshrews bury.co.uk; 2 Fish St; from s/d £55/75) Your hosts at this central and quaint establishment serve up a fabulous organic breakfast in a half-timbered gem blanketed in antiques.

Old Post Office Hotel (☎ 236019; www.oldpost officepub.com; Milk St; s/d/f £30/60/65) This 450-year-old Tudor gem has seven modernised rooms and a tasty pub-restaurant downstairs.

Traitor's Gate Brasserie (☎ 249152; Castle St, St Mary's Water Lane; mains £9-15, sandwiches £3-6) This brasserie beckons with fresh flowers and cosy tables tucked in an underground brick cavern.

Three Fishes (☎ 344793; 4 Fish St; mains £5-9; ✗) A rare chance to drink or dine at a smoke-free pub, this affable place serves quite decent pub fayre in a traditional Tudor setting.

Getting There & Away

National Express connects to London (£14.50, five hours, 1pm and 4pm) via Birmingham (£15.50, four hours).

For information on transport in Shropshire, contact **Traveline** (☎ 0870 6082608). Bus No 96 runs about every two hours between Shrewsbury and Telford via Ironbridge (35 minutes). Bus No 420 connects Shrewsbury with Birmingham twice daily. Bus No 435 runs regularly to and from Ludlow.

Shrewsbury is the best base for train journeys to North Wales. It has good connections to London's Euston station via Birmingham (£34.10, three hours, at least every half-hour), Chester (£6, one hour, 11 to 12 daily) and Snowdonia's Betsw-y-Coed (£19, three hours, six to seven daily).

Two fascinating small railways terminate at Shrewsbury, in addition to plenty of the usual main-line connections. It's possible to do a highly recommended rail loop from Shrewsbury around North Wales. Time-tabling is a challenge so phone ☎ 0845 7484950 for information. The journey is possible in a day as long as you don't miss any of the connections, but it's much better to allow at least a couple of days as there's plenty to see. The Freedom of North and Mid-Wales Flexi-Rover ticket is the most economical way of covering this route. It costs £29 and allows travel on three days out of seven.

From Shrewsbury you head due west across Wales to Machynlleth, past beautiful coastline, to Porthmadog, where you pick up the Ffestiniog Railway, a restored, narrow-gauge steam train that winds up into Snowdonia National Park to the slate-mining town of Blaenau Ffestiniog. From Blaenau, another small railway carves its way through the striking mountain and valley scenery to Llandudno and Conwy.

Another famous line, promoted as the Heart of Wales Line, runs southwest to Swansea (four hours), connecting with the main line from Cardiff to Fishguard (six hours).

PEAK DISTRICT

Squeezed between the industrial Midlands to the south, Manchester to the west and Sheffield to the east, the Peak District seems an unlikely site for one of England's most beautiful regions. Even the name is misleading, being derived from the tribes who once lived here, not from the existence of any significant peaks (there are none!). Nonetheless, the 542-sq-mile Peak District National Park is a delight, particularly for walkers and cyclists.

The Peak District divides into the green fields and steep-sided dales of the southern White Peak and the bleak, gloomy moors of the northern Dark Peak. Buxton, to the west, and Matlock, to the east, are good bases for exploring the park, or you can stay right in the centre at Bakewell or Castleton. In May and June the ancient custom of 'well dressing' can be seen in many villages. There are also prehistoric sites, limestone caves, the tragic plague village of Eyam and the fine stately homes of Chatsworth and Haddon Hall.

Castleton and nearby Edale are popular villages on the border between the White and Dark Peaks. From Edale, the Pennine Way starts its 250-mile meander northwards.

From the town of Castleton, the 25-mile Limestone Way is a superb day walk covering the length of the White Peak to Matlock. In addition, a number of disused railway lines in the White Peak have been redeveloped as walking and cycling routes, with strategically situated bicycle-rental outlets at old station sites.

Check online at www.peakdistrict.org for NPA info or www.thepeakdistrict.info for tourist information. Contact **National Park Information Centres** (Edale ☎ 01433 670207; next to train station; ⏲ 9am-5.30pm summer, to 5pm winter; Castleton ☎ 01433 620679; Castle St; ⏲ call for opening hrs; Bakewell (☎ 01629-813227; Old Market Hall; ⏲ 9am-5.30pm summer, 9.30am-5pm winter) for information on B&Bs, hiking, or camping barns in the area. Visitors to Bakewell should make sure to sample Bakewell pudding (not tart).

The regular Transpeak bus service cuts right across the Peak District from Nottingham and Derby to Manchester via Matlock, Bakewell and Buxton. Pick up a Derbyshire Wayfarer ticket (adult/concession or child £7.50/3.75) to explore the area. Pick one up at any TIC in the area or call **Traveline** (☎ 0870 6082608) for information.

EAST ENGLAND

Apart from the city of Cambridge, most of the eastern counties – such as Norfolk, Suffolk, Cambridgeshire and Lincolnshire – have been overlooked by tourists. Here you will find a softer England where picturesque medieval market towns straddle a gently undulating landscape that is criss-crossed by waterways and marshland and bordered by some stunning coastlines.

It's difficult to believe that this pastoral idyll was once the epicentre of economic power in England. Its heyday was in medieval times when its wool and weaving industry made Norwich one of the most prominent cities in England and King's Lynn a major port. The evidence of the region's busy medieval past is still here to charm the visitor.

Orientation & Information

Cambridge, Lincoln, Norwich and Kings' Lynn are all easily accessible from London by train or bus. Ely and King's Lynn are on a direct train line from Cambridge.

East of England Tourist Board (☎ 0870 225 4800; www.visiteastofengland.com) has a comprehensive website and a booklet called *Great Days Out* (£4.50) that covers all the attractions of the region.

Getting Around

Bus transport is aimed more at local needs than for visitors, so it can seem slow and complex. For regional timetables and information phone **Traveline** (☎ 0870 608 2608; www.traveline.org.uk).

If you are planning extensive rail travel, **Anglia Plus** (☎ 0845 484950; www.angliarailways .co.uk) passes offer three days travel out of seven for £20, and one day for £9. If you are from overseas, it may be cheaper using a BritRail pass (see Transport p258).

CAMBRIDGE

☎ 01223 / pop 130,000

Home to one of the world's greatest universities, Cambridge is steeped in history and learning. The lofty academia, architectural beauty and gentle Cam River bordered by meadows, gives Cambridge a sense of agelessness and tranquillity. Yet Cambridge has not rested on its historic laurels, it's also a lively market town with its fair share of designer boutiques and trendy cafés.

The university began in the early 13th century, about a century later than its arch academic rival Oxford. A must-see for any visitor to Britain is the choir and chapel of King's College.

Orientation & Information

Cambridge is 54 miles (87km) north of London. The central area lies in a wide bend of the Cam River, and is easy to get around on foot or bike (most of it is semipedestrianised).

The bus station is in the centre of town, but the train station is a 20-minute walk to the southeast. Sidney St is the main shopping street. The most important group of colleges (including King's) and the Backs (literally the stretch of the river at the 'backs' of the colleges with its adjoining grasslands) are to the west of Sidney St.

The **Cambridge Visitor Centre** (accommodation ☎ 457581, tours ☎ 457574; www.visitcambridge.org; Wheeler St; ⏲ 10am-5.30pm Mon-Sat, 11am-4pm Sun) organises two-hour **walking tours** (☎ 457574; adult/child under 12 yrs £8/4; ⏲ 1.30pm) around

Cambridge; it's recommended to buy your ticket in advance. **Drama tours** (☎ 457574; adult/child £5/free; ⏱ 6.30pm Tue & Fri, Aug, 90min) of historic Cambridge are also on offer, complete with costumed actors in Tudor dress There are also two-hour **walking and punt tours** (adult/child under 12 yrs £14/8; ⏱ 12.30pm Sat Apr-Oct).

The main college opening hours are detailed in the Sights section following, but in general most are closed to visitors for the Easter term (mid-April to mid-June), and all are closed for exams (mid-May to mid-June). Times sometimes change so verify with the visitor centre or the colleges directly on ☎ 337733.

The Internet café, **ITC Café** (☎ 377358; 2 Wheeler St; per 1hr £1; ⏱ 9am-9pm), is opposite the visitor centre.

Sights

Following is a walking tour of some of the main sights.

Starting at Magdalene Bridge, walk south down Bridge St until you reach the unmistakable **Round Church** (adult/concession/child £1/50p/free; ⏱ 10am-5pm Tue-Sat, 1-5pm Sun-Mon), one of only four surviving medieval round churches, dating from the 12th century. Turn right down St John's St (immediately across the road), which is named in honour of **St John's College** (☎ 338600; adult/concession/family £2.20/1.30/4.40; ⏱ 10am-5pm Mon-Fri, 9.30am-5pm Sat & Sun, March-end Oct) on the right. The gatehouse dates from 1510, walk through and find three beautiful courts, the second and third date from the 17th century. From the third court, the picturesque **Bridge of Sighs** (not open to the public) crosses the river.

Next door, **Trinity College** (☎ 338400; adult/concession/family £2/1/£4; ⏱ 10am-4.30pm, library noon-2pm Mon-Fri, closed 11-18 & 24 Jun) is one of the largest and most attractive colleges. It was established in 1546 by Henry VIII on the site of several earlier foundations. The Great Court, Cambridge's largest enclosed court, incorporates buildings from the 15th century. Beyond the Great Court is Nevile's Court and its western side – Sir Christopher Wren's library, built in the 1680s.

Next comes Caius (pronounced keys) College, and then **King's College** (☎ 331100; adult/concession £4/3; ⏱ during term 9.30am-3.30pm Mon-Sat, 1.15-2.30pm Sun, choral service 5.30pm Tue-Sat, 10.30am & 3.30pm Sun, btwn terms 9.30am-4.30pm Mon-Sat, 10am-5pm Sun, chapel open almost all year,

grounds closed mid-Apr–mid-Jun), one of Europe's greatest buildings with its perpendicular, late-Gothic style and its famous chapel. The chapel was begun in 1446 by Henry VI, but it wasn't completed until 1545. Majestic as this building is from the outside, its interior, with its breathtaking scale, stunning stained glass and intricate fan vaulting, makes the greater impact. It's amazing when the choir sings.

Continue south on King's Parade and turn right onto Silver St (St Catherine's College is on the corner), which takes you down to the Cam and the hiring point for punts.

Along the Backs, **punting** is at best sublime, but it can also be a wet and hectic experience, especially on a busy weekend. **Scudamore's** (☎ 359750; www.scudamores.com; Granta Place, Mill Lane; hire per hr Mon-Fri £12, Sat & Sun £14, deposit per punt £60/70, 45min tours adult/concession/child £12/10/6; ⏱ 9am-dusk Apr-Sep, 10am-dusk Oct-Mar) have various punt stations along the Cam. Punts hold up to six people. If you do wimp out, the Backs are also perfect for a walk or a picnic – cross the bridge and walk along the river to the right.

Festivals

Held over three days at the end of July in the fields around Cherry Hinton is the **Cambridge Folk Festival** (☎ 357851; www.cambridgefolkfestival.co.uk; Cherry Hinton; full festival £74, Fri/Sat/Sun £25/36/35, admission & camping per 2–3-person tent £107). This festival features the best of British and overseas folk musicians. There is a bus service to the site from Cambridge train station and the city centre.

Sleeping

The visitor centre has a booking service (☎ 457581, £3 fee). Cambridge's choice of good quality sleeping options is rather sparse; following is a selection of the best value, centrally located hotels.

BUDGET

Youth Hostel (☎ 354601; cambridge@yha.org.uk; 97 Tenison Rd; adults/under 18 yrs £16.50/12.40; ✗ ☐) Near the train station, this hostel has a lounge, games rooms, café, kitchen and laundry facilities. It's very popular – book ahead.

Tenison Towers Guest House (☎ 363924; www.cambridgecitytenisontowers.com; 148 Tenison Rd; B&B per person £25) There are several B&Bs on this road

BRITAIN

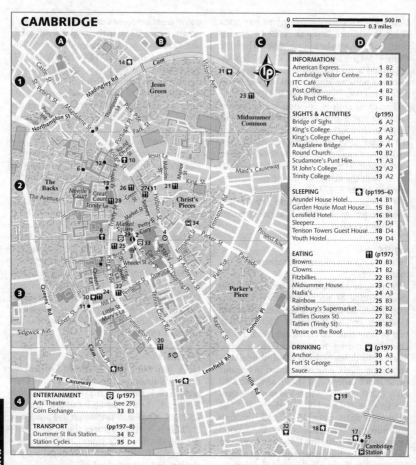

CAMBRIDGE

0 ———————— 500 m
0 ———————— 0.3 miles

INFORMATION
American Express.......................... **1** B2
Cambridge Visitor Centre................ **2** B2
ITC Café..................................... **3** B3
Post Office.................................. **4** B2
Sub Post Office............................ **5** B4

SIGHTS & ACTIVITIES (p195)
Bridge of Sighs............................. **6** A2
King's College.............................. **7** A3
King's College Chapel..................... **8** A2
Magdalene Bridge.......................... **9** A1
Round Church............................... **10** B2
Scudamore's Punt Hire.................... **11** A3
St John's College........................... **12** A2
Trinity College.............................. **13** A2

SLEEPING (pp195–6)
Arundel House Hotel...................... **14** B1
Garden House Moat House.............. **15** B4
Lensfield Hotel............................. **16** B4
Sleeperz..................................... **17** D4
Tenison Towers Guest House........... **18** D4
Youth Hostel............................... **19** D4

EATING (p197)
Browns....................................... **20** B3
Clowns....................................... **21** B2
Fitzbillies................................... **22** B3
Midsummer House......................... **23** C1
Nadia's....................................... **24** A3
Rainbow..................................... **25** B3
Sainsbury's Supermarket................ **26** B2
Tatties (Sussex St)........................ **27** B2
Tatties (Trinity St)........................ **28** B2
Venue on the Roof........................ **29** B3

DRINKING (p197)
Anchor....................................... **30** A3
Fort St George............................. **31** C1
Sauce.. **32** C4

ENTERTAINMENT (p197)
Arts Theatre................................ (see 29)
Corn Exchange............................. **33** B3

TRANSPORT (pp197–8)
Drummer St Bus Station.................. **34** B2
Station Cycles.............................. **35** D4

---

and this is the best of the bunch. Spotlessly clean and fresh-looking rooms with a blue and pine décor, this is a cosy and friendly establishment.

Sleeperz (☎ 304050; www.sleeperz.com; Station Rd; s/tw/d £35/45/55; P X) Just outside the train station in a converted railway warehouse, this great-value hotel has large, minimalist-style rooms with spacious bathrooms, but the hallways feel a bit hospital-like.

MID-RANGE & TOP END

Lensfield Hotel (☎ 355017; www.lensfieldhotel.co.uk; 53 Lensfield Rd; B&B s £65, d £98-105, f £120-130; P X) Although the Lensfield has gone a bit overboard on the frills and fake flowers, it's comfortable and just south of the city centre.

Arundel House Hotel (☎ 367701; www.arundel househotels.com.uk; 53 Chesterton Rd; B&B s £75-90, d £95-120, f £125-135; P X) This rather genteel hotel located near the centre has very large, pristine rooms with modem points overlooking the pretty Jesus Green. The décor, however, is aimed at the more senior clientele and the carpets can be headache-inducing.

Garden House Moat House (☎ 259988; www .moathousehotels.com; Grant Place, Mill Lane; s/d £170-200, with balcony £225-255; P X X ⬚ ⬚) This large hotel has rooms with their own balconies overlooking the Cam River. There is also a secluded private garden on the riverbank, as well as a swimming pool and gym. Make sure you ask for a river-view room, and also for their regular promotion prices.

BRITAIN

Eating

BUDGET

For self-caterers there's a **Sainsbury's** supermarket on Sidney St.

Nadia's (☎ 568335; 16 Silver St; sandwiches £2; 8am-5pm) For a picnic on the Backs try the excellent value rolls, baguettes, bagels and cakes here.

Clowns (☎ 355711; 54 King St; mains £3-6.50; 8am-midnight Mon-Sat, to 11pm Sun) Offering English breakfasts, toasted sandwiches and basic pasta dishes, this is a good place to refuel at a low price. Popular with students, it has a jovial atmosphere and colourful décor.

Tatties (baked potatoes £3-6; ☯ 8am-6pm Mon-Sat, 9am-5pm Sun) Trinity St (☎ 357766; No 15) Sussex St (☎ 323399; No 11) Sit down to their speciality of baked potatoes stuffed with a variety of tempting fillings, as well as breakfasts, filled baguettes, salads and cakes.

MID-RANGE

Rainbow (☎ 321551; 9A King's Parade; mains £7.25-8.25; 10am-10pm Tue-Sat; ✖) Opposite the King's College gates is this friendly vegetarian/vegan restaurant with healthy dishes from around the world.

Browns (☎ 461655; 23 Trumpington St; mains £7.95-14.95; ☯ 11am-10.30pm) The huge dining room and bar has a colonial feel with its ceiling fans, cream walls, plants and brown leather banquettes. The restaurant serves mainly British favourites, with some pasta dishes and vegetarian options.

Fitzbillies (☎ 352500; 52-54 Trumpington St; lunch mains £4.50-7.70, dinner £14.50-17.95; 10am-9.30pm Mon-Fri, 11am-5.30pm Sat, noon-5pm Sun) The combination of this light-filled modern European restaurant and its patisserie next door (chocolate cake £1) make for a sublime sensory experience.

TOP END

Venue on the Roof (☎ 367333; Arts Theatre, 6 St Edwards Passage; lunch mains £6.50-12.95, dinner £12.95-16.95; ☯ noon-3pm, 5.30-10.30pm Mon-Sat) This ultra cool, modern space is set in a rooftop conservatory above the Arts Theatre. Modern European cuisine is served, ranging from haddock and chips to roast guinea fowl with black cherry and lentil stew. Check out the stylish bar downstairs.

Midsummer House (☎ 369299; www.midsummer house.co.uk; Midsummer Common; 2-/3-course lunch menu £20/26, 3-course dinner menu £45; ☯ noon-2pm, 7-10pm

Tue-Sat) Awarded with a Michelin star, the finest restaurant in Cambridge serves exquisite French/Mediterranean meals by the banks of the Cam River. With its smart, contemporary dining room, conservatory, and private garden, this is the place for a special occasion.

Drinking & Entertainment

For local events pick up the free magazines, *Explorer* and *Agenda*.

Fort St George (☎ 354327; Midsummer Common) In a lovely riverside spot on the northern end of Midsummer Common, this 16th-century pub is said to be the oldest on the Cam.

The Anchor (☎ 353554; Silver St) This two-level traditional pub has views over the Cam River with willow trees and bobbing punts.

Sauce (☎ 360268; 3 Station Rd) Just near the train station, this minimalist style bar with '70s prints is a popular place with students and travellers.

Corn Exchange (☎ 357851; www.cornex.co.uk; Wheeler St) The main centre for arts and entertainment, it attracts pop, rock and classical music, as well as some theatre and ballet.

Arts Theatre (☎ 503333; www.cambridgeartstheatre .com; 6 St Edward's Passage) Cambridge's only real theatre, it puts on everything from pantomime to Shakespeare.

Getting There & Away

Cambridge can easily be visited as a day trip from London or en route to the north. It's well served by trains, but not so well by buses.

To London there are hourly National Express buses (one way/return £9/15, two hours). Direct buses go to King's Lynn at 7pm daily (one way/return £6.50/10.25, one hour 50 minutes). **Stagecoach Express** (☎ 01865 772250) goes to Oxford hourly (one way/return £5.99, 3½ hours).

National Express Airport (☎ 0870 575 7747) run buses to all London airports: Stansted (one way/return £8.50/10.50, one hour), Luton (£11/15, 1½ hours), Heathrow (£23.50/29.50, 2½ hours) and Gatwick (£27.50/33.50, 3½ hours).

There are trains every half-hour from London's King's Cross and Liverpool St stations (one way/return £16.40/21.70, one hour 20 minutes). There are also regular trains services to Ely (£3.60, 15 minutes) and King's Lynn (£8, one hour). There are connections at Peterborough with the main northbound trains to Lincoln, York and Edinburgh. If you want to head west to Oxford or Bath, you'll have to return to London first. For more information, phone ☎ 0845 7484950.

Getting Around

Stagecoach Cambus (☎ 423578) operates buses around town from Drummer St, including bus No 1 from the train station to the town centre.

If you're staying out of the centre, or plan to wander into the fens (fine flat country for the lazy cyclist), a bicycle can be hired from **Station Cycles** (☎ 307125; www.stationcycles .co.uk; Station Rd; per day £8; ☼ 8.30am-6pm Mon-Fri, 9am-5pm Sat all year, 10am-4pm Sun Mar-Oct) just outside the train station.

ELY

☎ 01353 / pop 9000

Ely is set on a low hill that was once an island deep in the watery world of the fens. It is dominated by the huge **Ely Cathedral** (☎ 667735; www.cathedral.ely.anglican.org; adult/concession/under 12 yrs £4.80/4.20/free; ☼ 7am-7pm May-Sep, 7.30am-6pm Mon-Sat, to 5pm Sun Oct-Mar), a superb example of the Norman Romanesque style, built between 1081 and 1200. Among Ely's narrow streets and lanes is the former home of Oliver Cromwell, which now houses the **Ely Visitor Centre** (☎ 662062; www.eastcambs.gov.uk; 29 St Mary's St), phone here for places to stay.

From Cambridge, there are trains twice an hour to Ely (one way/return £3.60/3.90, 20 minutes).

LINCOLNSHIRE
Lincoln

☎ 01522 / pop 85,500

Since it's not on a main tourist route, many people bypass Lincoln, missing a magnificent 900-year-old **cathedral** (☎ 544544; www.lin colncathedral.com; adult/concession/child/family £4/3/1/10; ☼ 7.15am-6pm), the third largest in Britain, and an interesting city with a compact medieval centre of narrow, winding streets.

Lincoln Visitor Centre (☎ 873213; www.lincoln .gov.uk; 9 Castle Sq) has information on B&Bs; the **Youth Hostel** (☎ 522076; lincoln@yha.org.uk; 77 South Park; dm adult/under 18 yrs £10.60/7.20) has kitchen and laundry facilities and a lovely park opposite.

Lincoln is 132 miles (212km) from London, with direct National Express coaches (one

way/return £19/24, 4¼ hours) and rail services (one way/return £31.50/32.50, 2¾ hours).

NORFOLK
Norwich

☎ 01603 / pop 170,000

This ancient capital was for many years larger than London, its prosperity based on trade with the Low Countries. Norwich's medieval centre has been retained along with its castle, cathedral and no fewer than 33 churches. There are numerous B&Bs – contact the **Norwich Visitor Centre** (☎ 727927; www.visitnorwich -area.co.uk; The Forum, Millennium Plain) for details.

Between London and Norwich there are direct rail (one way/return £31.50/46.80, two hours) and National Express coach links (one way/return £14/21, three hours).

King's Lynn

☎ 01553 / pop 37,500

King's Lynn is an interesting old port with some notable buildings, some of which were distinctly influenced by the trading links with Holland. Contact the **King's Lynn Visitor Centre** (☎ 763044; www.visitwestnorfolk.com; Custom House, Purfleet Quay) for tourist and accommodation information. There's a **Youth Hostel** (☎ 772461; kingslynn@yha.org.uk; College Lane; adult/under 18 yrs £10.60/7.20; ☼ 9 Apr-31 Sep) with kitchen facilities. There are regular trains from Cambridge (£8, one hour).

SUFFOLK
Sutton Hoo

Home to the 6th century burial grounds of Anglo-Saxon pagan kings is **Sutton Hoo** (☎ 01394-389700; near Woodbridge; www.nationaltrust .org.uk; adult/child £4/2; ☼ 10am-5pm Mar-Sep, winter hrs vary). Its 90ft timber ship and central burial chamber are among the most important archaeological discoveries ever made in Britain. There are walking tours of the burial site, and the **exhibition hall** houses a reconstruction of the chamber and some of its artefacts.

Take a train from London's Liverpool St station to Melton (every two hours, one way/return £20.50/21, 1¾ hours). From the station it's a half-mile walk to Sutton Hoo.

NORTHEAST ENGLAND

Rolling hills, craggy sea-fronts, turbulent history and some of England's most vibrant big cities, Northeast England is a region of rewarding contrasts. While many come to trek through three of the nation's best national parks, others come to explore Roman ruins or some of the world's finest cathedral architecture. But the area's once-depressed industrial cities are the best reason to visit, with a host of civic super-projects creating a renaissance in places that were on the scrap heap just a few years ago. For general information on visiting the region, check www.visitnorth umbria.com and www.yorkshirevisitor.com. For art, theatre and heritage information visit www.culturalyorkshire.com.

Activities

The Northeast is ideal rambling country with the ever-popular **Pennine Way** leading many walkers' top ten lists. Stretching from the Peak District to Scotland's Kirk Yetholm, it's a 268-mile hike easily broken into sections. Northumberland's 39-mile coastline is a designated Area of Outstanding Natural Beauty, offering breathtaking vistas of rocky cliffs, rolling dunes and isolated islands. For a simple escape from the city, the **Yorkshire Dales** national park is hard to beat.

Getting There & Around

Check in with **Traveline** (☎ 0870 6082608; www .traveline.org.uk) for up-to-the-minute answers to all regional transit questions.

YORK

☎ 01904 / pop 180,000

York wears its past on its sleeve and as one of Britain's most historic cities that works perfectly for most visitors. An important settlement since Roman times, its spectacular Minster and medieval wall show that it was also a key ecclesiastical and political centre before it become an entrepreneurial hub of the Industrial Revolution. All these layers are celebrated in today's York, a bustling, tourist-friendly city that's perfect for exploring on foot.

Orientation & Information

Although the city is relatively small, York's streets are a confusing medieval tangle. While here, keep in mind that 'gate' means street, and 'bar' means gate. There are five major landmarks: the walkable 2.5 miles of city wall; the Minster at the northern corner; Clifford's Tower, a 13th-century fortification

and mound at the southern end; the Ouse River that cuts the centre in two; and the train station just outside the western corner.

INTERNET ACCESS

Gateway Internet Café-Bar (☎ 646446; 26 Swinegate; ⏰ 10am-8pm Mon-Wed, to 11pm Thu-Sat, noon-4 Sun) Half an hour costs £2, or for a 5-minute email you'll pay 50p.

POST

Post Office (Lendal; ⏰ 8.30am-5.30pm Mon-Fri, to 6pm Sat)

TOURIST INFORMATION

TIC (☎ 621756; www.thisisyork.co.uk/www.visityork .org; De Grey Rooms, Exhibition Sq; ⏰ 9am-5pm Mon-Sat, 10am-4pm Sun Nov-Mar, 9am-6pm Mon-Sat, 10am-5pm Sun Apr-Oct) The website is useful for accommodation listings and special offers.
What's on York (www.whatsonyork.com) Up-to-date events listings.

Sights

YORK MINSTER

Northern Europe's largest Gothic cathedral and the highlight of the city, **York Minster** (☎ 557216; Minster Yard; adult/concession £4.50/3; ⏰ 9am-6.30pm Mon-Sat, noon-6.30 Sun) is a treasure house of architecture and richly coloured stained glass, especially the giant **Great Eastern Window** whose 117 detailed panels cost just £58 to create in 1408. Take an audio tour of the **Undercroft** (adult/concession £3/2) for an atmospheric exploration of an evocative site that's been an important religious centre since the 7th century.

JORVIK CENTRE

With its time machine ride through recreated Viking streets, the **Jorvik Centre** (☎ 543402; Coppergate; adult/concession/child £7.20/6.10/5.10; ⏰ 10am-5pm Apr-Oct, to 4pm Nov-Mar), York's most popular visitor attraction, is cheesy in a good way. Its animatronic citizens – including one grimacing toilet-sitter – illuminate the sights, sounds and unfortunate smells of the era while a newly displayed skeleton of an ancient multi-wounded resident shows that being a Viking wasn't all fun.

NATIONAL RAILWAY MUSEUM

Housed in several former train sheds near the train station, the giant **National Railway Museum** (☎ 621261; Leeman Rd; admission free;

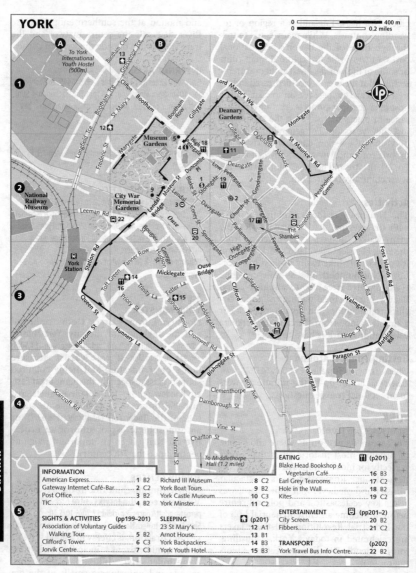

YORK

10am-6pm) is the home of dozens of legendary locomotives, each polished to a fine sheen. The **Great Hall** includes the record-breaking Mallard and the only Bullet Train outside Japan while the **Station Hall** offers a glimpse of luxury with royal trains through the ages. Trainspotters can hang around the trackside balcony overlooking nearby lines.

Also recommended are **York Castle Museum** (☎ 553125; Castle Area, Eye of York; adult/child £6/3.50; ☑ 9.30am-5pm Apr-Oct, to 4.30pm Nov-Mar), a labyrinth of rooms exploring 600 years of British life from medieval prisons to Victorian parlours and the tiny but fun **Richard III Museum** (☎ 634191; Monk Bar, Monkgate; adult/concession £2/1; ☑ 9.30am-4pm Nov-Feb, 9am-5pm Mar-Oct), which puts one of Britain's looniest kings on trial for his various alleged crimes.

Tours

The Association of Voluntary Guides offers free two-hour **walking tours** (10.15am & 2.15pm Apr-Oct & 6.45pm Jun-Aug), departing across the street from the TIC. There's fierce competition among the city's cut-throat ghost tour operators, which befits a city reputed to be Europe's most haunted. Among the best is the **Ghost Hunt of York** (608700; The Shambles; admission £3; 7.30pm), an entertaining 75-minute combination of horror and hilarity. The Ghost Cruise is also one of the packages offered by **York Boat** (628324; Lendal Bridge; from £6.50; from 10.30am).

Sleeping

York is always crowded in summer and finding a bed can be trying. Use the TIC's accommodation booking service (£3) or check options online at www.roomcheck.co.uk/yk.

BUDGET

York International Youth Hostel (653147; york@ yha.org.uk; 42 Water End, Clifton; dm £12.30-17;) Large and busy this hostel is reached via a river-side footpath from the city centre. Most rooms have four beds and there's a good café-bar and private garden. Book in advance to avoid the summer crush.

York Youth Hotel (625904; www.yorkyouthhotel .com; 11-13 Bishophill Senior; dm £12-18) Located in an impressive Georgian townhouse, this popular hotel has some smaller dorms and family rooms, and there's a comfortable bar serving hearty pub grub.

York Backpackers (627720; www.yorkbackpack ers.co.uk; 88-90 Micklegate; dm £13-14) The city's most sociable hostel thanks to its lively bar and large dorms. The impressive building was once the home of Yorkshire's High Sheriff, who reportedly did not sleep in a bunk.

MID-RANGE & TOP END

A gaggle of B&Bs are clustered along Bootham Terrace and Grosvenor Terrace, parallel to the railway line and just a few minutes' walk from the town centre.

Arnot House (641966; www.arnothouseyork.co.uk; 17 Grosvenor Tce; r £58-65;) A cosy, well-located heritage B&B within walking distance of the Minster. Rooms are en-suite (shower only) and some contain brass beds and other

Victorian-style knick-knacks. Some rooms overlook nearby Bootham Park.

23 St Mary's (622738; www.23stmarys.co.uk; 23 St Mary's, Bootham; s/d £34/60) A popular spot with *Lonely Planet* readers, this gem has won awards for its high-level hospitality, with good-sized rooms bursting with character and owners who are more than happy to help you plan your day.

Middlethorpe Hall (641241; www.middlethorpe.com; Bishopthorpe Rd; s/d £109/140) Set in 20 acres of parkland outside the city centre, this 17th-century option is like staying in an old-fashioned country manor. Bring your monocle and smoking jacket to feel right at home amid the leather chairs and oak panelling, top-notch restaurant and spa centre.

Eating & Drinking

Earl Grey Tea Rooms (654353; 13-14 The Shambles; tea & cake £3; 9am-5pm) Alongside ubiquitous street-corner pie shops serving good value stodge for those on the run, consider sinking into the grandmotherly ambience of this timber-framed place. It's a good place to write postcards while knocking-back a pot of strong Yorkshire tea.

Blake Head Bookshop & Vegetarian Café (623767; 104 Micklegate; mains £4.50; 9.30am-5pm Mon-Sat, 10am-5pm Sun) Offers a wide array of vegan and vegetarian dishes and a heaping main course salad option that can't be beaten. Popular with students and backpackers, it can fill up quickly during the summer.

Hole in the Wall (634468; 10 High Petergate; mains £5-7) Among the city's dozens of ancient pubs, this one attracts a comfortable mix of locals and visitors. A good selection of local tipples, including Yorkshire Terrier is complemented by a comfort-food menu that stretches way beyond the usual pub selection.

Kites (641750; 11-13 Grape Lane; mains from £13) Among the nook of great little restaurants along Grape Lane., despite its minimalist interior, Kites is characterised by comfortable service and a menu packed with unusual ingredients innovatively prepared, including pigeon. Save room for the sticky toffee pudding which is almost certainly illegally addictive.

Entertainment

Not a nightlife hotbed like Leeds or Newcastle, most visitors content themselves with a

BRITAIN

city-centre pub crawl. There are a few other options though and they're promoted in the Friday edition of the *Evening Press* and online at www.whatsonyork.com.

With the recent demise of the city's Odeon, York is relying on **City Screen** (☎ 541144; 13-17 Coney St; from £3.50) to keep the projectors rolling. Favouring a mix of mainstream and art house, there are also regular live music and comedy gigs here.

York's nightclub scene is laughably poor but one live music venue is a cut above the dreck. **Fibbers** (☎ 651250; Stonebow House; admission £5-15; ☒ 11am-1pm Mon-Sat, noon-11pm Sun) cranks up the amps every night with new and up-and-coming bands.

Getting There & Away

There are **National Express** buses arriving throughout the day from London (£22, five to seven hours). There are also six daily buses from Birmingham (£21.50, three to six hours) and four from Edinburgh (£28.50, six to eight hours).

There are numerous daily trains from London's King's Cross (£69, two hours) and from Edinburgh (£56, 2½ hours).

Getting Around

A great city for getting lost on foot, bike-friendly York also has lots of cycle routes; the TIC has network maps. You can hire bikes from **Europcar** (☎ 656161; York Railway Station) from £7.50 per day.

AROUND YORK

The 18th-century **Castle Howard** (☎ 648333; adult/concession/child £9.50/8.50/6.50; ☒ 10am-4pm Feb-Oct), 15 miles (24km) northeast of the city, has a greater claim to being a British Versailles than almost any stately home in the country. The most popular day out from York, its ostentatious Renaissance exteriors are complemented by sumptuous interiors of priceless art and artefacts. The surrounding landscaped parkland is also impressive, complete with temples, fountains and a formidable rose garden.

YORKSHIRE DALES & AROUND

Probably the most scenic and certainly the most popular part of the Pennine uplands, the Dales is a region of lush valleys crowned by craggy limestone cliffs. In between there are trickling streams, mossy

dry stone walls, sheep-strewn meadows and unspoilt villages with excellent pubs. Not surprisingly, it can get very crowded in the summer so pick up a good map from the nearest TIC and head off the beaten path. Check out the **Dales Way** (www.thedalesway .co.uk) for some recommended routes.

Orientation & Information

A national park of 700 sq miles (1126 sq km), the Dales is best explored from Grassington, home of the region's main TIC. For orientation, the Dales can be broken into northern and southern halves. In the north, the main dales run parallel and east to west and include Wensleydale, Teesdale and Swaledale. In the southern half, the north to south Ribblesdale with its famous viaduct is the route of the Leeds–Settle–Carlisle (LSC) railway. Pretty Wharfedale is parallel to the east.

Getting Around

Unless you're driving, the LSC is the best way to get to those places along its route. Settle, which has many accommodations and hiking options, is the best of these. Public transport is patchy across the region but cycling is a viable and more efficient alternative. Bikes can be hired in Skipton from **The Bicycle Shop** (☎ 01756 794386; 3-5 Water St) for £8 per half-day.

Good maps on local hiking and biking routes are available from the **National Park Centre** (☎ 01756 752774; Hebdon Rd, Grassington; ☒ 9.30am-5.15pm Apr-Oct), which is open for limited hours seasonally throughout the year.

Grassington

☎ 01756 / pop 1100

Arguably the prettiest Dale village, Grassington is centred on a cobbled market square ringed with stone cottages. A popular base for hikers, the **Dales Way** footpath passes through the village. There's a clutch of small B&Bs but **Kettlewell YHA** (☎ 0870 770 5896; kettlewell@yha.org.uk; dm £10.60; ☒ limited opening) is the nearest hostel, 6 miles away in sleepy Kettlewell. Catch the Pride of the Dales bus No 74.

Settle

☎ 01729 / pop 2400

This small but perfectly formed town is accessible by rail and shouldn't be missed. Hike up to **Castleberg Rock** overhanging the town for breathtaking views or tackle the 5-mile circular route to the gorgeous **Attermire**

Scar. Or check out the chapel in **Giggleswick School** (☎ 893000).

The **TIC** (☎ 825192; Town Hall; 🕐 10am-5pm Mar-Oct, to 4pm Nov-Feb) helps with maps and accommodation. Try the YHA **Stainforth Youth Hostel** (☎ 0870 770 6046; stainforth@yha.org.uk; dm £11.80), but opening times are limited so call ahead, or **Arbutus Guest House** (☎ 015242 51240; www.arbutus.co.uk; Riverside, Clapham; r per person £24.50-26) in nearby Clapham. Situated in a former Georgian vicarage, it's an excellent touring base and chefs-up a fab Yorkshire breakfast.

Skipton
☎ 01756 / 13,500

Skipton is worth a visit for its excellent **castle** (☎ 792442; adult/concession/child £5/4.40/2.50; 🕐 10am-6pm Mon-Sat, noon-6pm Sun). Check in at the **TIC** (☎ 792809; 35 Coach St) to make sure you're not missing anything else before heading to one of the most complete medieval fortresses in Britain. The giant complex was under siege for three years during the Civil War after which Cromwell ordered the removal of the roof to prevent its effective use as a fortress. Replaced 10 years later, the 'new' roof has kept the castle protected in the centuries since. There are B&Bs aplenty on Keighley Rd and the town is served by frequent trains from Leeds.

Haworth
☎ 01535 / pop 2750

Home of the legendary Bronte sisters, Haworth's cobbled streets and hillside vistas make it one of the Dales' hidden gems. A summer tourist magnet, the **Bronte Parsonage Museum** (☎ 642323; Church St; adult/concession/child £4.80/3.50/1.50; 🕐 10am-5.30pm Apr-Sep, 11am-5pm Oct-Mar) offers a fascinating trip back in time for literature buffs. The **TIC** (☎ 642329; Main St) can help with accommodation but **Haworth Youth Hostel** (☎ 642234; Haworth@yha.org.uk; Longlands Dr, Lees Ln; dm £11.80; 🕐 Feb-Oct) should be your first option. A former Victorian stately home, it has 100 beds and often attracts large groups. There are frequent buses from Keighley, which has train connections with Leeds. It is open at some other times also.

NORTH YORK MOORS NATIONAL PARK

One of Britain's finest natural treasures, the **North York Moors** is 550 sq miles (885 sq km) of wild and wonderful terrain coloured by purple heather, craggy coastline and old stone farmhouses where long-haired sheep wander freely. It's the perfect spot for a dramatic windswept run towards your lover but try not to fall over any escarpments or you might ruin the moment.

Orientation & Information

The moors run east to west, from the craggy coastline that includes Whitby and Scarborough to the gentle rolling hills and steep cliffs of Hambleton and Cleveland Hills. Pick up a copy of the tabloid-sized *Moors & Coast* (£0.50) from most newsagents in the region. With maps and information, it's the best-value park guide around. There are several TICs in the area but the **Moors Centre** (☎ 01439 772737; Lodge Ln, Danby; 🕐 10am-5pm Apr-Oct, 11am-4pm Nov-Dec & Mar, 11am-4pm Sat & Sun only Jan-Feb) is the best.

Activities

Walking is the best way to experience the park and the 110-mile **Cleveland Way** from Helmsley to Filey will take you via as many of its hills and coastal vistas as you can handle. The steam trains of the **North Yorkshire Moors Railway** (NYMR; ☎ 01751 473799; 1-day pass adult/concession/child £12.50/11/6.30; 🕐 Apr-Oct, limited winter services) offer a more sedate way to traverse the region, running the picturesque 18 miles (29km) between Pickering and Grosmont – look out for **Goathland Station**, transformed into Hogsmead Station for the *Harry Potter* movies. The **Moor to Sea** (www.moortoseacycle .net) cycle route links Scarborough, Pickering and Whitby via 80 miles (129km) of forest tracks and old railway lines. Rent mountain bikes from **Trailways Cycle Hire** (☎ 01947 829207; per day from £6.30) near Whitby, where hostel-style accommodation in the **old train station** (dm £19) is also available.

Getting Around

The **Moorbus** (☎ 01845 597426; rover ticket £3) services a network of stops (daily June to September, Sunday April to October) throughout the region.

Helmsley & Around
☎ 01439 / pop 1500

Starting point for the **Cleveland Way**, Helmsley's 13th-century ruined **castle** (☎ 770442; adult/concession/child £4/3/2; 🕐 10am-6pm Apr-Sep, to 4pm Oct-Mar) is the town's top visitor attraction. The locals focus more on the **marketplace**, where stallholders set-up shop every Friday. The nearby town hall houses the **TIC** (☎ 770173; ☺ 9.30am-5.30pm Mar-Oct, 10am-4pm Fri-Sun Nov-Feb).

Among Britain's most impressive monastics ruins, **Rievaulx Abbey** (☎ 798228; adult/concession/ child £4/3/2; ☺ 10am-6pm Apr-Sep, to 4pm Oct-Mar) has soaring arches and intricate decorative flourishes that are a testament to the wealth and power of the monks who once lived here. The 18th-century **Rievaulx Terrace & Temples** (☎ 01969 640382; admission £3.30; ☺ variable Mar-Nov) is also recommended for its glorious views overlooking the abbey.

There are several camping grounds in the area but it's worth pitching your tent at **Foxholme Caravan Park** (☎ 771241; www.ukparks.co.uk/foxholme; Harome; camp sites £8.50-12.50; ☺ Mar-Oct), only 4 miles from town. **Helmsley Youth Hostel** (☎ 770433; helmsley@yha.org.uk; Carlton Ln; dm £10.60; ☺ hrs vary) is a friendly backpacker option.

Scarborough & District buses (☎ 01723 507300) run a regular No 128 service from Scarborough via Pickering (£3, 90 minutes, hourly).

Pickering

☎ 01751 / pop 6600

An excellent gateway to the moors, Pickering is the terminus for the NYMR. The 1930s train station was recently restored to its former glory. The well-preserved ruins of Pickering's Norman **castle** (☎ 474989; adult/concession £3/2; ☺ 10am-6pm Apr-Sep, to 4pm Oct) are also well worth a visit, as are the 15th-century frescoes in the nearby **Church of St Peter and St Paul**. Pickering's helpful **TIC** (☎ 473791; The Ropery; ☺ 9.30am-6pm Mon-Sat, to 5pm Sun Mar-Oct, 10am-4.30pm Mon-Sat Nov-Feb) staff can assist with accommodation bookings.

The basic **Lockton Youth Hostel** (☎ 460376; Old School, Lockton; dm £10.60; ☺ Apr-Sep) is the nearest YHA offering, a 10-minute Yorkshire Coastliner bus ride away. Scarborough & District buses arrive from Scarborough and Helmsley while Yorkshire Coastliner services run from York and Whitby.

Scarborough

☎ 01723 / pop 38,000

A typically faded English seaside town, Scarborough is characterised by tacky amusement arcades, greasy fish and chip shops and pensioners looking for a good time. But with its extensive bus and rail links and myriad B&Bs, it's a useful base for exploring the region. After soaking up the paint-peeled ambience, head to **Scarborough Castle** (☎ 372451; Castle Rd; adult/concession/child £3/2.30/1.50; ☺ 10am-6pm Apr-Sep, to 5pm Oct, to 4pm Wed-Sun Nov-Mar) for great views across North Bay or take in the **Rotunda Museum** (☎ 374839; Vernon Rd; adult/concession £2/1.50; ☺ 10am-5pm Tue-Sun May-Sep, 11am-4pm Tue, Sat & Sun, Oct-Apr). One of the world's oldest museums, it's a typical Victorian menagerie of local history and archaeology. The **TIC** (☎ 373333) can help with accommodation recommendations, or just head straight for the YHA **White House Youth Hostel** (☎ 361176; scarborough@yha.org.uk; Burniston Rd; dm £10.60).

Whitby

☎ 01947 / pop 14,100

You have to be fit to climb the steep, winding streets of Whitby but since this is Yorkshire's most rewarding coastal town it's well worth it. The young Captain James Cook was apprenticed to a Whitby shipowner and HMS Endeavour was built here but much of the town's renown is based on the fictional character of Dracula: this is where Bram Stoker's dentally challenged villain swoops ashore on his travels to Britain. While tacky Dracula attractions are mercifully few, **Whitby Abbey** (☎ 603568; adult/concession/child £4/3/2; ☺ 10am-6pm Apr-Sep, to 5pm Oct, to 4pm Nov-Mar), accessible via 199 stone steps and through the graveyard of the church next door, is an evocative wind-whipped spot to let imagination take flight. A new **visitor centre** explains the rich history of the ruined cliff-top location founded in 657. Hold on to your hat for the 5.5-mile cliff-top walk south to beautiful **Robin Hood's Bay** but watch out for the marauding seagulls; they're ready to pick off lone hikers at a moment's notice.

SLEEPING

Across from the train station, the helpful staff at the **TIC** (☎ 602674; ☺ 9am-6pm May-Sep, 10am-4.30pm Oct-Apr) will book accommodation for free from the town's wide selection.

Whitby Youth Hostel (☎ 602878; East Cliff; dm £10.60; ☺ variable) Currently located next to the abbey but the hostel is planning to move to a nearby larger building in 2005.

Whitby Backpackers (☎ 601794; www.thewhitby backpackers.co.uk; 28 Hudson St; dm £10-15; ☺ Mar-Nov) Centrally located in a Victorian house, this is the town's best hostel, combining a friendly atmosphere with good-sized rooms and superior facilities.

Whitby Backpackers at Harbour Grange (☎ 60 0817; Spital Bridge; www.whitbybackpackers.co.uk; dm from £10; ✖) Confusingly and recently re-named, this is a separate operation from Whitby Backpackers, and has an 11.30pm curfew.

B&Bs abound throughout the town but some are closed off-season. Recommended year-round options include the neat, com-fortable and good-value **Sandpiper House** (☎ 600246; www.sandpiperhouse.co.uk; 4 Belle Vue Tce; B&B £25.50-29.50), where low prices don't affect the level of hospitality. Pay a little extra for a mesmerising view across the bay at the **Riviera Hotel** (☎ 602533; www.rivierawhitby.com; 4 Crescent Tce; B&B per person £26-35), where some rooms have four-poster beds and all are en suite. There's a good single room towards the top of the house where you can watch the sun rise or set from your window over-looking the sea.

EATING
Finley Café Bar (☎ 606660; 22-23 Flowergate; mains £4-6; ✖ 8am-11pm Mon-Sat, 11am-10pm Sun) is a sur-prising pocket of hipness, offering a good postcard-writing coffee stop by day and a cool hangout scene by night (live music Wednesdays).

Gourmet fish and chips are on the menu at the **Magpie Café** (☎ 602058; 14 Pier Rd; mains £7-14; ✖ 11.30am-9pm), where queues habitu-ally form for what may be Yorkshire's best seafood restaurant. Specialising in local catches, the service is super-friendly but it can get noisy when crowded and there isn't much elbow room. The fish platter sampler of Whitby cod, haddock, plaice and skate is highly recommended.

GETTING THERE & AWAY
Trains arrive via Middlesborough so you have to change if you're coming from York or Durham. It's a long journey but worth it for the hypnotic Dales' landscape along the way. Regular buses arrive from York and Scarborough.

DURHAM
☎ 0191 / pop 90,000
With its winding medieval streets and dra-matic skyline dominated by Britain's fin-est Norman cathedral, Durham is home to thousands of students at England's third-oldest university – they're the ones hanging around street corners with long scarves and plummy accents.

The **TIC** (☎ 3843720; www.durhamtourism.co.uk; Millennium Pla; ✖ 9.30am-5.30pm Mon-Sat, 10am-4pm Sun) can provide information. Internet access is available for free at **Clayport Library** (☎ 386 4003; Millennium Place; ✖ 9.30am-7pm Mon-Fri, 9am-5pm Sat) but photo ID is required and there is a 30-minute limit at peak times.

Sights
Taking 40 years to complete, the spectacular **Durham Cathedral** (☎ 3864266; Palace Green; admis-sion free; ✖ 9.30am-6.15pm Mon-Sat, 12.30-5pm Sun, to 8pm mid-Jun–Sep) is a Unesco-listed landmark of solemn, rib-vaulted architecture, part church and part fortress. Climb the 66m **tower** (adult/child £2.50/£1.50) for spectacular city views or take an illuminating **history tour**.

Nearby **Durham Castle** (☎ 3333800; Palace Green; adult/child £3/2; ✖ 10am-12.30pm & 2-4.30pm Jul-Sep), also a World Heritage Site, was com-pleted in 1072 and was the university's first home 800 years later. It's open longer hours at Easter and Christmas.

Sleeping
Accommodation options abound online at www.durham.gov.uk/tourism or call the TIC for their free booking service. Vacancies are virtually non-existent during university graduation in late June but 11 **colleges** (☎ 334 5878; www.dur.ac.uk/conference_tourism;r per person from £20) – including the castle's medieval Uni-versity College – offer a variety of rooms outside term.

There's no youth hostel, so the city's best B&B deal is **Mrs Koltai** (☎ 386 2026; 10 Gilesgate; s £20). Clean, somewhat clinical facilities, as well as rooms for the disabled, are available at the new **Travelodge Durham** (☎ 386 5461; www .travelodge.co.uk; Station Ln; r £54.95), a five-minute uphill walk from the centre. For a lot more character, a few more pounds and a cork-ing breakfast, **Farnley Tower** (☎ 3750011; www .farnley-tower.co.uk; The Avenue; s/d £50/78) is a former country house with castle and cathedral views from many rooms.

Eating & Drinking
Brown Sugar Bistro (☎ 3865050; 81-83 New Elvet; mains £4-8; ✖ 7am-11pm) In a former garage where you can still watch the cars go by. Heaping fried breakfasts – including a good selection of vegetarian options – are popular and it

BRITAIN

transforms during the day from coffee stop to sandwich bar and cosy evening lounge.

Numjai (☎ 3862020; 19 Milburngate Shopping Centre; mains £7-11; ☷ 5-11pm) Durham's best restaurant serves up Thai delicacies and sunset views of the Wear River. There's a great value early-bird special from 5pm to 7pm, where you can sample two-courses for £9.99.

Locals take over the bars on North Rd at the weekend – including the **Yates**, **Outback** and **Wetherspoons** mega-pub triumvirate – while students favour the kitschy **Klute Nightclub** (☎ 3869589; Elvet Bridge; admission £2.50-4.50). **Varsity** (☎ 3846704; 46 Saddler St) is a bright, backpacker-friendly three-level pub offering a good beer selection, cheap bar food and a covered garden.

Getting There & Away

Six National Express buses run from London daily (£25, six to eight hours) and three arrive from Edinburgh (£20, four to five hours). The Arriva X1 service runs throughout the day to Newcastle, excluding Sunday. On the main London–Edinburgh line, trains arrive from London (£88, three hours) and Edinburgh (£37.50, two hours) throughout the day. Trains also arrive every few minutes from York (£17, 45 minutes).

Getting Around

The compact town centre is best explored on foot and it's hard to get lost with the cathedral looming permanently above. The train station is above and northwest of the cathedral while the bus station is on the western side. For local bus information call ☎ 0870 608 2608.

NEWCASTLE GATESHEAD

☎ 0191 / pop 470,000

England's top two Geordie cities now market themselves as a unified entity but there's no denying that Newcastle-Upon-Tyne has the lion's share of attractions. While the city lost its way with the decline of UK manufacturing in the 1970s and 1980s, recent years have seen a major resurgence. Like Manchester and Glasgow, Newcastle is undergoing a mini cultural renaissance with major new art centres, a swanky bar and restaurant scene and a kicking nightlife. Walk the streets during the day and you can tell the locals are biding their time for an evening of alcoholic revelry.

Orientation & Information

Newcastle's compact city centre is easy to navigate on foot. The Central train and coach station is just south of the centre. Packed with chain stores, indoor markets and giant £1 shops, it's partly pedestrianised around Grainger St. A surprising number of buildings here are formidable 19th-century classical structures, with almost half heritage listed. Tourist information is available at the **TIC** (☎ 2778000; www.visitnewcastlegateshead .com; 132 Grainger St; ☷ 9.30am-5.30pm Mon-Sat, 10am-4pm Sun Jun-Sep), with an additional branch at Central train station (closed Sunday).

Sights

Despite losing a recent European City of Culture competition, Newcastle went ahead and built several impressive attractions. The **Sage Music Centre**, resembles a giant silver chrysalis on the banks of the Tyne.

BALTIC

A contemporary art centre housed in a former flourmill, **Baltic** (☎ 4781810; Gateshead Quay; admission free; ☷ 10am-7pm Mon-Sat, to 5pm Sun) is the North's answer to London's Tate Modern. While it's scandalised some stuffy locals with occasional shows of nude artworks, exhibitions change frequently and it's a great place to spend a couple of hours on a rainy day. The café is a perfect postcard-writing spot. It's reached from the Newcastle side of the river via the Gateshead Millennium Bridge, a curving movable pedestrian walkway that's a sci-fi artwork in itself.

LIFE SCIENCE CENTRE

Billing itself as a 'sexy' science museum, **Life** (☎ 2438210; Times Sq; adult/concession £6.95/5.50; ☷ 10am-6pm Mon-Sat, 11am-6pm Sun) takes a refreshing, high-tech look at the natural science of genetics. Check out the simulator that takes you on the kind of hair-raising taxi ride through Newcastle that you'd want to avoid in real life.

ANGEL OF THE NORTH

The most potent symbol of restored Northeast pride, the towering **Angel of the North** (☎ 4784222; A1, Gateshead; admission free) sculpture was built from 200 tonnes of steel by artist Antony Gormley. The roadside figure has a wingspan of 54m and has been quickly embraced by locals.

Sleeping

Never over-endowed with good value accommodation, the area has attracted some upmarket chains and boutique hotels in recent years to add to a traditional plethora of mediocre mid-market options.

Northumbria University (☎ 2274024; rc.conferences@northumbria.ac.uk; Ellison Tce; s with shared bathroom incl breakfast £17-28.50; ❤ Jun-Sep) Offers well-situated summer accommodation in the city centre. Most rooms are basic singles but a number of en suites are also available for a few pounds extra.

Bewick Hotel (☎ 4771809; bewickhotel@hotmail.com; 145 Prince Consort Rd, Gateshead; B&B s/d £25/46) Two miles from the city centre, this end-of-terrace family house in a residential street is welcoming but certainly on the quiet side. A favourite with older travellers who like to party before 9pm.

Malmaison (☎ 2455000; newcastle@malmaison.com; Quayside; d/tr £79/145) Newcastle's best boutique hotel is in the emerging Quayside area next to the Millennium Bridge. When you're not watching the bridge move up and down, there's a trendy hotel bar for hanging out with the visiting *nouveaux riches*. Rooms are bright, with high ceilings, and stripy bed linen that makes your bed look like a zebra crossing.

Eating

New restaurants have sprouted like mushrooms around the city centre in recent years with Grey St and the new Gate (p208) entertainment complex offering plenty of mid-priced options. Many Newcastle restaurants have early-bird dinner specials. For something fancier and more original, the Quayside is emerging as a gourmet destination. For food on the run, hot pie and sandwich shops are everywhere.

Café Blue (☎ 2220371; 9 Higham Pl; mains £4-6; ❤ 8am-6pm Mon-Sat) Like sipping an espresso in an Italian piazza, Café Blue is a great place to sit and watch the world go by. It's also a low-cost fuel-stop with surprisingly large breakfasts. A wide range of takeaway sandwiches is available for those who can't sit still.

Spice Cube (☎ 2221181; The Gate, Newgate St; early 2-course dinner £10.50; ❤ noon-2.30pm & 5.30-11.30pm Mon-Fri, noon-11.30pm Sat & Sun) The days of flock wallpaper and dodgy sitar muzak are over at this uber-modern reinvention of the Indian restaurant where the approach is laid-back lounge. The tangy lamb and mint curry *(nahari podina ghoust)* is highly recommended and there are several worthwhile vegetarian options. Service is friendly too so don't be afraid to ask for suggestions from the small but perfectly formed menu.

Paradiso Caffe Bar (☎ 2211240; 1 Market Lane; mains £5-17; ❤ 11am-10.30pm Mon-Fri, 12.30-3.30pm Sun) An atmospheric location in an old print-works adds to the Paradiso's warm yet modern Euro-ambience. Try to grab a booth and take your time checking out the imaginative menu – the juicy fillet of pork stuffed with dates is recommended. There's also a great balcony for relaxing summer dining.

Drinking

Newcastle's pub scene has moved on from the days when the Bigg Market area was little more than a nightly open-air vomitorium. There are still plenty of mini-skirted women and short-shirted lads hanging around here even in winter, and local pubs offer perhaps the UK's longest happy hours. But there are dozens of great options away from the obvious and ubiquitous big-box bars.

Popolo (☎ 2328923; 82-84 Pilgrim St; ❤ 11-1am) Away from the crowds, Popolo is an excellent bar that's something of a Newcastle secret so don't tell anyone about it. Large comfy chairs and two bars make this a good chill-out spot and the prices are reasonable, despite a wide selection of international beers and lip-smacking cocktails.

Bob Trollop's (☎ 2611037; Sandhill, Quayside) One of the Quayside area's most popular pubs, Bob Trollop's has a wide regional beer selection and regular drinks specials for those who want to get blotto on the cheap. The pub meals are good too, ranging from quality bangers and mash to a wider variety of vegetarian options than almost any pub in town.

The following are also recommended:
Intermezzo (☎ 2612072; 10 Pilgrim St; ❤ 8am-11pm Mon-Sat, 11am-11pm Sun)
Pitcher & Piano (☎ 2324100; 108 The Quayside; ❤ noon-11pm Mon-Thu, to midnight Fri & Sat, 11am-midnight Sun) Classy bar with views of the Baltic.

Entertainment

Since the Geordies know how to party. the city's nightlife is excellent – pick up a copy of *The Crack* for the latest listings. The **Gate**

(Newgate St; ✹ 10-2am Sun-Thu, to 3am Fri & Sat) the city centre's new nightlife attraction, offers restaurants, bars and cinemas in a venue resembling a swanky shopping centre but there are lots of other hip joints to check out.

NIGHTCLUBS

Foundation (☎ 2618985; Melbourne St; admission £8-10; ✹ 10pm-3am) From club classics to retro hip-hop and house and garage, Foundation offers some of the Northeast's best club nights. The UK's top club DJs are regularly scheduled but Monday night means school disco – indie style. Disabled access.

Powerhouse (☎ 2723621; Times Sq, Centre for Life; admission £7-8; ✹ 7pm-3am) Reflecting Newcastle's vibrant gay and lesbian scene, Powerhouse has two floors, four bars and music ranging from chart to trance. The city's only gay nightclub, it has an '80s techno feel, a wicked light system and theme nights throughout the week. For other gay venues, head to the Pink Triangle area near Central Station.

Getting There & Away
AIR
Located 20 minutes from the city centre, daily flights to Newcastle International Airport arrive from London's Heathrow and Gatwick airports, as well as Amsterdam and Paris, with other cities served on a less regular basis. Low-cost favourites **Ryanair** (☎ 0870 156 9569; www.ryanair.com) and **easyJet** (☎ 0870 600 0000; www.easyjet.com) ply their trade here, so check their websites for the latest deals.

BOAT
Regular ferries arrive at Royal Quays from Norway, Sweden and the Netherlands. See the Britain Transport section (p256) for more information.

BUS
National Express coaches arrive from many major UK cities (London, £24, 6½ hours; Edinburgh, £11, 2½ hours etc.). The excellent value Explorer Northeast ticket (£5.50) is valid on most local regional services. Bus No 505 arrives from Berwick-Upon-Tweed and No 685 comes from Hexham and Haltwhistle for Hadrian's Wall.

TRAIN
There are frequent trains from Edinburgh (£33.50, 1¾ hours), London (£83, three hours) and York (£15.50, one hour). Berwick-upon-Tweed and Alnmouth (for Alnwick) are also served.

Getting Around
The city centre is surprisingly easy to navigate on foot, and the excellent metro (underground railway) is quicker and more efficient than many local buses. Unlimited travel for one day is £3. For advice and information contact **Traveline** (☎ 0870 608 2608; www.traveline.org.uk).

NORTHUMBERLAND
With its haunting beauty and scant population, Northumberland offers a rare opportunity to really get away from it all. But it's not just breathtaking natural splendour that attracts visitors. There's almost an embarrassment of historic sites here that speak of centuries of bloody conflict, mostly with the Scots. Like old broken teeth, the horizon is full of the jagged remains of dozens of immense fortifications.

The most significant is **Hadrian's Wall**. Brainchild of Roman Emperor Hadrian in AD 122, it stretches for 73 miles (117km) from Newcastle to Bowness-on-Solway near Carlisle and was the northern frontier of the empire for almost 300 years. It was superseded in Norman times by dozens of castles and fortified houses, some of which remain intact while others lie half-eaten away on craggy hilltops. You'll stumble upon some of these by hiking in the wild and empty **Cheviot Hills** in **Northumberland National Park**, although it's not a terrain for amateurs.

There are 15 TICs around Northumberland, each offering maps, accommodation booking and transport information. Some are quite small and open only seasonally while **Alnwick** (☎ 01665 510665; 2 The Shambles) and **Hexham** (☎ 01434 652220; Wentworth Car Park) open year-round. Check www.visitnorth umberland.com for others.

Berwick-Upon-Tweed & Around
☎ 01289 / pop 26,000
A good stopover before heading up to Scotland, Berwick-upon-Tweed sits on the northern tip of England. The historic site of Scottish-English strife for centuries, it's now a peaceful market town set amid some beautiful countryside and characterised by some impressive ruins of a bygone age.

Tourist information is available from the **TIC** (☎ 330733; www.berwickonline.org.uk; 106 Marygate; ✆ 10am-5pm Mon-Sat, 11am-3pm Sun), which has a free town guide with accommodation listings.

SIGHTS & ACTIVITIES

While the town is pretty and its intact Elizabethan **wall** provides a nice walk with some good views of the region, the best attractions lie outside. A must-see for any Northumberland visit, the holy island of **Lindisfarne** (☎ 389244; adult/concession £3.50/2.61; ✆ 10am-6pm Apr-Sep, to 4pm Oct-Jan, to 4pm Sat & Sun only Feb-Mar) contains a castle and ancient Benedictine priory reached by a causeway at low tide (see TIC for tide times). Although often overrun with tourists in summer, this seat of Anglo-Saxon Christianity retains a calming element of peace and tranquillity at most other times.

Dominating the coastal skyline, the stunning **Bamburgh Castle** (☎ 01668 214515; adult/concession/child £3.50/2.50/1.50; ✆ 11am-5pm Mar-Oct) was the seat of Northumbria's Angle kings. The present 11th-century structure was a Norman stronghold that survived many sieges. Restored in the 19th century, there's an interesting collection of art and weaponry and the site is partially wheelchair accessible.

SLEEPING

Berwick is the main accommodation hub but there are other pockets of B&Bs throughout the region.

Berwick Backpackers (☎ 331481; www.berwick backpackers.co.uk; 56 Bridge St; dm £9-18) In a great location only five minutes from the bus and train stations, it's more like being in your own flat than a hostel and has single rooms if required.

Lindisfarne Guest House (☎ 01665 603430; 6 Bondgate, Alnwick; s from £19) Popular with the budget-minded but can fill up quickly in summer so book ahead.

Old Vicarage Guest House (☎ 306909; www .oldvicarageberwick.co.uk; Church Rd, Tweedmouth; B&B s/d £18-36) With its attention to service and good location, this place has been pulling in visitors for years.

GETTING THERE & AWAY

Berwick is on the main London to Edinburgh rail line and several trains arrive daily from each city (from London £90, 3½ hours; from Edinburgh £13.10, 45 minutes).

The main local bus (☎ 0870 608 2608) for travellers is the No 501, which runs to/from Alnwick via Bamburgh.

Hadrian's Wall

The most spectacular section of this World Heritage Site is between Hexham and Brampton.

Chesters Roman Fort (☎ 01434 681379; adult/concession £3.50/2.60; ✆ 9.30am-6pm Apr-Sep, 10am-4pm Oct-Mar) near Chollerford is a well-preserved fortification that includes an impressive bathhouse. Its museum displays a fascinating array of Roman sculptures and drawings found in the area.

Housesteads Roman Fort (☎ 01434 344363; adult/concession £3.50/2.60; ✆ 10am-6pm Apr-Sep, to 4pm Oct-Mar) northeast of Bardon Mill is the area's most dramatic and popular ruin. The well-preserved foundations include a famous latrine, which offered ancient users some great views over the Northumbrian countryside.

Roman Army Museum (☎ 01697 747485; adult/concession £3.30/2.90; ✆ from 10am, seasonal closing times Feb-Nov) offers a graphic reconstruction of military life, including a cool virtual reality flight over a reconstructed Hadrian's Wall.

SLEEPING

Corbridge, Hexham, Haltwhistle and Brampton make ideal bases for exploring the wall and are stuffed with B&Bs and a number of cheap, convenient YHA hostels. The following selection starts in the east.

Acomb Youth Hostel (☎ 01434 602864; acomb@yha .org.uk; Main St; dm £8.20; ✆ Apr-Nov) A basic, converted stable about 2.5 miles north of Hexham. Catch bus No 880 from Hexham.

Once Brewed Youth Hostel (☎ 01434 344360; oncebrewed@yha.org.uk; Military Rd, Bardon Mill; dm £11.80; ✆ Feb-Nov, closed Sun Feb & Oct & Mon Mar & Nov) Also basic but next door to a TIC and only 3 miles from Housesteads Roman Fort. Northumbria bus No 685 (from Hexham or Haltwhistle stations) drops you at Henshaw.

Greenhead Youth Hostel (☎ 016977 47401; greenhead@yha.org.uk; dm £10.60; ✆ Apr-Oct; Greenhead, Brampton) A charming chapel-conversion with better facilities than most. It's 3 miles west of Haltwhistle station and is also served by the trusty bus No 685 and the White Star bus No 185 from Carlisle. Opening hours vary so call ahead.

Holmhead Guest House (☎ 016977 47402; www .bandbhadrianswall.com; Castle Farm, Hadrian's Wall; r per person £30) A picturesque old farmhouse built from stones pillaged from the wall. The hosts are experts on local Roman life and can help you plan trips around the area.

GETTING THERE & AWAY
The Newcastle to Carlisle rail line has stations at Hexham, Haydon Bridge, Bardon Mill, Haltwhistle and Brampton but not all trains stop at all stations. There are hourly bus services from Carlisle and Newcastle on No 685. From June to September the hail-and-ride Hadrian's Wall Bus links Hexham, Haltwhistle and Carlisle with all the main sites. Call Hexham **TIC** (☎ 01434-652220) for information.

NORTHWEST ENGLAND

The southern part of this region is often dismissed as England's industrial back yard. The dense network of motorways you see on maps gives forewarning of both the level of development and the continuing economic importance of the region, despite the decline of some traditional industries. This said, there are still some beautiful corners, and the larger cities are cultural hubs with a legacy of brilliant Victorian architecture, and a population that really knows how to have a good time.

This is the working-class heartland of England. There's a big gap between these northern cities and those south of Birmingham. Since the Industrial Revolution created them, life for the inhabitants has often been an uncompromising struggle. The main industrial corridor runs from Merseyside (Liverpool) to the Humber River. The cities of Liverpool and Manchester sprawl into the countryside, burying it under motorways, grim suburbs, power lines, factories and mines. There are, nonetheless, some important exceptions, including walled Chester, which makes a good starting point for North Wales and the Lake District, (the most beautiful corner of England).

MANCHESTER
☎ 0161 / pop 390,000
Manchester decided to take its future as a cultural weigh station seriously after a 1996 IRA bombing destroyed a solid chunk of the city centre. Playing host to the 2002 Commonwealth Games gave Manchester an excuse to rebuild with a fervour. With its vibrant cultural diversity – including a large gay scene and active Chinatown, ample public space and art, and stunningly juxtaposed modern and Victorian architecture, Manchester is now famous for much more than the former Industrial Revolution headquarters. Its nightlife and music scenes are rivalled by few other cities. Visitors will find plenty to do and see, and can get around easily by foot or public transport, but any influx of tourists is still years away.

Orientation & Information
The University of Manchester lies to the south of the city centre (on Oxford St/Rd). To the west of the university is Moss Side, a ghetto with high unemployment and a thriving drug trade – keep clear. Victoria train station caps the city in the north. Internet access is available at **easyEverything** (☎ 8329200; St Anne's Sq). The **TIC** (☎ 2343157; www .destinationmanchester.com; Town Hall Extension, Lloyd St, St Peter Sq; ☺ Mon-Sat 10am-5.30pm, Sun & bank holidays 10.30am-4.30pm) also has branches in Terminals 1 and 2 at the airport.

Sights & Activities
Get in touch with your hooligan roots at the **Manchester United Football Museum & Tour** (☎ 0870 4421994; www.manutd.com; Old Trafford Stadium; adult/child £7.50/5). Hour-long tours run every 10 minutes and introduce fans to more information about Man United than anyone would ever, *ever* want to know. Call or email, as tour times depend on match days and times. For tickets, check the website months and months in advance, or, if you've been praying to your football altar, go to the box office early on match day and wait with thousands for a few cancelled tickets. Be very wary of scalpers, as most of the tickets they sell are not only expensive, but fake.

The **Castlefield Urban Heritage Park** is an extraordinary landscape made up of the remains of ancient Roman fortresses and newly constructed canal-side footpaths, pubs, hotels and a YHA hostel. The area also takes in the excellent **Museum of Science & Industry** (☎ 8322244; Liverpool Rd, Castlefield; admission free; ☺ 10am-5pm), where you'll discover that the history of fabric is actually interesting.

Dominating Albert Sq in the city centre is the enormous Victorian Gothic **Town Hall**, designed by Albert Waterhouse (of London's Natural History Museum fame) in 1876.

The recently renovated **Manchester Art Gallery** (☎ 2341456; cnr Nicholas & Mosley Sts; admission free; ☻ 10am-5pm Tue-Sun) has an impressive collection covering everything from early Italian, Dutch and Flemish painters to Gainsborough, Blake, Constable and the Pre-Raphaelites.

An eye-catching modern construction on Salford Quay, **The Lowry** has two theatres and a number of galleries (one devoted to LS Lowry himself). The galleries are free to enter. Take the Metrolink to either Broadway or Harbour City.

Sleeping

The TIC can arrange accommodation for a £2.50 booking fee, plus a 10% deposit.

The Hatters (☎ 2369500; ; www.hattersgroup.com; 50 Newton St dm £16-17; ⌨) The best low-priced option is equidistantly located between the railway and coach stations in the city centre, and offers 200 beds, cheap high-speed Internet access (£1 per 30 minutes), no lockout, plus a full restaurant and laundry facilities.

YHA Manchester (☎ 8399960; manchester@yha.org .uk; dm adult/under 18 yrs £19.50/14.40) Across the road from the Museum of Science & Industry in the Castlefield area (well signposted), this hostel has over 140 beds and full facilities.

The Mitre Hotel (☎ 8344128; www.mitrehotel .com; Cathedral Gates; s/d/f £45/62.50/79) The location (beside Manchester Cathedral and Arndale) and the charm (sloping 200-year-old floors and several competing floral wallpaper patterns) make this family-owned place your best mid-range bet in town.

Rembrandt (☎ 2361311; www.rembrandtmanchester .com; 33 Sackville St; s/d/tr/q £45/50/55/60, with shared bathroom £10 less) In the heart of the Gay Village, this place has a fabulous bar and restaurant downstairs making it a genial, if not particularly quiet, place to stay.

From mid-June to mid-September, the University of Manchester lets students' rooms to visitors from around £14 per person. Contact **St Anselm Hall** (☎ 2247327) or **Woolaton Hall** (☎ 2247244). The **Burton Arms Hotel** (☎ /fax 8343455; 31 Swan St; s/d/tr from £25/39/58.50) is a traditional pub close to the centre of town.

Eating

The most distinctive restaurant zones are Chinatown in the city centre and Rusholme

in the south, called the Curry Mile for its plethora of Indian restaurants, but cafés and restaurants cover the city centre, as well.

Chinatown is bounded by Charlotte, Portland, Oxford and Mosley Sts, and it has a number of restaurants, not all Chinese.

Little Yang Sing (☎ 2287722; 17 George St; set menu lunch £9, dinner £16) The most acclaimed of Chinatown, which specialises in Cantonese cuisine.

Tampopo (☎ 8191966; 16 Albert Sq; full backpacker menu £13.95) More affordable, with a special menu for backpackers, Tampopo serves up lots of vegetarian noodle and rice dishes inspired by Thai, Malaysian and Japanese cuisines.

Dimitri's (☎ 8393319; Campfield Arcade; mains £4-8) A hip place near the YHA for tapas or a few drinks.

Rusholme is to the south of the university on Wilmslow Rd, the extension of Oxford St/Rd known as the Curry Mile, and has numerous popular, cheap and very good Indian/Pakistani places.

Cafés are big business in Manchester these days, as the ubiquitous chain coffee houses will testify, however if you're looking for something less generic the **Earth Vegetarian Café** (☎ 8341996; 16-20 Turner St; mains £3-7), in the Northern Quarter, serves up an imaginative vegetarian selection and **Java Coffee Bar** (☎ 2364003; 8a Oxford Rd; snacks £1.95-4.95) has a good selection of pastries and decent coffee. There are several cafés in the indoor market of Affleck's Palace.

Drinking

There are several places to drink in Castlefield, including **Barça** (☎ 8397099) in Catalan Sq, with outdoor seating for sunny days. Two historic pubs are the **Old Wellington Inn** (☎ 8301440), built in 1530 and **Sinclairs Oyster Bar** (2 Cathedral Gates) at the top of New Cathedral St, where you can get great prices on beer in an establishment that was moved brick by brick to its new location.

Entertainment

You will be spoilt for choice in Manchester when it comes to after-dark entertainment. One of the best venues for live jazz, blues and funk is **Band on the Wall** (☎ 8326625; ticket info ☎ 2375554; 25 Swan St). For rock and pop, including big international acts, check out the **Manchester Academy** (☎ 2752930; 269 Oxford Rd), part of the University Students Union. Check out indie bands at the pulsating **Roadhouse** (☎ 2379789; 8 Newton St) before they make it big.

Mancunians, like hip young things the world over, have taken a strong liking to cocktail and wine bars. One of the first to emerge, **Dry Bar** (☎ 2369840; 28 Oldham St) is still popular and still cool.

Canal St is the centre of Manchester's enormous gay nightlife scene. There are over 20 bars and clubs in the so-called 'Gay Village'. **Paradise Factory** (☎ 2735422; 114-116 Princess St) is a cutting edge club, with gay nights at the weekend.

Getting There & Away

There are many coach links with the rest of the country. National Express operates out of Chorlton St station in the city centre to almost anywhere you'll want to go, including London's Victoria Station (£25 return, 4½ hours, seven to nine per day) and Edinburgh (£26.50, 6½ hours, about five per day).

Piccadilly is the main station for trains to and from the rest of the country, although Victoria serves Halifax and Bradford. The two are linked by **Metrolink** (☎ 0845 7484950). There are frequent services to London (£51.10, 2¾ hours, hourly) and Liverpool (£7.70, 45 minutes to one hour, three per hour).

Getting Around

Most sites are reachable by bus £1 or £2, both free (maps available at the TIC). For general inquiries about local transport, including night buses, phone ☎ 2287811 (8am to 8pm daily). A Day Saver ticket for £3 covers travel throughout the Great Manchester area on bus, train and Metrolink. Manchester's Metrolink light-railway (tram) makes frequent connections between Victoria and Piccadilly train stations and G-Mex (for Castlefield). Buy tickets from machines on the platforms.

Two free buses – the Nos 1 and 2 – make travelling anywhere in the city centre a breeze. Routes and schedules are available from the TIC.

CHESTER
☎ 01244 / pop 80,000

Chester is one of the oldest cities in England. Much of it is still ringed by the most complete city walls in Britain (much of its 2 miles is the original Roman construction)

which makes for a commendable stroll about town, and the eye-catching two-level shopping streets (known as the Rows) may date back to the post-Roman period. They now make convenient rainproof shopping arcades, which is one of modern Chester's biggest attractions. Chester caters to tourism, which can be overwhelming at times with all the High St shops, the noon-time town crier and international chain restaurants, but its sights and streets make it one of the most beautiful towns in the North, as well as the most child-friendly.

Orientation & Information

Built in a bow formed by the Dee River, the walled centre is now surrounded by suburbs. The train station is a 15-minute walk from the city centre; go up City Rd, then turn right onto Foregate at the large roundabout.

The **TIC** (☎ 402111; www.chestercc.gov.uk; Town Hall) is just opposite the cathedral, but the omnipresent **Chester Visitor Centre** (☎ 351609; tis@chestercc.gov.uk; Vicar's Lane) can book your accommodation and then keep you busy for days with guided walks, brass rubbing, ghost hunting, even a wall patrol with fully-clad Roman Legionaries.

For Internet access, head to the **library** (☎ 602611; Northgate St; ☽ 9.30am-7pm Mon & Thu, to 5pm Tue, Wed & Fri, to 4pm Sat).

Sights & Activities

The present **Chester Cathedral** (☎ 324756; requested donation £2) was originally a Saxon Minster, and with its cloisters, showcases the most complete monastic complex in Britain.

The **Dewa Roman Experience** (☎ 343407; Pierpoint Lane; adult/concession/child £3.95/3.50/2.25; ☽ 9am-5pm) is an interactive museum. Its simulated archaeological dig and reconstruction of typical Roman street life is especially great for kids, but, honestly, who doesn't want to try on a set of Roman armour?

From 2004 to 2006, a massive archaeological dig will be on display at the **Roman Amphitheatre**, next to the visitor's centre, which will have an exhibition hall and viewing platform.

Sleeping & Eating

There are numerous good-value B&Bs along Hoole Rd, the road into the city from the M53/M56 (check with the TIC).

YHA Chester (☎ 0870 7705762; chester@yha.org.uk; 40 Hough Green; dm adult/under 18 yrs £14.90/11.60; P ☒ ▣) Charming, amiable and in a large Victorian mansion, 1 mile from the centre, on the opposite side from the train station. Take bus Nos 3, 4, 4a or 16.

Chester Backpackers (☎ 400185; www.chester backpackers.co.uk; 67 Boughton St; dm/s/d £13/18.50/34; ▣) More central, this one is five minutes from both the train station and the city centre, most rooms are en suite and they offer free left luggage.

Commercial Hotel (☎ 320749; St Peter's Churchyard; s/d/f £37/50/66; P) Central and well-priced, the Commercial is also a quirky bar popular with local literati types.

Grove Villa (☎ 349713; grove.villa@tesco.net; 18 The Groves; s/d £23/46; P ☒) Not far from the city centre this place is quietly situated next to the Dee River.

Recorder Hotel (☎ 326580; 19 City Walls; d/tr from £60/75; P ☒) You can't get much closer to the city walls than on them; this is a sweet Georgian inn that overlooks the Dee River. Many rooms feature beautiful iron beds.

Café Venue – The Crypt (☎ 350001; 34-40 Eastgate Rd; sandwiches £3, salads £6; ☯ 9.30am-6pm Mon-Wed, to 7pm Thu, to 6.30pm Fri & Sat, 11am-5pm Sun) Built as a wine cellar around 1290 this cavernous place is great for either a bite to eat, throwing back a few drinks or checking your email (£1.50 for 30 minutes).

Blue Bell (☎ 317758; 65 Northgate St; ☯ lunch & dinner, closed Sun; mains dinner £10-16, lunch £6-8) One of the poshest restaurants in Chester excels at blending ingredients such as chive-crusted beef fillet or crab cakes with chilli jam.

Getting There & Around

Chester has excellent transport connections, especially to and from North Wales.

National Express has numerous connections with Chester, including Birmingham (£9.50, 2½ hours, four daily) and on to London (£16, 5½ hours), Manchester (£5.25, 1¼ hours, three daily), Liverpool (£5.75, one hour, four daily) and Llandudno (£8.25, 1½ hours, departs once daily at 4.55pm). For many destinations in the south or east it's necessary to change at Birmingham; for the north, change at Manchester.

For information on local bus services ring **Chester City Transport** (☎ 602666). Local buses leave from Market Sq behind the town hall.

Any bus from the station goes into the centre. There are numerous trains to Manchester (£9.50, one hour, hourly); Liverpool (£4.50, 40 minutes, half-hourly); Holyhead (£17.90, two hours, about hourly), via the North Wales coast, for ferries to Ireland; Shrewsbury (£6, one hour, hourly in morning); and London's Euston station (£51, 2½ to three hours, almost hourly, last one at 7.30pm). Phone ☎ 0845 7484950 for details.

LIVERPOOL
☎ 0151 / pop 510,000

Of all northern England's cities, Liverpool has perhaps the strongest sense of its own identity, an identity which is closely tied up with the totems of the Beatles (apparent to airplane visitors, at the Liverpool John Lennon Airport), the Liverpool and Everton football teams, and the Grand National steeplechase, run at Aintree since 1839.

Architecturally, the city is a striking mix of grandeur and decay, decrepit streets, boarded-up windows and massive cathedrals and imperious buildings. This juxtaposition is coupled with the city's dramatic site above the broad Mersey estuary, where industrial shipping and dramatic swathes of fog and light creates one of the most arresting sights in Britain.

Liverpool's dramatic economic collapse has given the whole city a sharp edge you'd do well not to explore. But on weekends the centre pumps to music from countless pubs and clubs, a testimony to the city's determinedly vibrant population.

However, Liverpool has been voted the European City of Culture 2008. The entire city will be covered in scaffolding and cranes for the next several years and the bus system is in flux, but watch as this backwater city starts to shine.

Orientation & Information

Lime St, the main train station, is just to the east of the city centre. The National Express coach station is on the corner of Norton and Islington Sts slightly northeast of the train station. The bus station is in the centre on Paradise St. The city is fairly compact, but a fairly sizable hill adds a good walk between the Albert Dock and the city centre.

You're advised to be a bit cautious while in Liverpool. It's best to avoid dark sidestreets even in the city centre.

Internet access is available from **Planet Electra** (☎ 7080303; 34-36 London Rd; ☼ 10am-5.30pm Mon-Wed, to 7.30pm Thu-Fri, noon-5pm Sun; per hr £2, 20% student discount). Information can be obtained from the **TIC** (☎ 0906 6806886, per min 50p; www.visitliverpool.com; Queen Square Centre; ☼ 9am-5.30pm Mon-Sat, 10.30am-4.30pm Sun), which also has a branch inside the Maritime Museum (both book accommodation).

Sights & Activities

A £100 million renovation helped make **Albert Dock** (☎ 7088854; all museums admission free; ☼ from 10am), deservedly, Liverpool's number one tourist attraction, housing several outstanding museums. The top-notch **Merseyside Maritime Museum** (☎ 4784499; ☼ 10am-5pm), teaches visitors about Liverpool's involvement in the transatlantic slave trade and the lives of emigrants, as well as housing a branch of the TIC. Re-creation buffs should visit the **Museum of Liverpool Life** (☎ 4784080; ☼ 10am-5pm), with stages in Liverpudlian history. There's a **Tate Gallery Liverpool** (☎ 7027400; ☼ 10am-6pm Tue-Sun & bank holiday Mon), as well as shops and restaurants. Avoid several tacky tourist attractions; the Beatles Story and the Fingerprints of Elvis are disappointing.

A visit to Liverpool wouldn't be complete without a Beatles tour. The **Magical Mystery Tour** (☎ 7093285; tickets £11.95; tours 2.10/2.30pm daily from the main TIC/Beatles Story, also 11.40am/noon during summer, weekends & hols) takes passengers by a really bright bus to the actual Penny Lane, Strawberry Fields and where the banker never wore a mac in the pouring rain (very strange).

A re-creation of the original music venue where the Beatles made their name, the **Cavern Club** (☎ 2361964; 10 Mathew St), still attracts a big crowd when hosting live bands or DJs.

Sleeping

For accommodation, ring ☎ 0845 6011125.

YHA Liverpool International (☎ 0870 7705924 7098888; liverpool@yha.org.uk; 25 Tabley St, at Wapping; dm adult/under 18 yrs £19/14; Ⓟ ▯) Right across the road from Albert Dock, with all the best hostel amenities: complete restaurant with breakfast included, 24-hour access, laundry facilities, etc.

Embassie Hostel (☎ 7071089; www.embassie.com; 1 Falkner Sq; dm 1st night, £13.50, subsequent nights £12.50) Named for its former life as the Venezuelan

consulate, this comfortable hostel is a labour of love for its owners, a former backpacker and his father, who provide a comfortable environment, summer barbecues on the patio, and free coffee, tea and toast.

International Inn (☎ 7098135; www.internationalinn.co.uk; 4 S Hunter St; dm/tw £15/36; Ⓟ ▯) Close to the city centre, off Hardman St, the International is well-equipped with a café, kitchen and games room.

There are several central hotels on Mount Pleasant, between the city centre and the Metropolitan Cathedral. The award-winning **Aachen Hotel** (☎ 7093477; www.aachenhotel.co.uk; s/d/f £34/50/65), at No 89, has comfortable rooms and an all-you-can-eat breakfast. The up-market **Britannia Adelphi Hotel** (☎ 7097200; www.britanniahotels.co.uk; Ranelagh Pl; s/d £99/115; Ⓟ ☲) was once the world's most luxurious hotel and is still an opulent experience with a health spa and several restaurants.

Eating

There's a plethora of places to eat down Bold St in the city centre.

The restaurants at the Albert Dock are geared towards fine dining, so if you're on a budget head to the **Royal Liver Building diner** (☎ 2550192; Pier Head; ☼ 8am-3pm Mon-Fri; light meals £2-4), set amid stained glass and a gushing fountain. Security will only allow dining visitors in the building. **Café 53** (☎ 7080482; 53 Bold St, Concert Sq; mains £3-7) is popular with locals for a hip snack. The famed **Flannagan's Apple** (☎ 2311957; 18 Mathew St; pub meals £5) is as proudly dank and smoky as Liverpool itself.

Entertainment

The entertainment guide *Itchy Liverpool*, £3 from TICs and major bookshops, can point you in the right direction, or just wander around Mathew St and southwest to Bold, Seel and Slater Sts and you'll stumble upon an amazing array of clubs and pubs catering to every style you can imagine. The **Philharmonic Dining Room** (☎ 7091163; cnr 36 Hope & Hardman), built in 1900, is one of Britain's most extraordinary pubs. The interior is resplendent with etched glass, stained glass, wrought iron, mosaics and ceramic tiling, and, if you're male, be sure to drink enough ales to use the one-of-a-kind toilets.

Everyman Theatre (☎ 7094776; Hope St) is one of the best repertory theatres in the country.

Getting There & Away

There are National Express services linking Liverpool to most major towns, including London's Euston station (£20, 5¼ hours, four daily), Manchester (£5.25, 1½ hours, hourly) and Chester (£4.10, 45 minutes, every half-hour).

Direct trains head to London's Euston station (£51.10, three hours, hourly) and Chester (£4.10, 45 minutes, every half-hour).

Getting Around

Public transport in the region is coordinated by **Merseytravel** (☎ 2367676). For day visitors, a Saveaway ticket (£3.20) covers zones B and E, which includes all city centre buses and the ferry.

Liverpool has no less than 18 bus companies operating, and these change every few months. Most services are quite frequent. Check the Queen St Travel Centre in the main TIC for up-to-date information.

The ferry across the Mersey, started 800 years ago by Benedictine monks but made famous by Gerry & the Pacemakers, still offers one of the best views of Liverpool. Boats depart from Pier Head ferry terminal, just north of Albert Dock. Special 50-minute commentary cruises run year-round, departing hourly from 10am to 3pm on weekdays and until 6pm on weekends (adult/concession/child £2.40/1.85/1.35). Phone **Mersey Ferries** (☎ 3301444) for more information.

LAKE DISTRICT

There are two reasons to go to the Lake District: to do some serious rambling (also known as walking, hiking or trekking) amid jagged peaks, picturesque lakes, stone wall–enclosed meadows and sheep, or to do some serious village ambling amongst tea shops, stone cottages and souvenir shops. The 14 million plus visitors each year seem to be about divided.

This is Wordsworth country, and his houses, Dove Cottage at Grasmere and Rydal Mount, between Ambleside and Grasmere, are literary shrines.

Note that the Lake District is home to both the highest peak (Scaffell, 978 metres) and the wettest inhabited place (Seathwaite, over 3 metres of rain a year) in England, so weather conditions should not be trifled with. Even in summer, day hikes on the mountains – with their swiftly changing micro-climates – have proved fatal to experienced hikers. Before heading out, prepare thoroughly and check the **Weatherline** (☎ 017687 75757).

Orientation & Information

The two principal bases for the Lake District are Keswick in the north (particularly for walkers) and Windermere/Bowness in the south. Kendal, Coniston, Ambleside, Grasmere and Cockermouth are less-hectic alternatives. All these towns have hostels, numerous B&Bs and places to eat.

Ullswater, Grasmere, Windermere, Coniston Water and Derwent Water are usually considered the most beautiful lakes, but they also teem with boats. Wastwater, Crummock Water and Buttermere are equally spectacular and less crowded.

TICs stock a frightening quantity of local guidebooks and brochures and both Windermere and Keswick have decent TICs with free booking services. If you're staying for a few days, buy any one of the dozens of books featuring information on walking, bicycling, travelling with children or driving. Those interested in Wordsworth's life might enjoy reading his sister Dorothy's *Grasmere Journals*.

The numerous walking/climbing shops in the region, particularly in Ambleside and Keswick, are good sources of local information. **George Fisher** (☎ 017687 72178; 2 Borrowdale Rd, Keswick) is an excellent shop for stocking up on equipment.

There are over 25 YHA hostels in the region, many of which can be linked by foot. The YHA also runs a shuttle-bus between eight of the Lake District hostels during summer. Call ☎ 0870 7705672 for more information.

The brochure 'Andy Goldsworthy Sheepfolds' allows those interested in the environmental sculptures to locate the artist's work through Cumbria. Check www.sheepfolds.org for more information.

Getting There & Away

National Express buses have direct connections from Windermere to Preston (£9.25, two hours, two daily) and Keswick to Birmingham (£29, 3½ hours, two daily).

For all public transport inquiries contact **Traveline** (☎ 0870 6082608). There are several important bus services in the Lake District, including bus No 555, which runs about once an hour all year and links Lancaster with Carlisle, via Kendal, Windermere, Ambleside, Grasmere and Keswick. No 599 is an open-top bus that runs during the summer between Windermere and Ambleside, via Grasmere. No 505/506, runs from Ambleside to Coniston via Hawkshead. Ask about Day Ranger and Explorer tickets, as single tickets can be £3 apiece.

Windermere is at the end of a spur off the main railway line between London's Euston station and Glasgow. London (£65.50, four hours, at least six daily), Manchester (£12.55, two hours, 15 daily).

Getting Around

Walking or cycling are the best ways to get around, but bear in mind that conditions can be treacherous, and the going can be very, very steep. **Alexander Sports** (☎ 01539 488891; Main Rd, Windermere; £12 per day) rents many sizes of bikes.

Windermere & Bowness
☎ 015394 / pop 8500

Thanks to the railway, the Windermere/ Bowness conglomerate is the largest tourist town in the Lake District. The two towns are quite strung out, with lakeside Bowness a 30-minute downhill walk from Windermere. The excellent **TIC** (☎ 46499; Victoria St, Windermere) is conveniently located near the train station at the northern end of town, and also offers **internet access** (£3 for 30 minutes).

Offering beds in small rooms and plenty of camaraderie, **Lake District Backpackers Lodge** (☎ 46374 or 44725; www.backpackers.co.uk/lakes; High St; dm £12.50) is 200m from the train station. Call ahead for reservations. Popular with families, **Windermere YHA** (☎ 43543; High Cross, Bridge Lane, Troutbeck; dm adult/under 18 yrs £11.80/8.50) commands a scenic spot on Lake Windermere in the Troutbeck Valley. Two miles from the train station, numerous buses run past Troutbeck Bridge, and in summer the hostel sends a minibus to meet trains.

Windermere is wall-to-wall B&Bs, which the TIC can book for you. The incomparably hospitable **Denehurst Guest House** (☎ 44710; www.denehurst-guesthouse.co.uk; 40 Queens Dr; r per person £25-40; **P**) is situated halfway between Bowness and Windermere. Guests can use the health spa facilities at a nearby four-star

hotel. There's a healthy smattering of cafés and restaurants in both townships. **The Bowness Kitchen** (☎ 45529; 4 Grosvenor Tce, Bowness) serves tasty toasted sandwiches for £3. The chef/owners of **Jambo** (☎ 43429; Victoria St, Windermere; 3-course dinner £17.50; 6-10.30pm, closed Mon winter) are foodies who know how to combine ingredients – like scallops and cauliflower or rhubarb and lemon curd ice cream – to create a taste sensation.

Grasmere
☎ 015394 / pop 2700

Grasmere is a picture-postcard village and a lovely place to stay out of season; in summer it's completely overrun with tourists. Information can be found at the **TIC** (☎ 35245; Red Bank Rd; 9.30am-5.30pm). The homes of poet William Wordsworth are the major attractions here. **Dove Cottage & Museum** (☎ 35544; www.wordsworth.org.uk; adult/concession/child £5.95/5/3; 9.30am-5.30pm) allows visitors to take a peek into the belongings of the poet. Just south of Grasmere, it's accessible by bus Nos 555 or 599 (in summer).

Grasmere Butterlip How YHA (☎ 35316; grasmere@ yha.org.uk; Easedale Rd; dm adult/under 18 yrs £13.40/9.30) is just north of the village. The lovely **How Foot Lodge** (☎ 35366) has rooms priced from £22 and is ideal for access to Dove Cottage, which is on the main A591 Kendal–Keswick Rd, just south of Grasmere village.

For an award-winning dining experience, try **The Jumble Room** (☎ 35188; Langdale Rd; mains £10-16; 10.30am-4.30pm Wed-Sun & from 6pm nightly), where the same family has been cooking for generations, with creations such as a smoked salmon tart infused with dill and mustard and cashew chicken curry with tiger prawns, ginger, coriander and saffron.

Keswick
☎ 017687 / pop 5000

Keswick is an important walking centre, and although the town centre lacks the green charm of Windermere, the lake is beautiful. The **TIC** (☎ 72645), in the middle of the pedestrianised town centre, books accommodation and runs guided tours of the area. Check email at **U-Compute Cyber Café** (☎ 75127; 48 Main St) above the post office.

The **Youth Hostel** (☎ 72484; keswick@yha.org.uk; dm adult/under 18 yrs £11.80/8.50), a short walk down Station Rd from the TIC, is open most of the year. Station Rd has a number of B&Bs, most charging around £24 per person.

Kendal
☎ 01539 / pop 27,100

On the eastern outskirts of the Lake District National Park, Kendal is a lively town and makes for a good base from which to explore the region. The TIC (☎ 725758; Highgate) is in the Town Hall.

Kendal Youth Hostel (☎ 724066; kendal@yha .org.uk; 118 Highgate; dm adult/under 18 yrs £14.90/11.60; ⌚ daily mid-Apr–Aug, Tue-Sat Sep–early Apr) is right next door to the Brewery, a wonderful arts complex with a theatre, cinema and bar/bistro.

Kendal is on the branch railway line from Windermere to Oxenholme, with connections north to Manchester and south to Lancaster and Barrow-in-Furness.

Ambleside
☎ 015394

Eponymously named for its best attraction, Ambleside is a good base for both hikers and village amblers.

Rydal Mount (☎ 33002; adult/student/child £4.50/3.50/1.50; ⌚ 9.30am-5pm Mar-Oct, 10am-4pm Nov-Feb), where Wordsworth lived for 37 years, still contains many effects from Wordsworth's life. Both the house and gardens are closed for the last three weeks of January.

CARLISLE
☎ 01228 / pop 73,000

Although Carlisle isn't known for much these days besides its proximity to Hadrian's Wall, for 1600 years Carlisle defended the north of England, or south of Scotland, depending on who was winning. In 1745 at the market cross Bonnie Prince Charlie proclaimed his father king.

Most visitors pass quickly through Carlisle, as it's a hub for five scenic railway journeys. Industrialisation in the 1900s diminished its character, but several museums make Carlisle worth a short stopover. It's also a useful base for getting to or from Northumberland, Dumfries & Galloway, the Borders (the beautiful Scottish border counties), and the Lake District.

The train station is a five- to 15-minute walk from all places listed. The well-stocked TIC (☎ 625600; Old Town Hall; ⌚ 9.30am-5.30pm Mon-Sat, 10am-4pm Sun May-Aug & Easter, shorter hrs Mon-Sat & closed Sun rest of year) has information for visiting Hadrian's Wall. A general information office at the train station is open until 7.30pm. For Internet access, head to Cyber Café (8-10 Devonshire St; per 30min £2). For more information about Carlisle, check out www .historic-carlisle.org.uk.

The 11th-century Carlisle Castle (☎ 591922; adult/concession/child £3.80/2.90/1.90) is to the north of the cathedral, overlooking the Eden River. The adjoining museum is a must for Roman history buffs. The excellent Tullie House Museum & Art Gallery (☎ 534781; Castle St; adult/concession/child £5.20/3.60/2.60; ⌚ 10am-5pm Mon-Sat, 11am-5pm Sun, Apr-Oct, to 4pm Nov-Mar), behind the Cathedral, reveals the region's history from the prehistoric Cumbrian tribes to the influence of the railway, and showcases local artists.

The university halls double as the Carlisle Youth Hostel (☎ 597352; dm £13; open mid-Jul–early Sep) in the Old Brewery Residences on Bridge Lane. There are plenty of comfortable B&Bs for around £16, especially along Warwick Rd, including the Georgian Ivy House B&B (☎ 530432; 101 Warwick Rd; per person £20-25).

National Express coaches have services to London (£28.20, 6½ hours, two daily), Edinburgh (£14.50, 3¾ hours, three daily), Glasgow (£14.50, two hours, 10 daily) and Manchester (£20.50, three hours, three daily). A Rail Link coach service runs to Galashiels in the Scottish Borders.

Carlisle is the terminus for six famous scenic railways; phone ☎ 0845 748 4950 for information. You can get anywhere easily from Carlisle, most notably London's Euston station (£41, four hours, 15/10 daily in summer/winter). Most of the following lines have Day Ranger tickets that allow you unlimited travel, ask for details.

Cumbrian Coast Line This line follows the coast in a great arc around to Lancaster, with views over the Irish Sea and back to the Lake District. Change at Barrow for trains to Lancaster on the main line. Ulverston, just north of Barrow, is the starting point for the Cumbria Way, which traverses the lakes to Carlisle.

Glasgow–Carlisle Line The main route north to Glasgow goes through Lockerbie and gives you a glimpse of the grand scale of Scottish landscapes.

GSW Line A slower lines veers west through Dumfries and takes about half an hour longer, if you've got the time and don't mind scenery of the gods.

Lake District Line This line branches off the main north–south line between Preston and Carlisle at

Oxenholme, just outside Kendal, for Windermere. The landscape on the main line is beautiful. The Windermere branch is only about 10 miles long but takes nearly half an hour.

Leeds–Settle–Carlisle Line (LSC) This famous line cuts southeast across the Yorkshire Dales through beautiful countryside and is one of the great engineering achievements of the Victorian railway age. Several stations make good starting points for walks in the Yorkshire Dales National Park.

Tyne Valley Line This line follows Hadrian's Wall to and from Newcastle. There are fine views; see p206 and p208.

SCOTLAND

Craggy snow-capped mountains, sapphire blue lochs and barren islands where seabirds easily outnumber the hardy locals, Scotland is dominated by huge swathes of picture-perfect wilderness as accessible to visitors as anywhere in the world. But alongside the dramatic Highlands and beautifully remote Orkneys and Shetlands, there's also a couple of world-class cities, dozens of appealing towns and a kaleidoscope of timeless, stone-hewn villages that look as if they've been around since the invention of the kilt.

Scotland, with its giant new parliament complex symbolising the country's increasing independence from its historic overlord to the south, should never be just a rushed addition to an England trip. With a proud and vital national identity that goes way beyond bagpipes and haggis, it's a most distinctive region of Britain and deserves at least as much attention as its noisy neighbour.

HISTORY

Scotland's early history is evoked by the ancient standing stones on Lewis (p241) but almost nothing is known about those who lived here around 3000 BC. The strongest indication of the unique and decidedly resolute early Scottish character came during the Roman invasion of Britain 2500 years later. Arriving in 55 BC, the Romans swept up from England only to meet fierce resistance from the wild Scots tribes that awaited them. After decades of clashes, Emperor Hadrian built his eponymous fortified wall (p208) to contain these clans, and evocative sections of it still exist throughout the region.

The Scandinavians, who dominated Northern Europe for much of the first millennium,

were the next big threat, causing the Celts from Ireland to arrive and form an alliance with the local Picts. The alliance began a unifying process in the region that saw Scotland beginning to see itself as a single nation for the first time. Scone became the first capital and the Stone of Destiny, now at Edinburgh Castle (p223), was launched into legend as a symbol of Scottish nationhood.

By the start of the next millennium, the Normans had conquered England but all they could do in Scotland was influence affairs. The outlying regions remained a law unto themselves, culminating in the first full-scale invasion from England in 1296. The resulting 1328 Treaty of Northampton recognised Robert the Bruce as king of an independent country.

By the 16th-century, Scotland was a strongly nationalistic society with its own close links to Europe and a visceral hatred of the English. It boasted universities at St Andrews, Glasgow, Edinburgh and Aberdeen (there were only two in England at the time), reflecting a rigorous and pioneering intellectual climate. The period's distinctive and imposing architecture can be seen today at palaces at Holyrood (p223) and Stirling (p234).

When the childless Queen Elizabeth I died in 1603, Mary Stuart's son united the crowns of Scotland and England for the first time, becoming James I of England and James VI of Scotland. In 1707, after complex bargaining and a modicum of double-dealing, England's government persuaded the Scottish Parliament to agree to the formal union of the two countries under a single parliament. But after a rebellion was buried at the Battle of Culloden (1746), the English set out to destroy the clans, prohibiting Highland dress, weapons and military service. They also cleared entire villages from the land to make way for sheep grazing, forcing thousands of families to abandon their traditional homes – the remains of destroyed houses from this time can still be seen throughout the Highland region. Mentioning this period of ethnic and economic ravaging can still raise the hackles of many Scots.

While its political power had been forcibly removed, Scotland's cultural and intellectual life flourished throughout the 18th century when Edinburgh became a hotbed of Enlightenment thinking. Philosophers Adam Smith and David Hume along with seminal

THE INVENTIVE SCOTS

The canny Scots have contributed much more than their fair share to the world, with dozens of major inventions of historic importance. James Watt (1736–1819) refined the steam engine, enabling it to become the catalyst of the Industrial Revolution, while William Symington (1763–1831) adapted the new technology to develop the first steam-powered boat. Kirkpatrick Macmillan (1813–78) invented a more relaxed form of transport, when he launched the pedal bicycle on an unsuspecting world. Alexander Graham Bell (1847–1922) enabled people to gossip about it by inventing the telephone. And John Logie Baird (1888-1946) created the most important communications medium of the 20th-century when he invented TV. Not content to put his feet up and wait for a football game to appear, he also co-produced the first TV broadcast with sound, the first TV outside broadcast and the concept of colour TV.

But Scotland's history of innovation doesn't end with these key inventions; the country has also contributed a wealth of important discoveries, mostly in the fields of science and medicine. Scotland's top five discoveries are:

- Identifying the nucleus in living cells (Robert Brown, 1773–1858)
- Pioneering the use of antiseptics (Joseph Lister, 1827–1912)
- Identifying mosquitos as the carriers of malaria (Sir Patrick Manson, 1844–1922)
- Discovering insulin (John JR Macleod, 1876–1935)
- Co-discovering penicillin (Sir Alexander Fleming, 1881–1955)

Scottish poet Robert Burns influenced generations of thinkers, and the city became one of Europe's most beautiful examples of the new rational approach to architecture. Much of this heritage is still intact, making modern-day Edinburgh one of the world's most picturesque cities.

The 19th century saw Scotland take a leading role in the Industrial Revolution, with Glasgow becoming an international powerhouse of commerce and the 'second city' in the British Empire after London. While generations of Scots now turned to heavy industry for their employment, Scottish industrialists moved around the world, leaving a lasting legacy of the period as far away as Canada and Australia.

Scotland escaped much of the devastation that saw English cities reduced to rubble in WWII, although there was some bombing, particularly in strategic shipbuilding areas. A gradual industrial decline followed after the war, along with a growing feeling that England was increasingly treating its brother nation as a second-class citizen.

Nationalistic fervour grew in the 1970s, with the Scottish Nationalist Party (SNP) using its newly won seats in the British Parliament as a soapbox to call for devolution. Separatist demands became louder throughout the 1980s when economic recession and cuts to government services had many Scots demanding change. Following-through on its election promise, Britain's new Labour government of 1997 announced a referendum on devolution among the Scots. The result was overwhelmingly in favour.

Representatives to the new Scottish Parliament – which has limited but increasing law-making powers – were elected in 1999. While temporary accommodation was found in the Assembly Rooms of the Church of Scotland at the end of Edinburgh's Royal Mile, plans for a new parliament building were quickly announced. It's hoped that the complex – which went controversially way over budget and missed its completion date several times – is not an indicator of the nature of Scottish self-rule to come.

ENVIRONMENT
The Land

The landscape of Scotland is divided into the Southern Uplands, Central Lowlands and the Highlands. The first is characterised by low, heather-covered hills; the second by the coal and oil deposits that fuelled the country's economic growth; the third by sword-shaped lochs, broad valleys and dramatic mountain peaks. Loch Awe is the longest loch (24 miles/39km), Ben Nevis is the highest peak (1341m) and there are 790 islands around

BRITAIN

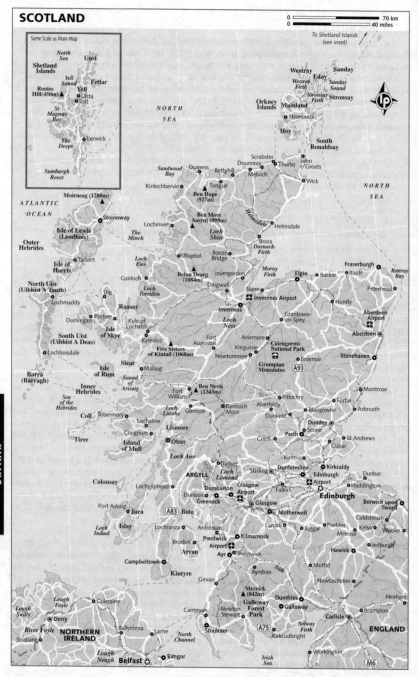

SCOTLAND

0 ——— 70 km
0 ——— 40 miles

Inset (Same Scale as Main Map):

To Shetland Islands (see inset)

Shetland Islands

North Sea

Unst

Fetlar

Yell Sound
Ronies Hill (450m)
Yell
Ulsta
Toft

St Magnus Bay

The Deeps

Lerwick

Sumburgh Roost

Main Map:

To Shetland Islands (see inset)

Westray
Westray Firth
Eday
Sanday
Sanday Sound
Stronsay
Orkney Islands
Mainland
Stronsay Firth
Stromness
Hoy
South Ronaldsay

NORTH SEA

Scrabster
Dounreay
Thurso
John o'Groats
Durness
Bettyhill
Melvich
Wick

Sandwood Bay
Kinlochbervie

Tongue
Ben Hope (927m)

NORTH SEA

Moirneag (1280m)

ATLANTIC OCEAN

Stornoway
Lochinver

Ben More Assynt (998m)
Loch Shin
Helmsdale
Brora

Isle of Lewis (Leodhais)
The Minch

Dornoch Firth
Bonar Bridge

Outer Hebrides

Tarbert
Loch Ewe
Ullapool

Isle of Harris
Gairloch

Beinn Dearg (1084m)
Invergordon
Moray Firth

Fraserburgh
Elgin
Buckie
Banff
Rattray Bay

North Uist (Uibhist A Tuath)
Loch Torridon

Dingwall
Nairn
Inverness Airport

Peterhead

Lochmaddy

Uig

Raasay

Portree

Inverness
Loch Ness

Grantown-on-Spey
Huntly

Aberdeen Airport

Dunvegan

Kyle of Lochalsh

Aviemore

South Uist (Uibhist A Deas)
Isle of Skye

Kyleakin
Fort Augustus
Kingussie
Cairngorms National Park

Aberdeen

Lochboisdale

Five Sisters of Kintail (1068m)
Newtonmore

Braemar
Stonehaven

Barra (Barragh)

Isle of Rum

Sleat

Mallaig

Sound of Arisaig

Grampian Mountains
A93

Inner Hebrides

Sea of the Hebrides

Fort William
Ben Nevis (1343m)

Coll
Tobermory

Lochaline
Lismore
Glencoe
Loch Linnhe

Rannoch Moor
Aberfeldy
Pitlochry
Dunkeld
Blairgowrie
Forfar
Montrose
Arbroath

Tiree

Craignure
Island of Mull
Oban

Loch Awe

Crieff
Perth
Scone
Dundee
St Andrews

Colonsay

Lochgilphead

Tarbet
Loch Lomond
ARGYLL

Kinross
Cupar

Stirling
Dunfermline
Kirkcaldy
Dunbar

Port Askaig

Jura

A83

Bute

Dumbarton
Glasgow Airport
Dunoon
Greenock
Glasgow
Falkirk

Edinburgh Airport
Edinburgh
Haddington

Islay
Loch Indaal

Lochranza

Ardrossan
Brodick
Arran
Prestwick Airport
Kilmarnock
Motherwell
Lanark
Biggar

Berwick upon Tweed
Coldstream
Peebles
Kelso
Wooler

Campbeltown

Prestwick
Ayr

Ayrshire

Melrose
Jedburgh

Kintyre

Girvan

Nith
Moffat
Hawick

Newcastleton

Merrick (842m)

Galloway Forest Park
Dumfries
Galloway

Hexham

Lough Foyle
Coleraine

Cairnryan
Newton Stewart
Stranraer

Solway Firth
A75
Kirkcudbright

Carlisle
Brampton

ENGLAND

Lough Swilly
Derry

River Foyle
Strabane

NORTHERN IRELAND

Ballymena

Larne

North Channel

Workington

Lough Neagh
Belfast
Bangor

Irish Sea

M6

the coast. While Scotland covers only half as much landmass as England (about 491,000 sq miles/79,000 sq km), almost 80% of Britain's coastline lies north of the English border.

National Parks & Conservation Areas

Huge areas of Scotland are naturally beautiful and 12.8% of the country is designated as areas of Specific Scientific Interest (SSI). This includes several categories of protected land, such as 73 National Nature Reserves, 40 National Scenic Areas and 51 Wetlands Areas of International Importance. There are also two national parks, Cairngorms National Park (p235) and Loch Lomond & the Trossachs National Park. In addition, Scotland houses several Unesco-designated World Heritage Sites, including Edinburgh, New Lanark and Orkney.

Environmental Issues

Despite its outstanding natural beauty, Scotland has historically suffered serious challenges to its natural environment. Forests and traditional farms were cleared by the English to make way for sheep grazing in the 18th-century, the Industrial Revolution saw heavy pollution seeping unchecked into the sea and the 1980s witnessed the introduction of giant non-native conifer plantations that destroyed huge areas of delicate ecosystem.

While the long-term effects of these are difficult to calculate, global warming is already taking its toll on the land: Scotland's delicate skiing sector is under threat due to decreasing snowfalls and the Cairngorm Railway (p235), built to service the slopes despite a huge environmentalist outcry, may become a white elephant if snowfall levels continue to decrease.

PEOPLE

The Scottish regard themselves as a separate race occupying the same island as the English and Welsh. While the English proudly term themselves as British, the Scots rarely do and mistakenly calling them English can cause anything from a sharp correction to a bar fight and possible lynching.

Scotland's strong sense of nationalistic pride features a rag-bag of cultural icons, including tartan, haggis, bagpipes, thistles (not the official Scottish flower – the bluebell is) and the Loch Ness Monster. Many of these were solidified as symbols during the Victorian era. The country's singular identity is also based on influential and conspicuous achievers, including poet Robert Burns, novelist Sir Walter Scott and an incredible roster of inventors and innovators (p219).

Scotland's population is five million (another 25 million around the world claim Scottish lineage), with more than 80% living in towns and cities in the Central Lowlands. Only 9% of Britain's population lives in Scotland.

LANGUAGE

A recent survey found that most British people regard the Scottish accent as the world's most trustworthy, with Sean Connery's rich brogue regarded as the most honourable of all. But 'Scottish' is more than just an accent. Gaelic is spoken here by 80,000 people, mainly in the Highlands and Islands, while Lallans, or Lowland Scots, is spoken in the south. It's not unusual to see bilingual road signs, Gaelic shows on TV and Gaelic words used in English conversation. For example, ceilidh (pronounced kay-lay), which translates as 'visit' but now means an evening of dance and live music, is in wide usage. There's an online Scots dictionary at www.scots-online.org.

EDINBURGH

☎ 0131 / pop 440,000

On the surface, Edinburgh is a foppish dandy compared to Glasgow, its earthy rival to the west. But its streets of Georgian townhouses, superb museums and its looming, rock-mounted castle make the country's capital a rewarding first stop for visitors north of Hadrian's Wall. This is the most tourist-friendly of locales, with attractions, restaurants and accommodation to cover every conceivable budget. But there's also plenty of history to get your teeth into: every building seems to have its own ghost story. And with arguably the UK's best festival scene, visitors who plan a brief stopover often end up staying longer.

Orientation

Edinburgh's two most distinctive landmarks are Arthur's Seat, the 251m-high rocky peak southeast of the centre, and the castle, which dominates Princes St Gardens. The Old and New Towns are separated by

CENTRAL EDINBURGH

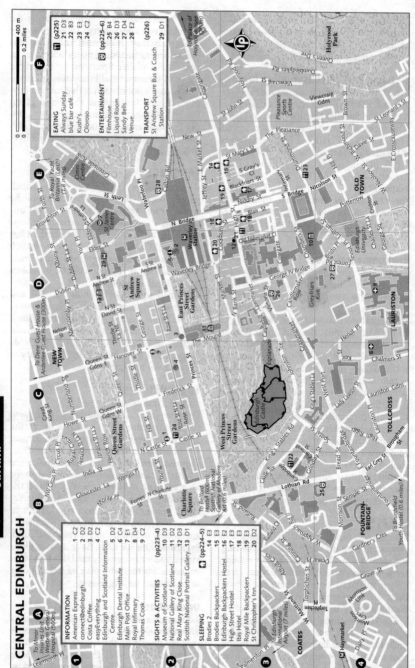

Princes St Gardens and Waverley train station. Buildings are restricted to the northern side of Princes St, which has the usual high-street shops. At the eastern end, Calton Hill is crowned by several monuments, including an incomplete war memorial modelled on the Parthenon, and a tower honouring Nelson. The Royal Mile (Lawnmarket, High St and Canongate) is Princes St's parallel equivalent in the Old Town. The bus station is in the New Town, off the southeastern corner of St Andrew Sq, north of Princes St.

Information

EMERGENCY

Emergency Services Call ☎ 999 for police, fire and ambulance.

Edinburgh Rape Crisis Centre (☎ 556 9437)

Lothian & Borders Police HQ (☎ 311 3131)

INTERNET ACCESS

connect@edinburgh (☎ 473 3800; 3 Princes St; per 20min £1; ☟ 9am-5pm, to 8pm Jul-Aug) Inside the TIC near Waverly train station.

Costa Coffee (☎ 226 4814; 1 Hanover St; per 20min £1; ☟ 7.30am-6.30pm Mon-Sat, 10am-6pm Sun)

easyEverything (☎ 220 3580; 58 Rose St; £1.60 per hour ☟ 8am-10.30pm)

MEDICAL SERVICES

Chemists/Pharmacies Operate standard shop hours, with 24-hour opening arranged on a rotating basis. Check information in chemist shop windows when closed.

Edinburgh Dental Institute (☎ 536 4958; Lauriston Pl; ☟ 9am-3pm Mon-Fri) For biting emergencies.

Edinburgh Royal Infirmary (☎ 536 1000; 51 Little France Cres, Old Dalkeith Rd) 24-hour accident and emergency.

Minor Injuries Unit (☎ Western General Hospital, Crew Rd South; ☟ 9am-9pm) Walk-in clinic for the slightly afflicted.

MONEY

American Express (☎ 718 2501; 69 George St; ☟ 9am-5pm Mon-Sat, 9.30am-5pm Wed)

Thomas Cook (☎ 226 5500; 52 Hanover St; ☟ 9am-5.30pm Mon, Tue & Thu-Sat, 10am-5.30pm Wed)

POST

Main post office (☎ 0845 722 3344; St James Centre, Leith St; ☟ 8.30am-5.30pm Mon-Fri, to 6pm Sat)

TOURIST INFORMATION

Edinburgh & Scotland Information Centre (☎ 0845 225 5121; www.edinburgh.org; 3 Princes St; ☟ 9am-8pm Jul-Aug, to 5pm Sep-Jun) Accommodation reservations, currency exchange and coach booking services. Free city guide and pocket map.

Eventful Ed (www.eventful-edinburgh.com) Guide to city festivals.

The List (www.list.co.uk) Local listings magazine's events site.

Sights

EDINBURGH CASTLE

Dominating the skyline like a city in the clouds, the hilltop complex of **Edinburgh Castle** (☎ 225 9846; Castle Hill; adult/concession/child £9.50/7/2; ☟ 9.30am-6pm Apr-Oct, to 5pm Nov-Mar) should be the first stop for any visitor. Perched on an extinct volcano, it's a hodge-podge of architectural styles, representing centuries of myriad historic uses. The Romanesque 11th-century **St Margaret's Chapel** is Edinburgh's oldest building, the **Scottish Crown Jewels** are among the oldest in Europe and the **Stone of Destiny**, symbol of Scottish nationhood, resides here. The castle's darker history is recorded in its newly opened permanent **Prisoners of War** exhibition, where disembodied wails permeate the shadows.

REAL MARY KING CLOSE

A formerly plague-ridden nest of hidden streets, homes and shops comes back to life at the **Real Mary King Close** (☎ 430160; adult/concession/child £7/6/5; 2 Warriston's Cl, High St; ☟ 10am-9pm Apr-Oct, to 4pm Nov-Mar) on the Royal Mile, a fascinating underground tour through the lives of the real residents who once lived here. Not officially a ghost tour, sightings have been numerous – especially in one room where visitors from around the world routinely leave gifts for one ghostly child resident. A great crash course in Edinburgh history, it's not recommended for claustrophobics.

PALACE OF HOLYROODHOUSE

At the foot of the Royal Mile, the **Palace of Holyroodhouse** (☎ 556 5100; Canongate; adult/concession/child £8/6/3.50; ☟ 9.30am-6pm Apr-Oct, to 4.30pm Nov-Mar) is a beautiful baroque confection mostly dating from a reconstruction by Charles II in 1671. Best known as the home of Mary Queen of Scots, it's the official Scottish residence of the British royal family – which means it's closed when the Queen turns up. Don't miss the extraordinary plaster ceiling and Brussels tapestries in the **State Apartments**. Nearby is the new **Scottish Parliament**.

BRITAIN

Controversially way over-budget, this is a slick uber-modern complex.

NATIONAL GALLERY OF SCOTLAND

Edinburgh has five impressive national galleries, linked by a free bus. First stop for many is the **National Gallery of Scotland** (☎ 624 6200; The Mound; admission free; 🕑 10am-5pm Fri-Wed, to 7pm Thu), a beautifully housed collection of European blockbusters by the likes of Titian, Rembrandt and Monet.

SCOTTISH NATIONAL GALLERY OF MODERN ART

Surrounded by an impressive modernist sculpture garden that's also a good packed lunch spot, the **Scottish National Gallery of Modern Art** (☎ 624 6200; 75 Belford Rd; admission free; 🕑 10am-5pm Fri-Wed, to 7pm Thu) houses an eclectic collection of 20th- and 21st-century works from Picasso and Mondrian to Brit Art favourites like Damian Hirst.

OTHER ATTRACTIONS

The following galleries and museums are also recommended:

Scottish National Portrait Gallery (☎ 624 6200; 1 Queen St; admission free; 🕑 10am-5pm Fri-Wed, to 7pm Thu) Portraits of famous tartan-lovers from Mary Queen of Scots to Sean Connery.

Museum of Scotland (☎ 247 4422; Chambers St; admission free; 🕑 10am-5pm Mon-Sat, noon-5pm Sun) Housed in a modern interpretation of castle architecture, is an evocative exploration of the country's colourful history.

Royal Yacht Britannia (☎ 555 5566; Ocean Terminal, Leith; adult/child £8/4; 🕑 9.30am-4.30pm Apr-Sep, 10am-3.30pm Oct-Mar) The Royal Family's luxury boat for 40 years now offers a fascinating museum-style glimpse into state visits and official receptions.

BRITAIN

Festivals & Events

The **Edinburgh International Festival** (☎ 473 2000; www.eif.co.uk; mid-Aug) takes over the city with three-weeks of world-class music, dance, drama and opera. Just to make sure every bed within a 40-mile radius is taken, the **Edinburgh Military Tattoo** (☎ 08707 555 1188; www.edinburgh-tattoo.co.uk) brings its pipe bands and pageantry to town at the same time. To add to the fun, the **Edinburgh Festival Fringe** (☎ 226 0026; www.edfringe.com) also chooses August for its revelries. Originally an offshoot of the International Festival, the Fringe is a semi-alternative arts festival focusing on theatre, comedy and music. While booking ahead is advised for the International Festival and Tattoo, tickets for many Fringe shows can often be purchased on the day.

Sleeping

It's essential to book for festival, New Year and peak summer periods and it's never too early to do so. The TIC can help with reservations (£3); it also has a good free listings brochure, and plenty of options online (www.edinburgh.org/accommodation).

Almost all the hostels have better locations than the B&Bs and guesthouses, which are mostly located outside the city centre.

BUDGET

Brodies Backpackers (☎ 556 6770; www.brodieshostels.co.uk; 12 High St, Royal Mile; dm £9.50-16.50; 💻) Central Edinburgh's best hostel has mixed dorms with superior mattresses and themed rooms that range from *Trainspotting* to traditional tartan. There's also a cosy, rustic feel – mostly due to its painted rock walls and roaring fireplace – and the recently upgraded facilities include free Internet access.

Brodies 2 (☎ 556 2223; www.brodieshostels.co.uk; 93 High St, Royal Mile; dm £10.50-19.50; 💻) A raid on the local IKEA store has given this property its clean and slightly more sophisticated appearance, helping to make it the city's first four-star hostel. Most rooms are spacious with a Royal Mile view.

St Christopher's Inn (☎ 226 1446; www.st-christophers.co.uk; 9-13 Market St; dm £13-19; 💻) With two bars and proximity to city centre nightlife, this is the party hostel. There's swipe-card entry for added security, all dorms have en-suite bathrooms and a continental breakfast is included. Book online for a discount.

The following are also recommended:

Edinburgh Backpackers Hostel (☎ 220 1717; www.hoppo.com; 65 Cockburn St; £13-15.50) Bright and friendly, close to pubs and nightlife.

High St Hostel (☎ 557 3984; www.scotlands-top-hostels.com; 8 Blackfriars St; dm £12-13) Ever-popular and sociable with a permanent aroma of backpackers' socks.

Royal Mile Backpackers (☎ 557 6120; www.scotlands-top-hostels.com; 105 High St, Royal Mile; dm £12-13) Small, great location, helpful staff, slightly downtrodden appearance.

Belford Hostel (☎ 225 6209; www.hoppo.com; 6/8 Douglas Gdns; dm incl breakfast £10-15.50; 💻) Church conversion with excellent bar lounge. Close to two major galleries and a 10-minute walk from the city centre.

Bruntsfield Youth Hostel (☎ 0870 004 1114; bruntsfield@syha.org.uk; 7 Bruntsfield Cres; dm £12-16; 🖥 ✗) Clean and bright SYHA hostel with no curfew.

MID-RANGE & TOP END
Dene Guest House (☎ 556 2700; deneguesthouse@yahoo.com; 7 Eyre Pl; s £20-35, d £40-65) The laid-back Dene Guest House is located in a high-ceilinged Georgian townhouse in New Town, about a mile's walk from the city centre.

Ardenlee Guest House (☎ 556 2838; info@ardenlee.co.uk; 9 Eyre Pl; s £50-59, d £50-90; ✗) The Ardenlee is a short walk from the centre in a listed Victorian townhouse. Family-run and informal, breakfast includes vegetarian options.

Ibis Hotel (☎ 240 7000; www.ibishotel.com; 6 Hunter Sq; r £50-70) Great value for its location, rooms at the Ibis are all en suite, clean and spacious. Despite having the slightly characterless look common to most chains, it's always popular so book well ahead at peak times. Continental buffet breakfast is an extra £4.95.

The Edinburgh Residence (☎ 622 5080; reserve@theedinburghresidence.com; 7 Rothesay Tce; r £112-395) If those Scottish banknotes are burning a hole in your pocket, the Edinburgh Residence is a superlative serviced apartment experience. High-ceilinged character suites and giant rooms are perfect for large groups or families and it's only a five-minute walk to the city centre.

Eating
The wide variety of eating establishments in Edinburgh should keep culinary adventurers happy, whatever their budget. Many of the city's 700 bars also offer good budget to mid-price meals.

BUDGET
Always Sunday (☎ 622 0667; 170 High St, Royal Mile; mains £4-6; 🕑 8am-6pm Mon-Fri, 9am-6pm Sun) Right in the centre of the Royal Mile, this is a sunny coffee stop where you'll end up staying for lunch. Fairtrade coffee, wheat-free dishes and plenty of vegetarian options suggest a grungy hangout for the worthy student set but the interior is all spa-like cool.

Kushi's (☎ 556 8996; 16 Drummon St; mains £3-5; 🕑 noon-3pm Mon-Sat, 5-9pm Mon-Thu, to 9.30pm Fri & Sat) The near-legendary Kushi's is a basic Punjabi restaurant serving great-value Indian curry dishes. Bring your own six-pack if you want a beer with your meal.

Favorit (☎ 221 1800; 30-32 Levan St; mains £4-6; 🕑 8am-3am Mon-Sun) The cost-conscious student set keeps on coming back for the simple dishes on offer at Favorit. Hummus and pita with a couple of beers is a common sight here while munchie-hunting nightclubbers often stagger in on their way home.

MID-RANGE & TOP END
blue bar café (☎ 221 1222; 10 Cambridge St; mains £11-14; 🕑 noon-3pm, 6-10.30pm Mon-Sat) Sophisticated without being uptight, blue bar café combines Continental influences with British favourites, creating a menu that mixes Toulouse cassoulet with sticky toffee pudding, although not on the same plate. Popular with visitors from the Traverse Theatre downstairs.

Walima (☎ 652 3764; 31a Dundas St; mains £12-18; 🕑 noon-2.30pm & 5-11pm Mon-Sat) As close as you'll come to Morocco this side of Hadrian's Wall, Walima offers authentic, spicy meat and fish dishes served in filo parcels and earthenware pots. If the food doesn't warm you up, the rich décor will.

Oloroso (☎ 226 7614; 33 Castle St; mains £14-22; 🕑 noon-2.30pm & 6-10.30pm) Accessed via a lift in an anonymous street-level foyer, Oloroso is Edinburgh's hottest new restaurant with the best views in town – especially from the terrace. The minimalist décor adds to an ever-changing menu that features delicately prepared reinventions of traditional Scottish ingredients like salmon and game.

Entertainment
Edinburgh has a vibrant arts and entertainment scene that stretches well beyond the traditional festival period. Pick up fortnightly local magazine *The List* (£2.20) for the latest info on Edinburgh and Glasgow happenings. It usually includes a few coupons with two-for-one offers.

Sandy Bells (☎ 225 2751; 25 Forrest Rd; 🕑 11.30-1am Mon-Sat, 12.30-11.30pm Sun) A gem of a pub and the best spot in the city to experience traditional Scottish music. Free performances almost every night and also on Sunday afternoons, it's small so it fills up quickly on weekends.

Liquid Room (☎ 225 2564; 9c Victoria St; £3-5; 🕑 10.30pm-3am Mon-Sat, 11pm-3am Sun) Popular mid-sized club, the subterranean Liquid Room has the best indie night in town every Friday. It's also a live venue that has attracted the likes of Coldplay and the Smashing Pumpkins.

BRITAIN

The Venue (☎ 557 3073; 17-21 Calton Rd; £3-10; ☽ 10pm-3am Thu-Sun) An Edinburgh legend, the three floors here rarely stray from the tried and tested house and techno formula – so long as you don't want any surprises, it virtually guarantees a great night out. Friday is the best night, with each floor hosting its own separate club.

Filmhouse (☎ 228 2688; www.filmhousecinema .com; 88 Lothian Rd; £5.50) Perhaps the UK's best regional movie house, Filmhouse's eclectic programme runs the gamut of classics, obscurities and the downright weird. Education plays a key role, with regular lectures and mini-festivals – this is the home of the Edinburgh International Film Festival every August.

Getting There & Away
AIR
There are flights to **Edinburgh International Airport** (☎ 333 1000) daily from major European cities, including Amsterdam, Paris and Madrid, while US flights also arrive from New York. There are many arrivals from the rest of the UK – via such hubs as London, Bristol, Birmingham, Cardiff, Luton and Manchester – and from other Scottish cities like Aberdeen and Inverness. Times and schedules change frequently on these competitive domestic routes but if you're flexible and book online a few weeks ahead, you can buy tickets for just a few pounds. See p254 for more information.

BUS
National Express and Scottish Citylink services arrive from a multitude of locations throughout the UK at St Andrew Sq bus and coach station. Citylink arrives from Aberdeen (£15.40, 3¼ hours, hourly) Glasgow (£4, 1¼ hours, every 20 minutes) and Inverness (£15, four hours, hourly) among others while National Express services arrive from London (£29, nine to 12 hours, seven daily), Newcastle (£14, three hours, three daily) and York (£28.50, 5½ to nine hours, four daily) for example.

New kid on the block, **Megabus** (☎ 01738 639 095; www.megabus.com), runs frequent refurbished double-decker bus services to Edinburgh from three Scottish cities (Glasgow, 1½ hours; Dundee two hours; and Perth, 1½ hours). Fares are as low as £1 (plus £0.50 booking fee).

TRAIN
There are up to 20 trains daily from London's King's Cross station (4½ to 5½ hours) and fares vary considerably (see Britain Transport p258 for more information). ScotRail runs two northern lines to Edinburgh from Inverness (£32.90, 3½ hours) and Aberdeen (£32.90, 2½ hours), with trains throughout the day. There are trains every 15 minutes from Glasgow (£8.60, 45 minutes).

Getting Around
An Airlink service, operated by **Lothian Buses** (www.lothianbuses.co.uk), from the airport (£3.30, 30 minutes, every 15 minutes). The main local buses for travelling around the city are operated by Lothian Buses and **First Edinburgh** (www.firstedinburgh.co.uk). Adult fares start at £0.80 and exact change is required. For full information – including details on the night bus system – pick up a free *Edinburgh Travelmap* from the TIC or call **Traveline** (☎ 0870 608 2608).

GLASGOW
☎ 0141 / pop 630,000
If Edinburgh is the historic heart of Scotland, Glasgow is its latter-day soul. Not as picturesque as its twee neighbour, it has an energy and vibrancy that can make it a more rewarding visit for those prepared to spend a little more time delving beneath its edgier surface. A recent designation as a European 'city of culture' helped Glasgow to see itself in a different light: this once maudlin industrial area is now overflowing with museums, galleries, a lively arts scene and the best nightlife in Scotland.

Orientation
The two train stations (Central and Queen St), Buchanan St bus station and the TIC are all within a couple of blocks of George Sq, the city's main public space. Running along a ridge in the northern part of the city, Sauchiehall (pronounced sokky-hall) St is a busy pedestrian mall with high street shops at its eastern end and pubs and restaurants to the west. In front of the Royal Concert Hall, it connects with Buchanan St, a second major pedestrian thoroughfare where shops, restaurants and coffee bars collide. The nearby Merchant City area contains streets cafés, swanky restaurants and popular bars.

GLASGOW

0 — 500 m
0 — 0.25 miles

BRITAIN

Information

EMERGENCY
Emergency Services Call ☎ 999 for fire, police and ambulance services.

INTERNET ACCESS
easyInternet (☎ 222 2364; 57 St. Vincent St; per hr £1.40; ☒ 24hr)
Gallery of Modern Art (☎ 229 1996; Queen St; admission free; ☒ 10am-5pm Mon-Thu & Sat, 11am-5pm Fri & Sun) In the basement library.

MEDICAL SERVICES
Glasgow Royal Infirmary (☎ 211 4000; 84-86 Castle St) 24-hour accident and emergency.
Glasgow Dental Hospital (☎ 211 9600; 378 Sauchiehall St)
Munro (☎ 339 0012; 693 Great Western Rd; ☒ 9am-9pm) Late-opening chemist.

MONEY
American Express (☎ 222 1401; 115 Hope St; ☒ 8.30am-5.30pm Mon-Fri, 9am-noon Sat)
Thomas Cook (☎ 207 3400; Central Station; ☒ 8.30am-5.30pm Mon-Fri, 9am-1pm Sat)

POST
Central post office (☎ 08457 223344; 47 St Vincent St; ☒ 8.30am-5.45pm Mon-Fri, 9am-5.30pm Sat) Also has currency exchange.

TOURIST INFORMATION
Glasgow Museums (www.glasgowmuseums.com) Great guide to city museums.
Glasgow TIC (☎ 204 4400; www.seeglasgow.com; 11 George Sq; ☒ 9am-6pm Mon-Sat Oct-Apr, to 7pm Mon-Sat, 10am-6pm Sun May, Jun & Sep, & to 8pm Mon-Sat, 10am-6pm Sun Jul & Aug) With currency exchange and postage stamps sales. The website offers online accommodation bookings.

Sights

GALLERY OF MODERN ART
Glasgow's **Gallery of Modern Art** (☎ 229 1996; Queen St; admission free; ☒ 10am-5pm Mon-Thu & Sat, 11am-5pm Fri & Sun) is a most accessible and very popular collection of works housed in a beautiful neo-classical building in the city centre. Exhibits here are aimed to please both art lovers and people who wouldn't normally set foot in a gallery, so humour is well-represented. This gallery is a highly recommended introduction to some of Scotland's finest contemporary artists.

ST MUNGO'S MUSEUM OF RELIGIOUS LIFE & ART
St Mungo's (☎ 553 2557; 2 Castle St; admission free; ☒ 10am-5pm Mon-Thu & Sat, 11am-5pm Fri & Sun) is a fascinating exploration of major world religions that includes medieval and modern stained glass windows, a magnificent bronze sculpture of Shiva and Salvador Dali's *Christ of St John of the Cross*. The **Gallery of Religious Life** illuminates disparate beliefs relating to birth, marriage, death and the afterlife. Wheelchair accessible.

GLASGOW SCIENCE CENTRE
The city's splendid **Science Centre** (☎ 420 5000; Pacific Quay; adult/child £6.95/4.95; ☒ 10am-6pm) is an excellent, hands-on day out. The city's newest uber-modern attraction houses more than 500 exhibits in its **Science Mall** – don't miss the 3D **Virtual Science Centre**. There's also an **IMAX cinema** showing mainstream and education movies. The 127m revolving **observation tower** is due to reopen soon after a period of reconstruction.

THE LIGHTHOUSE
Exploring Scotland's unique contribution to contemporary architecture and design, the **Lighthouse** (☎ 221 6362; 11 Mitchell Lane; adult/concession/child £3/1.50/1; ☒ 10.30am-5pm Mon & Wed-Sat, 11am-5pm Tue, noon-5pm Sun) presents a kaleidoscope of revolving exhibitions on six modernised floors of the old Glasgow *Herald* newspaper offices.

Celebrating the original architect of the building, there's a permanent **Interpretation Centre** on the work of Glasgow design god Charles Rennie Mackintosh. See if you can spot any of his Art Noveau cityscape flourishes around the area from the top floor observation deck.

GLASGOW NECROPOLIS
Looming on a hill above the nearby cathedral, Glasgow's 'City of the Dead' **necropolis** (☎ 287 3961; Castle St; admission free; ☒ dawn-dusk) is like no other cemetery in Scotland. Undulating turf and minor headstones on its lower reaches give way to giant Victorian temples built to house some of the city's great and good in the afterlife. A fascinating glimpse into the vanity and wealth of a bygone age, there are also some of the best views of the city from between the crooked tombs at the top.

OTHER SIGHTS

The following sights are also recommended:

Glasgow Cathedral (☎ 552 6891; Cathedral Sq; admission free; ◷ 9.30am-6pm Mon-Sat & 1-5pm Sun Apr-Sep, to 4pm Mon-Sat & 1-4pm Sun Oct-Mar) Scotland's most magnificent surviving medieval church.

Glasgow School of Art (☎ 353 4526; 167 Renfrew St; adult/child £5/4) Mackintosh's greatest architectural achievement. The hours vary throughout the year so call ahead.

Burrell Collection (☎ 287 2550; Pollok Country Park; admission free; ◷ 10am-5pm Mon-Thu & Sat, 11am-5pm Fri & Sat) Eclectic treasure trove of artworks, artefacts and ephemera.

McLellan Galleries (☎ 565 4137; 270 Sauchiehall St; admission free; ◷ 10am-5pm Mon-Thu & Sat, 11am-5pm Fri & Sun) Housing art treasures from the popular Kelvingrove Art Gallery & Museum, until it reopens in 2006.

Scottish Football Museum (☎ 616 6139; Hampden Park; adult/concession £5/2.50; ◷ 10am-5pm Mon-Sat, 11am-5pm Sun) Unmissable treat for all football nuts.

Sleeping

There's been a big increase in accommodation in Glasgow in the last few years but finding a decent B&B in July and August can still be difficult, so book well ahead for the summer peak. There are some good mid-range chain hotels offering flat-rate rooms throughout the year. Last-minute deals are also available via the TIC site at www.seeglasgow.com.

BUDGET

Glasgow Youth Hostel (☎ 0870 004 1119; 7-8 Park Tce; dm £13) the city's only SYHA has newly renovated facilities for upcoming visitors. Always busy in summer, so book ahead.

Euro Hostel (☎ 222 2828; www.euro-hostels.co.uk; 318 Clyde St; B&B £13.75-29; 🖳) Large, party-friendly hostel in a former student hall of residence. Located a few minutes' walk from Central Station, rooms – twins, families and dorms – are en-suite and prices are reduced depending on the number of people sharing the room. There are good weekly rates for longer stays and a 24-hour reception.

Campus Village (☎ 553 1448; www.rescat.strath .ac.uk; Cathedral St; ◷ Jun-Sep; r per person incl breakfast £22.75-32) A large, modern complex of student accommodation at the University of Strathclyde. Well-located near the cathedral, facilities are clean but basic. Some singles have shared bathrooms; phonecards have to be purchased to use the in-suite phones.

MID-RANGE

Belhaven Hotel (☎ 339 3222; www.belhavenhotel.com; 15 Belhaven Tce; s £35-50, d £45-60; ⊠) A cosy Art Noveau–inspired nook opposite the West End's Botanic Gardens. A comfortable bar lounge with fireplace makes it hard to leave this place during the evening but there are plenty of good pubs and restaurants in this area too. The two budget rooms share a bathroom.

Travel Inn Metro (☎ 0870 238 3320; glasgow.city .mti@whitbread.com; 187 George St; r £49.95) Brilliant location near George Sq for this bright and cheerful chain hotel. Rooms are spacious and some are designed specifically for disabled travellers. Family rooms are also available at no extra cost but book early for these. The all-you-can eat buffet breakfast (£6.50) is popular and there's also an on-site currency exchange.

The following are also recommended:

Old School House (☎ 332 7600; oschoolh@hotmail .com; 194 Renfrew St; B&B s/d £35/52) Good value accommodation in heritage-listed Georgian villa.

Willow Hotel (☎ 332 2323; 228 Renfrew St; s/d £30/48) Past its prime but clean, tidy and well-located.

Jurys Glasgow Hotel (☎ 334 8161; www.jurysdoyle .com; Great Western Rd; r £40-125) Large rooms and an on-site fitness centre.

TOP END

Langs Hotel (☎ 333 1500; www.langshotels.co.uk; 2 Port Dundas Pl; r £90-170) Swanky, modern, independent hotel brashly looming over the heart of the city centre. Fight your way through the power-dressing business-types shouting into their mobile phones in the lobby and you'll discover the best high-end rooms in the city. Power showers, PlayStations and satellite TVs are standard features in this stylish boutique hotel, as is an on-site spa.

Eating

Despite the disturbing prevalence of fast food joints on many streets, Glasgow's eating scene has been revitalised in recent years and now includes a growing number of excellent cafés and some of the best restaurants in Scotland. Check www.bestglasgowrestaur ants.com for its listings and useful People's Choice recommendations.

BUDGET

Willow Tea Rooms (☎ 332 0521; 217 Sauchiehall St; lunches £3-6; ◷ 9am-5pm Mon-Sat, 11am-4.30pm Sun)

Designed by Charles Rennie Mackintosh, this must-see Art Noveau café is often packed at peak times so plan to eat early or late to avoid the crowds. The afternoon tea is a local legend but avoid the recently opened branch on Buchanan St – it's nowhere near as authentic as the original.

Wee Curry Shop (☎ 353 0777; 7 Buccleuch St; lunch £4.75; ⏰ noon-2pm Mon-Sat, 5.30-10.30pm Sat) Glasgow often touts itself as Britain's curry capital; with this fabulous little south Indian restaurant who can argue? The two-course £4.75 special is the city's best lunch deal. At night, prices jump a bit but with a bring-your-own beer policy, you'll save anyway. Book ahead, it's not called 'wee' for nothing.

The following are also recommended:

Vancouver Muffin Company (☎ 221 9253; 73 St Vincent St; mains £3-5; ⏰ 8am-6pm Mon-Fri, 9am-6pm Sat, 10am-5pm Sun) Great coffee and postcard-writing pit stop in the centre of the action, also sells sandwiches.

Glasgow College of Food Technology (☎ 552 3751; 230 Cathedral St; mains from £3; ⏰ hrs vary) Two restaurants, a food court and a bakery staffed by students and open to the public.

MID-RANGE & TOP END

Grassroots Café (☎ 333 0534; 93-97 St Georges Rd; mains £5-12; ⏰ 10am-10pm) A laid-back restaurant using mainly organic ingredients on its eclectic vegetarian menu. Homely comfort dishes like veggie bangers and mash are popular, with the daily soup special often worth checking out. Organic beers – including the delicious Lomond Gold – or filling fruit smoothies are the perfect accompaniments.

Pancho Villas (☎ 552 7737; 26 Bell St; mains £5-15; ⏰ noon-10.30pm Mon-Thu, to 11pm Fri & Sat, 6-10.30pm Sun) Traditional Mexican food served in a strikingly colourful restaurant, Pancho Villas would be pure kitsch if not for the serious menu. Check out the ever-changing daily specials before ordering and be sure to try a cactus-tight tortilla with your margarita.

Ubiquitous Chip (☎ 334 5007; 12 Ashton Lane; 2-/3-course dinner £32.50/37.50; ⏰ noon-2.30pm & 5.30-11pm Mon-Sat, 12.30-3pm & 6.30-11pm Sun) Scottish cuisine served in an award-winning up-market restaurant that attracts Glasgow's high-flying VIPs. Using local produce and mixing traditional and original approaches, the Chip's mouth-watering fish and game dishes include a revelatory Perthshire pork dish served on crumbled black pudding.

Drinking

Glasgow has plenty of street cafés – the piazza around the Gallery of Modern Art is a great spot for sitting outside and watching the world go by – and it's full of great pubs, too. While the usual suspects, including Whetherspoons and Outback, are prominently positioned, there are dozens of interesting spots just waiting to be discovered. Happy hour is *de rigueur* and often lasts longer than it does elsewhere.

Fresh (☎ 552 5532; 51-53 Cochrane St; juices & smoothies £2.50; ⏰ 8am-7pm Mon-Fri, 9am-6pm Sat, 11am-6pm Sun) The city centre's only fresh juice bar has the décor of a day spa to complement its wide range of fruity pick-me-ups. At the favourite haunt of many an Australian backpacker, the Morning After beverage is particularly recommended – it's an apple, orange, carrot and ginger concoction that mercifully removes all thoughts of the previous night's 10-pint booze-fest.

Blackfriars (☎ 552 5924; 36 Bell St; ⏰ noon-midnight Mon-Sat, 12.30pm-midnight Sun) Glasgow's best traditional pub couldn't be more laid-back, attracting a healthy mix of locals, students and visitors. While some come for the giant meals (served until 7pm) or the weekend live jazz nights, most are here for a few sociable beers.

Bar 10 (☎ 572 1448; 10 Mitchell Ln; ⏰ 10am-midnight Mon-Sat, noon-midnight Sun) The brain-child of Ben Kelly, creator of Manchester's legendary Hacienda Club, this older, but surprisingly unpretentious, bar still beats most of Glasgow's up-and-coming trendy drinking holes. Capturing the essence of a busy, metropolitan Euro-bar, there are drinks specials and DJs on most nights.

The following are also recommended:

Waxy O'Connor's (☎ 354 5154; 46 West George St; ⏰ noon-11pm Mon & Tue, to midnight Wed-Sat, 12.30-11pm Sun) Friendly, often-crowded Irish pub with six bars.

Horse Shoe Bar (☎ 229 5711; 17 Drury St; ⏰ 11am-midnight Mon-Sat, 12.30pm-midnight Sun) Excellent real ale selection and value-priced pub meals.

Entertainment

Glasgow is Scotland's entertainment and nightlife capital and you can plug in to what's on by picking up *The List* (£2.20) or scanning local newspapers (especially the *Herald* and the *Evening Times*) throughout the week. The monthly *Gig Guide*, available free in many pubs, lists upcoming music concerts. Tickets can be booked via **Ticket Scotland** (☎ 204 5151; www.ticketsscotland.com).

LIVE MUSIC

King Tut's Wah Wah Hut (☎ 221 5279; 272a St Vincent St; ☽ noon-midnight Mon-Sat, 6pm-midnight Sun) A deservedly popular live music pub where the early Indie versions of Oasis and Radiohead started out. Live music nightly, King Tut's also has a good menu with many vegetarian options for those withered Morrissey fans.

Barrowlands (☎ 552 4601; www.glasgow-barrow land.com; 244 Gallowgate) Legendary old dance-hall venue where some of the larger visiting bands crack open their guitar cases. Check online and book ahead.

NIGHTCLUBS

The Tunnel (☎ 204 1000; 88 Mitchell St; admission £5; ☽ 11pm-3am Wed-Sat) Mainstream good-time club favouring house and trance where top UK DJs regularly appear in front of an adoring crowd. They're quite strict on the dress code, so smarten up before joining the queue outside.

The Cathouse (☎ 248 6606; 15 Union St; admission free-£5; ☽ 11pm-3am Thu & Sun, 10.30pm-3am Fri & Sat) Almost enough to make a Goth smile, this great indie and alternative nightspot is the perfect antidote to the usual sterile club experience. With two dance floors, the upper being for hardcore mosh pit freaks, the imaginative music selection is almost matched by some of the wacky outfits on display. If you're not wearing black, stay at home.

Getting There & Away

AIR

Ten miles west of the city, **Glasgow International Airport** (☎ 887 1111) receives flights from the UK and the rest of the world. Several no-frills airlines, including easyJet, bmiBaby and Ryanair, provide domestic services from London and other cities. See the Britain Transport section (p256) for more details.

BUS

All long-distance buses arrive and depart from **Buchanan bus station** (☎ 333 3708; Killermont St) and there are a number of competing services that keep the prices down.

The **Silver Choice** (☎ 01355 230403; www.silverchoice travel.co.uk) offers the best deal from London (£25, 8½ hours). There are daily departures at 10pm from London Victoria, but book well in advance because it's a popular service.

Seven **National Express** (☎ 0870 580 8080; www .nationalexpress.com) services arrive from London (single £29, 8½ to 10 hours) daily. The company also runs regular coaches from Birmingham (£39.50, seven to nine hours), Carlisle (£14.50, two hours) and York (£28.50, seven to 10 hours) among others.

Coaches run by **Scottish Citylink** (☎ 0870 550 5050; www.citylink.co.uk) arrive in Glasgow from most of Scotland's towns and cities. Services include the popular route from Edinburgh that runs every 20 minutes (£6, 1¼ hours). There are also daily arrivals from Aberdeen (£16, four hours), Fort William (£13, three hours), Inverness (£15.50, four hours), Oban (£12.20, three hours), Skye (£22, 6¼ hours) and Stirling (£4, 45 minutes).

Daily refurbished double-decker bus services owned by **Megabus** (☎ 01738 639 095; www.megabus.com) run to Glasgow from three Scottish cities (Dundee, two to three hours; Edinburgh, 1½ hours; Perth, two hours). Fares are as low as £1 (plus £0.50 booking fee) if you order far enough in advance.

TRAIN

As a general rule, Glasgow's Central station serves southern Scotland, England and Wales, while Queen St station serves the north and east. Trains arrive throughout the day from London Euston and London King's Cross. A much more comfortable ride than a long-haul bus trek, prices can vary considerably (from £25) for the five-hour direct trip.

The West Highland line north to Oban and Fort William is run by **ScotRail** (☎ 0845 748 4950; www.scotrail.co.uk), and direct links from Dundee (£21.60, 1½ hours), Aberdeen (£32.90, 3¼ to four hours) and Inverness (£32.90, 3½ hours). There are numerous trains from Edinburgh (£7.80 to £9, 50 minutes).

Getting Around

The **St Enoch Square Travel Centre** (☎ 226 4826, St Enoch Sq; ☽ 9.30am-5.30pm Mon-Sat) can help demystify the city's myriad transport options.

TO/FROM THE AIRPORT

The No 905 shuttle service runs from Glasgow International Airport to Buchanan bus station. It runs from 6am Monday (from 7am Sunday) to midnight Saturday, every 10 to 15 minutes during the week, every 30 minutes at weekends, and costs £3.30. A taxi on the same route costs £12 to £17.

BUS

The city is covered by a good bus system but passengers often need exact change. The main operator is **First Glasgow** (☎ 423 6600; www .firstglasgow.com), whose city centre fares average 70p. For multiple trips, the company's FirstDay ticket, purchased from the driver, allows unlimited all-day travel after 9.30am for £2.10. There are also several night bus routes, mostly alighting in George Sq.

TRAIN

There's an extensive suburban train network in Glasgow, which connects to another system – the highly efficient **SPT subway** (☎ 0870 608 2608; www.spt.co.uk) loop – at Buchanan station. Serving 15 stations in the centre, west and south of the city, single SPT tickets cost £1. For travel after 9.30am, there's an unlimited trip Discovery Ticket for £1.70. Alternatively, the Roundabout Glasgow ticket (£4) covers use of all train and subway routes in the city for one day.

SOUTHWEST SCOTLAND

Scotland's southwest corner, warmed by Gulf Stream currants, has the region's mildest climate. It's also a place of contrasts: from the bare hills, moors and woodlands nearer Glasgow to the ancient crags of a coastline that attracts those looking for Scottish scenery without the attendant crowds. They're not the only ones who've been lured here: this was the home of Robbie Burns, Scotland's national poet, and generations of Glaswegians have had their summer vacations here.

Ayrshire is immediately southwest of Glasgow, while Dumfries & Galloway covers the southern half of this western elbow. There are many notable historic and prehistoric attractions linked by the Solway Coast Heritage Trail. The Southern Upland Way links the region coast-to-coast. This is also great cycling country. Visit a local TIC for extensive information on these routes. The picturesque town of Kirkcudbright makes a good base, so consider starting your journey there. There are SYHA hostels throughout the region.

Isle of Arran

☎ 01770 / pop 4800

The region's best walking country, Arran is often described as 'Scotland in miniature' because of its compact reflection of a variety of scenery. This includes sheep-strewn farmland, rock-sheltered beaches, looming peaks such as **Goat Fell** and a coastal road that's perfect for cycling.

The main **TIC** (☎ 303774; www.ayrshire-arran .com; The Pier, Brodick; ☺ 9am-5pm Mon-Thu & Sat, to 7.30pm Fri, 10am-5pm Sun May-Sep, 9am-5pm Mon-Sat Oct-Apr) is helpfully stocked with information on how to experience the region, which includes the highly recommended **Brodick Castle** (☎ 302202; adult/child £7/5.25; 11am-4.30pm Apr-Sep, to 3.30pm Oct) 2.5 miles north. It's a magnificent 13th-century sandstone pile full of silver, porcelain and hunting trophies of the stuffed head variety. The landscaped gardens, featuring many exotic plants, are excellent.

Call the TIC for accommodation assistance or head for the **Belvedere Guest House** (☎ 302397; stb@vision-unlimited.co.uk; Alma Rd; s/d £20/40). The nearest **SYHA hostel** (0870 004 1140; dm £10.50-11; ☺ Mar-Oct) is 14 miles (22km) north in Lochranza.

GETTING THERE & AROUND

Conveniently accessible from Glasgow, Brodick is only an hour by **CalMac** (☎ 302166; passenger/car £4.70/33.50) ferry ride from Ardrossan (four to six daily). Six buses run daily from Brodick to Lochranza (£2, 45 minutes, Monday to Saturday) and there are additional services around the island. Ask for additional transport information at the TIC or consider renting a bike for your visit from **Mini Golf Cycle Hire** (☎ 07968 024040; Shore Rd) for £10 per day.

Stranraer & Cairnryan

☎ 01776 / pop 11,500

A transport hub and useful layover if you're between ferries, the bus and train stations as well as the TIC and some accommodation options are huddled around the sea terminals.

You can check email at the **library** (☎ 707400, North Strand St; ☺ 9.15am-7.30pm Mon-Wed & Fri, to 5pm Thu & Sat) for free before visiting the **TIC** (702595; 28 Harbour St), which specialises in booking Citylink/National Express journeys, as well as day trips across the Irish Sea: at less than 2½ hours, Stranraer offers the shortest links to Northern Ireland. Frequent **Stena Line** (☎ 0870 570 7070; www.stenaline .co.uk) services arrive from Belfast.

For an economical bed for the night, **Ivy House** (☎ 704176; 3 Ivy Pl; r per person £18-25) is the best B&B in town.

Coach services arrive from London, run by **National Express**, while **Stagecoach Western** (☎ 01387-253496) runs services from Glasgow (£8.25, three hours, six per day). ScotRail trains arrive from Glasgow throughout the day (£15, 2½ hours)

Kirkudbright
☎ 01557 / pop 3500

An ideal base for exploring the southern coast, Kirkudbright has dignified Victorian merchants' houses as well as a lively harbour. There is an excellent restaurant **Auld Alliance** (☎ 330569; 5 Castle St; mains £10-16; ☾ dinner daily & lunch Sun) that represents the historic allegiance between Scotland and France as it combines local produce with French cooking and wine. Booking advised. Call in at the **TIC** (☎ 330494, Harbour Sq; ☾ Mon-Sat Apr-Oct) for accommodation information.

Buses run by **National Express** arrive from London and Birmingham (via Manchester and Carlisle), servicing the main towns and villages along the A75 (including Ayr, Dumfries and Newton Stewart) en route. **Stagecoach Western** (☎ 01387-253496) provides local bus services.

SOUTHEAST SCOTLAND

The ancient abbeys, lush glens and proud forests of the Scottish Borders have a unique beauty and romance that's often missed by travellers rushing through on their way to Edinburgh. Those who do stop, discover the lovely valley of the Tweed River and a host of dramatic ruins kept alive by the charming stone towns and villages that cluster nearby. This is a great region to explore on foot or by bike: check local TICs for maps and options or head straight for the signposted **Tweed Cycleway** between Biggar and Berwick-Upon-Tweed.

Located between England's Cheviot Hills and Scotland's Pentland, Moorfoot and Lammermuir Hills, the Scottish Borders has a good network of local buses. **First** (☎ 01896 752237) runs numerous services from Galashiels, Melrose and Edinburgh and they offer a Rover ticket for unlimited travel in the region (£6.45).

Jedburgh & Around
☎ 01835 / pop 4000

The best base for exploring the Scottish Borders, Jedburgh is a bustling wee town that's well worth checking out on foot. Its

TIC (☎ 863170; Murray's Green; ☾ 9am-7pm Mon-Sat & 10am-6pm Jul & Aug, variable hrs rest of year) has plenty of maps and transport information for exploring the region but your first stop should be **Jedburgh Abbey** (☎ 863925; adult/concession/child £3.50/2.50/1.20; ☾ 9.30am-6.30pm Apr-Sep, to 4.30pm Mon-Sat, 2-4.30pm Sun Oct-Mar). The most complete of the ruined Border abbeys, this 12th-century red sandstone masterpiece was founded by David I as an Augustinian priory.

Local bus services arrive from Melrose (£2.60, 30 minutes; five daily Monday to Saturday) and Kelso (£1.50, 30 minutes, 11 daily Monday to Saturday, five on Sunday). **Munro** bus services from Edinburgh arrive throughout the day (£5.30, two hours, eight daily Monday to Saturday, five on Sunday).

Melrose & Around
☎ 01896 / pop 1650

Another popular base for exploring the Borders, Melrose is a pretty little village clustered around a perfectly formed market square. Check in with the **TIC** (☎ 0870 608 0404; Abbey St; ☾ 10am-5pm year-round, to 2pm Sun Apr-Oct) for local B&B options, or head to the **Melrose Youth Hostel** (☎ 0870 004 1141; Priorwood; dm £12; 🖳), a quiet, well-maintained option.

The main attraction here is **Melrose Abbey** (☎ 822562; adult/concession/child £3.50/2.50/1.20; ☾ 9.30am-6.30pm Apr-Sep, to 4.30pm Mon-Sat & 2-4.30pm Sun Oct-Mar). Repeatedly attacked by the English in the 14th-century, the abbey's highly decorative red sandstone husk is a potent symbol for many Scots. Rebuilt by Robert the Bruce – whose heart is reputedly buried here – this Gothic gem has great views from the top.

First buses arrive throughout the day from Jedburgh (£2.40, 30 minutes, 11 per day Monday to Saturday, five per day Sunday) and Edinburgh (£4.55, 2¼ hours, eight daily Monday to Saturday).

STIRLING
☎ 01786 / pop 45,000

With a fortress here since prehistoric times, Stirling has one of the most blood-drenched histories of any Scottish city – key victories over the English at the Battle of Stirling Bridge (1297) and the Battle of Bannockburn (1314) both happened in this area. With this in mind, most visitors head straight for the old town for a reminder of the past.

BRITAIN

Head up the steep streets from the train station and you'll find some fascinating old stone buildings, the SYHA hostel and the windswept castle itself, which offers spectacular panoramic views of the seemingly endless plains below. Take a slight detour to the **TIC** (☎ 08707 200620; 41 Dumbarton Rd; ☿ 9am-7.30pm Mon-Sat, 9.30am-6.30pm Sun Jul & Aug, varies rest of year) whose staff are not as helpful as their raft of free brochures.

The thick, grey walls of **Stirling Castle** (☎ 450000; adult/concession/child £8/6/2; ☿ 9.30am-6pm Apr-Oct, to 5pm Nov-Mar) are perched dramatically on an extinct volcano and the site rivals Edinburgh for the title of Scotland's best castle. But since it's always less crowded here than is its eastern neighbour, it's much easier to skulk into a corner and imagine yourself in centuries past. The current complex was conceived as a fortress in the 14th-century when a succession of Stuart monarchs began their residency.

One of Scotland's best SYHA properties, **Stirling Youth Hostel** (☎ 0870 004 1149; St John St; dm £11.50-13.50; ▣) occupyies a large old church building near the castle. Rooms are small and each has en-suite facilities. The huge dining room/lounge area is a great hangout spot.

Down near the train station, there's also the **Willy Wallace Hostel** (☎ 446773; www.willywall acehostel.com; 77 Murray Pl; dm £13), which is cosy, welcoming and closer to the modern heart of the city. When the tourists have left the castle for the day, head next door to the **Portcullis pub** (☎ 472290; Castle Wynd) for a wee dram. You're likely run into a castle employee who'll regale you with some great insider stories.

Scottish Citylink buses arrive during the day from Aberdeen (£14.50, 3½ hours, four daily), Edinburgh (£6.20, one hour, three daily), Glasgow (£5, 45 minutes, hourly) and other towns and cities. ScotRail services arrive from Dundee (£12.70, 50 minutes), Edinburgh (£5.50, 50 minutes, twice hourly), Glasgow (£5.70, 40 minutes, every two hours) and other cities during the day.

ST ANDREWS
☎ 01334/ pop 14,200

St Andrews' fascinating history casts a long shadow over its cobbled streets and ancient terrace cottages. Scotland's former ecclesiastical capital, the ruins of a cavernous cathedral and moody, seafront castle lurk on its outskirts while the town's university,

founded in 1410, is the country's oldest. While 6000 students fill St. Andrews during term, golfers annually flock here in even bigger numbers for the area's nine courses – especially the legendary Old Course, the sport's spiritual home.

Internet access is available from **Costa Coffee** (☎ 475986; 83 Market St; ☿ 8am-6pm Mon-Sat, 10am-1pm Sun) £1 for 20 minutes and the **TIC** (☎ 472021; www.visit-standrews.co.uk; 70 Market St; ☿ Mon-Sat Oct-Mar, daily Apr-Sep) has a free town guide with a street map.

Sights

Scotland's largest ever church, **St Andrews Cathedral** (☎ 472563; The Pends; adult/child incl castle £4/1.25; ☿ 9.30am-6.30pm Apr-Sep, to 4.30pm Oct-Mar) was reduced to rubble during the Reformation in 1559. Half-eaten walls detail its past splendour while a visitor centre explains its turbulent history. A 12th-century tower offers spectacular views – watch out for seals bobbing offshore. A short, windswept walk away is the ruined **St Andrews Castle** (☎ 477196; The Scores; adult/child incl cathedral £4/1.25; ☿ 9.30am-6.30pm Apr-Sep, to 4.30pm Oct-Mar). Perched on coastal rocks, this is a great spot for storm-watching. In contrast, the **British Golf Museum** (☎ 460046; Bruce Embankment; adult/child £4/2; ☿ 9.30am-5.30pm Easter–mid-Oct, 11am-3pm mid-Oct–Easter) is a modern, hands-on exhibition that, even for non-golfers, is worth visiting.

Sleeping

Golf nuts take over the town's accommodation during major tournaments and throughout the summer, so make peak bookings well in advance.

The **St Andrews Tourist Hostel** (☎ 479911; www .eastgatehostel.com; St Mary's Pl; dm £11-16; ☿ 7am-11pm) is clean and friendly and only five minutes from the bus station. **Meade B&B** (☎ 477350; 5 Albany Pl; r per person £20) is also a popular budget haunt but only has one room. Almost every house along Murray Pl and Murray Park offers accommodation, with off-season prices from £25. **Brownlees Guest House** (☎ 473868; www.brownlees.co.uk; 7 Murray Pl; r per person £25-32) provides maps for visitors and a rib-sticking breakfast.

Eating & Drinking

The Eating Place (☎ 475671; 177-179 South St; mains £4-7; ☿ 9.30am-5pm Mon-Sat, 11am-5pm Sun) is a good coffee stop with a bewildering selection of sweet and savoury Scottish pancakes – try the Applesin and you'll die happy. The charming **Brambles Bistro** (☎ 475380; 5 College St; mains £5-10; ☺ 9am-10pm) has hearty comfort-food, including good vegetarian options, while the ever-popular **Vine Leaf Restaurant** (☎ 477497; 131 South St; 2-course dinner £19.95; ☺ from 7pm Tue-Sat) is perfect for a gourmet splurge of seafood, game or Scottish beef.

The **Central Bar** (☎ 478296; Market St) is the town's top pub, with a lip-smacking array of Scottish ales to keep locals and visitors merry but it's the subterranean hot spot of **Ma Bells** (☎ 472611; 40 The Scores) where students and backpackers spend most of their drinking time. Escape the rabble at **Whey Pat Tavern** (☎ 477740; 1 Bridge St), where quieter drinks and chat are *de rigueur*.

Getting There & Around

Leuchars, the nearest train station (trains to/from Aberdeen, Dundee, Edinburgh, Inverness) is an £8.50 taxi or £1.75 bus (No 96 or 99) ride away. **Stagecoach Fife** (☎ 01592-642394) runs buses from Edinburgh (£6, two hours, hourly) and Dundee (£2.70, 30 minutes, half-hourly).

The compact town centre is best explored on foot, but **Spokes** (☎ 477835; 37 South St; ☺ 9am-5pm Mon-Sat) rents bikes from £6.50 per half day for those venturing further afield.

EASTERN HIGHLANDS

Like a craggy nose jutting defiantly into the North Sea, the land between Perth and the Firth of Tay in the south and Inverness and Moray Firth in the north is filled with a cornucopia of landscapes. From broad, un-peopled beaches and craggy cliffs teeming with seabirds to tiny stone fishing villages and the bare shoulders of the Cairngorm Mountains, it contains Britain's newest national park as well as two of Scotland's biggest cities, Aberdeen and Dundee.

Orientation & Information

The Grampian Mountains march from Oban in a great arc northeastward, becoming the Cairngorm Mountains in the eastern region. The Cairngorms are as dramatic and demanding as any of the Scottish ranges, and the coastline, especially from Stonehaven to Buckie, is exceptional. Aberdeen is the region's biggest city, providing the main

ferry port for Shetland. Reflecting the division between the Eastern and Western Highlands, there are few links between Perth and Inverness, the capital of the Highlands.

There are TICs in towns and cities throughout the region and a useful Highlands of Scotland tourism website at www .visithighlands.com.

Perthshire & Cairngorms

One of the region's most important towns (it's on the main train line from Edinburgh and Inverness) Perth became Scotland's capital in the 12th century. It's now a bustling settlement that celebrates its heritage without resting idly on it.

With its excellent visitor amenities, Aviemore makes a good base for exploring the region and is regarded as the gateway to the Cairngorms. This is where hikers, bikers and climbers congregate to take on the Scottish outdoors and, in winter, it's the centre of the country's skiing and snowboarding action. While the season traditionally runs from December until April, recent light snowfalls have seen closures as early as February. Check ski.visitscotland.com for the latest conditions.

The **Cairngorms National Park** (www.cairngorms .co.uk), Britain's newest, doesn't rely on snow to show its visitors a good time. Combining wild mountain tundras and secluded old pinewoods, the area bursts with ancient castles, unique wildlife and lush colours year-round. There are plenty of attractions and activities here, with the **Cairngorm Mountain Railway** (☎ 01479 861261; Cairngorm Ski Area; adult/concession £8/6.50; ☺ 10am-5pm), the UK's highest and longest funicular, a popular, though pricey, trip.

The modern **Aviemore Youth Hostel** (☎ 0870 004 1104; 25 Grampian Rd; dm £11.50-13; ☐) is well-equipped and close to both the local TIC and village centre.

Grampian Country Coast

On the coast between Perth and Aberdeen, Dundee is the region's second largest city. While an important ancient port and main player in Scotland's Industrial Revolution, its 20th-century fortunes flagged until the 1990s when it re-invented itself as a tourism destination. Check in at the **TIC** (☎ 01382 527527; www.angusanddundee.co.uk; 21 Castle St; ☺ 9am-6pm Mon-Sat, noon-4pm Sun Jun-Sep, 9am-5pm Mon-Sat

Oct-May) for accommodation options before heading to **Discovery Point**, where Scott's restored Antarctic ship **RRS Discovery** (☎ 01382 201245; adult/concession/child £6.25/4.70/3.85; ☺ 10am-6pm Mon-Sat, 11am-6pm Sun Apr-Oct & 10am-5pm zMon-Sat, 11am-5pm Sun Nov-Mar) is moored.

ABERDEEN

☎ 01224 / pop 205,000

With almost every building constructed from granite, Scotland's third largest city is a symphony in grey – shiny and almost silvery when it's sunny but dull and depressing when blustery rain rolls in from the North Sea. Fuelled by offshore oilfield money, there are plenty of services and amenities for visitors and, like many Scottish cities, there's a growing nightlife and cultural scene aided by a university population eager for ways to avoid assignments.

Orientation & Information

The city is built on a ridge that runs east–west to the north of the Dee River. Union St, the main shopping street, runs along the crest of this ridge. The train and bus stations are next to each other off Guild St and the **TIC** (☎ 288828; 23 Union St; www.aberdeen-grampian .com; ☺ 9am-7pm Mon-Sat, 10am-4pm Sun Jul & Aug, variable hrs rest of year) is on the corner of Union St and Shiprow. The Old Town, with its cobbled streets, old university and ecclesiastical buildings, is a mile north of the centre.

Sights

There's a fascinating modern exploration of the region's long association with the sea at **Aberdeen Maritime Museum** (☎ 337700; Shiprow; admission free; ☺ 10am-5pm Mon-Sat, noon-3pm Sun). There's plenty of high-tech, touch-screen action to keep most visitors engrossed and there's a three-storey replica of a North Sea oilrig in case you were in any doubt where the money in this part of the world comes from. Another gallery contains the non-replica **Provost Ross's House**, the city's third-oldest surviving home.

Sleeping

Oilfield workers monopolise much of the city's accommodation and their presence keeps many hotel prices artificially high. The imposing (yes, it's granite) **SYHA Aberdeen Youth Hostel** (☎ 0870 004 1100; 8 Queen's Rd; dm £11.50-13.50) is a mile west of the train

station. It's clean and welcoming but a bit too clinical to be truly cosy. Clusters of B&Bs line Bon Accord St and Springbank Terrace (both close to the centre), including the recommended **Dunrovin Guest House** (☎ 586081; 186 Bon Accord St; s/d £23/37), where the hearty Scottish breakfast includes vegetarian options. For a mid-range alternative, the **Brentwood Hotel** (☎ 595440; www.brentwood-hotel .co.uk; 101 Crown St; s/d £37/87; ✗) is a 66-room city institution that appeals to visiting yuppies. Single room rates are often dramatically lower on weekends.

Eating & Drinking

Close to the TIC and just off Union St, the scrubbed and refurbished Belmont St houses some of Aberdeen's best cafés, bars and restaurants.

Books and Beans (☎ 646438; 22 Belmont St; ☺ 8.30am-5.30pm Mon-Wed, Fri & Sat, to 8pm Thu, 11am-4pm Sun) Fortifying coffees combine with secondhand book sales. There are also poetry readings on the last Thursday of every month. Grab a well-filled sandwich for lunch on the run. The home-made soups and vegetarian options are recommended.

Prince of Wales (☎ 640597; 7 St Nicholas Ln; mains £5) The area's best pub for a cheap and cheerful lunch. The city centre institution offers some great Scottish ales to help the chips slip down.

Ashvale Fish Restaurant (☎ 596581; 42-48 Great Western Rd; mains £6-9, takeaway £3; ☺ 11.45am-11pm) A quality, award-winning fish-and-chip joint.

Nargile Restaurant (☎ 636093; 77-79 Skene St; mains £8-12 ☺ noon-3pm & 5.30-10.30pm Mon-Thu, to 11pm Fri & Sat) With much classier fayre, Nargile offers an incredible array of mouthwatering Turkish dishes. Locals regard it as one of the country's best restaurants.

Getting There & Away

AIR

Six miles northeast of the city centre, **Aberdeen Airport** (☎ 722331) receives flights from 26 destinations in eight countries. Ryanair and easyJet offer competitive and highly variable fares from London and other UK cities. See the Britain Transport section (p254) for further information. There are also regular but expensive **Loganair** (☎ 01856 872494; www.loganair.co.uk) flights from Orkney and Shetland.

BOAT

The passenger ferry terminal is a short walk east of the train and bus stations. **NorthLink Ferries** (☎ 0845 6000 449; www.northlinkferries.co.uk) runs services from Orkney (passenger only one way from £14.75, car and passenger from £58.25, 10 to 12 hours, daily) and Shetland (passenger only one way from £19.75, car and passenger from £78.50, eight hours, three weekly).

BUS

There are National Express buses from London (£37.50, 12 hours, five daily). In addition, Scottish Citylink runs frequent services from Edinburgh (£8, three hours), Glasgow (£8, four hours) and other Scottish cities.

TRAIN

Services from London Kings' Cross (£98.90, 7½ hours) and Scottish destinations including Dundee (£19.10, one hour) and Inverness (£19.90, 2¼ hours) arrive throughout the day.

Getting Around

First Aberdeen's (☎ 650065) bus No 27 (£1.30, 35 minutes) arrives frequently on Union St from the airport. The company runs an extensive service throughout the city and an unlimited one-day adult pass is £2.50.

WESTERN HIGHLANDS

Stretching from Rannoch Moor past Fort William on the west coast, this is a wild and woolly region of mist-covered glens, ice-cold lochs and wild, snow-covered mountains, including Ben Nevis, Britain's highest peak. While Fort William is the region's only town, Loch Lomond and the Isle of Mull provide the best natural eye-candy. The 95-mile **West Highland Way** between Fort William and Glasgow is a good hiking trail for moderately accomplished ramblers.

Orientation & Information

Fort William, at the southern end of the Great Glen, is the region's main base for visitors. Oban, on the west coast, is the key ferry port for the Inner Hebrides (Mull, Coll, Tiree, Colonsay, Jura and Islay) and the Outer Hebridean islands of South Uist and Barra. There's a reasonable scattering of SYHA accommodation and some independent hostels in locations including Glencoe, Oban, Tobermory, Crianlarich, Inchree and Corpach. Call in at the Fort William TIC for details.

Fort William

☎ 01397 / pop 9500

An attractive if somewhat touristy base for exploring the local mountains, Fort William is situated on the banks of Loch Linne. With a pedestrianised centre that's easily explored on foot, there's at least one of everything here that a visitor might need – including shops, cafés, pubs and accommodation. The **TIC** (☎ 703781; Cameron Sq; 9am-8pm Mon-Sat, 10am-6pm Sun) and www.discover-fortwilliam .com offer local information.

The lively **Fort William Backpackers** (☎ 700 711; www.scotlands-top-hostels.com; Alma Rd; dm £10-11;) is a short walk from the bus and train stations and has impressive hillside views. **Bank St Lodge** (☎ 700070; www.accommodation -fortwilliam.com; dm £10-12) has a wide variety of rooms, including dorms and twins, and enjoys a more central location, while **St. Andrew's Guesthouse** (☎ 703038; Fassifern Rd; r per person £18-24) retains many features from its former rectory days, including some stained-glass windows.

Four daily buses from Glasgow, run by Scottish Citylink, (£11.80, three hours) and two daily buses from Edinburgh (£16.50, 3¼ hours), both via Glencoe. The spectacular West Highland railway line runs three daily trains from Glasgow (£18.70, 3¾ hours).

Some local buses are run by **Rapsons/Highland Country** (☎ 702373) but call ahead for timetables since services are seasonal. **Off-Beat Bikes** (☎ 704008; 117 High St; 9am-5.30pm) offers an alternative method of travelling around the area, renting bikes from £10 per half day.

Oban

☎ 01631 / pop 8500

A hub for holidaymakers every summer, Oban is a traditional resort town combining pretty bay-front vistas with a raft of visitor amenities. The bus, train and ferry terminals are together beside the harbour and the **TIC** (☎ 563122; Argyll Sq; Mon-Sat May-Sep) is in a former church nearby.

Oban Backpackers Lodge (☎ 562107; www .scotlands-top-hostels.com; Breadalbane St; dm £11-12;) is less than a mile from the train station and has a welcoming ambience, including a friendly lounge area. The SYHA **Oban Youth Hostel** (☎ 0870 004 1144; Corran Esplanade; dm £10.50-13; ✗) is a little more institutional but has great views across the bay if you happen to be a ship spotter. There are several B&Bs along Corran Esplanade but these can fill up quickly in summer.

There are Scottish Citylink buses from Glasgow (£12.20, three hours, four daily), Fort William (£7.60, 1½ hours, four daily) and other Scottish destinations. There are also three daily trains from Glasgow (£15.60, three hours). **CalMac** (☎ 566688; www .calmac.co.uk) ferries link Oban with the Inner and Outer Hebrides.

Isle of Mull

Scotland's third-largest island is dripping with great mountain views and pretty seascapes, drawing thousands of Scots to its charming shores every summer. While most arrive at the Craignure ferry terminal, many quickly head north to Tobermory, the capital and a picturesque fishing port. There are TICs in both towns but only **Craignure's** (☎ 01680 812377; ☯ 8.30am-7pm Mon-Thu, to 5.15pm Fri, 9am-5pm Sat, 10am-5pm Sun) is open year-round. Call ahead for accommodation options.

Don't expect to turn up and easily find a bed in summer when accommodation is often booked out. Call in advance for the SYHA **Tobermory Youth Hostel** (☎ 0870 004 1151; Main St; dm £10-11), which is small enough to fill up quickly, or bring a tent and head for **Tobermory Campsite** (☎ 01688 302624; Newdale, Dervaig Rd; adult/child £3.50/2; ☯ Mar-Oct).

For a filling pub lunch or weekend evening of live music, **MacGochan's** (☎ 01688 302350; Ledaig, Tobermory; mains £3.50-£6) is popular with locals and visitors. It can get quite lively on Friday and Saturday nights, so don't come with a book to read. There are evening barbecues throughout the summer, a good time to chat to locals about what they think of Scottish devolution.

NORTHERN HIGHLANDS & ISLANDS

While much of Scotland's outdoors seems to be littered with crumbling old castles, the Northern Highlands and islands are all about wild and wonderful open space virtually untrammelled by human habitation. As one of Europe's last great wildernesses, this breathtakingly beautiful swathe of endless moors, glassy lochs and buffeted coastal cliffs is as close to nature as anyone could wish to be. And for those historically tenacious few who have lived here over the centuries – particularly on Orkney, Shetland and the Outer Hebrides – this is the ancient homeland of Gaelic culture.

It's easy to underestimate the size of the region, so give yourself extra time to explore here via air, bus, train or ferry. Public transport outside the main centres can be as rare as a wild haggis sighting and some services are severely curtailed after the tourists have packed up for the season. Check in with the **Highlands of Scotland Tourist Board** (☎ 0845 2255 121; www.visithighlands.com) for transport and accommodation advice throughout the region or drop by one of the local TICs that dot the area.

Inverness

☎ 01463 / pop 44,000

The capital of the Highlands, Inverness is the perfect base for plotting a trip through the region. It has few attractions of its own – even the red, Baronial-style castle is closed to visitors – but a stroll along the fast-moving Ness River which bisects Inverness is recommended. It's just 6 miles from the infamous **Loch Ness** and few visit here without making an excursion to the home of the elusive monster.

ORIENTATION & INFORMATION

The town centre resides on the river's eastern bank, along with the bus and train stations, new Eastgate shopping centre and several hostels. The **TIC** (☎ 234353; www .inverness-scotland.com; Castle Wynd; ☯ 9am-8pm Mon-Sat, 9.30am-5pm Sun) is near the castle and has probably the friendliest tourism bureau staff in Scotland. They can help with information on the entire Highlands region and they also offer a currency exchange and Internet access terminal (£1 for 20 minutes).

SIGHTS

One of Scotland's most entertaining spectral treks is offered by **Davy the Ghost Tours** (☎ 07730 831069; adult/child £6/4; ☯ 7pm), regaling visitors with a 75-minute walk through the town's colourful history, departing from the TIC. Expect plenty of jokes – including some good-natured anti-English jibes – along with a pint in a local pub to round-out the tour.

No visit to Inverness is complete without a trek to **Loch Ness**. While tourists by the coach load roll up here every few minutes in the summer, there's no doubt that a half-day excursion is worth the Citylink bus fare (adult £6.90 return). If you haven't had your fill of crumbling forts, get off at **Urquart Castle** (☎ 01456 450551; adult/concession/child £6/4.50/1.20; ☺ 9.30am-6.30pm Apr-Sep, to 4.30pm Mon-Sat & 2-4.30pm Sun Oct-Mar), where a new wheelchair-friendly interpretation centre and drum-rolling movie presentation enhance a dramatic loch-side setting. If the weather's good, walk the 2 miles back to Drumnadrochit where your search for Nessie can really begin.

Packed with monster gift shops and themed businesses, the best of the two Nessie exhibitions here is **Loch Ness 2000** (☎ 01456 450573; adult/concession/child £5.95/4.50/3.50; ☺ 9am-8pm Jul & Aug, to 6pm Jun & Sep, to 5.30pm Oct, 9.30am-5pm Easter-May, 10am-3.30pm Nov-Easter), which traces the historic hunts for the age-old scallywag. The headset narration is in 11 languages. Before picking up the bus back to town, check out the giant whisky selection in the gift shop.

SLEEPING

There are plenty of budget options and a good range of B&Bs and guesthouses in Inverness but the town fills quickly in the summer so book ahead.

Bazpackers Backpackers Hostel (☎ 717663; 4 Culduthel Rd; dm £9-11; ☐ ☒) Clean and compact with some great views across the river. The homely feel is enhanced by a wood-burning stove and Poppy, the hostel cat. There's an excellent bargain-basement downstairs suite available for £40 per week off-season.

Inverness Tourist Hostel (☎ 241962; 24 Rose St; dm £11-13; ☐) The town's newest backpacker option, located right at the bus station. With a swanky fitted kitchen and black leather couches, it has a helpful band of staff. There's a Sky-accessed, flat screen TV in the lounge and single-entry shower rooms.

Eastgate Backpackers Hostel (☎ 718756; www .eastgatehostel.com; 38 Eastgate; dm £9.50-13) Newly refurbished with the kind of jokey wall paintings common to many backpacker joints, it's a well-situated, lively hostel where the uber-friendly staff are happy to explain the recently upgraded power showers, metal bunks and difference between mixed and single-sex dorms. With only 47 beds, it's quite small, until July and August when a 60-bed annexe is opened.

Along the banks of the Ness and on Old Edinburgh Rd, there are also several mid-range and top-end options, including the **Ivybank Guest House** (☎ 232796; ivybank@talk21.com; 28 Old Edinburgh Rd; s £25-60, d £50-65; ☒), whose old-style character includes a great guest room with its own turret. The pricier **Glen Mhor Hotel** (☎ 234308; www.glen-mhor.com; s £59-75, d £88-118; ☒) has an oak-lined bistro and kitsch-cosy rooms. The restaurant (Nico's) is recommended for local Scottish cuisine.

The following budget accommodations are also recommended:

Inverness Millburn Youth Hostel (☎ 0970 004 2227; Victoria Dr; dm £11.50-13.50; ☒) Large, modern property that's one of the SYHA's best.

Inverness Student Hotel (☎ 236556; inverness@scotlands-top-hostels.com; 8 Culduthel Rd; dm £10-12; ☐) Eclectic lounge and student house feel.

HoHo Hostel (☎ 221225; www.hohohostel.force9.co.uk; 23a High St; dm £8.90-9.90; ☐) Grunge-comfort with free tea and coffee.

EATING & DRINKING

Castle Restaurant (☎ 230925; 41-43 Castle St; mains £4-7; ☺ 8am-8.30pm Mon-Sat) A backpacker favourite, this cheap and cheery café serves up heaping plates of simple comfort food that provides enough fuel for a giant hike around the region. Mountains of chips are *de rigueur* and come accompanied with fried fish or crusty meat pies.

Mustard Seed (☎ 220220; 16 Fraser St, mains £8-15; ☺ noon-3pm & 6-10pm) This is the town's most stylish restaurant, specialising in traditional French and Scottish produce prepared with a modern flare. The menu changes weekly but look out for the fish dishes, especially the finger-licking seared wild halibut in lobster oil.

Hootannay Cèilidh Café Bar (☎ 233651; 67 Church St; ☺ noon-midnight) For a real Scottish knees-up, this two-level bar can't be beaten. A host of Scottish beer specials are on offer, with the rust-coloured Red Kite from Black Isle Brewery particularly recommended. There's rip-roaring traditional music on the ground floor every night and a host of rock and comedy events upstairs almost as regularly. Shows are free throughout the week and there's a £2 charge, covering both floors, on Friday and Saturday.

BRITAIN

GETTING THERE & AROUND

Ten miles east of town **Inverness Airport** (☎ 01667-464000) receives flights from Edinburgh, Glasgow, London, Orkney and Shetland, among others.

National Express coach services arrive from London (£37.50; 13 hours; four daily), while Citylink buses arrive from Edinburgh (£15.50, four hours, hourly), Fort William (£8.20, two hours, six daily), Glasgow (£15.50, four hours, hourly) and other Scottish destinations.

There are several daily train services from London (£102, eight to 10 hours), including the overnight Caledonian Sleeper, along with services from Glasgow (£32.90, 3½ hours) and Edinburgh (£32.90, 3¼ hours), The highly picturesque Kyle of Lochalsh (£14.60, 2½ hours, two to four daily) line delivers passengers from the bridge across to the Isle of Skye while the line from Thurso (£13, 3½ hours, two to three daily) connects with the ferry from Orkney.

Highland Country (☎ 710555) operates local buses, with destination information and advice available at the TIC. A Rover ticket costs £6 for unlimited one-day travel.

Orkney Islands
☎ 01856 / pop 19,250

Just 6 miles off the north coast of Scotland, this magical group of islands is known for its dramatic coastal scenery (which ranges from soaring cliffs to white, sandy beaches, abundant marine bird life, and plethora of prehistoric sites. If you're in the area around mid-June, don't miss the **St Magnus Arts Festival** (www.stmagnusfestival.com), a lively celebration of arts, music and performance.

Sixteen of the 70 Orkney Islands are inhabited, but Kirkwall is the main town and Stromness is the major port. They're both on Mainland, the largest island. Contact Kirkwall's **TIC** (☎ 872856; 6 Broad St; ☺ Mon-Sat Oct-Apr, daily May-Sep) for more information or visit www.visitorkney.com for some pre-trip resources.

Stenness, a small village that's a short bus ride from Kirkwall or Stromness, is the most accessible spot for exploring prehistoric Orkney. The **Standing Stones of Stennes**, **Barnhouse Neolithic Village** and **Skara Brae** are all close by. Particularly recommended, though, is **Maes Howe** (☎ 761606; adult/child £3/1; ☺ 9.30am-6.30pm Apr-Sep, to 4.30pm Mon-Sat,

2-4.30pm Sun Oct-Mar), a 5000-year-old earthmound tomb. You can walk in and check out the engineering skills of the period and take a guided tour to find out more.

There's a good selection of low-priced B&Bs in the area – especially on Mainland – and numerous hostels dot the region. In Stromness, **Brown's Hostel** (☎ 850661; 45 Victoria St; dm £9-10) is popular and close to the ferry, while **Ness Caravan & Camping Park** (☎ 873535; tent sites £3.70-5.80) offers a low-cost option for tent-packers.

GETTING THERE & AWAY

Flights run by **Loganair** (☎ 0845 773 3377) arrive daily in Kirkwall from Aberdeen (£155, one hour), Edinburgh (£186, 1¾ hours) and other Scottish cities, while British Airways provides affiliated connections to London, Manchester and the rest of the UK.

Services operated by **Northlink Ferries** (☎ 0845 6000 449; www.northlinkferries.co.uk) run from Aberdeen, Scrabster and the Shetlands, while **John o'Groats Ferries** (☎ 01955 611353; www.jogferry.co.uk) also operates a passenger-only run from the mainland.

Shetland Islands
☎ 01595 / pop 23,000

Sixty miles (96km) north of Orkney, the Shetland Islands remained under Norse rule until 1469, when they were given to Scotland as part of a Danish princess' dowry. Even today, these remote, windswept, treeless islands are almost as much a part of Scandinavia as Britain. Lerwick, the capital, is less than 230 miles (370km) from Bergen in Norway. For some pre-trip information, visit www.shetland-tourism.co.uk.

Much bleaker than Orkney, Shetland is famous for its varied bird life, its rugged coastline and 4000-year-old archaeological heritage. There are 15 inhabited islands. Lerwick is the largest town on Mainland Shetland, which is used as a base for the North Sea oilfields. Oil has brought some prosperity to the islands – there are well-equipped leisure centres in many villages.

Small ferries connect a handful of the smaller islands. Contact the **TIC** (☎ 693434; ☺ 8am-6pm Mon-Fri, to 4pm Sat & 10am-1pm Sun Apr-Sep, 9am-5pm Mon-Fri Oct) for information on B&Bs and camping barns, or stay at **Lerwick Youth Hostel** (☎ 692114; King Harald St; dm £11; ☺ mid-Apr–Sep).

NorthLink Ferries (☎ 01856 851144; www.north linkferries.co.uk) runs services from Aberdeen to Lerwick and Kirkwall to Lerwick.

North Coast

The coast from Dounreay west around to Ullapool is nothing short of spectacular. Everything is on a massive scale: vast emptiness, enormous lochs and snow-capped mountains. Unreliable weather and limited public transport are the only drawbacks.

The **Dounreay Nuclear Power Station** (☎ 01847 802572; admission free; ☉ 10am-4pm May-Oct) is a highly unusual attraction where visitors can learn just how great nuclear power is.

Getting to Thurso by bus or train is no problem, but from there your troubles start. From June to September, **Rapsons/Highland Country Buses** (☎ 01847 893123) runs its Northern Explorer service once daily (except Sunday) from Thurso to Durness (£7.75, 2½ hours). The rest of the year, there are Monday to Saturday services from Thurso to Bettyhill.

West Coast

Ullapool is the jumping-off point for the Isle of Lewis; contact its **TIC** (☎ 01854-612135; 6 Argyle St; ☉ Apr-Sep daily, Mon-Sat Oct, Mon-Fri Nov-Mar) for information. The coastline keeps getting better round to Gairloch, along Loch Maree and down to the Kyle of Lochalsh and Skye. From there you're back in the land of the tour bus; civilisation (and main roads) can be a shock after all the empty space.

Kyle of Lochalsh ('Kyle') is a small village that overlooks the lovely island of Skye across narrow Loch Alsh. There's a **TIC** (☎ 01599-534276; ☉ 9am-5.30pm Mon-Sat Easter-Oct) beside the seafront car park but the nearest hostels are on Skye. Kyle can be reached by bus and train from Inverness and also by direct Citylink buses from Glasgow (£19.50, 5½ hours).

Isle of Skye

pop 8850

Skye is a large, rugged island, 50 miles (80km) north to south and 25 miles (40km) east to west. It's ringed by stunning coastline and dominated by the magnificent Cuillin Hills, popular for the sport of 'Munro bagging' – climbing Scottish mountains of 914m or higher. You can contact the **Portree TIC** (☎ 01478-612137; Bayfield Rd) for more information.

SLEEPING & EATING

There are more than a dozen SYHA and independent hostels on the island and numerous B&Bs. The SYHA hostels most relevant to ferry users are at **Uig** (☎ 0870 004 1155; dm £10.50; ☉ Apr-Sep) for the Outer Hebrides (Western Isles) and **Armadale** (☎ 0870 004 1103; dm £10.50; ☉ Apr-Sep) for Mallaig. The best independent hostel is the welcoming **Skye Backpackers** (☎ 01599 534510; www.scotlands -top-hostels.com; Kyleakin; dm £10-12), a short walk from the Skye Bridge.

In Portree, **Rosedale Hotel** (☎ 01478 613131; www.rosedalehotelskye.co.uk; Beaumont Cres; s £40-46, d £68-98) is popular, while **Portree House Hotel** (☎ 01478 613713; Home Farm Rd; s £24-28, d £50-70) is a great place for a hearty meal.

GETTING THERE & AWAY

The bridge toll on the Skye Bridge runs from £5.70 to £11.40 per car. **CalMac** (☎ 0147 844248; www.calmac.co.uk) operates a ferry service from the mainland between Mallaig and Armadale (passengers/cars £3/16.50, 30 minutes, eight daily). It's wise to book, especially during the summer. There's also a private **Glenelg to Kylerhea service** (☎ 01599-511302; www.skyeferry .co.uk) from mid-April to late October (not always on Sunday), taking 10 minutes (£0.70 for pedestrians, £6 for car and passengers).

Outer Hebrides (Western Isles)

The Outer Hebrides (Western Isles) are bleak, remote and treeless. The climate is fierce – the islands are completely exposed to the gales sweeping in from the Atlantic, and it rains more than 250 days of the year. Some people find the landscape mournful, but others find the stark beauty and isolated world of the crofters captivating. Check out www.witb.co.uk for resources.

Lewis is reached by ferry from Ullapool, and its largest town, Stornoway, has a **TIC** (☎ 01851 703088; 26 Cromwell St) and several banks. On Harris (which can be reached from Uig on Skye), the **TIC** (☎ 01859 502011; Pier Rd) is in Tarbert. North Uist sports a **TIC** (☎ 01876 50032i) in Lochmaddy, while South Uist has one (☎ 01878 700286) in Barra.

WALES (CYMRU)

There's a remarkably upbeat feeling in Wales today. In 1979 the majority of the people voted against home rule; yet in a 1997 referendum they said yes to a Welsh Assembly, and two years later its first members were elected. While less powerful than Scotland's and prone to false starts, Wales is developing its voice as a nation.

Despite a tumultuous history as the whipping boy of European invaders and English monarchs, Wales remains an intensely proud nation. The Welsh language, one of the oldest vernaculars in Europe, is gaining popularity. Millennia-long literary and musical traditions live on in villages and cities.

After years of environmental degradation from invasions, mining and unchecked seaside tourism, Wales is carefully guarding its natural landscape and historical architecture. The best way to appreciate the Great Welsh Outdoors is by walking, cycling or canal-boating, or using Wales' excellent public transport. Outdoors enthusiasts will be blown away by the beauty of Pembrokeshire or Snowdonia, and village amblers will enjoy Hay-on-Wye, Brecon, St David's, Dolgellau, Llanberis and Betws-y-Coed.

Check out information online at www .visitwales.com.

HISTORY

Wales was settled by Celts when Britain became an island, some time between 10,000 and 5000 BC. Wave after wave of armies, hordes, barbarians and sundry imperialistic types have washed upon its shore ever since.

In AD 43 the Romans invaded and for the next 400 years kept close control over the Welsh tribes from their garrison towns at Chester and Caerlon, guarding valuable deposits of lead, tin and gold. For the next few hundred years, Germanic Anglo-Saxon tribes attacked and many Celtic tribes fought back bravely. Some say one of those kings was named Arthur (*that* Arthur, thought by many to be Welsh). As far back as the Battle of Chester in AD 616, the Welsh thought of themselves as one people.

However, for the next few hundred years, internal struggles and the egalitarian but strategically unfortunate law of dividing land among all male heirs created a fractured Wales. The Normans invaded, setting up 'Marcher Lords' around the Marches to rule heavy-handedly over Wales. The Norman times brought relative peace, and a thriving Welsh literature movement was born.

After a short-lived bit of independence, the English Edward I ascended to the throne in 1272 with the goal of creating a united Britain. Famed Welsh Prince Llewellyn fought hard, but fell in battle after further internal squabbles.

Soon after, King Edward named his eldest son Prince of Wales, a tradition that continues to this day with Prince Charles. You can still visit the castles Edward built in Caernarfon, Conway, Harlech and Beaumaris, most a mile or so from a train station.

Wales unsuccessfully revolted against the English crown but having no capital city or central university, and being subject to English law, led to a reluctant acceptance of its British status.

Industry thrived throughout the 19th and 20th centuries. Mining villages emerged with a unique culture of Methodism, rugby and male voice choirs. However, natural resources were quickly depleted and the 1960s saw the start of a collapse in the coal and associated steel industry, bringing widespread unemployment and socioeconomic problems from which Wales is just now recovering.

In 1997, the people of Wales voted to be governed by a Welsh Assembly rather than from the House of Commons in London. In a self-confident step towards greater political autonomy, the first Assembly was put in place in May 1999 and it now meets in a new Assembly building at Cardiff Bay.

ENVIRONMENT
The Land

Wales has two major mountain systems: the Black Mountains and Brecon Beacons in the south, and the more dramatic mountains of Snowdonia in the northwest. The population is concentrated in the southeast along the coast between Cardiff (the capital) and Swansea and the old mining valleys that run north into the Brecon Beacons. Wales is approximately 170 miles (274km) long and 60 miles (96km) wide. About 20% of the country is designated as three national parks: Snowdonia, Pembrokeshire and Brecon Beacons.

Wildlife

Keep an eye open for peregrine falcons around Brecon Beacons and dolphins and seals off the coast of Pembrokeshire.

WALES

Irish
Sea

Liverpool
Bay

To Dublin &
Dun Laoghaire
(Ireland)

Isle of
Anglesey

Amlwch

Red
Wharf
Bay

Great
Orme

Llandudno
Colwyn
Bay

Prestatyn
Rhyl

Holyhead
Bay

Holyhead

ANGLESEY
Llangefni
Beaumaris

Menai
Bridge

Conwy
Abergele
Holywell

Dee
Estuary

Ellesmere
Port

M6

Holy
Island

A5

Bangor

A55

A470
CONWY

Elwy

Flint

FLINTSHIRE

Chester

Crewe

Caernarfon
Llanberis
Capel
Curig

Llanrwst
Betws-
y-Coed

Denbigh
DENBIGHSHIRE

Ruthin

Brymbo
Wrexham

A41

Waunfawr

Caernarfon
Bay

Pen-y-
Pass

Mt Snowdon
(1110m)

Blaenau
Ffestiniog
Ffestiniog

A5

Corwen

Conwy

Horseshoe
Pass

WREXHAM

Llangollen

Oswestry

A5

A49

A487

Porthmadog
Criccieth

Snowdonia
National
Park

Eden

A494

Llanfyllin

A483

Shrewsbury

Telford

Llyn
Peninsula

Pwllheli

Tremadog
Bay

Harlech

GWYNEDD

Dolgellau

Twrch

A458

Welshpool

ENGLAND

St
George's
Channel

Abersoch

Barmouth

Centre for
Alternative
Energy

Church
Stretton

Tywyn

Machynlleth

Glyndwr's
Way

Newtown

A470

Bishop's
Castle

A49

Cardigan
Bay

Borth

A487

Rheidol
Falls

Aberystwyth

Devil's
Bridge

Rheidol

Llanidloes

Severn

Ystwyth

A44

POWYS

Ludlow

Knighton

Leominster

Aberaeron

New Quay

Tregaron

Cambrian
Mountains

Llandrindod
Wells

Kington

A49

CEREDIGION

Lampeter

Llanwrtyd
Wells

Builth
Wells

A470

A438

Hereford

Ross-
on-Wye

Pembrokeshire
Coast Path

To Rosslare (Ireland)

Cardigan

A487

Teifi

Llandovery

Tywi

A483

Llanstephan

Hay-on-
Wye

Capel-
Ffin

A40

Newcastle
Emlyn

Gwili

Llandeilo

Brecon

Talgarth

A465

Pwll Deri
Trefin

Fishguard

Preseli
Hills

CARMARTHENSHIRE

Black
Mountains

Libanus

Black
Mountains

Crickhowell

Abergavenny

Monmouth

A40

St David's

A40

PEMBROKESHIRE

Carmarthen

National Botanic
Gardens of Wales

Ammanford

Brecon Beacons
National Park

Tredegar

Ebbw
Vale

MONMOUTH-
SHIRE

Newgale

Whitesands
Bay

Haverfordwest

Narberth

Laugharne

Kidwelly

Pontardulais

Clydach

NEATH &
PORT
TALBOT

Merthyr
Tydfil

Aberdare

A470

Blaenafon
BLAENAU
GWENT

Abersychan

Usk

Tintern
Abbey

Milford
Haven

Carew
Castle

Amroth

Carmarthen
Bay

Llanelli

Neath

Pontypridd

Cwmbran

Chepstow

To Rosslare
(Ireland)

Pembroke

Tenby

SWANSEA

Swansea
Airport

Swansea

Port
Talbot

RHONDDA
CYNON
TAFF

Bedwas
Caerphilly

Newport

Freshwater
West

Manorbier

Caldey
Island

Gower

Rhossili

The
Mumbles

M4

Pontypridd

CAERPHILLY

St Mellons

Pembrokeshire
Coast National Park

Oxwich
Bay

Bridgend

Llandaff
VALE OF
GLAMORGAN

Cardiff

Mouth
of the
Severn

Porthcawl

Penarth

Clevedon

To Cork (Ireland)

Barry

Cardiff
Airport

Weston-
super-
Mare

Bristol
Channel

ATLANTIC
OCEAN

Ilfracombe

Minehead

Bridgwater
Bay

Burnham

Wells

M5

Glastonbury

ENGLAND

Bridgwater

0 ___ 40 km
0 ___ 20 miles

Environmental Issues

Wales is extremely committed to preserving its natural heritage. The National Parks use a 'park and ride' system where drivers can hop on and hop off buses after leaving their cars in car parks. In Snowdonia, try the Snowdon Sherpa (p248) or the Puffin Shuttle in Pembrokeshire along the coast path.

PEOPLE

Wales has a population of 2.9 million, around 5% of the total population of Britain.

LANGUAGE

Welsh is spoken by over 20% of the population, mainly in the north. Recent efforts have been made to reverse its decline. Every Welsh person speaks English, but there's been a national push for Welsh TV and radio programmes, a more aggressive education policy and most signs are now bilingual.

At first sight, Welsh looks impossibly difficult to get your tongue around. Once you know that 'dd' is pronounced 'th', 'w' can also be a vowel pronounced 'oo', 'f' is 'v' and 'ff' is 'f', and you've had a native speaker teach you how to pronounce 'll' (roughly 'cl'), you'll be able to ask the way to Llanfairpwllgwyngyllgogerychwyrndrobwllllantysiliogogogoch (a village in Anglesey reputed to have Britain's longest place name – no joke) and be understood. Try the following (pronunciation in brackets):

- *Bore da* (bora-da) good morning
- *Peint o gwrw* (paint-o-guru) pint of beer
- *Diolch* (diolkh) thank you

ACTIVITIES
Hiking

Wales has many popular walks; the most challenging are in the rocky Snowdonia National Park (around Llanberis and Betwsy-Coed) and the grassy Brecon Beacons National Park (around Brecon). The three official National Trails in Wales are the Pembrokeshire Coast Path (p246), Offa's Dyke Path (p246) along the English border and Glyndwr's Way (p247) through mid-Wales.

See Lonely Planet's *Walking in Britain* for more information.

Cycling

Much of Wales is excellent for cycling. Two of the best known-routes are Lôn Las Cymru (the Welsh National Route), which takes in 260 miles (418km) from Holyhead to Cardiff, and the 227-mile (365km) Lôn Getaidd ('the Celtic Trail') from near Chepstow to Fishguard. Pick up the Wales Tourist Board's free *Cycling Wales* publication for an introduction to these and other routes. For more on cycling see p250.

Surfing

The southwest coast of Wales has a number of surf spots. From east to west, try Porthcawl, Oxwich Bay, Rhossili, Manorbier, Freshwater West and Whitesands. Call the backpackers in Fishguard (p247) to find out the newest breaks.

GETTING THERE & AWAY

Wales is easily accessible from Chester, Liverpool and Shrewsbury in the North, and Bristol in the South. Ferries leave Swansea, Fishguard and Holyhead for Cork, Rosslare and Dublin in Ireland.

GETTING AROUND

Wales is committed to creating better public transport, but in the meantime, you might have difficulty getting around, especially in the more rural areas.

Call the eternally helpful **Traveline** (☎ 0870 608 2608), which will give you everything you need to know about buses and trains (except prices).

Travel Passes

Four excellent passes are available that give free travel, in designated regions of Wales and immediately adjacent areas of England, on all rail routes and nearly all intercity bus routes. The passes, with high/low season prices (high season is late May–September and Christmas), are:

4 in 8 Flexi-pass Eight days' bus travel plus any four days' train travel throughout Wales (£55/45).

8 in 15 Flexi-pass Fifteen days' bus travel plus any eight days' train travel throughout Wales (£92/75).

Freedom of North and Mid-Wales 7-day Flexi Rover Any three days out of seven of bus and train travel in North and Mid-Wales (£30).

Freedom of South Wales 7-day Flexi-Rover Seven days' bus travel plus any three days' train travel in South Wales (£35/30).

These passes give various discounts including £1 off at YHA hostels in Wales and free or discounted travel on narrow-gauge railways. They are sold online at www.wales flexipass.co.uk, over the counter at most train stations and at many TICs.

Bus

Some 70 private bus companies operate in Wales. The biggest intercity operators are Arriva Cymru, First Cymru and Stagecoach.

For all public transport information call the UK-wide **Traveline** (☎ 0870 6082608; 8am-8pm).

Train

Wales has some fantastic train lines, both main-line services (☎ 0845 7484950) and narrow-gauge and steam train survivors (see www.greatlittletrainsofwales.co.uk for information on nine narrow-gauge railways). For details on passes see p244.

Tours

Several backpacker bus companies run three- to seven-day trips throughout Wales.
Bus Wales (☎ 0800 3280284; www.buswalestours.com) Leaves from Cardiff, Bath and Bristol and offers three-day All Wales Tours (£75) and four-day West & Wales (£99). Departs Monday and Friday, although it's possible to join just for one or two days.
Dragon Tours (☎ 01874 658124; www.dragonback packertours.co.uk) Picks up at Cardiff (incl hostels and train and bus stations). Trips usually leave Monday and include five- or six-day All-Wales Circuit (£129), four-day Welsh Highlights and three-day Weekend Mountain Breaks (£79).
Shaggy Sheep (☎ 07919 244549; www.shaggysheep .com) Leaves from London and offers three-day Merlin Backpacker weekends (£69, plus £39 kitty) and a four-day Dragon All-Wales Tour (£79 plus £59 kitty).

SOUTH WALES

The villages that form a continuous chain along the valleys have their own stark beauty and the people are very friendly, particularly in the traditional market town of Abergavenny.

Nestled in a beautiful valley is the breathtaking **Tintern Abbey** (☎ 051 562650; 9.30am-6pm, shorter in winter; adult/concession £2.50/2), Cistercian ruins on a grand scale.

The **Big Pit** (☎ 01495 790311; admission free), near Blaenafon, closed as a coal mine in 1980. These days it gives you a chance to experience life underground, and the guided tours conducted by former miners are highly recommended.

Cardiff (Caerdydd)

☎ 029 / pop 285,000
The Welsh are proudly defensive of their capital, which used to be thought of as a dull provincial backwater but is now a prosperous university city with an increasingly lively arts scene.

Stock up on maps and information from the **TIC** (☎ 2022 7281; www.visitcardiff.info; The Hayes) for all of Wales. Free Internet access is available at **Cardiff Central Library** (☎ 2038 2116; Frederick St).

Worth seeing for its outrageous interior refurbishment **Cardiff Castle** (☎ 2087 8100; Castle St) was revamped by the Victorians; it's more Hollywood than medieval. Nearby, the **National Museum & Gallery of Wales** (☎ 2039 7951; Cathays Park; admission free; 10am-5pm Tue-Sun & bank hols) packs in everything Welsh but also includes one of the finest collections of impressionist art in Britain. The **Museum of Welsh Life** (☎ 20573500; St Fagan's; admission free; 10am-5pm), 5 miles from the centre, is a popular open-air attraction with reconstructed buildings and craft demonstrations.

The **YHA Cardiff** (☎ 0870 7705750; cardiff@yha.org .uk; 2 Wedal Rd; dm £14.90 bus No 28 or 29) is in a hip student area. The lively **Cardiff Backpacker** (☎ 2034 5577; www.cardiffbackpacker.com; 98 Neville St, Riverside; dm from £15; P) is a five- to 10-minute walk from most sights in the city centre.

Famed Welsh singer Charlotte Church's mum runs the **Church Hotel** (☎ 340881; http:// homepage.ntlworld.com/church.hotel; 126 Cathedral Rd; s/d/f from £25/45/55), or try the **Town House** (☎ 2023 9399; www.thetownhousecardiff.co.uk; 70 Cathedral Rd; s/d £42.50/52.50; P) nearby.

National Express has buses to/from London (£17, 3¼ hours, seven daily) and Bristol (£7.40, 50 minutes, every half-hour). Trains come from all over the southeast.

Swansea (Abertawe)

☎ 01792 / pop 190,000
Swansea is the second-largest town (it would be stretching the definition to call it a city), and the gateway to the **Gower Peninsula** and its superb coastal scenery (crowded in summer). Brittany Ferries and Swansea Cork Ferries run between Swansea and Cork, Ireland.

For more information, contact the **TIC** (☎ 468321; www.swansea.gov.uk; Plymouth St). Take bus No 18A to get to **YHA Port Eynon** (☎ 0870 7705998), a converted lifeboat house, superbly situated right on the beach at Port Eynon.

National Botanic Garden of Wales

The **National Botanic Garden of Wales** (☎ 01558 668768; www.gardenofwales.org.uk; adult/concession/child £7/5/2; ✆ 10am-6pm Easter-Oct, to 4.30pm Nov-Easter) contains the world's largest single-span greenhouse, double-wall and Japanese gardens, and is home to endangered plants from around the globe. The garden is on the B4310, 7 miles east of Carmarthen. Call **Traveline** (☎ 0870 6082608) for information on how to arrive.

Brecon Beacons National Park

The Brecon Beacons National Park covers 519 sq miles (835 sq km) of high bare hills, surrounded on the northern flanks by a number of attractive market towns; Llandovery, Brecon, Crickhowell, Talgarth and Hay-on-Wye make good bases. The railhead is at Abergavenny (with a Norman castle). A 55-mile cycleway/footpath, the Taff Trail, connects Cardiff with Brecon.

The **National Park Visitor Centre** (☎ 01874 623366; www.visitbreconbeacons.com; near Libanus) is near many walking trails. Other information offices are in **Brecon** (☎ 01874 622485) and **Llandovery** (☎ 01550 720693; Kings Rd). All make B&B bookings.

Brecon (Aberhonddu)

☎ 01874 / pop 7000

Brecon is an attractive, historic market town, with a **cathedral** dating from the 13th century. The market is held on Tuesdays and Fridays. There's a highly acclaimed jazz festival in August.

The **TIC** (☎ 622485; brectic@powys.gov.uk) can help with further information. The **YHA Brecon** (☎ 0870 7705718; brecon@yha.org.uk; Groesffordd) is popular with trekkers and cyclists. In town there's **B&B Cantre Selyf** (☎ 622904; www.cantreselyf.co.uk; Lion St; s/d £40/60; ✗), a spacious Georgian townhouse with décor that harks back to the 17th century.

Brecon has no train station, but there are regular bus links. **Stagecoach Red & White** (☎ 01685 385539) has regular buses to Swansea and Abergavenny, and to Hereford via Hay-on-Wye.

Hay-on-Wye

☎ 01497 / pop 1600

At the northeastern tip of the Black Mountains there's Hay-on-Wye, an eccentric market village that is now known as the world

centre for **second-hand books** – there are over 35 shops and more than one million books, everything from first editions costing £1000 to books by the yard (literally).

Contact the **TIC** (☎ 820144) for information on the excellent restaurants and B&Bs in the neighbourhood. **Capel-y-Ffin Youth Hostel** (☎ 0870 7705748) is 8 miles south of Hay on the road to Abergavenny. The walk here from Hay follows part of Offa's Dyke and is highly recommended.

SOUTHWEST WALES

The coastline northeast of St David's to Cardigan is particularly beautiful and, as it is protected by the national park, it remains delightfully unspoilt. The Pembrokeshire Coast Path begins at Amroth, north of Tenby, on the western side of Carmarthen Bay and continues to St Dogmaels to the west of Cardigan. Tenby is an attractive holiday destination, a little overrun at times.

Carmarthen Bay is often referred to as Dylan Thomas Country; **Dylan's boathouse** (☎ 01994-427420; adult/concession £3/2; ✆ 10am-5.30pm May-Oct, 10.30am-3.30pm Nov-Apr) at Laugharne, where he wrote *Under Milk Wood*, has been preserved exactly as he left it, and it is a moving memorial. Llanstephan has a beautiful Norman castle overlooking sandy beaches. On west-facing beaches, there can be good surf.

From Pembroke Dock **Irish Ferries** (☎ 08705 171717) leave for Rosslare in Ireland; ferries connect with buses from Cardiff and destinations east. **Stena Line** (☎ 08705 707070) has ferries to Rosslare from Fishguard; these connect with buses and trains. See p677.

Pembrokeshire Coast National Park

The national park protects a narrow band of magnificent coastline, broken only by the more dense development around Pembroke and Milford Haven. The only significant inland portion is the mystical Preseli Hills to the southeast of Fishguard. There are National Park Information Centres and TICs at **Tenby** (☎ 01834 842402), **St David's** (☎ 01437 720392) and **Fishguard** (☎ 01348 873484), among others. Get a copy of the free paper, *Coast to Coast*, which has detailed local information. Contact **Traveline** (☎ 0870 6082608) for bus information . Apart from hostels, there are loads of B&Bs from around £20.

St David's (Tyddewi)

☎ 01437 / pop 1450

The linchpin for the southwest is beautiful St David's, one of Europe's smallest 'cities', referred to as such because of its cathedral. There's a web of interesting streets and, concealed in the Vale of Roses, beautiful **St David's Cathedral** (☎ 720517; ☺ 8am-6pm Mon-Sat, shorter in winter), an imposing structure, spectacularly well-preserved with a striking wood ceiling.

Contact the **TIC** (☎ 720392; www.stdavids.co.uk; High St) for more information. There are regular **Richards Bros** (☎ 01239 613756) buses to and from Fishguard (45 minutes, every two hours Monday to Saturday). The closest train station to St David's is Haverfordwest, from where bus No 411 runs hourly into town.

There are several handy **youth hostels**: near **St David's** (☎ 0870 7706042); at **Trefin** (☎ 0870 7706074), 11 miles (17.8km) from St David's; and the superb little **Pwll Deri** (☎ 0870 7706004), on the cliffs 8 miles from Trefin and just over 4.5 miles from Fishguard.

Fishguard (Abergwaun)

☎ 01348 / pop 3200

Fishguard is on a beautiful bay, and the old part of town, Lower Fishguard, was the location for the 1971 film version of *Under Milk Wood*, starring Richard Burton and Elizabeth Taylor. The train station and harbour (for ferries to Rosslare) are at Goodwick, a 20-minute walk from the town proper.

There's a **TIC** (☎ 873484; fishguard@pembrokeshire .gov.uk; ☺ daily summer), but the **Hamilton Guest House & Backpackers Lodge** (☎ 874797; www.fish guard-backpackers.com; 21 Hamilton St; dm/d £12/30) is even more helpful, and has a sauna.

MID-WALES

Most visitors to Wales head either for the easily accessible south or the scenically more dramatic north, leaving the quiet valleys of Mid-Wales to the Welsh.

Change the world one small step at a time by visiting arguably one of the more fascinating attractions in all of Wales at the **Centre for Alternative Technology** (☎ 01654 702400; www .cat.org.uk; adult/concession/child summer £7.20/5.10/4.10, winter £5.20/4.10/3.10; ☺ 10am-5pm, to 4pm in winter). Forty interactive acres bring to life the next generation of renewable energy and sustainable living, many ideas visitors can take back home. Courses and residential visits available. Countless special events. Great for kids.

The 120-mile **Glyndwr's Way** national trail visits sites associated with the Welsh hero between Knighton (on Offa's Dyke Path) and Welshpool via picturesque villages such as Machynlleth and stunning natural scenery. Leaflets are available from TICs in the area and are invaluable – route-finding is difficult in places.

Machynlleth is an attractive market town and a good base for exploring Mid-Wales. Check with the TIC (☎ 01654 702401; mactic@mail .powys.gov.uk).

A remarkably pleasant coastal university town, **Aberystwyth** has good transport connections. Contact the TIC (☎ 01970 612125; aberystwyth.tic@ceredigion.gov.uk) for B&Bs. **Borth Youth Hostel** (☎ 0870 7705708) is 8 miles north of Aberystwyth, near a wide sandy beach.

Running through the Vale of Rheidol to Devil's Bridge are **steam trains**, offering spectacular views of the waterfall.

NORTH WALES

North Wales is dominated by the Snowdonia Mountains, which loom over the beautiful coastline. The Red Rover day ticket (adult/child £4.80/2.40) covers most of the region. For information call **Traveline** (☎ 0870 6082608).

Holyhead (Caergybi)

☎ 01407 / pop 12,500

Holyhead is a grey and daunting ferry port. Both **Irish Ferries** (☎ 08705 171717) and **Stena Line** (☎ 08705 707070) run ferries to Dublin. Stena Line also sails to Dun Laoghaire, just outside Dublin.

The **TIC** (☎ 762622; holyhead@nwtic.com) is in ferry terminal 1. In the nearby township there's a batch of B&Bs that are used to dealing with late ferry arrivals (check with the TIC). Trains come from all over Britain, including London, Chester, Birmingham and Llandudno.

Llandudno

☎ 01492 / pop 22,000

Llandudno seethes with tourists in summer. It was developed as a Victorian holiday town and has retained much of its 19th-century architecture and antiquated atmosphere. There's a wonderful **pier and promenade** and donkeys on the beach.

Llandudno is on its own peninsula between two sweeping beaches, and is dominated by the spectacular limestone headland, the **Great Orme**, with the mountains of Snowdonia as a backdrop. The Great Orme, with its **tramway** (adult/child £3.95/2.80), superb views and Bronze Age mine, is fascinating.

There are hundreds of guesthouses, but it can be difficult to find somewhere in the peak July/August season. Contact the **TIC** (☎ 876413; www.llandudno-tourism.co.uk; 1/2 Chapel St) for more information.

Conwy
☎ 01492 / pop 3900

Conwy has been revitalised since the through traffic on the busy A55 was consigned to a tunnel, which burrows under the estuary of the Conwy River. It's a picturesque and interesting little town, dominated by superb **Conwy Castle** (☎ 592358; adult/concession £3.75/3.25; ◷ 9.30am-6pm), one of the grandest of Edward I's castles and a medieval masterpiece.

The **TIC** (☎ 592248; conwy.tic@virgin.net; Conwy Castle Visitor Centre) is in the castle. About 3 miles south of Llandudno, Conwy is linked to Llandudno by several buses an hour and a few trains. There are, however, numerous trains from Llandudno to Llandudno Junction, a 15-minute walk from Conwy.

Snowdonia National Park

Although the Snowdonia Mountains are fairly compact, they loom over the coast and are definitely spectacular. The most popular region is in the north around Mt Snowdon, at 1085m the highest peak in Britain south of the Scottish Highlands. Hikers must be prepared to deal with hostile conditions at any time of the year. Check www.visitsnowdonia.info or www.snowdonia-npa.gov.uk for more information.

There are several National Park Information Centres including **Betws-y-Coed** (☎ 01690 710426; ticbetws@hotmail.com), **Blaenau Ffestiniog** (☎ 01766 830360), and **Harlech** (☎ 01766 780658). They all have a wealth of information, and all make B&B bookings.

The beautiful, if crowded, hamlet of **Betws-y-Coed** is a lovely base from which to explore Snowdonia. The nearest hostel is **Capel Curig** (☎ 0870 7705746), 5 miles west.

B&Bs and hotels are plentiful. The intimate **Henllys Guest House** (☎ 710534; www.jhaddy.freeserve.co.uk; Old Church Rd; per person from £15) is a converted Victorian magistrate's court set next to the Conwy River. Another historic

building is the **Royal Oak Hotel** (☎ 710219; www.royaloakhotel.net; r per person £40-60; P), a former coaching inn located right in the heart of the village.

Snowdon Sherpa buses (day ticket adult/child £3/1.50) run along the major mountain routes within the national park, with connections to Llandudno from Betws-y-Coed, to Caernarfon from Waunfawr, and to Caernarfon/Bangor from Llanberis.

In Llanberis, you can take the **Snowdon Mountain Railway** (☎ 0870 458 0033) for the ride to the top and back. The **TIC** (☎ 870765; llanberis.tic@gwynedd.gov.uk; 41a High St) is helpful.

The best hostel in the area is the **Pen-y-Pas Youth Hostel** (☎ 0870 7705990; Nantgwynant, Caernarfon; dm adult/child £11.80/8.50), 6 miles up the valley in a spectacular site at the start of one of the paths up Snowdon. **Pete's Eats** (☎ 870358; mains £2-5) is a warm café opposite the TIC where hikers swap information over large portions of healthy food. In the evenings, climbers hang out in the **Heights** (☎ 871179; www.heightshotel.co.uk; 74 High St; dm/d £14/50, f £60-100; P), a hotel/hostel with a pub and restaurant that will arrange outdoor adventures for guests.

Llangollen
☎ 01978 / pop 2600

Famous for its **International Musical Eisteddfod** (☎ 862001; www.international-eisteddfod.co.uk), Llangollen is just 8 miles from the English border. This six-day music, song and dance festival, held in July, attracts folk groups from around the world.

The town makes an excellent base for outdoor activities – walks to ruined **Valle Crucis Abbey** and the Horseshoe Pass, horse-drawn canal-boat trips, and canoeing on the Dee River. **Plas Newydd** was the 'stately cottage' of the eccentric Ladies of Llangollen, fascinating as much for their unorthodox (for those days, 1780–1831) lifestyle as for the building's striking black-and-white decoration.

The **Llangollen Youth Hostel & Activity Centre** (☎ 0870 7705932; llangollen@yha.org.uk; Tyndwr Rd; adult/under 18 yrs £10.60/7.20) is 1.5 miles from the centre. Contact the TIC for B&Bs.

BRITAIN DIRECTORY

ACCOMMODATION

For most visitors to Britain, accommodation is the single biggest expense; even the cost of pitching your tent at a camping ground can be high. Alternatives for keeping costs to a minimum are hostels, university accommodation and B&Bs – although not all are budget-priced. In the mid-range, more characterful B&Bs share the bed with guesthouses, small hotels and a growing band of chain hotels offering good quality, flat-rate rooms in and around city centres. Most towns and cities also have larger hotels, sometimes occupying grand converted castles or mansions, for a top-end splurge. Accommodation has been listed in budget order throughout this chapter, with the lowest-priced first.

Remember that many TICs will search for and book accommodation for you ahead of your arrival if you tell them your budget and what you're looking. The service is sometimes free but usually costs around £3.

Camping

Free camping is rarely possible, except in Scotland. There are hundreds of official camping grounds throughout Britain, with sites usually running from £3 to £15 per night. *AA Caravan and Camping in Britain* (£9.99) is a comprehensive listing and is available in most bookshops.

Hostels

There are separate Youth Hostel Associations for **England & Wales** (☎ 0870 770 8868; www.yha .org.uk) and **Scotland** (☎ 0870 155 3255; www.syha .org.uk) but membership of either gives you access to both organisations' accommodation. European Community residents can join in England for £14 (£7 for under-18s) or in Scotland for £6 (£2.50 for under-17s), while overseas visitors who are not members of a YHA in their home country can join after six nights' residency.

Dorm beds in YHA and SYHA hostels range from £7 to £16 per night and there's a free Book a Bed Ahead scheme, which is highly recommended in summer. Not all hostels are open throughout the year and some also have curfews and are closed during the day. Check the website, call ahead for details or pick up the useful free brochures covering all English or Scottish hostels available from larger TICs.

There's also a growing number of independent hostels, particularly in large cities. Membership is not required and while dorms are still the norm, these hostels sometimes also offer good-value double or single rooms. Facilities and prices (typically from £8 to £23) vary widely: some are quiet and cosy while others are for serious party travellers. Check websites or pick up the useful *Independent Hostel Guide* (£4.95) from bookshops.

Hotels, Guesthouses & B&Bs

A great British institution and often the best value accommodation in town, B&Bs can range from £15 per person for a bedroom in a family home to more than £50 for a warm and fuzzy stay in a characterful old house that you won't want to leave. The common link is the heaping cooked breakfast that's intended to keep you fuelled until well into the afternoon. Solo travellers are unfortunately not well catered for in many B&Bs: single rooms are in short supply and can attract an ugly premium.

Guesthouses are a stepping-stone between B&Bs and hotels. They're often large houses converted to resemble small hotels and prices range towards the higher end of the B&B scale.

Hotels can range from small pub accommodation (£15to £50) to a night of a luxury in a giant converted castle (upwards of £80). In between are a plethora of chains including **Travelodge** (www.travelodge.co.uk), **Ibis** (www.ibishotel .com) and **Travel Inn** (www.travelinn.co.uk) providing good-value rooms for flat rates ranging from £39 to £69 per room per night. These are often located in city centres.

There are several competing grading systems for B&Bs, guesthouses and hotels, all of which are voluntary and some of which are paid for. While TICs only recommend accommodation that pay them a fee to be listed, these are always of an acceptable standard and a safe bet when you arrive in an unfamiliar region.

Rental Accommodation

Booking a self-catering, picture-postcard cottage in the heart of the British countryside can be one of the most cost-effective ways to experience a region. Prices, which start from £200 per week, are particularly appealing if you are travelling in a group of four or more. An online search will uncover dozens of rental agencies – **English Country Cottages** (☎ 01328 864 041; www.english-country -cottages.co.uk) and **Cottages 4 You** (☎ 08700 782 100;

www.cottages4you.co.uk) are good starting places, but you can also order a free copy of *Self-catering Holiday Homes* from **Visit Britain** (www.visitbritain.com).

Universities

Many universities offer student accommodation to visitors during Christmas, Easter and summer holidays. Usually in basic single study rooms, B&B here ranges from £17 to £35 per person. For more information, contact **Venuemasters** (☎ 0114 249 3090; www.venuemasters.com), which represents 100 British universities or call campuses directly.

ACTIVITIES

Britain is a great destination for outdoor enthusiasts, from daredevil rock climbers to beach bum surfer doods and leisurely day hikers. There are clubs and associations across the land, and useful brochures on many activities are available from **Visit Britain** (www.visitbritain.com/uk/outdoorbritain).

Cycling

Compact Britain is an excellent destination to explore by bike, but while not all cities are especially cycle-friendly, there are plenty of designated routes through some of the nation's best countryside. Popular cycle paths include the **Yorkshire Dales Cycleway**, the **Trans-Pennine Trail** and the challenging 1000-mile **Land's End to John o'Groats** trail through western Britain. The **National Cycle Network** (☎ 0845 113 0065; www.sustrans.co.uk) administers a host of smaller routes, many of them one-day rides, and is actively expanding all the time. They can provide free maps and other resources. The **Cyclists Touring Club** (☎ 0870 873 0060; www.ctc.org.uk) is the leading national organisation for biking enthusiasts and can help with route information and general inquiries about cycling in Britain.

Hiring bikes is easy in many towns and cities, with prices typically ranging from £6 for a half-day to £60 for a week. Britain's roads are best cycled in spring or late summer – July and August can be very busy, so always book ahead for rentals. You can take your bike on many rail services but always call ahead to check because the regulations are complex and inconsistent. Bikes are welcome on many local buses but not on inter-city coaches operated by National Express or Citylink.

Hiking

Britain's cornucopia of picturesque terrains makes for great hiking country and there's an age-old tradition of experiencing the land on foot. Day hikes are a popular and accessible way to escape from the crowded cities and there are hundreds of longer routes, either marked or waiting to be created by adventurous travellers.

Popular hiking routes include the 191-mile **Coast to Coast Walk** (☎ 01609 882800; www.coast2coast.co.uk) across three northern England national parks, and the 84-mile **Dales Way** (☎ 01609 883881; www.thedalesway.co.uk) through Yorkshire's charming countryside. Other routes crisscross **Exmoor National Park** in Devon, **Pembrokeshire National Park** in Wales and the highlands and islands of Scotland. Many of these are mentioned throughout this chapter.

The **Ramblers Association** (☎ 020-7339-8500; www.ramblers.org.uk) is a voluntary organisation with a wealth of experience and information on hiking and walking across Britain. They produce dozens of maps, guides and accommodation listings for local and visiting hoofers. **Visit Britain** (www.visitbritain.com/walking) also publishes a free folder of paths and trails.

Water Sports

Surrounded by water and dripping with lakes, lochs and canals, Britain offers a brimming bucket full of coastal and inland water-based activities.

Cornwall is England's surfing paradise, with rideable swells at more than 100 closely linked beaches, including Penhale, Droskyn and Holywell Bay (p177). Scotland is also opening up to its surfing potential, with the north and west coasts proving particularly popular with visitors. The **British Surfing Association** (☎ 01637 876 474; www.britsurf.org) should be your first stop for information and resources. Windsurfers can also check out their Brit-based options via the **Royal Yachting Association** (☎ 0845 345 0400; www.rya.org.uk).

A 2000-mile network of canals means that even budget travellers should consider the possibility of hiring a canal boat and cruising through Britain's inland waterways. If you hire a boat outside the high season, prices are quite reasonable, ranging from around £350 per week in April to £700 in August for a boat that sleeps four. Try **Hoseasons Holidays** (☎ 01502 501501; www.hoseasons.co.uk) and check-in with the

Inland Waterways Association (☎ 01923 711114; www.waterways.org.uk) for route information.

With Britain's rich naval history, diving is also an eye-opening day out for visitors. With hundreds of shipwrecks strewn around the coast, some of the most popular wetsuit haunts are along the English South Coast, where hapless medieval and WWII vessels reside together. The divable coast around St. Abbs, Scotland's first marine nature reserve, is also popular. The **British Sub-Aqua Club** (☎ 0151 350 6200; www.bsac.com) offers courses and information for visiting divers.

BUSINESS HOURS

Standard office hours are 9am to 5pm Monday to Friday. Restaurants often open daily for lunch (☺11am to 3pm) then reopen for dinner (☺6pm to 10pm). Pubs typically operate 11am to 11pm Monday to Saturday and noon to 10.30pm Sunday, with some closing in the afternoon and others (particularly in Scotland) staying open later. Some late-opening pubs charge for entry. Shops open from at least 9am to 5pm Monday to Saturday, while 10am to 4pm Sunday opening is increasingly common with larger shops. Many also stay open late one night per week, usually Thursday or Friday. Some city-centre supermarkets open 24 hours.

CUSTOMS

There is no tax or duty on personal-use goods for those arriving in Britain from another EU country. Those under 17 are not allowed to import alcohol or tobacco, but others can bring in up to 3200 cigarettes, 10L of spirits, 90L of wine and 110L of beer. Those arriving from outside the EU can import up to 200 cigarettes, 1L of spirits, 2L of wine and £145 of other goods without paying tax or duty. Contact **HM Customs and Excise** (☎ 0845 010 9000; www.hmce.gov.uk) for more information.

DISABLED TRAVELLERS

While newer hotels, shops and attractions are disabled-user-friendly as a matter of course, there are many old buildings in Britain that are not. Wheelchair travellers, in particular, are not well-served by pubs, B&Bs and most public transport systems. The Travelodge and Travel Inn chains have well-designed disabled rooms, particularly in their newer hotels, and many banks and ticket offices are fitted with hearing loops.

The **Royal Association for Disability & Rehabilitation** (☎ 020 7250 3222; www.radar.org.uk) publishes an invaluable guide on disabled travel in Britain, while **Holiday Care** (☎ 0845 124 9971; www.holidaycare.org.uk) provides lists of checked and accredited disabled accommodation across the country.

EMBASSIES & CONSULATES
British Embassies & Consulates
British embassies abroad include:
Australia (☎ 02-6270 6666; www.britaus.net; Commonwealth Ave, Yarralumla, Canberra, ACT 2600)
Canada (☎ 613-237 1530; www.britainincanada.org; 80 Elgin St, Ottawa, ON K1P 5K7)
France (☎ 01 44 51 31 00; www.amb-grandebretagne.fr, in French; 35 rue du Faubourg St Honore, 75383 Paris)
Germany (☎ 030-20457 0; www.britischebotschaft.de; Wilhelmstrasse 70, 10117 Berlin)
Ireland (☎ 01 205 3700; www.britishembassy.ie; 29 Merrion Rd, Ballsbridge, Dublin 4)
Japan (☎ 03-5211 1100; www.uknow.or.jp; 1 Ichiban-cho, Chiyoda-ku, Tokyo 102-8381)
The Netherlands (☎ 0 70 4270 427; www.britain.nl; Lange Voorhout 10, 2514 ED, The Hague)
New Zealand (☎ 04 924 2888; www.britain.org.nz; 44 Hill St, Wellington 1)
South Africa (☎ 012 421 7733; www.britain.org.za; 255 Hill St, Arcadia, 0002 Pretoria)
USA (☎ 202-588 6500; www.britainusa.com; 3100 Massachusetts Ave NW, Washington DC 20008)

Embassies & Consulates in Britain
Countries with diplomatic representation in London include the following:
Australia (Map pp142-4; ☎ 020-7379 4334; www.australia.org.uk; Australia House, The Strand, London WC2B 4LA)
Canada (Map pp142-4; ☎ 020-7258 6600; Macdonald House, 1 Grosvenor Sq, London W1K 4AB)
France (☎ 020-7073 1200; www.ambafrance-uk.org; 21 Cromwell Rd, London SW7 2EN)
Germany (☎ 020-7824 1300; www.german-embassy.org.uk; 23 Belgrave Sq, London SW1 8PZ)
Ireland (☎ 020-7235 2171; 17 Grosvenor Pl, London SW1X 7HR)
Japan (☎ 020-7465 6500; www.emb-japan.go.jp; 101-104 Piccadilly, London W1J 7JT)
The Netherlands (Map pp146-7; ☎ 020-7590 3200; www.netherlands-embassy.org.uk; 38 Hyde Park Gate, London SW7 5DP)
New Zealand (Map pp142-4; ☎ 020-7930 8422; www.nzembassy.com; New Zealand House, 80 Haymarket, London SW1Y 4TQ)
South Africa (Map pp142-4; ☎ 020-7451 7299;

BRITAIN

www.southafricahouse.com; South Africa House, Trafalgar Square, London WC2N 5DP)
Spain (☎ 020-7589 8989; 20 Draycott Pl, London SW3 2RZ)
USA (☎ 020-7499 9000; www.usembassy.org.uk; 24 Grosvenor Sq, London W1A 1AE)

FESTIVALS & EVENTS

There are countless diverse special events across Britain throughout the year, many based on traditional customs initiated centuries ago.

January

Hogmanay (www.edinburghshogmanay.org) Huge New Year street party in Edinburgh.
Chinese New Year (can be in February) Colourful London parade.

March

Oxford/Cambridge University Boat Race Traditional rowing face-off along the Thames.

April

London Marathon (www.london-marathon.co.uk) Giant annual jog-a-thon.
Grand National (www.aintree.co.uk) Britain's top annual horseracing event, held at Aintree, Liverpool.

May

English FA Cup Final Leading knock-out football club competition. Held in Cardiff while London's Wembley Stadium is rebuilt.
Glyndebourne Festival (www.glyndebourne.com) High-calibre opera and performing arts festival (runs to August).

June

Trooping the Colour Queen's birthday is marked with pomp and pageantry in London.
Lawn Tennis Championships (www.wimbledon.org) World's leading tennis event, served-up with strawberries and cream.
Glastonbury Festival (www.glastonburyfestivals.co.uk) Giant open-air music fest in Somerset.

July

Henley Royal Regatta (www.hrr.co.uk) Premier rowing and posh social event in Henley-on-Thames, Oxfordshire.

August

Cowes Week (www.cowesweek.co.uk) Yachting extravaganza around the Isle of White.
Edinburgh Fringe Festival (www.edfringe.com) Comedy and avant-garde theatre dominates this alternative event.

Edinburgh International Festival (www.eif.co.uk) World's leading performance arts festival.
Notting Hill Carnival (www.portowebbo.co.uk) Enormous multicultural street parade in London.
Reading Festival (www.readingfestival.com) Popular annual live music (and camping) fest in Berkshire.

September

Braemar Gathering Kilts and caber-tossing attended by the Queen (additional events held across Scotland June-September).

October

Cheltenham Festival (www.cheltenhamfestivals.co.uk) Celebration of literature and books in the Cotswolds.

November

Guy Fawkes Night Bonfires and fireworks on the 5th recall a failed anti-government plot from the 1600s.
Lord Mayor's Show (www.lordmayorsshow.org) Giant London street procession.

GAY & LESBIAN TRAVELLERS

Britain has an active and widespread gay and lesbian scene with most major cities – especially London, Brighton, Manchester, Birmingham and Glasgow – having the nightlife to prove it. Visit Britain operates an excellent website of resources for gay and lesbian travellers (www.gaybritain.org), while the **Gay Britain Network** (www.gaybritain .co.uk) website provides links to searchable databases of clubs and bars and gay-friendly travel options.

Gay Times, Britain's leading gay magazine, provides details of major happenings, including the annual summer Pride event in London. The **National Gay and Lesbian Switchboard** (☎ 020 7837 732) provides a 24-hour support service for residents and visitors throughout Britain.

HOLIDAYS

While bank holidays affect most businesses (increasingly excluding shops) in England and Wales, they have less impact in Scotland. In England and Wales, these official public holidays include January 1, Good Friday, Easter Monday, the first and last Mondays in May, the last Monday in August and Christmas Day and Boxing Day. Scotland's only official holidays are January 1, January 2, Good Friday, Easter Monday and Christmas Day, although many towns set their own additional one-day holidays twice a year.

LANGUAGE

Britain has several regional languages, including Cornish, Welsh and, in Scotland, Gaelic. While everyone you will meet also speaks English, you should expect to see bilingual road signs and placenames in many locations. There are also dozens of distinctive local accents and word choices that are unique to specific regions.

MEDIA
Newspaper & Magazines

Britain has a curious mix of some of the world's best and worst newspapers. At the top end, it's hard to beat the *Guardian, Telegraph, Times* and *Independent*. The *Sun, Star* and *Mirror* continue to mine the bottom of the barrel. The tabloid *Sun* remains Britain's most widely-read newspaper. The magazine sector is equally diverse with *GQ, Vogue* and *Cosmopolitan* producing UK versions very different from their US counterparts.

MONEY

Britain is still holding out against adopting the euro (€), which is only accepted at some major tourist attractions and large hotels. The currency of choice here is the pound sterling (£), split among a variety of coins and banknotes each bearing the Queen's image. Scotland also issues banknotes which are legal tender on both sides of the border: if you have any trouble using them in England, exchange them at any bank. Most banks are open Monday to Friday 9.30am to 4.30pm, with major city centre branches staying open later and on Saturday mornings.

ATMs

It's not hard to find an ATM – usually called cashpoints – in Britain, where they're often located outside banks, building societies and large supermarkets. They accept a wide variety of cards, including Visa, MasterCard and American Express (Amex). Some cashpoints, particularly those in unusual locations like pubs, charge a £1 fee for withdrawals.

Credit Cards & Travellers Cheques

MasterCard and Visa are the most acceptable cards in Britain, with Amex and Diners Club not far behind. Thomas Cook and Amex travellers cheques are commonly used but don't rely on exchanging them at businesses since they are rarely accepted. Instead, bring large denomination travellers cheques (in UK sterling) and cash them as needed at a Thomas Cook or Amex branch on your travels. Be aware that Amex offices are often located only in large cities while Thomas Cook branches are more numerous. Banks will also change your cheques for you but will charge a small commission.

Moneychangers

Be careful with bureaux de change: they may advertise good exchange rates but they frequently levy outrageous fees and commissions. The exchanges at airports are exceptions to the rule. They charge less than most banks and cash sterling travellers cheques for free. Always ask what the fees and commissions are before making a transaction.

POST

Most post offices are open 9am to 5pm Monday to Friday and Saturday until noon. Within the UK, 1st-class mail is quicker and more expensive (£0.28 per letter) than 2nd-class mail (£0.21). Postcards sent overseas cost £0.40 (Europe) and £0.43 (outside Europe). Stamp vending machines are located outside some post offices and larger newsagents and supermarkets sell them in books of four or 10. Single stamps are often available at larger attractions and some TICs.

STUDYING

There are thousands of language schools across Britain, not just the ones advertised on postcards handed out along London's Oxford St. Unfortunately some outfits are scams preying on impressionable wannabe-students. Fortunately, many schools do belong to an accreditation scheme administered by the **British Council** (www.britishcouncil.org). It guarantees that teachers are properly trained and schools have the required facilities. **English in Britain** (www.englishinbritain.co.uk) provides a general introduction to the field, while the **Association of Recognised English Language Services** (www.arels.org.uk) is more specific about the classes and programmes offered.

DEPARTURE TAX

Passengers flying from Britain need to pay an Air Passenger Duty. Those flying to other EU countries will pay £12 and those flying beyond will pay £24. This fee is usually included in the cost of your ticket. There is no departure tax if you leave by boat or train.

TELEPHONE

Call boxes are a common sight throughout Britain, although the beloved red telephone box has been largely usurped by a characterless steel and glass replacement. Most public payphones are operated by British Telecom (BT) and they take coins, credit cards, phonecards or a combination of all three. Coin phones do not give change and they charge a minimum of 20p. Local calls are charged by time while national calls are by time and distance: it's cheaper to call before 8am or after 6pm Monday to Friday or any time on weekends.

Mobile Phones

Codes for mobile phones usually begin with ☎ 07. Britain uses the GSM 900/18000 network, covering Europe, Australia and New Zealand. It's not generally compatible with North America. If you have a GSM phone, it's best to ask your service provider if it can be used in the UK. Consider buying a pay-as-you-go phone for as little as £50 for the duration of your visit.

Phone Codes

For international direct calls, dial ☎ 00 followed by the country code, area code (drop the first zero if there is one) and local number. Dial ☎ 155 for the international operator. For calls within Britain, dial ☎ 100 for operator assistance and ☎ 1188500 for directory enquiries. Useful codes to know are:

☎ 0800 – free call
☎ 0845 – local rate call
☎ 0870 – national rate call
☎ 0891 – premium rate call

TOURIST INFORMATION

The British Tourist Authority now brands itself **Visit Britain** (www.visitbritain.com). Its website alone is stuffed with resources and it is ever-eager to send brochures and information on request. **England** (www.visitengland .com), **Scotland** (www.visitscotland.com) and **Wales** (www.visitwales.com) also have dedicated tourism agencies. Britain has a good network of local TICs, although their opening hours and seasons vary widely. Some overseas Visit Britain contacts include:

Amsterdam (☎ 020 689 0002; britinfo.nl@bta.org.uk)
Auckland (☎ 09 3030 1446; bta.nz@bta.org.uk)
Dublin (☎ 01 670 8000; contactus@bta.org.uk)
New York (☎ 1 800 GO 2 BRITAIN; travelinfo@bta.org.uk)
Sydney (☎ 01 9377 4400; visitbritainaus@bta.org.uk)

VISAS

You don't need a visitor visa if you are a citizen of Australia, Canada, New Zealand, South Africa or the USA. Tourists are generally permitted to stay for up to six months, but are prohibited from working. The Working Holidaymaker scheme allows Commonwealth citizens aged 17 to 27 years to live and work here for up to two years, but arrangements must be made in advance via a British embassy overseas. Visiting full-time students from the USA are eligible to work in Britain for up to six months. Contact the **British North America Universities Club** (☎ 020 7251 3471; www.bunac.org.uk) for details. European Union (EU) citizens can visit, live and work in Britain without a visa.

All other nationalities should apply for a visitor visa through their nearest British diplomatic mission. These currently cost £36 to £60. For more information, visit www .ukvisas.gov.uk.

Current worldwide security issues mean that immigration officials at all ports of entry are stricter now than ever before. Be prepared to answer questions about your reasons for entering Britain and the date you expect to leave – show your outbound travel ticket if necessary.

TRANSPORT IN BRITAIN

GETTING THERE & AWAY
Air

Britain is a busy transport hub with five airports serving London alone. The following are Britain's biggest international airports:

Aberdeen (☎ 0870 040 0006; www.baa.com/aberdeen)
Cardiff (☎ 01446 711111; www.cial.co.uk)
Edinburgh (☎ 0870 040 0007; www.baa.com/edinburgh)

Glasgow (☎ 0870 040 0008; www.baa.com/glasgow)
London Heathrow (☎ 0870 0000 123; www.baa.com /heathrow)
London Gatwick (☎ 0870 000 2468; www.baa.com /gatwick)
London Stansted (☎ 0870 0000 303 www.baa.com /stansted)
London Luton (☎ 01582 405100; www.london-luton .co.uk)
Manchester (☎ 0161 489 3000; www.manairport.co.uk)
Southampton (☎ 020 7834 9449; www.baa.com/ southampton)

Some airlines flying to and from Britain are listed below:

Aer Lingus (code EI; ☎ 0845 973 7747; www.aer lingus.com)
Air Canada (code AC; ☎ 0870 524 7226; www.air canada .com)
Air France (code AF; ☎ 0845 084 5111; www.air france.com)
American Airlines (code AA; ☎ 0845 778 9789; www.aa.com)
British Airways (code BA; ☎ 0845 773 3377; www .britishairways.co.uk)
British Midland (code BD; ☎ 0870 607 0555; www.flybmi.com)
easyJet (code U2; ☎ 0870 600 0000; www.easyjet.com)
KLM (code KLM; ☎ 9870 507 4074; www.klm.com)
Lufthansa (code LH; ☎ 0845 773 7747; www.luft hansa.com)
Ryanair (code FR; ☎ 0870 156 9569; www.ryanair.com)
Scandinavian Airlines (code SK; ☎ 0845 6072 7727; www.sas.se)
Virgin Atlantic (code VS; ☎ 0293 747 747; www .virgin-atlantic.com)

Land

The Channel Tunnel provides Britain a land link with Europe (albeit rail only), but even without using the tunnel, you can still get to the continent by bus or train – there's just a short ferry ride thrown in. The ferries carry cars and motorcycles.

BUS

Servicing an enormous network of European destinations, including Ireland and Eastern Europe, **Eurolines** (London ☎ 0870 514 3219; www .eurolines.com; 52 Grosvenor Gardens, Victoria, London SW1; Amsterdam ☎ 020-560 8788; Brussels ☎ 02-203 07 07; Frankfurt ☎ 069-790 32 40; Madrid ☎ 091-327 1381; Paris ☎ 01 49 72 48 00; Rome ☎ 06-884 08 40) has regular daily services to London arriving from Amsterdam, Brussels, Frankfurt, Madrid, Paris

and Rome, and elsewhere. The company also operates six circular explorer routes, always starting and ending in London, the most popular of which is the London–Amsterdam–Brussels–Paris route (£62). You can book tickets through any National Express office, including Victoria coach station in London (where Eurolines' buses depart and arrive), and at many travel agencies.

CAR & MOTORCYCLE

You can bring a car to Britain via ferry or hovercraft services from several European nations or via the Channel Tunnel. See below for specific information on these options and refer to Getting Around (p257) for information on driving in Britain. If hiring, check with the company regarding insurance requirements and drop-off charges for travelling from Europe to Britain.

TRAIN

Three options exist for travel between England and Europe: Eurostar, Eurotunnel or train/ferry connections. Travellers aged under 26 years can pick up Billet International de Jeunesse (BIJ) tickets which cut train fares by up to 50%. Various agents issue BIJ tickets in London.

The high-speed **Eurostar** (☎ 0870 5186 186; www.eurostar.com) passenger train travels between London and Paris or Brussels via the Channel Tunnel. There are stops in Ashford (England) and in Lille and Calais (France). The London terminal is at Waterloo station. There are between 14 and 20 trains per day from Paris to London (£170 one way, three hours), and from eight to 12 trains daily between Brussels and London (£157, 2¾ hours). Holders of BritRail, Eurail and Euro passes are entitled to discounted fares.

Trains run by **Eurotunnel** (☎ 0870 535 3535; www.eurotunnel.com) carry vehicles and their passengers or freight through the Channel Tunnel between Folkestone in the UK and Calais in France. The specially designed shuttle trains run 24 hours, departing up to four times an hour in each direction between 6am and 10pm, and every hour from 10pm to 6am. A car and passengers costs between £185 and £220, depending on day and time of travel.

Rail/ferry links involve trains at either end and a ferry or high-speed catamaran across the Channel. Trains arrive at London's

BRITAIN

Victoria, Liverpool St or Charing Cross stations from points across Europe and are usually much cheaper than travelling by Eurostar. Contact **Rail Europe** (☎ 0870 584 8848; www.raileurope.com) for information. Remember that Eurail passes are not valid in Britain.

Sea

There's a bewildering array of car and passenger ferry and high-speed catamaran services between Britain and Europe, with prices changing rapidly to reflect the intense competition. Shop around for a bargain via operators' websites. The shortest crossing from mainland Europe is Calais to Dover on the English south coast. The main operators and some of the popular routes follow:

Brittany Ferries (☎ 08703 665 333; www.brittany -ferries.com) Operates from France (Caen or St Malo to Portsmouth: six–nine hours, one–three daily; Cherbourg–Poole: three hours, one–three daily and Roscoff–Plymouth: five hours, one–three daily) and from Spain (Santander–Plymouth: 24 hours, twice weekly)

DFDS Seaways (☎ 08705 333 000; www.dfdsseaways .co.uk) Operates from Denmark (Esbjerg–Harwich: 19½ hours, every two days), Germany (Hamburg–Harwich: 16½ hours, every two days), the Netherlands (Amsterdam–Newcastle: 15 hours, daily) and Sweden (Gothenburg–Newcastle: 17 hours, twice weekly).

Hoverspeed (☎ 0870 240 8070; www.hoverspeed.com) Operates from France (Calais–Dover: one hour, hourly).

P & O (☎ 0870 242 4999; www.poferries.com) Operates from France (Calais–Dover: 75 minutes, every 45 minutes; Cherbourg or Le Havre to Portsmouth: three–six hours; one–five daily). It also operates from Ireland (Dublin–Liverpool: 7½ hours, twice daily) and Spain (Bilbao–Portsmouth: 31 hours, twice weekly).

Stena Line (☎ 08704 006798; www.stenaline.com) operates from the Netherlands (Hook of Holland–Harwich: 3½ hours, three daily) and from Ireland (Dublin–Holyhead 1½–three hours, twice daily and Rosslare–Fishguard: 3½ hours, six daily).

Superfast Ferries (☎ 0870 410 6040; www.superfast .com) Operates from Belgium (Zeebrugge–Rosyth near Edinburgh: 17½ hours, daily).

GETTING AROUND

Britain's dense transport network diminishes to almost nothing in most remote areas and national parks where populations are low. But with some creative thinking, visitors can get almost anywhere via a combination of rail, road and cheap flights, with many areas crying out to be explored on foot or by

bike. Rental cars are an option but they are rarely cost-effective unless you're travelling in a group or to areas not well-served by other transport options. Contact **Traveline** (☎ 0870 608 2608; www.traveline.org.uk) for information on all air, train, coach, bus and ferry options throughout Britain. For Scotland-only transport options, check www.travel inescotland.com.

Your **International Student Identity Card** (www .isiccard.com) also qualifies you for discount travel passes – check bus (p257) and train (p258) sections for details.

Air

No-frills airlines offer some of the best potential bargains for travelling around Britain – especially on the London to Scotland route –but you'll have to be flexible to get the best deals and factor in the cost of travelling to and from airports. There are often additional charges for credit card bookings and ticket changes.

AIRLINES IN BRITAIN

The following airlines operate domestic flights:

Air Scotland (☎ 0141 848 4990; www.air-scotland.com)

bmiBaby (☎ 0870 264 2229; www.bmibaby.com)

British Airways (☎ 0845 773 3377; www.britishairways .co.uk)

British Midland (☎ 0870 607 0555; www.flybmi.com)

easyJet (☎ 0870 600 0000; www.easyjet.com)

Ryanair (☎ 0870 156 9569; www.ryanair.com)

ScotAirways (☎ 0870 606 0707; www.scotairways.co.uk)

Bicycle

Compact Britain is a bike-friendly destination. Keep in mind that many streets are narrow and you'll have to keep your wits about you as the cars whizz by. See the Cycling section in Activities (p250) for further information.

Boat

See p250 for information on accessing Britain's extensive canal boat network. Ferries are an important part of Scotland's transport network, with essential services linking islands such as Orkney, Skye and the Outer Hebrides to the mainland. The main operators include **Caledonian MacBrayne** (CalMac; ☎ 0870 565 0000; www.calmac.co.uk) and **Northlink Ferries** (☎ 0845 6000 449; www.northlinkferries.co.uk). CalMac offers a range of passes for those making multiple trips. See individual town, city and island listings for specific route and fare information.

Bus

Buses are the cheapest way to get around in Britain but they're slow, with many routes winding through several cities before reaching their destinations. While local services operate in each region, there's also a network of inter-city buses (usually referred to as coaches) covering longer distances. It's advisable to make coach reservations in advance during July and August, either online, by phone or at main bus stations.

Since Britain's bus and coach system is largely deregulated, some no-frills operators have begun emerging on the scene. These are worth checking out for a bargain if you enjoy sitting in a cramped and battered double-decker bus for several hours at a time. See individual sections for sample bus and coach routes and fares.

Contact **Traveline** (☎ 0870 608 2608; www .traveline.org.uk) for bus and coach options throughout England, Scotland and Wales. Britain's largest coach operators include **National Express** (☎ 0870 580 8080; www.national express.com) and its subsidiary **Scottish Citylink** (☎ 0870 550 5050; www.citylink.co.uk). **Megabus** (☎ 01738 639 095; www.megabus.com) is a popular no-frills provider with services between major cities and **MacBackpackers** (☎ 0131 558 9900; www.macbackpackers.com) runs a jump-on, jump-off service linking several Scottish destinations. It's targeted at hostel-dwellers and costs £65 for up to one year of travel. **Silver Choice** (☎ 01355 230403; www.silverchoicetravel .co.uk) also operates good-value services from London to Edinburgh and Glasgow.

BUS PASSES

The National Express Student/Young Persons Discount Coachcard costs £10 for one-year and provides discounts of up to 30% on all fares. It's available to 16- to 25-year-olds and all full-time students. There's a similar card for over-50s. Purchase one from any National Express agent using a passport (or an ISIC card for students). Discounts do not apply to travel in Scotland.

Scottish Citylink offers its own Young Person's Discount Card and 50+ Discount Card (£7, 20% discount on most fares). UK students qualify for a free version of the card.

See p257 for information about passes offered by Eurolines.

POSTBUS

Royal Mail postbuses provide a reliable service to remote areas and can be useful for wilderness hiking trips. For information and timetables, contact **customer service** (☎ 01246-546329; www.postbus.royalmail.com).

Car & Motorcycle

Often the quickest, most convenient way to travel around Britain is by car or motorcycle – particularly in remote areas. Cars are often inconvenient in city centres and parking can be troublesome and expensive. Petrol is also expensive, especially compared with North America.

DRIVING LICENCE

Your foreign driving licence is valid in Britain for up to 12 months from your date of entry.

HIRE

Car hire is expensive in Britain and it's often better to make arrangements in your home country for a fly/drive deal. Drivers are usually expected to be between the ages of 23 and 65 years, with special insurance conditions applying to those outside these limits.

Larger operators charge from around £120 per week for a small car (Ford Fiesta, Peugeot 106) but rates can vary considerably based on many factors including pick-up and drop-off locations, whether or not you're picking up on the weekend and how long you're renting for. Always ask for any special offers or mention that you're shopping around for the best rate. TICs can also suggest favoured local rental companies. Major operators are listed below:

Avis (☎ 0870 606 0100; www.avis.co.uk)

Budget (☎ 0845 606 6669: www.budget.co.uk)

Europcar (☎ 0870 607 5000; www.europecar)

Thrifty Car Rental (☎ 0870 066 0514; www.thrifty .co.uk)

ROAD RULES

The *Highway Code*, available in most bookshops, contains all you'll need to know about Britain's road rules. Vehicles drive on the left-hand side; seat belts are compulsory in the front seats (also in the back, where fitted); the speed limit is 30mph (48km/h) in built-up areas, 60mph (96km/h) on single carriageways and 70mph (112km/h) on dual carriageways. Remember to give way to your right at roundabouts.

The maximum blood-alcohol level for driving is 35mg/100ml. A yellow line along the edge of a road indicates parking restrictions – look for a sign nearby for exact limits. Motorcyclists must wear helmets.

Train

Trains, especially when you have a travel pass purchased in your home country, are a competitive option: they're also quicker and often take you through Britain's best scenery. While the network is extensive, covering all cities and most towns, it can be difficult to use the train to reach remote areas. Investment from private companies is bringing faster, more comfortable trains into service but the ancient infrastructure means repairs to the rails are ongoing: don't be surprised to see services delayed for engineering work, particularly on weekends. When services are cancelled, buses are provided to ensure passengers reach their destinations. For information, contact the **National Rail Enquiry Service** (☎ 0845 748 4950; www.nationalrail.co.uk).

CLASSES

There are myriad ticketing options for rail travel in Britain and the system can be quite complex. Call the **National Rail Enquiry Service** (☎ 0845 748 4950; www.nationalrail .co.uk) for details. The main difference is that 1st-class tickets are up to 50% more expensive than standard-class tickets for travel in separate carriages on the same trains.

RESERVATIONS

Recommended for summer, peak times and popular routes, advance reservations can be made at train stations or on the Web at www.thetrainline.com. Ticket prices usually depend upon the degree of flexibility you want, the availability of cheap tickets, and any passes you hold. Without a pass, the cheapest tickets must be bought at least a week ahead. Of the bewildering array of ticket options, some are listed below:

Apex The cheapest options for outward and return journeys (usually long-distance) on different days. They must be booked at least 48 hours in advance; availability is limited.

Cheap Day Return For outward and return journeys on the same day (usually limited to travel after 9.30am); often costs little more than a one-way fare and is a great deal for day-trippers.

Saver Open return but travel during weekday peak times is not permitted.

SuperSaver Return ticket but with weekday peak time travel, Friday travel and holiday travel not allowed.

TRAIN PASSES

The Young Persons Railcard (£14), Seniors Railcard (£18) and Disabled Persons Railcard (£14) are each valid for 12 months and give a one-third discount on most trips in Britain. Check the options at www.railcard.co.uk; your application can be processed over the counter at main train stations. You'll need proof of age (passport, birth certificate or driving licence) for the Seniors and Young Persons railcards (or proof of student enrolment) and proof of entitlement for the Disabled Persons Railcard.

The most convenient and cost-effective option for extensive travel is to purchase a rail pass. **BritRail** (www.britrail.com) has an excellent selection. You must buy them at home before you arrive in the UK – ask at your nearest British Tourist Authority (BTA) office – or from the British Travel Centre in Regent St London. You simply show your pass (and sometimes your passport) on the train, avoiding the confusing options and restrictions of most tickets. Remember your Eurorail pass is invalid in Britain; you'll need a separate BritRail pass. Options include the popular BritRail Consecutive Pass (unlimited four- to 31-day passes ranging from US$189 to US$605) and the BritRail Flexipass (travel four, eight or 15 days over a two-month period for US$239 to US$519). There are cheaper, regional versions of these two passes, including a popular Days Out from London pass (two to seven days of travel from $US59 to $US155); all passes have 1st-class options for an extra US$100 to US$300.

ScotRail (☎ 0845 755 0033; www.scotrail.co.uk) offers passes, available through BritRail or at rail stations across the UK, for travel in Scotland. The most convenient for many travellers the Freedom of Scotland pass (travel four days out of eight or eight days out of 15 for £89 to £119) is . Of other options, the Central Scotland Rover is popular, allowing unlimited travel for three days out of seven between Edinburgh, Fife, Glasgow, North Berwick and Stirling.

France

CONTENTS

FRANCE

Is it any wonder that France topped a 2004 list of most popular countries to visit? And is it a coincidence that so many holidaying French are such stay-at-homes? Surely not. They have everything they need right on their collective doorstep: mountains, beaches, countryside, vibrant cities, and national parks rich in natural wonders.

Strewn liberally around the place are remnants of a rich, often illustrious past: unimaginably old prehistoric cave paintings, mysterious dolmens, grand Roman ruins, awe-inspiring medieval cathedrals and grand public palaces. France retains a confident culture today with a strong sense of identity and a correspondingly rich treasure house of art and architecture.

French cuisine and wine are truly without peer. Few other European countries are as spoiled for choice by the bounty of farm, forest and vineyard, not to mention an ocean and a sea (the Atlantic and Mediterranean).

An old-style courtesy is still found in the daily interactions here (although perhaps less often in places like Paris) that many other countries have lost. A little French will take you a long way with the locals. At the very least make the effort with greetings and pleasantries. The more effort you make the more you will get back, just as the more you travel in France, the more wonders you'll discover.

FAST FACTS

- **Area** 551,000 sq km
- **Capital** Paris
- **Currency** euro (€); A$1 = €0.58; ¥100 = €0.76; NZ$ = €0.54; UK£1 = €1.50; US$1 = €0.83
- **Famous for** Napoleon Bonaparte, fabulous food, world-class wine, cheese, bad plumbing
- **Key Phrases** *merci* (thank you); *parlez-vous Anglais?* (do you speak English?); *excusez-moi* (excuse me); *s'il vous plaît* (please); *pardon* (sorry)
- **Official Language** French
- **Population** 60.2 million
- **Telephone Codes** country code ☎ 33; international access code ☎ 00
- **Visas** none needed for EU citizens, prospective EU member states, Switzerland, Iceland, Norway, Australia, the USA, Canada, New Zealand, Japan and Israel

FRANCE

HIGHLIGHTS

- Spoil yourself in chic, romantic, demure **Paris** (p268); you'll need several days just to scratch the cultural surface.
- Lavish treats on your tastebuds in **Burgundy** (p334) – in the Côe d'Or's world class wine country or the gastronomic powerhouse of Dijon.
- Drop in to **Nice** (p363) down south for mild climes, inexpensive accommodation, great art, good food and happening nightlife.
- Discover the wilder, more savage beauty and solitude of **Corsica** (p378), with its jagged coasts, magnificent harbours, spectacular mountain trails and dazzling seas.

ITINERARIES

- **One week** You'll find it hard to leave Paris, so stacked is it with beauty, charm and cultural riches. Four days is barely enough for an introduction to the museums and sights but make time for the Musée d'Orsay, the Louvre and for simply strolling its lovely boulevards and along the banks of the river Seine. Then explore the surrounding area on day trips out of town: Versailles, or Chartres' for its amazing cathedral. With your remaining time head a little further from Paris, either west to the Loire Valley's magnificent chateaux and wine country, or east to the lively streets of Strasbourg near the German border.
- **Two weeks** After Paris, choose a region or perhaps two: Normandy for amazing, tide-washed Mont St-Michel and the haunting military WWII memorials; or Brittany for rugged coast, Celtic culture and St-Malo's winding streets. Alternatively head to Burgundy for unbeatable food, wine and Dijon's historic streets, or further south for the Côte d'Azur's incredible sea vistas and stylish seaside resorts.

CLIMATE & WHEN TO GO

France's climate is generally temperate and mild except in mountainous areas. The Atlantic brings rain and persistent wind to the northwest. Except for when the sometimes fierce, often biting, Mistral blows in the south, a pleasant Mediterranean climate extends from the southern coast as far inland as the southern Alps, the Massif Central and the eastern Pyrenees.

HOW MUCH?

- **Loaf of bread** €1
- **Bottle of table wine** €3
- **Restaurant meal** €20-30
- **Espresso** €1.50
- **Breakfast** €4-5

LONELY PLANET INDEX

- **Litre of petrol** €1.15
- **Litre of bottled water** €0.80
- **Beer – at a bar** (25cl) €3
- **Souvenir T-shirt** €9
- **Street snack (pommes frites)** €1

The country is at its best in spring. Summer can be fiercely hot, especially in the south away from the coast. Even Paris can swelter in July and August. It can be a crowded, traffic choked and expensive time to travel, especially around the Mediterranean. Autumn by contrast is mellow and pleasant everywhere, and swimming and sunbathing are often viable until October. Winter provides excellent winter sport opportunities in the mountains.

HISTORY
Prehistoric People

Animal-hunting, cave-dwelling Neanderthals were the first to live in France (about 90,000 to 40,000 BC). Cro-Magnons, a taller *Homo sapiens* variety, followed 35,000 years ago and left behind cave paintings and engravings. Neolithic people (about 7500 to 4000 years ago) created France's incredible menhirs (single standing stones) and dolmens (monolithic tombs).

The Celtic Gauls moved into the region between 1500 and 500 BC. They were superceded by the Romans for five centuries after Julius Caesar took control around 52 BC, until the Franks (thus the name 'France') and the Alemanii overran the country from the east.

The Frankish Merovingian and Carolingian dynasties ruled from the 5th to the 10th century. In 732 Charles Martel defeated the Moors, thus preventing France from falling under Muslim rule as Spain had done.

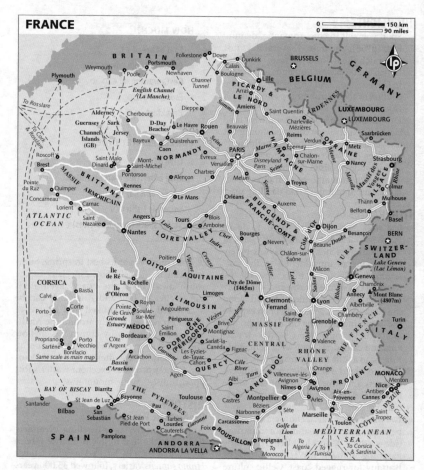

Martel's grandson, Charlemagne (742–814), extended the power and boundaries of the kingdom and was crowned Holy Roman Emperor (Emperor of the West) in 800.

William the Conqueror and his Norman forces occupied England in 1066, making Normandy (and, later, Plantagenet-ruled England) a formidable rival of the kingdom of France, a tale told on the Bayeux tapestry (p303). The subsequent rivalry between France and England for the vast English territories in France lasted three centuries, degenerating into the Hundred Years' War (1337–1453).

Five years later, the dukes of Burgundy (allied with the English) occupied Paris and in 1422 John Plantagenet, duke of Bedford,

was made regent of France for England's King Henry VI. Less than a decade later he was crowned king of France at Paris' Notre Dame (p273).

In 1429, a 17-year-old virginal warrior in the shape of Jeanne d'Arc (Joan of Arc) persuaded French legitimist Charles VII that she had a divine mission from God to expel the English from France and bring about Charles' coronation in Reims. Convicted of witchcraft and heresy following her capture and sale to the English, Joan was burned at the stake in Rouen in 1431.

The Reformation swept through Europe in the 1530s, the ideology of Jean (John) Calvin (1509–64) – a Frenchman born in Noyon (Picardie) but exiled to Geneva. The

Wars of Religion (1562–98) broke out between the Huguenots (French Protestants who received help from the English), the Catholic League (led by the House of Guise) and the Catholic monarchy.

The Sun King

Le Roi Soleil (the Sun King) ascended the throne as Louis XIV (ruled 1643–1715), involving France in wars that gained it territory, terrified its neighbours and nearly bankrupted the treasury. In Versailles, 23km southwest of Paris, Louis XIV built an extravagant palace and made his courtiers compete with each other for royal favour, reducing them to ineffectual sycophants.

Sun-king grandson Louis XV (who ruled from 1715 to 1774) was an oafish buffoon whose regent, the duke of Orléans, shifted the royal court back to Paris. As the 18th century progressed, the *ancien régime* (old order) became increasingly out of step with the needs of the country. Enlightened anti-establishment and anticlerical ideas expressed by Voltaire, Rousseau and Montesquieu further threatened the royal regime.

Revolution to Republic

Popular discontent plus the lack of political progress under Louis XVI culminated in a Parisian mob storming the prison at Bastille (now a busy roundabout; p276). France was declared a constitutional monarchy but before long, the moderate republican Girondins lost power to the radical Jacobins. Louis XVI was publicly guillotined in January 1793 on Paris' place de la Concorde (p276).

The terrifying Reign of Terror between September 1793 and July 1794 saw religious freedoms revoked, churches closed, cathedrals turned into 'Temples of Reason' and thousands beheaded. In the chaos a dashing young Corsican general named Napoleon Bonaparte (1769–1821) emerged.

Napoleon Bonaparte

In 1799 Napoleon assumed power as consul and in 1804 Pope Pius VII crowned him emperor of the French at Notre Dame. To consolidate and legitimise his authority, Napoleon waged several wars in which France gained control over most of Europe. Two years later, Allied armies entered Paris, exiled Napoleon to Elba and restored the

House of Bourbon to the French throne at the Congress of Vienna (1814–15).

In 1815 Napoleon escaped, entering Paris on 20 May. His glorious 'Hundred Days' back in power ended with the Battle of Waterloo and his return to exile where he died in 1821.

Second Republic to Second Empire

A struggle between extreme monarchists who sought a return to the *ancien régime,* people who saw the changes wrought by the Revolution as irreversible, and the radicals of the poor working-class neighbourhoods of Paris dominated the reign of Louis XVIII (ruled 1814–24). Charles X's rule (1824–30) was inept and he was overthrown.

Louis-Philippe (ruled 1830–48), a constitutional monarch of bourgeois sympathies and tastes, was subsequently chosen by parliament, only to be ousted by the 1848 Revolution. The Second Republic was established and elections brought in Napoleon's almost useless nephew, Louis Napoleon Bonaparte, as president. But in 1851 Louis Napoleon led a coup d'état and proclaimed himself Emperor Napoleon III of the Second Empire (1852–70).

France enjoyed significant economic growth at this time. Paris was transformed under urban planner Baron Haussmann (1809–91) who, among other things, created the 12 huge boulevards radiating from the Arc de Triomphe (p276).

But Napoleon III embroiled France in various catastrophic conflicts, including the Crimean War (1853–56) and the humiliating Franco-Prussian War (1870–71) which ended with Prussia taking the emperor prisoner. Upon hearing the news, defiant Parisian masses took to the streets demanding a republic be declared – the Third Republic.

The Great War

A trip to the Somme (p300) battlefields goes some way to revealing the unimaginable human cost of WWI. Of the eight million French men called to arms, 1.3 million were killed and almost one million crippled. Much of the war took place in northeastern France – trench warfare using thousands of soldiers as cannon fodder to gain a few metres of territory.

The Great War officially ended in November 1918 but the details were not meted out until 1919 at the Palace of Versailles (p287) when the Treaty of Versailles was signed. Its harsh terms included the return of Alsace-Lorraine to France and a reparations bill of US$33 billion for Germany.

WWII

In 1939, France joined Britain in declaring war on Germany. By June 1940, France had capitulated. Germany divided France into a zone under direct German occupation (in the north and along the western coast) and a puppet state centred on the spa town of Vichy.

An 80km-long stretch of beach (p303 and p304) and Bayeux's Musée Mémorial 1944 Bataille de Normandie (p303) tell the tale of the D-day landings on 6 June 1944 when Allied troops stormed the coastline to liberate most of Normandy and Brittany. Paris was liberated on 25 August.

The Fourth Republic

Elections in 1945 created a national assembly composed largely of pro-resistant Communists. The wartime leader of the Free French, General Charles de Gaulle, was appointed head of the government, but quickly sensed that the tide was turning against his idea of a strong presidency and in 1946 he resigned.

Progress rebuilding France's shattered economy and infrastructure was slow. By 1947 France was forced to turn to the USA for loans as part of the Marshall Plan to rebuild Europe. The economy gathered steam in the 1950s but the decade marked the end of French colonialism in Vietnam and in Algeria, where the struggle for independence was nastier. The resulting Algerian War (1954–62) was brutal, characterised by torture and massacre meted out to nationalist Algerians.

The Fifth Republic

De Gaulle assumed the presidency in 1958 and drafted a new constitution – the Fifth Republic – which gave considerable powers to the president at the expense of the National Assembly.

Georges Pompidou (1911–74), prime minister under de Gaulle, stepped onto the podium as president and was followed by Valéry Giscard d'Estaing (b 1926). In 1981 he was ousted by long-time head of the Parti Socialiste (Socialist Party), François Mitterrand (1916–96).

By 1986 the economy was weakening and in parliamentary elections that year the right-wing opposition led by Jacques Chirac (Paris mayor since 1977) won a majority in the National Assembly.

Presidential elections in 1995 ushered in Jacques Chirac who was re-elected with an overwhelming majority in 2002 after French voters boxed themselves into a corner by setting up National Front right winger Jean Marie Le Pen as the only alternative.

PEOPLE

France is not really densely populated – 107 people inhabit every square kilometre – although 20% of the national population is packed into the Paris area.

The last 10 years have seen rural and suburban areas steadily gaining population; and Paris and the northeast (except Alsace) losing inhabitants to southern France, where populations are predicted to rise by 30% over the next 30 years.

For much of the last two centuries, France has had a considerably lower rate of population growth than its neighbours. In the last decade, that trend has changed and the birth rate is now 2.1%. By 2050 the population of mainland France is expected to reach 64 million – five million more than in 2000.

Multicultural France has always drawn immigrants from other parts of Europe and more recently from Africa. Immigrants today form 7.4% (4.3 million) of the population yet only 36% have French citizenship, which is not conferred automatically at birth.

The French republican code, while inclusive and non-discriminatory on one hand, does little to accommodate a multicultural society. Racial tensions are fuelled by the extreme-right Front National (National Front).

This dichotomy exploded in a riot of demonstrations in 2004 when the Islamic headscarf (along with Jewish skullcaps, crucifixes and other religious symbols) was banned in French schools. The law, avowedly intended to protect the secular nature of state education, was also seen as proof that the French state is not prepared to integrate Muslims into French society.

Some 90% of France's Muslim community are non-citizens; many are illegal immigrants, and most live in depressing poverty-stricken *bidonvilles* (tinpot towns) surrounding major metropolitan centres.

RELIGION

Secular France maintains a rigid distinction between church and state. Some 55% of French identify themselves as Catholic, but no more than 10% attend church regularly. Another one million are Protestant.

Coexisting uneasily with this nominally Christian majority is France's five million-strong Muslim community. Over half of France's 600,000-strong Jewish population (Europe's largest) lives in and around Paris. Marseille has the next-largest Jewish community.

ARTS
Literature

The philosophical work of Voltaire (1694–1778), and of Swiss-born philosopher Jean-Jacques Rousseau, dominated the 18th century. A century on the poems and novels of Victor Hugo – *Les Misérables* and *Notre Dame de Paris* (The Hunchback of Notre Dame) among them – became landmarks of French Romanticism.

In 1857 two literary landmarks were published: *Madame Bovary* by Gustave Flaubert (1821–80) and Charles Baudelaire's collection of poems, *Les Fleurs du Mal* (The Flowers of Evil). Émile Zola (1840–1902) meanwhile strove to convert novel-writing from an art to a science in his powerful series, *Les Rougon-Macquart*.

Symbolists Paul Verlaine (1844–96) and Stéphane Mallarmé (1842–98) aimed to express mental states. Verlaine's poems, with those of Arthur Rimbaud (1854–91) are seen as French literature's first modern poems.

After WWII, existentialism developed around the lively debates of Jean-Paul Sartre (1905–80), Simone de Beauvoir (1908–86) and Albert Camus (1913–60) in Paris' left-bank cafés of St-Germain des Prés.

Contemporary authors include Françoise Sagan, Pascal Quignard, Jean Auel, Emmanuel Carrère and Stéphane Bourguignon. Also popular are Frédéric Dard (alias San Antonio), Léo Malet and Daniel Pennac.

Cinema

Cinematographic pioneers, the Lumière brothers, shot the world's first-ever motion picture in March 1895 and French film flourished in the following decades. The post-WWII *nouvelle vague* (new wave) filmmakers, such as Claude Chabrol and François Truffaut, produced uniquely personal films using real-life subject matter.

Big-name stars, slick production values and nostalgia were the dominant motifs in the 1980s as filmmakers switched to costume dramas, comedies and 'heritage movies'. Claude Berri's depiction of prewar Provence in *Jean de Florette* (1986), Jean-Paul Rappeneau's *Cyrano de Bergerac* (1990) and *Bon Voyage* (2003) set in 1940s Paris – all starring France's best known (and biggest-nosed) actor Gérard Depardieu – found huge audiences in France and abroad.

Le Fabuleux Destin de Amélie Poulain (*Amélie*; 2001) is a feel-good story about a winsome Parisian do-gooder. Directed by Jean-Pierre Jeunet, it proved an instant hit everywhere. French film has enjoyed a massive renaissance abroad ever since.

Music

There's more to French music than accordions and Edith Piaf.

French musical luminaries – Charles Gounod (1818–93), César Franck (1822–90) and *Carmen*-creator Georges Bizet (1838–75) among them – were a dime a dozen in the 19th century.

Claude Debussy (1862–1918) revolutionised classical music with *Prélude à l'Après-Midi d'un Faune* (Prelude to the Afternoon of a Faun), creating a light, almost Asian musical impressionism; while comrade impressionist Maurice Ravel (1875–1937) peppered his work, including *Boléro,* with sensuousness and tonal colour.

Jazz hit 1920s Paris, which post–WWI hoisted the likes of Sidney Bechet, Kenny Clarke, Bud Powell and Dexter Gordon.

The *chanson française* was revived in the 1930s by Piaf and Charles Trenet. In the 1950s the Left Bank cabarets nurtured *chansonniers* (cabaret singers) such as Léo Ferré, Georges Brassens, Claude Nougaro, Jacques Brel and Serge Gainsbourg.

French pop music has evolved massively since the 1960s *yéyé* (imitative rock) days of Johnny Halliday. Particularly strong is world music, from Algerian *rai* and other North African music (artists include Natacha Atlas) to Senegalese *mbalax* (Youssou N'Dour) and

West Indian *zouk* (Kassav, Zouk Machine). One musician who combines many of these elements is Paris-born Manu Chao.

Another hot musical export is Parisian electronic music from bands such as Daft Punk and Air. French rap was spearheaded in the 1990s by Senegal-born Paris-reared rapper MC Solaar, and today is a popular genre in its own right.

Architecture

Southern France is the place to find France's Gallo-Roman legacy: at the Pont du Gard (p377), amphitheatres in Nîmes and Arles and the theatre at Orange.

Several centuries later, architects adopted Gallo-Roman architectural elements to create *roman* (Romanesque) masterpieces such as Poitier's Église Notre Dame la Grande (p320).

Impressive 12th-century Gothic structures include Avignon's massive pontifical palace (p361) and the seminal cathedral at Chartres (p287).

Under Napoleon, many of Paris' best-known sights – the Arc de Triomphe, the Arc du Carrousel at the Louvre and the Assemblée Nationale building – were designed.

Art Nouveau (1850–1910) combined iron, brick, glass and ceramics in new ways. See for yourself in Paris's noodle-like metro entrances and in the Musée d'Orsay (p272).

French political leaders have long sought to immortalise themselves by building public edifices. Georges Pompidou commissioned the once-reviled – now much-revered – Centre Beaubourg (p273) in Paris while François Mitterrand commissioned several contemporary architectural landmarks, including IM Pei's glass pyramid (p273) at the Louvre.

Painting

An extraordinary flowering of artistic talent occurred in 19th- and 20th-century France. The Impressionists, who endeavoured to capture the ever-changing aspects of reflected light, included Edouard Manet, Claude Monet, Edgar Degas, Camille Pisarro, and Pieree-Auguste Renoir.

They were followed by the likes of Paul Cézanne, Paul Gauguin and Georges Seurat. A little later the Fauves, the most famous of whom was Henri Matisse, became known for their radical use of vibrant colour.

France was also where Cubism, a form of art based on abstract and geometric representation, was pioneered by Pablo Picasso and Georges Braque.

ENVIRONMENT
The Land

Hexagon-shaped France, Western Europe's largest country, is hugged by water or mountains along each side except its northeastern boundary, a relatively flat frontier abutting Germany, Luxembourg and Belgium. Inland, five major river systems cross the country.

Mountains run riot. Europe's highest peak, Mt Blanc (4807m), spectacularly tops the French Alps which stagger along France's eastern border from Lake Geneva to the Côte d'Azur. North of Lake Geneva the gentle limestone Jura Range runs along the Swiss frontier to reach heights of around 1700m, while the rugged Pyrenees lace France's entire 450km-long border with Spain.

The ancient Massif Central covers one-sixth (91,000 sq km) of the country and is renowned for its chain of extinct volcanoes.

Wildlife

France is blessed with a rich variety of flora and fauna, with more mammalian species to see (around 110) than other country in Europe. Couple this with its 363 bird species, 30 amphibian types, 36 varieties of reptiles and 72 kinds of fish, and wildlife watchers are in paradise.

The Alps and Pyrenees shelter the marmot, the nimble *chamois* (mountain antelope) with its dark-striped head and the *bouquetin* (Alpine ibex). Red and roe deer and wild boar are common in lower-altitude forested areas.

The wolf, which disappeared from France in the 1930s, was seen in the Parc National du Mercantour in 1992. The brown bear disappeared from the Alps in the mid-1930s; no more than five remain in France today.

National Parks

The proportion of land protected in France is low relative to the country's size: six small national parks *(parcs nationaux)* fully protect just 0.8% of the country. Another 7% is protected to a substantially lesser degree by 42 *parcs naturals régionaux* (regional parks) and a further 0.4% by 136 smaller *réserves naturelles* (nature reserves).

Environmental Issues

Summer forest fires are an annual hazard; great tracts of forest burn each year. Wetlands, essential for the survival of a great number of species, are shrinking. More than two million hectares – 3% of French territory – are considered important wetlands, but only 4% of this land is protected. Hunters with dogs and guns pose an equally big threat to French animal life. Many traditional animal habitats have been destroyed by the damming of rivers to produce electricity.

FOOD & DRINK
Staples & Specialities

French cuisine has long stood apart for its great use of a variety of foods – beef, lamb, pork, poultry, fish and shellfish, cereals, vegetables and legumes – but its staple 'trinity' is bread, cheese and *charcuterie* (cured, smoked or processed meat products).

Nothing is more French than *pain* (bread). More than 80% of all French people eat it at every meal. All bakeries have long thin *baguettes* (and the similar but fatter *flûtes*) and wider loaves which are simply called *pains*. There are countless other heavenly varieties.

France has nearly 500 varieties of *fromage* (cheese). The choice on offer at a *fromagerie* (cheese shop) can be overwhelming, but *fromagers* (cheese merchants) always allow you to sample and are usually happy to advise.

Traditionally charcuterie is made only from pork, though a number of other meats – from beef and veal to chicken and goose – are used in making sausages, blood puddings, hams and other cured and salted meats. *Pâtés, terrines* and *rillettes* are essentially charcuterie and are prepared in many different ways.

REGIONAL SPECIALTIES

There are all sorts of reasons for the amazing variety of France's regional cuisine. Climatic and geographical factors have been particularly important: the hot south tends to favour olive oil, garlic and tomatoes, while the cooler, pastoral northern regions favour cream and butter. Coastal areas specialise in mussels, oysters and saltwater fish.

French cuisine is typified by certain regions, most notably Normandy, Burgundy, Périgord, Lyon and, to a lesser extent, the Loire region, Provence and Alsace. Still others such as Brittany, the Auvergne, the Basque Country, Languedoc and Corsica have made incalculable contributions to what can generically be called French food.

DRINKS

There are dozens of wine-producing regions throughout France, but the seven principal regions are Alsace, Bordeaux, Burgundy, Champagne, Languedoc-Roussillon, the Loire region and the Rhône. Areas such as Burgundy comprise many well-known districts, including Chablis, Beaujolais and Mâcon, while Bordeaux encompasses Médoc, Saint Émilion and Sauternes – to name just a few of its many subregions.

The *bière à la pression* (draft beer) is served by the *demi* (about 33cl). Northern France and Alsace produce some excellent local beers.

The most popular nonalcoholic beverages consumed in France are coffee and mineral water. If you prefer tap water (perfectly safe) rather than pricey bottled water, make sure you ask for *de l'eau* (some water), or *une carafe d'eau* (a jug of water).

The most common coffee is espresso. A small espresso, served without milk, is called *un café noir, un express* or simply *un café. Café crème* is espresso with steamed milk or cream.

Where to Eat & Drink
BISTROS & BRASSERIES

A *bistro* (often spelled *bistrot*) is not clearly defined in France. It can be simply a pub or bar with snacks and light meals, or a fully fledged restaurant. *Brasseries* – which can look very much like cafés – serve full meals, drinks and coffee from morning till late at night.

RESTAURANTS

The *restaurant* comes in many guises and price ranges in France. Generally they specialise in a particular variety of food (eg regional, traditional, Vietnamese). You can generally get an excellent French meal for under €30.

Restaurants almost always have a *carte* (menu) posted outside so you can decide before going in whether the selection and prices are to your liking. Most offer at least one fixed-price, multicourse and usually good-value meal known in French as a *menu, menu à prix fixe* or *menu du jour* (daily menu), usually offering an entrée, such as salad, paté or soup; a main dish (several meat, poultry or fish dishes, including the *plat du jour* (daily special); and a final course (cheese or dessert).

Boissons (drinks), including wine, cost extra unless the menu says *boisson comprise* (drink included), in which case you may get a beer or a glass of mineral water. If the *menu* has *vin compris* (wine included), you'll probably be served a 25cl *pichet* (jug) of wine.

Restaurant meals are almost always served with bread.

Vegetarians & Vegans
Vegetarians and vegans are not particularly well catered for; specialist vegetarian restaurants are few and far between. On the bright side, more and more restaurants are offering vegetarian choices on their set menus, and *produits biologiques* (organic products) are springing up.

PARIS

pop 2.147 million
Everyone has an opinion on Paris, whether they have travelled there or not. Other towns are quick to adopt its moniker: Maastricht styles itself the 'Paris of the Netherlands'; Melbourne is affectionately referred to as 'Paris on the Yarra'; while Bucharest, St Petersburg, Shanghai and Hanoi all lay claim to being the 'Paris of the East'.

Oft imitated, but never duplicated, Paris remains the benchmark for beauty, culture and class the world over. Even the most cynical traveller, sceptical that any city could live up to Paris' reputation, can't help but be charmed by its magnificent avenues and cosy café life, its unparalleled arts scene and energetic but composed pace. Paris is the Paris of the Parisians, the Paris of France, the one and only Paris. Nothing comes close.

HISTORY
The Parisii, a tribe of Celtic Gauls, settled the Île de la Cité in the 3rd century BC. In 508 AD, Frankish king Clovis I made Paris his seat in the newly united Gaul. Paris prospered during the Middle Ages and flourished during the Renaissance when many of city's most famous buildings were erected.

The excesses of Louis XVI and his capricious queen, Marie-Antoinette, led to an uprising of Parisians on 14 July 1789 and the storming of the Bastille prison – kick-starting the French Revolution.

In 1851 emperor Napoleon III oversaw the building of a more modern Paris, with wide boulevards, sculptured parks and a sewer system. The disastrous 1870 war with Prussia led to the emperor's capture. When the news reached Paris, the masses took to the streets, demanding that the republic be restored.

This, the Third Republic, ushered in the glittering *belle époque* (beautiful era), famed for its Art Nouveau architecture and its artistic and scientific advances. By the 1930s, Paris had become a centre for the artistic avant-garde, an era cut short by the Nazi occupation of 1940 to 1944.

ORIENTATION
Central Paris is quite small: around 9.5km (north to south) by 11km (east to west). Excluding the Bois de Boulogne and the Bois de Vincennes, its total area is 105 sq km. Within the 'oval' of central Paris, which Parisians call *intra-muros* (Latin for 'within the walls'), the Rive Droite (Right Bank) is north of the Seine, while the Rive Gauche (Left Bank) is south since the river flows east to west.

Paris is divided into 20 *arrondissements* (districts), which spiral clockwise from the centre. City addresses always include the number of the arrondissement, as streets with the same name exist in different districts.

The city has 372 metro stations and there is almost always one within 500m of where you need to go.

Maps
The most useful map of Paris is the 1:10,000-scale *Paris Plan* published by Michelin.

INFORMATION
Emergency
SOS Helpline (☎ 01 47 23 80 80, in English)
SOS Médecins (☎ 01 47 07 77 77, 0 820 332 424) Provide 24-hour house calls.
Urgences Médicales de Paris (Paris Medical Emergencies; ☎ 01 53 94 94 94, 01 48 28 40 40) Provides 24-hour house calls.

Internet Access

Some metro and RER stations offer free Internet access. Fifty post offices have Internet centres called Cyberposte Internet, they're generally open between 8am or 9am and 7pm weekdays and till noon Saturday.

The following are among the best and/or most central commercial Internet cafés in Paris.

Access Academy (Map pp274-5; ☎ 01 43 25 23 80; www.accessacademy.com, in French; 60-61 rue St-André des Arts, 6e; metro Odéon; per hr €3.50, per day/week/month €6.80/14.90/35.70; ☺ 8-2am) This is France's largest Internet café, with 400 screens in the heart of St-Germain.

XS Arena Les Halles (Map pp274-5; ☎ 01 40 13 02 60; 43 rue Sébastopol, 1er; metro Les Halles) Just down from the Forum des Halles.

XS Arena Luxembourg (Map pp274-5; ☎ 01 43 44 55 55; 17 rue Soufflot, 5e; metro Luxembourg; per 1/2/3/4/5 hrs €3/6/8/10/12; ☺ 24hr) This mini-chain of Internet cafés is bright, buzzy and open round the clock.

Internet Resources

Metropole Paris (www.metropoleparis.com) Excellent online magazine in English.
Paris Pages (www.paris.org) Good links to museums and cultural events.
Paris tourist office (www.paris-touristoffice.com) Super site with more links than you'll ever need.

Laundry

There's a *laverie libre-service* (self-service laundrette) around every corner in Paris; your hotel or hostel can point you to one in the neighbourhood.

Left Luggage

All the train stations have left-luggage offices or lockers. Most are closed from about 11.15pm to about 6.30am.

Medical Services

There are some 50 *assistance publique* (public health service) hospitals in Paris. Major hospitals include:

American Hospital (Map pp270-1; ☎ 01 46 41 25 25; www.american-hospital.org; 63 blvd Victor Hugo, 92200 Neuilly-sur-Seine; metro Pont de Levallois Bécon) Offers emergency 24-hour medical and dental care.
Hertford British Hospital (Map pp270-1; ☎ 01 46 39 22 22; http://hbh.free.fr; 3 rue Barbès, 92300 Levallois-Perret; metro Anatole France) Less expensive English-speaking option than the American Hospital.

Money

In general, post offices in Paris can offer the best exchange rates, and accept banknotes in various currencies as well as travellers cheques issued by American Express or Visa. The commission for travellers cheques is 1.5% (minimum about €4).

Commercial banks usually charge a stiff €3 to €4.50 per foreign-currency transaction. The rates offered vary, so it pays to compare. In Paris, bureaux de change are faster and easier, open longer and give better rates than most banks. Some good central choices:

Best Change (Map pp274-5; ☎ 01 42 21 46 05; 21 rue du Roule, 1er; metro Louvre Rivoli; ☺ 10am-1pm & 2-7pm Mon-Sat) This bureau de change is three blocks southwest of Forum des Halles.
Bureau de Change (Map pp270-1; ☎ 01 42 25 38 14; 25 av des Champs-Élysées, 8e; metro Franklin D Roosevelt; ☺ 9am-8pm)
Thomas Cook (Map pp270-1; ☎ 01 47 20 25 14; 125 av des Champs-Élysées, 8e; metro Charles de Gaulle-Étoile; ☺ 9.15am-8.30pm)

Post

Most post offices (*bureaux de poste*) in Paris are open 8am to 7pm weekdays and 8am or 9am till noon on Saturday. *Tabacs* (tobacconists) usually sell postage stamps.

The **main post office** (Map pp274-5; ☎ 01 40 28 76 00; 52 rue du Louvre, 1er; metro Sentier or Les Halles; ☺ 24hr) opens round the clock for basic services such as sending letters and picking up poste restante mail (window Nos 5 to 7; €0.46 per letter). Other services, including currency exchange, are available during regular opening hours.

Tourist Information

Office de Tourisme et de Congrès de Paris (Paris Convention & Visitors Bureau; Map pp270-1; ☎ 0 892 683 3000; www.paris-touristoffice.com; 25-27 rue des Pyramides, 1er; metro Pyramides; ☺ 9am-8pm Apr-Oct, 9am-8pm Mon-Sat & 11am-7pm Sun Nov-Mar) This main branch is about 500m northwest of the Louvre. Closed 1 May only.

DANGERS & ANNOYANCES

Paris is generally a safe city. You'll notice that women *do* travel alone on the metro at night in most areas. Metro stations that are probably best avoided late at night include: Châtelet-Les Halles; Château Rouge in Montmartre; Gare du Nord; Strasbourg St-Denis; Réaumur Sébastopol; and Montparnasse Bienvenüe.

FRANCE

PARIS

See Montmartre Map (p281)

See Central Paris Map (pp274-5)

SIGHTS & ACTIVITIES	(pp272-7)
Arc de Triomphe	14 B3
Bateaux Mouches	15 B3
Catacombes	16 D6
Eiffel Tower	17 B4
Fat Tire Bike Tours Office	18 B4
Grand Palais	19 C3
Hôtel des Invalides	20 C4
Jardins du Trocadéro	21 B4
Musée d'Orsay	22 C4
Musée Rodin	23 C4
Parc de Bercy	24 G6
Petit Palais	25 C3
École Militaire	26 B4

SLEEPING	(pp277-80)
Auberge de Jeunesse Jules Ferry	27 F3
Auberge de Jeunesse Le D'Artagnan	28 H4
Hôtel Britannia	29 D2
Hôtel de l'Espérance	30 E5
Hôtel Eldorado	31 C2
Hôtel Favart	32 D3
Hôtel Français	33 E2
Hôtel La Vieille France	34 E2

Maison Internationale des Jeunes pour la Culture et la Paix	35 G4
Peace & Love Hostel	36 F2
Sibour Hôtel	37 E2

EATING	(pp280-2)
Franprix	38 G6
Le Dôme	39 D5

DRINKING	(pp282-3)
Gibus	40 F3
Le Batofar	41 F6
Le Cithéa	42 F3

ENTERTAINMENT	(pp283-4)
Palais Garnier	43 D3

SHOPPING	(p284)
Fnac Montparnasse	44 C5
Galeries Lafayette	45 D3
Le Bon Marché	46 C4

TRANSPORT	(pp284-6)
Aérogare des Invalides	47 C3
Gare Routière Internationale de Paris Galliéni	48 H3
OTU Voyages	49 D5

FRANCE

0 _____ 1 km
0 _____ 0.8 miles

E   **F**   **G**   **H**

R de la Chapelle

R Ordener

Blvd Barbès

Stephenson

Av de Flandre

Galerie de la Villette

Stade
Jules
Ladoumègue

Parc
de la Villette

Porte
de
Pantin

Square
Méhul

LA
GOUTTE
D'OR

Square
de la
Marseillaise

Cimetière
du Pré St
Gervais

Stade
Charles
Auray

Gare
du
Nord

R du Faubourg St Denis

R du Faubourg St Martin

Cimetière
de la
Villette

Blvd Sérurier

Place
Henri
Sellier

Cimetière
de
Pantin

34

36

5

Parc des
Buttes
Chaumont

Porte du
Pré St
Gervais

Cimetière
des
Lilas

R Marcin

Blvd de Magenta

33

R La Fayette

Gare
de
l'Est

37

R du Faubourg du Temple

St
Louis

R Claude
Velléraux

Blvd de la Villette

R Botzaris

R de Mouzaïa

Port
des
Lilas

Blvd de Sébastopol

Parc
de
Belleville

Belleville
Market

BELLEVILLE

R le Vau

Av Ibsen

Rue
Montorgueil
Market

R Beaubourg

R du Faubourg du Temple

Blvd du Temple

27

40

Av Parmentier

42

Av de la République

Av de Ménilmontant

Blvd de Ménilmontant

Av Gambetta

Gare Routière
Internationale
Paris-Galliéni

48

R Belgrand

Av Capitaine

R de Turenne

MARAIS

R Richard Lenoir

Square
de la
Roquette

Cimetière
du Père
Lachaise

R des Pyrénées

Centre
Sportif

28

Stade de
la Porte
de Bagnolet

Blvd Davout

Théâtre
Musical
de Paris

Théâtre
de
la Ville

Île
de
la Cité

Square R
Viviani

Île St
Louis

Blvd Henri IV

Blvd de la Bastille

Av Ledru Rollin

Blvd Voltaire

Blvd de Charonne

Stade
Louis
Lumière

R des Écoles

Q Henri IV

R de Turenne

R du Faubourg St Antoine

35

Blvd de Lyon

Jardin
des
Plantes

R Lacépède

Q St Bernard

Av Daumesnil

Gare
de
Lyon

Blvd Diderot

R de Bercy

R de Reuilly

R de Charenton

R Claude
Bernard

Gare
d'Austerlitz

Q d'Austerlitz

Blvd de
Bercy

Cimetière
sud de
St Mandé

30

Blvd St Marcel

Université Paris VI
Centre Hospitalier
Universitaire
Chevaleret

Le
Parc de
Bercy

38

41

24

Blvd
Poniatowski

Île de
Bercy

Parc
Zoologique

Île de
Reuilly

Av des Gobelins

Blvd de l'Hôpital

François

R Joseph Kessel

Lac Daumesnil

Blvd Vincent Auriol

Mauriac

Bois
de
Vincennes

Parc
de
Choisy

R de Tolbiac

R de Palay

et Panhard
et Levassor

Q de Bercy

Blvd
Masséna

Av de Gravelle

Av de Choisy

Av d'Ivry

INFORMATION	
American Hospital	**1** A1
Australian Embassy	**2** B4
Bureau de Change	**3** C3
Canadian Embassy	**4** B3
Club Alpin Française	**5** F2
German Embassy	**6** C3
Hertford British Hospital	**7** A1
Irish Embassy	**8** B3
Italian Embassy	**9** C4
Netherlands Embassy	**10** C4
New Zealand Embassy	**11** A3
Post Office	**12** B3
Thomas Cook	**13** B3

FRANCE

SIGHTS
Left Bank
MUSÉE D'ORSAY

The spectacular **Musée d'Orsay** (Orsay Museum; Map pp270-1; ☎ 01 40 49 48 84; www.musee-orsay.fr; 1 rue de la Légion d'Honneur, 7e; metro Musée d'Orsay or Solférino; adult/senior & 18-25 yrs/under 18 yrs €7/5/free, everyone free 1st Sun of month; ☺ 9am-6pm Tue, Wed, Fri & Sat, to 9.45pm Thu, to 6pm Sun late Jun-Sep, 10am-6pm Tue, Wed, Fri & Sat, 10am-9.45pm Thu, 9am-6pm Sun Oct-late Jun), housed in a former train station (1900) facing the Seine from quai Anatole France, displays France's national collection of paintings, sculptures, *objets d'art* and other works produced between the 1840s and 1914, including the fruits of the Impressionist, post-Impressionist and Art Nouveau movements. Many visitors head straight to the upper level (lit by a skylight) to see the famous Impressionist paintings by Monet, Renoir, Pissarro, Sisley, Degas and Manet and the post-Impressionist works by Gauguin, Cézanne, Van Gogh, Seurat and Matisse, but there's also a great deal to see on the ground floor, including some early works by Manet, Monet, Renoir and Pissarro.

EIFFEL TOWER

The **Tour Eiffel** (Eiffel Tower; Map pp270-1; ☎ 01 44 11 23 23; www.tour-eiffel.fr; metro Champ de Mars-Tour Eiffel or Bir Hakeim; lifts to 1st/2nd/3rd platforms €4/7.30/10.40, children 3-11 yrs €2.20/4/5.70, stairs to 1st & 2nd platforms only €3.50; ☺ lifts 9am-midnight mid-Jun–Aug, 9.30am-11pm Sep–mid-Jun, stairs 9am-midnight mid-Jun–Aug, 9.30am-6.30pm Sep–mid-Jun) faced opposition from Paris' artistic and literary elite when it was built for the 1889 Exposition Universelle (World Fair), marking the centenary of the Revolution. The 'metal asparagus', as some Parisians snidely called it, was almost torn down in 1909 but was spared as it proved an ideal platform for the transmitting antennas needed for the new science of radiotelegraphy.

CATACOMBES

In 1785, the hygienic (not to mention aesthetic) problems posed by Paris' overflowing cemeteries were solved by exhuming the bones and storing them in the tunnels of three disused quarries. One, created in 1810, is now known as the **Catacombes** (Map pp270-1; ☎ 01 43 22 47 63; www.paris.fr/musees/musee_carnavalet, in French; 1 pl Denfert Rochereau, 14e; metro Denfert Rochereau; adult/senior & student/14-25 yrs/under 14 yrs €5/3.30/2.60/free; ☺ 10am-5pm Tue-Sun). After descending 20m (130 steps) from street level, visitors follow 1.6km of underground corridors stacked with the bones and skulls of millions of Parisians.

MUSÉE NATIONAL DU MOYEN AGE

The **Musée National du Moyen Age** (National Museum of the Middle Ages; Map pp274-5; ☎ 01 53 73 78 16, 01 53 73 78 00; www.musee-moyenage.fr, in French; Thermes de Cluny, 6 pl Paul Painlevé, 5e; metro Cluny-La Sorbonne or St-Michel; adult/senior, student & 18-25 yrs €5.50/4, everyone free 1st Sun of month; ☺ 9.15am-5.45pm Wed-Mon), sometimes called the Musée de Cluny, is housed in two structures: the **frigidarium** (cooling room) and other remains of Gallo-Roman baths dating from around AD 200, and the late-15th-century Hôtel de Cluny, considered the finest example of medieval civil architecture in Paris. The spectacular displays include statuary, illuminated manuscripts, arms, furnishings and objects made of gold, ivory and enamel.

PANTHÉON

The domed landmark now known simply as the **Pantheon** (Map pp274-5; ☎ 01 44 32 18 00; www.monum.fr; pl du Panthéon, 5e; metro Luxembourg; adult/18-25 yrs/under 18 yrs €7/4.50/free, everyone free 1st Sun of month Oct-Mar; ☺ 9.30am-6.30pm Apr-Sep, 10am-6.15pm Oct-Mar) was commissioned around 1750 as an abbey church dedicated to Ste-Geneviève, but because of financial and structural problems it wasn't completed until 1789. The 80-odd permanent residents of the crypt include Voltaire, Jean-Jacques Rousseau, Victor Hugo, Émile Zola, Jean Moulin and Nobel Prize-winner Marie Curie.

JARDIN DU LUXEMBOURG

When the weather is fine Parisians of all ages flock to the formal terraces and chestnut groves of the 23-hectare **Jardin du Luxembourg** (Luxembourg Garden; Map pp270-1; metro Luxembourg; 🕑 7am-9.30pm Apr-Oct, 8am-sunset Mar-Nov) to read, relax and sunbathe.

MUSÉE RODIN

The **Musée Rodin** (Rodin Museum; Map pp270-1; ☎ 01 44 18 61 10; www.musee-rodin.fr; 77 rue de Varenne, 7e; metro Varenne; adult/seniors & 18-25 yrs/under 18 yrs €5/3/free, everyone free 1st Sun of month, garden only €1; 🕑 9.30am-5.45pm Apr-Sep, to 4.45pm Oct-Mar) is both a sublime museum and one of the most relaxing spots in the city, with a lovely **garden** full of sculptures and shade trees.

HÔTEL DES INVALIDES

The **Hôtel des Invalides** (Map pp270-1; metro Varenne or La Tour Maubourg) was built in the 1670s by Louis XIV to provide housing for 4000 *invalides* (disabled war veterans). On 14 July 1789, a mob forced its way into the building and, after fierce fighting, seized 28,000 rifles before heading on to the prison at Bastille, and revolution.

CHAMP DE MARS

Running southeast from the Eiffel Tower, the grassy **Champ de Mars** (Field of Mars; Map pp270-1; metro Champ de Mars-Tour Eiffel or École Militaire), named after the Roman god of war, was originally a parade ground for the cadets of the 18th-century **École Militaire** (Military Academy). This is a vast, French-classical building (1772) at the southeast end of the park, which counted Napoleon among its graduates.

The Islands

ÎLE DE LA CITÉ

The site of the first settlement in Paris around the 3rd century BC and later the Roman town of Lutèce (Lutetia), the **Île de la Cité** (Map pp274-5) remained the centre of royal and ecclesiastical power even after the city spread to both banks of the Seine during the Middle Ages.

CATHÉDRALE DE NOTRE DAME DE PARIS

The **Cathédrale de Notre Dame de Paris** (Cathedral of Our Lady of Paris; Map pp274-5; ☎ 01 42 34 56 10; pl du Parvis Notre Dame, 4e; metro Cité; 🕑 8am-6.45pm Mon-Fri, to 7.45pm Sat & Sun) is the true heart of Paris; in fact, distances from Paris to every part of metropolitan France are measured from **place du Parvis Notre Dame**, the square

in front of Notre Dame, and a bronze star, set in the pavement across the street from the cathedral's main entrance, marks the exact location of **point zéro des routes de France** (point zero of French roads).

Notre Dame is not only a masterpiece of French Gothic architecture but has also been the focus of Catholic Paris for seven centuries. Built on a site occupied by earlier churches – and, a millennium before that, a Gallo-Roman temple – it was begun in 1163 and largely completed by the middle of the 14th century.

STE-CHAPELLE

The most exquisite of Paris' Gothic monuments, **Ste-Chapelle** (Holy Chapel; Map pp274-5; ☎ 01 53 40 60 97; www.monum.fr; 4 blvd du Palais, 1er; metro Cité; adult/18-25 yrs/under 18 yrs €6.10/4.10/free, everyone free 1st Sun of month Oct-Mar, joint ticket with Conciergerie €10.40/7.40; 🕑 9.30am-6pm Mar-Oct, 9am-5pm Nov-Feb) is tucked within the walls of the **Palais de Justice** (Law Courts). Built in just under three years, Ste-Chapelle was consecrated in 1248. The chapel was conceived by Louis IX to house his personal collection of sacred relics.

Right Bank

MUSÉE DU LOUVRE

The vast Palais du Louvre was constructed as a fortress by Philippe-Auguste in the early 13th century and rebuilt in the mid-16th century. In 1793, the Convention turned it into the **Musée du Louvre** (Louvre Museum; Map pp274-5; ☎ 01 40 20 53 17 or ☎ 01 40 20 51 51; www.louvre.fr; metro Palais Royal-Musée du Louvre; permanent collections/permanent collections & temporary exhibits €7.50/11.50, after 3pm & all day Sun €5/9.50, everyone free on 1st Sun of month; 🕑 9am-6pm Thu-Sun, 9.45pm Mon & Wed).

The paintings, sculptures and artefacts on display include works of art and artisanship from all over Europe and important collections of Assyrian, Etruscan, Greek, Coptic and Islamic art and antiquities. Traditionally the Louvre's raison d'être is to present Western art from the Middle Ages to about the year 1848 (at which point the Musée d'Orsay takes over).

CENTRE GEORGES POMPIDOU

The **Centre National d'Art et de Culture Georges Pompidou** (Georges Pompidou National Centre of Art & Culture; Map pp274-5; ☎ 01 44 78 12 33; www.centre pompidou.fr; pl Georges Pompidou, 4e; metro Rambuteau) also known as the Centre Beaubourg, has

CENTRAL PARIS

INFORMATION

Access Academy	1 B4
Best Change	2 C2
Main Post Office	3 C1
Office de Tourisme et Congrès de Paris	4 A1
XS Arena Les Halles	5 D2
XS Arena Luxembourg	6 B5

SIGHTS & ACTIVITIES (pp272-7)

Cathédral de Notre Dame de Paris	7 D4
Centre Georges Pompidou	8 D2
Conciergerie Entrance	9 C3
Ed l'Epicier Supermarket	10 D3
Entrance to Opéra Bastille	11 G4
Musée du Louvre	12 B2
Musée National du Moyen Âge-Thermes de Cluny	13 C4
Musée Picasso	14 F2
Notre Dame North Tower Entrance	15 D4
Opéra Bastille Box Office	16 G4
Palais de Justice & Conciergerie	17 C3
Panthéon	18 C5
Préfecture de Police Entrance	19 C3
Ste Chapelle	20 C3
Union des centres de Rencontre Internationales de France (UCRIF)	21 D1

FRANCE

0 ——————— 400 m
0 ——————— 0.3 miles

SLEEPING 🏠 (pp277–80)
Blue Planet Hostel	22 H6
Centre International BVJ Paris-Louvre	23 B1
Centre International BVJ Paris-Quartier Latin	24 D5
Grand Hôtel du Progrès	25 C6
Hôtel Caron de Beaumarchais	26 E3
Hôtel Castex	27 F4
Hôtel de la Bretonnerie	28 E2
Hôtel de la Herse d'Or	29 G4
Hôtel de Lille Pélican	30 B1
Hôtel de Nice	31 E3
Hôtel Esmeralda	32 C4
Hôtel Gay Lussac	33 C6
Hôtel Henri IV	34 B3
Hôtel Minerve	35 D5
Hôtel St Honoré	36 C2
MIJE Fauconnier	37 E4
MIJE Fourcy	38 E3
MIJE Maubuisson	39 E3
Young & Happy Hostel	40 D6

EATING 🍴 (pp280–2)
Bacteria Alley Restaurants	41 C4
Bouillon Racine	42 C4
Café Marly	43 B2
Chez Léna et Mimille	44 D6
Crèmerie des Carmes (Fromagerie)	45 D4
Food Market	(see 45)
Franprix	46 C2
Franprix Marais	47 D2
Franprix Supermarket	48 E3
Fromagerie G Millet	49 F3
L'Ambassade d'Auvergne	50 D1
L'Épi d'Or	51 B1
Le Petit Mâchon	52 B2
Le Petit Picard	53 E2
Les Galopins	54 H3
Monoprix Supermarket	55 F3
Perraudin	56 C5

DRINKING 🍷 (p282)
Café de Flore	57 A3
L'Apparement Café	58 F2
Le Fumoir	59 B2
Le Piano Vache	60 C5
Le Vieux Chêne	61 D6
Les Deux Magots	62 A4

ENTERTAINMENT (pp283–4)
Le Caveau de la Huchette	63 C4
Opéra Bastille	64 G4

SHOPPING 🛍 (p284)
Forum des Halles	65 C2

TRANSPORT (pp284–6)
Eurolines Office	66 C4
Noctambus (Night Bus) Stops	67 D3
OTU Voyages	68 D2

FRANCE

amazed and delighted visitors since it was inaugurated in 1977, not just for its outstanding collection of modern art, but for its radical architectural statement; it was among the first buildings to have its 'insides' turned outside. The **Forum du Centre Pompidou** (admission free; ☾ 11am-10pm Wed-Mon), the open space at ground level, has temporary exhibits.

The 4th and 5th floors are taken up by the **Musée National d'Art Moderne** (MNAM, National Museum of Modern Art; adult/senior & 18-25 yrs/under 18 yrs €7/5/free, everyone free 1st Sun of month, day pass incl MNAM & temporary exhibits €10/8, permanent collection ☾ 11am-9pm Wed-Mon), which exhibits art dating from 1905 onward and including the work of the Surrealists and Cubists as well as pop art and contemporary works.

HÔTEL DE VILLE
Gutted during the Paris Commune of 1871, Paris' **Hôtel de Ville** (city hall; Map pp274-5; ☎ 0 820 007 575; www.paris.fr; pl de l'Hôtel de Ville, 4e; metro Hôtel de Ville; ☾ 9.30am-6pm to 7pm Mon-Sat) was rebuilt in the neo-Renaissance style (1874–82). The Hôtel de Ville faces the majestic **place de l'Hôtel de Ville**, used from the Middle Ages to the 19th century to stage many of Paris' celebrations, rebellions, book burnings and public executions.

MUSÉE PICASSO
The **Musée Picasso** (Picasso Museum; Map pp274-5; ☎ 01 42 71 25 21; 5 rue de Thorigny, 3e; metro St-Paul or Chemin Vert; adult/18-25 yrs/everyone Sun €6.70/5.20/5.20, everyone free 1st Sun of month; ☾ 9.30am-6pm Wed-Mon Apr-Sep, to 5.30pm Wed-Mon Oct-Mar), housed in the mid-17th-century Hôtel Salé, is one of Paris' best loved art museums and includes more than 3500 of the *grand maître's* works.

PLACE DE LA BASTILLE
The Bastille, built during the 14th century as a fortified royal residence, is the most famous monument in Paris that no longer exists; the notorious prison was demolished by a Revolutionary mob on 14 July 1789. The **place de la Bastille** (Map pp274-5; metro Bastille) in the 12e, where the prison once stood, is now a very busy traffic roundabout.

JARDINS DU TROCADÉRO
The **Jardins du Trocadéro** (Trocadero Gardens; Map pp270-1; metro Trocadéro), whose fountains and statue garden are grandly illuminated at night, are accessible across Pont d'Iéna from the Eiffel Tower.

ÉTOILE & CHAMPS-ÉLYSÉES
A dozen avenues radiate from the world's largest traffic roundabout, **place de l'Étoile** (Map pp270-1; metro Charles de Gaulle Étoile) – officially called place Charles de Gaulle; first among these is the av des Champs-Elysées. This broad boulevard, whose name refers to the 'Elysian Fields', where happy souls dwelt after death according to Greek mythology, links place de la Concorde with the Arc de Triomphe. Symbolising the style and *joie de vivre* of Paris since the mid-19th century, the avenue remains a popular tourist destination.

ARC DE TRIOMPHE
The **Arc de Triomphe** (Triumphal Arch; Map pp270-1; ☎ 01 55 37 73 77 or ☎ 01 44 95 02 10; www.monum. fr; metro Charles de Gaulle-Étoile; viewing platform adult/18-25 yrs €7/4.50, admission free for under 18 & everyone on 1st Sun of month; ☾ 9.30am-11pm Apr-Sep, 10am-10.30pm Oct-Mar) is 2.2km northwest of place de la Concorde in the middle of place Charles de Gaulle (or place de l'Étoile). Commissioned in 1806 by Napoleon to commemorate his imperial victories, it remained unfinished when he started losing battles and then entire wars. It was not completed until 1836.

GRAND & PETIT PALAIS
Erected for the 1900 Exposition Universelle, the **Grand Palais** (Great Palace; Map pp270-1; ☎ 01 44 13 17 17; www.rmn.fr; 3 av du Général Eisenhower, 8e; metro Champs-Élysées Clemenceau; adult without/with booking €9/10, student & senior €7/8, everyone Mon €7/8, free 1st Sun of month; ☾ without booking 1-8pm Thu-Mon, to 10pm Wed, with booking from 10am) houses the **Galeries Nationales du Grand Palais** beneath its huge, Art Nouveau glass roof.

PLACE DE LA CONCORDE
Place de la Concorde (Map pp270-1; metro Concorde) was laid out between 1755 and 1775. The 3300-year-old pink granite **obelisk** with the gilded top in the middle of the square once stood in the Temple of Ramses at Thebes (today's Luxor); Muhammad Ali, viceroy and pasha of Egypt gave it to France in 1831.

MONTMARTRE & PIGALLE
During the late 19th and early 20th centuries the bohemian lifestyle of **Montmartre** (Map p281)

in the 18e attracted a number of important writers and artists, including Picasso, who lived at the studio called **Bateau Lavoir** (Map p281; 11bis Émile Goudeau) from 1908 to 1912. Montmartre retains an upbeat ambience that all the tourists in the world couldn't spoil.

Only a few blocks southwest of the tranquil, residential streets of Montmartre is lively, neon-lit **Pigalle** (Map p281), 9e and 18e, a red-light district that also boasts plenty of trendy nightspots, including clubs and cabarets.

BASILIQUE DU SACRÉ CŒUR

The **Basilique du Sacré Cœur** (Basilica of the Sacred Heart; Map p281; ☎ 01 53 41 89 00; www.sacre-coeur -montmartre.com; pl du Parvis du Sacré Cœur, 18e; metro Anvers; ⏰ 6am-11pm), perched at the very top of the Butte de Montmartre (Montmartre Hill), was built from contributions pledged by Parisian Catholics as an act of contrition after the humiliating Franco-Prussian War of 1870 to 1871. Construction began in 1873, but the basilica was not consecrated until 1919. Some 234 spiralling steps lead you to the basilica's **dome** (admission €5; ⏰ 9am-7pm Apr-Sep, to 6pm Oct-Mar), which affords one of Paris' most spectacular panoramas.

CIMETIÈRE DU PÈRE LACHAISE

The world's most visited graveyard, the **Cimetière Père Lachaise** (Père Lachaise Cemetery; Map pp270-1; ☎ 01 55 25 82 10; metro Philippe Auguste, Gambetta or Père Lachaise; ⏰ 8am-6pm Mon-Fri, 8.30am-6pm Sat, 9am-6pm Sun mid-Mar–early Nov; 8am-5.30pm Mon-Fri, 8.30am-5.30pm Sat, 9am-5.30pm Sun early Nov–mid-Mar) opened its one-way doors in 1804. Its 70,000 ornate – even ostentatious – tombs form a verdant, open-air sculpture garden. Among the mortal remains of the one million people buried here are Chopin, Molière, Oscar Wilde, Balzac, Proust, Gertrude Stein, Colette, Pissarro, Seurat, Modigliani, Sarah Bernhardt, Yves Montand, Delacroix, Edith Piaf and even the immortal 12th-century lovers, Abélard and Héloïse. One particularly frequented grave is that of 1960s rock star **Jim Morrison** (1943–71), who is buried in division No 6.

TOURS

An English-speaking company that consistently gets rave reviews from readers is **Fat Tire Bike Tours** (Map pp270-1; ☎ 01 56 58 10 54; www .fattirebiketoursparis.com; 24 rue Edgar Faure, 15e; metro La Motte-Piquet Grenelle; ⏰ 9am-7pm), offering day tours of the city (adult/student €24/22) lasting about four hours from March to September.

Based on the Right Bank just east of Pont de l'Alma, **Bateaux Mouches** (Map pp270-1; ☎ 01 42 25 96 10; www.bateauxmouches.com; Port de la Conférence, 8e; metro Alma Marceau; adult/senior & child 4-12 yrs €7/4, child under 4 yrs free; ⏰ every half-hour 10am-8pm, every 20 min 8-11pm mid-Mar–mid-Nov, at 11am, 2.30pm, 4pm, 6pm & 9pm mid-Nov–mid-Mar), the most famous river boat company in Paris, runs 1000-seat tour boats.

SLEEPING

The student travel agency **OTU Voyages** (Central Paris Map pp274-5; ☎ 01 40 29 12 22, 0 825 004 024; www .otu.fr, in French; 119 rue St-Martin, 4e; metro Rambuteau; ⏰ 9.30am-6.30pm Mon-Fri, 10am-5pm Sat; Luxembourg Map pp270-1; ☎ 0 825 004 027; 39 av Georges Bernanos, 5e; metro Port Royal; ⏰ 9am-6.30pm Mon-Fri, 10am-noon & 1.15-5pm Sat), directly across the *parvis* (square) from the Centre Pompidou, can *always* find you accommodation.

An agency that arranges bed and breakfast accommodation in Paris and gets good reviews from readers is **Alcôve & Agapes** (☎ 01 44 85 06 05; fax 01 44 85 06 14; info@paris-bedandbreakfast .com). Expect to pay between €45 and €100 for a double. Prices for budget accommodation include shared bathroom unless stated. All mid-range and top end accommodation has en-suite bathroom unless stated.

Louvre & Les Halle

BUDGET

Centre International BVJ Paris-Louvre (Map pp274-5; ☎ 01 53 00 90 90; bvj@wanadoo.fr; 20 rue Jean-Jacques Rousseau, 1er; metro Louvre-Rivoli; dm €25, d per person €28; ⌧) This modern, 200-bed hostel run by the Bureau des Voyages de la Jeunesse, has bunks in a single-sex room for two to eight people; rates include breakfast. Guests should be aged under 35.

Hôtel de Lille Pélican (Map pp274-5; ☎ 01 42 33 33 42; 8 rue du Pélican, 1er; metro Palais Royal-Musée du Louvre; s/d/tr with washbasin €35/43/65, d with shower €50; ⌧) This old-fashioned but clean 13-room hotel down a quiet side street has recently been given a face-lift. The helpful manager speaks good English.

MID-RANGE

Between the Palais Royal and the Seine and at the eastern end of a very upmarket shopping

FRANCE

street, **Hôtel St-Honoré** (Map pp274-5; ☎ 01 42 36 20 38; paris@hotelsthonore.com; 85 rue St-Honoré, 1er; metro Châtelet; s/d/tw/q €59/74/83/92) offers some fairly cramped rooms and a few more spacious ones for three and four people.

Marais & Bastille
BUDGET
Maison Internationale de la Jeunesse et des Étudiants (MIJE; ☎ 01 42 74 23 45; www.mije.com) runs three hostels in attractively renovated 17th- and 18th-century *hôtels particuliers* (private mansions) in the heart of the Marais, and it's difficult to think of a better budget deal in Paris. Costs are the same for all three (see following listings); rooms are closed from noon to 3pm, and curfew is from 1am to 7am.

MIJE Le Fourcy (6 rue de Fourcy, 4e; metro St-Paul; dm with shower €27, s/d/tr €42/32/28; ✗ ⌨) This 207-bed branch is the largest of the three. There's a cheap eatery here called Le Restaurant with a three-course *menu* including a drink for €10.50 and a two-course *formule* plus drink for €8.50.

MIJE Le Fauconnier (11 rue du Fauconnier, 4e; metro St-Paul or Pont Marie; dm with shower €27, s/d/tr €42/32/28; ✗ ⌨) This 125-bed hostel is two blocks south of MIJE Le Fourcy.

MIJE Maubuisson (12 rue des Barres, 4e; metro Hôtel de Ville or Pont Marie; dm with shower €27, s/d/tr €42/32/28; ✗ ⌨) This 103-bed place – and the pick of the three in our opinion – is half a block south of the *mairie* (town hall) of the 4e.

Maison Internationale des Jeunes pour la Culture et la Paix (Map pp270-1; ☎ 01 43 71 99 21; mij .cp@wanadoo.fr; 4 rue Titon, 11e; metro Faidherbe Chaligny; dm €20; ✗ ⌨) This hostel with 166 beds is 1.3km east of place de la Bastille. It offers accommodation in comfortable but rather institutional dormitory rooms for up to eight people.

Hôtel de la Herse d'Or (Map pp274-5; ☎ 01 48 87 84 09; hotel.herse.dor@wanadoo.fr; 20 rue St-Antoine, 4e; metro Bastille; d €58/60, s/d with washbasin €38/45) This friendly, 35-room place on busy rue St-Antoine has serviceable rooms.

MID-RANGE
Hôtel de la Bretonnerie (Map pp274-5; ☎ 01 48 87 77 63; www.bretonnerie.com; 22 rue Ste-Croix de la Bretonnerie, 4e; metro Hôtel de Ville; s & d €110-145, tr & q €170, ste €180-205) A charming three-star hotel in the heart of the Marais nightlife area dating

from the 17th century. Decorations in each of the 22 rooms and seven suites are unique and some rooms have four poster and canopy beds.

Hôtel Caron de Beaumarchais (Map pp274-5; ☎ 01 42 72 34 12; www.carondebeaumarchais.com; 12 rue Vieille du Temple, 4e; metro St-Paul; d €120-152; ✗) You have to see this award-winning themed hotel to believe it. The hotel has a prized 18th-century pianoforte, gilded mirrors and candelabras in its front room and 44 stylish (though somewhat dated) guestrooms.

Hôtel Castex (Map pp274-5; ☎ 01 42 72 31 52; www.castexhotel.com; 5 rue Castex, 4e; metro Bastille; s €95-115, d €120-140, ste €190-220; ✗) This former budget hotel, equidistant from Bastille and the Marais, had a major face-lift in 2003 and has retained some of its 17th-century elements

Hôtel de Nice (Map pp274-5; ☎ 01 42 78 55 29; fax 01 42 78 36 07; 42bis rue de Rivoli, 4e; metro Hôtel de Ville; s/d/tr €65/100/120) This is an especially warm, family-run place with 23 comfortable rooms. Some rooms have balconies high above busy rue de Rivoli. Reception is on the 1st floor.

The Islands
BUDGET
Popular for its terrific location on the tip of the Île de la Cité, **Hôtel Henri IV** (Map pp274-5; ☎ 01 43 54 44 53; 25 pl Dauphine, 1er; metro Pont Neuf or Cité; s €24-31, d €31-36, tr with washbasin €42, d with shower €44, d with shower & toilet €55/68) is a decrepit place with 20 tattered and worn rooms. But it would be impossible to find something this romantic at such a price elsewhere. Hall showers cost €2.50. Breakfast included. Book well in advance.

Latin Quarter & Jardin des Plantes
BUDGET
Centre International BVJ Paris-Quartier Latin (Map pp274-5; ☎ 01 43 29 34 80; bvj@wanadoo.fr; 44 rue des Bernardins, 5e; metro Maubert Mutualité; 1-/2-/6-bed per person €35/28/26; ✗) This 38-bed Left Bank hostel is a branch of the Centre International BVJ Paris-Louvre (see p277) and has the same rules. All the rooms here have en-suite showers and telephones.

Grand Hôtel du Progrès (Map pp274-5; ☎ 01 43 54 53 18; fax 01 56 24 87 80; 50 rue Gay Lussac, 5e; metro Luxembourg; s/d/tr €35/42/55, s/d with shower & toilet €46/54) This budget, 26-room hotel has been a favourite of students for generations.

There are washbasin-equipped singles and large, old-fashioned doubles with a view and morning sun. Rates include breakfast. Hall showers are free.

Young & Happy Hostel (Map pp274-5; ☎ 01 47 07 47 07; www.youngandhappy.fr; 80 rue Mouffetard, 5e; metro Pl Monge; dm €20-22, d per person €23-25; ✕ 🖳) A friendly though slightly tatty place in the centre of the most happening area of the Latin Quarter. The 2am curfew is strictly enforced. Beds are in smallish rooms for two to four people. In summer, the best way to get a bed is to stop by at about 9am.

MID-RANGE

Hôtel Esmeralda (Map pp274-5; ☎ 01 43 54 19 20; fax 01 40 51 00 68; 4 rue St-Julien le Pauvre, 5e; metro St-Michel; s with washbasin/shower/bath €35/65/80, d with shower & toilet €80, d with bath & toilet €85-95, tr/q from €110/180) This renovated 19-room inn, tucked away in a quiet street with full views of Notre Dame, has been well and truly discovered, so book ahead.

Hôtel de l'Espérance (Map pp270-1; ☎ 01 47 07 10 99; hotel.esperance@wanadoo.fr; 15 rue Pascal, 5e; metro Censier Daubenton; s with shower/bath & toilet €68/76, d with shower/bath & toilet €73/84, tw €84, tr €99) The 'Hotel of Hope', just a couple of minutes' walk south of lively rue Mouffetard, is a quiet and immaculately kept 38-room place with faux antique furnishings and a warm welcome.

Hôtel Gay Lussac (Map pp274-5; ☎ 01 43 54 23 96; fax 01 40 51 79 49; 29 rue Gay Lussac, 5e; metro Luxembourg; s/d €33/49, s/d with shower €55/64, s/d with shower & toilet €59/68.50, tr/q with shower & toilet €90/95) A 35-room, family-run hotel with a lot of character in the southern part of the Latin Quarter.

Hôtel Minerve (Map pp274-5; ☎ 01 43 26 26 04; www.hotel-paris-minerve.com; 13 rue des Écoles, 5e; metro Cardinal Lemoine; s with shower & toilet €79-101, d with shower €93, d with bath €109-125, tr €145; 🖳) Reception is kitted out with Oriental carpets and antique books, attractive frescoes and reproduction 18th-century wallpaper. There are 10 rooms with small balconies, eight with views of Notre Dame and two have tiny courtyards that are swooningly romantic.

Clichy & Gare St-Lazare
BUDGET

A great find: the **Hôtel Eldorado** (Map pp270-1; ☎ 01 45 22 35 21; eldoradohotel@wanadoo.fr; 18 rue des Dames, 17e; metro Pl de Clichy; s/d/tr with shower €45/60/80) is a welcoming, well-run hotel with 40 colourfully decorated rooms on a quiet street with a private garden at the back. Is this really Paris?

MID-RANGE

Hôtel Britannia (Map pp270-1; ☎ 01 42 85 36 36; fax 01 42 85 16 93; 24 rue d'Amsterdam, 9e; metro St-Lazare; s & d with shower/bath €78/85, tr €94) A 46-room place with narrow hallways but pleasant, clean rooms just opposite the Gare St-Lazare and an easy walk to the *grands magasins* on blvd Haussmann.

Hôtel Favart (Map pp270-1; ☎ 01 42 97 59 83; www .hotel-paris-favart.com; 5 rue Marivaux, 2e; metro Richelieu Drouot; s/d/tr €85/108/130) With 37 rooms facing the Opéra Comique, the Favart is a stylish Art Nouveau hotel that feels like it never let go of the *belle époque*.

Gare du Nord, Gare de l'Est & République
BUDGET

Auberge de Jeunesse Jules Ferry (Map pp270-1; ☎ 01 43 57 55 60; www.fuaj.fr; 8 blvd Jules Ferry, 11e; metro République or Goncourt; dm €19.50, d per person €20; ✕ 🖳) It's somewhat institutional and the rooms could be cleaner, but the atmosphere is relaxed. Beds are in rooms for two to six people. There is no curfew. Those without a Hostelling International card or equivalent pay an extra €3 per night.

Auberge de Jeunesse Le D'Artagnan (Map pp270-1; ☎ 01 40 32 34 56; www.fuaj.fr; 80 rue Vitruve, 20e; metro Porte de Bagnolet; dm €20.60; ✕ 🖳) Far from the centre of the action but just one metro stop from the Gare Routière Internationale de Paris-Gallieni (international bus terminal), this is the largest hostel in France, with 439 beds. The D'Artagnan has rooms with two to eight beds, big lockers, laundry facilities, a bar and cinema.

Peace & Love Hostel (Map pp270-1; ☎ 01 46 07 65 11; www.paris-hostels.com; 245 rue La Fayette, 10e; metro Jaurès or Louis Blanc; dm €17-21, d per person €21-26; 🖳) This modern-day hippy hangout is rather chaotically run with beds in small-ish, shower-equipped rooms for two to four people. There's a great kitchen and eating area and a lively ground floor bar (open till 2am).

Sibour Hôtel (Map pp270-1; ☎ 01 46 07 20 74; sibour.hotel@wanadoo.fr; 4 rue Sibour, 10e; metro Gare de l'Est; s & d with washbasin €35, s & d with toilet €40, s/d/tr/q with shower & toilet €50/58/63/80; ℗) This homely and friendly place has 45 well-kept rooms, including some old-fashioned ones. Hall showers cost €3.

Hôtel La Vieille France (Map pp270-1; ☎ 01 45 26 42 37; la.vieille.france@wanadoo.fr; 151 rue La Fayette, 10e; metro Gare du Nord; d with washbasin €42, d with shower/bath & toilet €58/64, tr €78-90) 'The Old France' is a 34-room place with relatively spacious and pleasant rooms. At least one reader has written to complain about the noise, however. Hall showers are free.

MID-RANGE

Facing the Gare de l'Est, the two-star **Hôtel Français** (Map pp270-1; ☎ 01 40 35 94 14; www.hotelfrancais.com; 13 rue du 8 Mai 1945, 10e; metro Gare de l'Est; s €77-81, d €84-91, tr €109-116; 🗷 🖳 🅿) has 71 attractive, almost luxurious, rooms (some with balconies).

Gare de Lyon, Nation & Bercy
BUDGET

The 43-room **Blue Planet Hostel** (Map pp274-5; ☎ 01 43 42 06 18; www.hostelblueplanet.com; 5 rue Hector Malot, 12e; metro Gare de Lyon; dm €18.30-21; 🖳) is very close to Gare de Lyon – convenient if you're heading south or east. Dorm beds are in rooms for three or four people. There's no curfew.

Montmartre & Pigalle
BUDGET

Hôtel Bonséjour (Map p281; ☎ 01 42 54 22 53; fax 01 42 54 25 92; 11 rue Burq, 18e; metro Abbesses; s with washbasin €22-25, d with washbasin €30-32, d with shower €38-40, tr €53) The 'Good Stay' is at the end of a quiet street in Montmartre. Some rooms (eg No 14, 23, 33, 43 & 53) have little balconies and at least one room (No 55) offers a fleeting glimpse of Sacré Coeur. It's a simple place to stay – no lift, linoleum floors – but comfortable and very friendly. The hall showers cost €2.

Le Village Hostel (Map p281; ☎ 01 42 64 22 02; www.villagehostel.fr; 20 rue d'Orsel, 18e; metro Anvers; dm/d/tr per person €20/23/21.50 Nov–mid-Mar, €21.50/25/23 mid-Mar–Oct; 🖳) 'The Village' is a fine 25-room hostel with beamed ceilings and views of Sacré Cœur. Dorm beds are in rooms for four to six people and all rooms have showers and toilet. Kitchen facilities are available, and there is a lovely outside terrace. Curfew is 2am.

Woodstock Hostel (Map p281; ☎ 01 48 78 87 76; www.woodstock.fr; 48 rue Rodier, 9e; metro Anvers; dm/d per person Oct-Mar €15/17, Apr-Sep €20/23; 🖳) Woodstock is just down the hill from raucous Pigalle in a quiet, residential quarter. Dorm beds are in rooms for four to six people and there's a kitchen for self-catering. Curfew is at 2am.

MID-RANGE

Hôtel des Arts (Map p281; ☎ 01 46 06 30 52; www.arts-hotel-paris.com; 5 rue Tholozé, 18e; metro Abbesses or Blanche; s/d/tr €64/78/94; 🅿) Part of the Logis de France group, the 'Arts Hotel' is a friendly and attractive 50-room place convenient for both Pigalle and Montmartre. Towering over it is the old-style Moulin de la Galette windmill.

Hôtel des Capucines Montmartre (Map p281; ☎ 01 42 52 89 80; fax 01 42 52 29 57; 5 rue Aristide Bruant, 18e; metro Abbesses or Blanche; s €45-50, d €54-60, tr €60-70) A decent, family-run hotel with 30 rooms on a small street awash with places to stay.

EATING

Parisian restaurants generally specialise in a particular variety of food (eg traditional or regional French, north African, Vietnamese), whereas a brasserie always serves more standard French and/or Alsatian fare. One of the delights of visiting Paris is stocking up on fresh bread, pastries, cheese, fruit, and prepared dishes and sitting down for a gourmet *pique-nique*.

CAMPING IN PARIS

Camping du Bois de Boulogne (☎ 01 45 24 30 81; www.abccamping.com/boulogne.htm; 2 allée du Bord de l'Eau, 16e; camp sites Oct-Mar/Apr-Jun & Nov/Jul & Aug €11/14.20/15.40, per d with vehicle €18.50/22.50/24.50, per d with electricity €22.50/26.50/31.70, 1st-time booking fee €12; ☯ 6-2am) The only campsite within the Paris city limits lies along the Seine at the far western edge of the Bois de Boulogne. It gets crowded in the summer, but there's always space for a small tent. Fully equipped caravans sleeping four to five cost around €49 to €85. Porte Maillot metro station, 4.5km to the northeast through the wood, is linked to the site by RATP bus No 244, which runs from 6am to 8.30pm daily, and from April to October by a privately operated shuttle bus charging about €2.

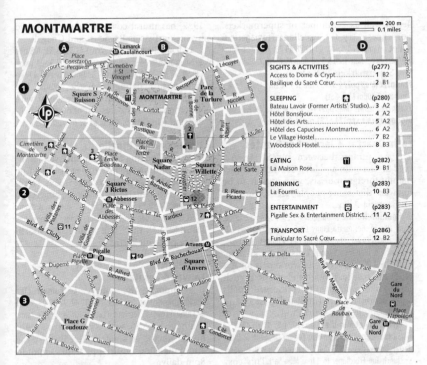

MONTMARTRE

SIGHTS & ACTIVITIES	(p277)
Access to Dome & Crypt.....................	1 B2
Basilique du Sacré Cœur.....................	2 B1

SLEEPING	(p280)
Bateau Lavoir (Former Artists' Studio)...	3 A2
Hôtel Bonséjour.................................	4 A2
Hôtel des Arts....................................	5 A2
Hôtel des Capucines Montmartre.........	6 A2
Le Village Hostel................................	7 B2
Woodstock Hostel..............................	8 B3

EATING	(p282)
La Maison Rose..................................	9 B1

DRINKING	(p283)
La Fourmi..	10 B3

ENTERTAINMENT	(p283)
Pigalle Sex & Entertainment District....	11 A2

TRANSPORT	(p286)
Funicular to Sacré Cœur......................	12 B2

Louvre & Les Halles

Café Marly (Map pp274–5; ☎ 01 46 26 06 60; cour Napoléon du Louvre, 93 rue de Rivoli, 1er; metro Palais Royal-Musée du Louvre; starters €8-21, sandwiches & snacks €10-14, mains €16-30; ☽ noon-1am) This classic venue serves contemporary French fare under the colonnades of the Louvre, and overlooks the glass pyramid.

L'Épi d'Or (Map pp274–5; ☎ 01 42 36 38 12; 25 rue Jean-Jacques Rousseau, 1er; metro Louvre-Rivoli; starters €5-15, mains €14-20, set menu €18; ☽ lunch & dinner Mon-Fri, Sat dinner only) This oh-so-Parisian bistro specialises in well-prepared, classic dishes such as succulent *gigot d'agneau* (leg of lamb), which is slowly cooked for seven hours.

Le Petit Mâchon (Map pp274–5; ☎ 01 42 60 08 06; 158 rue St-Honoré, 1er; metro Palais Royal-Musée du Louvre; starters €6.50-12.50, mains €14-21, lunch menu €16.50; ☽ lunch & dinner to 11pm Tue-Sun) This is an upbeat bistro convenient to the Louvre, with Lyon-inspired specialities.

Self catering options include **Ed l'Épicier** (Map pp274–5; 80 rue de Rivoli, 4e; ☽ 9am-8pm Mon-Sat) and **Franprix** (Map pp274–5; 35 rue Berger, 1er; ☽ 8.30am-7.50pm Mon-Sat).

Marais & Bastille

L'Ambassade d'Auvergne (Map pp274–5; ☎ 01 42 72 31 22; 22 rue du Grenier St-Lazare, 3e; metro Rambuteau; starters €9-18, mains €14-19, menu €27; ☽ lunch & dinner to 10.30pm) The place to go if you're really hungry; the sausages and hams of this region, the lentils from Puy and the *clafoutis*, a custard and cherry tart, are sublime.

Les Galopins (Map pp274–5; ☎ 01 47 00 45 35; 24 rue des Taillandiers, 11e; metro Bastille or Voltaire; starters €6-10.50, mains €11.50-18, lunch menu €11.50 & €15; ☽ lunch Mon-Fri, dinner to 11pm Mon-Thu, to 11.30pm Fri & Sat) This cute little neighbourhood bistro serves dishes in the best tradition of French cuisine: *poêlée de pétoncles* (pan-fried queen scallops), *magret de canard* (fillet of duck breast), *coeur de rumsteck* (tenderloin rump steak).

Le Petit Picard (Map pp274–5; ☎ 01 42 78 54 03; 42 rue Ste-Croix de la Bretonnerie, 4e; metro Hôtel de Ville; lunch menu €12, dinner menu €14.50 & €21.50; ☽ lunch Tue-Fri, dinner to 11pm Tue-Sun) This popular little restaurant in the centre of Marais serves traditional French cuisine. If you're very hungry, try the generous *menu traditionel* (€21.50).

In the Marais, there are several food shops and Asian delicatessens on rue St-Antoine,

FRANCE

4e, as well as a number of supermarkets. For cheese, try the excellent **Fromagerie G Millet** (Map pp274-5; ☎ 01 42 78 48 78; 77 rue St-Antoine, 4e; 🕑 7.30am-1pm & 3.30-8pm Mon-Fri, 7.30am-1pm Sat). Supermarkets include:

Franprix (Map pp274-5; 135 rue St-Antoine, 4e; 🕑 9am-8.30pm Mon-Sat)

Franprix Marais (Map pp274-5; 87 rue de la Verrerie, 4e)

Monoprix (Map pp274-5; 71 rue St-Antoine, 4)

Latin Quarter & Jardin Des Plantes

The restaurants between rue St-Jacques, blvd St-Germain and blvd St-Michel attract mainly foreign tourists, who appear to be unaware that some people refer to the area as 'Bacteria Alley'.

Bouillon Racine (Map pp274-5; ☎ 01 44 32 15 60; 3 rue Racine, 6e; metro Cluny La Sorbonne; starters €7-11.50, mains €12-17, lunch menu €15 & dinner menu €25; 🕑 lunch & dinner to 11pm) This 'soup kitchen' built in 1906 to feed city workers is an Art Nouveau palace, though the classic French dishes like *caille confite* (preserved quail) and *cochon de lait* (milk-fed pork) can't hold a candle to the surrounds.

Chez Léna et Mimille (Map pp274-5; ☎ 01 47 07 72 47; 32 rue Tournefort, 5e; metro Censier Daubenton; lunch starters/mains/desserts €7/14/7, dinner menu with wine €3; 🕑 lunch Tue-Fri, dinner to 11pm Mon-Sat) This cosy but elegant French restaurant has excellent food and one of the most fabulous terraces in Paris, overlooking a little park with a fountain.

Perraudin (Map pp274-5; ☎ 01 46 33 15 75; 157 rue St-Jacques, 5e; metro Luxembourg; starters €6-15, mains €14-23, lunch/dinner menu €18/26; 🕑 lunch & dinner to 10.30pm Mon-Fri) Perraudin is a traditional French restaurant that hasn't changed much since the late 19th century and is great for classics such as *bœuf bourguignon* (€14), *gigot d'agneau* (€15) or *confit de canard* (€15).

There's a lively **food market** (Place Maubert) in 5e four mornings a week. There are also some provisions shops here, including a cheese shop called **Crémerie des Carmes** (Map pp274-5; ☎ 01 43 54 50 93; 47 ter blvd St-Germain, 5e; metro Maubert Mutualité; 🕑 7.30am-1pm & 3.30-8pm Mon-Fri, to 1pm Sat).

Montparnasse

La Coupole (Map pp274-5; ☎ 01 43 20 14 20; 102 blvd du Montparnasse, 14e; metro Vavin; starters €7.50-12.50, mains €13.50-18.50, lunch menu €17.50, dinner menu €22.90 & €32.90; 🕑 8-1am Sun-Thu, to 1.30am Fri & Sat) This 450-seat brasserie, which opened in

1927, has mural-covered columns painted by such artists as Brancusi and Chagall.

Le Dôme (Map pp270-1; ☎ 01 43 35 25 81; 108 blvd du Montparnasse, 14e; metro Vavin; starters €12.50-23, mains €30.50-56; 🕑 lunch & dinner to 12.30am) An Art Deco extravaganza dating from the 1930s, The Dome is a monumental place for a meal, with the emphasis on the freshest of oysters, shellfish and fish dishes such as *sole meunière*.

Montmartre & Pigalle

If you are looking for the quintessential intimate Montmartre bistro, head for the tiny **La Maison Rose** (Map p281; ☎ 01 42 57 66 75; 2 rue de l'Abreuvoir, 18e; metro Lamarck Caulaincourt; starters €7.80-13, mains €14.50-16.50, menu €14.50; 🕑 lunch & dinner to 10.30pm Mar-Oct, lunch Thu-Mon, dinner to 9pm Mon, Thu-Sat Nov-Feb), the 'Pink House', just north of the place du Tertre.

DRINKING
Louvre & Les Halles

Just opposite the Louvre, **Le Fumoir** (The Smoking Room Map pp274-5; ☎ 01 42 92 00 24; 6 rue de l'Amiral Coligny, 1er; metro Louvre-Rivoli; 🕑 11-2am), is a huge bar/café with a gentleman's club/library theme. It's a friendly, lively place and quite good fun. Happy hour is 6pm to 8pm daily.

Marais & Bastille

An oasis of peace, **L'Apparement Café** (Map pp274-5; ☎ 01 48 87 12 22; 18 rue des Coutures St-Gervais, 3e; metro St-Sébastien Froissart; 🕑 noon-2am Mon-Fri, 4pm-2am Sat, 12.30pm-midnight Sun), tucked not so 'apparently' behind the Musée Picasso, looks like a private living room.

Latin Quarter & Jardin des Plantes

Le Piano Vache (Map pp274-5; ☎ 01 46 33 75 03; 8 rue Laplace, 5e; metro Maubert Mutualité; 🕑 noon-2am Mon-Fri, 9pm-2am Sat & Sun) Just down the hill from the Panthéon, 'The Mean Piano' plays great music (guest DJs) and attracts a good crowd of mixed ages. Happy hour is from opening to 9pm Monday to Friday.

Le Vieux Chêne (Map pp274-5; ☎ 01 43 37 71 51; 69 rue Mouffetard, 5e; metro Pl Monge; 🕑 4pm-2am Sun-Thu, to 5am Fri & Sat) 'The Old Oak' is popular with students and has jazz at the weekend. Happy hour is from opening to 9pm daily.

St-Germain, Odéon & Luxembourg

Café de Flore (Map pp274-5; ☎ 01 45 48 55 26; 172 blvd St-Germain, 6e; metro St-Germain des Prés; 🕑 7.30-

1.30am) The Flore is an Art Deco café where the red upholstered benches, mirrors and marble walls haven't changed since the days when Sartre, de Beauvoir, Camus and Picasso bent their elbows here. The terrace is a much sought-after place to sip beer (€7.50 for 400ml), the house Pouilly Fumé (€7.50 a glass or €29 a bottle) or coffee (€4).

Les Deux Magots (Map pp274-5; ☎ 01 45 48 55 25; 170 blvd St-Germain, 6e; metro St-Germain des Prés; ☽ 7-1am) This erstwhile literary haunt is best known as the favoured hangout of Sartre, Hemingway, Picasso and André Breton. Everyone has to sit on the terrace here at least once and have a coffee (€4), beer (€5.50) or the famous hot chocolate served in porcelain jugs (€6).

Montmartre & Pigalle

A trendy Pigalle hang-out, **La Fourmi** (Map p281; ☎ 01 42 64 70 35; 74 rue des Martyrs, 18e; metro Pigalle; ☽ 8-2am Mon-Thu, 10-4am Fri-Sun), the 'Ant', buzzes (marches?) day and night; it's a good place to meet before hitting the clubs.

ENTERTAINMENT

It's almost impossible to sample the richness of Paris' entertainment scene without first studying *Pariscope* (€0.40) or *Officiel des Spectacles* (€0.35); both come out on Wednesday. *Pariscope* includes a six-page insert in English at the back, courtesy of London's *Time Out* magazine. The weekly magazine *Zurban* (www.zurban.com – in French; €0.80) also appears on Wednesday, offering a fresher look at entertainment in the capital. For up-to-date information on clubs and the music scene, get a copy of *LYLO*

You can buy tickets for cultural events at many ticket outlets, including **Fnac** (☎ 08 92 68 36 22; www.fnac.com, in French) and **Virgin Megastore branches** (www.virginmega.fr, in French), for a small commission.

Cinemas

Expect to pay between €6 and €8 for a first-run film. Students and those aged under 18 or over 60 usually get discounts of about 25% except on Friday, Saturday and Sunday nights.

Live Music

OPERA & CLASSICAL

Opéra National de Paris (ONP; ☎ 08 92 89 90 90; www .opera-de-paris.fr, in French) splits its performance schedule between the Palais Garnier and the modern Opéra Bastille, which opened in 1989. Both opera houses also stage ballets and classical-music concerts (September to July) performed by the ONP's affiliated orchestra and ballet companies.

Opéra Bastille (Map pp274-5; 2-6 pl de la Bastille, 12e; metro Bastille) Tickets are available from the **box office** (Map pp274-5; 130 rue de Lyon, 12e; ☽ 11am-6.30pm Mon-Sat) some 14 days before the date of the performance, but the only way to ensure a seat is by **post** (120 rue de Lyon, 75576 Paris CEDEX 12) some two months in advance. Operas cost €6 to €114. Ballets cost €13 to €70; seats, with limited or no visibility, available at the box office only are €6 to €9. Unsold tickets are offered to people aged under 26 or over 65 and students for €20 only 15 minutes before the curtain goes up.

Palais Garnier (Map pp270-1; pl de l'Opéra, 9e; metro Opéra) Ticket prices and conditions (including last-minute discounts) at the **box office** (pl de l'Opéra, 9e; ☽ 11am-6.30pm Mon-Sat) of the city's original opera house are almost exactly the same as those at the Opéra Bastille.

JAZZ & BLUES

After WWII, Paris was Europe's most important jazz centre and it is again very much à la mode; the city's better clubs attract top international stars.

Le Caveau de la Huchette (Map pp274-5; ☎ 01 43 26 65 05; 5 rue de la Huchette, 5e; metro St-Michel; adult Sun-Thu €10.50, Fri & Sat €13, student €9; ☽ 9pm-2.30am Sun-Thu, to 3.30am Fri, 9pm-4am Sat) Housed in a medieval *caveau* (cellar) that was used as a courtroom and torture chamber during the Revolution, this club is where virtually all the jazz greats since the end of WWII have played.

Nightclubs

Paris is great for music (techno remains very popular) and there are some mighty fine DJs based here. Latino and Cuban salsa music is also huge.

Le Batofar (Map pp270-1; ☎ 01 56 29 10 33; www .batofar.net, in French; opposite 11 quai François Mauriac, 13e; metro Quai de la Gare or Bibliothèque; admission free-€12; ☽ 9pm-midnight Mon & Tue, 9pm or 10pm-4am, 5am or 6am Wed-Sun) What looks like an unassuming tugboat moored near the imposing Bibliothèque Nationale de France is a rollicking dancing spot that attracts some top international techno and funk DJ talent.

Le Cithéa (Map pp270-1; ☎ 01 40 21 70 95; www
.cithea.com, in French; 114 rue Oberkampf, 11e; metro Parmentier or Ménilmontant; admission free-€4; ⏰ 5pm-5.30am Tue-Thu, 10pm-6.30am Fri & Sat) This popular concert venue has bands playing soul, Latin and funk but especially world music and jazz, usually from 10.30pm, with DJs from 1am.

Gibus (Map pp270-1; ☎ 01 47 00 78 88; www.gibus .fr, in French; 18 rue du Faubourg du Temple, 11e; metro République; admission free-€18; ⏰ 11pm-dawn Tue-Sat) Gibus, an enormously popular cave-like venue halfway between the Canal St-Martin and place de la République, has hard techno on Tuesday, acid and trance on Wednesday, techno on Thursday.

SHOPPING

Le Bon Marché (Map pp270-1; ☎ 01 44 39 80 00; www .bonmarche.fr, in French; 24 rue de Sèvres, 7e; metro Sèvres Babylone; ⏰ 9.30am-7pm Mon-Wed & Fri, 10am-9pm Thu, 9.30am-8pm Sat) Opened by Gustave Eiffel as Paris' first department store in 1852.

Galeries Lafayette (Map pp270-1; ☎ 01 42 82 34 56; www.galerieslafayette.com; 40 blvd Haussmann, 9e; metro Auber or Chaussée d'Antin; ⏰ 9.30am-7.30pm Mon-Wed, Fri & Sat, to 9pm Thu) A vast grand magasin in two adjacent buildings, Galeries Lafayette features a wide selection of fashion and accessories.

GETTING THERE & AWAY
Air
AÉROPORT D'ORLY

The airport **Orly** (code ORY; ☎ 01 49 75 15 15, flight info 0 892 681 515; www.adp.fr) is about 18km south of the city.

AÉROPORT ROISSY CHARLES DE GAULLE

Located 30km northeast of Paris in the suburb of Roissy is **Roissy Charles de Gaulle** (code CDG; ☎ 01 48 62 22 80, 0 892 681 515; www.adp.fr). Terminals (Aérogares) 1 and 25 are used by international and domestic carriers.

AÉROPORT PARIS-BEAUVAIS

The international airport at **Beauvais** (code BVA; ☎ 03 44 11 46 86; www.aeroportbeauvais.com), 80km north of Paris, is used by the discount airline Ryanair for its European flights, including those between Paris and Dublin, Shannon and Glasgow.

Bus

Eurolines buses link Paris with points all over Western Europe, Central Europe,
Scandinavia and Morocco. The main **Eurolines office** (Map pp274-5; ☎ 01 43 54 11 99 or 0 892 899 091; www.eurolines.fr; 55 rue St-Jacques, 5e; metro Cluny-La Sorbonne; ⏰ 9.30am-6.30pm Mon-Fri, 10am-1pm & 2-6pm Sat) is in the central city.

The **Gare Routière Internationale** (Map pp270-1; ☎ 0 892 899 091; 28 av du Général de Gaulle; metro Gallieni) is the city's international bus terminal; it's in the inner suburb of Bagnolet.

Train

Mainline train information is available round the clock at **SNCF** (www.sncf.fr; ☎ 0 892 353 535). Paris has six major train stations, each of which handles passenger traffic to different parts of France and Europe.

Gare d'Austerlitz (Map pp270-1; blvd de l'Hôpital, 13e; metro Gare d'Austerlitz) For trains to Spain and Portugal; Loire Valley and non-TGV trains to southwestern France (eg Bordeaux and Basque Country).

Gare de l'Est (Map pp270-1; blvd de Strasbourg, 10e; metro Gare de l'Est) For Luxembourg, parts of Switzerland (Basel, Lucerne, Zurich), southern Germany (Frankfurt, Munich) and points further east; areas of France east of Paris (Champagne, Alsace and Lorraine).

Gare de Lyon (Map pp270-1; blvd Diderot, 12e; metro Gare de Lyon) Serves parts of Switzerland (eg Bern, Geneva, Lausanne), Italy and points beyond; regular and TGV Sud-Est trains to areas southeast of Paris, including Dijon, Lyon, Provence, the Côte d'Azur and the Alps.

Gare du Nord (Map p281; rue de Dunkerque, 10e; metro Gare du Nord) Serves the UK, Belgium, northern Germany, Scandinavia, Moscow etc (terminus of the high-speed Thalys trains to/from Amsterdam, Brussels, Cologne and Geneva and Eurostar to London); trains to the northern suburbs of Paris and northern France, including TGV Nord trains to Lille and Calais.

Gare Montparnasse (Map pp270-1; av du Maine & blvd de Vaugirard, 15e; metro Montparnasse Bienvenüe) Services to Brittany and places en route from Paris (eg Chartres, Angers, Nantes), TGV Atlantique trains to Tours, Nantes, Bordeaux and other destinations in southwestern France.

Gare St-Lazare (Map pp270-1; rue St-Lazare & rue d'Amsterdam, 8e; metro St-Lazare) For Normandy (eg Dieppe, Le Havre, Cherbourg).

GETTING AROUND
To/from the Airports
AÉROPORT D'ORLY

There are half a dozen public transport options for getting to or from Orly airport. Apart from RATP bus No 183, all services call in at both terminals.

Tickets for all bus services are sold on board the bus, rather than at offices.

FRANCE

Air France Bus No 1 (☎ 0 892 350 820; www
.cars-airfrance.com, in French; one way/return
€7.50/12.75; ⏰ every 15min 6am-11.30pm to Paris,
5.45am-11pm to Orly; journey time 30-45min) This
navette (shuttle bus) runs to/from the eastern side of Gare
Montparnasse as well as **Aérogare des Invalides** (Map
pp270-1; metro Invalides) in the 7e. On your way into the
city, you can ask to get off at metro Porte d'Orléans or
metro Duroc.

Jetbus (☎ 01 69 01 00 09; €5.15; ⏰ every 15-20min
6.43am-10.49pm to Paris, 6.15am-10.15pm to Orly;
journey time 55min) With the exception of RATP bus No
183, Jetbus is the cheapest way to get to/from Orly. It runs
to/from metro Villejuif Louis Aragon, south of the 13e on
the city's southern fringe.

Orlybus (☎ 0 892 687 714; €5.70; ⏰ every 15-20min
6am-11.30pm to Paris, 5.35am-11pm to Orly; journey time
30min) This RATP bus runs to/from metro Denfert Rochereau in the 14e and makes several stops in the eastern
14e in each direction.

Orlyval (☎ 0 892 687 714; €8.80 to/from Paris, €10.65
to/from La Défense; ⏰ every 4-12min 6am-11pm each
direction; journey time 33min to Paris, 50min to La
Défense) This RATP service links Orly with the city centre
via a shuttle train and the RER. A driverless shuttle train
runs between the airport and Antony RER station (eight
minutes) on RER line B, from where it's an easy journey
into the city; to get to Antony from the city (26 minutes),
take line B4 towards St-Rémy-lès-Chevreuse. Orlyval
tickets are valid for travel on the RER and for metro travel
within the city.

RATP Bus No 183 (☎ 0 892 687 714; €1.30 or one
metro/bus ticket; ⏰ every 35min 5.35am-8.35pm each
direction; journey time 1hr) This is a slow public bus that
links Orly-Sud (only) with metro Porte de Choisy, at the
southern edge of the 13e.

RER C (☎ 0 890 361 010; €5.35; ⏰ every 12-20min
5.45am-11pm each direction; journey time 50min) An
Aéroports de Paris (ADP) shuttle bus links the airport with
RER line C at Pont de Rungis-Aéroport d'Orly RER station.
From the city, take a C2 train towards Pont de Rungis or
Massy-Palaiseau. Tickets are valid for onward travel on
the metro.

Along with public transport the following
private options provide door-to-door service
for about €25 for a single person (from about
€15 to €18 per person for two or more). Book
in advance and allow for numerous pick-ups
and drop-offs:

Allô Shuttle (☎ 01 34 29 00 80; www.alloshuttle.com)
Paris Airports Service (☎ 01 46 80 14 67; www
.parisairportservice.com)
Shuttle Van PariShuttle (☎ 0 800 699 699; www
.parishuttle.com)

Taxi A taxi between central Paris and Orly costs about €40
and takes 20 to 30 minutes.
World Shuttle (☎ 01 46 80 14 67; www.worldshuttles
.com)

AÉROPORT ROISSY CHARLES DE GAULLE

Roissy Charles de Gaulle has two train stations – Aéroport Charles de Gaulle 1 (CDG1)
and Aéroport Charles de Gaulle 2 (CDG2) –
both served by commuter trains on RER line
B3. A free shuttle bus links the terminals and
train stations. There are various transport
options for travel between Aéroport Roissy
Charles de Gaulle and Paris. Tickets for the
bus services are sold on board.

Air France bus No 2 (☎ 0 892 350 820; www.cars
-airfrance.com, in French; one way/return €10/17;
⏰ every 15min 5.45am-11pm each direction; journey
time 35-50mins) Air France bus No 2 links the airport with
two locations on the Right Bank: near the Arc de Triomphe
just outside 2 av Carnot, 17e (metro Charles de Gaulle-
Étoile) and the Palais des Congrès de Paris (blvd Gouvion
St-Cyr, 17e; metro Porte Maillot).

Air France bus No 4 (☎ 0 892 350 820; www
.cars-airfrance.com, in French; one way/return
€11.50/19.55; ⏰ every 30min to Paris 7am-9pm, to
Roissy Charles de Gaulle 7am-9.30pm; journey time 45-
55min) Air France bus No 4 links the airport with Gare de
Lyon and with the Gare Montparnasse

RATP Bus Nos 350 (☎ 0 892 687 714; €3.90 or three
metro/bus tickets; ⏰ every 30min 5.45am-7pm each
direction; journey time 1¼hrs) This public bus links Aérogares 1 & 2 with Gare de l'Est and with Gare du Nord

RATP Bus No 351 (☎ 0 892 687 714; €3.90 or three
metro/bus tickets; ⏰ every 30min 6am-9.30pm to Paris,
6am-8.20pm to Roissy Charles de Gaulle; journey time
55min) Links the eastern side of place de la Nation with
the Roissy Charles de Gaulle.

RER B (☎ 0 890 361 010; €7.75; ⏰ every 4-15min
4.56am-11.40pm in each direction; journey time 30min)
RER line B3 links CDG1 and CDG2 with the city. To get to
the airport take any RER line B train whose four-letter
destination code begins with E (eg EIRE) and a shuttle bus
(every 5 to 8 minutes) will ferry you to the appropriate
terminal. Regular metro ticket windows can't always sell
RER tickets as far as the airport so you may have to buy
one at the RER station where you board.

Roissybus (☎ 0 892 687 714; €8.20; ⏰ every 15-20
min 5.45am-11pm in each direction; journey time 60min)
This public bus links both terminals with rue Scribe (metro
Opéra) behind the Palais Garnier in the 9e.

Shuttle Van The four companies in the Orly section (see
p284) will take you from Roissy Charles de Gaulle to your
hotel for similar prices. Book in advance.

Taxi Taxis to/from the city centre cost from €40 to €55.

FRANCE

Car & Motorcycle

While driving in Paris is nerve-racking, it can be done. The fastest way to get across the city by car is usually via the blvd Périphérique, the ring road that encircles the city.

In many parts of Paris you pay €1.50 to €2 an hour to park your car on the street. Large municipal parking garages usually charge €2.60 an hour and between €20 and €23 for 24 hours.

Car rental companies include:

Avis (☎ 0 802 050 505; www.avis.fr)

Budget (☎ 0 825 003 564; www.budget.fr, in French)

Europcar (☎ 0 825 358 358; www.europcar.fr, in French)

Hertz (☎ 0 825 861 861; www.hertz.fr)

Smaller agencies can offer much more attractive deals. Check the *Yellow Pages* under 'Location d'Automobiles: Tourisme et Utilitaires'.

Public Transport

BUS

Paris' bus system, also operated by the RATP, runs from 5.45am to 12.30am Monday to Saturday. Services are drastically reduced on Sunday. After the metro lines have finished their last runs at about 1am, the Noctambus network of night buses links the place du Châtelet (1er) and av Victoria just west of the Hôtel de Ville in the 4e with most parts of the city. Short bus rides cost one metro/bus ticket; longer rides require two. Whatever kind of single-journey ticket you have, you must cancel *(oblitérer)* it in the *composteur* (cancelling machine) next to the driver.

METRO & RER

Paris' underground network consists of two separate but interlinked systems: the **Métropolitain**, known as the metro, with 14 lines and 372 stations; and the **RER** (Réseau Express Régional), a network of suburban lines designated A to E and then numbered, that pass through the city centre.

Metro Network

Each metro train is known by the name of its terminus. On lines that split into several branches (eg line Nos 3, 7 and 13), the terminus served by each train is indicated with back-lit panels on the cars. The last metro trains run between 12.35am and 1.04am and start again around 5.30am.

RER Network

The RER is faster than the metro, but the stops are much further apart. RER lines are known by an alphanumeric combination – the letter (A to E) refers to the line, the number to the spur it will follow somewhere out in the suburbs. The same RATP tickets are valid on the metro, the RER (for travel within the city limits), buses, the Montmartre funicular and Paris' two tram lines. They cost €1.30 if bought individually, €10 (€5 per child aged four to 11) for a carnet of 10.

Always keep your ticket until you exit from your station; you may be stopped by a *contrôleur* (ticket inspector).

TOURIST PASSES

The Mobilis card and its coupon allows unlimited travel for one day in two to eight zones (€5.20 to €18.30), but you would have to make at least six metro trips in a day (based on the carnet price) in zones 1 and 2 to break even on this pass.

Paris Visite passes, which allow the holder discounted entry to certain museums and activities as well as discounts on transport fares, are valid for one, two, three or five consecutive days of travel in either three, five or eight zones. The version covering one to three zones costs €8.35/13.70/18.25/26.65 for one/two/three/five days.

TRAVEL PASSES

The cheapest and easiest way to use public transport in Paris is to get a Carte Orange, a weekly or monthly combined metro, RER and bus pass. The basic ticket valid for zones 1 and 2 should be sufficient. To buy your first Carte Orange, take a passport-size photograph to any metro or RER ticket window.

Taxi

The *prise en charge* (flag-fall) in a Parisian taxi is €2. Within the city limits, it costs €0.62 per kilometre for travel between 7am and 7pm Monday to Saturday and €1.06 per kilometre from 7pm to 7am at night, all day Sunday and on public holidays. Pick-ups from SNCF mainline stations cost another €0.70.

Radio-dispatched taxi companies, on call 24 hours, include:

Alpha Taxis (☎ 01 45 85 85 85)

Taxis Bleus (☎ 01 49 36 10 10)

Taxis Radio 7000 (☎ 01 42 70 00 42)

AROUND PARIS

The region encircling Paris is known as the Île de France because of its position between the rivers Epte, Aisne, Eure, Yonne and the Marne. The area's exceptional sights make it especially popular with day-trippers from Paris.

DISNEYLAND RESORT PARIS

It took almost €4.6 billion and five years of work to turn the beet fields east of the capital into Europe's first Disney theme park, which opened in 1992. One-day admission fees at **Disneyland Resort Paris** (☎ 01 60 30 60 30, UK ☎ 0 870 503 0305, USA ☎ 407-WDISNEY or 407-934 7639; www.disneylandparis.com or www.needmagic.com) include unlimited access to all rides and activities in either Disneyland Park or Walt Disney Studios Park.

VERSAILLES

pop 85,300

The prosperous, leafy and very bourgeois suburb of Versailles, 21km southwest of Paris, is the site of the grandest and most famous chateau in France. It served as the kingdom's political capital and the seat of the royal court for more than a century, from 1682 to 1789 – the year Revolutionary mobs massacred the palace guard and dragged Louis XVI and Marie-Antoinette back to Paris where they eventually had their heads lopped off.

The **Office de Tourisme de Versailles** (☎ 01 39 24 88 88; www.versailles-tourisme.com; 2bis av de Paris; 🕙 9am-7pm Apr-Oct, to 6pm Tue-Sat, to 5pm Sun & Mon Nov-Mar) has themed guided tours (adult/child €8/4) of the city and chateau.

Sights

CHÂTEAU DE VERSAILLES

The splendid and enormous **Château de Versailles** (Palace of Versailles; ☎ 01 30 83 78 00 or ☎ 01 30 83 77 77; www.chateauversailles.fr; adult/child Apr-Oct €20/6, Nov-Mar €14.50/4; 🕙 9am-5.30pm Tue-Sun Nov-Mar, to 6.30pm Tue-Sun Apr-Oct) was built in the mid-17th century during the reign of Louis XIV – the Roi Soleil (Sun King) – to project the absolute power of the French monarchy. The palace, a 580m-long structure with innumerable wings, grand halls and sumptuous bedchambers, has vast gardens (admission free Nov-Mar, adult €3, free for under 18 yrs &

all after 6pm Apr-Oct, 🕙 8am-5.30pm, to 6.30pm Nov-Mar, 9am-sunset Apr-Oct). Tickets are on sale at Entrée A (Entrance A), which is off to the right of the equestrian statue of Louis XIV as you approach the palace.

Getting There & Away

RER line C5 (€2.35) takes you from Paris' Left Bank RER stations to Versailles-Rive Gauche station, which is only 700m southeast of the chateau and close to the tourist office. The last train back to Paris leaves shortly before midnight.

SNCF operates 70 trains a day from Paris' Gare St-Lazare (€3.20) to Versailles-Rive Droite, 1.2km from the chateau. The last train to Paris leaves just after midnight.

CHARTRES

pop 40,250

The magnificent 13th-century cathedral of Chartres, crowned by two very different spires – one Gothic, the other Romanesque – rises from rich farmland 88km southwest of Paris and dominates the medieval town around its base. With its astonishing blue stained glass and other treasures, this cathedral is a must-see for any visitor to Paris.

Office de Tourisme de Chartres (☎ 02 37 18 26 26; info@otchartres.fr; pl de la Cathédrale; 🕙 9am-7pm Mon-Sat, 9.30am-5.30pm Sun Apr-Sep, 10am-6pm Mon-Sat, to 1pm & 2.30-4.30pm Sun Oct-Mar) provides information.

Sights

CATHÉDRALE NOTRE DAME DE CHARTRES

The 130m-long **Cathédrale Notre Dame de Chartres** (Cathedral of Our Lady of Chartres; ☎ 02 37 21 22 07; www.cathedrale-chartres.com, in French; pl de la Cathédrale; 🕙 8.30am-7.30pm), one of the crowning architectural achievements of Western civilisation, was built in the Gothic style during the first quarter of the 13th century.

English-language audioguide **tours** (per 25/45/70min €2.90/3.80/5.65) with three different themes can be hired from the cathedral bookshop. The cathedral's 172 extraordinary **stained-glass windows** form one of the most important ensembles of medieval stained glass in the world.

Sleeping & Eating

Auberge de Jeunesse (☎ 02 37 34 27 64; fax 02 37 35 78 85; 23 av Neigre; dm €11; ✗ 🖳) Reception at this hostel, which is about 1.5km east of the train station via blvd Charles Péguy and blvd Jean Jaurès, opens from 2pm to 10pm daily; curfew is 10.30pm in winter and 11.30pm in summer. To get there from the train station, take bus No 5 (direction: Mare aux Moines) to the Rouliers stop.

Hôtel du Bœuf Couronné (☎ 02 37 18 06 06; fax 02 37 21 72 13; 15 pl Châtelet; s/d with washbasin & toilet €27/30, s/d with shower €40/50, s/d with bath €43/57) This cosy, Logis de France-affiliated guesthouse in the centre offers excellent value and has a memorable **restaurant** (menu €22 & €26; ⏱ lunch & dinner to 11pm) with generous menus.

Le Tripot (☎ 02 37 36 60 11; 11 pl Jean Moulin; starters €11-19, mains €13.50-24, lunch menu €15, dinner menu €22.50, €28.50 & €37.50; ⏱ lunch Tue-Sun, dinner to 9.30pm Tue-Sat) This wonderful little place just down from the cathedral is one of the best bistros in Chartres.

Le Buisson Ardent (☎ 02 37 34 04 66; 10 rue au Lait; starters €9.50-16, mains €13-22, lunch menu €18, dinner menu 22; ⏱ lunch Thu-Tue & dinner to 10.30pm Mon, Tue, Thu-Sat) 'The Burning Bush' is a charming, old-style place with good-value menus.

There's a **covered market** (pl Billard; ⏱ 7am-1pm Sat), just off rue des Changes south of the cathedral. It dates from the early 20th century; there are many food shops surrounding it.

Getting There & Away
Some 30 SNCF trains a day (20 on Sunday) link Paris' Gare Montparnasse (€11.80, 55 to 70 minutes) with Chartres, all of which pass through Versailles-Chantiers (€9.90, 45 to 60 minutes).

SAVED BY RED TAPE

The magnificent cathedral at Chartres and its priceless stained glass managed to survive the ravages of the Revolution and the Reign of Terror for the same reason that everyday life in France can often seem so complicated: French bureaucracy.

As antireligious fervour reached fever pitch in 1791, the Revolutionary government decided the cathedral deserved demolition, not just desecration. But how to accomplish it? To find an answer, they appointed a committee, whose admirably thorough members deliberated for four or five years. By that time the Revolution's fury had been spent, and – to history's great fortune – the plan was shelved.

CHAMPAGNE

Only bubbly from the Champagne region – grown in designated areas, then aged and bottled according to the strictest standards – can be labelled as champagne. The town of Épernay, south of Reims, is the de facto capital of champagne (the drink) and is the best place to head for *dégustation* (tasting).

REIMS
pop 206,000
Meticulously reconstructed after the two world wars, Reims is a neat and orderly city with wide avenues and well-tended parks.

Orientation & Information
The train station is about 1km northwest of the cathedral, across square Colbert from place Drouet d'Erlon, the city's major nightlife centre. Virtually every street in the city centre is one-way.

The **tourist office** (☎ 03 26 77 45 00; www.reims -tourisme.com; 2 rue Guillaume de Machault; ⏱ 9am-7pm Mon-Sat, 10am-6pm Sun & hols early Apr–mid-Oct, 10am-5pm Mon-Sat, 11am-4pm Sun & hols mid-Oct–early Apr) has an Internet post that runs on a France Télécom *télécarte*.

The **post office** (2 rue Cérès; ⏱ 8.30am-6pm Mon-Fri, 8am-noon Sat) has currency exchange and a Cyberposte.

Clique et Croque Cybercafé (☎ 03 26 86 93 92; 27 rue de Vesle; per hr €4.20; ⏱ 10am-12.30am Mon-Sat, 2pm-9pm Sun) has Internet access.

Sights & Activities
The heavily restored Reims' **Cathédrale Notre Dame** (⏱ 7.30am-7.30pm except, closed Sun morning Mass) is a 138m-long Gothic edifice where the coronation of Charles VII took place – with Joan of Arc at his side – on 17 July 1429. The **Palais du Tau** (☎ 03 26 47 81 79; adult/18-25 yrs/under 18 yrs €6.10/4.10/free; ⏱ 9.30am-6.30pm Tue-Sun early May-early Sep, to 12.30pm & 2-5.30pm Tue-Sun early Sep-early May), displays truly exceptional statues, ritual objects and tapestries from the cathedral. Also see the **Basilique St-Rémi** (pl St-Rémi) – its Romanesque nave and transept date mainly from the mid-11th century.

CHAMPAGNE CELLARS
There are about a dozen champagne houses in the Reims area with *caves* (cellars) that offer tastings and guided tours in English.

Taittinger (☎ 03 26 85 84 33; www.taittinger.com; 9 place St-Niçaise; adult/child under 12 yrs €7/free; tours ⏰ 9.30-11.45am and 2-4.20pm, closed weekends Dec–mid-Mar) An excellent place for a straightforward presentation on how champagne is made.

Mumm (☎ 03 26 49 59 70; www.mumm.com; 34 rue du Champ de Mars; adult/child under 16 yrs €7/free; tours ⏰ 9-11am & 2-5pm Mar-Oct) Pronounced moom, this is now the world's 3rd-largest producer of champagne (eight million bottles a year).

Pommery (☎ 03 26 61 62 55; www.pommery.com; 5 pl du Général Gouraud; adult/student/child under 12 yrs €7.50/6/free; tours ⏰ 10am-5pm, to 4 or 4.30pm mid-Nov–Mar) Cellar tours take you 30m underground to Gallo-Roman quarries and 25 million bottles of bubbly.

Sleeping

Centre International de Séjour (CIS; ☎ 03 26 40 52 60; www.cis-reims.com; chaussée Bocquaine; s €28, per person in 2/3–5-bed dm €12/11, with shower & toilet 16/13; ⏰ 24hr; 💻) A friendly atmosphere makes up for the institutional rooms. To get there take bus B, K, M or N to the Comédie stop or bus H to the Pont De Gaulle stop.

Hôtel Alsace (☎ 03 26 47 44 08; fax 03 26 47 44 52; 6 rue du Général Sarrail; s/d/tr with shower from €26/29/34, with shower & toilet €29/32/37) The large rooms at this friendly family-run place have been recently redecorated.

Hôtel de la Cathédrale (☎ 03 26 47 28 46; fax 03 26 88 65 81; 20 rue Libergier; d/q from €56/77) This charming family-run two-star place, has 17 high-ceilinged rooms.

Grand Hôtel du Nord (☎ 03 26 47 39 03; www .hotelreims.com; 75 pl Drouet d'Erlon; d from €55) Boasts 50 cheerful, upbeat rooms, some with grand views of the square.

Eating & Drinking

Place Drouet d'Erlon, the focal point of Reims' nightlife, is lined with a profusion of pizzerias, brasseries, cafés, pubs and sandwich places.

L'Apostrophe (☎ 03 26 79 19 89; 59 pl Drouet d'Erlon; 2-course weekday menu €13, salads €11-14, mains €12.50-23) This bustling, book-lined brasserie serves generous portions of international cuisine and some mean cocktails. There's a chic atmosphere and a summertime terrace.

Hôtel Alsace (☎ 03 26 47 44 08; fax 03 26 47 44 52; 3-course menu €9.90; ⏰ lunch Mon-Sat) This hotel restaurant has one of the best midday deals in town.

Le Continental (☎ 03 26 47 01 47; 95 pl Drouet d'Erlon; menu €18.50-36, some incl wine; ⏰ noon-2.30pm

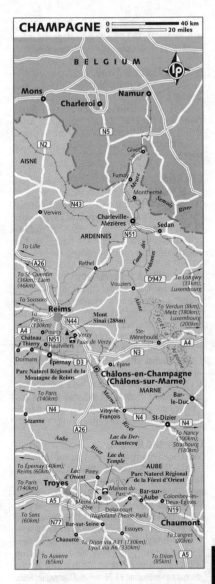

& 7-11pm or later) Panoramic views complement classic French dishes at Le Continental – seafood is the speciality from September to May here.

Brasserie Le Boulingrin (☎ 03 26 40 96 22; 48 rue de Mars; menu €16-23; ⏰ Mon-Sat). Check out the original 1920s décor here, including an old-time zinc bar.

Self caterers should try the **food market** (pl du Boulingrin; ☼ till 1.30pm Wed) or **Monoprix supermarket** (21 rue de Chativesle; ☼ 9am-8pm Mon-Sat).

Getting There & Away

Direct train destinations from Reims include Épernay (€5.20, 21 to 45 minutes, 23 daily weekdays, 14 daily weekends) and Paris' Gare de l'Est (€20.30, 1¾ hours, 12 to 16 daily). Information and tickets are available at the **Boutique SNCF** (1 cours JB Langlet; ☼ 10am-7pm Mon-Sat).

ÉPERNAY

pop 26,000

Home to some of the world's most famous champagne houses, Épernay, is 25km south of Reims. Beneath the streets, 200 million of bottles of champagne are being aged in 100km of subterranean cellars.

Orientation & Information

Mansion-lined ave de Champagne, where many of Épernay's champagne houses are based, stretches eastwards from the town's commercial heart (around place des Arcades), whose liveliest streets are rue Général Leclerc and rue St-Thibault.

The **tourist office** (☎ 03 26 53 33 00; www.ot-epernay.fr; 7 ave de Champagne; ☼ 9.30am-12.30pm & 1.30-7pm Mon-Sat, 11am-4pm Sun & hols mid-Apr–mid-Oct, 9.30am-12.30pm & 1.30-5.30pm Mon-Sat mid-Oct–mid-Apr) supplies details on activities in the region, including cellar visits.

Champagne Houses

Must-see champagne houses of Épernay include **Moët & Chandon** (☎ 03 26 51 20 20; www.moet.com; adult/12-16 yrs €7.50/4.50; 18 ave de Champagne; tours ☼ 9.30-11.30am & 2-4.30pm, closed weekends mid-Nov–mid-Mar), the number one champagne producer; **De Castellane** (☎ 03 26 51 19 19; www.castellane.com; 64 ave de Champagne; adult/10-18 yrs €6/4.50; tours ☼ 10.30-11.15am & 2.30-5.15pm Apr-Nov) is recommended for the panoramic view from the top of the 60m tower. **Mercier** (☎ 03 26 51 22 22; www.champagnemercier.com; 68-70 ave de Champagne; adult/12-15 yrs €6.50/3; ☼ mid-Jan–late Dec, closed Tue & Wed except mid-Mar–mid-Nov, tours 9.30-11.30am & 2-4.30pm) has the most glitzy and impressive tour

Sleeping

Épernay's hotels are especially full-on weekends from Easter to September and on weekdays in May, June and September.

Hôtel St-Pierre (☎ 03 26 54 40 80; fax 03 26 57 88 68; 1 rue Jeanne d'Arc; s/d from €21/24, d with shower & toilet from €34; **P**) Occupying an early–20th-century mansion that has hardly changed in half a century, this place has 15 simple rooms that retain the charm and atmosphere of yesteryear.

Hôtel de la Cloche (☎ 03 26 55 15 15; hotel-de-la-cloche.c.prin@wanadoo.fr; 5 pl Mendès-France; d from €39) This hotel has two stars and 19 cheerful, pastel rooms.

Hôtel Les Berceaux (☎ 03 26 55 28 84; les.berceaux@wanadoo.fr; 13 rue des Berceaux; d €66-75) The 27 rooms of this three-star institution, founded in 1889, are endowed with a certain Champenoise ambience.

Eating

La Cave à Champagne (☎ 03 26 55 50 70; 16 rue Gambetta; menu €14.50-28; ☼ Thu-Tue) Designed to look like a wine cellar, this place specialises in Champenoise cuisine.

Chez Ali (☎ 03 26 51 80 82; 27 rue de la Fauvette; mains €12-18.50; ☼ closed Sun night & Mon) Chez Ali serves up steaming Algerian couscous (€12 to €18.50).

Les Berceaux (weekday menu without/with wine €28/38, other menus €46 & €61; ☼ Wed-Sun) This sparklingly elegant *gastronomique* restaurant is inside the venerable Hôtel Les Berceaux (see Sleeping).

Le Sept (menu €16-22) is better priced and offers traditional French cuisine.

Self-catering options include the **covered market** (Halle St-Thibault; rue Gallice; ☼ 8am-noon Wed & Sat), and **Traiteur** (9 pl Hugues Plomb; ☼ 8am-12.45pm & 3-7.30pm daily except Sun & Wed), which sells scrumptious prepared dishes.

Getting There & Around

The **train station** (pl Mendès-France) has direct services to Reims (€5.20, 21 to 45 minutes, 23 daily weekdays, 14 daily weekends) and Paris' Gare de l'Est (€17.50, 1¼ hours, 10 to 16 daily). Cars can be hired from **Europcar** (☎ 03 26 54 90 61; 20 rempart Perrier).

TROYES

pop 123,000

Troyes is a lively old town graced with one of France's finest ensembles of medieval and Renaissance half-timbered houses. Several unique museums and ancient churches provide further reasons to spend time here.

Orientation & Information

The main commercial street is rue Émile Zola. Most of the city's sights and activities are in the Old City, centred on the 17th-century town hall and Église St-Jean.

There's a **tourist office** (☎ 03 25 73 36 88; www.tourisme-troyes.com; rue Mignard; ⏲ 10am-7pm Jul–mid-Sep, 9am-12.30pm & 2-6.30pm Mon-Sat, 10am-noon & 2-5pm Sun & hols May, Jun & mid-Sep–Oct) in the city centre, and another at the **train station** (☎ 03 25 82 62 70; 16 blvd Carnot; ⏲ 9am-12.30pm & 2-6.30pm Mon-Sat except hols year-round, 10am-1pm Sun Nov-Mar).

Sights

An architectural mishmash, **Cathédrale St-Pierre et St-Paul** (⏲ 10am-1pm & 2-6pm except Mon morning, longer in Jul–mid-Sep) incorporates elements from every period of Champenois Gothic architecture. In 1429, Joan of Arc and Charles VII stopped here on their way to his coronation in Reims.

The **Église Ste Madeleine** (Rue Général de Gaulle; ⏲ 10am-noon & 2-5pm except Sun & Mon mornings, longer hours Jul–mid-Sep) is Troyes' oldest and most interesting church.

The **Musée d'Art Moderne** (☎ 03 25 76 26 80; pl St-Pierre; adult/student under 25 yrs €5/free; ⏲ 11am-6pm except Mon & hols) features works by Derain, Dufy, Matisse, Modigliani, Picasso, Soutine and local favourite Maurice Marinot.

The **Musée St-Loup** (☎ 03 25 76 21 68; 1 rue Chrestien de Troyes; adult/student under 25 yrs €4/free; ⏲ 10am-noon & 2-6pm except Tue & hols) has a varied collection of medieval sculpture, enamel, archaeology and natural history.

Worth a look is the **Apothicairerie de l'Hôtel-Dieu-le-Comte** (☎ 03 25 80 98 97; quai des Comtes de Champagne). It is a fully outfitted, wood-panelled pharmacy from the early 1700s.

Sleeping

Hôtel Arlequin (☎ 03 25 83 12 70; www.hotelarlequin .com; 50 rue de Turenne; s/d €34/37; ⏲ reception 8am-12.30pm & 2-10pm Mon-Sat, 8am-12.30pm & 6.30-10pm Sun) The 22 cheerful rooms at this charming and very yellow two-star hostelry come with antique-style furnishings, high ceilings and commedia dell'arte playfulness.

Hôtel Les Comtes de Champagne (☎ 03 25 73 11 70; www.comtesdechampagne.com; 56 rue de la Monnaie; d from €28, with shower & toilet €37; **P**) This very welcoming 35-room place has a huge and romantic double with balcony for €60.

Royal Hôtel (☎ 03 25 73 19 99; www.royal-hotel -troyes.fr; 22 blvd Carnot; d from €70) With its 40 restrained rooms and bright, shiny bathrooms, the Royal has the usual three-star comforts. It's closed for three weeks around New Year.

Eating

Le Bistroquet (☎ 03 25 73 65 65; pl Langevin; menu €16.90-26.90; ⏲ closed Sun dinner, also closed Sun lunch mid-Jun–mid-Sep) Hugely popular Parisian-style brasserie offering excellent French dining value.

Le Jardin Gourmand (☎ 03 25 73 36 13; 31 rue Paillot de Montabert; menu €16.50; ⏲ closed Mon lunch & Sun) Elegant without being overly formal this places boasts a decent wine list including 25 vintages available by the glass; there is a terrace in summer.

L'Union (☎ 03 25 40 35 76; 34 rue Champeaux; 2-/3-course menu €12.50/18.50; ⏲ Mon-Sat) Suffused with the atmosphere of 1950s Paris – and just a touch of the classic American diner.

For self-catering try the **covered market** (⏲ 8am-12.45pm & 3.30-7pm Mon-Thu, 7am-7pm Fri & Sat, 9am-12.30pm Sun) or the **Monoprix supermarket** (71 rue Émile Zola; ⏲ 8.30am-8pm Mon-Sat).

Getting There & Away

The **bus station office** (☎ 03 25 71 28 42; ⏲ 8.30am-12.30pm & 2-6.30pm Mon-Fri), run by Courriers de l'Aube, is in a corner of the train station building. Troyes is on the rather isolated train line linking Basel (Bâle) with Paris' Gare de l'Est (€19.90, 1½ hours, 13 to 15 daily).

ALSACE & LORRAINE

Though often spoken of as if they were one, Alsace and Lorraine, neighbouring regions in France's northeastern corner, are linked by little more than a common border through the Vosges Mountains and the imperial ambitions of late-19th-century Germany. In 1871, after the Franco-Prussian War, the newly created German Reich annexed Alsace and part of Lorraine, making their return to rule from Paris a rallying cry of French nationalism.

STRASBOURG

pop 427,000

Situated just a few kilometres west of the Rhine, prosperous, cosmopolitan Strasbourg (City of the Roads) is France's great northeastern metropolis and the intellectual

FRANCE

and cultural capital of Alsace. Strasbourg serves as an important European crossroads thanks to the presence of the European Parliament, the Council of Europe, the European Court of Human Rights and 48,000 students.

Towering above the restaurants, *winstubs* (traditional Alsatian restaurants) and pubs of the lively old city is the cathedral, a medieval marvel in pink sandstone. Nearby you'll find one of the finest ensembles of museums anywhere in France.

Orientation

Strasbourg's train station is about 400m west of the Grande Île (Big Island), the core of ancient and modern Strasbourg. The quaint Petite France area in the Grande Île's southwestern corner is subdivided by canals. Much of the city centre is for pedestrians only. The European Parliament building and Palais de l'Europe are about 2km northeast of the cathedral. The city centre is about 3.5km west of pont de l'Europe, the bridge that links the French bank of the Rhine with the German city of Kehl.

Information

INTERNET ACCESS
NeT SuR CouR (☎ 03 88 35 66 76; 18 quai des Pêcheurs; tram stop Gallia; per hr €2; ⌚ 9.30am-9.30pm Mon-Fri, 2-8pm Sat & Sun) Situated at the end of a narrow courtyard.

TOURIST INFORMATION
Tourist office (☎ 03 88 52 28 28; www.ot-strasbourg .fr; 17 pl de la Cathédrale; ⌚ 9am-7pm) The Strasbourg Pass (€10.60), a coupon book valid for three consecutive days, may save you a fair bit of cash.
Tourist office annexe (☎ 03 88 32 51 49; tram stop Gare Centrale; ⌚ 9am-7pm Jun-Sep & Dec, to 12.30pm & 1.45-6pm Apr, May, Oct & Nov, closed Sun Jan-Mar & Nov) In the subterranean Galerie de l'En-Verre (underneath place de la Gare); there are plans to move it into the train station building.

Sights & Activities

The enchanting **Grande Île** is a paradise for an aimless amble through bustling public squares, busy pedestrianised areas and up-market shopping. The narrow streets of the **old city**, crisscrossed by narrow lanes, canals and locks, have a fairytale feel. The romantic Terrasse Panoramique atop **Barrage Vauban** (admission free; ⌚ 9am-7.30pm), a dam built

to prevent river-borne attacks on the city, affords panoramas of the Ill River.

Strasbourg's lacy, fragile-looking Gothic **Cathédrale Notre Dame** (⌚ 7am-7pm) is one of the marvels of European architecture. The west façade was completed in 1284, but the 142m spire, the tallest of its time, was not in place until 1439; its southern companion was never built. The 30m-high Gothic and Renaissance contraption just inside the southern entrance is the *horloge astronomique* (astronomical clock), a late-16th-century clock that strikes solar noon every day at 12.30pm. The 66m-high **platform** (☎ 03 88 43 60 40; adult/student & under 18 yrs €3/1.50; ⌚ 9am-5pm Mon-Fri, 10am-5pm Sat & Sun Apr-Oct, to 4.30pm Nov-Mar) above the façade affords a spectacular stork's-eye view of Strasbourg.

Occupying a group of magnificent 14th- and 16th-century buildings, the world-renowned **Musée de l'Œuvre Notre Dame** (☎ 03 88 32 88 17; 3 pl du Château; adult/student under 26 yrs & senior/under 18 yrs & disabled €4/2/free incl audioguide; ⌚ 10am to 6pm Tue-Sun) has one of Europe's premier collections of Romanesque, Gothic and Renaissance sculptures, 15th-century paintings and stained glass.

The outstanding **Musée d'Art Moderne et Contemporain** (☎ 03 88 23 31 31; pl Hans Jean Arp; tram stop Musée d'Art Moderne; adult/student/over 60 & under 18 yrs €5/2.50/free; ⌚ 11am-7pm Tue, Wed, Fri & Sat, noon-10pm Thu, 10am-6pm Sun) has an exceptionally diverse collection of works representing every major art movement of the past century.

The **Palais Rohan** (☎ 03 88 52 50 00; 2 pl du Château; adult/student under 26 yrs & senior/under 18 yrs & disabled €6/3/free for whole complex, €4/2/free for each museum; ⌚ 10am-6pm Wed-Mon) was built between 1732 and 1742 as a residence for the city's princely bishops. It houses several museums including the **Musée Archéologique**, which takes you from the Palaeolithic period to AD 800.

Tours

Boat excursions (70 minutes) that take in Petite France and the European institutions are run by **Strasbourg Fluvial** (☎ 03 88 84 13 13, 03 88 32 75 25; behind Palais Rohan; adult/student day €6.80/3.40, night €7.20/3.60; 4 tours daily).

The **Brasseries Kronenbourg** (☎ 03 88 27 41 59; siege.visites@kronenbourg-fr.com; 68 route d'Oberhausbergen; tram stop Ducs d'Alsace; adult/12-18 yrs €3/2) has interesting and thirst-quenching brewery tours. The office is about 1.2km northwest of town.

Located about 1.5km north of town is **Brasseries Heineken** (☎ 03 88 19 57 55; 4 rue St-Charles) which has free, two-hour brewery tours.

Sleeping

It is *extremely* difficult to find last-minute accommodation from Monday to Thursday when the European Parliament is in plenary session (generally for one week each month) – contact the tourist office for dates. Two- and three-star hotels line place de la Gare.

Camping de la Montagne Verte (☎ 03 88 30 25 46; 2 rue Robert Forrer; per camp site/adult €4.50/3.35; ☿ mid-Mar–Oct & late Nov–early Jan) The municipal Montagne Verte is a grassy place a short walk from the Nid de Cigognes stop on bus line No 2, about 2km southwest of town.

CIARUS (☎ 03 88 15 27 88; www.ciarus.com; 7 rue Finkmatt; per person in 8-/4-/2-bed dm incl breakfast €16.50/20/22.50; P ☐) This welcoming hostel is so stylish it even counts a few European parliament members among its regular clients.

Hôtel Le Colmar (☎ 03 88 32 16 89; hotel.le.colmar@ wanadoo.fr; 1 rue du Maire Kuss; tram stop Alt Winmärik; s/d €37/40, with shared bathroom €24.50/27.50; ☿ reception closed 1.30-5.30pm Sun) This 15-room cheapie isn't stylish but it's convenient and good value. Hall showers cost €2.50.

Hôtel du Rhin (☎ 03 88 32 35 00; www.hotel-du -rhin.com; 7-8 pl de la Gare; tram stop Gare Centrale; d €60, with shared bathroom €34) This 61-room two-star establishment has comfortable, sound-proofed rooms.

Hôtel Régent Petite France (☎ 03 88 76 43 43; www .regent-hotels.com; 5 rue des Moulins; s/d from €223/243, ste €366-455; P ✪) Guests of this luxurious four-star hotel enjoy romantic watery views, a sauna and marble bathrooms worthy of a Roman emperor.

Eating & Drinking

Just south of place Gutenberg, pedestrianised rue des Tonneliers is lined with mid-range restaurants of all sorts, both ethnic and French. Inexpensive places can be found northeast of the cathedral along rue des Frères. A few blocks south of the cathedral, pedestrianised rue d'Austerlitz is home to quite a few **food shops** (rue d'Austerlitz) also.

Au Crocodile (☎ 03 88 32 13 02; 10 rue de l'Outre; 3-/ 4-course weekday lunch menu €53/74, with wine €77/104, dinner menu €80 & €122; ☿ Tue-Sat) This elegant restaurant, holder of two Michelin stars, offers all-out gastronomique indulgence

and sophisticated elegance at a surprisingly reasonable price. Reservations are a good idea.

L'Assiette du Vin (☎ 03 88 32 00 92; 5 rue de la Chaîne; lunch menu €19.90, 2-/3-course menu €21/26, 4-course menu with 4 wines €45; ☿ closed lunch Mon & Sat, all day Sun) The cuisine changes with the seasons, inspired by what's available fresh in the marketplace. The wine list is extensive.

Au Renard Prêchant (☎ 03 88 35 62 87; 33 pl de Zurich; mains €9-16; ☿ closed lunch Sat & Sun) Occupying a 16th-century chapel, this convivial, often crowded restaurant, offers excellent, reasonably priced French fare. *Gibier* (game) is a seasonal speciality.

Winstub s'Muensterstuewel (☎ 03 88 32 17 63; 8 pl du Marché aux Cochons de Lait; lunch menu €23; ☿ Tue-Sat) This winstub has an excellent reputation – for mains and desserts – thanks to its English-speaking Paul Bocuse-trained owner, who's happy to whip up vegetarian options on demand.

Au Brasseur (☎ 03 88 36 12 13; 22 rue des Veaux; ☿ 11am-1am) Four beers – *brune*, *ambrée*, *blonde* and *blanche* – are brewed on the premises of this warm, dimly lit microbrewery, which also has some of the best deals in town on Alsatian treats.

Entertainment

Strasbourg's entertainment options are legion. Details on cultural events appear in the free monthly **Spectacles** (www.spectacles -publications.com), available at the tourist office.

La Salamandre (☎ 03 88 25 79 42; www.lasalamandre -strasbourg.fr, in French; 3 rue Paul Janet; adult/student incl drink €10/6; ☿ 10pm-4am Wed-Sun) Billed as a *bar-club-spectacles*, this discotheque has theme nights every Friday night (salsa, disco, 1980s etc).

Getting There & Away

Eurolines buses stop 2.5km south of the **Eurolines office** (☎ 03 90 22 14 60; 6D pl d'Austerlitz; ☿ 10am-6.30pm Mon-Fri, to noon & 2-5pm Sat) near Stade de la Meinau (the city's main football stadium), on rue du Maréchal Lefèbvre, about 200m west of avenue de Colmar and the Lycée Couffignal tram stop.

Strasbourg city bus No 21 (€1.20) links place Gutenberg with the Stadthalle in Kehl, the German town just across the Rhine.

Train information and tickets are available on the Grande Île at the **SNCF Boutique** (5 rue des France-Bourgeois; ☿ 10am-7pm Mon-Fri, to 5pm Sat).

STRASBOURG

INFORMATION
Main Post Office..................1 G3
NeT SuR CouR......................2 H4
Tourist Office Annexe..........3 A4

SIGHTS & ACTIVITIES   (p292)
Barrage Vauban...................4 B5
Cathédrale Notre Dame........5 F5
Musée d'Art Moderne et
  Contemporain...................6 B5
Musée de l'Œuvre Notre Dame..7 F5
Palais Rohan (Musée
  Archéologique)..................8 F5
Strasbourg Fluvial...............9 F5

SLEEPING   (p293)
CIARUS.............................10 E2
Hôtel du Rhin.....................11 B4
Hôtel Le Colmar..................12 B4
Hôtel Régent Petite France....13 C5

EATING   (p293)
Au Crocodile......................14 E4
Au Renard Prêchant.............15 G5
Food Shops........................16 F6
L'Assiette du Vin.................17 D5
Winstub s'Muensterstuewel...18 F5

DRINKING   (p293)
Au Brasseur.......................19 G4

ENTERTAINMENT   (p293)
La Salamandre.....................20 H5

TRANSPORT   (pp293–6)
CTS.................................21 D4
Eurolines Office..................22 F6
SNCF Boutique....................23 D4
Vélocation Bicycle Rental.....24 F6

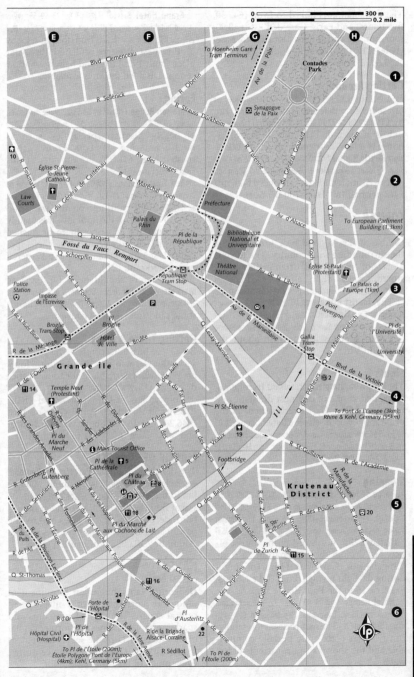

0   300 m
0   0.2 mile

E   **F**   **G**   **H**

Blvd Clemenceau

To Hoenheim Gare
Tram Terminus

Contades Park

R. Oberlin

R. Sellénick

R. Strauss Durkheim

Av. de la Paix

Synagogue de la Paix

Q. Zorn

1

10

Église St-Pierre-le-Jeune (Catholic)

R. Finkmatt

Av. des Vosges

R. du Général de Castelnau

R. du Maréchal Foch

R. Erienne

R. du Général Gouraud

Q. Zorn

2

Law Courts

Palais du Rhin

Préfecture

Av. d'Alsace

To European Parliment
Building (1.3km)

Q. Jacques Sturm

Pl de la République

Bibliothèque National et Universitaire

Q. Koch

Fossé du Faux Rempart

Q. Schoepflin

Théâtre National

Av. de la Liberté

Église St-Paul (Protestant)

To Palais de l'Europe (1km)

Police Station

R. de la Nuée Bleue

Impasse de l'Écrevisse

R. de la Fonderie

République Tram Stop

P

Av. de la Marseillaise

Pont d'Auvergne

3

Broglie Tram Stop

Pl Broglie

1

Q. Lezay-Marnésia

Gallia Tram Stop

Pl de l'Université

R. de la Mésange

Hôtel de Ville

R. Brûlée

Q. du Maire Dietrich

University

Grande Île

Blvd de la Victoire

R. de l'Outre

14

Temple Neuf (Protestant)

R. des Juifs

R. du Faisan

Pl St-Étienne

III

R. des Pêcheurs

@ 2

4

R. des Grandes-Arcades

Pl du Marché Neuf

R. des Hallebardes

R. des Frères

R. des Veaux

19

R. St-Guillaume

R. de l'Académie

Main Tourist Office

Pl de la Cathédrale

5

Pl du Château

8

Footbridge

Krutenau District

R. de la Manufacture des Tabacs

R. Gutenberg

Pl Gutenberg

7

R. Mercière

R. du Vieux-Hôpital

18

9

Pl du Marché aux Cochons de Lait

Q. des Bateliers

R. de Zurich

Ste-Catherine

R. de la Krutenau

R. des Poules

R. Paul Janet

20

5

R. des Serruriers

R. des Tonneliers

du Puits

R. de l'Écurie

R. du Vieux Marché aux Poissons

R. des Couples

R. des Orphelins

Pl de Zurich

15

R. de la Zürich

R. du Jeu de Paume

Q. St-Thomas

16

R. d'Austerlitz

R. des Bateliers

R. de St-Gothard

Q. St-Nicolas

Porte de l'Hôpital

24

Pl d'Austerlitz

R. de Berne

6

R d'Or

Pl de l'Hôpital

R. des Bouchers

R. de la 1ère Armée

R. de la Brigade Alsace-Lorraine

22

Hôpital Civil (Hospital)

To Pl de l'Étoile (200m);
Étoile Polygone Pont de l'Europe
(4km); Kehl, Germany (5km)

R. Sédillot

To Pl de l'Étoile (200m)

To Pont de l'Europe (3km);
Rhine & Kehl, Germany (95km)

LP

The train station is linked to Lyon (€42.30, five hours) and Paris' Gare de l'Est (€40.90, four hours); and, internationally, to Basel (Bâle; €17.40, 1¼ hours) and Frankfurt (€35.60, 2½ hours).

Getting Around

Four tram lines form the centrepiece of Strasbourg's public transport network, run by **CTS** (☎ 03 88 77 70 70; 31 pl Kléber). The main hub is at place de l'Homme de Fer. Strasbourg is a bicycle-friendly place and **Vélocation Bicycle Rental** (☎ 03 88 23 56 75; 4 rue du Maire Kuss; ⊙ 6am-7.30pm Mon-Fri, 9am-noon & 2-7.30pm Sat) rents well-maintained single-speed bikes for €4/7 per half/full day (€100 deposit).

COLMAR

pop 67,000

Colmar makes a good base for exploring the surrounding wine country. The town is a maze of cobbled pedestrian malls and restored, Alsatian-style half-timbered houses from the late Middle Ages or Renaissance.

The **tourist office** (☎ 03 89 20 68 92; www.ot-colmar.fr; 4 rue des Unterlinden; ⊙ 9am-noon & 2-6pm Mon-Sat, 10am-1pm Sun & hols, longer hrs depending on seasons) supplies information about the Route du Vin.

Sights

The **Issenheim Altarpiece** (Rétable d'Issenheim), acclaimed as one of the most dramatic and moving works of art ever created, is the pride and joy of the **Musée d'Unterlinden** (☎ 03 89 20 15 50; www.musee-unterlinden.com; adult/student 25 yrs & under incl audioguide €7/5; ⊙ 9am-6pm May-Oct, to noon & 2-5pm Wed-Mon Nov-Apr).

Sleeping

Auberge de Jeunesse Mittelhart (☎ 03 89 80 57 39; fax 03 89 80 76 16; 2 rue Pasteur; dm/d €11.65/28.30 incl breakfast; ⊙ reception 8-10am & 5-11pm, to midnight during daylight savings time; closed mid-Dec–mid-Jan) Situated 1.2km northwest of the tourist office, just around the corner from 76 route d'Ingersheim. Curfew is 11pm (midnight during daylight savings time). Take No 4, 5, 6, 12, or 15 to the Pont Rouge stop.

Hôtel Kempf (☎ 03 89 41 21 72; www.chez.com/mawo/kempf.html; 1 ave de la République; d €40, with shared bathroom €28) The mattresses at this family-run two-star place are especially comfortable and the showers squirt torrents of hot water.

Grand Hôtel Bristol (☎ 03 89 23 59 59; www.grand-hotel-bristol.com; 7 pl de la Gare; d from €75; **P**) A marble stairway leads from the plush lobby of this Best Western-affiliated three-star place (built 1925) to grand hallways and 71 rooms. Disabled facilities available.

Eating

La Maison Rouge (☎ 03 89 23 53 22; 9 rue des Écoles; menu €16.90-34.30; ⊙ Mon-Sat; ✗) A good variety of hearty Alsatian specialities, such as mouth-watering *jambon braisé* (spit-roasted ham; €10.90), are on offer at this rustic restaurant.

Aux Trois Poissons (☎ 03 89 41 25 21; 15 quai de la Poissonnerie; menu €21-45; ⊙ closed dinner Tue & Sun, all day Wed) Oil paintings on the walls and Persian carpets on the floor give this mainly fish restaurant an atmosphere of hushed and very civilised elegance. The chef's speciality is *sandre à la choucroute* (pike-perch with sauerkraut; €20).

Self-caterers should head for the **food markets** (pl de l'Ancienne Douane & rue des Écoles; ⊙ 8am-noon daily, to 12.30pm Thu) at the handsome sandstone marché couvert.

Getting There & Away

Buses and bus-train combos (via Breisach) serve the German city of Freiburg. Hours are posted and available at the tourist office or online at www.l-k.fr.

Colmar has rail links to Basel (Bâle; €10.20, 50 minutes), Paris' Gare de l'Est (€46.20, five to six hours via Strasbourg) and Strasbourg (€9.30, 31 to 60 minutes).

MASSIF DES VOSGES

The delightful, sublime **Parc Naturel Régional des Ballons des Vosges** covers about 3000 sq km in the south of the Vosges range. In the warm months, the gentle, rounded mountains, deep forests, glacial lakes and rolling pastureland are a walker's paradise, with an astounding 10,000km of marked trails.

NANCY

pop 331,000

Delightful Nancy has an air of refinement unique in Lorraine. With a magnificent central square, several fine museums and sparkling shop windows, the former capital of the dukes of Lorraine seems as opulent today as it did in the 16th to 18th centuries, when much of the centre was built.

DOUG MCKINLAY

Chocolates in a shop window in Brussels (p101), Belgium

SHANNON NACE

Hiking in the valleys around Canillo (p28), Andorra

Innsbruck (p72), Austria

CHRIS MELLOR

CHRISTIAN ASLUND

Off-piste skiing at St Anton am Arlberg (p80), Austria

MARK DAFFEY

Spectacular scenery at Exmoor
National Park (p178), Britain

MARTIN MOOS

The colourful fishing port of
Tobermory (p238), Isle of Mull, Britain

TONY WE

The grand interior of St Mary's Cathedral
(p172), Salisbury, Britain

Edinburgh Castle (p223), Scotland

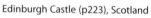

JONATHAN SMITH

Orientation & Information

Place Stanislas connects the narrow, twisting streets of the medieval Vieille Ville (Old Town), centred on the Grande Rue, with the rigid right angles of the 16th-century Ville Neuve (New Town) to the south. The train station is 800m southwest of place Stanislas.

There's a **tourist office** (☎ 03 83 35 22 41; www .ot-nancy.fr; pl Stanislas; ☺ 9am-7pm Mon-Sat, 10am-5pm Sun & hols Apr-Oct, 9am-6pm Mon-Sat, 10am-1pm Sun & hols Nov-Mar).

Sights

Beautifully proportioned, the neoclassical **place Stanislas** is impressively illuminated at night. The opulent buildings that surround the square, dazzling gilded wrought-iron gateways, rococo fountains and **d'Amphitrite** form one of the finest ensembles of 18th-century architecture and decorative arts anywhere in France.

The highlight of a visit to Nancy is the brilliant **Musée de l'École de Nancy** (School of Nancy Museum: ☎ 03 83 40 14 86; 36-38 rue du Sergent Blandan; adult/student & senior €4.75/2.29; ☺ 10.30am-6pm Tue-Sat), which brings together a collection of furnished rooms and glass produced by the Art Nouveau movement.

Star attractions at the excellent **Musée des Beaux-Arts** (☎ 03 83 85 30 72; 3 pl Stanislas; adult/student & senior €5.34/3.05; ☺ 10am-6pm Wed-Mon) include a superb collection of Art Nouveau glass and a rich and varied selection of paintings from the 14th to 18th centuries.

The 16th-century Palais Ducal, splendid former residence of the dukes of Lorraine, now houses the **Musée Historique Lorrain** (☎ 03 83 32 18 74; 64 & 66 Grande Rue; adult/student for both sections €4.60/3.10, for one section €3.10/2.30; ☺ 10am-12.30pm & 2-6pm Wed-Mon), dedicated to fine arts and history and to regional art and folklore.

Sleeping

Auberge de Jeunesse Château de Remicourt (☎ 03 83 27 73 67; aubergeremicourt@mairie-nancy.fr; 149 rue de Vandoeuvre in Villers-lès-Nancy; dm €13.50, d per person incl sheets & breakfast €15.50) This fantastic old chateau, with 60 beds, is 4km south of the centre.

Hôtel de l'Académie (☎ 03 83 35 52 31; fax 03 83 32 55 78; 7 bis rue des Michottes; s/d with shower from €23.50/26.50, with shower & toilet from €29.50) This offbeat place has 29 cheaply furnished rooms.

Hôtel des Portes d'Or (☎ 03 83 35 42 34; www .hotel-lesportesdor.com; 21 rue Stanislas; d from €51) This welcoming and very cosy two-star hostelry,

superbly situated just metres from place Stanislas, has 20 charming rooms.

Eating & Drinking

Rue des Maréchaux is lined with restaurants.

La Basse Cour (☎ 03 83 36 67 29; 23 Grande Rue; menu €16; ☺ 6.30-11pm or later Mon-Sat) A former 16th- and 17th-century townhouse, this homely place specialises in mouth-watering Lorraine-style *cuisine de campagne* (farm-fresh country cuisine).

There's a **covered market** (pl Henri Mangin; tram stop Point Central; ☺ 7am-6pm Tue-Thu, 7am-6.30pm Fri & Sat). The **Monoprix supermarket** (☺ 8.30am-8.30pm Mon-Sat) is inside the St-Sébastien shopping mall.

Le Ch'timi (☎ 03 83 32 82 76; 17 pl St-Epvre; ☺ 9am-2am Mon-Sat, to 8pm Sun) This unpretentious, mellow bar offers 200 different beers.

Getting There & Away

The **train station** (pl Thiers; tram stop Nancy Gare) is on the main line linking Paris' Gare de l'Est (€35.30, three hours, 12 to 14 daily) with Strasbourg (€18.40, 1¼ hours, nine to 12 daily).

FAR NORTHERN FRANCE

Le Nord de France, densely populated and laden with declining rust-belt industries, is made up of three historical regions, Flanders (Flandre or Flandres), Artois and Picardy (Picardie), and has lots to offer visitors willing to explore.

LILLE

pop 1 million

Long an industrial centre, Lille's recent history shows how a grimy metropolis, its economy based on declining technologies, can transform itself with the help of generous government investment into a glittering and self-confident cultural hub. Highlights include an attractive old town with a strong Flemish flavour, two renowned art museums, some fine dining and a happening student-driven nightlife scene.

Orientation

Lille is centred around three public squares: place du Général de Gaulle (also called the Grand' Place), place du Théâtre and place Rihour. The area of narrow streets north

FRANCE

of place du Général de Gaulle is known as Vieux Lille (Old Lille). Gare Lille-Flandres is about 400m southeast of place du Général de Gaulle; ultra-modern Gare Lille-Europe is 500m further east.

Information

INTERNET ACCESS
Cybercafé Le Smiley (☎ 03 20 21 12 19; 2 rue Royale; per hr €6.10; ⏰ noon-3am Mon-Sat, 4pm-midnight Sun)

TOURIST INFORMATION
Tourist office (☎ 03 59 57 95 00; www.lilletourism.com; pl Rihour; ⏰ 9.30am-6.30pm Mon-Sat, 10am-noon & 2-5pm Sun & hols).

Sights

North of place du Général de Gaulle, **Vieux Lille** gleams with restored 17th- and 18th-century houses. Other equally atmospheric streets include **rue de la Grande Chaussée** and **rue Esquermoise**.

The ornate, Flemish-Renaissance **Vieille Bourse** (Old Stock Exchange; pl du Général de Gaulle), built in 1652, actually consists of 24 separate buildings. The courtyard in the middle hosts a **book market** (⏰ 2-7pm Tue-Sun).

The world-renowned **Palais des Beaux-Arts** (☎ 03 20 06 78 00; pl de la République; metro République; adult/12-25 yrs/child under 12 yrs €4.60/3/free; ⏰ 2pm-6pm Mon, 10am-6pm Wed, Thu, Sat & Sun, to 7pm Fri) possesses a superb collection of 15th- to 20th-century paintings.

The innovative **La Piscine Musée d'Art et d'Industrie** (☎ 03 20 69 23 60; museeroubaix.free.fr; 23 rue de l'Espérance in Roubaix; metro Gare Jean Lebas; adult €3; ⏰ 11am-6pm Tue-Thu, to 8pm Fri, 1-6pm Sat & Sun), 11km northeast of central Lille, showcases fine arts, applied arts and sculpture in a delightful environment.

Sleeping

Auberge de Jeunesse (☎ 03 20 57 08 94; lille@fuaj.org; 12 rue Malpart; metro Mairie de Lille; dm 1st/subsequent nights incl breakfast €16.25/13.45; ⏰ closed late-Dec–late Jan) The spartan rooms house 165 beds (up to six beds per room).

Hôtel de France (☎ 03 20 57 14 78; fax 03 20 57 06 01; 10 rue de Béthune; s/d €39/46, with shared bathroom from €30/35) You can't get more central than this two-star place, whose 32 airy, functional rooms are one of the best deals in town.

Central Hôtel (☎ 03 20 54 64 63; centralhotel@club-Internet.fr; 91 rue Boucher de Perthes; s/d €32/40; ⏰ reception closed noon-7pm Sun) With one star and

12 spacious rooms, this place is peaceful, quiet and central.

Hôtel Faidherbe (☎ 03 20 06 27 93; fax 03 20 55 95 38; 42 pl de la Gare; d from €30, with shower & toilet €45) Cheerful, compact and well-designed rooms – but very simply furnished.

Hôtel Le Globe (☎ 03 20 57 29 58; 1 blvd Vauban; d/q €35/50.50) The 20 large rooms have French windows that look out on the Citadelle and (in most cases) chimneys, adding a dollop of old-fashioned charm.

Eating & Drinking

Rue Royale is *the* place for ethnic cuisine. The rue d'Amiens area is full of restaurants and pizzerias.

À l'Huîtrière (☎ 03 20 55 43 41; www.huitriere.fr; 3 rue des Chats Bossus; lunch menu €43, mains €30-48; ⏰ noon-2pm & 7-9.30pm except dinner Sun & 21 Jul-22 Aug). The original sea-themed Art-Deco mosaics, stained glass and ceramics haven't changed since this family-owned fish shop, situated in the heart of Vieux Lille, opened in 1928. Nor has the family's commitment to culinary excellence: the restaurant has held one or two Michelin stars continuously since 1930 for super-fresh seafood, accompanied by a wine or two from the 40,000-bottle cellar. Book ahead at weekends.

La Voûte (☎ 03 20 42 12 16; 4 rue des Débris St-Étienne; weekday lunch menu €9, other menus €12-16; ⏰ closed Mon dinner & Sun) The specialties of Flanders, including carbonnade (€11), are served in a classic bistro ambience.

Le Hochepot (☎ 03 20 54 17 59; 6 rue du Nouveau Siècle; menu €18-25; ⏰ closed Sat lunch & Sun) This rustic but elegant restaurant specialises in Flemish dishes such as *coq à la bière* (chicken cooked in beer) and carbonnade.

Brasserie La Chicorée (☎ 03 20 54 81 52; 15 pl Rihour; menu €9.50-25.50; ⏰ 10am-4.30am Sun-Thu, 10am-6.30am Fri & Sat) Dine on regional treats such as carbonnade and *waterzoë* (three kinds of fish prepared with beer) at practically any time of the day or night.

Aux Moules (☎ 03 20 57 12 46; 34 rue de Béthune; ⏰ noon-midnight) An informal, brasserie-style place specialising in Flemish dishes such as rabbit in *Kriek* beer sauce with frites (€9) and, of course, mussels (€10 to €11.50).

Self catering options include **Carrefour hypermarket** (⏰ 9am-10pm Mon-Sat), on the upper level of the Euralille shopping mall, and **Wazemmes food market** (pl Nouvelle Aventure; metro Gambetta; ⏰ 7am-6pm Tue-Thu, to 8pm Fri & Sat, to 2pm

Sun), a lively covered market 1.2km south-west of the centre.

L'Illustration Café (☎ 03 20 12 00 90; 18 rue Royale; 12.30pm-3am) This mellow but smoky bar is decorated with Art Nouveau woodwork and paintings by local artists.

Getting There & Away

Buses with **Eurolines** (☎ 03 20 78 18 88; 23 parvis St-Maurice; 9am-7pm Mon-Fri, to 6pm Sat Jun–mid-Sep) go to destinations that include Brussels (€10, two hours), Amsterdam (€34, six hours) and London (€39, six hours). Buses depart from the unsignposted bus parking lane on rue de Turin, on the northeast side of Gare Lille-Europe.

Lille's two train stations are one stop apart on metro line No 2. **Gare Lille-Flandres** is used by almost all regional services and most TGVs to Paris' Gare du Nord (€33.70 or €45.80, 62 minutes) while **Gare Lille-Europe** handles pretty much everything else, including Eurostar trains to London, TGVs/Eurostars to Brussels (weekdays/weekends €22.40/14.40, 38 minutes) and TGVs to Nice (€104.90 or €123.70, 7¼ hours).

Getting Around

Lille's two speedy metro lines, two tramways and bus lines – several of which cross into Belgium – are run by **Transpole** (☎ 08 20 42 40 40), which has an **information window** (closed Sunday) in the Gare Lille-Flandres metro station.

CALAIS

pop 75,000

Except for two small museums and Rodin's *The Burghers of Calais*, there's little to encourage the 22 million people who travel by way of grim, industrial Calais each year to linger any longer than necessary.

Orientation & Information

Gare Calais-Ville (the train station) is 650m south of the main square, place d'Armes, and 700m north of Calais' commercial district, which is centred around blvd Léon Gambetta and the Place du Théâtre bus hub. The Car Ferry Terminal is 1.5km northeast of place d'Armes; the Hoverport (for SeaCats) is an additional 1.5km further out. The Channel Tunnel's vehicle loading area is about 6km southwest of the town centre.

The **tourist office** (☎ 03 21 96 62 40; www.calais -cotedopale.com; 12 blvd Georges Clemenceau; 9am-7pm Mon-Sat, 10am-1pm Sun & hols Easter-August, 10am-1pm & 2-6.30pm Mon-Sat Sep-Easter) can provide information.

Sights

Calais's Flemish Renaissance-style **town hall** (1911–25) contains Rodin's famous sculpture *Les Bourgeois de Calais* (1895), honouring six local citizens who, in 1347, after eight months of holding off the besieging English forces, surrendered themselves and the keys of the starving city to Edward III of England. They hoped that by sacrificing themselves they might save the town and its inhabitants. Moved by his wife Philippa's entreaties, Edward eventually spared both the Calaisiens and their six brave leaders.

The exhibits at **Musée des Beaux-Arts et de la Dentelle** (Museum of Fine Arts & Lace; ☎ 03 21 46 48 40; 25 rue Richelieu; adult/student €3/1.50, free Wed; 10am-noon & 2-5.30pm Mon & Wed-Fri, to noon & 2-6.30pm Sat, 2-6.30pm Sun) focus on mechanised lacemaking.

Original WWII artefacts (uniforms, weapons, proclamations) fill the display cases of the **Musée de la Guerre** (☎ 03 21 34 21 57; adult/student/family €6/5/14 incl audioguide; 10am-6pm May-Aug, 11am-5.30pm Apr & Sep, 11am-5pm Wed-Mon mid-Feb–Mar, noon-5pm Wed-Mon Oct–mid-Nov), housed in a concrete bunker built as a German naval headquarters.

Sleeping

Camping Municipal (☎ 03 21 97 89 79; ave Raymond Poincaré; camp sites per adult/tent €3.24/2.27; year-round) This camping ground occupies a grassy but soulless site inside Fort Risban. It's served by bus No 3.

Auberge de Jeunesse (Centre Européen de Séjour; ☎ 03 21 34 70 20; www.auberge-jeunesse-calais.com; ave Maréchal de Lattre de Tassigny; dm incl breakfast €15.20; 24hr; P) This modern, well-equipped 162-bed hostel just 200m from the beach is a good source of information on local events.

Hôtel Richelieu (☎ 03 21 34 61 60; www.hotel richelieu-calais.com; 17 rue Richelieu; d/q from €46/92) At this quiet two-star place the 15 cheerful rooms, each one unique, are attractively outfitted with antique furniture redeemed and restored by the owner from the local markets.

Eating

Rue Royal and place d'Armes are lined with touristy places.

La Pléiade (☎ 03 21 34 03 70; 32 rue Jean Quéhen; 3-/4-/6-course menu €22/35/50; ☺ closed Sun & Mon) The *filet de bar rôti* (sea bass with almond sauce and a dollop of pistou) is very popular.

Aux Mouettes (☎ 03 21 34 67 59; 10 rue Jean Pierre Avron; menu €15-32; ☺ closed Sun dinner & Mon) Fishers sell their daily catch across the street at the quay – easy to see why this unassuming place is known for serving only the freshest fish.

There's a **food market** (pl d'Armes; ☺ Wed & Sat morning) and a **Match supermarket** (pl d'Armes; ☺ 9am-7.30pm Mon-Sat).

Getting There & Around

For details on getting across the Channel, see p391.

BOAT

Every day, 45 to 54 car ferries from Dover dock at the busy Car Ferry Terminal, about 1.5km northeast of place d'Armes. Companies at the ferry terminal are:

P&O Ferries (☎ 03 21 46 10 10; ☺ 24hr)
SeaFrance (☎ 03 21 46 80 05; ☺ 6am-10.45pm)

Their offices in town are:
P&O Ferries (☎ 01 55 69 82 28; 41 pl d'Armes)
SeaFrance (☎ 03 21 19 42 42; 2 pl d'Armes)

Shuttle buses (€1.50 for P&O), coordinated with departure times, link Gare Calais-Ville and each company's office at place d'Armes with the Car Ferry Terminal.

Hoverspeed's car-carrying SeaCats to Dover (operational from mid-March to 22 December) use the **Hoverport** (High Speed Ferry Terminal; ☎ 03 21 46 14 00 or ☎ 00800 1211 1211), which is 3km northeast of the town centre.

BUS

Inglard (☎ 03 21 96 49 54), at the Car Ferry Terminal, links Calais' train station with the beautiful Côte d'Opaleand Boulogne.

Cariane Littoral (☎ 03 21 34 74 40; 10 rue d'Amsterdam) operates express BCD services from Calais to Boulogne and Dunkirk.

CAR & MOTORCYCLE

To reach the Channel Tunnel's vehicle loading area at Coquelles, follow the signs on the A16 to the 'Tunnel Sous La Manche' (Tunnel under the Channel) at exit No 13.

TRAIN

Calais has two train stations: Gare Calais-Ville in the city centre; and Gare Calais-Fréthun, a TGV station 10km southwest of town near the Channel Tunnel entrance. They are linked by the free Navette TER, a bus service operated by Cariane Littoral.

Gare Calais-Ville has services to Boulogne (€6.60, 27 to 48 minutes, 15 to 19 daily Monday to Saturday, nine daily Sunday), Dunkirk (€7, 50 minutes, four daily Monday to Friday, two on Saturday) and Lille-Flandres (€14, 1¼ hours, 18 daily Monday to Friday, 11 on Saturday, seven on Sunday).

Calais-Fréthun is served by TGVs to Paris' Gare du Nord (€35.50 or €47.90, 1½ hours, five daily Monday to Saturday, two on Sunday) as well as the Eurostar to London.

DUNKIRK

pop 209,000

Dunkirk (Dunkerque), razed during WWII, was rebuilt during one of the most uninspired periods in Western architecture (the 1950s). Unless you want to hang out on Malo-les-Bains beach or join in a colourful pre-Lent carnival, there's little reason to stay.

Orientation & Information

The train station is 600m southwest of Dunkirk's main square, place Jean Bart. The beach and esplanade are 2km northeast of the centre in the rather faded resort of Malo-les-Bains.

There's a **tourist office** (☎ 03 28 66 79 21; www.ot-dunkerque.fr; rue de l'Amiral Ronarc'h; ☺ 9am-12.30pm & 1.30-6.30pm Mon-Fri, to 6.30pm Sat, 10am-noon & 2-4pm Sun & hols, no midday closure Jul & Aug).

The **Musée Portuaire** (Harbour Museum; ☎ 03 28 63 33 39; 9 quai de la Citadelle; adult/child €4/3; ☺ 10am-12.45pm & 1.30-6pm), housed in a one-time tobacco warehouse, will delight ship-model lovers.

Getting There & Away

For details on links to Calais, see p300. Almost all trains to Lille use Lille-Flandres (€11.60, 1¼ hours, nine to 21 daily).

Ferries run by **Norfolk Line** (☎ 03 28 59 01 01; www.norfolkline.com) link Loon Plage, about 25km west of the town centre, with Dover.

BATTLE OF THE SOMME MEMORIALS

The First Battle of the Somme, a WWI Allied offensive waged in the villages and woodlands northeast of Amiens, was designed to relieve pressure on the beleaguered French troops at Verdun. On 1 July 1916, British, Commonwealth and French troops 'went over the top' in a massive assault along a 34km front. But German positions proved virtually unbreachable, and on the first day of the battle an astounding 21,392 Allied troops were killed and another 35,492 were wounded.

By the time the offensive was called off in mid-November, some 1.2 million lives had been lost on both sides. The British had advanced 12km, the French 8km. The Battle of the Somme has become a metaphor for the meaningless slaughter of war and its killing fields have become a site of pilgrimage.

NORMANDY

Often compared with the countryside of southern England, Normandy (Normandie) is the land of the *bocage*, farmland subdivided by hedges and trees. Winding through these hedgerows are sunken lanes, whose grassy sides are covered with yellow primroses and gorse. In 911 the Rouen region became home to the invading Viking Norsemen (or Normans), who gave their name to the region.

ROUEN

The city of Rouen, for centuries the furthest point downriver where you could cross the Seine by bridge, is known for its many spires, church towers and half-timbered houses. Rouen also has a renowned Gothic cathedral and a number of excellent museums. The city was occupied by the English during the Hundred Years' War when the young Joan of Arc (Jeanne d'Arc) was tried for heresy and burned at the stake here.

Orientation & Information

The main train station (Gare Rouen-Rive Droite) is at the northern end of rue Jeanne d'Arc, the main thoroughfare running south to the Seine. The old city is centred around rue du Gros Horloge between the place du Vieux Marché and the cathedral.

The **tourist office** (☎ 02 32 08 32 40; www.mairie-rouen.fr; 25 pl de la Cathédrale; ☺ 9am-7pm Mon-Sat, 9.30am-12.30pm & 2-6pm Sun May-Sep, 9am-6pm Mon-Sat, 10am-1pm Sun Oct-Apr) is opposite the western façade of the Cathédrale Notre Dame.

Sights

The main street of the old city, rue du Gros Horloge, runs from the cathedral to **place du Vieux Marché**, where 19-year-old Joan of Arc was executed in 1431. The striking **Église Jeanne d'Arc** (☺ 10am-12.15pm & 2-6pm, closed Fri & Sun morning) marks the site; it has marvellous 16th-century stained-glass windows.

Rouen's **Cathédrale Notre Dame** (☺ 8am-6pm Tue-Sun, 2-6pm Mon) is considered a masterpiece of French Gothic architecture. There are several guided visits each day to the crypt and ambulatory.

The fascinating **Musée Le Secq des Tournelles** (☎ 02 35 71 28 40; 2 rue Jacques Villon; adult/student €2.30/1.55; ☺ 10am-1pm & 2-6pm Wed-Mon), devoted to the blacksmith's craft, displays some 12,000 locks, keys, scissors, tongs and other wrought-iron utensils made between the 3rd and 19th centuries.

The **Musée des Beaux-Arts** (Fine Arts Museum; ☎ 02 35 71 28 40; 26 bis rue Jean Lecanuet; adult/student €3/2; ☺ 10am-6pm Wed-Mon) features paintings from the 15th to the 20th centuries.

The **Tour Jeanne d'Arc** (☎ 02 35 98 16 21; rue du Donjon; adult/student €1.50/free; ☺ 10am-12.30pm & 2-6pm Mon & Wed-Sat, 2-6.30pm Sun Apr-Sep, 10am-12.30pm & 2-5pm Mon & Wed-Sat, 2-5.30pm Sun Oct-Mar) is where Joan of Arc was imprisoned before her execution.

Sleeping

If you're staying over a weekend, ask the tourist office about its 'Bon Weekend' offer of two nights for the price of one in some hotels, but you must book eight days ahead.

Camping Municipal (☎ 02 35 74 07 59; rue Jules Ferry; camp sites per tent/car/child €4/1.50/1; ☺ year-round). The camping ground is 5km northwest of Gare Rouen-Rive Droite in Déville-lès-Rouen.

Hôtel des Flandres (☎ /fax 02 35 71 56 88; 5 rue des Bons Enfants; d with shower/shower & toilet €26/29) This is the pick of the budget options with comfy, newly renovated doubles.

Hôtel Le Palais (☎ 02 35 71 41 40; 12 rue du Tambour; s/d €32/34, with washbasin only €25) Well-situated hotel near the Palais de Justice and the Gros Horloge.

Eating

Les Maraîchers (☎ 02 35 71 57 73; 37 pl du Vieux Marché; menu €14.95-21) Always busy and the best of the Vieux Marché's many restaurants, this place has a lively pavement terrace and varied *menus*.

ROUEN

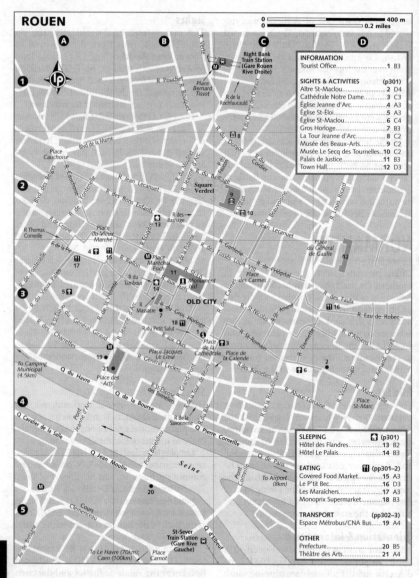

0		400 m
0		0.2 miles

Le P'tit Bec (☎ 02 35 07 63 33; 182 rue Eau de Robec; lunch menu €11 & €13.50, mains €7-9; ✆ closed dinner Mon-Thu & all day Sun) On a peaceful square, this restaurant offers a delicious array of dishes including some vegetarian specialities.

Dairy products, fish and fresh produce are on sale at the **covered food market** (pl du Vieux Marché; ✆ 6am-1.30pm Tue-Sun), and there's a **Monoprix supermarket** (65 rue du Gros Horloge; ✆ 8.30am-9pm Mon-Sat).

Getting There & Away

Regional bus information is dispensed by **Espace Métrobus** (☎ 02 35 52 92 00; 9 rue Jeanne d'Arc). Buses leave from quai du Havre and quai de la Bourse.

Trains to Paris and far-flung destinations depart from Gare Rouen-Rive Droite. The Gare Rouen-Rive Gauche south of the river has mainly regional services.

BAYEUX

pop 15,000

Bayeux is celebrated for two trans-Channel invasions: the conquest of England by the Normans under William the Conqueror in 1066 (an event chronicled in the celebrated Bayeux Tapestry) and the Allied D-day landings of 6 June 1944, which launched the liberation of Nazi-occupied France. It was the first town in France to be freed and, remarkably, survived virtually unscathed. Bayeux is a very attractive town with several excellent museums and serves as a good base for visits to the D-day beaches.

Orientation & Information

The Cathédrale Notre Dame, the major landmark in the centre of Bayeux and visible throughout the town, is 1km northwest of the train station.

Just off the northern end of rue Larcher is the **tourist office** (☎ 02 31 51 28 28; fax 02 31 51 28 29; www.bayeux-tourism.com; Pont St-Jean; 🕑 9.30am-12.30pm & 2-6pm Mon-Sat, 10am-12.30pm & 2-5.30pm Sun Apr-Jun, 9am-7pm Mon-Sat, 9am-12.30pm & 2-6.30pm Sun Jul-Sep, 9.30am-12.30pm & 2-5.30pm Mon-Sat Jan-Mar & Oct-Dec).

Sights

The world-famous Bayeux Tapestry was commissioned by Bishop Odo of Bayeux, half-brother to William the Conqueror, sometime between the successful Norman invasion of England in 1066 and 1082. The tapestry recounts the dramatic story of the Norman invasion and the events that led up to it (from the Norman perspective).

The tapestry is housed in the **Musée de la Tapisserie de Bayeux** (☎ 02 31 51 25 50; rue de Nesmond; adult/student €6.40/2.60; 🕑 9am-7pm May-Aug; 9am-6.30pm mid-Mar–Apr, Sep & Oct, 9.30am-12.30pm & 2-6pm Nov–mid-Mar).

The spectacular **Cathédrale Notre Dame** (🕑 8am-7pm July & Aug, 8.30am-6pm Sep-Jun) is a fine example of Norman Gothic architecture, dating from the 13th century.

Bayeux's huge war museum the **Musée Mémorial 1944 Bataille de Normandie** (☎ 02 31 51 46 90; blvd Fabien Ware; adult/student €5.40/2.50; 🕑 9.30am-6.30pm May–mid-Sep, 10am-12.30pm & 2-6pm

mid-Sep–Apr) displays thousands of photos, uniforms, weapons, newspaper clippings and lifelike scenes associated with D-day and the Battle of Normandy.

The peaceful **war cemetery** (☎ 02 21 21 77 00; blvd Fabien Ware), a few hundred metres west of the war museum, is the largest of the 18 Commonwealth military cemeteries in Normandy. It contains 4868 graves of soldiers from the UK and 10 other countries.

Sleeping

Camping Municipal de Bayeux (☎ 02 31 92 08 43; camp sites per adult/tent & car €2.85/3.50; 🕑 mid-Mar–mid-Nov; check-in 7am-9pm Jul & Aug, 8-9am & 5-7pm Sep-Jun) is about 2km north of the town centre, just south of blvd d'Eindhoven.

Centre d'Accueil Municipal (☎ 02 31 92 08 19; fax 02 31 92 12 40; 21 rue des Marettes; s €11.90) In a large, modern building, 1km southwest of the cathedral, the singles (all that's available) are a great deal and prices include breakfast.

Family Home (☎ 02 31 92 15 22; 39 rue du Général de Dais; dm with/without HI card €16/18, s €25) An excellent old hostel, this is a great place to meet other travellers. Dorm rates include breakfast. Multicourse French dinners cost €10 including wine. A few tents can be pitched in the back garden for €5 per person. There's a laundry.

Hôtel de la Gare (☎ 02 31 92 10 70; fax 02 31 51 95 99; 26 pl de la Gare; s/d/tr €22/37/64.50) Old but well-maintained, this hotel has recently installed showers and toilets in all the rooms.

Hôtel des Sports (☎ 02 31 92 28 53; fax 02 31 92 35 40; 19 rue St-Martin; s/d from €26/33.55) A cut above, with tastefully appointed rooms.

Eating

Le Petit Normand (☎ 02 31 22 88 66; 35 rue Larcher; lunch menu €8.85, dinner menu €12.95 & €22.10; 🕑 closed Thu Nov-Apr) Traditional Norman food is served here, including dishes such as mussels with apple cider, or ham with camembert sauce.

Le Petit Bordelais (☎ 02 31 92 06 44; 15 rue du Maréchal Foch; plat du jour €7.20; 🕑 noon-2pm Tue-Sat) This tiny extension of an old wine shop serves good home-cooked meals, local cheeses and homemade pâté for lunch only.

La Table du Terroir (☎ 02 31 92 05 53; Alleé de l'Orangerie; menu €11-20; 🕑 closed Sun dinner & Mon) Excellent Norman-style *menus*. Meat is king here.

The many takeaway shops on or near rue St-Martin and rue St-Jean, include **Le Petit Glouton** (42 rue St-Martin). Rue St-Jean has an

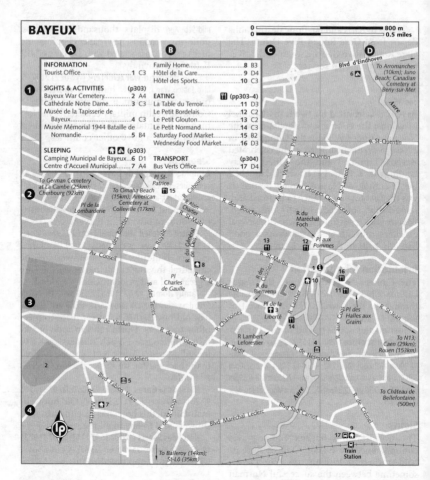

BAYEUX

0 _____ 800 m
0 _____ 0.5 miles

INFORMATION	
Tourist Office.....................1 C3	
SIGHTS & ACTIVITIES	(p303)
Bayeux War Cemetery...........2 A4	
Cathédrale Notre Dame........3 C3	
Musée de la Tapisserie de	
Bayeux.............................4 C3	
Musée Mémorial 1944 Bataille de	
Normandie.......................5 B4	
SLEEPING	(p303)
Camping Municipal de Bayeux..6 D1	
Centre d'Accueil Municipal.....7 A4	

Family Home........................8 B3	
Hôtel de la Gare...................9 D4	
Hôtel des Sports.................10 C3	
EATING	(pp303–4)
La Table du Terroir..............11 D3	
Le Petit Bordelais...............12 C2	
Le Petit Glouton.................13 C2	
Le Petit Normand...............14 C3	
Saturday Food Market..........15 B2	
Wednesday Food Market.......16 D3	
TRANSPORT	(p304)
Bus Verts Office..................17 D4	

open-air food market on Wednesday morning, place St-Patrice on Saturday morning.

Getting There & Away

Bus Verts (☎ 08 10 21 42 14; ✆ 10am-noon & 3-6pm Mon-Fri, closed most of July) runs services from the train station and place St-Patrice to Caen and the D-day beaches; its office is opposite the train station.

Train services include Paris' Gare St-Lazare (€28.50, 2½ hours) via Caen (€4.98, 20 minutes, 15 daily) as well as Cherbourg (€14.30, one hour, 10 daily).

D-DAY BEACHES

The D-day landings, codenamed 'Operation Overlord', were the largest military operation in history. Early on the morning of 6 June 1944, swarms of landing craft – part of a flotilla of almost 7000 boats – hit the beaches, and tens of thousands of Allied soldiers poured onto French soil.

Most of the 135,000 Allied troops stormed ashore along 80km of beaches north of Bayeux, that were codenamed Utah, Omaha, Gold, Juno and Sword. The landings on D-day were followed by the Battle of Normandy, which would lead to the liberation of Europe from Nazi occupation. Caen's Mémorial museum provides the best introduction to the history of what took place here. Once on the coast, take the well-marked circuit that links the battle sites.

FRANCE

Maps of the D-day beaches are available at *tabacs* (tobacconists), newsagents and bookshops in Bayeux and elsewhere.

Arromanches

To make it possible to unload the quantities of cargo necessary, the Allies established two prefabricated ports code-named **Mulberry Harbours**. One of them, Port Winston, can still be viewed at Arromanches, a seaside town 10km northeast of Bayeux. In the three months after D-day, 2.5 million men, four million tonnes of equipment and 500,000 vehicles were unloaded there. At low tide you can walk out to many of the caissons.

The well-regarded **Musée du Débarquement** (Invasion Museum; ☎ 02 31 22 34 31; pl de 6 Juin; adult/student €6/4; ⏰ 9.30am-5.30pm Mar-May & Sep, 9am-7pm Jun-Aug, 10am-5pm Feb & Oct-Dec), right in the centre of Arromanches, explains the logistics and importance of Port Winston and makes a good first stop before visiting the beaches.

Omaha & Juno Beaches

The most brutal fighting on D-day took place 15km northwest of Bayeux along 7km of coastline known as Omaha Beach. A memorial marks the site of the first US military cemetery on French soil, which contained the bodies of soldiers killed on the beach as they ran inland towards German positions on the nearby ridge. Dune-lined Juno Beach, 12km east of Arromanches, was stormed by Canadian troops on D-day.

Military Cemetery

The bodies of the American soldiers who died during the pivotal Battle of Normandy were either sent back to the USA or buried in the **American Military Cemetery** (☎ 02 31 51 62 00; ⏰ 9am-6pm mid-Apr–Sep, to 5pm Oct–mid-Apr) at Colleville-sur-Mer. The cemetery contains the graves of 9386 American soldiers and a memorial to 1557 others whose remains were never found. The huge, immaculately tended expanse of lawn, with white crosses and Stars of David set on a hill overlooking Omaha Beach, testifies to the extent of the killings that took place around here in 1944.

Tours

From Caen, the Mémorial museum offers a combined ticket that includes a visit to the museum and a half-day tour of the landing beaches for €64.80 (€52.68 for veterans, those under 18 and morning departures). The visit and tour can be done either separately or on the same day.

Getting There & Away

The rather infrequent Line No 70 operated by **Bus Verts** (☎ 08 10 21 42 14) from Bayeux goes westwards to the American Military Cemetery at Colleville-sur-Mer and Omaha Beach, and on to Pointe du Hoc and the town of Grandcamp-Maisy.

MONT ST-MICHEL

pop 42

It's difficult not to be impressed with your first sighting of Mont St-Michel. Covering the summit is the massive abbey, a soaring ensemble of buildings in a hotchpotch of architectural styles.

Mont St-Michel's fame derives equally from the bay's extraordinary tides. Depending on the gravitational pull of the moon and, to a lesser extent, the sun, the difference between low and high tides can reach 15m. The Mont either looks out onto bare sand stretching many kilometres into the distance or, at high tide (only about six hours later), the same expanse under water. However, the Mont and its causeway are completely surrounded by the sea only at the highest of tides, which occur at seasonal equinoxes.

The Mont's major attraction is the renowned **Abbaye du Mont St-Michel** (☎ 02 33 89 80 00; adult/student & under 25 yrs/child under 17 yrs €7/4.50/ free incl guided tour; ⏰ 9am-7pm May-Aug, 9.30am-6pm Sep-Apr). To reach it, walk to the top of the Grande Rue and then climb the stairway.

Pontorson (population 4100), the nearest town to Mont St-Michel, is 9km to the south and the base for most travellers. Route D976 from Mont St-Michel runs right into Pontorson's main thoroughfare, rue du Couësnon.

Information

The **tourist office** (☎ 02 33 60 14 30; fax 02 33 60 0675; www.mont-saint-michel.net; ⏰ 9am-noon & 2-6pm Easter-Jun, Sep-Oct, to 7pm July & Aug; to noon & 2-5.30pm Mon-Sat, 10am-noon & 2-6pm Sun Nov-Easter) is up the stairs to the left as you enter Porte de l'Avancée.

The friendly staff at Pontorson's **tourist office** (☎ 02 33 60 20 65; fax 02 33 60 85 67; mont .st.michel.pontorson@wanadoo.fr; pl de l'Église; ⏰ 9am-noon & 2-7pm Mon-Fri, 10am-noon & 3-6pm Sat, 10am-noon

FRANCE

Sun Apr-Sep, to 6pm, closed Sun Oct-Mar) provide tons of information about local walks, tours and events.

Sleeping

Camping Les Portes du Mont St-Michel (☎ 02 33 60 22 10; fax 02 33 60 20 02; camp sites per adult/tent & car €3/4.65; ☼ Mar-Oct) This grassy camping ground is on the shop-lined D976 to Pontorson, only 2km from the Mont. It also has bungalows with shower and toilet.

Centre Duguesclin (☎ /fax 02 33 60 18 65; aj@ville-pontorson.fr; blvd du Général Patton; dm €7.30) About 1km west of the train station, in Pontorson, this modern, newly renovated hostel is in an old three-storey stone building opposite No 26. Accommodation is in four- to six-bed rooms and there are kitchen facilities. The hostel closes from 10am to 6pm, but there's no curfew.

Hôtel Saint-Aubert (☎ 02 33 60 08 74; fax 02 33 60 35 67; d €29-54) A bland but adequate hotel with private facilities at the beginning of the 2km causeway that leads to Mont St-Michel.

The cheapest hotels are in Pontorson.
Hôtel Le Rénové (☎ 02 33 60 00 21; 4 rue de Rennes; s/d €23/35) has basic but adequate rooms.

Eating

La Mère Poulard (☎ 02 33 60 14 01; menu from €19) This is the place to come to for the world's most famous, and possibly fluffiest, omelettes. The cheapest *menu* (€19) is served between 2.30pm and 6.30pm and includes a plain omelette with a dessert. Check the prices of the menu you are handed inside the restaurant carefully; they may not correspond to the misleading menus displayed outside.

Hôtel de Bretagne (☎ 02 33 60 10 55; 59 rue du Couësnon; menu €14.50; ☼ Tue-Sun) For something a little more formal, Bretagne has a dining room with quality food and excellent service.

Getting There & Away

Courriers Bretons (☎ 02 33 60 11 43; 2 rue du Docteur Bailleul) runs fairly frequent buses from Pontorson train station to Mont St-Michel (€1.17, 30 minutes). From Paris, take the train to Caen (from Gare St-Lazare), to Rennes (from Gare Montparnasse), or travel directly to Pontorson via Folligny (from Gare Montparnasse; €35.60).

BRITTANY

Brittany stands slightly aloof from the rest of France, set apart by its Celtic roots and a stubborn independent streak. Brittany's shoreline possesses some of France's finest coastal scenery, while its traditional music and culture festivals are among the most colourful in Europe. Brittany boasts dozens of classic seaside resorts and offers some of the best yachting, windsurfing, sea-kayaking and coastal hiking in France. You might well hear Breton (Breiz), a Celtic language related to Cornish and Welsh, spoken in western Brittany (especially in Cornouaille).

QUIMPER
pop 59,400

Quimper (kam-*pair*), lying where the small rivers Odet and Steïr meet, takes its name from the Breton word *kemper*, meaning 'confluence'. Strongly Breton in character and the administrative capital of the *département* of Finistère, Quimper is very much the cultural and artistic capital, with its cobbled streets, half-timbered houses, waterways and magnolias imparting a pleasing village feel. The old city, much of it pedestrianised, clusters around the cathedral on the north bank of the Odet, overlooked by Mont Frugy on the south bank.

The **tourist office** (☎ 02 98 53 04 05; www.quimper-tourisme.com, in French; pl de la Résistance; ☼ 9am-7pm Mon-Sat, 10am-1pm & 3-5.45pm Sun Jul-Aug, 9.30am-12.30pm & 1.30-6pm or 6.30pm Mon-Sat Sep-Jun, 10am-12.45pm Sun Jun & 1-15 Sep) can arrange weekly guided city tours in English in July and August, and can reserve accommodation.

Sights

The twin spires and soaring vertical lines of Quimper's **Cathédrale St-Corentin** dominate the city centre. Begun in 1239, it wasn't fully completed until the 1850s. The inside gives an extraordinary feeling of light and space.

The **Musée Départemental Breton** (☎ 02 98 95 21 60; 1 rue du Roi Gradlon; adult/child €3.80/2.50; ☼ 9am-6pm Jun-Sep, to noon & 2-5pm Tue-Sat & 2-5pm Sun Oct-May) is in what used to be the bishop's palace, beside the cathedral. It has superb exhibits on the history, furniture, costumes, crafts and archaeology of the area. Adjoining the museum is the **Jardin de l'Évêché** (Bishop's Palace Garden; admission free; ☼ 9am-5pm or 6pm).

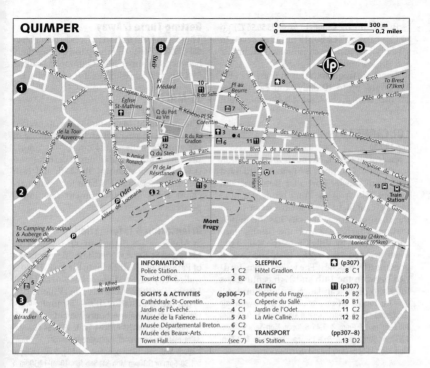

INFORMATION	**SLEEPING** (p307)
Police Station...............................1 C2	Hôtel Gradlon..............................8 C1
Tourist Office...............................2 B2	
	EATING (p307)
SIGHTS & ACTIVITIES (pp306–7)	Crêperie du Frugy.........................9 B2
Cathédrale St-Corentin.................3 C1	Crêperie du Sallé.........................10 B1
Jardin de l'Évêché........................4 C1	Jardin de l'Odet...........................11 C2
Musée de la Faïence......................5 A3	La Mie Câline.............................12 B2
Musée Départemental Breton.........6 C2	
Musée des Beaux-Arts...................7 C1	**TRANSPORT** (pp307–8)
Town Hall................................(see 7)	Bus Station.................................13 D2

The **Musée de la Faïence** (☎ 02 98 90 12 72; 14 rue Jean-Baptiste Bousquet; adult/child €4/2.30; ☒ 10am-6pm Mon-Sat mid-Apr–mid-Oct) occupies a one-time ceramics factory and displays over 2000 pieces of choice china.

The **Musée des Beaux-Arts** (☎ 02 98 95 45 20; 40 pl St-Corentin; adult/child €4/2.50; ☒ 10am-7pm Jul-Aug; to noon & 2-6pm Wed-Mon Apr-Jun & Sep-Oct, to noon & 2-6pm Wed-Sat & Mon, 2-6pm Sun Nov-Mar), in the town hall, displays European paintings from the 16th to early 20th centuries.

Sleeping

Camping Municipal (☎ /fax 02 98 55 61 09; ave des Oiseaux; person/tent/car €3.26/0.75/1.55; ☒ year-round) is 1km west of the old city. Take bus No 1 from the train station to the Chaptal stop.

Auberge de Jeunesse (☎ 02 98 64 97 97; quimper@ fuaj.org; 6 ave des Oiseaux; dm €8.90) Beside a camping ground, on the edge of a wooded park.

Hôtel Gradlon (☎ 02 98 95 04 39; www.hotel -gradlon.com, in French; 30 rue de Brest; d €82-99; ☒ closed 20 Dec-20 Jan) Rooms are set around a pretty courtyard with a rose garden at its heart, and there's a convivial bar with an open fire for winter evenings.

Eating

Crêperie du Frugy (☎ 02 98 90 32 49; 9 rue Ste-Thérèse; galettes €3.70-6.55; ☒ closed Sun & Mon lunch) This tiny place, in the shadow of Mont Frugy, serves excellent inexpensive crepes and galettes.

Crêperie du Sallé (☎ 02 98 95 95 80; 6 rue du Sallé; galettes €3-9; ☒ Tue-Sat) Locals crowd into this bright and breezy crêperie at lunchtime, so arrive early to guarantee a table. Sample some real Breton specialities such as *saucisse fumée* (smoked sausage; €6.60) and *coquilles St-Jacques* (scallops; €8.60).

Jardin de l'Odet (☎ 02 98 95 76 76; 39 blvd Amiral de Kerguélen; menu €19-35; ☒ Mon-Sat) This stylish Art Deco restaurant overlooks part of the Jardin de l'Évêché. Specialising in Breton and French cuisine, it takes familiar dishes and modifies them creatively.

La Mie Câline (14 quai du Steir) A hugely popular bakery where a whopping filled baguette, pastry and soft drink is only €5.20.

Getting There & Away

Bus destinations with **CAT** (☎ 02 98 90 68 40) include Brest (€13.30, 1¼ hours) and Douarnenez (€6, 35 minutes, six to 10 daily).

FRANCE

Buses run by **Caoudal** (☎ 02 98 56 96 72) go to Concarneau (€4.60, 45 minutes, seven to 10 daily); three daily continue to Quimperlé (€8.90, 1½ hours).

There are frequent trains to Brest (€13.80, 1¼ hours, up to 10 daily) and Paris (Gare Montparnasse; €63.30, 4¾ hours, eight daily).

CONCARNEAU

pop 18,600

Concarneau (Konk-Kerne in Breton), 24km southeast of Quimper, is France's third most important trawler port after Boulogne and Lorient. Much of the tuna brought ashore here is caught in the Indian Ocean or off the coast of Africa. The city has the unpretentious charm of a working fishing port, supplemented by Ville Close, the walled old town perched on a rocky islet, and several good nearby beaches. The walled town, fortified between the 14th and 17th centuries, is linked to place Jean Jaurès by a footbridge.

The **tourist office** (☎ 02 98 97 01 44; www.ville -concarneau.fr, in French; quai d'Aiguillon; ⏱ 9am-7pm Jul-Aug; to 12.30pm & 1.45-6.30pm Mon-Sat, 9.30am-12.30pm Sun Apr-Jun & 1-15 Sep, 9am-noon & 2-6pm Mon-Sat mid-Sep–Mar) has information.

Sleeping & Eating

Camping Moulin d'Aurore (☎ 02 98 50 53 08; www .moulinaurore.com, in French; 49 rue de Trégunc; per camp site/person €4/4; ⏱ Apr-Sep) This site is only 600m southeast of the harbour and a mere 50m from the sea.

Auberge de Jeunesse (☎ 02 98 97 03 47; concarneau .aj.cis@wanadoo.fr; quai de la Croix; dm €10) This friendly hostel is right on the waterfront.

Hôtel des Halles (☎ 02 98 97 11 41; www.hotel deshalles.com; pl de l'Hôtel de Ville; s €42 d €47-56) A quiet, older-style hotel with comfortable, renovated rooms, the Halles is only a few minutes' stroll from Ville Close.

Le Buccin (☎ 02 98 50 54 22; 1 rue Dougay Trouin; menu €16-34; ⏱ closed all day Thu, lunch Sat, dinner Sun except Jul-Aug) This elegant restaurant is where Concarneau's gourmets gather to enjoy whatever harvest of the sea has been landed at the Port de Pêche that morning.

Aux Remparts (☎ 02 98 50 65 66; 31 rue Théophile Louarn; ⏱ Easter-Oct) Enjoy the very Breton lunchtime *menu* (€11) of fish soup, *moules frites* and *far breton*.

There's a **covered market** on place Jean Jaurès.

Getting There & Away

There's no train station in Concarneau. **Caoudal** (☎ 02 98 56 96 72) runs up to 10 buses daily between Quimper and Quimperlé, calling by Concarneau (€4.60 to/from Quimper).

ST-MALO

pop 52,700

The port of St-Malo, famed for its walled city, fantastic nearby beaches – and one of the world's highest tidal ranges – is among Brittany's most popular tourist destinations. It was a key port during the 17th and 18th centuries, serving as a base for both merchant ships and government-sanctioned pirates.

Orientation & Information

St-Malo consists of the harbour towns of St-Malo and St-Servan plus the modern suburbs of Paramé and Rothéneuf to the east. The old walled city of St-Malo is known as Intra-Muros ('within the walls') or Ville Close. From the train station, it's a 15-minute walk westwards along ave Louis Martin.

There's a **tourist office** (☎ 02 99 56 64 48; www .saint-malo-tourisme.com; esplanade St-Vincent; ⏱ 9am-7.30pm Mon-Sat, 10am-6pm Sun Jul-Aug; 9am-12.30pm & 1.30-6pm or 6.30pm Mon-Sat Sep-Jun, 10am-12.30pm & 2.30-6pm Sun Easter-Jun & Sep).

Sights

The old walled city was originally an island, which became linked to the mainland by the sandy isthmus of Le Sillon in the 13th century. During 1944, the battle to drive German forces out of St-Malo destroyed around 80% of it. The main historical monuments were faithfully reconstructed, while the rest of the area was rebuilt in the style of the 17th and 18th centuries.

The town's centrepiece, **Cathédrale St-Vincent** (pl J de Châtillon; ⏱ 9.30am-6pm), constructed between the 12th and 18th centuries, was severely damaged by the 1944 bombing. If the narrow streets become claustrophobic, escape to the **ramparts**, constructed at the end of the 17th century. You can make a complete circuit (around 2km), and there's free access at several places, including all the main city gates. From their northern stretch, you can look across to the remains of **Fort National** (admission free; ⏱ Jun-Sep).

You can walk to the rocky islet of Île du Grand Bé, where the great 18th-century writer Chateaubriand is buried; go via the Porte des Bés. Once the tide rushes in, the causeway remains impassable for about six hours, so make sure you check tide times with the tourist office.

The **Musée International du Long Cours Cap-Hornier** (Museum of the Cape Horn Route; ☎ 02 99 40 71 58; adult/child €4.8/2.40; ☼ 10am-noon & 2-6pm Apr-Sep, Tue-Sun Oct-Mar) is in the 14th-century Tour Solidor. Presenting the life of the hardy sailors who followed the Cape Horn route, it offers superb views from the top of the tower.

Sleeping

Camping Aleth (☎ 02 99 81 60 91; camping@ville -saint-malo.fr; Allée Gaston Buy, St-Servan; camp sites €11.10; ☼ Apr-Sep) This camping ground enjoys an exceptional view in all directions. Take bus No 6.

Auberge de Jeunesse (☎ 02 99 40 29 80; info@ centrevarangot.com; 37 ave du Père Umbricht; dm €13.20, s €20.70-22, d €29.40-32) This place offers a considerably more luxurious stay than the usual French hostel. Take bus No 5 from the train station or No 1 (July and August only) from the bus station and tourist office.

Hôtel Le Neptune (☎ 02 99 56 82 15; 21 rue de l'Industrie; d €27-42, with shared bathroom €20-27.50) Close to the Grande Plage, this comfortable, family-run place is above a small, cheerful bar.

Hôtel Aux Vieilles Pierres (☎ 02 99 56 46 80; 4 rue des Lauriers; d €45, with shared bathroom €29) This friendly, intimate, family-run hotel, the cheapest in the old city, has a cosy downstairs restaurant but only six rooms, so book ahead.

Hôtel San Pedro (☎ 02 99 40 88 57; www.san-pedro .hotel.com; 1 rue Sainte-Anne; s/d €50/55; ☼ Feb-Nov) Tucked at the back of the old city, the San Pedro offers impeccable rooms, the warmest of welcomes and sea views.

Eating

Le Petit Crêpier (☎ 02 99 40 93 19; 6 rue Ste-Barbe; dishes €5.50-8; ☼ closed Tue-Wed except Jul-Aug) This famous creperie is known for its gourmet specialities such as a galette with plaice in a seaweed and Muscadet sauce, or a crepe with a mousse of dates and spices.

La Coquille d'Oeuf (☎ 02 99 40 92 62; 20 rue de la Corne de Cerf; menu €12-23.50) Neat, trim and with a nautical theme, this small restaurant with its tables for two makes for intimate, good-value dining.

Among the food shops along rue de l'Orme is a truly excellent **cheese shop** (☼ Tue-Sat) at No 9. Just down the street is **Hall au Blé**, a covered market.

Getting There & Away

The company **Brittany Ferries** (reservations France ☎ 08 25 82 88 28, UK ☎ 0870 556 1600; www .brittany-ferries.com) runs ferries between St-Malo and Portsmouth, and **Condor Ferries** (France ☎ 08 25 16 03 00, UK ☎ 0845 345 2000; www.condorferries .co.uk) to/from both Poole and Weymouth via Jersey or Guernsey.

Hydrofoils and catamarans depart from the Gare Maritime de la Bourse; car ferries leave from the Gare Maritime du Naye.

From April to September, **Corsaire** (☎ 02 23 18 15 15) runs the **Bus de Mer** (Sea Bus; adult/child return €5.90/3.60, 10 min, hourly) shuttle service between St-Malo and Dinard.

There are bus services with **Courriers Bretons** (☎ 02 99 19 70 80) to Cancale (€3.80, 30 minutes), Fougères (€13.90, 1¾ hours, one to three daily), and Pontorson (€8.30, one hour) and Mont St-Michel (€9.20, 1½ hours, three to four daily). Bretons also offers all-day tours to **Mont St-Michel** (return €25, Tue & Sat Jun-Sep).

Regular buses to Dinard (€3.40, 30 minutes, hourly) and Rennes (€9.90, one to 1½ hours, three to six daily) are run by **TIV** (☎ 02 99 82 26 26).

Bus No 10 for **CAT** (☎ 02 99 82 26 26) goes to Dinan (€5.70, 50 minutes, three to eight daily) via the Barrage de la Rance.

Frequent trains or SNCF buses run between St-Malo and Rennes (€11.40, one hour). Change at Rennes for Paris' Gare Montparnasse (€53, 4¼ hours, eight to 10 daily).

AROUND ST-MALO
Dinard
pop 10,100

Dinard has attracted a well-heeled clientele, especially from the UK, since the mid-19th century. Indeed, it still has something of the feel of a turn-of-the-century beach resort with its striped bathing tents, beachside carnival rides and pinnacled *belle époque* mansions. As befits a classic seaside resort, Dinard's main attractions are its beaches, cafés and waterfront walks. Take a stroll along the **promenade du Clair de Lune** (Moonlight promenade). With a free sound-and-light

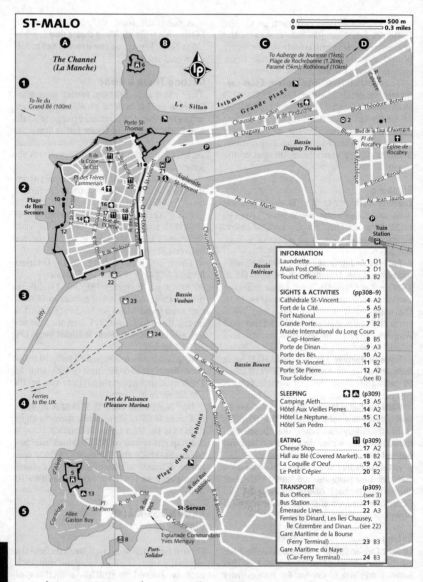

ST-MALO

0 — 500 m
0 — 0.3 miles

The Channel
(La Manche)

To Île du
Grand Bé (100m)

Le Sillon Isthmus

To Auberge de Jeunesse (1km);
Plage de Rochebonne (1.2km);
Paramé (5km); Rothéneuf (10km)

Grande Plage

Chaussée du Sillon

Q Duguay Trouin

R de l'Industrie

Blvd Théodore Botrel

Blvd de la Tour d'Auvergne

Pl de
Rocabey

Église de
Rocabey

Porte St-
Thomas

R de
la Corne
de Cerf

Pl des Frères
Lammenais

Plage
de Bon
Secours

Porte St-Vincent

Esplanade
St-Vincent

Bassin
Duguay Trouin

Av Louis Martin

R Ernest Renan

Av Jean Jaurès

Train
Station

Rue de
l'Orme

R de Toulouse

Chaussée des Corsaires

Bassin
Intérieur

Bassin
Vauban

Bassin
Bouvet

R de Trichet

R Georges Clemenceau

R Dauphine

Jetty

Ferries
to the UK

Port de Plaisance
(Pleasure Marina)

Plage des Bas Sablons

R des Bas
Sablons

R de la Cité

R du Dick

Pl St-Pierre

Allée
Gaston Buy

St-Servan

Q Solidor

Esplanade Commandant
Yves Menguy

Port-
Solidor

INFORMATION	
Laundrette	1 D1
Main Post Office	2 D1
Tourist Office	3 B2

SIGHTS & ACTIVITIES	(pp308–9)
Cathédrale St-Vincent	4 A2
Fort de la Cité	5 A5
Fort National	6 B1
Grande Porte	7 B2
Musée International du Long Cours	
Cap-Hornier	8 B5
Porte de Dinan	9 A3
Porte des Bés	10 A2
Porte St-Vincent	11 B2
Porte Ste Pierre	12 A2
Tour Solidor	(see 8)

SLEEPING	(p309)
Camping Aleth	13 A5
Hôtel Aux Vieilles Pierres	14 A2
Hôtel Le Neptune	15 C1
Hôtel San Pedro	16 A2

EATING	(p309)
Cheese Shop	17 A2
Hall au Blé (Covered Market)	18 B2
La Coquille d'Oeuf	19 A2
Le Petit Crêpier	20 B2

TRANSPORT	(p309)
Bus Offices	(see 3)
Bus Station	21 B2
Émeraude Lines	22 A3
Ferries to Dinard, Les Îles Chausey,	
Île Cézembre and Dinan	(see 22)
Gare Maritime de la Bourse	
(Ferry Terminal)	23 B3
Gare Maritime du Naye	
(Car-Ferry Terminal)	24 B3

spectacle in summer, it runs from just north of place Général de Gaulle to the Embarcadère, offering views of St-Malo's old city across the River Rance estuary. The **tourist office** (☎ 02 99 46 94 12; www.ville-dinard.fr; 2 blvd Féart; ⏰ 9.30am-7.30pm Jul-Aug, 9am-12.15pm & 2-6pm Mon-Sat Sep-Jun) will book accommodation at no charge.

THE LOIRE

Defensive fortresses thrown up in the 9th century to fend off marauding Vikings were superseded by whimsical pleasure palaces as this area became the playground of nobles who spent fortunes turning it into a vast neighbourhood of lavish chateaux. The result is a rich concentration of architectural treasures (Unesco has named the entire region a World Heritage site) that are great to explore by car and especially bicycle.

BLOIS

pop 49,300

From the 15th to the 17th century, Blois (pronounced blwah) was a hub of court intrigue, and during the 16th century it served as a second capital of France. Several dramatic events involving some of the most important personages in French history such as the kings Louis XII, François I and Henri III, took place inside the city's outstanding attraction, Château de Blois.

Orientation & Information

Blois, on the northern bank of the River Loire, is a compact town – almost everything is within 10 minutes' walk of the train station. The old city is the area south and east of Château de Blois, which towers over place Victor Hugo.

The **tourist office** (☎ 02 54 90 41 41; www.ville -blois.fr & www.loiredeschateaux.com; 23 pl du Château; ☼ 9am-7pm Mon-Sat, 10am-7pm Sun Apr-Sep, 9am-12.30pm & 2-6pm Mon-Sat, 9.30am-12.30pm Sun Oct-Mar) charges €2.30 to make hotel or B&B reservations.

Sights

The **Château de Blois** (☎ 02 54 90 33 32; adult/ student/child €6.50/4.50/2; ☼ 9am-7pm Jul & Aug; to 6pm Apr-Jun, Sep & Oct, to 12.30pm & 2-5.30pm Nov-Mar) consists of four distinct wings constructed around a central courtyard, each reflecting the favoured style of the period in which it was built. The distinctive brick-and-stone **Louis XII section**, which includes the hall where entrance tickets are sold, is ornamented with porcupines, Louis XII's heraldic symbol.

Opposite is the **Maison de la Magie** (House of Magic; ☎ 02 54 55 26 26; 1 pl du Château; adult/12-17 yrs/6-11 yrs €7.50/6.50/5; ☼ 10am-12.30pm & 2-6.30pm Jul & Aug, to 12.30pm & 2-6pm Tue-Sun Apr-Jun, to noon & 2-6pm Wed, Thu, Sat & Sun Sep-Mar) faces the chateau and has magic shows, interactive exhibits and displays of clocks invented by the Blois-born magician Jean-Eugène Robert-Houdin (1805-71), after whom the great Houdini named himself.

The **Cathédrale St-Louis** (☼ 7.30am-6pm) in the **old town** was rebuilt in a late Gothic

style after the devastating hurricane of 1678. There's a great view of Blois and the River Loire from the lovely **Jardins de l'Évêché** (Gardens of the Bishop's Palace), behind the cathedral.

The 15th-century **Maison des Acrobates** (House of the Acrobats; 3 bis rue Pierre de Blois), across the square from the cathedral, is so-named because its timbers are decorated with characters taken from medieval farces. It was one of the few medieval houses to survive the bombings of WWII.

Sleeping

Camping des Châteaux (☎ 02 54 78 82 05; camp sites €9; ☼ Jul-Sep) This two-star camping ground is in Vineuil, about 4km south of Blois.

Auberge de Jeunesse Les Grouëts (☎ 02 54 78 27 21; blois@fuaj.org; 18 rue de l'Hôtel Pasquier; dm €7, sheets €2.70, breakfast €3.20; ☼ Mar–mid-Nov) This youth hostel is in Les Grouëts, 4.5km southwest of Blois train station – call ahead as it's often full. Beds are in two 24-bed, single-sex dorms and kitchen facilities are available.

Hôtel du Bellay (☎ 02 54 78 23 62; www.hoteldu bellay.free.fr; 12 rue des Minimes; d/tr/q €35/45/55, d with shared bathroom €23-25) Some of the rooms are tiny, but all have charm, lovingly adorned with older-style, mumsy wallpaper.

Hôtel St-Jacques (☎ 02 54 78 04 15; www.hotel saintjacquesblois.com; 7 rue Ducoux; s/d €35/37, with shared bathroom with washbasin €25/27) A functional but friendly one-star hotel next to the station with ample-sized but uninspiring rooms.

Côté Loire (☎ 02 54 78 07 86; www.coteloire .com; 2 pl de la Grève; r from €39, Apr-Oct €46) Full of wooden-beamed character, this seven-room, higgledy-piggledy hotel has had a recent spruce-up with new beds, carpets and colour scheme.

Eating & Drinking

Popular restaurants line rue Foulerie and several café-brasseries dot place de la Résistance. There are several good bars in the old town.

Au Rendez-Vous des Pêcheurs (☎ 02 54 74 67 48; 27 rue du Foix; mains €21-28; ☼ Tue-Sat) Perhaps the finest seafood restaurant in town, this pretty cottage-style place specialises in fish from the River Loire and the Atlantic Ocean.

Le Triboulet (☎ 02 54 74 11 23; Pl du Château; menu €16.50-23.50; ☼ closed Sun & Mon) A busy restaurant right by the château offering traditional French dining. The tasty *menu du terroir*

BLOIS

To Centre Hospitalier & D149 (1.5km)

Place Jean Jaurès

Av du Maréchal Maunoury

Jardins de l'Évêché

R du Hauts Bourg

Place de la République

Place Guéry

R d'Angleterre

R des Rouillis

R des Minimes

R des Cordeliers

R du Bourg Neuf

Old Town

R Porte Clos Haut

R Pierre de Blois

Place St-Louis

Escalier Denis Papin

Place Avé Maria

R Denis Papin

R Henri Drussy

R Anne de Bretagne

Rond Point de la Résistance

R Franciade

R de la Paix

R Chambourdin

R Bretonnerie

R des Minimes

R St-Honoré

R Beauvoir

R Porte Côté

R Porte Chartraine

R du Commerce

R Denis Papin

Quai de l'Abbé Grégoire

Promenade du Mail

Pont Jacques Gabriel

Loire

To Château de Beauregard (6km); Cheverny (16km) & Romorantin-Lanthenay (36km)

To Cloître St-Saturnin (300m); Chaumont (17km); Amboise (34km)

To Cloître St-Saturnin & Église St-Saturnin (1.5km); Camping des Châteaux (4km); D951 & Chambord (16km)

Av Wilson

R du Commerce

R de la Voûte du Château

R des Violettes

R des Jacobins

Place Louis XII

Quartier St-Nicolas

R Anne de Bretagne

R St-Lubin

R des Fossés du Château

R des Trois Marchands

R des Marchands

R du Bourg St-Jean

Degrés St-Nicolas

R des Carmélites

R des Lices

R St-Lubin

Place Victor Hugo

Jardin des Simples et des Fleurs Royales

Av du Dr Jean Laigret

R Alfred Halou

Square Pasteur

Av Gambetta

Av Médicis

Blvd Daniel Dupuis

Place de la Gare

Train Station

R Ducoux

R Roberet

R du Semion

R André Gideon

R du Foix

Place de la Grève

To N152 & Auberge de Jeunesse Les Grouëts (4km); Tours (60km)

To Charcuterie (200m); A10, Tours (64km); Paris (180km)

INFORMATION
Tourist Office..............................1 C2

SIGHTS & ACTIVITIES   (p311)
Cathédrale St-Louis.....................2 F2
Château de Blois.........................3 D3
Église St-Nicolas.........................4 D4
Église St-Vincent........................5 C2
Maison de la Magie.....................6 D3
Maison des Acrobates..................7 E2

SLEEPING   (p311)
Côté Loire...................................8 C4
Hôtel du Bellay...........................9 D1
Hôtel St-Jaques........................10 B3

EATING   (pp311-13)
Au Rendez-Vous des Pêcheurs....11 C4
Charcuterie................................12 E3
Charcuterie................................13 D1
Food Market...............................14 E3
Intermarché..............................15 A3
Le Triboulet..............................16 D3

DRINKING   (p313)
Le St James...............................17 F2

TRANSPORT   (p313)
Bus Station................................18 B2
Bus Stop....................................19 E3
Bus Stop....................................20 D3
Bus Stop....................................21 E1
Point Bus Office........................22 D2

OTHER
Préfecture.................................23 E1

0   200 m
0   0.1 miles

(€23.50) showcases seasonal Loire area special-ties. There's a pleasant garden and terrace for warmer days.

Le St James (☎ 02 54 74 44 99; 50 rue Foulerie; ☷ 10pm-5am Thu-Sun) A lively bar serving 162 different cocktails with an atmospheric courtyard to enjoy them in.

As well as the **Intermarché supermarket** (ave Gambetta; ☷ 9am-12.30pm & 3-7.15pm Mon-Sat), in the old city, a food market fills rue Anne de Bretagne on Tuesday, Thursday and Saturday until 1pm. There are a number of charcuter-ies in the area around Place Louis XII offer-ing cold meats and prepared dishes.

Getting There & Away

The **TLC bus network** (☎ 02 54 58 55 44) has a very limited service, reduced further dur-ing the holidays and on Sunday. TLC buses to destinations around Blois leave from in front of the **Point Bus information office** (☎ 02 54 78 15 66; 2 pl Victor Hugo; ☷ 1.30-6pm Mon, 8am-noon & 1.30-6pm Tue-Fri, 1.30-4.30pm Sat) and the bus station – a patch of car park with schedules posted – in front of the train station.

The train station is on ave Dr Jean Lai-gret at the western end of the street. There are frequent trains to/from Tours (€8.30, 40 minutes, 11 to 17 daily) and the nearest TGV station, St-Pierre des Corps (€8, 25 to 35 minutes, half-hourly).

There are four direct non-TGV trains daily from Blois to Paris' Gare d'Austerlitz (€20.80, two hours), more if you change trains in Orléans. There are also direct trains to Nantes (€27.10, two hours, three daily).

AROUND BLOIS
Château de Chambord

The pinprick village of Chambord is domin-ated by the spectacular **Château de Chambord** (☎ 02 54 50 50 02; www.chambord.org; adult/18-25 yrs/child €7/4.50/free; ☷ 9am-6.15pm Apr-Sep, to 5.15pm Oct-Mar), which François I had built from 1519 as a base for hunting game in the Sologne forests. Ironically, the king chose the site for its easy two-day ride by horse and carriage from Paris, but he stayed here a total of only 42 days during his reign (1515-47).

The chateau's famed **double-helix staircase**, attributed by some to Leonardo da Vinci who lived in Amboise (34km southwest) from 1516 until his death three years later, consists of two spiral staircases that wind around a central axis but never meet.

Ticket sales end 30 minutes before the chateau closes. As well as free mini-guides in English distributed on arrival, you can rent an audioguide (€4).

GETTING THERE & AWAY

Chambord is 16km east of Blois and 20km northeast of Cheverny. To/from Blois there are TLC buses during the school year and coach tours to Chambord and Cheverny between mid-May and 31 August.

GETTING AROUND

Bicycles, perfect for exploring Forêt de Chambord and around, can be rented from the **Echapée Belle kiosk** (☎ 02 54 33 37 54; per hr/day/weekend €5.50/13/24) in Chambord, next to Pont St-Michel in the castle grounds.

Château de Cheverny

The elegant, perfectly symmetrical **Château de Cheverny** (☎ 02 54 79 96 29; www.chateau-cheverny .fr; adult/student/child €6.10/4.10/3; ☷ 9.15am-6.45pm Jul & Aug, to 6.15pm Apr-Jun & Sep, 9.30am-noon & 2.15-5.30pm Oct & Mar, 9.30am-noon & 2.15-5pm Nov-Feb), built between 1625 and 1634, is the region's most magnificently furnished chateau. Sit-ting like a sparkling white ship amid a sea of beautifully manicured gardens, the chateau is graced with a finely proportioned neoclas-sical façade. Inside, room after sumptuous room is fitted out with the finest of period appointments. In the 1st-floor dining room, 36 panels illustrate the story of *Don Quixote*. The grounds shelter the 18th-century **Orang-erie**, where Leonardo da Vinci's *Mona Lisa* was hidden during WWII. The château was also the inspiration for the mythical Marlin-spike Hall, home of French fictional favourite *Tintin*. It features in many of Tintin's adven-tures and in honour of this, a permanent Tintin exhibition, **Les Secrets de Moulinsart** (The Secrets of Marlinspike Hall; combined ticket for château & ex-hibition adult/student/child €10.50/8.40/6.20; ☷ 9.15am-6.45pm Jul & Aug, to 6.15pm Apr-Jun & Sep, 9.30am-noon & 2.15-5.30pm Oct & Mar, 9.30am-noon & 2.15-5pm Nov-Feb), has been created in the grounds.

GETTING THERE & AWAY

Cheverny is 16km southeast of Blois and 20km southwest of Chambord. The TLC bus No 4 from Blois to Villefranche-sur-Cher stops at Cheverny (€2.40, 25 to 35 minutes). Buses leave Blois at 12.25pm Monday to Fri-day. Returning to Blois, the last bus leaves

Cheverny at 6.52pm. Departure times can vary; check with TLC or the **Blois tourist office** (☎ 02 54 58 55 55).

Château de Chaumont

It's a short climb up to **Château de Chaumont** (☎ 02 54 51 26 26; adult/18-25 yrs/child €5.50/3.50/free; ⏰ 9.30am-6pm mid-Mar–mid-Oct, 10am-4.30pm mid-Oct–mid-Mar), set on a bluff overlooking the Loire. The entrance, across a wooden drawbridge between two wide towers, opens onto an inner courtyard from where there are stunning views. The building resembles a feudal castle and is modestly sized for a chateau. Opposite the main entrance are the luxurious **stables**, built in 1877.

GETTING THERE & AWAY

Chaumont-sur-Loire is 17km southwest of Blois and 20km northeast of Amboise, on the Loire's southern bank. The path leading to the park and chateau starts at the intersection of rue du Village Neuf and rue Maréchal Leclerc (D751).

By public transport, the only way to get to Chaumont-sur-Loire is via local train on the Orléans-Tours line. Get off at Onzain (10 minutes), from where it's about a 20-minute, 2km walk across the river to the chateau. Single rail fares are €2.80/6.60/10.30 to Onzain from Blois/Tours/Orléans.

By bicycle, the quiet back roads on the southern bank of the river are a tranquil option. The Chaumont-sur-Loire **tourist office** (☎ 02 54 20 91 73; 24 rue du Maréchal Leclerc) rents out bicycles for €10 per day.

Château de Beauregard

Built in the early 16th century to serve as a hunting lodge for François I, the most famous feature of **Château de Beauregard** (☎ 02 54 70 36 74; adult/student & child €6.50/4.50; ⏰ 9.30am-7.30pm Jul & Aug, to 12.30pm & 2-6.30pm Apr-Jun & Sep, to 12.30pm & 2-5pm Thu-Tue Oct-Dec & mid-Feb–Mar) is its **Galerie des Portraits**, the walls of which are plastered with 327 portraits from the 14th to 17th century.

GETTING THERE & AWAY

Beauregard is 6km south of Blois. It can also be reached via a pleasant 15km cycle ride through the forest from Chambord. There is road access to the chateau from the Blois-Cheverny D765 and the D956 (turn left at the village of Cellettes).

The **TLC bus** (☎ 02 54 58 55 44) from Blois to St-Aignan stops at Cellettes (€1.50), 1km southwest of the chateau, Monday to Friday at 7.50am and on Wednesday, Friday and Saturday; the first bus from Blois to Cellettes leaves at 12.25pm. Unfortunately, there's no afternoon bus back except for the Châteauroux-Blois line operated by **Transports Boutet** (☎ 02 54 34 43 95), which passes through Cellettes around 6.15pm Monday to Saturday, and – except during August – at about 6pm on Sunday.

TOURS
pop 270,000

Lively Tours has the cosmopolitan, bourgeois air of a miniature Paris, with wide 18th-century avenues, formal public gardens, café-lined boulevards and a thriving university. The French spoken in Tours is said to be the purest in France.

Twice in its history Tours briefly hosted the French government: in 1870 during the Franco-Prussian war and again in 1940, with the onset of WWII. Since then, it has become better known for its crisp white Vouvray and Montlouis wines.

Orientation & Information

The focal point is place Jean Jaurès, where the city's major thoroughfares – rue Nationale, blvd Heurteloup, ave de Grammont and blvd Béranger – meet. The train station is 300m east of place Jean Jaurès. The old city is centred on place Plumereau, which is about 400m west of rue Nationale. The northern boundary of the city is demarcated by the River Loire, which flows roughly parallel to the River Cher, 3km south.

The local tourist office is **Office de Tourisme de Tours** (☎ 02 47 70 37 37; www.ligeris.com; 78-82 rue Bernard Palissy; ⏰ 8.30am-7pm Mon-Sat, 10am-12.30pm & 2.30-5pm Sun mid-Apr–mid-Oct, 9am-12.30pm & 1.30-6pm Mon-Sat, 10am-1pm Sun mid-Oct–mid-Apr).

Sights

In an impressive 17th- to 18th-century archbishop's palace, the **Musée des Beaux-Arts** (☎ 02 47 05 68 73; 18 pl François Sicard; adult/student/child €4/2/free; ⏰ 9am-12.45pm & 2-6pm Wed-Mon) has an excellent collection of paintings, furniture and *objets d'art* from the 14th to 20th century.

Tours' Gothic-style **Cathédrale St-Gatien** (Pl de la Cathedral; ⏰ 9am-7pm, closed during services) dates from the 13th to the 16th centuries.

The spectacular exterior does not, however, overshadow the interior which is renowned for its marvellous 13th- to 15th-century **stained-glass windows**.

The **Musée de l'Hôtel Goüin** (☎ 02 47 66 22 32; 25 rue du Commerce; adult/child €3.50/2.60; ♥ 9.30am-12.30pm & 1.15-6.30pm Apr-Sep, to 12.30pm & 2-5.30pm Oct-Mar) is housed in a Renaissance residence built around 1510 for a wealthy merchant. Its façade is worth seeing, even if the eclectic assemblage of prehistoric, Gallo-Roman, medieval, Renaissance and 18th-century artefacts doesn't interest you.

Sleeping

Camping Municipal des Rives du Cher (☎ 02 47 27 27 60; fax 02 47 25 82 89; 61 rue de Rochpinard, St-Avertin; camp sites €11; ♥ Apr–mid-Oct) A three-star camping ground 5km south of Tours. To get there, take bus No 5 from place Jean Jaurès to the St-Avertin bus terminal, then follow the signs.

Auberge de Jeunesse du Vieux Tours (☎ 02 47 37 81 58; tours@fuaj.org; 5 rue Bretonneau; dm €12.70/15.60 HI members/nonmembers; ♥ 8am-12.30pm, 6-10pm; ☐) This new, well-equipped hostel is near the old town.

Hôtel Val de Loire (☎ 02 47 05 37 86; hotel.val .de.loire@club-Internet.fr; 33 blvd Heurteloup; r €29-40) A delightful two-star hotel in an old bourgeois home near the station. The rooms are simple, but with character.

Hôtel Mondial (☎ 02 47 05 62 68; www.hotelmondial tours.com; 3 pl de la Résistance; s/d from €34/40) A modern option with immaculate, carpeted rooms overlooking place de la Résistance. There's a sunny room to enjoy the generous buffet breakfast (€6).

Hôtel Régina (☎ 02 47 05 25 36; fax 02 47 66 08 72; 2 rue Pimbert; s/d/q from €25/29/38, r with shared bathroom €20.50-23.50) The best of the lower-priced options, this popular and good value hotel has a range of rooms depending on your budget.

Hôtel du Cygne (☎ 02 47 66 66 41; hotelcygne .tours@wanadoo.fr; 6 rue du Cygne; r €40-60; Ⓟ) A quiet, pretty hotel in the old town with lots of period detail. First-floor rooms are spacious.

Eating

In the old city, place Plumereau and nearby rue du Grand Marché and rue de la Rôtisserie are loaded with restaurants, cafés, creperies and *boulangeries* – many have lovely street terraces. Another tasty cluster graces rue Colbert.

Comme Autre Fouée (☎ 02 47 05 94 78; 11 rue de la Monnaie; lunch/dinner menu from €10/19.50) Take your time in this old stone building where your basket is constantly replenished with oven-fresh Fouée. It's an age-old regional speciality: a small disc of dough thrown into a wood-fired oven for 45 seconds and served immediately, piping hot. Use the pitta-like bread to scoop up fouéefuls of *rillettes* (spiced, potted meat), *haricots blanc* (white beans) or farmhouse goats' cheese.

L'Hedoniste (☎ 02 47 05 20 40; 16 rue Lavoisier; lunch/ dinner menu from €11/16) In this convivial, cave-like place, a regional French menu is enhanced by an exhaustive range of wines and the viticultural knowledge of the proprietor.

Le Picrocole (☎ 02 47 20 68 13; 28-30 rue du Grand Marché; lunch/dinner menu €11/17) This popular place serves regional and French specialties. Try *rillons* (crisp pork or duck) or their renowned *chocolate fondant cake*.

Le Petit Patrimoine (☎ 02 47 66 05 81; 58 rue Colbert; lunch menu €9, dinner menu €12-26) This simple but atmospheric place is excellent value with hearty portions of tasty, well-presented French food.

Sandwich stalls sell well-filled baguettes and pastries in the **Grand Passage shopping centre** (18 rue de Bordeaux). There's a large, permanent **covered market** (pl Gaston Pailhou) and an **Atac supermarket** (5 pl du Général Leclerc; ♥ 8.30am-8pm Mon-Sat, 9.30am-12.30pm Sun).

Drinking & Entertainment

It's easy to find bars and cafés in Tours, but a good starting point is place Plumereau. There are also some lively student bars along rue de la Longue Echelle and the southern strip of rue du Dr Bretonneau.

Le Vieux Mûrier (☎ 02 47 61 04 71; 11 pl Plumereau; ♥ 11am-midnight) This stylish place is a firm favourite.

Au Temps des Rois (☎ 02 47 05 04 51; 3 pl Plumereau; ♥ 11am-2am) Across the square, this bar has more of a student vibe.

Live jazz venues include alternative café-theatre **Le Petit Faucheux** (☎ 02 47 64 50 50; 12 rue Leonard de Vinci) and the brilliant **Bistro 64** (☎ 02 47 38 47 40; 64 rue du Grand Marché) – blues in a 16th-century interior.

Getting There & Away

There's a **Eurolines ticket office** (☎ 02 47 66 45 56; 76 rue Bernard Palissy; ♥ 2-6pm Mon, 9am-noon & 1.30-6.30pm Tue-Fri, 9am-noon & 1.30-5.30pm Sat).

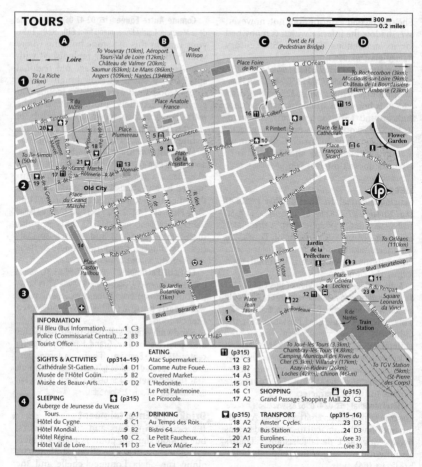

TOURS

INFORMATION
Fil Bleu (Bus Information)...........1 C3
Police (Commissariat Central)...2 B3
Tourist Office...........................3 D3

SIGHTS & ACTIVITIES   (pp314–15)
Cathédrale St-Gatien...............4 D1
Musée de l'Hôtel Goüin............5 B2
Musée des Beaux-Arts.............6 D2

SLEEPING   (p315)
Auberge de Jeunesse du Vieux
    Tours...................................7 A1
Hôtel du Cygne......................8 C1
Hôtel Mondial........................9 B2
Hôtel Régina.........................10 C2
Hôtel Val de Loire.................11 D3

EATING   (p315)
Atac Supermarket..................12 C3
Comme Autre Fouée..............13 B2
Covered Market......................14 A3
L'Hedoniste..........................15 D1
Le Petit Patrimoine................16 C1
Le Picrocole.........................17 A2

DRINKING   (p315)
Au Temps des Rois................18 A2
Bistro 64..............................19 A2
Le Petit Faucheux.................20 A1
Le Vieux Mûrier....................21 A2

SHOPPING   (p315)
Grand Passage Shopping Mall..22 C3

TRANSPORT   (pp315–16)
Amster' Cycles......................23 D3
Bus Station...........................24 D3
Eurolines.............................(see 3)
Europcar..............................(see 3)

Buses operated by **Touraine Fil Vert** (☎ 02 47 47 17 18) serve destinations around Tours and the Indre-et-Loire department, including Amboise (€2.10). They leave from the **bus station** (☎ 02 47 05 30 49; pl du Général Leclerc). There's an **information desk** (☎ 02 47 05 30 49; 7am-7pm Mon-Sat), but you can only buy tickets from the driver.

The station, overlooking place du Général Le-Clerc, has an **information office** (8.30am-6.30pm Mon-Sat, closed public hols). Tours is linked to St-Pierre des Corps (Tours' TGV train station) by shuttle train.

To get from Paris to Tours by rail take a TGV from Gare Montparnasse (€35 to €45, 1¼ hours, 10 to 15 daily) – often requiring a change of trains at St-Pierre des Corps; or

a direct non-TGV from Gare d'Austerlitz (€25.80, two to three hours, five to eight daily).

Car rental offices include **Europcar** (☎ 02 47 64 47 76; 76 blvd Bernard Palissy) and **Avis** (☎ 02 47 20 53 27) at the train station.

Getting Around
The bus network serving Tours and its suburbs is run by **Fil Bleu** (☎ 02 47 66 70 70), which has an information office at 5 bis rue de la Dolve. Most lines stop around the periphery of place Jean Jaurès.

From May to September, friendly **Amster' Cycles** (☎ 02 47 61 22 23; 5 rue du Rempart; €14/21/55 for 1/2/7 days) rents out road and mountain bikes.

TOURS AREA CHATEAUX

Some of the most interesting Loire chateaux make an easy day trip from Tours. Those accessible by train or SNCF bus from Tours include Chenonceau, Villandry, Azay-le-Rideau, Langeais, Amboise, Chaumont, Chinon and Saumur. The tourist office in Tours has details of son et lumières, medieval re-enactments, and other spectacles performed at the chateaux during summer.

Tours

Touring chateaux by public transport can be slow and expensive, so consider taking an organised bus tour. The interesting English-language tours are surprisingly relaxed and informal. Most allow you between 45 minutes and one hour at each chateau. Tour prices do not include entrance fees, but if you're part of a group you may be entitled to discounts. If you can get five to seven people together, you can design your own minibus itinerary. Try **Acco-Dispo** (☎ 06 82 00 64 51; www.accodispo-tours.com), **Quart de Tours** (☎ 06 85 72 16 22; www.quartdetours.com) and **St-Eloi Excursions** (☎ 02 47 37 08 04; www.saint-eloi.com). Typical prices are from €18 to €31 for a half-day trip to various chateaux, in a shared minibus for up to eight people. Reservations can be made at the Tours tourist office or via their website.

Services Touristiques de Touraine (STT; ☎ 02 47 05 46 09; www.stt-millet.fr) runs full-sized coaches for individuals rather than groups from April to mid-October. Many tours include wine tasting in Vouvray or Montlouis-sur-Loire. Afternoon/day tours taking in three chateaux cost €34, including admission fees.

Château de Chenonceau

With its stylised moat, drawbridge, towers and turrets, the 16th-century **Château de Chenonceau** (☎ 08 20 20 90 90; www.chenonceau.com; adult/student & child €8/6.50; ⏱ 9am-7pm mid-Mar–mid-Sep, to 4.30pm rest of year) is all a fairytale castle should be, although its crammed interior is only of moderate interest. Chenonceau's vast park, landscaped gardens and forests cover 70 hectares either side of the River Cher.

GETTING THERE & AWAY

Château de Chenonceau, in the town of Chenonceaux, is 34km east of Tours, 10km southeast of Amboise and 40km southwest of Blois.

Chenonceaux SNCF train station is in front of the chateau. Between Tours and Chenonceaux there are four to six trains daily (€5.20, 30 minutes).

Château d'Azay-le-Rideau

Azay-le-Rideau (☎ 02 47 45 42 04; adult/18-25 yrs/child €6.10/4.10/free; ⏱ 9.30am-6pm Apr-Jun & Sep-Oct, to 7pm Jul & Aug, to 12.30pm & 2-5.30pm Nov-Mar), built on an island in the River Indre, and adorned with stylised fortifications and turrets, is harmonious and elegant. Seven (rather disappointing) rooms are open to the public.

The bloodiest incident in the chateau's history occurred in 1418. During a visit to Azay, then a fortified castle, the crown prince (later King Charles VII) was insulted by the Burgundian guard. Enraged, he had the town burned and executed some 350 soldiers and officers.

GETTING THERE & AWAY

Château d'Azay-le-Rideau, 26km southwest of Tours, features on most tour itineraries from Tours. The D84 and D17, either side of the River Indre, are a delight to cycle along.

Azay-le-Rideau is on SNCF's Tours–Chinon line (four or five daily Monday to Saturday and one on Sunday). From Tours, the 30-minute trip (50 minutes by SNCF bus) costs €4.40; the station is 2.5km from the chateau. The last train/bus to Tours leaves Azay at about 6.35pm (8pm Sunday).

AMBOISE

pop 11,000

The picturesque town of Amboise, nestling under its fortified chateau on the southern bank of the Loire, reached its peak around 1500, when the luxury-loving King Charles VIII enlarged it and King François I held raucous parties here. Leonardo da Vinci lived his last years here under the patronage of François I.

Amboise is protected from the river by a dike, whose flower-covered heights are a fine place for a riverside promenade. Tours, 23km downstream, and Blois, 34km upstream, are easy day trips from here. Amboise makes a good base for visiting the chateaux east of Tours.

The **tourist office** (☎ 02 47 57 09 28; www.amboise -valdeloire.com; ⏱ 10am-1pm & 2-6pm Mon-Sat, to 1pm & 3-6pm Sun Apr-Jun & Sep, 9am-8pm Mon-Sat, 10am-6pm Sun Jul & Aug; 10am-1pm & 2-6pm Mon-Sat, to 1pm Sun

FRANCE

Oct-Mar) is in a pavilion opposite 7 quai du Général de Gaulle.

The rocky outcrop topped by **Château d'Amboise** (☎ 02 47 57 00 98; pl Michel Debré; adult/student/7-14 yrs €7.50/6.50/4.20; ☼ 9am-6.30pm Apr-Jun & Sep-Oct, to 7.30pm Jul & Aug, to noon & 2-5pm Nov-May) has been fortified since Roman times. Charles VIII (r 1483–98), who was born and brought up here, enlarged the chateau in 1492 after a visit to Italy, where he was impressed by that country's artistic creativity and luxurious lifestyle.

Today, just a few of the 15th- and 16th-century structures survive. These include the Flamboyant Gothic **Chapelle St-Hubert** and the **Salle des États** (Estates Hall). The chateau entrance is at the end of rampe du Château.

Leonardo da Vinci came to Amboise in 1516 at the invitation of François I. Until his death three years later at the age of 67, Leonardo lived and worked in the brick manor house called **Le Clos Lucé** (☎ 02 47 57 62 88; 2 rue du Clos Lucé; adult/student/6-15 yrs €9.50/7.50/5; ☼ 9am-5pm Jan, to 7pm Apr, Jun, Sep & Oct, to 8pm Jul & Aug, to 6pm Nov, Dec, Feb & Mar). It now contains restored rooms and fascinating scale models of Leonardo's inventions, including a proto-automobile, armoured tank, parachute and hydraulic turbine.

Getting There & Away

Buses to/from Amboise stop at the bus shelter opposite the tourist office.

CAT's line No 10 links the town with Tours' bus terminal (€2.10 one way, 30 to 50 minutes, eight daily Monday to Saturday, six daily during summer holidays).

The **train station** (☎ 02 47 23 18 23; blvd Gambetta), across the river from the centre of town, is served by trains from Paris' Gare d'Austerlitz (€24.20, 2¼ to three hours, 11 daily).

About three-quarters of the trains on the Blois-Tours line (11 to 17 daily) stop here. Fares are €5.50 to Blois (20 minutes) and €4.40 to Tours (20 minutes).

SOUTHWESTERN FRANCE

It may not have the glitz and glamour associated with its counterpart on the Mediterranean, but France's Atlantic coast is just as appealing: sunshine and sandy beaches, world-renowned wine-growing regions and about the best surf in Europe are just some of the coast's attractions.

NANTES
pop 550,000

The lively and relaxed university city of Nantes, historically part of Brittany, is France's seventh-largest metropolis. It has several fine museums and countless inexpensive cafés and restaurants. The Edict of Nantes, a landmark royal charter guaranteeing civil rights and freedom of conscience and worship to France's Protestants, was signed here by Henri IV in 1598.

Orientation & Information

The city centre's two main arteries, both served by tram lines, are the north–south, partly pedestrianised, cours des 50 Otages, and the east–west Cours Franklin Roosevelt that connects the train station (to the east) with quai de la Fosse (to the west).

The commercial centre runs from the Gare Centrale bus/tram hub northeast to rue de la Marne and northwest to rue du Calvaire. The old city is to the east, between cours des 50 Otages and the chateau. There is Internet access at **Cyber Planet** (☎ 02 51 82 47 97; 18 rue de l'Arche Sèche; Internet per hr €3; ☼ 10am-midnight Mon-Sat, 2-8pm Sun). The **tourist office** (☎ 02 40 20 60 00; www.nantes-tourisme.com; pl du Commerce; ☼ 10am-7pm Mon-Sat) is in the Palais de la Bourse. In July and August there is also an **annexe** (2 pl St-Pierre) next to the cathedral.

Sights

This renowned **Musée des Beaux-Arts** (☎ 02 51 17 45 00; adult €3.30; 10 rue Georges Clemenceau; ☼ 10am-6pm Wed-Mon, to 8pm Fri) showcases one of the finest French collections of paintings outside Paris, with works by Georges de La Tour, Ingres and Monet, Picasso and Kandinsky.

From the outside, the **Château des Ducs de Bretagne** (Chateau of the Dukes of Brittany; ☎ 02 51 17 49 00; adult/child €10/free, admission to grounds free; ☼ 10am-6pm) looks like your standard medieval castle. Inside, the parts facing the courtyard are in the style of a Renaissance pleasure palace. Walking along part of the ramparts is free.

Inside the flamboyant Gothic **Cathédrale St-Pierre et St-Paul** (pl St-Pierre), the **tomb of François II** (r 1458–88), duke of Brittany, and his second wife, Marguerite de Foix, is considered a masterpiece of Renaissance art. The statue facing the nave represents **Prudence**.

Sleeping

Hôtel de la Bourse (☎ 02 40 69 51 55; fax 02 40 71 73 89; 19 quai de la Fosse; d €24, with shared bathroom from €19) The emphasis here is on low prices rather than style and location. As a place to sleep though, the clean, tidy rooms here are a steal. Hall showers cost €2.20.

Hôtel St-Daniel (☎ 02 40 47 41 25; hotel.st.daniel@ wanadoo.fr; 4 rue du Bouffay; d from €29) In the heart of the old town, this great-value budget place offers rooms with un-budget extras like spaciousness, TV, hairdryer and double-glazing. Some rooms have been renovated and boast flashy wooden floors. There are a few family rooms for €39.

Hôtel Fourcroy (☎ 02 40 44 68 00; 11 rue Fourcroy; s/d with shower & toilet €30/32; **P**) In a nondescript building tucked away down a side-street, this great-value hotel has 19 exceptionally well-kept rooms, with modern bathrooms and upholstered doors.

Hôtel Pommeraye (☎ 02 40 48 78 79; www.hotel -pommeraye.com; 2 rue Boileau; s/d from €49/59 Mon-Fri, €35/43 Sat & Sun; **P** **💻**) A stylish boutique hotel within an older building, mixing the classic and the contemporary with great success in the heart of Nantes' shopping district. Comfortable, well-equipped rooms are presented in warm, modern colours. Cheaper rooms are a bit small but there's free lobby Internet.

Hôtel Graslin (☎ 02 40 69 72 91; fax 02 40 69 04 44; 1 rue Piron; d €57-70; **💻**) A modern three-star hotel with all the in-room facilities you could wish for including bathrobes, minibar and matching yellow curtains, bedspreads and chairs. Good location off Place Graslin.

Eating & Drinking

There are dozens of cafés, bars and small restaurants, many of them French-regional or ethnic, a couple of blocks west of the chateau in the lively area around rue de la Juiverie, rue des Petites Écuries and rue de la Bâclerie.

Brasserie La Cigale (☎ 02 51 84 94 94; 4 pl Graslin; menu €15.20-24.80; ☽ 7.30-12.30am) A trip to Nantes wouldn't be complete without a stop at the exquisite Cigale, grandly decorated with 1890s tilework and painted ceilings that mix baroque with Art Nouveau. If you can't

get there for a meal (traditional French), drop in for afternoon tea.

Chez Maman (☎ 02 51 72 20 63; 2 rue de la Juiverie; mains from €10; ☽ lunch & dinner Tue-Sun) Traditional home-style French cooking is served in this lively bistro-cum-junk-shop.

Chez Le Gaulois (☎ 02 40 08 22 98; 8 rue de la Paix; mains €9.50-17; ☽ Mon-Sat) You can't get any more 'French carnivore' than this place with giant legs of ham hanging from the rafters and piles of saucisson lying about. Specialties include *raclette* (hot melted cheese served with potatoes), fondue and *tartiflette* (potato, cheese and bacon pie). Speedy service and pack-'em-in tables keeps the atmosphere lively and the prices reasonable.

The small **covered market** (pl du Bouffay) and the huge **Marché de Talensac** (rue Talensac) are open until about 1pm (closed Monday).

There's also the **Monoprix supermarket** (2 rue du Calvaire; ☽ 9am-9pm Mon-Sat).

La Maison (☎ 02 40 37 04 12; 4 rue Lebrun; ☽ 3pm-2am) An entertaining send-up of a home furnished in very bad taste c 1970, this convivial bar plays mainly house music and is a lively place popular with students.

Entertainment

Listings of cultural events appear in *Nantes Poche* and *Pil'* (both €0.50). *Le Mois Nantais*, available at the tourist office and at tobacconists, has day-by-day details of cultural events. What's-on websites include www .vivanantes.com. The six-screen **Cinéma Katorza** (☎ 02 51 84 90 60; 3 rue Corneille) offers non-dubbed films.

Getting There & Away

The southbound **bus station** (☎ 0825 08 71 56), across from 13 allée de la Maison Rouge, is used by CTA buses serving areas of the Loire-Atlantique *département* south of the Loire River. The northbound **bus office** (☎ 0825 08 71 56; 1 allée Duquesne, on cours des 50 Otages), run by Cariane Atlantique, handles buses to destinations north of the Loire. There's also a **Eurolines office** (☎ 02 51 72 02 03; allée de la Maison Rouge; ☽ 8am-6pm Mon-Fri, to 12.30pm Sat).

The **train station** (☎ 36 35; 27 blvd de Stalingrad) is well connected to most of France. Destinations include Paris' Gare Montparnasse (€49.10 to €61.40, 2¼ hours by TGV, 15 to 20 daily), Bordeaux (€37, four hours, three or four daily) and La Rochelle (€21, 1¾ hours, three or four daily). Tickets and information are available at the **SNCF ticket office** (12 pl de la Bourse; ⊗ 10am-7pm Mon, 9am-7pm Tue-Sat; allée Brancas; ⊗ 8.30am-6.45pm Mon-Fri).

Getting Around

The **TAN network** (☎ 0801 44 44 44; www.tan.fr), which has an **information office** (2 allée Brancas, pl du Commerce; ⊗ Mon-Sat), includes three modern tram lines that intersect at the Gare Centrale (Commerce), the main bus/tram transfer point. Buses run from 7.15am to 9pm. Night services continue until 12.30am.

Bus/tram tickets, sold individually (€1.20) by bus (but not tram) drivers and at tram stop ticket machines, are valid for one hour after being time-stamped. A *ticket journalier*, good for 24 hours, costs €3.30; time-stamp it only the first time you use it.

POITIERS

pop 120,000

Poitiers, the former capital of Poitou, is home to some of France's most remarkable Romanesque churches. It is not a particularly fetching city although the pedestrian-only shopping precinct has its charms. In AD 732, somewhere near Poitiers (the exact site is not known), the cavalry of Charles Martel defeated the Muslim forces of Abd ar-Rahman, governor of Córdoba, thereby ending Muslim attempts to conquer France.

Orientation & Information

The train station is about 600m west and down the slope from the old city and commercial centre, which begins just north of Poitiers' main square, place du Maréchal Leclerc, and stretches northeast to Église Notre Dame la Grande. Rue Carnot heads south from place du Maréchal Leclerc.

The **tourist office** (☎ 05 49 41 21 24; accueil@ ot-poitiers.fr; 45 pl Charles de Gaulle; ⊗ 9.30am-7pm Mon-Sat, 10am-6pm Sun Jun-Sep, 10am-6pm Mon-Sat Oct-May) is near the Église Notre Dame.

Cybercafé Poitiers (☎ 05 49 39 51 87; www.cybercafé -poitiers.fr; 171 Grand'Rue; per hr €5.50; ⊗ 10am-8pm Mon-Sat, 4-8pm Sun, to 10pm Jul & Aug) is east of Église Notre Dame.

Sights

The renowned Romanesque **Église Notre Dame la Grande** (pl Charles de Gaulle; ⊗ 8.30am-7pm Mon-Sat, 2-5pm Sun) is in the pedestrianised old city. It dates mostly from the 11th and 12th centuries. The atrociously painted decoration in the nave is from the mid-19th century; the only original **frescoes** are the faint 12th- or 13th-century works that adorn the U-shaped dome above the choir.

The worthwhile **Musée Ste-Croix** (☎ 05 49 41 07 53; www.musees-poitiers.org; 3 rue Jean Jaurès; adult/ child €3.50/free; ⊗ 1.15-6pm Mon, 10am-noon & 1.15-6pm Tue-Fri, 10am-noon & 2-6pm Sat & Sun Jun-Sep, only to 5pm Mon-Fri & afternoons Sat & Sun Oct-May) is across the lawn from Baptistère St-Jean, and was built atop Gallo-Roman walls that were excavated and left *in situ*. It has exhibits on the history of Poitou from prehistoric times to the 19th century.

Sleeping

Other than a couple of nasty places near the station, Poitiers is fairly short on budget accommodation.

Hôtel de l'Europe (☎ 05 49 88 12 00; www.hotel deleuropepoitiers.com; 39 rue Carnot; s/d from €47.50/53; Ⓟ) A charming hotel worth more than its official two stars. The main building dates from 1710, with a sweeping staircase, large rooms and pleasing older-style décor. Breakfast is served in the lovely garden room.

Hôtel du Plat d'Étain (☎ 05 49 41 04 80; hotel duplatdetain@wanadoo.fr; 7-9 rue du Plat d'Étain; d €45-50; Ⓟ) In a pedestrian street half a block north of place du Maréchal Leclerc (through the arch next to the theatre), is this cosy two-star hotel, next to a late-opening bar.

Le Grand Hôtel (☎ 05 49 60 90 60; www.grand hotelpoitiers.fr; 28 rue Carnot; s/d €65.50/80.50; Ⓟ ⊠) Faux Art Deco furnishings and fittings give this three-star hotel some character. The rooms, popular with business travellers, are spacious and well-equipped.

Eating & Drinking

The most promising dining area is south of place du Maréchal Leclerc, especially rue Carnot. The Grand'Rue also has good eateries. Look for bars and pubs along rue Carnot and one block north of place du Maréchal Leclerc along rue du Chaudron d'Or.

La Serrurerie (☎ 05 49 41 05 14; 28 rue des Grandes Ecoles; mains €10-14) This atmospheric, lively and popular café bistro does great meals and huge weekend brunches (€14). Temporary exhibitions showcase local art and sculpture.

La Joyeuse Marmite (☎ 05 49 88 14 59; 66 Grand'Rue; menu €10; ⊗ lunch only Mon-Fri) A merry local bistro serving hearty lunch meals including wine. It's just north of Place de la Cathédrale.

The **Marché Notre Dame** (7am-1pm Tue-Sat) is right next to Église Notre Dame la Grande. About 200m to the south, the **Monoprix supermarket** (9am-7.30pm Mon-Sat) is across from 29 rue du Marché Notre Dame (behind the Palais de Justice).

Getting There & Away

The modern **train station** (0836 35 35 35; blvd du Grand Cerf) has direct links to Bordeaux (€28.70, 1¾ hours), La Rochelle (€19.80, one hour 20 minutes), Tours (€16, one hour) and many other cities. TGV tickets from Paris' Gare Montparnasse (1½ hours, 12 daily) cost from €43. SNCF buses go to Nantes (€23, 3¼ hours).

AROUND POITIERS

Futuroscope (05 49 49 30 80; www.futuroscope.com; Jaunay-Clan; adult/5-12 yrs Mon-Fri Oct-Mar €21/16, Apr-Sep & Sat & Sun €30/22; 10am-10.15pm Apr-Sep, to 6pm Sun-Fri, to 10pm Sat Feb, Mar, Oct & Nov, closed mid-Nov–mid-Feb) is a unique cinema theme park whose 22 attractions make for an entertaining day. There are evening lakeside laser and firework shows (Sat & Sun Mar-Nov, daily Apr-Aug) – as a result, closing times range from 6pm to 11pm. On show days, a ticket costs €15/9 if you arrive after 6pm. Allow at least five hours to see all the major attractions which include **Cyberworld**, an action-packed 3D trip inside a computer with a Lara Croft-style cyber-guide and a cameo appearance by the Pet Shop Boys, and **Cosmos** a journey through the solar system and beyond. A free headset provides soundtracks in English, German and Spanish.

Futuroscope is 10km north of Poitiers in Jaunay-Clan (take exit No 28 off the A10). TGV trains link the park's TGV station with Paris (€43.20, 1½ hours, three daily), Tours (€14.90, 30 minutes, three daily) and Bordeaux (€29.60, 1¾ hours, two to three daily).

Local STP buses (05 49 44 66 88) Nos 9, 16 and 17 (€1.30, 30 minutes) link Futuroscope (Parc de Loisirs stop) with Poitiers' train station (the stop in front of Avis car rental); there are one to two buses an hour from 6.15am until 7.30pm or 9pm.

LA ROCHELLE

pop 120,000

The focal point of La Rochelle, a lively and increasingly chic port city midway down France's Atlantic coast, is the old port lined with picturesque cafés and restaurants, which basks in the bright Atlantic sunlight by day and is grandly illuminated at night.

Orientation & Information

The train station is linked to the Vieux Port by the 500m-long ave du Général de Gaulle. Place du Marché and place de Verdun are at the northern edge of the old city. The **tourist office** (05 46 41 14 68; larochelle-tourisme.com or www .ville-larochelle.fr; 9am-8pm Mon-Sat, 11am-5.30pm Sun Jul & Aug; 9am-7pm Mon-Sat, 11am-5pm Sun Jun & Sep, 9am-6pm Mon-Sat, 10am-1pm Sun Oct-May) is on the southern side of the Vieux Port in an area of brightly painted wooden buildings known as Le Gabut.

Sights & Activities

To protect the harbour at night and defend it in times of war, an enormous chain used to be stretched between the two 14th-century stone towers at the harbour entrance. **Tour de la Chaîne** affords fine views from the top and has displays on the history of the local Protestant community in the basement. Across the harbour you can also climb to the top of the 36m-high pentagonal **Tour St-Nicolas**, if you don't get lost in the maze of stairs and corridors.

West of Tour de la Chaîne, the medieval wall leads to the steeple-topped, 15th-century **Tour de la Lanterne**, also known as Tour des Quatre Sergents in memory of four sergeants from the local garrison who were executed in 1822 for plotting to overthrow the newly reinstated monarchy.

The **three towers** (05 46 34 11 81; admission per tower adult/18-25 yrs/child €4.60/3.10/free; 10am-7pm Apr-Sep, to 12.30pm & 2-5.30pm Tue-Sun Oct-May, closed hols) can be visited on a combined ticket which costs €10/6.50.

South of Le Gabut is the impressive **Aquarium** (05 46 34 00 00; adult/student & child €10/7; 9am-11pm Jul & Aug, to 8pm Apr-Jun & Sep, 10am-8pm Oct-Mar) a relatively new attraction, thoughtfully laid-out and well-stocked with over 10,000 specimens of sea-based flora and fauna.

Easily visited on a day trip from La Rochelle is the flat island of **Île de Ré**, whose eastern tip, 9km west of the centre of La Rochelle, gets more hours of sunshine than any part of France away from the Mediterranean coast.

FRANCE

The island boasts 70km of coastline, including 20km to 30km of fine-sand beaches. Its western half curves around a bay known as the Fier d'Ars, which is lined with *marais salants* (salt evaporation pools), saltwater marshes and a nature reserve for birds, **Lilleau des Niges**.

Year-round, **Rébus** (☎ 05 46 09 20 15) links La Rochelle (the train station car park, Tour de la Grosse Horloge and place de Verdun) with all the major towns on the island.

Sleeping

Camping du Soleil (☎ 05 46 44 42 53; ave Marillac; bus No 10; ☺ mid-May–mid-Sep) Nearest camping ground to the city centre, but often full.

Centre International de Séjour-Auberge de Jeunesse (☎ 05 46 44 43 11; fax 05 46 45 41 48; ave des Minimes; bus No 10; dm/d €13/32; ☺ check-in 8am-midnight) This hostel is 2km southwest of the train station in Les Minimes.

Terminus Hôtel (☎ 05 46 50 69 69; hotel.terminus@tourisme-francais.com; 7 rue de la Fabrique; s/d low season from €39/47, high season €53/53; ☒) Near the tourist office, this welcoming hotel has 32 comfortable rooms. The bright, sunny ones at the front are the best.

Hôtel François 1er (☎ 05 46 41 28 46; www.hotelfrancois1er.fr; 15 rue Bazoges; d €50-85; **P**) A charming, quiet hotel with a cobbled courtyard entrance and traditionally furnished rooms. In the 15th and 16th centuries, a number of French kings stayed in this building.

Hôtel La Marine (☎ 05 46 50 51 63; www.hotel-marine.com; 30 quai Duperré; r May-Sep €70-95, Oct-May €59-75) This two-star hotel is in a fantastic location overlooking the port. Most rooms have recently been refurbished with neutral tones and designer furniture – rooms 1, 6, 9 and 13 stand out, with first class views.

Eating

André (☎ 05 46 41 28 24; 5 rue St-Jean du Perot; mains €12-22) Something of an institution, this restaurant has been serving up fresh seafood for more than 50 years, and is usually packed with fish-hungry punters enjoying innovative creations like Monkfish infused with mango and Indian spices, or the knockout *Cassate Charentaise* (regional fruit flan) both on the €35 menu.

Café de la Paix (☎ 05 46 41 39 79; 54 rue Chaudrier; breakfast €6.50, menu €14-19, children €8, mains €15-20; ☺ 7am-9.30pm) This century-old place is a grand, atmospheric brasserie-bar with high,

painted ceilings, gold-edged mirrors and all the traditional choices: beef, duck, foie gras and salads. Also a good spot for breakfast or afternoon tea.

Le Champêtre (☎ 05 46 41 12 17; 22 rue Verdière; menu €22, mains around €12; ☺ dinner only from 7.30pm Tue-Sat) An unfussy, intimate little place away from the main restaurant strips, but worth seeking out. You'll find classic (mainly meat-based) French dishes and an enthusiastic patron.

The best place to pick up your own edibles is at the lively, 19th-century **covered market** (pl du Marché; ☺ 7am-1pm). Food shops in the vicinity include two cheap East Asian **takeaways** (4 & 10 rue Gambetta). In the old city, there's **Monoprix supermarket** (30-36 rue du Palais; ☺ 8.30am-8pm Mon-Sat).

Getting There & Away

From **La Rochelle Airport** (☎ 05 46 42 30 26; www.larochelle.aeroport.fr), north of the city centre off the N237, there are flights throughout France and to London (with Ryanair) and Southampton (with Flybe) in the UK.

The **bus station** and bus information offices are at place de Verdun. Eurolines ticketing is handled by **Citram Littoral** (☎ 05 46 50 53 57; 30 cours des Dames; ☺ closed Sat afternoon, Mon morning & all day Sun).

The **train station** (☎ 0836 35 35 35) is linked by TGV to Paris' Gare Montparnasse (€53.60, three hours, five or six direct daily). Other destinations served by direct trains include Nantes (€22, two hours, five or six daily), and Bordeaux (€22.60, two hours, five to seven daily).

Getting Around

Autoplus (☎ 05 46 34 02 22), the innovative local transport system, has a bus hub and **information office** (pl de Verdun; ☺ 7am-7.30pm Mon-Sat). Tickets are €1.20. Bus No 21 runs from place Verdun to the train station, returning via the Vieux Port. No 10 links place de Verdun with the youth hostel and Les Minimes.

At **Les Vélos Autoplus** (☎ 05 46 34 02 22) you can hire a bike for free for the first two hours; after that the charge is €1 per hour. Child seats, but not bike helmets, are available for no extra charge. Bikes, as well as electric motorcars for €16 per day, are available at the **Electrique Autoplus office** (☎ 05 46 34 84 58; pl de Verdun; ☺ 7.30am-7pm Mon-Sat, 1-7pm Sun).

BORDEAUX

pop 735,000

Bordeaux is buzzing thanks, in part, to a massive renovation programme: streets have been pedestrianised, squares re-paved, trees planted and a state-of-the-art tram system installed. Against a backdrop of neoclassical architecture, wide avenues and pretty parks, the city boasts excellent museums, a vibrant nightlife, an ethnically diverse population and a lively university community.

Orientation

The city centre lies between place Gambetta and the tidal, 350m- to 500m-wide Garonne. From place Gambetta, place de Tourny is 500m northeast, and the tourist office is 400m to the east.

The train station, Gare St-Jean, is in a seedy area about 3km southeast of the city centre. Cours de la Marne stretches from the train station to place de la Victoire, which is linked to place de la Comédie by the long and straight pedestrianised shopping street, rue Ste-Catherine. Banks offering currency exchange can be found near the tourist office on cours de l'Intendance, rue de l'Esprit des Lois and cours du Chapeau Rouge.

Information

Laundrette (31 rue du Palais Gallien; ⏱ 8am-9pm)
Self-service (32 rue des Augustins; ⏱ 7am-9pm) Also at 5 rue de Fondaudège and 8 rue Lafaurie de Monbadon.
Main post office (37 rue du Château d'Eau)
NetZone (☎ 05 57 59 01 25; 209 rue Ste-Catherine; Internet access per hr €3; ⏱ 9.30am-midnight)
Tourist office (☎ 05 56 00 66 00; www.bordeaux -tourisme.com; 12 cours du 30 Juillet; ⏱ 9am-7.30pm Mon-Sat Jul-Aug, to 7pm May-Jun & Sep-Oct, 9.30am-6.30pm Sun May-Oct, 9am-6.30pm Mon-Sat, 9.45am-4.30pm Sun Nov-Apr) Next to the tram stop Comédie.

Sights

The sights mentioned below appear pretty much from north to south.

Entrepôts Lainé was built in 1824 as a warehouse for the rare and exotic products of France's colonies (such as coffee, cocoa, peanuts and vanilla). Its capacious spaces now house the **CAPC Musée d'Art Contemporain** (Museum of Contemporary Art; ☎ 05 56 00 81 50; Entrepôt 7, rue Ferrère; ⏱ 11am-6pm Tue, Thu-Sun, to 8pm Wed, closed Mon). Most of the exhibits and installations are temporary, presenting major artistic movements over the last 30 years.

The beautifully landscaped **Jardin Public** (cours de Verdun), established in 1755 and laid out in the English style a century later, includes the meticulously catalogued **Jardin Botanique** (☎ 05 56 52 18 77; admission free; ⏱ 8.30am-6pm), founded in 1629 and at its present site since 1855; and the nearby **Musée d'Histoire Naturelle** (Natural History Museum; ☎ 05 56 48 29 86; ⏱ 11am-6pm Mon & Wed-Fri, 2-6pm Sat & Sun). There's a **children's playground** on the island.

Nearby, off rue de Fondaudège, is the city's most impressive Roman site, the **Palais Gallien** (rue du Dr Albert Barraud; adult/under 12 yrs €1.50/free; ⏱ 3-7pm Jun-Sep), the ruins of a 3rd-century amphitheatre.

The most prominent feature of **esplanade des Quinconces**, a vast square laid out in 1820, is the fountain monument to the Girondins, a group of moderate, bourgeois National Assembly deputies during the French Revolution, 22 of whom were executed in 1793 after being convicted of counter-revolutionary activities.

Nowadays, **place Gambetta** is an island of greenery in the midst of the city centre's hustle and bustle, but during the Reign of Terror that followed the Revolution, a guillotine placed here severed the heads of 300 alleged counter-revolutionaries.

A few blocks south of place Gambetta, the **Musée des Arts Décoratifs** (Museum of Decorative Arts; ☎ 05 56 00 72 50; 39 rue Bouffard; museum ⏱ 2pm-6pm Wed-Mon, temporary exhibits from 11am Mon-Fri) specialises in faïence, porcelain, silverwork, glasswork, furniture and the like.

The **Musée des Beaux-Arts** (☎ 05 56 10 20 56; 20 cours d'Albret; ⏱ Wed-Mon 11am-6pm) occupies two

---

MUSEUM PRICES & PASSES

Bordeaux' municipal museums, including the Musée d'Art Contemporain (CAPC), Musée d'Histoire Naturelle, Musée des Arts Décoratifs, Musée des Beaux-Arts and Musée d'Aquitaine, are free to those under 18 and students holding a valid student card. They're also free for everyone on the first Sunday of each month.

Admission for adult/concession is €4/2.50 for each museum's permanent collections and €5.50/3 for temporary exhibits. Concession prices refer to people over 60 yrs or under 25 (though sometimes under 25s can enter free, even without a student card).

FRANCE

BORDEAUX

0	200 m
0	0.1 miles

Jardin Botanique

Jardin Public

R. d'Aviau

R. Constantin

R. Note

R. du Maréchal Foch

Cours Xavier Amozan

R. Foy

To Croiseur Colbert (500m);
Le Nautilus Disco (2.1km);
D209 to the Médoc;
A10 to Poitiers (248km);
Paris (580km)

18

17

R. de Fondaudège

To UK Consulate
(1.2km); N215 to
D1, Lesparre (65km);
The Médoc

19

R. Emile Fourcand

R. Ferrère

Q. des Chartrons

Allées de Chartres

P

39

R. Charles GRt

R. Turenne

R. de l'Abbé de l'Epée

R. Leflaive de Monbadon

R. du Palais Gallien

Cours de Verdun

R. Boudet

Allées de Bristol

Esplanade des
Quinconces

2

Pl de Tourny

Cours de Tournon

Cours de Tourny

Allées de Tourny

13

Q. Louis XVIII

25

Huguerie

24

5

R. Rousseau

R. Cordiliac

22

Cours du 30 Juillet

Quinconces

Allées de Munich

Garonne

9

1

Pl Casteja

Cours Georges Clemenceau

Cours Montesquieu

Pl des Grands Hommes

7

Allées d'Orléans

10

23

R. de l'Esprit des Lois

Pl Jean Jaurès

Riverfront Esplanade

To Bordeaux
Airport (10km)

R. Judaique

37

R. Mautrec

R. de la Comédie

Cours du Chapeau Rouge

Q. de la Douane

R. St-Sernil

Pl Gambetta

Cours de l'Intendance

R. de Grassi

Grand Théâtre

R. du Port de la Mousque

36

27

St-Rém

33

Pl de la Bourse

Place de la Bourse

6

Pl du Colonel Raynal

R. la Boëtie

Porte Dijeaux

R. de la Porte Dijeaux

Gambetta

Ste-Catherine

Pl du Parlement

Pl St-Pierre

Line C

R. Richelieu

R. du Château d'Eau

14

R. des Remparts

R. Vital Carles

Line B

R. des Cheverus

R. des Piliers de Tutelle

R. du Cancera

R. des Bahutiers

12

26

21

R. Boulan

R. Montbazon

15

City Hall

Jardin de
la Mairie

11

20

Pl Jean Moulin

R. des Trois Conils

Pl St-Projet

R. de la Merci

38

30

Pl Camille Jullian

32

Pl du Palais

R. du Chapeau Fermé

Porte Cailhau

To N89 to Libourne
(31km) St-Emilion (40km),
Pont de Pierre, A10 to
Poitiers (248km) & Paris
(580km)

Line A

Hôtel de Ville

Cours d'Alsace et Lorraine

Ste-Catherine

Place du Palais

Palais de Justice

Line A

R. D. Diderot

R. des Frères Bonie

Cours du Maréchal Juin

R. du Ha

R. du Mirail

R. Ste-Catherine

R. Bouquière

R. Neuve

Porte de
Bourgogne

Porte des Salinières

R. de Bellort

R. Lacornée

Pl de la
République

16

Musée
d'Aquitaine

R. de Cursol

Porte de la
Grosse Cloche

R. St-James

Cours Victor Hugo

R. des Faures

To Quai de
la Paludate
(Bars & Discos;
1.3km)

29

St-Michel

R. St-François

R. des Menuts

R. Mouneyra

Cours d'Albret

Cours Pasteur

Cours de la Libération

R. Jean Burgnet

R. Paul Louis Lande

8

R. Crabosne

R. Bergeret

R. du Tondu

R. Henri IV

Cours Aristide Briand

3

R. des Augustins

Line B

Victoire

R. de Pessac

To Arcachon
via N250

R. Villedieu
To A630; A62 to
Spa de Vinothérapie
Caudalie (15km);
A63 to Arcachon
(74km); Bayonne (190km);
Toulouse (248km)

28

Porte d'Aquitaine

Pl
de la
Victoire

R. Elie Gintrec

Cours de la Marne

4

Pl des
Capucins

31

35

34

To Auberge
de Jeunesse (800m);
Gare St-Jean
(1.4km)

FRANCE

wings of the Hôtel de Ville (city hall) complex (built in the 1770s); between them is a verdant public park, the **Jardin de la Mairie**. Founded in 1801, the museum has a large collection of paintings, including Flemish, Dutch and Italian works from the 17th century and a particularly important work by Delacroix.

In 1137 the future King Louis VII married Eleanor of Aquitaine in **Cathédrale St-André** (☎ 05 56 81 26 25; admission free; ⊙ 10-11.30am & 2-6.30pm Mon, 7.30-11.30am & 2-6pm Tue-Fri, 9-11.30am & 2-7pm Sat, 8am-12.30pm Sun, 2.30-5.30pm 1st Sun of month), now a Unesco World Heritage site. Behind the choir, the 50m-high belfry, 15th-century **Tour Pey-Berland**, has a panoramic view at the top of 232 narrow steps.

The outstanding **Musée d'Aquitaine** (Museum of Aquitaine; ☎ 05 56 01 51 00; 20 cours Pasteur; ⊙ 11am-6pm Tue-Sun) presents 25,000 years of Bordeaux's history and ethnography. Its exceptional artefacts include several stone carvings of women and a collection of Gallo-Roman steles, statues and ceramics. A detailed, English-language catalogue is worth borrowing at the ticket counter (€1.50 deposit).

Sleeping

Auberge de Jeunesse (☎ 05 56 33 00 70; fax 05 56 33 00 71; 22 cours Barbey, annexe at 208 cours de l'Argonne; dm HI member/nonmember incl breakfast €16/17.50; ▯) Ultra-modern, well-equipped and open 24 hours, there's a café-bar, kitchen, laundry and facilities for the disabled. All the rooms are dorms, but most are for four people or fewer. Take bus Nos 7 or 8 to the Meunier stop.

Hôtel Boulan (☎ 05 56 52 23 62; fax 05 56 44 91 65; 28 rue Boulan; s/d €28.25/28.50, with shared bathroom €20.25/23.50) Tucked away in a quiet side-street, but still handy for many of the sights, this friendly place has rooms of a good standard for this price.

Hôtel Excelsior (☎ 05 56 48 00 14; www.hotel-bordeaux.com; 26 rue Huguerie; d/tw/tr €22.80/24.40/ 27.50) The simple, functional rooms are larger and brighter than those at its sister property up the road, Hôtel Studio, where you'll need to go to check in.

Hôtel de Famille (☎ 05 56 52 11 28; fax 05 56 51 94 43; 76 cours Georges Clemenceau; s & d €29-36, with shared bathroom €18-22) A variety of ordinary but comfy rooms. There's no lift, so the higher your room, the cheaper (and smaller) it is. Light sleepers beware – there's no double-glazing.

La Maison du Lierre (☎ 05 56 51 92 71; www .maisondulierre.com; 57 rue Huguerie; s/d €63/73; Ⓟ) A delightful hotel occupying a sympathetically restored townhouse with a beautiful Bordeaux stone staircase and pretty courtyard for breakfast in summer. The 12 mid-sized rooms are nicely decorated with warm colours and parquet floors.

Hôtel des 4 Soeurs (☎ 05 57 81 19 20; http://4soeurs .free.fr; 6 cours du 30 Juillet; s/d from €60/70; ☒ ☒ ▯) An appealing three-star hotel in a great location. The very comfortable rooms boast extras such as hairdryers and English-language TV channels and some overlook place de la Comédie.

Eating & Drinking

Claret's (☎ 05 56 01 21 21; 46 rue du Pas St Georges; lunch menu €10, dinner menu €16-20; ⊙ closed Sat lunch & all day Sun) A chic, smart but reasonably priced little venue on place Camille-Jullian, offering an interesting selection of southwestern French and Japanese specialities.

Cassolette Café (☎ 05 56 92 94 96; www.cassolette café.com; 20 pl de la Victoire; cassolette (of which there are five) €10.50, lunch/dinner menu €8.50/10.50; ⊙ noon-midnight) Extremely popular and great value, you order your menu or the ingredients of your *cassolette* (casserole cooked on a terra-cotta plate) using a check-off form – and your choices appear promptly.

Le Bistrot d'Édouard (☎ 05 56 81 48 87; 16 pl du Parlement; menu €11-20) The great-value three-course menu at €11 (available lunch and dinner) keeps this bistrot packed. Outside tables are in a calming spot by the fountain in place du Parlement.

La Petite Brasserie (☎ 05 56 52 19 79; 43 rue du Pas St Georges; menu €25/35; ☺ Wed-Sun) An unpretentious place offering fine brasserie-style dining in a relaxed and cosy atmosphere. The traditional bordelaise cuisine, extensive wine list and attentive service all get top marks.

Le Fournil des Capucins (62-64 cours de la Marne) Near place de la Victoire, this bakery never closes.

Bodega Bodega (☎ 05 56 01 24 24; 4 rue des Piliers de Tutelle; ☺ noon-3.15pm & 7pm-2am Mon-Sat, 7pm-2am Sun) With two floors of tapas, tunes and trendy types, this is the biggest and best Spanish bar in town.

Café Brun (☎ 05 56 52 20 49; 45 rue St-Rémi; ☺ 10-2am) This bar-bistro with a warm atmosphere and cool jazz is great for an evening aperitif.

Marché des Capucins (☺ 6am-1pm Tue-Sun) is a few blocks east of place de la Victoire, and is a one-time wholesale market. Nearby rue Élie Gintrec has super-cheap **fruit & vegie stalls** (☺ to 1pm or 1.30pm Mon-Sat).

Also recommended:

Champion supermarket (pl des Grands Hommes; ☺ 8.30am-7.30pm Mon-Sat) In the basement of the Marché des Grands Hommes.

Auchan supermarket (Centre Commercial Mériadeck; ☺ 8.30am-10pm Mon-Sat) Opposite 58 rue du Château d'Eau.

Entertainment

Bordeaux has a vibrant nightlife scene; details of events appear in *Bordeaux Plus* and *Clubs & Concerts* (French website at www.clubsetconcerts.com), both free and available at the tourist office.

Nondubbed films are screened at two art cinemas, **Centre Jean Vigo** (☎ 05 56 44 35 17; 6 rue Franklin), and the popular, five-screen **Cinéma Utopia** (☎ 05 56 52 00 03; 3 pl Camille Jullian).

Getting There & Away

Bordeaux airport (☎ 05 56 34 50 50; www.bordeaux.aeroport.fr) is in Mérignac, 10km west of Bordeaux. **Ryanair** (www.ryanair.com) and Air France

operate regular flights from the UK and low-cost Dutch airline **Basiq Air** (www.basiqair.com) flies from Amsterdam.

Buses to places all over the Gironde (and parts of nearby *départements*) leave from the **Halte Routière** (bus terminal; allées de Chartres), in the northeast corner of esplanade des Quinconces; schedules are posted. **Citram Aquitaine** runs buses to destinations in the Gironde and has an **information kiosk** (☎ 05 56 43 68 43; ☺ 1-8pm Mon-Fri, 9am-1.30pm & 5-8pm Sat) at the Halte Routière.

Facing the train station is **Eurolines** (☎ 05 56 92 50 42; 32 rue Charles Domercq; ☺ Mon-Sat).

Train station **Gare St-Jean**, about 3km from the city centre, is at the southern terminus of cours de la Marne. Destinations include Paris' Gare Montparnasse (€58.90, three hours, at least 16 daily), Bayonne (€24.40, 1¾ hours, eight daily), La Rochelle (€22.50, two hours, five to seven daily) and Toulouse (€27.70, two to three hours, nine to 14 daily).

BORDEAUX WINE-GROWING REGION

The 1000-sq-km wine-growing area around the city of Bordeaux is, along with Burgundy, France's most important producer of top-quality wines. Bordeaux has over 5000 chateaux (also known as *domaines, crus* or *clos*), the properties where grapes are raised, picked, fermented and then matured as wine. The smaller chateaux often accept walk-in visitors, but at many places, especially the better-known ones, you have to make advance reservations by phone. Many chateaux are closed during the *vendange* (grape harvest) in October.

Information & Tours

In Bordeaux, the **Maison du Vin de Bordeaux** (☎ 05 56 00 22 88; 3 cours du 30 Juillet; ☺ 8.30am-4.30pm Mon-Fri), across the street from the tourist office, can supply you with a free, colour-coded map of production areas, details on chateau visits, and the addresses of local *maisons du vin* (tourist offices that deal mainly with winery visits).

On Wednesday and Saturday (daily from May to October) at about 1.30pm, the Bordeaux tourist office runs five-hour bus tours in the area (adult/student/child under 12 €26/23/11.50). From May to October, all-day trips (adult/student/child €47/40/23.50) to wine chateaux, starting with a tour and lunch in Bordeaux, begin at 9.15am on Wednesday and Saturday.

THE MÉDOC

Northwest of Bordeaux lie some of Bordeaux's most celebrated vineyards. To the west, fine-sand beaches, bordered by dunes and *étangs* (lagoons), stretch for some 200km from Pointe de Grave south along the Côte d'Argent (Silver Coast) to the Bassin d'Arcachon and beyond; seaside resorts include Soulac-sur-Mer, Carcans Plage, Lacanau-Océan and Cap Ferret. The coastal dunes abut a vast pine forest planted in the 19th century to stabilise the drifting sands and prevent them from encroaching on areas further inland.

The Pauillac tourist office houses the Maison du Tourisme et du Vin (☎ 05 56 59 03 08; www.pauillac-medoc.com; ☙ 9am-7pm Jul–mid-Sep, 9.30am-12.30pm & 2-6.30pm Jun & mid-Sep–Nov; 9.30am-12.30pm & 2-6pm Mon-Sat, 10.30am-12.30pm & 3-6pm Sun Dec-May), an excellent centre for information about the Médoc region.

Vineyards & Chateaux

The gravelly soil of the Médoc's gently rolling hills supports neat rows of meticulously tended grape vines (mainly cabernet sauvignon) that produce some of the world's most sought-after red wines. Chateaux in the Pauillac appellation that welcome visitors by appointment include Château Lafite Rothschild (☎ 05 56 73 18 18; www.lafite.com; admission free; ☙ Mon-Fri Nov-Jul), famed for its premier *grand cru classé*, with free, bilingual, one-hour tours (including a tasting session) on weekdays; and the equally illustrious Château Mouton Rothschild (☎ 05 56 73 21 29; fax 05 56 73 21 28; ☙ Mon-Fri Jan-Dec, daily Apr-Nov), whose tours, frequently in English, cost €5 (tasting session extra). Book ahead for both.

ST-ÉMILION

pop 2500

The medieval village of St-Émilion, 39km east of Bordeaux, is surrounded by vineyards renowned for their full-bodied, deeply coloured red wines.

The tourist office (☎ 05 57 55 28 28; www.saint-emilion-tourisme.com; pl des Créneaux; ☙ 9.30am-7pm mid-Jun–mid-Sep, to 12.30pm & 1.45-6pm mid-Sep–mid-Jun) has brochures in English and details on visiting almost 100 nearby chateaux.

St-Émilion's most interesting historical sites can only be visited with one of the tourist office's 45-minute guided tours (adult/student/child €5.50/3.60/2.90, plus entry to sites) run several times daily. Most are in French. Check ahead for English tour times (usually 1pm). The tour is the only way to see the astounding Église Monolithe, carved out of solid limestone from the 9th to the 12th centuries.

ARCACHON

pop 11,800

The coastal resort of Arcachon became popular with bourgeois residents of Bordeaux at the end of the 19th century. It's not hard to see why – beach lovers can frolic away sunny days on the long, sandy seashore and nearby Dune de Pyla, Europe's highest sand dune. The town itself is not overly attractive but it does have a certain laid-back charm, and a pretty inner suburb of heyday villas harks back to its golden era.

Arcachon makes an easy day trip from Bordeaux, meaning it's often crowded in summer. To escape the hoards, grab a bike and explore the practically deserted out-of-town beaches. Arcachon is on the southern side of the triangular Bassin d'Arcachon (Arcachon Bay), which is linked to the Atlantic by a 3km-wide channel just west of town.

The flat area that abuts the Plage d'Arcachon (the town's beach) is known as the Ville d'Été (Summer Quarter). The liveliest section is around Jetée Thiers, one of the two piers.

The Office de Tourisme d'Arcachon (☎ 05 57 52 97 97; www.arcachon.com; pl Président Roosevelt; ☙ 9am-7pm July & Aug, to 6.30pm Mon-Fri, to 5pm Sat, 10am-noon & 1-5pm Sun Apr-Jun & Sep, 9am-6pm Mon-Fri, to 5pm Sat Oct-Mar) is a few hundred metres from the train station.

Sleeping

The steep, inland side of the Dune de Pyla, 10km south of town, is gradually burying five large and rather pricey camping grounds, most of them half-hidden in a forest of pine trees. Of these, La Forêt (☎ 05 56 22 73 28; www.campinglaforet.fr; route de Biscarosse; camp sites €12.25-26.50; ☙ Apr–mid-Oct; ⧉) is a well-run, three-star place with plenty of shade and good amenities.

Hôtel La Paix (☎ 05 56 83 05 65; fax 05 56 83 05 65; 8 ave de Lamartine; s/d from €25.80/28.90, with shower & toilet €33.30/36.10, d half-board €54-62, studio apt per week €152.40-290, in July & Aug €320-487; ☙ late Apr-Nov) A charming, friendly and down-to-earth place in a quaint old house, near the beach. From June to September (peak season), half-board is obligatory.

Hôtel St-Christaud (☎ /fax 05 56 83 38 53; 8 allée de la Chapelle; d with washbasin €21-35, with shower & toilet €31-47) A rambling old house with a maze of rooms in varying states of renovation. Facilities are basic, but prices are reasonable.

Getting There & Away

Some of the trains from Bordeaux to Arcachon (€8.60, 50 minutes, 11 to 18 daily) are coordinated with TGVs from Paris' Gare Montparnasse. The last train back to Bordeaux usually leaves Arcachon at 8.15pm (9.51pm on Sundays and holidays).

BAYONNE
pop 42,000

The cultural and economic capital of the French Basque Country Bayonne, unlike the upmarket seaside resort of Biarritz, retains much of its Basqueness: you'll hear almost as much Euskara (the Basque language) as French in certain quarters. The town's premier fiesta is the five-day **Fêtes de Bayonne** in early August – like Pamplona's running of the bulls, only with cows.

Orientation & Information

The Rivers Adour and Nive split Bayonne into three: St-Esprit, the area north of the Adour; Grand Bayonne, the oldest part of the city, on the western bank of the Nive; and the very Basque Petit Bayonne quarter to its east. Check your email at **Cyber Net Café** (☎ 05 59 50 85 10; pl de la République; Internet per hr €4.50; ☼ 7am-11pm Mon-Sat, noon-11pm Sun) or visit the **tourist office** (☎ 05 59 46 01 46; www.bayonne-tourisme.com; pl des Basques; ☼ 9am-7pm Mon-Sat, 10am-1pm Sun Jul & Aug, 9am-6.30pm Mon-Fri, 10am-6pm Sat Sep-Jun) for free brochures including *Fêtes*, listing French Basque Country cultural and sporting events and *Tout à Loisir*, and information on hiking, biking and other activities.

Sights

Construction of Bayonne's Gothic **Cathédrale Ste-Marie** (☼ 7.30-11.45am & 3-5.45pm Mon-Sat, 3.30-5.45pm Sun) began in the 13th century, when Bayonne was ruled by the Anglo-Normans, and was completed well after France assumed control in 1451.

The **Musée Basque et de l'Histoire de Bayonne** (☎ 05 59 46 61 90; 37 quai des Corsaires; adult/student/under 18 yrs €5.50/3/free; ☼ 10am-6.30pm Tue-Sun May-Oct, to 12.30pm & 2-6pm Tue-Sun Nov-Apr) presents exhibits and information about the history and culture of this unique people.

There is a **combined ticket** (adult/student €9/4.50) to both the Musée Basque and **Musée Bonnat** (☎ 05 59 59 08 52; 5 rue Jacques Lafitte; adult/student/child €5.50/3/free; ☼ 10am-6.30pm Wed-Mon May-Oct, to 12.30pm & 2-6pm Wed-Mon Nov-Apr), an art gallery featuring canvases by El Greco, Goya and Degas, and Rubens.

Sleeping

Auberge de Jeunesse (☎ 05 59 58 70 00; anglet@fuaj.org; 19 route des Vignes, Anglet; dm 1st night/subsequent nights €17/14.20; ☼ mid-Feb–mid-Nov) This hostel, in Anglet, complete with a Scottish pub, is lively and popular. Reservations are essential in summer. The hostel has **camping** (sites per adult incl breakfast €10). From Bayonne station, take STAB bus No 2 towards Anglet. At the Cinq Cantons stop, change to No 72, direction Les Plages, which stops outside the hostel. Alternatively – and in high season when bus No 72 doesn't run – take No 2 to the Moulin Barbot stop, from where the hostel is a 10-minute signposted walk. On Sunday take line C from the town hall.

Hôtel Paris-Madrid (☎ 05 59 55 13 98; sorbois@wanadoo.fr; pl de la Gare; d from €25, s/d with shared bathroom from €16/22; P) This friendly place is highly recommended, especially for those arriving at the station opposite. The owners speak English and the rooms, decorated with flair, are good value.

Hôtel des Arceaux (☎ 05 59 59 15 53; hotel.arceaux@wanadoo.fr; 26 rue Port Neuf; r with washbasin/shower €28/38) Inexpensive and recently undergone a complete overhaul, so by the time you read this the rooms should be sparkling new.

Adour Hôtel (☎ 05 59 55 11 31; www.adourhotel.fr; 13 pl Ste-Ursule; d/tr/q from €47/50/64) Just north of the River Adour and convenient for the station, this welcoming establishment has bright, airy rooms decorated with bull-fighting, rugby and gastronomy memorabilia.

Eating & Drinking

A good selection of medium-priced restaurants surround the covered market and all along quai Amiral Jauréguiberry.

Bodega Ibaia (☎ 05 59 59 86 66; 45 quai Jauréguiberry; mains €8-12; ☼ closed Sun & Mon lunch) Here

ROB FLYNN

Artist painting in the main square of Montmartre (p276), Paris, France

Musée du Louvre (p273), Paris, France
GREG ELMS

DAVID TOMLINSON

The island of Mont St-Michel (p305), Normandy, France

The citadel of Bonifacio, Corsica (p383), France

OLIVIER CIRENDINI

MARK AVELLINO

Fresco on outside walls of the Altes Rathaus (p465), Bamberg, Germany

DAVID PEEVERS

The modern Jüdisches Museum (p411), Berlin, Germany

Bar scenes in Berlin (p419), Germany

RICHARD NEBESKY

CHRIS

The fantastical Neuschwanstein Castle (p470), Bavaria, Germany

is an atmospheric Basque restaurant/tapas bar with wooden benches, sawdust on the floor and traditional Spanish tiling.

Bistrot Ste-Cluque (☎ 05 59 55 82 43; 9 rue Hugues; menu €16) There's only one *menu* here on a large chalkboard. Noisy, smoky and bustling, it's atmospheric and unpretentious.

Restaurant Koskera (☎ 05 59 55 20 79; 2 rue Hugues; menu around €10; ☽ lunch Mon-Sat) A dark, cave-like place serving inexpensive daily specials of hearty Basque fare.

The **covered market** (quai Commandant Roquebert; ☽ 7am-1pm & 3.30-7pm Fri, 8am-1pm Mon-Thu & Sat) occupies an imposing riverside building. There are several tempting food shops and delicatessens along rue Port Neuf and rue d'Espagne. The greatest concentration of pubs and bars is in Petit Bayonne, especially along rue Pannecau, rue des Cordeliers and quai Galuperie. Every Thursday in July and August, there's traditional **Basque music** (admission free; ☽ 9.30pm) in place Charles de Gaulle.

Getting There & Away
The **Biarritz-Anglet-Bayonne airport** (☎ 05 59 43 83 83; www.biarritz.aeroport.fr) is 5km southwest of central Bayonne and 3km southeast of Biarritz. Air France flies to/from Paris Orly about eight times daily and less frequently to Lyon and Geneva. Ryanair flies daily to/from London Stanstead.

From place des Basques, **ATCRB buses** (☎ 05 59 26 06 99) follow the coast to the Spanish border. Transportes Pesa buses leave twice a day for Irún and San Sebastián in Spain (€6.20, 1¾ hours). **Eurolines** (☎ 05 59 59 19 33; 3 pl Charles de Gaulle) buses stop opposite the company office.

TGVs run between Bayonne and Paris' Gare Montparnasse (€71.60, five hours, five daily). There are frequent trains to Biarritz (€2.10, 10 minutes), Bordeaux (€24.40, 2¼ hours, at least 10 daily), Lourdes (€17.80, 1¾ hours, six daily) and Toulouse (€33.10, 3¾ hours, at least four daily).

BIARRITZ
pop 30,000

The stylish coastal town of Biarritz, 8km west of Bayonne, is known for its fine beaches and some of Europe's best surfing. If you're travelling on a budget, consider staying in Bayonne and visiting Biarritz from there. Many surfers camp or stay at one of the two excellent youth hostels in Biarritz and in Anglet.

Orientation & Information
Place Clemenceau, at the heart of Biarritz, is just south of the main beach (Grande Plage). Pointe St-Martin, topped with a lighthouse, rounds off Plage Miramar, the northern continuation of the Grande Plage. Both train station and airport are about 3km southeast of the centre.

The **tourist office** (☎ 05 59 22 37 10; www.biarritz.fr; 1 square d'Ixelles; ☽ 8am-8pm Jul & Aug; 9am-6pm Mon-Sat, 10am-5pm Sun Sep-Jun) publishes *Biarritzcope*, a free monthly what's-on guide.

For surfing of the electronic kind, visit **Génius Informatique** (☎ 05 59 24 39 07; 60 ave Édouard VII; per hr €5).

Sights
Musée de la Mer (☎ 05 59 22 75 40; www.museedelamer.com; Esplanade de la Vierge; adult/child €7.20/4.60; ☽ 9.30am-12.30pm & 2-6pm Tue-Sat) has an aquarium seething with underwater life from the Bay of Biscay (Golfe de Gascogne) plus exhibits on commercial fishing and Biarritz' whaling past.

Biarritz' fashionable beaches – the **Grande Plage** and **Plage Miramar** to its north – are lined with striped bathing tents and are often packed in summer. Beyond Pointe St-Martin, the superb surfing beaches of **Anglet** stretch northwards for over 4km. Take eastbound bus No 9 from place Clemenceau. The best board rental and instruction bargains are to be had at the **Auberge de Jeunesse** in Anglet. The French-language **Swell Line** (☎ 08 36 68 40 64; www.swell-line.com) details surf conditions.

Sleeping
Camping de Parme (☎ 05 59 23 03 00; www.campingdeparme.com; route de l'Aviation; camp sites €15.50-23) The area's only year-round camp site is in a quiet, leafy spot 1.25km northeast of the train station. It's normally fully booked months in advance for July and August.

Biarritz Camping (☎ 05 59 23 00 12; www.biarritz-camping.fr; 28 rue d'Harcet; camp sites €13.50-19.50; ☽ mid-May–mid-Sep; ☒) This summer campsite has spacious and shady sites, 3km southwest of the centre. Take westbound bus No 9 to the Biarritz Camping stop.

Auberge de Jeunesse (☎ 05 59 41 76 00; biarritz@fuaj.org; 8 rue Chiquito de Cambo; dm €14.90; ☽ mid-Jan–mid-Dec) This popular place offers a host of outdoor activities including surfing and sailing. To get here, follow the railway westwards from the train station for 800m.

Villa Etche-Gorria (☎ 05 59 24 00 74; www.hotel -etche-gorria.com; 21 ave du Maréchal Foch; r €60, with shared bathroom €35; ⊗ mid-Dec–late Nov) This pretty Basque villa has a friendly English-speaking owner, huge 1st-floor rooms, some with large balconies. The small, cheaper attic rooms are about the best value in town.

Hôtel Maïtagaria (☎ 05 59 24 26 65; www.hotel -maitagaria.com; 34 ave Carnot; d from €56) Spotless, modern rooms and swish bathrooms make this friendly place good value. There's an intimate garden at the rear for summer breakfasts (€6).

Hôtel Plaza (☎ 05 59 24 74 00; hotel.plaza.biarritz@ wanadoo.fr; 20 ave Edouard VII; s/d from €81/103; ⊠) A three-star Art Deco delight overlooking Grande Plage with the feel of a glamorous heyday hotel. The spacious rooms (many with beach views) are decked out in grand style.

Eating

Le Corsaire (☎ 05 59 24 63 72; Port des Pêcheurs; mains €9-22) It's all about seafood down here by the waters edge on a delightful harbour-side terrace, with dishes including *dorade à l'Espagnole* (€14.50) and grilled cod with chorizo (€12.20).

Le Lodge (☎ 05 59 24 73 78; 1 rue de Port-Vieux; mains €13-17) A buzzing new restaurant and gallery featuring traditional cuisine and contemporary art.

Bistrot des Halles (☎ 05 59 24 21 22; 1 rue du Centre; mains €13-17) One of a cluster of decent little restaurants in this precinct that obtain their produce fresh from the nearby **covered market** (⊗ 7am-1.30pm).

Just downhill from Bistrot des Halles, **La Table de Don Quichotte** (12 ave Victor Hugo) sells Spanish hams and sausages. There's a tempting array of cheeses, wines and pâtés at nearby **Mille et Un Fromages** (8 ave Victor Hugo).

Drinking & Entertainment

There are several good bars along rue du Port Vieux and the streets radiating from it. **Le Surfing** (☎ 05 59 24 78 72; 9 blvd Prince des Galles) is the place to come to discuss waves and wipe-outs. There's an outside terrace with decent views.

Two discos near the town centre are **Le Caveau** (☎ 05 59 24 16 17; 4 rue Gambetta; ⊗ 11pm-5am) and the **Biarritz Latino** (☎ 05 59 22 77 59; ⊗ 11pm-5am Tue-Sat), in the Casino Municipal.

Getting There & Away

Stopping outside the tourist office, nine **ATCRB buses** (☎ 05 59 26 06 99) daily follow the coast southwestwards. For other destinations, it's better to go from Bayonne – not least to ensure a seat in high season. Biarritz-La Négresse train station is about 3km from the town centre. Bus Nos 2 and 9 connect the two. **SNCF** has a town-centre office (13 ave du Maréchal Foch; ⊗ Mon-Fri).

LOURDES

pop 15,000 / elevation 400m

Lourdes, 43km southeast of Pau, was just a sleepy market town until 1858 when Bernadette Soubirous (1844-79), a near-illiterate, 14-year-old peasant girl, saw the Virgin Mary in a series of 18 visions that came to her in a grotto. The Vatican declared her Saint Bernadette in 1933.

Five million visitors now flock here annually. Well over half are pilgrims, including many invalids seeking cures. In counterpoint to the fervent, almost medieval piety of the pilgrims, visitors will witness astounding displays of tacky merchandising – shake-up snow domes, baseball caps, cuckoo clocks and plastic bottles in the shape of the Virgin (just add holy water at the shrine) are but a sample.

Orientation & Information

Lourdes' two main east–west streets are rue de la Grotte and blvd de la Grotte, both leading to the Sanctuaires Notre Dame de Lourdes. The principal north–south thoroughfare, called Ave Général Baron Maransin where it passes above blvd de la Grotte, connects the train station with place Peyramale, where you'll find the **tourist office** (☎ 05 62 42 77 40; www.lourdes-infotourisme .com; pl Peyramale; ⊗ 9am-7pm Mon-Sat, 10am-6pm Sun Jul-Aug, 9am-6.30pm Mon-Sat, 10am-12.30pm Sun Apr-Jun & Sep–mid-Oct, 9am-noon & 2-6pm Mon-Sat Jan-Mar & mid-Oct–Dec).

The huge religious complex that has grown up around the original cave where Bernadette's visions took place is across the River Pau, west of the town centre.

Sights

The Sanctuaries of Our Lady of Lourdes were developed within a decade of the events of 1858. The most revered site is the **Grotte de Massabielle** (Massabielle Cave or Grotto) or the Grotte des Apparitions (Cave of the Apparitions), its walls worn smooth by the touch of millions of hands. Nearby are 19 **pools** in which 400,000 pilgrims seeking cures immerse themselves each year.

The main 19th-century section of the sanctuaries includes the neo-Byzantine **Basilique du Rosaire** (Basilica of the Rosary), the **crypt** and above it the spire-topped, neo-Gothic **Basilique Supérieure** (Upper Basilica).

Visitors to the sanctuaries should dress modestly. All four places of worship open 6am to 10pm in summer and 7am to 7pm in winter.

Sleeping & Eating

Camping de la Poste (☎ 05 62 94 40 35; 26 rue de Langelle; camp sites €9, ste d/tr/q €25/32/40; ⓨ Easter–mid-Oct) Right in the heart of town, this tiny, friendly camping ground is often full. It also rents eight excellent-value en-suite rooms.

Hôtel du Viscos (☎ 05 62 94 08 06; fax 05 62 94 26 74; 6 bis ave St-Joseph; d €34, with shared bathroom €29; ⓨ Feb–mid-Dec) This friendly, family-run place near the station has a bustling bar for guests and offers great value.

Grand Hôtel de la Grotte (☎ 05 62 94 58 87; www .hotel-grotte.com; 66 rue de la Grotte; s €66-113, d €74-140; ⓨ Apr–Oct; Ⓟ ⓧ) Established in 1872, this charming *fin de siècle* place has belonged to the same family for four generations. A gorgeous garden, bar and a couple of prestige restaurants make it an excellent choice.

Le Cardinal (☎ 05 62 42 05 87; 11 pl Peyramale; salads €5.50-6, menu du jour €8.50; ⓨ Mon-Sat) This unpretentious bar/brasserie is where the staff of the tourist office lunch – and they should know what's best. Tuck into steak, chips and salad for only €6.50.

La Rose des Sables (☎ 05 62 42 06 82; 8 rue des Quatre Frères Soulas; dishes €12-14; ⓨ Tue-Sun) This North African restaurant specialises in couscous.

Lourdes' **covered market** (place du Champ Commun) occupies most of the square.

Getting There & Away

The **bus station** (pl Capdevieille) has services northwards to Pau (€7.20, 1¼ hours, four to six daily). SNCF buses to Cauterets (€6.10, one hour, six daily) leave from the train station.

Lourdes is well connected by train to cities all over France, including Bayonne (€17.80, 1¾ hours, three to four daily) and Toulouse (€20.90, 1¾ hours, seven daily). There are four daily TGVs to Paris' Gare Montparnasse (€72.40 to €81.40, six hours).

THE DORDOGNE

Known to the French as Périgord, this region was one of the prehistoric cradles of human civilisation. The remains of Neanderthal and Cro-Magnon people have been discovered throughout the area and quite a number of local caves, including the world-famous Lascaux, are decorated with extraordinary works of prehistoric art. During the warmer months the Dordogne, famed for its rich cuisine (such as truffles and *foie gras*), attracts vast numbers of tourists. In winter, the region goes into deep hibernation, and many hotels, restaurants and tourist sites close.

PÉRIGUEUX

pop 33,294

Founded over 2000 years ago on a hill bounded by a curve in the gentle River Isle, Périgueux has one of France's best museums of prehistory. The city is at its liveliest during the Wednesday and Saturday truffle and *foie gras* markets. The medieval and Renaissance old city, Puy St-Front, is on the hillside between the Isle (to the east) and blvd Michel Montaigne and place Bugeaud (to the west). The train station is about 1km northwest of the old city. The **tourist office** (☎ 05 53 53 10 63; tourisme.perigueux@perigord.tm.fr; 26 pl Francheville; ⓨ 9am-1pm & 2-6pm Mon-Sat year-round, 10am-1pm & 2-6pm Sun mid-Jun–mid-Sep) is next to the medieval Tour Mataguerre.

Hôtel des Voyageurs (☎ 05 53 53 17 44; 26 rue Denis Papin; s/d from €14/16) is one of half a dozen inexpensive hotels near the train station, along rue Denis Papin and rue des Mobiles de Coulmiers. The rock-bottom prices here mean tiny rooms, flimsy furniture and noise from the rowdy bar next door.

Hôtel de l'Univers (☎ 05 53 53 34 79; fax 05 53 06 70 76; 18 cours Michel Montaigne; s €42.70, d €45-53.35; ⓨ Feb-Dec) is a welcoming two-star hotel with a varied selection of generously sized rooms. Most have high ceilings and bathrooms; the two attic rooms are a touch cheaper. There's a decent restaurant downstairs.

The **bus station** (pl Francheville) is on the southern side of the square; hours are posted at the bus stops. One of the carriers, **CFTA** (☎ 05 53 08 43 13; ⓨ Mon-Fri), has an office on the

FRANCE

storey overlooking the waiting room. The tourist office and the train station information office can supply you with schedules.

The **train station** (rue Denis Papin) is served by local bus Nos 1, 4 and 5. Destinations with direct services include Bordeaux (€16.30, 1¼ hours, nine to 13 daily). Services to Paris' Gare d'Austerlitz (€45.90, three to five hours, 12 to 16 daily) are via Limoges. To get to Sarlat-la-Canéda (€12) you have to change at Brive.

SARLAT-LA-CANÉDA
pop 10,000

The beautiful, well-restored town of Sarlat, administratively twinned with nearby La Canéda, is the capital of Périgord Noir. Its medieval and Renaissance townscape, much of it built of tan sandstone in the 16th and 17th centuries, attracts large numbers of tourists, especially for the year-round Saturday market.

Orientation & Information

The heart-shaped Medieval Town (Cité Médiévale) is bisected by the ruler-straight rue de la République (La Traverse), which (along with its continuations) stretches for 2km north from the viaduct and nearby train station to the Auberge de Jeunesse. The Medieval Town is centred on place de la Liberté, rue de la Liberté and place du Peyrou. Sarlat is an excellent base for car trips to the prehistoric sites of the Vézère Valley.

Sarlat's **main tourist office** (☎ 05 53 31 45 45; www.ot-sarlat-perigord.fr; rue Tourny; ☼ 9am-7pm Mon-Sat, 10am-noon Sun Apr-Oct, 9am-noon & 2-7pm Mon-Sat Nov-Mar) is in a building attached to the cathedral. In summer, it charges €2 for hotel and B&B bookings.

Sleeping & Eating

Auberge de Jeunesse (☎ 05 53 59 47 59, 05 53 30 21 27; 77 ave de Selves; dm €10) At this modest but friendly 15-bed hostel kitchen facilities are available; call ahead for a reservation.

Hôtel Les Récollets (☎ 05 53 31 36 00; www.hotel-recollets-sarlat.com; 4 rue Jean-Jacques Rousseau; d from €39) Lost in the narrow alleys of the Medieval Town, this delightful old building has been freshly renovated inside with 18 fully-equipped two-star rooms.

La Maison des Peyrat (☎ 05 53 59 00 32; www.maisondespeyrat.com; Le Lac de la Plane; r €47-95, half-board per person €51-75) This tastefully renovated

17th-century house with tranquil gardens is set on a hill about 1.5km from the town centre, with great views over the surrounding countryside. It's one of the most charming hotels in the area, renowned for its good food and welcoming atmosphere.

Getting There & Away

Bus services are very limited; schedules are available at the tourist office. Departures are from the train station, place Pasteur or place de la Petite Rigaudie. There are one or two buses daily (fewer in July and August) to Périgueux (€6.80, 1½ hours) via Montignac.

The **train station** (☎ 05 53 59 00 21), 1.3km south of the old city at the southern end of ave de la Gare, is poorly linked with the rest of the region.

Destinations served include Bordeaux (€19.90, 2½ hours, two to four direct daily) which is on the same line as Bergerac, Périgueux (change at Le Buisson; €12.00, 1½ hours, two daily). The SNCF bus to Souillac (€4.90, 40 minutes, two to four daily) links up with trains on the Paris (Gare d'Austerlitz)-Limoges-Toulouse line.

PREHISTORIC SITES & THE VÉZÈRE VALLEY

Of the Vézère Valley's 175 known prehistoric sites, the most famous ones, including the world-renowned cave paintings in Lascaux, are situated between Le Bugue (near where the Vézère conflows with the Dordogne) and, 25km to the northeast, Montignac. Most of the valley's sites are closed in winter.

Les Eyzies de Tayac
pop 850

The two museums in the one-street touristy village of Les Eyzies de Tayac provide an excellent introduction to the valley's prehistoric legacy. The very interesting **Musée National de Préhistoire** (National Museum of Prehistory; ☎ 05 53 06 45 45; adult/18-25 yrs/under 18 yrs €4.50/3/free, adults on Sunday €3; ☼ 9.30am-6.30pm Jul & Aug, to noon & 2-5.30pm Wed-Mon Sep-Jun) is built into the cliff above the tourist office. Its well-presented collection of artefacts provides a great introduction to the area's prehistoric human habitation.

About 250m north of Musée National de Préhistoire along the cliff face is the **Abri Pataud** (☎ 05 53 06 92 46; adult/6-12 yrs €5.20/3.20; ☼ 10am-7pm except Mon, Fri & Sat Sep-Jun), a Cro-Magnon shelter *(abri)* inhabited over a period of 15,000 years starting some 37,000 years ago.

Montignac
pop 3101

The relaxing and picturesque town of Montignac, on the Vézère 25km northeast of Les Eyzies, achieved sudden fame after the discovery of the nearby Grotte de Lascaux.

The **tourist office** (☎ 05 53 51 82 60; www .bienvenue-montignac.com; pl Bertrand de Born; ☼ 9am-7pm Jul-Sep, to noon & 2-6pm Mon-Sat Oct-Jun), 200m west of place Tourny, is next to the 14th-century Église St-Georges le Prieuré. IGN maps and topoguides are sold at the **Maison de la Presse** (☼ closed Sun Sep-Jun) located just across the street.

The banks, including three right around the tourist office, open Tuesday to Saturday. The **post office** (pl Tourny) offers currency exchange.

This dramatic **Château de Beynac fortress** (☎ 05 53 29 50 40; adult/5-11 yrs €7/3; ☼ 10am-6pm) is perched atop a sheer cliff, dominating a strategic bend in the Dordogne.

In a stunning spot with the château high above and the river just below is the stylish **Hôtel-Restaurant du Château** (☎ 05 53 29 19 20; www.hotelduchateau-dordogne.com; d from €50; ☼ Feb-Dec), with spacious rooms. The attached **restaurant** (menu €17.50-22) specialises in traditional Périgord cuisine. It's on the main road through Beynac.

QUERCY

Southeast of the Dordogne *département* lies the warm, unmistakeably southern region of Quercy, many of whose residents still speak Occitan (Provençal). The dry limestone plateau in the northeast is covered with oak trees and cut by dramatic canyons created by the serpentine River Lot and its tributaries. The main city, Cahors, is not far from some of the region's finest vineyards.

CAHORS
pop 21,432

Cahors, nestled on a bend in the River Lot and ringed by hills, is a quiet town with a relaxed Midi atmosphere.

The main commercial thoroughfare is the north–south oriented blvd Léon Gambetta. It divides Vieux Cahors (Old Cahors) to

the east, from the new quarters to the west. Place François Mitterrand is home to the **tourist office** (☎ 05 65 53 20 65; cahors@wanadoo.fr; pl François Mitterrand; ☼ 9am-12.30pm & 1.30-6pm Mon-Sat, 10am-noon Sun & hols Jul-Aug) which has several excellent brochures in English on offer.

Sights

The cavernous nave of the Romanesque-style **Cathédrale St-Étienne**, consecrated in 1119, is crowned with two 18m-wide cupolas (the largest in France), inspired by the architecture of the Near East.

The small **Musée de la Résistance** (☎ 05 65 22 14 25; pl Général de Gaulle; admission free; ☼ 2-6pm), on the northern side of the square, presents illustrated exhibits on the Resistance, the concentration camps and the liberation of France.

Sleeping & Eating

Auberge de Jeunesse (☎ 05 65 35 64 71; fax 05 65 35 95 92; 20 rue Frédéric Suisse; dm €9.30; ☼ check-in 24hr; ▣) The 40-bed youth hostel is in the same building as the Foyer des Jeunes Travailleurs. There's a cheap canteen. Smaller rooms for one or two people are often full, so accommodation is usually in dorms of four to 10 beds; telephone reservations advisable.

Hôtel La Bourse (☎ /fax 05 65 35 17 78; 7 pl Claude Rousseau; d from €28) The 10 rooms here are all spacious and clean. It's also the only decent budget option in the medieval quarter.

Grand Hôtel Terminus (☎ 05 65 53 32 00; terminus .balandre@wanadoo.fr; 5 ave Charles de Freycinet; d €60-160; ℗ ✗) This luxurious and characterful 1920s place has been refurbished to a high standard with period detail including ornamental radiators, stained-glass windows and roll-top baths. The rooms are beautifully furnished and have huge beds.

Restaurant Marie Colline (☎ 05 65 35 59 96; 173 rue Clemenceau; mains €7; ☼ noon-2pm Tue-Fri) This is a rarity in France – a fantastic vegetarian restaurant. Choose from a changing menu of just two or three delicious dishes such as aubergine lasagne or *dauphinois* of pumpkin. Book ahead.

Marché Couvert (pl des Halles; ☼ 7.30am-12.30pm & 3-7pm Tue-Sat, 9am-noon Sun & most hols) A covered market also known as Les Halles.

Getting There & Away

Cahors' **train station** (pl Jouinot Gambetta, aka pl de la Gare) is on the main SNCF line (four to nine daily) linking Paris' Gare d'Austerlitz (€59.60, five hours) with Limoges (€23.30, two hours), and Toulouse (€14.70, 1½ hours). To get to Sarlat-la-Canéda, take a train to Souillac and an SNCF bus from there (€13.80, three hours, three daily).

AROUND CAHORS

The limestone hills between Cahors and Figeac are cut by the dramatic, cliff-flanked Rivers Lot and Célé. The spectacular, 1200m-long **Grotte de Pech Merle** (☎ 05 65 31 27 05; www .pechmerle.com; adult/5-18 yrs €7/4.50; mid-Sep–mid-Jun €6/3.80), 30km northeast of Cahors, is a natural wonder, with thousands of stalactites and stalagmites of all varieties and shapes. It also has dozens of paintings of mammoths, horses and 'negative' human handprints, drawn by Cro-Magnon people 16,000 to 20,000 years ago. Get there early as only 700 people daily are allowed to visit. Telephone reservations are accepted.

St-Cirq Lapopie, 25km east of Cahors and 44km southwest of Figeac, is perched on a cliff top 100m above the River Lot. The spectacular views and the area's natural beauty make up for the village's self-conscious charm.

The harmonious riverside town of Figeac, on the River Célé 70km northeast of Cahors, has a picturesque **old city**, with many houses dating from the 12th to 18th centuries. Four SNCF buses daily go to Cahors and Figeac.

BURGUNDY & THE RHÔNE

Best-known for its cooking and its world class wine, you'll find Burgundy is also one of France's most varied *départements* – an enticing blend of hilltop villages and bustling market towns, grand châteaux and tiny churches, rolling fields and abandoned abbeys.

DIJON

pop 230,000

Dijon is one of France's most appealing provincial cities, with an inviting centre graced by elegant medieval and Renaissance buildings. It served as the capital for the dukes of Burgundy from the 11th to 15th centuries during which time Dijon was turned into one of the great centres of European art. Modern Dijon is a lively, dynamic city with 24,000 university students and a thriving cultural scene. It also makes a great base for touring the world-class wine country nearby.

Orientation

Dijon's commercial centre stretches from the tourist office eastwards to Église St Michel; the main shopping streets are rue de la Liberté and rue du Bourg. Place Grangier is north of rue de la Liberté, while the train station is at the western end of ave Maréchal Foch. The old city is around place François Rude and the surrounding streets.

Information

Laundrette (41 rue Auguste Comte; ☽ 7.30am-9pm) Also at 28 rue Berbisey, 55 rue Berbisey and 8 pl de la Banque.
Main post office (pl Grangier; ☽ 8am-7pm Mon-Fri, to noon Sat)
Multi-Rezo (☎ 03 80 66 33 21; 74 rue Vannerie; Internet per 12min/hr €1/5; ☽ 9am-midnight Mon-Sat, 2-10pm Sun)
Tourist office (☎ 03 80 44 11 44; www.dijon-tourism .com; pl Darcy; ☽ 9am-7pm May–mid-Oct, 10am-6pm mid-Oct–Apr)

Sights & Activities

Once home to the region's rulers, the elaborate **Palais des Ducs et des États de Bourgogne** palace complex lies at the heart of old Dijon. The eastern wing houses the Musée des Beaux-Arts (see p335). The 46m-high, 15th-century **Tour Philippe-le-Bon** (Tower of Philip the Good; adult/concession €2.30/1.20; ☽ 9am-noon, 1.45-5.30pm Easter-end Nov, to 11pm, 1.30-3.30pm Wed afternoon, Sat & Sun Nov-Easter) affords fantastic views over the city.

A little way north of the Palais des Ducs, **Église Notre Dame** was built between 1220 and 1240. The façade's three tiers are decorated with leering gargoyles. Outside, **rue de la Chouette** is named after the small stone *chouette* (owl) carved into the north wall of the church. It is said to grant happiness and wisdom to those who stroke it.

Situated above the tomb of St Benignus (who brought Christianity to Burgundy in the 2nd century), Dijon's 13th-century **Cathédrale St Bénigne** was originally built as an abbey church.

Dijon has several outstanding museums. The Dijon Card (€8/11/14 for 24/48/72 hours) gets you into the main ones, and includes a guided city tour and use of public transport. Several museums are free to students and to everyone on Sunday.

Housed in the eastern wing of the Palais des Ducs, **Musée des Beaux-Arts** (☎ 03 80 74 52 70; adult/senior/student €3.40/1.60/free, admission free Sun; ⏰ 9.30am-6pm Wed-Mon May-Oct, 10am-5pm Wed-Mon Nov-Apr) is one of the most renowned museums in France – considered by many to be second only to the Louvre. The museum has important collections of French, Flemish and Italian art.

The city's archaeological museum, **Musée Archéologique** (☎ 03 80 30 88 54; 5 rue du Docteur Maret; adult/senior/student €2.20/1.10/free, free Sun; ⏰ 9.30am-12.30pm & 1.30-6pm Wed-Sun Oct-May, to 6pm Jun-Sep) displays Celtic artefacts and a particularly fine 1st-century bronze of the goddess Sequana standing on a boat. The 11th-century chamber on the lowest level was once part of a Benedictine abbey.

Housed in a 17th-century *hotel particulier*, **Musée National Magnin** (☎ 03 80 67 11 10; 4 rue des Bons Enfants; adult/student €3/2.30, Sun €2.30, 1st Sun of the month free; ⏰ 10am-noon & 2-6pm Tue-Sun) displays works of art donated to the city in 1938 by the brother and sister team of Jeanne and Maurice Magnin.

In the copper-domed chapels of a neoclassical church (1709), the **Musée d'Art Sacré** (☎ 03 80 44 12 69; 15 rue Ste Anne; adult/senior/student €2.80/1.60/free, free Sun; ⏰ 9am-noon & 2-6pm Wed-Mon) displays ecclesiastical objects from the 12th to 19th centuries. Nearby and included in the ticket price, the **Musée de la Vie Bourguignonne** (☎ 03 80 44 12 69; 17 rue Ste Anne; ⏰ 9am-noon & 2-6pm Wed-Mon) occupies a 17th-century Cistercian convent and explores rural life in Burgundy in past centuries.

You couldn't really leave Dijon without paying homage to the city's most famous export. Visits to the **Musée de la Moutarde** (48 quai Nicolas Rolin; adult/child €3/free) at the factory of Amora, Dijon's main mustard company, can be arranged at the tourist office.

Sleeping

Centre de Rencontres Internationales et de Séjour de Dijon (CRISD; ☎ 03 80 72 95 20; reservation@auberge-cri -dijon.com; 1 blvd Champollion; s/d/q per person €26/16/13.50) An institutional 260-bed place 2.8km northeast of the centre. Take bus No 5 (towards Épirey) from place Grangier; at night take line A to Épirey.

Hôtel Lamartine (☎ 03 80 30 37 47; ot-dijon.fr; 12 rue Jules Mercier; s/d €31/47; ⏰ reception closed noon-3pm) On a shabby backstreet just off rue du Bourg, the 14 rooms are plain and the street views are uninspiring, but the location is unbeatable – the Palace des Ducs is a few steps from the front door.

Hôtel du Palais (☎ 03 80 67 16 26; fax 03 80 65 12 16; 23 rue du Palais; s €30-37, d with shower €34-43, s/d/tr with bath €40-45/48-65/52-70) One of Dijon's best-kept secrets oozes old-fashioned charm in a former *hotel particulier* near the Quartier d'Antiquaires. The rooms are spacious and welcoming (the best are on the first floor).

Hôtel le Chambellan (☎ 03 80 67 12 67; hotel chambellan@aol.com; 92 rue Vannerie; s €34-48, d €42-52) A great deal on one of the city's oldest streets. The pretty building is typical of the area, with flower-boxes and shuttered windows, and there is a small 17th-century courtyard where breakfast is served in summer.

Hostellerie du Sauvage (☎ 03 80 41 31 21; hotel dusauvage@free.fr; 64 rue Monge; d from €41; P) On an idyllic cobbled courtyard in a 15th-century *relais de poste* (relay posthouse), this great-value hotel is off buzzy rue Monge. Parking is available in the old carriage-houses for €4.

Eating & Drinking

Au Moulin à Vent (☎ 03 80 30 81 43; 8 pl François Rude; ⏰ closed Sun dinner & Mon) A quintessentially French street-side café opposite the fountain on place François Rude. There's a large terrace outside and a snug restaurant upstairs, serving local specialities.

Chez Nous (☎ 03 80 50 12 98; 8 impasse Quentin; plat du jour €7; ⏰ Tue-Sat) A tiny neighbourhood bistro down an alleyway off place du Marché. Locals come for the coffee and lunch-time menu; the décor and atmosphere could have been lifted from a café on Paris' Left Bank.

Hostellerie du Chapeau Rouge (☎ 03 80 50 88 88; bourgogne.net/chapeaurouge; 5 rue Michelet; menu without/with wine €35/42) Bold, creative French cuisine based on traditional ingredients and top-quality local produce. For gastrophiles, the restaurant offers two gourmet menus; €75 buys seven sumptuous courses, while €100 gets a belt-busting 11.

La Dame d'Aquitaine (☎ 03 80 30 45 65; 23 pl Bossuet; menu €18-35.90; ⏰ closed lunch Sun & Mon) Excellent Burgundian and southwestern French cuisine and the atmospheric location in a vaulted 13th-century cellar make this one of Dijon's most renowned restaurants.

DIJON

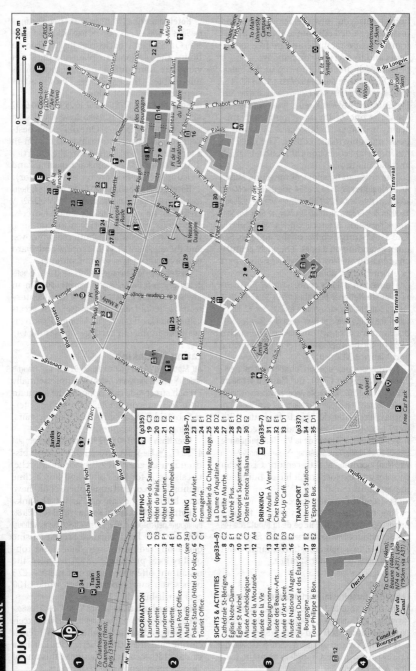

La Petite Marche (☎ 03 80 30 15 10; 27-29 rue Mu-sette; menu €10-15; ⏰ 7am-9pm Mon-Sat, 9am-noon Sun) Vegetarians tired of Burgundy's meat-heavy menus should head for this popular organic restaurant.

Osteria Enoteca Italiana (☎ 03 80 50 07 36; 32 rue Amiral Roussin; lunch menu €14; ⏰ Tue-Sun) A small Italian diner with delicious pasta and fish dishes.

Pick-Up Café (☎ 03 80 30 61 44; 9 rue Mably; ⏰ 8am-2am) A typically French idea of an American bar-diner, complete with juke-boxes and pinball machines.

Coco-Loco (☎ 03 80 73 29 44; 18 ave Garibaldi; ⏰ 6pm-2am Tue-Sat) This friendly, noisy bar attracts legions of students.

For picnic treats, head for the 19th-century **covered market** (Halles du Marché; ⏰ until 1pm Tue, Thu-Sat) and the nearby **fromagerie** (28 rue Mu-sette; ⏰ closed Sun & Mon morning). Supermarkets include **Monoprix** (11-13 rue Piron; ⏰ 9am-9pm Mon-Sat) and **Marché Plus** (Rue Bannelier; ⏰ 7am-9pm Mon-Sat, 9am-noon Sun).

Entertainment

For the latest on Dijon's cultural scene, pick up *Spectacles*, available free from the tourist office. Dijon's club scene is centred on place de la République.

L'An-Fer (☎ 03 80 70 03 69; 8 rue Marceau; Wed-Thu €5-7, Fri €9.50, Sat & Sun €8; ⏰ 11pm-5am Wed-Sun, closed Wed mid-Jul–mid-Sep) achieved fame for pioneering techno music (Laurent Garnier worked here for four years); house music takes centre stage on Saturday.

Getting There & Away

Five km southeast of the city centre, **Dijon-Bourgogne airport** (☎ 03 80 67 67 67) has regu-lar flights to many French cities, as well as Strasbourg and Amsterdam.

The bus station is in the train station complex. Details on services are available at the **Transco information counter** (☎ 03 80 42 11 00; ⏰ 5.30am-8.30pm Mon-Fri, 6.45am-12.30pm & 4-8.30pm Sat, 10am-1pm & 4-8.30pm Sun). Timetables are posted on the platforms; tickets are sold on board.

Lines to the Côte d'Or include No 44 to Beaune and No 60, which serves Gevrey-Chambertin (€1.70, 30 minutes, 15 to 18 Monday to Saturday, fewer on Sunday). For details on Transco buses to Autun, Avallon, Châtillon-sur-Seine, Saulieu and Semur-en-Auxois consult the relevant sections.

Paris' Gare de Lyon is just 1¾ hours away by TGV (€46.20, nine to 16 daily). Most trains to Lyon (€22.50, two hours, at least 12 daily) go to Gare de la Part-Dieu. Other long-haul destinations include Nice (€76.20, six hours, two daily) and Strasbourg (€34.60, four hours, three or four non-direct daily).

Getting Around

To get to the airport, take bus No 1 (towards Longvic) and get off at the Longvic Mairie stop, from where it's a 500m walk Details on Dijon's bus network, operated by **STRD**, are available from **L'Espace Bus** (☎ 03 80 30 60 90; pl Grangier; ⏰ 7.15am-7.15pm Mon-Fri, to 12.15pm & 2.15-7.15pm Sat). Single tickets, sold by drivers, cost €0.80 and last for an hour; a Forfait Journée ticket is valid all day and costs €2.70 (avail-able from the tourist office or Espace Bus).

CÔTE D'OR VINEYARDS

Burgundy's finest vintages come from the vine-covered Côte d'Or (Golden Hillside), the narrow, eastern slopes of a limestone, flint and clay ridge that runs south from Dijon for about 60km. The northern section, the **Côte de Nuits**, stretches from the village of Fixin south to Corgoloin and produces full-bodied, robust reds. The southern section, the **Côte de Beaune** between Aloxe-Corton and Santenay produces great reds and whites.

Wine & Voyages (☎ 03 80 61 15 15; www.wineand voyages.com) runs minibus tours from Dijon in French and English, including two-hour/three-hour/full-day circuits to the Côte de Nuits vineyards (€45/50/95) from early March to mid-December. It's essential to reserve ahead.

BEAUNE
pop 22,000

Beaune (pronounced similarly to 'bone') is the unofficial capital of the Côte d'Or. This thriving town's *raison d'être* is wine – making it, tasting it, selling it, but most of all, drinking it.

Orientation & Information

The old city is partly enclosed by ramparts and encircled by a one-way boulevard. The train station is 1km east of the **tourist office** (☎ 03 80 26 21 30; www.beaune-burgundy.com; 1 rue de l'Hôtel-Dieu; ⏰ 9.30am-8pm Mon-Sat 21 Jun-21 Sep, to 7pm Mon-Sat Apr-20 Jun & 22 Sep–mid-Nov, 10am-6pm Mon-Sat mid-Nov–Mar, 10am-12.30pm & 2-5pm or 6pm

Sun year-round), and most of the town's sights. The main commercial area centres on place Carnot. Rue Monge and rue Carnot are pedestrianised.

Sights & Activities

Beaune's celebrated charity hospital, **Hôtel-Dieu des Hospices de Beaune** (☎ 03 80 24 45 00; rue de l'Hôtel-Dieu; adult/student/under 18 yrs €5.40/4.50/2.60; ☼ 9am-6.30pm Easter–mid-Nov, to 11.30am & 2-5.30pm mid-Nov–Easter) was founded in 1443 by Nicolas Rolin (chancellor to Philip the Good). Behind the imposing Gothic frontage, the hospice opens into an amazing stone courtyard surrounded by ornate balconies, turrets and pitched rooftops covered in multicoloured glazed tiles. Another highlight is the graphic **Polyptych of the Last Judgement** (1443), an ornate altar-piece by the Flemish painter Roger van der Weyden.

Underneath Beaune, millions of dusty bottles of wine are being aged to perfection in cool, dark, cobweb-lined cellars.

During the **Marché aux Vins** (☎ 03 80 25 08 20; www.marcheauxvins.com; 2 rue Nicolas Rolin; ☼ tastings 10-11am & 2-5pm mid-Sep–mid-Jun, 9.30am-5.45pm mid-Jun–mid-Sep) tour, using a *tastevin* (a flat metal cup whose shiny surfaces help you admire the wine's colour) you'll sample 18 wines in the candle-lit Église des Cordeliers and its cellars. Tastings last an hour.

Patriarche Père et Fils (☎ 03 80 24 53 78; www.patriarche.com; 5 rue du Collège; tours z; ☼ tastings 9.30-11.30am & 2-5.30pm) The largest cellars in Beaune are rather like Paris' Catacombs, except that the corridors are lined with dusty wine bottles instead of human bones. An audio-guided tour, and the opportunity to compare 13 wines, takes 40 minutes.

Bourgogne Randonnées (☎ 03 80 22 06 03; www.bike-in-france.com; 7 ave du 8 Septembre; day tours incl lunch & tastings €65; ☼ 9am-noon & 1.30-7pm Mon-Sat, 10am-noon & 2-7pm Sun Apr-Oct) arranges tailor-made bike tours around the Côte d'Or. Bikes can be rented for €15/69/170 per day/week/month.

Sleeping & Eating

Other than camping, budget deals are tough to find in Beaune.

Camping ground (☎ 03 80 22 03 91; 10 rue Auguste Dubois; adult/tent €3/4; ☼ mid-Mar–Oct) This four-star site is 700m north of the centre.

Hôtel Rousseau (☎ 03 80 22 13 59; 11 pl Madeleine; s from €24-40, d from €30-50, tr from €47-55) The endearingly shabby Rousseau is the best option. Some of the old-fashioned rooms, all with hardwood floors, have shower or toilet.

Hôtel Au Grand St Jean (☎ 03 80 24 12 22; hotel-au-grand-st-jean@wanadoo.fr; 18 rue du Faubourg Madeleine; d/q from €41/51; ☼ Jan–mid-Nov) This big, institutional hotel has lots of plain rooms and it's cheap – at least for Beaune.

Restaurant Maxime (☎ 03 80 22 17 82; 3 pl Madeleine; menu €16-28; ☼ closed Sun night & Mon) A reasonably priced Burgundy restaurant serving delicacies including traditional *coq au vin* in a small dining room. Other restaurants surround the square.

Ma Cuisine (☎ 03 80 22 30 22; passage Ste Hélène; menu €16; ☼ lunch & dinner Mon-Fri, closed lunch Wed) Excellent French and Burgundian dishes are good value at this busy bistro, and there's a nice outdoor terrace.

For self-caterers the covered market in place de la Halle hosts a **food market** (☼ to 1pm Sat) and a smaller **marché gourmand** (gourmet market; ☼ Wed morning). The **Casino supermarket** (28 rue du Faubourg Madeleine; ☼ 8.30am-7.30pm Mon-Sat) is through an archway on rue Faubourg Madeleine.

Wine can be purchased *en vrac* (in bulk) for as little as €1.10 per litre (from €3.40 per litre for AOC vintages), not including the container, at **Cellier de la Vieille Grange** (27 blvd Georges Clemenceau; ☼ closed Sun afternoon).

Getting There & Away

Service No 44 run by **Transco** (☎ 03 80 42 11 00) links Beaune with Dijon (€5.80, one hour, six to nine daily, two on Sunday and holidays), stopping at wine-growing villages such as Vougeot, Nuits-St-Georges and Aloxe-Corton. Certain buses serve villages south of Beaune (eg Pommard, Volnay, Meursault and Rochepot). In Beaune, buses stop along the boulevards around the old city. The tourist office has timetables.

From Beaune frequent trains depart for Dijon (€6, 20 minutes, 15 to 20 daily) and the Côte d'Or village of Nuits-St-Georges (€3, 10 minutes, 15 to 20 daily). The last train from Beaune to Dijon leaves at about 11.20pm.

Other destinations include Paris' Gare de Lyon (from €35.30, two direct TGVs daily); Mâcon (€11.60, one hour, 11 to 15 daily) and one or both of Lyon's train stations (€19.20, 1½ to 2¼ hours, seven to nine daily).

LYON

pop 415,000

Grand old Lyon (Lyons in English) is the hub of a prosperous urban area of almost two million people, France's second-largest conurbation. Lyon boasts outstanding museums, a dynamic cultural life, a hot clubbing and bar scene, a large university, fantastic shopping and a historical centre that's a Unesco world heritage site. Gourmets can indulge their wildest gastronomic fantasies here. The city centre is on the Presqu'île, a 500m- to 800m-wide peninsula bounded by the Rivers Rhône and Saône. On the western bank of the Saône, Vieux Lyon (Old Lyon) sits between the river and the hilltop area of Fourvière.

Information
INTERNET ACCESS
The Albion (☎ 04 78 28 33 00; 12 rue Ste-Catherine, 1er; metro Hôtel de Ville; ☉ 7pm-2am Sun-Thu, to 3am Fri & Sat) English pub with free WiFi zone and free Internet access on two terminals.

LAUNDRY
Laundrette (10 rue Ste-Catherine, 1er; metro Hôtel de Ville; ☉ 6.30am-8.30pm)

MONEY
Commercial banks abound on rue Victor Hugo, 2e; rue du Bât d'Argent, 1er; and rue de la République, 1er.
AOC Exchange (20 rue Gasparin, 2e; metro Bellecour; ☉ 9.30am-6.30pm Mon-Sat)

POST
Central post office (10 pl Antonin Poncet, 2e; metro Bellecour)

TOURIST INFORMATION
Tourist office (☎ 04 72 77 69 69; www.lyon-france.com; pl Bellecour, 2e; metro Bellecour; ☉ 9am-7pm Mon-Sat, 10am-6pm Sun mid-Apr–mid-Oct, 10am-6pm Mon-Sat, 5.30pm Sun mid-Oct–mid-Apr) Buy the **Lyon City Card** (€15/25/30 for 1/2/3 days) here. It allows entry to every museum in Lyon, onto the roof of Basilique Notre Dame de Fourvière, and up Fourvière's Tour de l'Observatoire; also unlimited travel on buses, trams, the funicular and the metro, guided or audioguided city tours, and – between April and October – a free river excursion.

Sights
VIEUX LYON
Old Lyon, with its cobbled streets and **medieval** and **Renaissance houses** below Fourvière

hill, is split into three quarters: St-Paul at the northern end, St-Jean in the middle and St-Georges in the south. Facing the river is the **Palais de Justice** (Law Courts; quai Romain Rolland).

The partly Romanesque **Cathédrale St-Jean** (pl St-Jean, 5e; metro Vieux Lyon; ☉ 8am-noon & 2-7.30pm Mon-Fri, to noon & 2-5pm Sat & Sun), seat of Lyon's 133rd bishop, was built from the late 11th to the early 16th centuries. The portals of its Flamboyant Gothic façade (completed in 1480) are decorated with 280 square stone medallions (early 14th century).

FOURVIÈRE
Over two millennia ago, the Romans built the city of Lugdunum on the slopes of Fourvière. Today, Lyon's 'hill of prayer' – topped by a basilica and the **Tour Métallique**, a grey, Eiffel Tower-like structure erected in 1893 and used as a TV transmitter – affords spectacular views of Lyon and its two rivers. The funicular departing from place Édouard Commette in Vieux Lyon is the easiest way up; use a metro ticket or buy a funicular return ticket (€2.20).

Crowning the hill is the ornate **Basilique Notre Dame de Fourvière** (www.lyon-fourviere.com; ☉ 8am-7pm), a superb example of the exaggerated enthusiasm for embellishment that dominated French ecclesiastical architecture during the late 19th century. **Guided tours** (☎ 04 78 25 86 19; adult/child €4/2.50; ☉ 2.30pm & 4pm Mon-Sun Jun-Sep, 2.30pm Oct & Nov, 2.30pm & 4pm Apr-May) last 1¼ hours and take in the roof and various bits inside, and end up at the top of the **Tour de l'Observatoire** (Observatory Tower).

Several sumptuous mosaics and lots of Latin inscriptions are displayed in the **Musée de la Civilisation Gallo-Romaine** (Museum of Gallo-Roman Civilisation; ☎ 04 72 38 81 90; 17 rue Cléberg, 5e; Fourvière funicular station; adult/under 18 yrs €3.80/free, admission free Thu; ☉ 10am-6pm Tue-Sun Mar-Oct, to 5pm Tue-Sun Nov-Feb). Next door to the museum is the **Théâtre Romain,** built around 15 BC and enlarged in AD 120 to seat an audience of 10,000, and the smaller **odéon** where Romans held poetry readings and musical recitals.

PRESQU'ÎLE
The centrepiece of beautiful **place des Terreaux** (metro Hôtel de Ville) is a 19th-century fountain made of 21 tonnes of lead and sculpted by Frédéric-Auguste Bartholdi, creator of New York's Statue of Liberty.

LYON

| 0 | 400 m |
| 0 | 0.2 miles |

Arrondissement
Boundary

A To Modern Art Café

B To Hôtel de la
Poste; Hôtel de la
Croix Rousse; Aux7
Pêchés du Plateau

C

D To N83; N84;
Pérouges (27km);
La Dombes

Pont Morand

Saône

Q Pierre Scize

To L'Ouest (3km);
Colonges-au-Mont- d'Or (10km)

R du
Griffon

Pl Louis
Pradel

Pl de la
Comédie

City Hall

Hôtel
de Ville

Rhône

R des Capucins

29

22

26

R de la Martinière

27

R d'Algérie

Pl des
Terreaux

11

21

R Ste-Catherine

3

6

R Romarin

R Terme

To Cité Internationale
& Musée d'Art
Contemporain
(2km)

Pont Lafayette

To Les Halles
de Lyon (1km)

Pl de
la Bourse

R de la Bourse

Pont Wilson

To Gare de
la Part Dieu

R Constantine

R d'Octavio Mey

Pl St-
Paul

Gare St-Paul

R François Vernay

St-Paul

Pl du
Change

Pl du
Gouvernement

Église
St Nizier

R Neuve

R Gentil

Cordeliers

Pl
Francisque
Regaud

R de Brest

R de Dubois

R Mercière

23 25

17

MERCIÈRE-
ST-ANTOINE

Pl des
Jacobins

Pl de la
République

R Childebert

R Ferrandière

Pont
Alphonse
Juin

24

VIEUX LYON

Pl Neuve
St-Jean

15

FOURVIÈRE
HILL

Jardin du
Rosaire

Fourvière Funicular
Station

8

13

Pl
St-Jean

9

St-Jean

Pl Édouard
Commette

Vieux Lyon

18

Pl des
Célestins

R Émile Zola

R Gasparin

R des
Archers

PRESQU'ÎLE

1

5

Pl Bellecour

Bellecour

Bellecour

7

Pl Antonin
Poncet

2

28

R de la Barre

R des
Marronniers

10

14

Minimes
Funicular
Stop

16

To St-Just
Funicular
Station

Église
St Georges

St-Georges

Pont
Bonaparte

Quartier
Auguste Comte

R Ste-Hélène

R Sala

To Hôtel de Noailles (500m);
Musée Lumière;
Hangar du Premier Film &
Mur du Cinema Mural (3km);
Hôpital Édouard Herriot (3.5km);
Grande Mosquée de Lyon (4.5km)

Rhône

University

To Camping
International de la
Porte de Lyon (10km);
Beaujolais (40km);
A6 to Paris (460km)

N7

30

Pl
Ampère

Ampère

12

R des Remparts d'Ainay

R Franklin

A6

Pl
Carnot

ramp

R de Condé

R Duhamel

20

To Centre d'Histoire de
la Résistance et de la
Déportation (150m); A43
to Lyon St-Exupéry
Airport (25km);
Grenoble (110km)

31

Perrache

Gare de
Perrache

To Marseilles
(315km via the A7)

Av Perrache

Q Claude Bernard

R de l'Université

R Chevreul

R Pasteur

Next door is the **Musée des Beaux-Arts** (Museum of Fine Arts; ☎ 04 72 10 17 40; 20 pl des Terreaux, 1er; metro Hôtel de Ville; adult/under 18 yrs €6/free; ⏰ 10am-6pm Wed-Mon, from 10.30am Fri) showcasing France's finest collection of sculptures and paintings, from every period of European art, outside Paris. The free **cloister garden** is a great picnic venue.

Extraordinary Lyonnais silks, French and Asian textiles, and carpets are included in the collection of the **Musée des Tissus** (Textile Museum; ☎ 04 78 38 42 00; www.musee-des-tissus.com; 34 rue de la Charité, 2e; metro Ampère; adult/under 18 yrs €4.60/free; ⏰ 10am-5.30pm Tue-Sun). Next door, the **Musée des Arts Décoratifs** (Decorative Arts Museum; free with Textile Museum ticket; ⏰ 10am-noon & 2-5.30pm Tue-Sun) showcases 18th-century furniture, tapestries, wallpaper, ceramics and silver.

OTHER ATTRACTIONS

The brick-and-glass **Cité Internationale** was designed by Italian architect Renzo Piano to host the G7 summit in 1996. Inside, the **Musée d'Art Contemporain** (Museum of Contemporary Art; ☎ 04 72 69 17 17; www.moca-lyon.org; 81 quai Charles de Gaulle, 6e; adult/under 18 yrs €3.80/free; ⏰ noon-7pm Wed-Sun) displays works created after 1960.

The WWII headquarters of Gestapo chief Klaus Barbie house the evocative **Centre d'Histoire de la Résistance et de la Déportation** (☎ 04 78 72 23 11; 14 ave Berthelot, 7e; metro Perrache or Jean Macé; adult/under 18 yrs €3.80/free; ⏰ 9am-5.30pm Wed-Sun). Multimedia exhibits present the history of Nazi atrocities and the heroism of French Resistance fighters.

Cinema's glorious beginnings are featured at the **Musée Lumière** (☎ 04 78 78 18 95; www .institut-lumiere.org; 25 rue du Premier Film, 8e; metro Monplaisir-Lumière; adult/student €6/5; ⏰ 11am-6.30pm Tue-Sun), 3km southeast of place Bellecour along cours Gambetta. It occupies the home of Antoine Lumière who, together with his

sons Auguste and Louis, shot the first reels of the world's first motion picture, *La Sortie des Usines Lumières* (Exit of the Lumières Factories) on 19 March 1895. Classic films are screened at the **Hangar du Premier Film**.

Sleeping

Camping International de la Porte de Lyon (☎ 04 78 35 64 55; camping-lyon@marie-lyon.fr; allée du Camping, Portes de Lyon; camp sites €13.70; reception ⏰ 8am-8pm Mon-Fri, 12.30-8pm Sat & Sun; 🐾) About 10km northwest of central Lyon in Dardilly, this 215-place camping ground can be reached by bus No 3 from metro Hôtel de Ville or bus No 89 from metro Gare de Vaise.

Auberge de Jeunesse du Vieux Lyon (☎ 04 78 15 05 50; lyon@fuaj.org; 41-45 montée du Chemin Neuf, 5e; metro Vieux Lyon; dm €12.70; reception ⏰ 7am-1pm & 9pm or 10pm-1am) Rates include breakfast at this superbly located hostel above Vieux Lyon. Its 180 beds are split between rooms for two to seven people.

Hôtel de la Poste (☎ /fax 04 78 28 62 67; 1 rue Victor Fort, 4e; metro Croix Rousse; d/tr €33/46, s/d/q with shared bathroom from €17/17/33; reception ⏰ 6.30am-8.30pm) Rooms share toilets on the corridor (some showers too) at this back-to-basics hotel where price – not prettiness – pulls in the punters.

Hôtel Iris (☎ 04 78 39 93 80; hoteliris@freesurf.fr; 36 rue de l'Arbre Sec, 1er; metro Hôtel de Ville; s/d from €36/39, with shared bathroom €29/32) The location of this two-star hotel, inside a wonderful, four-century-old convent, could not be better – so get in quick to snag one of its 11 simple rooms overlooking a quiet courtyard.

Hôtel de la Croix Rousse (☎ 04 78 28 29 85; 157 blvd de la Croix Rousse, 4e; metro Croix Rousse; d €46; P) Croix Rousse's simple, village-style hotel touts 18 rooms. Although furnished several decades ago the rooms here are well presented and spotlessly clean

FRANCE

Hôtel de Noailles (☎ 04 78 72 40 72; hotel-de
-noailles-lyon@wanadoo.fr; 30 cours Gambetta, 7e; metro
Saxe-Gambetta; s/d from €54/62; ✖ P) This charming 24-room hotel is a comfortable choice
for those seeking a bed on the *rive gauche*
(left bank).

Comfort Hôtel St-Antoine (☎ 04 78 92 91 91; www
.hotel-saintantoine.fr; 1 rue du Port du Temple, 2e; metro
Cordeliers; s/d from €63/66; ✖ P ▢) A stylish mix
of old and new – a WiFi zone and period
furnishings – greet guests at this thoroughly
modern hotel which languishes inside an
18th-century townhouse.

Hotel des Artistes (☎ 04 78 42 04 88; www.hotel
desartistes.fr; 8 rue Gaspard André, 2e; metro Bellecour or
Hôtel de Ville; s €70-102, d €79-108) Theatrically furnished rooms are the trademark of this very
red, very charming, three-star pad in the
heart of Presqu'île shopping land.

Sofitel Royal Lyon (☎ 04 78 37 57 31; fax 04 78
37 01 36; H2952@accor-hotels.com; 20 pl Bellecour, 2e;
metro Bellecour; s/d from €136/150, lux s/d from €215/241,
ste €492; P ✖ ✖ ▢) The most prestigious
address on place Bellecour has lavished loving luxurious care on its guests since 1895.

Eating

Café des Fédérations (☎ 04 78 28 26 00; www.lesfedes
lyon.com; 8 rue Major Martin, 1er; metro Hôtel de Ville; dinner menu €23; ☾ Mon-Fri) For proof of the pudding that some things never change, plop
yourself down at this splendid little place
and feast on *caviar de la Croix Rousse* (lentils dressed in a creamy sauce) and other
age-old dishes.

Café-Restaurant des Deux Places (☎ 04 78 28 95
10; 5 pl Fernand Rey, 1er; metro Hôtel de Ville; menu €22;
☾ Mon-Fri) Checked curtains and an interior
crammed with antiques and old photographs contribute to the overwhelmingly
traditional feel of this well-placed *bouchon*.
Its pavement-terrace beneath trees on a quiet
village-like square is a major drawcard.

L'Ouest (☎ 04 37 64 64 64; www.bocuse.com; 1 quai
du Commerce, 9e; metro Gare de Vaise; starters/mains around
€14/20; ☾ lunch & dinner) Run by the legendary
chef Paul Bocuse, one of the oldest and most
respected names in the business, the focus
is on everything from crab 'n saffron soup
to Indonesian-inspired cod and straightforward lamb chops prepared in front of
diners in a state-of-the-art open kitchen.
Décor is minimalist and avant garde (think
glass and wood), and a vast decking space
outside overlooks the Saône.

Aux 7 Péchés du Plateau (☎ 04 78 28 48 82; pl Tapis
3, 4e; metro Croix Rousse; menu €18 & €30; ☾ Mon-Sat)
Make no bones about it – diners come here
for the meat, not the décor. This butcher's
restaurant serves *salade de rognons blancs et
ris d'agneau* (white kidney salad with sweet
breads), *tête de veau* (calf's head) and several
beef cuts.

Commanderie des Antonins (☎ 04 78 37 19 21;
www.commanderie-antonons.fr; 30 quai St-Antoine, 2e;
metro Cordeliers; lunch/dinner menu €15/19.90) Another
meaty choice, albeit it a highly refined one,
this ode to the carnivorous sees meat cooked
the old-fashioned way – slowly over a low
heat in a wood-burning oven and serves it
with a flourish in a medieval banquet hall.

La Table d'Hippolyte (☎ 04 78 27 75 59; 22 rue
Hippolyte Flandrin, 1er; metro Hôtel de Ville; lunch menu €17,
full dinner around €45; closed Sat lunch, Sun & Mon) Traditional French cuisine is concocted with the
freshest seasonal ingredients at this pocket-
sized place with a pocket-sized pavement
terrace in summer. What's at the market
dictates what is chalked up on the board.

Gaston Restaurant Agricole (☎ 04 72 41 87 86; 41
rue Mercière, 2e; metro Cordeliers; lunch buffet €12; ☾ Mon-
Sat) You need a hearty thirst and giant-sized
appetite for this feisty agricultural restaurant
complete with rusty old tractor out front
and a liberal scattering of veg-filled wheel-
barrows. Dining is around shared wooden
tables and the feast-until-you're-full lunch-
time buffet of cold meat and veg is a steal.

Maison Perroudon (☎ 04 78 37 37 56; 6 rue de la
Barre, 2e; metro Bellecour; ☾ 7am-7.30pm Tue-Sun ✖)
A predominantly female crowd lunches on
light salads. Its cakes are to die for.

Central Lyon has two fantastic **outdoor
food markets** (☾ Tue-Sun morning; quai St-Antoine, 2e;
metro Bellecour or Cordeliers; blvd de la Croix Rousse, 4e; metro
Croix Rousse). The main indoor food markets
are **Les Halles de Lyon** (102 cours Lafayette, 3e; metro
Part-Dieu; ☾ 7am-noon & 3-7pm Tue-Thu, to 7pm Fri & Sat,
to noon Sun) and **La Halle de la Martinière** (24 rue de
la Martinière, 1er; metro Hôtel de Ville; ☾ 8am-12.30pm &
4-7.30pm Tue-Sun).

Drinking

The bounty of café-terraces on place des Ter-
reaux, 1er, buzz with drinkers day and night.
English-style pubs are clustered on rue Ste-
Catherine, 1er (metro Hôtel de Ville) and in
Vieux Lyon.

Modern Art Café (☎ 04 72 87 06 82; www.modern
artcafé.net; 65 blvd de la Croix Rousse, 4e; metro Croix Rousse;

FRANCE

⊗ 5-1am Mon-Fri, 11-1am Sat & Sun) Retro furnishings, changing art on the walls, a *plage* (beach) with deckchairs, weekend brunch and a clutch of music- and video-driven happenings make this art bar one cool place to lounge.

Palais de la Bière (☎ 04 78 27 94 00; 1 rue Terme, 1er; metro Hôtel de Ville; ⊗ 6pm-2am Tue-Thu, 6pm-3am Fri & Sat) With 15 beers on tap (€3.40/4.20 for a 25cl glass before/after 9pm) and 300 different types of bottled beers, pint lovers won't go thirsty. An Ardèche-brewed *bière aux marrons* (chestnut beer) is about the only beer produced in the wine-loving Rhône Valley. The truly thirsty can embark on a 15-beer *tour du monde* (world tour).

Thé Cha Yuan (☎ 04 72 41 04 60; 7-9 rue des Remparts d'Ainay, 2e; metro Ampère; ⊗ 9am-7pm Tue-Sat) Some 300 kinds of tea are brewed at this tea room which also serves dim sum – a sublime combination of French elegance and traditional Chinese serenity.

Entertainment

The tourist office has loads of information on Lyon's rich and varied entertainment scene. Locally published listings guides include the weekly *Lyon Poche* (www.lyon poche.com; €1 at newsagents); the quarterly *Progrescope* (www.progrescope.com) distributed every three months with the local daily newspaper *Le Progrès* (www.leprogres.fr; €0.80 at newsagents); and the free weekly *Le Petit Bulletin* (www.petit-bulletin.fr) available at the tourist office.

Getting There & Away

Flights from cities around Europe land at **Lyon-St Exupéry airport** (formerly Lyon-Satolas; ☎ 0800 826 826; www.lyon.aeroport.fr), 25km east of the city.

In the Perrache complex, **Eurolines** (☎ 04 72 56 95 30), **Intercars** (☎ 04 78 37 20 80) and Spain-oriented **Linebús** (☎ 04 72 41 72 27) have offices on the bus-station level of the Centre d'Échange – to find them follow the 'Lignes Internationales' signs.

Lyon has two mainline train stations: **Gare de la Part-Dieu** (metro Part-Dieu), 1.5km east of the Rhône, which handles all long-haul trains; and **Gare de Perrache** (metro Perrache), on the Presqu'île, which is increasingly becoming just a regional station. Many long-distance trains stop at both. Just a few local trains stop at **Gare St-Paul** (metro Vieux Lyon) in Vieux Lyon.

Tickets are sold at all three stations and in town at the **SNCF Boutique** (2 pl Bellecour, 2e; metro Bellecour; ⊗ 9am-6.45pm Mon-Fri, 10am-6.30pm Sat).

Destinations accessible by direct TGV include Paris' Gare de Lyon (€55.60, two hours, every 30 to 60 minutes), Nantes (€102.20, 4¾ hours, six daily), Dijon (€24.20, 1¾ to two hours, at least 12 daily) and Strasbourg (€42.30, five hours, four or five direct daily).

Getting Around

Public transport – buses, trams, a four-line metro and two funiculars linking Vieux Lyon to Fourvière and St-Just – is run by **TCL** (☎ 08 20 42 70 00, www.tcl.fr; 17 bis blvd Vivier Merle, 3e; metro Part-Dieu; ⊗ 8.30am-5pm Mon-Fri). It operates from around 5am to midnight. Tickets cost €1.40/11.50 for one/10 and are available from bus and tram drivers and from machines at metro entrances. Tickets allowing unlimited travel for two hours/one day €2/4.20 are also available, as are *tickets jumelés* which combine a return a public transport ticket with admission to the Musée Lumière (adult/child €7/6) or aquarium (€11/7).

THE FRENCH ALPS

The French Alps, where green valleys meet soaring peaks with craggy, snowbound summits, are one of the most awesome mountain ranges in the world. Skiing and snowboarding are the region's most obvious attractions, but in summer, visitors can explore hundreds of kilometres of hiking trails and engage in warm-weather sports ranging from paragliding to white-water rafting. History buffs can head for the medieval towns of Annecy and Chambéry, while big-city thrills can be found in the dynamic capital of the Alps, Grenoble. Expect to pay at least €45 daily to ski or snowboard, more for high altitude stations. There are good deals in January between the school holidays.

CHAMONIX
pop 10,000 / elevation 1037m
Chamonix is surrounded by the most spectacular scenery in the French Alps. It's almost Himalayan: deeply crevassed glaciers point towards the valley from the icy crown of Mont Blanc, which soars 3.8km above the valley floor.

Information

INTERNET ACCESS

Le CyBar (☎ 04 50 53 69 70; www.cybarchamonix.com; 80 rue des Moulins; ☺ 10am-1.30am; per min €0.10) Computers spread over two floors.

LAUNDRY

Laundromats (40 impasse Primavère; ☺ 9am-8pm) Also a branch at 174 ave de l'Aiguille du Midi.

MONEY

Le Change (21 pl Balmat; ☺ 9am-1pm & 3-7pm May, Jun, early Sep-Nov, 8am-8pm Jul-early Sep & Dec-Apr) Generally offers the best rate in town. A 24-hour automated exchange machine accepts banknotes in 15 currencies.

POST

Post office (pl Balmat; ☺ 8am-noon & 2-6pm Mon-Fri, to noon Sat Sep-Jun, to 7pm Mon-Fri, to noon Sat Jul-Aug)

TOURIST INFORMATION

Centrale de Réservation (☎ 04 50 53 23 33 reservation@chamonix.com; ☺ 24hr) Usually takes accommodation bookings for stays of three nights minimum.

Maison de la Montagne (190 pl de l'Église) Across the square from the tourist office, this should be your first port of call for finding out about the Mont Blanc area and about winter sports, ski lessons and guided tours and activities.

Office de Haute Montagne (☎ 04 50 53 22 08; www.ohm-chamonix.com; 2nd fl, 190 pl de l'Église; ☺ 9am-12.30pm & 2.30-6.30pm Mon-Sat) Serves walkers, hikers and mountain climbers, providing information on trails, hiking conditions and *refuges* (huts).

Tourist office (☎ 04 50 53 00 24; www.chamonix.com; 85 pl du Triangle de l'Amitié; ☺ 8.30am-12.30pm & 2-7pm Jun-Sep & Dec-Apr, 9am-12.30pm & 2-6.30pm offseason) Offers hundreds of brochures on accommodation and activities, and also sells ski passes. Weather bulletins are posted here.

Sights

AIGUILLE DU MIDI

A jagged pinnacle of rock rising above glaciers, snowfields and rocky crags, 8km from the domed summit of Mont Blanc, the Aiguille du Midi is one of Chamonix's most famous landmarks. The panoramic views from the summit are absolutely breathtaking.

Return cable-car tickets from Chamonix to the Aiguille du Midi cost adult/child €34/24. A ride to the téléphérique's halfway point, Plan de l'Aiguille (2317m) – an excellent place to start hikes in summer – costs €12.30/14.40 one way/return.

The *téléphérique*, which leaves from the end of ave de l'Aiguille du Midi, runs year-round from 8am (7am in summer). The last ride up is at 3.30pm (5.30pm in summer). Be prepared for long queues. You can make advance reservations 24 hours a day (☎ 08 92 68 00 67 premium rate number; booking fee €2).

From the Aiguille du Midi, between May and September, you can make the 5km ride in the Panoramic Mont Blanc cable car to **Pointe Helbronner** (3466m) on the Italian border, crossing a vista of glaciers, snow plains and shimmering ice-fields en route.

LE BRÉVENT

The highest peak on the western side of the valley (2525m) has fabulous views of the Mont-Blanc massif. It can be reached by **télécabine** and **téléphérique** (☎ 04 50 53 13 18; adult/child return €15.50/11) from the end of Chemin de la Mollard. The lifts are open 8am-5.45pm in summer, 9am-5pm in winter.

Several hiking trails can be picked up at Le Brévent or at the *télécabine*'s midway station, **Planpraz** (1999m; €8.50/10.50 one way/return).

MER DE GLACE

The Mer de Glace (Sea of Ice), the second largest glacier in the Alps, is 14km long, 1800m wide and up to 400m deep. The glacier moves 45m a year at the edges, and up to 90m a year in the centre, and has become a popular tourist attraction thanks to the rack-and-pinion railway line built between 1897 and 1908.

Since 1946, the **Grotte de la Mer de Glace** (ice cave; ☺ late May-late Sep) has been carved every spring – work begins in February and takes three months. The interior temperature is between -2 and -5°C. Look down the slope for last year's cave to see how far the glacier has moved.

With avalanche proofing over parts of the tracks, the train – which leaves from **Gare du Montenvers** (☎ 04 50 53 12 54) in Chamonix and creeps up to Montenvers (1913m) – runs year-round. Trains run from 10am to 4pm in winter (longer in summer). The 20-minute trip costs €14 return. From Montenvers, a *téléphérique* takes tourists to the cave. A combined ticket valid for the train, *téléphérique*, and admission to the cave costs adult/child €21/15.

The Mer de Glace can be reached on foot via the Grand Balcon Nord trail from Plan de l'Aiguille. The uphill trail from Chamonix (two hours) begins near the summer luge track. Traversing the glacier and its crevasses requires proper equipment and an experienced guide.

Activities

In late spring and summer (about mid-June to October), 310km of spectacular walking trails open up around Chamonix. The most rewarding are the high-altitude trails reached by cable car. The *téléphériques* shut down in the late afternoon, but in June and July there is enough light to walk until 9pm or later.

The combined map and guide *Carte des Sentiers du Mont Blanc* (Mountain Trail Map; €4) is ideal for straightforward day walks. The most useful map is the 1:25,000 IGN map entitled *Chamonix-Massif du Mont Blanc* (No 3630OT; €9). Both are sold at Photo Alpine Tairraz. *The Most Beautiful Hikes for Everyone* (Editions Aio; €4.50) details easy day hikes in the Mont Blanc region.

The **Grand Balcon Sud** trail along the western side of the valley stays at around 2000m and affords great views of Mont Blanc. On foot, it can be reached from behind Le Brévent's *télécabine* station. For less uphill walking, take either the Planpraz or La Flégère lifts.

CANYONING

Summer canyoning expeditions are offered by **Yannick Seigneur** (mobile ☎ 06 09 48 51 77; info@ yannickseigneur.com), in the Mont Blanc mountains. A half-/full day canyoning course costs €54.90/83.85.

Sleeping

BUDGET

Because of the altitude, it's nearly always chilly at night if you're camping. Most mountain *refuges* (huts; €14-20 a night) are accessible to hikers, though some can be reached only by mountain climbers. Breakfast and dinner, prepared by the warden, are often available for an extra fee. It's essential to reserve a place – you don't want to hike halfway across Mont Blanc to find the *refuge* full. For information, contact the CAF (see Maison de la Montagne, p344). *Gîte* accommodation can also be a good way to cut costs.

L'Île des Barrats (☎ 04 50 53 51 44; 185 chemin d'Île des Barrats; ☼ May-Oct) This three-star site is in a quiet clearing, near the base of the Aiguille du Midi *téléphérique*.

Les Deux Glaciers (☎ 04 50 53 15 84; glaciers@ clubInternet.fr; 80 route des Tissières; ☼ closed mid-Nov– mid-Dec) Another three-star place in Les Bossons, 3km south of Chamonix. To get there, take the train to Les Bossons or the Chamonix Bus to the Tremplin-le-Mont stop.

Auberge de Jeunesse (☎ 04 50 53 14 52; chamonix@ fuaj.org; 127 montée Jacques Balmat; dm with breakfast €17; ☼ check-in 8am-noon & 5-10pm, closed early May & Oct–mid-Dec) In Les Pélerins, 2km southwest of Chamonix, this hostel can be reached by bus. Take the Chamonix-Les Houches line and get off at the Pélerins École stop. In winter, only weekly packages are available, including bed, food, ski pass and ski hire for six days. There's no kitchen.

Gîte La Montagne (☎ 04 50 53 11 60; www.levaga bond.co.uk; 789 promenade des Crémeries; dm €12; ☼ closed 11 Nov-20 Dec) An attractive *gîte* in a traditional alpine-style building on a forested site, 1.5km north of the train station (near La Frasse bus-stop).

Gîte Vagabond (☎ 04 50 53 15 43; fax 04 50 53 68 21; 365 ave Ravanel-le-Rouge; dm €12.50, half-board €28; ☐) A neat hostelry with a kitchen, bar/ restaurant with Internet access, BBQ area, climbing wall and parking. Beds are in four- or six-person dorms.

MID-RANGE

During July, August and the ski season, most hotels are heavily booked, so reserve ahead.

Hôtel Boule de Neige (☎ 04 50 53 04 48; 362 rue Joseph Vallot; s/d from €36/56) A chalet-style hotel halfway up the lively rue Joseph Vallot. The rooms are as basic as they come, but there's an attractive mountain-town feel helped by the little local bar downstairs.

Au Bon Coin (☎ 04 50 53 15 67; hotelauboncoin@ wanadoo.fr; 80 ave de l'Aiguille du Midi; d €54.50-62; Ⓟ) One of the best year-round deals in Chamonix. Perched above busy shops, it looks drab from the front; but the rear rooms are south-facing, and most have small balconies offering views of Mont Blanc.

Hôtel Richemond (☎ 04 50 53 08 85; fax 04 50 55 91 69; 228 rue du Docteur Paccard; d low/high €66/80; Ⓟ) A vast, austere hotel where the prices stay low even in high season, which means it's nearly always full. The best rooms have mountain views; the worst overlook the car park.

Eating

Neapolis (☎ 04 50 53 98 41; 79 Gallerie Alpina; pizza & pasta €6.40-9.90; ☼ Mon-Sat) This simple Italian

FRANCE

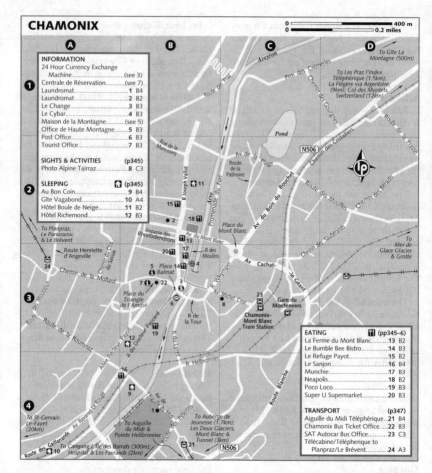

CHAMONIX

0 — 400 m
0 — 0.2 miles

INFORMATION
24 Hour Currency Exchange
Machine..........................(see 3)
Centrale de Réservation...........(see 7)
Laundromat...........................**1** B4
Laundromat...........................**2** B2
Le Change............................**3** B3
Le Cybar.............................**4** B3
Maison de la Montagne..............(see 5)
Office de Haute Montagne............**5** B3
Post Office..........................**6** B3
Tourist Office.......................**7** B3

SIGHTS & ACTIVITIES   (p345)
Photo Alpine Tairraz................**8** C3

SLEEPING   (p345)
Au Bon Coin..........................**9** B4
Gîte Vagabond.......................**10** A4
Hôtel Boule de Neige................**11** B2
Hôtel Richemond.....................**12** B3

EATING   (pp345–6)
La Ferme du Mont Blanc.............**13** B2
Le Bumble Bee Bistro..............**14** B3
Le Refuge Payot....................**15** B2
Le Sanjon..........................**16** B4
Munchie............................**17** B3
Neapolis...........................**18** B2
Poco Loco..........................**19** B3
Super U Supermarket................**20** B3

TRANSPORT   (p347)
Aiguille du Midi Téléphérique......**21** B4
Chamonix Bus Ticket Office.........**22** B3
SAT Autocar Bus Office.............**23** C3
Télécabine/Téléphérique to
Planpraz/Le Brévent...............**24** A3

---

restaurant overlooks the river and has cheap, wholesome cooking – which makes it very popular.

Le Sanjon (☎ 04 50 53 56 44; 5 ave Ravanel-le-Rouge; menu €15-25) Le Sanjon is a picturesque wooden chalet restaurant serving *raclette* (a block of melted cheese), usually eaten with potatoes and cold meats (€12) and fondue (€11 to €21).

Munchie (☎ 04 50 53 45 41; 87 rue des Moulins; mains €10-25; � closed lunch) A trendy place with excellent pan-Asian food, exciting mains include blackened salmon *sashimi*, Thai Chicken with pimento and ginger and sushi.

Le Bumble Bee Bistro (☎ 04 50 53 50 03; 65 rue des Moulins) A tiny, welcoming café which serves

hot, hearty meals throughout the day. Cod fritters, chargrilled chicken, steak and ale pie and potato wedges are ideal after a hard day on the slopes, but veggies should try the Red Dragon Pie, stuffed full of vegetables, lentils and spicy beans.

Poco Loco (☎ 04 50 53 43 03; 47 rue du Docteur Paccard; pizza €5-7, menu from €7) One of several sandwich shops near place Balmat, with hot paninis (from €3.80), sweet crepes (from €1.50) and huge burgers.

There's a **Super U Supermarket** (117 rue Joseph Vallot; �8.15am-7.30pm Mon-Sat, to 12.45pm Sun in winter). **Le Refuge Payot** (166 rue Joseph Vallot) and **La Ferme du Mont Blanc** (202 rue Joseph Vallot) stock an excellent range of cheeses, meats and other local products.

FRANCE

Getting There & Away

The bus station is in the train-station building. The office of **SAT Autocar** (☎ 04 50 53 01 15; satobus-alps.com; ⏰ 6.45-10.30pm & 1.25-4.45pm Mon-Fri, to 11pm & 1.25-4.45pm Sat & Sun in winter, hrs vary in summer) is near the train station entrance. Buses operate to Geneva bus station (€33, 1½ to two hours) and Geneva airport (€33, 2¼ hours). Services to Italy, through the Mont Blanc tunnel, include Courmayeur (€18 return) and Aoste (€22 return).

The Chamonix-Mont Blanc **train station** (☎ 04 50 53 12 98) is at the end of ave Michel Croz. There's a **left-luggage counter** (⏰ 6am-8pm).

Major destinations include Paris' Gare de Lyon (€86.50, six to seven hours, five daily), Lyon (€31.70, 4½ hours via Annecy), Geneva (€16.60, four hours via Annecy or Chambéry), and Grenoble (27.90, five hours via Annecy). There's an overnight train to Paris (€98.90. 10 hours) year-round.

Getting Around

Bus transport is handled by **Chamonix Bus** (☎ 04 50 53 05 55; pl du Triangle de l'Amitié; ⏰ 7am-7pm in winter, 8am-noon & 2-7pm Jun-Aug).

ANNECY

pop 50,000 / elevation 448m

Annecy, the chic capital of Haute-Savoie, is an unquestionably pretty lakeside town, criss-crossed with ancient canals and lined with arched alleyways and medieval houses. Visitors in a languid mood can stroll along the lakefront or mosey around the old city, admiring the Alpine peaks or the geranium-covered bridges, while more active types can take to the waters of Lac d'Annecy in pedalos, canoes and cruise-boats.

Orientation

The train and bus stations are 500m northwest of the Vieille Ville (Old City), which is huddled around the River Thiou (split into Canal du Thiou to the south and Canal du Vassé to the north). The town centre is between the post office and the purpose-built Centre Bonlieu, which houses the city's theatre and the tourist office, near the shores of Lac d'Annecy.

Information

Main post office (4 bis rue des Glières; ⏰ 8am-7pm Mon-Fri, 9am-noon Sat)

Syndrome Cybercafé (☎ 04 50 45 39 75; infos@syndrome.com; 3 bis ave de Chevêne; Internet per 15min/hr €2/6; ⏰ noon-midnight)

Tourist office (☎ 04 50 45 00 33; www.lac-annecy.com; 1 rue Jean Jaurès; ⏰ 9am-12.30pm & 1.45-6pm Mon-Sat mid-Sep–mid-May, to 6.30pm Mon-Sat mid-May–mid-Sep, to 12.30pm & 1.45-6pm Sun Jul-Sep, 10am-1pm Sun Oct) In the Centre Bonlieu.

Sights & Activities

The **Vieille Ville**, a warren of narrow streets and colonnaded passageways, retains much of its 17th-century appearance. On the central island, the imposing **Palais de l'Isle** (☎ 04 50 33 87 31; adult/student €3.05/0.75; ⏰ 10am-6pm Jun-Sep, to noon & 2-6pm Wed-Mon Oct-May) was once a prison, but now houses local history displays.

Located in the 13th-16th century castle above town, **Musée Château** (☎ 04 50 33 87 30; adult/student €4.70/1.60; ⏰ 10am-noon & 2-6pm Wed-Mon Oct-May, 10.30am-6pm Jun-Sep) offers a great view over the old city's tightly packed rooftops. The fine museum explores traditional Savoyard art and crafts, and has a display on the natural history of the Alps.

The lakefront is lined with parks and grassy areas where you can picnic, sunbathe and swim in the warm months. **Plage d'Annecy-le-Vieux** is 1km east of the Champ de Mars. Closer to town is **Plage Impérial** (€3), which has changing rooms. **Plage des Marquisats** is 1km south of the Vieille Ville along rue des Marquisats. The beaches are officially open from June to September.

Sleeping

Cheap hotels are hard to find from mid-July to mid-August – book in advance.

Camping Municipal Le Belvédère (☎ 04 50 45 48 30; fax 04 50 45 55 56; camp sites €13) In the Forêt du Crêt du Maure, 2.5km south of the train station. There are several other camping grounds near the lake in Annecy-le-Vieux.

Auberge de Jeunesse (☎ 04 50 45 33 19; annecy@fuaj.com; 4 route du Semnoz; dm €12) This hostel is situated about 1km from Camping Municipal Le Belvédère in the Forêt du Semnoz. Take bus No 1 to the Marquisats stop.

Hôtel du Château (☎ 04 50 45 27 66; fax 04 50 52 75 26; 16 rampe du Château; s/d €45-60; P) Just below one of the towers of the château, this small, hilltop hotel is hard to beat for a serene view over Annecy's lantern-lit lanes. The rooms are cosy and there's a great terrace overlooking the city's rooftops.

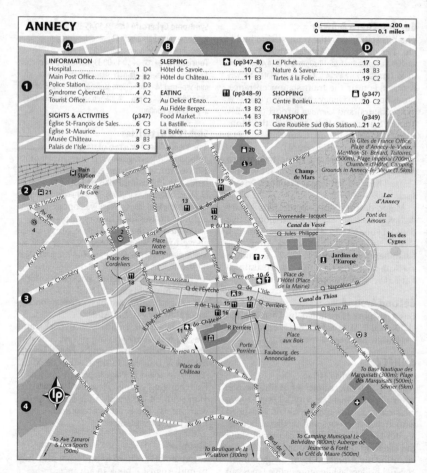

ANNECY

INFORMATION
Hospital................................1 D4
Main Post Office....................2 B2
Police Station.......................3 D3
Syndrome Cybercafé.............4 A2
Tourist Office.......................5 C2

SIGHTS & ACTIVITIES   (p347)
Église St-François de Sales.....6 C3
Église St-Maurice..................7 C3
Musée Château.....................8 B3
Palais de l'Isle......................9 C3

SLEEPING   (pp347-8)
Hôtel de Savoie...................10 C3
Hôtel du Château.................11 B3

EATING   (pp348-9)
Au Delice d'Enzo..................12 B2
Au Fidéle Berger...................13 B2
Food Market........................14 B3
La Bastille...........................15 C3
La Bolée..............................16 C3

Le Pichet.............................17 C3
Nature & Saveur...................18 B3
Tartes á la Folie....................19 C2

SHOPPING   (p347)
Centre Bonlieu.....................20 C2

TRANSPORT   (p349)
Gare Routière Sud (Bus Station)...21 A2

Chambre d'hôte (☎ 04 50 45 72 28; rampe du Château; d €60-80) A good choice in a big period house next to Hôtel du Château.

Hôtel de Savoie (☎ 04 50 45 15 45; fax 04 50 45 11 99; 1 pl de St-François; s/d €45-70) Once a convent, this characterful little hotel has its entrance on the left side of Église St-François de Sales. It's a small, friendly place with simple rooms and a great location.

Eating

In the Vieille Ville, the quays along both sides of Canal du Thiou are lined with cafés and restaurants. There are lots of cheap places along rue du Pâquier.

Au Delice d'Enzo (☎ 04 50 45 35 36; 17 rue du Pâquier; pizza & pasta €6.50-10) One of several res-

taurants under the arched colonnades of rue du Paquier, this tiny little Italian joint has a streetside terrace and serves good, simple pizza and pasta.

La Bolée (☎ 04 50 45 26 62; 14 rue de l'Isle; crepes €7-9; ⏰ Thu-Tue May-Sep) A simple Breton creperie with regional variations on the theme. Try the *Savoyard*, served with bacon and local *reblochon* cheese.

Le Pichet (☎ 04 50 45 32 41; 13 rue Perrière; menu €18-29; ⏰ Thu-Mon) Next door to the Hôtel du Palais de L'Isle, Le Pichet has a big terrace and a range of Savoyard dishes, including delicious, diet-busting *tartiflette* (sliced potatoes and *reblochon* cheese baked in the oven).

La Bastille (☎ 04 50 45 09 37; 3 quai des Vieilles Prison; menu €11-20; ⏰ lunch & dinner) A great little canalside restaurant with a sheltered terrace, opposite the old city prison. Tartiflette, steaks and Savoyard fondues are all delicious.

Tartes à la Folie (7-9 rue Vaugelas) Sweet and savoury tarts are on offer at this little café – don't miss the scrumptious rhubarb and nut tarts.

Au Fidèle Berger (cnr rue Royale & rue Carnot; 9.15am-7pm Tue-Fri, 9am-7.30pm Sat) A traditional tearoom and patisserie with a fantastic old-world feel.

Nature & Saveur (pl des Cordeliers; 8.30am-7pm Tue-Sat) A cosy organic café with a quayside terrace, offering smoothies, fresh juices, organic salads and snacks.

In the Vieille Ville, there's a popular **food market** (rue Faubourg Ste-Claire; 8am-noon Sun, Tue & Fri).

Getting There & Away

Annecy's small **airport** (04 50 27 30 06; 8 route Côte Merle) is north of the city in Meythet, just west of the autoroute to Geneva. The airport has daily flights to Paris' Orly Sud, Lilles, Nantes, Bordeaux and Toulouse.

The bus station, **Gare Routière Sud** (rue de l'Industrie) is next to the train station. Exits from the train-station platforms lead directly to the bus station.

Voyages Crolard (04 50 45 08 12; 7.15am-12.15pm & 1.30-7.30pm Mon-Sat, 7.45am-noon Sun) serves various points around Lake Annecy, including Menthon, Talloires and Roc de Chère on the eastern shore; Sévrier on the western shore; and Bout du Lac on the lake's southern tip. Other destinations include La Clusaz (€9.20, 50 minutes), Albertville (€7.70, 1¼ hours) and Chamonix (€15.80, two hours).

Autocars Frossard (04 50 45 73 90; 7.45-11am & 2-7.15pm Mon-Fri, to 1pm Sat) sells tickets to Annemasse, Chambéry, Évian, Geneva, Grenoble, Nice and Thonon.

The information counters at the **train station** (08 36 35 35 35; pl de la Gare) are open 9am to noon and 2pm to 7pm daily, and the ticket windows are open 5am to 10.30pm Monday to Friday, 9am to 7.30pm Saturday and Sunday.

There are frequent trains to Paris' Gare de Lyon (€76.40 by TGV, 3¾ hours), Nice (€65.50, 7½ hours), Lyon (€19, three hours). The night train to Paris (€70.30, eight hours), often full at weekends, leaves between 9pm and 10pm.

GRENOBLE
pop 156,000

Elegant, modern Grenoble is the intellectual and economic capital of the Alps, spectacularly set in a broad valley surrounded by snow-capped mountains. The city's modern shops, broad boulevards and varied architecture make it a great place to spend a few days soaking up the big-city atmosphere. The university serves a student body of 50,000.

Orientation

The old city is centred on place Grenette and place Notre-Dame, both about 1km east of the train and bus stations. The main university campus is around 2km east of the old centre on the southern side of the River Isère.

Information
INTERNET ACCESS

Neptune Internet Services (04 76 63 94 18; 2 de la Paix; per 15min/hr €2/3.50; 9am-9pm Mon-Fri, to 8pm Sat, 1-8pm Sun; salle-Internet@neptune.fr) Wireless networking and laptop connection points. Discounts from noon to 2pm and 7pm to 9pm.

LAUNDRY

Lavomatique (14 rue Thiers; 7am-10pm) Opposite Hôtel Victoria.

POST

Main post office (7 blvd Maréchal Lyautey; 8am-6.45pm Mon-Fri, to noon Sat)

TOURIST INFORMATION

Cargo Kiosk (1pm-6.30pm Tue-Sat) Events tickets.

SNCF Counter (8.30am-6.30pm Mon-Fri, 9am-6pm Sat) For train information.

TAG office (8.30am-6.30pm Mon-Fri, 9am-6pm Sat) Local bus information.

Tourist office (04 76 42 41 41; grenoble-isere.info; 14 rue de la République; 9.30am-6pm year-round, 10am-1pm Sun Oct-Apr, 10am-1pm & 2-4pm May-Sep) Located inside the large purpose-built Maison du Tourisme on rue de la Republique.

Sights

Looming above the old city on the northern side of the Isère river, the 16th century **Fort de la Bastille** is Grenoble's best-known landmark. The views are spectacular, with vast mountains on every side and the bridges and grey waters of the Isère river below. To get to the fort, a **téléphérique** (04 76 44 33 65; one way/return €3.80/5.50, students €3/4.40) leaves from Quai

FRANCE

GRENOBLE

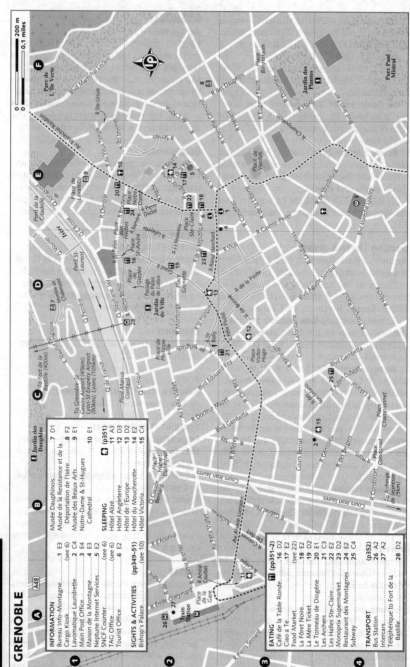

A	**B**	**C**	

INFORMATION
Bureau Info-Montagne..........................1	E3
Cargo Kiosk.................................(see 6)	
Lavomatique Laundrette......................2	C4
Main Post Office.............................3	E4
Maison de la Montagne......................4	E3
Neptune Internet Services...................5	E2
SNCF Counter................................(see 6)	
TAG Office...................................(see 6)	
Tourist Office................................6	E2

SIGHTS & ACTIVITIES   (pp349–51)
Bishop's Palace..............................(see 10)	

Musée Dauphinois..........................7	D1
Musée de la Resistance et de la	
Déportation de l'Isère......................8	F2
Musée des Beaux Arts.......................9	E1
Notre-Dame & St-Hugues	
Cathedral....................................10	E1

SLEEPING   (p351)
Hôtel Alizé..................................11	A3
Hôtel Angleterre............................12	D3
Hôtel de l'Europe...........................13	D2
Hôtel du Moucherotte......................14	E2
Hôtel Victoria...............................15	C4

EATING   (pp351–2)
Café de la Table Ronde.....................16	D2
Ciao a Te....................................17	E2
Food Market...............................(see 22)	
La Fôret Noire..............................18	E2
La Mère Ticket..............................19	D2
Le Tonneau de Diogène.....................20	E1
Les Archers.................................21	C3
Les Halles Ste-Claire........................22	E2
Monoprix Supermarket......................23	D2
Restaurant des Montagnes..................24	E2
Subway.....................................25	C4

TRANSPORT   (p352)
Bus Station..................................26	A2
Intercars....................................27	A2
Téléphérique to Fort de la	
Bastille......................................28	D2

Stéphane Jay between the Marius Gontard and St-Laurent bridges. It gets crowded in summer – leave early to avoid the worst queues.

The sleek glass and steel exterior of Grenoble's boldest museum, the **Musée des Beaux-Arts** (☎ 04 76 63 44 44; 5 pl de Lavalette; www.museede grenoble.fr; adult/student €5/2; ⏱ 10am-6.30pm, closed Tue), stands at the southern end of place Notre-Dame. It's renowned for its distinguished modern collection, which includes work by Chagall, Matisse, Modigliani, Monet, Picasso, Pissaro, Gauguin and others.

Musée Dauphinois (☎ 04 76 85 19 01; www.musee -dauphinois.fr; 30 rue Maurice Gignoux; ⏱ 10am-7pm Wed-Mon May-Oct, to 6pm Nov-Apr) documents the cultures, crafts and traditions of Alpine life. The museum occupies a beautiful 17th-century convent, nestled at the foot of the hill below Fort de la Bastille. From the city centre, it is most easily reached by the Pont St-Laurent footbridge.

The **Notre Dame and St-Hugues Cathedral** (pl Notre Dame) and the adjoining 14th-century **Bishop's Palace** (☎ 04 76 03 15 25; 2 rue Très Cloîtres; www.ancien-eveche-isere.com; admission free; ⏱ 9am-6pm Mon-Sat except Tue, 10am-7pm Sun) have had complete facelifts and now contain three museums: the **crypte archéologique**, with Roman walls and a baptistery dating from the 4th to 10th century; the **Musée d'Art Sacré**, which contains liturgical and religious objects; and the **Centre Jean Achard**, with exhibits of art from the Dauphiné region.

This moving **Musée de la Résistance et de la Déportation de l'Isère** (☎ 04 76 42 38 53; 14 rue Hébert; admission free; ⏱ 9am-7pm Wed-Mon Jun-Aug, 9-noon & 2-6pm Wed-Mon, from 10am Sun Sep-May) examines the deportation of Jews and other 'undesirables' from Grenoble to Nazi camps during WWII, and explores the role of the Vercors region in the French Resistance. Captions are in French, English and German.

Activities

For information on outdoor activities, head for the **Maison de Montagne** (☎ 08 25 82 55 88; 3 rue Raoul Blanchard). All the main organisations are housed under one roof. The **Bureau Info-Montagne** (☎ 04 76 42 45 90; fax 04 76 42 87 08; ⏱ 9am-noon & 2-6pm Mon-Fri, 10am-1pm & 2-6pm Sat) can give advice on just about every imaginable mountain activity except skiing. It sells hiking maps and has information on *gîtes d'étape* and *refuges* (huts).

The tourist office has comprehensive information, including accommodation lists, for all of Grenoble's surrounding ski resorts.

Sleeping

Auberge de Jeunesse (☎ 04 76 09 33 52; grenoble@ fuaj.org; 10 ave du Grésivaudan; dm incl breakfast €12; reception ⏱ 7.30am-11pm) This hostel is 5km south of the train station in the Echirolles district. From Cours Jean Jaurès, take bus No 1 to the Quinzaine stop (look for the Casino supermarket).

Hôtel du Moucherotte (☎ 04 76 54 61 40; fax 04 76 44 62 52; 1 rue Auguste Gaché; s/d from €28.20/30.25) If you're on a tight budget, the murky Moucherotte is one of the cheapest options near the city centre. Despite its dingy exterior, the rooms are clean but basic.

Hôtel de l'Europe (☎ 04 76 46 16 94; hoteleurope.fr; 22 pl Grenette; s €26-53, d €28-59) One of the city's oldest establishments, housed in a classic Grenoblois building above pl Grenette. It's a great value hotel with big rooms and a fabulous spiral staircase to the top floor. The front rooms have balconies with great views.

Hôtel Alizé (☎ 04 76 43 12 91; fax 04 76 47 62 79; 1 rue Amiral Courbet; s/d €31/36, tr €44-48) Small, simple and very cheap hotel which makes its popular – book in advance.

Hôtel Victoria (☎ 04 76 46 06 36; 17 rue Thiers s/d from €32/36.30; ⏱ Sep-Jul; P) Tucked away in a quiet courtyard in the Place Condorcet Area, this place has old-fashioned floral décor and friendly owners. The lively place Condorcet area has lots of low-rent restaurants and scruffy bars.

Hôtel Angleterre (☎ 04 76 87 37 21; www.hotel -angleterre.fr; 5 pl Victor-Hugo; s/d €88-150) The pick of several three-star hotels in the area, thanks to its luxurious rooms and a great location opposite the fountain-adorned pl Victor-Hugo. Accepts 'Bon-Weekend' reservations.

Eating

Le Tonneau de Diogène (☎ 04 76 42 38 40; 6 pl Notre Dame; menu from €6, plat du jour €10; ⏱ 8.30-1am) A cramped, wonderfully atmospheric place, decked out with polished wood, leather booths, and lots of tightly packed tables.

Café de la Table Ronde (☎ 04 76 44 51 41; 7 pl St-André; lunch menu €10; ⏱ 7am-midnight Mon-Sat) Another of Grenoble's most famous cafés, it was a favoured haunt of Stendhal and Rousseau, and the old-world atmosphere and period furnishings don't seem to have changed much since they were around.

La Forêt Noire (pl Ste-Claire) A Grenoble institution for afternoon tea. The café serves a lavish range of cakes, tarts and *viennoiseries*, as well as light meals. Look no further for something sweet and sticky.

La Mère Ticket (☎ 04 76 44 45 40; 13 rue Jean-Jacques Rousseau; ☽ lunch & 8-11pm Mon-Sat) A tiny, traditional French restaurant tucked away on a busy shopping street. The homely country cooking is fantastic value, especially at lunchtime (€10, 11 with dessert). The delicious *poulet aux écrevisses* (chicken with crayfish) and *gratin dauphinois* come highly recommended.

Restaurant des Montagnes (☎ 04 76 15 20 72; 5 rue Brocherie; ☽ 7pm-midnight Sep-Jun) Grenoble's premier place for fondue and *tartiflette*. Loosen your belt and order one of the 13 kinds of sumptuous fondue (€12.50 to €21 per person – minimum two people).

Les Archers (☎ 04 76 46 27 76; 2 rue Docteur Bailly; ☽ 11-1am) A brasserie with great outside seating in summer. Fish and seafood are especially good, with delicacies including pan-fried trout and grilled sea bass.

Ciao a Te (☎ 04 76 42 54 41; 2 rue de la Paix; ☽ Tue-Sat) A vibrant Italian restaurant which serves great pasta from around €10. If you're feeling hungry, try the filling, delicious cannelloni.

Les Halles Ste-Claire (☽ 6am-1pm Tue-Sun) is Grenoble's lovely old covered market. Even if you're not going there to shop, the market atmosphere is worth investigating.

There's also a busy **food market** (place Ste-Claire ; ☽ Wed-Mon), and a **Monoprix supermarket** (cnr rue de la République & rue Lafayette; ☽ 8.30am-7.30pm Mon-Sat).

Getting There & Away
AIR
Domestic flights are handled by **Grenoble-St-Geoirs airport** (☎ 04 76 65 48 48), 41km northwest of Grenoble. All international flights operate to/from **Lyon-St Exupéry airport** (☎ 08 26 80 08 26), 90km from the city off the A43 to Lyon.

BUS
The **bus station** (☎ 04 76 87 90 31; rue Émile Gueymard; ☽ 6.30am-7pm Mon-Sat, 7.15am-7pm Sun) is next to the train station, and is the main terminus for several bus companies. **VFD** (☎ 08 20 83 38 33; http://vfd.fr, in French; ☽ 8am-6pm Tue-Fri, to noon &

1.30-4.30pm Sat & Mon) serves most Alpine destinations; tariffs are worked out on a zone system according to how far you travel. Destinations include the Vercors ski stations.

Intercars (☎ 04 76 46 19 77; www.intercars.fr; station office ☽ 9am-noon & 2-6pm Mon-Fri, to noon & 2-5pm Sat) handles long-haul destinations including Budapest (€88, 22 hours), Munich (€72, 10½ hours), Rome (€48, 13½ hours), Milan (€23, 5½ hours), Zurich (€31, five) and Geneva (€12, 2½ hours).

TRAIN
The huge, modern **train station** (☎ 08 36 35 35 35; rue Émile Gueymard; ☽ 4.30am-2am) is next to the Gare Europole tram stop, which is served by both tramlines (see Getting Around).

Destinations served include Paris' Gare de Lyon (from €63.30, 3½ hours by TGV), Chambéry (€9, one hour, 14 daily) and Lyon (€16.30, 1½ hours, five daily), from where you can catch trains to Nice and Monaco. There are also daily trains to Turin (€44), Milan (€54, change at Chambéry), and Geneva (€19.70, two hours).

Getting Around
TO/FROM THE AIRPORT
The bus (☎ 04 76 87 90 31) to Lyon-St Exupéry airport stops at the bus station (one way/return €20/30, 65 minutes). Buses to the Grenoble-St-Geoirs domestic airport depart from the bus station (one way/return €13/20, 45 minutes).

BUS & TRAM
Grenoble's two tram lines – sensibly called A and B – both stop at the tourist office and the train station, and run through the heart of town. Bus and tram tickets cost €1.20 and are available from ticket machines at tram stops or from drivers. They must be time-stamped in the blue machines located at each stop before boarding. Tickets are valid for transfers – but not return trips – within one hour.

A *carnet* of 10 tickets costs €9.50. Daily/five-day passes (Visitag) are available for €3.20/11 at the **TAG information desk** (☎ 04 76 20 66 66) at the tourist office, or from the TAG office outside the train station.

Most of the buses on the 20 different lines stop running quite early, usually between 6pm and 9pm. Trams run daily from 5am (6.15am on Sunday) to just after midnight.

FRANCE

THE JURA

The dark wooded hills and granite plateaus of the Jura Mountains stretch for 360km along the Franco-Swiss border from the Rhine to the Rhône. Part of the historic Franche-Comté region, the Jura is one of the least explored regions in France, which makes it a fine place to escape the Alpine crowds. If you're looking for a taste of traditional mountain life, the Jura makes a far better destination than the ruthlessly modernised and tourist-orientated resorts elsewhere in the Alps.

The Jura – from a Gaulish word meaning 'forest' – is an important agricultural area, best known for its unique wines and cheeses. It is also France's premier cross-country skiing area and popular for its superb hiking and nature trails.

BESANÇON
pop 125,000

Noted for its vast parks, clean streets and few tourists, Besançon is considered one of the most liveable cities in France. It has one of the country's largest foreign student populations and the old town's cobbled streets hum with bars and bistros. Victor Hugo, author of *Les Misérables*, and the film-pioneering Lumière brothers, were all born on the square now known as place Victor Hugo in Besançon's old town.

Orientation

Besançon's old city is neatly encased by the curve of the River Doubs called the Boucle du Doubs. The tourist office and train station are both just outside this loop to the northwest and north. The Battant quarter straddles the northwest bank of the river around rue Battant. Grande Rue, the pedestrianised main street, slices through the old city from the river to the gates of the citadel.

Information
INTERNET ACCESS
Optimum (☎ 03 81 82 13 07; www.optimum.fr; 31 rue d'Arènes; Mon-Sat, 2-10pm Sun per 10min/hr €1/3.50; ☯ 10am-10.30pm)

LAUNDRY
Blanc-Matic (14 rue de la Madeleine; ☯ 7am-8pm)

POST
Post office (23 rue Proudhon; ☯ 9am-noon & 2-6pm) In the old city. There is another branch on rue Battant.

TOURIST INFORMATION
Tourist office (☎ 03 81 80 92 55; besancon-tourisme .com; 2 place de la 1ère Armée Française; ☯ 10am-7pm Mon, 9am-7pm Tue-Sat, 10am-noon & 3-5pm Sun Apr-Sep, 10am-6pm Mon, 9am-6pm Tue-Sat Oct-Mar, 10am-noon Sun mid-Sep–mid-Jun)

Sights

Thought to be France's oldest museum, the **Musée des Beaux-Arts** (☎ 03 81 87 80 49; 1 pl de la Révolution; adult/student €3/free; ☯ 9.30am-noon & 2-6pm Wed-Mon) houses an impressive collection of paintings, including primitive and Renaissance works. Franche-Comté's long history of clock-making is also displayed here.

Built by Vauban for Louis XIV between 1688 and 1711, Besançon's **citadel** (☎ 03 81 87 83 33; adult/concession/child €7/6/4; ☯ 9am-7pm Jul-Aug, to 6pm Apr-Jun, Sep & Oct, 10am-5pm Nov-Mar) sits at the top of rue des Fusillés de la Résistance. It's a steep 15-minute walk from the **Porte Noire** (Black Gate), a triumphal arch left over from Besançon's Roman days, dating from the 2nd century AD.

Inside the walls of citadel, there are three museums focusing on local culture: the **Musée Comtois**, the **Musée d'Histoire Naturelle** (Natural History Museum) and the **Musée de la Résistance et de la Déportation**.

Sleeping

Auberge de Jeunesse Les Oiseaux (☎ 03 81 40 32 00; 48 rue des Cras; dm €20) The hostel is 2km east of the train station. Rates include breakfast and bedding; subsequent nights cost €2 less. Take bus No 7 from the tourist office toward Orchamps and get off at Les Oiseaux.

Hôtel Regina (☎ 03 81 81 18 30; 91 Grande Rue; d €35-50) Down a quiet alley in the heart of the old city, this two-star hotel offers cosy, floral rooms with shower, toilet and TV.

Hôtel de Paris (☎ 03 81 81 36 56; hoteldeparis@ hotmail.com; 33 rue des Granges; d €45-60; P) One of the best deals in Besancon, this efficient, comfortable hotel has 60 rooms which vary in quality; we recommend you ask to see a couple before you choose.

Hôtel Castan (☎ 03 81 65 02 00; fax 03 81 83 01 02; 6 square Castan; d €65-95) Housed in an ivy-covered 18th-century townhouse on a little shaded square in the old city, this is one of the nicest

FRANCE

places to stay in town, with tastefully furnished rooms. Book well ahead.

Eating & Drinking

Carpe Diem (☎ 03 81 83 11 18; 2 pl Jean Gigoux; salads from €2.60, plats du jour €8) A small, rough-and-ready café-bar with a smoky atmosphere, wooden bar, and tattered posters.

La Femme du Boulanger (☎ 03 81 82 86 93; 6 rue Morand) Scrumptious bakery and coffee bar offering homemade breads, sweet and savoury tarts, healthy breakfasts and not-so-healthy cakes.

Boîte à Sandwichs (21 rue du Lycée) Cheap, filling sandwiches from €2.80 to €4.50.

Au Feu Vert (☎ 03 81 82 17 20; 11 pl de la Révolution; menu from €9; ☷ noon-10.30pm) A simple, local restaurant with a bright colourful dining room and a cheap and generous menu, offering regional specialities such as *gratin de saucisse de Morteau* (a cheesy potato and sausage bake).

Al Sirocco (☎ 03 81 82 24 05; 1 rue Chifflet; ☷ closed lunch Sun & Mon) Great, traditional Italian diner with little tables and fishing nets hanging from the ceiling. Locals come here for the best pizza and pasta in Besançon.

Le Vin et l'Assiette (☎ 03 81 81 48 18; 97 rue Battant; menu €18; ☷ Tue-Sat) An intimate bistro and wine bar, located above the Caves Marcellin (Marcellin wine cellars). Sample local Jura wine accompanied by meats and cheeses.

Pierre qui Mousse (☎ 03 81 81 15 25; 1 pl Jouffroy; ☷ daily until late) A popular bar-brasserie right on the riverfront, where you can sup Belgian beer (€3.50) under low wooden beams. Happy hour is usually from 6pm to 7pm.

Les Passagers du Zinc (☎ 03 81 81 54 70; 5 rue de Vignier; ☷ 5pm-1am Tue-Fri, to 2am Sat & Sun) A grungy bar and club that hosts tapas nights, live bands, and music nights.

Fresh fish, meat, vegetables and cheeses are sold at the large **indoor market** (cnr rue Paris & rue Claude Goudimel). The nearby **outdoor market** (pl de la Révolution) sells mainly fresh fruit and vegetables.

Getting There & Away

Buses operated by **Monts Jura** (☎ 08 25 00 22 44) depart from the **bus station** (9 rue Proudhon; ☷ 8-10am & 4-6.30pm Mon-Fri, 8am-1pm & 2.30-5.30pm Sat). There are daily services to Ornans and Pontarlier.

Uphill, 800m from the city centre, is **Besançon Gare Viotte** (☎ 08 36 35 35 35; ticket office

☷ 5am-10.30pm). Train tickets can be bought in advance at the **SNCF office** (44 Grande Rue). Major connections include Paris' Gare de Lyon (from €45.10 non-TGV, three hours, three daily), Dijon (€13.80, 50 minutes, 20 daily), Lyon (€31.40, three hours, eight daily).

Getting Around

Local buses are run by **CTB** (☎ 03 81 48 12 12), which has a **ticket/information kiosk** (pl du 8 Septembre; ☷ 9am-12.30pm & 1-7pm Mon-Sat). A single ticket/day ticket/*carnet* of 10 costs €0.95/3.20/8. Bus Nos 8 and 24 link the train station with the centre.

AROUND BESANÇON

Saline Royal

Envisaged by its designer, Claude-Nicolas Ledoux, as the 'ideal city', the 18th-century Saline Royale (Royal Salt Works; ☎ 03 81 54 45 45; adult/student/child €7/4.50/2.80; ☷ 9am-7pm Jul-Aug, to 6pm Jun & Sep, to noon & 2-6pm Apr-May & Oct, 10am-noon & 2-5pm Nov-Dec, Jan-Mar) at **Arc-et-Senans**, 30km southwest of Besançon, is a showpiece of early Industrial Age town planning. Although his urban dream was never realised, Ledoux's semicircular saltworks is now listed as a Unesco World Heritage site.

Route Pasteur & Route du Vin

Nearly every town in the Jura seems to have a street, square or garden (sometimes all three) named after Louis Pasteur, the great 19th century chemist, born and raised in the Jura, who invented pasteurisation and developed the first rabies vaccine.

Pasteur grew up in **Arbois**, a rural community 35km east of Dole. His laboratory and workshops in Arbois are on display at **La Maison de Louis Pasteur** (☎ 03 84 66 11 72; 83 rue de Courcelles; adult/child €5.50/2.80; ☷ 9.45am-6.15pm Jun-Sep). The house is still decorated with its original 19th century fixtures and fittings. There are hourly tours from 2.15pm to 5.15pm in April to October, with extra morning tours between June and September.

No visit to Arbois, the wine capital of the Jura, would be complete without sampling a glass of *vin jaune*. The history of this nutty 'yellow wine', which is matured for six years in oak casks, is recounted at the **Musée de la Vigne et du Vin** (☎ 03 84 66 26 14; percee@jura.vins.com; ☷ 10am-noon & 2-6pm Wed-Mon Feb-Jun & Sep, to 6pm Wed-Mon Jul & Aug) inside the restored **Château**

Pécaud, a turreted mansion which once formed a part of the city's fortifications.

The **tourist office** (☎ 03 84 37 47 37; http://arbois .com; rue de l'Hôtel de Ville; ☼ 9.30am-noon & 2-6pm Sep-Easter, 9am-12.30pm & 2-6.30pm Easter-Sep) offers advice on cycling routes in the Arbois area. The **SNCF office** is housed in the same building. There are regular trains to Arbois from Besançon via Mouchard (€14.80, 40 minutes, eight to 10 daily).

MÉTABIEF MONT D'OR
pop 700 / elevation 1000m

Métabief Mont d'Or, 18km south of Pontarlier on the main road to Lausanne, is the region's leading cross-country ski resort. Year-round, lifts take you almost to the top of Mont d'Or (1463m), the area's highest peak, from where a fantastic 180-degree panorama stretches over the foggy Swiss plain to Lake Geneva and from the Matterhorn all the way to Mont Blanc. Métabief is famed for its unique *vacherin Mont d'Or* cheese.

The main lift station for downhill skiers is in Métabief. There are smaller lifts in Les Hôpitaux Neufs, 2km northeast.

In Métabief, the **tourist office** (☎ 03 81 49 16 79; ot@metabief-montdor.com; ☼ 9am-noon & 2-5pm, closed Sun Sep–mid-Dec) and **École du Ski Français** (ESF; ☎ 03 81 49 04 21; ☼ 9am-noon & 2-5pm) are inside the **Centre d'Accueil** (6 pl Xavier Authier).

PROVENCE

First-time visitors may be as captivated by this ruggedly lovely chunk of France as the painter Van Gogh was. 'What intensity of colours, what pure air, what vibrant serenity,' he wrote on arrival from a gloomy Paris. 'Nature here is extraordinarily beautiful, everything and everywhere.'

It's a culturally and historically rich region too. The Romans were among the earliest to spot its charms, invading it then sending their favourite legions to retire here. They left many unmissable monuments behind, including theatres and thermal baths (some still in use) in places like Arles and Aix.

MARSEILLE
pop 807,071

In parts African, in others Middle-eastern but in its entirety unmistakeably French, the cosmopolitan port of Marseille is a brusque, bustling place full of character. There's the attractive old port, gritty (often stinking) back streets, markets reminiscent of Moroccan *souks* and great harbourside restaurants.

France's second city and its third-largest metropolitan area, Marseille has not been prettified for the benefit of tourists and its old (and mostly outdated) reputation as a place of crime and racial tension dies hard. Yet visitors who enjoy exploring on foot will be rewarded with more sights, sounds, smells and big-city commotion than almost anywhere else in the country.

Orientation & Information

The city's main thoroughfare, the boulevard called La Canebière, stretches eastwards from the Vieux Port (Old Port). The train station is north of La Canebière at the northern end of blvd d'Athènes. A few blocks south of La Canebière is the bohemian cours Julien, a large pedestrianised square. The ferry terminal is west of place de la Joliette, a few minutes' walk north of the Nouvelle Cathédrale. Addresses below include arondissements (1er being the most central).

Surf the Web at **Info Cafe** (☎ 04 91 33 74 98; 1 quai du Rive Neuve, 1e; Internet per hr €3.60; ☼ 9am-10pm Mon-Sat, 2.30pm-7.30pm Sun). The often overwhelmed and understaffed **tourist office** (☎ 04 91 13 89 00; www.marseille-tourisme.com; 4 La Canebière, 1er; ☼ 9am-7pm Mon-Sat, 10am-5pm Sun, 9am-7.30pm daily mid-Jun–mid-Sep) can make hotel reservations. There's an **annexe** (☎ 04 91 50 59 18; ☼ 10am-1pm & 2-6pm Mon-Sat) at the main train station.

DANGERS & ANNOYANCES

Despite its reputation for crime, Marseille is not significantly more dangerous than other French cities. Avoid walking alone at night in the Belsunce area, a poor neighbourhood southwest of the train station bounded by La Canebière, cours Belsunce and rue d'Aix, rue Bernard du Bois and blvd d'Athènes.

Sights

Unless noted otherwise, the museums open from 10am to 5pm Tuesday to Sunday October to May and 11am to 6pm June to September. Admission to each museum's permanent exhibitions cost adult/child €2/1.

The **Centre de la Vieille Charité** (Old Charity Cultural Centre; ☎ 04 91 14 58 80; 2 rue de la Charité, 2e) in the mostly North African Panier Quarter is

FRANCE

FRANCE

MARSEILLE

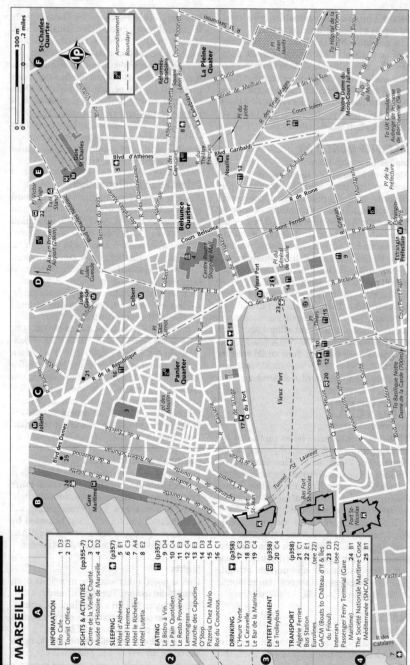

home to **Musée d'Archéologie** (☎ 04 91 14 58 80) with some worthwhile exhibits on ancient Egypt and Greece.

A relatively small place just north of La Canebière, **Musée d'Histoire de Marseille** (☎ 04 91 90 42 22; Centre Bourse shopping centre, 1er; ☯ noon-7pm Mon-Sat) gives a good overview of the cultures that have made their home in Marseille, and the crafts they practised over the centuries, including the remains of a 3rd century AD merchant vessel.

Not to be missed for great panoramas and some handsome, if overwrought, 19th-century architecture is the **Basilique Notre Dame de la Garde** (☎ 04 91 13 40 80; admission free; basilica & crypt ☯ 7am-8pm, to 10pm mid-Jun–mid-Aug, to 7pm in winter). Dress conservatively when you visit. Bus No 60 links the old port (from cours Jean Ballard) with the basilica.

Château d'If (☎ 04 91 59 02 30; adult/student €4.60/3.10; ☯ 9.30am-6pm Sep-Mar, to 6.30pm Jun-Aug), the 16th-century fortress-turned-prison made infamous by Alexandre Dumas' classic novel, *Le Comte de Monte Cristo* (The Count of Monte Cristo), is on a 30-sq-km island, 3.5km west of the entrance to the old port. In reality all sorts of political prisoners, hundreds of Protestants (many of whom perished in the dungeons), the Revolutionary hero Mirabeau, the rebels of 1848 and the Communards of 1871 were imprisoned here.

GACM (☎ 04 91 55 50 09; www.answeb.net/gacm; 1 quai des Belges, 1er) runs boats to the Château d'If at 9am, 10.30am, noon, 2pm, and 3.30pm (€9 return, 20 minutes).

Sleeping

Generally, the better hotels cluster around the old port (where budget options are pretty much non-existent) and as you head east out of the centre along the corniche.

Auberge de Jeunesse de Bonneveine (☎ 04 91 17 63 30; fax 04 91 73 97 23; impasse du Docteur Bonfils, 8e; dm €14.55; ☯ Feb-Dec) About 4.5km south of the centre, rates at this hostel include breakfast. Take bus No 44 from the Rond Point du Prado metro stop and get off at the place Bonnefons stop.

Le Richelieu (☎ 04 91 31 01 92; hotelmer@club-Internet.fr; 52 Corniche Président John F Kennedy, 7e; r €34-41, sea-facing €41-53) An idyllic, two-star place with ace views, built onto the rocks right next to plage des Catalans. Road-facing rooms can be noisy. Some sea-facing rooms have balconies. Book ahead.

Hôtel d'Athènes (☎ 04 91 90 12 93; fax 04 91 90 72 03; 37-39 blvd d'Athènes, 1er; s/d with shower €24/34, s/d/tr with shower & toilet 39/46/56) At the foot of the grand staircase leading from the train station into town you'll find average but well-kept rooms and an elevator here. It also runs the adjoining one-star **Hôtel Little Palace** (r with shower only €25-34).

Hôtel Lutetia (☎ 04 91 50 81 78; www.hotellutetia13.com; 38 allées Léon Gambetta, 1er; s/d/tr from €46/51/70) Homely and spotless, the smallish rooms are equipped with TV and phone.

Hôtel Hermes (☎ 04 96 11 63 63; hotel.hermes@wanadoo.fr; 2 rue Bonneterie, 1er; s/d from €45/67; ☒ ☒ ☒ P) Right on the quayside, bright, cheerful and good value given the location overlooking the harbour and Basilique Notre Dame.

Eating

No trip to Marseille is complete without sampling *bouillabaisse*, a rich red soup full of chunks of Mediterranean fish – the old port area is a good hunting ground.

Lemongrass (☎ 04 91 33 97 65; 8 rue Fort-Notre-Dame, 1er; menu €20; ☯ closed Sun) An exciting newcomer serving inexpensive and interesting menus of fusion Asian/French food.

Le Bistro à Vin (☎ 04 91 54 02 20; 17 rue Sainte, 6e; mains around €12; ☯ closed lunch Sat & all day Sun) The wine selection is excellent and the accompaniments – *tapenade*, artisanal cheeses and unusual meat parts – are equally enticing.

Le Resto Provençal (☎ 04 91 48 85 12; 64 cours Julien, 1er; ☯ closed lunch Sat & all day Sun) A winning combination of an outside dining terrace, a *menu* offering regional fare for €21, a *plat du jour* for around €9 and a good-value lunchtime *menu* for €12.

Get your fresh fruit and veg at the **Marche des Capucins** (place des Capucins; ☯ Mon-Sat), a block south of La Canebiére. For snackier fare take your pick:

Le Pain Quotidien (☎ 04 91 33 55 00; 18 Pl Aux Huiles; breakfast €5-8) For a decent breakfast.

Pizzeria Chez Mario (☎ 04 91 54 48 54; 8 rue Euthymènes, 1er; mains €8.50-15) Good fish, grilled meats, pizza and pasta.

Roi du Couscous (☎ 04 91 91 45 46; 63 rue de la République, 2e; couscous €8-12; ☯ Tue-Sun) Serves large and delicious portions of steamed semolina with meats and vegetables.

O'Stop (☎ 04 91 33 85 34; 15 rue Saint-Saëns, 1er; menu €9; ☯ 24hr) Non-stop sandwiches, pasta and simple, authentic regional specialities.

Drinking & Entertainment

Cultural event listings appear in the monthly *Vox Mag* and weekly *Taktik* and *Sortir*, all distributed free at the tourist office. It's also worth consulting the website www.marseille bynight.com.

There are plenty of venues (and lots of variety) to check out. Two hotspots are the bars and clubs around quayside, especially along the Quai de Rive Neuve, and, a fair hike away, the bars and cafés around Place Jean Jaurès

Le Trolleybus (☎ 04 91 54 30 45; 24 Quai Rive Neuve; ⏳ 11pm–dawn Wed-Sat) Inside the various sections of this tunnel-like club by the harbour there could be techno, funk and indie playing at the same time.

Le Bar de la Marine (☎ 04 91 54 95 42; 15 Quai de Rive Neuve) Chic metropolitan espresso sippers mix it with grizzled pastis-gulping sailor types at this gregarious bar right on the water.

La Caravelle (☎ 04 91 90 36 64, 34 quai du Port, 2e) Upstairs at the Hôtel Bellevue, this is in a marvellous location overlooking the port with a small balcony.

L'Heure Verte (☎ 04 91 90 12 73; 108 quai du Port; ⏳ 11am-11pm high season) The place to go to sample many different types of pastis and some fierce absinthe.

Getting There & Away

AIR

The **Marseille-Provence airport** (☎ 04 42 14 14 14), also known as the Marseille-Marignane airport, is 28km northwest of the city in Marignane.

BOAT

Marseille's **passenger ferry terminal** (gare maritime; ☎ 04 91 56 38 63; fax 04 91 56 38 70) is 250m south of place de la Joliette, 2e.

The **Société Nationale Maritime Corse Méditerranée** (SNCM; ☎ 08 36 67 95 00; fax 04 91 56 35 86; 61 blvd des Dames, 2e; ⏳ 8am-6pm Mon-Fri, 8.30am-noon & 2-5.30pm Sat) links Marseille with Corsica, Sardinia and Tunisia.

There is an office for **Algérie Ferries** (☎ 04 91 90 64 70; 29 blvd des Dames, 2e; ⏳ 9am-11.45 & 1-4.45pm Mon-Fri). Ticketing and reservations for the Tunisian and Moroccan ferry companies, **Compagnie Tunisienne de Navigation** (CTN) and **Compagnie Marocaine de Navigation** (COMANAV; ☎ 04 67 46 68 00), departures from 4 quai d'Alger in Sète, are handled by SNCM.

BUS

The **bus station** (gare des autocars; ☎ 04 91 08 16 40; 3 pl Victor Hugo, 3e) is 150m to the right as you exit the train station. Services include Aix-en-Provence (€4.20, 35 minutes via the autoroute or one hour via the N8, every five to 10 minutes); Avignon (€17, 35 minutes, one daily); and Nice (€22, 2¾ hours).

Eurolines (☎ 08 92 28 99 091, 04 91 50 57 55) has buses to Spain, Belgium, the Netherlands, Italy, Morocco, the UK and other countries. **Intercars** (☎ 04 91 50 08 66), whose office is next to Eurolines in the bus station, has buses to the UK, Spain, Portugal, Morocco, Poland and Slovakia. Both firms share offices at the bus station and at 3 alles Leon Gambetta (☎ 04 91 50 57 55).

TRAIN

Marseille's passenger train station, served by both metro lines, is **Gare St-Charles.** There's a large information and ticket **reservation office** (⏳ 9am-8pm Mon-Sat, ticket sales 4pm-1am). Trains run to Paris' Gare de Lyon (€83.90, three hours, 17 daily); Avignon (€19.40, 30 minutes, 27 daily); Lyon (€39.40, 3¼ hours, 16 daily) and Nice (€25, 2½ hours, 21 daily).

Luggage may be left at the **left-luggage office** (⏳ 7.15am-10pm; €3.40 for 72hr), which is next to platform A.

Getting Around

TO/FROM THE AIRPORT

Navette Shuttle Buses (Marseille ☎ 04 91 50 59 34, airport ☎ 04 42 14 31 27) link the Marseille-Provence airport (€8.50, one hour) with Marseille's train station. Airport-bound buses leave from the train station's main entrance every 20 minutes.

BUS & METRO

Marseille is served by two well-maintained, fast metro lines (Métro 1 and Métro 2) and an extensive bus network. The metro and most buses run from about 5am to 9pm. From 9.25pm to 12.30am, metro and tram routes are covered every 15 minutes by buses M1 and M2.

Bus/metro tickets cost €1.50. A pass for one/three days costs €4/9.50.

AIX-EN-PROVENCE

pop 137,067

Aix-en-Provence, or just Aix (pronounced like the letter 'x'), is one of France's most graceful and popular cities, boasting the art heritage of Cezanne who lived and painted here (although sadly the Musée Granet which exhibits some of his work is closed until at least 2006), a lively nightlife (much of it sustained by the presence of 30,000 students) and plenty of charm.

The Cours Mireabeau, a graceful plane tree-lined boulevard is the perfect place to watch the world pass as you nurse a slow espresso on one of the many large cafés lining it. The warren of streets running off it into the old town are full of ethnic restaurants and specialist shops, mingled with handsome old 17th- and 18th-century mansions. Aix's **Cathédrale St-Sauveur** (rue J de Laroque; 🕑 8am-noon & 2-6pm) is an interesting rag-tag of styles through the ages, incorporating architectural features of every major period from the 5th to 18th centuries stuck onto one another.

Aix is easy to see on a day trip from Marseille, and frequent buses (€4.20) make the 35-minute trip.

Sleeping

Despite being a student town, Aix is not cheap. Even so, the centre can fill up fast so book ahead.

Camping Arc-en-Ciel (🕿 04 42 26 14 28; route de Nice; camp sites €17.10; 🕑 Apr-Sep) There are peaceful wooded hills out back but a busy motorway out front. It's 2km southeast of town, at Pont des Trois Sautets. Take bus No 3 to Les Trois Sautets stop

Auberge de Jeunesse du Jas de Bouffan (🕿 04 42 20 15 99; fax 04 42 59 36 12; 3 ave Marcel Pagnol; dm incl breakfast & sheets €15) A smart, modern place with great views of a distant Mont Ventoux. It's 2km west of the centre. Rooms are locked between 9am and 5pm. Take bus line No 4 from La Rotonde to the Vasarely stop.

Hôtel Paul (🕿 04 42 23 23 89; hotel.paul@wanadoo.fr; 10 ave Pasteur; s/d/tr €35/45/55) Welcoming rooms and a pleasant courtyard garden make this an appealing budget option just north of blvd Jean Jaurès and a 10-minute walk from the tourist office, or take minibus No 2 from La Rotonde or the bus station.

Hôtel Cardinal (🕿 04 42 38 32 30; fax 04 42 26 39 05; 24 rue Cardinale; s/d €47/60, self-catering ste €76) A charming place with large (mostly) en-suite rooms and a mix of modern and period furniture. The upper rooms offer pretty views across town.

Eating

Aix is known for its superb markets. A mass of fruit and vegetable stands are set up each morning on place Richelme, just as they have been for centuries.

Aix's cheapest dining street is rue Van Loo, lined with tiny restaurants offering Italian, Chinese, Thai and other Asian cuisines.

Le Dernier Bistrot (🕿 04 42 21 13 02; 15-19 rue Constantin; lunch menu €10, dinner menu €16-23; 🕑 Mon-Sat) Mixes traditional bistro recipes with Provençal culinary fodder such as beef *daubes* (stew) and carpaccios, *soupe au pistou* (pesto soup) and courgette flan.

Yôji (🕿 04 42 38 84 48; 7 ave Victor Hugo; lunch menu from €9.50, dinner menu €16-20) Often packed and you'll taste why if you can get in (book ahead). The sushi is first rate but for real theatre choose the sizzling Korean barbecues brought to your table. There are some great fusion twists too, including the toothsome green tea brulée.

AVIGNON
pop 88,312

Avignon is synonymous in France with the annual performing arts festival held here each summer, but there's plenty to see in this bustling walled city year-round, including a number of interesting museums and the massive fortress of the medieval popes, the Palais des Papes.

The city first acquired wealth and power, its mighty ramparts and its reputation as a city of art and culture during the 14th century, when Pope Clement V and his court fled political turmoil in Rome and established themselves near Avignon. From 1309 to 1377 seven French-born popes based themselves here. Even after the pontifical court returned to Rome, Avignon remained under papal rule until 1791.

Orientation & Information

The main avenue within the walled city *(intra-muros)* runs northwards from the train station to place de l'Horloge; it's called cours Jean Jaurès south of the tourist office and rue de la République north of it.

Place de l'Horloge is 300m south of place du Palais, which abuts the Palais des Papes. The city gate nearest the train station is Porte de la République, while the city gate next to pont Édouard Daladier, which leads to Villeneuve-lès-Avignon, is Porte

FRANCE

AVIGNON

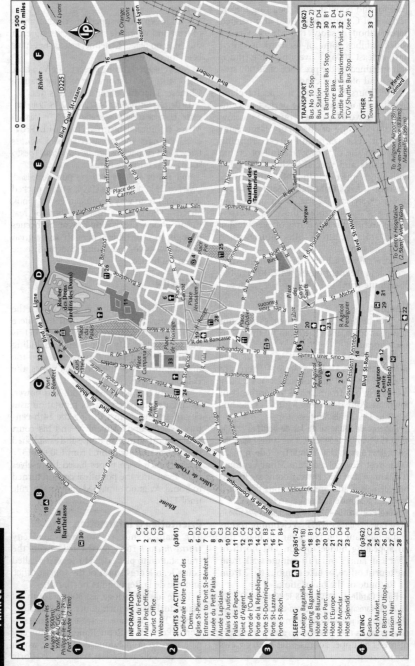

0 .... 500 m
0 .... 0.3 miles

To Villeneuve-les
Avignon (500m);
YMCA-UCJG; Tour
Philippe-le-Bel (1.2km);
Fort St-André (2.1km)

To Lyons

To Orange;
Lyons

To Avignon Airport (8km);
Aix-en-Provence (83km);
Marseilles (99km)

To Centre Hospitalier
(2.5km); Arles (36km)

INFORMATION
Bureau du Festival.....................	1 C4
Main Post Office........................	2 C4
Tourist Office...........................	3 C3
Webzone.................................	4 D2

SIGHTS & ACTIVITIES   (p361)
Cathédrale Notre Dame des Doms....	5 D1
Église St-Pierre.........................	6 D2
Entrance to Pont St-Bénézet..........	7 C1
Musée du Petit Palais..................	8 C1
Musée Lapidaire........................	9 C3
Palais de Justice........................	10 D2
Palais des Papes........................	11 D2
Point d'Argent..........................	12 C4
Porte de l'Oulle.........................	13 C2
Porte de la République.................	14 C4
Porte St-Dominique....................	15 B3
Porte St-Lazare.........................	16 F1
Porte St-Roch..........................	17 B4

SLEEPING   (pp361-2)
Auberge Bagatelle...............	(see 18)
Camping Bagatelle....................	18 B1
Hôtel de Blauvac......................	19 C2
Hôtel du Parc..........................	20 D3
Hôtel L'Europe.........................	21 C2
Hôtel Mignon..........................	22 D4
Hôtel Splendid........................	23 D4

EATING   (p362)
Casino...................................	24 C2
Food Market............................	25 D3
Le Bistrot d'Utopia....................	26 D1
Maison Nani............................	27 C3
Tapalocas..............................	28 D2

TRANSPORT   (p362)
Bus No 10 Stop.....................	(see 2)
Bus Station............................	29 D4
La Barthelasse Bus Stop..............	30 B1
Provence Bike.........................	31 D4
Shuttle Boat Embarkation Point......	32 C1
TGV Shuttle Bus Stop................	(see 2)

OTHER
Town Hall..............................	33 C2

de l'Oulle. Check out the Internet at **Web-zone** (☎ 04 32 76 29 47; 3 rue St Jean le Vieux; Internet per hr €4.57; ☺ 11am-10pm Mon-Sat, noon-5pm Sun). For local information visit the **tourist office** (☎ 04 32 74 32 74; fax 04 90 82 95 03; www.ot-avignon.fr; 41 cours Jean Jaurès; ☺ 9am-6pm Mon-Sat, 9am-5pm Sun Apr-Jun & Aug-Oct, to 6pm Mon-Fri, to 5pm Sat, 10am-noon Sun Nov-Mar, to 7pm Mon-Sat, 10am-5pm Sun Jul), 300m north of the train station; during the Avignon Festival it opens 9am to 7pm daily (till 5pm on Sunday).

Sights

Ask at the tourist office about the Avignon Passion museum pass, which entitles you to special discounts.

The **Pont St Bénézet** (Le Pont d'Avignon; ☎ 04 90 27 51 16; full price/pass €3.50/3; ☺ 9am-7pm Apr-May, Oct-Nov, to 8pm Jul-Sep, 9.30am-5.45pm Nov-Mar) was built between 1177 and 1185 to link Avignon with the settlement across the Rhône that later became Villeneuve-lès-Avignon. Yes, this is also the **Pont d'Avignon** in the French nursery rhyme. Many people find a distant view of the bridge from the Rocher des Doms (also known as the Pont Édouard Daladier) much more interesting (and it's free).

The huge **Palais des Papes** (☎ 04 90 27 50 00; pl du Palais; full price/pass €9.50/7.50; ☺ 9am-7pm Apr-May, Oct-Nov, to 8pm Jul-Sep, 9.30am-5.45pm Nov-Mar) was built during the 14th century as a fortified palace for the pontifical court. The cavernous stone halls testify to the enormous wealth amassed by the papacy while it resided here.

The **Musée du Petit Palais** (☎ 04 90 86 44 58; pl du Palais; full price/pass €6/3; ☺ 10am-1pm & 2-6pm Wed-Mon Jun-Sep, 9.30am-1pm & 2-5.30pm Wed-Mon Oct-May), a former archbishop's palace, houses an outstanding collection of lavishly coloured 13th- to 16th-century Italian religious paintings.

Just up the hill from the cathedral is **Rocher des Doms**, a delightful bluff-top park that affords great views of the Rhône, Pont St-Bénézet, Villeneuve-lès-Avignon and the Alpilles. There's shade, breeze and benches aplenty up here – a good spot for a picnic.

The **Musée Lapidaire** (☎ 04 90 86 33 84; 27 rue de la Republic; full price/pass €2/1; ☺ 10am-1pm & 2-6pm Wed-Mon), close to the tourist office, is well worth a quick look for its somewhat random collection of Egyptian, Roman, Etruscan and early Christian marble statuary, delicate vases and bronze figurines.

Founded in the late 13th century, the charming **Villeneuve-lès-Avignon**, across the

Rhône from Avignon (and in a different *département*), is home of the **Musée Pierre de Luxembourg** (☎ 04 90 27 49 66; rue de la République; full price/pass €3/1.90; ☺ 10am-12.30 & 2-6.30pm, closed Mon mid-Sep–mid-Jun). If you're remotely interested in religious art it's well worth the visit for Enguerrand Quarton's lavish and dramatic 1453 painting *The Crowning of the Virgin*.

Tour Philippe-le-Bel (☎ 04 32 70 08 57; full price/pass €1.60/0.90; ☺ 10am-12.30pm & 2-6.30pm, closed Mon mid-Sep–mid-Jun), a 14th century defensive tower offering great views of Avignon's walled city, the river and the surrounding countryside, is a five-minute walk away. The spiral stairs up are narrow and numerous.

Festivals & Events

Avignon's streets buzz with life, street theatre, buskers and leafleters enticing you into the hundreds of shows held during the city's now world-famous **Festival d'Avignon**, held every year from early July to early August. Information on the official festival can be obtained from the **Bureau du Festival** (☎ 04 90 27 66 50; www.festival-avignon.com; Espace St-Louis, 20 rue du Portail Boquier) and for the fringe events contact **Avignon Public Off** (☎ 01 48 05 01 19; www.avignon-off.org).

Sleeping

During the festival it's practically impossible to find a hotel room at short notice. Rooms are readily available in August, however.

Camping Bagatelle (☎ 04 90 86 30 39; camping.bagatelle@wanadoo.fr; Île de la Barthelasse; s/d camp sites €11/13; ☺ year-round, reception 8am-9pm) An attractive, shaded camping ground just north of pont Édouard Daladier, 850m from the walled city. Take bus No 10 to the La Barthelasse stop. Follow the river to the camp site.

Auberge Bagatelle (☎ 04 90 85 78 45; auberge.bagatelle@wanadoo.fr; Île de la Barthelasse; dm €11-11.50, d €34, d with shared bathroom €26.50) This hostel has 210 beds and is part of a large, park-like area that includes Camping Bagatelle.

YMCA-UCJG (☎ 04 90 25 46 20; www.ymca-avignon.com; 7 bis Chemin de la Justice; s/d/tr €33/42/51, s/d/tr/q with shared bathroom €22/28/33/44) A good hostel in Villeneuve-lès-Avignon offering well-maintained rooms in a variety of sizes. Take bus No 10 to the Pont d'Avignon stop Monteau.

Hôtel Monclar (☎ 04 90 86 20 14; www.hotel-monclar.com; 13 Ave Monclar; s/d €26/45, with shared bathroom €20/30; P) Occupies a handsome, peppermint-shuttered 18th-century building by the train station (next to the tracks in fact, so noise can be a problem).

Hôtel du Parc (☎ 04 90 82 71 55; www.hotelduparc .fr.fm; 18 rue Agricol Perdiguier; s/d with shower €35/43, with shower & toilet €47/47) Comfortable one-star rooms and its location close to the tourist office are the main attractions for staying at this hotel.

Hôtel Splendid (☎ 04 90 86 14 46; www.avignon -splendid-hotel.com; 17 rue Agricol Perdiguier; s/d with shower €37/49, with shower & toilet €43/54). Near the Hôtel du Parc, this is a friendly hotel with recently renovated rooms.

Hôtel de Blauvac (☎ 04 90 86 34 11; www.hotel -blauvac.com; 13 rue Joseph Vernet; s/d/tr €48/51/65) Just off the main square you'll find the lovely 17th century former townhouse of the Marqui de Blauvac, now a friendly, comfortable and central hotel with convivial and stylish rooms.

Hôtel L'Europe (☎ 04 90 14 76 76; www.heurope .com; 12 pl Crillon; r €129-410; ✄ 🅿 ✕) A great four-star place with bags of charm. Napoleon Bonaparte is just one of the famous folk to have stayed here.

Eating

From Easter until mid-November, half of place de l'Horloge is taken over by tourist restaurants and cafés. *Menus* start at about €14.

Tapalocas (☎ 04 90 82 56 84; 15 rue Galante; dishes from €2; ✇ 11.45-1am) A down-to-earth Spanish tapas bar selling cheap, beer-session ballast.

Maison Nani (☎ 04 90 82 60 90; 29 rue Théodore Aubanel; plat du jour €9; ✇ lunch Mon-Sat, dinner Fri-Sun) A cheerful, popular bistro serving Provençal salads, grilled meat and fresh fish.

Le Bistrot d'Utopia (☎ 04 90 27 04 96; 4 rue des Escaliers Ste-Anne; mains from €13) Great for atmosphere and simple, tasty food like mushroom tarts with buttery pastry and ace desserts such as a slender lemon curd tart topped with a sliver of crystallised orange.

Les Halles has a great **food market** (pl Pie; ✇ 7am-1pm Tue-Sun). For groceries there's **Casino** (22 rue St-Agricol; ✇ 8am-12.45pm & 3-7.30pm Mon-Sat).

Getting There & Away
BUS

The **bus station** (halte routière; ☎ 04 90 82 07 35; information window ✇ 10.15am-1pm Mon-Fri, 2-6pm Mon-Fri) is in the basement of the building down the ramp to the right as you exit the train station on blvd St-Roch. Destinations include Aix-en-Provence (via the highway €13.90, one hour; on secondary roads €11.70, 1½ hours, four to six daily); Arles (€8.50, 1½ hours, six daily); Marseille (€16.40, 35 minutes direct, one daily) and Nice (€27, three hours, one daily).

Long-haul bus companies **Linebus** (☎ 04 90 85 30 48) and **Eurolines** (☎ 04 90 85 27 60; www .eurolines.fr) have offices at the far end of the bus platforms.

TRAIN

The **main train station** (information counters ✇ 9am-6.15pm Mon-Sat) is located across blvd St-Roch from Porte de la République. The **left-luggage** (from €3; ✇ 6am-10pm) is to the left as you exit the station

The brand new **TGV station** is a few kilometres from town. A **shuttle bus** (€2; ✇ half-hourly 5.30am-10.50pm) takes you from the TGV station to the bus stop just outside the main post office.

There are trains to Arles (€5.70, 20 minutes, 14 to 18 daily); Marseille (€15.50, 40 minutes); Nice (€38.80, three hours); Nîmes (€7.40, 30 minutes, 15 daily); and, by TGV, Paris' Gare de Lyon (€67, 2½ hours) and Lyon (€29.60, one hour).

Getting Around

Local TCRA bus tickets cost €1.05 each if bought from the driver. The two most important bus transfer points are the Poste stop at the main post office and place Pie. Bus No 10, which stops in front of the main post office and on the western side of the walled city near Porte de l'Oulle, heads to Villeneuve-lès-Avignon.

Rent a bike, scooter and larger motorbike from **Provence Bike** (☎ 04 90 27 92 61; 52 bd St Roch).

AROUND AVIGNON
Arles
pop 51,614

Arles began its ascent to prosperity and political importance in 49 BC, when the victorious Julius Caesar – to whom the city had given its support – captured and plundered Marseille, which had backed Caesar's rival, the general and statesman Pompey the Great.

Arles soon replaced Marseille as the region's major port, becoming the sort of Roman provincial centre that, within a century and a half, needed a 12,000-seat theatre and a 20,000-seat amphitheatre to entertain its citizens. Known as the **Arénes** and the **Théâtre Antique** they are still used for cultural events and bullfights. Vincent van Gogh (1853-90), Arles' most famous resident, painted many of his most celebrated works here.

The **tourist office** (☎ 04 90 18 41 20; www .tourisme.ville-arles.fr; Esplanade Charles de Gaulle; ☺ 9am-6.45pm Apr-Sep, to 4.45pm Mon-Sat, 10.30am-2.30pm Sun Oct-Mar) is a short trip along blvd des Lices. There is a **tourist office annexe** (☎ 04 90 49 36 90; ☺ 9am-1pm Jun-Sep) at the train station.

Arles' **train station** (information office ☺ 9am-12.30pm & 2-6.30pm Mon-Sat) is opposite the bus station. Major rail destinations include Nîmes (€6.60, 30 minutes), Montpellier (€12.20, one hour), Marseille (€11.60, 40 minutes) and Avignon (€5.70, 20 minutes).

The **bus station** (information office ☎ 08 00 19 94 13, 08 10 00 08 16; ☺ 7.30am-4pm Mon-Sat), at the end of ave Paulin Talabot, is about 1km north of les Arènes. **Telleschi** (☎ 04 42 28 40 22; 16 blvd de la Durance) runs services to Aix-en-Provence (€11.30, 1¾ hours).

CÔTE D'AZUR

The beautiful Côte d'Azur (Azure Coast), also known as the French Riviera, stretches along the Mediterranean coast from Toulon to the Italian border. Many towns along the coast – Nice, Monaco, Cannes, St Tropez – are well known as the playgrounds of the rich, famous and tanned. The reality is usually less glamorous but the Côte d'Azur still has a great deal to attract visitors: sun, 40km of beach, sea water as warm as 25°C, and numerous cultural activities.

East of Nice, the foothills of the Alps plunge into the Mediterranean. Three heart-stopping roads, known as *corniches*, take you eastwards from Nice to Menton and the Italian border. The Principality of Monaco is about midway between Nice and Menton.

NICE

pop 345,892

The capital of the Riviera, Nice makes a great base from which to explore the rest of the Côte d'Azur. The city has lots of relatively cheap places to stay and is only a short train or bus ride from Monaco, Cannes and other Riviera hot spots. It's also blessed with fine museums, a lively night life in the old city's narrow warren of streets, an old harbour and great markets.

Orientation

Ave Jean Médecin runs south from near the train station to place Masséna. The modern city centre, the area north and west of place Masséna, includes the upmarket pedestrianised streets of rue de France and rue Masséna. The Station Centrale and intercity bus station are three blocks east of place Masséna. The famous promenade des Anglais follows the gently curved beachfront from the city centre to the airport, 6km west.

Information

Le Change (☎ 04 93 88 56 80; 17 ave Thiers; ☺ 7.30am-8pm) Opposite the Gare Nice Ville, to the right as you leave the terminal building; offers decent rates.

Main post office (23 ave Thiers; ☺ 8am-7pm Mon-Fri, to noon Sat) Exchanges foreign currency.

Tourist office (☎ 04 92 70 74 07; www.nicetourism.com; ave Thiers; ☺ 8am-8pm Mon-Sat, 9am-7pm Sun Jun-Sep, 8am-7pm Mon-Sat, 9am-6pm Sun Oct-May) Next to the Gare Nice Ville (main train station).

Tourist office (☎ 08 92 70 74 07; fax 04 92 14 48 03; 5 promenade des Anglais; ☺ 8am-8pm Mon-Sat, 9am-7pm Sun Jun-Sep, 9am-6pm Mon-Sat Oct-May) Less crowded.

Worldwide Web Service (☎ 04 93 80 51 12; 32 rue Assalit; ☺ 10am-7pm Mon-Sat)

Sights

An excellent-value pass that gives free admission to some 60 Côte d'Azur museums is the Carte Musées Côte d'Azur. It costs €8/15/25 for one/five/seven days and is available at tourist offices and participating museums. Alternatively the Carte Musées Ville de Nice, which allows entry into all of Nice's museums except the Chagall, costs €6/18.30 for seven/15 days.

The **Musée d'Art Moderne et d'Art Contemporain** (☎ 04 93 62 61 62; ave St-Jean Baptiste; adult/student €4/2.50; ☺ 10am-6pm Wed-Mon) specialises in French and American avant-garde works from the 1960s to the present, which explode with colour in the light, large display spaces. Featured artists include Nice-born Yves Klein (1928-62), Andy Warhol, Christo, Marseille-born sculptor César and sculptor Nikki St-Phalle.

The **Musée National Message Biblique Marc Chagall** (☎ 04 93 53 87 20; adult/student €5.50/4, Jul & Aug €5.80/4.25; ☺ 10am-6pm Wed-Mon Jul-Sep, to 5pm

NICE

INFORMATION

Le Change.....................................1	D3
Main Post Office...........................2	C3
Main Tourist Office.......................3	D2
Police Headquarters.....................4	F3
Tourist Office Annexe...................5	D5
Worldwide Web Service................6	D2

SIGHTS & ACTIVITIES (pp363-6)

Flower Market...............................7	F5
Musée d'Art Moderne et d'Art	
Contemporain.............................8	G3
Musée National Message Biblique Marc	
Chagall.......................................9	E1
Russian Orthodox Cathedral of	
St-Nicolas.................................10	B2
WW1 Memorial...........................11	G5

To Blvd Auguste Reynard; Autoroute A8; Villa Saint Exupery (4km)

Blvd Joseph Garnier

Gare Nice Ville (Train Station)

Sud Train Station

Baie des Anges

To Airport (5km); Nice Ferber Office

To Cannes (34km)

SLEEPING (pp366-7)

Backpackers Chez Patrick........12	E2
Hôtel Belle Meunière...............13	D3
Hôtel Claire Meublé................14	D3
Hôtel du Centre......................15	D3
Hôtel Félix..............................16	D4
Hotel Hi.................................17	B4
Hôtel L'Oasis.........................18	C3
Hôtel Les Orangers.................19	D3
Hôtel Notre Dame...................20	D3
Hôtel Plaisance......................21	E2

Villa Eden..............................22	A5
Villa la Tour...........................23	H1

EATING (p367)

Chez Rene Socca....................24	H1
Fruit & Vegetable Market........25	D2
Le Merenda...........................26	F5
Le Pain Quotidien..................27	E5
Le Safari...............................28	G2
Monoprix Supermarket............29	E3
Nissa Socca..........................30	G2

DRINKING (pp367-8)

Chez Wayne's........................31	F4
Jonathan's.............................32	G2
Le Bar des Oiseaux................33	G2
Nocy-Bé...............................34	G2

TRANSPORT (p368)

ANT Airport Buses..................35	C5
ANT Airport Buses..................36	B5
Corsica Ferries Terminal...........37	G5
Corsica Ferries Terminal...........38	H6
Corsica Ferries Ticket Office......39	H5
Ferry Terminal.......................40	H6
Intercity Bus Station...............41	G1

FRANCE

0 |————————| 300 m
0 |————————| 0.2 miles

E

To Cimiez (1.2km); Musée Matisse (1.3km);
Musée est Site Archéologique (1.4km);
Monastère de Cimiez (1.5km)

F

Blvd Ymélénois
Mareuil

G

0 |——————| 100 m
0 |——————| 0.1 miles

H

24

23

1

Av Raymond
Comboul

Av Georg V

Av Dr V
de l'Olivetto

Av e de l'Olivetto

Ménard
9

Blvd de Cimiez

Montée de Cimiez

R du Collet

Paillon
41

Pl
St François

R de Pétrolière

R Marceau

Autoroute Urbaine Sud

Blvd Raimbaldi

Av de Cimiez

Av R Monez

Av de Normandie

Av Émile Chemin du Bois

Promenade du
Blvd Jean Jaurès

R Ste Claire

R de la Boucherie
32

R de la Loge

Parc du
Château

2

R Assalit

Av Pertinax

Blvd de Cimiez
Av Desambrois

Pl
Rossetti
33

R Centrale
R Benoit Bunico

R Rossetti

Allée Professeur Bérault

R Pertinax

R de la Préfecture
30

R Droite

Colline du
Château

12

21
R de Paris

R R Miron

R Notre
Dame
Foch

R de la Barillerie
34

VIEUX
NICE

R Av Maréchal

R E Trianu Lamartine

R Biscarra

4

Blvd Carabacel

Blvd Péghienatti

Av Gallieni

Cours Saleya
28

Av Auguste Gal

3

Av Jean Médecin

R Pastorelli

R Deloye

Dubouchage

R Pierre Dévoluy

R Delille

R Tonduti de l'Escarène

R A Mortier

Av St Jean Baptiste

R Gubernatis

R Alberti

R Gioffrédo

Esplanade des
Victoires

Av de la République

R Barla

Pl Arson

R Arson

Blvd Riquier

4

R Cassini

R de l'Hôtel des Postes

R Chauvain

8

Pl
Garibaldi

R Bonaparte

To Auberge de
Jeunesse (2.5km)

R de la
Liberté

Pasg Émile
Négrin

Pl
Masséna

Espace
Masséna

Sq
Général
Leclerc

R Félix Faure

Promenade du Paillon

Blvd Jean Jaurès

R Rossetti

Parc du
Château

Pl Île
de Beauté

R Foderé

Blvd

5

Av de Verdun

R Paradis

Jardin
Albert
1er

R St François de Paule

31

26
R A Mari

27

Préfecture

Pl Pierre
Gautier

VIEUX
NICE

Pl
Robilante

Q Papacino

Q Lunel

Bassin
Lympia

Q des Docks

Bassin
des
Amiraux

Q des Deux
Emmanuel

39

Carnot

6

Cours Saleya

Q des États - Unis

Colline du
Château

11

Q Rauba Capeu

37

Q Infernet

Bassin
du Commerce

38

Q du Commerce

40

To Monaco
via Corniche
Inférieure (N98)
(18km)

See Enlargement

Baie des Anges

*MEDITERRANEAN
SEA*

LP

FRANCE

Wed-Mon Oct-Jun) contains a series of large, impressive and colourful series of paintings of Old Testament scenes. Take bus No 15 from place Masséna to the front of the museum or walk.

The **Musée Matisse** (☎ 04 93 81 08 08; 164 ave des Arènes de Cimiez; adult/student €4/2.50; ☿ 10am-6pm Wed-Mon) houses a fine collection of works by Henri Matisse in the bourgeois district of Cimiez. Well-known pieces in the permanent collection include Matisse's blue paper cutouts of *Blue Nude IV* and *Woman with Amphora*. Take bus No 15, 17, 20, 22 or 25 from the Station Centrale to the Arènes stop.

The multicoloured **Russian Orthodox Cathedral of St-Nicolas** (☎ 04 93 96 88 02; ave Nicolas II; ☿ 9am-noon & 2.30-6pm, closed Sun morning), crowned by six onion domes, is opposite 17 blvd du Tzaréwich. Step inside and you're transported to Imperial Russia. Shorts, miniskirts and sleeveless shirts are forbidden.

Activities

A good way to see Nice is aboard the open-topped buses of **Le Grand Tour** (☎ 04 92 29 17 00; adult/student/child €17/13/9). Tours, with headphone commentary, last 1½ hours.

Free sections of **public beach** alternate with 15 **plages concédées** (private beaches), for which you have to pay by renting a chair (around €11 a day) or mattress (around €9).

On the beach you can hire a catamaran, paddleboats, sailboards and jet skis, go parascending and water-skiing, or give paragliding a shot. There are outdoor showers on every beach, and indoor showers and toilets opposite 50 promenade des Anglais.

Festivals & Events

The colourful **Carnaval de Nice**, held every spring around Mardi Gras (Shrove Tuesday), fills the streets with floats and musicians. The week-long **Nice Jazz Festival** (www.nicejazzfest.com) takes up the entire Arènes de Cimiez, Roman ruins and all.

Sleeping

Nice has a surfeit of reasonably priced places to stay, particularly in the city centre, around the main railway station, and along rue d'Angleterre, rue d'Alsace-Lorraine and ave Durante. Accommodation is plentiful (and pricier) close to and on the seafront. In summer budget places can be hard to find after 10am or 11am.

BUDGET

Auberge de Jeunesse (☎ 04 93 89 23 64; fax 04 92 04 03 10; route Forestière de Mont Alban; dm €14; ☿ curfew midnight) This is 4km east of the Gare Nice Ville. Rooms are locked from noon to 5pm. Take bus No 14 (last one at 8.20pm) from the Station Centrale bus terminal on place Général Leclerc, which is linked to the Gare Nice Ville by bus Nos 15 and 17, and get off at L'Auberge stop.

Villa St Exupery (☎ 04 93 84 42 83; www.villasaintexupery.com; 22 ave Gravier; dm/s/d from €18/28/44; P ☐) Out of town, this hostel in a lovely old former monastery has been recommended by a number of readers. There's no curfew, a friendly vibe and free Internet access, breakfast and station shuttle.

Backpackers Chez Patrick (☎ 04 93 80 30 72; chezpatrick@voila.fr; 32 rue Pertinax; dm €18-21, 2–3-bed r per person €20-25) A popular 24-bed spot. There's no curfew and Patrick, who runs the place, can direct party-mad backpackers to the hot spot of the moment.

The following budget hotels are near the train station – walk straight down the steps opposite the Gare Nice Ville onto ave Durante:

Hôtel Belle Meunière (☎ 04 93 88 66 15; fax 04 93 82 51 76; 21 ave Durante; dm with shower & toilet for under 26 yrs €15, d with shower €47, dm with shower & toilet €51) A great and central option. The large four-bed dorm rooms are posh, panelled affairs and the place touts a tree-studded garden to lounge in. Rates include breakfast.

Hôtel Les Orangers (☎ 04 93 87 51 41; fax 04 93 82 57 82; 10 bis ave Durante; dm €16, s/d with shower €25/40) Les Orangers is recommended for its large-windowed, sunlit rooms, although this scruffy old place could do with a refit. Rooms come with a fridge (and a hotplate on request).

MID-RANGE & TOP END

Hôtel du Centre (☎ 04 93 88 83 85; hotel-centre@webstore .fr; 2 rue de Suisse; s/d €50/59, d with hall shower €28.50) This is an attractively renovated place with very neat rooms.

Hôtel Notre Dame (☎ 04 93 88 70 44; fax 04 93 82 20 38; 22 rue de Russie; s/d/q €39/42/60) A basic but popular place (so book ahead) offering spacious rooms.

Hôtel Claire Meublé (☎ 04 93 87 87 61; hotel_clair _meuble@hotmail.com; 6 rue d'Italie; 2-/3-/4-/5-person studios €42/50/64/70) A spotless place near the train station with compact, fully equipped studios well suited for self-catering families and couples.

Hôtel Plaisance (☎ 04 93 85 11 90; hotelplaisance@ wanadoo.fr; 20 rue de Paris; s/d from €46/56; ❄ P) Soundproofed modern rooms with TVs, and modern bathrooms.

Hôtel L'Oasis (☎ 04 93 88 12 29; www.hotel-oasis -nice.com.fr; 23 rue Gounod; s/d from €43/84; ❄ P ✗) An attractive period house where the playwright Chekhov wrote his play *The Three Sisters*. In a quiet close near the sea, it has a verdant, shady garden, appealing rooms and parking (€8).

Hôtel Félix (☎ 04 93 88 67 73; www.hotel-felix. com; 41 rue Masséna; r low season €50, high season €70; ❄ 🖳) This hotel has considerable appeal, with small brightly coloured rooms equipped with hairdryers, air-con and satellite TV.

Villa Eden (☎ 04 93 86 53 70; hotelvilllaeden@caramail .com; 99 bis promenade des Anglais; s/d/tr €50/75/90; ❄ P) Across the street from the beach, this is a good option for beach bums. Some of the comfortable, old-fashioned rooms have sea-facing terraces.

Villa la Tour (☎ 04 93 80 08 15; www.villa-la-tour .com; 4 rue de la Tour; r from €56; ❄) A great new place in old Nice. Rooms are individually decorated with contemporary flair, there's a cute little roof patio, a good breakfast (continental/buffet €3.50/7) and, best of all, you're just a stumble from the bars and *socca* joints of the old town.

Hotel Hi (☎ 04 97 07 26 26; www.hi-hotel.com; 3 ave des Fleurs; rooms €175-500; 🖳 ❄ 🖳 ✗) Step inside this modern, hi-tech place and you could be forgiven for thinking you've somehow boarded an ultra-stylish, candy-coloured, inter-stellar spaceship. Philippe Starck had a hand in designing the functional, modular panelling in ice-cream limes and purples. There's a modish roof-top plunge pool overlooking town and the Alps.

Rooms are similarly striking with bright panels of colour and modern entertainment systems. A rather glam clientele, such as fashion designer Jean Paul Gaultier or rock stars like the band REM, may teleport in to join you.

Eating

The cours Saleya and the narrow streets of Vieux Nice are lined with restaurants, cafés and pizzerias. Local specialities to watch out for include *socca* (a thin layer of chickpea flour and olive oil batter fried on a griddle and served with pepper), *salade Niçoise*,

ratatouille and *farcis* (stuffed vegetables, especially stuffed zucchini flowers).

Nissa Socca (☎ 04 93 80 18 35; 5 rue Ste-Réparate; menu €13, dishes from €6; ⏰ closed Mon lunch & all day Sun) This is a good place to try many of those local specialties. It's a perennial favourite with locals.

Chez Rene Socca (☎ 04 93 92 05 73; rue Pairoliére; ⏰ 9am-10.30pm Jul-Aug, to 9pm rest of the year, closed Mon) A lively, rough and ready place to sample oily, tapas-style dishes for around €2, including good portions of *socca* (crepe). Order and take your food from the window but get your drinks from the waiters when seated.

Le Merenda (4 rue de la Terrasse; starters from €9, mains around €16; ⏰ Mon-Fri) Tiny and annoying (no phone, no credit cards, no phone reservations) but you won't be disappointed by the first-rate specialities including *pâte au pistou* (pasta with pesto sauce), stockfish and a range of French/Provençale dishes.

Le Safari (☎ 04 93 80 18 44; 1 cours Saleya; menu €28, mains from €14) Avoiding the heaviness of cheaper Provençale food, this local favourite brings a lighter touch to specialities such as *farcis* and stockfish. Good seafood choices include octopus salad and langoustine pasta.

Le Pain Quotidien (cnr rue Louis Gassin & Cours Saleya; breakfast from €6, brunch €18) *The* place in town to breakfast, perhaps by tackling the mother of all brunches. Choose your breakfast *formule*, enjoy the excellent hot chocolate, take in the colour and fragrance of the adjacent flower market from the terrace (or inside through the large windows) and be happy.

There's a fantastic **fruit & vegetable market** (⏰ 7am-1pm Tue-Sun) in front of the prefecture on cours Saleya. There are two **Monoprix supermarkets** (33 ave Jean Médecin; ⏰ 8.30am-8.30pm Mon-Sat; pl Garibaldi; ⏰ 8.30am-8pm Mon-Sat).

Drinking & Entertainment

Terraced cafés and bars, perfect for quaffing beers and sipping pastis, abound in Nice. Almost all nightlife is in Vieux Nice, which throbs with activity on summer nights. The most popular pubs in Nice are run by Anglophones, with happy hours and live music.

Chez Wayne's (☎ 04 93 13 46 99; 15 rue de la Préfecture; ⏰ 3pm-midnight) The best-known place for liquor-fuelled carousing. It opens later at weekends. Happy 'hour' is until 9pm.

FRANCE

Nocy-Bé (rue de la Prefecture) This is a cool, dark Moroccan-style tea house where you can sit low on cushions and sip sweet, refreshing mint teas.

Le Bar des Oiseaux (☎ 04 93 80 27 33; 5 rue St-Vincent; ✆ Mon-Sat) Offers a changing programme of music, theatre and philosophical discussion sessions. Jazz is the strong point. Expect to pay around €5 for admission when there's live music.

Jonathan's (☎ 04 93 62 57 62; 1 rue de la Loge) Another live music hot spot every night in summer.

Getting There & Away

AIR

Nice's international airport, **Aéroport International Nice-Côte d'Azur** (☎ 08 20 42 33 33), is located about 6km west of the city centre. The free shuttle bus connects both terminals.

BUS

Lines operated by some two dozen bus companies stop at the **intercity bus station** (☎ 04 93 85 61 81; 5 blvd Jean Jaurès). There's a busy information counter.

There are slow but frequent services until about 7.30pm daily to Cannes (€5.90, 1½ hours), Menton (€5.10, 1¼ hours) and Monaco (€3.90 return, 45 min). For long-haul travel, **Intercars** (☎ 04 93 80 08 70), at the bus station, takes you to various European destinations; it sells Eurolines tickets for buses to London, Brussels and Amsterdam.

TRAIN

Nice's main train station, **Gare Nice Ville** (Gare Thiers; ave Thiers), is 1.2km north of the beach. There are fast and frequent services (up to 40 trains a day in each direction) to towns along the coast including Cannes (€5.20, 40 minutes), Menton (€3.90, 35 minutes) and Monaco (€3, 20 minutes).

Two or three TGVs link Nice with Paris' Gare de Lyon (€81, 5½ hours), via Lyon (€55.50, 4½ hours).

Getting Around

Sunbus route No 23 (€1.30), which runs to the airport every 20 or 30 minutes from about 6am to 8pm, can be picked up at the Gare Nice Ville or on blvd Gambetta, rue de France or rue de la Californie.

Local buses, operated by Sunbus, cost €1.30/16 for a single/14 rides. After you

time-stamp your ticket, it's valid for one hour and can be used for one transfer or return. The Nice by Bus pass, valid for one/five/seven days costs €4/12.95/16.75 and includes a return trip to the airport. You can buy single trips, 14-trip cards and a day card on the bus.

CANNES
pop 68,214

The harbour, the bay, the hill west of the port called Le Suquet, the beachside promenade, the beaches and the people sunning themselves provide more than enough natural beauty to make at least a day trip here worth the effort.

Cannes is famous for its cultural activities and many festivals, the most renowned being the 10-day **Cannes Film Festival** in mid-May, which sees the city's population treble overnight.

The **tourist office** (☎ 04 92 99 84 22; www.cannes .com; ✆ 9am-8pm daily Jul-Aug, to 7pm Mon-Sat Sep-Jun) is on the ground floor of the Palais des Festivals. There's an **annexe** (☎ 04 93 99 19 77; ✆ 9am-7pm Mon-Sat) next to the train station.

Check email at **Cybercafé Webstation** (☎ 04 93 68 72 37; 26 rue Hoche; Internet per 30min/hr €3/6; ✆ 10am-11pm Mon-Sat).

Sights & Activities

One of the best ways to spend time here is to meander aimlessly east from the **Vieux Port** and its massive yachts, along the **Croisette** where you can sit and watch Cannes' human circus pass by in all its expensively-but-strangely-dressed, perma-tanned, facelifted, small-yappy-dog-carrying glory.

Housed in the chateau atop Le Suquet, the **Musée de la Castre** (☎ 04 93 38 55 26; adult/concession €3/2; ✆ 10am-1pm & 3-7pm Tue-Sun Jun-Aug, to 1pm & 2-6pm Tue-Sun Apr, May & Sep, to 1pm & 2-5pm Wed-Mon Oct-Mar) has a diverse collection of Mediterranean and Middle Eastern antiquities, as well as objects of ethnographic interest from all over the world.

Unlike Nice, Cannes is endowed with sandy **beaches**, most of which are sectioned off for guests of the fancy hotels lining blvd de la Croisette. Sun worshippers pay around €19 a day for the privilege of stretching out on a lounge chair. There's only a small strip of public sand near the Palais des Festivals. However, free public beaches, **Plages du Midi** and **Plages de la Bocca**, stretch westward from

CANNES

INFORMATION	
Cannes Réservation........1 D1	
Cybercafe Webstation.....2 D2	
Tourist Office Annexe......3 D1	
Tourist Office................4 D3	
SIGHTS & ACTIVITIES (pp368-70)	
Musée de la Castre..........5 A3	
Palais des Festivals et des	
Congrès........................6 D3	
SLEEPING (p370)	
Hôtel Florella.................7 F1	
Hôtel Florian..................8 E2	
Hôtel National................9 C2	
Le Chanteclair..............10 A2	

EATING (p370)	
Astoux & Brun..............11 B2	
Food Market.................12 E1	
La Piazza.....................13 B2	
Le Petit Lardon.............14 E2	
Lenôtre.......................15 D2	
Monoprix Supermarket....16 D1	
Sushikan.....................17 E2	
TRANSPORT (p371)	
Bus Station (to Nice).......18 B3	
CMC Ticket Office..........19 C2	
Trans Côte d'Azur Ticket Office..20 B4	
OTHER	
Palais Underground Car Park....(See 6)	

the Vieux Port along blvd Jean Hibert and blvd du Midi.

Cannes makes a good base for boat trips up and down the coast. **Trans Côte d'Azur** (☎ 04 92 98 71 30; www.trans-cote-azur.com; quai St-Pierre) runs boats to St Tropez or Monaco (adult/child €31/16 return), Île de Porquerolles (€46/21) and San Remo (€41/19.50) in Italy.

A good trip from Cannes is to the nearby **Îles de Lérins**. The eucalyptus- and pine-covered **Île Ste-Marguerite**, 1km from the mainland is where the enigmatic Man in the Iron Mask – immortalised by Alexandre Dumas in his novel *Le Vicomte de Bragelonne* (The Viscount of Bragelonne) – was held during the late 17th century. The **Musée de la Mer** (☎ 04 93 38 55 26; adult/child €3/2; museum & cells ❧ 10.30am-1.15pm & 2.15-5.45pm Wed-Mon Apr-Sep, closes 4.45pm Wed-Mon Oct-Mar), in the Fort Royal, has interesting exhibits dealing with the fort's history.

The smaller, forested 1.5km long and 400m wide **Île St-Honorat** is home to Cistercian monks who own the island but welcome people to visit their monastery and seven small chapels dotted around the island.

All boats for the isles leave from the same point on the quai des îles at the far end of the western arm of the harbour. **Compagnie Maritime Cannoise** (CMC; ☎ 04 93 38 66 33) runs ferries to Île Ste-Marguerite (€9 return, 20 minutes) and **Compagnie Esterel Chanteclair** (☎ 04 93 39 11 82) runs boats to Île St-Honorat (€10 return, 20 minutes).

Sleeping

Tariffs rise by up to 50% in July and August. During the film festival hotel rooms, many booked months in advance, are virtually impossible to find.

Parc Bellevue (☎ 04 93 47 28 97; fax 04 93 48 66 25; 67 ave Maurice Chevalier; camp sites per €20; ❧ Apr-Sep) In Cannes-La Bocca, this is the nearest place to camp, 5.5km west of the centre. Take No 9 from the bus station on place Bernard Cornut Gentille stops 400m away.

Le Chalit (☎ 04 93 99 22 11; www.lechalit.com; 27 ave du Maréchal Galliéni; bed in 4-/6-person dm €16/20; ❧ Jan-Oct, ❧ reception 8.30am-7.30pm) Around 300m northwest of the station, this is a friendly, pleasant private hostel. Sheets cost €3. There is no curfew.

Le Chanteclair (☎ /fax 04 93 39 68 88; 12 rue Forville; s/d €40/42, with shared bathroom €33/36) A well-run hotel with functional whitewashed rooms

in the colourful Le Suquet area. It's well located for many of the restaurants and the harbour.

Hôtel Florella (☎ 04 93 38 48 11; fax 04 93 99 22 15; 55 blvd de la République; s/d €60/64, with shared bathroom €40/45) A slightly tatty hotel but friendly, homely and good value.

Hôtel National (☎ 04 93 39 91 92; fax 04 92 98 44 06; 8 rue Maréchal Joffre; s/d 45/60; 🅿) The newly refurbished and well equipped rooms at this friendly hotel are soundproofed and have TVs and hairdryers. Book ahead and try to get a room overlooking the courtyard.

Hôtel Florian (☎ 04 93 39 24 82; fax 04 92 99 18 30; 31 rue Commandant André; s/d €62/72; 🅿) Neat and modern, all rooms at this central hotel have private bath, TV, telephone and hairdryers.

Hôtel Moliére (☎ 04 93 38 16 16; www.hotel-moliere .com; 5 rue Moliére; s/d from €79/97; 🅿) This immaculate, comfortable period place has a picture-postcard garden and a pastel-pink wedding cake exterior. Some rooms have balconies.

Eating

Le petit Lardon (☎ 04 93 39 06 28; 3 rue du Batéguier; menu €21) A small, intimate, friendly and reliable place for reasonably priced local fare, such as *soupe de poisson* and *anchoiade*.

Astoux & Brun (☎ 04 93 39 21 87; 21 rue Félix Faure; menu €28; ❧ 10am-1am) This is the place for seafood. Every type and size of oyster is available by the dozen here, as well as elaborate fish platters, scallops, and mussels stuffed with garlic and parsley. In summer, chefs draw the crowds by preparing the shellfish out front.

La Piazza (☎ 04 92 98 60 80; 9 pl Bernard Cornut Gentille; menu €19, mains €12) This sprawling, friendly establishment offers the best homemade pasta, risotto and pizza in town.

Sushikan (☎ 04 93 39 86 13; 5 rue Florian; dishes €2.50-4.50) A smart sushi-on-a-conveyor-belt place, which also does takeaways.

Lenotre (☎ 04 92 92 56 00; 63 rue d'Antibes; breakfast €7, lunch €12 ❧ 8am-4.30pm) With a serene, classy dining room above the patisserie counter, this is a great place to sip espresso, take breakfast or enjoy a light lunch of tarts and pastries among well-to-do ladies who lunch.

Food markets (pl Gambetta & rue du Marché Forville) are held every morning except Monday. Large supermarkets include **Monoprix** (9 rue Maréchal Foch).

Getting There & Away

Buses to Nice (€5.90, 1½ hours, every 20 minutes) leave from place Bernard Cornut Gentille. There is an **information office** (☎ 04 93 39 11 39).

From the **train station** (☎ 36 35; rue Jean Jaurès) there are regular services to Nice (€5.20, 40 minutes, two an hour) and Marseille (€22.30, two hours).

ST TROPEZ

pop 5542

A destination for the jet set – and in summer too many visitors for comfort – St Tropez has long since ceased to be the quiet, charming, isolated fishing village that attracted artists, writers and the gliteratti here in the 20th century. The year things really changed for good was 1956, when *Et Dieu Créa la Femme* (And God Created Woman) starring Brigitte Bardot was shot here. Its stunning success brought about St Tropez' rise to stardom – or destruction, depending on your point of view.

Away from the conspicuous consumption going on aboard the harbourside yachts, it can still be a place of charm. Sitting in a café on place des Lices in late May, watching the locals play *pétanque* (bowls) in the shade of the age-old plane trees, you could be in any little Provençal village (if you squint to ignore those exclusive boutiques). There is a helpful **tourist office** (☎ 04 94 97 45 21; www .saint-tropez.st; quai Jean Jaurès; ☒ 9.30am-8.30pm Jul-Aug, to 12.30pm & 2-7pm Apr-Jun, Sep & Oct, to 12.30pm & 2-6pm Nov-Mar) overlooking the boats.

Sights & Activities

The **Musée de l'Annonciade** (☎ 04 94 97 04 01; pl Grammont, Vieux Port; adult/student €4.50/2.50; ☒ 10am-noon & 3-7pm Wed-Mon Jun-Sep, to noon & 2-6pm Wed-Mon Oct-May, closed Nov) contains an impressive collection of modern art, including works by Matisse, Bonnard, Dufy, Derain and Rouault and Signac.

If you're bored with watching the antics of the rich and (maybe not so) famous, the **Citadelle de Saint Tropez** (☎ 04 94 97 59 43; adult/concession €4/2.50; ☒ 10am-12.30pm & 1.30-6.30pm Apr-Sep, to 12.30pm & 1.30-5.30pm Oct-Mar) is worth strolling to for the views across the bay, a view you may share with the resident peacocks. Inside the citadelle there are displays on the town's maritime history and the Allied landings that took place here in 1944.

About 4km southeast of the town is the start of a magnificent sandy beach, **Plage de Tahiti**, and its continuation, Plage de Pampelonne. It runs for about 9km between Cap du Pinet and the rocky Cap Camarat.

Sleeping & Eating

There's not a cheap hotel to be found in St Tropez. However, to the southeast along Plage de Pampelonne there are plenty of multi-star camping grounds.

Le Baron (☎ 04 94 97 06 57; fax 04 94 97 58 72; 23 rue de l'Aïoli; r €54-100; ☒) Well worth the cash, Le Baron is calm and quiet. Rooms – all with TV and private bath – overlook the citadel. Some have balconies. You will need to book ahead.

Lou Cagnard (☎ 04 94 97 04 24; www.hotel-lou -cagnard.com; 18 ave Paul Roussel; rooms €44-100; ☒ P) A very pleasant option with attractive rooms containing TV and telephone in a traditional Provençale *mas* (farmhouse), surrounded by shrubs and plants.

Hôtel La Méditerranée (☎ 04 94 97 00 44; www .hotelmediterranee.org; 21 blvd Louis Blanc; r low/high season €50/150; ☒) This solid, period house has recently refurbished rooms, a cosy restaurant and courtyard garden, and a proprietor who can tell you exactly where all the St Tropez' hotspots are.

La Table du Marché (☎ 04 94 97 85 20; 38 rue Georges Clemenceau; lunch/dinner formule of main, dessert & glass of wine €18, menu €25; ☒ lunch & dinner) A stylish place for great pastries in the café at the front (daytime only), for sushi upstairs (summer only) or excellent, reasonably priced brasserie-style food (like scallop raviolis in thyme butter or tomato and basil tart) at the back.

Le Fregate (☎ 04 94 97 07 08; 52-54 rue Allard; menu €19-27; ☒ Thu-Tue) The blue and white décor heralds excellent fish dishes. Try the *aïoli* at €15 if it's on the daily menu.

Le Café (☎ 04 94 97 44 69; pl des Lices) St Tropez' most historic café was one of the former haunts of BB and her glam friends.

Getting There & Away

St Tropez' **bus station** (ave Général de Gaulle) is on the southwest edge of town on the main road out. There's an **information office** (☎ 04 94 54 62 36; ☒ 8am-noon & 2-6pm Mon-Fri, to noon Sat). A day trip by boat from Nice or Cannes can be a good way to avoid St Tropez' notorious traffic jams and high hotel prices.

MENTON

pop 29,266

Menton, a confection of elegant historic buildings in sugared-almond pastels a few kilometres from the Italian border, is said to be the warmest spot on the Côte d'Azur (especially in winter). It's popular with older holiday-makers, making the town's nightlife a tad tranquil compared to other spots along the coast. Artist Jean Cocteau lived here from 1956 to 1958. Today, Menton retains a sedate charm free of the pretensions found elsewhere on the Côte d'Azur.

The **tourist office** (☎ 04 92 41 76 76; www.menton .fr; 8 ave Boyer; ☒ 9am-7pm Mon-Sat, 10am-noon Sun Jul-Aug; 8.30am-12.30pm & 2-6pm Mon-Fri, 9am-noon & 2-6pm Sat low season) is inside the Palais de l'Europe.

The early-17th-century **Église St-Michel** (Church of St Michael; ☒ 10am-noon & 3-5.15pm, closed Sat morning), the grandest and possibly prettiest Baroque church in this part of France, is perched in the centre of the Vieille Ville.

Sleeping

Camping Saint Michel (☎ 04 93 35 81 23; route des Ciappes de Castellar; ☒ 1 Apr-15 Oct) This two-star camping ground is 1km northeast of the train station up Plateau St-Michel, close to the youth hostel.

Auberge de Jeunesse (☎ 04 93 35 93 14; fax 04 93 35 93 07; Plateau St-Michel; dm with breakfast €14.40; ☒ closed noon-5pm, 10am to 5pm in winter; ℗) In a lovely spot on a hill overlooking town and bay. From the train station this hostel's quite a hike uphill or take a Line 6 bus to the camping ground. Curfew is midnight (10pm in winter).

Hôtel Le Terminus (☎ 04 92 10 49 80; fax 04 92 10 49 81; pl de la Gare; s/d €30/40, with shared bathroom €28/31; ℗) A welcoming, clean place with a few rooms right next to the station. Hall showers are free.

Hôtel de Londres (☎ 04 93 35 74 62; www.hotel -de-londres.com; 15 ave Carnot; s/d from €53/58, with shared bathroom from €35/38; ℗ ☒) An appealing place with a dining terrace and garden near the seafront.

Getting There & Away

The **bus station** (☎ 04 93 28 43 27) is next to 12 promenade Maréchal Leclerc, the northern continuation of ave Boyer. There's an **information office** (☎ 04 93 35 93 60). Buses run to Monaco (€2.10 return, 30 minutes), Nice (€5.10 return, 1¼ hours). Trains to Ventimiglia cost €2.10 and take 10 minutes.

MONACO

pop 30,000

Tiny, glamorous Monaco (Principauté de Monaco), covering a mere 1.95 sq km, is a fantasy land of perfectly groomed streets, lush gardens, chic boutiques and extravagantly opulent 19th-century pleasure palaces. With a photogenic royal family whose heritage stretches back to the 13th century and a continual stream of high-rollers filling Monte Carlo's famous casino or gathering for the annual Formula One Grand Prix race, Monaco never seems to go out of style.

The Principality of Monaco has been under the rule of the Grimaldi family for most of the period since 1297 and is a sovereign state with close ties to France. It has been ruled since 1949 by Prince Rainier III (b1923), whose sweeping constitutional powers make him much more than a mere figurehead. Rainier's rule modernised Monaco and weaned it from its dependence on gambling revenue, and his marriage to the much beloved Grace Kelly (remembered from her Hollywood days as an actress) restored Monaco's glamour.

Direction du Tourisme et des Congrès de la Principauté de Monaco (☎ 92 16 61 16; www.monaco-tourisme.com; 2a blvd des Moulins; ☒ 9am-7pm Mon-Sat, 10am-noon Sun) is across the public gardens from the casino. From mid-June to late-September several tourist information kiosks open around the harbour.

SIGHTS & ACTIVITIES

The changing of the guard takes place daily outside the **Palais du Prince** (☎ 93 25 18 31), at the southern end of rue des Remparts in Monaco Ville, at precisely 11.55am. You can also visit the **state apartments** (adult/child €6/3; ☒ 9.30am-6.30pm Jun-Sep, 10am-5pm Oct, closed Nov-May) with commentary through audioguides.

If you're planning to see just one aquarium during your whole trip, the world-renowned **Musée Océanographique de Monaco** (☎ 93 15 36 00; ave St-Martin, Monaco Ville; adult/student €11/6; ☒ 9.30am-7pm Jul-Aug, to 6.30pm Apr-Jun, to 7pm Sep) should be it. The aquarium has 90 tanks, and upstairs there are all sorts of exhibits on ocean exploration. Bus Nos 1 and 2 are the alternatives to a relatively long walk up the hill.

MONACO

| 0 | 300 m |
| 0 | 0.2 miles |

INFORMATION
Centre Hospitalier Princess Grace..1 A6
Direction du Tourisme et des Congrès
  de la Principauté de Monaco....2 C2
Tourist Information Kiosk............3 C4
Tourist Information Kiosk............4 C4

SIGHTS & ACTIVITIES (pp372-4)
Cathedral.....................................5 C5
Musée Océanographique de
  Monaco.....................................6 C5
Palais du Prince...........................7 B5
Rowing Club...............................8 C4

SLEEPING (p374)
Azur Hotel...................................9 C2
Hôtel Cosmopolite.....................10 C2

EATING (p374)
Planet Pasta..............................11 B4
U Cavagnetu.............................12 C5

ENTERTAINMENT (p372)
Casino de Monte Carlo.............13 D3

SHOPPING (p374)
Centre Commercial Le
  Métropole................................14 D2

OTHER
Casino Parking...........................15 C3
Public Lift Entrance....................16 B5
Public Lift Entrance....................17 A5
Public Lift Entrance....................18 A4
Public Lift Entrance....................19 B4
Public Lift Entrance....................20 C5
Public Lift Entrance....................21 B3
Public Lift Entrance....................22 D1
Public Lift Entrance....................23 D1
Public Lift.................................24 A5
Public Lift.................................25 D1

FRANCE (Beausoleil)

Monte Carlo

Monaco Train Station

La Condamine

Moneghetti

Port de Monaco

Monaco Ville

Port de Fontvieille

Fontvieille

Parc Fontvieille

MEDITERRANEAN SEA

To Nice (16km)

FRANCE

Although rather unspectacular, the 1875 Romanesque-Byzantine **cathedral** (4 rue Colonel) has one draw: the grave of former Hollywood film star Grace Kelly (1929–82), which lies on the western side of the cathedral choir. Her modest tombstone, which is inscribed with the Latin words *Gratia Patricia Principis Rainerii III,* is heavily adorned with flowers.

SLEEPING

Monaco has no hostels or cheap hotels so neighbouring Beausoleil is where to head for accommodation. When calling these hotels from Monaco (eg from the train station), dial 00 33, then the listed phone number (dropping the first 0).

Azur Hotel (☎ 04 93 78 01 25; www.azurhotel.biz; 12 blvd de la Republique; s/d/tr from €42/52/62; 🗷) This is probably the pick of places in the area for value, appealing décor and location.

Hôtel Cosmopolite (☎ 04 93 78 36 00; fax 04 93 41 84 22; 19 blvd du Général Leclerc; s/d €51/54) Cosmopolite has comfortable rooms with TV, telephone, minibars and hairdryers.

EATING

There are a few sandwich and snack places inside the Centre Commercial Le Métropole. One closely kept local secret, until now, is the very reasonable food available in the quiet little bar above the **rowing club** (quai des Etats Unis; mains €9-12), where locals smoke and play cards.

Planet Pasta (☎ 93 50 97 02; 6 rue Imberty; pizza/pasta €9-13, mains €17-22) This is a reliable choice, serving filling portions of what its name advertises in a busy, often hot and stuffy dining room.

U Cavagnetu (☎ 93 30 35 80; 14 rue Comte Félix-Gastaldi; lunch menu €14.50, dinner menu €20-25) One of the few affordable restaurants specialising in Monégasque dishes.

GETTING THERE & AWAY

Intercity buses depart from various stops around the city. There's an **information desk** (ave Prince Pierre) at Monaco train station. Taking the train along the coast is a highly recommended experience – the sea and the mountains provide a truly magnificent sight. There are frequent trains eastwards to Menton (€1.70, 10 minutes), Nice (€2.90, 20 minutes) and Ventimiglia in Italy (€3, 25 minutes).

LANGUEDOC-ROUSSILLON

pop 2.295 million

Languedoc-Roussillon is something of a three-eyed hybrid, cobbled together in the 1960s by the merging, for administrative purposes, of two historic regions. **Bas Languedoc** (Lower Languedoc), land of bullfighting, rugby and robust red wines and home to all the major towns, such as Montpellier, the region's vibrant capital, sun-baked Nîmes with its magnificent Roman amphitheatre – and fairytale Carcassonne, with its witches' hat turrets, hovering over the hot plain like a medieval mirage. On the coast, good beaches abound.

Deeper inland, **Haut Languedoc** (Upper Languedoc) occupies rugged, sparsely populated mountainous terrain, great for trekking, mountain pasture, forests and hearty cuisine while **Roussillon**, abutting the Pyrenees, constantly glances over the frontier to Catalonia, in Spain, with which it shares a common language and culture.

MONTPELLIER

pop 230,000

The 17th-century philosopher John Locke may have had one glass of Minervois wine too many when he wrote: 'I find it much better to go twise (sic) to Montpellier than once to the other world'. Paradise it ain't, but Montpellier continues to attract visitors with its reputation for innovation and vitality and a public transport system second to none. Students form nearly a quarter of the population.

Orientation & Information

Montpellier's mostly pedestrianised historic centre, girdled by wide boulevards, has place de la Comédie at its heart. Northeast of this square is esplanade Charles de Gaulle, a pleasant tree-lined promenade. Westwards, between rue de la Loge and Grand Rue Jean Moulin, sprawls the city's oldest quarter, a web of narrow alleys and fine *hôtels particuliers* (private mansions). There's Internet at **Point Internet** (☎ 04 67 54 57 60; 54 rue de l'Aiguillerie; per hr €1.60; 🕑 9.30am-midnight Mon-Sat, 10.30am-midnight Sun). The **tourist office** (☎ 04 67 60 60 60; www.ot-montpellier.fr; 🕑 9am-6.30pm or 7.30pm Mon-Fri,

10am-6pm Sat, 10am-1pm & 2-5pm Sun) is at the southern end of esplanade Charles de Gaulle.

Sights

Musée Languedocien (☎ 04 67 52 93 03; 7 rue Jacques Cœur; adult/student €5/3; ☼ 3-6pm Mon-Sat Jul-Aug, 2-5pm Mon-Sat Sep-Jun) displays the area's rich archaeological finds as well as *objets d'art* from the 16th to 19th centuries.

Sleeping

The closest camping grounds are around the suburb of Lattes, some 4km south of the city centre.

Oasis Palavasienne (☎ 04 67 15 11 61; www.oasis -palavasienne.com; route de Palavas; camp sites €16.70-24.50; ☼ mid-May–Aug; ☒) This shady camping ground has a large pool. Prices vary according to the season. Take bus No 17 from Montpellier bus station.

Auberge de Jeunesse (☎ 04 67 60 32 22; montpel lier@fuaj.org; 2 impasse de la Petite Corraterie; dm €8.90; ☼ mid-Jan–mid-Dec) Montpellier's HI-affiliated youth hostel is just off rue des Écoles Laïques. The grandiose mosaic entrance contrasts with its basic dorms but who can complain when there's a friendly bar and a cheap bed? Take the tram to the Louis Blanc stop.

Hôtel des Étuves (☎ 04 67 60 78 19; www.hotel desetuves.fr, in French; 24 rue des Étuves; s €20.50-31, d €32-38) This welcoming, 13-room family hotel creeps around a spiral staircase like a vine.

Hôtel Le Guilhem (☎ 04 67 52 90 90; www.hotel -le-guilhem.com; 18 rue Jean-Jacques Rousseau; s €71-78, d €71-135; ☒) Occupying a couple of interconnecting 16th-century buildings, Hôtel Le Guilhem's rooms are exquisitely and individually furnished. Nearly all have views of the cathedral and overlook a tranquil garden. Room 100 (€135) has its own little terrace and garden.

Eating & Drinking

You'll find plenty of cheap and cheerful places on rue de l'Université, rue des Écoles Laïques and the streets interlinking them. Place de la Comédie is alive with cafés where you can drink and watch street entertainers strut their stuff. Smaller, more intimate, squares include place Jean Jaurès and place St-Ravy. With over 60,000 students, Montpellier has a profusion of places to drink and dance.

Roule Ma Poule (☎ 04 67 60 36 15; 20 pl Candolle; plat du jour €7.50) Like most places in this area, Roule Ma Poule pulls in a mainly student crowd with its decent, cheap fare and a quiet, atmospheric location in a shady old town square.

Le Ban des Gourmands (☎ 04 67 65 00 85; 5 pl Carnot; menu €25, mains €16-18; ☼ Tue-Fri & Sat dinner Sep-Jul) South of the train station and a favourite of locals in the know, this appealing restaurant, run by a young family team, serves delicious local cuisine.

Tripti Kulai (☎ 04 67 66 30 51; 20 rue Jacques Cœur; salads €8.50, menu €11 & €15; ☼ noon-9.30pm Mon-Sat) Barrel-vaulted and cosy, this popular vegetarian place stands out for the inventiveness of many of its dishes.

Mannekin-Pis (110 rue des Balances) This little neighbourhood bar serves eight brands on draught and around 100 in bottles.

The city's **food markets** include **Halles Castellane** (rue de la Loge), the biggest, and **Halles Laissac** (rue Anatole France).

Getting There & Away

Montpellier's **airport** (☎ 04 67 20 85 00) is 8km southeast of town. British Airways flies three times per week (daily in summer) to/from London (Gatwick) and Ryanair operates daily to/from London (Stansted). Air France has up to 10 daily flights to Paris.

The **bus station** (☎ 04 67 92 01 43; rue du Grand St-Jean) is an easy walk from the train station. **Hérault Transport** (☎ 08 25 34 01 34) runs hourly buses to La Grande Motte (No 106; €1.25, 35 minutes) from Odysseum at the end of the tram line.

Eurolines (☎ 04 67 58 57 59; ticketing & information office 8 rue de Verdun) has buses to most European destinations including Barcelona (€27, five hours), London (€93, 17 hours) and Amsterdam (€87, 21 hours). **Linebus** (☎ 04 67 58 95 00) mainly operates services to destinations in Spain.

Major destinations from Montpellier's two-storey **train station** include Paris' Gare de Lyon by TGV (€70 to €83, 3½ hours, 12 daily), Carcassonne (€19.50, 1½ hours, six to eight daily), Millau (€21.80, 1½ hours, two daily). Over 20 trains daily go northwards to Nîmes (€7.50, 30 minutes).

CARCASSONNE

pop 46,250

From afar, Carcassonne looks like some fairy-tale medieval city. Bathed in late-afternoon sunshine and highlighted by dark clouds, La Cité, as the old walled city is known, is truly breathtaking. Once you're inside the fortified walls, La Cité is far less magical. Luring over two million visitors each year, it can be a tourist hell in high summer.

Orientation & Information

The River Aude divides the Ville Basse from the Cité, on a hill 500m southeast. Pedestrianised rue Georges Clemenceau leads from the train station and Canal du Midi southwards through the heart of the lower town.

The **tourist office** (☎ 04 68 10 24 30; www.carcassonne-tourisme.com; 28 rue Verdun; ♥ 9am-7pm Jul-Aug, to 6pm Sep-Jun) has local information.

Sights

Dramatically illuminated at night, **La Cité** is one of Europe's largest city fortifications. Only the lower sections of the walls are original; the rest, including the anachronistic witch's-hat roofs (the originals were altogether flatter and weren't covered with slate), were stuck on by Viollet-le-Duc in the 19th century.

The entry fee to the 12th-century **Château Comtal** (adult/student/child €6.10/4.10/free; ♥ 9.30am-6.30pm Apr-Sep, to 5pm Oct-Mar) lets you visit the castle itself and also join a 30- to 40-minute **guided tour** of both castle and ramparts.

Sleeping

Camping de la Cité (☎ 04 68 25 11 77; www.campeoles .com; route de St-Hilaire; camp sites €13.50-19 ♥ mid-Mar–mid-Oct) A walking and cycling trail from the camping ground leads to La Cité and the Ville Basse. From mid-June to mid-September, bus No 8 connects it with La Cité and the train station.

Auberge de Jeunesse (☎ 04 68 25 23 16; carcassonne@fuaj.org; rue Vicomte Trencavel; dm €15.50; ♥ Feb–mid-Dec; 🖳) Carcassonne's cheery, welcoming, HI-affiliated youth hostel is in the heart of La Cité. It has a members kitchen, snack bar offering light meals and a great outside terrace. Breakfast is included. Although it has 120 beds, it's smart to reserve year-round.

Hôtel Astoria (☎ 04 68 25 31 38; hotel-astoria@ wanadoo.fr; 18 rue Tourtel; d €20, with shower €29, with bathroom €32-36; 🅿) The new owners have re-painted all the rooms and laid fresh tiles or parquet at this hotel and its equally agreeable annexe. Great value.

Hôtel au Royal (☎ 04 68 25 19 12; godartcl@wanadoo .fr; 22 blvd Jean Jaurès; d €36-65; ♥ Jan-Nov; 🅿) At this attractive mid-range option you're guaran-

teed a copious, varied breakfast. Rooms are comfortable, well appointed and equipped with ceiling fans and those facing the busy street all have double glazing.

Eating

Au Bon Pasteur (☎ 04 68 25 49 63; 29 rue Armagnac; menu €13-22; ♥ closed Sun-Mon Jul-Aug, Sun & Wed Sep-Jun) At this welcoming, intimate family restaurant, you can warm yourself in winter with their yummy cassoulet or *choucroute* (sauerkraut). Year-round, their *menu classique* (€13) and *formules de midi* (lunch specials; €9.50 to €11) both represent excellent value.

La Divine Comédie (☎ 04 68 72 30 36; 29 blvd Jean Jaurès; pizzas €8-9.50, mains €12.50-14.50; ♥ Mon-Sat) Beside Hôtel Central, this restaurant serves both pizzas and regional dishes on its pleasant outside terrace.

Restaurant Gil (☎ 04 68 47 85 23; 32 route Minervoise; menu €15-33, mains €9-19) Here you'll enjoy quality, Catalan-influenced cuisine. Of note is the quality of its fresh seafood (€10 to €15), mostly served grilled and unsmothered by superfluous sauces or adornment.

There's a **covered market** (rue Verdun; ♥ Mon-Sat) and an **open-air market** (pl Carnot; ♥ Tue, Thu & Sat).

Getting There & Away

Carcassonne-Salvaza airport (☎ 04 68 71 96 46), 5km from town, has precisely two flights daily – **Ryanair** (☎ 04 68 71 96 65) to/from London (Stansted) and to/from Brussels (Charleroi). Carcassonne is on the main line linking Toulouse (€12.10, 50 minutes) and Montpellier (€18.90, 1½ hours).

NÎMES

pop 134,000

Nîmes is graced by some of France's best-preserved Roman buildings. Founded by Emperor Augustus, the Roman Colonia Nemausensis reached its zenith during the 2nd century AD, receiving its water from a Roman aqueduct system that included the Pont du Gard, a magnificent arched bridge 23km northeast of town. Ransacked by the Vandals in the early 5th century, the city began a decline, and has never quite recovered. For information drop in to the **tourist office** (☎ 04 66 58 38 00; www.ot-nimes.fr; 6 rue Auguste; ♥ 8.30am-7pm Mon-Fri, 8am-8pm Jul-Aug, 9am-7pm Sat & 10am-5pm Sun year-round).

Sights

A **combination ticket** (adult/child €5.70/4.65) admits you to both Les Arènes and Tour Magne. Alternatively, pick up a **three-day pass** (adult/child €10/5), giving access to all of Nîmes' museums and sites, from the tourist office or the first place you visit.

LES ARÈNES

This superb Roman amphitheatre (adult/child €4.65/3.40; ☼ 9am-7pm mid-Mar–mid-Oct, 10am-5pm mid-Oct–mid-Mar), built around AD 100 to seat 24,000 spectators, is wonderfully preserved, even retaining its upper storey, unlike its counterpart in Arles.

MAISON CARRÉE

This well-preserved rectangular Roman temple, today called the Maison Carrée (Square House; ☼ as for Les Arènes), was built around AD 5 to honour Emperor Augustus' two adopted sons. It has survived the centuries as a medieval meeting hall, private residence, stable, church and, after the Revolution, archive.

The striking glass and steel building across the square, completed in 1993, is the **Carré d'Art** (Square of Art), housing the municipal library and Musée d'Art Contemporain. Designed by British architect Sir Norman Foster, it's a wonderful, airy building.

FÉRIAS & BULLFIGHTS

Nîmes becomes more Spanish than French during its *férias*. Each – the three-day Féria Primavera (Spring Festival) in February, the five-day Féria de Pentecôte (Whitsuntide Festival) in June, and the three-day Féria des Vendanges coinciding with the grape harvest on the third weekend in September – is marked by daily *corridas* (bullfights). The **Bureau de Locations des Arènes** (☎ 04 66 02 80 90; 2 rue de la Violette) sells tickets.

Sleeping

Auberge de Jeunesse (☎ 04 66 68 03 20; nimes@fuaj .org; 257 chemin de l'Auberge de Jeunesse, la Cigale; dm €13.25) Freshly and comprehensively renovated, this hostel is in a lovely park 3.5km northwest of the train station. Take bus No 2, direction Alès or Villeverte, and get off at the Stade stop.

Hôtel de La Mairie (☎ 04 66 67 65 91; fax 04 66 76 07 92; 11 rue des Greffes; s €23, with shower €30, d with bathroom €39-42; ☼ closed 15-31 Oct) Several rooms in this hyperfriendly two-star, 13-room hotel

have separate toilet. Ceilings are high and rooms cool, even in high summer.

Hôtel Amphithéâtre (☎ 04 66 67 28 51; hotel-amphitheatre@wanadoo.fr; 4 rue des Arènes; s €37-40, d €47-59; ☼ Feb-Dec; ☒ ☒) The friendly Amphithéâtre, once a pair of 18th-century mansions, is now run by a young family. Rooms are decorated in warm, woody colours and named after writers or painters; we suggest Montesquieu or Arrabal (€59), both large, with balconies overlooking pedestrian place du Marché.

Eating

La Truye qui Filhe (☎ 04 66 21 76 33; 9 rue Fresque; menu €8.70; ☼ noon-2pm Mon-Sat, closed Aug) Within the vaults of a restored 14th-century inn, this, the bargain of Nîmes, blends a self-service format with a homely atmosphere and does a superb-value *menu*.

Restaurant Le Menestrel (☎ 04 66 67 54 45; 6 rue École Vieille; menu €15-22; ☼ closed all day Mon & Tue lunch) *The* place for quality local cuisine.

There are colourful Thursday markets in the old city in July and August. The large covered food market is in rue Général Perrier.

Getting There & Away

Nîmes' **airport** (☎ 04 66 70 49 49), 10km southeast of the city on the A54, handles precisely one plane daily – the Ryanair flight to/from London Stansted.

The **bus station** (rue Ste-Félicité) is just south of the train station. Regional destinations include Pont du Gard (€5.40, 45 minutes, up to seven daily). There are also buses to/from Avignon (€7.30, 1½ hours, seven daily).

Long-haul operator **Eurolines** (☎ 04 66 29 49 02) covers most European destinations including London (€95) and Amsterdam (€87) and, together with **Line Bus** (☎ 04 66 29 50 62), services to/from Spain.

There's an **SNCF sales office** (11 rue de l'Aspic). Ten TGVs daily run to/from Paris' Gare de Lyon (€68.90 to €82.80, three hours). There are frequent services to/from Arles (€6.60, 30 minutes), Avignon (€7.40, 30 minutes), Marseille (€16.20, 1¼ hours) and Montpellier (€7.50, 30 minutes).

AROUND NÎMES
Pont du Gard

The Pont du Gard, a Unesco World Heritage site, is an exceptionally well-preserved, three-tiered Roman aqueduct that was once part of a 50km-long system of canals built

FRANCE

about 19 BC by the Romans to bring water from near Uzès to Nîmes. The scale is huge: the 35 arches of the 275m-long upper tier, running 50m above the River Gard, contain a watercourse designed to carry 20,000 cubic metres of water per day and the largest construction blocks weigh over five tonnes.

From car parks (€5) either side of the River Gard, you can walk along the road bridge, built in 1743 and running parallel to the aqueduct's lower tier. The best view of the Pont du Gard is from upstream, beside the river, where you can swim on hot days.

CORSICA

Though Corsica (Corse) has been governed by mainland France for over 200 years, the island remains a nation apart, with its own distinctive language, customs and character and an entirely unique landscape: 1000km of seaswept coastline, snowcapped mountain-ranges, a world-renowned marine reserva-tion, uninhabited desert and a 'continental divide' running down the island's centre.

A single day's travel can carry you through secret coves, booming waterfalls, plunging canyons, sweeping bays, megalithic men-hirs and dense forests of chestnut and pine. Away from the main holiday resorts, you'll discover the quiet fishing villages, remote mountain towns and deserted beaches that died out in the rest of the Mediterranean long ago.

Dangers & Annoyances
When Corsica makes the headlines, it's often because nationalist militants have turned nasty (previous acts include bombings, bank robberies and the murder of the prefect). But the violence is not targeted at tourists, and visitors have no need to worry about their safety.

BASTIA
pop 37,800

Bustling Bastia, once the seat of Corsica's Genoese governors and retaining a distinctly Italian atmosphere, is Corsica's main centre of business and commerce. Little effort has been made to smarten up the city for tour-ists, making it an authentic and atmospheric introduction to modern-day Corsica. You can easily spend a day exploring – the old

port being Bastia's highlight – but most visitors move on pretty quickly. The focal point of the city is place St-Nicolas. Bastia's main thoroughfares are the busy shopping street of boulevard Paoli and ave Maréchal Sébastiani, which links the ferryport with the train station.

Information
Cyber Space (☎ 04 95 30 70 83; 3 blvd Paoli; Internet per 15min/hr €1/3.80; ☺ 9am-midnight Mon-Sat, 4pm-midnight Sun)

Oxy Cybercafé (☎ 04 95 58 27 96; rue Salvatore Viale; Internet per hr €3.10; ☺ 9am-midnight Mon-Sat)

Post office (ave Maréchal Sébastiani; ☺ 8am-7pm Mon-Fri, to noon Sat)

Tourist office (☎ 04 95 55 96 85; bastia-tourisme.com; pl St-Nicolas; ☺ 8am-6pm Mon-Sat, to 1pm Sun)

Sights & Activities
Bastia can be covered in a half-day stroll starting with **place St-Nicolas**, a vast seafront esplanade laid out in the 19th century. The square is lined with trees and cafés, and at the southern end, a bizarre statue of **Napo-leon Bonaparte** depicted as a muscle-bound Roman emperor stands guard.

Between place St-Nicolas and the old port lies **Terra Vecchia**, a historic neighbourhood of old houses and tumbledown tenement blocks.

The **old port** is an atmospheric jumble of boats, restaurants and crumbling buildings, dominated by the twin towers of the **Eglise St-Jean-Baptiste**, which loom over the north side of the harbour.

Bastia's most historic quarter juts out above the old port. The **citadel** (Terra Nova), built by the Genoese between the 15th and 17th centuries to protect Bastia's harbour, can be reached by climbing the stairs through **Jardin Romieu**, the hillside park on the southern side of the harbour.

Sleeping
Camping San Damiano (☎ 04 95 33 68 02; www.camp ingsandamiano.com; camp sites low/high season €5.50/6.50; ☺ Apr-Oct) A shady seaside camping ground 5km south of Bastia, with furnished bunga-lows available. Served by the airport bus.

Hôtel Central (☎ 04 95 31 71 12; www.centralhotel .fr; 3 rue Miot; s €40-55, d €50-78, apt per day €5-65, per week €305-420; ☒) As its name suggests, it's right in the city centre and the rooms have all been refurbished: the best have balconies and kitchenettes. Prices vary depending on high/low season.

Hôtel d'Univers (☎ 04 95 31 03 38; fax 04 95 31 19 91; 3 ave Maréchal Sébastiani; s/d/tr low season €45/55/65, high season €60/70/80; ☒) The pick of Bastia's mid-range hotels, tucked between old and new towns. The tasteful rooms have white walls, colourful bedspreads and wood floors.

Eating
Cafés and restaurants line place St-Nicolas, the old port, quai des Martyrs and place de l'Hôtel de Ville.

La Marine (☎ 06 12 21 38 09; 8 rue St-Jean; menu €12-21; ☼ Mon-Sat) An informal seafood restaurant which also offers pizzas and Corsican fare on its portside terrace: most of the fish comes literally straight off the boats.

Chez Mémé (☎ 04 95 31 44 12; quai des Martyrs; menu €14-17) One of many seafront restaurants near the old port, this is a simple, unpretentious place that specialises in fish and shellfish: the €14 *Menu Corse* includes Corsican meats and cheeses.

There's a lively **food market** (☼ Tue-Sun) on place de l'Hôtel de Ville. The large **Spar supermarket** (rue César Campinchi) is the most convenient place for supplies. Out of town, there is a **Casino supermarket** (Géant Port Toga Centre Commercial).

Getting There & Away
AIR
Bastia-Poretta airport (☎ 04 95 54 54 54; bastia.aero port.fr) is 24km south of the city. Buses (€8, seven to nine daily, fewer on Sunday) depart from outside the prefecture building. The tourist office has schedules, and timetables are posted at the bus stop. A taxi to the airport costs €20 to €30.

BOAT
The southern ferry terminal is at the eastern end of ave François Pietri. There's an **SNCM office** (☎ 04 95 54 66 81; www.sncm.fr; ☼ 8am-11.45am & 2-5.45pm Mon-Fri, to noon Sat) in the southern terminal. **Moby Lines** (☎ 04 95 34 84 94; www.mobylines .it; 4 rue du Commandant Luce de Casabianca; ☼ 8am-noon & 2-6pm Mon-Fri, to noon Sat) has a bureau in the ferry terminal, open two hours before each sailing. **Corsica Ferries** (☎ 04 95 32 95 95; www.corsicaférries .com; 15 bis rue Chanoine Leschi; ☼ 8.30am-noon & 2-6pm Mon-Fri, 9am-noon Sat) is across the road from the ferry terminal.

BUS
Buses leave from several locations around town – consult the tourist office. **Eurocorse** (☎ 04 95 31 73 76) travels to Ajaccio (€18, three hours) via Corte (€10, two hours) twice daily except Sunday. **Rapides Bleus** (☎ 04 95 31 03 79; 1 ave Maréchal Sébastiani) runs buses to Porto-Vecchio (€18.50) with connections to Bonifacio and Sartène. It sells tickets for the Eurocorse service to Corte and Ajaccio. **Les Beaux Voyages** (☎ 04 95 65 11 35) travels to Calvi (€12.50, two hours) daily except Sunday.

TRAIN
The **train station** (☎ 04 95 32 80 61; ave Maréchal Sébastiani; ☼ 6am-8.40pm Mon-Sat, 8.40am-12.40pm & 4.15-8.40pm Sun) is beside the large roundabout on Square Mal-Leclerc. Main destinations include Ajaccio (€20.70, four hours) via Corte, and Calvi (€15.70, four hours).

CALVI
pop 4800
On a sparkling crescent-shaped bay and backed by snowy peaks, Calvi is a thriving pleasure port that attracts sun-seekers and weekend sailors from all over the Mediterranean, though the towers, bastions and clustered houses of its 15th-century citadel remain as relics of its martial past.

In 1794, a British expeditionary fleet assisting Pasquale Paoli's Corsican nationalist forces besieged and bombarded Calvi during which the legendary British sailor Horatio Nelson was wounded and lost the use of his right eye.

Orientation & Information
The citadel – also known as the Haute Ville (upper city) – is on a rocky promontory northeast of the Basse Ville (lower city). Blvd Wilson, the major thoroughfare through town, is uphill from the marina.

The **main tourist office** (☎ 04 95 65 16 67; omt .calvi@wanadoo.fr; ☼ 8.30am-1pm & 2.30-7pm Jun–mid-Sep, 9am-noon & 2-6pm Mon-Sat Oct-May) is near the marina.

Sights & Activities
Calvi's massively fortified 15th-century **citadel** dominates the harbour skyline and affords great harbour views. The **Palais des Gouverneurs** (Governors' Palace; pl d'Armes), once the seat of power for the Genoese administration, now serves as a base for the French Foreign Legion.

Uphill from Caserne Sampiero is the 13th-century **Église St-Jean Baptiste**, rebuilt in 1570.

Calvi's 4km of beach begins at the marina and stretches east around the Golfe de Calvi. Other good beaches are west of town, including **Algajola**.

Sleeping

Calvi's hotels aren't cheap at any time of year, and most are closed in winter.

Camping La Clé des Champs (☎ 04 95 65 00 86; camagni2@wanadoo.fr; route de Pietra Maggiore; adult/car/tent €6/2/2.50; ⊗ Apr-Oct, reception 9am-10.30pm) South of Les Castors, but still only a short walk to the beach.

Auberge de Jeunesse BVJ Corsotel (☎ 04 95 65 14 15; bvjhotel.com; ave de la République; dm €22; ⊗ Mar-Nov) The hostel offers 120 budget beds, including breakfast.

Hôtel Le Magnolia (☎ 04 95 65 19 16; fax 04 95 65 08 02; cnr pl du Marché & rue Alsace-Lorraine; s/d low season €65/77-97, high season €85/100-120; ⊗ Apr-Jan; ⚄) An elegant hotel ideally placed just behind the harbour, near Église Ste-Marie. The impeccable rooms have garden or sea views, and you can have breakfast or supper in the tree-covered courtyard.

Hôtel Le Rocher (☎ 04 95 65 20 04, hotel.lerocher@wanadoo.fr; blvd Wilson; d €90-190; 2-person apt per week €389-793, 4-person apt per week €645-1080; ⊗ Apr-Sep; ⚄) Provides rooms and mini-apartments with kitchenettes, fridges, TVs and phones.

Eating

Île de Beauté (☎ 04 95 65 00 46; quai Landry; menu €20) The best of the romantic cafés and restaurants along Calvi's waterfront. It specialises in fish and Corsican cuisine: delicacies include red mullet salad, sea bream in pesto sauce, and crab soup.

U Minellu (☎ 04 95 65 05 52; Traverse á l'Église; menu €14-16; ⊗ closed Sun in winter) A delightful family-run restaurant opposite Église Ste-Marie, serving Corsican dishes under a wooden awning lit by lanterns. The menu Corse (€16) includes regional specialties such as *brocciu* cannelloni, Corsican cooked pork, and chestnut and apple cake.

Best Of (1 rue Clemenceau; snacks €4-6; ⊗ 11.30am-10pm) Head here for something light, such as sandwiches and paninis.

The **Marché Couvert** (covered market; ⊗ 8am-noon Mon-Sat) is near Église Ste-Marie Majeure. There's a large **Casino Supermarket** (ave Christophe Colomb) south of the train station. Alternatively, try the well-stocked **Alimentation du Golfe** (rue Clemenceau).

Getting There & Away

The tourist office can supply timetables. Buses to Bastia (€12.50, 2¼ hours) are run by **Les Beaux Voyages** (☎ 04 95 65 15 02; pl de la Porteuse d'Eau). From mid-May to mid-October, **Autocars SAIB** (☎ 04 95 22 41 99) runs buses from Calvi's Monument aux Morts (war memorial) to Galéria (1¼ hours) and Porto (three hours). There are no buses on Sunday.

Calvi's **train station** (☎ 04 95 65 00 61; ⊗ until 7.30pm) is off ave de la République. There are two departures daily to Ajaccio (€24.10), Bastia (€15.70) and the stations between. From April to October, the single-car trains of CFC's **Tramway de la Balagne** make 19 stops along the coast between Calvi and Île Rousse (45 minutes).

The ferry terminal is below the southern side of the citadel. From Calvi there are express NGV ferries to Nice (2½ hours, five weekly). Ferry tickets can be bought at the port two hours before departure. At other times, SNCM tickets are handled by **Tramar** (☎ 04 95 65 01 38; quai Landry; ⊗ 9am-noon & 2-6pm Mon-Fri, to noon Sat). Tickets for Corsica Ferries are handled by Les Beaux Voyages.

PORTO

pop 460

The seaside village of Porto (Portu), which nestles among huge outcrops of red granite and fragrant groves of eucalyptus, is renowned for its fiery sunsets and proximity to the Scandola nature reserve. Hotel prices are reasonable, making it a good base for exploring Les Calanques, a spectacular mountain landscape of orange and red granite, and the mountain villages of Ota and Évisa.

Orientation & Information

Porto is split into three sections: the marina area, the Vaita quarter further uphill, and the main road from Calvi. All three districts have shops, hotels and restaurants. From the Calvi road to the marina is about 1km.

The **main tourist office** (☎ 04 95 26 10 55; www.porto-tourisme.com; ⊗ 9am-noon & 2-6pm Mon-Sat Apr-Jun, Sep & Oct, to 6pm Jul-Aug) is built into the wall below the marina's upper car park. It publishes a good English brochure, *Hikes & Walks in the Area of Porto* (€2.50).

Sights & Activities

A short trail leads up the rocks to a **Genoese tower** (€2.50; 🕙 10am-noon & 2-7pm Apr-Jun, Sep & Oct, 9am-9pm Jul-Aug). Nearby, the marina overlooks the estuary of the Porto river. On the far side, across a footbridge, there's a modest pebbly **beach** and one of Corsica's best-known **eucalyptus groves**.

From April to October, **Nave Va Promenades en Mer** (☎ 04 95 26 15 16; www.naveva.com) and **Porto Linéa** (☎ 04 95 26 11 50, ☎ 06 08 16 89 71) offer excursions (€35 to €40 depending on season) to the **Réserve Naturelle de Scandola** (Scandola Nature Reserve), listed by Unesco for its unique marine environment.

Sleeping

Le Funtana al' Ora (☎ 04 95 26 11 65; fax 04 95 26 15 48; per person/tent/car €5.50/2.20/2.20; 🕙 Apr-Oct) This camping ground, 2km east of Porto on the road to Évisa, has four-person bungalows from €300/540 in low/high season

Le Golfe (☎ 04 95 26 13 33; Marina; r low, high season €35-50 €55-70) This cheap hotel above a café offers basic rooms, some with little balconies overlooking the bay.

Le Colombo (☎ 04 95 26 10 14; www.hotelcolombo .com; route de Calvi; d incl breakfast low/high season €59/120; 🕙 Apr-Oct; P ✿) Charming little hotel on the Calvi road, with quirky décor and valley views. Get a balcony if you can.

Getting There & Away

The **Autocars SAIB** (☎ 04 95 22 41 99) has two buses daily, linking Porto and Ota with Ajaccio (€11, two hours, none on Sunday). From May to October a bus runs from Porto to Calvi (€16, three hours). **Transports Mordiconi** (☎ 04 95 48 00 44) connects Porto with Corte (€19, 2½ hours, one daily) via Évisa and Ota.

PIANA

pop 500 / elevation 438m

The quiet hillside village of Piana affords breathtaking views of the Golfe de Porto and the soaring central mountains, and makes an excellent base for exploring Les Calanques.

Hôtel Continental (☎ 04 95 27 83 12; continental piana.com; d low, high season €29-35, €32-38, 🕙 Apr-Sep) An old, converted townhouse 100m uphill from the church, with 17 old-fashioned rooms and antique décor to match.

Hôtel des Roches Rouges (Red Rocks; ☎ 04 95 27 81 81; fax 04 95 27 81 76; d from €69; 🕙 Apr-mid-Nov) A

grand old 30-room hotel dating from 1912, and without doubt one of Corsica's most romantic places to stay. The elegant double rooms have panoramic views of sea and hills while the antique dining room and period furnishings conjure the air of a bygone age.

Buses between Porto and Ajaccio stop near the church and the post office.

LES CALANQUES

One of Corsica's most stunning natural sights is just outside Piana: Les Calanques de Piana (E Calanche in Corsican), a spectacular landscape of red granite cliffs and spiky outcrops, carved into bizarre shapes by the forces of wind, water and weather. Less rocky areas support pine and chestnut forests, whose green foliage contrasts dramatically with the technicoloured granite.

AJACCIO

pop 60,000

The pastel-shaded port of Ajaccio (Ajacciu, pronounced Ajaxio)is the most cosmopolitan city in Corsica. with designer shops, fashionable restaurants and hectic traffic. Inland from the harbour, the modern shopping streets lead into the alleyways and narrow lanes of the old city crowded with 18th-century townhouses. For educational value there are several museums dedicated to Ajaccio's most famous native son, Napoleon Bonaparte.

Orientation

Ajaccio's main street is cours Napoléon, stretching from place de Gaulle north to the train station and beyond. The old city is south of place Foch. The port is on the east side of town, from where a tree-lined promenade leads west along plage St-Francois.

Information

Game Net (☎ 04 95 50 72 79; 2 ave de Paris; Internet per 15min/1hr €2/5; 🕙 9am-noon & 2-9pm Mon-Fri, 2-9pm Sat & Sun)

Main post office (13 cours Napoléon; 🕙 8am-6.45pm Mon-Fri, to noon Sat)

Tourist office (☎ 04 95 51 53 03; www.tourisme .fr/ajaccio; 3 blvd du Roi Jérôme; 🕙 8am-7pm Mon-Sat, 9am-1pm Sun)

Sights

You can't walk far in Ajaccio without stumbling across a reference to the Ajaccio-born

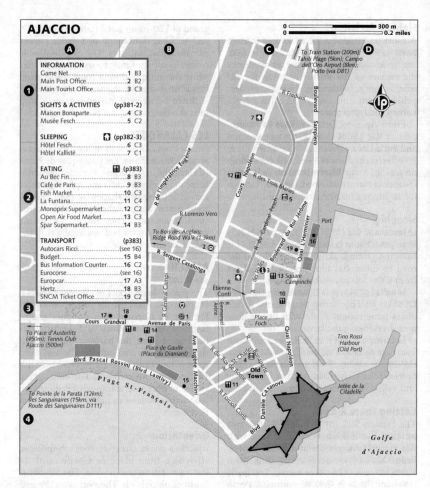

AJACCIO

INFORMATION	
Game Net	1 B3
Main Post Office	2 B2
Main Tourist Office	3 C3

SIGHTS & ACTIVITIES	(pp381-2)
Maison Bonaparte	4 C3
Musée Fesch	5 C2

SLEEPING	(pp382-3)
Hôtel Fesch	6 C3
Hôtel Kallisté	7 C1

EATING	(p383)
Au Bec Fin	8 B3
Café de Paris	9 B3
Fish Market	10 C3
La Funtana	11 C4
Monoprix Supermarket	12 C2
Open Air Food Market	13 C3
Spar Supermarket	14 B3

TRANSPORT	(p383)
Autocars Ricci	(see 16)
Budget	15 B4
Bus Information Counter	16 C2
Eurocorse	(see 16)
Europcar	17 A3
Hertz	18 B3
SNCM Ticket Office	19 C2

boy who became Emperor of France. In fact, Napoleon spent little of his adult life in Corsica. After crowning himself Emperor of France in 1804, he never returned.

The saga begins at the **Maison Bonaparte** (☎ 04 95 21 43 89; rue St-Charles; adult/concession €4/2.60; �9am-noon & 2-6pm Tue-Sun, 2-6pm Mon Apr-Sep, 10am-noon & 2-5pm Tue-Sat, 2-5pm Mon Oct-Mar), the grand building in the old city where Napoleon was born and spent the first nine years of his childhood.

Impressive **Musée Fesch** (☎ 04 95 21 48 17; 50-52 rue du Cardinal Fesch; adult/student €5.35/3.80; � 1.15-5.15pm Mon, 9.15am-12.15pm & 2.15-5.15pm Tue-Sun Apr-Jun & Sep, 1.30-6pm Mon, 9am-6pm Tue-Fri, 10.30am-6pm Sat & Sun Jul-Aug, 9.15am-12.15pm & 2.15-5.15pm Tue-Sat

Oct-Mar), established by Napoleon's uncle, has the finest collection in France of 14th- to 19th-century Italian art outside the Louvre (mostly looted during Napoléon's foreign campaigns), including works by Titian, Botticelli, Raphael, Poussin and Bellini.

Sleeping

There are no budget options in Ajaccio so make sure to reserve ahead in summer.

Hôtel Kallisté (☎ 04 95 51 34 45; 51 cours Napoléon; s/d low season €51/56, high season €58/68; ☒ ☒ ☐) An excellent city hotel with contemporary bedrooms. Stylish features like the glass elevator, terracotta floors and exposed brickwork don't normally come this cheap.

FRANCE

Hôtel Fesch (☎ 04 95 51 62 62; www.hotel-fesch .com; 7 rue du Cardinal Fesch; s/d low season €54/63, high season €73/84; ❄) On one of Ajaccio's oldest streets, the period building, grand rooms and old-fashioned service make this a favourite with regulars, so book ahead.

Eating

Café de Paris (☎ 04 95 51 03 90; pl de Gaulle; dishes €8-15;) A traditional café and brasserie with a fine terrace overlooking place de Gaulle.

Au Bec Fin (☎ 04 95 21 30 52; 3 bis blvd du Roi-Jérôme; menu €13.90; ❄ closed Sun & Mon) A relaxed restaurant near the market, decked out as a 1930s brasserie. The excellent-value menu includes grilled tuna, salmon fillet and *carpaccio de boeuf*.

La Funtana (☎ 04 95 21 78 04; 7 rue Notre Dame; lunch/ dinner menu €25/55, à la carte dishes €24-30; ❄ lunch & dinner Tue-Sat, dinner only Jul & Aug) One of Ajaccio's grandest *grandes tables*, regularly featured in gourmet guides. The grilled lobster and *l'anima Corse* (a pudding made with chestnut flour and brocciu cheese) are renowned.

Ajaccio's **open-air food market** (pl Campinchi; ❄ closed Monday) fills the square with Corsican atmosphere most mornings until noon. There's a daily **fish market** (pl Campinchi) in the building behind the food market. Near place de Gaulle, the **Spar Supermarket** (❄ 8.30am-12.30pm & 3-7.30pm Mon-Sat) is opposite 4 cours Grandval. **Monoprix Supermarket** (❄ 8.30am-7.15pm Mon-Sat) is on cours Napoléon.

Getting There & Away

The **Aéroport d'Ajaccio-Campo dell'Oro** (☎ 04 95 23 56 56; ajaccio.aeroport.fr) is 8km east of the city centre.

Bus companies operate from Terminal Maritime et Routier on quai l'Herminier. Most have ticket kiosks on the right as you enter the station. The **information counter** (☎ 04 95 51 55 45; ❄ 7am-7pm) provides schedules.

Companies **Eurocorse** (☎ 04 95 21 06 30) and **Autocars Ricci** (☎ 04 95 51 08 19) serve the main destinations, including Bastia (€18, three hours, two daily); Bonifacio (€19.50, four hours, two or three daily); Calvi (€19.85, change at Ponte Leccia); Corte (€10.50, 2¾ hours, two daily); Porto (€11.45, 2½ hours, two daily). Services run Monday to Saturday.

The **train station** (☎ 04 95 23 11 03; pl de la Gare ❄ until 6.30pm, to 8pm May-Sep) services Bastia (€20.70, four hours, three to four daily),

Corte (€11, two hours, four daily), and Calvi (€24.10, five hours, two daily; change at Ponte-Leccia).

The main car-rental companies have airport bureaus. In town you'll find **Hertz** (☎ 04 95 21 70 94; 8 cours Grandval); **Europcar** (☎ 04 95 21 05 49; 16 cours Grandval); and **Budget** (☎ 04 95 21 17 18; 1 blvd Lantivy).

Hôtel Kallisté (see p382) rents cars at cheap rates. A three-door car costs €49/227 per day/week including unlimited mileage. Prices rise in July and August.

The ferry terminal is in the same building as the bus station. The **SNCM ticket office** (☎ 04 95 29 66 99; 3 quai l'Herminier; ❄ 8am-6pm Mon, to 8pm Tue-Fri, to 1pm Sat) is across the street.

BONIFACIO
pop 2700

The citadel of Bonifacio (Bunifaziu) sits 70m above the Mediterranean on a rock promontory called 'Corsica's Gibraltar'. On all sides, white limestone cliffs drop vertically into the sea, while the tall houses of the old city lean precariously over the water. The citadel's northern side overlooks Bonifacio Sound (Goulet de Bonifacio) with the **marina** at the southeastern corner; the southern ramparts give views of Sardinia, 12km away across the Strait of Bonifacio (Bouches de Bonifacio).

The **tourist office** (☎ 04 95 73 11 88; bonifacio .com; 2 rue Fred Scamaroni; ❄ 9am-8pm Jul-Aug, to noon & 2-6pm Mon-Fri, to noon Sat Sep-Jun) is inside the citadel.

Sights
CITADEL

The steps linking rue St-Érasme with Porte de Gênes are known as Montée Rastello and Montée St-Roch further up. At the top of Montée St-Roch stands the **Porte de Gênes**. Just inside the gateway, you can visit the **Grand Bastion** (admission €2; ❄ 9am-6pm Mon-Sat Apr-May & Sep-Oct, daily Jul-Aug) above Porte de Gênes.

Nearby, along the citadel's ramparts, there are great views from **place du Marché** and **place Manichella**.

Criss-crossed by meandering alleyways lined with tall stone houses, the old city has a distinctly medieval feel. **Rue des Deux Empereurs** is so named because Charles V and Napoleon once slept in the houses at Nos 4 and 7. **Église Ste-Marie Majeure**, a 14th-century Romanesque church, is known for its loggia (roofed porch).

From the citadel, the **Escalier du Roi d'Aragon** (Staircase of the King of Aragon; admission €2; 9am-6pm Mon-Sat Apr-May & Sep-Oct, daily Jul-Aug) leads down the cliff.

Outside the citadel, west along the limestone headland, stands **Église Ste-Dominique** – one of the only Gothic buildings in Corsica. Further west, near three ruined **mills**, the elaborate tombs of the **Cimetière Marin** stand out against a backdrop of crashing waves and wheeling gulls.

Sleeping

Camping L'Araguina (04 95 73 02 96; ave Sylvére Bohn; per person/tent/car €5.50/1.70/1.85; Mar-Oct) Near the Hôtel des Étrangers, shaded by olive trees and conveniently, just a short walk into town.

Hôtel des Étrangers (04 95 73 01 09; fax 04 95 73 16 97; ave Sylvére Bohn; d €43-71; Apr-Oct; P) The best deal in Bonifacio is just outside town. This large hotel offers 30 plain rooms and there's plenty of onsite parking – a rare treat in Bonifacio.

Hotel du Roy d'Aragon (04 95 73 03 99; royaragon .com; 13 quai Camporetti; d low season €45-79, high season €90-145;) A refined hotel that stands out on the crowded quay. The lovely rooms with portside balconies are the best value in Bonifacio – book well ahead.

Eating

Le Voilier (04 95 73 07 06; quai Jérôme Comparetti; menu €24.50, two courses €19) A reliable restaurant offering top-quality fish dishes, from *langoustines* (lobster) roasted in butter to sea bream cooked with basil sauce.

L'Archivolto (04 95 73 17 58; rue de l'Archivolto; plats du jour €7-14; Mon-Sat) A wonderfully quirky restaurant-cum-antique shop in the citadel, serving imaginative food. Try the chicken in pietra beer and the fresh herb tart with brocciu.

Super Marché Simoni (93 quai Jérôme Comparetti; 8am-12.30pm & 3.30-7.30pm Mon-Sat, to 12.30pm Sun) is on the marina. Next door, **Coccinelle supermarket** (quai Jérôme Comparetti) has a fresh bakery counter.

Getting There & Away

There are two buses to Ajaccio (€19.50, three to four hours) via Sartène from Monday to Saturday, run by Eurocorse (04 95 70 13 83 in Porto-Vecchio). For Bastia, change at Porto-Vecchio (€6.50, 45 minutes, two to four daily). Buses leave from near the Eurocorse kiosk on the marina in summer only

Daily ferries to Santa Teresa in Sardinia are offered by **Saremar** (04 95 73 00 96) and **Moby Lines** (04 95 73 00 29) from Bonifacio's ferry-port (50 minutes, two to seven daily). Saremar charges €6.70/8.50 one way in low/high season, while Moby Lines charges €22/30 return. Cars cost between €21 and €43. Port taxes are €3.

CORTE

pop 5700 / elevation 400m

When Pasquale Paoli led Corsica to independence in 1755, one of his first acts was to make this fortified town at the centre of the island the country's capital. To this day, Corte (Corti) remains a potent symbol of Corsican independence. Paoli founded a national university here in 1765, with 3000 students today.

Ringed with mountains and bordered eastwards by the forest region of Castagniccia, it's also an excellent base for hiking. Some of the island's highest peaks are just west of town. There is Internet access at the **Grand Café** (04 95 46 00 33; 22 cours Paoli; per 15min/hr €1/3.50; 7pm-2am). The **tourist office** (04 95 46 26 70; corte.tourisme@wanadoo.fr; La Citadelle; 9am-noon & 2-6pm Mon-Sat Apr & May, to 1pm & 2-7pm Mon-Sat Jun & Sep, to 8pm daily Jul & Aug, to noon & 2-6pm Mon-Fri Oct-Mar) can provide good local information.

Sights

CITADEL

Corte's citadel juts from a rocky outcrop above the Tavignanu and Restonica Rivers and the cobbled alleyways of the Ville Haute. The highest point is the **chateau** (known as the Nid d'Aigle, or Eagle's Nest), built in 1419 by a Corsican nobleman allied with the Aragonese. It was expanded during the 18th and 19th centuries and served as a Foreign Legion base from 1962 until 1983.

The **Museu di a Corsica** (Musée de la Corse; 04 95 45 25 45; museu@sitec.fr; adult/student €3/2.30; 10am-6pm Tue-Sun, to 5pm Nov-Apr, daily late Jun-late Sep) houses an outstanding exhibition (in French and Corsican) on Corsican traditions, crafts, agriculture, and anthropology. Outside the ramparts, a path leads to the **belvédére** (viewing platform), which has views of the city and the Eagle's Nest. Nearby, a precarious staircase leads down to the river.

Sleeping

Camping Alivetu (☎ 04 95 46 11 09; fax 04 95 46 12 34; faubourg de St-Antoine; per person/car/tent €5/2/2; ⏰ Apr-Oct) Attractive and shaded by olive trees.

Hôtel de la Paix (☎ 04 95 46 06 72; fax 04 95 46 23 84; ave du Général de Gaulle; s/d/tr from €35/42/55; P) A big, comfortable hotel with 60 spic-and-span rooms on a quiet square off cours Paoli. The inhouse Corsican restaurant (*menu* €13) is decent too.

Hôtel de la Poste (☎ 04 95 46 01 37; 2 pl du Duc de Padoue; r €33.50) On the same square as Hôtel de la Paix, but looking rather worse for wear, this is a typically Corsican no-frills hotel with mismatched décor and run-down charm.

Eating

A Merenda (☎ 04 95 46 30 99; 3 cours Paoli; ⏰ 9am-midnight Mon-Sat) A popular café-bar and *salon du thé* with delicious coffee and light meals, including salads and *croques-monsieurs*.

Grand Café (☎ 04 95 46 00 33; 22 cours Paoli; ⏰ 7-2am) A cosy student hangout underneath the Hotel du Nord where you can leave your backpacks for free.

U Museu (☎ 04 95 61 08 36; rampe Ribanelle; menu €13-15; ⏰ closed Sun Oct-Jun) Corte's outstanding Corsican restaurant serves traditional cuisine on a gazebo-covered terrace. Its menus include *civet de sanglier aux myrtes sauvages* (wild boar with myrtle), *soissons Corses* (Corsican lima beans), and *truite au peveronata* (trout in red pepper sauce).

La Trattoria (☎ 04 95 46 00 76; 6 cours Paoli; menu €9-14; ⏰ closed Sun) A family-run restaurant loved by locals, which serves up classic Corsican meat dishes and enormous salads. The next-door patisserie is the best in town.

Corte's top boulangerie is **Casanova** (cours Paoli), next door to La Trattoria; practically the whole town comes here to buy their cakes. There's also a **Eurospar** (7 ave Xavier Luciani) and a **Casino Supermarket** (allée du 9 Septembre).

Getting There & Away

Eurocorse travels through town twice daily from Ajaccio (€9.90, 2¾ hours) towards Bastia (€8.40, 1¼ hours) except Sunday.

The **train station** (☎ 04 95 46 00 97; ⏰ 6.30am-8.30pm Mon-Sat, 9.45am-noon & 4.45-8.35pm Sun) is 1km east of the city centre. Destinations include Bastia (€9.70, two hours, three to four daily) and Ajaccio (€11, two hours, three to four daily).

FRANCE DIRECTORY

ACCOMMODATION

Accommodation is listed in this chapter in ascending order of price (ie from budget to top end). Hotels listed under 'budget' have doubles up to €40 (€50 in Paris). Most are equipped with a wash basin but lack private bath/shower or toilet. Hall showers usually cost €2. Prices quoted in this chapter for budget listings are for shared bathroom facilities unless otherwise stated.

Hotels listed under 'mid-range' are usually in the range of €40 to €100 for a double (up to €150 in Paris) and always have en-suite bathroom facilities. These places are comfortable and good value. 'Top end' accommodation will cost more than €100 (€150 in the capital). Prices quoted in this chapter for mid-range and top-end accommodation include en-suite bathroom unless stated.

During periods of heavy domestic or foreign tourism, popular destinations are packed out. Tourist offices will often reserve rooms (generally for a fee).

Camping & Caravan Parks

Camping is immensely popular in France, and many of the thousands of camping grounds are near rivers, lakes or oceans. Most close from October or November to March or April. Hostels sometimes let travellers pitch tents in their grounds. Gîtes de France coordinates farm camping and publishes an annual guide *Camping à la Ferme*.

Camping in non-designated spots, or *camping sauvage*, is usually illegal. Camping on the beach is not a good idea in areas with high tidal variations.

Gîtes Ruraux & B&Bs

A *gîte rural* is a self-contained holiday cottage (or part of a house) in a village or on a farm. A *chambre d'hôte*, basically a B&B (bed and breakfast), is a room in a private house, rented by the night. The website www.bbfrance.com is useful for arranging B&Bs and vacation rentals.

Ask about Gîtes de France offices and brochures and guides at local tourist offices, or contact the **Fédération Nationale des Gîtes de France** (☎ 01 49 70 75 75; www.gites-de-france.fr).

Hostels & Foyers

Official hostels are known as *auberges de jeunesse*. A hostel bed generally costs around €20 (including breakfast) in Paris, and €8 to €13 in the provinces.

France's major hostel associations, **Fédération Unie des Auberges de Jeunesse** (FUAJ; ☎ 01 48 04 70 30; www.fuaj.org) and **Ligue Française pour les Auberges de la Jeunesse** (LFAJ; ☎ 01 44 16 78 78; www .auberges-de-jeunesse.com) require you to have or buy a Hostelling International (HI) card or a nightly Welcome Stamp. Bring your own sleeping sheet or rent one for a small fee.

The non-profit organisation **Union des Centres de Rencontres Internationales de France** (UCRIF; ☎ 01 40 26 57 64; www.ucrif.asso.fr) has 'international holiday centres' with private rooms, dorms and restaurant facilities.

In university towns, student dormitories *(foyers d'étudiant)* are sometimes converted for travellers during summer. Relatively unknown, these places frequently have space when other hostels are full.

Hotels

A double has one double bed, so specify if you prefer twin beds *(deux lits séparés)*. Look out for great weekend deals to 33 cities and towns at www.bon-week-end-en-villes.com. **Logis de France** (☎ 01 45 84 83 84; www.logis-de-france .fr) publishes an annual guide with maps.

ACTIVITIES

France's varied geography and climate make it a superb place for a wide range of outdoor pursuits. France's stunning scenery lends itself to adventure sports and exhilarating outdoor activities of all kinds.

Cycling

Some of the best areas for cycling (with varying grades of difficulty) are in the French Alps, the Jura, and the Pyrenees, the Dordogne, Quercy, Brittany, Normandy and the Atlantic coast. Lonely Planet's *Cycling France* includes essential maps, directions, technical tips and advice.

Hiking

France is crisscrossed by a staggering 120,000km of *sentiers balisés* (marked walking paths), which pass through every imaginable kind of terrain (note that there are restrictions on where you can camp, especially in national parks).

Probably the best-known trails are the *sentiers de grande randonnée*, long-distance footpaths marked by red-and-white striped track indicators.

The **Club Alpin Français** (Map pp270-1; ☎ 01 53 72 87 00; www.clubalpin.com; 24 ave de Laumiére, 19e Paris; metro Laumiére) has a centre with useful information in Paris – joining is probably worthwhile if you're planning to do a great deal of hiking.

Lonely Planet's *Walking in France* is packed with essential practical information.

Skiing

France has more than 400 ski resorts in the Alps, the Jura, the Pyrenees, the Vosges, the Massif Central and even Corsica. The ski season generally lasts from December to March or April. January and February tend to have the best overall conditions.

The Alps have some of Europe's finest – and priciest – ski facilities. Much cheaper and less glitzy, smaller, low-altitude stations are in the Pyrenees and the Massif Central.

Ski de fond (cross-country skiing) is possible at high-altitude resorts but is usually much better in the valleys. Undoubtedly some of the best trails are in the Jura range.

One of the cheapest ways to ski in France is to buy a package deal before leaving home. Websites for online bookings include www .ski-europe.com and www.alpsweek.com.

Watersports

France has lovely beaches. The fine, sandy beaches along the family-oriented Atlantic coast (eg near La Rochelle) are less crowded than their often pebbly counterparts on the Côte d'Azur. Corsica has some magnificent spots. Brittany and the north coast are also popular (though cooler) beach destinations.

The best surfing in France is on the Atlantic coast around Biarritz, where waves can reach heights of 4m. Windsurfing is popular wherever there's water and a breeze, and renting equipment is often possible on lakes.

White-water rafting and kayaking are practised on many French rivers, especially in Massif Central and the Alps. The **Fédération Française de Canoë-Kayak** (FFCK; ☎ 01 45 11 08 50; www.ffck.org) can supply information on canoeing and kayaking clubs around the country.

Adventure Sports

France is a top spot for adventurous activities. In big cities and picturesque places, especially the Côte d'Azur and the Alps, local companies offer high adrenaline pursuits such as canyoning and bungy jumping.

BUSINESS HOURS

Shop hours are usually 9am or 10am to 6pm or 7pm, often (except in Paris) with a break from noon or 1pm to 2pm or 3pm. Most businesses close on Sunday; exceptions include grocery stores, *boulangeries* and patisseries. Many will also close on Monday.

Restaurants are usually open for lunch between noon and 2pm and for dinner from 7.30pm. Cafés open from early morning until around midnight. Bars usually open early evening and close at 1am or 2am.

Banks usually open from 9am to 1pm and 2pm to 5pm, Monday to Friday or Tuesday to Saturday. Post offices usually open 8.30am or 9am to 5pm or 6pm on weekdays (often with a midday break) and Saturday morning.

Supermarkets open Monday to Saturday from about 9.30am to 7pm (plus a midday break in smaller towns); some open on Sunday morning.

EMBASSIES & CONSULATES
French Embassies & Consulates

France's diplomatic and consular representatives abroad are listed on the website www .france.diplomatie.fr.

Australia Canberra (☎ 02-6216 0100; www.ambafrance -au.org; 6 Perth Ave, Yarralumla, ACT 2600); Sydney (☎ 02-9261 5779; www.consulfrance-sydney.org; 20th floor, St Martin's Tower, 31 Market St, Sydney, NSW 2000)

Canada Ottowa (☎ 613-789 1795; www.ambafrance -ca.org; 42 Sussex Drive, Ottawa, Ont K1M 2C9); Toronto (☎ 416-925 8041; www.consulfrance-toronto.org; 130 Bloor West, Suite 400, Ont M5S 1N5)

Germany Berlin (☎ 030-590 039 000; www.botschaft -frankreich.de; Parizer Platz 5, 10117); Munich (☎ 089-419 4110; Möhlstrasse 5, 81675)

Italy (☎ 06-686 011; www.ambafrance-it.org; Piazza Farnese 67, Rome 00186)

The Netherlands The Hague (☎ 070-312 5800; www .ambafrance-nl.org; Smidsplein 1, 2514 BT); Amsterdam (☎ 020-530 6969; www.consulfrance-amsterdam.org; Vijzelgracht 2, 1017 HR)

New Zealand (☎ 04-384 2555; www.ambafrance-nz.org; Rural Bank Building, 34-42 Manners St, Wellington)

UK London (☎ 020-7073 1000; www.ambafrance-uk.org;

58 Knightsbridge, London SW1X 7JT); Consulate (☎ 020-7073 1200; 21 Cromwell Rd, London SW7 2EN); Visa section (☎ 020-7838 2051; 6A Cromwell Place SW7 2EW)

USA Washington (☎ 202-944 6000; 4101 Reservoir Rd NW, DC 20007); New York (☎ 212-606 3600/89; www .consulfrance-newyork.org; 934 Fifth Ave, NY 10021); San Francisco (☎ 415-397 4330; www.consulfrance-sanfrancisco .org; 540 Bush St, CA 94108)

Embassies & Consulates in France

All foreign embassies can be found in Paris. Many countries – including the USA, Canada and most European countries – also have consulates in other major cities. To find an embassy or consulate not listed here, look up 'Ambassades et Consulats' in the *Yellow Pages* (*Pages Jaunes*; www.pagesjaunes.fr) for Paris.

Countries represented in Paris include:

Australia (Map pp270-1; ☎ 01 40 59 33 00; www.austgov.fr; 4 rue Jean Rey, 15e; metro Bir Hakeim)

Canada (Map pp270-1; ☎ 01 44 43 29 00; www .amb-canada.fr; 35 ave Montaigne, 8e; metro Franklin D Roosevelt); Nice (☎ 04 93 92 93 22; 10 rue Lamartine)

Germany (Map pp270-1; ☎ 01 53 83 45 00; www .amb-allemagne.fr; 13-15 ave Franklin D Roosevelt, 8e; metro Franklin D Roosevelt)

Ireland (Map pp270-1; ☎ 01 70 20 00 20; 33 rue Miromesnil, 8e; metro Miromesnil)

Italy (Map pp270-1; ☎ 01 49 54 03 00; www.amb -italie.fr; 51 rue de Varenne, 7e; metro Rue du Bac)

The Netherlands (Map pp270-1; ☎ 01 40 62 33 00; www.amb-pays-bas.fr; 7 rue Eblé, 7e; metro St-François Xavier)

New Zealand (Map pp270-1; ☎ 01 45 01 43 43; www .nzembassy.com; 7 ter rue Léonard de Vinci, 16e; metro Victor Hugo)

UK Paris (☎ 01 44 51 31 00; www.amb-grandebretagne.fr; 35 rue du Faubourg St-Honoré, 8e; metro Concorde); Paris (☎ 01 44 51 31 02; 16 bis rue d'Anjou, 8e metro Madeleine); Nice (☎ 04 93 62 13 56; 26 ave Notre Dame); Marseille (☎ 04 91 15 72 10; 24 ave du Prado)

USA Paris (Map pp270-1; ☎ 01 43 12 22 22; www.amb -usa.fr; 2 ave Gabriel, 8e metro Concorde); Paris (☎ 01 43 12 47 08; 2 rue St-Florentin, 1er metro Concorde); Nice (☎ 04 93 88 89 55; 7 ave Gustav V, 06000); Marseille (☎ 04 91 54 92 00; place Varian Fry)

FESTIVALS & EVENTS

Most French cities, towns and villages have at least one major arts festival each year.

May/June

May Day (France; 1 May) Workers day is celebrated with trade union parades, and diverse protests. People give each other *muguet* (lilies of the valley) for good luck. No-one works (except waiters and muguet sellers).

Cannes Film Festival (Cannes; mid-May; www.festival-cannes.com) The stars walk the red carpet at Cannes, the epitome of see-and-be-seen cinema events in Europe.

Fête de la Musique (France; 21 June; www.fetedela musique.culture.fr) Bands, orchestras, crooners, buskers and spectators take to the streets for this national celebration of music.

July

National Day (France; 14 July) Fireworks, parades and all-round hoo-ha to commemorate the storming of the Bastille in 1789, symbol of the French Revolution.

Gay Pride (Paris and other cities; www.gaypride.fr) Effervescent street parades, performances and parties through Paris and other major cities.

August/September

Festival Interceltique (Lorient; www.festival-interceltique.com) This massive August event pulls hundreds of thousands of Celts from all over Brittany and the UK for a massive celebration of their shared celtic culture.

December

Christmas Markets (Alsace) Alsace is the place to be for a traditional-style festive season, with world-famous Christmas markets, decorations and celebrations.

GAY & LESBIAN TRAVELLERS

France is one of Europe's most liberal countries when it comes to homosexuality. Paris has been a thriving gay and lesbian centre since the late 1970s. Montpellier, Lyon, Toulouse, Bordeaux and many other towns also have significant active communities. Predictably, attitudes towards homosexuality tend to become more conservative in the countryside and villages. France's lesbian scene is much less public than its gay counterpart and is centred mainly around women's cafés and bars, which are the best places to find information.

Online, www.gayscape.com has hundreds of links, while www.france.qrd.org is a 'queer resources directory' for gay and lesbian travellers. Another good sight for finding out about gay events is http://citegay.fr.

HOLIDAYS

The following *jours fériés* (public holidays) are observed in France.

New Year's Day (Jour de l'An) 1 January – Parties in larger cities; fireworks tend to be subdued by international standards.

Easter Sunday and Monday (Pâques & lundi de Pâques) Late March/April

May Day (Fête du Travail) 1 May – Traditional parades.

Victoire 1945 8 May – The Allied victory in Europe that ended WWII.

Ascension Thursday (L'Ascension) May – Celebrated on the 40th day after Easter.

Pentecost/Whit Sunday and Whit Monday (Pentecôte & lundi de Pentecôte) Mid-May to mid-June – Celebrated on the seventh Sunday after Easter.

Bastille Day/National Day (Fête Nationale) 14 July – The national holiday.

Assumption Day (L'Assomption) 15 August

All Saints' Day (La Toussaint) 1 November

Remembrance Day (L'onze novembre) 11 November – Celebrates the WWI armistice.

Christmas (Noël) 25 December

LEGAL MATTERS

French police have wide powers of search and seizure, and can ask you to prove your identity at any time. Foreigners must be able to prove their legal status in France (eg passport, visa, residency permit) without delay. If the police stop you for any reason, be polite and remain calm. You may refuse to sign a police statement, and have the right to ask for a copy. French law does not officially distinguish between 'hard' and 'soft' drugs.

MONEY

The official currency of France is the euro. You always get a better exchange rate in-country, though it's a good idea to arrive with enough local currency to take a taxi to a hotel. Automated Teller Machines (ATMs), or *distributeurs automatiques de billets* (DAB) are plentiful in all major cities and towns. Visa and MasterCard (Access or Eurocard) are widely accepted. In general cards can be used in shops, supermarkets, for train travel, car rentals, autoroute tolls and cash advances. Don't assume that you can pay for a meal or a budget hotel with a credit card – inquire first. For lost travellers cheques call **AmEx** (☎ 0 800 90 86 00) or **Thomas Cook** (☎ 0 800 90 83 30). For lost cards, these numbers operate 24 hours:

AmEx (☎ 01 47 77 72 00; AmEx offices arrange on-the-spot replacements)

Diners Club (☎ 0810 314 159)

MasterCard, Eurocard & Access (Eurocard France; ☎ 0 800 90 13 87)

Visa (Carte Bleue; ☎ 0 800 90 20 33)

POST

Each of France's 17,000 post offices is marked with a yellow or brown sign reading 'La Poste'. Since La Post also has banking, finance and bill-paying functions, queues can be very long, but there are automatic machines for postage.

Postal Rates

Domestic letters of up to 20g cost €0.50. Internationally, there are three different zones: a letter/package under 20g/2kg costs €0.50/12.50 to Zone A (EU, Switzerland, Iceland, Norway); €0.75/14 to Zone B (the rest of Europe and Africa); and €0.90/20.50 to Zone C (North and South America, Asia and Middle East, Australasia). Worldwide express mail delivery, called **Chronopost** (☎ 0 825 80 18 01), costs a fortune and is not as rapid as advertised.

Receiving Mail

Picking up poste-restante mail costs €0.50; you must show your passport or national ID card. Mail will be kept for 15 days. Poste-restante mail not addressed to a particular branch goes to the city's main post office.

TELEPHONE
International Dialling

Phone cards offer better international rates than Country Direct services (which allow you to be billed by the long-distance carrier you use at home). To make a reverse-charges (collect) call *(en PCV)* or a person-to-person call *(avec préavis)*, dial ☎ 3123 or ☎ 0 800 990 011 (for the USA and Canada) and ☎ 0 800 990 061 for Australia. Expect about €12 for a three-minute call.

National Dialling Areas

France has five telephone dialling areas. You dial the same 10-digit number no matter where you are, but it is cheaper to call locally. The five regional area codes are:
- ☎ 01 Paris region
- ☎ 02 the northwest
- ☎ 03 the northeast
- ☎ 04 the southeast (including Corsica)
- ☎ 05 the southwest

For France Telecom's directory inquiries *(services des renseignements)*, dial ☎ 12 (around €0.45 per minute). Not all operators speak English. Emergency numbers

---

EMERGENCY NUMBERS

- Ambulance (SAMU) ☎ 15
- Fire ☎ 18
- Police ☎ 17
- EU-wide emergency hotline ☎ 112
- Rape crisis hotline ☎ 0 800 059 595

---

and 0800 numbers can be dialled free from public and private telephones.

Public Phones & Telephone Cards

Almost all public telephones in France are card-operated. Cards can be purchased for €7.50 or €15 at post offices, *tabacs* (tobacconists) and anywhere that you see a blue sticker reading *'télécarte en vente ici'*. A whole bevy of other cards are available for cheap international calls.

Mobile Phones

France uses GSM 900/1800, which is compatible with the rest of Europe and Australia but not with the North American GSM 1900 (though some North Americans have GSM 1900/900 phones that do work here).

The three major mobile networks are **Bouygues** (☎ 0 810 63 01 00; www.bouygtel.com), France Telecom's **Orange** (☎ 0 800 83 08 00; www.orange.fr) and **SFR** (0800 10 60 00; www.sfr.com). If you already have a compatible phone, you can buy a pre-paid phone SIM-card with a mobile phone number. When these run out you purchase a recharge card at most *tabacs*.

VISAS

EU nationals and citizens of Switzerland, Iceland and Norway need only a passport or national identity card to enter France. Citizens of Australia, the USA, Canada, New Zealand, Japan and Israel do not need visas to visit France as tourists for up to three months; the same goes for citizens of EU candidate countries (except Turkey).

Those not exempt will need a visa allowing unlimited travel throughout the entire zone for 90 days. Apply to the consulate of the country you are entering first, or the country that will be your main destination. You will need medical insurance and proof of sufficient funds to support yourself. See www.eurovisa.com for information.

TRANSPORT IN FRANCE

GETTING THERE & AWAY
Air
AIRPORTS
Air France (www.airfrance.com), France's national carrier, and scores of other airlines link Paris with every part of the globe. France's two major international airports are Roissy-Charles de Gaulle (CDG, ☎ 01 48 62 12 12) and Orly (ORY; ☎ 01 49 75 15 15), both run by **Aeroports de Paris** (☎ 01 43 35 70 00; www.adp.fr). For details on these airports see the Paris chapter.

The other airports with significant international services (mainly within Europe) include:

Bordeaux (code BOD; ☎ 05 56 34 50 50; www.bordeaux.aeroport.fr)

Lyon (code LYS; ☎ 0826 800 826; www.lyon.aeroport.fr)

Marseille (code MRS; ☎ 04 42 14 14 14; www.marseille-provence.aeroport.fr)

Nice (code NCE; ☎ 0820 423 333; www.nice.aeroport.fr)

Strasbourg (code SXB; ☎ 03 88 64 67 67 www.strasbourg.aeroport.fr)

Toulouse (code TLS; ☎ 0825 380 000; www.toulouse.aeroport.fr)

Some airlines and budget carriers use minor provincial airports for flights to the UK, continental Europe and, sometimes, North Africa. Smaller airports taking international flights include Biarritz, Caen, Carcassone, Metz-Nancy-Lorraine, Montpellier, Rennes, Tours and Quimper.

AIRLINES
Most of the world's major carriers serve Paris at the very least. Airlines flying to and from France include:

Aer Lingus (code EI; ☎ 01 70 20 00 72; www.aerlingus.com; hub Dublin)

Air Canada (code AC; ☎ 0 825 880 881; www.aircanada.ca; hub Toronto)

Air France (code AF; ☎ 0 820 820 820; www.airfrance.com; hub Paris)

Alitalia (code AZ; ☎ 0 820 315 31; www.alitalia.com; hub Rome)

American Airlines (code AA; ☎ 0 810 872 872; www.americanairlines.com; hub Dallas)

Basiqair (code HV; www.basiqair.com; hub Amsterdam)

BMI BritishMidland (code BD; ☎ www.flybmi.com; hub London)

British Airways (code BA; ☎ 0 825 825 400; www.britishairways.com; hub London)

Easyjet (code EZY; ☎ 023-568 4880; www.easyjet.com; hub London Luton)

Iberia (code IB; ☎ 0 820 075 075; www.iberia.com; hub Madrid)

Lufthansa (code LH; ☎ 0 820 020 030; www.lufthansa.com; hub Frankfurt)

Ryanair (code FR; www.ryanair.com; hub London Stansted & Dublin)

Land
If you are doing a lot of travel around Europe, look for discount bus and train passes, which can be conveniently combined with discount air fares.

BUS
Buses are slower and less comfortable than trains, but they are cheaper, especially if you qualify for discount rates (youths under 26, seniors over 60, teachers and students).

The company **Eurolines** (☎ 08 92 69 52 52, 01 43 54 11 99; www.eurolines.com) groups together 31 European coach operators and links points all across Europe as well as Morocco and Russia. Eurolines' all-Europe website has links to each national company's site and gives detailed information on fares, routes, bookings and special deals. You can usually book online. Return tickets cost about 20% less than two one-ways. In summer, make reservations at least two working days in advance. The main hub is Paris.

French coach company **Intercars** (www.intercars.fr, in French) links France with cities throughout Europe, including Eastern Europe and Russia. The office in **Paris** (☎ 01 42 19 99 35; 139 bis rue de Vaugirard, 15e; metro Falguière) links with Berlin (€77, 13 hours), Moscow (€234, 50 hours), and many places in between. From **Lyon** (☎ 04 78 37 20 80; Perrache bus station) you can reach Venice, Naples, Porto, Minsk or Zagreb. From **Nice** (☎ 04 93 80 08 70; Nice bus station) you can reach San Sebastian, Casablanca and Warsaw. Reserve by emailing the agency closest to your place of departure.

CAR & MOTORCYCLE
Arriving in France by car is easy to do. At some border points you may be asked for your passport or identity card (your drivers' licence will not be sufficient ID). Police searches are not uncommon for vehicles entering France, particularly from Spain and Belgium.

Eurotunnel

The Channel Tunnel, inaugurated in 1994, is the first dry-land link between England and France since the Ice Age.

High-speed **Eurotunnel shuttle trains** (UK ☎ 0870 535 3535, France ☎ 03 21 00 61 00; www .eurotunnel.com) whisk cars, motorbikes and coaches from Folkestone via the Channel Tunnel to Coquelles, 5km southwest of Calais. Shuttles run daily 24 hours a day, with up to five departures an hour in peak periods.

Prices vary with market demand, but the regular one-way fare for a car and passengers costs from UK£150 (in February or March) to UK£250 (in July or August); return passage costs twice as much. Return fares valid for less than five days are much cheaper.

TRAIN

Rail services link France with every country in Europe; schedules are available from major train stations in France and abroad. You can book tickets and get information from **Rail Europe** (www.raileurope.com) up to two months ahead. In France, ticketing is handled by the **SNCF** (☎ 08 92 35 35 35; www.sncf.fr).

Eurostar

On the highly civilised **Eurostar** (France ☎ 08 92 35 35 39, UK ☎ 08705 186 186; www.eurostar.com), the trip from London to Paris will take just two hours and 35 minutes. There are direct services from London and Ashford to Paris and the three other stations in France: Calais-Fréthun, Lille and Disneyland Paris. A full-fare, 2nd-class ticket from London to Paris can be as low as UK£50 (and as high as UK£300). Student travel agencies often have youth fares unavailable directly from Eurostar.

Sea

Tickets for ferry travel to/from the UK, Channel Islands and Ireland are available from most travel agencies in France. In some cases, return fares cost less than two one-way tickets.

IRELAND

Eurail pass holders pay 50% of the adult pedestrian fare for crossings between Ireland and France on Irish Ferries (book ahead).

Irish Ferries (Ireland ☎ 01-638 3333, France ☎ 01 43 94 46 94; www.irishferries.ie) has overnight runs from Rosslare to either Cherbourg (18 hours)

or Roscoff (16 hours) every other day. A pedestrian/car with two adults costs around €90/389.

From April to September, **Brittany Ferries** (Ireland ☎ 0870 366 5333, France 0825 828 828; www .brittany-ferries.com) runs a car ferry every Saturday from Cork (Ringaskiddy) to Roscoff (14 hours) and on Friday in the other direction.

Freight ferries run by **P&O Irish Sea** (Ireland ☎ 0870 242 4777; www.poirishsea.com) link Rosslare with Cherbourg (18 hours, three per week); cars with two passengers cost from €154. From April to September there is also a weekly Dublin–Cherbourg route (18 hours); cars with two adults cost €174. Foot passengers are not accepted.

ITALY

From late April to mid-October, the **Société Nationale Maritime Corse Méditerranée** (SNCM; ☎ 0891 70 18 01; www.sncm.fr) has five or six car ferries per week from Marseille or Toulon to Porto Torres on the island of Sardinia (Sardaigne in French). The one-way adult pedestrian fare is around €100 and takes about 11 hours.

NORTH AFRICA

The SNCM and the **Compagnie Tunisienne de Navigation** (CTN; www.ctn.com.tn) link Marseille with the Tunisian capital, Tunis (about 24 hours, three or four a week). The standard adult fare is €300 one way with discounts for seniors and those under 25. In France, ticketing is handled by the SNCM. The SNCM also links Marseille with Alger (Algeria).

Compagnie Marocaine de Navigation (CoMaNav; www.comanav.co.ma) links Sète, 29km (20 minutes by train) southwest of Montpellier, with Morocco's port of Tangier (Tanger; 36 hours, five to seven monthly). The cheapest berth costs €168 (€228 in August and for some other summer sailings) one way; return tickets cost 15% to 20% less than two one-ways. In France, ticketing is handled by SNCM.

UK

Fares vary widely. Three- or five-day excursion (return) fares generally cost about the same as regular one-way tickets; special promotional return fares, often requiring advance booking, are sometimes cheaper than a standard one-way fare. Check out **Ferry Savers** (☎ 0870 990 8492; www.ferrysavers.com),

FRANCE

which guarantees the lowest prices on Channel crossings.

Normandy

The Newhaven–Dieppe route is handled by **Hoverspeed** (☎ 0870 240 8070, France 00 800 1211 1211; www.hoverspeed.co.uk) and **Transmanche Ferries** (☎ 0800 917 1201; www.transmancheferries.com). The hovercraft trip (one to three daily) takes 2¼ hours, while the ferry trip (two daily) takes four hours. Pedestrians pay from UK£30 one way, with special deals available.

Brittany Ferries also has car ferries from Portsmouth to Caen (Ouistreham; six hours, three per day). Tickets cost the same as for Poole–Cherbourg.

The 4¼-hour crossing (two or three per day) from Poole to Cherbourg is with **Brittany Ferries** (UK ☎ 0870 366 5333, France ☎ 0825 82 88 28; www.brittany-ferries.com). Foot passengers pay from UK£33 one way.

On the Portsmouth–Cherbourg route, Brittany Ferries, Condor Ferries and **P&O Portsmouth** (UK ☎ 0870 598 0555, France ☎ 08 25 01 30 13; www.poferries.com) have two or three car ferries a day (five hours by day, eight hours overnight) and, from April to September, two faster catamarans a day. Foot passengers pay from UK£29 one way.

The Portsmouth–Le Havre crossing is handled by P&O Portsmouth (5½ hours by day, 7¾ hours overnight, three car ferries a day, fewer in winter). Passage costs somewhat more than Portsmouth–Cherbourg, check the website for details.

Far Northern France

The fastest way to cross the English Channel is between Dover and Calais, served by Hoverspeed's SeaCats (catamarans), which take 50 minutes. For foot passengers, a one-way trip (or a return completed within five days) costs UK£39. From Calais, there are five daily trains to Le Tréport, the northernmost town in Normandy (€19, five hours).

The Dover–Calais crossing is also handled by car ferries, run by **SeaFrance** (UK ☎ 0870 571 1711, France ☎ 08 04 04 40 45; www. seafrance.com; 1½hr, 15 daily) and **P&O Ferries** (UK ☎ 0870 520 20 20; www.posl.com; 1-1¼hr, 29 daily) for about the same price.

A new 50-minute catamaran service between Dover and Boulogne is operated by **Speed One** (UK ☎ 01304 203000; www.speedferries .com) which makes five crossings daily and costs from £60 return for five passenger and car. It's cheaper the earlier you book.

Brittany

From mid-March to mid-November, Plymouth is linked to Roscoff (six hours for day crossings, one to three per day) by Brittany Ferries. The one-way fare for foot passengers is around UK£35.

Brittany Ferries also links Portsmouth and Plymouth with St-Malo (8¾ hours for day crossing, one per day). Pedestrians pay from UK£27 one way.

From April to September, **Condor Ferries** (UK ☎ 0845 345 2000, France ☎ 02 99 20 03 00; www .condorferries.com) has at least one daily ferry linking Weymouth with St-Malo (UK£35) that can take anywhere from seven to 10 hours, including a stopover in Guernsey.

GETTING AROUND
Air

The long-established **Air France** (☎ 0820 820 820; www.airfrance.com) continues to control the lion's share of France's long-protected domestic airline industry, although British budget carrier Easyjet has introduced flights linking Paris with Marseille, Nice and Toulouse.

Any French travel agency or Air France office can make bookings for domestic flights and supply details on the complicated fare options. Outside France, Air France representatives sell tickets for many domestic flights.

Up to 84% reduction is available if you fly during the week and purchase your ticket three weeks in advance. Significant discounts are available to children, young people, families and seniors. Special last-minute offers are posted on the Air France website every Wednesday.

Bus

Within France, bus services are provided by numerous different companies, usually based within one *département*. For travel between regions, a train is your best bet since inter-regional bus services are limited. Buses are used quite extensively for short-distance travel within *départements*, especially in rural areas with relatively few train lines (eg Brittany and Normandy) – but services are often slow, and few and far between.

Car & Motorcycle

Having your own wheels gives you exceptional freedom and allows you to visit more remote parts of France. Unfortunately, it can be expensive, and in cities parking and traffic are frequent headaches. Motorcyclists will find France great for touring. The websites www.viamichelin.com and www.autoroutes .fr both calculate how much you will pay in petrol and tolls for specified journeys.

DRIVING LICENCE & DOCUMENTS

All drivers must carry at all times: a national ID card or passport; a valid driver's licence; car ownership papers, known as a *carte grise* (grey card); and proof of third-party (liability) insurance.

FUEL

Essence (petrol or gasoline), also known as *carburant* (fuel) costs around €1.10 a litre for 95 unleaded.

HIRE

To hire a car in France you'll generally need to be over 21 years old and hold a valid drivers' licence and an international credit card. Arranging your car rental or fly/drive package before you leave home is often considerably cheaper. Major rental companies include:

ADA (☎ 08 25 16 91 69; www.ada.fr)
Avis (☎ 08 02 05 05 05; www.avis.com)
Budget (☎ 08 00 10 00 01; www.budget.com)
Easycar (☎ 09 06 33 33 33 3; www.easycar.com) Cheap rates and offices in Paris and Nice.
Europcar (☎ 08 03 35 23 52; www.europcar.com)
Hertz (☎ 08 25 34 23 43; www.hertz.com)
OTU Voyages (☎ 01 40 29 12 12; www.otu.fr) For students.

Deals can be found on the Internet, with travel agencies and through companies like **Auto Europe** (☎ 1-888 223 5555; www.autoeurope .com) in the US, or **Holiday Autos** (☎ 08 70 5300 400; www.holidayautos.co.uk) in the UK.

INSURANCE

Unlimited third-party liability insurance is mandatory for all vehicles entering France, whether the owner accompanies the vehicle or not. Third-party liability insurance is provided by car-rental companies, but collision-damage waivers (CDW) vary greatly. When comparing rates check the *franchise* (excess/

deductible), which is usually €350 for a small car. Your credit card may cover CDW if you use it to pay for the car rental.

ROAD RULES

Cars drive on the right in France. All passengers must wear seat belts, and children weighing less than 18kg must travel in backward-facing child seats. You will be fined for going 10km/h over the speed limit.

Any car entering an intersection (including a T-junction) from a road on your right has right-of-way, unless the intersection is signposted *vous n'avez pas la priorité* (you do not have right of way) or *cédez le passage* (give way). *Priorité à droite* (give way to the right) is also suspended on priority roads, which are marked by an up-ended yellow square with a black square in the middle.

It is illegal to drive in France with a blood-alcohol concentration (BAC) over 0.05% (0.5g per litre of blood) – the equivalent of two glasses of wine for a 75kg adult. Mobile phones may only be used with a hands-free kit or speakerphone.

Riders of any type of two-wheeled vehicle that has a motor (except for motor-assisted bicycles) must wear a helmet.

Train

France's superb rail network reaches almost every part of the country. Many towns and villages not on the SNCF train and bus network are linked by intra-departmental bus lines.

France's most important train lines radiate from Paris like the spokes of a wheel, making train travel between provincial towns situated on different spokes infrequent and rather slow. In some cases you have to transit through Paris.

TGV Atlantique Sud-Ouest & TGV Atlantique Ouest These link Paris' Gare Montparnasse with western and southwestern France, including Brittany (Rennes, Quimper, Brest), Nantes, Tours, Poitiers, La Rochelle, Bordeaux, Biarritz and Toulouse.

TGV Nord, Thalys & Eurostar These link Paris' Gare du Nord with Arras, Lille, Calais, Brussels, Amsterdam, Cologne and, via the Channel Tunnel, Ashford and London Waterloo.

TGV Sud-Est & TGV Midi-Méditerranée These link Paris' Gare de Lyon with the southeast, including Dijon, Lyon, Geneva, the Alps, Avignon, Marseille, Nice and Montpellier.

FRANCE

A train that is not a TGV is often referred to as a *corail,* a *classique* or a TER *(train express régional).*

Fantastic deals are available exclusively on the website www.sncf.com: last minute offers at up to 50% off, published on the site every Tuesday; and *Prem's* early bird deals (eg Paris–Nice €25), available only through online bookings made at least three weeks in advance

Before boarding the train you must validate your ticket by time-stamping it in a *composteur,* one of those orange posts situated at the start of the platform. If you forget, find a conductor on the train so they can punch it for you (otherwise you're likely to be fined). Tickets *can* be purchased on board the train (straight away from the conductor) with cash but there is a surcharge.

Germany

CONTENTS

Germany is the powerhouse of Central Europe, geographically, politically and culturally. Its legendary economy may be struggling, but few countries have contributed quite so much to the current state of the continent – both positively and negatively – since the start of the 20th century.

Most visitors are very conscious of the country's catastrophe-strewn history, but then so are the Germans themselves, and there is no denying the remarkable resilience of a nation that has come through two world wars and 40 years of division. The many museums confronting the Nazi and German Democratic Republic (GDR) eras are highly recommended as an insight into current attitudes as well as the traumas of the past.

Today Germany can easily rival France as an accessible, popular, fascinating tourist destination, with centuries' worth of culture, no end of spectacular castles and palaces, and some of Europe's most dramatic scenery. Its major cities, too, can hold their own with the world's best, and visitors are seldom stuck for entertainment in the charismatic capital Berlin (or in Frankfurt, or Hamburg, Munich, Dresden, or…). With the EU opening up to Eastern Europe, Germany has never been more central, and bypassing it would really be a crime.

FAST FACTS

- **Area** 356,866 sq km (138 Luxembourgs, two-thirds of France)
- **Capital** Berlin
- **Currency** euro (€); A$1 = €0.58; ¥100 = €0.76; NZ$1 = €0.54; UK£1 = €1.50; US$1 = €0.83
- **Famous for** sausages, beer, culture, cars, history
- **Key Phrases** Guten Tag (good day); Auf Wiedersehen (goodbye); Ja/Nein (yes/no); Danke (thank you); Sprechen Sie Englisch? (Do you speak English?)
- **Official Language** German
- **Population** 82.5 million
- **Telephone Codes** country code ☎ 49; international dialling code ☎ 00
- **Visa** none usually required

HIGHLIGHTS

- Burn the candle at both ends in **Berlin** (p406), with culture by day and clubs by night.
- Stack up the steins with your fellow tourists at the Munich **Oktoberfest** (p460), Europe's biggest beer festival.
- Sharpen your architectural eye either side of the Elbe in **Dresden** (p426), Saxony's baroque'n'roll capital.
- Hike, bike or ski the well-trodden trails of the famous **Black Forest** (p480).
- Seek out the furthest corners of **Rügen Island** (p453) to strike out from the beaten track, on foot, bike or canoe.

ITINERARIES

- **Two weeks** Starting in Berlin, spend a day in Potsdam then head south towards Munich, stopping off in Dresden and Leipzig or Bamberg and Freiburg. From Munich, venture west to the Rhine or Moselle Valley.
- **One month** Following the route above, you should have time to include Meissen and the Harz Mountains on the way south, then take in the Alps, Lake Constance and the Black Forest; alternatively, head back up north to explore Lübeck, Hamburg and the Baltic coast.

CLIMATE & WHEN TO GO

German weather can be variable, so it's best to be prepared for many conditions throughout the year. The most reliable weather is from May to October, coinciding with the standard tourist season (except for skiing). The shoulder periods (late March to May and September to October) can bring fewer tourists and surprisingly pleasant weather. Camping season is from May to September. See Climate Charts p1054.

HISTORY

Events in Germany have often dominated the European stage, but the country itself is a relatively recent invention: for most of its history Germany has been a patchwork of semi-independent principalities and city-states, occupied first by the Roman Empire, then the Holy Roman Empire and finally the Austrian Habsburgs. Perhaps because of this, many Germans retain a strong regional identity, despite the momentous events that have occurred since.

HOW MUCH?

- Budget hotel room €60
- Two-course meal €15
- Loaf of bread €0.80
- Caipirinha cocktail €4.50
- Newspaper €0.60

LONELY PLANET INDEX

- Litre of petrol €1.10
- Litre of bottled water €2
- Beer (0.3L local Pils) €2
- Souvenir T-shirt €15
- Street snack (döner kebab) €2.40

The most significant medieval events in Germany were pan-European in nature – Martin Luther, a monk from Erfurt, brought on the Protestant Reformation with his criticism of the Catholic Church in Wittenberg in 1517, a movement which in turn sparked the Thirty Years' War. Germany became the battlefield of Europe, and only began to regain stability after the Napoleonic Wars with increasing industrialisation and the rise of the Kingdom of Prussia. In 1866 legendary Prussian 'Iron Chancellor' Otto von Bismarck succeeded in bringing the German states together, largely by force, and a united Germany emerged for the first time in 1871, under Kaiser Wilhelm I.

WWI & the Rise of Hitler

With the advent of the 20th century, Germany's rapid growth soon overtaxed the political talents of Kaiser Wilhelm II and led to mounting tensions with England, Russia and France. When war broke out in 1914, Germany's only ally was a weakened Austria-Hungary. Gruelling trench warfare on two fronts sapped the nation's resources, and by late 1918 Germany sued for peace. The Kaiser abdicated and escaped to Holland. Amid widespread public anger and unrest a new republic, which became known as the Weimar Republic, was proclaimed.

The Treaty of Versailles in 1919 chopped huge areas off Germany and imposed heavy reparation payments. These were impossible to meet, and when France and Belgium

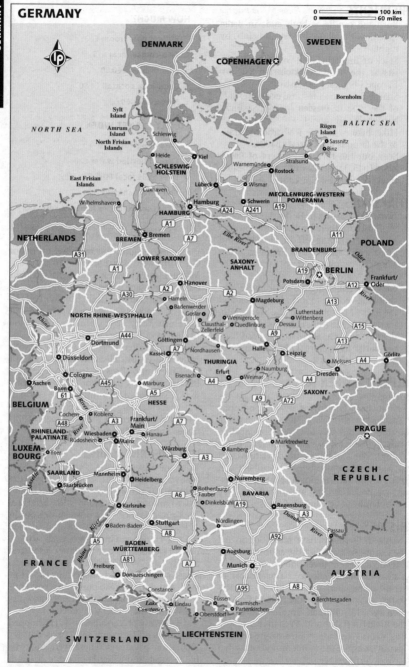

occupied the Rhineland to ensure continued payments, the subsequent hyperinflation and miserable economic conditions provided fertile ground for political extremists. One of these was Adolf Hitler, an Austrian drifter, would-be artist and German army veteran.

Led by Hitler, the National Socialist German Workers' Party (or Nazi Party) staged an abortive coup in Munich in 1923. This landed Hitler in prison for nine months, during which time he wrote *Mein Kampf.*

From 1929 the worldwide economic depression hit Germany hard, leading to unemployment, strikes and demonstrations. The Communist Party under Ernst Thälmann gained strength, but wealthy industrialists began to support the Nazis and police turned a blind eye to Nazi street thugs.

The Nazis increased their strength in general elections and in 1933 replaced the Social Democrats as the largest party in the *Reichstag* (parliament), with about one-third of the seats. Hitler was appointed chancellor and one year later assumed absolute control as *Führer* (leader).

WWII & the Division of Germany

From 1935 Germany began to re-arm and build its way out of depression with strategic public works such as the autobahns. Hitler reoccupied the Rhineland in 1936, and in 1938 annexed Austria and, following a compromise agreement with Britain and France, parts of Czechoslovakia.

All of this took place against a backdrop of growing racism at home. The Nuremburg Laws of 1935 deprived non-Aryans – mostly Jews and Roma (Gypsies) – of their German citizenship and many other rights. On 9 November 1938, the horror escalated into *Kristallnacht* ('night of broken glass'), in which synagogues and Jewish cemeteries, property and businesses across Germany were desecrated, burnt or demolished.

In September 1939, after signing a pact that allowed both Stalin and himself a free hand in the east of Europe, Hitler attacked Poland, which led to war with Britain and France. Germany quickly occupied large parts of Europe, but after 1942 began to suffer increasingly heavy losses. Massive bombing reduced Germany's cities to rubble, and the country lost 10% of its population. Germany accepted unconditional surrender in May 1945, soon after Hitler's suicide.

At the end of the war, the full scale of Nazi racism was exposed. 'Concentration camps', intended to rid Europe of people considered undesirable according to Nazi doctrine, had exterminated some six million Jews and one million more Roma, communists, homosexuals and others in what has come to be known as the Holocaust, history's first 'assembly line' genocide.

At conferences in Yalta and Potsdam, the Allies (the Soviet Union, the USA, the UK and France) redrew the borders of Germany, making it around 25% smaller than it had become after the Treaty of Versailles 26 years earlier. Germany was divided into four occupation zones.

In the Soviet zone of the country, the communist Socialist Unity Party (SED) won the 1946 elections and began a rapid nationalisation of industry. In September 1949 the Federal Republic of Germany (FRG) was created out of the three western zones; in response the German Democratic Republic (GDR) was founded in the Soviet zone the following month, with (East) Berlin as its capital.

From Division to Unity

As the West's bulwark against communism, the FRG received massive injections of US capital, and experienced rapid economic development (the *Wirschaftswunder,* or 'economic miracle') under the leadership of Konrad Adenauer. The GDR, on the other hand, had to pay US$10 billion in war reparations to the Soviet Union and rebuild itself from scratch.

A better life in the west increasingly attracted skilled workers away from the miserable economic conditions in the east. As these were people the GDR could ill afford to lose, in 1961 it built a wall around West Berlin and sealed its border with the FRG.

In 1971 a change to the more flexible leadership of Erich Honecker in the east, combined with the *Ostpolitik* (East Politics) of FRG chancellor Willy Brandt, allowed an easier political relationship between the two Germanys. In the same year the four occupying powers formally accepted the division of Berlin.

Honecker's policies produced higher living standards in the GDR, yet East Germany barely managed to achieve a level of prosperity half that of the FRG. After Mikhail

Gorbachev came to power in the Soviet Union in March 1985, the East German communists gradually lost Soviet backing.

Events in 1989 rapidly overtook the GDR government, which resisted pressure to introduce reforms. When Hungary relaxed its border controls in May 1989, East Germans began crossing to the west. Tighter travel controls resulted in would-be defectors taking refuge in the FRG's embassy in Prague. Meanwhile, mass demonstrations in Leipzig spread to other cities and Honecker was replaced by his security chief, Egon Krenz, who introduced cosmetic reforms. Then suddenly on 9 November 1989, a decision to allow direct travel to the west was mistakenly interpreted as the immediate opening of all GDR borders with West Germany. That same night thousands of people streamed into the west past stunned border guards. Millions more followed in the next few days, and dismantling of the Berlin Wall began soon thereafter.

The trend at first was to reform the GDR but, in East German elections held in early 1990, citizens voted clearly in favour of the prereunification Christian Democratic Union (CDU). A Unification Treaty was drawn up to integrate East Germany into the Federal Republic of Germany, enacted on 3 October 1990. All-German elections were held on 2 December that year and, in the midst of national euphoria, the CDU-led coalition, which strongly favoured reunification, soundly defeated the Social Democrat opposition. CDU leader Helmut Kohl earned the enviable position of 'unification chancellor'.

Into the Millennium

In 1998, a coalition of Social Democrats, led by Gerhard Schröder, and Bündnis 90/die Grünen (the Greens party) took political office from Kohl and the CDU amid allegations of widespread financial corruption in the unification-era government.

At reunification, it was said that 10 years would bring the two Germanys to parity, but now it's generally considered that another 10 years will be needed. The German economic miracle has largely petered out, and with 4.5 million people out of work, social problems are an increasing fact of life, especially in the hard-hit eastern states. Most disturbingly, racism appears to be on the rise, and government attempts to ban the neo-Nazi National Democratic Party in 2003 were deemed unconstitutional, a symbolic victory for right-wing groups everywhere.

Schröder and the SDP-Greens only narrowly managed to retain office in the 2002 general election. In 2004 things looked even worse, largely thanks to the chancellor's pet Agenda 2010 project, which aimed to lower taxes by cutting public spending in key areas. The slashing of university funding brought students out in protest for several weeks, and a botched reform of the public health insurance system was one of the most unpopular pieces of legislation ever, resulting in massive gains for the supposedly discredited CDU at subsequent local elections. With both presidential and national elections due in the next couple of years, the ruling coalition has a lot to do if they wish to regain favour.

On an international level, however, Germany has transformed itself from two squabbling states into one of Europe's leading nations and arguably the driving force in EU politics. The government's forthright opposition to the US-led Iraq war in 2003 was a major indication of how far the country has come, challenging the old Cold War lines of allegiance and hinting at the potential of Europe to rival the USA's influence on the world stage in years to come. As a firm believer in the European superstate, Germany will doubtless be at the forefront of any such development.

PEOPLE

Germany has a population of around 83 million, making it the most populous in Europe after Russia. Germany's main native minority is the tiny group of Slavonic Sorbs in the eastern states of Saxony and Brandenburg, who maintain their own folk traditions. In political and economic terms, Germany is Europe's most decentralised nation, but considerable variation in population density exists. The Ruhr district in the northern Rhineland has Germany's densest concentration of people and industry, while Mecklenburg–Western Pomerania in the northeastern corner is relatively sparsely settled. About one-third of the population lives in 84 cities, each with more than 100,000 people.

Immigration compensates for the extremely low birth rate among the established

German population, and more than seven million foreigners now live in Germany. Most hail from Turkey, Italy, Greece and the former Yugoslavia, and have arrived as 'guest workers' in the FRG since the early 1960s to work in lower-paid jobs. In 1999 archaic immigration laws dating back to 1913 were changed to make it easier for residents without German ancestry to gain citizenship. Integration is generally fairly successful, although larger immigrant communities tend to stick together.

RELIGION

The majority religions in Germany are Protestantism and Catholicism, which claim roughly equal numbers of followers. Some regions have higher concentrations of one branch – Bavaria is staunchly Catholic, for example.

The most significant minority religion is Islam, with about 1.8 million adherents, many of them immigrants. Islamic fundamentalism has become an increasing issue since the start of the global 'war on terror': extremist groups have become more vocal recently, and several of the perpetrators of the September 11th suicide attacks in 2001 were German residents. Politically, this has often led to calls for conservative integration measures such as banning headscarves in schools, causing further friction with Muslim communities.

Around 61,000 Jews also live in Germany, little more than a tenth of pre-WWII numbers. Many are actually from the former Soviet Union, attracted by the relaxed immigration and citizenship deals offered around the time of reunification.

Germans who belong to a registered denomination have to pay a church tax on top of their income tax, usually around 10% of their salary. Unsurprisingly, fewer and fewer people are choosing to declare their religious affiliation!

ARTS

Germany's meticulously creative population has made major contributions to international culture, particularly during the 18th century when the Saxon courts at Weimar and Dresden attracted some of the greatest minds of Europe. With such rich traditions to fall back on, inspiration has seldom been in short supply for the new generations of German artists and artistes, despite the upheavals of the country's recent history.

Literature

The undisputed colossus of the German arts was Johann Wolfgang von Goethe: poet, dramatist, painter, politician, scientist, philosopher, landscape gardener and perhaps the last European to achieve the Renaissance ideal of excellence in many fields. His greatest work, the drama *Faust,* is the definitive version of the legend, showing the archetypal human search for meaning and knowledge.

Goethe's close friend Friedrich Schiller was a poet, dramatist and novelist. His most famous work is the dramatic cycle *Wallenstein,* based on the life of a treacherous general of the Thirty Years' War who plotted to make himself arbiter of the empire. Schiller's other great play, *William Tell,* dealt with the right of the oppressed to rise against tyranny.

On the scientific side, Alexander von Humboldt contributed much to environmentalism through his studies of the relationship of plants and animals to their physical surroundings. His contemporary, the philosopher Georg Wilhelm Friedrich Hegel, created an all-embracing classical philosophy that is still influential today.

Postwar literature in both Germanys was influenced by the politically focused Gruppe 47. It included writers such as Günter Grass, winner of the 1999 Nobel Prize for Literature, whose modern classic, *Die Blechtrommel* (The Tin Drum), humorously follows German history through the eyes of a young boy who refuses to grow up. Christa Wolf, an East German novelist and Gruppe 47 writer, won high esteem in both Germanys. Her 1963 story *Der geteilte Himmel* (Divided Heaven) tells of a young woman whose fiancé abandons her for life in the West.

A wave of recent novelists have addressed modern history in a lighter fashion.

Helden wie wir (Heroes Like Us) by Thomas Brussig, an eastern German, tells the story of a man whose penis brings about the collapse of the Berlin Wall, while the GDR's demise is almost incidental to the eponymous barfly in Sven Regener's *Herr Lehmann* (Mr Lehmann). Also from Berlin is Russian-born Wladimir Kaminer, whose books *Russendisko* (Russian Disco) and *Schönhauser Allee* document the stranger-than-fiction lives of his many friends and acquaintances in the capital.

Cinema & TV

Since the foundation of the UFA studios in Potsdam in 1917 Germany has had an active and successful film industry. Marlene Dietrich (1901–92) became the country's first international superstar and sex symbol, starting out in silent films and later moving to Hollywood. Director Fritz Lang, too, made a name for himself with complex films like *Metropolis* (1926) and *M* (1931).

During the Third Reich, the arts were devoted mainly to propaganda, with grandiose projects and realist art extolling the virtues of German nationhood. The best-known Nazi-era director was Leni Riefenstahl (1902–2003) whose *Triumph of the Will* (1934), depicting the Nuremberg rallies, won great acclaim but later rendered her unemployable. The controversy surrounding her personal politics dogged her for much of her life.

The 1960s and 1970s saw a great revival of German cinema, spearheaded by energetic, politically aware young directors such as Rainer Werner Fassbinder, Wim Wenders, Volker Schlöndorff and Margarethe von Trotta. Fassbinder died in 1980 and Wenders moved to the USA, but Schlöndorff and von Trotta are still key figures in the industry, joined by newer faces such as Dorris Dörrie, Tom Tykwer, Detlev Buck, Leander Haussmann and Sylke Enders.

Most recently, Wolfgang Becker's GDR comedy *Good Bye Lenin!* (2003) was a surprise smash hit worldwide, while Turkish-German director Fatih Akin's bleak *Gegen die Wand* (Against the Wall; 2003) won the top prize at the 2004 Berlin film festival to great acclaim.

Music

Forget brass bands and oompah music – few countries can claim the impressive musical heritage of Germany. Even a partial list of household names would have to include Johann Sebastian Bach, Georg Friedrich Händel (Handel), Ludwig van Beethoven, Richard Strauss, Robert Schumann, Johannes Brahms, Felix Mendelssohn-Bartholdy, Richard Wagner and Gustav Mahler, all of whom are celebrated in museums, exhibitions and festivals around the country.

These musical traditions continue to thrive: the Berlin Philharmonic, Dresden Opera and Leipzig Orchestra are known around the world, and musical performances are hosted almost daily in every major theatre in the country.

Germany has also made significant contributions to the contemporary music scene. Internationally renowned artists include punk icon Nina Hagen – '80s balloon girl Nena – and rock bands from the Scorpions to Die Toten Hosen and current darlings Wir sind Helden. Gothic and hard rock are disproportionately well-followed in Germany, largely thanks to the success of death-obsessed growlers Rammstein.

For real innovation, though, the German dance music scene is second to none, particularly in the party cities of Frankfurt-

REALITY BITTEN

Flick on the telly at any time of day and you'll probably come to the same conclusion: Germany is obsessed with reality TV. Wherever you look, sarcastic presenters are ripping out people's kitchens, disparaging their cooking skills, mediating with their neighbours or telling them how to become pop stars. Worse, there is even a whole sub-genre of tenuous real-ish shows attempting to cash in – teenagers learn life lessons from groups of 'real-life' students (bad actors shot with a camcorder for authenticity), and there are even several screen judges who try 'real-life' cases (even worse, actors shot in a fake courtroom).

Of course, the fault lies with the original. Germany was one of the first countries to buy into Dutch company Endemol's phenomenally successful *Big Brother* franchise, and the obsession with other people's dull lives doesn't seem to have waned since the first series came out back in 1999. The latest instalment started in March 2004 with an all-new cast of exhibitionists and a massive one million euros prize money; the real novelty, however, is that it will now last a whole *year*. With half the population glued to the couch and Endemol busy counting the cash, reality itself may start to feel a little neglected.

am-Main and Berlin. Kraftwerk pioneered the original techno sounds, which were then popularised in raves and clubs such as Berlin's Tresor in the early '90s. Paul van Dyk was among the first proponents of euphoric trance, which pushed club music firmly into the commercial mainstream; DJs like Ian Pooley, Westbam and Ellen Allien now play all over the world, and labels such as !K7, Ongaku (Klang/Playhouse) and Shitkatapult continue to turn out cutting-edge leftfield electronic music. Producers and remixers Jazzanova also have a great worldwide reputation on the more jazzy, downtempo side of things.

Even German hip-hop is well represented and increasingly recognised internationally – German performers such as DJ Tomekk, Simon Vegas and Kool Savas have all recently produced tracks with hot US acts.

Of course, what's good isn't always what's popular, and you'll still encounter plenty of naff pop, Pop Idol-style unit-shifters and the peculiarly German *Schlager* genre, with its schmaltzy lyrics and mullet-sporting performers.

Architecture

The scope of German architecture is such that it could easily be the focus of an entire visit. The first great wave of buildings came with the Romanesque period (800–1200), examples of which can be found at Trier Cathedral, the churches of Cologne and the chapel of Charlemagne's palace in Aachen.

The Gothic style (1200–1500) is best viewed at Freiburg's Münster cathedral, Cologne's Dom (cathedral) and the Marienkirche in Lübeck. Red-brick Gothic structures are common in the north of Germany, with buildings such as Schwerin's Dom and Stralsund's Nikolaikirche.

For classic baroque, Balthasar Neumann's superb Residenz in Würzburg, the magnificent cathedral in Passau and the many classics of Dresden's old centre are must-sees. The neoclassical period of the 19th century was led by Karl Friedrich Schinkel, whose name crops up all over Germany.

In 1919, Walter Gropius founded the Bauhaus movement in an attempt to meld theoretical concerns of architecture with the practical problems faced by artists and craftspeople. The Bauhaus flourished in Dessau, but with the arrival of the Nazis, Gropius left for Harvard University.

Albert Speer was Hitler's favourite architect, known for his pompous neoclassical buildings and grand plans to change the face of Berlin. Most of his epic works ended up unbuilt or flattened by WWII.

Dresden's transparent VW factory is a prime example of modern style. For a glimpse of the future of German architecture, head to Potsdamer Platz, Leipziger Platz and the new government area north of the Reichstag in Berlin, which are all being developed into space-age swathes of glass, concrete and chrome.

Visual Arts

The Renaissance came late to Germany but flourished once it took hold, replacing the predominant Gothic style. The draughtsman Albrecht Dürer of Nuremberg was one of the world's finest portraitists, as was the prolific Lucas Cranach the Elder, who worked in Wittenberg for more than 45 years. The baroque period brought great sculpture, including works by Andreas Schlüter in Berlin, while romanticism produced some of Germany's most famous paintings, best exemplified by Caspar David Friedrich and Otto Runge.

At the turn of the 20th century, expressionism established itself with great names like Paul Klee and the Russian-born painter Wassily Kandinsky, who were also associated with the Bauhaus design school. By the 1920s, art had become more radical and political, with artists like George Grosz, Otto Dix and Max Ernst exploring the new concepts of dada and surrealism. Käthe Kollwitz is one of the era's few major female artists, known for her social realist drawings.

The only works encouraged by the Nazis were of the epic style of propaganda artists like Mjölnir; non-conforming artists such as sculptor Ernst Barlach and painter Emil Nolde were declared 'degenerate' and their pieces destroyed or appropriated for secret private collections.

Since 1945 abstract art has been the mainstay of the German scene, with key figures like Joseph Beuys and Anselm Kiefer achieving worldwide reputations. The latest young artist to emerge is Italian-German Monica Bonvicini, whose acclaimed installations address themes of space and destruction.

Theatre & Dance

In the 1920s, Berlin was the theatrical capital of Germany; its most famous practitioner was the poet and playwright Bertolt Brecht (1898–1956). Brecht introduced Marxist concepts into his plays, aiming to encourage moral debate by detaching the audience from what was happening on stage.

Today Berlin once again has the most dynamic theatre scene in the country, as Volksbühne director Frank Castorf vies with Schaubühne head Thomas Ostermeier to capture the attention of young audiences neglected by the major stages, choosing mainly modern, provocative works. Dance, too, is undergoing a renaissance – Ostermeier's co-director is renowned dancer and choreographer Sascha Waltz (yes, that really is her name), and several other venues offer unparalleled opportunities to see experimental and avant-garde performances.

SPORT

Football (soccer) is the number one spectator sport in Germany, as in most other European countries. The German national team has won the World Cup twice (don't remind the English!) and is still rated among the world's best teams. The Bundesliga is the top national league, with seasons running from September to June; notable top-flight teams include Bayern München, Borussia Dortmund and Hertha BSC (Berlin's major team). The DFB (www.dfb.de) is the national body responsible for all levels of the game.

Ice hockey is very popular in certain parts of the country, attracting many professional Canadian and American players as well as some vocal fans. The two Berlin teams, the Capitals and the Eisbären, are generally good teams to follow. The DEB (www.deb.de, in German) is the governing body.

International sports are also well-attended, especially when the relevant national teams are in form; major tennis, athletics, Grand Prix, swimming, cycling and water polo events are all features of the German calendar.

ENVIRONMENT
The Land

Germany covers 356,866 sq km and can be divided from north to south into several geographical regions.

The Northern Lowlands are a broad expanse of flat, low-lying land that sweeps across the northern third of the country from the Netherlands into Poland. The landscape is characterised by moist heaths interspersed with pastures and farmland.

The complex Central Uplands region divides northern Germany from the south. Extending from the deep schisms of the Rhineland massifs to the Black Forest, the Bavarian Forest, the Ore Mountains and the Harz Mountains, these low mountain ranges are Germany's heartland. The Rhine and Main Rivers, important waterways for inland shipping, cut through the southwest of this region. With large deposits of coal as well as favourable transport conditions, this was one of the first regions in Germany to undergo industrialisation.

The Alpine Foothills, wedged between the Danube and the Alps, are typified by subalpine plateaus and rolling hills, and moors in eastern regions around the Danube.

Germany's Alps lie entirely within Bavaria and stretch from the large, glacially formed Lake Constance in the west to Berchtesgaden in Germany's southeastern corner. Though lower than the mountains to their south, many summits are well above 2000m, rising dramatically from the Alpine Foothills to the 2966m Zugspitze, Germany's highest mountain.

Wildlife

Few species of flora and fauna are unique to Germany. Unique, however, is the importance Germans place on their forests, the prettiest of which are mixed-species deciduous forests planted with beech, oak, maple and birch. You'll find that many cities even have their own city forest (*Stadtwald*). Alpine regions bloom in spring with orchids, cyclamen, gentians, edelweiss and more; and the heather blossom on the Lüneburg Heath, north of Hanover, is stunning in August.

Apart from human beings, common mammals include deer, wild pigs, rabbits, foxes and hares. The chances of seeing these in summer are fairly good, especially in eastern Germany. The wild pig population is particularly thriving – foraging porkers have even become a regular nuisance in the suburbs of Berlin! On the coasts you will find seals and, throughout Germany, falcons, hawks, storks and migratory geese are a common sight.

National Parks

Berchtesgaden (in the Bavarian Alps), the Wattenmeer parks in Schleswig-Holstein, Lower Saxony and Hamburg, and the Unteres Odertal, a joint German-Polish endeavour, are highlights among Germany's 13 national parks. There are also a number of Unesco-listed sites in Germany, including the Wartburg castle in Eisenach.

Environmental Issues

Germans are fiercely protective of their natural surroundings. Households and businesses participate enthusiastically in waste-recycling programmes. A refund system applies to a wide range of glass bottles and jars, while containers for waste paper and glass can be found in each neighbourhood. The government is a signatory of the major international treaties on climate change and runs its own campaigns to save energy and reduce CO_2 emissions domestically; a controversial 'eco-tax' was recently added to the price of petrol.

Times have changed since the violent clashes between police and antinuclear protestors in the 1980s. Germany still generates about one-third of its energy from its 19 atomic plants, but a deal has been struck with the powerful energy lobby to close the plants over the next three decades. In the meantime, nuclear waste remains a sticky, unresolved issue.

FOOD & DRINK
Where to Eat & Drink

Mid-priced Italian, Turkish, Greek and Chinese restaurants can be found in every town, and most pubs serve basic German food. If you're on a low budget, you can get a feed at stand-up food stalls (*Schnellimbiss* or *Imbiss*). The food is usually quite reasonable and filling, ranging from döner kebabs to Chinese stir-fries and traditional German sausages with beer.

Much of the German daily and social life revolves around daytime cafés, which often serve meals and alcohol as well as coffee. The late-opening variety are great places to meet people.

For self-caterers, supermarkets such as Penny Markt, Kaiser's, Aldi, Rewe and Plus are cheap and have quite a good range. Make a point of buying your drinks in supermarkets if your budget is tight.

Students can eat cheaply (though not always well) at university *Mensa* (cafeterias). ID is not always checked.

Staples & Specialities

Wurst (sausage), in its hundreds of forms, is by far the most universal main dish. Regional favourites include bratwurst (spiced sausage), *Weisswurst* (veal sausage) and *Blutwurst* (blood sausage). Other popular main dishes include *Rippenspeer* (spare ribs), *Rotwurst* (black pudding), *Rostbrätl* (grilled meat), *Putenbrust* (turkey breast) and many forms of *Schnitzel* (breaded pork or veal cutlet).

Potatoes feature prominently in German meals, as *Bratkartoffeln* (fried), *Kartoffelpüree* (mashed), Swiss-style *Rösti* (grated then fried) or *Pommes Frites* (french fries); a Thuringian speciality is *Klösse,* a ball of mashed and raw potato that is then cooked into a dumpling. A similar Bavarian version is the *Knödel. Spätzle,* a noodle variety from Baden-Württemberg, is a common alternative.

Germans are keen on rich desserts. Popular choices are the *Schwarzwälder Kirschtorte* (Black Forest cherry cake) – one worthwhile tourist trap – as well as endless varieties of *Apfeltasche* (apple pastry). In the north you're likely to find berry *mus,* a sort of compote. Desserts and pastries are also often enjoyed during another German tradition, the 4pm coffee break.

DRINKS

Beer is the national beverage and it's one cultural phenomenon that must be adequately explored. The beer is excellent and relatively cheap. Each region and brewery has its own distinctive taste and body.

Vollbier is 4% alcohol by volume, *Export* is 5% and *Bockbier* is 6%. *Helles Bier* is light, while *dunkles Bier* is dark. *Export* is similar to, but much better than, typical international brews, while the *Pils* is more bitter. *Alt* is darker and more full-bodied. A speciality is *Weizenbier,* which is made with wheat instead of barley malt and served in a tall, 500mL glass. Nonalcoholic beers such as *Clausthaler* are also popular.

Eastern Germany's best beers hail from Saxony, especially Radeberger from near Dresden and Wernesgrüner from the Erzgebirge on the Czech border. *Berliner Weisse*

GERMANY

is a low-alcohol wheat beer mixed with woodruff or raspberry syrup, seen as a bit of a tourist drink by locals. The breweries of Cologne produce *Kölsch,* always served in 0.2L glasses to keep it fresh; in Bamberg *Schlenkerla Rauchbier* is smoked to a dark-red colour.

German wines are exported around the world, and for good reason. They are inexpensive and typically white, light and intensely fruity. A *Weinschorle* or *Spritzer* is white wine mixed with mineral water. The Rhine and Moselle Valleys are the classic wine-growing regions. The *Ebbelwei* of Hesse is a strong apple wine with an earthy flavour, and the Saale-Unstrut region around Naumburg in Saxony-Anhalt is famous for tart wines and Rotkäppchen *Sekt* (sparkling wine).

The most popular nonalcoholic choices are mineral water and soft drinks, coffee and fruit or black tea. Bottled water almost always comes bubbly *(mit Kohlensäure)* – order *ohne Kohlensäure* if you're bothered by bubbles.

Vegetarians & Vegans

Most German restaurants will have at least a couple of vegetarian dishes on the menu, although it is advisable to check anything that doesn't specifically say it's meat-free, as bacon and chicken stock both seem to be common undeclared ingredients in German cuisine. Asian and Indian restaurants will generally be quite happy to make vegetarian dishes on demand. Vegans may find themselves having to explain exactly what they do and don't eat to get something suitable.

Habits & Customs

Restaurants always display their menus outside with prices, but watch for daily or lunch specials chalked onto blackboards. Beware of early closing hours, and of the *Ruhetag* (rest day) at some establishments. Lunch is the main meal of the day; getting a main meal in the evening is never a problem, but you may find that the dish or menu of the day only applies to lunch.

Rather than leaving money on the table, tip when you pay by stating a rounded-up figure or saying *'es stimmt so'* (that's the right amount). A tip of 10% is generally more than sufficient.

BERLIN

☎ 030 / pop 3.45 million

Berlin, Germany's largest city, has more to offer visitors than almost any city in Europe, and is rapidly maturing into a major world capital. Historically, culturally and politically this is a unique place and a must for anyone passing through Germany.

Literally split in two for 40 years, the city has reintegrated far more quickly and easily than the country as a whole, and has resumed its role as capital almost effortlessly. You can still tell the difference between the old eastern and western districts, but this is now less a matter of division and more one of individual identity; Berliners have never been much for running with the crowd, and the city's relentless diversity pervades every aspect of life here, from the broad ethnic spectrum to the unrivalled nightlife.

Above all, the city is characterised by an endless capacity to surprise. History may not have been kind, but the future is a blank canvas – as the tourist office proudly proclaims, Berlin is 'different every hour', and its constant reinvention of itself is without a doubt the city's best feature.

HISTORY

Berlin started life as two separate trading posts, Berlin and Cölln, which merged in 1432. The city's importance began in 1470 when the Hohenzollern Elector moved his residence here from Brandenburg. By the end of the 17th century Berlin was in its heyday as the capital of Prussia under Friedrich I, whose wife Sophie Charlotte patronised the arts and sciences. Friedrich II fostered further cultural and political development.

The 19th century began with seven years of French occupation, but Berlin and Prussia remained strong. The city's population doubled between 1850 and 1870 as the Industrial Revolution took hold. By 1900, Berlin was home to almost two million people; in 1920, when Greater Berlin was created, that figure doubled again.

Before WWI Berlin had become an industrial giant, but the war and its aftermath led to revolt throughout Germany. On 9 November 1918 Philipp Scheidemann, leader of the Social Democrats, proclaimed

GREATER BERLIN

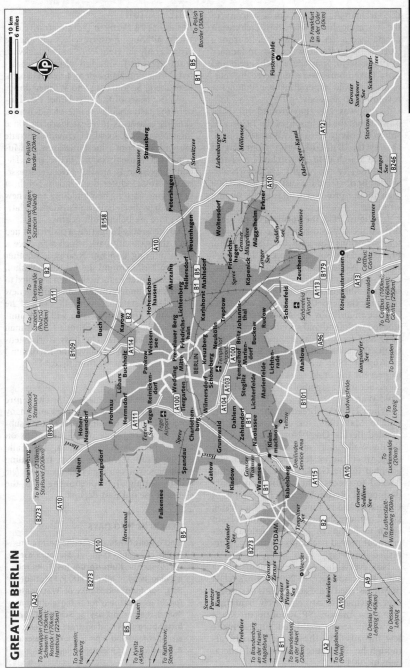

10 km
6 miles

To Neuruppin (20km);
Schwerin (150km);
Rostock (170km);
Hamburg (225km)

To Schwerin;
Hamburg

To Kyritz
(45km)

To Rathenow;
Stendal

B273

B5

A24

B5

B273

B273

A10

B96

Oranienburg

Nauen

Trebbin

Scharow-
Paretzer
Kanal

Havelkanal

Havel

Velten

Hennigsdorf

Falkensee

Fahrländer
See

Grosser
Zernsee

Grosser
Plessower See

To Brandenburg
an der Havel;
Magdeburg

To Brandenburg
an der Havel
(20km)

To Magdeburg
(90km)

B1

B273

A2

A9

A10

Werder

Schwielow-
see

POTSDAM

Templiner
See

Babelsberg

Dreilinden
Service Area

Wann-
see

Grosser
Wannsee

Kladow

Gatow

Spandau

Grunewald

Tegeler
See

Tegel
Airport

Spree

Charlotten-
burg

Hohen
Neuendorf

Frohnau

Hermsdorf

Lübars

Reinicken-
dorf

Buchholz

Pankow

Weissen-
see

Karow

Buch

Prenzlauer Berg

Wedding

Mitte

Tiergarten

BERLIN

Friedrichs-
hain

Kreuzberg

Schöneberg

Wilmersdorf

Dahlem

Zehlendorf

Nikolassee

Klein-
machnow

Teltow

Steglitz

Tempelhof
Airport

Neukölln

Britz

Marienfelde

Lichterfelde

Lichten-
rade

Buckow

Rudow

Treptow

Johannis-
thal

Schönefeld
Airport

Schönefeld

Mahlow

Ludwigsfelde

Grosser
Seddiner See

Rangsdorfer
See

A115

A10

B2

A100

A103

A104

A111

A114

A100

A100

B1

B1

B101

A96

A113

A117

Mittenwalde

Königswusterhausen

A10

A12

Zeuthen

B179

A10

A10

Köpenick

Mahlsdorf

Karlshorst

Lichtenberg

Marzahn

Hohenschön-
hausen

B1

B5

B2

Bernau

B109

B158

A11

A10

Wolters-
dorf

Erkner

Friedrichs-
hagen

Müggelheim

Müggelsee

Grosser
Müggelsee

Langer
See

Seddin-
see

Seddin-
see

Neuenhagen

Hellersdorf

Petershagen

Strausberg

Strausee

Sienitzsee

Liebenberger
See

Möllensee

Oder-Spree-Kanal

Spree

Fürstenwalde

Storkow

Grosser
Storkower
see

Schurmützel-
see

Langer
See

Dolgensee

Krossinsee

B246

B179

To Cottbus;
Görlitz

To Cottbus (100km);
Dresden (160km);
Görlitz (250km)

To Dresden

To Leipzig

To Luckenwalde
(20km)

To Lutherstadt-
Wittenberg (50km)

To Dessau (75km);
Leipzig (140km)

To Dessau;
Leipzig

To Frankfurt
an der Oder
(30km)

To Polish
Border (30km)

To Polish
Border (20km)

To Stralsund; Rügen;
Szczecin (Poland)

To Szczecin
(Poland;
100km)

To Eberswalde
(15km)

To Rostock;
Stralsund

the German Republic from a balcony of the Reichstag; hours later, Karl Liebknecht proclaimed a free socialist republic from a balcony of the Berliner Schloss. In January 1919 the Berlin Spartacists, Liebknecht and Rosa Luxemburg, were murdered by remnants of the old imperial army, bringing the revolution to a bloody end.

Berlin was the showground for Nazi power from the beginning of the 1930s, and suffered heavily during WWII as a result. During the 'Battle of Berlin' from August 1943 to March 1944, British bombers hammered the city every night. The Soviets also shelled Berlin from the east, and lost 18,000 men in the prolonged final battle on the streets.

In August 1945, the Potsdam Conference divided the city into zones, occupied by the four victorious powers – the USA, Britain, France and the Soviet Union. In June 1948 the three Western Allies introduced a western German currency and established a separate administration in their sectors. In response the Soviets blockaded West Berlin, but an airlift by the Allies kept the city stocked with food and supplies. In October 1949 East Berlin became the capital of the GDR. The construction of the Berlin Wall in August 1961 was originally intended to prevent the drain of skilled labour, but soon became a symbol of the escalating Cold War.

When Hungary breached the Iron Curtain in May 1989, the end was nigh for divided Berlin. On 9 November 1989 the Berlin Wall finally opened and by 1 July 1990, when the western Deutschmark was adopted in the GDR, the Wall was being hacked to pieces. The Unification Treaty designated Berlin the official capital of Germany, and in June 1991 the Bundestag voted to move the seat of government from Bonn to Berlin. In 1999, the federal government moved back into the newly refurbished Reichstag.

Not everything has been plain sailing since then, however: in 2001 Berlin's CDU mayor resigned amid accusations of corruption, leaving the city effectively bankrupt. The new mayor, SPD politician Klaus Wowereit, seems well liked but has made few inroads into the financial crisis, although he did secure a promise of federal help in 2004.

ORIENTATION

Berlin has 23 *Bezirken* (administrative districts), although most travellers will end up visiting only the eight 'core' ones (clockwise from the west): Charlottenburg, Tiergarten, Mitte, Prenzlauer Berg, Friedrichshain, Kreuzberg, Schöneberg and Wilmersdorf.

At the heart of the city, Unter den Linden, the fashionable avenue of old Berlin, extends eastwards to Alexanderplatz, once the centrepiece of socialist Germany. En route are some of Berlin's finest museums, on Museuminsel (Museum Island) in the Spree. The cultural centre is around Friedrichstrasse, which crosses Unter den Linden. South of here, some startling new buildings and a new station have been built on Potsdamer Platz, and more are being built nearby.

To the west is Tiergarten, a district named after the vast city park which was once a royal hunting domain. Nearby is another vast work site around the Lehrter Bahnhof, where the Spree has actually been rerouted to allow a vast underground tunnel for the new central train station. On the other side of the park, near Zoo station, you will find hundreds of shops and the Europa-Center mall on Breitscheidplatz. The busy Kurfürstendamm (known colloquially as the 'Ku'damm') runs 3.5km southwest from here.

Maps

Excellent free tourist maps of the city centre are available from tourist offices and many hotels. If you're heading to the outer suburbs there are plenty of full-size maps on sale in bookshops and newsagents; Falk, Michelin and ADAC are among the leading publishers. You can even pick up an *Ostalgie* (GDR nostalgia) map showing you the sights of the old East Berlin!

BERLIN IN TWO DAYS

Step on bus No 100 to see the best of the Berlin cityscape, then hit **Museuminsel** (p410) or the **Kulturforum** (p411). In the evening, head to **Miro** (p418) in Prenzlauer Berg for food and drinks or **Watergate** (p420) in Krenzberg for a big night out. Spend the second day at **Schloss Charlottenburg** (p411), then treat yourself to a proper feed and a posh drink in **Galerie Bremer** (p419), Charlottenburg.

INFORMATION
Bookshops
Books in Berlin (Map p417; ☎ 313 1233; Goethestrasse 69, Charlottenburg)

Hugendubel (Map p417; ☎ 214 060; Tauentzienstrasse 13, Charlottenburg)

Discount Cards
Berlin-Potsdam Welcome Card (72hr card €18)

SchauLust Museen Berlin (72hr €10) Free admission to over 50 museums.

Emergency
Ambulance ☎ 112

Fire ☎ 112

Police ☎ 110

Internet Access
Al Hamra (Map p410; ☎ 4285 0095; Raumerstrasse 16, Prenzlauer Berg; per 15min €1; ⏰ from 10am)

Netz Galaxie (Map p417; ☎ 7870 6446; Joachimsthaler Strasse 19, Charlottenburg; per hr €1; ⏰ 11-2am)

Plan@t Internettreff (Map pp412-13; ☎ 209 488; Niederbarnimstrasse 4, Friedrichshain; per hr €2; ⏰ from 11am)

Surf & Sushi (Map pp414-15; ☎ 2838 4898; Oranienburger Strasse 17, Mitte; per 30min €2.50; ⏰ from noon Mon-Sat, from 1pm Sun)

Laundry
Schnell & Sauber (€5; ⏰ 6am-11pm) Charlottenburg (Map p417; Uhlandstrasse 53); Mitte (Map pp414-15; Torstrasse 115)

Medical Services
Kassenärztliche Bereitschaftsdienst (Public Physicians' Emergency Service; ☎ 310 031)

Money
American Express (Map pp414-15; ☎ 2045 5721; Friedrichstrasse 172, Mitte; ⏰ 9am-7pm Mon-Fri, 10am-1pm Sat)

Reisebank Zoo station (Map p417; ☎ 881 7117; Hardenbergplatz; ⏰ 7.30am-10pm); Ostbahnhof (Map pp412-13; ☎ 296 4393; ⏰ 7am-10pm Mon-Fri, 8am-8pm Sat & Sun)

Thomas Cook/Travelex (Map pp414-15; ☎ 2016 5916; Friedrichstrasse 56, Mitte; ⏰ 9am-6.30pm Mon-Fri, 9.30am-1pm Sat)

Post
Main post office (Map p417; Joachimstalerstrasse 7, Charlottenburg; ⏰ 8am-midnight Mon-Sat, 10am-midnight Sun)

Tourist Information
Berlin Tourismus Marketing (☎ 250 025; www .berlin-tourist-information.de) Europa-Center (Map p417;

Budapester Strasse 45; ⏰ 10am-7pm Mon-Sat, 10am-6pm Sun); Brandenburger Tor (Map pp414-15; ⏰ 10am-6pm); Fernsehturm (Map pp414-15; ⏰ 10am-6pm)

EurAide (Map p417; www.euraide.de; Zoo station; ⏰ 8.30am-noon Mon-Sat, 1-4.30pm Mon-Fri) English-language service.

Travel Agencies
Alternativ Tours (Map p417; ☎ 881 2089; Wilmersdorfer Strasse 94, Wilmersdorf) Unpublished discount air fares.

Atlas Reisewelt (Map pp414-15; ☎ 247 5760; Galeria Kaufhof, Alexanderplatz 9, Mitte)

STA Travel Prenzlauer Berg (Map p410; ☎ 2859 8264; Gleimstrasse 28); Charlottenburg (Map p417; ☎ 311 0950; Goethestrasse 73)

DANGERS & ANNOYANCES
Berlin is generally safe and tolerant. Walking alone at night on city streets shouldn't be considered a risk. Begging on the street and in the U-Bahn is increasing, but aggressive demands are very rare. Take the usual precautions against robberies in the Zoo station area.

SIGHTS
Monuments & Landmarks
The buildings and structures that shape the Berlin skyline are also an integral part of the city's cultural make-up, and many count among the capital's foremost attractions.

The ultimate symbol of Berlin, Karl Gotthard Langhans' **Brandenburger Tor** (Brandenburg Gate; Map pp414-15; Pariser Platz, Mitte) built in 1791, was once the boundary between east and west and now stands proudly at the centre of the united city (and in the background of a million tourist photos).

Not as universally loved as the Brandenburger Tor but considerably more visible, Berlin's favourite 368m eyesore, **Fernsehturm** (TV Tower; Map pp414-15; ☎ 242 3333; Panoramastrasse 1A, Mitte; adult/concession €6/3; ⏰ 10-1am), was built in 1969. If it's a clear day and the queue isn't too long, it's worth paying to go up the tower or have a drink in the revolving Telecafé at 207m.

The third in the holy trinity of structures that are synonymous with Berlin, the **Reichstag** (Map pp414-15; ☎ 2273 2152; Platz der Republik 1, Tiergarten; ⏰ 8am-midnight, last admission 10pm) is where the reunification of Germany was enacted, at midnight on 2 October 1990. Once again the seat of the German parliament, the building is Berlin's number one

PRENZLAUER BERG

INFORMATION		
Al Hamra	1	B2
STA Travel	2	A1

SLEEPING		(p415)
Lette'm Sleep	3	B1
Pension Amsterdam	4	A1

EATING		(pp416-18)
Buddha Lounge	5	B1
Intersoup	6	B1
Miro	7	B2

DRINKING		(p419)
X Bar	8	B2

ENTERTAINMENT		(pp419-21)
Kulturbrauerei	9	A2
nbi	10	A3

visitor attraction, thanks to Sir Norman Foster's stunning 1999 reconstruction. The lift to the distinctive glass cupola is free and doesn't require reservations; to avoid the hordes, arrive first thing in the morning or just before closing. Tours of the interior can be arranged by writing to Deutscher Bundestag, Besucherdienst, Platz der Republik 1, 11011 Berlin.

A British bombing on 22 November 1943 left only the broken west tower of this 1895 church standing, and the stark ruins of the **Kaiser-Wilhelm-Gedächtniskirche** (Map p417; ☎ 218 5023; Breitscheidplatz, Charlottenburg; Memorial Hall ☽ 10am-4pm Mon-Sat, Hall of Worship ☽ 9am-7.30pm) have remained a world-famous landmark and memorial since then. The newer glass-panelled hall of worship next door provides relief from the rampant commercialism outside.

Europe's busiest square until WWII, **Potsdamer Platz** (Map pp412-13) was occupied by the Wall and death strip until reunification. Now it's a vast urban development and one of the city's main tourist attractions, with striking buildings by some world-famous

architects. The two sections, Daimler-City and Sony Center, feature shopping, theatres, a hotel and office buildings, plus the **Panorama Observation Deck** (Map pp414-15; adult/concession €3.50/2.50; ☽ 11am-8pm Tue-Sun), reached by what is billed as Europe's fastest lift.

Museums

Among Berlin's 170 museums, the **state museums** (marked 'SMB') are reliable highlights. Unless otherwise noted, SMB museums are closed Monday and are free the first Sunday of each month; admission is by day pass (adult/concession €6/3, on Museuminsel €8/4), which generally allows admission to other nearby or related SMB museums.

MUSEUMINSEL

Widely considered one of the city's finest museums, the huge 1930s **Pergamonmuseum** (SMB; Map p414-15; ☎ 2090 5555; Am Kupfergraben; ☽ 10am-6pm Tue-Sun, to 10pm Thu) is a feast of classical Greek, Babylonian, Roman, Islamic and Oriental antiquity. The world-renowned Ishtar Gate from Babylon (580 BC), the reconstructed Pergamon Altar from Asia Minor

(160 BC) and the Market Gate from Greek Miletus (Asia Minor, 2nd century AD) are among the Middle Eastern artefacts.

The **Alte Nationalgalerie** (Old National Gallery; SMB; Map pp414-15; ☎ 2090 5801; Bodestrasse 1-3; ⏰ 10am-6pm Tue-Sun, to 10pm Thu), houses sculpture and paintings by 19th-century. European masters in dozens of tiny galleries. Inside the stairwell is a massive frieze by Otto Geyers, depicting a cavalcade of great German philosophers, thinkers, writers and patrons.

KULTURFORUM

Plans for a cultural centre in the southeastern corner of Tiergarten were born as early as the 1950s. One of the premier architects of the time, Hans Scharoun, was given the job of coming up with the design of what would be known as **Kulturforum** (Map pp412-13), a cluster of museums and concert halls. The first building constructed was the gold-plated **Berliner Philharmonie** (1961; see p420).

If you only have time for one Kulturforum museum, it should probably be the **Gemäldegalerie** (Picture Gallery; SMB; ☎ 2090 5555; Matthäikirchplatz 4-6; ⏰ 10am-6pm Tue-Sun, to 10pm Thu), a spectacular showcase of European painting from the 13th to the 18th centuries. More than 1300 works are on view.

Mies van der Rohe's split-level glass building, the **Neue Nationalgalerie** (New National Gallery; SMB; ☎ 266 2651; Potsdamer Strasse 50; ⏰ 10am-6pm Tue-Fri, to 10pm Thu, 11am-6pm Sat & Sun) houses a major collection of 19th- and 20th-century paintings and sculptures by Picasso, Klee, Miró and many German expressionists.

Dedicated to the artists of the Bauhaus school, who developed the central tenets of modern architecture and design, the **Bauhaus Archiv/Museum für Gestaltung** (Bauhaus Archive/Design Museum; ☎ 254 0020; Klingelhöferstrasse 14; adult/concession €4/2; ⏰ 10am-5pm Wed-Mon) was designed by founder Walter Gropius, though it was only built 40 years after his death.

SCHLOSS CHARLOTTENBURG

Completed in 1699 as a summer residence for Queen Sophie Charlotte, the **Schloss Charlottenburg** (☎ 320 911; Luisenplatz; day pass adult/concession €7/5), just north of Charlottenburg, is one of the few remaining sites in Berlin still reflecting the former splendour and grandeur of the Hohenzollern dynasty. The palace was bombed in 1943 but has been completely rebuilt. Before the entrance is an equestrian

statue of the Great Elector (1620–88), Sophie Charlotte's father-in-law. Along the Spree River behind the palace are extensive French and English **gardens** (admission free).

In the central building below the dome are the former royal living quarters. The **winter chambers** of Friedrich II, upstairs in the new wing (1746) to the east, are highlights, as well as the **Schinkel Pavilion**, the neoclassical **Mausoleum** and the rococo **Belvedere pavilion**. Huge crowds are often waiting for the guided tour of the palace and it may be difficult to get a ticket, especially on weekends and holidays in summer. If you can't get into the main palace, content yourself with the façades and gardens. Each section charges separately and has different hours, or a palace day card is good for all the tours and attractions.

OTHER MUSEUMS

Even before it opened in 2001, the zinc-clad shell of the Daniel Libeskind–designed **Jüdisches Museum** (Jewish Museum; Map pp412-13; ☎ 2599 3300; Lindenstrasse 9-14, Kreuzberg; adult/concession €5.50/2.50; ⏰ 10am-10pm Mon, to 8pm Tue-Sun) drew flocks of visitors. Now its collection covers

KREUZBERG

INFORMATION
Plan@t Internettreff.....................1 H3

SIGHTS & ACTIVITIES (pp409–13)
Checkpoint Charlie.......................2 C1
East Side Gallery..........................3 H2
Gemäldegalerie............................4 A1
Haus am Checkpoint Charlie.........5 C1
Jüdisches Museum........................6 C2
Neue Nationalgalerie....................7 A1

SLEEPING (pp414–16)
East-Side-City Hotel......................8 H2
Gasthaus Dietrich Herz.................9 C4
Hotel Riehmers Hofgarten..........10 B4
Meininger City Hostel.................11 C3
Meininger City Hostel.................12 C3
Odyssee Globetrotter Hostel......13 G4

1000 years of Jewish history in Germany in a manner that's both admiring and wistful.

Potsdamer Platz's major highlight, the **Filmmuseum** (Map pp414–15; ☎ 300 9030; Potsdamer Strasse 2, Tiergarten; adult/concession €6/4; ☒ 10am-6pm Tue-Sun, to 8pm Thu), provides an excellent multimedia journey through German film history, with lots on the big Berlin names (heaven for Marlene Dietrich fans) and a behind-the-scenes look at special effects.

A fascinating insight into the practices of the GDR's secret police, the regime's 'sword and shield', is at the **Stasi – Die Ausstellung** (Stasi Exhibition; Map pp414–15; ☎ 2324 7951; Mauerstrasse 38, Mitte; ☒ 10am-6pm Mon-Sun). Miniature cameras, bugs and body odour samples are just some of the surprises.

Lofty ceilings and plentiful natural light make **Hamburger Bahnhof** (SMB; Map pp414-15; ☎ 3978 3412; Invalidenstrasse 50, Mitte; ☒ 10am-6pm Tue-Fri, 11am-6pm Sat & Sun), a former station building, a surprisingly fitting showcase for Berlin's premier post-1950s art collection. Displays take in Warhol, Lichtenstein, Rauschenberg and a whole wing of Joseph Beuys.

With an extensive collection on German history from AD 900 to the present in a former *Zeughaus* (armoury), the **Deutsches Historisches Museum** (Map pp414-15; ☎ 203 040; Unter den Linden 2, Mitte; admission €2; ☒ 10am-6pm Tue-Sun) was built in 1706 and renovated in 2004. Special exhibits are housed in a spectacular extension by modernist architect IM Pei.

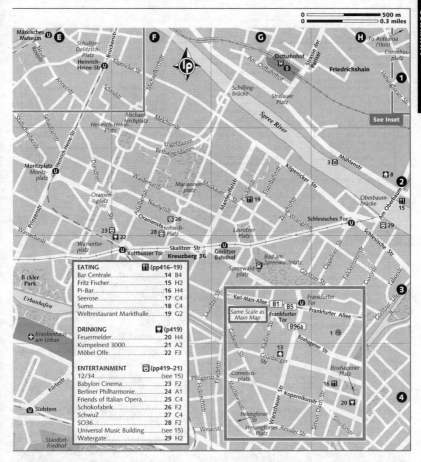

Berlin Wall

The longest surviving stretch of the **Berlin Wall** (Map pp412-13) runs west from near Warschauer Strasse station in Friedrichshain. This 300m section was turned over to graffiti writers and artists who created the **East Side Gallery** (Map pp412-13), a permanent open-air art gallery along the side facing Mühlenstrasse. The gallery also has a showcase in Ostbahnhof.

Almost nothing remains of the famous **Checkpoint Charlie** (Map pp412-13), a major crossing between east and west during the Cold War. However, the Wall's history is commemorated nearby in the fascinating **Haus am Checkpoint Charlie** (Map pp412-13; ☎ 253 7250; Friedrichstrasse 43-45, Mitte; adult/concession €9.50/5.50;

☼ 9am-10pm), with countless tales of successful and failed escape attempts.

FESTIVALS & EVENTS
February

International Film Festival Berlin (☎ 259 200; www.berlinale.de) Also known as the Berlinale, this is Germany's answer to the Cannes and Venice film festivals.

June

Christopher Street Day (☎ 0177-277 3176; www.csd-berlin.de) Held on the last weekend in June, this is by far the largest gay event in Germany.

July

Berlin Love Parade (☎ 284 620; www.loveparade.de) The largest techno party in the world.

GERMANY

MITTE

SLEEPING

If you're travelling to Berlin on weekends and between May and September, especially during big events, be sure to make reservations at least several weeks in advance. From November to March, on the other hand, visitor numbers plunge significantly (except over Christmas and New Year) and you may be able to get very good deals at short notice.

Budget

DJH HOSTELS

Berlin's official hostels are extremely popular, especially at the weekend and between March and October; they are often booked

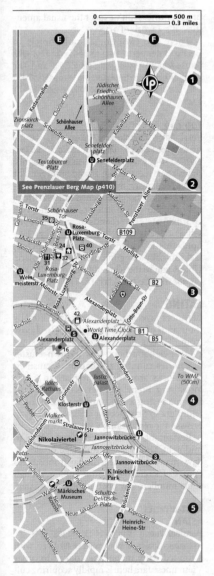

out by noisy school groups until early July. None offer cooking facilities, but breakfast is included. Reserve several weeks in advance (www.hostel.de). Phone reservations can only be made two weeks in advance. The **Jugendherberge Berlin International** (☎ 261 1098; Kluckstrasse 3, Schöneberg; juniors dm €12-19, d €23.50, seniors dm €16-23.10, d €27.60; P 🖳) is the only

DJH hostel within the city centre, near the Landwehrkanal. A total of 364 beds are available, but it's not really keeping pace with the competition.

INDEPENDENT HOSTELS

Berlin's independent hostel scene is booming, with new competition constantly springing up to vie for the lucrative backpacker market – you won't find as many school groups here. Breakfast costs extra unless indicated. Some hostels give student discounts.

Odyssee Globetrotter Hostel (Map pp412-13; ☎ 2900 0081; www.globetrotterhostel.de; Grünberger Strasse 23, Friedrichshain; dm €13-19, s €35, d €45-52; 🖳) Energetic, welcoming and a perfect base for those intent on investigating Friedrichshain's nightlife. Perks include free linen, late checkout and a bustling bar-lounge.

Meininger City Hostel (Map pp412-13; ☎ 6663 6100; www.meininger12.com; Hallesches Ufer 30, Kreuzberg; dm €13.50, s/d €49/66; P ✗ 🖳) This small, well-run chain sports modern rooms and a comfort level that rivals small hotels. There's lots of free stuff, including breakfast, linen and lockers, plus a fun bar and rooftop terrace. There are also hostels at **Tempelhofer Ufer 10** (Map pp412-13) and **Meininger Strasse 10** (Map p411).

Circus Hostels (Map pp414-15; ☎ 2839 1433; www .circus-hostel.de; Rosa-Luxemburg-Strasse 39 & Weinberg-sweg 1a, Mitte; dm €15-20, s/d €32/48, 2-/4-person apt €75/130; 🖳) Leading the hostel renaissance, these two excellent locations count cheerful rooms, great showers, free lockers and competent staff among their many good qualities. The fantastic penthouse apartments are amazing value.

Lette'm Sleep (Map p410; ☎ 4473 3623; www.back packers.de; Lettestrasse 7, Prenzlauer Berg; dm €15-19, d €44-66; 🖳) One for the traditionalists, this is a hostel as hostels used to be: low-key, low-tech and sociable, with shared kitchen and common room. The location on trendy Helmholtzplatz puts you right in the middle of the Prenzlberg action.

HOTELS & GUESTHOUSES

Pension Amsterdam (Map p410; ☎ 448 0792; Gleim-strasse 24, Prenzlauer Berg; s €25-33, d €50-67; 🖳) There's plenty to like about this contemporary *pension*: big apartments, full kitchens, rooms with four-poster beds and a buzzy downstairs café popular with a mixed gay crowd.

Gasthaus Dietrich Herz (Map pp412-13; ☎ 691 7043; Marheinekeplatz 15, Kreuzberg; s €28-53, d €45-75)

Located above the historic Marheineke covered market, Herr Herz's is the kind of place your mum would just love for its Old Berlin colour. The noise starts early but the charm is always there, and the restaurant does a good line in schnitzel.

Pension Kettler (Map p417; ☎ 883 4949; Bleibtreu-strasse 19, Charlottenburg; s €50-75, d €60-90) If you want quirk and true Berlin character, you'll find heaps of it at this nostalgic retreat, strewn with objects best described as 'esoterica'. The place's most eccentric and memorable feature, though, is its owner!

Mid-Range

Andechser Hof (Map pp414-15; ☎ 2809 7844; www .andechserhof.de; Ackerstrasse 155, Mitte; s €65-70, d €80-90) Run with heart, soul and enthusiasm, this is an oasis of charm in ageing Mitte. Rooms are spread over two buildings linked by a nice courtyard; the restaurant is recommended.

East-Side-City Hotel (Map pp412-13; ☎ 293 833; www .eastsidehotel.de; Mühlenstrasse 6, Friedrichshain; s €60-100, d €70-110) The East-Side's ultramodern rooms are a meditation in understatement. Singles all face the Spree River and East Side Gallery, the longest remaining stretch of the Wall, while deluxe rooms feature generous marble baths and a couch. Video and PC rentals are available.

Hotel-Pension Art Nouveau (Map p417; ☎ 327 7440; www.hotelartnouveau.de; Leibnizstrasse 59, Charlottenburg; s/d €95/110; ✗) One of Berlin's best *pensions*, offering a unique blend of youthful flair and tradition. The affable owners have made creative use of colour and furnished each room with handpicked antiques and heavenly beds. Bonuses include the sunny breakfast room and honour bar.

Hotel Riehmers Hofgarten (Map pp412-13; ☎ 7809 8800; www.riehmers-hofgarten.de; Yorckstrasse 83, Kreuzberg; s €98-108, d €123-138; ✗) Near the popular Viktoriapark, Riehmers offers 20 rooms in a listed 1891 building with a lush traditional *Hinterhof* (inner courtyard) certain to delight romantics. Custom-made furniture and original contemporary art grace the rooms; the restaurant is equally elegant.

Propellor Island City Lodge (Map p417; ☎ 891 9016; www.propeller-island.de; Albrecht-Achilles-Strasse 58, Wilmersdorf; s €65-110, d €90-180; ℗ ✗) Berlin's most eccentric hotel is the brainchild of artist/musician Lars Stroschen, who crafted these 30 rooms into a unique series of surreal environments perfect for those with a sense of adventure. Don't expect the usual amenities: it's a work of art.

There are two women-only hotels in Berlin, **Intermezzo** (Map pp414-15; ☎ 2248 9096; Gertrud-Kolmar-Strasse 5, Mitte; s/d €56/90) and the smaller but smarter **Artemisia** (Map p417; ☎ 873 8905; Brandenburgische Strasse 18, Wilmersdorf; s €64-79, d €89-104; ✗).

Top End

Hotel Adlon Kempinski (Map pp414-15; ☎ 226 10; www.hotel-adlon.de; Unter den Linden 77; s/d from €300/350; ℗ ✗ ✗ ▯ ▣) With lavish rooms, slavish service and the Brandenburger Tor about 50m away, this replica of Berlin's original 1st-class hotel reopened in 1997 after a hiatus of more than half a century and took approximately 30 seconds to re-establish itself as the city's top billet. Music fans take note: this is where the infamous Michael Jackson baby-dangling incident took place. Unless you're the King of Pop yourself, rates do *not* include breakfast (€27).

EATING

Berliners love eating out and have literally thousands of restaurants and cafés to choose from. There's no need to travel far, since every neighbourhood has its own cluster of eateries running the gamut of cuisines. The blocks around Savignyplatz in Charlottenburg, Prenzlauer Berg's Kollwitzplatz, Bergmannstrasse in Kreuzberg and Winterfeldtplatz in Schöneberg are great places to browse for restaurants with character.

Restaurants usually open from 11am to midnight, with varying Ruhetage or closing days; many close during the day from 3pm to 6pm. Cafés often close around 8pm, though equal numbers stay open until 2am or later.

Restaurants

ASIAN

Monsieur Vuong (Map pp414-15; ☎ 3087 2643; Alte Schönhauser Strasse 46, Mitte; mains €6.40) Even with a limited daily menu, the cooked-to-order Vietnamese fare here is rapidly acquiring cult status – be prepared to queue for a seat.

Sumo (Map pp412-13; ☎ 6900 4963; Bergmannstrasse 89, Kreuzberg; mains €7-11) With its sleek, stylish looks and top-notch Japanese food, Sumo has long been a favourite among Kreuzberg chopstick-wielders.

Buddha Lounge (Map p410; ☎ 4471 6024; Stargarder Strasse 60, Prenzlauer Berg; mains €10-13) This little

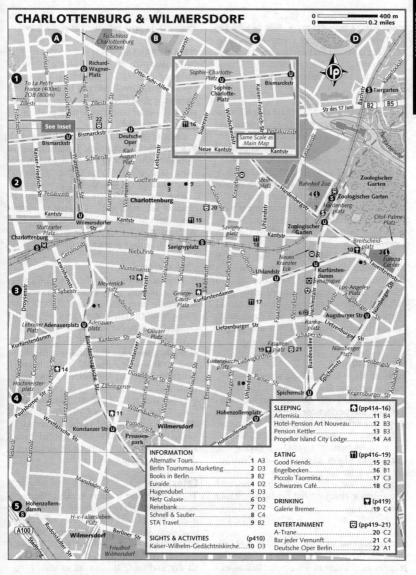

CHARLOTTENBURG & WILMERSDORF

INFORMATION	
Alternativ Tours	1 A3
Berlin Tourismus Marketing	2 D3
Books in Berlin	3 B2
Euraide	4 D2
Hugendubel	5 D3
Netz Galaxie	6 D3
Reisebank	7 D2
Schnell & Sauber	8 C4
STA Travel	9 B2

SIGHTS & ACTIVITIES	(p410)
Kaiser-Wilhelm-Gedächtniskirche	10 D3

SLEEPING	(pp414–16)
Artemisia	11 B4
Hotel-Pension Art Nouveau	12 B3
Pension Kettler	13 B3
Propellor Island City Lodge	14 A4

EATING	(pp416–19)
Good Friends	15 B2
Engelbecken	16 B1
Piccolo Taormina	17 C3
Schwarzes Café	18 C3

DRINKING	(p419)
Galerie Bremer	19 C4

ENTERTAINMENT	(pp419–21)
A-Trane	20 C2
Bar jeder Vernunft	21 C4
Deutsche Oper Berlin	22 A1

Asian restaurant-bar is crammed at weekends for its table-bending buffet of vegetarian sushi, Thai risotto and other goodies.

Good Friends (Map p417; ☎ 313 2659; Kantstrasse 30, Charlottenburg; mains €7-19) Near Savignyplatz, this is a proper Chinese restaurant with plenty of authentic dishes alongside the Westernised standards.

FRENCH
La Petite France (☎ 325 8242; Knobelsdorffstrasse 27, Charlottenburg; mains €14-18; ☽ dinner only, closed Tue) Within walking distance of Schloss Charlottenburg, La Petit France is a fantastic, convincing slice of Gallic gourmandise, with some quality red wine to help things along.

Margaux (Map pp414-15; ☎ 2265 2611; Unter den Linden 78, Mitte; mains €24-40; ☺ closed for lunch Sun) Michelin-starred within a year of opening, Margaux is Mitte's best new gourmet hotspot, with avant-garde interpretations of classic French cuisine in sensuous surrounds.

GERMAN
Engelbecken (Map pp412-13; ☎ 615 2810; Witzleben-strasse 31, Charlottenburg; mains €8-16; ☺ dinner only) It's no Munich beer hall, but this corner restaurant serves what many rate as Berlin's best Bavarian food. All meats are organic.

Fritz Fischer (Map pp412-13; ☎ 520 072 202; Stral-auer Allee 1, Friedrichshain; mains €13-20; ☺ dinner only) In the Universal Music building, part of the hip new Oberbaum City development next to Warschauer Strasse station, Franz Fischer is the last word in cool modern German food and design.

Weltrestaurant Markthalle (Map pp412-13; ☎ 617 5502; Pücklerstrasse 34, Kreuzberg; mains €8-15) Any time of day is good for dropping into this century-old pub, as featured in the 2003 cult flick *Herr Lehmann*. It draws a mixed clientele of ageing hipsters and neighbour-hood folk with its relaxed vibe and simple no-nonsense food.

INTERNATIONAL
Intersoup (Map p410; ☎ 2327 3045; Schliemannstrasse 31, Prenzlauer Berg; soups €4-6; ☺ noon-3am) The dozen soups on offer in this self-service chill-out den are perfect for nursing hangovers or staving off the winter chills.

Aotearoa (Map pp412-13; ☎ 2977 0582; Weichsel-strasse 26a, Friedrichshain; mains €7-15) Taking the indigenous Maori name for New Zealand, the family-friendly Aotearoa is a home away from home for Kiwi lamb-lovers, and also offers a cheeky twist on British staple fish and chips.

ITALIAN
Piccolo Taormina (Map p417; ☎ 881 4710; Uhland-strasse 29, Charlottenburg; pizzas €3-12) Join the leagues of Ku'damm shoppers, Italian ex-pats, families and office folk here for the generously topped wafer-thin pizzas in this cobalt-blue self-service Italian.

Bar Centrale (Map pp412-13; ☎ 786 2989; Yorckstrasse 82, Kreuzberg; pasta €9-12, mains €13-20) Proper cre-ative Italian cooking (not a pizza in sight) is the name of the game at this attractive mod-ern eatery, apparently a favourite of Berlin

mayor Klaus Wowereit. Much of the chef's imagination goes into the antipasto menu.

MEDITERRANEAN
Ousies (Map p411; ☎ 216 7957; Grunewaldstrasse 16, Schöneberg; dishes €2.60-7; ☺ dinner only) This is not your typical Greek taverna but a so-called *ouzeria*, sort of Greek-style tapas bar where you build your meal from small portions of hot and cold dishes.

Kasbah (Map pp414-15; ☎ 2759 4361; Gipsstrasse 2, Mitte; mains €8-15; ☺ dinner only) Tantalising tastes from the other side of the Med, from *tajine* (stew) to *b'stilla* (chicken in pastry), served as you lounge on low-slung pillows.

Miro (Map p410; ☎ 4473 3013; Raumerstrasse 29, Prenzlauer Berg; mains €6-15) The name means 'hero', and Miro does indeed serve up epic portions of delicious Anatolian dishes, and a killer appetiser platter.

VEGETARIAN
In general Berlin caters fairly well for veg-etarians, though you still need to be wary of seemingly innocent German dishes. Most Asian and Indian restaurants will make vegetarian dishes on demand.

Seerose (Map pp412-13; ☎ 6981 5927; Mehringdamm 47, Kreuzberg; dishes €3-7) Vegetarians in the know flock to this little café, which tempts taste-buds with delicious casseroles, soups, salads, pasta and juices.

Pi-Bar (Map pp412-13; ☎ 2936 7581; Gabriel-Max-Strasse 17, Friedrichshain; mains €7-17) Preaching to the clubbed-out as well as the converted, Pi has all the ingredients to do well with F'hain's alternative elements: tasty casseroles, inven-tive creations and a cocktail bar.

Cafés
The number and variety of cafés in Berlin is astonishing. They're wonderful places to relax over a cup of coffee and some cake, while ploughing through a newspaper or chatting with friends. Many of these places honour the great Berlin tradition of serving breakfast all day, and some also do full meals.

Beth Café (Map pp414-15; ☎ 281 3135; Tucholsky-strasse 40, Mitte; mains €2-9; ☒) This is a good-value kosher café-bistro with a pretty inner courtyard, perfect for enjoying a leisurely lunch.

Schwarzes Café (Map p417; ☎ 313 8038; Kantstrasse 148, Charlottenburg; dishes €4.50-9) Founded in 1978, this 24-hour food'n'booze institution must have seen half of Berlin pass through it (or out in it) at some point.

Quick Eats & Self-Catering
Berlin is paradise for snackers on the go, with Turkish (your best bet), wurst, Greek, Italian, Chinese, even Sudanese, all available at *Imbiss* (snack) stands throughout the city. Good areas to look include Budapester Strasse in Tiergarten, the eastern end of Kantstrasse near Zoo station, Wittenbergplatz in Schöneberg, Alexanderplatz in Mitte and around Yorckstrasse or Schlesisches Tor in Kreuzberg.

Self-catering isn't hard in Berlin either, and the Aldi, Lidl, Plus and Penny Markt discount supermarket chains have outlets throughout Berlin. There are also farmers' markets around town; the most famous is Schöneberg's Winterfeldtplatz **farmer's market** (Map p411; ☽ Wed & Sat). More ambitious self-caterers shouldn't miss the food floor of KaDeWe (see p421).

DRINKING
Berlin's boozing scene is defined by its diversity, with each district offering something different. For fancy, fairly upmarket venues, go to Savignyplatz in Charlottenburg. Around Mehringdamm and Bergmannstrasse, Kreuzberg is alternative with some trendy touches, while further east, along Oranienstrasse and Wiener Strasse, it acquires a more grungy feel. In Schöneberg, you'll find few tourists and plenty of the 30-something brigade around Winterfeldtplatz, as well as a high concentration of gay venues.

In the eastern districts, the nightlife is far more earthy and experimental. New bars and restaurants are constantly springing up, bringing previously dull streets to life overnight – the area around Simon-Dach-Strasse and Boxhagener Platz in Friedrichshain is the latest to emerge. Prenzlauer Berg is another dynamic quarter, particularly up Schönhauser Allee, with energetic student and gay populations. More established clubs and bars can be found in Mitte along Oranienburger Strasse, Rosenthaler Platz and in the Scheunenviertel area. Bars that don't serve food open between 5pm and 8pm and may close as late as 5am (if at all).

Erdbeer (Map pp414-15; Max-Beer-Strasse 56, Mitte) The red colour scheme and €7 pints of daiquiri make drinking here pretty sweet,

and the no-frills approach separates it from standard scene cocktail joints. Exhibitionists should note the webcam in the toilet.

Feuermelder (Map pp412-13; Krossener Strasse 21, Friedrichshain) Defiantly not part of the cocktail lounge explosion, punks, rockers and other leather-clad folk seek solace in this loud music and games bar.

Galerie Bremer (Map p417; ☎ 881 4908; Fasanenplatz 37, Charlottenburg) Art-lovers should make a beeline for this gallery-bar where proprietor Rudolf van der Lak has been in charge since 1955, serving up sophisticated drinks and modernist art like a Zen Morgan Freeman.

Kumpelnest 3000 (Map pp412-13; ☎ 8891 7960; Lützowstrasse 23, Tiergarten) Once a brothel, always an experience – the Kumpelnest has been famed since the '80s for its wild, inhibition-free nights. Much of the original whorehouse décor remains intact.

Möbel Olfe (Map pp412-13; ☎ 6165 9612; Reichenberger Strasse 177, Kreuzberg) Livening up the flagging Kottbusser Tor area, this sparsely furnished beer hall is good for Polish beer and table football at least a couple of hours after the regular places close.

X Bar (Map p410; ☎ 443 4909; Raumerstrasse 17, Prenzlauer Berg) Not for the indecisive, this smart cocktail/sushi bar has possibly the biggest drinks menu you'll ever see. Of course, with drinks containing up to eight different spirits it's probably a good idea to take your time choosing.

ENTERTAINMENT
Berliners take culture and fun seriously, and everything from the impenetrably highbrow to the unashamedly populist crops up here in the course of an average month. Music dominates the after-dark landscape, with an active theatre scene close behind.

Nightclubs
Berlin nightlife is an education in musical styles, with an incredible range of venues putting on everything from techno to ska nights – you can take your pick from at least 130 different parties on any given Friday or Saturday. Clubs rarely open before 11pm (though earlier 'after-work' clubs and Sunday sessions are also popular) and stay open well into the early hours. Admission charges, when they apply, range from €3 to €15.

As the fastest-changing scene in a fast-changing city, some of these places will

GERMANY

inevitably have changed by the time you get to them. Seek out flyers and word-of-mouth tips for the most up-to-date, cutting-edge locations.

12/34 (Map pp412-13; ☎ 5200 72301; Stralauer Allee 1, Friedrichshain) The new sister club of famous techno haunt Tresor (see following) has a more housey vibe and a top riverside setting in the Universal Music building.

Kaffee Burger (Map pp414-15; ☎ 2804 6495; Torstrasse 60, Mitte) A cornerstone of Berlin's alternative scene, decked out in original GDR '60s wallpaper. Come here for indie, rock, punk and the legendary *Russendisko* (Russian disco).

nbi (Map p410; Schönhauser Allee 157, Prenzlauer Berg) For a new club, the décor here looks quite shabby, but that's all part of its slightly retro charm – sink into the sofas and admire the egg cartons on the walls while DJs spin the latest house and electro tracks.

S036 (Map pp412-13; ☎ 6140 1307; Oranienstrasse 190, Kreuzberg) Kreuzberg's punk heart is still going strong, with thrashy live gigs and a hugely popular range of gay and lesbian nights.

Tresor/Globus (Map pp414-15; ☎ 609 3702; Leipziger Strasse 126a, Mitte) Some tastes may have changed but Berlin is still the home of techno, and this long-term survivor from the early rave days keeps flying the flag, though its location is threatened.

Watergate (Map pp412-13; ☎ 6128 0394; Falckensteinstrasse 49a, Kreuzberg) Berlin's hottest recent arrival, in a fantastic location with a downstairs lounge overlooking the Spree – it's just opposite 12/34. The music is mainly electro, drum'n'bass and hip-hop, and it seldom closes early.

WMF (Map pp414-15; ☎ 2838 8850; Karl-Marx-Allee 34, Mitte) This classic electro/downtempo club is now on its sixth location, a great spacious ex-GDR lounge. Regular appearances by remix gods Jazzanova count among the best nights anywhere in Germany; Sunday is GayMF.

Berlin also has a thriving scene of no-holds-barred sex clubs and parties catering for both gays and straights. The notorious **KitKat Club** (Map p411; ☎ 7889 9704; Bessemerstrasse 2-14, Schöneberg) is the original and best.

Music

Berliner Philharmonie (Map pp412-13; ☎ 2548 8132; Herbert-von-Karajan Strasse 1, Tiergarten) The Pots-

---

GAY & LESBIAN BERLIN

Roll over, Amsterdam – Berlin is reclaiming its crown as the gayest city in Europe, with a wild scene recapturing the anything-goes vibe of the liberal 1920s. Venues are concentrated around Nollendorfplatz in Schöneberg and Schönhauser Allee station in northern Prenzlauer Berg. Consult gay and lesbian freebie *Siegessäule* or strictly gay *Sergej* magazine to bone up on the scene, or contact **Mann-O-Meter** (Map p411; ☎ 216 8008; Bülowstrasse 106, Schöneberg).

Schokofabrik (Map pp412-13; ☎ 615 1561; Mariannenstrasse 6, Kreuzberg) You don't have to be a lesbian to hang out at the Chocolate Factory (oo-er) cultural centre, but being a woman really helps, especially in the *hammam* (Turkish bath).

SchwuZ (Map pp412-13; ☎ 693 7025; Mehringdamm 61, Kreuzberg) On Saturdays the Melitta Sundström café at the front fuses warm-up bar for this mainstream dance club, with flamboyant drag queens and two dancefloors.

Sonntags-Club (☎ 449 7590; Greifenhagener Strasse 28, Prenzlauer Berg) This relaxed gay-friendly café-bar project is open to all and holds frequent events.

---

damer Platz 'circus tent' is famous for its acoustics; current director Sir Simon Rattle has consolidated its supreme musical reputation. All seats are excellent.

Konzerthaus (Map pp414-15; ☎ 250 025; Gendarmenmarkt, Mitte) Berlin's second major classical venue, and home to the world-renowned Berlin Symphony Orchestra.

A-Trane (Map p417; ☎ 313 2550; Bleibtreustrasse 1, Charlottenburg; admission €5-20) Safeguarding all the best live traditions, A-Trane is still *the* place in Berlin for jazz. Admission is often free on Monday and Tuesday when local musicians perform.

Staatsoper Unter den Linden (Map pp414-15; ☎ 2035 3455; Unter den Linden 5-7, Mitte) The city's central prestige opera house hosts lavish productions with international talent in an exquisite building dating from 1743.

Deutsche Oper Berlin (Map p417; ☎ 343 8401; Bismarckstrasse 35, Charlottenburg) Specialising in Wagner, the staple diet here includes classical works by mostly Italian and French composers, plus contemporary works.

Theatre

Berlin has around 150 theatres, so there really should be something for everybody. In the former eastern section, they cluster around Friedrichstrasse; in the western part they're concentrated along the Ku'damm. A number of venues are also helping to revive the lively and lavish variety shows of 1920s Berlin. Programmes include dancers, singers, jugglers, acrobats and other entertainers, who each perform a short piece; expect to pay around €14. Don't confuse cabaret with *Kabarett*, political and satirical revues.

Deutsches Theater (Map pp414-15; ☎ 250 025; Schumannstrasse 13a, Mitte) The historic German National Theatre offers classic as well as modern productions.

Volksbühne (Map pp414-15; ☎ 247 6772; Rosa-Luxemburg-Platz, Mitte) Nonconformist, radical and intense, director Frank Castorf's provocative programming pulls in a sharp young audience, with moments of genius amid the frequent controversy.

Friends of Italian Opera (Map pp412-13; ☎ 691 1211; Fidicinstrasse 40, Kreuzberg) Berlin's only English-language theatre venue.

Bar jeder Vernunft (Map p417; ☎ 883 1582; Schaperstrasse 24, Wilmersdorf) With an emphasis on entertainment rather than varieté, most performers at this wonderful offbeat venue have cult followings.

Cultural Centres

Berlin's cultural centres are a unique by-product of the old squat scene, 'repurposing' all manner of derelict buildings for gigs, readings, plays, exhibitions and all kinds of cultural events.

Tacheles (Map pp414-15; ☎ 282 6185; Oranienburger Strasse 54-56, Mitte) Berlin's original and most famous alternative art, culture and entertainment centre has occupied a bombed-out department store since the *Wende* (fall of the Wall). It's run by a self-governed nonprofit organisation.

Kulturbrauerei (Map p410; ☎ 441 9269; Knaackstrasse 97, Prenzlauer Berg) On the commercial side, the 'Culture Brewery' is exactly that, 8000 sq m of renovated former beer factory with a cinema, several bars, nightclubs and music venues, two theatres and artists' studios.

Cinemas

Cinema tickets cost up to €10, and foreign films are usually dubbed into German. In listings, films screened in the original language are marked 'OF' or 'OV', and 'OmU' if they're shown with German subtitles.

Cinemas with original-language showings include **Babylon** (Map pp412-13; ☎ 6160 9193; Dresdner Strasse 126, Kreuzberg) and **Cinestar** (Map pp412-13; ☎ 2606 6260; Potsdamer Strasse 4, Potsdamer Platz).

SHOPPING

Berlin's decentralised character is reflected in the fact that it doesn't have a clearly defined shopping artery like London's Oxford Street or New York's Fifth Avenue. Rather, the numerous shopping areas are in various neighbourhoods, many of which have a local speciality and 'feel'. For art galleries and *haute couture*, for instance, you should head for posh Charlottenburg, while multi-ethnic Kreuzberg is known for its eclectic second-hand and junk stores.

The closest Berlin gets to an international shopping strip is the area along Kurfürstendamm and its extension, Tauentzienstrasse. The star of this area is **KaDeWe** (Map p411; Tauentzienstrasse 21), the Harrods of Germany. The gourmet food halls on the 6th floor are extraordinary. Equally upmarket is the chic indoor shopping complex outside Französische Strasse station in Mitte, anchored by **Galeries Lafayette** (Map pp414-15; ☎ 209 480; Friedrichstrasse 76-78; ☯ 10am-8pm Mon-Sat), a branch of the famous Parisian department store.

When they're not on eBay, thrifty Berliners head for the many fleamarkets around town. The **Berlin Art and Nostalgia Market** (Map pp414-15; Georgenstrasse, Mitte; ☯ 8am-5pm Sat & Sun) is heavy on collectibles, books, ethnic crafts and possibly authentic GDR memorabilia.

GETTING THERE & AWAY
Air

For now, Berlin has three airports.

Tegel (TXL) primarily serves destinations within Germany and Europe.

Schönefeld (SXF) mostly operates international flights to/from Europe, Asia, Africa and Central America. Tegel is due to close within a few years, leaving a revamped and expanded Schönefeld as the new airport hub, to be called Berlin-Brandenburg-International (BBI).

Berlin-Tempelhof (THF) became famous as the landing hub for Allied airlifts during the Berlin blockade of 1948 to 1949, but will also be closing within the next few years.

Bus

Berlin is well connected to the rest of Europe by long-distance bus. Most buses arrive at and depart from the **Zentraler Omnibusbahnhof** (ZOB; ☎ 302 5361; Masurenallee 4-6, Charlottenburg), opposite the stately Funkturm radio tower; the U2 to Kaiserdamm or S45 to Witzleben. Tickets are available from travel agencies or at the bus station.

Car

Lifts can be organised by **ADM Mitfahrzentrale** (ride-share agencies; ☎ 194 40; Zoo station Map p417; ☎ 9am-8pm Mon-Fri, 10am-6pm Sat & Sun; Alexanderplatz U-Bahn Map pp414-15; ☺ 10am-6pm Mon-Fri, 11am-4pm Sat & Sun), who charge a fixed amount payable to the driver, plus commission ranging from €6 for short distances to €10.50 for longer trips (including outside Germany).

Train

ICE and IC trains have hourly services to every major city in Germany. There are night trains to the capitals of most major central European countries. Until the opening of the huge new centralised Lehrter Bahnhof (scheduled for 2007), visitors may find train services to and from Berlin confusing, as different services use different stations. Zoo station is the principal station for long-distance travellers going to/from the west, while Ostbahnhof and Lichtenberg generally handle trains to/from the old east and countries beyond, as well as night trains. Check your schedules carefully and be aware that you may need to switch stations.

GETTING AROUND

Berlin's public transport system is excellent and a much better option than trying to drive around the city. Roughly one billion passengers annually ride the comprehensive network of U-Bahn and S-Bahn trains, buses, trams and ferries, which covers nearly every corner of Berlin and surrounding areas.

To/From the Airport

Schönefeld airport is reached in 30 minutes by Airport Express trains leaving from Zoo station every 30 minutes. The train also stops at the rest of the stations along the central train line including Friedrichstrasse and Ostbahnhof. The station is about 300m from the terminal and there's a free shuttle bus. A taxi to Zoo station costs between €25 and €35.

The Tegel airport is connected by bus No 109 to Zoo station (€2.10), via Kurfürstendamm and Luisenplatz. JetExpress Bus TXL (€3.10) goes via Unter den Linden, Potsdamer Platz and the Reichstag. A taxi between Tegel airport and Zoo station will cost around €20.

Tempelhof airport is reached by the U6 (Platz der Luftbrücke) and by bus No 119 from Kurfürstendamm via Kreuzberg. A taxi to/from Zoo station will cost about €16.

Car & Motorcycle

You'll soon want to ditch your wheels in Berlin. Garage parking is expensive (about €1.50 per hour), but it's often your only choice if you want to be near main attractions. Few hotels have their own garages.

Public Transport

Services are provided by **Berliner Verkehrsbetriebe** (BVG; ☎ 194 49), which operates the U-Bahn, buses, trams and ferries, and **Deutsche Bahn** (DB; www.bahn.de), which runs the S-Bahn and regional RE, SE and RB trains. One type of ticket is valid on all forms of transport.

Berlin's metropolitan area is divided into three tariff zones – A, B and C. Unless you're venturing to Potsdam or the very outer suburbs, you'll only need an AB ticket. The following types of tickets and passes are available:

Ticket type	AB	BC	ABC
Single	€2	€2.25	€2.60
Day Pass	€5.60	€5.70	€6
Group Day Pass (up to 5 people)	€14	€14.30	€15
7-Day Pass	€23.40	€24	€29

Most types of tickets are available from vending machines in U-/S-Bahn stations. Tickets must be validated before use. If you're caught without a ticket (or with an unvalidated one), there's a €30 on-the-spot fine.

U-Bahn and S-Bahn services operate from 4am until just after midnight on weekdays; some 70 night bus (*Nachtbus*) lines fill the gap until normal morning services resume. At weekends, major U-Bahn lines run every 15 minutes all night, while most S-Bahns operate hourly.

Taxi

Taxi stands with call columns are located beside all main train stations and throughout the city. Basic flag fall fare is €2.50, then it's €1.50 per kilometre for the first 7km and €1 thereafter; short trips (less than 2km) cost €3, but must be requested before the meter goes on. If you order a taxi by phone, flag fall goes up to €3. Ring **TAXIfon** (☎ 0800-8001 1554), **Funk Taxi** (☎ 0800-026 1026) or **Würfelfunk** (☎ 0800-222 2255).

BRANDENBURG

Despite its proximity to the ever-popular Berlin, Brandenburg has suffered from a poor reputation since reunification. Many western Germans still think of the Brandenburgers as archetypal Ossis, ambivalent about the demise of the GDR and perhaps even a touch xenophobic; declining population figures, economic depression and high unemployment have also contributed to social problems in urban areas. However, the situation is nowhere near as bad as some would have you believe – in fact, most travellers are pleasantly surprised at the wealth of attractions and the friendliness of the locals in this much-maligned state, and the pride people take in their home towns here can be amazingly infectious.

POTSDAM

☎ 0331 / pop 131,000

Potsdam, on the Havel River just beyond the southwestern tip of Greater Berlin, is the capital of Brandenburg state. In the 17th century, Elector Friedrich Wilhelm of Brandenburg made it his second residence. With the creation of the Kingdom of Prussia, Potsdam became a royal seat and garrison town; in the mid-18th century, Friedrich II (Frederick the Great) built many of the marvellous palaces which visitors flock to today.

In April 1945, Royal Air Force bombers devastated the historic centre of Potsdam, including the City Palace on Alter Markt, but fortunately most other palaces escaped undamaged. To emphasise their victory over the German military machine, the Allies chose Schloss Cecilienhof for the Potsdam Conference of August 1945, which set the stage for the division of Berlin and Germany into occupation zones.

The Potsdam suburb of Babelsberg is the site of a historic – and now once again functioning – film studio (with less historic theme park). In 2001, Potsdam hosted the Bundesgartenschau (National Garden Show), for which this already lovely metropolis was further spruced up; whatever your tastes, a visit here is essential if you're spending any time in the area at all.

Orientation

Potsdam Hauptbahnhof is just southeast of the city centre, across the Havel River. The next two stops are Charlottenhof and Sanssouci, which are closer to Sanssouci Park and the palaces; however, these are served only by RB trains, not the RE or S-Bahn, which most people use to get here from Berlin. It's about 2km to Charlottenhof on foot.

Information

Potsdam Information (☎ 275 580; www.potsdam tourismus.de, in German; Neuer Markt 1; ☺ 9am-7pm Mon-Fri, 10am-6pm Sat & Sun Apr-Oct; 10am-6pm Mon-Fri, to 2pm Sat & Sun Nov-Mar)

Sanssouci Besucherzentrum (☎ 969 4202; www .spsg.de; An der Historischen Windmühle; ☺ 8.30am-5pm Mar-Oct, 9am-4pm Nov-Feb)

Sights

SANSSOUCI PARK

This large park west of the city centre is open from dawn till dusk year-round; the palaces and outbuildings all have different hours and admission prices, and many only open on weekends and holidays outside the main season. A two-day pass including all palaces and other sights in the park costs €15 for adults, and various other combination tickets are available.

The park itself is a sprawling beast, with crisscrossing trails strewn throughout; take along the free map provided by the tourist office or you'll find yourself up the wrong path at almost every turn. The palaces are spaced fairly far apart – for example, it's 2km between the Neues Palais and Schloss Sanssouci, and about 15km to complete the entire circuit. Sadly, cycling in the park is strictly *verboten* (forbidden).

At the heart of the park, Georg Wenzeslaus von Knobelsdorff's celebrated rococo palace **Schloss Sanssouci** (☎ 969 4190; mandatory tour adult/concession €8/5; ☺ 9am-5pm Tue-Sun Apr-Oct, to 4pm Nov-Mar), built in 1747, has some

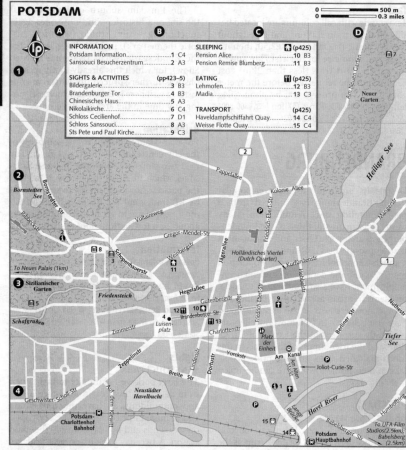

POTSDAM

0 ____ 500 m
0 ____ 0.3 miles

INFORMATION	
Potsdam Information	1 C4
Sanssouci Besucherzentrum	2 A3

SIGHTS & ACTIVITIES	(pp423–5)
Bildergalerie	3 B3
Brandenburger Tor	4 B3
Chinesisches Haus	5 A3
Nikolaikirche	6 C4
Schloss Cecilienhof	7 D1
Schloss Sanssouci	8 A3
Sts Pete und Paul Kirche	9 C3

SLEEPING	(p425)
Pension Alice	10 B3
Pension Remise Blumberg	11 B3

EATING	(p425)
Lehmofen	12 B3
Madia	13 C3

TRANSPORT	(p425)
Haveldampfschiffahrt Quay	14 C4
Weisse Flotte Quay	15 C4

glorious interiors and should be your first stop. Only 2000 visitors a day are allowed entry (a rule laid down by Unesco), so tickets are usually sold out by 2.30pm, even in the quiet seasons – arrive early and avoid weekends and holidays. Tours run by the tourist office guarantee entry.

The late-baroque **Neues Palais** (New Palace; ☎ 969 4255; adult/concession €5/4; 10am-5pm Sat-Thu) was built in 1769 as the summer residence of the royal family. It's one of the most imposing buildings in the park and the one to see if your time is limited. The tour takes in about a dozen of the palace's 200 rooms.

Germany's first purpose-built art museum, the **Bildergalerie** (Picture Gallery; ☎ 969 4181; adult/concession €2.50/1.50; 10am-5pm Tue-

Sun, 15 May–15 Oct) was completed in 1764. It contains a rich collection of 17th-century paintings by Rubens, Caravaggio and other big names.

Spare time for what many consider to be the pearl of the park: **Chinesisches Haus** (Chinese Teahouse; ☎ 969 4222; admission €1; 10am-5pm Tue-Sun, 15 May–15 Oct) is a circular pavilion of gilded columns, palm trees and figures of Chinese musicians and animals, built in 1757. Look out for a monkey with Voltaire's face!

NEUER GARTEN
Northeast of the centre, the New Garden is another sprawling park on the bank of the Heiliger See and a fine place to relax after Sanssouci.

At the northern end of the park is **Schloss Cecilienhof** (☎ 969 4244; adult/concession €4/3; ☒ 9am-5pm Tue-Sun), an English-style country manor, incongruous in rococo-heavy Potsdam. The palace was the site of the 1945 Potsdam Conference, where territorial divisions were decided after WWII, and large photos of the participants – Stalin, Truman and Churchill – are displayed inside. The conference room can be visited on a guided tour.

FILMPARK BABELSBERG
Germany's one-time response to Hollywood, the **UFA film studios** (☎ 721 2755; www.filmpark .de; Grossbeerenstrasse; adult/concession/child €15/14/9; ☒ 10am-6pm 15 Mar–2 Nov), are east of the city centre. Shooting began in 1912 but the studio had its heyday in the 1920s, when such silent-movie epics as Fritz Lang's *Metropolis* were made, along with some early Greta Garbo films. Nowadays the place resembles a mini–Universal Studios theme park, with haunted house, volcano, live shows, signings, an impressive stunt show and a few poky rides. During the studio tour, staff whisk you around the backlot for a peek at the film sets and production, as well as into the props and costumes room.

ALTSTADT
The baroque arch on Luisenplatz, at the western end of the old town, **Brandenburger Tor** (Brandenburg Gate) doesn't cut as much of a dash as its larger namesake in Berlin but is actually older (1770). From here, pedestrian Brandenburger Strasse runs due east, providing the town's main shopping and eating drag.

Standing out from its surroundings, the **Holländisches Viertel** (Dutch Quarter), towards the northern end of Friedrich-Ebert-Strasse, is a pretty area with some 134 gabled red-brick houses, built for Dutch workers who came to Potsdam in the 1730s at the invitation of Friedrich Wilhelm I. The homes have been well restored and now house all kinds of interesting galleries, cafés and restaurants.

Tours
Weisse Flotte (☎ 275 9210; www.schiffahrt-in-pots dam.de; Lange Brücke 6; ☒ 8.45am-4.15pm Apr-Oct) Boats cruising the Havel and the lakes around Potsdam depart regularly from the dock near Lange Brücke, with frequent trips to Wannsee (€7) and Spandau (€15 return). Sister company **Haveldampfschiffahrt** (☎ 275 9233; www.schiffahrt-in-potsdam.de; Lange Brücke 6; tours from €9.50) has steamboat tours of the same areas. See the website for boat and steamboat departure times.

Sleeping & Eating
While most people visit Potsdam as a day trip from Berlin, accommodation can still be pretty scarce in high season. Conversely, low season prices can be great bargains.

Pension Alice (☎ 292 304; Lindenstrasse 16; s/d €25/50) This is Potsdam's most central budget option, with a few quirky rooms above a busy café.

Pension Remise Blumberg (☎ 280 3231; Wein-bergstrasse 26; s/d €55/68; ☒ ☒) Well-placed for Sanssouci, the large apartment-style rooms here are ideal for self-caterers (breakfast isn't included). Bike hire is available, and the garden café sports an almost cheery mural of Caspar David Friedrich's *Isle of the Dead*.

Madia (Lindenstrasse 53; food from €3.50; ☒ noon-7pm) A fair-trade haven for vegos and hippies, tucked away in a nice courtyard behind a record store and a dubious 'headshop'.

Lehmofen (☎ 280 1712; Hermann-Elflein-Strasse 10; mains €10-17) This smart Turkish place may do kebabs, but it's a world away from your average döner shop, serving up tasty, authentic dishes from its eponymous clay oven.

Getting There & Away
S-Bahn line S7 links central Berlin with Potsdam Hauptbahnhof about every 10 minutes. Some regional (RB/RE) trains from Berlin-Zoo stop at all three stations in Potsdam, and RB22 trains connect to Berlin-Schönefeld airport. Berlin transit passes must cover Zones A, B and C (€2.60) to get you here.

Getting Around
Potsdam is part of Berlin's S-Bahn network but has its own local trams and buses; these converge on Lange Brücke near the Hauptbahnhof. A two-zone ticket costs €1.40 and a day pass €3.

SACHSENHAUSEN CONCENTRATION CAMP
In 1936 the Nazis opened a 'model' *Konzentrationslager* (concentration camp) for men

in a disused brewery in Sachsenhausen, near the town of Oranienburg (population 30,000), about 35km north of Berlin. By 1945 about 220,000 men from 22 countries had passed through the gates – labelled, as at Auschwitz in southwestern Poland, *Arbeit Macht Frei* (Work Sets You Free). About 100,000 were murdered here, their remains consumed by the fires of the horribly efficient ovens.

After the war, the Soviets and the communist leaders of the new GDR set up Speziallager No 7 (Special Camp No 7) for political prisoners, ex-Nazis, monarchists and anyone else who didn't happen to fit into their mould. An estimated 60,000 people were interned at the camp between 1945 and 1950, and up to 12,000 are believed to have died here.

The **Sachsenhausen Memorial and Museum** (☎ 03301-200 200; ⏰ 8.30am-6pm Tue-Sun Apr-Sep, 8.30am-4.30pm Oct-Mar) consists of several parts. The **Neues Museum** (New Museum) has some excellent exhibits, including a history of anti-Semitism and audiovisual material. East of it are **Barracks 38 & 39**, reconstructions of two typical huts housing most of the 6000 Jewish prisoners brought to Sachsenhausen after Kristallnacht (9–10 November 1938). Number 38 was rebuilt after being torched by neo-Nazis in September 1992. Inside the prison yard is a **memorial** to the homosexuals who died here, one of the few monuments you'll see anywhere to these 'forgotten victims' (there's another one at Nollendorfplatz U-Bahn station in Berlin).

The easiest way to get to Sachsenhausen from Berlin is to take the frequent S1 to Oranienburg (€6.45, 50 minutes). There are also RB trains from Berlin-Lichtenberg (€6, 30 minutes, hourly). The walled camp is an easy, signposted 20-minute walk northeast of Oranienburg train station.

SAXONY

Saxony is densely populated, highly industrialised and, along with Bavaria, somehow the most German of the German states, taking great pride in its unique identity. Known as the birthplace of the German language, the impenetrable local dialect is a treasured artefact, and rich veins of history in all its forms run through the region. With

Poland and the Czech Republic entering the EU, Saxony is also an increasingly important gateway to Eastern Europe.

The Elbe River is Saxony's lifeline, bisecting the state north–south. The region was hit hard by the *Jahrhundertflut* (the 'flood of the century' or 100-year flood) in August 2002, when the river reached its highest level for 100 years (up to 9.5m in places), causing millions of euros worth of damage; Meissen and state capital Dresden, which straddle the river, were among the worst sufferers. A costly clean-up operation was completed admirably quickly, and you can now see plaques in many affected towns commemorating this (hopefully) once-in-a-lifetime event. As an ironic footnote, the river hit almost record low levels during the scorching summer of 2003.

DRESDEN
☎ 0351 / pop 479,000
In the 18th century Dresden was famous throughout Europe as 'Florence on the Elbe', as Italian artists, musicians, actors and master craftsmen flocked to the court of Augustus the Strong, bestowing countless masterpieces upon the city. Today, however, it's best known for the controversial carpet-bombing of February 1945, when Allied aircraft levelled much of the city, killing at least 35,000 people at a time when the war was almost over.

Luckily you can't keep a great city down, and many of Dresden's stunning baroque buildings have been restored, putting the Saxon capital firmly back at the forefront of Germany's tourist towns. With major restoration work going on for its 800th anniversary in 2006 and a strong bid for European Capital of Culture 2010 in the offing, the coming years should see Dresden garner more fans. Take a few days to enjoy what this monumental city has to offer.

Orientation
The Elbe River splits the town in a rough V-shape, with the Neustadt to the north and the Altstadt to the south.

Dresden has two main train stations: the Hauptbahnhof on the southern side of town, and the more contemporary Dresden-Neustadt north of the river. Most trains stop at both. Dresden-Mitte is little more than a forlorn platform between the two.

GERMANY

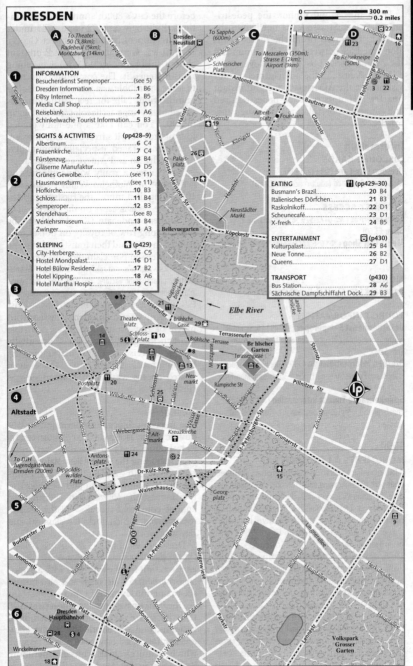

DRESDEN

| 0 | 300 m |
| 0 | 0.2 miles |

INFORMATION
Besucherdienst Semperoper...............(see 5)
Dresden Information..............................**1** B6
E@sy Internet...**2** B5
Media Call Shop....................................**3** D1
Reisebank..**4** A6
Schinkelwache Tourist Information......**5** B3

SIGHTS & ACTIVITIES (pp428–9)
Albertinum..**6** C4
Frauenkirche...**7** C4
Fürstenzug..**8** B4
Gläserne Manufaktur.............................**9** D5
Grünes Gewölbe................................(see 11)
Hausmannsturm.................................(see 11)
Hofkirche..**10** B3
Schloss..**11** B4
Semperoper...**12** B3
Stendehaus...(see 8)
Verkehrsmuseum.................................**13** B4
Zwinger...**14** A3

SLEEPING (p429)
City-Herberge.....................................**15** C5
Hostel Mondpalast..............................**16** D1
Hotel Bülow Residenz..........................**17** B2
Hotel Kipping......................................**18** A6
Hotel Martha Hospiz............................**19** C1

EATING (pp429–30)
Busmann's Brazil..................................**20** B4
Italienisches Dörfchen..........................**21** B3
Raskolnikoff..**22** D1
Scheunecafé..**23** D1
X-fresh..**24** B5

ENTERTAINMENT (p430)
Kulturpalast..**25** B4
Neue Tonne...**26** B2
Queens..**27** D1

TRANSPORT (p430)
Bus Station..**28** A6
Sächsische Dampfschiffahrt Dock........**29** B3

To Theater
50 (3.8km);
Radebeul (5km);
Moritzburg (14km)

Dresden-
Neustadt

To Sappho
(600m)

To Mezcalero (350m);
Strasse E (2km);
Airport (9km)

To Reisekneipe
(50m)

Katharinenstr
Louisenstr

Dr-Friedrich-Wolf-Str
Schlesischer
Platz

Antonstr

Bautzner Str

Albert-
platz

Fountains

Leipziger Str

Fischhaus
Allee

Theresienstr

Hainstr

Nieritzstr

Königstr

Palais-
platz

Grosse Meissner Str

Grosse Meissner Str

Hauptstr

Neustädter
Markt

Bellevuegarten

Köpckestr

Elbe River

Augustus-
brücke

Theater-
platz

Terrassenufer

Brühlsche
Gasse

Terrassenufer

Brühlsche Terrasse

Brühlscher
Garten

Br hlscher
Garten

Terrassengasse

Schloss-
platz

Augustusstr

Munzgasse

Am Schiesshaus

Sophienstr

Neu-
markt

Rampische Str

Landhausstr

Schlossstr

Schweriner Str

Postplatz

Wilsdruffer Str

Galeriestr

Landhaus Schlossgasse

Pillnitzer Str

Altstadt

Annenstr

Am See

Walstr

Marienstr

Webergasse

Altmarkt

Weisse
Gasse

Kreuzstr

Kreuzkirche

St-Petersburger Str

Grunaerstr

To DJH
Jugendgästehaus
Dresden (200m)

Josephinenstr

Lilienstr

Antons-
platz

Dippoldis-
walder
Platz

Dr-Külz-Ring

Georg-
platz

Zirkusstr

Budapester Str

Ammonstr

Waisenhausstr

Prager Str

Reitbahnstr

St-Petersburger Str

Zinzendorfstr

Bürgerwiese

Sidonienstr

Lindenaustr

Parkstr

Blüherstr

Lingnerallee

Dresden
Hauptbahnhof

Wiener Platz

Bayrische Str

Winckelmannstr

Wiener Str

Mary-Wigman-Str

Mosczinsky Str

Sidonienstr

**Volkspark
Grosser
Garten**

Hauptallee

Herkulesallee

Hauptallee

From the Hauptbahnhof, the pedestrianised Prager Strasse leads north into the Altstadt. The lovely Brühlsche Terrasse runs along the Elbe between the Albertinum and the Zwinger, with boat docks below.

In the Neustadt, the main attractions for visitors are the Albertplatz and Antonstadt quarters. Hauptstrasse is pedestrianised and connects Albertplatz with the Augustusbrücke.

Information

DISCOUNT CARDS

Dresden City-Card (48hr card €18)
Museums day card (adult/concession €10/6)

INTERNET ACCESS

E@sy Internet (☎ 0172-579 5652; Pfarrgasse 1; per hr €3.60)
Media Call Shop (☎ 656 7277; Rothenburger Strasse; per hr €3)

MONEY

Reisebank (☎ 471 2177; Hauptbahnhof)

TOURIST INFORMATION

Besucherdienst Semperoper (☎ 491 10; Schinkelwache, Theaterplatz 2; ✆ 10am-6pm Mon-Fri, 10am-1pm Sat)
Dresden Information (☎ 4919 2100; www.dresden-tourist.de; Prager Strasse 21; ✆ 9.30am-6pm Mon-Fri, 9.30am-4pm Sat)
Schinkelwache Tourist Information (☎ 491 1705; Theaterplatz 2; ✆ 10am-6pm Mon-Fri, 10am-4pm Sat & Sun)

Sights

MONUMENTS & LANDMARKS

The neo-Renaissance opera house, **Semperoper** (☎ 491 1496; www.semperoper.de; Theaterplatz; tour adult/concession €5/3; ✆ varies), designed by Gustav Semper, *is* Dresden. The original building opened in 1841 but burned down less than three decades later; rebuilt in 1878, it was pummelled in WWII and reopened only in 1985, after the communists invested millions in restoring it. Flooding closed it down again briefly in 2002. Thanks to a recent beer commercial, the Semperoper is probably one of the best-known buildings in Germany.

Another of Dresden's most beloved symbols, the **Frauenkirche** (Church of Our Lady; ☎ 439 3934; www.frauenkirche-dresden.org; Neumarkt; ✆ tours 10am-4pm) is rapidly emerging from its scaffolding shroud and should be restored well before the city's 800th anniversary celebrations. Built between 1726 and 1743 under the direction of baroque architect George Bähr, it was Germany's greatest Protestant church until February 1945, when bombing raids flattened it. The communists decided to leave the rubble as a war memorial; after reunification, calls for reconstruction prevailed and a huge archaeological dig began in 1992. You can take a one-hour guided tour of the site – it's free, but donations are greatly encouraged, especially from guilty-looking British and American visitors.

You'd need a really wide-angle lens to get a shot of Wulhelm Walther's amazing 102m-long tiled mural, the **Fürstenzug** (Procession of Princes; Augustusstrasse), on the outer wall of the former Stendehaus (Royal Stables). The scene, a long row of royalty on horses, was painted in 1876 and then transferred to some 24,000 Meissen porcelain tiles in 1906.

Volkswagen's striking **Gläserne Manufaktur** (Transparent Factory; ☎ 0180-589 6268; www.glaesernemanufaktur.de; Grosser Garten; adult/concession €5/4; ✆ 8am-8pm) opened in 2001 as a blast of modernity amid Dresden's classics, with much of the production process visible through the great glass panels. Essentially a huge exercise in brand marketing, the building made such an impact that it even hosted operas while the Semperoper was closed in 2002!

MUSEUMS

The imposing block, **Albertinum** (☎ 491 4619; Brühlsche Terrasse; adult/child €4/2.50; ✆ 10am-6pm Fri-Wed), houses many of Dresden's art treasures, including the **Galerie Neue Meister**, with renowned 19th- and 20th-century paintings from leading French and German Impressionists, the **Münzkabinett** collection of antique coins and medals, and the **Skulpturensammlung**, which includes classical and Egyptian works.

Dresden's elaborate 1728 fortress **Zwinger** (☎ 491 4622; Theaterplatz 1; ✆ 10am-6pm Tue-Sun) is an attraction in its own right, with a popular ornamental courtyard, and also houses six major museums. The most important are the **Rüstkammer** (armoury; adult/concession €3/2), with its superb collection of ceremonial weapons, and the **Galerie Alte Meister** (adult/concession €6/3.50, incl entry to Rüstkammer; ✆ daily), which features masterpieces including Raphael's *Sistine Madonna*. The dazzling

Porzelansammlung (Porcelain Collection; adult/concession €5/3) is another highlight.

Schloss (☎ 491 4619; Schlossplatz) Restoration of this massive neo-Renaissance palace is scheduled, a bit optimistically, to finish in 2006. At the time of writing, the **Hausmannsturm** (Servants' Tower; adult/concession €4/2.50; ⊙ 10am-6pm Tue-Sun) and the baroque Catholic **Hofkirche** (⊙ 9am-5pm Mon-Thu, 1-5pm Fri, 10.30am-4pm Sat, noon-4pm Sun), which contains the heart of Augustus the Strong, were open to the public. Also here is the **Grünes Gewölbe** (Green Vault; adult/concession €6/3.50; ⊙ 10am-6pm Wed-Mon), one of the world's finest collections of jewel-encrusted precious objects. Treasures include the world's biggest green diamond, tiny pearl sculptures and a stunning group of 137 gem-studded figures by Johann Melchior Dinglinger, court jeweller of Augustus the Strong.

Verkehrsmuseum (Transport Museum; ☎ 864 40; Augustusstrasse 1; adult/concession €2/1; ⊙ 10am-5pm Tue-Sun) Motoring back towards the 20th century, this is a fascinating collection including penny-farthings, trams, dirigibles and carriages. Included in the admission is a great 40-minute film with original black-and-white footage of 1930s Dresden.

Tours
Cruise the Elbe on the world's oldest fleet of paddle-wheel steamers with **Sächsische Dampfschiffahrt** (☎ 866 090; www.saechsische-dampfschiffahrt .de; adult/child €10/5). Ninety-minute tours leave from the Terrassenufer dock at 11am, 1pm, 3pm and 5pm daily.

Sleeping
BUDGET
Accommodation in Dresden can be horrendously overpriced, with hotel rates among the highest in Germany. Luckily, several good-value budget places have emerged in or near the centre; the Neustadt is particularly strong on interesting, youth-oriented hostels. Breakfast is not included unless otherwise stated.

DJH Jugendgästehaus Dresden (☎ 492 620; jghdresden@djh-sachsen.de; Maternistrasse 22; s/d €24/36; ☒ ▣) This tower block was once a Communist Party training centre; now it's a great hostel, with small dorms and a bistro (breakfast included), plus wheelchair access and lift. Take tram No 7 or 10 to the corner of Ammonstrasse and Freiberger Strasse.

Hostel Mondpalast (☎ 804 6061; www.mondpalast .de; Louisenstrasse 77; dm €13.50, s €29-39, d €37-50; ☒) Looking even better after a quick move and a TV appearance, the Moon Palace has bedrooms decorated by theme (Australia, Greece, space travel) and a great bar/café.

Mezcalero (☎ 810 770; www.mezcalero.de; Königsbrücker Strasse 64; dm €15-23, s €30-45, d €50-60; ℗) Definitely one for the 'oddities' basket: how often do you get to stay in a Mexican/Aztec B&B, complete with sombreros, red-yellow colour scheme, tiles and tequila bar? Very random, very cool.

City-Herberge (☎ 485 9900; www.city-herberge.de; Lingnerallee 3; s/d €36.50/63; ℗) Large and in a central location, this basic tourist hotel is a good bet if you arrive at a busy time.

MID-RANGE
Hotel Kipping (☎ 478 500; www.hotel-kipping.de; Winckelmannstrasse 6; s €70-95, d €85-115; ℗ ☒) Just south of the Hauptbahnhof, this is a family-run, family-friendly hotel which comes with fervent reader recommendations.

Hotel Martha Hospiz (☎ 817 60; marthahospiz .dresden@t-online.de; Nieritzstrasse 11; s €54-84, d €102-118; ℗) Quiet reigns in this ample yet lovely inn with country furnishings, once owned by a church.

Rothenburger Hof (☎ 812 60; www.rothenburger -hof.de; Rothenburger Strasse 15-17; s/d €95/130; ℗ ☒ ☻) In the middle of Neustadt you'll find this place with a clean, bright atmosphere and lots of beauty treatments, including steam room and sauna.

TOP END
If you've got the cash to flash, Dresden is a fantastic place to live it up. Wheelchair access comes as standard, and all the top-flight places offer *Arrangements* combining several nights' stay with attractions such as hard-to-come-by Semperoper tickets.

Hotel Bülow Residenz (☎ 800 30; buelow-residenz .de; Rähnitzstrasse 19; s/d €180/220; ℗ ☒ ☻) A real gem, tucked away on a quiet street near Palaisplatz. Breakfast is extra but the minibar is included (priorities!), and the Caroussel restaurant is rated one of the best in Saxony, run by award-winning young chef Stefan Hermann.

Eating
It's no problem finding somewhere to eat in the Neustadt, with multifarious cafés and

restaurants taking up most streets. South of the river, Weisse Gasse, near the Altmarkt, and Münzgasse/Terrassengasse, between Brühlsche Terrasse and the Frauenkirche, are crammed with restaurants representing all kinds of local and international cuisine.

Italienisches Dörfchen (☎ 498 160; www.italienisches-doerfchen.de, in German; Theaterplatz 3; mains €5-20) This collection of four restaurants offers stylish surroundings and varied cuisine, from bargain barbecue on the terrace to swish Italian and Saxon dishes inside.

Raskolnikoff (☎ 804 5706; www.raskolnikoff.de, in German; Böhmische Strasse 34; mains €5.20-7) This place couldn't be more bohemian if it tried – it's even on Bohemian Street! The menu sorts its good-value light meals by compass direction, and includes Eastern European dishes such as *borscht* (beetroot soup) and *pelmeni* (Russian ravioli). There's a gallery and *pension* (rooms €30 to €45) upstairs.

Scheunecafé (☎ 802 6619; Alaunstrasse 36-40; mains €6.40-10.10) Indian food in an alternative rock venue? Way better than it sounds – just watch the crowds gather in the beer garden.

X-fresh (☎ 484 2791; Altmarkt Galerie; mains €6.50-14.90) Billed as a 'Wellness-bistro', the food here is refreshingly healthy, with a good range of salads and shakes and a *prosecco*-tinged Sunday breakfast buffet (€7.80, 9am to 2pm).

Busmann's Brazil (☎ 862 1200; Kleine Brüdergasse 5; mains €9.60-21.20) For a taste of Brazilian culture beyond the usual *caipirinha*, try this huge, swish place, which boasts such strange delicacies as frogfish and rattlesnake (€40.90).

Drinking & Entertainment

The finest all-round listings guide to Dresden is *SAX* (€1.50), available at newsstands around the city.

Dresden is synonymous with opera, and performances at the spectacular **Semperoper** (☎ 491 1496; www.semperoper.de; Theaterplatz), opposite the Zwinger, are brilliant. Tickets cost from €15, but they're usually booked out well in advance. Some performances by the renowned Philharmonic are also held there, but most are in the **Kulturpalast** (☎ 486 60; www.kulturpalast-dresden.de, in German; Schlossstrasse 2), which hosts a wide range of concerts and events.

Neue Tonne (☎ 802 6017; www.jazzclub-tonne.de, in German; Königstrasse 15; entry free-€15) Dresden's best jazz club, now in a new, more central location.

Reisekneipe (☎ 889 4111; Görlitzerstrasse 15) Experience Africa, Asia, Arabia, Russia and Europe just by wandering through this massively popular bar and trying its exotic imported beers. Hardened globetrotters give talks (with slides, of course) every Wednesday.

Strasse E (www.strasse-e.de, in German; Werner-Hartmann-Strasse 2) Six thousand square metres of 'cultural centre' comprising no fewer than eight different club spaces, this complex north of town offers a wide range of nights, from disco to drum'n'bass. Take tram No 7 to Industriegelände.

Queens (☎ 803 1650; Görlitzerstrasse 3) A young crowd hangs out at this noisy gay bar/lounge/disco.

Sappho (☎ 404 5136; Hechtstrasse 23) This new women's café is an excellent addition to Dresden's thriving gay map.

Getting There & Around

Dresden-Klotzsche airport, served by Lufthansa, KLM and other major airlines, is 9km north of the city centre, on S-Bahn line 2 (€1.50, 30 minutes). The Airport City Liner bus serves Dresden-Neustadt (€3) and the Hauptbahnhof (€4), with stops at key points in town. A taxi to the Hauptbahnhof is about €10.

Dresden is two hours south of Berlin-Ostbahnhof by IC/EC train (€30.20, every two hours). The Leipzig-Riesa-Dresden service (€16.80, 70 minutes) operates hourly. The S-Bahn runs half-hourly to Meissen (€4, 45 minutes). There are hourly connections to Frankfurt-am-Main (€66.80, 4½ hours) and Munich (€97.60, 6¾ hours) and daily direct international services to Vienna (€110, 7¾ hours) and Prague (€25, three hours).

Dresden's public transport network charges €1.50 for a single ticket; day tickets cost €4. The family day ticket, for two adults and up to four kids, is a good deal at €5.

AROUND DRESDEN
Meissen
☎ 03521 / pop 29,000

Some 27km northwest of Dresden, Meissen is a compact, perfectly preserved old town and the centre of a rich wine-growing region, with red-tiled roofs reminiscent of coastal Croatia.

Meissen's medieval fortress, the Albrechtsburg, crowns a ridge high above the Elbe River and contains the former ducal palace and Meissen Cathedral, a magnificent Gothic structure. Augustus the Strong of Saxony created Europe's first porcelain factory here in 1710. The town celebrated its 1075th anniversary in 2004.

Like Dresden, Meissen straddles the Elbe, with the old town on the western bank and the train station on the eastern. Both sides were struck by record flood levels in 2002, with water pushing quite a distance into the Altstadt; look out for plaques marking the highest points.

The tourist office is at **Meissen-Information** (☎ 419 40; www.touristinfo-meissen.de, in German; Markt 3; ☼ 10am-6pm Mon-Fri, 10am-4pm Sat & Sun, closed Sun Nov-Mar).

SIGHTS

Steep stepped lanes lead up to Meissen's towering medieval **Albrechtsburg Cathedral** (☎ 452 490; Domplatz 7; adult/concession €2/1.50; ☼ 10am-6pm Mar-Oct, to 4pm Nov-Feb), which contains an altarpiece by Lucas Cranach the Elder.

Beside the cathedral is the remarkable 15th-century **palace** (☎ 470 70; Domplatz 1; adult/concession €3.50/2.50; ☼ 10am-6pm Mar-Oct, to 5pm Nov-Feb), widely seen as the birthplace of Schloss architecture, with its ingenious system of internal arches. A combined ticket for both buildings costs €5/2.50.

Meissen has long been renowned for its chinaware, with its trademark insignia of blue crossed swords. The Albrechtsburg palace was originally the manufacturing site, but the factory is now 1km southwest of the Altstadt in an appropriately beautiful building, the **Porzellan Manufaktur** (Porcelain Factory; ☎ 468 700; Talstrasse 9; collection adult/concession €4.50/4, workshop €3; ☼ 9am-6pm May-Oct, to 5pm Nov-Apr), which dates to 1916. There are often long queues for the workshop demonstrations, but you can view the porcelain collection upstairs at your leisure.

SLEEPING & EATING

Hotel Am Markt Residenz (☎ 415 10; residenz@ meissen-hotel.com; An der Frauenkirche 1; s €60, d €95-125; P) This smart, stately hotel, along with its sister Am Markt 6, offers classic rooms with multiple shades of green and all kinds of art around the place. The rock-hewn wine cellar here is particularly atmospheric.

Gaststätte Winkelkrug (☎ 453 711; Schlossberg 13; mains €4-7.50; ☼ evenings only, Wed-Sun) Eschew the posh Albrechtsburg eateries for this quaint wine house on the way up, in a lovely old building with a flourishing garden section.

GETTING THERE & AWAY

Half-hourly S-Bahn trains run from Dresden's Hauptbahnhof and Neustadt train stations (€4.50, 30 minutes). To visit the porcelain factory, get off at Meissen-Triebischtal (one stop after Meissen).

A more interesting way to get here is by steamer (between May and September). Boats leave from the Sächsische Dampfschiffahrt dock in Dresden at 9.15am and head back at 3pm (€15 return, two hours).

Saxon Switzerland

Sächsische Schweiz (Saxon Switzerland) is a 275 sq km national park 50km south of Dresden, near the Czech border. Its wonderfully wild, craggy country is dotted with castles and tiny towns along the mighty Elbe. The landscape varies unexpectedly and radically: its forests can look deceptively tropical, while the worn cliffs and plateaus recall the parched expanses of New Mexico or central Spain (generally without the searing heat).

The highlight of the park is the **Bastei** lookout, on the Elbe some 28km southeast of Dresden. One of the most breathtaking spots in the whole of Germany, it features towering outcrops 305m high and unparalleled views of the surrounding forests, cliffs and mountains, not to mention a magnificent sightline right along the river itself.

LEIPZIG
☎ 0341 / pop 493,000

Dresden may be Saxony's capital, but Leipzig is bigger, livelier and less stuffy than its museum-jammed neighbour. It's an important business and transport centre, a trade-fair mecca and arguably the most dynamic city in eastern Germany.

Leipzig also has some of the finest classical music and opera in the country, and its art and literary scenes are flourishing. It was once home to Bach, Wagner and Mendelssohn, and to Goethe, who set a key scene of *Faust* in the cellar of his favourite watering hole. More recently, it earned the sobriquet *Stadt der Helden* (City of Heroes) for its leading role in the 1989 democratic revolution. It's the kind of city you just can't help liking.

The big news for Leipzig, however, is its Olympic bid for 2012, gleefully backed by chancellor Gerhard Schröder, which could rocket the city to international stardom alongside Berlin, Munich and Frankfurt-am-Main, as well as boosting the Saxon economy by millions of euros.

Big things are expected here in the next few years, and we can only recommend that you get a piece of the action.

Orientation

Leipzig's centre lies within a ring road that outlines the town's medieval fortifications. To reach the city centre from the Hauptbahnhof, cross Willy-Brandt-Platz and continue south along Nikolaistrasse for five minutes.

The central Markt (square), which was being redeveloped for a new station at the time of writing, is a couple of blocks southwest, and east down Grimmiasche Strasse is the massive Augustusplatz, home to some of the city's most important (if not prettiest) GDR-era buildings and also the modern MDR Tower.

Information

Leipzig Card (24/72hr card €5.90/11.50)
Leipzig Tourist Service (☎ 710 4260; www.leipzig.de; Richard-Wagner-Strasse 1; ☺ 9am-7pm Mon-Fri, 9am-4pm Sat, 9am-2pm Sun)
Reisebank (☎ 980 4588; South Hall, Hauptbahnhof)
Webcafé (☎ 0700-1999 3000; Reichsstrasse 18; Internet per hr €2.60-4)

Sights

Don't rush from sight to sight – wandering around Leipzig is a pleasure in itself, with many of the blocks around the central Markt crisscrossed by amazingly designed internal shopping passages.

MONUMENTS & LANDMARKS

Off the southern ring road is the impressive 108m-high tower of the baroque **Neues Rathaus** (New Town Hall; ☎ 1230; Martin-Luther-Ring; ☺ 6.45am-4.30pm Mon-Fri). Although the building's origins date back to the 16th century, its current manifestation was completed in 1905. The interior makes it one of the finest municipal buildings in Germany; the lobby houses rotating art exhibitions, mostly on historical themes.

Located 4km southeast of the centre, the **Völkerschlachtdenkmal** (Battle of Nations Monument;

Strasse des 18 Oktober; adult/concession €2.50/1.25; ☺ 10am-6pm Apr-Oct, to 4pm Nov-Mar) is a massive 91m-high monument commemorating the decisive victory here by the combined Prussian, Austrian and Russian forces over Napoleon's army in 1813. The blackened dome looms like a glowering skull over its surroundings, looking particularly moody in winter. Take tram No 15 from the station.

MUSEUMS

Haunting and uplifting by turns, the **Zeitgeschichtliches Forum** (Forum of Contemporary History; ☎ 222 20; Grimmaische Strasse 6; admission free; ☺ 9am-6pm Tue-Fri, 10am-6pm Sat & Sun) tells the story of the GDR from division and dictatorship to resistance and reform. You can see legendary GDR products and footage of families stifling tears as the Berlin Wall was built between them, and it's hard not to feel moved by the Gentle Revolution that started right here in Leipzig. An English-language pamphlet translates the main captions.

Former headquarters of the East German secret police, the **Stasi Museum** (☎ 961 2443; Dittrichring 24; admission free; ☺ 10am-6pm) has exhibits on propaganda, disguises, surveillance photos and other forms of 'intelligence'. There are also mounds of papier-mâché that were created when officers shredded and soaked secret documents before the fall of the GDR.

Opposite the Thomaskirche, is the **Bach Museum** (☎ 964 110; Thomaskirchhof 16; adult/concession €3/2; ☺ 10am-5pm), where JS Bach worked from 1723 until his death in 1750. This excellent collection focuses on the composer's busy life in Leipzig. There are portraits, manuscripts and other Bach memorabilia.

Leipzig's finest museum, the **Museum der Bildenden Künste** (Museum of Fine Arts; ☎ 216 990; Grimmaische Strasse 1-7; adult/concession €2.50/1; ☺ 10am-6pm Tue & Thu-Sun, 1-8pm Wed), is temporarily housed in the Handelshof building, with an excellent collection of old masters. If all goes well, in 2005 it should have moved to a new building on Sachsenplatz.

Sleeping

BUDGET

Camping Am Auensee (☎ 465 1600; Gustav-Esche-Strasse 5; adult/child €4/3, car €3, tent €3-5, cabins €20-35) This camping ground is in a pleasant wooded spot on the city's northwestern outskirts (take tram No 10 or 28 to Wahren). The cabins are A-frame bungalows.

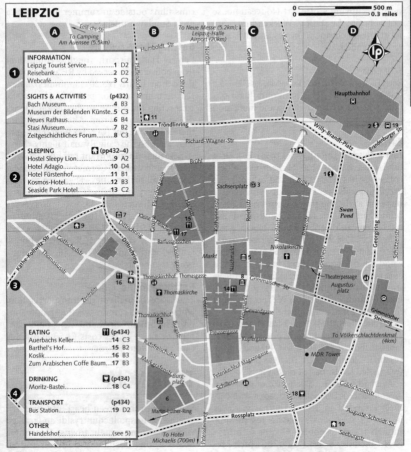

LEIPZIG

INFORMATION	
Leipzig Tourist Service...............1	D2
Reisebank...............2	D2
Webcafé...............3	C2
SIGHTS & ACTIVITIES	(p432)
Bach Museum...............4	B3
Museum der Bildenden Künste...5	C3
Neues Rathaus...............6	B4
Stasi Museum...............7	B2
Zeitgeschichtliches Forum...............8	C3
SLEEPING	(pp432–4)
Hostel Sleepy Lion...............9	A2
Hotel Adagio...............10	D4
Hotel Fürstenhof...............11	B1
Kosmos-Hotel...............12	B3
Seaside Park Hotel...............13	C2

EATING	(p434)
Auerbachs Keller...............14	C3
Barthel's Hof...............15	B2
Koslik...............16	B3
Zum Arabischen Coffe Baum...17	B3
DRINKING	(p434)
Moritz-Bastei...............18	C4
TRANSPORT	(p434)
Bus Station...............19	D2
OTHER	
Handelshof...............(see 5)	

Hostel Sleepy Lion (☎ 993 9480; www.hostel-leipzig.de; Käthe-Kollwitz-Strasse 3; dm €14-15, s/d €24/36; ☒ 🖵) This lively hostel is in a nicer location than its new sister Globetrotter near the station. Breakfast costs an extra €3.

Kosmos-Hotel (☎ 233 4422; www.kosmos-hotel.de; Gottschedstrasse 1; s/d €40/75) Ever fancied waking up next to James Dean or Marilyn Monroe? You can in this imaginative hotel, which seems to have taken inspiration from the theatre next door when decorating its highly individual rooms. Baroque, Arabian, jungle, cow print...take your pick.

MID-RANGE

Mid-range accommodation in the centre is fairly unexciting and usually the preserve of the big chains (particularly the many Accor brands); for something a little more individual you'll have to look a bit further afield.

Hotel Adagio (☎ 216 699; www.hotel-adagio.de; Seeburgstrasse 96; s/d €67/79; **P**) You get convenience and character in a quiet area at this small, stylish private hotel. Rooms are smartly decked out with a black-and-white theme.

Hotel Michaelis (☎ 267 80; www.hotel-michaelis.de; Paul-Gruner-Strasse 44; s €70-95, d €85-125; **P** ☒) Just south of the ring road, this is a superior three-star townhouse establishment with well-equipped rooms.

Seaside Park Hotel (☎ 985 20; info@parkhotelleipzig.de; Richard-Wagner-Strasse 7; s €105-125, d €126-140; **P** 🕸) Leipzig could hardly be further from the real seaside, but this Seaside isn't a bad swap, occupying a nice Art Nouveau house just opposite the station. Weekend rates are substantially cheaper. The restaurant is also recommended.

TOP END

Hotel Fürstenhof (☎ 1400; Tröndlinring 8; s €125-270, d €151-300; P X ⚒) This is an ultra-luxurious hotel with a 200-year tradition and more mod cons than you can shake a stick at.

Eating

Zum Arabischen Coffe Baum (☎ 965 1321; Kleine Fleischergasse 4; mains €7.50-15) Leipzig's oldest coffee bar has a restaurant and café offering excellent meals over three floors, plus a coffee museum at the top (free). Composer Robert Schumann met friends here, and if you ask nicely you can sit at his regular table.

Koslik (☎ 998 5993; cnr Gottschedstrasse & Zentralstrasse; mains €7.80-13, pizza/pasta €5.60-8.90) A stylish wood interior complements excellent mixed cuisine here, with great breakfasts and meals from Italian standards to duck *à l'orange*. Jazz on Sunday and DJs on Wednesday night throw in a bit of atmosphere.

Barthel's Hof (☎ 141 310; Hainstrasse 1; mains €8-14) This is a sprawling, historic place with some fantastic buffets (€8.30 to €11.99) and quirky seasonal Saxon dishes such as *Heubraten* (marinated lamb roasted on hay).

Auerbachs Keller (☎ 216 100; www.auerbachs -keller-leipzig.de, in German; Mädlerpassage; mains €10.50-20.60) Founded in 1525, Auerbachs Keller is one of Germany's classic restaurants, though it's not snobby. Goethe's *Faust – Part I* includes a scene here, in which Mephistopheles and Faust carouse with some students before they ride off on a barrel. The historic section of the restaurant includes the Goethe room and the Fasskeller; note the carved tree-trunk in the latter, depicting the whole barrel-riding shenanigans.

Drinking

Barfussgässchen and Kleine Fliescherstrasse, west of the Markt, form one of Leipzig's two 'pub miles', packed with outdoor tables that fill up the second the weather turns warm. The other is on Gottschedstrasse, a wider cocktail strip just west of the Altstadt.

Moritz-Bastei (☎ 702 590; Universitätsstrasse 9) One of the best student clubs in Germany, located in a spacious cellar below the old city walls. It has live music or DJs most nights,

runs films outside in summer and serves a great Sunday brunch.

Getting There & Away

Leipzig-Halle airport, roughly equidistant from both cities, is served by RE and IC trains three times hourly (€3.20, 15 minutes); a new ICE terminal was completed in June 2003, connecting the airport to the national long-distance network. From Altenburg airport, there's a shuttle bus (€12, 1¾ hours) timed to coincide with the daily Ryanair flights.

Leipzig is an important rail link between eastern and western Germany, with connections to all major cities. There are services to Frankfurt-am-Main (€54.60, 3½ hours, hourly), Munich (€65.20, five hours, every two hours), Dresden (€16.80, 70 minutes, hourly), Berlin (€33.20, 1½ hours, every two hours), Hanover (€38.40, 2¾ hours, hourly) and Hamburg (€65.80, 4¼ hours, every two hours).

Getting Around

Trams are the main public transport option, with most lines running via the Hauptbahnhof. The S-Bahn circles the city's outer suburbs. A single ticket costs €1.50 and a day card €4.40; four-journey strips cost €5.40.

THURINGIA

Welcome to the 'green heart' of Germany: swathed in unspoilt countryside and packed with charming small towns, Thuringia boasts a long hospitality tradition and an excellent tourist infrastructure. Despite the years of GDR rule, much of the state has stayed relatively untouched for centuries, and the rich history of towns such as Erfurt, Weimar and Eisenach is a big part of Thuringia's appeal.

History does, however, bring its own problems – Thuringia had a dubious reputation for receiving the National Socialist regime particularly warmly, and the grim memorial of the Buchenwald concentration camp, scant kilometres from the humanist haven of Weimar, brings home the atrocities of both the Nazis and their successors.

Today the state has largely escaped the shadows of its recent past and is a huge favourite with travellers from all over the world, revelling in the cultural traditions that inspired Goethe, Schiller, Thomas Mann and so many other great figures.

ERFURT

☎ 0361 / pop 202,000

Thuringia's charming capital was founded by St Boniface as a bishopric in 742. In the Middle Ages the city shot to prominence and prosperity as an important trading post. The Altstadt's many well-preserved buildings attest to that period's wealth; however, none are from before the 15th century, due to a major fire that raged through the city in 1472.

During WWII, damage was extensive, and the GDR regime did little to restore the city's former glories. Over the past decade, however, Erfurt has become an extremely attractive, lively town that deserves a day or two of exploration and makes a good central base for exploring the rest of the state.

Orientation

Most of the car traffic is routed around the Altstadt via two ring roads, making it a pleasure to walk between the main sights (watch out for fast-moving trams, though). The train and bus stations are just beyond the southeastern edge of the town centre, and were undergoing a massive reconstruction at the time of writing. It's a five-minute walk north along Bahnhofstrasse to Anger, the main shopping and business artery. The little Gera River bisects the Altstadt, spilling off into numerous creeks.

Information

ErfurtCard (24/72hr card €7/14)

Erfurt Family Card (72hr card €33) Two adults and all children.

Erfurt Tourismus (☎ 664 00; www.erfurt-tourist-info .de; Benediktsplatz 1; ⏰ 10am-7pm Mon-Fri, to 4pm Sat & Sun)

Lokal-Global (☎ 262 3834; Ratskellerpassage, Fischmarkt 5; Internet per hr €1.30; ⏰ 1-8pm Mon-Sat)

Reisebank (☎ 643 8361; Hauptbahnhof; ⏰ 8am-7pm Tue-Fri, 8am-4pm Sat & Mon)

Sights

It's hard to miss Erfurt's cathedral, **Dom St Marien** (☎ 646 1265; Domplatz; ⏰ 9-11.30am & 12.30-5pm Mon-Fri, to 4pm Sat, 2-4pm Sun), which casts its massive shadow over Domplatz from an artificial hill built specially to hold it. Ironically, it was originally only planned

as a simple chapel in 752; by the time it was completed in the 14th century someone had obviously changed the design! In July, the stone steps leading up to the cathedral are the site of the **Domstufenfestspiele**, where operas are performed against the dramatic background.

Next to the cathedral, the 1280 **Severikirche** (☎ 576 960; ⏰ 9am-12.30pm & 1.30-5pm Mon-Fri) is an impressive five-aisled church hall boasting a stone Madonna (1345) and a 15m-high baptismal font (1467), as well as the sarcophagus of St Severus, whose remains were brought to Erfurt in 836.

Now a nunnery, the **Augustinerkloster** (☎ 576 600; Augustinerstrasse; adult/concession €5/4.50; ⏰ tours 10am-noon & 2-5pm Tue-Sat, 11am Sun) has a strong pedigree: Martin Luther was a monk here from 1505 to 1511 and read his first mass after being ordained beneath the chapel's striking stained-glass windows. You can view Luther's cell, an exhibit on the Reformation, and the main buildings. The grounds and church are free of charge.

North of the Dom complex and west of Andreasstrasse, many of the city's lesser churches were demolished to erect the impressively tough-looking **Citadelle Petersberg** (Petersberg fortress; ☎ 211 5270; tour adult/concession €4.50/2.50; ⏰ 10am-6pm Tue-Sun, tour 2pm) – hence the reason why Erfurt has so many steeples without churches attached. There is a fascinating series of subterranean tunnels within the thick walls, which can only be seen on a guided tour from the tourist office.

Unique in this part of Europe, the medieval **Krämerbrücke** (Merchants' Bridge) is an 18m-wide, 120m-long curiosity spanning the Gera River. Quaint houses and shops line both sides of the narrow road.

Sleeping

Pension am Dom (☎ 5504 8660; Lange Brücke 57; s/d €39/55; P ✗) True to its name, this friendly little central *pension* has superb views of the cathedral – but only from the breakfast room and terrace. Still, it's good value whichever way you look at it.

Hotel Grenzenlos (☎ 6013 2600; www.behinderten verband-erfurt.de, in German; Moskauerstrase 114; s €35-45, d €50-70; P ✗) Sensitively designed and run, this excellent establishment just outside the ring road is aimed particularly at physically disabled guests, with easy wheelchair access and other facilities.

GERMANY

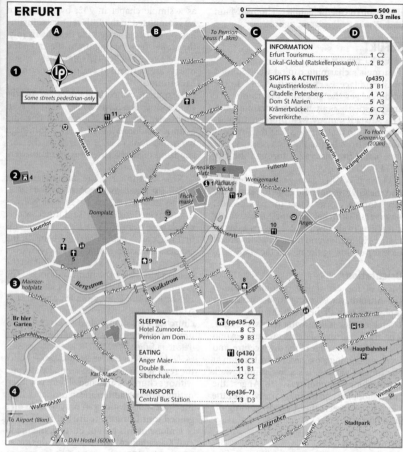

ERFURT

INFORMATION
Erfurt Tourismus...............................1 C2
Lokal-Global (Ratskellerpassage)........2 B2

SIGHTS & ACTIVITIES (p435)
Augustinerkloster.............................3 B1
Citadelle Petersberg.........................4 A2
Dom St Marien................................5 A3
Krämerbrücke..................................6 C2
Severikirche...................................7 A3

SLEEPING (pp435–6)
Hotel Zumnorde...............................8 C3
Pension am Dom..............................9 B3

EATING (p436)
Anger Maier...................................10 C3
Double B.......................................11 B1
Silberschale...................................12 C2

TRANSPORT (pp436–7)
Central Bus Station..........................13 D3

Hotel Zumnorde (☎ 568 00; www.hotel-zumnorde .de; Anger 50/51; s €100-120, d €120-150; P ☒ ☒) One of Erfurt's finest independent hotels, filled with character and amenities, the Zumnorde has a lovely courtyard, conservatory and roof garden. Enter from Weitergasse.

Eating

Anger Maier (☎ 566 1058; www.angermaier.de; Schlösserstrasse 8; mains €3.30-9.80) This tunnel-like restaurant is an Erfurt institution, with cheap, quality eats – prices have apparently risen by just 1.1% since 2001. It's always busy, often smoky, and you may get on TV just by being here.

Double B (☎ 642 1671; Marbacher Gasse 10; mains €4.30-8.90) This cosy pub-restaurant is a stu-

dent favourite for its all-day breakfasts offering everything from a VIP *Sekt*'n'brie blowout to the 'hangover breakfast': 2 aspirin and a glass of water.

Silberschale (☎ 654 7723; Kürschnergasse 3; mains €8-9.50) Patrons of all ages and budgets enjoy this friendly restaurant-pub, with German and international bistro fare. Seating is spread over three levels, including a conservatory and a wooden terrace overhanging the Gera River.

Getting There & Around

Erfurt's Hauptbahnhof has regular direct IR and ICE links to Berlin-Zoo (€41.20, 3¼ hours), Dresden (€39, 2¼ hours) and Frankfurt-am-Main (€41.80, 2¼ hours).

There are trains to Weimar (€4, 15 minutes) and Eisenach (€8.10, 50 minutes) running several times hourly.

Public transport is divided into three zones, but you're likely to travel only within the city centre (yellow zone). Tickets are €1.20 and €3 for a day pass. Bus No 99 runs frequently from the Hauptbahnhof to the small Erfurt airport (€1.20, 16 minutes). A taxi to town should cost around €10.

WEIMAR

☎ 03643 / pop 62,000

Neither a monumental town nor a medieval one, Weimar's many-splendoured selection of museums, parks and biographical exhibits appeals to intellectual tastes, and the town is something of a pilgrimage site for cultured Germans. Its position as the epicentre of this country's Enlightenment and the birthplace of much that is considered great in German thought and deed is unrivalled.

Because of its historical significance, Weimar has received particularly large hand-outs for the restoration of its many fine buildings, and in 1999 it was the European Capital of Culture. While the city can sometimes feel like a giant museum teeming with tourists, it is one of Germany's most fascinating places and belongs on any itinerary.

Information

Buchenwald Information (☎ 430 200; Markt 6;
☺ 10am-12.30pm & 1-5pm Mon-Fri, 10am-3pm Sat, 10am-2pm Sun)

Sparkasse (☎ 01803-236 000; Graben 4)

Stiftung Weimarer Klassik (Weimar Classics Foundation; ☎ 545 401; www.swkk.de; Frauentorstrasse 4;
☺ 8.30am-4.45pm) Museum tickets and literature.

Tourist Information (☎ 240 00; www.weimar.de, in German; Markt 10; ☺ 9.30am-6pm Mon-Fri, 9.30am-3pm Sat & Sun)

Vobis (☎ 902 925; Schwanseestrasse; Internet per hr €1.80)

WeimarCard (72hr card €10)

Sights

Museums and sights administered by the Stiftung Weimarer Klassik are open 9am to 6pm April to October and 9am or 10am to 4pm November to March. These hours apply to the Goethe Nationalmuseum, Goethe Haus, Schiller Haus and Liszt Haus. A combined ticket for all except the Goethe Haus costs adult/concession €20/15.

MUSEUMS

Those who visit the **Goethe Nationalmuseum** (☎ 545 401; Frauenplan 1; adult/concession €2.50/2; ☺ Tue-Sun) expecting to learn all about the great man of letters will probably be disappointed. Rather than focusing on Goethe himself, the museum offers a broad overview of German Classicism, from its proponents to its patrons. The **Faustina café** is more topical, with its controversial Christoph Hodgson mural depicting Weimar's glorious Who's Who – lurking among the famous faces is one Adolf Hitler.

The Bauhaus School and movement was founded in Weimar in 1919 by Walter Gropius, who managed to draw top artists including Kandinsky, Klee, Feininger and Schlemmer as teachers. The exhibition at the **Bauhaus Museum** (☎ 545 401; Theaterplatz; adult/concession €4/3; ☺ 10am-6pm Tue-Sun) chronicles the evolution of the group, explains their innovations and spotlights the main players. In 1925 the Bauhaus moved to Dessau and in 1932 to Berlin, where it was dissolved by the Nazis.

If you're feeling stifled by artefacts and display cases, the half-hour Disneyland-style multimedia tour at the **Weimar Haus** (☎ 901 890; www.weimarhaus.de; Schillerstrasse 16-18; adult/concession €6.50/5.50; ☺ 10am-7pm Apr-Oct, to 6pm Nov-Mar) takes you through the Weimar of old from prehistory to classicism, with an animatronic clone of none other than Goethe as your guide (yes, you did read that right). Sophisticates may roll their eyes, but it's a decent, basic introduction and available in English.

Housed in the **Stadtschloss**, the former residence of the ducal family of Saxe-Weimar, the **Schlossmuseum** (☎ 5460; Burgplatz; adult/concession €4.50/3.50; ☺ 10am-6pm Tue-Sun Apr-Oct, to 4.30pm Nov-Mar) displays encompass sculpture, paintings, and arts-and-craft objects. Highlights include the Cranach Gallery, several portraits by Albrecht Dürer, and collections of Dutch masters and German romanticists. Several restored residence rooms can also be seen.

HOUSES

No other individual is as closely associated with Weimar as Johann Wolfgang von Goethe, who lived at the **Goethe Haus** (☎ 545 401; Frauenplan 1; adult/concession €6/4.50; ☺ Tue-Sun) from 1775 until his death in 1832. In 1792 his sponsor and employer, Duke Carl August, gave him a house as a gift, and it was

WEIMAR

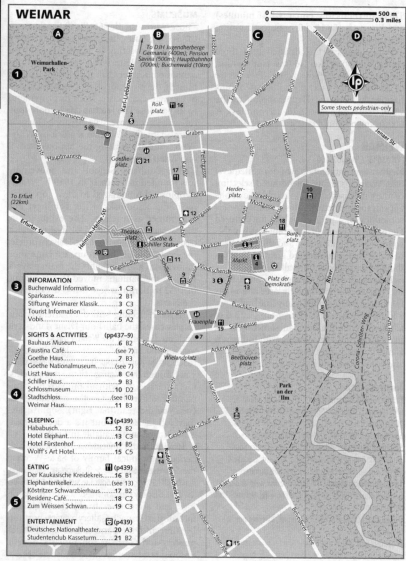

here that he worked, studied, researched and wrote such immortal works as *Faust*.

Goethe's original 1st-floor living quarters are reached via an expansive Italian Renaissance staircase decorated with sculpture and paintings brought back from his travels to Italy. You'll see his dining room, study and the bedroom with his deathbed. Because

demand often exceeds capacity, you'll be given a time slot to enter. Once inside, you can stay as long as you want.

Goethe's fellow dramatist Friedrich von Schiller lived in Weimar from 1799 until his early death in 1805; unlike his mentor, he had to buy his own house, now known as **Schiller Haus** (☎ 545 401; Schillerstrasse 12; adult/

concession €3.50/2.50; ⊙ Wed-Mon). The study at the end of the 2nd floor contains the desk where he penned *Wilhelm Tell* and other works, and also holds his deathbed.

Liszt Haus (☎ 545 401; Marienstrasse 17; adult/concession €2/1.50; ⊙ Tue-Sun) On the western edge of the Ilm park, composer and pianist Franz Liszt lived here in 1848 and again from 1869 to 1886, when he wrote *Hungarian Rhapsody* and *Faust Symphony*. It's the usual biographical stuff, but at least you get a break from Goethe.

Sleeping

Hababusch (☎ 850 737; Geleitstrasse 4; dm €10, s/d €15/24; ☒) Undercutting even the DJH hostels, this independent establishment is run by student volunteers in an unrestored 19th-century house. Luxury it ain't, but you won't find a cheaper bed anywhere.

Jugendherberge Germania (☎ 850 490; www .djh-thueringen.de, in German; Carl-August-Allee 13; juniors/seniors €17/20; ☒) The central Germania, south of the station, is the most convenient DJH for new arrivals.

Pension Savina (☎ 866 90; Meyerstrasse 60 & Rembrandtweg 13; s €40-45, d €55-75; ☒) On quiet side streets near the Hauptbahnhof, this *pension* and its annexe are excellent value, with sauna, solarium and a station shuttle service.

Hotel Fürstenhof (☎ 833 231; www.fuerstenhof -weimar.de, in German; Rudolf-Breitscheid-Strasse 2; s €52-72, d €80-100; ▢) A nice modern alternative to the ubiquitous 'period' décor elsewhere, with abstract prints scattered around and an almost startlingly yellow breakfast room.

Wolff's Art Hotel (☎ 540 60; www.wolffs-art-hotel .de; Freiherr-vom-Stein-Allee 3a/b; s €69-85, d €99-110; ℗ ☒) Quiet, classy and very contemporary, Wolff's has a fully equipped spa/fitness area (with treatments), and is also known for its gourmet restaurant.

Hotel Elephant (☎ 8020; elephant.weimar@arabella sheraton.com; Markt 19; s €179-219, d €205-245; ℗ ▢) A true classic, the marble Bauhaus-Deco splendour of the Elephant has seen most of Weimar's great and good come and go; just to make the point, a golden Thomas Mann looks out over the Markt from a balcony in front. The Elephantenkeller restaurant is also a local institution.

Eating

Residenz-Café (☎ 594 08; Grüner Markt 4; mains €4.90-15) Known as the 'Resi' by regulars, this is one of Weimar's most popular haunts and has been for more than 160 years. Food comes in super-sized portions, with a top-notch Sekt/champagne brunch for two (€45.50).

Der Kaukasische Kreidekreis (☎ 493 922; Rollplatz 12; mains €6-10) As you'd expect from anything named after a Brecht play, intelligence and imagination are manifest in this modern Georgian restaurant, which must be the best of the many Russian and Eastern European places in town.

Köstritzer Schwarzbierhaus (☎ 779 337; Scherfgasse 4; mains €6.90-13.50) Fans of dark beer and substantial traditional Thuringian cooking are in exactly the right place here – the listed half-timbered house has been converted into a restaurant and *pension* (d €75) by one of Germany's biggest *Schwarzbier* breweries.

Zum Weissen Schwan (☎ 202 521; Frauentorstrasse 23; mains €8-16; ⊙ Wed-Sun) Looking for inspiration? Goethe, Schiller and Liszt all dined here, and apparently it worked for them. The gourmet menu highlights Thuringian cuisine, and the kitchen also caters for the renowned Elephantenkeller (see Hotel Elephant earlier).

Entertainment

Deutsches National Theater (German National Theatre; ☎ 755 334; Theaterplatz; ⊙ closed Jul-Aug) This historic venue was used to draft the constitution of the Weimar Republic in 1919, and it hasn't been idle since then. Expect a grabbag of classic and contemporary plays, plus ballet, opera and classical concerts.

Studentenclub Kasseturm (☎ 851 670; www .kasseturm.de, in German; Goetheplatz 10) A Weimar classic, the Kasseturm is a historic round tower with three floors of live music, DJs, cabaret or just games nights.

Getting There & Away

Weimar is on the ICE route from Frankfurt-am-Main (€44.20, 2½ hours) to Leipzig (€22.40, 50 minutes) and Dresden (€36.40, two hours), and on the IC route to Berlin (€39.20, three hours). All leave at two-hour intervals. Erfurt (€4, 15 minutes) and Eisenach (€10.70, one hour) are served several times hourly.

The town centre is a 20-minute walk south of the Hauptbahnhof. Most buses serve Goetheplatz, on the northwestern edge of the Altstadt.

AROUND WEIMAR

The **Buchenwald** (☎ 03643-4300; www.buchenwald.de; bus No 6; ☺ 9.45am-6pm May-Sep, 8.45am-5pm Oct-Apr) concentration camp museum and memorial are 10km north of Weimar. You first pass the memorial erected atop the mass graves of some of the 56,500 victims from 18 nations. The concentration camp and museum are 1km beyond the memorial.

After 1943, prisoners here were exploited in the production of weapons. Shortly before the end of the war, some 28,000 were sent on death marches. Between 1937 and 1945, more than one-fifth of the 250,000 people incarcerated here died. On 11 April 1945, as US troops approached and the SS guards fled, the prisoners rebelled, overwhelmed the remaining guards and liberated themselves.

After the war, the Soviet victors turned the tables by establishing Special Camp No 2, in which 7000 so-called anticommunists and ex-Nazis were literally worked to death. Their bodies were found after the *Wende* in mass graves north of the camp and near the Hauptbahnhof.

EISENACH

☎ 03691 / pop 44,000

Composer Johann Sebastian Bach was born in Eisenach, a small, pretty city on the edge of the Thuringian Forest; but the town's big-ticket attraction is the Wartburg, the only German castle to be named a Unesco World Heritage Site. The historical associations of the place must rival just about any other single building in Thuringia. The modest size and charming atmosphere of the town itself make it a very pleasant alternative to the larger, more popular destinations of Weimar and Erfurt.

Information

Tourist Information (☎ 792 30; www.eisenach.de, in German; Markt 9; ☺ 10am-6pm Mon, 9am-6pm Tue-Fri, 10am-2pm Sat & Sun)

Wartburg Information (☎ 2500; Schlossberg; ☺ 9am-12.30pm & 1-5pm Tue-Fri)

Wartburg

This superb medieval **castle** (☎ 2500; www.wartburg-eisenach.de; tour adult/concession €6/3; ☺ tours 8.30am-5pm), perched high above the town on a wooded hill, is said to go back to Count Ludwig der Springer (the Jumper); you'll hear the story of how the castle got its name

many times, but listen out for how Ludwig got his peculiar moniker as well.

The castle thanks its huge popularity to Martin Luther, who went into hiding here from 1521 to 1522 after being excommunicated; during this time he translated the entire New Testament from Greek into German, contributing enormously to the development of the written German language. His modest, wood-panelled **study** is part of the guided tour (available in English), which is the only way to view the interior. The **museum** houses the famous Cranach paintings of Luther and important Christian artefacts from all over Germany. Most of the rooms you'll see here are extravagant 19th-century impressions of medieval life rather than original fittings; the reimagined Great Hall in turn inspired Richard Wagner's opera *Tannhäuser*. Between Easter and October, crowds can be horrendous; arrive before 11am.

Sleeping & Eating

Pension Mahret (☎ 742 744; www.puppenstuben-hotel.de, in German; Neustadt 30; r per person €22.50-44) East of the centre, on the edge of the Wartburg woods, this is a self-confessed 'dolls house hotel' offering apartment-style rooms of varying sizes.

Hotel Haus Hainstein (☎ 2420; www.hainstein.de, in German; Am Hainstein 16; s €45-50, d €70-80; P ✗) One of a cluster of handsome Art Nouveau villas in the hilly south of town, this fantastic church-affiliated mansion has a park-like setting, great views of the Wartburg, light, stylish rooms and a nice restaurant.

Brunnenkeller (☎ 212 358; Markt 10; mains €7-9) For good hearty Thuringian dishes in an authentic Weinkeller setting, try the old monastery cellars on the south side of the Georgenkirche.

Getting There & Away

Direct trains run to Erfurt (€8.10, 50 minutes) and Weimar (€10.70, one hour) several times hourly. ICE trains to Frankfurt-am-Main (€35.80, 1¾ hours, hourly) and IC trains to Berlin-Zoo (€47.40, 3¾ hours, every two hours) also stop here.

SAXONY-ANHALT

Once the GDR's industrial cornerstone, Sachsen-Anhalt (Saxony-Anhalt) has found reunification something of a two-edged sword. On the one hand, the area's bleak, polluted landscape seems transformed: environmentally friendly wind turbines now dot the countryside and the cities have been spruced up. On the other hand, much of the clean-up has come about because the industries that once pumped thick, caustic smoke into the atmosphere have closed. As unemployment has risen above 20% in some areas, locals have suffered and population figures are in freefall as people move west.

Still, the state has plenty of appeal reaching further back into its history: 16th-century reformer Martin Luther carried out most of his life's work in and around Wittenberg, and Dessau's strong links with the seminal Bauhaus school of design is another selling point. Visitors can also investigate reminders of the GDR, stretch their legs in the Harz Mountains or retreat to the southeastern wine region of the Saale Valley. Saxony-Anhalt may not be Germany's best-kept state, but there's certainly no need to bypass it.

MAGDEBURG

☎ 0391 / pop 228,000

Sometimes in Magdeburg just turning the corner can transport you into another century. The Sachsen-Anhalt capital is largely a very modern city of wide boulevards, shopping centres and huge concrete *Plattenbauten* apartment complexes. However, step onto tree-lined Hegelstrasse and you find yourself on pristine cobbled footpaths, surrounded by immaculately restored terraced buildings from the early 1900s. Looking north, you see Magdeburg's famous medieval cathedral. Continue south to Hasselbachplatz and you remain in an enclave of pretty-as-a-picture historic streets, like a film set plonked down in the middle of a GDR-style town.

The city's other beauty spots are its parks, from the Stadtpark Rotehorn, on an island in the Elbe River, to the Elbauenpark on the opposite bank.

Orientation

To reach the town centre from the Hauptbahnhof, turn left (north) out of the main Kölner Platz exit, cross the square and turn right (east) into Ernst-Reuter-Allee. The tourist office is just after Ernst-Reuter-Allee meets the major north–south artery, Breiter Weg. From here, you can walk a

block north to the Alter Markt or carry on east across the Neue Strombrücke (bridge) and the Elbe River to the Stadthalle.

Northwards, Breiter Weg leads to Universitätsplatz; heading south it takes you to the Dom and Hasselbachplatz.

Information

Commerzbank (☎ 592 30; Breiter Weg 200)
Orbit Internet (☎ 620 9835; Keplerstrasse 7; per hr €3)
Tourist Information Magdeburg (TIM; ☎ 5404 9000; www.magdeburg-tourist.de; Ernst-Reuter-Allee 12; ☺ 10am-6pm Mon-Fri, to 1pm Sat)

Sights

Apparently the first of its kind on German soil when built (1209–1363), Magdeburg's Gothic **Dom** (☎ 543 2414; admission free; ☺ 10am-4pm Mon-Sat, 11.30am-4pm Sun), features an impressive, high-ceilinged interior. Here you'll find the **tomb of Otto I** and art spanning eight centuries. Notable works include a pensive **WWI memorial** by Ernst Barlach and, through the doors beside it, the sculpture of the **Magdeburger Virgins**.

South of Ernst-Reuter-Allee, near the river, stands Magdeburg's oldest building, **Kloster Unser Lieben Frauen** (☎ 565 020; Regierungstrasse 4-6; ☺ 10am-5pm Tue-Sun) which also houses a **museum** (adult/concession €2/1). There's not much in the 12th-century Romanesque cloister apart from the courtyard and pleasant café, but the museum has religious relics and rotating exhibits. The front door, designed by popular local artist Heinrich Apel (1935–), is fun: you knock with the woman's necklace and push down on the man's hat to enter.

With its recreation of Roman streets, model of the solar system and all manner of wacky scientific contraptions, the interior of the conical wooden **Jahrtausendturm** (Millennium Tower; ☎ 01805-251 999; www.elbauenpark .de, in German; Tessenowstrasse 5a; ☺ 10am-6pm Tue-Sun Apr-Oct; adult/child incl park admission €2.60/2) makes a memorable sight. German-speakers will be even more thrilled by the museum of science history to which these exhibits belong, as staff demonstrate experiments first performed by the likes of Galileo and Otto von Guericke.

Sleeping & Eating

DJH Jugendherberge Magdeburg (☎ 532101; jh-magdeburg@djh-sachsen-anhalt.de; Leiterstrasse 10; juniors/seniors €18/20.70; P ⊠) Its combination of modern premises and a central, but quiet, location make this possibly the best hostel in Sachsen-Anhalt. The staff are friendly and there is a late curfew.

Hotel Stadtfeld (☎ 506 660; www.hotelstadtfeld .de; Maxim-Gorki-Strasse 31/37; s/d €55/70; P ⊠) There's a gentleman's-club feel to this pleasant three-star business hotel. That's partly because of the no-nonsense, masculine furnishings, but the location atop an apartment building and the top-floor reception also create a sense of chummy privacy.

Oma & Opa (☎ 543 9419; cnr Einsteinstrasse & Leibnizstrasse; mains €4.40-13) Located in a popular eating area, Grandma and Grandpa's cosy little place is festooned with odd bric-a-brac (a stuffed fox, for example) and has a straightforward menu of good ol' dishes like spaghetti and wurst.

Getting There & Away

Regional trains to/from Berlin-Zoo take about 1½ hours (€20.20, hourly). Magdeburg is on direct IC routes to Rostock (€39.80, three hours, daily) and Leipzig (€22.20, 1½ hours, hourly) and the RE line to Erfurt (€22.40, 2½ hours, every two hours).

QUEDLINBURG

☎ 03946 / pop 23,600

Unspoilt Quedlinburg is a popular year-round destination, especially since being added to Unesco's World Heritage List in 1994. Almost all the buildings in the historic town centre are half-timbered – street after cobbled street of them – and they are slowly being restored. There are also plenty of cultural offerings to complement the atmospheric Altstadt.

Orientation & Information

The circular medieval centre of the old town is a 10-minute walk from the Hauptbahnhof along Bahnhofstrasse. To reach the Markt, turn left onto Heiligegeiststrasse after the post office. Hohe Strasse, off the Markt, leads south to the castle. The tourist office is **Quedlinburg-Tourismus** (☎ 905 625; www .quedlinburg.de, in German; Markt 2; ⊗ 9am-7pm Mon-Fri, 10am-4pm Sat & Sun Apr-Oct; 9.30am-5.30pm Mon-Fri, to 2pm Sat Nov-Mar).

Sights & Activities

The castle district, perched above Quedlinburg on a 25m-high plateau, was established

during the reign of Heinrich I, from 919 to 936. The present-day Renaissance **Schloss** (⊗ 6am-10pm) partly built upon earlier foundations, dates from the 16th century and offers good views over the town. The north wing houses the **Schlossmuseum** (☎ 2730; adult/ concession €2.50/1.50; ⊗ 10am-6pm), which has some mildly interesting exhibits on local natural and social history. The centrepiece, however, is the restored baroque **Blauer Saal** (Blue Hall).

The 12th-century Romanesque church, **Stiftskirche St Servatius** (☎ 709 900; adult/concession €3/2; ⊗ 10am-6pm Tue-Fri, to 4pm Sat, noon-6pm Sun), part of the castle complex, is one of Germany's most significant of the period. Its treasury contains valuable reliquaries and early Bibles. The crypt has some early religious frescoes and contains the graves of Heinrich and his widow, Mathilde, along with those of the abbesses.

The work of influential Bauhaus artist Lyonel Feininger (1871–1956), who was born in Germany and became an American citizen, is in the **Lyonel-Feininger-Galerie** (☎ 2238; Finkenherd 5a; adult/concession €3/1.25; ⊗ 10am-6pm Tue-Sun). The original graphics, drawings, watercolours and sketches on display are from 1906 to 1936 and were hidden from the Nazis by a Quedlinburg citizen. A highlight is the much-reproduced *Selbstbildnis mit Tonpfeife* (Self-Portrait with Clay Pipe).

For **hiking**, head 10km southwest to **Thale**, the starting point for hikes along the lovely Bode Valley. From here there's a lift to Hexentanzplatz, the site of raucous Walpurgisnacht celebrations every 30 April, believed in German folklore to be the night of a witches' sabbath.

Sleeping & Eating

Zum Alten Fritz (☎ 704 880; Pölkenstrasse 18; s/d €45/55; P) Less tradition-steeped than the competition, this hotel is still a pleasant place, and offers some newly renovated deluxe 'Romantik' rooms for €95/125.

Romantik Hotel Theophano (☎ 963 00; www.hotel theophano.de; Markt 13-14; s €62, d €93-113; P ⊠ 🖳) The Theophano's historic building is highly recommended for a night of rustic luxury; individually decorated rooms have four-poster beds, the vaulted cellar restaurant-bar is excellent and the staff are very friendly. One drawback: there are lots of steep, creaky stairs and no lift.

Zum Roland (☎ 4532; Breite Strasse 2-6; mains €5.75-14.75) Spread over seven different houses, this quirky but charming café-restaurant can seat up to 736 people for traditional meals, pasta and international dishes.

Getting There & Away
Hourly trains run to Magdeburg (€11.10, 1¼ hours). For trains to Wernigerode (€6.60, 50 minutes), change at Halberstadt.

WERNIGERODE
☎ 03943 / pop 35,000
Flanked by the foothills of the Harz Mountains, Wernigerode is a busy tourist centre attracting thousands of German holidaymakers in summer. A romantic ducal castle rises above the Altstadt, which counts some one-thousand half-timbered houses spanning five centuries. The town is the northern terminus of the steam-powered narrow-gauge Harzquerbahn railway, which has chugged the breadth of the Harz for almost a century; the trail to the summit of the Brocken, the highest mountain in northern Germany, also starts here.

Orientation & Information
The bus and train stations are on the northern side of town. From Bahnhofplatz, Rudolf-Breitscheid-Strasse leads southeast to Breite Strasse, which runs southwest to the Markt. The tourist office is **Wernigerode Tourismus** (☎ 633 035; www.wernigerode.de, in German; Nicolaiplatz 1; ☺ 9am-7pm Mon-Fri, 10am-4pm Sat, 10am-3pm Sun).

Sights
On the Markt, the spectacular towered **Rathaus** began life as a theatre around 1277, but what you see today is mostly late-Gothic from the 16th century. Legend tells us that the artisan who carved the town hall's 33 wooden figures fell out with the authorities and added a few mocking touches.

First built in the 12th century, Wernigerode's **Schloss** (☎ 553 030; adult/concession/child €4.50/4/2.50; ☺ 10am-6pm Tue-Sun Nov-Apr) has been restored and enlarged over the centuries, and is now one of the most-visited museums in Germany. It got its fairy-tale façade from Count Otto of Stolberg-Wernigerode in the last century. The museum includes portraits of Kaisers, beautiful panelled rooms with original furnishings and the opulent **Festsaal**.

Sleeping & Eating
Jugendgästehaus (☎ 632 061; Friedrichstrasse 53; s €16, dm juniors/seniors €19.80/16; P) Better located than its DJH counterpart, this city hostel has a few quirks: junior price is for under-18s only, and includes full board.

Altwernigeroder Aparthotel (☎ 949 260; www .appart-hotel.de, in German; Marktstrasse 14; s/d €51/75; P ✗) This large central building has stylish apartment rooms of varying sizes, plus extended sauna area and a popular potato-based restaurant out front.

Ins kleine Paradies (☎ 632 050; Unterengengasse 6-8; mains €6.15-14.60) Just off the Markt, it may not be paradise but you do get excellent authentic Harz specialities here.

Getting There & Away
There are frequent trains to Halle (€16, 1¼ hours). Direct buses run to most major towns in the region.

DESSAU
☎ 0340 / pop 79,500
Dessau will forever be linked to the 20th century's most influential school of architecture and art, the Bauhaus. The seven years (1925–32) the eponymous institute of design was based here proved to be its heyday, and by the time the Nazis drove its leading exponents to Berlin and into US exile, the block-faced signet 'Bauhaus Dessau' had already won a place in history.

But the town has even more to offer than some of the earliest buildings by Walter Gropius & Co. Although much of its centre was reconstructed after WWII and is typically Eastern Bloc uninspiring, Dessau is also surrounded by a thick green belt of 18th-century, English-style landscaped parks.

Orientation
The town is south of the confluence of the Elbe and Mulde Rivers. The leading Bauhaus sights are west of the Hauptbahnhof, within easy walking distance. The town centre lies east, reachable on foot or by tram.

Information
Dessau Card (72hr card €8)
Tourist Office (☎ 204 2242; www.dessau.de, in German; Rathaus, Zerbster Strasse 4; ☺ 9am-6pm Mon-Fri, to 1pm Sat Apr-Oct; 9am-5pm Mon-Fri, 10am-1pm Sat Nov-Mar)
Worldnet Internet (☎ 220 23 81; Ferdinand von Schiller Strasse 28a; per hr €3)

Sights

Not only an example of Walter Gropius' handiwork and a forerunner of untold buildings worldwide, this **Bauhaus Building** (☎ 650 8251; Gropiusallee 38; tour adult/concession €5/4, with Meisterhäuser €8/6; ⏰ 10am-6pm Tue-Sun) was the very Hochschule für Gestaltung (Institute for Design) where the architect and his colleagues taught a whole generation of young modernists. Today it houses the small post-grad **Bauhaus Kolleg** (☎ 650 8403; www.bauhaus-dessau.de); the three-sectioned ensemble of glass, steel and concrete (built from 1925 to 1926) remains open to the public. Tours take place daily, and on weekdays you can wander inside by yourself.

Since a key Bauhaus aim was to provide housing appropriate for a modern, industrial lifestyle, the three white, concrete 'master craftsmen's houses', the **Meisterhäuser** (Ebertallee 63-71; admission to all three houses adult/concession €5/4; ⏰ 10am-5pm Tue-Sun, to 6pm mid-Feb–Oct), are in a sense more illuminating than the Bauhausgebäude. The houses were built by Gropius for senior institute staff, and while parts of their interiors are given over to administrative or museum purposes and the rest is largely unfurnished, photos help recall what it must have been like, say, at home with the Kandinskys.

Sleeping & Eating

Bauhaus Gästehaus (☎ 650 8318; oede@bauhaus-dessau.de; Heidestrasse 33; r per person from €15) Book in advance if you want to live the Bauhaus dream. The Bauhaus Stiftung has its own 1970s *Plattenbau* apartment complex south of the centre, with some great views.

An den 7 Säulen (☎ 619 620; www.pension7saeulen.de, in German; Ebertallee 66; s €47-52, d €65-72; P ✗) Not the most luxurious, but certainly the most memorable option in town, this pleasant *pension* has a garden and glass-fronted breakfast room overlooking the Meisterhäuser across the leafy street.

Kornhaus (☎ 640 4141; Kornhausstrasse 146; mains €7-13) Kill several birds with one stone at the Kornhaus: see the remarkable Bauhaus dining room, enjoy the view over the Elbe banks and acquaint yourself with local specialities from the hands of an acclaimed chef.

Getting There & Away

IC and RE trains run to Berlin every two hours (€21.60/16.80, 1½ hours). Regional trains serve Wittenberg (€5.70, 35 minutes, hourly). Dessau is almost equidistant from Leipzig, Halle and Magdeburg (all €8.40, one hour), with at least one service hourly to each.

LUTHERSTADT-WITTENBERG

☎ 03491 / pop 53,000

As the crucible of the Reformation, where Protestant Christians first split from the Roman Catholic Church, Wittenberg is Sachsen-Anhalt's most popular destination. Religious pilgrims, scholars, fans of the Joseph Fiennes film *Luther* and the merely curious all swarm here to follow in the footsteps of Martin Luther, whose campaigning zeal changed the face of Catholic Europe.

It's hard to imagine now, but 16th-century Wittenberg was a genuine hotbed of progressive ideas. Long-term resident Luther wrote his *95 Theses* here in 1517, challenging what he regarded as the Catholic Church's corruption, in particular the selling of 'indulgences' (absolution from sin); meanwhile local priests got married and delivered services in German, not Latin, and educators like Philipp Melanchthon argued for schools to teach in German and to accept female pupils.

Quaint, quiet and picturesque, Wittenberg can be seen in a day from Berlin, but it is worth a longer look. The town is busiest in June, during the Luther's Wedding festival, and on 31 October, the date of publication of the *95 Theses*.

Orientation & Information

Hauptbahnhof Lutherstadt-Wittenberg is the stop for regional trains; some also stop at Wittenberg-Altstadt. Bus No 304 (€1.10, every 15 minutes) goes from the Hauptbahnhof to the city centre; otherwise it's a sign-posted 15- to 20-minute walk down the main street, Collegienstrasse. Most major sights are within the Altstadt ring. The tourist office is **Wittenberg-Information** (☎ 498 610; www.wittenberg.de; Schlossplatz 2; ⏰ 9am-6pm Mon-Fri, 10am-3pm Sat, 11am-4pm Sun).

Sights

If you only visit one of the several museums in Germany devoted to the father of the Reformation, make it the **Lutherhaus** (☎ 420 30; www.martinluther.de; Collegienstrasse 54; adult/concession €5/3; ⏰ 9am-6pm Apr-Oct, 10am-5pm Tue-Sun Nov-Mar). The exhibition in Luther's one-time home was revamped in 2003 to the tune of €17.5 million, and it shows. Even those with no previous interest in the subject will be drawn in by the accessible narrative (in German and English), personal artefacts, oil paintings by Lucas Cranach and interactive displays. There's also an original room furnished by Luther in 1535, decorated with a bit of royal graffiti from Russian Tsar Peter the Great in 1702.

Legend has it that it was the door of the **Schlosskirche** (Schlossstrasse; 10am-5pm Mon-Sat, 11.30am-5pm Sun) where Luther nailed the *95 Theses*. There's no hard evidence this happened, especially as the door in question was destroyed by fire in 1760, but there is now an impressive bronze memorial (1858). Inside the church is Luther's tombstone; it lies below the pulpit, opposite that of his friend and fellow reformer Philipp Melanchthon.

If the Schlosskirche was the billboard used to advertise the forthcoming Reformation, its sister the **Stadtkirche St Marien** (Kirchplatz; 9am-5pm Mon-Sat, 11.30am-5pm Sun) was where the ecumenical revolution began, with the world's first Protestant worship services in 1521. It was also here that Luther preached his famous Lectern sermons in 1522 and three years later married ex-nun Katharina von Bora. The centrepiece is the large altar, designed jointly by Lucas Cranach the Elder and his son.

To see another side to Luther-obsessed Wittenberg, check out the strangely heartwarming **Haus der Geschichte** (House of History; 409 004; Schlossstrasse 6; adult/concession/family €3/2/6; 10am-5pm Tue-Fri, 11am-6pm Sat & Sun), a museum of everyday life in the GDR. The ground floor is devoted to temporary exhibitions, while living rooms, kitchens, bedrooms and bathrooms on the next two levels have been reconstructed in various styles from the 1940s to 1980s.

Sleeping & Eating

Pension am Schwanenteich (402 807; Töpferstrasse 1; s €31-36, d €50-59;) This small *pension* has much nicer rooms than you'd expect for the price, plus a convenient location. That and the charming owners make this Wittenberg's best budget option, despite its inability to accept credit cards.

Stadthotel Wittenberg Schwarzer Baer (420 4344; www.stadthotel-wittenberg.de; Schlossstrasse 2; s/d €56/69;) In the heart of the old town, the

Black Bear has clean, modern rooms. At the same time, there's just enough old-world charm in the public areas to keep it atmospheric and interesting.

Café Hundertwasserschule (410 685; Markt 15; mains €4-14;) Named for the famous Wittenberg school designed by out-there Viennese architect Friedensreich Hundertwasser, this is the best spot in town for home-made, healthy and vegetarian food, with plenty of more indulgent treats for the unrepentant.

Zur Schlossfreiheit (402 980; Coswigerstrasse 24; mains €6.25-10.50; closed Sun) Wittenberg's favourite pub enjoys considerable local fame and pulls in plenty of tourists as well, with historical theme dishes such as *Lutherschmaus* (scrumptious duck in peppery sultana sauce) spicing up the menu.

Getting There & Away

Wittenberg is on the main train line to Halle, Leipzig (€9, one hour) and Berlin (€16.20, 1½ hours), with hourly services. All Berlin-bound trains stop at Schönefeld airport. Coming here, make sure you board for 'Lutherstadt-Wittenberg' – there's also a Wittenberge west of Berlin.

HALLE

0345 / pop 239,500

Halle has never exactly had good press, despite a long history as a university town, and many feel the city's privileged status as a key GDR base led to a certain amount of pointed neglect after reunification. Certainly the old centre is not as shiny and well-preserved as many in the region, with a jumble of grimy medieval buildings jutting out amid the concrete communist efforts; however, with some surprisingly amenable pedestrian areas and busy student-driven nightlife, you may well find yourself liking Halle more than you expect.

Orientation & Information

The Altstadt, northwest of the Hauptbahnhof, is circled by a road known as the Stadtring. To walk to the centre from the Bahnhof takes about 15 to 20 minutes; head left from the main entrance and turn left into the underpass and graffiti showcase known as Der Tunnel. Continue along pedestrianised Leipziger Strasse to the Markt, Halle's central square. Take care when entering the Markt, as trams careen through here at speed.

The tourist information office is **Halle Tourist** (☎ 472 330; www.halle-tourist.de; Stadtcenter Rolltreppe, Grosse Ulrichstrasse 60; ⌚ 10am-6pm Mon-Fri, 10am -2pm Sat).

Dangers & Annoyances

Undesirables hang around the Hauptbahnhof at all hours. Use common sense, particularly in and around Der Tunnel.

Sights

Halle's most famous son is composer George Friedrich Handel (Händel in German), who was born in the **Händelhaus** (☎ 500 900, www.haendelhaus.de; Grosse Nikolai Strasse 5-6; adult/concession €2.60/1.60; ⌚ 9.30am-5.30pm, to 7.30pm Thu) in 1685. The main exhibition charts the composer's life, through moves to Hamburg, Hanover, Italy and eventually London. More interesting for non-German speakers, however, is the newly revamped collection of antique musical instruments, which has English captions, interactive displays and a peek inside a cut-away organ.

In one tower of the atmospheric 15th-century **Schloss Moritzburg** (☎ 212 590; www .moritzburg.halle.de, in German; Friedemann-Bach-Platz 5; adult/concession €5/3, free Tue; ⌚ 11am-8.30pm Tue, 10am-6pm Wed-Sun) you'll find a small but well-presented collection of German Expressionism and other contemporary art. Works include several by Franz Marc, Ernst Ludwig Kirchner, Erich Heckel and influential Bauhaus devotee Lyonel Feininger, who painted many scenes of Halle. There are also single pieces by Edvard Munch and Emil Nolde, while temporary exhibitions occupy other halls.

Sorry entomologists, it is all about the Fab Four at the **Beatles Museum** (☎ 290 3900; www .beatlesmuseum.halle.de, in German; Alter Markt 12; adult/ concession €2.50/1.50; ⌚ 10am-6pm Wed-Sun, closed Sep). There's no real Halle connection; owner Rainer Moers moved his memorabilia here when rents in Cologne became prohibitive. Even in this roomy, three-storey building only a fraction of the 10,000 items he's accumulated since 1964 are displayed – from legendary photos, record covers and film posters to merchandise like wigs, jigsaws and even talcum powder.

Sleeping & Eating

DJH hostel (☎ 202 4716; August-Bebel-Strasse 48a; dm juniors/seniors €17.50/21.20; 🖳) The high point of this converted old house is the dining room, with a distinct 1930s flashback vibe. The hostel's a 15-minute walk north of the centre, close to the nightlife of Kleine Ulrichstrasse.

Zum Kleinen Sandberg (☎ 682 5913; Kleiner Sandberg 3; s/d €40/80) In a quiet location just off the main pedestrian thoroughfare of Leipziger Strasse, this is easily the best-situated mid-range option in town. The incongruous half-timbered house has a rustic restaurant and spotless, if fairly basic, modern rooms.

Ökoase (☎ 290 1604; Kleine Ulrichstrasse 2; mains €2.50-5.60; ⌚ 10am-7pm Mon-Fri) A rare healthy stop on Halle's main eating street, the 'Eco-Oasis' lives up to its name, with changing weekly menus of inventive vegetarian and vegan food made from organic produce.

Drei Kaiser (☎ 203 1868; Bergstrasse 1; mains €8-15) Service here is very old-school German, with just the right amount of gravitas for the weighty imperial-themed menu. The healthy options are offset by cholesterol-packed specialities like *Ofenfrischer Brotlaib* – smoked pork, white wine and crème fraîche baked in a hollow loaf.

Getting There & Away

Leipzig and Halle are linked by several trains an hour (€5.20, 30 minutes). Halle is also on direct routes to Magdeburg (€16.80, 45 minutes, hourly), Erfurt (€15, 1½ hours, hourly) and Berlin-Zoo (€28.40, two hours, every two hours). Local trains serve Wittenberg (€9.40, one hour) every two hours.

NAUMBURG

☎ 03445 / pop 31,500

Charming Naumburg, in the heart of German wine country, is best known for its huge cathedral and the fact that philosopher Friedrich Nietzsche spent some of his final years here while dying of syphilis. The town also coined its own architectural style, known as 'Naumburg Renaissance' – see the Rathaus for a typical example. Perhaps most importantly, though, Naumburg is an ideal base for hiking, cycling, kayaking and vineyard excursions in the Saale-Unstrut region.

Orientation & Information

The Hauptbahnhof is 1.5km northwest of the old town, which is encircled by a ring road. Rossbacher Strasse leads into town past the cathedral.

The local tourist office is **Naumburg-Information** (☎ 201 614; www.naumburg-tourismus.de, in German; Markt 6; ☺ 9am-6pm Mon-Fri, 10am-2pm Sat).

Sights

In the western quarter of town stands the enormous medieval cathedral, **Dom St Peter und Paul** (☎ 230 110; Domplatz 16-17; adult/concession €4/3; ☺ 9am-6pm Mon-Sat, noon-6pm Sun). Its size is impressive enough, but the cathedral is also possibly unique in having two choirs. The western one, built in 1250–60 in late-Romanesque style, is the more interesting: considered the magnum opus of the anonymous 'Master of Naumburg', it contains some of Germany's oldest and most valuable stained glass windows and some celebrated 13th-century statues. The stair rails leading up to the raised east choir are also worth a closer look.

Sleeping & Eating

Hotel Garni St Marien (☎ 235 40; Marienstrasse 12; s €41-49, d €59-72; P) A few welcoming touches, like the magazine rack and the honour bar, plus this hotel's small size, offset the fairly impersonal (but comfortable) modern rooms. Set back from the street, it ensures a good night's rest.

Zur Alten Schmiede (☎ 243 60; www.hotel-zur-alten-schmiede.de; Lindenring 36-37; s/d €60/85) Combining the smiley service of a family-run business with effortless, unstuffy elegance, this is the most chic place to stay in Naumburg. The **restaurant** (mains €7.20 to €11.80) shares all the hotel's good qualities.

Getting There & Away

There are fast trains to Naumburg from Halle (€6.60, 40 minutes, twice hourly) and Weimar (€6.60, 30 minutes, hourly). ICE trains serve Frankfurt-am-Main (€52, 3½ hours), Berlin (€39, 2½ hours), Hamburg (€71.40, five hours) and Munich (€70.50, 4½ hours) every two hours.

MECKLENBURG-WESTERN POMERANIA

Mecklenburg-Vorpommern is Germany's finest domestic holiday spot. In summer thousands of visitors descend on the resort island of Rügen to enjoy the sparkling sand and all-too-brief swimming season, as well as touring pretty coastal towns like Wismar and Warnemünde and red-brick classics such as Stralsund and Schwerin.

Dog lovers might also care to know that this is where Pomeranians come from (they're descended from the region's ancient Spitz breeds, apparently); despite this, dogs are only allowed on certain marked stretches of beach.

SCHWERIN

☎ 0385 / pop 100,000

State capital Schwerin has to be one of the prettiest cities in northern Germany. The oldest city in Mecklenburg-Western Pomerania, it has so many lakes that locals and officials can't even agree on the number! The centre, an interesting mix of 16th-, 17th- and 19th-century architecture, is small enough to explore on foot, but you can easily take two or three days to get to know the city and its environs properly. Schwerin's beauty and charm are invariably infectious, and few people regret spending a bit of extra time here.

Orientation

The Altstadt is a 10-minute walk south from the Hauptbahnhof along Wismarsche Strasse. A couple of blocks east of the Hauptbahnhof is the rectangular Pfaffenteich, a pretty artificial pond with the ludicrously orange Arsenal (now government offices) at its southwest corner. Heading east from here will take you to the central Markt.

Information

HypoVereinsbank (☎ 530 30; Mecklenburger Strasse)
In-Ca Internet (☎ 500 7883; Wismarsche Strasse 123; per hr €2.50; ☺ 1pm-midnight)
Schwerin-Information (☎ 592 5212; www.schwerin .de, in German; Rathaus, Markt 10; ☺ 9am-7pm Mon-Fri, 10am-6pm Sat & Sun)

Sights

Southeast of the Alter Garten, over the causeway on the Burginsel (Burg Island), Schwerin's superb neo-Gothic palace, the **Schloss Schwerin** (☎ 525 2920; www.schloss-schwerin .de, in German; adult/concession €4/2.50; ☺ 10am-6pm Tue-Sun 15 Apr–14 Oct, to 5pm 15 Oct–15 Apr), was built around the chapel of a 16th-century ducal castle and is quite rightly the first attraction visitors head to upon arrival.

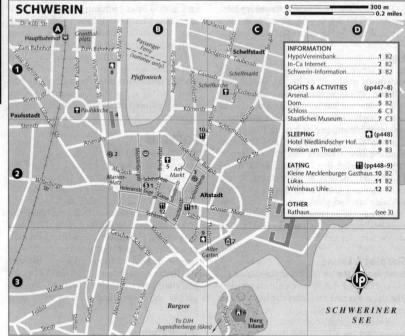

SCHWERIN

0		300 m
0		0.2 miles

INFORMATION
HypoVereinsbank..................................1 B2
In-Ca Internet.......................................2 B2
Schwerin-Information............................3 B2

SIGHTS & ACTIVITIES (pp447–8)
Arsenal..4 B1
Dom...5 B2
Schloss..6 C3
Staatliches Museum...............................7 C3

SLEEPING (p448)
Hotel Niederländischer Hof....................8 B1
Pension am Theater...............................9 B3

EATING (pp448–9)
Kleine Mecklenburger Gasthaus..........10 B2
Lukas...11 B2
Weinhaus Uhle...................................12 B2

OTHER
Rathaus...(see 3)

The causeway is overlooked by a statue of **Niklot**, an early Slavic prince, who was defeated by Heinrich der Löwe in 1160. The huge, graphic picture of his death is a highlight of the castle interior.

You don't get much better examples of north German red-brick architecture than this 14th-century Gothic **Dom** (☎ 565 014; Am Dom 4; tower €1; ❧ 10am-5pm Mon-Fri, noon-5pm Sun), towering above the Markt. You can climb up to the viewing platform in the 19th-century tower (118m), which locals hotly point out is a whole 50cm taller than Rostock's Petrikirche (see p450).

The enormous neoclassical building in the Alter Garten, the **Staatliches Museum** (☎ 595 80; Alter Garten 3; adult/concession €6/4; ❧ 10am-8pm Tue, to 6pm Wed-Sun), couldn't really be anything other than a museum, and the contents fit the imposing exterior well: the permanent displays showcase old Dutch masters including Rembrandt, Rubens and Brueghel, as well as oils by Lucas Cranach the Elder and collections of more modern works by Marcel Duchamp and Ernst Barlach.

Sleeping

Jugendherberge (☎ 326 0006; jh-schwerin@djh-mv.de; Waldschulweg 3; juniors/seniors €14.50/17.50) This hostel is about 4km south of the city centre, just opposite the zoo. Take bus No 14, which has stops at the Hauptbahnhof and Marienplatz.

Pension am Theater (☎ 593 680; www.pension amtheater.m-vp.de, in German; Theaterstrasse 1-2; r €50-82; **P**) In the shadow of the huge theatre building and (just) within sight of the castle, you get a friendly welcome and big, comfortable rooms here, although you may miss little things like soap in the bathrooms.

Hotel Niederländischer Hof (☎ 591 100; www .niederlaendischer-hof.de; Karl-Marx-Strasse 12-13; s/d from €90/118; **P**) You can't beat the Pfaffenteich location or the swank rooms and marble bathrooms at this exceedingly classy hotel. There's even a library with an open fire for those contemplative German winters.

Eating

Lukas (☎ 565 935; Grosser Moor 5; mains €6.90-17) Fish-lovers should head straight to this top conservatory restaurant, with a great range of dishes and some extravagant prawn and lobster options. See if you can look at the aquarium without feeling guilty.

Weinhaus Uhle (☎ 562 956; Schusterstrasse 13-15; mains €9-17.50) This long-standing traditional family wine merchant has vaulted ceilings in the downstairs restaurant and a lovely Weinstube upstairs.

Kleine Mecklenburger Gasthaus (☎ 555 9666; Puschkinstrasse 37) This modern restaurant, run by the owners of Uhle, has excellent food, and its wine list is practically encylopaedic.

Getting There & Away
Direct trains leave for Rostock (€12.90, 1¼ hours) and Stralsund (€21.60, two hours) at least every two hours, and for Wismar (€5.50, 30 minutes) throughout the day. Trains to Berlin (€27.20, 2½ hours, every two hours) go via Wittenberge.

WISMAR
☎ 03841 / pop 46,500
Wismar, about halfway between Rostock and Lübeck, joined the powerful Hanseatic trading league in the 13th century – the first town east of Lübeck to do so. For centuries the town was in and out of Swedish control, and traces of that rule can still be seen, particularly in the colourful 'Swedish heads' all over town. Quieter than Rostock or Stralsund, Wismar can still fill up with visitors pretty quickly in high season; it's definitely worth an overnight stay, and is also the gateway to **Poel Island**, a lovely little piece of green to the north.

Orientation & Information
The Altstadt is the city centre, built up around the Markt, which is said to be the largest medieval town square in northern Germany. The Bahnhof is at the northeastern corner of the Altstadt and the Alter Hafen port is in the northwest.

In the Altstadt is the **tourist Information** (☎ 251 3025; www.wismar.de, in German; Am Markt 11; ⏱ 9am-6pm).

Sights & Activities
The old harbour, **Alter Hafen** (☎ 389 082; www.alterhafenwismar.de, in German), featured in the 1922 film *Nosferatu*, is still a focal point of activity in Wismar. **Clermont Reederei** (☎ 224 646; www.reederei-clermont.de, in German) operates hour-long harbour cruises five times daily from May to September, leaving from Alter

Hafen (adult/concession €6/3). Daily boats also go to Poel Island (€10/5 return). Various other companies run tours on historic ships during the summer; contact the harbour for details.

The town's historical museum **Schabbell-haus** (☎ 282 350; www.schabbellhaus.de, in German; Schweinsbrücke 8; adult/concession €2/1, free Fri; ⏱ 10am-8pm Tue-Sun May-Oct, to 5pm Nov-Apr) has taken over a former Renaissance brewery (1571), just south of the Nikolaikirche across the canal. The museum's pride and joy is the large tapestry *Die Königin von Saba vor König Salomon* ('The Queen of Sheba before King Solomon'; 1560–75).

CHURCHES
Wismar was a target for Anglo-American bombers just a few weeks before the end of WWII. Of the three great red-brick churches that once rose above the rooftops, only the **St-Nikolai-Kirche** (St-Nikolai-Kirchhof; admission €1; ⏱ 8am-8pm May-Sep, 10am-6pm Apr & Oct, 11am-4pm Nov-Mar) built from 1381 to 1487, was left intact. The massive red shell of **St-Georgen-Kirche** is being restored for use as a church, concert hall and exhibition space, and was partially opened in 2002 (completion by 2010). Cars now park where the 13th-century **St-Marien-Kirche** once stood, although its great brick steeple (1339), now partly restored, still towers above the city.

Sleeping & Eating
Pension Chez Fasan (☎ 213 425; www.pension-chez-fasan.de, in German; Bademutterstrasse 20a; s/d €25/50; P) The best budget deal in town, with en suite rooms, TVs and a great central location.

Hotel Alter Speicher (☎ 211 746; www.hotel-alter-speicher.de; Bohrstrasse 12; s €66-105, d €90-140; P ✗ 🛏) Another good upmarket option, the Old Warehouse is a striking red building with lots of wood fittings and the budget guesthouse **Wismaria** (s/d €21/31) next door.

Zum Weinberg (☎ 283 550; Hinter dem Rathaus 3; mains €6.80-16.10) This lovely Renaissance house serves gargantuan portions of fruity Mecklenburg specialities, including a corking duck, and throws in some nice wines too.

Brauhaus am Lohberg (☎ 250 238; Kleine Hohe Strasse 15; mains €7-17.50) On Wismar's picturesque 'restaurant row', pedestrianised Am Lohberg, this was once home to the town's first brewery. Restored in 1995, it's now brewing again, taking up three floors and offering a good seafood menu. Look out for the painted penguins.

Getting There & Away

Trains travel to Rostock (€8.10, 70 minutes) and Schwerin (€5.50, 30 minutes) every hour. There's also a direct service to Berlin-Zoo (€30.40, three hours) every two hours.

ROSTOCK & WARNEMÜNDE

☎ 0381 / pop 199,000

Rostock, the largest city in sparsely populated northeastern Germany, is a major Baltic port and shipbuilding centre. First mentioned in 1161 as a Danish settlement, the city began taking shape as a German fishing village around 1200. In the 14th and 15th centuries, Rostock was an important Hanseatic trading city; parts of the city centre, especially along Kröpeliner Strasse, retain the flavour of this period.

Rostock hosted the Internationale Gartenausstellung (IGA; International Garden Show) in 2003, giving the local tourist industry a massive boost and raising the international profile of a city often just thought of as a port. Many of the centre's pretty gabled structures have been spruced up, the general infrastructure is excellent and the nightlife is the busiest in the state – it's definitely worth spending some time here.

Rostock's chief suburb is Warnemünde, 12km north of the centre. Counted among eastern Germany's most popular beach resorts, it's hard to see it as a small fishing village these days, but the boats still bring in their catches, and some charming streets and buildings persist amid the tourist clutter.

Orientation

The city begins at the Südstadt (Southern City), south of the Hauptbahnhof, and extends right the way north to Warnemünde on the Baltic Sea. Much of the city is on the western side of the Warnow River, which creates a long shipping channel practically due north to the sea.

The Altstadt is an oval area approximately 1.5km north of the Hauptbahnhof. Rosa-Luxemburg-Strasse runs north from the station to Steintor, which unofficially marks the southern boundary of the old town.

Information

Citibank (☎ 459 0081; Kröpeliner Strasse)

Das Netz (☎ 490 0270; Grubenstrasse 49; Internet per hr €2; ✆ 2-8pm Tue-Thu & Sun, 2pm-midnight Fri & Sat)
Rostock Card (48hr card €8)
Tourist-Information (☎ 381 2222; www.rostock.de; Neuer Markt 3; ✆ 10am-7pm Mon-Fri, 10am-4pm Sat & Sun)
Warnemünde-Information (☎ 548 000; www .warnemuende.de; Am Strom 59; ✆ 10am-7pm Mon-Fri, 10am-4pm Sat & Sun)

Sights

Kröpeliner Strasse, a broad, lively, cobbled pedestrian street lined with 15th- and 16th-century burghers' houses, runs west from Neuer Markt to the **Kröpeliner Tor**, a 55m-high tower, which contains the city's **Regional History Museum** (☎ 454 177; adult/concession €3/1.50; ✆ 10am-6pm Wed-Sun). The top floor is dedicated to the GDR days, and includes a leather jacket given to Politbüro supremo Erich Honecker in 1980 by West German rocker Udo Lindenberg.

The **Kloster Zum Heiligen Kreuz** (Holy Cross convent; ☎ 203 590; Klosterhof 18), was established in 1270 by Queen Margrethe II of Denmark; today it houses the **Cultural History Museum** (adult/concession €3/1.50; ✆ 9am-6pm Tue-Sun), with an excellent and varied collection including sculptures by Ernst Barlach and Victorian furniture. A combined ticket with the Kröpeliner Tor costs €4.50.

Rostock's pride and joy, the **Marienkirche** (☎ 453 325; Am Ziegenmarkt; admission €1; ✆ 10am-5pm Mon-Sat, 11.15am-noon Sun), built in 1290, was the only one of Rostock's four main churches to survive WWII unscathed. The long north–south transept was added after the ceiling collapsed in 1398. Notable features include the 12m-high astrological clock (1470–72), the Gothic bronze baptismal font (1290), the baroque organ (1770) and some fascinating tombstones in the floor.

The crowded seafront promenade to the north at **Warnemünde**, lined with hotels and restaurants, is where the tourists congregate. Its broad, sandy beach stretches west from the **lighthouse** (1898) and the **Teepott** exhibition centre, and is chock-a-block on hot summer days with bathers.

Sleeping

Baltic-Freizeit Camping und Ferienpark (☎ 04544-800 30; www.baltic-freizeit.de, in German; Dünenweg 27, Markgrafenheide; camp sites €9-28) On the east side of Warnow River, this enormous city-run affair has 1200 sites. Take tram No 4 to Dierkower Kreuz, then bus No 18 (45 minutes).

Jugendgästeschiff (☎ 670 0320; ms-georg -buechner@t-online.de; Am Stadthafen 72-3; s/d €27.50/50, dm juniors/seniors €17/20) Bed down on board the 1950s Belgian cargo ship MS *Georg Büchner*, which offers hostel-style dorms as well as spacious standard rooms and an amazing wood-panelled dining room. In the next berth, **Jugendschiff** (☎ 495 8107; r €52-62) is a much smaller boat with some nice doubles.

City-Pension (☎ 252 260; Krönkenhagen 3; s €44-55, d €66-88; P) A small family *pension* occupying a lovely quiet street near the harbour, in the heart of the old-fashioned northern Altstadt.

Hotel Kleine Sonne (☎ 497 3153; www.die-kleine -sonne.de; Steinstrasse 7; s/d €79/99; P   🖥) The 'budget' offshoot of the fancier Hotel Sonne across the street, this is actually an excellent place in its own right, with a very modern style and art by Nils Ausländer dotted around.

Accommodation in Warnemünde can be like gold dust in summer. For private rooms, contact the tourist office or **Warnemünde Zimmervermittlung & Reisedienst** (☎ 0700-9276 3683; www.zimmervermittlung-wde.m-vp.de, in German; Am Bahnhof 1; d €26-70).

Eating

Krahnstöver Likörfabrik (☎ 252 3551; Grosse Wasserstrasse 30/Grubenstrasse 1; mains €4.80-8.40) A restaurant of Rostock's oldest family-run wine merchant, you can choose between hearty German pub grub in the *Kneipe* and more sophisticated wine-bar fare round the corner.

Tre Kronor (☎ 490 4260; Hansepassage, Lange Strasse; mains €7.50-15.70) Set in a strange split-level glass-fronted pillar box at the back of a shopping centre, the Three Crowns serves up good interesting Swedish dishes, including the classic elk steak.

Fischerklause (☎ 525 16; Am Strom 123, Warnemünde; mains €9-15.10) Hungry? Try the DIY *Steuerrad* ('steering wheel'; €21.50) at this well-respected seafood restaurant: a whopping 300g of freshly smoked fish with bread, fried potatoes and a local digestif.

Smoked fish fans will be in heaven in Warnemünde, as many of the boats lining the Alter Strom smoke their catch on site and sell it cheaply.

Getting There & Around

Trains run to Berlin (€29.60, three hours, every two hours), Stralsund (€11.10, one

hour, hourly), Schwerin (€12.90, 1¼ hours, hourly) and Hamburg (€26, 2¼ hours, hourly).

Various ferry companies operate from Rostock seaport. **Scandlines** (☎ 673 1217; www .scandlines.de, in German) has daily services to Trelleborg in Sweden (€15-20, 5¾ hours) and Gedser in Denmark (€5-8, two hours). **TT-Line** (☎ 670 790; www.ttline.de) departs for Trelleborg several times daily (€18-30, three to six hours). **Silja Line** (☎ 350 4350; www.siljaline .de) sails to St Petersburg (€90 to €211, 39 hours) and Helsinki (€67 to €87, 24 hours), both via Tallinn, once or twice a week.

For local transport a *Tageskarte* (day ticket) costs €3.10. For two zones (covering Rostock and Warnemünde), single rides cost €1.50; for one zone it's €1.20.

STRALSUND

☎ 03831 / pop 60,000

Seventy kilometres east of Rostock on the Baltic coast, Stralsund was the second-most powerful member of the medieval Hanseatic League, after Lübeck. In 1648 Stralsund, Rügen and Pomerania came under the control of Sweden, which had helped in their defence. The city remained Swedish until it was incorporated into Prussia in 1815.

Stralsund is an attractive, accessible town of imposing churches and elegant townhouses, boasting more examples of classic red-brick Gothic gabled architecture than almost anywhere else in northern Germany. While it lacks the bijou Schloss of Schwerin and the all-in nightlife of Rostock, it's worth at least as much time as either of them.

Orientation

The Altstadt is effectively on its own island, surrounded by lakes and the sea. Its main hubs are Alter Markt in the north and Neuer Markt in the south. The Hauptbahnhof is across the Tribseer Damm causeway, west of the Neuer Markt. The harbour is on the Altstadt's eastern side.

Information

INTERNET ACCESS

M@trix (☎ 278 80; Wasserstrasse 8-9; per hr €4; 🕑 2pm-midnight)

MONEY

Sparkasse (☎ 221 516; Neuer Markt 7)

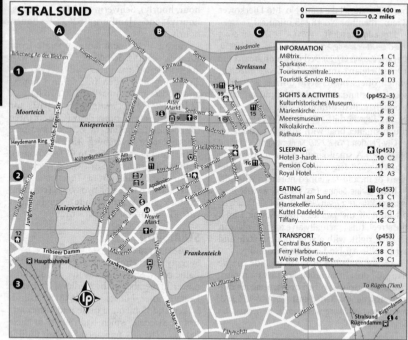

STRALSUND

INFORMATION
M@trix	1 C1
Sparkasse	2 B2
Tourismuszentrale	3 B1
Touristik Service Rügen	4 D3

SIGHTS & ACTIVITIES (pp452-3)
Kulturhistorisches Museum	5 B3
Marienkirche	6 B3
Meeresmuseum	7 B2
Nikolaikirche	8 B1
Rathaus	9 B1

SLEEPING (p453)
Hotel 3-hardt	10 C2
Pension Cobi	11 B2
Royal Hotel	12 A3

EATING (p453)
Gastmahl am Sund	13 B1
Hansekeller	14 B2
Kuttel Daddeldu	15 B2
Tiffany	16 C2

TRANSPORT (p453)
Central Bus Station	17 B3
Ferry Harbour	18 C1
Weisse Flotte Office	19 C1

TOURIST INFORMATION

Tourismuszentrale (☎ 246 90; www.stralsund.de, in German; Alter Markt 9; ☺ 9am-7pm Mon-Fri, 9am-2pm Sat, 10am-2pm Sun May-Sep; 9am-5pm Mon-Fri, 10am-2pm Sat Oct-Apr; ☐)

Touristik Service Rügen (☎ 285 70; www.insel-ruegen .com, in German; Bahnhof Rügendamm, Werftstrasse 2; ☺ 8am-9pm Mon-Fri, 9am-8pm Sat, 10am-7pm Sun)

Sights

One of the two structures dominating the Alter Markt is the splendid **Rathaus**, with its late-Gothic decorative façade. The upper portion has slender copper turrets and gables which have openings to prevent strong winds from knocking over the façade; this ornate design was Stralsund's answer to its rival city, Lübeck, which has a similar town hall. The sky-lit gallery overhanging the vaulted walkway is held aloft by shiny black pillars on carved and painted bases.

Exit through the eastern walkway to the main portal of the other dominant presence in the Alter Markt, the 1270 **Nikolaikirche** (☎ 299 799; Alter Markt; ☺ 10am-5pm Mon-Sat, 11.15am-noon & 2-4pm Sun). Modelled after the

Marienkirche in Lübeck and bearing a fleeting resemblance to Notre Dame, it's filled with art treasures. Also worth a closer look are the **high altar** (1470), 6.7m wide and 4.2m tall, showing Jesus' entire life, and the **astronomical clock** (1394), allegedly the oldest in the world – sadly it's never worked very well.

The Neuer Markt is dominated by the massive 14th-century **Marienkirche** (☎ 298 965; Neuer Markt; ☺ 10am-6pm Mon-Fri, to 5pm Sat & Sun), another superb example of north German red-brick construction. Its main draw is the huge **F Stellwagen organ** (1659), festooned with music-making cherubs. You can climb the steep wooden steps up the tower (€1) for a sweeping view of the town and Rügen Island.

MUSEUMS

North of Neuer Markt, a former 13th-century convent church, the **Meeresmuseum** (Oceanographic Museum; ☎ 265 010; www.meeres museum.de; Katharinenberg 14-20; adult/concession €4/2.50; ☺ 9am-6pm Jun-Sep, 10am-5pm Oct-May) now houses displays on all things fishy.

There's a large natural history section and tanks with live tropical fish, coral and scary Baltic creatures.

Stralsund's cultural history museum, **Kulturhistorisches Museum** (☎ 287 90; Mönchstrasse 25-27; adult/concession €3/1.50; ☻ 10am-5pm Tue-Sun), has a large historical collection, paintings by Caspar David Friedrich and Philipp Otto Runge, *faïence* (tin-glazed earthenware), playing cards and Gothic altars, as well as various outlying exhibitions in restored houses.

Tours

Ferries operate seven times daily by **Weisse Flotte** (☎ 268 138; www.weisse-flotte.com, in German; Fährstrasse 16; one way €2.30; ☻ May-Oct) to the scenic fishing village of Altefähr on Rügen. One-hour **harbour cruises** depart four times daily (€6). The ferry harbour is on the northeastern edge of the Altstadt.

Sleeping

Pension Cobi (☎ 278 288; www.pension-cobi.de, in German; Jakobiturmstrasse 15; s €32-42, d €46-62; ℗) In the shadow of the Jakobikirche, this is a great location for exploring the Altstadt, and also offers bike hire to get a bit further afield. Rooms are smart, clean and some have balconies.

Hotel 3-hardt (☎ 285 658; Heilgeiststrasse 50; s/d €45/70; ☒) A stone's throw from both the docks and the centre, the 3-hardt is a friendly, cosy operation with a nice restaurant and an Irish cellar pub.

Royal Hotel (☎ 295 268; www.royal-hotel.de, in German; Tribseer Damm 4; s/d €65/80, ste from €90; ℗) A regal Art Nouveau building opposite the train station houses this excellent-value hotel; buffet meals and lovely, big suites make up for a bit of street noise.

Eating

Tiffany (☎ 3090 088; Am Langenwall; buffet €4.99) This breakfast bar (geddit?) is simply fantastic, darling. If you're not a morning person, try the Audrey Hepburn drink-all-you-can champagne buffet (€28, including bowl of fruit).

Hansekeller (☎ 703 840; Mönchstrasse 48; mains €7.50-13) In an old guardhouse near Neuer Markt, the Hansekeller serves up hearty regional dishes at moderate prices in its vaulted brick cellar.

There are plenty of fish (and tourist) restaurants around the harbour. Try **Gastmahl**

am Sund (☎ 306 209; Seestrasse 2), with its 40-odd dishes, or the eccentric **Kuttel Daddeldu** (☎ 299 526; Hafenstrasse), which has little lighthouses on every table.

Getting There & Away

Regional trains travel to/from Rostock (€10.70, 1¼ hours), Berlin-Ostbahnhof (€30.80, 3½ hours) and Hamburg (€33, 4hrs) at least every two hours. There are lots of trains to Sassnitz (€8.10, 50 minutes) and Binz (€8.10, 50 minutes), on Rügen Island. International trains between Berlin and Stockholm or Oslo use the car-ferry connecting Sassnitz Fährhafen on Rügen with Trelleborg and Malmö in Sweden.

RÜGEN ISLAND

Germany's largest island, Rügen has 574km of coast and a resort tradition reflecting all sides of Germany's recent past. In the 19th century, luminaries such as Einstein, Bismarck and Thomas Mann came to unwind in the fashionable coastal resorts. Later, both Nazi and GDR regimes made Rügen the holiday choice for dedicated comrades.

The island's highest point is the **Königstuhl** (king's throne, 117m), reached by car or bus from Sassnitz. The **chalk cliffs** that tower above the sea are the main attraction. Much of Rügen and its surrounding waters are either national park or protected nature reserves. The **Bodden** inlet area is a bird refuge popular with bird-watchers. **Kap Arkona**, on Rügen's north shore, is famous for its rugged cliffs and two lighthouses, one designed by Karl Friedrich Schinkel.

The main resort area is in eastern Rügen, around the towns of Binz, Sellin and Göhren. A lovely hike from Binz to Sellin skirts the cliffs above the sea through beech and pine forest, offering great coastal views. Another popular destination is **Jagdschloss Granitz** (1834), surrounded by lush forest; Prora, up the coast from Binz, is the site of a 2km-long workers' retreat built by Hitler before the war, now housing several museums.

Information

RügenCard (www.ruegencard.de; 3/7/14 days €9/19/35)
Tourismus Rügen (☎ 03838-807 70; www.ruegen.de; Am Markt 4, Bergen)
Verbund Rügener Zimmervermittlungen (☎ 01805-334 433; www.insel-ruegen.org, in German) Island-wide reservation service.

Sleeping & Eating

Jugendherberge Binz (☎ 325 97; jh-binz@djh-mv .de; Strandpromenade 35, Binz; dm juniors/seniors €18.50/22.50) A beachside location means that this high-spirited hostel is always popular – book ahead.

Pension Haus Colmsee (☎ 325 56; www.haus colmsee.de, in German; Strandpromenade 8, Binz; d €73; P ✕) A big, pleasant villa by the beach at the eastern edge of town, with some of the best high-season prices around.

Panorama-Hotel Lohme (☎ 038302-9221; www .lohme.com; Dorfstrasse 35, Lohme; s €60, d €80-106; P) This hotel west of the Stubbenkammer has what may be the island's most romantic restaurant, particularly when the sun sets over Kap Arkona on summer nights.

Ostsee-Campingplatz Göhren (☎ 038308-90120; www.ostseecampingplatz-goehren.de; Am Kleinbahnhof 18586 Ostseebad Göhren; adult/6-16 yrs/2-person tent low season €2.50/1.50/2, high season €3/2/2.50; ⌣ Apr-Oct) With a good choice of settings, this is probably the best spot among Rügen's 21 official camping grounds.

Getting There & Away

A new IC train connects Binz to Hamburg (€44.20, four hours), Cologne (€82.60, 8½ hours) and Frankfurt-am-Main (€89.80, nine to 10 hours) every two hours. Local trains run hourly from Stralsund to Sassnitz (€8.10, 50 minutes) and also to Binz (€8.10, 1¼ hours). To get to Putbus, change in Bergen; for Sellin, Baabe and Göhren, you can catch the historic Rasender Roland narrow-gauge train in Putbus or Binz.

Five **Scandlines** (☎ 01805-7226 3546 37) car ferries run from Sassnitz Mukran, several kilometres south of Sassnitz, to Trelleborg (one way €15 June to August and €10 September to May, 3¾ hours, daily). Ask about special round-trip packages. Scandlines also runs ferries between Sassnitz and Rønne on Bornholm Island (one way €17, Thursday, Saturday and Sunday April to mid-June and September to November, daily mid-June to September, 3¾ hours).

BAVARIA

For many visitors to Germany, Bavaria (Bayern) is a microcosm of the whole country. Here are the German stereotypes of lederhosen, beer halls, oompah bands and romantic castles. However, it's more accurate to say Bavaria is the exception, that it is in fact unique and not representative of the rest of the country. It has a long history of conservative politics, Munich being a periodic exception, and a reputation for being culturally closer to Italy than parts of Germany to the north.

Bavaria was ruled for centuries as a duchy under the line founded by Otto I of Wittelsbach, and eventually graduated to the status of kingdom in 1806. The region suffered amid numerous power struggles between Prussia and Austria and was finally brought into the German Empire in 1871 by Bismarck. The last king of Bavaria was Ludwig II (1845–86), who earnt the epithet the 'mad king' due to his obsession with building fantastic fairy-tale castles at enormous expense. He was found drowned in Starnberger See in suspicious circumstances and left no heirs.

Bavaria draws visitors year-round. If you only have time for one part of Germany after Berlin, this is it. Munich, the capital, is the heart and soul. The Bavarian Alps, Nuremberg and the medieval towns on the Romantic Road are other important attractions.

MUNICH

☎ 089 / pop 1.3 million

Munich (München) is the Bavarian mother lode. This beer-quaffing, sausage-eating city can be as cosmopolitan as anywhere in Europe. Munich residents have figured out how to enjoy life – in fact Munich consistently ranks near the top in quality-of-life surveys – and are perfectly happy to show outsiders, as a visit to a beer hall will confirm. But Munich is more than a beer mecca as the 11 universities, 300 churches and many fine museums attest – um, OK and six large breweries. Throw in one of the largest parks in all of Europe and it's easy to understand why it's the number one destination for foreign visitors in all of Germany.

History

Originally settled by monks from the Benedictine monastery at Tegernsee in the 7th and 8th century, the city itself wasn't founded until 1158 by Henry the Lion. In 1255 Munich became the home for the Wittelsbach dukes, princes and kings who ruled for the next 700 years. The city suffered through the Black Plague first in 1348 and again in 1623 when two-thirds of the population died.

Munich has been the capital of Bavaria since 1503, but didn't really achieve prominence until the 19th century under the guiding hand of Ludwig I. Ludwig became more conservative and repressive, and carried on an affair with the actress and dancer Lola Montez. He was forced to abdicate in favour of his son, Maxmilian II, who started a building renaissance, promoting science, industry and education.

At the turn of the last century there were half a million residents, but in the aftermath of WWI Munich became a hotbed of right-wing political ferment. Hitler staged a failed coup attempt in Munich in 1923 but the National Socialists seized power only a decade later. WWII brought bombing and more than 6000 civilian deaths until American forces entered the city in 1945. The 1972 Olympics turned disastrous when 11 Israeli athletes were murdered.

Today it is the centre of Germany's burgeoning high-tech industries and the largest publishing industry in Germany and all of Europe, besides being the home of Siemens and BMW. Munich will serve as one of the hosts of the 2006 World Cup games.

Orientation

The main train station is just west of the centre. From the station, head east along Bayerstrasse, through Karlsplatz, and then along Neuhauser Strasse and Kaufingerstrasse to Marienplatz, the hub of Munich.

North of Marienplatz are the Residenz (the former royal palace), Schwabing (the famous student section) and the parklands of the Englischer Garten through which the Isar River runs. East of Marienplatz is the Platzl quarter for beer houses and restaurants, as well as Maximilianstrasse, a fashionable street that is ideal for simply strolling and window-shopping.

Information

BOOKSHOPS

Anglia English Bookshop (Schellingstrasse 3) Overflowing with English titles; northeast of the Hofgarten.
Geobuch (Rosental 6) Opposite Viktualienmarkt.
Hugendubel (Marienplatz; Karlsplatz) Has a good selection of guides and English-language offerings.

EMERGENCY

Ambulance (☎ 112)
Home Medical Service (☎ 55 17 71, 724 20 01)
Police (☎ 110)

INTERNET ACCESS

easyEverything (☎ 55 99 96 96; Bahnhofplatz 1; per 80min €2; ⏰ 24hr) In the post office building, part of a chain of Internet cafés. Has hundreds of terminals and is normally packed with cyber surfers.
Internet Café (Altheimer Eck 12; per 30min €2.50; ⏰ 11am-1am)
Internet-Point (☎ 20 70 27 37; Marienplatz 20; ⏰ 24hr) In the subway directly in front of the stairway up to the Viktualienmarkt.
Times Square Online Bistro (Hauptbahnhof) In the southern part of the train station, just before the exit to Bayerstrasse.

INTERNET RESOURCES

English Magazine (www.munichfound.de) Website for monthly events, restaurants, entertainment and more.
Munich Fair Schedule (www.messe-muenchen.de)
Munich Transport (www.mvv-muenchen.de/en) Everything you need to know about Munich's transport system.

LAUNDRY

City SB-Waschcenter (Paul-Heysestrasse 21; ⏰ 7am-11pm; €4) Close to the Hauptbahnhof.
Schnell & Sauber Laundrette (Klenzestrasse; ⏰ 7am-11pm)

MONEY

American Express Promenadeplatz (☎ 2280 14 65; Promenadeplatz 6); Neuhauserstrasse (☎ 2280 13 87; Neuhauserstrasse 47)
Reisebank (☎ 55 108 30) Has two offices at the main train station.
Sparkasse (Sparkassenstrasse 2) On the southeast side of Marienplatz.
Thomas Cook (☎ 23 50 92 0; Kaiserstrasse 45, Schwabing)

POST

Main post office (Bahnhofplatz 1; ⏰ 7.30am-8pm Mon-Fri, 9am-4pm Sat) The poste restante address is: Hauptpostlagernd (Poste Restante), Bahnhofplatz 1, 80074 München.

TOURIST INFORMATION

The excellent *Young People's Guide* (€ 0.50) is available from information offices. The English-language monthly *Munich Found* (€3) is also useful, as is the annual *Visitors' Guide* (free).

GERMANY

CENTRAL MUNICH (MÜNCHEN)

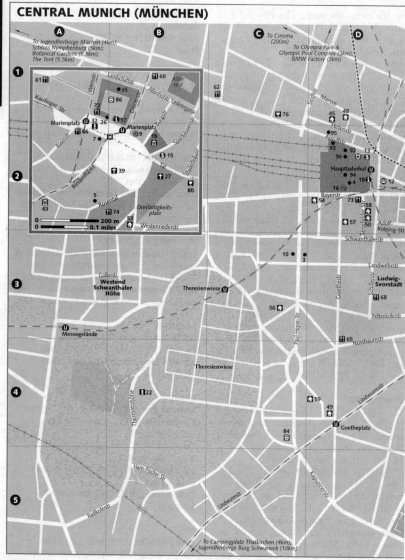

To Jugendherberge München (4km);
Schloss Nymphenburg (5km);
Botanical Gardens (5.5km);
The Tent (5.5km)

To Cinema (200m)

To Olympia Park & Olympic Pool Complex (3km); BMW Factory (3km)

Landschaftstr
Alter Hof
Weinstr
Kaufinger Str
Altenhofstr
Ledererstr
Burgstr
Sparkassenstr

Marienplatz
Marienplatz
Rosenstr
Rindermarkt
Tal
Rosental
Dreifaltigkeits-platz
Westenriederstr

0 ————— 200 m
0 ————— 0.1 miles

Hauptbahnhof
Bayerstr
Adolf-Kolping-Str
Schwanthalerstr

Landwehrstr
Ludwig-Svorstadt
Schillerstr
Pettenkoferstr
Nussbaumstr

Gollierstr
Westend Schwanthaler Höhe

Theresienwiese

Messegelände

Paul-Heyse-Str

Theresienwiese

Theresienhöhe

Goetheplatz
Lindwurmstr

Hans-Fischer-Str

Lindwurmstr
Kapuzinerstr

Radlkoferstr

To Campingplatz Thalkirchen (4km);
Jugendherberge Burg Schwaneck (10km)

EurAide (☎ 59 38 89; www.euraide.com; Hauptbahnhof; ☼ 7.45am-noon & 1-6pm Jun) Near platform 11 at the main train station, Euraide is a one-stop shop for all your travel needs.

Jugendinformationszentrum (Youth Information Centre; ☎ 51 41 06 60; Paul-Heyse-Strasse 22; ☼ noon-6pm Mon-Fri, to 8pm Thu) This centre has a wide range of information for young people, as well

as an extensive library of periodicals and fast, cheap Internet access.

Tourist office (☎ 23 33 03 00; www.muenchen-tourist .de) Main tourist office (Hauptbahnhof; ☼ 8am-8pm Mon-Sat, 10am-6pm Sun); Branch office (Marienplatz; ☼ 10am-8pm Mon-Fri, to 4pm Sat) Both offices sell the Munich Welcome Card (€16), which allows three days unlimited travel on public transport, plus discounts for many

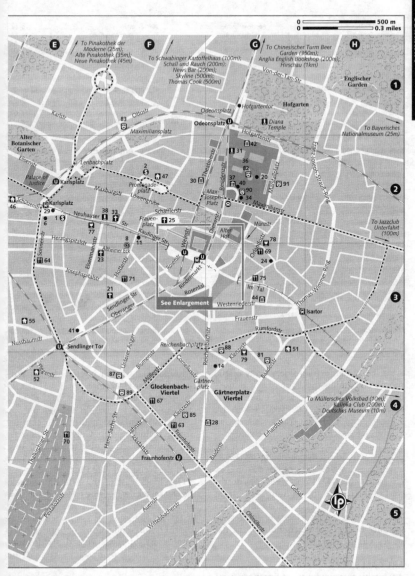

museums, galleries and other attractions. The main tourist office is to the right as you exit the Hauptbahnhof via the eastern entrance; its room-finding service is free. The branch office is beneath the Neues Rathaus (New Town Hall).

TRAVEL AGENCIES
DER Reisebüro (☎ 120 40; Hauptbahnhof)

Sights
PALACES

The huge **Residenz** (Max-Joseph-Platz 3) housed Bavarian rulers from 1385 to 1918 and features more than 500 years of architectural history. Apart from the palace itself, the **Residenzmuseum** (☎ 29 06 71; www.schloesser.bayern.de; Residenzstrasse 1; adult/concession €6/5; ☼ 9am-6pm Tue-Sun,

GERMANY

to 8pm Thu) has an extraordinary array of 100 rooms containing the Wittelsbach house's belongings, while in the same building, the **Schatzkammer** (☎ 29 06 71; enter from Max-Joseph-Platz 3; adult/concession €4/2; ☼ 9am-6pm Tue-Sun, to 8pm Thu) exhibits jewels, crowns and ornate gold.

If this doesn't satisfy your passion for palaces, visit **Schloss Nymphenburg** (☎ 17 90 80; www.schloesser.bayern.de; adult/concession museum €3.60/2.60, museum & gallery €7.70/6.15; ☼ 9am-6pm), north-west of the city centre via tram No 17 from the main train station (Hauptbahnhof). This was the royal family's equally impressive summer home. The surrounding park deserves a long, regal stroll.

ART GALLERIES

A veritable treasure house of European masters from the 14th to 18th centuries, the **Alte Pinakothek** (☎ 23 80 52 16; www.alte-pinakothek.de, in German; Barer Strasse 27; adult/concession €5/3.50, free Sun; ☼ 10am-5pm Tue-Sun, to 10pm Thu), a stroll northeast of the city, includes highlights such as Dürer's Christ-like *Self Portrait* and his *Four Apostles*, Rogier van der Weyden's *Adoration of the Magi* and Botticelli's *Pietà*.

Immediately north of the Alte Pinakothek, the **Neue Pinakothek** (☎ 23 80 51 95; www.neue-pinakothek.de, in German; Barer Strasse 29; adult/concession €5/3.50, free Sun; ☼ 10am-5pm Wed-Sun, to 10pm Thu) contains mainly 19th-century works, including Van Gogh's *Sunflowers*, and sculpture. A combined card costing €8/5 per adult/concession gets you into both the Neue and Alte Pinakotheks.

One block east of the Alte Pinakothek, the **Pinakothek der Moderne** (☎ 23 80 53 60; www.pinakothek-der-moderne.de, in German; Barer Strasse 40; ☼ 10am-5pm Tue-Sun, to 8pm Thu & Fri) brings together four collections of modern art, graphic art, applied art and architecture from galleries and museums around the city.

MUSEUMS

An enormous science and technology museum, **Deutches Museum** (☎ 217 91; www.deutsches-museum.de; Museumsinsel 1; adult/concession €7.50/5, planetarium €2 extra; ☼ 9am-5pm Tue-Sun) is like a combination of Disneyland and the Smithsonian Institution all under one huge roof. Take the S-Bahn or tram No 18.

The **Bayerisches Nationalmuseum** (☎ 211 24 01; www.bayerisches-nationalmuseum.de; Prinzregentenstrasse 3; adult/concession €3.10/1.80; ⊙ 10am-6pm Tue-Sun, to 8pm Thu), east of the Hofgarten, houses an impressive collection of Bavarian and southern German artefacts.

North of the city, auto-fetishists can thrill to the **BMW Factory** (☎ 3822 3306), adjacent to the BMW headquarters and museum (museum closed until 2007), which offers free tours of the factory line (in German and English). Take the U3 to Olympiazentrum.

At the **Zentrum für Aussergewöhnliche Museen** (Centre for Unusual Museums; ☎ 290 41 21; www .zam-museum.de; Westenriederstrasse 26; adult/concession €4/2.50; ⊙ 10am-6pm Tue-Sun), you'll find displays on everything from the Easter Bunny to Austrian Empress Elisabeth.

PARKS & GARDENS

One of the largest city parks in Europe, the **Englischer Garten**, west of the city centre, is a great place for strolling, especially along the Schwabinger Bach. In summer, nude sunbathing is the rule rather than the exception. It's not unusual for hundreds of naked people to be in the park during a normal business day, with their clothing stacked primly on the grass. If they're not doing this, they're probably drinking merrily at one of the park's three **beer gardens** (p462).

Munich's beautiful **Botanical Gardens** (adult/concession €2/1; ⊙ 9am-6pm) are two stops past Schloss Nymphenburg on tram No 17.

SWIMMING POOLS

The following pools are open year-round:
Cosima Wellenbad (☎ 23 61 79 21; Cosimastrasse 5; admission €3; ⊙ 7.30am-11pm)
Müllersches Volksbad (☎ 23 61 34 34; Rosenheimerstrasse 1; admission €3; ⊙ 7.30am-11pm)
Olympic Pool Complex (☎ 30 67 22 90; Olympic Park; admission €3; ⊙ 7am-11.30pm) Northeast of the city.

OLYMPIATURM

If you like heights, then go up the lift of the 290m Olympiaturm (tower) situated in the **Olympia Park complex** (☎ 67 27 50; www .olympiapark-muenchen.de; adult/concession €3/2.50; tower ⊙ 9am-midnight). Take the U3 to Olympiazentrum.

Walking Tour

The pivotal **Marienplatz** is a good starting point. Dominating the square is the tower-ing neo-Gothic **Neues Rathaus** (New Town Hall; Marienplatz), with its incessantly photographed **Glockenspiel** (carillon) which performs at 11am and noon (also at 5pm from May to October), bringing the square to an expectant standstill. Two important churches are on this square: **St Peterskirche** (Rindermarket 1; ⊙ 9am-7pm Apr-Oct, to 6pm Nov-Mar) and, behind the Altes Rathaus, the **Heiliggeistkirche** (Tal 77; ⊙ 7am-6pm). Head west along shopping street Kaufingerstrasse to the late-Gothic **Frauenkirche** (Church of Our Lady; ☎ 42 34 57; Frauenplatz; tower adult/concession €3/1.50), the landmark church of Munich. Go inside and join the hordes wandering in stupefied awe at the grandeur of the place, or climb the tower for majestic views of Munich. Continue west to the large grey **Michaelskirche** (☎ 609 02 24; Neuhauserstrasse 52; ⊙ 8am-7pm), Germany's grandest Renaissance church.

Further west is the **Richard Strauss Fountain** and the medieval **Karlstor**, an old city gate. Double back towards Marienplatz and turn right onto Eisenmannstrasse, which becomes Kreuzstrasse and converges with Herzog-Wilhelm-Strasse at the medieval gate of **Sendlinger Tor**. Go down the shopping street Sendlinger Strasse to the **Asamkirche** (Sendlinger Strasse 34), a remarkable rococo church designed by brothers Cosmas Damian and Egid Quirin Asam. The ornate marble façade won't prepare you for the opulence inside, where scarcely an inch is left unembellished.

Continue along Sendlinger Strasse and turn right on Hermann-Sack-Strasse to reach the **Stadtmuseum** (☎ 233; St-Jakobs-Platz 1; adult/concession €2.50/1.50; ⊙ 10am-6pm Tue-Sun), where outstanding exhibits cover beer brewing, fashion, musical instruments, photography and puppets.

Tours

Following are some recommended tour companies.
Mike's Bike Tours (☎ 25 54 39 87; www.mikesbiketours .com; ½-/full-day tours €22/33) Highly recommended (and leisurely) city cycling and walking tours in English. Tours depart from the archway at the Altes Rathaus on Marienplatz – feel free to just show up.
Panorama Tours (☎ 55 02 89 95; stadtrundfahrten@ t-onlind.de; Arnulfstrasse 8; €11) Double-decker buses whisk you through the city. Tours last an hour and depart from outside the Hauptbahnhof.
Radius Tours (☎ 55 02 93 74; www.radiusmunich.com; Arnulfstrasse 3) Runs excellent English-language tours: a

two-hour walk of the city heart, and a tour of the Third Reich sites (both €9). Tours leave from its office near track 30 at the Hauptbahnhof. It also offers five-hour trips to Dachau at €18, including transport.

Festivals & Events

Hordes come to Munich for the **Oktoberfest** (its origins are in the marriage celebrations of Crown Prince Ludwig in 1810), one of the Continent's biggest and most drunken parties, running the 15 days before the first Sunday in October. Reserve accommodation well ahead and go early in the day so you can grab a seat in one of the hangar-sized beer 'tents'. The action takes place at the Theresienwiese grounds, about a 10-minute walk southwest of the Hauptbahnhof. While there is no entrance fee, those €6 1L steins of beer add up fast.

Sleeping

BUDGET

Munich's youth hostels that are DJH and HI affiliated do not accept guests over age 26, except group leaders or parents accompanying a child.

Campingplatz Thalkirchen (☎ 724 308 08; fax 724 31 77; Zentralländstrasse 49; per person/tent €4.40/3.60, heated cabin per person €10.50; ☜ mid-Mar–end Oct) To get to this camping ground, southwest of the city centre, take the U3 to Thalkirchen and then catch bus No 57 (about 20 minutes).

Tent (☎ 141 43 00; www.the-tent.com; In den Kirschen 30; bed in main tent €9, camp site €5.50; ☜ Jun-Sep) Roll out of your tent to this camping ground's own beer garden. Take tram No 17 to the Botanic Gardens then follow the signs.

Jugendherberge München (☎ 13 11 56; www.djh .de, in German; Wendl-Dietrich-Strasse 20; dm €19.20) Northwest of the centre (U1 to Rotkreuzplatz), this DJH hostel lacks atmosphere, but has plenty of beds.

Jugendherberge Burg Schwaneck (☎ 74 48 66 70; www.burgschwaneck.de, in German; Burgweg 4-6; dm €15.50) No that's not a fantastic old castle, it's your DJH hostel; take the S7 to Pullach, then it's a 10-minute walk.

Euro Youth Hotel (☎ 59 90 88 11; www.euro-youth -hotel.de; Senefelderstrasse 5; dm €17, s/d with shared bathroom €35/50) The party never stops at the friendly Euro Youth Hotel, where Euro and non-Euro youths alike work on international relationships in the bar and lounge. Rooms and facilities are well maintained, and the

staff are a good source for info on Munich and other destinations.

Jaeger's (☎ 55 52 81; www.jaegershotel.de; Senefelderstrasse 3; dm €15, s/d with shared bathroom €45/80) Next door to the Euro, Jaeger's is more subdued.

Easy Palace International Youth Hostel (☎ 55 87 97 0; www.easypalace.com; Mozartstrasse 4; dm/s/d €17/29/50) This place gets noisy when school groups are in, otherwise it's on a nice quiet block. The attached restaurant cooks up good pizza.

4 you München (☎ 55 21 66 0; www.the4you .de; Hirtenstrasse 18; dm under/over 27s €17/19, s/d incl breakfast €44/70) The 4 you is rightfully proud of its eco-friendly practices, it also boasts a location just a short walk from the train station.

MID-RANGE

Hotel Pension Central (☎ 543 98 46; pension.central@ t-online.de; Bayerstrasse 55; s/d €34/52) The Central has adequate rooms across from the train station.

Hotel Pension Utzelmann (☎ 59 48 89; www .hotel-utzelmann@t-online.de; Pettenkoferstrasse 6; s/d incl breakfast €33/53) This hotel is housed in an attractive pastel-painted home; it's best to call or book ahead to make sure someone's there when you arrive.

Pension Haydn (☎ 54 40 47 03; www.pension -haydn.de, in German; Haydnstrasse 9; s/d incl breakfast €38/52) Not far from the Goetheplatz U-Bahn station on a nice, quiet residential street, the Haydn's superior rooms are tended with love and care.

Hotel Pension am Markt (☎ 22 50 14; hotel-am -markt.muenchen@t-online.de; Heiliggeiststrasse 6; s/d incl breakfast €38/68) Near the Viktualienmarkt, Hotel Pension am Markt has a pleasant feel and lovely rooms.

Creatif Hotel Elephant (☎ 55 57 85; www.munich -service.de/elephant.htm; Lämmerstrasse 6; s/d €69/89) Just around the corner from 4 you München, the Creatif is becoming slightly more upmarket, undergoing an Art Deco transformation. It also does a good breakfast buffet.

TOP END

Hotel Uhland (☎ 54 33 50; www.hotel-uhland.de; Uhlandstrasse 1; s/d €64/77) Behind a beautiful neo-Renaissance façade near the Oktoberfest site, you'll find all the mod cons and an inspirational breakfast buffet.

Hotel Müller (☎ 232 38 60; www.hotel-mueller .inmuenchen.de; Fliegenstrasse 4; s/d €70/90) The Müller is roomy and weekend deals are available but it's not as luxurious as the others in this category.

Advokat Munchen (☎ 21 63 10; www.hotel-advokat.de; Baaderstrasse 1; s/d €130/150) Though the design scheme is minimalist, your stay here is anything but – with a complimentary self-service lobby bar, roof garden, and all-you-can-eat breakfast spread, this hotel is a work of art in itself.

Anna Hotel (☎ 59 99 40; www.geisel-hotels.de, in German; Schützenstrasse 1; s/d €145/165) Form follows function at this meticulously designed luxury hotel. All guests have access to the health club and wireless Internet access.

Hotel Bayerischer Hof (☎ 212 00; www.bayerischerhof.de; Promenadeplatz 2-6; s/d €182/232) Opened in 1841, generations of world leaders have made the Bayerischer Hof their home in Munich. No doubt you too will appreciate the beautiful glass domed atrium, marble, gold leaf and bustling efficiency.

Eating
RESTAURANTS
Bergwolf (☎ 232 59 858; Fraunhoferstrasse 17; meals €5) Inexpensive wurst, fries and beer are the speciality at this informal hang-out.

Bon Valeur (☎ 54 88 39 94; Sonnenstrasse 17; mains €7) Try here for organic food and freshly squeezed fruit juices in a casual setting.

Fraunhofer (☎ 26 64 60; Fraunhoferstrasse 9; mains €8-13) The highly recommended and always crowded Fraunhofer serves up good Bavarian cuisine. While you'll probably be sharing your table with a young crowd, the wood and stuccoed ceiling give it a decidedly aged look.

Schwabinger Kartoffelhaus (☎ 30 36 77; Hohenzollernplatz 4; mains €5-15) Large potato-oriented portions in Schwabing.

Andechser Am Dom (☎ 29 84 81; Weinstrasse 7; mains €9-14) Slip behind the Frauenkirche for hearty Bavarian chow at its best.

Prinz Myschkin (☎ 26 55 96; Hackenstrasse 2; mains €9-14) For the stylish vegetarian in you, Myschkin provides a tasty selection of pizza and pasta.

Weisses Brauhaus (☎ 29 01 38 0; www.weisses-brauhaus.de, in German; Tal 7; mains €10-15) In one of the oldest breweries in Munich, the waitresses, dressed as you might imagine a Fräulein to look like, serve up specials like boiled ox cheeks.

Myra (☎ 26 01 83 84; Pestalozzistrasse 32; mains €10-19) South of Sendlinger Tor has a menu of meat, seafood and vegetarian dishes infused with a Turkish tang, and an awe-inspiring cocktail list.

CAFÉS
Most of Munich's café culture centres on Schwabing, the university haunt. Here you'll find plenty of snug little spots that are filled with laid-back laureates and lively lingo.

Café Am Beethovenplatz (☎ 54 40 43 48; Goethenstrasse 51; dishes €7-10) A casual hang-out with no airs and graces. It serves great, affordable food, and there's live music from 7.30pm.

Schall und Rauch (☎ 288 09 57; Schellingstrasse 22; dishes €5) This small unpretentious café has its own CD shop, a short stroll north of the city. The menu changes daily but the soups are always good.

News Bar (☎ 28 17 87; Amalienstrasse 55; sandwiches €5) Besides food and drinks, newspapers (some in English) and magazines are available at this spot in Schwabing, north of the city.

Café Glockenspiel (☎ 26 42 56; Marienplatz 28; dishes €7) In the Altstadt, a window seat at the Glockenspiel is a much-sought, if ambitious, goal – here you can view the café's namesake at eye level.

Stadt Café (☎ 26 69 49; St-Jakobsplatz 1; cakes €3) At the Stadtmuseum, this café has funky décor, an intellectual crowd and a pleasant courtyard.

QUICK EATS
Mensas (Schillerstrasse 47; meals €2) Student cardholders can fill up very cheaply at this university café. There are also other cafés at Leopoldstrasse 13B, Arcisstrasse 17B and Lothstrasse 13D.

Ristorante Ca'Doro (Bayerstrasse 31; pizza slices €1.90) The food and service are better than you might expect at this streetside restaurant in the middle of the train station traffic.

Munchen Strudelstube (☎ 53 86 87 10; Orlandostrasse; 3 strudels €6) Eat your fill of greasy fritters and strudels here.

SELF-CATERING
Viktualienmarkt, just south of Marienplatz, is a large open-air market open every day except Saturday afternoon and Sunday, where you can put together a picnic feast to take to the Englischer Garten. The fresh produce, cheese and baked goods are hard to resist.

Alois Dallmayr (☎ 213 50; Dienerstrasse 14), one of the world's greatest (and priciest) delicatessens, with an amazing range of exotic foods imported from every corner of the earth.

Drinking
BEER HALLS & BEER GARDENS
Beer-drinking is an integral part of Munich's entertainment scene. Germans drink an average of 130L of the amber liquid each per year, while Munich residents manage to drink much more than this!

Hofbräuhaus (☎ 29 01 36 10; www.hofbraeuhaus .de, in German; Am Platzl 9) Though tourists come by the busload, it's still a good time. Expect singing, drinking and loud merriment.

Augustiner Grossgaststätte (☎ 55 19 92 57; Neuhauser Strasse 27) What you probably imagine an old-style Munich beer hall looks like, filled with laughter, smoke and clinking glasses.

Augustiner Keller (☎ 59 43 93; Arnulfstrasse 52) Only five minutes from the Hauptbahnhof, the Keller has a large and leafy beer garden and a fine beer when the weather keeps you indoors.

Paulaner im Tal (☎ 219 94 00; Tal 12) If you've had your fill of beer, the Paulaner, whose interior is more elegant than most, also has an extensive wine menu.

On a summer's day there's nothing better than sitting and sipping among the greenery at one of Munich's beer gardens. In the Englischer Garten is the classic **Chinesischer Turm** (☎ 383 87 30) beer garden, while the nearby **Hirschau** (☎ 36 99 42) beer garden on the banks of Kleinhesseloher See is less crowded.

PUBS
Munich has no shortage of lively pubs. Dozens are clustered in industrial buildings in the Kunstpark Ost neighbourhood southeast of the Aldstadt on the other side of the Isar River. The *Young People's Guide* (p455) keeps abreast of the hot spots to party.

Klenze 17 (☎ 228 57 95; Klenzestrasse 17) The extensive whisky selection is almost as large as Klenze 17's two small rooms, usually populated with students.

Bar Triana (☎ 55 26 91 22; Schleissheimerstrasse 19) In the Max Vordstadt neighbourhood north of the train station, Triana's tapas and wine is a nice change of pace if you've had your fill of wurst and beer.

Killians Irish Pub (☎ 24 21 98 99; Frauenplatz 11) In a cellar behind the Frauenkirche, Killians is a roomy, casual drinking hole. There's live Irish music but, unusual for an Irish pub, no TVs to catch football on the tube.

Entertainment
PERFORMING ARTS, CINEMAS & JAZZ
Munich is one of the cultural capitals of Germany; the publications listed in the Information section (p455) can guide you to the best events.

Residenztheater (☎ 21 85 19 20; Max-Joseph-Platz 2) Home of the Bavarian State Opera and the site of many cultural events (particularly during the opera festival in July). You can buy tickets at the box office or book by telephone.

Cinema (☎ 55 52 55; www.cinema-muenchen.com; Nymphenburger Strasse 31) Current films in English are screened here. Take the U1 to Stiglmaier Platz, exit at Nymphenburgerstrasse.

CLUBS
Jazzclub Unterfahrt (☎ 448 27 94; Kirchenstrasse 42-44) Near the Max-Weber-Platz U-Bahn station. It has live music every night from 7.30pm, and open jam sessions on Sunday night.

Mister B's (☎ 53 49 01; Herzog-Heinrichstrasse 42) Take the U-Bahn to Goetheplatz to hear live jazz Thursdays to Sundays at this tiny club.

Skyline (☎ 33 31 31; Leopoldstrasse 82) In northern Schwabing, Skyline plays hip-hop on the top floor of the Hertie department store.

Kalinka Club (☎ 40 90 72 60; Grafingerstrasse 6; ☽ 10pm-late Thu-Sat) This Russian club in the Kultafabrik, southeast of the city, attracts an eclectic mix.

GAY & LESBIAN
Much of Munich's gay and lesbian nightlife is in the area just south of Sendlinger Tor, especially around Gärtnerplatz. *Our Munich* is a monthly guide to gay and lesbian life, and is available at **Our Munich Shop** (☎ 26 01 85 03; Müllerstrasse 36). Resembling a Paris bar, **Morizz** (☎ 201 67 76; Klenzestrasse 43) is a popular haunt for gay men, serving food and cocktails and cranking up later in the night. **Bei Carla** (☎ 227 901; Buttermelcherstrasse 9) is an exclusively lesbian bar-café with a friendly atmosphere and lots of regulars.

Shopping
All shoppers converge on the Marienplatz to buy designer shoes or kitschy souvenirs. For the well-heeled, check out the *haute couture*

shops on Maxmilianstrasse, while Schwabing boasts its fair share of boutiques. **Christkindlmarkt** (Marienplatz) in December is large and well stocked but often expensive, so buy a warm drink and just wander around. A huge flea market, the **Auer Dult** (Mariahilfplatz), has great buys and takes place during the last weeks of April, July and October.

Getting There & Away
AIR
Munich is second in importance only to Frankfurt-am-Main for international and national connections. Flights will take you to all major destinations worldwide. Main German cities are serviced by at least half a dozen flights daily.

BUS
Munich is linked to the Romantic Road by the Deutsche-Touring (also known as the Europabus) Munich–Frankfurt service (see p464). Inquire at **Deutsche-Touring** (☎ 545 87 00; www.deutsche-touring.com), near platform 26 of the Hauptbahnhof, about its international services to destinations such as Prague and Budapest. Buses stop along the northern side of the train station.

CAR & MOTORCYCLE
Munich has autobahns radiating out on all sides. Take the A9 to Nuremberg, the A92 to Passau, the A8 east to Salzburg, the A95 to Garmisch-Partenkirchen and the A8 west to Ulm or Stuttgart. The main rental companies have counters together on the second level of the Hauptbahnhof. For arranged rides, the **ADM-Mitfahrzentrale** (☎ 194 40; www.mitfahrzentralen.de; Lämmerstrasse 4; ☺ 8am-8pm Mon-Sat) is near the Hauptbahnhof. Destinations and sample charges (including booking fees) include Berlin €32, Frankfurt €25 and Hamburg €39.

TRAIN
Train services to/from Munich are excellent. There are rapid connections at least every two hours to all major cities in Germany, as well as frequent EC trains to other European cities such as Zurich (€61, five hours, four per day), Vienna (€62, five hours, hourly), Prague (€72, seven hours, two per day), Paris (€105, nine hours, three per day) and Amsterdam (€143, nine hours, hourly).

High-speed ICE services from Munich include Frankfurt (€69, 3½ hours, hourly),

Hamburg (€111, six hours, hourly) and Berlin (€111, seven hours, hourly).

Getting Around
TO/FROM THE AIRPORT
Munich's gleaming Flughafen Franz Josef Strauss is connected by the S8 and the S1 to Marienplatz and the Hauptbahnhof (€8). The service takes 40 minutes and runs every 20 minutes from 4am until around 12.30am.

The airport bus also runs at 20-minute intervals from Arnulfstrasse on the north side of the Hauptbahnhof (€9, 45 minutes) between 6.50am and 7.50pm. Forget taxis (at least €50!).

BICYCLE
Pedal power is popular in relatively flat Munich. **Radius Bike Rental** (☎ 59 61 13; Hauptbahnhof) rents out two-wheelers from €14/43 per day/week.

CAR & MOTORCYCLE
It's not worth driving in the city centre – many streets are pedestrian only. The tourist office has a map that shows city parking places (€1.50 or more per hour).

PUBLIC TRANSPORT
Munich's excellent public transport network (MVV) is zone-based, and most places of interest to tourists (except Dachau and the airport) are within the 'blue' inner zone (*Innenraum*). MVV tickets are valid for the S-Bahn, U-Bahn, trams and buses, but must be validated before use. The U-Bahn stops operating around 12.30am Monday to Friday and 1.30am Saturday and Sunday, but there are some later buses and S-Bahns. Rail passes are valid only on the S-Bahn.

Kurzstrecke (short rides) cost €1 and are good for no more than four stops on buses and trams, and two stops on the U and S-Bahns. Longer trips cost €2. It's cheaper to buy a strip-card of 10 tickets (*Mehrfahrtenkarte*) for €9 and stamp one strip per adult on short rides, two strips for longer rides in the inner zone. *Tageskarte* (day passes) for the inner zone cost €4.50, while three-day tickets cost €11, or €15 for two adults.

TAXI
Taxis are expensive (€2.50 flag fall, plus €1.30 per kilometre) and not much more

convenient than public transport. For a radio-dispatched taxi dial ☎ 216 10.

DACHAU

The first Nazi concentration camp was **Dachau** (☎ 08131 66 99 70; www.cc-memorial-site -dachau.org; Alte-Roemerstrasse 75; admission free; ⊗ 9am-5pm Tue-Sun), built in March 1933. Jews, political prisoners, homosexuals and others deemed 'undesirable' by the Third Reich were imprisoned in the camp. More than 200,000 people were sent here; more than 30,000 died at Dachau and countless others died after being transferred to other death camps. An English-language documentary is shown at 11.30am and 3.30pm. A visit includes camp relics, a memorial and a very sobering museum. Take the S2 to Dachau and then bus No 726 or 724 (Sunday and holidays) to the camp. A Gesamtnetz (total area) ticket (€9) is needed for the trip.

ROMANTIC ROAD

Originally conceived as a way of promoting tourism in western Bavaria, the popular Romantic Road (Romantische Strasse) links a series of picturesque Bavarian towns and cities.

The road runs north–south through western Bavaria, from Würzburg to Füssen near the Austrian border, passing through Rothenburg ob der Tauber, Dinkelsbühl and Augsburg.

Locals get their cut of the Romantic Road hordes through, among other things, scores of good-value private accommodation offerings – expect to pay around €15 to €25 per person. Tourist offices are efficient at finding accommodation in almost any price range. DJH hostels listed in this section only accept people aged under 27.

Getting There & Away

In the north of the Romantic Road route, Würzburg is well-served by trains. To start at the southern end, take the hourly RE train from Munich to Füssen (€18.20, two hours). Rothenburg is linked by train to Würzburg, Nuremberg and Munich via Steinach. To reach Dinkelsbühl, take a train to Ansbach and from there a frequent bus onwards. Nördlingen has train connections to Stuttgart and Munich.

There are four daily buses between Füssen and Garmisch-Partenkirchen (€7; all stop at

Hohenschwangau and Oberammergau), as well as several connections between Füssen and Oberstdorf (€9.40; via Pfronten). Deutsche-Touring runs a daily 'Castle Road' coach service in each direction between Mannheim and Rothenburg via Heidelberg (€29, 5½ hours).

Getting Around

It is possible to do this route using train connections, local buses or by car (just follow the brown 'Romantische Strasse' signs), but most train pass-holders prefer to take the Deutsche-Touring (also known as Europabus) bus. From April to October Deutsche-Touring runs one coach daily in each direction between Frankfurt and Munich (12 hours), and another in either direction between Dinkelsbühl and Füssen (4½ hours). The bus makes short stops in some towns, but it's silly to do the whole trip in one go, since you can break the journey at any point and continue the next day (reserve a seat for the next day as you disembark).

The full fare from Frankfurt to Füssen is €74 (change buses at Rothenburg). Eurail and German Rail passes are valid and Inter-Rail pass-holders receive a 50% discount, as do those over 60, while those under 26 save 10%. Tickets are available for short segments and reservations are only necessary on summer weekends. Bike transport is €6 for up to 12 stops. Contact **Deutsche-Touring GmbH** (☎ 069-79 03 50; www.deutsche-touring.com; Am Römerhof 17, 60486 Frankfurt/Main).

With its ever-changing scenery and gentle gradients, the Romantic Road makes a good bike trip. **Radl-Tours** (☎ 09341-53 95) offers nine-day cycling packages from Würzburg to Dinkelsbühl from €398.

WÜRZBURG

☎ 0931 / pop 130,000

Over 1300 years old, surrounded by forests and vineyards – including three of the four largest wine growing estates in all of Germany – the charming city of Würzburg straddles the upper Main River. Rebuilt after bombings late in the war (it took only 17 minutes to almost completely destroy the city), Würzburg is a centre of art, beautiful architecture and delicate wines.

The **tourist office** (☎ 37 23 35; www.wuerzburg .de, in German; Oberer Markt; ⊗ 10am-6pm Mon-Fri, to

2pm Sat), in the rococo masterpiece Haus zum Falken. On the 1st floor of the same building, the **Stadtbücherei** (☎ 37 34 38) provides 20 minutes of Internet access for €1.

Sights

The magnificent, sprawling **Residenz** (☎ 35 51 70; www.schloesser.bayern.de; Residenzplatz 2; adult/ concession €5/3.50; ☼ 9am-6pm Apr-Oct, 10am-4pm Nov-Mar), a baroque masterpiece by Neumann, took a generation to build and boasts the world's largest ceiling fresco painting; the **Hofgarten** at the back is a beautiful spot. The interior of the **Dom St Kilian** (☎ 386 261; www. museum-am-dom.de, in German; Kiliansplatz; admission €4; ☼ 10am-7pm Apr-Oct, to 5pm Nov-Mar) and the adjacent **Neumünster**, an 11th-century church in the old town housing the bones of St Kilian – the patron Saint of Wurzburg – continue the baroque themes of the Residenz.

Neumann's fortified **Alter Kranen** (old crane), which serviced a dock on the riverbank south of Friedensbrücke, is now the **Haus des Frankenweins** (☎ 390 11 11; Kranenkai 1), where you can taste Franconian wines (for around €3 per glass).

The medieval fortress **Marienberg**, across the river on the hill, is reached by crossing the 15th-century stone **Alte Mainbrücke** (bridge) from the city and walking up Tellstiege, a small alley. It encloses the **Fürstenbau Museum** (☎ 438 38; admission €2.50; ☼ 9am-6pm Tue-Sun Apr-Oct, 10am-4pm Tue-Sun Nov-Mar) featuring the episcopal apartments, and the regional **Mainfränkisches Museum** (☎ 430 16; adult/concession €3/1.50; ☼ 10am-6pm Tue-Sun Apr-Sep, to 4pm Tue-Sun Oct-Mar). See both on a combined card (€4). For a simple thrill, wander the walls enjoying the panoramic views.

Sleeping & Eating

Kanu-Club (☎ 725 36; Mergentheimer Strasse 13b; per person/tent €3.50) A camping ground on the west bank of the Main; take tram No 3 or 5 to Jugendbühlweg.

Jugendgästehaus Würzburg (☎ 425 90; www .djh.de/jh/wuerzburg; Burkarderstrasse 44; dm €18) This hostel looks like a mini-version of the fortress that looms above; take tram No 3 or 5 from the train station.

Pension Spehnkuch (☎ 547 52; www.pension -spehnkuch.de, in German; Röntgenring 7; s/d/tr from €29/52/75) A nice spot near the river and park. Rooms are spotless and the welcome friendly.

Hotel Alter Kranen (☎ 351 80; mail@hotel-alter -kranen.de; Kärrnerpetrolse 11; s/d €60/80) The Alter Kranen offers lovely lodgings overlooking the river and fort. Breakfast is included.

Schloss Steinburg (☎ 970 20; hotel@steinburg.com; Auf dem Steinburg; s/d €80/120) High on a hill overlooking the city, you can peacefully watch the boat traffic on the Main below from one of the turrets in this castle-cum-hotel. If you stay long enough you'll feel like royalty.

Café Klug (Peterstrasse 2; dishes €6) A student café/bar/restaurant with a rock and roll theme.

Bürgerspital (☎ 35 28 80; Theaterstrasse 19; mains €5-18) The atmosphere, food and the local wines are all first class in this former medieval hospice.

Getting There & Away

Würzburg is two hours by frequent RE trains from Frankfurt (€19.20) and one hour from Nuremberg (€14.40). It's a major stop-off for the ICE trains on the Hamburg–Munich line. It is also on the Deutsche-Touring Romantic Road bus route (2½ hours to/from Rothenburg by bus). The main bus station is next to the train station off Röntgenring. Both Frankfurt and Bamberg are about one hour away by car.

BAMBERG

☎ 0951 / pop 70,000

Tucked away from the main routes in northern Bavaria, Bamberg is practically a byword for magnificence – an untouched monument to the Holy Roman Emperor Heinrich II (who conceived it), to its princebishops and clergy, patriciate and townsfolk. It is a fun and beautiful town recognised by Unesco as a World Heritage Site.

The **tourist office** (☎ 87 11 61; www.bamberg .info, in German; Geyerswörthstrasse 3; ☼ 9am-6pm Mon-Fri, to 3pm Sat year-round, 10am-2pm Sun May-Oct) is situated on an island in the Regnitz River.

Sights

Bamberg's main appeal is its fine buildings – their sheer number, their jumble of styles and the ambience this creates. Most attractions are spread either side of the Regnitz River, but the colourful **Altes Rathaus** (Obere Brücke; ☼ 9am-6pm Apr-Sep, 10am-4pm Oct-Mar) is actually precariously perched on its own islet.

The princely and ecclesiastical district is centred on Domplatz, where the Romanesque and Gothic **cathedral** (Domplatz; ⏰ 9am-6pm Apr-Sep, 10am-4pm Oct-Mar), housing the statue of the chivalric king-knight, the *Bamberger Reiter*, is the biggest attraction.

Above Domplatz is the former Benedictine monastery of St Michael, at the top of Michaelsberg. The **Kirche St Michael** (Franziskanergasse 2; ⏰ 9am-6pm) is a must-see for its baroque art and the herbal compendium painted on its ceiling. The garden terraces afford another marvellous overview of the city's splendour.

The **Fränkisches Brauereimuseum** (☎ 530 16; Michaelsberg 10f; adult/concession €2/1.50; ⏰ 1-5pm Wed-Sun Apr-Oct) shows how the monks brewed their robust *Benediktiner Dunkel* beer.

Sleeping & Eating

Campingplatz Insel (☎ 563 20; campinginsel@web .de; Am Campingplatz 1; per person/tent €3.50/6) A well-equipped place in a tranquil spot right on the river. Take bus No 18 to Campingplatz.

Jugendherberge Wolfsschlucht (☎ 560 02; www .djh.de, in German; Oberer Leinritt 70; dm €13.70; closed mid-Dec–mid-Jan) On the river's west bank, take bus No 18 to Rodelbahn, walk northeast to the riverbank, then turn left.

Petrolthof Fässla (☎ 265 16; kasparźschultz@ t-online.de; Hallstadter Strasse 174; s/d €34/52) A drinker's dream – a bed in a brewery. The rooms are large, clean and comfy.

Hotel Graupner (☎ 980 400; www.hotel-graupner .de; Langestrasse 5; s/d with shared bathroom €35/50) The Graupner, which has been around for a hundred years, has individually decorated rooms and an elegant café with seating indoors and out.

Barock Hotel (☎ 540 31; fax 540 21; Vorderer Bach 4; s/ d €57/80) Near the Dom (cathedral), the quaint Barock offers lovely rooms in a quiet spot.

Fränkischer Gästhaus (Obere Sandstrasse 1; mains €5-15) Serves hearty mains and excellent bratwurst on outdoor tables.

Wirsthaus zum Schlenkerla (Dominikanerstrasse 6; mains €7-12) Zum Schlenkerla has been brewing its extraordinary *Rauchbier* since 1678. A menu of Franconian specialities accompanies the beer.

Getting There & Away

There are hourly RE and RB trains to/from both Würzburg (€14) and Nuremberg (€9), taking one hour. Bamberg is also served by ICE trains running between Munich (€45.20, 2½ hours) and Berlin (€68.80, 4½ hours) every two hours.

ROTHENBURG OB DER TAUBER
☎ 09861 / pop 12,000

Not a single modern building is within sight in Rothenburg and it's soon obvious why this charmingly preserved medieval town is continually under siege from tourists. Granted 'free imperial city' status in 1274, it's an enchanting place of twisting cobbled lanes and strikingly pretty architecture enclosed by towered stone walls. The town's museums only open in the afternoon from November to March. There's a **tourist office** (☎ 404 92; www.rothenburg.de; Marktplatz 2; ⏰ 9am-noon, 1-6pm Mon-Fri, 10am-3pm Sat May-Oct; 9am-5pm Mon-Fri, 10am-1pm Sat Nov-Apr).

Sights

The **Rathaus on Markt** was commenced in Gothic style in the 14th century but completed in Renaissance style. The **tower** (admission €1) gives a majestic view over the town and the Tauber Valley. According to legend, the town was saved during the Thirty Years' War when the mayor won a challenge by the Imperial general Tilly and downed more than 3L of wine at a gulp. The **Meistertrunk** scene is re-enacted by the clock figures on the tourist office building (eight times daily in summer).

The **Puppen und Spielzeugmuseum** (Doll & Toy Museum; ☎ 73 30; Hofbronnengasse 13; adult/concession €4/2.50; ⏰ 9.30am-6pm Mar-Dec, 11am-5pm Jan-Feb) is the largest private doll and toy collection in Germany. The **Reichsstadt Museum** (☎ 93 90 43; www.reichsstadtmuseum.rothenburg.de; Klosterhof 5; adult/concession €3/2; ⏰ 10am-5pm Apr-Oct, 1-4pm Nov-Mar), in the former convent, features the superb *Rothenburger Passion* in 12 panels and the Judaica room, with a collection of gravestones with Hebrew inscriptions. Get a gruesome glimpse of the past at the **Kriminalmuseum** (☎ 53 59; www.kriminalmuseum .rothenburg.de; Burggasse 3-5; adult/concession €3.20/1.70; ⏰ 9.30am-6pm Apr-Oct, 2-4pm Nov-Mar), which houses all manner of devices with which to torture and shame medieval miscreants.

Sleeping & Eating

Resist the temptation to try a *Schneeball*, a crumbly ball of bland dough with the taste and consistency of chalk – surely one of Europe's worst 'local specialities'.

Tauber-Romantik (☎ 61 91; fax 868 99; Detwang 39; per person/tent €3.75/4; ⏰ Apr-Nov) This camping option is 1km to 2km north of the town walls at Detwang, west of the road on the river.

Youth Hostel (☎ 941 60; www.jugenherberge.de, in German; Mühlacker 1; dm €18) This hostel is housed in two enormous renovated old buildings in the south of the old town.

Das Lädle (☎ 61 30; www.das-laedle.de, in German; Spitalgasse 18; s/d incl breakfast €22/38) A good budget option, with casual, comfortable rooms in a central location.

Gasthof Am Siebersturm (☎ 33 55; www.sie bersturm.de; Spitalgasse 6; s/d €25/60) Located just outside the southern gate to the city, Am Siebersturm also has a good restaurant that cooks up Franconian specials.

Hotel Garni Hornburg (☎ 84 80; www.hotelhornburg .rothenburg.de; Hornburgweg 28; s/d €49/69) The striking Hornburg, formerly a private villa, has 10 extremely spacious rooms.

Altfrankische Weinstube (☎ 64 04; Klosterhof 7; mains €6-13) Vine covered and cosy, the Altfrankische Weinstube is justifiably popular, with a varied and well-priced menu, and fantastic atmosphere.

NÖRDLINGEN

☎ 09081 / pop 20,000

Nördlingen is encircled by its original 14th-century walls and lies within the basin of the **Ries**, a huge crater created by a meteor more than 15 million years ago. The crater is one of the largest in existence (25km in diameter) and the **Rieskrater Museum** (☎ 273 82 20; Eugene-Shoemaker-Platz 1; adult/concession €3/1.50; ☺ 10am-noon, 1.30-4.30pm Tue-Sun) gives details. For a bird's-eye view of the town, climb the tower of **St Georg Kirche**. You'll find the **tourist office** (☎ 43 80; www.noerdlingen .de, in German; Marktplatz 2) very helpful. The **Youth Hostel** (☎ 27 18 16; Kaiserwiese 1; dm €11.25) is a signposted 10-minute walk from the centre. **Altreuter Garni** (☎ 43 19; fax 97 97; Markt 11; s/d €38/52) has simple, pleasant rooms.

NUREMBERG

☎ 0911 / pop 500,000

Nuremberg's relatively oversized historical old town – imposing and picturesque – attests to the fact that it is the largest city of the Franconia region of northern Bavaria. It's also why tourists flock here, especially during its world-famous Christmas market. Nuremberg played a major role during the Nazi years, as documented in Leni Riefenstahl's film *Triumph of Will* and during the war crimes trials afterwards. The city was rebuilt after Allied bombs reduced it to rubble on 2 January 1945.

Orientation

The main train station is just outside the city walls of the old town. The main artery, the mostly pedestrian Königsstrasse, takes you through the old town and its major squares.

Information

Both tourist offices sell the two-day Nuernberg Card (€18) which provides free public transport and entry to all museums and attractions, including those in nearby Fürth.

Flat-S (☎ 815 75 21; 2nd fl, middle hall, Hauptbahnhof; ☺ 24hr; per hr €4) Internet access available inside the train station.

Netzkultur (☎ 211 07 82; 3rd fl, Maximum Bldg, Färberstrasse 11; 9-1am Mon-Sat, 1.30pm-1am Sun; Internet per hr €3.50)

Post office (Bahnhofplatz 1)

Reisebank (Hauptbahnhof) Operates inside the station.

Schnell und Sauber Laundry (☎ 180 9400; Sulzbacher Strasse 86; €4 per load; ☺ 6am-midnight)

Tourist office (www.tourismus.nuernberg.de) Main office (☎ 233 61 32; Königsstrasse 93; ☺ 9am-7pm Mon-Sat); Branch office (☎ 233 61 35; Hauptmarkt 18; ☺ 9am-6pm Mon-Sat, 10am-4pm Sun May-Sep)

Sights

The spectacular **Germanisches Nationalmuseum** (☎ 133 10; www.gnm.de, in German; Kartäusergasse 1; adult/concession €4/3, free 6-9pm Wed; ☺ 10am-5pm Tue-Sun, 10am-9pm Wed) is the most important general museum of German culture. It displays works by German painters and sculptors, an archaeological collection, arms and armour, musical and scientific instruments and toys. Close by, the sleek and harmonious **Neues Museum** (☎ 24 02 00; Luitpoldstrasse 5; adult/concession €3.50/2.50; ☺ 10am-8pm Tue-Fri, to 6pm Sat & Sun) contains a superb collection of contemporary art and design.

The scenic **Altstadt** is easily covered on foot. On Lorenzer Platz there's the **St Lorenz-kirche**, noted for the 15th-century tabernacle that climbs like a vine up a pillar to the vaulted ceiling.

To the north is the bustling **Hauptmarkt**, where the most famous Christkindlesmarkt in Germany is held from the Friday before Advent to Christmas Eve. The church here is the ornate **Pfarrkirche Unsere Liebe Frau**; the clock's figures go strolling at noon. Near the Rathaus is **St Sebalduskirche**, Nuremberg's oldest church (dating from the 13th century), with the shrine of St Sebaldus.

Climb up Burgstrasse to the enormous **Kaiserburg complex** (☎ 22 57 26; Burg 13; adult/concession €5/4; ☼ 9am-6pm Apr-Sep, 10am-4pm Oct-Mar) for good views of the city. The walls spread west to the tunnel-gate of **Tiergärtnertor**, where you can stroll behind the castle to the gardens. Nearby is the renovated **Albrecht-Dürer-Haus** (☎ 231 25 68; Albrecht-Dürer-Strasse 39; adult/concession €5/2.50; ☼ 10am-5pm Tue-Sun, to 8pm Thu), where Dürer, Germany's renowned Renaissance draughtsman, lived from 1509 to 1528.

Nuremberg's role during the Third Reich is well known. The Nazis chose this city as their propaganda centre and for mass rallies, which were held at **Luitpoldhain**, a (never completed) sports complex of megalomaniac proportions. After the war, the Allies deliberately chose Nuremberg as the site for the trials of Nazi war criminals. Not to be missed is the **Dokumentationzentrum** (☎ 231 56 66; www.museen.nuernberg.de; Bayernstrasse 110; adult/concession €5/2.50; ☼ 9am-6pm Mon-Fri, 10am-6pm Sat & Sun) in the north wing of the massive Congress Hall. The museum houses a permanent exhibition, *Fascination and Terror*, which features mesmerizing film and audio footage dealing with the causes, relationships and consequences of the Nazi ideology, and its links with Nuremberg. Take tram No 9 or No 6 to Doku-Zentrum.

Sleeping

Lette'm Sleep (☎ 99 28 128; www.backpackers.de; Frauentormauer 42; dm/s/d €15/30/48) Dorms are available as well as quirky private rooms designed with a flair not often seen in hostels. Tea, coffee, free Internet access and personal attention add to the positive vibe.

Jugendherberge Nürnberg (☎ 230 93 60; www.djh.de; Burg 2; dm with linen €19) This hostel has more character than most.

Hotel Pension Vater Jahn-Parma (☎ 44 45 07; fax 43 15 236; Jahnstrasse 13; s/d €20/31) No-frills and friendly, the Vater Jahn isn't in the centre but offers clean rooms with shared facilities.

Pension Zum Schwänlein (☎ 22 51 62; fax 241 90 08; Hintere Sterngasse 11; s/d €26/42) Conveniently located in the Altstadt a short walk from the train station, Zum Schwänlein has small, comfy rooms with shared facilities. There's a pub attached.

Pension Sonne (☎ 0175 982 37 37; Königstrasse 45; s/d incl breakfast €30/60) It's a steep climb up three flights of stairs to the cosy and bright rooms with high ceilings.

Hotel Agneshof (☎ 21 44 40; info@agneshof-nuernberg.de; Agnesgasse 10; s/d €90/105) In the middle of Nuremberg's well-preserved historic centre, the Agneshof has welcoming rooms with an extra touch of comfort and wireless Internet access. The small sauna is a plus.

Knaus-Campingpark 'Am Dutzendteich' (☎ 981 27 17; Hans-Kalb-Strasse 56; site plus one person/each additional person €8/5) Southeast of the centre (U1 to Messezentrum), this camping ground is open year-round.

Eating

Don't leave Nuremberg without trying its famous bratwurst.

Landbierparadies (☎ 28 78 673; Rothenburgerstrasse 26; meals €6) Inexpensive Franconian food only a 15-minute walk west of the train station. Big portioned meals and 16 kinds of locally brewed beers make for a good combination.

Bratwursthäusle (☎ 22 76 95; Rathausplatz 2; 10 for €8.30) Here the bratwurst are flamegrilled and scrumptious, and served with *Meerettich* (horseradish) and *Kartoffelsalat* (potato salad).

Kaiserburg (☎ 22 12 16; Obere Krämerspetrolse 20; mains €8-17) For medieval ambience and a Franconian/international menu, try the Kaiserburg.

Also recommended are **Barfüber** (☎ 204 242; Hallplatz 2; mains €7-13) and for Japanese fare, **Sushi Glas** (☎ 205 99 01; www.sushi-glas.de; Kornmarkt 5; lunch special €9).

Getting There & Around

Nuremberg is well-connected by public transport. IC trains run hourly to/from Frankfurt-am-Main (€36, 2¼ hours) and Munich (€38, 1½ hours). IR trains run every two hours to Stuttgart (€28, two hours) and ICE trains every two hours to Berlin Ostbahnhof (€78.20, five hours). Several daily EC trains travel to Vienna (seven hours) and Prague (5½ hours). Buses to regional destinations leave from the station just east of the main train station.

Tickets on the bus, tram and U-Bahn system cost €1.35/1.75 for each short/long ride in the central zone. A day pass is €3.50.

REGENSBURG

☎ 0941 / pop 145,000

On the Danube River, Regensburg has relics of all periods, yet lacks the packaged feel of some other German cities. It escaped the carpet bombing, and here, as nowhere else in Germany, you enter the misty ages between the Roman and the Carolingian, albeit with a healthy dose of young students thrown in the mix.

From the main train station, you walk up Maximillianstrasse for 10 minutes to reach the centre.

Information

City Point (☎ 09 41; Wahlenstrasse; ⏰ 9am-10.30pm; Internet per hr €3.50)

Surf City (☎ 69 85 857; Speicherpetrolse 1; ⏰ 10am-1am Mon-Sat, 2pm-1am Sun; Internet per hr €3.50)

Tourist office (☎ 507 44 10; www.regensburg.de; Altes Rathaus; ⏰ 9.15am-6pm Mon-Fri, to 4pm Sat & Sun)

Sights

Dominating the skyline are the twin spires of the Gothic **Dom St Peter** (☎ 597 10 02; Domplatz; admission free; tours in German adult/concession €2.50/1.50; ⏰ tours 10am, 11am, 2pm Mon-Fri & noon, 2pm Sun May-Nov; 11am Mon-Fri & noon Sun Dec-Apr) built during the 14th and 15th centuries from unusual green limestone.

The **Altes Rathaus** (Rathausplatz 1; guided tours €2.50; ⏰ tours 9.30-11.30am & 2-4pm Mon-Sat, 10am-noon Sun) was progressively extended from medieval to baroque times and remained the seat of the Reichstag for almost 150 years. Guided tours in English are available through the tourist office.

The **Roman wall**, with its **Porta Praetoria** arch, follows Unter den Schwibbögen onto Dr-Martin-Luther-Strasse.

Lavish **Schloss Thurn und Taxis** (☎ 504 81 33; Emmeramsplatz 6; adult/concession €10/8.50; ⏰ 11am-5pm Mon-Fri, 10am-5pm Sat & Sun) is near the train station and is divided into three separate sections: the castle proper (Schloss), the monastery (Kreuzgang) and the royal stables (Marstall).

Sleeping & Eating

Azur-Camping (☎ 27 00 25; fax 29 94 32; Weinweg 40; per person/site €4.50/5.50) Bus No 6 from the train station goes to the entrance.

DJH Hostel (☎ 574 02; www.djh.de; Wöhrdstrasse 60; dm €16) Regensburg's modernised hostel is in a beautiful old building on Unterer Wöhrd island about a 10-minute walk north of the Altstadt. Take bus No 3 from Albertstrasse to Eisstadion.

Spitalgarten Hotel (☎ 847 74; www.spitalgarten.de, in German; St Katharinenplatz 1; s/d €23/46) Across the river is the Spitalgarten, with basic rooms in a large imposing building. A beer garden is attached.

Hotel Am Peterstor (☎ 545 45; www.hotel-am-peterstor.de; Fröliche-Türkenstrasse 12; s/d €35/40) A good value place, with clean, basic rooms.

Hotel Weidenhof (☎ 530 31; www.hotel-weidenhof.de; Maximilianstrasse 23; s/d €50/72) A well-located friendly place to sleep.

Orphée (☎ 59 60 20; www.hotel-orphee.de; Wahlenstrasse 1; s/d €69/80) Each of the 15 rooms is unique – one has a four-poster bed and another a great balcony – and there's a common room with a large terrace. The reception is in the restaurant of the same name around the corner.

Carlitos (Am Wiedfang 2) On the Danube next to the Steinerne bridge, Carlitos is a lively Latin bar.

Hemingway's (☎ 56 15 06; Obere Bachgasse 5) A trendy Art Deco–style bar with lots of photos of the bar's namesake.

Neue Filmbüche (☎ 5 70 37; Bismarckplatz 9) Students and families alike come to the Filmbüche for its great terrace and theatrical décor.

Historische Wurstküche (☎ 5 90 98; Thundorferstrasse 3; dishes €6) This is the best spot for a snack of bratwurst on the banks of the Danube.

Getting There & Away

Regensburg is on the train line between Nuremberg (€19, one hour) and Austria, and there are EC/IC trains in both directions every two hours, as well as RB/RE trains to Munich (€19.20, 1½ hours). EC/IC services run every two hours to Passau (€20.20, one hour). Regensburg is a major stop on the Danube bike route. If you're driving it's around an hour to both Munich and Nuremberg.

FÜSSEN

☎ 08362 / pop 14,000

Just short of the Austrian border and the foothills of the Alps, Füssen has a monastery, a castle and splendid baroque architecture, but it is primarily visited for the two castles in nearby Schwangau associated with King Ludwig II. There's a **tourist office**

(☎ 938 50; www.fuessen.de; Kaiser-Maximillian-Platz 1; ◷ 9am-5pm Mon-Fri, 10am-1pm Sat).

Neuschwanstein & Hohenschwangau Castles

The castles provide a fascinating glimpse into the romantic king's state of mind (or lack thereof) and well-developed ego. **Hohenschwangau** (☎ 811 27; info@ticket-center-hohen schwangau.de; adult/concession €9/8, combination €17/15; ◷ 9am-6pm mid-Apr–mid-Oct, 10am-4pm mid-Oct–mid-Apr) is where Ludwig lived as a child, but more interesting is the adjacent **Neuschwanstein** (☎ 810 35; ◷ 9am-6pm mid-Apr–mid-Oct, 10am-4pm mid-Oct–mid-Apr), his own creation (albeit with the help of a theatrical designer). Although it was unfinished when he died in 1886, there is plenty of evidence of Ludwig's twin obsessions: swans and Wagnerian operas. The sugary pastiche of architectural styles, alternatively overwhelmingly beautiful and just a little-too-much, reputedly inspired Disney's Fantasyland castle. To get to the top from the ticket centre you can walk (30 minutes), take a bus (€2.60) or horse and buggy carriage (€7.50). There's a great view of Neuschwanstein from the Marienbrücke (bridge) over a waterfall and gorge just above the castle. From here you can hike the Tegelberg for even better vistas.

Take the bus from Füssen train station (€2.80 return), share a **taxi** (☎ 77 00; €8.50) or walk the 5km. The only way to enter the castles is with a 35-minute guided tour, which can be purchased from the ticket centre at Alpseestrasse 12, near Hohenschwangau. Go early to avoid the massive crowds.

Sleeping & Eating

A pavillion near the tourist office has a computerised list of vacant rooms in town; most of the cheapest rooms, at around €12 per person, are located in private homes just a few minutes from the Altstadt. Nearby Bad Faulenbach, Hopfen Am See and Weissensee also have plenty of affordable and pleasant hotels and *pensions*.

DJH Hostel (☎ 77 54; www.djh.de; Mariahilferstrasse 5; dm €15) It gets a bit loud with groups in residence otherwise it's quiet and only a signposted 10-minute walk from the train station.

Hotel Filser (☎ 912 50; Saulingerstrasse 3; s/d €49/86) This a quiet, comfortable place with clean rooms, a good restaurant downstairs

(mains €7 to €15) and a health spa in the basement.

Hotel Sonne (☎ 90 80; www.hotel-sonne.de; Reichenstrasse 37; s/d €59/83) Just across from the tourist office, the pastel-coloured Sonne is hard to miss.

Try the **Aquila Restaurant** (Brotmarkt 9; lunch special €5) and **Römerkeller** (Drehergasse 48; dishes €6) for top cuisine.

BAVARIAN ALPS

While not quite as high as their sister summits further south in Austria, the Bavarian Alps (Bayerische Alpen) rise so abruptly from the rolling hills of southern Bavaria that their appearance seems all the more dramatic. Stretching westward from Germany's southeastern corner to the Allgäu region near Lake Constance, the Alps take in most of the mountainous country fringing the southern border with Austria.

Activities

The Bavarian Alps are extraordinarily well organised for outdoor pursuits, with skiing, snowboarding and hiking being the most popular. The ski season usually runs from mid-December to April. Ski gear is available for hire in all the resorts, with the lowest daily/weekly rates including skis, boots and stocks at around €12/48 (downhill), €7/32 (cross-country) and €16/57 (snowboard). Five-day skiing courses start at around €100.

During the warmer months, the activities include hiking, canoeing, rafting, biking and paragliding.

Getting There & Around

While the public transport network is very good, the mountain geography means there are few direct routes between main centres; sometimes a short cut via Austria is quicker (such as between Füssen and Oberstdorf). Road rather than rail routes are often more practical. For those driving, the German Alpine Rd (Deutsche Alpenstrasse) is a scenic way to go, though obviously much slower than the autobahns and highways that fan out across southern Bavaria.

Regional RVO (☎ 089-55 16 40) bus passes giving free travel on the network between Füssen, Garmisch and Mittenwald are excellent value; the day pass is €7 and a pass for five days' travel to be used any time within one month costs €22.50.

BERCHTESGADEN

☎ 08652 / pop 8200

Berchtesgaden is perhaps the most romantically scenic place in the Bavarian Alps. To reach the centre from the train station, cross the footbridge and walk up Bahnhofstrasse. The helpful **tourist office** (☎ 96 70; www.berchtes gaden.de, in German; Königsseer Strasse 2; ⊙ 8am-6pm Mon-Fri, to 5pm Sat, 9am-3pm Sun mid-Jun–Sep) is just across the river from the train station.

Sights

A tour of the **Salzbergwerk** (☎ 600 220; Berg werkstrasse 83; adult/concession €12.50/6.80; ⊙ 9am-5pm May–mid-Oct; 12.30-3.30pm Mon-Sat mid-Oct–Apr) combines history with a carnival (rides and games to amuse you). Visitors descend into the salt mine for a 1½-hour tour.

Nearby **Obersalzberg** is an innocent-looking place with a creepy legacy as the second seat of government for the Third Reich. Hitler, Himmler, Goebbels and the rest of the Nazi hierarchy all maintained homes here. The **Dokumentation Obersalzberg Museum** (☎ 94 79 60; www.obersalzberg.de; Salzbergstrasse 41; adult/concession €2.50/1.50; ⊙ 9am-5pm Tue-Sun mid-May–mid-Nov, 10am-3pm Tue-Sun mid-Nov–mid-May) documents their time in the area, as well as the horrors their policies produced, through photos, audio and film. Ask for the free brochure in English (the explanatory captions and audio are in German). The admission fee also gets you into the eerie **Hitler's bunker**. Catch bus No 9538 (€3.70 return) from the Nazi-constructed Berchtesgaden train station to Obersalzberg-Hintereck. Take the first major street on the right after alighting from the bus and follow it for five minutes.

Kehlstein (☎ 29 69; admission €12; buses run 7.40am-4.25pm; ⊙ May-Oct) is a spectacular meeting house built for, but seldom used by, Hitler. Despite its reputation as the 'Eagle's Nest', it's a popular destination because of the stunning views. Entry includes transport on special buses which link the summit with Obersalzberg-Hintereck, as well as the 120m lift through solid rock to the peak. Or you can make the steep ascent or descent on foot in two to three hours.

The best way to see Obersalzberg and Kehlstein is with **Eagle's Nest Tours** (☎ 649 71; www.eagles-nest-tours.com; €36), which has English-language tours lasting four hours and covering the entire history of the area during WWII.

You can forget the horrors of war at the **Königssee**, a beautiful alpine lake situated 5km south of Berchtesgaden (and linked by hourly buses in summer). There are frequent boat tours across the lake to the quaint chapel at St Bartholomä (€10.50), or all the way to Obersee (€13.50).

The wilds of Berchtesgaden National Park offer some of the best **hiking** in Germany. A good introduction to the area is a 2km path up from St Bartholomä beside the Königssee to the Watzmann-Ostwand, a massive 2000m-high rock face where scores of ambitious mountaineers have died.

Berchtesgaden has five major **skiing** resorts, and you can buy five-day lift passes that cover them all (€98). Rossfeld is the cheapest for day passes (€13), while Götschen, with a permanent half-pipe, is the destination for snowboarders (€20 per day).

Sleeping & Eating

Youth Hostel (☎ 943 70; www.djh.de; Gebirgsjägerstrasse 52; dm €13.10) Closed in November and December. Take bus No 9539 to Jugendherberge.

Hotel Watzmann (☎ 20 55; fax 51 74; Franziskan erplatz 2; s/d €28/50) Decorated in traditional upper-Bavarian style, the Watzmann has comfortable rooms and an excellent outdoor terrace with top food (mains €9 to €11).

Hotel Bavaria (☎ 966 10; Sunklergaesschen 11; s/d €46/80) Ask for a room with a balcony at the charming Bavaria, just 400m from both the bus and train station. A sauna is there for your pleasure after a long day of hiking.

Hotel Floriani (☎ 660 11; www.hotel-floriani .de; Königsseer Strasse 37; s/d €33/56) The cheerful rooms all have spectacular vistas.

Alt Berchtesgaden (☎ 45 19; Bahnhofstrasse 3; schnitzel €4.99) Choose from 15 varieties of schnitzel.

Of the five camping grounds around Berchtesgaden, the nicest are at Königssee:

Grafenlehen (☎ 41 40; www.camping-grafenlehen .de; per person/site €4.50/6)

Mühlleiten (☎ 45 84; www.camping-muehlleiten .de; per person/site €4.35/5.11)

Getting There & Away

Both RB and RE trains run hourly to Munich and cost €25.

GARMISCH-PARTENKIRCHEN

☎ 08821 / pop 27,000

The towns of Garmisch and Partenkirchen were merged by Hitler for the 1936 Winter Olympics. Munich residents' favourite getaway spot, this often-snooty, year-round resort is also a big draw for skiers, snowboarders, hikers and mountaineers.

Sights & Activities

The huge **ski stadium** outside town hosted the Olympics. From the pedestrian Am Kurpark, walk up Klammstrasse, cross the tracks and veer left on the first path to reach the stadium and enjoy the spectacular views. The **tourist office** (☎ 18 07 00; tourist-info@garmisch-partenkirchen.de; Richard Strauss Platz 2; � 8am-6pm Mon-Sat, 10am-noon Sun) is in the centre of town.

An excellent short hike from Garmisch is to the **Partnachklamm gorge**, via a winding path above a stream and underneath the waterfalls. You take the Graseck cable car and follow the signs.

An excursion to the **Zugspitze** summit, Germany's highest peak (2963m), is a popular outing from Garmisch. There are various ways up, including a return trip by rack-railway (just west of the main train station), summit cable car or Eibsee cable car for €43, or you can scale it in two days. For detailed information concerning guided hiking or mountaineering courses, check with **Bergsteigerschule Zugspitze** (☎ 589 99; Am Gudiberg 7, Garmisch).

Garmisch is bounded by three separate ski areas – **Zugspitze plateau** (the highest), **Alpspitze/Hausberg** (the largest), **Eckbauer** (the cheapest). Day ski passes range from €16 for Eckbauer to €34 for Zugspitze. The Happy Ski Card covers all four areas and is valid for a minimum of three days (€77). A web of cross-country ski trails runs along the main valleys.

Flori Wörndle (☎ 583 00) has ski-hire outlets at the Alpspitze and Hausbergbahn lifts. For detailed skiing information and instruction (downhill), contact the **Skischule Garmisch-Partenkirchen** (☎ 49 31; Am Hausberg 4), or (cross-country) the **Skilanglaufschule** (☎ 15 16; Olympia-Skistadion).

Sleeping & Eating

Zugspitze (☎ 31 80; fax 94 75 94; Griesener Strasse 4, Grainau; per person/tent/vehicle €5.50/3.50/3.50) To get to this camping ground along Hwy B24, take the blue-and-white bus (outside the train station and left across the street) towards Eibsee.

DJH Hostel (☎ 29 80; www.djh.de; Jochstrasse 10; dm €15.10) Situated in the suburb of Burgrain, this hostel is closed from mid-November to Christmas. From the train station take bus No 3 or 4 to the Burgrain stop.

Gästehaus Becherer (☎ 547 57; www.gaestehaus -becherer.de, in German; Höllentalstrasse 4; s/d €23/46) The Becherer treats you to a warm welcome and spotless comfort.

Hotel Schell (☎ 95 750; www.hotel-schell.de, in German; Partnachauenstrasse 3; s/d €26/50) In a lovely house a short walk from the train station, the Schell has well-maintained snug rooms.

Hotel Zugspitze (☎ 90 10; www.hotel-zugspitze .de; Klammstrasse 19; s from €72) Cosy timber-lined rooms and an elegant indoor pool make you feel at home – a very nice home.

Café Mukkefuck (☎ 73 440; Zugspitzstrasse 3; meals €6-12) If you can get past the double-take name, an outdoor courtyard and a tasty array of light meals await.

St Martin Am Grasberg (☎ 49 70; Am Grasberg; mains €7-15) An eatery perched an hour's climb in the mountains, northwest of the centre, Am Grasberg boasts spectacular views.

Getting There & Away

Garmisch is serviced from Munich by hourly trains (€14, 1½ hours). Trains from Garmisch to Innsbruck (1½ hours) pass through Mittenwald (€3.10, 20 minutes). RVO bus No 1084, from in front of the train station, links Garmisch with Füssen (€7, two hours) four times daily via Oberammergau.

OBERSTDORF

☎ 08322 / pop 10,400

Over in the western part of the Bavarian Alps, Oberstdorf is a car-free resort. Like Garmisch, it is surrounded by towering peaks and offers superb hiking.

There's a main **tourist office** (☎ 70 00; www .oberstdorf.de; Marktplatz 7; � 8.30am-6pm Mon-Fri, 9.30am-noon Sat). There's another office near the train station (☎ 70 02 17; Bahnhofplatz 3).

For an exhilarating day **hike**, ride the Nebelhorn cable car to the upper station then walk down via the Gaisalpseen, two lovely alpine lakes. In-the-know skiers value Oberstdorf for its friendliness, its lower prices and the generally uncrowded slopes.

The village is surrounded by several ski areas: the **Nebelhorn, Fellhorn/Kanzelwand** and **Söllereck**. Combined daily/weekly ski passes that include all three areas (plus the adjoining Kleinwalsertal lifts on the Austrian side) cost €30/160. For ski hire and tuition, try Neue Skischule, which has convenient outlets at the valley stations of the **Nebelhorn** (☎ 27 37) and **Söllereck** (☎ 51 54) lifts.

There's a **camping ground** (☎ 65 25; www .camping-oberstdorf.de; Rubingerstrasse 16; per tent €2.60-4.60, per person €4.60-5.10, per car €2.60; ☼ year-round) 2km north of the station beside the train line, and a **youth hostel** (☎ 22 25; www.djh.de; Kornau 8; dm €14.10) on the outskirts of town near the Söllereck chairlift – take the Kleinwalsertal bus to the Reute stop.

Gästhaus Gaymann (☎ 964 00; www.oberstdorf .com/gaesthaus/gaymann.htm, in German; Am Stiegle 5; s/d €32/60) is a small welcoming home with pleasant rooms. Or head to the **Hotel Traube** (☎ 809 940; www.hotel-traube.de, in German; Hauptstrasse 6; s/d €57/136) for delightful rooms with four-poster beds and a large Bavarian-style restaurant downstairs (mains €10 to €20).

Paulaner Bräu (☎ 96 760; Kirchstrasse 1; meals €7.50) is a simple, cheap Bavarian restaurant.

There are hourly RB trains to/from Immenstadt where you connect to Lindau (€13.50, two hours) and Munich (€24, 2½ hours; IR train). Direct RE trains to/from Ulm run hourly (€17.80, 1¾ hours). On weekdays, several bus connections to Füssen go via Pfronten (€8.10).

BADEN-WÜRTTEMBERG

Baden-Württemberg is deservedly one of Germany's main tourist regions. With recreational centres such as the Black Forest and Lake Constance, medieval towns like Heidelberg and the health spa of Baden-Baden, it's one of the most varied parts of Germany.

The prosperous modern state of Baden-Württemberg was created in 1951 out of three smaller regions: Baden, Württemberg and Hohenzollern. Baden was first unified and made a grand duchy by Napoleon, who was also responsible for making Württemberg a kingdom in 1806. Both areas, in conjunction with Bavaria and 16 other states, formed the Confederation of the Rhine under French protection. Baden and Württemberg both sided with Austria against Prussia in 1866,

but were ultimately drafted into the German Empire in 1871.

STUTTGART
☎ 0711 / pop 590,000

Hemmed in by vine-covered hills and full of greenery, residents of prosperous Stuttgart enjoy a high quality of life. Nevertheless it is Baden-Württemberg's state capital and the hub of its industries. At the forefront of Germany's economic recovery from the ravages of WWII, Stuttgart started life less auspiciously in AD 950 as a horse stud farm. About 80% of the city centre was destroyed in the war, but there are still some fine historical buildings left.

Information
Level One Cyber Bar (☎ 120 46 65; Königstrasse 22; ☼ noon-midnight; Internet per 30min €3)
Post office (Bolzstrasse 3)
Reisebank (Hauptbahnhof) At the main train station
Tourist office (☎ 22 280; www.stuttgart-tourist.de; Königstrasse 1a; ☼ 9.30am-8.30pm Mon-Fri, 9.30am-6pm Sat, 10.30am-6pm Sun) Opposite the main train station on the main pedestrian strip, the office sells the three-day StuttCard plus (€17), which allows free public transport and free entry to some museums.
Waschsalon (Hohenheimer Strasse 33) For your laundry needs.

Sights
The tower at the main train station sports the three-pointed star of the Mercedes-Benz. It's also an excellent vantage point for the sprawling city and surrounding hills, and is reached via a **lift** (free; ☼ 10am-10pm Tue-Sun).

Stretching southwest from the Neckar River to the city centre is the **Schlossgarten**, an extensive strip of parkland divided into three sections (Unterer, Mittlerer and Oberer), complete with ponds, swans, street entertainers and modern sculptures. At their northern edge the gardens take in the **Wilhelma zoo & botanical gardens** (☎ 540 20; Neckarstrasse; adult/concession €9/4.50; ☼ 8.15am-6pm May-Aug, to 5.30pm Apr & Sep, to 5pm Mar & Oct, to 4pm Nov-Feb). At the gardens' southern end they encompass the sprawling baroque **Neues Schloss** (Schlossplatz) and the Renaissance **Altes Schloss**, which houses a **regional museum** (☎ 279 34 00; Schillerplatz 6; adult/concession €2.60/1.50; ☼ 10am-5pm Wed-Sun, to 1pm Tue).

Next to the Altes Schloss is the city's oldest square, Schillerplatz, with its monument

STUTTGART

| | 0 | 500 m |
| 0 | 0.3 miles |

INFORMATION		Neues Schloss................................**16** C5	Cortijo.............................**30** B6
Das Bistro..**1** C6	Rathaus.............................**17** B6	Iden..................................**31** B6
i-Punkt Tourist Office....................**2** C4	Staatsgalerie.....................**18** D4	Markthalle.......................**32** B5
Internet Cafe...................................**3** B4	Stadtbücherei (City Library)...**19** C5	Mensa..............................**33** A4
Katharinen Hospital......................**4** A4	Stiftskirche........................**20** B5	Weistube Zur Kiste.........**34** C6
Level One Cyber Bar.....................**5** B4		
Post Office......................................**6** B4	**SLEEPING** (p475)	**DRINKING** (pp475–6)
Waschsalon.....................................**7** D6	Der Zauberlehrling..........**21** C6	Beer Garden....................**35** C3
	DJH Hostel........................**22** D4	Biddy Earlys....................**36** A6
SIGHTS & ACTIVITIES (pp473–5)	Hotel Espenlaube............**23** D6	High Bar...........................**37** B6
Alexander Calder's Mobile..........**8** B5	Hotel Unger.....................**24** B4	Palast der Republik.........**38** B4
Altes Schloss...................................**9** B5	Museumstube...................**25** A5	Tea Room.........................**39** A5
Börse (Stock Exchange)...............**10** B5		
Friedrich Schiller Statue...............**11** B5	**EATING** (p475)	**ENTERTAINMENT** (p476)
Hans im Glück Statue...................**12** B6	Alte Kanzlei......................**26** B5	Staatstheater...................**40** C4
Haus der Geschichte....................**13** C5	Bovie................................**27** C6	
Königsbau.....................................**14** C4	Brunnenwirt.....................**28** B6	**TRANSPORT** (p476)
Kunstverein (Municipal Art Gallery)..**15** B4	Calwer-Eck-Bräu..............**29** A5	Bus Station......................**41** C3

to the poet **Schiller**, and the 12th-century **Stiftskirche** (Stiftstrasse 12; 9am-5.30pm Mon-Wed, Fri & Sun, noon-5.30pm Thu). Adjoining the park you'll find the **Staatsgalerie** (212 40 50; Konrad-Adenauer-Strasse 30; adult/concession €4.50/2.50; 10am-6pm daily, to 9pm Thu), which houses an excellent collection from the Middle Ages to the present.

Next door there's the **Haus der Geschichte** (House of History; 212 39 50; Urbansplatz 2; admission €3). This is an eye-catching postmodern museum which covers the past 200 years of the Baden-Württemburg area in film, photography, documents and multimedia.

MOTOR MUSEUMS

The motor car was first developed by Gottlieb Daimler and Carl Benz at the end of the 19th century. The impressive **Mercedes-Benz Museum** (172 25 78; Mercedesstrasse 137; admission free; 9am-5pm Tue-Sun) is in the suburb of Bad-Cannstatt; take S-Bahn No 1 to Neckarstadion. Mercedes-Benz also runs free weekday tours of its Sindelfingen plant, but you must reserve a spot in advance (07031 907 04 03; children under 6 not allowed). For even faster cars, cruise over to the **Porsche Museum** (911 56 85; Porscheplatz 1; admission free; 9am-4pm Mon-Fri, to 5pm Sat & Sun); take S-Bahn No 6 to Neuwirtshaus, north of the city. Sadly, neither place offers free samples.

Sleeping

Campingplatz Stuttgart (55 66 96; info@camping platz-stuttgart.de; Mercedesstrasse 40; per person/site €4.60/4.10) Situated beside the river and 500m from the Bad Cannstatt S-Bahn station.

DJH Hostel (24 15 83; www.djh.de; Haussmannstrasse 27; dm juniors/seniors €14.30/19) It's a steep climb to this hostel, which is a signposted 15-minute walk from the train station.

Museumstube (29 68 10; www.museumstube.de; Hospitalstrasse 9; s/d €35/55) The rooms are pretty much no-frills at the Museumstube but it's only a short walk to several nearby bars and clubs.

Hotel Espenlaube (22 28 233; www.stuttgart -tourist.de, in German; Charlottenstrasse 27; s/d €30/40) Take S-Bahn No 5, 6 or 7 from the train station to reach this hotel.

Pension am Heusteig (23 93 00; www.central -classic.de, in German; Heusteigstrasse 30; s/d €50/67) Only a few minutes southeast of the city centre, rooms here are comfortable despite the out-of-place wicker.

Hotel Unger (209 90; www.hotel-unger.de, in German; Kronenstrasse 17; s/d €75/100) A step up in quality, the Unger has all the conveniences you'd expect.

Der Zauberlehrling (237 77 70; www.zauberlehr ling .de; Rosenstrasse 38; s/d €100/160) This innovative place has nine distinctly different thematic rooms that marry contemporary design with tasteful old-fashioned touches.

Eating

Stuttgart is a great place to sample Swabian specialities such as *Spätzle* (home-made noodles) and *Maultaschen* (similar to ravioli).

Markthalle (Dorotheenstrasse 4; 7am-6.30pm Mon-Fri, to 4pm Sat) An excellent Art Nouveau–style market that's jam-packed with fresh fare.

Mensa (Holzgartenstrasse 11; dishes €2.50) Fill up at the university eatery which has a downstairs cafeteria for the uneducated masses.

Iden (235 989; Eberhardtsrasse 1; dishes €1.50-2.50) Vegetarians (and those who have overdosed on German sausages) should try Iden, which serves cheap, self-serve salad (€1.50), 100g of vegetarian lasagne (€1.50) and soup (€2.50).

Alte Kanzlei (29 44 57; Schillerplatz 5a; dishes €6-17) Excellent for a sunny lunch, with pastas, wraps and salads.

Weinstube Zur Kiste (24 40 02; Kanalstrasse 2; mains €8-17) Generations of Stuttgarters have patronised this wine tavern in the Bohnenviertel (Bean Quarter), but the delicious menu is still fresh.

Calwer-Eck-Bräu (22 24 94 40; www.calwereck .de, in German; Calwerstrasse 31; mains €9-12) You can't beat a restaurant that brews its own beer, and the kitchen serves up top-notch regional fare.

Bovie (23 37 78; Eslinger Strasse 8; dishes €9-16) Offers an international selection with Swabian influences.

Drinking & Entertainment

Though in German, *Lift Stuttgart*, a comprehensive guide to local entertainment and events (€1) is useful.

There are several funky drinking holes around Hans-im-Glück-Platz, a small square that's often packed with party-goers.

There's a **beer garden** (226 12 74; Canstatterstr 18) in the Mittlerer Schlossgarten northeast of the main train station, with beautiful views over the city.

Tea Room (Theodor-Heussstrasse 4) Good cocktails and a DJ keep a hip crowd at the Tea Room till late.

Bar Code (☎ 88 78 104; Theodore-Heuss-Strasse 30) A cool modern bar with a young crowd.

Biddy Early's (☎ 615 98 53; www.biddyearlys.com; Marienstrasse 28) This Irish pub has live music four nights a week and karaoke every Wednesday.

Palast der Republik (☎ 22 64 887; Friedrichstrasse 27) A tiny bar that pulls a huge crowd of laid-back drinkers.

Staatstheater (☎ 20 20 90; Oberer Schlossgarten 6) Home of the famous Stuttgart Ballet, this theatre holds regular symphony, ballet and opera performances.

Getting There & Around

Stuttgart's international airport is south of the city and is served by S2 and S3 trains (30 minutes from the main train station). There are frequent train departures for all major German and many international cities. ICE trains run to Frankfurt (€45, 1½ hours), Berlin (€109, 5½ hours) and Munich (€44, two hours). Regional and long-distance buses leave from the station next to the main train station.

One-way fares on Stuttgart's public transport network are €1.10/5.30 for short/long trips. A four-ride strip ticket costs €5.80 and a central zone day pass is €4.70.

AROUND STUTTGART
Tübingen

☎ 07071 / pop 80,000

This gentle, picturesque university town is a perfect place to spend a day wandering winding alleys of half-timbered houses and old stone walls, and taking a leisurely boat ride down the Neckar River. On **Marktplatz**, the centre of town, is the 1435 **Rathaus** with its ornate baroque façade and astronomical clock. The nearby late-Gothic **Stiftkirche** (Am Holz-markt; ☼ 9am-5pm Feb-Oct, to 4pm Nov-Jan) houses the tombs of the Württemberg dukes and has excellent medieval stained-glass windows. From the heights of the Renaissance **Schloss Hohentübingen** (Burgsteig 11), now part of the university, there are fine views over the steep, red-tiled rooftops of the old town. **Burg Hohenzollern** (☎ 074 71 24 28; ☼ 9am-5.30pm). The **tourist office** (☎ 913 60; www.tuebin gen-info.de; An der Neckarbrücke; ☼ 9am-7pm Mon-Fri, to 5pm Sat) is beside the bridge.

The **DJH Hostel** (☎ 230 02; www.djh.de; Gartenstrasse 22/2; dm juniors/seniors €19/22) has a delightful location by the river. **IB Viktor-Renner-Haus** (☎ 55 90 20; Frondsbergstrasse 55; s/d €26/47) is a good deal with well-kept rooms just north of the Altstadt.

Hotel Am Schloss (☎ 929 40; www.hotelam schloss.de; Burgsteige 18; s/d incl breakfast €51/76) is an attractive hotel with simple and pleasant rooms. Its restaurant, **Maultaschen** (meals €6-10), serves almost 30 varieties of, yes, *Maultaschen*, a delicious stuffed pasta.

X Grill-Bar (☎ 2 49 02; Kornhausstrasse 6; hamburgers €2.50) is popular with students for its cheap hamburgers and sandwiches.

Neckar Muller (☎ 2 78 48; www.neckarmueller.de, in German; Gartenstrasse 4) is a beer garden across the river from the tourist office. **Wurstküche** (☎ 9 27 50; www.wurstkueche.com, in German; Am Lustnauer Tor 8) specialises in typical Swabian noodles.

There are regular RE trains between Tübingen and Stuttgart (€9; one hour).

HEIDELBERG
☎ 06221 / 140,000

The French destroyed Heidelberg in 1693; they may have been the last visitors to dislike this charming town on the Neckar River. Its magnificent castle and medieval town are irresistible drawcards for most travellers in Germany. Mark Twain began his European travels here and recounted his comical observations in *A Tramp Abroad*. Britain's JMW Turner loved Heidelberg and it inspired him to produce some of his finest landscape paintings. Throw in nice weather and lively pubs, and you understand why many of Heidelberg's students (attending the oldest university in the country) rarely graduate on time. But be warned: this place is chock-a-block with tourists during July and August.

Orientation

Heidelberg's captivating old town starts to reveal itself after a 15-minute walk west of the main train station, along the Kurfürsten-Anlage. Hauptstrasse is the pedestrian way leading eastwards through the heart of the Altstadt from Bismarckplatz via Marktplatz to Karlstor.

Information

Main post office (Sophienstrasse) Near the Altstadt.
Main tourist office (☎ 194 33; www.cvb-heidelberg.de;

Willy-Brandt-Platz 1; 9am-7pm Mon-Sat year-round, 10am-6pm Sun Apr-Nov) Outside the train station. There are smaller private tourist offices at the funicular train station near the castle and on Neckarmünzplatz that keep reduced hours. The €12 Heidelberg Card on sale here offers unlimited public transport and free admission to many sights.

Office Shop GmbH (Plock 85; Internet per 15min €1.30)

Post office (Kurfürsten) Across from train station.

Reisebank (Hauptbahnhof) In the train station, west of town.

Schnell & Sauber Waschcenter (Poststrasse 44; per wash €3.50)

Waschsalon Wojtala (Ketterpetrolse 17; per wash & dry €8) This is a convenient, if expensive, laundry.

Sights

Heidelberg's imposing **Schloss** (53 84 21; adult/concession €2.50/1.20; 10am-5.30pm) is one of Germany's finest examples of grand Gothic-Renaissance architecture. The building's half-ruined state actually adds to its romantic appeal. Seen from anywhere in the Altstadt, this striking red-sandstone castle dominates the hillside. The entry fee covers the castle, the **Grosses Fass** (Great Vat), an enormous 18th-century keg capable of holding 221,726L, and **Deutsches Apotheken-museum** (German Pharmaceutical Museum; 258 80; www.deutsches-apotheken-museum.de; Schlosshof 1; 10am-5.30pm).

You can take the **funicular railway** (adult/concession return €3/2) to the castle from lower Kornmarkt station, or enjoy an invigorating 10-minute walk up steep, stone-laid lanes. The funicular continues up to the **Königstuhl**, where there's a TV and **lookout tower** (adult/concession return incl castle stop €5.10/3.60).

Dominating Universitätsplatz are the 18th-century **Alte Universität** and the **Neue Universität**. Nearby there's the **Studentenkarzer** (student jail; 54 35 54; Augustinergasse 2; adult/concession €2.50/2; 10am-noon & 2-5pm Tue-Sat Apr-Oct, 10am-2pm Tue-Fri Nov-Mar). From 1778 to 1914 this jail was used for uproarious students. Sentences (usually two to 10 days) were earned for 'heinous' crimes such as drinking, singing and womanising. The **Marstall** is the former arsenal, now a student *mensa*.

The **Kurpfälzisches Museum** (Palatinate Museum; 58 34 02; Hauptstrasse 97; adult/concession €2.50/1.50; 10am-5pm Tue-Sun, to 9pm Wed) contains paintings, sculptures and the jawbone of the 600,000-year-old Heidelberg Man.

A stroll along the **Philosophenweg**, north of the Neckar River, gives a welcome respite from Heidelberg's tourist hordes.

Sleeping

Finding any accommodation during Heidelberg's high season can be difficult. Arrive early in the day or book ahead.

Camping Haide (80 25 06; www.camping-heidelberg.de; Schlierbacher Landstrasse 151; per person €5.50, tent €2.50-6) These grounds are in a pretty spot on the river. Take bus No 35 to Orthopädische Klinik.

DJH Hostel (65 11 90; www.djh.de; Tiergartenstrasse 5; dm juniors/seniors €13.35/16.05) Across the river from the train station. From the station or Bismarckplatz, take bus No 33 towards Ziegelhausen.

Pension Jeske (237 33; www.pension-jeske-heidelberg.de, in German; Mittelbadgasse 2; dm/d €20/50) Pension Jeske is a labyrinthine backpacker favourite, still the cheapest in the Altstadt.

Pension Astoria (40 29 29; Rahmengasse 30; s/d €40/65) Quaint and friendly, the Astoria has comfy rooms with character. It's north of the river, across Theodor-Heuss-Brücke.

Hotel am Kornmarkt (243 25; hotelamkornmarkt@web.de; Kornmarkt 7; s/d with shared bathroom €49/80) This pleasant hotel has spacious rooms and a superb breakfast buffet.

Hotel Vier Jahreszeiten (241 64; www.4-jahreszeiten.de; Haspelgasse 2; s/d €60/100) Goethe himself reputedly once slumbered here, so you know it's good.

Gasthaus Hackteufel (905 380; www.hackteufel.de; Steingasse 7; s/d €70/105) Each room is distinctive and full of character at the Hackteufel, in the middle of the romantic old town.

Hotel Zum Ritter (13 50; www.ritter-heidelberg.de; Hauptstrasse 178; s/d €92/155) Ornate Hotel Zum Ritter is close to the cathedral and provides grand accommodation. There's also an excellent restaurant attached.

Eating

Raja Rani (244 84; Mitelbadgasse 5; dishes €5) For fast-food Indian just off the Marktplatz.

Vetter im Schöneck (16 58 50; Steingasse 9; mains €10) Somehow meat and potatoes just seem appropriate surrounded by massive brewing kettles. Groups of six or more can order the Brewer's feast, a sausage, pretzels, radishes, meat and cheese smorgasbord.

Kulturbrauerei Heidelberg (50 29 80; www.heidelberger-kulturbrauerei.de; Leyergasse 6; mains €11)

GERMANY

HEIDELBERG

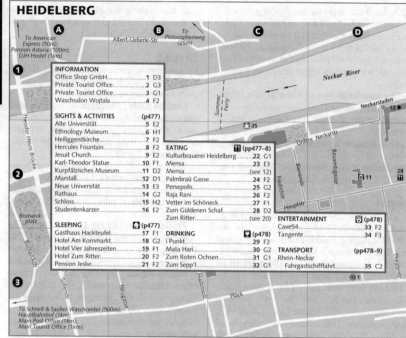

INFORMATION
Office Shop GmbH...............................1 D3
Private Tourist Office..........................2 G3
Private Tourist Office..........................3 G1
Waschsalon Wojtala............................4 F2

SIGHTS & ACTIVITIES (p477)
Alte Universität..................................5 E2
Ethnology Museum.............................6 H1
Heiliggeistkirche................................7 F2
Hercules Fountain...............................8 F2
Jesuit Church.....................................9 E2
Karl-Theodor Statue..........................10 F1
Kurpfälzisches Museum......................11 D2
Marstall...12 D1
Neue Universität...............................13 E3
Rathaus...14 G2
Schloss..15 H2
Studentenkarzer...............................16 E2

SLEEPING (p477)
Gasthaus Hackteufel..........................17 F1
Hotel Am Kornmarkt..........................18 G2
Hotel Vier Jahreszeiten......................19 F1
Hotel Zum Ritter...............................20 F2
Pension Jeske...................................21 F2

EATING (pp477–8)
Kulturbrauerei Heidelberg..................22 G1
Mensa...23 E3
Mensa..(see 12)
Palmbräu Gasse................................24 F2
Persepolis..25 G2
Raja Rani...26 F2
Vetter im Schöneck...........................27 F1
Zum Güldenen Schaf..........................28 D2
Zum Ritter....................................(see 20)

DRINKING (p478)
iPunkt...29 F2
Mata Hari..30 G2
Zum Roten Ochsen............................31 G1
Zum Sepp'l......................................32 G1

ENTERTAINMENT (p478)
Cave54..33 F2
Tangente...34 F3

TRANSPORT (pp478–9)
Rhein-Neckar
  Fahrgastschifffahrt.........................35 C2

The classic-looking Kulturbrauerei is highly recommended, with a delightful garden at the back. For a pork alternative, try the duck.

Zum Güldenen Schaf (☎ 208 79; Hauptstrasse 115; mains €13) If you can, make reservations with a group, to experience the cuisine, music and costumes of previous centuries. There's a quirky museum attached.

Palmbräu Gasse (☎ 285 36; Hauptstrasse 185; mains €8-16) Looking a little like a medieval dungeon – a pleasant, non-punitive one – Palmbräu Gasse wins for ambience, service and food.

Also recommended are the **Mensa** (Universitätsplatz; meals €3), which cater to students – there's another one that's not as nice in the Marstall, a short walk north of the University on Marstallstrasse – and **Persepolis** (☎ 16 46 46; Zwingerstrasse 21; dishes €4-7), fast food for vegetarians.

Drinking & Entertainment

This being a university town, you won't have to go far to find a happening backstreet bar. Lots of the action centres on Unterestrasse.

Mata Hari (☎ 18 18 08; Oberbadgasse 10) Mata Hari is a mellow place open till 3am.

Tangente (☎ 169 444; Kettengasse 23) A small discotheque in the old part of town.

iPunkt (☎ 124 41; Unterestrasse 30) Modern and popular with a young crowd.

Zum Roten Oschen (☎ 209 77; www.roterochsen .de; Hauptstrasse 213) One of Heidelberg's most famous historic student pubs, now frequented by tourists, some of whom have already graduated.

Zum Sepp'l (☎ 230 85; Hauptstrasse 217) Also gets much of the tourist trade these days, though the wear and tear and graffiti collected over the centuries attest to a colourful history.

Cave54 (☎ 278 40; Krämerpetrolse 2; ⌚ Thu-Sun) For live jazz and blues, head to this underground stone cellar that oozes character, and once hosted Louis Armstrong.

Getting There & Around

Heidelberg is on the Castle Rd route from Mannheim to Nuremberg. From mid-May through till the end of September Deutsche-Touring has a daily coach service, with one bus in either direction between Heidelberg

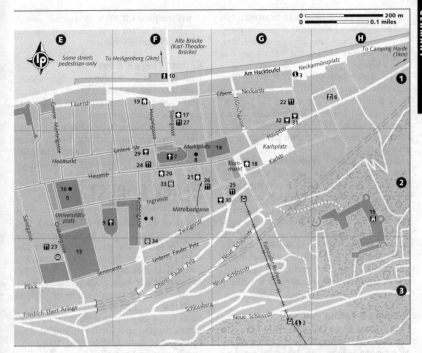

and Rothenburg ob der Tauber (€29, five hours); see p464.

There are ICE/IC trains that operate to/from Frankfurt (€17.20, one hour, two per hour), Stuttgart (€20, 40 minutes, one per hour) and Munich (€53, three hours, hourly). Mannheim, 12 minutes to the west by frequent trains, has connections to cities throughout Germany.

Bismarckplatz is the main local transport hub. One-way tickets for the excellent bus and tram system are €1.80 and a 24-hour pass costs €5.90.

BADEN-BADEN
☎ 07221 / pop 50,000

Baden-Baden's natural hot springs have attracted visitors since Roman times, but this small city, close to France, Luxembourg and Switzerland, only really became fashionable in the 19th century when the likes of Victor Hugo came to bathe in and imbibe its therapeutic waters. Today, though Baden-Baden is Germany's premier (and ritziest) health spa, it still has many other salubrious activities to offer to the traveller.

Orientation & Information

The train station is 7km northwest of town. Bus Nos 201, 205 and 216 run frequently to/from Leopoldsplatz, the heart of Baden-Baden. From here, Sophienstrasse leads eastwards to the more historic part of town. North of Sophienstrasse are the baths, the Stiftskirche and the Neues Schloss. Across the river to the west you will find the Trinkhalle (pump room) and the tourist office, and past Goetheplatz both the Kurhaus and Spielhalle (casino).

The **tourist office** (☎ 27 52 00; www.baden-baden .com; Kaiserallee 3; ⏱ 10am-5pm Mon-Sat, 2-5pm Sun) is in the Trinkhalle. There is a spa *Kurtaxe* (visitors' tax) of €2.80, entitling you to a *Kurkarte* from your hotel that brings various discounts. The tax doesn't apply to those staying at the hostel.

Sights & Activities

The 2000-year-old **Römische Badruinen** (Roman Bath Ruins; ☎ 27 59 34; Römerplatz 1; adult/child €2/1) are worth a quick look, but for a real taste of Baden-Baden head to the **Kurhaus**, built in the 1820s which houses the opulent **casino**

(☎ 302 40; Kaiserallee 1; admission €3, guided tours adult/child €4/2; ☯ tours 9.30am-noon) which inspired Dostoyevsky to write *The Gambler*. Men seeking similar inspiration must wear ties (€3 to hire).

The **Merkur Cable Car** (☎ 27 71; €4; ☯ 10am-10pm) takes you up to the 670m summit, where there are fine views and numerous walking trails (bus No 204 or 205 from Leopoldplatz takes you to the cable-car station). A good hiking-driving tour is to the wine-growing area to the west.

The 19th-century **Friedrichsbad** (☎ 27 59 20; www.roemisch-irisches-bad.de; Römerplatz 1; bathing programme €21; ☯ 9am-10pm Mon-Sat, noon-8pm Sun) is decadently Roman in style and provides a muscle-melting 16-step bathing programme. No clothing is allowed inside, and several bathing sections are mixed on most days. **Caracalla-Therme** (☎ 27 59 40; Römerplatz 11; €12 for 2hr; ☯ 8am-10pm) is a vast, modern complex of outdoor and indoor pools, hot- and cold-water grottoes. You must wear a bathing costume and bring your own towel.

Sleeping & Eating

Campingplatz Adam (☎ 07223-231 94; www.campingplatz-adam.de; Campingplatzstrasse 1, Bühl-Oberbruch; per person/tent €6.50/8) This lakeside camping ground has its own small beach and offers swimming, tennis, beach volleyball and clean, well kept facilities. It's about 12km outside town.

DJH Hostel (☎ 522 23; www.djh.de; Hardbergstrasse 34; dm juniors/seniors €17/20) This modern three-story hostel is on a hillside 3km northwest of the centre – it's a steep hike up a long flight of stairs to the entrance. The attic-like upper rooms let in lots of sun; take bus No 201 to Grosse Dollenstrasse then walk for 10 minutes.

Hotel Bischoff (☎ 223 78, www.hotelsbaden-baden.de; Römerplatz 2; s/d €40/65) Centrally located close to the spas, the Bischoff is a comfortable choice.

Holland Hotel Sophienpark (☎ 35 60; www.holland-hotel.de; Sophienstrasse 14; s/d €98/140) The Sophienpark is for those who want a taste of luxury. It has its own park, and bright and sunny rooms.

Leo's (☎ 380 81; Luisenstrasse 8; lunch special €9) A great spot for a long, leisurely meal, especially for lunch which includes soup, salmon and coffee. The bouillabaisse (€12) is also recommended.

Rathausglöckl (☎ 906 10; Steinstrasse 7; mains €8-17) This restaurant serves excellent regional fare in a historic setting.

Getting There & Away

Baden-Baden is on the busy Mannheim-Basel train line. Fast trains in either direction stop every two hours. Frequent local trains serve both Karlsruhe and Offenburg, from where you can make connections to much of Germany. For those driving, Baden-Baden is just off the A5 running between Frankfurt and Basel, both 180km away.

BLACK FOREST

Home of the cuckoo clock, the Black Forest (Schwarzwald) gets its name from the dark canopy of evergreens, though it's also dotted with open slopes and farmland. The fictional Hansel and Gretel characters encountered their wicked witch in these parts, but modern-day hazards are more likely to include packs of tourists piling out of buses. However, a 20-minute walk from even the most crowded spots will put you in quiet countryside dotted with huge traditional farmhouses and patrolled by amiable dairy cows. It's not nature wild and remote, but serene and picturesque.

Orientation

The Black Forest is east of the Rhine between Karlsruhe and Basel. It's roughly triangular in shape, about 160km long and 50km wide. Baden-Baden, Freudenstadt, Titisee and Freiburg act as convenient information posts for Black Forest excursions but smaller towns generally have tourist offices as well.

Information

Freudenstadt is a good place for information on the northern section.

Feldberg tourist office (☎ 07655-80 19; www.feldberg.de, in German; Kirchpetrolse 1; ☯ 8am-5.30pm Mon-Fri year-round, Sat Jun-Sep, Sun July-Aug) Can supply ski information.

Hintzerzarten Breitnau's tourist office (☎ 07652 1206 0; www.hinterzarten-breitnau.de; Freiburgerstrasse 1) This also covers the southern Black Forest.

Titisee tourist office (☎ 07651 980 40; www.titisee.de, in German; Strandbadstrasse 4, Kurhaus; ☯ 8am-noon & 1.30-5.30pm Mon-Fri year-round, 10am-noon Sat & Sun May-Oct)

Tourist office (☎ 07441-86 40; www.freudenstadt.de; Am Markt-platz; ☼ 9am-6pm Mon-Fri, 10am-2pm Sat & Sun Mar-Nov; 10am-5pm Mon-Fri, 10am-1pm Sat & Sun Dec-Feb)

Sights

Enjoying the natural countryside will be the main focus: you can take a plunge in a lake or down a ski slope. Alternatively, lose yourself in shops full of cuckoo clocks.

Roughly halfway between Baden-Baden and Freudenstadt – along the Schwarzwald-Hochstrasse (Black Forest Hwy) – the first major tourist sight is the **Mummelsee**, south of the Hornisgrinde peak. It's a small and deep lake steeped in folklore (legend says an evil sea king inhabits the depths).

Further south, **Freudenstadt** is mainly used as a base for excursions into the countryside; however, the central marketplace, the largest in Germany, is worth a look.

The area between Freudenstadt and Freiburg is cuckoo-clock country, a name that takes on new meaning when you see the prices people are willing to pay. A few popular stops are **Schramberg**, **Triberg** and **Furtwangen**. In Furtwangen, visit the **Deutsches Uhrenmuseum** (German Clock Museum; ☎ 07723-92 01 17; www.deutsches-uhrenmuseum.de, in German; Gerwigstrasse 11; adult/concession €3/2.50; ☼ 9am-6pm Apr-Oct, 10am-5pm Nov-Mar) for a look at the traditional Black Forest skill of clock-making.

Titisee boasts its namesake natural lake where you can take a **cruise** (€4; 25min) or rent a boat in summer. The engines are all electric to preserve the lake's serenity.

Activities

With more than 7000km of marked trails, hiking possibilities during summer are, almost literally, endless. Three classic long-distance **hiking trails** run south from the northern Black Forest city of Pforzheim as far as the Swiss Rhine: the 280km Westweg to Basel; the 230km Mittelweg to Waldhut-Tiengen; and the 240km Ostweg to Schaffhausen.

The southern Black Forest, especially the area around the 1493m Feldberg summit, offers some of the best hiking; small towns such as Todtmoos or Bonndorf serve as useful bases for those wanting to get off the more heavily trodden trails. The 10km Wutachschlucht (Wutach Gorge) outside Bonndorf is justifiably famous.

You can also try windsurfing, boating or swimming on the highland lakes, though some may find the water a bit cool. Titisee boasts several small **beaches**.

The Black Forest **ski season** runs from late December to March. While there is some good downhill skiing, the area is more suited to cross-country skiing. The main centre for winter sports is around Titisee, with uncrowded downhill runs at **Feldberg** (day passes €20; rental equipment available) and numerous graded cross-country trails.

Sleeping

Away from the major towns you can find scores of simple guesthouses where the rates are cheap and the welcome warm. The Black Forest is also good for longer stays, with holiday apartments and private rooms available in almost every town.

BUDGET

Campingplatz Wolfsgrund (☎ 07656-573; per person €4.25-4.75; per site €5-6) A modern camping ground on the eastern shore of the Lake Schluchsee, just north of the town centre.

Terrassencamping Sandbank (☎ 07651-82 43; fax 82 86; Seerundweg; per person €3.25-4.25, site €5-6.50) One of four camping grounds on the Titisee.

Bergpetrolthof Wasmer (☎ 07676-230; fax 430; An der Wiesenquelle 1; s/d €23/46) When in Feldberg, try the Wasmer for small, comfortable timber-lined rooms.

Petrolthof Pension Traube (☎ 07441-91 74 50; fax 853 28; Markt 41; s/d €30/57) In Freudenstadt, Traube has simple rooms.

Hotel Pfaff (☎ 07722-44 79; www.hotel-pfaff.com; Hauptstrasse 85; s/d €38/66) The Pfaff in Triberg offers comfortable lodgings near the waterfall.

The DJH net is extensive in the southern Black Forest but limited in the north. Dorms are €14.30 throughout:

Freudenstadt (☎ 07441-77 20; www.djh.de; Eugen-Nägele-Strasse 69)

Titisee (☎ 07652-238; www.djh.de; Bruderhalde 27)

Triberg (☎ 07722-41 10; www.djh.de; Rohrbacher Strasse 3)

Zuflucht (☎ 07804-611; www.djh.de; Schwarzwald-hochstrasse)

MID-RANGE

Hotel Sonneneck (☎ 07651 82 46; fax 881 74; Parkstrasse 2; s/d €44/88) Provides spacious comfort

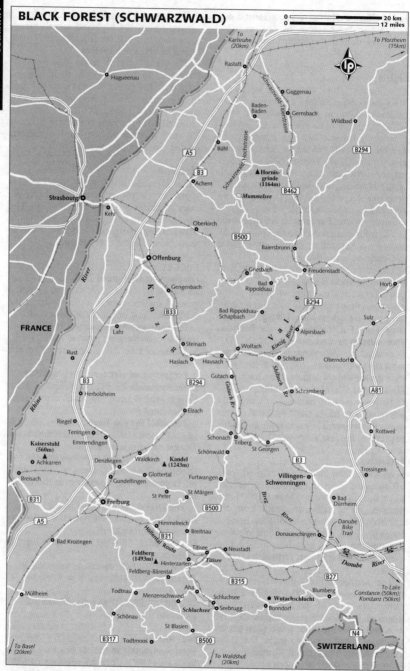

BLACK FOREST (SCHWARZWALD)

0 _____ 20 km
0 _____ 12 miles

To Karlsruhe (20km)

To Pforzheim (15km)

Hagueenau

Rastatt

Gaggenau

Baden-Baden

Gernsbach

Wildbad

B294

A5

Bühl

Schwarzwald-Hochstrasse

Schwarzwald-Talerstrasse

B3

Achern

▲ Hornis-grinde (1164m)

B462

Strasbourg

Kehl

Mummelsee

Oberkirch

B500

Baiersbronn

Freudenstadt

Offenburg

Gnesbach

Bad Rippoldsau

Horb

Gengenbach

K
i
n
z
i
g

B33

Bad Rippoldsau-Schapbach

V
a
l
l
e
y

B294

Sulz

Lahr

Steinach

Wolfach

Alpirsbach

Kinzig River

Schiltach

Oberndorf

Rust

Haslach

Hausach

FRANCE

Gutach

B294

Schramberg

A81

Herbolzheim

Schiltach Rv

Elzach

Gutach Rv

Rhine River

Riegel

Teningen

Schonach

Triberg

St Georgen

Rottweil

Kaiserstuhl (560m) ▲

Emmendingen

Waldkirch

Kandel (1243m) ▲

Schönwald

B3

Villingen-Schwenningen

Trossingen

Achkarren

Denzlingen

Furtwangen

Breisach

Gundelfingen

Glottertal

St Peter

Breg River

Bad Dürrheim

Freiburg

St Märgen

B500

B31

Himmelreich

Breitnau

A5

Höllental Route

B31

Donaueschingen

Danube Bike Trail

Bad Krozingen

Feldberg (1493m) ▲ Hinterzarten

Titisee

Neustadt

Titisee

Danube River

Feldberg-Bärental

B315

B27

Müllheim

Todtnau

Aha

Schluchsee

Blumberg

To Lake Constance (50km); Konstanz (50km)

Menzenschwand

Wutachschlucht

Schönau

Schluchsee

Seebrugg

Bonndorf

N4

St Blasien

B500

B317

Todtmoos

SWITZERLAND

To Basel (20km)

To Waldshut (20km)

when in Titisee and boasts an excellent restaurant downstairs.

Hotel Adler-Post (☎ 07651 50 66; fax 37 29; Hauptstrasse 16; s/d €49/83) The Adler-Post in Neudstadt has charming rooms furnished in period style; the price includes use of the luxurious indoor pool, sauna and solarium.

Parkhotel Adler (☎ 07652-127 0; www.parkhotel adler.de; Adlerplatz 3; s/d €100/190) Top-flight luxury in Hinterzarten.

Eating

Regional specialities include *Schwarzwälderschinken* (ham), which is smoked and served in a variety of ways. Rivalling those ubiquitous clocks in fame (but not price), *Schwarzwälderkirschtorte* (Black Forest cake) is a chocolate and cherry concoction. Most hotels and guesthouses have restaurants serving traditional hearty but expensive German fare.

Getting There & Away

The Mannheim to Basel train line has numerous branches that serve the Black Forest. Frequent trains for Freudenstadt (€13, 1¾ hours) and the north leave from Karlsruhe. Triberg is on the busy line linking Offenburg and Constance. Titisee has frequent services from Freiburg with some trains continuing to Feldberg and others to Neustadt, where there are connections to Donaueschingen.

The rail network for the area is extensive and where trains don't go, buses do. However, be aware that travel times can be slow and service infrequent, so check the schedules at bus stops which are usually located outside train stations. There's a variety of group and multiday deals valid on trains and buses; these are sold from ticket machines at the stations.

To reach Feldberg, take one of the frequent buses from the train stations in Titisee or Bärental.

Drivers will enjoy their flexibility. The main tourist road is the Schwarzwald-Hochstrasse (B500), which runs from Baden-Baden to Freudenstadt and from Triberg to Waldshut. Other thematic roads with maps provided by tourist offices include Schwarzwald-Bäderstrasse (spa town route), Schwarzwald-Panoramastrasse (panoramic view route) and Badische Weinstrasse (wine route).

FREIBURG

☎ 0761 / pop 200,500

Nestled between hills and vineyards and the southern Black Forest, both of which serve as wonderful refuges, Freiburg im Breisgau is a fun place, thanks to the city's large and thriving university community. Founded in 1120 and ruled for centuries by the Austrian Habsburgs, Freiburg has retained many traditional features, although major reconstruction was necessary following severe bombing damage during WWII. The monumental 13th-century cathedral is the city's key landmark but the real attractions are the vibrant cafés, bars and street-life, plus the local wines. The best times for tasting are early July for the four days of *Weinfest* (Wine Festival), or early August for the nine days of *Weinkost* (loosely meaning 'wine as food').

Orientation

The city centre is a convenient 10-minute walk from the train station. Walk east along Eisenbahnstrasse to the tourist office, then continue through the bustling pedestrian zone to Münsterplatz, dominated by the red stone cathedral.

Information

Alexis (Marienstrasse 10; ☷ 10-1am Mon-Sat, noon-1am Sun; Internet per hr €2.40)

Deutsche Bank (Rotteckring 1-3) Across from Colombiapark.

Main post office (Eisenbahnstrasse 58-62)

Tourist office (☎ 388 18 80; www.freiburg.de, in German; Rotteckring 14; ☷ 9.30am-8pm Mon-Fri, to 5pm Sat, 10am-noon Sun Jun-Sep, 9.30am-6pm Mon-Fri, to 2pm Sat, 10am-noon Sun Nov-Apr) Has reams of information on the Black Forest.

Volksbank Freiburg (Bismarckalle 10) Opposite the train station.

Wash & Tours (Salzstrasse 22; wash €4, Internet per 30min €1; ☷ 9am-7pm Mon-Fri, to 4pm Sat, to 10pm Sun) A combined laundry and Internet café.

Sights

The major sight in Freiburg is the 700-year-old **Münster** (Cathedral; Münsterplatz; steeple adult/child €1.30/0.80; ☷ 9.30am-5pm Mon-Sat, 1-5pm Sun Easter-Oct, 10am-4pm Tue-Sat, 1-5pm Sun Nov-Easter), a classic example of both high and late-Gothic architecture which looms over Münsterplatz, Freiburg's market square. Ascend the tower to the stunning pierced spire for great views of Freiburg and, on a clear day,

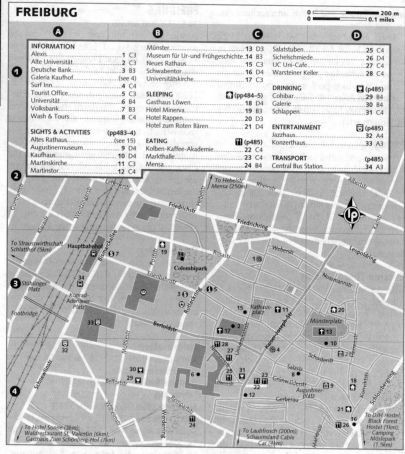

FREIBURG

INFORMATION		
Alexis	1	C3
Alte Universität	2	C3
Deutsche Bank	3	B3
Galeria Kaufhof	(see 4)	
Surf Inn	4	C4
Tourist Office	5	C3
Universität	6	B4
Volksbank	7	B3
Wash & Tours	8	C4

SIGHTS & ACTIVITIES	(pp483–4)	
Altes Rathaus	(see 15)	
Augustinermuseum	9	D4
Kaufhaus	10	D4
Martinskirche	11	C3
Martinstor	12	C4

Münster	13	D3
Museum für Ur-und Frühgeschichte	14	B3
Neues Rathaus	15	C3
Schwabentor	16	D4
Universitätskirche	17	C3

SLEEPING	(pp484–5)	
Gasthaus Löwen	18	D4
Hotel Minerva	19	B3
Hotel Rappen	20	D3
Hotel zum Roten Bären	21	D4

EATING	(p485)	
Kolben-Kaffee-Akademie	22	C4
Markthalle	23	C4
Mensa	24	B4

Salatstuben	25	C4
Sichelschmiede	26	D4
UC Uni-Cafe	27	C4
Warsteiner Keller	28	C4

DRINKING	(p485)	
Cohibar	29	B4
Galerie	30	B4
Schlappen	31	B4

ENTERTAINMENT	(p485)	
Jazzhaus	32	A4
Konzerthaus	33	A3

TRANSPORT	(p485)	
Central Bus Station	34	A3

---

the Kaiserstuhl and the Vosges. South of the Münster stands the picturesque **Kaufhaus**, the 16th-century merchants' hall.

The bustling **university quarter** is northwest of the Martinstor (one of the old city gates).

Freiburg's main museum, the **Augustinermuseum** (☎ 201 25 31; Salzstrasse 32; adult/concession €2/1; ☼ 10am-5pm Tue-Sun) has a fine collection of medieval art.

The popular trip by **cable car** (one way/return €6.60/10.20, concession €3.60/5.60; ☼ 9am-5pm) to the 1286m Schauinsland peak is a quick way to reach the Black Forest highlands. Numerous easy and well-marked trails make the Schauinsland area ideal for day walks. From Freiburg take tram No 4 south to Günterstal and then bus No 21 to Talsta-

tion. The five-hour hike from Schauinsland to the Untermünstertal offers some of the best views with the fewest people; return to Freiburg via the train to Staufen and then take the bus.

Sleeping

Camping Möslepark (☎ 729 38; campingfreizeit@aol .com; Waldseestrasse 77; per person €5, tent €2.10-2.60) Take tram No 1 to Stadthalle (direction: Littenweiler), turn right under the road, go over the train tracks and follow the bike path.

Black Forest Hostel (☎ 675 65; www.blackforest -hostel.de; Kartäuserstrasse 33; dm/s/d €12/22/27) Take tram No 1 to Römerhof (direction: Littenweiler) then follow the signs down Fritz-Geigesstrasse.

Hotel Sonne (☎ 40 30 48; fax 409 88 56; Basler Strasse 58; s/d €35/52) A 15-minute walk south of the centre, friendly Sonne has decent, simple rooms and a magnificent breakfast buffet.

Gasthaus Löwen (☎ 331 61; fax 362 38; Herrenstrasse 47; s/d €35/80) For clean, basic rooms in a busy part of the Altstadt.

Hotel Rappen (☎ 313 53; www.hotelrappen.de; Münsterplatz 13; s/d €55/70) Lovely rooms done 'Black Forest' style with close-up views of the Münster.

Hotel Minerva (☎ 38 64 90; Poststrasse 8; s/d €72/90) The Minerva, only a block from the train station, is a restful hotel with enthusiastic staff who aim to please.

Hotel Zum Roten Bären (☎ 38 78 70; www .roter-baeren.de; Oberlinden 12; s/d €100/138) Prices were undoubtedly more reasonable when the Roten Bären originally opened its doors early in the 12th century, but it's still a good value for those looking for luxury. The restaurant is first class as well.

Eating

There's a good selection of wurst and other quick eats from stalls set up in the market square during lunch.

Some restaurants located outside the city centre, while not easy to get to using public transport, are highly recommended.

UC Uni-Café (☎ 38 33 55; Niemensstrasse 7; meals €3-7) A popular hang-out that serves light bites on its highly visible outdoor terrace.

Laubfrosch (Kaiser Josephstrasse 273; pizzas €3.80) A cheap pizzeria popular with students just past the Martinstor on the river.

Warsteiner Keller (☎ 329 29; Niemensstrasse 13; meals €7.50) A bar/café that oozes atmosphere, and has an excellent range of cheap chow.

Salatstuben (Löwenstrasse 1; 100g salad €1.20, hot meal €4.10) There's a great range of cheap vegetarian dishes at this self-serve place.

Sichelschmiede (☎ 350 37; Insel 1; mains around €12) Substantial portions in the eastern Altstadt.

Strausswirthschaft Schlatthof (☎ 418 47; www .weingut-schlatthof.de, in German; Schlatthöfe 3; mains €5) You'll likely be the only nonlocal washing down the cheap but filling schnitzel with *wein schorle* (watered-down wine) at this farm/vineyard a 10-minute drive from town.

Waldrestaurant St Valentin (☎ 388 41 31; www .restaurant-valentin.de, in German; Valentinstrasse 100; mains €9) Halfway up a mountain, surrounded by a forest, romantic St Valentin feels like a well-kept secret.

Gasthaus Zum Schönberg-Hof (☎ 07664 72 22; 79285 Ebringen; mains €6) Besides the usual fare, Schönberg-Hof has fresh air and beautiful vistas of the surrounding countryside.

Drinking

Schlappen (Lowenstrasse 2) A happening student nightspot. It's a large, sprawling bar with a lively vibe, a budget menu and late closing.

Galerie (Milchstrasse 7) An intimate watering hole with a nice courtyard and cheap Spanish eats.

Cohibar (Milchstrasse 9) Mellow and candlelit, this bar doesn't close till 3am at weekends.

Entertainment

Konzerthaus (☎ 388 85 52; Konrad-Adenauer-Platz 1) An impressive range of orchestral performances.

Jazzhaus (☎ 34 973; Schnewlinstrasse 1) Live jazz every night. Admission starts at €6, depending on who's playing.

Getting There & Around

Freiburg is situated on the Mannheim-Basel train corridor and is served by numerous ICE and EC trains in both directions. The trains to Titisee leave every 30 minutes (€9). The regional bus station is next to Track 1. For ride-sharing information contact the **Citynetz Mitfahr-Service** (☎ 194 44; Belfortstrasse 55).

Single rides on the efficient local bus and tram system cost €1.75. A 24-hour pass costs €4.60. Trams depart from the bridge over the train tracks.

LAKE CONSTANCE

Often jokingly called the 'Swabian Ocean', Lake Constance (Bodensee) is an oasis in landlocked southern Germany. Even if you never make contact with the water, this giant bulge in the sinewy course of the Rhine can breathe life into the weary traveller. The many historic towns around its periphery, which can be explored by boat or bicycle and on foot, while inviting in their own right are enhanced by the breeze and the possibility of getting wet.

The lake's southern side belongs to Switzerland and Austria, where the snow-capped mountain tops provide a perfect backdrop when viewed from the northern (German) shore. The German side of Lake Constance features three often-crowded tourist centres in Constance, Meersburg and the island of Lindau. It's essentially a summer area, when it abounds with liquid joy, and is too often foggy, or at best hazy, in winter.

Activities

A 270km international bike track circumnavigates Lake Constance through Germany, Austria and Switzerland, tracing the often steep shoreline beside vineyards and pebble beaches. The route is well signposted, but you may want one of the many widely sold cycling maps. The tourist booklet *Rad Urlaub am Bodensee* lists routes, rental places and a wealth of other information for the region.

In Constance, **Velotours** (☎ 07531-982 80; Fritz-Arnold-Strasse 2b; bike rental daily/weekly €11/52) rents out bikes and organises cycling tours.

Getting There & Around

Constance has train connections every one to two hours to Offenburg (€25.40) and Stuttgart (€34). Meersburg is easily reached by bus No 7395 from Friedrichshafen (€6.40, every 30 minutes), or by **Weisse Flotte** (☎ 07531-28 13 98) boats from Constance (€3.40, several times daily in season).

The Constance to Meersburg **car-ferry** (☎ 07531-80 36 66; person/ bicycle/car €1.40/0.75/4.65) runs every 15 minutes year-round from the northeastern Constance suburb of Staad.

Lindau has trains to/from Ulm (€17.80), Munich (€28) and Bregenz (€2.10), where you can connect to the rest of Austria.

Trains link Lindau, Friedrichshafen and Constance, and buses fill in the gaps. By car, the B31 hugs the northern shore of Lake Constance, but it can get rather busy.

The most enjoyable, albeit slowest, way to get around is on the Weisse Flotte boats which, from Easter to late October, call several times a day at the larger towns along both sides of the lake; there are discounts for rail pass-holders.

The **Erlebniskarte** (3/7/14 days €47/60/87) is a handy pass that allows free boat travel and free access to a host of activities around the lake.

The seven-day **Bodensee-Pass** (€30) gives half-price fares on all boats, buses, trains and mountain cableways on and around Lake Constance (including its Austrian and Swiss shores).

CONSTANCE

☎ 07531 / pop 78,000

The town of Constance (Konstanz) achieved historical significance in 1414 when the Council of Constance convened to try to heal huge rifts in the Church. The consequent burning at the stake of the religious reformer Jan Hus as a heretic, and the scattering of his ashes over the lake, failed to block the impetus of the Reformation.

In the west, Constance straddles the Swiss border, a good fortune that spared it from Allied bombing in WWII.

The **tourist office** (☎ 13 30 30; www.konstanz .de/tourismus; Bahnhofplatz 13; ☽ 9am-6.30pm Mon-Fri, to 4pm Sat, 10am-1pm Sun Apr-Oct; 9.30am-12.30pm, 2-6pm Mon-Fri Nov-Mar) is 150m to the right from the train station exit. **Clixworkx.net** (☎ 99 12 11; Badanstrasse 21; ☽ 10am-8pm Mon-Sat) charges €3 for half an hour of Internet access.

Sights & Activities

The city's most visible feature is the Gothic spire of the cathedral, added only in 1856 to a church that was started in 1052, which gives excellent views over the old town. Visit the old **Niederburg** quarter or relax in the parklands of the **Stadtgarten**. If you have time, head across to **Mainau Island** (☎ 30 30; adult/concession €10/5, after 4pm €5/2.50; ☽ 7am-8pm mid-Mar–Nov, 9am-6pm Nov–mid-Mar), with its baroque castle set among vast and gorgeous gardens that include a butterfly house. Take bus No 4 (€1.60, 25 minutes) or a Weisse Flotte boat (€5.20, one hour) from the harbour behind the station. Five public **beaches** are open from May to September, including the Strandbad Horn with shrub-enclosed nude bathing. Take bus No 5 or walk for 20 scenic minutes around the shore.

Sleeping & Eating

Campingplatz Bodensee (☎ 330 57; www.kanu.de, in German; Fohrenbühlweg 45; per person €3.50) A lovely spot to camp. Take bus No 1 to the car-ferry terminal, then walk south along the shore for 10 minutes.

DJH Hostel (☎ 322 60; www.djh.de; Zur Allmannshöhe 16; dm juniors/seniors €19/22) Take bus No 1 or 4 from the station to the Jugendherberge stop to stay in this converted water tower.

Hotel Sonnenhof Garni (☎ 222 57; www.hotel -sonnenhof-konstanz.de, in German; O Raggenbasstrasse 3; s/d €35/70) Centrally located, the Sonnenhof Garni has basic but decent rooms.

Hotel Barbarossa (☎ 12 89 90; www.barbarossa -hotel.com, in German; Obermarkt 8-12; s/d €38/85) A charming old place with period furniture and creaky floors. There's also a **restaurant** (mains €10-19) downstairs with local specialities.

Hotel Gasthof Linde (☎ 974 20; www.hotel-linde .com; Radolfzellerstrasse 27; s/d €45/65) There's a modern guesthouse attached to the older hotel. Both share a restaurant and beer garden. Take bus No 2 or 13 from the train station to the Linde on the other side of the Rhein from the Altstadt.

Exxtra (☎ 23 39 4; Hussenstrasse 21; lunch special €5) You can't beat Exxtra for tasty *kässpätzle*. Popular with students and others interested in a leisurely meal.

Hafenalle Biergarten (☎ 211 26; Hafenstrasse 10) A perfect spot for a beer garden, Hafenalle catches the breeze off the lake. Pretzels and wurst make for good snacking.

Latinos (☎ 173 99; Am Fischmarkt; all-you-can-eat €7.80) Latinos serves an eclectic mix of Mexican food, sushi and barbecue spare ribs.

Restaurant Elefanten (☎ 221 64; Salmannsweiler-petrolse 34; mains €10-21) This restaurant offers a cosy dining room, an international menu and elephant-sized servings.

MEERSBURG
☎ 07532 / pop 5200

Constance seems positively urban when compared to enchanting Meersburg across the lake. It's hard not to smile as the ferry approaches, and winding cobblestone streets, vine-patterned hills and a sunny lakeside promenade come into focus.

The helpful **tourist office** (☎ 01805 63 37 72; www.meersburg.de, in German; Kirchstrasse 4; ☼ 9am-noon & 2-6pm Mon-Fri, 10am-2pm Sat) is in the Altstadt.

Steigstrasse is lined with delightful half-timbered houses, each boasting a gift shop. The 11th-century **Altes Schloss** (☎ 800 00; adult/concession €5.50/4; ☼ 9am-6pm Mar-Oct, 10am-6pm Nov-Feb) is the oldest structurally intact castle in Germany. Baroque **Neues Schloss** (☎ 40 49 00; adult/concession €4/3; ☼ 10am-1pm & 2-6pm) houses the town's art collection.

Meersburg is a good base for watery pursuits and is popular with windsurfers. **Rudi Thum's** (☎ 73 11) at the yacht harbour, rents out equipment and offers sailing courses.

There are no handy camping grounds or DJH hostels, but relatively inexpensive accommodation can still be found. There's

no shortage of gastronomic options on the promenade, with dozens of cafés and restaurants jostling for attention; meals average about €9.

Inside the pink pastel façade, upstairs from the über traditional restaurant, rooms at the **Hotel Weinstube** (☎ 65 11; fax 62 24; Unterstadtstrasse 35; s/d €30/65) are spacious and comfortable.

Gästehaus Am Hafen (☎ 70 69; www.amhafen .de.vu, in German; Spitalgasse 3; s/d €33/54) looks a little like a narrow Swiss chalet. It has potted flowers in the windows and charming, small spiffy rooms.

Seehotel zur Münz (☎ 43 59 0; www.seehotel -zur-muenz.de, in German; Seepromenade 7; s/d €36/72) is situated on the lakefront promenade. Some of the rooms have balconies with marvellous views.

Hotel Seehof (☎ 07545 936 0; www.seehof-hotel.de; Unterstadtstrasse 36; s/d €50/92) is large compared to some of the other hotels. It's just around the corner from the promenade fronting one of the ferry docks, and some of the rooms have balconies.

The best place for cheap eats from the ocean is **Ins Fischernetz** (☎ 58 45; Unterstadtstrasse 32; fish sandwiches €4).

Besides the excellent menu of Lake Constance fish, pastas, pizza and tasty desserts, you can't beat the setting, directly on the lake promenade, of **Seerestaurant Stärk** (☎ 49 58 43; www.staerk-meersburg.de, in German; Seepromenade 7; dishes €9).

Winzerstube Zum Becher (☎ 075 32 90 09; www .winzerstube-zum-becher.de, in German; Höllgasse 4; mains €12) does traditional dishes with flair in the Oberstadt (upper town).

LINDAU
☎ 08382 / pop 26,000

Most of the German part of Lake Constance lies within Baden-Württemberg, but Lindau in the east is just inside Bavaria, near the Austrian border. The **tourist office** (☎ 26 00 30; www.lindau-tourismus.de; Ludwigstrasse 68; ☼ 9am-noon & 2-5pm Mon-Fri year-round, 10am-2pm Sat & Sun Apr-Oct) is directly opposite the train station.

Connected to the nearby lakeshore by bridges, key sights of this oh-so-charming island town have murals: **Altes Rathaus** (Reichsplatz), the **city theatre** (Barfüsser-platz) and the harbour's **Seepromenade**, with its Bavarian Lion monument and lighthouse. When the haze clears, the Alps provide a stunning backdrop for photos.

Park Camping Lindau am See (☎ 722 36; www .park-camping.de, in German; Fraunhoferstrasse 20; per person/tent €5.50/2.50) is on the foreshore 3km southeast of Lindau. Take bus No 1 or 2 to the bus station, then bus No 3.

The **DJH Hostel** (☎ 96 71 0; www.djh.de; Herbergsweg 11; dm €18) is only open to under 27s. Take bus No 1 or 2 to the bus station, then bus No 3.

Gasthof Engel (☎ 52 40; fax 56 44; Schafgasse 4; s/d €27/80) is a quaint, good-value hotel.

The attractive-looking façade of **Hotel Gasthof Goldenes Lamm** (☎ 57 32; Schafgasse 3; s/d €40/80) is mirrored by the quality rooms and restaurant inside.

The **Alte Post** (☎ 934 60; www.alte-post-lindau.de, in German; Fischergasse 3; s/d €44/80) has beautifully maintained rooms and a Bavarian/Austrian restaurant (mains €7 to €17).

Choose from rooms with balconies, terraces, park or lake views, or even the double with a sauna at the **Hotel Schreier Am See** (☎ 94 44 84; www.hotel-schreier.de; Färbergasse 2; s/d €65/110).

Petrolthaus zum Sünfzen (Maximillianstrasse 1; dishes €7) is a popular island institution.

RHINELAND-PALATINATE

Rhineland-Palatinate (Rheinland-Pfalz) has a rugged topography characterised by thinly populated mountain ranges and forests cut by deep river valleys. Created after WWII from parts of the former Rhineland and Rhenish Palatinate regions, its turbulent history resulted in the area being settled by the Romans and later hotly contested by the French and a variety of German states. The state capital is Mainz.

This land of wine and great natural beauty reaches its apex in the enchanted Moselle Valley towns such as Cochem, and along the heavily touristed Rhine, where verdant hillside vineyards twine around the foundations of noble castles and looming medieval fortresses.

MOSELLE VALLEY

Exploring the vineyards and wineries of the Moselle (Mosel) Valley is an ideal way to get a taste of German culture and people – and, of course, the wonderful wines. Take the time to slow down and do some sipping, but note that most wineries are closed from November to March.

The Moselle is bursting at the seams with historical sites and picturesque towns built along the river below steep rocky cliffs planted with vineyards (they say locals are born with one leg shorter than the other so that they can easily work the vines). It's one of the country's most romantically scenic regions, with stunning views rewarding the intrepid hikers who brave the hilly trails.

Many wine-makers have their own small *pensions* but accommodation is hard to find in May, on summer weekends or during the local wine harvest (mid-September to mid-October).

Getting There & Away

The most scenic part of the Moselle Valley runs 195km northeast from Trier to Koblenz; it's most practical to begin your Moselle Valley trip from either of these two. If you have private transport and are coming from the north, however, you might head up the Ahr Valley and cut through the scenic Eifel Mountain area between the A61 and A48.

Getting Around

It is not possible to travel the length of the Moselle River via rail. Local and fast trains run every hour between Trier and Koblenz (€15.60, 1½ hours), but the only riverside stretch of this line is between Cochem and Koblenz. Apart from this run – and the scenic Moselweinbahn line taking tourists between Bullay and Traben-Trarbach (€2.50, 20 minutes) – travellers must use buses, ferries, bicycles or cars to travel between Moselle towns.

Moselbahn (☎ 0651 14 77 50; www.moselbahn .de, in German) runs eight buses on weekdays (fewer at weekends) between Trier and Bullay (three hours each way), a very scenic route following the river's winding course and passing through numerous quaint villages. Buses leave from outside the train stations in Trier, Traben-Trarbach and Bullay. Frequent buses operate between Kues (Alter Bahnhof) and the Wittlich main train station (€3.60, 30 minutes one way), and connect with trains to Koblenz and Trier.

A great way to explore the Moselle in the high season is by boat. Just make sure you have enough time to relax and enjoy the languorous pace; getting from Koblenz to Trier using scheduled ferry services takes two days. Between early May and mid-October,

Köln-Düsseldorfer (KD) Line (☎ 0221 208 8318; www
.k-d.com) ferries sail daily between Koblenz
and Cochem (€20.20 one way, 4½ hours),
and the **Gebrüder Kolb Line** (☎ 02673 15 15) runs
boats upriver from Cochem to Trier and back
via Traben-Trarbach and Bernkastel. Various
smaller ferry companies also operate on the
Moselle. Eurail and German Rail passes are
valid for all normal KD Line services, and
travel on your birthday is free.

The Moselle is a popular area among
cyclists, and for much of the river's course
there's a separate 'Moselroute' bike track.
Touren-Rad (☎ 0261 911 60 16; Hohenzollernstrasse
127), six blocks from the main train station in
Koblenz, rents quality mountain and touring
bicycles from €6 to €10 per day. It has a deal
with the rental shop at Trier's main **train
station** (☎ 0651 14 88 56), so you can pick up
or return bikes at either. In Bernkastel, **Fun-
Bike Team** (☎ 06531 940 24; Schanzstrasse 22) rents
standard bikes from €8 per day.

Koblenz
☎ 0261 / pop 109,000
While not to be compared with Trier or
Cochem, Koblenz is a nice enough place to
spend around half a day or so. The **tourist
office** (☎ 30 38 80; www.koblenz.de; Bahnhofsplatz 7)
is in front of the Hauptbahnhof.

The **Deutsches Eck** is a park at the sharp
confluence of the Rhine and Moselle Rivers
dedicated to German unity. Immediately
across the Rhine is the impressive **Festung
Ehrenbreitstein fortress** (☎ 974 24 45; adult/concession
€1.10/0.50), which houses both the DJH hostel
and the rather staid **Landesmuseum** (☎ 970 30;
adult/concession €2/1.50).

South of Koblenz, at the head of the
beautiful Eltz Valley, **Burg Eltz** (☎ 02672-95
05 00; adult/concession €5/3; ☼ Apr-Nov) is not to be
missed. Towering over the surrounding hills,
this superb medieval castle has frescoes,
paintings, furniture and ornately decorated
rooms. Burg Eltz is best reached by train
to Moselkern, from where it's a 50-minute
walk up through the forest. Alternatively,
you can drive via Münster-Maifeld to the
nearby car park.

Koblenz has a wonderful **DJH Hostel** (☎ 97
28 70; www.djh.de; dm €14.20-17.50) housed in the
old Ehrenbreitstein fortress. From the main
train station take bus No 7, 8 or 9; there's
also a chairlift (€4/6 one way/return) from
Ehrenbreitstein station by the river.

Hotel und Weinstube Kornpforte (☎ 311 74;
Kornpfortstrasse 11; s/d €38/80) is a good choice.

Altenhof and the area around Münzplatz
in the Altstadt offer a variety of good eating options.

Cochem
☎ 02671 / pop 5300
This pretty picture-postcard German town
has narrow alleyways and one of the most
beautiful castles in the region. It's also a
good base for hikes into the hills. The staff
are very helpful in Cochem's **tourist office**
(☎ 600 40; www.cochem.de; Endertplatz) next to the
Moselbrücke bridge.

For a great view, head up to the **Pinnerkreuz**
with the chairlift on Endertstrasse (€4). The
stunning **Reichsburg Castle** (☎ 255; ☼ 9am-5pm
mid-Mar–mid-Nov) is just a 15-minute walk
up the hill from town. There are regular
daily tours (adult/concession €3/1.60) and
English translation sheets are available. Cochem's **HH Hieronimi** (☎ 221; Stadionstrasse 1-3),
just across the river is a friendly, family-run
vineyard that offers tours for €5, including
two tastings, a bottle of its own wine and
a souvenir glass. Also in Cochem there's
Weingut Rademacher (☎ 41 64; Pinnerstrasse 10),
diagonally behind the train station, where
you can tour its vineyard and cellar (an
old WWII bunker) for €5/7 with four/six
wine tastings.

Campingplatz Am Freizeitszentrum (☎ 44 09;
Stadionstrasse; per person/tent/car €4/4/6) is downstream from the northern bridge, alongside
the river.

DJH Hostel (☎ 86 33; www.djh.de; Klottener Strasse
9; dm €16.90-22.90) is beautifully situated on the
banks of the river, the spotless rooms in this
hostel have only four beds and their own
private bathrooms.

Hotel Noss (☎ 36 12; www.noss-live.de; Mosel-
promenade 17; s/d €44/86) is a large hotel on the
waterfront.

Kochlöffel (Am Markt 10) is a cheap fast-food
choice where you can eat well for less than
€5 (chicken halves €2.50). **Zom Stüffje** (☎ 72
60; Oberbachstrasse 14; mains €8-18) is a traditional
eating house.

Bernkastel-Kues
☎ 06531 / pop 7500
The twin town of Bernkastel-Kues is at the
heart of the middle Moselle region. On
the right bank, Bernkastel has a charming

Markt (square), a romantic ensemble of half-timbered houses with beautifully decorated gables. For a primer on the local vino, try Bernkastel's **Weingut Dr Willkomm** (☎ 80 54; Gestade 1). Located in a lovely old arched cellar, the vineyard also distils its own brandy. For a more thorough course, head across the river to Kues' **Vinothek** (☎ 41 41; Cusanusstrasse 2; admission €1.50, with tastings €9), where €9 entitles you to taste as much or as little of the 130 wines and sparkling wines as you wish. The **tourist office** (☎ 40 23; www.bernkastel-kues.de, in German; Am Gestade 6) is on the Bernkastel side.

The **Campingplatz Kueser Werth** (☎ 82 00; Am Hafen 2) has pleasant camp sites by the river. The **DJH Hostel** (☎ 23 95; www.djh.de; Jugendherbergsstrasse 1; dm €12.70) is near the castle. **Hotel Bären** (☎ 95 04 40; www.hotel-baeren.de; Schanzstrasse; s/d €48/88) has first-rate, modern rooms, some with river views.

Traben-Trarbach

☎ 06541 / pop 5800

Full of fanciful Art Nouveau villas, the smart double town of Traben-Trarbach is a welcome relief from the 'romantic-half-timbered-town' circuit. Pick up a map at the **tourist office** (☎ 839 80; www.traben-trarbach.de, in German; Bahnstrasse 22), a five-minute walk south of Traben's train station.

For camping, there's the **Rissbach** (☎ 31 11; Rissbacher Strasse 170; ☀ Apr–mid-Oct). The **DJH Hostel** (☎ 92 78; www.djh.de; Hirtenpfad 6; dm €15.90) has small, modern dorms.

The **Central-Hotel** (☎ 62 38; www.central-hotel-traben.de, in German; Bahnstrasse 43; s/d €33/60) is clean, friendly and provides a good breakfast, and rooms come with toilet and shower.

Unusual and popular with the locals, the restaurant **Alte Zunftscheune** (☎ 97 37; Neue Rathausstrasse) serves steak with horseradish sauce, salad and fried potato for €14.

TRIER

☎ 0651 / pop 100,000

Vineyards line the Moselle River on the way to Trier and Luxembourg. Trier is touted as Germany's oldest town and you'll find more Roman ruins here than anywhere else north of the Alps. Although settlement of the site dates back to 400 BC, Trier itself was founded in 15 BC as Augusta Treverorum, the capital of Gaul, and was second in importance only to Rome in the Western Roman Empire. Its proximity to France can be tasted in its cuisine, while its large student population injects life among the ruins.

Orientation & Information

From the main train station head west along Bahnhofstrasse and Theodor-Heuss-Allee to the Porta Nigra, where you'll find Trier's **tourist office** (☎ 97 80 80; www.trier.de; ☀ 9am-6pm Mon-Sat, 10am-3pm Sun Apr-Oct; 10am-5pm Mon-Sat, to 1pm Sun Nov-Mar). Ask about the Saturday guided **city walking tours** in English (€6), and the three-day Trier-Card (€9), a combined ticket for the city's main sights, museums and public transport. From Porta Nigra, walk along Simeonstrasse's pedestrian zone to Hauptmarkt, the heart of the old city. Most of the sights are within this area of roughly 1 sq km. There's a convenient and cheap **Wasch Salon** (Brückenstrasse 19-21). The **main post office** is near the station.

Sights

The town's chief landmark is the **Porta Nigra** (adult/concession €2.10/1.60; ☀ 9am-6pm Apr-Sep, to 5pm Oct-Mar), the imposing city gate on the northern edge of the town centre, which dates back to the 2nd century AD. The interesting **Rheinisches Landesmuseum** (Weimarer Allee 1; admission €5.50; ☀ 9.30am-5pm Tue-Fri, 10.30am-5pm Sat & Sun, 9.30am-5pm Mon May-Oct) has works of art dating from Paleolithic, Roman and modern times.

Trier's massive Romanesque **Dom** (www.dominformation.de; Liebfrauenstrasse 12; ☀ 6.30am-6pm Apr-Oct, to 5.30pm Nov-Mar) shares a 1600-year history with the nearby and equally impressive **Konstantin Basilika** (☎ 724 68; Konstantinplatz; tours by appt €25; ☀ 10am-6pm Mon-Fri, noon-6pm Sun Apr-Oct). Also worth visiting are the ancient **Amphitheater** (Olevigerstrasse), the **Kaiserthermen** (Im Palastgarten) and **Barbarathermen** (Roman baths; Südallee). The early-Gothic **Dreikönigenhaus** (Simeonstrasse 19) was built around 1230 as a protective tower; the original entrance was on the second level, accessible only by way of a retractable rope ladder.

History buffs and nostalgic socialists can visit the **Karl Marx Haus Museum** (☎ 97 06 80; Brückenstrasse 10; adult/concession €2/1; ☀ 10am-6pm Tue-Sun, 1-6pm Mon Apr-Oct) the birthplace of the man.

Sleeping

Trier-City (☎ 869 21; Luxemburger Strasse 81; per person/tent/car €6/4/4; ☀ Apr-Oct) Central and located

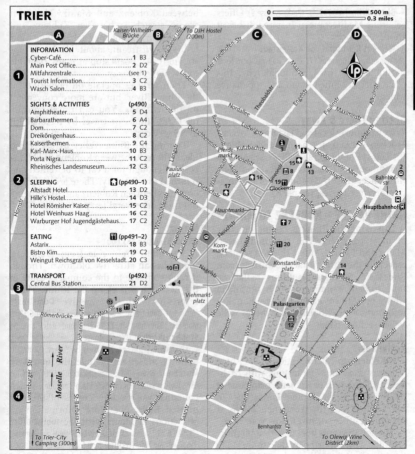

TRIER

INFORMATION	
Cyber-Café	1 B3
Main Post Office	2 D2
Mitfahrzentrale	(see 1)
Tourist Information	3 C2
Wasch Salon	4 B3

SIGHTS & ACTIVITIES	(p490)
Amphitheater	5 D4
Barbarathermen	6 A4
Dom	7 C2
Dreikönigenhaus	8 C2
Kaiserthermen	9 C4
Karl-Marx-Haus	10 B3
Porta Nigra	11 C2
Rheinisches Landesmuseum	12 C3

SLEEPING	(pp490-1)
Altstadt Hotel	13 D2
Hille's Hostel	14 D3
Hotel Römisher Kaiser	15 C2
Hotel Weinhuas Haag	16 C2
Warburger Hof Jugendgästehaus	17 C2

EATING	(pp491-2)
Astarix	18 B3
Bistro Kim	19 C2
Weingut Reichsgraf von Kesselstadt	20 C3

TRANSPORT	(p492)
Central Bus Station	21 D2

beside the Moselle River. Ask at the tourist office for pleasant spots further afield.

DJH Jugendgästehaus (☎ 14 66 20; www.djh-info .de; An der Jugendherberge 4; dm/s/d €16/22/60) Located by the Moselle River.

Hille's Hostel (☎ 71 02 78 5; www.hilles-hostel-trier .de; Gartenfeldstrasse 7; dm €14) The rooms, furnished with Ikea-like bunk beds, are set back from the road and quiet, but the building itself and the facilities feel somewhat neglected.

Warberger Hof Jugendgästehaus (☎ 97 52 50; www.warsberger-hof.de; Dietrichstrasse 42; dm/s/d €15/ 25/42) A large old mansion with a nice bar attached.

Hotel Weinhaus Haag (☎ 97 57 50; www.hotel -weinhuas-haag.de, in German; Stockplatz 1; s/d €25/50) The best value for staying in the Altstadt.

Altstadt Hotel (☎ 14 55 60; www.hotels-trier.de; Am Porta-Nigra-Platz; s/d €67/98) In the centre, the Altstadt has spacious rooms.

Hotel Römischer Kaiser (☎ 977 00; hotels-trier.de; Am Porta-Nigra-Platz 6; s/d €66/96) Across the road from the Altstadt, the Kaiser has even better rooms.

Eating

The narrow Judenpetrolse, near the Markt, has several bars and cafés for tipples and nibbles, whereas a slicker crowd gravitates towards a cluster of bars on Viehmarktplatz.

Astarix (☎ 722 39; Karl-Marx-Strasse 11) This is a favourite student hang-out back in an arcade that serves large salads and main dishes for under €6.

Bistro Krim (☎ 739 43; Glockenstrasse 7) Offers generous Mediterranean-inspired dishes at affordable prices.

Weingut Reichsgraf von Kesselstadt (☎ 411 78; Liebfrauenstrasse 10; mains €7) In a casual outdoor setting beside the Liebfrauenkirche, this place offers a limited menu and superlative wines.

Getting There & Away

Trier has hourly local and fast trains to Saarbrücken (€12.90, 1½ hours) and Koblenz (€15.60, 1½ hours), as well as services to Luxembourg (€7.40, 45 minutes) and Metz (in France; €18.20, 2½ hours). For information on river ferries, see p488.

RHINE VALLEY – KOBLENZ TO MAINZ

A trip along the Rhine is on the itinerary of most travellers. The section between Mainz and Koblenz offers the best scenery, especially the narrow tract downriver from Rüdesheim. Spring and autumn are the best times to visit; in summer it's over-run and in winter most towns go into hibernation. For information on Koblenz, see the Moselle Valley section, p488.

Activities

The Koblenz-to-Mainz section of the Rhine Valley is great for wine tasting, with Bacharach, 45km south of Koblenz, being one of the top choices for sipping. For tastings in other towns, ask for recommendations at the tourist offices or just follow your nose.

Though the trails here may be a bit more crowded with day-trippers than those along the Moselle, hiking along the Rhine is also excellent. The slopes and trails around Bacharach are justly famous.

Getting There & Away

Koblenz and Mainz are the best starting points. The Rhine Valley is also easily accessible from Frankfurt on a long day trip, but that won't do justice to the region.

Getting Around

Each mode of transport on the Rhine has its own advantages and all are equally enjoyable. Try combining several of them by going on foot one day, cycling the next, and then taking a boat for a view from the river. The **Köln-Düsseldorfer (KD) Line** (☎ 0221 208 83 18; www.k-d .com) runs many slow and fast boats daily

between Koblenz and Mainz. The most scenic stretch is between Koblenz and Rüdesheim; the journey takes about four hours downstream, about 5½ hours upstream (€24). Boats stop at many riverside towns along the way.

Train services operate on both sides of the Rhine River, but are more convenient on the left bank. You can travel nonstop on IC/EC trains or travel by regional RB or SE services.

Touring the Rhine Valley by car is also ideal. The route between Koblenz and Mainz is short enough for a car to be rented and returned to either city. There are no bridge crossings between Koblenz and Rüdesheim, but there are several ferry crossings.

Mainz

☎ 06131 / pop 183,000

A 30-minute train ride from Frankfurt, Mainz has an attractive old town. Though it can't compare to the compact beauty of the nearby towns along the Rhine, Mainz impresses with its massive **Domstrasse** (cathedral; Domstrasse 3; admission free; ☽ 9am-6.30pm Mon-Fri, 10am-4pm Sat, 12.45-3pm Sun) and the **St Stephanskirche** (Weisspetrolse 12; admission free), with stained-glass windows by Marc Chagall. Mainz's museums include the **Gutenberg Museum** (☎ 26 40; Liebfrauenplatz 5; adult/concession €3/1.30; ☽ 9am-5pm Tue-Sat, 11am-3pm Sun), which contains two precious copies of the first printed Bible. For more information on attractions in Mainz, visit the **tourist office** (☎ 28 62 10; www.mainz.de; Brückenturm am Rathaus; ☽ 9am-6pm Mon-Fri, 10am-3pm Sat).

If you are staying overnight, try the **Jugendgästehaus** (☎ 853 32; www.djh.de; Otto-Brunfels-Schneise 4; dm €16.10-21.20); take bus No 62, 63 or 92 towards Weisenau. The **Hotel Stadt Coblenz** (☎ 22 76 02; fax 22 33 07; Rheinstrasse 49; s/d €52/68, with shared bathroom €42/55) has hostel-quality rooms.

The **Augustiner Keller** (☎ 22 26 62; Augustinerstrasse 26; mains €6-14) serves tasty Alsatian-style pizzas in a homy, old-fashioned setting.

St Goar/St Goarhausen

☎ 06741 / pop 3500

Where the slopes along the Rhine aren't covered with vines, you can bet they built a castle. One of the most impressive is **Burg Rheinfels** (☎ 383; adult/concession €4/2; ☽ 9am-5pm Apr-Oct, 10am-4pm Sat & Sun in good weather Nov-Mar) in St Goar. An absolute must-see, the labyrinthine ruins reflect the greed and ambition of Count Dieter V of Katzenelnbogen, who built the castle in 1245 to help levy tolls on passing ships. Across the river, just south of St Goarshausen, is the Rhine's most famous sight, the **Loreley Cliff**. Legend has it that a maiden sang sailors to their deaths against its base. It's worth the trek to the top of the Loreley for the view.

For camping, **Campingplatz Loreleyblick** (☎ 20 66; camp sites €2.20, plus per person €3; ☯ Mar-Oct) is on the banks of the Rhine, opposite the legendary rock. St Goar's **Jugendherberge** (☎ 388; www.djh.de; Bismarckweg 17; dm €12.70) is right below the castle. More restful accommodation can be found at **Knab's Mühlenschänke** (☎ 16 98; fax 16 78; Gründelbachtal 73; s/d €30/52) about 1.5km north of St Goar. You can sip the house wine here in a rural atmosphere. The **Schlosshotel Rheinfels** (☎ 80 20; www .schlosshotel-rheinfels.de, in German; s/d €85/128) in the castle is the top address in town, with rooms and a fine restaurant with prices to match.

Bacharach

☎ 06743 / pop 2400

The town of Bacharach hides its not inconsiderable charms behind a time-worn wall and is therefore easily bypassed.

Walk beneath one of its thick arched gateways, however, and you'll find yourself in a beautifully preserved medieval village. Drop by the **tourist office** (☎ 91 93 03; www.bacharach .de, in German; Oberstrasse 45; ☯ 9am-5pm Mon-Fri, 10am-4pm Sat Apr-Oct) for information on Bacharach's sights and lodging.

The **Sonnenstrand** (☎ 17 52; www.camping -sonnenstrand.de; per person/tent/car €4.20/3/6; ☯ Apr-mid-Oct) offers riverside camping just 500m south of the centre. Bacharach's **Jugendherberge** (☎ 12 66; www.djh.de; dm €15.90) is a legendary facility housed in the Burg Stahleck castle. In town, **Irmgaard Orth** (☎ 15 53; Spurgasse 2; s/d €20/34) offers good budget rooms.

Kurpfälzische Münze (☎ 13 75; Oberstrasse 72; dishes €7-20) serves traditional dishes, including game. **Zum Grünen Baum** (☎ 12 08; Oberstrasse 63; mains €7) is a wonderful place to sample the region's abundance of top-notch wines.

HESSE

The Hessians, a Frankish tribe, were among the first to convert to Lutheranism in the early 16th century. Apart from a brief period of unity in that same century under Philip the Magnanimous, Hesse (Hessen) remained a motley collection of principalities and, later, of Prussian administrative districts until proclaimed a state in 1945. Its main cities are Frankfurt-am-Main, Kassel and the capital, Wiesbaden.

As well as being a transport hub, the very un-German city of Frankfurt-am-Main can also be used as a base to explore some of the smaller towns in Hesse. The beautiful Taunus and Spessart regions offer quiet village life and hours of scenic walks.

FRANKFURT-AM-MAIN

☎ 069 / pop 650,000

They call it 'Bankfurt', 'Mainhattan' and much more. It's on the Main (pronounced 'mine') River, and is generally referred to as Frankfurt-am-Main, or Frankfurt/Main, since there is another large city called Frankfurt (Frankfurt-an-der-Oder) that is near the Polish border.

Frankfurt is the financial and geographical centre of western Germany, as well as the host of important trade fairs. Thanks to generous funding in the 1980s and early 1990s, Frankfurt also has some excellent museums.

It is Germany's most important transport hub for air, train and road connections so you'll probably end up here at some point. Don't be surprised if you find this cosmopolitan melting pot much more interesting than you had expected.

Orientation

The airport is 11 minutes by train southwest of the city centre. The Hauptbahnhof is on the western side of the city, but within walking distance of the old city centre.

The safest route to the city centre through the sleazy train station area is along Kaiserstrasse. This leads to Kaiserplatz and on to a large square called An der Hauptwache. The area between the former prison/police station (Hauptwache), and the Römerberg, in the tiny vestige of Frankfurt's original old city, is the centre of Frankfurt. The Main River flows just south of the Altstadt, with several bridges leading to one of the city's livelier areas, Sachsenhausen. Its northeastern corner, behind the youth hostel (see p495), is known as Alt-Sachsenhausen and is full of quaint old houses and narrow alleyways.

Information

BOOKSHOPS

British Bookshop (Börsenstrasse 17) Provides a wide range of English-language fiction and nonfiction.

Hugendubel (Beiberpetrolse) Between the Hauptwache and Rathenauplatz stocks guidebooks and has a café downstairs.

Südseite (☎ 25 29 14; Kaiserstrasse 55) Near the train station, a good selection of new and used books in English.

DISCOUNT CARDS

Frankfurt-am-Main Card (one day/two days €7.80/11.50) Give 50% off admission to important museums, the zoo and Palmengarten; unlimited travel on public transport.

INTERNET ACCESS

CyberRyder (☎ 39 67 54; Töngesgasse 31; per 30min €3.20)

Prepaidmarkt.de (☎ 24 24 79 39; Kaiserstrasse 81; per hr €3)

Telebistro (☎ 61 99 11 87; Poststrasse 2; per 30min €2.10)

LAUNDRY

Miele Wash World (Moselstrasse; wash/dry €3/0.50) A few blocks from the train station.

SB Waschcenter (Grosse Seestrasse 46; wash/dry €3-4/0.50; ☽ 6am-11pm) An option in Bockenheim.

SB Waschcenter (Wallstrasse 8) In Sachsenhausen.

MEDICAL SERVICES

Doctor (☎ 192 92; ☽ 24hr)

Uni-Klinik (☎ 630 10; Theodor Stern Kai, Sachsenhausen; ☽ 24hr)

MONEY

American Express (Kaiserstrasse 10)

Reisebank Train station (☽ 6.30am-10pm); Airport (Terminal 1, arrival hall B; ☽ 6am-11pm) The train station branch is near the southern exit at the head of platform No 1.

Thomas Cook (Kaiserstrasse 11)

POST

Main post office (Zeil 90; Ground fl, Karstadt department store; ☽ 9.30am-8pm)

Post office Hauptbahnhof (☽ 7am-7.30pm Mon-Fri, 8am-4pm Sat); Airport (Departure Lounge B; ☽ 7am-9pm)

TOURIST INFORMATION

CityInfo Zeil (☎ 21 23 88 00; cnr Zeil & Stiftstrasse; ☽ 10am-6pm Mon-Fri, to 4pm Sat & Sun) Another conveniently located branch.

German National Tourist Office (☎ 974 64; www .deutschland-tourismus.de, in German; Beethovenstrasse 69) Just northwest of the centre, this is a good place to contact if you're still planning your trip to Germany; it has brochures on all areas of the country.

Römer Tourist Office (☎ 21 23 88 00; Römerberg 27; ☽ 9.30am-5.30pm Mon-Fri, 10am-4pm Sat & Sun) Occupies the northwest corner of the Römerberg square.

Tourist office (☎ 21 23 88 00; www.frankfurt -tourismus.de; ☽ 8am-9pm Mon-Fri; 9am-6pm Sat, Sun & hols) In the main hall of the train station. For its efficient room-finding service there's a charge of €3.

Sights

About 80% of the old city was wiped off the map by two Allied bombing raids in March 1944, and postwar reconstruction was subject to the demands of the new age. Rebuilding efforts were more thoughtful, however, in the **Römerberg**, the old central area of Frankfurt west of the cathedral, where restored 14th- and 15th-century buildings provide a glimpse of the beautiful city this once was. The old town hall, or **Römer**, is in the northwestern corner of Römerberg and consists of three 15th-century houses topped with Frankfurt's trademark stepped gables.

East of Römerberg, behind the Historischer Garten (Historical Garden), which has the remains of Roman and Carolingian foundations, is the **Fankfurter Dom** (Domplatz 14; tour adult/concession €3/2; ☽ 9am-noon Mon-Thu, Sat & Sun; 2.30-6pm daily), the coronation site of Holy Roman emperors from 1562 to 1792. It's dominated by the elegant 15th-century Gothic **tower** (completed in the 1860s) – one of the few structures left standing after the 1944 raids.

Anyone with an interest in German literature should visit **Goethe Haus** (☎ 13 88 00; Grosser Hirschgraben 23-25; adult/concession €5/3; ☽ 9am-6pm Mon-Fri Apr-Sep, to 4pm Mon-Fri Oct-Mar, 10am-4pm Sat & Sun year-round). Johann Wolfgang von Goethe was born in this house in 1749.

A little further afield, there's the botanical **Palmengarten** (☎ 21 23 66 89; www.palmengarten-frank furt.de; Siesmayerstrasse 63; adult/concession €3.50/1.50; ☽ 9am-6pm), next door to **Grüneburg Park**. The creative **Frankfurt Zoo** (☎ 212 337 35; www.zoo -frankfurt.de; Alfred-Brehm-Platz 16; adult/concession €8/4) is also a good place to unwind. It is also a nice 40-minute walk east along the south bank of the Main River to the **lock** in Offenbach – just before it there's a good beer garden.

There's a great **flea market** along Museumsufer that's open between 8am and 2pm every Saturday.

MUSEUMS

North of the cathedral, the **Museum für Moderne Kunst** (☎ 21 23 04 47; Domstrasse 10; adult/concession €5/2.50) features works of modern art by Joseph Beuys, Claes Oldenburg and many others.

Also on the north bank there's the **Jüdisches Museum** (Jewish Museum; ☎ 21 23 50 00; Untermainkai 14-15; adult/concession €2.60/1.30, free Sat; ☸ 10am-5pm Tue-Sun), a huge place with exhibits on Jewish life in the city from the Middle Ages to present.

Numerous museums line the south bank of the Main River along the so-called **Museumsufer** (Museum Embankment). Pick of the crop is the **Städelsches Kunstinstitut** (☎ 605 09 80; www.staedelmuseum.de; Schaumainkai 63; adult/concession €6/5; ☸ 10am-5pm Tue, Fri-Sun; to 9pm Wed & Thu), with a world-class collection of paintings by artists from the Renaissance to the 20th century, including Botticelli, Dürer, Van Eyck, Rubens, Rembrandt, Vermeer, Cézanne and Renoir.

Other highlights include the **Deutsches Filmmuseum** (☎ 21 23 88 30; Schaumainkai 41; adult/concession €2.50/1.30; ☸ 10am-5pm Tue, Thu-Fri & Sun; to 8pm Wed; 2-8pm Sat); the fascinating, design-oriented **Museum für Angewandte Kunst** (Museum of Applied Arts; ☎ 21 23 40 37; Schaumainkai 17; admission €5); and the **Deutsches Architekturmuseum** (☎ 212 388 44; Schaumainkai 43; admission €8).

Sleeping

Some of the best *pensions* are in Frankfurt's posh Westend. Predictably, most of Frankfurt's budget accommodation is in the sleazy Bahnhofsviertel which surrounds the station.

BUDGET

Campingplatz Heddernheim (☎ 57 03 32; An der Sandelmühle 35; camp sites €3.50, plus per person/car €5.20/4.50; ☸ year-round) In the Heddernheim district northwest of the city centre. It's a 15-minute ride on the U1, U2 or U3 from the Hauptwache U-Bahn station – get off at Heddernheim.

DJH Hostel (☎ 610 01 50; www.djh.de; Deutschherrnufer 12; dm juniors/seniors €16/20) Within walking distance of the city centre and Sachsenhausen's nightspots, this well-run hostel is a good choice. From the train station take bus No 46 to Frankensteinerplatz, or take S-Bahn No 2, 3, 4, 5 or 6 to Lokalbahnhof, then walk north for 10 minutes. Check-in begins at 1pm, curfew is 2am.

Pension Backer (☎ 74 79 92; fax 74 79 00; Mendelssohnstrasse 92; s/d €25/40) The Backer has basic rooms but is located in a nice residential neighbourhood.

Hotel Glockshuber (☎ 74 26 28; fax 74 26 29; Mainzer Landstrasse 120; s/d €35/60) North of the main train station, the Glockshuber is another pleasant option.

Stay & Learn Alliance (☎ 25 39 52; www.room-frankfurt.de; Kaiserstrasse 74; s/d €35/45) Only two minutes from the train station, the large and rambling Stay & Learn has slightly deteriorating rooms. German language classes are conducted on the premises.

MID-RANGE

Hotel-Pension Bruns (☎ 74 88 96; fax 74 88 46; Mendelssohnstrasse 42; s/d €50/65, with shared bathroom €40/50) Simple rooms in a spacious house, but the highlight is breakfast in bed.

Hotel Münchner Hof (☎ 23 00 66; fax 23 44 28; Münchener Strasse 46; s/d €49/65) Just a short walk from the train station, the Münchner Hof is a basic option.

Hotel Memphis (☎ 242 609 0; www.memphis-hotel.de; Münchenerstrasse 15; s/d €60/80) The stylish modern rooms are fully equipped and the front desk is trained to assist with all your needs, business or otherwise.

Hotel Wiesbaden (☎ 23 23 47; fax 25 28 45; Baselerstrasse 52; s/d €65/75) One of the better options in the area around the train station.

Hotel Hamburger Hof (☎ 271 39 69 0; www.hamburgerhof.com; Poststrasse 10-12; s/d €69/79) Another excellent choice, the Hamburger Hof's rooms are immaculate and modern.

Hotel Beethoven (☎ 74 60 91; www.hotelbeethoven.de, in German; Beethovenstrasse 44; s/d €70/145) The elegant Beethoven is in a quiet neighbourhood north of the train station.

TOP END

Bristol Hotel (☎ 242 39 0; www.bristol-hotel.de; Ludwigstrasse 15; s/d €70/80) With a hip sophisticated aesthetic, and fantastic outdoor garden, the Bristol is a standout in the neighbourhood around the train station. International newspapers and Internet access are free for guests.

Hotel Mozart (☎ 156 80 60; www.hotelmozart.de; Parkstrasse 17; s/d €95/125) A 10-minute walk north from the Opera House, the Mozart is nicely furnished, has excellent breakfasts and is directly across the street from peaceful Grüneburg Park.

FRANKFURT-AM-MAIN

Some streets pedestrian-only

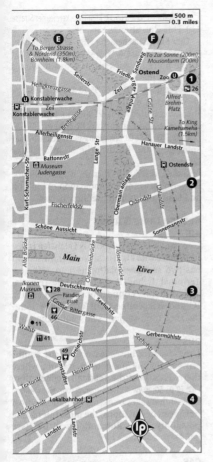

Strasse in particular has a Middle Eastern tone. Wallstrasse and the surrounding streets in Alt-Sachsenhausen also have lots of ethnic mid-priced restaurants.

Another good place for ravenous hunters and gatherers is the cosmopolitan Berger Strasse and Nordend areas north of the Zeil.

CAFÉS

Stattcafé (☎ 70 89 07; Grempstrasse 21; mains €6) In Bockenheim, offers vegetarian and meat dishes, as well as good coffee and cakes.

Metropol (☎ 288 287; Weckmarkt 13-15; mains €7) Serves up well-priced and filling salads and casseroles until late. It's near the Dom and you can sit unharrassed for hours with a book.

Café Laumer (☎ 727 912; Brockheimer Landstrasse 67; mains €9-15) The philosopher Theodor Adorno used to drink coffee at this café; reminiscent of old-school Vienna. Grab one of the few outdoor tables but be aware that it closes at 7pm.

Café Karin (☎ 295 217; Grosser Hirschgraben 28; mains €9-15) Breakfast and whole-grain baked goods are the specialities at this understated place near the Zeil.

RESTAURANTS

Da Cimino (☎ 77 11 42; Abdelstrasse 28; pizza €4-8) Customise your pizza at this small neighbourhood spot which gets especially busy during lunch time.

Zum Gemalten Haus (Schweizer Strasse 67; mains €7) A lively place full of paintings of old Frankfurt, where you can try apple wine with your meal.

Zur Sonne (☎ 45 93 96; Berger Strasse 312; mains €7) This has a gorgeous yard for summer tippling in Bornheim. To get there take the U-4 to Bornheim-Mitte.

Pielok (Jordanstrasse 3; mains €7) Looks like your grandmother had a hand in the decorations; it's cosy and the food is traditional, filling and very popular with students. Take the U-4 to Merianplatz.

Eckhaus (☎ 49 11 97; Bornheimer Landstrasse 45; meals from €7) A relaxed restaurant and bar that serves well-priced salads and main dishes in the evening. Take the U-4 to Merianplatz.

Fichte-Kränzi (Wallstrasse 5; mains €8) Recommended for its friendly atmosphere and well-priced food.

Steigenberger Frankfurter Hof (☎ 215 02; frank furter-hof@steigenberger.de; Am Kaiserplatz; s/d Mon-Fri €335/385, Sat & Sun €160/210) Schopenhauer used to lunch here but his pessimism is unlikely to dampen your enthusiasm for this elegant and cosmopolitan 19th-century neo-renaissance institution.

Eating

Known to the locals as Fresspetrols (Munch-Alley), the Kalbächer Petrolse and Grosse Bockenheimer Strasse area, between Opernplatz and Börsenstrasse, has some medium-priced restaurants and fast-food places with outdoor tables in summer.

The area around the main train station has lots of ethnic eating options. Baseler

GERMANY

SELF-CATERING

Off Hasenpetrolse, **Kleinmarkthalle** (Hasengasse 5-7; 7.30am-6pm Mon-Fri, to 3pm Sat) is a great produce market with loads of fruit, vegetables, meats and hot food.

There are also good fresh-produce markets at **Bockenheimer Warte** (8am-6pm Thu) and **Südbahnhof** (8am-6pm Fri).

Drinking

Apple-wine taverns are a Frankfurt eating and drinking tradition. They serve *Ebbelwoi* (Frankfurt dialect for *Apfelwein*), an alcoholic apple cider, along with local specialities like *Handkäse mit Musik* (literally, 'hand-cheese with music'). This is a round cheese soaked in oil and vinegar and topped with onions; your bowel supplies the music. Some good *Ebbelwoi* are situated in Alt-Sachsenhausen – the area directly behind the DJH hostel – which bulges with eateries and pubs.

Bar Oppenheimer (62 66 74; Oppenheimerstrasse 41) The drinks and clientele are both cosmopolitan and the décor minimalist at this bar, and at next door Orion which is under the same management.

Zur Germania (61 33 36; Textorstrasse 16) This is an apple-wine tavern in Sachsenhausen.

Keeper's Lounge (60 60 72 10; Schweizerstrasse 78) Another Sachsenhausen joint, the extensive drinks menu at Keeper's will keep you occupied for most of the night.

Zum Schwejk (29 31 66; Schäfferpetrolse 20) This is a popular gay bar.

Living XXL (242 93 710; Kaiserstrasse 29) Living large – think three bars and huge video screens – is what it's all about at Frankfurt's largest nightclub located on the ground floor of the Eurotower.

Entertainment

Ballet, opera and theatre are strong features of Frankfurt's entertainment scene. *Journal Frankfurt* (€1.50) and *Fritz* have good listings in German of what's on in town. For information and bookings, go to **Städtische Bühnen** (134 04 00; Willy-Brandt-Platz), or the **Karstadt concert and theatre booking service** (29 48 48; Zeil 90; commission charged).

Turm-Palast (28 17 87; Am Eschenheimer Turm) Multiscreen cinema with films in English.

English Theatre (24 23 16 20; Kaiserstrasse 34) English-language plays and musicals are staged every evening (except Monday).

Jazzkeller (28 85 37; Kleine Bockenheimer Strasse 18a) This club attracts top acts.

Club King Kamehameha (480 03 70; Hanauer Landstrasse 192; cover €10; Wed-Sat) Come dressed to the nines if you want to get in to what's known as the 'Kingka'.

Mousonturm (40 58 95 20; Waldschmidtstrasse 4) Arty rock, dance performances and politically oriented cabaret are on tap at this converted soap factory in Bornheim.

Cave (28 38 08; Brönnerstrasse 11) A club that spins goth and features the occasional live concerts.

Cooky's (Am Salzhaus 4) Open until the wee hours, delivering a winning combination of hip-hop and house nights, and live indie bands.

Getting There & Away

AIR

Germany's largest airport is **Flughafen Frankfurt/Main** (69 01). The airport train station has two sections: platforms 1 to 3 (below Terminal 1, hall B) both handle regional and S-Bahn connections, whereas IR, IC and ICE connections are in the long-distance train station; signs point the way.

BUS

Long-distance buses leave from the southern side of the main train station, where there is a **Deutsche Touring/Eurolines office** (79 03 50; www.deutsche-touring.com; Mannheimerstrasse 4) that takes bookings. It handles most European destinations; the most interesting possibility is the Romantic Road bus (see p464).

CAR

Frankfurt-am-Main features the famed Frankfurter Kreuz, the biggest autobahn intersection in the country. All the main car rental companies have offices in the main hall of the train station and at the airport. The **ADM-Mitfahrzentrale** (194 40; Baselerplatz), is a three-minute walk south of the train station.

TRAIN

The Hauptbahnhof handles more departures and arrivals than any other station in Germany. For rail information, call 01805-99 66 33. The **DB Lounge** (6am-11pm) above the information office is a comfortable retreat for anyone with a valid train ticket. Hourly IC or EC trains go to Cologne (€51, two hours) and Nuremberg (€39, 2½ hours) and ICEs run to/from Hamburg on weekdays (€90, five hours).

Getting Around
TO/FROM THE AIRPORT
The S-Bahn's S8/S9 train runs every 15 minutes between the airport and Frankfurt Hauptbahnhof (11 minutes), usually continuing via Hauptwache and Konstablerwache to Offenbach; a fixed fare of €3.25 applies. Taxis (about €25 and taking 30 minutes without traffic jams) or the frequent airport bus No 61 (from Südbahnhof; €3.10) take longer.

PUBLIC TRANSPORT
Both single or day tickets for Frankfurt's excellent transport network (RMV) can be purchased from automatic machines at almost any train station or stop. The peak period short-trip tickets (*Kurzstrecken*) cost €1.05, single tickets cost €1.60 and a *Tageskarte* (24-hour ticket) costs €4.35 without a trip to the airport and €6.65 with an airport trip.

TAXI
Taxis are slow compared with public transport and expensive at €2.05 flag fall plus a minimum of €1.48 per kilometre. There are numerous taxi ranks throughout the city, or you can book a cab (☎ 23 00 01, 25 00 01, 54 50 11).

NORTH RHINE-WESTPHALIA

The North Rhine-Westphalia (Nordrhein-Westfalen) region was formed in 1946 from a hotchpotch of principalities and bishoprics, most of which had belonged to Prussia since the early 19th century. One-quarter of Germany's population currently lives here. The Rhine-Ruhr industrial area is Germany's economic powerhouse and is one of the most densely populated conurbations in the world. Though the area is dominated by bleak industrial centres and connected by a maze of train lines and autobahns, some of the cities are steeped in history and their attractions warrant an extensive visit.

COLOGNE
☎ 0221 / pop 1 million
Located at a major crossroads of European trade routes, Cologne (Köln) was an important city even in Roman times. It was then known as Colonia Agrippinensis, the capital of the province of Germania, and had no fewer than 300,000 inhabitants. In later years it remained one of northern Europe's main cities (the largest in Germany until the 19th century), and is still the centre of the German Roman Catholic church. Almost completely destroyed in WWII, it was rebuilt and many of its old churches and monuments have been meticulously restored. It's worth making the effort to visit this lively, relaxed city, especially for its famous cathedral, interesting museums and vibrant nightlife.

Orientation
Situated on the Rhine River, the skyline of Cologne is dominated by the cathedral. The pedestrianised Hohe Strasse runs north–south through the middle of the old town and is Cologne's main shopping street. The main train station is just north of the cathedral. The main bus station is just behind the train station, on Breslauer Platz.

Information
BOOKSHOPS
Ludwig im Bahnhof (Hauptbahnhof) Stocks international press and books.

EMERGENCY & MEDICAL SERVICES
Fire & Ambulance (☎ 112)
Doctor (☎ 192 92)
Police (☎ 110)

INTERNET ACCESS
Future Point (☎ 206 72 51; Richmodstrasse 13; per 30min €1.50; 🕒 8-1am Mon-Sat, 10-1am Sun)
Jetzt Dom Internet Café (☎ 277 99 32; Komödienstrasse 37; per hr €2; 🕒 9am-8pm Mon-Fri)
Surf Inn (Hohestrasse; per 30min €2; 🕒 9am-8pm Mon-Fri)

LAUNDRY
Eco-Express Waschsalon (cnr Händelstrasse & Richard-Wagner-Strasse; 🕒 6am-11pm Mon-Sat)

MONEY
American Express (Burgmauer 14)
Reisebank (Hauptbahnhof; 🕒 8am-10pm)
Thomas Cook (Burgmauer 4)

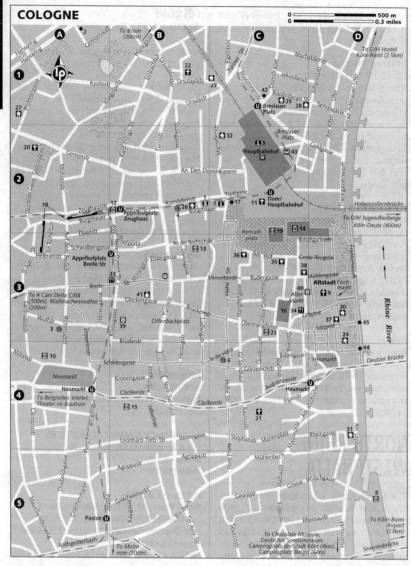

COLOGNE

POST

Main post office (Hauptbahnhof; 🕑 6am-10pm Mon-Sat, 7am-10pm Sun) Inside the Ludwig im Bahnhof bookshop near Track 6.

TOURIST INFORMATION

Tourist office (☎ 22 13 04 00; www.koelntourismus.de, in German; Unter Fettenhennen 19; 🕑 9am-9pm Mon-Sat, 10am-6pm Sun & hols Oct-Jun; 9am-10pm Mon-Sat, 10am-6pm Sun & hols Jul-Sep) Helpful office; the room-finding service (€3) is a bargain when the city is busy with trade fairs; offers a one-day Cologne Welcome Card (€9).

Sights

Cologne has a large town centre and the cathedral (Dom) is its heart, soul and tourist

INFORMATION		Praetorian Palace	(see 16)	Gaffel Haus	34 C3
American Express	1 B2	Rathaus	16 C3		
Eco-Express Waschsalon	2 A1	Roman Arch	17 C2	DRINKING	(p503)
Future-Point	3 A3	Roman Wall	18 A2	Biermuseum	(see 37)
Jetzt Dom Internet Cafe	4 B2	Römerturm	(see 18)	Brauhaus Sion	35 C3
Ludwig in Bahnhof	(see 5)	Römisch-Germanisches Museum	19 C2	Früh am Dom	36 C3
Post Office	(see 5)	St Gereon	20 A2	Papa Joe's Em Streckstump	37 D3
Reisebank	5 C2	St Maria im Kapitol	21 C4	Peter's Brauhaus	38 C3
Surf Inn	6 C4	St Ursula	22 B1		
Thomas Cook	(see 1)	Wallraf-Richartz-Museum-Fondation		ENTERTAINMENT	(p503)
Tourist Office	7 C2	Corboud	23 C3	Köln Ticket	(see 14)
				Opernhaus	39 B3
SIGHTS & ACTIVITIES	(pp500-2)	SLEEPING	(pp502-3)	Papa Joe's Klimperkasten	40 C3
Deutsches Sport und Olympia		Hayk Hotel	24 D3		
Museum	8 D5	Hotel Berg	25 C1	SHOPPING	(p503)
Diözesanmuseum	(see 19)	Hotel Good Sleep	26 B2	4711 Perfumery & Gift	
Domschatzkammer	(see 11)	Hotel Im Kupferkessel	27 A1	Shop	41 B3
Gross St Martin	9 D3	Hotel Ludwig	28 C1		
Käthe Kollwitz Museum	10 A4	Hotel Madison	29 C1	TRANSPORT	(pp503-4)
Kölner Dom	11 C2	Rhein-Hotel St Martin	30 D3	ADM-Mitfahrzentrale	42 C1
Kölnisches Stadtmuseum	12 B2	Station Hostel & Bar	31 D4	Central Bus Station	43 C2
Mikwe	(see 16)	Station	32 C2	Rent-A-Bike	44 D4
Museum für Angewandte Kunst	13 B3				
Museum Ludwig	14 C2	EATING	(p503)	OTHER	
Museum Schnütgen	15 B4	Buffet Chang	33 B3	KD River Cruises	45 D3

draw. Combined with the excellent museums next door, plan to spend at least one full day inside and around the Dom.

DOM

Head first to the southern side of the **Kölner Dom** (admission free; 7am-7.30pm) for an overall view. The structure's sheer size, with spires rising to 157m, is overwhelming. Building began in 1248 in the French Gothic style. The huge project was stopped in 1560 but started again in 1842, in the style originally planned, as a symbol of Prussia's drive for unification. It was finally finished in 1880. Miraculously, it survived WWII's heavy night bombing intact.

When you reach the transept you'll be overwhelmed by the sheer size and magnificence of it all. The five **stained-glass windows** along the north aisle depict the lives of the Virgin and St Peter. Behind the high altar you can see the **Magi's Shrine** (c 1150–1210), believed to contain the remains of the Three Wise Men, which was brought to Cologne from Milan in the 12th century. Guided tours in English are held at 10.30am and 2.30pm Monday to Saturday (at 2.30pm only on Sunday) and cost €4/2 per adult/concession; meet inside the main portal. Tours in German are more frequent and cost €3/2.

For a fitness fix, climb 509 steps up the Dom's south tower to the base of the stupendous **steeples** (adult/concession €2/1; 9am-5pm Mar-Sep, to 4pm Oct-Feb), which towered over all of Europe until the Eiffel Tower was erected. Look at the 24-tonne **Peter Bell**, the largest

working bell in the world, on your way up. At the end of your climb, the view from the vantage point, 98.25m up, is absolutely stunning; on a clear day you can see all the way to the Siebengebirge Mountains beyond Bonn. The cathedral **treasury** (27 28 01 0; www.koelner -dom.de, in German; adult/concession €4/2; 10am-6pm) has a small but valuable collection of reliquaries. Cologne's archbishops are interred in the crypt.

MUSEUMS

Next to the cathedral there's the **Römisch-Germanisches Museum** (Roman Germanic Museum; 221 223 04; Roncalliplatz 4; adult/concession €4/2; 10am-5pm Tue-Sun), which displays artefacts from all aspects of the Roman settlement in the Rhine Valley.

The **Wallraf-Richartz-Museum** (221 211 19; Martinstrasse 39; adult/concession €5.80/2.90; 10am-6pm Wed-Fri, to 8pm Tue, 11am-6pm Sat & Sun) has a fantastic collection of artworks that includes paintings by Rubens, Rembrandt and Monet.

The **Museum Ludwig** (221 223 79; www.mu seenkoeln.de, in German; Bischofsgartenstrasse 1; adult/concession €5.80/2.90; 10am-6pm Wed-Fri, to 8pm Tue, 11am-6pm Sat & Sun) displays prime pieces from Kirchner, Kandinsky and Max Ernst, as well as pop-art works by Rauschenberg and Andy Warhol.

The former church of St Cecilia houses the **Museum Schnütgen** (Cäcilienstrasse 29; adult/concession €2.50/1.25; 10am-5pm Tue-Fri, 11am-5pm Sat & Sun), an overwhelming display of church riches, including many religious artefacts as well as early ivory carvings.

At the **Diözesanmuseum** (Roncalliplatz; admission free; ⊗ Fri-Wed) you can see religious treasures.

The multimedia **Deutsches Sport und Olympia Museum** (☎ 336 09 0; www.sportmuseum-koeln.de, in German; Rheinauhafen 1; adult/concession €4/3.50; ⊗ 10am-6pm Tue-Fri, 11am-7pm Sat & Sun) is a great place to find out all about the history of sport from ancient times to the present.

Other museums worth visiting are **Käthe Kollwitz Museum** (Neumarkt 18-24; adult/concession €2.50/1), with some fine sculpture and graphics by this acclaimed socialist artist; and the **Chocolate Museum** (☎ 93 18 88 0; Rheinauhafen; adult/ concession €5.50/5; ⊗ 10am-6pm Tue-Fri, 11am-7pm Sat & Sun), on the river in the Rheinauhafen near the Altstadt, where you will learn everything about the history of making chocolate – as if you cared beyond the taste.

Tours

The summer daily **city tour** in English lasts two hours; a bus departs from the tourist office at 10am, 12.30pm and 3pm (at 11am and 2pm from November to March). The cost is a steep €14. You can also make day trips to nearby cities with **KD River Cruises** (see p503). A trip down the Rhine to Bonn is €10.40 and to Koblenz it's €32.80 one way.

Festivals & Events

Visit Cologne during the wild and crazy period of the **Cologne Carnival** (Karneval), rivalled only by Munich's Oktoberfest. People dress in creative costumes, clown suits, and whatever else their alcohol-numbed brains may invent. The streets explode with activity on the Thursday before the seventh Sunday before Easter. On Friday and Saturday evening the streets pep up, Sunday is like Thursday and on Monday (Rosenmontag) there are formal and informal parades, and much spontaneous celebrating.

Sleeping

Cheap accommodation in Cologne is not plentiful, but there are a couple of good pensions around the city, and you should be able to get private rooms unless there's a trade fair on.

BUDGET

Accommodation prices in Cologne increase by at least 20% when fairs are on. If you have private transport, a night in a car park will set you back €15 or more (and not all of them operate 24 hours). The tourist office has a room-finding service that can help with hotel rooms in the lower price range. A lot of budget and mid-range hotels cluster in the streets just north and east of the main train station.

Campingplatz der Stadt Köln (☎ 83 19 66; camp sites €4, plus per person €4; ⊗ Easter–mid-Oct) On the banks of the river on Weidenweg in Poll, 5km southeast of the city centre. Excellent kitchen facilities and a small shop selling wine and other necessities. Take the U16 to Marienburg and cross the Rodenkirchener bridge.

Campingplatz Berger (☎ 39 22 11; Uferstrasse 71; camp sites per person/car €4.50/6; ⊗ year-round) This camping ground is 7km southeast of the city in Rodenkirchen. Take the U16 to Heinrich-Lübke-Ufer and from there bus No 130.

Jugendgästehaus Köln-Riehl (☎ 76 70 81; www .djh.de; An der Schanz 14; dm €19.90) North of the city, this hostel has one- to six-bed rooms and a disco in the basement. Take the U15 or U16 to Boltensternstrasse.

Jugendherberge Köln-Deutz (☎ 81 47 11; www .djh.de; Siegesstrasse 5a; dm €19.90) Has over 500 beds and large clean bathrooms. An easy 15-minute walk east from the main train station over the Hohenzollernbrücke.

Station (☎ 912 53 01; www.hostel-cologne.de; Marzellenstrasse 44-48; dm/s €15/27) Just a short walk from the main train station, this is a good place to meet fellow travellers although the rooms are cramped.

Station Hostel & Bar (☎ 221 23 02 47; www.hostel -cologne.de; Rheingasse 34-36; dm/s €16/27) The hostel's other branch is closer to Cologne's pubs.

Hotel Im Kupferkessel (☎ 270 796 0; www.im-kup ferkessel.de; Probsteigasse 6; s/d €30/60) The cheaper rooms at the Kupferkessel have shared facilities but all are well-kept and it's just a 15-minute walk west of the train station.

Hotel Good Sleep (☎ 257 22 57; www.goodsleep .de, in German; Komödienstrasse 19-21; s/d €35/50) The Dom looms majestically just a block away and the rooms are bright and clean.

Hotel Berg (☎ 12 11 24; www.hotel-berg.com, in German; Brandenburger Strasse 6; s/d €50/60, with shared bathroom from €40/50) Basic but small rooms and Internet access are here just a short walk from the train station.

MID-RANGE

Hotel Ludwig (☎ 160 540; www.hotelludwig.de; Brandenburgerstrasse 22-24; s/d €65/85) Rooms on the fourth floor have balconies with views of the Dom.

Hotel Madison (☎ 13 29 91; contact@hotelmadison .de; Ursulaplatz 10-12; s/d €40/60) The Madison's large rooms have wireless Internet access.

Hayk Hotel (☎ 92 57 44 0; www.koeln-altstadt.de/ hayk; Frankenwerft 9; s/d €50/70) Rooms are basic here but the real draw is the location along the promenade on the Rhein.

Rhein-Hotel St Martin (☎ 257 78 98; www.koeln -altstadt.de/rheinhotel; Frankenwerft 31-33; s/d €34/70) One of the better choices along the Rhein, the St Martin is modern and has a nice restaurant.

Eating

Cologne's beer halls serve cheap and filling meals to go with their home brew (see below). The Belgisches Viertel (Belgian Quarter) around and west of Hahnentor is packed with restaurants. To put together a picnic, visit a market; the biggest is held on Tuesday and Friday at the Aposteln-Kloster near Neumarkt.

Gaffel Haus (☎ 257 7692; Alter Markt 20-22) A nice place to sample the local concoction.

Buffet Chang (☎ 250 99 09; Breitestrasse 80-90; all-you-can-eat buffet €6) Stuff yourself full of Chinese cuisine here, located in the DuMont Carré centre.

4 Cani Della Città (☎ 257 40 85; Benesisstrasse 61; pizza €6) This busy café attracts a fashionable clientele with its lively streetside seating.

Drinking

As in Munich, beer in Cologne reigns supreme. There are more than 20 local breweries, all producing a variety called *Kölsch*, which is relatively light and slightly bitter. The breweries run their own beer halls and serve their wares in skinny glasses holding a mere 200mL, but you'll soon agree it's a very satisfying way to drink the stuff.

Peter's Brauhaus (☎ 257 3950; Mühlengasse 1) In the heart of the Altstadt, Peter's serves up their own brew.

Biermuseum (☎ 257 7802; Buttermarkt 39) Next door to Papa Joe's – this beer museum has 18 varieties on tap.

Brauhaus Sion (☎ 257 8540; Unter Taschenmacher 9) A big beer hall, packed most nights and for good reason: a couple of beers and a full meal will only set you back €12.

Früh am Dom (☎ 258 0394; Am Hof 12-14) Rightly famous for its own-brew beer.

Entertainment

Evenings and weekends in the Altstadt are like miniature carnivals, with bustling crowds and lots to do.

Papa Joe's Klimperkasten (☎ 258 2132; Alter Markt 50) A lively jazz pub with a wonderful pianola.

Papa Joe's Em Streckstrump (☎ 257 7931; Buttermarkt 37) More intimate and more traditional.

Metronom (☎ 21 34 65; Weyerstrasse 59) Near the Kwartier Latäng (Latin Quarter), the Metronom is Cologne's most respected evening bar for jazz enthusiasts, with live performances mainly weekdays.

Wallmachenreuther (Brüsseler Platz 9) is an offbeat bar in the Belgisches Viertel that also serves food. The gay scene also centres on the Belgisches Viertel.

Köln Ticket (☎ 28 02 80; Roncalliplatz) Next to the Römisch-Germanisches Museum, has tickets and information on classical music and theatre performances in town.

Theater im Bauturm (☎ 52 42 42; Aachener Strasse 24) This is one of Cologne's more innovative theatres.

Shopping

A good Cologne souvenir might be a small bottle of *eau de Cologne*, which is still produced in its namesake city. The most famous brand is called 4711, after the house number where it was invented. There's still a **perfumery and gift shop** (cnr Glockenpetrolse & Schwertnerpetrolse) by that name.

Getting There & Away

AIR

Cologne/Bonn airport has many connections within Europe and to the rest of the world. For more detailed flight information phone ☎ 02203-40 40 01/02.

BOAT

An enjoyable way to travel to/from Cologne is by boat. **KD River Cruises** (☎ 208 83 18; www .k-d.com; Frankenwerft 35) has its headquarters in the city, and has services all along the Rhine.

BUS

Deutsche Touring's Eurolines (☎ 13 52 52; www .deutsche-touring.com) offers overnight trips to Paris (€34, 6½ hours). The office is at the main train station at the Breslauer Platz exit.

CAR

The city is on a main north–south autobahn route and is easily accessible for drivers and hitchhikers. The **ADM-Mitfahrzentrale** (☎ 194 40; www.citynetz-mitfahrzentrale.de; Maximinen Strasse 2) is near the train station.

TRAIN

There are frequent services operating to both nearby Bonn (€6, 18 minutes) and Düsseldorf (€7, 40 minutes) as well as to Aachen (€11, one hour). Frequent direct IC/EC (€47.80, 3¼ hours) and ICE (€53.40, 2¾ hours) trains go to Hanover. There are ICE links with Frankfurt-am-Main (€38, 2¼ hours, three per hour) and Berlin (€85, 4½ hours, hourly). The Thalys high-speed train connects Paris and Cologne via Aachen and Brussels (€75/67 weekdays/weekends, four hours, seven times daily), with only a small discount for rail pass-holders.

Getting Around
TO/FROM THE AIRPORT

Bus No 170 runs between Cologne/Bonn airport and the main bus station every 15 minutes from 5.30am to 11.20pm daily (€5, 20 minutes).

PUBLIC TRANSPORT

Cologne offers a convenient and extensive mix of buses, trams and local trains – trams travel underground in the inner city, and trains handle destinations up to 50km around Cologne. The best ticket option is the one-day pass: €5.50 if you're staying near the city (one or two zones); €9 for most of the Cologne area (four zones); and €12 including Bonn (seven zones). Single city trips cost €1.20 and 1½-hour two-zone tickets are €1.90.

TAXI

To order a taxi call ☎ 194 10 or ☎ 28 82.

AROUND COLOGNE
Bonn

☎ 0228 / pop 293,000
This friendly city on the Rhine south of Cologne became West Germany's temporary capital in 1949 but now hosts international associations and large corporations after the seat of government and embassies moved to Berlin. Settled in Roman times, Bonn was the seat of the electors of Cologne in the 18th century, and some of their baroque architecture survived the ravages of WWII and the postwar demand for modern government buildings. Organise a day trip out here and to the nearby spa town of Bad Godesberg. Classical music buffs can pay homage to Bonn's most famous son – Ludwig van Beethoven.

The **tourist office** (☎ 77 50 00; www.bonn-regio.de, in German; Windeckstrasse 1; ⏰ 9am-6.30pm Mon-Fri, to 4pm Sat, 10am-2pm Sun) is a three-minute walk along Poststrasse from the Hauptbahnhof.

SIGHTS

Bonn is a city that lives and breathes Beethoven, and you can visit the **Beethoven-Haus** (☎ 981 75 25; www.beethoven-haus-bonn.de; Bonngasse 20; adult/concession €4/3; ⏰ 10am-6pm Mon-Sat Apr-Oct, to 5pm Mon-Sat Nov-Mar, 11am-4pm Sun year-round), where the composer was born in 1770. The house contains memorabilia concerning his life and music, including his last piano, specially made with an amplified sounding board to accommodate his deafness. The annual Beethoven Festival takes place September to October.

The **Münsterbasilika** (Münsterplatz; ⏰ 7am-7pm) has a splendid interior and honours Sts Cassius and Florentius, two martyred Roman officers who became the patron saints of Bonn.

Bonn also boasts several interesting museums. The **Frauenmuseum** (☎ 69 13 44; Im Krausfeld 10; adult/concession €8/free; ⏰ 2-6pm Tue-Sat, 11am-6pm Sun) promotes and exhibits art created by women. Take bus No 625, 626, 627 or 635 to Kaiser-Karl-Ring.

The **Haus der Geschichte der Bundesrepublik Deutschland** (FRG History Museum; ☎ 916 50; Willy-Brandt-Allee 14; admission free; ⏰ 9am-7pm Tue-Sun) covers the history of Germany from 1945; it is part of the **Museumsmeile**, a row of four museums that also includes the **Kunstmuseum** (☎ 77 62 60; Friedrich-Ebert-Allee 2; ⏰ 10am-6pm Tue & Thu-Sun, to 9pm Wed) with its collection of 20th-century art; and exhibitions at the **Kunst- und Ausstellungshalle der Bundesrepublik Deutschland** (☎ 917 12 00; Friedrich-Ebert-Allee 2; ⏰ 10am-9pm Tue & Wed, 10am-7pm Thu-Sun).

EATING & DRINKING

Pawlow (☎ 65 36 03; Heerstrasse 64) This is a relaxed place for a beer or late breakfast in the Altstadt. Located across from the Hofgarden/university field, and with views up and down the Rhine, it's the best outdoor beer garden in Bonn. It also has pizza, salad and pretzels, but no wursts...which can be a plus or a minus, depending on your view of things.

Tacos (☎ 655 185; Bongasse 7) In the centre of town, between Marktplatz and Oxford-strasse. Mexican food and salsa/*cumbia*/merengue dance floor on Tuesday and at the weekend. It even has mescal!

GETTING THERE & AWAY
There are frequent trains to Cologne in the north and to Koblenz (€12.80, 30 minutes) in the south. For river cruises to and from Bonn, see p502. The Bonn transit system is linked with Cologne's and a one-way train ride between the two cities costs only €7 (see p504 for passes covering both).

DÜSSELDORF
☎ 0211 / pop 571,000
This elegant and wealthy capital of North Rhine-Westphalia is an important centre for fashion and commerce, and a charming example of big-city living along the Rhine River. Banks and large corporations have their headquarters here but the visitor will want to concentrate on the area between the train station and Rhine.

Information
Internet Café World (Worringer Platz 21; per 30min €2) Three blocks north of the train station.
Main post office (Immermannstrasse 1) Across the street from the train station.
Reisebank (Hauptbahnhof; ☒ 8am-10pm Mon-Fri, to 9pm Sat & Sun) In the train station's main hall.
SB Waschsalon (Charlottenstrasse 87)
Surf Inn (☎ 139 12 13; Galeria Kaufhof; Internet per hr €3)
Tourist office (www.duesseldorf-tourismus.de, in German; ☒ 8am-8pm Mon-Sat, 4-8pm Sun) Main office (☎ 17 202 22; Immermannstrasse 65B); Branch office (☎ 60 257 53; Burg Platz)

Sights & Activities
To catch a glimpse of Düsseldorf's swish lifestyle, head for the famed Königsallee, or 'Kö', with its stylish (and pricey) boutiques and arcades. Stroll north along the Kö to the **Hofgarten**, a large park in the city centre.

The city has several interesting museums. These include the **Kunstmuseum Düsseldorf** (☎ 899 24 60; adult/concession €8/4.50; ☒ 11am-8pm

Tue-Sun) at Ehrenhof north of the Oberkasse-ler Brücke, with a comprehensive European collection, and the incorporated **Glasmuseum Hentrich** (☒ 10am-6pm Tue-Sun).

The quite expansive modern art collection in the **Kunstsammlung Nordrhein-Westfalen** is displayed in two different galleries: **K20** (☎ 838 12 04; Grabbeplatz 5; adult/concession €6.50/4.50; ☒ 10am-6pm Tue-Fri, 11am-6pm Sat & Sun) features works by 20th-century masters; **K21** (☎ 838 16 42; Ständehausstrasse 1; adult/concession €6.50/4.50) specialises in art from 1990 onwards. A combined ticket to both costs €10/8.

The **Goethe-Museum Düsseldorf** (☎ 899 62 62; Jacobistrasse 2; adult/concession €2/1; ☒ 11am-5pm Tue-Fri & Sun, 1-5pm Sat) in Schloss Jägerhof, pays tribute to the life and work of one of Europe's great men of letters. Any German-literature buff will also want to visit **Heinrich-Heine-Institut** (Bilker Strasse 12-14; adult/concession €2/1; ☒ 11am-5pm Tue-Fri & Sun, 1-5pm Sat), which documents this Düsseldorfer's career, or his house at Bolker-strasse 53, now a literary pub.

On Marktplatz, the restored **Rathaus** looks onto the **statue of Prince Elector Johann Wilhelm**, known locally as 'Jan Wellem'.

Nearby, the reconstructed **Schlossturm** of the long-destroyed Residenz stands on Burg-platz as a forlorn reminder of the Palatine elector's glory. In summer, the town's youth congregate on the steps below the tower.

The nearby pedestrian-only **Rheinufer-promenade** provides perfect strolling along the river. **Schloss Benrath** (☎ 899 72 71; www .schloss-benrath.de; Benrather Schlossallee 104; adult/ concession €4/2; ☒ 10am-6pm Tue & Thu-Sun, 5-8pm Wed), a late-baroque pleasure palace with a park, located 12km south of the city, makes for a lovely excursion. Take tram No 701 from Jan-Wellem-Platz.

Sleeping
There are two camping grounds relatively close to the city.

Campingplatz Nord Unterbacher See (☎ 899 20 94; camp sites €5.50, plus per person/car €3.25/4; ☒ 4 Apr–27 Sep) This camping ground is at Kleiner Torfbruch in Düsseldorf-Unterbach (take S-Bahn No 7 to Eller, and then bus No 735 to Seeweg).

Camping Oberlörick (☎ 59 14 01; camp sites €4, plus per person/car €3/4.50; ☒ year-round) In Lut-ticherstrasse, just beside the Rhine in Düs-seldorf-Lörick (U-Bahn No 70, 74 or 76 to Löricker Strasse, and then bus No 833 to

GERMANY

DÜSSELDORF

| 0 | 500 m |
| 0 | 0.3 miles |

INFORMATION		Schlossturm	13 A2	Brauerei Zur Uer	21 B2
Internet Cafe World	1 D3	Theatermuseum	14 C2	Fischhaus	22 B3
SB Waschsalon	2 D3			Zum Schlüssel	23 B3
Surf Inn	3 C3	SLEEPING	(pp505–6)		
Tourist Office Altstadt	4 B2	Hotel an der Kö	15 C4	DRINKING	(p507)
Tourist Office Hauptbahnhof	5 D4	Hotel Haus Hillesheim	16 C4	Et Kabüffke	24 B3
		Hotel Komet	17 D4	Night Live/dä Spiegel	25 B3
SIGHTS & ACTIVITIES	(p505)	Madison Hotel	18 D4	Zum Uerige	26 B3
Andreaskirche	6 B2				
Goethe Museum	7 D1	EATING	(pp506–7)		
Heinrich Heine Institut	8 B3	Anadolou	19 B3		
K20 Kunstsammlung am Grabbeplatz	9 B2	Bäckerei Hinkel	20 B3		
K21 Kunstsammlung im Ständehaus	10 B4				
Kunsthalle	11 B2				
Rathaus	12 A3				

Strandbad Lörick). The trek to the Altstadt is particularly inconvenient from either camping ground.

Jugendgästehaus (☎ 55 73 10; www.djh.de; Düsseldorfer Strasse 1; dm/s/d €21/26/48) This hostel is in posh Oberkassel across the Rhine from the Altstadt. Take U-Bahn No 70, 74, 75, 76 or 77 from the main train station to Luegplatz. From there it's a short walk.

Backpackers-Düsseldorf (☎ 302 08 48; www .backpackers-duesseldorf.de; Fürstenwall 180; dm/s €20/29) This hostel rents bicycles, has free Internet access and is only a kilometre from the train station. Take bus No 725 to Kirchplatz.

Hotel Komet (☎ 17 87 90; info@hotelkomet.de; Bismarckstrasse 93; s/d €33/44) Within walking distance of the train station, the bathrooms in

some of Komet's small, efficient rooms are luxurious.

Hotel Haus Hillesheim (☎ 38 68 60; rezeption@ hotel-hillesheim.de; Jahnstrasse 19; s/d €60/70, with shared bathroom €40/55) A good value option.

Hotel an der Kö (☎ 37 10 48; fax 37 08 35; Talstrasse 9; s/d €78/87) and **Madison Hotel** (☎ 168 50; www .madison-hotels.com, in German; Graf-Adolfstrasse 47; s/d €85/105) are also recommended.

Eating

Anadolou (Mertenspetrolse 10; mains €4) Delicious Anatolian sit-down and takeaway food including vegetarian dishes are available at Anadolou.

Brauerei zur Uer (Ratinger Strasse 16) is a rustic place to fill up for less than €10. Ratinger

Strasse is also home to a couple of other pub-style places where you can eat and drink.

Zum Schlüssel (☎ 828 955; Bolkerstrasse 43-47; dishes €5-11) Good food and good beer. No wonder it's popular.

Bäckerei Hinkel (☎ 32 87 58; Hohestrasse 31) Don't be surprised to find a queue at Hinkel, the oldest bakery in the city

Fischaus (☎ 854 98 64; Bergerstrasse 3-7; mains €8-25) Enjoy Mediterranean-style fish dishes, including delicious soup at this large restaurant in the Altstadt.

Drinking

The Altstadt, affectionately referred to as the 'longest bar in the world' sees drinkers spill out onto the streets on evenings and weekends. Favoured streets include Bolkerstrasse, Kurze Strasse, and Andreasstrasse as well as the surrounding side streets. The beverage of choice is Alt beer, a dark and semisweet brew typical of Düsseldorf.

Zum Uerige (☎ 866 990; Bergerstrasse 1) The only place where you can buy Uerige Alt beer. It's €1.40 per 250mL glass, and the beer flows so quickly that the waiters just carry around trays and give you a glass when you're ready or not.

Et Kabüffke (☎ 13 32 69; Flingerstrasse 1) Taste *Killepitsch*, a herb liqueur sold only here and in the shop next door.

Night-Live (Bolkerstrasse 22) has live bands; **dä Spiegel** (Bolkerstrasse 22), upstairs from Night-live, is itself a popular bar.

Getting There & Away

Düsseldorf's Lohausen airport is busy with national and international flights. S-Bahn trains run every 20 minutes between the airport and the main train station. Düsseldorf is part of a dense S-Bahn and train network in the Rhine-Ruhr region, and there are regular IC/EC services to/from Hamburg (€63, 3½ hours), ICE services to Hanover (€46, 2¾ hours) and Frankfurt-am-Main (€44, 2½ hours), and trains to Cologne (€8.40, 40 minutes) and most other major German cities.

Getting Around

As Düsseldorf is very spread out, it's easiest to get around by public transport. A short-trip ticket up to 1.5km (destinations are listed on the machines) costs €2. A single ticket for Zone A, which includes all of Düsseldorf proper, is €3.30. Better value is the 24-hour *TagesTicket* for €12, valid for up to five people in Zone A.

AACHEN
☎ 0241 / pop 244,000

Aachen was famous in Roman times for its thermal springs. The great Frankish conqueror Charlemagne was so impressed with their revitalising qualities that he settled here and made it the capital of his kingdom in AD 794. Ever since, Aachen has held special significance among the icons of German nationhood. It is now an industrial and commercial centre, and its proximity to the Netherlands, Belgium and the country's largest technical university give it a dynamic international flare.

Orientation

Aachen's compact old centre is contained within two ring roads that roughly follow the old city walls. The inner ring road, or Grabenring, changes names – most ending in 'graben' – and encloses the old city proper. To get to the tourist office from the Hauptbahnhof, turn left on leaving the main entrance, cross Römerstrasse, follow Bahnhofstrasse north and then go left along Theaterstrasse to Kapuzinergraben.

Information

Main post office (An den Frauenbrüdern 1; ☯ 9am-6pm Mon-Fri, to 2pm Sat) Three blocks northwest of the train station.

Tourist office (☎ 180 29 60/1; www.aachen-tourist.de; Kapuzinergraben, Atrium Elisenbrunnen; ☯ 9am-6pm Mon-Fri, to 2pm Sat, 10am-2pm Sun)

Sparkasse Bank (Lagerhausstrasse 12; ☯ 8.30am-4.30pm Mon-Wed, to 5.30pm Thu, to 4pm Fri) One block west of the train station.

Web (Kleinmarschierstrasse 74-76; Internet per 30min €2)

Sights
DOM

Aachen's drawing card is its **Dom** (Kaiserdom or Münster; ☯ 7am-7pm). The cathedral's subtle grandeur, its historical significance and interior serenity make a visit almost obligatory – it's a Unesco World Heritage Site. No fewer than 30 Holy Roman emperors were crowned here from 936 to 1531.

The heart of the cathedral is a Byzantine-inspired **octagon**, built on Roman foundations. It was the largest vaulted structure north of the Alps when it was consecrated as Charlemagne's court chapel in AD 805. He lies buried here in the golden **shrine**, and the cathedral became a site of pilgrimage after his death, not least for its religious relics. The Gothic **choir** was added in 1414; its massive stained-glass windows are impressive even though some date from after WWII. The octagon received its **folded dome** after the city fire of 1656 destroyed the original tent roof.

Worth noting is the huge brass **chandelier**, which was added to the octagon by Emperor Friedrich Barbarossa in 1165; the **high altar** with its 11th-century gold-plated Pala d'Oro (altar front) depicting scenes of 'the Passion'; and the gilded copper ambo, or **pulpit**, donated by Henry II.

The entrance to the **Domschatzkammer** (cathedral treasury; adult/concession €2.50/2; 10am-1pm Mon; to 6pm Tue, Wed & Fri-Sun; to 9pm Thu), with one of the richest collections of religious art north of the Alps, is on nearby Klosterpetrolse.

OTHER ATTRACTIONS
North of the cathedral, the 14th-century **Rathaus** (adult/concession €2/1; 10am-5pm Mon-Fri, to 1pm & 2-5pm Sat & Sun) overlooks the Markt, a lively gathering place in summer, with its fountain statue of Charlemagne.

Foremost among Aachen's worthwhile museums is the **Ludwig Forum for International Art** (180 71 04; Jülicherstrasse 97-109; adult/concession €3/1.50; 10am-4pm Tue & Thu, 10am-7.30pm Wed & Fri, 11am-4.30pm Sat & Sun) with works by Warhol, Lichtenstein, Baselitz and others.

THERMAL BATHS
The 8th-century Franks called the town 'Ahha', which is supposed to mean water. A visit to the city-owned **Carolus Thermen** (18 27 40; www.carolus-thermen.de; Passstrasse 79) costs €9 for 2½ hours (€17 with the sauna), or €13 for up to five hours (€23 with sauna). It's in the city garden, northeast of the centre.

Sleeping
To book a room in advance, call Aachen's reservation line 180 29 50/1 (weekdays).

Hoeve de Petroltmolen (0031-433 06 57 55; Lemierserberg 23; camp sites incl car €7, plus per person €2.50) About 6km outside Aachen in the town of Vaals. Take bus No 15 or 65 and get off at the 'Heuvel' stop.

Jugendgästehaus (71 10 10; www.djh.de; Maria-Theresia-Allee 260; dm/s/d €21/33.80/38.80) This DJH

outpost is 4km southwest of the train station on a hill overlooking the city. Take bus No 2 to Ronheide, or bus No 12 to the closer Colynshof at the foot of the hill.

Hotel Marx (375 41; info@hotel-marx.de; Hubertusstrasse 33-35; s/d €49/67, with shared bathroom €34/62) Good cheap rooms but the facilities are a little cramped.

Hotel Drei Könige (483 93; fax 361 52; Büchel 5; s/d €60/75, without bathroom €35/55) Centrally located, the Drei Könige has a few rather basic rooms.

Hotel am Marschiertor (319 41; hotel.marschiertor@t-online.de; Wallstrasse 1-7; s/d €62/75) A definite step up in quality, am Marschiertor is only a short walk from the train station. Breakfast is €8.50 extra.

Eating
Being a university town, Aachen is full of spirited cafés, restaurants and pubs, especially along Pontstrasse, referred to by locals as the 'Quartier Latin'.

Café Kittel (Pontstrasse 39; mains €6) Vegetarians and those seeking lighter options than your average wurst should stop by Café Kittel, a cosy hang-out with a lively garden area.

Petroltstätte Labyrinth (Pontstrasse 156-158; dishes €7-11) You may have trouble finding your way back to your table if you drink too much at this labyrinthine beer hall. Good, filling meals should provide sustenance for your journey.

Alt Aachener Kaffeestuben (Büchel 18) An old-world coffee house (where wine also is served) that does a traditional lunchtime dish for €7.

Entertainment
Domkeller (Hof 1) Students have frequented this pub since the 1950s. Jazz or blues is usually featured on Monday nights.

B9 (Blondelstrasse 9) The style of music changes nightly, but you can count on young patrons every night.

Club Voltaire (Friedrichstrasse 9) A slightly older crowd comes to the Voltaire.

City Theatre (478 42 44; Theaterplatz) Concerts and opera are performed almost nightly.

Getting There & Away
Aachen is well served by road and rail. There are fast trains almost every hour to Cologne (€11.10, 43 minutes) and Liège (€9.90, 40 minutes). The high-speed Thalys train

passes through seven times daily on its way to Brussels and Paris. There's also a frequent bus service to Maastricht (€5, 55 minutes). The bus station is at the northeastern edge of Grabenring on the corner of Kurhausstrasse and Peterstrasse.

Getting Around

Aachen's points of interest are clustered around the city centre, which is covered easily on foot. A 24-hour Familienkarte und Gruppenkarte is valid for up to five people and costs €4.85.

BREMEN

The federal state of Bremen covers only the 404 sq km comprising the two cities of Bremen (the state capital) and Bremerhaven. In medieval times Bremen was Europe's northernmost archbishopric. The city was ruled by the Church until joining the Hanseatic League in the 14th century. Controlled by the French from 1810 to 1813, Bremen went on to join the German Confederation in 1815. In 1871 the city was made a state of the German Empire. In 1949 Bremen was officially declared a state of the Federal Republic of Germany.

BREMEN

☎ 0421 / pop 550,000

Bremen is, after Hamburg, the most important harbour in Germany, even though the sea lies 113km to the north. Once known as the 'Rome of the North' because it was used as a base for Christianising Scandinavia, from 1646 to the present it has enjoyed its status as a free imperial city and its reputation for liberal politics and a congenial atmosphere.

The Altstadt is an enjoyable place to explore on foot, and Bremen's vibrant student population ensures the fun continues long after dark.

Orientation

The heart of the city is Am Markt, but its soul is the port. City walks (English explanations provided) leave at 2pm daily from the tourist office at the station (€6). A Bremen tourist card (from €8.50 for two days) offers unlimited public transport and substantial discounts on city sights.

Information

Internet Café/Callshop (Internet per hr €4)
Main post office (Domsheide 15) Branch office (Bahnhofplatz 21)
Reisebank (Bahnhofplatz 15)
Tourist office (☎ 30 80 00; www.bremen-tourism.de, in German; Hauptbahnhof; ☼ 8am-8pm Mon-Thu, 9am-6pm Fri-Sun) There is also a booth at the Rathaus opposite the smaller of the main Altstadt churches, Unser Lieben Frauen Kirche.

Sights & Activities

Around Am Markt don't miss the splendid and ornate **Rathaus**, the cathedral **Dom St Petri**, which has a tower **lookout** (admission €1; ☼ 10am-5pm Mon-Fri, to 2pm Sat, 2-5pm Sun) and **museum** (adult/concession €1.50/1; ☼ 10am-5pm Mon-Fri, to 2pm Sat, 2-5pm Sun). The lookout, though is only open half the year. There's also the large statue of the knight **Roland**, Bremen's sentimental protector, which was erected in 1404.

Walk down **Böttcherstrasse**, a must-see recreation of a medieval alley, complete with tall brick houses, shops, galleries, restaurants and several **museums** (adult/concession combined ticket €6/3; ☼ 11am-6pm Tue-Sun). The **Paula Modersohn-Becker Museum**, at No 8, has works by its namesake contemporary painter. The **Museum im Roselius-Haus** is at No 6, with a collection of paintings and applied arts from the 12th to 19th centuries. The **Glockenspiel**, active in summer hourly from noon to 6pm (in winter at noon, 3pm and 6pm), plays an extended tune between rooftops and an adjacent panel swivels to reveal a rotating cast of fearless explorers, from Leif Erikson to Charles Lindbergh.

The nearby **Schnoorviertel** area features fishing cottages that are now a tourist attraction, with shops, cafés and tiny lanes.

An excellent walk around the Altstadt is along the **Wallanlagen**, peaceful parks stretching along the old city walls and moat. Backing onto the parkland is Bremen's **Kunsthalle** (adult/concession €5/2.50; ☼ 10am-5pm Wed-Sun, to 9pm Tue) art gallery.

Tours

BECK'S BREWERY

Tours of **Beck's Brewery** (☎ 50 94 55 55; www.becks .de; Am Deich 18-19; tours in German €3; 10am-5pm Tue-Sat, to 3pm Sun) are available (take tram No 1 or 5 from the train station to Westerstrasse). English-language tours run at 1.30pm Tuesday to Sunday.

BREMEN

0 — 300 m
0 — 0.2 miles

INFORMATION
Internet Café/Callshop.............................1 C2
Tourist Info Bremen................................2 C2
Tourist Info Stand....................................3 B4

SIGHTS & ACTIVITIES (p509)
Bleikeller..4 B3
Dom St Petri...5 B3
Dommuseum..(see 5)
Glockenspiel..(see 7)
Kunsthalle...6 C4
Museum im Roselius-Haus.................(see 7)
Paula Modersohn-Becker Museum....7 B3

Rathaus..8 B3
Statue of Knight Roland.........................9 B3

SLEEPING (p510)
Bremer Backpacker Hostel..................10 C2
Jugendgästehaus Bremen....................11 A2
Hotel Am Hillmannplatz.......................12 B2

EATING (p511)
Captain Sushi...13 B3

Casablanca...14 C4
Katzen Café...15 B4
Savarin...16 D3
Schnoor Teestübchen...........................17 B4

TRANSPORT (p511)
Central Bus Station................................18 C2

Sleeping

Campingplatz Bremen (☎ 21 20 02; Am Stadtwaldsee 1; camp sites €4, plus per person/car €4/2) Take tram No 6 from the train station to the Klagenfurter Strasse stop.

Jugendgästehaus Bremen (☎ 17 13 69; www .djh.de; Kalkstrasse 6; dm juniors/seniors €17/22) Only a short swim across the river to Beck's Brewery. Take tram No 3 or 5 from the train station to Am Brill.

Bremen Backpacker Hostel (☎ 223 80 57; www .bremer-backpacker-hostel.de; Emil-Waldmannstrasse 5-6; dm/s/d €16/27/44) This well-maintained hostel is conveniently located just a few minutes from the train station.

Hotel-Pension Weidmann (☎ 498 44 55; www .white-pleasure.de; Am Schwarzen Meer 35; s/d €21/42)

This place offers warm hospitality and great value. Take tram No 2 from Domsheide or No 10 from the station.

Hotel Garni Gästehaus Walter (☎ 55 80 27; fax 55 80 29; Buntentorsteinweg 86-88; s/d €25/40) This pleasant guesthouse is on the other side of the Wester River. Take tram No 4 or 5 from the main train station.

Gästehaus Peterswerder (☎ 44 71 01; www.gaeste hauspeterswerder.de, in German; Cellerstrasse 4; s/d €28/50) A welcoming option not far from the Weidmann, the Peterswerder has excellent rooms including a small but cosy attic.

Turmhotel Weserblick (☎ 94 94 10; fax 949 41 10; Osterdeich 53; s/d €67/82) has nice views and **Hotel Am Hillmannplatz** (☎ 132 58; Hillmannplatz 1; s/d €50/72) is just a short walk from the train station.

Eating

A prowl around Ostertorsteinweg (near Am Dobben) will offer all sorts of gastronomic possibilities. The long courtyard of Auf den Höfen, north of Ostertorsteinweg, has several restaurants and bars, and serves as one of the epicentres of Bremen's nightlife.

Casablanca (☎ 32 64 29; Ostertorsteinweg 59; mains €5-12) is known for its breakfast; it also has cheap pastas and soups.

Piano (☎ 785 46; Fehrfeld 64; mains €5.50-7.50) Just east of Am Dobben, Piano serves huge Mediterranean-inspired salads and tasty baked casseroles.

Savarin (☎ 769 77; Auf Den Häfen; mains €6) serves good casseroles by candlelight.

Katzen Café (☎ 326 621; Schnoor 38; mains €6-15) There's a kind of French Moulin Rouge tone to this basement restaurant and its open-air terrace. Oysters, bouillabaisse, and salmon are all available.

Captain Sushi (☎ 25 67 89; www.captain-sushi.de, in German; Böttcherstrasse 2; lunch specials €8) High-quality authentic Japanese sushi. Service is quick and friendly.

Schnoor Teestübchen (Wüstestätte 1; lunch dishes €6) Specialises in tea and cakes, but it also serves vegetarian soups and quiche in a low-ceilinged, hobbit-like setting.

Getting There & Away

There are frequent regional and IC trains servicing Hamburg (€16.80, one hour). There are hourly IC trains to Cologne (€47, three hours). A couple of ICE trains run direct to Frankfurt-am-Main (€78, 3½ hours) and Munich (€111, six hours) daily. Change trains in Hanover for Berlin (€65, 3½ hours). For Amsterdam (€54, four hours), you change in Osnabrück.

Getting Around

To get to Am Markt follow the tram route from directly in front of the train station. The tourist office stocks good public transport maps. Short trips on buses and trams cost €1.85, a four-trip transferable ticket is €5.60 and a day pass is €4.50.

LOWER SAXONY

Lower Saxony (Niedersachsen) has much to offer, and it's a quick train ride or autobahn drive from the tourist centres down south. The scenic Harz Mountains, the old student town of Göttingen, and the picturesque towns along the Fairy-Tale Road are the most popular tourist attractions. British occupation forces created the federal state of Lower Saxony during 1946, when the states of Braunschweig (Brunswick), Schaumburg-Lippe and Oldenburg were amalgamated with the Prussian province of Hanover.

HANOVER

☎ 0511 / pop 523,000

Hanover has few architectural gems but plenty of parks and greenery. In 1714, the eldest son of Electress Sophie of Hannover, a granddaughter of James I of England and VI of Scotland, ascended the British throne as King George I. This Anglo-German union lasted through several generations until 1837. Savaged by heavy bombing in 1943, Hanover was rebuilt into a prosperous city known throughout Europe for its trade fairs.

Information

The **tourist office** (☎ 12 23 55 55; www.hannover -tourism.de; Ernst-August-Platz 2; 🕑 9am-6pm Mon-Fri, to 2pm Sat) is next to the main post office and near the main train station.

Sights

The chief attractions are the glorious parks of the **Herrenhäuser Gärten** (☎ 16 84 77 43; www .herrenhaeuser-gaerten.de; 🕑 9am-sunset), especially the baroque **Grosser Garten** and the **Berggarten** (admission for both €4; 🕑 9am-8pm in summer), with its newly installed rainforest exhibit, the **Regenwald Haus** (adult/concession €9/6).

Sprengel Museum (☎ 16 84 38 75; Kurt-Schwitters-Platz; adult/concession €3.50/1.80; 🕑 Tue-Sun) exhibits contemporary works, the highlights being Picasso and Max Beckmann.

At Am Markt in the old town is the 14th-century **Marktkirche** (Hanns-Lilje-Platz 2; 🕑 9am-12.30pm Mon-Fri & 2-4pm Thu). Apart from its truncated tower, it is characteristic of the northern red-brick Gothic style; the original stained-glass windows are particularly beautiful. The **Altes Rathaus** – across the marketplace – was built in various sections over a century.

Sleeping

The tourist office only offers a private room-finding service during trade fairs but will arrange a hotel room year-round for €6.50.

WHEN FAIRY TALES GO BAD

The more familiar certain stories and figures are, the more shrouded their actual origins become. Two names that have entered our collective mythology and two expressions that have become part of our lexicon happen to originate from Hameln and Bodenwerder, two small towns just south of Hanover. Generations of citizens of both have taken a certain amount of civic pride and even attract tourists through their association despite the fact that both 'fairy tales' deal with practices we usually condemn – lying and mass murder.

Karl Friedrich Hieronymous Baron von Munchausen (1720–97), born in Bodenwerder, served first as page to a prince, then rose to a calvary captain fighting in two Turkish wars. Following the death of his first wife, his second marriage, to a 17 year old, was troubled and led to debt and scandal. In order to amuse friends visiting his country estate and to relieve the tedium of retirement, the Baron made up fantastic tales of war, travel and hunting. The first of these was published anonymously in a Berlin magazine in 1781. Soon after, an aquaintance of the Baron's, Rudolph Erich Raspe, a scholar, librarian, poet and thief, translated the stories into English and with his own additions published them under the Baron's name, who understandably soured at this public caricature. Later editions were illustrated, adapted and expanded by other authors. The stories – one of which has the Baron dancing in the belly of a whale, in another he rides a cannonball – were especially popular at the time because they were seen as anti-rationalist and anti-Enlightenment, although all fiction of course involves lying.

There have been over 20 film adaptations of the Baron's stories, including *Adventures of Baron von Munchausen Capturing the North Pole* (1909), *The Three Stooges Meet the Baron* (1933), a costly Joseph Goebbels funded film (1933) and more recently Terry Gilliams' 1988 stab at the archetypal myth. But most people now think of him as one of his fictional creations or of the psychiatric disorder Munchausen Syndrome, in which the 'patient' feigns a severe illness, or Munchausen Syndrome by Proxy, in which a parent claims a child is sick or deliberately makes the child sick. At least one partial explanation for the 'lie' is the desire for attention and sympathy.

The nearby town of Hameln is maybe even more surprisingly proud of the story of the Pied Piper, despite the fact that the eponymous piper killed all but two of the town's children out of revenge after being cheated by the Hameln mayor – thus the expression 'to pay the piper'.

The history of the story is obscure, but it's generally agreed that something happened in 1284 involving the exodus of children from the area – most probably a stranger was hired by a sovereign to recruit settlers for parts further east. The oldest written source, not discovered until 1936, was a short piece written in Latin prose in 1430. It took the Brothers Grimm to add the rat-catcher theme in 1816, the horrors of the plague even then still part of the collective memory. Poems by Goethe, Brecht and Robert Browning further popularised the tale. But one only needs to look to the world of rock and pop to know that the piper has survived the transition from medieval times to the modern world – Jethro Tull and Abba have immortalised him in song.

Jugendherberge (☎ 131 76 74; www.djh.de/jh /hannover; Ferdinand-Wilhelm-Fricke-Weg 1; dm juniors/ seniors €17/20) Look for the space-lab looking structure 3km out of town, near the Maschsee, an artificial lake. Take the U3 or U7 from Hauptbahnhof to Fischerhof, then cross the river on the Lodemannbrücke bridge and turn right.

Hotel Flora (☎ 38 39 10; www.hotel-flora-hannover .de; in German; Heinrichstrasse 36; s/d €47/75, with shared bathroom €33/62) At the edge of the city forest, the Flora provides pleasant rooms.

Hotel am Thielenplatz (☎ 32 76 91; hotel.am .thielenplatz@t-online.de; Thielenplatz 2; s/d €45/68) is centrally located.

Hotel Gildehof (☎ 36 36 80; www.gildehof.de; Joachimstrasse 6; s/d €50/70, with shared bathroom €35/60) The Gildehof is centrally located and has clean, modern rooms. The restaurant downstairs serves well-priced traditional dishes.

Eating

The Altstadt area behind Marktkirche has plenty of well-priced restaurants offering German cuisine.

Markthalle (cnr Karmarschstrasse & Leinestrasse) A gourmand's paradise – it keeps normal shop hours and has lots of budget ethnic food stalls, some vegetarian offerings and fresh produce.

Brauhaus Ernst August (Schmiedestrasse 13a; mains €5-17) A Hanover institution, the Brauhaus Ernst August brews its own Hannöversch beer and also serves German dishes.

Sawaddi (☎ 34 43 67; Königstrasse 7; mains €11) A Thai restaurant, behind the train station; its all-you-can-eat lunch buffet is good value.

Getting There & Away
Hanover's spruced-up train station is a major hub. ICE trains to/from Hamburg (€34.40, 1½ hours), Frankfurt-am-Main (€65, 2½ hours), Munich (€95, 4½ hours), and Cologne (€51, 2¾ hours) leave hourly, and every two hours to Berlin-Zoo (€49, 1¾ hours). A web of services fills in the gaps locally.

GÖTTINGEN
☎ 0551 / pop 130,000
This leafy university town is an ideal stopover on your way north or south; it's on the direct train line between Munich and Hamburg. Though small, Göttingen is lively, mostly because of its large student population. A legion of notables, including Otto von Bismarck and the Brothers Grimm, studied and worked here, and the university has produced more than 40 Nobel Prize winners.

Information
Computerwerk (☎ 48 80 50 90; Düsterestrasse 20; Internet per 30min €2)
Main tourist office (☎ 49 98 00; www.goettingen-tourismus.de; Markt 9; 9.30am-6pm Mon-Fri, 10am-4pm Sat) This is in the old Rathaus.
Post office (Gronerstrasse 15) Left (north) of the old Rathaus. There's another in the Altstadt at Groner Strasse 15-17.
Waschcenter Laundry (Ritterplan 4)

Sights
When visiting the Markt, don't miss the **Great Hall** (9.30am-1pm & 2-6pm Mon-Fri, 10am-2pm Sat) in the Altes Rathaus where colourful frescoes cover every centimetre of wall space. Just outside, students and a colourful assortment of harmless punk rockers mill about the **Gänseliesel** fountain, the town's symbol. The bronze beauty has a reputation as 'the most kissed girl in the world' because every student who obtains a doctor's degree must then plant a kiss on her cheek.

The 15th-century **Junkernschänke** (Barfüsserstrasse 5), with its colourful carved façade, is the most stunning of the town's half-timbered

buildings. A walk on top of the old **town wall** along Bürgerstrasse takes you past **Bismarckhäuschen** (admission free; 10am-1pm Tue; 3-5pm Wed, Thu & Sat), a modest building where the Iron Chancellor lived in 1833 during his wild student days, and the pretty **Botanical Gardens**.

Sleeping
Camping am Hohen Hagen (☎ 05502 21 47; camping.lesser@t-online.de; Hoher-Hagen-strasse; bus No 120; camp sites €3, plus per person €5; year-round) This camping ground is about 10km west of town in Dransfeld.

Jugendherberge (☎ 576 22; www.djh.de; Habichtsweg 2; dm juniors/seniors €15/18) This hostel is in a quiet residential tree-filled neighbourhood northeast of the centre. From the train station's main entrance take bus No 6 to the Jugendherberge stop.

Hotel Weender Hof (☎ 50 37 50; www.weender-hof.de, in German; Hannoverschestrasse 150; s/d €35/65) Situated on the edge of town, the Weender Hof has simple rooms.

Conveniently situated in the middle of town is the **Hotel Central** (☎ 571 57; info@hotel-central.com; Jüdenstrasse 12; s/d €58/78), while another option is the **Hotel-Gasthaus Zum Weissen Ross** (☎ 316 11; fax 37 37 48; Hannoverschestrasse 128; s/d €28/67).

Eating
Nikolaistrasse and Goethe Allee offer loads of takeaway options.

Salamanca (Gartenstrasse 21b; mains €5-10) Come here for the affordable and tasty food but stay a long time for the boho, politically conscious conversation.

Zum Schwarzen Bären (☎ 573 20; Kurzstrasse 12; mains €9-15) Dating back to the 16th century, the stained-glass windows and cosy alcoves here enhance the dining experience.

Naturell (Lange-Seismarstrasse 40; mains €7-12) Inventive vegetarian restaurant.

Cron & Lanz (☎ 560 22; Weenderstrasse 25; cakes from €2.50) Wonderful cakes are served at this traditional café with a roof terrace.

Entertainment
Göttingen's nightlife give this small university town a lively, big-city atmosphere.

Blue Note (☎ 469 07; Wilhelmsplatz 3) The salsa, hip-hop and funk dance nights at the Blue Note are popular with students and non-students alike.

Tangente (☎ 463 76; Goetheallee 8a) An older crowd – OK, graduate students – make Tangente popular.

Elektroosho (☎ 531 49 70; Weender Strasse 38) Göttingen's hippest dance club, tiny Elektroosho specialises in house music. Things don't get started here until late.

Getting There & Away

Hourly ICE trains pass through on their way to/from Hanover (€26, 30 minutes), Berlin (€62, 2¼ hours), Hamburg (€53, two hours), Frankfurt-am-Main (€48, two hours) and Munich (€93, 4½ hours). Direct RB trains depart every two hours from Göttingen for Goslar in the Harz Mountains (€12, 1¼ hours).

GOSLAR

☎ 05321 / pop 48,000

Goslar is a centre for Harz Mountains tourism, but this 1000-year-old city with its beautifully preserved half-timbered buildings has plenty of charm in its own right. It's especially peaceful to wander the cobblestone streets at night. The town and the nearby Rammelsberg Mine is listed as a World Heritage Site by Unesco.

Information

The **tourist office** (☎ 780 60; www.goslar.de, in German; Markt 7; ☼ 9.15am-6pm Mon-Fri, 9.30am-4pm Sat, to 2pm Sun May-Oct; 9.15am-5pm Mon-Fri, 9.30am-2pm Sat Nov-Apr) can help when the area's accommodation is packed. For information on the Harz Mountains go to **Harzer Verkehrsverband** (☎ 340 40; www.harzinfo.de, in German; Marktstrasse 45; ☼ 8am-4pm Mon-Thu, to 1pm Fri).

Sights

The **Marktplatz** has several photogenic houses. The one opposite the Gothic **Rathaus** has a chiming clock depicting four scenes from the history of mining in the area. It struts its stuff at 9am, noon, 3pm and 6pm. The **market fountain** dates from the 13th century and is crowned by an eagle.

Usually jammed with tour-bus visitors, the **Kaiserpfalz** (Kaiserbleek 6; adult/concession €4.50/2.50) is a reconstructed Romanesque 11th-century palace. Just below there's the restored **Domvorhalle** which displays the 11th-century 'Kaiserstuhl' throne, used by German emperors. At the **Rammelsberger Bergbaumuseum** (Rammelsberger Strasse; adult/concession €8.50/5.50; ☼ 9am-6pm), about 1km south of the town

centre, you can delve into the 1000-year mining history of the area and descend into the shafts on a variety of tours.

Sleeping

Jugendherberge (☎ 222 40; www.djh.de; Rammelsbergerstrasse 25; dm juniors/seniors €19/22) Situated up the hill near the Kaiserpfalz (take bus No 803 to Theresienhof from the train station), this hostel is a peaceful refuge when not full of high-school students.

Hotel und Campingplatz Sennhütte (☎ 225 02; Clausthaler Strasse 28; camp sites €2.50, plus per person/car €3.30/2, s/d €20/40; ☼ Fri-Wed) These camping grounds are 3km south on Route B241. Take bus No 830 from the train station to Sennhütte. There are also several clean, simple rooms and you'll find lots of trails nearby.

Hotel Zur Börse (☎ 345 10; www.hotel-boerse -goslar.de, in German; Bergstrasse 53; s/d with shared bathroom €25/50) Housed in a traditional Goslar home, Hotel Zur Börse is just a short walk from the market square.

Gästehaus Schmitz (☎ 234 45; fax 30 60 39; Kornstrasse 1; s/d €30/40) Centrally located, Schmitz offers the best value with cheerful rooms.

Die Tanne (☎ 343 90; www.die-tanne.de, in German; Bäringerstrasse 10; s/d €30/60) The Die Tanne is another excellent choice. The rooms are homy but modern and there's even a small, private sauna for guests.

Hotel Kaiserworth (☎ 70 90; www.kaiserworth.de; Markt 3; s/d €58/101) It's a thrill to sleep in this magnificent 500-year-old building right on the market square.

Eating

Altdeutsches Kartoffelhaus (☎ 454 25; Breite Strasse; mains €4-11) Can one ever tire of the potato? The Kartoffelhaus, in the Kaiserpassage shopping arcade says no.

Brauhaus Wolpertinger (☎ 221 55; Marstallstrasse 1; mains €5-15) A restaurant with whimsical décor and a beer garden in summer.

Didgeridoo (☎ 468 37; Hoher Weg 13; mains €7-10) Come for the Aussie 'cuisine' such as well-priced kangaroo burgers and barbecue meals (also has some good Australian wines).

Getting There & Away

Goslar is regularly connected by train to Göttingen (€12.90, 1¼ hours), Hanover (€12.90, one hour) and Wernigerode (€6.90, 30 minutes). For information on getting to/from the eastern Harz region, see p443.

HAMBURG

☎ 040 / pop 1.7 million

One of the few growing cities in Germany, Hamburg has flourished since reunification, and still maintains its reputation as one of the most important media and cultural centres in Germany. While a massive multibillion-dollar port project, expected to take decades to complete, gets under way, vibrant and casually fashionable neighbourhoods such as Schanzenvertiel, St Pauli and Altoona express Hamburg's personality and self-image.

The first recorded settlement on the present site of Hamburg was the moated fortress of Hammaburg, built in the first half of the 9th century. The city that developed around it became the northernmost archbishopric in Europe, to facilitate the conversion of the northern peoples.

The city was burned down many times, but in the 13th century it became the Hanseatic League's gateway to the North Sea and was second in importance and influence only to Lübeck. With the decline of the Hanseatic League in the 16th century, Lübeck faded into insignificance but Hamburg continued to thrive.

Hamburg strode confidently into the 20th century but WWI stopped all trade and most of Hamburg's merchant shipping fleet (almost 1500 ships) was forfeited to the Allies as reparation payment. In WWII, more than half of Hamburg's residential areas and port facilities were demolished and 55,000 people killed in Allied air raids that spawned horrific firestorms.

Today this is a sprawling port city and a separate state of Germany, with a stylish shopping district, numerous waterways (with more bridges than Venice), and even a beach (in Blankenese, which is one of Germany's most exclusive suburbs).

ORIENTATION

The Hauptbahnhof is very central, near Aussenalster Lake and fairly close to most of the sights. These are south of Aussenalster and north of the Elbe River, which runs all the way from the Czech Republic to Hamburg before flowing into the North Sea. The city centre features the Rathaus and the beautiful Hauptkirche St Michaelis. The port is southwest of the city centre, facing the Elbe.

Stadtpark, the biggest part in the city, is a popular meeting point in summer.

INFORMATION
BOOKSHOPS
Dr Götze Land & Karte (Alstertor 14-18) Claims to be the biggest specialist map and travel bookshop in Europe.
English Bookstore (Stresemannstrasse 169; S-Bahn to Holstenstrasse) Sells second-hand books.
Thalia Bücher (Grosse Bleichen 19) Has a large selection of English-language books and some guidebooks.

EMERGENCY
Ambulance (☎ 112)
Police (☎ 110) There is a police station in St Georg at Steindamm 82 and another in St Pauli at Spielbudenplatz 31, on the corner of Davidstrasse.

INTERNET ACCESS
Spiele Netzwerk (☎ 450 38 210; www.spielenetzwerk .com, in German; Kleiner Schäferkamp 24)

LAUNDRY
Schnell & Sauber Laundrette (Nobistor 34, St Pauli) There's also a branch at Neuer Pferdemarkt 27 (U3 to Feldstrasse).
Waschalon St Georg (Hanseplatz 12)

MEDICAL SERVICES
Dental Treatment (☎ 33 11 55)
Medical Emergency Service (☎ 22 80 22)

MONEY
American Express (☎ 303 938 11; Rathausmarkt 10; ☽ 9.30am-6pm Mon-Fri)
Reisebank (☽ 7.30am-10pm) Above the Kirchenallee exit of the main train station, and others at Altona train station (☽ Mon-Sat) and in Terminal 4 at the airport (☽ 6am-10pm).

POST
Main post office (cnr Dammtorstrasse & Stephansplatz; U-Bahn Stephansplatz); Branch post office (Hauptbahnhof, Kirchenallee exit; ☽ 8am-8pm Mon-Fri, 9am-6pm Sat, 10am-6pm Sun)

TOURIST INFORMATION
Both tourist offices stock the Hamburg Card, which offers unlimited public transport and free or discounted admission to many attractions, museums and cruises. The 'day card' costs €6.80 (single) or €12.70 (groups of up to five people). The 'multiday card' is valid for three days (single/group €14/22.50). An even better deal is the Power Pass, which

GERMANY

HAMBURG

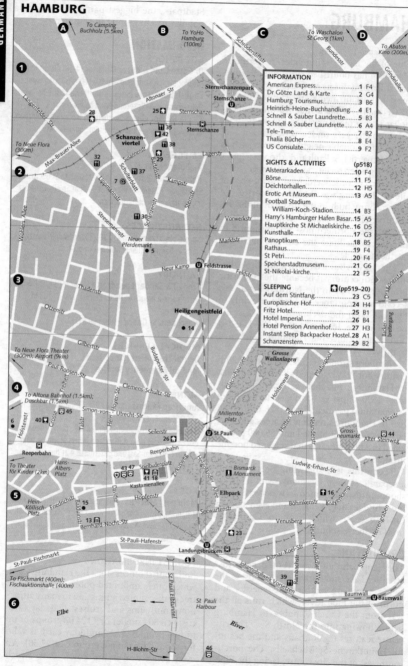

INFORMATION
American Express	1 F4
Dr Götze Land & Karte	2 G4
Hamburg Tourismus	3 B6
Heinrich-Heine-Buchhandlung	4 E1
Schnell & Sauber Laundrette	5 B3
Schnell & Sauber Laundrette	6 A4
Tele-Time	7 B2
Thalia Bücher	8 E4
US Consulate	9 F2

SIGHTS & ACTIVITIES (p518)
Alsterarkaden	10 F4
Börse	11 F5
Deichtorhallen	12 H5
Erotic Art Museum	13 A5
Football Stadium William-Koch-Stadion	14 B3
Harry's Hamburger Hafen Basar	15 A5
Hauptkirche St Michaeliskirche	16 D5
Kunsthalle	17 G3
Panoptikum	18 B5
Rathaus	19 F4
St Petri	20 F4
Speicherstadtmuseum	21 G6
St-Nikolai-kirche	22 F5

SLEEPING (pp519–20)
Auf dem Stintfang	23 C5
Europäischer Hof	24 H4
Fritz Hotel	25 B1
Hotel Imperial	26 B4
Hotel Pension Annenhof	27 H3
Instant Sleep Backpacker Hostel	28 A1
Schanzenstern	29 B2

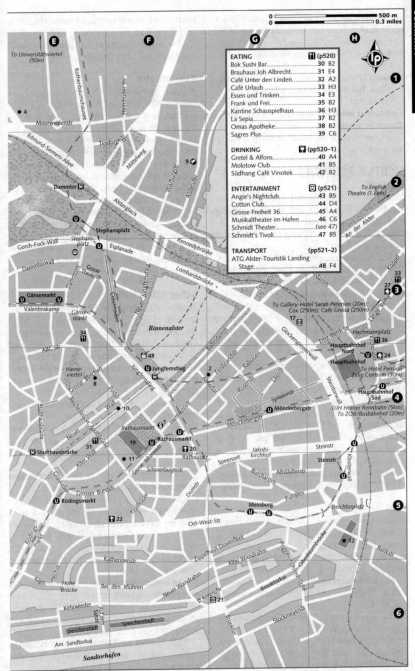

```
0                    500 m
0                    0.3 miles
```

EATING 🍴 (p520)
Bok Sushi Bar	**30** B2
Brauhaus Joh Albrecht	**31** E4
Café Unter den Linden	**32** A2
Café Urlaub	**33** H3
Essen und Trinken	**34** E3
Frank und Frei	**35** B2
Kantine Schauspielhaus	**36** H3
La Sepia	**37** B2
Omas Apotheke	**38** B2
Sagres Plus	**39** C6

DRINKING 🍺 (pp520–1)
Gretel & Alfons	**40** A4
Molotow Club	**41** B5
Südhang Café Vinotek	**42** B2

ENTERTAINMENT 🎭 (p521)
Angie's Nightclub	**43** B5
Cotton Club	**44** D4
Grosse Freiheit 36	**45** A4
Musikaltheater im Hafen	**46** C6
Schmidt Theater	(see 47)
Schmidt's Tivoli	**47** B5

TRANSPORT (pp521–2)
ATG Alster-Touristik Landing Stage	**48** F4

To Universitätsviertel (50m)

To English Theatre (1.8km)

Moorweidenstr

Edmund-Siemers-Allee

Rothenbaumchaussee

Heimhuder Str

Tesdorpfstr

Mittelweg

Warburgstr

Alsterufer

Dammtor

Alsterglacis

Stephansplatz

Stephans-platz

Esplanade

Kennedybrücke

Gorch-Fock-Wall

Dammtorwall

Grosse Theaterstr

Neuer Jungfernstieg

Lombardsbrücke

Ferdinandstr

An der Alster

Koppel

Linke Reihe

Ernst-Merck-Str

Hachmannstr

To Gallery-Hotel Sarah Petersen (20m); Cox (250m); Cafe Gnosa (250m)

Hauptbahnhof Nord

Hauptbahnhof

To Hotel Pension Zelig Centrum (30m)

Hauptbahnhof Süd

DJH Horner Rennbahn (5km); To ZOB/Busbahnhof (20m)

Gänsemarkt

Valentinskamp

Gänse-markt

ABC-Str

Binnenalster

Ballindamm

Glockengiesserwall

Steintorwall

Klosterwall

Steinstr

Hanse-viertel

Grosse Bleichen

Poststr

Bleichenbrücke

Neuer Wall

Alter Wall

Adolphsbrücke

Jungfernstieg

Hermannstr

Alsterstr

Rosenstr

Spitalerstr

Mönckebergstr

Mönckebergstr

Rathausmarkt

Rathausmarkt

Rathausstr

Grosse Johannisstr

Schauenburgerstr

Domstr

Speersort

Jakobi-kirchhof

Altstädterstr

Steinstr

Stadthausbrücke

Stadthausbrücke

Neuer Wall

Rödingsmarkt

Rödings-markt

Grosser Burstah

Trostbrücke

Ost-West-Str

Bankstr

Schauenburgerstr

Burchardstr

Pumpen

Messburg

Deichtorplatz

Katherinenstr

Zippelhaus

Dovenfleet

Alter Wandrahm

Deichtorhauptbrücke

Brücktorbrücke

Brooktorkai

Kajen

Deichstr

Hohe Brücke

Bei den Mühren

Neuer Wandrahm

St Annenufer

Brooktor

Stockmeyerstr

Kehrwieder

Auf dem Sande

Speicherstadt

Speicherstadt

Am Sandtorkai

Sandtorhafen

gives steep discounts to anyone under 30 for €6.70 (extendable for an extra €3 per day). For cultural events and lifestyle information, look for the monthly magazines *Morgan Post* (€0.50), *Szene* (€2.50) and *Prinz* (€1).

Hamburg Tourismus (St Pauli Harbour, btwn piers 4 & 5; ⊗ 8am-8pm Mon-Sat, to 7pm Sun Apr-Sep; 10am-5.30pm Oct-Mar)

Main tourist office (☎ 30 05 12 00; www.hamburg -tourism.de; Hauptbahnhof; ⊗ 7am-11pm) Near the Kirchenallee exit at the train station; offers a room-finding service (€4).

SIGHTS & ACTIVITIES
Altstadt

Much of Hamburg's old city centre was lost in WWII, but it's still worth a walking tour. The area is laced with wonderful canals (called 'fleets') running from the Alster lakes to the Elbe.

The Altstadt is centred on Rathausmarkt, where the large **Rathaus** (tours adult/concession €1/0.50, ⊗ tours in English hourly from 10.15am-3.15pm Mon-Thu, to 1.15pm Fri-Sun), with 647 rooms – six more than Buckingham Palace – and the huge clock tower overlook the lively square. This is one of the most interesting city halls in Germany, and the 35-minute tour is worthwhile.

It is a moving experience to visit the remaining tower of the devastated **St-Nikolai-Kirche**, now an antiwar memorial, nearby on Ost-West-Strasse. From there, walk a few blocks west to the baroque **Hauptkirche St Michaeliskirche** and take the lift up the **tower** (adult/concession €2.50/1.25; ⊗ 10am-6pm Apr-Oct, to 5pm Nov-Mar); enter through portal No 3 for a great view of the city and the port. Inside, the beautiful interiors and the crypt (a donation of €1.25 is requested) are open for viewing.

Port

After exploring the Altstadt, stroll down to one of the busiest ports in the world. It boasts the world's largest carpet warehouse complex, while the Free Port Warehouses stockpile goods from all continents.

The **port cruises** are touristy but still worthwhile. There are many options; for details see p519.

If you're in the port area early on a Sunday (5am to 10am, from 7am October to March), head for **Fischmarkt** (Fish Market) in St Pauli, right on the Elbe. Hamburg's oldest market (established 1703) is popular with locals and tourists alike and everything under the sun is sold here. Cap your morning with a visit to the live music session at the **Fischauktionshalle** (Fish Auction Hall; Grosse Elbstrasse 9).

Reeperbahn

Among Hamburg's biggest tourist attractions is the famous Reeperbahn red-light district. It is 600m long and is the heart of the St Pauli entertainment district, which includes shows, bars, cabarets, clubs, theatres and a casino. The Reeperbahn sex establishments have been gradually moving over for popular restaurants and bars, with a dwindling number of peep shows and sex shops plying a 'traditional' trade.

On **Grosse Freiheit**, Safari is one of the more famous clubs. Notorious **Herbertstrasse** is where prostitutes pose in windows offering their wares. It is fenced off at each end and off-limits to men under 18 and women of all ages.

Other Attractions

Hamburg's **Kunsthalle** (Glockengiesserwall; adult/concession €7.50/5; ⊗ 10am-6pm Tue-Sun, to 9pm Thu) has old masters and a large collection of German paintings from both the 19th and 20th centuries. Contemporary art is housed next door in the modern **Galerie der Gegenwart** (adult/concession €7.50/5; ⊗ 10am-6pm Tue-Sun, to 9pm Thu).

The waxworks museum **Panoptikum** (Spielbudenplatz 3; adult/concession €4/2.50; ⊗ 11am-9pm Mon-Fri, to midnight Sat, 10am-9pm Sun early Feb–mid-Jan) is kitschy fun; don't miss the gruesomely realistic syphilitic hands in the 'medical history' wing.

A fascinating 'shop' is **Harry's Hamburger Hafen Basar** (Balduinstrasse 18; admission €2.50). It's the life's work of Harry, a bearded character known to seamen all over the world, who for decades bought trinkets and souvenirs from sailors and others. Now run by Harry's daughter, the shop has a wealth of curiosities and the entry fee is refunded with a €5 purchase.

The **Erotic Art Museum** (☎ 317 841 26; www.eroticart museum.de; Bernhard-Nochtstrasse 69; adult/concession €8/5; ⊗ 10am-midnight Sun-Thu, to 2am Fri & Sat) contains some 1800 paintings, drawings and sculptures by artists from Delacroix to Picasso.

The **Planten un Blomen** is a gorgeously landscaped city park with a large Japanese garden.

Blankenese, a rocky beach west of the city centre, is worth a visit. Take the S-Bahn to the Blankenese stop. Small former fishers' houses line the steep path to the water.

TOURS

Stattreisen Hamburg (☎ 430 34 81; www.stattreisen -hamburg.de) runs a variety of highly recommended city walking tours in German, French and English.

Basic city sightseeing **bus tours** (adult/concession €12/6.50) in English run at least twice daily from April to October, and every 30 minutes from 9.30am to 4.45pm the rest of the year. They leave from Kirchenallee next to the main train station and last 1¾ hours; you can add a harbour cruise for an extra €7.

Two-hour 'Fleet' (inner canal) **cruises** (adult/concession €14/7) depart from Jungfernstieg three times daily. The 50-minute Alster lakes tour departs at least three times daily from Jungfernstieg and costs adult/concession €9/4.50. Both of these operate from April to October. There are also special summer cruises.

Port Cruises

Port cruises in sightseeing boats and the unusual **Barkassen wooden boats** (adult/concession €8.50/4.50; 1hr) built to navigate the Speicherstadt's canals operate throughout the year from St Pauli-Landungsbrücken, piers 1 to 9. They depart half-hourly from 9am to 6pm from April to October, and hourly from 10.30am to 3.30pm from November to March. Tours with English commentary run at 11am daily from April to September from pier 1.

SLEEPING

The tourist office at the main train station charges €4 for accommodation bookings. You can also call the **Hamburg-Hotline** (☎ 30 05 13 00; ☉ 8am-8pm) for availability and reservations.

Many budget hotels are along Steindamm and a few blocks east of the main train station along Bremer Reihe, but the concentration of junkies and prostitutes make the streets feel unsafe, especially at night.

Budget

Campingplatz Buchholz (☎ 540 45 32; Kielerstrasse 374; camp sites €7-10, plus per person/car €4/4) Though inconvenient and catering mainly for caravans, the Buchholz can be reached from the

Hauptbahnhof by taking the S-Bahn No 2 or 3 to Stellingen. You can also take bus No 183 from Hamburg-Altona train station towards Schnelsen.

Auf dem Stintfang (☎ 31 34 88; jh-stintfang@ t-online.de; Alfred-Wegener-Weg 5; dm juniors/seniors €17.30/20) Modern and clean, this hostel has superb views of the Elbe and the harbour. Large, noisy school groups regularly stay here. You can take the U-/S-Bahn to St Pauli-Landungsbrücken.

Instant Sleep Backpacker Hostel (☎ 43 18 23 10; www.instantsleep.de; Max Brauer Allee 277; dm/s/d €15/28/44) The accommodation is spartan and yes those are school lockers for your things, but the Instant Sleep is cheap, friendly and just a few blocks from the action in the Schanzenviertel.

Schanzenstern (☎ 439 84 41; www.schanzenstern .de; Bartelsstrasse 12; dm €17, s/d/tr €35/50/60) Smack dab in the middle of this lively neighbourhood, the Schanzenstern, some of whose rooms have seen better days, has a hip café attached.

Mid-Range

Hotel Pension Selig Zentrum (☎ 24 46 90; fax 24 98 45; Bremer Reihe 23; s/d €31/61) One of the best values close to the train station.

Hotel Pension Annenhof (☎ 24 34 26; www.hotel annenhof.de, in German; Lange Reihe 23; s/d €35/65) Don't be discouraged by the rather grubby façade. Annenhof's attractive rooms have polished wooden floorboards and brightly painted colour schemes.

Hotel Imperial (☎ 319 60 21; info@hotel-imperial -hamburg.de; Millerntorplatz 3-5; s/d Mon-Fri €50/77, Sat & Sun €60/85) Some rooms face away from the Reeperbahn, and are spacious and well furnished.

Gallery-Hotel Sarah Petersen (☎ 24 98 26; www .galerie-hotel-sarah-petersen.de; Lange Reihe 50; s/d €45/65) Designed and decorated with paintings by the owner/artist, every aesthetic detail of this charmingly unique hotel delights. More expensive rooms have video, fax and other practical comforts.

YoHo Hamburg (☎ 28 41 91 0; www.yoho-hamburg .de; Moorkamp 5; juniors s/d €57/67, seniors €77/87) Don't let the name fool you, there's nothing hostel-like about this renovated former mansion. A team of young architects has attended to every detail including Mazza, the Syrian restaurant that offers a delectable five-course meal (€20).

Fritz Hotel (☎ 822 22 83 0; www.fritzhotel.com; Schanzenstrasse 101-103; s/d €60/90) This friendly and professional boutique-style hotel is an oasis of calm and luxury. Rooms fronting the street have small balconies, fantastic for people-watching or sipping an early morning espresso. Rooms at the back are quieter.

Europäischer Hof (☎ 24 82 48; www.europaeischer -hof.de; Kirchenallee 45; s/d €103/133) Directly across from the train station; ask for a room that's quiet and has been renovated.

EATING

Under the elevated U-Bahn train on Isestrasse, there's a food market, which would seem picturesque if you weren't so focused on your stomach. Take the U-3 to Hohe Luftbrücke on Tuesday and Friday between 8.30am and 2pm.

Hauptbahnhof Area

Kantine im Schauspielhaus (Kirchenallee; lunches €6) One of the best-kept secrets in this part of town with plain but filling lunches, the Kantine is downstairs in the Deutsches Schauspielhaus.

Café Gnosa (☎ 24 30 34; Lange Reihe 93; mains €6) It has good lunch specials, wonderful homemade cakes, and is nice for an evening meal or drink.

Café Urlaub (Lange Reihe 63; dishes €7; ⏰ until 2am) This student café, open from breakfast until late, is a good eating and drinking option. Here you can find good salads and pasta dishes.

Cox (☎ 24 94 22; Lange Reihe 68; mains €16) An upmarket bistro with stylish Continental décor and friendly staff, the Cox is a great place to spend an hour or three.

Gänsemarkt & Around

You'll find a wide choice around Gänsemarkt and Jungfernstieg near the Binnenalster lake.

Essen und Trinken (Gänsemarkt 21) Choose from Asian, Mediterranean and German cuisine at budget prices at this food hall.

Brauhaus Joh Albrecht (Adolfsbrücke 7; dishes less than €10) A bustling microbrewery with a few canal-side tables.

Schanzenviertel

The lively Schanzenviertel neighbourhood lies west of the TV tower and north of St Pauli (take the U-Bahn or S-Bahn to Stern-schanze), and is shared by students and immigrants. Lots of cosy cafés and restaurants string along Schanzenstrasse and Susannenstrasse.

Omas Apotheke (☎ 43 66 20; Schanzenstrasse 87; mains €7) Alcohol is the hardest drug available at Omas, a former pharmacy that now prescribes good international fare.

Frank und Frei (☎ 43 48 03; Schanzenstrasse) Just opposite Omas is Frank und Frei, a student hang-out offering a small menu.

Café Unter Der Linden (☎ 43 81 40; Juliusstrasse 16) This is a popular gay hang-out doling out big bowls of coffee and bistro fare.

Bok Sushi Bar (☎ 430 67 80; Schanzenstrasse 27; mains around €8) A young crowd frequents Bok, with an array of Thai, Korean and Japanese dishes. A delicious 18-piece Bento II sushi platter costs €32.

La Sepia (☎ 432 24 84; Schulterblatt 36; dishes around €13) La Sepia offers terrific seafood in a Mediterranean atmosphere, and it sometimes has live music.

St Pauli/Port Area

There is a cluster of good Portuguese and Spanish restaurants along Ditmar-Koel-Strasse and Reimarus-Strasse near St Pauli Landungsbrücken.

Ristorante L'Incontro da Cosimo (☎ 430 02 46; Wiedenallee 25; pizza €7) Just off the Reeperbahn, this is good choice for relaxed Italian fare at reasonable prices.

Sagres Plus (☎ 37 12 01; Vorsetzen 52; mains €10) Always packed Sagres specialises in fresh-off-the-boat fish dishes done Portuguese style.

Freudenhaus (☎ 31 46 42; Hein-Hoyerstrasse 7-9; mains €13-17) The ubiquitous angel designs and delicate German cuisine make this an oasis off the Reeperbahn.

DRINKING

Not surprisingly, St Pauli is the flash point for nightclubs. Young people meet in Hans Albersplatz, especially during the summer, before heading off to the pubs and cafés for the night.

Duschbar (☎ 39 90 40 06; Bahrenfelderstrasse 168) Washing is the theme at this quirky boho hangout in Ottensen, replete with a shower-curtain door, sink tables and shower-head lamps.

Molotow Club (☎ 31 08 45; Spielbudenplatz 5) An alternative, independent music scene –

indie, electro, garage and punk – thrives at Molotow.

Gretel & Alfons (☎ 31 34 91; Grosse Freiheit 29) Across from Grosse Freiheit 36, you can have a drink where the Beatles once quaffed.

Südhang Café Vinotek (☎ 43 09 90 99; Susannenstrasse 29) Above a shoe store in the Schanzenviertel, casual and sophisticated Südhang has an excellent wine selection and is an Internet hotspot for those laptop carriers who must check thier email.

ENTERTAINMENT

Hamburg has a lively jazz scene, as well as an excellent alternative and experimental theatre scene. For central theatre or concert bookings, go to the **Theaterkasse** (☎ 35 35 55; Grosse Bleichen) in the basement of the Alsterhaus shopping complex.

Grosse Freiheit 36 (☎ 36 31 77 780; Grosse Freiheit 36) Wedged between live sex theatres and peep shows, this is one of the most popular places for live rock and pop. The Beatles played in the Kaiserkeller, the disco in the basement.

Abaton Kino (☎ 41 32 03 20; Allende-Platz 3) Screens English-language films here.

Cotton Club (☎ 34 38 78; Alter Steinweg 10) Traditional jazz tunes. On weekends, reservations are recommended.

Angie's Nightclub (☎ 31 77 88 16; Spielbudenplatz 27-28) A classy, sweaty local favourite for live music and dancing.

English Theatre (☎ 227 70 89; Lerchenfeld 14) Good for a language fix.

Theater für Kinder (☎ 38 25 38; Max-Brauer-Allee 76) Great for kids – or children of all ages (in German only).

Schmidt Theater (☎ 31 77 88 99; Spielbudenplatz 27) The Schmidt Theater's wild variety shows (in German only) are decidedly adult.

Schmidt's Tivoli (☎ 317 78 99; Spielburdenplatz 24) For cabaret and musical productions.

Neue Flora Theater (☎ 0180 544 44; Stresemannstrasse 159a) Take the S-Bahn to Holstenstrasse for musical extravaganzas.

Musikaltheater im Hafen (☎ 0180 519 97; Norderelbstrasse 6; shuttle service from pier 1 of St Pauli Landungsbrücken) Tickets, which start at around €26, can be reserved at the tourist offices or on the hotline ☎ 30 05 13 00.

GETTING THERE & AWAY

Air

Hamburg's **international airport** (☎ 50 75 25 57), located in Fuhlsbüttel, has frequent flights to domestic destinations as well as cities in Scandinavia and elsewhere in Europe.

Bus

The **Berlin Linienbus** (☎ 030 861 93 31; www.berlinlinienbus.de) goes to, you guessed it, Berlin every two hours (€37, three hours) from the central bus station.

International destinations that aren't served directly by train from Hamburg, such as Amsterdam (€44.50, 6½ hours) and London (€61.50, 17½ hours), are served by **Eurolines** (www.eurolines.com) buses. A good option for getting to London is **Rainbow Tours** (☎ 32 09 33 09; www.rainbowtours.de, in German; Gänsemarkt 45), which offers return trips without an overnight stay from €55 – a cheap way to get to London, even if you don't use the return portion of the ticket. The central bus station is southeast of the main train station on Adenauerallee.

Car & Motorcycle

The autobahns of the A1 (Bremen-Lübeck) and A7 (Hanover-Kiel) cross south of the Elbe River. Hamburg's only **Mitfahr-Zentrale** (☎ 194 40; Ernst-Merck-Strasse 8) is near the train station.

Ferry

A busy car and passenger ferry run by **Scandlines** (☎ 01805 72 26 35 46 37; www.scandlines.com) goes from the German harbour town of Puttgarden to Rodby in Denmark, which leaves every half-hour 24 hours a day and takes 45 minutes. The cost is €60 each way for a car including up to five people. A bicycle costs €7, including one person. A single passenger pays €3 (€6 mid-June to August) each way. If you're travelling by train, the cost of the ferry is included in your ticket.

FRS (☎ 1080 320 20 25; www.frs.de) runs one trip daily from Hamburg to the outlying island of Helgoland.

Train

Hamburg's Hauptbahnhof is one of the busiest in Germany. There are frequent RE/RB trains to Lübeck (€9, 45 minutes) and Kiel (€15, 1¼ hours), various services to Hanover (€29, 1½ hours) and Bremen (€16.80, 1¼ hours), as well as ICE trains to Berlin (€49, 2½ hours) and Frankfurt-am-Main (€86, 3½ hours). There are overnight services to Munich, Vienna, Paris and Zurich via Basel as well as trains to Copenhagen. Hamburg-Altona station is quieter but has a monopoly on some services to the north. Carefully read the timetables when booking to/from Hamburg stations or you could finish up at the wrong station at the wrong time. Hamburg-Harburg handles some regional services (for instance to/from Cuxhaven, the main port for Helgoland).

GETTING AROUND
To/From the Airport
A taxi from the main train station costs around €30 (one easy number to use is ☎ 21 12 11). A better airport option is to take the U1 from the main train station to Ohlsdorf and from there the No 110 express bus (€2.20). Airport buses (€4.25) make the 25-minute trip between the airport and the train station every 25 minutes between 5am and 9.20pm.

Bus
A day pass for travel after 9am in most of Hamburg is €4.25 (€6.85 if you include the surrounding area) and there are various family passes. From midnight to dawn the night-bus network takes over from the trains, converging on the main metropolitan bus station at Rathausmarkt. For transport options with a Hamburg Card see p515 .

SCHLESWIG-HOLSTEIN

Schleswig-Holstein is Germany's northern-most state and borders Denmark at the southern end of the Jutland Peninsula. Although most travellers rarely make it this far north, there are many attractions including the North Frisian Islands, the historical city of Lübeck and the straw-roofed beautiful old farm houses that dot the landscape. The further north you go the flatter the land gets until it meets the North Sea.

The northern dialect called 'Plattdeutsch' (low-German) sounds a lot like English and shares many similar words.

Schleswig and Holstein began breaking away from Denmark with the help of Sweden in the mid-17th century, a process which took until 1773. When Holstein joined the German Confederation in 1815, Denmark attempted to lure Schleswig back to the motherland.

Three wars were fought over the region between Germany and Denmark until the third in 1866, when Bismarck annexed it to unify Germany. Under the Treaty of Versailles in 1919, North Schleswig was given to Denmark. Finally, in 1946, the British military government formed the state of Schleswig-Holstein from the Prussian province of the same name.

LÜBECK
☎ 0451 / pop 215,000
Medieval Lübeck was known as the Queen of the Hanseatic League, as it was the capital of this association of towns that ruled trade on the Baltic Sea from the 12th to the 16th centuries. This beautiful city, with its red-stone buildings, is a highlight of the region and well worth taking the time to explore.

Orientation
Lübeck's old town is set on an island ringed by the canalised Trave River, a 15-minute walk east from the main train station. To get there, just take Konrad-Adenauer-Strasse across the pretty Puppenbrücke (Doll Bridge) to Holstentor, the city's western gateway. Then follow Holstenstrasse east from An der Untertrave to Kohlmarkt, from where Breite Strasse leads north to the Markt and the historic Rathaus.

Information
Central post office (Königstrasse 46) Across from the Katarinenkirche.
Lübeck-Information (☎ 122 54 19; www.luebeck -tourism.de; Breite Strasse 62; ◯ 9.30am-6pm Mon-Fri, 10am-2pm Sat & Sun) Near the Rathaus. Both city tourist offices run a room-finding service.
Room-Finding Office (☎ 86 46 75; fax 86 30 24) At the train station, this private office charges €3 (free if reserved by phone).

Sights
The landmark **Holstentor** (☎ 122 41 29; adult/ concession €5/3; ◯ 10am-6pm Tue-Sun Apr-Sep, 10am-4pm Tue-Sun Oct-Mar), a fortified gate with huge twin towers, serves as the city's symbol as well as its museum, but for a literary kick, visit the **Buddenbrookhaus** (☎ 122 4190; www.budden brookhaus.de; Mengstrasse 4; adult/concession €6/3.60; ◯ 10am-6pm, to 5pm Nov-Mar), the family house where Thomas Mann was born and which he made famous in his novel *Buddenbrooks*. The literary works and philosophical rivalry

of the brothers Thomas and Heinrich are commemorated here. The must-see **Marienkirche** (Markt; 🕑 10am-6pm) contains a stark reminder of WWII; a bombing raid brought the church bells crashing to the stone floor and the townspeople have left the bell fragments in place, with a small sign saying: 'A protest against war and violence'. Also on the Markt is the imposing **Rathaus** (☎ 122 1005; adult/concession €2.60/1.50; guided tours 🕑 11am, noon & 3pm Mon-Fri).

Lübeck's **Marionettentheater** (Puppet Theatre; ☎ 700 60; cnr Am Kolk & Kleine Petersgrube; 🕑 Tue-Sun) is a must. Usually there is a daily afternoon performance for children (€4, 3pm) and an evening performance (€11, 8pm) for adults only on Saturday.

The tower lift at the partly restored **Petrikirche** (adult/concession €2/1.20; 🕑 9am-7pm May-Oct, shorter hrs other months, closed Jan & Feb) affords a superb view over the Altstadt.

Sleeping

Campingplatz Schönböcken (☎ 89 30 90; Steinrader Damm 12; tent site/person/car €3.50/4.50/1; 🕑 Apr-Oct) This ground is located in a western suburb of Lübeck. For camping grounds in the nearby coastal resort of Travemünde ask at the tourist office.

Jugendgästehaus Lübeck (☎ 702 03 99; www .djh.de; Mengstrasse 33; dm juniors/seniors €17.40/20.10, s/tw €25.60/51.20) Clean, comfortable and well situated in the middle of the old town.

Jugendherberge 'Vor dem Burgtor' (☎ 334 33; fax 345 40; Am Gertrudenkirchhof 4; dm juniors/seniors €15.40/18.10) To get to this hostel, a little outside the old town, take bus No 1, 3, 11, 12 or 31 to Gustav-Radbruch-Platz.

Sleep-Inn (☎ 719 20; fax 789 97; Grosse Petersgrube 11; dm €10, d €30, apt per person €32; 🕑 mid-Jan–mid-Dec) This centrally located YMCA charges €4 extra for breakfast and €4.50 extra for sheets.

Hotel Stadt Lübeck (☎ 838 83; fax 86 32 21; Am Bahnhof 21; s/d €43/63) Fairly good rooms come with shower and toilet at the Stadt Lübeck, just outside the main train station.

The **Klassik Altstadt Hotel** (☎ 720 83; www .klassik-Altstadt-hotel.de, in German; Fischergrube 52; s/d €44/75) is also recommended.

Eating

The best eating and drinking options are in the area directly east of the Rathaus. Save room for a dessert or a snack of marzipan, which was invented in Lübeck (local legend has it that the town ran out of flour during a long siege and resorted to grinding almonds to make bread).

Tipasa (Schlumacherstrasse 12-14; mains €4.40) Whatever your taste, tandoori to tacos, Tipasa is a great place to eat and drink in the evening.

Hieronymus (☎ 706 30 17; Fleischhauerstrasse 81; mains €4.50-19.40) Spread over three floors of a 15th-century building, Hieronymus is relaxed and the menu creative. The lunch specials are good value.

Also recommended: **Schiffergesellschaft** (Breite Strasse 2; mains €14.80) for maritime atmosphere and **JG Niederegger** (Breite Strasse 89), directly opposite the Rathaus, is Lübeck's mecca of marzipan.

Getting There & Away

Lübeck is close to Hamburg, with at least one train every hour (€9, 45 minutes). There are also frequent services to Kiel (€12, 1¼ hours) and Schwerin (€11, 1¼ hours). Trains to/from Chhagen also stop here.

The central bus station is next to the main train station. Services to/from Wismar stop here, as well as Autokraft buses to/from Hamburg, Schwerin, Kiel, Rostock and Berlin.

Getting Around

Frequent double-decker buses run to Travemünde (€3.50, 45 minutes) from the central bus station. City buses also leave from here; a single journey costs €1.35.

NORTH FRISIAN ISLANDS

The Frisian Islands reward those who make the trek with sand dunes, sea, pure air and, every so often, sunshine. Friesland covers an area stretching from the northern Netherlands along the coast up into Denmark. North Friesland (Nordfriesland) is the western coastal area of Schleswig-Holstein up to and into Denmark. The sea area forms the National Park of Wattenmeer, and the shifting dunes, particularly on the islands of Amrum, Föhr and Langeness, are sensitive and cannot be disturbed; paths and boardwalks are provided for strolling. The most popular of the North Frisian Islands is the glamorous resort of Sylt, which gets very crowded from June to August; the neighbouring islands of Föhr and Amrum are far more relaxed and less touristy.

Nature is the prime attraction on the North Frisian Islands. Beautiful dunes stretch out for kilometres, red and white cliffs border wide beaches, and bird lovers will be amply rewarded. Amazingly, when the tide is out it's possible to walk from the mainland to the islands, however several people die every year making this trek. Civilisation has also taken hold here, especially in Westerland on Sylt. After WWII, the German jet-set invaded the island, which explains the abundance of luxury homes, cars and expensive restaurants, particularly around Kampen.

Low-budget accommodation is hard to find on the islands, but the tourist offices can help with private rooms from €20 per person. Some proprietors may be reluctant to rent for fewer than three days.

All communities charge visitors a so-called *Kurtaxe*, a resort tax of about €3 a day, depending on the town and the season. Paying the tax gets you a *Kurkarte* which you need on Sylt even just to get onto the beach. Day passes are available from kiosks at beach entrances, but if you're spending more than one night, your hotel can obtain a pass for you for the length of your stay (not included in the room rate).

Getting There & Around

Sylt is connected to the mainland by a scenic train-only causeway right through the Wattenmeer. Around seven trains leave from Hamburg-Hauptbahnhof daily for Westerland (€33, 3¼ hours). If you are travelling by car, you must load it onto a train in the town of Niebüll near the Danish border. There are about 26 crossings in both directions every day and no reservations can be made. The cost per car is a shocking €77 return, but that includes all passengers.

To get to Amrum and the island of Föhr, you must board a ferry in Dagebüll Hafen. To get there, take the Sylt-bound train from Hamburg-Altona and change in Niebüll. In summer, there are also some through trains. A day-return from Dagebüll costs €18, which allows you to visit both islands. If you stay overnight, return tickets cost €18 (bicycle €4). The trip to Amrum takes around two hours, stopping at Föhr on the way.

There are daily flights between Westerland airport and Hamburg, Munich and Berlin, and several flights weekly from other German cities.

Sylt's two north–south bus lines run every 20 to 30 minutes, and three other frequent lines cover the rest of the island. There are seven price zones, costing from €1.30 to €5.60. Some buses have bicycle hangers. On Amrum, a bus runs from the ferry terminal in Wittdün to Norddorf and back every 30 to 60 minutes, depending on the season. The slow, fun interisland options are the day-return cruises to Föhr (Wyk) and Amrum (Wittdün) from the harbour at Hörnum on Sylt. Day-return cruises through shallow banks that attract both seals and sea birds are offered by **Adler-Schiffe** (☎ 04651 836 10 28 in Westerland; €18.50). Bicycles are an extra €5.

SYLT
☎ 04651 / pop 21,600

The excellent **tourist office** (☎ 99 88; www.sylt .de, in German; ☷ 9am-6pm Mon-Fri, to 4.30pm Sat year-round, to 2pm Sun Jun-Sep) is inside Westerland's train station on Sylt.

In Westerland, a visit to the indoor water park and health spa **Sylter Welle** (☎ 99 82 42; admission €9, with sauna €13; ☷ 10am-9pm) is fun, especially when it's too cold for the beach. It includes saunas, solariums, a wave pool and a slide (and there's no time limit). For a real thrill, though, visit one of Sylt's **beach saunas** – the tourist office can point you in the right direction, or **Heiko's Reitwiese** (☎ 56 00) in Westerland for **horse riding**.

For **cycling**, in Westerland, **Fahrrad am Bahnhof** (☎ 58 03; per day €5) is conveniently situated at the train station.

Sylt has seven camping grounds; **Campingplatz Kampen** (☎ 420 86; Möwenweg 4; per person/ tent car site €3.50/4.50/1.50; ☷ Easter-Oct) is one of the best, set beautifully amid dunes near the small town of Kampen.

Hotel Garni Diana (☎ 988 60; fax 98 86 86; Elisabethstrasse 19; s/d €46/87, with shared bathroom €41/72) is close but not quite on the beach.

Landhaus Nielsen (☎ 986 90; fax 98 69 60; Bastianstrasse 5; s/d €65/75) is a good deal, especially in the winter when prices are lowered.

For good, inexpensive fare, try **Toni's Restaurant** (Norderstrasse 3; dishes €5.80-12.80); it also has a pleasant garden.

Blum's (Neue Strasse 4; soups from €4, mains €8) has some of the freshest fish in town.

On Kampen, in Stapelhooger Wai, **Kupferkanne** (☎ 410 10; Stapelhooger Wai, Kampen; meals €5.50-9) is a beautiful stop during a bike tour with a great view of the Wattenmeer.

There are two DJH options: **Jugendherberge** (☎ 88 02 94; www.djh.de; Friesenplatz 2; dm €15.30), in the south of the island of Hörnum, and List's **Jugendherberge** (☎ 87 03 97; www.djh.de; List; dm €15.30). Neither is very central, but bus services bring you close.

List's harbour sports a number of colourful food kiosks. **Gosch** (List Harbour) prides itself on being Germany's northernmost fish kiosk, and is an institution well known beyond Sylt.

AMRUM
☎ 04682 / pop 2100
On Amrum, the friendly **tourist office** (☎ 940 30; www.amrum.de, in German) is at the harbour car park. The spa administration's **Kurverwaltungen** at the various resorts are also useful sources of information.

You'll find signs of traditional Frisian life around the village of **Nebel**. The **lighthouse** (adult/concession €2/0.50; ☼ 8.30am-12.30pm Mon-Fri), the tallest in northern Germany at 63m, affords a spectacular view of the dunes from the southwest of the island and over to the islands of Sylt, Föhr and Langeness.

Reiterhof Jensen (☎ 20 30) on Amrum offers horse riding. One of several excellent **hikes** on Amrum (8km return) is from Norddorf along the beach to the tranquil Odde **nature reserve**. The tourist office can help with information on guided hikes in summer across the Watt to Föhr and where to rent bikes.

Amrum has only a few restaurants and many of them close early or are closed entirely in the low season.

A budget option is **Campingplatz Schade** (☎ 22 54; camp sites €4, per person €5) at the northern edge of Wittdün; alternatively there are over 200 beds at **Jugendherberge** (☎ 20 10; www.djh.de; Mittelstrasse 1; dm juniors/seniors €15.30/18). It's best to book ahead with this hostel, even in the low season.

The historic **Hotel Ual Öömrang** (☎ 836; fax 14 32; Bräätlun 4; s/d €51/102; ☼ Mar-Dec) has a sauna.

The **Hotel Ual Öömrang** (☎ 836; Bräätlun 4; dishes €14; ☼ Mar-Dec) serves filling traditional dishes and **Haus Burg** (☎ 23 58; Boragwai 2; cakes €3; ☼ 3pm-10.30pm) built on an old Viking hill-fort above the eastern beach at Norddorf, has a teahouse atmosphere and home-made cakes.

GERMANY DIRECTORY

ACCOMMODATION
Local tourist offices are great resources for accommodation in Germany – almost all offer a *Gastgeberverzeichnis* (accommodation list) and a *Zimmervermittlung* (room-finding service), and staff will usually go out of their way to find something in your price range.

In this book, options are listed by price, with the cheapest first. Accommodation usually includes breakfast, except in camping grounds and holiday apartments.

Germany has more than 2000 organised camping grounds, several hundred of which stay open throughout the year. Prices are around €3 to €5 for an adult, plus €3 to €7 for a car and/or tent. Look out for ecologically responsible camping grounds sporting the Green Leaf award from the ADAC motoring association.

The **Deutsches Jugendherbergswerk** (DJH; www.djh.de) coordinates the official Hostelling International (HI) hostels in Germany. Guests must be members of an HI-affiliated organisation, or join the DJH when checking in. The annual fee is €10/17.50 for juniors/seniors, which refers to visitors below/above 26 years old. Bavaria is the only state that enforces a strict maximum age of 26 for visitors. A dorm bed ranges from around €12 to €20 for juniors and €15 to €25 for seniors. Camping at a hostel (where permitted) is generally half price. Sheet hire costs from €2.50 to €3.50.

Private rooms and guesthouses can be excellent value, especially for lone travellers, with prices starting as low as €10. Budget hotels and *pensions* typically charge under €60 for a double room (under €45 with shared bathroom), while good-value midrange options come in around €70 to €130. Anything over €130 can generally be considered top end, and should offer enough amenities to justify the price – spa facilities are a common extra.

Renting an apartment for a week or more is a popular option, particularly for small groups. Again, tourist offices are generally the best source of information, or have a look in newspaper classifieds under *Ferienwohnungen* (FeWo) or *Ferien-Apartments*. Rates vary widely but decrease dramatically with the length of stay. Local *Mitwohnzentralen* (accommodation-finding services) can help in finding shared houses and longer-stay rentals.

ACTIVITIES

Germany, with its rugged alps, picturesque uplands and fairy-tale forests, is ideal for hiking and mountaineering. There are well-marked trails crisscrossing the countryside, especially in popular areas such as the Black Forest (see p480), the Harz Mountains (p443), the Saxon Switzerland area (p431) and the Thuringian Forest. The Bavarian Alps (p470) offer the most dramatica and inspiring scenery, however, and are the centre of mountaineering in Germany. Good sources of information on hiking and mountaineering are: **Verband Deutscher Gebirgs-und Wandervereine** (Federation of German Hiking Clubs; ☎ 0561-938 730; Wilhelmshöher Allee 157-159, 34121 Kassel); and **Deutscher Alpenverein** (German Alpine Club; ☎ 089-140 030; Von-Kahr-Strasse 2-4, 80997 Munich).

The Bavarian Alps are the most extensive area for winter sports. Cross-country skiing is also good in the Black Forest and Harz Mountains. Ski equipment starts at around €12 per day, and daily ski-lift passes start at around €13. Local tourist offices are the best sources of information.

Cyclists will often find marked cycling routes, and eastern Germany has much to offer in the way of lightly travelled back roads. There's an extensive cycling trail along the Elbe River, and islands like Rügen Island (p453) are also good for cycling. For more details and tips, see Getting Around (p531).

Railway enthusiasts will be excited by the wide range of excursions on old steam trains organised by the Deutsche Bahn and local services. Ask for the free booklet *Nostalgiereisen* at any large train station in Germany.

Water rats shouldn't feel left out either, as there's no shortage of opportunities for messing about in boats on Germany's northern coasts and in wetland areas like the Spreewald, south of Berlin.

BOOKS

For a more detailed guide to the country, pick up a copy of Lonely Planet's *Germany*. Lonely Planet also publishes *Bavaria,* and *Berlin* and *Munich* city guides.

The German literary tradition is strong and there are many works that provide excellent background to the German experience. Mark Twain's *A Tramp Abroad* is recommended for his comical observations on German life.

For a more modern analysis of the German character and the issues that are facing Germany, dip into *Germany and the Germans* by John Ardagh.

BUSINESS HOURS

By law, shops in Germany may open from 6am to 8pm on weekdays and until 4pm on Saturday. In practice, however, only department stores and some supermarkets and fashion shops stay open until 8pm; most open at 8am or 9am. Bakeries are open 7am to 6pm on weekdays, until 1pm on Saturday, and some open for the allowable maximum of three hours on Sunday.

Banking hours are generally 8.30am to 1pm and 2.30pm to 4pm weekdays, but many banks remain open all day, and until 5.30pm on Thursday. All shops and banks are closed on public holidays. Government offices close for the weekend at 1pm or 3pm on Friday. Museums are generally closed on Monday; opening hours vary greatly, although many art museums are open later one evening per week.

Restaurants are usually open from 11am to midnight, with varying *Ruhetage* or closing days; many close for lunch during the day from 3pm to 6pm. Cafés often close around 8pm, though equal numbers stay open until 2am or later. Bars that don't serve food open between 5pm and 8pm and may close as late as 5am (if at all) in the larger cities.

CUSTOMS

See the Regional Directory (p1055).

DANGERS & ANNOYANCES

Although the usual cautions should be taken, theft and other crimes against travellers are relatively rare in Germany. Africans, Asians and southern Europeans may encounter racial prejudice, especially in eastern Germany, where they can be singled out as convenient scapegoats for economic hardship. However, the animosity is usually directed against immigrants, not tourists.

DISABLED TRAVELLERS

Germany caters reasonably well to the needs of physically disabled travellers, with access ramps for wheelchairs and/or lifts in most public buildings.

Bahn operates a **Mobility Service Centre** (☎ 01805-512 512; ⏱ 8am-8pm Mon-Fri, 8am-2pm Sat) whose operators can answer questions about station and train access. With one day's notice, they can also arrange for someone to meet you at your destination.

DISCOUNT CARDS

Many cities, particularly those that are on popular tourist routes, offer discount cards. These cars will usually combine up to three days' free use of public transport with free or reduced admission to major local museums and attractions. They're generally a good deal if you want to fit a lot in; see the Information section under the relevant destination and ask at tourist offices for full details.

EMBASSIES & CONSULATES
German Embassies & Consulates

Australia (☎ 02-6270 1911; 119 Empire Circuit, Yarralumla, ACT 2600)

Canada (☎ 613-232 1101; 1 Waverley St, Ottawa, Ont K2P 0T8)

France (☎ 01-53 83 45 00; 13-15 Ave Franklin Roosevelt, 75008 Paris)

Ireland (☎ 01-269 3011; 31 Trimleston Ave, Booterstown, Dublin)

The Netherlands (☎ 070-342 0600; Groot Hertoginnelaan 18-20, 2517 EG The Hague)

New Zealand (☎ 04-473 6063; 90-92 Hobson St, Wellington)

UK (☎ 020-7824 1300; 23 Belgrave Square, London SW1X 8PZ)

USA (☎ 202-298 4000; 4645 Reservoir Rd, NW Washington, DC 20007-1998)

Embassies & Consulates in Germany

The following embassies are all in Berlin. Many countries also have consulates in cities such as Frankfurt-am-Main and Munich.

Australia (Map pp414-15; ☎ 880 0800; Wallstrasse 76-78)

Canada (Map pp414-15; ☎ 203 120; Friedrichstrasse 95)

France (Map pp414-15; ☎ 590 039 000; Pariser Platz 5)

Ireland (Map pp414-15; ☎ 220 720; Friedrichstrasse 200)

The Netherlands (Map pp414-15; ☎ 209 560; Klosterstrasse 50)

New Zealand (Map pp414-15; ☎ 209 560; Friedrichstrasse 60)

South Africa (Map pp414-15; ☎ 220 730; Tiergartenstrasse 18)

UK (Map pp414-15; ☎ 204 570; Wilhelmstrasse 70-71)

USA (Map pp414-15; ☎ 238 5174; Neustädtische Kirchstrasse 4-5)

FESTIVALS & SPECIAL EVENTS
January-February

Carnival season Shrovetide, known as '*Fasching*' or '*Karneval*', sees many carnival events begin in large cities, most notably Cologne, Munich, Düsseldorf and Mainz. The partying peaks just before Ash Wednesday.

International Film Festival Held in Berlin (see p413).

March

Frankfurt Music Fair
Frankfurt Jazz Fair
Spring Fairs Held throughout Germany.
Bach Festival

April

Munich Ballet Days
Mannheim May Fair
Stuttgart Jazz Festival
Walpurgisnacht Festivals Held the night before May Day in the Harz Mountains.

May

Dresden International Dixieland Jazz Festival
Dresden Music Festival Held in last week of May into first week of June.
Red Wine Festival Held in Rüdesheim.

June

Händel Festival Held in Halle.
International Theatre Festival Held in Freiburg.
Moselle Wine Week Held in Cochem.
Munich Film Festival
Sailing regatta Held in Kiel.

July

Berlin Love Parade See p413.
Folk festivals Held throughout Germany.
International Music Seminar Held in Weimar.
Kulmbach Beer Festival
Munich Opera Festival
Richard Wagner Festival Held in Bayreuth.

August

Heidelberg Castle Festival
Wine festivals Held throughout the Rhineland area.

September

Berlin Festival of Music & Drama
Oktoberfest Held in Munich (see p460).

October
Bremen Freimarkt
Berlin Jazzfest
Frankfurt Book Fair

November-December
Christmas fairs Held throughout Germany, most famously in Munich, Nuremberg, Berlin, Essen and Heidelberg.
St Martin's Festival Held throughout Rhineland and Bavaria.
Silvester New Years Eve, celebrated everywhere.

GAY & LESBIAN TRAVELLERS
Germans are generally fairly tolerant of homosexuality, but gays (*Schwule*) and lesbians (*Lesben*) still don't enjoy quite the same social acceptance in Germany as in some other northern European countries. Most progressive are the larger cities, particularly Berlin and Frankfurt-am-Main, which have dozens of gay and lesbian bars and meeting places. The age of consent is 18 years. Christopher Street Day, in June, is the biggest Pride festival in Germany, with events held in Berlin and many other major towns.

HOLIDAYS
Germany has many public holidays, some of which vary from state to state. Holidays include:
New Year's Day 1 January
Easter March/April
Labour Day 1 May
Ascension Day 40 days after Easter
Whitsun/Pentecost May/June
Day of German Unity 3 October
All Saints' Day 1 November
Day of Prayer & Repentance 18 November
Christmas 24-26 December

INTERNET ACCESS
Internet cafés abound in every large town and most smaller ones. If you can't find a dedicated Internet shop, connections are often available in Vobis computer stores, amusement arcades (*Spielotheke*) and public libraries.

MEDIA
Magazines
Germany's most popular magazines are *Der Spiegel, Focus* and *Stern. Die Zeit* is a weekly publication about culture and the arts.

Newspapers
The most widely read newspapers in Germany are *Die Welt, Frankfurter Allgemeine,* Munich's *Süddeutsche Zeitung* and the left-leaning *Die Tageszeitung (Taz). Bild* is Germany's favourite sensationalist tabloid, part of the Axel Springer publishing empire.

Radio
German radio sticks to a fairly standard diet of news and discussion or Europop, inane chatter and adverts, though most regions and cities have their own stations so quality can vary. The BBC World Service (on varying AM wavelengths) broadcasts in English.

Television
Germany's two national TV channels are the government-funded ARD and ZDF. They are augmented by a plethora of regional broadcasters, plus private cable channels such as Pro7, SAT1 and RTL, which show a lot of dubbed US series and films with long ad breaks. You can catch English-language news and sports programmes on cable or satellite TV in most hotels and *pensions.*

MONEY
The easiest places to change cash in Germany are banks or foreign exchange counters at airports or train stations, particularly those of the Reisebank. Main banks in larger cities generally have money-changing machines for after-hours use, though they don't often give good rates. The Reisebank charges a flat €2.50 to change cash. Some local Sparkasse banks have good rates and low charges.

There are international ATMs virtually everywhere in Germany. Typically, with drawals over the counter against cards at major banks cost a flat €5 per transaction. Check other fees and the availability of services with your bank before you leave home.

Travellers cheques can be cashed at any bank and the most widely accepted are AmEx, Thomas Cook and Barclays. A percentage commission (usually a minimum of €5) is charged by most banks on any travellers cheque, even those issued in euros. The Reisebank charges 1% or a minimum of €5 (€2.50 on amounts less than €50) and €3.75 for AmEx. Note that AmEx does not charge commission on its own cheques.

Credit cards are especially useful for emergencies, although they are rarely accepted by budget hotels and restaurants outside major cities. Cards most widely accepted for payment for goods and services are Eurocard (linked to Access and MasterCard), Visa and AmEx.

POST

Standard post office hours are 8am to 6pm weekdays and to noon on Saturday. Many train station post offices stay open later or offer limited services outside these hours.

Within Germany and the EU, standard-sized postcards cost €0.45 and a 20g letter is €0.55. Postcards to North America and Australasia cost €1, a 20g airmail letter is €1.55. Surface-mail parcels up to 2kg within Europe are €8.20, €12.30 to destinations elsewhere. Airmail parcels up to 1kg are €10.30/21 within Europe/elsewhere.

TELEPHONE

Calling from a private phone is most expensive between 9am and 6pm. From telephone boxes, city calls cost €0.10 per minute, calls to anywhere else in Germany €0.20 per minute.

Reverse-charge (collect) calls can be made to some countries through home-direct services. For these dial ☎ 0800 plus: USA 888 0013 (Sprint), 225 5288 (AT&T) or 888 8000 (MCI); Canada 080 1014; UK 0800 044; or Australia 0800 061 (Telstra).

For directory assistance within Germany call ☎ 118 33 (☎ 118 37 in English); both cost €0.25 plus €0.99 per minute. International information is ☎ 118 34 (€0.55 per 20 seconds).

Mobile Phones

Mobile phones are as ubiquitous in Germany as elsewhere; the main operators are T-Mobile, Vodafone (D2), O2 and E-Plus. You can pick up a pre-pay SIM card for around €30; top-up cards are available from kiosks, various shops and vending machines

---

EMERGENCY NUMBERS

- Ambulance ☎ 112
- Fire ☎ 112
- Police ☎ 110
- ADAC breakdown service
  ☎ 0180-222 2222

(including certain ticket machines on the Berlin U-Bahn). Mobile numbers generally begin with a ☎ 016 or ☎ 017 prefix. Calling from a landline costs up to €0.54 per minute.

Phone Codes

The country code for Germany is ☎ 49. To ring abroad from Germany, dial ☎ 00 followed by the country code, area code and number. An operator can be reached on ☎ 0180-200 1033.

Phonecards

Most pay phones in Germany accept only phonecards, available for €5, €10 and €20 at post offices, news kiosks, tourist offices and banks. One call unit costs a little more than €0.06 from a private telephone and €0.10 from a public phone.

TIME

Germany runs on Western European time, one hour ahead of GMT – see the World Map (p1084).

TOURIST INFORMATION

German tourist offices are almost invariably super-efficient mines of information, offering everything from free maps and information to tours, books and souvenirs.

VISAS

Citizens of the EU and some other Western European countries can enter on an official identity card. Americans, Australians, Canadians, Israelis, Japanese, New Zealanders and Singaporeans require only a valid passport (no visa). Germany is also part of the Schengen visa scheme (see p1063). Three months is the usual limit of stay, less for citizens of some developing countries.

WORK

With unemployment remaining high, Germany offers limited prospects for employment unless you have high-level specialist skills such as IT expertise. EU citizens can work in Germany with an *Aufenthaltserlaubnis* (residency permit); non-EU citizens require a work permit as well. Citizens of Australia, New Zealand and Canada between the ages of 18 and 30 may apply for a Working Holiday Visa, which entitles them to work anywhere in

Germany for up to 90 days in a 12-month period.

To look for a job, consult your local *Arbeitsamt* (employment office); it will have an excellent databank of vacancies, internships and seasonal positions, or try major newspapers. Private language teaching is another option. Numerous approved agencies can help you find work as an au pair.

TRANSPORT IN GERMANY

GETTING THERE & AWAY
Departure Tax

The international airport departure tax is included in the price of all air tickets when purchased.

Air

The main arrival and departure points in Germany are Frankfurt-am-Main, Munich, Düsseldorf and Berlin. Germany's national carrier Lufthansa is rapidly becoming Europe's biggest airline; British Airways provides its main competition. Both airlines have solid safety records. Prices are generally competitive among all major airlines, though scheduled flights from Western Europe tend to be more expensive than the train or bus.

Airline deregulation has encouraged cheap, no-frills deals, especially between London and Frankfurt-am-Main, Berlin or Düsseldorf. Ryanair, Easyjet, Air Berlin and Germanwings are among the foremost cheap options, serving destinations throughout Europe from smaller regional airports as well as the major terminals.

Lufthansa has many flights to Eastern Europe, but the region's national carriers are cheaper. The following airlines fly to/from Germany:

Air Berlin (code AB; ☎ 01805-737 800; www.airberlin.de)
Alitalia (code AZ; ☎ 01805-074 747; www.alitalia.it)
British Airways (code BA; ☎ 01805-266 522; www.britishairways.com)
Czech Airlines (code OK; ☎ 01803-006 737; www.csa.cz)
Easyjet (code BH; ☎ 01803-654 321; www.easyjet.com)
Germania Express (code ST; ☎ 01805-737 100; www.gexx.de)
Germanwings (code 4U; ☎ 01805-955 855; www.germanwings.com)

Iberia (code IB; ☎ 01803-000 613; www.iberia.es)
LOT (code LO; ☎ 01803-000 336; www.lot.com)
Lufthansa (code LH; ☎ 01803-803 803; www.lufthansa.com)
Ryanair (code FR; ☎ 0190-170 100; www.ryanair.com)
SAS (code SK; ☎ 01803-234 023; www.scandinavian.net)
Vbird (code 5D; ☎ 0190-172 500; www.vbird.com)
Volare (code VA; ☎ 0800-101 4169; www.volareweb.com)

Land
BUS

Travelling by bus between Germany and the rest of Europe is cheaper than by train or plane, but journeys are a lot longer.

Eurolines is a consortium of national bus companies operating routes throughout the continent. Sample one-way fares and travel times include: London–Frankfurt (€76, 16 hours); Amsterdam–Frankfurt (€39, eight hours); Paris–Hamburg (€62, 11½ hours); Paris–Cologne (€39, 6½ hours); Prague–Berlin (€31, seven hours), and Barcelona–Frankfurt (€81, 20 hours). Eurolines has a youth fare for under-26s that saves around 10%. Tickets can be bought in Germany at most train stations. Eurolines' German arm is **Deutsche-Touring** (☎ 069-790 350; www.deutsche-touring.com), a subsidiary of Deutsche Bahn.

CAR & MOTORCYCLE

Germany is served by an excellent highway system. If you're coming from the UK, the quickest option is the Channel Tunnel. Ferries take longer but are cheaper. Choices include hovercraft from Dover, Folkestone or Ramsgate to Calais in France. You can be in Germany three hours after the ferry docks.

Within Europe, autobahns and highways become jammed on weekends in summer and before and after holidays. This is especially true where border checks are still carried out, such as going to/from the Czech Republic and Poland. For road rules when driving in Germany, see p532.

The cheapest way to get to Germany from elsewhere in Europe is as a paying passenger in a private car. Leaving Germany, or travelling within the country, such rides are arranged by *Mitfahrzentrale* (ride-sharing agencies) in many German cities. You pay a reservation fee to the agency and a share of petrol and costs to the driver. Tourist offices can direct you to local agencies, or call ☎ 194 40 in large German cities. Individual agencies are listed in the relevant Getting There & Away sections.

TRAIN

Another good way to get to Germany from elsewhere in Europe is by train. It's a lot more comfortable (albeit more expensive) than the bus.

Long-distance trains between major German cities and other countries are called EuroCity (EC) trains. The main German hubs with the best connections for major European cities are Hamburg (Scandinavia); Cologne (France, Belgium and the Netherlands, with Eurostar connections from Brussels or Paris going on to London); Munich (southern and southeastern Europe); and Berlin (Eastern Europe). Frankfurt-am-Main has the widest range of international connections, but these are not always the quickest.

Generally the longer international routes are served by at least one day train and often a night train as well. Many night trains only carry sleeping cars; a bunk is more comfortable than sitting up in a compartment but can add around €21 to the cost of a 2nd-class ticket.

Sea

If you're heading to or from the UK or Scandinavia, the port options are Hamburg, Lübeck, Rostock, Sassnitz and Kiel. The Hamburg–Harwich service operates at least three times a week. The Puttgarden–Rodbyhavn ferry is popular with those heading to Copenhagen. In eastern Germany, ferries run daily year-round between Trelleborg (Sweden) and Sassnitz, on Rügen Island (p453).

There are daily services between Kiel and Gothenburg (Sweden) and Oslo. The Kiel–Gothenburg trip takes 13½ hours and costs from €37 to €85. A ferry between Travemünde (near Lübeck) and Trelleborg (Sweden) runs one to four times daily. The journey takes seven hours and costs from €20 to €40. Ferries also run between the Danish island of Bornholm and Sassnitz. Car-ferry service is good from Gedser (Denmark) to Rostock. Silja Line serves Tallin, Helsinki and St Petersburg from Rostock in summer (p450). Finnlines has daily sailings from Lübeck to Helsinki. Consult www .finnlines.fi for details.

GETTING AROUND

Air

There are lots of flights within the country, but costs can be prohibitive compared to other modes of transport. Lufthansa has the most frequent air services within Germany, though deregulation has brought some competition, particularly from the budget airlines.

Bicycle

Radwandern (bicycle touring) is very popular in Germany. Pavements are often divided into separate sections for pedestrians and cyclists – be warned that these divisions are taken very seriously. Favoured routes include the Rhine, Moselle, Elbe and Danube Rivers and the Lake Constance area. Of course, cycling is strictly *verboten* (forbidden) on the autobahns. Hostel-to-hostel biking is an easy way to go, and route guides are often sold at DJH hostels. There are well-equipped cycling shops in almost every town, and a fairly active market for used touring bikes.

Simple three-gear bicycles can be hired from around €8/32 per day/week, and more robust mountain bikes from €10/48. DB publishes *Bahn&Bike*, an excellent annual handbook (in German) covering bike rental and repair shops, routes, maps and other resources.

A separate ticket must be purchased whenever you carry your bike on trains (generally €3 to €6). Most trains (excluding ICEs) have at least one 2nd-class carriage with a bicycle compartment.

Germany's main cycling organisation is the **Allgemeiner Deutscher Fahrrad Club** (ADFC; ☎ 0421-346 290; www.adfc.de).

Boat

Boats are most likely to be used for basic transport when travelling to or between the Frisian Islands, though tours along the Rhine, Elbe and Moselle Rivers are also popular. In summer there are frequent services on Lake Constance but, except for the Constance to Meersburg and the Friedrichshafen to Romanshorn car ferries, these boats are really more tourist craft than a transport option. From April to October, excursion boats ply lakes and rivers throughout Germany and can be a lovely way to see the country.

GERMANY

Bus

The bus network in Germany functions primarily in support of the train network. That is, they go to destinations that aren't serviced by trains. Bus stations or stops are usually located near the train station in any town. Consider buses when you want to cut across two train lines and avoid long train rides to and from a transfer point. A good example of this is in the Alps, where the best way to follow the peaks is by bus.

Within Germany **Eurolines** (☎ 069-790 350) operates as Deutsche-Touring GmbH; services include the Romantic and Castle Roads buses in southern Germany, as well as organised bus tours of Germany lasting a week or more.

Car & Motorcycle

AUTOMOBILE ASSOCIATIONS

Germany's main motoring organisation is the Munich-based **Allgemeiner Deutscher Automobil Club** (ADAC; ☎ 089-767 60), which has offices in all major cities.

DRIVING LICENCE

Visitors do not need an international driving licence to drive in Germany; technically you should carry an official translation of your licence with you, but in practice this is rarely necessary.

FUEL & SPARE PARTS

Prices for fuel vary from €1.05 to €1.15 per litre for unleaded regular. Avoid buying fuel at the more expensive autobahn filling stations. Petrol stations are generally easy to find, although they can be scarce in the centres of many towns.

HIRE

You usually must be at least 21 years of age to hire a car in Germany. You'll need to show your licence and passport, and make sure you keep the insurance certificate for the vehicle with you at all times.

Germany's four main rental companies are **Avis** (☎ 0180-555 77), **Europcar** (☎ 0180-580 00), **Hertz** (☎ 0180-533 3535) and **Sixt** (☎ 0180-526 0250).

INSURANCE

You must have third-party insurance to enter Germany with a vehicle.

ROAD CONDITIONS

The autobahn system of motorways runs throughout Germany. All road signs (and most motoring maps) indicate national autobahn routes in blue with an 'A' number, while international routes have green signs with an 'E' number. Though efficient, the autobahns are often busy, and visitors frequently have trouble coping with the very high speeds. Secondary roads (usually designated with a 'B' number) are easier on the nerves and much more scenic, but these can be slow going.

Cars are impractical in urban areas. Vending machines on many streets sell parking vouchers which must be displayed clearly behind the windscreen. Leaving your car in a central *Parkhaus* (car park) costs roughly €10 per day or €1.25 per hour.

To find passengers willing to pay their share of fuel costs, drivers should contact the local *Mitfahrzentrale* (see p530).

ROAD RULES

Road rules are easy to understand and standard international signs are in use. You drive on the right, and most cars are right-hand drive. Right of way is usually signed, with major roads given priority, but on unmarked intersections traffic coming from the right always has right of way.

The usual speed limits are 50km/h in built-up areas and 100km/h on the open road. The speed on autobahns is unlimited, though there's an advisory speed of 130km/h; exceptions are clearly signposted.

The blood-alcohol limit for drivers is 0.05%. Obey the road rules carefully: the German police are very efficient and issue heavy on-the-spot fines. Germany also has one of the highest concentrations of speed cameras in Europe.

Local Transport

Local transport is excellent within big cities and small towns, and is generally based on buses, *Strassenbahn* (trams), S-Bahn and/or U-Bahn (underground trains). Tickets cover all forms of transit; fares are determined by zones or time travelled, sometimes both. Multiticket strips and day passes are generally available offering better value than single-ride tickets.

Make certain that you have a ticket when boarding – only buses and some trams let you buy tickets from the driver. In some cases you will have to validate it on the platform or once aboard. Ticket inspections are frequent (especially at night and on holidays) and the fine is a non-negotiable €30.

Train

Operated almost entirely by Deutsche Bahn (DB), the German train system is arguably the finest in Europe, and is generally the best way to get around the country.

Trains run on an interval system, so wherever you're heading, you can count on a service at least every two hours. Schedules are integrated throughout the country so that connections between trains are timesaving and tight, often only five minutes. Of course this means that when a train is late, connections are missed and you can find yourself stuck waiting for the next train.

CLASSES

It's rarely worth buying a 1st-class ticket on German trains; 2nd class is usually quite comfortable. There's more difference between the train classifications – basically the faster a train travels, the plusher (and more expensive) it is.

Train types include:

ICE InterCityExpress services run at speeds up to 280km/h. The trains are very comfortable and feature restaurant cars. Main routes link Hamburg to Munich, Cologne to Berlin, Frankfurt-am-Main to Berlin and Frankfurt-am-Main to Munich.

IC/EC Called InterCity or EuroCity, these are the premier conventional trains of DB. When trains are crowded, the open-seating coaches are much more comfortable than the older carriages with compartments.

RE RegionalExpress trains are local trains that make limited stops. They are fairly fast and run at one- or two-hourly intervals.

RB RegionalBahn are the slowest DB trains, not missing a single cow town.

S-Bahn These DB-operated trains run frequent services in larger urban areas. Not to be confused with U-Bahns, which are run by local authorities who don't honour rail passes.

EN, ICN, D These are night trains, although an occasional D may be an extra daytime train.

COSTS

Standard DB ticket prices are distance-based. You will usually be sold a ticket for the shortest distance to your destination.

Sample fares for one-way, 2nd-class ICE travel include Hamburg to Munich €111, Frankfurt-am-Main to Berlin €92 and Frankfurt-am-Main to Munich €69. Tickets are good for four days from the day you tell the agent your journey will begin, and you can make unlimited stopovers along your route during that time (if you break your journey, it's wise to inform the conductor).

There are hosts of special fares that allow you to beat the high cost of regular tickets. The following are the most popular special train fares offered by DB (all fares are for 2nd class):

BahnCard 25/50/100 Only worthwhile for extended visits to Germany, these discount cards entitle holders to 25/50/100% off regular fares and cost €50/200/3000.

Länder Tickets Good within individual German states, for up to five people travelling together, or one or both parents and all their children. Tickets cost €21, and are valid weekdays from 9am until 3am the next day. Other conditions vary by state.

Schönes Wochenende 'Good Weekend' tickets allow unlimited use of RE, RB and S-Bahn trains on a Saturday or Sunday between midnight and 3am the next day, for up to five people travelling together, or one or both parents and all their children/grandchildren for €28. They are best suited to weekend day trips from urban areas.

In addition, check the website (www.bahn .de) and ask about the various *Sparpreis* schemes that offer big savings on return tickets booked three days in advance.

For schedule and fare information (available in English), call ☎ 01805-996 633 (€0.13 per minute).

RESERVATIONS

Nearly every DB station offers the option of purchasing tickets with credit cards at ticket machines for longer haul trains; these usually have English-language options, but when in doubt consult the ticket window. Buying a ticket or supplement (*Zuschlag*) from a conductor carries a penalty (€1.50 to €4.50). If you're really stuck you can *technically* use a credit card on the train, but in practice it may not be possible.

On some trains there are no conductors at all, and roving inspectors enforce compliance. If you are caught travelling without a valid ticket the fine is €30, no excuses.

During peak travel periods, a seat reservation (€2.50) on a long-distance train can mean the difference between squatting near the toilet or relaxing in your own seat. Express reservations can be made at the last minute.

TRAIN PASSES

Travel agencies outside Germany sell German Rail Passes valid for unlimited travel on all DB trains for a given number of days within a 30-day period. Sample 2nd-class prices (in US$) for adults/two adults together/individuals under 26 are $180/270/142 for four days and $324/486/220 for 10 days. Eurail and Inter-Rail passes are also valid in Germany.

Greece

CONTENTS

GREECE

Perennially popular, Greece has been saying *yasas* (hello) to travellers for thousands of years. Indeed, it's been almost 2000 years since the Greek geographer and historian Pausanias penned the first travel guide to Greece. Today, visiting the country's magnificent archaeological sites leads travellers on a journey not only through the landscape but also through time, witnessing the legacy of Europe's greatest ages – the Mycenaean, Minoan, classical, Hellenistic and Byzantine. You cannot wander far in Greece without stumbling across a broken column, a crumbling bastion or a tiny Byzantine church, each perhaps neglected and forgotten but retaining an aura of its former glory.

A trip through time isn't the only attraction of Greece – an island-hop around Greece's over 1400 islands is equally as popular. Greece has more coastline than any other country in Europe and a breathtaking variety of island experiences await the visitor, from the relentless party atmosphere of Mykonos to the medieval splendour of Rhodes' old town.

The allure of Greece is also due to less tangible attributes – the dazzling clarity of the light, the floral aromas that permeate the air, the spirit of places – for there is hardly a grove, mountain or stream that is not sacred to a deity, and the ghosts of the past still linger.

Amongst the myriad attractions, travellers to Greece inevitably end up with a favourite location they long to return to – it's just up to you to find yours.

FAST FACTS

- **Area** 131,900 sq km
- **Capital** Athens
- **Currency** euro (€); A$1 = €0.58; ¥100 = €0.76; NZ$1 = €0.54; UK£1 = €1.50; US$1 = €0.83
- **Famous for** ancient ruins, beautiful beaches
- **Key Phrases** *yasas* (hello); *andio* (goodbye); *parakalo* (please); *efharisto* (thank you); *ne* (yes); *ohi* (no)
- **Official Language** Greek
- **Population** 11 million
- **Telephone Codes** country code ☎ 30; international access code ☎ 00; area codes are part of the 10-digit number within Greece – landline prefix ☎ 2, mobiles ☎ 6
- **Visas** visitors from most countries don't need a visa

HIGHLIGHTS

- Explore the most famous monument of the ancient world, the **Acropolis** (p546), towering above Athens.
- Soak in the history of **Rhodes** (p588), built by the Knights of St John and the largest inhabited medieval town in Europe.
- Visit **Olympia** (p565), the evocative birthplace of the games.
- Experience the spectacular sight of Santorini's **volcanic caldera** (p579).
- Drink and dine in the gorgeous old Venetian town of **Nafplio** (p561), one of Greece's most romantic destinations.

ITINERARIES

- **One week** Spend a day in Athens seeing its museums and ancient sites, then two days in the Peloponnese visiting Nafplio, Mycenae and Olympia, and four days in the Cyclades.
- **One month** Spend some extra time in both Athens and the Peloponnese, then catch an overnight ferry from Patra to Corfu for a couple of days. Head to Ioannina to explore the Zagoria villages of northern Epiros for two days before travelling back to Athens via Meteora and Delphi over three days. Take a ferry from Piraeus to Chios, then island-hop your way back through the northeastern Aegean Islands, the Dodecanese and the Cyclades over two weeks.

CLIMATE & WHEN TO GO

Greece's climate is typically Mediterranean with mild, wet winters followed by very hot, dry summers. Spring and autumn are the best times to visit – the weather's fine and there's a relative lack of tourists. Winter is quiet and the islands are in hibernation between late November and early April. The cobwebs are dusted off in time for Easter, and while everything is open the crowds have yet to arrive. From July until mid-September, it's summer madness and if you want to party, this is the time to go. The flipside is that everywhere is packed and rooms can be hard to find.

HISTORY

Occupying a strategic position at the crossroads of Europe and Asia, Greece has endured a long and turbulent history.

During the Bronze Age (3000 to 1200 BC in Greece), the advanced Cycladic, Minoan

HOW MUCH?

- Local telephone call €0.20
- Minimum taxi fare €2
- Herald Tribune newspaper €2
- Coffee €2.50-3.50
- Can of soft drink €0.80

LONELY PLANET INDEX

- Litre of petrol €0.70-0.85
- Litre of bottled water €1
- Bottle of beer €2
- Souvenir T-shirt €12
- Street snack (gyros) €1.30

and Mycenaean civilisations flourished. The Mycenaeans were swept aside in the 12th century BC and replaced by the Dorians, introducing Greece to the Iron Age. The next 400 years are often referred to as the Dark Ages, a period about which very little is known.

By 800 BC, when Homer's *Odyssey* and *Iliad* were first written down, Greece was undergoing a cultural and military revival with the evolution of the city-states, the most powerful of which were Athens and Sparta. Greater Greece, Magna Graecia, was created, with southern Italy as an important component. The unified Greeks repelled the Persians twice, at Marathon (490 BC) and Salamis (480 BC). Victory over Persia was followed by unparalleled growth and prosperity known as the classical (or golden) age.

The Golden Age

During this period, Pericles commissioned the Parthenon, Sophocles wrote *Oedipus the King* and Socrates taught young Athenians to think. The golden age ended with the Peloponnesian War (431–404 BC), when the militaristic Spartans defeated the Athenians. They failed to notice the expansion of Macedonia under King Philip II, who easily conquered the war-weary city-states.

Philip's ambitions were surpassed by those of his son, Alexander the Great, who marched triumphantly into Asia Minor, Egypt, Persia and what are now parts of Afghanistan and

GREECE

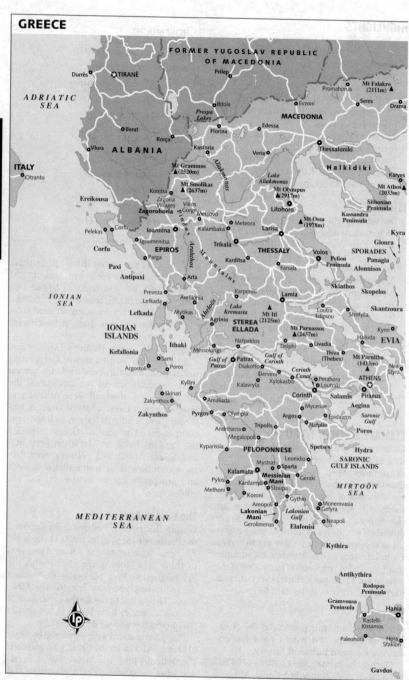

India. In 323 BC he met an untimely death at the age of 33, and his generals divided his empire between themselves.

Roman Rule & the Byzantine Empire

Roman incursions into Greece began in 205 BC; by 146 BC, Greece and Macedonia had become Roman provinces. After the subdivision of the Roman Empire into eastern and western empires in AD 395, Greece became part of the eastern (Byzantine) Empire, based at Constantinople.

In the centuries that followed, Venetians, Franks, Normans, Slavs, Persians, Arabs and, finally, Turks took turns chipping away at the Byzantine Empire.

The Ottoman Empire & Independence

After the end of the Byzantine Empire in 1453, when Constantinople fell to the Turks, most of Greece soon became part of the Ottoman Empire. Crete was not captured until 1670, leaving Corfu as the only island never occupied by the Turks. By the 19th century the Ottoman Empire was in decline. The Greeks, seeing nationalism sweep through Europe, fought the War of Independence (1821–32). The great powers – Britain, France and Russia – intervened in 1827, and Ioannis Kapodistrias was elected the first Greek president.

Kapodistrias was assassinated in 1831 and the European powers stepped in once again, declaring that Greece should become a monarchy. In January 1833, Otho of Bavaria was installed as king. His ambition, called the Great Idea, was to unite all the lands of the Greek people to the Greek motherland. In 1862 he was peacefully ousted and the Greeks chose George I, a Danish prince, as king.

During WWI, Prime Minister Venizelos allied Greece with France and Britain. King Constantine (George's son), who was married to the Kaiser's sister Sophia, disputed this and left the country.

Smyrna & WWII

After the war, Venizelos resurrected the Great Idea. Underestimating the newfound power of Turkey under the leadership of Atatürk, he sent forces to occupy Smyrna (the present-day Turkish port of İzmir), with its large Greek population. The army was heavily defeated and this led to a brutal population exchange between the two countries in 1923.

In 1930 George II, Constantine's son, was reinstated as king and appointed the dictator General Metaxas as prime minister. Metaxas' grandiose ambition was to combine aspects of Greece's ancient and Byzantine past to create a Third Greek Civilisation. However, his chief claim to fame is his celebrated *ohi* (no) to Mussolini's request to allow Italian troops into Greece in 1940 (p607).

Greece fell to Germany in 1941 and resistance movements, polarised into royalist and communist factions, staged a bloody civil war lasting until 1949. The civil war was the trigger for a mass exodus that saw almost one million Greeks head off to places such as Australia, Canada and the USA. Entire villages were abandoned as people gambled on a new start in cities such as Melbourne, Toronto, Chicago and New York.

The Colonels' Coup

Continuing political instability led to the colonels' coup d'etat in 1967. King Constantine (son of King Paul, who succeeded George II) staged an unsuccessful counter-coup, and fled the country. The colonels' junta distinguished itself with its appalling brutality, repression and political incompetence. In 1974 they attempted to assassinate Cyprus' leader, Archbishop Makarios, and when he escaped, the junta replaced him with the extremist Nikos Samson, prompting Turkey to occupy North Cyprus. The continued Turkish occupation of Cyprus remains one of the most contentious issues in Greek politics. The junta had little choice but to hand back power to the people. In November 1974 a plebiscite voted against restoration of the monarchy. Greece became a republic with the right-wing New Democracy (ND) party taking power.

The Socialist 1980s

In 1981 Greece entered the then EC (European Community, now the EU). Andreas Papandreou's Panhellenic Socialist Movement (Pasok) won the next election, giving Greece its first socialist government. Pasok promised the removal of US air bases and withdrawal from NATO, but delivered only rising unemployment and spiralling debt.

Forced to step aside in 1989 during a scandal involving the Bank of Crete, an unprecedented conservative and communist coalition took over. Papandreou and four ministers were ordered to stand trial, and the coalition ordered fresh elections in October 1990.

The 1990s & Beyond
The elections brought the ND party back to power with a slight majority. Tough economic reforms introduced by Prime Minister Konstantinos Mitsotakis soon made his government unpopular and corruption allegations forced Mitsotakis to call an election in October 1993.

Greeks again turned to Pasok and the ailing Papandreou, who was eventually cleared of all charges. He had little option but to continue with the austerity programme begun by Mitsotakis, quickly making his government equally unpopular.

Papandreou stood down in January 1996 due to ill health and the party abandoned its leftist policies, electing economist and lawyer Costas Simitis as leader. Simitis romped to a comfortable majority at a snap poll called in October 1996.

His government focused strongly on further integration with Europe. In January 2001, the EU agreed that Greece had met the economic requirements for monetary union and Greece duly adopted the euro as its currency in 2002.

Simitis was rewarded with a further four-year mandate in April 2000, but after suffering a serious popularity slump he announced an election as well as his retirement. Andreas Papandreou went to the polls as the prospective new leader in March 2004. The ND party led by Costas Karamanlis soundly defeated Pasok.

Recent Foreign Policy
Greece's foreign policy is dominated by its sensitive relationship with Turkey. Greece has also had its hands full coping with events to the north precipitated by the break-up of former Yugoslavia and the collapse of the communist regimes in Albania and Romania.

Greece was a somewhat low-key member of the 'coalition of the willing' invasion of Iraq in March 2003. Faced with strong domestic opposition to the war, the government kept the role played by US forces based at Souda Bay in Crete very low key.

PEOPLE
Greece's population was 10,939,771 according to the 2001 census. About one third of these inhabitants live in the Greater Athens area and more than two thirds of the population live in cities – confirming that Greece is now a primarily urban society. Less than 15% now live on the islands, the most populous being Crete, Evia and Corfu. There are 100,000 foreigners officially living permanently in Greece and an estimated one million living in Greece illegally.

SPORT
Football (soccer) is by far the most popular spectator sport in Greece – not least since the shock victory of the Greek national team in Euro 2004. The season runs from September to mid-May, and the two most popular domestic teams are Olympiakos of Piraeus and Panathinaikos of Athens. The aforementioned clubs are also the main players in Greece's other main sport, basketball. These teams fare well in European competition, achieving more consistent success than their soccer-playing counterparts.

RELIGION
About 98% of the Greek population belongs to the Greek Orthodox Church. The remainder are split between the Roman Catholic, Protestant, Evangelist, Jewish and Muslim faiths. While older Greeks and those in rural areas tend to be deeply religious, most young people are decidedly more secular.

ARTS
The arts have been integral to Greek life since ancient times. Of all the ancient Greek arts, architecture has had the most profound influence. Greek temples, seen throughout history as symbolic of democracy, have been the inspiration for architectural movements such as the Italian Renaissance. Today masses of cheap concrete apartment blocks built in the 20th century in Greece's major cities belie this architectural legacy.

Thankfully, the great works of Greek literature are not as easily besmirched. The first and greatest ancient Greek writer was Homer, author of *Iliad* and *Odyssey*. Little is known of Homer's life; where or when he lived, or whether, as it is alleged, he was blind.

Pindar (c518–438 BC) is regarded as the pre-eminent lyric poet of ancient Greece and was commissioned to recite his odes at the Olympic Games. The great writers of the tradition of love poetry were Sappho (6th century BC) and Alcaeus (5th century BC), both of whom lived on Lesvos. Sappho's poetic descriptions of her affections for women gave rise to the term 'lesbian'.

The Alexandrian, Constantine Cavafy (1863–1933), revolutionised Greek poetry by introducing a personal, conversational style. He is considered to be the TS Eliot of Greek literary verse. Poet George Seferis (1900–71) won the Nobel Prize for literature in 1963, and Odysseus Elytis (1911–96) won the same prize in 1979.

Nikos Kazantzakis, author of *Zorba the Greek* and numerous other novels, plays and poems, is the most famous of 20th-century Greek novelists.

The country's most famous painter was a young Cretan called Domenikos Theotokopoulos, who moved to Spain in 1577 and became known as the great El Greco. Famous painters of the 20th century include Konstantinos, Partenis and, later, George Bouzianis, whose work can be viewed at the National Art Gallery in Athens.

Musical instruments have been an integral part of Greek life since ancient times. In more recent times, the plucked-string sound of the ubiquitous bouzouki provides the background music of a thousand tavernas. The bouzouki is one of the main instruments of *rembetika* music – which is in many ways the Greek equivalent of the American blues. *Rembetika* has its roots in the sufferings of the refugees from Asia Minor in the 1920s and is now enjoying a revival. Alongside the bouzouki, *rembetika* music is accompanied by the guitar, violin and accordion. See p554 for venues to see live *rembetika* music.

Alongside music, dance is an integral part of Greek life. Whether at a wedding, nightclub or a village celebration, traditional dance is still widely practiced. If you don't see folk dancing on your travels, try to catch the Dora Stratou Dance Company (p554), in Athens.

In summer, Greek dramas are staged in the ancient theatres where they were originally performed. Drama continues to feature in domestic arts, but predominantly in Athens and Thessaloniki.

Greek film has for many years been associated with the earnest work of film maker Theo Angelopoulos, who won Cannes' Palme d'Or in 1998 with *An Eternity and One Day*. Since the late '90s, Greek cinema has witnessed a minor renaissance, with films such as *Safe Sex* (2000) luring Greek moviegoers back to the cinema.

Greek TV is dominated by chat shows, sport and foreign movies, only to be interrupted by localised versions of the latest American 'reality TV' hit.

ENVIRONMENT
The Land

Greece sits at the southern tip of the Balkan Peninsula and of its 1400 islands, only 169 are inhabited. The land mass is 131,900 sq km and Greek territorial waters cover a further 400,000 sq km.

Around 80% of Greece is mountainous. The Pindos Mountains in Epiros are the southern extension of the Dinaric Alps, which run the length of former Yugoslavia. The range continues down through central Greece and the Peloponnese, and re-emerges in the mountains of Crete. Less than a quarter of the country is suitable for agriculture.

Greece lies in one of the most seismically active regions in the world, recording over 20,000 earthquakes in the last 40 years – most of them very minor. The activity occurs because the eastern Mediterranean lies at the meeting point of three continental plates: the Eurasian, African and Arabian.

Wildlife

The variety of flora in Greece is unrivalled in Europe. Spectacular wild flowers thrive in Greece and the best places to see the dazzling array of flowers are the mountains of Crete and the southern Peloponnese.

You won't encounter many animals in the wild, mainly due to hunting. Wild boar, still found in the north, is a favourite target. Squirrels, rabbits, hares, foxes and weasels are all fairly common on the mainland. Reptiles are well represented by snakes, including several poisonous viper species.

Lake Mikri Prespa in Macedonia has the richest colony of fish-eating birds in Europe, while the Dadia Forest Reserve in Thrace numbers such majestic birds as the golden eagle and the giant black vulture among its residents.

The brown bear, Europe's largest land mammal, still survives in very small numbers in the mountains of northern Greece, as does the grey wolf.

Europe's rarest mammal, the monk seal, was once very common in the Mediterranean Sea, but is now on the brink of extinction in Europe. There are about 400 left in Europe, half of which live in Greece. About 40 frequent the Ionian Sea and the rest are found in the Aegean.

The waters around Zakynthos are home to Europe's last large sea turtle colony, that of the loggerhead turtle (*Careta careta*). The **Sea Turtle Protection Society of Greece** (☎ /fax 2105 231 342; www.archelon.gr) runs monitoring programmes and is always looking for volunteers.

National Parks

Visitors who expect Greek national parks to provide facilities on par with those in countries such as Australia and the USA will be disappointed. Although they all have refuges and some have marked hiking trails, facilities are limited.

The most visited parks are Mt Parnitha, just north of Athens, and the Samaria Gorge on Crete. The others are Vikos-Aoös and Prespa national parks in Epiros; Mt Olympus on the border of Thessaly and Macedonia; and Parnassos and Iti national parks in central Greece.

If you want to see wildlife, the place to go is the Dadia Forest Reserve, and there is also a national marine park off the coast of Alonnisos, and another around the Bay of Laganas area off Zakynthos.

Environmental Issues

Greece is belatedly becoming environmentally conscious but, regrettably, it's too late for some regions. Deforestation and soil erosion are problems that go back thousands of years. Olive cultivation and goats have been the main culprits, but fire-wood gathering, shipbuilding, housing and industry have all taken their toll.

Forest fires are also a major problem, with an estimated 25,000 hectares destroyed every year. Epiros and Macedonia in northern Greece are the only places where extensive forests remain.

General environmental awareness remains at a depressingly low level, especially where litter is concerned. The problem is particularly bad in rural areas, where roadsides are strewn with soft-drink cans and plastic packaging hurled from passing cars. Environmental education has begun in schools, but it will be some time before community attitudes change.

The news from the Aegean Sea is both good and bad. According to EU findings, it is Europe's least-polluted sea – apart from areas immediately surrounding major cities – but like the rest of the Mediterranean, it has been overfished.

FOOD & DRINK
Staples & Specialities
SNACKS

Greece has a great range of fast-food options. Foremost among them are the *gyros* and the souvlaki. The *gyros* is a giant skewer laden with seasoned meat that grills slowly as it rotates, the meat being steadily trimmed from the outside. Souvlaki are small, individual kebabs (the Turkish name). Both are served wrapped in pitta bread with salad and lashings of tzatziki (a yoghurt, cucumber and garlic dip). Other snacks are pretzel rings, *spanakopitta* (spinach and cheese pie) and tyropitta (cheese pie).

STARTERS

Greece is famous for its appetisers, known as *mezedes* (literally, 'tastes'; *meze* for short). Standards include tzatziki, *melitzanosalata* (aubergine or eggplant dip), taramasalata (fish-roe dip), *dolmades* (stuffed vine leaves), *fasolia* (beans) and *oktapodi* (octopus). A selection of three or four starters represents a good meal and can be a very good option for vegetarians.

MAIN DISHES

You'll find moussaka (layers of aubergine and mince, topped with béchamel sauce and baked) on every menu, alongside a number of other taverna staples. They include *moschari* (oven-baked veal and potatoes), *keftedes* (meatballs), *stifado* (meat stew), *pastitsio* (baked dish of macaroni with minced meat and béchamel sauce) and *yemista* (either tomatoes or green peppers stuffed with minced meat and rice). Most mains cost between €4 and €8.

The most popular fish are *barbouni* (red mullet) and *sifias* (swordfish) and they tend to be more expensive than meat dishes. Prices start at about €10 a serve. *Kalamaria* (fried squid) is readily available and cheap at about €5.

Fortunately for vegetarians, salad is a mainstay of the Greek diet. The most popular is *horiatiki salata*, normally listed on English-language menus as Greek salad. It's a mixed salad comprising cucumbers, peppers, onions, olives, tomatoes and feta cheese.

DESSERTS

Turkish in origin, most Greek desserts are variations on pastry soaked in honey. Popular ones include baklava (thin layers of pastry filled with honey and nuts) and *kadaïfi* (shredded wheat soaked in honey).

DRINKS

Bottled mineral water is cheap and available everywhere, as are soft drinks and packaged juices. Greece is traditionally a wine-drinking society. Retsina, wine flavoured with pine tree resin, is somewhat of an acquired taste. Fortunately, Greece also produces an increasingly good range of wines from traditional grape varieties.

Mythos, in its distinctive green bottle, is the most common Greek beer, but in many places the choice is either Amstel or Heineken. You can expect to pay about €0.80 in a supermarket, €2 in a restaurant and from €5 in a club. The most popular aperitif is the aniseed-flavoured ouzo, which is mixed with water to taste.

Where to Eat & Drink

There are several varieties of restaurants in Greece. The most common is the taverna, traditionally an extension of the Greek home table. *Estiatorio* is Greek for restaurant and often has the same dishes as a taverna but with higher prices. A *psistaria* specialises in charcoal-grilled dishes while a *psarotaverna* specialises in fish. *Ouzeria* (ouzo bars) often have such a range of *mezedes* that they can be regarded as eating places.

Kafeneia are the smoke-filled cafés where men gather to drink 'Greek' coffee, play backgammon and cards, and engage in heated political discussion.

Buying and preparing your own food is easy in Greece – every town of consequence has a supermarket, as well as fruit-and-vegetable shops.

ATHENS AΘHNA

pop 3.7 million

Named in honour of Athena, the goddess of wisdom, ancient Athens ranks alongside Rome for its glorious past and its influence on Western civilisation. But it's just as well Athens wasn't named after Eros, the god of love, for it's a city that, until recently, few visitors fell in love with.

Today, however, Athens is undergoing a revival. The 2004 Olympics saw a slew of new public works projects, hotel renovations, new shops and restaurants that have made Athens worthy of more time than most visitors give it.

Still, Athens isn't a Greek goddess in the looks department. The surrounding urban sprawl, the appalling traffic congestion and pollution still plague the city. But delve a little deeper and Athens reveals the complexities that only a city with such a long history can. Tavernas now compete with hip new restaurants; *rembetika* is heard alongside DJs playing the latest lounge compilations; and exciting contemporary art can be seen as well as the wonderful Islamic art of the Benaki Museum (p549).

Instead of just relying on the past to attract visitors, Athens has finally started working on its future.

ORIENTATION

Although Athens is a huge, sprawling city, nearly everything of interest to travellers is located within a small area bounded by Omonia Sq (Plateia Omonias) to the north, Monastiraki Sq (Plateia Monastirakiou) to the west, Syntagma Sq (Plateia Syntagmatos) to the east and the Plaka district to the south. The city's two major landmarks, the Acropolis and Lykavittos Hill, can be seen from just about everywhere in this area.

Syntagma is the heart of modern Athens. Flanked by luxury hotels, banks and fast-food restaurants, the square is dominated by the old royal palace – home of the Greek parliament since 1935.

Once a smart address, Omonia is known today for its prostitutes and pickpockets rather than its position as a central square. All the major streets of central Athens meet here. Panepistimiou (El Venizelou) and Stadiou run parallel southeast to Syntagma, while

ATHENS IN TWO DAYS

Rise early and beat the crowds and heat at the **Acropolis** (p546) before retiring to the shade of Byzantino (p553) for lunch or a quick *gyros*. Explore **Plaka** (p555) in the afternoon and have dinner with a view of the Parthenon at **Pil Poul** (p553). On the second day take in the **National Archaeological Museum** (p549) and the **Benaki Museum** (p549) and head to **Plateia Kolonakiou** (p554) for people watching and shopping.

Athinas leads south to the market district of Monastiraki. Monastiraki is in turn linked to Syntagma by Ermou – home to some of the city's smartest shops – and Mitropoleos.

Mitropoleos skirts the northern edge of Plaka, the delightful old quarter, which was virtually all that existed when Athens was declared the capital of independent Greece. Its labyrinthine streets are nestled on the northeastern slope of the Acropolis, and most of the city's ancient sites are close by.

Streets are clearly signposted in Greek and English. If you do get lost, it's very easy to find help. A glance at a map is often enough to draw an offer of assistance. Anyone you ask will be able to direct you to Syntagma (*syn*-tag-ma).

INFORMATION
Bookshops

The bigger *periptera* (kiosks) stock a good range of English-language magazines as well as international newspapers.

Compendium Books (Map p551; ☎ 2103 221 248; Nikis 28, Plaka) Specialises in English-language books and has a popular second-hand section.

Eleftheroudakis Books Syntagma (Map p551; ☎ 2103 314 180; Panepistimiou 17); Plaka (Map p551; ☎ 2103 229 388; Nikis 20) While the Panepistimiou shop is huge, both branches stock a good range of English-language books.

Cultural Centres

The centres listed here hold concerts, screen films and have occasional exhibitions. Check the *Kathimerini* section of the *International Herald Tribune* newspaper for listings.

British Council (Map pp548-9; ☎ 2103 692 314; www .britishcouncil.gr; Plateia Kolonakiou 17, Kolonaki)

French Institute of Athens (Map pp548-9; ☎ 2103 624 301; www.ifa.gr; Sina 31, Kolonali)

Hellenic-American Union (Map pp548-9; ☎ 2103 629 886; Massalias 22) Holds frequent concerts and shows films, exhibitions and the like.

Goethe Institut (Map p551; ☎ 2103 608 115; Omirou 14-16, Kolonaki)

Emergency

Athens Central Police Station (Map pp548-9; ☎ 2107 705 701/717; Leof Alexandras 173, Ambelokipi)

Fire brigade (☎ 199)

First-aid service (☎ 166)

Police emergency (☎ 100)

Tourist police (☎ 2108 707 000; Tsoha7, Ambelokipi; ☺ 24hr)

Tourist police information service (☎ 171; ☺ 24hr) Offers general tourist information as well as emergency help.

Internet Access

The following selection of Internet cafés around the city centre charge about €3 per hour.

Arcade Internet Café (Map p551; ☎ 2103 210 701; Stadiou 5, Syntagma; ☺ 10am-10pm Mon-Sat, noon-8pm Sun) Has dedicated laptop connections.

Bits & Bytes Internet Café Exarhia (Map pp548-9; ☎ 2103 306 590; Akadimias 78; ☺ 24hr); Plaka (Map p551; Kapnikareas 19; ☺ 24hr)

C@fe4U (Map pp548-9; ☎ 2103 611 981; Ippocratous 44, Exarhia; ☺ 24hr)

Plaka Internet World (Map p551; Pandrosou 29, Monastiraki; ☺ 11am-11pm)

Laundry

Plaka Laundrette (Map p551; Angelou Geronta 10, Plaka; 5kg wash & dry €8; ☺ 10am-6pm Mon-Sat, 10am-2pm Sun)

Left Luggage

Many hotels store luggage free for guests, but be aware that it is usually nothing more than leaving them unsecured in a hallway. Left-luggage facilities are available at the airport and train station.

Medical Services

Duty doctor (☎ 105; ☺ 2pm-7am)

Duty hospital (☎ 106)

Duty pharmacy (☎ 107)

SOS Doctors (☎ 2103 220 046/015; ☺ 24hr) Call-out service with multilingual doctors.

Money

Most banks have branches around Plateia Syntagmatos. Bank hours are generally 8am to 2pm Monday to Thursday and 8am to 1.30pm Friday. The following services are useful for travellers:

Acropole Foreign Exchange (Map p551; ☎ 2103 312 765; Kydathineon 23, Plaka; ☼ 9am-midnight)

American Express (Map p551; ☎ 2103 223 380; Ermou 7, Syntagma; ☼ 8.30am-4pm Mon-Fri, 8.30am-1.30pm Sat)

Eurochange Syntagma (Map p551; ☎ 2103 220 155; Karageorgi Servias 4; ☼ 8am-8pm Mon-Fri, 10am-6pm Sat & Sun); Plaka (Map p551; ☎ 2103 243 997; Filellinon 22; ☼ 8am-8pm Mon-Fri, 9am-7pm Sat, 10am-7pm Sun) Exchanges Thomas Cook travellers cheques without commission.

Post

Athens' Central Post Office (Map pp548-9; Eolou 100, Omonia; ☼ 7.30am-8pm Mon-Fri, to 2pm Sat) Unless specified otherwise all poste restante will be sent here.

Parcel post office (Map p551; Stadiou 4, Syntagma; ☼ 7.30am-2pm Mon-Fri) Parcels over 2kg going abroad must be taken here, unwrapped for inspection. The office is in the arcade.

Syntagma post office (Map p551; cnr Mitropoleos & Plateia Syntagmatos; ☼ 7.30am-8pm Mon-Fri, to 2pm Sat, 9am-1pm Sun) If you're staying in Plaka, it's easier to get poste restante sent here.

Telephone

Public phones are everywhere and only take phonecards – readily available from kiosks. See p608 for card denominations.

Toilets

Public toilets are thin on the ground in Athens, but fast-food outlets around the city have clean toilets that come in handy. You can also try a café, but without buying anything you're testing the hospitality of the tourist-tired Athenians.

Tourist Information

EOT Head Office (Greek National Tourist Organisation; Map pp548-9; ☎ 2108 707 000; www.gnto.gr; Tsoha 7, Ambelokipi; ☼ 9am-4pm Mon-Fri); EOT tourist office (Map p551; ☎ 2103 310 561/562; Amerikis 2; ☼ 9am-4pm Mon-Fri); EOT airport office (☎ 2103 530 445; Arrivals Hall, Eleftherios Venizelos International Airport; ☼ 9am-7pm Mon-Fri, 10am-3pm Sat & Sun) Each of these offices stocks a fairly useful map featuring public transport routes around the city.

DANGERS & ANNOYANCES

Athens has its fair share of problems that are associated with most big cities. Many of Athens' footpaths are marble, so it's important to wear a good pair of shoes and be very careful when these surfaces are wet.

Pickpockets are a major problem in Athens. Be aware on the metro system, the crowded streets around Omonia and the Sunday market on Ermou. Make sure your important documents are not in an outer pocket of a day-pack.

When you get in a taxi, either ensure the driver turns the meter on, negotiate a fair price or wait for another taxi. Be aware that some drivers use that age-old ruse of telling you that the hotel you have directed them to is closed or full. Insist on going where you want.

Some travel agents in the Plaka/Syntagma area employ touts that wander the streets promoting 'cheap' packages to the islands. Slick salespeople at the agency pressure you into buying packages that are outrageously overpriced .

Bar Scams

Lonely Planet continues to receive readers' reports warning about bar scams, particularly around Syntagma. The most common ruse runs something like this: friendly Greek approaches solo male traveller and discovers that the traveller knows little about Athens; friendly Greek then reveals that he, too, is from out of town. However, he's found this great little bar and offers to take the visitor for a drink. They order, and the equally friendly owner offers another drink. Women appear, more drinks are provided and the visitor relaxes as he realises that the women are not prostitutes, just friendly Greeks. The crunch comes at the end of the evening when the traveller is presented with an exorbitant bill and the smiles disappear.

SIGHTS
The Acropolis

The defining feature of Athens is the **Acropolis** (Map p551; ☎ 2103 210 291; sites & museum adult/concession €12/6; ☼ 8am-6.30pm Apr-Oct, 8am-4.30pm Nov-Mar). It's arguably the most important ancient monument in the Western world, a fact not lost on the multitudes of tourists who converge on the Acropolis every day, so it's best to visit first thing in the morning or late in the afternoon.

Pericles commissioned most of the buildings here during the golden age of Athens in the 5th century BC. The site had been cleared

CHEAPER BY THE HALF DOZEN

The €12 admission charge at the Acropolis buys a collective ticket that also gives entry to all the other significant ancient sites: the ancient agora, the Roman agora, the Keramikos, the Temple of Olympian Zeus and the Theatre of Dionysos. The ticket is valid for 48 hours, otherwise individual site fees apply. If you plan to see them, it's a bargain.

for him by the Persians, who destroyed an earlier temple complex on the eve of the Battle of Salamis.

The entrance to the Acropolis is through the **Beule Gate**, a Roman arch that was added in the 3rd century AD. Beyond this is the **Propylaia**, the monumental gate that was the entrance to the city in ancient times. It was damaged in the 17th century when lightning set off a Turkish gunpowder store, but it has since been restored. To the south of the Propylaia is the small, graceful **Temple of Athena Nike**, which is not accessible to visitors.

Standing supreme over the Acropolis is the monument that more than any other epitomises the glory of ancient Greece – the **Parthenon**. Completed in 438 BC, this building is unsurpassed in grace and harmony. To achieve perfect form, its lines were ingeniously curved to counteract optical illusions. The base curves upward slightly towards the ends, and the columns become slightly narrower towards the top, to achieve the overall effect of making them look straight.

Above the columns are the remains of a Doric frieze, which was partly destroyed by Venetian shelling in 1687. The best surviving pieces are the controversial Elgin Marbles, carted off to Britain by Lord Elgin in 1801. The Parthenon, dedicated to Athena, contained an 11m-tall gold-and-ivory statue of the goddess completed in 438 BC by Phidias of Athens (only the statue's foundations exist today).

To the north is the **Erechtheion** and its much-photographed Caryatids, the six maidens who support its southern portico. These are plaster casts – the originals (except for the one taken by Lord Elgin) are in the **Acropolis Museum** (noon-6.30pm Mon, 8am-6.30pm Tue-Sun Apr-Oct, 8am-4.30pm Nov-Mar).

South of the Acropolis

The importance of theatre in the life of the Athenian city-state is evident from the dimensions of the enormous **Theatre of Dionysos** (Map pp548-9; 2103 224 625; adult/concession €2/1; 8am-7pm May-Oct, to sunset Nov-Apr), just south of the Acropolis; enter via Dionysiou Areopagitou. Built between 342 and 326 BC on the site of an earlier theatre, in its time it could hold 17,000 people spread over 64 tiers of seats, of which about 20 tiers survive.

The **Stoa of Eumenes**, built as a shelter and promenade for theatre audiences, runs west from the Theatre of Dionysos to the **Theatre of Herodes Atticus**, which was built in Roman times. It is used for performances during the Athens Festival, but is closed at other times.

Temple of Olympian Zeus

Begun in the 6th century BC, this massive **temple** (Map pp548-9; 2109 226 330; adult/concession €2/1; 8.30am-3pm Tue-Sun) took more than 700 years to complete. Emperor Hadrian eventually finished the job in AD 131. It was the largest temple in Greece, impressive for the sheer size of its 104 Corinthian columns (17m high with a base diameter of 1.7m). The site is just southeast of Plaka, and the 15 remaining columns are a useful landmark.

Roman Stadium

This **stadium**, east of the Temple of Olympian Zeus, hosted the first modern Olympic Games in 1896. It was originally built in the 4th century BC as a venue for the Panathenaic athletic contests. The seats were rebuilt in Pentelic marble by Herodes Atticus in the 2nd century AD, and then faithfully restored in 1895.

Ancient Agora

The **ancient agora** (Map pp548-9; 2103 210 185; adult/concession €4/2; 8.30am-3pm Tue-Sun) was the marketplace of ancient Athens and the focal point of civic and social life. Socrates spent much time here expounding his philosophy. The main monuments are the well-preserved **Temple of Hephaestus**, the 11th-century **Church of the Holy Apostles** and the reconstructed **Stoa of Attalos**, which houses the site's museum.

Roman Agora

The Romans built their **agora** (Map p551; 2103 245 220; cnr Pelopida Eolou & Markou Aureliou; adult/

GREECE

CENTRAL ATHENS

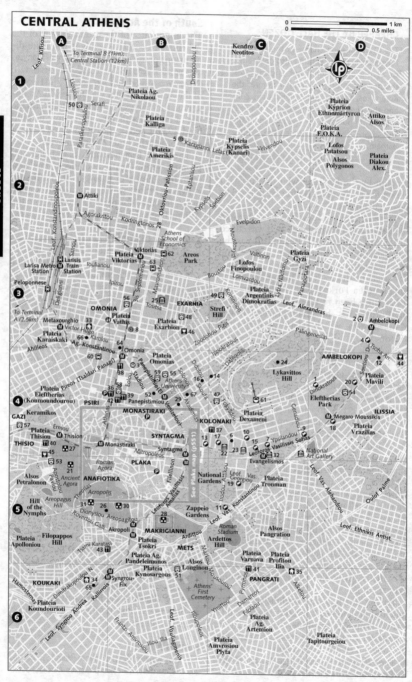

GREECE

concession €2/1; ☼ 8.30am-3pm Tue-Sun) just west of its ancient counterpart. Its principal monument is the wonderful **Tower of the Winds**, built in the 1st century BC by a Syrian astronomer named Andronicus. Each side represents a point of the compass, and has a relief carving depicting the associated wind.

National Archaeological Museum

One of the world's great museums, the **National Archaeological Museum** (Map pp548-9; ☎ 2108 217 717; 28 Oktovriou-Patission 44; www.culture .gr; adult/concession €6/3; ☼ 12.30-7pm Mon, 8am-7pm Tue-Sun Apr-Oct, 10.30am-5pm Mon, 8am-5pm Tue-Sun Nov-Mar) contains important finds from all the major archaeological sites around the country. The crowd-pullers are the magnificent, exquisitely detailed gold artefacts from Mycenae and spectacular Minoan frescoes from Santorini (Thira). There is also a wonderful collection of sculpture, including the superb Cycladic collection of figurines.

Benaki Museum

The **Benaki Museum** (Map pp548-9; ☎ 2103 671 000; cnr Leof Vasilissis Sofias & Koumbari 1, Kolonaki; adult/concession €6/3; ☼ 9am-5pm Mon, Wed, Fri & Sat, to midnight Thu, to 3pm Sun) houses the sumptuous collection of Antoine Benaki, the son of an Alexandrian cotton magnate named Emmanual Benaki. The collection includes ancient sculpture, Persian, Byzantine and Coptic objects, Chinese ceramics, icons, two

El Greco paintings and a superb collection of traditional costumes.

Goulandris Museum of Cycladic & Ancient Greek Art

This private **museum** (Map pp548-9; ☎ 2108 015 870; Neofytou Douka 4; adult/concession €3.50/2; ☼ 10am-4pm Mon & Wed-Fri, to 3pm Sat) was custom-built

---

FREE MUSEUMS

Athens has nearly 30 museums and the following free museums are interesting and well worth a visit.

Museum of Greek Popular Instruments (Map p551; ☎ 2103 254 119; Diogenous 1-3, Plaka; ☼ 10am-2pm Tue & Thu-Sun, noon-6pm Wed) This popular museum has displays and recordings of traditional instruments.

War Museum (Map pp548-9; ☎ 2107 290 543/544; cnr Leof Vasilissis Sofias & Rizari 2; ☼ 9am-2pm Tue-Fri, 9.30am-2pm Sat & Sun) Displays an interesting historical record of Greece in war through the ages.

Theatre Museum (Map pp548-9; ☎ 2103 629 430; Akadimias 50, Syntagma; ☼ 9am-2pm Mon-Fri) Contains memorabilia from Greek theatre in the 19th and 20th centuries, including photographs, costumes and props.

Centre of Folk Arts & Traditions (Map p551; ☎ 2103 243 987; Hatzimihali Angelikis 6, Plaka; ☼ 9am-1pm daily & 5-9pm Tue-Fri) Good displays of costumes, embroideries, musical instruments and pottery.

to display a fabulous collection of Cycladic art, with an emphasis on the early Bronze Age. The marble figurines are beautiful.

Lykavittos Hill

Pine-covered **Lykavittos** (Hill of Wolves; Map pp548-9) is the highest of the eight hills dotted around Athens. From the summit, there are all-embracing views of the city, the Attic basin and the islands of Salamis and Aegina – pollution permitting of course. The open-air Lykavittos Theatre, northeast of the summit, is used for concerts in summer.

The main path to the summit starts at the top of Loukianou, or you can take the **funicular railway** (Map pp548-9; one way/return €2/4; 9.15am-11.45pm), from the top of Ploutarhou.

Changing of the Guard

Every Sunday at 10.45am a platoon of traditionally costumed *evzones* (guards), accompanied by a band, marches down Vasilissis Sofias to the Tomb of the Unknown Soldier, in front of the parliament building on Syntagma. The guards also change every hour on the hour.

FESTIVALS & EVENTS

The annual **Hellenic Festival** (www.greekfestival.gr) is the city's most important cultural event, running from mid-June to late September. It features a line-up of international music, dance and theatre at the Theatre of Herodes Atticus. The setting is superb, backed by the floodlit Acropolis. Get information from the **festival box office** (Map pp548-9; 2103 221 459; fax 2103 235 172; Stadiou 39, Syntagma; 8.30am-4pm Mon-Fri, 9am-2.30pm Sat). Tickets are not available for events until three weeks beforehand, but you'll find details of the year's events from February on the festival website.

SLEEPING

Athens is a late-night and noisy city so we've made an effort to select accommodation that is central to the action, but lets you get some sleep. There's a good range of sleeping options around Plaka, the most popular place to stay due to its proximity to the sights. It fills up quickly in July and August and you should book ahead for this time of year.

Camping

There are no camping grounds in central Athens, but the EOT has a brochure listing sites in Attica. There are several camping grounds southeast of Athens on the coast road to Cape Sounion.

Athens Camping (2105 814 114; fax 2105 820 353; Leof Athinon 198; per adult/tent €5/3; year-round) Located 7km west of the city centre on the road to Corinth, this is the closest camping ground to Athens. It has reasonable facilities, but little else going for it.

Hostels

Athens International Youth Hostel (Map pp548-9; 2105 234 170; fax 2105 234 015; Victor Hugo 16; dm HI members €8.66, dm nonmembers incl joining fee €15, daily stamp €2.50) While it's long been popular with travellers, the HI's dodgy location is a drawback. As long as you're not intimidated by the junkies and prostitutes that inhabit the area, the rooms are good value.

Youth Hostel No 5 (Map pp548-9; 2107 519 530; y-hostel@otenet.gr; Damareos 75; dm with shared bathroom €10) The rooms here are basic, but this pleasant hostel is in a quiet neighbourhood. Facilities include coin-operated hot showers, a communal kitchen, TV room and washing machine. Take trolleybus No 2 or 11 from Syntagma to the Filolaou stop on Frinis, or walk from Evangelismos metro station.

Hotels

BUDGET

Hotel Tempi (Map p551; 2103 213 175; www.travelling.gr/tempihotel; Eolou 29, Monastiraki; s/d/tr €40/48/60, s/d with shared bathroom €30/42) This friendly, family-run hotel is a quiet place on the pedestrian part of Eolou. Rooms at the front overlook pretty Plateia Agia Irini. It has a small communal kitchen with refrigerator and being close to the markets makes it a good choice for self-caterers.

Student & Travellers' Inn (Map p551; 2103 244 808; www.studenttravellersinn.com; Kydathineon 16, Plaka; d/tr €60/75, dm with shared bathroom €15-22, s/d with shared bathroom €45/50;) Despite a small hike in prices this place is still a backpacker favourite. It's well-run, with rooms that range widely in size. Facilities include a courtyard with big-screen TV, and a travel service. It's also heated in winter.

Marble House Pension (Map pp548-9; 2109 234 058; www.marblehouse.gr; Zini 35A, Koukaki; s/d/tr €35/43/50, d/tr with shared bathroom €37/44;) Located on a quiet cul-de-sac off Zini, this long-standing pension is one of Athens'

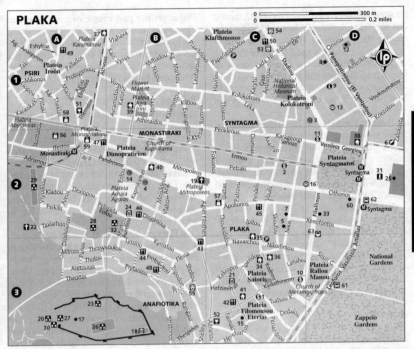

PLAKA

better budget hotels. All rooms have a bar fridge, ceiling fans and safety boxes for valuables. Breakfast is an extra €4.

MID-RANGE
Acropolis House Pension (Map p551; ☎ 2103 222 344; fax 2103 244 143; Kodrou 6-8, Plaka; s/d/tr from €64/80/96, s/d with shared bathroom €38.90/51.55; ✷) A beautifully preserved 19th-century house, this well-situated pension is a pretty good deal once you get your head around the price structure. There are discounts for longer stays, supplements for the air-conditioning etc. Rooms are heated in winter.

Hotel Adonis (Map p551; ☎ 2103 249 737; fax 2103 231 602; Kodrou 3, Plaka; s/d from €44/59; ❄) Opposite the Acropolis House Pension, this comfortable, friendly hotel is one of the best deals around. There are excellent views of the Acropolis from the 4th-floor rooms and the rooftop bar, which doubles as the breakfast room. All rooms have a TV and prices includes breakfast.

Hotel Cecil (Map p551; ☎ 2103 217 909; www.cecil.gr; Athinas 39, Monastiraki; s/d/tr €55/80/105; ❄) Occupying a fine old classical building with beautiful high, moulded ceilings and polished floors, this hotel looks immaculate. Rooms are tastefully furnished and come equipped with a TV. Rates include breakfast.

Hotel Plaka (Map p551; ☎ 2103 222 096; www.plaka hotel.gr; cnr Kapnikareas 7 & Mitropoleos, Monastiraki; s/d/tr €99/125/145; ❄) With its great position right on the Ermou St shopping strip, it's little wonder this hotel is so popular with clued-up tour operators. Don't let that put you off though. The rooms are stylishly minimalist and there's a great rooftop garden.

TOP END

Electra Palace (Map p551; ☎ 2103 370 000; www .electrahotels.gr; Navarchou Nikodimou 18-20, Plaka; s/d/ ste €158/186/320; P ✗ ❄ ▣) After a lengthy renovation, the best address in Plaka finally reopened in time for the Olympics. Resplendent with its new neoclassical façade, the well-overdue makeover appears to be a winner. The almost comical service of the past appears to have been jettisoned as well. The rooftop area and pool remained unfinished at the time of writing.

Hotel Grand Bretagne (Map p551; ☎ 2103 330 000; www.grandebretagne.gr; Vassileos Georgiou 1, Plateia Syntagmatos; s/d from €470/510; P ✗ ❄ ▣) Built in 1842 as a residence, this wonderful hotel has a commanding presence – made even more so by its recent renovation. Restored to the opulence of its original transformation to a hotel (in 1874), it has no peer in Athens. Nonsmoking floors, rooms for disabled guests, 24-hour butler service and a gymnasium are just some of the extras on offer. Add to this its prime position off Plateia Syntagmatos and it's a winning combination in this price category.

EATING

For travellers, eating in Athens has been traditionally associated with a taverna meal in Plaka, yet the past couple of years has seen city eating become both more diversified and sophisticated. While every visitor should experience the traditional taverna meal, there's now some French-influenced fine dining and Asian and fusion food on offer.

Budget

Athens has plenty of places where you can eat and run. Locals in a hurry grab a coffee and a snack from one of the popular branches of the ubiquitous Flocafé's and a quick bite from a branch of the Everest sandwich shops.

Savas (Map p551; ☎ 2103 245 048; Mitropoleos 86; gyros €1.30; ❄ 9pm-3am) One of the best places to try a *gyros* – either pork, beef or chicken, all equally greasy and equally good. Eat in or takeaway.

O Platanos (Map p551; ☎ 2103 220 666; Diogenous 4, Plaka; mains €7; ❄ noon-4.30pm & 7.30pm-midnight Mon-Sat, noon-4.30pm Sun) A taverna without touts, O Platanos serves some of the best home cooking around. Try one of the lamb dishes and the barrel retsina that for once is more suited for drinking than stripping the paint off a car. While the service is leisurely, the shady outdoor courtyard is a pleasant and tranquil retreat. No credit cards.

Noodle House (Map p551; ☎ 2103 318 585; Apollonos 11, Plaka; mains €8; ❄ 11am-midnight Mon-Sat, from 5pm Sun) The pick of several Asian restaurants around Plaka, Noodle House serves up tasty noodles and soups at honest prices. The menu features a mix of mainly Thai- and Singapore-based dishes and you can order it for takeaway or home delivery.

Eden Vegetarian Restaurant (Map p551; ☎ 2103 248 858; Lyssiou 12, Plaka; mains €4.70-8.50; ❄ 11am-midnight Wed-Mon) Eden is the long-standing champion of vegetarian restaurants in Athens, serving up vegetarian versions of Greek classics, such as moussaka (€6.80) and a mushroom *stifado* (cooked in a tomato puree, €8.80). There's also organic wine and beer on offer. No credit cards.

Mid-Range

Taverna tou Psiri (Map pp548-9; ☎ 2103 214 923; Eshylou 12, Psiri; meals for 2 people €25; ❄ noon-1am) This taverna is a local favourite, both for its cheerful atmosphere and below-average prices for a Psiri eatery. The daily menu is full of Greek taverna specials – all good stuff. It's tucked away off Plateia Iroön; look for the apt mural of a drunk leaning against a lamppost.

Eat (Map pp548-9; ☎ 2103 249 129; Adrianou 91, Plaka; mains €12; ⏰ 10-12.30am) A stylish antidote to the endless tavernas in Plaka, Eat offers salads, pastas and modern interpretations of some Greek classics, as well as good wines by the glass. Try the *haloumi* salad with balsamic vinaigrette (€8) or just drop in for coffee and listen to the great music selection.

Byzantino (Map p551; ☎ 2103 227 368; Kydathineon 18, Plaka; mains €11; ⏰ 9-2am Mon-Sat) One of the better choices for the obligatory Plaka taverna meal, Byzantino offers good-value traditional cuisine. The fish soup and the starters are excellent and it's popular with tourists and locals alike who take an outside table to watch the passing Plaka parade.

Taverna tou Psara (Map p551; ☎ 2103 218 734; Eretheos 16, Plaka; mains €5-18; fish from €40 a kg; ⏰ 11-1am) This refurbished taverna is one of the best around, serving up fabulous *mezedes* – try the *melizanokeftedes* (eggplant croquettes, €5.30) – and excellent meat or fish grills. Secure a table on the terrace with city views and you've scored one of the best taverna experiences in the city.

Top End
Here's a small selection from Athens' increasingly impressive fine-dining scene. All accept credit cards, are only open for dinner (keep in mind most Athenians don't arrive before 10pm), and bookings are essential.

Pil Poul (Map pp548-9; ☎ 2103 423 665; Apostolou Pavlou 51, Thisio; mains €30; ⏰ 8pm-12.30am Mon-Sat) Arguably the best 'great food and great view' combination in Athens. A creative Franco-Mediterranean menu featuring ingredients such as lobster and foie gras, coupled with Acropolis views, makes this an excellent choice for a romantic dinner.

Spondi (Map pp548-9; ☎ 2107 520 658; Pyrronos 5, Pag12, Plaka; mains €30; ⏰ 8.30pm-12.30am) Perhaps Athens' own temple of gastronomy, Spondi earns its Michelin star for a creative menu combining French technique with fresh ingredients. The starters, such as sea bass with rose petal sauce (€25), are superb, but pace yourself because the desserts are a knock-out. Refreshingly for a restaurant of this pedigree, the staff are friendly and helpful and the atmosphere relaxed.

Self-Catering
You'll find the best selection of fresh produce at the **fruit and vegetable market** (Map pp548-9)

on Athinas, which is opposite the **meat market** (Map pp548-9). The following are among the main supermarkets in central Athens: **Bazaar Discount Supermarket** (Map pp548-9; Eolou 104, Omonia), **Marinopoulos** (Map pp548-9; Athinas 60, Omonia), **Marinopoulos** (Map p551; Kanari 9, Kolonaki), **Vasilopoulou** (Map pp548-9; Stadiou 19, Syntagma) and **Veropoulos** (Map pp548-9; Parthenos 6, Koukaki).

DRINKING
Athens has more than its fair share of drinking establishments. There are casual, grungy student hang-outs, pubs for the expats, and bars where you can flash your cash. During the summer months, however, most of the action heads to the islands. Outside summer, the bars of Kolonaki and Psiri are very popular.

Bars & Pubs
Brettos (Map p551; ☎ 2103 232 110; Kydathineon 41, Plaka; ⏰ 10am-midnight) A distillery and bottle shop by day, at night this old family-run place is a popular stop to imbibe and to check out its eye-catching, back-lit collection of coloured bottles. Right in the heart of Plaka, it's a good stop for a nightcap – just watch those shots of Brettos-brand spirits (€1.50); they're lethal.

Bee (Map p551; ☎ 2103 212 624; cnr Miaouli & Themidos, Psiri; ⏰ 8pm-1am Tue-Sun, lunch from noon Sat & Sun) A popular bar/restaurant (with good food), Bee attracts a mixed crowd that spills out onto the street when it gets late. Also great for a Sunday-afternoon drink after the markets.

GREECE

Mike's Irish Bar (Map pp548-9; ☎ 2107 776 797; Sinopsis 6, Ambelokipi; ⊙ 8pm-4am) For those who can't go too long without a pint of Guinness or Murphy's (both €7), Mike's is where you can satisfy that need. A favourite watering hole of the expat community, you can play darts or listen to live music nightly from 11.30pm.

Stavlos (Map pp548-9; ☎ 2103 452 502; Iraklidon 10, Thisio; ⊙ 10-4am) One of the originals in Thisio, Stavlos is an arty venue with an internal courtyard and a café/brasserie outside. It has a laid-back, cool vibe during the day, while the DJ sets the mood as the night goes on.

Wonderbar (Map pp548-9; ☎ 2103 818 577; Themistokleous 80, Exarhia; ⊙ 10-3.30am) Cool by day, packed by night, this café/lounge bar attracts hip young Athenians to the emerging area of Exarhia.

Cafés

Athens café society is as strong as ever, despite having some of the highest prices for a coffee in Europe. To best experience the Athens café scene, head to Kolonaki, where a mind-boggling array of cafés run off Plateia Kolonakiou, on Skoufa and Tsakalof Sts. Take whatever free seats you can find and settle in for some slow *frappé* (frothy ice coffee) drinking and plenty of people watching.

ENTERTAINMENT

The best source of entertainment information is the weekly *Athenorama*, but it's in Greek only. The *Kathimerini* supplement that accompanies the *International Herald Tribune* has daily event listings and the weekly *Athens News* carries an entertainment guide.

Cinemas

Most cinemas show recent releases in English and admission prices are €6 to €8. Two of the major cinemas in central Athens are **Apollon** (Map p551; ☎ 2103 236 811; Stadiou 19) and the **Astor** (Map p551; ☎ 2103 231 297; Stadiou 28).

Classical Music, Opera and Dance

Dora Stratou Dance Company (Map p551; ☎ 2109 216 650; Filopappos Hill; tickets €13; ⊙ 9.30pm Tue-Sat, 8.15pm Sun May-Sep) A colourful 1½-hour traditional folk dancing show featuring over 75 dancers and musicians.

Megaron Mousikis (Athens Concert Hall; Map pp548-9; ☎ 2107 282 333; www.megaron.gr; Leof Vasilissis Sofias, Ambelokipi; ⊙ box office 10am-6pm Mon-Fri, to 2pm Sat)

An excellent concert venue hosting performances by local and international artists. Tickets generally go on sale three weeks before the performance and range from €10 to €40.

Olympia Theatre (Map pp548-9; ☎ 2103 611 516; www.nationalopera.gr; Akadimias 59, Exarhia) The Greek National Opera season runs from November to June, featuring works by artists such as Verdi, Handel and Puccini. Tickets range from €17 for students to €50 for box seats.

Gay & Lesbian Venues

The greatest concentration of gay bars is to be found around Makrigianni, south of the Temple of Olympian Zeus. Most places don't get moving until midnight. Here's a small selection of the scene:

Alekos' Island (Map pp548-9; ☎ 2103 640 249; Tsakalof 42, Kolonaki; ⊙ 6pm-late) One of Athens' longstanding gay bars, it attracts an older crowd to its candle-lit interior.

Aroma Gynekas (Map pp548-9; ☎ 2103 819 615; Tsamadou 15, Exarhia; ⊙ 10.30pm-late) Packed on weekends, this lesbian dance club is one of the busiest in Athens, playing both mainstream and Greek music.

Kirkis & Lizard (Map pp548-9; ☎ 2103 466 960; Apostolou Pavlou 31, Thisio; Kirkis ⊙ 10-3am, Lizard ⊙ 11pm-late Fri-Sun) A popular gay and lesbian hang-out, Kirkis café is busy from late afternoon onwards. Lizard, the club upstairs, is busy over the weekend.

Live Music
POP, ROCK & JAZZ

Tickets for concerts are sold at **Ticket House** (Map pp548-9; ☎ 2103 608 366; Panepistimiou 42). Venues include:

Rodon Club (Map pp548-9; ☎ 2105 247 427; Marni 24, Omonia; ⊙ from 10pm) The city's main rock venue.

Gagarin 205 Club (Map pp548-9; ☎ 2108 547 601; Liossion 205; ⊙ from 9.30pm) A newer, more intimate live venue.

Half Note (Map pp548-9; ☎ 2109 213 310; Trivonianou 17, Mets; ⊙ from 10.30pm) The principal jazz venue in Athens.

REMBETIKA

Rembetika Stoa Athanaton (Map pp548-9; ☎ 2103 214 362; Sofokleous 19; ⊙ 3-6pm & midnight-6am Mon-Sat Oct-Apr) Located above the meat market, this is *the* place to experience the Greek version of the blues.

Nightclubs

The clubs don't get busy until midnight, with most people staying at bar-restaurants until then. Expect to pay at least €5 for a beer. A cover charge usually applies, especially later in the week and when there's a guest DJ.

+ Soda (Map pp548-9; ☎ 2103 456 187; Ermou 161, Thisio; admission incl one drink €10-20; ☼ midnight-late Sep-May) This multilevel superclub features international guest DJs and attracts a young group of clubbers who come for progressive and hard-core house and techno.

Decadence (Map pp548-9; ☎ 2108 823 544; cnr Pouliherias & Voulgaroktonou 69, Lofos Strefi; admission incl one drink €6-8; ☼ 10.30pm-4am) For indie and alternative music lovers, Decadence has two levels of sonic mayhem, with a quieter bar scene on the lower floor and club upstairs.

SHOPPING

Athens offers excellent shopping opportunities for Greek jewellery, shoes and clothes, as well as souvenirs. The most concentrated shopping is on Ermou, from Syntagma to Monastiraki, with clothes and shoes being the major attraction. The clothes boutiques are scattered around Kolonaki; designers and jewellers are on Voukourestiou. Plaka and Monastiraki are full of souvenir and gift shops. Here you can pick up common souvenirs such as backgammon sets, olive-wood gift items, key rings, worry beads and silver and gold jewellery.

For folk art and other crafts visit the **National Welfare Organisation** (Map p551; ☎ 2103 218 272; cnr Apollonos & Ipatias, Plaka), which has a great selection of hand-woven carpets, tapestries and tablecloths. Sandal wearers head to **Stavros Melissinos' Store** (Map p551; ☎ 2103 219 247; Aghias Theklas 2, Monastiraki) for some custom Jesus sandals and some poetry from the poet sandal maker. If you're in Athens on a Sunday, it's obligatory to visit the **Sunday market** (Map p551; ☼ 7am-2pm) near the Athens flea market, starting at Plateia Monastiraki and onto Ermou.

GETTING THERE & AWAY

Air

Athens is served by **Eleftherios Venizelos International Airport** (☎ 2103 530 000; www.aia.gr) at Spata, 27km east of Athens.

Facilities at the new state-of-the-art airport are excellent, with a good selection of reasonably priced cafés and some decent duty free,

including local goods and foodstuffs. See p556 for information on getting to/from the airport. International-airline phone numbers in Athens are listed on p609.

The vast majority of domestic flights are handled by Greece's much-maligned national carrier, **Olympic Airways** (toll free ☎ 8011 144 444, flight information ☎ 2109 666 666; www.olympic-airways.gr); Koukaki head office (Map pp548-9; ☎ 2103 569 111; Leof Syngrou Andrea 96); Syntagma (Map p551; ☎ 2109 264 444; Filellinon 15); Omonia (Map pp548-9; ☎ 2109 267 218; Kotopouli Merakas 1).

Crete-based competitor **Aegean Airlines** (reservations ☎ 8011 120 000; www.aegeanair.com) offers flights to many of the same destinations as Olympic. It has a city **sales office** (Map p551; ☎ 2103 315 502; Othonos 10) at Syntagma.

Bus

Athens has two main intercity bus stations. EOT gives out schedules for both stations detailing departure times, journey times and fares.

Terminal A (☎ 2105 298 740; Kifissou 100), northwest of Omonia, has buses to the Peloponnese, Ionian Islands and western Greece. To get to Terminal A, take bus No 015 from the junction of Zinonos and Menandrou, near Plateia Omonia.

Terminal B (☎ 2108 317 096), off Liossion, is north of Omonia and has departures to central and northern Greece, as well as to Evia. To get to Terminal B, take bus No 024 from outside the main gate of the National Gardens on Amalias. Get off the bus at Liossion 260, turn right onto Gousiou and you'll see the bus terminal at the end of the road.

Buses for Attica leave from the **Mavromateon bus terminal** (Map pp548-9; cnr Alexandras & 28 Oktovriou-Patission). Buses to Rafina and Marathon leave from the bus stops 10m north of Mavromateon.

Car & Motorcycle

National Rd 1 is the main route north from Athens. It starts at Nea Kifissia. To get there from central Athens, take Vasilissis Sofias from Syntagma and follow the signs. National Rd 8, which begins beyond Dafni, is the road to the Peloponnese; take Agiou Konstantinou from Omonia.

The northern reaches of Syngrou, just south of the Temple of Olympian Zeus, are packed solid with car-rental firms.

GREECE

Ferry

See p557 for information on ferries travelling to and from the islands.

Train

At the time of writing, the city's new Central Station, 12km north of the city at Arharnon, was not yet operational. Access to the station will be by suburban train and all intercity train services will leave from there. Until this opens, trains to central and northern Greece leave from Larisis train station (Map pp548-9), and trains to the Peloponnese leave from the Peloponnese station 200m away.

More information on the services is available from **OSE offices** Omonia (Map pp548-9; ☎ 2105 240 647; Karolou 1; ⏲ 8am-6pm Mon-Fri, to 3pm Sat); Syntagma (Map pp548-9; ☎ 2103 624 402; Sina 6; ⏲ 8am-3.30pm Mon-Fri, to 3pm Sat). Both offices handle advance bookings.

GETTING AROUND

The new metro system has made getting around central Athens (and to Piraeus) very easy, but Athens' road traffic is still horrendous. Most of Athens' public-transport services were being upgraded for the Olympics at the time of writing. A daily travel pass (€2.90) is valid for all forms of public transport, including a trip to/from the airport.

To/From the Airport
BUS

Bus E94 (25 minutes, every 16 minutes 6am to midnight) operates between the airport and the eastern terminus of metro Line 3 at Ethniki Amyna.

Bus E95 (one to 1½ hours, every 30 minutes) operates between the airport and Plateia Syntagmatos. The bus stop is outside the National Gardens on Amalias on the eastern side of Plateia Syntagmatos.

Bus E96 (one to 1½ hours, every 40 minutes) operates between the airport and Plateia Karaïskaki in Piraeus.

Tickets for all these services cost €2.95, are valid for 24 hours and can be used on all forms of public transport in Athens – buses, trolleybuses and the metro.

METRO

Completed just in time for the Olympics, Line 3 of the metro is now linked to the airport via the train system and can take you to the city centre in under 30 minutes.

TAXI

Taxi fares vary according to the time of day and level of traffic, but you should expect to pay €20 to €30 from the airport to the city centre, and €20 to €25 from the airport to Piraeus, depending on traffic conditions. Both trips can take anywhere between one and 1½ hours.

Bus & Trolleybus

Blue-and-white suburban buses operate every 15 minutes from 5am to midnight. Route numbers and destinations, but not the actual routes, are listed on the free EOT map. Timetables can be obtained from the **GNTO** (www.gnto.gr) in EOT tourist offices, or the **Athens Urban Transport Organisation** (OASA; ☎ 8836 076; www.oasa.gr). The EOT map does, however, mark the routes of the yellow trolleybuses, making them easy to use. They also run from 5am to midnight.

There are special buses that operate 24 hours to Piraeus. Bus No 040 leaves from the corner of Syntagma and Filellinon, and No 049 leaves from the Omonia end of Athinas. The buses run every 20 minutes from 6am to midnight, and then hourly until 6am.

Tickets for all these services cost €0.45, and must be purchased before you board – either from a ticket booth or from a *periptero* (kiosk). The same tickets can be used on either buses or trolleybuses and must be validated as soon as you board.

Metro

The opening of the first phase of the long-awaited new metro system transformed travel around central Athens. Coverage is still largely confined to the city centre, but that's good enough for most visitors. For the latest on the metro, visit www.ametro.gr. The following is a brief outline of the three lines that make up the network:

Line 1 (Green) This line is the old Kifissia-Piraeus line and is indicated in green on maps and signs. Useful stops include Piraeus (for the port), Monastiraki and Omonia (city centre), Plateia Viktorias (National Archaeological Museum) and Irini (Olympic Stadium). Omonia and Attiki are transfer stations with connections to Line 2; Monastiraki will eventually become a transfer station with connections to Line 3.

Line 2 (Red) This line runs from Sepolia in the northwest to Dafni in the southeast and is indicated in red on maps and signs. Useful stops include Larisa (for the train stations), Omonia, Panepistimiou and Syntagma (city centre) and Akropoli (Makrigianni). Attiki and Omonia are transfer stations for Line 1, while Syntagma is the transfer station for Line 3.

Line 3 (Blue) This line runs northeast from Syntagma to Ethniki Amyna. It is indicated in blue on maps and signs. Useful stops are Evangelismos (for the museums on Vasilissis Sofias) and Ethniki Amyna (buses to the airport). Syntagma is the transfer station for Line 2.

Travel on Lines 2 and 3 costs €0.75, while Line 1 is split into three sections: Piraeus–Monastiraki, Monastiraki–Attiki and Attiki–Kifissia. Travel within one section costs €0.60 and a journey covering two or more sections costs €0.75. The same conditions apply everywhere: tickets must be validated at the machines at platform entrances before travelling. The penalty for travelling without a validated ticket is €23.50.

The metro operates from 5am to midnight. Trains run every three minutes during peak periods and every 10 minutes at other times.

Taxi

Athenian taxis are yellow. The flag fall is €0.75 and there's an additional surcharge of €0.60 from ports and train and bus stations, as well as a €0.90 surcharge from the airport. After that, the day rate (tariff 1 on the meter) is €0.23 per kilometre. The rate doubles between midnight and 5am (tariff 2 on the meter). Baggage is charged at the rate of €0.30 per item over 10kg. The minimum fare is €1.50, which covers most journeys in central Athens.

AROUND ATHENS

Piraeus Πειραιάς

pop 175,697

Greece's main port, and one of the main ports of the Mediterranean, Piraeus is the hub of the Aegean ferry network. Piraeus has been the port of Athens since classical times, but these days it's more like an outer suburb of the space-hungry capital. The streets that most travellers see on their way to a ferry are every bit as traffic-clogged as in Athens, but a trip to tranquil and picturesque Mikrolimano (Small Harbour), with its cafés and fish restaurants, reveals another side to Piraeus.

ORIENTATION & INFORMATION

Piraeus consists of a peninsula surrounded by harbours. The largest of its three harbours is the Megas Limin (Great Harbour), on the western side, where all the ferries leave from, along with hydrofoil and catamaran services to Aegina and the Cyclades. Zea Marina (Limin Zeas) and Mikrolimano (Small Harbour), on the eastern side of the peninsula, are for private yachts.

An Internet café, **Internet Center** (☎ 2104 111 261; Akti Poseidonos 24; ⏰ 10am-11pm) is on the main road, across from the main harbour.

EATING

If you're in Athens for more than a few days, a seafood meal on the harbour at Mikrolimano is a must. **Jimmy & the Fish** (☎ 2104 124 417; Koumoundourou 46; mains €16; ⏰ 1pm-1am) is the most reliable of the harbour-front restaurants, serving up excellent seafood in stylish surrounds. There are also a couple of good cafés along this strip. Trolleybus No 20 runs past the harbour.

GETTING THERE & AWAY
Bus

Two 24-hour bus services operate between central Athens and Piraeus. Bus No 049 runs from Omonia to the bus station at the Great Harbour, and bus No 040 runs from Syntagma to the tip of the Piraeus peninsula. No 040 is the service to catch from Athens for Zea Marina – get off at the Hotel Savoy on Iroön Polytehniou – though the trip can take over an hour in bad traffic. The fare is €0.45 for each service. There are no intercity buses to or from Piraeus. The E96 buses to the airport leave from the southern side of Plateia Karaïskaki.

Ferry

The following information is a guide to ferry departures between June and mid-September. Schedules are similar in April, May and October, but are radically reduced in winter – especially to smaller islands. The main branch of EOT in Athens (see p546) has a reliable schedule, updated weekly. The departure points for the ferry destinations are shown on the map of Piraeus (p557). Check where to find your boat when you buy your ticket. See the Getting There & Away sections for each island for more details.

Crete There are two boats a day to Hania and Iraklio, a daily service to Rethymno, and three a week to Agios Nikolaos and Sitia.

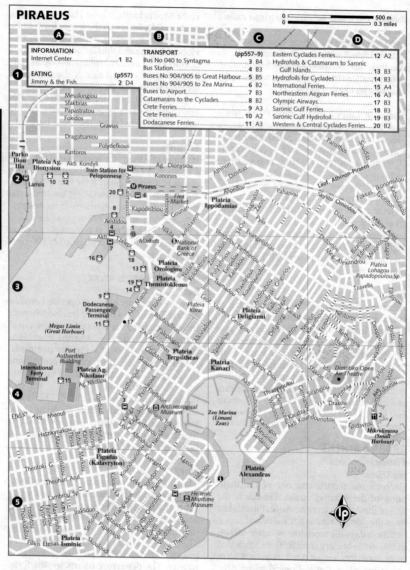

PIRAEUS

0 — 500 m
0 — 0.3 miles

INFORMATION	
Internet Center	1 B2

EATING	(p557)
Jimmy & the Fish	2 D4

TRANSPORT	(pp557–9)
Bus No 040 to Syntagma	3 B4
Bus Station	4 B3
Buses No 904/905 to Great Harbour	5 B5
Buses No 904/905 to Zea Marina	6 B2
Buses to Airport	7 B3
Catamarans to the Cyclades	8 B2
Crete Ferries	9 A3
Crete Ferries	10 A2
Dodecanese Ferries	11 A3

Eastern Cyclades Ferries	12 A2
Hydrofoils & Catamarans to Saronic Gulf Islands	13 B3
Hydrofoils for Cyclades	14 B3
International Ferries	15 A4
Northeastern Aegean Ferries	16 A3
Olympic Airways	17 B3
Saronic Gulf Ferries	18 B3
Saronic Gulf Hydrofoil	19 B3
Western & Central Cyclades Ferries	20 B2

Cyclades There are daily ferries to Amorgos, Folegandros, Ios, Kimolos, Kythnos, Milos, Mykonos, Naxos, Paros, Santorini (Thira), Serifos, Sifnos, Sikinos, Syros and Tinos; two or three ferries a week to Iraklia, Shinoussa, Koufonisi, Donoussa and Anafi; and none to Andros or Kea.
Dodecanese There are daily ferries to Kalymnos, Kos, Leros, Patmos and Rhodes; three a week to Karpathos and Kassos; and weekly services to the other islands.

Northeastern Aegean Islands Daily ferries to Chios, Lesvos (Mytilini), Ikaria and Samos; twice weekly to Limnos.
Saronic Gulf Islands Daily ferries head to Aegina, Poros, Hydra and Spetses year-round.

Hydrofoil & Catamaran
Hellas Flying Dolphins (www.www.dolphins.gr) operates high-speed hydrofoils and catamarans

to the Cyclades from early April to the end of October, and year-round services to the Saronic Gulf Islands. All services to the Cyclades and Aegina leave from Great Harbour. Some services to Poros, Hydra and Spetses also leave from here, but most leave from Zea Marina.

Metro
The fastest and most convenient link between the Great Harbour and Athens is the metro (€0.60, 20 minutes). The station is close to the ferries, at the northern end of Akti Kalimassioti. There are metro trains every 10 minutes from 5am to midnight.

Train
At the time of research, all services to the Peloponnese from Athens start and terminate at the Piraeus train station. With the advent of the new Central Station at Arharnon, this is expected to change.

GETTING AROUND
Local bus Nos 904 and 905 run between the Great Harbour and Zea Marina. They leave from the bus stop beside the metro at Great Harbour, and drop you by the maritime museum at Zea Marina.

THE PELOPONNESE
ΠΕΛΟΠΟΝΝΗΣΟΣ

The Peloponnese is a region of outstanding beauty situated at the southern extremity of the rugged Balkan Peninsula. It's linked to the rest of Greece by the narrow Isthmus of Corinth, but technically became an island after the completion of the Corinth Canal across the isthmus in 1893 and is now linked to the mainland by road and rail bridges.

The Peloponnese has played a major role in Greek history, particularly at Olympia, birthplace of the Olympic Games. Other highlights are Mycenae, Epidavros and Corinth in the northeast, all close to the pretty Venetian town of Nafplio.

In the south, Monemvasia is one of the most romantic spots in Greece. The rugged Mani Peninsula is famous for its spectacular wild flowers in spring, as well as for the peculiar tower settlements sprinkled across its landscape.

PATRA ΠΑΤΡΑ
pop 160,400
Patra, Greece's third-largest city, is the principal port for ferries to Italy and the Ionian Islands. Despite its long history, stretching back 3000 years, today few travellers hang around any longer than it takes to catch that next connection.

Orientation
The city is easy to negotiate and is laid out on a grid stretching uphill from the port to the old *kastro* (castle). Most services of importance to travellers are to be found along the waterfront (Othonos Amalias) in the middle of town, and Iroön Politehniou to the north. The **train station** (Othonos Amalias) is right in the middle of town, and the bus stations are close by.

Information
EOT (☎ 2610 620 353; 7am-8pm) Outside the international arrival terminal.
Info Centre (☎ 2610 461 740; infopatras@hol.gr; Othonos Amalias 6; 8am-10pm) Friendly, well-organised local information.
Main post office (cnr Zaïmi & Mezonos; 7.30am-8pm Mon-Fri, 7.30am-2pm Sat, 9am-1.30pm Sun)
National Bank of Greece (Plateia Trion Symahon; 8am-2pm Mon-Thu, 8am-1.30pm Fri & 6-8.30pm Mon-Fri) Open weekends 11am-1pm & 6-8.30pm for foreign exchange only.
Netrino Internet Café (☎ 2610 623 344; Karaïskaki 133; 10-2am) There are other Internet cafés in the surrounding area.
Tourist police (☎ 2610 451 833; 7am-9pm) Upstairs in the embarkation hall at the port.

Sights
The city's old **kastro** (8am-7pm Tue-Sun Apr-Oct, 8.30am-5pm Tue-Fri, 8.30am-3pm Sat & Sun Nov-Mar) stands on the site of the acropolis of ancient Patrai. This Byzantine fortress has great views of Zakynthos and Kefallonia. The small **archaeological museum** (☎ 2610 275 070; Mezonos 42; 8.30am-2.30pm Tue-Sun) houses a collection from the Mycenaean, Hellenic and Roma periods. Labels are in English.

Sleeping & Eating
Pension Nicos (☎ 2610 623 757; cnr Patreos & Agiou Andreou 121; s/d/tr €20/35/45, d/tr with shared bathroom €30/40) The best budget choice in town, with hot water and clean sheets. It's just up from the waterfront.

GREECE

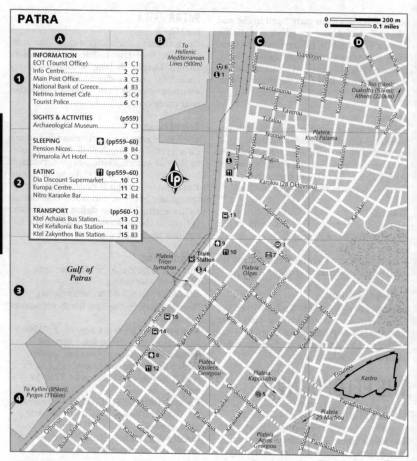

PATRA

INFORMATION
EOT (Tourist Office)..................1	C1
Info Centre.............................2	C2
Main Post Office......................3	C3
National Bank of Greece...........4	B3
Netrino Internet Café...............5	C4
Tourist Police.........................6	C1

SIGHTS & ACTIVITIES (p559)
Archaeological Museum............7	C3

SLEEPING (pp559–60)
Pension Nicos........................8	B4
Primarolia Art Hotel.................9	C3

EATING (pp559–60)
Dia Discount Supermarket........10	C3
Europa Centre.......................11	C2
Nitro Karaoke Bar..................12	B4

TRANSPORT (pp560-1)
Ktel Achaias Bus Station..........13	C2
Ktel Kefallonia Bus Station.......14	B3
Ktel Zakynthos Bus Station.......15	B3

Gulf of Patras

Primarolia Art Hotel (☎ 2610 624 900; www.arthotel .gr; Othonos Amalias; d €118-177; ☒ ▢) At the opposite end of the accommodation scale, Primarolia is a beautifully designed boutique hotel featuring original Greek art. Prices vary depending on whether you have a sea or city view.

Europa Centre (☎ 2610 437 006; Othonos Amalias 10; mains €5.50-7; ☽ 7am-midnight) A convenient cafeteria-style place close to the international ferry dock, serving up decent taverna fare and vegetarian meals.

Nitro Karaoke Bar (☎ 2601 279 357; Pantanasis 9; mains €8-10; ☽ 1pm until late) A well set up bar for transitory travellers, offering Internet access and a shower room. You'll find daily specials such as steak-and-kidney pie or shepherd's pie, Sunday roasts and a choice of English beers.

Dia Discount Supermarket (Agiou Andreou 29) Ideally located for travellers planning to buy a few provisions and keep moving.

Getting There & Away

Train is the best way to travel to Athens. Buses are faster but drop you a long way from the city centre at Terminal A on Kifissou. Trains take you close to the city centre, five minutes from Syntagma on the metro.

There are nine trains a day to Athens. Four are slow trains (€5.30, five hours) and five are intercity express trains (€10, 3½ hours). Trains also run south to Pyrgos and Kalamata.

The **Ktel Achaias bus station** (☎ 2610 623 888; Othonos Amalias) services Athens (€12.90, three hours, half-hourly) via Corinth. There are also 10 buses daily to Pyrgos (for Olympia).

Buses to the Ionian islands of Kefallonia and Lefkada leave from the **Ktel Kefallonia bus station** (☎ 2610 277 854; Othonos Amalias). Buses to Zakynthos leave from the **Ktel Zakynthos bus station** (☎ 2610 220 219; Othonos Amalias 58). These services travel via the port of Kyllini.

Daily ferries depart for Kefallonia (€11.50, 2½ hours), Ithaki (€11.70, 3¾ hours) and Corfu (€21, seven hours). Services to Italy are covered on p610. Ticket agencies line the waterfront.

DIAKOFTO–KALAVRYTA RAILWAY
ΔΙΑΚΟΦΤΟ–ΚΑΛΑΒΡΥΤΑ

This spectacular rack-and-pinion line climbs up the deep gorge of the Vouraikos River from the small coastal town of Diakofto to the mountain resort of Kalavryta, 22km away. It is a thrilling one-hour journey, with dramatic scenery all the way and it's best viewed from 1st class (€4.40) rather than 2nd (€3.70). There are four trains a day in each direction.

Diakofto is one hour east of Patra on the main train line to Athens.

CORINTH ΚΟΡΙΝΘΟΣ
pop 29,787

Modern Corinth (*ko*-rin-thoss), 6km west of the Corinth Canal, is an uninspiring town, in part due to the devastating earthquakes it has suffered through its history. It is, however, a convenient base from which to visit nearby ancient Corinth.

About 4km west of town, near the ancient port of Lecheon, the **Blue Dolphin Campground** (☎ 2741 025 766; skoupos@otenet.gr; per adult/tent €5.50/4; 🚿) is a well-organised site with its own stretch of Gulf of Corinth pebble beach. Buses from Corinth to Lecheon can drop you here.

Hotel Apollon (☎ 2741 022 587; hotapol@otenet.gr; Pirinis 18; s/d €40/50; 🚗) , near the train station, is the best of Corinth's budget hotels. The rooms are equipped with air-con and TV and rooms can go for as low as €25/30, making it good value.

As the name suggests, **Restaurant To 24 Hours** (☎ 2741 083 201; Agiou Nikolaou 19; mains €3.25-7.35) never closes, turning out an ever-changing selection of taverna favourites.

Buses to Athens (€6, 1½ hours) leave every 30 minutes from the **Ktel Korinthos bus station** (☎ 2741 075 424; Dimocratias 4) opposite the train station. This is also the departure point for buses to ancient Corinth (€0.90, 20 minutes, hourly) and Lecheon. Buses to Nafplio leave from the **Argolis bus station** (cnr Ethnikis Antistaseos & Aratou).

There are 14 daily trains to Athens, five of which are intercity services. Trains service Kalamata, Nafplio and Patra.

ANCIENT CORINTH & ACROCORINTH
ΑΡΧΑΙΑ ΚΟΡΙΝΘΟΣ & ΑΚΡΟΚΟΡΙΝΘΟΣ

The ruins of **ancient Corinth** (☎ 2741 031 207; site & museum €4; ⏰ 8am-7pm Apr-Oct, 8am-5pm Nov-Mar) lie 7km southwest of the modern city. Earthquakes and sacking by a series of invaders have left little standing of the ancient Greek city, which was one of ancient Greece's wealthiest and most wanton cities. The only ancient Greek monument remaining is the imposing **Temple of Apollo**; the others are Roman. Towering over the site is **Acrocorinth**, the ruins of an ancient citadel built on a massive outcrop of limestone.

NAFPLIO ΝΑΥΠΛΙΟ
pop 13,822

Nafplio is one of Greece's prettiest towns. The narrow streets of the old quarter are filled with elegant Venetian houses and neoclassical mansions and the setting is dominated by the towering Palamidi Fortress.

There is a **municipal tourist office** (☎ 2752 024 444; 25 Martiou; ⏰ 9am-1.30pm & 4-8pm) and **tourist police** (☎ 2752 028 131; Kountouridou 16). Good holiday reading can be found at **Odyssey Bookshop** (☎ 2752 023 430; Plateia Syntagmatos).

Sights

There are terrific views of the old town and the surrounding coast from the magnificent hill-top Palamidi Fortress (☎ 2752 028 036; admission €4; ⏰ 8am-6.45pm summer, 8am-5pm at other times), built by the Venetians between 1711 and 1714. There are also a number of small museums. Contact the tourist office for information.

Sleeping

The cheapest rooms are in the new part of town along Argous, the road to Argos. Most people prefer to stay in the old town, which is the most interesting place to be.

Unfortunately, there is very little budget accommodation here.

Hotel Economou (☎ 2752 027 721; Argonafton 22; dm €8, d/tr €30/35) This hotel is very accommodating to groups of backpackers, being flexible with sleeping arrangements depending on the number of guests.

Dimitris Bekas (☎ 2752 024 594; Efthimiopoulou 26; s/d/tr with shared bathroom €16/22/27) This is the only decent budget option in the old town. It offers top value for a great location above the church on the slopes of the Akronafplia, and the rooftop terrace has great views over the old town.

Pension Marianna (☎ 2752 024 256; www.pension marianna.gr; Potamianou 9; s/d/tr €55/60/70; 🅿) Tucked beneath the walls of the Akronafplia, at the top of Potamianou, this is the best location in town. All the rooms have wonderful views and the place is spotlessly clean.

Eating

The streets of Nafplio's old town are filled with restaurants. Staïkopoulou, in particular, is a very busy eat street.

Taverna Paleo Arhontiko (☎ 2752 022 449; cnr Ypsilandou & Sofroni; mains €4.40-7.65) One of the best tavernas in town and very popular with locals. The food's excellent and there's live music after 10pm in summer. Reservations essential on weekends.

Taverna O Vassilis (☎ 2752 025 334; Staïkopoulou 20-24; mains €4-8.50) A busy family-run place at the heart of the restaurant strip. It has a large choice of starters and a good selection of main dishes, including a very tasty rabbit *stifado* (€4.85).

Getting There & Away

The **Ktel Argolis bus station** (☎ 2752 027 323; Syngrou 8) has hourly buses to Athens (€9, 2½ hours) via Corinth, as well as services to Argos (for Peloponnese connections), Mycenae and Epidavros.

EPIDAVROS ΕΠΙΔΑΥΡΟΣ

One of the most renowned of Greece's ancient sites, World Heritage–listed **Epidavros** (☎ 2753 022 006; admission €6; 🕑 8am-7pm Apr-Oct, 8am-5pm Nov-Mar) was the sanctuary of Asclepius, the god of medicine. The **theatre** is the star of the show, but don't miss the more peaceful **Sanctuary of Asclepius** nearby, which was once a flourishing spa and healing centre.

You can enjoy the theatre's astounding acoustics first-hand during the annual Hellenic Festival, from July to August.

There are buses to Athens (€8.80, 2½ hours, two daily) and Nafplio (€2, 40 minutes, four daily), which is 30km away.

MYCENAE ΜΥΚΗΝΕΣ

Ancient Mycenae (☎ 2751 076 585; admission €6; 🕑 8am-7pm Apr-Oct, 8am-5pm Nov-Mar) was the most powerful influence in Greece from 1600–1200 BC. The rise and fall of Mycenae is shrouded in myth, but the site was settled as early as the sixth millennium BC. Described by Homer as 'rich in gold', Mycenae's entrance, the **Lion Gate**, is Europe's oldest monumental sculpture.

Excavations of **Grave Circle A** by Heinrich Schliemann in the 1870s uncovered magnificent gold treasures (such as the Mask of Agamemnon) that are now on display at the National Archaeological Museum (p549).

Most people visit on day trips from Nafplio, but there are several hotels in the modern village below the site. The **Belle Helene Hotel** (☎ 2751 076 225; fax 2751 076 179; Christou Tsounta; s/d €30/45), located on the main street, is where Schliemann stayed during the excavations.

There are three buses daily to Mycenae from Argos (€1.35, 30 minutes) and Nafplio (€2, one hour).

SPARTA ΣΠΑΡΤΗ
pop 14,817

Modern, neat and relaxed, Sparta (*spar*-tee) is in stark contrast to the ancient image of discipline and deprivation. While the Spartans left little in the way of monuments, modern Sparta makes a convenient base from which to visit Mystras.

Sparta's street grid system sees Palaeologou running north-south through the town, and Lykourgou running east-west.

Cosmos Club Internet Café (☎ 2731 021 500; Palaeologou 34; 🕑 8.30am-11pm) is located on Palaeologou, as is the **National Bank of Greece** (Palaeologou 84), which has an ATM. Tourist information is available from the **municipal tourist office** (☎ 2731 024 852; Town Hall, Plateia Kentriki; 🕑 8am-2.30pm Mon-Fri) and the **tourist police** (☎ 2731 020 492; Theodoritou 20) are also helpful. The **post office** (Archidamou 10; 🕑 7.30am-2pm Mon-Fri) is at Archidamou.

A friendly, well-organised camping ground with good facilities is **Camping Paleologou**

Mystras (☎ 2731 022 724; fax 2731 025 256; per adult/tent €4/3.50; ☺ year-round; ☒), 2km west of Sparta. It's located on the road to Mystras and buses travelling to Mystras can drop you there.

Most travellers head to the family-run **Hotel Cecil** (☎ 2731 024 980; fax 2731 081 318; Palaeologou 125; s/d €35/45; ☒) for its clean, comfortable rooms with TV.

Restaurant Elysse (☎ 2731 029 896; Palaeologou 113; mains €4.50-8.90) is run by a helpful Greek-Canadian family. It offers Lakonian specialities such as chicken *bardouniotiko* (chicken cooked with onions and feta cheese, €4.90).

Sparta's well-organised **Ktel Lakonias bus station** (☎ 2731 026 441; cnr Lykourgou & Thivronos) has buses to Athens (€13.30, 3¼ hours, 10 daily); three go to Monemvasia and two to Kalamata. There are also frequent buses to Mystras (€0.90, 30 minutes).

MYSTRAS ΜΥΣΤΡΑΣ

The magnificent **ruins of Mystras** (☎ 2731 083 377; adult/concession €6/3; ☺ 8am-6pm Apr-Oct, 8am-3.30pm Nov-Mar), 7km from Sparta, were once the shining light of the Byzantine world. The large site needs at least half a day to do it justice. The streets of Mystras are lined with palaces, monasteries and churches, most of them dating from the period between 1271 and 1460, when the town was the effective capital of the Byzantine Empire.

GEFYRA & MONEMVASIA
ΓΕΦΥΡΑ & ΜΟΝΕΜΒΑΣΙΑ

Monemvasia, 99km southeast of Sparta, might no longer be an undiscovered paradise, but tourism hasn't lessened the impact of the first encounter with this extraordinary town – nor the thrill of exploring it.

Separated from mainland Gefyra by an earthquake in AD 375, Monemvasia occupies a great outcrop of rock rising dramatically from the sea. From the causeway, a road curves around the base of the rock for about 1km, then it comes to a narrow L-shaped tunnel in the massive fortifying wall, where you emerge, blinking, into the magical town of Monemvasia.

The cobbled main street is flanked by stairways leading to a complex network of stone houses with tiny walled gardens and courtyards. Signposted steps lead to the ruins of the **fortress** built by the Venetians in the 16th century. The views are amazing, and from here you can explore the Byzantine

Church of Agia Sophia, perched precariously on the edge of the cliff.

All the practicalities are based in Gefyra. Malvasia Travel, just up from the causeway, acts as the bus stop and the National Bank of Greece and **post office** (☺ 7.30am-2pm Mon-Fri) are opposite.

Sleeping & Eating

There is no budget accommodation in Monemvasia, although there are *domatia* in Gefyra, as well as cheap hotels. If you're going to break the budget at least once in Greece though, romantic Monemvasia is certainly the place to do it.

Camping Paradise (☎ 2732 061 123; paradise@otenet .gr; per adult/tent €5/3; ☺ year-round) This pleasant, well-shaded camping ground on the coast 3.5km from Gefyra has its own minimarket, bar and big screen TV.

Hotel Monemvasia (☎ 2732 061 381; fax 2732 061 707; s/d €30/40) A small, modern hotel 500m north of Gefyra on the road to Molai. It has large balconies looking out to Monemvasia, and prices include breakfast.

Malvasia Hotel (☎ 2732 061 113; fax 2732 061 722; d €45-78, tr €60, 4-person apt €70-150; ☒) This hotel offers a variety of excellent rooms spread around the old town. Prices include an excellent breakfast. The hotel's office is on the main street of the old town.

Taverna O Botsalo (☎ 2732 061 491; Gefyra; mains €5.90-23.50) Serves up tasty meals overlooking the port in Gefyra.

Matoula (☎ 2732 061 660; Monemvasia; mains €6-12) The pick of the bunch in the old town, Matoula is on the main street and especially good if you score a table on the terrace. It's a great place to try the tasty local *barbounia* (red mullet, €10).

Getting There & Away

Buses leave from outside **Malvasia Travel** (☎ 2732 061 752), where you can pick up tickets. Four daily buses travel to Athens (€20, 5½ hours) via Sparta, Tripolis and Corinth.

The **Flying Dolphin** (www.dolphins.gr) hydrofoil service to Monemvasia has been suspended, but this may change.

GYTHIO ΓΥΘΕΙΟ

pop 4489

Once the port of ancient Sparta, Gythio (*yee-thih-o*) is a bustling and attractive fishing town at the head of the Lakonian Gulf. It is

GREECE

the gateway to the rugged Mani Peninsula to the south.

Access the Internet at **Café Mystery** (☎ 2733 025 177; cnr Kapsali & Grigoraki; ☯ 9am-1pm); there's a **post office** (cnr Ermou & Arhaia Theatrou; ☯ 7.30am-2pm Mon-Fri).

Sights

The main attraction is the picturesque **Marathonisi Islet**, linked to the mainland by a causeway. According to mythology, this islet is ancient Cranae, where Paris (prince of Troy) and Helen (the wife of Menelaus of Sparta) consummated the love affair that sparked the Trojan War. An 18th-century tower on the islet has been turned into the **Museum of Mani History** (☎ 2733 024 484; admission €1.50; ☯ 9am-7pm).

Sleeping & Eating

Camping Meltemi (☎ 2733 022 833; www.camping meltemi.gr; per adult/tent €5/4; ☯ year-round) Situated right behind the beach, 3km south of Gythio, this is the pick of the camp sites along the coast south of town. Buses to Areopoli stop outside.

Xenia Karlaftis Rooms to Rent (☎ 2733 022 719; s/d/tr €25/35/40) Opposite the causeway to Marathonisi, this is the pick of the budget options, with clean rooms and a communal kitchen.

The waterfront is lined with countless fish tavernas with similar menus. For something completely different, head inland to the tiny **General Store & Wine Bar** (☎ 2733 024 113; Vasileos Georgiou 67; mains €3.50-13; ☯ 6-11pm Mon-Sat). It has an imaginative menu featuring dishes like orange-and-pumpkin soup and fillet of pork with black pepper and ouzo.

Getting There & Away

The **Ktel Lakonias bus station** (☎ 2733 022 228; cnr Vasileos Georgios & Evrikleos) has buses to Athens (€16.30, 4¼ hours, five daily) via Sparta (€2.90, one hour), south to Areopoli (€1.80, 30 minutes, four daily), Gerolimenas (€4, 1¼ hours, two daily) and the Diros Caves (€2.50, one hour, one daily).

ANEN Lines (www.anen.gr) runs five ferries weekly to Kissamos on Crete (€19.20, seven hours) via Kythira (€8.90, 2½ hours) between June and September. The schedule varies often, so check with **Rozakis Travel** (☎ 2733 022 207; rosakigy@otenet.gr) on the waterfront before coming here to catch a boat.

THE MANI Η ΜΑΝΗ

The region referred to as the Mani covers the central peninsula in the south of the Peloponnese and is divided into two regions, the Lakonian (inner) Mani in the south and Messinian (outer) Mani in the northwest below Kalamata.

Lakonian Mani

The wild and remote Lakonian Mani has a landscape dotted with the striking stone-tower houses that are a feature of the region. The best time to visit is in spring, when the barren countryside briefly bursts into life with a spectacular display of wild flowers.

The region's principal village is **Areopoli**, about 30km southwest of Gythio. There are a number of fine towers on the narrow, cob-bled streets of the old town at the lower end of the main street, Kapetan Matepan.

Just south of here are the magnificent **Diros Caves** (☎ 2733 052 222; adult/concession €12/6; ☯ 8am-5.30pm Jun-Sep, 8am-3pm Oct-May), where a subterranean river flows. **Gerolimenas**, 20km further south, is a tranquil fishing village built around a sheltered bay.

Most of the accommodation in the Lako-nian Mani is found in Areopoli.

Tsimova Rooms (☎ 2733 051 301; Kapetan Matepan; s/d €25/40, apt €45) has cosy rooms tucked away behind the Church of Taxiarhes.

Pyrgos Kapetanakas (☎ 2733 051 233; fax 2733 051 401; s/d/tr €40/60/80; ☒) is an excellent place occupying the tower house built by the powerful Kapetanakas family at the end of the 18th century. It's signposted to the right at the bottom of Kapetan Matepan.

Popular **Nicola's Corner Taverna** (☎ 2733 051 366; Plateia Athanaton; mains €4-7), on the central square, has a good choice of tasty taverna staples.

The **bus station** (☎ 2733 051 229; Plateia Athana-ton) in Areopoli is the focal point of the local bus network. There are buses to Gythio and Sparta, two to Gerolimenas and Itilo, and one to Diros Caves. Crossing to the Messinian Mani involves changing buses at Itilo.

Messinian Mani

The Messinian Mani runs north along the coast from Itilo to Kalamata. The beaches here are some of the best in Greece, set against the dramatic backdrop of the Tay-getos Mountains.

The picturesque coastal village of **Kardam-yli**, 37km south of Kalamata, is a favourite destination for trekkers. The walks are well organised and colour-coded, and many incorporate the spectacular **Vyros Gorge**. Kardamyli has a good choice of accommodation to suit all budgets, starting with several *domatia*.

Olympia Koumounakou rooms (☎ 2721 073 623; s/d €20/28), signposted opposite the post office, is a favourite with budget travellers and has clean, comfortable beds and a communal kitchen.

Anniska Apartments (☎ 2721 073 600; anniska@ otenet.gr; studio/apt €85/90; 🎗) has a range of spacious, well-appointed studios and apartments, all with kitchen facilities. The studios sleep two people, while the larger apartments accommodate up to four.

There are several tavernas around the village, the best being **Lela's Taverna** (☎ 2721 073 541).

There are two daily buses from Kalamata to Itilo, stopping at Kardamyli and Stoupa.

OLYMPIA ΟΛΥΜΠΙΑ
pop 1286

The site of ancient Olympia lies 500m beyond the modern town of the same name, surrounded by the foothills of Mt Kronion. In ancient times, Olympia was a sacred place of temples, priests' dwellings and public buildings, as well as being the venue for the quadrennial Olympic Games. The first Olympics were staged in 776 BC, reaching the peak of their prestige in the 6th century BC. The city-states were bound by a sacred truce to stop fighting for three months and compete.

Ancient Olympia (☎ 2624 022 517; adult/concession €6/3, combined site & museum admission €9/5; 🕙 8am-7pm daily Apr-Oct, 8am-5pm Mon-Fri, 8.30am-3pm Sat & Sun Nov-Mar) is dominated by the immense, ruined **Temple of Zeus**, to whom the games were dedicated. In the **museum** (adult/concession €6/3), which keeps similar hours as the site, don't miss the statue of **Hermes of Praxiteles**, a classical sculpture masterpiece. The well-organised **municipal tourist office** (☎ 2624 023 100; Praxitelous Kondyli; 🕙 9am-9pm daily Jun-Sep, 8am-2.45pm Mon-Sat Oct-May), on the main street, changes money.

Camping Diana (☎ 2624 022 314; fax 2624 022 425; per adult/tent €5/3.85; 🕙 year-round; 🎗), located 250m west of town, is the most convenient of the three camping grounds around Olympia; it has excellent facilities.

The **youth hostel** (☎ 2624 022 580; Praxitelous Kondyli 18; dm €8) has free hot showers. There are two more good budget options around the corner on Stefanopoulou: **Pension Achilleys** (☎ 2624 022 562; Stefanopoulou 4; s/d/tr €20/30/35), a small, family-run pension (breakfast €5), and **Pension Posidon** (☎ 2624 022 567; Stefanopoulou 9; s/d/tr €20/28/36), which is good value with its clean and airy rooms.

Taverna To Steki tou Vangeli (Stefanopoulou 13; mains €2.95-6.75) represents better value than most of the tavernas around town.

There are four buses a day to Olympia from Athens (€20, 5½ hours) and regular buses to Pyrgos, 24km away on the coast.

CENTRAL GREECE
ΚΕΝΤΡΙΚΗ ΕΛΛΑΔΑ

Central Greece has a dramatic landscape and history, exemplified by its rugged mountains and fertile valleys and the ruins of ancient Delphi, where Alexander the Great sought the advice of the Delphic Oracle. Further to the north, the intriguing rock monasteries of Meteora are another highlight of this less-travelled region.

DELPHI ΔΕΛΦΟΙ
pop 2373

Like so many of Greece's ancient sites, the setting of Delphi – overlooking the Gulf of Corinth from the slopes of Mt Parnassos – is stunning. Modern Delphi is very much geared towards the number of tourists that come to visit one of Greece's major tourist attractions, but ancient Delphi is still a special place to visit.

The bus station, post office, OTE, National Bank of Greece and **EOT** (☎ 2265 082 900; Vasileon Pavlou 44; 🕙 7.30am-2.30pm Mon-Fri) are all on modern Delphi's main street, Vasileon Pavlou.

Sights
ANCIENT DELPHI

By the 6th century BC, **ancient Delphi** (☎ 2265 082 312; site or museum €6, combined admission €9, EU/ non-EU students free/€3, free Sun Nov-Mar; 🕙 7.30am-7pm Apr-Oct, 8.30am-6.45pm Tue-Fri, 8.30am-2.45pm Sat, Sun & holidays Nov-Mar) had become the Sanctuary of Apollo. Thousands of pilgrims would come to consult the oracle, who was always a peasant woman of 50 years or more. She sat at the mouth of a chasm that emitted fumes. These she inhaled, causing her to gasp, writhe and shudder in divine frenzy. After sacrificing a sheep or goat, the pilgrim would deliver a question, and a priest would translate the oracle's incoherent mumbling. Wars were fought, voyages embarked upon and business transactions undertaken on the strength of these prophecies.

The **Sacred Way** leads up from the entrance of the site to the **Temple of Apollo**. It was here that the oracle supposedly sat, and from here the path continues to the **theatre** and **stadium**. Opposite this sanctuary is the **Sanctuary of Athena** and the much-photographed **Tholos**, a 4th-century-BC columned rotunda of Pentelic marble.

Sleeping & Eating

There are lots of hotels in the modern town, catering for the many tour groups that stop overnight.

Apollon Camping (☎ 2265 082 762; apollon4@otenet .gr; per adult/tent €5/3.50; ⊠) Located 1.5km west of the modern town, Apollon is the closest camping ground to Delphi. The first-rate facilities include a restaurant, minimarket and barbecue.

Hotel Hermes (☎ 2265 082 318; cnr Vasileon Pavlou & Friderikis 27; s/d €34/40, ste €75; ⊠) A tastefully furnished and welcoming hotel in the town centre. There are some two-room family suites and many rooms have balcony views. Breakfast included.

Taverna Vakhos (☎ 2265 083 186; Apollonos 31; mains €4.50-11) This taverna turns out honest and tasty dishes such as lamb in lemon sauce with rice and potatoes (€6.50). Check out the excellent house wine and the great views.

Getting There & Away

The **bus station** (☎ 2266 082 317) sells bus tickets as well as snacks. There are six buses a day to Delphi from Athens (€10.90, three hours).

METEORA ΜΕΤΕΩΡΑ

The jutting pinnacles of Meteora (meh-*teh*-o-rah) with their stunning late-14th-century monasteries perched atop are one of Greece's most extraordinary sights. Meteora is just north of the town of Kalambaka, on the Ioannina–Trikala road. The rocks behind the town are spectacularly floodlit at night. **Kastraki**, which is 2km from Kalambaka, is a charming village of red-tiled houses just west of the monasteries.

There were once monasteries on each of the 24 pinnacles, but only six are still occupied. They are **Megalou Meteorou** (Grand Meteoron; ☻ 9am-5pm Wed-Mon), **Varlaam** (☻ 9am-2pm & 3.20-5pm Fri-Wed), **Agiou Stefanou** (☻ 9am-2pm & 3.30-6pm Tue-Sun), **Agias Triados** (Holy Trinity; ☻ 9am-12.30pm & 3-5pm Fri-Wed), **Agiou Nikolaou Anapafsa** (☻ 9am-3.30pm Sat-Thu) and **Agias Varvaras Rousanou** (☻ 9am-6pm). Admission is €2 for each monastery; free for Greeks. Bear in mind that they are religious grounds; strict dress codes apply. Women must wear skirts that reach below their knees, men must wear long trousers, and arms must be fully covered.

When looking for somewhere to stay, Kastraki is the best base for visiting Meteora.

Vrachos Camping (☎ 2432 022 293; camping-kastraki@kmp.forthnet.gr; per adult & tent €3.50, per car €1; ⊠) is an excellent camping ground on the edge of the village, with good facilities, including a market, restaurant and a barbecue.

Dupiani House (☎ 2432 075 326; dupiani-house@kmp.forthnet.gr; s/d/tr €30/45/55) is a welcoming guesthouse situated only 500m from the town square. It has spotless rooms with balconies and splendid views from the attractive garden.

Excellent traditional dishes are served at the large and lively **Taverna Paradisos** (☎ 2432 022 723; mains €4-6.50) with its superb views of the Meteora from the large terrace.

Hourly buses travel to Trikala (€1.50, 30 minutes), the region's major transport hub. There are buses to Ioannina (€8.10, three hours, two daily). Local buses shuttle constantly between Kalambaka and Kastraki; five a day continue to Metamorphosis. From Trikala, there are buses to Athens (€19.10, 5½ hours, eight daily). From Kalambaka's new station, there are express trains to Athens (€19.10, five hours, two daily). Trains also run to Thessaloniki (€9.50, four hours, two daily) and Volos (€5, 1½ hours, two daily), both changing at Paliofarsalos.

NORTHERN GREECE
ΒΟΡΕΙΑ ΕΛΛΑΔΑ

Northern Greece rewards those travellers who take the time to explore this vast region. The area comprises Epiros, with its stark and rugged mountains, Macedonia with its rich archaeological sites and shimmering lakes, and Thrace, where rolling plains front forested mountains threaded with rivers. The best reason to visit, however, is that it doesn't take much of an adventure to escape the tourist trail. Your reward is experiencing an aspect of Greece that's noticeably different to other mainland areas and islands of Greece.

IGOUMENITSA ΗΓΟΥΜΕΝΙΤΣΑ
pop 9104

The west-coast port of Igoumenitsa (ih-goo-meh-*nit*-sah), is generally known as the outpost where you catch ferries to Corfu and Italy. Few people stay here any longer than it takes to buy a ticket out.

If you need to stay the night, you'll find signs for *domatia* around the port. Try the aptly named **Rooms to Let** (☎ 2665 023 612; Xanthou 12; s/d €30/38), which is handy for the ferry and has decent enough rooms.

Alekos (☎ 2665 023 708; Ethnikis Andistasis 84; mains €3.50-5.50) is a local favourite eatery 500m north of the Corfu ferry quay. It does a fine moussaka (€3.80) and other taverna favourites.

From the **bus station** (☎ 2665 022 309; Kyprou 29), there are buses to Ioannina (€6.40, two hours, nine daily) and Athens (€29.80, eight hours, five daily).

Ferries to Corfu (€5.10, 1¾ hours, every hour) operate between 5am and 10pm.

There are international ferry services to the Italian ports of Ancona, Bari, Brindisi, Trieste and Venice. Ticket agencies are opposite the port.

IOANNINA ΙΩΑΝΝΙΝΑ
pop 61,629

Ioannina (ih-o-*ah*-nih-nah), the capital and largest town in Epiros, lies on the western shore of Lake Pamvotis. During Ottoman rule, it became a major commercial and intellectual centre. Today, Ioannina is a thriving commercial centre and university town.

The town centre is around Plateia Dimokratias where the main streets of the new town meet. All facilities of importance to travellers are nearby; there's Internet access at **The Web** (☎ 2651 026 813; Pyrsinella 21; per hr €2.50; ⏰ 24hr), regional information at the **EOT office** (☎ 2651 041 142; Dodonis 39; ⏰ 7.30am-2.30pm), and you can find out about treks in the Zagoria region with **Robinson Expeditions** (☎ 2651 029 402; www.robinson.gr; Mitropoleos 23).

Sights

The **old town** juts out into the lake on a small peninsula. Inside the impressive fortifications lies a maze of winding streets flanked by traditional Turkish houses.

The **Nisi** (island) is a serene spot in the middle of the lake, with four monasteries set among the trees. Ferries (€1) to the island leave from just north of the old town. They run half-hourly in summer and hourly in winter. For information on the decent archaeological museum and Byzantine museum, visit the EOT office.

Sleeping & Eating

Limnopoula Camping (☎ 2651 020 541; Kanari 10; per adult/tent €4.40/3; ⏰ year-round) An open, breezy camping ground right on the edge of the lake, 2km northwest of town. There's a restaurant and bar and sites are shaded.

Rooms to Rent (☎ 2651 081 786; Spileou 76, Perama; s/d €22/27) In Perama (take bus No 8), this is one of many *domatia* in the neighbourhood. Rooms are smallish but clean and pleasant and have private bathrooms.

GREECE

Galaxy Hotel (☎ 2651 025 432; fax 2651 030 724; Plateia Pyrrou; s/d €45/60; **P** ✲) On the south side of the main square, it's a pleasant modern hotel with TV and telephone. Most rooms have fine views over the lake.

To Rembetiko (☎ 2651 075 535; Plataia Georgiou 14; mains €3.50-6.50) While live *rembetika* music isn't on the menu, this eatery serves up delicious mixed platters, grills and *mezedes*.

Presveia (☎ 2651 026 309; Karamanli 17; platters €5-15; ☿ evenings) Serves up over 100 beers and good pub food to boot.

Getting There & Away

Aegean Airlines (☎ 2651 064 444) and **Olympic Airways** (☎ 2651 026 518) both fly twice a day to Athens, and Olympic has a daily flight to Thessaloniki.

The **main bus station** (☎ 2651 026 404; Zossimadon) is 300m north of Plateia Dimokratias. There are buses to Athens (€26, 7½ hours, 10 daily), Igoumenitsa (€6.40, 2½ hours, nine daily), Thessaloniki (€21.45, seven hours, five daily) and Trikala (€10, 3½ hours, two daily) via Kalambaka. For details of ferries to Italy see p610.

ZAGORIA VILLAGES & VIKOS GORGE
ΤΑ ΖΑΓΟΡΟΧΩΡΙΑ & ΧΑΡΑΔΡΑ ΤΟΥ ΒΙΚΟΥ

The Zagoria region covers a large expanse of the Pindos Mountains north of Ioannina. It's a wilderness of raging rivers, crashing waterfalls and deep gorges. Here, snow-capped mountains rise out of dense forests and the remote villages that dot the hillsides are famous for their impressive grey-slate architecture.

The fairy-tale village of **Monodendri** is the starting point for treks through the dramatic **Vikos Gorge**, with its awesome sheer limestone walls. It's a strenuous 7½-hour walk from Monodendri to the twin villages of **Megalo Papingo** and **Mikro Papingo**. The trek is very popular and the path is clearly marked. Ioannina's EOT office has more information. Other walks start from Tsepelovo, near Monodendri.

There are some wonderful places to stay, but none of them are particularly cheap. The options in Monodendri include cosy **To Kalderimi** (☎ 2653 071 510; d/tr €35/41). For food, **Haradra tou Vikou** (☎ 2653 071 559) in Monodendri specialises in fabulous *pittes* (pies).

In Megalo Papingo, you can check out **Xenonas Kalliopi** (☎ /fax 2653 041 081; s/d €34/42). It

also has a small restaurant-bar serving meals and *pittes*. Mikro Papingo has the pleasant **Xenonas Dias** (☎ 2653 041 257; www.touristorama .com; s/d €40/54). Its restaurant serves breakfast and excellent meals.

There are buses from Ioannina to Megalo and Mikro Papingo (€3.65, two hours) at 5am and 3pm Monday, Wednesday and Friday, and to Monodendri (€2.50, one hour) at 5.30am and 4.15pm daily.

THESSALONIKI ΘΕΣΣΑΛΟΝΙΚΗ
pop 788,551

Thessaloniki (thess-ah-lo-*nee*-kih), also known as Salonica, was the second city of Byzantium and is the second city of modern Greece. It's a bustling, sophisticated place with good restaurants and a busy nightlife and while it doesn't possess the monuments of the capital, it has some wonderful Byzantine churches, and a scattering of Roman ruins.

Orientation

Thessaloniki is laid out on a grid system. The main thoroughfares – Tsimiski, Egnatia and Agiou Dimitriou – run parallel to Leof Nikis, on the waterfront. Plateias Eleftherias and Aristotelous, both on Leof Nikis, are the main squares. The city's most famous landmark is the White Tower at the eastern end of Nikis.

The train station is on Monastiriou, the westerly continuation of Egnatia beyond Plateia Dimokratias, and the airport is 16km to the southeast.

Information

Bianca Laundrette (Panagias Dexias 3; ☿ 8am-8.30pm Tue, Thu & Fri, 8.30am-3pm Mon, Wed & Sat; per 6kg load €6)

Enterprise Internet Café (☎ 2310 211 722; Gounari 52; per hr €2; ☿ 9-3am)

First-aid centre (☎ 2310 530 530; Navarhou Koundourioti 10) Near the port.

Main post office (Aristotelous 26; ☿ 7.30am-8pm Mon-Fri, 7.30am-2.15pm Sat, 9am-1.30pm Sun)

National Bank of Greece (Tsimiski 11) Open Saturday and Sunday for currency exchange. There are other branches throughout the city.

Tourist information office (☎ 2310 500 310; passenger terminal Thessaloniki port; ☿ 7.30am-3pm Mon-Fri, 8am-2pm Sat)

Tourist police (☎ 2310 554 871; 5th fl, Dodekanisou 4; ☿ 7.30am-11pm)

THESSALONIKI

Eptapyrgio

Kastra (Ana Polis)

Gulf of Thessaloniki

INFORMATION	
Bianca Laundrette	1 E3
Enterprise Internet Café	2 E3
First-aid Centre	3 B4
Main Post Office	4 B4
National Bank of Greece	5 C3
Tourist Information Office	6 C3
Tourist Police	7 B2

SIGHTS & ACTIVITIES	(p570)
Archaeological Museum	8 F4
White Tower	9 E4

SLEEPING	(p570)
Hotel Acropol	10 C2
Hotel Tourist	11 C3

EATING	(p570)
Ta Nea Ilysia	12 C2
Zythos	13 B4

TRANSPORT	(p570)
Aegean Airlines	14 C3
Karaharisis Travel & Shipping Agency	15 B4
Main Bus Station	16 A2
Olympic Airways	17 A4
Smaller Bus Terminal	18 D2
Train Tickets Office (OSE)	19 D3

GREECE

See Enlargement

Ladadika

Sights

The **Archaeological Museum** (☎ 2310 830 538; Manoli Andronikou 6; ⊕ 10.30am-5pm Mon, 8.30am-3pm Tue-Sun) lost much of its lustre when the treasures of the Vergina tombs were relocated to Vergina. At the time of research, the museum was being renovated.

The 15th-century **White Tower** (☎ 2310 267 832; Lefkos Pyrgos; ⊕ 8am-6pm Tue-Sun) is the city's most prominent landmark – but be aware that it's not white. It was whitewashed after independence as a symbolic gesture, but the whitewash has now been removed.

Sleeping

Hotel Acropol (☎ 2310 536 170; fax 2310 528 492; Tandalidou 4; s/d with shared bathroom €18/26) The best budget option in town is on a quiet side street with basic but comfortable rooms.

Hotel Tourist (☎ 2310 270 501; fax 2310 226 865; Mitropoleos 21; s/d €53/67.50; ⌘) Hotel Tourist is a fine old neoclassical hotel, which has comfortable rooms with TV and air-con. Prices include buffet breakfast.

Eating & Drinking

Ta Nea Ilysia (☎ 2310 536 996; Leotos Sofou 17; mains €4-6) A popular place with travellers and locals alike, it serves up a good choice of daily specials as well as decent moussaka.

Zythos (☎ 2310 540 284; Katouni 5; mains €8) This pub-restaurant does a roaring trade, with excellent pub food and pastas and an impressive beer and wine list. It serves a decent pint of Guinness and with its outside tables, it's a great place to settle in for a couple of hours.

Mylos (☎ 2310 525 968; Andreou Georgiou 56; admission free) This huge old mill, 1km west of town, has been converted into an entertainment complex with an art gallery, restaurant, bar and live-music club (classical and rock). Catch a cab here for €8.

Getting There & Away

AIR

Olympic Airways (☎ 2310 368 666; Navarhou Koundourioti 1-3) and **Aegean Airlines** (☎ 2310 280 050; Venizelou 2) both have several flights a day to Athens (€96). Olympic also has daily flights to Ioannina, Lesvos and Limnos; three weekly to Corfu, Iraklio and Mykonos; and two weekly to Chios, Hania and Samos. Aegean also has two flights a day to Iraklio on Crete, and daily flights to Lesvos, Rhodes and Santorini.

BUS

Most of Thessaloniki's buses depart from the new **main bus station** (☎ 2310 595 408; Monastiriou 319). Destinations include Athens (€30.80, 13 daily), Ioannina (€21.45, five daily) and Volos (€12.45, seven daily).

Buses to the Halkidiki Peninsula leave from the smaller **bus terminal** (☎ 2310 924 445; Karakasi 68) in the eastern part of the city. To get there, take local bus No 10 from Egnatia to the Botsari stop.

FERRY & HYDROFOIL

There's a Sunday ferry to Lesvos (€30, 13 hours), Limnos (€20, eight hours) and Chios (€30, 18 hours) throughout the year. In summer there are at least three ferries a week to Iraklio (Crete), stopping in the Sporades and the Cyclades on the way. There are also daily hydrofoils to Skiathos, Skopelos and Alonnisos. **Karaharisis Travel & Shipping Agency** (☎ 2310 524 544; fax 2310 532 289; Navarhou Koundourioti 8) handles tickets for both ferries and hydrofoils.

TRAIN

All domestic trains leave from the **train station** (☎ 2310 517 517; Monastiriou). There are four regular trains a day to Athens (€14, 7½ hours) and seven IC or ICE services (€27.60, six hours). There are also five trains to Alexandroupolis, two of which are IC services (€16.20, 5½ hours). All international trains from Athens stop at Thessaloniki. You can get more information from the **OSE** (☎ 2310 598 120; Aristotelous 18) office or from the train station.

Getting Around

Bus No 78 plies the airport bus route – slowly. A taxi to the train station through the centre of town from the airport costs about €9 and takes about 20 minutes.

MT OLYMPUS ΟΛΥΜΠΟΣ ΟΡΟΣ

Greece's highest mountain, Mt Olympus was chosen by the ancients as the abode of their gods and assumed to be the exact centre of the earth. Olympus has eight peaks, the highest of which is Mytikas (2918m). The area is popular with trekkers, most of whom use the village of Litohoro as a base. Litohoro is 5km inland from the Athens–Thessaloniki highway. The **EOS office** (☎ 2352 084 544; Plateia Kentriki; ⊕ 9.30am-12.30pm & 6-8pm Mon-Sat) has information on various treks.

The main route to the top takes two days, with a stay overnight at one of the refuges on the mountain. Good protective clothing is essential, even in summer.

Olympios Zeus (☎ 2352 022 115; Plaka Litohorou; per adult/tent €4.50/3.20) is one of several good camping grounds with a taverna, snack bar and minimarket.

Hotel Enipeas (☎ 2352 084 328; fax 2352 081 328; Plateia Kentriki; d/tr €35/40) is bright, breezy and squeaky clean. Rooms have balconies with some of the best views of Olympus in town.

Psistaria Dias (☎ 2352 082 225; Agiou Nikolaou 36; grills €5-6) attracts hordes of locals who order the popular grills. It gets busy at night, so get in early for a table.

From the **bus station** (☎ 2352 081 271) in Litohoro there are buses to Thessaloniki (€6.20, 1½ hours, 10 daily) and Athens (€25.90, 5½ hours).

HALKIDIKI ΧΑΛΚΙΔΙΚΗ

Halkidiki is a three-pronged peninsula that extends into the Aegean Sea, southeast of Thessaloniki. It's the main resort area of northern Greece, with superb sandy beaches right around its 500km of coastline.

Kassandra, the southwestern prong of the peninsula, has surrendered irrevocably to mass tourism and is not of much interest to the independent traveller.

The **Sithonia Peninsula**, the middle prong, is not as over the top and has some spectacular scenery.

Mt Athos Αγιος Ορος

Halkidiki's third prong is occupied by the all-male Monastic Republic of Mt Athos (known in Greek as the Holy Mountain), where monasteries full of priceless treasures stand amid an impressive landscape of gorges, wooded mountains and precipitous rocks.

Obtaining a four-day visitor permit involves a bit of work. Only 10 foreign adult males may enter Mt Athos per day and there are long waiting lists in summer. You can start the process from outside Thessaloniki, but you need to travel to Thessaloniki to pick up your reservation.

You must first book a date for your visit with the **Mt Athos Pilgrims' Office** (☎ 2310 861 611; fax 2310 861 811; Leoforos Karamanli 14; ⏰ 8.30am-1.30pm & 6-8pm Mon, Tue, Thu & Fri), east of the International Exhibition Fairground in Thessaloniki. Make a telephone booking first. You

need to supply a photocopy of your passport details and, if you are Orthodox, a photocopied certificate showing your religion.

You must visit the Pilgrims' Office in person to collect the forms confirming your reservation. You can then proceed from Thessaloniki to the port of Ouranoupolis, the departure point for boats to Mt Athos, where you will be given your actual permit. Armed at last with a permit, you can explore, on foot, the 20 monasteries and dependent religious communities of Mt Athos. You can stay only one night at each monastery.

ALEXANDROUPOLIS ΑΛΕΞΑΝΔΡΟΥΠΟΛΗ
pop 49,176

While there are few sights in Alexandroupolis, its lively student atmosphere makes for a pleasant stopover on the way to Turkey or Samothraki.

One block north of the bus station, **Hotel Lido** (☎ 2551 028 808; fax 2551 025 156; Paleologou 15; s/d €35/43, with shared bathroom €27/35) has comfortable rooms and makes a good budget option.

Nea Klimataria Restaurant (☎ 2551 026 288; Plateia Polytehniou; mains €5-7) is an attractive dining space with good home-cooked fare and draught wine.

Olympic Airways and Aegean Airlines both have several flights a day to Athens (€75, 55 minutes) from the airport, 7km west of town. Several trains and buses a day travel to Thessaloniki (€20). There's also a daily train and a daily OSE bus to Istanbul.

In summer at least two boats a day head to Samothraki, dropping to one boat a day in winter. There are also hydrofoils to Samothraki and Limnos.

SARONIC GULF ISLANDS
ΝΗΣΙΑ ΤΟΥ ΣΑΡΩΝΙΚΟΥ

The five Saronic Gulf Islands are the closest island group to Athens. Their proximity to the congested capital makes them a popular escape, so accommodation is scarce between mid-June and September, and at weekends year-round.

AEGINA ΑΙΓΙΝΑ
pop 13,552

Aegina (*eh-yee-nah*) is the closest island to Athens and a popular destination for day trips. The lovely **Temple of Aphaia** (☎ 2279 032 398; adult/concession €4/2; ◷ 8am-7pm), a well-preserved Doric temple 12km east of Aegina town, is worth visiting. Buses from Aegina town to the small resort of Agia Marina can drop you at the site.

Most travellers prefer to stay in Aegina town, where the **Hotel Plaza** (☎ 2297 025 600; plazainaegina@yahoo.co.uk; s/d €20/25, d with sea view €30) is a popular choice.

HYDRA ΥΔΡΑ
pop 2719

Hydra (ee-drah) is the most stylish destination of the island group. Its gracious stone mansions are stacked up the rocky hillsides that surround the fine natural harbour. The main attraction is the tranquillity as there are no motorised vehicles – apart from sanitation and construction vehicles.

Accommodation is expensive, but of a high standard. **Pension Erofili** (☎ 2298 053 984; www.pensionerofili.gr; Tombazi; s/d/tr €40/50/60; 🌐) is a popular choice, with clean, comfortable rooms, including TV and fridge. It's about 300m from the harbour.

Once the residence of a wealthy Hydriot sea captain, the **Hotel Miranda** (☎ 2298 052 230; mirhydra@hol.gr; Miaouli; s/d/tr €75/100/150; 🌐) is a beautifully renovated mansion that has been converted to a very smart hotel.

SPETSES ΣΠΕΤΣΕΣ
pop 3916

Pine-covered Spetses is perhaps the most beautiful island in the group. Having the best beaches means it's also packed with tourists in summer. The **old harbour** in Spetses town is a delightful place to explore.

Villa Marina (☎ 2298 072 646; s/d €40/56; 🌐), located just off Plateia Agios Mamas, beyond the row of restaurants, is a small place with good rooms containing a fridge, and there's a well-equipped communal kitchen.

CYCLADES ΚΥΚΛΑΔΕΣ

The Cyclades (kih-klah-dez), named after the rough circle (kyklos) they form around the island of Delos, are what Greek island dreams are made of – rugged outcrops of rock, appealing beaches, azure waters, white cubist buildings and blue-domed Byzantine churches.

Some of the islands, such as Mykonos, Ios and Santorini (Thira), have seized tourism with great enthusiasm, while others are little more than clumps of rock, each with a village, secluded coves and a few curious tourists. Ferry services rarely run in winter, while from July to September the Cyclades are vulnerable to the *meltemi*, a fierce northeasterly wind that can cull ferry schedules.

For detailed information on the islands, check out Lonely Planet's *Greek Islands*.

History

The Cyclades enjoyed a flourishing Bronze Age civilisation (3000 to 1100 BC), more or less concurrent with the Minoan civilisation. Between the 4th and 7th centuries AD, the islands, like the rest of Greece, suffered a series of invasions and occupations. During the Middle Ages they were raided by pirates – hence the labyrinthine character of their towns, which was meant to confuse attackers. On some islands the whole population would move into the mountainous interior to escape the pirates, while on others they would brave it out on the coast. On some islands the *hora* (main town) is on the coast, and on others it is inland.

The Cyclades became part of independent Greece in 1827. Before the revival of the islands' fortunes by the tourist boom that began in the 1970s, many islanders lived in poverty and many more headed for the mainland or emigrated to America and Australia in search of work.

MYKONOS ΜΥΚΟΝΟΣ
pop 9300

The most visited and expensive of the Cyclades, Mykonos survives on tourism. The island has marvellous variety. Sun worshippers will love its beaches, party animals will struggle to escape its bars, shoppers will be trapped by its boutiques, and romantics will savour its sunsets. Add in the nearby sacred island of Delos and the fact that Mykonos is a mecca for gay travellers, and it's clear that the island has something for everybody.

Orientation & Information

Mykonos town has two ferry quays. The old quay, where most of the conventional ferries and some fast ferries dock, is 400m north of the town waterfront. The new quay is 2.5km north of town, where buses meet arriving

MYKONOS

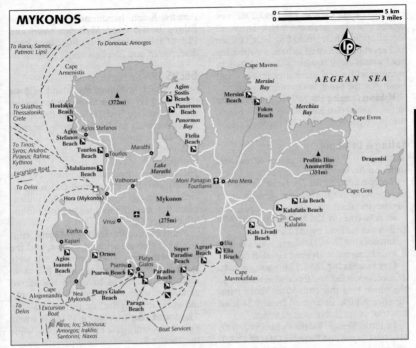

0 ————— 5 km
0 ————— 3 miles

To Ikaria; Samos;
Patmos; Lipsi

To Donousa; Amorgos

Cape
Armenistis

Cape Mavros

Mersini
Bay

AEGEAN SEA

To Skiathos;
Thessaloniki;
Crete

Houlakia
Beach

▲
(372m)

Agios
Sostis
Beach

Panormos
Beach

Mersini
Beach

Fokos
Beach

Merchias
Bay

Cape Evros

Agios Stefanos

To Tinos;
Syros; Andros;
Piraeus; Rafina;
Kythnos

Agios
Stefanos
Beach

Tourlos
Beach

Panormos
Bay

Ftelia
Beach

Marathi

Tourlos

Lake
Marathi

Profitis Ilias
Anomeritis
(351m)

Dragonisi

Excursion Boat

Malaliamos
Beach

Vothonas

Moni Panagias
Tourlianis

Ano Mera

To Delos

Cape Goni

Hora (Mykonos)

Mykonos

Lia Beach

Kalafatis Beach

Korfos

Vrissi

▲
(275m)

Cape
Kalafatis

Kapari

Kalo Livadi
Beach

Agios
Ioannis
Beach

Ornos

Psarou

Platys
Gialos

Super
Paradise
Beach

Agrari
Beach

Elia

Elia
Beach

Psarou Beach

Paradise
Beach

Cape
Mavrokefalas

Cape
Alogomandra

Nea
Mykonos

Platys Gialos
Beach

To
Delos

Excursion
Boat

Paraga
Beach

To Paros; Ios; Shinousa;
Amorgos; Iraklio;
Santorini; Naxos

Boat Services

ferries. When buying outgoing tickets, check which quay the ferry leaves from.

Angelo's Internet Café (☎ 2289 024 106; Xenias; per hr €3.50) is on the road between the southern bus station and the windmills. The post office is near the southern bus station. **Island Mykonos Travel** (☎ 2289 022 232; www.discovergreece. org; Taxi Sq), where the port road meets the town, is helpful for travel information.

Sights & Activities

Summer crowds consume the island's capital and port, shuffling through snaking streets of chic boutiques and blinding white walls with balconies of flowers. **Little Venice**, where the sea laps up to the edge of the buildings, and Mykonos' famous hill-top row of **windmills** should be included in a stroll.

The most popular beaches are **Platys Gialos**, with its wall-to-wall sun lounges, the often-nude **Paradise Beach** and mainly gay **Super Paradise**, **Agrari** and **Elia**. The less-squashy ones are **Panormos**, **Kato Livadi** and **Kalafatis**.

The amazing World Heritage–listed ancient site on nearby Delos (p574) should not be missed.

Sleeping

Rooms in town fill up quickly in high season so it's wise to go with the first *domatia* owner who accosts you. Be aware that room rates can change by the day. Outside July and August, rooms are as cheap as chops.

At the old port, the same building houses the **Hoteliers Association of Mykonos** (☎ 2289 024 540; www.mykonosgreece.com; ⏰ 9am-11pm) and the **Association of Rooms, Studios & Apartments** (☎ 2289 026 860; ⏰ 9am-10pm); both can book accommodation.

Hotel Philippi (☎ 2289 022 294; fax 2289 024 680; 25 Kalogera; s/d €60/75) Has spacious rooms and garden.

Zorzis Hotel (☎ 2289 022 167; www.zorzishotel.com; 30 Kalogera; s/d €92/115; ❄) An impressive place run by Aussie/Greek owner Jonathan. The rooms are immaculate, and if you turn up outside July/August, you'll get a bargain.

Hotel Apollon (☎ 2289 022 223; fax 2289 024 237; Paralia; s/d with shared bathroom €50/65) On the waterfront, Apollon has old-world charm.

Mykonos has two camping areas, both on the south coast. Minibuses from both meet the ferries and buses go regularly into town.

Paradise Beach Camping (☎ 2289 022 852; www .paradisemykonos.com; per person/tent €8/4) There are lots of options here, including beach cabins and apartments, as well as bars, a swimming pool, games etc. It is skin-to-skin mayhem in summer with a real party atmosphere – and nudity on the beach is not uncommon!

Mykonos Camping (☎ 2289 024 578; www.mycamp .gr; per person/tent €8/4) Near Platys Gialos beach, this place parties but is a bit more relaxed.

Eating & Drinking

There is no shortage of places to eat and drink on Mykonos.

Madupas (☎ 2289 022 224; Paralia; dishes €5-12) On the waterfront, Madupas serves a mean Mykonian sausage for €8.

Nikos Taverna (☎ 2289 024 320; Porta; dishes €4-13) Dishes out seafood by the kilo.

Antonini's (☎ 2289 022 319; Taxi Sq; dishes €3.50-12.50) A local hang-out with great Greek food.

Cavo Paradiso (☎ 2289 027 205; www.cavoparadiso .gr; admission from €20) For those who want to go the whole hog, this club 300m above Paradise Beach picks up around 2pm. A 24-hour bus transports clubbers in summer.

In Little Venice, **Katerina's Bar** (☎ 2289 023 084; Agion Anargion) and **Verandah Café** (☎ 2289 027 400; Agion Anargion) are bars with huge views.

Long feted as a gay travel destination, Mykonos has plenty of gaycentric clubs and hang-outs. **Kastro** (☎ 2289 023 072; Agion Anargion), **Diva** (☎ 2289 027 271) and **Pierro's** (☎ 2289 022 177), just near Taxi Sq, are particularly popular.

Getting There & Around

Olympic Airways (☎ 2289 022 490; Plateia Remezzo) is by the southern bus station, or call **Aegean Airlines** (☎ 2289 028 720). There are daily flights from Mykonos to Athens (€76) and to Santorini (Thira; €65). In summer, there are flights to and from Rhodes and Thessaloniki. Daily ferries arrive from Piraeus (€18.20, six hours). From Mykonos, there are daily ferries and hydrofoils to most major Cycladic islands, three services weekly to Crete (€20.50, nine hours), and less-frequent services to the northeastern Aegean Islands and the Dodecanese. Head to Island Mykonos Travel (p572) for details and tickets.

The northern bus station is near the old port. It serves Agios Stefanos, Elia, Kalafatis and Ano Mera. The southern bus station, southeast of the windmills, serves Agios Ioannis, Psarou, Platys Gialos, Ornos and Paradise Beach. In summer, *caiques* (small fishing boats) from Mykonos town and Platys Gialos putter to Paradise, Super Paradise, Agrari and Elia beaches.

DELOS ΔΗΛΟΣ

Southeast of Mykonos, the island of **Delos** (☎ 2289 022 259; admission €5; ☼ 9am-3pm Tue-Sun) is the Cyclades' archaeological jewel, and the opportunity to clamber among the ruins shouldn't be missed.

According to mythology, Delos was the birthplace of Apollo – the god of light, poetry, music, healing and prophecy. The island flourished as an important religious and commercial centre from the 3rd millennium BC, reaching its apex of power in the 5th century BC.

Ruins include the **Sanctuary of Apollo**, containing temples dedicated to him, and the **Terrace of the Lions**. These proud beasts were carved in the early 6th century BC using marble from Naxos to guard the sacred area. The original lions are in the island's museum, with replicas on the original site. The **Sacred Lake** (dry since 1926) is where Leto supposedly gave birth to Apollo, while the **Theatre Quarter** is where private houses were built around the **Theatre of Delos**.

The climb up **Mt Kynthos** (113m), the island's highest point, is a highlight. The view of Delos and the surrounding islands is spectacular, and it's easy to see how the Cyclades got their name – for the circle (*kyklos*) they form around Delos.

Numerous companies offer excursion boats from Mykonos to Delos (€7 return, 30 minutes) between 9am and 12.50pm. The return boats leave Delos between 12.20pm and 3pm. To appreciate the site, pick up a guidebook or take a guided tour. Take a sunhat, sunblock, sturdy footwear and water.

PAROS ΠΑΡΟΣ

pop 12,850

Paros is an attractive island with good swimming beaches and terraced hills that build up to Mt Profitis Ilias (770m). It is more open and laid-back than Mykonos, and is famous for its pure white marble, from which the *Venus de Milo* was sculpted.

Orientation & Information

Paros' main town and port is Parikia, on the west coast. Agora, also known as Market St,

PAROS & ANTIPAROS

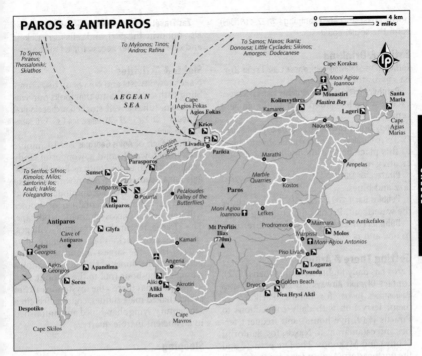

0 ——— 4 km
0 ——— 2 miles

To Syros; Piraeus; Thessaloniki; Skiathos

To Mykonos; Tinos; Andros; Rafina

To Samos; Naxos; Ikaria; Donousa; Little Cyclades; Sikinos; Amorgos; Dodecanese

Cape Korakas

AEGEAN SEA

Cape Agios Fokas
Agios Fokas

Krios

Livadia
Parikia

Pa[r]asporos

Excursion Boat

To Serifos; Sifnos; Kimolos; Milos; Santorini; Ios; Anafi; Iraklio; Folegandros

Sunset

Antiparos

Pounta

Antiparos

Antiparos

Glyfa

Cave of Antiparos

Agios Georgios

Agios Georgios

Soros

Apandima

Despotiko

Cape Skilos

Moni Agiou Ioannou

Monastiri

Kolimvythres
Plastira Bay
Kamares

Santa Maria

Lageri

Cape Agias Marias

Naoussa

Marathi

Marble Quarries

Kostos

Ampelas

Petaloudes (Valley of the Butterflies)

Paros

Moni Agiou Ioannou

Lefkes

Kamari

Mt Profitis Ilias (770m)

Prodromos

Marpissa

Marmara

Molos

Cape Antikefalos

Moni Agiou Antonios

Piso Livadi

Angeria

Aliki
Aliki Beach

Akrotiri

Dryos

Logaras

Pounda

Golden Beach

Nea Hrysi Akti

Cape Mavros

GREECE

is Parikia's main commercial thoroughfare, running from the main square, Plateia Mavrogenous (opposite the ferry terminal).

Opposite the ferry quay, to the left, is **Memphis.net** (☎ 2284 022 878; ☟ 9am-midnight; per 15min €1), which provides Internet access. There is no tourist office, but travel agencies such as **Santorineos Travel** (☎ 2284 024 245), on the waterfront, oblige with information.

Check also the **island website** (www.paros .web.com).

Sights & Activities

One of the most notable churches in Greece is Parikia's **Panagia Ekatontapyliani** (Our Lady of the Hundred Gates; ☎ 2284 021 243; ☟ 7.30am-9.30pm) for its beautiful, ornate interior.

A great option on Paros is to rent a scooter at one of the many outlets in Parikia and ride around the island. There are sealed roads the whole way round, and the opportunity to explore villages such as **Naoussa**, **Marpissa** and **Aliki**, and swim at beaches such as **Logaras**, **Pounda** and **Golden Beach**. Naoussa is a cute little fishing village that is all geared up to welcome tourists.

Less than 2km from Paros, the small island of **Antiparos** has fantastic beaches, which have made it wildly popular. The chief attraction is its **cave** (admission €3; ☟ 10.15am-3pm summer), considered to be one of Europe's best.

Sleeping

Domatia owners meet the ferries. The **Rooms Association** (☎ 2284 022 861; ☟ 9-1am) has a helpful kiosk on the quay.

Rooms Mike (☎ 2284 022 856; s/d/tr €25/35/45) Mike is a brilliant host. Walk 50m left from the port and it's next to Memphis.net.

Rooms Rena (☎ 2284 021 427; Epitropakis; s/d €25/35) These quiet and well-kept rooms are excellent value. To get here, turn left from the pier then right at the ancient cemetery.

Hotel Argonauta (☎ 2284 021 440; www.argonauta .gr; d €60; ﹟) On the main square, Argonauta has a more traditional feel.

There's loads of camping around Paros, with charges of around €6 per person and €4 per tent. **Koula Camping** (☎ 2284 022 081; Livadia beach) is about 1km north of Parikia's waterfront, **Naoussa Camping** (☎ 2284 051 565) is on the north coast and **Alyki Camping** (☎ 2284 091 303) is on the south coast.

Eating & Drinking

Zorba's (Plateia Mavrogenous; gyros €1.80) Trust Zorba's *gyros* for a quick fix.

Porphyra (☎ 2284 023 410; dishes from €5) Serves excellent fresh seafood next to the ancient cemetery.

Happy Green Cows (☎ 2284 024 691; dishes from €5; ❤ 7pm-midnight) Vegetarians should head to this place behind the main square for a creative menu.

Pirate (☎ 2284 021 114; Market St) Plays great jazz and blues.

Pebbles Bar (☎ 2284 022 283) Perched above the waterfront, Pebbles has stunning views.

Dubliner (☎ 2284 021 113) Houses three bars in one and is loud and large.

Getting There & Around

Paros has daily flights to/from Athens (€72); contact **Olympic Airways** (☎ 2284 021 900; Plateia Mavrogenous, Parikia) for details. Parikia is a major ferry hub with daily connections to Piraeus (€19, five hours) and frequent ferries and catamarans to Naxos, Ios, Santorini (Thira) and Mykonos. The Dodecanese and the northeastern Aegean Islands are also well serviced from here. Head to Santorineos Travel (p574) for tickets.

The bus station, 100m left from the port, has frequent services to the entire island. In summer there are hourly excursion boats to Antiparos from Parikia port, or you can catch a bus to Pounta and ferry it across.

NAXOS ΝΑΞΟΣ
pop 18,200

Naxos, the biggest and greenest of the Cyclades, enjoys its reputation as a family destination. The island is well worth taking time to explore with its fascinating main town, excellent beaches and striking interior.

Orientation & Information

Naxos town, on the west coast, is the island's capital and port. Court Sq is also known as Plateia Protodikiou. The island website is www.naxos-greece.net.

Naxos Tourist Information Centre (NTIC; ☎ 2285 025 201; www.naxostownhotels.com; ❤ 8am-midnight), a privately owned organisation just opposite the port, offers help with accommodation, tours, luggage storage and laundry.

Zas Travel (☎ 2285 023 330; ❤ 8am-midnight) is also opposite the port, and sells ferry tickets and offers Internet access for €4 an hour.

Sights & Activities

Naxos town twists and curves up to a crumbling 13th-century **kastro** that looks out over the town. It has a well-stocked **archaeological museum** (☎ 2285 022 725; admission €3; ❤ 8.30am-3pm Tue-Sun).

The beach of **Agios Georgios** is a 10-minute walk from town. Beyond it, wonderful sandy beaches stretch as far south as **Pyrgaki Beach**. **Agia Anna Beach**, 6km from town, and **Plaka Beach** are lined with accommodation and packed in summer. A rental car or scooter will help reveal Naxos' dramatic landscape. The **Tragea region** has tranquil villages, churches atop rocky crags and huge olive groves. **Filoti**, the largest inland settlement, perches on the slopes of **Mt Zeus** (1004m). It's a tough three-hour trail to the summit.

In Apollonas there's the mysterious 10.5m **kouros** (naked male statue), constructed circa 7th century, lying abandoned and unfinished in an ancient marble quarry.

Sleeping

Owners of *domatia* and camping grounds meet ferries, picking up those with a booking and competing for those who don't.

Pension Irene (☎ 2285 023 169; irenepension@hotmail.com; d & tr €30-60) Two locations in town – one old with OK rooms, the other one new, with a pool.

Pension Sofi (☎ 2285 023 077; www.pensionsofi.gr; d & tr €30-60) and **Studios Panos** (☎ 2285 026 078; www.studiospanos.com; Agios Georgios Beach; d & tr €30-60; ❄) are run by members of the friendly Koufopoulos family. All guests are met with a glass of family-made wine or ouzo, and rooms are immaculate with bathroom and kitchen. Rates halve out of the high season.

The three camping grounds are all south of town, charging around €5 per person. **Camping Naxos** (☎ 2285 023 500) is in a bit of a lonely spot, 2km from town. Better options are **Camping Maragas** (☎ 2285 042 552) on Agia Anna Beach, and **Plaka Camping** (☎ 2285 042 700) at Plaka Beach. There are plenty of eating options around both.

Eating & Drinking

Naxos' waterfront is lined with eating and drinking establishments.

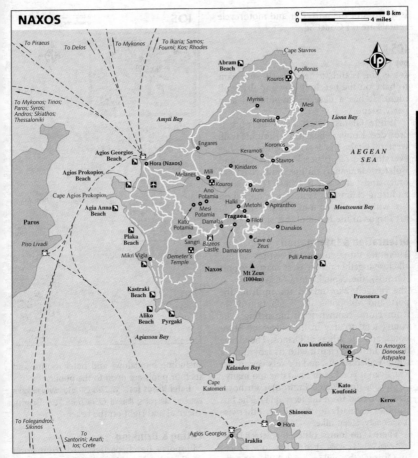

NAXOS

0 — 8 km
0 — 4 miles

To Piraeus
To Delos
To Mykonos
To Ikaria; Samos;
Fourni; Kos; Rhodes

Cape Stavros

Abram
Beach

Apollonas
Kouros

To Mykonos; Tinos;
Paros; Syros;
Andros; Skiathos;
Thessaloniki

Myrisis

Mesi

Amyti Bay

Koronida

Liona Bay

Engares
Keramoti
Koronos

Agios Georgios
Beach

Hora (Naxos)
Melanes
Mili
Kinidaros
Stavros

AEGEAN
SEA

Agios Prokopios
Beach

Kouros
Ano
Potamia
Moni
Moutsouna

Cape Agios Prokopios

Agia Anna
Beach

Halki
Metohi
Apiranthos

Moutsouna Bay

Paros

Mesi
Potamia
Tragaea
Filoti

Kato
Potamia
Damalas
Danakos

Plaka
Beach

Sangri
Bazeos
Castle

Piso Livadi

Mikri Vigla
Demeter's
Temple
Damarionas

Cave of
Zeus

Psili Amas

Naxos

Mt Zeus
(1004m)

Prassoura

Kastraki
Beach

Aliko
Beach
Pyrgaki

Agiassou Bay

Ano koufonisi
Hora
To Amorgos
Donousa;
Astypalea

Kalandos Bay

Kato
Koufonisi

Cape
Katomeri

Keros

To Folegandros;
Sikinos

Shinousa

To
Santorini; Anafi;
Ios; Crete

Agios Georgios
Hora

Iraklia

Taverna O Apostolis (☎ 2285 026 777; dishes
€1.50-2.50) A good place to try for ouzo and
mezedes. Head up the street adjacent to Zas
Travel and spot the signs.

Nikos Restaurant (☎ 2285 023 153; dishes from
€3) Seafood addicts will rave over this place
overlooking the waterfront. Fish swim in a
tank before your eyes one minute and are
on your plate the next.

Picasso Mexican Bistro (☎ 2285 025 408; dishes
€3.50-9) A stylish place that does sensational
Tex-Mex 20m off Court Sq.

A good nightlife clusters around the
southern end of the waterfront. There's
the tropical **Med Bar** and **Caesar's Club**, and if
you're up for dancing, the club **Ocean** (☺ from
11pm) goes wild after midnight. **Super Island**

Dance Club, on the Grotto Beach waterfront,
is also lively.

Getting There & Around

Naxos has daily flights to Athens (€64),
and Olympic Airways is represented by
Naxos Travel (☎ 2285 022 095). There are daily
ferries to Piraeus (€21.50, six hours) and
good ferry and hydrofoil connections to
most Cycladic islands. Boats depart once
a week to Crete, Thessaloniki and Rhodes,
and two to three times a week to Samos.
Zas Travel (p576) can provide details and
sells tickets.

Buses travel to most villages regularly
(including Apollonas and Filoti) and to the
beaches towards Pyrgaki. The bus terminal

is in front of the port. Car and motorcycle rentals are off Court Sq.

IOS ΙΟΣ
pop 1850

Ios is the island to head for if you want to bake on the beach all day and drink all night. It has a deserved reputation as a party island.

While Gialos Beach near the port is crowded, Koubara Beach, a 20-minute walk west of Gialos, is less so. Milopotas has everything a resort beach can ask for, and isolated Manganari on the south coast has four sandy crescent beaches. There is an enduring claim that Homer was buried on Ios, with his alleged tomb on the slopes of Mt Pirgos in the north of the island.

Orientation & Information

There are three population centres on Ios, all close together on the west coast: the port (Ormos); the capital, Hora (also known as 'the village'), 2km inland and up from the port; and Milopotas, the beach 1km down from Hora, renown for windsurfing. The young tend to stay in the village or Milopotas, and the others at Ormos. The village has an intrinsic charm with its labyrinth of white-walled streets, and it's very easy to get lost, even if you haven't had one too many.

The bus stop (Plateia Emirou) in Ormos is straight ahead from the ferry quay. The bus trundles regularly to the village; otherwise it's a nasty, steep hike.

There is no tourist office, but **Acteon Travel** (☎ 2286 091 343; www.acteon.gr) has four offices in Ormos, the village and Mylopotas to keep busy. Internet access costs around €4 an hour, and is scattered among hotels, cafés, bars and Acteon Travel.

Sleeping

Francesco's (☎ 2286 091 223; www.francescos.net; Hora; dm/d €10/50, d with shared bathroom €30; 🖳) A lively meeting place with superlative views from its terrace bar. All rooms have TV. Very convenient for party going, and the rates halve out of high season.

Camping los (☎ 2286 092 035; www.campingios.com; Ormos; per person €6; 🖳) Clearly visible just right of the port.

Far Out Beach Club (☎ 2286 091 468; www.farout club.com; Milopotas; camping per person €7, bungalows €15, r €25-60; 🖳🖳) This place has tons of facilities, including bungalows and hotel rooms, and its four pools are open to the public.

Hotel Nissos los (☎ 2286 091 610; www.nissosios hotel.gr; Milopotas; dm/s/d €25/55/75; 🖳) Bright, cheerful and right on the beach.

Eating & Drinking

Milopotas Beach parties hard from noon until midnight with up to 3000 people. In the village, **Porky's**, just off the main square, is a legend for cheap eats.

Ali Baba's (☎ 2286 091 558; Hora; dishes €6.50-9) Popular and parties until late. It has huge meals and a funky ambience.

Fiesta (☎ 2286 091 766; Hora; dishes from €3) A short tumble down the hill from Francesco's, Fiesta has great wood-oven pizzas.

Susana (☎ 2286 051 108; Ormos; dishes from €2.50) Hit this spot for an honest feed.

At night, the compact little village erupts with bars to explore. Perennial favourites include **Red Bull** (☎ 2286 091 019), **Slammers** (☎ 2286 092 119) and **Blue Note** (☎ 2286 092 271). Opposite the central car park, **Sweet Irish Dreams** (☎ 2286 091 141) is a crowd pleaser with table dancing.

Getting There & Around

Ios has daily ferry connections to Piraeus (€18.80, seven hours) and there are frequent hydrofoils and ferries to the major Cycladic islands. There are buses every 20 minutes between the port, the village and Milopotas Beach until early morning, and two to three a day to Manganari Beach (45 minutes). Head to Acteon Travel (p578) for details and tickets.

SANTORINI (THIRA) ΣΑΝΤΟΡΙΝΗ (ΘΗΡΑ)
pop 13,400

Stunning Santorini is something special. Visitors cannot help but gaze at the startling sight of the submerged caldera almost encircled by sheer cliffs.

Orientation & Information

The capital, Fira, perches on top of the caldera on the west coast, with the port of Athinios 10km away by road. The bus station and taxi station are located just south of Fira's main square, Plateia Theotokopoulou.

Dakoutros Travel (☎ 2286 022 958; www.dakoutros travel.gr; ◷ 8.30am-10pm), opposite the taxi sta-

tion, is extremely helpful, and there are a batch of other agencies around the square. Internet access is readily available around Fira. **Lava Internet Café** (☎ 2286 025 551; 25 Martiou; per 15min €1.50) is funky and just up from the square. The post office is one block south of the taxi station.

On the main street of Perissa, on the southeast coast, **Santosun Travel** (☎ 2286 081 456; www .santosun.gr) can book and rent you anything, and has Internet access at €3 per hour.

Sights & Activities
FIRA

The shameless commercialism of Fira has not quite reduced its all-pervasive dramatic aura. The exceptional **Museum of Prehistoric Thira** (☎ 2286 023 217; admission €3; ◷ 8.30am-3pm Tue-Sun), which has wonderful displays of artefacts predominantly from ancient Akrotiri, is two blocks south of the main square. The **Megaron Gyzi Museum** (☎ 2286 022 244; admission €3; ◷ 10.30am-1.30pm & 5-8pm Mon-Sat, 10.30am-4.30pm Sun), behind the Catholic cathedral, houses local memorabilia, including photographs of Fira before and after the 1956 earthquake.

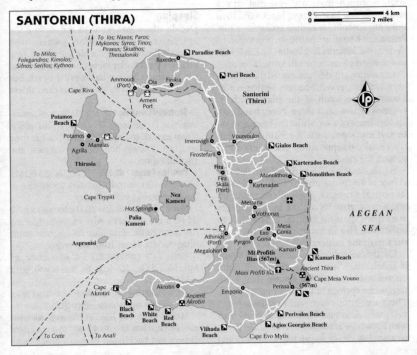

SANTORINI (THIRA)

SANTORINI'S BIG BANGS

Santorini, officially known as Thira, is regarded by many as the most spectacular of all the Greek islands. Its violent volcanic past is visible everywhere, and through the centuries eruptions have regularly changed the shape of the island.

First inhabited around 3000 BC, Santorini was circular and known as Strongili (the Round One). About 1650 BC, a massive volcanic explosion – speculated to be the biggest such explosion in recorded history – caused the centre of the island to sink, producing a caldera that the sea quickly filled in. The explosion generated a huge tsunami that caused havoc around the Aegean, and it is widely believed that the catastrophe was responsible for the demise of Crete's powerful Minoan culture.

In 236 BC further volcanic activity separated Thirasia from the main island. The islet of Palia Kameni appeared in the caldera in 197 BC, and in AD 726 a major blast catapulted pumice as far as Asia Minor. The island's south coast collapsed in 1570, while an eruption created the islet of Nea Kameni in 1707.

In 1956 an earthquake measuring 7.8 on the Richter scale pummelled the island, killing scores of people and destroying most of the houses in Fira and Oia.

One thing is for certain – it isn't over yet. Minor tremors are fairly common. Santorini is incomparable when it comes to a sense of impermanence and precariousness.

Those wishing to play in the volcanic wonderland can bake on Santorini's sizzling black-sand beaches, clamber around on volcanic lava on Nea Kameni or swim into the warm sea at Palia Kameni.

AROUND THE ISLAND

Santorini's **beaches** of black volcanic sand sizzle – beach mats are essential. It's a strange feeling to walk over black sand then out onto smooth lava when going for a dip. **Perissa** and **Kamari** are particularly popular. In Perissa, the **Santorini Dive Centre** (☎ 2286 083 190; www.divecenter.gr) can look after divers' needs.

Excavations in 1967 uncovered the remarkably well-preserved Minoan settlement of **Akrotiri** at the south of the island with its remains of two- and three-storey buildings, and evidence of a sophisticated drainage system. It's a popular site for visitors, though it's visually disappointing due to efforts to protect the ruins.

At the north of the island, the flawless village of **Oia** (pronounced ee-ah), famed for its postcard sunsets, is less hectic than Fira and a must-visit. Its caldera-facing tavernas are superb spots for brunch. It's possible to walk from Fira in about three hours along the top of the caldera.

Of the surrounding islets, only **Thirasia** is inhabited. Visitors can clamber around on volcanic lava on **Nea Kameni** then swim into warm springs in the sea at **Palia Kameni**. There are various excursions available to get you there. Also possible is a submarine tour with **Submarine Santorini** (☎ 2286 082 577; 1hr tour per person €50), or sea-kayak tours, horse riding

and wine-tasting tours. Bookings are possible at most travel agencies.

Sleeping

Decide where you want to stay before the aggressive accommodation owners who meet the boats try to decide things for you. Fira has spectacular views, but is miles from the beaches. Perissa has a great beach but is on the east coast, away from the caldera views.

Santorini Camping (☎ 2286 022 944; www.santorini camping.gr; Fira; per person €7; P ⚐) This place, 500m east of the main square, is a bit tired and lacks views, but has a restaurant and swimming pool.

Pension Petros (☎ 2286 022 573; fax 2286 022 615; Fira; s/d €55/60) Centrally located, 250m east of the square, but without views.

Maria's Rooms (☎ 2286 025 143; Agiou Mina; d €50; ⚐) On the southern edge of town, Maria's has small but immaculate rooms, and stunning caldera views from its terrace.

Hotel Keti (☎ 2286 022 324; www.hotelketi.gr; Agiou Mina; d €70; ⚐) Just to the north with caldera views to die for.

Perissa Camping (☎ 2286 081 343; Perissa; per person €7; P) Right on Perissa's beach.

Stelio's Place (☎ 2286 081 860; www.steliosplace .com; Perissa; d from €25; P ⚐ ⚐) An excellent option just back from Perissa's beach, with very friendly service and port and airport transfers.

Eating & Drinking

Taverna Lava (☎ 2286 081 776; Perissa; dishes €3-8) On Perissa's waterfront, this island-wide favourite has a mouthwatering menu. You can visit the kitchen and pick what looks good.

Naoussa (☎ 2286 024 869; Erythrou Stavrou; dishes €3-20) Excellent-value Greek classics.

Stani Taverna (☎ 2286 023 078; Erythrou Stavrou; dishes €4-15) Has a wide-ranging menu and a rooftop setting.

Nikolas (☎ 2286 024 550; Erythrou Stavrou; dishes €5-10) Receives rave reviews from diners.

Cheap eateries such as Grill House are in abundance around the square in Fira.

Most of the popular bars and clubs in Fira are clustered along Erythrou Stavrou. **Kira Thira** (☎ 2286 022 770) plays smooth jazz. Once things hot up, **Koo Club** (☎ 2286 022 025), **Enigma** (☎ 2286 022 466) and **Murphys** (☎ 2286 022 248) more than meet late-night requirements. In Perissa, the **Full Moon Bar** (☎ 2286 081 177; ⏰ 9pm-late), on the main street, goes off.

Getting There & Around

Santorini's international airport has daily flights to Athens (€85), and less regular ones to Rhodes (€90) and Mykonos (€65); call **Olympic Airways** (☎ 2286 022 493) or **Aegean Airlines** (☎ 2286 028 500) for details.

There are daily ferries to Piraeus (€22.50, nine hours), daily connections in summer to Mykonos, Ios, Naxos, Paros and Iraklio, and ferries to the smaller islands in the Cyclades. Large ferries use Athinios port, where they are met by buses (€1.20) and taxis. Get your tickets from Dakoutros Travel (p579) or Santosun Travel (p579). Small boats use Fira Skala port, where the mode of transport up to Fira is by donkey or cable car (€3); otherwise, it's a clamber up 600 steps.

Buses go frequently to Oia, Kamari, Perissa, Akrotiri, ancient Thira and Monolithos. Port buses usually leave Fira, Kamari and Perissa one to 1½ hours before ferry departures. A rental car or scooter is a great option on Santorini.

CRETE ΚΡΗΤΗ

Greece's largest and most southerly island, Crete hosts a quarter of all visitors to the country. The island is split by a spectacular chain of mountains east to west. Major towns are on the more hospitable northern coast; package-tourism industry thrives here. Most of the south coast is too precipitous to support large settlements. The mountainous interior offers rigorous trekking and climbing.

For more detailed information, snap up a copy of Lonely Planet's *Crete*. Good websites on Crete include www.interkriti.org, www.infocrete.com and www.explorecrete.com.

History

Crete was the birthplace of Minoan culture, Europe's first advanced civilisation, which flourished from 2800 to 1450 BC. Very little is known of Minoan civilisation, which came to an abrupt end, possibly destroyed by Santorini's volcanic eruption in around 1650 BC. Later, Crete passed from the warlike Dorians to the Romans, and then to the Genoese, who in turn sold it to the Venetians. Under the Venetians, Crete became a refuge for artists, writers and philosophers who fled Constantinople after it fell to the Turks. Their influence inspired the young Cretan painter Domenikos Theotokopoulos, who moved to Spain and there won immortality as the great El Greco.

The Turks conquered Crete in 1670. In 1898 it became a British protectorate after a series of insurrections and was united with independent Greece in 1913. There was fierce fighting during WWII when a German airborne invasion defeated Allied forces in the 10-day Battle of Crete. An active resistance movement drew heavy reprisals from the German occupiers.

IRAKLIO ΗΡΑΚΛΕΙΟ

pop 133,000

Iraklio, Crete's capital, is a bustling modern city and the fifth-largest in Greece. It has a lively city centre, an excellent archaeological museum and is close to Knossos, Crete's major tourist attraction.

Information

The city centre is about 500m west of the port. Banks, a stack of travel agencies and Olympic Airways are on 25 Avgoustou.

Post office (Plateia Daskalogiani)

Skoutelis Travel (☎ 2810 280 808; www.skoutelis.gr; 25 Avgoustou) Handles airline and ferry bookings, and rents cars.

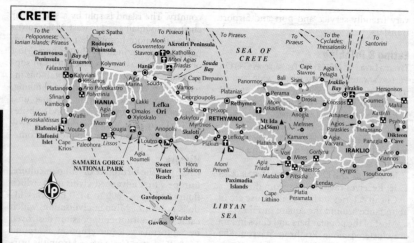

CRETE

SportC@fé (25 Avgoustou; per hr €2; 24hr) Internet access.

Tourist police (2810 283 190; Dikeosynis 10; 7am-11pm) Helpful with maps and information.

Sights & Activities

Iraklio's **archaeological museum** (2810 226 092; Xanthoudidou; adult/student €6/3; 12.30-7pm Mon, 8am-7pm Tue-Sun) has an outstanding Minoan collection, second only to the national museum in Athens. Even a superficial perusal will take half a day.

At the end of the old harbour's jetty is the impressive fortress **Rocca al Mare** (2810 246 211; adult/student €2/1; 8am-6pm Mon-Sat, 10am-3pm Sun), which, like the city walls, was built by the Venetians in the 16th century. The **Battle of Crete Museum** (2810 346 554; cnr Doukos Beaufort & Hatzidaki; admission free; 8am-3pm) chronicles the historic WWII battle with photographs, letters, uniforms and weapons.

Sleeping

Near the old harbour and bus stations is a cluster of decent mid-range hotels.

Rent Rooms Hellas (2810 288 851; Handakos 24; dm/d €10/25) A popular budget choice. It's clean, with packed dorms, a rooftop bar and a bargain breakfast.

Hotel Kronos (2810 282 240; www.kronoshotel .gr; Sofokli Venizelou 2; s/d €35/45;) This waterfront place has large, airy rooms and includes breakfast.

Hotel Mirabello (2810 285 052; www.mirabello -hotel.gr; Theotokopoulou 20; s/d €38/50;) A pleasant place in the centre of town, run by an ex-sea captain who has travelled the world. Check out the excellent website.

Hotel Kastro (2810 284 185; www.kastro-hotel .gr; Theotokopoulou 22; s/d €80/95;) Next to Mirabello, this upmarket place has large rooms with fridges, TV, phones and ISDN Internet connectivity.

Eating & Entertainment

There's a congregation of cheap eateries in the Plateia Venizelou and El Greco Park area, as well as a bustling, colourful market all the way along 1866.

Giakoumis Taverna (2810 280 277; Theodosaki 5-8; dishes €2.50-8) With its full menu of Cretan specialities, Giakoumis is the best of a bunch of cheap tavernas in the market area.

Ippokampos Ouzeri (2810 280 240; Mitsotaki 2; dishes €3.50-8) On the waterfront, this place serves up a popular, well-priced menu.

Istioploikos (2810 228 118; dishes €3-10) In an old warehouse on the harbour, this is perfect for fish lovers.

Take Five (2810 226 564; Akroleondos 7) On El Greco Park, this gay-friendly place has low-key music and ambience.

Jasmin (2810 288 880; Handakos 45) A DJ spins nightly.

Guernica (2810 282 988; Apokoronou Kritis 2) Plays contemporary music.

Getting There & Around

There are several flights a day to Athens (€76) and, in summer, regular flights to

his wife Pasiphae to fall in love with the animal. The result of this odd union was the Minotaur – half-man and half-bull – who lived in a labyrinth beneath the king's palace, munching on youths and maidens.

In 1900 Arthur Evans uncovered the ruins of Knossos. Although archaeologists tend to disparage Evans' reconstruction, the buildings – an immense palace, courtyards, private apartments, baths, lively frescoes and more – give a fine idea of what a Minoan palace might have looked like.

A whole day is needed to see the site and a guidebook is essential. Arrive early to avoid the jam. From Iraklio, local bus No 2 goes to Knossos (€0.95) every 10 minutes from Bus Station A; it also stops on 25 Avgoustou.

PHAESTOS & OTHER MINOAN SITES ΦΑΙΣΤΟΣ

Phaestos (☎ 2982 042 315; admission €4; ☉ 8am-7pm May-Oct, 8am-5pm Nov-Apr), 63km from Iraklio, is Crete's second-most important Minoan site; while not as impressive as Knossos, it's still worth a visit for its stunning views of the surrounding Mesara plain and Mt Ida. Crete's other important Minoan sites are **Malia**, 34km east of Iraklio, where there's a palace complex and adjoining town, and **Zakros**, 40km from Sitia, the smallest and least impressive of the island's palace complexes.

RETHYMNO ΡΕΘΥΜΝΟ

pop 29,000

Rethymno's gracious old quarter of crumbling Venetian and Turkish buildings is on a peninsula that juts out into the Sea of Crete; the ferry quay is on its eastern side. Hassle from restaurant touts is likely to take some of the enjoyment out of a stroll around the old quarter. El Venizelou is the main strip by the waterfront. Running parallel behind it is Arkadiou, the main commercial street.

The **Venetian fortress** (☎ 2831 028 101; Paleokastro Hill; admission €3; ☉ 8am-8pm) affords great views across the town and mountains. **Happy Walker** (☎ 2831 052 920; www.happywalker.com; Tombazi 56) runs a programme of daily walks in the countryside (€25 per person).

Galero Café (☎ 2831 054 345; per hr €4), beside the Rimondi fountain with its spouting lion heads, has Internet access. The **municipal tourist office** (☎ 2831 029 148; Eleftheriou Venizelou; ☉ 8.30am-2pm Mon-Fri) is on the beach side of El Venizelou, but is next to useless. **Ellotia Tours**

Thessaloniki and Rhodes. Get tickets from **Olympic Airways** (☎ 2810 229 191; 25 Avgoustou 27) and **Aegean Airlines** (☎ 2810 344 324; Leof Dimokratias 11). Both also have offices at the airport.

Daily ferries service Piraeus (€29.50, 10 hours), and most days boats go to Santorini (Thira) and continue on to other Cycladic islands. Head to Skoutelis Travel (p581) for schedules and tickets.

Iraklio has two bus stations. Bus Station A is just inland from the new harbour and serves eastern Crete (Agios Nikolaos, Ierapetra, Sitia, Malia and the Lasithi Plateau). The Hania and Rethymno terminal is also opposite Bus Station A.

Bus Station B, 50m beyond the Hania Gate, serves the southern route (Phaestos, Matala and Anogia). Check out www.ktel.org for long-distance bus information.

Bus No 1 travels to and from the airport (€0.70) every 15 minutes from 6am to 1am. It stops at Plateia Eleftherias, across the road from the archaeological museum.

KNOSSOS ΚΝΩΣΣΟΣ

Five kilometres south of Iraklio, **Knossos** (☎ 2810 231 940; admission €6; ☉ 8am-7pm Apr-Oct, 8am-5pm Nov-Mar) is the most famous of Crete's Minoan sites and is the inspiration for the myth of the Minotaur. According to legend, King Minos of Knossos was given a bull to sacrifice to the god Poseidon, but decided to keep it (as you would). This enraged Poseidon, who punished the king by causing

IRAKLIO

0 — 300 m
0 — 0.2 miles

SEA OF CRETE

INFORMATION	
Post Office................................1	C3
Skoutelis Travel..........................2	C1
SportC@fé................................3	C1
Tourist Police...........................4	C3

SIGHTS & ACTIVITIES	(p582)
Archaeological Museum..............5	D2
Battle of Crete Museum.............6	D2
Rocca al Mare..........................7	C1

SLEEPING	(p582)
Hotel Kastro............................8	B2
Hotel Kronos...........................9	C1
Hotel Mirabello......................10	B2
Rent Rooms Hellas...................11	B2

EATING	(p582)
Food Market..........................12	C3
Giakoumis Taverna..................13	D2
Ippokambos Ouzeri.................14	C1
Istioploïkos...........................15	D1

ENTERTAINMENT	(p582)
Guernica...............................16	B2
Jasmin..................................17	B2
Take Five..............................18	C2

TRANSPORT	(pp582–3)
Aegean Airlines.......................19	D3
Bus Station A..........................20	D2
Buses to Airport......................21	D3
Buses to Hania & Rethymno.......22	D1
Buses to Knossos....................23	D2
Buses to Knossos....................24	D2
Olympic Airways.....................25	C2

Old Harbour

New Harbour

Quay

To Ferries to Piraeus (200m);
Hersonisos (26km); Agios
Nikolaos (67km)

National Bank of Greece

El Greco Park

Morosini Fountain

Basilica of San Marco

Plateia Venizelou

Mirabelou

To Hania Gate; Bus Station B;
University Hospital at Voutes;
Rethymno (85km);
Hania (142km)

Agios Minos Cathedral

Plateia Eleftherias

To Airport (3km)

Bembo Fountain

Plateia Kornarou

(☎ 2831 051 981; www.forthnet.gr/elotia; Arkadiou 155) will answer all transport, accommodation and tour inquiries.

Elizabeth Camping (☎ 2831 028 694; per person/tent €6.30/4.20) is situated on Mysiria Beach, 4km east of town, and is accessible by the bus that goes to and from Iraklio. **Rethymno Youth Hostel** (☎ 2831 022 848; www.yhrethymno .com; Tombazi 41; dm €7) is a well-run place with crowded dorms. **Rent Rooms Sea Front** (☎ 2831 051 981; www.forthnet.gr/elotia; Arkadiou 159; 🗙), run by Ellotia Tours, has all sorts of options and is ideally positioned with beach views and spacious rooms.

Gounakis Restaurant & Bar (☎ 2831 028 816; Koroneou 6; mains from €5) is the place to go for live Cretan music and reasonably priced food. **Restaurant Symposium** (☎ 2831 050 538; www.sypo sium-kriti.gr; dishes from €3.50), near the Rimondi fountain, takes its food seriously but has good prices.

There are daily ferries from Piraeus to Rethymno (€24, 10 hours). Buses depart regularly to Iraklio (€5.90, 1½ hours), Hania (€5.30, one hour), Agia Galini, Moni Arkadiou and Plakas.

HANIA XANIA
pop 53,500

Hania (often spelt Chania) is the former capital of Crete and is the island's second-largest city. The Venetian quarter that surrounds the old harbour lures the tourists in droves. The city is a good base for exploring nearby idyllic beaches and a glorious mountain interior.

Information

Central post office (Tzanakaki 3)

Elyros Travel (☎ 2821 074 191; Plateia 1866) Can help with schedules and ticketing. There are a stack of other agencies on Halidon, the street leading down to the old harbour.

Hotel Manos (Zambeliou 24; Internet per hr €4)

Tourist information office (☎ 2821 036 155; www.chania.gr; Kydonias 29; 🕘 9am-8pm Mon-Fri, to 2pm Sat) Near Plateia 1866; very helpful staff.

Sights

The **archaeological museum** (☎ 2821 090 334; Halidon 21; admission €2; 🕘 8.30am-3pm Tue-Sun) used to be the Venetian Church of San Francesco, until the Turks made it into a mosque.

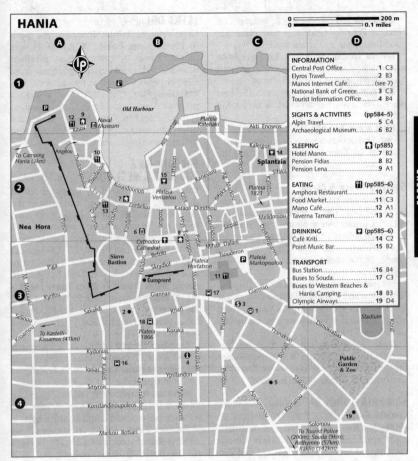

HANIA

| | 0 | 200 m |
| | 0 | 0.1 miles |

INFORMATION
Central Post Office...............1 C3
Elyros Travel...........................2 B3
Manos Internet Cafe.........(see 7)
National Bank of Greece........3 C3
Tourist Information Office........4 B4

SIGHTS & ACTIVITIES (pp584–5)
Alpin Travel...........................5 C4
Archaeological Museum........6 B2

SLEEPING (p585)
Hotel Manos..........................7 B2
Pension Fidias........................8 B2
Pension Lena.........................9 A1

EATING (pp585–6)
Amphora Restaurant.............10 A2
Food Market........................11 C3
Mano Café...........................12 A1
Taverna Tamam....................13 A2

DRINKING (pp585–6)
Café Kriti.............................14 C2
Point Music Bar...................15 B2

TRANSPORT
Bus Station..........................16 B4
Buses to Souda....................17 C3
Buses to Western Beaches &
  Hania Camping..................18 B3
Olympic Airways...................19 D4

GREECE

Hania's spectacular covered **food market** is worth a visit, even if you aren't self-catering. Part of the city wall was demolished in 1911 to make way for this cruciform creation.

Sleeping

There is a swath of sleeping options around the Venetian port.

Camping Hania (☎ 2821 031 138; per person/tent €5/3.50) Take the Hania–Stalos bus from the southeast corner of Plateia 1866 to get to this camping ground. It's 3km west of town on the beach.

Pension Fidias (☎ 2821 052 494; Sarpaki 6; dm/d/tr €9/18/27) Despite its position behind the Orthodox cathedral, Pension Fidias is still a budget choice.

Pension Lena (☎ 2821 086 860; www.travelling-crete.com/lena; Ritsou 3; s/d €28/50; ✉) A friendly pension in an old Turkish building near the mouth of the old harbour.

Hotel Manos (☎ 2821 094 156; www.manoshotel.gr; Zambeliou 24; s/d €45/55; ✉ 🖳) Big, airy rooms and an Internet café; on the waterfront.

Eating & Drinking

The entire waterfront of the old harbour is lined with restaurants and tavernas, many of which qualify as tourist traps. Watch out for touts trying to reel you in.

Amphora Restaurant (☎ 2821 093 224; Akti Koundourioti 49; mains €4.50-7) Under the hotel of the same name, you'll find this place with excellent pasta dishes and a fine reputation.

Mano Café (☎ 2821 072 265; Theotokopoulou 62) Next to Pension Lena, this tiny place has good breakfasts and snack food.

Taverna Tamam (☎ 2821 096 080; Zambeliou 49; mains €4-6.50) A taverna in an old converted Turkish bathhouse that has tasty soups.

Café Kriti (☎ 2821 058 661; Kalergon 22) The best place to hear live Cretan music while having a drink.

Point Music Bar (☎ 2821 057 556; Sourmeli 2; 🕙 9pm-2am) Serves up good rock and has an excellent 1st-floor balcony overlooking the harbour.

Getting There & Away
There are several flights a day to Athens (€74) and two flights a week to Thessaloniki (€110). Contact **Olympic Airways** (☎ 2821 057 701) or **Aegean Airlines** (☎ 2821 063 366). Daily ferries to Piraeus (€22) depart from the port of Souda, 7km east of town. Get your tickets at Elyros Travel (p584).

Frequent buses plough daily to Iraklio, Rethymno and Kastelli-Kissamos; buses run less frequently to Paleohora, Omalos, Hora Sfakion and Elafonisi from the main bus station on Kydonias.

Buses for Souda (the port) leave frequently from outside the food market. Buses for the beaches west of Hania leave from the southeastern corner of Plateia 1866.

SAMARIA GORGE ΦΑΡΑΓΓΙ ΤΗΣ ΣΑΜΑΡΙΑΣ
Samaria Gorge (☎ 2825 067 179; admission €5; 🕙 6am-3pm May–mid-Oct) is one of Europe's most spectacular gorges. Walkers should take rugged footwear, food, water and sun protection for this strenuous five- to six-hour trek, which is not recommended for inexperienced walkers.

You can do the walk as part of an excursion tour, or do it independently by taking the Omalos bus from the main bus station in Hania (€4.70, one hour) to the head of the gorge at Xyloskalo (1230m) at 6.15am, 7.30am, 8.30am or 1.45pm. It's a 16.7km walk out to Agia Roumeli on the coast, from where you take a boat to Hora Sfakion (€5, 1¼ hours, three daily) and then a bus back to Hania (€5.65, two hours, four daily).

There are daily excursions from Hania and other cities that do the whole route, and shorter ones that walk about 4km into the gorge. Check out the travel agencies in Hania and other cities for information.

LEFKA ORI ΛΕΥΚΑ ΟΡΟΙ
Crete's rugged 'White Mountains' are south of Hania. **Alpine Travel** (☎ 2821 053 309; www .alpine.gr; Bouniali 11-19, Hania) offers excellent one- to 15-day trekking programmes from €58 per person, as well as trail advice.

Trekking Plan (☎ /fax 2821 060 861; www.cycling .gr), based in Agia Marina, 8km west of Hania, is next to Santa Marina Hotel and offers mountain biking, trekking and mountaineering tours.

PALEOHORA & THE SOUTHWEST COAST ΠΑΛΑΙΟΧΩΡΑ
Paleohora, discovered by hippies back in the 1960s, has a relaxing 'at the end of the line' feel about it. Isolated and a bit hard to get to, the village is on a peninsula with a beach on each side. There's a welcoming **tourist office** (☎ 2823 041 507) three blocks south of the bus stop, but don't expect it to be up and running before June. In the main street, **Notos Rentals/Tsiskakis Travel** (☎ 2823 042 110; notosgr@yahoo.gr; Eleftheriou Venizelou) handles everything, including tickets, rental cars/scooters, laundry and Internet access (€4 per hour).

Camping Paleohora (☎ 2823 041 225; per person/ tent €4/2.50) is 1.5km northeast of town, near the pebble beach. There's also a restaurant and nightclub here.

Homestay Anonymous (☎ 2823 041 509; Paleohora; s/d €14/18) is a great place for backpackers with its warm service and communal kitchen.

Poseidon Hotel (☎ 2823 041 374; www.c-v.net /hotel/paleohora/poseidon; s/d €25/35; 🖭) is right on the beach. Rooms are equipped with kitchen facilities.

Domatia and tavernas dot the harbour. Vegetarians rave about the **Third Eye** (☎ 2823 041 234; mains €4-6). The special omelette at **Coconuts Cafetéria** (☎ 2823 041 523; dishes €3-8) is a winner.

Further east along Crete's southwest coast are **Sougia**, **Agia Roumeli** (at the mouth of the Samaria Gorge), **Loutro** and **Hora Sfakion**. Coastal paths lead from Paleohora to Sougia and from Agia Roumeli to Loutro. Both walks take a hefty six to seven hours. No road links the coastal resorts but daily boats from Paleohora to Elafonisi, Agia Roumeli and Hora Sfakion connect the villages in summer.

There are at least five buses daily between Hania and Paleohora (€5.65, two hours).

LASITHI PLATEAU ΟΡΟΠΕΔΙΟ ΛΑΣΙΘΙΟΥ

The first view of this mountain-fringed plateau, laid out like an immense patchwork quilt in eastern Crete, is marvellous. The plateau, 900m above sea level, is a vast flat expanse of orchards and fields, which was once dotted with some 1000 stone windmills with white canvas sails. Now, sadly, there are few of the originals left; most have been replaced by mechanical pumps.

The **Dikteon Cave** (☎ 2844 031 316; admission €3; ☼ 8am-4pm) is where, according to mythology, the Titan Rhea hid the newborn Zeus from Cronos, his offspring-gobbling father. The cave is just outside the small village of Psyhro, which is the best place to stay. **Zeus Hotel** (☎ 2844 031 284; s/d €23/30) is near the start of the Dikteon Cave road. On the main street, **Stavros** (☎ 2844 031 453; dishes €3-5) and **Platanos** (☎ 2844 031 668; dishes €3-5) tavernas serve decent food at OK prices.

There are daily buses to the area from Iraklio (€5.15, two hours) and three a week from Agios Nikolaos (€6.30, 2½ hours).

AGIOS NIKOLAOS ΑΓΙΟΣ ΝΙΚΟΛΑΟΣ

pop 11,000

Agios Nikolaos (ah-yee-os nih-ko-laos) may be touristy but it is an undeniably pretty former fishing village on Crete's northeast coast that is well worth a visit. The bulk of the action is around the picturesque Voulismeni Lake, about 200m from the main square of Plateia Venizelou. The lake is ringed with cafés and tavernas, and is linked to the sea by a short canal. The ferry port is 150m past the canal.

There are plenty of Internet access options at €4 per hour. The very helpful **municipal tourist office** (☎ 2841 022 357; www.aghiosnikolaos.gr; ☼ 8am-9.30pm 1 Apr-15 Nov) is on the north side of the bridge over the canal and does a good job of finding sleeping options. **Mirabello Travel** (☎ 2841 022 144; www.mirabellotravelagency .com; 13 M Sfakianakistr) handles ticketing, accommodation and car rentals.

The two nice little beaches in town get a bit crowded in summer. **Almyros Beach**, about 1km south, gets less so. Agios Nikolaos acts as a base for excursion tours to **Spinalonga Island**. The island's massive fortress was built by the Venetians in 1579, but taken by the Turks in 1715. It later became a leper colony, but nowadays is a fascinating place to explore. Tours run for around €20.

For accommodation, **Pergola Hotel** (☎ 2841 028 152; Sarolidi 20; s/d €22/32) is a good deal with clean rooms and sea views out near the ferry port. **Afrodite Rooms** (☎ 2841 028 058; Korytsas 27; s/d with shared bathroom €18/25) is comfortable.

Finding a place to eat will not be a problem. **Migomis** (☎ 2841 024 353; N Plastira 20; mains €5-10) overlooks the lake from high on the south side, providing great views and ambience. **Itanos** (☎ 2841 025 340; Kyprou 1; mains €3-10), tucked away on a back street off the main square, is superb. Head for the kitchen and pick what looks good.

Ferries depart for Rhodes (€25.80, 11 hours) via Kasos and Karpathos three times a week. There are also three weekly ferries to Piraeus (€27, 12 hours). Buses from Iraklio run every 30 minutes (€5) and six times daily to Sitia (€5.25).

SITIA ΣΗΤΕΙΑ

pop 8750

Sitia is a lovely little town in the northeastern corner of Crete that has escaped much of the package tourism along the north coast. It is on an attractive bay flanked by mountains, and is an easy place to unwind. There are good ferry connections to the Dodecanese islands.

The main square is on the waterfront, in the corner of the bay, recognisable by its palm trees and statue of a dying soldier. The ferry port is about 500m to the north, while the post office is just off the back of the square.

Porto Belis Travel (☎ 2843 022 370; www.portobelis -crete.gr; Karamanli Aven 34; ☼ 9am-8.30pm), on the waterfront just before the start of the town beach, is a one-stop shop, handling ticketing, rental cars and scooters and accommodation bookings in town. It also runs **Porto Belis Rooms and Apartments** (d/q €34/57; ✢) above the travel agency. These rooms are immaculate, have kitchens and look straight out onto the beach.

Hotel Arhontiko (☎ 2843 028 172; Kondylaki 16; s/d with shared bathroom €25/30), two streets uphill from the port, is basic but spotless.

Itanos Hotel (☎ 2843 022 900; www.itanoshotel .com; Karamanli 4; s/d €30/50; ✢ 🖳) is an upmarket establishment next to the square. It includes breakfast and a drink with dinner if you eat at its excellent **Itanos Taverna** (dishes €3-12), on the waterfront outside the front door.

The waterfront is lined with tavernas. Popular with locals is **Gato Negro** (☎ 2843 025 873;

GREECE

dishes €3-12), serving Cretan specialities. It's the closest taverna to the ferry quay. **Kali Kardia** (☎ 2843 022 249; Foundalidou 22; mains €4-6), a couple of streets back from the waterfront, is also excellent.

Sitia airport has three flights a week to Athens (€75) with **Olympic Airways** (☎ 2843 022 270). There are regular ferries from Piraeus to Sitia (€27.50, 14 hours), and three ferries per week via Karpathos to Rhodes (€23, 10 hours). Porto Belis Travel (p587) has details and sells tickets.

There are six buses daily to Ierapetra, and five to Iraklio via Agios Nikolaos. In peak season, there are four buses daily to Vaï Beach.

DODECANESE
ΔΩΔΕΚΑΝΗΣΑ

Closer to Asia Minor than mainland Greece, the 18 islands of the Dodecanese are strung out along the coast of western Turkey. Due to their strategic position they have suffered a turbulent past of invasions and occupations that has endowed them with a fascinating wealth of diverse archaeological remains.

The islands themselves are verdant and mountainous with appealing beaches. There is something for everyone in the Dodecanese. While Rhodes and Kos host highly developed tourism, the more remote islands await those in search of traditional island life.

RHODES ΡΟΔΟΣ

Rhodes (ro-dos in Greek) is the largest island in the Dodecanese and has a population of nearly 100,000. According to mythology, the sun god Helios chose Rhodes as his bride and bestowed light, warmth and vegetation upon her. The blessing seems to have paid off, for Rhodes produces more flowers and sunny days than most Greek islands.

The ancient sites of Lindos and Kamiros are legacies of Rhodes' importance in antiquity. In 1291, the Knights of St John, having fled Jerusalem, came to Rhodes and established themselves as masters. In 1522, Süleyman I, sultan of the Ottoman Empire, staged a massive attack on the island and took Rhodes City. The island, along with the other Dodecanese islands, then became part of the Ottoman Empire.

In 1912 it was the Italians, and in 1944 the Germans took over. The following year Rhodes was liberated by British and Greek commandos. In 1948 the Dodecanese became part of Greece. These days, tourists rule.

Rhodes City
pop 54,000
Rhodes' capital and port is Rhodes City, on the northern tip of the island. Almost everything of interest lies in the old town, enclosed within massive walls. The new town to the north is a monument to package tourism.

The main port, Commercial Harbour, is east of the old town, and north of here is Mandraki Harbour, the supposed site of the Colossus of Rhodes, a 32m-high bronze statue of Apollo built over 12 years (294–282 BC). The statue stood for a mere 65 years before being toppled by an earthquake. There are no remains and no tangible evidence that it actually existed, but these days you will see it on a lot of souvenir T-shirts.

INFORMATION
For information about the island, visit www .rodosisland.gr.

Main post office (Mandraki Harbour)
Mango Café Bar (☎ 2241 024 8770; Plateia Dorieos 3; per hr €5) In the old town, with Internet access.
Municipal tourist office (☎ 2241 035 945; Plateia Rimini; ☼ 8am-8pm summer only)
National Bank of Greece (Mandraki Harbour)
Tourism Directorate for the Dodecanese Islands (☎ 2241 044 335; www.ando.gr/eot; cnr Makariou & Papagou; ☼ 7.30am-3pm Mon-Fri)
Tourist police (☎ 2241 027 423) Next door to the tourism directorate.
Triton Holidays (☎ 2241 021 690; www.tritondmc.gr; 1st fl, Plastira 9) In the new town and extremely helpful, handling accommodation bookings, ticketing and rental cars. To get there, turn left after the bank.

SIGHTS & ACTIVITIES
The old town is reputedly the world's finest surviving example of medieval fortification. The 12m-thick walls are closed to the public but you can take a **guided walk** (☎ 2241 023 359; tours €6; ☼ 2.30pm Tue & Sat) along them, starting in the courtyard of the Palace of the Knights.

Odos Ippoton (Ave of the Knights) is lined with magnificent medieval buildings, the most imposing of which is the **Palace of the Knights** (☎ 2241 023 359; admission €6; ☼ 8.30am-3pm

RHODES

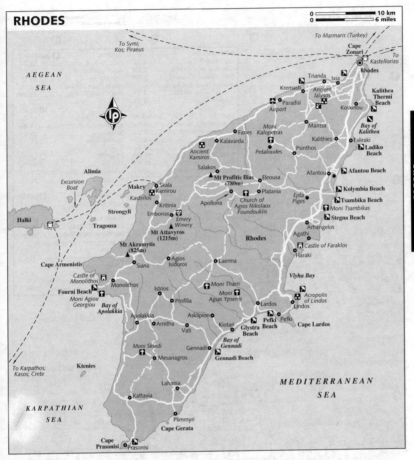

To Symi;
Kos; Piraeus

To Marmaris (Turkey)

Cape
Zonari

To
Kastellorizo

Rhodes

*AEGEAN
SEA*

Trianda   Ixia

Kremasti

Ancient
Ialysos

Kalithea
Thermi
Beach

Paradisi
Airport

Koskinou

Moni
Kalopetras

Maritsa

Bay of
Kalithea

Fanes

Kalithies

Faliraki

Kalavarda

Psinthos

Ladiko
Beach

Ancient
Kamiros

Petaloudes

Salakos

Afantou

Afantou Beach

Skala
Kamirou

▲Mt Profitis Ilias
(780m)

Eleousa

Kolymbia Beach

Makry

Platania

Epta
Piges

Tsambika Beach

Alimia

Excursion
Boat

Kastellos

Kritinia

Apollona

Church of
Agios Nikolaos
Foundoukli

Moni Tsambikas

Stegna Beach

Strongyli

Embonas

Emery
Winery

Arhangelos

Halki

Tragousa

Mt Attavyros
(1215m)

Rhodes

Agathi

Castle of Faraklos

Haraki

Mt Akramytis
(825m)

Agios
Isidoros

Laerma

Cape Armenistis

Siana

Vlyha Bay

Castle of
Monolithos

Monolithos

Istrios

Moni Tharri

Moni
Agias Ypsenis

Acropolis
of Lindos

Fourni Beach

Profilia

Lardos

Lindos

Moni Agiou
Georgiou

Bay of
Apolakkia

Apolakkia

Asklipion

Kiotari

Pefki
Beach

Pefki

Cape Lardos

Amitha

Vati

Glystra
Beach

Moni Skiadi

Gennadi

Bay of
Gennadi

*MEDITERRANEAN
SEA*

Mesanagros

Gennadi Beach

To Karpathos;
Kasos; Crete

Ktenies

Lahania

*KARPATHIAN
SEA*

Kattavia

Plimmyri

Cape Gerata

Cape
Prasonisi

Prasonisi

GREECE

0 ━━━━ 10 km
0 ━━━━ 6 miles

Tue-Sun), which was restored, but never used, as a holiday home for Mussolini.

The 15th-century Knight's Hospital now houses the **archaeological museum** (☎ 2241 027 657; Plateia Mousiou; admission €3; ⏰ 8am-5.40pm Tue-Sun). The splendid building was restored by the Italians and has an impressive collection that includes the ethereal marble statue *Aphrodite of Rhodes*. The pink-domed **Mosque of Süleyman** at the top of Sokratous was built in 1522 to commemorate the Ottoman victory against the knights, then rebuilt in 1808. The **Kahal Shalom synagogue** (www.rhodesjewishmuseum .org; Dosiadou) in the Jewish quarter has a plaque to the members of the old town's Jewish population who were sent to Auschwitz during the Nazi occupation.

SLEEPING

Rodos Youth Hostel (☎ 2241 030 491; Ergiou 12, Old Town; dm/d €8/25) Off Agio Fanouriou, this hostel has a lovely garden and a couple of excellent-value studios out the back.

Mango Rooms (☎ 2241 024 877; karelas@hotmail .com; Plateia Dorieos 3, Old Town; s/d €30/45; 🖳) Mango has a restaurant, bar and Internet café down below, and six well-kept rooms above.

Hotel Andreas (☎ 2241 034 156; www.hotelandreas .com; Omirou 28d, Old Town; s/d €50/60) Small, pleasant rooms and terrific views from its terrace.

Pink Elephant Pension (☎ 2241 022 469; www .pinkelephantpension.com; Irodotou 42, Old Town; d €32-53; ❄) Down a side street at the back of the old town, this pension has compact but clean rooms around a communal courtyard.

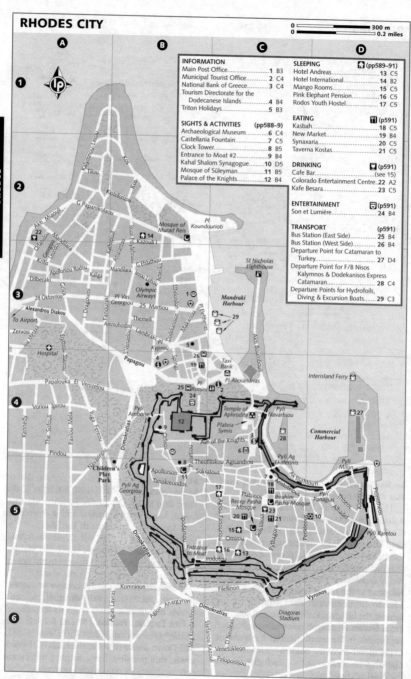

RHODES CITY

0 — 300 m
0 — 0.2 miles

INFORMATION
Main Post Office.................................1 B3
Municipal Tourist Office....................2 C4
National Bank of Greece....................3 C4
Tourism Directorate for the
  Dodecanese Islands.......................4 B4
Triton Holidays..................................5 B3

SIGHTS & ACTIVITIES   (pp588–9)
Archaeological Museum.....................6 C4
Castellania Fountain..........................7 C5
Clock Tower......................................8 B5
Entrance to Moat #2.........................9 B4
Kahal Shalom Synagogue................10 D5
Mosque of Süleyman.......................11 B5
Palace of the Knights.......................12 B4

SLEEPING   (pp589–91)
Hotel Andreas................................13 C5
Hotel International..........................14 B2
Mango Rooms.................................15 C5
Pink Elephant Pension....................16 C5
Rodos Youth Hostel.......................17 C5

EATING   (p591)
Kasbah...18 C5
New Market....................................19 B4
Synaxaria.......................................20 C5
Taverna Kostas..............................21 C5

DRINKING   (p591)
Cafe Bar..(see 15)
Colorado Entertainment Centre....22 A2
Kafe Besara....................................23 C5

ENTERTAINMENT   (p591)
Son et Lumiére...............................24 B4

TRANSPORT   (p591)
Bus Station (East Side)...................25 B4
Bus Station (West Side)..................26 B4
Departure Point for Catamaran to
  Turkey...27 D4
Departure Point for F/B Nisos
  Kalymnos & Dodekanisos Express
  Catamaran...................................28 C4
Departure Points for Hydrofoils,
  Diving & Excursion Boats.............29 C3

Hotel International (☎ 2241 024 595; diethnes@ otenet.gr; Ioannou Kazouli 12, New Town; s/d €25/35; ⊠) A real bargain in the new town with excellent facilities and a friendly owner in Prokopis.

EATING & DRINKING

There is food and drink every way you look in Rhodes. Outside the city walls, there are a lot of cheap places in the **New Market** (Mandraki Harbour), at the southern end of the harbour.

Taverna Kostas (☎ 2241 026 217; Pythagora 62, Old Town; mains €5-10) This good-value spot has stood the test of time and can't be beaten on quality.

Synaxaria (☎ 2241 036 562; Aristofanous 47, Old Town; mains €4-8) A cosy little place.

Kasbah (☎ 2241 078 633; Platonos 4-8; mains from €10; ☷ dinner) Serves some huge Moroccan-influenced meals in a refined atmosphere.

Kafe Besara (☎ 2241 030 363; Sofokleous 11, Old Town) One of the Old Town's liveliest bars.

Mango Café Bar (☎ 2241 024 877; Plateia Dorieos 3, Old Town) Mango claims to have the cheapest drinks.

Colorado Entertainment Centre (☎ 2241 075 120; cnr Akti Miaouli & Orfanidou) This enormous palace of hype consists of three drinking venues.

In the new town, head to Orfanidou in the city's northwest. The usual drink-till-you-droppers are there, and there is a bar for every nationality.

ENTERTAINMENT

Rhodes' impressive **Son et Lumière** (Sound & Light Show; ☎ 2241 021 922; www.hellenicfestival.gr; adult/concession €5/3; ☷ Mon-Sat) is held by the walls of the Old Town off Plateia Rimini. English-language sessions are staggered, but are generally at 9.15pm or 11.15pm.

AROUND THE ISLAND

The **Acropolis of Lindos** (☎ 2244 031 258; admission €6; ☷ 8.30am-6pm Tue-Sun), 47km from Rhodes City, is Rhodes' most important ancient city and is spectacularly perched atop a 116m-high rocky outcrop. Below is **Lindos** town, a tangle of streets with elaborately decorated 17th-century houses. It's beautiful but tainted by tourism. The bus to Lindos (€3.40) departs from Rhodes City's east-side station.

The extensive ruins of **Kamiros** (admission €4; ☷ 8am-5pm Tue-Sun), an ancient Doric city on the west coast, are well preserved, with the remains of houses, baths, a cemetery and

a temple, but the site should be visited as much for its lovely setting on a gentle hillside overlooking the sea.

Between Rhodes City and Lindos the **beaches** are choked. If you prefer space, venture south to the bay of **Lardos**. Even further south, between Genardi and Plimmyri, you'll find good stretches of deserted sandy beach.

GETTING THERE & AWAY

There are daily flights from Rhodes to Athens (€90) and Karpathos (€28) with **Olympic Airways** (☎ 2241 024 571) and **Aegean Airlines** (☎ 2241 024 400). In summer there are regular flights to Iraklio and Kastellorizo. Contact Triton Holidays (p588).

There are daily ferries from Rhodes to Piraeus (€33, 15 to 18 hours). Most sail via the Dodecanese north of Rhodes, but at least three times a week there is a service via Karpathos, Crete and the Cyclades.

Excursion boats (€20 return) and hydrofoils (€12.50 one way) travel daily to Symi. Ferries (€8 one way) travel less often. Similar services also run to Kos, Kalymnos, Nisyros, Tilos, Patmos and Leros.

Between April and October, there are daily boats from Rhodes to Marmaris in Turkey (one way/return €45/60).

GETTING AROUND

There are frequent buses between the airport and Rhodes City's west-side bus station (€1.70).

Rhodes City has two bus stations. The west-side bus station, next to the New Market, serves the airport, the west coast, Embona and Koskinou; the **east-side bus station** (Plateia Rimini) serves the east coast and the inland southern villages.

Car- and motorcycle-rental outlets compete for business in Rhodes City's new town, on and around 28 Oktovriou. Cars are forbidden in most of the old town but there are small car parks around the periphery.

KARPATHOS ΚΑΡΠΑΘΟΣ

pop 6000

Karpathos is an elongated, mountainous island that lies midway between Crete and Rhodes. It's a scenic, hype-free place with a cosy port, numerous beaches and unspoilt villages. It is a wealthy island, reputedly receiving more money from emigrants living abroad (mostly in the USA) than any other Greek island.

Karpathos has lovely beaches, particularly **Apella**, **Kyra Panagia**, **Lefkos** on the west coast and **Ammoöpi**, 8km south of Pigadia. The northern village of **Olympos** is like a living museum. Locals wear traditional outfits and the façades of houses are decorated with bright plaster reliefs, though with more and more tourists arriving, the village is becoming less and less 'traditional'. The main port and capital of Karpathos is Pigadia.

Enter Café (☎ 2245 029 053; 28 Oktovriou; per hr €4; ☼ 9am-2pm & 6pm-1am) has Internet access. For more information on the island, check out the websites www.inkarpathos.com and www.karpathos .com.

A booth on the harbour serves as **municipal tourist office** (☎ 2245 023 835; ☼ Jul & Aug). **Possi Travel** (☎ 2245 022 148; possitvl@hotmail.com) on the waterfront can suggest local tours and handles travel arrangements.

Pigadia accommodation owners usually meet the boats.

Elias Rooms (☎ 2245 022 446; www.eliasrooms tripod.com; Dimokratias; s/d €21/25) is a good option. Owner Elias is a mine of information for travellers, and his rooms have great views.

Harry's Rooms (☎ 2245 022 188; Kyprou 21; s/d €20/25) are central and spotless.

Hotel Titania (☎ 2245 022 144; www.titaniakar pathos.gr; Dimokratias; s/d €35/50; ❄) has spacious rooms with fridge, phone and TV.

Head for **Taverna I Orea Karpathos** (☎ 2245 022 501; mains €4-6) near the quay for traditional Karpathian dishes. Try the Karpathian goat *stifado* at **To Helliniko** (☎ 2245 023 932; dishes €3-8) on the harbour.

Karpathos has daily flights to Rhodes (€29) and five a week to Athens (€75); there is an **Olympic Airways** (☎ 2245 022 150) office on the central square in Pigadia. There are three ferries a week to Rhodes (€15.60, four hours) and four to Piraeus (€29, 19 hours) via the Cyclades and Crete. The ferries between Rhodes and Crete stop at Pigadia and the small northern port of Diafani on Karpathos. In summer there are daily excursion boats from Pigadia to Apella and Kyra Panagia beaches.

There are also excursions from Pigadia to Diafani that include a bus trip to Olympos. Local buses drop you at Lefkos and Ammoöpi beaches.

SYMI ΣΥΜΗ

pop 2600

Symi is superb. While the island itself is rocky and dry, the port town of Gialos is a Greek treasure. Pastel-coloured mansions are heaped up the hills surrounding the protective little harbour. The island is swamped by day-trippers from Rhodes; it's worth staying over to enjoy Symi in cruise control. The town is divided into Gialos, the harbour, and the tranquil *horio* (village) above it, accessible by taxi, bus, or 360 steps from the harbour.

For Internet access head to **Orange & Lemon Café** (☎ 2246 071 988; per hr €4) on the waterfront. There is no tourist office or tourist police. The best source of information is the free and widely available monthly English-language **Symi Visitor** (www.symivisitor.com), which includes maps of the town.

Kalodoukas Holidays (☎ 2246 071 077; www.symi -greece.com) handles accommodation bookings, ticketing and has a book of trails on the island that you can walk independently. **Symi Tours** (☎ 2246 071 307; www.symitours.com) runs a trip to Datça in Turkey (€35) on Saturdays.

Budget accommodation is scarce. **Rooms Katerina** (☎ 2246 071 813, 6945 130 112; d €25-30) is excellent, but get in quick as there are only three rooms. There is a communal kitchen with breathtaking views. **Pension Catherinettes** (☎ 2246 071 671; marina-epe@rho.forthnet.gr; d €55) has airy rooms. It's in the building on the waterfront where the treaty surrendering the Dodecanese to the Allies was signed in 1945. Located back from the excursion boats is **Hotel Albatros** (☎ 2246 071 707; www.albatrosymi.gr; d €50), where breakfast is included.

Bella Napoli (☎ 2246 072 456; pizzas from €5) serves exceptional wood-fired pizzas while, next door, **Vapori Bar** (☎ 2246 072 082) is open all day. Drop by to use the Internet or read the free newspapers by day, or for drinks and cruising at night. **Taverna Neraida** (☎ 2246 071 841; mains from €5), back from the waterfront by the square, has good food and intriguing old photos of Symi on its walls.

There are frequent ferries and hydrofoils between Rhodes and Kos that also call at Symi, as well as less-frequent services to Tilos, Nisyros, Kalymno, Leros and Patmos. The bus and taxi stop is at the east end of the harbour, past the restaurants. Excursion boats visit inaccessible east-coast beaches daily in summer, including spectacular **Agios Georgious**, backed by a 150m sheer cliff.

KOS ΚΩΣ

pop 17,900

Only 5km from the Turkish peninsula of Bodrum, Kos is a long, narrow island with a mountainous spine. Hippocrates, the father of medicine, was born on Kos, but that's as Greek as this place gets. With its ruins and Turkish buildings on a backdrop of pretty palm-lined streets, neon cafés, pulsing clubs and tourist trains, Kos town, the main town and port, exudes an aura of mini Las Vegas.

Information

Café Del Mare (☎ 2242 024 244; Megalou Alexandrou 4; per hr €4) The best-equipped Internet café.

Municipal tourist office (☎ 2242 024 460; www .hippocrates.gr; Vasileos Georgiou 1; ☺ 8am-8pm Mon-Fri, 8am-3pm Sat May-Oct) On the waterfront directly south of the port, it provides maps and accommodation information.

Pulia Tours (☎ 2242 026 388; www.laumzis.gr) Handles schedules, ticketing, money exchange, excursions and rental cars.

Tourist police (☎ 2242 022 444) Housed with the regular police, just opposite the quay.

Sights & Activities

The focus of the **archaeological museum** (☎ 2242 028 326; Plateia Eleftherias; adult/student €3/2; ☺ 8am-2.30pm Tue-Sun) is sculpture from excavations around the island. The **ancient agora**, with the ruins of the **Shrine of Aphrodite** and **Temple of Hercules**, is just off Plateia Eleftherias. It's free but has zero data. North of the agora is the **Hippocrates Plane Tree**, under which the man himself is said to have taught his pupils.

On a pine-clad hill, 4km southwest of Kos town, stand the extensive ruins of the re-nowned healing centre of **Asklipieion** (☎ 2242 028 763; adult/student €4/3; ☺ 8.30am-6pm Tue-Sun), where Hippocrates practised medicine.

At the southern end of Kos is **Kefalos Bay**, a long stretch of beach swamped in sun lounges and rippling with water sports.

Sleeping

Pension Alexis (☎ 2242 028 798; fax 2242 025 797; Iro-dotou 9; s/d €23/29) This highly-recommended place has long been a budget favourite with travellers. It has large rooms and shared fa-cilities. Try the legendary feta omelette for breakfast. It's back behind Dolphin Sq.

Hotel Afendoulis (☎ 2242 025 321; afendoulishotel@ kos.forthnet.gr; Evripilou 1; s/d €29/42) Looking for a superior hotel with well-kept rooms in

a quieter area? Head south from the ferry quay, walk about 500m to Evripilou and turn right.

Nitsa Studios (☎ 2242 025 810; Averof 37; d €30-50) North of the harbour and a street back from the beach, Nitsa's rooms have a bathroom, kitchen and balcony.

Kos Camping (☎ 2242 023 910; per adult/tent €4.50/2.50) This spot, 3km along the eastern waterfront, has good shade and a mini-market. Hop on any of the buses going to Agios Fokas from the harbour.

Eating & Drinking

Restaurants line the central waterfront, but you might want to hit the backstreets for value. There are a dozen discos and clubs catering to the different music moods of the crowd around the streets of Diakon and Nafklirou, just north of the agora.

Barbas (☎ 2240 027 856; Evripilou 6; mains €4-7) Opposite Hotel Afendoulis, Barbas special-ises in grills and has an excellent chicken souvlaki.

Taverna Hirodion (☎ 2242 026 634; Artemisias 27; mains €5-8) This place serves good, inexpensive food. Try the pork fillet in brandy sauce.

Olympiada (☎ 2242 023 031; mains €4-6) Back in the ruins area, Olympiada serves up reliable Greek dishes.

Fashion Club (☎ 2242 022 592; Kanari 2) Off Dol-phin Sq, this monster has three bars.

Kalua (☎ 2242 024 938; Akti Zouroudi 3) You'll find Kalua by the beach to the north of the harbour. No shortage of bars around that area either.

Getting There & Around

There are daily flights to Athens (€82) from Kos' international airport with **Olympic Air-ways** (☎ 2242 028 330). The airport is 28km from Kos town.

There are frequent ferries from Rhodes that continue on to Piraeus (€27, 12 to 15 hours) via Kalymnos, Leros and Patmos, and less-frequent connections to Nisyros, Tilos, Symi, Samos and Crete. Daily excursion boats visit Nisyros, Kalymnos, Patmos and Rhodes. In summer, ferries depart daily for Bodrum (ancient Halicarnassus) in Turkey (one way/return €20/34). Get details and tickets at Pulia Tours (see above).

Next to the tourist office is a blue mini-train for Asklipion (€3, hourly) and a green mini-train that does city tours (€2).

Buses for Agios Fokas leave from opposite the town hall on the harbour; all other buses (including those to Kefalos Bay) leave from the bus station on Kleopatras, near the ruins at the back of town.

PATMOS ΠΑΤΜΟΣ
pop 3050

Orthodox and Western Christians have long made pilgrimages to Patmos, for it was here that St John wrote his revelations. Not only the religiously motivated will enjoy Patmos, though. It has a mix of qualities that are instantly palatable.

Information

For information on the island, visit www .patmosweb.gr. The *Patmostimes*, an excellent English-language magazine, is readily available.

Blue Bay Hotel (per hr €4), 200m south from the port, has Internet access. The **tourist office** (☎ 2247 031 666; ☾ 8am-6pm Mon-Fri summer only), post office and police station are in the white building at the island's port and capital of Skala. Buses leave regularly for the *hora*, 4.5km inland.

Apollon Travel (☎ 2247 031 324; apollon@12net .gr), on the waterfront, handles schedules and ticketing.

Sights & Activities

The **Cave of the Apocalypse** (☎ 2247 031 234; ☾ 8am-1.30pm daily, 4-6pm Tue, Thu & Sun), where St John wrote the divinely inspired *Book of Revelations*, is halfway between the port and *hora*. Take a bus or make the pilgrimage via the **Byzantine path**. To do this, walk up the Skala–Hora road and take the steps to the right 100m beyond the far side of the football field. The path begins opposite the top of the steps.

The **Monastery of St John the Theologian** (☎ 2247 031 223; admission monastery/treasury free/€5; ☾ 8am-1.30pm daily, 4-6pm Tue, Thu & Sun) looks more like a castle than a monastery and crowns the island. It exhibits monastic treasures: early manuscripts, embroidered robes, incredible carvings and an El Greco painting.

Patmos' coastline provides secluded coves, mostly with pebble beaches. The best is **Psili Ammos**, in the south, reached by excursion boat from Skala port. **Lambi Beach**, on the north coast, is a pebble-beach lover's dream come true.

Sleeping & Eating

There is a cluster of sleeping options about 500m to the north of the port.

Hotel Australis (☎ 2247 031 576; www.patmosweb .gr/australis; d incl breakfast €40-60) This place has private facilities, a family church on site and an oasis-like garden that has featured in *Garden Design* magazine. Australis also has apartments in town.

Villa Knossos (☎ 2247 032 189; fax 2247 032 284; d €25-50; ✕) Next door to Australis, this place has exceptional rooms.

Blue Bay Hotel (☎ 2247 031 165; www.bluebay.50g .com; s/d €54/68; ✕ ▢) There are great rooms here, 200m south of the port.

Stefanos Camping (☎ 2247 031 821; per person/ tent €6/3) On the pleasant tree-shaded Meloi Beach, 2km northeast of Skala, this spot has a minimarket and café-bar.

Grigoris Taverna (☎ 2247 031 515; mains €4-8) Opposite the port gate, this is a popular spot.

Kipos Garden Restaurant (☎ 2247 031 884; dishes €3-8) Head here for home-grown vegetable dishes such as fried aubergines.

Aman (☎ 2247 032 323) Has a tree-shaded patio and relaxing music.

Getting There & Away

Patmos is well connected, with ferries to Piraeus (€22, eight hours) and to Rhodes (€19, 7½ hours) via Leros, Kalymnos and Kos. In summer, there are daily Flying Dolphin hydrofoils to Leros, Kalymnos, Kos, Rhodes, Fourni, Ikaria, Agathonisi and Samos. Head to Apollon Travel (see above) for details and tickets.

NORTHEASTERN AEGEAN ISLANDS
ΤΑ ΝΗΣΙΑ ΤΟΥ ΒΟΡΕΙΟΑΝΑΤΟΛΙΚΟ ΑΙΓΑΙΟΥ

This group consists of seven major islands that are strewn across the northeastern corner of the Aegean, closer to Turkey than mainland Greece. Turkish influence is barely visible, despite the islands being part of the Ottoman Empire until 1912. Though island-hopping can be tricky due to their far-flung nature, these islands remain relatively calm even in the heights of summer and reward exploration with wonderful hiking, crowd-free beaches and unique villages.

SAMOS ΣΑΜΟΣ
pop 32,800

Birthplace of mathematician Pythagoras and storyteller Aesopus, Samos was an important centre of Hellenic culture. A mountainous island only 3km from Turkey, it is lush and humid with spectacular beaches, a huge variety of flora and fauna, and is worth more than a casual glance.

Samos has two main ports: Vathy (Samos town) in the northeast and Pythagorio on the southeast coast. Those coming from the south generally arrive in Pythagorio. Big ferries use Vathy. Once you're there and have onward tickets, double-check where your boat is leaving from. Buses between the two take 25 minutes. **By Ship Travel** (☎ 2273 025 065; www.byshiptravel.gr) has offices at both ports that handle schedules and ticketing.

Pythagorio Πυθαγόρειο

Pretty Pythagorio, where you'll disembark if you've come from Patmos, is small and attractive. The bus stop is on the main street, about 300m from the waterfront heading inland, on your left.

The cordial **municipal tourist office** (☎ 2273 061 389; deap5@otenet.gr; Lykourgou Logotheti; ⏰ 8am-10pm) is two blocks from the waterfront on the main street. By Ship Travel is next door. **Digital World** (☎ 2273 062 722; per hr €5; ⏰ 11am-2pm & 5-11pm) provides Internet access across the street.

The **Evpalinos Tunnel** (☎ 2273 061 400; adult/student €4/2; ⏰ 8.45am-2.45pm Tue-Sun), built in the 6th century BC, is a 1km tunnel dug by political prisoners and used as an aqueduct to bring water from the springs of Mt Ampelos (1140m). Part of it can still be explored. It's a 20-minute walk north of town. If you feel like reminiscing about maths study, there's an excellent **statue of Pythagoras** and his triangle on the waterfront opposite the ferry quay.

Pension Sydney (☎ 2273 061 733; Pythagora; d €30), a block in from the waterfront, is immaculate with private facilities. **Pension Philoxenia** (☎ 2273 061 055; Polykratous; s/d €20/30; ✶), on the road to Vathy, but still close, also has private bathrooms, a huge communal kitchen and dining room, and is a good option.

Iliad Café-Bar (☎ 2273 062 207), on the waterfront and run by Sandy, a Kiwi, is an excellent spot to start or finish the evening. Try the Pythogorian Sunset. Mama's Plate of the Day at **Espirides Garden-Tavern** (☎ 2273 061 767; Pythagora; mains from €5) is the stuff legends are made of, while the food at **Poseidonas Neptune Taverna** (☎ 2273 062 530; mains from €5), on the small town beach, is superb.

Vathy (Samos) Βαθύ Σάμος

Busy Vathy, 25 minutes from Pythagorio by bus, is more of a working town. Its **archaeological museum** (☎ 2273 027 469; adult/student €3/2; ⏰ 8.30am-3pm Tue-Sun), by the municipal gardens, is first rate. The highlight is a 4.5m male *kouros* statue.

The rarely open and hard-to-find **tourist office** (☎ 2273 028 530; ⏰ summer only) is in a side street one block north of the main square, Plateia Pythagorou. **ITSA Travel** (☎ 2273 023 605; www.itsatravel.com), opposite the quay, is helpful with travel inquiries, excursions, accommodation and luggage storage. To get to Vathy's bus station, follow the waterfront and turn left onto Lekati, 250m south of Plateia Pythagorou (just before the police station). **Diavlos NetCafé** (☎ 2273 022 469; per hr €3), beside the bus station, offers Internet access.

Pythagoras Hotel (☎ 2273 028 601; www.pythagorashotel.com; Kallistratou; s/d/tr/q €20/26/33/36; 💻) is a friendly, great-value place with a convivial atmosphere. There is a restaurant, bar, satellite TV and Internet access on site. Facing inland, the hotel is 500m to the left of the quay. Call ahead for pick up on arrival. **Pension Avli** (☎ 2273 022 939; Areos 2; d €28), back up to the left behind the main square, is in a former Roman Catholic convent and built around a lovely courtyard.

The Garden (☎ 2273 024 033; Manolis Kalomiris; mains €4-9) serves good Greek food in a lovely garden setting up to the left behind the main square. **La Calma** (☎ 2273 022 654; Kefalopoulou 7; mains from €6), to the north of the port, has outstanding views. **Ovaga** (☎ 2273 025 476; Kefalopoulou 13), near La Calma, serves up tasty cocktails on its stunning terrace by the water.

Around Samos

Ireon (☎ 2273 095 277; adult/student €3/2; ⏰ 8.30am-3pm Tue-Sun), the legendary birthplace of the goddess Hera, is 8km west of Pythagorio. The temple at this World Heritage site was enormous – four times the Parthenon – though only one column remains.

GREECE

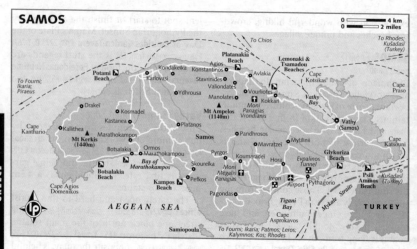

The captivating villages of **Vourliotes** and **Manolates**, on the slopes of imposing Mt Ampelos, northwest of Vathy, provide excellent walking territory and have many marked pathways.

Choice beaches include **Tsamadu** and **Platanakia** on the north coast, **Botsalakia** in the southwest and **Psili Amos** to the east of Pythagorio.

Getting There & Around

There are daily flights to Athens (€75) from the airport at Pythagorio, and twice weekly to Thessaloniki (€90) with **Olympic Airways** (☎ 2273 027 237).

There are daily ferries for Piraeus (€24, 13 hours) – most via Paros and Naxos, and some via Mykonos – and Ikaria, but only three a week visit Chios (€10.70, four hours). Daily hydrofoils ski to Patmos (€13.20, 1¼ hours), carrying on to Leros, Kalymnos and Kos. There are daily ferries to Kuşadası (for Ephesus) in Turkey (€45 return plus €21 port taxes). Day excursions are also available from April to October.

You can get to most of the island's villages and beaches by bus, except for Manolates. Agios Konstantinos, 4km away, is its closest bus stop. Rental cars and scooters are readily available around the island.

CHIOS ΧΙΟΣ
pop 54,500

Due to its thriving shipping and mastic industries (mastic produces the resin used in chewing gum) Chios (*hee*-os) has never really bothered much with tourism. The chief attraction lies in exploring its inland villages.

Information

Chios town is a working port and not really a place to linger. It is, however, a good base for day trips to Turkey.

Aegan Travel (☎ 2271 041 277; aegeantr@otenet.gr; Leof Aigaiou 14) On the waterfront; handles ticketing.

Enter Internet Café (☎ 2271 026 108; Leof Aigaiou 48; per hr €3.60) Slick café upstairs on the southern waterfront.

Municipal tourist office (☎ 2271 044 389; infochio@ otenet.gr; Kanari 18; ☼ 7am-10pm Apr-Oct, 7am-4pm Nov-Mar) On the main street that runs from the waterfront to Plateia Vounakiou, the main square. Staff members are extremely helpful and provide information on accommodation, schedules and rentals. The publication *Hiking Routes on Chios* is available at no charge.

Post office (Rodokanaki) One block back from the waterfront.

Sights & Activities

In Chios town, **Philip Argenti Museum** (☎ 2271 023 463; admission €1.50; ☼ 8am-2pm Mon-Fri, 5-7.30pm Fri, 8am-12.30pm Sat) contains the treasures of the wealthy Argenti family.

World Heritage–listed **Nea Moni** (New Monastery; ☼ 8am-1pm & 4-8pm) is 14km west of Chios town and reveals some of the finest Byzantine art in the country, with mosaics dating from the 11th century. The mosaics survived, but the resident monks were massacred by the Turks in 1822. Those in the ghost village of **Anavatos**, 10km from Nea Moni and built on a precipitous cliff, preferred a different fate, hurling themselves off the cliff rather than being taken captive by the Turks. Currently the village is being spruced up in the hope of attracting visitors.

Chios' southern Mastihohoria (mastic villages) were spared in the 1822 massacres thanks to the Turkish fondness for mastic chewing gum. **Pyrgi**, 24km southwest of Chios town, is one of Greece's most unusual villages. The façades of the town's dwellings are decorated with intricate grey and white geometric patterns and motifs. The tiny medieval town of **Mesta**, 10km from Pyrgi and nestled within fortified walls, has four entry gates, two ornate churches and cobbled streets connected by overhead arches.

Sleeping & Eating

The tourist office gives out a practical accommodation guide for the town and villages.

Chios Rooms (☎ 2271 020 198; Leoforos Aigaiou 110; s/d/tr with shared bathroom €20/26/35) On the waterfront at the opposite end of the harbour from the ferry dock, Chios Rooms has bright, airy rooms in a building that oozes rustic charm.

Hotel Kyma (☎ 2271 044 500; kyma@chi.forthnet.gr; Evgenias Chandris 1; s/d incl breakfast €46/60; 🔌) Around the corner from Chios Rooms, this place has helpful owners and tons of character.

To Meliotiko Ouzeri (☎ 2271 040 407; dishes from €3) On the waterfront to the right of the ferry disembarkation point, you'll get huge helpings of Greek classics.

Taverna Hotzas (☎ 2271 042 787; Kondyli 3; dishes from €3.50) Excellent food and ambience 15 minutes' walk south of the town crush.

Getting There & Around

There are daily flights from Chios to Athens (€69) with **Olympic Airways** (☎ 2271 020 359). Ferries sail daily to Piraeus (€19.50, eight hours) via Lesvos (€12, three hours), and weekly to Thessaloniki (€30, 18 hours) via Lesvos and Limnos. There are three ferries a week to Samos (€10.70, four hours).

Boats to Turkey run all year from Chios, with daily sailings from July to September to Çeşme (one way/return €40/50 plus €9 port tax). For details, check out **Miniotis Lines** (☎ 2271 024 670; www.miniotis.gr; Neorion 24).

Chios has two bus stations. Blue buses go regularly to local villages and Karfas and Kontari beaches, and leave from the right side (coming from the waterfront) of

Plateia Vounakiou, by the garden. Green long-distance buses to Pyrgi and Mesta leave from the station one block back to the left of Plateia Vounakiou.

LESVOS (MYTILINI) ΛΕΣΒΟΣ (ΜΥΤΙΛΗΝΗ)

The third largest of the Greek islands, fertile Lesvos has always been a centre of philosophy and artistic achievement and still attracts creative types on sabbatical. Spoil yourself with a taste of the island's prized olive oil, ouzo and sardines, or relax in its therapeutic hot springs. An excellent source of information on the island is www.greeknet.com.

Mytilini Μυτιλήνη
pop 27,250

The capital and main port, Mytilini, is a large, dreary working town. **Sponda** (☎ 2251 041 007; Komninaki; per hr €2), has impressive Internet access a block back from the waterfront in a pool bar. The **tourist police** (☎ 2251 022 776) are at the entrance to the quay. The **tourist office** (☎ 2251 042 511; 6 Aristarhou; 🕑 9am-1pm Mon-Fri), 50m up Aristarhou by the quay, offers brochures and maps, but is open limited hours.

Samiotis Tours (☎ 2251 042 574; samiotistours@ hotmail.com; Kountourioti 43), 400m from the ferry on the waterfront, handles flights, boat schedules, ticketing and excursions to Turkey.

SIGHTS & ACTIVITIES

Mytilini's excellent neoclassical **archaeological museum** (☎ 2251 022 087; 8 Noemvriou; adult/senior for both museums €3/2; 🕑 8.30am-7pm Tue-Sun) has a fascinating collection from Neolithic to Roman times. The **new archaeological museum** (8 Noemvriou; 🕑 8.30am-7pm Tue-Sun) displays spectacular mosaics from ancient households. Follow the signposts from the ferry.

Theophilos Museum (☎ 2251 041 644; admission €2; 🕑 9am-2.30pm & 6-8pm Tue-Sun), 4km south of Mytilini in Varia village, is a shrine to the prolific folk painter Theophilos.

Five kilometres from Mytilini, on the Gulf of Year, are the **Therma hot springs** (☎ 2251 024 575; admission €2.50; 🕑 8am-6pm), where you can bathe in a steamy white room overlooking the water and mountains. The experience is highly recommended.

SLEEPING

Salina's Rooms (☎ 2251 024 640; cnr Fokeas & Kinikiou; s/d €25/30) Clean rooms, a garden and a kitchen for guest use.

Pension Thalia (☎ 2251 042 073; Kinikiou 1; s/d €25/30) Virtually next door and run by the same people as Salina's, this pension has clean, bright rooms in a large house. It is about a five-minute walk north of the main square, up Ermou.

Porto Lesvos Hotel (☎ 2251 022 510; www .portolesvos.gr; Komninaki 21; s/d €60/90; 🖳) A newish hotel in a restored building one block back from the waterfront.

EATING & DRINKING

Ocean Eleven Bar (Kountourioti 17) In the corner on the waterfront, this is an excellent place to start or end the evening.

Restaurant Averof (☎ 2251 022 180; Ermou 52; mains from €4) Hearty Greek staples such as *patsas* are dished up just back from the main square.

Via Alla Pasta (☎ 2251 037 717; Mitropoleous 22; mains from €7) Top-quality Italian dishes are served in this place behind Ocean Eleven Bar just off the waterfront.

GETTING THERE & AROUND

There are daily flights to Athens (€78) and to Thessaloniki (€88), five a week to Limnos (€46) and two a week to Chios (€28) with **Olympic Airways** (☎ 2251 028 659) and **Aegean Airlines** (☎ 2251 061 120).

In summer, there are daily boats to Piraeus (€24, 12 hours), some via Chios, Mykonos and Syros, and one boat a week to Thessaloniki (€30, 13 hours). There is also one ferry a week to Skiathos (€26) in the Sporades group. There are four ferries a week to Ayvalik in Turkey (one way/return

€30/45). Stop by Samiotis Tours (p597) for ticketing and schedules.

Mytilini has two bus stations. For local buses, walk along the waterfront to the main square, where buses leave regularly for Therma and Varia. For long-distance buses, walk 600m from the ferry along the waterfront to El Venizelou and turn right until you reach Agia Irinis park, which is next to the station. There are regular services in summer to Mithymna, Petra, Agiasos, Skala Eresou, Mantamados and Agia Paraskevi.

Mithymna Μήθυμνα
pop 1500

The gracious, preserved town of Mithymna (known by locals as Molyvos) is 62km north of Mytilini. Cobbled streets canopied by flowering vines wind up the hill below the impressive castle. The town is full of cosy tavernas and genteel stone cottages. You'll be tempted never to leave this scenic place.

ORIENTATION & INFORMATION

There are three Internet cafés along the port road. From the bus stop, walk straight ahead towards the town for 100m to the helpful **municipal tourist office** (☎ 2253 071 347; www .mithymna.gr; 🕑 8am-9pm Mon-Fri, 9am-7pm Sat & Sun), which has good maps. A further 50m on, take the right fork onto 17 Noemvriou, the cobbled main thoroughfare, or continue straight ahead to reach the colourful fishing port.

Panatella Holidays (☎ 2253 071 520; www.pana tella-holidays.com), just before the fork, handles bookings and runs all kinds of local trips, including Donkey Days (ride a donkey!).

SAPPHO, LESBIANS AND LESVOS

If you saw *My Big Fat Greek Wedding*, you may remember that Toula's father had a passion for showing how virtually every word in common usage in English today can be traced back to Greek. He even found a way to show that the word *kimono* has Greek origins. One he didn't come up with at the wedding party though was the word lesbian. He would undoubtedly be aware, however, of the word's origins.

One of Greece's great ancient poets, Sappho, was born on the island of Lesvos during the 7th century BC, in the town of Eresos. Her poetry quickly became famous for its lyrically evocative style and richly sumptuous imagery. Most of Sappho's work was devoted to love and desire and the objects of her affection were often female. Owing to this last fact, her name and birthplace have come to be associated with female homosexuality. There is an excellent statue of Sappho taking pride of place in the main square on the waterfront in Mytilini.

These days, Lesvos is visited by many lesbians paying homage to Sappho. The whole island is very gay-friendly, in particular the southwestern beach resort of Skala Eresos, which is built over ancient Eresos, Sappho's birthplace.

SIGHTS & ACTIVITIES

The noble **Genoese castle** (☎ 2253 071 803; admission €2; ☺ 8am-7pm Tue-Sun) sits above the town like a crown and affords tremendous views out to Turkey.

Eftalou hot springs (☎ 2253 071 245; public/private baths per person €3.50/5; ☺ public baths 10am-2pm & 4-8pm, private baths 9am-4pm), 4km from town on the beach, is a superb bathhouse complex with a whitewashed dome and steaming, pebbled pool. The views are new private baths where you don't need a bathing suit.

Pebbly **Mithymna Beach** sits below the town. Don't forget to stroll down to the harbour.

SLEEPING & EATING

There are over 50 *domatia* in Mithymna.

Nassos Guest House (☎ 2253 071 432; nassosguesthouse@hotmail.com; Arionis; d/tr €25/30) An airy, friendly, traditional place with shared facilities and a communal kitchen. The views are rapturous. To get there, head up 17 Noemvriou and take the second right (a sharp switchback).

Marina's Rooms (☎ 0253 071 470; d €26-30) On the main road just short of the port, Marina's has excellent facilities.

Betty's Restaurant (☎ 2253 071 421; Agora; mains from €5) Betty's has superb views and atmosphere in a building that was once a notorious bordello. Ask Betty about the old photos on the wall.

Captain's Table (☎ 2253 071 241; mains from €5) At the end of the port road, this busy spot does Greek fare with flair. There is a swath of bars down at the port.

GETTING AROUND

In summer, buses go regularly to Petra Beach and Eftalou. Excursion boats leave the port daily for Skala Sykaminias. Car- and scooter-hire outlets line the port road.

Around the Island

East of Mithymna, the traditional picturesque villages surrounding Mt Lepetymnos (**Sykaminia**, **Mantamados** and **Agia Paraskevi**) are worth your time.

Southern Lesvos is dominated by **Mt Olympus** (968m) and the very pretty day-trip destination of **Agiasos**, which has good artisan workshops.

SPORADES ΣΠΟΡΑΔΕΣ

There are 11 islands in the Sporades group, four of which are inhabited. Skiathos has the best beaches and a throbbing tourist scene, while Skopelos is more relaxed, with a postcard waterfront, sandy bays and lush forest trails. Alonnisos is far less visited and retains more local character. The National Marine Park of Alonnisos, encompassing seven islands, is aimed at protecting the Mediterranean monk seal – a welcome innovation in a country not noted for protecting its fauna.

The main ports for the Sporades are Volos and Agios Konstantinos on the mainland.

SKIATHOS ΣΚΙΑΘΟΣ
pop 6150

Lush and green, Skiathos has a beach-resort feel about it. An international airport has brought loads of package tourists, but the island still oozes enjoyment. There are plenty of good beaches with water sports on the south coast, particularly Koukounaries.

Orientation & Information

Skiathos town's main thoroughfare is Papadiamanti, running inland opposite the quay. **Internet Zone Café** (☎ 2427 022 767; per hr €3; ☺ 10.30-1am) is off Papadiamanti, 100m up Evangelistrias, on your right just before you reach the post office, and the helpful **tourist police** (☎ 2427 023 172; ☺ 8am-9pm).

There's a **tourist information booth** (☎ 2427 023 172) to the left as you leave the port, but it opens irregularly. **Travel Agency Skiathos** (☎ 2427 022 209; www.skiathosoe.com; cnr Papadiamantis & waterfront) organises travel schedules and tickets. **Heliotropio Travel** (☎ 2427 022 430; helio@skiathos.gr), just nearby, runs excellent excursions, including a day trip to Skopelos and Alonnisos (€20).

Skiathos has excellent beaches, particularly on the south coast. **Koukounaries** is popular with families. A stroll over the headland, **Big Banana Beach** is superb, but if you want an all-over tan, head a tad further to **Little Banana Beach**, where bathing suits are a rarity.

Sleeping

The **Rooms to Let** (☎ 2427 022 990) bookings kiosk on the waterfront opens when ferries and hydrofoils arrive. *Domatia* owners meet ferries.

Pension Pandora (☎ 2427 024 357, 6979 156 019; www.skiathosinfo/accommodation/pansionpandora; Paleokastro; s/d/q €30/45/60; **P** **✺**) Run by the effervescent Georgina, this superb place is 10 minutes' walk north of the quay. The 14 rooms have TV, kitchens and balconies. Georgina also has two exceptional apartments just off Papadiamanti.

Apartments Filitsa (☎ 2427 021 185; Metaxa; apt €30-100; **✺**) In the old part of town near Panagia Theotokos church, these two-bedroom apartments sleep from two to six people, have fully-equipped kitchens and are perfect for a long stay.

Hotel Marlton (☎ 2427 022 552; fax 2427 022 878; s/d €40/55) This place is friendly and has fresh, pine-furnished rooms. To get there from Papadiamanti, turn right onto Evangelistrias and walk 50m.

Camping Koukounaries (☎ 2427 049 250; per person/ tent €6/3) This camping ground, 30 minutes away by bus at Koukounaries Beach, has a minimarket, taverna and good facilities.

Eating & Drinking

Skiathos is brimming with eateries. Nightlife sprawls along Politehniou; to find it, turn left off Papadiamanti at Evangelistrias and walk 100m.

Taverna Dionysos (☎ 2427 022 675; Panora) Heading up Papadiamanti, turn right opposite the National Bank to find this place, which has tasty three-course menus from €7. Taverna Dionysos presents you with an ouzo before dinner and a *metaxa* with coffee to finish. Bring your appetite.

Taverna Misogia (☎ 2427 021 440; Grigoriou; mains €3-8) Turn left at the National Bank and walk 150m to get to this taverna, which has great grills of lamb, pork and chicken.

Psaradiki Ouzeri (☎ 2427 023 412; Paralia; mains €3.50-10) By the fish market at the far end of the old port, this is the seafood winner.

La Skala Bar (☎ 2427 023 102; Politehniou) Check out Skiathos' low-key gay and lesbian scene above the old port.

Kahlua Bar (☎ 2427 023 205) On the club strip at the eastern waterfront end of town, Kahlua is popular and pulses with mainstream DJ sets.

Getting There & Around

In summer, there are daily flights from Athens to Skiathos (€55). There is an **Olympic Airways** (☎ 2427 022 200) office at the airport.

There are frequent ferries to the mainland ports of Volos (€11.60) and Agios Konstantinos (€20.80), and frequent hydrofoils each day to Skopelos (€9.10) and Alonnisos (€13). In summer, there are two boats a week to Thessaloniki (€16.80).

Crowded buses ply the south-coast road between Skiathos town and Koukounaries every 20 minutes, stopping at all the beaches along the way. The bus stop is at the eastern end of the harbour.

SKOPELOS ΣΚΟΠΕΛΟΣ
pop 4700

Mountainous and forest-covered Skopelos is less commercialised than Skiathos. Skopelos Town skirts a semicircular bay and clambers in tiers up a hillside, culminating in a ruined fortress.

Velanio Beach on the south coast is the island's nudie spot. On the west coast, pebbled **Panormos Beach**, with its sheltered emerald bay surrounded by pine forest, is superb. The 2km stretch of **Milia Beach**, a few kilometres further on, is considered the island's best.

Head 50m up the road opposite the port entrance to find Platanos Sq. Along Doulidi, the street to the left after Gyros.gr, is the **Internet @ Café** (☎ 2424 023 093; 🕘 9am-2.30pm & 5pm-midnight), post office and a stack of popular nightspots. The bus station is next to the port.

There is no tourist office or tourist police, but **Thalpos Leisure & Services** (☎ 2424 022 947; www.holidayislands.com), on the waterfront between the ferry quay and the excursion-boat quay, is handy for accommodation and tours.

Domatia owners meet the boats. **Pension Sotos** (☎ 2424 022 549; www.skopelos.net/sotos; s/d €25/50), in the middle of the waterfront, has big rooms in an enchanting building. There's also a communal kitchen and courtyard. **Pension Soula** (☎ 2424 022 930; d/tr €25/55), a 10-minute walk out of town, is a welcoming place with airy rooms; you'll awake in rural bliss to donkeys braying and birdsong. To find it, walk left from the port and turn left at Hotel Amalia. Follow the road, bearing right after about 200m; it's on your right. **Hotel Adonis** (☎ 2424 022 231; s/d €50/90) is more upmarket and in a prime spot overlooking the waterfront.

The top spot in town to chill out is under the huge plane tree at **Platanos Jazz Bar** (☎ 2424

023 661), opposite the excursion-boat quay. It's open all day, serves a mean omelette (€3) for breakfast, and plays wicked jazz and blues until the late hours. Next door is **Taverna Ta Kimata** (☎ 2424 022 381; mains from €4), started by the current owner's grandfather in 1928. Try the *yuvetsi* (claypot pasta). **Perivoli Taverna** (☎ 2424 023 758; mains €6-13), 50m inland from Platanos Sq, serves great vegetarian dishes.

Oionos Blues Bar (☎ 2424 023 731) offers excellent jazz, blues and soul in a traditional Skopelean house. From the waterfront, turn inland next to Pension Sotos and take the second right. On Doulidi there is a clutch of popular bars, including **Dancing Club Kounos** (☎ 2424 023 623).

In summer, there are daily ferries to Volos (€15.10) and Agios Konstantinos (€28.40) that also call at Skiathos. Flying Dolphin hydrofoils dash several times a day to Skiathos, Alonnisos, Volos and Agios Konstantinos. Most hydrofoils also call in at Loutraki, the port below Glossa on the northwest coast. For schedules and tickets, see **Skopelos Ferry Office** (☎ 2424 022 767), opposite the port. There are frequent buses from Skopelos town to Glossa stopping at all beaches along the way.

ALONNISOS ΑΛΟΝΝΗΣΟΣ
pop 2700

Green, serene Alonnisos is the least visited of the Sporades. The area surrounding the island has been declared a marine park and reputedly has the cleanest waters in the Aegean.

The port village of Patitiri isn't particularly attractive. Its concrete buildings were slapped together in 1965 after an earthquake destroyed the hill-top capital of Alonnisos Town. There are two main thoroughfares; facing inland from the ferry quay, Pelasgon is to the left and Ikion Dolopon is to the far right.

There is no tourist office or tourist police but the post office, police and Internet access at **Il Mondo Café** (☎ 2424 065 834; per hr €4) are on Ikion Dolopon. On the waterfront itself, **Alonnisos Travel** (☎ 2424 065 188; www.alonnisostravel .gr) handles boat scheduling and ticketing. **Ikos Travel** (☎ 2424 065 320; www.ikostravel.com) runs a popular round-the-island excursion. The bus stop is on the corner of Ikion Dolopon and the waterfront.

The tiny *hora*, **Old Alonnisos**, is a few kilometres inland. Its streets sprout a profusion of plant life, alluring villas of eclectic design and dramatic vistas.

Alonnisos is ideal for walking. Waterfront travel agencies offer guided tours or there's an excellent trail guide called *Alonnisos on Foot: A Walking & Swimming Guide* by Bente Keller & Elias Tsoukanas which is available at newsstands for €9.

The **Rooms to Let service** (☎ 2424 066 188; fax 2424 065 577; ⏰ 10am-2pm, 6.30-10.30pm), opposite the quay, books accommodation all over the island. **Camping Rocks** (☎ 2424 065 410; per person €5) is a shady, basic site. It is a steep hike about 1.5km from the port; go up Pelasgon and take the first road on your left. **Pension Pleiades** (☎ 2424 065 235; pleiades@internet.gr; s/d €25/45; ❄) looks out over the harbour and is visible from the quay. The rooms are bright and cheerful. **Illias Rent Rooms** (☎ 2424 065 451; Pelasgon 27; d €25-40) has good-value rooms 300m up Pelasgon.

To Kamaki Ouzeri (☎ 2424 065 245; Ikion Dolopon; mains €4-10) is a traditional island eatery. Check the ready-to-eat dishes out in the kitchen.

Café Flisvos (☎ 2424 065 307; mains from €5) is the pick of the waterfront restaurants, under the canopy opposite the dock. **Symvolo Bar** (☎ 2424 066 156; Ikion Dolopon) plays jazz and blues, while **Club Enigma** (☎ 2424 065 307; Pelasgon) rocks once the tourist season kicks in.

Up in the old town, **Fantasia House** (☎ 2424 065 186; Plateia Hristou; s/d €30/40) has sweet rooms and a verdant terrace. **Astrofengia** (☎ 2424 065 182; mains €5-12), signposted from the bus stop, serves scrumptious alternative fare.

There are daily ferries from Alonnisos to Volos (€15.70) and Agios Konstantinos (€28.40) via Skiathos and Skopelos. Flying Dolphin hydrofoils travel several times a day to Volos and Agios Konstantinos and between the islands.

The local bus (€0.90) runs to the *hora* every hour. Car- and scooter-hire outlets are on Pelasgon and Ikion Dolopon, but only one main road spans the island!

IONIAN ISLANDS
ΤΑ ΕΠΤΑΝΗΣΑ

The idyllic Ionian group of islands stretch down the western coast of Greece from Corfu in the north to Kythira, off the southern tip of the Peloponnese. These mountainous islands, with their soft light and Italian influence, offer quite a contrasting experience to other island groups in Greece.

CORFU ΚΕΡΚΥΡΑ
pop 109,540

Corfu is the second-largest and most important island in the group and many consider it to be Greece's most beautiful island.

Corfu Town
pop 28,200

The island's capital is built on a promontory and the old town, wedged between two fortresses, offers up a medley of occupying influences. While the narrow alleyways of high, shuttered tenements are an immediate reminder of the town's long association with Venice, the Liston, a row of arcaded buildings, was based on the Rue de Rivoli in Paris.

ORIENTATION

The town's old fortress (Palaio Frourio) stands on an eastern promontory, separated from the town by an area of parks and gardens known as the Spianada. The new fortress (Neo Frourio) lies to the northwest. Ferries dock at the new port, just west of the new fortress. The **long-distance bus station** (Avrami) is inland from the port.

INFORMATION

National Bank of Greece (cnr Voulgareos & Theotoki)
On Line Internet Café (Kapodistria 28; per hr €4)
Tourist police (☎ 2661 030 265; 3rd fl, Samartzi 4)
A good source of information.

SIGHTS

The **Archaeological Museum** (☎ 2661 030 680; P Vraili 5; admission €3; ☜ 8.30am-3pm Tue-Sun) houses a collection of finds from Mycenaean to classical times. The star attraction is the pediment from the Temple of Artemis, decorated with gorgons.

Corfu's most famous church, the **Church of Agios Spiridon**, has a richly decorated interior. Pride of place is given to the remains of St Spiridon, displayed in a silver casket; four times a year it is paraded around town.

SLEEPING & EATING

Hotel Hermes (☎ 2661 039 268; G Markora 14; s/d with shared bathroom €28/33, s/d €36/44) Hotel Hermes is

a tad noisy, has a certain shabby charm and is popular with backpackers.

Hotel Konstantinoupolis (☎ 2661 048 716; www .konstantinoupolis.com.gr; K Zavitsianou 11; s/d/tr €55/80/96; 😢) This renovated hotel has an unbeatable position overlooking the old harbour (ask for a front room). The rooms are spotless, all have TV and there are good discounts off season.

No matter where you eat in Corfu, a must is to sit on the Liston nursing a *frappé* (€3.50) and indulging in some people watching.

To Dimarchio (☎ 2661 039 031; Plateia Dimarchio; mains €7-20) Located in a pleasant square, this place serves up the best food in town. The seafood's excellent and there are also some less expensive pasta and salad dishes.

Around the Island

There is hardly anywhere in Corfu that hasn't made a play for the tourist dollar, but the north is over the top. The only real attraction there is the view from the summit of **Mt Pantokrator** (906m), Corfu's highest mountain. There's a road to the top from the village of Strinila.

The main resort on the west coast is **Paleokastritsa**, built around a series of pretty bays. Further south, there are good beaches around the small village of **Agios Gordios**. Between Paleokastritsa and Agios Gordios is the hill-top village of **Pelekas**, one of the best places on Corfu to watch the sunset.

SLEEPING

Pink Palace (☎ 2661 053 103; www.thepinkpalace .com; A-/B-class room incl breakfast & dinner per person €32/25; 😢 🖳) This huge, garish complex on the main road into Agios Gordios is like a summer camp, with organised activities such as theme parties and water sports. The A-class rooms are hotel-style; B-class rooms are hostel-style and sleep up to four people. Long considered an obligatory stop on the European backpacker circuit, it attracts an uninhibited, hard-partying crowd.

Sunrock (☎ 2661 094 637; www.geocities.com/sun rock_corfu; r per person with shared bathroom €18, r per person with bathroom incl breakfast & dinner €24; 🖳 🐾) At the southern end of Pelekas Beach is family-run Sunrock, with excellent facilities and activities that have earned it a place as a firm backpacker favourite. Open year-round, it will arrange for you to be picked up at the port.

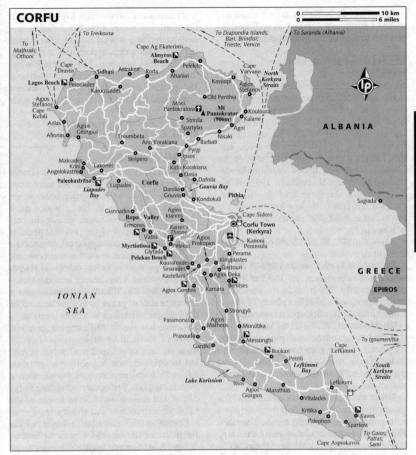

CORFU

0 _____ 10 km
0 _____ 6 miles

GREECE

Getting There & Away

Three flights daily to Athens are offered by both **Olympic Airways** (☎ 2661 038 694; Polila 11, Corfu town) and **Aegean Airlines** (☎ 2661 027 100). Olympic also flies to Thessaloniki three times a week.

There are daily buses to Athens (€29.50, 8½ hours) and Thessaloniki (€28.50, eight hours) from the Avrami terminal in Corfu town. Fares include the ferry to Igoumenitsa.

There are hourly ferries to Igoumenitsa (€5.10, 1½ hours) and a daily ferry to Paxoi. In summer, there are daily services to Patra (€21.50 to €25, six hours) on the international ferries that call at Corfu on their way from Italy. See p610 for more details about international ferry services.

Getting Around

Buses for villages close to Corfu town leave from Plateia San Rocco. Services to other destinations leave from the station on Avrami. There's no bus from the airport and a taxi to the old town costs around €9.

ITHAKI IΘAKH

pop 3080

Ithaki, or ancient Ithaca, was Odysseus' long-lost home in Homer's *Odyssey*. Ithaki doesn't attract large crowds, mainly because of its lack of good beaches, but it's perfect for a quiet holiday. From the main town of Vathy, you can walk to the **Fountain of Arethousa**, the fabled site of Odysseus' meeting with the swineherd Eumaeus on his return to Ithaki.

Ithaki has daily ferries to the mainland ports of Patra and Astakos, as well as daily services to Kefallonia and Lefkada.

KEFALLONIA ΚΕΦΑΛΛΟΝΙΑ
pop 35,600

After years of relative obscurity, quiet Kefallonia found itself thrust into the international spotlight following the success of the book and film *Captain Corelli's Mandolin*. Unfortunately for visitors to the island's capital, Sami, the old Venetian streets featured in the movie were as fake as Nicholas Cage's accent – a major earthquake destroyed the original streets in 1953. While Kefallonia is the largest of the Ionians, tourism remains fairly low-key outside the resort areas near the capital and on the beaches in the southwest.

There's an **EOT** (☎ 2671 022 248) on the waterfront in Argostoli.

Karavomilos Beach Camping (☎ 2674 022 480; www.camping-karavomilos.gr; per adult/tent €6/3.50; ▣) is located 800m from Sami. This site is well-maintained and offers plenty of shade, a minimarket, laundry and restaurant.

Hotel Melissani (☎ 2674 022 464; Sami; d €53; ✖) is a slightly eccentric and pleasant older-style hotel offering such comforts as TV and fridge. Some rooms have air-con. Follow the signposts from the eastern end of the waterfront.

Riviera (☎ 2674 022 777; r €45, mains €3.50-8.50) is a welcoming café-pizzeria on the waterfront with good coffee and light meals. There are also simple rooms available above the café.

There are daily flights to Athens (€65) from the airport, 9km south of Argostoli. Daily ferries operate from Sami to Patra (€11.50, 2½ hours); others depart from Argostoli and the southeastern port of Poros for Kyllini on the Peloponnese. There are also ferry connections to the islands of Ithaki, Lefkada and Zakynthos. See p611 for details about international ferry services.

ZAKYNTHOS ΖΑΚΥΝΘΟΣ
pop 39,020

Zakynthos, or Zante, is a beautiful island resplendent with gorgeous beaches – but during summer it's completely overrun with tourists. Its capital and port, Zakynthos town, is an imposing old Venetian town that has been painstakingly reconstructed after being levelled by an earthquake in 1953.

The area around the huge **Bay of Laganas** in the south has some of the best beaches, but endangered loggerhead turtles come ashore here to lay their eggs in August – at the peak of the tourist invasion. The Greek government has declared this area a national marine park. There are regular ferries between Zakynthos and Kyllini on the Peloponnese.

GREECE DIRECTORY

ACCOMMODATION

There is a range of accommodation in Greece to suit every taste and pocket. All accommodation is subject to strict price controls set by the tourist police. By law, a notice must be displayed in every room, stating the category of the room and the seasonal price. If you think you've been ripped off, contact the tourist police. Prices quoted in this book are for the high season, unless otherwise stated. Prices are about 40% cheaper between October and May. It's difficult to generalise about accommodation prices in Greece because of the seasonal variations as well as location

Greece has almost 350 camping grounds, many of them in great locations. Lots of these are only open April to October. Standard facilities include hot showers, kitchens, restaurants and minimarkets – and often a swimming pool. Prices vary according to facilities, but reckon on €4.50 to €6 per adult, €3.50 for a small tent and €6 for a large one.

Greece has 55 mountain refuges, which are listed in the booklet *Greece Mountain Refuges & Ski Centres*, available free of charge at EOT and EOS (Ellinikos Orivatikos Syndesmos, the Greek Alpine Club) offices.

You'll find youth hostels in most major towns and on half a dozen islands. The only place affiliated to Hostelling International (HI) is the Athens International Youth Hostel (p550).

Most other hostels throughout Greece are run by the **Greek Youth Hostel Organisation** (☎ 210 7 519 530; y-hostels@otenet.gr). There are affiliated hostels in Athens, Olympia, Patra and Thessaloniki on the mainland, and on the islands of Crete and Santorini (Thira). Most charge €8 to €10, and you don't have to be a member to stay in any of them.

Domatia are the Greek equivalent of a bed and breakfast – minus the breakfast. *Domatia* initially consisted of little more than spare rooms rented out in summer. Nowadays many of these *domatia* are purpose-built appendages to the family house, but can still represent good value. Expect to pay about €25 to €35 for a single and €40 to €50 for a double. Don't worry about finding them – the owners will find you as they greet ferries and buses shouting 'room!'.

Hotels in Greece are classified as deluxe, A, B, C, D or E class. The ratings seldom seem to have much bearing on the price, but expect to pay €18/25 for singles/doubles in D and E class, and anything from €35/45 to €60/80 for singles/doubles with a private bathroom in a decent C-class place.

Some places are classified as pensions and are rated differently. Both are allowed to levy a 10% surcharge for stays of less than three nights, but they seldom do. It normally works the other way – you can bargain a cheaper rate if you're staying more than one night.

ACTIVITIES
Diving & Snorkelling
Snorkelling can be enjoyed just about wherever there's coastline in Greece. Corfu (p602), Mykonos (p572), and Santorini (p579) are just some of the good areas to snorkel; diving schools operate from these sites as well. Diving outside the organised supervision of a dive school is forbidden in order to protect the aquatic environment. For a complete list of diving possibilities, visit www.isdc.gr.

Sailing & Yachting
Sailing facilities are generally found at the same locations recommended for windsurfing. Hrysi Akti (p574) on Paros and Mylopotas Beach on Ios (p578) are two of the best locations. Hire charges for catamarans range from €20 to €25.

Yachting is an excellent way to see the Greek islands. If you have a couple of certified sailors in your group, you can hire a 28-foot bare boat (without crew) that sleeps six for around €1000 per week. Hiring a skipper will nearly double that price. You can find more information at www.yachting.gr.

Skiing
Greece offers some of the cheapest skiing in Europe with 16 resorts dotted around the mainland, mainly in the north. The resorts are basic and cater mainly to Greek skiers.

The season can start late (January) and generally runs through to late March or early April, depending on conditions. The *Greece Mountain Refuges & Ski Centres* brochure is available from EOT offices. Check out www.snowreport.gr for information about snow conditions.

Trekking
Greece could be a trekkers' paradise if trekking organisations received better funding. Outside the main popular routes, the trails are generally overgrown and poorly marked. Several companies run organised treks; the biggest is **Trekking Hellas** (Map p551; ☎ 2103 310 323; www.trekking.gr; Filellinon 7, Athens 105 57).

Windsurfing
Windsurfing is the most popular water sport in Greece. Sailboards are widely available for hire, priced at €12 to €15 per hour. The top spots for windsurfing are Hrysi Akti (p575) on Paros, and Ios (p578) on Lefkada, which is a popular place to learn.

BUSINESS HOURS
Banks are open from 8am to 2pm Monday to Thursday, and 8am to 1.30pm Friday. Some banks in the larger cities and towns are also open from 3.30pm to 6.30pm and on Saturday morning. Post offices are open from 7am to 2pm Monday to Friday; in major cities they're open until 8pm and also open from 7.30am to 2pm on Saturday.

In summer, the usual opening hours for shops are from 8am to 1.30pm and 5.30pm to 8.30pm on Tuesday, Thursday and Friday, and 8am to 2.30pm on Monday, Wednesday and Saturday. Shops generally open 30 minutes later during winter.

Restaurants in tourist areas generally open at 11am and stay open through to midnight; normal restaurant hours are 11am to 2pm and from 7pm to midnight or 1am. Cafés tend to open between 9am and 10am and stay open until midnight. Bars open around 8pm and close late; and while discos might open at 10pm, you'll drink alone until midnight. Discos generally close around 4am, but many go through to dawn during summer.

DANGERS & ANNOYANCES
Greece has the lowest crime rate in Europe. Athens is developing a reputation for petty theft and scams, but elsewhere crimes are

most commonly committed by other travellers. See p546 for scam warnings.

DISABLED TRAVELLERS

If mobility is a problem, the hard fact is that most hotels, museums and ancient sites are not wheelchair accessible. While facilities in Athens are improving (thanks to the 2004 Olympics), elsewhere the uneven terrain is an issue for even able-bodied people.

Useful information on disabled travel is available on the Internet at www.sath.org and www.access-able.com.

EMBASSIES & CONSULATES
Greek Embassies & Consulates

Greek diplomatic missions abroad include:

Australia (☎ 02-6273 3011; 9 Turrana St, Yarralumla, ACT 2600)
Canada (☎ 613-238 6271; 76-80 Maclaren St, Ottawa, Ontario K2P 0K6)
Cyprus (☎ 02-680 670/671; Byron Bvld 8-10, Nicosia)
France (☎ 01-47 23 72 28; www.amb-grece.fr/presse; 17 Rue Auguste Vaquerie, 75116 Paris)
Germany (☎ 0228-83010; www.griechische-botschaft.de; Jaegerstrasse 54-55, 10117 Berlin-Mitte)
Italy (☎ 06-854 9630; Via S Mercadante 36, Rome 3906)
Japan (☎ 03-3403 0871/2; www.greekemb.jp; 3-16-30 Nishi Azabu, Minato-ku, Tokyo 304-5853)
New Zealand (☎ 04-473 7775; 5-7 Willeston St, Wellington)
South Africa (☎ 12-430 7351; 1003 Church St, Hatfield, Pretoria 0028)
Spain (☎ 01-564 4653; Ave Doctor Arce 24, Madrid 28002)
Turkey (☎ 312-436 8860; Ziya-ul-Rahman Caddesi 9-11, Gaziosmanpasa 06700, Ankara)
UK (☎ 020-7229 3850; www.greekembassy.org.uk; 1A Holland Park, London W11 3TP)
USA (☎ 202-939 1300; www.greekembassy.org; 2221 Massachusetts Ave NW, Washington, DC 20008)

Embassies & Consulates in Greece

All foreign embassies in Greece are in Athens and its suburbs.
Australia (Map pp548-9; ☎ 2106 450 404; Dimitriou Soutsou 37, 115 21)
Canada (Map pp548-9; ☎ 2107 273 400; Genadiou 4, 115 21)
Cyprus (Map pp548-9; ☎ 2107 237 883; Irodotou 16, 106 75)
France (Map pp548-9; ☎ 2103 611 663; Leof Vasilissis Sofias 7, 106 71)
Germany (Map pp548-9; ☎ 2107 285 111; cnr Dimitriou 3 & Karaoli, Kolonaki 106 75)

Italy (Map pp548-9; ☎ 2103 617 260; Sekeri 2, 106 74)
Japan (Map pp548-9; ☎ 2107 758 101; Athens Tower, Leoforos Messogion 2-4, 115 27)
New Zealand (Map pp548-9; ☎ 2106 874 701; Kifissias 268, Halandri)
South Africa (Map pp548-9; ☎ 2106 806 645; Kifissias 60, Maroussi, 151 25)
Turkey (Map pp548-9; ☎ 2107 245 915; Vasilissis Georgiou 8, 106 74)
UK (Map pp548-9; ☎ 2107 236 211; Ploutarhou 1, 106 75)
USA (Map pp548-9; ☎ 2107 212 951; Leoforos Vasilissis Sofias 91, 115 21)

FESTIVALS & EVENTS

In Greece, it's probably easier to list the dates when festivals and events are *not* on! Some are religious, some cultural and others seemingly just an excuse to party. It's worth timing at least one part of your trip to coincide with one as you'll be warmly invited to join in the revelry. The following list is by no means exhaustive and more details can be found at www.cultureguide.gr.

January
Epiphany (Blessing of the Waters) Christ's baptism is celebrated on the 6th when seas, lakes and rivers are blessed. The largest ceremony occurs at Piraeus.

February
Carnival Season The three-week period before the beginning of Lent is celebrated all over Greece with fancy dress, feasting and traditional dance.

March
Independence Day On 25 March, parades and dancing mark the anniversary of the hoisting of the Greek Flag that started the War of Independence.

April
Easter The most important festival of the Greek Orthodox religion. The emphasis is on the Resurrection rather than the Crucifixion so it's a celebratory event. The most significant part of the event is midnight on Easter Saturday when candles are lit (symbolising the Resurrection) and a fireworks and candle-lit procession hits the streets.

May
May Day The celebrations on 1 May see a mass exodus from towns to the country. During picnics, wild flowers are gathered and made into wreaths for decoration.

June
Hellenic Festival The most important of festivals staged throughout Greece during summer. The Theatre of Herodes

Atticus in Athens and the Theatre of Epidavros, near Nafplio, are venues for traditional events.

July

Feast of Agia Marina (St Marina) This feast day is celebrated on 17 July in many parts of Greece, and is a particularly important event on the Dodecanese island of Kasos.

August

Feast of the Assumption Greeks celebrate this day (15 August) with family reunions. There's generally transport chaos on the days before and after the event so it's wise to stay put for a couple of days.

Samothraki Dance Festival The northeastern Aegean island of Samothraki plays host to Greece's biggest rave party for a week starting at the end of August.

September

Genesis tis Panagias The birthday of the Virgin Mary is celebrated on 8 September with religious services and feasting.

October

Feast of Agios Dimitrios This feast day, on 26 October, is celebrated in Thessaloniki with much revelry.

Ohi (No) Day Metaxas' refusal to allow Mussolini's troops free passage through Greece in WWII is commemorated on 28 October with military parades, folk dancing and feasting.

GAY & LESBIAN TRAVELLERS

In a country where the church plays a major role in shaping society's views on issues such as sexuality, it should come as no surprise that homosexuality is generally frowned upon. While there is no legislation against homosexual activity, it is wise to be discreet and to avoid open displays of togetherness.

However, Greece is a popular destination for gay travellers. Athens has a busy gay scene – but most people head for the islands. Mykonos (p572) has long been famous for its bars, beaches and hedonism and the town of Eresos (p597) on Lesvos has become something of a pilgrimage for lesbians.

HOLIDAYS

New Year's Day 1 January
Epiphany 6 January
First Sunday in Lent February
Greek Independence Day 25 March
Good Friday/Easter Sunday March/April
Spring Festival/Labour Day 1 May
Feast of the Assumption 15 August

Ohi Day 28 October
Christmas Day 25 December
St Stephen's Day 26 December

INTERNET ACCESS

Greece was slow to embrace the Internet, but now Internet cafés are springing up everywhere and are listed in this book under Information for cities and islands where available. Charges differ radically – from less than €3.50 per hour in big cities up to €15 per hour on Mykonos.

There has been a huge increase in the number of hotels and businesses using email, and addresses have also been listed in this chapter where available.

INTERNET RESOURCES

Culture Guide (www.cultureguide.gr) Plenty of information about contemporary culture and the arts.
Greek Ferries (www.greekferries.org) Get all your ferry information from the source. Covers international and domestic ferries.
Greek National Tourist Organisation (www.gnto.gr) Concise tourist information.
Lonely Planet (www.lonelyplanet.com) Has postcards from other travellers and the Thorn Tree bulletin board, where you can pose those tricky questions or help answer other travellers' questions on your return.
Ministry of Culture (www.culture.gr) Information on ancient sites, art galleries and museums.

LANGUAGE

Greeks are naturally delighted if you can speak a little of their language, but you don't need Greek to get around. English is almost a second language, especially among younger people. Many Greeks have lived abroad, usually in Australia or the USA, so even in remote villages there are invariably one or two people who can speak English.

MAPS

Unless you are going to trek or drive, the free maps given out by the tourist offices will probably suffice. The best motoring maps are produced by local company Road Editions, which also produces a good trekking series.

MONEY

Banks will exchange all major currencies, in either cash or travellers cheques and also Euro-cheques. Post offices charge less commission than banks, but won't cash travellers cheques.

GREECE

All major credit cards are accepted, but only in larger establishments. You'll find ATMs everywhere, particularly in tourist areas.

Costs

Greece is still a cheap destination by northern European standards, but it's no longer dirtcheap. A rock-bottom daily budget would be €40. This would mean hitching, staying in youth hostels or camping, staying away from bars, and only occasionally eating in restaurants or taking ferries. Allow at least €80 per day if you want your own room and plan to eat out regularly as well as seeing the sights. If you really want a holiday – comfortable rooms and restaurants all the way – you will need closer to €120 per day.

Your money will go a lot further if you travel in the quieter months as accommodation is generally much cheaper outside the high season. There are fewer tourists around and more opportunities to negotiate even better deals.

Currency

Greece adopted the euro in 2002, and the Greek drachma disappeared after a twomonth period of dual circulation.

Taxes & Refunds

Value-added tax (VAT) varies from 15% to 18%. A tax-rebate scheme applies at a restricted number of shops and stores; look for a Tax Free sign in the window. You must fill in a form at the shop and then present it with the receipt at the airport on departure. A cheque will (hopefully) be sent to your home address.

Tipping & Bargaining

In restaurants the service charge is included on the bill, but it is the custom to leave a small tip – just round off the bill. Accommodation is nearly always negotiable outside peak season, especially if you are staying more than one night. Souvenir shops will generally bargain. Prices in other shops are normally clearly marked and non-negotiable.

POST

Post offices (*tahydromia*) are easily identified by the yellow sign outside. Regular post boxes are yellow as well; red post boxes are for express mail only. The postal rate for postcards and airmail letters within the EU is €0.60. To other destinations the rate is €0.65. Post within Europe takes five to eight days and to the USA, Australia and New Zealand, nine to 11 days. Some tourist shops also sell stamps, but with a 10% surcharge.

Mail can be sent poste restante to any main post office and is held for up to one month. Your surname should be underlined and you will need to show your passport when you collect your mail. Parcels are not delivered in Greece – they must be collected from a post office.

SOLO TRAVELLERS

Greece is a great destination for solo travellers, particularly in summer when the islands are full of travellers meeting and making friends. Hostels and other backpacker-friendly accommodation are excellent places to meet other travellers. Solo women are quite safe – which is not to say that problems don't occur, but violent offences are rare.

TELEPHONE

The Greek telephone service is maintained by Organismos Tilepikoinonion Ellados, a public corporation always referred to by its acronym OTE (o-*teh*). Public phones are easy to use and pressing the 'i' button brings up the operating instructions in English. Public phones are everywhere and all use phonecards.

Mobile Phones

Mobile phones have become the must-have accessory in Greece. If you have a compatible GSM phone from a country with a global roaming agreement with Greece, you will be able to use your phone in Greece. Make sure you have global roaming activated before you leave your country of residence.

Phonecards

All public phones use OTE phonecards, sold at OTE offices and *periptera* (street kiosks). These cards are sold in €3, €5, and €9 versions and a local call costs €0.30 for three minutes. There are also discount-card schemes available that give you double the time for your money.

TIME

Greece is two hours ahead of GMT/UTC and three hours ahead during daylight-saving time, which is in effect between the last Sunday in March and the last Sunday in October.

TOURIST INFORMATION

Tourist information is handled by the Greek National Tourist Organisation (GNTO), known as EOT in Greece. There is either an EOT office or a local tourist office in almost every town of consequence and on many of the islands. Popular destinations have tourist police who can often help in finding accommodation.

Tourist Offices Abroad

Australia (☎ 02-9241 1663/5; hto@tgp.com.au; 51-57 Pitt St, Sydney, NSW 2000)

Canada Toronto (☎ 416-968 2220; gnto.tor@simpatico .ca; 91 Scollard St, Toronto, Ontario M5R 1G4); Montreal (☎ 514-871 1535; 1170 Pl Du Frere Andre, Montreal, Quebec H3B 3C6)

France (☎ 1-42 60 65 75; eot@club-Internet.fr; 3 Ave de l'Opéra, Paris 75001)

Germany Berlin (☎ 30-217 6262; Wittenbergplatz 3a, 10789 Berlin 30); Frankfurt (☎ 69-236 561; info@gzf-eot .de; Neue Mainzerstrasse 22, 60311 Frankfurt); Hamburg (☎ 40-454 498; info-hamburg@gzf-eot.de; Neurer Wall 18, 20254 Hamburg); Munich (☎ 89-222 035/6; Pacellistrasse 5, 2W 80333 Munich)

Italy Rome (☎ 06-474 4249; www.ente-tourismoellenico .com; Via L Bissolati 78-80, Rome 00187); Milan (☎ 02-860 470; Piazza Diaz 1, 20123 Milan)

Japan (☎ 03-350 55 917; gnto-jpn@t3.rim.or.jp; Fukuda Bldg West, 5th fl 2-11-3 Akasaka, Minato-ku, Tokyo 107)

UK (☎ 020-7734 5997; 4 Conduit St, London W1R ODJ)

USA Chicago (☎ 312-782 1084; www.greektourism.com; ste 600, 168 North Michigan Ave, Chicago, IL 60601); Los Angeles (☎ 213-626 6696; ste 2198, 611 West 6th St, Los Angeles, CA 92668); New York (☎ 212-421 5777; Olympic Tower, 645 5th Ave, New York, NY 10022)

VISAS

The list of countries whose nationals can stay in Greece for up to three months include Australia, Canada, all EU countries, Iceland, Israel, Japan, New Zealand, and the USA. For the full list, contact a Greek embassy or visit www.lonelyplanet.com/ subwwway for updated visa information. For longer stays, apply at a consulate abroad or at least 20 days in advance to the **Aliens Bureau** (Map pp548-9; ☎ 2107 705 711; Leoforos Alexandras 173, Athens; ☼ 8am-1pm Mon-Fri) at the Athens Central Police Station. Elsewhere in Greece, apply to the local authority.

EMERGENCY NUMBERS

- Ambulance ☎ 166
- Fire ☎ 199
- Police ☎ 100
- Roadside Assistance (ELPA) ☎ 104
- Tourist Police ☎ 171

In the past, Greece has refused entry to those who have visited Turkish-occupied North Cyprus. Play safe and ask the North Cyprus immigration officials to stamp a piece of paper instead of your passport. If you enter North Cyprus from the Greek Republic of Cyprus (only possible for a day visit at present), no exit stamp is put in your passport.

TRANSPORT IN GREECE

GETTING THERE & AWAY

Air

There are no less than 16 international airports in Greece, but most of them handle only summer charter flights to the islands. **Eleftherios Venizelos International Airport** (code ATH; ☎ 2103 530 000; www.aia.gr), near Athens, handles the vast majority of international flights, including all intercontinental flights, and has regular scheduled flights to all the European capitals.

Thessaloniki is also well served by **Macedonia International Airport** (code SKG; ☎ 2310 473 700), and there are scheduled flights to/from Iraklio (Crete) from **Nikos Kazantzakis International Airport** (code HER; ☎ 2810 228 401).

Airlines that fly to and from Greece:

Aegean Airlines (code A3; www.aegeanair.com)

Air France (code AF; ☼ 2103 220 986; www.airfrance .com)

British Airways (code BA; ☼ 2108 906 666; www .britishairways.com)

Delta Airlines (code DL; ☼ 2103 311 660; www.delta .com)

easyJet (code EZY; ☼ 2109 670 000; www.easyjet.com)

Emirates (code EK; ☼ 2019 333 400; www.emirates.com)

Iberia (code IB; ☼ 2103 234 523; www.iberia.com)

Japan Airlines (code JL; ☼ 2103 248 211; www.jal.com)

KLM (code WA; ☼ 2103 531 295; www.klm.com)

Lufthansa (code IH; ☼ 2106 175 200; www.lufthansa .com)

GREECE

Olympic Airways (code OA; www.olympic-airways.gr)
Virgin Express (code TV; ☎ 2106 175 200; www.virgin
-express.com)

Land

NORTHERN EUROPE

Overland travel between northern Europe and Greece is virtually a thing of the past. Buses and trains can't compete with cheap air fares. All bus and train services now go via Italy and take the ferries over to Greece.

Unless you have a Eurail pass (p1080), travelling to Greece by train is prohibitively expensive. Greece is part of the Eurail network, and passes are valid on the ferries operated by Adriatica di Navigazione and Hellenic Mediterranean Lines from Brindisi to Corfu, Igoumenitsa and Patra.

NEIGHBOURING COUNTRIES

The OSE operates a bus from Athens to Istanbul (€67.50, 22 hours) daily except Wednesday. There are daily trains between Athens and Istanbul (€63, 22 hours) via Thessaloniki (€42.50, 5½ hours).

The crossing points into Turkey are at Kipi and Kastanies, the crossings into the Former Yugoslav Republic of Macedonia (FYROM) are at Evzoni and Niki, and the Bulgarian crossing is at Promahonas. All crossings are open 24 hours. The crossing points to Albania are at Kakavia and Krystallopigi.

Sea

You'll find all the latest information about ferry routes, schedules and services online. For an overview try www.greekferries.gr. Most of the ferry companies have their own websites, including the following:
Agoudimos Lines (www.agoudimos-lines.com)
ANEK Lines (www.anek.gr)
Blue Star Ferries (www.bluestarferries.com)
Fragline (www.fragline.gr)
Hellenic Mediterranean Lines (www.hml.gr)
Italian Ferries (www.italianferries.it)
Minoan Lines (www.minoan.gr)
Superfast (www.superfast.com)
Ventouris Ferries (www.ventouris.gr)

The following ferry services are for high season (July and August), and prices are for one-way deck class. Prices are about 30% less in the low season.

ALBANIA

Corfu-based Petrakis Lines has daily ferries to the Albanian port of Saranda (€15, 25 minutes), plus twice-weekly services to Himara (€25, 1¼ hours) and Vlora (€38, 2½ hours).

CYPRUS & ISRAEL

Passenger services from Greece to Cyprus and Israel had been suspended at the time of research. **Salamis Lines** (www.viamare.com/Salamis) was still operating on the route, but carrying only vehicles and freight, while **Poseidon Lines** (www.ferries.gr/poseidon) had stopped all services.

ITALY

There are ferries to the Italian ports of Ancona, Bari, Brindisi, Trieste and Venice from Patra, Igoumenitsa, Corfu and Kefallonia. If you want to take a vehicle across, it's a good idea to make a reservation beforehand. In the UK, reservations can be made on almost all of these ferries through **Viamare Travel Ltd** (☎ 020-7431 4560; ferries@viamare.com).

Ancona

Blue Star Ferries and **Superfast Ferries** have two boats daily, taking 19 hours direct to Patra, or 21 hours via Igoumenitsa. Both charge €80 and also sell tickets through **Morandi & Co** (☎ 071- 20 20 33; Via XXIX Settembre 2/0). Superfast accepts Eurail passes. **ANEK Lines** (☎ 071-207 23 46; Via XXIX Settembre 2/0; €68) and **Minoan Lions** (☎ 071-201 708; Via Astagno 3; €72) do the trip daily in 19½ hours via Igoumenitsa.

Bari

Minoan Lines(☎ 080 52 10 266; Via Latilla 14) and **Superfast Ferries** (☎ 080 52 11 416; Corso de Tullio 6) have daily sailings to Patra via Igoumenitsa. **Ventouris Ferries** (☎ 080-521 7609) has daily boats to Corfu (10 hours) and Igoumenitsa (11½ hours) for €45.

Brindisi

The trip from Brindisi operates only between April and early October. **Med Link** (Discovery Shipping, ☎ 0831-54 81 16/7; Costa Morena) and **Hellenic Mediterranean Lines** (☎ 0831 54 80 01; Costa Morena) offer at least one boat a day to Patra between them.

Hellenic Mediterranean calls at Igoumenitsa on the way, and also has services that call at Corfu, Kefallonia, Paxi and

Zakynthos, while Medlink calls at Kefallonia during July and August. All these services cost €50.

Agoudimos Lines (☎ 0831-550180; Via Provinciale per Lecce 29) and **Fragline** (☎ 0831-54 85 40; Via Spalato 31) sail only to Igoumenitsa.

Italian Ferries (www.italianferries.it) operates high-speed catamaran services to Corfu (€57 to €85, 3¼ hours) and Paxi (€73 to €110, 4¾ hours) daily from July to mid-September.

Trieste
ANEK Lines (☎ 040-32 20 561; Via Rossini 2) has boats to Patra (€68, 32 hours) every day except Thursday, calling at Corfu and Igoumenitsa.

Venice
Minoan Lines (☎ 041-24 07 177; Stazione Marittima 123) has boats to Patra (29 hours, €75) every day except Wednesday, calling at Corfu and Igoumenitsa. **Blue Star Ferries** (☎ 041-277 0559; Stazione Marittima 123) sails the route four times weekly for €64.

TURKEY
Five regular ferry services operate between Turkey's Aegean coast and the Greek islands. Tickets for all ferries to Turkey must be bought a day in advance. For more information about these services, see Rhodes (p588), Chios (p596), Kos (p593), Lesvos (p597) and Samos (p595).

GETTING AROUND
Greece is an easy destination to travel around thanks to a very comprehensive transport system. On the mainland, buses travel to just about every town on the map and trains offer a good alternative where available. Island-hopping is what most people think of when travelling within Greece and there are myriad ferries that crisscross the Adriatic and Aegean Seas. If you're in a hurry, there's also an extensive and well-priced domestic air network. Timetables are seasonal and change in at least some way every year.

Air
The vast majority of domestic flights are handled by Greece's much-maligned national carrier, **Olympic Airways** (☎ 8011 144 444; www .olympic-airways.gr).

Crete-based competitor **Aegean Airlines** (☎ 8011 120 000; www.aegeanair.com) is the sole survivor of the deregulation of domestic air travel. It offers flights to many of the same destinations as Olympic, and has the same fares, but Aegean often has great discount fares as well as youth and senior discounts.

Bicycle
Given Greece's hilly terrain, stifling summer heat and rather wayward four-wheeled friends, cycling is not that popular a form of transport. You can hire bicycles at most tourist centres, but these are generally for pedalling around town rather than for serious riding. Prices generally range from €5 to €12 per day. If you wish to do a cycling tour of Greece, bicycles are carried for free on ferries.

Boat
CATAMARAN
High-speed catamarans have become an important part of the island travel scene. They are just as fast as hydrofoils, if not faster, and are much more comfortable. They are also much less prone to cancellation in rough weather and the fares are generally the same as hydrofoils. The main players are Hellas Flying Dolphins and Blue Star Ferries.

FERRY
Every island has a ferry service of some sort, although in winter these are pared back. Services pick up from April, and during July and August Greece's seas are a mass of wake and wash. The ferries come in all shapes and sizes, from the state-of-the-art 'superferries' that run on the major routes to the ageing open ferries that operate local services to outlying islands.

The main ferry companies in Greece include:

ANEK (☎ 2104 197 420; www.anek.gr)
Blue Star Ferries (☎ 2108 919 800; www .bluestarferries.com)
GA Ferries (☎ 2104 199 100; www.gaferries.com)
Hellas Flying Dolphins (☎ 2104 199 000; www .dolphins.gr)
LANE Lines (☎ 2104 274 011; www.lane.gr)
Minoan Lines (☎ 2104 145 700; minoan.gr)
NEL Lines (☎ 2251 026 299; www.nel.gr)

Classes
Large ferries usually have four classes: 1st class has air-con cabins and a decent lounge and restaurant; 2nd class has smaller cabins

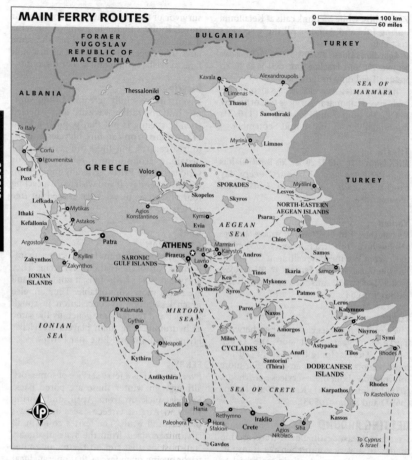

MAIN FERRY ROUTES

0 ———— 100 km
0 ———— 60 miles

Map shows ferry routes across Greece including locations: Former Yugoslav Republic of Macedonia, Bulgaria, Turkey, Albania, Thessaloniki, Kavala, Limenas, Thasos, Alexandroupolis, Samothraki, Sea of Marmara, Myrina, Limnos, To Italy, Corfu, Igoumenitsa, Corfu, Paxi, Greece, Volos, Alonnisos, Sporades, Skopelos, Skyros, Mytilini, Lesvos, North-Eastern Aegean Islands, Lefkada, Mytikas, Astakos, Ithaki, Kefallonia, Agios Konstantinos, Kymi, Evia, Psara, Chios, Chios, Turkey, Argostoli, Patra, Athens, Marmari, Karystos, Andros, Samos, Zakynthos, Kyllini, Zakynthos, Saronic Gulf Islands, Piraeus, Ratina, Lavrio, Kea, Tinos, Ikaria, Samos, Ionian Islands, Aegean Sea, Kythnos, Syros, Mykonos, Patmos, Peloponnese, Kalamata, Gythio, Mirtoön Sea, Paros, Naxos, Amorgos, Leros, Kalymnos, Kos, Ionian Sea, Neapoli, Milos, Ios, Kos, Nisyros, Symi, Kythira, Cyclades, Anafi, Astypalea, Tilos, Rhodes, Santorini (Thira), Dodecanese Islands, Antikythira, Rhodes, Sea of Crete, Karpathos, To Kastellorizo, Kastelli, Hania, Rethymno, Iraklio, Kassos, Paleohora, Hora Sfakion, Crete, Agios Nikolaos, Sitia, To Cyprus & Israel, Gavdos

and sometimes a separate lounge; tourist class gives you a berth in a shared four-berth cabin; and the last class, 3rd, is 'deck', which gets you a seat, restaurant, lounge/bar and (drum roll) the deck.

Deck class is an economical way to travel and is the class that most travellers use; 1st class is almost the same price as the equivalent air fare on some routes. Children under four years travel free, between four and 10 years pay half-fare. Children over 10 years pay full fare. When buying tickets you will automatically be given deck class.

Costs

Fares are fixed by the government. The small differences in price you may find be-

tween ticket agencies are the result of some agencies sacrificing part of their designated commission to qualify as a discount service. The discount offered seldom amounts to much.

Tickets can be bought at the last minute from quayside tables set up next to the boats. Prices are the same, contrary to what you will be told by agencies.

Routes

The hub of the vast ferry network is Piraeus, the main port of Athens. It has ferries to the Cyclades, Crete, the Dodecanese, the Saronic Gulf Islands and the northeastern Aegean Islands. Patra is the main port for ferries to the Ionian Islands, while Volos and Agios

Konstantinos are the ports for the group of islands called Sporades.

HIGH-SPEED FERRY
New high-speed ferries are slashing travel times on some of the longer routes. **NEL Lines** (☎ 2251 026 299; www.nel.gr), for example, does Piraeus to Chios in 4½ hours – nearly half the time of a normal ferry and twice the price.

HYDROFOIL
Hydrofoils offer a faster alternative to ferries on some routes, particularly to islands close to the mainland. They take half the time, but cost twice as much. Most routes operate only during high season. **Hellas Flying Dolphins** (☎ 2104 199 000; www.dolphins.gr) travels from Piraeus to the Saronic Gulf Islands and the ports of the eastern Peloponnese, as well as to the Sporades from Agios Konstantinos and Volos.

Kyriacoulis Hydrofoils (☎ 2241 024 000), based in Rhodes, serves the Dodecanese and provides connections to the northeastern Aegean Islands of Ikaria and Samos as well as other routes.

Tickets for hydrofoils must be bought in advance and there is seat allocation.

Bus
All long-distance buses on the mainland and the islands are operated by regional collectives known as **KTEL** (Koino Tamio Eispraxeon Leoforion; www.ktel.org). Fares are fixed by the government and service routes can be found on the website.

Greece's buses are comfortable, they run on time and there are frequent services on all the major routes. The buses are reasonably priced, with journeys costing about €4 per 100km. Fares and journey times on a couple of the major routes are Athens–Thessaloniki (€29.40, 7½ hours) and Athens–Patra (€12.25, three hours). Tickets should be bought at least an hour in advance to ensure a seat. Buses don't have toilets and refreshments, but stop around every three hours for those needs.

Car & Motorcycle
A great way to explore areas in Greece that are off the beaten track is by car. However, it's worth bearing in mind that Greece has the highest road-fatality rate in Europe. The road network has improved dramatically

in recent years and places that were little more than a one-lane dirt track masquerading as a road have now been widened and asphalted.

Almost all islands are served by car ferries, but they are expensive. For example, the cost for a small vehicle from Piraeus to Mykonos is €66.60. Petrol in Greece is expensive at around €0.70 per litre in the big cities, but you'll pay €0.90 in remote areas.

The Greek automobile club, ELPA, offers reciprocal services to members of other national motoring associations. If your vehicle breaks down, dial ☎ 104.

You can bring a vehicle into Greece for four months without a carnet – provided you have a Green Card (international third-party insurance).

HIRE
Rentals cars are available just about anywhere in Greece. All the major multinational companies are represented in Athens and in most major tourist destinations. You can generally get a much better rate with local companies. Their advertised rates are about 25% lower and they're often willing to bargain. Make sure to check the insurance waivers on these companies closely and check how they can assist in case of a breakdown.

High-season weekly rates with unlimited mileage start at about €280 for the smallest models, dropping to €200 in winter – and that's without tax and extras. Major companies will request a credit card deposit. The minimum driving age in Greece is 18, but most car-hire firms require a driver of 21 or over.

Mopeds and motorcycles are available for hire everywhere. There are, however, recently introduced regulations stipulating that you need a valid motorcycle licence stating proficiency for the size of motorcycle you wish to rent – from 50cc upwards.

Motorcycles are a cheap way to get around Greece. Mopeds and 50cc motorcycles range from €10 to €15 per day or from €25 per day for a 250cc motorcycle. Outside high season, rates drop considerably. Ensure the bike is in good working order and the brakes work well.

If you plan to hire a motorcycle or moped, check that your travel insurance does cover you for injury resulting from motorcycle accidents.

ROAD RULES

While it sometimes appears that there aren't any road rules in Greece, you are apparently supposed to drive on the right and overtake on the left. No casual observer would ever guess that it is compulsory to wear seat belts in the front seats of vehicles, and in the back if they are fitted.

The speed limit for cars is 120km/h on toll roads, 90km/h outside built-up areas and 50km/h in built-up areas. For motorcycles up to 100cc, the speed limit outside built-up areas is 70km/h and for larger motorbikes, 90km/h. Drivers exceeding the speed limit by 20/40% receive a fine of €60/150.

Drink-driving laws are strict; a blood alcohol content of 0.05% incurs a fine of around €150 and over 0.08% is a criminal offence.

Local Transport

BUS

Most Greek towns are small enough to get around on foot. All major towns have local bus systems, but the only place that you'll probably need them are Athens, Kalamata and Thessaloniki.

METRO

Athens is the only city large enough to warrant a metro system – and it finally has one. See p556 for details.

TAXI

Taxis are widely available in Greece and they are reasonably priced. Yellow city cabs are metered. Flag fall is €0.75, followed by €0.24 per kilometre in towns and €0.44 per kilometre outside towns. The rate doubles from midnight to 5am. Additional charges are €1.18 from airports, €0.60 from ports, bus stations and train stations, and €0.30 per luggage item over 10kg.

Taxi drivers in Athens are gifted in their ability to make a little extra with every fare. If you have a complaint, note the cab number and contact the tourist police. In rural areas taxis don't have meters, so make sure you agree a price before you get in – drivers are generally honest, friendly and helpful.

Train

The main problem with train travel in Greece is that there are only two main lines: north to Thessaloniki and Alexandroupolis, and to the Peloponnese. In addition there are a number of branch lines, such as the Pyrgos–Olympia line and the spectacular Diakofto–Kalavryta mountain railway. There are two distinct levels of service: the painfully slow, dilapidated trains that stop at all stations, and the faster, modern intercity trains.

Inter-Rail and Eurail passes are valid in Greece, but you still need to make a reservation. In summer, make reservations at least two days in advance.

Ireland

CONTENTS

IRELAND

After centuries of suffering, it's finally Ireland's day in the sun. Money has arrived – and it's changing everything. Cities are becoming more and more cosmopolitan, small towns suddenly do lattes, and farmers are building dream homes that don't look like anything the Irish countryside has ever seen.

No amount of money will ever wipe away Ireland's long and tragic history; its traces appear at every turn: Stone Age passage tombs and ring forts, medieval monasteries and castles, the stately homes and splendid Georgian architecture of the 18th and 19th centuries, as well as the ubiquitous reminders of Ireland's long and difficult relationship with Britain. Nor will any amount of money change the Irish. Famously friendly and down-to-earth, they'll draw you into their circle like the nice kid at the new school. You may find yourself feeling oddly at home here rather quickly, as though you belong right there in that old pub, among those patchwork green hills spotted with sheep, along those moody coastlines of rocks and flowers, and over that long, chatty cup of tea.

The northeastern corner of Ireland is part of the United Kingdom (UK) and its official name is Northern Ireland. It's also referred to as 'the North', or Ulster, a reference to the historical province of Ulster that was ceded to Britain following the partition of Ireland in 1921. The rest of Ireland is known as the Republic of Ireland, although on your travels you may hear it referred to as Éire, the Irish Republic, the Republic, Southern Ireland or 'the South'. This chapter covers both the independent Republic of Ireland and Northern Ireland.

FAST FACTS

- **Area** 84,421 sq km
- **Capitals** Dublin, Belfast (NI)
- **Currency** euro (€) Republic/pound sterling (£) NI; €1 = £0.68; £1 = €1.50; A$1 = €0.58/£0.39; ¥100 = €0.76/£0.49; NZ$1 = €0.54/£0.35; US$1 = €0.83/£0.56
- **Famous for** James Joyce, St Patrick, pub life, rolling green hills
- *Key Phrases craic* (gossip/good time); bleedin' (bloody); *slàinte* (drinking toast; cheers); shorts (shots); deadly (brilliant); *Erin go Brágh* (Ireland Forever)
- **Official Languages** English, Irish Gaelic
- **Population** 3.9 million
- **Telephone Codes** country code ☎ 353; Northern Ireland ☎ 44 28; international access code ☎ 00
- **Visas** no visa necessary for citizens of the EU, Australia, Canada, New Zealand or the USA

HIGHLIGHTS

- Soak up the Georgian architecture, literary ghosts, Guinness and *craic* of the nouveau **Dublin** (p624), where the optimism will get you as tipsy as the pints.
- Admire the pretty medieval streets, lively arts scene and spectacular castle at **Kilkenny** (p638).
- Discover the Burren's dramatic **Cliffs of Moher** (p647), the top-notch traditional music in **Doolin** (p654) and the trippy lunar landscape, home to millions of wildflowers and fairy trees.
- Cycle across one of the windswept and starkly beautiful **Aran Islands** (p657) in search of magical Stone Age forts.
- Spend time seeking enlightenment – as many have done before you – in the monastic environments of **Glendalough** (p635) or the **Beara Peninsula** (p647).

ITINERARIES

- **One week** Spend a couple days in Dublin to wander around Trinity College, marvel at the Chester Beatty Library's *objets* and have a meal and a pint in Temple Bar. Ponder solitude at magical Glendalough, and continue south to magnificent Kilkenny Castle. Deconstruct the landscape on a hike through the Burren and watch performance art on the streets of Galway.
- **One month** With your own car you can cover most of the main attractions around the coast. Follow the one-week itinerary, adding in Cork, Killarney and the Ring of Kerry before hitting the Burren. From Galway, spend a couple of days on one of the rugged, beautiful Aran Islands and then another few days in enchanting Connemara. Move up to the pristine northwestern region, stopping at Sligo and Donegal to take in these charming towns and the natural beauty nearby. Explore Northern Irish history walking Derry's city walls, and Northern Irish legend at the Giant's Causeway. Hike for a couple of days along the northern coast before letting it all hang out in Belfast's clubs and restaurants.

CLIMATE & WHEN TO GO

Ireland has a relatively mild climate. Average temperatures range from 4°C to 7°C in January and February and from 14°C to 16°C in July and August. June, July and August are

---

HOW MUCH?

- Cup of coffee €2
- Irish Times (newspaper) €1.50
- Umbrella €10
- Cinema ticket €8
- Aran sweater €50+

LONELY PLANET INDEX

- Litre of petrol €0.95
- Litre of bottled water €1.25
- Pint of Guinness €4
- Souvenir T-shirt €15
- Pub sandwich €3.50

---

the sunniest months; December and January are the gloomiest. Snow is scarce, but rain is plentiful – about 1000mm annually.

The tourist season begins the weekend before St Patrick's Day (17 March) and is in full swing from Easter onward. Crowds are at their biggest – and prices at their highest – in July and August.

HISTORY
Very Early Irish, Celts & Vikings

Our turbulent tale begins about 10,000 years ago, as the last ice caps melted and the rising sea level cut Ireland off from Britain. Hunters and gatherers may first have traversed the narrowing land bridge, but many more crossed the Irish Sea in small hide-covered boats. Farming did not reach Ireland until around 4000 BC. Bronze Age gold working was of a very high quality in Ireland and stimulated trade with the rest of Europe.

The Celtic warrior tribes who had such an influence on Irish culture came from central Europe. They had conquered large sections of southern Europe and plundered Rome in the 4th century AD. Known as 'Galli' (Gauls) by the Romans and 'Keltoi' by the Greeks, they were feared by both. They were an imaginative race who put great store in spirituality and the supernatural.

The Celts probably reached Ireland from mainland Europe around 300 BC and were well ensconced by 100 BC. Christian monks, including St Patrick, arrived in Ireland around the 5th century AD and, as the Dark Ages enveloped Europe, Ireland

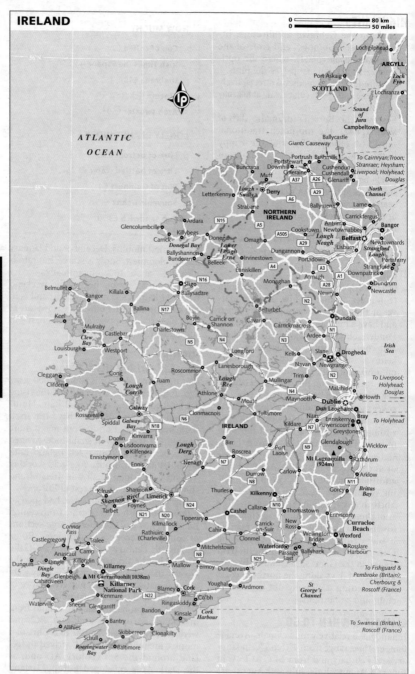

IRELAND

| 0 | 80 km |
| 0 | 50 miles |

ATLANTIC OCEAN

SCOTLAND

ARGYLL

Loch Fyne

Lochgilphead

Port Askaig

Lochranza

Sound of Jura

Campbeltown

Ballycastle

Giants Causeway

Bushmills

Portrush

Portstewart

Downhill

Coleraine

Cushendun

Cushendall

Glenariff

To Cairnryan; Troon; Stranraer; Heysham; Liverpool; Douglas

North Channel

Buncrana

Mulff

Derry

Lough Swilly

Letterkenny

Strabane

NORTHERN IRELAND

Ballymena

Antrim

Newtownabbey

Larne

Carrickfergus

Bangor

Newtownwards

Belfast

Lisburn

Strangford Lough

Portaferry

Strangford

Downpatrick

Dundrum

Newcastle

Glencolumbcille

Ardara

Killybegs

Carrick

Donegal Bay

Donegal

Ballyshannon

Bundoran

Belleek

Omagh

Cookstown

Dungannon

Portadown

Armagh

Newry

Lower Lough Erne

Irvinestown

Enniskillen

Monaghan

Cavan

Belturbet

Carrickmacross

Ardee

Dundalk

Irish Sea

Belmullet

Killala

Bangor

Keel

Ballina

Sligo

Ballysadare

Boyle

Carrick on Shannon

Slane

Kells

Navan

Trim

Drogheda

Newgrange

To Liverpool; Holyhead; Douglas

Mulrany

Castlebar

Charlestown

Longford

Lanesborough

Malahide

Clew Bay

Louisburgh

Westport

Roscommon

Lough Ree

Mullingar

Howth

Dublin

Dun Laoghaire

Cleggan

Clifden

Cong

Tuam

Athlone

Moate

Maynooth

Rossaveal

Spiddal

Galway

Galway Bay

Clonmacnois

Tullamore

Naas

Enniskerry

Powerscourt

Bray

Greystones

To Holyhead

Kinvarra

Doolin

Lisdoonvarna

Kilfenora

Lough Corrib

Lough Derg

Birr

Roscrea

Kildare

Port Laoise

Glendalough

Wicklow

Ennistymon

Ennis

Nenagh

Mt Lugnaquilla (924m)

Rathdrum

Durrow

Carlow

Arklow

Brittas Bay

Kilrush

Shannon River

Shannon

Foynes

Limerick

Thurles

Kilkenny

Callan

Gorey

Enniscorthy

Tarbet

Kilmallock

Tipperary

Cashel

Thomastown

New Ross

Curracloe Beach

Rathluirc (Charleville)

Cahir

Carrick-on-Suir

Wellington Bridge

Wexford

Connor Pass

Castlegregory

Tralee

Mitchelstown

Clonmel

Waterford

Ballyhack

Rosslare Harbour

Camp

Anascaul

Dingle

Killorglin

Killarney

Mallow

Fermoy

Dungarvan

Passage East

To Fishguard & Pembroke (Britain); Cherbourg & Roscoff (France)

Dunquin

Dingle Bay

Glenbeigh

Mt Carrantuohil (1038m)

Killarney National Park

Blarney

Youghal

Ardmore

St George's Channel

Cahirciveen

Waterville

Sneem

Kenmare

Glengarriff

Cork

Co'bh

Ringaskiddy

Kinsale

Cork Harbour

To Swansea (Britain); Roscoff (France)

Allihies

Bantry

Skibbereen

Clonakilty

Bandon

Schull

Baltimore

Roaringwater Bay

became an outpost of European civilisation. A land of saints, scholars and missionaries, its thriving monasteries produced beautiful illuminated manuscripts, some of which survive to this day.

From the end of the 8th century, the rich monasteries were targets of raids by Vikings until they, too, began to settle. At the height of their power the Vikings ruled Dublin, Waterford and Limerick, but they were eventually defeated by the legendary Celtic hero Brian Ború, the king of Munster, at the battle of Clontarf in 1014.

The British Arrive

In 1169 the Norman conquest of England spread to Ireland when Henry II, fearful of the growing power of the Irish kingdoms, dispatched his forces to the island – the legendary figure Strongbow among them. Yet, over the centuries, Anglo-Norman control gradually receded to an area around Dublin known as 'the Pale'.

Oppression of the Catholic Irish got seriously under way in the 1500s under Elizabeth I. Huge swathes of Irish land were confiscated and given to Protestant settlers, sowing the seeds of the divided Ireland that exists today. A 1641 Catholic rebellion in Ulster led to violent massacres of Protestant settlers. Later in the decade the English Civil War ended in victory for Oliver Cromwell, who began a two-year rampage through Ireland in 1649, leaving a trail of blood and smoke behind him.

In 1685 James II (a Scotsman) became King, but angered his English Protestant subjects with his outspoken Catholicism and was forced to flee the country. He sought unsuccessfully to regain his throne, which had been handed over to the Protestant William of Orange (a Dutchman) and his wife Mary (James' daughter). William's victory over James at the Battle of the Boyne on 12 July 1690 is commemorated to this day by northern Protestants as a pivotal triumph over 'popes and popery'.

By the early 18th century, the dispirited Catholics in Ireland held less than 15% of the land and suffered brutal restrictions in employment, education, land ownership and religion. An organisation known as the United Irishmen began agitating for Irish civil rights under the leadership of a young Dublin Protestant and republican, Theobald Wolfe Tone

(1763–98). The group was effectively dissolved in 1798 with Wolfe Tone's capture by the British and subsequent suicide, but it had stirred the cause of Irish nationalism – and provoked the government's wrath.

Ireland's Protestant gentry, alarmed at the level of unrest, sought the security of closer ties with Britain. In 1800 the Act of Union was passed, joining Ireland politically with Britain. The Irish Parliament duly voted itself out of existence and around 100 of the Irish MPs moved to the House of Commons in London.

In the first half of the 19th century Daniel O'Connell (1775–1847) seemed to be succeeding in moving Ireland towards greater independence by peaceful means and in 1828 won a seat in the British Parliament. Rather than risk a Catholic rebellion, the British Parliament passed the 1829 Act of Catholic Emancipation, allowing Catholics limited voting rights and the right to be elected as MPs. O'Connell later died as Ireland was suffering its greatest tragedy.

The easily grown potato had been the staple food of a rapidly growing but desperately poor Irish population. By 1840 the population had reached eight million, but successive failures of the potato crop, caused by a blight between 1845 and 1851, resulted in the mass starvation and emigration known as Ireland's Great Famine, also known as the Potato Famine.

Shamefully, during these years there were excellent harvests of other crops such as wheat and dairy produce – the country was producing more than enough grain to feed the entire population and it's said that more cattle were sold abroad than there were people on the island. But while millions of its citizens were starving, Ireland was forced to export its food to Britain and overseas. About one million people died from disease or starvation – some of them buried in mass graves, others left to rot in the fields where they had dropped. Another million emigrated, and migration continued to reduce the population during the next 100 years.

In the late 19th and early 20th centuries, the British Parliament began to contemplate Irish home rule, but WWI interrupted the process. Ireland might still have moved, slowly but peacefully, towards some sort of accommodation but for a bungled uprising in 1916. Though it is now celebrated as a

IRELAND

IRELAND

glorious bid for freedom, the Easter Rising was, in fact, heavy with rhetoric, light on planning and lacking in public support. The British response was just as badly conceived. After the insurrection had been put down, a series of trials and executions (15 in all) transformed the ringleaders into martyrs and roused international support for Irish independence.

The Road to Independence

In the 1918 general election, Irish republicans stood under the banner of Sinn Féin ('We Ourselves' or 'Ourselves Alone') and won a majority of the Irish seats. Ignoring London's Parliament, where technically they were supposed to sit, the newly elected Sinn Féin deputies, many of them veterans of the 1916 Easter Rising, declared Ireland independent and formed the first Dáil Éireann (Irish assembly or lower house), led by Eamon de Valera. The British had by no means conceded independence, however, and confrontation was inevitable.

The Anglo-Irish War (1919–21) pitted Sinn Féin and its military wing, the Irish Republican Army (IRA), against the British. The increasingly brutal responses of Britain's hated Black and Tans infantry further roused anti-British sentiment, and atrocity was met with atrocity. This was the period when Michael Collins came to the fore, a charismatic and ruthless leader who masterminded the IRA's campaign of violence against the British (while serving as finance minister in the new Dáil).

After months of negotiations in London, Michael Collins and Arthur Griffith led the delegation that signed the Anglo-Irish Treaty on 6 December 1921. The treaty gave 26 counties of Ireland independence and allowed six largely Protestant counties in Ulster the choice to opt out (a foregone conclusion).

The treaty was ratified by the Dáil in January 1922, but passions were so inflamed that within weeks a civil war broke out. At issue was not so much the future of Protestant Ulster, but rather that, under the Anglo-Irish Treaty, the British monarch remained the (nominal) head of the new Irish Free State and Irish MPs were required to swear allegiance. To de Valera and many Irish Catholics, these compromises were a betrayal of IRA and republican principles. In the violence that followed, Michael Collins was assassinated in Cork by anti-Treaty forces, while the Free State government briefly imprisoned de Valera.

By 1923 the civil war had ground to a halt, and for nearly 50 years development in the Republic of Ireland was slow and relatively peaceful. After boycotting the Dáil for a number of years, de Valera founded a new party called Fianna Fáil (Warriors of Ireland), which won a majority in the 1932 election. De Valera introduced a new constitution in 1937 that abolished the oath of British allegiance and claimed sovereignty over the six counties of Ulster. In 1948 the Irish government declared the country a republic and, in 1949, left the British Commonwealth.

The Troubles

While the Anglo-Irish Treaty granted independence to 26 counties, six counties in the north were governed by a Northern Irish Parliament sitting at Stormont, near Belfast, from 1920 until 1972.

The Protestant majority made its rule absolute by systematically excluding Catholics from power. This led to the formation of an initially nonsectarian civil rights movement in 1967 to campaign for fairer representation for Northern Irish Catholics. In January 1969 civil rights marchers walked from Belfast to Derry to demand a fairer division of jobs and housing. Just outside Derry a Protestant mob attacked the mostly Catholic marchers. Further marches and protests and violence followed. Far from keeping the two sides apart, Northern Ireland's mainly Protestant police force, the Royal Ulster Constabulary (RUC), was becoming part of the problem.

Finally, in August 1969 British troops were sent into Derry and (two days later) Belfast to maintain law and order. Though the Catholics initially welcomed it, the army soon came to be seen as a tool of the Protestant majority. The peaceful civil rights movement lost ground and the IRA, which had been hibernating, found itself with new and willing recruits for an armed independence struggle.

Thus the so-called Troubles rolled back and forth throughout the 1970s and into the 1980s. Passions reached fever pitch in 1972 when 13 unarmed Catholics were shot dead by British troops in Derry on 'Bloody

Sunday' (30 January). Then in 1981 IRA prisoners in Northern Ireland went on a hunger strike to demand the right to be recognised as political prisoners (rather than as terrorists). Ten of them fasted to death, the best known being an elected MP, Bobby Sands.

The waters were further muddied by the IRA splitting into 'official' and 'provisional' wings, from which sprang even more violent republican organisations. Protestant paramilitary organisations such as the Ulster Volunteer Force (UVF) sprang up in opposition to the IRA and its splinter groups, and violence was met with violence.

Giving Peace a Chance

In 1985 the Anglo-Irish Agreement gave the Dublin government an official consultative role in Northern Irish affairs for the first time. The Downing St Declaration of December 1993, signed by Britain and the Republic, moved matters forward, with Britain declaring it had no 'selfish, economic or military interest' in preserving the division of Ireland.

In August 1994 a 'permanent cessation of violence' by the IRA, announced by Sinn Féin's leader Gerry Adams, offered the almost unimagined prospect of peace in Ulster. When Protestant paramilitary forces responded with their own cease-fire in October 1994, most British troops were withdrawn to barracks and roadblocks were removed.

In 1995 the British and Irish governments published two 'framework documents' to lay the groundwork for all-party peace talks. The subsequent negotiations stalled when Britain's Conservative prime minister, John Major, refused to allow all-party talks to start until the IRA decommissioned its weapons. An IRA bomb in the Docklands area of London shattered the negotiations in February 1996. In June 1996, with the IRA's refusal to restore its cease-fire, 'all-party' talks on Ulster's future convened without Sinn Féin.

The peace process regained momentum with the landslide victory in May 1997 of Tony Blair's Labour Party, its massive majority enabling it to act with a freer hand than the previous Conservative government. In June 1997 Britain's new Northern Ireland Secretary, Dr Mo Mowlam, promised to admit Sinn Féin to all-party talks following any new cease-fire. Encouraged by this, the IRA declared another cease-fire on 20 July 1997.

To worldwide acclaim these talks produced the Good Friday Agreement on 10 April 1998. This complex agreement allows the people of Northern Ireland to decide their political future by majority vote and commits its signatories to 'democratic and peaceful means of resolving differences on political issues'. It established a new Northern Irish Parliament and high-level political links between the Republic and Northern Ireland. In May 1998, the agreement was approved by 71% of voters in the North and 94% in the South in simultaneous referendums. However, despite these moves towards peace, later that year a bomb planted by the 'Real IRA' killed 28 people in Omagh.

Since the Good Friday Agreement the peace process has stopped and started, with the new Parliament being suspended then reinstated, largely over wrangles about how and when the IRA should 'decommission' its weapons stockpiles, an unknown quantity of which it has voluntarily 'put beyond use'.

Devolution was most recently suspended in October 2002 following allegations of intelligence-gathering at Stormont by the IRA and had still not resumed at the time of research. November 2003 elections did not bode well for further negotiations, either. The leaders of the newly elected majority parties – Reverend Ian Paisley of the hardline Democratic Unionist Party and Sinn Féin's Gerry Adams – are widely considered the two figures least likely to collaborate in forming a new devolved administration, with Paisley essentially refusing to share power with Adams.

A very cautious optimism seems to prevail, however, and although it often seems bickering of one sort or another will continue forever, most agree (with fingers crossed perhaps) that the 'war' is over. The question now is how far optimism can take the process, and how long it will last.

PEOPLE

The total population of Ireland is around 5.6 million: 3.9 million in the Republic and nearly 1.7 million in Northern Ireland. Prior to the 1845–51 Great Famine, the population was around eight million; death and emigration reduced it to around six million, and emigration continued at a high level for the next 100 years. It wasn't until the 1960s that Ireland's population finally began to recover.

Lately, economic migrants, including relatively wealthy Western European nationals and poorer migrants from elsewhere, have had a minor but palpable impact on the population.

RELIGION

Religion has always played a pivotal role in Irish history. About 90% of residents in the Republic are Roman Catholic, followed by 3% Protestant, 0.1% Jewish and the rest with no professed religious belief. In the North the breakdown is about 53% Protestant and 44% Catholic.

The Catholic Church has always opposed attempts to liberalise laws governing contraception, divorce and abortion. Today, condom machines can be found all over Ireland and divorce is legal, but abortion remains illegal in the Republic. Though still wielding considerable influence in the South, the Catholic Church has been weakened recently by drastically declining attendance, falling numbers of young men and women entering religious life and by damaging paedophile sex scandals. It's now treated with a curious mixture of respect and derision by various sections of the community.

ARTS

Literature

The Irish have made an enormous impact on world literature. Important writers include Jonathan Swift, Oscar Wilde, WB Yeats, George Bernard Shaw, James Joyce, Sean O'Casey, Samuel Beckett and Roddy Doyle, whose *Paddy Clarke Ha Ha Ha* won the Booker Prize in 1993. The Ulster-born poet Seamus Heaney was awarded the Nobel Prize for Literature in 1995. Earlier Irish Nobel laureates include Shaw (1925), Yeats (1938) and Beckett (1969). Frank McCourt became a world favourite with his autobiographical *Angela's Ashes*, which won the Pulitzer Prize, and *'Tis*.

Music

Traditional Irish music – played on instruments such as the *bodhrán* (a flat, goatskin drum), *uilleann* (or 'elbow') pipes, flute and fiddle – is an aspect of Irish culture that visitors are most likely to encounter. Almost every town and village in Ireland seems to have a pub renowned for its trad-

---

THE GAELTACHT

Were you to limit your travels in Ireland to what was once called the Pale (including Dublin and Counties Wexford and Waterford), or much of the east and south for that matter, you would be forgiven for thinking you were in a monolingual, English-speaking country. But the Republic is officially bilingual: in pockets of the Republic known as the Gaeltacht, Irish (or Gaelic as it is sometimes called) remains, at least in theory, the first language of communication and commerce among the majority of the population.

You are likely to hear Irish in your travels – on the Aran Islands, the Dingle Peninsula or in Connemara, where you may find the language's domination of street signs less than romantic. A Celtic language closely related to Scottish Gaelic (and less so to Welsh), Irish is an attractive but difficult tongue with a unique orthographic system. For example, 'mh' is pronounced like 'v', 'bhf' is a 'w', and 'dh' is like 'g'.

Sadly, the Gaeltacht represents only a tiny area of Ireland's linguistic past. If you were to look at a map of Ireland dating from the early 19th century that had been shaded to show the areas in which Irish was spoken as a first language, and then compared it with one marking today's Gaeltacht, you would be shocked to see the extent that the language has lost ground over the past 200 years.

The older map would incorporate more than two-thirds of the island, representing some 2.4 million people. On the more recent map there would be just a dozen small smudges in seven counties, mostly along the west coast. Some 90,000 people live in the Gaeltacht today, with the majority of them – just over 70% – *Gaeilgeoirí* (Irish speakers). But according to the most recent census (2002), only 55.6% of adults there speak Irish on a daily basis.

More than 1.5 million people in the Irish Republic claim to have an ability to speak Irish, but the vast majority say so only because they were required to study it for up to 12 years at school.

itional music. Of the Irish music groups, perhaps the best-known are the Chieftains, the Dubliners, Altan, De Danann and the wilder Pogues. Among popular Irish singers/ musicians who have made it on the international stage are Van Morrison, Enya, Sinéad O'Connor, Bob Geldof, U2, the Cranberries and, more recently, The Corrs, Westlife and half-Zambian Samantha Mumba.

Architecture

Ireland is packed with archaeological sites, prehistoric graves, ruined monasteries, crumbling fortresses, abandoned manor houses and many other firm reminders of its long and usually dramatic history. You may encounter the following terms on your travels:

cashel – a stone *ring fort* or *rath*

dolmen – a portal tomb or Stone Age grave consisting of stone 'pillars' supporting a stone roof or capstone

ogham stone – a memorial stone of the 4th to 9th centuries, marked on its edge with groups of straight lines or notches to represent the Latin alphabet

passage tomb – a megalithic mound-tomb with a narrow stone passage that leads to a burial chamber

ring fort or **rath** – a circular fort, originally constructed of earth and timber, but later made of stone

round tower – a tall tower or belfry built as a lookout and place of refuge from the Vikings

Theatre

Ireland has a rich theatrical history. Dublin's first theatre was founded in Werburgh St in 1637. The literary revival of the late 19th century resulted in the establishment of Dublin's Abbey Theatre, now Ireland's national theatre, which presents works by former greats – WB Yeats, George Bernard Shaw, JM Synge and Sean O'Casey – and promotes modern Irish dramatists. One of the most outstanding playwrights of the last two decades is Frank McGuinness (born 1956), whose plays explore the consequences of 1972's Bloody Sunday on the people of Derry. Other playwrights to watch out for are Martin McDonagh, Brian Friel (of *Dancing at Lughnasa* fame), Conor McPherson, Donal O'Kelly, Enda Walsh and Damian Gorman.

ENVIRONMENT

Ireland is divided into 32 counties: 26 in the Republic and six in Northern Ireland. The island measures 84,421 sq km (about 83% is the Republic) and stretches 486km north to south and 275km east to west. The jagged

coastline extends for 5631km. The midlands of Ireland are flat, generally rich farmland with huge swaths of brown peat (which is rapidly being depleted for fuel).

Carrantuohill (1038m) on the Iveragh Peninsula, County Kerry, is the highest mountain on the island. The Shannon River, the longest in Ireland, flows for 259km before emptying into the Atlantic west of Limerick.

Ireland's rivers and lakes are well stocked with fish, such as salmon and trout, and the island is home to some three dozen mammal species, including the Irish hare and Irish stoat. The Office of Public Works (OPW) maintains five national parks and 76 nature reserves in the Republic; the Department of the Environment owns or leases more than 40 nature reserves in Northern Ireland.

FOOD & DRINK

In Irish B&B accommodation, breakfasts almost inevitably include 'a fry', that heart attack on a plate that consists of fried eggs, bacon, sausages, the ubiquitous black pudding (a blood sausage) and tomatoes as well as toast and butter. A bowl of the day's soup with some excellent soda or brown bread can be an inexpensive lunch that'll take the chill out of a rainy day. Traditional meals (like Irish stew, often found in pubs) are also cheap and hearty. Potatoes are everywhere, colcannon and champ being two of the tastiest mashes. Seafood, long neglected in Ireland, is often excellent, especially in the west, and there are some good vegetarian restaurants in cities and larger towns.

In Ireland a drink means a beer, either lager or stout. Stout is usually Guinness, the famous black beer of Dublin, although in Cork it can mean a Murphy's or a Beamish. If you haven't developed a taste for stout, a wide variety of lagers are available, including Harp and Smithwicks (don't pronounce the 'w'!). Simply asking for a Guinness will get you a pint (570ml); if you want a half-pint, ask for a 'glass' or a 'half'.

Listening to traditional music in a pub while nursing a Guinness is a popular form of entertainment in Ireland. If someone suggests visiting a pub for its good *craic*, it means a good time, convivial company, sparkling conversation and scintillating music. In the Republic, cigarettes are not part of the mix: smoking in all public places was banned in March 2004.

DUBLIN

☎ 01 / pop 1.1 million

If it seems like Dubliners are all young, hip and international, that's because they are. Ireland's young population (41% of the country is under 25) combined with a manic dual influx of money and immigrants has created a town full of energy, amnesia, optimism and more foreign languages floating through the air than you can identify. Dublin (Baile Átha Cliath), like a kid that's just discovered she can walk, is bustling, growing and revising her identity with abandon.

And it's contagious. Visitors swarm in droves to Dublin like moths to a light bulb – for the historic museums, top-class attractions and Georgian architecture, sure. But they also come for the humour and warmth of the people: they come, in a word, for the *craic*. Some come to party (weekends can be boisterous), but the social draw is more than that. Dublin, in all its quickening pace and bursting prosperity, somehow retains its legendary kindness and relaxed feel, which, in an ever fast-paced world, are worth their weight in gold.

ORIENTATION

Dublin is neatly divided by the Liffey River into the more affluent 'south side' and the grittier, less prosperous 'north side'.

North of the river important landmarks are O'Connell St, the major shopping thoroughfare, and Gardiner St, with its many B&Bs and guesthouses. Pedestrianised Henry St, running west off O'Connell St, is the main shopping precinct. The main bus station, Busáras, and Connolly station, one of the city's two main train stations, are near the southern end of Gardiner St.

Immediately south of the river is the bustling, sometimes raucous, Temple Bar district, Dame St, Trinity College and just below it, the lovely St Stephen's Green. The pedestrianised Grafton St and its surrounding streets and lanes are crammed with shops and are always busy. About 2km west is Heuston station, the city's other main train station.

INFORMATION
Bookshops

Easons (Map p630; ☎ 873 3811; 40 O'Connell St) One of the biggest magazine stockists in Ireland.

Hodges Figgis (Map p630; ☎ 677 4754; 56-58 Dawson St) With a large selection of books on things Irish.

Sinn Féin Bookshop (Map pp626-7; ☎ 872 7096; 44 Parnell Sq West)

Emergency

For emergency assistance phone ☎ 999 or ☎ 112 for *gardai* (police), ambulance or fire brigade. Both numbers are free.

Internet Access

Both Talk Shop and Wired have a couple of branches around town, all with cheap international calling and Internet access.

Talk Shop (per hr €3.50) Dame St (Map p630; ☎ 1890-890 200); Temple Lane (Map p630; ☎ 672 7212; No 20); Upper O'Connell St (Map pp626-7; ☎ 872 0200; No 5)

Wired (http://mail.wired.ie; per hr €2.50) Aungier St (Map p630; ☎ 405 4814; No 15); Dame St (Map pp626-7; ☎ 679 0950; No 76) Open till midnight.

Medical Services

Eastern Regional Health Authority (Map pp626-7; ☎ 679 0700; www.erha.ie; Dr Steevens's Hospital, 138 Thomas St) Opposite Heuston station; can advise you on a suitable doctor from 9am to 5pm Monday to Friday.

Doctors on Call (☎ 453 9333; ☽ 24hr) Request a doctor to come to your accommodation (€60-75).

O'Connell's Pharmacy (Map p630; ☎ 873 0427; 55-56 O'Connell St; ☽ 7.30am-10pm Mon-Fri, 8am-10pm Sat, 10am-10pm Sun)

Well Women Clinic (Map p630; ☎ 872 8051, 688 3714; 35 Lower Liffey St) Handles women's health issues and can supply contraception.

Money

The Dublin airport and Dublin Tourism Centre have currency-exchange counters, and numerous banks around the city centre have exchange facilities, open during regular bank hours. The central bank offers the best exchange rates, while the airport and ferry terminal bureaus offer the worst. ATMs are everywhere.

Post

Dublin's famous **General Post Office** (GPO; Map pp626-7; ☎ 705 7000; O'Connell St; ☽ 8am-8pm Mon-Sat) is north of the river. South of the river there are post offices on Anne St South and St Andrew's St.

Tourist Information

Dublin Tourism, a branch of Fáilte Ireland (pronounced 'fawlcha'), runs a fantastic toll-free **information line** (☎ 1850-230 330). The offices provide walk-in services only.

Dublin Tourism Centre (Map p630; ☎ 605 7700; www.visitdublin.com; St Andrew's Church, 2 Suffolk St; ☽ 9am-7pm Mon-Sat, 10.30am-3pm Sun Jul & Aug, 9am-5.30pm Mon-Sat Sep-Jun) A sort of tourist information complex. Services include accommodation bookings, car rentals, maps, tickets for tours, concerts and more.

Dublin Tourism City Centre (Map pp626-7; 14 O'Connell St; ☽ 9am-5pm Mon-Sat); Dun Laoghaire (Dun Laoghaire ferryport; ☽ 10am-1pm & 2-6pm)

Fáilte Ireland (Map pp626-7; Baggot St; ☽ 9am-5pm Mon-Fri) Less conveniently situated about 500m southeast of town, but much less crowded than the other centres.

Northern Ireland Tourist Board (NITB; Map p630; ☎ 679 1977; http://discovernorthernireland.com; 16 Nassau St; ☽ 9.15am-5.30pm Mon-Fri, 10am-5pm Sat) Information and free booking services.

SIGHTS
Trinity College & Book of Kells
Ireland's premier university was founded by Queen Elizabeth I in 1592. Its full name is the University of Dublin, but Trinity College is the institution's sole college. Until 1793 its students were all Protestants, but today most of its 9500 students are Catholic. Women were first admitted to the college in 1903 – earlier than at most British universities.

In summer, **walking tours** (per person €10; ☽ 10.45am-3.40pm Mon-Sat, 10.15am-3pm Sun mid-May–Sep) depart every 40 minutes from College St (inside the main gate on College Green). The tour's a good deal since it includes the fee to see the *Book of Kells*, an elaborately illuminated manuscript dating from around AD 800, and one of Dublin's prime attractions. It's on display in the East Pavilion of the **Colonnades** (Map p630; adult/concession €7.50/6.50; ☽ 9.30am-5pm Mon-Sat year-round, to 4.30pm Sun Jun-Sep, noon-4.30pm Sun Oct-May) together with the 9th-century *Book of Armagh*, the even older *Book of Durrow* (AD 675) and the harp of Brian Ború, who led the Irish against the Vikings in the Battle of Clontarf.

Trinity's other big attraction is the **Dublin Experience** (Map p630; ☎ 608 1688; admission €5, adult/concession incl Book of Kells €10.50/8.50; ☽ 10am-5pm mid-May–Sep), a 45-minute audiovisual introduction to the city.

Museums
Among the highlights of the exhibits at the impressive **National Museum** (Map pp626-7; ☎ 667 7444; www.museum.ie; Kildare St; admission by donation; ☽ 10am-5pm Tue-Sat, 2-5pm Sun) are the superb collection of Bronze Age, Iron Age and medieval gold objects in the treasury, the skeleton of a once tall, mighty Viking and the slighter but incredibly well-preserved 'Bog Body'. Other exhibits focus on the Viking period, the 1916 Easter Rising and the struggle for Irish independence. The nearby **Natural History Museum** (Map pp626-7; ☎ 677 7444; www.museum.ie; Merrion St; admission free; ☽ 10am-5pm Tue-Sat, 2-5pm Sun), aka the 'dead zoo', has hardly changed since it opened in 1857, its Victorian charm even more beautifully preserved than the exhibits.

The **Chester Beatty Library** (Map p630; ☎ 407 0750; www.cbl.ie; Dublin Castle; admission free; ☽ 10am-5pm Mon-Fri, to 1am Sat, to 1pm Sun, closed Mon Oct-Apr) houses a breathtaking collection of more than 20,000 manuscripts, rare books, miniature paintings, clay tablets, costumes and other objects spread across two floors. The 270 illuminated Qur'ans are just one draw.

Dublin Writers Museum (Map pp626-7; ☎ 872 2077; 18-19 Parnell Sq; adult/student €6.25/5.25; ☽ 10am-5pm Mon-Sat, 11am-5pm Sun), north of the river, celebrates the city's long and continuing role as a literary centre, with displays on Joyce, Swift, Yeats, Wilde, Beckett and others.

Galleries
The **National Gallery** (Map pp626-7; ☎ 661 5133; www.nationalgallery.ie; Merrion Sq West; admission & guided tours free; ☽ 9.30am-5.30pm Mon-Wed, Fri & Sat, to 8.30pm Thu, noon-5.30pm Sun, guided tours 3pm, 4pm & 5pm Sun) has a fine collection strong in Irish art. The impressive new Millennium wing has a small collection of contemporary Irish works. The gallery has wheelchair access.

On Parnell Sq, north of the river, **Dublin City Gallery, The Hugh Lane** (Map pp626-7; ☎ 874 1903; www.hughlane.ie; admission free; ☽ 9.30am-6pm Tue-Thu, to 5pm Fri & Sat, 11am-5pm Sun), has works by French Impressionists and by 20th-century Irish artists and is wheelchair accessible.

The **Irish Museum of Modern Art** (IMMA; ☎ 612 9900; www.imma.ie; admission free; ☽ 10am-5.15pm Tue-Sat, noon-5.15pm Sun), at the old Royal Hospital Kilmainham, is renowned for its conceptual installations and temporary exhibitions. It has wheelchair access and bus No 51 or 79 from Aston Quay will get you there.

In Temple Bar, around Meeting House Sq, are the **National Photographic Archives** (Map p630; ☎ 603 0374; www.nli.ie; admission free; ☽ 10am-5pm Mon-Fri, to 2pm Sat), with rotating exhibitions,

DUBLIN

300,000 photo negatives with a viewing room to look at them all, and the **Gallery of Photography** (Map p630; ☎ 671 4654; www.irish-photography.com; admission free; ✆ 11am-6pm Tue-Sat, 1-6pm Sun), which shows contemporary local and international photographers in its light and airy space. In and around Meeting House Sq is a feast of cultural activities. **Temple Bar Information Centre** (Map p630; www.templebar.ie; 12 East Essex St; ✆ 9am-5.30pm Mon, to 6pm Tue-Fri, 10am-6pm Sat, 12.30-4.30pm Sun, closed Sun Oct-May) provides free maps, guides and information on them all.

Christ Church Cathedral & Around

Christ Church Cathedral (Map p630; ☎ 677 8099; www.cccdub.ie; Christ Church Pl; adult/concession €5/2.50; ✆ 9.45am-5pm Mon-Sat, 12.30-3pm Sun) was a simple structure of wood until 1169, when the present stone church was built. In the southern aisle is a monument to the 12th-century Norman warrior Strongbow. Note the church's precariously leaning northern wall (it's been that way since 1562).

Next door and connected to the Cathedral by an elegant arched walkway, **Dublinia** (Map pp626-7; ☎ 679 4611; www.dublinia.ie; adult/child €5.75/4.25, incl Cathedral €8.75/5.75; ✆ 10am-5pm Apr-Sep, 11am-4pm Mon-Sat, 10am-4.30pm Sun Oct-Mar) is a lively attempt to bring medieval Dublin to life, with models of 10 episodes in Dublin's history. It has wheelchair access.

St Patrick's Cathedral & Around

A church was on the site of **St Patrick's Cathedral** (Map pp626-7; ☎ 475 4817; www.stpatrickscathedral.ie; St Patrick's Close; adult/concession €4.20/3.20; ✆ 9am-5pm year-round, to 6pm Sat Mar-Oct, closed during times of worship) as early as the 5th century, but the present building dates from 1191. St Patrick's choir was part of the first group to perform Handel's *Messiah* in 1742, and you can hear their successors sing the 5.45pm evensong most weeknights.

The oldest public library in the country, **Marsh's Library** (Map pp626-7; ☎ 454 3511; www.marshlibrary.ie; adult/concession €2.50/1.50; ✆ 10am-1pm & 2-5pm Mon & Wed-Fri, 10.30am-1pm Sat), contains 25,000 books dating from the 16th to early 18th century, as well as numerous maps and manuscripts. The friendly librarians are full of interesting facts about the library.

Kilmainham Gaol

The grey, threatening **Kilmainham Gaol** (☎ 453 5984; Inchicore Rd; adult/child €5/2; ✆ 9.30am-6pm Apr-Sep, to 5.30pm Mon-Fri, 10am-6pm Sun Oct-Mar), a couple of kilometres east of the city centre, played a key role in Ireland's struggle for independence and was the site of mass executions following the 1916 Easter Rising. An excellent audiovisual introduction to the building, covering its opening in 1796 to its 1924 closure, is followed by a thought-provoking tour. Arrangements can be made for a wheelchair-accessible tour with advance booking. Bus Nos 79, 78A and 51B from Aston Quay all pass by here.

O'Connell St

The 1815 **General Post Office** (GPO; Map pp626-7; ☎ 705 7000; O'Connell St; ✆ 8am-8pm Mon-Sat) is an important landmark, both physically and historically. During the 1916 Easter Rising the Irish Volunteers used the GPO as a base for attacks against the British army. After a fierce battle the GPO was almost totally destroyed. Upon surrendering, the leaders of the Irish rebellion and 13 others were taken to Kilmainham Gaol and executed.

The nearby **Monument of Light** (Map pp626-7), better known as 'The Spire', soars 120m over O'Connell St. The gigantic knitting needle was erected here in 2003 in a flashy homage to that most humble of exports, the Aran sweater. The teeny 15cm tip is a beam of light.

Guinness Brewery

The **Guinness Storehouse** (Map pp626-7; ☎ 408 4800; www.guinness-storehouse.com; Market St; adult/child €13.50/5; ✆ 9.30am-9pm Jul-Aug, to 5pm Sep-Jun) sits in the malty fug of the mighty **Guinness brewery** southeast of the centre. The tour is uninspired, but the building is impressive and you won't get a better Guinness than the free pint served at the end of the tour. It has wheelchair access; take bus No 51B or 78A from Aston Quay, or No 123 from O'Connell St.

Other Attractions

Dublin Castle (Map p630; ☎ 677 7129; www.dublincastle.ie; adult/concession €3.50/2; ✆ 10am-4.45pm Mon-Fri, 2-5pm Sat & Sun) dates back to the 13th century, when it was the centre of British power.

Dublin's finest Georgian architecture, including its famed doorways, is found around the handsome **St Stephen's Green** and **Merrion Sq**, both of which are prime picnic spots when the sun shines.

Tours of the **Old Jameson Distillery** (Map pp626-7; ☎ 807 2355; www.whiskeytours.ie; Bow St; adult/child €8/3.50; tours 9am to 5.15pm) cover the entire whiskey-distilling process; tastings follow. At the back of the distillery is the **Chimney** (Map pp626-7; ☎ 817 3820; Smithfield Village; adult/concession €5/3.50; ⛎ 10am-5pm Mon-Sat, 11am-5pm Sun), an old distillery chimney converted into a 360-degree observation tower.

TOURS

Gray Line (☎ 872 9010; www.grayline.com), **Irish City Tours** (☎ 872 9010; www.irishcitytours.com) and **Dublin Bus** (Map pp626-7; ☎ 873 4222; www.dublinbus.ie) run a variety of coach tours in and around Dublin, including frequent daily hop-on hop-off services from €14 that complete 1½-hour city circuits with commentary.

It's certainly worth considering one of the many walking tours and pub crawls of the city. The **Dublin Literary Pub Crawl** (☎ 670 5602; www.dublinpubcrawl.com), led by actors performing pieces from Irish literature, and the well-reviewed **1916 Rebellion Walking Tour** (☎ 086-858 3847; www.1916rising.com), which visits key sites in the rebellion, are two of the best. Others include the **Musical Pub Crawl** (☎ 475 3313; mpc@discoverdublin.ie) and the more scholarly 'seminar on the street' with **Historical Walking Tours of Dublin** (☎ 878 0227; www.historicalinsights.ie). Each lasts about two hours and costs around €10. Bookings can be made with Dublin Tourism (p624), hostels or by calling direct.

SLEEPING

At weekends and other unexpected times Dublin beds fill up fast so reserve in advance, even for hostels. Don't forget that Dublin Tourism offices can find and book accommodation for €4 plus a 10% deposit for the first night's stay.

North of the Liffey
BUDGET

Mount Eccles Court (Map pp626-7; ☎ 873 0826; info@ecclescourt.com; 42 Nth Great George's St; dm €11-27.50, d €34-37; 🖳) In a renovated Georgian town house on one of the north side's most beautiful streets, this pristine place with dorms and doubles mostly with en suites is a great choice.

Isaacs Hostel (Map pp626-7; ☎ 855 6215; www.isaacs.ie; 2-5 Frenchman's Lane; dm/d from €16.50/52.50; 🖳) This busy, grungy hostel in a 200-year-old wine vault has loads of character and prob-

ably the cheapest beds in town. Summer barbecues and live music in the foyer are added features. A recent face-lift added a new hang-out area, Internet facilities and a disabled-access room.

Globetrotters Tourist Hostel (Map pp626-7; ☎ 878 8088; gtrotter@indigo.ie; 46-48 Lower Gardiner St; dm €21.50-24) This friendly, city-centre place has 94 beds in a variety of dorms, all with under-bed storage. Décor is funky and there's a little patio garden to the rear for the elusive sunny day. A full Irish breakfast is included.

Other recommendations:

Abbey Court Hostel (Map p630; ☎ 878 0700; www.abbey-court.com; 29 Bachelor's Walk; dm/d €21/88) Clean dorms with good storage.

Jacob's Inn (Map pp626-7; ☎ 855 5660; www.isaacs.ie; 21-28 Talbot Pl; dm/d from €16.50/72; 🖳) Just behind Busáras, with some wheelchair-accessible rooms.

MID-RANGE & TOP END

Clifden Guesthouse (Map pp626-7; ☎ 874 6364; www.clifdenhouse.com; 32 Gardiner Pl; s/d €60/110; Ⓟ) Over 200 years old, this refurbished Georgian house is a great place to stay in the area. Its 14 tastefully decorated rooms are immaculately clean and extremely comfortable. There's no lift, however, to 4th-floor rooms.

Townhouse (Map pp626-7; ☎ 878 8808; www.townhouseofdublin.com; 47-48 Lower Gardiner St; s/d from €67/110) The Townhouse has all the hallmarks of a great guesthouse – 80 individually designed, comfortable rooms, friendly and efficient staff and a city centre location. It's fantastic value for the money.

Castle Hotel (Map pp626-7; ☎ 874 6949, www.castle-hotel.ie; Great Denmark St; s/d/tr from €69/115/155; Ⓟ) Established in 1809, the Castle Hotel claims to be Dublin's oldest. Many rooms are generous in size and retain their lovely Georgian cornicing and proportions. The house, though rough around the edges, still feels like a 19th-century home.

Modest options on Upper Gardiner St (north of the city centre) include the friendly **Fatima House** (Map pp626-7; ☎ 874 5410; 17 Upper Gardiner St; s/d €48/84; Ⓟ) and **Marian Guesthouse** (Map pp626-7; ☎ 874 4129; 21 Upper Gardiner St; s/d from €35/60; Ⓟ).

South of the Liffey
BUDGET

Ashfield House (Map p630; ☎ 679 7734; ashfield@indigo.ie; 19-20 D'Olier St; dm/d from €15/80; 🖳) A stone's throw from Temple Bar and O'Connell

Bridge, this relatively new hostel has one 14-bed dorm; its 25 other rooms include four-bed family rooms and doubles. It feels more like a small hotel, without the price tag.

Avalon House (Map pp626-7; ☎ 475 0001; www .avalon-house.ie; 55 Aungier St; dm/d from €17/64; 🖳) A megahostel near St Stephen's Green with four-, 12- and 20-bed mixed dorms on two levels, offering some privacy. There's a large kitchen, several lounges and a pool room.

Barnacles Temple Bar House (Map p630; ☎ 671 6277; www.barnacles.ie; 19 Temple Lane; dm/d from €17.50/78; 🖳) Bright and spacious in the heart of Temple Bar, Barnacles has immaculate dorms and doubles with in-room storage. Rooms are quieter in the back. Probably the best hostel south of the river.

Other recommendations:

Brewery Hostel (Map pp626-7; ☎ 453 8600; brew eryh@indigo.ie; 22-23 Thomas St; dm/d from €20/75; 🅿 🖳) Small and family-run, with a patio out back.

Kinlay House (Map p630; ☎ 679 6644; www.kinlayhouse .ie; 2-12 Lord Edward St; dm/d from €16/62; 🖳) Huge, mixed 24-bed dorms and smaller rooms. Not for the faint-hearted.

MID-RANGE & TOP END

Grafton Guesthouse (Map p630; ☎ 679 2041; grafton guesthouse@eircom.net; 26-27 Sth Great George's St; s/d €60/100) In a Gothic-style building over the George's St Arcade market, this friendly guesthouse has 16 cheerful rooms, if you don't mind the old-school chintz and brocade décor.

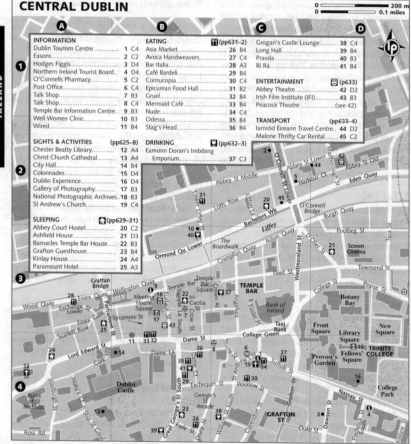

CENTRAL DUBLIN

INFORMATION		
Dublin Tourism Centre	1	C4
Easons	2	C2
Hodges Figgis	3	D4
Northern Ireland Tourist Board	4	D4
O'Connells Pharmacy	5	C2
Post Office	6	C4
Talk Shop	7	B3
Talk Shop	8	C4
Temple Bar Information Centre	9	B3
Well Women Clinic	10	B3
Wired	11	B4

SIGHTS & ACTIVITIES	(pp625-8)	
Chester Beatty Library	12	A4
Christ Church Cathedral	13	A4
City Hall	14	B4
Colonnades	15	D4
Dublin Experience	16	D4
Gallery of Photography	17	B3
National Photographic Archives	18	B3
St Andrew's Church	19	C4

SLEEPING	(pp629-31)	
Abbey Court Hostel	20	C2
Ashfield House	21	D3
Barnacles Temple Bar House	22	B3
Grafton Guesthouse	23	B4
Kinlay House	24	A4
Paramount Hotel	25	A3

EATING	(pp631-2)	
Asia Market	26	B4
Avoca Handweavers	27	C4
Bar Italia	28	A3
Café Bardeli	29	B4
Cornucopia	30	C4
Epicurean Food Hall	31	B2
Gruel	32	B4
Mermaid Café	33	B4
Nude	34	C4
Odessa	35	B4
Stag's Head	36	B4

DRINKING	(pp632-3)	
Eamonn Doran's Imbibing Emporium	37	C3

Grogan's Castle Lounge	38	C4
Long Hall	39	B4
Pravda	40	B3
Rí Rá	41	B4

ENTERTAINMENT	(p633)	
Abbey Theatre	42	D2
Irish Film Institute (IFI)	43	B3
Peacock Theatre	(see 42)	

TRANSPORT	(pp633-4)	
Iarnród Éireann Travel Centre	44	D2
Malone Thrifty Car Rental	45	C2

Number 31 (Map pp626-7; ☎ 676 5011; www
.number31.ie; 31 Leeson Close; s/d/tr from €105/150/210)
The coach house and former home of mod-
ernist architect Sam Stephenson (of Central
Bank fame) still feel like a real 1960s home intact, with sunken sitting room, leather sofas,
mirrored bar, Perspex lamps and ceiling-to-
floor windows. A hidden oasis of calm, a
five-minute walk from St Stephen's Green.
Children under 10 are not permitted.

La Stampa Hotel (Map pp626-7; ☎ 677 4444; www.la
stampa.ie; 35 Dawson St; s/d from €120/160) La Stampa
is a wonderful, atmospheric little hotel on
trendy Dawson St. There are plans to extend
afoot, but at the moment it has 24 lovely
Asian-influenced white rooms with Oriental
rattan furniture, exotic velvet throws, TV and
minibar. Excellent value for its location.

Paramount Hotel (Map p630; ☎ 417 9900; www
.paramounthotel.ie; Parliament St & Essex Gate; s/d/tr
€140/200/250) Behind the Victorian façade is
a genuine re-creation of a 1930s-style hotel,
complete with stained-wood floors, deep-red
leather couches and heavy velvet curtains.
The 70 rooms are decorated along similar
lines, with plenty of dark wood and subtle
colours, and some are wheelchair accessible.

EATING

Dubliners' increased spending power in
recent years has spawned a proliferation of
new restaurants around the capital, while
the city's influx of immigrants has created
a market for ethnically diverse eateries.
Around Parnell St you'll find a spate of new
international spots, and the numbers of
decent-quality restaurants and cafés north
of the Liffey are growing steadily. Many
of the mid-range options are concentrated
around the southern side of the city centre,
and Temple Bar is awash with eateries of
mixed quality. Dublin has a reputation for
being an expensive place to eat, but with so
many places to choose from, you'll find
something to suit both your budget and palate.

North of the Liffey

Epicurean Food Hall (Map p630; Lower Liffey St; mains
€3.50-12; ⏱ 9.30am-5.30pm Mon-Sat) You'll be spoilt
for choice in this refurbished arcade that has
almost every imaginable type of food stall.
The quality varies, but good choices include
Itsabagel, Taco Taco and Istanbul House.

Cobalt Café & Gallery (Map pp626-7; ☎ 873 0313;
16 Nth Great George's St; mains €4-7; ⏱ 10.30am-4.30pm

Mon-Fri) This gorgeous, elegant café in a bright
and airy Georgian drawing room is a must if
you're in the 'hood. It's almost opposite the
James Joyce Cultural Centre. The menu is
simple but you'll be welcomed with hearty
soups and a roaring fire in winter or fresh
sandwiches in the garden on warmer days.

Alilang (Map pp626-7; ☎ 874 6766; 102 Parnell St;
mains €6-15; ⏱ noon-3pm & 5-11.30pm, to 12.30am Fri &
Sat) With elements of Chinese, Japanese and
Thai cuisine, this new Korean restaurant has
plenty to whet Western appetites. Tasty dishes
like *padun* (a seafood pancake), cod and tofu
hotpot or barbecued meats brought to your
table with gas burner, skillet and spicy mari-
nade make the food a talking piece.

Chapter One (Map pp626-7; ☎ 873 2266; 18-19
Nth Parnell Sq; mains €22-32; ⏱ 12.30-2.30pm Tue-Fri,
6-11pm Tue-Sat) Savour classic French cuisine
like *foie gras*, duck confit or rabbit cassoulet
to the tinkle of the grand piano in the vaulted
basement of the Dublin Writers Museum.
This is one of the city's top 10 restaurants.
Get there before 7pm for the three-course
Pre-Theatre Special (€29).

South of the Liffey
BUDGET

Gruel (Map p630; ☎ 670 7119; 68a Dame St; mains
€3.50-12; ⏱ 10am-9.30pm Sun-Wed, to 10.30pm Thu-Sat)
Gruel offers more sophisticated food than
its name suggests. This funky place, which
wouldn't look amiss in downtown New York,
sells good food that bursts with flavour: sandwiches to die for (slow-roast organic meats or
veggies in a bap), zinging salads, and a mix
of risotto, baked fish or its trademark bangers
and mash in the evening.

Nude (Map p630; ☎ 677 4804; 21 Suffolk St; snacks
€5-8; ⏱ 8am-9pm Mon-Sat, 11am-7pm Sun) This ul-
tracool place (owned by Bono's brother) just
off Grafton St has been a huge hit since it
opened, serving tasty wraps with all kinds of
Asian fillings. You can eat in or take away,
but be sure to try one of the freshly squeezed
fruit juices.

Govinda's (Map pp626-7; ☎ 475 0309; 4 Aungier St;
mains €5-9; ⏱ noon-9pm Mon-Sat) The soup at this
branch of the Hare Krishna chain is so subtle
and flavourful you'll think Krishna himself
cooked it. The place is totally vegetarian,
with a wholesome mix of salads and Indian-
influenced hot daily specials.

Stag's Head (Map p630; ☎ 679 3701; 1 Dame
Ct; mains from €7) For a good pub lunch, we

recommend the Stag's Head. Apart from being a popular drinking spot, this place turns out simple, well-prepared, filling meals in elegant Victorian surroundings.

Bar Italia (Map p630; ☎ 679 5128; 4 Essex Quay; mains €7.50-9; ☺ 8am-6pm Mon-Fri, 9am-6pm Sat) This little café with big windows and a terrace on the quay serves proper Italian risotto, a couple of daily pasta dishes and delicious panini with Italian fillings. The real McCoy.

Cornucopia (Map p630; ☎ 677 7583; 19 Wicklow St; mains €9.75; ☺ 9am-8pm Mon-Sat, to 9pm Thu, noon-7pm Sun) For those escaping the Irish cholesterol habit, Cornucopia is a popular wholefood café turning out scrumptious healthy goodies. There's even a hot vegetarian breakfast as an alternative to muesli.

Self-caterers should wander the aisles of **Asia Market** (Map p630; ☎ 677 9764; 18 Drury St; ☺ 10am-7pm) and try to figure out what all the products are. Heaps of fresh produce and stir-fry sauces in addition to the usual Asian grocery standbys.

MID-RANGE & TOP END

Café Bardeli (Map p630; ☎ 677 1646; 12-13 Sth Great George's St; mains €6.50-13; ☺ 12.30-11pm Mon-Sat, 2-10pm Sun) The pizzas have imaginative toppings such as potato and rosemary or roasted pepper and goats cheese, and the home-made pasta menu is equally enticing. Favourites such as spag bol or fettuccine amatriciana are sold by the family-size bowl.

Avoca Handweavers (Map p630; ☎ 672 6019; 11-13 Suffolk St; mains €9-14; ☺ 11am-4.30pm Mon-Fri, to 5pm Sat & Sun) This light-filled café above the Avoca shop is a lively place, usually filled with gorgeous young mothers and their exceedingly cute offspring. It serves fabulous lunches with Italian leanings – smoked chicken, roasted red pepper and chèvre tartlet, for example. Salads are fresh and creative, and vegetarians will do fine.

Odessa (Map p630; ☎ 670 7634; 13 Dame Ct; mains €15-20; ☺ 6-10pm Mon-Wed, to 11pm Thu-Fri, 11.30am-4.30pm & 6-11pm Sat & Sun) Just off Exchequer St, Odessa's loungy atmosphere with comfy sofas and retro standard lamps attracts Dublin's hipsters, who flock in for its brunch (€9 to €12), home-made burgers, steaks or daily fish specials. You might not escape the sofa after a few of Odessa's renowned cocktails, quaffed over a game of backgammon.

Mermaid Café (Map p630; ☎ 670 8236; 22 Dame St; brunch €8-15; mains €19-30; ☺ 12.30-2.30pm &

6-10.30pm Mon-Sat, 12.30-3.30pm & 6-9pm Sun) The Mermaid caters mainly to a hip gourmand crowd who appreciate inventive organic food such as monkfish with buttered red chard or braised lamb shank with apricot couscous. Its informal atmosphere, pure food and friendly staff make it difficult to get a table without notice.

DRINKING

Dublin's 'party district' is undoubtedly Temple Bar, which can devolve into debauchery after sundown. If that's not your style, don't despair: there's plenty to do beyond Temple Bar. In fact, most of the best old-fashioned pubs are outside the district. Note that smoke-filled pubs are a thing of the past, with smoking banned in all public places in the Irish Republic in March 2004.

Grogan's Castle Lounge (Map p630; ☎ 677 9320; 15 Sth William St) Grogan's has long been a favourite haunt of Dublin's writers and painters as well as others from the bohemian, alternative set, but also of young people who don't care how they look and hip retired fishermen. It's atmospheric and unpretentious, with random art on the walls.

Long Hall (Map p630; ☎ 475 1590; 51 Sth Great George's St) Luxuriating in full Victorian splendour, this is one of the city's most beautiful and best-loved pubs. Check out the ornate carvings in the woodwork behind the bar, and the elegant chandeliers.

Stag's Head (Map p630; ☎ 679 3701; 1 Dame Ct) Built in 1770, remodelled in 1895 and unbeatable in 2005, the Stag's Head is the best pub in Dublin (and therefore the world). You may find yourself philosophising in the ecclesiastical atmosphere, as James Joyce did. Some of the fitters that worked on this pub probably also worked on churches in the area, so the stained-wood-and-polished-brass similarities are no accident.

Hipster spots include **Dice Bar** (Map pp626-7; ☎ 674 6710; 79 Queen St), the decadent **Voodoo Lounge** (Map pp626-7; ☎ 873 6013; 37 Arran Quay), the hip-hop **Forum Bar** (Map pp626-7; ☎ 878 7084; 144 Parnell St) and the north side's USSR-style **Pravda** (Map p630; ☎ 874 0076; 35 Lower Liffey St).

ENTERTAINMENT

For events, reviews and club listings, pick up a copy of the bimonthly freebie *Event Guide* (www.eventguide.ie) or the weekly *In Dublin*, available at cafés and hostels. Thursday's

Irish Times has a pull-out section called *The Ticket* that has reviews and comprehensive listings of all things arts.

Cinema

Irish Film Institute (IFI; Map p630; ☎ 679 3477; www .irishfilm.ie; 6 Eustace St; wheelchair access) The fantastic IFI has two screens showing classic and art-house films. It also has a decent bar, a café and bookshop.

Savoy (Map pp626-7; ☎ 874 6000; Upper O'Connell St) The Savoy, a traditional four-screen first-run cinema, has late-night shows at weekends.

Nightclubs

Eamonn Doran's Imbibing Emporium (Map p630; ☎ 679 9773; 3a Crown Alley) This is a large place with food, drink and live indie music, followed by DJs. Sunday night alternates between R&B and hip-hop.

Gaiety Theatre (Map pp626-7; ☎ 677 1717; www .gaietytheatre.com; King St Sth) The Gaiety is a sort of grown-ups' amusement park on Friday (€9 cover) and Saturday) (€14 cover), with a salsa bar, nightclub, live bands and bad movies all at the same time in its many rooms. It's open till 4am.

Rí Rá (Map p630; ☎ 677 4835; Dame Ct; ☒ closed Sun) Rí Rá is one of the friendlier clubs in the city centre and is full nearly every night with a diverse crowd who come for the mostly funk music downstairs or more laid-back lounge tunes and movies upstairs.

Theatre & Classical Music

Abbey Theatre (Map p630; ☎ 878 7222; www.abbey theatre.ie; Lower Abbey St) The famous Abbey Theatre near the river is Ireland's national theatre. It puts on new Irish works as well as revivals of classic Irish works. Seamus Heaney's translation of *Antigone* was playing when we last checked. The smaller and less expensive **Peacock Theatre** (Map p630; ☎ 878 7222) is part of the same complex.

Gaiety Theatre (Map pp626-7; ☎ 677 1717; www .gaietytheatre.com; King St Sth) This popular theatre hosts, among other things, a programme of classical concerts and opera. Free pre-opera lectures are sometimes held on weeknights.

National Concert Hall (☎ 417 0000; www.nch.ie; Earlsfort Tce) Just south of the city, Ireland's premier orchestral hall hosts a variety of concerts year-round, including a series of lunch-time concerts from 1.05pm to 2pm on Tuesday, June to August.

GETTING THERE & AWAY

Air

Dublin airport (☎ 814 1111), about 13km north of the city centre, is Ireland's major international gateway airport, with direct flights from Europe, North America and Asia. See p677 for more details.

Boat

There are two direct services from Holyhead on the northwestern tip of Wales – one to Dublin Port and the other to Dun Laoghaire at the southern end of Dublin Bay. Boats also sail direct to Dublin Port from Liverpool and from Douglas, on the Isle of Man. See p677 for more details.

Bus

At Bus Éireann's central bus station, just north of the Liffey on Store St, is **Busáras** (Map pp626-7; ☎ 836 6111; www.buseireann.ie). Standard one-way fares from Dublin include Belfast (€19, three hours, five to seven daily), Cork (€20.50, 3½ hours, six daily), Galway (€13, 3¾ hours, 15 daily), and Rosslare Harbour (€14.50, three hours, 12 daily).

The private company **Citylink** (☎ 626 6888) has slightly cheaper daily services to Galway; see p657.

Train

Just north of the Liffey is **Connolly station** (Map pp626-7; ☎ 703 2358), the station for Belfast, Derry, Sligo, other points north and Wexford. **Heuston station** (Map pp626-7; ☎ 703 2131), south of the Liffey and well west of the centre, is the station for Cork, Galway, Killarney, Limerick, Waterford and most other points to the south and west. For travel information and tickets, contact the **Iarnród Éireann Travel Centre** (Map p630; ☎ 836 6222, 703 4070 for booking; www.irishrail.ie; 35 Abbey St Lower). Regular one-way fares from Dublin include Belfast (€31, two hours, up to eight daily), Cork (€50, three hours, up to nine daily) and Galway (€25, three hours, five daily).

GETTING AROUND

To/From the Airport

Dublin Bus (Bus Átha Cliath; Map pp626-7; ☎ 873 4222; www.dublinbus.ie; 59 O'Connell St) runs a frequent Airlink Express service to/from Busáras, Heuston train station and various points around the city for €5 (30 to 40 minutes from the stations). Alternatively, the slower

IRELAND

(one-hour) bus No 41, 41A, 16 or 16A costs €1.65. A taxi to the centre should cost around €22. Some Dublin airport taxi drivers can be as unscrupulous as their brethren anywhere else in the world: make sure the meter is on and mention up front that you'll need a meter receipt.

To/From the Ferry Terminals

Bus Nos 53 and 53A go to Busáras from the **Dublin Ferryport terminal** (☎ 855 2222; Alexandra Rd) after all ferry arrivals (€1.25). Buses also run from Busáras to meet Irish Ferries departures. To travel between Dun Laoghaire's ferry terminal and Dublin, take bus No 46A to Fleet St in Temple Bar, bus No 7 to Eden Quay or the Dublin Area Rapid Transport (DART) rail service to Pearse station (for south Dublin) or Connolly station (for north Dublin).

Bicycle

Most rental places open during high season only, and daily rental costs can reach €25 per day. Try **MacDonalds Cycles** (☎ 475 2586; 38 Wexford St), just south of town, or **Cycleways** (Map pp626-7; ☎ 873 4748; 185-186 Parnell St).

Car

All the major car-hire companies have offices at Dublin airport and in the city centre. See p679 for details.

Public Transport

Dublin Bus local buses cost €0.85 for one to three stages, up to a maximum of €1.75 (23 or more stages). You must tender exact change when boarding; drivers can't give change.

One-day passes cost €5 for bus (including Airlink), or €7.70 for bus and DART. Late-night Nitelink buses (€4) operate from the College St/Westmoreland St/D'Olier St triangle, south of the Liffey, until 4.30am on Thursday, Friday and Saturday nights.

DART provides quick rail access to the coast as far north as Howth (€1.80) and south to Bray (€2.60). Pearse station is handy for central Dublin. Bicycles cannot be taken on the DART, but may travel on suburban trains.

LUAS (from the Irish word for 'light'; www .luas.ie) is a new light rail system that is currently running on two (unconnected) lines; the green line runs from the eastern side of St Stephen's Green southeast to Sandyford,

and the red line runs from Tallaght to Connolly station, with stops at Heuston station, the National Museum and Busáras.

Taxis in Dublin are expensive, and flag fall costs €2.75. Call **National Radio Cabs** (☎ 677 2222).

AROUND DUBLIN

Dun Laoghaire
☎ 01

Dun Laoghaire (pronounced dun leary), only 13km south of central Dublin, is a popular resort and a busy harbour with ferry connections to Britain. The B&Bs are slightly cheaper than in central Dublin, and the fast and frequent rail connections make it convenient to stay out here.

On the southern side of the harbour is the **Martello Tower**, where James Joyce's epic novel *Ulysses* opens. It now houses the **James Joyce Museum** (☎ 280 9265; adult/child €6.50/4; 🕑 10am-1pm & 2-5pm Mon-Sat, 2-6pm Sun Apr-Oct, by arrangement only Nov-Mar). If you fancy a cold saltwater dip, Dun Laoghaire's famous **Forty Foot Pool** is the place.

The chilled-out **Marina House** (☎ 284 1524; www.marinahouse.com; 7 Old Dunleary; dm €19-21, d €45), about a 10-minute walk west of town near the Monkstown DART station, has a congenial atmosphere. The patio is perfect for the weekly hostel-hosted dinner (€5).

The Rosmeen Gardens area south of the ferry pier is packed with B&Bs. To get there, walk south along George's St, the main shopping street; Rosmeen Gardens is the first street after Glenageary Rd Lower. The best of the Rosmeen Gardens B&Bs is **Rosmeen House** (☎ 280 7613; 13 Rosmeen Gardens; s/d €50/70), a lovely Spanish villa with four elegant bedrooms that are supremely comfortable.

Bus No 7, 7A or 46A or the DART rail service (€1.70, 20 minutes), will take you from Dublin to Dun Laoghaire. For information on Dun Laoghaire ferries, see p677.

Malahide Castle
☎ 01

Despite the vicissitudes of Irish history, the Talbot family managed to keep **Malahide Castle** (☎ 846 2184; adult/child €6.25/3.75; 🕑 10am-5pm Mon-Sat, 11am-6pm Sun Apr-Oct, 11am-5pm Sun Nov-Mar) from 1185 through to 1973. The castle is packed with furniture and paintings, and Puck, the family ghost, is still in residence. The extensive **Fry Model Railway** (☎ 846 3779; adult/child

€6.25/3.75; 10am-1pm & 2-5pm Mon-Thu & Sat, 2-6pm Sun Apr-Sep, closed Oct-Mar) in the castle grounds covers 240 sq metres and re-creates Ireland's rail and public transport system (it's better than it sounds). Combined admission tickets and wheelchair access are available.

To reach Malahide, take bus No 42 from beside Busáras, or a Drogheda-bound suburban train or DART from Connolly station. Malahide is 13km northeast of Dublin.

Brú na Bóinne
☎ 041

A thousand years older than Stonehenge, the extensive Neolithic necropolis known as Brú na Bóinne (the Boyne Palace) is, quite simply, one of the most extraordinary sites in Europe. Its tombs date from about 3200 BC, predating the great pyramids of Egypt by some six centuries. The entire complex, including the Newgrange and Knowth passage tombs (access to the latter is limited) can only be visited on a tour run by the **Brú na Bóinne visitor centre** (☎ 988 0300; Donore; adult/student visitor centre only €2.75/1.50, centre & Newgrange €5.50/2.75, centre & Knowth €4.25/1.50; ☉ 9.30am-7pm May-Sep, to 5.30pm Oct & Mar-Apr, to 5pm Nov-Feb). At 8.20am during the winter solstice, the rising sun's rays shine directly down Newgrange's long passage and illuminate the chamber for a magical 17 minutes. Arrive early in the summer months as tours tend to fill up.

Day tours run by **Mary Gibbons** (☎ 01-283 9973; tour & admission fees €35; ☉ Mon-Fri) come highly recommended.

Bus Éireann's service to Donore (via Drogheda; €15 return, 1½ hours, five daily) stops at the gates of the visitor centre.

THE SOUTHEAST

The Southeast doesn't just seem sunnier – it is. Counties Waterford and Wexford are the warmest and driest in Ireland and have drawn Vikings and working Dubliners alike to its beaches for centuries. The pastoral wonderland of County Kilkenny, with its verdant fields, stone walls and horse farms, dresses up for Kilkenny Castle's backyard, a 20-hectare park where families smell the roses and sunbathe amidst the ghosts of wealthy families past. The Wicklow Way is Ireland's most popular walking trail and the best way to travel to the splendid gardens of Powerscourt, the magical early-Christian ruins of Glendalough and the rugged mountain tops, deep wooded valleys, cascading waterfalls and still lakes of County Wicklow, the Garden of Ireland.

COUNTY WICKLOW

County Wicklow, less than 20km south of Dublin, has three contenders for the 'best in Ireland': best garden (at Powerscourt), best monastic site (at Glendalough) and best walk (the Wicklow Way). Its main towns, many of them dormitory communities for Dublin, hug the coast south of the capital. Pleasant seaside resorts and beaches sit between Bray and Arklow, especially at Brittas Bay. West towards Sally Gap and due south from here is a striking, sparsely populated mountainous wasteland, which includes the black waters of Lough Tay.

Powerscourt

In 1974, after major renovations, the 18th-century mansion at Powerscourt Estate was burned to the ground when a bird's nest in a chimney caught fire. One wing of the building remains, now revamped with exhibition room, café and shop, but people come for the 19th-century, 20-hectare formal gardens. Five strollable terraces extend for more than 500m down to Triton Lake, with views east to the Great Sugar Loaf Mountain.

The **estate** (☎ 01-204 6000; www.powerscourt.ie; house & gardens adult/child €8/4.50, gardens only €6/3.50; ☉ 9.30am-5.30pm Mar-Oct, to dusk Nov-Feb) is 500m south of Enniskerry's main square and about 22km south of Dublin and is wheelchair accessible. Dublin Bus No 44 runs regularly from Hawkins St in Dublin to Enniskerry (€1.70, 1¼ hours, every 20 minutes).

From the estate, a scenic 6km trail leads to **Powerscourt Waterfall** (☎ 01-204 6000; adult/child €4/3; ☉ 9.30am-7pm Mar-Oct, to dusk Nov-Feb), at 130m the highest in Ireland. You can reach the waterfall by road (5km), following signs from the estate entrance.

Glendalough
☎ 0404

Haunting Glendalough (Gleann dá Loch), pronounced glen-da-lock, is one of the most historically significant monastic sites in Ireland and one of the loveliest spots in the country, nestled as it is between two lakes at the foot of a deep valley.

IRELAND

It was founded in the late 6th century by St Kevin, a bishop who established a monastery on the Upper Lake's southern shore. It is said that St Kevin stood in one of the lakes long enough for birds to nest in his hands, and made his bed in the hollow of a tree.

During the Middle Ages, when Ireland was known as 'the island of saints and scholars', Glendalough became a monastic city catering to thousands of students and teachers. The site is entered through the only surviving monastic gateway in Ireland.

The **Glendalough Visitor Centre** (☎ 45325; adult/child €2.75/1.25; ☿ 9.30am-6pm mid-Mar–mid-Oct, to 5pm mid-Oct–mid-Mar), opposite the Lower Lake car park, overlooks a round tower, a ruined cathedral and the tiny Church of St Kevin. It has historical displays and a good 20-minute audiovisual, and staff can help plan half-hour to half-day hikes. From the centre a trail leads 1.5km west to the panoramic Upper Lake, with a car park and more ruins nearby.

Visitors swarm to Glendalough in summer so it's best to arrive early and/or to stay late, preferably on a weekday, as the site is free and open 24 hours. The lower car park gates are locked when the visitor centre closes.

SLEEPING

Glendalough Hostel (☎ 45342; glendaloughyh@ireland .com; dm/d €22/50; **P** ☐) This modern An Óige hostel is near the round tower, 600m west of the visitor centre and has wheelchair access.

Glendalough Cillíns (☎ 45777; www.hermitage .dublindiocese.ie; St Kevin's Parish Church; s/tw bungalows €45/65, min 2 nights; **P**) Designed for contemplation, these modest, self-catering dwellings are open to people of all faiths. The Glendalough area also has plenty of moderately priced B&Bs.

GETTING THERE & AWAY

St Kevin's Bus Service (☎ 01-281 8119) runs daily to Glendalough (one way/return €10/16, 1½ hours) from outside Dublin's College of Surgeons, across from St Stephen's Green. Buses leave daily at 11.30am and 6pm (11.30am and 7pm on Sunday), returning to Dublin at 7.15am and 4.15pm Monday to Friday (9.45am and 4.15pm on Saturday and 9.45am and 5.30pm on Sunday).

The Wicklow Way

Running for 132km from Marlay Park, Rathfarnham, in southern County Dublin through to County Carlow, the Wicklow Way is the oldest and most popular of Ireland's long-distance walks. The route is clearly signposted and is documented in leaflets and guidebooks; one of the better ones is *The Complete Wicklow Way* by JB Malone. Much of the trail traverses countryside above 500m, so pack boots with grip, a walking stick and clothing for Ireland's fickle weather.

The most attractive section of the walk is from Enniskerry to Glendalough (three days). Camping is possible along the route, but you'll need to ask permission from local farmers. An Óige's **Lacken House Hostel** (☎ 01-286 4036; dm €14; ☿ closed 10am-5pm; **P**) is 7km west of Enniskerry. The village of Roundwood, a good stopover, has a camp site and some B&Bs.

WEXFORD

☎ 053 / pop 9443

Little remains of Wexford's Viking past apart from its narrow streets and name, Waesfjord, or 'Ford of Mud Flats'. Cromwell was in one of his most destructive moods when he included Wexford on his 1649–50 Irish tour, destroying the churches and 'putting to the sword' three-quarters of the town's 2000 inhabitants.

Wexford is a convenient stopover for those travelling to France or Wales via the Rosslare Harbour ferry port, 21km southeast of town. Wexford's more colourful draw, though, is its world-famous opera festival, held every October (see p637).

Orientation & Information

The train and bus stations are at the northern end of town, on Redmond Pl. Follow the Slaney River 700m south along the waterfront quays to reach the **tourist office** (☎ 23111; www .southeastireland.com; The Crescent; ☿ 9am-6pm Mon-Sat May-Sep, to 5pm Oct-Apr). The curiously tight North Main and South Main Sts are a block inland and parallel to the quays.

The main post office is northwest of the tourist office on Anne St. Internet access is available at the **Westgate Computer Centre** (☎ 46291; Westgate; ☿ 9am-1pm & 2-5pm Mon-Fri; per hr €5).

Sights

Of the six original town gates, only the 14th-century **West Gate** (Slaney St) survives. Nearby is **Selskar Abbey**, founded by Alexander de la Roche in 1190 after a crusade to the Holy Land. Its present ruinous state is a result of Cromwell's 1649 visit. The **Bullring** (cnr Cornmarket & Nth Main St) was the site of one of Cromwell's massacres, but it gets its name from the now-defunct sport of bull-baiting. Today a market is held here on Friday and Saturday mornings.

About 4km northwest of Wexford, on the Dublin–Rosslare (N11) road at Ferrycarrig, the **Irish National Heritage Park** (☎ 20733; www.inhp.com; adult/concession €7/5.50; ☻ 9.30am-6.30pm Apr-Nov, to 5.30pm Dec-Mar) is an outdoor theme park that re-creates dwellings and life from the Stone Age to the early Norman period. Last admission is 1½ hours before closing. Taxis from town cost about €6.

Sleeping

Ferrybank Camping & Caravan Park (☎ 42611; nfo@wexfordcorp.ie; camp site €12; ☻ Easter-Oct; ☻) Location and luxury, right across the river from the town centre.

Kirwan House (☎ 21208; kirwanhostel@eircom.net; 3 Mary St; dm/s/d €15/25/40; ℗) A lovely old Georgian building houses this Independent Holiday Hostels (IHH) hostel.

Westgate House (☎ 22167; www.wexford-online.com/westgate; s/d €45/75; ℗) With Selskar Abbey and West Gate right across the road you won't lack for a good view from this refurbished family guesthouse.

Talbot Hotel (☎ 22566; www.talbothotel.ie; Trinity St; s/d €105/170; ℗ ☻) The bar at the Talbot is a favourite with locals, but the big, stylish bedrooms and the pool are the real attractions.

Eating

Cappuccino's (☎ 23669; 25 Nth Main St; mains €4-12; ☻ 8am-6pm Mon-Fri, to 6.30pm Sat, 10am-6.30pm Sun) From heart stopper to healthy, this little eatery is perfect for bagel breakfasts or lasagne lunches.

La Riva (☎ 24330; The Crescent; mains €18-22; ☻ 6-11pm) This 1st-floor bistro is casual about everything but the food. The menu is modern with French, Italian and Asian influences. Sunday brunch is a three-course affair (€18, 1pm to 4pm).

North and South Main Sts have something for most tastes, including a delicious range of picnic supplies at **Greenacres Food Hall** (☎ 22975; 54 Nth Main St; 9am-6pm Mon-Sat).

Drinking

Sky & the Ground (☎ 21273; 112-113 Sth Main St) A great place to eat and one of the most popular pubs in town, this family establishment has traditional music sessions almost nightly.

Thomas Moore Tavern (☎ 24348; Cornmarket) Locals call this an 'old man's pub', meaning it's good for a quiet drink and a chat.

Entertainment

Wexford hosts the **Wexford Festival Opera** (☎ 22400; www.wexfordopera.com; Theatre Royal; 27 High St) in late October. The 18-day extravaganza presents many rarely performed operas and shows to packed audiences. Theatre and dance productions are put on year-round at the **Wexford Arts Centre** (☎ 23764; www.wexford artscentre.ie; Cornmarket).

Getting There & Away

On the Dublin–Rosslare line is Wexford's **O'Hanrahan train station** (☎ 22522), which is served by three trains daily in each direction. The three-hour trip to Dublin costs €16.50 (more at weekends); to Rosslare Harbour (30 minutes) it's €4.50. **Bus Éireann** (☎ 23939, 051-879 000) runs from the train station to Rosslare Harbour (€3.80, 30 minutes, every 45 minutes Monday to Saturday, 10 on Sunday), Dublin (€11.50, 2¼ hours, 10 Monday to Saturday, eight Sunday) and beyond.

WATERFORD

☎ 051 / pop 44,564

Waterford (Port Láirge) is a busy port and modern commercial centre, retaining vestiges of its Viking and Norman past in its narrow streets and old town walls. Strongbow took the city in 1170, and in later centuries it was the most powerful political centre in Ireland.

Today Waterford is famed for its crystal but little else, apart from a few lively pubs. Despite a recent face-lift it's an unlovely town with little to offer beyond a couple of mildly interesting heritage sites. Budget travellers, beware: Waterford has no hostels.

Orientation & Information

The main shopping street runs directly back from the Suir River, beginning as Barronstrand St and changing names as it runs south to intersect with Parnell St, which runs northeast back up to the river, becoming The Mall on the way.

The **tourist office** (☎ 870 800; www.southeastire land.com; The Granary, 41 Merchant's Quay; ⏱ 9am-6pm Mon-Sat May-Sep, to 5pm Mon-Sat Oct-Apr) is near the river.

Sights & Activities

The **Waterford Crystal Factory Visitor Centre** (☎ 373311; www.waterfordvisitorcentre.com; ⏱ 8.30am-6pm Mar-Oct, 9am-5pm Nov-Feb) is 2km out on the road to Cork (N25). A guided tour (adult/student €7.50/3.50) takes you through the factory to see big-cheeked glass blowers and fragile exhibits. Bus No 3 runs from the Clocktower to the factory every 15 minutes (€2.40 return).

The **old quarter** is good for a stroll, and several handsome sections of the old city wall still stand. **Reginald's Tower**, on the corner of The Mall and Parade Quay, was built in 1003 and now has a **museum** (☎ 304 220; adult/student €2/1; ⏱ 10am-5.15pm Wed-Sun May-Sep).

On Merchants Quay, **Waterford Treasures** (☎ 304 500; www.waterfordtreasures.com; The Granary; adult/child €6/3.20; ⏱ 9.30am-6pm Mon-Sat, 11am-6pm Sun Apr-Sep, 10am-5pm Mon-Fri, 11am-5pm Sat & Sun Oct-Mar) is an impressive, hi-tech, wheelchair-accessible museum exhibition documenting Waterford's 1000-year history.

Sleeping & Eating

Mayor's Walk House (☎ 855 427; mayorswalkbandb@ eircom.net; 12 Mayor's Walk; s/d €26/46) This quiet B&B serves up big welcomes and bigger breakfasts near the police station, about 10 minutes out of town.

Portree Guesthouse (☎ 874 574; Mary St; s/d €45/75, with shared bathroom €35/50; P) The Portree is in an attractive Georgian house closer to the town centre.

Haricot's Wholefood (☎ 841 299; 11 O'Connell St; mains €8-10; ⏱ 9am-8pm) Haricot's serves generous portions of vegetarian and meat dishes. The chocolate cake is a gooey delight.

Wine Vault (☎ 853 444; 2 High St; mains €11-18; ⏱ 12.30-2.30pm Tue-Sat, 5.30-10.30pm Mon-Sat) In the old quarter, the Wine Vault serves great food, such as escalope of beef with spinach on home-made bread, with 350 wine accompaniments to choose from.

Drinking & Entertainment

Henry Downes (☎ 874 118; 10 Thomas St) A drink at Downes' – with its dark, echoey interior, a well, and whiskey blended on site – is more like a visit to the 18th century.

T & H Doolan (☎ 872 764; 32 George's St) The venerable T & H Doolan is packed at weekends and hosts some good traditional musicians.

Garter Lane Arts Centre (☎ 855 038; www.garter lanewaterford.com; 22a O'Connell St) This theatre stages plays, poetry readings and contemporary and cutting-edge films and exhibitions.

Getting There & Around

Waterford airport (☎ 875 589) is 7km south of the city at Killowen. **Aer Arann** (☎ 0818-210 210, 01-814 5240; www.aerarann.com) has a daily flight (one way €45 to €85) to Luton airport, outside London, and a Manchester service three times a week (one way €25 to €60).

The **train station** (☎ 873 401) is across the river from the town centre. Trains run regularly to Dublin (€20, three hours, five daily), Rosslare Harbour (€8.50, 1½ hours, two daily), Kilkenny (€8, 45 minutes, five daily) and Cork, via Limerick Junction (€14.50, three to five hours, four daily).

From the **Bus Éireann** (☎ 879 000) depot, opposite the tourist office, plenty of buses run daily to Dublin (€10, three hours), Wexford (€11, 1½ hours), Rosslare Harbour (€14, 1½ hours), Kilkenny (€19, one hour) and Cork (€15, 2¼ hours). **Rapid Express Coaches** (☎ 872 149; Parnell St) runs several services daily to Dublin and Dublin airport for €10 and €14.

BnB Cycles (☎ 870 356, 22 Ballybricken), up Patrick St and past the police station, rents bikes for €15 per day.

KILKENNY

☎ 056 / pop 8594

Kilkenny (Cill Chainnigh) is perhaps the most attractive city in the country. Even though Cromwell ransacked it during his 1650 campaign, Kilkenny retains some of its medieval ground plan, particularly the narrow streets. Kilkenny Castle is a magnificent fortress overlooking a bend of the river and nestling in lush, expansive grounds, while the town has an excellent selection of eating, drinking and accommodation options. Kilkenny is renowned throughout Ireland for its devotion to the arts, and it hosts several world-class festivals throughout the year that attract thousands of people.

Orientation & Information

Most places of interest can be found on or close to Parliament St and its continuation (High St), which runs parallel to the Nore

River; and along Rose Inn St, which changes its name to John St, and leads away from the river to the northeast. The **tourist office** (☎ 775 1500; www.southeastireland.com; Rose Inn St; ☺ 9am-6pm Mon-Sat May-Sep, 9am-1pm & 2-5pm Mon-Sat Oct-Apr) is a short walk from the castle. Internet access is plentiful; the **Kilkenny e.centre** (☎ 776 0093; 26 Rose St; per hr €5; ☺ 10am-9pm Mon-Sat, 11am-8pm Sun) is comfy and central.

Sights

KILKENNY CASTLE

Stronghold of the powerful Butler family, **Kilkenny Castle** (☎ 772 1450; adult/child incl tour €5/2; ☺ 9.30am-7pm Jun-Aug, 10am-6.30pm Sep, 10.30am-5pm Oct-May, closed 12.45-2pm Oct-Mar) has a history dating back to 1172, when the legendary Anglo-Norman Strongbow erected a wooden tower on the site.

The **Long Gallery**, with its vividly painted ceiling and extensive portrait collection of Butler family members over the centuries, is quite remarkable.

The castle hosts contemporary art exhibitions in the **Butler Gallery** (☎ 776 1106; www.butler gallery.com; admission free), with opening times the same as for the castle.

ST CANICE'S CATHEDRAL

The approach on foot from Parliament St leads over Irishtown Bridge and up **St Canice's Steps**, which date from 1614. Around the **cathedral** (☎ 776 4971; www.cashel.anglican.org; adult/concession €3/2; ☺ 9am-6pm Mon-Sat & 2-6pm Sun Apr-Sep, 10am-1pm & 2-4pm Mon-Sat & 2-4pm Sun Oct-Mar) is a wheelchair-accessible **round tower** (which you can climb – if you're over 12 – for €2). Although the present cathedral dates from 1251, it has a much lengthier history and contains some remarkable tombs and monuments that are decoded on a board in the southern aisle.

OTHER ATTRACTIONS

Rothe House (☎ 772 2893; Parliament St; adult/child €3/1; ☺ 10.30am-5pm Mon-Sat, 3-5pm Sun Apr-Oct, 1-5pm Mon-Sat, 3-5pm Sun Nov-Mar) is a restored 1594 Tudor house. Its original owner, the wealthy John Rothe, lived here with his wife and 12 children.

The **National Craft Gallery** (☎ 776 1804; www .ccoi.ie; Castle Yard; admission free; ☺ 10am-6pm, closed Sun Jan-Mar) showcases contemporary Irish crafts, many of which are more 'art' than 'craft'.

Tynan walking tours (☎ 087-265 1745; www .tynantours.com; adult/student €6/5) conducts hour-long tours of Kilkenny, departing from the tourist office several times a day (weekends only November to March).

Sleeping

Tree Grove Caravan & Camping Park (☎ 777 0302; www.camping-ireland.ie; camp site €12.50; ☺ Mar-mid-Nov) You can walk into town along the river from this full-facilities park. By car, it's 1.5km south of Kilkenny on the New Ross (R700) road.

Foulksrath Castle (☎ 776 7674; foulksrath@eircom .net; dm €14; ☺ closed 10am-5pm) An Óige's out-of-the-way hostel is beautifully situated in a stout 16th-century Norman castle 13km north of Kilkenny in Jenkinstown, near Ballyragget (watch for the sign). **Buggy's Coaches** (☎ 774 1264) has a service between The Parade in Kilkenny and the hostel (€3, 20 minutes), leaving at 11.30am and 5.30pm Monday to Saturday. Taxis cost about €10.

Kilkenny Tourist Hostel (☎ 776 3541; kilkenny hostel@eircom.net; 35 Parliament St; dm/tw €15/38) This IHH hostel is friendly, clean and central. Check the excellent information board for happenings.

Rose Inn (☎ 777 0061; 9 Rose Inn St; dm/d €15/50) Little Rose Inn, opposite the tourist office, is a serviceable cheapie. It's central and cheerful, and rooms in the back are quiet.

Bregagh Guesthouse (☎ 772 2315; www.bregagh house.com; Dean St; s/d €45/80; P) This central B&B near St Canice's Cathedral is comfortably furnished with sturdy antiques.

Lacken House (☎ 776 1085; www.lackenhouse.ie; Dublin Rd; s/d incl breakfast €79/138; P) Just out of town, this beautiful 1847 Victorian guesthouse is highly rated. The breakfast is superb; for €125, throw in a five-course dinner in the restaurant (see p640).

Eating

ML Dore (☎ 776 3374; 65 High St; mains €8-17; ☺ 8am-9pm, to 10pm May-Oct) ML Dore is funny, with its over-the-top kitsch décor with price stickers. It's an old standby for traditional Irish grub, with a smattering of veggie dishes.

Marble City Bar (☎ 776 1143; 66 High St; lunch €8-13, dinner €10-14; ☺ 10am-9pm) Sleek meets cosy at this bar that looks more expensive than it is. You may not be able to get the deep-fried brie in filo pastry (with mixed wild berries) out of your mind. Jazz and blues on Friday.

IRELAND

Ristorante Rinuccini (☎ 776 1575; 1 The Parade; lunch €8-14, dinner €15-25; ☼ noon-2.30pm & 6.30-10.30pm Mon-Fri, 5.30-10.30pm Sat, to 9.30pm Sun) This upmarket Italian restaurant has delicious pasta dishes, all freshly prepared.

Lacken House (☎ 776 1085; Dublin Rd; mains €23-27, 5-course menu €45; ☼ 6-9pm) The celebrated Lacken House dishes out such appetising original creations as pork with cider potato, and ostrich fillet with aubergine caviar.

Gourmet Store (☎ 777 1727; 56 High St; ☼ 9am-6pm Mon-Sat) A good option for classy picnickers and hostellers.

Drinking & Entertainment

John Cleere's (☎ 776 2573; 22 Parliament St) Cleere's often has good alternative bands – and the occasional poetry reading – in its theatre out the back.

Kyteler's Inn (☎ 772 1064; 27 St Kieran's St) The old house of Dame Kyteler (aka the Witch of Kilkenny) is a tourist magnet but atmospheric all the same.

Maggie's (☎ 776 2273; St Keiran's St) Little Maggie's is the best pub in town for traditional Irish music.

Watergate Theatre (☎ 776 1674; www.watergate kilkenny.com; Parliament St) The Watergate hosts musical and theatrical productions throughout the year.

Getting There & Around

McDonagh train station (☎ 772 2024; Dublin Rd) is east of the town centre via John St. At least four trains a day link Dublin's Heuston station to Kilkenny (€18.50) and then on to Waterford (€8). Fares are higher on Friday and Saturday.

Bus Éireann (☎ 776 4933, 051-879 000) operates out of the train station. There are eight buses a day (five on Sunday) to Dublin (€11, 2¼ hours), four to Cork (one on Sunday, €17), and one or two to Wexford, Waterford and Rosslare Harbour.

JJ Wall (☎ 772 1236; 86 Maudlin St) rents bikes for €15 per day with photo identification.

AROUND KILKENNY
Kells Priory

Only 13km south of Kilkenny, Kells Priory is one of Ireland's most impressive and romantic monastic sites. Set by rolling fields and a babbling brook, the earliest remnants of the priory date from the late 12th century, with the bulk of the present ruins from the 15th century. Extraordinarily, it's free and there are no set opening hours, which makes it ideal for a private monastic adventure and a great picnic destination. Unfortunately, unless you've got a car, the site is difficult to get to. A taxi will cost approximately €20 from Kilkenny.

CASHEL
☎ 062 / pop 2403

The **Rock of Cashel** (☎ 61437; www.heritageireland .ie; adult/student €5/2; ☼ 9am-7pm Jun–mid-Sep, to 4.30pm mid-Sep–mid-Mar, to 5.30pm mid-Mar–May), in the town of Cashel 18km north of Cahir, is a striking archaeological site. On the outskirts of town rises a huge lump of limestone bristling with ancient fortifications. Mighty stone walls encircle a complete round-tower, a roofless abbey and the country's finest 12th-century **Romanesque chapel**. Final admission is 45 minutes before closing time.

IHH's **Cashel Holiday Lodge** (☎ 61003; Dundrum Rd; dm/s/d from €15/30/50, camp site per person €7; P), at the northwestern edge of town, has fantastic views of the Rock. The **tourist office** (☎ 61333; ☼ 9am-1pm & 2-6pm Mon-Sat May-Sep) is in the town hall, on Cashel's main street. Six Dublin–Cork buses pass through Cashel daily.

THE SOUTHWEST

The Southwest reflects Ireland in all its rich diversity, from lively regional city to seaside resort, green pastures to rugged mountains, river to roaring sea. Cork is buzzing, crammed with historic and cultural venues, and with a growing number of terrific restaurants to match Dublin's. The southern coast is a fascinating trail of sea inlets, seaside resorts, historic towns and medieval castles that leads the traveller enticingly towards the fabled world of County Cork's western shores. And it's here, in the Southwest's islands and eroding peninsulas, that the seductive beauty of Atlantic Ireland captivates.

CORK
☎ 021 / pop 123,338

Cork (Corcaigh), the Irish Republic's second-largest city, buzzes with the energy and the promise of a city on the rise. This upbeat renaissance includes a stint as European Capital of Culture 2005, while a university and a burgeoning arts and music scene give this once hard-nosed commercial centre a vibrant cosmopolitan edge.

Cork has long been a significant city in Ireland, not least during the Anglo-Irish War. The Black and Tans were at their most brutal in Cork. The city was also a centre for the civil war that followed independence (Irish leader Michael Collins was ambushed and killed nearby). Today Cork is noted for its hurling and Gaelic-football teams, and its fierce rivalry with Dublin.

Orientation & Information

The city centre is an island between two channels of the Lee River. Oliver Plunkett St and the curve of St Patrick's St are the main shopping/eating/drinking areas. The train station and several hostels are north of the river; MacCurtain St and Glanmire Rd Lower are the main thoroughfares there.

The **Internet Exchange** (☎ 425 4666; 5 Woods St; per hr €3; ☒ 9am-midnight Mon-Fri, from 10am Sat, from 11am Sun), has a second **internet branch** (Paul St; ☒ 9am-10pm Mon-Sat, 10am-10pm Sun) near the Gingerbread House. The main post office is on Oliver Plunkett St.

The Bank of Ireland and Allied Irish Bank, both on St Patrick's St, have ATMs and currency-exchange facilities.

The **tourist office** (☎ 425 5100; www.corkkerry .ie; Grand Pde; ☒ 9.15am-5.15pm Mon-Fri 9.30am-4.30pm Sat, to 6pm Sat Jun-Aug), awash in souvenirs, has plenty of brochures, books and maps about the city and county.

Sights

The brick, glass and steel **Crawford Municipal Art Gallery** (☎ 427 3377; www.crawfordartgallery .com; Emmet Pl; admission free; ☒ 10am-5pm Mon-Sat) is an impressive blending of cutting-edge architecture with an existing 18th-century building. The small but excellent permanent collection includes pieces by such Irish artists as Jack Yeats and Seán Keating, as well as works of the British Newlyn and St Ives schools. The museum also puts on contemporary shows and retrospectives and is wheelchair accessible.

Cork's notable churches include the fairytale riot of spires and buttresses of the 1879 Protestant **St Fin Barre's Cathedral** (☎ 496 3387; www.cathedral.cork.anglican.org; Bishop St; adult/child €3/1; ☒ 10am-5.30pm Mon-Fri Apr-Sep, 10am-12.45pm & 2-5pm Mon-Fri Oct-Mar), south of the centre; par-

ticularly impressive are the huge pulpit and colourful chancel ceiling. North of the river there's a fine view from the tower of the 18th-century **St Anne's Church** (☎ 450 5906; www .shandonbells.org; Shandon; adult/student €6/5; ☒ 9am-5pm Mon-Sat). Admission lets you climb the tower, ring the Shandon Bells (which were being refurbished at the time of research) and watch an audiovisual presentation about the Shandon area.

The **Cork Public Museum** (☎ 427 0679; Fitzgerald Park; museum@corkcity.ie; admission Mon-Fri free, adult Sun €1.50; ☒ 11am-1pm & 2.15-5pm Mon-Fri, 3-5pm Sun, to 6pm Sun-Fri Jun-Aug) has a fine collection of artefacts that trace Cork's history from prehistory to the present, including the city's role in the fight for independence. Bus No 8 goes to the UCC main gates nearby.

Cork City Gaol (☎ 430 5022; www.corkcitygaol.com; adult/child €6/3.50; ☒ 9.30am-5pm) received its first prisoners in 1824 and its last in 1923, including many prominent independence fighters. The impressive 35-minute taped tour around the restored and refurnished cells is very moving. The gaol is off Sunday's Well Rd.

Sleeping

BUDGET

Kinlay House Shandon (☎ 450 8966; www.kinlay house.ie; Bob & Joan's Walk; dm €14-16, s/d with shared bathroom incl breakfast €30/45, d €50; ☐) This excellent hostel has a smart décor and a fun but sensible atmosphere.

Sheila's Hostel (☎ 450 5562; www.sheilashostel .ie; 4 Belgrave Pl; dm €14-16.50, s €28-30, d €44-50; ☐) Sheila's is a big and busy place with lots of young travellers passing through. Facilities include a sauna (!), currency exchange and bike hire (€14 per day).

Cork International Hostel (☎ 454 3289; 1-2 Western Rd; dm €18-20, tw €44; ☐) The cheerful staff at this bright and busy An Óige hostel do a great job coping with the flow of young travellers and lively groups. Bus No 8 stops outside the hostel.

MID-RANGE & TOP END

Garnish House (☎ 427 5111; www.garnish.ie; Western Rd; s €60-70, d €90-120; ☐) An outstanding B&B of increasing fame, the Garnish has comfy rooms and charming little touches everywhere. You get welcoming tea and treats on arrival and breakfasts are delish.

Victoria Hotel (☎ 427 8788; www.thevictoriahotel .com; St Patrick's St; s/d €65/90) You won't get more

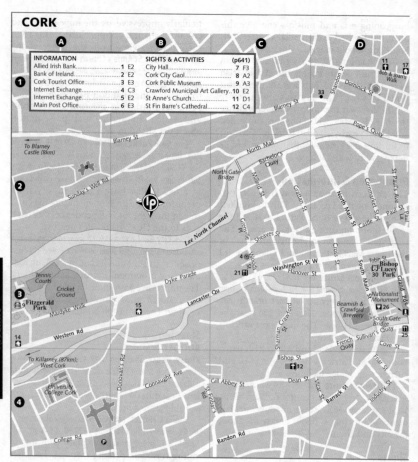

CORK

INFORMATION		SIGHTS & ACTIVITIES	(p641)
Allied Irish Bank	1 E2	City Hall	7 F3
Bank of Ireland	2 E2	Cork City Gaol	8 A2
Cork Tourist Office	3 E3	Cork Public Museum	9 A3
Internet Exchange	4 C3	Crawford Municipal Art Gallery	10 E2
Internet Exchange	5 E2	St Anne's Church	11 D1
Main Post Office	6 E3	St Fin Barre's Cathedral	12 C4

central than this old established hotel that once saw Charles Stuart Parnell and James Joyce as guests. Rooms are big and comfortable, and rates include breakfast.

Gresham Metropole Hotel (☎ 450 8122; www .gresham-hotels.com; MacCurtain St; s/d €110/140; P ☻) Following a full refurbishment, the Metropole now allows you to pad around soundlessly on lush carpets and feel comfortably corporate in the lavish rooms, swimming pool, health club and elegant bars and restaurant. One room here is wheelchair accessible.

Close to the train station at the northeastern end of town there's a handful of basic but perfectly fine B&Bs, including **Auburn House** (☎ 450 8555, auburnhouse@eircom.net;

Wellington Rd; s/d €52/75, with shared bathroom €42/66; P) and **Oaklands** (☎ 450 0578; oaklandsbandb@o2 .ie; Glanmire Rd; d €60).

Eating

Gingerbread House (☎ 427 6411; Paul St; snacks €3-6; ☺ 8am-10.30pm Mon-Tue, to 12.30am Wed-Thu, to 5am Fri & Sat, 9-12.30am Sun) Good coffee, pastries, and pizza are served up in this huge but comfy cafeteria that never seems to close. Try the home-made organic juices.

Quay Co-op Café (☎ 431 7026; 24 Sullivan's Quay; mains €7.50-9; ☺ 9am-9pm Mon-Sat) Flying a cheerful flag for alternative Cork, this enduring favourite rattles out delectable veggie options. The environment is chic and homy, with plants and art on the walls depicting

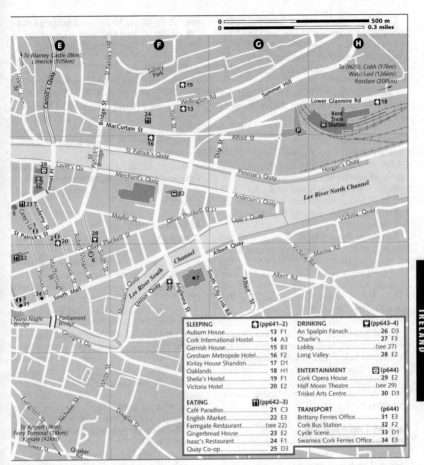

SLEEPING	⌂(pp641-2)
Auburn House	13 F1
Cork International Hostel	14 A3
Garnish House	15 B3
Gresham Metropole Hotel	16 F2
Kinlay House Shandon	17 D1
Oaklands	18 H1
Sheila's Hostel	19 F1
Victoria Hotel	20 E2

EATING	🍴(pp642-3)
Café Paradiso	21 C3
English Market	22 E3
Farmgate Restaurant	(see 22)
Gingerbread House	23 E2
Isaac's Restaurant	24 F1
Quay Co-op	25 D3

DRINKING	🍺(pp643-4)
An Spailpín Fánach	26 D3
Charlie's	27 F3
Lobby	(see 27)
Long Valley	28 E2

ENTERTAINMENT	🎭(p644)
Cork Opera House	29 E2
Half Moon Theatre	(see 29)
Triskel Arts Centre	30 D3

TRANSPORT	(p644)
Brittany Ferries Office	31 E3
Cork Bus Station	32 F2
Cycle Scene	33 D1
Swansea Cork Ferries Office	34 E3

IRELAND

the universal life force. The shop next door has loads for green self-caterers.

Farmgate Restaurant (☎ 427 8134; English Market; mains €8.50-12; 🕙 8.30am-5pm Mon-Sat) An unmissable Cork experience at the heart of the colourful English Market. Filling breakfasts, coffee and lunches (bouncing fresh salads, shepherd's pie) draw a regular Cork clientele to the Farmgate's balcony, which overlooks the market below, source of the food on your plate.

Isaac's Restaurant (☎ 450 3805; MacCurtain St; lunch mains €9-11, dinner €14-24; 🕙 10am-2.30pm & 6.30-10.30pm, to 9pm Sun) Housed in a converted 18th-century warehouse, Isaac's has a nostalgic Mediterranean ambience to go with its lively menu.

Café Paradiso (☎ 427 7939; 16 Lancaster Quay; mains €16-22; 🕙 12.30-3pm & 6.30-10.30pm Tue-Sat) Top-class vegetarian dishes that will seduce the most committed carnivore make this cheerful restaurant a busy place. Creativity maintains the standard of dishes, and the wine list is terrific.

For self-catering, head for the well-stocked food stalls inside the English Market.

Drinking

Cork's pub life is brimming. Locally brewed Murphy's is the stout of choice here, not Guinness.

An Spailpín Fánach (☎ 427 7949; 28 Sth Main St) The 'wandering labourer' hosts trad sessions almost every night.

The Lobby (☎ 431 9307; 1 Union Quay) The Lobby gets traditional at weekends and has an upstairs space (€5 to €15 cover) that hosts a range of performers. Tuesday is jazz night. Sister pub **Charlie's** (☎ 496 5272) next door has music every night.

Long Valley (☎ 427 2144; Winthrop St) This Cork institution has been going strong more or less since the mid-19th century.

Entertainment

Cork's cultural life is generally of a high calibre. *WhazOn*, a free monthly publication available from the tourist office, newsagencies, shops, hostels and B&Bs, lists it all. The Cork International Jazz Festival and the International Film Festival both take place in October.

Cork Opera House (☎ 427 0022; www.corkopera house.ie; Emmet Pl) Staging everything from opera to stand-up, the Opera House has seen performances as varied as *Carmen*, Oumou Sangaré and the *Vagina Monologues*. It has wheelchair access. The **Half Moon Theatre** (☎ 427 0022), behind it, hosts live bands and DJs.

Triskel Arts Centre (☎ 427 2022; www.triskelarts centre.com; Tobin St) At the time of research the Triskel was being refurbished and expanded as part of Cork's European Capital of Culture 2005 campaign. It's an important venue for contemporary art, film, theatre, music, and other media arts.

Getting There & Away

Cork airport (☎ 431 3131) is 8km south of the city on the N27. There are direct flights into Dublin, London, Birmingham, Manchester, Jersey, Paris, Rennes, Milan, Barcelona and Amsterdam.

The **bus station** (☎ 450 8188; cnr Merchants Quay & Parnell Pl) is east of the centre. You can get to almost anywhere in Ireland by bus from Cork: Dublin (€20.50, 4¼ hours, six daily), Killarney (€13.50, two hours, 12 daily), Waterford, Wexford and more.

Cork's **Kent train station** (☎ 450 4777; Glanmire Rd Lower) is across the river. Trains go to Dublin (€50, three hours, nine daily), Limerick (€20, 1½ hours, seven daily) and Killarney (€20, 1½ hours, five daily).

Cork's ferry terminal, with regular boats to Swansea and Roscoff, is at Ringaskiddy, about 15 minutes by car southeast of the city centre along the N28. **Swansea Cork Ferries** (☎ 427 6000; 52 Sth Mall) and **Brittany Ferries** (☎ 427 7801; 42 Grand Pde) both have offices in town. See p677 for more details.

Getting Around

Frequent buses head from the bus station to the airport (€3.50, 25 minutes) from April to September (fewer off season). Otherwise, a taxi costs around €15. Buses also run fairly often to the ferry terminal (€5, 40 minutes).

Parking discs (€1.25 per hour) are sold at newsagencies.

Hire a bike for €15/80 per day/week from **Cycle Scene** (☎ 430 1183; 396 Blarney St). Return it almost anywhere in the country for another €25.

AROUND CORK
Blarney
☎ 021

Just northwest of Cork, Blarney (An Bhlarna) is a village with one reason to visit – the tall imposing walls of 15th-century **Blarney Castle** (☎ 438 5252; www.blarneycastle.ie; adult/child €7/2.50; ☼ 9am-7pm Mon-Sat, 9.30am-5.30pm Sun Jun-Aug, to 6.30pm Mon-Sat May & Sep, 9am-6pm or to sunset Mon-Sun Oct-Apr). If you don't mind putting your lips where millions of others have been, you can kiss the castle's legendary **Blarney Stone** on the high battlements and get the 'gift of the gab'. It was Queen Elizabeth I, exasperated with Lord Blarney's ability to talk endlessly without ever actually agreeing to her demands, who invented the term. Bending over backwards to kiss the sacred rock requires a head for heights, although there's someone there to hold you in position. Getting there at opening time is one way to beat the crowds.

Myriad B&Bs surround the castle, including The **White House** (☎ 438 5338; www.thewhite houseblarney.com; s/d €50/68; ℗), which tends to fill up quickly. The basic, unaffiliated **Blarney Tourist Hostel** (☎ 438 5580; www.blarneyhostel.com; dm/d €12/35; ℗) is a few kilometres west on the road to Killarney.

Buses run regularly from the Cork bus station (€4.70 return, 30 minutes).

Cobh
☎ 021 / pop 6771

The small town of Cobh (pronounced cove) is worth a day trip from Cork for its picture-postcard looks and rich maritime history, celebrated in the excellent **Cobh, The**

Queenstown Story (☎ 481 3591; www.cobhheritage .com; adult/child €5/2.50; ⏲ 10am-6pm May-Oct, to 5pm Nov-Apr) heritage centre in the town's old train station. It tells the story of the migrants who sailed from here and of the town's links with the *Titanic* and the *Lusitania*. Last admission is one hour before closing and the centre has wheelchair access. The old Cunard buildings in town have been converted into a pub and restaurant.

Cobh is 24km southeast of Cork via the N25. Hourly trains (€4.60 return, 30 minutes) also connect with Cork.

Kinsale
☎ 021 / pop 3035
Kinsale (Cionn tSáile) is the quintessential Irish seaside town. People come for the coastal scenery and for the town's reputation as Ireland's gourmet capital.

The **tourist office** (☎ 477 2234; www.corkkerry .ie/kinsaletic; 1 Pier Rd; ⏲ 9.15am-5.15pm Jul-Aug, closed Sun Mar-Jun & Sep-Nov, closed Sun-Wed Dec-Feb) can help with visitor inquiries.

Southeast of Kinsale, a scenic 2.5km walk from the town centre, stand the stout ruins of **Charles Fort** (☎ 477 2263; www.heritageireland.ie; adult/student €3.50/1.25; ⏲ 10am-6pm mid-Mar–Oct, to 5pm Nov–mid-Mar). Built in the 1670s, it's one of the best-preserved star forts in Europe. On a sunny day the views from the hill-top battlements are lovely.

SLEEPING & EATING
The only hostel accommodation in the immediate area is **Dempsey's Hostel** (☎ 477 2124; Eastern Rd; dm/d €16/40), an uphill walk from the centre on the Cork road (most buses will drop you off in front). Herbs from the garden are yours for the cooking.

B&Bs in town are pricey. Two of the good ones in handsome Georgian houses are the friendly **Captain's Quarters** (☎ 477 4549; www .captains-kinsale.com; 5 Denis Quay; s/d €39/92; ⏲ closed Feb-Mar), which has two wheelchair-accessible rooms, and the sumptuously decorated **Chart House** (☎ 477 4568; www.charthouse-kinsale.com; 6 Denis Quay; s/d €50/120).

Diva's (☎ 086-852 2420; 40 Main St; snacks €3.50-7; ⏲ 8.30am-9pm Mon-Sat May–mid-Oct, 9am-7pm Mon-Sat mid-Oct-Apr, 11am-6pm Sun year-round) is a little oasis of affordable, healthy food: American-style Asian salads, home-made pastries and bottomless cups of coffee. No-fuss **Dino's** (☎ 477 4561; Pier Rd; mains €8-10; ⏲ 9am-midnight) turns

out fish and chips galore and an all-day four-courser (€17.50). **Max's Wine Bar** (☎ 477 3677; 48 Main St; lunch €5-12, dinner €17-22; ⏲ 12.30-2.45pm & 6.30-10.30pm Wed-Mon), with a Brittany coast vibe, serves close-to-affordable Irish-French dishes. If you really want to push the boat out, the **Vintage Restaurant** (☎ 477 2502; 50 Main St; mains €32-45; ⏲ 6.30-9.30pm Tue-Sat) is one of Kinsale's best and most creative places.

GETTING THERE & AWAY
Buses connect Kinsale with Cork (€6.90 return, 45 minutes, 10 daily Monday to Saturday, five on Sunday) and stop near the tourist office. To head west by bus you'll have to go back to Cork.

WEST COUNTY CORK
Travelling west by public transport from Cork can be tough. There are at least two daily bus services in summer connecting towns, but some routes are not serviced at all the rest of the year. The trick is to plan ahead at Cork, have the timetables committed to memory, and be prepared to change buses and backtrack. Make friends with **Bus Éireann** (in Cork ☎ 021-450 8188; www.buseireann.ie).

Baltimore
☎ 028
Just 13km down the Ilen River from Skibbereen, sleepy Baltimore has a population of around 250 that swells enormously during summer. Its main attraction is its proximity to Cape Clear Island. The **tourist office** (☎ 21766; ⏲ 9.15am-5.15pm Mon-Fri Oct-May, 9am-6pm Mon-Sat Jun & Sep, to 7pm Jul-Aug) in Skibbereen can handle questions about the area. The **Baltimore Diving Centre** (☎ 20300; Harbour Dr) arranges diving expeditions (€80 for two dives, including gear).

Baltimore has plenty of B&Bs, plus the excellent IHH **Rolf's Hostel** (☎ 20289; www.rolfs holidays.com; dm/d €15/60, d with shared bathroom €40); follow the signs up a hill about 700m east of town. Whether or not you're staying, Rolf's terrific **café/restaurant** (mains €7-24; ⏲ 8.30am-9.30pm, closed Mon & Tue in winter) is the place to eat in town.

Clear & Sherkin Islands
☎ 028
Cape Clear Island, or Cape Clear as the locals call it, is the most southerly point of

Ireland (apart from Fastnet Rock, 6km to the southwest). Clear Island is a Gaeltacht area with about 150 Irish-speaking inhabitants, one shop and three pubs. The **camping ground** (☎ 39119; www.oilean-chleire.ie; per person €6; ☿ Jun-Sep) is signposted from the shop. An Óige's basic **Cape Clear Island Hostel** (☎ 39198; anoige@fenlon.net; dm €15; ☿ Jun-Oct; 🖵) is a short walk from the pier. **Cluain Mara** (☎ 39153; www .capeclearisland.com; Nth Harbour; s/d €30/60; 🅿) and **Ard Na Goithe** (☎ 39160; The Glen; s/d €30/60; 🅿) are both friendly places in typical island houses.

The ferry **Naomh Ciarán II** (☎ 39159; www .capeclearferry.info) sails between Baltimore and Cape Clear (weather permitting) three to four times daily in the summer months and less frequently off season. The trip takes 45 minutes and costs €11.50 return (bikes go free). **West Cork Coastal Cruises** (☎ 39153; www .westcorkcoastalcruises.com) runs a similar service. In summer, boats to Clear Island also leave from Schull (see below).

If Cape Clear seems a long ride, consider heading to tiny Sherkin Island, its friendly neighbour with a couple of convivial pub/restaurants, several decent B&Bs and a few good beaches.

The homy **Horseshoe Cottage B&B** (☎ 20598; chris@sherkintefl.com; s/d €35/70) has bay views and one wheelchair-accessible room. Try the **Jolly Roger Tavern** (☎ 20379) for fresh mussels and a great atmosphere.

Ferries (☎ 20218) sail from Baltimore nine times daily in summer and reasonably frequently in winter (€7 return, 10 minutes).

Mizen Head Peninsula
☎ 028

Mizen Head is a scenic alternative to the better known and more touristy Ring of Kerry and Dingle Peninsula to the north.

At least two buses a day leave Cork (via Skibbereen) for the small village of **Schull** at the foot of Mt Gabriel (407m). In summer, Schull's pubs and restaurants are packed with tourists, but the rest of the year it's blissfully quiet.

Schull Backpackers' Lodge (☎ 28681; www.schull backpackers.com; Colla Rd; camp site per person €7.50, d €44, dm/s/d with shared bathroom €15/20/40; 🖵) is excellent and has wheelchair access. It rents bikes (€10) and organises diving, kayaking, and horse-riding trips. From mid-June to mid-September **boats** (☎ 39153) leave from

Schull's pier for Clear Island at 2pm and 4.30pm, returning at 3.30pm and 5.30pm. The one way/return fare is €6.50/11.50.

The road south from Schull leads to **Mizen Head** and its 1910 **signal station**, now a **visitors centre** (☎ 35115; www.mizenhead.net; adult/child €4.50/2.50; ☿ 10am-6pm Jun-Sep, 11am-4pm Sat & Sun Nov–mid-Mar, 10.30am-5pm mid-Mar–May & Oct), which is on a small island connected to the mainland by a 45m-high suspension bridge. From here you can look down on pounding seas, striking layered rock formations and maybe the odd seal. It's a great place to just come and experience the mighty Atlantic winds and seas as they strike land.

Bantry
☎ 027 / pop 2936

Bantry is famed for its mussels and wedged between hills and the waters of Bantry Bay. The **tourist office** (☎ 63084; www.corkkerry.ie; 9am-6pm Mon-Sat & 10am-5pm Sun Jun-Aug, 9.15am-5.15pm Mon-Sat Apr-May & Sep-Oct, closed Mar-Nov) is on the east end of Wolfe Tone Sq.

The colourful old **Bantry House** (☎ 50047; www.bantryhouse.ie; adult/concession €10/8, gardens & French Armada Centre only €4; ☿ 10am-6pm mid-Mar–Oct) is superbly situated overlooking the bay. The gardens are beautifully kept, and the house is noted for its French and Flemish tapestries. In the courtyard a **French Armada exhibit** recounts France's failed 1796 attempt to aid the Irish independence struggle.

The IHH **Bantry Independent Hostel** (☎ 51050; bantryhostel@eircom.net; Reenrour East; dm/d €11/24; ☿ Apr-Sep) is off Glengarriff Rd, about 600m northeast of the town centre. **Eagle Point Camping** (☎ 50630; www.eaglepointcamping.com; Glengarriff Rd, Ballylickey; camp site €18; ☿ end-Apr–Sep) is on a promontory about 6km north of Bantry. There are plenty of B&Bs in Bantry, including a few around Wolfe Tone Sq.

The place to go to for those famous mussels is definitely the wheelchair-accessible **O'Connor's Seafood Restaurant** (☎ 50221; Wolfe Tone Sq; lunch €6-9, mains €18-27; ☿ 12.15-4pm & 6-10pm). **Pantry** (☎ 52181; New St; snacks €3-8; ☿ 9am-5pm Mon-Sat) is a great little café near Vickery's Inn.

Frequent buses to Cork (€13.50, 2½ hours), Killarney (summer only), Glengarriff and beyond stop just off the main square at Barry Murphy's pub.

Beara Peninsula

☎ 027

From Bantry, the N71 follows the coast northwest to Glengarriff from where the R572 runs southwest to the Beara Peninsula, a wild, handsome, rocky landscape that's ideal for exploring by foot or bike. The Beara is far less on the tourist trail than the Ring of Kerry or the Dingle and is a great place to spend a few relaxing days. It's possible to drive the 137km 'Ring of Beara' in one day although that would be missing the point. If you're driving or cycling (leg power permitting) don't miss the beautiful Healy Pass.

Walkers might like to tackle ruggedly beautiful Hungry Hill, made famous by Daphne DuMaurier's book of the same name, just outside the pleasant fishing town of Castletownbere, itself a good place to stop for a bite or a pint.

Murphy's Village Hostel (☎ 63555; murphyshostel@ eircom.net; Main St; dm/d €13/35; ⌨ P) in the heart of Glengarriff is cheerful, bright and wheelchair accessible. Westwards, **Adrigole** is a tiny hamlet with lots of rocks and **Hungry Hill Lodge** (☎ 60228; www.hungryhilllodge.com; camping per person €7, dm/s/d €15/20/40; ☽ Mar-Oct; P). Staff here can arrange diving and boat trips. Reception is in the Glenbrook Bar next door.

Garranes Hostel (☎ 73147; dm/s €12/17) between Castletownbere and Allihies has a breathtaking location perched high above Bantry Bay. The atmosphere is quiet and meditative here, appropriately so as it's run by the **Dzogchen Buddhist Retreat Centre** (☎ 73032; www.dzogchenbeara.ie) next door. Guests can join daily meditation sessions. Given the reflective atmosphere, this is not a place to come to party. Inquire first by phone.

Among the copper mines surrounding the lovely, sleepy village of **Allihies** is An Óige's friendly **Allihies Hostel** (☎ 73014; www.anoige.ie; dm €14.50; ☽ Jun-Sep; P). **Glanmore Lake Hostel** (☎ 064-83181; www.anoige.ie; dm €14; ☽ Jun-Sep; P) is in an old schoolhouse 5km from Lauragh, nestling in stunning Healy Pass.

Bus Éireann's No 46 runs from Cork to Castletownbere, via Bantry, Glengarriff and Adrigole, once or twice a day. The No 282 serves Castletownbere and Kenmare with a stop at Lauragh twice a day, Monday to Saturday, from mid-June to August only. Though most people walk or hitch to Allihies, it's served by the privately run **O'Donoghue bus company** (☎ 027-70007).

THE WEST COAST

Ireland's west coast has everything you could possibly want in a coastal landscape. The Iveragh and Dingle Peninsulas, with their awesome mountains, picturesque lakes, wild and dramatic terrain and misty islands, fulfil the romantic dream of Ireland. Another kind of dream – the surreal one – plays itself out in the Burren, paradoxically both moonlike and bursting with colour: its million-year-old rocks live in harmony with the new spring's junipers, its massive sea cliffs and roadside boulders assume an otherworldly presence. The nearby Aran Islands take this rocky dream into another time, another tempo, another language; the ancient forts look out silently over the sea in restful retirement. Silent too is Connemara's patchwork of bogs, windswept hills and jagged beaches. Then you wake up in Galway – that curved, cobbled, eccentric, café'd, pubbed and clubbed city of buskers, fishermen, bohemians and swans.

KILLARNEY

☎ 064 / pop 9470

By the time you reach Killarney (Cill Airne) you will have seen plenty of touristy Irish towns, but nothing will prepare you for a Killarney summer weekend chock-a-block with tour coaches. Cynics may find Killarney little more than a charmless and pricey Irish theme-park. But it's become so popular for a reason: it has a national park and three lakes on its doorstep, providing endless escapes for walkers and cyclists, and is a convenient base for touring the Ring of Kerry (p650). Killarney is also a transport hub for the area.

Information

Killarney's **tourist office** (☎ 31633; www.corkkerry .ie; Beech Rd; ☽ 9am-8pm Mon-Sat & 10am-6pm Sun Jul-Aug, 9am-6pm Mon-Sat & 10am-6pm Sun Sep & Jun, 9.15am-5.15pm Mon-Sat Oct-May) is busy. Send mail at the **main post office** (☎ 31461; New St). Internet access is free at the **Killarney Library** (☎ 32655; Rock Rd; ☽ 10am-5pm Mon, Wed, Fri & Sat, to 8pm Tue & Thu), but you should book ahead. Otherwise, no-frills **Leaders** (☎ 39635; Beech Rd; ☽ 10am-9pm Mon-Sat, 10.30am-9pm Sun, to 6.30pm Nov-Apr; per hr €3.60) is the cheapest. *Where Killarney* (€5) is a good monthly 'what's on' guide, available at your B&B or hostel or at the tourist office.

IRELAND

Sights

WITHIN KILLARNEY

Most of Killarney's attractions are just outside the town, not actually in it. The 1855 **St Mary's Cathedral** (☎ 31014; Port Rd) is worth a look, as is the **Museum of Irish Transport** (☎ 34677; Scott's Gardens, East Ave Rd; adult/child €5/2; ⏰ 10am-6pm Jun-Aug, 11am-5pm Sep-Oct), which has an interesting assortment of old cars and bikes and is wheelchair accessible.

KILLARNEY NATIONAL PARK

The picture-perfect backdrop of mountains (well, big hills) beyond town are in fact part of Killarney's huge 10,236-hectare national park. Within the park are beautiful Lough Leane, Muckross Lake and Upper Lake. There's a pedestrian entrance opposite St Mary's Cathedral, and a drivers' entrance off the N71.

As well as ruins and ex-gentry housing, the park has much to explore by foot, bike or boat – plenty of options to last a day or longer. The *Killarney Area Guide* (€1.90 at the tourist office) has some ideas.

The restored 14th-century **Ross Castle** (☎ 35851; www.heritageireland.ie; adult/concession €5/2; ⏰ 9am-6.30pm Jun-Aug, 9.30am-5.30pm Sep–mid-Oct & mid-Mar–May, to 4.30pm Tue-Sun mid-Oct–mid-Nov, closed mid-Nov–mid-Mar) is a 2.5km walk from St Mary's Cathedral. Hour-long **cruises on Lough Leane** leave the castle daily in summer; make bookings at the tourist office. From late September to May boats depart only on demand.

Inisfallen Island, Lough Leane's largest, is where the 13th-century *Annals of Inisfallen* were written. The annals, now in the Bodleian Library at Oxford, remain a vital source of information about early Irish history. From Ross Castle you can hire a boat and row to the island to inspect the ruins of a 12th-century **oratory**. Alternatively, boatmen charge around €8 per person for the crossing.

The core of Killarney National Park is **Muckross Estate** (☎ 31440; www.muckross-house.ie; adult/child €5.50/2.25; ⏰ 9am-6pm Jul-Aug, to 5.30pm Sep-Jun), donated to the government in 1932 by Arthur Bourn Vincent. You can walk around the estate's rooms and view their faded 19th-century fittings free of guided tours. The estate is 5km from Killarney, set in beautiful gardens; in the summer a tourist bus leaves for the house at 1.45pm

from O'Connor's pub (High St), returning at 5.15pm (€8).

GAP OF DUNLOE

In summer the Gap, a heather-clad valley at the foot of Purple Mountain (832m), is Killarney tourism at its worst. Rather than following the hordes on one-hour horse-and-trap rides through the Gap (per person €15 to €18), consider hiring a bike and cycling to Ross Castle. From here take a boat across to Lord Brandon's Cottage and cycle down through the Gap and back into town via the N72 and a path through the golf course. Including bike hire, this should cost you about €25. The 1½-hour boat ride alone justifies the trip.

Sleeping

Wherever you stay, book ahead from June to August. Hostels in Killarney generally rent out bikes and offer discounted tours.

BUDGET

Killarney Railway Hostel (☎ 35299; railwayhostel@eircom.net; Fair Hill; dm/s/d €13.50/25/36; P) A handy position close to the train and bus stations and the centre of town makes this a useful stopover. It's also well equipped, has cheerful, clean rooms, good kitchen facilities and wheelchair access.

Killarney International Hostel (☎ 31240; anoige@killarney.iol.net; dm €14-16; ⏰ Easter-Sep; P ▣) Occupying a splendid 18th-century manor house on 28 hectares of lakes and forests, this An Óige's hostel is 5km west of the centre and off the N72 to Killorglin. A complimentary bus service runs to/from the bus and train stations in summer.

About 2.5km from town on the banks of the Flesk River is **Fleming's White Bridge Caravan & Camping Park** (☎ 31590; www.killarneycamping.com; White Bridge, Ballycasheen Rd; camp site €17.50; ⏰ mid-Mar–Oct). Head south out of town along Muckross Rd and turn left at Woodlawn. **Flesk Muckross Caravan Park** (☎ 31704; www.campingkillarney.com; Muckross Rd; camp site €17; ⏰ mid-Apr–Sep), with great views of the mountains, is 1.5km out on the Kenmare road (N71).

MID-RANGE & TOP END

In high season finding a room can be tricky, so it may be worth the €4 booking fee to have the tourist office do the hunting.

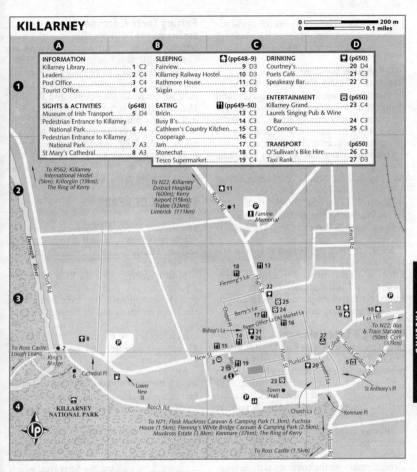

KILLARNEY

0 — 200 m
0 — 0.1 miles

INFORMATION
Killarney Library.............................1 C2
Leaders...2 C4
Post Office......................................3 C4
Tourist Office.................................4 C4

SIGHTS & ACTIVITIES (p648)
Museum of Irish Transport..........5 D4
Pedestrian Entrance to Killarney
    National Park.............................6 A4
Pedestrian Entrance to Killarney
    National Park.............................7 A3
St Mary's Cathedral......................8 A3

SLEEPING (pp648–9)
Fairview..9 D3
Killarney Railway Hostel.............10 D3
Rathmore House...........................11 C2
Súgán..12 D3

EATING (pp649–50)
Brícin...13 C3
Busy B's...14 C3
Cathleen's Country Kitchen........15 C3
Cooperage....................................16 C3
Jam..17 C3
Stonechat.....................................18 C3
Tesco Supermarket.....................19 C4

DRINKING (p650)
Courtney's....................................20 D4
Poets Café....................................21 C3
Speakeasy Bar..............................22 C3

ENTERTAINMENT (p650)
Killarney Grand............................23 C4
Laurels Singing Pub & Wine
    Bar..24 C3
O'Connor's...................................25 C3

TRANSPORT (p650)
O'Sullivan's Bike Hire..................26 C3
Taxi Rank.....................................27 D3

IRELAND

Rathmore House (☎ 32829; rathmorehousekly@iol
.ie; Rock Rd; s/d €42/70; P) There's a real Irish
welcome at this long-established family-run
B&B at the entrance to town.

Fuchsia House (☎ 33743; www.fuchsiaguesthouse
.com; Muckross Rd; s/d €80/118; P) Rooms here
are huge with plush carpets, sparkling bathrooms (with towel warmers), gorgeous antique furniture, and elegant, original décor.
Some look out over the back yard, a lush
garden in rich greens and pinks; room No 9
may be the quietest in Killarney.

Fairview (☎ 34164; www.fairviewkillarney.com;
Lewis Rd; s/d €110/150; P) The Fairview never
ceases to keep ahead of things, and lavish
refurbishment has ensured high standards in
the smart but comfy rooms, some of which

are wheelchair accessible. Rates are substantially discounted off season.

Eating
BUDGET

Jam (☎ 31441; High St; snacks €2.50-7.50; ☺ 8am-
5pm Mon-Sat) The cutest coffee shop in town
has bottomless cups and high-calibre sandwiches and quiches.

Busy B's Bistro (☎ 31972; 15 New St; mains €3-10;
☺ 11am-9pm) This all-purpose, refreshingly
unhip diner has veggie burgers, spaghetti
and baked potatoes. It also boasts a separate
calorie-counter menu.

Cathleen's Country Kitchen (☎ 33778; New St;
mains €6.50-9; ☺ 8am-8pm Apr-Sep, 9am-6.30pm Oct-
Mar, closed Sun) Down the road and similarly

pretensionless, Cathleen's serves up sandwiches and Irish stew. It's worth visiting for some tough love from Cathleen.

MID-RANGE & TOP END

Stonechat (☎ 34295; Flemings Lane; mains €7-15; ☯ noon-10pm) Deep-red walls, plants and skylights in this little stone house make for a hip and homy dining room. The many veggie options include a tagliatelle in a creamy mushroom and bean sauce.

Cooperage (☎ 37716; Old Market Lane; lunch €4-9.50, dinner €14-22; ☯ 12.30-3pm & 6.30-10pm, closed Mon Oct-Easter) Studio chic surroundings here are matched by the imaginative menu of modern European cuisine (with little for vegetarians). The early-bird dinner, to 7.30pm, is a €20 three-courser. The restaurant is wheelchair accessible.

Brícín (☎ 34902; High St; lunch €7-8, dinner €17-24; ☯ noon-3pm & 6-9.30pm Tue-Sat) The food at Brícín is a great mix of traditional Kerry cooking and international influences; the stuffed *boxty* (potato pancake) will leave you all warm and fuzzy inside.

Drinking & Entertainment

Laurels Singing Pub & Wine Bar (☎ 31149; Main St) Much of what's played at Killarney's music pubs is tourist-oriented. Laurels makes no bones about catering for coach parties, but it's all good fun nevertheless. The musical part (€6 cover) is behind the main pub via a side alley.

Killarney Grand (☎ 31159; Main St) More authentic music, if you can hear it over the hubbub, is on at the Grand, which has interesting takes on the traditional thing from 9pm. At 11pm, modern bands take over (€6 cover).

O'Connor's (☎ 30200; 7 High St) Reliable O'Connor's puts on a mix of trad, stand-up comedy, readings, and pub theatre.

Enough with the music already. Pubs with good atmosphere include **Courtney's** (☎ 32689; Plunkett St) and the friendly **Speakeasy Bar** (☎ 32540; High St), which, oblivious to the hordes, is filled with men watching horse races.

A good pub alternative is the tiny **Poets Café** (☎ 31954; Bishop's Lane; light meals €2.80-9.50; ☯ 9am-10pm, noon-10pm Sun), which has great organic coffees to go with its open-mike poetry readings and prose and film nights. Food's good, too.

Getting There & Around

Bus Éireann (☎ 30011) operates from the **train station** (☎ 31067), with regular services to Cork (€13.50, two hours, four daily), Dingle (€13, 2½ hours, three daily), Galway via Limerick (€19, five hours, six daily), Dublin (€20.50, six hours, five daily) and Rosslare Harbour (€22, seven hours, one to two daily). Travelling by train to Cork (€20, 2¼ hours, three daily) or Dublin (€52.50, six hours, three daily) usually involves changing at Mallow.

O'Sullivan's (☎ 22389; Bishop's Lane) rents bikes for €12/70 per day/week.

THE RING OF KERRY

☎ 066

The Ring of Kerry, a 179km circuit around the Iveragh Peninsula with dramatic coastal scenery, clearly is one of Ireland's premier tourist attractions.

Most travellers tackle the Ring by bus on a guided day trip from Killarney. The tourist coaches approach the Ring in an anticlockwise direction and in summer it's hard to know which is more unpleasant – driving/cycling behind the buses or travelling in the opposite direction and meeting them on blind corners.

Eliminate some of these frustrations by leaving the main highway. The **Ballaghbeama Pass** cuts across the peninsula's central highlands and has spectacular views and remarkably little traffic.

The shorter **Ring of Skellig**, at the end of the peninsula, has fine views of the Skellig Rocks and is less touristy. You can forgo roads completely by walking the **Kerry Way**, which winds through the Macgillycuddy's Reeks mountains past Carrantuohill (1038m), Ireland's highest mountain.

Sights

Daniel O'Connell (see p619) was born near **Cahirciveen**, one of the Ring's larger towns. The excellent, wheelchair-accessible **Barracks Heritage Centre** (☎ 947 2777; adult/student €4/3; ☯ 10am-5pm Mon-Sat & 2-5pm Sun Jun-Sep, 10am-5pm Mon-Fri Apr-May & Oct) off Bridge St occupies what was once an intimidating Royal Irish Constabulary (RIC) barracks. Exhibits focus on Daniel O'Connell and moving material on the local impact of the famine.

South of Cahirciveen the R565 branches west to the 11km-long **Valentia Island**, a jumping-off point for one of Ireland's most unforgettable experiences: the **Skellig Rocks**, two tiny islands 12km off the coast. The vertiginous climb up uninhabited Skellig Michael inspires a mild terror and an awe that monks could have clung to life in the meagre beehive-shaped stone huts that stand on the only flat strip of land on top. On a clear day the views from the summit are astounding.

Calm seas permitting, boats run from spring to late summer from Portmagee, just before the bridge to Valentia, to Skellig Michael. The standard fare is €35 return. Advance booking is essential; contact **Joe Roddy & Sons** (☎ 947 4268; www.skelligtrips.com) or **Des Lavelle** (☎ 947 6124; lavelles@indigo.ie).

The **Skellig Experience** (☎ 947 6306; www.skellig experience.com; adult/child €4.40/2.20; ❤ 10am-5pm Sat-Wed Apr & Oct-Nov, to 6pm May-Jun & Sep, to 7pm Jul-Aug), on Valentia Island across from Portmagee, has exhibits on the life and times of the monks who lived on Skellig Michael from the 7th to the 12th centuries. It is wheelchair accessible.

The pretty pastel-coloured town of **Kenmare** is an excellent alternative base for exploring the Ring of Kerry. Kenmare is somewhat touristy, but it's nothing like Killarney.

Sleeping

It's wise to book your next night as you make your way around the Ring; some places are closed out of season, others fill up quickly.

Cycling hostel-to-hostel around the Ring, there's the IHH **Laune Valley Farm** (☎ 976 1488; dm €13-17, d €35-44), 2km east of Killorglin, with wheelchair-accessible rooms; the IHO **Cáitín Hostel** (☎ 947 7614; patscraftshop@eircom.net; dm €13) in Kells; the meagre IHH **Sive Hostel** (☎ 947 2717; dm/d €15/36) in Cahirciveen; IHO's **Ring Lyne Hostel** (☎ 947 6103; dm/d €12/30) in Chapeltown; the large **Royal Pier Hostel** (☎ 947 6144; www.royalpiervalentia.com; dm €15-20, d €45-50) in Knightstown on Valentia Island; An Óige's **Baile an Sceilg** (☎ 947 9229; dm €14; ❤ Jun-Sep) in Ballinskelligs; and the **Travellers' Rest Hostel** (☎ 947 5175; www.caherdanielhostel.com; dm/d €13/33).

An Óige's **Black Valley Hostel** (☎ 064-34712; dm €15; ❤ Apr-Oct), in the Macgillycuddy's Reeks mountains, is a good starting point for walking the Kerry Way.

Getting There & Around

If you're not up to cycling, **Bus Éireann** (☎ 064-30011) has a Ring of Kerry bus service daily from late May to mid-September. In June, buses leave Killarney at 8.30am, 1.30pm and 3.45pm (at 9.40am and noon on Sunday), and stop at Killorglin, Glenbeigh, Kells, Cahirciveen, Waterville, Caherdaniel and Sneem, before returning to Killarney (the 3.45pm service terminates at Waterville).

Travel agencies in Killarney, including **Destination Killarney Tours** (☎ 064-32638; Scott's Gardens), offer daily tours of the Ring for about €20. Hostels in Killarney arrange tours for around €18.

THE DINGLE PENINSULA
☎ 066

The Dingle Peninsula is far less crowded and just as beautiful as the Ring of Kerry, with narrow roads that discourage heavy bus traffic.

The region's main hub, Dingle Town (An Daingean), is a workaday fishing village with a dozen good pubs. The western tip of the peninsula, noted for its extraordinary number of ring forts and high crosses, is predominantly Irish-speaking.

The **tourist office** (☎ 915 1188; www.corkkerry.ie; ❤ 9am-7pm Mon-Sat & 10am-5pm Sun-Aug, 9.15am-1pm & 2-5.15pm, closed Wed & Sun, Sep-May) is at the Dingle Town pier. **Dingle Internet Café** (☎ 915 2478; Lower Main St; per hr €5; ❤ 10am-8pm Mon-Sat, 1-6pm Sun, closed Sun Nov-Feb) also has cheap international calling.

Dingle Town

In the winter of 1984 fisher folk noticed a solitary bottlenose dolphin that followed their vessels and sometimes leapt over their boats. **Dingle Boatmen's Association** (☎ 915 2626) leaves Dingle's pier for one-hour trips to find Fungie the dolphin. The cost is €12 (free if Fungie doesn't show, but he usually does). You can swim with him for €25; wetsuit hire is extra. The **Peig Sayers** (☎ 915 1344; www.great blasketisland.com) also leaves from the harbour for the Blasket Islands (€30 return).

Dingle Oceanworld (☎ 915 2111; www.dingle -oceanworld.ie; adult/child €8.50/5.50; ❤ 10am-8.30pm Jul-Aug, to 6pm May-Jun & Sep, to 4.30pm Oct-Apr), opposite the harbour, has a walk-through tunnel and touch pool and it's wheelchair accessible.

IRELAND

Ride a horse through the peninsula for €20 per hour with **Dingle Horse Riding** (☎ 915 2199; www.dinglehorseriding.com).

East of Dingle

From Tralee the N86 heads west along the coast. The 'quick' route to Dingle Town is southwest from Camp via Anascaul and the N86. The scenic route follows the R560 northwest crossing the wildly scenic **Connor Pass** (456m).

West of Dingle

From Dingle follow signs for the 'Slea Head Drive', a scenic coastal stretch of the R559. To the southwest, **Slea Head** offers some of the peninsula's best views.

Ferries (☎ 915 6422, 915 4864) run from Dunquin to the bleak, uninhabited (since 1953) **Blasket Islands** (€20 return, 20 minutes), off the tip of the peninsula. Subtly powerful exhibits at Dunquin's excellent, wheelchair-accessible **Blasket Centre** (☎ 915 6444; adult/child €3.50/1.25; ⏰ 10am-7pm Jul-Aug, to 5.15pm Apr-Jun & Sep-Oct) feature the lives of the islanders, many of them celebrated musicians, storytellers and writers.

Sleeping

Ballintaggart Hostel (☎ 915 1454; www.dingleaccommodation.com; camp site €12, dm €14-18, d €54; ⏰ Apr-Oct) About 1.5km east of Dingle on the Tralee road is this IHH hostel in an old 18th-century hunting lodge. Buses to town will stop in front.

Grapevine Hostel (☎ 915 1434; Dykegate St, Dingle Town; dm €14-16) The Grapevine, with its faint but ominous smell of beer, has a cosy salon where guests bond before the fireplace.

Café Mhártan (☎ 087-631 9933; Goat St, Dingle Town; s/d €20/40) This little café has converted upstairs space into some cute and good-value rooms, painted spiritedly in bright colours.

Ocean View (☎ 915 1659; www.oceanviewdingle .com; 133 The Wood, Dingle Town; s/d €26/46) This is one of the many B&Bs in town; rooms in the back have the eponymous views.

Kirrary (☎ 915 1606; collinskirrary@eircom.net; Dingle Town; s/d €45/70) Another homely B&B in town where you'll feel like part of the family.

Hostels east of Dingle include the IHH **Fuchsia Lodge** (☎ 915 7150; fuchsia@eircom.net; camp site per person €6, dm/s/d €14/25/35) in Anascaul, and IHH **Connor Pass Hostel** (☎ 713 9179; dm €13; ⏰ Apr-Oct) in Stradbally.

West of Dingle, look for An Óige's **Dunquin Hostel** (☎ 915 6121; dm/d €14/30; ⏰ closed 10am-5pm) across from the Blasket Centre; the fantastic **Ballybeag Hostel** (☎ 915 9876; dm/d 15/42) in Ventry, with bike hire, cheap laundry, wheelchair access, and a swing in the garden; and the IHO **Black Cat Hostel** (☎ 915 6286; dm/d €12/24) in Ballyferriter.

Eating

An Café Liteártha (☎ 915 2204; Dykegate Lane, Dingle Town; snacks €3-7; ⏰ 9am-6pm) Allow the spirit of literary Dingle to engulf you as you eat your soup in this café, nestled at the back of an excellent bookshop.

Homely House (☎ 915 2431; Dick Mack's Yard, Green St, Dingle Town; snacks €3.50-9; ⏰ noon-5pm Mon-Sat) Tiny Homely House serves soups, wraps and burritos in colourful surroundings.

John Benny's Pub (☎ 915 1215; Strand St, Dingle Town; snacks €3-5, mains €8-17; ⏰ 12.30-9.30pm) A good bet for soup, chowder and sandwiches, or quality fish and chips. There's music most nights, too.

Vegetarians are well taken care of at both **Midi** (☎ 915 1988; Green St, Dingle Town; mains €9.50-14.50; ⏰ 5pm-late Wed-Sun), which counts hot red-onion, leek and parmesan tart among its offerings, and **Global Village Restaurant** (☎ 915 2325; Main St, Dingle Town; mains €16.50-21.50; ⏰ 6-9.30pm), which specialises in imaginative modern Irish cuisine.

Getting There & Around

Buses stop outside the car park at the back of the Super Valu store in Dingle Town. Killarney–Tralee–Dingle buses run four times daily Monday to Saturday (€13, 2½ hours). Dingle has several bike-rental places. **Paddy Walsh** (☎ 915 2311; Dykegate St), near the Grapevine Hostel, has bikes for €12/70 per day/week.

LIMERICK

☎ 061 / pop 54,058

Limerick (Luimneach) is the Irish Republic's third-largest city with a reputation as rather a rough old place. The squalor depicted in Frank McCourt's *Angela's Ashes* didn't help matters any, either. Limerick's picked up in recent years, though, with better restaurants and a lively music scene. The delightful Hunt Museum is the jewel in Limerick's tarnished crown. It's mostly an unremarkable place so if you're pressed for time, skip it.

Orientation & Information

The main street through town changes name from Rutland St to Patrick St, then O'Connell St, The Crescent and Quinlan St as it runs south. The train and bus station are situated to the southeast, off Parnell St. The **tourist office** (☎ 317522; Arthur's Quay; ⌚ 9.30am-6pm Jun-Aug, to 5.30pm Mon-Sat May & Sep, 9.30am-5.30pm Mon-Fri, to 1pm Sat Oct-Apr) is near the Shannon River.

Sights

The fascinating **Hunt Museum** (☎ 312833; www .huntmuseum.com; Rutland St; adult/child €6.50/3.20; ⌚ 10am-5pm Mon-Sat, 2-5pm Sun) has contemporary art shows and a superb collection of Bronze Age, Celtic and medieval artefacts. Half the fun of a visit to this museum is opening the drawers, in which much of the collection is kept, to discover random treasures within. It is also wheelchair accessible.

The lofty, echoing rooms of the restored **Georgian House** (☎ 314130; 2 Perry Sq; adult/child €5/3; ⌚ 10am-4pm Mon-Fri) are charmingly eerie. The back garden leads to a coach house that contains a photographic memoir of Limerick and a small but evocative **Ashes Exhibition**, including a reconstruction of Frank McCourt's childhood home.

Across the Shannon is the sturdy but underwhelming **King John's Castle** (☎ 411201; adult/child €10.50/5.95; ⌚ 9.30am-5.30pm, last admission 4pm). Limerick's oldest building, **St Mary's Cathedral** (☎ 310293; admission €2; ⌚ 9am-4pm), was founded in 1168; parts of the original survive.

Sleeping & Eating

Cherry Blossom (☎ 469449; www.cherryblossomlimerick .com; 3 Alexandra Tce, O'Connell Ave; dm/s/d/q €20/30/50/72) Your best budget option in town is small and friendly, but it has only one dorm room, a single-sex six-bedder.

Alexandra (☎ 318472; 6 Alexandra Tce, O'Connell Ave; s/d €35/70, with shared bathroom €30/60; ⓟ) There's an upbeat, caring attitude at this happily rambling house run by the same family that operates the Cherry Blossom. Rooms are no-frills but comfy and bright.

Java's Café & Wine Bar (☎ 418077; 5 Catherine St; mains €6-8; ⌚ 9am-10pm Mon-Sat, 10.30am-8pm Sun) Stylish Java's has tons of teas and coffees and fresh wraps and salads at good prices. The walls are red and it's all very hip and busy.

Furze Bush (☎ 411733; 12 Glentworth St; mains €7-13; ⌚ 10am-4.30pm Mon-Sat, & 6.30-8pm Sat) Furze Bush is a little bit of old Paris, and after a lunch of triple Mediterranean veggie crepe, you'll be tempted to stay all afternoon with your coffee and cream and your newspaper. Saturday dinners (€20) are special, as in Barbary duck breast with caramelised apples and port and berry sauce.

Getting There & Around

Shannon airport (☎ 712000), 24km from Limerick, handles domestic and international flights. **Bus Éireann** (☎ 313333) services operate from Colbert train station, with hourly connections to Dublin (€15, 1¼ hours), Cork (€13.50, two hours) and Galway (13.50, 2½ hours). Direct buses also run from the airport to Dublin, Cork and Killarney. By **train** (☎ 315555) it costs €38 to Dublin (10 daily) and €20 to Cork (seven daily). Hourly buses connect Shannon with the bus and train station (€5.20).

Emerald Alpine Cycles (☎ 416983; 1 Patrick St) hires bikes for €20/100 per day/week. For an extra €25, return or pick up the bike in any other town nationwide.

THE BURREN

County Clare's greatest attraction is the haunting Burren, a harsh and bleakly beautiful stretch of country. *Boireann* is Irish for 'Rocky Country', and the name is no exaggeration. Unwelcoming from the surface, the Burren transforms upon entering into a complex landscape littered with ancient dolmens, ring forts, round towers, high crosses and a surprisingly diverse range of flora, while rocky foreshores, occasional beaches and splendid limestone cliffs line its coast. Oh, and among the stunning scenery are some of the best music pubs in Ireland.

Tim Robinson's excellent *Burren Map & Guide* is available at bookshops or tourist offices. If you're stuck for transport, a number of bus tours leave the Galway tourist office every morning for the Burren and Cliffs of Moher, including **O'Neachtain Tours** (☎ 091-553188; www.oneachtaintours.com). They all cost around €25. A much better way to explore the Burren, however, is on foot: **Burren Hill Walks** (☎ 065-707 7168) based in Ballyvaughan and **Burren Wild** (☎ 087-877 9565; www.burrenwalks .com) near Kinvara both offer half-day guided walks for €20 per person.

IRELAND

Doolin

☎ 065 / pop 200

Tiny Doolin, famed for its music pubs, is a convenient base for exploring the Burren and the awesome Cliffs of Moher. It's also a gateway for boats to Inisheer, the easternmost and smallest of the Aran Islands. In summer it can be difficult to get a bed in Doolin, so book ahead. Some of the hostels rent bikes for around €8 a day plus deposit.

Doolin's reputation for top-notch traditional Irish music has spread like wildfire, and with it, its popularity among holidaymakers from around the world. At night the three pubs are packed with an appreciative cosmopolitan crowd.

SLEEPING

Aille River Hostel (☎ 707 4260; www.esatclear.ie /ailleriver; dm/d €12/28; ☺ closed Jan; P ☐) In a picturesque spot by the river in the upper village this converted 17th-century farmhouse is the best budget choice. It has turf fires, hot showers, free laundry and good company.

Rainbow's End (☎ 707 4415; www.rainbowhostel .com; s/d €45/60; P) Lots of exposed wood and light and airy rooms make this friendly, family-run B&B a good choice. It's run by the owners of the Rainbow Hostel next door, also highly recommended, and free walking tours take place every evening.

Other recommendations:

O'Connors Riverside Camping & Caravan Park (☎ 707 4314; www.oconnorsdoolin.com; camp site €12; ☺ May-Sep; P) A friendly camping ground with immaculate facilities.

Doolin Activity Lodge (☎ 707 4888; www.doolinlodge .com; s/d €35/70; P ☐) Modern and spacious B&B rooms and good-value self-catering apartments.

EATING

Doolin Cafe (☎ 707 4795; lunch €3.50-9.50, dinner €17-22.50; ☺ 10am-3pm & 6-10pm Fri-Wed, closed Feb) There's a great atmosphere – homy but elegant – at this friendly place. With the fantastic food, including everything from steaks to veggie options, it could get away with being pretentious, but chooses not to.

Flagship Restaurant (☎ 707 4309; mains €8-11; ☺ 10am-6pm Easter-Sep) In a little garden 400m along the Lisdoonvarna road, the Flagship serves home-cooked snacks and light meals. Save room for Guinness cake.

Doolin's three pubs serve basic, cheap pub food.

GETTING THERE & AWAY

There are direct buses to Doolin from Limerick, Ennis, Galway and even Dublin; the main Bus Éireann stop is across from Paddy Moloney's Doolin Hostel. See p658 for information on ferries to and from the islands.

Cliffs of Moher

About 8km south of Doolin are the towering Cliffs of Moher, at 203m one of Ireland's most famous natural features. In summer the cliffs are overrun by day-trippers, so consider staying in Doolin and hiking or biking along the Burren's quiet country lanes, where the views are just as good and crowds are never a problem. Either way, be careful walking along these sheer cliffs, especially in wet or windy weather.

Near the **Cliffs of Moher tourist centre** (☎ 065-708 1171; ☺ 9.30am-5.30pm May-Sep) is **O'Brien's Tower**, which you can climb for €1. Apparently, local landlord Cornelius O'Brien (1801–57) raised it to impress 'lady visitors'. From the tower walk south or north and the crowds soon disappear. You can also avoid the crowds – and the €4 charge for the car park – by visiting after the tourist centre closes.

GALWAY

☎ 091 / pop 65,774

The city of Galway (Gaillimh) is a pleasure, with its narrow streets, fast-flowing river, ramshackle shop fronts, and good restaurants and pubs. At weekends people come from as far as Dublin for the nightlife, and during the city's festivals the streets are bursting. Galway is also a departure point for the rugged Aran Islands.

Orientation & Information

Galway's tightly packed town centre is spread evenly on both sides of the Corrib River. The bus and train stations are within a stone's throw of Eyre Sq.

The **tourist office** (☎ 53 7700; www.irelandwest .ie; Forster St; ☺ 9am-5.45pm daily Jul-Sep, 9am-5.45pm Mon-Fri, to 12.45pm Sat Oct-May) is a short way off Eyre Sq. In summer there can be a long wait to make accommodation bookings.

Send mail at the **main post office** (Eglinton St) and email at **Clan Video** (☎ 588710; 11 Upper Dominick St; per hr €4; ☺ 8am-midnight Mon-Sat, noon-midnight Sun) or **iSupply** (☎ 585770; 10-12 Sea Rd; per hr €2; ☺ 9am-6pm Mon-Fri, 10am-4pm Sat). The

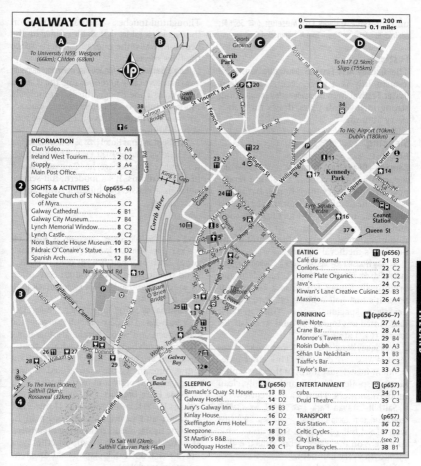

GALWAY CITY

0 — 200 m
0 — 0.1 miles

To University; N59; Westport (66km); Clifden (68km)

Corrib Park

To N17 (2.5km); Sligo (155km)

Sports Ground

Town Hall

To N6; Airport (10km); Dublin (180km)

Salmon Weir Bridge

Kennedy Park

Corrib River

King's Gap

Eyre Square Centre

Ceannt Station

Queen St

Nun's Island Rd

William O'Brien Bridge

The Cornstore

Churchyard St

Galway Bay

Wolfe Tone Bridge

Galway Bay

Canal Basin

To The Ivies (500m); Salthill (2km); Rossaveal (32km)

To Salt Hill (2km); Salthill Caravan Park (4km)

INFORMATION		
Clan Video	1	A4
Ireland West Tourism	2	D2
iSupply	3	A4
Main Post Office	4	C2

SIGHTS & ACTIVITIES	(pp655–6)	
Collegiate Church of St Nicholas of Myra	5	C2
Galway Cathedral	6	B1
Galway City Museum	7	B4
Lynch Memorial Window	8	C2
Lynch Castle	9	C2
Nora Barnacle House Museum	10	B2
Pádraic O'Conaire's Statue	11	D2
Spanish Arch	12	B4

EATING		(p656)
Café du Journal	21	B3
Conlons	22	C2
Home Plate Organics	23	C2
Java's	24	C2
Kirwan's Lane Creative Cuisine	25	B3
Massimo	26	A4

DRINKING		(pp656–7)
Blue Note	27	A4
Crane Bar	28	A4
Monroe's Tavern	29	B4
Roisín Dubh	30	A3
Séhán Ua Neáchtain	31	B3
Taaffe's Bar	32	C3
Taylor's Bar	33	A3

SLEEPING		(p656)
Barnacle's Quay St House	13	B3
Galway Hostel	14	D2
Jury's Galway Inn	15	B3
Kinlay House	16	D2
Skeffington Arms Hotel	17	D2
Sleepzone	18	D1
St Martin's B&B	19	B3
Woodquay Hostel	20	C1

ENTERTAINMENT		(p657)
cuba	34	D1
Druid Theatre	35	C3

TRANSPORT		(p657)
Bus Station	36	D2
Celtic Cycles	37	D2
City Link		(see 2)
Europa Bicycles	38	B1

cathedral car park, just east of the Corrib, costs just €2 for the night, but the gate doesn't open until 9.30am.

Sights

Eyre Sq is the uninspired focal point of the eastern part of the city centre. In the centre of the square is **Kennedy Park**, honouring a visit by John F Kennedy in 1963. To the north of the square is a controversial statue to the Galway-born writer and hell-raiser Pádraic O'Conaire (1883–1928). Southwest of the square, the **Collegiate Church of St Nicholas of Myra** (Shop St) dates from 1320 and has several interesting tombs.

Also on Shop St, parts of **Lynch Castle**, now a bank, date back to the 14th century. Lynch,

so the story goes, was a mayor of Galway in the 15th century who, when his son was condemned for murder, personally acted as hangman since nobody else was willing to do the job. The stone façade that is the **Lynch Memorial Window** (Market St) marks the spot of the sorrowful deed.

Across the road, in the Bowling Green area, is the **Nora Barnacle House Museum** (☎ 564743; www.norabarnacle.com; 8 Bowling Green; admission €2.50; ☼ 10am-1pm & 2-5pm Tue-Sat mid-May–mid-Sep or by appointment), the former home of the wife and lifelong muse of James Joyce. The small museum is dedicated to the couple.

Little remains of Galway's old city walls apart from the **Spanish Arch**, right beside the river mouth. Next to the arch is the small and unimpressive **Galway City Museum** (☎ 567641; adult/child €2/1; ☒ 10am-1pm & 2-5pm Wed-Sun).

Festivals

The **Galway Arts Festival** (www.galwayartsfestival .com) in July is a huge event. The **Galway Oyster Festival** (www.galwayoysterfest.com), going strong for over 50 years, draws thousands every autumn.

Sleeping

BUDGET

Barnacle's Quay Street House (☎ 568644; www.barn acles.ie; 10 Quay St; dm €15.50-22, d €53) In a repurposed 16th-century town house, Barnacle's is at the heart of the action on the pedestrian mall, surrounded by all the pubs, cafés and restaurants you came to Galway for. Rooms are modernised with no hint of the building's medieval history.

Kinlay House (☎ 565244; www.kinlayhouse.ie; Merchant's Rd; dm €16-21, d €49-52; ☒) Modern and brightly lit Kinlay House is a convenient base. It's just half a block off Eyre Sq and has clean, spacious rooms. You can book discounted bus tours (€20) and Aran Islands ferries (€12) at reception.

Woodquay Hostel (☎ 562618; www.woodquayhostel .ie; 23-24 Wood Quay; dm €18-20) This quiet independent hostel, just north of the city centre, keeps a spotless kitchen and equally clean modern showers. There's a 3am curfew.

Salthill Caravan Park (☎ 523972; www.salthill caravanpark.com; camp site €15, ☒ Apr-Sep; ℗) Just west of Salthill, off Salthill Rd, is this scenic spot right on the water. A bus runs the 4km into town every half hour.

Other recommendations:

Sleepzone (☎ 566999; www.sleepzone.ie; Bóthar na mBan, Wood Quay; dm €15-18, s/d €35/50; ℗ ☒)

Galway Hostel (☎ 566959; www.galwayhostel.com; Frenchville Lane; dm €15-20, d €40)

MID-RANGE & TOP END

St Martin's B&B (☎ 568286; 2 Nun's Island Rd; s/d €35/65) St Martin's is in an ideal spot, with back-window views overlooking the William O'Brien Bridge and a simple garden that reaches the banks of the Corrib. It's in a well-kept, older town house, and the home cooking, comfortable rooms, friendliness and central location put it above everything else.

Ivies (☎ 583257; 1 Montpelier Tce, Sea Rd; s/d €40/75; ℗) Rooms at this small, friendly B&B are elegantly furnished with family antiques.

Thoughtful touches – such as the tulips on the breakfast table, that shade of lilac on the bedroom walls, the piles of pillows – make the Ivies special.

Jury's Galway Inn (☎ 566444; www.bookajurysinn .com; Quay St; r €115) Overlooking the Corrib and Wolfe Tone Bridge, this is a completely modern, full-service hotel. Rooms can accommodate three adults or a family of four at no additional charge.

Skeffington Arms Hotel (☎ 563173; www.skeffing ton.ie; Eyre Sq; d incl breakfast €140) The Skeffington, right on the square, has 23 spacious and luxurious rooms. It's a modern, full-service hotel in a classic old building with an attractive pub.

Eating

Java's (☎ 567400; Upper Abbeygate St; snacks €4-7; ☒ 11-3am Mon-Sat, 2pm-3am Sun) This small room, with an open fire on cold days, is a good spot to head to for an afternoon coffee, or to revive yourself with a sweet snack long after midnight.

Massimo (☎ 582239; 10 West William St; mains €3.50-8; ☒ noon-3pm) The décor is pub nouveau; the dark-green and wood booths are there, but they're aerodynamically shaped and there's inventive art on the walls. The important thing, though, is the char-grilled veggies sandwich with pesto and mixed leaves.

Home Plate Organics (☎ 561475; 13 Mary St; mains €4-10; ☒ 10am-9.30pm Mon-Sat) Home Plate is smart and homy and serves up high-quality, hearty meals in heaping quantities. It's the best deal in town, whether you crave roasted meat, a ciabatta sandwich or a veggie omelette.

Kirwan's Lane Creative Cuisine (☎ 568266; Kirwan's Lane; lunch €8-12, dinner €15-25; ☒ 12.30-2pm & 6-9.30pm, closed lunch Sun) A stylish, somewhat formal restaurant with devoted followers, Kirwan's Lane spruces up Irish cuisine with international ingredients. Reservations advised.

Other recommendations:

Café du Journal (☎ 568426; Quay St; mains €4-8; ☒ 9am-6pm winter, 10am-10pm summer) Sandwiches, strong coffee and animated bavardage.

Conlons (☎ 562268; Eglinton St; mains €8-17; ☒ 11am-midnight Mon-Sat, 4-10pm Sun) Nobody does fish and chips better.

Drinking & Entertainment

The free *Galway Advertiser* includes listings of what's on in the city. It's available on Thursday at the tourist office and newsstands around town.

Crane Bar (☎ 587419; 2 Sea Rd) The Crane is an atmospheric old pub that's good for a quiet pint even though a top-notch *ceilidh* (traditional music) session is usually on.

Róisín Dubh (☎ 586540; Upper Dominick St) Appearing like a reliable local boozer, Róisín Dubh is better known as *the* place to see new rock and roll talents before they get too big for such intimate venues. On occasion it's also good for traditional music.

Séhán Ua Neáchtain (☎ 568820; 17 Upper Cross St) Known simply as Neáchtains, this dusty old pub has a truly fabulous atmosphere and attracts an eccentric, mixed crowd.

Other good spots to hear trad sessions include **Monroe's Tavern** (☎ 583397; Upper Dominick St), which has set dancing on Tuesday, **Taaffe's Bar** (☎ 564066; 19 Shop St) and **Taylor's Bar** (☎ 587239; Upper Dominick St).

NIGHTCLUBS

Blue Note (☎ 589116; 3 West William St) DJs spin every night in this slightly grungy club, and an interesting, mixed crowd generally makes the scene. There's usually no cover charge.

cuba (☎ 565991; www.cuba.ie; Eyre Sq) Exuding Latin swank and attracting exuberant crowds, cuba has three cavernous floors with soulful DJs and live bands, often going simultaneously.

THEATRE

Druid Theatre (☎ 568660; Courthouse Lane) The long-established Druid is famed for its experimental works by young Irish playwrights.

Getting There & Around

The **bus station** (☎ 562000) is just behind the Great Southern Hotel, off Eyre Sq, and next to the **Ceannt train station** (☎ 561444). Bus Éireann operates services to Doolin (€12, 1½ hours, five daily Monday to Saturday in summer), Dublin (€13, 3¾ hours, 15 daily), Killarney (€19, 4¾ hours, three daily), Limerick, Sligo and beyond.

Private bus companies, generally a bit cheaper than Bus Éireann, also operate from Galway. **Citylink** (☎ 564163; www.citylink.ie) runs 13 buses a day to Dublin airport (€16) via the city centre (€11).

Four or more trains run to and from Dublin (€25 but €35 on Friday and Sunday, 2¾

hours, six daily). You can connect with other trains at Athlone.

Celtic Cycles (☎ 566606; Queen St), a Raleigh rent-a-bike outlet, hires bikes for €20/80 a day/week. **Europa Bicycles** (☎ 563355), on Earl's Island opposite Galway Cathedral, charges €10/50 per day/week.

ARAN ISLANDS

☎ 099

In recent years the windswept, starkly beautiful Aran Islands have become one of western Ireland's major attractions. Apart from natural beauty, the Irish-speaking islands have some of the country's oldest Christian and pre-Christian ruins.

On the islands, particularly on tiny **Inisheer**, the abundance of stone walls is almost absurd, with countless kilometres of stone walls separating every little patch of rocky land. Inhospitable though these rocky patches may appear, the islands were settled at a much earlier date than the mainland, since agriculture was easier to pursue here than in the densely forested Ireland of the pre-Christian era.

There are three main islands in the group, all inhabited year-round. Most visitors head for long and narrow (14.5km by a maximum 4km) **Inishmór** (or Inishmore). The land slopes up from the relatively sheltered northern shores of the island and plummets on the southern side into the raging Atlantic. **Inishmaan** and **Inisheer** are much smaller and receive far fewer visitors.

Although day trips to the islands are feasible, Inishmór alone is worth a few days of exploration. The islands can get crowded at holiday times (St Patrick's Day, Easter) and in July and August, when accommodation is at a premium and advance reservations are advised.

Orientation & Information

The **tourist office** (☎ 61263; ✆ 10am-5pm May-Aug, 11am-5pm Sep-Apr) operates year-round on the waterfront at Kilronan, the arrival point and major village of Inishmór. You can change money there and at some of the local shops. Around the corner is Spar Supermarket, which has an ATM, and about 150m to the north is a small post office. The Ionad Árann heritage centre has Internet access.

JM Synge's *The Aran Islands* is the classic account of life on the islands and is readily

IRELAND

available in paperback. A much less accessible (but more recent) tribute to the islands is map-maker Tim Robinson's *Stones of Aran*. For detailed exploration, pick up a copy of his *The Aran Islands: A Map and Guide*.

Getting There & Away

AIR

If time is important or if seasickness is a concern on the often-rough Atlantic, you could fly to the islands and back with **Aer Arann** (☎ 091-593034; www.aerarannislands.ie) for €44. Flights operate to all three islands at least six times a day (hourly in summer) and take less than 10 minutes. The mainland departure point is Connemara regional airport at Minna, near Inverin, 38km west of Galway. A connecting bus from outside the Galway tourist office costs €3 one way.

BOAT

All three islands are served year-round by **Island Ferries** (☎ 091-568903; www.aranislandferries .com; adult/child €19/10 return) and the trip takes around 40 minutes. Unfortunately the boat leaves from Rossaveal, 37km west of Galway. It's an extra €5 to catch an Island Ferries bus from outside the tourist office in Galway. Buses leave 1½ hours before ferry departure time and are scheduled to meet arriving ferries. If you have a car you can go straight to Rossaveal and leave it free in the car park there.

InisMór Ferries (☎ 091-566535; www.queeno faran2.com), billed as the islanders' ferry company, runs a nearly identical operation.

If you have time only for a tiny taste of the islands, **O'Brien's Shipping** (☎ 091-567676) sails several mornings a week from Galway's docks. The trip costs €12, and stops on Inishmór for two hours and each of the other islands for one hour, returning to Galway in the evening. The 46km sea crossing to Inishmór takes two hours (sensitive stomachs beware). Call in the morning for information.

Another option is to leave from Doolin in County Clare (see p654). **Doolin Ferries** (☎ 065-707 4455, 091-567676; www.doolinferries.com) runs to Inishmór (€32 return, 55 minutes) and Inisheer (€25 return, 40 minutes).

Inter-island services are limited in winter.

Getting Around

Inisheer and Inishmaan are small enough to explore on foot, but on larger Inishmór

bikes are definitely the way to go. **Aran Cycle Hire** (☎ 61132), just up from Kilronan's pier, is one of many bike shops that charges €10 per day. The islands are tough on bikes, so check your cruiser carefully before renting it.

Plenty of small operators offer island bus tours for around €10.

Inishmór

The 'Big Island' has four impressive stone forts of uncertain age, though 2000 years is a good guess. Halfway down the island and about 8km west of Kilronan, semicircular **Dún Aengus** (☎ 61008; adult/child €2/1; 10am-6pm May-Jun & Sep, to 7pm Jul-Aug, to 4pm Oct-Apr), perched on the edge of the sheer southern cliffs, is the best known of the four. It's an amazing place, but take great care near the cliff edge as there are no guard rails.

About 1.5km north is **Dún Eoghanachta**, while halfway back to Kilronan is **Dún Eochla**; both are smaller but perfectly circular ring forts. Directly south of Kilronan and dramatically perched on a promontory is **Dún Dúchathair**, surrounded on three sides by cliffs.

Ionad Árann (☎ 61355; www.visitaranislands.com; adult/child €3.50/2, incl film €5.50/4; 10am-7pm Jun-Aug, to 5pm Apr-May & Sep-Oct), just off the main road leading out of Kilronan, introduces the geology, wildlife, history and culture of the islands. Robert Flaherty's 1934 film *The Man of Aran* is shown five times daily.

SLEEPING & EATING

An Aharla (☎ 61305; dm €12) In a laid-back former farmhouse, quietly positioned in a grove of trees (a rarity on these islands), An Aharla has three four-bed dorms and lots of good vibes.

Mainistir House (☎ 61169; www.mainistirhouse aran.com; dm/s/d incl breakfast €15/30/45;) This colourful 60-bed hostel is in a scenic spot on the main road north of Kilronan. The shuttle from the pier is €2.50.

St Brendan's House B&B (☎ 61149; stbrendans aran@eircom.net; s/d €25/50) A cheerful old house with views of Kilronan harbour. It's extremely rough around the edges, but the hundred layers of pink paint, plethora of knick-knacks and mismatched drawer handles are why we love it.

Kilmurvey House (☎ 61218; www.kilmurveyhouse .com; s/d €50/80; Easter-Sep) This B&B is in a lovely, old stone mansion on the path leading to Dún Aengus and close to a Blue Flag beach.

Lios Aengus (☎ 61030; snacks €5-8; ☽ 9.30am-5pm) is a simple coffee shop with OK soups and sandwiches. Book ahead for the great-value organic, largely vegetarian buffet dinners at **Mainistir House Hostel** (☎ 61169; mains €12; ☽ 8pm-close summer, 7pm-close winter). **Man of Aran Cottage** (☎ 61301; sandwiches from €2.50, mains €20; ☽ 11.30am-7.30pm Apr-Sep) serves fresh fish and veggies and herbs from the owners' garden.

Inishmaan

The least visited of the three islands is Inishmaan (Inis Meáin, or 'Middle Island'). High stone walls border its fields, and it's a delight to wander along the lanes and take in some of the tranquillity. The main archaeological site here is **Dún Chonchúir**, a massive oval-shaped stone-fort built on a high point and offering good views of the island.

There are no hostels on Inishmaan, but B&Bs are relatively cheap, at about €30 per person. Try **Angela Faherty's** (☎ 73012; ☽ Mar-Oct) in Creigmore, about 500m northwest of the pier.

Inisheer

The smallest island, only 8km off the coast from Doolin, is Inisheer (Inis Oírr, or 'Eastern Island'). The 15th-century **O'Brien Castle** (Caislea'n Uí Bhriain) overlooks the beach and harbour.

Brú Radharc Na Mara (☎ 75024; maire.serraigh@ oceanfree.net; dm/s/d from €13/28/50; ☽ Mar-Oct) is an IHH hostel near the pier with ocean views. Also near the pier, **Ard Mhuire B&B** (☎ 75005; s/d €30/60) has home-baked goods.

CONNEMARA

☎ 095

The northwestern corner of County Galway is the wild and barren region known as Connemara. It's a stunning patchwork of bogs, lonely valleys, pale-grey mountains and small lakes that shimmer when the sun shines. Connemara's isolation has allowed Irish to thrive and the language is widely spoken here; the lack of English signposting can be a little confusing at times.

By car or bicycle the most scenic routes through Connemara are Oughterard–Recess (via the N59), Recess–Kylemore Abbey (via the R344) and the Leenane–Louisburgh

route (via the R335). From Galway, **Lally Tours** (☎ 091-562905; www.lallytours.com) and **O'Neachtain Tours** (☎ 091-553188; www.oneachtaintours.com) run day-long bus trips through Connemara for around €25.

Sights

Aughanure Castle (☎ 091-552214; adult/child €2.75/ 1.25; ☽ 9.15am-6pm May-Sep), 3km east of Oughterard, is a 16th-century tower house on a rocky outcrop overlooking Lough Corrib.

Just west of **Recess** (Straith Salach) on the N59, the turn north at the R334 takes you through the stunning Lough Inagh Valley. At the end of the R334 is the equally scenic **Kylemore Abbey** (☎ 41146; www.kylemoreabbey.com; adult/child €10/free; ☽ 9.30am-5.30pm mid-Mar–Nov, 10.30am-4pm Nov–mid-Mar) and its adjacent lake. The neo-Gothic 19th-century abbey is run by nuns.

From Kylemore, take the N59 east to Leenane (An Líonán), then detour north on the R335 to Louisburgh and onwards to Westport (p660); or travel 17km southwest along the N59 to **Clifden** (An Clochán), Connemara's largest town. Clifden is quiet, pleasant and has a few good pubs and restaurants. The **Connemara Walking Centre** (☎ 21379; www.walking ireland.com; Island House, Market St) runs guided walking trips from €20.

Sleeping

Oughterard has numerous B&Bs and a good hostel. **Canrawer House Hostel** (☎ 091-552388; www.oughterardhostel.com; dm/d €13/34; ☽ Feb-Oct) is an attractive place at the Clifden end of town, just over 1km down a signposted turning. It rents bikes for €15 per day. In town, the **Jolly Lodger** (☎ 091-552682; jollylodger@eircom .net; s/d €30/54; P) is in an old town house and serves up excellent breakfast pancakes.

An Óige's excellent and super-friendly **Ben Lettery Hostel** (☎ 51136; dm/tw €15/32; ☽ Mar-Nov; P ▯) is on the N59 halfway between Recess and Clifden.

In Clifden, the IHH **Clifden Town Hostel** (☎ 21076; Market St; dm/d €13/34; P) is in the centre of town. The IHH/IHO **Brookside Hostel** (☎ 21812; Hulk St; dm/d from €11.50/30; ☽ Mar-Oct; P) is by the Owen Glin River.

Two kilometres out of town on 14 hectares of woodland, **Mallmore House** (☎ 21460; mallmorecountryhouse.com; d €64; ☽ Mar-Oct) is a lovingly restored and tastefully furnished Georgian manor house.

IRELAND

Getting There & Away

Galway–Westport buses stop in Clifden, as well as Oughterard, Maam Cross and Recess; a few lines also stop in Cong and Leenane. There are three express buses a day between Clifden and Galway (one on Sunday).

WESTPORT

☎ 098

The beautiful town of Westport (Cathair na Mairt) is a popular stop on the way to/from Sligo or Donegal. It has a tree-lined mall running along the Carrowbeg River, handsome Georgian buildings and a handful of good pubs.

North over the Carrowbeg is a small **tourist office** (☎ 25711; www.irelandwest.ie; James St; ☾ 9am-6pm Jul-Aug, to 5.45pm Mon-Sat May-Jun & Sep, to 5.45pm Mon-Fri & 10am-1pm Sat Oct-Apr).

Sights

Westport's major attraction, **Croagh Patrick**, about 7km west of the town, is the hill from which St Patrick performed his snake expulsion (Ireland has been serpent-free ever since). Climbing the 765m peak is a ritual for thousands of pilgrims on the last Sunday of July.

Sleeping

Westport has two IHH hostels: the **Old Mill Hostel** (☎ 27045; http://ireland.iol.ie/~oldmill; dm €14-16), in a courtyard off James St, and the almost-luxurious **Club Atlantic Holiday Hostel** (☎ 26644; Altamount St; dm/s/d €11/16/32; ☾ Mar-Oct) near the train station.

Getting There & Away

Buses depart from Mill St for just about everywhere, including Cork (€22, six hours, two daily), Dublin (€15, four hours, five daily), Galway (€13, two hours, five daily) and Sligo (€15, two hours, two daily), where there are connections to Belfast (€27). Bus Éireann has a counter at the tourist office. The **train station** (☎ 25253; Altamount St) is southeast of the town centre. Rail connections to Dublin (€25, €35 on Friday and Sunday, 3½ hours) go via Athlone.

THE NORTHWEST

The Northwest is tourism's last frontier. The hordes haven't yet hit Counties Sligo and Donegal, so you can still get good-and-lost here if you're looking to get off the tourist trail. Sligo is somewhat known to travellers from the evocative poetry of WB Yeats, but its cute main town, the stunning scenery surrounding it and its megalithic cemetery are still among Ireland's better-kept secrets. Donegal, with its magnificent coastline of precipitous cliffs and golden beaches, has an especially wild feel to it; no other county in Ireland can boast such remoteness – or such unspoilt splendour.

SLIGO

☎ 071 / pop 18,429

William Butler Yeats (1865–1939) was born in Dublin and educated in London, but his poetry is infused with the wild landscapes, bitter history and rich folklore of his mother's native Sligo (Sligeach). He returned here many times, and reminders of his presence in this sweet, sleepy town, and the rolling green hills around it, are plentiful.

The **North West Regional Tourism office** (☎ 916 1201; www.irelandnorthwest.ie; Temple St; 9am-5pm daily mid-Jun–Aug, to 5pm Mon-Fri Sep–mid-Jun) is just south of the centre. The **main post office** (Wine St) is east of the train and bus station. **Café Online** (☎ 914 4892; Stephen St; ☾ 10am-10pm Mon-Sat, noon-8pm Sun), across from the library, has Internet access for €5 per hour.

Sights

Sligo's two major attractions are outside town. **Carrowmore**, 5km to the southwest, is the site of a **megalithic cemetery** (☎ 916 1534; carrowmoretomb@duchas.ie; adult/child €2/1; ☾ 10am-5.15pm Easter-Oct) with more than 60 stone rings, passage tombs and other Stone Age remains. The cemetery is one of the largest Stone Age necropolises in Europe.

If it's a fine day don't miss the hill-top cairn-grave **Knocknarea**, a few kilometres northwest of Carrowmore. About 1000 years younger than Carrowmore, the huge cairn is said to be the grave of the legendary Maeve, 1st century AD Queen of Connaught. Several trails lead to the 328m summit, which commands amazing views over the surrounding country and shore.

Sleeping & Eating

The very popular IHH **White House Hostel** (☎ 914 5160; Markievicz Rd; dm €12.50; ℗) is just north of the town centre. About 1km northeast of the centre, IHH's comfortable, wheelchair-accessible **Harbour House** (☎ 917 1547; www.harbourhousehostel.com; Finisklin Rd; dm/s/d €18/25/40; **P**) is modern and well-equipped. **Clarence Hotel** (☎ 914 2211; fax 914 5823; Wine St; s/d €60/110; **P**) is one of Sligo's best, even though the rooms are decorated in standard business-hotel style.

Café Bar Deli (☎ 914 0101; 15-16 Rear Stephen St; mains €8-20; ♥ 6-10pm Mon-Sat, noon-3pm Sun), a popular pasta-and-pizza place, is upstairs from the equally popular **Garavogue Bar** (mains €4-9; ♥ food served noon-6pm), which serves superior bar food – outside on the river, if the weather agrees. **Bistro Bianconi** (☎ 914 1744; 44 O'Connell St; mains €9-19; ♥ noon-2.30pm & 5.30-11.30pm Mon-Sat) serves pizzas from its wood-fired oven, and fresh pasta.

Getting There & Around

Flights to Dublin run out of **Sligo airport** (☎ 916 8280). **Bus Éireann** (☎ 916 0066) has six services a day to/from Dublin (€15, four hours). The Galway–Sligo–Donegal–Derry service runs five times daily; it's €12.50 and 2½ hours to Galway and €15 and 2½ hours to Derry. Buses operate from below the **train station** (☎ 916 9888), which is just west of the centre along Lord Edward St. Trains to Dublin (€22, three hours, three daily) pass by Boyle, Carrick-on-Shannon and Mullingar.

Flanagan's Cycles (☎ 914 4477; Market Yard) rents bikes by the week (€80) only.

DONEGAL

☎ 074 / pop 3723

Donegal Town (Dún na nGall) is not the major centre in County Donegal, but it's a pleasant and laid-back place and well worth a visit.

The triangular Diamond is the centre of Donegal; a few steps south along the Eske River is the **tourist office** (☎ 972 1148; www.ireland northwest.ie; Quay St; ♥ 9am-6pm Mon-Sat, 10am-4pm Sun Jun-Aug, to 5.30pm Mon-Fri Sep-May).

Donegal Castle (☎ 972 2405; donegalcastle@duchas .ie; adult/child €3.50/1.25; ♥ 10am-6pm mid-Mar–Oct, 9.30am-4.30pm Sat & Sun Nov-Dec), on a rocky outcrop over the Eske River, stands in ruins but is impressive all the same. Notice the floral decoration on the corner turret and the decorated fireplace on the 1st floor.

The comfortable IHH/IHO **Donegal Town Independent Hostel** (☎ 972 2805; www.donegal

hostel.com; camp site per person €6, dm/d €12/28; **P**) is 1km northwest of town on the Killybegs road (N56). An Óige's **Ball Hill** (☎ 972 1174; dm €14.50; ♥ Easter-Sep; **P**) has a beautiful setting at the end of a quiet road, on the shores of Donegal Bay. To get here, take the Killybegs road (N56) and, 5km out, look for the signs on the left-hand side of the road. The location is pretty remote, so stock up on food before arriving.

Busy **Blueberry Tearoom** (☎ 972 2933; the Diamond; mains €5-8; ♥ 9am-7pm) has substantial sandwiches and excellent baked goods. The **Famous Donegal Chipper** (☎ 972 1428; Upper Main St; fish & chips from €5; ♥ 4.30-11pm Mon-Tue, to 11.30pm Thu-Sun) isn't kidding: it's well-known throughout the area for its fabulous fish and chips.

Bus Éireann (☎ 972 1101) goes to Derry (€11.50, 1½ hours, six daily), Enniskillen (€7.20, 1¼ hours, six daily), Sligo (€11, one hour, five daily), Galway (€20.50, four hours, four daily) and Dublin (€15, 4¼ hours, five daily). The bus stop is on the Diamond, outside the Abbey Hotel. **McGeehan Coaches** (☎ 954 6150; www.mcgeehancoaches.com) does a quicker Donegal–Dublin return trip once or twice daily, departing from the police station opposite the tourist office. It's €16.50 and the trip takes 3½ hours.

AROUND DONEGAL

The awe-inspiring cliffs at **Slieve League**, dropping 300m straight into the Atlantic Ocean, are a recommended side trip from Donegal. To drive to the cliff edge, take the Killybegs–Glencolumbcille road (R263) and, at Carrick, take the turn-off signposted 'Bunglas'. Continue beyond the narrow track signposted for Slieve League (this trail is good for hikers) to the one signposted for Bunglas. Starting from Teelin, experienced walkers can spend a day walking via Bunglas and the somewhat terrifying One Man's Path to Malinbeg, near Glencolumbcille.

IHH's **Derrylahan Hostel** (☎ 973 8079; derryla han@eircom.net; camp site per person €6, dm/s/d €12/21/32; **P**), on a working farm 2km southeast of Carrick and 3km northwest of Kilcar, is a convenient base for walkers. Call for free pick-up from Kilcar or Carrick. IHO's remote **Dooey Hostel** (☎ 973 0130; tent/dm/d €5/10/22) at tiny Glencolumbcille is built into the hillside and has great views down onto the sea, and wheelchair access.

Daily **Bus Éireann** coaches (three a day in summer) stop in Kilcar and Carrick on the Donegal–Glencolumbcille route.

NORTHERN IRELAND

☎ 028

First of all, Northern Ireland is part of the UK. The accent here is distinctly different, the currency is pounds sterling, people smoke *inside* bars and not on the footpath, and petrol – along with everything else – is pricier; otherwise, cross-border differences are minimal. After all, verdant fields, grazing sheep, breathtaking coastlines and moody old castles pay little mind to politics.

Travellers do, though, and decades of internal strife have seriously damaged Northern Ireland's image – and tourism figures. The first declared IRA cease-fire in 1995 and, more significantly, the 1998 ratification of the Good Friday Agreement provided doses of positive international press, though, and visitors are finally coming back.

And the North has plenty to come back to. The coastal scenery of the Causeway Coast ranks among the most beautiful in Ireland: dramatic sea cliffs, caves and rock pinnacles, broad, sweeping beaches, picturesque harbours and of course, the surreal geological centrepiece of the Giant's Causeway. In the southeast, the lush, green landscape and Early Christian sites around Lough Erne make for a watery wonderland. The urban centres of Derry, the historic walled city with modern flair, and booming Belfast, with its eyes firmly on the future, are good bets for a good time. Even the few signs of the Troubles that remain – the powerful street murals in Belfast and Derry, for example – are an integral part of the North, reminders that peace is fragile and hope priceless.

BELFAST

pop 277,390

Imposing architecture, foot-stomping music in packed-out pubs and the UK's second-biggest arts festival – Belfast (Béal Feirste) is a city that confounds expectations. Massive investment in recent years, combined with the optimism engendered by the peace process, have transformed Belfast into something of a boom town. Walking its handsome Victorian town hall square, its lovely Botanic

Gardens or past the smart and extensive new waterfront developments, today there's little sign of the daily tension once engendered by bomb threats and army checkpoints. First-time visitors soon cast aside their preconceptions and immerse themselves in a city that is rapidly rebuilding and reinventing itself.

The city is compact and easy to get around, with most points of interest within easy walking distance of each other. Nightlife is vibrant and inspired, and a colourful new wave of stylish bars and restaurants has emerged to complement the splendid Victorian pubs that have been a mainstay for the capital's social life for decades.

Belfast has not shaken its past altogether, however, and the passions that have torn Northern Ireland apart over the decades still run deep. But despite occasional setbacks, the prevailing atmosphere of determined optimism will hopefully propel Belfast towards a peaceful future.

Orientation

The city centre is a compact area with the imposing City Hall in Donegall Sq as the central landmark. Belfast's principal shopping district is north of the square. North of that, around Donegall St and St Anne's Cathedral, is the bohemian Cathedral Quarter.

South of the square lies the Golden Mile, a restaurant- and pub-filled stretch of Dublin Rd, Shaftesbury Sq, Bradbury Pl and Botanic Ave. To the east, most of Belfast's smart new hotel, leisure and arts developments line the banks of the Lagan. East of the river rise the huge yellow cranes of the Harland & Wolff shipyards.

Information

Belfast Welcome Centre (☎ 9024 6609; www.goto belfast.com; 47 Donegall Pl; ☺ 9am-5.30pm Mon-Sat Sep-May, to 7pm Mon-Sat & noon-5pm Sun Jun-Aug) Efficient and extremely helpful.

Fáilte Ireland (☎ 9032 7888; www.ireland.ie; 53 Castle St; ☺ 9am-5pm Mon-Fri year-round, to 12.30pm Sat Jun-Sep) Has information on the Irish Republic.

Hostelling International Northern Ireland (HINI; ☎ 9032 4733; www.hini.org.uk; 22-32 Donegall Rd) Has its offices at the Belfast International Youth Hostel.

Internet café (☎ 9043 4058; per hr £3) Send email and have a coffee; next to the Belfast Welcome Centre. It's open when the centre is.

Main post office (Castle Pl) There is a smaller branch at the top end of Botanic Ave by Shaftesbury Sq.

Sights

CITY CENTRE

The wheelchair-accessible classical Renaissance–style **City Hall** (☎ 9027 0456; admission free; guided tours ☺ 11am, 2pm & 3pm Mon-Fri & 2.30pm Sat Jun-Sep, 11am & 2.30pm Mon-Fri & 2.30pm Sat Oct-May), completed in 1906, is a testament to the city's Industrial Revolution success. At the northeastern corner is a statue of Sir Edward Harland – the Yorkshire-born engineer who founded Belfast's Harland & Wolff shipyards – whose famous yellow twin cranes **Samson and Goliath** tower above the city. The yards' most famous construction was the ill-fated *Titanic*, the 'unsinkable' ship that sank in 1912. A memorial to the disaster and its victims stands on the eastern side of City Hall.

City Hall is fronted by an especially dour statue of Queen Victoria. To the northeast – between High St and Queen's Sq – the queen's consort, Prince Albert, also makes his Belfast appearance at the slightly leaning **Albert Memorial Clocktower** (1867).

Across from the Europa Hotel, the famed **Crown Liquor Saloon** (☎ 9027 9901; 46 Great Victoria St; ☺ 11.30am-midnight Mon-Sat, 12.30-10pm Sun) was built by Patrick Flanagan in 1885 and displays Victorian architecture at its most extravagant. The snugs are equipped with bells that were once connected to a board behind the bar, enabling drinkers to demand more drink without leaving their seats. The Crown was lucky to survive a 1993 bomb that devastated the (now fully restored) **Grand Opera House** (☎ 9024 1919; www.goh.co.uk) across the road.

MUSEUMS & GARDENS

Belfast's biggest tourist attraction, the **Ulster Folk & Transport Museums** (☎ 9042 8428; www .magni.org.uk; adult/child 1 museum £5/3, both museums £6.50/3.50; ☺ 10am-5pm Mon-Fri, to 6pm Sat, 11am-6pm Sun Mar-Jun, 10am-6pm Mon-Sat, 11am-6pm Sun Jul-Sep, 10am-4pm Mon-Fri, to 5pm Sat, 11am-5pm Sun Oct-Feb), one of the finest museums in Northern Ireland, is 11km northeast of the centre beside the Bangor road (A2) near Holywood. The 30 buildings on the 60-hectare site range from urban terrace homes to thatched farm cottages. A bridge crosses the A2 to the Transport Museum, a sort of automotive zoo, which contains various Ulster-related vehicles, including a prototype of the vertical take-off and landing (VTOL) aircraft. From Belfast take Ulsterbus No 1 or any Bangor-bound train that stops at Cultra station.

The wheelchair-accessible **Ulster Museum** (☎ 9038 3000; www.magni.org.uk; admission free; ☺ 10am-5pm Mon-Fri, 1-5pm Sat, 2-5pm Sun), in the **Botanic Gardens** (☎ 9032 4902; admission free; ☺ 8am-sunset) near the university, has excellent exhibits on Irish art, wildlife, dinosaurs, steam and industrial machines, and more. The gardens themselves are well worth a wander. The grand glass **Palm House** contains a luxuriant riot of greenery.

W5 (☎ 9046 7700; www.w5online.co.uk; 2 Queen's Quay; adult/child/concession £6/4/4.50; ☺ 10am-6pm Mon-Sat, noon-6pm Sun), aka the whowhatwhere-whenwhy, is an interactive science centre with fun exhibits such as a laser harp, a lie detector and a wind tunnel. The centre is wheelchair accessible.

FALLS & SHANKILL RDS

The Catholic Falls Rd and the Protestant Shankill Rd have been battlefronts since the 1970s. Even so, these areas are quite safe and worth venturing into, if only to see the large **murals** expressing local political and religious passions. King Billy riding to victory in 1690 on his white steed, and hooded IRA gunmen are two of the more memorable images.

If you don't fancy an organised tour (see below), the best way to visit the sectarian zones of the Falls and Shankill Rds is by what is known locally as the 'people's taxi'. These black former London cabs run a bus-like service up and down their respective roads from terminuses in the city. Shankill Rd taxis go from North St, and Falls Rd taxis from Castle St. The Falls Rd taxis occupy the first line at the Castle St taxi park, with signs in Gaelic. Taxis depart when full, dropping off and picking up passengers as they go; fares on both services run around £1 per person.

Tours

Black Taxi Tours (☎ 9064 2264; www.belfasttours.com) and **Original Belfast Black Taxi Tours** (☎ 0800 032 2003), running daily, are organised 'people taxi' tours. An even-sided account of the Troubles is given in a refreshingly down-to-earth way. Prices are £8 per person based on four sharing and pick-up can be arranged.

IRELAND

IRELAND

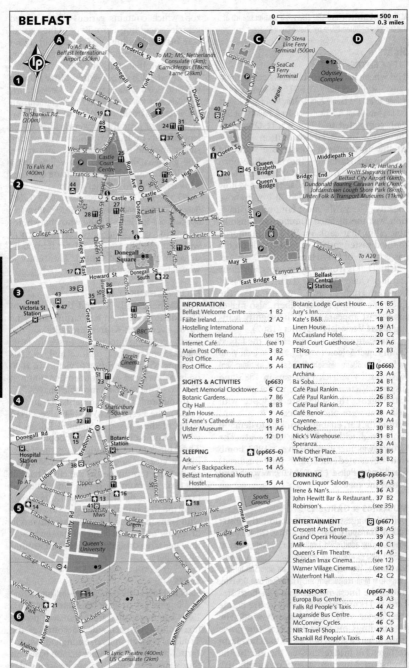

BELFAST

0 — 500 m
0 — 0.3 miles

To A6, A52;
Belfast International
Airport (30km)

Frederick St

To M2; M5; Netherlands
Consulate (6km);
Carrickfergus (18km);
Larne (28km)

Corporation St

To Stena
Line Ferry
Terminal (500km)

SeaCat
Ferry
Terminal

Odyssey
Complex

Donegall St

York St

Donegall Quay

Albert Sq

Dunbar Link

Library St

Kent St

Peter's Hill

To Shankill Rd
(200m)

West St

Orchard

Castle
Court
Centre

To Falls Rd
(400m)

Francis St

North St

Royal Ave

Waring St

Bridge St

High St

Queen Sq

Queen
Elizabeth
Bridge

Queen's
Bridge

Middlepath St

Bridge End

To A2, Harland &
Wolff Shipyards (1km);
Belfast City Airport (6km);
Dundonald Touring Caravan Park (7km);
Jordanstown Lough Shore Park (8km);
Ulster Folk & Transport Museums (11km)

Castle St

Castle
Pl

Ann St

Oxford St

Castle La

Victoria Sq

Chichester St

College St North

College St

Fountain St

Upper Arthur St

Arthur St

Cornmarket

Donegall Pl

May St

Lanyon Pl

Laganbank Rd

To A20

Donegall
Square

Donegall Sq
South

Howard St

Bedford St

Adelaide St

East Bridge St

Belfast
Central
Station

Queen St

Upper Queen St

College Sq East

Great Victoria St
Station

Brunswick St

Clarence St

BBC

Ormeau Ave

Great Victoria St

Bruce St

Virgin
Cinema

Salisbury St

Dublin Rd

Apsley St

Shaftesbury
Square

Ventry St

Sandy Row

Botanic
Station

Bradbury Pl

Donegall Rd

Hospital
Station

To A1

Lisburn Rd

Lower Crewe

Cromwell Rd

Lawrence St

University St

Fitzroy Ave

Ormeau Rd

Sports
Ground

Camden St

Claremont St

Mount Charles

University Sq

University
Mws

College
Green

College Park

University Rd

Fitzwilliam St

Rugby Ave

Queen's
University

Elmwood Ave

College Gdns

Camden St

Wellesley Ave

Wellington
Park

Malone Rd

Malone
Ave

Stranmillis Rd

Lansdowne St

Agincourt Ave

Stranmillis Embankment

To Lyric Theatre (400m);
US Consulate (2km)

INFORMATION		
Belfast Welcome Centre	1	B2
Fáilte Ireland	2	A2
Hostelling International		
Northern Ireland	(see 15)	
Internet Café	(see 1)	
Main Post Office	3	B2
Post Office	4	A6
Post Office	5	A4

SIGHTS & ACTIVITIES	(p663)	
Albert Memorial Clocktower	6	C2
Botanic Gardens	7	B6
City Hall	8	B3
Palm House	9	A6
St Anne's Cathedral	10	B1
Ulster Museum	11	A6
W5	12	D1

SLEEPING	(pp665-6)	
Ark	13	A5
Arnie's Backpackers	14	A5
Belfast International Youth		
Hostel	15	A4

Botanic Lodge Guest House	16	B5
Jury's Inn	17	A3
Kate's B&B	18	B5
Linen House	19	A1
McCausland Hotel	20	C2
Pearl Court Guesthouse	21	A6
TENsq	22	B3

EATING	(p666)	
Archana	23	A4
Ba Soba	24	B1
Café Paul Rankin	25	B2
Café Paul Rankin	26	B3
Café Paul Rankin	27	B2
Café Renoir	28	A2
Cayenne	29	A4
Chokdee	30	B3
Nick's Warehouse	31	B1
Speranza	32	A4
The Other Place	33	B5
White's Tavern	34	B2

DRINKING	(pp666-7)	
Crown Liquor Saloon	35	A3
Irene & Nan's	36	A3
John Hewitt Bar & Restaurant	37	B2
Robinson's	(see 35)	

ENTERTAINMENT	(p667)	
Crescent Arts Centre	38	A5
Grand Opera House	39	A3
Milk	40	C1
Queen's Film Theatre	41	A5
Sheridan Imax Cinema	(see 12)	
Warner Village Cinemas	(see 12)	
Waterfront Hall	42	C2

TRANSPORT	(pp667-8)	
Europa Bus Centre	43	A3
Falls Rd People's Taxis	44	A2
Laganside Bus Centre	45	C2
McConvey Cycles	46	C5
NIR Travel Shop	47	A3
Shankill Rd People's Taxis	48	A1

Mini Coach (☎ 9031 5333; www.minicoachni.co.uk; 22 Donegall Rd) conducts two-hour city tours (£8 per person) that include Falls and Shankill Rds, St Anne's Cathedral and Harland & Wolff shipyards. Tours leave at 10.30am daily and 12.30pm Monday to Friday from the Belfast International Youth Hostel (see p665).

There are a number of walking tours on offer, including the two-hour **Bailey's Historical Pub Tour** (☎ 9268 3665). It costs £6, and begins at Flannigan's (above the Crown Bar on Great Victoria St) on Thursday at 7pm and Saturday at 4pm.

Festivals

For three weeks in late October and early November, Belfast hosts the UK's second-largest arts festival, the **Festival at Queen's** (☎ 9066 7687; www.belfastfestival.com), in and around Queen's University. Also worth checking out is the fantastic **Cathedral Quarter Arts Festival** (☎ 9023 2403; www.cqaf.com) in early May, which attracts pioneering writers, comedians, musicians and artists and theatre productions.

Sleeping

BUDGET

Linen House (Paddy's Backpackers; ☎ 9058 6400; www.belfasthostel.com; 18-20 Kent St; dm £6.50-9, tw £30; P ☒ ▣) In a former linen factory in the Cathedral Quarter, the Linen House comes well recommended by readers and has wheelchair access but lacks the cosy feel of Arnie's and the Ark.

Arnie's Backpackers (☎ 9024 2867; www.arnies backpackers.co.uk; 63 Fitzwilliam St; dm £7-9.50; ☒) This long-established, exceedingly friendly hostel is set in a quiet terraced house in the university area with plenty of lively bars and restaurants nearby. A bit on the cramped side, but lots of fun.

Ark (☎ 9032 9626; www.arkhostel.com; 18 University St; dm/s/d £9.50/20/32; ☒ ▣) The Ark is a cosy, compact hostel in a pleasant terraced house in a quiet street. It's a good place to look for temporary work, and long-term accommodation is available.

Belfast International Youth Hostel (☎ 9032 4733, 9031 5435; www.hini.org.uk; 22-32 Donegall Rd; dm/s/d £9.50/17/26; P ☒ ▣) HINI's 112-bed Belfast International is conveniently sited on the Golden Mile, which means it can be a bit noisy at night when the pubs and clubs empty. It's modern, though, very clean and has a small café.

Camping options include **Jordanstown Lough Shore Park** (☎ 9086 3133; camp site £10), 8km north of town on Shore Rd (A2) in Newtownabbey, and **Dundonald Touring Caravan Park** (☎ 9080 9100; www.theicebowl.com; 111 Old Dundonald Rd; camp site £7-13; ☽ Apr-Sep) in a park next to the Dundonald Icebowl, 7km east of the centre (take bus No 21 from the Laganside Bus Centre).

MID-RANGE

Many B&Bs are in the university area, which is close to the centre, safe and well-stocked with restaurants and pubs. Botanic Ave, Malone Rd, Wellington Park and Eglantine Ave are good hunting grounds.

Botanic Lodge Guesthouse (☎ 9032 7682; 87 Botanic Ave; s/d £25/40) All rooms at this university-district bargain, in a handsome red-brick house, have a basin, but most bathrooms are shared; the two doubles with en suites cost £45.

Kate's B&B (☎ 9028 2091; katesbb127@hotmail .com; 127 University St; s/d £25/50) Clean and friendly Kate's, in a lovingly restored 1860 town house, will make you feel right at home. Kate advertises her breakfast fry with 'go on – kill yourself!' Discounted weekly rates are available.

Pearl Court Guesthouse (☎ 9066 6145; pearl courtgh@hotmail.com; 11 Malone Rd; s £25-35, d £52) Expect big bedrooms and bigger breakfasts at this elegantly old-fashioned B&B in a 200-year-old terrace south of Queen's University. Six of the 10 rooms have en suites.

TOP END

Jury's Inn (☎ 9053 3500; www.bookajurysinn.com; College Sq; r £75-85; ☒) Jury's bland modernity is more than made up for by its location (three minutes from City Hall) and excellent value – room rates include anything up to three adults or two adults and two kids. Some rooms are wheelchair accessible.

McCausland Hotel (☎ 9022 0200; www.mccaus landhotel.com; 34-38 Victoria St; r £120-190; ☒) This elegant hotel occupies two beautifully restored Italianate warehouses built for rival firms in the 1850s. Many period features have been retained and the rooms, though equipped with all mod cons, have a pleasantly sepia-tinted feel. Some rooms are wheelchair accessible

TENsq (☎ 9024 1001; www.tensquare.co.uk; 10 Donegall Sq; r £160-200; ☒) The chichi 'Ten square'

IRELAND

(*not* 'Tensk') aspires to old Shanghai. The former bank building across from City Hall has been given a luxurious *feng shui* makeover with dark lacquered wood, cream carpets and low-slung futon-style beds. It has wheelchair access.

Eating
BUDGET
Café Paul Rankin (☎ 9031 5090; 27-29 Fountain St; snacks £2-5.25; ⊙ 7.30am-5.30pm Mon-Sat, to 7.30pm Thu; ☒) Owned by Northern Ireland's top celebrity chef, this café serves quality coffee, cakes, *focaccia*, soups, pastas and salads, with comfy benches and sofas for lounging on. Other branches are at **12 Upper Arthur St** (☎ 9031 0108) and Castle Court Centre.

Café Renoir (☎ 9032 5592; 5 Queen St; snacks £4-6; ⊙ 9am-5pm Mon-Sat, to 7pm Thu; ☒) Renoir tempts hungry shoppers with decent coffee, home-baked bread and a range of filling vegetarian and wholefood dishes.

White's Tavern (☎ 9024 3080; 1-4 Wine Cellar Entry; mains £6-7; ⊙ food served noon-6pm Mon-Sat) Historic White's, on a cobbled alley off High St, is a popular lunch-time meeting spot, serving down-to-earth pub food such as baked potatoes, fish dishes, Irish stew, and sausage and champ. It's also a great place for a pint.

MID-RANGE
Ba Soba (☎ 9058 6868; 38 Hill St; mains £6-10; ⊙ noon-3pm Tue-Fri, 5.30-10pm Mon-Thu, to 11pm Fri & Sat) This bright and breezy Asian noodle bar dishes up fragrant, steaming bowls of Japanese *ramen* (noodle broth), prawn tempura, Thai warm salad and a host of other Oriental dishes.

The Other Place (☎ 9020 7200; 79 Botanic Ave; mains £7-10; ⊙ 8am-10pm) Another student favourite where you can linger over the Sunday paper amid red brick, orange pine and antiques, or get full on big plates of lasagne, cajun pita or home-made hamburger.

Archana (☎ 9032 3713; 53 Dublin Rd; mains £5-11; ⊙ noon-2pm & 5.30-11pm Mon-Sat) A cosy and unpretentious Indian restaurant, Archana has a good range of vegetarian dishes. The lunch *thali* – a platter of two curries with rice and salad – is good value at £2.50/6 for the veggie/meat version.

Chokdee (☎ 9032 3211; 44 Bedford St; mains £6-12; ⊙ 11am-11pm Mon-Sat, 4-10pm Sun) Cute little Chokdee (it means 'good luck' in Thai) serves up a variety of Western-inspired

Asian food and Asian-inspired Western food in a stylish setting saturated with colour. It has plenty for vegetarians (no 'bang bang chicken' for you).

TOP END
Speranza (☎ 9023 0213; 16-19 Shaftesbury Sq; mains £8-13; ⊙ 5-10pm Mon-Thu, to 11pm Fri & Sat, 3-9pm Sun; ☒) A local institution – it's been around for more than 20 years – Speranza is a big, buzzing Italian restaurant that complements the traditional pastas with more sophisticated dishes.

Nick's Warehouse (☎ 9043 9690; 34-39 Hill St; mains £6-15; ⊙ noon-3pm Mon-Fri, 6-9.30pm Tue-Sat) A Cathedral Quarter pioneer (opened in 1989), Nick's is an enormous wine bar and restaurant buzzing with happy diners. The menu is strong on inventive seafood and veggie dishes, and the wine list is excellent.

Cayenne (☎ 9033 1532; 7 Ascot House, Shaftesbury Sq; mains £10.50-17; ⊙ noon-2.30pm Mon-Fri, 6-10pm Mon-Thu, to 11pm Fri & Sat, 5-8.45pm Sun; ☒) Behind an anonymous frosted-glass façade lurks this award-winning restaurant serving quality Irish produce prepared with an Asian or Mediterranean twist. Cayenne is owned by TV celebrity chef Paul Rankin. Reservations recommended.

Drinking
Pubs are generally open until 11pm Monday to Saturday, though pubs with an entertainment licence stay open to 1am or 1.30am and to 11pm Sunday.

Crown Liquor Saloon (☎ 9024 9476; 46 Great Victoria St) Belfast's most famous bar has a wonderfully ornate Victorian interior with discreet panelled snugs. Despite being a tourist attraction, it fills up with crowds of locals at lunch time and in the early evening.

Irene & Nan's (☎ 9023 9123; 12 Brunswick St) Named after two pensioners from a nearby pub who fancied themselves as glamour queens, I & N's, with its 1950s retro theme, is dripping with designer chic. It's a laid-back place though, and its in-bar bistro will tempt your taste buds.

John Hewitt Bar & Restaurant (☎ 9023 3768; 51 Donegall St) The John Hewitt is one of those treasured bars that have no TV; the only noise here is the murmur of conversation. The bar has gained a reputation for its music sessions – jazz on Friday and folk several nights a week.

Robinsons (☎ 9024 7447; 38-40 Great Victoria St) Next door to the Crown, this is a theme pub spread over four floors with music – from traditional music in Fibber Magee's to DJs in the Mezzanine club – most nights.

Entertainment

The Belfast Welcome Centre issues *Whatabout?*, a free monthly guide to Belfast events. The website www.wheretotonight.com is another useful guide.

CINEMAS

Queen's Film Theatre (☎ 0800 328 2811; www.qftbelfast.info; 20 University Sq) The QFT is a two-screen art-house cinema close to the university and a major venue for the Belfast Film Festival.

The Odyssey Pavilion has two monster cinemas:

Sheridan Imax Cinema (☎ 9046 7000; www.belfastimax.com)

Warner Village Cinemas (☎ 0870 155 5176; www.theodyssey.co.uk) Belfast's biggest multiplex, with 12 screens and stadium seats throughout.

LIVE MUSIC & NIGHTCLUBS

Crescent Arts Centre (☎ 9024 2338; www.crescentarts.org; 2 University Rd) The Crescent puts on some excellent concerts, from New York jazz to top-rate Irish music. It also stages a literary festival called Between the Lines each March, and a dance festival, City Dance, in June.

Waterfront Hall (☎ 9033 4400; www.waterfront.co.uk; Lanyon Pl) The impressive 2235-seat Waterfront is Belfast's flagship concert venue, hosting local, national and international performers from pop stars to symphony orchestras.

Milk (☎ 9027 8876; www.clubmilk.com; 10-14 Tomb St; admission £2-10) Milk, in a converted warehouse, is one of Belfast's hottest and most sophisticated clubs. Monday is gay night, with cabaret acts hosted by Baroness Titty Von Tramp.

THEATRE

Grand Opera House (☎ 9024 1919; www.goh.co.uk; 2-4 Great Victoria St) This grand old venue plays host to a mixture of opera, popular musicals and comedy shows.

Lyric Theatre (☎ 9038 1081; www.lyrictheatre.co.uk; 55 Ridgeway St) The Lyric, south of the city, stages serious drama; Hollywood star Liam Neeson first trod the boards here.

Getting There & Away

For all Ulsterbus, Northern Ireland Railways (NIR) and local bus information call **Translink** (☎ 9066 6630; www.translink.co.uk). The **NIR Travel Shop** (☎ 9023 0671, 9024 2420; Great Victoria St station; ☻ 9am-5pm Mon-Fri, to 12.30pm Sat) can book and provide information on trains, buses and ferries.

AIR

There are flights from some regional airports in Britain to the convenient **Belfast city airport** (☎ 9093 9093; www.belfastcityairport.com; Airport Rd), but everything else, including flights from the Republic, Britain, Amsterdam, Brussels and New York, goes to **Belfast international airport** (☎ 9448 4848, 9442 2888; www.belfastairport.com), 30km north of the city in Aldergrove by the M2. For more information, see p677.

BOAT

See p677 for more details on ferries to/from Northern Ireland. Three main ferry routes connect Belfast to Stranraer, Liverpool and the Isle of Man.

Steam Packet/SeaCat (☎ 0870 552 3523; www.seacat.co.uk) catamaran car ferries dock at Donegall Quay, a short walk north of the city centre. **P&O European** (☎ 01-407 3434, 0870 242 4777; www.poirishsea.com) ferries to and from Scotland dock at Larne, 30km north of Belfast.

Norse Merchant Ferries (☎ 9077 9090, 0870 600 4321) to Liverpool leave from Victoria terminal, 5km north of central Belfast; take a bus from Europa Bus Centre or catch a taxi (£4). **Stena Line** (☎ 0870 570 7070; www.stenaline.co.uk) services to Stranraer leave from nearby Corry Rd.

BUS

Belfast has two separate bus stations. The smaller of the two is the **Laganside Bus Centre** (Oxford St), near the river, with bus connections to counties Antrim, Down and Derry. Buses to everywhere else in Northern Ireland, the Republic, the international airport and the Larne ferries, leave from the bigger **Europa Bus Centre** (Glengall St). Regional bus timetables are free at the bus stations.

Ulsterbus has seven daily Belfast–Dublin buses (six on Sunday) that take about three hours and start at £13 one way. The service to Derry (£9, 1¾ hours) is even more frequent.

IRELAND

TRAIN

Belfast has two main train stations – **Great Victoria St**, next to the Europa Bus Centre, and the **Belfast Central** (East Bridge St), east of the city centre.

Destinations served from Belfast Central include Derry and Dublin. Belfast–Dublin trains (£22/32 one way/return, two hours) run up to eight times a day (five on Sunday). From Belfast Central a free (with your bus or train ticket) Centrelink bus to Donegall Sq in the city centre leaves every 10 minutes. A local train also connects with Great Victoria St.

Great Victoria St station has services to Derry (£8.20, 2¼ hours, about every two hours) and Larne Harbour (£4.10, one hour, hourly).

Getting Around

Airbus buses link Belfast international airport with the Europa Bus Centre every 30 minutes (£6, 30 minutes). Alternatively, a taxi costs about £25.

The Belfast city airport is only 6km northeast of the centre. Take a shuttle bus from the terminal to the Sydenham Halt station, from which trains (£1.10, every half hour) run to Central station, Botanic station or Great Victoria St station. The taxi fare is about £7.

A short trip on a bus costs £0.70 to £1.20. Most local bus services depart from Donegall Sq, near the City Hall, where there's a ticket kiosk.

If you're driving, be fastidious about where you park; car theft is a serious problem here. The tourist office has a free leaflet showing all the multistorey car parks.

McConvey Cycles (☎ 9033 0322; www.mcconvey cycles.com; 182 Ormeau Rd) rents bikes for £10 a day or £40 a week. A £50 deposit is required.

THE BELFAST–DERRY COASTAL ROAD

Ireland isn't short of fine stretches of coast, but the Causeway Coast stretching from Portstewart in County Derry to Ballycastle in County Antrim, and the Antrim Coast stretching from Ballycastle to Belfast, taking in the striking rock formations of the Giant's Causeway, are as magnificent as they come.

From late May to late September, Ulsterbus' Antrim Coaster bus No 252 operates twice daily (except Sunday) between Belfast and Coleraine (four hours), stopping at all

the main tourist sights. An open-topped Bushmills Bus (No 177) runs from the Giant's Causeway to Coleraine five times daily in July and August. The trip takes just over an hour. Bus No 172 runs year-round along the coast between Ballycastle and Portrush. **Translink** (☎ 9066 6630; www.translink.co.uk) handles all bookings and inquiries.

Carrickfergus

Only 13km northeast of Belfast is Carrickfergus and its impressive Norman **castle** (☎ 9335 1273; adult/concession £3/1.50; ☼ 10am-6pm Mon-Sat, 2-6pm Sun Apr-Sep, 10am-4pm Mon-Sat, 2-4pm Sun Oct-Mar), which was built in 1180 by John de Courcy and overlooks the harbour where William III landed in 1690. A small museum documents the castle's long history (it was occupied until 1928).

There are no hostels in Carrickfergus; the cheapest B&B is **Langsgarden** (☎ 9336 6369; 72 Scotch Quarter; s/d £23/48; P ✗).

Glens of Antrim

Between Larne and Ballycastle, the nine Glens of Antrim are extremely picturesque stretches of woodland and downland where streams cascade into the sea. The port of **Cushendall** has been dubbed the 'Capital of the Glens', while **Glenariff**, a few kilometres to the south, is 'Queen of the Glens'. Between Cushendun and Ballycastle, eschew the main A2 road for the narrower and more picturesque B92, and take the turnoff down to sweeping Murlough Bay.

A good bet for a budget bed, and possibly a bedtime story, is at the modern **Ballyeamon Camping Barn** (☎ 2175 8699; www.taleteam.demon .co.uk; dm £8-12; P ✗ ▢) near Cushendall on the B14. The proprietor is a professional storyteller.

Ballycastle

Ballycastle, where the Atlantic Ocean meets the Irish Sea, is a quiet harbour town and a natural base for exploring the coasts to the west or south.

The IHH/IHO **Castle Hostel** (☎ 2076 2337; www.castlehostel.com; 62 Quay Rd; dm/s/d £8/12/20; P ✗) is just past the Marine Hotel. It's clean, welcoming and spacious with wheelchair access. The IHO **Ballycastle Backpackers** (☎ 2076 3612; www.bcbackpackers.com; 4 North St; dm £8, d £20-30; P ✗) is near the waterfront and the main bus stop.

Carrick-a-Rede Island

The 20m **rope bridge** (☎ 2076 9839; adult/child £2/1; ☼ 10am-6pm Mar-Sep), connecting Carrick-a-Rede Island to the mainland and swaying some 25m above pounding waves, is fun to stagger across. The island is the site of a salmon fishery and a nesting ground for gulls and fulmars. It's a scenic 1.25km walk from the car park to the bridge. Note that the bridge is closed in high winds.

Giant's Causeway

Chances are you've seen pictures of the Giant's Causeway (Clochán an Aifir), Northern Ireland's main tourist attraction. The hexagonal basalt columns, all 38,000 of them (counting the ones under the water), are amazingly uniform. Legend has it that the giant in question, Finn McCool, built the Causeway to get to Scottish rival giant Benandonner on the Scottish island of Staffa (which has similar rock formations).

The more prosaic explanation is that lava erupted from an underground fissure and crystallised some 60 million years ago. The phenomenon is explained in an audiovisual (£1) at the **Causeway Visitors Centre** (☎ 2073 1855; causewaytic@hotmail.com; ☼ 10am-5pm Mar-Jun & Sep-Oct, to 6pm Jul-Aug, to 4.30pm Nov-Feb).

It costs nothing to visit the site, but car parking is an exorbitant £5. It's an easy 10- to 15-minute walk downhill to the Causeway itself. A better approach, though, is to follow the cliff-top path northeast for 2km to the Chimney Tops headland, which has excellent views of the Causeway and the coastline. For the less mobile or the downright lazy, a minibus shuttles from the visitors centre to the Causeway for £0.70 one way or £1.40 return.

Bus No 172 runs about four times a day (more often in summer and fewer on Sunday) between Portrush and Ballycastle passing by the Giant's Causeway. If you can, try to visit the Causeway midweek or out of season to avoid the crowds and experience it at its most evocative.

A recommended walk is from the Giant's Causeway 16km east along the coast (not the highway), past Dunseverick Castle to the beach at Whitepark Bay. Be careful if you walk this route: the windy cliff-top conditions have been known to send walkers over the edge. A great place to crash at the end is the terrific, modern HINI **Whitepark Bay Hostel** (☎ 2073 1745; dm/d £13/30; ☼ closed Dec-Feb; **P** ✗), with bay views and smart dorms and rooms.

Bushmills

Bushmills, 4km southwest of the Giant's Causeway, is a small town off the A2 between Portrush and Ballycastle. The town makes a good base for visits to the Causeway Coast, but its real attraction is the **Old Bushmills Distillery** (☎ 2073 1521; www.bushmills.com; adult/child £5/2.50; ☼ 9.30am-5.30pm Mon-Sat, noon-5.30pm Sun, last tour 4pm Apr-Oct, tours 10.30 & 11.30am, 1.30, 2.30 & 3.30pm Mon-Fri, 1.30, 2.30 & 3.30pm Sat & Sun Nov-Mar), 500m south of the main square. After a noisy tour of the industrial process (it's quieter at weekends, when production is halted), there's a whiskey-tasting session.

The excellent HINI **Mill Rest Hostel** (☎ 2073 1222; 49 Main St; dm/s/tw £12/30; ☼ closed 11am-5pm Oct-Mar; ✗ ▯) has small dorms and one wheelchair-friendly twin room (reserve in advance).

Dunluce Castle

Abandoned in 1641, the ruins of 14th-century **Dunluce Castle** (☎ 2073 1938; adult/child £2/1; ☼ 10am-6pm Mon-Sat, 2-6pm Sun Apr-Sep, noon-6pm Sun Jun-Aug, 10am-4pm Mon-Sat, 2-4pm Sun Oct-Mar), between Bushmills and Portrush, are dramatically sited right on the cliff edge – so close, in fact, that the castle's kitchen once collapsed into the sea. Perched 30m above the sea, the castle was of obvious military value, and the extensive remains inside the walls give a good idea of what life was like here.

Portstewart & Downhill

These seaside resorts are only a few kilometres apart. Pleasant Portstewart has a slightly decayed, early-20th-century feel to it, while Downhill has a lovely long stretch of beach.

Portstewart's friendly **Causeway Coast Hostel** (☎ 7083 3789; 4 Victoria Tce; dm/s £8/12, d £20-24; ✗) is at the eastern end of town. The Belfast–Portrush bus, No 218, stops about 100m away.

Harder to get to, but well worth the effort, is the **Downhill Hostel** (☎ 7084 9077; www.downhillhostel.com; 12 Mussenden Rd; dm/d £8/25; **P** ✗), a lovely converted period house on the beach with open fires and a good library of books and vinyl. Pick-ups can be arranged from Castlerock train station. The Coleraine–Limavady bus (No 134) also passes nearby.

DERRY

pop 83,100

Derry. Londonderry. Even the name you use for Northern Ireland's second-largest city can be a political statement. In practice it's better known as Derry, whatever your politics.

Doire, the original Irish name, means 'oak grove', and the 'London' prefix was added after settlers from London Guilds, the companies that built the city walls, were granted much of the land in the area by James I.

In the 1960s, resentment at the long-running Protestant domination and gerrymandering of the city council boiled over in the (Catholic-dominated) civil rights marches of 1968. In August 1969, fighting between police and local youths in the poor Catholic Bogside district prompted the UK government to send British troops into Derry. In January 1972, 'Bloody Sunday' resulted in the deaths of 13 unarmed Catholic civil rights marchers in Derry at the hands of the British army, an event that marked the beginning of the Troubles in earnest. At the time of research the lengthy inquiry into the events of Bloody Sunday was continuing in Derry's Guildhall.

Today Derry is as safe to visit as anywhere else in Northern Ireland, while the Bogside and the inner city have been redeveloped. The town's long, dramatic history is still palpable – in the 17th-century city walls, in the captivating Bogside murals – but it's also a laid-back place with a well-founded reputation for musical excellence, from traditional to cutting-edge contemporary, and a lively arts scene that thrives in the town's many innovative venues.

Orientation

The old centre of Derry is the small, walled city on the western bank of the Foyle River. The heart of the walled city is The Diamond, intersected by four main roads: Shipquay St, Ferryquay St, Bishop St Within, and Butcher St. The Catholic Bogside area is below the walls to the northwest. To the south is a Protestant estate known as the Fountain. The Waterside district across the river is mostly Protestant.

Information

bean-there.com (☎ 7128 1303; 20 The Diamond; Internet per hr £3.50; ☺ 8.30am-5.30pm Mon-Fri, 10am-5.30pm Sat) Internet access as well as snacks and coffee.

Central Library (☎ 7127 2310; 35 Foyle St; Internet per hr £3; ☺ 9.15am-5.30pm Tue, Wed & Fri, to 8pm Mon & Thu, to 5pm Sat) Internet access available.

Derry Visitor & Convention Bureau (☎ 7126 7284; www.derryvisitor.com; ☺ 9am-5pm Mon-Fri, 10am-5pm Sat mid-Mar–Jun & Oct, 9am-7pm Mon-Fri, 10am-6pm Sat, to 5pm Sun Jul-Sep, 9am-5pm Nov–mid-Mar) Handles all of Northern Ireland and the Republic as well as Derry.

Main post office (Custom House St) Just north of the Tower Museum.

Sights

Derry's magnificent **city walls**, built between 1613 and 1618, were the last to be constructed in Europe, and Ireland's only city walls to survive almost intact. They're about 8m high, 9m thick, and encircle the old city for 1.5km. The walls make for a fantastic walk, and the gates give an excellent overview of Bogside (itself worth a closer look on foot) and its defiant **murals**, one notably proclaiming 'You Are Now Entering Free Derry'. From the city walls between Butcher's Gate and the army barracks, you can see many of the darkly beautiful buildingside murals.

Just inside Coward's Bastion to the north, O'Doherty's Tower is home to the excellent **Tower Museum** (☎ 7137 2411; tower.museum@derry city.gov.uk; adult/child £4.20/1.60; ☺ 10am-5pm Mon-Sat, 2-5pm Sun Jul-Aug, 10am-5pm Tue-Sat Sep-Jun), which traces the story of Derry from the days of St Columbcille to the present. At the time of research, the museum was being renovated and expanded to include an interactive Spanish Armada exhibition. If it hasn't reopened by the time you arrive, see the modified Story of Derry exhibition at the **Harbour Museum** (☎ 7137 7331; Harbour Sq; admission free; ☺ 10am-1pm & 2-4.30pm Mon-Fri).

The fine red-brick **Guildhall** (☎ 7137 7335; admission free; ☺ 9am-5pm Mon-Fri) just outside the city walls, was originally built in 1890 and is noted for its stained-glass windows. Guided tours are available in July and August.

Austere **St Columb's Cathedral** (☎ 7126 7313; requested donation £1; ☺ 9am-5pm Mon-Sat Apr-Oct, to 4pm Nov-Mar) dates from 1628 and stands at the southern end of the walled city, off Bishop St Within.

Near Bishop's Gate, the **Verbal Arts Centre** (☎ 7126 6946; www.verbalartscentre.co.uk; Stable Lane; ☺ 9am-5.30pm Mon-Thu, to 4pm Fri) focuses on the literary tradition of Derry and its surrounds. It has wheelchair access.

Tours

Both **City Tours** (☎ 7127 1996; derrycitytours@aol.com; 11 Carlisle Rd) and the **Derry Visitor & Convention Bureau** (☎ 7126 7284; www.derryvisitor.com; 44 Foyle St; ☒ 9am-5pm Mon-Fri, 10am-5pm Sat mid-Mar–Jun & Oct, 9am-7pm Mon-Fri, 10am-6pm Sat, to 5pm Sun Jul-Sep, 9am-5pm Nov–mid-Mar) have walking tours of the city walls and around for £4. Readers have also recommended Bogside tours (£3.50) by **Free Derry Tours** (☎ 0779 328 5972; www.freederry.net).

Sleeping

Derry City Independent Hostel (Steve's Backpackers; ☎ 7137 7989; www.derryhostel.com; 44 Great James St; dm/d incl breakfast £10/28; ☒ ▢) It's a little cramped but funky and fun, with an eating nook covered in Indian paintings and pillows. There's free Internet access, no checkout time, and the fifth night is free. Steve also runs Derry Backpackers, a smaller, cosier hostel on quiet Asylum Rd, a little further from the walled city. These are the only hostels in town so consider booking ahead.

Saddler's House (☎ 7126 9691; www.thesaddlers house.com; 36 Great James St; s/d £27.50/45; Ⓟ ☒) Centrally located just a few minutes' walk from the walled city, this friendly place is set in a lovely Victorian town house. It's almost worth visiting Derry just to stay here or at its sister B&B, **Merchant's House** (16 Queen St; s £20-27.50, d £40-45), a Georgian-style town house around the corner. Both places are extremely comfortable and artfully decorated with antiques and interesting *objets*. The friendly, witty owners are fun to talk to.

Tower Hotel (☎ 7137 1000; www.towerhotelderry .com; Butcher St; s/d £89/110 incl breakfast; Ⓟ ☒) The flashy new Tower is the only hotel within the old city walls, with plush wheelchair-accessible rooms and business suites, a fitness centre and a good restaurant.

Eating

An Bácús (☎ 7126 4678; 37 Great James St; snacks £1.50-2.50; ☒ 7.30am-5pm Mon-Fri, 9am-5pm Sat) The bilingual menu at this Irish language café is a little confusing to read, but you'll learn the Irish words for egg (ubh) and Coke (Cóca). It's a cute place for a coffee and a pastry or sandwich.

Sandwich Co (☎ 7137 2500; The Diamond; snacks £2-3; ☒ 9am-5pm Mon-Sat) The Sandwich Co offers good-value, choose-your-own sandwiches and salads. It has a second location (☎ 7126 6771) at the corner of Clarendon St and Strand Rd.

Lloyd's No 1 Bar/Ice Wharf (☎ 7127 6610; 22 Strand Rd; mains £5-7; ☒ 10am-10pm Mon-Sat) Big, bustling Lloyd's serves a meat or veggie breakfast fry, tasty bar snacks and hearty meals like steaks, burgers, pastas and a range of veggie dishes.

La Sosta (☎ 7137 4817; 45A Carlisle Rd; mains £9-15; ☒ 6-9.30pm Tue-Sat) This small new *ristorante* cooks up serious dishes with quality ingredients – lamb with leeks, garlic, lemon juice and white wine, for example.

Mange 2 (☎ 7136 1222; 2 Clarendon St; lunch £5, dinner mains £12-15; ☒ noon-2.30pm & 5.30-10pm) The candle-lit, Georgian-style dining room here is an elegant spot for a splurge. The interesting fusion menu includes a handful of good veggie options.

Tesco has a large supermarket in the Quayside Shopping Centre on Strand Rd.

Drinking

Mullan's Bar (☎ 7126 5300; 13 Little James St) Mullan's is a good live-music venue, with jazz, blues and traditional sessions on Wednesday and Thursday nights. DJs spin Friday to Sunday. The lavish interior was rebuilt after a petrol bomb set the roof on fire during the Troubles.

Peadar O'Donnell's (☎ 7126 2318; 63 Waterloo St) Peadar's goes for traditional music sessions every night starting around 11pm.

Sandino's (☎ 7130 9297; 1 Water St) This alternative Latin American-themed venue (named after Nicaraguan guerrilla leader Augusto Sandino) is popular with up-and-coming bands and visiting musicians. It hosts regular theme nights, fundraising and political events.

Entertainment

Millennium Forum (☎ 7126 4455; www.millennium forum.co.uk; New Market St) Ireland's biggest theatre auditorium has several wheelchair-accessible spaces for dance, drama, concerts, opera and musicals.

Nerve Centre (☎ 7126 0562; www.nerve-centre.org .uk; 7-8 Magazine St) The ever-expanding Nerve Centre is a multimedia venue with music, art-house cinema and café and bar. It also has workshops and studios for animation, film and music.

IRELAND

Getting There & Away

City of Derry airport (☎ 7181 0784) is about 13km east of Derry along the A2. There are direct flights daily to London Stanstead (Ryanair), Dublin, Glasgow and Manchester (British Airways), and Birmingham (Aer Arann).

The **bus station** (☎ 7126 2261) is just outside the city walls, on Foyle St near the Guildhall. Ulsterbus's No 212, the *Maiden City Flyer*, is the fastest service between Belfast and Derry (£8.60, 1¾ hours, every half hour, six daily on Sunday). Bus No 234 runs to Portrush and Portstewart in July and August (£6.50, 1½ hours, four daily). Five buses daily (four on Sunday) go to Dublin (£12.80, 4¼ hours).

Lough Swilly Bus Service (☎ 7126 2017), with an office upstairs at the Ulsterbus station, serves County Donegal across the border.

Air Porter Buses (☎ 7126 9996; www.airporter .co.uk) runs eight daily services (four at weekends) between Belfast airport and Derry's Quayside Shopping Centre for £15.

Derry's **Waterside train station** (☎ 7134 2228) lies across the Foyle River from the centre, but is connected to it by a free Linkline bus that leaves the bus station 15 minutes before each train departure. Nine trains run daily (four on Sunday) to Belfast (£8.20, three hours) via Portrush.

ENNISKILLEN & LOUGH ERNE

Enniskillen, the main town of County Fermanagh, is handy for activities on Upper and Lower Lough Erne. Enniskillen itself has only one notable sight, **Enniskillen Castle** (☎ 6632 5000; www.enniskillencastle.co.uk; adult/child £2.50/1.50; ☿ 10am-5pm Tue-Fri, 2-5pm Sat-Mon, closed Sun Sep-May, closed Sat Oct-Apr), home to the Fermanagh County Museum, with displays on the county's history, landscape and wildlife, and the Museum of the Royal Inniskilling Fusiliers.

The town centre is on an island in the Erne River, which connects the upper and lower lakes. The very helpful **tourist office** (☎ 6632 3110; Wellington Rd; ☿ 9am-7pm Mon-Fri Jul-Aug, to 5.30pm Sep-Jun, 10am-6pm Sat & 11am-5pm Sun Easter-Sep) is about 100m from the centre.

Between May and September – from the Round 'O' Jetty at Brook Park – the **MV Kestrel waterbus** (☎ 6632 2882) operates 1½-hour tours (£7) of the lower lough, which include a visit to **Devenish Island**, with its 9th-century church and one of the best round-towers in Ireland.

At White Island, close to the eastern shore of the lough, there's a line of six mysterious statues, dating from around the 6th century. At weekends from April to September, and daily in July and August, a ferry runs across to White Island from the Castle Archdale marina, 20km north of Enniskillen on the Kesh road. The return fare is £3. Contact the tourist office for bookings.

Marble Arch Caves (☎ 6634 8855; www.marble archcaves.net; adult/child £6/3; ☿ 10am-4.30pm Apr-Sep), 16km southwest of Enniskillen via the A4 and A32, is Ireland's most extensive cave network. The 1½-hour tours are popular and it's wise to book ahead.

If you're driving through County Fermanagh to/from Derry, don't miss the excellent **Ulster-American Folk Park** (☎ 8224 3292; www.folk park.com; adult/child £4/2.50; ☿ 10.30am-6pm Mon-Sat, 11am-6.30pm Sun Apr-Sep, 10.30am-5pm Mon-Fri Oct-Mar) on the A5 in Castletown, 8km northwest of Omagh. This open-air museum has impressive life-size exhibits: a forge, weaver's cottage, 19th-century Ulster street, and an early street from the US state of Pennsylvania (where many Ulster emigrants settled). The last admission is 1½ hours before closing.

Sleeping

Lakeland Canoe Centre (☎ 6632 4250; camp site/dm per person £4.50/10) Take a free ferry from the Fermanagh Lakeland Forum southeast of the tourist office to get to this place on Castle Island (press the bell on the jetty or call to be picked up). It has hostel-style accommodation and a camping ground.

Bridges Hostel (☎ 6634 0110; Belmore St; dm/tw £12/26; ☐) With 4- and 6-bed dorms and a restaurant, the fresh and modern Bridges is part of the Bill Clinton Peace Centre in central Enniskillen. Two twin rooms are wheelchair accessible.

Rossole House B&B (☎ 6632 3462; 85 Sligo Rd; s/d £27/40; P ☒) Rossole, on the edge of town, overlooks a lake and has its own rowing boat that you can use for free.

Getting There & Around

Enniskillen's **Ulsterbus station** (☎ 6632 2633; Shore Rd) is across from the tourist office. There are up to 10 services a day (fewer at weekends) to Belfast via Dungannon (£8.60, 2½ hours). Buses also run to Derry (£8.20, 2½ hours, once daily Monday to Friday) via

Omagh. Bus Éireann has express buses to Dublin (£15, three hours, five daily, fewer at weekends).

IRELAND DIRECTORY

ACCOMMODATION

The sleeping listings in this chapter include the high-season price. In the off season, rates are generally 15% to 25% lower.

Booking ahead is essential in peak season. Fáilte Ireland (Irish Tourist Board) will book accommodation for a 10% room deposit and a fee of €4 (£2). The **Northern Ireland Tourist Board** (NITB; www.discovernorthernireland.com) books accommodation at no cost with a 10% room deposit. This can be handy when it may take numerous phone calls to find a free room. Accommodation for the Republic and the North may also be booked online, via the **Gulliver booking service** (www.gulliver.ie). A deposit of 10% and a €4 fee is payable.

B&Bs

The bed and breakfast is as Irish a form of accommodation as there is. It sometimes seems that every other house is a B&B, and you'll stumble upon them in the most unusual and remote locations. Typical costs are around €35 per person a night, though more-luxurious B&Bs can cost from €55 or more per person. Most B&Bs are small, so in summer they can quickly fill up.

Camping & Hostels

Commercial camping grounds typically charge €12 to €18 for a tent and two people, and some hostels also have space for tents. Unless indicated otherwise prices given in this chapter for 'camp site' are for a tent plus two people.

Hostels in Ireland can be booked heavily in summer. An Óige (meaning 'youth') and Hostelling International Northern Ireland (HINI) are branches of Hostelling International (HI); An Óige has 33 hostels scattered around the Republic, while HINI administers another seven in the North. Other hostel associations include Independent Holiday Hostels (IHH), a cooperative group with about 120 hostels in both Northern Ireland and the Republic, and the Independent Hostels Owners (IHO) association, which has more than 100 members around Ireland.

From June to September nightly costs at most hostels are €15 to €20, except for the more expensive hostels in Dublin, Belfast and a few other places.

An Óige (Map pp626-7; ☎ 01-830 4555; www.anoige.ie; 61 Mountjoy St, Dublin 7)

Hostelling International Northern Ireland (HINI; ☎ 028-9032 4733; www.hini.org.uk; Belfast International Youth Hostel, 22-32 Donegall Rd, Belfast BT12 5JN)

Independent Holiday Hostels (IHH; ☎ 01-836 4700; www.hostels-ireland.com)

Independent Hostel Owners in Ireland (IHO; ☎ 074-973 0130; www.holidayhound.com/ihi; Dooey Hostel, Glencolumbcille, County Donegal)

ACTIVITIES

Ireland is a great place for outdoor activities, and the tourist boards put out a wide selection of information sheets covering bird-watching (County Donegal, p661, and County Wexford, p636), surfing (great along the west coast, p647), scuba diving (West Cork, p645), rock climbing, trout and salmon fishing, ancestor tracing, horse riding, sailing, canoeing and many other activities.

Walking is particularly popular although, of course, you must come prepared for wet weather. There are now well over 20 waymarked trails throuoghout the country, one of the most popular being the 132km Wicklow Way.

BOOKS

Lonely Planet's *Ireland, Dublin, Cycling Ireland, Walking in Ireland* and *World Food Ireland* guides offer comprehensive coverage of the island and its most visited city.

One of the better books about Irish history is *The Oxford Companion to Irish History* (1998) edited by SJ Connolly.

BUSINESS HOURS

Offices are open 9am to 5pm Monday to Friday, shops a little later. On Thursday and/ or Friday, shops stay open later. Many are also open on Saturday. In winter, tourist attractions are often open shorter hours, fewer days per week or may be shut completely. In Northern Ireland some tourist attractions are closed on Sunday morning.

Restaurants north and south tend to close around 9pm or 10pm. In the Republic, pubs close at 11.30pm Monday to Thursday, 12.30am Friday and Saturday and 11pm on Sunday; some pubs have licences allowing them to stay open till 2.30am Thursday to Saturday. In the North, pubs close at 11pm Monday to Saturday and 10pm on Sunday, and those with late licences stay open until 1am Monday to Friday and to midnight on Sunday.

DISABLED TRAVELLERS

Guesthouses, hotels and sights throughout Ireland are increasingly being adapted for people with disabilities. In Northern Ireland, this became compulsory under the Disability Discrimination Act of 1995, and service providers across the North worked to make the necessary adjustments by the 2004 deadline. Fáilte Ireland's various accommodation guides indicate which places are wheelchair accessible, and the NITB publishes *Accessible Accommodation in Northern Ireland*. Comhairle publishes detailed accessibility information in the Republic and the North. Travellers to Northern Ireland should also check out www.everybody.co.uk.

Comhairle (Map pp626-7; ☎ 01-874 7503; www .comhairle.ie; 44 Nth Great George's St, Dublin 1)

Disability Action (☎ 028-9029 7880; www.disability action.org; Portside Business Park, 189 Airport Rd West, Belfast BT3 9ED)

EMBASSIES & CONSULATES
Irish Embassies & Consulates

Irish diplomatic missions overseas include the following:

Australia (☎ 02-6273 3022; irishemb@cyberone.com.au; 20 Arkana St, Yarralumla, ACT 2600) There is also a consulate in Sydney.

Canada (☎ 613-233 6281; embassyofireland@rogers.com; 130 Albert St, Suite 1105, Ottawa, Ontario K1P 5G4)

France (☎ 01 44 17 67 00; paris@iveagh.irlgov.ie; 4 rue de Paris, 75116 Paris)

Germany (☎ 030-220 720; Friedrichstrasse 200, D-10117 Berlin)

The Netherlands (☎ 070-363 09 93; www.irish embassy.nl; Dr Kuyperstraat 9, 2514 BA The Hague)

New Zealand (☎ 09-977 2252; consul@ireland.co.nz; 6th fl, 18 Shortland St, 1001 Auckland)

UK (☎ 020-7235 2171; 17 Grosvenor Pl, London SW1X 7HR) There are consulates in Edinburgh and Cardiff.

USA (☎ 202-462 3939; 2234 Massachusetts Ave NW, Washington, DC 20008-2849) Boston, Chicago, New York and San Francisco have consulates.

Embassies & Consulates in Ireland

The following countries have diplomatic offices in Dublin:

Australia (☎ 01-676 1517; www.australianembassy.ie; 2nd fl, Fitzwilton House, Wilton Tce, Dublin 2)

Canada (☎ 01-478 1988; www.canada.ie; 4th fl, 65-68 St Stephen's Green, Dublin 2)

France (☎ 01-277 5000; www.ambafrance.ie; 36 Ailesbury Rd, Dublin 4)

Germany (☎ 01-269 3011; www.germanembassy.ie; 31 Trimleston Ave, Booterstown, Co Dublin)

The Netherlands (☎ 01-269 3444; www.netherlands embassy.ie; 160 Merrion Rd, Dublin 4)

New Zealand (☎ 01-660 4233; 37 Leeson Park, Dublin 6)

UK (☎ 01-205 3700; www.britishembassy.ie; 29 Merrion Rd, Ballsbridge, Dublin 4)

USA (☎ 01-668 7122; www.dublin.usembassy.gov; 42 Elgin Rd, Ballsbridge, Dublin 4)

In Northern Ireland, nationals of most countries should contact their embassy in London. Consulates in the North include:

Germany (☎ 028-7034 0403; Hillman's Way, Ballycastle Rd, Coleraine)

The Netherlands (☎ 028-9037 0223, fax 028-9037 1104; 14-16 West Bank Rd, Belfast, BT3 9JL)

New Zealand (☎ 028-9264 8098; The Ballance House, 118A Lisburn Rd, Glenavy BT29 4NY)

USA (☎ 028-9038 6100; www.americanembassy.org.uk; Danesfort House, 223 Stranmillis Rd, Belfast BT9 5GR)

FESTIVALS & EVENTS

Annual celebrations include the following.

St Patrick's Day is a cacophony of parades, fireworks and light shows for three days around 17 March in Dublin; Cork, Armagh and Belfast also have parades. The **All-Ireland hurling** and **football finals** both take place in Dublin in September. There are some great regional cultural events around the island, like the **Galway Arts Festival** (p656) in late July and the **Kilkenny Arts Festival** in late August. In Dublin, Leopold Bloom's Joycean journey around the city is marked by various events on **Bloomsday** (16 June). The **Dublin International Film Festival** in April is also a highlight. In Northern Ireland, July is **marching month** and every Orangeman in the country hits the streets on the 'glorious 12th' (see p619). Other events include the **Galway Oyster Festival** in September and the **Belfast Festival** at Queen's in November.

GAY & LESBIAN TRAVELLERS

Despite the decriminalisation of homosexuality for people more than 17 years of age (Northern Ireland in 1982 and the Republic in 1993), gay life is generally neither acknowledged nor understood. Only Dublin and, to a lesser extent, Belfast, Cork, Galway, Waterford and Limerick have open gay and lesbian communities. The monthly *Gay Community News* (www.gcn.ie), available at bars and cafés, is a free publication of the **National Lesbian & Gay Federation** (☎ 01-671 9076; Unit 2, Scarlet Row, West Essex St, Dublin 8). Information is also available from **Outhouse Community Centre** (☎ 01-873 4932; www.outhouse .ie; 105 Capel St, Dublin 1), a gay, lesbian and transgender community centre.

HOLIDAYS

Public holidays in the Republic, Northern Ireland or both are:

New Year's Day 1 January
St Patrick's Day 17 March
Easter (Good Friday to Easter Monday inclusive) March/April
May Holiday 1 May
Christmas Day 25 December
St Stephen's Day (Boxing Day) 26 December

NORTHERN IRELAND

Spring Bank Holiday Last Monday in May
Orangemen's Day 12 July
August Bank Holiday 1st Monday in August

REPUBLIC

June Holiday 1st Monday in June
August Holiday 1st Monday in August
October Holiday Last Monday in October

INTERNET RESOURCES

Ireland is well wired, so there's a lot of useful information available online. **CIE Group** (www.cie.ie) and **Translink** (www.translink.co.uk) are handy for planning transport in the south and north, respectively.

Blather (www.blather.net) This wry webzine dishes out healthy portions of irreverent commentary on all things Irish.

Entertainment Ireland (www.entertainmentireland.ie) Countrywide listings for clubs, theatres, festivals, cinemas, museums and much more.

Irish Tourist Board (www.ireland.ie) The Republic's tourist information site has heaps of practical info. It features a huge accommodation database with photos.

Irish Times (www.ireland.com) Get up to speed on the latest news before you leave home with Ireland's largest daily newspaper.

Lonely Planet (www.lonelyplanet.com) Comprehensive travel information and advice.

Northern Ireland Tourism (www.discovernorthern ireland.com) Northern Ireland's official tourism information site is particularly strong on activities and accommodation.

Office of Public Works (www.heritageireland.ie) The Republic's heritage sites – castles, churches and abbeys, parks, cemeteries and the like.

MAPS

Good-quality maps of Ireland include the Lonely Planet *Dublin City Map*, Michelin *Ireland Motoring Map* No 923 (1:400,000) and Ordnance Survey's (OS) four Ireland *Holiday Maps* (1:250,000). The more detailed OS *Discovery* series (1:50,000) covers the entire country with 89 maps.

MEDIA
Newspapers

The main papers in the Republic are the Dublin-based *Irish Times* and *Irish Independent*, and the *Examiner*. In the North the three main papers are, with the highest circulation, the *Belfast Telegraph*, and the popular pro-Unionist *Newsletter* and pro-Nationalist *Irish News*. British newspapers are available, as is the *International Herald Tribune*.

Radio & Television

The Republic has three national TV stations: the relatively conservative State-funded RTE, the purely commercial TV3, and the critically acclaimed Irish-language TG4. It has three radio stations. Northern Ireland's two TV channels are BBC Northern Ireland and Ulster Television. Britain's BBC and some other stations can be picked up throughout most of the North. Raidió na Gaeltachta (92.5/96 FM or 540/828/963 MW) is the national Irish-language service.

MONEY

The Irish Republic is part of the euro zone, while Northern Ireland uses the British pound sterling (£). Banks offer the best exchange rates; exchange bureaus, open longer, have worse rates and higher commissions. Post offices generally have exchange facilities and open on Saturday morning.

In Northern Ireland several banks issue their own Northern Irish pound notes, which are equivalent to sterling but not readily accepted in Britain.

Ireland is an expensive place, marginally more costly than Britain, but prices vary around the island. Entry prices to sites and museums are usually 20% to 50% lower for children, students and senior citizens (OAPs).

For the budget traveller, €65 per day should cover hostel accommodation, getting around and a meal in a restaurant leaving just (barely) enough for a pint at the end of the day.

Fancy hotels and restaurants usually add a 10% or 15% service charge onto the bill. Simpler places usually do not add service; if you decide to tip, just round up the bill (or add 10% at most). Taxi drivers do not have to be tipped, but if you're feeling flush, 10% is more than generous.

POST

The post offices (An Post) throughout the Republic are generally open from 9am to 5.30pm Monday to Friday, and from 9am to 1pm Saturday; smaller offices close for lunch.

Letters weighing less than 50g cost €0.60 to Britain and €0.65 to continental Europe and the rest of the world.

Post-office hours and postal rates in Northern Ireland are the same as in Britain. Mail can be addressed to poste restante at post offices, but is officially held for only two weeks. Writing 'hold for collection' on the envelope may help.

TELEPHONE

Local telephone calls from a public phone in the Republic cost €0.25 for around three minutes (around €0.50 to a mobile). In Northern Ireland a local call costs a minimum of £0.20. Some pay phones in the North take euros. Pre-paid phonecards by Eircom or private operators, available in newsagencies and post offices, work from all payphones and dispense with the need for coins.

To call Northern Ireland from the Republic, you do not use ☎ 0044 as for the rest of the UK. Instead, you dial ☎ 048 and then the local number.

You can dial direct to your home country operator and then reverse charges (collect) or charge the call to a local phone-credit card.

EMERGENCY NUMBERS

Dial ☎ 999 for police, ambulance or fire brigade in both the Republic and NI.

From the Republic, dial the following codes, then the area code and number you want. Your home-country operator will come on the line before the call goes through.

Australia ☎ 1800 550061
France ☎ 1800 551033
New Zealand ☎ 1800 550064
UK (BT) ☎ 1800 550044
USA (AT&T) ☎ 1800 550000
USA (MCI) ☎ 1800 551001
USA (Sprint) ☎ 1800 552001

Reverse-charge calls can also be made from the North using the same numbers as from the UK.

Mobile Phones

The mobile (cell) phone network in Ireland runs on the GSM 900/1800 system compatible with the rest of Europe and Australia, but not the USA. Ireland's three service providers are Vodafone (087), O2 (086) and Meteor (085). A new SIM for your mobile, generally around €30, may be free after the standard phone-credit refund. Pay-as-you-go phones run from €100.

TOURIST INFORMATION

The Irish tourist board, **Fáilte Ireland** (www.failteireland.ie), and the **Northern Ireland Tourist Board** (NITB; www.discovernorthernireland.com) operate separate offices. Both are usually well organised and helpful, though Fáilte Ireland will not provide any information on places (such as B&Bs and camping grounds) that it has not approved. Every town big enough to have half-a-dozen pubs will certainly have a tourist office, although smaller ones may close in winter. Most will find you a place to stay for a fee of €2 to €4.

Tourism Ireland (www.tourismireland.com) handles tourist information for both tourist boards overseas.

Tourist Offices Abroad

Overseas offices of Tourism Ireland include:
Australia (☎ 02-9299 6177; 5th fl, 36 Carrington St, Sydney, NSW 2000)
Canada (☎ 1 800 223 6470; Suite 3403, 2 Bloor St W, Toronto M4W 3E2
New Zealand (☎ 09-977 2255; Level 6, 18 Shortland St, Private Bag, 92136 Auckland)
UK (☎ 0800 039 7000; Nations House, 103 Wigmore St, London W1U 1QS)
USA (☎ 1 800 223 6470; 345 Park Ave, New York, NY 10154)

VISAS

Citizens of the EU and most other Western countries do not need a visa to visit either the Republic or Northern Ireland. EU nationals are allowed to stay indefinitely, while other visitors can usually remain for three to six months.

UK nationals born in Britain or Northern Ireland do not need a passport, but should carry some form of identification.

TRANSPORT IN IRELAND

GETTING THERE & AWAY
Air

The Fáilte Ireland **online tourist office** (www .ireland.ie) has useful information on getting to Ireland from a number of countries. International departure tax is normally included in the price of your ticket.

There are scheduled nonstop flights from Britain, continental Europe and North America to Dublin and Shannon, and good nonstop connections from Britain and continental Europe to Cork.

International airports in the Republic include the following:

Cork (code ORK; ☎ 021-431 3131; www.corkairport.com)
Dublin (code DUB; ☎ 01-814 1111; www.dublinairport .com)
Kerry (code KIR; ☎ 066-976 4644; www.kerryairport .ie; Farranfore)
Knock (code NOC; ☎ 094-67222; www.knockairport.com)
Shannon (code SNN; ☎ 061-712 000; www.shannon airport.com)
Waterford (code WAT; ☎ 051-875 589; www.flywater ford.com)

International airports in Northern Ireland include the following:
Belfast city (code BHD; ☎ 028-9093 9093; www.belfast cityairport.com) Serves Britain.
Belfast international (code BFS; ☎ 028-9448 4848; www.belfastairport.com) Serves Britain, Europe and the USA.
Derry (code LDY; ☎ 028-7181 0784; www.cityofderry airport.com) Serves Britain.

See p1066 for a comprehensive list of airlines serving Ireland from outside Western Europe. Airlines that fly to and from Ireland from within Western Europe include the following:
Aer Arann (☎ 01-814 5240; www.aerarann.ie) A small carrier that operates flights within Ireland and also to Britain.

Aer Lingus (☎ 01-886 8844; www.aerlingus.com) The Irish national airline, with direct flights to Britain, continental Europe and the USA.
Air France (☎ 01-605 0383; www.airfrance.com)
Alitalia (☎ 01-844 6035; www.alitalia.com)
BMI British Midland (UK ☎ 01332-854 854; www .flybmi.com)
British Airways (in the UK ☎ 0845-773 3377; www .ba.com)
easyJet (☎ 048-9448 4929; www.easyjet.com)
Finnair (☎ 01-844 6565; www.finnair.com)
Flybe (in the UK ☎ 0870-567 6676; www.flybe.com)
Iberia (☎ 01-407 3017; www.iberia.com, in Spanish)
KLM (☎ 01-663 6900; www.klm.nl)
Lufthansa (☎ 01-844 5544; www.lufthansa.com)
Ryanair (☎ 01-609 7800; www.ryanair.com) Ireland's budget carrier, flying to Britain and continental Europe.
Scandinavian Airlines (☎ 01-844 5888; www .scandinavian.net)

Land

Because of cheap flights, getting to Ireland by land is not very popular. National Express and Bus Éireann's Eurolines operate services direct from London and other UK centres to Dublin, Belfast and other cities. For details in London, contact **National Express** (☎ 0870-514 3219; www.nationalexpress.com); in Dublin, contact **Bus Éireann** (☎ 01-836 6111; www.buseireann .ie). London to Dublin by bus takes about 11 hours and costs £25/39 one way/return (more for the evening bus). To Belfast it's 13 hours and £40/54.

Sea

There's a great variety of ferry services from Britain and France to Ireland. Prices vary drastically, depending on season, time of day, day of the week and length of stay. One-way fares for an adult foot passenger can be as little as £20, but nudge close to £50 in summer. For a car plus driver and up to four adult passengers, prices can range from £130 to £250.

Keep an eye out for special deals, discounted return fares and other money savers. And plan ahead – some services are booked up months in advance.

BRITAIN

Regular ferry services run to ports in the Republic and Northern Ireland from Scotland (Cairnryan–Larne, Stranraer–Belfast, Troon–Belfast and Troon–Larne), England (Heysham–Belfast, Liverpool–Belfast and

IRELAND

Liverpool–Dublin), Wales (Fishguard–Rosslare Harbour, Holyhead–Dublin, Holyhead–Dun Laoghaire, Pembroke–Rosslare Harbour and Swansea–Cork) and from the Isle of Man (Douglas–Dublin, Douglas–Belfast).

Irish Ferries (☎ 0818-300 400, 01-638 3333, in the UK ☎ 0870-517 1717; www.irishferries.com) For ferry and fast-boat services from Holyhead to Dublin (two or 3¼ hours), and ferry services from Pembroke to Rosslare Harbour (3¾ hours).

Isle of Man Steam Packet Company/Sea Cat (☎ 1800-805 055, in the UK ☎ 0870-552 3523; www.steam-packet.com) Ferry and fast-boat services from Douglas (Isle of Man) to Belfast (2¾ hours, Easter to September) and Dublin (2¾ hours, Easter to September); Liverpool to Dublin (3¾ hours, February to October); and Troon to Belfast (2½ hours).

Norse Merchant Ferries (☎ 028-9077 9090, in the UK ☎ 0870-600 4321; www.norsemerchant.com) Ferries from Liverpool to Belfast (8½ hours).

P&O European Ferries (☎ 01-407 3434, in the UK ☎ 0870-242 4777; www.poirishsea.com) Ferry and fast-boat services from Cairnryan to Larne (one or 1¾ hours), Troon to Larne (two hours, April to September), and Liverpool to Dublin (eight hours).

Stena Line (☎ 01-204 7777, in the UK ☎ 0870-570 7070; www.stenaline.co.uk) Ferry and fast-boat services from Holyhead to Dublin (three hours) and Holyhead to Dun Laoghaire (1¾ hours); Fishguard to Rosslare Harbour (1¾ or 3½ hours); and Stranraer to Belfast (1¾ or 3¼ hours).

Swansea Cork Ferries (☎ 021-427 6000, in the UK ☎ 01792-456116; www.swanseacorkferries.com) Ferry services from Swansea to Cork (10 hours).

FRANCE

Ferries run between Roscoff and Cherbourg to Rosslare Harbour and Cork.

Brittany Ferries (in France ☎ 021-427 7801, 02-9829 2800; www.brittanyferries.com) Services from Roscoff to Cork once weekly (11 hours, April to September).

Irish Ferries (in France ☎ 01-4394 4694) Ferries from Roscoff/Cherbourg to Rosslare Harbour (17½/20½ hours, April to December).

P&O European Ferries Services from Cherbourg to Rosslare Harbour (19 hours).

GETTING AROUND

Travelling around Ireland looks very simple, as the distances are short and there's a dense network of roads and railways. But in Ireland, from A to B is seldom a straight line, and public transport can be expensive (particularly trains), infrequent or both. For

these reasons having your own transport – car or bicycle – can be a major advantage.

Passes & Discounts

Eurail passes are valid for train travel in the Republic of Ireland but not in Northern Ireland and will get you a 50% discount on Irish Ferries crossings to France. **InterRail passes** give you a 50% reduction on train travel within Ireland and on Irish Ferries and Stena Line services. Both Bus Éireann and Iarnród Éireann offer discounts to ISIC holders.

Irish Rambler tickets are available from Bus Éireann for bus-only travel in the Republic. They cost €53 (for travel on three out of eight consecutive days), €116 (eight out of 15 days) or €168 (15 out of 30 days). The similar **Open Road pass** costs €42 for travel on three out of six consecutive days and is extendable.

Irish Rover tickets combine services on Bus Éireann and Ulsterbus. They cost €68 (for three days travel out of eight consecutive days), €152 (eight days out of 15) and €226 (15 out of 30 days).

For train-only travel within the Republic, **Iarnród Éireann Explorer tickets** are good for five travel days out of 15 (€115.50) or 15 out of 30 (€341). It's €143 (five travel days out of 15) to include Northern Ireland.

Irish Explorer Rail and Bus tickets (€176) allow you eight days' travel out of 15 consecutive days on trains and buses in the Republic.

In Northern Ireland, the **Freedom of Northern Ireland ticket** is good for unlimited travel on Ulsterbus and Northern Ireland Railways for one day (£13), three days out of eight (£32) or seven consecutive days (£47).

Air

There are flights within Ireland between Dublin and Belfast, Cork, Derry, Donegal, Galway, Kerry, Shannon and Sligo, as well as a Belfast–Cork service. Most domestic flights take 30 to 50 minutes. See the list of airlines p677).

Bicycle

Ireland is a great place for cycling, despite bad road surfaces in places and inclement weather. You can either bring your bike with you on the ferry or plane, or rent one in Ireland. Typical rental costs are €10 to €20 a day or around €50 to €100 a week. Bags and other equipment can also be rented. Raleigh

Rent-a-Bike agencies are all over Ireland. Contact them at **Eurotrek** (☎ 01-456 8847; www .eurotrekraleighgroup.com). Like many local bike shops, they offer one-way rentals for an extra charge.

Bicycles can be transported by bus if there's enough room; it usually costs €10 per trip. By train, costs start at €2.50 for a one-way journey, but bikes are not allowed on certain routes, including the Dublin Area Rapid Transit (DART).

Bus

Bus Éireann (☎ 01-836 6111; www.buseireann.ie) is the Republic's national bus line, and it operates services all over the Republic and into Northern Ireland. Fares are much cheaper than regular rail fares. Returns are usually only slightly more expensive than one-way fares, and special deals (eg same-day returns) are often available. Most intercity buses in Northern Ireland are operated by **Ulsterbus** (☎ 028-9066 6630; www.translink.co.uk).

Car & Motorcycle

AUTOMOBILE ASSOCIATIONS

Automobile association members should ask for a Card of Introduction entitling you to services offered by sister organisations, usually free of charge.

Automobile Association (AA; www.aaireland.ie) Northern Ireland (☎ 0870-950 0600, breakdowns ☎ 0800-667788); The Republic (☎ 01-677 9481; breakdowns ☎ 1800-667788)

Royal Automobile Club (RAC; www.rac.ie) Northern Ireland (☎ 0800-029 029); The Republic (☎ 1800-483 483)

HIRE

Car rental in Ireland is expensive so you'll often be better off booking a package deal from your home country, though in the off season, prices plunge. In the high season it's wise to book ahead. Extra daily fees may apply if you cross the North-South border.

People under 21 cannot hire a car; for most rental companies you must be at least 23 and have had a valid driving licence for one year. Some companies will not rent to those aged over 70 or 75. Your own local licence is usually sufficient to hire a car for up to three months.

In the Republic, typical weekly high-season rental rates – with insurance, VAT, unlimited distance and collision-damage waiver – range from €300 for a small car

to €450 for a larger one. **Nova Car Hire** (www .rentacar-ireland.com) acts as an agent for Alamo, Budget, European and National and offers greatly discounted rates.

The international rental companies and the major local operators have offices all over Ireland. Recommended Dublin-based operators:

Argus Rent-A-Car (Map p626-7; ☎ 01-490 4444, 01-862 3811; www.argusrentals.com; Dublin Tourism Centre, Suffolk St)

Malone Thrifty Car Rental (☎ 01-874 5844; www .thrifty.ie) 26 Lombard St East (Map p626-7); 33 Bachelors Walk (Map p630)

Murrays Europcar (☎ 01-614 2800, 01-812 0410; www.europcar.com; Baggot St Bridge) Just southeast of the city.

ROAD RULES

As in Britain, driving is on the left and you should only overtake (pass) to the right of the vehicle ahead of you. The driver and all passengers must wear safety belts, and children under 12 cannot sit in the front. Motorcyclists and their passengers must wear helmets; headlights should be dipped.

Minor roads can be potholed and narrow, but the traffic is rarely heavy except through popular tourist or busy commercial towns. Speed limits in both Northern Ireland and the Republic appear in kilometres, miles or both: 112km/h (70mph) on the motorways, 96km/h (60mph) on other roads and 48km/h (30mph) or as signposted in towns. On quiet, narrow, winding rural roads it's simply foolish to speed. Ireland's blood-alcohol limit is 0.08% and strictly enforced.

Parking in car parks or other specified areas in Ireland is regulated by the 'pay and display' tickets or disc parking. Available from newsagencies, discs are good for one hour and usually cost around €1.25 each. In Northern Ireland beware of the Control Zones in town centres where, for security reasons, cars absolutely must not be left unattended. Double yellow lines by the roadside mean no parking at any time; single yellow lines indicate restrictions, which will be signposted.

Train

Iarnród Éireann (☎ 1850-360 222, 01-836 6222; www .irishrail.ie), the Republic of Ireland's railway system, has routes fanning out from Dublin. Tickets can be twice as expensive as the bus, but travel times may be dramatically reduced. Special fares are often available, and a midweek return ticket sometimes costs just a bit more than the single fare; the flip side is that fares may be significantly higher on

Friday or Sunday. A 1st-class ticket costs an extra €10. **Northern Ireland Railways** (in Dublin ☎ 028-9066 6630, 01-679 1977; www.translink.co.uk) has four routes from Belfast, one of which links up with the Republic's rail system.

Italy

CONTENTS

ITALY

Rare is the traveller who isn't smitten by Italy. Everyone loves the Italians – their quirky, outspoken zest for life – and their gorgeous country. Teeming with ancient history, artistic splendour, divine food and wine, and a romantic olive-grove dappled landscape, Italy hits the heart and soul fast. It's an intoxicating place, swooning with raw beauty and simple *passione*, but also rough around the edges, frustrating at times, and exceptionally humorous. Where else would a wine maker conduct a contest for the ideal breast, the winning form to serve as the shape for a new line of wine glasses?

From the dazzling Renaissance and baroque masterpieces, to the stunning natural beauty, Italy offers tangible pleasures to all. Whether you're cycling through Tuscany, ancient ruins-hopping through Rome, sunning on the Amalfi coast or hiking in the Dolomites, the cities and landscapes will undoubtedly enrapture you, and a first visit soon grows into an unquenchable thirst for more.

Natural and historic beauties aside, modern Italy is exceptionally vibrant and simmers with a hedonistic passion – for food and wine, soccer and women, the everyday happenings of the dolce vita. If you come looking for efficient systems, fast-paced living and a low-carb menu, best leave your expectations and diets at the border. It's a moveable feast – prepare to indulge yourself.

FAST FACTS

- **Area** 301, 230 sq km
- **Capital** Rome
- **Currency** euro (€); A$1 = €0.58; ¥100 = €0.76; NZ$1 = €0.54; UK£1 = €1.50; US$1 = €0.83
- **Famous for** emperors, gladiators, Renaissance art, food and wine, romantic countryside, resplendent seaside
- **Key Phrases** *buongiorno* (hello); *grazie* (thanks); *mi scusi* (excuse me); *come si chiama?* (what's your name?); *prego* (no problem); *andiamo* (let's get going)
- **Official Language** Italian
- **Population** 57.8 million
- **Telephone Codes** country code ☎ 39; international access code ☎ 00; non-Europe reverse-charge code ☎ 170; Europe reverse-charge code ☎ 15
- **Visa** citizens of many countries, including the USA, Australia, Canada and New Zealand, don't need visas to enter Italy as tourists; a *permesso di soggiorno* is necessary if you plan to study, work or live in Italy; EU citizens with a passport or national identity card can stay in Italy for as long as they like

ITALY

HIGHLIGHTS

- Savour **la cucina** (p688): classics such as *mozzarella di bufala,* bruschetta, pizza margherita, *insalata caprese* and pasta bolognese (washed down with chianti or *brunello*).
- Love it or leave it, edgy **Naples** (p756) and its sparkling bay (not to mention the most perfect pizza) is sure to elicit strong emotions.
- Island-hop around the the sun-splashed **Aeolian Islands** (p771), with their lush lemon groves, aquamarine coves and steaming volcano.
- Get off the beaten track to proud Puglia, with its crowd-free coastline, delicious cuisine, and the baroque treasures of delightful, spunky **Lecce** (p767).
- Immerse yourself in more than 2500 years of visible archaeological and anthropological history in **ancient Rome** (p689).

ITINERARIES

- **One week** Start with a Renaissance fix in Florence, with Tuscan detours to Siena and San Gimignano. Head south to Rome and immerse yourself in the sights for two days. Wind down the coast to Naples, sampling Italy's best pizza and hopping over to Capri for a day trip.
- **Two weeks** Start with a few days exploring Venice, Verona and Bologna. Next, jump into the Renaissance for three days, visiting Florence and environs, including Siena and San Gimignano. Dally in Rome for two days, then skirt to the coast to cover Naples and the Amalfi coast. Spend your final two days soaking up the sun on Sicily, in Palermo and Taormina, Italy's first resort town.

CLIMATE & WHEN TO GO

Italy lies comfortably in a temperate zone, but the climates of the north and south can vary considerably. Summers are hot (and sticky), and winters can be chilly and finicky, though mild in the south. May and October are the best months to visit – gentle weather, few crowds and better rates. Virtually all of Italy goes on vacation during the month of August – if you're planning a summer trip, book well in advance. Winter is a peaceful and cost-effective time to visit the cities, with elbowroom to spare at star sights.
See the Climate Charts p1055.

HISTORY

According to legend, the she-wolf-reared Romulus founded Rome in 753 BC, but the country had already been inhabited for thousands of years. By the start of the Bronze Age, around 2000 BC, the peninsula had been settled by several Italic tribes. From 900 BC, the Etruscan civilisation developed, while the southern reaches were settled by Greek traders in the 8th century BC, their independent city-states forming Magna Graecia. Etruscan civilisation flourished until the end of the 3rd century BC, when the Romans took over the last of the Etruscan cities.

The New Roman Republic

Despite an occasional blow – such as the invasion of the Gauls in 390 BC – Rome steadily garnered strength and expanded south, claiming Sicily in 241 BC and Spain and Greece in 202 BC. Romans left their mark everywhere, planting olive trees and grape vines, establishing trade networks, building roads and aqueducts, and settling prosperous towns on the plains. Under Julius Caesar's rule, Rome conquered Gaul and moved into Egypt in the 1st century BC. After Caesar's assassination, his adopted son Octavius defeated rivals Mark Antony and Cleopatra. He established the Roman Empire in 27 BC and adopted the title of Augustus Caesar, kicking off a time of significant advancement in engineering and the arts.

ITALY

ITALY

0 — 100 km
0 — 60 miles

FRANCE
Basel
GERMANY
Munich
Vienna
Budapest
Zurich
Lucerne
Vaduz
LIECHTENSTEIN
Innsbruck
AUSTRIA
Bern
SWITZERLAND
Bolzano
HUNGARY
Mont Blanc (4807m)
Courmayeur
Verbania
Sondrio
TRENTINO-ALTO ADIGE
Trento
Belluno
FRIULI-VENEZIA GIULIA
SLOVENIA
Ljubljana
Zagreb
SERBIA & MONTENEGRO
Aosta
VALLE D'AOSTA
VENETO
Bassano
Trieste
Rijeka
Karlovac
CROATIA
Turin
PIEDMONT
Milan
LOMBARDY
Brescia
Verona
Vicenza
Padua
Venice
Gulf of Venezia
Monviso (3841m)
Piacenza
Mantua
BOSNIA HERZEGOVINA
Cuneo
Alessandria
Parma
Modena
Ferrara
Banja Luka
FRANCE
Savona
LIGURIA
EMILIA-ROMAGNA
Bologna
Ravenna
Genoa
Gulf of Genova
La Spezia
Cesena
Forlì
Rimini
Zadar
Sarajevo
Nice
Imperia
Lucca
Pistoia
Pesaro
Ligurian Sea
Pisa
Florence
SAN MARINO
Ancona
Split
Capraia
TUSCANY
Siena
Arezzo
Gubbio
LE MARCHE
MONACO
Livorno
Perugia
Assisi
Bastia
Piombino
Grosseto
UMBRIA
Spoleto
Dubrovnik
Elba
Viterbo
L'Aquila
Pescara
To Greece, Turkey & Albania
CORSICA (Fr)
Civitavecchia
LAZIO
Chieti
ABRUZZO
ADRIATIC SEA
Fiumicino
ROME
Lido di Ostia
Frosinone
MOLISE
Campobasso
Promontorio del Gargano
LAZIO
Latina
Foggia
Asinara
Porto Torres
Olbia
Golfo Aranci
Gulf of Gaeta
CAMPANIA
Benevento
Andria
Bari
To Greece
Sassari
Alghero
Nuoro
Naples
Avellino
Vesuvio (1277m)
Potenza
Matera
PUGLIA
Brindisi
Bosa
Dorgali
Ischia
Pompeii
Salerno
BASILICATA
Taranto
Lecce
Oristano
Arbatax
Capri
Gulf of Salerno
Paestum
Otranto
Gallipoli
SARDINIA
Gulf of Taranto
CALABRIA
Cagliari
Cosenza
Sant'Antioco
Tyrrhenian Sea
AEOLIAN ISLANDS
Salina
Stromboli
Catanzaro
Crotone
Capo Rizzuto
Gulf of Squillace
Ionic Sea
Filicudi
Alicudi
Panarea
Lipari
Vulcano
Messina
Reggio di Calabria
Trapani
Palermo
Mt Etna (3330m)
Marsala
Cefalù
Catania
ALGERIA
Tunis
SICILY
Agrigento
Syracuse
Ragusa
MEDITERRANEAN SEA
Pantelleria
TUNISIA
MALTA
Valletta

The Emergence of City-States & the Renaissance

By the end of the 3rd century AD, the Roman empire was so big that Emperor Diocletian divided it between east and west. His successor, Constantine, ruled from Byzantium (Istanbul) and was the first Christian emperor. From the 5th to 9th centuries, Goths, Huns and Arabs beset the empire from the south.

The Middle Ages were marked by the development of powerful city-states in the north. In the 15th century the Renaissance spread throughout the country, fostering artistic geniuses such as Brunelleschi, Donatello, Bramante, Botticelli, da Vinci, Masaccio, Lippi, Raphael and Michelangelo. By the early 16th century much of Italy was under Habsburg rule. After Napoleon's invasion in 1796, a degree of unity was introduced for the first time in centuries. In the 1860s the unification movement (the Risorgimento) gained momentum, and in 1861 the Kingdom of Italy was declared under the rule of King Vittorio Emanuele. Venice was wrested from Austria in 1866, and Rome yanked from the papacy four years later and named the country's capital.

Fascism, WWII & the Italian Republic

In 1921 Benito Mussolini's Fascist Party took control, and became a German ally in WWII. After several military disasters, the king led a coup against Mussolini and had him arrested. Italian partisans killed Mussolini in April 1945, and the monarchy was abolished a year later.

In 1957, Italy was a founding member of the European Economic Community, the forerunner of the European Union (EU). The '70s were marked by a spate of terrorism, including the assassination of Prime Minister Aldo Moro in 1978, but the following decade saw increased stability and significant economic growth, with Italy for a short time one of the world's leading economies.

Modern Times

The country enjoyed economic growth for a while, but the 1990s heralded a period of crisis, both economically and politically. A national bribery scandal known as Tangentopoli ('kickback city') rocked the nation. Investigations implicated thousands of politicians, public officials and businesspeople, and left the main parties in tatters after the 1992 elections. A programme of fiscal austerity was ushered in to guarantee Italy's entry into the EMU, and Italy also moved decisively against the Sicilian Mafia.

Since 2001, media magnate Silvio Berluschoni – dubbed Il Cavaliere ('the Knight') by the press – has been prime minister, with his right-wing Forza Italia party. His tenure thus far has disappointed many and been marred by continued allegations of corruption, a well-worn path.

La Mafiosa

Once a powerful entity, the Sicilian Mafia has gradually lost its steam. During the 1990s, Italy took decisive steps against La Cosa Nostra ('Our Thing'), prompted by the 1992 assassinations of two prominent anti-Mafia judges. Numerous testimonies took place, leading to several important arrests, including the life sentencing of Salvatore 'Toto' Riina, the Sicilian godfather himself. Riina's suspected successor, Giovanni Brusca, was arrested in 1996, implicated for murder and imprisoned for 30 years in 1999. While the high-profile arrests continue, and some claim the Mafia's confidence and power have been seriously undermined, others believe the entrenched system and family *segreti* (secrets) are far from cracked. However, the April 2004 death of a former leader, serving a life sentence in America, led to a public declaration that the *mafiosa* had seen its last days of power.

PEOPLE

Italians have a legendary reputation for being impassioned, fiery, love-struck individuals who drive with reckless abandon, ooze charm, wear their hearts on the sleeve, siesta away the workday and feast daily on sinfully good food and wine. Scratch the stylish veneer and get to know Italy's remarkably diverse, and vigorously proud, inhabitants. Amongst one another, Italians are fiercely protective of their home towns, of regional dialects and cuisine; either Sicilian or Roman, but not both. Yet when faced with a foreigner, Italians exude more of a national pride, making those strong regional distinctions harder to discern for the unaware visitor.

Italy's population hovers around 57.8 million, and the country has the lowest birth rate in Europe.

Italians are supremely family oriented, and 'mamma's boys' do exist, with a high percentage of men living at home until married. Grandmothers *(nonne)* are downright revered, and there's even a 'coolest granny' title doled out annually (the most recent winner beat the competition by dancing a barefoot tarantella).

SPORT

Football (soccer) is a national love, and there are stadiums in all major towns. Italy's club teams have traditionally done well in European tournaments. Check newspapers for details of who's playing where.

In May, the *Gazzetta dello Sport* sponsors the *Giro d'Italia,* held annually since 1909. This long-distance, multi-staged cycle race covers a great swatch of the countryside and draws legions of cheering fans.

Italy hosts two major motor races each year: the Italian Formula One Grand Prix is held each September at Monza, just north of Milan; and the San Marino Grand Prix is held at Imola in May. Team Ferrari is the long-time favourite; securing tickets can be a challenge.

RELIGION

To most foreigners, Italy is synonymous with Catholicism. Just shy of 85% of Italians profess to be Catholic. While millions still flock to Rome to catch a glimpse of the pope each year, the role of religion in Italy has lessened in recent years, with more attention put towards formalities than actual faith. Still, first Communions, church weddings and regular feast days are an integral part of daily life, and pilgrimages continue to be big business. Beyond Catholics, there are about 700,000 Muslims, making Islam Italy's second religion. Italy is also home to 400,000 evangelical Protestants, 350,000 Jehovah's Witnesses and smaller numbers of Jews and Buddhists.

ARTS
Literature

Before Dante wrote his *Divina Commedia* (Divine Comedy) in the early 1300s, Latin was the language of writers. Among ancient Rome's greatest writers were Cicero, Ovid, Petronius and Virgil, whose *Aeneid* – an epic of the founding of Rome – is the most famous work of that time. Petrarch (1304–74) was a contemporary of Dante's. Giovanni Boccac-

cio (1313–75), author of the *Decameron,* is considered the first Italian novelist. Machiavelli's *The Prince,* a purely political work, has proved a lasting Renaissance piece.

Italy's richest contribution to modern literature has been in the novel and short story. Leonardo Sciascia's taut writings on Sicilian themes are enigmatically beautiful. Umberto Eco's best-known work, *The Name of the Rose,* is a highbrow murder mystery.

Cinema

Despite a few popular contemporary Italian films, such as Robert Benigni's Oscar-winning *Life is Beautiful* (1998) and *Cinema Paradiso,* the real heyday for Italian films was during the postwar 1940s, when a trio of brilliant neorealists – Roberto Rossellini (1906–77), Vittorio de Sica (1901–74) and Luchino Visconti (1907–76) – turned the camera on the everyday struggles of warworn Italians and churned out classic masterpieces such as *Bicycle Thieves* (1948) and *Rome Open City* (1945). Schooled with the neorealist stars, Federico Fellini carried the creative torch onward with gems such as *La Dolce Vita* (1959). Other notable directors and films include Michelangelo Antonioni, with the 1967 hit *Blow-up* (1966); Bernardo Bertolucci, with *Last Tango in Paris* (1972), *The Last Emperor* (1987), *Stealing Beauty* (1996) and *Besieged* (1999); and Franco Zeffirelli, whose film *Tea with Mussolini* (1998) was an international hit.

Contemporary directors worth a look include the Taviani brothers, Giuseppe Tornatore, and Nanni Moretti. *L'Ultimo Bacio,* produced in 2001 by Gabriele Muccino, and a smash hit in Italy and abroad, portrayed a group of 30-something men grappling with life's poignant questions and a lack of ideals.

Music & Theatre

Italian artists have taken a dominant place in the realms of opera and instrumental music. Antonio Vivaldi (1675–1741) created the concerto in its present form. Verdi, Puccini, Bellini, Donizetti and Rossini, composers from the 19th and early 20th centuries, are all stars of the modern operatic era. Tenor Luciano Pavarotti (1935–) has recently had his crown as 'King of Mother's Day CD Sales' taken by Andrea Bocelli (1958–), who soared to international stardom in the 1990s. With his bluesy voice, Zucchero (Adelmo Fornaciari) has also had a few international hits.

Sicilian Luigi Pirandello (1867–1936), author of the influential *Six Characters in Search of an Author*, is Italy's most renowned playwright and won the Nobel Prize in Literature in 1934. On the contemporary scene, actor/director Dario Fo (who won the Nobel Prize in Literature in 1998) is the most noteworthy, with luminous works such as *Mistero Buffo*, laced with social and political commentary.

Architecture, Painting & Sculpture

Take a walk through any Italian town – Palermo, Siena, Florence, Pienza, Venice, Lecce, Rome – and you'll see glistening examples of Italy's rich artistic past before even stepping into a museum. In the south, where the Greeks left an indelible mark prior to Roman domination, there are important archaeological sites, with well-preserved temples at Paestum, in Campania, and the Valley of the Temples in Agrigento, Sicily. Pompeii and Herculaneum glean insight on the day-to-day lives of ancient Romans. In Ravenna, Venice and Palermo, gilded Byzantine mosaics adorn churches.

Patronised mainly by the Medici family in Florence and the popes in Rome, painters, sculptors, architects and writers flourished during the Renaissance. Filippo Brunelleschi's greatest achievement – the distinct red dome on the Florence Duomo – represented the greatest artistic feat of the day. The High Renaissance (1490–1520) was dominated by three brilliant artists: Leonardo da Vinci (1452–1519), Michelangelo Buonarrotti (1475–1564) and Raphael (1483–1520).

The baroque period followed in the 17th century, spawning numerous buildings with elaborately sumptuous façades and richly decorative painting and sculpture. Florence and the small city of Lecce, in the southern region of Puglia, offer countless displays of this luxuriant architectural style, while Rome literally teems with masterpieces by the brilliant baroque sculptor and architect Gianlorenzo Bernini (1598–1680) and Michelangelo Merisi da Caravaggio (1573–1610). During the neoclassic period, Canova (1757–1822) emerged as a star sculptor, his smooth white marble works sensual masterpieces. Rome's Spanish Steps and Trevi Fountain both date from this period, a reaction to the frivolous excesses of the baroque works.

Of Italy's modern artists, Amedeo Modigliani (1884–1920) is most famous. The early 20th century also produced a movement known as the futurists, which rejected the sentimental art of the past and was infatuated by new technology, including modern warfare. Fascism produced its own style of architecture, characterised by the EUR satellite city and the work of Marcello Piacentini (1881–1960).

ENVIRONMENT

Boot-shaped Italy incorporates Sicily and Sardinia and is bound by the Adriatic, Ligurian, Tyrrhenian and Ionian Seas. There is more than 8000km of coastline. Inland, about 75% of the peninsula is mountainous, with the Alps dividing the country from France, Switzerland and Austria, and the Apennines forming a backbone that extends from the Alps into Sicily.

Italy has 20 national parks, with several more on the way, and over 400 smaller nature reserves, natural parks and wetlands. The national parks cover about 5% of the country's land, and include: Parco Nazionale del Gran Paradiso and Parco Nazionale dello Stelvio, both in the Alps; Parco Nazionale d'Abruzzo; Parco Nazionale del Pollino, straddling Basilicata and Calabria; and Umbria's Parco Nazionale dei Monti Sibillini, home to over 50 species of mammals and over 150 types of bird.

Not known for environmental awareness, Italy's major cities, and much of the industrialised north, suffer from air pollution, attributed to high car usage. Aesthetically, the result of industrious humankind is not always displeasing – much of Tuscany's beauty lies in the mazing of olive groves with vineyards. But centuries of tree clearing,

TOP TEN ITALY

- **Top Small Towns** – San Gimignano (p752) and Lecce (p767)
- **Top Festival** – Siena's Il Palio (p751)
- **Top Walks** – Cinque Terre (p714)and Positano to Nocelle (p764)
- **Top Piazza for a Cocktail** – Campo de'Fiori (p706)
- **Top Ancient Ruins** – the Forum in Rome (p692) and Agrigento in Sicily (p775)
- **Top Coastal Stretch** – Amalfi Coast (p764)
- **Top Sights** – Florence's Duomo (p741) and Sardinia's Grotte di Nettuno (p780)
- **Top Islands** – Aeolian Islands (p771)
- **Top Coffee** – Tazza d'Oro, Rome (p707)
- **Top Alpine Views** – Dolomites (p738)

combined with illegal building, have also led to severe land degradation and some serious erosion woes. Coupled with some people's passion for hunting, this has had a dire effect on native animals and birds, many now endangered. Fortunately, new laws are far more progressive, partly in response to EU directives. Italy also has its share of natural hazards, including landslides, mudflows, floods, earthquakes and volcanic eruptions, thanks to six active volcanoes. A rumble of quakes in the autumn of 1997 left severe damage and 10 dead in Umbria, particularly in the town of Assisi, and another devastating quake in 2002 killed 29 in Molise. Sicily and the Aeolian Islands have seen much nonfatal volcanic action since then, including a Stromboli eruption that caused an eight-metre tidal wave.

FOOD & DRINK

Food enthusiasts will have a gastronomic heyday in Italy, where *la cucina* (the kitchen) revolves around season and region with additional variances between north and south. While rustic Tuscan cooking is characterised by simplicity and distinct flavours, in the south dishes are usually spicier. During spring, you'll see lots of fava beans, courgette (zucchini) flowers and asparagus pepper dishes, while autumn brings *porcini* (funghi)

and *cinghiale* (wild boar). Vegetarians won't have a problem foraging in Italy, which prides itself on using fresh garden produce and which has open-air produce markets countrywide.

A full meal consists of an antipasto such as bruschetta, followed by the *primo piatto*, a pasta dish, and the *secondo piatto*, meat or fish. Next comes an *insalata* (salad) or *contorni* (side vegetable) before finishing with with *dolci* (cake) and *caffè* (coffee).

Italian wine is delicious, abundant, justifiably world-famous and reasonably priced, with a very drinkable bottle costing as little as €7. In Tuscany, sample chianti, *sangiovese* and *brunello* for reds, and *vernaccia* for white; Piedmont produces excellent Barolo, Sicily terrific *nero di avola*, and crisp *vermentino* hails from Sardinia and Liguria. Peroni is the national beer; for a draft, order it *alla spinna*.

Where to Eat & Drink

Dining options are divided into several categories. A pizzeria serves the obvious, but sometimes a full menu as well, and the best sport a *forno a legna* sign, indicating a wood-fire oven. An *osteria* is the Italian equivalent of a tavern, with an equal doling of wine and local dishes, while an *enoteca* (wine library) specialises in wines by the glass accompanied by savoury pairings, such as platters of cheese, olives and cured meats. Trattorias are traditional neighbourhood eateries, often family-run with simple home cooking. A *ristorante* tends towards a more formal ambience and higher price bracket. For fast, cheap eating, there's *pizza a taglio* (pizza by the slice) and the *tavola calda* (literally 'hot table'), offering inexpensive dishes served caféteria-style. A *rosticceria* specialises in grilled meats and take-away food, *alimentari* and *salumerie* are small, delicatessen-style grocers, and fresh bread is baked at a *forno* or *panetteria*. Cafés serve any number of beverages and snacks, and often stay open from morning until late at night.

Keep an eye out for recent stickers from Italian restaurant guides (such as *Gambero Rosso*) posted in eating-establishment windows – almost always a sign of excellent, well-valued food.

Restaurants are usually open for lunch from 12.30pm to 3pm. For dinner, opening hours can vary from north to south but are generally from 7.30pm to 11.30pm. Restaurants are closed one night a week and for much of August; in seasonal tourist areas, many also close between Christmas and April.

Most eating establishments charge a *pane e coperto* (cover charge), ranging from €1 to €4; some tack on a *servizio* (service charge) of 10% to 15% but when it's not included, tourists are expected to round up the bill or leave 10% (locals, however, don't).

Habits & Customs

Italians don't tend to eat a sit-down *colazione* (breakfast), preferring instead a quick cappuccino and *cornetto* (croissant) grabbed at the bar. *Pranzo* (lunch) is traditionally the main meal, although more Italians are taking speedy lunches these days, and *cena* (dinner) is becoming the bigger meal. Italians are late diners, often not eating dinner until after 9pm.

ROME

pop 2.8 million

If you had time for just one city in life, Rome's your spot – gloriously artistic, romantically beautiful, and endearingly *pazzo* (crazy). No other city so stylishly meshes its significant, visible history with its hip, contemporary, fun-loving self. Rome's more than 2500 years of history have produced a veritable archive of Western culture. There is simply a dizzying amount to see, between the remnants of ancient Rome and the artistic splendours from the Renaissance and baroque periods.

Whether you've got a weekend or a month, this beguiling city will swallow you whole, charm you to pieces, then leave you craving more.

HISTORY

Rome's origins date to a group of Etruscan, Latin and Sabine settlements, scattered across the city's hills, but it is the legend of the she-wolf-reared twins – Romulus and Remus – that's the pervading tale. Having killed his brother over governing rights, Romulus established the city on the Palatine, one of the famed Seven Hills of Rome, and seeded an empire that eventually controlled almost all of Europe.

Modern Rome still gleams with evidence of the Western world's two great rulers: the Roman Empire and the Christian Church. The sprawling Forum and majestic Colosseum are balanced by St Peter's and the Vatican, which give off a decidedly powerful energy. Between the two are countless layers of history, displayed in every piazza and church, some visible, some not. For example, St Peter's Basilica stands on the site of an earlier basilica built by the Emperor Constantine on top of the necropolis where St Peter himself was buried.

ORIENTATION

Despite Rome's vast size, it's a very walking-friendly city, with most of the major sights within the relatively small *centro storico* (historic centre), just west of Stazione Termini, the central train station. The Tiber River cuts through the city, with Vatican City and Trastevere lying on its west bank. Rome's best-known geographical features are its seven hills: Palatine, Capitoline, Aventine, Celian, Esquiline, Viminal and Quirinal – all part of the ancient city.

Rome's main bus terminus is in Piazza del Cinquecento, directly in front of the train station. Many intercity buses arrive and depart from the Piazzale Tiburtina, in

---

ROME IN TWO DAYS

Visit the **Sistine Chapel** (p698), the **Vatican Museums** (p695) and **St Peter's Basilica** (p695), then recover over a leisurely lunch around **Piazza Navona** (p698). Traipse the afternoon away at the **Roman Forum** (p692) and **Colosseum** (p699), stopping for a *caffè* at **Café Café** (p706) before hitting vivacious **Trastevere** (p699) for dinner, an evening *passeggiata* and a final nightcap at **Stardust** (p707).

On day two, take in the Roman morning vibe at the **Campo de'Fiori market** (p698), then tackle the **Musei Capitolini** (p694) and the **Pantheon** (p698) – with a *granita* break at **Tazza D'Oro** (p707). Refresh on a siesta walk to **Villa Borghese** (p698), via **Trevi Fountain** (p699) and **Piazza di Spagna** (p699), then window shop on **Via Condotti** (p708) and gallery hop on **Via Giulia** (p700). Eat hip at **'Gusto** (p705) then stroll back to **'Il Campo'** (p698) for the night vibe.

ROME

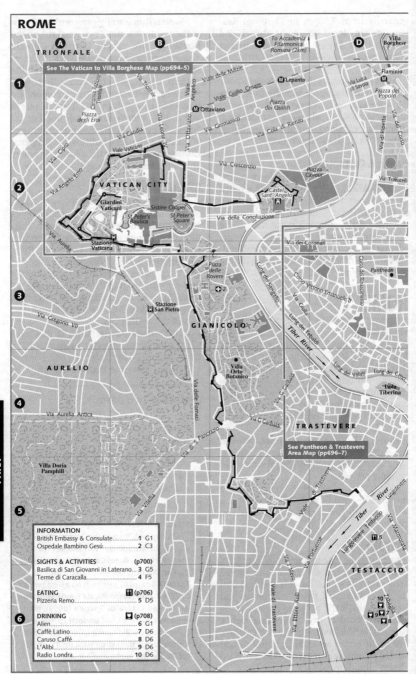

See The Vatican to Villa Borghese Map (pp694–5)

TRIONFALE

VATICAN CITY

Giardini Vaticani

St Peter's Basilica

Sistine Chapel

St Peter's Square

Stazione Vaticana

Castel Sant'Angelo

GIANICOLO

Stazione San Pietro

Villa Orto Botanico

AURELIO

Villa Doria Pamphilj

TRASTEVERE

See Pantheon & Trastevere Area Map (pp696–7)

Tiber River

TESTACCIO

To Accademia Filarmonica Romana (2km)

Villa Borghese

INFORMATION	
British Embassy & Consulate.............1	G1
Ospedale Bambino Gesù....................2	C3

SIGHTS & ACTIVITIES	(p700)
Basilica di San Giovanni in Laterano...3	G5
Terme di Caracalla............................4	F5

EATING	(p706)
Pizzeria Remo...................................5	D5

DRINKING	(p708)
Alien..6	G1
Caffè Latino.....................................7	D6
Caruso Caffè....................................8	D6
L'Alibi...9	D6
Radio Londra..................................10	D6

ITALY

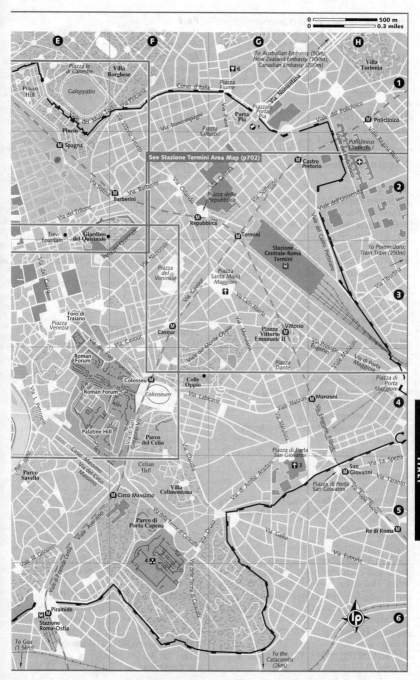

front of Stazione Tiburtina, accessible from Termini on the Metro Linea B.

If your time is limited, it helps to plan an itinerary. Most of the major museums and galleries are open all day until 7pm or 8pm; some museums are closed on Monday, so check ahead.

INFORMATION
Bookshops
Feltrinelli International (Map p702; Via VE Orlando 84; ☉ 9am-8pm) An extensive selection of maps, travel books and titles in many different languages.

Emergency
Foreigners' Bureau (Map p702; ☎ 06 468 62 977; Via Genova 2) Report thefts here.
Police station (Questura; Map p702; ☎ 06 468 61; Via San Vitale 11; ☉ 24hr)

Internet Access
There are Internet cafés scattered all over town.
Easy Internet Café (Map pp694-5; Via Barberini 2; per 30min €1) Plenty of terminals, around-the-clock access, an actual café and good prices.

Medical Services
A list of all-night pharmacies in the city centre is posted on www.romaturismo.it and in all pharmacy windows.
24-hour Pharmacy (Map p702; ☎ 06 488 00 19; Piazza del Cinquecento 51) Opposite Stazione Termini.
Ospedale Bambino Gesù (Map pp690-1; ☎ 06 685 92 351; Piazza di Sant'Onofrio 4) Rome's paediatric hospital.
Ospedale San Gallicano (Map pp696-7; ☎ 06 588 23 90; Via di San Gallicano 25a, Trastevere)
Ospedale San Giacomo (Map pp964-5; ☎ 06 362 61; Via Canova 29) Near Piazza del Popolo.
Ospedale Santo Spirito (Map pp694-5; ☎ 06 65 09 01; Lungotevere in Sassia 1) Near the Vatican; multilingual staff.

Money
Banks are open from 8.45am to 1.30pm and 2.45pm to 4pm Monday to Friday. There's a bank and exchange booths at Stazione Termini, and an exchange booth and ATMs at Fiumicino. There are numerous Bancomats (ATMs) and exchange booths throughout the city.
American Express (Map pp694-5; ☎ 06 676 41; Piazza di Spagna 38)
Thomas Cook (Map pp694-5; ☎ 06 482 81 82; Piazza Barberini 21)

Post
Main post office (Map pp694-5; Piazza di San Silvestro 20; ☉ 9am-6.30pm Mon-Fri, 9am-1pm Sat) Off Via del Tritone.
Vatican post office (Map pp694-5; ☎ 06 69 88 34 06; Piazza di San Pietro; ☉ 8.30am-6pm Mon-Fri, to 1pm Sat) Said to offer faster and more reliable service.

Tourist Information
Enjoy Rome (Map p702; ☎ 06 445 18 43; www.enjoy rome.com; Via Marghera 8a; ☉ 8.30am-7pm Mon-Sat, to 2pm Sun) Five minutes' walk northeast of the station; a well-run private tourist office with a free hotel-reservation service and travel agency. The English-speaking staff can help you find or book nearly anything and offer great biking and walking tours (in English) that cover all sorts of interests.
Rome Online (www.romatourismo.com) Everything you need to know about Rome.
Tourist offices Stazione Termini (Map p702; ☎ 06 48 90 63 00; ☉ 8am-9pm); Via Parigi 5 (Map p702; ☎ 06 36 00 43 99; ☉ 9am-7pm Mon-Sat) Good information on hotels and sights. Both offices provide maps and printed information about bus services.
Vatican tourist office (Map pp694-5; ☎ 06 69 88 16 62; Piazza San Pietro; ☉ 8.30am-7pm Mon-Sat) To the left of the basilica.

SIGHTS & ACTIVITIES
When it comes to seeing the sights, that old adage, *Roma, non basta una vita* (Rome, a lifetime is not enough), couldn't be more true. It would take 900 days alone to visit all of Rome's churches, one per day. Whew, time for another espresso. Fortunately, you can briskly cover many of the important sights in three days. Entry to various attractions is free for EU citizens aged under 18 and over 65, and half-price for EU citizens aged between 18 and 25 plus those from countries with reciprocal arrangements and many university students. Cumulative tickets can represent good value, with discounts for multiple main attractions. A good pick is the €20 ticket, getting you into nine important attractions, including the Colosseum, Palatine and some of the Museo Nazionale Romano locations. These tickets can be purchased at the sites they cover, or by calling ☎ 06 39 96 77 00.

Roman Forum & Palatine Hill
The ancient Roman commercial, political and religious centre, the **Roman Forum** (Map pp696-7; ☎ 06 399 67 700; free admission to Roman Forum, admission to Palatine Hill with Colosseum €8; ☉ 9am-1hr before sunset Mon-Sat), stands in a valley between the Capitoline and Palatine hills. Originally

marshland, the area was drained during the early republican era and started out as a typical piazza, a public centre for political rallies, public ceremonies and senate meetings. Its importance declined along with the empire after the 4th century, and the temples, monuments and buildings constructed by successive emperors, consuls and senators over a period of 900 years fell into ruin, until eventually the site was used as pasture land.

During medieval times the area was extensively plundered for its stone and precious marble. Many temples and buildings were converted to other uses, while some monuments lay half-revealed. The area was systematically excavated in the 18th and 19th centuries, and excavations are continuing. You can enter the Forum from Via dei Fori Imperiali, which leads from Piazza Venezia to the Colosseum.

As you enter, to your left is the **Tempio di Antonino e Faustina**, erected by the senate in AD 141 and transformed into a church in the 8th century. To your right are the remains of the **Basilica Aemilia**, built in 179 BC and plundered for marble during the Renaissance. The **Via Sacra**, which traverses the Forum from northwest to southeast, runs in front of the basilica. Towards the Campidoglio is the **Curia**, once the meeting place of the Roman senate and converted into a church. In front of the Curia

is the **Lapis Niger**, a large piece of black marble that purportedly covered Romulus' grave.

The **Arco di Settimo Severo** was erected in AD 203 in honour of this emperor and his sons, and is considered one of Italy's major triumphal arches. A circular base stone beside the arch marks the *umbilicus urbis,* the symbolic centre of ancient Rome.

Just to the southwest of the arch is the **Tempio di Saturno**, one of the most important ancient Roman temples, used as the state treasury. The **Basilica Giulia**, in front of the temple, was the seat of justice, and nearby is the **Tempio di Giulio Cesare**, erected by Augustus in 29 BC on the site where Caesar's body was burned and Mark Antony read his famous speech.

Back towards the Palatine Hill is the **Tempio dei Castori**, built in 489 BC in honour of the Heavenly Twins, or Dioscuri. It is easily recognisable by its three remaining columns.

In the area southeast of the temple is the **Chiesa di Santa Maria Antiqua**, the oldest Christian church in the Forum, now closed to the public. Back on Via Sacra is the **Casa delle Vestali**, home of the virgins who tended the sacred flame in the adjoining **Tempio di Vesta**. If the flame went out, it was seen as a bad omen. The next major monument is the vast **Basilica di Costantino**. Its impressive design inspired Renaissance architects. The **Arco di Tito**, at the Colosseum end of the Forum, was built in AD 81 in honour of the victories of the emperors Titus and Vespasian against Jerusalem.

From here, climb the **Palatine** (admission costs apply from here; entrances are along Via di San Gregorio and Piazza dei Santa Maria Nova), where wealthy Romans built their homes and legend says that Romulus founded the city. Archaeological evidence shows that the earliest settlements in the area were in fact on the Palatine. Like the Forum, the buildings of the Palatine fell into ruin and in the Middle Ages the hill became the site of convents and churches. During the Renaissance, wealthy families established gardens here. The Farnese gardens were built over the ruins of the Domus Tiberiana.

Worth a look is the impressive **Domus Augustana**, the private residence of the emperors; the **Domus Flavia**, the residence of Domitian; the **Tempio della Magna Mater**, built in 204 BC; and the fresco-adorned **Casa di**

Livia, thought to belong to the wife of Emperor Augustus.

Piazza del Campidoglio

Perched atop Capitoline Hill, this elegant **piazza** (Map pp696-7) was designed by Michelangelo in 1538. Formerly the seat of the ancient Roman government, it is now the seat of the city's municipal government. Michelangelo also designed the façades of the three palaces bordering the piazza. A modern copy of the bronze equestrian statue of Emperor Marcus Aurelius is at its centre; the original is on display in the ground-floor portico of the **Palazzo Nuovo** (Palazzo del Museo Capitolino; Map pp696-7). This forms part of the **Musei Capitolini** (Map pp696-7; ☎ 06 67 10 20 71; admission €6.20; ☺ 9am-8pm Tue-Sun), well worth visiting for the collections of ancient Roman sculpture.

Walk to the right of the Palazzo Senatorio for a lovely panorama of the Roman Forum. Walk to the left of the same building to reach the ancient Roman **Carcere Mamertino** (Mamertine Prison; Map pp696-7; ☺ 9am-noon & 2-5pm), where it's believed St Peter was imprisoned.

The **Chiesa di Santa Maria d'Aracoeli** (Map pp696-7) is between Piazza del Campidoglio and the Monumento Vittorio Emanuele II, at the highest point of the Capitoline Hill. It is built on the site where legend says the Tiburtine Sybil told the Emperor Augustus of the coming birth of Christ.

Vatican City

After Italian unification in 1861, the Papal States of central Italy became part of the new Kingdom of Italy, causing a considerable rift between church and state. In 1929, Mussolini, under the Lateran Treaty, gave the pope full sovereignty over what is now called Vatican City. The smallest independent state in existence, the Vatican has considerable influence, along with its own postal service, currency, newspaper, radio station and even an army of Swiss Guards to watch over the pope's personal safety.

Guided tours of the Vatican City **gardens** (Map pp694-5; ☎ 06 69 88 44 66; €10) can be organised at the Vatican tourist office (p692) in advance.

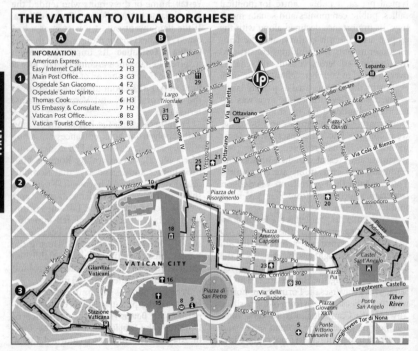

THE VATICAN TO VILLA BORGHESE

INFORMATION
American Express	1 G2
Easy Internet Café	2 H3
Main Post Office	3 G3
Ospedale San Giacomo	4 F2
Ospedale Santo Spirito	5 C3
Thomas Cook	6 H3
US Embassy & Consulate	7 H2
Vatican Post Office	8 B3
Vatican Tourist Office	9 B3

ST PETER'S BASILICA & SQUARE

Whatever your faith, the most famous, but no longer largest, church in Christendom will likely leave you awestruck. **St Peter's Basilica** (Map pp694-5; Piazza San Pietro; admission free; ⏲ 7am-7pm Apr-Sep, to 6pm Oct-Mar) stands on the site where St Peter was buried. The first church on the site was built during Constantine's reign in the 4th century, and in 1506 work started on a new basilica, designed by Bramante.

Final kudos, however, went to Michelangelo, who took over the project in 1547, at the age of 72, and was responsible for the design of the grand dome, which soars 120m above the altar and was completed in 1590, long after the genius artist had died. The cavernous interior contains numerous treasures, including Michelangelo's superb *Pietà*, sculpted when he was only 24 years old and the only work to carry his signature.

Entrance to the dome is to the right as you climb the stairs to the basilica's atrium. Make the climb on foot (€4) or by lift (€5). Dress rules and security are stringently enforced – no shorts, miniskirts or sleeveless tops, and be prepared to have your bags searched.

Equally impressive is Bernini's masterpiece **Piazza San Pietro**, laid out in the 17th century. The vast piazza is bound by two semicircular colonnades, each comprised of four rows of Doric columns, and in its centre stands an obelisk brought to Rome by Caligula from Heliopolis (in ancient Egypt). The pope usually gives a **public audience** at 10am every Wednesday in the Papal Audience Hall or St Peter's Square. You must make a booking, in person or by fax to the **Prefettura della Casa Pontifica** (Map pp694-5; ☎ 06 69 88 46 31; fax 06 69 88 38 65) on the Monday or Tuesday beforehand, between 9am and 1pm. To go in person, enter via the bronze doors under the colonnade to the right of St Peter's (facing the church); you can also apply in writing to Prefettura della Casa Pontifica, 00120 Citta del Vaticano.

VATICAN MUSEUMS

From St Peter's, follow the wall of the Vatican City to the **Vatican Museums** (Map pp694-5; admission €12, free last Sun of month; ⏲ 8.45am-4.45pm Mon-Fri, to 1.45pm Sat & last Sun of month). The buildings that house the Vatican Museums, known

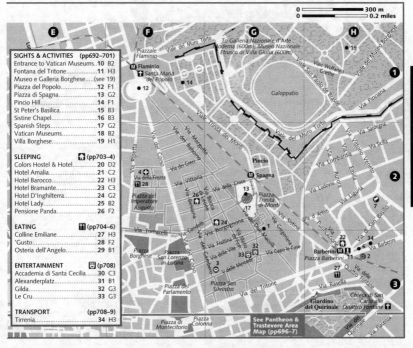

SIGHTS & ACTIVITIES	(pp692–701)
Entrance to Vatican Museums..10	B2
Fontana del Tritone.................11	H3
Museo e Galleria Borghese.....(see 19)	
Piazza del Popolo....................12	F1
Piazza di Spagna.....................13	G2
Pincio Hill..............................14	F1
St Peter's Basilica....................15	B3
Sistine Chapel........................16	B3
Spanish Steps.........................17	G2
Vatican Museums....................18	B2
Villa Borghese........................19	H1

SLEEPING	(pp703–4)
Colors Hostel & Hotel..............20	D2
Hotel Amalia..........................21	C2
Hotel Barocco........................22	H3
Hotel Bramante......................23	C3
Hotel D'Inghilterra..................24	G2
Hotel Lady.............................25	B2
Pensione Panda......................26	F2

EATING	(pp704–6)
Colline Emiliane......................27	H3
'Gusto...................................28	F2
Osteria dell'Angelo.................29	B1

ENTERTAINMENT	(p708)
Accademia di Santa Cecilia......30	C3
Alexanderplatz.......................31	B1
Gilda....................................32	G3
Le Cru..................................33	G3

TRANSPORT	(pp708–9)
Tirrenia.................................34	H3

See Pantheon & Trastevere Area Map (pp696–7)

ITALY

PANTHEON & TRASTEVERE AREA

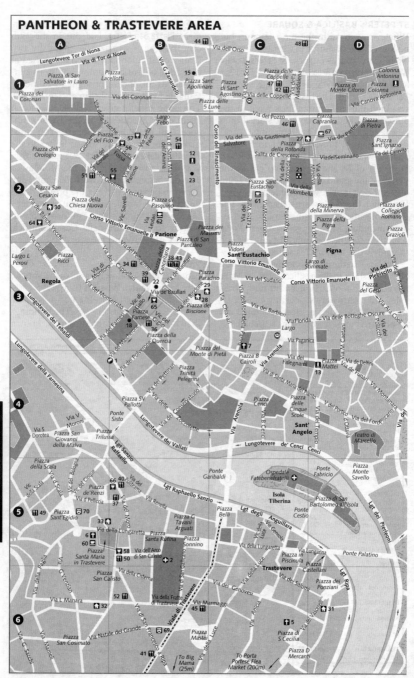

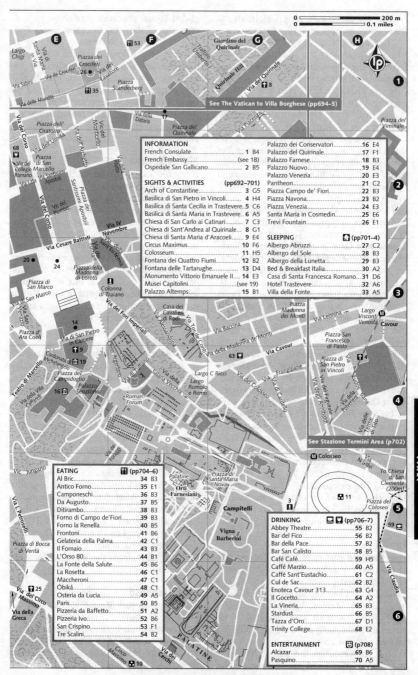

INFORMATION
French Consulate...............................1 B4
French Embassy............................(see 18)
Ospedale San Gallicano....................2 B5

SIGHTS & ACTIVITIES   (pp692–701)
Arch of Constantine..........................3 G5
Basilica di San Pietro in Vincoli..........4 H4
Basilica di Santa Cecilia in Trastevere..5 C6
Basilica di Santa Maria in Trastevere...6 A5
Chiesa di San Carlo ai Catinari...........7 C3
Chiesa di Sant'Andrea al Quirinale......8 G1
Chiesa di Santa Maria d'Aracoeli.........9 E4
Circus Maximus.............................10 F6
Colosseum...................................11 H5
Fontana dei Quattro Fiumi...............12 B2
Fontana delle Tartarughe.................13 D4
Monumento Vittorio Emanuele II......14 E3
Musei Capitolini........................(see 19)
Palazzo Altemps..........................15 B1

Palazzo dei Conservatori.................16 E4
Palazzo del Quirinale.....................17 F1
Palazzo Farnese............................18 B3
Palazzo Nuovo.............................19 E4
Palazzo Venezia............................20 E3
Pantheon....................................21 C2
Piazza Campo de' Fiori...................22 B3
Piazza Navona.............................23 B2
Piazza Venezia.............................24 E3
Santa Maria in Cosmedin................25 E6
Trevi Fountain..............................26 E1

SLEEPING   (pp701–4)
Albergo Abruzzi...........................27 C2
Albergo del Sole...........................28 B3
Albergo della Lunetta.....................29 B3
Bed & Breakfast Italia.....................30 A2
Casa di Santa Francesca Romano.......31 D6
Hotel Trastevere...........................32 A6
Villa della Fonte...........................33 A5

EATING   (pp704–6)
Al Bric.......................................34 B3
Antico Forno...............................35 E1
Camponeschi..............................36 B3
Da Augusto................................37 B5
Ditirambo...................................38 B3
Forno di Campo de' Fiori................39 B3
Forno la Renella...........................40 B5
Frontoni....................................41 B6
Gelateria della Palma.....................42 C1
Il Fornaio...................................43 B3
L'Orso 80...................................44 B1
La Fonte della Salute......................45 B6
La Rosetta..................................46 C1
Maccheroni................................47 C1
Óbikà.......................................48 C1
Osteria da Lucia...........................49 A5
Paris..50 B5
Pizzeria da Baffetto.......................51 A2
Pizzeria Ivo................................52 B6
San Crispino...............................53 F1
Tre Scalini.................................54 B2

DRINKING   (pp706–7)
Abbey Theatre.............................55 B2
Bar del Fico................................56 B2
Bar della Pace.............................57 B2
Bar San Calisto............................58 B5
Café Café...................................59 H5
Caffè Marzio...............................60 A5
Caffè Sant'Eustachio......................61 C2
Cul de Sac.................................62 B2
Enoteca Cavour 313......................63 G4
Il Gocetto..................................64 A2
La Vineria..................................65 B3
Stardust....................................66 B5
Tazza d'Oro................................67 D1
Trinity College.............................68 E2

ENTERTAINMENT   (p708)
Alcazar.....................................69 B6
Pasquino...................................70 A5

collectively as the Palazzo Apostolico Vaticano, cover an area of 5½ hectares.

The Vatican Museums contain an astonishing collection of art and treasures collected by the popes, and you'll need several hours to see the most important areas. Make sure you pick up a floor-plan leaflet. There are four very helpful 'one-way' itineraries, lasting from 1½ to five hours, mapped out with the aim of simplifying visits and containing the huge number of visitors. The Sistine Chapel comes towards the very end of a full visit; otherwise, you can walk straight there, but if you'd like to visit the Stanze di Raffaello, do so first as you can't backtrack once in the chapel.

The **Museo Pio-Clementino**, containing Greek and Roman antiquities, is on the ground floor near the entrance. Through the superb **Galleria delle Carte Geografiche** (Map Gallery) and the **Galleria degli Arazzi** (Tapestry Gallery) are the magnificent **Stanze di Rafaello**, once the private apartments of Pope Julius II, decorated with frescoes by Raphael. Of particular interest is the magnificent **Stanza della Segnatura**, which features Raphael's masterpieces *The School of Athens* and *Disputation on the Sacrament.*

From Raphael's rooms, go down the stairs to the sumptuous **Appartamento Borgia**, decorated with frescoes by Pinturicchio, and then down another flight of stairs to the **Sistine Chapel**, the private papal chapel built in 1473 for Pope Sixtus IV. Michelangelo's wonderful frescoes, *Creation* and *Last Judgment,* have been superbly restored to their original brilliance. It took Michelangelo four years, at the height of the Renaissance, to paint the *Creation;* 24 years later he painted the extraordinary *Last Judgment.* The other walls of the chapel were painted by artists including Botticelli, Ghirlandaio, Pinturicchio and Signorelli.

Pantheon

The **Pantheon** (Map pp696-7; Piazza della Rotonda; admission free; 8.30am-7.30pm Mon-Sat, 9am-6pm Sun) is the best-preserved building of ancient Rome. The original temple was built in 27 BC by Marcus Agrippa, son-in-law of Emperor Augustus, and dedicated to the planetary gods. Agrippa's name remains inscribed over the entrance.

Over the centuries the temple has been consistently plundered and damaged. The gilded-bronze roof tiles were removed by an emperor of the eastern empire, and Pope Urban VIII had the bronze ceiling of the portico melted down to make the canopy over the main altar of St Peter's and 80 cannons for Castel Sant' Angelo. The Pantheon's extraordinary dome is considered the most important achievement of ancient Roman architecture. The Italian kings Vittorio Emanuele II and Umberto I, and the painter Raphael, are buried here.

Piazza Navona

A few blocks west of the Pantheon, this vast and beautiful **square** (Map pp696-7), lined with baroque palaces, was laid out on the ruins of Domitian's stadium and features three fountains. In its centre is Bernini's masterpiece, **Fontana dei Quattro Fiumi** (Fountain of the Four Rivers; Map pp696-7). Visit at different times of the day, and be sure to grab a *gelato,* relax on one of the stone benches in the sun, or enjoy a cappuccino at one of the many cafés – the expense is worth it to watch the various artists mingling in the piazza and to absorb the ever-vibrant hum.

Campo de'Fiori

The colourful **Piazza Campo de'Fiori** (Map pp696-7), affectionately called 'Il Campo', was a place of execution during the Inquisition, and Caravaggio went on the run after killing a man who had the gall to beat him in tennis on this piazza. Nowadays a **flower and vegetable market** is held here Monday to Saturday, and revellers fill the many bars at night.

The **Palazzo Farnese** (Map pp696-7), in the piazza of the same name, is just off the Campo. A magnificent Renaissance building, it was started in 1514 by Antonio da Sangallo, carried on by Michelangelo and completed by Giacomo della Porta. Built for Cardinal Alessandro Farnese (later Pope Paul III), the palace is now the French embassy. The piazza has two fountains, which are enormous granite baths taken from the Baths of Caracalla (see p700).

Villa Borghese

This gorgeous **park** (Map pp694-5) was once the estate of Cardinal Scipione Borghese. His 17th-century villa houses the **Museo e Galleria Borghese** (Map pp694-5; ☎ 06 3 28 10; www.ticketeria.it; admission €8.50; 9am-7pm Tue-Sat), an impressive collection of paintings and sculptures. Take a walk through the lovely, leafy park, which has a zoo and a lake full of ducks, swans and turtles. You can hire boats at the lake and bicycles near the Porta Pinciana entrance. Just north of the park is the **Galleria Nazionale d'Arte Moderna** (☎ 06 32 34 000; Viale delle Belle Arti 131; admission €6.50; ⏱ 8.30am-7.30pm Tue-Sun), a *belle époque* palace housing 19th- and 20th-century paintings. The Etruscan museum, **Museo Nazionale Etrusco di Villa Giulia** (admission €4; ⏱ 8.30am-7.30pm Tue-Sun), is on the same street in Piazzale di Villa Giulia, in the former villa of Pope Julius III.

Trevi Fountain

The high-baroque **Fontana di Trevi** (Map pp696-7; Piazza di Crociteri), about six blocks northeast of the Pantheon, was designed by Nicola Salvi in 1732 and immortalised in Fellini's *La Dolce Vita*. It sprawls over almost the entire piazza and depicts Neptune's chariot being led by Tritons, with sea horses representing the moods of the sea. Its water was supplied by one of Rome's earliest aqueducts, and the name refers to the three roads *(tre vie)* that converged here. The custom is to throw a coin into the fountain (over your shoulder while facing away) to ensure your return to Rome; a second coin grants a wish.

Colosseum & Arch of Constantine

Originally known as the Flavian Amphitheatre, Rome's best-known monument, the **Colosseum** (Map pp696-7; ☎ 06 399 67 700; admission with Palatine Hill €8; ⏱ 9am-1hr before sunset), was begun by Emperor Vespasian in AD 72. The massive structure could seat 80,000 and featured gory and deadly gladiatorial combat and wild beast shows.

During the Middle Ages, the Colosseum became a fortress, then later a quarry for travertine and marble to build Palazzo Venezia and other buildings. Restoration works have been under way since 1992. Skip paying the entrance fee for the barren interior.

On the west side of the Colosseum is the triumphal arch built to honour Constantine following his victory over his rival Maxentius at the battle of Milvian Bridge in AD 312. Its decorative reliefs were taken from earlier structures.

Piazza di Spagna & Spanish Steps

The exquisite **Piazza di Spagna** (Map pp694-5), church and famous **Spanish Steps** (Scalinata della Trinità dei Monti; Map pp694-5) have long provided a major gathering place for foreigners and locals alike. Built with a legacy from the French in 1725, but named after the Spanish embassy to the Holy See, the steps lead to the church; the steps were constructed to link the piazza with the well-heeled folks living above it.

In the 18th century, beautiful Italians gathered here, hoping to be chosen as artists' models. Today, beauties of both sexes still abound. To the right as you face the steps is the house where Keats spent the last three months of his life, in 1821. In the piazza is the boat-shaped fountain of the **Barcaccia**, believed to be by Pietro Bernini, father of the famous Gian Lorenzo. One of Rome's most elegant and expensive shopping streets, **Via Condotti** (p708), runs off the piazza towards Via del Corso.

Piazza del Popolo

The vast and impressive **Piazza del Popolo** (Map pp694-5) was laid out in the 16th century at the point of convergence of three roads – Via di Ripetta, Via del Corso and Via del Baubino – which form a trident at what was the city's main entrance from the north. Giuseppe Valadier redesigned it three centuries later, and today this neighbourhood is called 'the trident'. Rainaldi designed the seemingly twin baroque churches in the 17th century, and Bernini worked on the gate around the same time. **Santa Maria del Popolo** houses two magnificent Caravaggio paintings (of St Peter and of St Paul). The piazza is at the foot of the **Pincio Hill** (Map pp694-5), which affords a *bella vista* of the city, especially in the early hours; Keats, Strauss, Ghandi and Mussolini liked strolling here.

Trastevere

Separated from *centro storico* by the Tiber, picturesque Trastevere exudes a sense of bonhomie. Wander through the narrow medieval streets, which retain the air of a typical Roman neighbourhood despite the influx of foreigners. Especially beautiful at night, this is a great area for eating and bar hopping.

Don't miss the **Basilica di Santa Maria in Trastevere** (Map pp696-7), in the lovely piazza of the same name, believed to be the oldest Roman church dedicated to the Virgin. Although the first church was built on the site in the 4th century, the present structure was built in

ITALY

the 12th century and features a Romanesque bell tower and façade, with a mosaic of the Virgin. Its interior was redecorated during the baroque period, but the vibrant mosaics in the apse and on the triumphal arch date from the 12th century. Also take a look at the **Basilica di Santa Cecilia in Trastevere** (Map pp696-7; admission free; ☯ 9am-12.30pm & 4.15-6.30pm Mon-Sat), with its magnificent 13th-century fresco.

Via Giulia

Bramante designed this elegant street for Pope Julius II as a new approach to St Peter's. It runs parallel to the Tiber, south of Vittorio Emanuele II, and is lined with Renaissance palaces, antique shops and art galleries. Spanning the southern end is Michelangelo's ivy-draped **Arco Farnese.**

Catacombs

There are several catacombs in Rome, consisting of miles of tunnels carved out of volcanic rock, which were the meeting and burial places of early Christians. The largest are along the Via Appia Antica (Appian Way), just southeast of the city and accessible on Metro Linea A to Colli Albani, then bus No 660. Via Appia Antica is traffic-free on Sundays if you want to walk or cycle it. The **Catacombs of San Callisto** (admission €5; ☯ 8.30am-noon & 2.30-5pm Thu-Tue Mar-Jan) and **Catacombs of San Sebastiano** (admission €5; ☯ 8.30am-noon & 2.30-5pm Mon-Sat mid-Dec–mid-Nov) are almost next to each other. Admission to each is with a guide only.

Terme di Caracalla

The huge **Baths of Caracalla** (Map pp690-1; ☎ 06 399 67 70; Via delle Terme di Caracalla 52; admission €5; ☯ 9am-1hr before sunset Tue-Sun, to 2pm Mon) complex, covering 10 hectares, could hold 1600 people and included shops, gardens, libraries and entertainment. Begun by Antonius Caracalla and inaugurated in AD 217, the baths were used until the 6th century.

Churches & Cathedrals

Down from Stazione Termini is the massive **Basilica di Santa Maria Maggiore** (Map p702; Via Cavour; ☯ 7am-6.30pm), originally named Santa Maria della Neve and built by Pope Liberius in 352 after the Virgin Mary instructed him to construct a church on the spot where the next snow fell. Its main baroque façade was added in the 18th century, preserving the 13th-century mosaics of the earlier façade. Its bell tower is Romanesque and the interior is baroque. There are 5th-century mosaics decorating the triumphal arch and nave.

Rome's cathedral, **Basilica di San Giovanni in Laterano** (Map pp690-1; Via Merulana; ☯ 7am-12.30pm & 3.30-7pm), was originally a church built in the 4th century, the first Christian basilica in Rome. Largely destroyed over a long period of time, it was rebuilt in the 17th century.

Basilica di San Pietro in Vincoli (Map pp696-7), just off Via Cavour, is worth a visit because it houses Michelangelo's *Moses* and his unfinished statues of Leah and Rachel, as well as the chains worn by St Peter during his imprisonment before being crucified; hence the church's name (St Peter in Chains).

Chiesa di San Clemente (Via San Giovanni in Laterano), east from the Colosseum, defines how history in Rome exists on many levels. The 12th-century church at street level was built over a 4th-century church that was, in turn, built over a 1st-century Roman house containing a temple dedicated to the pagan god Mithras.

STAY COOL UNDERGROUND

While visitors queue on the streets for star attractions, head underground for some funky sights. Check out the underbellies of four cities while exploring Roman cisterns, former bomb shelters, haunted freezer chambers and rows of mummies. Added bonus: this makes a very cool activity on hot summer days.

Naples (www.napolisotterranea.com) An amazing 40m beneath the city streets are underground passages totalling more than 400km.

Rome (www.catacombe.roma.it, in Italian) The eternal city has over 50 catacombs, of which five are open for public visits – try a night-time foray.

Palermo (☎ 091 21 21 17) Lined with adorned mummies sitting upright, the Catacombe dei Cappuccini are bizarrely ghoulish; there's even a separate section for virgins.

Turin (www.somewhere.it) Hidden passages tucked into 19th-century *palazzi* lead to a labyrinth of war-time shelters and tunnels, including the Porta Palazzo's natural ice caves, rumored to be haunted.

Santa Maria in Cosmedin (Map pp696-7; Via del Circo Massimo; 🕙 10am-1pm & 2.30-6pm), northwest of **Circus Maximus** (Map pp696-7; Via del Circo Massimo), is regarded as one of the finest medieval churches in Rome. It has a seven-storey bell tower and its interior is heavily decorated with Cosmatesque inlaid marble, including the beautiful floor. The main attraction for masses of tourists is, however, the **Bocca della Verità** (Mouth of Truth). Legend has it that if you put your right hand into the mouth and tell a lie, it will snap shut.

Piazza Venezia

A neoclassical monument dedicated to Vittorio Emanuele II overshadows the **Piazza Venezia** (Map pp696-7). Built to commemorate Italian unification, the piazza incorporates the **Altare della Patria** and the **tomb of the unknown soldier**, as well as the **Museo del Risorgimento** (admission free; 🕙 10am-6pm). Also in the piazza is the 15th-century **Palazzo Venezia** (🕙 9am-2pm Tue-Sat, to 1pm Sun), partially built with material quarried from the Colosseum, was once Mussolini's official residence and is now a museum housing medieval and Renaissance art.

Baths of Diocletian & Basilica di Santa Maria degli Angeli

Just across the piazza from Termini, the **Baths of Diocletian** (Map p702; ☎ 06 488 05 30; Viale E De Nicola 79; admission €5; 🕙 9am-7.45pm Tue-Sun) were built at the turn of the 3rd century. Rome's largest baths could accommodate 3000 people; the complex also included libraries, concert halls and gardens and covered about 13 hectares. In AD 536, invaders destroyed the aqueduct that fed the baths and the complex fell into decay. Parts of the ruins are incorporated into the **Basilica di Santa Maria degli Angeli** (Map p702; Piazza della Repubblica; 🕙 7.30am-6.30pm).

Designed by Michelangelo, the basilica incorporates what was the great central hall and *tepidarium* (lukewarm room) of the original baths. Over the centuries his original work was drastically changed and little evidence of his design, apart from the great vaulted ceiling of the church, remains. An interesting feature of the church is a double meridian in the transept, one tracing the polar star and the other telling the precise time of the sun's zenith (visible at noon).

Museo Nazionale Romano-Palazzo Altemps

This museum, in two separate buildings, houses an important collection of ancient art, including Greek and Roman sculpture. The restored 15th-century **Palazzo Altemps** (Map pp696-7; ☎ 06 683 37 59; Piazza Sant'Apollinare 44; admission €5; 🕙 9am-7.45pm Tue-Sun), near Piazza Navona, is home to most of the art, with numerous important pieces from the Ludovisi collection. **Palazzo Massimo alle Terme** (Map p702; ☎ 06 48 90 35 00; Largo di Villa Peretti 1; admission €6; 🕙 9am-7.45pm Tue-Sun), just off Piazza del Cinquecento, houses another part of the same museum and contains a collection of frescoes and mosaics from the Villa of Livia, excavated at Prima Porta, and a knockout numismatic (coin) collection.

Villa Doria Pamphill

Rome's largest park, **Villa Doria Pamphill** (Via di San Pancrazio; 🕙 sunrise-sunset), west of Trastevere, was laid out by Algardi in the 16th century, and offers a rejuvenating reprieve from the heady city pace. Relax by a baroque fountain, nap under a parasol pine or enjoy a stroll along the lovely walkways. To get there, you can take a bus to Via di San Pancrazio.

SLEEPING

Rome has a wide range of accommodation, much of it charming, but the most popular and best-value options fill fast; book well ahead. The municipal government keeps a full list of accommodation options, including prices, on its excellent and very helpful website www.romaturismo.it.

The head office of the **Italian Youth Hostel Association** (Map p702; ☎ 06 487 11 52; www.ostellionline.org; Via Cavour 44; 🕙 9am-5pm Mon-Fri) has information about all the hostels in Italy and will assist with bookings to stay at universities during summer. You can also join HI here.

Still a new concept in Rome, B&Bs are growing in popularity. The tourist office has a list of private B&B operators, as does **Bed & Breakfast Italia** (Map pp696-7; ☎ 06 68 80 15 13; www .bbitalia.it; Palazzo Sforza Cesarini, Corso Vittorio Emanuele II 282, 00186 Rome; s/d €50/40, with shared bathroom €37/28).

North of Stazione Termini

Most of the less-expensive options near the station are along Via Castro Pretorio, to the right as you leave the train platforms.

ITALY

STAZIONE TERMINI AREA

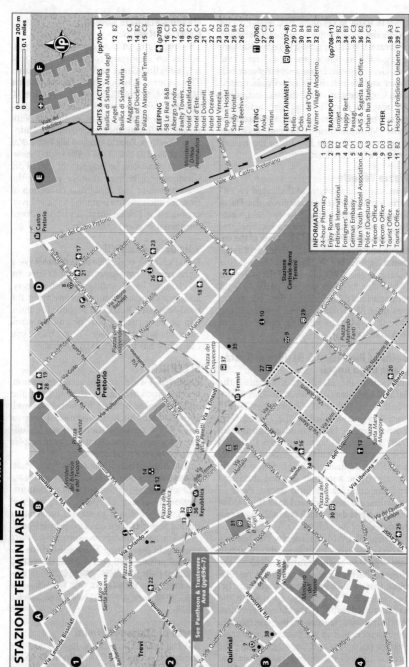

0   200 m
0   0.1 miles

SIGHTS & ACTIVITIES	(pp700–1)
Basilica di Santa Maria degli Angeli	12 B2
Basilica di Santa Maria Maggiore	13 C4
Baths of Diocletian	14 B2
Palazzo Massimo alle Terme	15 C3

SLEEPING	(p703)
58 Le Real B&B	16 C3
Albergo Sandra	17 D1
Fawlty Towers	18 D2
Hotel Castelfidardo	19 C1
Hotel d'Este	20 C4
Hotel Dolomiti	21 D1
Hotel Oceania	22 A2
Hotel Venezia	23 D2
Pop Inn Hostel	24 D3
Sandy Hostel	25 B4
The Beehive	26 D2

EATING	(p706)
Moka	27 C3
Trimani	28 C1

ENTERTAINMENT	(pp707–8)
Hello	29 D3
Orbis	30 B4
Teatro dell'Opera	31 B3
Warner Village Moderno	32 B2

TRANSPORT	(pp708–11)
Eurojet	33 B2
Happy Rent	34 B3
Passagi	35 D1
SAIS & Segesta Bus Office	36 B2
Urban Bus Station	37 C3

OTHER	
CTS	38 A3
Hospital (Policlinico Umberto I)	39 F1

INFORMATION	
24-hour Pharmacy	1 C3
Enjoy Rome	2 D2
Feltrinelli International	3 B2
Foreigners' Bureau	4 A3
German Embassy	5 D1
Italian Youth Hostel Association	6 C3
Police (Questura)	7 A3
Telecom Office	8 D1
Telecom Office	9 D3
Tourist Office	10 D3
Tourist Office	11 B2

Fawlty Towers (Map p702; ☎ 06 445 03 74; www .fawltytowers.org; Via Magenta 39; dm/s/d €23/55/70, with shared bathroom €20/47/65; 🖳) This ever-popular spot offers hostel-style accommodation, lots of information about Rome, cheap Internet access and a lively common room with satellite TV – the flower-filled terrace and lack of curfew are icing on the cake.

Beehive (Map p702; ☎ 06 447 04 553; www.the-bee hive.com; Via Marghera 8; dm €20, d per person €40, with shared bathroom per person €35) This clean, cheery spot with a friendly American couple at the helm has a nice garden and communal kitchen. Walk-ins are not accepted, and party animals will be happier elsewhere.

Albergo Sandra (Map p702; ☎ 06 445 26 12; albergo sandra@libero.it; Via Villafranca 10; s/d €45/65) A mere 10-minute walk from Termini, this medium-sized *pensione* has clean and pleasant rooms and is lorded over by a house-proud Italian mamma and her English-speaking son.

Pop Inn Hostel (Map p702; ☎ 06 495 98 87; www .popinnhostel.com; Via Marsala 80; dm €17-25, s €35-95, d €20-49; 🖳) Comfortable and squeaky clean, this notch-above hostel has exceptionally helpful, friendly and multilingual staff; other simpatico features include no curfew, free breakfast, free luggage storage, and laundry.

Hotel Castelfidardo (Map p702; ☎ 06 446 46 38; castelfidardo@italmarke.it; Via Castelfidardo 31; s/d €55/74, with shared bathroom €46/65) Just off Piazza dell'Indipendenza, this well-run spot is one of Rome's better one-star hotels. The English-speaking staff are friendly and helpful.

Hotel Dolomiti (Map p702; ☎ 06 49 10 58; www .hotel-dolomiti.it; Via San Martino della Battaglia 11; s €58-90, d €78-125; 🔀) Two former run-down *pensioni* merged into one airy, good-value hotel with spotless, spacious and well-outfitted rooms. There's a snug bar, and the welcoming staff speak English, French and Spanish.

Hotel Venezia (Map p702; ☎ 06 445 71 01; www .hotelvenezia.com; Via Varese 18; s €200-215, d €180-205; 🔀) The elegant Venezia is a delightful haven, beautifully furnished with antiques and pretty fabrics, and with a charming multilingual staff. It's excellent value, and the best spot in this hood; good for families too.

South of Stazione Termini

This area can be a bit seedy but gets noticeably better closer to the Colosseum.

Sandy Hostel (Map p702; ☎ 06 488 45 85; www .sandyhostel.com; Via Cavour 136; dm €18, with bathroom €20) Rome's version of a backpackers' crash pad

is on the 5th floor (no lift), has no curfew, not-great bathrooms, metal lockers without keys and a party atmosphere for the young and tolerant crowd; cash only.

58 Le Real B&B (Map p702; ☎ 06 48 23 566; www .58viacavour.it; Via Cavour 58; s €65-75, d €85-95; 🔀) Close to the Colosseum, this is a clean and pretty apartment, with airy rooms and a sun-drenched terrace. The friendly owners treat guests like friends, offering free access to a fridge loaded with juices, yogurt and water.

Hotel Oceania (Map p702; ☎ 06 482 46 96; www .hoteloceania.it; Via Firenze 38; s €52-104, d €62-135) You'll be greeted with a warm welcome at this small hotel with outstanding hospitality, smart rooms, wonderful owners and thoughtful extras such as English newspapers in the morning.

Hotel d'Este (Map p702; ☎ 06 446 56 07; d.este@ italyhotel.com; Via Carlo Alberto 4b; s €72-145, d €83-196; 🔀) A short skip from Piazza Santa Maria Maggiore, this friendly spot with eager-to-please staff has nicely furnished rooms and a pleasant roof garden.

City Centre

Truly budget rooms don't exist once you foray from the noisy Termini area. But what you lose in euros, you more than make up for in convenience and the unbeatable pleasure of staying in the heart of historic Rome.

Albergo della Lunetta (Map pp696-7; ☎ 06 686 10 80; Piazza del Paradiso 68; d/tr €110/130, s/d/tr with shared bathroom €57/85/115) This old-school *pensione* is managed by *signori* who will either charm or irritate you; the maze-like corridors and staircases lead to small, spotless rooms.

Albergo Abruzzi (Map pp696-7; ☎ 06 679 20 21; Piazza della Rotonda 69; s €125-150, with shared bathroom €55-75, d €175-195, with shared bathroom €90-115) There's nothing special about the rooms, but the position – overlooking the Pantheon – is hard to beat, even if the piazza can be noisy. Bookings are essential, and the chatty management makes this a perennial favourite.

Pensione Panda (Map pp694-5; ☎ 06 678 01 79; www .pensionepanda.com; Via della Croce 35; s/d €65/98, with shared bathroom €48/68) Close to the Spanish Steps, this 2nd-floor *pensione* has comfortable rooms with arched ceilings and helpful, English-speaking staff.

Albergo del Sole (Map pp696-7; ☎ 06 687 94 46; www.solealbiscione.it; Via del Biscione 76; s/d €83/125, with shared bathroom €65/95; 🅿) A short walk from Campo de'Fiori, this sunny spot dates from

1462. Cheery rooms, some with antiques, lots of communal space, a pretty patio and rooftop terrace make this hotel, one of Rome's oldest, a standout.

Hotel Barocco (Map pp694-5; ☎ 06 48 72 001; www .hotelbarocco.com; Piazza Barberini 9; s/d €170/250; ⓟ ⓧ) Tucked into a quiet street off Piazza Barberini, this intimate and elegant pad has gentle staff and pretty rooms, some with a view of Bernini's baroque Triton fountain.

Hotel D'Inghilterra (Map pp694-5; ☎ 06 699 81 204; www.charminghotels.com; Via Bocca di Leone 14; d from €260; ⓟ ⓧ ⌨) This fashionable boutique hotel near the Spanish Steps is housed in a 16th-century *palazzo* and steeped in literary history – Hemingway, Twain and Henry James all bedded down here.

Near the Vatican

Staying in this area is a good choice for those looking for quiet not too far from the main sights. Alas, bargains are rare, and bookings necessary because rooms are often filled with people attending Vatican conferences. The easiest way to reach the area is on Metro Linea A to Ottaviano; bus No 64 from Termini stops at St Peter's.

Colors Hostel & Hotel (Map pp694-5; ☎ 06 687 40 30; www.colorshotel.com; Via Boezio 31; dm/d/tr €22/85/90, d/tr with shared bathroom €75/85; ⌨) Run by the people at Enjoy Rome (p692), Colors offers tidy rooms, a mini-gym and cooking facilities; the owners are opening a new mid-range hotel next door.

Hotel Lady (Map pp694-5; ☎ 06 324 21 12; 4th fl, Via Germanico 198; d €125, with shared bathroom €90) A quiet, old-world *pensione* with pleasant rooms and rustic antiques. The friendly and loquacious owners don't speak much English, but it's a good chance to practise *la lingua*.

Hotel Amalia (Map pp694-5; ☎ 06 397 23 356; www .hotelamalia.com; Via Germanico 66; s €95-130, d €150-210; ⓧ) Bright, clean rooms a coin's toss from the Vatican make this a popular, good-value option; look for last-minute specials online.

Hotel Bramante (Map pp694-5; ☎ 06 688 06 426; www.hotelbramante.com; Via delle Palline 24; s €105-150, d €150-210; ⓧ) With marble bathrooms and antique furnishings, this charming hotel is the nicest sleep spot in the area.

Trastevere

One of Rome's most vibrant neighbourhoods makes an excellent base for the young (or young at heart).

Casa di Santa Francesca Romano (Map pp696-7; ☎ 06 581 21 21; istituto@sfromana.it; Via dei Vascellari 61; s/d/tr incl breakfast €70/100/123) This former noble home is now a gracious inn with pretty rooms and a cloistered garden.

Hotel Trastevere (Map pp696-7; ☎ 06 581 47 13; hoteltrastevere@tiscalinet.it; Via L Manara 24a-25; s €77-83, d €103-119, tr & q €129-154) This little gem offers great value and friendly service; many of the spotless rooms look out over Piazza San Cosimato.

Villa della Fonte (Map pp696-7; ☎ 06 580 37 97; www.villafonte.com; Via della Fonte d'olio 8; s/d €95/145; ⓧ) Five pretty and pristine rooms a hop from Piazza Santa Maria; the sunny garden terrace is lovely.

EATING

Romans take visible pride in their *cucina* and traditional recipes. The roots of the local cuisine are the diet of the poor, hence a preponderance of *trippa* (tripe), and the Roman-Jewish tradition, with legacies such as stuffed *fiori di zucca* (zucchini/courgette flowers) and *carciofi alla romana* (artichokes with garlic, mint and parsley). Antipasto is a standout, particularly bruschetta, and classic Roman pastas include *cacio e pepe* (with pecorino, black pepper and olive oil) and the snappy *all'amatriciana* (with tomato, pancetta and chilli). The most beloved *secondo* is *saltimbocca alla romana* (escalopes of veal sautéed with white wine, sage and prosciutto).

Restaurant hours are generally noon to 3pm for lunch, and 7.30pm to 11.30pm for dinner; locals rarely eat dinner before 9pm.

Snacks & Self-Catering

For quick and cheap eats, head to a bar, where you can wolf a *panini* (sandwich) for under €3, or a *pizza al taglio*, where a slab of oven-hot pizza, sold by weight, can cost as little as €1.50.

Antico Forno (Map pp696-7; Via del Muratte 8) Head here for delicious oven-hot slices and hearty sandwiches.

Frontoni (Map pp696-7; Viale di Trastevere) Good sandwiches made from local delicacies and sold by weight.

Forno la Renella (Map pp696-7; Via del Moro 15-16) This tiny spot churns out has some of Trastevere's top-notch slices.

Forno di Campo de'Fiori (Map pp696-7; Campo de'Fiori 22) Rome's best spot for metres of

MOZZARELLA DI BUFALA

Springy on the outside, tantalisingly moist and buttery on the inside, *mozzarella di bufala* is a most singular (and surprisingly low-fat) cheese. And, to settle the debate, it really is made with milk from water buffalos, which have grazed the countryside south and west of Naples since the 2nd century AD. When the prized herds were destroyed during WWII, Italy brought in more water buffalos from India. Today, thanks to increasingly healthy herds, there is a thriving water buffalo–milk industry ensuring a plentiful supply of the cheese. Although mozzarella is made from cow's milk as well, it lacks the nuttiness and depth of flavour.

You'll see fresh *mozzarella di bufala* on menus all over Italy, often tucked into *insalata caprese*, and in shops. Buy a mozzarella ball and eat it like an apple, doused with a little salt. Then head to the recently opened **Óbikà** (Map pp696-7; Via dei Prefetti 26a; tasting plates from €12), a sushi-style 'mozzarella bar', to hone your taste.

pizza bianca (white pizza; that is without tomato sauce).

Foragers will be orgasmic in the lively food markets, held off Viale delle Millizie, just north of the Vatican, and in Piazza Vittorio Emanuele, near Termini. There's also a well-stocked **24-hour supermarket** (Map p702; Stazione Termini) underneath the main concourse of the station, which is a handy stop for self-caterers.

Restaurants, Trattorias & Pizzerias

With a few exceptions, eating near Stazione Termini is to be avoided, unless you're okay about paying high prices for mediocre food. In the historic centre, you'll pay dearly to eat in the A-list piazzas, sometimes a worthy splurge. For better value, hit the side streets off 'Il Campo' and Piazza Navona. San Lorenzo, to the east of Termini, and Testaccio are currently hot dining spots with locals. Trastevere simmers with eating options, but dodge the soulless tourist menus; expect to pay more near the Vatican.

CITY CENTRE

'Gusto (Map pp694-5; ☎ 06 322 62 73; Piazza Augusto Imperatore 9; pastas from €6) Slick and savvy, this place is a melange of pizzeria, *osteria*, wine bar and kitchen shop. It's a worthy stop any time, with an excellent wine list, an enormous cheese selection and good people-watching.

Pizzeria da Baffetto (Map pp696-7; ☎ 06 686 16 17; Via del Governo Vecchio 114; pizza about €7) Any self-respecting pizza fan will make a stop at this Roman institution, always packed to the beams. Come very early or very late if you don't want to queue or share a table.

Ditirambo (Map pp696-7; ☎ 06 687 16 26; Piazza della Cancelleria 72; mains about €9) With wood-beamed ceilings, this cosy trattoria serves largely organic fare with funky twists, such as ravioli with *taleggio* (pungent soft cheese) and *radicchio* (chicory); the tall, dark and handsome waiters will charm you silly.

Maccheroni (Map pp696-7; ☎ 06 683 07 895; Piazza delle Coppelle 44; mains from €9) A hip trattoria that serves traditional Roman fare with new flair to the trendy set; on a hot night, the outdoor tables are coveted.

Al Bric (Map pp696-7; ☎ 06 687 95 33; Via del Pellegrino 51-52; mains from €9) This snug dining space, with wood beams, wine box–lined walls and soft lighting, combined with excellent pastas served in big bowls, will make you feel like you're in a friend's home.

Colline Emiliane (Map pp694-5; ☎ 06 481 75 38; Via degli' Avignonesi 22; mains from €12) This small trattoria tucked into a cheerless street off Piazza Barberini serves superb Emilia-Romagnan food such as home-made pasta stuffed with pumpkin.

L'Orso 80 (Map pp696-7; ☎ 06 686 4904; Via dell Orso 33; antipasti from €15) Delicious and plentiful antipasti are the stars at this popular spot, and the friendly waiters are happy to keep bringing small plates until you yell *basta* (enough); a good option for vegetarians.

Camponeschi (Map pp696-7; ☎ 06 687 49 27; Piazza Farnese 50; mains from €15) Politicians, diplomats and glitterati swear by this spot, which has an ideal location – tucked onto Michelangelo's impossibly pretty piazza – and excellent Mediterranean fare served up with French flair.

La Rosetta (Map pp696-7; ☎ 06 686 10 02; Via della Rosetta 8-9; mains €25) Near the Pantheon, this oft-lauded star serves the best seafood in Rome. Trust your palate to owner-chef Massimo Riccioli, regarded as one of Italy's best, and his deliciously creative dishes such as fried *moscardini* (octopus) and mint. Expensive but oh so memorable.

THE AUTHOR'S CHOICE

Tram Tram (☎ 064 470 25 85; Via dei Reti 44; mains from €10) In the heart of funky San Lorenzo, 500m east of Stazione Termini, this small trattoria is worth the trek: friendly and *molta carina* (very sweet/charming), with high ceilings, big windows, cosy bar and loyal local clientele. The menu changes daily, but seafood dishes from southern Italy are the speciality; the swordfish is sublime and the excellent wine list lauds small producers.

WEST OF THE TIBER: TRASTEVERE, TESTACCIO & THE VATICAN

Café Café (Map pp696-7; ☎ 06 700 87 43; Via dei Santi Quattro 44; salads & lights meals from €4) This low-key neighbourhood joint is not far from the Colosseum and offers excellent salads, light meals and sandwiches – as well as international newspapers, cups of brew and wines by the glass. So likeable and comfortable, in fact, you may have trouble leaving.

Pizzeria Remo (Map pp690-1; ☎ 06 574 62 70; Piazza Santa Maria Liberatice 44; pizzas from €4.50) This place is loud and rowdy – filling with party types on weekend nights – but the cheap prices, pizza and *bruschette al pomodoro* (bruschettas with tomato) make the chaos and obligatory queues worth it.

Pizzeria Ivo (Map pp696-7; ☎ 06 581 70 82; Via di San Francesco a Ripa 158; pizza €4.75) Nice outdoor tables, excellent bruschetta and a spirited local crowd, who gather to watch soccer games, make up for the too-small-but-tasty pizzas and long queues.

Da Augusto (Map pp696-7; ☎ 06 580 37 98; Piazza de'Renzi 15; mains from €8) This bare-bones-but-beloved mamma's kitchen serves Roman classics – occasionally accompanied by a surly attitude.

Osteria da Lucia (Map pp696-7; ☎ 06 580 36 01; Via del Mattinato 2; mains from €8) Dine under the stars, laundry flittering on the line, at this terrific neighbourhood trattoria serving a *trippa alla romano* (Roman tripe) that may well make you a convert.

Osteria dell'Angelo (Map pp694-5; ☎ 06 372 94 70; Via G Bettolo 24; mains from €12) Offering the best value near the Vatican, this popular spot serves delicious authentic Roman fare such as *salsicce al cinghiale* (wild boar sausage), and is run by a former rugby player.

Paris (Map pp696-7; ☎ 06 581 53 78; Piazza San Calisto 7; mains from €10) This elegant, old-world restaurant serves excellent Roman-Jewish cuisine such as *fritto misto con baccalà* (fried vegetables with salted cod).

AROUND STAZIONE TERMINI & SAN LORENZO

Trimani (Map p702; ☎ 06 446 96 630; Via Cernaia 37; mains from €7) Rome's biggest *enoteca* (wine bar) has a vast selection of regional wines along with excellent soups, pasta and *torta rustica* (quiche).

Pommidoro (☎ 06 445 26 92; Piazza dei Sanniti 44; mains from €11) This San Lorenzo trattoria, 500m east of the Termini, is popular with artists and intellectuals; the grilled meats are particularly good.

Moka (Map p702; ☎ 06 474 22 11; Via Giovanni Giolitti 34; ☾ 24hr) If you've got some time at Termini, head to platform 24 for tasty, ready-made food.

Gelati

San Crispino (Map pp696-7; Via della Panetteria 42) The rumour that this *gelateria*, near Trevi Fountain, has some of Rome's best *gelato* is in fact true. The delicious fruit sorbets change with the season – try *fichi* (fig) – but it's the divine cream-based flavours – such as ginger, honey, whisky and cinnamon – that will make you an instant addict.

Tre Scalini (Map pp696-7; Piazza Navona 30) While ogling in Piazza Navona, swing by Tre Scalini for good *gelato* and a memorable *tartufo nero* (black truffle) concoction.

Also recommended (though not for the indecisive), **Gelateria della Palma** (Map pp696-7; Via della Maddalena 20) has 100 flavours – the creamy mousses are a sure bet – and Trastevere's **La Fonte della Salute** (Map pp696-7; Via Cardinale Marmaggi 2-6) has excellent *gelati* (try the *marron glace*) and generous scoops.

DRINKING

Rome has an array of watering holes worthy of the gods. Much of the activity is in the centre, where Campo de'Fiori fills with young revellers, and there are nifty late-night spots nestled in the alleyways fringing Piazza Navona. Trastevere is packed with friendly bars and co-mingling tourists and locals; the Monti, Esquilino and Testaccio districts also have lots of bars, including some gay venues. Romans love their *enotecas,* and these cool places can offer a good-value way to sample *vini* (wine) and meet locals over a glass.

Just remember, the same cappucino taken at the bar will cost less – but passing an hour or so watching the world go by over a wine in a beautiful location is hard to beat and, despite what you may have heard, Italians do it too. Often.

Cafés

Tazza d'Oro (Map pp696-7; ☎ 06 679 27 68; Via degli Orfani; ✆ Mon-Sat) Locals claim it's the water from one of the city's original aqueducts that makes the coffee here so outstanding; in summer, try the *granita di caffè*.

Caffè Sant'Eustachio (Map pp696-7; ☎ 06 686 13 09; Piazza Sant'Eustachio 82) Also excellent, with sublime, creamy coffee, served extra sweet.

Caffè Marzio (Map pp696-7; Piazza Santa Maria) This place in Trastevere has terrific coffee and views onto one of Rome's prettiest piazzas; perfection comes with a price, though.

Bars & Pubs

Bar del Fico (Map pp696-7; ☎ 06 06 687 55 68; Piazza del Fico 24; ✆ 8-2am Mon-Sat, from 6pm Sun) Popular with local actors and artists, this pretty bar has tables beneath its namesake fig tree – providing shade on sunny days and a hit of romance at night – and a snug interior with tasteful music and local art.

Cul de Sac (Map pp696-7; Piazza Pasquino; ✆ noon-4pm & 6-12.30am Tue-Sat) Tucked into a nook off Piazza Navona, this *carina* wine bar has communal wood benches out front, a chattery interior, simple but good *enoteca* fare and a robust wine list.

Enoteca Cavour 313 (Map pp696-7; Via Cavour 313) With wine-packed shelves, wood benches, good antipasti and a very knowledgeable owner, this simple and *buono* wine bar is one of Rome's best.

Bar della Pace (Map pp696-7; ☎ 06 686 12 16; Via della Pace 3-7) With its gilded ambience and

dashing in-crowd, this is an atmospheric drinking spot.

La Vineria (Map pp696-7; ☎ 06 68 80 32 68; Campo de'Fiori 15; ✆ 9.30am-2pm & 6-1am Mon-Sat, to 2am Sun) Hit the cosy Vineria on the Campo, once the gathering place of the Roman literati.

Bar San Calisto (Map pp696-7; ☎ 06 583 58 69; Piazza San Calisto) The slacker Trastevere set hangs out at unglamorous Calisto. Besides the cheap drinks and arty crowd, it has memorable chocolate offerings.

Il Gocetto (Map pp696-7; ☎ 06 686 42 68; Via dei Banchi Vecchi 14; ✆ 5.30-10pm Mon-Sat) This club-like wine bar – one of the city's best – always attracts locals dropping by after work. Slip in and enjoy some of the 20 wines by the glass.

Trinity College (Map pp696-7; ☎ 06 678 64 72; Via del Collegio Romano 6; ✆ 11-3am) If you're hankering for pub night, try Trinity College; it has a good selection of imported brews, great food and an easy-going ambience; it also gets packed at weekends.

ENTERTAINMENT

Even if you can no longer see gladiators fighting to their deaths, Rome has a lively entertainment scene. Though clubbing isn't as big in Rome as in other European capitals, sophisticates and hipsters are still well served.

The best entertainment guide is *Roma C'è* (www.romace.it, in Italian), with an English-language section, published on Thursday; *Wanted in Rome* (www.wantedinrome.com), published on alternate Wednesdays, is also good; *La Repubblica* and *Il Messagero*, daily newspapers, have cinema, theatre and concert listings. All are available at newsstands. Rome's entertainment schedule is particularly heady in summer, with numerous alfresco performances; be sure to catch one if possible.

For theatre, opera and sporting events, book ahead through **Hello** (Map p702; Stazione Termini) or **Orbis** (Map p702; Piazza dell'Esquilino 37).

Nightclubs & Live Music

For jazz and blues featuring top international musicians, head to **Alexanderplatz** (Map pp694-5; ☎ 06 397 42 171; Via Ostia 9; ✆ 8.30am-2.30am Mon-Sat), near the Vatican, or **Big Mama** (☎ 06 581 24 51; Via San Francesco a Ripa 18; ✆ 9pm-1.30am), just south of Piazza Mastai in Trastevere. At Roman nightclubs, expect to pay upwards

---

THE AUTHOR'S CHOICE

Stardust (Map pp696-7; ☎ 06 583 20 875; Viccolo dei Renzi 4; ✆ 7.30pm-2am Mon-Sat, from noon Sun) is a tiny Trastevere pub-meets-jazz bar. This funky haunt purrs with sultry jazz and impromptu jam sessions, and doesn't close until the last customers tumble out the door.

of €20 just to get in, which may or may not include one drink.

Radio Londra (Map pp690-1; ☎ 06 575 00 44; Via di Monte Testaccio 65b, Testaccio) Popular and decked out like an air-raid shelter, with live music four nights a week.

Caruso Caffè (Map pp690-1; Via di Monte Testaccio 36) Nearby and more sedate, with live music twice weekly and good DJs.

Caffè Latino (Map pp690-1; Via di Monte Testaccio 36) Live Latin music and a disco of Latin and funk.

Gilda (Map pp694-5; ☎ 06 679 73 96; Via Mario de'Fiori 97) With its plush décor and vast dance floor, Gilda attracts a slightly older, jackets-required crowd.

Le Cru (Map pp694-5; ☎ 06 678 48 38; Via della Mercede 10/d) A newcomer, next door to Gilda, oozing smoke and bedecked with tapestries, mirrors, candle-lit tables and kissing couples; there's no cover, but the cocktails, served in voluptuous glasses, are steep.

L'Alibi (Map pp690-1; ☎ 06 574 34 48; Via di Monte Testaccio 44) Regarded as Rome's premier gay venue.

Popular stayers include **Alien** (Map pp690-1; ☎ 06 841 22 12; Via Velletri 13; ⏳ 10.30pm-4am Tue & Thu-Sun), for sci-fi décor, dancers on raised platforms and hip-hop rhythms, and the far-flung **Goa** (☎ 06 574 82 77; Via Libetta 13; 11pm-3am Tue & Thu-Sun Oct-May), with its groovy ethnic décor and glam crowd but a distant location south of the city near metro stop Garbatella.

Cinema
Several cinemas show films in English, including **Pasquino** (Map pp696-7; ☎ 06 580 36 22; Piazza Sant'Egidio), just off Piazza Santa Maria, and **Warner Village Moderno** (Map p702; ☎ 06 588 00 99; Via Merry del Val 14), a mega-plex showing Hollywood blockbusters and Italian films. Expect to pay €7, with discounts on Wednesday.

Opera & Classical Music
Teatro dell'Opera (Map p702; ☎ 06 481 60 28 706; www .operaroma.it, in Italian; Piazza Beniamino Gigli) Rome's finest opera offerings from December to June; ticket prices are steep.

For a full season of concerts, there's the **Accademia di Santa Cecilia** (Map pp694-5; ☎ 06 361 10 64; Via della Conciliazione 4) and the **Accademia Filarmonica Romana** (☎ 06 323 48 90; www.teatroolimpico .it; Teatro Olimpico, Piazza Gentile da Fabriano 17), about 2km north of the city – take the bus from Piazza Manzini.

SHOPPING
Shopping in Rome is undeniably fun and will no doubt lure your attention from ancient ruins. It's a very popular local pastime, with traffic banned on Saturdays to accommodate the thousands of window shoppers traipsing down the three ancient Roman roads radiating from Piazza del Popolo, the main shopping district.

Fashionistas will be happiest on Via Condotti and the narrow streets fanning from Piazza di Spagna to Via del Corso, lined with expensive boutiques full of clothing, footwear and accessories; most major designer labels are represented here. Via del Corso, with a nice mix of shops featuring designer knock-offs, is easier on the wallet, as is Via Nazionale. Via del Governo Vecchio is home to second-hand shops and up-and-coming designers.

If you're after art and antiques, wander the streets around Via Margutta, Via Ripetta, Via del Babuino, and Via dei Coronari, near Piazza Navona. For jewellery, the area between Ponte Sisto and Campo de'Fiori shines.

Across the Tiber, head to Via Cola di Rienzo, near the Vatican, for a good selection of clothing, shoes and food shops; the twisty streets of Trastevere harbour lots of little boutiques and design shops.

For funky finds and great bargains, head to Trastevere's **Porta Portese flea market** (⏳ 6.30am-2pm Sun), Rome's biggest and best known. It's just 400m southeast of Basilica di Santa Cecilia in Trastevere – even if you don't want to buy an antique vase or doll parts, go for the scene (but be aware of pickpockets). The excellent **market** (Via Sannio; ⏳ Mon-Sat morning) near Porta San Giovanni sells new and second-hand clothes.

GETTING THERE & AWAY
Air
Rome's main airport is Leonardo da Vinci, at Fiumincino. Once in town, you'll find the main airline offices just north of Stazione Termini, in the area around Via Bissolati and Via Barberini.

Boat
Tirrenia and the Ferrovie dello Stato (FS) ferries leave for various points in Sardinia (see p775) from Civitavecchia. A Tirrenia fast ferry leaves from Fiumincino and Civitavecchia in summer only. Bookings can be

made at the Termini-based agency **Passagi** (Map p702; ⏰ 7.15am-9pm), or any travel agency displaying the Tirrenia or FS sign. You can also book directly with **Tirrenia** (Map pp694-5; ☎ 06 42 00 98 03; Via San Nicola da Tolentino 5) or at the Stazione Marittima (ferry terminal) at the ports. Bookings can be made at Stazione Termini for FS ferries.

Bus

The main terminal for intercity buses is in Piazzale Tiburtina, in front of the Stazione Tiburtina. Catch Metro Linea B from Termini to Tiburtina, or bus No 649 or 492 from the piazza in front of the station.

Numerous bus lines run services to cities throughout Italy; all depart from the same area and the relevant ticket offices or agents are next to the bus terminus. For general information of which company services what area, go to the tourist office or Enjoy Rome (p692); for information and to make bookings, it's best and easiest to go through a travel agent.

Cotral (☎ 800 15 00 08; www.cotralspa.it, in Italian) services the Lazio region and departs from numerous points throughout the city, depending on the destinations.

Lazzi (☎ 06 884 08 40) runs services to other European cities and northern and central Italy.

Eurojet (Map p702; ☎ 06 474 28 01; Piazza della Repubblica 54) runs services to Bari, Brindisi, Sorrento, the Amalfi Coast and Pompeii, as well as to Matera. **SAIS & Segesta** (Map p702; ☎ 06 481 96 76; Piazza della Repubblica 42) has services to Sicily, and **SENA** (☎ 06 440 44 95) has services to Siena.

Sulga Trioviaggi (☎ 06 440 27 38) or **Sulga Perugia** (☎ 075 575 96 41) offer services to Perugia, Assisi and Romagna.

Car & Motorcycle

It's no holiday trying to motor yourself into Rome's centre, which has many traffic restrictions and can be exceedingly nerve fraying to navigate. If you insist, the main road connecting Rome to the north and south is the Autostrada del Sole (A1), which extends from Milan to Reggio di Calabria. On the outskirts of the city it connects with the Grande Raccordo Anulare (GRA), the ring road encircling Rome. It's best to enter or leave Rome via the GRA and the major feeder roads that connect it to the city. If approaching from the north, take the Via Salaria, Via Nomentana or Via Flaminia exits. From the south, Via Appia Nuova, Via Cristoforo Colombo and Via del Mare (which connects Rome to the Lido di Ostia) all provide reasonably direct routes into the city. The A12 connects the city to both Civitavecchia and Fiumincino airport.

Car-rental offices at Stazione Termini include **Avis** (☎ 800 86 30 63; www.avis.com), **Europcar** (☎ 800 014410; www.europcar.com), **Hertz** (☎ 06 474 03 89; www.hertz.com) and **Maggiore National** (☎ 06 488 00 49; www.maggiore.it, in Italian). All have offices at both airports as well. **Happy Rent** (Map p702; ☎ 06 481 81 85; www.happyrent.com; Via Farini 3) hires scooters (from €31 per day), motorcycles (around €104 and up) and bicycles (from €62 per week).

Train

Almost all trains arrive at and depart from Stazione Termini, though some depart from the stations at Ostiense and Tiburtina. There are regular connections to all major cities in Italy and throughout Europe. The tourist office in Stazione Termini (p692) can provide all timetables (English is spoken), however reservations must be made outside at Sportello 8. Italian speakers can book by phone on the **reservations line** (☎ 848 88 80 88; ⏰ 7am-9pm). Most travel agents with a Trenitalia sign in the window can make reservations for you as well, and the **Trenitalia** (www.trenitalia.it) website is highly useful. You can also pick up an *orario* (timetable) at most newsstands in and around Termini for €4; this is particularly handy and a worthwhile investment if you are making multiple train journeys.

Services at Termini include telephones, money exchange, tourist information, post office, shops and **luggage storage** (per piece for 5hrs €3.10, per piece per hr thereafter €0.52; ⏰ 7am-midnight).

GETTING AROUND
To/From the Airport

There are several options for getting to and from Rome's main airport, Leonardo da Vinci (often simply called Fiumincino), about 30km southwest of the city centre. The least expensive transport is the convenient Leonardo Express train service (follow the signs to the station from the airport arrivals hall), which costs €8.80, arrives at and leaves from platform Nos 25 to 29 at Termini and takes 35 minutes. The first direct train leaves

ITALY

the airport at 6.37am, and then trains run half-hourly until the last one at 11.37pm. From Termini to the airport, trains start at 5:51am and run half-hourly until the last train at 10.51pm. Another train (€4.70) from Fiumincino (with destination Orte or Fara Sabina) stops at Trastevere, Ostiense and Tiburtina stations, but not at Termini, with a service from the airport every 20 minutes from 5.57am to 11.27pm, and from Tiburtina from 5.06am until 10.36pm. From midnight to 5am, an hourly bus runs from Stazione Tiburtina to the airport. Taxis from the airport to city centre run to about €47.

The **Airport Shuttle** (☎ 06 420 14 507; www .airportshuttle.it) offers transfers to/from Fiumincino for €28.50 for one or two passengers, €35 for three and €46.50 for four.

Airport Connection Services (☎ 06 338 32 21; www.airportconnection.it) offers a minivan shuttle to either airport for €30 per person, minimum two passengers. If driving yourself, the airport is connected to Rome by an autostrada, accessible from the GRA.

The other airport is Ciampino, 15km southeast of the city centre and used for most domestic and international charter flights. Blue Cotral buses (running from 6.50am to 11.40pm) connect with the Metro Linea A at Anagnina, where you can catch the subway to Termini or the Vatican. If you arrive very late at night, a taxi is your best bet. The FM4 metro line connects Termini with the Ciampino airport and Albano Laziale. The airport is connected to Rome by Via Appia Nuova.

Car & Motorcycle

Negotiating Roman traffic by car is difficult enough, but you are in for enormous life-risking stress if you ride a motorcycle or Vespa. The rule in Rome is to look straight ahead to watch the vehicles in front and pray those behind are watching you. Pedestrians should always watch out for motorcycles, which often skip red lights.

Most of the historic centre is closed to normal traffic, and you are not permitted to drive into the centre from 6.30am to 6pm Monday to Friday and 2pm to 6pm Saturday without residency or special permission.

If your car goes missing after being parked illegally, check with the **traffic police** (☎ 06 6 76 91). It will cost about €95 to get it back, plus a hefty fine.

The major parking area closest to the centre is at the Villa Borghese; entrance is from Piazzale Brasile at the top of Via Vittorio Veneto. There is also a supervised car park at Stazione Termini. Other car parks are at Piazza dei Partigiani, just outside Stazione Ostiense, and at Stazione Tiburtina, from where you can also catch the metro into the centre.

See p709 for information about car and scooter rental.

Public Transport

Rome has an integrated public transport system, so the same **Metrebus** (www.metrebus.it) ticket is valid for all modes of transport. You can buy tickets at all *tabacchi*, newsstands and from vending machines at main bus stops. Single tickets cost €0.75 for 75 minutes, daily tickets cost €3.10 and weekly tickets cost €12.40. Tickets must be purchased before you get on and validated in the orange machine as you board. Ticketless riders risk a hefty €53 fine – there's zero tolerance for tourists being or acting dumb.

ATAC (☎ 800 43 17 84; www.atac.roma.it) is the city's public transport company. Free transport maps and details on bus routes are available at the **ATAC information booth** (Piazza dei Cinquecento), where many of the main bus routes terminate. Largo di Torre Argentina, Piazza Venezia and Piazza San Silvestro are other hubs. Buses generally run from about 6am to midnight, with limited services throughout the night on some routes. A fast tram service, the No 8, connects Largo Argentina with Trastevere, Porta Portese and Monteverde Nuovo.

The Metropolitana has two lines, A and B. Both pass through Stazione Termini. Take Linea A for Piazza di Spagna, the Vatican (Ottaviano) and Villa Borghese (Flaminio), and Linea B for the Colosseum and Circus Maximus. Trains run approximately every five minutes between 5.30am and 11.30pm (12.30am on Saturday).

Taxi

Roman taxi drivers can be at the top of the fleecing-foreigners game, so understand the rules before you and your bags get in the car. Make sure your taxi is licensed and metered, and always go with the metered fare, never an arranged price. Daytime trips within the centre can cost from €5 to €15.

Cooperativa Radio Taxi Romana (☎ 06 35 70) oversees many operators. Major taxi ranks are at the airports, Stazione Termini and Largo Argentina in the historical centre (look for the orange-and-black taxi signs). There are surcharges from €1 to €3 for luggage, night service, Sunday and public holidays; travel to/from Fiumicino airport has a surcharge of €7.45/6.10. The flagfall is around €2.75 (for the first 3km), then €0.75 for every kilometre. Taxis are on radio call 24 hours a day.

AROUND ROME
Ostia Antica

The Romans founded this port city at the mouth of the Tiber in the 4th century BC and it became a strategically important centre of defence and trade. It was populated by merchants, sailors and slaves, and the ruins of the city provide a fascinating contrast to the ruins at Pompeii, which was a resort town for the wealthy. Barbarian invasions and the outbreak of malaria led to Ostia Antica's eventual abandonment, but Pope Gregory IV re-established the city in the 9th century AD.

Information about the town and ruins is available from the Rome tourist office or Enjoy Rome (p692).

Of particular note in the **excavated city** (☎ 06 56 35 80 99; admission €4.20; ⏱ 9am-5pm Tue-Sun winter, to 7pm summer) are the mosaics of the **Terme di Nettuno** (Baths of Neptune); a **Roman theatre** built by Agrippa; the **forum** and **Capitolium temple**, dedicated to Jupiter, Juno and Minerva; and the **Piazzale delle Corporazioni**, the offices of Ostia's 70 merchant guilds, distinguished by mosaics depicting their different trades.

To get to Ostia Antica from Rome, take the Metro Linea B to Piramide or Magliana, then the Ostia Lido train (getting off at Ostia Antica). By car, take the Via del Mare or the parallel-running Via Ostiense.

Tivoli
pop 53,000

Set on a hill by the Aniene River, Tivoli was a resort town of the ancient Romans and became popular as a summer playground for the wealthy during the Renaissance. While the terraced gardens and fountains of the Villa d'Este are the main tourist draw, the ruins of Villa Adriana, built by the Roman emperor Hadrian, are far more interesting.

The **tourist office** (☎ 0774 31 12 49; Largo Garibaldi; ⏱ 8.30am-2.30pm Tue-Sat & 3-6pm Tue-Thu) is near the Cotral bus stop.

SIGHTS

Hadrian's spectacular summer villa, **Villa Adriana** (☎ 0774 53 02 03; admission €6.50; ⏱ 9am-1hr before sunset), built in the 2nd century AD, was one of the largest and most sumptuous in the Roman Empire. Although successively plundered by barbarians and Romans for building materials (many of its original decorations were used to embellish the Villa d'Este), enough resplendence remains to convey the villa's magnificence.

The Renaissance **Villa d'Este** (admission €6.50; ⏱ 9am-1hr before sunset Tue-Sun) was built in the 16th century for Cardinal Ippolito d'Este. Situated on the site of a Franciscan monastery, the villa's wonderful gardens are decorated with numerous fountains, which are its main attraction.

GETTING THERE & AWAY

Tivoli is 30km east of Rome and accessible by Cotral bus from outside the Ponte Mammolo station on Metro Linea B. Buses depart every 20 minutes, stopping at Villa Adriana, about 1km from Tivoli, along the way; the trip takes about one hour. Local bus No 4 goes to Villa Adriana from Tivoli's Piazza Garibaldi. The fastest route by car is on the Rome-L'Aquila autostrada (A24).

Tarquinia
pop 15,300

Believed to have been founded in the 12th century BC, and home of the Tarquin kings who ruled Rome before the creation of the republic, Tarquinia was an important economic and political centre of the Etruscan League. The major attractions here are the painted tombs of its *necropoli* (burial grounds), although the town itself is quite pretty and has a small medieval centre. There's a **tourist information office** (☎ 0766 85 63 84; Piazza Cavour 1; ⏱ 8am-2pm Mon-Sat) just past the medieval ramparts.

Tarquinia is about 90km northwest of Rome.

SIGHTS

The 15th-century Palazzo Vitelleschi houses the **Museo Nazionale Tarquiniense** (☎ 0766 85 60

36; admission incl necropolis €6.20; 🕙 9am-7pm Tue-Sun), a significant collection of Etruscan treasures, including frescoes from the tombs. Keep an eye out for a few red-and-black plates featuring acrobatic sex acts. The **necropolis** (☎ 0766 85 63 08; 🕙 8.30am-6.30pm Tue-Sun) is a 15- to 20-minute walk away (or catch one of four daily buses). Ask at the tourist office for directions. Some of the tombs are richly painted with frescoes, although many have deteriorated.

SLEEPING & EATING

Tarquinia has limited accommodation, so it's best to book ahead; it makes a very fine day trip from Rome.

Hotel San Marco (☎ 0766 84 22 34; Piazza Cavour 10; s/d €52/67) In the medieval centre, this pleasant hotel is the closest to the sights.

Trattoria Arcadia (Via Mazzini 6) Friendly and affordable for a good meal.

GETTING THERE & AWAY

Cotral buses leave every hour for Tarquinia from outside the Lepanto stop on Metro Linea A, arriving at Barriera San Giusto, a short distance from the tourist office.

Cerveteri

Ancient Caere, founded by the Etruscans, was one of the most important commercial centres in the Mediterranean from the 7th to 5th century BC. The present-day lures are the atmospheric tombs, known as *tumoli*, great mounds of earth with carved stone bases. Treasures taken from these tombs can be seen in the Vatican Museums, the Villa Giulia Museum and the Louvre. There is a **tourist office** (☎ 06 994 06 72; Piazza Risorgimento 19).

Once inside the main necropolis area, **Banditaccia** (☎ 06 994 00 01; Via del Necropoli; admission €4.20; 🕙 9am-7pm Tue-Sun summer, 9am-4pm Tue-Sun winter), the *tumoli* are laid out in the form of a town. The best-preserved example is the 4th-century-BC **Tomba dei Rilievi**, adorned with painted reliefs depicting household items.

Antica Locanda Le Ginestre (☎ 06 994 06 72; Piazza Santa Maria 5) draws Romans just for a meal on the outdoor terrace; the pastas are especially good.

Cerveteri is accessible from Rome by Cotral bus (1¼ hours, every 30 minutes) from outside the Lepanto stop on Metro Linea A.

Banditaccia is accessible by local bus (summer only) from the main square; otherwise it's a pleasant 2km walk west from town.

NORTHERN ITALY

Italy's 'well-heeled' north isn't short of finery; from the imposing Alps to the jewelled beaches of Liguria and fairy-tale beauty of *La Serenissima* (Venice), its physical riches are matched only by the cultural treasures concentrated here, due to Florence's role as the epicentre of the Renaissance. The only danger is lingering in bigger cities, when there are equal delights awaiting throughout Piedmont, Lombardy, Emilia-Romagna and the Veneto.

GENOA

pop 628,800

Liguria's capital, the busy port of Genoa is simultaneously aristocratic, grandiose and dingy. Amid the contradictions, however, the mighty maritime republic once lauded as 'La Superba' retains a salty exuberance its most famous son, Christopher Columbus (1451–1506), would surely salute.

Vibrant Genoa was an EU–designated European City of Culture in 2004. It justly rewards a stop on anyone's northern Italy itinerary.

Orientation

Most trains stop at Genoa's main stations, Principe and Brignole. Brignole is closer to Genoa's centre and convenient to slightly better accommodation. Principe, nearer to the port, has many cheaper, if somewhat dingy, options nearby. It's no war zone, but it's somewhere best avoided at night by women travelling alone. From Brignole walk down Via Fiume towards Via XX Settembre and the historic centre. Local ATM buses service both stations.

Information

In-Centro IT (Via XX Settembre 17-21; per hr €4; 🕙 10am-1pm & 2.30-7.30pm Mon-Fri, 10am-1pm & 3.30-7.30pm Sat) A tourism 'shop' with Internet access and good maps upstairs.

Main post office (☎ 5318708; Via Dante 4a; 🕙 8am-6.30pm Mon-Sat) Just off Piazza de Ferrari.

Ospedale San Martino (☎ 010 55 51; www.hsan martino.liguria.it, in Italian; Largo Rosanna Benzi 10) East of the centre.

Telecom office (Piazza Verdi; 🕙 8am-9pm) To the left of Stazione Brignole.

Tourist information office Stazione Principe (☎ 010 2462633; www.apt.genova.it; 🕙 9.30am-1pm & 2.30-6pm

Mon-Sat); Stazione Marittima (☎ 010 2463686; ☿ based on ship arrivals/departures); Airport (☎ 010 6015247; ☿ 9.30am-12.30pm & 1.30-5.30pm Mon-Sat)

Sights

Any tour of Genoa should start in the back-streets around the old port. Newer parts of the harbour also appeal at night, when the hill-top lights form an appealing backdrop for the popular evening *passeggiata*.

Search out the gorgeous 12th-century, black-and-white marble **Cattedrale di San Lorenzo** (Piazza San Lorenzo; ☿ 8am-noon & 3.30-7pm) and the huge **Palazzo Ducale** (☎ 010 5574000; www.palazzoducale.genova.it; Piazza Matteotti 9; admission varies; ☿ 9am-9pm, ticket office to 8pm Tue-Sun), which doubles as the region's major exhibition space/arts hub.

Palaces line Via Garibaldi, many of which house galleries, including the 16th-century **Palazzo Bianco** (☎ 010 5572013; www.museopalazzobianco.it; Via Garibaldi 11; 1-day/3-day card €8/12, bus surcharge €1/3; ☿ 9am-8pm Tue-Sun) and the 17th-century **Palazzo Rosso** (☎ 010 2476351; www.palazzorosso.it; Via Garibaldi 18; admission €3.10; ☿ 9am-7pm Tue-Fri, 10am-7pm Sat & Sun). **Galleria Nazionale di Palazzo Spinola** (☎ 010 2477061; Piazza Pellicceria 1; admission €4; ☿ 8.30am-7.30pm Tue-Sat, 1-8pm Sun) displays major Italian and Flemish Renaissance works, including Caravaggio's *Ecce Homo*.

Acquario Di Genova (☎ 010 234 52 67; www.acquario.ge.it; Ponte Spinola; adult/child €12.50/7.50; ☿ 9.30am-7.30pm Mon-Wed & Fri, to 10pm Thu, to 8.30pm Sat & Sun) is a highlight. The eye-catching Renzo Piano–designed aquarium jutting into the harbour is Europe's biggest, with typical beasties on display in an atypically interesting example of the genre.

Sleeping

Ostello Genova (☎ 010 242 2457; hostelge@iol.it; Via Costanzi 120; dm incl breakfast €13-18, dinner €8; ☿ closed Jan) In Righi, outside Genoa, is the nearest AIG (HI) hostel. Typically clean, but a little soulless (11.30pm curfew). There's a terrace with spectacular views of Genoa, though. Take bus No 40 from Brignole.

Carola (☎ 010 839 13 40; Via Gropallo 4; d/tr €55/70, s/d/tr with shared bathroom €30/45/60) On the 3rd floor of a gracious old *palazzo* near Brignole, Carola offers simple rooms and a warm welcome. Basic but functional, it's comfortable enough and a steal at the price. On a pleasant street north of Piazza Brignole, 1km from the old port.

Hotel Bel Soggiorno (☎ 010 542880; www.belsoggiornohotel.com; Via XX Settembre 19; s/d €73/93; ⊠ ▯) The charming owner of this enchanting hotel works hard to ensure a pleasant stay, and rooms are bright and airy, if a little chintzy. Superbly located in the historic centre, a stone's throw from Brignole. The multilingual staff (Italian, German, French, English) are helpful, and there's a decent buffet breakfast. Ask about discounts for multinight stays.

Eating

Genoa offers many Ligurian specialities, including the eponymous local 'dish', *pesto Genovese*. There's also delicious *pansoti* (ravioli in ground walnut sauce) and focaccia.

Threegaio (☎ 010 2465793; Piazza delle Erbe 17/19r; snacks €5-10; ☿ lunch & dinner Mon-Sat) Hip without being pretentious, accessible without being boring, and nicely placed on one of Genoa's coolest little piazzas, Threegaio is a bit of everything – bar, café, restaurant, meeting point. Best at *aperitivo* (cocktail hour) time.

Il Panson (☎ 010 2468903; Piazza delle Erbe 5; mains €9-11; ☿ dinner Mon-Sat) Il Panson has been serving up superb seafood to Genovese diners since 1790. Try the handmade basil ravioli in prawn sauce– insanely delicious and amazing value.

Il Barbarossa (☎ 010 2465097; Piano di Sant Andrea 21/23r; 2-course menu €12-18; ☿ 7.30-3.30am Mon, to 2.30am Tue-Fri, 12.30pm-2.30am Sat & Sun) In the shadows of the Porta Soprana, metres from Columbus' house, Barbarossa is small, popular and deliciously atmospheric. The fab wine and cocktail list offsets a menu of local specialities, though it's also great for a quick *panini* and a beer.

Antica Cantina i Tre Merli (The Three Crows; ☎ 010 2474095; www.itremerli.it; Vico dietro il Coro Maddalena 26r; 2-course menu €15-20; ☿ noon-3pm & 7pm-1am Mon-Fri, dinner Sat) For a protracted dining experience, this *antica cantina* (old-style eatery) offers moody, rustic ambience and serves up great, hearty Ligurian food with a sensational wine list; try the fantastic tomato pasta with *seppia* (cuttlefish ink) sauce.

Oriental market (Via XX Settembre) Fantastic fresh produce.

Drinking & Entertainment

Dueseiuno (☎ 010 2511558; Mura della Marina, 21r; ☿ noon-2am) Genoa's nightlife is subdued; try the three floors here.

ITALY

Cosa Zapata (Via Sampierdarena 36; 9pm-3am Fri & Sat) Live music fans should seek this place out, where a younger crowd mosh to modern music within medieval walls.

There are good bars clustered around Piazza Raibetta and Piazza delle Erbe – great for an aperitif. There's also a cinema multiplex and abundant mainstream shops in the huge **Magazin del Cotone** (Cotton Shop; Porto Antico).

Getting There & Around

AIR

There are regular domestic and international flights from **Cristoforo Colombo Airport** (010 601 54 10; Sestri Ponente), 6km west of the city. The **Volabus** (558 24 14; 5.30am-11pm) airport bus service (line No 100) leaves from Piazza Verdi (€2.20, 25 minutes, every 30 minutes), just outside Stazione Brignole, also stopping at Stazione Principe.

BUS

Buses for Rome, Florence, Milan and Perugia leave from Piazza della Vittoria, south of Stazione Brignole, where Eurolines coaches also depart for Barcelona, Madrid and Paris. Book tickets at **Geotravels** (010 58 71 81) in the piazza.

FERRIES

Genoa is a major embarkation point for ferries to Sicily, Sardinia and Corsica. Major companies are **Corsica Ferries** (019 21 55 11; www.corsicaférries.com) in Savona; **Moby Lines** (010 254 15 13; www.moby.it) at Ponte Asserato for Corsica; **Tirrenia** (199 12 31 99, 800 82 40 79; www.gruppotirrenia.it) at the Stazione Marittima, Ponte Colombo, for Sicily and Sardinia; and Grandi Navi Veloci and **Grandi Traghetti** (010 58 93 31; Via Fieschi 17) for Sardinia, Sicily, Malta and Tunisia.

TRAIN

Genoa has services to Turin (€15.86, 1¾ hours, seven to 10 daily), Milan (€12.86, 1½ hours, up to eight daily), Pisa (€15.86, two hours, up to eight daily) and Rome (€34.51, 5¼ hours, six daily); it makes little difference whether you leave from Principe or Brignole train station, except for trips along the two Rivieras. Fares quoted are Intercity fares.

RIVIERA DI LEVANTE

The Ligurian coast from Genoa south to La Spezia is spectacular, rivalling the Amalfi Coast in its sheer beauty. Summer here is congested; it's advisable to go in spring or autumn when smaller crowds make sightseeing easier and the heat is less stifling. A good option is using either Santa Margherita Ligure in the north as a base or La Spezia in the south.

The **tourist office** (0185 28 74 85; www.aptcin queterre.sp.it; Via XXV Aprile 4) in Santa Margherita is central; the one in **La Spezia** (0187 77 09 00; Via Mazzini 45) is near the waterfront. Both have information on the Cinque Terre and surrounding coastal towns.

Sights & Activities

From pretty Santa Margherita Ligure you can explore the nearby resorts of **Portofino**, a haunt of the glamour set, and **Camogli**, a gorgeous fishing village turned resort town. The medieval Benedictine monastery of **San Fruttuoso** is a hilly 2½-hour walk from Camogli or Portofino, with sensational views along the way; it's possible to catch the ferry back.

Don't miss the **Cinque Terre**, five tiny villages – Riomaggiore, Manorola, Corniglia, Vernazza and Monterosso – clustered along a section of eye-popping Unesco-protected coastline, easily among the most beautiful regions in Italy. Individually charming, collectively breathtaking, all are easily reached by train from La Spezia. Linked by a 12km path, the remarkable scenery of the **Via dell'Amore** (Lovers' Lane; toll €3) is a perfect, mildly challenging day walk.

Don't limit your sightseeing to land; in summer, swimming's permitted in some bays and coves, so bring snorkelling gear for an often-overlooked treat.

Sleeping

La Dolce Vita (0187 760044; fax 0187 920935; Via Colombo 120; bed from €20) Giacomo Natale runs this bed-booking service in Riomaggiore, and he knows everyone and everywhere worth remembering in the area. Call him first or ask for him at Bar Centrale; if he can't find you a bed, no-one can. Rooms are generally excellent (most with views).

Ostello 5 Terre (0187 92 02 15; www.cinqueterre .net/ostello; Via B Riccobaldi 21; dm €17-22, breakfast €3.50, dinner €14) This is an orderly, well-run hostel in Manorola. Always crowded, so reserve. Manorola is a 15-minute, clearly-marked walk from Riomaggiore.

Nuova Riviera (☎ 0185 28 74 03; info@nuovariviera .com; Via Belvedere 10/2; s/d €75/90; P ⊠ ⊠) In Santa Margherita, this lovely old hotel is only metres from the water and highly atmospheric for a seaside rendezvous. Splash out!

Eating & Drinking

A Pie De Ma (☎ 338 2220088; Via dell' Amore; snacks €5-8; ⊙ breakfast, lunch & dinner) Perched on a cliffside above the perfect teal of a tiny Riomaggiore bay, you'll seldom find a more beautiful backdrop for a snack, coffee or wine – or just whiling away hours – than the divine terrace vista here. Food and service are tops, too.

Bar Centrale (☎ 0187 920208; barcentr@tin.it; Via Colombo 144; Internet per hr €6) On the main drag, this hub of Riomaggiore hijinks is always open. Your only real carousing option in the off-season, certainly the most raucous one in summer; barman Ivo serves up drinks and sarcasm equally.

Getting There & Away

All the coastal towns are easily accessible by train from Genoa. Buses leave from Santa Margherita's Piazza Martiri della Libertà for Portofino. **Servizio Marittimo del Tigullio** (☎ 0185 28 46 70; www.traghettiportofino.it) runs summer ferries from Santa Margherita to Portofino, San Fruttuoso and the Cinque Terre. From La Spezia many ferry routes service the coast. For the Cinque Terre, a *biglietto giornaliero Cinque Terre* (24-hour Cinque Terre rail pass; €5.80) allows unlimited travel between Monterosso and La Spezia.

TURIN

pop 898,400

Set to host the 2006 Winter Olympics, Turin is a grand old city. The former capital of Italy (until 1945) and seat of the Savoys feels like a once-regal place whose glory won't *quite* fade; mostly thanks to the era of the Agnelli family's Fiat automobile empire, and to Italy's most notorious football team, Juventus. Memorable products occasionally originate in unexpected places, and Turin is the birthplace of Ferrero Rocher chocolates, Nutella and Tic Tacs. Turin's other famous icon is Il Sindone, or the Shroud of Turin, believed to be Christ's burial cassock.

Orientation

Porta Nuova train station is the usual point of arrival. For the centre, cross Corso Vittorio Emanuele II and walk through the grand Carlo Felice and San Carlo piazzas toward Piazza Castello.

Information

Tourist offices Piazza Castello (☎ 011 53 51 81; www .turismotorino.org; Piazza Castello 161; ⊙ 9.30am-7pm Mon-Sat, to 3pm Sun); Porta Nuova train station (☎ 011 53 13 27); Airport (☎ 011 567 81 24) Museum enthusiasts should consider the **Torino Card** (48/72hr card €15/17), available at the Piazza Castello tourist office and valid for all public transport and discounts/entry to 120 museums, monuments and castles.

Sights

Start at the central Piazza San Carlo, known as 'Turin's drawing room' and capped by the baroque churches of **San Carlo** and **Santa Cristina**.

Nearby, the majestic **Piazza Castello** features the sumptuous **Palazzo Madama**, home to the **Museo Civico d'Arte Antica** (☎ 011 442 99 12; Piazza Castello; adult/child €6.20/3.10; ⊙ 10am-8pm Tue-Fri & Sun, to 11pm Sat) and the 17th-century **Palazzo Reale** (Royal Palace; ☎ 011 436 14 55; Piazza Castello; adult/child €6.50/free; ⊙ 9am-7pm Tue-Sun), where the gardens were designed in 1697 by Louis le Nôtre, noted for his work at Versailles.

Film buffs shouldn't miss the **Museo Nazionale del Cinema** (☎ 011 8125658; www.museo nazionaledelcinema.it; Via Montebello 20; adult/concession €5.20/4.20; ⊙ 9am-8pm Tue-Fri & Sun, to 11pm Sat), Italy's most comprehensive archive of imaging history/materials. There are presound 'magic lantern' exhibits, original Charlie Chaplin storyboards, HR Giger–designed *Aliens* props and more, all in a cutting-edge gallery. It's 20 minutes from Porta Nuova on foot, or take bus No 61 (alight Via Po) or 68 (alight Via Rossini).

The nearby **Cattedrale di San Giovanni Battista** is home to a Catholic curiosity, the Shroud of Turin, the linen cloth purportedly used to wrap the crucified Christ. Carbon dating challenges this, showing the cloth to be from the 13th century, and, in 2004, Italian scientists discovered what appears to be a secondary image on the reverse of the iconograph. Rarely shown, check ahead if you're determined to see it. There's a copy displayed in the cathedral.

The **Museo della Sindone** (Museum of the Shroud; ☎ 011 436 58 32; Via San Domenico 28; adult/child €5.50/2.50; ⊙ 9am-noon & 3-7pm) answers most questions.

ITALY

Turin's **Museo Egizio** (Egyptian Museum; ☎ 011 561 77 76; www.museoegizio.org; Via Accademia delle Scienze 6; admission €6.50; ☾ 8.30am-7.30pm Tue-Sun) is considered to be among the best museums of Egyptian artefacts after those in London and Cairo.

Outside town is the **Palazzina di Caccia di Stupinigi** (Savoy Hunting Lodge; ☎ 011 358 1220; www .stupinigi.it, in Italian; Piazza Principe Amedeo 7; ☾ 10am-5pm Tue-Sun, to 6pm summer), a stupefyingly rococo example of the French baroque architecture the Savoys applied to Turin more broadly during their reign.

Sleeping

Bologna (☎ 011 562 02 90; www.hotelbolognasrl.it, in Italian; Corso Vittorio Emanuele II 60; s/d/tr €57/88/100) Near the station, and deservedly popular. Looking grim at first, rooms are actually clean and comfortable, if a little exposed to street noise.

Hotel Roma e Rocco Cavour (☎ 011 561 27 72; hotel@roma.tin.it; Piazza Carlo Felice 60; s/d/tr €70/88/99, s/d with shared bathroom €50/68) Something for everyone right on Turin's most engaging square. Basic décor and adequate service don't detract from a fundamentally pleasant night's accommodation.

Dogana Vecchia (☎ 011 436 67 52; Via Corte D'Appello 4; s/d €83/104; ✗ ✗ ▢) Dogana Vecchia has accommodated the likes of Verdi and Mozart. Rooms have all mod cons, yet still make you feel like you've stepped back in time. Splurge and see how it feels to live like minor royalty.

Ostello Torino (☎ 011 660 29 39; www.ostellion line.org; Via Alby 1; dm/d €12/17, dinner €8.50; ☾ closed 9.30am-2pm; ✗) To get to this quiet HI hostel, walk 1.5km up a steep hill or catch bus No 52 from Porta Nuova (No 64 on Sunday). Book ahead to snag a double room.

Campeggio Villa Rey (☎ 011 819 01 17; Strada Superiore Val San Martino 27; per person/tent €3.65/6; ☾ Mar-Oct) This camping ground in the hills east of the Po has access and bathrooms for disabled travellers. Bus No 52 from Porta Nuova (No 64 on Sunday).

Eating

Al Pigaron (☎ 011 8125018; Via Accademia Albertina 27; set menus €8; ☾ lunch & dinner) The cheapest good three-course lunch in Turin. Décor is '70s shabby-tacky, but the service is excellent and the simple Piemontese dishes are delicious and served in decent portions.

La Stua (☎ 011 8178339; Via Giuseppe Mazzini 46; pizzas €7-9; ☾ noon-2pm & 6.45pm-midnight Tue-Sun) Wonderful pizzeria offering a fantastic range of the trademark dish, as well as excellent pasta and main meals. Warm atmosphere, great prices and friendly staff.

Ristorante Perbacco (☎ 011 882110; Via Giuseppe Mazzini 31; set menus €28; ☾ 7.45pm-1am Tue-Sun) Super stylish. Think low light, deep-red furnishings, first-rate cooking with the best local produce and a wine list longer than the Po. Try the rabbit with *dolcelatte* (sweet blue cheese), or the outstanding salmon in rocket sauce.

For *gelati* and chocolate you're spoiled for choice; get revolutionary at **Caffè Fiorio** (Via Po 8), which was good enough for Camillo Cavour, the father of Italian unification.

Getting There & Around

Turin is serviced by the **Turin International Airport** (☎ 011 567 63 61; www.turin-airport.com) in Caselle, with flights to European and national destinations. **Sadem** (☎ 011 300 01 66) runs buses to the airport (€5.40, 40 minutes, every 45 minutes) from the corner between Via Sacchi and Corso Vittorio Emanuele II, west of Porta Nuova. National and international buses use the terminal on Corso Castelfidardo. Regular daily trains connect with Milan (€14.57, 1¾ hours), Aosta (€6.80, two hours), Venice (€25, five hours), Genoa (€15.86, 1¾ hours) and Rome (€40.45, seven hours). The city is well serviced by buses and trams.

MILAN

pop 1.3 million

Milan is a glitzy city, obsessed with money, looks and glamour. Sure enough, it offers the best in Italian theatre, nightlife and clothes, but little else. And you almost require the salary of one of its top models or football stars to fully indulge in its other world-famous diversion: shopping.

Originally believed to be Celtic, Milan was conquered by the Romans in 222 BC and then developed into a major trading and transport centre. From the 13th century, the city flourished under the rule of two powerful families: the Visconti, followed by the Sforza.

Milan closes down almost completely in August, when most of the city's inhabitants take their buff bodies away to the nearby coastline for annual holidays.

Orientation

From Milan's central train station (Stazione Centrale), approach the centre on its efficient underground railway, the Metropolitana Milanese (MM). Use the Duomo (cathedral) and the Castello Sforzesco as your landmarks; the main shopping areas and sights are around and between the two.

Information

BOOKSHOPS

Feltrinelli International (☎ 02 6595644; www.la feltrinelli.it, in Italian; Piazza Cavour 1) The foreign-language arm of Italy's best book chain.

EMERGENCY

Ambulance & Fire (☎ 118)
Milan City Council (☎ 02 54 66 81 18; Via Friuli 30) For lost property.
Police headquarters (Questura; ☎ 02 622 61; Via Fatebenefratelli 11) English spoken.
Ufficio Stranieri (Foreigners' office; ☎ 02 622 61; Via Montebello 26)

INTERNET ACCESS

Grazia Internet (☎ 02 6700543; Piazza Duca D'Aosta 40; per hr €4; ⏲ 8-2am) Next to Stazione Centrale, this place is orange, like a mini Easy Internet.

LAUNDRY

Lavanderia Self Service (Via Tadino 4; small/large load €3.10/6.10; ⏲ 7.30am-9.30pm)

MEDICAL SERVICES

Farmacia Carlo Erba (☎ 02 87 86 68; Piazza del Duomo 21; ⏲ 24hr)
Ospedale Maggiore Policlinico (☎ 02 550 31; Via Francesco Sforza 35) A central public hospital.
Pharmacy (☎ 02 669 07 35; Stazione Centrale; ⏲ 24hr)

MONEY

American Express (Via Larga 4; ⏲ 9am-5.30pm Mon-Fri)
Banca Cesare Ponte (19 Piazza del Duomo) Has an ATM.
Exchange offices (Stazione Centrale)

POST

Main post office (Via Cordusio 4; ⏲ 8am-7pm Mon-Fri, 8.30am-noon Sat) Off Via Dante, near Piazza del Duomo. There are other offices at the station and Linate airport.

TELEPHONE

Telecom office Stazione Centrale (Upper level; ⏲ 8am-9.30pm); Galleria Vittorio Emanuele II (⏲ 8am-9.30pm) Both offices have international telephone directories. The Galleria Vittorio Emanuele II branch also has fax services and phonecards.

TOURIST INFORMATION

Tourist offices Piazza del Duomo (☎ 02 72 52 43 01; www.milanoinfotourist.com; Via Marconi 1; ⏲ 8.45am-1pm & 2-6pm Mon-Sat, 9am-1pm & 2-5pm Sun); Stazione Centrale (☎ 02 72 52 43 60; ⏲ 9am-6.30pm Mon-Sat, 9am-12.30pm & 1.30-5pm Sun) Pick up free guides *Hello Milano* and *Milano Mese* here, and a *Milan is Milano* map. There are also tourist offices at both airports.

Dangers & Annoyances

Milan's main shopping areas are haunts for thieves; some teams employ diversionary tactics. Be alert, particularly around Stazione Centrale, to people crowding you around the underground, especially when the platform seems oddly uncrowded.

Sights

The city's landmark **Duomo** (stairs/lift to roof €3.50/5; ⏲ 9am-5.30pm) looks like the backdrop for an animated story (and seats 40,000!). Commissioned in 1386 to a florid French-Gothic design and finished nearly 600 years later, the resulting façade is an unforgettable marble mass of statues, spires and pillars. The view from the roof is wonderful.

Join the throngs for a *passeggiata* through the magnificent **Galleria Vittorio Emanuele II** towards **Teatro alla Scala** (see p720), the world's most famous opera house, recently reopened after – appropriately enough for Milan – a facelift.

The immense **Castello Sforzesco** (☎ 02 801 410; www.milanocastello.it; Piazza Castello 3; admission free; ⏲ 9.30am-5.30pm Tue-Sun), once a Visconti fortress, rebuilt by Francesco Sforza in 1450, now houses collections of furniture, artefacts and sculpture, notably Michelangelo's unfinished *Pietà Rondanini*. Nearby, on Via Brera, is the 17th-century Palazzo di Brera, home to the **Pinacoteca di Brera** (☎ 02 86 07 96; www.amicidibrera.milano.it, in Italian; Via Brera 28; admission €5; ⏲ 8.30am-7.30pm Tue-Sun), whose collection includes Mantegna's masterpiece, the *Dead Christ*.

Leonardo's *Last Supper* is in the **Cenacolo Vinciano** (☎ 02 89 42 11 46; www.cenacolovinciano.org; Piazza Santa Maria delle Grazie 2; admission €6.50; ⏲ 8am-7.30pm Tue-Sun), just west of the city centre. Phone ahead to book; decide for yourself whether or not the apostle to Christ's left really is a woman (or Mary Magdalene), as

CENTRAL MILAN

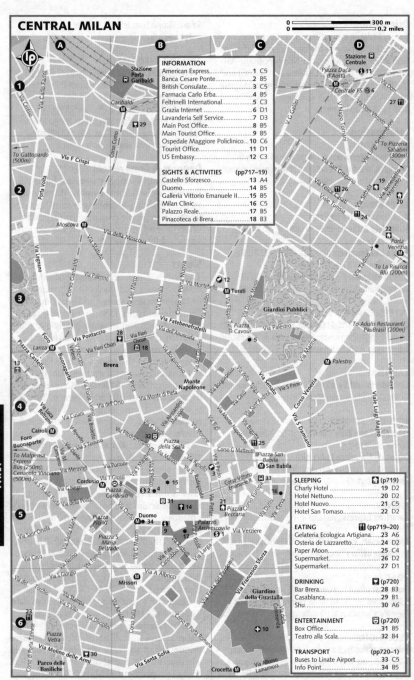

| 0 | 300 m |
| 0 | 0.2 miles |

INFORMATION

American Express.................................	1 C5
Banca Cesare Ponte...........................	2 B5
British Consulate................................	3 C5
Farmacia Carlo Erba.........................	4 B5
Feltrinelli International.......................	5 C3
Grazia Internet...................................	6 D1
Lavanderia Self Service.....................	7 D3
Main Post Office................................	8 B5
Main Tourist Office...........................	9 B5
Ospedale Maggiore Policlinico.........	10 C6
Tourist Office.....................................	11 D1
US Embassy..	12 C3

SIGHTS & ACTIVITIES (pp717–19)

Castello Sforzesco.............................	13 A4
Duomo..	14 B5
Galleria Vittorio Emanuele II............	15 B5
Milan Clinic.......................................	16 C5
Palazzo Reale.....................................	17 B5
Pinacoteca di Brera...........................	18 B3

SLEEPING (p719)

Charly Hotel	19 D2
Hotel Nettuno....................................	20 D2
Hotel Nuovo.......................................	21 C5
Hotel San Tomaso..............................	22 D2

EATING (pp719–20)

Gelateria Ecologica Artigiana...........	23 A6
Osteria de Lazzaretto........................	24 C4
Paper Moon..	25 D2
Supermarket.......................................	26 D2
Supermarket.......................................	27 D1

DRINKING (p720)

Bar Brera..	28 B3
Casablanca...	29 B1
Shu...	30 A6

ENTERTAINMENT (p720)

Box Office...	31 B5
Teatro alla Scala................................	32 B4

TRANSPORT (pp720–1)

Buses to Linate Airport......................	33 C5
Info Point...	34 B5

ITALY

Dan Brown implied in his controversial bestseller *The Da Vinci Code*.

Festivals

St Ambrose's Day (7 December) is Milan's major festival, with celebrations at the Fiera di Milano (MM1 – red line: stop Amendola Fiera).

Sleeping

Milan's hotels are among the most expensive and heavily booked in Italy, due to frequent trade fairs held here. Budget hotels of widely varying quality are concentrated around Stazione Centrale.

Ostello Piero Rotta (☎ 02 39 26 70 95; Viale Salmoiraghi 1; dm €16; ◷ lockout 9am-3.30pm, curfew 12.30am) An HI hostel northwest of the centre near San Siro; there are friendly multilingual staff and typically sterile ambience. Take the MM1 (red line, direction Molino Dorino) to stop QT8.

Hotel Due Giardini (☎ 02 29 52 10 93; duegiardini hotel@libero.it; Via B Marcello 47; s/d/tr €68/115/155; ☒) One of Milan's nicest one-star hotels has delightful rooms overlooking a tranquil back garden. Turn right off Via D Scarlatti, to the left as you leave the station. Note that these prices may be negotiable depending on season/trade fairs.

Hotel Bagliori (☎ 02 29 52 68 84; www.hotelme .it; Via Boscovich 43; s €80-140, d €130-200) For some three-star comfort, try the schmick Bagliori with its pretty little walled garden and attentive service. The tastefully decorated rooms have fridge, TV, direct-dial phone and the breakfast buffet is fab. The hotel is located about 15 minutes out of the city centre.

Hotel Nettuno (☎ 02 29 40 44 81; Via Tadino 27; s/d/tr/q €50/95/125/165, s/d/tr with shared bathroom €45/68/87; ☒ ☒) This modest outfit is much nicer than its spartan foyer might suggest. The gracious multilingual staff ensure a pleasant stay.

Charly Hotel (☎ /fax 02 20 47 190; www.hotelcharly .com; Via Settala 76; s €62-90, d €68-130, s with shared bathroom €45-60, d with shared bathroom €57-100; Ⓟ ☒ ☒) Small, friendly two-star on a quiet street, Charly Hotel is a bargain gem worth ferreting out. The terrace is dinky, but pleasant in fine weather.

Hotel San Tomaso (☎ 02 29 51 47 47; hotelsan tomaso@tin.it; Viale Tunisia 6; d from €65, s/d with shared bathroom from €30/45; ☒ ▢) Just off Corso Buenos Aires, this super-friendly place is

well located for shopping, and cosy as you like. Room prices vary because some have views, but all have TV and phone. It was renovated in 2004.

Hotel Serena (☎ 02 29404958; www.hotelserena .com; Via Boscovich 59; s €50-135, d €75-210, tr €101-289; ☒ ☒ ▢) Rates vary hugely with tradefair/seasonal demand at the neat, luxurious Serena. Rooms are excellent, the staff gruff yet likeable. Buffet breakfast included.

Hotel Nuovo (☎ 02 86 46 05 42; fax 02 72 00 17 52; Piazza Beccaria 6; d/tr €93/124, s/d with shared bathroom €31/51) Just off Corso Vittorio Emanuele II and the Duomo, you'll need to call ahead; the Nuovo is a perennial budget favourite in a city that doesn't care much for 'cheap'. A good deal at great rates for the simple yet comfortable rooms.

Eating

If you're looking for a traditional trattoria, try streets south of the station and along Corso Buenos Aires.

Osteria del Lazzaretto (☎ /fax 02 669 6234; Via Lazzaretto 15; 3-course menu €9; ◷ lunch & dinner) Fantastic, understated restaurant whose daily special is a gobsmacking bargain. Heaping portions and gracious service, all in a rustic dining room on a quiet street off Viale Tunisia. Try the authentically eggy carbonara – it's a myth the dish contains cream.

La Risacca Blu (☎ 02 20480964; www.larisaccablu .it, in Italian; Viale Tunisia 13; mains €12-15; ◷ lunch Wed-Sun, dinner Tue-Sun) Splash out on a fish or shellfish feast at La Risacca, a fabulous seafood restaurant serving delights such as crayfish with *pilaf* rice (€16). The mouth-watering marine morsels are augmented `by a great wine list and elegant, semi-formal dining rooms.

Ristorante Pizzeria Sabatini (☎ 02 29 40 28 14; www.ristorantesabatini.com; Via Boscovich 54; pizzas €15; ◷ lunch & dinner Mon-Sat) Around the corner from Corso Buenos Aires, this large, bland place does superior pizzas, more than compensating for the lack of ambience. Pasta and other mains are also available; seafood is a speciality.

Adulis Restaurant/Pau Brasil (☎ 02 29 51 58 16; Via Melzo 24; mains €12-16; ◷ lunch & dinner Tue-Sun) This Brazilian/Eritrean restaurant is great when you're all pizza and pastad out. A social and dining hub for afro-*sudamericano* expats, the atmosphere is as warm and inviting as the food. Great spicy rice and meat dishes at fair prices.

ITALY

Paper Moon (☎ 02 796 083; Via Bagutta 1; mains €10-15; ✓ Mon-Sat) It may be 'only' a paper moon, but it's well worth seeking for its understated dishes, many vegetarian.

Pastarito (☎ 02 86 22 10; Via Verdi 6; mains €10) A chain restaurant (along with Pizzarito, usually adjacent) that compensates for a subdued atmosphere with huge portions and dependable quality. It's €1 to €2 extra for fresh (handmade) pasta; pay – it tastes better and cooks faster.

There are two supermarkets in Stazione Centrale, one on the upper level and one on the western side, as well as other **supermarkets** (Via D Vitruvio 32 & Via Casati 30) close by.

Drinking

Bar Brera (☎ 02 877091; Via Brera 23; cocktail €6) Relaxed rendezvous nook before a night's dining and dancing, in the artsy precinct. Low-key and friendly.

Casablanca (☎ 02 62690186; Corso Como 14) 'Loop it, Sam' – a more appropriate paraphrase at this DJ-fuelled doof-den evoking the Bogey classic. Faux colonial décor; chic despite the potted palms.

Gattopardo (☎ 02 34537699; www.gattopardocafé .com; Via Piero della Francesca 47; ✓ 6pm-4am; happy-hour buffet €6) Elitist, looks-based entry is the only admission price to one of Milan's hottest nightspots; if you got 'it', bring it!

Shu (☎ 02 58315720; www.shucafé.it, in Italian; Via della Chiusa) This place is awesomely hipper than thou but bearably so, with cool art on the walls and foxy cocktails. If you're feeling fly – Shu.

Entertainment

Music, theatre and cinema dominate Milan's entertainment calendar. The opera season at **Teatro alla Scala** (☎ 02 86 07 75; www.teatroallascala.org) runs from 7 December through to July. The **box office** (☎ 02 72 0 37 44; Galleria del Sagrato, Piazza del Duomo; ✓ noon-6pm Sep–mid-Jul) is in the metro underpass beneath Piazza del Duomo.

Nightlife is centred on Brera and, further south, Navigli. The club scene is exclusive, policed vigilantly by local fashionistas. Consult *Hello Milano* or *Milano Mese*, or ask in hip shops about what's on. Note that most Italian bartenders don't use spirit measures, preferring the showy skilfulness of free-pouring, so cocktails can be 'potent'!

Football fans must visit the San Siro (official name Stadio Olympico Meazza), home-

ground of both AC Milan (the *rossoneri*, 'red and blacks') and Inter (the *ner'azzuri*, 'black and blues'). Local rivalry is savage: confusing the two *will* offend. Tickets (from €15) are available at branches of Cariplo (AC Milan) and Banca Popolare di Milano (Inter) banks.

Shopping

Looking good is religion; shopping is nearly a blood sport in Milan, and it's not cheap. Hit the streets behind the Duomo around Corso Vittorio Emanuele II for clothing, footwear and accessories, or window-shop along Via Monte Napoleone, Via della Spiga and Via Borgospesso. Street markets are held around the canals, notably on Viale Papiniano on Tuesday and Saturday morning. There's a **flea market** (Viale Gabriele d'Annunzio) each Saturday, and an **antique market** (Via Fiori Chiari) in Brera every third Saturday.

Getting There & Away

AIR

Most international flights use Malpensa Airport, about 50km northwest of Milan. Domestic and some European flights use Linate Airport, about 7km east of the city. Call **flight information** (☎ 02 74 85 22 00).

CAR & MOTORCYCLE

Milan is the major junction of Italy's motorways: the A1 (Rome), A4 (Milan–Turin), A7 (Milan–Genoa), the Serenissima (Verona and Venice) and the A8/A9 north to the lakes and Swiss border. All these join the Milan ring road – the Tangenziale Est and Tangenziale Ovest (the east and west bypasses). All roads are well marked. The A4 is very busy; accidents delay traffic interminably. In winter all roads can become hazardous.

TRAIN

Regular trains depart Stazione Centrale for Venice, Florence, Bologna, Genoa, Turin, Rome and major European cities. For **timetable information** (☎ 848 88 80 88; ✓ 7am-9pm), call or visit the office in Stazione Centrale (English spoken). Regional trains stop at Stazione Porta Garibaldi and Stazione Nord in Piazzale Cadorna on the MM2 line.

Getting Around

TO/FROM THE AIRPORT

STAM buses leave for Linate Airport from Piazza Luigi di Savoia, on the east side of

Stazione Centrale (€1.80, every 30 minutes 5.40am to 9.35pm) or use local bus No 73 from Piazza San Babila (€1, 20 minutes). For Malpensa Airport, the Malpensa Shuttle and Malpensa Bus Express both depart from Piazza Luigi di Savoia (€4 to €5, 50 minutes to one hour, every 20 minutes 4.30am to 12.15am). Buses also link the airports (hourly, 8am to 9.30pm). The Malpensa Express train connects Malpensa Airport with Cadorna underground station (€9.30, 40 minutes, 5.50am to 8.20pm from Cadorna, buses 8.20pm to 11.10pm).

BUS & METRO
Milan's public transport is excellent, with underground (MM), tram and bus services (tickets €1 for one ride and/or 75 minutes on buses and trams). Buy tickets at MM stations and most tobacconists and newsstands.

CAR & MOTORCYCLE
Entering Milan by car or motorcycle niggles, and the city car parks are expensive. An alternative is using one of the supervised car parks at the last stop on each MM line. In the centre there are private garages (€3 per hour). If your car is clamped or towed, call the **Polizia Municipale** (☎ 02 772 72 59). Hertz, Avis, Maggiore and Europcar all have offices at Stazione Centrale.

TAXI
Don't hail passing taxis; they won't stop. Head for the taxi ranks, which have telephones, or call one of numerous radio **taxi companies** (☎ 02 40 40, 02 52 51, 02 53 53, 02 83 83 or 02 85 85).

MANTUA
pop 48,000
Poised quietly beside Lake Superior, Mantua is associated with the Gonzaga family, who ruled from 1328 until 1707. These days, Mantua is considered a stronghold of Umberto Bossi's separatist *Lega Nord* party, though you'd barely notice in this sleepy township if it weren't for the odd spot of tepid graffiti. The sumptuous Gonzaga palaces justify a detour.

Information
Tourist office (☎ 0376 32 82 53; www.aptmantova.it, in Italian; Piazza Andrea Mantegna 6; ☙ 8.30am-12.30pm & 3-6pm Mon-Sat, 9.30am-12.30pm Sun) A short walk from the station along Corso Vittorio Emanuele, which becomes Corso Umberto 1.

Sights
Impressive buildings surround Piazza Sordello, including the eclectic **cattedrale**, but the focal point is the **Palazzo Ducale** (adult/concession €6.50/3.25; ☙ 8.45am-7.15pm Tue-Sun), the massive former seat of the Gonzaga family. Amongst its 500 rooms and 15 courtyards, its showpieces include the Gonzagas' private apartments and art collection, and the **Camera degli Sposi** (Bridal Chamber), with frescoes by Mantegna. The weekend **market** sprawls across four piazzas, and is more diverse than similar fare in cities twice Mantua's size.

Sleeping & Eating
Hotel ABC (☎ 0376 32 23 29; www.hotelabcmantova.it; Piazza Don Leoni 25; s €44-77, d €66-110) Conveniently located opposite the train station, Hotel ABC is basic but sufficient. Breakfast is included. All rooms feature TV, telephone and en-suite bathroom.

Osteria Vecchia Mantova (Piazza Sordello 26; 2-course menu €13-20; ☙ lunch & dinner Tue-Sun) This place is small and elegant, with rustic local specialities – such as the sensational pumpkin tortellini (€6.50) – at unbeatable prices.

Ristorante Pavesi (☎ 0376 32 36 27; Piazza delle Erbe 13; set menu €34) If all the Gonzaga luxury has stirred your sense of indulgence, Pavesi is the place; the classic Lombardy menu oozes as much class as the ambience, complemented by a fab wine list.

Getting There & Away
Mantua is accessible by train and bus from Verona (40 minutes), and by train from Milan and Bologna (change at Modena).

VERONA
pop 256,100
One of Italy's prettiest cities, Verona is perpetually associated with Romeo and Juliet. But the city was an important Roman centre long before the Della Scala (aka the Scaligeri) family took the reins around the mid-13th century, a period noted for the savage feuding between families, particularly the Guelphs and Ghibellines, on which Shakespeare based his tragedy. In centuries past, Verona was even referred to as *piccola Roma* ('little Rome').

ITALY

Leave your preconceptions about *that* balcony aside, however, and you may just fall in love with Verona's real stars – its charming pedestrianised centre and amazing amphitheatre.

Buses to the centre leave from the train station; otherwise, it's a 2km walk. Turn right to leave the station, cross the river and follow Corso Porta Nuova to Piazza Brà.

Information
Ask at the tourist office about the **Verona Card** (1/3 days €8/12) if you're cramming lots of sightseeing into a short time.

Internet Fast (☎ 045 803 32 12; Via Oberdan 16/b; per hr €4; ☼ 10am-10pm Mon-Fri, to 8pm Sat & 2-8pm Sun)

Post office (Piazza Viviani)

Tourist offices Via degli Alpini 9 (☎ 045 806 86 80; info@tourism.verona.it; ☼ 9am-6pm Mon-Sat, to 2pm Sun); Train station (☎ 045 800 08 61; ☼ 9am-6pm Mon-Sat); Airport (☎ 045 861 91 63; ☼ 11am-5pm Mon-Sat)

Sights
Piazza Brà's Roman **amphitheatre**, known simply as the 'Arena', dates from the 1st century and is the world's third largest. Not as big as Rome's, but well preserved, it's now Verona's opera house, and regularly hosts contemporary artists from Pink Floyd to Bjork.

Walk along Via Mazzini to Via Cappello and the **Casa di Giulietta** (Juliet's House; ☎ 045 803 5645; Via Capello 23; courtyard free; Capulet museum €3; ☼ 9am-6.30pm Tue-Sun), where the balcony overlooks a graffiti-covered courtyard and statue of Juliet. Romantic superstition suggests that rubbing Juliet's 'heart' brings you a new lover. Further along the street is **Porta Leoni**, one of the gates to the old Roman Verona; the other, **Porta Borsari**, is north of the Arena.

The former site of the Roman forum, **Piazza delle Erbe** is lined with palaces and filled with questionable market stalls. Nearby is the elegant (and much quieter) **Piazza dei Signori**, flanked by the medieval town hall and the Della Scala (Scaligeri) residence, partly decorated by Giotto and nowadays known as the **Governor's Palace**.

Sleeping
Ostello Villa Francescatti (☎ 045 59 03 60; fax 045 800 9127; Salita Fontana del Ferro 15; dm incl breakfast €14, 2-course menu €8.50) Among the best HI hostels in Italy, this 500-year-old former church has vaulted roofs and remnants of original frescoes on some walls. Wonderfully evocative. A hostel/student card is required. Take bus No 73 from the station.

Hotel Aurora (☎ 045 597 834; www.hotelaurora.biz; Piazza Erbe; d €117, s/d with shared bathroom €56/108; ☒ ☒ ▢) Right on the city's prettiest piazza is this fantastic option. Most rooms have views and all are well-appointed. Great buffet breakfast included.

Hotel All'Antica Porta Leona (☎ 045 59 54 99; fax 045 59 52 14; htlanticaportaleona@tiscalinet.it; Corticella Leoni 3; s/d €91/129; ℗ ☒ ☒) Bright, airy rooms are the signature of the once glorious, still good Porta Leona. Well located with superb amenities.

Eating
Boiled meats are a Veronese speciality, as is the crisp Soave white wine.

Hosteria All'Orso (☎ 045 597214; Via Sottoriva 3/c; mains €14-20; ☼ lunch Tue-Sat, dinner Mon-Sat) A warm, friendly restaurant nestled under the Sottoriva porticoes, serving hearty Veronese and northern Italian staples within a shout of the river. In the heart of Verona's nightlife district, it's the perfect place to kick off with a substantial meal and drinks.

Trattoria All'Isolo (☎ 045 59 42 91; Piazza dell'Isolo 5a; menus €12) Dodge the tourist crowds and eat with a Veronese one, across the river at this pleasant place, which has challenging meat dishes: adventurers could try the horse-meat pie or the donkey stew.

Il Desco (☎ 045 801 00 15; Via Dietro San Sebastiano 7; mains €60-90; ☼ Tue-Sat & lunch Sun) Among Italy's finest restaurants, this Michelin-starred stunner is the perfect place to dine. Il Desco's reputation is as grand as the décor. Try the amazing *petto di faraone con purea di topinambur, salsa all'aceto balsamico e cioccolato* (breast of guinea fowl with Jerusalem artichoke purée and a chocolate and balsamic sauce).

Drinking & Entertainment
Verona hosts events throughout the year, culminating in a season of opera and drama at the **Arena** (www.arena.it; tickets from €21.50; ☼ Jul-Sep). There is a winter lyric-symphonic season at the 18th-century **Teatro Filarmonico** (☎ 800 28 80; Via dei Mutilati 4; Box Office ☎ 045 8005151; www.arena.it; Via Dietro Anfiteatro 6b).

For bar/late action, head for Via Sottoriva, which has a variety of carousing options.

Two goodies are the bizarrely cool 'life-style-bar' **square** (☎ 045 597 120; Via Sottoriva 15; ❤ 6.30pm-2am Mon-Fri, 3.30pm-2am Sat & Sun), whose DJ-assisted options include shiatsu massage, perusing elegant homewares, sipping swanky cocktails, fusion snacks and free Internet, or the more traditional **Sottoriva 23** (☎ 045 800 99 04; Via Sottoriva 23; ❤ 10-2am), a cosy, low-lit cavern for drinks and chatter, usually rammed with friendly locals.

Getting There & Around

The **Verona-Villafranca airport** (☎ 045 809 56 66) is 16km away, accessible by bus and train. The APT airport bus (€4.20, every 20 minutes) departs from the train station. Bus Nos 11, 12, 13 and 14 (Nos 91, 92 and 98 on Sunday) connect the station (bus stop A) with Piazza Brà, and Nos 72 and 73 go to Piazza delle Erbe. The main bus station is in the piazza in front of Porta Nuova train station. Buses service surrounding towns, including Mantua, Ferrara and Brescia.

Verona is on the Brenner Pass train line to Austria/Germany, and directly linked by rail to Milan, Venice, Florence and Rome. There's a free car park in Via Città di Nimes.

PADUA

pop 211,500

In millennia past, the most compelling reason to visit Padua was to see the tomb of Saint Anthony. These days, it's to marvel at Giotto's restored frescoes in the Cappella degli Scrovegni (Scrovegni Chapel), among the world's greatest works of figurative art. Masterpieces aside, Padua is a pleasant city, and – thanks to the students attending its university – always lively and engaging.

Orientation & Information

It's a 15-minute walk from the train station to the centre, or take bus No 3 or 8 along Corso del Popolo (which becomes Corso Garibaldi). Padua's centre is easily covered on foot.

The **padovacard** (1 adult & 1 child €13) provides discounts on many sights and all public transport for 48 hours. Pick one up at the tourist office.

There is a **post office** (Corso Garibaldi 33), and a number of **tourist offices** (Train station ☎ 049 875 20 77; ❤ 9.15am-6.30pm Mon-Sat, 9am-12.30pm Sun); Galleria Pedrocchi (☎ 049 876 79 27; ❤ 9am-12.30pm & 3-7pm Mon-Sat) around town.

Sights

The **Cappella degli Scrovegni** (☎ 049 201 00 20; www.cappelladegliscrovegni.it; Piazza Eremitani 8; admission €12, free Mar 25; ❤ 9am-7pm, 30 min entry) is Padua's highlight, housing Giotto's transcendent frescoes. The 38 glorious panels movingly depict Christ's life. Booking ahead is mandatory, as is arriving at the chapel 10 minutes prior to your appointed time. The ticket accesses the neighbouring **Musei Civici agli Eremitani** (☎ 049 829 4550; www.padovanet.it/museicivici, in Italian; ❤ 9am-6pm Tue-Sun winter, to 7pm spring-autumn).

Thousands of pilgrims annually seek out Padua's **Basilica di Sant'Antonio** (St Anthony's Basilica) in the hope that St Anthony, patron saint of lost things (and Padua), will help them find whatever they're looking for. The saint's gaudy **tomb** is in the basilica, along with 14th-century frescoes, and sculptures by Donatello adorning the high altar. Just outside the basilica is an equestrian statue, the *Gattamelata* (Honeyed Cat), also by Donatello.

Sleeping

Ostello della Città di Padova (☎ /fax 049 654 210; www.ctgveneto.it/ostello, in Italian; Via A Aleardi 30; dm incl breakfast €15.50) The HI hostel is a five-minute bus ride from the station. Take bus No 3, 8 or 12 to Prato della Valle and then ask for directions.

Hotel Sant'Antonio (☎ 049 875 13 93; www.hotelsantantonio.it; Via Santo Fermo 118; s/d €60/80, s with shared bathroom €40; ✜) In a fabulous central location near the river, all of the rooms in this neat-as-a-pin place are as comfy as they are charming, and all have TV, telephone and en-suite facilities.

Koko Nor Association (☎ 049 864 33 94; www.bandb-veneto.it/kokonor; Via Selva 5; s/d from around €35/60) This is a good organisation to consult if you're after the privacy (and often friendlier touch) of lodging in *affittacamere* – rented rooms in private family homes. Also try the tourist office, which keeps similar lists of families offering such services.

Eating

Dalla Zita (Via Gorizia 16; panini from €2.30) A great sandwich bar, popular with local workers and skint students alike. Value and quality are matched only by the variety; the details of over 100 types of *panini* cover the place more like wallpaper than a menu.

Godenda (☎ 049 877 41 92; www.godenda.it, in Italian; Via Squarcini 4/6; mains €10-15; ☺ lunch & dinner) A combination gourmet-everything locale, including a wine bar (more than 300 labels), a great sampling/tasting restaurant, and dozens of delicious pre-prepared takeaway dishes (sold by weight) to tempt the taste buds.

Pe Pen (☎ 049 875 94 83; www.pepen.it, in Italian; Piazza Cavour 15; pizza & pasta €10-12; ☺ lunch & dinner) This is the last word in Padua posh nosh. Try Umbrian speciality *tagliolini* (hand-cut fresh pasta) with stunning variations such as *con ostriche e porri* (with oysters and leeks).

Getting There & Away

Padua has direct rail links to Milan, Venice and Bologna, and is easily accessible from other major cities. Buses serve Venice, Milan, Trieste and surrounding towns. The **bus terminal** (Piazzale Boschetti) is off Via Trieste, near the train station. There is a car park in Prato della Valle, a massive piazza near the Basilica del Santo.

VENICE

pop 272,100

It throws one of the best parties on earth (Carnevale), and you can drown crossing its roads. There's no doubt that Venice is extraordinary. In no other city is fantasy and reality so artfully combined. Ever since Casanova set the romance myth rolling, travellers, writers and even dictators have been beguiled by La Serenissima (the Most Serene Republic). Writers from Byron to Henry James to contemporary best-seller Jeanette Winterson have used Venice to bewitching effect. Even Napoleon pronounced Piazza San Marco (St Mark's Square) 'the finest drawing room in Europe'.

Obviously Venice wasn't always a living museum. The lagoon's islands were settled during barbarian invasions around 1500 years ago, when the Veneto's inhabitants sought refuge in the area, building the city on pole foundations pounded into the marshy subsoil. Following centuries of Byzantine rule, Venice evolved into a republic ruled by a succession of doges (chief magistrates) and enjoyed a period of independence that lasted 1000 years. It was the point where east met west, and the city grew in power to dominate half the Mediterranean, the Adriatic and the trade routes to the Levant. It was from Ven-

ice that Marco Polo set out on his voyage to China in 1271

Today, delivery boats jostle chintzy gondolas, endless stalls tout bogus Carnevale masks, and the pigeons are only outnumbered by the swarms of tourists picking through all the wonderment. Regular flooding (*acqua alte*, 'high tides') and sky-high property prices make it a difficult place to actually live: most 'locals' commute from Mestre, linked by the bridge across the lagoon.

The secret to discovering Venice is walking. Dorsoduro and Castello rarely see many tourists; you can lose yourself for hours in the streets between the Accademia and the train station. Another groovy gambit is choosing your hours strategically; even San Marco, the glorious centrepiece heaving with thousands daily, is basically empty from midnight to dawn. At such moonlit moments, you'll be suddenly and irrevocably seduced by the Queen of the Seas.

Orientation

Venice is built on 117 islands with 150-odd canals and 400 bridges. Only three bridges cross the Canal Grande (Grand Canal): the Rialto, the Accademia and, at the train station, the Scalzi. To cross the Grand Canal between the bridges, use a *traghetto* (basically a public gondola, but much cheaper).

The city is divided into six *sestieri* (quarters): Cannaregio, Castello, San Marco, Dorsoduro, San Polo and Santa Croce. A street can be a *calle, ruga* or *salizzada;* beside a canal it's a *fondamenta*. A canal is a *rio;* a filled canal-turned-street a *rio terra*. The only square in Venice called a *piazza* is San Marco – all the others are called *campo*. Venice's street numbering is unique, too. Instead of a system based on individual streets, each *sestiere* has a series of numbers; addresses are virtually meaningless unless you're a Venetian postie. Getting lost is inevitable – enjoy!

Public transport is via the canals, on *vaporetti* (water buses). The other mode of transportation is your feet. Walking from the *ferrovia* (train station) to San Marco along the main thoroughfare, Lista di Spagna (whose name changes frequently), takes about 30 minutes – follow the signs to San Marco. From San Marco the routes to the Rialto, the Accademia and the train station are well signposted but confusing, particularly in Dorsoduro and San Polo.

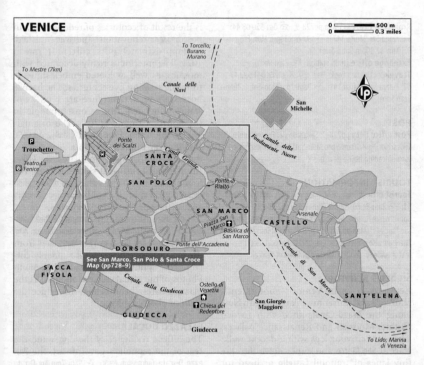

VENICE

0 — 500 m
0 — 0.3 miles

To Torcello;
Burano;
Murano

To Mestre (7km)

Canale delle
Navi

San
Michelle

P
Tronchetto

Ponte
dei Scalzi

CANNAREGIO

Canale delle
Fondamente
Nuove

Teatro La
Fenice

SANTA
CROCE

Canal Grande

SAN POLO

Ponte di
Rialto

SAN MARCO

Piazza San
Marco

Basilica di
San Marco

Arsenale

CASTELLO

DORSODURO

Ponte dell'Accademia

See San Marco, San Polo & Santa Croce
Map (pp728–9)

SACCA
FISOLA

Canale della Giudecca

Ostello di
Venezia

Chiesa del
Redentore

San Giorgio
Maggiore

Canale di San Marco

SANT'ELENA

GIUDECCA

Giudecca

To Lido; Marina
di Venezia

Information

There are two types of discount cards available from tourist offices and various outlets. The **Rolling Venice Card** (☎ 041 241 39 08; €3) is for visitors aged 14 to 29; it offers discounts on food, accommodation, shopping, transport and museums. You'll need your passport and a colour photograph. The **Venice Card** (☎ 041 2424; www.venicecard.it; blue card under 29 yrs 1/3/7 days €9/22/49, over 29 yrs €14/29/51; orange card under 29 yrs €18/35/61, over 29 yrs €28/47/68) is a multipurpose pass for museums, public transport, car parks and restrooms. The Venice Card *isn't* always a saving, so check its coverage against your itinerary before spending.

INTERNET ACCESS

There are tons of Internet cafés in Venice, none cheap. The airport is a Wi-Fi hotspot.
Casanova (Map pp728–9; ☎ 041 524 06 64; Rio Tera Lista di Spagna, Cannaregio 158/a; per hr €7; ⏱ 9am-11.30pm) A cheesy club and combined webcafé in one, close to the station.
Netgate (Map pp728–9; ☎ 041 244 02 13; Calle dei Preti Crosera 3812, Dorsoduro; per hr €6; ⏱ 10.15am-8pm Mon-Fri, to 10pm Sat, 2.15-10pm Sun)

Nethouse (Map pp728–9; ☎ 041 277 11 90; Campo Santo Stefano 2967; per 20min/1hr €3/9; ⏱ 24hr) Nethouse has tons of screens, plus printing and fax services.
Planet Internet (Map pp728–9; ☎ 041 524 41 88; Rio Tera San Leonardo, Cannaregio 1520; per hr €7; ⏱ 8am-11pm) Good central location; the perfect place to surf while doing laundry.

LAUNDRY

Speedy Wash (Map pp728–9; Rio Tera San Leonardo, Cannaregio 1520; 8kg wash/dry €4.50/3; ⏱ 9am-10pm) Strangely, laundry is cheaper here than anywhere else in Italy.

MEDICAL & EMERGENCY SERVICES

Emergency (☎ 112) An emergency service in foreign languages run by the *carabinieri*.
Ospedale Civile (Map pp728–9; ☎ 041 529 41 11; Campo SS Giovanni e Paolo)
Police station (Questura; Map pp728–9; ☎ 041 271 55 11; Fondamenta di San Lorenzo, Castello 5053) Handles thefts etc.

MONEY

Most major banks have branches in the area around the Rialto and San Marco.

American Express (Map pp728-9; ☎ 041 520 08 44; Salizzada San Moisè 1471; ☑ 9am-5.30pm Mon-Fri, 9.30am-12.30pm Sat & Sun)
Exchange office (train station; ☑ 7am-9pm)
Travelex (Thomas Cook; Map pp728-9; ☎ 041 522 47 51; Piazza San Marco 141; ☑ 9am-7pm Mon-Sat, 9.30am-5pm Sun)

POST
Post office (Map pp728-9; Salizzada del Fontego dei Tedeschi; ☑ 8.10am-7pm Mon-Sat) In an atmospheric former trading house near the Rialto.

TOURIST INFORMATION
Tourist offices Train station (Map pp728-9; ☎ 041 529 87 11; ☑ 8am-8pm); Piazzale Roma (Map pp728-9; ☑ 8am-8pm); Venice Pavilion (Map pp728-9; ☑ 10am-6pm); Piazza San Marco 71f (Map pp728-9; ☑ 9.45am-3.15pm Mon-Sat) There are also offices at the Lido and the airport. Get the useful guide *Un Ospite di Venezia* (A Guest of Venice).

Sights & Activities
Before you visit Venice's monuments, churches and museums, take vaporetto No 1 along the **Grand Canal**, lined with rococo Gothic, Moorish and Renaissance palaces. Then stretch your legs with a decent walk: start at **San Marco** and either delve into the tiny lanes of tranquil **Castello** or head for the **Ponte dell'Accademia** (Accademia Bridge) to reach the narrow streets and squares of **Dorsoduro** and **San Polo**.

Most museums are closed Monday.

PIAZZA & BASILICA DI SAN MARCO
The stunning Piazza San Marco is enclosed by the basilica and the elegant arcades of the **Procuratie Vecchie** and **Procuratie Nuove**. While you're taking it all in, you might see the bronze *mori* (Moors) strike the bell of the 15th-century **Torre dell'Orologio** (clock tower). Venice's lowest point, the Piazza is the first place to flood when tides rise. In *acque alte* of epochs past, the *gondolieri* could punt across the square itself!

From a distance, it looks like some sort of glorious ice-cream cake, but the **Basilica di San Marco** (St Mark's Basilica; Map pp728-9) was built to house St Mark's body. Stolen from his Egyptian burial place and smuggled to Venice in a barrel of pork, the saint has been reburied several times, his body now resting under the high altar. The present basilica, with its spangled spires, Byzantine domes and façade of mosaics and marble,

is the result of centuries of redesigning and postdisaster renovations and was 'finished' in (approximately) its current form in 1071. The interior is richly decorated with mosaics, as well as looted embellishments from the ensuing five centuries. The bronze horses above the entrance are replicas of statues 'liberated' from Constantinople in the Fourth Crusade (1204). The originals are in the basilica's **Galleria** (admission €1.55). You'll never forget you're in a floating city; the 12th-century floor undulates, wavelike, from centuries of tidal shifts affecting the foundation. Don't miss the **Pala d'Oro** (adult/child €1.50/1), a stunning gold altarpiece decorated with countless priceless jewels.

The 99m freestanding **campanile** (bell tower; Map pp728-9; adult/child €6/3; ☑ 9am-9pm late Jun-Aug, to 7pm Apr-Jun & Sep-Oct, to 4pm Nov-Mar) dates from the 10th century, although it suddenly collapsed on 14 July 1902 and had to be rebuilt. Photos of the actual collapse abound, as the piazza's barely been camera-free since the birth of photography.

PALAZZO DUCALE
The official residence of the doges and the seat of the republic's government, the **Palazzo Ducale** (admission €9.50; ☑ 9am-7pm Apr-Oct, to 5pm Nov-Mar, ticket office closed 4.30pm) also housed municipal officials and Venice's prisons. The **Sala del Maggior Consiglio** features paintings by Tintoretto and Veronese. Tickets also cover entry to the Museo Correr (for Venetian art and history), Biblioteca Marciana and Museo Archeologico. A surcharge (€6) covers the Palazzo Mocenigo (San Stae area), and Burano and Murano museums.

The **Ponte dei Sospiri** (Bridge of Sighs) connects the palace to the old dungeons, and evokes romantic images, possibly through association with Casanova, a Venetian native who languished in the cells. Far bleaker is the real reason for the sighing; the sadness of condemned prisoners en route to their executions, seeing Venice for the last time.

GALLERIA DELL'ACCADEMIA
Tracing the development of Venetian art, the **Galleria dell'Accademia** (Academy of Fine Arts; Map pp728-9; ☎ 041 522 2247; adult €6.50, EU citizens 18-25 yrs €3.25, child under 12 yrs & EU citizens under 18 & over 65 yrs free; ☑ 8.15am-2pm Mon, to 7.15pm Tue-Sun) includes masterpieces by Bellini, Titian, Carpaccio, Tintoretto, Giorgione and Veronese.

COLLEZIONE PEGGY GUGGENHEIM

For a change of pace and style, visit the **Collezione Peggy Guggenheim** (Map pp728-9; ☎ 041 240 54 11; www.guggenheim-venice.it; Palazzo Venier dei Leoni, Dorsoduro 701; adult €8, student & child €5; ☺ 10am-6pm Wed-Fri & Sun-Mon, to 10pm Sat), displayed in the American heiress' former home. The brilliant collection runs the gamut of modern art (Bacon, Pollock, Picasso, Dali, Magritte and more) and the *palazzo* is in a sculpture garden where Peggy and her dogs are buried.

CHURCHES

Venice has many gorgeous churches, most boasting an art treasure or two. The excellent **Chorus Pass** (adult €8, student & child €5) gets you into 15 of them; ask at a tourist office.

The **Chiesa del Redentore** (Church of the Redeemer; Map p725; Giudecca) was built by Palladio to commemorate the end of the great plague (1576) and is the scene of the annual Festa del Redentore (see p727). Longhena's **Chiesa di Santa Maria della Salute** (Map pp728-9) 'guards' the Grand Canal's entrance and contains works by Tintoretto and Titian. Definitely visit the great Gothic churches **SS Giovanni e Paolo** (Map pp728-9), with its glorious stained-glass windows, and the **Frari** (pp728-9), home to Titian's tomb and his uplifting *Assumption*.

THE LIDO

This thin strip of land separating Venice from the Adriatic is easily accessible by vaporetto Nos 1, 6, 14, 61 and 82. Once *the* most fashionable resort and still very popular – it's almost impossible to find a space on the beach in summer.

ISLANDS

The island of **Murano** is the home of Venetian glass. Tour a factory for a behind-the-scenes look at production, or visit the **Glassworks Museum** to see its exquisite historical pieces. **Burano**, still a relatively sleepy fishing village, is renowned for its lace and colourful houses. **Torcello**, the republic's original island settlement, was abandoned due to malaria. Little remains on the hauntingly deserted island besides the Byzantine cathedral, its mosaics intact. Vaporetto No 12 services all three from Fondamente Nuove.

GONDOLAS

Ask yourself what price for romance, and the rather alarming answer is €62 (€77.45 after 8pm) for a 50-minute ride. These are the official rates and are valid for the gondola (which can carry six people), not per person; it's entirely acceptable to split a gondola with friends.

Festivals & Events

Carnevale Venice's famed last-knees-up-before-Lent. Everyone dons spectacular masks and costumes for a 10-day street party.

Feste del' Laure Students lampoon their graduating comrades in March and November by putting up caricatured posters all over town, and singing while parading drunkenly through the streets.

Festa del Redentore (Festival of the Redeemer) Held on the third weekend in July to celebrate the plague's end; features a spectacular fireworks display.

Regata Storica A wildly colourful gondola race on the Grand Canal; held on the first Sunday in September.

Venice Biennale A major, year-long exhibition of international visual arts; held every even-numbered year.

Venice International Film Festival Italy's take on Cannes; held in September at the atmospheric Palazzo del Cinema, on the Lido

Sleeping

Venice is Italy's most pricey city. Prices are highest in peak periods (Christmas, Carnevale, Easter and the height of summer). Always book ahead. Litorale del Cavallino, northeast of the city on the Adriatic coast, has numerous camping grounds, many with bungalows.

BUDGET

Ostello di Venezia (Map p725; ☎ 041 523 82 11; fax 041 523 56 89; Fondamenta delle Zitelle 86; dm €16, dinner €8; ☺ curfew 11.30pm) On the island of Giudecca, the HI hostel is for members only, although you can buy membership there. Take vaporetto No 41, 42 or 82 from the station, alighting at Zitelle.

Foresteria Valdese (Map pp728-9; ☎ 041 528 67 97; fax 041 241 6238; Castello 5170; dm €20, d €75, d with shared bathroom €55) Behave yourself at this popular option in the former Palazzo Cavagnis. Follow Calle Lunga from Campo Santa Maria Formosa.

Ostello Santa Fosca (Map pp728-9; ☎ 041 71 57 75; cpu@iuav.unive.it; Cannaregio 2372; dm €18, s/d with shared bathroom €21; ☺ check-in 5pm-8pm) Students and travellers on the cheap will feel at home in these basic university dorms less than 15 minutes from the station through Campo Santa Fosca.

SAN MARCO, SAN POLO & SANTA CROCE

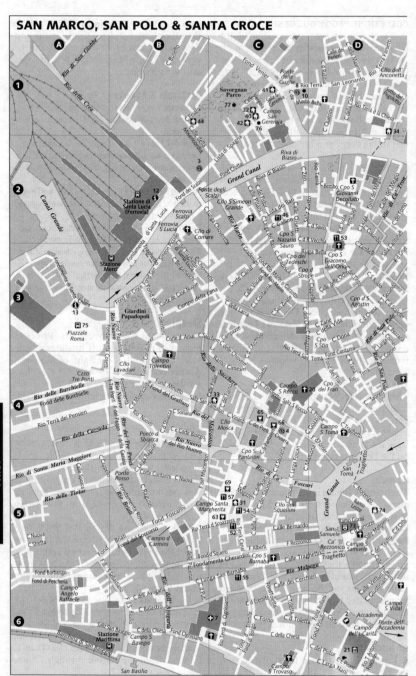

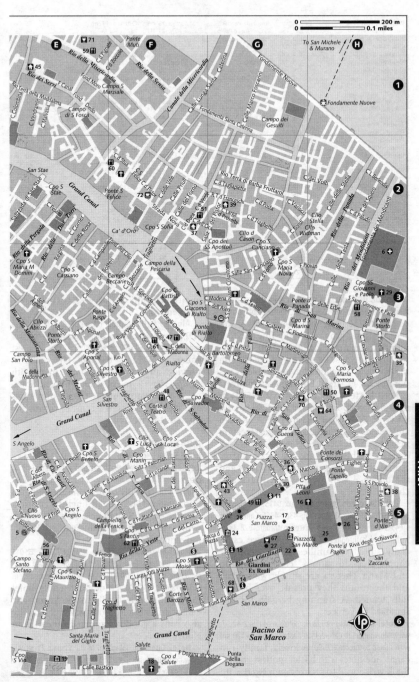

Marina di Venezia (☎ 041 530 09 55; camping@marinadivenezia.it; Via Montello 6, Punta Sabbioni; per person/tent €7.50/19; ⊗ mid-Apr–end Aug) A decent camping ground for the fine weather months, with many facilities (shop, cinema, playground) close by. It's out of the way, on the Littorale Cavallino, but accessible by vaporetto No 12 (from Fondamenta Nuove).

Hotel Marte & Biasin (☎ 041 522 72 57; Fondamenta di Cannaregio 338; d €65, s/d with shared bathroom €35/45; ✗ 😺) A pair of very basic but clean and friendly one-star hotels in a great location near the Ponte delle Guglie in Cannaregio. Beds are slightly limp and the appointments spartan, but rooms are clean and quiet and the bilingual staff are just lovely. It's also cheap.

Hotel Bernardo Semenzato (☎ 041 522 72 57; www.hotelbernardi.com; SS Apostoli, 4363-4366 Cannaregio; s €45-50, d €78-88, s with shared bathroom €28-33, d with shared bathroom €58-68) Sweet place especially suited to families, with a popular couple-plus-kids annex. Hosts Leonardo and Maria Theresa are simply wonderful, and the rooms they preside over beautifully tended. A stunning bargain for this standard in Venice.

Hotel Doni (Map pp728-9; ☎ /fax 041 522 42 67; www.albergodoni.it; Calle del Vin, Castello 4656; d €120, s/d with shared bathroom €60/90) A lovely, family-run canal-side hotel with basic, spotless rooms. Book well ahead to secure room No 8, with

an original 18th-century fresco. Highly recommended.

Albergo Antico Capon (Map pp728-9; ☎ 041 528 5292; www.casaperon.com; Campo Santa Margherita, Dorsoduro 3004b; s €25-90, d €45-90) In the coolest square in Venice, 'the old (fat) cockerel' provides airy, colourful rooms – many with *campo* views – to roost in. Opposite some of Venice's most understatedly fun cafés and cheap eateries, it's central, yet off the obvious tourist trail.

MID-RANGE

Hotel Santa Lucia (Map pp728-9; ☎ 041 71 51 80; www.hotelslucia.com; Calle della Misericordia, Cannaregio 358; d/tr/q from €110/140/170, s/d with shared bathroom from €60/70) The friendly owners and multilingual staff (Italian, French and English) ensure a carefree stay at Santa Lucia. Ask for a room with a view of the charming garden. Breakfast is included.

Hotel Minerva & Nettuno (Map pp728-9; ☎ 041 71 59 68; www.minervaenettuno.it; Lista di Spagna, Cannaregio 230; s/d/tr/q €58/92/114/136, with shared bathroom €50/61/80/98; ✗ 😺) Modest, friendly hotel run by the same family for 66 years. The half-board rates are worthwhile; the family also runs a good restaurant in the Ghetto Nuovo.

Hotel Guerrini (Map pp728-9; ☎ 041 71 53 33; www.hotelguerrini.it; Lista di Spagna, Cannaregio 265; d €110-140, tr €130-160, q €140-170, s with shared bathroom

€45-60, d with shared bathroom €65-85) With rooms ranging from simple singles without bathroom to lushly appointed suites, Guerrini has something for everyone.

Casa Gerotto & Alloggi Calderan (Map pp728-9; ☎ 041 71 55 62; www.casagerottocalderan.com; Campo San Geremia 283; dm/s/d/tr €21/46/90/108, s/d with shared bathroom €36/65) A popular choice, whether for the prices or location on a buzzing *campo* near a morning produce market. A pleasantly ramshackle atmosphere most suited to travellers used to the delightful chaos of hostelling. Single-sex dorms.

Hotel Noemi (Map pp728-9; ☎ 041 523 81 44; www.hotelnoemi.com; Calle dei Fabbri, San Marco 909; s/d/tr €100/150/200, s/d with shared bathroom from €40/50; ☒ ☒ ☐) Superbly located just 50m from Piazza San Marco is this comfy hotel. All rooms with en-suite bathroom, TV, telephone and pleasant décor.

Casa Peron (Map pp728-9; ☎ 041 71 10 21; www.casaperon.com; Salizzada San Pantalon, San Polo 84; s/d/tr €48/75/105) You get some idea of the relaxed atmosphere at Casa Peron after being greeted by Pierino, the owner's enormous parrot, presiding calmly over the reception. The place is no menagerie, though. Neat as a pin and in a lovely area close to happenin' Campo Santa Margherita.

Hotel ai Do Mori (Map pp728-9; ☎ 041 520 48 17; www.hotelaidomori.com; Calle Larga San Marco 658; s €50-100, d €80-135, d with shared bathroom €60-90; ☒ ☒) Up some alarmingly steep stairs, the rooms here have views of St Mark's, plus there's a breakfast terrace practically in the shadow of the campanile. Simple rooms and friendly staff make this sensational for the price.

TOP END

Hotel Giorgione (Map pp728-9; ☎ 041 522 58 10; www.hotelgiorgione.com; Calle Larga dei Proverbi, Campo SS Apostoli 4587; s from €105-173, d from €120-200, ste from €250; ☒ ☒ ☐) A sybaritic sensation, superb for splurging, this former 15th-century palace impresses. When you're not sightseeing, you can sip Bellinis in the billiard room, or a *sprizze* on the sun deck. Conservatively decorated rooms sport every luxury.

Ca' San Marcuola (Map pp728-9; ☎ 041 71 60 48; www.casanmarcuola.com; Cannaregio 1763; s €70-150, d €100-200, tr €130-250, q €160-300; ☒ ☒ ☐) Newly expanded, the marble interior of Ca' San Marcuola leads to fabulous rooms – many with *campo* views – matching varied budgets, but all featuring rococo Venetian décor and

mod cons. Free Internet and great breakfast included.

Eating

Wherever you choose to eat in Venice it will be expensive, but quality can vary greatly, so sniff around and be selective.There are good-value restaurants tucked away from the big landmarks, and excellent self-catering options. Staples of Venetian cuisine are rice and beans, and, naturally, seafood. Try *risotto con piselli* (risotto with baby peas) followed by a glass of *fragolino*, a fragrant strawberry wine.

RESTAURANTS

Pizza al Volo (Map pp728-9; ☎ 041 522 54 30; Campo Santa Margherita, Dorsoduro 2944; pizza slice €1.50, whole pizzas €4-6; ☯ lunch & dinner) Venice's favourite cheapie pizza takeaway serves slices the size of sails for under €2. The 'normal' pizza is enormous; don't even contemplate the *familiare* (family-size) unless you have friends handy.

Cip Ciap (Map pp728-9; ☎ 041 523 66 21; Calle del Mondo Novo, Castello, 5799; pizza slice €2.30) Cip Ciap is cheap and cheerful, just right for a quick takeaway pizza slice, and near buzzy Campo Santa Maria Formosa.

Ae Oche (Three Geese; Map pp728-9; ☎ 041 524 11 61; Calle del Tintor, Santa Croce 1552a/b; pizzas €7; ☯ lunch & dinner) Venice's best pizzeria; easily the most welcoming and always busy. Enjoy one of 90 (!) pizzas or its excellent pastas in the cosy saloon-style dining room. Then chase it all down with a little dollop of Venetian wonder: *sgroppino*. This cool, creamy, alcoholic lemon sorbet is *heavenly* after a meal.

Sahara (Map pp728-9; ☎ 041 72 10 77; Fondamenta della Misericordia, Cannaregio 2519; mains €10, set menus €20; ☯ lunch & dinner Tue-Sun) In what passes for a nightlife district in Cannaregio, Sahara is an excellent Arabic eatery offering an alternative to Italian food. The Syrian cooking is delicious, and there's belly dancing every Saturday night.

Vino Vino (Map pp728-9; ☎ 041 523 70 27; www.vinovino.co.it; Calle della Veste, San Marco 2007; mains €10; ☯ 10.30am-midnight Wed-Mon) At Ponte Veste, near Teatro La Fenice, this fantastic wine bar also does excellent food. Typical Venetian specialities abound; a great, moodily evocative place to try some polenta or *pasta con nero di seppia* (pasta in shellfish ink).

There's a choice of 350 wines available by the bottle/glass.

La Zucca (The Pumpkin; Map pp728-9; ☎ 041 524 15 70; San Giacomo dell'Orio, Santa Croce 1762; mains €10-16; 🕑 lunch & dinner Mon-Sat) A smashing *hosteria*, purveying innovative dishes using seasonal vegetables. The veg lasagne is stunning, the fennel in spicy olive sauce transcendent. Rabbit, wild fowl and even horse are also offered. Lovely rustic ambience and magnificent service make this tiny restaurant worth seeking. Book ahead.

Osteria ai 4 Ferri (Map pp728-9; ☎ 041 520 69 78; Calle Lunga San Barnaba, Dorsoduro 2754/a; mains €12-17; 🕑 lunch & dinner) A great *osteria* off Campo San Barnaba. 'The Four Irons' is well-respected for its regional seafood delights (fantastic scampi, prawns and shellfish). The mix of young owners and traditional outlook is successful; booking required.

Al Buso (Map pp728-9; ☎ 041 528 90 78; Ponte Di Rialto, San Marco 5338; set menus €15; 🕑 lunch & dinner) If you must eat by the Grand Canal, Venetians themselves recommend Al Buso, in the shadow of the Rialto (literally). The set menu is good; try the *spaghetti al scoglio* (spaghetti with seafood) for an ample, tasty meal.

Hosteria Ai Promessi Sposi (Map pp728-9; ☎ 041 522 86 09; Calle De L'Oca 4367; mains €15-20; 🕑 lunch & dinner Tue-Sun) Tucked away down a tiny alley is this lovely place where the mixed fish antipasti – among the many mouthwatering Venetian specialities displayed – is a thing of particular wonder. You're on Venetian time in this place where the old boys serving you glide around with graceful, practised ease.

Antica Carbonera (Map pp728-9; ☎ 041 22 54 79; Calle Bembo, San Marco 4648; mains €30; 🕑 lunch & dinner) This popular bar/*osteria* on the continuation of Calle dei Fabbri has old-school charm in spades. Ambience in abundance lies within its little booths, but at a price. Seafood is a speciality – the *tagliolini ai granseola* (hand-cut pasta with spider crab) is outstanding.

Trattoria alla Madonna (Map pp728-9; ☎ 041 522 38 24; Calle della Madonna 594; meal about €30; 🕑 lunch & dinner Thu-Tue) In a city of seafood restaurants, this one is among the best. You'll spend a bit, but there's no faulting the food or super-friendly service – it's great value at the price.

GELATI & PASTRIES

There's no shortage of great pastries and *gelato* in Venice.

Il Doge (Map pp728-9; ☎ 041 523 46 07; Campo Santa Margherita, Dorsoduro 3058/a; small/large gelato €1.50/3; 🕑 10-2am Feb-Nov) The finest *gelato* on the sweetest piazza.

Pasticceria Marchini (Map pp728-9; ☎ 041 522 91 09; www.golosessi.com; Calle Spadaria, San Marco 2769; 🕑 9am-10pm Mon-Sat) Popular, pricey spot for pastries just off Campo Santo Stefano. Kitschy but cute are Le Baute Veneziane – chocolates shaped like Carnevale masks.

Rosa Salva (Map pp728-9; ☎ 041 522 79 49; rsalva@doge.it; Campo SS Giovanni e Paolo, Castello 6779; 🕑 7.30am-8.30pm Thu-Tue) More than 100 years after launching as a 'travelling kitchen', delivering hot meals by gondola, Rosa Salva's reputation is unmatched; some of the best coffee and pastries in Venice can be enjoyed while perusing local artists' exhibits.

SELF-CATERING

For fruit and vegetables, as well as deli items, head for the markets in the streets on the San Polo side of the Rialto, or the Rio Terrà San Leonardo in Cannaregio. There are also supermarkets: Mega 1, off Campo Santa Margherita, and **Standa** (Strada Nova).

Drinking
BARS

Around 4pm you'll notice everyone drinking *sprizze* – an aperitif of *prosecco* (Venetian sparkling white), soda and a bitter mixer (usually the gaudy Aperol) giving the drink its trademark colour. The best ones come with a fat olive. Delicious!

Harry's Bar (Map pp728-9; ☎ 041 528 57 77; www.cipriani.com; Calle Vallaresso, San Marco 1323; cocktails €8-13; 🕑 10.30am-11.15pm) Venice's star-magnet seems stalled in time, a sepia-toned scene, gilt-edged but amber-mellow. The ambience in Harry's isn't really inviting, but it oozes style. Writers and celebrities from Hemingway and Capote to Woody Allen, Orson Welles and Marlene Dietrich have all dined here. Although Harry's is first and foremost a bar, the menu's star is the Bellini (€13) – a divine cocktail of white-peach pulp and *prosecco*, invented here.

Il Caffè (Map pp728-9; ☎ 041 528 79 98; Campo San Margherita, Dorsoduro 2963; 🕑 late) Better known as Café Rosso because of its big red sign, this fantastic hub on Venice's most delightful square is popular with young and old. The cool staff make great *sprizze* and might even let you assault the piano if you can convince them you can wail – jams aren't uncommon.

Café Blue (Map pp728-9; ☎ 041 71 02 27; café bluevenezia@hotmail.co; Salizzada San Pantalon, Dorsoduro 3778; ☼ late Mon-Sat) A pub-like drinking den not far from Santa Margherita, Café Blue usually figures somewhere in a Dorsoduro *giro d'ombra* (Venetian-style low-key pub crawl). Dark and atmospheric, it's a slightly shabby option, but still warm and inviting. Free Internet access is a cool feature.

Café Noir (Map pp728-9; ☎ 041 71 09 25; Calle San Pantalon 3805; ☼ 7am-2am Mon-Sat, 9am-2am Sun) A laid-back, more studenty hang-out, usually occupied night and day with locals catching up on gossip, flirting, drinking, eating and generally enjoying the wonderfully casual atmosphere of this pub-like bar/café.

Paradiso Perduto (Paradise Lost; Map pp728-9; ☎ 041 72 05 81; Fondamenta della Misericordia, Cannaregio 2540; ☼ 7pm-late, happy hour 6.30-7.30pm Thu-Mon, lunch Sat & Sun) Popular dim, bohemian bar/eatery/club with live and DJ-fuelled music. It's queer-friendly, self-consciously outré and does an awesome quasi-buffet lunch on weekends.

Inishark (Map pp728-9; ☎ 041 523 53 00; Calle Mondo Novo, Castello 5787; ☼ 5.30pm-2am Tue-Sun, closed Aug) A fun Irish bar so low-lit you'll need the light from the TV screens showing football (soccer) games to even *see* your Guinness.

Bar Du Champ (Map pp728-9; ☎ 041 528 62 55; Campo Santa Margherita, Dorsoduro 3019; ☼ 10-2am) Hip bar considered studenty because of the location, but really pulling a mixed crowd. Cheap *panini* for €1 to €2 and Tetley's on tap. It's swisher than it sounds.

Barbanera (Map pp728-9; ☎ 041 541 07 17; Calle de le Bande, Castello 5356; ☼ 11am-midnight) A *birreria/enoteca* (specialist wine and beer bar) also doing good food. The fish soup is cheap (€5) and authentic, and the deep-fried olives (€3) are pure salty deliciousness. Try them with warm crusty bread and a cold ale.

CAFÉS
Caffè Florian (Map pp728-9; ☎ 041 520 56 41; www .caffeflorian.com; Piazza San Marco 56/59; coffee €7-10; ☼ late daily) If you can cope with paying at least €7 for a cappuccino, spend an hour or so sitting at an outdoor table in Piazza San Marco, listening to the orchestra and taking in the sights at leisure.

Caffè Quadri (Map pp728-9; ☎ 041 528 92 99; www .quadrivenice.com; Piazza San Marco 120; coffee €7-10;

☼ late) Another piazza café with a pedigree stretching back centuries.

Torrefazione Costarica (Map pp728-9; ☎ 041 716 371; Strada Nuovo, Cannaregio 1337; ☼ 8am-6.30pm) Perhaps surprisingly, Venice's best coffee is also the cheapest, prepared by the sweetest, most unassuming purveyors. Camillo Marchi and family do espresso for €0.65, cappuccino for €1.05.

Entertainment
Teatro La Fenice (Map p725; ☎ 041 78 6511; www .teatrolafenice.it; Campo San Fantin, San Marco 1970) Like the phoenix it's named after, Venice's opera house recently re-emerged – literally – from the ashes of its previous incarnation: fire damage in 1996 saw the theatre closed for repairs for seven years. Back to its sumptuous best, it's once again the nexus of grand musical and theatrical performances in Venice.

Palazzo Grassi (Map pp728-9; www.palazzograssi .it; San Samuele, San Marco 3231; tickets adult/concession €9/6.50; ☼ 10am-7pm) Palazzo Grassi is *the* schmick venue for major art exhibitions, from ancient to modern, in the city throughout the year.

Shopping
Venice is synonymous with elaborate crafts, primarily glassware from the island of Murano and Venetian lace. Marbled paper and luscious velvet fabrics are other Venetian specialities, as are hand-bound books. There are several workshops and showrooms in Venice, but quality's inconsistent – there are a lot of knock offs. A good rule of thumb is to go to the source. If you're after Murano glass, visit Murano. If it's lace, just remember that the authentic stuff is expensive – if it ain't pricey, it ain't genuine.

For designer-label clothing, shoes, accessories and jewellery, head for the narrow streets between San Marco and the Rialto. Luxury items can be found in the area near La Fenice. **Studio Livio De Marchi** (Map pp728-9; ☎ 041 528 56 94; www.liviodemarchi.com; Salizzada San Samuele, San Marco 3157/a) Step into the fairy-tale world of surrealist sculptor Livio De Marchi, a dazzling showcase of his playfulness with wood and glass. When not turning trees into treasures, he's sometimes found 'driving' on the canals in his 'car': a vaporetto that's an exact, life-size, hand-carved wooden replica of a Ferrari F50!

ITALY

Getting There & Away

Some 12km from Venice is **Marco Polo Airport** (☎ 041 260 61 11, flight info ☎ 041 260 92 60), servicing domestic and European flights. From Piazzale Roma use **ATVO** (☎ 041 520 55 30; €2.70) buses or **ACTV** (☎ 899 90 90 90; Intercity Bus Station) bus No 5 (€0.80).

The ACTV buses also service surrounding areas, including Mestre and Chioggia, a fishing port at the southernmost point of the lagoon, and also Padua and Treviso. Tickets and information are available at the office in Piazzale Roma.

The train station, **Stazione Santa Lucia** (☎ 848 88 80 88) is directly linked to Padua, Verona, Trieste, Milan and Bologna, and easily accessible for Florence and Rome. You can also reach points in France, Germany, Austria, Switzerland, Slovenia and Croatia. The Venice Simplon *Orient Express* (London ☎ 020 7805 5100; www.orient-express.com) runs twice weekly between Venice and London, via Innsbruck, Zurich and Paris.

Minoan Lines (☎ 041 240 71 01; Porto Venezia, Zona Santa Marta) run ferries to Greece (one way summer €72, daily in summer and four times a week in winter).

Getting Around

Cars must be parked on Tronchetto or at Piazzale Roma (cars are allowed on the Lido – take car ferry No 17 from Tronchetto). The car parks are not cheap – €18 per day – so leave the car at Fusina, near Mestre, and catch vaporetto No 16 to Zattere, then No 82 either to Piazza San Marco or the train station. Ask for information at the tourist office just before the bridge to Venice.

The city's mode of public transport is the vaporetti (single/return ticket €3.10/5.20, and a 24-/72-hour unlimited-use ticket €19/31). A full timetable (€0.50) is available at vaporetto ticket offices. The most useful vaporetti are:

No 1: From Piazzale Roma, the No 1 zigzags along the Grand Canal to San Marco, then the Lido.

No 12: Departs from Fondamenta Nuove for the islands of Murano, Burano and Torcello.

No 82: Faster than the No 1 if you are in a hurry to get to St Mark's. Also services Giudecca.

Traghetti (€0.50 per crossing) are the public gondolas used by Venetians for crossing the Grand Canal – they get you a less romanticised gondola experience. Use them;

they're quick, cheap, fun and you'll be getting around Venetian-style.

FERRARA

pop 131,600

The lovely township of Ferrara outshines some bigger-named neighbours. The colourful medieval centre retains the vibe of its heyday as a seat of the Este family (1260–1598) when the town was a dynamic force. Castello Estense remains the imposing landmark in this charming town, though its friendly people are reason enough to visit. The **tourist office** (☎ 0532 29 93 03; www.ferrara terraeacqua.it; 🕑 9am-1pm & 2-6pm Mon-Sat, 9.30am-1pm & 2-5.30pm Sun) is inside Castello Estense.

Sights

The small historic centre encompassing medieval Ferrara lies south of **Castello Estense** (☎ info 0532 29 93 03, tickets ☎ 0243 353 522; www.castelloestense.it; Viale Cavour; adult €10, under 18 & over 65 €8.50, reservation €1; 🕑 9am-8pm Mon-Thu, to 10pm Fri-Sun). Complete with moat and drawbridges, the castle was begun by Nicolò II d'Este in 1385. The foreboding atmosphere of its interior isn't mirrored outside, where there's a bustling marketplace.

The pretty pink-and-white-striped **Duomo** dates from the 12th century, with Gothic and Renaissance additions. Its **museum** (☎ 0532 76 12 99; Via San Romano 1-9; entry €4.20; 🕑 9am-1pm & 3-8pm Tue-Sun) is worth seeing, with some Renaissance works. The **Palazzo Schifanoia** (☎ 0532 20 99 88; Via Scandiana 23; entry €4.20; 🕑 9am-6pm Tue-Sun) is one of the city's earliest major Renaissance buildings and another of the Este palaces. Head for the 'Room of the Months' for Ferrara's finest frescoes.

Sleeping

You won't need to overnight to see Ferrara's sights, but it's a cheap alternative to Bologna, and a viable base for visiting Venice. It's also small; tourist information can help you find *affittacamere*.

Albergo Lupa (☎ 0532 76 00 70; Vicolo della Lupa 8; s/d €35/45, with shared bathroom €30/40) This is a fantastic bargain in a quiet street minutes from great nightlife and eating. The rooms are lovely enough, but exceptional at the price.

Pensione Artisti (☎ 0532 76 10 38; Via Vittoria 66; d €57, s/d with shared bathroom €22/40) A fabulously friendly place on a medieval street, with attentive hosts ensuring the warmest welcome.

Clean, bright rooms are secure and comfy. With a good guest kitchen available, this is Ferrara's choicest cheapie.

Eating & Drinking

Woodpecker (☎ 0532 20 94 63; Via Saraceno 14; pizzas €7, pastas €8-10; ☽ dinner) The Woodpecker is a popular pizzeria/*ristorante* with a buoyant ambience and crisp, typically Italian décor. The pizzas are fine but try local speciality *cappellacci di zucca*, a hat-shaped pasta filled with pumpkin that is superb, sauced simply with butter, sage and *grana* (parmesan).

Fusion (☎ 0532 20 14 73; www.viascienze8.it, in Italian; Via Delle Scienze 8/a; ☽ 7.30-1.30am Tue-Sat, 6pm-1.30am Sun & 7.30am-3.30pm Mon) Personal grooming is a contact sport for Ferrara's fashionistas at this slick wine bar. Warm colours, comfy décor and chilled DJ-ing (and occasional live jazz) provide entertainment, but ogling's the real action. There are great snacks, and that inimitable Italian *style*.

Messisbugo (☎ 0532 76 40 60; www.messisbugo.com; ☽ late Tue-Sun) The cooler big sister to the strutting style warfare at Fusion. Boisterously casual without being raucous, sophisticated without being self-important, Messisbugo is a bar for grown-ups. Unpretentious, friendly staff keep the snacks and wonderful wines coming.

Getting There & Away

Ferrara is on the Bologna–Venice train line, with regular trains to both (40 minutes to Bologna, 1½ hours to Venice) plus nearby Ravenna. Buses run from the train station to Modena (also in the Emilia-Romagna region).

BOLOGNA

pop 381,000

Bologna is vibrant, beautiful and *red* – and it's often joked that its politics are reflected in the predominant colour of its buildings. Traditionally well to the Left, Bologna's reputation for spawning fiery rhetoric and socialist sympathies has mutated into a more agreeable one of open-ness and tolerance, reinforced by thousands of progressive-thinking students and teachers who come to study or work at Europe's oldest university, founded here in 1088.

The capital of Emilia-Romagna is further lauded as one of the greatest culinary cities in a great culinary nation. Bologna's traditional nickname was La Grassa ('Fatty'), for the richness of the food, rather than the circumference of its bellies. Besides the eponymous spaghetti bolognese (known as *spaghetti al ragù*), Bologna also gave the world tortellini and lasagne. Wonderful displays fill many a restaurant window – many still hand-cut their pasta under public scrutiny.

Bologna's a beautiful town, fantastic for a few days. Just like the food, however much you have, you'll probably want more.

Information

Ambulance (☎ 118)

Easy Internet (☎ 051 23 1074; www.easyInternetcafé.it; Via Rizzoli 9; ☽ 9am-11pm) The big orange purveyors of Internet access complement Bologna's existing colour scheme.

Ospedale Maggiore (☎ 051 647 8111)

Police station (Questura; ☎ 051 640 1111; Piazza Galileo 7)

Post office (☎ 051 23 0699; Piazza Minghetti 1; ☽ 8am-6pm Mon-Fri, to noon Sat)

Tourist information (call centre ☎ 051 24 65 41); Piazza Maggiore 1 (☽ 9am-7pm Mon-Sat); Train station (☽ 8.30am-7.30pm Mon-Sat); Airport (☽ 8am-8pm Mon-Sat, 9am-3pm Sun)

Sights & Activities

Simply strolling Bologna's porticoes is lovely as there's abundant atmosphere to be absorbed in the architecture.

Start in the pedestrianised centre formed by **Piazza Maggiore**, the adjoining **Piazza del Nettuno** and **Fontana del Nettuno** (Neptune's Fountain), sculpted in bronze by Giambologna. Arriving at **Piazza di Porta Ravegnana**, climb the 498 steps up the 97m **Torre Asinelli** (€3; ☽ 9am-6pm), the larger of Bologna's leaning towers, for wonderful views. The **Basilica di San Petronio** (☎ 051 22 5422; Piazza Maggiore; ☽ 7.30am-1pm & 2-6pm, free tours 11.30am Tue, Thu & Sat) is dedicated to the city's patron saint, Petronius. Its partially complete state, most detectable in the cracked façade, doesn't diminish its status as the fifth largest basilica in the world. The chapels contain many notable artworks.

The adjacent **Palazzo Comunale** (Town Hall; admission free) combines disparate architectural styles harmoniously. There's a statue of the Bolognese pope, Gregory XIII (creator of the Gregorian calendar), an impressive staircase attributed to Bramante and Bologna's collection of art treasures.

The 16th-century Nicoló Pisano–designed **Basilica di San Domenico** (☎ 051 640 0411; Piazza San

ITALY

BOLOGNA

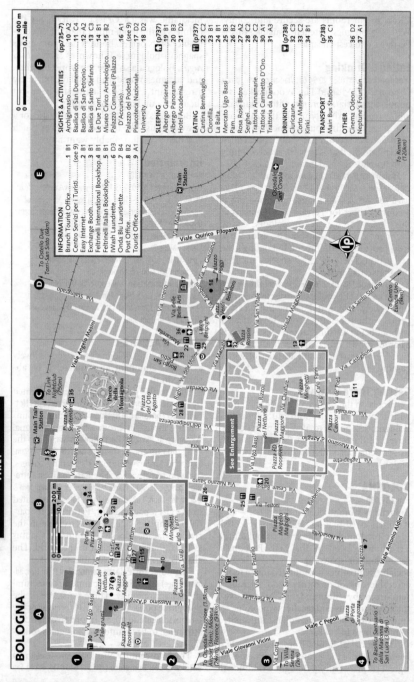

Domenico; admission free; 8am-1.30pm & 2.30-7.30pm) houses the sarcophagus of St Dominic, namesake of the Dominican order: its shrine features carvings by a young Michelangelo, and Mozart once played the church's organ.

The **Museo Civico Archeologico** (051 23 3849; Via dell'Archiginnasio 2; entry adult/concession €4/2; 9am-6.30pm Tue-Sat & 10am-6.30pm Sun) houses one of Italy's best Etruscan collections.

Sleeping

Bologna's budget hotels are in perpetual demand. Finding a room can be nightmarish, especially during the conventions and conferences often held here.

Ostello Due Torri/San Sisto (/fax 051 50 1810; Via Viadagola 5; dm/d €13.50/15, sheets €1.50; curfew 11pm) Two HI hostels beside each other, so inconveniently located they're nearly redundant. If circumstances necessitate penny-pinching, take bus No 93 (or No 301 Sundays, and 21b daily after 8.30pm) from Via Irnerio to San Sisto. There's nothing notable nearby; bring everything with you.

Albergo Garisenda (051 22 4369, fax 051 22 1007; Via Rizzoli 9, Galleria del Leone 1; s/d/tr with shared bathroom €45/65/90) In the shadow of the two towers, Garisenda has some rooms with a view of Torre Asinelli, as well as buzzing Via Rizzoli. It's conveniently located for pretty much everything, and good value for the unfussy rooms. Small breakfast included.

Albergo Panorama (051 22 1802; www.hotel panoramabologna.it; Via Livraghi 1; s/d/tr/q with shared bathroom €55/75/85/95) Lovely family-run place with spacious, clean rooms, all with TV and phone. You can glimpse the towers from some rooms. It's friendly and inviting – take bus No 25 four stops from the train station.

Hotel Accademia (051 23 2318; www.hotelaccad emia.it; Via delle Belle Arti 6; s €70-90, with shared bathroom €45-70, d €80-125, with shared bathroom €65-100) Good rooms with satellite TV, phone and decent breakfast make the Accademia great value. There's also uncommonly good disabled access. In the thick of the university quarter, it's great for people watching and close to excellent eating options.

Eating

Lively and moreish is how you'd describe both Bologna's eating and entertainment scenes. Sample the following if you can.

Trattoria da Danio (051 55 5202; Via San Felice 50a; menus €11.50; lunch & dinner) The quintes-

sential Bolognese trattoria; atmospheric, unpretentious and with quality food that would cost double in other cities. The three-course lunch special includes 500ml of mineral water or a *quartino* (250ml) of house wine. Perfect for authentic *tagliatelle al ragu*.

Rosa Rose Bistro (051 22 5071; www.rosarose.it, in Italian; Via Clavature 18; lge salad €7; lunch & dinner) Surprisingly, the stars of Rosa Rose's menu are 'her' lush, enormous salads. Maybe it's something to do with the floral décor. This is a great café with a gorgeous terrace for fine-weather alfresco dining.

Trattoria Caminetto D'Oro (051 26 3494; www .caminettodoro.it, in Italian; Via Falegnami 4; mains €14-18; lunch Thu-Tue & dinner Thu-Mon) Higher up the luxury scale is this award-winning trattoria, cosily ensconced under a portico in a pleasant part of town. Staff fire up the fondo in winter, and the earthy smell of grilling fills the intimate dining rooms.

Trattoria Annamarie (051 26 6894; Via delle Belle Arti 17; mains €20-30; lunch Thu-Tue & dinner Thu-Mon) Unbelievably good handmade pastas and sauces accompany the freshest produce in this lovely restaurant. Keep it basic like the Bolognese do: try the *tortellini alla gorgonzola* (meat-filled pasta with blue cheese) – rich, filling, tasty but, above all, simple.

Serghei (051 23 3533; Via Piella 12; mains €15-20; lunch Mon-Sat & dinner Mon-Fri) Don't be fooled by the Baltic sobriquet – this small place used to be a card room in the former Palazzo Piella, but it's definitely a safe bet dining here. These days it's two generations into serving heaped, authentic Emilia-Romagna specialities to a diverse clientele. Reserve.

Cantina Bentivoglio (051 26 54 16; Via Mascarella 4b; mains €12-15; 8pm-2am) A liberal sauce of live jazz (nightly) and a selection of over 500 wines can accompany your excellent meal at this mid-range marvel.

Clorofilla (051 235 53 43; Strada Maggiore 64/c) An uncommon thing in Italy: a specialist vegetarian restaurant! Lots of great dishes made with locally grown ingredients and all manner of fab cheeses. This is a wonderful alternative for vegetarians.

Self caterers should hit **Mercato Ugo Bassi** (Via Ugo Bassi 27; Mon-Sat), a covered market offering all sorts of local fare, supermarket **Pam** (Via Marconi 28a) for staple items, or the extravagant **La Baita** (Via Pescheria Vecchie) for deluxe ingredients.

ITALY

Drinking

Cluricaune (☎ 051 26 34 19; www.cluricaune.com; Via Zamboni 18/b; ☼ noon-2am Mon-Thu, noon-2.30am Fri, 2.30pm-2.30am Sat & 2.30pm-2am Sun) Deep in student territory, this Irish pub is heavily popular, and rightly so.

Corto Maltese (☎ 051 22 97 46; Via Borgo San Pietro 9/2; ☼ till late) Fantastic bar/pub/dancing spot with pool tables, free pasta and an inclusive vibe.

Kinki (☎ 051 587 5178; www.kinkidisco.com, in Italian; Via Zamboni 1; ☼ 7pm-4am, happy hour 7-9pm) It's hot! It's vinyl! Gays, lesbians and über-cool straights are welcome to work it until all hours at Kinki's themed nights. Wicked fun.

Getting There & Around

Bologna's **Guglielmo Marconi Airport** (☎ 051 647 9615) is northwest of the city. On land, Bologna is a major transport hub. Trains from around the country stop here. National and international coaches depart from the main **bus station** (Piazza XX Settembre) around the corner from the **train station** (Piazza delle Medaglie d'Oro).

The city is linked to Milan, Florence and Rome by the A1 (Autostrada del Sole). The A13 services Venice and Padua, and the A14 handles Rimini and Ravenna. Traffic is restricted in Bologna's centre; park cars outside city walls.

The bus system is efficient. To get to the centre from the station take bus No 25 or 27, or enjoy a 10-minute walk.

RAVENNA

pop 139,800

Ravenna's exquisite mosaics, relics of the time it was capital of the Western Roman Empire and western seat of the Byzantines, are the big drawcards. Dante (Alighieri) arrived in 1302 after being exiled from Florence, writing most of *The Divine Comedy* here before his death in 1321. Easily accessible from Bologna, this perfectly manicured, stress-free town is worth a day trip at the very least.

Visit the **IAT tourist information office** (☎ 0544 354 04; Via Salara 12; ☼ 8.30am-7pm Mon-Sat Apr-Sep, to 6pm Mon-Sat Oct-Mar, 10am-4pm Sun year-round); for medical assistance, see **Ospedale Santa Maria delle Croci** (☎ 0544 409 111; Via Missiroli 10).

Sights

You can buy a combination ticket (€8.50) at the tourist office to visit Ravenna's famed mosaics at **Basilica di Sant'Apollinare Nuovo**

(☼ 9am-7pm; Via di Roma); the **Basilica di San Vitale** (☼ 9am-7pm), the oldest of them all; **Mausoleo di Galla Placidia** (☼ 9am-7pm); the **Battistero Neoniano** (Via Battistero; ☼ 9am-7pm); and the **Museo Arcivescovile**.

Itself fairly unremarkable, **Dante's tomb** (Via Dante Alighieri 9; admission free; ☼ 9am-7pm) is worth noting for the 'perpetual' lamp – a belated admission from Florence that it had fumbled in exiling the 'father of modern Italian (language)' – which is kept permanently alight in tribute.

Sleeping & Eating

Ostello Dante (☎ 0544 42 11 64; Via Aurelio Nicolodi 12; dm incl breakfast €12.50, f per person €14) The HI hostel is neat as a pin, with friendly staff and good evening meals. It's 1km out of town; take bus No 1 from Viale Pallavacini, by the train station. A taxi costs €6.

Albergo Al Giaciglio (☎ /fax 0544 394 03; Via Rocca Brancaleone 42; s/d/tr €36/51/65, with shared bathroom €30/42/55) Small family-run hotel near the station with bright blue rooms and a good restaurant (set menus €13).

Cá de Vén (☎ 0544 301 63; Via Corrado Ricci 24; pastas €6-8, mains €9-14; ☼ Tue-Sun) The best all-round eating option in Ravenna offers good regional dishes and an extensive wine list in monastic surroundings, with a big non-smoking section. Pasta courses are ample for a small meal, but the tempting menu encourages lingering.

Getting There & Around

Ravenna is accessible by train from Bologna (1½ hours, €7 to €15), sometimes involving a change at Castel Bolognese. Cycling is a popular way to get around; Ravenna's fairly flat. Rental is available from **COOP San Vitale** (Piazza Farini XX; per hr/day €1.20/8) outside the station, or the **tourist office** (free; ☼ spring & summer only).

THE DOLOMITES

The limestone Dolomites stretch across Trentino–Alto Adige and into the Veneto. Characterised by the reddish glow of the rock formations that jut into the sky like jagged teeth, this spectacular Alpine region is the Italians' favoured area for skiiing and, in summer, hiking.

Information about Trentino–Alto Adige can be obtained in Trent (Trento) at the **APT** del Trentino (☎ 0461 83 90 00; www.trentino.to; Via Romagnosi 11); Rome (☎ 06 36 09 58 42; Via del Babuino 20); Milan (☎ 02 86 46 12 51; apt.milano@trentino.to; Piazza Diaz 5). Bolzano's **tourist office** (☎ 0471 30 70 00; www .bolzano-bozen.it; Piazza Walther 8) also has information on the region. The **APT Dolomiti** (☎ 0436 32 31/2/3; fax 0436 32 35) at Cortina can provide details on trekking and skiing in the Veneto. An excellent website for planning your trip is www.dolomiti.org, which has compehensive information, including maps.

Activities
SKIING
The Dolomites' many resorts range from posh Cortina d'Ampezzo in the Veneto to more family-oriented resorts in the Val Gardena (Trentino–Alto Adige). Most resorts have helpful tourist offices.

High season (Christmas to early January, and early February to April) costs will hit your pocket hard. Buy a *settimana bianca* (literally 'white week') – a package deal including seven days' worth of accommodation, food and ski passes, available throughout Italy.

Most resort areas also offer their own passes for unlimited use of lifts within nominated periods. Prices vary with resort (six days from €130 to €160). Average cost of ski-plus-boot hire (downhill/cross-country €15/10) is bearable. The **Superski Dolomiti pass** (www.dolomitisuperski.com; high season 3/6 days €100/175) accesses 464 lifts and 1220km of runs in 12 valleys.

TREKKING
Without doubt, the Dolomites provide the most breathtaking opportunities for walking in the Italian Alps (the season is from the end of June to September) – from basic half-day strolls with the kids to hardcore trekking and mountaineering. Alpine refuges *(rifugi)* usually close around 20 September. Trails are well marked with numbers on red-and-white bands on trees and rocks, or by numbers inside coloured triangles for the four Alte Vie ('High Routes') through the Dolomites.

The best maps are the Tabacco 1:25,000 series, widely available at bookshops throughout the region. Lonely Planet's *Walking in Italy* outlines several treks in detail; the *Italy* guide also suggests hikes.

Recommended hiking areas include:
Alpe di Siusi – a vast plateau above the Val Gardena, at the foot of the spectacular Sciliar.

Cortina area – featuring the magnificent Parco Naturale di Fanes-Sennes-Braies.
Pale di San Martino – accessible from San Martino di Castrozza.

WARNING
Even in summer the weather is extremely changeable in the Alps; though it may be sweltering when you set off, be prepared for very cold, wet weather on even the shortest walks. Essentials include good-quality, worn-in walking boots, an anorak or wind jacket, lightweight backpack, warm hat and gloves, waterproof poncho, light food and plenty of water.

Getting There & Away
The region has excellent public transport. The two principal bus companies are **SAD** (☎ 800 84 60 409) in Alto Adige and the Veneto, and **Atesina** (www.atesina.it) in Trentino. A network of long-distance buses operated by various companies (eg Lazzi, SITA, Sena, STAT and ATVO) connects major towns and resorts with big cities (Rome, Florence, Venice, Bologna, Milan and Genoa). Information is available from tourist offices and regional *autostazioni* (bus stations). For long-distance travel information, try **Lazzi Express** Rome (☎ 06 884 08 40; Via Tagliamento 27b); Florence (☎ 055 28 71 18; Piazza Stazione 47r). There is a **SITA office** (☎ 055 29 49 55; Via Santa Caterina da Siena 15) in Florence.

Getting Around
If you're planning an Alpine hike during warmer months, you'll find that hitching is no problem; normal caution should still apply. Areas near major resorts are well serviced by local buses, and tourist offices have information on routes. During winter, most resorts have 'ski bus' shuttle services to the main facilities.

CORTINA D'AMPEZZO
pop 6570
The ski resort for Italy's elite, Cortina is excruciatingly fashionable with matching prices. It's also one of the best-equipped, most picturesque resorts in the Dolomites. The area is popular for trekking and climbing, with well-marked trails and numerous *rifugi*.

The **main tourist office** (☎ 0436 32 31; Piazzetta San Francesco 8) has information on Cortina's

ITALY

accommodation options. **International Camping Olympia** (☎ /fax 0436 50 57; per person €8.50, tent & car €9; ⊗ year-round) is 3.5km north of Cortina at Fiames. **Casa Tua** (☎ 0436 22 78; www.casatuacortina .com; Via Zuel 100; r per person €34-50) in Cortina has season-dependent rates.

SAD buses connect Cortina with Bolzano, via Dobbiaco; ATVO travels to Venice, and Zani to Milan and Bologna.

CANAZEI

pop 1780

Set in the Fassa Dolomites, Canazei has over 100km of trails and is linked to a challenging network of runs, the **Sella Ronda**. Canazei also offers cross-country and summer skiing on Marmolada (3342m), the highest peak in the Dolomites.

Spend a cheap night at the Marmolada **camping ground** (☎ 0462 60 16 60; per person/tent €8/8; ⊗ year-round), or contact the **tourist office** (☎ 0462 60 11 13; Via Roma 34) for further details on accommodation. The resort is accessible by Atesina bus from Trent and SAD bus from Bolzano.

VAL GARDENA

A popular area in the Alps, with reasonable prices and top facilities. There are superb walking trails in the Sella Group and the Alpe di Siusi. The Vallunga, behind Selva, is great for family walks and cross-country skiing.

The valley's main towns are Ortisei, Santa Cristina and Selva, all offering plenty of accommodation and easy access to runs. Each town has a **tourist office** (Ortisei ☎ 0471 79 63 28, Santa Cristina ☎ 0471 79 30 46, Selva ☎ 0471 79 51 22) with extensive information on local facilities. Staff speak English and send details on request. The Val Gardena is accessible from Bolzano by SAD bus, and connected to major Italian cities by coach (Lazzi, SITA and STAT).

SAN MARTINO DI CASTROZZA

pop 700

In a sheltered position beneath the Pale di San Martino, this resort is popular among Italians, offering good skiing and a toboggan run. The **tourist office** (☎ 0439 76 88 67) provides lists of accommodation. **Hotel Suisse** (☎ 0439 680 87; Via Dolomiti 1; r incl breakfast from €33) is a pleasant one-star. Buses travel regularly from Trent, Venice and Padua.

CENTRAL ITALY

Tuscan light is a thing of unfettered beauty, playing over the rolling green landscapes in a million shades of gorgeous, and the hill towns of Umbria and the Marches (Le Marche) are worth the ankle strain for some of Italy's sweetest vistas. Though you'll be cheek by jowl with the hordes of culture-vultures in buzzing hubs such as Florence – and even some of the smaller towns just hours away – it's still possible to lose yourself down a medieval side street and get a little closer to a sense of Italy's fabled *la dolce vita* ('the good life').

FLORENCE

pop 375,000

Italy's been successfully selling itself on Florence's appeal for centuries. And although everything they claim is true – that it's a beautiful city with an artistic heritage unrivalled anywhere else in the world – it can also be disheartening. For most of the year, you'll overhear more conversations in English than Italian, and in summer the heat, pollution and crowds are stifling. Griping apart, Florence remains among the most enticing cities in Italy. Cradle of the Renaissance, home of Dante, Machiavelli, Michelangelo, the Medici and Carlo Collodi (who created Pinocchio), the wealth of history, art and culture still overwhelms.

Florence was founded as a colony of the nearby Etruscan city Fiesole around 200 BC, later becoming the strategic Roman settlement of Florentia. In the Middle Ages the city developed a flourishing mercantile economy, sparking a period of building and growth previously unequalled in Italy. But Florence truly flourished under the Medici family (1469–1737), its cultural, artistic and political fecundity culminating in the Renaissance.

The Grand Duchy of the Medici was succeeded in the 18th century by the House of Lorraine (related to the Habsburgs). Following unification, Florence was the capital of the new kingdom of Italy (1865–71). During WWII, parts of the city were destroyed by bombing, including all Florence's bridges except the Ponte Vecchio, and in 1966 a devastating flood destroyed or severely damaged many important works of art.

Orientation

However you arrive, Florence's main train station, Santa Maria Novella, is a good reference point. The main thoroughfare to the centre is Via de' Panzani and then Via de' Cerretani.

Once at Piazza del Duomo, Florence is easy to negotiate, as most major sights are within comfortable walking distance. Many museums close on Mondays, but you won't waste your time just strolling.

A good map of the city, on sale at newsstands, is *Firenze: Pianta della Città* (€3.50).

Information

BOOKSHOPS

Feltrinelli International (Map p742; ☎ 055 21 95 24; Via Cavour 12r) Italy's best foreign-language bookstore has a huge outlet here.

Paperback Exchange (Map pp744-5; ☎ 055 247 81 54; Via Fiesolana 31r) Huge range of new and second-hand books.

EMERGENCY

Ambulance & Fire (☎ 118)

Police station (Questura; Map pp744-5; general ☎ 055 497 71, lost property ☎ 055 328 39 42, towed vehicles ☎ 055 41 57 81; Via Zara 2) Has a foreigners' office.

INTERNET ACCESS

Internet Train (www.Internettrain.it, in Italian; from per hr €4) Via Oriuolo (Map p742; ☎ 055 263 89 68); Via Guelfa 24a (Map pp744-5; ☎ 055 21 47 94); Borgo San Jacopo 30r (Map p742; ☎ 055 265 79 35); Stazione Santa Maria Novella (Map pp690-1; ☎ 055 239 97 20) This Internet chain has 15 branches.

Netgate (Map p742; ☎ 055 658 02 07; www.thenetgate .it; Via Sant' Egidio 10-20r; ☒ 10am-10.30pm, free Internet ☒ 10.30-11am & 2-2.30pm Sat)

LAUNDRY

Wash & Dry (☎ 800 23 11 72; ☒ 8am-10pm) Via Nazionale 129r (Map pp744-5); Via del Sole 29r (Map p742); Via della Scala 52-54r (Map pp744-5); Via dei Servi 105r (Map p742); Via de Seragli 87r (Map pp744-5)

MEDICAL SERVICES

Farmacia Comunale (Map pp744-5; ☎ 055 28 94 35; Stazione Santa Maria Novella) A late-night pharmacy inside the station.

Misericordia di Firenze (Map p742; ☎ 055 21 22 22; Vicolo degli Adimari 1; ☒ 1.30pm-5pm Mon-Fri) A tourist medical service, just off Piazza Duomo.

Tourist Medical Service (Map pp744-5; ☎ 055 47 54 11; Via Lorenzo il Magnifico 59; ☒ 24hr) Has doctors who speak English, French and German.

MONEY

American Express (Map p742; ☎ 055 509 81; Via Dante Alighieri 22r; ☒ 9am-5.30pm Mon-Fri, 9.30am-12.30pm Sat)

Thomas Cook (Map p742; ☎ 055 28 97 81; Lungarno degli Acciaiuoli 6r)

POST

Main post office (Map p742; Via Pellicceria 3; ☒ 8.15am-7pm Mon-Fri, to 12.30pm Sat)

TELEPHONE & FAX

Telecom office (Map pp744-5; Via Cavour 21r; ☒ 7am-11pm)

TOURIST INFORMATION

Tourist offices Main office (Map pp744-5; ☎ 055 29 08 32; www.firenzeturismo.it; Via Cavour 1r; ☒ 8.30am-6.30pm Mon-Sat, to 1.30pm Sun); Piazza della Stazione 4 (Map pp744-5; ☎ 055 21 22 45; ☒ 8.30am-7pm Mon-Sat, to 2pm Sun); Borgo Santa Croce 29r (Map p742; ☒ 8.30am-7pm Mon-Sat, to 2pm Sun); Amerigo Vespucci Airport (☎ 055 31 58 74; ☒ 7.30am-11.30pm)

Sights & Activities

Enjoying Florence's sights can be taxing, as lengthy queues stretch patience. Entry to all state museums is half-price for EU passport holders (make sure you have it with you); if you're an EU passport holder under 18 or over 65 years of age, they're are free. You'll still have to wait, though.

But don't despair; **Firenze Musei** (☎ 055 29 48 83; www.firenzemusei.it; fee per museum €3; ☒ 8.30am-6.30pm Mon-Fri, to 12.30pm Sat) advance books tickets for all state museums, including the Uffizi, Palazzo Pitti, Museo del Bargello, Galleria dell'Accademia and Cappelle Medicee.

Take the city ATAF buses to **Piazzale Michelangelo** or the nearby suburb of **Fiesole**, both offering panoramic views.

DUOMO

The terracotta-orange roof contrasts dramatically with the red, green and white marble façade of the skyline-dominating cathedral, the **Duomo** (Map p742; ☎ 055 230 28 85; ☒ 10am-5pm Mon-Sat) – among Italy's most beloved monuments, and the world's fourth-largest cathedral. Officially the Cattedrale di Santa Maria del Fiore, the breathtaking structure was begun in 1294 by Sienese architect Arnolfo di Cambio, taking almost 150 years to complete.

ITALY

AROUND THE DUOMO

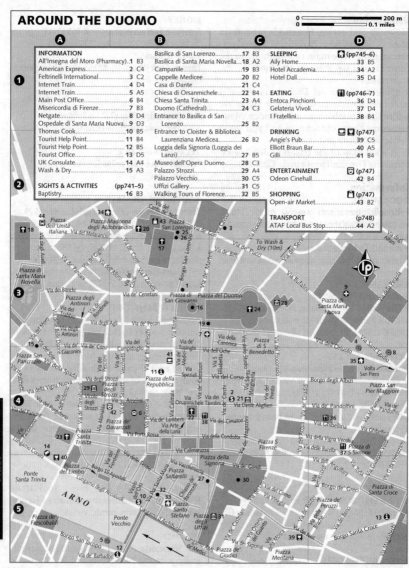

INFORMATION	Basilica di San Lorenzo......17 B3	**SLEEPING** 🏠 (pp745–6)
All'Insegna del Moro (Pharmacy)..1 B3	Basilica di Santa Maria Novella...18 A2	Aily Home.............................33 B5
American Express.....................2 C4	Campanile..............................19 B3	Hotel Accademia.....................34 A2
Feltrinelli International...............3 C2	Cappelle Medicee.....................20 B2	Hotel Dali..............................35 D4
Internet Train...........................4 D4	Casa di Dante.........................21 C4	
Internet Train...........................5 A5	Chiesa di Orsanmichele............22 B4	**EATING** 🍴 (pp746–7)
Main Post Office.......................6 B4	Chiesa Santa Trinita.................23 A4	Entoca Pinchiorri.....................36 D4
Misericordia di Firenze...............7 B3	Duomo (Cathedral)..................24 C3	Gelateria Vivoli.......................37 D4
Netgate...................................8 D4	Entrance to Basilica di San	I Fratellini...............................38 B4
Ospedale di Santa Maria Nuova..9 D3	Lorenzo............................25 B2	
Thomas Cook...........................10 B5	Entrance to Cloister & Biblioteca	**DRINKING** 🍷 (p747)
Tourist Help Point....................11 B4	Laurenziana Medicea.........26 B2	Angie's Pub............................39 C5
Tourist Help Point....................12 B5	Loggia della Signoria (Loggia dei	Elliott Braun Bar......................40 A5
Tourist Office...........................13 D5	Lanzi)...............................27 B5	Gilli......................................41 B4
UK Consulate...........................14 A4	Museo dell'Opera Duomo........28 C3	
Wash & Dry............................15 A3	Palazzo Strozzi........................29 A4	**ENTERTAINMENT** 🎭 (p747)
	Palazzo Vecchio......................30 C5	Odeon Cinehall......................42 B4
SIGHTS & ACTIVITIES (pp741–5)	Uffizi Gallery...........................31 C5	
Baptistry.................................16 B3	Walking Tours of Florence........32 B5	**SHOPPING** 🛍 (p747)
		Open-air Market......................43 B2
		TRANSPORT (p748)
		ATAF Local Bus Stop...............44 A2

Brunelleschi won a competition in 1420 to design the enormous octagonal dome, the first of its kind since antiquity. The interior is decorated with frescoes by Vasari and Zuccari, and the stained-glass windows are by Donatello, Paolo Uccello and Lorenzo Ghiberti. The façade is a 19th-century replacement of the unfinished original, pulled down in the 16th century. For a bird's-eye view of Florence, climb to the top of the **cupola** (admission €6; 🕙 8.30am-6.20pm Mon-Fri, to 5pm Sat).

Giotto designed and began building the graceful 82m **campanile** (Map p742; climb €6; 🕙 8.30am-6.50pm) beside the cathedral in 1334, but died before it was completed. The climb to the top yields gorgeous views.

The Romanesque **battistero** (baptistry; Map p742; admission €3; ☼ noon-6.30pm Mon-Sat, 8.30am-1.30pm Sun & hols), believed built between the 5th and 11th centuries on the site of a Roman temple, is the oldest building in Florence. The infant Dante was baptised here, and it's famous for its gilded-bronze doors. The celebrated *Gates of Paradise* by Lorenzo Ghiberti face the Duomo to the east. The south door (1336), by Andrea Pisano, is the oldest.

GALLERIA DEGLI UFFIZI (UFFIZI GALLERY)

Unless you book ahead (which costs an extra €1.55), you may find yourself waiting at the end of a very long queue for **Palazzo degli Uffizi** (Map p742; ☎ 055 238 86 51, reservations ☎ 055 294 883; www.uffizi.firenze.it; Piazza degli Uffizi; admission €8; ☼ 8.15am-6.50pm Tue-Sun, ticket office closes 6.05pm) – but it's worthwhile. Begun by Vasari in 1560 and ultimately bequeathed to the city by the Medici family in 1743, it houses the greatest collection of Italian and Florentine art in existence, including many of the world's most recognisable Renaissance paintings.

The gallery's seemingly endless masterpieces include 14th-century gems by Giotto and Cimabue; Botticelli's *Birth of Venus* and *Allegory of Spring* (rooms 10 to 14); plus works by Filippo Lippi, Fra Angelico and Paolo Uccello. *The Annunciation* by Leonardo da Vinci is here (room 15), along with Michelangelo's *Holy Family* (room 25), Titian's *Venus of Urbino* (room 28) and renowned works by Raphael, Andrea del Sarto, Tintoretto and Caravaggio.

PIAZZA DELLA SIGNORIA & PALAZZO VECCHIO

Designed by Arnolfo di Cambio and built between 1298 and 1340, **Palazzo Vecchio** (Map p742; Piazza della Signoria; adult/child €5.70/4.30; ☼ 9am-7pm Fri-Wed, to 2pm Thu) is the traditional seat of the Florentine government. In the 16th century it became the ducal palace of the Medici (before they occupied the Palazzo Pitti), and was given an interior facelift by Vasari. Visit the Michelozzo courtyard just inside the entrance, and the lavish apartments upstairs.

The **Loggia della Signoria** stands at right angles to the Palazzo Vecchio, displaying sculptures. The statue of *David* is a fine copy of Michelangelo's masterpiece; the original was once here (1504), but is now safely indoors in the Galleria dell'Accademia (opposite).

PONTE VECCHIO

The 14th-century **Ponte Vecchio** (Map p742), lined with gold and silversmiths' shops, was the only one to survive Nazi bombing in WWII. Originally, the shops housed butchers, but when a corridor along the 1st floor was built by the Medici to link the Palazzo Pitti and Palazzo Vecchio, they ordered that goldsmiths rather than noisome butchers should trade on the bridge. The area south of the river after crossing the Ponte Vecchio is the 'Oltrarno' (literally, 'beyond the Arno').

PALAZZO PITTI

This immense *palazzo* was built for the Pitti family, great rivals of the Medici, who moved in a century later. The **Galleria Palatina** (Palatine Gallery; Map p744-5; admission before/after 4pm €8.50/4; ☼ 8.15am-6.50pm Tue-Sun) has works by Raphael, Filippo Lippi, Titian and Rubens, hung in lavishly decorated rooms. The gallery and luxuriant decoration of the **royal apartments** are worth seeing. The palace also houses the **Museo degli Argenti** (Silver Museum; Map pp744-5; ☼ 8.15am-4.20pm Tue-Sun, 2nd & 3rd Mon each month), the **Galleria d'Arte Moderna** (Modern Art Gallery; Map pp744-5; admission €5; ☼ 8.15am-1.50pm Tue-Sat) and the **Galleria del Costume** (Costume Gallery; Map pp744-5; admission €5; ☼ 8.15am-1.50pm Tue-Sat).

Don't leave without visiting the Renaissance **Giardino di Boboli** (Boboli Gardens; Map pp744-5; admission €4; ☼ 8.15am-7.30pm Jun-Aug, to 6.30pm Apr-May & Sep, to 5.30pm Mar & Oct, to 4.30pm Nov-Feb), with secluded grottoes, fountains, leafy walkways and panoramic views.

GALLERIA DELL'ACCADEMIA

Michelangelo's *David*, arguably the most famous sculpture in the Western world, is housed in this **gallery** (Map pp744-5; ☎ 055 238 86 09; Via Ricasoli 60; admission €6.50; ☼ 8.15am-6.50pm Tue-Sun). *David* truly is an amazing work close-up; it's much bigger and more intricately detailed than many might imagine. Be sure you're keen – a two-hour wait is typical, rain or shine.

BASILICA DI SAN LORENZO & CAPPELLE MEDICEE (MEDICI CHAPELS)

The **Basilica di San Lorenzo** (Map p742; admission €2.50; ☼ 10am-5pm Mon-Sat) was built by Brunelleschi in the 15th century for the Medici and includes his **Sagrestia Vecchia** (Old Sacristy), with sculptural decoration by Donatello. The cloister leads to the **Biblioteca Laurenziana**,

ITALY

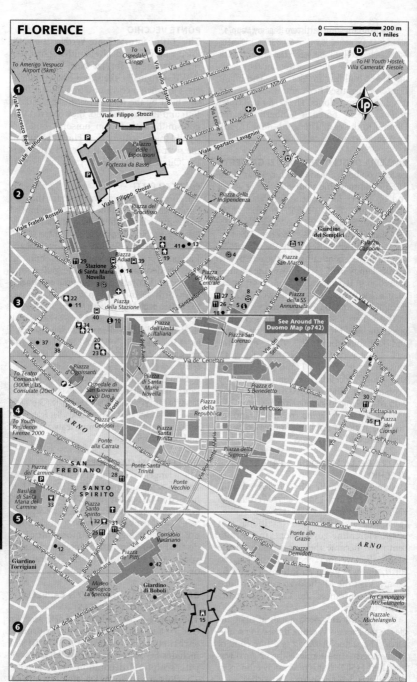

FLORENCE

0 —————— 200 m
0 —————— 0.1 miles

To Amerigo Vespucci
Airport (5km)

To
Ospedale
Careggi

To HI Youth Hostel;
Villa Camerata; Fiesole

Via della Cernaia

Via dello Statuto

Via Francesco Puccinotti

Via XX Settembre

Viale Giovanni Milton

Via Cosseria

Viale Filippo Strozzi

Via Leone X

Il Magnifico

Via Lorenzo X

Viale Spartaco Lavagnini

Palazzo
delle
Esposizioni

Fortezza da Basso

Via Enrico
Poggi

Via C. Dolfi

Via C. Ridolfi

Piazza della
Indipendenza

Giardino
dei Semplici

Palazzo
Capponi

Viale Filippo Strozzi

Via della
Fortezza

Piazza del
Crocifisso

Via Guelfa

Via XXVII Aprile

Via Nazionale

Via San Gallo

Via Cavour

Via Fratelli Rosselli

24

41 ● 13

19

Piazza
Adua

39

Stazione
di Santa Maria
Novella

36

● 14

Via Fiume

Piazza del
Mercato
Centrale

Piazza
San Marco

17

Via Ricasoli

16

Piazza
della Stazione

3

1

Via Sant'Antonino

27

26

8

5

18

Piazza
dei SS
Annunziata

22

11

Piazza
dell'Unità
Italiana

Piazza San
Lorenzo

See Around The
Duomo Map (p742)

40

34

21

10

20

23

Via de' Panzani

Via de' Cerretani

Piazza di
S Benedetto

37

38

Piazza
d'Ognissanti

Piazza di Santa
Maria
Novella

Piazza
della
Repubblica

Via del Corso

6

30

Via Pietrapiana

To Teatro
Comunale
(300m); US
Consulate (20m)

2

Ospedale di
San Giovanni
di Dio

Piazza
Santa
Trinità

Piazza della
Signoria

35

Piazza
dei
Ciompi

Via dell'Agnolo

To Youth
Residence
Firenze 2000

ARNO

Piazza C
Goldoni

Ponte
alla Carraia

Ponte Santa
Trinità

Ponte
Vecchio

Via Ghibellina

28

SAN
FREDIANO

SANTO
SPIRITO

Piazza
del Carmine

33

Basilica
di Santa
Maria del
Carmine

Piazza
Santo
Spirito

32

31

25

12

Corridóio
Vasariano

Lungarno delle Grazie

Ponte alle
Grazie

Piazza
Demidoff

ARNO

Via Tripoli

Via de' Renai

Giardino
Torrigiani

Piazza
de' Pitti

42

Museo
Zoologico
La Specola

Giardino
di Boboli

15

To Campéggio
Michelangelo

Piazzale
Michelangelo

9

4

ITALY

INFORMATION				
Farmacia Comunale	**1** B3	Passamaneria Toscana	**18** C3	Supermarket	**30** D4
French Consulate	**2** A4			Trattoria Casalinga	**31** B5
Internet Train	**3** A3	SLEEPING (pp745–6)			
Internet Train	**4** C3	Albergo Anna	(see 19)	DRINKING (p747)	
Main Tourist Office	**5** C3	Albergo Armonia	(see 19)	Cabiria	**32** A5
Paperback Exchange	**6** D4	Albergo Azzi	**19** B3	La Dolce Vita	**33** A5
Police (Questura)	**7** C2	Albergo Margaret	**20** A3	The Joshua Tree Pub	**34** A3
Telecom Office	**8** C3	Albergo Merlin	(see 19)		
Tourist Medical Service	**9** C1	Albergo Minerva	(see 19)	SHOPPING (p747)	
Tourist Office	**10** B3	Albergo Montreal	**21** A3	Flea Market	**35** D4
Wash & Dry	**11** A3	Albergo Paola	(see 19)		
Wash & Dry	**12** A5	Hotel Aprile	**22** A3	TRANSPORT (p748)	
Wash & Dry	**13** B2	La Scala	**23** A3	ATAF Local Bus Station	**36** B3
		Ostello Archi Rossi	**24** B2	Avis	**37** A3
				Hertz	**38** A3
SIGHTS & ACTIVITIES (pp741–5)		EATING (pp746–747)		Lazzi Bus Station	**39** B3
ATAF Ticket & Information		Borgo Antico	**25** A5	SITA Bus Station	**40** A3
Booth	**14** A3	da Garibardi	**26** C3		
Forte di Belvedere	**15** B6	Mario's	**27** C3	OTHER	
Galleria dell'Accademia	**16** C3	Ristorante Beccofino	**28** B5	Alinari	**41** B2
Museo di San Marco	**17** C2	Supermarket	**29** A3	Palazzo Pitti	**42** B5

the library built to house the Medici collection of some 10,000 manuscripts. You enter the library via Michelangelo's flowing Mannerist stairway.

The **Cappelle Medicee** (Map p742; ☎ 055 238 86 02; Piazza Madonna degli Aldobrandini; admission €6; 8.15am-5pm Tue-Sat, 1st, 3rd & 5th Sun of the month, 2nd & 4th Mon of the month) are around the corner. The **Cappella dei Principi** was the principal burial place of the Medici grand dukes. The incomplete **Sagrestia Nuova** was Michelangelo's first architectural effort, and contains his *Medici Madonna, Night & Day* and *Dawn & Dusk* sculptures, which adorn the Medici tombs.

Festivals & Events

The **Scoppio del Carro** (Explosion of the Cart) is held in front of the Duomo on Easter Sunday, and involves igniting a cart full of fireworks. Yes – as noisy, colourful and popular as it sounds.

The **Festa di San Giovanni** (Feast of St John), honouring Florence's patron saint, is held on 24 June and includes *calcio storico* ('period football') – soccer matches played in 16th-century costume on the Piazza Santa Croce.

Maggio Musicale Fiorentino (April to June) is Italy's longest-running music festival. For information call the **Teatro Comunale** (☎ 800 11 22 11).

Sleeping

BUDGET

Budget hotels and *pensioni* are concentrated around Via Nazionale, to the east of the station, and Piazza Santa Maria Novella, to the south. Despite there being over 150 budget hotels in Florence, it's still prudent to book. Arrive by late morning to claim your room.

Ostello Villa Camerata (Map pp744-5; ☎ 055 60 14 51; fax 055 61 03 00; Viale Augusto Righi 2-4; dm €15, dinner €8; lockout 9am-2pm) This HI hostel, a converted 17th-century villa, is superbly located. If it's not enough being drunk on the sheer beauty of your surrounds, it also has a bar. Take bus No 17 (€1, 30 minutes) from the station. Members only; reservations essential in summer.

Ostello Archi Rossi (Map pp744-5; ☎ 055 29 08 04; ostelloarchirossi@hotmail.com; Via Faenza 94r; dm €16-19; lockout 9am-2pm;) Hugely popular is this fun place, great for meeting other travellers – if privacy and quiet matter, look elsewhere. Good breakfast is included and bright, faux-frescoed décor – three floors of traveller graffiti – adorns the walls. Arrive before 9am to get a bed.

Campeggio Michelangelo (Map p742; ☎ 055 681 19 77; Viale Michelangelo 80; per person/tent €8/5) The camping ground closest to town is near Piazzale Michelangelo. Take bus No 13 from the station.

MID-RANGE

Albergo Azzi (Map pp744-5; 055 21 38 06; hotel azzi@hotmail.com; Via Faenza 56; bed in shared room €30, s/d incl breakfast €60/90, with shared bathroom incl breakfast €42/67) One of six basic, comfy and clean hotels operating in the same building; a great bargain option. Upstairs are the very similar Albergo Anna, Paola, Minerva, Merlin and Armonia. Prices flex a bit, so bargain.

Accademia (Map p742; ☎ 055 29 34 51; www.hotel accademia.it; Via Faenza 7; s €40-85, d €60-150;) This two-star is in an 18th-century palace, complete with magnificent stained-glass doors, carved wooden ceilings and a grand staircase straight out of a Ziegfield number.

ITALY

It's a great all-round option with website-only specials, so get surfing.

La Scala (Map pp744-5; ☎ 055 21 26 29; Via della Scala; d €85, s with shared bathroom €60; ✗ ✗) Gabriele Bini is the charming host of this wonderfully unpretentious place. Rooms are lovely, and value at these prices. There are portions of original frescoes on some ceilings, and the whole place is neat as a pin. Jovial Gabriele may be open to a spot of haggling, so don't hesitate.

Albergo Margaret (Map pp744-5; ☎ 055 21 01 38; www.dormireintoscana.it/margaret; Via della Scala 25; d €90, s with shared bathroom €60; ✗ ✗) A simple but functional place with pleasantly decorated rooms, serviced by helpful staff. It's possible to negotiate discounts for multinight stays at this recommended one-star.

Albergo Montreal (Map pp744-5; ☎ 055 238 23 31; www.hotelmontreal.com; Via della Scala 43; d €100, s/d with shared bathroom €55/85; P ✗ ✗ □) A well-appointed option, with sound-proofed, air-conditioned rooms featuring TV, phone and fridge. A decent buffet breakfast available.

Aily Home (Map p742; ☎ 055 239 65 05; Piazza Santo Stefano 1; s/d with shared bathroom €35/45) A great budget option with disproportionately large rooms overlooking the river. You'll struggle with the tiny lift, but the rooms at the top are worth it.

Hotel Dalì (Map p742; ☎ 055 234 07 06; www.hotel dali.com; Via dell'Oriuolo 17; d €75, s/d with shared bathroom €40/60) The only thing melting here will be your heart, as owners Marco and Samanta bend over backwards to ensure a pleasant stay in a city indifferent to some visitors. Rooms are as attractive and relaxing as the charming staff.

TOP END

Bencistà (h055 591 63; pensionebencista@iol. it; Via Benedetto da Maiano 4; s/d €150/160) A gorgeous villa about 1km from Fiesole in the hills overlooking Florence. It's as close as you'll get to *la dolce vita* without restoring your own ramshackle Tuscan cottage.

Hotel Aprile/Palazzo del Borgo (Map pp744-5; ☎ 055 21 62 37; www.hotelaprile.it; Via della Scala 6; s/d €120/180; P ✗ ✗ □) If you're in the mood to lash out, look no further than this former Medici palace, gorgeously appointed yet disarmingly low-key. Some rooms feature frescoes by Masaccio and Masolino and there's a gorgeous courtyard garden. A worthwhile indulgence.

Eating

Tuscan cuisine is all about simplicity and quality, exemplified in the staple *fettunta*, crusty bread rubbed with garlic and dripping with virgin olive oil. Other delights include *ribollita*, a heavy soup of vegetables and *canellini* (white beans), and the eponymous, usually enormous, *bistecca alla Fiorentina* (Florentine steak).

You can stock up at the **food market** (Map pp744-5; Piazza San Lorenzo; ☺ 7am-2pm Mon-Sat) or at the **supermarket** (Map pp744-5; Stazione Santa Maria Novella) on the western side of the train station, or the **supermarket** (Map pp744-5; Via Pietrapiana 94) east of Piazza Duomo.

RESTAURANTS

Mario's (Map pp744-5; Via Rosina 2r; pastas & mains €5; ☺ lunch Mon-Sat) Two generations of expertise fuel this cheap-but-great diner perpetually heaving with hungry locals. Delicious authentic pastas can be had for (nearly) a song. Whether you're budgeting or not, Mario's is worth a look for a glimpse of a typical Italian eatery in all its glory – the value's a welcome bonus!

Borgo Antico (Map pp744-5; ☎ 055 21 04 37; Piazza Santo Spirito 6r; mains €7-10; ☺ lunch & dinner) Heaping portions may be part of the draw at this great eatery, popular with a hip crowd. It could also be the excellent Tuscan dishes, the prime terrace space on a lovely piazza or the frankly unbelievable prices. Whatever it is, they should bottle it – it's a local favourite.

Ristorante Beccofino (Map pp744-5; ☎ 055 29 00 76; Piazza degli Scarlatti 1r; 1st & 2nd course €10-20; ☺ Tue-Sun) In all but quality, chef Francesco Berardinelli always planned to turn Tuscan tradition upside down with Beccofino's modern mojo. From the cyber-toilets to the bold menu, the new kid on Florence's culinary block rocks.

Trattoria Casalinga (Map pp744-5; ☎ 055 21 86 24; Via dei Michelozzi 9r; mains €16) The pick of the Piazza Santo Spirito trattorias is rammed with locals for lunch and dinner. There's a bit of a 'hurry-up!' feel to it, but you won't mind being nudged along for food this good at these prices. Fantastic friendly service, flamboyant Florentine clientele, and delicious dishes. Don't miss.

da Garibardi (Map pp744-5; ☎ 055 21 22 67; www .garibardi.it; Piazza del Mercato Centrale 38r; mains €15-20; ☺ noon-11pm) A great, authentic trattoria just a spit away from more the obvious stuff on the piazza. Indulge your Asterix-comic fantasies with *pasta al cinghiale* (wild boar) – a Tuscan speciality – augmented with *alla caccia* (hunter-style) accompaniments: olives, bay leaves, mushrooms and peppercorns. Service is friendly, the dining rooms cobblestone cosy and wood-fired warm.

Enoteca Pinchiorri (Map p742; ☎ 055 24 27 77; www .enotecapinchiorri.com; Via Ghibellina 87; mains €80-100) Nothing obvious on Via Ghibellina suggests the presence of possibly Italy's best restaurant, but it's there. Hostess Annie Feolde and sommelier Giorgio Pinchiorri deliver an unparalleled dining experience by combining a daring, innovative menu and jaw-dropping wine list with traditional surrounds and service evocative of fine dining from eras past. Book well ahead, and check online for its latest stunning menu.

SNACK BARS & GELATI

Gelateria Vivoli (Map p742; ☎ 055 29 23 34; Via dell'Isola delle Stinche 7) South of Via Ghibellina, this is widely considered the city's best *gelati*.

I Fratellini (Map p742; ☎ 055 239 60 96; Via dei Cimatori 38r; panini €2-3) A Florence institution; for nearly 130 years it's been dishing up the freshest (and quickest!) made-to-order takeaway *panini*. The only place to go if you need a snack to go. Brave the hordes.

Drinking

Drinking alcohol in Florence can be pricey (from €5). Stick to cocktails or the *aperitivo/* happy hours.

Gilli (Map p742; ☎ 055 21 38 96; Piazza della Repubblica 39r; ☿ Wed-Sun) The city's grandest café. Gloriously evocative, Gilli sends you straight back to the *belle époque*.

Cabiria (Map pp744-5; ☎ 055 21 53 72; Piazza Santa Spirito 4/r; ☿ late Wed-Mon) Blissful bar with an understated vibe lending itself perfectly to hours of languid people watching. Popular for all the right reasons, pulling a diverse crowd.

La Dolce Vita (Map pp744-5; ☎ 055 28 45 95; Piazza del Carmine 6/r; ☿ Mon-Thu, to 3am Fri-Sun) Check your style meter – go toe to toe with the fashionistas at this great cocktail bar. Fab décor and swish drinks make a grand night out at this hipster magnet.

Elliot Braun Bar (Map pp744-5; ☎ 055 35 23 52; Via Ponte alle Mosse 117r; ☿ 10am-4pm Mon-Fri & 6pm-2am Mon-Sat, aperitivo 6-8pm) An alt-cool mishmash that's a unique treat: art exhibits,

cocktails, food, live music and renowned for its *aperitivo;* buy a drink and gorge on the monster buffet at the bar. Anywhere else it would be freeloading – in Italy, it's called 'timing'.

Angie's Pub (Map p742; ☎ 055 28 37 64; Via De Neri 35r; snacks €3-5; ☿ noon-1am Mon-Sat, 6pm-1am Sun) One of Florence's better pubs does great on-the-cheap lunches, with a huge *panini* list. There's cold beer to hand, as well as other light meal options and plentiful good cheer.

Entertainment

Firenze Spettacolo, the definitive monthly entertainment guide, is sold at newsstands (€1.75). Concerts, opera and dance are performed year-round at the **Teatro Comunale** (☎ 800 11 22 11; Corso Italia 16). Original-language films screen at the **Odeon Cinehall** (Map p742; ☎ 055 21 40 68; www.cinehall.it, in Italian; Piazza Strozzi; tickets €7.20; ☿ Mon, Tue & Thu, other days Italian only).

Shopping

Shopping is concentrated between the Duomo and the Arno, with boutiques along Via Roma, Via dei Calzaiuoli and Via Por Santa Maria, leading to the goldsmiths lining the Ponte Vecchio.

Open-air market (Map p742; Piazza San Lorenzo; ☿ Mon-Sat) Just north of the Duomo and offering leather goods, clothing and jewellery, sometimes of dubious quality.

Flea market (Map pp744-5; Piazza dei Ciompi; ☿ daily) Off Borgo Allegri and north of Santa Croce, is better for finding genuine bargains.

Getting There & Away

Florence is served by two airports. **Amerigo Vespucci** (☎ 055 306 15, flight info ☎ 055 306 13 00/02), 5km northwest of the city centre, serves domestic and European flights. **Galileo Galilei** (☎ 050 84 92 02) is 50 minutes away, near Pisa, and one of northern Italy's main air-transport hubs.

The **SITA bus station** (Map pp744-5; ☎ 800 37 37 60; Via Santa Caterina da Siena 17) is just west of the train station. Buses leave for Siena, San Gimignano and Volterra. **Lazzi** (Map pp744-5; ☎ 055 35 10 61; Piazza Adua 1), next to the station, runs services to Rome, Prato (€2.20, 45 minutes, every 30 minutes), Pistoia (€2.70, 50 minutes, nine daily), Lucca (€4.70, 1½ hours, 18 daily) and Pisa (€6.20, two hours, hourly).

Florence is on the main Rome–Milan train line; call ☎ 848 88 80 88 for details or visit the **train information office** (☎ 7am-9pm) at the station.

Florence is connected by the Autostrada del Sole (A1) to Bologna and Milan in the north and Rome and Naples to the south. The Firenze-Mare motorway (A11) links Florence with Prato, Pistoia, Lucca, Pisa and the Versilia coast, and a *superstrada* (dual carriageway) joins the city to Siena.

Getting Around

TO/FROM THE AIRPORT

Regular trains to Pisa airport (1½ hours, 6.45am to 5pm) leave from platform five at Santa Maria Novella station. Check your bags in at the **air terminal** (☎ 21 60 73) near platform five at least 15 minutes before departure time. You can get to Amerigo Vespucci Airport (€4, 25 minutes, half-hourly 6am to 11.30pm) by the Vola in Bus shuttle, which departs from the SITA coach depot in Via Santa Caterina da Siena. Buy tickets onboard.

BUS

ATAF buses service the city centre and Fiesole. The most useful terminal is in a small piazza to the left as you exit the station onto Via Valfonda. Bus No 7 leaves for Fiesole and stops at the Duomo. Tickets (one/three/24 hours €1/1.80/4) must be bought prior to boarding and are sold at most tobacconists and newsstands.

CAR & MOTORCYCLE

There are several car parks dotted around the city centre. A good choice is **Fortezza da Basso** (per hr €1.10; ☎ 24hr). Further details are available from **Firenze Parcheggi** (☎ 055 500 19 94). To rent a car, try **Hertz** (☎ 055 239 82 05; Via M Finiguerra 33r) or **Avis** (☎ 055 21 36 29; Borgo Ognissanti 128r).

PISA
pop 92,000

Pisa's iconic leaning tower is among Italy's most popular sights, and a godsend to producers of tourist kitsch.

Today it's a fairly quiet university town, but Pisa was once a maritime power rivalling Genoa and Venice, and the home of Galileo Galilei (1564–1642). Levelled by the Genoese in the 13th century, its history eventually merged with that of Florence, its bigger neighbour up the River Arno. You'd be pressed to find reasons for an extended stay, but the city retains a certain charm.

Orientation

The Campo dei Miracoli is a 1.5km walk from the train station across the Arno. Bus No 3 will save time. The medieval town centre around Borgo Stretto is 1km or so from the station.

Information

Internet Planet (☎ 050 83 07 02; Piazza Cavallotti 3-4; Internet per hr €3.10; ☎ 10am-midnight Mon-Sat, 2pm-midnight Sun)
Onda Blu (☎ 800 86 13 46; Via San Francesco 8a; 7kg wash/dry €5/5; ☎ 8am-10pm) Cheap laundrette.
Tourist offices Piazza del Duomo (☎ 050 56 04 64; ☎ 9am-6pm Mon-Sat, 10.30am-4.30pm Sun); Piazza della Stazione (☎ 050 4 22 91; ☎ 9am-7pm Mon-Sat, 9.30am-3.30pm Sun); Airport (☎ 050 50 37 00)

Sights

Pisans claim their **Campo dei Miracoli** (Field of Miracles) is among the most beautiful squares in the world. It's debatable: while the immaculately manicured lawns provide a gorgeous backdrop for the cathedral, baptistry and bell tower – *all* leaning – you do have to grit your teeth through throngs of tat-waving hawkers to approach them. It's a little underwhelming precisely because the square is so spartan – there's nothing going on apart from slanting.

And enchanting. The buildings are gorgeous. The candy-striped **cathedral** (admission €2; ☎ 10am-7.40pm Mon-Sat, 1pm-7.40pm Sun summer, 10am-12.45pm & 3-4.45pm Sun winter), begun in 1063, has a graceful façade and cavernous interior. The transept's bronze doors, facing the tower, are by Bonanno Pisano, while the 16th-century bronze entrance doors are by Giambologna. The cathedral's cupcake-like **battistero** (baptistry; admission €5; ☟ 8am-7.40pm summer, 9am-4.40pm winter), begun in 1153 (completed 1260), contains a pulpit by Nicola Pisano.

The irony is, Bonnano's biggest mistake ended up being his signature work. The campanile, better known as the **Leaning Tower** (Torre Pendente; www.opapisa.it; admission €15; ☟ 8am-8pm summer, 9am-7pm winter), was wonky immediately; just three of the tower's eventual seven tiers were completed before it started tilting, continuing at a rate of about 1mm per year.

British engineer John Burland was given the task of saving the tower in the early '90s. Burland marvelled at how the tower hadn't fallen; computer models showed the landmark should've toppled once the lean hit 5.4 degrees. In 1990, it was already at 5.5 degrees. But by 2001, 'the old lady of Pisa' was restored to her (secure) 1838 angle by Burland's cunning use of biased weighting and soil drilling, making her sink back into a safer position. In theory, the tower might be in 1990-like peril again in about 300 years. Today it is almost 4.1m off the perpendicular, despite the 11 years of ground-levelling work.

Visits are limited to groups of 30; entry times are staggered and waiting is inevitable. There are many combo-tickets, but admission to the Leaning Tower is always separate.

Sleeping

Ostello per la Gioventù (☎ /fax 050 89 06 22; Via Pietrasantina 15; dm €22; ☟ closed 9am-6pm) The youth hostel is basic but friendly and clean. Take bus No 3 from the station, or it's an easy 10-minute walk from the Campo dei Miracoli.

Hotel di Stefano (☎ 050 55 35 59; www.hoteldi stefano.pisa.it; Via Sant'Apollonia 35-37; s/d/tr/q €70/85/110/120, s/d with shared bathroom €45/60) Simply decorated rooms and a lovely breakfast terrace are just two features of this good hotel. It's walking distance from all sights, in a calm street behind lovely Piazza dei Cavalieri.

Hotel Francesco (☎ 050 55 54 53; www.hotel francesco.com; Via Santa Maria 129; s/d from €75/110; ☐) Fantastic three-star with good disabled access, friendly service and comfortable rooms that feature every imaginable convenience.

There's a great buffet breakfast and you're literally down the road from the Campo dei Miracoli. It also hires bikes and scooters; a great way to see Pisa.

Villa Kinzica (☎ 050 56 04 19; fax 050 55 12 04; Piazza Arcivesovado 2; s/d/tr incl breakfast €77/103/123) Lovely refurbished place, souvenir-throwing distance from the tower – some rooms have views of Pisa's centrepiece (ask when you book). Pleasant decorations won't distract from the comforts afforded by the good appointments and polite service.

Eating

Antica Trattoria il Campano (☎ 050 58 05 85; Vicolo Santa Margherita; mains €25; ☟ Thu-Tue) Outstanding Tuscan grub in a dungeon-esque, vaulted-ceilinged, medieval atmosphere. If you and a friend are really hungry, kick off with the *Tagliere del Re* ('cut of the king') – a staggering platter of 12 kinds of regional antipasti. You shouldn't need a second course.

La Tana (☎ 050 58 05 40; Vicolo San Frediano 6; 1st course €4, mains €10-14; ☟ Sat-Thu) Studenty hot spot dishing up voluminous pizza and pasta options. Atmospheric and friendly, with tasty food and fab service. It'll be hard to stay vewy qwiet after sampling its delicious *spaghetti al coniglio* (spaghetti with rabbit).

Trattoria La Buca (☎ 050 56 06 60; Via Gallit Tussi 6; mains €6-10, pizzas €6; ☟ Sat-Thu) Highly recommended trattoria doing hearty Tuscan fare at reasonable prices. Cheap pizzas are a budget winner, but the whole menu's great. Subdued ambience.

Getting There & Away

The airport, with domestic and European flights, is minutes away by train, or bus No 3 from the station. **Lazzi** (☎ 050 462 88) buses run to Florence via Lucca. Pisa is linked by train to Florence, Rome and Genoa.

SIENA
pop 54,350

Don't miss Siena. Despite being surrounded by glamorous neighbours, it's a captivating and beautifully preserved town. Surrounded by mostly intact ramparts, its corkscrew-coiled streets and labyrinthine centre are jam-packed with majestic Gothic buildings in various shades of 'burnt sienna'. It's also usually teeming with visitors.

According to legend, Siena was founded by the sons of Remus (who was one

ITALY

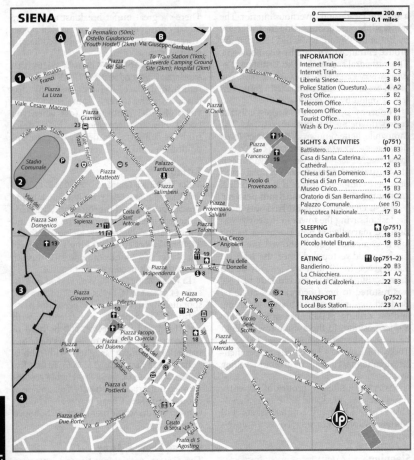

SIENA

0 ——— 200 m
0 ——— 0.1 miles

of Rome's founders). In the Middle Ages the city became a free republic, its dramatic rise – on the back of banking skill – causing political and cultural friction with Florence. Painters of the Sienese School (most notably the 13th to 15th centuries) produced significant works of art, and the city was home to St Catherine and St Benedict.

Orientation

Leaving the train station, cross the concourse to the bus stop opposite for bus No 3, 9 or 10 to central Piazza Gramsci, then walk along Via dei Termini (10 minutes to Piazza del Campo). Visitors' cars aren't permitted in the centre.

Information

Ambulance (☎ 118)

Internet Train Via di Città 12 (per hr €5); Via di Pantaneto 57 (per hr €5)

Libreria Senese (☎ 0577 28 08 45; libreria_senese@ libero.it; Via di Città 62/66) A fantastic bookshop with English books and, more interestingly, a professional-standard language-instruction section.

Police station (Questura; ☎ 0577 20 11 11; Via del Castoro 23) Near the Duomo.

Post office (Piazza Matteotti 1) North of the centre.

Tourist office (☎ 0577 28 05 51; www.terresiena.it; Piazza del Campo 56; ⏰ 9am-7pm) Can explain the chicanery of the myriad tickets permitting entry to Siena's sights.

Wash & Dry (Via di Pantaneto 38; wash/dry €3.50/€3.50; ⏰ 8am-10pm)

Sights

Siena's uniquely shell-shaped **Piazza del Campo** (simply, Il Campo) has been the city's focus for 700 years. The piazza's base is formed by the nobly proportioned **Palazzo Pubblico** (Town Hall; admission/tower/both €5.50/6.50/9.50; 🕐 10am-7pm mid-Mar–end Oct, to 5.30pm end Nov–mid-Feb, to 6.30pm rest of the year), also known as Palazzo Comunale, which was once seen as one of Italy's most graceful Gothic buildings. Climb the 102m-high **Torre del Mangia** (bell tower) for a pigeon's-eye view of proceedings, as well as those pretty red roofs.

The spectacular **Duomo** (admission free; 🕐 7.30 am-7.30pm Mon-Sat, 2-7.30pm Sun mid-Mar–Oct, 7.30am-5pm Mon-Sat, 2-5pm Sun Nov–mid-Mar) is another Gothic masterpiece. Begun in 1196, extravagant expansion plans were stymied by the niggling arrival of the Black Death in 1348, claiming nearly 70,000 of Siena's 100,000 people. Venice's aside, Siena has the most striking cathedral interior in northern Italy. The green-red-and-white-striped marble of the exterior is, incredibly, maintained throughout – a noteworthy distinction from comparable – or even grander, cathedrals; Florence's Duomo, despite dramatic external decoration, is bland inside.

The Romanesque lower section has carvings by Giovanni Pisano, and the inlaid-marble floor features 56 biblical panels. Other artworks include a bronze of St John the Baptist by Donatello, and statues of St Jerome and Mary Magdalene by Bernini. The **battistero** (baptistry; Piazza del Duomo; admission €2.50; 🕐 9am-7.30pm mid-Mar–Sep, to 6pm Oct, 10am-1pm & 2.30-5pm Nov–mid-Mar) behind the cathedral has a Gothic façade and 15th-century frescoes.

Want to see the preserved head of a saint? Head for the **Chiesa di San Domenico & Santuario di Santa Caterina** (shop ☎ 0577 28 68 48; Piazza San Domenico; free; 🕐 7.30am-1pm & 3-6.30pm), where St Catherine's is displayed (plus part of her thumb). The church itself is tranquil and airy, and friendly Federico Muzzi in the souvenir shop sells some funky Christian kitsch.

Festivals & Events

Siena is divided into 17 *contrade* (districts) and 10 are chosen annually to contest the **Palio**, a tumultuous horse race (and pageant) held in the Piazza del Campo on 2 July and 16 August. Securing accommodation during the Palio will require foresight or luck as it's very heavily touristed.

Sleeping

It's always advisable to book in advance, but for August and the Palio, it's essential.

Colleverde Camping Ground (☎ 0577 28 00 44; Strada di Scacciapensieri 47; per person/tent €8/8; 🕐 late Mar-early Nov) Siena's handiest camping ground is 2km north of the historic centre (take bus No 3 from Piazza Gramsci). Tell the driver you're headed for the *campeggio* (cam-*peh*-gee-oh).

Ostello Guidoriccio (☎ 0577 522 12; Via Fiorentina; dm incl breakfast €16.50) The HI hostel is an inconvenient 2.5km haul north of the centre, up a hill in Stellino. It's clean and bland, but cheap. Take bus No 3 from Piazza Gramsci and tell the driver you're after the *ostello* (hostel). Rooms are quiet, and shutters afford pitch-black rooms, at least ensuring a good night's sleep.

Piccolo Hotel Etruria (☎ 0577 28 80 88; fax 0577 28 84 61; Via delle Donzelle 3; s/d/tr/q €44/73/96/119, s with shared bathroom €39) Siena's best all-round value (despite breakfast not being included); you practically exit onto the Campo! Basic, large rooms are passable, and the 12.30am curfew won't hinder as Siena rarely kicks on that long. Location doesn't get any better than this.

Locanda Garibaldi (☎ 0577 28 42 04; Via Giovanni Dupré 18; d/tr/q €70/89/108, menus €15) Fresh from a facelift a few years back, this good option with passable rooms behind the town hall also has a good trattoria. Marcello is an amiable host, flitting fluidly between running his eatery and managing the accommodation. He'll bargain in nonpeak times, too, so call ahead.

Eating

Osteria di Calzoleria (☎ 0577 28 90 10; Via di Calzoleria 12; mains €15-20; 🕐 dinner) Fantastic hole in the wall on a winding street meandering off the Campo, with evocative Tuscan fare and exceptionally good *contorni* (vegetable side dishes); two or three make a great vegetarian meal. A great place to slurp some *ribollita*, a dense vegetable soup, or twirl perfect *pici*, the traditional Sienese thick pasta, round yer fork.

La Chiacchiera (The Chatterbox; ☎ 0577 28 06 31; Costa di Sant'Antonio 4; mains €15-20; 🕐 lunch & dinner) This rustic place has wooden stools and handwritten menus. An evocative setting for an ideal meal; try the *trippe* (tripe) if you're game – it's a serious threat to offal's bad culinary rep. Served in a garlicky sauce, it's an aeons-old Tuscan traditional dish too few have the audacity to try.

Permalico (☎ 0577 411 05; www.permalico.net; Via di Camollia 193; mains €15; ✆ lunch & dinner Mon-Sat) Just north of the centre is this great little medieval cavern/tavern serving simple Tuscan grub, and complete with vaulted ceilings. A fine place to grab a *panini* and a beer, or something more substantial. Also has an excellent wine list.

Bandierino (☎ 0577 28 22 17; Piazza del Campo 66; pizza/pasta from €8/10; ✆ lunch & dinner) The best if you must eat on Il Campo. Prices are steepish but the pastas and risotti are excellent, particularly the *ai funghi porcini,* with rich, musty mushrooms; worth opting for over the popular (and cheaper) pizzas. Your politeness will be matched by the brisk staff; just don't slow them down.

Getting There & Away

Regular Tra-In buses run from Florence to Siena, arriving at Piazza Gramsci. Local buses also go to San Gimignano (€5, 1½ hours, hourly), Volterra (€4.50, 50 minutes, hourly) and other points in Tuscany, and there are daily buses to Rome (€16, three hours, 10 daily). For Perugia (€11, two hours), buses leave infrequently from the train station; inquire at the tourist office. Siena is not on a main train line; from Rome you'll have to change at Chiusi (from Florence, at Empoli).

SAN GIMIGNANO
pop 7100

In a region famed for its beauty, this tiny hill-top town deep in the Tuscan countryside is still gaspworthy. It's not really the town itself – these days custom-built for tourists – that appeals but some of the incredible vistas available from climbing its steep walkways or remaining towers (of an original 72 built as fortified homes for the town's 11th-century feuding families, 13 remain). The best time to visit is midweek, preferably in deepest winter.

The **Pro Loco tourist office** (☎ 0577 94 00 08; Piazza del Duomo 1; ✆ 9am-1pm & 3-7pm, to 6pm in winter) is in the town centre.

Climb San Gimignano's tallest tower, **Torre Grossa,** off Piazza del Duomo, for utterly stunning views of the hills. Entrance is via the **Palazzo del Popolo,** which houses the **Museo**

Civico (☎ 0577 94 00 08; adult/child €5/4; ✆ 9.30am-7.20pm Mar-Oct, 10am-5.50pm Nov-Feb). The **Duomo,** known also as the Collegiata, has a Romanesque interior, frescoes by Ghirlandaio in the **Cappella di Santa Fina** and a gruesome *Last Judgment* by Taddeo di Bartolo.

San Gimignano is generally visited from Florence or Siena. Hotels are expensive but there are *affittacamere,* and *agriturismo* is well-organised locally; see the tourist office.

If budget's the priority and you don't mind moderating your behaviour, the lovely nuns at the **Foresteria Monastero di San Girolamo** (☎ 0577 94 05 73; Via Folgore 26-32; dm incl breakfast €23) run the best budget option in town. Mind your Ps & Qs, now.

If you can afford a splurge, soak up the medieval ambience and awesome views on offer at the excellent **Hotel La Cisterna** (☎ 0577 94 03 28; www.hotelcisterna.it; Piazza della Cisterna 24; s/d/tr incl breakfast €70/90/120; Ⓟ ⓧ ▢). After all, if you've decided to stay, you may as well go the whole hog.

For good pasta and decent local wines, stop at **Il Castello** (☎ 0577 94 08 78; Via del Castello 20; pastas €5-6), a fine way to punctuate a day's walking, while **Gelateria di Piazza** (☎ 0577 94 22 44; Piazza della Cisterna 4; ✆ Mar–mid Nov) provides the obligatory *gelato.*

Regular buses link San Gimignano with Florence and Siena, arriving at Porta San Giovanni.

UMBRIA & MARCHE

Umbrians consider their hilly region the green heart of Italy. Exemplified in its many medieval hill towns – any of which makes a fantastic excursion – the area's noted for its Romanesque and Gothic architecture. Assisi, Gubbio, Spello, Spoleto, Todi and Orvieto are all accessible from Perugia, the region's sedate but beguiling capital.

Mountainous Marche is more appealing than the mildly grim coastal capital Ancona suggests; nothing can mar the prettiness of its elevated northern villages, particularly the medieval centre of gorgeous Urbino.

PERUGIA
pop 158,300

Perugia is a well-preserved hill town offering sweeping panoramas at every turn. Best known for its University for Foreigners (established 1925), attracting many international students, the city is also noted for the Umbria Jazz Festival (July) and another excessive indulgence: chocolate.

Highlights, or lowlights, of Perugia's history, bloody even by medieval standards, include the vicious internal feuding of the Baglioni and Oddi families, and the death of a few popes. Art and culture, however, have thrived: painter Perugino and Raphael, his student, both worked here.

Orientation

Perugia's hub is Corso Vannucci, running north-south from Piazza Italia, through Piazza della Repubblica, ending at Piazza IV Novembre. Get to the centre from the train station with any bus to Piazza Italia, where you then get a **scala mobila** (public escalator; free; 6.45-1.45am) uphill to the medieval heart.

Information

InfoUmbria (☎ 075 57 57; Largo Cacciatori delle Alpi 3b) An excellent independent tourist office.
Internet Train (Via Ulisse Rocchi 30; per hr €4)
Post office (Piazza Matteotti; 8.10am-6pm Mon-Sat)
Tourist office (☎ 075 572 33 27; Palazzo Dei Priori, Piazza IV Novembre 3; 8.30am-1.30pm & 3.30-6.30pm Mon-Sat, 9am-1pm Sun) Opposite the Duomo.

Sights

Perugia's austere **Duomo** (☎ 075 572 38 32; Piazza IV Novembre; admission free; 8am-noon & 4pm-sunset) has an unfinished two-tone façade. Inside

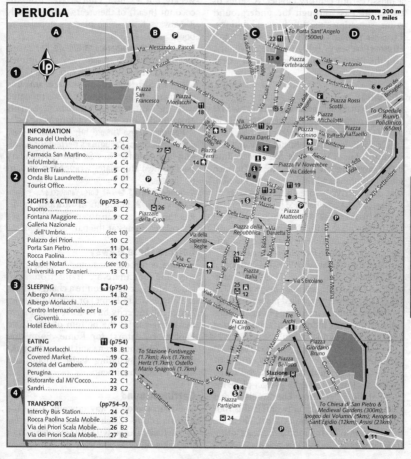

PERUGIA

0 — 200 m
0 — 0.1 miles

INFORMATION	
Banca del Umbria	1 C2
Bancomat	2 C4
Farmacia San Martino	3 C2
InfoUmbria	4 C4
Internet Train	5 C1
Onda Blu Laundrette	6 D1
Tourist Office	7 C2

SIGHTS & ACTIVITIES	(pp753-4)
Duomo	8 C2
Fontana Maggiore	9 C2
Galleria Nazionale dell'Umbria	(see 10)
Palazzo dei Priori	10 C2
Porta San Pietro	11 D4
Rocca Paolina	12 C3
Sala dei Notari	(see 10)
Università per Stranieri	13 C1

SLEEPING	(p754)
Albergo Anna	14 B2
Albergo Morlacchi	15 C2
Centro Internazionale per la Gioventù	16 D2
Hotel Eden	17 C3

EATING	(p754)
Caffe Morlacchi	18 B1
Covered Market	19 C2
Osteria del Gambero	20 C2
Perugina	21 C2
Ristorante dal Mi'Cocco	22 C2
Sandri	23 C2

TRANSPORT	(pp754-5)
Intercity Bus Station	24 C4
Rocca Paolina Scala Mobile	25 C3
Via dei Priori Scala Mobile	26 B2
Via dei Priori Scala Mobile	27 B2

ITALY

are artworks from the 15th to 18th centuries, as well as the Virgin Mary's wedding ring, unveiled every 30 July. The **Palazzo dei Priori** is a rambling 13th-century palace housing the impressively frescoed **Sala dei Notari** (☎ 075 573 03 66; Corso Vanucci 15; admission free; ⏱9am-1pm & 3-7pm Tue-Sun, daily Jun-Sep) and the **Galleria Nazionale dell'Umbria** (☎ 075 572 10 09; www.gallerianazionaledellumbria.it, in Italian; Corso Vanucci 19; adults €6.50, 18-25 yrs €3.25, EU citizens under 18 & over 65 free; ⏱8.30am-7.30pm), with works by Perugino and Fra Angelico. The fountain in Piazza IV Novembre is the 13th-century **Fontana Maggiore**, designed by Fra Bevignate (1278) and carved by Nicola and Giovanni Pisano.

At the other end of Corso Vannucci is the **Rocca Paolina** (Paolina Fortress), the ruins of a massive 16th-century citadel. A series of escalators pass through the underground ruins, sometimes used to host exhibitions. Etruscan remains in Perugia include the **Arco Etrusco** (Etruscan Arch), near the university, and the **Pozzo Etrusco** (Etruscan Well), near the Duomo.

Sleeping

Centro Internazionale per la Gioventù (☎ 075 572 28 80; www.ostello.perugia.it; Via Bontempi 13; dm €11.50, sheets €1.50; ⏱from 4pm, midnight curfew, closed Dec-Jan) Possibly Italy's best hostel for value and comfort. The TV room's frescoed ceiling beats anything on the screen, the terrace view's fabulous and there's a guest kitchen. Just don't arrive before 4pm.

Albergo Anna (☎ 075 573 63 04; www.albergoanna.it; Via dei Priori 48; s/d €40/58, with shared bathroom €30/48) Charming place with delightful rooms off Corso Vannucci, full of character and antiques, and a super-friendly owner (Signora Emma Citti). Great value for this comfort.

Albergo Morlacchi (☎ 075 572 03 19; Via Leo Tiberi 2; s/d from €38/65, s with shared bathroom from €28; P X 🐾) A lovely, art-filled place with well-maintained rooms, including phone, TV, antique furnishings, indoor plants and subdued elegance. Pretty and peaceful.

Hotel Eden (☎ 075 572 81 02; www.hoteleden.191.it; Via Cesare Caporali 9; s/d/tr/q €36/57/77/103; P X 🐾 🖥) If brightness appeals, the white rooms at Hotel Eden are a perfect place for 'tired starlings' to nest. They're also great value and tended by friendly staff in this 700-year-old building on a quiet street. There are modem points in the rooms for tech-toting travellers, too – rare at this price.

Eating

Mercato Coperto (covered markets; ⏱7am-1.30pm Mon-Sat) Downstairs from Piazza Matteotti, you can buy fresh vegetables, bread, meat and condiments.

Caffe Morlacchi (☎ 075 572 17 60; Piazza Morlacchi 8; snacks €7-12; ⏱8-1am Mon-Sat) The meeting place in Perugia and kick-off place for many a *festa dell' laurea* (graduation celebration) is also a great spot to grab a light meal. Absolutely packed at peak times, with good reason.

Ristorante dal Mi'Cocco (☎ 075 573 25 11; Corso Giuseppe Garibaldi 12; mains €6-7, set menus €13; ⏱Tue-Sun) Super place near the university with long communal tables and an *antica taverna* vibe. The set menu (written in local dialect) means you eat what's dished up, and changes weekly, but it's always *dal' cocco* – from the coconut (head) of the creative chef. Luckily it's always tasty – the place is popular, so book.

Osteria del Gambero (☎ 075 572 19 76; Piazza Danti 16; mains €20-30, set menus €35) Traditional Umbrian dishes are well represented. The land- or sea-themed menus are amazing showcases of the finest ingredients prepared with the best regional know-how. Equally amazing desserts and a cracking wine list.

Perugina (Corso Vannucci 101; ⏱9.30am-7.45pm, closed Mon mornings) Perugina's perfect for handling sublimated desires. Sample its legendary Baci (kisses) chocolates wrapped in romantic quotes.

Sandri (☎ 075 44 9 41; Corso Vannucci 32; ⏱8am-11pm Tue-Sun) A Perugian institution, Sandri has the best cakes in town, as well as free chocolate nibbles at the bar.

Getting There & Away

Perugia is not on the Rome–Florence railway line, but there are trains from both cities. Most services require a change, either at Foligno (from Rome) or Terontola (from Florence). Intercity buses leave from Piazza dei Partigiani (at the bottom of the Rocca Paolina escalators) for Rome, Fiumicino Airport, Florence, Siena and towns throughout Umbria, including Assisi, Gubbio and nearby Lake Trasimeno.

Getting Around

The train station is way downhill from the historic centre. Catch any bus heading for Piazza Italia. Tickets (€0.80) are available from the ticket office as you leave the station.

The centre is mostly closed to cars; that's a good thing – driving in Perugia frustrates. Park downhill and take the pedestrian escalator up to the centre. There's a supervised **car park** (Piazza dei Partigiani; 1st hr €0.80, per hr thereafter €1.05; 24hr), from where you can catch the Rocca Paolina escalator to Piazza Italia, and two more car parks beside the Via dei Priori escalator.

ASSISI

pop 25,500

Birthplace and spiritual home of animal-loving St Francis, picturesque Assisi is a major destination for millions of pilgrims wishing to retrace holy footsteps. Somehow this hamlet halfway up Mt Subasio manages to maintain a tranquil air regardless, particularly in the lanes off the central streets.

In September 1997, an earthquake rocked Assisi, causing damage to the upper church of the Basilica di San Francesco (St Francis' Basilica), but nowadays there is little evidence of the destruction.

The **tourist office** (075 81 25 34; info@iat.assisi .pg.it; Via S Croce; 8am-6.30pm Mon-Sat, 10am-1pm & 2-5pm Sun summer, 8am-2pm & 3-6pm Mon-Sat, 9am-1pm Sun winter) has information.

Sights

If you're intending to visit the religious sites, look the part, as dress rules are applied rigidly – absolutely no shorts, miniskirts, low-cut dresses or tops allowed.

The **Basilica di San Francesco** (075 81 90 01; Piazza di San Francesco; admission free; 7am-7pm Apr-Sep, to 5pm Oct-Mar) comprises two churches, one above the other. The lower church is decorated with frescoes by Simone Martini, Cimabue and a pupil of Giotto, and contains the crypt where St Francis is buried. The Italian Gothic upper church has a stone-vaulted roof and decoration by Giotto and Cimabue. The frescoes in the apse and entrance were damaged in the 1997 quake.

The frescoed 13th-century **Basilica di Santa Chiara** (St Clare's Basilica; 075 81 22 82; Piazza Santa Chiara; admission free; 7am-noon & 2-7pm) contains the remains of St Clare, friend of St Francis and founder of the Order of Poor Clares. For spectacular valley views, the massive 14th-century fortress **Rocca Maggiore** (075 81 52 92; Via della Rocca; admission €2.60; 10am-sunset) is perfect.

Sleeping & Eating

Assisi is well geared for tourists. Peak periods are Easter, August, September and the Feast of St Francis (3 to 4 October). The tourist office has extensive *affittacamere* listings and religious information.

Fontemaggio (075 81 36 36; Via Eremo delle Carceri 8; dm €18.50) The non-HI hostel also has camping facilities. From Piazza Matteotti, at the far end of town from the basilica, it's a 30-minute uphill walk.

Pensione La Rocca (/fax 075 81 22 84; Via Porta Perlici 27; s/d €38/45; P X X) Tucked away in a quiet corner, with sunny rooms, some with awesome valley views. All have en-suite facilities.

Pizzeria Flipper (Via San Francesco 2/d; pizza slice €2; 9am-7.30pm Thu-Tue) Fab, cheap, convenient *pizze al taglio* and calzone.

Cantine Di Oddo (Via San Francesco; mains €7-8; Thu-Tue) An apt and excellent mostly vegetarian place with mouthwateringly good spinach-and-ricotta ravioli in a basic sauce of butter and lightly fried sage. Even carnivores won't miss the meat.

Getting There & Away

Buses connect Assisi with Perugia, Foligno and other local towns, leaving from Piazza Matteotti. Buses for Rome and Florence leave from Piazzale dell'Unità d'Italia. Assisi's train station is in the valley, in Santa Maria degli Angeli on the Perugia line; a shuttle bus (€0.60, every 30 minutes) runs between Piazza Matteotti and the station.

ANCONA

pop 100,100

Ancona, a largely industrial port city and capital of the Marches, is worth mentioning mostly because you may find yourself here waiting for onward ferries to Croatia, Greece or Turkey.

Bus No 1 goes from the train station to the port. The main **tourist office** (071 35 89 91; www .comune.ancona.it, in Italian; Via Thaon de Revel 4; 9am-2pm & 3-6pm Mon-Fri, 9am-1pm & 3-6pm Sat, to 1pm Sun; limited in winter) is out of the way. Stazione Marittima also has a **tourist office** (071 20 11 83; 8am-8pm Tue-Sat & 2-8pm Sun & Mon summer). There's a **post office** (Largo XXIV Maggio; 8.15am-7pm Mon-Sat).

Sleeping

Many backpackers sleep at the ferry terminal, but Ancona does have cheap hotels.

ITALY

Ostello della Gioventú (☎/fax 071 422 57; Via Lamaticci 7; dm €12) Around 400m from the station, clean, quiet and cheap, with a lift and bathrooms big enough for wheelchair access.

Hotel della Rosa (☎ 071 413 88; www.hoteldella rosa.it, in Italian; Piazza Rosselli 3; s/d €55/88; P ⊠ ☐) A recently spruced-up three-star opposite the station and offering comfort in the event of an overnight stay. Rooms are adequate with all mod cons.

Getting There & Away
Buses depart from Piazza Cavour for towns throughout the Marches. Rome is served by **Marozzi** (☎ 071 280 23 98). Ancona is on the Bologna–Lecce train line and easily accessible from major towns. Connect to Rome via Foligno.

Ferry operators have booths at the terminal, off Piazza Kennedy. Companies include **Superfast** (☎ 071 207 02 40) to Patra in Greece (€78), **Minoan Lines** (☎ 071 20 17 08) to Igoumenitsa and Patra (€68) and **Adriatica** (☎ 071 20 49 15) to Durrës in Albania (€86) and Split in Croatia (€47). Prices are one-way deck class in high season.

URBINO
pop 6000
This beautiful medieval town can be tricky to reach, but the 'pride of the Marches' rewards the effort. Birthplace of Raphael and Bramante, university-town Urbino remains a bustling centre of culture and learning. It's small, steep and the streets meander snakily around a gorgeous cobbled core that's been World Heritage listed by Unesco.

The **IAT tourist office** (☎ 0722 26 13; Via Puccinoti 3; ☤ 9am-1pm Mon-Sat, 9am-1pm & 3-6pm Sun & hols May-Sep) is central. There is a **post office** (☎ 0722 37 79 17; Via Bramante 18; ☤ 8.30am-6.30pm Mon-Sat).

Urbino's centrepiece is the **Palazzo Ducale** (☎ 0722 32 90 57; Piazza Duca Federico; adult/child incl Galleria Nazionale €4.15/free; ☤ 8.30am-7.15pm Tue-Sun, to 2pm Mon), designed by Laurana and completed in 1482. Enter from Piazza Duca Federico and visit the **Galleria Nazionale delle Marche**, within the *palazzo*, which features works by Raphael, Paolo Uccello and Verrocchio.

Visit the **Casa di Raffaello** (☎ 0722 32 01 05; Via Rafaello 57; admission €2.60; ☤ 9am-1pm & 3-7pm Mon-Sat, 10am-1pm Sun spring & summer, morning only Nov-early Mar), where Raphael was born.

The tourist office has an *affittacamere* list for accommodation.

Albergo Italia (☎ 0722 27 01; www.albergo-italia -urbino.it; Corso Garibaldi 32; s/d €41/62, breakfast €8; P ⊠ ⊠) is a good mid-range hotel covering a range of needs from cheap singles to deluxe doubles. Rooms are super-neat and comfortable.

Gula (☎ 0722 26 94; Corso Garibaldi 23; mains €6-10; ☤ lunch & dinner) is a sprawling *birreria/osteria* serving fantastic meals that are cheap, but very good, attracting a broader clientele than just local students.

Trains don't run to Urbino. Buses (Monday to Friday) connect to cities including Ancona, Pesaro and Arezzo. There's a bus link to the train station at Fossato di Vico, on the Rome–Ancona line, or to Pesaro on the Bologna–Lecce line. Buses to Rome (€18.10, five hours) run twice daily. Buses arrive at Piazza Mercatale, down Via Mazzini from Piazza della Repubblica.

SOUTHERN ITALY

While not as wealthy as the north in the traditional sense, you'll be well rewarded by the south's abundant riches. The land of the *mezzogiorno* (midday sun) sizzles with palpable passion, has a rich history and honours deep cultural traditions. Here, the food is magnificent, the people can seem more open and friendly and the varied landscape is resplendently pretty. Campania, Puglia and Basilicata are still under the tourist radar in many parts, and Naples is as unforgettable as your first love.

NAPLES
pop 1.04 million
Stunningly situated on the Bay of Naples, and lorded over by Mt Vesuvius, Naples (Napoli) has a wily, scrappy and ultimately irresistible charm. The Campania region's capital is edgy, raucous, overwhelming and, above all, fun. Come with your preconceptions – it's hard not to – but expect to be blown away by the disarming energy this city exudes. And yes, the drivers can be reckless and petty thieves are rampant, so look both ways and watch your back.

Orientation
Naples lazes along the waterfront and is divided into *quartieri* (districts). Both the Stazione Centrale and the main bus terminal

are off Piazza Garibaldi, east of Spaccana-poli, the city's ancient heart. Corso Umberto I, the main shopping thoroughfare, heads southwest from Piazza Garibaldi to Piazza Bovio, skirting Spaccanapoli. To the south and west, on the bay, are Santa Lucia and Mergellina, both fashionable and picturesque and a contrast with the chaotic historical centre. In the hills above is the serene and affluent Vomero district, a natural balcony with grand Vesuvian views.

Information

EMERGENCY
Police station (Questura; ☎ 081 794 11 11, to report a stolen car ☎ 081 794 14 35; Via Medina 75) Just off Via Armando Diaz.

INTERNET ACCESS
Internetbar (☎ 081 29 52 37; Piazza Belllini 74; per hr €3; ⏰ 9-2am Mon-Sat, from 8pm Sun).

MEDICAL SERVICES
Ambulance (☎ 081 752 06 96)
Guardia Medica After-hours medical service; phone numbers are listed in *Qui Napoli* (Here Naples).
Ospedale Loreto-Mare (☎ 081 254 27 01; Via A Vespucci) On the waterfront, near the station.
Pharmacy (Stazione Centrale; ⏰ 8am-8pm)

MONEY
There are plenty of ATMs throughout the city, as well as foreign-exchange booths.
Every Tour (☎ 081 551 85 64; Piazza Municipio 5-6) Represents American Express, changes money and is a Western Union agent.

POST
Main post office (Piazza G Matteotti; ⏰ 8.15am-7pm Mon-Sat) Off Via Armando Diaz.

TELEPHONE
Telecom office (Via A Depretis 40; ⏰ 9am-1pm & 2-5.30pm Mon-Fri)

TOURIST INFORMATION
Ask for *Qui Napoli* (Here Naples), published monthly in English and Italian, listing events in the city, as well as information about transport and other services.
Tourist offices Stazione Centrale (☎ 081 20 66 66; ⏰ 9am-7.30pm Mon-Sat, to 1.30pm Sun); Piazza del Gesù Nuovo (☎ 081 552 33 28; ⏰ 9am-8pm Mon-Sat, to 3pm Sun) The office at the train station will make hotel bookings.

Dangers & Annoyances
Although the city's home-grown Mafia, the Camorra, is still a pervasive local force, you're more likely to encounter a thief. The petty-crime rate is very high, and pickpockets, moped bandits and bag-snatchers abound, stealing at any opportunity (including from the car when stopped at a red light). Car theft is also a major problem. Pay attention at night near the station, Piazza Dante, the area west of Via Toledo and as far north as Piazza Carità.

Sights
A good investment is the **Campania artecard** (☎ 800 600 601; www.napoliartecard.com; €13), giving access to six museums at reduced rates and public transport; purchase at the airport, train and metro stations and selected museums.

Start your sightseeing at Spaccanapoli, the historic centre of Naples. From the station and Corso Umberto I, turn right onto Via Mezzocannone, taking you to Via Benedetto Croce, the bustling main street of the quarter. To the left is spacious Piazza del Gesù Nuovo, with the 15th-century rusticated façade of **Chiesa di Gesù Nuovo** and the 14th-century **Basilicata di Santa Chiara**, restored to its original Gothic-Provençal style after being severely damaged by WWII bombing. The beautifully tiled **Chiostro delle Clarisse** (Nuns' Cloisters; Piazza del Gesù Nuovo; admission €4; ⏰ 9.30am-1pm daily & 2.30-5.30pm Mon-Sat) is also worth visiting.

The **Duomo** (☎ 081 44 90 97; Via Duomo; ⏰ 8am-12.30pm & 4.30-7.30pm Mon-Sat, 8.30am-1pm & 5-8pm Sun) has a 19th-century façade but was built by the Angevin kings at the end of the 13th century on the site of an earlier basilica. Inside is the **Cappella di San Gennaro**, containing the head of St Januarius (the city's patron saint) and two vials of his congealed blood. The saint is said to have saved the city from disasters such as plague and volcanic eruptions.

Turn off Via Duomo and onto the very characteristic **Via Tribunali** and head for Piazza Dante, through the 17th-century **Port'Alba**, one of the city's gates. Via Roma, the most fashionable street in old Naples, heads to the left (becoming Via Toledo) and ends at Piazza Trento e Trieste and **Piazza del Plebiscito**.

In the piazza is the **Palazzo Reale** (☎ 081 794 40 21; admission €4.50; ⏰ 9am-8pm Thu-Tue), the former official residence of the Bourbon and Savoy

NAPLES

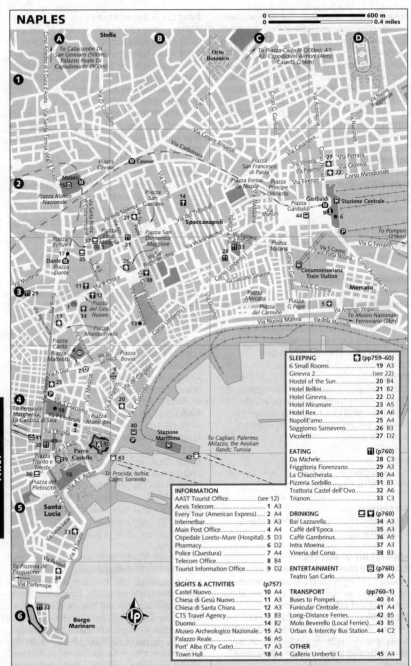

0 ——————— 600 m
0 ——————— 0.4 miles

To Catacombe Di
San Gennaro (500m);
Palazzo Reale Di
Capodimonte (900m)

Stella

Orto
Botanico

To Piazza Carlo III (200m); A1;
A3; Capodichini Airport (4km);
Caserta (25km)

Corso Amedeo di S Duca d'Aosta

Via Santa Teresa degli Scalzi

Via D Cirillo

Via Foria

Via Cesare Rosaroli

Via Carbonara

Piazza
Cavour

Museo
15

Piazza Museo
Nazionale

Via della Sapienza

Via S Paolo

Piazza
San Gaetano

Via del Tribunali

Spaccanapoli

Piazza
San Domenico
Maggiore

Piazza San
Luigi
Miraglia

Piazza
Bellini

Dante
17
Piazza
Dante

Via Benedetto Croce

Via S
Sebastiano

Piazza
del Gesù
Nuovo

Via Pignasecca

Via Monteoliveto

Piazza
Monteoliveto

Piazza
Carità

Piazza
Matteotti

Via A Diaz

Via Medina

Via G
Sanfelice

Piazza
Bovio

Piazza
Trieste

Via de' Gasperi

Via C Colombo

Stazione
Marittima

To Cagliari; Palermo;
Milazzo; the Aeolian
Ilands; Tunisia

Parco
Castello

Piazza
Municipio

Via A F Acton

To Procida; Ischia;
Capri; Sorrento

Santa
Lucia

Piazza del
Plebiscito

To Pizzeria de
Pasqualino

Via Partenope

Borgo
Marinaro

Piazza
San Francesco
di Paola

Piazza Enrico
de Nicola

Corso G Garibaldi

Via Casanova

Via Venezia

Via Palermo

Via Firenze

Via Ferrara

Via Genova

Corso Meridionale

Piazza
Principe
Umberto

Garibaldi

Stazione Centrale

Piazza
Garibaldi

To Pompeii
(25km)

Via G Ferraris

Piazza
Nolana

Circumsuuviana
Train Station

Via E Cosenz

Mercato

Corso Arnaldo Lucci

Piazza
Mercato

Piazza
G Pepe

Piazza
del Carmine

Via Nuova Marina

Via della Marinella

To Museo Nazionale
Ferroviario (2km)

To Amerigo Vespucci

Corso Umberto I

Via Maddalena

Via Marina

ITALY

kings, now a museum. Just off the piazza is the world-renowned **Teatro San Carlo** (☎ 081 791 21 11; guided tours €5; Via San Carlo 98), famed for its perfect acoustics and lavish interior and now a ballet school.

The 13th-century **Castel Nuovo** with the **Museo Civico** (☎ 081 795 58 77; admission €5; ☾ 9am-7pm Mon-Sat, to 2pm Sun) on the first three floors, overlooks the ferry port. The early Renaissance triumphal arch commemorates the entry of Alfonso I of Aragon into Naples in 1443. Situated southwest along the waterfront, at Santa Lucia, is the **Castel dell'Ovo** (☎ 081 764 05 90; Borgo Marinaro; admission free; ☾ 9am-6pm Mon-Fri, to 1pm Sat & Sun), originally a Norman castle, surrounded by **Borgo Marinaro**, a tiny fishing village.

North of Piazza Dante, the **Museo Archeologico Nazionale** (☎ 081 44 01 66; Piazza Museo Nazionale; admission €6.50; ☾ 9am-7.30pm Wed-Mon) contains one of the most important collections of Greco-Roman artefacts in the world, mainly the rich collection of the Farnese family, and the art treasures discovered at Pompeii and Herculaneum. Book a (free) tour to see the **Gabinetto Segreto** (Secret Cabinet), reopened to the public in 2000. The ancient smut is heady stuff!

Catch the Funicolare Centrale (funicular), on Via Toledo, to Vomero and the **Certosa di San Martino**, a 14th-century Carthusian monastery, rebuilt in the 17th century in Neapolitan-baroque style. It houses the **Museo Nazionale di San Martino** (☎ 081 578 17 69; Via Tito Angelini; admission €6; ☾ 8.30am-7.30pm Tue-Sun). Worth a visit, the monastery's church has exquisite marble work and frescoes and magnificent views from the terraced gardens.

Festivals & Events

The **Festa di San Gennaro** honours the city's patron saint and is held three times a year (first Sunday in May, 19 September and 16 December). Thousands swarm the Duomo to witness the saint's blood, held in two vials, liquefy, a miracle said to save the city from potential disasters. Don't miss it.

Sleeping

While accommodation in Naples is plentiful, and can be charming, quality varies considerably, particularly around Stazione Centrale and Piazza Garibaldi, which can be seedy. Our recommendations in this zone are clean, safe and reliable.

To best experience the historic centre, stay in convenient and festive Spaccanapoli. Those seeking a peaceful reprieve will be happiest staying in Mergellina, Vomero or Santa Lucia.

AROUND STAZIONE CENTRALE

Hotel Ginevra (☎ 081 28 32 10; www.hotelginevra.it; Via Genova 116; d/tr €60/100, s/d/tr with shared bathroom €30/50/70) This long-time favourite is tidy and lovingly kept by the exuberant owners; the same holds true for the same-floor sister hotel, Ginevra 2, with plusher rooms.

Vicoletti (☎ 081 56 41 156; Via S Domenico Soriano 46; s/d/tr €55/78/100, with shared bathroom €42/62/90) This cheery spot has a sunny, colourful décor, pretty terrace, spacious rooms and friendly owners.

AROUND SPACCANAPOLI

6 Small Rooms (☎ 081 790 13 78; www.at6smallrooms .com; Via Diodato Lioy 18; dm/d incl breakfast €18/25) This friendly and sociable hostel has sun-lit rooms, a spacious kitchen and an excellent reputation with travellers.

Hotel Bellini (☎ 081 45 69 96; Via San Paolo 44; s/d €51/70) Tucked away in the heart of the old centre, this snug hotel oozes Neapolitan charm.

Napolit'amo (☎ 081 552 36 26; www.napolitamo.it, in Italian; Via Toledo 148; s/d incl breakfast €65/90) Feel like royalty in this 16th-century palace, packed with faded glory and stylish décor.

Soggiorno Sansevero (☎ 081 551 57 42; www .albergosansevero.it; Piazza San Domenico Maggiore 9; s/d €80/100, with shared bathroom €58/68) One of a three-property chain, this tasteful hotel is housed in a historic building and offers excellent value for money.

MERGELLINA, VOMERO & SANTA LUCIA

Pensione Margherita (☎ 081 556 70 44; Via D Cimarosa 29; s/d/tr €35/62/87) Just near the funicular station, this is a no-frills place in a pretty part of town; ask for a room with a bay view, and have a coin handy for the lift.

Hostel of the Sun (☎ /fax 081 420 63 93; www .hostelnapoli.com; Via Melisurgo 15; d €70, dm/s/d with shared bathroom €18/40/50; ▣) Handy for ferry travellers, this popular 7th-floor hostel has a ready-to-please young staff, and offers the use of kitchen and laundry. Internet per 30 minutes costs €2.

Hotel Rex (☎ 081 764 93 89; www.hotel-rex.it; Via Palepoli 12; d incl breakfast €125; ❁) A relaxed

ITALY

three-star near the sea; breakfast is served in your room.

Hotel Miramare (☎ 081 764 75 89; Via Nazario Sauro 24; s/d €149/203; 🅿 🖵) With perfect bay views, breakfast (and hammocks) on the rooftop terrace, funky Art Deco décor and free Internet, this former villa offers an airy splurge and delightful reprieve from the frenetic centre.

Eating

It would take serious effort not to eat well in Naples, and the centre is packed with good options. Pizza was created here during the 18th century, and once you sample a classic *margherita* – with fresh mozzarella, tomato sauce, olive oil and sea salt – you'll want one every meal. Save room for *calzone* (puffed-up dough stuffed with toppings), *misto di frittura* (deep-fried vegetables) and the excellent local seafood; it's worth sinning for the coffee and cakes. Naples has many good *alimentari* and food stalls – try **Friggitoria Fiorenzano** (Piazza Montesanto 6) and gorge yourself silly on heavenly fried vegetables at bargain prices.

CITY CENTRE

Da Michele (☎ 081 55 39 204; Via Cesare Sersale 1; pizzas €5-7) A top contender for world's best pizza, this unpretentious place draws legions of fans who queue patiently for the masterpieces.

La Chiacchierata (☎ 081 41 14 65; Piazzetta Matilde Serao 37; mains from €8; ☽ lunch & Fri pm) This Bijou, family-run cosy spot has a loyal local following, simple and delicious fare and an on-view kitchen.

Trianon (☎ 081 553 94 26; Via P Colletta 46; pizzas €5-10) This local institution, with marble-topped tables and a warm welcome, has been tossing very good pizzas since 1923.

Pizzeria Sorbillo (☎ 081 44 66 43; Via dei Tribunali; pizzas from €5) A long lineage of talented *pizza-ioli* have secured this always-packed place as a shoe-in contender for Naples' No 1 pizza parlour.

MERGELLINA, VOMERO & SANTA LUCIA

Pizzeria da Pasqualino (☎ 081 68 15 24; Piazza Sannazzaro 79; pizzas €5) Near the Mergellina station, this likeable trattoria has outdoor tables on the busy square; restore your faith in the world with its *margherita* pizza and an *insalata caprese*.

Trattoria Castel dell'Ovo (☎ 081 76 46 352; Via Luculliana 28; mains from €8) This unpretentious spot, southwest of Santa Lucia, serves well-priced, delicious seafood at harbour-side tables with lovely views of Borgo Marinaro.

Cantina di Sica (☎ 081 556 75 20; Via C Bernini 17; mains from €10) This beloved Vomero trattoria has a vaulted ceiling and serves excellent Neapolitan fare; try the *spaghetti alle vongole e pomodorini* (with clams and cherry tomatoes).

Drinking

BARS

There is a handful of lively bars in Piazza Gesù Nuovo.

Bar Lazzarella (Calata Trinita Maggiore 7-8) A popular watering hole.

Vineria del Corso (Via Paladino 8a) Snug, with a good wine list, welcoming lighting, charming décor and low-key electronica played at a polite volume.

CAFÉS

Caffè Gambrinus (☎ 081 41 41 33; Via Chiaia 12) Naples' oldest and most posh café remains a beloved haunt for artists, intellectuals and musicians – including saxophonist and former US president Bill Clinton.

Intra Moenia (☎ 081 29 07 20; Piazza Bellini 70; salads from €5) Tucked onto a beautiful piazza, this café/bookshop/publishing house hosts the city's intellectual elite; it's arty, literary, left leaning – with excellent salads to boot.

Caffè dell'Epoca (☎ 081 29 17 22; Via Santa Maria di Constantinopoli 81-82) Serving up Naples' best coffee in a hip way.

Entertainment

The monthly *Qui Napoli* and local newspapers are the best guides to what's on when. In May the city organises Maggio dei Monumenti, a month of mostly free concerts and cultural events. Ask at the tourist offices for details. **Teatro San Carlo** (☎ 081 797 21 11; www .teatrosancarlo.it, in Italian; Via San Carlo 98; tickets from €20) has year-round concerts and performances of opera and ballet.

Getting There & Away

AIR

Capodichino Airport (☎ 081 789 62 59) is about 6km northeast of the city centre and links Naples with most Italian and several European cities. Take an **ANM** (☎ 800 63 95 25) city bus No 3S (€0.77, 30 minutes, every 15 minutes) from Piazza Garibaldi or the Alibus airport bus (€3, 20 minutes, at least hourly) from Piazza Municipio. A taxi will cost about €30.

BOAT

Naples is above all a water city, and *traghetti* (ferries), *aliscafi* (hydrofoils) and *navi veloci* (fast ships) leave for Sorrento and the islands of Capri, Ischia and Procida from Molo Beverello, in front of Castel Nuovo. Some hydrofoils leave for the bay islands from Mergellina, and ferries for Ischia and Procida also leave from Pozzuoli. All operators have offices at the various ports from which they leave. Hydrofoils cost around double the price of ferries but take half the time. **Tirrenia** (☎ 199 12 31 99) operates ferries to Palermo (€45, 9¾ hours, daily) and Cagliari (€39, 13½ hours, weekly) while **Siremar** (☎ 081 580 03 40) services the Aeolian Islands and Milazzo. **SNAV** (☎ 081 428 51 11) runs hydrofoils to the islands of Capri (€12, 30 minutes), Procida and Ischia, and a daily Sicilia Jet to Palermo mid-April to September. **Caremar** (☎ 081 551 38 82) services Capri (hydrofoil €12, 30 minutes; ferry €6, 1½ hours), Procida and Ischia by ferry and hydrofoil.

BUS

Buses leave from Piazza Garibaldi, in front of the train station, for nearby destinations, including Salerno, the Amalfi Coast and Caserta, as well as far-flung Bari (€20, three hours), Lecce (€25, 5½ hours) and Brindisi (€23, five hours). Signage is sparse, so check destinations carefully or ask at the information kiosk.

CAR & MOTORCYCLE

If you value your sanity and life, skip driving in Naples. The traffic is constant and chaotic, theft is rife and the street plan does not lend itself to easy navigation. But if you want to tempt fate, the city is easily accessible from Rome on the A1. The Naples–Pompeii–Salerno road (A3) connects with the coastal road to Sorrento and the Amalfi Coast.

TRAIN

Naples is the rail hub for the south, and regular trains for most major Italian cities arrive and depart from Stazione Centrale. There are up to 30 trains daily to/from Rome.

Getting Around

You can make your way around Naples by bus, tram, metro and funicular. City **ANM** (☎ 800 63 95 25) buses leave from Piazza Garibaldi for the centre of Naples and Mergellina. You can buy 'Giranapoli' tickets at stations, ANM booths and tobacconists. A ticket costs €0.77 and is valid for 1½ hours of unlimited public transit. A daily ticket is good value at €2.32. Useful buses include No 3S to the airport; the R1 to Piazza Dante; the R3 from Mergellina; and No 110 from Piazza Garibaldi to Piazza Cavour and the archaeological museum. Tram No 1 leaves from east of Stazione Centrale for the city centre. To get to Molo Beverello and the ferry terminal, take bus No R2 or M1.

The metro station is downstairs at the train station. Line one runs north from Piazza Dante, with stops at Piazza Cavour, Salvator Rosa, Cilea, Piazza Vanvitelli, Piazza Medaglie d'Oro and seven stops beyond. Line two heads west to Mergellina, with stops at Piazza Cavour, Piazza Amedeo and the funicular to Vomero, and on to the Campi Flegrei and Pozzuoli.

The main funicular connecting the city centre with Vomero is located in Piazza Duca d'Aosta, next to Galleria Umberto I, on Via Toledo.

The Ferrovia Circumvesuviana operates trains for Herculaneum, Pompeii and Sorrento. The station is about 400m southwest of Stazione Centrale, in Corso Garibaldi (take the underpass from Stazione Centrale). The Ferrovia Cumana and the Circumflegrea, based at Stazione Cumana in Piazza Montesanto, operate services to Pozzuoli, Baia and Cumae every 20 minutes.

AROUND NAPLES

From Naples, it's a short jaunt to **Campi Flegrei**, with volcanic lakes and mud baths that provided inspiration for the writings of both Homer and Virgil. Though now an overdeveloped suburb, the area still has tinges of its ancient Greek and Roman past, making it a worthwhile half-day trip. Take metro line two.

In the Greek colony of Cuma, visit the **Cave of the Cumaean Sybil**, home of one of the ancient world's greatest oracles. Nearby are **Lake Avernus**, a crater lake marking the mythical entrance to the underworld (and a nice picnic spot), and **Baia**, once a fashionable and debaucherous Roman resort whose submerged remains are viewable from a glass-bottomed boat.

Reached by CPTC bus (€2.70, every 30 minutes) from Naples' Piazza Garibaldi, or by train from the Stazione Centrale, is the lovely **Palazzo Reale** (☎ 0823 44 74 47; admission €6; ☙ 8.30am-7pm Tue-Sun) at Caserta. Built in the 18th century under the Bourbon king Charles III, who wanted his own Versailles, this imposing 1200-room palace is set in elegant gardens.

Pompeii

In AD 79 Mt Vesuvius blew its top and buried Pompeii under layers of lapilli (burning fragments of pumice stone), killing 2000 in the deluge. The world's most famous volcano disaster left behind fascinating **ruins** (☎ 081 857 53 47; www.pompeiisites.org; admission €10, combined ticket incl Herculaneum & 3 minor sites €18; ☙ 8.30am-7.30pm Apr-Oct, 8.30-5pm Nov-Mar) that provide insight into the daily life of ancient Romans. Once a resort town for the wealthy, the vast ruins include impressive temples, a forum, an amphitheatre, and streets lined with shops and luxurious homes. Most of the site's original mosaics and frescoes are on view at Naples' Museo Archeologico Nazionale (p759), but those adorning Villa dei Misteri have stayed intact. Many ruins are open to the public and allow about four hours to visit; bring a hat or umbrella, depending on the weather.

There is a **tourist office** (☎ 081 850 72 55; Via Sacra 1; ☙ 8am-3.30pm Mon-Sat Oct-Mar, 8am-7pm Mon-Sat Apr-Sep) in Pompeii town, and another **tourist office** (☎ 800 01 33 50; Piazza Porta Marina Inferiore 12; ☙ 8am-3.30pm Mon-Sat) just outside the excavations at Porta Marina.

Catch the Ferrovia Circumvesuviana train from Naples and get off at the Pompeii Scavi-Villa dei Misteri stop; the Porta Marina entrance is nearby.

CAPRI
pop 7270

Gorgeous Capri has been charming holiday seekers since Emperor Augustus and Tiberius made it their summer play pad around AD 27. Come summer, hordes of chatty day-trippers and swanky jetsetters pack onto the island, less than an hour by boat from Naples and heavily geared towards tourism. Nonetheless, like a deep golden tan, the place never seems to lose its appeal and remains fetchingly beautiful. Famed for its grottoes, Capri also has fantastic walking.

Online information can be found at www .capri.it and www.capritourism.com. There are also numerous **tourist offices** (Marina Grande ☎ 081 837 06 34; ☙ 8.30am-8.30pm; Capri town ☎ 081 837 06 86; Piazza Umberto I; ☙ 8.30am-8.30pm; Anacapri ☎ 081 837 15 24; Piazza Vittoria 4; ☙ 8.30am-8.30pm) in town.

Sights & Activities

Capri's craggy coast is studded with dozens of sea caves, visitable by boat, of which the sparkling **Blue Grotto** (admission €4; ☙ visits 9am-1hr before sunset) is the most famous. Boats leave to visit the cave from the Marina Grande and a return trip will cost €15.30, including the return motor boat to the grotto, rowing boat in, admission fee and singing captains; allow an hour for the trip. You'll save little money and spend more time if you catch a bus from either town, as you still have to pay for the rowing boat and admission.

You can walk to most of the interesting points on the island. Close to Capri centre is the commanding **Giardini d'Augusto**. One hour uphill, along Via Tiberio, is **Villa Jovis** (admission €2; ☙ 9am-1hr before sunset), the ruins of one of Tiberius' villas. It's a gorgeous walk along Via Matrimonia to the **Arco Naturale** – follow the spur trail, marked by splashes of paint, winding up the piny hillside. Near Anacapri, the resplendent **Villa San Michele** (☎ 081 837 14 01; Viale Axel Munthe; admission €5; ☙ 9am-6pm May-Sep, 10.30am-4.30pm Oct-Apr) was the home of Swedish writer and dog-lover Dr Axel Munthe.

Sleeping & Eating

If you come in spring or autumn, you'll find good off-season rates.

Albergo Stella Maris (☎ 081 837 04 52; Via Roma 27; s/d €45/80) Right in the noisy heart of town and just off Piazza Umberto I, this place is convenient, with functional but small rooms.

Hotel La Minerva (☎ 081 837 03 74; www.laminerva capri.com; Via Occhiio Marino; s/d incl breakfast €80/150; ☒) This lovely three-star with gorgeous views, bright rooms and sunny tiles everywhere is good value, Capri-style.

Loreley (☎ 081 837 14 40; fax 081 837 13 99; Via G Orlandi 16; s/d incl breakfast €75/115; ☙ Mar-Nov) In Anacapri, this above-average hotel has decent rooms, some with views.

ITALY

Pulalli Wine Bar (☎ 081 837 4108; Piazza Umberto I; mains from €4) Perched in the clock tower overlooking Capri's main piazza, this great spot serves light meals and good vino.

La Grottelle (☎ 081 837 57 19; Via Arco Naturale 13; pasta from €8) Tucked inside a couple of small caves near Arco Naturale, this popular spot has simple and tasty dishes.

Villa Brunella (☎ 081 837 01 22; www.villabrunella .it; Via Tragara 24a; mains from €14) Away from the din, this very pretty restaurant has top service, good sea views and some of the best seafood around; the attached **hotel** (d €240; [icon] [icon]) is equally elegant, with a nice terrace pool.

Il Saraceno (☎ 081 837 20 99; Via Trieste e Trento 18; pasta from €7) A pleasant Anacapri spot with tasty *ravioli caprese* and the proprietor's own wine and *limoncello*.

Getting There & Around
There are hydrofoils and ferries virtually every hour from Naples' Molo Beverello and Mergellina, especially in summer. In Naples, pick up the daily *Il Mattino* for sailing times. Several companies make the trip; see p761. Hydrofoils cost about €12 each way and take about 30 minutes; ferries cost €6 each way and take about 1½ hours.

From Marina Grande, a funicular takes you to the town of Capri, at the top of a steep hill some 3km from the port up a winding road. Local buses connect the port with Capri, Anacapri and other points around the island, and run between the two main towns until past midnight. Tickets for the funicular and buses cost €1.30 each trip or €6.71 per daily ticket.

SORRENTO
pop 17,450

A shameless resort town, pretty Sorrento gazes out over the Bay of Naples and lures throngs of holiday seekers to its sunny, crowded streets. Still, southern Italian charm goes straight to the soul – come off season or use as a fun, handy pause before heading to Capri and the Amalfi Coast.

Orientation
The centre of town is Piazza Tasso, a short walk from the train station along Corso Italia. If you arrive by boat at Marina Piccola, walk south along Via Marina Piccola then climb the 200 steps to reach the piazza.

Information
EMERGENCY
Ospedale Civile (☎ 081 533 11 11; Corso Italia 1)
Police station (Questura; ☎ 081 807 44 33; Corso Italia 236)

INTERNET ACCESS
Sorrento Info (Via Tasso 19; per hr €6)

MONEY
Deutsche Bank (Piazza Angelina Laura) Has an ATM.

POST
Post office (Corso Italia 210)

TELEPHONE
Telecom office (Piazza Tasso 37)

TOURIST INFORMATION
Tourist information office (☎ 081 807 40 33; www .sorrentotourism.it; Via Luigi de Maio 35; [icon] 8.45am-6.15pm Mon-Sat) An excellent office inside the Circolo dei Forestieri complex.

Sleeping & Eating
Nube d'Argento (☎ 081 878 13 44; www.nubedargento .com; Via del Capo 21; per person/tent €9/9.50) This nearby camping ground is tucked into a sea of olive trees and 200m from the beach; head south along Corso Italia, then follow Via Capo.

Villa Elisa (☎ 081 878 27 92; Piazza S Antonino 2; s/d €70/90) Five pretty rooms surround a courtyard at this convenient, pleasant spot with a sweet rooftop terrace and in-room kitchen facilities.

Pensione Linda (☎ 081 878 29 16; Via degli Aranci 125; s/d €35/70) This modest hotel has good value, old-fashioned courtesy, nice spacious rooms and eclectic and attractive furnishings.

Hotel La Tonnarella (☎ 081 878 11 53; www.laton narella.com; Via Capo 31; d €140) This elegant roost sports pretty lemon and blue tiles, sweeping sea views and a private lift to the beach.

Self-Service Angelina Lauro (☎ 081 807 47 08; Piazza Angelina Lauro 39; pastas from €4) An economical snack venue with a nice selection for vegetarians.

Pizzeria Gastronomia (☎ 081 807 40 97; Via degli Aranci; pizzas from €3) A tasty and cheery spot opposite Pensione Linda.

Bollicine (☎ 081 878 46 16; Via dell'Accademia 9; glass of wine from €2) This snug wine bar serves good local varietals and light meals.

ITALY

La Fenice (☎ 081 878 16 52; Via degli Aranci 11; mains from €8, pizzas from €4) Rightfully popular, this pretty spot serves delicious fresh seafood and good pizzas.

Getting There & Away

Circumvesuviana trains run every 30 minutes between Sorrento and Naples via Pompeii and Ercolano. At least 12 SITA buses a day leave from outside the train station for the Amalfi Coast (€3). Hydrofoils and ferries leave for Capri (€20 return, 20 minutes), Napoli (€15 return, 35 minutes) and Ischia from the port at Marina Piccola; the tourist office has timetables.

AMALFI COAST

This 50km of cliff-hugging coastline is some of Europe's most dazzling, luring wealthy holiday seekers who pay skyrockethigh prices in summer. Nonetheless, the natural beauty is dazzling and the lemonterraced land and aquamarine coves aren't to be missed – save money and patience by visiting in spring or autumn.

There are tourist offices in the individual towns. For itinerary planning, www.amalficoast.com is useful.

Getting There & Away

SITA buses head to Sorrento (€2.30, more than 10 daily) via Positano (€1.30), and hourly to Salerno (€1.80), which is a 40-minute train trip from Naples. Buses stop in Amalfi at Piazza Flavio Gioia, from where you can catch a bus to Ravello.

The narrow, spectacular and tortuous coastal road is clogged with traffic in summer; be prepared for delays. Things are a little quieter at other times. **Sorrento Rentacar** (☎ 081 878 13 86; Corso Italia 210a, Sorrento) rents scooters and cars.

Hydrofoils and ferries service the coast between April and mid-September, leaving from Salerno and stopping at Amalfi and Positano. There are also boats between Positano and Capri, and to Naples.

Positano
pop 3900

With its Moorish flair and colourful houses, Positano is the most photographed, fashionable and expensive town on the coast. The colourful centre is laden with boutiques (selling locally made clothing) and has more steps than streets. The hills behind the town are full of wonderful walks; pick up a hiking map at the **tourist office** (☎ 089 87 50 67; Via del Saracino 4; ☺ 8am-2pm & 3.30-8pm Mon-Sat year-round, 3.30-8pm Jul & Aug).

Villa Nettuno (☎ 089 87 54 01; www.villanettuno positano.it; Via Pasitea 208; s/d €70/80) On the south end of town, this cheery hotel is tucked into a pretty garden and most rooms have balconies.

Villa Rosa (☎ 089 81 19 55; www.villarosapositano.it; Via C Colombo 127; d incl breakfast €149) This charming family-run villa at the other end of town has very pretty rooms, all with terraces.

Il Saraceno d'Oro (Viale Pasitea 254; pizza about €6) A popular eatery with decent pizzas and exceptional profiteroles.

Nearby, the new **2next2** (Via Pasitea 242) bar has a glitterati crowd, while closer to town **Caffè Positano** (Viale Pasitea) has a small terrace ideal for a sunny cappuccino or *aperitivo* under the stars.

AROUND POSITANO

Hikers will love the classic **Sentiero degli Dei** (Path of the Gods; five to 5½ hours) – ask at the tourist office. For a shorter option, head to **Nocelle**, a tiny village above Positano, accessible by walking track from the stairs near Bar Internazionale. Have lunch at **Trattoria Santa Croce** (☎ 089 81 12 60; pastas from €6; ☺ lunch & dinner spring-autumn), with panoramic views. Nocelle is accessible by local bus from Positano via Montepertuso.

Just south of Positano is the town of **Praiano**, less scenic but with the only camping ground on the Amalfi Coast. **La Tranquillità** (☎ 089 87 40 84; www.continental.praiano.it; Via Roma 21; 2 people & tent €39, bungalows €90) has many sleeping options, and the SITA bus stops outside.

Amalfi
pop 5528

A maritime superpower during the 11th century, Amalfi is now a legendary tourist resort. Despite being packed to the gills in summer, the town retains an appealing vibe. In the centre is an impressive **Duomo** (☎ 089 87 10 59) and nearby is the **Grotta dello Smeraldo** (admission €5; ☺ 9am-4pm), a rival to Capri's Blue Grotto. This is excellent walking terrain. The **tourist office** (☎ 089 87 11 07; Corso Roma 19; ☺ 8.30am-1.30pm & 3-5.30pm Mon-Fri, to 12.30pm Sat) can provide details.

In the hills behind Amalfi is delightful and breezy **Ravello**, accessible by bus and walking paths, with magnificent 11th-century **Villa Rufolo** (admission €4; ☼ 9am-6pm), once the home of popes and later of the German composer Wagner. The 20th-century **Villa Cimbrone**, a Greta Garbo hideaway, is also set in pretty gardens, which end at a terrace offering a spectacular view of the Gulf of Salerno.

There are numerous walking paths in the hills between Amalfi and Ravello; you can also visit the vineyards surrounding the towns.

SLEEPING & EATING

Locanda Costa d'Amalfi (☎ 089 83 19 50; Via G Augustariccio 50; s/d incl breakfast €55/60) This well-priced newcomer, a few kilometres before town, has six well-appointed rooms and a sunny air. You can get there by bus or taxi.

Hotel Lidomare (☎ 089 87 13 32; www.lidomare.it; Largo Duchi Piccolomini 9; s/d incl breakfast €50/90) This lovely family-run hotel is excellent value – romantic rooms, elegant furnishings and kind service.

Hotel Toro (☎ 089 85 72 11; www.hoteltoro.it; s/d incl breakfast €74/105) In Ravello, just off Piazza Duomo, this hotel is pleasant with nice rooms and a pretty walled garden.

Trattoria San Giuseppe (Salita Ruggerio II 4; pizza & pasta from €7) A tasty, family-run joint hidden away in Amalfi's maze-like alleyways; follow signs from Via Lorenzo d'Amalfi.

Pizzeria al Teatro (Via E Marini 19; pizza & pasta from €7) Good local dishes and a welcoming ambience. Follow the signs to the left from Via Pietro Capuana, the main shopping street.

Cantina S Nicola (Salita Marino Sebaste 8) This new wine bar, with vaulted ceilings and a robust by-the-glass list, is excellent for light meals.

The best pastries are at **Pasticceria Andrea Pansa** (Piazza Duomo 40), with luxe charm, and **Casbahr** (Piazza Umberto 1) gets the local vote for friendliest coffee spot.

The warm and bustling **Cumpa Cosimo** (Via Roma 44-6; mains from €8) has great food and friendly service, plus everything you eat and drink is from the family farm.

PAESTUM

One of southern Italy's most lasting images is that of three stark white Greek **temples** (☼ 9am-1hr before sunset; admission €4, with museum €6.50) towering in a field of bright red pop-

pies. This majestic trio, just south of Salerno, are among the best-preserved temples of Magna Graecia, a Unesco World Heritage site, and well worth a visit. At the site, there's an informative **tourist office** (☎ 0828 81 10 16; ☼ 9am-4pm) and an evocative **museum** (☼ 9am-7pm; admission €4, with temples €6.50). Buy a combined entrance ticket (€6.50), covering the temples and museum; separate admissions are €4 each.

Paestum is accessible by **CSTP** (☎ 800 01 66 59) and **SCAT** (☎ 0974 83 4 15) buses, departing hourly from Salerno's Piazza della Concordia, and by train.

MATERA

pop 57,315

Unique and ancient Matera delicately balances its peasant-class past with its burgeoning modern face. Its famous *sassi* – stone houses carved into the two ravines that slice through town – were home to half the town's population through the 1950s, when the peasant class was relocated to new government housing just outside of the town. Now a Unesco World Heritage site, the cave homes still evoke a powerful image of a poverty that's difficult to imagine in a developed European country. Mel Gibson filmed *The Passion of the Christ* in Matera, which has added a new dimension of tourism, and an additional step away from the town's poverty-stricken and malaria-ridden roots. For a refresher course, Francesco Rosi's excellent film *Cristo si é Fermato a Eboli* (Christ Stopped at Eboli), originally a book by Carlo Levi, is a poignant illustration of what life was once like in Basilicata. Today people are returning to live in the *sassi* – but as a trend rather than a necessity.

There's a **tourist office** (☎ 0835 33 19 83; Via De Viti De Marco 9; ☼ 9am-1pm Mon-Sat & 4-6.30pm Mon & Thu), off the main Via Romas. It's easy enough to navigate yourself through the *sassi*, particularly with the helpful map *Matera: Percorsi Turistici* (€1.30), with four easy-to-follow itineraries.

Sights & Activities

The two *sassi* areas, **Barisano** and **Caveoso**, had no electricity, running water or sewerage system until well into the 20th century. The oldest *sassi* (dating from medieval times or earlier) are at the top of the ravines, while the dwellings in the lower sections, which appear to be the oldest, were in fact established in the 1920s – as space ran out, the population began moving into hand-hewn or natural caves. The *sassi* zones are accessible from Piazza Vittorio Veneto and Piazza del Duomo in the centre of Matera. Caveoso is the more picturesque and its highlights include the rock churches or **Santa Maria d'Idris** and **Santa Lucia alla Malve**, both with well-preserved Byzantine frescoes. The 13th-century Puglian-Romanesque **cathedral**, which overlooks Sasso Barisano, also warrants a stop. A couple of *sassi* have been refurnished as they were when the last peasant inhabitants occupied them, of which **Casa-Grotta di Vico Solitario** (admission €1.50) is worth a visit.

Sleeping & Eating

Albergo Roma (☎ /fax 0835 33 39 12; Via Roma 62; s/d €22/32) This very central hotel has basic rooms at unbeatable prices.

Locanda Di San Martino (☎ /fax 0835 25 66 00; Via San Martino 22; s/d incl breakfast €60/80) This new *sassi* hotel elegantly meshes the past and present; very pretty rooms, balconies and a cave bar.

Le Botteghe (☎ 0835 34 40 72; Piazza San Pietro Barisano 22; pastas from €6) Tasty local dishes, salads and excellent wines.

Il Cantuccio (☎ 0835 33 20 90; Via delle Beccherie 33; secondo from €7) Serves cavarie pastas to a local clientele – try the delicious *cavatelli al frantoio*, a local pasta dish with olives.

Fresh-produce market (Via A Persio) Daily market, just south of Piazza Vittoria Veneto.

Getting There & Away

SITA buses connect Matera with Taranto and Metaponto. The town is on the private Ferrovie Apulo-Lucane train line, which connects with Bari, Altamura and Potenza. There are also three Marozzi buses a day between Rome and Matera (€30). Buy tickets at **Biglietteria Manicone** (☎ 0835 332 86 21; Piazza Matteoti 3).

PUGLIA

The province of Puglia comprises the hardscrabble heel of Italy's boot, bound by the Adriatic and Ionian Seas. Oft dismissed as an impoverished backwater by northerners, the region knows better and seems content to quietly harbour its natural beauty and artistic brilliance. In the past, this coastline was fought over by virtually every major colonial

power, from the Greeks to the Spanish, all intent on establishing a strategic foothold in the Mediterranean and leaving their architectural stamp. Today, there's a strong regional pride, the cuisine is exceptional and the area remains relatively untouristed. A helpful source for planning is www.pugliaturismo.com, in Italian.

Brindisi

pop 90,020

Despite its shady reputation, Brindisi is probably more boring than dangerous. The major embarkation point for ferries to Greece, the city swarms with people in transit – and there's little to do here but wait for your boat. Most backpackers gather at the train station or ferry terminal, or in pedestrianised Piazza Cairoli or Piazza del Popolo. The old port is a 10-minute walk from the station, along Corso Umberto I, which leads into Corso Garibaldi; the new port (Costa Morena) is east of town, 7km from the station, with free bus connections linking the two.

Be exceedingly mindful of your possessions at all times, but particularly in the areas around the train station and ports.

There's a helpful **tourist office** (☎ 0831 52 30 72; Viale Regina Margherita 44; ☒ 8.30am-2pm & 3.30-7pm Mon-Fri, 8.30am-1pm Sat).

Carpe Diem (☎ 0831 59 79 54; Via N Brandi 2; dm €14) is a cheery private hostel 2km from town with laundry facilities and offering an evening meal (€7); hop on bus No 3 from Via Cristoforo Colombo near the train station or call for a pick-up.

Tucked off Corso Garibaldi, and a five-minute walk from the port bus stop, the modest **Hotel Altair** (☎ 0831 56 22 89; Via Giudea 4; s/d €30/50, with shared bathroom €20/37) with high-ceilinged rooms is ideal for early-morning departures.

The popular **Iaccato** (☎ 0831 52 40 84; Via Lenio Flacco 32; mains from €7) has happy owners and terrific seafood specialities.

For boat-trip supplies, hit the morning **market** (Piazza Mercato) or the **supermarket** (Corso Garibaldi 106).

GETTING THERE & AWAY
Boat

Ferries, all of which take vehicles and have snack bars and restaurants, leave Brindisi for Greek destinations, including Corfu (10 to 15 hours), Igoumenitsa (nine to 12 hours) and Patra (15 to 20 hours). Boats also service Albania (daily) and Turkey (seasonal).

Most ferry companies operate only in summer. All have offices at Costa Morena, and the major ones also have offices in town along Corso Garibaldi.

Major ferry companies are **Hellenic Mediterranean Lines** (HML; ☎ 0831 52 85 31; www.hml.gr; Corso Garibaldi 8), **Blue Star Ferries** (☎ 0831 56 22 00; www.bluestarferries.com; Corso Garibaldi 65), **Italian Ferries** (☎ 0831 59 08 40; www.italianferries.it; Corso Garibaldi 96) and **Med Link Lines** (☎ 0831 52 76 67; www.ferries.gr/medlink; Corso Garibaldi 49).

The largest, most expensive and most reliable of the lines, HML also officially accepts Eurail and Inter-Rail passes, entitling you to travel free in deck class (paying a €15 supplement in July and August). If you intend to use your pass, it is best to reserve in advance in summer.

Discounts are available for travellers under 26 years of age and holders of some Italian rail passes. Fares generally increase by up to 40% on peak travel days in July and August, and you might save 20% on a round-trip ticket. At the time of writing, HML's low-/high-season fares for one-way deck-class service to Greece were €30/49; for a car €29/55; and for a motorcycle €12/20.

Look up details of fares and timetables on www.ferries.gr. Be wary of any too-good-to-be-true offers from fly-by-night operators claiming your Eurail and Inter-Rail pass is accepted by them or invalid with anyone else.

The port tax is €6, payable when you buy your ticket. Check in at least two hours before departure or risk losing your reservation. To get to the new port of Costa Morena from the train station take the free Portabagagli bus, departing a handy two hours before boat departures.

Bus

Marozzi runs four buses daily to Stazione Tiburtina in Rome (€32.55, nine hours), leaving from Viale Arno. **Appia Travel** (☎ 0831 52 16 84; Viale Regina Margherita 8-9) sells tickets. There are rail connections to major cities in northern Italy, as well as to Bari, Lecce, Ancona, Naples and Rome, and you can fly to/from Rome, Naples, Milan, Bologna and Pisa from Brindisi's small airport, Papola Casale (BDS).

Lecce
pop 97,462
This sparkling little city hosts an astonishing array of baroque architecture and the effect is of a crazy but delightful architect gone a bit mad. Unabashedly opulent, the local style is known to Italians as *barocco leccese* (Lecce baroque), and Lecce is oft referred to as the 'Florence of the South'. The university town exudes a sassy charm and sports a vibrant bar scene at weekends. It's also home to a high population of lawyers, but don't let that discourage you from visiting this elegant surprise.

There is a sleepy **tourist office** (☎ 0832 24 80 92; Corso Vittorio Emanuele 24) near Piazza Duomo. The historic centre is a five-minute walk from the station, or take bus No 1, 2 or 4 from the station to Viale Marconi.

SIGHTS
Lecce's baroque style is most famously on display at the **Basilica della Santa Croce** (☎ 0832 24 19 57; Via Umberto I; admission free; ☽ 8am-1pm & 4-7.30pm). A team of artists worked throughout the 16th and 17th centuries to decorate the building and its extraordinarily ornate façade. In the **Piazza del Duomo** are the 12th-century **cathedral** (admission free; ☽ 6.30am-noon & 5-7.30pm), completely restored in baroque style by Giuseppe Zimbalo, and its 70m-high **bell tower**; the 15th-century **Palazzo Vescovile** (Bishop's Palace); and the **Seminario**, with its elegant façade and baroque well in the courtyard. The piazza is particularly beautiful at night, illuminated by floodlights. In **Piazza Sant'Oronzo** are the remains of a 2nd-century-AD **Roman amphitheatre**.

SLEEPING & EATING
Centro Storico Prestige (☎ 0832 24 33 53; www.bbprestige-lecce.it; Via S Maria del Paradiso; per person incl breakfast €40) On the 3rd floor of a 16th-century palazzo, this gem has elegantly furnished and balconied rooms, a roof garden and a hip owner.

Azzurretta B&B (☎ 338 258 59 58; www.bblecce.it, in Italian; Via Vignes 2; s/d incl breakfast €35/63) On the same floor as the Centro Storico Prestige, and run by the same family; both are excellent city-centre options.

Hotel Cappello (☎ 0832 30 88 81; Via Montegrappa 4; s/d €30/45) For station convenience, this is your best option.

Trattoria Casereccia (☎ 0832 24 51 78; Via Colonello Costadura 19; pasta from €6) This family-run favourite serves home cooking at good value.

Ristorante Da Guido e Figli (☎ 0832 30 58 68; Via XXV Luglio 14; antipasti from €2) Both the formal dining room and take-away area have delicious food; for good value, hit the delicious self-service antipasto buffet.

ENTERTAINMENT
Seemingly sedate Lecce comes alive on weekend nights, and there are some great little bars in its historic centre. Try **Caffè Letterario** (Via Paladini 46), where you can enjoy wine by the glass in colourful surrounds, **Al di Vino Bicchiere** (Via S Maria del Paradiso 4), an elegant little *enoteca*, **I Merli** (Via Federico D'Aragona), where locals crowd nightly, and **B Lounge** (Via Federico D'Aragona), just across the street.

GETTING THERE & AWAY
STP bus services connect Lecce with towns throughout the Salentine peninsula, departing from Via Adua.

There are frequent trains to Brindisi (€3, 40 minutes), Bari (€8, 2¼ hours), Rome (€40, seven hours), Naples (€30.50, six hours) and Bologna (€42.30, 8½ hours), as well as to points throughout Puglia.

SICILY

Sun-baked Sicily shines with visible layers of its rich and often turbulent history. Afloat in the Mediterranean, Italy's largest island coddles Greek temples, Arab domes, Byzantine mosaics, Norman churches and baroque architecture. Its magnificent landscape is dominated by Mt Etna (3350m) on the east coast, laced with fertile citrus groves, fringed with dazzling coastline, and with a vast plateau at its heart.

With a population of just over five million, Sicily has a mild climate in winter and a relentlessly hot summer. The best times to visit are spring and autumn.

Most ferries from Italy arrive at Sicily's capital, Palermo, which is convenient as a jumping-off point. If you're short on time, spend a day in Palermo and then hit Taormina, Syracuse or Agrigento.

No need to worry about a *Godfather*-style confrontation, though the Mafia does remain a powerful, if crumbling, force. Car thieves

and the occasional overly friendly male local are the only safety concerns.

Getting There & Away
AIR
Flights from all over mainland Italy and from major European cities land at Palermo (PMO) and Catania (CTA). For information on flights to/from Sicily, contact **Alitalia** (☎ 00 39 06 65 641; www.alitalia.com).

BOAT
Sicily is accessible by ferry from Genoa, Livorno, Naples, Reggio di Calabria and Cagliari, and also from Malta and Tunisia. The main companies servicing the Mediterranean are **Tirrenia** (☎ 199 12 31 99; www.tirrenia .it) and **Grimaldi** (☎ 091 58 74 04; www.grimaldi.it), which runs Grandi Navi Veloci. **SNAV** (Palermo ☎ 091 58 60 66, Naples ☎ 081 761 23 48; www.snav .com) runs a summer ferry between Naples and Palermo. Prices vary by season and are highest July to September. Timetables vary, and it's best to check with a travel agency. Book well in advance during summer, particularly if you have a car.

At the time of writing, high-season fares for a *poltrona* (airline-type seat) were: Genoa to Palermo (€75, 18 hours) and Livorno to Palermo (€80, 19 hours) with Grimaldi's Grandi Navi Veloci; and Naples to Palermo (€45, 9¾ hours) and Cagliari to Palermo (€39, 13½ hours) with Tirrenia.

Virtu Ferries (www.virtuferries.com) serves Sicily to Malta March through October.

For information on ferries going from the mainland directly to the Aeolian Islands, see p773.

BUS
Direct bus services between Rome and Sicily are operated by **SAIS** (☎ 091 616 60 28; www .saistrasporti.it, in Italian; Via P Balsamo 20, Palermo) and **Segesta** (☎ 091 616 90 39; Via P Balsamo 16, Palermo), departing from Rome's Piazza Tiburtina. Buses service Messina (€27, 9¼ hours), Catania (€30, 11 hours), Palermo (€35, 12 hours) and Syracuse (€32.50, 11½ hours).

TRAIN
For train information, call ☎ 147 88 80 88 (7am to 9pm) or go to the information office at any station; the ticket cost includes the 3km ferry crossing from Villa San Giovanni (Calabria) to Messina.

Getting Around

Bus is the most common and convenient mode of public transport in Sicily. There are numerous services between Syracuse, Catania and Palermo, as well as to Agrigento and towns in the interior. The coastal train services between Messina and Palermo and Messina to Syracuse vary from efficient and reliable to delayed and unpredictable, as does the run between Palermo and Agrigento.

PALERMO

pop 750,000

Once regarded as Europe's grandest city, Palermo today on first glance is more decrepit than dazzling, due to heavy WWII bombing and years of neglect. But look closer and this dignified city's gilded 3000-year history – with stints as an Arab emirate and the seat of a Norman kingdom – shines through the fray. It's a fascinating city, and you'll eat like a king.

Orientation

Palermo is a large but easily manageable city. The main streets of the historic centre are Via Roma and Via Maqueda, which extend from the central station to Piazza Castelnuovo, a vast square in the modern part of town.

Information

EMERGENCY

Police station (Questura; theft & lost documents ☎ 091 21 01 11, foreigners office ☎ 091 651 43 30; Piazza della Vittoria; 🕑 24hr)

MEDICAL SERVICES

Ambulance (☎ 091 30 66 44)
Lo Cascio (☎ 091 616 21 17; Via Roma 1) A late-night pharmacy near the train station.
Ospedale Civico (☎ 091 666 11 11; Via Carmelo Lazzaro)

MONEY

Exchange offices Stazione Centrale (🕑 8am-8pm); Airport (🕑 8am-7pm)
Ruggieri & Figli (☎ 091 58 71 44; Via Enrico Amari 40; 🕑 9am-1pm & 4-7pm Mon-Fri, to 1pm Sat) Represents American Express and will cash travellers cheques for cardholders only.

POST

Palazzo delle Poste (Via Roma 322; 🕑 8.30am-6.30pm Mon-Fri, to 12.30pm Sat)

TELEPHONE

Aexis Telecom (Via Maqueda 347; Internet per hr €5) Has Internet, fax and phone services.

TOURIST INFORMATION

Tourist offices Piazza Castelnuovo 35 (☎ 091 605 81 11; 🕑 8.30am-2pm & 2.30-6pm Mon-Fri, 8.30am-2pm Sat); Stazione Centrale (☎ 091 616 59 14; 🕑 8.30am-2pm & 2.30-6pm Mon-Fri, 8.30am-2pm Sat); Airport (☎ 091 59 16 98; 🕑 8am-noon) All branches have brochures and the helpful bimonthly *Agenda*.

Sights

The intersection of Corso Vittorio Emanuele and Via Maqueda marks the **Quattro Canti**, the ideal and actual centre of historic Palermo. Called *il teatro*, it's marked by four 17th-century Spanish baroque façades, each decorated with a statue. Nearby Piazza Pretoria houses the beautifully ornate **Fontana Pretoria**, created by Florentine sculptors in the 16th century and dubbed the Fountain of Shame because of the cavorting nude statues; despite restoration work, you can still grab a peek.

Also in the piazza are the baroque **Chiesa di Santa Caterina** and the **Palazzo del Municipio** (town hall). Around the corner in Piazza Bellini is Palermo's top wedding spot, the famous **La Martorana** (☎ 091 616 1692; admission free; 🕑 8am-1pm & 3.30-5.30pm Mon-Sat, to 1pm Sun) church, with a striking Arab-Norman bell tower and stunning Byzantine mosaic interior, and next to the red-domed **Chiesa di San Cataldo**, which meshes Arab and Norman styles.

In Piazza Giuseppe Verdi is the grand neoclassical **Teatro Massimo** (☎ 091 605 35 15; www.teatromassimo.it, in Italian; guided tours €3; 🕑 10am-4pm Tue-Sun). Built between 1875 and 1897 to celebrate the unification of Italy, the theatre has become a symbol of the triumph and tragedy of Palermo itself; appropriately, the closing scene of *The Godfather III* was filmed here.

The huge **cathedral** (☎ 091 33 43 76; Corso Vittorio Emanuele; admission free; 🕑 7am-7pm Mon-Sat, 8am-1.30pm & 4-7pm Sun & hols), modified many times over the centuries, is a good example of Sicily's unique Arab-Norman style. At Piazza Indipendenza is **Palazzo Reale**, also known as the Palazzo dei Normanni, now the seat of the Sicilian parliament. Step inside and downstairs to see the **Cappella Palatina** (☎ 091 705 48 79; admission free; 🕑 9am-11.45am &

ITALY

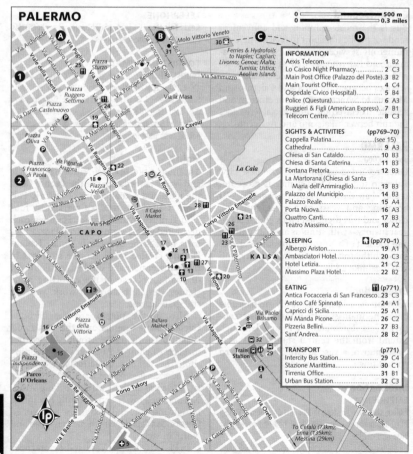

PALERMO

3-4.45pm Mon-Fri, 9am-11.45am Sat, 9-10am & noon-1pm Sun), a truly jaw-dropping example of Arab-Norman architecture, designed by Roger II in 1130 and lavishly decorated with exquisite mosaics. King Roger's former bedroom, **Sala di Ruggero** (☎ 091 705 43 17; admission free; ⏰ 9am-noon Mon, Fri & Sat), is adorned with 12th-century mosaics; you can only visit the room with a guide (free).

For a worthy foray, take bus No 389 from Piazza Indipendenza to the nearby town of **Monreale**, just 8km southwest of Palermo, to see the gorgeous mosaics in the world-famous 12th-century **Duomo** (☎ 091 640 44 13; admission free; ⏰ 8am-6pm), plus its **cloisters** (admission €4.50; ⏰ 9am-7pm Mon-Sat, 9am-1.30pm Sun).

Sleeping

Trinacria (☎ /fax 091 53 05 90; Via Barcarello 25; per person/site €4.10/7.50) The area's best camping is at Sferracavallo, by the sea. Catch bus No 628 from Piazzale Alcide de Gasperi, reached by bus No 101 or 107 from the station.

Albergo Ariston (☎ 091 33 24 34; Via Marino Stabile; s/d €40/55) Tucked into an unattractive apartment block is Palermo's best lower-priced hotel: great location, sparkling-clean rooms and an exceedingly polite (non-English-speaking) staff.

Ambasciatori Hotel (☎ 091 610 66 881; 5th fl, Via Roma 111; s/d €47/67; ❄) Previously known as the Hotel Azzuro di Lampedusa, this recently revamped hotel resides in an old *palazzo*; it's friendly, convenient and good value.

Hotel Letizia (☎ 091 58 91 10; www.hotelletizia .com; Via dei Bottai 30; s/d €78/110; 🗙) This lovely little hotel off the quaint Piazza Marina has pretty rooms with wood floors, an airy ambience, a cheery reading nook and a breakfast terrace.

Massimo Plaza Hotel (☎ 091325657; www.massimo plazahotel.com; Via Maqueda 437; s/d €130/190; P 🗙) As close as you can stay to the theatre without sleeping on stage, one of Palermo's more intimate luxe hotels is extremely comfortable and boasts impeccable service.

Eating

Palermo guards its tantalising cuisine with pride, and traditional dishes feature both sweet and spicy flavours reflecting the area's Arab past. A popular Palermitan dish is *pasta con le sarde* (with sardines, fennel, peppers, capers and pine nuts). Locals dine late and restaurants rarely open for dinner before 8.30pm.

Antico Café Spinnato (☎ 091 58 32 31; Via Principe di Belmonte 107-15) This elegant pastry shop has been serving its loyal clientele since 1860; the cakes are works of art, the *gelato* heavenly and the shaded outdoor tables ideal for a coffee *granita*.

Antica Focacceria di San Francesco (☎ 091 32 02 64; Via A Paternostro 58; mains €7) A local institution that's popular with workers and families alike, this fast-food spot has a bustling atmosphere and serves delicious calzone, pizza slices and some Palermitan speciality snacks such as *panini* stuffed with ricotta and steaming veal innards.

Pizzeria Bellini (☎ 091 616 56 91; Piazza Bellini 6) This popular pizzeria has a coveted spot, nestled in the shadow of La Martorana; come to eat at night, when the churches glow with floodlights.

Mi Manda Picone (☎ 091 616 06 60; Via A Paternostro 59; mains from €10) Nestled in a 13th-century building on Piazza San Francesco, this terrific restaurant serves top-notch contemporary cuisine in an airy arched interior. It doubles as an *enoteca*, where you can opt for generous platters of cheese and salami while sipping Sicilian vino.

Capricci di Sicilia (☎ 091 32 77 77; Via Instituto Pignatelli 6; secondo from €7) Once a puppet theatre, this cosy restaurant serves typical Sicilian fare, with an excellent selection of antipasto; always whirring with locals, so make a reservation in summer.

Sant'Andrea (☎ 091 33 49 99; Piazza Sant'Andrea 4; mains from €9) In the heart of the Vucciria market, the chef crafts produce and seafood fresh from the market into superb dishes with innovative twists; the pastas are sublime.

Palermo's best open-air markets are the **Vucciria** (🕙 Mon-Sat), in the narrow streets around Piazza San Domenico, and Il Ballaro, held in the Albergheria quarter off Via Maqueda; both have excellent offerings and unbeatable local colour.

Getting There & Away

Falcone-Borsellino Airport (☎ 091 702 01 11) is at Punta Raisi, 32km west of Palermo. For 24-hour information on domestic flights, ring **Alitalia** (☎ 00 39 06 65 641), and for international flights call the airport.

The main intercity bus station is around Via P Balsamo, to the right as you leave the train station. Offices for the various companies are all in this area, including **SAIS Trasporti** (☎ 091 617 11 41; www.saistrasporti.it; Via Balsamo 20), **SAIS Autolinee** (☎ 091 616 60 28; www.saisauto linee.it, in Italian; Via Balsamo 18) and **Segesta** (☎ 091 616 90 39; www.segesta.it, in Italian; Via Balsamo 26).

Regular trains leave from the Stazione Centrale for Milazzo, Messina, Catania, Trapani, Syracuse and Agrigento, as well as for nearby towns such as Cefalù. Direct trains go to Reggio di Calabria, Naples and Rome.

Boats leave from the port (Molo Vittorio Veneto) for Sardinia and the mainland (see p768). The **Tirrenia office** (☎ 091 602 11 11) is at the port.

Getting Around

Taxis to the airport cost about €40. A better option is to hop on one of the blue Prestia e Comande buses, which leave from outside the station every 30 minutes from 5am to 10.45pm. Tickets for the 45-minute trip cost €4.65 and can be purchased on the bus. There's also an hourly train service from the airport to Stazione Centrale (€4.50) between 5.40am and 10.40pm. Most of Palermo's city buses stop outside or near the train station. You must buy tickets before you get on the bus; they cost €0.80 and are valid for two hours, or €2.60 for a day pass.

AEOLIAN ISLANDS

These seven breezy islands – volcanic spurs strewn in the cobalt sea north of Milazzo –

are stunning. Also known as the Liparis, they display an extraordinary range of landscapes, from lush Lipari, a well-honed resort, to tiny and exclusive Panarea, to rugged Vulcano, the gorgeous scenery of Stromboli (with its fiercely active volcano), fertile vineyards of Salina, and tranquil Alicudi and Filicudi, relatively undeveloped. The islands have been inhabited since the Neolithic era, when migrants sought the valuable volcanic glass, obsidian. The Isole Eolie are so named because the ancient Greeks believed they were the home of Aeolus, the god of wind; Homer wrote of their natural beauties in the *Odyssey*. Today they have divine stature among the hordes of summer hedonists – best come in spring or autumn.

There is a **tourist information office** (☎ 090 988 00 95; www.netnet.it/aasteolie, in Italian; Via Vittorio Emanuele 202, Lipari; ☽ 8am-2pm Mon-Sat & 4.30-7.30pm Mon-Fri) in Lipari. Other offices are open on Vulcano, Salina and Stromboli during summer.

Sights & Activities

On **Lipari** visit the **citadel** (☽ 9am-7pm), with its fabulous **Museo Archeologico Eoliano** (☎ 090 988 01 74; admission €4.50; ☽ 9am-1.30pm & 3-7pm Mon-Sat) and museum. There are excellent walks on the island, as well as good snorkelling and scuba diving. The tourist office has information on trails, beaches and excursions.

With its pungent sulphurous odour, **Vulcano** is a short boat trip from Lipari. The main volcano, **Vulcano Fossa**, is still active, although the last recorded period of eruption was 1888–90. You can make the one-hour hike to the crater, or take a bath in the therapeutic hot muds.

On the most spectacular of the islands, **Stromboli**, you can climb the volcano. While recent activity has made it too dangerous to hike to the volcano's 2760-foot summit, you can still hike 1200 feet up the craters with a guide (or 900 feet without) and view the impressive Trail of Fire (Sciara del Fuoco) lava streaming down the side of the volcano. Contact **Magmatrek** (☎ 090 98 65 768; www.magmatrek.it) for guided treks to the crater (they only depart if groups are large enough).

Sleeping & Eating

Camping facilities are available on Lipari, Salina and Vulcano. Most accommodation in summer is booked out well in advance on the smaller islands, particularly on Stromboli, and many places close during winter. Prices skyrocket during summer, but you can find good deals otherwise.

LIPARI

Lipari has the most options and greatest range of accommodation, and from here the other islands are easily accessible by regular hydrofoil. Don't dismiss outright offers for *affittacamere* (room rentals) by touts when you arrive at the port – they're often genuine.

Diana Brown (☎ 090 981 25 84; dbrown@netnet.it; Vico Himera 3; s/d €62/68) has comfortable rooms that are centrally located and Diana is a fountain of local expertise; she and her husband also run **Gruppo di Navigazione** (www.navigazioniregina.com), featuring boat tours of all the islands.

Lazing over half the piazza, Lipari's classiest joint, **Filippino** (☎ 090 981 10 02; Piazza Municipo; mains from €16), has superb seafood and top-notch service; dress to show off your tan and make a reservation. For pizza, hit the rightfully popular **La Piazzetta** (☎ 090 981 25 22; pizzas from €5), off Corso Vittorio with piazza-side tables; also recommended is tiny **La Cambusa** (☎ 349 476 60 61; Via Garibaldi 72; mains from €12), serving delicious pastas and fish.

STROMBOLI

La Sirenetta (☎ 090 98 60 25; lasirenetta@netnet.it; Via Marina 33; s/d €99/212, half-board €132) is a serene pad perfectly located in front of Stròmbolicchio, a towering rock rising out of the sea at San Vincenzo; the panoramic terrace with a great restaurant encourages lingering.

VULCANO

You'll find good value at **Hotel Torre** (☎ /fax 090 985 23 42; Via Favaloro 1; d low/high season €38/75) with its large rooms, kitchens and terraces and close beach access.

ALICUDI & FILICUDI

If you want seclusion and still-wild beauty, head for Alicudi or Filicudi. The former offers the simple but nice **Ericusa** (☎ 090 988 99 02; fax 090 988 96 71; Via Regina Elena; d €62, half-board per person €60), while Filicudi has the truly delightful **La Canna** (☎ 090 988 99 56; vianast@tin.it; Via Rosa 43; s/d €40/80). There are good restaurants at both.

Getting There & Away

Ferries and hydrofoils leave for the islands from Milazzo (easily reached by train from Palermo and Messina) and all ticket offices are along Corso dei Mille at the port. If arriving at Milazzo by train, catch a Giunta bus to the port. **SNAV** (☎ 081 428 51 11) and **Siremar** (☎ 081 580 03 40) run hydrofoils (€10.10), and the latter also has ferries (€7.50). SNAV also runs hydrofoils between the islands and Palermo (summer only).

You can also travel directly to the islands from the mainland. Siremar runs regular ferries from Naples, and SNAV runs hydrofoils from Naples, Messina and Reggio di Calabria. Occasionally, rough seas cancel sailings.

Getting Around

Regular hydrofoil and ferry services operate between the islands. Both Siremar and SNAV have booths at Lipari's port, where you can get full timetable information.

TAORMINA
pop 10,700

Spectacularly located on a mountain terrace, with resplendent views of the glistening sea and Mt Etna, beautiful Taormina has been charming mortals for centuries. Sicily's glitziest resort was long ago discovered by the European jet set, and the chic town is expensive and touristy. But even trinket shops and crowds can't hamper the allure, and its magnificent setting, Greek theatre, medieval centre and great beaches are as seductive now as they were for Goethe and DH Lawrence.

The **tourist office** (☎ 0942 2 32 43; www.gate 2taormina.com; Palazzo Corvaja; ☯ 8.30am-2pm & 4-7pm) has extensive information on the town and its wealth of sights.

Sights & Activities

The **Teatro Greco** (☎ 0942 2 32 20; admission €4.50; ☯ 9am-7pm Mon-Sat, 9am-1pm Sun), a perfect horseshoe theatre, was built in the 3rd century BC and later expanded and remodelled by the Romans. Concerts, theatre and festivals are staged here in summer and wonderful views of Mt Etna abound.

From the colourful and well-tended gardens of **Villa Comunale** (☯ 9am-7pm), there's a panoramic view of the sea. Along Corso Umberto I is **Piazza del Duomo**, with a baroque fountain and Norman-Gothic cathedral. The postcard-perfect local beach is **Isola Bella**, accessible by cable car (€2.70 return, 8am to 1am).

Mt Etna trips (€27) can be organised through **CST** (☎ 0942 62 60 88; Corso Umberto I 101).

Sleeping & Eating

The tourist office has a list of *affittacamere* in Taormina.

Pensione Svizzera (☎ 0942 237 90; svizzera@tao.it; Via Pirandello 26; s/d €70/90; ☯ Feb-Nov) Teetering on the edge of the cliff, this cheery *pensione* is convenient and comfortable. The views and breakfast served in a pretty garden terrace are bonuses.

Hotel Belvedere (☎ 094223791; www.villabelvedere .it; Via Bagnoli Croce 79; s/d €80/110) One of the first hotels in town, this family-run spot has an enviable location; the high charm, pretty citrus gardens and pool-side lunch service make it a holiday idyll.

Maffei's (☎ 0942 240 55; Via San Domenico de Guzman 1; mains from €20) With a handful of tables and some of the best seafood in Taormina, this great spot is very popular: book a table and order the evening special.

Granduca (☎ 0942 249 83; Corso Umberto 172; pizzas from €5) Excellent pizza and a spectacular terrace make this a consistently good choice.

Arco Rosso (Via Naumachie 7) This is a good spot for a stiff drink any time.

DiVino Wine Bar (Piazza Raggia 4) Has local wines, terrific owners and nice plates of cheese.

Café Wunderbar (Piazza IX Aprile) Posers will be well rewarded at this café, sporting Taormina's best view and serving a mean *granita*.

Getting There & Away

Bus is the easiest way to get to and from Taormina. Interbus services leave for Messina (€2.50, 1½ hours, 12 per day) and Catania (€3.80, 1½ hours, hourly). Taormina is on the main train line between Messina and Catania.

MT ETNA

Dominating the landscape in eastern Sicily between Taormina and Catania, Mt Etna (3350m) is Europe's largest live volcano, and is also one of the world's most active. Eruptions occur frequently, both from the four live craters at the summit and on the volcano's slopes, which are littered with fissures and extinct cones.

Recent activity has meant more disruption to services, and visitors should be aware that excursions are at the mercy of volcanic activity. Due to the volcano's unpredictability, you can no longer climb to the craters, although it is still possible to climb one of the peaks in front of the Rifugio Sapienza to get a small taste of the real thing. **Gruppo Guide Alpine Etna Sud** (☎ 095 791 47 55) or **Natura e Turismo** (☎ 095 33 35 43) organise excursions involving trekking and 4WD vehicles, led by a vulcanologist or alpine guide.

Mt Etna is best approached from Catania by **AST bus** (☎ 095 746 10 96), which departs from the car park in front of the main train station at 8.30am, and leaves from Rifugio Sapienza at about 4.45pm (€4.65 return). The private **Ferrovia Circumetnea train line** (☎ 095 54 12 50; www.circumetnea.it) circles Mt Etna from Catania to Riposto, a 3½-hour trip. You can reach Riposta from Taormina by train or bus if you want to make the trip from that direction.

The classic **Agora Hostel** (☎ 095 723 30 10; agorahostel@hotmail.com; Piazza Curro 6, Catania; dm/d €15.50/40) in Catania is known for its live music, cheap eats and good bar; proximity to La Pescheria market is an added boon.

SYRACUSE
pop 126,000

Once rivalling Athens in power and prestige, Syracuse is a highlight of a visit to Sicily. Founded in 734 BC by Corinthian settlers, the city became a sultry and dominant Mediterranean power, prompting Athens to attack in 413 BC. Syracuse was the birthplace of Archimedes, Cicero frequented town and Plato attended the court of the tyrant Dionysius, who ruled from 405 BC to 367 BC.

Orientation & Information

The main sights are on the island of Ortygia and the archaeological park 2km across town. There are two **tourist offices** (Via San Sebastiano 45 ☎ 0931 48 12 00; www.apt-siracusa.it; 8.30am-1.30pm & 3.30-6.30pm; Ortygia ☎ 0931 46 42 55; Via Maestranza 33; 8.30am-2pm & 2.30-5pm Mon-Fri, mornings only Sat). The Via San Sebastiano office has English-speaking staff and a useful city map.

Sights
ORTYGIA

The island of Ortygia is the spiritual and physical heart of Syracuse. Despite eye-catching baroque palaces and churches, its Greek essence is everywhere. The **cathedral** (admission free; 8am-noon & 4-7pm) was built in the 7th century on top of the Temple of Athena, incorporating most of the original columns in its three-aisled structure. The splendid **Piazza del Duomo** is lined with baroque palaces. Just down the winding street from the cathedral is the **Fontana Aretusa**, a natural freshwater spring. Greek legend has it that the goddess Artemis transformed her handmaiden Aretusa into the spring to protect her from the unwelcome attention of the river-god Alpheus. Undeterred, Alpheus turned himself into the river that feeds the spring.

NEAPOLIS-PARCO ARCHEOLOGICO

To get to the **Neapolis-Parco Archeologico** (☎ 093 1 6 62 06; Viale Paradisa; admission €4.50; 9am-2hrs before sunset), catch bus No 1 or 2 from Riva della Posta on Ortygia. The main attraction here is the sparkling-white 5th-century-BC **Greek theatre**, entirely hewn out of solid rock and gazing seaward over the city. Nearby is the **Orecchio di Dionisio**, an ear-shaped artificial grotto used by Syracuse's resident tyrant Dionysius to eavesdrop on his prisoners. The impressive 2nd-century **Roman amphitheatre** is well preserved.

The excellent **Museo Archeologico Paolo Orsi** (☎ 0931 46 40 22; admission €4.50; 9am-1pm Tue-Sat), about 500m east of the archaeological zone, contains Sicily's best-organised and most interesting archaeological collection.

Sleeping & Eating

Fontane Bianche (☎ 0931 79 03 33; Via dei Lidi 476; per person/tent €6/4.50; May-Sep) About 15km southwest of town, this camping ground is near a beach that teems with active bars come summer; catch bus No 21 or 22 from Corso Umberto.

B&B Casa Mia (☎ 0931 46 33 49; Corso Umberto 112; s/d €45/75) You'll feel right at home in this comfy old mansion with nicely decorated rooms and a breakfast area designed for lingering.

Hotel Gutkowski (☎ 0931 46 58 61; www.guthotel .it; Lungomare Vittorini 26; s/d €65/90) This lovely pastel-blue, sea-fronting hotel has an appealing minimalist décor and a helpful entrepreneurial family at the helm, doing its part to help revive the city's crumbling *palazzi*.

There is no shortage of good dining on Ortygia, where all the best eateries are located.

Trattoria Archimede (☎ 0931 697 01; Via Gemellaro 8; mains from €8) This authentic spot has a daily changing menu featuring excellent seafood and pastas, served smartly in three airy dining rooms.

Don Camillo (☎ 0931 6 71 33; Via Maestranza 96; mains from €9) Sitting pretty in the old guild quarter, this popular upmarket trattoria serves traditional Sicilian fare matched by excellent wines; it's packed at weekends so book ahead.

For scrumptious Sicilian sweets, head to **Pasticceria Tipica Catanese** (Corso Umberto 46); for good local wines, accompanied by hearty cheese and ham platters, try **Fermento** (Via Crocifisso 44/46), a terrific vaulted wine bar.

Getting There & Away

Services with **Interbus** (☎ 0931 6 67 10) leave from Via Trieste for Catania (€4.60, one hour, Monday to Saturday), Palermo (€14.20, four hours), Enna (€3, one hour) and surrounding towns. The service for Rome (€38, 12 hours) also leaves from here, connecting with the Rome bus at Catania. **AST** (☎ 0931 46 48 20) buses service the town and the surrounding area from Riva della Posta. Syracuse is easy to reach by train from Messina (€8.75, three hours) and Catania (€4.70, 1½ hours).

AGRIGENTO

pop 55,500

Founded around 582 BC, Agrigento is today a pleasant (if a little brutish) medieval town, but the Greek temples strewn in the valley below are the reason to visit. Goethe first put Agrigento on the map in the 18th century, which makes it Sicily's oldest tourist site. The Italian novelist and dramatist Luigi Pirandello (1867–1936) was born here, as was the Greek philosopher and scientist Empedocles (c 490–430 BC).

There's a so-so **tourist office** (☎ 0922 2 04 54; Via Cesare Battisti 15; ⌚ 8.30am-1.30pm Mon-Fri).

Sights

Agrigento's **Valley of the Temples** (☎ 0922 261 91; admission €2, with museum €6; ⌚ 8.30am-1hr before sunset) is one of the major Greek archaeological sights in the world. Despite its name, the five main Doric temples stand along a ridge, designed to be visible from afar. In varying states of ruin, the 5th-century-BC temples offer a tantalising glimpse of one of the most luxurious cities in Magna Graecia. The only temple to survive relatively intact was **Tempio della Concordia**, transformed into a church. **Tempio di Giunone**, a short walk uphill to the east, has an impressive sacrificial altar. **Tempio di Ercole** is the oldest of the structures. Across the main road that divides the valley is the imposing **Tempio di Giove**, which used to cover an area measuring 112m by 56m, with columns 18m high. *Telamoni*, colossal statues of men, were used in the structure, and the remains of one are in the **Museo Archeologico** (☎ 0922 40 15 65; admission €4.50, with temples €6; ⌚ 9am-1.30pm & 2-7.30pm Tue-Sat, 9am-1.30pm Sun & Mon), just north of the temples on Via dei Templi. Nearby is the **Tempio di Castore e Polluce**, partly reconstructed in the 19th century.

The temples are beautifully lit up at night. To get to the temples from the town, catch bus No 1, 2 or 3 from the train station.

Sleeping & Eating

Bella Napoli (☎ 0922 2 04 35; Piazza Lena 6; s/d/tr €22/54/75) This friendly hotel has clean, comfortable if unremarkable rooms

Antica Foresteria Catalana (☎ 0922 204 35; s/d €45/75) With the same owners as Bella Napoli, this has newer rooms that are not necessarily worth the price jump.

La Corte degli Sfizzi (☎ 0922 59 55 20; Via Atenea 4; pizzas from €5) A popular pizzeria with a pretty garden setting and good value.

Café Girasole (Via Atenea 68-70) This is a great little wine bar in the heart of the medieval town.

Getting There & Away

Intercity buses leave from Piazza Rosselli, just off Piazza Vittorio Emanuele, for Palermo, Catania and surrounding towns.

SARDINIA

The Mediterranean's second largest island feels like a mini-continent all to itself. Sardinia was colonised by the Phoenicians and Romans, the Pisans and Genoese, and the Spaniards. Despite constant domination, the proud locals (Sardi) have retained a strong sense of identity, far removed from mainland

ITALY

influences. The striking landscape ranges from a wild interior pocked with gorges and valleys, to stunning stretches of unspoiled coastline. The gorgeous island gets overrun with sun seekers in August.

Getting There & Away
AIR
The airports at Cagliari, Olbia, Alghero and Arbatax-Tortoli link Sardinia with major Italian and European cities. Discount airlines, including Air One and Ryanair, are servicing the island more and more.

BOAT
Sardinia is accessible by ferry from Genoa, Livorno, Fiumicino, Civitavecchia, Naples, Palermo, Trapani, Bonifacio and Porto Vecchio (both Corsica) and Tunis. Departure points in Sardinia are Olbia, Golfo Aranci, Palau, Santa Teresa di Gallura and Porto Torres in the north, Arbatax on the east coast and Cagliari in the south.

The main company, **Tirrenia** (www.tirrenia .com, in Italian), runs a service between Civitavecchia and Olbia, Arbatax or Cagliari, and between Genoa and Porto Torres, Olbia, Arbatax or Cagliari. There are fast ferries between Fiumicino and Golfo Aranci/Arbatax and Civitavecchia and Olbia (both summer only). The national railway, Ferrovie dello Stato (FS), also runs a service between Civitavecchia and Golfo Aranci. **Moby Lines** (www.mobylines.it) and **Sardinia Ferries** (www.sardiniaferries.com), also known as Elba and Corsica Ferries, both operate services from the mainland to Sardinia, as well as to Corsica and Elba. They depart from Genoa, Livorno, Civitavecchia and arrive at Olbia, Cagliari or Golfo Aranci. **Grandi Navi Veloci** (www.gnv.it) runs a service between Genoa and Olbia (June to September) or Porto Torres (year-round). Most Italian travel agencies have brochures on the different services.

Timetables change and prices fluctuate with the season. Prices for a *poltrona* (seat) on Tirrenia ferries are: Genoa to Porto Torres or Olbia (€46, 13 hours); Naples to Cagliari (€41, 16¼ hours); Palermo to Cagliari (€39, 13½ hours, weekly); Civitavecchia to Olbia (€25, eight hours); and Civitavecchia to Cagliari (€41, 14½ hours).

The cost of taking a small car from Civitavecchia to Cagliari in the high season is €78. A motorcycle (over 200cc) costs €40 year-round for the same trip.

Getting Around
The two main bus companies are state-run **ARST** (☎ 0800 86 50 42; www.arst.sardegna.it, in Italian), which operates extensive services throughout the island, and privately owned **PANI** (☎ 070 65 23 26), which links main towns.

The main **Trenitalia** (www.trenitalia.it) train lines link Cagliari with Oristano, Sassari and Olbia, and are generally reliable but can be very slow. The private railways that link smaller towns throughout the island can be *very* slow. However, the *Trenino Verde* (Little Green Train), which runs a scenic route from Cagliari to Arbatax through the Barbagia, is a relaxing and lovely way to see part of the interior.

The best way to explore Sardinia properly is by road, and all the major international car-rental agencies are represented at the main airports.

CAGLIARI
pop 176,000
Sardinia's capital and largest city is an attractive, friendly and cosmopolitan enclave, with a beautifully preserved medieval section, the delightful beach of Poetto and salt lakes that are home to pink flamingos.

Orientation
The main port, bus and train stations are near Piazza Matteotti, where the useful city tourist office is as well. The main street along the harbour is Via Roma, and the old city stretches up the hill behind it to the castle. There are several hotels and restaurants near the port, normally not a great place in most cities, but perfectly safe and pleasant here.

Information
EMERGENCY
Police station (Questura; ☎ 070 49 21 69; Via Amat 9) Tucked behind the imposing law courts.

INTERNET ACCESS
Web Travel Point (☎ 070 65 93 07; Via Maddalena 34; per 30min €2.60)

LAUNDRY
Lavanderia Ghilbi (Via Sicilia 20; ☼ 8am-10pm; per 6kg €3) Laundrettes are a rarity on the island.

CAGLIARI

0   1 mile
0   2 km

0   800 m
0   0.5 miles

See Enlargement

To Grotta della Vipera (600m);
Tuvixeddu (700m); Elmas Airport (5km);
Pula (32km); Iglesias (60km);
Oristano (100km); Sassari (217km)

MEDICAL SERVICES
Ospedale San Giovanni di Dio (☎ 070 66 32 37; Via Ospedale)
Guardia Medica (☎ 070 50 29 31) For after-hour emergencies.

POST
Main post office (☎ 070 6 03 11; Piazza del Carmine 27; ⊗ 8.15am-6.40pm Mon-Fri, to 1.20pm Sat)

TOURIST INFORMATION
Main tourist office (☎ 070 66 92 55; Piazza Matteotti 9; ⊗ 9am-2pm & 3-6pm Mon-Sat) There are additional information offices at the airport and in the Stazione Marittima.

Sights & Activities
In the Citadella dei Musei, the **Museo Archeologico Nazionale** (☎ 070 68 40 00; Piazza Arsenale; admission €4; ⊗ 9am-8pm Tue-Sun) has a fascinating collection of Nuraghic bronzes. These bronzes are objects found in stone constructions all over Sardinia (there are about 7000), a legacy of the island's native culture.

It's enjoyable to wander through the medieval quarter. The Pisan-Romanesque **Duomo** (Piazza Palazzo) was built in the 13th century and has an interesting Romanesque pulpit.

There are good sea and city views from **Bastione San Remy** (Piazza Costituzione), in the town's centre, which once formed part of the fortifications of the old city.

The **Torre di San Pancrazio** (Piazza Indipendenza; ⊗ 9am-5pm Tue-Sun) is also worth a look. The **Roman amphitheatre** (Viale Buon Cammino; admission free; ⊗ 9am-5pm Tue-Sun) is considered the most important Roman monument in Sardinia. During summer, opera is performed here.

A day on the **Spiaggia di Poetto**, east of the centre, is a day well spent, and you can wander across to the salt lakes to view the flamingos.

Festivals & Events
The **Festival of Sant'Efisio**, a colourful celebration mixing the secular and the religious, is held annually for four days from 1 May.

Sleeping & Eating
Hotel A&R Bundes Jack (☎ /fax 070 66 79 70; Via Roma 75; s/d €47/72, with shared bathroom €40/60) The Marina's choice spot has a warm welcome and high-ceilinged rooms that are spotless and comfortable.

Hotel Regina Margherita (☎ 070 67 03 42; www .hotelreginamargherita.com; Viale Regina Margherita 44; s/d €128/165) This well-managed hotel has nice views and comfortable, modern rooms.

Lillicu (☎ 070 65 29 70; Via Sardegna 78; mains from €9) An authentic trattoria that's often packed with happy locals downing good seafood dishes at large communal marble tables.

Antica Hostaria (☎ 070 66 58 60; Via Cavour 60; mains from €15) Cagliari fine dining at its finest, this antique-laden restaurant has a warm ambience and classic Italian cuisine.

Il Buongustaio (☎ 070 66 81 24; Via Concezione 7; pasta from €7) This home-spun spot for foodies serves equally good fish and fowl, and the home-made pastas are particularly tasty.

Trattoria GennarGentu (☎ 070 67 20 21; Via Sardegna 60; pasta from €8) At this welcoming spot, try the Sardinian specialities such as *spaghetti bottarga* (spaghetti with dried tuna roe).

The Marina area is riddled with good little spots to suit all tastes and budgets. Also worth a mention are **Antico Caffè** (☎ 070 65 82 96; Piazza Costituzione), Cagliari's most elegant café with a terrace and marble-topped tables, and **Brasserie Vecchia Bruxelles** (☎ 070 68 20 37; Via Sulcis 4; ⊗ Mon-Sat), with stone vaults and long comfy sofas, an excellent choice for a beer, snack or nip of whiskey.

Getting There & Away
Some 8km northwest of the city at Elmas is Cagliari's airport. ARST buses leave regularly from Piazza Matteotti to coincide with flight arrivals and departures. **Alitalia** (☎ 070 24 00 79) is at the airport.

Departing from Piazza Matteotti are **ARST** (☎ 070 409 83 24) buses servicing nearby towns, the Costa del Sud and the Costa Rei. **PANI** (☎ 070 65 23 26) buses leave from Stazione Marittima for towns including Sassari (€15, 3¼ hours), Oristano (€6.10, 1½ hours) and Nuoro (€6.10, 3½ hours).

The main train station is also in Piazza Matteotti, with regular service to Oristano (€4.85, two hours), Sassari (€12.80, 4¼ hours) and Porto Torres via Oristano and Olbia (€13.25, four hours). The private **Ferrovie della Sardegna** (FdS; ☎ 070 49 13 04) train station is in Piazza Repubblica.

Ferries arrive at the port adjacent to Via Roma. Bookings for **Tirrenia** (☎ 070 66 60 65) can be made at the Stazione Marittima in the port area. See p776 for details of services.

For rental cars, try **Hertz** (☎ 070 66 81 05; Piazza Matteotti 1), which also has a branch at the airport, while **Autonoleggio Cara** (☎ 070 66 34 71) can deliver a scooter or bike to your hotel.

CALA GONONE
pop 1010
This attractive seaside resort makes a good base from which to explore the coves along the Golfo di Orosei's coastline, as well as the Nuraghic sites and rugged terrain inland. Major points are accessible by bus and boat, but you'll need a car to really explore.

Information
Coop Ghivine (☎ 0784 9 67 21; www.ghivine.com; Via Montebello 5, Dorgali) Organises excellent guided treks and farm stays in the region from €30 per person.

Tourist office Cal Gonone (☎ 0784 9 36 96; Viale Bue Marino 1a; 🕙 9am-6pm Apr-Oct, to 11pm Jul & Aug); Dorgali (☎ 0784 9 62 43; Via Lamarmora 181; 🕙 9am-1pm & 3.30-7pm Mon-Fri) The Cala Gonone office has maps, a list of hotels and plenty of local information.

Sights & Activities
From Cala Gonone's tiny port, catch a boat to the **Grotta del Bue Marino** (admission €5.50), where a guide will take you on a 1km walk to see vast caves with stalagmites and stalactites. Sardinia's last colony of monk seals once lived here but have not been seen for quite some time. Boats also leave for **Cala Luna**, an isolated beach where you can walk along **Codula di Luna**, a fabulous gorge. The beach is packed with day-tripping tourists in summer. The boat trip to visit the grotto and beach costs around €20.

A **walking track** along the coast links Cala Fuili, about 3.5km south of Cala Gonone, and Cala Luna (about 1½ hours one way). There's also some good mountain biking and diving in the area. Ask at the tourist office for information on outfitters and rentals.

If you want to descend the impressive **Gorropu Gorge**, ask for information from the team of expert guides based in Urzulei – **Società Gorropu** (☎ 0782 64 92 82, 0347 775 27 06; francescomurru@virgilio.it) – who also offer a wide range of guided walks in the area. It is necessary to use ropes and harnesses to traverse the Gorropu Gorge.

Sleeping & Eating
Camping Gala Gonone (☎ 0784 9 31 65; www.camping calagonone.it; per person €16, 4-bed bungalows up to €135;

🕙 Apr-Oct) Along the main road from Dorgali, this camping ground has good-quality and shady sites, plus a pool and restaurant, but gets overrun in August.

Pop Hotel (☎ 0784 9 31 85; lfancel@box1.tin.it; s/d €59/93) Despite the ugly sign, this terracotta-hued hotel near the port has clean, pleasant rooms and a decent restaurant.

Hotel Costa Dorada (☎ 0784 9 33 32; www.hotel costadorada.it; Via Lungomare Palmasera 45; d incl breakfast from €74) Has a swatch of beach across the street, flower-laced terraces and lovely rooms.

Hotel Su Gologone (☎ 0784 28 75 12; www.sugol ogone.it; s/d €80/120; **P**) If you have your own transport, don't miss the opportunity to stay here, at the base of Sardinia's second-highest peak, about 20 minutes west, near Dorgali. This gorgeous white-washed hacienda has pretty rooms decorated with locally crafted furnishings, walking trails, pool and a fabulous restaurant serving classic Sardinian mountain cuisine.

Getting There & Away
Catch a PANI bus to Nuoro from Cagliari (€12, 3½ hours), Sassari (€7.20, 2½ hours) or Oristano (€6.20, two hours) and then take an ARST bus to Cala Gonone via Dorgali (€85, 20 minutes). If you are travelling by car, you will need a proper road map of the area.

ALGHERO
pop 40,600
With a distinctive Spanish flair, this colourful resort town is on the west coast, known as the Coral Riviera. The town makes a good base for exploring the magnificent coastline to the south, and the famed Grotte di Nettuno on the Capo Caccia to the north. The medieval centre, with its sea walls intact, is one of Sardinia's most charming towns. Visit off-season to see pretty Alghero at its peaceful best.

Orientation
Alghero's historic centre is on a small promontory jutting into the sea, with the new town stretching out behind and along the coast north.

Information
Main post office (Via Carducci 35)
Medical attention (☎ 079 98 71 61)

ITALY

Ospedale Civile (☎ 079 99 62 33; Via Don Minzoni)
Police (☎ 113)
Public telephones (Via Vittorio Emanuele)
Tourist office (☎ 079 97 90 54; www.infoalghero.it, in Italian; Piazza Porta Terra 9; ☒ 8am-8pm Mon-Sat) Near the port and just across the gardens from the bus station, this is an exceedingly helpful office.

Sights & Activities

The narrow streets of the old city and around the port are lovely. The most interesting church is the **Chiesa di San Francesco** (Via Carlo Alberto; ☒ 7.30am-noon & 5-8.30pm). Although constant remodelling has ruined the cathedral, the **bell tower** (admission €1.50; ☒ 7am-9.30pm Jun-Sep) remains a fine example of Gothic-Catalan architecture.

Near Alghero at the dramatic cape, **Capo Caccia**, are the **Grotte di Nettuno** (☎ 079 94 65 40; admission adult/child €8/4; ☒ 9am-7pm Apr-Sep, 10am-5pm Oct, 9am-2pm Nov-Mar), an underground fairyland accessible by boat (€10, not including grotto admission, 2½ hours, hourly 8am to 7pm June to September) from the port, or by the FdS bus from Via Catalogna (€3.25 return, 50 minutes, three daily trips June to September).

If you have a car, don't miss the **Nuraghe di Palmavera** (☎ 079 95 32 00; admission €2.10; ☒ 9am-7pm), a ruined palace 10km out of Alghero on the road to Porto Conte.

Rugged cliffs stretch down to solitary beaches, and near **Bosa** is one of the last habitats of the griffon vulture. The best way to see the coast is by car or motorcycle. If you want to rent a bicycle (from €9) or motorcycle (from €70) to explore the coast, try **Cicloexpress** (☎ 079 98 69 50; Via Garibaldi) at the port.

Festivals & Events

In summer Alghero stages a music festival in the cloisters of the church of San Francesco. A festival, complete with fireworks display, is held on 15 August for the Feast of the Assumption.

Sleeping & Eating

It is virtually impossible to find a room in August unless you book in advance. At other times of the year you'll be fine.

Camping La Mariposa (☎ 079 95 03 60; Via Lido 22; per person/tent €10.50/5; bungalows up to €72; ☒ Apr-Oct) About 2km north of the centre, this low-key camping ground is on the beach.

Hotel San Francesco (☎ /fax 079 98 03 30; Via Ambrogio Machin 2; s/d €47/85; ℗) In the old town, this hotel exudes charm and is housed in a former convent; the rooms are simple but comfortable, and there's a cloistered courtyard shared with the church of the same name.

Villa Las Tronas (☎ 079 98 18 18; www.hotelvillalastronas.it; Lungomare Valencia 1; s/d €170/200; ℗ ☐ ☒) On its own private promontory, this former summer residence of the Italian royalty has a pool and very pretty rooms, but an overly formal feel elsewhere. Still, the views are stupendous, the breakfasts enough to cover lunch, and there are mountain bikes for pedalling the coast.

Trattoria Maristella (☎ 079 97 81 72; Via Fratelli Kennedy 9; mains from €10) This popular spot, with Mediterranean-splashed décor, offers good value, reliable grub and alfresco dining.

Da Ninetto (☎ 079 97 80 62; Via Gioberti 4; mains from €12) Locals swear by the lobster served at this unassuming hole-in-the-wall.

Al Tuguri (☎ 079 97 67 72; Via Maiorca 113; mains from €15) Although this oft-lauded restaurant sometimes rests on its many laurels, and the service can be puffy, the seafood is memorable.

Focacce Sarde Ripiene (Via Garibaldi 11; ☒ until 1.30am) Serves delicious sandwiches, fronts the sea and is always packed with locals.

Caffè Costantino (Piazza Civica 30) A classy coffee stop in the historic centre that also serves good wine and tantalising cakes.

Getting There & Away

Alghero is accessible from Sassari by train (€2.20, 35 minutes) and bus (€2.60, one hour). The main bus station is on Via Catalogna, next to the public park. The **train station** (Via Don Minzoni) is about 1km north of town and is connected to the centre by a regular bus service. **ARST** (☎ 079 95 01 79) buses leave for Sassari and Porto Torres. **FdS** (☎ 079 95 04 58) buses also service Sassari, Macomer and Bosa. **PANI** (☎ 079 23 69 83) buses serve Cagliari, Nuoro and Macomer from Sassari.

ITALY DIRECTORY

ACCOMMODATION

Accommodation in Italy ranges from the magnificent to the ridiculous with prices to match. Hotels and *pensioni* make up the bulk of accommodation, with a vast gulf between top-end luxury and budget options that can be pricey and pokey. Fortunately, there's a growing range of good and characterful B&Bs, villa rentals, hostels and *agriturismo* (farm stays) options to fill the void.

Prices fluctuate throughout the country and depend on the season, with Easter and the summer and Christmas holidays being peak tourist times. During low season, prices can be 20% cheaper. Tourist offices have listings for all local accommodation, including prices. In this chapter listings are categorised roughly as budget (under €100), mid-range (€100 to 190) and top end (€190 and up).

Agriturismo

Farm stays are increasingly popular, particularly in Tuscany and on the islands. For a countrywide directory, contact **Agriturist** (☎ 06 685 23 42; www.agriturist.it, in Italian; Corso Vittorio Emanuele II 89, 00186 Rome).

B&Bs

Bed and breakfast options range from city *palazzi* to seaside bungalows. Prices are typically between €70 and €150. For information contact **Bed & Breakfast Italia** (Map pp696-7; ☎ 06 68 80 15 13; www.bbitalia.it; Palazzo Sforza Cesarini, Corso Vittorio Emanuele II 282, 00186 Rome).

Camping

Most camping grounds in Italy have a swimming pool, tennis court and restaurant, and are graded according to a star system. Prices range from €4 to €10 per person and €5 to €12 or more for a site. Lists of sites are available from local tourist offices or can be looked up on the website of **Touring Club Italiano** (TCI; www.touringclub.it).

Independent camping is not permitted in many of the more beautiful parts of Italy but if you choose spots not visible from the road and don't light fires you shouldn't have trouble off season. Always get permission from the landowner if you want to camp on private property.

Hostels

Hostels in Italy are called *ostelli per la gioventù* and are run by the Associazione Italiana Alberghi per la Gioventù (Italian Youth Hostel Association), affiliated with **Hostelling International** (HI; www.iyhf.org). A valid HI card is required, which you can get in your home country, at the youth hostel in Rome, from CTS offices and from the hostel association offices throughout Italy. The national head office of the **Italian Youth Hostel Association** (Map p702; ☎ 06 487 11 52; www.ostellionline.org; Via Cavour 44, Rome; ☺ 9am-5pm Mon-Fri) has a booklet detailing all Italian hostels.

Accommodation is in segregated dormitories, although some hostels offer higher-priced doubles. Nightly rates, often including breakfast, range from €10 to €20. Lockout times are usually from 9am to 5pm. Check-in is 6pm to 10.30pm and curfews are around midnight.

Hotels & Pensioni

There is often no difference between a *pensione* and an *albergo*. However, the former will generally be of one- to three-star quality, while the latter can be awarded up to five stars. *Locande* (inns) and *affittacamere* (rooms for rent) are cheaper and not included in the star classification system, although the standard can be very high (particularly on the Aeolian Islands and in the Alps).

Always check on prices before committing to stay in a place. Proprietors have been known to pad bills, so make a complaint to the local tourist office if you believe you're being overcharged.

Prices are higher in northern Italy and highest in major tourist destinations. Rates can soar in the high season. A *camera singola* (single room) costs from €40, and quite a number of establishments do not bother catering to the single traveller; a double room with *camera doppie* (twin beds) or *camera matrimoniale* (double bed) will cost from about €55.

Mountain Refuges

Before hiking in the Alps, Apennines, or other mountains in Italy, obtain information about Italy's wonderful network of *rifugi* (alpine refuges) from local tourist offices. The *rifugi* are generally open from July to September, and dorm-style accommodation prevails, though some larger ones have double rooms. The price per person for a night with breakfast is around €20, with dinner another €15.

The locations of *rifugi* are marked on good hiking maps. The **Club Alpino Italiano** (CAI; www.cai.it, in Italian) owns and runs many of the refuges. CAI offers discounts to members of associated foreign alpine clubs.

Rental Accommodation

Finding rental accommodation in the major cities can be difficult, time-consuming and prohibitively costly. Major resort areas, such as the Aeolian Islands, coastal Sardinia and the Alps offer rental accommodation that's more reasonably priced and readily available. Many tourist offices will provide information by mail, fax or email.

Cuendet & Cie Spa (☎ 0577 57 63 30; www.cuendet .com; Strada di Strove 17, 53035 Monteriggioni, Siena) organises charming (and often pricey) villa rentals throughout Italy.

ACTIVITIES
Cycling

Cycling is an excellent way to see Italy's gorgeous countryside. Classic areas include Tuscany and Umbria. Lonely Planet's *Cycling in Italy* is a terrific reference with detailed itineraries.

There is good mountain biking in Sardinia, Sicily and around Maratea. Tourist offices offer information on trails, guided rides and rentals.

Hiking & Walking

Italy is a walker's paradise with thousands of kilometres of *sentieri* (marked trails). The **Club Alpino Italiano** (CAI; www.cai.it, in Italian) is a useful resource. There are plenty of organised hiking trips, but solo trekkers will find easy-to-follow trails and refuges; the magnificent Dolomites are the most popular area. On Sardinia, head for the coastal gorges between Dorgali and Baunei, and on Sicily for Mt Etna. Coastal walkers will enjoy Liguria and the Amalfi Coast. Check out Lonely Planet's *Walking in Italy* for detailed descriptions of more than 50 walks.

Skiing

The numerous excellent ski resorts in the Alps and the Apennines offer dramatic scenery and usually good conditions from December to April. See p739 for skiing destinations in the Dolomites.

BUSINESS HOURS

Hours can vary, but generally shops and businesses are open from 9am to 1pm and 3.30pm to 7.30pm Monday to Saturday, with some also open on Sunday morning. They may close on Saturday afternoon and on Thursday or Monday afternoon.

Restaurants are usually open for lunch from 12.30pm to 3pm. For dinner, opening hours vary from north to south but are generally from 7.30pm to 11.30pm. Restaurants are closed one night a week and for much of August; in seasonal tourist areas, many also close between Christmas and April.

Banks tend to open from 8.30am to 1.30pm and 3.30pm to 4.30pm Monday to Friday. Major post offices open from 8.30am to 6pm Monday to Friday, and until 1pm on Saturday. Most museums are now opening from 9.30am to 7pm, later in summer; many close on Monday.

CUSTOMS

There is no limit on the amount of euros brought into the country, and duty-free sales within the EU no longer exist. Travellers coming from outside the EU can import, duty-free 200 cigarettes, 1L of spirits, 2L of wine and other goods up to a total value of €175.

DANGERS & ANNOYANCES

It can require buckets of patience to deal with the Italian concept of service. What for Italians is part of daily life can be horrifying for the foreigner. Long queues are the norm in banks, post offices and any government offices. It definitely pays to remain calm and patient, as a demanding tone can be met with utter indifference.

Theft is the main problem for travellers in Italy, mostly in the form of petty thievery and pickpocketing, especially in the bigger cities. Carry your valuables in a moneybelt and avoid flashing your dough in public. Pickpockets operate in crowded areas, such as markets, and on buses headed for major tourist attractions.

Never leave valuables in a parked car – in fact, try not to leave anything visible in the car if you can help it and it's a good idea to park your car in a supervised car park.

Italy is not a dangerous country for women, however women travelling solo may find themselves plagued by unwanted attention, which can get annoying and tiresome fast. Get used to being ogled and yelled at because it's likely to happen, particularly the further south you travel. It's handy to toss out references to your (real or imagined) *marito* (husband) or *fidanzato* (boyfriend). And if a man's wandering hands find you on the bus, a loud '*Che schifo!*' (How disgusting!) usually does the trick.

EMBASSIES & CONSULATES
Italian Embassies & Consulates

Italian diplomatic missions abroad include:

Australia Canberra (☎ 02-6273 3333; www.ambitalia.org .au; 12 Grey St, Deakin ACT 2600); Melbourne (☎ 03-9867 5744; itconmel@netlink.com.au; 509 St Kilda Rd VIC 3004); Sydney (☎ 02-9392 7900; itconsyd@armadillo.com.au; Level 43, The Gateway, 1 Macquarie Pl NSW 2000)

Canada Ottawa (☎ 613-232 2401; www.italyincanada.com; 21st fl, 275 Slater St, Ontario, K1P 5H9); Vancouver (☎ 604-684 7288; consolato@italianconsulate.bc.ca; Standard Bldg 1100-510 West Hastings St, BC V6B IL8); Toronto (☎ 416-977 1566; consolato.it@toronto.italconsulate.org; 136 Beverley St, Ontario M5T 1Y5); Montreal (☎ 514-849 8351; cgi@italconsul.montreal.qc.ca; 3489 Drummond St, Quebec H3G 1X6)

France Paris (☎ 01 49 54 03 00; ambasciata@amb-italie.fr; 7 rue de Varenne 75007); Paris (☎ 01 44 30 47 00; italconsul parigi@mailcity.com; 5 Blvd Emile Augier 75116)

New Zealand (☎ 04-473 5339; www.italy-embassy.org .nz; 34 Grant Rd, Thorndon, Wellington)

UK London (☎ 020-7312 2200; www.embitaly.org.uk; 14 Three Kings Yard, W1Y 4EH); London (☎ 020-7235 9371; 38 Eaton Place, SW1X 8AN)

USA Washington (☎ 202-328 5500; www.italyemb.org; 1601 Fuller St, NW Washington, DC 20009); New York (☎ 212-737 9100; www.italconsulnyc.org; 690 Park Ave, 10021); Los Angeles (☎ 310-820 0727; www.italyemb .org/onsolati.htm; ste 300, 12400 Wilshire Blvd, 90025)

Embassies & Consulates in Italy

The headquarters of most foreign embassies are in Rome, although there are generally British and US consulates in other major cities. The following information is for Rome unless otherwise stated:

Australia (☎ 06 85 27 21; Via Alessandria 215, 00198)

Canada (☎ 06 44 59 81; Via G B de Rossi 27, 00161)

France Rome (Map pp696-7; ☎ 06 68 60 11; Piazza Farnese 67, 00186); Rome (Map pp696-7; ☎ 06 688 02 152; Via Giuila; 251; ⏲ 9am-12.30pm Mon-Fri); Florence (Map pp690-1; ☎ 055 230 25 56; Piazza Ognissanti 2)

Germany (Map p702; ☎ 06 49 21 31; Via San Martino della Battaglia 4, 00185)

New Zealand (☎ 06 441 71 71; Via Zara 28, 00198)

UK Rome (Map pp690-1; ☎ 06 42 20 00 01; Via XX Settembre 80a, 00187); Florence (Map p742; ☎ 055 28 41 33; Lungarno Corsini 2)

USA Rome (Map pp694-5; ☎ 06 4 67 41; www.usis.it; Via Veneto 119a, 00187); Florence (☎ 055 239 82 76; Lungarno Vespucci 38)

For a complete list of all foreign embassies in Rome and other major cities throughout Italy, look in the local telephone book under *ambasciate* or *consolati*, or ask for a list at a tourist office.

FESTIVALS & EVENTS

Italy's calendar teems with cultural events ranging from colourful traditional celebrations with a religious and/or historical flavour, to festivals of the performing arts, including opera, music and theatre. Annual events worth catching include:

Late February-Early March
Carnevale During the 10 days before Ash Wednesday, many towns stage carnivals. Venice's is the best known, but there are others, including at Viareggio in Tuscany and Ivrea near Turin.

April
Holy Week There are important festivals during this week countrywide; of note are Sicily's colourful and sombre traditional festivals and Assisi's rituals, attracting thousands of pilgrims.

Scoppio del Carro Literally 'Explosion of the Cart', this event, held in Florence on Easter Sunday, features the explosion of a cart full of fireworks and dates back to the Crusades. If all goes well, it is seen as a good omen for the city.

May
Corso dei Ceri One of Italy's strangest festivals is held in Gubbio on 15 May and features a race run by men carrying enormous wooden constructions called *ceri*, in honour of the town's patron saint, Sant'Ubaldo.

July & August
Il Palio On 2 July and 16 August, Siena stages this extraordinary horse race in the town's main piazza.

December
Natale (Christmas) During the weeks preceding Christmas, there are numerous processions and religious events. Many churches set up elaborate cribs or nativity scenes – Naples is famous for these.

HOLIDAYS

Italy's national public holidays include:
Epiphany 6 January
Easter Monday March/April
Liberation Day 25 April

Labour Day 1 May
Ferragosto 15 August
All Saints' Day 1 November
Feast of the Immaculate Conception 8 December
Christmas Day 25 December
Feast of St Stephen 26 December

Individual towns also have public holidays to celebrate the feasts of their patron saints. These include the Feast of St Mark in Venice on 25 April; the Feast of St John the Baptist on 24 June in Florence, Genoa and Turin; the Feast of St Peter and St Paul in Rome on 29 June; the Feast of St Rosalia in Palermo on 15 July; the Feast of St Januarius in Naples on 19 September; and the Feast of St Ambrose in Milan on 7 December.

INTERNET RESOURCES

Following are some websites that will be useful planning tools for your trip to Italy:
www.beniculturali.com – museum information and online reservation options.
www.cts.it – CTS is Italy's leading student travel organisation.
www.italianmade.com or www.deliciousitaly.com – recipes galore.
www.parks.it – for nature lovers, information on Italy's national parks.
www.vatican.va – all about Vatican City, including virtual tours of the main sights.
www.zoomata.com – a close-up on Italy's pop culture.

MONEY

Italy's currency since 2002 is the euro. There is little advantage in bringing foreign cash into Italy. A combination of travellers cheques and credit cards is the best way to take your money. If you buy travellers cheques in euro there should be no commission charged for cashing them. There are exchange offices at all major airports and train stations.

Major credit cards, including Visa, Master-Card and American Express, are widely accepted. They can also be used to get money from ATMs or, if you don't have a PIN, over the counter in major banks. If your credit card is lost, stolen or swallowed by an ATM, you can telephone toll free to have an immediate stop put on its use. For MasterCard the number in Italy is ☎ 800 87 08 66; for Visa ☎ 800 87 72 32; and for American Express, in Rome, call ☎ 06 722 82, which is a 24-hour card-holders' service.

You are not expected to tip in restaurants, but it's common to leave around 10%. In bars, leave small change. Bargaining is common in flea markets, but not in shops.

POST

Italy's postal system is notoriously unreliable. It can take up to two weeks for mail to arrive in the UK or USA, while a letter to Australia will likely take up to three weeks. Postcards take even longer. Put them in an envelope and send them as letters.

The most efficient service to use is *posta prioritaria* (priority mail). Registered mail is known as *raccomandato*, insured mail as *assicurato* and express post as *postacelere*. Stamps *(francobolli)* are available at post offices and tobacconists (*tabacchi* – look for the official sign, a big 'T', usually white on black). The cost of sending a letter *via area* (airmail) depends on its weight, destination and method of postage. Information about postal services and rates can be obtained on ☎ 800 22 26 66 or at www.poste.it, in Italian.

TELEPHONE

Italy's country code is ☎ 39. Area codes are an integral part of the telephone number, even if you're dialling a local number.

Local and long-distance calls can be made from a Telecom office or public phones. Italy's rates, particularly long-distance, are among the highest in Europe. Most public phones accept only *carte/schede telefoniche* (telephone cards), sold at tobacconists and newsstands. Off-peak hours for domestic calls are between 10pm and 8am, and for international calls from 11pm to 8am and Sunday.

To make a reverse-charge (collect) international call from a public phone, dial ☎ 170. For European countries, call ☎ 15. All operators speak English. For international directory inquiries, call ☎ 176. To call Italy from

---

EMERGENCY NUMBERS

- Ambulance ☎ 118
- Automobile Club d'Italia (ACI) ☎ 116
- Carabinieri (Police with military and civil duties) ☎ 112
- Fire Brigade ☎ 115
- Police (Questura) ☎ 113

ITALY

abroad, dial ☎ 39 and then the area code, including the 0.

Italy has one of the highest levels of mobile phone penetration in Europe, and there are several companies, including Telecom Italia Mobile, through which you can get a temporary or prepaid account if you already own a GSM, dual- or tri-band cellular phone. You will usually need your passport to open an account.

VISAS

EU citizens require a national identity card or passport to stay in Italy for as long as they like. Citizens of many other countries, including the USA, Australia, Canada and New Zealand, don't need visas if they are entering as tourists. Visitors are technically obliged to report to a police station if they plan to stay at the same address for more than one week. Tourists staying in hotels or hostels are not required to do this since proprietors need to register guests with the police. A *permesso di soggiorno* is necessary (for non-EU citizens) if you plan to study, work (legally) or live in Italy. Non-EU citizens who want to study at a university or language school in Italy must have a study visa, which can be obtained from your nearest Italian embassy or consulate (see p783).

TRANSPORT IN ITALY

GETTING THERE & AWAY

A recent influx of low-cost airlines, and competition this has stirred, means you should be able to track down a decent fare to Italy. If you live in Europe, you can also travel overland by car, bus or train.

Air

High season in Italy is June to September and bargains are hard to find during this period. Two months either side of this is the shoulder season, with low season officially November to March. Christmas and Easter can also cause fares to spike. The Internet can be the easiest way to locate and book reasonably priced tickets.

Full-time students and those under 26 years are eligible for discounted fares (see p1057). Other cheap deals include the ever-expanding no-frills carriers, which sell direct to travellers.

Italy's main intercontinental gateway is the **Leonardo da Vinci Airport** (Fiumicino; ☎ 06 659 51; www.adr.it) in Rome, but regular intercontinental flights also serve Milan's **Linate Airport** (☎ 02 748 522 00; www.sea-aeroportimilano.it). Plenty of flights from other European cities also go direct to regional capitals around the country.

Many European and international airlines, as well as discount carriers, compete with the country's national carrier, Alitalia. International airlines flying to/from Italy from Western Europe include:

Air Canada (code AC; ☎ 06 55 112, toll free ☎ 91 90 91; www.aircanada.ca)
Air France (code AF; ☎ 848 88 44 66; www.airfrance.com)
Air New Zealand (code NZ; ☎ 06 48 79 11; www.airnz.co.nz)
Alitalia (code AZ; ☎ 06 6 56 41, 848 86 56 41; www.alitalia.it)
American Airlines (code AA; Milan ☎ 02 69 68 24 64; Rome ☎ 06 66 05 31 69; www.aa.com)
British Airways (code BA; ☎ 199 712 266; www.britishairways.com)
British Midland (code BD; ☎ 44-1332 854 000; www.flybmi.com)
Delta Air Lines (code DL; ☎ 800-477-999; www.delta.com)
easyJet (code U2; ☎ 848 88 77 66; www.easyjet.com)
KLM (code KL; ☎ 06 6501 1147; www.klm.com)
Lufthansa (code LH; ☎ 06 6568 4004; www.lufthansa.com)
Meridiana (code IG; ☎ 199 11 13 33; www.meridiana.it)
Qantas (code QF; ☎ 06 529 22 87; www.qantas.com)
Ryanair (code FR; ☎ 889 89 98 44; www.ryanair.com)
Singapore Airlines (code SQ; ☎ 06 478 55 360; www.singaporeair.com)
Thai Airways International (code TG; ☎ 06 47 81 31; www.thaiair.com)
United Airlines (code UA; ☎ 02 69 63 37 07; www.ual.com)
Virgin Express (code TV; Milan ☎ 02 48 29 60 00, rest of Italy ☎ 800 097 097; www.virgin-express.com)

If you have patience, you can find good fares online. An excellent Italian site for low-cost travel is www.volareweb.com, in six different languages and adding new destinations rapidly (such as Warsaw, thanks to the expanding EU).

Land

BUS

A consortium of European coach companies, **Eurolines** (www.eurolines.com), operates across

ITALY

Europe with offices in all major European cities. You can contact it in your own country or in Italy and the multi-language website gives details of prices, passes and travel agencies where you can book tickets.

Covering at least 60 European cities and towns, **Busabout** (☎ 020 7950 1661; www.busabout .com) offers passes of varying duration, allowing you to use its hop-on hop-off bus network in Western in Central Europe. You can even book onward travel and accommodation on the bus or on the website.

TRAIN

Trains run from major destinations throughout Europe direct to major Italian cities through **Eurostar** (ES; ☎ 0870 518 6186; www.euro star.com). On overnight hauls, you can book a couchette for around €25. Travellers can take advantage of a range of passes, including the **Inter-Rail** (www.interrailnet.com) and **Eurail** (www.eurail.com) passes (see p1080). For prices and purchasing details, visit the websites. You can book local tickets at train stations and most travel agencies. For the latest fare information on journeys to Italy, contact the **Rail Europe Travel Centre** (☎ 0870 848 848; www.raileurope.co.uk).

Sea

Numerous ferry services connect Italy with other Mediterranean countries. Tickets are the most expensive in summer and prices for vehicles vary according to their size. Eurail and Inter-Rail pass holders pay only a supplement on the Italy to Greece routes from Ancona and Bari.

The incredibly helpful search engine **Traghettionline** (www.traghettionline.net) covers all the ferry companies in the Mediterranean; you can also book online. See individual town entries for ferry company details and services.

Blue Star Ferries (www.greekferries.gr) and **Minoan Lines** (☎ 210 414 57 00; www.minoan.gr) service Venice, Brindisi and Ancona from Igoumenitsa, Corfu or Patra, while **Fragline Ferries** (☎ 210 821 41 71; www.fragline.gr) connects Corfu to Brindisi. Turkish **Marmara Lines** (www.marara lines.com) connects Cesme to Brindisi and on to Venice.

Tirrenia Navigazione (☎ 199 12 31 99 call centre; www.tirrenia.it) services all major Italian ports and connects them with Tunisia, while **Grandi Navi Veloci** (www.grimaldi.it, Italian only; Livorno ☎ 058

640 98 94; Genoa ☎ 010 58 93 31; Palermo ☎ 091 58 74 04) services Barcelona and Valencia in Spain.

The **Maltese Virtu Ferries** (☎ 356 31 88 54; www .virtuferries.com) has ferries from Malta to Catania between March and October. Prices for an airline-style seat range from €40 to €90. There are a burgeoning number of ferries between Croatia (Split and Dubrovnik) and Slovenia and the Italian ports of Ancona, Bari and Pescara.

GETTING AROUND

Italy's extensive network of train and bus services means you can reach almost any destination fairly efficiently; for longer distances there are good domestic air and boat services. Renting a car obviously gives you the most freedom, but be prepared for shockingly expensive petrol and tolls, and you'll likely need a massage (or at least a stiff drink) from the stress of driving and parking in a big Italian city.

Air

Travelling by plane can be expensive within Italy, but it's becoming more reasonable. The domestic airlines are **Alitalia** (www.alitalia .it), **Meridiana** (www.meridiana.it) and **Air One** (www .flyairone.it). The main airports are in Rome, Pisa, Milan, Bologna, Genoa, Turin, Naples, Catania, Palermo and Cagliari, but there are other, smaller airports throughout Italy. Domestic flights can be booked directly with the airlines or through any travel agency (listed throughout this guide).

Bicycle

Bikes are available for rent in many Italian towns (about €10 a day) and can travel in the baggage compartment of some Italian trains (but not on Eurostar or Intercity trains); bikes travel free on ferries.

Boat

Navi (large ferries) service Sicily and Sardinia, and *traghetti* (smaller ferries) and *aliscafi* (hydrofoils) service the smaller island routes, including Elba, the Aeolian Islands, Capri and Ischia. The main embarkation points for Sicily and Sardinia are at Genoa, La Spezia, Livorno, Civitavecchia, Fiumicino and Naples. **Tirrenia Navigazione** (www.tirrenia.it) services nearly all the Italian ports and has offices throughout the country. Most long-distance ferries travel overnight.

Bus

Numerous bus companies operate within Italy. It is usually necessary to make reservations only for long trips, such as Rome–Palermo. Buses can be a cheaper and faster way to get around if your destination is not on major rail lines, such as from Umbria to Rome, and in the interior areas of Sicily and Sardinia. Major companies that run long-haul services include Marozzi (Rome to Brindisi), Interbus (Rome to Sicily) and Lazzi (from Lazio, Tuscany and other regions to the Alps).

Car & Motorcycle

Roads are generally good throughout the country and there is an excellent network of autostrade. The main north-south link is the Autostrada del Sole, which extends from Milan to Reggio di Calabria (called the A1 from Milan to Naples and the A3 from Naples to Reggio). There's a toll to use most of Italy's autostrade, and you can pay by cash or credit card as you leave it. If you've got time, follow the *strade statali* (state roads), toll free and often very scenic; these are designated by an 'S' or 'SS' on maps.

HIRE

The most competitive multinational car-rental agencies are:

Autos Abroad (☎ 44-8700 667 788; www .autosabroad.com)

Avis (☎ 02 754 197 61; www.avis.com)

Budget (☎ 1-800 472 33 25; www.budget.com)

Europcar (☎ 06 481 71 62; www.europcar.com)

Europe by Car (☎ 1-800 223 15 16; www.europe bycar.com)

Hertz (☎ 199 11 22 11; www.hertz.com)

To hire a car or motorcycle, you have to be aged over 21 and have a credit card, along with a valid EU driving licence, an International Driving Permit or your driving licence from your own country. If you're driving your own car, you'll need an international insurance certificate, known as a Carta Verde (Green Card), which can be obtained from your insurer.

Check with your car insurance, and credit cards, to find out what kind of coverage you have internationally. For the best rental rates, book your car before leaving home. The **Automobile Club d'Italia** (ACI; ☎ 06 4 99 81, 24hr info line ☎ 166 66 44 77) can be a helpful source of assistance once in Italy.

You'll have no trouble hiring a small Vespa or moped, as well as motorcycles for touring (provided you're over 18 years of age); there are numerous rental agencies in all Italian cities.

ROAD RULES

In Italy people drive on the right-hand side of the road and pass on the left. Unless otherwise indicated, you must give way to cars coming from the right. It is compulsory to wear seat belts if they are fitted to the car. If you are caught not wearing your seat belt, you will be required to pay an on-the-spot fine.

Random breath tests now take place in Italy; the blood-alcohol limit is 0.05%, and the penalities are severe.

Wearing a helmet is compulsory for every motorcycle and moped rider and passenger – although you won't necessarily see this.

Some of the Italian cities, including Rome, Bologna, Florence, Milan and Turin, have introduced restricted access to both private and rental cars in their historical centres. The restrictions, however, do not apply to vehicles with foreign registrations. *Motorini* (mopeds) and scooters (such as Vespas) are able to enter the zones without any problems (and park on footpaths).

Speed limits, unless otherwise indicated by local signs, are: on autostrade 130km/h; on non-urban roads 110km/h; on secondary non-urban highways 90km/h; and in built-up areas 50km/h.

Petrol prices are high in Italy. Petrol is called *benzina*, unleaded petrol is *benzina senza piombo* and diesel is *gasolio*.

Train

The partially privatised state train system that runs most of the services in Italy is **Trenitalia** (☎ 848 88 80 88; www.trenitalia.com, Italian only). There are several types of trains. Some stop at all the stations, such as *regionale* or *interregionale*, while faster trains, such as the Intercity (IC) and the fastest Eurostar Italia (ES), stop only at major cities. It is cheaper to buy all local train tickets in the country.

For details on timetables, services and prices, visit www.fs-on-line.com.

ITALY

There are 1st and 2nd classes on all Italian trains, with the former costing almost double the latter. Intercity and Eurostar trains require a supplement (usually €4 to €16), determined by the distance of travel.

All tickets must be validated – in the yellow machines at the entrance to all train platforms – before you board the train.

Trenitalia offers its own discount passes for travel within Italy, available at major train stations. These include the Carta Verde, which offers a 20% discount for people aged from 12 to 26 years, and the Carta d'Argento offers the same discount to people aged 60 years and over; both cost €26 and are valid for one year.

The new Trenitalia Pass allows for four to 10 days of travel within a two-month period. At the time of writing, passes for 1st/2nd class cost €349/282.

Liechtenstein

Blink and you'll miss Liechtenstein: the pocket-sized principality is so small (just 25km north to south and about 6km west to east) that if you went for a long run you could end up at the other side of the country.

You might easily think you're still in Switzerland: the currency is the Swiss franc, travel documents are the same for both countries and the only border regulations are on the Austrian side. Switzerland even represents Liechtenstein abroad. Even if you think you've never left Heidi's home turf, don't let the locals know this: they'd never forgive you. Generally eager to underscore its independent status, Liechtenstein often takes a different route to its big sister (seemingly just to be difficult) and, although the countries share the Swiss postal system, Liechtenstein still issues its own stamps.

In fact, many tourists come to Liechtenstein for the stamps – in the passport for themselves and on a postcard for the folks back home. But it's also worth heading to the hills: there are numerous hiking trails offering spectacular views of craggy cliffs, quaint villages and lush green forests.

FAST FACTS

- **Area** 150 sq km
- **Capital** Vaduz
- **Currency** Swiss franc (Sfr); A$1 = Sfr0.90; €1 = Sfr1.54; ¥100 = Sfr1.17; NZ$1 = Sfr0.84; UK£1 = Sfr2.29; US$1 = Sfr1.28
- **Famous for** sending postcards stamped by the country's postal service, dentures
- **Official Language** German
- **Population** 32,860
- **Telephone Codes** country code ☎ 423; international access code ☎ 00
- **Visas** none required for passport holders of the UK, Ireland, the USA, Canada, Australia, New Zealand and South Africa

LIECHTENSTEIN

HIGHLIGHTS

- Visit **Vaduz** (p791), the tiny village masquerading as a capital, and make sure to snap a picture of the royal castle with its stunning mountain backdrop.
- Just to say you did, write a postcard home from the ski resort of **Malbun** (p793); how many people really can say they were skiing in Liechtenstein?
- Check out the country's 400km of **hiking trails** (p793) through stunning Alpine scenery – this can be accomplished from anywhere in the tiny principality.

CLIMATE & WHEN TO GO

Visit Liechtenstein from December to April for skiiing, and May to October for general sightseeing and hiking. Alpine resorts all but close down in late April, May and November.

HISTORY

An merger of the domain of Schellenberg and the county of Vaduz in 1712 by the powerful Liechtenstein family created the country. A principality under the Holy Roman Empire from 1719 to 1806, it achieved full sovereign independence in 1866. A modern constitution was drawn up in 1921, but even today the prince retains the power to dissolve parliament and must approve every act before it becomes law. Prince Franz Josef II was the first ruler to live in the castle above the capital city of Vaduz. He died in 1989 and was succeeded by his son, Prince Hans-Adam II.

After a decade-long constitutional debate, a March 2003 referendum approved giving the Prince more powers and a larger role in running the principality. The referendum passed with a landslide two to three majority.

Liechtenstein has no military service and its minuscule army (80 men!) was disbanded in 1868. It is best known for wine production, postage stamps, dentures (an important export) and its status as a tax haven. In 2000, Liechtenstein's financial and political institutions were rocked by allegations that money laundering was rife in the country. In response to international outrage, banks agreed to stop allowing customers to bank money anonymously.

PEOPLE & CULTURE

Liechtenstein does not have a strong tradition in the arts. The language is German, although it has its own quirks and variants. The architecture varies according to region, but houses generally have ridged roofs with wide, overhanging eaves, and balconies and verandas enlivened by colourful displays of flowers.

FOOD & DRINK

Liechtenstein's cuisine borrows from its larger neighbours, and it is generally good quality but expensive. Basic restaurants provide simple but well-cooked food, although budget travellers may want to live out of the supermarket fridge. Soups are popular and usually very filling, and cheeses form an important part of the diet, as do *rösti* (fried shredded potatoes) and *wurst* (sausage).

Wine is considered an integral part of the meal. The local wines are good, but as they're rarely exported you'll probably never have heard of them.

VADUZ

pop 4930

Despite being a capital, Vaduz does a really good impersonation of a village. You can jog end-to-end in five minutes, although you'll want to walk slowly to appreciate its points of interest.

Two adjoining streets beneath the castle, Äulestrasse and pedestrian-only Städtle, enclose the town centre. Everything of importance is within this small area. The postal bus stops in the centre of town.

INFORMATION

The **Telecom FL shop** (☎ 237 74 74; Austrasse 77; 🕑 9am-noon & 1.30-6.30pm Mon-Fri, 9am-1pm Sat), 1km south of Vaduz, provides free Internet access. Send postcards at the **main post office** (Äulestrasse 38; 🕑 7.45am-6pm Mon-Fri, 8am-11am Sat). For medical attention, contact the **Vaduz Hospital** (☎ 235 44 11; Heiligkreuz 25).

Liechtenstein Tourism (☎ 239 63 00; www.touris mus.li; Städtle 37; 🕑 9am-noon & 1.30-5pm May-Oct, closed Sat & Sun Nov-Apr) has plenty of useful information; for Sfr2, staff will stamp your passport with a souvenir entry stamp.

SIGHTS & ACTIVITIES

Although the **Schloss Vaduz** (Vaduz Castle) is not open to the public, the exterior graces many a photograph, and it is worth climbing up the hill for a closer look. At the top, there's a magnificent vista of Vaduz with a spectacular backdrop of the mountains.

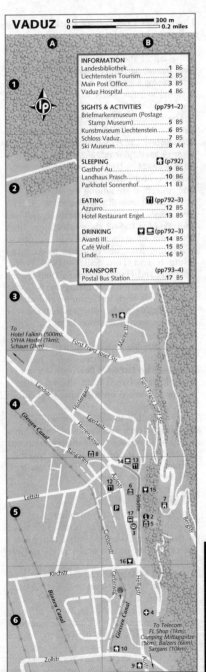

VADUZ

0 300 m
0 0.2 miles

INFORMATION
Landesbibliothek.....................1 B6
Liechtenstein Tourism...............2 B5
Main Post Office.....................3 B5
Vaduz Hospital.......................4 B6

SIGHTS & ACTIVITIES   (pp791-2)
Briefmarkenmuseum (Postage
  Stamp Museum).....................5 B5
Kunstmuseum Liechtenstein.........6 B5
Schloss Vaduz........................7 B5
Ski Museum...........................8 A4

SLEEPING 🛏   (p792)
Gasthof Au...........................9 B6
Landhaus Prasch.....................10 B6
Parkhotel Sonnenhof................11 B3

EATING 🍴   (pp792-3)
Azzurro.............................12 B5
Hotel Restaurant Engel.............13 B5

DRINKING 🍷 🖥   (pp792-3)
Avanti III..........................14 B5
Café Wolf...........................15 B5
Linde...............................16 B5

TRANSPORT   (pp793-4)
Postal Bus Station..................17 B5

There's also a network of marked walking trails along the ridge.

Keen philatelists will lick their lips in anticipation of the **Briefmarkenmuseum** (Postage Stamp Museum; ☎ 236 61 05; Städtle 37; admission free; 🕑 10am-noon & 1-5pm), where 300 frames of national stamps issued since 1912 are on display.

The national art collection is housed in a sleek modern building at the **Kunstmuseum Liechtenstein** (☎ 235 030 00; Städtle 32; www.kunst museum.li; adult/student/child Sfr8/5/5; 🕑 1-8pm Tue & Thu, to 5pm Wed & Fri, 11am-5pm Sat & Sun). Sixteenth-to 18th-century works from the prince's private collection are among the highlights.

The **Ski Museum** (National Museum; ☎ 232 15 02; www.skimuseum.li, in German; Bangarten 10; adult/child Sfr6/4; 🕑 2-6pm Mon-Fri) showcases more than 100 years of skiing history in Europe – everything from old bindings to Austrian skiing legend Toni Sailer's 1958 World Cup skis and Hanni Wenzel's 1980 Olympic gear. Wenzel, a sporting hero in the country, was born in Germany and moved to Liechtenstein when she was just one year old. She's won numerous Olympic skiing medals.

Look out for processions and fireworks on 15 August, Liechtenstein's national holiday. The **Little Big One** open-air music festival draws bands from all over when it sweeps into town on the third weekend in June.

It is possible to sample the wines from the prince's own vineyard, but only with a group of 10 or more. Advance reservations are essential. If you get a group together, contact the **Hofkellerei** (☎ 232 10 18; www.hofkel lerei.li; Feldstrasse 4).

SLEEPING

You can base yourself anywhere and still be within easy cycling or postbus distance of the centre. Ask the tourist office for a list of private rooms and chalets outside Vaduz.

Camping Mittagspitz (☎ 392 26 86; per adult/child/tent/car Sfr8.50/4/5/4, dm Sfr22; 🕑 year-round) Located on a hillside terrace overlooking the Rhine valley, this is Liechtenstein's only camping ground. Check out the comfortable dorms. It's south of Triesen, so not exactly in Vaduz.

SYHA Hostel (☎ 232 50 22; schaan@youthhostel.ch; Untere Rütigasse 6; dm from Sfr29, d with shared bathroom

---

> ### IT'S LIECHTENSTEIN TRIVIA TIME
>
> ■ If you ever meet the prince in the pub make sure he buys a round. The royal family is estimated to be worth UK£3.3 billion.
>
> ■ There are 80,000 companies registered in the principality – that's nearly double the population of Vaduz.
>
> ■ Liechtenstein bites into a large chunk of the false teeth market – it is the world's largest exporter of the product.

Sfr75, d Sfr87; 🕑 mid-Mar–Nov) This hostel is in a quiet rural setting between Vaduz and nearby Schaan. Take the postbus to the Muhleholz stop; it's a five-minute walk (signposted) from there.

Hotel Falknis (☎ 232 63 77; Landstrasse 92; s/d with shared bathroom Sfr55/110) With a pub and smart if rather basic rooms, this is a cheapish option just outside Vaduz. It's a 15-minute walk north from the centre (or take the postbus).

Gasthof Au (☎ 232 11 17; fax 232 11 68; Austrasse 2; s/d Sfr90/130, s/d with shared bathroom Sfr65/70) Intimate and warmly decorated rooms, some with balcony, are featured at this hotel south of the centre. There is an attached garden restaurant.

Landhaus Prasch (☎ 232 46 63; www.news.li/touri /prasch; Zollstrasse; s/d Sfr95/130; 🕑 Apr-Oct; 🔊) This is a quaint place with a sauna and indoor swimming pool. When it's quiet, ask about cheaper rates.

Parkhotel Sonnenhof (☎ 232 11 92; www.sonnen hof.li; Mareestrasse 29; s/d Sfr220/330; 🔊) This hotel is Liechtenstein's contribution to luxury accommodation. Rooms are brightly painted and offer excellent views. Pamper yourself in the large indoor swimming pool or top-class sauna.

EATING & DRINKING

The pedestrian-only Städtle street has a clutch of pavement restaurants and cafés to choose from.

Azzurro (☎ 232 48 18; cnr Äulestr & Badwegli; mains Sfr8; 🕑 9am-7pm) This takeaway stand delivers quick sandwiches, kebabs, small pizzas and salads.

Avanti III (Städtle 5; mains Sfr5-14; 🕑 9am-9pm) Serving cheap but filling snacks and meals, this place doubles as a souvenir shop. Sit at the outside tables.

Linde (☎ 233 10 05; Kirchstrasse 2; mains Sfr16-32; ⊙ 8.30am-11pm Mon-Sat) A trendy bar popular with locals, it has a great '70s retro vibe. The bamboo décor is slightly kitschy, but grows on you. Mexican and Asian dishes are served in heaped portions.

Hotel Restaurant Engel (☎ 236 17 17; Städtle 13; mains from Sfr17; ⊙ daily) A popular option inside the hotel, Engel serves Swiss meals that prove to be just as tasty as those found across the border. There also is a range of Chinese food.

Café Wolf (1st fl, Städtle 29; mains from Sfr24; ⊙ daily) Head here for live music in the evenings, when the place fills quickly. There is also a range of dishes if you are hungry.

AROUND VADUZ

In summer, skis give way to mountain boots as the hiking fraternity hits town. Northern Liechtenstein is dotted with small, tranquil communities with pleasant village churches. **Schellenberg** has a Russian monument, commemorating the night in 1945 when a band of 500 heavily armed Russian soldiers crossed the border.

Triesenberg, on a terrace above Vaduz, commands excellent views over the Rhine valley. It has a pretty onion-domed church and the **Heimatmuseum** (☎ 262 19 26; adult/student Sfr2/1; ⊙ 1.30-5.30pm Tue-Sat), which is devoted to the Walser community, whose members came from Switzerland's Valais to settle in the 13th century. Apparently, the Walser dialect is still spoken here.

Dominated by the soaring sides of the Gutenberg Castle is **Balzers**, in the extreme south of the country.

MALBUN
pop 100

Nestled amid the mountains in the southeast is tiny Malbun, Liechtenstein's one and only ski resort.

The road from Vaduz terminates at Malbun. The **tourist office** (☎ 263 65 77; ⊙ 9am-noon & 1.30-5pm Mon-Fri, 1-4pm Sat, closed mid-Apr–May & Nov-Dec) is by the first bus stop. Malbun has no bank, but the sports shop changes money. The ATM by the tourist office doesn't accept Visa cards.

> **EMERGENCY NUMBERS**
>
> The same emergency numbers apply as in Switzerland:
>
> ▪ Police ☎ 117
> ▪ Ambulance ☎ 144
> ▪ Fire ☎ 118

Although rather limited in scope – the runs are mostly novice and intermediate – the skiing is inexpensive for this region of the world and it does offer some bragging rights.

The resort has ski and snowboard schools. A one-day/week-long ski pass costs Sfr36/164 for adults and just Sfr30/136 for students under 28. Skis, shoes and poles cost Sfr44 for a day, and can be hired from the **sports shop** (☎ 263 37 55) in town.

Liechtenstein has some 400km of hiking trails through alpine scenery. Worthwhile treks in the area include the **Panorama** and **Furstin-Gina** paths, which start and finish in Malbun. A chairlift at the resort operates in the summer (one way/return Sfr8/12), so you can ride up and hike down. The village has eight hotels, each with a restaurant. Try the **Alpenhotel Malbun** (☎ 263 11 81; fax 263 96 46; s/d with shared bathroom from Sfr45/90; ☕), by the bus stop, for cosy, wooden rooms.

LIECHTENSTEIN DIRECTORY

Liechtenstein and Switzerland share almost everything – a postal system, a currency, an airport – so for more information about Liechtenstein basics check out the Switzerland Directory p1042.

TRANSPORT IN LIECHTENSTEIN

GETTING THERE & AWAY

Liechtenstein has no airport (the nearest is in Zürich); instead, get there by postbus. There are usually three buses an hour from the Swiss border towns of Buchs (Sfr2.40) and Sargans (Sfr3.60) that stop in Vaduz.

There are trains from Zürich to Sargans (Sfr27, one hour, hourly).

Buses run half-hourly from the Austrian border town of Feldkirch; you may have to change at Schaan to reach Vaduz (the Sfr3.60 ticket is valid for both buses).

By road, route 16 from Switzerland passes through Liechtenstein via Schaan and terminates at Feldkirch. The N13 follows the Rhine along the Swiss–Liechtenstein border; minor roads cross into Liechtenstein at each motorway exit.

GETTING AROUND
Postbus travel within Liechtenstein is cheap and reliable; all fares cost Sfr2.40 or Sfr3.60, with the higher rate for journeys exceeding 13km (such as Vaduz to Malbun). A weekly/monthly pass is only Sfr10/20 (half-price for students and seniors).

The only drawback is that some services finish early; the last of the hourly buses from Vaduz to Malbun, for example, leaves at 6.20pm. Grab a timetable from the Vaduz tourist office.

Luxembourg

FAST FACTS

- **Area** 2586 sq km
- **Capital** Luxembourg City
- **Currency** euro (€); A$1 = €0.58; ¥100 = €0.76; NZ$1 = €0.54; UK£1 = €1.50; US$1 = €0.83
- **Famous for** banking
- **Key Phrases** *moien* (hello); *äddi* (goodbye); *merci* (thanks)
- **Official Languages** Luxemburgian, French, German
- **Population** 440,000
- **Telephone Codes** country code ☎ 352; international access code ☎ 00; reverse-charge call ☎ 80 02 00
- **Visas** citizens of Australia, Canada, Israel, Japan, New Zealand and the USA do not need a visa to visit for up to three months; there are no entry requirements or restrictions on EU nationals

The Grand Duchy of Luxembourg (Luxemburg, Lëtzebuerg) has long been a transit land. For centuries, ownership passed from one superpower to another; and for decades travellers wrote it off as merely an expensive stepping stone to other destinations.

It's true that this tiny country is more a tax shelter for financial institutions than a budget haven for travellers, but many miss the best by rushing through. The beautiful countryside is dotted with feudal castles, deep river valleys and quaint wine-making towns, while the capital, Luxembourg City, is often described as the most dramatically situated in Europe.

HIGHLIGHTS

- Stroll the capital's **Chemin de la Corniche** (p799), a pedestrian promenade hailed as 'Europe's most beautiful balcony'.
- **Admire Vianden** (p803), Luxembourg's most popular countryside town, crowned by a picture-perfect castle.
- Explore the primeval landscape of the Müllerthal from **Echternach** (p804).

ITINERARIES

- **Two days** Explore the ancient core of Luxembourg City, taking in the Musée National d'Histoire et d'Art and the beautiful Chemin de la Corniche.
- **One week** This is ample time to tour the whole country. Don't miss Echternach, a little town steeped in Christian history, and a positively delightful little place to kick back. Vianden is another must. Move onto Diekirch for its fascinating WWII museum, and Remich for wine tasting.

CLIMATE & WHEN TO GO

Luxembourg's climate is temperate – warm summers and cold winters. The sunniest months are May to August, although April and September can be fine also. If you're into flowers, spring is the time to be here. For festivals and outdoor dining, come in summer. To enjoy wine-making, plan for autumn when the Moselle villages move into harvest celebrations.

HISTORY

Luxembourg's history reads a little like the fairy tale its name evokes. More than 1000 years ago, in 963, a count called Sigefroi (or Siegfried, Count of Ardennes) built a castle high on a promontory, laying the foundation of the present-day capital and the beginning of a dynasty that spawned rulers throughout Europe.

HOW MUCH?

- **Mid-range hotel double** €65-80
- **Restaurant meal** €12-35
- **Loaf of bread** €1.20
- **Local phone call** €0.30 per minute
- **Taxi ride from airport** €20

LONELY PLANET INDEX

- **Litre of petrol** €0.90
- **Litre of bottled water** €0.60
- **Beer – bottle of Diekirch** €0.85
- **Souvenir T-shirt** €15
- **Street snack (baguette)** €3

By the end of the Middle Ages the strategically placed, fortified city was much sought after – the Burgundians, Spanish, French, Austrians and Prussians all waged bloody battles to secure it. Besieged, devastated and rebuilt more than 20 times in 400 years, it became the strongest fortress in Europe after Gibraltar, hence its nickname, 'Gibraltar of the North'.

In 1814, it was included in the newly formed United Kingdom of the Netherlands, along with Belgium, and 25 years later, present-day Luxembourg was born. But its potentially perilous position between France and Germany led to the major European powers declaring the country neutral in 1867. As a result, much of its historic fortifications were dismantled, though you can still visit the damp galleries known as the Bock Casemates (p799).

Luxembourg's neutrality was quashed in 1914 when Germany invaded. It was occupied for the whole of WWI and again in WWII – for insight into the 1944 Battle

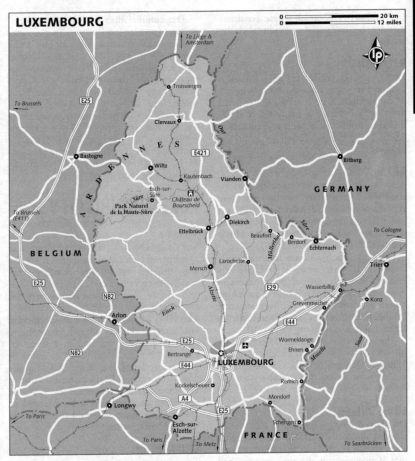

LUXEMBOURG

of the Ardennes, see the Musée National d'Histoire Militaire in Diekirch (p805).

After the war, Luxembourg dumped its useless neutral status and joined NATO and the EU. The government diversified the economy, enabling the little country to ride the depression in the iron and steel industries in the 1970s and to become a noted financial centre and tax haven. It's now home to some key EU institutions and has entered the 21st century with one of Europe's healthiest economies.

The Grand Duchy's royal family is on a similar high. Grand Duke Henri and Grand Duchess Maria Teresa, a Cuban-born commoner whom Henri met at university, have brought new life to the role

of the ducal family since coming to the throne in 2000.

PEOPLE

Luxembourg's 440,000 inhabitants are a confident and proud people who have no problem with the fact that they live in a seriously diminutive country. A motto that's occasionally seen carved in stone walls sums up the people's character: *Mir wëlle bleiwe wat mir sin* (We want to remain what we are).

More than a third of Luxembourg's population are immigrants, predominantly Portuguese and Italian. The Italians came a century ago to work in the mines; the Portuguese arrived in the 1970s when the iron and steel industries boomed. These communities are well integrated and cultural clashes are rare.

RELIGION

Christianity was established early, and today Catholicism reigns supreme. More than 95% of the population are Roman Catholic, with the church influencing many facets of life, including politics, the media and education. About 3% of the population are Protestant or Jewish.

ARTS

Arriving from any of its neighbouring countries, Luxembourg can be seen as an art breather. No great collections or 'must-see' galleries here, though it's possible to get among local art at the capital's Musée National d'Histoire et d'Art (p799).

Few Luxembourgers are internationally known in the arts, which is probably why Edward Steichen, one of the pioneers of American photography, is held in such high regard in his native land. See his fascinating exhibition in Clervaux (p803) and a display on his life in Luxembourg City (p801).

The expressionist painter Joseph Kutter introduced modern art to Luxembourg.

Roger Manderscheid is a contemporary author who writes in Luxemburgian, the national language.

ENVIRONMENT

On maps of Europe the Grand Duchy usually gets allocated a 'Lux' tag – and even that abbreviation is often too big to fit the space that it occupies on the map, sandwiched between Belgium, Germany and France. At only 82km long and 57km wide, it's divided between the forested Ardennes highlands to the north, and farming and industrial country to the south.

About a third of Luxembourg is covered by forests, home to wild boar, fox and deer. There are no national parks. The main environmental concerns are air and water pollution in urban areas.

FOOD & DRINK

Luxembourg is carnivore capital – game, pork and freshwater fish dominate. While French- and German-style foods are most common, there's modest culinary diversity in Luxembourg City.

The national dish is *judd mat gaardebounen* (smoked pork served in a cream-based sauce with chunks of potato and broad beans). Other specialities include *ferkelsrippchen* (grilled spareribs), *liewekniddelen mat sauerkraut* (liver meatballs with sauerkraut), *traipen* (black pudding), *kuddelfleck* (boiled tripe) and *kachkeis* (a cooked cheese).

Luxembourg's wine industry, based along the west bank of the Moselle River, is known for fruity white and sparkling wines at affordable prices. Try those made by Bernard-Massard at Grevenmacher and St Martin at Remich – for more details see p805.

LUXEMBOURG CITY

pop 80,176

The Grand Duchy's 1000-year-old capital is a composed blend of old and new. It's strikingly situated high on a promontory overlooking deep valleys carved by the Pétrusse and Alzette Rivers. These gorges were for centuries the key to the city's defence. Nowadays they provide visitors with spectacular vistas over parklands and old, atmospheric quarters, and are spanned by a series of imposing bridges, all of which combine to give the capital its unique and charming appeal. Aesthetics aside, the historical value of Luxembourg City's remaining fortifications and older quarters were acknowledged in 1994 when Unesco added them to its list of World Heritage sites.

ORIENTATION

The gorges that hampered invading armies for centuries define the face of the modern-day capital, dividing the central area into four distinct sections – the Old Town north of the Pétrusse Valley, the train station area, the river valley quarters and Kirchberg.

The pedestrianised Old Town is based around two squares – Place d'Armes and Place Guillaume II. To the south – across Pont Adolphe and Viaduc, two bridges spanning the Pétrusse Valley – is the train station quarter, an area of no appeal. The station, Gare Centrale, is 1.25km from Place d'Armes.

Below the Old Town's fortifications are the river valley neighbourhoods of the Grund, Clausen and Pfaffenthal. Easy access to the Grund is provided by an elevator on Plateau du St Esprit. To the northeast of the Old Town is Kirchberg, a boring business district that's slowly coming to life with the building of modern new art complexes (see p801).

Maps

The tourist office hands out a free map of the central area and also sells a more detailed map (scale: 1:15,000).

INFORMATION
Emergency
Ambulance & Fire ☎ 112
Emergency Roadside Service (☎ 45 00 45 1) Club Automobile de Luxembourg's 24-hour service.
Police ☎ 113

Internet Access
Centre Information Jeunes (CIJ; ☎ 26 29 32 00; www.youth.lu, no English; Galerie Kons, 26 Place de la Gare; ☼ 10am-6pm Mon-Fri) Youth information centre providing free Internet access (bookings necessary).
Sparkey's (☎ 26 20 12 23; 11a Ave Monterey; per hr €6; ☼ 7am-1am Mon-Sat) Bar with two Internet terminals.

Medical Services
Clinique Ste Thérèse (☎ 49 77 61; 36 Rue Ste Zithe) Central hospital providing emergency service.

Money
ATMs Inside Gare Centrale; outside main post office; inside Findel airport terminal.
Kredietbank Luxembourg (Place de la Gare; ☼ 8.30am-4.30pm Mon-Fri)

Post
Main post office (☎ 47 65 44 51; 25 Rue Aldringen; ☼ 7am-7pm Mon-Fri, 7am-5pm Sat)

Tourist Information
Centre Information Jeunes (CIJ; ☎ 26 29 32 00; www.youth.lu, no English; Galerie Kons, 26 Place de la Gare; ☼ 10am-6pm Mon-Fri) Youth information centre.
Luxembourg City Tourist Office (☎ 22 28 09; www .lcto.lu; Place d'Armes; ☼ 9am-6pm Mon-Sat & 10am-6pm Sun) Free city maps, walking tour pamphlets and events guides.
Luxembourg National Tourist Office (☎ 42 82 82 20; www.ont.lu; Place de la Gare; ☼ 8.30am-6.30pm Mon-Sat, 9am-12.30pm & 2-6pm Sun Jun-Sep, 9.15am-2.30pm & 1.45-6pm daily Oct-May) City and national information.

SIGHTS

Start at **Place d'Armes**, Luxembourg's central pedestrianised square, from where it's an

---

LUXEMBOURG CITY IN TWO DAYS

Place d'Armes, the pedestrianised core, is not to be missed. Neither are the **Musée National d'Histoire et d'Art** (p799) or the **Musée d'Histoire de la Ville de Luxembourg** (p799). For an alfresco lunch there's **Café Am Musee** (p801). Explore the **Bock Casemates** (p799) then stroll the **Chemin de la Corniche** (p799) which ends near an elevator that goes down to the **Grund** (p802), a great area for a drink. Dine at **Breedewee** (p801) for an unbeatable view.

---

easy walk to the **Musée National d'Histoire et d'Art** (☎ 47 93 30 1; www.mnha.lu, in French; Marché-aux-Poissons; adult/family €5/10; ☼ 10am-5pm Tue-Sun). This is the country's principal museum, and houses permanent collections of Roman and medieval relics, fortification models and art dating from the 13th century.

From the museum, it's a short walk to the **Bock Casemates** (☎ 22 28 09; Montée de Clausen; adult/child €1.75/1; ☼ 10am-5pm Mar-Oct), a honeycomb of rock galleries carved out under the Bock by the Spaniards in 1744. Over the years the casemates have housed everything from bakeries to slaughterhouses and garrisons of soldiers; during WWI and WWII they were used as a bomb shelter for 35,000 locals.

Exit the casemates and wander the city's beautiful **Chemin de la Corniche**. This promenade offers fab views over the Grund quarter and eventually leads up to Rue du St Esprit, home to Luxembourg's other main museum, the **Musée d'Histoire de la Ville de Luxembourg** (☎ 47 96 45 00; 14 Rue du St Esprit; www.musee-hist.lu, no English; adult/student/child €5/3.70/free; ☼ 10am-6pm Tue-Sun, until 8pm Thu). This multilevel complex explores the history of the city, using a glass elevator that beautifully reveals the Old Town's rocky geology.

The Moorish-style **Palais Grand-Ducal** (Rue du Marché-aux-Herbes; adult/child €5.50/2.75; ☼ mid-Jul–early-Sep, guided tours in English 4.30pm Mon-Fri & 1.30pm Sat) was built in the 1570s during Spanish rule. The royals no longer reside here; instead it's used as the Grand Duke's office.

Cathédrale Notre Dame (Blvd Roosevelt; ☼ 10am-noon & 2-5.30pm) is worth a peak to see the nation's most revered idol, the *Lady Comforter of the Afflicted,* a small, elaborately dressed statue of the Virgin and child.

LUXEMBOURG CITY

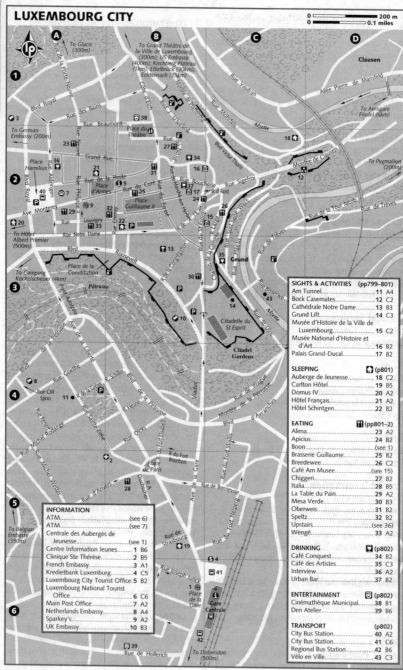

SIGHTS & ACTIVITIES		(pp799–801)
Am Tunnel	**11**	A4
Bock Casemates	**12**	C2
Cathédrale Notre Dame	**13**	B3
Grund Lift	**14**	C3
Musée d'Histoire de la Ville de Luxembourg	**15**	C2
Musée National d'Histoire et d'Art	**16**	B2
Palais Grand-Ducal	**17**	B2

SLEEPING		(p801)
Auberge de Jeunesse	**18**	C2
Carlton Hôtel	**19**	B5
Domus IV	**20**	A2
Hôtel Français	**21**	A2
Hôtel Schintgen	**22**	B2

EATING		(pp801–2)
Alima	**23**	A2
Apicius	**24**	B2
Boon	(see 1)	
Brasserie Guillaume	**25**	B2
Breedewee	**26**	C2
Café Am Musee	(see 15)	
Chiggeri	**27**	B2
Italia	**28**	B5
La Table du Pain	**29**	A2
Mesa Verde	**30**	B3
Oberweis	**31**	B2
Speltz	**32**	B2
Upstairs	(see 36)	
Wengé	**33**	A2

DRINKING		(p802)
Café Conquest	**34**	B2
Café des Artistes	**35**	C3
Interview	**36**	A2
Urban Bar	**37**	B2

ENTERTAINMENT		(p802)
Cinémathèque Municipal	**38**	B1
Den Atelier	**39**	B6

TRANSPORT		(p802)
City Bus Station	**40**	A2
City Bus Station	**41**	C6
Regional Bus Station	**42**	B6
Vélo en Ville	**43**	C3

INFORMATION

ATM	(see 6)
ATM	(see 7)
Centrale des Auberges de Jeunesse	(see 1)
Centre Information Jeunes	**1** B6
Clinique Ste Thérèse	**2** B5
French Embassy	**3** A1
Kredietbank Luxembourg	**4** C5
Luxembourg City Tourist Office	**5** B2
Luxembourg National Tourist Office	**6** C6
Main Post Office	**7** A2
Netherlands Embassy	**8** A4
Sparkey's	**9** A2
UK Embassy	**10** B3

Am Tunnel (☎ 40 15 24 50; 16 Rue Ste Zithe; admission free; ☿ 9am-5.30pm Mon-Fri, 2-6pm Sun) is in the depths of the BCE, one of Luxembourg's 180 banks. This underground art gallery devotes itself to temporary exhibitions but also has an interesting permanent display on Edward Steichen (see p798).

Pont Grand-Duchesse Charlotte connects the Old Town with the **Kirchberg Plateau** to the northeast. This plateau is home to EU institutions but it also accommodates the striking new **Musée d'Art Moderne Grand-Duc Jean** and the elegant oval **Salle Philharmonique de Luxembourg** (Luxembourg Philharmonic Hall), both due for completion in 2005. Bus No 18 from Gare Centrale or Place Hamilius tours the plateau.

SLEEPING
Budget
Camping Kockelscheuer (☎ 47 18 15; www.camp-kockelscheuer.lu; 22 Route de Bettembourg; adult/child/camp sites €3.50/1.75/4; ☿ Easter-31 Oct) Pleasantly sited between a forest and a sports centre, 4km southwest of the city. To get there, take bus No 5 from Gare Centrale or Place Hamilius.

Auberge de Jeunesse (☎ 22 68 89; luxembourg@youthhostels.lu; 2 Rue du Fort Olizy; dm/s/d €16.50/24.50/45; P ☒) Great location at the base of the Old Town and, by the time you read this, Luxembourg City's hostel should be fully operational again following extensive renovation. Bus No 9 from the airport or Gare Centrale stops nearby. Alternatively it's a 40-minute walk from Gare Centrale.

Hôtel Schintgen (☎ 22 28 44; schintgn@pt.lu; 6 Rue Notre Dame; s/d/tr €67/85/90) Handy location in the Old Town compensates for ordinary rooms.

Mid-Range & Top End
Carlton Hôtel (☎ 29 96 60; www.carlton.lu; 9 Rue de Strasbourg; s/d from €75/90) This atmospheric old place, c 1920, tucked away on a backstreet in the train station quarter, is a little gem, with stained-glass windows and modern rooms.

Hôtel Français (☎ 47 45 34; www.hotelfrancais.lu; 14 Place d'Armes; s/d Mon-Fri €97/125, Sat & Sun €90/118) Intimate hotel dotted with *objets d'art* and with a prized location overlooking the Old Town's main square.

Domus IV (☎ 46 78 78 1; www.domus.lu; 37 Ave Monterey; d with/without kitchen €130/115, breakfast €10.50; P €12; ☒ ☒ ☒) Offers zany decora-

tions and innovative rooms – expect beds that fold into the wall, vogue furnishings and modern art.

Hôtel Albert Premier (☎ 44 24 42 1; www.albert1er.lu; 2a Rue Albert 1er; ste Mon-Thu from €215, continental breakfast €12.50, ste Fri-Sun incl breakfast from €145; P ☐) The city's most charming hotel, located 750m west of Place d'Armes on an unassuming backstreet. The swanky rooms burst with Gothic excesses.

EATING
The Old Town, Grund and Clausen are the go for dining. In summer these areas turn into open-air terraces with tables spilling out onto pavements and tree-lined squares.

Budget
La Table du Pain (☎ 24 16 08; 19 Ave Monterey; ☿ 7am-7pm; ☒) Convivial, completely nonsmoking café doing baguette sandwiches (€4.50 to €6) and big salads (€10).

Café Am Musee (☎ 26 20 25 95; 14 Rue du St Ésprit; mains €10-12; ☿ 10am-6pm Tue-Sun, to 8pm Thu) Well-hidden local favourite, attached to the Musée d'Histoire de la Ville de Luxembourg, but easily overlooked. At its best for a casual lunch on a warm day (reservations needed).

Apicius (☎ 22 02 24; 26 Rue de l'Eau; mains €10-18; ☿ lunch daily, dinner Wed-Sun, closed Aug) Down-to-earth brasserie that's slightly off the beaten tourist track. Mainly French and Italian cuisine, but Luxembourg specialities also get a look in.

Brasserie Guillaume (☎ 26 20 20 20; 12 Place Guillaume II; mains €12-18; ☿ 10am-1am) Best brasserie in the Old Town and great for a late-night bite. Modern, big and slightly brash, it caters eclectically.

Also recommended:
Oberweis (☎ 47 07 03; 19 Grand Rue) Moreish cakes, chocolates and ice cream at this tearoom.
Boon (Place de la Gare) Supermarket opposite Gare Centrale.
Alima (Rue Neuve) Supermarket in the Old Town.

Mid-Range
Breedewee (☎ 22 26 96; 9 Rue Large; mains €19-22, 3-course menu €22, 6-course menu €54; ☿ lunch & dinner) No restaurant in Luxembourg can match the view. This modern but elegant little place has a terrace perched high on the Corniche in a setting that's unique (and dependent on fine weather). Great French food too.

Upstairs (☎ 26 27 01 12; 21 Rue Aldringen; mains €20; ⊙ lunch Tue-Sat, dinner Tue-Fri) This well-hidden, 1st-floor local eatery (entry at the back of the pub, Interview) does great Vietnamese and Japanese dishes in no-fuss surroundings. The lunch-time *plat du jour* (nonvegetarian or vegetarian dishes; €10) is superb value.

Mesa Verde (☎ 46 41 26; 11 Rue du St Esprit; mains €18-24; ⊙ lunch Wed-Fri, dinner Tue-Sat, closed lunch Aug; ✗) Imaginative vegetarian and seafood dishes are the mainstay of this exotic restaurant. It's often full, and deservedly so.

Also recommended:

Italia (☎ 48 66 26 1; 15 Rue d'Anvers; mains €12-20; ⊙ lunch & dinner) Crisp Italian restaurant known for its fresh, home-made pasta. Close to Gare Centrale.

Chiggeri (☎ 22 82 36; 15 Rue du Nord; mains €22-25; ⊙ lunch & dinner) Hip café/restaurant with an extraordinary wine list.

Top End

Wengé (☎ 26 20 10 58; 15 Rue Louvigny; mains €23-30; ⊙ 8am-7pm Mon-Sat plus dinner Wed & Fri) Top-notch food store-cum-restaurant that offers excellent French cuisine.

Speltz (☎ 47 49 50; www.restaurant-speltz.lu; 8 Rue Chimay; mains €25-35, 4-/6-course menu €40/63; ⊙ lunch Mon-Fri, dinner Mon-Sat) Proud new holder of one Michelin star, this delightful restaurant does seafood and French *haute cuisine* with aplomb.

DRINKING

The Old Town, Grund, Clausen and Hollerich are the most popular spots for a drink.

Café des Artistes (☎ 46 13 27; 22 Montée du Grund; ⊙ evenings Tue-Sun) Nostalgic Grund café that has been around since 1968 and has candles that almost prove its age.

Pygmalion (☎ 42 08 60; 19 Rue de la Tour Jacob; ⊙ 4pm-1am, until 3am Fri & Sat) This moody little Irish haunt is one of several good pubs in Clausen, an area favoured by late-night revellers. Take bus No 9 or night bus CN1 to get there.

Urban Bar (☎ 26 47 85 78; 2 Rue de la Boucherie) One of the newest addresses in the Old Town and unashamedly hip.

Interview (☎ 47 36 65; 19 Rue Aldringen) Raw café close to Place Hamilius and a great place to hang with a drink.

Café Conquest (☎ 22 21 41; 7 Rue du Palais de Justice) This popular gay pub is in the heart of the city.

ENTERTAINMENT

The entertainment guide, *Luxembourg Weekly*, is available free from the tourist office.

Cinémathèque Municipal (☎ 47 96 26 44; 17 Place du Théâtre; adult/concession €3.80/2.50) Closest thing in Luxembourg to an arthouse cinema and cheap to boot.

Den Atelier (☎ 49 54 66; www.atelier.lu; 56 Rue de Hollerich) The main venue for live music, located about 500m west of Gare Centrale in Hollerich, an off-the-beaten-track nightlife area.

Didjeridoo (☎ 44 00 49; 41 Rue de Bouillon; ⊙ Fri & Sat) Funky Hollerich nightclub; into techno and house.

Grand Théâtre de la Ville de Luxembourg (☎ 47 08 95 1; www.luxembourgticket.lu; 1 Rond Point Schuman) The nation's biggest performing arts complex, renovated in 2003 and offering state-of-the-art facilities.

GETTING THERE & AWAY

See p808 for information on both international flights and train services.

GETTING AROUND
To/From the Airport

Bus No 9 and 16 (€1, 20 minutes) connect Findel airport with Place Hamilius and Gare Centrale. Buses run from 5am to 11pm. Alternatively the Luxair bus (€3.70, 20 minutes, hourly) picks up from Place Hamilius or Gare Centrale.

A taxi to Findel costs €20.

Bicycle

The topography's not flat, but those with decent muscles will find Luxembourg City great for biking. **Vélo en Ville** (☎ 47 96 23 83; fax 22 27 52; 8 Bisserwée; half-/full-day €12.50/20; ⊙ 10am-noon & 1-8pm Apr-Oct) offers 20% discount (not available on half-day rentals) to people under 26.

Car & Motorcycle

The cheapest open-air car park is Glacis, about 800m northwest of Place d'Armes. For details on car rental agencies, see p808.

Public Transport

The main bus stations are Place Hamilius in the Old Town and Gare Centrale. For all ticket information see p808. Buses run from 5am to 10pm when a limited **late night bus service** (☎ 47 96 29 75) takes over (Friday and Saturday nights only).

AROUND LUXEMBOURG CITY

The rest of the country is easily accessible from Luxembourg City. The verdant forests of the Ardennes stretch over the country's northern tip and hide beguiling towns such as Vianden. To the east is the enchanting Müllerthal region and its ancient base, Echternach. Central Luxembourg is home to the famous war museum at Diekirch; in the southeast is the wine-producing Moselle Valley.

THE ARDENNES

The Grand Duchy's northern region is spectacular country – winding valleys with fast-flowing rivers cut deep through green tablelands crowned by castles. Of the main towns, Vianden is understandably Luxembourg's most touristy town while Clervaux is the most easily accessible by train. The tiny nearby hamlet of Esch-sur-Sûre attracts hordes of tourists due to its picturesque location, as does Wiltz, the Ardennes' capital, during July's open-air festival of music (see p804).

Getting There & Away

To reach Vianden from Luxembourg City, take the train to Ettelbrück (30 minutes) and then a bus (30 minutes, 10 buses per day).

Clervaux is easily reached from Luxembourg City by train (one hour, every two hours).

To get to Esch-sur-Sûre, take a bus from Ettelbrück (40 minutes, five per day).

Wiltz is easily accessible by train from Luxembourg City (1½ hours) – take the train (direction Clervaux) to Kautenbach, and catch another train from there.

Vianden

pop 1600

Vianden is Luxembourg's most dramatically sited countryside town. Its picturesque location – nestled in the valley of the Our River, framed by verdant wooded hills and overseen by its impeccably restored castle – has made it a favourite base for exploring the Ardennes.

Vianden's **tourist office** (☎ 83 42 57 1; www.vianden.lu, in French; 1a Rue du Vieux Marché; ☒ 8am-6pm Mon-Fri, 10am-2pm Sat & Sun Apr-Aug, 9am-noon & 1-5pm Mon-Fri Sep-Mar), is down by the river, next to the bridge over the Our.

Looming over the town is the **château** (☎ 83 41 08 1; www.castle-vianden.lu; Grand Rue; ☒ 10am-4pm Jan-Feb & Nov-Dec, 10am-5pm Mar & Oct, 10am-6pm Apr-Sep). The oldest part of the castle dates to the 11th century, although a much older Roman fort is thought to have occupied the craggy outcrop in the 4th century.

Vianden's picturesque position can be photographed from the **télésiège** (chairlift; ☎ 83 43 23; 39 Rue du Sanatorium; adult/child €4.50/2.50; ☒ 10am-6pm daily Jun-Sep, closed Mon Easter-May & Oct), which takes off from the lower bank of the river at the end of Rue Victor Hugo.

Directly opposite the tourist office is **Maison de Victor Hugo** (☎ 26 87 40 88; www.victor-hugo.lu, in French; 37 Rue de la Gare; adult/child €4/2.50; ☒ 11am-5pm Tue-Sun Easter–mid-Oct). Vianden was briefly home to author Victor Hugo during his 19-year exile from France and the town makes much ado about the three months he stayed here in 1871.

SLEEPING & EATING

Camping de l'Our (☎ 83 45 05; www.camping-our-vianden.lu, no English; 3 Route de Bettel; adult/child/camp sites €4/2/3.50; ☒ closed Nov-Easter) Camping ground draped along the riverbank to the south of town.

Auberge des Jeunesse (☎ 83 41 77; vianden@youthhostels.lu; 3 Montée du Château; dm/s/d €14.50/22.50/41; ☒ closed Jan-Mar & Dec; ☒) Pleasant hostel located in the shadow of the château (and a long 1km uphill walk from the bus station).

Hôtel Petry (☎ 83 41 22; www.hotel-petry.com; 15 Rue de la Gare; s/d from €35/50; mains €12-20; P) Rambling old hotel with a new wing that offers modern rooms with castle or river views. The restaurant does good French cuisine, and there are also cheaper pizzas.

Hôtel Heintz (☎ 83 41 55; www.hotel-heintz.lu; 55 Grand Rue; s/d from €59/77; mains €13-20; ☒ Easter–mid-Nov; P) Arguably the most distinguished hotel/restaurant in town. The public rooms and restaurant exude subtle charm, though the rooms are less atmospheric.

Clervaux

pop 1800

Hidden deep in the valley of the Clierf River, Clervaux is best associated with a permanent photographic exhibition that draws visitors from far afield.

The **tourist office** (☎ 92 00 72; ☙ 2-5pm Mon-Fri Easter-Jun, 9.45-11.45am & 2-6pm Jul-Aug, 9.45-11.45am & 1-5pm Sep-Oct) is housed in a side turret of Clervaux's castle.

The **castle**, razed in 1944, is visited mostly for the famous exhibition, **'Family of Man'** (☎ 92 96 57; adult/child €4.50/2.50; ☙ 10am-6pm daily Mar-Sep, Tue-Sun Mar & Oct-Dec), collated by Edward Steichen (1879–1973). Steichen compiled the 500 black-and-white photos in 1955 at the age of 76 and the exhibition travelled the world for years before coming to rest in Clervaux.

Clervaux's turreted **Benedictine Abbey of St Maurice** pokes out of the forest high above the town and is accessible by a 1km track from the castle. Time your visit to hear one of their **Gregorian Masses** (☙ 10.30am & 6pm Mon-Fri, 5pm Sat & Sun).

SLEEPING & EATING
Hôtel/Restaurant du Parc (☎ 92 06 50; www.hotel duparc.lu; 2 Rue du Parc; s/d €44/70; ☙ Feb-Dec; P) Full of character and perhaps the odd ghost. An old whitewashed mansion, sitting part way up a forested hill overlooking the town, it has seven rooms, fitted with a mix of modern and old, and a fab old restaurant serving well-priced French/Luxembourg cuisine.

Esch-sur-Sûre
pop 240
The tiny village of Esch-sur-Sûre, built on a rocky loop in the Sûre River, is surrounded by soft distant hills that drop to steep cliffs as they reach the river. Cushioned in among all this is a true 'crumbly' – a ruined **castle** dating from 927, around which visitors are free to wander. All in all it's very picturesque – some say it's one of Europe's prettiest villages – and in summer the day-trippers descend on Esch in droves.

Around Esch-sur-Sûre
Roughly halfway between Esch and Ettelbrück, a road winds up to the magnificent **Château de Bourscheid** (☎ 99 05 70; 1 Schlasswee; adult/child €3/1.50; ☙ 11am-5pm Apr, 10am-6pm May-Jun & Sep, 10am-7pm Jul-Aug, 11am-4pm Oct, 11am-4pm Sat & Sun Nov-Mar), a 1000-year-old castle superbly situated on a rocky bluff overlooking farmland and the Sûre River. It's one of the most beautiful castles in the Grand Duchy and, indeed, affords the best views.

Wiltz
pop 4600
Wiltz is the so-called capital of the Luxembourg Ardennes. In the Middle Ages it was a busy trading town and by the 19th century had become an important centre for textiles and tanning. These days it's a relatively quiet place, not all that big on the tourist circuit and with just a handful of local industries such as brewing to keep it afloat. It's worth a visit in July for the Grand Duchy's biggest theatre and musical event, the **Festival de Théâtre et de Musique** (www.festivalwiltz.online .lu, in French).

MÜLLERTHAL
The Müllerthal region occupies a pocket of land in the central east. It's a fabulous area for hikers, distinguished by an almost primeval landscape of deep gorges scoured by ancient streams through sandstone plateaux.

Echternach
pop 5100
The ancient town of Echternach flanks the western bank of the Sûre River and makes a superb base for exploring the Müllerthal.

The **tourist office** (☎ 72 02 30; Parvis de la Basilique; ☙ 9am-noon & 2-5pm Mon-Fri year-round, also Sat & Sun Jul-Aug) is in a courtyard next to the town's huge basilica.

SIGHTS & ACTIVITIES
If you happen to be in Echternach on the Tuesday after Whit Sunday, look out for the handkerchief pageant in honour of St Willibrord, an Anglo-Saxon monk who founded Echternach's abbey in the 7th century. If not, you can visit the **basilica** (☙ 9.30am-6.30pm), the country's most important religious building, where St Willibrord's remains lie in a primitive stone coffin covered by a marble canopy.

Marked **hiking trails** start from near the town's bus station. The best is path 'B', which winds up via Troosknepchen and Wolfsschlucht to the **Gorge du Loup**, a sheer-sided canyon flanked by dramatic sandstone formations; it takes 2½ hours round-trip.

SLEEPING & EATING
Camping Officiel (☎ 72 02 72; www.camping-echter nach.lu, no English; 5 Route de Diekirch; adult/child/camp sites €4/2/4; ☙ Easter-Oct; ☙) About 200m from the bus station, draped along the hillside.

Auberge de Jeunesse (☎ 72 01 58; echternach@ youthhostels.lu; 9 Rue André Duchscher; dm/s/d €14.50/ 22.50/41; ❤ Feb-Oct; ✗) Wonderfully sited hostel, right in the centre of town.

Hôtel Le Pavillon (☎ 72 98 09; www.lepavillon.lu; 2 Rue de la Gare; s/d €62/72; **P** €7) Little corner hotel with just 10 well-equipped rooms.

Hostellerie de la Basilique (☎ 72 98 83; www .hotel-basilique.lu; 7 Place du Marché; s/d/tr €91/108/135; ❤ Easter–mid-Nov) This is the best address in town. Fourteen tidy rooms that don't suffer decoration overkill.

Giorgio (☎ 72 99 34; 4 Rue André Duchscher; pizza €7-12, pasta €8-12; ❤ noon-2pm & 6-11.30pm, closed Tue Nov-Mar) Casual Italian restaurant that's always full.

Café de Philo'soff (☎ 72 00 19; 31 Rue de la Gare; ❤ closed Tue) Art Nouveau showpiece with laid-back music and a good range of Belgian beers.

GETTING THERE & AWAY

Only buses connect Echternach with Luxembourg City – the trip takes 40 minutes. From Echternach, buses head out to other towns.

CENTRAL LUXEMBOURG

Immediately north of Luxembourg City is a heavily farmed region known locally as the Gutland. The towns of Mersch and Ettelbrück don't rate much time but Diekirch definitely merits an overnight stay.

Diekirch

pop 6000

This pleasant little town on the banks of the gushing Sûre River is home to the country's main wartime museum.

The **tourist office** (☎ 80 30 23; www.diekirch.lu; 3 Place de la Libération; ❤ 9am-noon & 2-5pm Mon-Fri, 2-4pm Sat Sep-Jun, 9am-5pm Mon-Fri, 10am-4pm Sat & Sun Jul-Aug) is a 10-minute walk from the train station.

SIGHTS & ACTIVITIES

An excellent collection of wartime memorabilia detailing the WWII Battle of the Bulge and the liberation of Luxembourg by US troops is presented at Diekirch's **Musée National d'Histoire Militaire** (☎ 80 89 08; 10 Rue Barnertal; adult/child €5/3; ❤ 10am-6pm Apr-Nov, 2-6pm Dec-Mar).

Diekirch has one of Luxembourg's few bike rental outfits, **Speicher Sport** (☎ 80 84 38; 56 Rue Clairefontaine; half-/full-day €10/15; ❤ 8.30am-noon & 1.30-6pm Tue-Sat). Good cycling paths follow

the river all the way from Diekirch to Echternach (27km).

SLEEPING & EATING

Camping de la Sûre (☎ 80 94 25; fax 80 27 86; 34 Route de Gilsdorf; adult/child/camp sites €4.50/2.50/4.50; ❤ Apr-Sep) By the river and within a few minutes' walk from the town centre.

Hotel/Restaurant de la Gare (☎ 80 33 05; jamper@ sl.lu; 73 Ave de la Gare; s/d €42/73; **P**) Family-run establishment opposite the train station that offers simple rooms and a restaurant favoured by the locals; try the ham.

Hôtel/Restaurant Hiertz (☎ 80 35 62; fax 80 88 69; 1 Rue Clairefontaine; s/d €60/75; mains €25-30; ❤ closed late Dec-early Jan, restaurant closed Mon, lunch Sat & dinner Sun) A delight. The whole place oozes understatement and the restaurant does the region's best French food.

The region's only hostel is at Ettelbrück, a 5km train ride west of Diekirch. This **Auberge des Jeunesse** (☎ 81 22 69; ettelbruck@youth hostels.lu; Rue Josephine-Charlotte, Ettelbrück; dm/s/d €14.50/22.50/41; ✗) occupies a salmon-toned house some 20 minutes' walk from Ettelbrück train station.

GETTING THERE & AROUND

There are hourly trains from Luxembourg City to Diekirch (40 minutes).

MOSELLE VALLEY

Less than half an hour's drive east of the capital, the Luxembourg section of the Moselle Valley is one of Europe's smallest wine regions. More than a dozen towns and hamlets are draped along the **Route du Vin** (Wine Road), which meanders from the southern border town of Schengen, past the waterfront playground of Remich, through the region's capital at Grevenmacher.

There are only two tourist offices en route from Luxembourg City: the **Grevenmacher tourist office** (☎ 75 82 75; 10 Route du Vin; open 8am-noon & 1-5pm Mon-Fri), and the **Remich tourist office** (☎ 69 84 88; Esplanade; open 9am-5pm July-Aug).

Sights & Activities

Wine tasting is the premier attraction and several *caves* (cellars) give tours. The tour at **St Martin** (☎ 23 69 97 74; 53 Route de Stadtbredimus; adult/child €2.50/1.50; ❤ 10am-noon & 1.30-6pm Apr-Oct), 1.5km north of Remich, winds through damp tunnels hewn in the rock. Bus No 450 to Grevenmacher stops there.

Caves Bernard-Massard (☎ 75 05 45 1; 8 Rue du Pont; adult/child €2.75/1.75; ☒ 9.30am-6pm Apr-Oct) at Grevenmacher is one of the region's largest producers of sparkling wine (four million bottles per year). Tours take in the slick, fully-mechanised cellar.

Sleeping & Eating

Camping Route du Vin (☎ 75 02 34; fax 75 86 66; Route du Vin; adult/child/camp sites €3.50/2/4; ☒ Apr-Sep; ☒) Well located right on the river bank at Grevenmacher.

Auberge de Jeunesse (☎ 75 02 22; grevenmacher@ youthhostels.lu; 15 Gruewereck; dm/s/d €14.50/22.50/41; ☒ closed Jan-15 Mar & 15 Nov-Dec; ☒) This small hostel perches on the hill behind central Grevenmacher.

Auberge des Cygnes (☎ 23 69 88 52; hpcygnes@ pt.lu; 11 Esplanade; s/d/tr €48/65/83; ☒ closed mid-Jan–mid-Feb; ☒) One of several water-front hotels in Remich. It has calm, pastel-toned rooms and a restaurant doing good wood-fire-baked pizzas.

Bamberg's (☎ 76 00 22; bamberg@pt.lu; Route du Vin; s/d €65/90; mains €20-26; ☒ closed Tue) Located in the village of Ehnen, between Remich and Grevenmacher, this hotel/restaurant is one of the best places to eat on the Route du Vin. The blue European lobster is delicious.

Getting There & Away

The Moselle Valley region is difficult to explore without your own transport. Trains from Luxembourg City stop at the northern town of Wasserbillig only; buses from the capital go twice daily to Grevenmacher and Remich from where there are connections to other towns.

LUXEMBOURG DIRECTORY

ACCOMMODATION

The national tourist office (see p799) provides free hotel, B&B, camping and farm-stay brochures, and staff will book accommodation.

Camping grounds are abundant, although mainly in the central and northern regions. Grounds are graded: 'Category 3' grounds have basic facilities only and are quite scarce; 'Category 2' are mid-range in price and facilities; 'Category 1' grounds are the most expensive and profuse.

A dozen hostels are operated by **Centrale des Auberges de Jeunesse** (☎ 26 29 35 00; www .youthhostels.lu; Galerie Kons, 24-26 Place de la Gare, L-1616 Luxembourg City), which is affiliated with Hostelling International (HI). Most hostels do close irregularly throughout the year, so ring ahead. The nightly dorm rate, including breakfast and sheets, is from €14.50 to €16.50. Single/double rooms start at €22/20 per person.

B&Bs are very light on the ground but there are plenty of hotels, most in the mid-range (€80) or top-end (€150) brackets.

ACTIVITIES

With a 5000km network of marked walking paths, the Grand Duchy is a hiking haven. Tracks are marked by white triangles and connect the HI hostels. Local tourist offices always stock regional walking maps. The Müllerthal region offers amazing hiking tracks (see p804).

Cycling is a popular pastime but rental outfits are few – see Vélo en Ville (p802) or Speicher Sport (p805). Bikes can be taken on trains for €1.10.

BOOKS

For a humorous look at Luxembourg ways, get hold of *How to Remain What You Are* by George Müller, a Luxembourg psychologist. An excellent multilingual publication for walkers is *182 × Luxembourg*, which describes 182 hiking trails; *40 Cycle Routes* is the cyclist's equivalent. Both are published by Éditions Guy Binsfield and are widely available in bookstores.

BUSINESS HOURS

Trading hours are 9am to 5.30pm weekdays (except Monday when some shops open about noon). On Saturdays, shops can trade for either half a day or a full day. Many shops close for lunch between noon and 2pm. Banks have shorter hours: 8.30am to 4.30pm Monday to Friday and, in the capital, banks open Saturday mornings. Country branches close for lunch.

CUSTOMS

Petrol, alcohol, tobacco and perfume products are relatively cheap in Luxembourg, and people from neighbouring countries often come here to stock up on these items.

DISCOUNT CARDS

The **Luxembourg Card** (adult 1/2/3 days €9/16/22, family of 2 adults & up to 5 kids €18/32/44) gives free admission to attractions throughout the country plus unlimited use of public transport. It's valid from Easter to 31 October, and is available from tourist offices.

EMBASSIES & CONSULATES
Luxembourg Embassies & Consulates

In countries where there is no representative, contact the nearest Belgian or Dutch diplomatic missions. Visa information can be obtained online from www.mae.lu.

Diplomatic missions abroad include:

France (☎ 01 45 55 13 37; fax 01 45 51 72 29; 33 Ave Rapp, F-75005 Paris)

Germany (☎ 030-26 39 570; fax 030-26 39 5727; Klingelhöferstrasse 7, D-10785 Berlin)

The Netherlands (☎ 070-360 75 16; fax 070-356 33 03; Nassaulaan 8, NL-2514 JS The Hague)

UK (☎ 020-7235 6961; fax 020-7235 9734; 27 Wilton Crescent, London SW1X 8SD)

USA (☎ 202-265 4171; fax 202-328 8270; 2200 Massachusetts Ave NW, Washington DC 20008)

Embassies & Consulates in Luxembourg

The nearest Australian, Canadian and New Zealand embassies are in Belgium (see p121). The following foreign embassies are in Luxembourg City (Map p800):

Belgium (☎ 44 27 46 1; 4 Rue des Girondins, L-1626)

France (☎ 45 72 71 1; 8 Blvd Joseph II, L-1840)

Germany (☎ 45 34 45 1; 20-22 Ave Émile Reuter, L-2420)

Ireland (☎ 45 06 10; 28 Route d'Arlon, L-1140)

The Netherlands (☎ 22 75 70; 5 Rue C M Spoo, L-2546)

UK (☎ 22 98 64; 14 Blvd Roosevelt, L-2450)

USA (☎ 46 01 23; 22 Blvd Emmanuel Servais, L-2535)

FESTIVALS & EVENTS

Carnival (www.ont.lu/events.htm) One of the nation's biggest festivals, held six weeks before Easter.

Buergsonndeg (www.ont.lu/events.htm) Bonfire Day started in pagan times; held the first weekend after Carnival.

Octave (www.ont.lu/events.htm) This pilgrimage dates back to the 17th century and is held from the 3rd to 5th Sunday after Easter.

Luxembourg National Day (www.ont.lu/events.htm) Held on 23 June but festivities start in Luxembourg City the previous evening.

Schueberfouer (www.schueberfouer.lu, in French) One of Europe's biggest annual fun fairs. Takes over a parking lot in Luxembourg City for a fortnight from the last week in August.

HOLIDAYS

New Year's Day 1 January
Easter Monday March/April
May Day 1 May
Ascension Day Fortieth day after Easter
Whit Monday Seventh Monday after Easter
National Day 23 June
Assumption 15 August
All Saints' Day 1 November
Christmas Day 25 December

LANGUAGE

Luxembourg has three official languages – French, German and Luxemburgian (Lëtzebuergesch). The latter is most closely related to German and it was proclaimed as the national tongue in 1984. English is widely spoken in the capital and by the younger people around the countryside.

Luxembourgers speak Luxemburgian to each other but generally switch to French when talking to foreigners. A couple of Luxemburgian words you will probably overhear are *moien* (good morning/hello) and *äddi* (goodbye). For a rundown on basic French and German grammar, see the Language chapter (p1085).

MONEY

Banks are the best place to change money – you'll have no trouble finding one in Luxembourg. ATMs are common enough in Luxembourg City, but few and far between around the countryside.

Tipping is not obligatory as service and VAT are included in hotel and restaurant prices.

POST

Post offices are generally open from 9am to 5pm Monday to Friday and 9am to noon Saturday. Letters (under 20g) cost €0.60 to send to EU countries and €0.80 to non-EU countries.

The most useful poste restante address is: Poste Restante, Luxembourg-Centre Bureau de Post, L-1118 Luxembourg 2.

EMERGENCY NUMBERS

▪ Ambulance ☎ 112
▪ Fire ☎ 112
▪ Police ☎ 113

TELEPHONE

Luxembourg's international country code is ☎ 352. To telephone abroad, the international access code is ☎ 00. Call ☎ 12410 for an international operator. Numbers prefixed with ☎ 0800 are toll-free. Collect calls can be made by dialling ☎ 80 02 00.

VISAS

Citizens of Australia, Canada, Israel, Japan, New Zealand and the USA do not need a visa to visit as tourists for up to three months. There are no entry requirements or restrictions on EU nationals.

TRANSPORT IN LUXEMBOURG

GETTING THERE & AWAY
Air

Luxembourg's only international airport is **Aérogare Findel** (www.luxair.lu; ☎ 47 98 50 50), 6km east of the capital. Departure tax for airline passengers departing from Luxembourg is included in the ticket price.

The national carrier, Luxair, flies to a number of European destinations, including London, Paris and Frankfurt. In 2002, a Luxair plane landing at Findel crashed killing 15 people and bringing to an end the airline's four decades of accident-free flying.

Airlines flying into Luxembourg:

British Airways (☎ 34 20 80 83 23; www.britishairways .com)

Lufthansa (☎ 47 98 50 50; www.lufthansa.com)

Luxair (☎ 24 56 1, ☎ 24 56 50 50 for flight arrival and departure information; www.luxair.lu)

VLM Airlines (☎ 49 33 95; www.vlmairlines.com)

Land

Into Luxembourg, the main routes are the E411 from Brussels, the A4 from Paris, the E25 from Metz, and the E44 from Trier in Germany. Note that Eurolines buses do not pass through Luxembourg.

River

From Easter to September it's possible to take a boat from various points along the

Moselle to destinations in Germany (for example, Remich to Bernkastel costs €16 and takes four hours). For more details contact **Navitours** (☎ 75 84 89).

Train

International train services include to Brussels (€26 for a one-way 2nd-class ticket, 2¾ hours, hourly), Amsterdam (€46.40, 5½ hours, hourly), Paris (€43, four hours, six daily) and Trier in Germany (€8.40, 40 minutes, 11 daily). For details on the Benelux Tourrail pass, see p124. For all international enquiries, contact the **station office** (☎ 49 90 49 90; ⏱ 24hr) in Luxembourg City.

GETTING AROUND
Bus & Train

Luxembourg does not have an extensive rail system and getting around by bus once you leave the main north–south train line can take time. Both buses and trains are operated by **Société Nationale des Chemins de Fer Luxembourgeois** (CFL; www.cfl.lu; ☎ 49 90 55 44). The fare system is simple: €1.40 for a 'short' trip of about 10km or less (this ticket is valid for one hour) or €4.60 for a 2nd-class unlimited day ticket (known as a *Billet Réseau*). The latter is good for travelling on buses and trains anywhere in the country and is valid from the first time you use it until 8am the next day.

Many visitors opt for the Luxembourg Card which gives free bus and train travel plus discounted admissions to various sights – for details see p807.

Car & Motorcycle

Road rules are easy to understand and standard international signs are in use. The blood-alcohol limit for drivers is 0.08%. The speed limit on motorways is 120km. Fuel prices are among the lowest in Western Europe: lead-free costs €0.90 per litre and diesel is €0.65.

The country's only motoring club is **Club Automobile de Luxembourg** (☎ 45 00 45 1; 54 Route de Longwy, L-8007 Bertrange).

For car rental try:

Autolux (☎ 22 11 81; 33 Blvd Prince Henri)

Avis (☎ 48 95 95; Gare Centrale)

Budget (☎ 44 19 38; 300 Route de Longwy)

Hertz (☎ 43 46 45; Findel airport)

WAYNE WALTON

Cottages at Inishmór (p658), Aran Islands, Ireland

WAYNE WALTON

Temple of Apollo (p565), Delphi, Greece

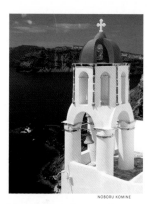
NOBORU KOMINE

The church belltower of
Santorini (p579), Greece

Stag's Head pub (p631), Dublin, Ireland

OLIVER STREWE

JON C

The Colosseum (p699), Rome, Italy

MARTIN MOOS

Schloss Vaduz (p791), Liechtenstein

A gondola gliding through Venice (p724), Italy

GLENN BEA

JEFF CANTARUTTI

Villa and vineyards of Central Italy (p740)

The Netherlands

CONTENTS

THE NETHERLANDS

'God created the world but the Dutch created the Netherlands' – it's a hoary old chestnut, but it can tell you a lot about this country. It's a metaphor for the uniqueness of the culture, but it also reads quite literally: the Dutch reclaimed much of their land from the sea, forging one of the most distinctive of all European states.

The Netherlands is small and is served by an efficient rail network, so its attractions are very accessible. While Amsterdam has understandable appeal, the rest of the country more than stacks up. Leiden, Haarlem and Delft are beguiling, well-preserved historical cities. Maastricht is a symbol of pan-European identity, hemmed in by the German and Belgian borders and sharing the best qualities of each nation. Rotterdam has a long-standing rivalry with Amsterdam for the title of the Netherlands' 'first city'; bombed flat during WWII, it's rebuilt itself with inimitable architecture and a gutsy vibe. Groningen swarms with university students and a spirited lifestyle, while refined Den Haag is the royal home and seat of government. In the north, the windswept islands of Noord Holland and the Frisian chain boast an exclusive language and lifestyle.

FAST FACTS

- **Area** 41,526 sq km
- **Capital** Amsterdam
- **Currency** euro (€); A$1 = €0.58; ¥100 = €0.76; NZ$1 = €0.54; UK£1 = €1.50; US$1 = €0.83
- **Famous for** extraordinary paintings, volatile footballers, cheese, liberal attitudes
- **Key Phrases** *hallo* (hello); *dag* (goodbye); *ja* (yes); *nee* (no); *alsjeblieft* (please); *bedankt* (thanks)
- **Official Languages** Dutch, Frisian
- **Population** 16.3 million
- **Telephone Codes** country code ☎ 31; international access code ☎ 00
- **Visas** not needed for passport holders of Australia, Canada, Israel, Japan, South Korea, New Zealand, Singapore, the USA and most of Europe

HIGHLIGHTS

- Ride a bike around Amsterdam's beautiful **old town** (p819).
- Soak up the refined pan-European flavour of **Maastricht** (p845).
- Do as the Dutch do: go **mud-flat walking** (p842) in Groningen.
- Admire the **architecture** (p837) of the Netherlands' second-largest city, Rotterdam.
- Fill your lungs on the isolated, windswept island of **Texel** (p843).

ITINERARIES

- **One week** Spend two days in Amsterdam, one day each in Den Haag and Delft, two days in Rotterdam and the last day in Maastricht.
- **Two weeks** Spend three days in Amsterdam, one day each in Haarlem, Den Haag, Delft and Leiden, two days in Rotterdam, one day each in Ameland, Texel and Groningen, and the last two days in Maastricht.

CLIMATE & WHEN TO GO

The warmest months are June to September. July and August are the wettest months. Daffodils bloom in April and tulips from late April to mid-May. High season is June to August and shoulder seasons mid-March to May and September to mid-October. Easter is busy, and tourists swarm throughout the country in summer; if driving, be wary of traffic in the last weekend of July. School holidays fall around mid-February, early May, most of July and August, and the second half of October.

HOW MUCH?

- **Hostel dormitory bed** €20
- **Average restaurant meal** €15-20
- **Local phone call** €0.30 per minute
- **Cup of coffee** €1.50-2
- **Bicycle hire** €7 per day

LONELY PLANET INDEX

- **Litre of petrol** €1.50
- **Litre of bottled water** €1.85
- **Can of beer** €.30
- **Souvenir T-shirt** €18.50
- **Vlaamse frites (Flemish fries)** €2

HISTORY

The Netherlands is geographically tiny, but it has been a major player in world affairs throughout the ages – often unwittingly. While the nation's borders have been repeatedly sliced and diced, the Dutch themselves have barnstormed distant lands. Away from conflict, the Netherlands has made a stellar contribution to the visual arts and has initiated many world firsts in 'social engineering'.

The Netherlands' early history is bound with that of Belgium and Luxembourg – the three were known as the Low Countries until the 16th century. In 1579, provinces in the northern Low Countries formed the United Provinces, the basis for the Netherlands today. They were opposed to the Spanish rule that was in place, while the southern regions, which eventually became Belgium, were open to compromise. The United Prov-

inces fought the Spanish in the 80-year-long Revolt of the Netherlands, which ended in 1648 with a treaty that recognised them as an independent republic.

The Netherlands' Golden Age lasted from about 1580 to 1740. The era's wealth was generated by the Dutch East India Company, which sent ships to the Far East for spices and other exotic goods, while colonising the Cape of Good Hope and Indonesia and establishing trading posts throughout Asia. Later the West Indies Company sailed to West Africa and the Americas. A number of Caribbean islands were also captured in a bid to thwart the Spanish. One unfortunate by-product of Dutch colonisation was the extinction of the dodo in Mauritius, largely due to introduced species.

The wealthy merchant class supported scores of artists, including Vermeer, Steen, Hals and Rembrandt. The sciences thrived: Christiaan Huygens, for example, discovered Saturn's rings and invented the pendulum clock.

In 1795 the French invaded. When the occupation ended in 1815, the United Kingdom of the Netherlands – incorporating Belgium and Luxembourg – was born. Earlier that year prostitution had been legalised in the Netherlands by Napoleon (who wanted to control STDs), although it took until 1988 for the Dutch to define it as a legal profession and to allow prostitutes to join trade unions.

In 1830 the Belgians rebelled and became independent, and Luxembourg was split between Belgium and the Netherlands. Nine years later the Dutch portion gained independence and became Luxembourg.

The Netherlands stayed neutral in WWI and tried to repeat the feat in WWII, only to be invaded by the Germans. Rotterdam was levelled, Dutch industry was commandeered for war purposes and thousands of Dutch men were sent to work in Nazi factories in Germany. Most of the country's Jews were murdered.

Indonesia won independence from the Netherlands in 1949, despite Dutch military opposition. Surinam followed, peacefully, in 1975. The Antilles has close ties with the Netherlands but is self-ruled.

In 1953 a high spring tide and severe storm breached Zeeland's dikes, drowning 1835 people. Under the Delta Plan (p841) a massive engineering project was built to prevent the tragedy from repeating.

In the 1960s Amsterdam became Europe's radical heart, giving rise to the riotous squatter's movement and the promiscuity that lingers today.

Although cannabis was decriminalised in the Netherlands in 1976, it took 27 years for this ruling to be taken to its logical conclusion; in 2003 the Netherlands became the first country to legalise prescriptions of medicinal cannabis, intended as a pain reliever for cancer and multiple sclerosis sufferers, among others.

Perhaps because of the devastating Nazi occupation, the Dutch have largely embraced European integration. In 1992 European Community members met in Maastricht to sign the treaty that created the EU.

In 1993 the Netherlands became the first country to regulate doctor-assisted euthanasia, and in 2000 the practice was legalised under stringent guidelines. That year the Netherlands also became the first nation in the world to legalise same-sex marriages.

As the Netherlands has become ever more crowded, immigration has become a political hot potato. Admission is now subject to rigid guidelines, and a new bill has been passed to deport 26,000 immigrants (including long-term residents) from the country.

In 2002 right-wing politician Pim Fortuyn was shot dead a few days before the Dutch general election. Fortuyn became a posthumous candidate and his party, Lijst Pim Fortuyn, with its zero-immigration policies, went on to win 17% of the seats in the lower house of parliament.

PEOPLE

Nine-tenths of the population are of Dutch stock, and around half of the 16.2 million people live in the western loop around Amsterdam, Den Haag and Rotterdam. Ethnic communities are concentrated in the Randstad (p828) cities. People from the former colonies of Indonesia, Surinam and the Dutch Antilles, along with recent arrivals from Turkey and Morocco, account for about 6% of the population, a result of a push in the 1960s and '70s to recruit migrant workers to boost labour forces.

Around 400,000 people in the northern Fryslân province speak their own language, Frisian.

RELIGION

There's another way you can read that old cliché about God doing one thing while the Dutch do another: nearly 40% of Dutch people over 18 years of age claim no religious affiliation. Of the remainder, 31% are Catholic, 21% are Protestant, 5% are Muslim and the remaining 3% are split among other denominations. Only six out of 10 Dutch regularly attend church.

Hindus and Muslims began arriving in the mid-20th century from former Dutch colonies Indonesia and Surinam, and a second wave since the 1960s included immigrants from Morocco and Turkey. The Islamic community has almost doubled in size in the last decade to 920,000, or 5.7% of the population. There are more than 300 mosques.

ARTS
Visual Arts

The Netherlands claims a superb artistic heritage: many non-Dutch would be able to name at least one famous Dutch painter, for example.

From the 15th century, Hieronymus Bosch's nightmarish works can be seen as an antecedent of surrealism.

During the Golden Age, Rembrandt emerged with the brightest glow of all, creating shimmering religious scenes, in-demand portraits and contemplative landscapes; Frans Hals (1582–1666) captured his subjects in unguarded moments; and Jan Vermeer (1632–75) concentrated on everyday occurrences in middle-class homes, giving a proto-cinematographic quality to his compositions.

Vincent Van Gogh's (1853–90) revolutionary use of colour, coarse brushwork and

---

VERMEER RIDES AGAIN

Jan Vermeer has become a media darling of late. In 2003, the film *Girl with a Pearl Earring* (based on Tracy Chevalier's novel) speculated on his relationship with the subject of his painting of that name. In 2004 a work long thought to be a forgery was finally confirmed as authentic – *Young Woman Seated at the Virginals*, the first Vermeer to be auctioned in more than 80 years, was sold to an anonymous buyer for £16 million (€24 million).

THE NETHERLANDS

layered contours established him on a higher plane than his contemporaries, yet he only sold one work while alive.

Piet Mondrian (1872–1944), along with Theo van Doesburg, founded the De Stijl movement; his style of abstract rectangular compositions came to be known as neo-plasticism.

MC Escher's (1902–72) graphic art still has uncanny power: a waterfall simultaneously flows up and down; a building folds in on itself. It's popular with mathematicians and stoners alike.

WWII gave birth to the CoBrA group (Copenhagen, Brussels and Amsterdam), who saw the conflict as pitching civilised society into severe moral decline. Their antidote was to embrace the mindset of children and the mentally ill in their art.

Music

Den Haag hosts the North Sea Jazz Festival, the world's largest jazz fest, each summer.

Rotterdam, Maastricht and Den Haag have a full calendar of performances by local orchestras and groups, and Amsterdam's Royal Concertgebouw Orchestra frequently performs abroad.

In the pop world, Golden Earring's *Eight Miles High* album went gold in the USA in 1969.

Herman Brood burst onto the scene in the '70s, morphing into a professional junkie/rock and roll star and later killing himself.

The Nits formed in 1974 and have since released a varied body of work, flirting with '60s pop, '80s new wave, and electronica stylings.

In the early '90s gabber was unleashed, an extreme mutation of techno originating in Rotterdam. It raised beats per minute to heart-attack levels, giving the finger to purists with its sheer fetishisation of sensation. The hip-hop of Urban Dance Squad made America's Top 20 during the decade.

The Dutch have a major presence in the populist world DJ rankings with the likes of Tiësto; DJ Speedy J's crunchy beats burrow deeper underground.

Pop festivals flourish in the warmer months, including Pinkpop in Landgraaf, Parkpop in Den Haag and Dynamo Open Air at Neunen. Dance Valley near Haarlem pulls over 100 bands and even more DJs to one of Europe's biggest open-air dance fests. Lowlands is a three-day alternative-music fest held at Six Flags in Flevoland.

Dance

The Dutch are world leaders in modern dance. Den Haag's Nederlands Dans Theater troupe was established in 1959, melding modern dance with classical ballet. In Rotterdam, Dansacadamie is the nation's largest dance school. Amsterdam's National Ballet performs mainly classical ballets, as well as 20th-century Dutch works.

Film & TV

The Netherlands' film industry is humble, producing around 20 feature films a year. Yet the Dutch have won four Best Foreign Language Film Academy Awards – the third-best tally in Oscar history.

Joris Ivens won an international peace prize for Song of the Rivers (1954), a global comparison of workers' conditions.

In the 1970s, Paul Verhoeven made earthy films, including Turks Fruit, the Netherlands' most popular film. He later moved to Hollywood, serving up the sardonic, ultra-violent satires Robocop and Starship Troopers, and the ultimate revenge thriller, Basic Instinct.

Leading Dutch actors include Rutger Hauer (an early Verhoeven favourite), Jeroen Krabbé and Famke Janssen.

The Rotterdam International Film Festival is held in February, the Amsterdam Fantastic Film Festival in April, Utrecht's Netherlands Film Festival in September and Amsterdam's International Documentary Film Festival in December.

SHAPING WORLDS

Many people are surprised to learn that the reality-TV franchise Big Brother is a Dutch invention, when it seems quintessentially American. But if you delve into the undercurrents of the Dutch social order, the concept of peering into the lives of a group of strangers makes sense. At only 41,526 sq km, the Netherlands is Europe's most densely populated country. While this adds immeasurably to its vibrancy, it can often seem that your neighbour is looking right over your shoulder. Maybe that's why many Dutch leave their curtains open at night so all can see inside: in a nation of 16.2 million, with space at a premium, there's nowhere to hide, really. No doubt the admirable Dutch trait of tolerance stems from this fact, too: when you're standing cheek-by-jowl, 'love thy neighbour' is a very sensible motto.

Perhaps because their country is so small, and therefore familiar in all its parts, the Dutch find it irresistible to recreate it – Big Brother, with its contestants from different walks of life, can be seen as a miniaturised cross-section of Dutch society.

Similarly, the popular theme park, Madurodam (p832), is a mini-Netherlands, containing 1:25 scale versions of every recognisable Dutch landmark: Schiphol airport, Amsterdam with its canals, sundry windmills and bicycles. More bizarrely, Amsterdam's Holland Experience theatre (p822) screens a kooky 30-minute film – a tour of the Netherlands – that's like a 3D-Madurodam: when dikes burst onscreen, water sprays the audience. Then there's Hendrik Willem Mesdag's massive 360-degree painting of Scheveningen beach (1881; p832). Inside an enclosed dome, real sand dunes and beach furniture are surrounded by this epic vision; with its amazing command of perspective it's an eerily realistic experience.

But then again, from a nation that recovered much of its land from the sea (p815), none of this should be surprising: the Dutch were shaping worlds many, many centuries ago.

Dutch TV is saturated with foreign programming, but one notable local product is the reality series *Big Brother,* now a worldwide franchise (see p814).

Theatre

Contemporary Dutch theatre didn't really produce anything of note until the 1960s, when companies such as Mickery and Shaffy made Amsterdam a centre for experimental theatre. Today, De Dogtroep tours abroad and stages fancy and unpredictable 'happenings' in quirky venues, like Amsterdam's ship passenger terminal.

Robodock, held at Rotterdam's former ADM shipyards in late September, features robots and choreographed pyrotechnics.

Literature

Dutch literature flourished in the 17th century with writers such as Vondel (the Dutch Shakespeare), Bredero and Hooft. Post-war literature was dominated by Willem Frederik Hermans, Harry Mulisch and Gerard Reve, and later by Jan Wolkers, Maarten 't Hart and Frederik van der Heijden.

Tim Krabbe writes dark, complex novels about love, suffering and utter futility. *The Golden Egg* was made into a compelling Dutch film, *Spoorloos,* and later a bad Hollywood remake.

Photography

Documentary is a specialty of contemporary Dutch photographers. Ed van der Elksen's most famous work is *Love on the Left Bank* from 1954, a photographic novel featuring a cast of Paris bohemians. Anton Corbijn is famous for his portraits of top-shelf artists and celebrities.

ENVIRONMENT

Acid, nitrate and phosphate levels in the Dutch biosphere are Europe's highest. The great European rivers Rijn (Rhine), Maas and Schelde (Scheldt) carry pollutants via the Netherlands into the North Sea, while the coastal situation of low-lying lands means that soil salination is a persistent problem.

In the late 20th century, Dutch awareness of the environment grew by leaps and bounds. Citizens now sort their rubbish, support pro-bicycle schemes and protest over scores of potentially detrimental projects. Congestion has been eased by cutting city parking spaces and erecting speed bumps. Country roads tend to favour bike lanes at the cost of motor vehicles.

Billions spent on sewage treatment means that Amsterdam's canals are now fairly clean, and agriculture and industry have been presented with mandatory goals to reduce run-off and pollution.

The Land

Much of the Netherlands' land mass has been reclaimed from the sea over many centuries. The country now encompasses 41,526 sq km, roughly half the size of Scotland, and half of it lies at or below sea level in the form of polders (stretches of land reclaimed from the sea). If the Netherlands lost its 2400km of dykes and dunes, the large cities would be inundated, so pumping stations run around the clock to drain off excess water. The danger of floods is most acute in Zeeland, a sprawling estuary for the rivers Schelde, Maas, Lek and Waal.

The Netherlands' highest point, the Vaalserberg, is in the province of Limburg, at a grand elevation of 321m.

Wildlife

Human encroachment has meant few wildlife habitats are left intact. Birds offer the greatest breadth of species, now heavily protected in sanctuaries and nature reserves. The Netherlands is a paradise for birdwatchers, and the wetlands are a major migration stop for European birds, particularly in the Wadden Islands, Flevoland and the Delta.

Plants

Tulips were imported from elsewhere and then commercially exploited, as were fruits, vegetables and other flowers; tomatoes and sweet peppers are among the Netherlands' biggest hothouse products but originated from Central America.

The remnants of oak, beech, ash and pine forests are carefully managed. Wooded areas such as Hoge Veluwe National Park are mostly products of recent forestation, so trees tend to be young and of a similar age. Even the vegetation on islands such as Ameland is monitored to control erosion.

National Parks

Some 1065 sq km (nearly 3%) of the Netherlands is protected in the form of national parks. The first publicly funded national park was established in 1984, and most average 5000 hectares. Little of the Netherlands is left untouched, so the Dutch cherish what's left.

The Hoge Veluwe (p844), established in the 1930s, is one of the largest and oldest parks. Forestation is maintained and it's a good place to see the sandy hills that once were prevalent in these parts.

Weerribben in Overijssel preserves a landscape once heavily scarred by the peat harvest. Off the coast of Friesland, Schiermonnikoog occupies a good portion of an island once used by a sect of monks. Reed farmers formerly inhabited the Biesbosch near Rotterdam.

Environmental Issues

Private car ownership has risen to about 50% over late-1980s levels; motorways could become gridlocked very soon.

Winters have become shorter and milder; three of the warmest years on record occurred in the past decade. If sea levels rise, the Netherlands could suffer annual flooding. Dykes and storm barriers will be extended if necessary.

North Sea water quality appears to be declining, and pesticides and unfiltered runoff industrial waste have been blamed. The Foundation for Environmental Education awarded its coveted 'blue flag' to just 12 Dutch beaches in 2003.

Pressure from the government and Greenpeace has forced Shell and the like to invest heavily in developing clean energy. Wind parks in Flevoland and Noord Holland generate a significant amount of electricity.

FOOD & DRINK
Staples & Specialities

Dutch food is very hearty and designed to line the stomach; favourite dishes include *stamppot* (mashed pot), potatoes mashed with kale, endive or sauerkraut and served with smoked sausage or pork strips; and *hutspot* (hotchpotch), similar to *stamppot*, but with potatoes, carrots, onions and braised meat.

The Netherlands is famous for cheese, and the Dutch consume 16.5kg per person of various varieties annually (nearly two-thirds of it is *gouda*).

Vlaamse frites (Flemish fries) are French fries made from whole potatoes. They're typ-ically smothered in mayonnaise, and stands are everywhere.

Seafood is found at street stalls in every town, including raw, slightly salted herring cut into bite-sized pieces and served with onion and pickles; smoked eel; and *kibbeling* (deep-fried cod parings).

International

Lebanese and Turkish snack bars specialise in *shwarma*, pitta bread filled with sliced lamb from a spit, and falafel.

The Netherlands' colonial legacy has introduced Indonesian and Surinamese cooking to the Dutch palate, and the cuisines of many other nations are also well represented, notably Japanese and Greek.

Indonesian cooking blends Thai chilli peppers, peanut sauce and stewed curries; lemongrass and fish sauces from Vietnam; Indian spice mixes; and Asian cooking methods. A popular dish is *rijsttafel* (rice table), an array of savoury dishes such as braised beef, pork satay and ribs served with white rice.

Surinamese dishes blend African and Indian flavours with Indonesian; chicken, lamb and beef curries are common. *Roti kip* is curried chicken served with potatoes, long beans, bean sprouts and a delicious *roti* (chickpea-flour pancake).

Drinks
NON-ALCOHOLIC

Tea is usually served Continental-style – a cup or pot of hot water with a tea bag on the side. Many locals add a slice of lemon rather than milk.

The Dutch consume more *koffie* (coffee) per capita than anywhere in Europe, except Denmark; it's drunk with *koffiemelk,* like condensed milk. *Koffie verkeerd* is similar to latte, served in a big mug with plenty of real milk.

ALCOHOLIC

The Dutch love a beer, and lager is the staple brew, topped by a large head of froth, which supposedly contains 'flavour bubbles' to enhance your drinking experience (so don't complain). *Een bier* or *een pils* is a normal glass, *een kleintje pils* a small glass, and *een fluitje* a tall, thin glass. Half-litre mugs are also available.

Jenever (gin), made from juniper berries, is drunk chilled from a shot glass filled to the brim; it's a creeper. The smoother *jonge* (young) *jenever* is good for beginners; the *oude* (old) *jenever* is an acquired taste. Dutch liqueurs include *advocaat* (a kind of eggnog) and the herb-based Beerenburg, a Frisian schnapps.

Wine has become popular, even though Dutch import duties keep prices high, particularly in restaurants.

Where to Eat & Drink

As well as restaurants, there are *eetcafés*, which are affordable, small and popular pub-like eateries.

'Café' means a pub, also known as a *kroeg*. They generally serve food, and many have outdoor terraces. The most famous type is the cosy *bruin café* (brown café); the name comes from smoke stains on the walls, although pretenders make do with brown paint.

Grand cafés are more spacious, have comfortable furniture and are very popular.

Theatre cafés are also popular and there are also a few *proeflokalen* (tasting houses), where you can sample from dozens of *jenevers* and liqueurs.

Broodjeszaken (sandwich shops) and snack bars are everywhere.

Vegetarians & Vegans

Many restaurant menus may have one or two veggie dishes, but they might not be 100% meat- or fish-free (meat stock is a common culprit). Vegetarian restaurants often rely on organic ingredients and generally make everything from bread to cakes in-house.

Habits & Customs

The Dutch eat dinner early – popular places fill up by 7pm. If you miss out, you could aim for the 'second sitting', around 8.30pm to 9.30pm, although many kitchens tend to close by 10pm.

Lunch tends to be more of a snack, and just a half-hour break is common. Coffee breaks are frequent.

Service is included in the bill and tipping is at your discretion, though most people round up 5% to 10%. In cafés and pubs it's common to put drinks on a tab and pay when you leave.

Many restaurants don't accept credit cards, so make sure your wallet is full.

AMSTERDAM

☎ 020 / pop 731,000

Amsterdam ranks as one of Europe's most eccentric cities. With its beautiful, heritage-protected 17th-century housing, museums and galleries – and notorious sleaze – it's known as the 'Venice of the North', a spot-on tribute. It's perfect for travellers, with enough sensory delights to keep the shortest attention spans occupied, while the endless cafés and bars provide welcoming havens from the rampant crowds and perpetual buzz. Amsterdam is compact and user-friendly – walk or ride a bike around the canal grid and bask in the many worlds-within-worlds that make this city so addictive.

Amsterdam has glowed since the Golden Age, when it led European art and trade. Centuries later, in the 1960s, it again led the pack – this time in the principles of tolerance, with broad-minded views on drugs and same-sex relationships taking centre stage. Amsterdam was then known as Europe's 'Magic Centre', the crux of a utopian dream where people believed anything could happen. Although the days of excess have been somewhat neutered, much of that famous swagger is still evident (and in some cases, institutionalised and parodied, like in the Red Light district).

Above all, the people of Amsterdam remain urbane and welcoming. Travellers, fringe-dwellers and the merely curious have flocked like moths to Amsterdam's flame since the Middle Ages, so chances are you'll fit in somewhere.

HISTORY

A small fishing town named Aemstelredamme emerged in around 1200. The community was freed by the count of Holland from paying tolls on its locks and bridges, and 'Amsterdam' developed into a major seaport.

Calvinist brigands captured Amsterdam in 1578 and the seven northern provinces, led by Holland and Zeeland, declared themselves a republic. The stage was set for the Golden Age, when merchants and artisans flocked to Amsterdam and a new class of monied intellectuals was born.

By the late 17th century Holland couldn't match the might of France and England, but

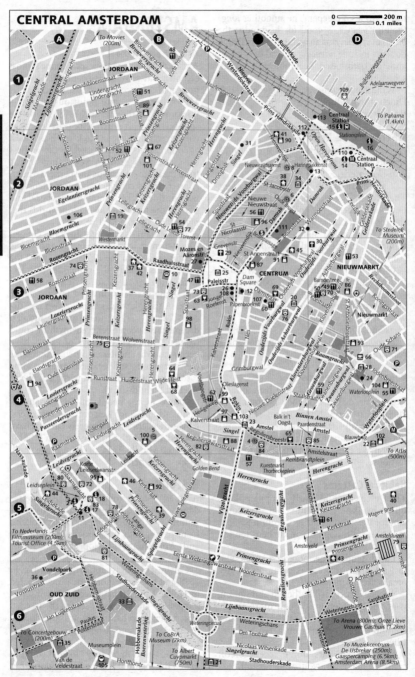

CENTRAL AMSTERDAM

when the country's first railway opened in 1839 the city was revitalised in a stroke.

After WWII, growth resumed with US aid (the Marshall Plan).

In the 1960s students occupied the administrative centre of the University of Amsterdam, and the women's movement began a campaign that fuelled the abortion debate throughout the next decade.

In the '70s, city planners proposed a metro line through the Nieuwmarkt neighbourhood, earmarking a large portion of the derelict district to be razed. When the inhabitants turned to squatting, the district was violently cleared on 24 March 1975: 'Blue Monday'.

In the '60s families and small manufacturers dominated inner-city neighbourhoods; by the early '90s they'd been replaced by professionals and a service industry of pubs, coffeeshops, restaurants and hotels. Non-Dutch nationalities comprised 45% of the population and the city's success in attracting large foreign businesses resulted in an influx of higher-income expatriates.

ORIENTATION

Amsterdam's old town is so compact you'll be able to get to all the major sights on foot or by bike. Centraal Station is the hub. From the station the streets radiate outward across a network of *grachten* (concentric canals).

Dam Square is Amsterdam's heart, five minutes' walk down Damrak from Centraal Station. Leidseplein is the centre of Amsterdam nightlife, and Nieuwmarkt is a vast cobblestone square with open-air markets and popular pubs. The Red Light District is a law unto itself.

Lush 17th-century homes occupy the western canals Prinsengracht, Keizersgracht and Herengracht. The Jordaan is filled with quirky shops, bohemian bars and art galleries. Outside the canal belt is ethnic-influenced De Pijp; posh and residential Oud Zuid, east of the Damrak-Rokin axis; and Nieuw Zuid, to the west of the axis, with its 20th-century housing projects. The Eastern Docklands is a showcase of modern Dutch architecture.

THE NETHERLANDS

INFORMATION		
American Express	1	C2
Amsterdam Uitburo	2	A5
Centrale Bibliotheek	3	A4
easyInternetcafé	4	C4
easyInternetcafé	5	B4
easyInternetcafé	6	C2
French Consulate	7	C5
Internet City	8	C2
Main Police Station	9	A4
Main Post Office	10	A5
Thomas Cook	11	D2
Thomas Cook	12	C3
Thomas Cook	13	D2
Tourist Office	14	D2
Tourist Office	15	D1
Tourist Office	16	D2
Tourist Office	17	A5
Tourist Office	18	A5

SIGHTS & ACTIVITIES	(pp820–2)	
Anne Frankhuis	19	B2
Hash, Marihuana & Hemp Museum	20	C3
Heineken Experience	21	C6
Hermitage Amsterdam	22	D4
Het Oranje Voetbal Museum	23	C4
Holland Experience 3D	24	D4
Koninklijk Paleis	25	C3
Madame Tussaud's	26	C3
Magna Plaza	27	B3
Museum Het Rembrandthuis	28	D4
Nieuwe Kerk	29	C3
Oude Kerk	30	D3
Poezenboot	31	C2
Prostitution Information Centre	32	C2
Rijksmuseum	33	B6
Sexmuseum Amsterdam	34	C2
Van Gogh Museum	35	A6
Vondelpark	36	A6

SLEEPING	(pp822–3)	
Budget Hotel Clemens	37	B3
Flying Pig Downtown Hostel	38	C2

Hans Brinker Budget Hotel	39	B5
Hotel Fantasia	40	D5
Hotel Groenendael	41	C2
Hotel Pax	42	B3
Hotel Prinsenhof	43	D5
Hotel Quentin	44	A5
Hotel Winston	45	C3
Seven One Seven	46	B5

EATING	(pp823–4)	
Albert Heijn	47	B3
Albert Heijn	48	B1
Albert Heijn	49	D3
Blauw aan de Wal	50	D3
Casa Juan	51	B1
De Bolhoed	52	B2
Eat Mode	53	D3
Foodism	54	B2
Gary's Muffins	55	D4
Hiyashi	56	C2
Memories of India	57	C5
Nomads	58	A3
Puccini	59	D4
Sukasari	60	C3
Tempo Doeloe	61	D5
Vlaams Friteshuis	62	C4

DRINKING	(p824)	
Absinthe	63	B3
Café Dante	64	B4
Café De Kroon	65	C4
Café de Sluyswacht	66	D4
Café de Vergulde Gaper	67	B2
Hoppe	68	B4
Proeflokaal Wijnand Fockinck	69	C3

ENTERTAINMENT	(pp824–6)	
Bethaniënklooster	70	D3
Bimhuis	71	D4
Boom Chicago	72	A5
Bulldog	73	A5
Club Zyon	74	B3
COC	75	A3

Felix Meritis	76	A3
Greenhouse	77	C3
Grey Area	78	B2
Jazz Café Alto	79	B5
Koninklijk Theater Carré	80	D5
Melkweg	81	A5
Paradiso	82	A5
Soho	83	B4
Tuschinskitheater	84	C4
Viva la Vie	85	D4
Winston International	(see 45)	

SHOPPING	(p826)	
Antiques Market	86	D3
Bijenkorf	87	C3
Bloemenmarkt	88	C4
Boerenmarkt	89	B1
Chills & Thrills	90	C2
Condomerie Het Gulden Vlies	91	C3
Conscious Dreams	92	B5
De Klomponboer	93	D3
De Looier	94	A4
Heinen	95	A5
Hema	96	C2
Kalvertoren Shopping Centre	97	C4
Magic Mushroom Gallery	98	B3
Maison de Bonneterie	99	C4
Metz & Co	100	B4
Pollinator	101	D4
Santa Jet	102	B2
Vroom & Dreesmann	103	C4
Waterlooplein flea market	104	D4

TRANSPORT	(pp826–7)	
ANWB	105	A6
Bike City	106	A2
Damstraat Rent-a-Bike	107	C3
Eurolines	108	C3
Fast Flying Ferries	109	D1
GVB	110	D2
Holland Rent-a-Bike	111	C2
Lovers Museum Boat	112	C2
MacBike	113	D1

Maps

Lonely Planet's *Amsterdam City Map* has a street index that covers most of the town in detail. The tourist offices also sell good, indexed maps, as do many bookshops and newsstands.

INFORMATION

Emergency

De Eerste Lijn (The First Line; ☎ 613 02 45) Sexual violence hotline.

Main police station (☎ 0900 8844)

Internet Access

Centrale Bibliotheek (Main Library; ☎ 523 09 00; Prinsengracht 587; ☿ 1-9pm Mon, 10am-9pm Tue-Thu, 10am-5pm Fri & Sat, 1-5pm Sun) Free Internet.

EasyInternet Café (www.easyeverything.com/map/ams) Reguliersbreestraat 22 (☿ 9am-10pm); Damrak 33 (☿ 9am-10pm); Leidsestraat 24 (☿ 11am-7pm Mon, 9.30am-7pm Tue-Sat, 11am-6pm Sun)

Internet City (☎ 620 12 92; Nieuwendijk 76; ☿ 10am-midnight)

Medical Services

Centrale Doktersdienst (Central Doctors' Service; ☎ 592 34 34; ☿ 24hr) Can refer you to a doctor, dentist or pharmacy.

Onze Lieve Vrouwe Gasthuis (☎ 599 91 11; Oosterpark 9) This is a 24-hour public hospital.

Money

American Express (☎ 504 87 77; Damrak 66; ☿ 9am-5pm Mon-Fri, to noon Sat)

GWK (☎ 627 27 31; Centraal Station; ☿ 7am-10.45pm) Converts travellers cheques and books hotel reservations; also at Schiphol.

Thomas Cook (☎ 625 09 22; Dam 23-25; ☿ 9am-7pm) Also branches at Damrak 1-5 (opposite Centraal Station) and Leidseplein 31A.

Post

Main post office (Singel 250; ☿ 9am-7pm Mon-Fri, to noon Sat)

Tourist Information

Amsterdam Tourist Board (☎ 0900-400 40 40; ☿ 9am-5pm Mon-Fri) Information line for hotel reservations and general queries.

Amsterdam Uitburo (☎ 0900-0191; www.aub.nl, in Dutch; Leidseplein 26; ☿ 10am-6pm Mon-Fri, to 9pm Thu, info & ticket line 9am-9pm) For cultural events, with free magazines and tickets at small discounts.

Tourist office (☎ 0900-400 40 40; www.vvvamsterdam .nl); Stationsplein 10 (☿ 9am-5pm); Centraal Track 2 (**Centraal**

Station; ☿ 8am-7.45pm Mon-Sat, 9am-5pm Sun); Leidseplein 1 (☿ 9am-7pm Mon-Fri, to 5pm Sat & Sun); Stadionplein (☿ 9am-5pm) The Stadionplein office is next to the old Olympic Stadium.

DANGERS & ANNOYANCES

Amsterdam is reasonably safe, but be sensible all the same: watch for pickpockets in crowded areas, don't leave valuables in cars and *always* lock your bike. Be wary of the old fake policeman trick – these types, invariably plain clothed, harass foreigners for drugs and ID. Dutch coppers rarely do this and they don't carry badges, so if your interrogator flashes one, be alert.

SIGHTS & ACTIVITIES

Museums & Galleries

The **Museum Het Rembrandthuis** (Rembrandt House Museum; ☎ 520 04 00; www.rembrandthuis.nl; Jodenbreestraat 4; adult/child €7/1.50; ☿ 10am-5pm Mon-Sat, 1-5pm Sun) is where Rembrandt ran the Netherlands' largest painting studio, only to lose it all when bankruptcy threatened. Today, the museum has almost every etching he's known to have made, and it houses guest artists on occasion.

Each year 1.2 million people visit the **Rijksmuseum** (☎ 674 70 47; www.rijksmuseum.nl; Stadhouderskade 42; adult/under 19 €9/free; ☿ 10am-5pm); its collection is valued in the billions. Until renovations finish in 2008, there'll only be 200 masterpieces displayed, but at least that includes the museum's crowning glory – Rembrandt's *Nightwatch* (1650).

The **Stedelijk Museum** (☎ 573 27 37; www.stedelijk .nl; Oosterdoksijk 5; adult/child €7/3.50; ☿ 11am-5pm) is in a temporary home; the original building is undergoing renovation until 2007. The collection holds around 100,000 pieces, including impressionist works from Monet, Cézanne, Matisse, Picasso and Chagall; sculptures from Rodin, Renoir and Moore; De Stijl landmarks by Piet Mondrian; abstract works by Appel and the CoBrA movement; and pop art from Andy Warhol and Roy Lichtenstein.

The **Van Gogh Museum** (☎ 570 52 00; www.van goghmuseum.nl; Paulus Potterstraat 7; adult/child €9/2.50; ☿ Sun-Thu 10am-6pm, to 10pm Fri) houses the world's largest Van Gogh collection: around 200 paintings and 500 drawings by the artist and his contemporaries, including Gauguin, Toulouse-Lautrec, Monet and Bernard.

St Petersburg's Hermitage collection is so massive it has had to expand abroad, with permanent annexes in London and Las Vegas, and the latest: **Hermitage Amsterdam** (☎ 626 81 68; www.hermitage.nl; Nieuwe Herengracht 14; adult/child €6/free; ☒ 10am-5pm). There are six galleries housing exhibitions twice a year; the inaugural exhibit in 2004 was Greek Gold, jewellery from 6th to 2nd century BC Greek colonies.

The **CoBrA Museum** (☎ 547 50 50; www.cobra -museum.nl; Sandbergplein 1-3; adult/child €6/2.50; ☒ 11am-5pm Tue-Sun) houses paintings, ceramics and statues from the CoBrA movement (p813). Take bus No 170, 171 or 172 from Amsterdam Centraal Station.

The **Anne Frankhuis** (Anne Frank House; ☎ 556 71 00; www.annefrank.nl; Prinsengracht 267; adult/child €7.50/3.50; ☒ 9am-7pm Sep-Mar, 9am-9pm Apr-Aug) is where Anne wrote her famous diary. A compelling reminder of Nazi horrors, it lures 900,000 visitors each year, so consider going in the early evening when crowds are lightest.

There are some interesting artefacts from the history of sexual entertainment at the **Sexmuseum Amsterdam** (☎ 622 83 76; Damrak 18; admission €2.50; ☒ 10am-11.30pm) – Pompeiian erotica, for example. But with wall-mounted plastic derrieres passing wind at passers-by and an animatronic flasher accosting all-comers, it's more like a tribute to Benny Hill.

For many Dutch, football isn't a matter of life or death: it's more important than that. **Het Oranje Voetbal Museum** (Orange Football Museum; ☎ 589 89 89; www.supportersclub-oranje.nl, in Dutch; Kalverstraat 236; ☒ 11am-5pm Sat & Sun) tells the story of orange maestros like Cruyff, Van Basten and Gullit, and the revolution that was Total Football.

The zealous though informative **Hash, Marihuana & Hemp Museum** (☎ 623 59 61; www.hash museum.com; Oudezijds Achterburgwal 130; admission €5.70; ☒ 11am-10pm) has many exhibits on the uses and history of cannabis (Queen Victoria used marijuana for menstrual cramps, it says here), as well as a seed shop, a greenhouse and a large selection of bongs.

At the **Heineken Experience** (☎ 523 94 36; www .heinekenexperience.com; Stadhouderskade 78; admission €7.50; ☒ 10am-6pm Tue-Sat) you can peer inside the malt silos and at memorabilia, although the brewery itself is long gone. Admission includes three glasses of Heineken.

Other Attractions

The **Koninklijk Paleis** (Royal Palace; ☎ 620 40 60; www .koninklijkhuis.nl; Dam 1; adult/child €4.50/3.60; ☒ 12.30-

5pm Sep-Jun, 11am-5pm Jul & Aug) is Queen Beatrix's official residence, even though she lives in Den Haag. The lavish interior has Empire carvings, sculptures, chandeliers and all the trappings of your average royal.

If the Queen isn't in, try her simulacrum across the way at **Madame Tussaud's** (☎ 522 10 10; www.madame-tussauds.com; Dam 20; adult/child €22.50/10; ☒ 10am-6.30pm Sep-Jun, 9.30am-10.30pm Jul & Aug). The queues will be deep.

Just north of the Royal Palace, the late-Gothic basilica **Nieuwe Kerk** (New Church; ☎ 638 69 09; www.nieuwekerk.nl; the Dam; admission from €5; ☒ 10am-6pm Fri-Wed, to 10pm Thu) is the coronation church of Dutch royalty. It features a carved oak chancel, a bronze choir screen, a massive, gilded organ and stained-glass windows. It's now used for exhibitions and organ concerts.

Amsterdam's oldest building, the **Oude Kerk** (Old Church; ☎ 625 82 84; www.oudekerk.nl; Oudekerksplein 23; adult/child €4/3; ☒ 11am-5pm Mon-Sat, 1-5pm Sun) was built to honour the city's patron saint, St Nicholas. Inside there's a dramatic Müller organ, gilded oak vaults and impressive stained-glass windows. The tower offers a magnificent view.

The neo-Gothic extravaganza, **Magna Plaza** (☎ 626 91 99; www.magnaplaza.nl; Nieuwezijds Voorburgwal 182; ☒ 11am-7pm Mon, 10am-7pm Tue, Wed, Fri & Sat, 10am-9pm Thu, noon-7pm Sun), behind the Royal Palace, was the central post office in the 19th century. Today it's a ritzy shopping complex with a grand interior (a Dutch video artist devoted a project to the Plaza's escalators in 2001).

Artis (☎ 523 34 00; www.artis.nl; Plantage Kerklaan 38-40; adult/child €14.50/11; ☒ 9am-5pm Oct-May, 9am to 6pm Jun-Sep) is the oldest zoo on the European continent. Besides the well-rounded animal population, it's also home to a planetarium, a petting zoo and themed habitats. The aquarium complex has coral reefs, shark tanks and an Amsterdam canal displayed from a fish-eye view.

Vondelpark (www.vondelpark.nl, in Dutch) is an English-style park with free concerts, ponds, lawns, thickets, winding footpaths and three outdoor cafés. It was named after the poet and playwright Joost van den Vondel, the 'Dutch Shakespeare', and is popular with joggers, skaters, buskers and lovers.

The **Red Light District** is bound by Zeedijk/Nieuwmarkt/Kloveniersburgwal in the east, Damstraat/Oude Doelenstraat/Oude

Hoogstraat in the south, and Warmoesstraat in the west. The area retains the power to bewilder, even if near-naked prostitutes propositioning passers-by from back-lit windows is the oldest Amsterdam cliché. Among the usual oddball assortment, you'll find middle-class tourists gawping at the blatant displays of sexual currency.

You can view a re-creation of a working girl's place of employment at the **Prostitution Information Centre** (☎ 420 73 28; www.pic-amsterdam.com; Enge Kerksteeg 3; ☻ noon-7pm Tue, Wed, Fri & Sat). The centre also organises evening Red Light walks and sells a handy map of the Red Light District.

The **Poezenboot** (Cat Boat; ☎ 625 87 94; www.poezenboot.nl; Singel 40; ☻ 1-3pm) is one of Amsterdam's more unusual 'flea markets'. This barge began life as a shelter for hundreds of homeless cats in the 1960s. It's now a registered charity – pat and pet the current feline inhabitants for a small donation.

Holland Experience 3D (☎ 422 22 33; www.holland-experience.nl; Waterlooplein 17; adult/child €8.50/7.25; ☻ 10am-6pm) screens a decidedly odd 30-minute film about Dutch life, presented in the third dimension: when tulips appear, you get sprayed with perfume; when dykes burst, you get sprayed with water. It's all part of that curious Dutch tendency to put the nation under a microscope (see p814).

SLEEPING
BUDGET
Gaaspercamping (☎ 696 73 26; www.gaaspercamping.nl; Loosdrechtdreef 7, Gaasperdam; camp sites €5-6, plus person €4.25, car €3.75, caravan €5-6; ☻ mid-Mar–Dec) Take a breather from Amsterdam's multitudes. This large park/recreation area, originally built to host 1982's International Horticultural Exhibition, has a café, a restaurant, a bar, barbecues, a supermarket, a lake and a beach.

Flying Pig Downtown Hostel (☎ 420 68 22; www.flyingpig.nl; Nieuwendijk 100; dm €19.70-25.70; ☐) Popular with unhurried dopers, who lounge around the throbbing lobby and bar. Decide whether it's your cup of tea by visiting the Pig's website: the message board has lively debate on the virtues (or otherwise) of the facilities.

Hans Brinker Budget Hotel (☎ 622 06 87; www.hans-brinker.com; Kerkstraat 136; dm €21-24) There's a hyperactive 'frat house' feel to the Brinker, with its bouncy bar and disco. Again, decide by visiting its unflattering (quite deliberately

so) website, where the art of self-mockery is taken to very Dutch extremes.

Hotel Groenendael (☎ 624 48 22; www.hotelgroenendael.com; Nieuwendijk 15; s/d/tr with shared bathroom incl breakfast €29/45/68) A bargain: a central location, neat (though small) rooms, charming owners. As always in this part of town, the quietest rooms are at the back.

Hotel Pax (☎ 624 97 35; Raadhuisstraat 37; s €25-45, d €45-95) Run by a pair of affable brothers, the Pax features eight brightly decorated rooms with a TV in each. There's a trade-off with the larger rooms: they face the busy street and noisy trams.

MID-RANGE & TOP END
Hotel Quentin (☎ 626 21 87; www.quentinhotels.com; Leidsekade 89; s with shared bathroom €45, d/tr incl breakfast from €90/125) This one has a reputation with lesbians and thespians swinging through town. It's done up in bright murals and handmade furniture. Some rooms have balconies, canal views and TVs.

Hotel Winston (☎ 623 13 80; www.winston.nl; Warmoesstraat 129; s €62-65, d €83-89, tr €110-118, s with shared bathroom €60-62, d with shared bathroom €75-83) How to make a lot out of a little: take some functional rooms and get local artists to imaginatively theme them with motifs including Arabian typography, jigsaw puzzles, and, fittingly for the Red Light location, bizarre sex. There's a jolly bar and the Winston's own club (p824) next door.

Hotel Fantasia (☎ 623 82 59; www.fantasia-hotel.com; Nieuwe Keizersgracht 16; s €55-65, d €84-94, tr €120, f €140) The owner grew up on a farm and has parlayed that into a workable obsession: this bovine-themed 18th-century canal house. Bucolic prints and cow motifs gleefully decorate the 19 rooms and breakfast area, complementing the peaceful location.

Hotel Prinsenhof (☎ 623 17 72; www.hotelprinsenhof.com; Prinsengracht 810; s/d incl breakfast €75/80, with shared bathroom $40/60) Dating from the 17th century, the Prinsenhof is wonderfully preserved, with spacious rooms. The attic quarters (slanted ceiling and unbeatable canal views) are booked way in advance by honeymooners. The breakfast policy promises that 'no one's allowed to leave until he or she is completely satiated'.

Budget Hotel Clemens (☎ 624 60 89; www.clemenshotel.com; Raadhuisstraat 39; s €55, d €70-110, tr €125-150) With rooms lavishly decorated in creams and yellows (or golds and reds, burgundies etc), along with antique furniture and marble fireplaces, it's a hit. Each room has a TV, phone and safe. Your hostess has boundless love for Amsterdam. All prices include breakfast.

Seven One Seven (☎ 427 07 17; www.717hotel.nl; Prinsengracht 717; ste €390-640; 🌐) These suites, hopelessly devoted to elegant luxury, are named after an eclectic group of cultural icons. Mahler, Shakespeare, Stravinsky – that should give you an idea of the refined tastes on display. The Picasso suite is indicative, with its high ceiling, antique décor and voluminous bathroom.

EATING

Amsterdam has a sizzling culinary scene with hundreds of restaurants and *eetcafés* catering to all tastes.

Restaurants

Eat Mode (☎ 330 08 06; www.eatmode.nl; Zeedijk 107; mains €4.50-12; 🌐 lunch & dinner) Billed as an 'Asian Fusion Kitchen: First in Chinatown', it's small and bright, with casual ambience, but the Thai, Chinese, Vietnamese and Japanese meals are filling and tasty. There's a good vegetarian selection, including seaweed salad, and a sushi happy hour.

Sukasari (☎ 624 00 92; Damstraat 26-28; mains €4.75-18.50; 🌐 lunch & dinner) Decorated with Indonesian artefacts and suffused in golden lighting, Sukasari is a quiet, contemplative oasis just off the manic Dam. The excellent menu serves fragrant, authentic Indonesian, like coconut chicken with rice.

De Bolhoed (☎ 626 18 03; Prinsengracht 60-62; mains €6-14; 🌐 lunch & dinner) Amsterdam's best-known vegetarian restaurant, with a prime canalside location. The food is fresh, organic, and often Mexican- and Italian-inspired: pancakes, salads, burritos, home-made breads, biological wines, organic beers and cakes.

Hiyashi (☎ 528 78 18; Nieuwe Nieuwstraat 16; mains €7-21; 🌐 dinner) A small Japanese restaurant serving small but very tasty portions, like great squid balls.

Casa Juan (☎ 623 78 38; Lindengracht 59; tapas €3-8, mains €12-17; 🌐 dinner) The signature dish is the paella, and it's deservedly popular. *Very* popular. Be sure to book.

Memories of India (☎ 623 57 10; www.memories ofindia.nl; Reguliersdwarsstraat 88; mains €11.50-22.75; 🌐 dinner) Stylish, friendly, relaxed. That's the winning combination, especially when combined with reasonable prices and dishes from all over India, including *paneerwala murg*: chicken pieces tossed with homemade cottage cheese, spring onion and ginger.

Tempo Doeloe (☎ 625 67 18; www.tempodoeloe restaurant.nl; Utrechtsestraat 75; mains €18-22; 🌐 dinner) The name means 'The Old Days' (ring a bell to gain entry) and the spice levels range from mild to *very* hot. Yet all the subtle flavours remain intact. How extraordinary. Reservations are essential.

Blauw aan de Wal (☎ 330 22 57; Oudezijds Achterburgwal 99; mains €24-26; 🌐 dinner Mon-Sat; 🌐) Tucked away in a little alley in the Red Light District, this charming 17th-century herb warehouse is the setting for modern Dutch dishes like suckling pig or wild bass. The leafy courtyard backs onto a monastery.

Nomads (☎ 344 64 01; www.restaurantnomads.nl; Rozengracht 131-133; set menu €42.50; 🌐 dinner) It's like a boudoir: eat your Middle Eastern food while taking it easy on stuffed cushions in a hall festooned with Moroccan curtains and oversized chandeliers. Belly dancers and DJs entertain late in the evening.

Quick Eats

Puccini (☎ 626 54 74; www.puccini.nl; in Dutch; Staalstraat 21; mains €5.30-12.50; 🌐 lunch & dinner Tue-Sun) This is where modish crowds refuel on Italian panini rolls and salads with sun-dried ingredients. Puccini also runs the chocolate and cake shop next door, where handmade sweets (like chocs blended with tamarind or lemongrass) induce rapture.

Foodism (☎ 427 51 03; www.foodism.nl; Oude Leliestraat 8; mains €6-8; 🌐 lunch & dinner) A groovy little lounge bathed in garish colours. It dishes out all-day breakfasts, healthy filled sandwiches and salads, and various pasta dishes.

Gary's Muffins (☎ 421 59 30; www.garys-muffins.nl; Jodenbreestraat 15; 🌐 9am-5.30pm) Gary used to be a professional ballet dancer; now he gets the nod for delectable fresh bagels, warm chocolate brownies, and sweet and savoury muffins. There must be a connection.

Vlaams Friteshuis (Voetboogstraat 31) This hole in the wall is Amsterdam's best-loved fries joint, an institution since 1887. The default topping is mayonnaise, but there's a full arsenal of alternatives – peanut, say, or green peppercorns.

Self-Catering

Albert Heijn (Nieuwezijds Voorburgwal 226) This upmarket supermarket chain sells takeaway meals and has branches at Koningsplein 6 and Museumplein.

DRINKING

Absinthe (☎ 320 6780; www.absinthe.nl; Nieuwezijds Voorburgwal 171) Devoted to the once-banned, brain-numbing liquor of the same name (popular among 19th-century artists and academics, and reputed to be the cause of Van Gogh's self-mutilation). There's trendy multi-ethnic décor and the staff can teach you all about their signature drink, although the jury's out on whether it's as potent as the old days.

Café de Sluyswacht (☎ 625 76 11; Jodenbreestraat 1) A pretty drinking spot, built on foundations that lean dramatically, with secluded tables overlooking a broad canal.

Hoppe (☎ 420 44 20; Spuistraat 18) This gritty brown café has been luring drinkers for more than 300 years and has one of Amsterdam's highest beer turnovers. In summer the energetic crowd spills onto the streets.

Café Dante (☎ 638 88 39; www.dante.nl; Spuistraat 320) A large, Art Deco–style space with an art gallery upstairs (where Dutch artist-rocker Herman Brood kept a studio). Peaceful during the day, in the evening it's filled with a boisterous, chic clientele.

Café De Kroon (☎ 625 20 11; www.dekroon.nl, in Dutch; Rembrandtplein 17) This neocolonial gem has a covered terrace, sumptuous velvet armchairs, high ceilings and wall-mounted taxidermic specimens.

Café de Vergulde Gaper (☎ 624 89 75; Prinsenstraat 30) Decorated with old chemist bottles and vintage posters, this ex-pharmacy has a pleasant terrace that fills for afternoon drinks.

Proeflokaal Wijnand Fockinck (☎ 639 26 95; www.wynand-fockink.nl, in Dutch; Pijlsteeg 31) This small tasting house (dating from 1679) serves scores of *jenevers* and liqueurs and has an appealing courtyard serving lunch and snacks.

ENTERTAINMENT
Cinemas

Find out what's on in Thursday's paper.

Movies (☎ 638 60 16; www.themovies.nl; Haarlemmerdijk 161) Art-house films mixed with independent American and British at a beautiful Art Deco cinema, just north of the centre.

Tuschinskitheater (☎ 626 26 33; Reguliersbreestraat 26) Mainstream blockbusters. Worth visiting for its sumptuous Art Deco interior, especially in its main auditorium No 1.

Nederlands Filmmuseum (☎ 589 14 00; www.filmmuseum.nl; Vondelpark 3) Maintains a priceless archive of films, sometimes screening with live music (a recent program included a retrospective of Dutch silent film). In summer films are shown on the outdoor terrace at the museum's café.

Clubs

Winston International (www.winston.nl; Warmoesstraat 125) Next to the Hotel Winston, it has everything from electronica to spoken word to punk to graffiti art. On Sundays, there's Club Vegas, where the dress code is 'jet set' (sequins, suits, stilletos, bow ties, tiaras) and the music is lounge. Kooky fun.

Paradiso (☎ 626 45 21; www.paradiso.nl, in Dutch; Weteringschans 6) This converted church is legendary. Saturday's Paradisco draws smart dressers for a sharp line-up of international DJs, while the monthly Kindred Spirits is hip-hop to the max.

Panama (☎ 311 86 86; www.panama.nl, in Dutch; Oostelijke Handelskade 4) This complex has a salsa-tango dance salon, a restaurant and a glam nightclub that programs Cuban big bands, Brazilian circus acts, a soulful selection of DJ talent, and ladies' night Club Lust.

Arena (☎ 694 74 44; www.hotelarena.nl; 's-Gravesandestraat 51) Just east of the city, Arena offers everything from dance classics to salsa. It's worth visiting for the interior; the chapel of this one-time orphanage has been given a lush redo.

Club Zyon (www.clubzyon.nl; Nieuwezijds Voorburgwal 161) With silver walls and queasy pink lighting, the décor is '70s sci fi. It claims to promote exclusiveness above all (fight the 'door bitch' to get in) but the music policy is more accessible: Latin and R&B on Thursday, salsa Friday, commercial house Saturday.

Coffeeshops

As opposed to 'cafés', a term used to mean pubs in the Netherlands, 'coffeeshops' here applies to establishments in the cannabis trade.

Grey Area (☎ 420 43 01; www.greyarea.nl; Oude Leliestraat 2) Owned by a couple of laid-back American guys, this tiny shop introduced the extra-sticky, flavourful 'Double Bubble Gum' weed to the city. The relaxed staff will advise on the lengthy menu.

Greenhouse (☎ 627 17 39; Oudezijds Voorburgwal 191) Winner of many awards at the annual High

Times festival, it charms smokers with its undersea mosaics, psychedelic stained-glass windows and high-quality weed and hash.

Bulldog (☎ 627 19 08; www.bulldog.nl; Leidseplein 13-17) Amsterdam's most famous coffeeshop chain has five branches. This is the largest, with Internet facilities, two bars, pool tables, fluorescent décor and a café.

Gay & Lesbian Venues

COC (☎ 626 30 87; www.cocamsterdam.nl; Rozenstraat 14) Amsterdam's gay and lesbian social centre, with a café and a nightclub.

Soho (☎ 626 15 73; www.reguliersdwars.nl/soho; Reguliersdwarsstraat 36) This enormous two-storey bar hums with a young, gay clientele and an increasing number of straights.

Vive la Vie (☎ 624 01 14; Amstelstraat 7) This popular 'lipstick lesbian' café has loud music, large windows and flirty girls, though men are also welcome. In summer patrons pack the outdoor terrace.

Live Music
CLASSICAL & CONTEMPORARY

Concertgebouw (Concert Building; ☎ 671 83 45 for tickets 10am-5pm; www.concertgebouw.nl; Concertgebouwplein 2-6) Each year, this neo-Renaissance centre presents around 650 concerts attracting 840,000 visitors, making it the world's busiest concert hall (with, reputedly, the best acoustics). Classical musicians consider the Concertgebouw a very prestigious gig indeed, as do some rock bands with classical pretensions (King Crimson, take a bow).

Muziekcentrum De IJsbreker (☎ 693 90 93; www.ysbreker.nl; Weesperzijde 23; ticket office ✆ 9.30am-5.30pm) Centre for contemporary music, where you might hear avant-garde jazz, modern Turkish guitar or atonal works. It's moving to the Muziekgebouw complex in the Eastern Docklands in late 2004.

Bethaniënklooster (☎ 625 00 78; www.bethanienklooster.nl, in Dutch; Barndesteeg 6B) Free lunchtime concerts on Fridays at 12.30pm – anything from medieval to contemporary – in this small former monastery near Nieuwmarkt.

JAZZ

Bimhuis (☎ 623 33 73; www.bimhuis.nl; Oude Schans 73-77; ✆ 8pm-2am Thu-Sat, closed Jul-Aug) Amsterdam's main jazz venue for nearly 30 years has intimate stage-side seating. Big names like Branford Marsalis, Mike Manieri, Dave Holland and Nicholas Payton appear regularly. It's moving to the Eastern Docklands in 2005.

Jazz Café Alto (☎ 626 32 49; www.jazz-café-alto.nl; Korte Leidsedwarsstraat 115) A slightly older crowd frequents this brown café, where tenor saxophonist Hans Dulfer performs frequently.

ROCK & POP

Paradiso (☎ 626 45 21; www.paradiso.nl, in Dutch; Weteringschans 6) This converted church has long been a premier rock venue since the '60s, hosting big names like Sonic Youth, David Bowie and the Rolling Stones.

Melkweg (Milky Way; ☎ 624 17 77; www.melkweg.nl; Lijnbaansgracht 234A) This former milk factory off Leidseplein has been a top cultural venue since the 1970s. It's an all-in-one entertainment complex with an art gallery, a café, a multimedia centre and top live music almost every night. On Saturdays there are two dance floors with a huge variety of beats.

Loungeroom Concerts (www.liveinthelivingroom.com, in Dutch) It's true what they say: 'Staying in is the new going out'. On Sunday evenings, local musicians stage intimate concerts in private homes – but open to the public. Hosts provide food and drink, and three performers play for 30 minutes each to a maximum of 50 people. Book well ahead.

Sport
FOOTBALL

Ajax is the Netherlands' most famous team: it's won the European Cup four times and launched Johan Cruyff to stellar heights in the '70s. Ajax plays in the **Amsterdam ArenA** (☎ 311 13 33; www.amsterdamarena.nl; Arena Blvd 11, Bijlmermeer), usually on Saturday evenings and Sunday afternoons August to May.

KORFBALL

A cross between netball, volleyball and basketball, this sport has a lively local club scene. Contact the **Amsterdam Sport Council** (☎ 552 24 90).

Theatre

Boom Chicago (☎ 423 01 01; www.boomchicago.nl; Leidseplein 12) English-language stand-up and improvised comedy is performed here year-round; the best way to see it is over dinner and a few drinks. The food is decent, as is the café, boomBar.

Koninklijk Theater Carré (☎ 622 52 25; www.theatercarre.nl, in Dutch; Amstel 115-125; ticket office

THE NETHERLANDS

🕐 10am-7pm Mon-Sat, 1-7pm Sun) The largest theatre in town, with mainstream international shows, musicals, cabaret, opera, operetta, ballet and circuses. Backstage tours are at 3pm on Saturday and Wednesday.

Felix Meritis (☎ 623 13 11; www.felix.meritis.nl, in Dutch; Keizersgracht 324) A hub of experimental theatre, music and dance, with a bevy of co-productions between Eastern and Western European artists.

SHOPPING
Department Stores
There are upmarket fashion, gift and jewellery shops in **Kalvertoren shopping centre** (www.kalvertoren.nl; Singel 457) and **Magna Plaza** (☎ 626 91 99; www.magnaplaza.nl; Nieuwezijds Voorburgwal 182).

Bijenkorf (☎ 621 80 80; www.bijenkorf.nl, in Dutch; Dam 1) Fashionable, tasteful designer items.

Hema (☎ 638 99 63; www.hema.nl, in Dutch; Nieuwendijk 174) Reasonable prices and wide-ranging stock.

Maison de Bonneterie (☎ 531 34 00; www.maison debonneterie.nl, in Dutch; Rokin 140) Exclusive, classic garments.

Metz & Co (☎ 520 70 36; Keizersgracht 455) Upmarket furnishings, homewares, clothes and gifts.

Vroom & Dreesmann (☎ 622 01 71; www.vroomen dreesmann.nl, in Dutch; Kalverstraat 201) Popular clothing and cosmetics.

Markets
Albert Cuypmarkt (www.decuyp.nl; Albert Cuypstraat; 🕐 10am-5pm, closed Sun) Cheap food, flowers, souvenirs, clothing, hardware and household goods.

Antiques market (Nieuwmarkt; 🕐 9am-5pm Sun May-Sep) Antiques, books, bric-a-brac.

Bloemenmarkt (Singel; 🕐 9am-5pm, closed Sun in winter) 'Floating' flower market (actually on pilings).

Boerenmarkt (Farmers' Market; www.boerenmarkt amsterdam.nl, in Dutch; Noordermarkt & Nieuwmarkt; 🕐 10am-3pm Sat) Homegrown produce, organic foods and picnic provisions.

De Looier (www.looier.nl, in Dutch; Elandsgracht 109; 🕐 11am-5pm Sat-Thu) Jewellery, furniture, art and collectibles.

Waterlooplein flea market (Waterlooplein; 🕐 9am-5pm Mon-Fri, 8.30am-5.30pm Sat) Curios, second-hand clothing, music, used footwear, ageing electronic gear, New Age gifts, cheap bicycle parts.

Smart Drugs
Should you purchase goods from the following establishments, please remember that importing drugs is illegal. In other words, don't take them out of the Netherlands.

Chills & Thrills (☎ 638 00 15; Nieuwendijk 17; 🕐 noon-8pm Mon-Wed, 11am-9pm Thu, to 10pm Fri-Sun) Herbal trips, mushrooms, psychoactive cacti, novelty bongs and life-sized alien sculptures.

Conscious Dreams (☎ 626 69 07; Kerkstraat 117; 🕐 11am-7pm Mon-Wed, to 8pm Thu-Sat, 2-6pm Sun) Magic mushrooms and other natural products.

Magic Mushroom Gallery (☎ 427 57 65; Spuistraat 249; 🕐 11am-10pm Sun-Thu, 10am-10pm Fri & Sat) Fresh and dried mushrooms, growing kits, herbal ecstasy, smart drinks.

Pollinator (☎ 470 88 89; Nieuwe Herengracht 25; 🕐 11am-7pm Mon-Sat) Potent psychoactive plants and a huge range of hemp products.

Speciality
Condomerie Het Gulden Vlies (☎ 627 41 74; www.condomerie.nl; Warmoesstraat 141) Hundreds of novelty condoms, lubricants and saucy gifts.

Santa Jet (☎ 427 20 70; Prinsenstraat 7) Mexican shrines, religious icons, lanterns, candles, love potions.

Souvenirs
De Klompenboer (☎ 623 06 32; Sint Antoniesbreestraat 51) Hand-painted wooden shoes and a tiny clog museum.

Heinen (☎ 627 82 99; Prinsengracht 440) Four floors of Delftware; all major factories represented.

GETTING THERE & AWAY
Air
Most major airlines fly directly to **Schiphol** (☎ 0900-0141; www.schiphol.nl), 18km southwest of the city centre. Luggage may be deposited at the **left-luggage office** (☎ 601 24 43). For information about getting to and from the Netherlands, including Amsterdam airline offices, see p850.

Boat
Fast Flying Ferries (☎ 639 22 47; adult/child return €7.45/4.35) runs a hydrofoil (25 minutes) from Pier 7 behind Amsterdam Centraal Station to Velsen, 3km short of IJmuiden, where you can catch Connexxion bus No 82 or 83 into IJmuiden. For travellers to the UK and beyond, Scandinavian Seaways sails from IJmuiden to Newcastle.

Bus
For details of regional buses, call the **transport information service** (☎ 0900-9292, per min €0.50).

Eurolines (☎ 560 87 87; www.eurolines.nl; Rokin 10) tickets can be bought at this office, at most travel agencies and at the NS Reisburo in Centraal Station. For further details on coach services, see p850.

Car & Motorcycle

Motorways link Amsterdam to Den Haag and Rotterdam in the south, and to Utrecht and Amersfoort in the southeast. Amsterdam is about 480km from Paris, 840km from Munich, 680km from Berlin and 730km from Copenhagen. The Hoek van Holland ferry port is 80km away; IJmuiden is just up the road along the Noordzeekanaal.

The Dutch automobile association, **ANWB** (☎ 673 08 44; Museumplein 5), provides information and services if you prove membership of your own association.

Train

Amsterdam's main train station is called Centraal Station (CS). See p850 for general information about international trains. The **NS international office** (Centraal Station; www.ns.nl; ☺ 6.30am-10.30pm) has information on international train information and reservations.

GETTING AROUND
To/From the Airport

A taxi into Amsterdam from Schiphol airport takes 20 to 45 minutes and costs about €40. Trains to Centraal Station leave every 15 minutes, take 15 to 20 minutes, and cost €3.10/5.50 per single/return.

Bicycle

Amsterdam is cycling nirvana: flat, beautiful, with dedicated bike paths. About 80,000 bicycles are stolen each year in Amsterdam alone, so always lock up. The Dutch automobile association, **ANWB** (☎ 673 08 44; Museumplein 5), provides cycling maps and information.

BICYCLE RENTAL

These companies require a passport/ID and a credit-card imprint or cash deposit.

Bike City (☎ 626 37 21; www.bikecity.nl; Bloemgracht 68-70; day/week €7.50/40) Inconspicuous bikes.

Damstraat Rent-a-Bike (☎ 625 50 29; www.bikes.nl; Damstraat 20; day/week €7/31)

Holland Rent-a-Bike (☎ 622 32 07; Damrak 247; day/week €6.25/32.50)

MacBike (☎ 624 83 91; www.macbike.nl; Stationsplein 12; day/week €6.50/29.75) Bikes have massive logos; you'll stand out.

Boat
FERRIES

Two free ferries to Amsterdam North leave every six to 10 minutes from the piers directly behind Centraal Station. Cars and motorbikes aren't allowed and the crossing takes only a couple of minutes.

CANAL BOAT, BUS & BIKE

Canal bikes (2-/4-seaters per person per hr €8/7) These paddle-boats can be hired from kiosks at Leidseplein, the corner of Keizersgracht and Leidsestraat, the Anne Frankhuis and the Rijksmuseum.

Canal bus (☎ 623 98 86; day pass adult/child €15/10.50; ☺ 9.50am-8pm) Several circuits between Centraal Station and the Rijksmuseum.

Lovers Museum Boat (☎ 622 21 81; www.lovers.nl, in Dutch; day pass adult/child €14.25/9.50) Stops at the Scheepvaartmuseum, Rembrandthuis, Bloemenmarkt, Leidseplein, Rijksmuseum and Anne Frankhuis.

Car & Motorcycle

Parking is not cheap and there are dire penalties for nonconformists: a wheel clamp and a €69 fine. The best place to park is the **Transferium parking garage** (☎ 400 17 21) at Amsterdam ArenA stadium, which charges €19 per day including two return metro tickets to the city centre.

Public Transport

Amsterdam's comprehensive public transport network is operated by the **GVB** (Amsterdam Transport Authority; ☎ 460 59 59; www.gvb.nl; Stationsplein; ☺ 7am-9pm Mon-Fri, 8am-9pm Sat & Sun); there's an information office in front of Centraal Station.

The best ticketing deal is the *strippenkaart*, a multifare 'strip ticket' valid on all buses, trams and metros (p852). The GVB office also sells a one-week pass valid in all zones for €16. If you board without a ticket, the driver sells one-/two-/three-zone tickets for €1.60/2.40/3.20. Ticketing is based on zones.

Night buses take over shortly after midnight when the trams and regular buses stop running. Drivers sell single tickets for €2.50, or you can stamp three strips off your strip card and pay a €1.50 surcharge (which is marginally more expensive). Day passes are valid on night buses but the surcharge still applies.

Taxi & Watertaxi

Amsterdam taxis are expensive, even over short journeys. Try **Taxicentrale Amsterdam** (☎ 677 77 77).

WielerTaxi (☎ 06-28247550) has covered three-wheelers for a flat €2.50 plus €1 per kilometre

THE NETHERLANDS

per person, or €15 for a half-hour tour with two passengers. Kids get discounts.

AROUND AMSTERDAM
Aalsmeer
The world's biggest **flower auction** (☎ 39 21 85; www.aalsmeer.com; Legmeerdijk 313; adult/child €4/2; ☼ 7.30-11am Mon-Fri) is held here, a few kilometres southwest of Amsterdam. Bidding starts early, so arrive between 7.30am and 9am. Take bus Nos 171 and 172 from Amsterdam Centraal Station (50 minutes).

Alkmaar
This picturesque town, an hour north of Amsterdam by train, stages its famous **cheese market** (Waagplein; ☼ 10am-noon Fri Apr-Sep) in the main square. It dates from the 17th century and is a theatrical sight, incomprehensible to first-timers. Dealers, in officious white smocks, insert a hollow rod to extract cheese samples, sniffing and crumbling for fat and moisture content. After the deals are made, the porters, wearing colourful hats to signify their cheese guild, heft the cheeses on wooden sledges to a large scale.

Arrive early if you want to get more than a fleeting glimpse. There are two trains per hour from Centraal Station (€5.40, 30 minutes) and it's a 15-minute walk at the other end.

THE RANDSTAD

The Randstad (literally 'Rim City') is the Netherlands' most densely populated region, with two-thirds of the country's 16 million people. It stretches from Amsterdam to Rotterdam and also includes Den Haag, Utrecht, Haarlem, Leiden, and Delft.

HAARLEM
☎ 023 / pop 148,000
Haarlem is an attractive, refined town. It's only 15 minutes by train from Amsterdam and, with its reasonably priced accommodation, makes a fine stopover should the capital's hotels be over-run. But, ideally, Haarlem should be thought of as an attraction in its own right, with an intriguing restaurant scene and a 17th-century layout

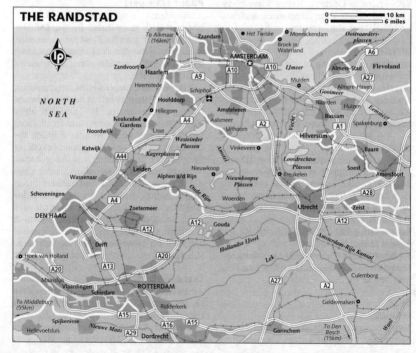

THE RANDSTAD

that's better preserved than many other Randstad cities.

Information

GWK exchange office (train station)
Library (☎ 515 76 00; Doelenplein 1; 🕑 10am-6pm Mon-Fri, noon-5pm Sat) Free Internet.
Main post office (Gedempte Oude Gracht 2)
Tourist office (☎ 0900-616 16 00; www.vvvzk.nl; Stationsplein 1; 🕑 9.30am-5.30pm Mon-Fri, 10am-2pm Sat)

Sights

Kept in an almshouse where Frans Hals spent his final, impoverished years, the superb collection at the **Frans Hals Museum** (☎ 511 57 75; www.franshalsmuseum.nl; Groot Heiligland 62; adult/child €5.40/free; 🕑 11am-5pm Mon-Sat, noon-5pm Sun) features his two paintings known collectively as the *Regents & the Regentesses of the Old Men's Alms House* (1664). Among other treasures are ceiling-high illustrations of the human anatomy with Biblical and mythological allusions.

Teylers Museum (☎ 531 90 10; www.teylersmuseum .nl; Spaarne 16; adult/child €5.50/1; 🕑 10am-5pm Tue-Sat, noon-5pm Sun) is the oldest museum in the country (1778), with an array of kooky inventions, like the 18th-century electrostatic machine that ran on batteries the size of a milk wagon. The museum also has works by Michelangelo and Raphael.

Grote Kerk (☎ 553 20 40; www.grotekerk.nl; Oude Groenmarkt 23; adult/child €1.50/1; 🕑 10am-4pm Mon-Sat) is a Gothic cathedral with a 50m-high steeple that can be seen from almost anywhere in Haarlem. It has a striking Müller organ, 30m high with around 5000 pipes.

Sleeping

Haarlem Stayokay (☎ 537 37 93; www.stayokay.com /haarlem; Jan Gijzenpad 3; d incl breakfast €21-24; 🖳) On the edge of the Noorder sports park, with a waterside terrace, this is Haarlem's version of the nationwide Stayokay hostel brand. The hostel hires out bicycles, canoes and scooters. Take bus No 2 (direction Haarlem Noord) from the train station (10 minutes).

Hotel Carillon (☎ 531 05 91; www.hotelcarillon .com; Grote Markt 27; s €55, with shared bathroom €33, d €76) The single beds may be the thinnest in the Netherlands, but the atmosphere is fine, friendly and fun, with a bar/sidewalk café downstairs, and your grand neighbour, the Grote Kerk, next door. All prices include breakfast.

Hotel Amadeus (☎ 532 45 30; www.amadeus-hotel .com; Grote Markt 10; s/d incl breakfast €57.50/80; 🖳) The Amadeus, snug in a prime location (nestled among a row of old gabled houses on the main square), has an exceedingly comfortable buffet area, tuliped windows, helpful staff and cheap Internet access.

Eating

Eko Eetkafé (☎ 532 65 66; Ziljstraat 39; mains €7-15.50; 🕑 lunch & dinner) This organic restaurant attracts a diverse crowd: singletons, suits, grannies, groovers. The menu is also eclectic (and tasty): fried trout, yakitori, Singapore noodles and more.

Pieck Jacobus (☎ 532 61 44; Warmoesstraat 18; mains €12-17; 🕑 lunch & dinner, Mon-Sat) A chic, intimate little *eetcafé* down a gorgeous side street. There's a superb lunchtime sandwich menu and appealing mains like kebab sausages.

Getting There & Away

Haarlem is served by frequent trains on the Amsterdam–Rotterdam line, including Alkmaar (€5.20, 30 minutes), Amsterdam (€3.10, 15 minutes), Den Haag (€6.40, 35 minutes) and Rotterdam (€9.00, 55 minutes).

KEUKENHOF GARDENS

Near the town of Lisse, between Haarlem and Leiden, you'll find the **Keukenhof gardens** (www.keukenhof.nl; adult/child under 11 €12/5.50; 🕑 8am-7.30pm late-Mar–May, cashier to 6pm), where a beautiful enigma unfurls for just two months each year: the blooming of millions of multicoloured tulip, daffodil and hyacinth bulbs.

Netherlands Railways sells a ticket (€15.50) that combines entrance to the gardens and travel by express bus from Leiden CS (20 minutes).

Bus No 54 travels from Leiden through Lisse to Keukenhof. Bus No 50 travels from Haarlem to Lisse, from where you can meet No 54.

LEIDEN

☎ 071 / pop 118,000

Leiden, Rembrandt's birthplace, is home to the Netherlands' oldest university – and 20,000 students. The university was a gift from Willem de Silent for withstanding two Spanish sieges in 1574. The Spanish must have legged it in a hurry because (so the story goes) they abandoned a kettle of *hutspot* (hotchpotch) – a Dutch culinary mainstay

THE NETHERLANDS

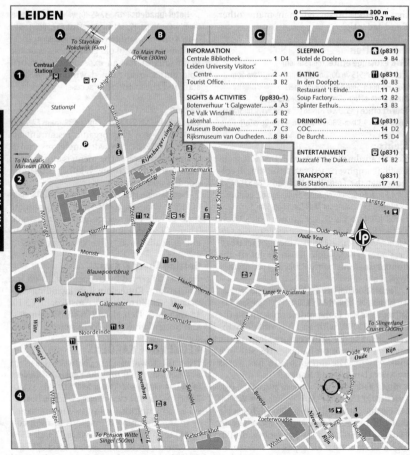

LEIDEN

INFORMATION		SLEEPING	🛏 (p831)
Centrale Bibliotheek................1 D4		Hotel de Doelen.................9 B4	
Leiden University Visitors'			
Centre..................2 A1		EATING	🍴 (p831)
Tourist Office.................3 B2		In den Doofpot.................10 B3	
		Restaurant 't Einde.................11 A3	
SIGHTS & ACTIVITIES (pp830–1)		Soup Factory.................12 B2	
Botenverhuur 't Galgewater......4 A3		Splinter Eethuis.................13 B3	
De Valk Windmill.................5 B2			
Lakenhal.................6 B2		DRINKING	🍷 (p831)
Museum Boerhaave.................7 C3		COC.................14 D2	
Rijksmuseum van Oudheden.....8 B4		De Burcht.................15 D4	
		ENTERTAINMENT	🎭 (p831)
		Jazzcafé The Duke.................16 B2	
		TRANSPORT	(p831)
		Bus Station.................17 A1	

ever since. The university culture gives Leiden a refreshing, vibrant bounce; there's loads of energy in the air. Look for the literary quotes painted on the walls, in everything from Russian to Hebrew to Spanish.

Information

Central post office (☎ 514 17 88; Breestraat 46; 🕘 9am-6pm Mon-Fri, 10am-1.30pm Sat)
Centrale Bibliotheek (Central Library; ☎ 514 99 43; Nieuwstraat 4; Internet per hr €2; 🕘 11am-5pm Oct-Apr, closed Sun Jun-Sep)
Doctor (☎ 0900-7763337) After-hours and public holidays.
GWK money exchange (🕘 7am-9pm) In the train station.
Leiden University Visitors' Centre (☎ 527 88 80; www.visitors.leidenuniv.nl; Stationsplein 3C) General tourist information.

Police (☎ 525 88 88)
Tourist office (☎ 0900-2222333; www.leidenpromotie .nl; Stationsweg 2D; 🕘 11am-5.30pm Mon, 9.30am-5.30pm Tue-Fri, 10am-4.30pm Sat)

Sights & Activities

The 17th-century **Lakenhal** (Cloth Hall; ☎ 516 53 60; www.lakenhal.nl, in Dutch; Oude Singel 28-32; adult/child €2/1; 🕘 10am-5pm Tue-Fri, noon-5pm Sat & Sun) houses the Municipal Museum, with an assortment of works by old Masters – including a smattering of Rembrandt – as well as period rooms and temporary exhibits.

The **Rijksmuseum van Oudheden** (National Museum of Antiquities; ☎ 516 31 63; www.rmo.nl; Rapenburg 28; adult/child under 18 €6/5.50; 🕘 10am-5pm Tue-Fri, noon-5pm Sat & Sun) has a classy collection of hieroglyphs – and 94 human and animal mummies. The entrance hall contains the actual Temple of Taffeh, a gift from Egypt for Dutch help in saving ancient monuments when the Aswan High Dam was built.

Leiden's trademark windmill, **De Valk** (Falcon; ☎ 516 53 53; http://home.wanadoo.nl/molenmuseum; 2e Binnenvestgracht 1; adult/child €2.50/1.50; ⏰ 10am-5pm Tue-Sat, 1-5pm Sun), has been carefully restored; its construction and operation highlight the wonders of pre-industrial engineering. There are many presentations, including one that laments the fact that local boy Rembrandt, as a miller's son, didn't paint many windmills. The upper levels afford an inspired view of the old town.

Leiden University was an early centre for Dutch medical research, and the **Museum Boerhaave** (National Museum of the History of Science and Medicine; ☎ 521 42 24; www.museumboerhaave.nl; Lange St Agnietenstraat 10; adult/under 18 & over 65/child under 5 €5/2.50/free; ⏰ 10am-5pm Tue-Sat, noon-5pm Sun) gathers together five centuries of pickled organs, surgical tools and skeletons in its Anatomy Theatre (it's morbid, but just try to look away).

Rent a canoe or kayak from **Botenverhuur 't Galgewater** (☎ 514 97 90; per hr €3.50; ⏰ 11am-6pm Oct-May, 11am-10pm Jun-Sep) and explore the canals.

Sleeping

Stayokay Noordwijk (☎ 0252-37 29 20; www.stayokay .com/noordwijk; Langevelderlaan 45; dm from €22) The hostel is 45 minutes away, next to a popular beach. Take bus No 57 or 90 (last bus at 11pm) to Sancta Maria hospital and walk for 10 minutes.

Pension Witte Singel (☎ 512 45 92; www.pension -ws.demon.nl; Witte Singel 80; s/d incl breakfast €36/66) Warm and welcoming, the Witte Singel has fresh, spacious rooms with large windows overlooking most agreeable scenery: the perfectly peaceful Singel canal in front and a typically Dutch garden at the back. Outstanding value.

Hotel de Doelen (☎ 512 05 27; www.dedoelen.com; Rapenburg 2; s/d/extra bed €70/90/15) Some of the canalside rooms border on palatial opulence, and even the more basic rooms have bath, phone and TV.

Eating

Soup Factory (cnr Steenstraat & Narmstraat; small/large soups €3/3.90; ⏰ noon-10pm) This small corner shop is unfussy in its décor, instead reserving its creative energy for healthy, delicious soups in imaginative variations, like Tandoori chicken.

Splinter Eethuis (☎ 514 95 19; Noordeinde 30; two-course meals €9.95-13.25; ⏰ Thu-Sun) A popular student haunt, with generous two-course meals featuring rotating ethnic cuisines. Good vegetarian options.

In den Doofpot (☎ 512 24 34; www.indendoofpot .nl, in Dutch; Turfmarkt 9; mains €10.50-43.50; ⏰ dinner) The interior is regal and airy, a sensuous setting for the menu's filling, French-tinged twists on Dutch cooking.

Restaurant 't Einde (☎ 512 21 15; Rembrandtstraat 2; mains from €15; ⏰ dinner Tue-Sun) Small and sophisticated, with an excellent menu: exquisite meat, fish, poultry and seafood variations.

Drinking

De Burcht (☎ 514 23 89; www.deburchtleiden.nl, in Dutch; Burgsteeg 14) This bar/café is in a picturesque spot, next to the Burcht fortification. It's popular with arty subcults, and has live music some nights.

COC (☎ 522 06 40; Langegracht 65) Run by the national gay and lesbian organisation, this bar is a focal point of the local scene.

Entertainment

Jazzcafé The Duke (☎ 566 15 85; www.jazzcaféthe duke.nl, in Dutch; Oude Singel 2) No windows, but loads of yellowing, vintage jazz posters on the walls. Their motto is, 'If we don't have it, you don't need it'. It's true: you don't need windows to enjoy this atmospheric den, with its fine live jazz every night, and suitably appreciative crowds.

Getting There & Away

Train service is frequent in all directions, including Amsterdam (€5.80, 34 minutes) and Den Haag (€2.80, 10 minutes). Regional and local buses leave from the bus station directly in front of Centraal Station.

DEN HAAG (THE HAGUE)

☎ 070 / pop 464,000

Officially known as 's-Gravenhage ('the Count's Domain'), Den Haag is the Dutch seat of government and residence of the royal family; the stately mansions and palatial embassies lining its green boulevards are suitably regal. Den Haag has a reputable culinary scene and a clutch of tasty museums, and

> **WHO GOES THERE?**
>
> During WWII, Dutch resistance fighters used 'Scheveningen' as a password. While the Germans could easily mimic Dutch, they couldn't learn the proper accent to pronounce Scheveningen. Give it a go: say *s'CHay-fuh-ninger*.

plays host to the world's biggest jazz festival, the North Sea Jazz Festival, held annually near the seaside suburb of Scheveningen (itself worth a visit for its lively kitsch).

Information

Connexion Plazza (cnr Stationsweg & Stationsplein) Internet access.

GWK money exchange (Centraal Station; ☻ 7am-9pm Mon-Sat, 8am-9pm Sun)

General medical information (☎ 0900-8600, after hours ☎ 346 96 69)

Police (☎ 310 49 11)

Post office (☎ 365 38 43; Kerkplein 6; ☻ 9am-6pm Mon-Wed & Fri, to 8pm Thu, to 4pm Sat)

Tourist office (☎ 0900-3403505; www.denhaag.com; Koningin Julianaplein 30; ☻ 8.30am-5.30pm Mon-Sat year-round, 10am-2pm Sun Jul & Aug)

Sights & Activities

The **Mauritshuis** (☎ 302 34 56; www.mauritshuis.nl; Korte Vijverberg 8; adult/under 18 €7.50/free; ☻ 10am-5pm Tue-Sat, 11am-5pm Sun) is a small but grand museum, housing Dutch and Flemish works (and Andy Warhol's *Queen Beatrix*). Highlights include Vermeer's *Girl with a Pearl Earring* (the painting that inspired the recent film) and Rembrandt self-portraits at ages 20 and 63.

The Lange Voorhout Palace was once Queen Emma's residence. Now it's home to the work of Dutch graphic artist MC Escher. **Escher in Het Paleis Museum** (☎ 338 11 20; Lange Voorhout; www.escherinhetpaleis.nl; adult/child €7.50/5; ☻ 11am-5pm Tue-Sun) is a permanent exhibition featuring notes, letters, drafts, photos and fully mature works covering Escher's entire career, from his early realism to the later phantasmagoria. There are some imaginative displays, including a virtual reality reconstruction of Escher's impossible buildings and 4D spatial dynamics.

The **Gemeentemuseum** (Municipal Museum; ☎ 338 11 20; www.gemeentemuseum.nl; Stadhouderslaan 41; adult/under 18 yrs €7.50/free; ☻ 11am-5pm Tue-Sat) has an extensive collection of works by Piet Mondrian and the De Stijl movement, as well as exhibits of applied arts, costumes and musical instruments, works from Picasso and a fabulous Photography Museum.

The **Panorama Mesdag** (☎ 364 45 44; www.panorama-mesdag.nl; Zeestraat 65; adult/child €4/2; ☻ Mon-Sat 10am-5pm, Sun & hols noon-5pm) contains the *Panorama* (1881), a gigantic 360-degree painting of Scheveningen, painted by Hendrik Willem Mesdag. It's another kind of virtual reality: the panorama is viewed from a constructed dune, with real sand and beach chairs, and birdsong and wave sounds piped through. Mesdag's command of perspective and minute detail was masterly: it's a fully immersive experience.

More virtual reality? **Madurodam** (☎ 355 39 00; www.madurodam.nl; George Maduroplein 1; adult/child under 11 yrs €12/8.75; ☻ 9am-8pm) is a miniaturised Netherlands, complete with 1:25 scale versions of Schiphol, Amsterdam, windmills and tulips, Rotterdam harbour, the Delta dikes, and so on. It's yet another enlightening example of the Dutch tendency to put their world under a microscope (see p814).

The long beach at **Scheveningen** (www.scheveningen.nl) attracts nine million visitors per year. Crowds can get up close and personal when the weather gets warm and the shopping strip gets crassly commercial, but the attraction of sea and sand keeps the peace, with a palpable frisson of frivolity sweetenening the air.

Sleeping

Stayokay Den Haag (☎ 315 78 88; www.stayokay.com/denhaag; Scheepmakerstraat 27; dm from €22.85) This branch of the Stayokay hostel chain has all the usual facilities including a bar, a restaurant, Internet and games. It's around 15 minutes' walk from Hollands Spoor station.

Strandhotel (☎ 354 01 93; www.strandhotel.demon.nl; Zeekant 111 & Gevers Deynootweg 1344 Scheveningen; s/d €37.50/62.50; Ⓟ ⊠ ⊠) It's on the beach, and the rooms have an unreconstructed 1950s motif. Book ahead and keep an eye on the weather – prices soar in summer.

Hotel Astoria (☎ 384 04 01; Stationsweg 139; s/d €35.50/56.70) The rooms are small and a touch bleak (although they do have private facilities, which sweetens the deal), but it's one of Den Haag's few budget options.

Paleis Hotel (☎ 362 46 21; www.paleishotel.nl; Molenstraat 26; s/d €125/165; Ⓟ ⊠) It has an austere style, a fine, central location near Noord-

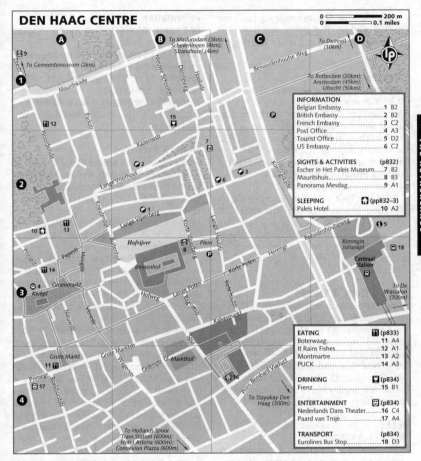

DEN HAAG CENTRE

0 -------- 200 m
0 -------- 0.1 miles

To Gemeentemuseum (2km)

To Madurodam (3km);
Scheveningen (4km);
Strandhotel (4km)

To Duinrell
(10km)

To Rotterdam (20km);
Amsterdam (45km);
Utrecht (50km)

To De
Wassalon
(700m)

To Stayokay Den
Haag (300m)

To Hollands Spoor
Train Station (600m);
Hotel Astoria (600m);
Connexion Plaza (600m)

INFORMATION

Belgian Embassy	1 B2
British Embassy	2 B2
French Embassy	3 C2
Post Office	4 A3
Tourist Office	5 D2
US Embassy	6 C2

SIGHTS & ACTIVITIES (p832)

Escher in Het Paleis Museum	7 B2
Mauritshuis	8 B3
Panorama Mesdag	9 A1

SLEEPING (pp832–3)

Paleis Hotel	10 A2

EATING (p833)

Boterwaag	11 A4
It Rains Fishes	12 A1
Montmartre	13 A2
PUCK	14 A3

DRINKING (p834)

Frenz	15 B1

ENTERTAINMENT (p834)

Nederlands Dans Theater	16 C4
Paard van Troje	17 A4

TRANSPORT (p834)

Eurolines Bus Stop	18 D3

THE NETHERLANDS

einde, and a solarium. The rooms are well equipped and comfortable.

Eating & Drinking

Montmartre (☎ 365 64 54; Molenstraat 4C; snacks €4.30-12.50; ☽ lunch) This brasserie has décor that's a little bit lacy and a lunch menu that's very French: understated, yet refined, with lavish attention to detail. The baguettes are seriously pleasing, with all kinds of cheeses and extras like marinated eggplant.

PUCK (Pure Unique Californian Kitchen; ☎ 427 76 49; www.puckfoodandwines.nl; Prinsestraat 33; mains €17.50-23.50; ☽ lunch & dinner Tue-Sat) The restaurant's vibrant paint job is apparently a tribute to the owner's daughter's love of M&Ms, and that refreshing lack of attitude and formality

carries over to the fusion menu. A case in point: pan-sauteed duck breast over oven-roasted rosenval fries, with napa cabbage and maple syrup.

It Rains Fishes (☎ 365 25 98; www.itrainsfishes.nl, in Dutch; Noordeinde 123; mains €18.50-24; ☽ lunch & dinner) It's the 'restaurant on the sunny side of the street', a multi-award-winning seafood concern serving grilled, fried and poached fish, mussels and scallops.

Boterwaag (☎ 365 96 86; www.september.nl, in Dutch; Grote Markt 8a; ☽ lunch & dinner) This cavernous old weighhouse serves as a café/restaurant and provides a distinctive drinking and eating experience, with its high ceilings, large windows, candle fetish, nooks and crannies to hide out in, and great beer list.

Frenz (☎ 363 66 57; Kazernestraat 106) Look for the big rainbow flag flying out the front of this friendly gay bar that's open until late.

Entertainment

Nederlands Dans Theater (☎ 360 49 30, reservations ☎ 360 38 73; www.ndt.nl; Schedeldoekshaven 60; ☺ box office 10am-6pm) This dance company has gained worldwide fame since its inception in 1959. There are three companies: NDT1, the main troupe of 32 dancers; NDT2, a small group of 12 dancers under 21; and NDT3, a group of dancers over age 40 who perform more dramatic works.

Paard van Troje (☎ 360 18 38; Prinsegracht 12) This recently renovated emporium has club nights and live music, as well as a café. Recent musical guests include Dutch art-pop legends The Nits, the English-but-aptly-named Jools Holland, and a posse of cool industrial-funk DJs.

Getting There & Around

Some sample train services, good for Den Haag's Centraal and Hollands Spoor stations, are Amsterdam (€8.50, 50 minutes), Leiden (€2.50, 13 minutes), Rotterdam (€3.50, 22 minutes) and Utrecht (€8.50, 40 minutes). Tram Nos 1, 8 and 9 link Scheveningen with Den Haag; the fare is three strips. The last tram at night runs in either direction at about 1.30am.

DELFT

☎ 015 / pop 96,000

Delft, founded around 1100, is compact and charming – a very popular tourist destination. With its narrow, canal-lined streets and remarkable old buildings, it's a gentle and relaxed stopover (except when the crowds are at their peak).

The town is famous for its 'delftware', the distinctive blue-and-white pottery originally duplicated from Chinese porcelain by 17th-century artisans (in a strange twist of fate, some of it is now mass-produced in China).

Delft was also the home of Golden Age painter Jan Vermeer. *View of Delft* is the title of one of Vermeer's best-loved works, an enigmatic, nonrealist vision of the town; *A Clear View from Delft* is the title of a recent Vermeer biography, attempting to sort through the enigma of Vermeer's life.

Information

GWK money exchange (☺ 8am-7pm Mon-Fri, to 6pm Sat & Sun) At the station.

Library (☎ 212 34 50; Kruisstraat 71; Internet per hr €2; ☺ 10am-7pm Mon-Fri, to 3pm Sat)

Post office (☎ 212 45 11; Hippolytusbuurt 14; ☺ 9am-5pm Mon-Fri, 10am-1.30pm Sat)

Tourist office (☎ 0900-515 15 55; www.delft.nl; Hippolytusbuurt 4; ☺ 11am-4pm Mon, 10am-4pm Tue-Sat, 10am-3pm Sun)

Sights & Activities

The 14th-century **Nieuwe Kerk** (☎ 212 30 25; www.nieuwekerk-delft.nl; Markt; admission €2.50; ☺ 9am-6pm Apr-Nov, 11am-4pm Nov-Apr, closed Sun) houses the crypt of the Dutch royal family and the mausoleum of Willem the Silent. There are exhibitions about the House of Orange and the church, and the fee includes entrance to the Oude Kerk (and vice versa).

The Gothic **Oude Kerk** (☎ 212 30 15; www.oudekerk-delft.nl; Heilige Geestkerkhof; admission €2.50; ☺ 9am-6pm Apr-Oct, 11am-4pm Nov-Mar, closed Sun) is 800 years old, and is quite a surreal sight: its tower leans 2m from the vertical. Among the tombs inside is Vermeer's.

Municipal Museum Het Prinsenhof (☎ 260 23 58; www.prinsenhof-delft.nl, in Dutch; St Agathaplein 1; adult/child €5/free; ☺ 10am-5pm Tue-Sat, 1-5pm Sun) is a former convent, where Willem the Silent was assassinated in 1584 (the bullet hole in the wall is covered in Perspex to protect against inquisitive visitors). The museum displays various objects telling the story of the 80-year war with Spain, as well as a selection of 17th-century paintings.

The **Museum Nusantara** (☎ 260 23 58; www.nusantara-delft.nl, in Dutch; St Agathaplein 4; adult/child €3.50/3; ☺ 10am-5pm Tue-Sat, 1-5pm Sun) is worth a look for the light it sheds on the Netherlands' colonial past. There's a collection of furniture and other lifestyle artefacts from 17th-century Batavia (now Jakarta), as well as a 'colonial department', detailing the beginnings of Dutch rule in the region.

Delftware manufacturer **Aardewerkatelier de Candelaer** (☎ 213 18 48; Kerkstraat 14; ☺ 9am-5pm Mon-Sat Nov-Feb, to 6pm Mon-Sat, 9am-5pm Sun Mar-Oct) allows you to peer behind the veil of artistry: it has five practitioners who often work in full view of customers, and the staff sometimes arrange tours on request.

See Delft on a **canal boat tour** (☎ 212 63 85; adult/child €4.50/2.50; ☺ 9.30am-6pm mid-Mar–Oct), departing from Koornmarkt 113.

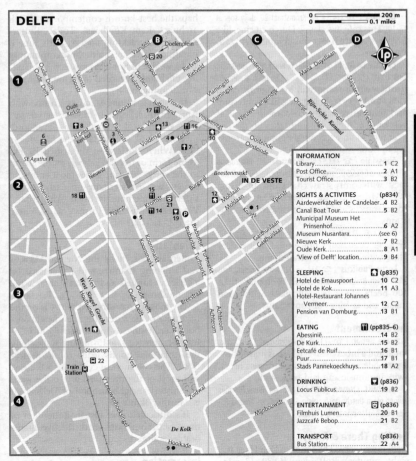

DELFT

0	200 m
0	0.1 miles

INFORMATION
Library	1 C2
Post Office	2 A1
Tourist Office	3 B2

SIGHTS & ACTIVITIES (p834)
Aardewerkatelier de Candelaer	4 B2
Canal Boat Tour	5 B2
Municipal Museum Het Prinsenhof	6 A2
Museum Nusantara	(see 6)
Nieuwe Kerk	7 B2
Oude Kerk	8 A1
'View of Delft' location	9 B4

SLEEPING (p835)
Hotel de Emauspoort	10 C2
Hotel de Kok	11 A3
Hotel-Restaurant Johannes Vermeer	12 C2
Pension van Domburg	13 B1

EATING (pp835–6)
Abessinië	14 B2
De Kurk	15 B2
Eetcafé de Ruif	16 B1
Puur	17 B1
Stads Pannekoeckhuys	18 A2

DRINKING (p836)
Locus Publicus	19 B2

ENTERTAINMENT (p836)
Filmhuis Lumen	20 B1
Jazzcafé Bebop	21 B2

TRANSPORT (p836)
Bus Station	22 A4

Sleeping

Pension van Domburg (☎ 212 30 29; Voldersgracht 24; s/d without bathroom €35/40) No frills but centrally located.

Hotel de Kok (☎ 212 21 25; www.hoteldekok.nl; Houttuinen 15; s/d incl breakfast from €66/80; P) Managed by an affable family, it has substantial, elegant rooms and an attractive garden terrace.

Hotel De Emauspoort (☎ 219 02 19; www.emauspoort.nl; Vrouwenregt 9-11; s/d €77.50/87.50, s/d caravan incl breakfast €72.50/82.50) Besides the comfy, old-style rooms, you have the option of staying in two attentively restored gypsy caravans at the back. Bonus: the bakery/confectionery store next door provides the big breakfast.

Hotel-Restaurant Johannes Vermeer (☎ 212 64 66; www.hotelvermeer.nl; Molslaan 18; s/d €112/125) This one's an ersatz Vermeer museum: it has immaculate views of old Delft (canals, churches and street scenes on all sides) and rooms decorated with Vermeer prints. The intriguing restaurant features rare kettles hanging from the roof and reproductions of all of Vermeer's known work, including a wall-length *Girl with a Pearl Earring* surrounded by (deliberately) unfinished brickwork.

Eating & Drinking

Stads Pannekoeckhuys (☎ 213 01 93; Oude Delft 113; €3-10; ❂ lunch & dinner) This typical pancake kitchen offers 90 pancake varieties; it also serves the old Dutch favourite, pea soup.

De Kurk (☎ 214 14 74; Kromstraat 20; daily special €8-10) This café has classic Dutch cuisine, like *broodjes*, meaty treats and ubiquitous potato variations.

Eetcafé De Ruif (☎ 214 22 06; www.ruif.nl, in Dutch; Kerkstraat 22; mains €11.80-15.80; ☽ lunch & dinner) Rustic, with a wonderful low ceiling, canal views and very tasty lunches, like lamb soup and innovative sandwich combinations. It gets busy at night, when it takes on the appearance of an exceedingly popular carousing option.

Abessinië (☎ 213 52 60; Kromstraat 21; dish/combo of 4 specials €13/29; ☽ dinner) Ethiopian establishment with comfy straw chairs and appetising West African cuisine: tubers, meats, pulses, spices, sauces and herbs in creative combinations.

Puur (☎ 213 70 15; Vrouw Juttenland 17; mains €17; ☽ dinner, closed Mon) Choice food in a cheery place with a long vegetarian menu.

Locus Publicus (☎ 213 46 32; www.locuspublicus .nl, in Dutch; Brabantse Turfmarkt 67) With more than 200 beers, it's a friendly place with good music and lashings of conviviality.

Entertainment

Jazzcafé Bebop (☎ 213 52 10; Kromstraat 33) Dark, small and a bit exclusive, which is maybe how a jazz café should be. Many different beers, swinging music and laid-back staff.

Filmhuis Lumen (☎ 214 02 26; www.filmhuis -lumen.nl, in Dutch; Doelenplein 5; screenings around €5) Screens alternative films.

Getting There & Away

Delft is well served by trains to Den Haag (€2, eight minutes), Rotterdam (€2.80, 13 minutes) and Amsterdam (€8.50, 50 minutes).

ROTTERDAM

☎ 010 / pop 600,000

Rotterdam, the Netherlands' second-largest city, has a long history as a major shipping hub, stretching back to the 14th century. It's had dark times, too. In 1940 the invading Germans issued an ultimatum to the Dutch: surrender, or Rotterdam (among other cities) would be destroyed. The government capitulated, but the raid was carried out anyway and the historic centre was razed.

Rotterdam spent the following decades rebuilding the harbour and the centre, and the result is an architectural aesthetic that's unique in Europe (the city is home to per-haps the best-known contemporary Dutch architect, Rem Koolhaas). Today, Rotterdam has a crackling energy, with superb nightlife, a diverse, multiethnic community and a wealth of top-class museums, including the highly regarded Museum Boijmans van Beuningen.

It also has a long-standing rivalry with Amsterdam, reflected in most aspects of culture. When local football team, Feyenoord, meets Ajax of Amsterdam, the fur *always* flies. When Rotterdam unleashed its extreme form of techno, gabber, on the world in the early '90s, one of its most enduring targets was Amsterdam: an early gabber single was memorably titled 'Amsterdam, Waar Lech Dat Dan?' ('Amsterdam, Where the F*** is That?').

Orientation

Rotterdam is split by the Nieuwe Maas, a vast shipping channel, and it's crossed by a series of tunnels and bridges, notably the Erasmusbrug.

The mostly reconstructed centre is on the north side of the water. Huge new neighbourhoods are rising to the south. From Centraal Station (CS), a 15-minute walk along the canal-like ponds leads to the waterfront. The commercial centre is to the east and most of the museums are to the west. The historic neighbourhood of Delfshaven is a further 3km west.

It's difficult to get lost in Rotterdam as many of the buildings are distinctive, memorable landmarks.

Information
EMERGENCY
Police (☎ 247 991) For reporting crimes after the event.

INTERNET ACCESS
EasyInternetcafé (www.easyeverything.com/map/rot; Stadhuisplein 16-18; ☽ noon-8pm Mon & Sun, 9.30am-8pm Tue-Thu & Sat, to 9pm Fri, noon-8pm Sun)

MEDICAL SERVICES
Erasmus MC (☎ 463 92 22; Dr Molenwaterplein 40)

MONEY
GWK money exchange (☽ 7am-9pm) In CS.

POST
Post office (☎ 233 02 55; Coolsingel 42; ☽ 9am-6pm Mon-Wed & Fri, to 8.30pm Thu, 9.30am-3pm Sat)

THE NETHERLANDS

TOURIST INFORMATION
Tourist office (☎ 0900-4034065; www.rotterdam.nl; Coolsingel 67; ☺ 9am-6pm Mon-Fri, to 5pm Sat & Sun)
Use-It (☎ 240 91 58; www.use-it.nl; Conradstraat 2; ☺ 9am-6pm Tue-Sun mid-May–mid-Sep, to 5pm Tue-Sat mid-Sep–mid-May) Aimed at young travellers.

Sights & Activities
MUSEUMS
Museum Boijmans van Beuningen (☎ 441 94 00; Museumpark 18-20; adult/child under 18 yrs €7/free; ☺ 10am-5pm Tue-Sat, 11am-5pm Sun & hols) is probably the finest museum in the country (some say Europe). Its permanent collection takes in Dutch and European art (Bosch, Van Eyck, Rembrandt, Tintoretto and Titian, etc), and there's an utterly absorbing Surrealist wing, featuring ephemera, paraphernalia and famous works from Duchamp, Magritte, Man Ray and more. Salvador Dali has a dedicated room, among the largest collections of his work outside Spain and France.

The museum has what it terms a 'Data Cloud', a holographic map allowing visitors to find the location of any item in the 120,000-piece collection.

The **Historisch Museum Het Schielandhuis** (☎ 217 67 67; Korte Hoogstraat 31; adult/child €3/1.50; ☺ 10am-5pm Tue-Sat, 11am-5pm Sun & hols) is in one of the city's few surviving 17th-century buildings. Its exhibits focus on everyday life through the ages, such as the (purportedly) oldest surviving wooden shoe.

The **Wereldmuseum** (World Museum; ☎ 270 71 72; www.wereldmuseum.rotterdam.nl; Willemskade 25; adult/child €6/3; ☺ 10am-5pm Tue-Sat) aims to provide a cross-cultural experience, with contemporary and historical exhibits from all over the globe, including photographs, books and maps.

Kunsthal (☎ 440 03 00; www.kunsthal.nl; Westzeedijk 341; adult/under 18 €7.50/free; ☺ 10am-5pm Tue-Sat, 11am-5pm Sun & hols) hosts around 20 temporary exhibitions (including art and design) each year.

EUROMAST
The 185m-high **Euromast** (☎ 436 48 11; www.euromast.com; Parkhaven 20; adult/child €7.75/5; ☺ 9.30am-11pm Apr-Sep, 10am-11pm Oct-Mar) offers unparalleled 360-degree views of Rotterdam, with its rotating, glass-walled 'Euroscope' contraption ascending to near the summit (scored to the tune of Bowie's 'Space Oddity').

From there, it's possible to fully appreciate just how mighty the harbour is.

There's also a luxury accommodation suite near the top, and the Panorama restaurant (see p838).

ARCHITECTURE
You won't fail to notice Rotterdam's highest building (152m), right next to Centraal Station: the **Nationale Nederlanden** skyscraper, designed by Abe Bonnema, has two glass-encased office wings that reflect each other and the sky, seemingly disappearing into each other and the elements.

The 800m-long **Erasmusbrug** (1996), with its spread-eagled struts, was designed by Ben van Berkel; nicknamed 'The Swan', it's near the Leuvehaven metro station.

To the south of there is **KPN Telecom headquarters** (2000), designed by Renzo Piano (who also designed Paris's Pompidou Centre). The building leans to a sharp angle and rests on a long pole.

Near Blaak metro station is the **Overblaak development** (1978–84), designed by Piet Blom. This postmodern extravaganza – marked by its pencil-shaped tower and up-ended, cube-shaped apartments – seems to be plucked straight from the novels of JG Ballard. One apartment, the **Show Cube** (☎ 414 22 85; www.cubehouse.nl; adult/child under 12 yrs €1.80/1.35; ☺ 11am-5pm, closed Mon-Thu Jan & Feb), is open to the public.

Learn more at the **Nederlands Architectuur Instituut** (☎ 440 12 00; www.nai.nl; Museumpark 25; ☺ 10am-5pm Tue-Sat, 11am-5pm Sun & hols).

DELFSHAVEN
Delfshaven was once the official seaport for the city of Delft. A reconstructed 18th-century **windmill** overlooks the water at Voorhaven 210, while the **Oude Kerk** on Voorhaven is where the Pilgrim Fathers prayed for the last time before leaving the city on 22 July 1620.

HARBOUR
Spido (☎ 275 99 88; www.spido.nl; Willemsplein 85; adult/child €8.20/5.10; ☺ 9.30am-5pm Jun-Sep, 11am-3.30pm Oct, to 2pm Thu-Sun Nov-Mar) offers daily harbour tours.

Sleeping
The tourist office makes reservations for a small fee, as does **Use-It** (see earlier).

Stayokay Rotterdam (☎ 436 57 63; www.stayokay .com/rotterdam; Rochussenstraat 107-109; dm from €20.25; ☻ reception until 1am; ▯) Well placed for the museums, with a low-key bar.

Hotel Boat De Clipper (☎ 331 42 44; Scheepmaker-shaven; bed & breakfast €22.50) This 'botel', docked in Rotterdam's old harbour, is perfect for soaking up the city's maritime atmosphere, even if the quarters are, inevitably, a little cramped.

Hotel Amar (☎ 425 57 95; www.amarhotel.nl; Ma-thenesserlaan 316; s/d €30/50) This friendly, small place is in a leafy neighbourhood close to the Museumplein and to good shopping and nightlife. The rooms are simple but comfy, and guests can use bikes for free. All rooms have TV.

Hotel Bazar (☎ 206 51 51; www.hotelbazar.nl; Witte de Withstraat 16; s/d/tr incl breakfast €60/75/120) The Bazar is deservedly popular for its Middle Eastern–themed rooms: lush, brocaded curtains, exotically tiled bathrooms, comfy beds, and copies of *Tales from the Arabian Nights* scattered about. Breakfast is spectacular, too: Turkish breads, international cheeses, yogurt, fruit, cold cuts and coffee. An exceptional place to wind down, particularly as its ground-floor bar and restaurant (below) is among the town's best.

Hotel New York (☎ 439 05 00; www.hotelnewyork .nl; Koninginnenhoofd 1; r €93-220) The city's favourite hotel is housed in the former headquarters of the Holland-America passenger ship line, and has excellent service and facilities. Often booked far in advance, it's noted for its views, café and boat shuttle taking guests across the Nieuwe Maas to the centre. The Art Nouveau rooms – with many original and painstakingly restored décor items and fittings – are divine.

Eating & Drinking

Café Gallery Abrikoos (☎ 477 41 40; www.abrikoos .com, in Dutch; Aelbrechtskolk 51; tapas from €4.50; ☻ lunch & dinner Tue-Sun) This bright, cheery tapas place has a variety of soups, salads, mains and Mediterranean mini-meals.

Bazar (☎ 206 51 51; www.hotelbazar.nl; Witte de Withstraat 16; mains €8-13.90) On the ground floor of the inventive Hotel Bazar (above), this eatery also comes up trumps, with similarly stylised Middle Eastern décor and matching menu: dolmades, falafel, mussels, sardines, couscous and kebabs served up in tangy, attention-grabbing combinations.

Panorama (☎ 436 48 11; www.euromast.nl; Euro-mast, Parkhaven 20; mains €9.50-19; ☻ lunch & dinner) This brasserie has the best location, in the midsection of the Euromast tower. At 100m it almost doesn't matter about the food, with that kind of view and a design to maximise it (the angled windows impart the odd sensation of eating in mid-air). It's a bonus, then, that the menu is good: Thai salad, croquets, soups, casseroles, pasta dishes.

Rotown (☎ 436 26 69; www.rotown.nl, in Dutch; Nieuwe Binnenweg 19; mains €10-13.50) Part of the Rotown bar/live music venue, the restaurant is in a rustic, wood-panelled extension. The menu alternates between hearty (red apple steak) and arty (herbal green tuna), and is delicious at each extreme.

Café Restaurant De Unie (☎ 414 16 66; Maurits-weg 35; mains €12-20; ☻ dinner) The original building on this site, dating from the 1920s and destroyed during WWII, has been faithfully reproduced here – this charming place has a red, yellow and blue facade, and the huge windows open onto the ponds.

Kip (Chicken; ☎ 436 99 23; Van Vollenhovenstraat 25; mains €15-25; ☻ dinner Tue-Sun) An elegant dining establishment with a large fireplace and a broad menu featuring immaculately prepared meat, poultry and vegetable dishes.

Stalles (☎ 436 16 55; Nieuwe Binnenweg 11a) This classic brown café is on a great stretch of road near plenty of good shops, cafés and bars. It has an extensive range of single malt whiskeys and some reasonable food, including pizza and lasagne.

Locus Publicus (☎ 433 17 61; www.locus-publicus. com, in Dutch; Oostzeedijk 364) With more than 200 beers on its menu, it's an outstanding specialist beer café.

Entertainment

Jazzcafé Dizzy (☎ 477 30 14; www.dizzy.nl, in Dutch; 's-Gravendijkwal 129) Live music Tuesday nights and Sunday afternoons. The evening performances are scorching: everything from hot jazz to fast and funky Brazilian and salsa, with a very lively, sweaty crowd jumping out of their skins.

Rotown (☎ 436 26 69; www.rotown.nl, in Dutch; Nieuwe Binnenweg 19) A smooth bar, a dependable live rock venue, an agreeable restaurant (above), a popular meeting place. The musical program features new local talent, established international acts and crossover experiments.

Off-Corso (☎ 411 38 97; www.off-corso.nl, in Dutch; Kruiskade 22) This is pretty much where it's at, with bleeding-edge local and international DJs mashing up a high-fibre diet of techno, house, trance and hip hop.

Desire (Nieuwe Binnenweg 148; ☺ 7am-4am) One of Rotterdam's many coffeeshops.

Luxor Theater (☎ 413 83 26; www.luxortheater .nl; Posthumalaan 1) A major new performance venue (2001), the Luxor features diverse theatrical entertainment.

Getting There & Away
TRAIN
Rotterdam Centraal Station is on the main line from Amsterdam south. Services are frequent to all points on the railway network, including Amsterdam (€11.20, 62 minutes), Den Haag (€3.50, 15 minutes), Middelburg (€7.50, 90 minutes) and Utrecht (€8.10, 40 minutes).

BUS
Rotterdam is a hub for Eurolines bus services to the rest of Europe (p850). The long-distance bus stops are immediately west of CS. The **Eurolines office** (☎ 412 44 44; Conradstraat 20; ☺ 9.30am-5.30pm Mon-Fri, to 3pm Sat) is there as well.

Getting Around
Bus No 33 makes the 15-minute run from the airport to CS every 12 minutes throughout the day. A taxi takes 10 minutes to the centre and costs around €20.

Most of Rotterdam's trams, buses and metro converge in front of CS, where there's an **information office** (☺ 6am-11pm Mon-Fri, 8am-11pm Sat & Sun) that also sells tickets.

For a taxi, call ☎ 462 60 60.

The **bicycle shop** (☎ 412 62 20) at CS is underground off the metro station.

AROUND ROTTERDAM
Kinderdijk
Named a Unesco World Heritage Site in 1997, the **Kinderdijk** (Child's Dyke; www.kinderdijk .nl) features 19 working windmills that date from the 18th century and stretch for 3km. It's a starkly beautiful area, with the windmills rising above the empty marshes and waterways.

There are hollow post mills and rotating cap mills, the latter among the highest in the country (they were designed to better catch the wind), and on Saturdays in July and August from 2pm to 5pm, all 19 windmills are in operation, an unforgettable sight (and unique, in this day and age). One of the mills functions as a **visitors centre** (☎ 078-613 28 00; admission €2.50; ☺ 9.30am-5.30pm Mon-Sat Apr-Sep).

To reach the Kinderdijk, take a local train from Rotterdam CS to Rotterdam Lombardijen station, then catch the hourly bus No 154. By car, take the N210 12km east from Rotterdam. There's a car ferry (€2) across the Lek River to the parking area.

UTRECHT
☎ 030 / pop 256,000
Utrecht has hosted many key moments in Dutch history. In 1579, the Union of Utrecht was signed here, uniting Holland, Zeeland, Utrecht, Gelderland, Overijssel, Groningen and Friesland, and paving the way for the modern Dutch state.

The city grew as a political power, having been a dominant bishopric since medieval times, and two centuries later it again gave its name to a landmark decision, when the Treaty of Utrecht was signed in 1713, ending the War of the Spanish Succession.

Utrecht has a great deal of intact religious edifices, including the tower of the storm-ravaged Dom and its church spire – the country's tallest. The striking canal wharves, built in the 13th century, are well below street level, a feature unique to Utrecht, and the streets along the canals bristle with chic shops, restaurants and cafés. Utrecht University was founded in 1663, and now has a student community of 40,000, the country's largest.

Information
GWK currency exchange (Centraal Station) Near platform No 12.

Municipal library (☎ 286 18 00; Oudegracht 167; ☺ 10am-9pm Mon, 11am-6pm Tue-Fri, 10am-5pm Sat) Offers Internet access for €0.20 per six minutes.

Post office (Neude 11)

Tourist office (☎ 0900-128 87 32; www.utrecht-city.com; Vinkenburgstraat 19; ☺ 9.30am-6.30pm Mon-Wed & Fri, to 9pm Thu, to 5pm Sat) Get the free map with street index.

Sights & Activities
The **Domtoren** (cathedral tower; ☎ 233 30 36; www .domtoren.nl, in Dutch; Domplein; adult/child €6/3.60; ☺ 10am-5pm Mon-Sat, noon-5pm Sun) is 112m high, with 465 steps. It's a tough haul to the top,

THE NETHERLANDS

but well worth the exertion: the tower will give you unbeatable views of the city. The guided tour, in Dutch and English, is detailed and gives privileged insight into this beautiful structure.

The **Museum Catharijneconvent** (☎ 231 72 96; www.catharijneconvent.nl; Nieuwegracht 63; adult/child €7/3.50; ☽ 10am-5pm Tue-Fri, 11am-5pm Sat & Sun) has the finest collection of medieval religious art in the Netherlands, housed in a Gothic former convent and an 18th-century canal-side house.

There are one-hour **canal boat trips** (☎ 272 01 11; adult/child €6.25/4.70; ☽ 11am-6pm) that trace a circular route through the old town. The landing is on Oudegracht just south of Lange Viestraat. You can also rent **canal bikes** (paddleboats; per person per hr €6) from in front of the municipal library.

Sleeping

Stayokay Hostel Ridderhofstad (☎ 656 12 77; www .stayokay.nl; Rhijnauwenselaan 14; dm €22-24) This charming old mansion overlooks a canal on the fringes of a nature reserve, 6km east of the city centre in Bunnik. Rooms are newly renovated and upgraded. Take bus No 40, 41 or 43.

Park Hotel (☎ 251 67 12; fax 254 04 01; Tolsteegsingel 34; s/d €50/63; P) You'll sleep right in this comfy eight-room guesthouse occupying a canal house. It's not far from Utrecht's buzzing nightlife, and breakfast can be taken in the pretty garden at the back.

Grand Hotel Karel V (☎ 233 75 55; Geertebolwerk 1; www.karelv.nl; s/d from €210/235; P ✕ 🖳) This 14th-century former knights' hall has understated, though excellent, service and décor. Rates plummet on the weekend.

Eating & Drinking

Lokaal de Reunie (☎ 231 01 00; 't Wed 3A; mains €8-15; ☽ lunch & dinner) One of many atmospheric cafés on this street near the cathedral tower. There's sawdust on the floors to soak up spilled beer, and it has an attractive airy interior. The menu has salads, sandwiches and more.

Dendermonde (☎ 231 46 99; www.dendermonde.nl, in Dutch; Biltstraat 29; mains €14.70; ☽ dinner) Delectable three-course Belgian meals (€24.80) are served here in a stylish interior with buffed parquet or in the bright rear hall with a sliding roof. Traditional Belgian dishes like *waterzooi* (chicken casserole) are usually

given a modern twist and the quality is consistently good.

Polman's (☎ 231 33 68; www.polmanshuis.nl; cnr Jansdam & Keistraat; mains €18-25; ☽ lunch & dinner Mon-Sat) Diners are welcomed in an elegant former ballroom with ceiling frescos, a hangover from its days as an elite gentlemen's club. The French and Italian menus are honed for the discriminating palate.

Café Springhaver (☎ 231 37 89; www.springhaver .nl, in Dutch; Springweg 50-52) This incredibly cosy bar next to the Springhaver Theater is a perfect spot to order a drink before the main feature, or just to pore over the daily news.

't Oude Pothuys (☎ 231 89 70; www.pothuys.nl, in Dutch; Oudegracht 279) Small and dark, this basement pub has nightly music – jam sessions with locals trying their hand at rock and jazz, but also touring pro bands.

Entertainment

Springhaver Theater (☎ 231 37 89; www.springhaver .nl, in Dutch; Springweg 50-52) This Art Deco complex has two intimate cinemas showing arthouse and independent films.

Tivoli (☎ 231 14 91; www.tivoli.nl; Oudegracht 245) This former monastery remains a fixture on Utrecht's student-oriented music scene. Whether it's for old rockers like REM, or big-band jazz, events at this cavernous dance hall are often sold out.

Getting There & Away

Some of the main train services include Amsterdam (€5.60, 35 minutes), Den Helder (€15, 110 minutes), Groningen (€22.30, 120 minutes), Maastricht (€21, 120 minutes) and Rotterdam (€7.50, 35 minutes).

Eurolines buses stop at Jaarbeursplein behind the train station. Tickets can be bought from its office on the covered walkway that joins Centraal Station to Jaarbeursplein.

THE DELTA REGION

The province of Zeeland (Sea Land) makes up most of the Delta region. Zeeland's three fingers of land are really just islands set in the middle of a vast delta through which many of Europe's rivers drain, including the Rijn (Rhine), Schelde and Maas.

For centuries Zeelanders have been battling the North Sea waters. The St Elizabeth's Day flood of 1421 killed over 100,000 and

JON DAVISON

Canal-side living in Amsterdam (p817), the Netherlands

OLIVER STREWE

Basque country tapas bar in San Sebastián (p944), Spain

The Alhambra (p975) in Granada, Spain

GREG ELMS

La Sagrada Familia (p930),
Barcelona, Spain

BETHUNE CARMICHAEL

Fortified hilltop village of Marvão
(p877), Portugal

Riverfront of Porto (p881), Portugal

Château overlooking Vianden (p803),
Luxembourg

Hiking beneath the Matterhorn (p1021), Switzerland

forever altered the landscape (and some would argue the disposition) of the Netherlands and its people. More recently, the huge flood of 31 January 1953 killed almost 2000, left 500,000 homeless and destroyed 800km of dykes.

This last calamity gave rise to the Delta Project, an enormous engineering feat spanning decades to ensure the security of these lands.

MIDDELBURG
☎ 0118 / pop 45,000
Middelburg, the capital of Zeeland, is a pleasant and prosperous town, and makes a good stopover before exploring the countryside. It holds a popular market on Thursday, attracting locals wearing traditional garb.

Information
Post office (☎ 64 22 88; Lange Noordstraat 48; ☸ 8am-5.30pm Mon-Fri, 9am-1pm Sat)
Tourist Shop (☎ 67 43 00; www.visitmiddelburg.nl, in Dutch; Markt 65c; ☸ 9.30am-5.30pm Mon-Fri, 10.30am-5pm Sat)
Zeeland Regional Library (☎ 64 40 00; Kousteensedijk 7; Internet per hr €3; ☸ 5-9pm Mon, 10am-9pm Tue-Fri, to 1pm Sat)

Sights
Abdij (☎ 61 35 96) is a sizable abbey complex dating from the 12th century. It houses the regional government as well as three churches and two museums. Climb **Lange Jan** (€1.50), a 91m-high tower dating from the 14th century, or visit the **Zeeuws Museum** (☎ 62 66 55; www.zeeuwsmuseum.nl), housed in the former monks' dormitories; it has some of the best first-hand accounts and archival information on the 1953 disaster. (At the time of research it was closed until 2005 for refurbishment.)

The **town hall** (☎ 67 54 52; admission €2; ☸ 11am-5pm Mon-Sat year-round, noon-5pm Sun Apr-Oct) is a pastiche of styles: the Gothic side facing the Markt is from the 1400s, while the portion on Noordstraat is more classical and dates from the 1600s.

The area around **Damplein** (east of the Abdij) preserves many 18th-century houses, some of which have recently been turned into interesting shops and cafés.

Sleeping & Eating
De Kaepstander (☎ 64 28 48; www.kaepstander.nl; Koorkerkhof 10; s/d with shared bathroom €35/60) This amiable place has four rooms with B&B-style accommodation.
Nieuwe Doelen (☎ 61 21 21; Loskade 3-7; low/high season €71/91) All rooms are simply, yet pleasantly, decorated. There's also an enclosed garden, perfect for breakfast in fine weather.
Jazz Eetcafé Desafinado (☎ 64 07 67; www.desafinado.nl; Koorkerkstraat 1; mains €15.40; ☸ lunch & dinner) It has a lovely wood dining room and laid-back staff. The menu incorporates local and French flavours and there's a refreshing variety of good value, delicious meals. There's live jazz and blues Wednesday nights.
De Mug (The Mosquito; ☎ 61 48 51; Vlasmarkt 54; mains €17; ☸ dinner Tue-Sat) De Mug is famous beyond Middelburg for its menu of dishes prepared with unusual beers. It shouldn't be a surprise that the beer list is long (72 kinds) and boasts many rare Trappist brews.
De Tuin van Broeder Ludovicus (☎ 62 60 11; Lange Delft 2a) A health-food store that's excellent for picnickers, with pre-made dishes, cooked meats and salads sold by weight.

Getting There & Away
Sample train fares and schedules include Amsterdam (€11, 150 minutes), Roosendaal (€4.60, 45 minutes) and Rotterdam (€7.50, 90 minutes). Regional buses, including No 104, stop along Kanaalweg in front of the train station.

AROUND MIDDELBURG
Delta Project
The disastrous 1953 flood was the impetus for the Delta Project: the southwest river deltas were blocked using a network of dams, dikes and a remarkable 3.2km storm-surge barrier. Lowered only in rough conditions, the barrier was built following environmental opposition to plans to dam the Eastern Schelde (Oosterschelde). It can be dropped during abnormally high tides but generally remains open to allow normal tidal movements and the survival of the region's shellfish. It was finished in 1986.

The **Delta Expo** (☎ 0187-49 99 13; www.expoharingvliet.nl; Haringvlietplein 3; adult/child under 12 yrs €4.30/3.30; ☸ 10am-5pm) is an excellent museum and visitors' centre explaining the project. Several floors deal with the effects of the floods and construction of the project. It's also possible to visit one of the storm-surge barrier's nearby pylons and see how the huge movable gate works.

THE NETHERLANDS

Bus No 104 stops at the Expo on its run between Rotterdam's Spijkenisse metro station (25 minutes from Rotterdam CS) and Vlissingen. The buses take about an hour from Rotterdam and 30 minutes from Middelburg and run every 30 minutes.

THE NORTH & EAST

The Netherlands' northern and eastern region is made up of several provinces, including Fryslân and Groningen, and is capped by the Frisian (or Wadden) Islands, a group of five islands that are popular escapes for stressed southerners. The region's shores are washed by the shallow Waddenzee, home to a small number of seals and the unique Dutch pastime of *wadlopen* (see p843).

The Frisian state used to incorporate regions of the Netherlands, northern Germany and Denmark, until it became part of the united Netherlands. Frisians are not backwards about coming forwards: they're determined to preserve their fiercely independent heritage, and in this they appear to have the support of the Dutch government. There have been radio broadcasts in Frisian since 1945 and a Frisian regional TV network since 1994; road signs are in Dutch and Frisian; in 1996 the province's name was officially changed from Friesland to Fryslân (as it is spelt in Frisian); and the national anthem cheekily proclaims Fryslân to be *it beste lan fan d'ierde* (the best land on earth).

LEEUWARDEN

☎ 058 / pop 90,500

Leeuwarden is a pleasant, sleepy place reflecting the serenity of the surrounding farmland. Not as vivacious as Groningen to the east, the city's quiet old streets are good for wandering. There's just enough action to provide interest, though in the thick of holiday season it can seem a bit of a ghost town. Its most famous daughter is WWI spy Mata Hari.

Information

Library (☎ 234 77 77; Wirdumerdijk 34; Internet per hr €2; ☺ 12.30-5.30pm Mon & Thu, 10am-1pm & 7-9pm Tue & Fri, 10am-1pm Wed & Sat)

Post office (☎ 213 09 98; Oldehoofster Kerkhof 4; ☺ 7.30am-6pm Mon-Fri, 7.30am-1.30pm Sat)

Tourist office (☎ 0900-2024060; www.vvvleeuwarden.nl; Sophialaan 4; ☺ 9am-5.30pm Mon-Fri, 10am-2pm Sat)

Sights

The **Fries Museum** (☎ 255 55 00; www.friesmuseum .nl; Turfmarkt 11; adult/child under 18 yrs €5/2.50; ☺ 11am-5pm, closed Mon) traces Frisian culture. The huge collection of silver items – long a local specialty – is spectacular, and there's a section on the life of Mata Hari.

The **Princessehof Museum** (☎ 294 89 58; www .princessehof.nl, in Dutch; Grote Kerkstraat 11; adult/child €3.50/2; ☺ 11am-5pm Tue-Sun) is the official museum for ceramics and has an impressive selection of Delftware and works from around the globe.

Sleeping

Hotel 't Anker (☎ 212 52 16; www.hotelhetanker.nl, in Dutch; Eewal 73; s/d from €26/47) The Anchor is in a fun and pretty part of town, close to the nightlife district.

Stadhouderlijk Hof (☎ 216 21 80; www.stadhouder lijkhof.nl, in Dutch; Hofplein 29; r €90-275; P ✿) Once the residence of local royalty, Stadhouderlijk Hof is luxuriously appointed. The genuinely elegant rooms start fairly basic, eventually hitting some sumptuous heights (the Imperial de Luxe Suite). Breakfast and other extravagant add-ons are available.

Getting There & Away

Train fares and schedules include to Amsterdam (€23.50, 140 minutes), Groningen (€7.30, 55 minutes) and Utrecht (€21.30, 120 minutes).

GRONINGEN

☎ 050 / pop 177,000

Groningen was founded around 1000 and has been a crucial centre for trade since the 13th century. The Netherlands' second university was built here in 1614, and like all of the country's large university towns, the student culture gives the place an upbeat, irreverent air.

Information

Call Shop (Herestraat 94; Nieuwe Ebbingestraat 80) Internet access and cheap international calls.

Tourist office (☎ 0900-2023050; www.vvvgroningen.nl; Gedempte Kattendiep 6)

Sights & Activities

Groninger Museum (☎ 366 65 55; www.groninger -museum.nl, in Dutch; adult/child €7/3.50; ☺ 10am-5pm Tue-Sun year-round, 1-5pm Mon Jul-Aug), built on the canal islands, hosts contemporary design and photography exhibitions alongside classic Golden Age Dutch paintings.

Perhaps you'd like to indulge in the curious Dutch activity of **wadlopen** (mudwalking) on mud flats stretching all the way to the Frisian islands. Treks of up to 12km are enthusiastically undertaken by many Dutch, with the 7km walk to Schiermonnikoog the most popular.

Never embark without a skilled guide, though, or you may end up washed away by the tides. Contact Groningen-based **Wadloopcentrum** (☎ 0595-52 83 00; www.waarnaartoe.nl, in Dutch; Hoofdstraat 105) and **Dijkstra's Wadlooptochten** (☎ 0595-52 83 45; www.wadloop-dijkstra.nl, in Dutch; Hoofdstraat 118) for assistance.

Sleeping & Eating

Hotel Friesland (☎ 312 13 07; www.hotelfriesland.nl, in Dutch; Kleine Pelsterstraat; s/d €28/48) The rooms here are just about as sparse as they come, but the price can't be beaten and the location is central.

City Hotel (☎ 588 65 65; fax 311 51 00; Gedempte Kattendiep 25; s/tw €109/124; **P** ✕) The hotel boasts a rooftop deck with good views and free coffee and tea on every floor. All rooms have baths and TV with in-house movies.

Ugly Duck (☎ 312 31 92; Zwanestraat 28; mains €10.30-14.20; ☯ lunch & dinner) An appealing street café/restaurant down a sweet street. The food is chunky and filling: Provençale beef stew and grilled monkfish share the stage with good veggie options like spanakopita and pies.

De 7e Hemel (7th Heaven; ☎ 314 51 41; www.zevende hemel.nl, in Dutch; Zuiderkerkstraat 7; 2-course meal €14-15.50; ☯ dinner Tue-Sat) Great vegetarian and organic eatery serving fantastic food. The restaurant also serves meat dishes, using only organically farmed meats. The delicious mains and set-menu combinations are served in a comfortable, uncluttered dining room.

Getting There & Away

Some train fares and schedules include: Amsterdam (€24.50, 140 minutes), Leeuwarden (€7.30, 50 minutes), Rotterdam (€27.30, 160 minutes) and Utrecht (€22.30, 120 minutes).

TEXEL

☎ 0222 / pop 13,500

Texel (pronounced *tes*-sel) is about 3km north of the coast of Noord Holland. It's remarkably diverse, with broad white beaches,

lush nature reserves, forests and picture-book villages. Now 25km long and 9km wide, it consisted of two islands until 1835, when a spit of land to Eyerland Island was pumped dry.

The island makes a superb getaway from the mainland rush, with beauty and isolation in abundance – except in mid-June, when spectators line the beaches for the largest catamaran race in the world, the Cisco Trophy.

Information

Library (Drijverstraat 7, Den Burg; ☯ 2-5pm Tue-Fri, 10.30am-12.30pm Sat & Mon) Has Internet access.

Tourist office (☎ 31 47 41; www.vvv-texel.nl; Emmalaan 66, Den Burg; ☯ 9am-6pm Mon-Fri, to 5pm Sat, 10.30am-1.30pm Sun)

Sights

Duinen van Texel National Park is a patchwork of varied dunescape running along the entire western coast of the island. Salt fens and heath alternate with velvety, grass-covered dunes; plants endemic to this habitat include the dainty marsh orchid and the sea buckthorn. Much of the area is bird sanctuary and accessible only on foot.

Sleeping

Hotel De 14 Sterren (☎ 32 26 81; www.14sterren.nl, in Dutch; Smitsweg 4, Den Burg; d €53-59; ✕) On the edge of De Dennen forest, it has 14 rooms decorated in warm Mediterranean hues, most with a terrace or balcony with garden views.

Hotel Koogerend (☎ 31 33 01; www.fletcher.nl, in Dutch; Kogerstraat 94, Den Burg; d €61/71; ✕) This large hotel is a few minutes' walk from the town centre. The rooms are small but well equipped; all include a TV. There's a large restaurant downstairs serving functional food, with Herman Brood prints festooning the walls.

Getting There & Away

Trains from Amsterdam to Den Helder (€10.90, one hour) are met by a bus that connects with the **car ferry** (☎ 36 96 00; adult/child/car return €4/2/38; ☯ 6.35am-9.35pm), which then makes the crossing in 20 minutes.

AMELAND

☎ 0519 / pop 3600

The 85sq km island of Ameland has two distinct centres: picturesque Nes, near the ferry dock, and Hollum, at the west end. Of

Ameland's four villages, the 18th-century former whaling port of Nes is the most carefully preserved, its streets lined with tidy little brick houses.

Nes hosts Ameland's **tourist office** (☎ 54 65 46; www.ameland.nl, in Dutch; Rixt van Doniastraat, Nes; ☼ 9am-12.30pm & 1.30-6pm Mon-Fri, 10am-3pm Sat), and there's a **Stayokay Ameland** (☎ 55 53 53; www .stayokay.com/ameland; Oranjeweg 59; dm from €18.10) near the lighthouse outside Hollum.

Hotel Restaurant de Jong (☎ 54 20 16; http://hotel dejong.vvv-ameland.nl, in Dutch; Reeweg 29; s/d from €45/60) has decent rooms and a swish café-dining room, and **Herberg De Zwaan** (☎ 55 40 02; www.ameland.net/dezwaan, in Dutch; Zwaneplein 6) is a popular restaurant in Hollum.

Wagenborg (☎ 54 61 11; www.wpd.nl) operates ferries between Nes and Holwerd. The ferries (45 minutes) run about every two hours all year. Schedules fluctuate with demand; call to confirm, or check the website. Return fares start at €9.10 for adults and €4.84 for children. There are surcharges for bicycles, dogs and cars.

To reach the Holwerd ferry terminal from Leeuwarden, take bus No 60 or 66 (40 minutes, hourly). From Groningen, take bus No 34 (80 minutes, four or five daily).

HOGE VELUWE NATIONAL PARK

The **Hoge Veluwe** (☎ 0318-59 16 27; www.hoge -veluwe.nl; adult/child €6/3, park & museum €12/6, car €6; ☼ 9am-5.30pm Nov-Mar, 8am-8pm Apr, 8am-9pm May & Aug, to 10pm Jun & Jul, 9am-8pm Sep, to 7pm Oct) is the Netherlands' largest national park. It was purchased in 1914 by a wealthy German-Dutch couple: Anton Kröller-Müller, who wanted hunting grounds, and wife Helene, who wanted a museum site. It was given to the state in 1930. It's best to explore on foot or by one of the park's famous white bicycles, available free at the park entrances or from the visitors centre inside.

The park is a mix of forests and woods, shifting sands and heathery moors, along with red deer, wild boar and moufflon (a Mediterranean goat). It also features the **Kröller-Müller Museum** (☎ 0318-59 12 41; www.kmm .nl; Houtkampweg 6; adult/child under 12 yrs €5/2.50; ☼ 10am-5pm Tue-Sun & public hols), with its world-class collection of Van Gogh paintings and works by Picasso, Renoir and Manet.

From Arnhem, take bus No 2 (direction: Deelevy OC) to the Schaarsbergen entrance and on to the Kröller-Müller Museum. The first bus leaves at 10.10am (April to October) and there are three more through the day (one per hour in July and August). From Apeldoorn, bus No 110 leaves the station every hour from 8.42am to 4.42pm.

THE SOUTHEAST

The Netherlands' southeastern corner is made up of Noord Brabant, the country's largest province, and Limburg province.

DEN BOSCH

☎ 073 / pop 132,500

Although 's-Hertogenbosch (The Duke's Forest) is the official name, the town is commonly known as Den Bosch (den boss). Noord Brabant's capital, it has a remarkable church, a good museum, some fine cafés and ancient streets. Den Bosch was the birthplace of 15th-century painter Hieronymous Bosch (who took the name of the town), and the proto-Surrealist is honoured with a statue in front of the town hall.

Information

Tourist office (☎ 0900-1122334; www.vvvs-hertogen bosch.nl; Markt 77; ☼ 11am-5.30pm Mon, 9am-5.30pm Tue-Fri, 9am-4pm Sat)

Sights

St Janskathedraal (admission €27; ☼ 10am-4.30pm Mon-Sat, 1-4.30pm Sun) is one of the finest Gothic churches in the Netherlands; it took from 1336 to 1550 to complete.

The **Noordbrabants Museum** (☎ 687 78 77; www .noordbrabantsmuseum.nl, in Dutch; Verwersstraat 41; adult/ child €5.70/3; ☼ 10am-5pm Tue-Fri, noon-5pm Sat), in the former governor's residence, features exhibits about Brabant life and art, and works by Bosch.

Boat tours (☼ Apr-Oct) leave from the canal by Sint Janssingel. Check the pier for times.

Sleeping & Eating

Hotel Terminus (☎ 613 06 66; fax 613 07 26; Boschveld-weg 15; r from €27) Decent rooms, an appealing bar and regular live folk music.

Hotel Euro (☎ 613 77 77; www.eurohotel-denbosch .com; Hinthamerstraat 63; s/d from €65/85; P ☒) Standard rooms and a great central location.

Café September (☎ 613 03 08; Verwersstraat 55-57; meals €4-8; ☼ lunch & dinner) In a little white building, serving simple meals.

Samtosa (☎ 612 51 22; Vughterstraat 161; mains €28; ☺ dinner) A fantastic vegetarian restaurant on a lovely street, with an extensive menu featuring Mediterranean and Indian influences.

Getting There & Away
Train fares and schedules include Amsterdam (€11, 60 minutes), Maastricht (€16, 90 minutes) and Utrecht (€6.50, 30 minutes).

MAASTRICHT
☎ 043 / pop 122,000
Maastricht, possibly the Netherlands' oldest city (Nijmegen is the other contender for the title), is unique. It exists as a kind of 'interzone', a hybrid of European influences, hemmed in by Belgium and Germany right near the southernmost point of the Dutch border.

In centuries past, Maastricht was captured at various times by most of Europe's powers, and this legacy as a crossroads for invaders has also bequeathed it a pan-European flavour. Appropriately, the city hosted a decisive moment in the history of the European Union: in 1992 the 12 members of the then European Community signed the Maastricht Treaty, thereby creating the EU.

Maastricht has an energy belying its size. Spanning both banks of the Maas River, with a host of pavement cafés and lovely old cobblestone streets, it's renowned for sparkling nightlife, world-class dining and an elegant atmosphere that is quite exquisitely addictive.

Orientation
Maastricht's centre is bisected by the Maas river. The area on the east side is known as Wyck, and to the south of here is the new area of Céramique. The walk from the train station to the Vrijthof, the cultural heart, takes 15 minutes.

Information
Academisch Ziekenhuis Maastricht (Hospital; ☎ 387 65 43; P Debyelaan 25)
easyInternetcafé (www.easyeverything.com/map/mas.html; Wolfstraat 8; ☺ 9am-6pm Mon-Wed & Fri, 9am-9pm Thu, 9am-5pm Sat)
GWK money exchange office (☺ 8am-9pm Mon-Sat, 8am-6pm Sun) In the train station.
Post office Statenstraat 4 (☎ 329 91 99; ☺ 9am-6pm Mon-Fri, 9am-1.30pm Sat); Stationsstraat 60 (☎ 321 45 11; ☺ 9am-6pm Mon-Fri, 9am-1.30pm Sat)

Tourist office (☎ 325 21 21; www.vvvmaastricht.nl; Kleine Staat 1; ☺ 9am-6pm Mon-Fri, to 5pm Sat, 11am-3pm Sun)

Sights & Activities
The **Bonnefantenmuseum** (☎ 329 01 90; www.bonnefantenmuseum.nl; Ave Céramique 250; adult/child under 12 €7/3.50; ☺ 11am-5pm Tue-Sun) features a 28m tower that's now a local landmark. Designed by Aldo Rossi, the museum opened in 1995 and is well laid out with collections divided into departments, each on its own floor – Old Masters and medieval sculpture on one floor, contemporary art by Limburg artists on the next.

The 16th-century **Spanish Government Museum** (☎ 321 13 27; www.museumspaansgouvernement.nl, in Dutch; Vrijthof 18; admission €2.50; ☺ 1-5pm Wed-Sun) is where Philip II outlawed his former lieutenant Willem the Silent at the start of the Eighty Years' War. The exhibits feature statues and 17th-century paintings.

At the end of Sint Bernardusstraat, the **Helpoort** is the oldest surviving town gate in the Netherlands (1229). Across the Maas in the new Céramique district, you can see the remains of the **13th-century ramparts and fortifications**.

Much of Maastricht is riddled with defensive tunnels dug into the soft sandstone over the centuries. The best place to see the tunnels is **Sint Pietersberg**, 2km south of Helpoort. The large fort has tunnels throughout the hill. The tourist office leads **cave tours** (☎ 321 78 78; adult/child €3/1.75; ☺ 3.30pm daily Jul-Aug & school hols). Bus No 29 goes past the fort from Vrijthof. Thirteen species of bats have been found living below the surface.

Stiphout Cruises (☎ 351 53 00; Maaspromenade 27; adult/child €5/3; ☺ daily Apr-Oct, Sat & Sun Nov-Dec) runs boat cruises on the Maas.

Sleeping
Stayokay Maastricht (☎ 346 67 77; www.stayokay.com/maastricht; Dousbergweg 4; dm €23.75; ☺) This hostel is on the perimeter of a nature reserve, which is a point in its favour; however, it's a 40-minute walk from the town centre. Take bus No 11 (Monday to Friday) or No 8 or 18 (Saturday and Sunday) from Maastricht station to the Dousberg stop.

Hotel Randwyck (☎ 361 68 35; www.hotelrandwyck.nl; Dousbergweg 102; s/d €57.50/67.50; ☺) The rooms here are more like units, and they represent pretty good value: all are equipped with TV

THE NETHERLANDS

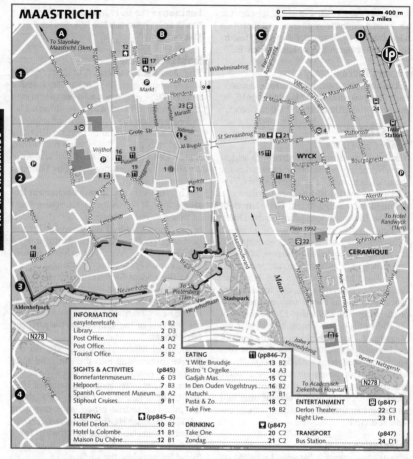

MAASTRICHT

INFORMATION	
easyInteretcafé	1 B2
Library	2 D3
Post Office	3 A2
Post Office	4 D2
Tourist Office	5 B2

SIGHTS & ACTIVITIES	(p845)
Bonnefantenmuseum	6 D3
Helpoort	7 B3
Spanish Government Museum	8 A2
Stiphout Cruises	9 B1

SLEEPING	(pp845–6)
Hotel Derlon	10 B2
Hotel la Colombe	11 B1
Maison Du Chêne	12 B1

EATING	(pp846–7)
't Witte Bruudsje	13 B2
Bistro 't Orgelke	14 A3
Gadjah Mas	15 C2
In Den Ouden Vogelstruys	16 B2
Matuchi	17 B1
Pasta & Zo	18 B2
Take Five	19 B1

DRINKING	(p847)
Take One	20 C2
Zondag	21 C2

ENTERTAINMENT	(p847)
Derlon Theater	22 C3
Night Live	23 B1

TRANSPORT	(p847)
Bus Station	24 D1

and bathroom, and there's a communal laundry. In perhaps a world first, dogs are also allowed to stay – for an extra €5. It's around a 20-minute walk from Centraal Station, or you can take the train for one stop to Randwyck Station.

Maison Du Chêne (☎ 321 35 23; www.maastricht hotel.com; Boschstraat 104; s/d from €40/58) This is a fine option in an elegant 1855 building. The rooms have baths and are very clean, and there is a good brasserie on the ground floor.

Hotel la Colombe (☎ 321 57 74, www.hotella colombe.nl; Markt 30; s/d from €59/75) This hotel is in a simple, white building on the Markt. The rooms are equally unadorned but all have TV and bath. Has a decent café.

Hotel Derlon (☎ 321 67 70; Onze Lieve Vrouweplein 6; r from €155; ⊠ ⚅ 🖵) The hotel boasts lovely rooms and enthusiastic staff. The breakfast room in the basement is built around Roman ruins.

Eating & Drinking

't Witte Bruudsje (☎ 321 00 57; Platielstraat 12; soups €3.50; ⓨ 10am-2am) Serves cheap, filling salads and soups, in a wide-ranging selection.

Take Five (☎ 321 09 71; Bredestraat 14; lunch €6; ⓨ lunch & dinner) Situated on a quiet street parallel to the cramped terraces of heaving Platielstraat, it combines fusion cooking with a stark interior, chill-out music and engaging staff. On many nights there's live jazz.

Pasta & Zo (☎ 325 41 54; Rechtstraat 38; mains from €7; ☒ lunch Mon-Sat, dinner) Pasta combinations with around 10 different homemade sauces mean you're backing the right horse. Fresh, flavoursome and filling (there's a takeaway option, too).

Gadjah Mas (☎ 321 15 68; www.gadjahmas.nl, in Dutch; Rechtstraat 42; mains from €12.10-15; ☒ lunch & dinner) This fabulous restaurant has many vegetarian options among its menu of authentic Indonesian food (as carefully presented as the artistic interior).

In Den Ouden Vogelstruys (☎ 321 48 88; www .vogelstruys.nl, in Dutch; Vrijthof 15) On the main drag, this antique bar is a little bit naughty and a little bit nice. The entrance has big, old, heavy red curtains, and inside there are photos of big, old, heavy men on the wall, big, old, heavy light fittings, and big, old, heavy Trappist beer.

Take One (☎ 321 64 23; www.takeonebiercafé.nl, in Dutch; Rechtstraat 28) Cramped and narrow from the outside, this 1930s tavern is a bit like Dr Who's Tardis: the inside is much more expansive. The beer list has well over 100 beers from the most obscure parts of Europe. The owner (who encourages the clientele to leave their peanut shells on the floor) gleefully refers to his customers as 'victims'. Relax: he'll willingly help you select the beer most appropriate to your tastes.

Matuchi (☎ 354 06 92; Kleine Gracht 34) They bill themselves as an 'Orient Style Lab', but it's a bit more than that: there's a dash of *A Clockwork Orange* in the interior design, mixed with *de rigueur* Arabian themes.

Zondag (Sunday; ☎ 321 93 00; www.cafézondag.nl, in Dutch; Wyckerbrugstraat 42) Here the cool is a bit more standard: the interior is a little more old-fashioned, though still jaw-achingly hip. Chow down on light lunches, tapas and other bar snacks, as well as musical accompaniment such as live Latin music or breakbeat DJs.

Entertainment

Night Live (☎ 0900-2020158; www.nightlive.nl, in Dutch; Kesselskade 43) 'If dance is your religion' – that's the motto at this disco in an old church. It opens after midnight on weekends, and everything from hard house to R&B to trance gets an airing here.

Derlon Theater (☎ 350 71 71; Plein 1992) Near the new library, with drama and music. The café has fine river views from the terrace.

Getting There & Away

Maastricht has a grand old train station with numerous services. Some fares and schedules are Amsterdam (€24.50, 155 minutes), Rotterdam (€23.50, 140 minutes) and Utrecht (€21, 120 minutes).

THE NETHERLANDS DIRECTORY

ACCOMMODATION

It is essential to always book your accommodation ahead anywhere in the Netherlands, especially during high season; note that many visitors choose to stay in Amsterdam even if travelling elsewhere. The tourist offices and Amsterdam Centraal Station's GWK exchange office operate hotel-booking services (see p820); when booking for two people, make it clear whether you want two single (twin) beds or a double bed.

In cities you should expect to pay under €50 for a double room in a budget hotel, up to €125 in a mid-range hotel and from €125 for the top end.

Many Dutch hotels have steep stairs but no lifts, although most top-end and some mid-range hotels are exceptions.

B&Bs are mostly found in the country – local tourist offices keep a list on file.

Lists of camp sites are available from the ANWB (p851) and tourist offices. Expect to pay roughly €8 to €20 for two people and a tent overnight, plus €3 to €6 for a car. The camping grounds have plenty of caravan hook-ups.

Stayokay (☎ 020-501 31 33; www.stayokay.com) is the Dutch hostelling association. A youth hostel card costs €14.50 at the hostels; non-members pay an extra €2.50 per night and after six nights you're a member. The usual HI discounts apply.

Apart from the usual dormitories, there are rooms for one to eight people depending on the hostel. Nightly rates range from €17 to €26 per person for dorm beds.

ACTIVITIES

Cycling, skating, windsurfing, sailing, boating and hanging out at the beach are popular Dutch pastimes. Check the tourist offices for further information.

BUSINESS HOURS

The working week starts around lunchtime on Monday. For the rest of the week most shops open at 8.30am or 9am and close at 5.30pm or 6pm, except Thursday when many close at 9pm, and on Saturday at 5pm. In Amsterdam and tourist centres you will find many shops open on Sunday. Supermarkets often have extended trading hours.

Banks are generally open 9am to 4pm or 5pm Monday to Friday. Many museums close on Monday.

Restaurants are usually open from 11am to 2.30pm or 3pm for lunch and 5.30pm to 10pm or 11pm for dinner. Most bars open by 11am and close between midnight and 2am. Nightclubs tend to open at 9pm or 10pm and close at 3am or 4am.

DISCOUNT CARDS

Available from the museums themselves, a *Museumkaart* gives access to 400 museums across the country for €30 (€17 for those under 26).

Tourist offices and some large Amsterdam hotels sell the Amsterdam Pass: 32 vouchers giving free public transport, free entry to most museums and a 25% discount on some attractions and restaurants. It's €26/36/46 for one/two/three days.

There's also a Rotterdam Card (www.rotterdamcard.nl), available from the Rotterdam tourist office and Use-It (p837). It offers similar discounts to the Amsterdam pass.

The **Cultureel Jongeren Paspoort** (Cultural Youth Passport, CJP; €11), available from tourist offices, gives people aged under 27 discounts to museums and cultural events around the country.

EMBASSIES & CONSULATES
Dutch Embassies & Consulates

Dutch embassies abroad include:

Australia (☎ 02-6220 9400; www.netherlands.org.au /index.html; 120 Empire Circuit, Canberra, ACT 2600)

Belgium (☎ 02-679 17 11; www.nederlandseambassade .be, in Dutch & French; ave Herrmann-Debroux 48, Brussels, 1160)

Canada (☎ 613-237 50 30; www.netherlandsembassy.ca; Suite 2020, 350 Albert St, Ottawa, Ont K1R 1A4)

Germany (☎ 030-20 95 60; www.dutchembassy.de, in Dutch & German; Friedrichstrasse 95, Berlin, 10117)

New Zealand (☎ 04-471 6390; www.netherlands embassy.co.nz; Investment House, cnr Ballance & Featherston Sts, Wellington)

UK (☎ 020-7590 3200; www.netherlands-embassy.org.uk; 38 Hyde Park Gate, London, SW7 5DP)

USA (☎ 202-244 5300; www.netherlands-embassy.org; 4200 Linnean Ave NW, Washington, DC 20008)

Embassies & Consulates in the Netherlands

The following embassies are located in Den Haag unless otherwise stated:

Australia (☎ 070-310 82 00; www.australian-embassy.nl; Carnegielaan 4)

Belgium (☎ 070-312 34 56; www.diplomatie.be/the hague; Alexanderveld 97)

Canada (☎ 070-311 16 00; www.dfait-maeci.gc.ca /canadaeuropa/netherlands; Sophialaan 7)

Germany (☎ 070-346 9754; www.duitse-ambassade.nl, in German; Groot Hertoginnelaan 18-20); Amsterdam (☎ 020-673 62 45; Honthorststraat 36-38)

New Zealand (☎ 070-346 93 24; www.nzembassy.com; Carnegielaan10-IV)

UK (☎ 070-427 04 27; www.britain.nl; Lange Voorhout 10); Amsterdam (☎ 020-676 43 43; Koningslaan 44)

USA (☎ 070-310 92 09; www.usemb.nl; Lange Voorhout 102); Amsterdam (☎ 020-575 53 09; Museumplein 19)

FESTIVALS & EVENTS
February/March
Carnaval Weekend before Shrove Tuesday.

March
Maastricht Art Show (☎ 041-164 50 90; www.tefaf.com)

April
Koninginnedag (Queen's Day) 30 April
Amsterdam Fantastic Film Festival (www.afff.nl) European and international fantasy, horror and science fiction movies.

May
Herdenkingsdag & Bevrijdingsdag (Remembrance Day & Liberation Day) 4 & 5 May
Nationale Molendag (National Mill Day) Second Saturday. Nearly every working windmill in the country open its doors to visitors.

June
Holland Festival (www.hollandfestival.nl) Virtually all month.

July
North Sea Jazz Festival (www.northseajazz.nl) World's largest jazz festival, held near Den Haag.

August

Gay Pride Canal Parade (First Saturday)
FFWD Dance Parade (☎ 010-433 13 00; www
.ffwdheinekendanceparade.nl, in Dutch)
Uitmarkt (www.uitmarkt.nl, in Dutch) The re-opening of
Amsterdam's cultural season for three days in late August.

November

Sinterklaas Intocht (Mid-November) The Dutch Santa
Claus arrives 'from Spain' with his staff.

December

Sinterklaas (5 December) Families exchange small gifts
ahead of Christmas religious celebrations.

HOLIDAYS
Public Holidays

Nieuwjaarsdag New Year's Day
Goede Vrijdag Good Friday
Eerste Paasdag Easter Sunday
Tweede Paasdag Easter Monday
Koninginnedag (Queen's Day) 30 April
Bevrijdingsdag (Liberation Day) 5 May
Hemelvaartsdag Ascension Day
Eerste Pinksterdag Whit Sunday (Pentecost)
Tweede Pinksterdag Whit Monday
Eerste Kerstdag (Christmas Day) 25 December
Tweede Kerstdag (Boxing Day) 26 December

School Holidays

Spring Holiday Two weeks in mid-February.
May Holiday First week of the month.
Summer Holiday July, August and sometimes the first
few days of September.
Autumn Holiday Second half of October.
Christmas Holiday Two weeks through the first full
week of January.

LEGAL MATTERS

Dutch police are helpful, with a sense of
humour most of the time. One of their leaflets urges foreigners to seek help if they
find themselves in trouble, like falling into
a canal stoned: 'Don't be embarrassed,' they
say, 'we've seen it all before'. They can hold
you for six hours for questioning, though, if
you break the law.

Drugs are actually illegal in the Netherlands. Possession of soft drugs up to 5g is
tolerated but larger amounts can get you
jailed. Hard drugs are treated as a serious
crime. Never buy drugs on the street: you'll
get ripped off or mugged. And don't light
up just anywhere without checking that it's
OK to do so.

MONEY
ATMs

Automatic teller machines can be found outside most banks, at airports and at most train
stations. Credit cards like Visa and Master-
Card/Eurocard are widely accepted, as well as
cash cards that access the Cirrus network.

Credit Cards

Report lost or stolen cards to the following
24-hour numbers:
American Express (🕑 9am-6pm; ☎ 020-504 80 00;
other times ☎ 020-504 86 66)
Diners Club (☎ 020-654 5511)
Eurocard and MasterCard (☎ 030-283 55 55)
Visa (☎ 020-660 06 11)

Moneychangers

Avoid the private exchange booths dotted
around tourist areas. Banks and the Postbank
(at post offices) stick to official exchange
rates and charge a sensible commission, as
does the **GWK** (Grenswisselkantoor; ☎ 0900-0566; www
.gwk.nl).

Travellers Cheques

Banks charge a commission to cash travellers cheques (with ID such as a passport).
American Express and Thomas Cook don't
charge commission on their own cheques
but their rates might be less favourable.
Shops, restaurants and hotels always prefer
cash; a few might accept travellers cheques
but their rates will be anybody's guess.

POST

Post offices are generally open 9am to 6pm
weekdays and 10am to 1pm Saturday. Poste
restante is best handled in Amsterdam. Letters up to 20g within Europe cost €0.59 (air
mail, known as 'priority') or €0.55 (standard); beyond Europe they are €0.75 (priority)
or €0.70 (standard). Postcards cost €0.59 to
anywhere outside the country. A *priorityblad*
(aerogramme) is €0.50. Within the country,
letters up to 20g or postcards cost €0.39.

TELEPHONE

Most public phones accept credit cards as
well as various phonecards. The official
KPN-Telecom public phone boxes charge
€0.30 per minute for all national calls. The
minimum charge from a public phone is
€0.20. Calling from private phones is considerably cheaper.

For mobile phones the Netherlands uses GSM 900/1800, compatible with Europe and Australia but not the North American GSM 1900.

To ring abroad dial ☎ 00 followed by the country code for your target country, the area code (you usually drop the leading 0 if there is one) and the subscriber number. The country code for calling the Netherlands is ☎ 31.

Numbers beginning with ☎ 06 are mobile or pager numbers.

EMERGENCY NUMBERS

Police, fire, ambulance ☎ 112

VISAS

Travellers from Australia, Canada, Israel, Japan, New Zealand, the USA and many other countries need only a valid passport (no visa) for a stay of up to three months. EU nationals can enter for three months with just their national identity card or a passport expired for no more than five years. Nationals of most other countries need a so-called Schengen visa, valid for 90 days within a six-month period. After three months, extensions can be sought through the **Vreemdelingenpolitie** (Aliens' Police; ☎ 020-559 63 00; Johan Huizingalaan 757; ✆ 8am-5pm Mon-Fri), but you'll need a good reason for an extension to be granted.

TRANSPORT IN THE NETHERLANDS

GETTING THERE & AWAY
Air

Schiphol Airport (www.schiphol.nl) is the Netherlands' main international airport. **Rotterdam Airport** (www.rotterdam-airport.nl) is much smaller. **Eindhoven** (www.eindhovenairport.nl), **Groningen** (www.gae.nl) and **Maastricht** (www.maastrichtairport.nl) act as feeder airports to Schiphol.

The following airlines fly to and from the Netherlands (offices are in Amsterdam unless stated).

Air France (code AF; ☎ 654 57 20; www.airfrance.nl; Evert van der Beekstraat 7, Schiphol)
British Airways (code BA; ☎ 346 95 59; www.britishairways.com; Neptunusstraat 33, Hoofddorp)

British Midland (code BD; ☎ 1332 854 321; www.flybmi.com)
Cathay Pacific (code CX; ☎ 653 20 10; www.cathaypacific.nl, in Dutch; Evert van der Beekstraat 18, Schiphol)
easyJet (code EZY; ☎ 023-568 48 80; www.easyjet.com)
KLM (code WA; ☎ 474 77 47; www.klm.nl; Amsterdamseweg 55, Amstelveen)
Lufthansa (code IH; ☎ 582 94 56; www.lufthansa.nl; Wibautstraat 129)
Northwest Airlines (code WH; ☎ 474 77 47; www.nwa.com; Amsterdamseweg 55, Amstelveen)
Qantas (code QF; ☎ 569 82 83; www.qantas.com.au; Neptunsstraat 33, Hoofddorp)
Ryanair (☎ 0900-2022184; www.ryanair.com)
Transavia (code HV; ☎ 406 04 06; www.transavia.nl; Westelijke Randweg 3)
United Airlines (code UA; ☎ 201 37 08; www.unitedairlines.nl; Strawinskylaan 831)

Land
BUS

The most extensive European bus network is maintained by **Eurolines** (UK ☎ 08705 143219; www.eurolines.com). It offers a variety of passes with prices that vary by time of year.

Busabout (UK ☎ 020-7950 1661; www.busabout.com) is a UK-based budget alternative to Eurolines. It runs coaches on circuits in Continental Europe including one through Amsterdam; a pass costs €359 (€329 for youth- and student-card holders) for two weeks, and passes are available for three weeks to three months. Services to/from Amsterdam run from April to October.

Gullivers Reisen (Berlin ☎ 030-3110 2110; www.gullivers.de, in German) links Berlin to Amsterdam (€49/89 for single/return, nine hours, once daily).

CAR & MOTORCYCLE

You'll need the vehicle's registration papers, third-party insurance and an international drivers permit in addition to your domestic licence. The ANWB (see p851) provides a wide range of information and services if you can show a letter of introduction from your own automobile association.

TRAIN FERRY

Stenaline (☎ 08705-70 70 70; www.stenaline.com) sails between Harwich and Hoek van Holland, west of Rotterdam. The fast HSS ferries take only three hours and depart in each direction twice a day. Foot passengers pay upwards of UK£26 return. Fares for a car with up to five people range from UK£250 to UK£303 return, depending on the season and day of week. A motorcycle and driver cost UK£98 to UK£154.

Train-boat-train combos are cheaper but take two to three hours longer. Stenaline has return fares from London to Amsterdam starting at UK£64 (for those aged under 26) or UK£79 (for everyone else). Special return deals cost £50. The train links go via Harwich in the UK and Hoek van Holland in the Netherlands and take about eight hours.

GETTING AROUND
Air
Domestic commercial flights link Amsterdam Schiphol to Eindhoven and Maastricht airports. They're chiefly used by business passengers transferring to international flights at Schiphol and are relatively expensive.

Bicycle
The Netherlands has 20,000km of cycling paths. The ANWB (p851) publishes cycling maps for each province, and tourist offices have numerous routes and suggestions. Major roads have separate bike lanes, and, except for motorways, there's virtually nowhere bicycles can't go. You'll often need legs like tree trunks to combat the North Sea headwinds.

Over 100 stations throughout the country have bicycle facilities for rental, protected parking, repair and sales. To hire, in most cases you'll need to show your passport and leave an imprint of your credit card or a deposit (€25 to €100). Private operators charge €4 to €7 per day, and €25 to €30 per week. Train station hire shops may be slightly cheaper.

Boat
Ferries connect the mainland with the five Frisian Islands. Other ferries span the Westerschelde in the south of Zeeland, providing road links to the bit of the Netherlands south of here and Belgium. These are popular with people using the Zeebrugge ferry terminal and run frequently year-round. There is also a frequent ferry service on the IJsselmeer linking Enkhuizen with Stavoren and Urk. You'll also find a few small river ferries providing crossings for remote stretches of the IJssel and other rivers.

Renting a boat is a popular way to tour the many rivers, lakes and inland seas. Boats come in all shapes and sizes from canoes to motor boats to small sailing boats to large and historic former cargo sloops. Prices vary widely, and there are hundreds of rental firms throughout the country.

Bus
Buses are used for regional transport rather than for long distances. The national *strippenkaart* (see p852) is used on most regional buses. The fares are zone-based, but figure on roughly one strip for every five minutes of riding. There are no special passes and only one class of travel. Reservations aren't possible on either regional or municipal lines, most of which run quite frequently.

Car & Motorcycle
AUTOMOBILE ASSOCIATIONS
Contact the **ANWB** (Royal Dutch Touring Association; ☎ 070-314 71 47; www.anwb.nl, in Dutch; Wassenaarseweg 220, Den Haag).

DRIVING LICENCE
You'll need to show a valid driving licence when hiring a car in the Netherlands. Visitors from outside the EU should also consider an international driving permit (IDP). Car rental firms will rarely ask for one, but the police might do so if they pull you up. An IDP can be obtained for a small fee from your local automobile association – bring along a valid licence and a passport photo – and is valid for one year together with your original licence.

FUEL
As in much of Western Europe, petrol is very expensive. Gasoline (petrol) is *benzine* in Dutch, while unleaded fuel is *loodvrij*. Leaded fuel is no longer sold in the Netherlands. Liquid petroleum gas can be purchased at petrol stations displaying LPG.

HIRE
Outside Amsterdam, the car hire companies can be in inconvenient locations if you're arriving by train. You must be at least 23 years of age to hire a car in the Netherlands. Some car-hire firms levy a small surcharge for drivers under 25. Most will ask either for a deposit or a credit card imprint as a guarantee of payment.

THE NETHERLANDS

INSURANCE

When hiring a car we strongly recommend you take out collision damage waiver (CDW), an insurance policy that limits your financial liability for damage. Note that at most car rental firms, CDW does not cover the first €500 to €1000 of damages incurred, so you're liable for this amount.

ROAD RULES

As in the rest of Continental Europe, traffic travels on the right. The minimum driving age is 18 for vehicles and 16 for motorcycles. Seat belts are required for everyone in a vehicle, and children under 12 must ride in the back if there's room.

The standard European road rules and traffic signs apply. Trams always have the right of way. If you are trying to turn right, bikes have priority. One grey area is at traffic circles: in principle, approaching vehicles have right of way, but in practice they yield to vehicles already travelling on the circle.

Speed limits are 50km/h in built-up areas, 80km/h in the country, 100km/h on major through-roads and 120km/h on freeways (sometimes 100km/h, clearly indicated). The blood-alcohol limit when driving is 0.05%.

Local Transport

BUS & TRAM

Buses and trams operate in most cities, and Amsterdam and Rotterdam also have metro networks.

There is a national fare system. You buy a *strippenkaart* (strip card), valid throughout the country, and stamp off a number of strips depending on how many zones you plan to cross. The ticket is then valid on all buses, trams, metro systems and city trains for an hour, or longer depending on the number of strips you've stamped. In most towns you punch two strips (one for the journey and one for the zone), with an additional strip for each additional zone. In the central areas of cities and towns, you usually will only need to stamp two strips – the minimum fee. A 15-strip card costs €6.20 and is available at tobacco shops, post offices, train-station counters, bookshops and newsagencies.

The buses are more conventional, with drivers stamping the strips as you get on. Bus and tram drivers sell two-/three-strip cards for €1.60/2.40.

RESERVATIONS

Ring the national **public transport number** (☎ 0900-9292; per min €0.50; ☷ 6am-midnight Mon-Fri, 7am-midnight Sat & Sun). The **NS website** (www.ns.nl) has complete schedules.

TAXI

Usually booked by phone – officially you're not supposed to wave them down on the street – taxis also hover outside train stations and hotels, and cost roughly €12 for 5km. Even short trips in town can be expensive.

TRAIN

Trains are frequent and serve domestic destinations at regular intervals, sometimes five or six times an hour. Rush-hour periods around the Randstad seem to notch up the most delays. The network is run by **Nederlandse Spoorwegen** (Netherlands Railways, NS; national inquiries ☎ 0900-9292, international inquiries ☎ 0900-9296; www.ns.nl, in Dutch).

Trains have 1st-class sections but these are often little different from the 2nd-class areas and not worth the extra cost.

Tickets cost the same during the day as in the evening, and can be bought at the window or ticketing machines. Buying a ticket on board means you'll pay almost double the normal fare.

Many stations rely on ticketing machines to cut personnel costs and queues at the counters, and there's now an additional charge when buying tickets at windows: €0.50 for one ticket, €1 for two or more. At the machine, check your destination on the alphabetical list of place names and enter the relevant code; then choose 1st/2nd class, *zonder/met korting* (without/with discount) and *vandaag geldig/zonder datum* (valid today/without date). With the tickets without date, you can travel on another day but you'll have to stamp the ticket in a yellow punch gadget near the platforms.

If you plan to do a lot of travelling, consider investing €49 in a *Voordeel-Urenkaart* valid for one year, which gives 40% discount on train travel weekdays after 9am, as well as weekends, public holidays and the whole months of July and August. The discount also applies to up to three people travelling with you on the same trip. As well, the card gives access to evening returns valid from 6pm (but not on Fridays) that are up to 65% cheaper than normal returns.

Portugal

PORTUGAL

854

Portugal's reserve, especially when compared with its exuberant neighbour, Spain, conceals a quiet confidence. Things are pretty good for the country right now: EU funding has brought the infrastructure up to speed and several recent big-time international events have led to a little well-deserved showing off.

The country is small enough to explore with ease and the landscape appealingly changeable. The far north is wonderfully remote with forested mountains dappled with tumbledown stone hamlets while, a short jaunt southwards, Porto attempts the swagger of a big city, yet remains emphatically and indelibly medieval.

In comparison, Lisbon is a hussy of a capital: easy on the eye with an upbeat atmosphere that is appealingly rough around the edges. Nearby, smaller towns like Coimbra, Sintra and Tomar are headily historic while, to the far south, the Algarve has virtual year-round sunbed appeal with a rural flip-side where you still need a phrasebook to order a beer.

FAST FACTS

- **Area** 92,389 sq km
- **Capital** Lisbon
- **Currency** euro (€); A$1 = €0.58; ¥100 = €0.76; NZ$1 = €0.54; UK£1 = €1.50; US$1 = €0.83
- **Famous for** port wine, fado music, Algarve beaches, *azulejo* tiles, Manueline architecture
- **Key Phrases** *bom dia* (hello); *obrigado/a* (thank you); *por favor* (please); *desculpe* (excuse me)
- **Official Language** Portuguese
- **Population** 10 million
- **Telephone Codes** country code ☎ 351; international access code ☎ 00; reverse-charge call ☎ 171; area codes are always dialled in Portugal and are listed with all numbers
- **Visas** EU nationals don't need a visa; most other nationalities can stay for up to 90 days in any half-year without a visa

HIGHLIGHTS

- Saunter around the fabulous palaces, villas and pampered gardens of **Sintra** (p868), a wooded hilltop retreat and seductive must-see on everyone's itinerary.
- Get lost in Lisbon's fascinating **Alfama district** (p862), a medieval tangle of narrow alleys and steep streets.
- Watch the sunset from the stunning hilltop village of **Marvão** (p877), which is encircled by ancient walls with a dramatic castle crown.

- Sample some of the local tipple at a **port lodge** (p883) in Vila Nova de Gaia, across the water from Porto.
- Stock up on muesli bars and take a hike in the wild and beautiful **Parque Nacional da Peneda-Gerês** (p887).

ITINERARIES

Portugal is not a big country – if you have your own wheels you could cover it within a month. Alternatively, the following two itineraries may help you plan your time.

- **One week** Devote two days to Porto in the historic Ribeira area on the waterfront or the port lodges across the way. Allow three days for Lisbon, including the *fado* in the Alhama, and Belém. Sidestep to gorgeous Sintra and spend the rest of the week in Óbidos and Nazaré.
- **Two weeks** The same as for one week, plus two days in sumptuous Évora and the rest exploring the Algarve (including a day each in Tavira, Lagos and Sagres).

CLIMATE & WHEN TO GO

The midsummer heat is searing in the Algarve, the Alentejo and in the upper Douro Valley, but tolerable elsewhere. The north is rainy and chilly in winter with snowfalls common in the Serra da Estrela. Avoid Algarve's packed beach resorts in July and August. You can often also save up to 50% for accommodation out of season (prices in this chapter are for peak season). See Climate Charts p1054 for more information.

HOW MUCH?

- **Loaf of bread** €0.65
- **Ice-cream** €1
- **Beach towel** €6
- **Gin and tonic** (or similar) €3.50
- **Underground parking** €1 per hour

LONELY PLANET INDEX

- **Litre of petrol** €0.97
- **Litre of bottled water** €0.40
- **Beer** €1
- **Souvenir T-shirt** €10
- **Street snack (sandwich)** €1.75

HISTORY

Portugal is a holiday-brochure 'land of contrasts' cliché and has enjoyed a similarly chequered history, stretching back to 700 BC when the Celts arrived on the Iberian Peninsula, followed by the Phoenicians, Greeks, Romans and Visigoths.

In the 8th century the Moors conquered Portugal. Their influence lingers in the culture, architecture and dark features of the people, particularly in the Algarve where the Moors established their capital in Silves

(see p873). After the Christian conquest, new trade routes were discovered in the 15th century, creating an empire that, at its peak, extended to four continents and launched Lisbon as the wealthiest city in Europe. Portugal's exuberant Gothic-style Manueline architecture dates from this time. This period of opulence was short-lived; in 1580 Spain occupied the Portuguese throne and, although the Portuguese regained it within 90 years, their imperial momentum had been lost forever.

In 1755 a massive earthquake tragically destroyed most of Lisbon followed, around 50 years later, by Napoleon's thwarted invasion, which further weakened and destabilised the country. A period of civil war and political mayhem followed, culminating in the abolition of the monarchy in 1910 and the founding of a democratic republic.

In 1926 a military coup set the stage for the dictatorship of António de Oliveira Salazar, who clung to power until his death in 1970. General dissatisfaction with his regime and a ruinous colonial war in Africa led to a peaceful military coup on 25 April 1974.

The subsequent granting of independence to Portugal's African colonies produced a flood of nearly a million refugees into the country. Today, the influence of these distant worlds, particularly Brazil, Cape Verde and Mozambique, are reflected in the music and food, especially in Lisbon and Porto.

The 1970s and early 1980s saw extreme swings between political right and left, and strikes over state versus private ownership. Portugal's entry into the EU in 1986 secured a measure of stability, although the 1990s remained consistently troubled by recession and rising unemployment.

Expo '98 gave the country an essential boost, triggered vast transport and communications' projects and launched Portugal into a new era of economic success. This was further advanced by Porto's status as a European Capital of Culture in 2001, followed in 2004 by Portugal playing host to the Euro 2004 football championships. The ensuing high international profile contributed further to a vast injection of funds into the country's infrastructure, including a Porto metro, 10 new/refurbished stadia and plans for a second international airline terminal to be built northwest of Lisbon in 2010.

PORTUGAL

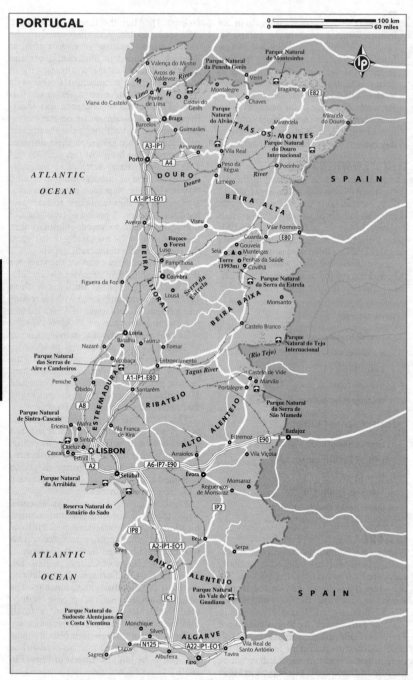

PORTUGAL

0 — 100 km
0 — 60 miles

ATLANTIC OCEAN

SPAIN

ATLANTIC OCEAN

SPAIN

Parque Natural da Peneda Gerês
Parque Natural de Montesinho
Valença do Minho
Arcos de Valdevez
Lima River
Montalegre
Verin
Bragança
E82
MINHO
Ponte de Lima
Caldas do Gerês
Chaves
Viana do Castelo
Parque Natural do Alvão
TRÁS-OS-MONTES
Mirandela
Miranda do Douro
Barcelos
Braga
Guimarães
Amarante
Vila Real
Parque Natural do Douro Internacional
A3-IP1
Porto
A4
Peso da Régua
Pocinho
DOURO
Douro River
Lamego
BEIRA ALTA
A1-IP1-E01
Aveiro
Viseu
Vilar Formoso
Buçaco Forest
Luso
Guarda
E80
Gouveia
Seia
Manteigas
Torre (1993m)
Penhas da Saúde
Pampilhosa
Covilhã
Figueira da Foz
Coimbra
Serra da Estrela
Parque Natural da Serra da Estrela
BEIRA LITORAL
Lousã
Monsanto
BEIRA BAIXA
Castelo Branco
Leiria
Batalha
Fátima
Tomar
Parque Natural do Tejo Internacional
Nazaré
(Rio Tejo)
Parque Natural das Serras de Aire e Candeeiros
Alcobaça
Entroncamento
Tagus River
Castelo de Vide
Marvão
Peniche
A1-IP1-E80
Santarém
Portalegre
Óbidos
RIBATEJO
ESTREMADURA
Parque Natural da Serra de São Mamede
A8
Parque Natural de Sintra-Cascais
Ericeira
Mafra
ALTO ALENTEJO
Vila Franca de Xira
Estremoz
E90
Badajoz
Sintra
Queluz
Arraiolos
Vila Viçosa
Cascais
LISBON
Estoril
A6-IP7-E90
A2
Évora
Monsaraz
Parque Natural da Arrábida
Setúbal
Reguengos de Monsaraz
Reserva Natural do Estuário do Sado
IP2
IP8
Beja
A2-IP1-EO1
Sines
Serpa
BAIXO
IC1
ALENTEJO
Parque Natural do Vale do Guadiana
Parque Natural do Sudoeste Alentejano e Costa Vicentina
Monchique
Silves
ALGARVE
Lagos
N125
A22-IP1-EO1
Vila Real de Santo António
Sagres
Albufeira
Faro
Tavira

PORTUGAL

PEOPLE

Portugal's population of 10.3 million excludes the estimated three million Portuguese living abroad, but includes the considerable number of African and Brazilian immigrants. There has also been an influx of new immigrants post-May 2004 when the European community embraced 10 new member countries.

RELIGION

Portugal is 98% Roman Catholic, with around 120,000 Protestants, of which a large percentage are evangelical Protestants from Brazil. There are approximately 5000 Jews.

ARTS
Music

The best-known form of Portuguese music is the melancholy, nostalgic songs called *fado* (fate), popularly considered to have originated from the Portuguese sailors expressing the swell of the seamen's emotions on the high seas. They sang of loneliness, danger, nostalgia, the joy of survival; and, although their accounts could be graphic and literal, the voyage was also a metaphor for the greater passage of life. The late Amália Rodrigues was the Edith Piaf of Portuguese *fado*. Today it is Mariza who has captured the public's imagination with her heart-wrenching voice, passionate recordings and blonde cornrows of hair contrasting with her dramatic dark colouring. Lisbon's Alfama district has plenty of *fado* houses (p862), ranging from the grandiose and tourist-conscious to small family affairs; the tourist office can supply you with a list.

Literature

Two of Portugal's finest 20th century writers are poet–dramatist Fernando Pessoa (1888–1935), author of the 1934 *Message*; and the 1998 Nobel Prize–winning novelist José Saramago, whose novels (notably *Baltasar and Blimunda* and *The Year of the Death of Ricardo Reis*) weave together the real and imaginary. Others to try are Eça de Queiroz (*The Maias*) and Fernando Namora (*Mountain Doctor*). A contemporary Portuguese 'whodunnit', close to the political bone, is *The Ballad of Dog's Beach* by José Cardoso Pires.

Architecture

Unique to Portugal is Manueline architecture, named after its patron King Manuel I (1495–1521). It symbolises the zest for discovery of that era and is hugely flamboyant, characterised by fantastically spiralling columns and elaborate carving and ornamentation.

Visual Arts

The most striking Portuguese visual art is pottery, with superb examples of the decorative blue-and-white *azulejo* tiles based on traditional 15th-century Moorish designs. Lisbon has its own *azulejo* museum (p863).

ENVIRONMENT
The Land

Portugal stretches 560km from north to south and 220km at its widest east–west point. The country is bordered on the north and east by Spain and on the south and west by the Atlantic.

National Parks

Portugal has one international-standard national park (70,290-hectare Peneda-Gerês), 12 *parques naturais* (natural parks), nine nature reserves and several other protected areas. The government's **Instituto da Conservação Wasteels** (ICN; Information Division ☎ 213 523 317; Rua Ferreira Lapa 29-A, Lisbon) manages them all, though information is best obtained from each park's headquarters. There are 12 **World Heritage Sites** in Portugal, including the Monastery of Batalha, the historic centre of Évora, and Sintra. For a complete list check the website http://whc.unesco.org/pg.cfm?cid=30.

Environmental Issues

Portugal's most heated environmental issue concerns the Alqueva dam that opened in February 2002 as Europe's largest artificial lake. Over a million trees were cut down to create the dam, and some 160 rocks covered with Stone Age drawings were submerged. Environmentalists also voiced concern at the inevitable destruction of rare species, including kites, wild boars and the Iberian lynx.

On a more positive note, Portugal has fast come up to speed in the recycling department with colour-coded receptacles in every town and city.

FOOD & DRINK

In the larger towns and cities, restaurants in this chapter are divided into budget (€2 to €7), mid-range (€8 to €12), and top end (€13 to €20) for the average price of a main dish.

PORTUGAL

PORTUGAL

Staples & Specialities

Seafood offers exceptional value, especially *caldeirada* (seafood stew), *sardinhas assadas* (grilled sardines) and the omnipresent *bacalhau* (dried cod) reputedly prepared in some 365 ways.

Meat dishes can be a letdown; among the safer bets are local *presunto* (ham), *borrego* (roast lamb) and *cabrito* (kid). Main-dish prices start around €6.

Diet-defying cafés and *pastelarias* (pastry shops) are everywhere in Portugal and offer splendid desserts and cakes. Try a delicious – and addictive – *pastel de nata* (custard tart).

Portuguese coffee is always good, in even the grungiest bar. In Lisbon, a small black espresso is known as a *bica,* and elsewhere simply as a *café.* Half coffee/milk is *café com leite.* Local beers *(cerveja)* include Sagres in the south and Super Bock in the north.

Portuguese *vinho* (wine) offers great value in all varieties: *tinto* (red), *branco* (white) and *vinho verde* (semi-sparkling young), which is usually white. Restaurants often have *vinho da casa* (house wine) for as little as €2.50 per 350ml jug, although sometimes it would be better suited for pickling onions. Port, synonymous with Portugal, is produced in the Douro Valley east of Porto and drunk in three forms: ruby, tawny and white.

Where to Eat & Drink

The line between snacks and meals is blurred. Bars and cafés offer snacks or even a small menu. For full meals try a *casa do pasto* (simple, cheap eatery), a *restaurante cervejaria* (bar-restaurant) or a *marisqueira* (seafood restaurant). Lunch time typically lasts from noon to 3pm, and evening meals from 7pm to 10.30pm.

The *prato do dia* (dish of the day) is often a bargain at around €6; the *ementa turística* (tourist menu) rarely is. A full portion or *dose* is ample for two decent appetites; a *meia dose* (half-portion) is a quarter to a third cheaper. The *couvert* – the bread, cheese, butter, olives and other titbits at the start of a meal – costs extra, sometimes a hefty sum. You can send it back without causing offence, although you should do this right away, rather than wait until the end of the meal! All restaurants in this chapter are open daily for lunch (noon to 3pm) and dinner (7pm to 10pm) unless otherwise noted.

Vegetarians & Vegans

The typical Portuguese menu does not cater to vegetarians, although the ubiquitous *sopa de legumes* (vegetable soup) is often included as a starter, together with the inevitable *salada* (salad). In general, the only other option (for vegetarians) is an *omeleta simple* (plain omelette) or the marginally more exciting *omeleta com queijo* (cheese omelette). Vegans have an even tougher time, although larger cities and the Algarve have a handful of vegetarian restaurants. Chinese restaurants are more common and always have plenty of vegetarian (and vegan) options. Where available, vegetarian restaurants are listed throughout this chapter.

LISBON

pop 720,000

Lisbon is one of Europe's smallest and most beguiling capitals; a life-affirming, lung-busting city of hills offering views over the sparkling Tagus River (Rio Tejo). The narrow streets and alleys of this once-great port city exude a sense of history with traditional shops and cafés, and ancient street trams that rattle up the steep gradients. Away from the centre are great stroll-around districts, like Moorish Alfama with its crumbling pastel-coloured houses packed into a steep shoulder of the city between the river and the castle.

Aside from the spoilt-for-choice nightlife, restaurants and entertainment, Lisbon has been busy playing host to the 2004 European Football Championships with preparations including a spanking new stadium and a general scrub-and-brush-up throughout town.

HISTORY

Lisbon's history is a roller coaster of power and poverty. Until the 1755 earthquake destroyed most of the centre – and killed some 40,000 people – the capital was one of Europe's most prosperous port cities with thriving trade routes to India, Africa and Brazil. Post-quake there was the inevitable backlash of political upheaval and suffering. Only in the last couple of decades has Lisbon begun to flex its muscles on the international power front, most noticeably in its recognition as the European City of Culture in 1994 and as the venue for the 1998 Expo and the 2004 European Football Championships.

ORIENTATION

Baixa is the heart of the modern city with its grid of wide streets and huge square, Praça do Comércio, to the south on the river's edge. To the north stands its second main square, Praça Dom Pedro IV, better known as Rossio and the commercial hub of the city, surrounded by cafés, bars and shops.

Chiado and Bairro Alto districts lie above the Baixa to the west. The Chiado is the affluent quarter with sophisticated shops, restaurants and cafés, while the Bairro Alto, the upper town, is famed for its lively nightlife and narrow 17th-century streets.

Alfama, northeast of the Baixa, is the oldest part of Lisbon with its warren of medieval streets plunging from the castle to the river and its animated, traditional life.

Belem, a peaceful suburb 6km west of Rossio, is home to Lisbon's finest monument, the Mosteiro dos Jerónimos, and several other historical sights.

Saldanha district is around a kilometre northeast of Marquês de Pombal; it has a couple of great museums (see p863) and a metro stop, but not much else.

Maps

Instituto Português de Cartográfia e Cadastro (Map pp860-1; ☎ 213 819 600; ipcc@ipcc.pt; Rua Artilharia Um 107) Publishes and sells topographic maps.

INFORMATION
Bookshops

The English Bookshop (Map pp864-5; ☎ 213 428 472; Rua do S. Marçal 83) Has a vast choice of English books ranging from blockbusters to the classics.
Livraria Buchholz (Map pp860-1; Rua Duque de Palmela 4) Has multilingual literature, including English, French and German.

Internet Access

Great Western (Map pp864-5; ☎ 213 431 004; Rua das Portas de Santo Antão 54; ꩜ 9am-10pm Mon-Fri, 10am-7pm Sat & Sun)
Lisboa Welcome Center (Map pp864-5; ☎ 210 312 810; 2nd fl Praça do Comércio; ꩜ 9am-8pm)
Web Café (Map pp864-5; ☎ 213 421 181; Rua do Diário de Notícias 126; ꩜ 4pm-2am)

Medical Services

British Hospital (Map pp860-1; ☎ 213 955 067; Rua Saraiva de Carvalho 49) English-speaking staff.

Money

Cota Câmbios (Map pp864-5; ☎ 213 220 470; Rossio 41; ꩜ 8am-10pm) One of the best exchange rates in town, hence the queue.
Top Atlântico (Map pp860-1; ☎ 213 108 800; Avenida Duque de Loulé 108; ꩜ 9am-8pm Mon-Fri) Commission-free currency exchange for AMEX cardholders; help with lost cards or cheques.

LISBON IN TWO DAYS

Start at **Rossio** (p859), walk to **Alfama** (p862) and the heady castle views. Tram it back and on to **Belém** (p862) and the **Mosteiro dos Jerónimos** (p862). Duck into **Confeitaria de Belém** (p866) for a custard tart (or three) and return via the **Museu de Arte Antiga** (p863).

Explore the **Bairro Alto** (p859) and **Chiado** (p859) popping into the **Solar do Vinho do Porto** (p866) for a port pick-me-up. Return to Baixa via the **Elevador da Glória** then take a bus or the metro to the **Museu Calouste Gulbenkian** (p863) and **Modern Art Centre** (p863) for the rest of the day.

PORTUGAL

PORTUGAL

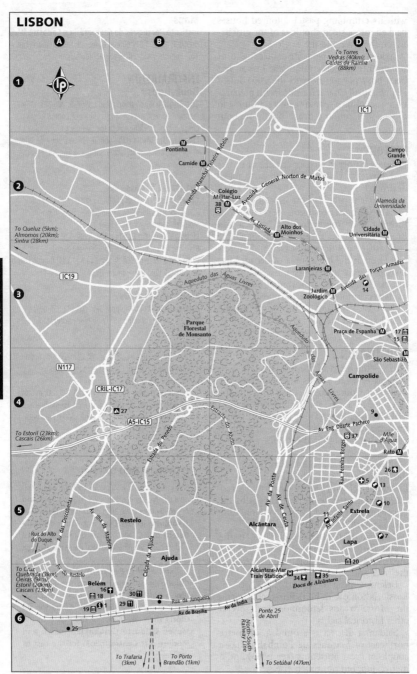

LISBON

To Torres
Vedras (40km);
Caldas da Rainha
(88km)

IC1

Pontinha M

Carnide M

Campo
Grande M

Colégio
Militar-Luz
38 M

Avenida Marechal Teixeira Rebelo

Avenida General Norton de Matos

Av Lusíada

Alto dos
Moinhos M

Alameda da
Universidade

To Queluz (5km);
Almornos (20km);
Sintra (28km)

Cidade
Universitária M

IC19

Aqueduto das Águas Livres

Laranjeiras M

Avenida das Forças Armadas

Parque
Florestal
de Monsanto

Jardim
Zoológico M

14

N117

Praça de Espanha M

17
15

São Sebastião M

Campolide

CRIL-IC17

27

A5-IC15

9

Estrada do Alvito

Estrada do Penedo

Av Eng Duarte Pacheco

37

Mãe
d'Água

Rato M

26

To Estoril (23km);
Cascais (26km)

5

13

Rua Ferreira Borges

10

Av da Ponte

Av de Ceuta

11

Infante Santo

Estrela

Restelo

Av das Descobertas

Av da Ilha da Madeira

Alcântara

7

Lapa

Rua do Alto
do Duque

Ajuda

Calçada da Ajuda

20

Av do Restelo

Alcântara-Mar
Train Station

34

35

Doca de Alcântara

To Cruz
Quebrada (3km);
Oeiras (9km);
Estoril (20km);
Cascais (23km)

Belém

16

18

30

42

19

1

29

Rua da Junqueira

Av da Índia

25

Av de Brasília

Ponte 25
de Abril

North-South
Railway Line

To Trafaria
(3km)

To Porto
Brandão (1km)

To Setúbal (47km)

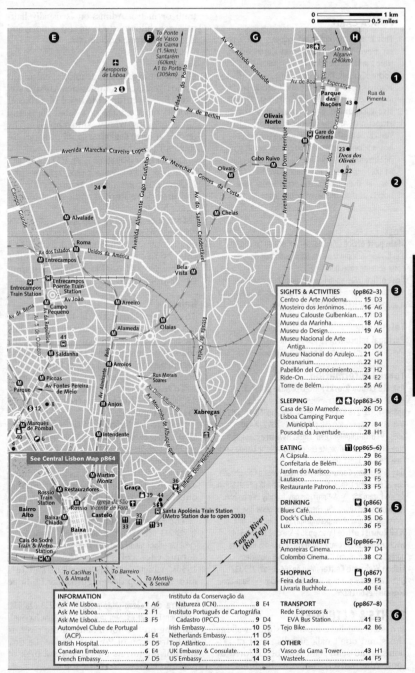

0	1 km
0	0.5 miles

SIGHTS & ACTIVITIES (pp862–3)
Centro de Arte Moderna..................15 D3
Mosteiro dos Jerónimos..................16 A6
Museu Calouste Gulbenkian..........17 D3
Museu da Marinha..........................18 A6
Museu do Design............................19 A6
Museu Nacional de Arte
  Antiga..20 D5
Museu Nacional do Azulejo............21 G4
Oceanarium....................................22 H2
Pabellón del Conocimiento............23 H2
Ride-On..24 E2
Torre de Belém...............................25 A6

SLEEPING (pp863–5)
Casa de São Mamede.....................26 D5
Lisboa Camping Parque
  Municipal.....................................27 B4
Pousada da Juventude....................28 H1

EATING (pp865–6)
A Cápsula.......................................29 B6
Confeitaria de Belém......................30 B6
Jardim do Marisco..........................31 F5
Lautasco...32 F5
Restaurante Patrono.......................33 F5

DRINKING (p866)
Blues Café......................................34 C6
Dock's Club....................................35 D6
Lux...36 F5

ENTERTAINMENT (pp866–7)
Amoreiras Cinema...........................37 D4
Colombo Cinema.............................38 C2

SHOPPING (p867)
Feira da Ladra.................................39 F5
Livraria Buchholz............................40 E4

TRANSPORT (pp867–8)
Rede Expressos &
  EVA Bus Station............................41 E3
Tejo Bike..42 B6

OTHER
Vasco da Gama Tower.....................43 H1
Wasteels...44 F5

INFORMATION
Ask Me Lisboa....................................1 A6
Ask Me Lisboa....................................2 F1
Ask Me Lisboa....................................3 F5
Automóvel Clube de Portugal
  (ACP)..4 E4
British Hospital...................................5 D5
Canadian Embassy..............................6 E4
French Embassy...................................7 D5
Instituto da Conservação da
  Natureza (ICN)................................8 E4
Instituto Português de Cartográfia
  Cadastro (IPCC)...............................9 D4
Irish Embassy....................................10 D5
Netherlands Embassy........................11 D5
Top Atlântico....................................12 D5
UK Embassy & Consulate..................13 D5
US Embassy.......................................14 D3

LISBOA CARD

This is a nifty, cost-saving pass that covers travel on the metro, on Carris buses, trams and lifts, and on trains between Cais Sodre, Cascais, Rossio and Sintra, as well as admission to 28 museums, historic buildings and other places of interest. There's also discounted entry to about 40 other attractions. Another perk of the pass is that you can usually skip the queue for tickets – not to be underestimated, especially in peak season. A 24-/48-/72-hour card costs €13/21.50/26.55. You can buy the *Lisboa Card* at the airport, tourist offices, several hotels and from travel agencies.

Post

Main post office (Map pp864-5; Praça do Comércio; 8.30am-6.30pm Mon-Fri, 9am-noon Sat) Handles poste restante collection.

Post office (Map pp864-5; Praça dos Restauradores; 8am-8pm Mon-Fri, 9am-noon Sat) This second branch is opposite the ICEP tourist office.

Telephone

Portugal Telecom (Map pp864-5; Rossio 68; 8am-11pm) Telephone booths and phonecards for sale.

Tourist Information

Ask Me Lisboa kiosks Palácio Foz (Map pp864-5; ☎ 213 463 314); Santa Apolónia train station (Map pp860-1; ☎ 218 821 606); Belém (Map pp860-1; ☎ 213 658 435); Lisbon airport (Map pp860-1; ☎ 218 450 660; 6am-midnight). All kiosks have free maps, the bimonthly guide *Follow Me Lisboa* and sell the Lisboa Card (see the boxed text above).

Gay & Lesbian Community Center (Centro Comunitário Gay e Lésbico de Lisboa; Map pp864-5; ☎ 218 873 918; Rua de São Lazaro 88; 5-9pm) Has gay-friendly info on bars, restaurants and clubs. Also check websites: www.ilga -portugal.org and www.portugalgay.pt.

ICEP tourist office (Map pp864-5; ☎ 213 463 314; www.askmelisboa.com; Palácio Foz, Praça dos Restauradores; 9am-8pm) Deals with national inquiries.

Lisboa Welcome Center (Map pp864-5; ☎ 210 312 810; www.visitlisboa.com; Praça do Comércio; 9am-8pm) Concentrates on Lisbon.

SIGHTS & ACTIVITIES

Provided you have a pair of sturdy walking shoes and don't balk at hills, most of Lisbon's grand-slam sights can be explored by foot. Alternatively, hop on the funicular, tram or metro. Admission is usually half-price for children, students and seniors, and free for everyone on Sundays.

Alfama

Despite the discouraging multilingual menus at most restaurants, this ancient district still looks like a set for a medieval blockbuster with its moody maze of twisted alleys and ancient strung-with-washing houses. The terrace at **Largo das Portas do Sol** provides *the* souvenir snapshot of the city.

Casa do Fado (Map pp860-1; ☎ 218 823 470; Largo do Chafariz de Dentro 1; admission €2.50; 10am-1pm & 2-5.30pm) is set in a former Alfama bathhouse and provides a spirited audiovisual look at *fado's* history.

Castelo de São Jorge (Map pp864-5; ☎ 218 800 620; admission free; 9am-6pm), dating from Visigothic times, sits high above the city like a cherry on a cake. If you can't hack the hike, take bus No 37 from Plaça Figueira or tram No 28 from Largo Martim Moniz.

Belém

This quarter 6km west of the Rossio has loads of charm, chairs on squares and reputedly the best *pasteis de nata* (custard tarts) in the country (see p866). On a loftier note, Belém (Bethlehem in English) is also home to Lisbon's most emblematic religious building.

To reach Belém take the train, or bus No 43, from Cais do Sodré, or tram No 15 from Praça da Figueira.

Mosteiro dos Jerónimos (Map pp860-1; ☎ 213 620 034; Praça do Império; admission Tue-Sat €3, Sun free; 10am-5pm Tue-Sun) dates from 1496 and is a soaring extravaganza of Manueline architecture with rich carvings and stunning *azulejos*. There's a funky craft market outside here on the first Sunday of each month.

The must-see **Museu do design** (Map pp860-1; ☎ 213 612 934; Praça do Império; admission €3; 11am-8pm Mon-Fri, 10am-7pm Sat & Sun) has a cutting-edge collection dating from the 1930s, which includes jewellery and furniture from top design gurus like Philippe Starck.

Torre de Belém (Map pp860-1; ☎ 213 620 034; admission Tue-Sat €3, Sun free; 10am-5pm Tue-Sun), standing on the north bank of the river, is *the* tourist icon of Portugal. Brave the tiny steps of the turrets for the natural high of panoramic views from the top.

The **Museu da Marinha** (Maritime Museum; Map pp860-1; ☎ 213 620 019; admission €3; ☼ 10am-6pm Tue-Sun, to 5pm winter) is a winner for nautical types, with all kinds of seafaring paraphernalia, including model ships.

Saldanha

The celebrated **Museu Calouste Gulbenkian** (Map pp860-1; ☎ 217 823 461; Ave de Berna 45; admission Tue-Sat €3, Sun free; ☼ 10am-6pm Tue-Sun) has an astounding collection that formerly belonged to an oil tycoon. There are Egyptian, Asian, Greek and Islamic artefacts and wonderfully contemplative paintings by such beret-and-smock masters as Renoir, Rembrandt and Monet. Families can drop off their kiddies for *free* at the on-site childcare centre.

Lisbon's **Centro de Arte Moderna** (Modern Art Centre; Map pp860-1; ☎ 217 823 474; Rua Dr Nicaulau de Bettencourt; admission Tue-Sat €3, Sun free; ☼ 10am-6pm Tue-Sun) is prettily approached via the gardens of the above museum. The centre includes most of the biggies from Portugal's modern-art scene, including London-based Paula Rego whose childhood in Portugal is strongly reflected in her dreamlike and theatrical themes.

Museums

The following two museums are away from the centre, but well worth the detour time.

The **Museu Nacional do Azulejo** (Map pp860-1; ☎ 218 100 340; Rua Madre de Deus 4; admission €2.50, Sun free; ☼ 10am-6pm Wed-Sun, 2-6pm Tue) has an evocative 17th-century convent setting, plus magnificent display of tiles, including a 36m panel of Lisbon dating from 1730.

The **Museu Nacional de Arte Antiga** (Ancient Art Museum; Map pp860-1; ☎ 213 962 825; Rua das Janelas Verdes; admission €3, 10am-2pm Sun free; ☼ 10am-5pm Wed-Sun, 2-6pm Tue) houses a beautifully displayed collection of works by Portuguese painters.

Parque das Nações

The former Expo '98 site, a revitalised 2km-long waterfront area in the northeast, has a range of attractions, including Europe's biggest **Oceanarium** (Map pp860-1; ☎ 218 917 002; adult/child €9/4.50; ☼ 10am-7pm) and a **Pabellón del Conocimiento** (Living Science Centre; Map pp860-1; ☎ 218 917 100; adult/child €5/2.50; ☼ 10am-7pm) with over 300 interactive exhibits for kids of all ages. Take the metro to Oriente station – an equally impressive Expo project.

Alcântara

The old wharves have been slickly revamped into a swanky strip of bars and restaurants with tables sprawling out onto the promenade. After your blow-out brunch, enjoy the half-hour stroll along the waterfront to Belém.

TOURS

Carris (Map pp864-5; ☎ 966 298 558; Praça da Figueira; adult/child from €13/6.50) offers various bus, tram and walking tours. **Transtejo** (Map pp864-5; Terreiro do Paço ferry terminal; ☎ 218 820 348; adult/child €15/8; ☼ Mar-Oct) runs cruises on the Tagus. There are great views of the city from this watery perspective.

FESTIVALS

The **Festa do Santo António** (Festival of Saint Anthony) fills the streets of Lisbon on 13 June.

SLEEPING
Budget

Lisboa Camping Parque Municipal (Map pp860-1; ☎ 217 623 100; Parque Florestal de Monsanto; camp sites €5) This is a well-treed spot 6km northwest of town. Take bus No 43 from Cais do Sodré.

Pensão Tomar (Map pp864-5; ☎ 218 888 484; Poço do Borraté; s/d €20/30) The high ceilings, large rooms and chandeliers here create an ambience of luxury accommodation for bargain-basement prices.

Pensão Globo (Map pp864-5; ☎ 213 462 279; www .pglobo.com; Rua do Teixeira 37; d from €30) Globo is no-frills with a range of prices, although you need a mountaineering degree to reach the best rooms at the top with their vast windows overlooking the leafy street.

Pousada da Juventude (Map pp860-1; ☎ 218 920 890; Via de Moscavide; dm/d €13/35) Pick-of-the-hostel bunch with a welcoming vibe and well-maintained rooms.

Pensão Prata (Map pp864-5; ☎ 213 468 908; 3rd fl Rua da Prata 71; s/d €20/35) Bland and institutional but very central if all you're looking for is a cheap sleep.

Pensão Imperial (Map pp864-5; ☎ 213 420 166; 4th fl Praça dos Restauradores 78; d €35) Charismatic owner and spotless comfortably worn rooms overlooking the city's main square.

Also recommended is **Pensão Norte** (Map pp864-5; ☎ 218 878 941; 2nd fl, Rua dos Douradores 159; d €35).

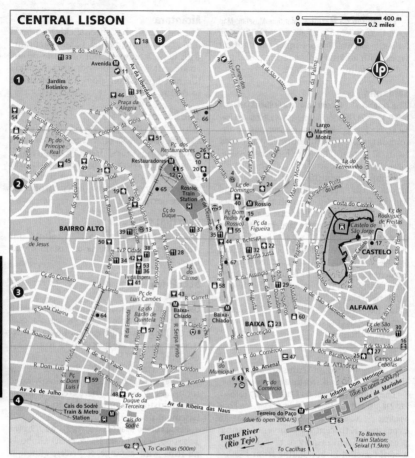

CENTRAL LISBON

Mid-Range

Residencial Florescente (Map pp864-5; ☎ 213 463 517; www.residencialflorescente.com; Rua Portas de Santo Antão 99; s/d €45/55; ※) Comfortable hotel on pedestrian cobbles a short suitcase trundle from the Praça dos Restauradores underground car park. Rooms are light and bright.

Pensão Residencial Gerês (Map pp864-5; ☎ 218 810 497; www.pensaogeres.web.pt; Calçada do Garcia 6; s/d €50/60) Religious pics, traditional tiles and carpeted comfy rooms. Go for corner room number 104 with its five-star view.

Pensão Londres (Map pp864-5; ☎ 213 462 203; Rua Dom Pedro V 53; s/d €50/65) Old-fashioned appeal with large, high-ceiling, carpeted rooms that have small balconies with neck-craning views of a bustling tree-lined street.

Sé Guest House (Map pp864-5; ☎ 218 864 400; 2nd fl Rua São João da Praça 97; s/d €40/70) Owner Luis is a keen traveller and cultural buff, hence the intriguing clutter of global artefacts and antiques throughout this historic, homy lodging.

Top End

Casa de São Mamede (Map pp860-1; ☎ 213 963 166; fax 213 951 896; Rua Escola Politécnica 159; s/d €75/80; ※) A soothing stay in 18th-century surroundings; this former magistrate's house has gorgeous original tiles and elegant antique-clad rooms.

Hotel Britania, (Map pp864-5; ☎ 213 155 016; www.heritage.pt; Rua Rodrigues Sampaio 17; s/d €146/156; ※ ▯ ⓟ)Classic Art Deco touches and massive luxury rooms in this go-for-the-splurge hotel a short walk from the centre.

EATING

All ages and incomes socialise over food in Lisbon. Watch out for tourist rip-offs like some of the energetic stretch of restaurants on Baixa's Correeiros (that *is* how it is spelt). Seafood is widely available and locals have an insatiable appetite for all things Brazilian including *feijoada* (bean stew) – and the daily dose of soap operas. The Bairro Alto has some good-value eateries while the Alfama has some of the most characterful restaurants, but can be touristy on the main castle route. The main market, Mercado da Ribeira, is near Cais do Sodré station. **Pingo Doce** (Rua de Dezembro 73) is a good central supermarket, with the Celeira Health Shop right next door.

Baixa & Alfama

Restaurante O Sol (Map pp864-5; ☎ 213 471 944; Calçada do Duque 23; mains €4; ☺ closed Sun) A rare fast-food vegetarian restaurant with outside seating, heady views and takeaways including soy burgers, pasties and (even) seaweed cannelloni.

Gingvinga (Map pp860-1; ☎ 218 850 377; Rua das Canastras 14; mains €6) Chow down on spicy African fare typical of Madagascar at this funky swing-a-cat-size restaurant with its suitably soul-searching surrounds.

Nilo (Map pp864-5; ☎ 213 467 014; Rua dos Correeiros 217; mains €6) No-frills Nilo is one of the better-

priced eateries on this restaurant strip. The pork with spicy *piri-piri* is recommended.

Restaurante Patrono (Map pp860-1; ☎ 218 868 887; Largo Chafariz de Dentro 20; mains €7) Ideally situated for a spot of refuelling, this is one of the cheapest restaurants in the nucleus of eateries in the winding backstreets of Alfama. It's usually packed with cheerful locals feasting on such specialities as hearty *aroz detamboril* (stew of monkfish and· rice).

Gandhi Palace (Map pp864-5; ☎ 218 873 839; Rua dos Douradores 214-216; mains €9) Good central choice for those suffering from curry-house withdrawal, and popular with intrepid Portuguese. If you like it hot, ask – local tastes are mild.

Lautasco (Map pp860-1; Beco do Azinhal 7-7A; mains €9; ☺ closed Sun; 🍴) Full points for atmosphere with seating on a secluded square in the shade of a magnificent rubber tree. The usual suspects are on the menu, including cod fritters and the ubiquitous *bacalhau*.

Jardim do Marisco (Map pp860-1; ☎ 218 824 242; Avenida Infante Dom Henrique, Doca Jardim do Tobaco; mains €10; 🍴) Large, airy warehouse conversion in a slick dock development on the river. The diverse menu includes grilled meats, seafood and pasta, plus cut-price kiddie choices.

Avenida de Liberdade

Os Tibetanos (Map pp864-5; ☎ 213 142 038; Rua do Salitre 117; mains from €6; ☺ closed Sat & Sun; 🍴 🍴) Doubles as a Tibetan Buddhist school with Zen-style surroundings, a leafy patio and diverse meatless menu; try the Japanese mushrooms with seaweed and tofu.

La Caffé (Map pp864-5; ☎ 213 256 736; Ave de Liberdade 129B; mains €8; 🕑 12.30-3.30pm & 8pm-11pm Tue-Sun; 🔀) Upbeat minimalist décor plus free Internet, giant fashion TV screens and a creative twist on Med cuisine, like cream of parsnip soup with green apple, Roquefort and walnuts, and black spaghetti with smoked salmon.

Bairro Alto & Saldanha

Restaurante a Primavera (Map pp864-5; ☎ 213 420 477; Travessa da Espera 34; mains from €6; 🔀) Hugely popular with a homey informality. Try the clams in garlic and coriander followed by a girth-expanding creamy dessert.

Cervejaria da Trindade (Map pp864-5; ☎ 213 423 506; Rua Nova da Trindade 20-C; mains €7) This vaulted restaurant in a former convent has nothing-fancy food, but the setting, in a former convent with dazzling pictorial tilework, provides serious food for thought.

Stravaganza (Map pp864-5; ☎ 213 468 868; Rua do Grémio Lusitano 18; mains €7-10; 🔀) A stylish Italian restaurant serving a better class of pizza and pasta, including seven vegetarian pasta choices. The goldfish bowls suspended on the wall are serious double-take stuff.

Restaurante Sinal Vermelho (Map pp864-5; ☎ 213 461 252; Rua das Gáveas 89; mains €8.50-11.50; 🕑 closed Sat lunch & Sun; 🔀) This elegant restaurant is decorated with breezy-blue *azulejos* and shelves of dusty bottles. Menu is reassuringly traditional and generous with groaning plates of seafood, rice (and the like).

Pap 'Acorda (Map pp864-5; ☎ 213 464 811; Rua da Atalaia 57-59; mains €12-15; 🔀) Lisbon luvvies lord it up in this former bakery now hung with thick curtains and chandeliers. The house speciality is various takes on *acorda*, a type of puree with lots of coriander and garlic.

Belém

Confeitaria de Belém (Map pp860-1; ☎ 213 637 423; Rua de Belém 86-88) A classic-tiled rabbit warren with reputedly the best *pasteis de nata* (custard tarts) in Portugal. Delicious!

A Cápsula (Map pp860-1; ☎ 213 648 768; Rua Vieira Portuense 72; mains €8; 🕑 Wed-Sun) This popular meet-and-greet place serves simple calorie-stoking food including Brazilian steak with rice and beans.

DRINKING

Lisbon is great if you suffer a perpetual sugar low with fabulous Art-Deco cafés particularly around Bairro Alto and Rossio. The Alcântara and Oriente area bars attract a well-heeled set while Alfama has plenty of gluggable choices, including moody low-lit places for locked-eyes-over-cocktails types. Gay and lesbian bars are mainly concentrated around the Príncipe Real area.

Café Nicola (Map pp864-5; ☎ 213 460 579; Rossio 24; 🕑 closed Sat pm & Sun) This sumptuous Art Deco café is past winner of the Café of the Year award.

Martinho da Arcada (Map pp864-5; ☎ 218 879 259; Praça do Comércio 3; 🕑 closed Sun) Former haunt of writer Pessoa; grab a coffee and head for an outdoor table under the arches.

Café a Brasileira (Map pp864-5; ☎ 213 469 547; Rua Garrett 120) Another historic watering hole for Lisbon's 19th-century greats with warm wooden innards and a busy counter serving daytime coffees and pints at night.

A Ginjinha (Map pp864-5; Largo de Domingos) Titchy, crusty local specialising in powerful *ginjinha* (cherry brandy).

Solar do Vinho do Porto (Map pp864-5; ☎ 213 475 707; Rua de São Pedro de Alcântara 45; 🕑 closed Sun) While away an evening in soft chairs with a lengthy list of white and red ports.

Pavilhão Chines (Map pp864-5; ☎ 213 424 729; Rua Dom Pedro V 89) A global mishmash of bizarre ornaments, including a roomful of war helmets, and legendary cocktails.

ENTERTAINMENT

Pick up the free monthly *Follow me Lisboa*, *Agenda Cultural Lisboa* or quarterly *Lisboa Step By Step* from the tourist office for what's on listings. Also, check out www .visitlisboa.com (Lisbon tourist office website), www.lisboacultural.pt (cultural events) and www.ticketline.pt (concert information and reservations).

Live Music

Adega Machado (Map pp864-5; ☎ 213 224 640; Rua do Norte 91; 🕑 8pm-3am, closed Mon) Earthy and authentic, run by Rita, goddaughter of the legendary Amalia Rodrigues; the walls are papered with signed photos of *fado* enthusiasts – including Kirk Douglas.

Adega do Ribatejo (Map pp864-5; ☎ 213 468 343; Rua Diário de Notícias 23; 🕑 8pm-2am) High on atmosphere with nightly *fado*.

Hot Clube de Portugal (Map pp864-5; ☎ 213 467 369; Praça da Alegria 39; ⏰ 10pm-2am, closed Sun & Mon) Hot, sweaty and packed with nightly gigs and raw new jazz sounds.

Ó Gilíns Irish Pub (Map pp864-5; ☎ 213 421 899; Rua dos Remolares 8-10; ⏰ 11am-2am) Predictable blarney atmosphere with live music on Friday and Saturday evenings.

Tertúlia (Map pp864-5; ☎ 213 462 704; Rua do Dia'rio de Noticias 60; ⏰ 8pm-2am Mon-Sun) Low-lit bar with newspapers, live jazz, exhibitions and – for those who can't resist a tinkle – a piano for customer use.

Nightclubs

Lux (Map pp860-1; ☎ 218 820 890; Armazém A, Cais da Pedra; ⏰ midnight-5am) Part-owned by John Malkovich, it's a trendy club with towering ceilings, river-side terraces and dance floors.

Dock's Club (Map pp860-1; ☎ 213 950 856; Rua da Cintura do Porto de Lisboa 226; ⏰ 11pm-6am Tue-Sat) Another river-side dance temple attracting a voguish clientele.

Blues Café (Map pp860-1; ☎ 213 957 085; Rua da Cintura do Porto; ⏰ 11pm-6am Tue-Sat) Jazz, blues and club nights, plus dock-side drinking in cool warehouse development.

Ritz Club (Map pp864-5; ☎ 213 425 140; Rua da Glória 57; ⏰ 9pm-3am) The city's largest African club, it's an atmospheric place with pulsating music and a friendly vibe.

Gay & Lesbian Venues

Lisbon has a relaxed yet flourishing gay scene, with an annual Gay Pride Festival at the end of June.

Portas Largas (Map pp864-5; ☎ 218 461 379; Rua da Atalaia 105) A tiled bar with barn-size doors attracting a mainly gay crowd with its giant carafes of sangria.

Trumps (Map pp864-5; Rua da Imprensa Nacional 104B) Not much elbow space in these two bars; one has a dance floor to get jiggy.

Finalmente (Map pp864-5; Rua da Palmeira 38) A heaving dance floor and nightly drag shows.

Cinemas

Lisbon has dozens of cinemas, including the multiscreen **Amoreiras** (Map pp860-1; ☎ 213 878 752) and **Colombo** (Map pp860-1; ☎ 217 113 222), both located within shopping centres.

Sport

Lisbon's football teams are Benfica, Belenenses and Sporting. Preparations for Euro 2004 led to the upgrading of the 65,000-seat Esta'dio da Luz and the construction of a new 54,000-seat Estadio Nacional. Bullfights are staged at Campo Pequeno between April and October. Tickets for both are available at **ABEP ticket agency** (Map pp864-5; Praça dos Restauradores). The tourist office can help with transport and locations of the city's stadia.

SHOPPING

One of the delights of shopping in Lisbon is exploring the idiosyncratic small shops. Many have remained in the same family for several generations; the personalised service is an added plus. In contrast, the shopping malls are packed with glossy new boutiques, familiar chains and snack bars for those shopping on the go. Antique shops are mainly in the Barro Alto district. Hand-painted ceramics can be found around Baixa and Chiado. Don't miss the flea market **Feira da Ladra** (Map pp860-1; Campo de Santa Clara; ⏰ Tue & Sat). For designer boutiques take a high-heeled strut down swanky Rua Garrett.

Grandes Armazens do Chiado (Map pp864-5; Rua do Carmo) is artfully concealed behind the restored façade of the historic main department store. FNAC is good for electronic items, music and booking concert tickets.

Fabrica Sant'Ana (Map pp864-5; Rua do Alecrim 95) and **Santos Ofícios** (Map pp864-5; Rua da Madalena 87) are touristy but have an eclectic range of Portuguese folk art.

GETTING THERE & AWAY

Air

Lisbon is connected by daily flights to Porto, Faro and many European centres. For arrival and departure information call ☎ 218 413 700.

Bus

A dozen different companies, including **Renex** (☎ 222 003 395), operate from Gare do Oriente. The Arco do Cego terminal is the base for **Rede Expressos** (☎ 707 223 344) and **EVA** (☎ 213 147 710), who cover the whole country.

Train

Santa Apolónia station (Map pp860-1; ☎ 218 816 121) is the terminus for northern and central Portugal, and for all international services (trains also stop en route at the better

PORTUGAL

connected Gare do Oriente). Cais do Sodré station is for Belém, Cascais and Estoril. Rossio station serves Sintra.

Barreiro station, which is across the river, is the terminus for southern Portugal; connecting ferries leave frequently from the pier at Terréiro do Paço. The north–south railway line, over the Ponte de 25 Abril, goes to suburban areas and will eventually carry on further to southern Portugal.

For more detailed information on all above modes of transport see p891.

GETTING AROUND
To/From the Airport

The AeroBus runs every 20 minutes from 7.45am to 8.45pm, taking 30 to 45 minutes between the airport and Cais do Sodré, including a stop by the ICEP tourist office. A €2.35/5.50 ticket is good for one/three days on all buses, trams and funiculars. Local bus Nos 44 and 45 also run near the ICEP tourist office; No 44 links the airport with Gare do Oriente too. A taxi into town is about €10, plus €1.50 for luggage.

Bicycle

Tejo Bike (Map pp860-1; ☎ 218 871 976), 300m east of Belém, rents out bicycles for €5 an hour to ride along the waterfront.

Car & Motorcycle

Car rental companies at Lisbon airport include **Avis** (☎ 800 201 002; www.avis.com), **Europcar** (☎ 218 410 163; www.europcar.com) or the nearby (and cheaper) **Ride-On** (☎ 218 452 811; Rua Reinaldo Ferreira 29; ride_on@netcabo.pt). The most central underground car park is at Praça dos Restauradores, costing around €0.75 an hour. There are cheaper (or free) car parks near Parque das Nações or Belém, from where you can catch a bus or tram to the centre.

Public Transport
BUS & TRAM

Two-journey bus and tram tickets are €0.93 from Carris kiosks, most conveniently at Praça da Figueira and the Santa Justa Elevador, or €0.90 per ride from the driver. A one-/four-/seven-day Passe Turístico, valid for trams, buses and the metro, costs €2.55/ 9.25/13.10. The *Lisboa Card* is good for unlimited travel on nearly all city transport (see p862).

Buses and trams run from 6am to 1am, with some night services. Pick up a transport map from tourist offices or Carris kiosks.

FERRY

Cais da Alfândega is the terminal for several ferries, including to Cacilhas (€0.60), a transfer point for some buses to Setúbal. A car (and bike) ferry runs from Cais do Sodré terminal.

METRO

The metro is useful for hops across town and to the Parque das Nações. Individual tickets cost €0.65; a *caderneta* of 10 tickets is €6. A return ticket *(allé et retour)* is €1.20. The metro operates from 6.30am to 1am.

Taxi

Lisbon's taxis are metered and best hired from taxi ranks. Confusingly, when the green light is on, it means the taxi is already occupied. Some at the airport are less than scrupulous. From the Rossio to Belém is around €6 and to the castle about €4.50.

AROUND LISBON
Sintra
pop 20,000

This hilltop town, less than an hour west of Lisbon, has traditionally been the holiday home for royalty, the rich and the famous. With stunning palaces and manors surrounded by lush green countryside it is a captivating camera-clicking place. Word is out, so visit out of season if you can.

The **tourist office** (☎ 219 231 157; www.cm-sintra .pt; Praça da República 23; ⏱ 9am-7pm) sells tourist passes and has a list of accommodation. Check your emails at the **Internet Lounge** (☎ 219 109 078; Rua Dr Alfredo da Costa 76; ⏱ 10.30am-midnight Mon-Fri, 11.30am-11pm Sat, 12.30am-10pm Sun) near the centre.

SIGHTS & ACTIVITIES

Although the whole town resembles a historical theme park, there are several compulsory eye-catching sights. Most are free or discounted with the *Lisboa Card* (see the boxed text p862); pensioners, students and children pay half-price.

The **Palácio Nacional de Sintra** (☎ 219 106 840; admission €3; ⏱ 10am-5.30pm Thu-Tue) is a dizzy mix of Moorish and Gothic architecture with twin chimneys that dominate the town.

The **Museu do Brinquedo** (☎ 219 242 172; Rua Visconde de Monserrate; admission €3; ☼ 10am-6pm Tue-Sun) offers serious playtime stuff with 20,000 toys from all over the world.

An energetic 3km greenery-flanked hike from the centre, the 8th-century ruined ramparts of **Castelo dos Mouros** (☎ 219 237 300; admission €3; ☼ 9am-7pm) provide fine views.

Trudge on for 20 minutes more to the exuberantly kitsch **Palácio da Pena** (☎ 219 105 340; admission €6; ☼ 10am-5.30pm Tue-Sun). Alternatively, take the cop-out bus No 434 (€3.20) from the station, via the tourist office.

Monserrate Gardens (☎ 219 237 116; admission €3; ☼ 9am-7pm) are fabulously lush botanical gardens 4km from town.

En route to the gardens is **Quinta da Regaleira** (☎ 219 106 650; admission €10; ☼ 10am-6pm, to 3.30pm winter), a World Heritage site. Visits to this extraordinary mansion must be prearranged.

Cabra Montêz (☎ 917 446 668; www.cabramontez .com) organises trekking, mountain biking and canoeing excursions.

SLEEPING
Residencial Adelaide (☎ 219 230 873; Rua Guilherme Gomes Fernandes 11; d from €25) A lick of paint could do wonders for this great-value accommodation, a 10-minute walk from the centre, with its pretty garden and large, well-worn rooms.

Estrada Velha (☎ 219 234 355; Consiglieri Pedroso 16; s/d €40/50; 🍴) Just five meticulously decorated rooms with wood-panelling and wrought-iron beds; the downstairs bar-restaurant is excellent for light tasty fare like sweet and savoury crepes.

Lawrence's Hotel (☎ 219 105 500; www.lawrences hotel.com; Rua Consiglieri Pedroso 38-40; s/d €180/235; P 🍴 💻) Shift your credit card into overdrive to stay at Iberia's oldest hotel, certainly vintage enough to have bedded Lord Byron and William Beckford, and more recently revamped to five-star luxury by its Dutch owners.

EATING
Xentra (☎ 219 240 759; Rua Consiglieri Pedroso 2-A; mains €6) Has a beamed cavernous bar and restaurant, rock music on Sunday nights and karaoke on Mondays.

Tulhas (☎ 219 232 378; Rua Gil Vicente 4-6; mains €7) Typically full of happily chomping locals, it dishes up comfort food like *bacalhau* with

cream and at least one vegetarian dish in rustic surrounds.

Taverna Bar (☎ 219 233 587; Escadinhas do Teixeira 3; mains €7) Homy place serving traditional dishes with salutary (and salivary) attention to detail. Try the roast pork.

GETTING THERE & AWAY
The Lisbon–Sintra railway terminates in Estefânia, 1.5km northeast of the town's historic centre. Sintra's bus station, and another train station, are a further 1km east in the new-town district of Portela de Sintra. Frequent shuttle buses run to the historic centre from the bus station.

Trains run every 15 minutes from Lisbon's Rossio station (€1.30, 45 minutes). Buses run hourly from Sintra to Estoril (€2.50, 40 minutes) and Cascais (€2.50, 45 minutes).

GETTING AROUND
A taxi to Pena or Monserrate costs around €10 return. Horse-drawn carriages are a spoil-her-rotten alternative: expect €55 to get to Monserrate and back. Old trams run from Ribeira de Sintra (1.5km from the centre) to Praia das Maças, 12km to the west.

Cascais
pop 30,000
Cascais has grown from a fishing village into a sunbed-and-sandcastle resort that is packed in summer. The **tourist office** (☎ 214 868 204; www.estorilcoast-tourism.com; Rua Visconde de Luz 14; ☼ 9am-7pm Mon-Fri Sep-Jun, 9am-8pm Mon-Fri Jul-Aug, 10am-6pm Sat & Sun year-round) has accommodation lists and bus timetables; there's also a **tourist police post** (☎ 214 863 929). You can slurp a soft drink while checking your emails at **Golfinho** (☎ 214 840 150; Sebastião Carvalho e Melo 17; ☼ 10am-midnight Mon-Sat May-Sep, 10am-8pm Mon-Sat Oct-Apr).

SIGHTS & ACTIVITIES
Estoril is an old-fashioned resort 2km east of Cascais with a superb sandy beach and Europe's largest **casino** (☎ 214 667 700; www.casino -estoril.pt, in Portuguese; ☼ 3pm-3am, floor show 11pm).

Praia Tamariz has an ocean swimming pool. The sea roars into the coast at **Boca do Inferno** (Hell's Mouth), 2km west of Cascais. Spectacular **Cabo da Roca**, Europe's westernmost point, is 16km from Cascais and Sintra and is served by buses from both towns.

Wild **Guincho** beach, 3km from Cascais, is a popular surfing venue.

SLEEPING & EATING

Residencial Avenida (☎ 214 864 417; Rua da Palmeira 14; d €30) Sparkling clean, well-placed accommodation efficiently run by English-speaking owners.

Casa da Pergola (☎ 214 840 040; www.ciberguia .pt/casa-da-pergola; Avenida Valbom 13; d €99; 🔀) Well worth the splurge, this elegant 19th-century home is tastefully done up with expensive art and antiques. Enjoy breakfast and bird-song in the pretty garden.

Dom Grelhas (☎ 214 839 963; Rua Sebastião JC Melo 35, Casa da Guia; mains €8) En route to Guincho, Casa da Guia is a fashionable small complex of edgy boutiques, art galleries, bars and restaurants, including this one with healthy salad and seafood choices accompanied by seamless sea views.

GETTING THERE & AROUND

Trains run frequently to Cascais, via Estoril (€1.30, 30 minutes) from Cais do Sodré station in Lisbon. **Transrent** (☎ 214 864 566; www .transrent.pt; Centro Commercial Cisne, Avenida Marginal) rents cars, bicycles and motorcycles.

Setúbal
pop 110,500

Portugal's third-largest port has a stunning church, a spectacular castle and a largely pedestrianised centre packed with good-looking shops and cafés. Pity about the in-your-face piped music over the city sound system.

INFORMATION

Instituto Português da Juventude (IPJ; ☎ 265 534 431; Largo José Afonso) Has free Internet access for limited periods on weekdays.

Municipal tourist office (☎ /fax 265 534 402; Praça do Quebedo; ❤ 9am-7pm) Is a five-minute walk east from the bus station (Avenida 5 de Outubro).

Regional tourist office (☎ 265 539 130; www .mun-setubal.pt; Travessa Frei Gaspar 10) With the oddity of a Roman fish-preserving factory under its glass floor.

SIGHTS & ACTIVITIES

Portugal's first Manueline building, the stunning **Igreja de Jesus** (Praça Miguel Bombarda), has maritime motifs and twisted pillars that resemble coiled ropes. The **Galeria da Pintura Quinhentista** (admission free; ❤ 9am-noon & 2-5pm Tue-

Sat), just around the corner, has a renowned collection of 16th-century paintings.

Good **beaches** west of town include Praia da Figuerinha (accessible by bus in summer). Across the estuary at Tróia is a more developed beach, plus the ruins of a Roman settlement. On the ferry trip across you may see some of the estuary's 30 or so bottle-nosed dolphins.

SAL (☎ 265 227 685; www.sal.pt, in Portuguese; ❤ Sat) organises walks from €5 per person. For jeep safaris, hiking and biking in the Serra da Arrábida, or canoe trips through the Reserva Natural do Estuário do Sado, contact **Planeta Terra** (☎ 919 471 871; Praça General Luís Domingues 9). **Vertigem Azul** (☎ 265 238 000; www.vertigemazul.com; Avenida Luísa Todi 375) offers canoe and dolphin-spotting excursions.

SLEEPING

Pousada da Juventude (☎ 265 534 431; setubal@ movijovem.pt; Largo José Afonso; dm/d €11/35) Well-equipped tidy hostel with a buzzy vibe.

Pensão Bom Regresso (☎ 265 229 812; Praça de Bocage 48; d €40) Overlooks the main square; about as close to church as you can get without attending confession. Rooms are clean but monastically basic.

Bom Amigo (☎ 265 526 290; Rua do Concelho 7; s/d €36/48) Pristine, down to the freshly dusted plastic flowers. Room 4 has lovely contemplative views of the plaza.

Residencial Bocage (☎ 265 543 080; fax 265 543 089; Rua São Cristovão 14; s/d €27/45) Fairly forgettable rooms in a newish building; satellite TV and nearby parking are the major perks for the price.

EATING

O Beco (☎ 265 524 617; Largo da Misericordia 24; mains €10) Locals rate this restaurant as one of the city's best. Go for one of the cockle dishes for that special seafood moment.

Peregrina (☎ 265 230 602; Rua dos Almocreves 74; mains €10) One of three vegetarian restaurants in town, although all close at an unsociable 6pm. Quiche, *seitan* (wheat gluten), nut rissoles and more salads than you can shake a carrot stick at.

Xica Bia (☎ 265 522 559; Ave Luisa Todi 131; mains from €10) Xiaca Bia has a lovely dinner-for-two setting with barrel-vault brick ceiling, candles and a wallet-slimming menu of dishes. Don't leave without trying the *arroz de marisco* (shellfish rice).

GETTING THERE & AWAY

Buses leave every half-hour from Lisbon's Praça de Espanha (€3.10, one hour). Ferries shuttle across the estuary to Tróia approximately every 45 minutes (€1.10, 15 minutes).

THE ALGARVE

The Algarve is popular not only as a sun-and-sea holiday resort, but also as home to an increasing number of permanent residents, particularly from Germany and the UK. While this may sound depressing, the good news is that away from the coastal strip (and the golf courses) you are back in Portugal again with attractions that include the forested slopes of Monchique, the fortified village of Silves and windswept, historic Sagres. Faro is the regional capital.

Getting There & Around

Air Portugal (TAP; ☎ 707 205 700; www.tap.pt) has daily Lisbon–Faro flights (under an hour) year-round.

There is no direct rail link from Lisbon to the Algarve. There are some regional services but these are generally slower than the long-distance buses. For drivers a speedy 235km toll road (around €20) links Lisbon with the Algarve.

EVA (☎ 289 899 740) and **Rede Expressos** (☎ 289 899 760) operate frequent and efficient bus services between Lisbon and major cities and various Algarve resorts. The IP1/EO1 super highway runs the length of the coast.

Bicycles, scooters and motorcycles can be rented everywhere; see town listings or check the nearest tourist office.

FARO

pop 45,000

Aside from midsummer when it is heaving, with no towel space on the beach, Faro is pleasantly low-key, as well as being the main transport hub and commercial centre. Expat-oriented, English-language newspapers with entertainment information include the *Algarve Good Life* and *The Resident*. Go online at the good and central **Self-Service Internet** (☎ 289 873 731; Largo Pé da Cruz 1; ☼ closed Sun). The central **tourist office** (☎ 289 803 604; www.rtalgarve.pt; Rua da Misericórdia) has informative leaflets and maps.

Sights & Activities

The palm-clad **waterfront** around Praça de Dom Francisco Gomes has pleasant kick-back cafés. Faro's beach, **Praia de Faro** (Ilha de Faro), is 6km southwest of the city; take bus No 16 from opposite the bus station. Less crowded is the unspoilt **Ilha Desserta** in the nature park **Parque Natural da Ria Formosa** (☎ 917 811 856); ask about lagoon tours. Access is by ferry from June to mid-September from Cais da Porta Nova.

At Estói, 12km north of Faro, the romantically ruined **Estói Palace** has a surreal garden

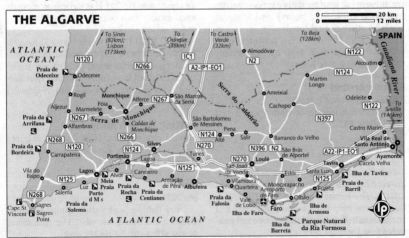

THE ALGARVE

of statues, balustrades and *azulejos*. It's ear-marked for a government-run pousada so visit soon.

Sleeping & Eating

Avoid midsummer when many of the hotels are block-booked by tour groups.

Pousada da Juventude (☎ 289 826 521; Rua da Polícia de Segurança Pública 1; dm/d €12/25) Welcoming low-key accommodation if you're euro economising.

Pensão Residencial Central (☎ 289 807 291; Largo Terreiro do Bispo 10; s/d €30/40) Squeaky clean if characterless, although it has a great position overlooking the jacaranda-fringed square.

Residencial Adelaide (☎ 289 802 383; fax 289 826 870; Rua Cruz dos Mestres 7; d €45) Lots of clinical white here, with large rooms, balconies, rooftop terrace and chatty owner. Disabled unit available.

Sol e Jardim (☎ 289 820 030; Praça Ferreira de Almeida 22; mains €9) Atmospheric seafood restaurant decorated with nets, jolly murals and aquariums. Try the seafood spaghetti.

Velha Casa (☎ 289 824 719; Rua do Pé da Cruz 33, mains €7) Solidly reliable traditional fare is on offer here, including mixed kebabs, pork with pineapple, and creamy, gut-sticking rice pudding.

Getting There & Away

Faro airport has both domestic and international flights (see p891).

From the bus station, just west of the centre, there are at least six daily express coaches to Lisbon (€14, four hours) and frequent buses to other coastal towns.

The train station is a few minutes' walk west of the bus station. Four trains run daily to Lisbon (€10, five hours).

Getting Around

The airport is 6km from the centre. Bus Nos 14 and 16 run into town until 9pm. A taxi costs about €12.

TAVIRA

pop 12,000

Lovely Tavira is in the process of being discovered by visitors, but still oozes old-world charm. The **tourist office** (☎ 281 322 511; Rua da Galeria 9) can help with accommodation and the **town hall** (Praça da Republica; ☺ closed Sun) provides free Internet access.

Sights & Activities

One of the town's 30-plus churches, the **Igreja da Misericórdia** has a striking Renaissance doorway and is a concert venue during the **Algarve International Classical Music Festival** (☺ May-July). Tavira's ruined **castle** (Rua da Liberdade; admission free; ☺ 8am-4.30pm Mon-Fri, 10am-5.30pm Sat & Sun) dominates the town.

Ilha da Tavira is an island beach connected to the mainland by a ferry at Quatro Águas. Walk the 2km or take the (summer only) bus from the bus station.

Enjoy pedal power with a rented bike from **Casa Abilio** (☎ 281 323 467). For walking or biking trips call **Exploratio** (☎ 919 338 226). To sail contact **Clube Náutico** (☎ 281 326 858). Jose Salvador Rocha organises **diving trips** (☎ 939 017 329).

Sleeping & Eating

Camping ground (☎ 281 324 455; camp sites €9) Ilha da Tavira has this summer-only budget option.

Pensão Residencial Lagoas (☎ 281 322 252; Almirante Cândido dos Reis 24; d €40) Handy for self-catering across the road from a supermarket. Rooms are dingy but clean.

Residencial Imperial (☎ 281 322 234; José Pires Padinha 24; d €40) Plain, no-nonsense *pensão* with balconies and a downstairs restaurant overlooking the river.

Marés (☎ 281 325 815; José Pires Padinha 134; s/d €40/60; ☒) Snazzy modern rooms with balconies and CNN. The restaurant is good.

Restaurante Bica (☎ 281 332 483; below Residencial Lagoas; mains €7; ☒) Has delicious specials such as sole with orange followed by own-made almond cake.

Patio (☎ 281 323 008; António Cabreira 30; mains €8-10; ☒) Fatten your credit card at the town's most famous restaurant dishing up traditional cuisine like octopus-studded sole. Terrace with panoramic views and vegetarian dishes.

Getting There & Away

Some 15 trains and at least six express buses run daily between Faro and Tavira (€1.80, 45 minutes).

LAGOS

pop 20,000

A busy fishing port with popular beaches, Lagos has a laid-back vibe. The municipal **tourist office** (☎ 282 764 111; www.lagosdigital.com, in Portuguese; Largo Marquês de Pombal; ☼ 10am-6pm Mon-Sat) is the more convenient tourist office; the other is 1km northeast of the centre. Surf through a cappuccino while checking your email at cool **Bora Café** (☎ 282 083 438; Conselheiro Joaquim Machado 17).

Sights & Activities

The **municipal museum** houses an assortment of archaeological finds and ecclesiastical treasures. The adjacent **Igreja de Santo António** has some intricate baroque woodwork.

The beach scene includes **Meia Praia**, a vast strip to the east; **Praia da Luz** to the west; and the smaller **Praia do Pinhão**.

Blue Ocean (☎ 282 782 718; www.blue-ocean-divers .de) organises diving, kayaking and snor- kelling safaris. On the seaside promenade, fishermen offer motorboat jaunts to nearby grottoes. For horse riding in the Algarve interior ring **Tiffany's** (☎ 282 697 395).

Sleeping

Campismo da Trindade (☎ 282 763 893; camp sites €4) Not much tent-peg space in summer at this small camping ground 200m south of town walls.

Pensão Caravaela (☎ 289 763 361; 25 de Abril 16; d from €32) Plain comfy rooms on a busy pe- destrian street; you may need earplugs on a Saturday night.

Pousada da Juventude (☎ 282 761 970; Rua Lançarote de Freitas 50; dm/d €16/44) Up there with the best, the rooms are light and airy and there's a cosy kitchen and garden.

Eating & Drinking

Maharaja de Lagos (☎ 282 761 507; Dr Jose Formoz- inho; mains €7) High above the old town with all those spicy Indian standards such as baltis, biryanis and *bhunas*.

Taberna de Lagos (☎ 282 084 250; 25 de Abril; mains €7) This former warehouse serves up a diet of pizzas, pastas, salads and vegetarian dishes in a grand space with beams and arches.

Lounge www.Cocktail (☎ 963 821 067; Sr da Graç 2; snacks €3) Funky English-run bar with chicken tikka, quiche and piled-high nachos. DJs weekend nights.

Getting There & Away

Bus and train services depart frequently for other Algarve towns and around six times daily to Lisbon (€14, four hours).

Getting Around

You can rent bicycles, mopeds and motorcy- cles from **Motoride** (☎ 289 761 720; Rua José Afonso 23; per day from €5) or agents in town.

MONCHIQUE
pop 6840

The rural B-side to the clamour and crowds of the coast, pretty Monchique is surrounded by the forested Serra de Monchique. The **tour- ist office** (☎ 282 911 189; ☼ 9.30am-1pm & 2-5.30pm Mon-Fri, 9.30am-noon Sat) is bang on the square.

Sights & Activities

Igreja Matriz has a stunning Manueline por- tal, its stone seemingly tied in knots. Fol- low the brown pedestrian signs up from the bus station, around the old town's narrow streets.

Caldas de Monchique, 6km south, is a mildly heritaged yet still quaint hot-spring hamlet. Some 8km west is the Algarve's 'rooftop', the 902m **Fóia** peak atop the Serra de Mon- chique, with heady views through a forest of radio masts.

Omega Parque Monchique (☎ 282 911 327; admis- sion €8; ☼ 10am-6pm) is an eco-friendly small zoo with animals kept in as near a natural environment as possible.

Alternativtour (☎ 282 420 800; from €25) organ- ises bike and walking tours.

Sleeping & Eating

Residencial Estrela de Monchique (☎ 282 913 111; Rua do Porto Fundo 46; s/d €20/35) Small scrubbed pine rooms with homy views of neighbour- ing gardens.

Restaurante A Charrete (☎ 282 912 142; Rua Dr Samora Gil 30; mains €7.50) Worth the climb; try the beans with cabbage followed by rice-and- honey pudding.

Getting There & Away

Over a dozen buses run daily from Lagos to Portimão, from where five to nine services run daily (€2.30, 45 minutes) to Monchique.

SILVES
pop 10,500

It's hard to believe that this small, genteel town was once the capital of Moorish Al- garve. Take a deep breath and climb up to the fairy-tale castle on the hill. The **tourist office** (☎ 289 442 255; Rua 25 de Abril; ☼ Mon-Fri & Sat morn- ing) can help with accommodation. The main

post office (Rua do Correio) has a Netpost (Internet) kiosk.

Sleeping & Eating

Residencial Sousa (☎ 282 442 502; Rua Samoura Barros 17; s/d €15/30) Plain, no-frills rooms in the centre of town.

Residencial Ponte Romana (☎ 282 443 275; d €30) Ace location beside the Roman bridge with castle views, Sky TV, good-size rooms and a cavernous bar-restaurant that packs them in at weekends.

Café Ingles (☎ 282 442 585; mains €8) Just below castle entrance, this English-owned funky place has vegetarian dishes, home-made soups, pasta and wood-fired pizza, plus live music at weekends, including sultry Brazilian café music on Sunday summer afternoons.

Restaurante Rui (☎ 282 442 682; Rua C Vilarinho 27; mains from €9) Push the boat out at this superb fish restaurant with everything from spider crab to cockles on the menu.

Getting There & Away

Silves train station is 2km from town; trains from Lagos (€1.50, 35 minutes) stop nine times daily (from Faro, change at Tunes), to be met by local buses. Six buses run daily to Silves from Albufeira (€2.75, 40 minutes).

SAGRES

pop 2500

Tucked away in Portugal's southwestern corner, Sagres is all drama and history with its evocative albeit bleak fort perched high above the thundering surf. There is a central **tourist office** (☎ 282 624 873; Rua Comandante Matoso; ⊗ 10am-1.30pm & 2.30-6pm Mon-Fri, 10am-1.30pm Sat) plus **Turinfo** (☎ 282 620 003; Praça da República), which rents cars and bikes, books hotels and arranges jeep and fishing trips.

Sights & Activities

The **fort** (admission €3; ⊗ 10am-6.30pm Mon-Sat, to 8.30pm Sun) has a 12-minute slide show on the history; Henry the Navigator established his navigation school here and primed the explorers who later founded the Portuguese empire.

This coast is ideal for the surfing set; hire windsurfers at sand-dune fringed **Praia do Martinhal**.

Surfcamp (Mestre António Galhardo; from €30) organises canoeing trips plus surfing and body-board classes.

Visit Europe's southwestern-most point, the **Cabo de São Vicente** (Cape St Vincent), 6km to the west. A solitary lighthouse stands on this barren cape.

Sleeping & Eating

Parque de Campismo Sagres (☎ 282 624 351; camp sites €5) This is 2km from town, off the Vila do Bispo road.

Mar à Vista (☎ 282 624 247; Praia da Mareta; mains €8) Sea-and-surf views from the terrace. Med cuisine includes pasta with lobster and eight different salads.

Getting There & Away

Frequent buses run daily to Sagres from Lagos (€2.50, 50 minutes), with fewer on Sunday. Three continue out to Cabo de São Vicente on weekdays.

CENTRAL PORTUGAL

The central slice of Portugal has a raw, rugged beauty with tumbling rivers, dense forests and stuck-in-a-time-warp stone villages where local women still carry their shopping on their head. The coast, too, has more sunbed space than further south, while the energetic can enjoy hiking and skiing in the dramatic Beiras region. The sense of history is everywhere, with castles, fortresses and even Roman temples, while the more modern gourmet can enjoy the fine local wines from the Dão region.

ÉVORA

pop 50,000

A Unesco World Heritage Site, Évora is walled and medieval with cobblestones, narrow alleys and arches, plus some blockbuster mansions and palaces. Hugely atmospheric and popular, Évora is well worth a stroll around, despite its mild overdose of souvenir shops. The **tourist office** (☎ 266 702 671; www.cm-evora.pt, in Portuguese; Praça do Giraldo 73; ⊗ 9am-7pm Mon-Sat) has an excellent city map. Log on at the **Cyber Center** (☎ 266 746 923; Rua dos Mercadores 42; ⊗ 9am-2am).

Sights & Activities

Sé (Largo do Marquês de Marialva; admission €2.25; ⊗ 9am-noon & 2-5pm), Évora's cathedral, has fabulous cloisters and a museum jam-packed with ecclesiastical treasures.

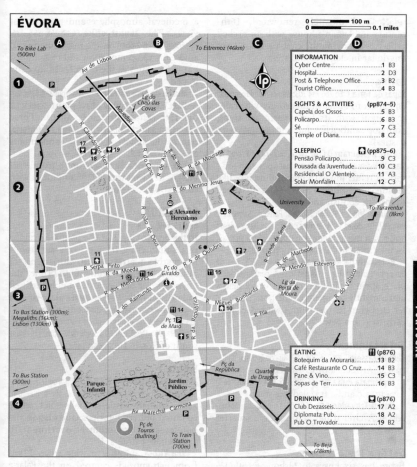

ÉVORA

INFORMATION
Cyber Centre	.................1 B3
Hospital	.......................2 D3
Post & Telephone Office	....3 B2
Tourist Office	................4 B3

SIGHTS & ACTIVITIES (pp874–5)
Capela dos Ossos	...........5 B3
Policarpo	.....................6 B3
Sé	............................7 C3
Temple of Diana	............8 C2

SLEEPING (pp875–6)
Pensão Policarpo	............9 C3
Pousada da Juventude	.....10 C3
Residencial O Alentejo	....11 A3
Solar Monfalim	.............12 C3

EATING (p876)
Botequim da Mouraria	....13 B2
Café Restaurante O Cruz	..14 B3
Pane & Vino	................15 C3
Sopas de Terr	..............16 B3

DRINKING (p876)
Club Dezasseis	.............17 A2
Diplomata Pub	.............18 A2
Pub O Trovador	............19 B2

The **Temple of Diana** with its graceful Corinthian columns is definitely worth some camera clicking. At the time of research, the museum opposite the temple was closed for renovations.

Capela dos Ossos (☎ 266 744 307; Largo Conde de Vila Flor; admission €2; � 9am-1pm & 2.30-6pm) was discovered in 1958 during restoration work. This ghoulish Chapel of Bones is constructed from the bones and skulls of several thousand people; not for the faint-hearted.

Turaventur (☎ 266 743 134; www.evora.net/turaven tur; Qta Serrado, Sr Aflitos) offers a whole range of adrenaline-fuelled activities, including canoeing (half-day, €60), mountain biking (four hours, €35) and 4WD safari tours (full day, €60).

Sleeping

Pousada da Juventude (☎ 266 744 848; Rua Miguel Bombarda 40; dm/d €14/35) Recently renovated with a bright imaginative interior, providing excellent cut-price accommodation.

Residencial O Alentejo (☎ 266 702 903; Rua Serpa Pinto 74; s/d €30/35) Nothing fancy but with a certain charm thanks to the folksy painted furniture and courtyard with cats.

Pensão Policarpo (☎ 266 702 424; www.localnet .pt/residencialpolicarpo; Rua da Freiria de Baixo 16; s/d €30/40; ☒) Hats off for the setting: a 17th-century manor house complete with Roman columns and part of the original city wall in the foyer. Large pleasant rooms with views.

Solar Monfalim (☎ 266 750 000; www.monfalim tur.pt/monfalim/ingles; Largo da Misericórdia 1; s/d €70/80;

P 🔀 🖳) Exquisitely renovated, 16th-century nobleman's house with an arched gallery overlooking the cobbles. Rooms are top dollar in elegance and style.

Eating

Sopas da Terra (☎ 266 744 703; Rua da Moeda 5; snacks €3) Expect to queue at this young-vibe café-restaurant with its belly-warming soups, doorstop sandwiches and *salgados* (savoury pasties).

Café Restaurant O Cruz (☎ 266 747 228; Praça 1 de Maio 20; mains €6) Earthy and inexpensive for a spot of refuelling with plain filling fare like *acorda com bacalhau e ovo escalfado* (bread soup with codfish and egg).

Pane & Vino (☎ 266 746 960; Páteo do Salema 22; mains €7; ⏱ closed Mon) Sunny colours, cheery staff and a vast menu including upper-class pizzas, swanky salad bar and creamy tiramisu.

Botequim da Mouraria (☎ 266 746 775; Rua da Mouraria 16a; mains €8; ⏱ closed Sun) A real insider's place; there are just a dozen bar-stool places and a nightly set menu of creations by master chef-cum-barman-cum-owner. Get here early to grab a pew.

Entertainment

Club Dezasseis (☎ 266 706 559; Rua do Escrivão da Câmara 16) Attracts a mix of suits and scruffs.

Diplomata Pub (☎ 266 705 675; Rua do Apóstolo 4) Live music and a frazzled bar staff.

Pub O Trovador (☎ 266 707 370; Rua da Mostardeira 4) A chilled-out setting for a smarter crowd.

Getting There & Away

Évora has six buses to Lisbon (€9.50, 1½ hours) Monday to Friday and two to Faro (€11.50, four hours), departing from the station off Avenida Túlio Espanca (700m southwest of the centre). Three daily trains run from Lisbon (€7.10, 2½ hours).

Getting Around

Bike Lab (☎ 266 735 500; ⏱ summer only) rents out bicycles. **Policarpo** (☎ 266 746 970; www.policarpo-viagens.pt, in Portuguese; Rua 5 de Outubro 63) organises city tours and jaunts to megaliths and other nearby attractions.

MONSARAZ

pop 100

In an exceptional setting, high above the plain, this swoonsome walled village has a medieval atmosphere and magnificent views. The **tourist office** (☎ 266 557 136; ⏱ 10am-1pm & 2-6pm) on the main square can advise on accommodation and restaurants. Eat before 8pm as the town tucks up early to bed.

Museu de Arte Sacra (⏱ 10am-1pm & 2-6pm; admission €1) has a display of religious artefacts; the 15th-century fresco is superb. Three kilometres north of town is **Menhir of Outeiro**, one of the tallest megalithic monuments ever discovered.

Up to four daily buses run to/from Reguengos de Monsaraz (€2, 35 minutes), with connections to Évora.

ESTREMOZ

pop 15,460

In the heart of the Alentejo plains, Estremoz is a shimmering tribute to its surrounding marble quarries, albeit with a sense of mildly fading grandeur. In its prime, the town was one of the most strongly fortified in Portugal with its very own palace (now a luxurious pousada). The **tourist office** (☎ 268 333 541; www.cm-estremoz.pt, in Portuguese; Largo da República 26; ⏱ 9.30am-12.30pm & 2-6pm) is just south of Rossio (main square).

Sights

Museu Municipal (☎ 268 339 200; Largo D Dinis; admission €1.10; ⏱ 9am-12.30pm & 2-5.30pm Tue-Sun), across from the castle, specialises in brightly coloured pottery figurines, and also incorporates an art museum of contemporary Portuguese painters.

Vila Viçosa, another marble town 17km from Estremoz, is centred on the **Palácio Ducal** (☎ 268 980 659; Terreiro do Paça; admission €5 plus €2.50 for armoury museum; ⏱ 9am-1pm & 3-5.30pm Tue-Sun), the magnificent ancestral home of the dukes of Bragança. It's rich with *azulejos*, frescoed ceilings, elaborate tapestries and the like.

Sleeping & Eating

Residencial Carvalho (☎ 268 339 370; Largo da República 27; s/d €20/40) Next to the tourist office, rooms are well dusted and spacious with newly tiled bedrooms. Larger rooms cost more.

Adega do Isaías (☎ 268 322 318; Rua Almeida 21; mains €6.50-8; ⏱ closed Sun) Huge wooden vats of wine cosy-in on the dining room. Expect a good grilling; it specialises in steaks.

Getting There & Away

Estremoz is linked to Évora by four local buses (€3.20, 1¼ hours) and two *expressos* (€6.20, 45 minutes), Monday to Saturday.

CASTELO DE VIDE & MARVÃO

pop 4000

A good-time detour, north of Estremoz, is the hilltop spa town, **Castelo de Vide**, which is noted for its picturesque houses with Gothic doorways. Highlights are the **Judiaria** (Old Jewish Quarter), the medieval backstreets and (yet another) castle-top view. Try to spend a night here before sidestepping to **Marvão**, a fabulous mountain-top walled village (population 190) 12km from Castelo de Vide. The **tourist offices** (Castelo de Vide ☎ 245 901 361; Rua de Bartolomeu Álvares da Santa 81; Marvão ☎ 245 993 886; Largo de Santa Maria) can help with beds.

On weekdays only, three buses run from Portalegre to Castelo de Vide (€4.65, 20 minutes) and two to Marvão (€2.10, 45 minutes). Two daily bus links the two villages (with a change at Portagem, a junction 5km from Marvão).

NAZARÉ

pop 16,000

A real seaside resort, it's predictably impossible to park here in summer. Locals wear national dress to charm the tourists and the restaurants use tiresome hassle techniques to lure in diners. On the plus side, the beach is sweeping and sandy and the seafood is some of the best on the coast. The **tourist office** (☎ 262 561 194; ♥ 10am-8pm May-Sep, 10am-1pm & 3-7pm Oct-Apr) is at the end of Avenida da República.

Sights & Activities

The **beaches** are the main attraction, although swimmers should beware of dangerous currents. Climb or take the funicular to the cliff-top **Sítio** with its cluster of fisherman's cottages and great view.

Two of Portugal's big-time architectural masterpieces are close by. Follow the signs to **Alcobaça** where, right in the centre of town, is the immense **Mosteiro de Santa Maria de Alcobaça** (☎ 262 505 120; admission €3, church free; ♥ 9am-7pm, to 5pm winter) dating from 1178; don't miss the colossal former kitchen!

Batalha's massive Gothic **Mosteiro de Santa Maria de Vitória** (☎ 244 765 497; admission to Cloisters & Unfinished Chapels €3; ♥ 9am-6pm, to 5pm winter),

dating from 1388, is home to the tomb of Henry the Navigator.

Sleeping & Eating

Many townspeople rent out rooms; doubles start from €35.

Vale Paraíso (☎ 262 561 800; camp sites €3.50) A well-equipped camping ground with bikes to hire.

Ribamar (☎ 262 551 158; fax 262 562 224; Rua Gomes Freire 9; d €45; ♣) A sunny yellow-and-white frontage a towel's throw from the beach, this 25-room hotel has sea-view balconies and spacious bijou rooms.

Casa Marques (☎ 262 551 680; Rua Gil Vicente 37; mains €5) Kitchen-sink informal with reliably good traditional dishes. There are kebab and pizza takeaways on the same street – fussy families take note.

Nova Casa Caçao (☎ 262 551 035; Rua das Caldeiras 1; mains €7) In a small square away from the main strip, choose from 40-plus seafood dishes, including black clams, lobster and sea bass.

A Tasquinha (☎ 262 551 945; Rua Adrião Batalha 54; mains €7) Breezy blue-and-white décor. Try the grilled squid or pork stew.

Getting There & Away

The nearest train station, 6km away at Valado, is connected to Nazaré by frequent buses. Nazaré has numerous bus connections to Lisbon (€7, two hours).

ÓBIDOS

pop 600

This tiny walled village is over-heritaged, but is still well worth a couple of rolls of film. Highlights include the **Igreja de Santa Maria**, with fine *azulejos*, and **views** from the walls. The **tourist office** (☎ 262 959 231; www.cm-obidos.pt, in Portuguese; Rua Direita) can advise on private rooms to rent.

Sleeping & Eating

Casa dos Castros (☎ 262 959 328; Direita 83-85; d €30) Bargain price for these homy large rooms right on the main street. Chilly in winter.

Casa do Poço (☎ 262 959 358; Travessa da Mouraria; d €60; ♣) Sumptuous elegant rooms with lashings of white linen and fabulous location down a wiggly flower-flanked side street.

Bar Lagar da Mouraria (☎ 919 937 601; Rua da Mouraria; snack €3) This 1770 *lagar* (winery) makes a moody setting for this multi-level

---

THE FÁTIMA FAITHFULS

If you want to channel Dylan and buy one of the souvenir 'flesh-colored Christs that glow in the dark' then check out Fátima, located in between Leiria and Tomar and one of the largest religious shrines in Western Europe. Aside from gawping at the super-kitsch religious souvenirs, the place itself is pretty extraordinary with its dazzling white basilica fronted by a vast concrete forecourt. Suspiciously reminiscent of an airport runway, this was built to hold more than a million devotees and is essential during the annual pilgrimages on May 12–13 and October 12–13 when this many pilgrims arrive from all over the country, some walking barefoot or on padded knees in penance.

The story behind Fátima dates back to 13 May, 1917, when the Virgin appeared to three children on top of a tree. The Virgin promised to return on the 13th of each month for the next five months, and amid much scepticism (yet each time accompanied by increasingly larger crowds) the three children reported successive apparitions. The word spread and by the final appearance on 13 October some 70,000 devotees had gathered and witnessed the so-called Miracle of the Sun. According to eyewitnesses, there were shooting beams of multicoloured light, and the sun intensified to a blinding swirling ball of fire. Disabilities and illnesses were miraculously cured: the blind could see, the dumb could talk and the crippled could walk (get the picture…?).

Three secrets of Fátima were also revealed to the children. The first foretold WWII and the spread of atheism. The second message was more prophetic concerning Russia and the spread of communism. The third secret was revealed in May 2000 by the Vatican, apparently predicting the attempt on the life of Pope John Paul II in 1981.

The exact site where the Virgin appeared is now a small chapel, always packed with devotees offering flowers and lighting candles. Seven masses are held here daily, including two in English; check the information booth for details. The basilica is surrounded by hotels, souvenir shops and a park with picnic tables – a popular spot on Sundays for coach-loads of Portuguese families.

Whatever your religious convictions, Fátima is an extraordinary place and well worth the detour if you have a couple of hours to spare.

---

bar and restaurant dishing up stacked sandwiches in combos like avocado, peppers and cheese.

Café-Restaurante 1 de Dezembro (☎ 262 959 298; Largo de São Pedro) A swallow's swoop from the lovely Igreja de São Pedro with pleasant out-door seating to kick back with a coffee or beer.

Getting There & Away
There's a direct bus Monday to Friday from Lisbon (€7.10, two hours) or via Caldas da Rainha, 10 minutes away.

TOMAR
pop 17,000
A town with history, charm – and a rare vegetarian restaurant. Tomar reached dizzy historical heights as the headquarters of the Knights Templar and is home to the outstanding Unesco-listed **Convento de Cristo**. Cradling the monastery's southern walls is the awesome 17th-century **Aqueduto de Pegões** (aquaduct), beyond which extends the dense greenery of the **Mata Nacional dos Sete Montes**

(Seven Hills National Forest). Tomar's **tourist office** (☎ 249 329 000; www.rttemplarios.pt, in Portuguese; Serpa Pinto) can provide town and forest maps.

Sleeping & Eating
Pensão Residencial União (☎ 249 323 161; Rua Serpa Pinto 94; d €35) Within a reasonable baggage-lug from the main car park, this gracious older home has dark wood furnishing, creaky floor boards and old-fashioned bathrooms.

Estalagem de Santa Iria (☎ 249 313 326; Mouchão Parque; s/d €65/85; **P** 😟) Boutique hotel with just 13 large sunny rooms with balconies overlooking the park and river beyond.

Gaia (☎ 249 311 109; Rua dos Moínhos 75; mains €6; 🕘 9am-8pm Mon-Fri, to 2pm Sat) Just a few tables and daily dishes that can include *seitan* stew, tofu burgers or meatless *feijada* (Brazilian bean stew).

Casinha d'Avó Bia (☎ 249 323 828; Rua Dr Joaquim Jacinto 16; mains €8) The quality is good, despite the mildly disquieting multilingual menu. Try the seafood *açorda* (fish and bread stew).

Getting There & Away

There are at least four express buses daily to Lisbon (€6.20, two hours) and even more frequent trains (€5.60, two hours).

COIMBRA

pop 150,000

Coimbra has a lively young vibe thanks to the student life centred on the magnificent 13th-century university. It is a handsome, eclectic city with elegant shopping streets, ancient stone walls and narrow cobbled backstreets. Coimbra played a key role in the country's history and was the birth and burial place of Portugal's first king.

Information

Esp@ço Internet (Praça 8 de Maio; ☽ 10am-8pm Mon-Fri, to 10pm Sat & Sun) Free Internet access for 30 minutes.
Regional tourist office (☎ 239 855 930; www.turismo-centro.pt; Largo da Portagem) Has pamphlets and cultural-events information.
Municipal tourist office (☎ 239 832 591; Praça Dom Dinis)
Tourist office (☎ 239 833 202; Praça da República)

Sights & Activities

Mosteiro de Santa Cruz (☎ 239 822 941; Rua Visconde da Luz; admission €1; ☽ 9am-noon & 2-5pm) has a fabulous ornate pulpit and medieval royal tombs. Located at the bottom of the hill in the old town, you can reach the monastery via the **elevator** (one way €1; ☽ daily) by the market; tickets are available from the booth or kiosks.

University Velha (☎ 239 822 941; www.uc.pt/sri; admission €3; ☽ 10am-noon & 2-5pm) is unmissable in its grandeur. You can visit the library with its gorgeous book-lined hallways and the Manueline chapel dating back to 1517.

Machado de Castro Museum (☎ 239 823 727; Largo Dr José Rodrigues; admission €3; ☽ 9.30am-12.30pm & 2-5.30pm) has a diverse collection of sculpture and paintings, and the 12th-century building is itself a work of art.

Conimbriga, 16km south of Coimbra, is the site of the well-preserved ruins of a **Roman town** (☽ 9am-8pm summer, 10am-6pm winter), including mosaic floors, baths and fountains. There's a good **site museum** (admission €3; ☽ 9am-8pm summer, 10am-6pm winter) with restaurant. Frequent buses run to Condeixa, 2km from the site; direct buses depart at 9.05am and 9.35am (only 9.35am at weekends) from the **AVIC terminal** (Rua João de Ruão 18) returning at 1pm and 6pm (only 6pm at weekends).

Odabarca (☎ 966 040 695; Parque Dr Manuel Braga; from €18) is just one of several companies that rents canoes and kayaks for paddling the Mondego River – the tourist office can provide you with a list. A free minibus takes you to Penacova for the 25km river journey.

Festivals & Events

Coimbra's annual highlight is **Queima das Fitas**, a boozy week of *fado* and revelry that begins on the first Thursday in May when students celebrate the end of the academic year.

Sleeping

Pousada da Juventude (☎ 239 822 955; coimbra@movijovem.pt; Rua António Henriques Seco 12-14; dm/d €12/29) Solid, efficiently run hostel; take bus No 7 from outside the Astoria hotel on Avenida Emídio Navarro 50m south of Coimbra A train station.

Pensão Santa Cruz (☎ 239 826 197; Praça 8 de Maio; d €32) Threadbare, large rooms in this old building in a great position, overlooking one of the city's most dynamic squares.

Pensão Flôr de Coimbra (☎ 239 823 865; fax 239 821 545; Rua do Poço 5; d from €35) Loads of *fin de siècle* atmosphere in this renovated family home run by sons; the restaurant has a small daily vegetarian menu.

Casa Pombal Guesthouse (☎ 239 835 175; www.casa.pombal@oninet.pt; Rua das Flores 18; d from €38) Has pretty rooms painted in pastel colours with roof-top views. The Dutch owner includes a blowout breakfast in the price.

Pensão Residencial Larbelo (☎ 239 829 092; fax 239 829 094; Largo da Portagem 33; d €45) The owner can seem a little cool, but the rooms are formula standard and large with a couple of good bars within stumbling distance.

Residência Coimbra (☎ 239 837 996; fax 239 838 124; Rua das Azeiteiras 55; s/d €35/45) Freshly redecorated carpeted rooms with shiny-white bathrooms, satellite TV and fridges.

THE AUTHOR'S CHOICE

Zé Manel (☎ 239 823 790; Beco do Forno 12; mains €5; ☽ Mon-Fri, lunch Sat) Great food, huge servings and a zany atmosphere with walls papered with diners' comments, cartoons and poems. There's just a few tables so arrive before 8pm to beat the crowds. Vegetarian choices include meatless bean stew.

Eating

Head to the lanes west of Praça do Comércio, especially Rua das Azeiteiras, for cheap eats.

O Cantinho das Escadas (☎ 239 820 578; Rua dos Gato 29; mains €4) House wine would be better for pickling onions, but the stews (fish, pork and veal) are excellent value at this brightly lit caf.

Restaurante Democrática (☎ 239 823 784; Travessa da Rua Nova; mains €6) Barrel-lined rustic restaurant dishing up stoking chow like *caldo verde* (potato soup with cabbage and sausage) in a low-key chummy atmosphere.

Restaurante Jardim da Manga (☎ 239 829 156; Rua Olímpio Nicolau Rui Fernanda; mains €7; ☾ closed Sat) A better breed of self-service restaurant at the back of the Mosteiro de Santa Cruz. Vegetarian dishes are available.

Café Santa Cruz (☎ 239 833 617; Praçca Maio) Former chapel that has been resurrected into one of Portugal's most atmospheric cafés.

Zé Carioca (☎ 239 835 450; Avenida Sá da Bandeira 89; mains €9-15). Chow down on fruity Brazilian dishes at this mellow restaurant northwest of Praça da República.

Entertainment

Coimbra-style fado is more cerebral than the Lisbon variety, and its adherents staunchly protective. **Bar Diligência** (☎ 239 827 667; Rua Nova 30) and **Boémia Bar** (☎ 239 834 547; Rua do Cabido 6) are popular *casas de fado*.

Á Capella (☎ 239 833 985; Capela de Nossa Senhora de Victória, Rua Corpo de Deus, Largo da Victória; ☾ 10.30pm Thu-Sat) is a fabulous new fado place attracting a groovy young crowd with nightly shows in a former chapel.

Vinyl (☎ 239 404 047; Avenida Afonso Henriques 43) and **Via Latina** (☎ 239 833 034; Rua Almeida Garrett 1) are a couple of popular discos for the bump and grinders.

Getting There & Away

At least a dozen buses and as many trains run daily from Lisbon (€9.20, 2½ hours) and Porto (€8.50, 1½ hours), plus frequent express buses from Faro and Évora, via Lisbon. The main long-distance train stations are Coimbra B, 2km northwest of the centre, and central Coimbra A (on timetables this is called just 'Coimbra'). Most long-distance trains call at both. Other useful connections are to Figueira da Foz and eight daily buses to Luso/Buçaco (from Coimbra A).

LUSO & THE BUÇACO FOREST

pop 2000

This region has an other-worldly appeal with a dense forest of century-old trees surrounded by an impressionist-style landscape dappled with heather, wild flowers and leafy ferns. Buçaco was chosen as a retreat by 16th-century monks and surrounds the pretty spa town of Luso.

The **tourist office** (☎ /fax 231 939 133; Avenida Emídio Navarro; ☾ 9.30am-12.30pm & 2-6pm) has maps and leaflets about the forest and trails, as well as free Internet access. The **Termas** (thermal baths; ☎ 231 937 910; Avenida Emídio Navarro; ☾ May-Oct) offers a range of treatments.

Sleeping & Eating

The Luso tourist office has a list of *pensãos* with an average cost of €30.

Astória (☎ 231 939 182; Avenida Emídio Navarro; s/d €20/30) Dark wood and beams equal cosy surroundings at this well-situated *pensão* near the baths.

Palace Hotel do Buçaco (☎ 231 930 101; www .almeidahotels.com; s/d from €145/185) If this is a hunting lodge – bring on the palace! A truly sumptuous pile with gargoyles, Manueline extravagance, an ornamental garden and Edwardian-style gracious rooms. The equally elegant restaurant here offers set menus for €40.

Restaurante O Cesteiro (☎ 231 939 360; EN 234; mains €7) Large dining room with extensive menu of confident traditional dishes. The grilled chicken is a winner.

Getting There & Away

There are three buses daily Monday to Friday, two on Saturdays and one on Sundays from Coimbra (€2.50, 50 minutes). Just one train, departing around 10.30am from Coimbra B (€1.30, 30 minutes) provides enough time to take a day trip.

SERRA DA ESTRELA

The forested Serra da Estrela has a raw natural beauty and offers some of the country's best hiking. This is Portugal's highest mainland mountain range (1993m), and the source of its two great rivers: Mondego River and Zêzere River. The **main park office** (☎ 275 980 060; fax 275 980 069; Manteigas) has plenty of information on the Parque Natural da Serra da Estrela; additional offices are at Gouveia and Guarda – claimed to be the highest city in Europe. Other good sources for regional information are the local **tourist offices** (Guarda ☎ 271 205 530; www.domdigital.pt/cm-guarda/english; Covilhã ☎ 275 319 560).

The park administration publishes *À Descoberta da Estrela,* a walking guide with maps and narratives. Park offices and some tourist offices sell an English edition (€4.25), plus a detailed topographic map of the park (€6).

Sleeping

The **Pousada da Juventude** (☎ /fax 275 335 375; penhas@movijem.pt; Penhas da Saúde; dm/d from €10/25) Located 10km above Covilhã, this is an excellent hostel and good excursion base, providing meals or kitchen facilities. Buses come from Covilhã (twice daily, July to September only). The only other options are your feet or bike, or a taxi (about €10).

At Guarda there's another **Pousada da Juventude** (☎ /fax 271 224 482; guarda@movijovem.pt; dm/d from €9/22), while Seia, Gouveia, Guarda and Covilhã have some modestly priced guesthouses.

Getting There & Away

Several buses run daily from Coimbra along the park's perimeter to Seia, Gouveia, Guarda or Covilhã. Others go via Covilhã (€4, 45 minutes) to Castel Branco (€7.50, 1¾ hours) and Lisbon, and several times daily to Viseu (€6.20, 1½ hours), Porto and Coimbra.

The twice-daily IC Line 110 train links Lisbon and Coimbra to Guarda (€12.80, 4¼ hours).

Getting Around

No buses cross the park, although you can go around it: Seia-Covilhã takes two hours via Guarda. At least two buses link Seia, Gouveia and Guarda daily, and considerably more run between Guarda and Covilhã.

THE NORTH

Portugal's northern Minho region is a colourful patchwork of rolling country, dense forests and dramatic mountains. This is also *vinho verde* country, that wholly addictive young green wine, while its capital Porto is named after another tipple and is a fascinating mix of the medieval and modern. Also here are two more must-see historical cities: Braga, the country's religious heart, and the finely situated Viana do Castelo.

PORTO

pop 305,000

Portugal's second-largest city, Porto has real charm, combining its slick commercial hub with the charmingly dilapidated riverfrontage district – a well-deserved World Heritage Site. Across the water is Vila Nova de Gaia, the headquarters of a thriving port trade since a 1703 agreement with England. More recently, Porto's role as one of the prime venues for the Euro 2004 football championships equalled a healthy boost to the economy and infrastructure.

Orientation

Porto centre is small enough to cover mainly by foot. The city clings to the north bank of the Rio Douro, spanned by five bridges across from Vila Nova de Gaia, home to the port wine lodges. Central Porto's axis is Avenida dos Aliados. Major shopping areas are eastward around the Bolhão Market and Rua Santa Catarina, home to the glassy shopping complex Via Catarina, and westward along Rua dos Clérigos. At the southern end of Avenida dos Aliados, Praça da Liberdade and São Bento train station are major local bus hubs. Another is Jardim da Cordoaria (called Jardim de João Chagas on some maps), about 400m westward.

The picturesque Ribeira district lies along the waterfront, in the shadow of the great Ponte de Dom Luís I bridge.

Information

INTERNET ACCESS

Portweb (☎ 222 005 922; Praça General Humberto Delgado 291; ⏰ 10-2am Mon-Sat, 3pm-2am Sun) Central, cheap Internet access.

MEDICAL SERVICES

Santo António Hospital (☎ 222 077 500; Largo Prof Abel Salazar) Has English-speaking staff.

MONEY

Intercontinental (Rua de Ramalho Ortigão 8) Exchange facilities.

Portocâmbios (Rua Rodrigues Sampaio 193)

Top Atlântico (☎ 222 074 020; trinidade@top atlantico.com; Rua Alferes Malheiro 96) Doubles as an Amex representative.

PORTUGAL

PORTO

POST

Main post office (Praça General Humberto Delgado) Across from the main tourist office.

Telephone office (Praça da Liberdade 62; 10am-10pm) Where faxes also can be sent.

TOURIST INFORMATION

ICEP tourist office (☎ 222 057 514; fax 222 053 212; Praça Dom João I 43; 9am-7pm Mon-Fri, 9.30am-3.30pm Sat & Sun) The national tourist office.

Municipal tourist office (☎ 223 393 472; www.porto turismo.pt; Rua Clube dos Fenianos 25; 9am-5.30pm Mon-Fri, 9.30am-4.30pm Sat & Sun Oct-Jun, 9am-7pm daily July-Sep) Next door to the tourist police office.

Tourist office (☎ 222 009 770; Rua Infante Don Henrique 63; 9am-5.30pm Mon-Fri)

TRAVEL AGENCIES

Montes d'Aventura (☎ 228 305 157; Alameda Dr Antonio Macedo 19) Organises walking, cycling and canoeing trips.

Tagus (☎ 226 094 146; fax 226 094 141; Rua Campo Alegre 261) Youth-oriented agency.

Top Atlântico (☎ 222 074 020; trinidade@topatlantico .com; Rua Alferes Malheiro 96)

Trilhos (☎ /fax 225 020 740; www.trilhos.pt, in Portuguese; Rua de Belém 94) Another option for canoe and hydrospeed excursions.

Wasteels (☎ 225 194 230; fax 225 194 239; Rua Pinto Bessa 27/29) Near Campanhã station and also youth oriented.

Sights & Activities

Head for the river-front Ribeira district for an atmospheric stroll around, checking out the gritty local bars, superb restaurants and river cruises. Note that for most museums and attractions, admission is half-price for children, students and seniors, and free for everyone on Sundays.

Torre dos Clérigos (Rua dos Clérigos; admission €1; 10am-noon & 2-5pm) rewards the 225 steep steps with the best panorama of the city.

Sé (☎ 222 059 028; Terreiro da Sé; cloisters €2; 9am-12.30pm & 2.30-7pm Apr-Oct, to 6pm rest of the year, closed Sun morning) dominates Porto. The cathedral is worth a visit for its mixture of architectural styles and vast ornate interior.

Many port-wine lodges (Vila Nova de Gaia) offer daily tours and tastings, including **Croft** (☎ 223 742 800; www.crofttport.com; admission €3) and **Osborne** (☎ 223 757 517; www.osborne .es, in Spanish; admission free).

Museum of Contemporary Art (☎ 226 156 571; www.serralves.pt, in Portuguese; Rua Dom João de Castro 210; admission €5; 10am-7pm Tue-Fri, 10am-8pm Sat

& Sun Apr-Sep, 10am-7pm Oct-Mar) is enclosed by pretty gardens and has works by contemporary Portuguese artists.

Museu do Vinho (Wine Museum; ☎ 222 076 300; museuvinhoporto@cm-porto.pt; Rua de Monchique 45-52; admission free; 11am-7pm Tue-Sun), Porto's newest museum, traces the history of wine- and port-making with an informative short film, models and exhibits, plus tastings.

Soares dos Reis National Museum (☎ 223 393 770; Rua Dom Manuel II 44; admission €3; 10am-6pm Wed-Sun) offers masterpieces of 19th- and 20th-century Portuguese painting and sculpture. Take bus No 78 from Praça da Liberdade.

Festivals & Events

Porto's big festivals are the **Festa de São João** (St John's Festival) in June and the international film festival **Fantasporto** in February. Also worth catching are the **Celtic music festival** in April/May, and the **rock festival** in August.

Sleeping

BUDGET

Campismo Salgueiros (☎ 227 810 500; fax 227 718 239; Praia de Salgueiros; camp sites €2.50) One of three camping grounds near the sea; all get packed in summer. Note that the coast here is too rocky and polluted for swimming.

Camping da Prelada (☎ 228 312 616; Rua Monte dos Burgos; camp sites €3.50) Basic, big and open year-round, 4km northwest of the centre. Take bus No 6 from Praça de Liberdade or bus No 54 from Jardim da Cordoaria.

Pousada da Juventude (☎ 226 177 257; porto@ movijovem.pt; Rua Paulo da Gama 551; dm/d €18/35) is a tastefully spruced-up hostel 4km west of the centre. Reservations are essential. Take bus No 35 from Praça de Liberdade or No 1 from São Bento station.

Residencial União (☎ 222 003 078; Rua Conde de Vizela 62; d from €25) Faded large rooms; the approach is via a gloomy backstreet, which could be dodgy after dark.

Pensão Astória (☎ 222 008 175; Rua Arnaldo Gama 56; d €35) Next to a handy car park or approach via the steep steps from the river front. Elegant old doubles, some with river views.

Pensão Mira Norte (☎ 222 001 118; Rua de Santa Catarina 969; d €30) Basic rooms, well placed for shopaholics, but not so good at siesta time.

Pensão Santa Luzia (☎ 222 001 119; Rua da Alegria; d €35;) Very pleasant, spotless rooms run

---

THE AUTHOR'S CHOICE

O Muro (☎ 222 083 426; Muro dos Bacalhoeiros 88; mains €7; ⊙ noon-2am) Top-notch, well-priced restaurant with five-star river views. The charismatic owner is an ex-professional soccer player who, together with his Mozambican wife, prepares delicious, filling food, including several vegetarian choices. Delightful wacky décor ranges from dried bacalhau to Che Guevara; ask to see the guest book!

---

by an elderly senhora who is still charging escuda-era rates.

Also recommended is **Pensão Porto Rico** (☎ 223 394 690; Rua do Almada 237; d €30; ✗).

MID-RANGE
Pensão Residencial Paulista (☎ 222 054 692; Avenida dos Aliados 214; s/d €40/50; ✗) Small shiny-wood rooms with balconies overlooking a tree-lined avenue crowned by the majestic city hall.

Pensão Sã Marino (☎ 223 325 499; Praça Carlos Alberto 59; s/d €38/45; ✗) Seductive 19th-century building overlooking the square with the airport bus stop outside. Carpeted good-sized rooms.

Also recommended is **Pensão Estoril** (☎ 222 002 751; fax 222 082 468; Rua de Cedofeita 193; d €40; ✗).

TOP END
Pensão Pão de Açucar (☎ 222 002 425; Rua do Almada 262; d €75; P ✗) Upbeat Art Nouveau décor. Go for the top floor with rooms opening onto the palm-fringed terrace.

Pestana Porto Carlton (☎ 223 402 300; www.residencialpaodeacucar.com, in Portuguese; Praça da Ribeira 1; s/d €118/140; P ✗ ✗ ☐) Red-carpet service in a gorgeous 16th-century setting. Rooms have city or river views and sleek glossy furnishings with all the extras.

Eating
RESTAURANTS
Restaurante Romão (☎ 222 005 639; Praça Carlos Alberto 100; mains €7) Agreeable little restaurant with northern specialities such as tripe and roast kid. Leave room for the *torta de noz* (walnut tart).

Geometria (☎ 222 030 398; Infante D Henrique 133; mains €9; ⊙ closed Mon) Dress-for-dinner style place with two candlelit dining rooms overlooking the river. Reasonably priced

pizza and pasta dishes and classy downstairs bar.

Casa Filha da Mãe Preta (☎ 222 055 515; Cais da Ribeira 40; mains €10; ⊙ closed Sun) Don't confuse this place with the same-name but less salubrious café one street back! Head upstairs for Douro views from the *azulejo*-lined dining room. Simple fish and meat dishes served with veggies, rice and boiled potatoes.

CAFÉS, QUICK EATS & SELF-CATERING
Café Majestic (☎ 222 003 887; Rua Santa Catarina 112; ⊙ closed Sun) An extravagant Art Nouveau relic where powdered ladies enjoy afternoon teas.

Confeitaria Império (149 Rua Santa Catarina; snacks €2.50) Brilliant bites like delicious *pasteis de carne* (meat and veggie filled pasties) and custard tarts.

Café Ancôra Douro (☎ 222 003 749; Praça de Parada Leitão 49; snacks €3) Heaving with peckish students, the vast menu includes veggie burgers, hotdogs and crepes.

Bolhão market (Rua Formosa; ⊙ closed Sun) Sells fruit and veggies in season, plus cheese and deli goodies.

Drinking
Solar do Vinho do Porto (☎ 226 094 749; Rua Entre Quintas 220; ⊙ 11am-midnight Mon-Sat) Laid-back yet elegant setting for tasting the port made just across the river.

La Maison des Porto (☎ 936 057 340; Rua São Joã 46; ⊙ closed Sun) French-owned vinotheque where you can taste and be educated about port by the charming multilingual owner.

Ryan's Irish Pub (☎ 222 005 366; Rua Infante Dom Henrique 18) Has the usual range of gluggable beer in blarney surroundings.

Entertainment
Academia (☎ 222 005 737; Rua São João 80) Stylishly hip and smoky disco-bar.

Taverna do Infante (☎ 205 49 86; Rua da Alfándega 13) Atmospheric macho den with Brazilian dancers.

Mexcal (☎ 226 009 188; Rua da Restauração 39) The Latino music here is good for a little late-night hip swinging.

Club Mau-Mau (☎ 226 076 660; Rua do Outeiro 4) A dodging-elbows disco with live music on Thursday nights.

Maré Alta (☎ 226 162 540; Alameda Basilio Teles) Nail-bitingly trendy disco with occasional live gigs.

Shopping

The best central shopping mall is **Via Catarina Shopping Centre** (Rua Santa Catarina) in a tasteful building. Port is, naturally, a popular purchase in this town. Shops with a broad selection include knowledgeable **Garrafeira do Carmo** (Rua do Carmo 17), the deli **Casa Januário** (Rua do Bonjardim 352) and **Casa Oriental** (Campo dos Mártires de Pátria 111). Other good buys are shoes and gold-filigree jewellery. For handicrafts, visit **Arte Facto** (Rua da Reboleira 37; ☉ Tue-Sun) in the Ribeira.

Getting There & Away

AIR

Porto is connected by daily flights from Lisbon and London, and almost-daily direct links from other European centres (see p891). For flight information call ☎ 229 413 260.

BUS

Porto has a baffling number of private bus companies; the main tourist office has a designated department for transport, which can assist with timetables and fares. In general, for Lisbon and the Algarve the choice is **Renex** (☎ 222 003 395; Rua das Carmelitas 32) or **Rede Expressos** (☎ 222 052 459).

Three companies operate from or near Praceto Régulo Magauanha, off Rua Dr Alfredo Magalhães: **REDM** (☎ 222 003 152) goes to Braga; **AV Minho** (☎ 222 006 121) to Viana do Castelo; and **Carlos Soares** (☎ 222 051 383) to Guimarães.

Rodonorte (☎ 222 004 398; Rua Ateneu Comércial do Porto 19) departs from its own terminal, mainly to Vila Real and Bragança.

Northern Portugal's main international carrier is **Internorte** (☎ 226 093 220; www.internorte.com, in Portuguese; Praça da Galiza 96) whose coaches depart from its booking office.

TRAIN

Porto is a northern Portugal rail hub with three stations. Most international trains, and all intercity links, start at Campanhã, 2km east of the centre. Inter-regional and regional services depart from either Campanhã or the central **São Bento station** (☎ 225 364 141; ☉ 8am-11pm); bus Nos 34 and 35 run frequently between these two.

At São Bento station you can book tickets to any destination from any other Porto station.

Getting Around

TO/FROM THE AIRPORT

The **AeroBus** (☎ 808 200 166; www.stcp.pt; €2.60; ☉ 7.30am to 7pm) runs every half-hour between Avenida dos Aliados and the airport via Boavista. The ticket, purchased on the bus, also serves as a free bus pass until midnight of the day you buy it.

City buses 56 and 87 run about every half-hour until 8.30pm to/from Jardim da Cordoaria, and until about 12.30am to/from Praça da Liberdade.

A taxi costs around €12.50 plus a possible €1.50 baggage charge.

BUS

Central hubs of Porto's extensive bus system include Jardim da Cordoaria, Praça da Liberdade and São Bento station (Praça Almeida Garrett). Tickets are cheapest from STCP kiosks (eg opposite São Bento station, beside Bolhão market and at Boavista) and many newsagents and tobacconists: €0.70 for a short hop, €0.90 to outlying areas or €2.05 for an airport return trip. Tickets bought on the bus are always €1.20. There's also a €2.10 day pass available.

METRO

Work is well away on Porto's **metro** (1-2 zones €0.80, 3 zones €1), a combination of upgraded and new track that will reach Campanhã, Vila Nova de Gaia and several coastal resorts to the north. The Blue Line was due to open mid-2005 (from Trindade to Gondomar) and already runs from Trindade to Sr Matosinhos in the northwest.

TAXI

To cross town, expect to pay about €5. An additional charge is made to leave the city limits, including across the Ponte Dom Luís I to Vila Nova de Gaia.

TRAM

Porto has one remaining tram, the No 1E, trundling daily from the Ribeira to the coast at Foz do Douro.

ALONG THE DOURO

Portugal's rural heartland of the Douro Valley stretches some 200km to the Spanish border. In the upper reaches, port-wine vineyards wrap around every hillside punctuated by wonderfully remote stone villages and, in spring, splashes of dazzling white almond blossom.

The Douro River, tamed by eight dams and locks since the late 1980s, is navigable right across Portugal. Highly recommended is the train journey from Porto to Peso da Régua (about a dozen trains daily, 2½ hours), the last 50km clinging to the river's edge; four trains continue daily to Pocinho (4½ hours). **Douro Azul** (☎ 223 393 950; www.douroazul.com) and other companies run one- and two-day river cruises, mostly from March to October. Cyclists and drivers can choose river-hugging roads along either bank, although they're crowded at weekends. The elegant, detailed colour map *Rio Douro* (€3) is available from Porto bookshops.

VIANA DO CASTELO
pop 18,000

This gracious port town with striking 16th-century buildings is regarded as the region's folk capital, specialising in making (and selling) the traditional embroidered costumes. The **tourist office** (☎ 258 822 620; www .rtam.pt; Rua Hospital Velho; ☘ 9am-12.30pm & 2.30-6pm Mon-Fri, 9am-1pm Sat) has information on festivals and the region in general. In August Viana hosts the **Festas de Nossa Senhora da Agonia** (p890).

Sights
The stately heart of town is Praça da República, with its delicate fountain and elegant buildings, including the 16th-century **Misericórdia**.

Atop Santa Luzia Hill, the **Templo do Sagrado Coração de Jesus** offers a grand panorama across the river. The funicular railway was temporarily closed at the time of research. Check at the tourist office for an update – or prepare for a 5km uphill climb.

Sleeping
Pousada da Juventude (☎ 258 800 260; vianacastelo@ movijovem.pt; Rua da Argaçosa; dm/d €13/35) A friendly clean place about a kilometre east of the town centre.

Residencial Magalhães (☎ 258 823 293; Avenida Combatentes da G. Guerra 215; s/d €30/38) One of a best of a handful of inexpensive *pensãos* on this street. Good-size rooms with wardrobes and lacy curtains.

Residencial Viana Mar (☎ 258 828 962; Avenida Combatentes da G Guerra 215) Well positioned with comfortable chintzy rooms and a sunken bar that dates from the sixties when it was Viana's first nightclub; the décor remains captivatingly unchanged.

Eating
A Gruta Snack Bar (☎ 258 820 214; Rua Grande 87; mains €5) Canteen-style surrounds with light lunches including a good salad choice.

Dolce Vita (☎ 258 820 214; Rua do Poço 44; mains €6) Wood-fired pizza and innovative pasta sauces make this *the* obligatory refuelling spot in town.

O Grelhador (☎ 258 825 219; Rua do Anjinho 17; mains €7) Not much elbowroom at this small bar-restaurant but its speciality – crepes – makes a change if you're suffering from *bacalau* burn out.

O Pipo (☎ 258 825 097; Rua Prior do Crato 68; mains €9) Octopus-studded rice, veal in green sauce and almond cake are just some of the traditional goodies available at this earthy restaurant in the centre of town.

Getting There & Away
Half a dozen express coaches daily go to Porto (€6.20, two hours) and Lisbon (€14, 5½ hours) Monday to Friday, with fewer at weekends.

BRAGA
pop 80,000

It's a pity about the brash new McDonald's restaurant stuck in the middle of Braga's most beautiful square; otherwise the religious capital of Portugal is monolithic in its ecclesiastical architecture with a contemporary contrast of pedestrian streets flanked with classy cafés, shops and boutiques. The **tourist office** (☎ 253 262 550; Praça da República; ☘ 9am-7pm Mon-Fri, 9am-12.30pm & 2-5.30pm Sat) can help with accommodation and maps.

Sights & Activities
In the centre of Braga is the **Sé** (museum & chapels €2; ☘ 8.30am-5.30pm), an elegant cathedral complex.

At Bom Jesus do Monte, a hilltop pilgrimage site 5km from Braga, is an extraordinary stairway, the **Escadaria do Bom Jesus**, with allegorical fountains, chapels and a superb view. Buses run frequently from Braga to the site, where you can climb the steps (pilgrims sometimes do this on their knees) or, alternatively, ascend by funicular railway (€1).

It's an easy day trip to **Guimarães**, considered the cradle of the Portuguese nation, with a medieval town centre and a palace of the dukes of Bragança.

Sleeping

Pousada da Juventude (☎ 253 616 163; braga@ movijovem.pt; Rua de Santa Margarida 6; dm/d €10/26) This bright and cheerful hostel is a 10-minute walk from the city centre.

Hotel Francfort (☎ 253 262 648; Avenida Central 7; d €35) Large rooms, lofty ceilings, antiques and an extremely elderly owner equal the mildly threadbare state of the place.

Grande Residência Avenida (☎ 253 609 020; fax 253 609 028; Avenida da Liberdade 738; d €50; 🅿) Had a glossy makeover with shiny white bathrooms and good-sized plushly carpeted rooms.

Eating & Drinking

Ruby (☎ 253 263 030; Avenida da Liberdade 74; mains €3.50) About as atmospheric as a railway waiting room, but good for burgers, pizza, sandwiches and all kinds of sugary treats.

Restaurante Pópulo (☎ 253 215 147; Praça Conde de Agrolongo 116; mains €11) Menu is heavy on regional classics including duck, veal and pork dishes. Ask for the daily specials when the chef likes to indulge in a little nouvelle innovation.

D. Diogo (☎ 253 262 297; RD Diogo de Sousa 81-83; mains €15) Go for the splurge at this classy candlelit restaurant with its limited menu of refined fish, meat and rice dishes.

Café Vianna (☎ 253 262 336; Praça da República) A classic 19th-century café. Good for breakfast.

A Brazileira (☎ 253 262 104; Largo do Barã de S Martinho) Mildly decadent corner bar attracting effortlessly stylish regulars.

Getting There & Away

The motorway from Porto puts Braga within easy day-trip reach. Intercidade trains arrive twice daily from Lisbon (€15, five hours), Coimbra (€10, three hours) and Porto (€2, 1¾ hours), and there are daily connections north to Viana do Castelo. Daily bus services link Braga to Porto (€3.80, 1½ hours) and Lisbon (€14.20, five hours).

PARQUE NACIONAL DA PENEDA-GERÊS

This magnificent park, northeast of Braga, has some of the most stunning scenery in the country. It's a popular holiday spot for Portugal's happy campers and also appeals to hikers with its wilder northern region around Serra de Peneda. The area has an ancient history with dolmens, stone circles and standing stones; most are marked on tourist maps of the area. The park's main centre is at **Caldas do Gerês**, a sleepy, hot-spring village.

Orientation & Information

Gerês' **tourist office** (☎ 253 391 133; fax 253 391 282) is in the colonnade at the upper end of the village and can provide information on activities and accommodation.

Other park offices are at Arcos de Valdevez, Montalegre. All have a map of the park (€3) with some roads and tracks marked but no trails, and a free English-language booklet on the park's features. A more detailed topographical map can be bought in Lisbon or Porto or ordered online (www .igeoe.pt, in Portuguese).

Activities

HIKING

There are trails and footpaths through the park, some between villages with accommodation. Leaflets detailing these are available from the park offices.

Day hikes around Gerês are popular. An adventurous option is the old Roman road from Mata do Albergaria (10km up-valley from Gerês by taxi or hitching), past the **Vilarinho das Furnas** reservoir to Campo do Gerês. More distant destinations include **Ermida** and **Cabril**, both with simple cafés and accommodation. Guided walks are organised by several outfits, including **Incentivos Outdoors** (☎ 914 863 353) at Gerês and **Trote-Gerês** (☎ /fax 253 659 860) at Cabril.

CYCLING

Mountain bikes can be hired from **Incentivos Outdoors** (☎ 914 863 353) or the German-run **Pensão Carvalho Araújo** (☎ 253 391 185; 🕑 May-Sep).

HORSE RIDING

The national park operates **horse riding facilities** (☎ 253 390 110) from beside its Vidoeiro camping ground, near Gerês. Incentivos Outdoors also has horses for hire.

WATER SPORTS

Rio Caldo, 8km south of Gerês, is the base for water sports on the Caniçada reservoir.

PORTUGAL

Agua Montanha Lazer (☎ 253 391 779; www.agua montanha.com) rents out canoes and other boats. For paddling the Salamonde reservoir, Trote-Gerês rents out canoes from its camp site at Cabril.

Gerês' **Parque das Termas** (admission €1; ☺ Sat & Sun Apr, daily May-Oct) has a **swimming pool** (Mon-Fri €3.50, Sat & Sun €5).

Sleeping

Although Gerês has plenty of pensões, you may find vacancies are limited as many are block-booked by spa patients in summer.

Pousada da Juventude (Campo do Gerês; ☎ /fax 253 351 339; dm/d €10/24) A former dam workers' camp offering comfortable, sprawling accommodation.

Cerdeira Camping Ground (Campo do Gerês; ☎ 253 351 005; fax 253 353 315; camp sites €4) Cerdeira has shady camp sites, a laundry and a mini-supermarket.

Vidoeiro Camping Ground (Gerês; ☎ 253 391 289; camp sites €4) Open year-round, Vidoeiro is just out of town and beside the river.

Pensão Adelaide (☎ 253 390 020; fax 253 390 029; d €40; ☒) Bit of a hike from the centre but the views are a suitable reward. Rooms are clean and bright.

Pensão Casa da Ponte (☎ 253 391 125; s/d €20/45; ☒) One of the longest established and could do with a makeover, but the rooms are good-sized and airy and the riverside location is ace.

Hotel Universal (☎ 253 390 020; ehgeres@netc .pt; s/d €58/70; ☒) A leafy inner patio lends an air of elegance to this main-street hotel with its comfortable carpeted rooms and energetic swimming pool and tennis court extras.

Eating

Most of Gerês pensões serve hearty meals to guests and nonguests. There are several restaurants, plus shops in the main street for stocking up on picnic provisions. The Cerdeira Camping Ground at Campo do Gerês has a cheap restaurant of a reasonable standard.

Getting There & Away

From Braga, at least six coaches daily run to Rio Caldo and Gerês, and seven to Campo do Gerês (fewer at weekends). If you are coming from Lisbon or Porto, change at Braga.

PORTUGAL DIRECTORY

ACCOMMODATION

Most tourist offices have lists of accommodation to suit a range of budgets, and can help you find and book it. Although the government uses stars to grade some types of accommodation, criteria seem erratic. In this chapter the Budget category is up to €35, Mid-Range is between €36 and €70 and Top End is over €71. The cheapest accommodation is listed first.

Camping

If you are seriously economising, camping is always the cheapest option, although some camping grounds close out of season. The multilingual, annually updated *Roteiro Campista* (€5), sold in larger bookshops, contains details of nearly all Portugal's camping grounds.

Guesthouses

The most common types of guesthouse, the Portuguese equivalent of B&Bs, are the *residencial* and the *pensão*. Both are graded from one to three stars, and the best are often cheaper and better run than some hotels. High-season *pensão* rates for a double start from around €35; a residencial, where breakfast is normally included, is a bit more. Many have cheaper rooms with shared bath.

Hotels

The government grades hotels with one to five stars. For a high-season double expect to pay €60 up to as much as €250. *Estalagem* and *albergaria* refer to upmarket inns. Prices drop considerably in low season. Breakfast is usually included.

Pousadas

Pousadas are government-run former castles, monasteries or palaces, often in spectacular locations. For details contact tourist offices, or **Pousadas de Portugal** (☎ 218 442 001; www.pousadasjuventude.pt; Avenida Santa Joana Princesa 10, 1749 Lisbon).

Private counterparts are operated under a scheme called Turismo de Habitação and a number of smaller schemes (often collectively called 'Turihab'), which allow you to stay in anything from a farmhouse to a manor house; some also have self-catering cottages. The tourist offices can tell you about local Turihab properties.

Youth Hostels

Portugal has 41 *pousadas da juventude* (youth hostels), all part of the Hostelling International (HI) system. You can reserve in advance for a €1.50 fee by contacting their central reservations office: **Movijovem** (☎ 213 524 072; reservas@movijovem.pt; Avenida Duque d'Ávila 137, Lisbon).

If you don't already have a card from your national hostel association, you can pay a €2 supplement per night (and have a one-night, six-night or year-long 'guest card').

Another cheaper option is a private room (*quarto particular*), usually in a private house, with shared facilities. Homeowners may approach you at the bus or train station; otherwise watch for 'quartos' signs or ask at tourist offices. Rooms are usually clean and cheap (€25 to €50 for a double in summer). You may be able to bargain in the low season.

ACTIVITIES

Off-road cycling (BTT; *bicyclete tudo terrano*, all-terrain bicycle) is booming in Portugal, with bike trips on offer at many tourist destinations (see Tavira p872, Setúbal p870, Évora p874 and Parque Nacional da Peneda-Gerês p887).

Despite some fine rambling country, walking is not a Portuguese passion. Some parks are establishing trails, though, and some adventure travel agencies offer walking tours (see p863, p870, p873, p874, p883 and p887).

Popular water sports include surfing, windsurfing, canoeing, white-water rafting and water-skiing. For information on local specialists, see Lagos (p873), Sagres (p874), Évora (p874), Tavira (p874), Coimbra (p879) and Parque Nacional da Peneda-Gerês (p887).

Alpine skiing is possible at Torre in the Serra da Estrela usually from January through to March.

The **Instituto Português da Juventude** (☎ 218 920 800; www.sej.pt, in Portuguese; Rua de Moscavide 47, Lisbon) offers holiday programmes for 16- to 30-year-olds (visitors too), including BTT, canoeing and rock climbing.

BUSINESS HOURS

Banks are open 8.30am to 3pm weekdays. Museums and tourist attractions are open between 10am and 5pm Tuesday to Friday, but are often closed at lunch. Shopping hours are generally 9am to 7pm weekdays, and 9am to 1pm Saturday. Lunch is given lingering and serious attention between noon and 3pm.

DANGERS & ANNOYANCES

Petty theft is the main problem in Portugal. Be wary of anyone asking you directions or the time, which may just be a distraction while an accomplice snatches your bag.

Scams

A common scam takes place predominantly at supermarket (or similar) car parks. After you have deposited your shopping in the trunk of the car and your bag on the passenger seat, someone will approach and inform you that you have a puncture in your back tyre. When you get out to investigate, the accomplice opens the passenger door and swipes your bag.

Despite all the adverse publicity and warnings from local tourist offices, timeshare touts on the Algarve continue to convince tourists that *their* scratch card is the one-in-a-hundred/thousand/million winner. And the prize (usually a bottle of cheap champagne) can, of course, only be collected in person from the resort – after several hours of being on the hard-sell receiving end. If you do end up there, don't sign anything until a week's 'cooling off' period and leave your credit cards at home.

EMBASSIES & CONSULATES
Portuguese Embassies & Consulates

Portuguese embassies abroad include:

Australia (☎ 026-2901 733; 23 Culgoa Circuit, O'Malley, Canberra ACT 2606)

Canada (☎ 613-7290 883; 645 Island Park Dr, Ottawa Ont K1Y 0B8)

France (☎ 01 47 27 35 29; 3 Rue de Noisiel, 75116 Paris)

Germany (☎ 030-590 063 500; Zimmerstrasse 56, Berlin 10117)

Ireland (☎ 012-894 46; Knocksinna House, Foxrock, Dublin 18)

New Zealand (☎ 09-309 1454; PO Box 305, 33 Garfield St, Parnell, Auckland)

Spain (☎ 915 617 800; Calle Castello 128, 28006 Madrid)

Netherlands (☎ 070-363 02 17; Bazarstraat 21, The Hague 2518)

UK (☎ 0207-235 5331; 11 Belgrave Square, London SW1X 8PP)

PORTUGAL

USA (☎ 202-328 8610; 2125 Kalorama Rd NW, Washington DC 20008)

Embassies & Consulates in Portugal

The following are embassies unless otherwise stated:

Canada Lisbon (Map pp860-1; ☎ 213 164 600; Avenida da Liberdade 196); Faro (☎ 289 521 120; Rua Frei Lourenço de Santa Maria 1)
France Lisbon (Map pp860-1; ☎ 226 939 292; Calçada a Marques de Abrantes 123); Porto (☎ 226 094 805; Rua Eugénio de Castro 352)
Germany (Map pp864-5; ☎ 213 810 210; Campo dos Mártires da Pátria 38, Lisbon)
Ireland (Map pp860-1; ☎ 213 929 440; Rua da Imprensa à Estrela 1, Lisbon)
Spain Lisbon (Map pp864-5; Consulate ☎ 213 472 792; Rua do Salitre 1); Porto (Map p882; ☎ 225 101 685; Rua de Dom João IV 341); Vila Real de Santo António (☎ 281 544 888; Avenida Ministro Duarte Pacheco)
Netherlands Lisbon (☎ 213 914 900; Avenida Infante Santo 43); Porto (Consulate ☎ 222 080 061; Rua da Reboleira 7)
UK Lisbon (Map pp860-1; ☎ 213 924 000; Rua de São Bernardo 33); Porto (☎ 226 184 789; Avenida da Boavista 3072); Portimão (☎ 282 417 800; Largo Francisco a Maurício 7) The UK consulate also oversees consular matters for New Zealand.
USA (Map pp860-1; ☎ 217 273 300; Avenida das Forças Armadas, Lisbon)

FESTIVALS & EVENTS
April
Holy Week Festival Easter week in Braga features colourful processions, including Ecce Homo, with barefoot penitents carrying torches.

May
Festas das Cruzes Held in Barcelos in May, the Festival of the Crosses is known for processions, folk music and dance, and regional handicrafts.

June
Feira Nacional da Agricultura In June, Santarém hosts the National Agricultural Fair, with bullfighting, folk singing and dancing.
Festa do Santo António The Festival of Saint Anthony fills the streets of Lisbon on 13 June.
Festas de São João Porto's big street bash is the St John's Festival, from 16 to 24 June.

August
Festas da Nossa Senhora da Agonia Viana do Castelo's Our Lady of Suffering Festival runs for three days, including

the weekend nearest to 20 August, and is famed for its folk arts, parades and fireworks.

HOLIDAYS
New Year's Day 1 January
Carnival Shrove Tuesday; February/March
Good Friday and the following Saturday March/April
Liberty Day 25 April (commemorating the 1975 Revolution)
Labour Day 1 May
Corpus Christi May/June (the ninth Thursday after Easter)
National Day 10 June
Feast of the Assumption 15 August
Republic Day 5 October
All Saints' Day 1 November
Independence Day 1 December (celebrating independence from Spain in 1640)
Immaculate Conception 8 December
Christmas Day 25 December

MONEY
ATMs
There are dozens of banks with ATMs throughout Portugal. However, some only accept credit (rather than debit) cards.

Credit Cards
Credit cards are increasingly accepted in hotels, restaurants and shops, however, you will normally be asked to provide some form of photo identification (ie passport).

Moneychangers
Exchange bureaux are common throughout Portugal; often located near to or even within the same building as the tourist offices. Unusually, they often offer a better rate of exchange for cash and travellers cheques than the banks.

POST
Portuguese post offices (correios) are open Monday to Friday 8.30am to 6pm. In Lisbon and Porto they are also open on Saturday mornings. Stamps can be bought over the counter or from an automatic dispensing machine (Correio de Portugal – Selos). Depending on the size of the city/town, there are usually several in and near the centre. A letter within Europe costs €0.56, or €0.72 to anywhere else. An increasing number of post offices also have a Netpost Internet kiosk (€5.50 for three hours).

EMERGENCY NUMBERS

Ambulance, fire, police ☎ 112

TELEPHONE
Mobile Phones
Mobile phone numbers within Portugal have nine digits and begin with ☎ 9.

Phone Codes
All Portuguese phone numbers have nine digits. These include area codes which always need to be dialled. For general information dial ☎ 118, for international inquiries dial ☎ 179, and for reverse-charge (collect) calls dial ☎ 120.

Phonecards
Phonecards are the most reliable and cheap way of making a phone call from a telephone booth. They are sold at post offices, newsagents and tobacconists in denominations of €5 and €10.

VISAS
EU nationals need only a valid passport or identity card for entry to Portugal, and may stay indefinitely. Citizens of Australia, Canada, New Zealand and the United States can stay for up to 90 days in any half-year without a visa. Check out www.travisa.com/visa1.htm for more visa information.

TRANSPORT IN PORTUGAL

GETTING THERE & AWAY
Air
Portugal's main gateway is the **Aeroporto Portela** (☎ 218 413 700) in Lisbon approximately 8km north of the city centre.

Porto's Aeroporto **Francisco Sá Carneiro** (☎ 229 432 400) also handles international flights, as does the **Aeroporto de Faro** (☎ 229 800 801) in the Algarve, which has the largest number of charter flights. The website for all three airports is www.ana-aeroportos.pt, in Portuguese.

Air Portugal (TAP; ☎ 289 800 218; www.tap.pt, in Portuguese) is the main international airline. **Portugália Airlines** (PGA; ☎ 218 425 559; www.pga.pt, in Portuguese) is primarily a domestic airline,

but is increasingly opening up international routes including to/from Manchester, Brussels, Nice and Lyon. Both airlines have an excellent safety record.

Following is a list of the major carriers serving Portugal with the airports they use: Lisbon, Porto or Faro. For details of carriers to/from outside Western Europe see the Transport chapter (p1066).

Air France (code AF; ☎ 218 482 177; www.airfrance.com) Lisbon, Porto.

Air Portugal (code TAP; ☎ 289 800 218; www.tap.pt) Lisbon, Porto, Faro.

British Airways (code BA; ☎ 214 154 151; www.ba.com) Lisbon, Porto, Faro.

British Midlands/bmibaby (code WW; UK ☎ 0870 264 2229; www.bmibaby.com) Lisbon, Porto, Faro.

EasyJet (code EZY; UK ☎ 0870 600 000; www.easyjet.com) Lisbon, Faro.

Iberia (code IB; ☎ 808 261 261; www.iberia.com, in Spanish) Lisbon, Porto.

Lufthansa (code IH; London ☎ 020-8750 3460; www.lufthansa.com, in German)

Monarch Airlines (code ZB; ☎ 289 889 475; www.fly-monarch.com) Faro.

Portugália Airlines (code PGA; ☎ 218 425 559; www.pga.pt, in Portuguese) Lisbon, Porto, Faro.

Spanair (code JK; ☎ 218 4998 578; www.spanair.com) Lisbon.

There are scheduled year-round flights from the UK to Lisbon, Porto and Faro with BA, PGA and TAP, and from Frankfurt (Germany) with Lufthansa.

TAP and Continental Airlines both have a daily flight from New York to Lisbon with connections to Faro and Porto. Air France has multiple daily non-stop Paris–Lisbon and Paris–Porto connections, while PGA has a daily flight from Paris to Porto. From neighbouring Spain, TAP, Iberia and Spanair have daily Madrid–Lisbon flights. Elsewhere in Europe, KLM and TAP fly to Lisbon and Porto daily from Amsterdam, while PGA has regular direct flights to Lisbon from Berlin, Stuttgart, Cologne and Hamburg.

There are no direct flights from Australia/New Zealand to Portugal, but dozens of indirect routes via third countries. TAP has regular routes to Lisbon from South America, including Rio and Recife (Brazil) and Caracas (Venezuela).

Among the cheaper scheduled options – if you want to use the UK as a base or transfer point – is the no-frills carrier Easyjet, which offers flights from London, Stanstead, Bristol and East Midland to Faro. Prices for Easyjet start as low as UK£100 return. British Midland's budget carrier bmibaby also has inexpensive flights from the East Midlands to Faro, and Monarch Airlines flies from Luton and Manchester.

Land

BUS

UK & France

Eurolines (UK ☎ 08705-143 219; www.eurolines.co.uk), now operated by National Express, offers departures for Portugal once a week, with several stops that include Lisbon (42 hours) and Porto (40 hours). Buses depart from Victoria coach station, travelling via the Channel ferry and there is a 7½-hour stopover and change of coach in Paris. The current return fare London–Lisbon is UK£145.

Busabout (UK ☎ 020 7950 1661; www.busabout .com) is a Europe-wide hop-on–hop-off coach network with passes that let you travel as much as you want within a set period. It stops in Lisbon and Lagos in Portugal. The current eight-day under-26 Flexipass costs UK£249.

IASA (Paris ☎ 014 353 9082; fax 014 353 4957) have several different routes within Portugal departing from Paris. The current return fare Paris–Lisbon is €135, with discounts for seniors and students.

Spain

Eurolines (Madrid ☎ 915 063 360; www.eurolines.es, in Spanish) operates several services from Spain to Portugal, including Madrid–Lisbon (€38, eight hours), Madrid–Porto (€38, seven hours), Seville–Lisbon (€35, four hours) and Barcelona–Lisbon (€74, 16 hours), all going at least three times weekly.

ALSA (Madrid ☎ 902 422 242) has twice-daily Madrid–Lisbon services, while **Damas** (Huelva ☎ 959 256 900) runs twice daily Monday to Saturday from Seville to Faro and Lagos via Huelva, jointly with the Algarve line EVA.

CAR & MOTORCYCLE

There is no border control in Portugal. For more information about driving in Portugal see p893.

TRAIN

UK & France

In general, it's only worth taking the train from the UK if you can use under-26 rail passes such as **Inter-Rail**. See p1079.

All services from London to Portugal go via Paris, where you change trains (and stations) for the *TGV Atlantique* to Irún in Spain (change trains again). From Irún there are two standard routes: the *Sud-Expresso* across Spain to Coimbra in Portugal, where you can continue to Lisbon or change for Porto; and an express service to Madrid, changing there to the overnight *Lusitânia* to Lisbon. Change at Lisbon for the south of Portugal.

Buying a one-way, 2nd-class, adult/youth London–Lisbon ticket (seat only) for the cheapest route, via the channel ferry, costs around UK£120; you'll need to allow at least 24 hours. Tickets for this route are available from bigger train stations or from **Trains Europe** (UK ☎ 01354-660 222; www.trains europe.co.uk). The Eurostar service to Paris via the Channel Tunnel cuts several hours off the trip but bumps up the cost. Contact **Rail Europe** (UK ☎ 08705-848 848; www.raileurope .co.uk) for details.

Spain

Renfe (Spain ☎ 902 240 202; www.renfe.es, in Spanish; return ticket €118) has a nightly sleeper service between Madrid and Lisbon. Badajoz–Elvas–Lisbon is slow and there is only one regional service daily, but the scenery is stunning. There are no direct southern trains: from Seville you can ride to Huelva (three daily), catch a bus for Ayamonte, change buses to cross the border to Vila Real de Santo António then catch one of the frequent trains to Faro and Lagos.

Sea

UK

There are no ferries from the UK to Portugal, but you can travel to northern Spain with the following operators and then hit the road to Portugal.

P&O Ferries (UK ☎ 0870 520 2020; www.poef .com; adult one way from UK£125) operates the Ports-mouth–Bilbao route (30 hours) with crossings twice weekly throughout the year except for three weeks in January.

Brittany Ferries (UK ☎ 0870 366 5333; www.brit tanyferries.com; from UK£110/per adult one way) operates between Plymouth and Santander twice weekly. The 24-hour crossing can be rough.

GETTING AROUND
Air
AIRLINES IN PORTUGAL
Flights within Portugal are poor value unless you have a youth/student card.

Portugália Airlines (PGA; Lisbon ☎ 218 425 559; www.pga.pt) and **TAP** (Lisbon ☎ 808 205 700; www .tap.pt) both have multiple daily Lisbon–Porto and Lisbon–Faro links for around €105. Portugália offers a 50% youth discount. TAP has a daily Lisbon–Faro service connecting with its international arrivals and departures at Lisbon. Portugal's domestic departure tax is €7 and is generally included in the ticket price. Both airlines have good safety records, marred only by a 1977 TAP accident in Madeira when there were 131 fatalities.

Bicycle
Mountain biking is popular in Portugal and a great way to explore the country, although given the Portuguese penchant for overtaking on blind corners, it can be dangerous on lesser roads. Bicycle lanes are rare, aside from in the natural parks: veteran pedallers recommend the Parque Nacional da Peneda-Gare (p887). A growing number of towns have bike-rental outfits (around €10 a day). If you're bringing your own, pack plenty of spares. Bicycles can't be taken with you on trains, although most bus lines will accept them as accompanied baggage, subject to space and sometimes for an extra fee.

Boat
Portugal is not big on waterborne transport, other than river cruises along the Douro River from Porto (p883), Lisbon's river trips (p863) and commuter ferries.

Bus
Portugal's buses are generally modern and comfortable. However, there is a baffling number of privatised bus companies operating across the country. In Porto alone there are at least 18 bus companies, most based at different terminals.

Unless you're a local or speak fluent Portuguese, the only company really worth worrying about is the national network **Rede Expressos** (☎ 969 502 050; www.rede-expressos .pt, in Portuguese), which has a fleet of 100 buses, a comprehensive website and provides connections to 300 locations throughout the country. Portugal's main Eurolines agents are **Internorte** (Porto ☎ 226 052 420), **Intercentro** (Lisbon ☎ 213 571 745) and **Intersul** (Faro ☎ 289 899 770), serving north, central and southern Portugal, respectively.

CLASSES
There are three classes of bus service: *expressos* are comfortable, fast, direct buses between major cities; *rápidas* are fast regional buses; and *carreiras* stop at every crossroad. *Expressos* are generally the best cheap way to get around (particularly for long trips, where per-kilometre costs are lowest). An under-26 card should get you a discount of around 20%, at least on the long-distance services.

COSTS
Travelling by bus in Portugal is comparatively inexpensive – especially when compared with the UK. Refer to the Getting There & Away section of the respective city or town you are travelling to or from for more information, including fares.

RESERVATIONS
Advance reservations are only really necessary on the longer routes of the *expresso* service.

Car & Motorcycle
AUTOMOBILE ASSOCIATIONS
ACP (Automóvel Clube de Portugal; head office ☎ 213 180 100; emergency help number for the south ☎ 219 429 103; emergency help number for the north ☎ 228 340 001; www .acp.pt, in Portuguese; Rua Rosa Araújo 24, Lisbon) has a reciprocal arrangement with many of the better-known foreign automobile clubs, including AA and RAC. ACP provides medical, legal and breakdown assistance.

FUEL & SPARE PARTS
Fuel is expensive, costing around €0.97 for a litre of 95-octane *sem chumbo* (unleaded petrol) and €0.71 for a *gasóleo* (diesel). There are plenty of self-service stations; some have garages that can replace batteries, repair punctures and do minor mechanical repairs, as well as carry some spare parts. Alternatively, they can direct you to the nearest car workshop.

PORTUGAL

HIRE

To hire a car in Portugal you must be at least 25 and have held your home licence for over a year (some companies allow younger drivers at higher rates). To hire a scooter of up to 50cc you must be over 18 years old and have a valid driving licence. For more powerful scooters and motorbikes you must have a valid driving licence covering these vehicles from your home country.

INSURANCE

Although most car insurance companies within the EU will cover taking your car to Portugal, it is prudent to consider extra cover for assistance in case your car breaks down. The minimum insurance required is third party. **ACP Insurance** (☎ 217 991 200; www

.acp.pt, in Portuguese) can advise members on car and motorcycle insurance.

ROAD RULES

Driving is on the right side of the road. Speed limits for cars and motorcycles are 50km/h in cities and public centres, 90km/h on normal roads and 120km/h on motorways (but 50km/h, 70km/h and 100km/h for motorcycles with sidecars). Drivers and front passengers in cars must wear seat belts. Motorcyclists and passengers must wear helmets, and motorcycles must have headlights on day and night. Using a mobile phone while driving could result in a fine.

Drink-driving laws are strict here with a maximum legal blood-alcohol level of 0.05%.

Spain

CONTENTS

896

Yes, this is the land of flamenco, fiestas and fun in the sun, but peer past Spain's tourist-brochure image and you'll find a fascinating country rich in history and culture.

A mammoth peninsula jutting out from southern Europe, Spain is home to just about every imaginable landscape, from the beaches of the Costa de la Luz to the rugged peaks of the Pyrenees, from the damp green of Galicia to the sunburnt plains of Castilla. This varied landscape was the backdrop of a long and turbulent history that reveals its presence at every turn.

Mudéjar (Islamic architecture in Christian-held territory) buildings in Andalucía and the medieval Jewish temples in Toledo are relics of an era when these cultures coexisted peacefully in Spain. Move on to the breathtakingly beautiful Catholic cathedrals of Burgos, León and Santiago de Compostela for a glimpse of the Church's tremendous power in this historically Catholic country.

Yet not all of Spain's glory lies in its past. The vibrant nightlife in cities such as Madrid and Barcelona is proof of the country's boundless energy, and international acclaim in art, design and cuisine show that Spain's creative juices are flowing.

FAST FACTS

- **Area** 505,000 sq km
- **Capital** Madrid
- **Currency** euro (€); A$1 = €0.58; ¥100 = €0.76; NZ$1 = €0.54; UK£1 = €1.50; US$1 = €0.83
- **Famous for** sunshine, late nights, bullfighting, *jamón serrano* (cured ham), *Don Quixote*, Pedro Almodóvar films
- **Key Phrases** *hola* (hello); *gracias* (thanks); *adios* (goodbye)
- **Official Languages** Spanish (Castilian or *castellano*), Catalan, Basque, Galician *(gallego)*
- **Population** 40.2 million
- **Telephone Codes** country code ☎ 34; international access code ☎ 00
- **Visas** EU, Norway and Iceland citizens do not need a visa; nationals of Australia, Canada, Israel, Japan, New Zealand, Switzerland and the USA need no visa for stays of up to 90 days, but must have a passport valid for the whole visit; South Africans are among nationalities that do need a visa

SPAIN

HIGHLIGHTS

- Admire the wonderfully weird architecture of **Gaudí** (p930) in Barcelona.
- Relax in *Grande dame* **San Sebastián** (p944), with her perfect beaches and tasty tapas.
- Sip a glass of chilled gazpacho under the shade of an orange tree in **Andalucía** (p970).
- Explore the beaches, pine forests and laid-back lifestyle of Tarifa and the luminous **Costa de la Luz** (p983).
- Soak up the sun on Galicia's pristine **Islas Cíes** (p951), Atlantic beaches far from the southern coast's crowds.

ITINERARIES

- **One week** Start in Barcelona, spending two days soaking up modernist architecture and seaside life before zipping up to graze on *pinxos* (tapas) in San Sebastián. Take a short side trip to Bilbao's Guggenheim Museum, and end your trip testing your endurance on Madrid's legendary night scene.
- **Two weeks** From Madrid, catch the train to Seville. Stay two days, then head south to Tarifa via Cádiz and the Costa de la Luz. Jump on the bus to Granada and visit the Alhambra, then hop on an overnight train to Valencia before returning to Madrid via the historic town of Cuenca.

CLIMATE & WHEN TO GO

Most of Spain is drenched with healthy doses of sunshine year-round, though the rainy north and snowcapped Pyrenees don't always comply. Along the coasts, beach weather begins in late May and lasts through September. In the north, the summer season is a little shorter, while Andalucía's summer often lasts longer.

The Mediterranean coast enjoys mild winters, rarely freezing, but central Spain (Madrid, Ávila, Segovia and around) and the Pyrenees get downright cold. The rains and winds along the Atlantic coasts make winters in Galicia, Cantabria, Asturias and the Basque Country occasionally unpleasant. See Climate Charts p1054 for more information.

HISTORY
Ancient History

The bridge between Africa and Europe, Spain has always been a meeting point for peoples and cultures, though not necessarily a peace-

---

HOW MUCH?

- Leg of Jamón Jabugo €225
- Bottle of Torres wine €9
- Bullfighter's suit €2500
- Camper shoes €120
- Ceramic plate from Andalucía €40

LONELY PLANET INDEX

- Litre of petrol €0.80
- Litre of bottled water €1.50
- Glass of Spanish beer €1.75
- Souvenir T-shirt €16
- Plate of churros €1.50

---

ful one. North African pioneers first began to settle the peninsula around 8000 BC, and in the millennia that followed, Celtic tribes, Phoenician merchants, Greeks and Carthaginians trickled in. The Romans arrived in the 3rd century BC but took 200 years to subdue the peninsula. Peace was short-lived; by AD 419 the Christian Visigoths had established a kingdom that lasted until 711.

Muslim Spain & the Reconquista

By 714 Muslim armies had occupied nearly the entire peninsula. Muslim dominion was to last almost 800 years in parts of Spain. In Islamic Spain (known as al-Andalus) arts and sciences prospered, new crops and agricultural techniques were introduced and palaces, mosques, schools, public baths and gardens were built.

In 1085 Alfonso VI, king of León and Castilla, took Toledo, the first definitive victory of the Reconquista (the struggle to wrestle Spain into Christian hands). By the mid-13th century, the Christians had taken most of the peninsula, except for the state of Granada.

In the process, the kingdoms of Castilla and Aragón emerged as Christian Spain's two main powers, and in 1469 they were united by the marriage of Isabel, princess of Castilla, and Fernando, heir to Aragón's throne. Known as the Catholic Monarchs, they laid the foundations for the Spanish golden age, but they were also responsible for one of the darkest hours in Spain's history – the Inquisition, a witch-hunt to expel or execute Jews and non-Christians. In 1492 the last Muslim

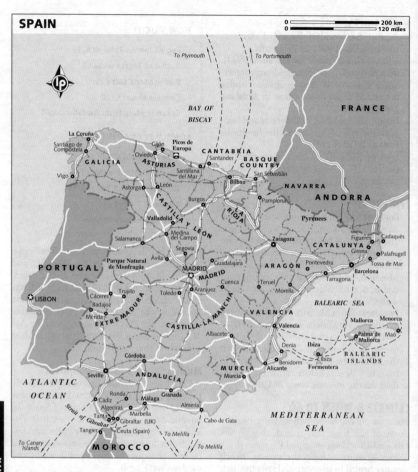

SPAIN

0 — 200 km
0 — 120 miles

To Plymouth
To Portsmouth

FRANCE

BAY OF
BISCAY

La Coruña
Santiago de
Compostela
GALICIA
Vigo

Gijón
Oviedo
Picos de
Europa
CANTABRIA
Santander
BASQUE
COUNTRY
San Sebastián
Bilbao
NAVARRA
Santillana
del Mar
Pamplona
ANDORRA

Astorga
León
Burgos
LA
RIOJA
Pyrenees

Valladolid
Medina
del Campo
Zaragoza
CATALUNYA
Figueres
Cadaqués
Girona
Palafrugell
Tossa de Mar
Barcelona

Salamanca
CASTILLA Y LEÓN
Segovia
Guadalajara
ARAGÓN
Pontevedra
Tarragona

PORTUGAL
Parque Natural
de Monfragüe
Ávila
MADRID
MADRID
Cuenca
Teruel
Morella
BALEARIC
SEA

Cáceres
Trujillo
Toledo
Aranjuez
VALENCIA
Mallorca
Menorca

LISBON
Badajoz
Mérida
EXTREMADURA
CASTILLA-LA MANCHA
Valencia
Palma de
Mallorca
Maó

Albacete
Denia
Ibiza
BALEARIC
ISLANDS

Córdoba
MURCIA
Benidorm
Alicante
Ibiza
Formentera

ATLANTIC
OCEAN
ANDALUCÍA
Murcia

Seville
Ronda
Cádiz
Algeciras
Tarifa
Gibraltar (UK)
Marbella
Málaga
Granada
Almería
Cabo de Gata
MEDITERRANEAN
SEA

Ceuta (Spain)
Tangier
To Melilla

To Canary
Islands
MOROCCO
To Melilla

Strait of Gibraltar

ruler of Granada surrendered to them, marking the end of the Reconquista.

The Golden Age

Christopher Columbus' so-called discovery of the Americas in 1492 kicked off Spain's golden age. Befuddled Columbus (Colón in Castilian), trying to find a new route to India, stumbled upon the Bahamas, though he never guessed he'd discovered new continents and changed the course of history. His voyages sparked a period of exploration and exploitation that was to yield Spain enormous wealth, while destroying the ancient American empires. For three centuries, gold and silver from the New World were used to finance the rapid expansion and slow decline of the Spanish empire. By the 18th century, the mighty Spanish empire was on its way out, the life sucked out of it by a series of unwise kings, self-seeking noblemen and unsuccessful wars that left the empire in shambles.

The 18th & 19th Centuries

The 18th century dawned with a war over the succession to the throne when Carlos II died heirless, but all was soon put right when Felipe V, the first Bourbon king, took control and ushered in a period of stability. Peace would last until the end of the century, when Spain declared war on France and then on Britain and Portugal. The wars proved disastrous, and Spain ultimately lost several colonies and nearly all its sea power.

In 1807–08 Napoleon's forces occupied a weakened Spain, and King Carlos IV abdicated without a fight. In his place Napoleon installed his own brother, Joseph Bonaparte. The Spaniards retaliated with a five-year war of independence, and in 1815 Napoleon was defeated by the Duke of Wellington, who had united with the Portuguese and Spanish troops. A Bourbon, Fernando VII, was restored to the Spanish throne.

Fernando's reign was a disastrous advertisement for monarchy: the Inquisition was re-established, liberals were persecuted, Spain entered a severe recession and the American colonies officially won their independence in 1824. After Fernando's death in 1833 came the First Carlist War (1834–39), which ended with Isabel II, Fernando's daughter, taking the throne. In 1868 the monarchy was overthrown during the Septembrina Revolution and Isabel II was forced to flee from Madrid. The First Republic was declared in 1873, but within 18 months the army had restored the monarchy, with Isabel's son Alfonso XII on the throne. Despite political turmoil, Spain's economy prospered in the second half of the 19th century, fuelled by industrialisation.

The disastrous Spanish-American War of 1898 marked the end of the Spanish empire. Spain was defeated by the USA and lost its last overseas possessions – Cuba, Puerto Rico, Guam and the Philippines.

The 20th Century

The early 20th century was characterised by growing instability, as anarchists and radicals struggled to overthrow the established order. In 1923, with Spain on the brink of civil war, Miguel Primo de Rivera made himself military dictator, ruling until 1930. In 1931 King Alfonso XIII fled the country and the Second Republic was declared.

Like its predecessor, the Second Republic fell victim to internal conflict. The 1936 elections split the nation in two, with the Popular Front (an uneasy alliance of leftist parties) on one side and the right-wing Nationalists (an alliance of the army, Church and the Fascist-style Falange Party) on the other.

Nationalist plotters in the army rose against the Republican government in July 1936, launching a civil war (1936–39) that would further sink the country in poverty and create bitter wounds that are still healing today. The Nationalists, led by General Francisco Franco, received military support from Nazi Germany and Fascist Italy, while the elected Republican government received support from the Soviet Union and foreign leftists.

The war ended in 1939, with Franco the victor. Some 350,000 Spaniards died in the war, most of them on the battlefield but many others in executions, prison camps or simply from starvation. After the war, thousands of Republicans were executed, jailed or forced into exile, and Franco's 36-year dictatorship began with Spain isolated internationally and crippled by recession. It wasn't until the 1950s and '60s, when the rise in tourism and a treaty with the USA combined to provide much-needed funds, that the country began to recover.

Franco died in 1975, having named Juan Carlos, the grandson of Alfonso XIII, as his successor. Instead of accepting power, King Juan Carlos handed it over to a newly created democratic government, earning the lasting respect of the country. The first elections were held in 1977 and a new constitution was drafted in 1978. Spain joined the European Community (EC) in 1986 and celebrated its return to the world stage in style in 1992, with Expo '92 in Seville and the Olympic Games in Barcelona.

Spain Today

The modern, forward-thinking Spain of today has long since thrown off the dark cloud of Franco's dictatorship. In 1996 the centre-right Partido Popular (Popular Party; PP), led by José María Aznar, took control of the nation after the long-ruling Socialist party was voted out under accusations of corruption. The PP went on to establish programmes of economic decentralisation and liberalisation, paving the way for economic success.

In 2003 Aznar's government declared its support for the US-led war on Iraq, against the wishes of more than 90% of the Spanish populace. The PP's popularity began to decline, eventually plummeting when it came to light, just days before the 2004 elections, that the PP had misled the Spanish people about the circumstances surrounding the 11 March train bombings in Madrid, leading them to believe the Basque separatist group

SPAIN

ETA was the author of the attack when all along evidence pointed to Al Qaeda. The terrorist bombings killed 200 people.

The Socialist party, led by José Luís Rodríguez Zapatero, was voted into power a few days after the bombings, and newly elected president Zapatero immediately made the call to withdraw Spanish troops from Iraq, a decision applauded by his countrymen. Another plus for Zapatero is the fact that his cabinet is the first in the world to have absolute parity between men and women; there are eight female ministers and eight male ministers.

PEOPLE

Spain has a population of 40 million, descended from all the many peoples who have settled here over the millennia, among them Iberians, Celts, Romans, Jews, Visigoths, Berbers, Arabs and 20th-century immigrants from across the globe. The biggest cities are Madrid (three million), Barcelona (1.5 million), Valencia (750,000) and Seville (700,000). Each region proudly preserves its own unique culture, and some – Catalonia and the País Vasco (Basque Country) in particular – display a fiercely independent spirit.

Most Spaniards are economical with etiquette, but this does not signify rudeness. They're gregarious people, on the whole very tolerant and easy-going towards foreigners. It's not easy to give offence. However, obviously disrespectful behaviour, including excessively casual dress in churches and boisterous behaviour in public, won't go down well.

RELIGION

Only about 20% of Spaniards are regular churchgoers, but Catholicism is deeply ingrained in the culture. As the writer Unamuno said, 'Here in Spain we are all Catholics, even the atheists'.

However, many Spaniards have a deepseated scepticism about the Church. During the Civil War, anarchists burned churches and shot clerics because they represented repression and corruption. Later, during Franco's rule, church-going was practically obligatory and those who shunned the Church were often treated as outcasts or targeted as delinquents by Franco's police. Understandably, many people began to see

the Church as a haven for hypocrites, and the image still hasn't completely worn off.

ARTS
Cinema

Classic Spanish directors include Luis Buñuel, whose films include *Un Chien Andalou* (1928), *L'Age d'Or* (1930), *Tierra sin Pan* (Land Without Bread; 1932), Juan Antonio Bardem, who made *Muerte de un Ciclista* (Death of a Cyclist; 1955) and Luis Berlanga, of *Bienvenido Mr Marshall* (Welcome Mr Marshall; 1953) fame.

Modern cinema's best-known director is Pedro Almodóvar, who broke away from the trend that focused only on Franco with humorous films set amid the Movida, the social and artistic revolution of the late 1970s and '80s. Winner of Oscars for *Todo Sobre Mi Madre* (All About My Mother; 1999) and *Habla Con Ella* (Talk to Her; 2002), Almodóvar is Spain's most internationally successful filmmaker.

Painting

The giants of Spain's golden age (1550–1650) were Toledo-based El Greco (originally from Crete) and Diego Velázquez, perhaps Spain's most revered painter. Both excelled with insightful portraits. The genius of both the 18th and 19th centuries was Francisco Goya, whose versatility ranged from unflattering royal portraits and anguished war scenes to bullfight etchings.

Catalonia was the powerhouse of early-20th-century Spanish art, claiming the hugely prolific Pablo Picasso (although he was born in Andalucía), the colourful symbolist Joan Miró and surrealist Salvador Dalí. Important artists of the late 20th century include Catalan abstract artist Antoni Tàpies and Basque sculptor Eduardo Chillida. Works by these and other major Spanish artists can be found in galleries throughout the country.

Architecture

Spain's earliest architectural relics are the prehistoric monuments on Menorca. Reminders of Roman times include the ruins of Mérida and Tarragona, and Segovia's amazing aqueduct. The Muslims left behind some of the most splendid buildings in the entire Islamic world, including Granada's Alhambra, Córdoba's awe-inspiring Mezquita and Seville's Alcázar – the latter an example of *Mudéjar* architecture, the name given to Islamic work done throughout Christian-held territory.

The first main Christian architectural movement was Romanesque. Surviving examples include many country churches and several cathedrals, notably that of Santiago de Compostela. Later came the great Gothic cathedrals (such as Toledo, Barcelona, León, Salamanca and Seville) of the 13th to 16th centuries, Renaissance styles such as the plateresque work so prominent in Salamanca and the austere work of Juan de Herrera, responsible for El Escorial (see p916). Spain then followed the usual path to baroque (17th and 18th centuries) and neoclassicism (19th century), before Catalonia produced its startling modernist (roughly Art Nouveau) movement around the turn of the 20th century, of which Antoni Gaudí's Sagrada Familia church is the most stunning example.

Literature

One of the earliest works of Spanish literature is the *Cantar de Mío Cid* (Song of My Cid), an anonymous epic poem describing the life of El Cid, an 11th-century Christian knight buried in the Burgos cathedral. Miguel de Cervantes' novel *Don Quixote de la Mancha* is the masterpiece of the literary flowering of the 16th and 17th centuries, as well as one of the world's great works of fiction. The playwrights Lope de Vega and Pedro Calderón de la Barca were also leading lights of the age.

The next high point, in the early 20th century, grew out of the crisis of the Spanish-American War that spawned the intellectual Generation of '98. Philosophical essayist Miguel de Unamuno was prominent, but the towering figure was poet and playwright Federico García Lorca, who won international acclaim before he was murdered in the civil war for his Republican sympathies.

Camilo José Cela, author of the civil war–aftermath novel *La Familia de Pascal Duarte* (The Family of Pascal Duarte), won the 1989 Nobel Prize for literature. Contemporary author Juan Goytisolo is one of the country's premier writers; his most approachable work is his autobiography, *Forbidden Territory*. There has been a proliferation of women – particularly feminist writers – during the past 25 years, among whose prominent representatives are Ana María Matute, known for her novels on the civil war, such as *Los Hijos Muertos* (The Lost Children), and Rosa Montero, known for works such as *Historias de Mujeres* (Stories of Women).

Flamenco

Getting to see real, deeply emotional flamenco can be hard, as it tends to happen semispontaneously in little bars. Andalucía is its traditional home and you'll find plenty of clubs there and elsewhere offering flamenco shows; these are generally aimed at tourists and are expensive, but some are good. Your best chance of catching the real thing is probably at one of the flamenco festivals in the south, usually held in summer. You'll also find quality *tablaos* (flamenco stages) in Madrid and throughout Andalucía.

ENVIRONMENT

Spain is probably Europe's most geographically diverse country, with landscapes ranging from the near-deserts of Almería to the green, Welsh-like countryside and deep coastal inlets of Galicia, and from the sun-baked plains of Castilla-La Mancha to the rugged mountains of the Pyrenees.

Nearly 5000km of coastline rings the country with yet more scenic variety. Spain's shore encompasses the rocky cliffs of the Costa Brava, the endless sandy beaches of the Costa de Luz and the pounding Atlantic waves of the Basque Country.

The country covers 84% of the Iberian Peninsula and spreads over some 505,000 sq km, more than half of which is high tableland (*meseta*). This is supported and divided by several mountain chains, making Spain Europe's second-hilliest country, after Switzerland. The main mountains are the Pyrenees, along the border with France; the Cordillera Cantábrica, backing the northern coast; the Sistema Ibérico, from the central north towards the middle Mediterranean coast; the Cordillera Central, from north of Madrid towards the Portuguese border; and three east-west chains across Andalucía, one of which is the highest range of all – the Sierra Nevada.

The major rivers are the Ebro, Duero, Tajo (Tagus), Guadiana and Guadalquivir, each draining a different basin between the mountains and all flowing into the Atlantic Ocean (except for the Ebro, which reaches the Mediterranean Sea).

The brown bear, wolf, lynx and wild boar all survive in Spain, although only the boar exists in abundance; farmers delight in shoot-

SPAIN

ing and roasting the tasty pest. Spain's high mountains harbour the goat-like chamois and Spanish ibex (the latter is rare) and big birds of prey such as eagles, vultures and the lammergeier. The marshy Ebro delta and Guadalquivir estuary are important for water birds, among them the spectacular greater flamingo. Many of Spain's 5500 seed-bearing plants occur nowhere else in Europe, due to the barrier of the Pyrenees. Spring wild flowers are magnificent in many country and hilly areas.

The conservation picture has improved by leaps and bounds in the past 25 years and Spain now has 25,000 sq km of protected areas, including 10 national parks. However, overgrazing, reservoir creation, tourism, housing developments, agricultural and industrial effluent, fires and hunting all still threaten plant and animal life.

FOOD & DRINK
Specialities
It's a good idea to reset your stomach's clock in Spain, unless you want to eat alone or with other tourists. Most Spaniards start the day with a light *desayuno* (breakfast), perhaps coffee with a *tostada* (piece of toast) or *pastel* (pastry). *Churros con chocolate* (long, deep-fried dough with hot chocolate) are a delicious start to the day and unique to Spain.

Almuerzo or *la comida* (lunch) is usually the main meal of the day, eaten between about 1.30pm and 3.30pm. The *cena* (evening meal) is usually lighter and may be eaten as late as 10pm or 11pm; meals out with friends may well last until 1am or later. It's common to go to a bar or café for tapas around 11am and again around 7pm or 8pm.

Spain has many local cuisines, and each region has its speciality. One of the most characteristic dishes, from the Valencia region, is paella – rice, seafood, the odd vegetable and often chicken or meat, all simmered together and traditionally coloured yellow with saffron. Another dish, of Andalucían origin, is gazpacho, a cold soup made from tomatoes, breadcrumbs, cucumber and green peppers. Tortillas are an inexpensive stand-by snack and come in many varieties. *Jamón serrano* (cured ham) is a delicacy for meat eaters.

Drinks
Start the day with a strong coffee, either as a *café con leche* (half-coffee, half-milk), *café*

solo (short black, espresso-like) or *café cortado* (short black with a little milk.)

The most common way to order a beer (*cerveza*) is to ask for a *caña*, which is a small draught beer. In the Basque Country this is called a *zurrito*. A larger beer (about 300mL) is often called a *tubo,* or (in Catalonia) a *jarra.* All these words apply to draught beer (*cerveza de barril*) – if you just ask for a *cerveza* you're likely to get bottled beer, which is more expensive.

Vino (wine) comes in *blanco* (white), *tinto* (red) or *rosado* (rosé). Exciting wine regions include Penedès, Priorat and Ribera del Duero. *Tinto de verano,* a kind of wine shandy, is good in summer. There are also many regional grape specialities, such as *jerez* (sherry) in Jerez de la Frontera and *cava* (a sparkling wine) in Catalonia. Sangría, a sweet punch made of red wine, fruit and spirits, is refreshing and very popular with tourists and in summer.

Agua del grifo (tap water) is usually safe to drink but it may not be very tasty in cities or near the coast. *Agua mineral con gas* (sparkling mineral water) and *agua mineral sin gas* (still mineral water) cost about €1 for a small bottle.

Where to Eat & Drink
Bars and cafés are open all day, serving coffees, pastries, *bocadillos* (long sandwiches) and usually tapas, which cost around €2. In the evenings these same bars fill with regulars looking for a quick beer or glass of house wine. Groups can order *raciónes,* a large-sized serving of these snacks; a *media ración* is half a *ración.* You can often save 10% to 20% by ordering and eating food at the bar rather than at a table.

Self-caterers will be delighted with Spain's fresh-produce markets, which you'll find near the centre of just about every city and town. Load up on colourful veggies, fresh bread and Spanish cheeses.

Spaniards like to eat out, and restaurants abound even in small towns. At lunch time, most places offer a *menú del día* – a fixed-price lunch menu and the budget traveller's best friend. For €7 to €12 you typically get three courses, bread and a drink. The *plato combinado* (combined plate) is a cousin of the *menú* and usually includes a meat dish and a couple of side dishes. Check out the crowd before sitting down; if it's full of locals, that's a good sign. If all the diners speak English, you may want to head elsewhere.

After dinner, you can head to a *bar de copas* (pub), where hard drinks are pretty much the only thing on offer.

Vegetarian Food

Vegetarians may have to be creative in Spain. Though in larger cities and important student centres there's a growing awareness of vegetarianism, traditional restaurants often offer salads and egg tortillas, but little else for noncarnivores. Even salads may come laden with sausages or tuna. Pasta and pizza are readily available, as is seafood.

MADRID

pop 3.09 million

Madrid's role as the capital of Spain and administrative headquarters of the country requires it to be somewhat serious-faced and austere; yet anyone who's been here on a Friday night knows that few cities let down their hair like Madrid. Plan to check out the anything-goes nightlife, but save energy for visits to the city's amazing art museums and busy historic centre.

HISTORY

Madrid was little more than a muddy, mediocre village when King Felipe II declared it Spain's capital in 1561. The obvious choice for the capital was nearby Toledo, but Felipe didn't like the fact that the stuck-up clergy already had the upper hand there, so no-name Madrid took the prize.

The city was a squalid grid of unpaved alleys and dirty buildings until the 18th century, when King Carlos III turned his attention to public works. Madrid grew in spurts, and it wasn't until the early 20th century that it began to take on the look of a proper capital.

The post–civil war 1940s and '50s were trying times for the capital, with poverty being a given for many people. Nowhere was Franco's thumb as firmly pressed down as on Madrid, and the city lived under a blanket of fear and forced austerity for nearly four decades. When the dictator died in 1975 the city exploded with creativity and life, giving Madrileños the party-hard reputation they still cherish.

MADRID IN TWO DAYS

Start with breakfast in the **Plaza de Santa Ana** (p913) and then a visit to the **Museo del Prado** (p906). Afterwards, walk around El Retiro (P907) but save energy for the **Palacio Real** (p907) and afternoon shopping and tapas in **Chueca** (p912). At night, catch a **flamenco show** (p913).

On day two, sign up for the tourist office's **walking tour** (p909) of historic Madrid, and then visit either the **Thyssen-Bornemisza** (p907) or the **Reina Sofía** (p906) art museums. At night, head to **Viva Madrid** (p912) for drinks in uniquely *madrileño* style.

ORIENTATION

In Spain's case, all roads lead to Madrid, more specifically to the Puerta del Sol – kilometre zero – the city's physical and emotional heart. Radiating out from this harried plaza are the main arteries – Calle Mayor, Calle Arenal, Calle Preciados, Calle Montera and Calle Alcalá – that stretch into the city.

South of Puerta del Sol is the oldest part of the city, with the Plaza Mayor to the southwest and the busy streets of the Huertas district to the southeast. North of the plaza is a modern shopping district and, beyond that, the east-west thoroughfare Gran Vía and the bohemian barrio Chueca. To the east is the stately Palacio Real, while to the west lies the city's green lung, El Retiro.

INFORMATION
Bookshops

La Casa del Libro (Map pp908-9; ☎ 91 524 19 00; Gran Vía 29; metro Gran Vía; ☒ 9.30am-9.30pm Mon-Fri, 11am-9pm Sun) Spain's answer to Barnes & Noble has a large English- and foreign-language literature section.

Petra's International Bookshop (Map pp908-9; ☎ 91 541 72 91; Calle Campomanes 13; metro Ópera or Santo Domingo; ☒ 11am-9pm Mon-Sat) A lively expat community hosts conversation groups in this English bookshop.

Emergency

Ambulance ☎ 061
Medical & Fire ☎ 112
Police ☎ 091
Red Cross ☎ 91 522 22 22

Internet Access

Nets (Map pp904-5; ☎ 91 522 20 17; Calle Palma 24; ☒ noon-1am Mon-Sat, noon-midnight Sun; per hr €1.50;

SPAIN

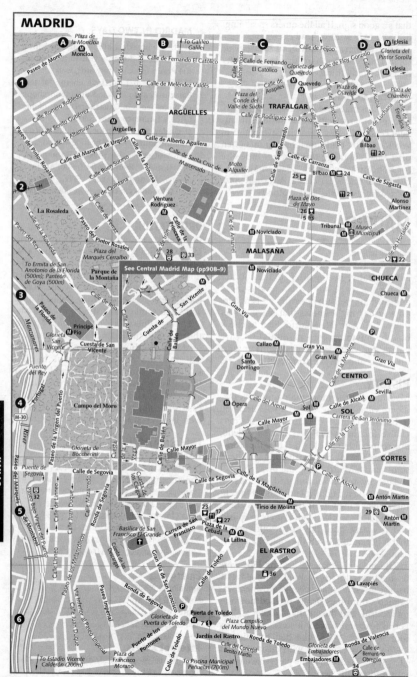

MADRID

Ⓐ Plaza de la Moncloa
Moncloa
Paseo de Moret
Calle Hilarión Eslava
Calle de Gaztambide
Calle de Fernando El Católico
Ⓑ To Galileo Galilei
Calle de Meléndez Valdés
Calle de Vallehermoso
Calle de Fernando El Católico
Ⓒ Calle de Feijoo
Glorieta de Quevedo
Calle de Eloy Gonzalo
Ⓓ Ⓜ Iglesia
Glorieta del Pintor Sorolla
Ⓜ Iglesia
Quevedo

① Calle Romero Robledo
Calle Benito Gutiérrez
Calle de Altamirano
Ⓜ Argüelles
Calle de Alberto Aguilera
ARGÜELLES
Plaza del Conde del Valle de Suchil
Calle de Araples
TRAFALGAR
Calle de Olavide
Ⓟ Plaza de Olavide
Calle de Juan de Austria
Plaza de Chamberí
Calle de Luchana
Calle de Santa Engracia

Paseo del Pintor Rosales
Calle del Marqués de Urquijo
Calle Buen Suceso
Calle de la Princesa
Calle de Santa Cruz de Marcenado
Moto Alquiler
Calle de Rodríguez San Pedro
Ⓜ San Bernardo
Calle de Carranza
Calle de Cardenal Cisneros
Calle de Fuencarral
Ⓟ
Ⓜ Bilbao
🏨 20

② Calle de Quintana
Calle de Ferraz
Ventura Rodríguez
Calle de la Princesa
25 ⬜
Ⓜ Bilbao Ⓜ 🖪 24
Calle de Sagasta
🏨 21
Ⓜ Alonso Martínez

La Rosaleda
Ⓗ
Paseo de la Rosaleda
Paseo del Rey
Paseo de Pintor Rosales
Plaza del Marqués Cerralbo
28 🖪
🖪 33
Calle de Amaniel
Plaza de Dos de Mayo
26 🖪 🏠
5 @
Ⓜ Noviciado
MALASAÑA
Tribunal Ⓜ
Museo Municipal
Ⓜ 🏛
Calle de Hortaleza
🖪 22

To Ermita de San Antonio de la Florida (500m); Panteón de Goya (500m)
Parque de la Montaña
Calle de Irún
③
Paseo de la Florida
Príncipe Pío
Ⓜ Príncipe Pío
Glorieta San Vicente
Cuesta de San Vicente
See Central Madrid Map (pp908–9)
San Vicente
Gran Vía
Ⓜ Noviciado
CHUECA
Chueca Ⓜ

Manzanares
Cuesta de la Vega
Calle de Bailén
Campo del Moro
Callao Ⓜ
Santo Domingo
Gran Vía Ⓜ
Gran Vía
Gran Vía
CENTRO
Ⓟ

④ M-30
Puente del Rey
Portugal
Paseo de la Virgen del Puerto
Glorieta de Boccherini
Ópera Ⓜ
Calle del Arenal
Ⓜ Sol
Calle Mayor
SOL
Carrera de San Jerónimo
Calle de Alcalá
Sevilla Ⓜ
Ⓜ
Calle de la Cruz

Río
Paseo del Marqués de Monistrol
Puente de Segovia
Calle de Segovia
Calle de Bailén
Calle Mayor
Calle de Segovia
Calle de la Magdalena
CORTES
Ⓟ
Calle de Atocha
Ⓜ Antón Martín

⑤ Calle Limneo
Calle Juan Duque
Ronda de Segovia
Basílica de San Francisco El Grande
23 🖪 17
Plaza de la Cebada
🖪 27
Carrera de San Francisco
Ⓜ Ⓜ
La Latina
Tirso de Molina Ⓜ
29 🖪
Antón Martín

Paseo Bajo Virgen del Puerto
🖪 32
Calle de los Metalúrgicos
Cuesta de los Descargas
Gran Vía de San Francisco
EL RASTRO
🖪 36
Ⓜ Lavapiés

⑥ Vía Interior al Paseo Imperial
Calle Juan Duque
Ronda de Segovia
Paseo Imperial
Ronda de Segovia
Puerto de los Pontones
Glorieta de Puerta de Toledo
Ⓜ
7 🏠
Puerta de Toledo
Calle de Toledo
Plaza Campillo del Mundo Nuevo
Ronda de Toledo
Glorieta de Embajadores
Ⓜ Embajadores
Ronda de Valencia
Calle de Bernardino Obregón
34 🖪

To Estadio Vicente Calderón (200m)
Plaza de Francisco Morano
To Piscina Municipal Peñuelas (700m)
Jardín del Rastro
Calle del Concejal Benito Martín

SPAIN

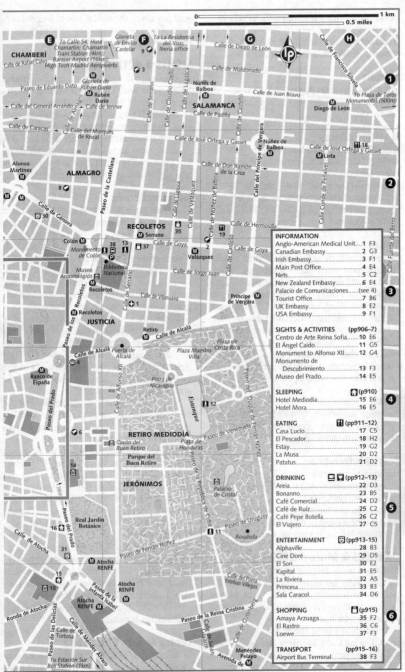

SPAIN

metro Tribunal) To just skim email, you can log on for up to five minutes for free.

Work Center (Map pp908-9; ☎ 91 360 13 95; Calle Príncipe 1; ⏱ 24hr; per hr €2; metro Sevilla)

Laundry

Lavandería Cervantes (Map pp908-9; ☎ 91 429 92 16; Calle León 6; ⏱ 9am-9pm; per load €2; metro Antón Martín)

Medical Services

Anglo-American Medical Unit (Map pp904-5; ☎ 91 435 18 23; Calle Conde de Aranda 1; metro Retiro) For medical help in English.

Farmacia del Globo (Map pp908-9; ☎ 91 369 20 00; Plaza Antón Martín 46; metro Antón Martín) For help with minor medical problems, ask a pharmacist. This is one of several 24-hour pharmacies.

Money

Large banks such as Caja de Madrid usually have the best rates, but check commissions. Banks generally open from 8.30am to 2pm Monday to Friday and, during winter, to 1pm on Saturday. Using your ATM card will usually give you the same bank rates, no matter where or what time of day you use it.

If you're desperate, there are plenty of *bureaux de change* around Puerta del Sol and Plaza Mayor, which have the predictable rip-off rates but are often open until midnight.

Post

Post office (Map pp904-5; ☎ 91 396 24 43; Plaza Cibeles; ⏱ 8.30am-9.30pm Mon-Sat; metro Banco de España) In the gigantic Palacio de Comunicaciones.

Tourist Information

Municipal tourist office (Map pp908-9; ☎ 91 366 54 77; www.munimadrid.es; Plaza Mayor 3; ⏱ 10am-8pm Mon-Sat, 10am-3pm Sun; metro Sol)

Regional tourist office (Map pp908-9; ☎ 91 429 49 51 or 902 10 00 07; www.madrid.org; Calle Duque Medinaceli 2; ⏱ 9am-7pm Mon-Sat, 9am-3pm Sun; metro Sevilla)

DANGERS & ANNOYANCES

Madrid is not a dangerous city but you need to constantly be aware of pickpockets, especially in touristy areas like Plaza Mayor (where thieves are astonishingly brash), Huertas and Chueca.

Prostitution (and the slimy clients it attracts) along Calle Montera and in the Casa del Campo park means that you need to exercise extra caution in these areas. Females

walking alone should try not to linger here, even if you're just looking at a map, as it could give the wrong idea.

SIGHTS & ACTIVITIES

Madrid's big three (the outstanding Prado, Reina Sofía and Thyssen-Bornemisza museums) should be the first things on your to-do list. If you still have energy left after soaking up the majestic art on display here, the city's monasteries, palace and luscious gardens promise to keep you busy for days. For information about even more museums and sights, ask at the tourist office (p906).

Museo del Prado

The **Prado** (Map pp904-5; ☎ 91 330 28 00; http://museo prado.mcu.es; Paseo del Prado s/n; metro Banco de España; adult/child €3.01/1.50, free Sun; ⏱ 9am-7pm Tue-Sun) is not just the best-known museum in Madrid, it's one of the most elite art collections in the world. The main emphasis is on Spanish, Flemish and Italian art from the 15th to 19th centuries, with generous coverage of Spanish greats Goya, Velázquez and El Greco.

Velázquez's masterpiece *Las Meninas* is one of the museum's prized works. This painting depicts maids of honour attending the daughter of King Felipe IV, and Velázquez himself painting portraits of the queen and king (through whose eyes the scene is witnessed).

Virtually the whole southern wing of the 1st floor is given over to Goya. His portraits include the pair *Maja Desnuda* and *Maja Vestida*; legend has it that the woman depicted here is the Duchess of Alba, Spain's richest woman in Goya's time. Goya was commissioned to paint her portrait by her husband and ended up having an affair with her, so painted an extra portrait for himself. In room 39 are Goya's masterpieces depicting the horrors of the Spanish War of Independence (1808–14). There are more Goya works on the ground floor.

Other well-represented artists include El Greco, the Flemish masters Hieronymus Bosch and Pieter Paul Rubens, and the Italians Tintoretto, Titian and Raphael.

Guided visits are available; ask for details at the ticket booth.

Centro de Arte Reina Sofía

A fantastic collection of modern, predominantly Spanish art, the **Centro de Arte Reina**

Sofía (Map pp904–5; ☎ 91 467 50 62; http://museo reinasofia.mcu.es; Calle Santa Isabel 52; metro Atocha; admission €3.01, free Sat 2.30–9pm & Sun, ☼ 10am–9pm Mon-Sat, 10am–2.30pm Sun) showcases Spanish contemporary culture. The exhibition includes Picasso's famous *Guernica*, his protest at the German bombing of the Basque town of Guernica during the Spanish Civil War in 1937.

The museum also contains further works by Picasso, as well as works by surrealist Salvador Dalí and the remarkably simple paintings of Joan Miró.

Museo Thyssen-Bornemisza

Sitting just opposite the Prado, the **Thyssen-Bornemisza** (Map pp908–9; ☎ 91 369 01 51; Paseo del Prado 8; metro Banco de España; adult/child €4.80/3; ☼ 10am–7pm Tue-Sun) is a themeless collection of priceless works, offering one of the most comprehensive art-history lessons you'll ever have. Starting with medieval religious art, it moves on through Titian, El Greco and Rubens to Cézanne, Monet and Van Gogh, then from Miró, Picasso and Gris to Pollock, Dalí and Lichtenstein. Formerly the private collection of the German-Hungarian family of magnates, the Thyssen-Bornemiszas, the collection was purchased by Spain in 1993 for a mere US$300 million.

Palacio Real

Madrid's 18th-century **Palacio Real** (Map pp908–9; ☎ 91 542 00 59; Calle Bailén s/n; metro Ópera; adult/child €9/3.50; ☼ 9.30am–5pm Mon-Sat, 9am–2pm Sun Oct-Mar, 9am–6pm Mon-Sat, 9am–3pm Sun Apr-Sep) is a lesson in what can happen if you give your interior decorators a free hand. You'll see some of the most elaborately decorated walls and ceilings imaginable, including the sublime Throne Room (and other rooms of more dubious merit). This over-the-top palace hasn't been used as a royal residence for some time and today is used only for official receptions and, of course, tourism.

Shuffle through the official tour to see a good selection of Goyas, 215 absurdly ornate clocks from the Royal Clock Collection and five Stradivarius violins, still used for concerts and balls. Most of the tapestries in the palace were made in the Royal Tapestry Factory (10 minutes southeast of the Atocha train station), and all the chandeliers are original and absolutely unique.

Outside the main palace you can also see the **Farmacia Real** (Royal Pharmacy), with an unending array of medicine jars and stills for mixing royal concoctions, and the **Armería Real** (Royal Armoury), a shiny collection of mostly 16th- and 17th-century weapons and royal suits of armour.

Monasterio de las Descalzas Reales

This ornate **monastery** (Convent of the Barefoot Royals; Map pp908–9; ☎ 91 542 00 59; www.patrimonio nacional.es; Plaza de las Descalzas; metro Sol; adult/child €5/2.50; ☼ 10.30am–12.45pm & 4–5.45pm Tue-Thu & Sat, 10.30am–12.45pm Fri, 11am–1.45pm Sun) was founded in 1559 by Juana of Austria, daughter of Spain's King Carlos I, and became one of Spain's richest religious houses thanks to gifts from noblewomen. Much of the wealth came in the form of art; on the obligatory guided tour you'll be confronted by a number of tapestries based on works by Rubens and a wonderful painting entitled *The Voyage of the 11,000 Virgins*.

Panteón de Goya

Home to Goya's *panteón* (tomb), the **Ermita de San Antonio de la Florida** (☎ 91 542 07 22; Glorieta San Antonio de la Florida 5; metro Príncipe Pío; admission free; ☼ 10am–2pm & 4–8pm Tue-Fri, 10am–2pm Sat & Sun), 500m east of the Príncipe Pío metro, is one of the artist's greatest works. The entire ceiling and dome is beautifully painted with religious scenes. The images on the dome depict the miracle of St Anthony.

Parque del Buen Retiro

A Sunday stroll in **El Retiro** (Map pp904–5; metro Retiro; ☼ 7am–midnight summer, 7am–10pm winter) is as much a Madrid tradition as tapas and *terrazas* (terrace cafés). Time it right and you may even catch a puppet show during summer.

Walk along **Paseo de las Estatuas**, a path lined with statues originally from the Palacio Real. It ends at a lake (Estanque) overlooked by a **statue of Alfonso XII**. There are rowing boats for rent at the northern end. Also search out the **El Ángel Caído** (The Fallen Angel), the first ever statue dedicated to the devil, and gardens such as **La Rosaleda** (rose garden).

Campo del Moro

This stately **garden** is directly behind the Palacio Real, and the palace is visible through the trees from just about all points. A couple of fountains and statues, a thatch-roofed pagoda

CENTRAL MADRID

and a carriage museum provide artificial diversions, but nature is the real attraction.

TOURS

The tourist office (p906) organises English-language **walking tours** (☎ 902 221 622; adult/child €3/2.50) around the centre of Madrid. You can reserve tickets by telephone or simply show up at the main tourist office on Plaza Mayor 15 minutes before the tour begins. One of the most popular walks is 'Madrid of the Court', a tour of the old quarter starting 10am Saturday. Other tour times vary with the season, so check with the office before you make your plans.

FESTIVALS & EVENTS

Madrid takes its partying seriously, and festive events are generously sprinkled over the year's calendar. Look out for:

Día de los Reyes (Three Kings' Day, Jan 6) The three kings bring gifts to children and a mammoth parade takes over the city centre.

Fiesta de San Isidro (May 15) Madrid's patron saint is honoured with nonstop processions, parties and bullfights.

Fiesta de Otoño (mid-Oct through mid-Nov) Music, dance and theatre take over Madrid during the fantastically cultural weeks of the Autumn Festival.

SLEEPING

You're spoiled for choice in Madrid. The city is packed with hotels and *hostales* (cheap hotels) of all shapes and sizes, but booking ahead is always a good idea and may be necessary in summer or during holidays.

Budget accommodation (doubles €50 and under) includes informal youth hostels, cheap *pensiones* (guesthouses) and slightly more upscale *hostales*. Even in this category many places offer private bathrooms and TVs in the rooms. Mid-range (doubles €51 to €90) are more comfortable and usually offer a touch of charm. Top-end hotels (doubles from €91) include everything from business-style three-stars to rooms worthy of royalty.

Los Austrias & Centro
BUDGET

Los Amigos Backpackers' Hostel (Map pp908-9; ☎ 91 547 17 07; www.losamigoshostel.com; Calle Campo-manes 6, 4th fl; metro Oriente; dm with shared bathroom €15; 🖳) Clean, friendly and English-speaking, this is one of the city's best budget options. Cheerful, well-kept rooms have four to 10 bunk beds and free lockers.

Hostal Orly (Map pp908-9; ☎ 91 531 30 12; 7th fl; Calle Montera 47; metro Gran Vía; s/d/tr with shared

SPAIN

bathroom €29/39/51) In a grand 19th-century building, this quiet hostel is excellent value (especially room No 11). Rooms are cheerful, with tall ceilings and wooden floors.

Also recommended:

Hostal Triana (Map pp908-9; ☎ 91 532 68 12; www
.hostaltriana.com; 1st fl, Calle Salud 13; metro Gran Vía;
s/d €35/47; P) Tidy rooms with bathroom.

Hostal Cruz Sol (Map pp908-9; ☎ 91 532 71 97; www
.hostalcruzsol.com; 3rd fl, Plaza Santa Cruz 6; metro Sol;
s/d €38/48; ✖) Cheery. Great location.

MID-RANGE

Hotel Plaza Mayor (Map pp908-9; ☎ 91 360 06 06;
www.h-plazamayor.com; Calle Atocha 2; metro Sol or Tirso
de Molina; s/d €48/70) Original elements of this 150-year-old building have been left intact, while the décor itself is stylish. Great value.

Hostal La Macarena (Map pp908-9; ☎ 91 365 92 21;
macarena@silserranos.com; Cava San Miguel 8; metro Ópera;
s/d €57/70) Near Plaza Mayor, this charming *hostal* is one of the best in the barrio. Rooms are quiet and welcoming.

Hostal Madrid (Map pp908-9; ☎ 91 522 00 60; www
.hostal-madrid.info; 2nd fl, Calle Esparteros 6; metro Sol;
s €50-58, d/tr €70/88; ✖) Rooms here are simple, with rustic décor and fully equipped bathrooms. The owner also rents apartments.

TOP END

Hotel HH Campomanes (Map pp908-9; ☎ 91 548 85 48;
www.hhcampomanes.com; Calle Campomanes 4; metro Ori-
ente; s €77-99, d €87-111; ✖ ✖ 💻) The ultimate in minimalism, with black walls and red lighting in the lobby. Rooms are spacious, with high ceilings and simple furniture.

Hotel Intur Palacio San Martín (Map pp908-9;
☎ 91 701 50 00; www.intur.com; Plaza San Martín 5; metro
Callao; s €109-165, d €109-204; P ✖) Set on a picturesque plaza, in the former US embassy, this lovely hotel offers simple luxury.

Sol, Huertas & Atocha
BUDGET

Hostal Internacional La Posada de Huertas (Map
pp908-9; ☎ 91 429 35 26; www.posadadehuertas.com;
Calle Huertas 21; metro Antón Martín; dm with shared
bathroom from €16) This simple youth hostel offers dorm-style rooms with metal beds and lockers. Though the place is clean, with warm blankets and decent (if tiny) bathrooms, it rates a zero on the charm scale.

Hostal Aguilar (Map pp908-9; ☎ 91 429 59 26; www
.hostalaguilar.com; 2nd fl, Carrera San Jerónimo 32; metro
Sol; s/d/tr with shared bathroom €40/47/63; 💻) Tacky

décor but pluses include the double-glazed, noise-blocking windows and a computer offering Internet access for €3 per hour.

MID-RANGE

Hotel Mediodia (Map pp904-5; ☎ 91 527 30 60; fax 91
530 70 08; Plaza Emperador Carlos V 8; metro Atocha; s/d/tr
€54/64/82; ✖) Just across from Atocha station, this attractive hotel is perfect if you're arriving on a late train.

Hotel Mora (Map pp904-5; ☎ 91 420 15 69; Paseo del
Prado 32; metro Atocha; s/d €57/75; ✖) Near the main museums, this simple hotel offers great value. Rooms are a bit sparse but some overlook the Real Jardine Botanico (botanical gardens).

Hostal Martín (Map pp908-9; ☎ 91 429 95 79; www
.hostalmartin.com; Calle Atocha 43; metro Antón Martín; s €36-
58, d €45-70; ✖) This fine *hostal* is luminous and sparklingly clean, with a look you'd expect to see in a two- or three-star hotel.

TOP END

Hotel Miau (Map pp908-9; ☎ 91 369 71 20; www
.hotelmiau.com; Calle Príncipe 26; metro Sol or Antón Martín;
s/d incl breakfast €88/98; P ✖) A boutique hotel overlooking the Plaza Santa Ana. Rooms are airy but can be noisy.

Catalonia Moratín (Map pp908-9; ☎ 91 369 71 71;
www.hoteles-catalonia.es; Calle Atocha 23; metro Antón
Martín; s/d €136/177; ✖ 💻) In a carefully restored 18th-century palace, this is one of the most charming places to stay in Madrid. Rooms are rustic-chic, with pretty balconies.

Malasaña & Chueca

Hostal Don Juan (Map pp908-9; ☎ 91 522 77 46; 2nd
fl, Plaza Vazquez de Mella 1; metro Gran Vía; s/d €34/48)
This elegant *hostal* is filled with art (each room has original works) and antique furniture. Rooms are simple but luminous.

Hostal La Zona (Map pp908-9; ☎ 91 521 99 04; www
.hostallazona.com; 1st fl, Calle Valverde 7; metro Gran Vía;
d €45-65) Catering to gay clientele, rooms are simple but stylish and very well kept. Spacious room 203 is one of the best.

Hostal San Lorenzo (Map pp908-9; ☎ 91 521 30 57;
www.hostal-lorenzo.com; Calle Clavel 8; metro Gran Vía; s €45-
50, d €55-65, tr €75-90; ✖) The original stone walls of this 19th-century building have been left exposed, adding unique character. Renovated in 2003, rooms are small but modern.

Also recommended:

Hostal El Catalan (Map pp908-9; ☎ 91 532 30 17;
2nd fl, Calle Hortaleza 17; metro Gran Vía; s €27-30,
d/tr €42/54) Clean, quiet, good value.

Hostal Maria Cristina (Map pp908-9; ☎ 91 531 63 00; www.iespana.es/hostalmariacristina; Calle Fuencarral 20; metro Gran Vía; s/d/tr €32/44/62) Friendly with lots of light.

Beyond the Centre

Husa Chamartín (☎ 91 334 49 00; www.hotelchamartin .com; Calle Augustín de Foxá; metro Chamartín; s €60-111, d €60-130; ⌘ ☐) A great option if you're arriving late to the Chamartín train station; rooms have all the comforts.

High Tech Madrid Aeropuerto (☎ 91 564 59 06; www.hthoteles.com; Calle Galeón 25; metro Aeropuerto; s €100-135, d €120-150; ☐ ⌘ ☐ ⌘) Within shouting distance of the airport (it provides free airport transport), the High Tech has stylish rooms, free Internet access and an outdoor pool.

La Residencia del Viso (☎ 91 564 03 70; www.resi denciadelviso.com; Calle Nervión 8; metro Republica Argentina; s €77-103, d €129; ⌘) Northeast of the centre, this quiet little city oasis has rooms that look rather like a favourite aunt's guest quarters.

EATING

Madrid's specialities include *cochinillo asad* (roast suckling pig) and *cocido madrileño*, a hearty stew made of beans and various animals' innards (it's tasty, honest). Snacky tapas range from olives and potato chips to sausages, tortillas and grilled meat on a stick. At this point, vegetarians may be questioning what local cuisine has to offer them: little, it's true. Look out for pastas, salads and *bocadillos vegetales* (vegetable sandwiches), which usually have cheese.

Lunch hour runs from about 1.30pm to 3.30pm, and dinner starts at 9pm and lasts until late – any variance in these general opening hours will be stated in reviews. Before meal times, many Madrileños head out for a *caña* and a tapas or two.

Tapas

Before lunch, before dinner, before the club, after the club…anytime is a good time for tapas! Heading into La Latina, you'll find oodles of tapas bars.

La Casa del Abuelo (Map pp908-9; ☎ 91 521 23 19; Calle Victoria 12; metro Sol) Taste the garlicky prawns (€4.35) at this famous bar in the centre of town.

Las Bravas (Map pp908-9; ☎ 91 532 26 20; Calle Espoz y Mina 13; metro Sol) Head to this caféteria-style joint known for its patented version of the classic Spanish *salsa brava*, a spicy

sauce slathered over fried potatoes, tortillas and even seafood.

La Chata (Map pp908-9; ☎ 91 366 14 58; Calle Cava Baja 24; metro La Latina) Enjoy the great cheese plate (€11) and bullfighter-themed décor.

Angel Sierra (Map pp908-9; ☎ 91 531 01 26; Calle Gravina 11; metro Chueca) Munchers at this Chueca classic spill onto the Plaza de Chueca with their tapas and drinks.

Stop Madrid (Map pp908-9; ☎ 91 521 88 87; Calle Hortaleza 11; metro Gran Vía) Known for its *jamón serrano*.

Restaurants

LOS AUSTRIAS & CENTRO

La Mallorquina (Map pp908-9; ☎ 91 521 12 01; Puerta del Sol 8; metro Sol; pastries around €1.50) Start the day sweet here, where a throng of white-jacketed waiters serve up pastries, truffles and candies.

La Gloria de Montera (Map pp908-9; ☎ 91 523 44 07; Calle Caballero de Gracia 10; metro Gran Vía; menú €6.60) For sit-down fare, there's no beating this place. It's oh-so-stylish, oh-so-cheap and oh-so-popular.

Sobrino de Botín (Map pp908-9; ☎ 91 366 42 17; Calle Cuchilleros 17; metro La Latina; mains €11-18) The oldest restaurant in Madrid couldn't be more atmospheric. The delicious speciality is roast suckling pig.

SOL, HUERTAS & ATOCHA

Cuevas El Secreto (Map pp908-9; ☎ 91 531 82 91; Calle Barcelona 2; metro Sol; mains €4-8; ⏲ 6.30pm-2am; ⏲ 6.30pm-2am;) A tavern serving tasty grilled meat and a few basic tapas. Everything is fresh and served with style, but it's refreshingly cheap.

La Finca de Susana (Map pp908-9; ☎ 91 369 35 57; Calle Arlaban 4; metro Sevilla; menú €7) This well-known place is priced right, serving a mix of Spanish and international fare to a professional crowd.

La Trucha (Map pp908-9; ☎ 91 532 0890; Calle Núñez de Arce 6) For fish, traditional dishes and tasty tapas, head to this classic.

Lhardy (Map pp908-9; ☎ 91 522 22 07; Carrera San Jerónimo 8; metro Sevilla; mains €12-20) Just as emblematic as La Trucha but with a more elegant touch, Lhardy has been in business since 1839.

LA LATINA & LAVAPIÉS

Casa Lucio (Map pp904-5; ☎ 91 365 32 52; Calle Cava Baja 35; metro La Latina; mains €9-18) Popular with

SPAIN

politicians, the traditional Casa Lucio is famous for its *huevos rotos,* fried eggs served runny over potatoes.

MALASAÑA & CHUECA

Patatus (Map pp904–5; ☎ 91 532 6129; Calle Fuencarral 98; metro Bilbao; for 2 people €9–16) Open late and where you go after hours for cheap, filling fare.

Bazaar (Map pp908–9; ☎ 91 523 39 05; Calle Libertad 21; metro Chueca; menú €7) For more formal meals, this funky fusion is a great bet for Mediterranean-style dishes with an international flair.

Omertà (Map pp908–9; ☎ 91 701 02 42; Calle Gravina 17; metro Chueca; menú €7.50) Bare brick walls and a tall ceiling give Omertà the feel of an old warehouse, though the friendly service and piping-hot square pizzas prove its worth as a pizzeria.

Wokcafé (Map pp908–9; ☎ 91 422 90 69; Calle Infantas 44; metro Sevilla; ☺ closed Sun) This chic Chinese-fusion restaurant lives by the motto *sexy y sano* (sexy and healthy). The romantic atmosphere and light dishes live up to the claim.

SALAMANCA & VENTAS

Estay (Map pp904–5; ☎ 91 578 04 70; Calle Hermosilla 46; metro Velázquez; tapas €2–5; ☺ 9–1am) 'Fine dining in miniature' is the claim to fame here. In food terms that means tiny tapas-like dishes of yummy things such as foie gras with raspberry sauce, and zucchini stuffed with shrimp.

El Pescador (Map pp904–5; ☎ 91 402 12 90; Calle José Ortega y Gasset 75; metro Núñez de Balboa; mains €10–18) High-end but worth a splurge, this is one of the city's best spots for seafood.

DRINKING

Bars are something Madrid has plenty of, and finding your favourite shouldn't take long. For traditional style, wander the streets of Huertas. For gay-friendly locales, Chueca is the place. Malasaña caters to a grungy, funky crowd, while La Latina has friendly, no-frills bars that guarantee atmosphere every night of the week. In summer, head to the outdoor cafés in the city's plazas.

Although many bars are open all day, functioning alternately as breakfast cafés, luncheon spots and bars, the night-time crowd starts showing up by 8pm for pre-dinner drinks. The mood really gets rolling around

midnight, and the bars all close by about 3am on weekends, or 2am on weekdays.

Bars

LOS AUSTRIAS, CENTRO & LA LATINA

Café del Nuncio (Map pp904–5; ☎ 91 366 09 06; Calle Segovia 9; metro La Latina) Straggling down a stairway passage to Calle Segovia, Nuncio has several cosy levels inside and an outdoor *terraza.*

Chocolatería San Ginés (Map pp908–9; ☎ 91 365 65 46; Pasadizo San Ginés 5; metro Sol or Ópera) You've got to end the night at this mythic bar at least once – it's famous for its freshly fried *churros* and syrupy hot chocolate.

El Viajero (Map pp904–5; ☎ 91 366 90 64; Plaza Cebada 11; metro La Latina) If you wander down and around the Calle Cava Baja there are myriad options such as this one, where you can get an informal dinner downstairs (tapas €3.50 to €8) or head to the bar upstairs, which has a fantastic rooftop terrace.

SOL, HUERTAS & ATOCHA

Casa Alberto (Map pp908–9; ☎ 91 429 93 56; www .casaalberto.es; Calle Huertas 18; metro Antón Martín) Since 1827 Madrileños have been getting their vermouth from the lovely Casa Alberto. Stop by on Sunday for a traditional pre-lunch apéritif.

Cervecería Alemana (Map pp908–9; ☎ 91 429 70 33; Plaza Santa Ana 6; metro Antón Martín or Sol; ☺ closed Aug) Another classic, this place is renowned for its cold, frothy beers and delicious tapas. It was one of Hemingway's haunts, and the wood-lined bar seemingly hasn't changed since his day.

Los Gabrieles (Map pp908–9; ☎ 91 429 62 61; Calle Echegaray 17; metro Sevilla) For a bit of Andalucían flavour, try this tile-covered bar, where you can catch midweek flamenco shows.

Matador (Map pp908–9; ☎ 91 531 89 81; Calle Cruz 39; metro Sol) A smoky, dark bar, this is the spot for soulful flamenco music and a totally unpretentious crowd.

Viva Madrid (Map pp908–9; ☎ 91 429 36 40; www .barvivamadrid.com; Calle Manuel Fernandez y González 7; metro Sol) Tapas and beer are the staples at this colourful landmark. The beautifully tiled bar is sure to earn oohs and ahs.

MALASAÑA & CHUECA

One of the liveliest nightlife areas of Madrid, gay-friendly Chueca and let-it-all-hang-loose Malasaña are packed with bars.

Areia (Map pp904-5; ☎ 91 310 03 07; www.areia chillout.com; Calle Hortaleza 92; metro Chueca) There's no better place to chill out than at this restaurant-cum-bar, where an Arabian vibe dominates the décor and chill-out music drifts up to the rafters.

Café Pepe Botella (Map pp904-5; ☎ 91 522 43 09; Calle San Andrés 12; metro Bilbao or Tribunal) This funky bar has cosy velvet benches and marble-topped tables that give it a quirky charm.

Museo Chicote (Map pp908-9; ☎ 91 532 67 37; Gran Vía 12; metro Gran Vía) A city classic popular with socialites and film stars, the Museo Chicote has a lounge atmosphere late at night and a stream of famous faces all day.

Finnegan's (Map pp908-9; ☎ 91 310 05 21; Plaza Salesas 9; metro Chueca; ☺ 1pm-2am) The friendliest pub in town, this Irish haven is full of regulars who'll make you feel at home.

Cafés

Salon del Prado (Map pp908-9; ☎ 91 429 33 61; Calle Prado 4; metro Antón Martín) Curl up with a tea and a book at the elegant Prado, just off Plaza de Santa Ana.

Café Comercial (Map pp904-5; ☎ 91 521 65 55; Glorieta de Bilbao 7; metro Bilbao) You can get a mean coffee and plenty of ambience here.

Café de Ruiz (Map pp904-5; ☎ 91 446 12 32; Calle Ruiz 11; metro Bilbao) The cosy Ruiz looks like it was lifted out of a 1930s movie, with marble tables, velvet-covered seats and a welcoming attitude.

Mamá Inés (Map pp908-9; ☎ 91 523 23 33; www .mamaines.com; Calle Hortaleza 22; metro Chueca) In Chueca, this romantic place is popular with gay men. By day, get yummy pastries and all the gossip on where that night's hot spot will be.

ENTERTAINMENT

The entertainment bible is the *Guía del Ocio*, a weekly magazine sold at newsstands for €1. Highlights are given in English at the back. The best gay guide is *Shanguide*, which you can pick up free in bars around town.

Cinemas

Several movie theatres are huddled around Gran Vía and Calle Princesa. For a selection of original-version flicks in this area, head to **Princesa** (Map pp904-5; ☎ 91 541 41 00; Calle Princesa 3; metro Plaza España) or **Alphaville** (Map pp904-5; ☎ 91 559 38 36; Calle Martín de los Heros 14; metro Plaza de España).

The National Film Library offers fantastic classic and vanguard films at **Cine Doré** (Map pp904-5; ☎ 91 549 00 11; Calle Santa Isabel 3; metro Antón Martín).

Gay & Lesbian Venues

Chueca is Madrid's lively, gay-friendly neighbourhood, and you'll find gay and lesbian bars and clubs on nearly every street. Some of the bigger-name gay dance clubs are along Gran Vía.

Ohm (Map pp908-9; ☎ 91 541 35 00; Plaza Callao 4; metro Callao) A weekend party hosted by Sala Bash, Ohm is a hit on the gay and straight scenes.

Cool (Map pp908-9; ☎ 91 542 34 39; Calle Isabel la Católica 6; metro Santo Domingo) One of Madrid's swankier clubs, Cool guarantees a sexy night for a well-heeled crowd.

Café Acuarela (Map pp908-9; ☎ 91 522 21 43; Calle Gravina 10; metro Chueca) For something low-key, head to this quiet bar.

Live Music
FLAMENCO

Madrid is a good place to see professional interpretations of this Andalucían art. Most shows are set up like a dinner theatre and are squarely aimed at tourists, but the quality is generally top-notch.

Casa Patas (Map pp908-9; ☎ 91 369 04 96; www .casapatas.com; Calle Cañizares 10; metro Antón Martín; admission about €30; ☺ noon-5pm & 8pm-3am, shows 10.30pm Mon-Thu, 9pm & midnight Fri & Sat) One of the best *tablaos* in the city, this is a great place to see passionate dancing and get in a good dinner too.

Las Tablas (Map pp908-9; ☎ 91 542 05 20; Plaza España 9; metro España; admission €12-15; ☺ from 7pm, show 10.30pm) Less established (but far cheaper) than other *tablaos*, this intimate spot is nevertheless a great place to see a variety of flamenco styles.

JAZZ

Café Central (Map pp908-9; ☎ 91 369 41 43; www .cafécentralmadrid.com; Plaza del Angel 10; metro Antón Martín; admission €10-12; ☺ 1.30pm-2.30am Sun-Thu, to 3.30am Fri & Sat, shows nightly at 10pm) This Art Deco bar is worth a visit on its own, but the live shows, which range from classic jazz to Latin, fusion or tango-style jazz, are what has made it one of the most popular bars in the city.

Populart (Map pp908-9; ☎ 91 429 84 07; www .populart.es; Calle Huertas 22; metro Antón Martín or Sol;

SPAIN

admission free; ☺ 6pm-2.30am Mon-Thu, to 3.30am Fri & Sat, shows nightly at 11pm) Get here early if you want a seat because this smoky, atmospheric jazz bar is always packed with fans yearning for some soothing live jazz.

Calle 54 (☎ 91 561 28 32; Paseo de la Habana 3; metro Nuevos Ministerios) Just north of the centre, this has got to be the best Latin jazz in Madrid, an ultra-cool club and restaurant started by film maker Fernando Trueba.

ROCK

Sala Caracol (Map pp904-5; ☎ 91 527 35 94; Calle Bernardino Obregón 18; metro Embajadores) A temple to variety, this club hosts a different style every night of the week.

Galileo Galilei (☎ 91 534 75 57; Calle Galileo 100; metro Islas Filipinas) This city classic, just north of Argüelles, has been known to stage everything from comedy acts to magic shows, though its strength is up-and-coming bands.

La Riviera (Map pp904-5; ☎ 91 365 24 15; Paseo Bajo de la Virgen del Puerto; metro Puerta del Ángel) A club and concert venue all in one, La Riviera has a pretty Art Deco interior and open-air concerts in summer.

Clubs & Discos

There's no barrio in Madrid without a decent club or disco, but the most popular dance spots are along and around Gran Vía. For intimate dancing, head to Chueca or Malasaña, especially the Calle Palma, which is lined with quirky clubs.

Club prices vary wildly, but most charge between €8 and €12, though you can get discounts for arriving early or if you're a girl (sorry guys). Keep your eyes open for discount tickets given out in bars or on the street. Most places, dancing starts at around 1am and lasts until daybreak. Come Thursday through Saturday for the best atmosphere.

El Sol (Map pp908-9; ☎ 91 532 64 90; Calle Jardines 3; metro Gran Vía) For guaranteed great dancing on weekends, check out this popular club near Gran Via.

Palacio Gaviria (Map pp908-9; ☎ 91 526 60 69; Calle Arenal 9; metro Sol) This palace-turned-club is atmospheric but pricier than most. Thursday is international student night.

Teatro Joy Eslava (Map pp908-9; ☎ 91 366 37 33; www.joy-eslava.com; Calle Arenal 11; metro Sol or Ópera) An old theatre that's gotten a new lease on life as one of Madrid's more popular clubs, this is a great place to meet people.

El Son (Map pp908-9; ☎ 91 532 32 83; Calle Victoria 6; metro Sol). Here you'll find the best Latino grooves. There are live shows Monday through Thursday.

Kapital (Map pp904-5; ☎ 91 420 29 06; Calle Atocha 125; metro Atocha) If you can't make up your mind about dance styles, this seven-storey mega disco is the place for you. Every floor offers a different mood.

Sport
FOOTBALL

Madrid's three major football clubs and accompanying delirious fans are a guarantee that football fever runs high in the city. The mythic Real Madrid plays at the **Santiago Bernabéu Stadium** (Map pp904-5; ☎ 91 398 43 00; www.realmadrid.com; metro Santiago Bernabéu; ☺ 10.30am-6.30pm except day after game), and the also-celebrated Atlético de Madrid plays at the **Vicente Calderón Stadium** (Map pp904-5; ☎ 91 366 47 07; www.at-madrid.com; Calle Virgen del Puerto; metro Pirámides). Though it's no match for these first-division teams, the Rayo Vallecano also plays in the city.

Get tickets (€10 and up) from box offices or through agents such as **Localidades Galicia** (Map pp908-9; ☎ 91 531 27 32 or 629 21 82 91; Plaza Carmen 1; metro Sol; ☺ 9.30am-1pm & 4.30-7pm Tue-Sat).

BULLFIGHTING

Some of Spain's top *matadores* (bullfighters) swing their capes in **Plaza de Toros de Las Ventas** (Map pp904-5; ☎ 91 356 22 00; www.las-ventas.com; Calle Alcalá 237; metro Ventas), the largest ring in the bullfighting world. You can see them every Sunday afternoon from mid-May through October, when fights are held in the plaza.

Get tickets (from €3.60 in the sun, from €6.60 in the shade) at the plaza box office or at official ticket agents along the Calle Victoria.

Theatre & Opera

Madrid has a lively cultural scene, with concerts and shows going on throughout the city.

Teatro Albéniz (Map pp908-9; ☎ 91 531 83 11; Calle Paz 11; metro Sol) Staging both commercial and vanguard drama, this is just one of Madrid's quality theatres. For more listings, check out the *Guía del Ocio* or local newspapers.

Teatro Real (Map pp908-9; ☎ 91 516 06 06; www.teatro-real.com; Plaza Oriente; metro Ópera) This is Madrid's opulent opera house, and the city's grandest stage. Here you can see opera, dance or theatre, depending on the offerings.

Teatro de la Zarzuela (Map pp908-9; ☎ 91 524 54 00; Calle Jovellanos 4; metro Banco de España) Come here for *zarzuela*, a very Spanish mixture of dance, music and theatre.

SHOPPING

For artisan goods and typically Spanish items, explore the maze of streets in Huertas and Los Austrias. Alternative, offbeat fashion is found in Chueca; this lively barrio is also a magnet for shoe shops – there are a dozen of them along and around Calle Augusto Figueroa. Roam Calle Fuencarral and Calle Hortaleza for funky clothing stores.

The glitziest shopping district is Salamanca, where all the designer labels show off for drooling window shoppers. This is also the district to find top art, antique and furniture galleries.

José Ramírez (Map pp908-9; ☎ 91 531 42 29; Calle Paz 8) Find handmade guitars at this family-run shop. There's a small museum of old guitars in the back.

Justo Algaba (Map pp908-9; ☎ 91 523 35 95; Calle Paz 4) The place to buy authentic bullfighters' suits; everything from capes to those sexy pink tights.

Gil (Map pp908-9; ☎ 91 521 25 49; Carrera San Jerónimo 2) Spanish shawls and veils are the speciality at this historic shop.

Divina Providencia (Map pp908-9; ☎ 91 522 02 65; Calle Fuencarral 45) At Divina you'll find fun clothes for women, with lots of retro and Asian styles.

Mercado de Fuencarral (Map pp908-9; ☎ 91 521 41 52; Calle Fuencarral 45) Clubbers should head to this small mall, where at least half the clothes on sale have silver studs or leather accents.

Loewe (Map pp904-5; ☎ 91 426 35 88; Calle Serrano 34) One of Spain's classiest fashion labels, Loewe is the place for leather handbags and accessories.

Amaya Arzuaga (Map pp904-5; ☎ 91 426 28 15; Calle Lagasca 50) Also top end but rather less austere, this shop has sexy, bold options for women.

El Rastro (Map pp904-5; metro La Latina; ⏰ 8am-3pm Sun) The city's main market, El Rastro is a throbbing mass of vendors, browsers, buyers and pickpockets. The madness begins at the Plaza Cascorro and worms its way downhill along the Calle Ribera Curtidores and the streets branching off it.

El Corte Ingles (Map pp908-9; ☎ 91 418 88 00) Spain's enormous department store has branches all over the city and sells everything from food and furniture to clothes, appliances and toiletries. It's truly one-stop shopping.

GETTING THERE & AWAY
Air

Madrid's international **Barajas Airport** (☎ 902 35 35 70), 16km northeast of the city, is a busy place, with flights coming in from all over Europe and beyond.

Most national flights are run by **Iberia** (☎ 902 40 05 00; www.iberia.com; Calle Velázquez 130); find the best deals on its website.

Bus

Though there are several bus stations dotted around the city, most out-of-town buses use the **Estación Sur** (☎ 91 468 42 00; Calle Méndez Álvaro; metro Méndez Álvaro). The largest bus company here is **Alsa** (☎ 902 42 22 42; www.alsa.es), north of the city.

Car & Motorcycle

If you arrive by car, be prepared to face gridlocked traffic. The city is surrounded by three ring roads, the M-30, M-40 and brand-new M-50 (still not 100% completed). You'll likely be herded onto one of these, which in turn give access to the city centre.

Car rental companies abound in Madrid; most have offices both at the airport and in town. See p997 for more information.

Train

Renfe (☎ 902 24 02 02; www.renfe.es) trains connect Madrid to just about every other point in Spain. There are two main rail stations: Atocha, south of the centre; and Chamartín, to the north. Both *cercanías* (regional trains) and long-distance trains pass through these stations. For ticket information, visit the Renfe offices inside the stations.

GETTING AROUND
To/From the Airport

The metro (line 8) zips you into the city from the airport's terminal two. The 12-minute trip to the Nuevos Ministerios station costs €1.15; from there, you can easily connect to all other stations.

There's also an airport bus service that makes a run to the Plaza de Colón every

10 minutes. The trip takes 30 minutes and costs €2.50.

A taxi ride to the centre should cost about €20 and the trip takes around 20 minutes.

Car & Motorcycle

Public transport in Madrid is excellent, so having a car or motorcycle is not usually necessary. If you do have a car, be prepared to face plenty of traffic and high parking prices. Public parking is available in the city centre; a big white 'P' on a blue sign denotes a car park.

Driving around the Plaza Mayor and the centre is especially challenging, as several roads dive underground and following them can be tricky.

Public Transport

Madrid's extensive **metro** (www.metromadrid.es) can get you to just about any corner of the city. It's quick, clean, relatively safe and runs from 6am until 2am.

The bus system is also good, but working out the maze of bus lines can be a challenge. Contact **EMT** (☎ 914 06 88 10; www.emtmadrid.es) for more information.

Taxi

Madrid's taxis are inexpensive by European standards. They're handy late at night, although in peak hours it's quicker to walk or get the metro. Flag fall is €1.55, after which you are charged by time, so avoid rush hour.

AROUND MADRID

The Comunidad de Madrid, the province surrounding the capital, is home to some of Spain's finest royal palaces and gardens, all of which make easy day trips from the capital.

San Lorenzo de El Escorial

Home to the majestic monastery-and-palace complex of **San Lorenzo de El Escorial** (☎ 918 90 59 02; www.patrimonionacional.es; admission €6; ⏱ 10am-6pm Apr-Sep, 10am-5pm Oct-Mar, closed Mon), this one-time royal getaway is now a prim little town overflowing with cutesy shops, restaurants and hotels (many of them closed in the low season).

El Escorial was built by Felipe II to commemorate his victory over the French in the battle of St Quentin (1557) and as a mausoleum for his father Carlos I, the first of

Spain's Habsburg monarchs. It's a quintessential monument of Spain's golden age.

Find more information at the **tourist office** (☎ 918 90 53 13; Calle Grimalidi 2; ⏱ 10am-6pm Mon-Thu, 10am-7pm Fri-Sun).

The **Hotel Parrilla Príncipe** (☎ 918 90 16 11; www .inicia.es/de/parrillaprincipe; Calle Floridablanca 6; s €42-44, d €53-59) has bare but clean rooms, some with views of the monastery. The **restaurant** (meals around €30) here – an unpretentious place with great grilled meats – is one of the best in town.

Herranz (☎ 918 96 90 28) has buses to El Escorial (€2.85, one hour, every 15 minutes, every hour weekends) from the bus depot outside Moncloa metro station, platform three. A few dozen of Renfe's C8 *cercanías* trains make the one-hour trip (€2.10) daily from Madrid to El Escorial.

Valle de los Caídos

Just 9km north of El Escorial is the **Valle de los Caídos** (☎ 918 90 13 98; Carretera 600; admission €5; ⏱ 10am-6pm Apr-Oct, 10am-5pm Nov-Mar), the ostentatious memorial that dictator Francisco Franco built to honour those who died in Spain's civil war. Franco himself is buried in the bunker-like basilica here, a cold church that's been built right into the mountainside. Above, an enormous granite cross marks the sight. You can take a **funicular** (one way €2.50; ⏱ 11am-5.30pm Apr-Oct, 11am-4.30pm Nov-Mar) to the base of the cross for fabulous views.

CASTILLA Y LEÓN

The huge region of Castilla y León is splashed across the Spanish heartland. This is the fabled Spain of castles, knights and strong stone bridges, a hilly landscape that's home to some of the country's most historic towns and prettiest architecture.

ÁVILA

Its old town huddled behind pristine medieval walls, Ávila is a remarkable, romantic city perfect for simply strolling and soaking up history. The city is most proud of its claim as the birthplace of Santa Teresa, a mystical writer and reformer of the Carmelite order.

Information

Cybernet (☎ 92 035 23 52; Ave de Madrid 25; per hr €2.50; ⏱ 11.30am-2.30pm & 4.30pm-1am)

Post office (☎ 92 031 35 06; Plaza de la Catedral 2; ⊗ 8.30am-8.30pm Mon-Fri, 9.30am-2pm Sat)

Tourist office (☎ 92 021 13 87; www.avilaturismo.com; Plaza de la Catedral 4; ⊗ 9am-2pm & 5-8pm 15 Sep-Jun, 9am-8pm Sun-Thu, 9am-9pm Fri & Sat Jul-Sep 14) In summer, there are also information kiosks set up at the Renfe train station and just outside the Puerta de San Vincente.

Sights

A walk along the top of Ávila's splendid 12th-century **walls** (murallas; ☎ 92 021 13 87; admission €3.50; ⊗ 11am-5.15pm winter, 10am-7.15pm summer) should be at the top of your list of things to do. More than 1km of wall-top is open to the public, though it's divided into two sections broken up by the cathedral. Made of 2500 turrets and 88 towers, Ávila's walls are some of the best-preserved in Spain.

Embedded into the eastern city walls, the **cathedral** (☎ 92 021 16 41; Plaza de la Catedral; admission €3; ⊗ 10am-5pm Mon-Fri, noon-5pm Sat & Sun Nov-Mar, until 7pm Mar-Oct) is the first Gothic church in Spain. It boasts rich walnut choir stalls and a long, narrow central nave that makes the soaring ceilings seem all the more majestic.

Even more beloved by locals than the cathedral is the **Convento de Santa Teresa** (☎ 92 021 10 30; Plaza de la Santa; Museum admission €2; ⊗ museum 10am-2pm & 4-7pm, relic room 9.30am-1.30pm & 3.30-7pm, church 8.30am-1.30pm & 3.30-8.30pm), built in 1636 at the birthplace of 16th-century mystic and ascetic, St Teresa. It has a simple interior and a gold-smothered chapel that sits atop Teresa's former bedroom; more interesting are the relics (including a piece of the saint's ring finger) and the small museum about her life.

Sleeping

Pensión Continental (☎ 92 021 15 02; Plaza de la Catedral 6; s €15, d €26-33, tr €39) Modest but offering unbeatable vistas of the cathedral and charming (if aged) décor. Shared bathrooms.

Hospedería La Sinagoga (☎ 92 035 23 21; www .lasinagoga.com; Calle Reyes Católicos 22; s €48-54, d €66-75; 🕸) More stylish and housed in a 15th-century synagogue.

Hostería de Bracamonte (☎ 92 025 12 80; Calle Bracamonte 6; s €36, d €50-73) Offers great value and old-world charm at every turn. Rooms boast shiny hardwood floors and antique furniture. The restaurant (above) is top too.

Eating

El Fogón de Santa Teresa (☎ 92 021 10 23; Plaza de la Catedral 9; mains €6-15, menú €14) Inside the Palacio Valderrabanos Hotel, with local dishes at reasonable prices and cushy seats perfect for a relaxing meal.

Hostería de Bracamonte (☎ 92 025 12 80; Calle Bracamonte 6; mains €8-18; ⊗ closed Tue) This is one of Ávila's most atmospheric spots for a meal. Old tapestries and photos fill the walls, setting the tone for the traditional Castilian food to come.

Mesón del Rastro (☎ 92 021 12 18; Plaza del Rastro 4; mains €7-14, menú €14) The spot for simple, tasty home-style cooking. You'll find plenty of local specialities and for noncarnivores there are tortillas and a few veggie dishes.

Entertainment

There are several good nightlife options just outside the Puerta del Peso de la Harina, along Calle San Segundo; try the **Bodeguito de San Segundo** (☎ 92 021 42 47; Calle San Segundo 19; ⊗ 11am-1am) for a great selection of Spanish wines and tapas.

Getting There & Away

Renfe trains come and go from Madrid (€5.60 to €7.15, up to two hours, at least 24 daily), León (€15.75 to €23.50, about three hours, seven daily) and other cities.

At least four buses connect Madrid's Estación Sur and Ávila (€6.26, 1½ hours) daily. Contact the **bus station** (☎ 92 025 05; Ave de Madrid 2) for more information.

Ávila is an hour's drive from Madrid, off the N-110 highway.

SALAMANCA

A university town through-and-through, fun, fairy-tale Salamanca is a historic city that's still very much in swing. Sitting on the Tormes River, the old city is a showcase of Spanish building styles, with some of the country's best examples of plateresque, Churrigueresque and Spanish Gothic architecture.

Salamanca's destiny was changed forever in 1218, when King Alfonso XI founded what was to become Spain's greatest university. Illustrious scholars passed through, giving the city a rich cultural life. Though today the university isn't considered one of Spain's most elite, it still draws scholars from throughout Spain and beyond.

Information

Come On (☎ 92 321 56 25; Calle de Palominos 21; Internet per hr €1.50; ⊗ 10am-midnight)

SPAIN

FIND THE FROG

The university's façade is an ornate mass of sculptures and carvings, and hidden amongst this 16th-century plateresque creation is a tiny stone frog. Legend says that those who find the frog will have good luck in studies, life and love. A hint: it's sitting on a skull on the pillar that runs up the right-hand side of the façade.

Cyberplace (☎ 92 326 42 81; Plaza Mayor 10; Internet per hr €1.20; ⏱ 10.30am-2pm)
Municipal tourist office (☎ 92 321 83 42; www .aytosalamanca.es; Plaza Mayor 32; ⏱ 9am-2pm & 4-6.30pm Mon-Fri, 9am-6.30pm Sat, 9am-2pm Sun)
Regional tourist office (Casa de las Conchas; ☎ 92 326 85 71; www.turismocastillayleon.com; Rúa Mayor; ⏱ 9am-2pm & 5-8pm daily Sep-Jun, 9am-8pm Sun-Thu, 9am-9pm Fri & Sat Jul & Aug)

Sights & Activities

The spirit of Salamanca isn't found inside museums or churches, it's out in the streets and plazas, where students from all over the globe walk busily and café tables spill onto the footpaths.

Start with a stroll in the harmonious **Plaza Mayor**, designed in 1755 by José Churriguera, founder of the architectural style that carries his name. From here, head up the busy Rúa Mayor to marvel at the **Casa de las Conchas** (House of Shells), a city symbol since it was built in the 15th century and now home to a tourist office and the library.

The **University** (☎ 92 329 44 00; Calle Libreros; adult/child €4/2; ⏱ 9.30am-1.30pm & 4-7pm Mon-Fri, 9.30am-1.30pm & 4-6.30pm Sat, 10am-1pm Sun), with its ubiquitous presence, is worth a visit. You can peek in the old classrooms (complete with torturous-looking original wooden benches), chapel, library and small museum.

Curiously, Salamanca is home to two cathedrals; the new, larger cathedral was built beside the old Romanesque one instead of on top of it, as was the norm. The **Catedral Nueva** (New Cathedral; ☎ 92 321 74 76; Plaza Anaya; ⏱ 9am-1pm & 4-6pm Oct-Mar, 9am-2pm & 4-8pm Apr-Sep), completed in 1733, is a Gothic masterpiece that took 220 years to build. From inside, you can head to the **Catedral Vieja** (Old Cathedral; adult/child €3/2.25; ⏱ 10am-12.30pm & 4-5.30pm Oct-Mar, 10am-1.30pm & 4-7.30pm Apr-Sep), a 12th-century temple with

a stunning altar and several noteworthy chapels.

Tours

Tourist offices (Casa de las Conchas; ☎ 92 326 85 71; Rúa Mayor) The tourist offices often organise guided tours (€6 and up) of the city. Times vary so ask for details.
Tren Turística (☎ 64 962 57 03; Plaza Anaya; adult/child €3/1.50; ⏱ 10am-2pm & 4-8pm, departures every 30min) Hop aboard this tourist train for an overview of the city's major sights.

Sleeping

Pensión Feli (☎ 92 321 60 10; Calle Libreros 58; per person with shared bathroom €12) One of the best-value places in town, with cheerful rooms (some with balconies), although the cramped shared baths are 1960s relics.

Hostal Catedral (☎ 92 321 14 27; fax 92 327 06 14; Rúa Mayor 46; s/d €30/45) We can't gush enough over this *hostal*. Its immaculate and quiet rooms have sparkling bathrooms and some have cathedral views.

Hostal Plaza Mayor (☎ 92 321 75 48; Plaza Corrillo 20; s/d/tr €36/60/90) More upscale, the classy Plaza Mayor offers 19 elegant rooms with all the extras. Marbled bathroom, hardwood floors and antique-style furniture show impeccable taste.

There are several good budget *hostales* on Calle Meléndez, in the centre.

Eating

Café El Ave (☎ 92 326 45 11; Calle Libreros 24; menú €9.90; ⏱ noon-midnight) This bright café is good for a quick lunch or afternoon coffee. The lunch *menú* offers plenty of variety and by night there's a wide range of speciality coffees.

El Patio Chico (☎ 92 326 51 03; Calle Meléndez 13; mains €5.90-11; ⏱ 1-4pm & 8pm-midnight) Good for rustic charm and offering everything such as international standards, such as T-bone steaks, to decidedly local dishes such as 'stewed tongue'.

Also recommended:
El Bardo (☎ 92 325 92 65; Ave Portugal 88; mains €8.40-13; ⏱ 1-4pm & 9-11.30pm) Castilian food, rustic air.
El Pecado (☎ 92 326 65 58; Plaza Poeta Iglesias 12; mains €14-21; ⏱ 1.30-3pm & 9-11pm) Upscale and ultra-stylish.

Entertainment

Salamanca's student population ensures that there's always something going on after classes. Wander around the university and

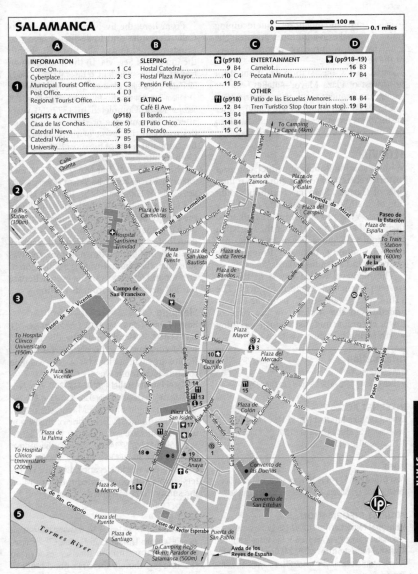

SALAMANCA

0 — 100 m
0 — 0.1 miles

INFORMATION
Come On.............................1 C4
Cyberplace.........................2 C3
Municipal Tourist Office.....3 C3
Post Office.........................4 D3
Regional Tourist Office......5 B4

SIGHTS & ACTIVITIES   (p918)
Casa de las Conchas............(see 5)
Catedral Nueva..................6 B5
Catedral Vieja...................7 B5
University..........................8 B4

SLEEPING   (p918)
Hostal Catedral..................9 B4
Hostal Plaza Mayor............10 C4
Pensión Feli.....................11 B5

EATING   (p918)
Café El Ave.......................12 B4
El Bardo...........................13 B4
El Patio Chico...................14 B4
El Pecado.........................15 C4

ENTERTAINMENT   (pp918–19)
Camelot............................16 B3
Peccata Minuta..................17 B4

OTHER
Patio de las Escuelas Menores..........18 B4
Tren Turístico Stop (tour train stop)..19 B4

SPAIN

---

the Plaza Mayor for low-key bars; **Peccata Minuta** (☎ 92 312 34 47; Calle Francisco Vitoria 3; ⏰ 9am-11pm Sun-Thu, 11am-1pm Fri & Sat) is a good option for drinks and special coffees. Later on, head to the popular disco **Camelot** (☎ 92 321 21 84; Calle Bordadores 3; ⏰ 8pm-2am Sun-Wed, to 4am Thu, to 6am Fri & Sat), which is housed in a former convent.

Getting There & Away

Renfe trains trickle in from Madrid (€14.15, 2½ hours, six daily), Valladolid (€5.60, one hour, one daily), Bilbao (€24.50, 5½ hours, one daily) and Ávila (€7.15, 1½ hours, seven daily). The main train station is northwest of the centre (catch bus No 1 or 1B from Gran Vía to get there), and that's where you'll have to catch trains and buy tickets, but incoming trains *only* make an additional stop near the Plaza España, within easy walking distance of the centre.

Salamanca's bus station is about 1km northwest of Plaza Mayor. **AutoRes** (www.auto-res.net) has frequent services to Madrid (€10 to €15, 2½ to three hours, eight daily). Other destinations served regularly include Santiago de Compostela, Ávila, Segovia and León.

SEGOVIA

With its soaring Roman aqueduct, compact historic centre and setting amid the rolling hills of Castilla, Segovia is without doubt one of Spain's most enchanting cities. The Romans, Visigoths and Muslims all tried their hand at ruling, but after the Christian Reconquista Segovia began to come into its own, building beautiful Romanesque churches and splendid palaces.

The medieval walled city is in the far-western corner of modern Segovia. The 11th-century walls stretch from the Roman aqueduct to the Alcázar on the edge of town, encompassing just about everything worth seeing in a short visit.

Information

EMERGENCY
Police (☎ 091; Paseo de Ezequiel González 22)

INTERNET ACCESS
Cyber Graphika Internet (☎ 92 146 09 66; 1st fl, Ave Fernández Ladreda 12; per hr €1.80; ☼ 11am-2pm & 3-10pm Mon-Fri, 4-10pm Sat)

POST
Post Office (☎ 92 146 16 16; www.correos.es; Plaza Doctor Laguna 5; ☼ 8.30am-8.30pm Mon-Fri, 9am-2pm Sat)

TOURIST INFORMATION
Municipal tourist office (☎ 92 146 29 14; www.segoviaturismo.es; Plaza Axoguejo 1; ☼ 10am-8pm)
Regional tourist office (☎ 92 146 03 34 or 902 20 30 30; www.turismocastillayleon.com; Plaza Mayor; ☼ 9am-2pm & 5-8pm)

Sights

Start your visit at the **Roman aqueduct**, an 894m-long engineering wonder that looks like an enormous comb plunged into the centre of Segovia. It's 28m high and was built without a drop of mortar – just good old Roman know-how.

From here, the lively commercial streets Calle Cervantes and Calle Juan Bravo (together referred to as Calle Real) climb into the innards of Segovia. In the heart of town towers the resplendent **cathedral** (☎ 92 146 22 05; Plaza de la Catedral; admission €2, free from 1.30pm Sun; ☼ 10am-2pm & 4-8pm Tue-Fri Sep-July, 10am-2pm Sat & Sun year-round). Completed in 1577, 50 years after its Romanesque predecessor had been destroyed in the revolt of the Comuneros, the cathedral is one of the most homogenous Gothic churches in Spain.

The fortified **Alcázar** (☎ 92 146 07 59; www.alcazarsegovia.com; Plaza Reina Victoria Eugenia; admission €3.50; ☼ 10am-6pm Oct-Mar, 10am-7pm Apr-Sep) is a fairy-tale castle perched dramatically on the edge of Segovia. Roman foundations are buried somewhere underneath this splendour, but what we see today is a 13th-century structure that burned down in 1862 and was subsequently rebuilt. Inside is a collection of armour and military gear, but even better are the 360-degree views from its rooftop.

Sleeping

Hostal Fornos (☎ 92 146 01 98; Calle Infanta Isabel 13; s €32-38, d €45-51) Hand-painted headboards and wall decorations give this place a cheerful air. Rooms are small but for a bit of extra wiggling room request room Nos 5 or 8.

Hotel Infanta Isabel (☎ 92 146 13 00; www.hotelinfantaisabel.com; Plaza Mayor 12; s €50-73, d €74-108; ☒) Sitting right on Plaza Mayor, the utterly charming Infanta Isabel is one of the best in town. Rooms are spacious and full of light.

Las Sirenas (☎ 92 146 26 63; www.hotelsirenas.com; Calle Juan Bravo 30; s €40-53, d €60-70, tr €80-90; ☒) Exuding old-world elegance, Las Sirenas offers simple but sophisticated rooms right off the sunny Plaza Medina del Campo.

Eating

Casa Duque (☎ 92 146 24 87; www.restauranteduque.es; Calle Cervantes 12; mains €5.70-21, menú €21; ☼ noon-11pm) A local institution that serves a mean suckling pig, though there is a good range of salads too. Downstairs is the informal tavern, where you can get tapas and yummy *cazuelas* (stews).

La Cordorniz (☎ 92 146 38 07; Calle Hermanos Barral 3; mains €9.50-12; ☼ 1.30-4pm & 8-11.30pm) For traditional fare at slightly cheaper prices, head here; the €9 lunch *menú* is a tasty deal.

Cueva de San Esteban (☎ 92 146 09 82; Calle Valdelaguila 15; menú €7.70-12.15; ☼ 1pm-11pm) One of the only restaurants in Segovia not pushing suckling pig, this place offers seasonal dishes and an excellent wine list.

Entertainment

After dark, the action is centred around the Plaza Mayor (especially along Calle Escuderos and Calle Isabel Católica). Some of the best nightspots are **Bar Santana** (☎ 92 146 35 64; Calle Infanta Isabel 18; ☼ 10.30-3am, until 4am Fri & Sat) and **El Purgatorio** (Calle Escuderos 26; ☼ 1pm-2am Mon-Fri, 5pm-3.30am Sat, 5pm-2am Sun).

Getting There & Away

If you're driving, take the A-6 motorway north from Madrid towards the N-603 national highway, which will take you to the city centre. The trip takes about an hour.

Buses (€5.68, 1¼ hours) leave every half-hour from Madrid's Paseo de la Florida bus stop and arrive to Segovia's central **bus station** (☎ 92 142 77 07; Paseo Ezequiel González). Renfe trains come in from Madrid (€5.10, two hours, seven daily) and elsewhere.

LEÓN

León has been called 'the beautiful unknown', and with good reason. This once-mighty city is often overlooked by travellers, but its long boulevards, open squares and historic Barrio Húmedo (Damp District) invite you to pause for a day or two.

León saw its heyday from the 10th to 13th centuries as capital of the expanding Christian kingdom of the same name. As a stop on the Camino de Santiago, it never fell into complete ruin, but it's been little more than a stopover city for centuries.

Information

Cafeteria Santo Domingo (☎ 98 726 13 84; Ave Ordoño II 3; Internet per hr €1; ☼ 8am-11pm Mon-Fri, 9am-11pm Sun) At the back of this caféteria is a well-run Internet centre.

Tourist office (☎ 98 723 70 82; www.aytoleon.com; Plaza Regla 3; ☼ 9am-2pm & 5-7pm Mon-Fri, 10am-2pm & 5-8pm Sat & Sun)

Sights

León's best and best-known monument is its breathtaking 13th-century **cathedral** (☎ 98 787 57 70; www.catedralleon.org; admission museum €3.50; ☼ cathedral 8.30am-1.30pm & 4-7pm Mon-Sat, 8.30am-2.30pm & 5-7pm Sun Oct-Jun, 8.30am-8pm Mon-Sat, 8.30am-2.30pm & 5-8pm Sun Jul-Sep, museum 9.30am-1.30pm & 4-6.30pm Mon-Fri, 9.30am-1.30pm Sat Oct-May,

9.30am-7.30pm Mon-Fri Jul-Sep). A marvel of Gothic architecture, it has an extraordinarily intricate façade with a rose window, three richly sculptured doorways and two muscular towers. The most outstanding feature, though, is the 128 radiant stained-glass windows (with a surface of 1800 sq metres), which give the place an ethereal quality.

Nearby is the **Real Basílica de San Isidoro** (☎ 98 787 61 61; www.sanisidorodeleon.org; admission €3, Thu afternoon free; ☼ 10am-1.30pm & 4-6.30pm Mon-Sat, 10am-1.30pm Sun Jan-Jun, 9am-8pm Mon-Sat, 9am-2pm Sun Jul & Aug), a simple Romanesque church that houses the interesting **Panteón Real**, where Leonese royalty lie buried beneath a canopy of some of the finest frescoes in all of Spain.

Across town is the equally worthwhile **Hostal de San Marcos**, a former pilgrims' hospital that now houses a luxury parador. The sumptuous interior can only be visited during free **tours** (☼ 1pm & 8.30pm Mon-Thu, 1pm Fri & Sat, 9.30am & 5pm Sun) but the **Museo de León** (☎ 98 724 50 61; adult/child €1.20/free, Sun free; ☼ 10am-2pm & 4-7pm Tue-Sat, 10am-2pm Sun Sep-Jun, 10am-2pm & 5-8pm Tue-Sat, 10am-2pm Sun Jul & Aug), also housed here, gives access to some parts of the building. Don't miss the façade, 100m of ornate golden-hued carvings.

Sleeping & Eating

Don Suero (☎ 98 723 06 00; Suero de Quiñones 15; s/d €21.10/40, s with shared bathroom €17.70) A clean, attractive place in the heart of town that could easily pass for a one- or two-star hotel.

La Posada Regia (☎ 98 721 31 73; www.regialeon .com; Calle Regidores 9-11; s/d incl breakfast €55/90) Offering more comfort, this quaint inn has pretty period furniture decorating every room and a great restaurant downstairs.

The Plaza San Martín is packed with bars and restaurants, many with terraces.

Café Gótico (☎ 98 708 49 56; Calle Varillas 5; menú €8; ☼ noon-midnight Sun-Thu, noon-2am Fri & Sat) Tasty but no-frills, inexpensive fare, including an all-vegetarian daily lunch *menú*.

Palomo (☎ 98 725 42 25; Calle Escalerilla 8; mains €5.50-14, menú €9-15; ☼ 1.30-4pm & 9pm-midnight, closed Wed & Sun dinner) Cosy, with traditional Castilian dishes.

Vivaldi (☎ 98 726 00 94; Calle Platerías 4; mains €11-18; ☼ 1-3.30pm, 9-11.30pm Tue-Sat, closed Sun dinner & all day Mon) For a treat, head to upscale Vivaldi in the Barrio Húmedo. You'll find seasonal dishes based on local products. There's also a bar area with some great gourmet tapas.

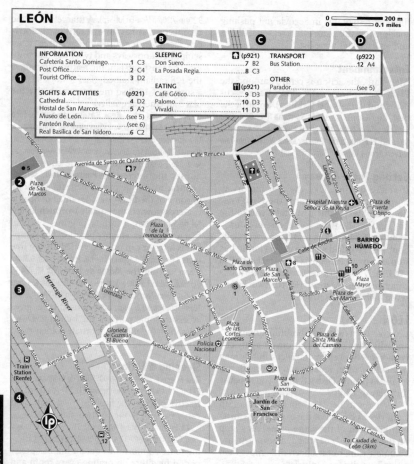

LEÓN

0 — 200 m
0 — 0.1 miles

INFORMATION		SLEEPING	(p921)	TRANSPORT	(p922)
Cafetería Santo Domingo	1 C3	Don Suero	7 B2	Bus Station	12 A4
Post Office	2 C4	La Posada Regia	8 C3		
Tourist Office	3 D2			OTHER	
		EATING	(p921)	Parador	(see 5)
SIGHTS & ACTIVITIES	(p921)	Café Gótico	9 D3		
Cathedral	4 D2	Palomo	10 D3		
Hostal de San Marcos	5 A2	Vivaldi	11 D3		
Museo de León	(see 5)				
Panteón Real	(see 6)				
Real Basílica de San Isidoro	6 C2				

Getting There & Away

Renfe train station has trains to and from Madrid (€19.20 to €29, at least four hours, seven daily), Ávila (€15.75 to €23.50, at least 2½ hours, up to nine daily), Burgos (€15.50 to €21, two hours, four daily) and Santiago de Compostela (€24.50, six hours, one daily).

The **bus station** (☎ 98 721 10 00; Paseo Ingeniero Saenz de Miera) connects with many Spanish cities, including Madrid (€18.31 to €31, at least 3½ hours, up to 12 daily), Burgos (€11.75, two to four hours, three daily) and Ávila (€14.18, 3½ hours, one daily). For more details contact the bus company, **Alsa** (www.alsa.es).

León is on the N-630 highway, 64km north of the A-6 motorway that cuts through the region.

BURGOS

With its grand riverside promenades and outstanding collection of churches and monasteries, Burgos is one of Spain's hidden gems. Marvel at the gleaming white cathedral (one of Christendom's most splendid) and spend the day strolling the characterful boulevards of the centre.

Information

Locutorio Capitanía (☎ 94 726 42 28; Plaza Alonso Martínez 3; per hr €1) Good for Internet access.

Municipal tourist office (☎ 94 728 88 74; www.ayto burgos.es; Teatro Principal, Paseo Espolón 1; ⊙ 10am-2pm & 4.30-7.30pm Mon-Sat, 10am-2pm Sun Oct-Jun, 10am-2pm & 5-8pm Mon-Sat, 10am-2pm Sun Jul-Sep)

Police (☎ 94 728 88 39, ☎ 091)

Sights

Burgos' claim to fame is its majestic 1261 Gothic **cathedral** (☎ 94 720 47 12; adult/child €3/1, guided tour €1.50; 🕙 10am-1.15pm & 4-6.45pm Sep-Jun, 9.30am-1.15pm & 4-7.15pm Jul & Aug, guided tour 5pm Mon-Fri & 11am Sun), a gleaming-white Gothic masterpiece. On this site, a modest Romanesque church once stood, but today we see ornate spires piercing the skyline, each representing 84m of richly decorated fantasy. Inside, the highlight is the Escalera Dorada (Gilded Staircase) by Diego de Siloé. The famed warrior El Cid lies buried beneath the central dome.

If you have time, visit the **Monasterio de las Huelgas** (☎ 94 720 16 30; adult/child €5/2.50; 🕙 10am-1.15pm & 4-5.45pm Tue-Sat, 10.30am-2.15pm Sun), an elegant Cistercian order founded in 1187 by Eleanor of Aquitaine and still home to 35 Cistercian nuns. You can get here by a 30-minute walk west along the southern bank of the Arlanzón River.

Sleeping & Eating

Pensión Peña (☎ 94 720 63 23; Calle Puebla 18; s €15-17, d €22-24) You'll pay amazingly low prices for well-kept, cheerful rooms here. All have pretty décor and shared baths.

Hotel Norte y Londres (☎ 94 726 41 25; www .hotelnorteylondres.com; Plaza Alonso Martínez 10; s €43-49.50, d €61-73.50) Great value and in an unbeatable location, this classy hotel boasts lovely rooms with hardwood floors and fine furnishings. Some rooms have balconies.

Restaurante La Riojana (☎ 94 720 61 32; Calle Avellanos 10; menú €6; 🕙 1.30-4pm & 8-10.30pm) Home to the cheapest lunch *menú* in town, this no-frills spot has a solid selection of Spanish dishes such as paella and Rioja-style codfish.

Prego (☎ 94 726 04 47; Huerto del Rey 4; salads & pasta €5-7, pizza €10; 🕙 noon-4pm, 8pm-midnight) One of the few good options for vegetarians. It's an elegant Italian restaurant with impressive prices and tasty dishes.

Mesón del Cid (☎ 94 720 87 15; www.mesondelcid.es; Plaza Santa María 8; mains €11-20; 🕙 1pm-4pm & 8.30-11pm) For traditional fare, try the kitschy but atmospheric El Cid, offering roasted meats and waiters in costume.

Getting There & Away

Trains come and go from cities including Salamanca (€17.50, about three hours, four daily), Madrid (€19.90 to €23, up to five hours, nine daily). The train station is connected to town by bus Nos 3, 5 and 7.

The bus station is just across the river from the cathedral and is home to several companies. One of the largest, **Alsa** (☎ 94 726 63 70; www .alsa.es), makes runs to Salamanca (€13 to €16, four hours, three daily), Valladolid (€7 to €9, two to three hours, three to four daily) and other destinations.

CASTILLA-LA MANCHA

Best known as the home of Don Quixote, Castilla-La Mancha conjures up images of lonely windmills and bleak, treeless plains giving way to pretty villages and medieval castles. It is also home to two of Spain's most fascinating cities: Toledo and Cuenca.

TOLEDO

pop 72,549

A jumble of narrow, winding streets, perched on a small hill above the Tajo River, Toledo is crammed with museums, churches and other monumental reminders of its splendid and turbulent past. It's also quite expensive and terribly touristy. If you can, try to stay overnight to really appreciate the spark and soul of this remarkable city.

Information

Main tourist office (☎ 92 522 08 43; www.jccm.es; Puerta Bisagra; 🕙 9am-6pm Mon-Sat, 9am-3pm Sun) At the northern end of town.

Scorpions (☎ 92 521 25 56; Calle Matías Moreno 10; Internet per hr €2; 🕙 12.30pm-2am)

Tourist office (☎ 92 525 40 30; 🕙 10.30am-2.30pm & 4.30-7pm Tue-Sun, 10.30am-2.30pm Mon) Opposite the cathedral and more helpful.

Sights & Activities

Toledo has lots to see. As well as the historical sights, its tourist shops are fun, many reflecting the city's swashbuckling past with suits of armour and swords for sale. More conventional souvenirs include *damasquinado* (damascene), the Moorish art of inlaying gold thread against matte black steel, available in the form of jewellery, boxes and ornaments. Toledo is also famed for its *mazapán* (marzipan).

You could happily spend an afternoon in Toledo's **cathedral** (☎ 92 522 22 41; Calle Cardenal Cisneros; 🕙 10.30am-6.30pm Mon-Sat, 2-6pm Sun), admiring the glorious stone architecture, stained-glass windows, tombs of kings in the Capilla

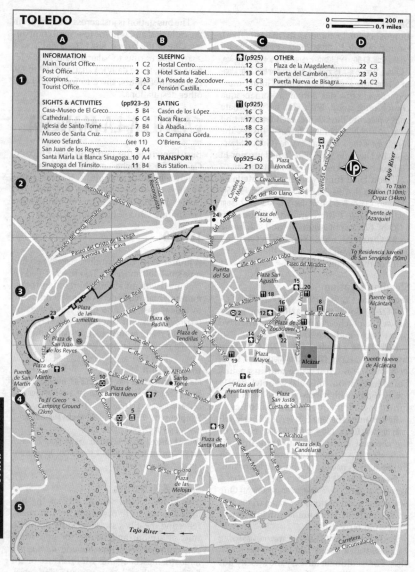

TOLEDO

0 ———— 200 m
0 ———— 0.1 miles

INFORMATION
Main Tourist Office..................1 C2
Post Office.............................2 C3
Scorpions..............................3 A3
Tourist Office.........................4 C4

SIGHTS & ACTIVITIES (pp923–5)
Casa-Museo de El Greco.........5 B4
Cathedral..............................6 C4
Iglesia de Santo Tomé............7 B4
Museo de Santa Cruz.............8 D3
Museo Sefardí.......................(see 11)
San Juan de los Reyes............9 A4
Santa María La Blanca Sinagoga..10 A4
Sinagoga del Tránsito.............11 B4

SLEEPING (p925)
Hostal Centro........................12 C3
Hotel Santa Isabel.................13 C4
La Posada de Zocodover........14 C3
Pensión Castilla....................15 C3

EATING (p925)
Casón de los López................16 C3
Ñaca Ñaca............................17 C3
La Abadia.............................18 C3
La Campana Gorda................19 C4
O'Briens...............................20 C3

TRANSPORT (pp925–6)
Bus Station...........................21 D2

OTHER
Plaza de la Magdalena............22 C3
Puerta del Cambrón................23 A3
Puerta Nueva de Bisagra.........24 C2

Mayor and art by the likes of El Greco, Velázquez and Goya. You have to buy a ticket (€5.50) to enter four areas – the **Coro**, **Sacristía**, **Capilla de la Torre** and **Sala Capitular**, which contain some of the finest art and artisanship.

The **Museo de Santa Cruz** (☎ 92 522 10 36; Calle Cervantes 3; admission free; ⊗ 10am-6.30pm Mon-Sat, 10am-2pm Sun) contains a large collection of fur-

niture, faded tapestries, military and religious paraphernalia, and paintings. Upstairs is an impressive collection of El Greco's works, including the masterpiece *La Asunción* (Assumption of the Virgin).

In the southwestern part of the old city, the queues outside an otherwise unremarkable church, the **Iglesia de Santo Tomé** (☎ 92 525 60 98;

Plaza Conde; admission €1.50; ⊙ 10am-6pm Oct-Jun, 10am-7pm Jul-Sep), betray the presence of El Greco's masterpiece *El Entierro del Conde de Orgaz*. The painting shows the burial of the Count of Orgaz in 1322 by St Stephen and St Augustine, observed by a heavenly entourage.

The **Casa-Museo de El Greco** (☎ 92 522 40 46; Calle Samuel Leví; admission €2.40; ⊙ 10am-2pm & 4-9pm Tue-Sat, 10am-2pm Sun), in Toledo's former Jewish quarter, contains the artist's famous *Vista y Plano de Toledo*, plus about 20 of his minor works. Although El Greco lived in Toledo from 1577 to 1614, it is unlikely he ever lived in this building.

The **Museo Sefardi** (☎ 92 522 36 65; www.museosefardi.net; Calle Samuel Leví s/n; admission €4.50; ⊙ 10am-6pm Tue-Sat, 10am-2pm Sun) is housed in the beautiful 14th century **Sinagoga del Tránsito**. Toledo's other synagogue, **Santa María La Blanca** (☎ 92 522 72 57; Calle Reyes Católicos 4; admission €1.50; ⊙ 10am-6pm), a short way north, dates back to the beginning of the 13th century.

A little further north is one of the city's most visible sights, **San Juan de los Reyes** (☎ 92 522 38 02; admission €1.50; ⊙ 10am-6pm Oct-Jun, 10am-7pm Jul-Sep), the Franciscan monastery and church founded by Fernando and Isabel. The prevalent late Flemish-Gothic style is tarted up with lavish Isabelline ornamentation and counterbalanced by *Mudéjar* decoration. Outside hang the chains of Christian prisoners freed after the fall of Granada in 1492.

Sleeping

Cheap accommodation is not easy to come by and is often full, especially from Easter to September.

Camping El Greco (☎ 92 522 00 90; per person/tent/car €4.75/4.55/4.55; ⊙ year-round; 🐾) The nearest camping ground, well signposted 2.5km southwest of town.

Residencia Juvenil de San Servando (☎ 92 522 45 54; fax 92 521 39 54; dm 25 yrs & under/26 yrs & over €8.70/11.30) Toledo's HI hostel is beautifully located in the Castillo de San Servando, a castle that started life as a Visigothic monastery.

Pensión Castilla (☎ 92 525 63 18; Calle Recoletos 6; s/d with shared bathroom €15/25) With its wooden floors, ceiling fans and bright rooms, this is one of Toledo's best budget options.

Hostal Centro (☎ 92 525 70 91; www.hostalcentro.com; Calle Nueva 13; s/d/tr €30/45/60; 🐾) Just off the social hang-out that is Plaza Zocodover, the *hostal* has wonderful spacious rooms, some with balconies, and a fabulous rooftop terrace.

La Posada de Zocodover (☎ 92 525 58 14; Calle Condonerias 6; d €37.30; 🐾) In an old, narrow building with timbered ceilings, pretty brass beds and tiled floors, the hotel's seven exquisite rooms get snapped up fast.

Hotel Santa Isabel (☎ 92 525 31 20; www.santa-isabel.com; Calle Santa Isabel 24; s/d €30/45; P 🐾) Well placed near the cathedral, this comfortable hotel offers impeccable service in a grand 14th-century building, with rooms around a stunning wooden gallery.

Eating & Drinking

Ñaca Ñaca (☎ 92 525 35 59; Plaza Zocodover 7; bocadillos €2-3; ⊙ 9am-11pm Mon-Thu, 9-4am Fri, 9am Sat-11pm Sun) For late-night munchies or midday snacks, this place does chunky *bocadillos* (filled rolls) to take-away.

O'Briens (☎ 92 521 26 65; Calle Cuesta de las Armas 12; mains €4-5; ⊙ noon-2am Sun-Thu, noon-4am Fri & Sat) O'Briens is a friendly Irish pub with good grub, including burgers and hefty club sandwiches (except on Saturday when the kitchen is closed).

La Campana Gorda (☎ 92 521 01 46; Calle Hombre de Palo 13; mains €9-14; ⊙ 9am-11pm) A tavern-style restaurant specialising in roast meats and fish, and football on the telly. It's popular with smartly dressed locals and does a very reasonable €9 *menú*.

La Abadia (☎ 92 525 07 46; Plaza San Nicolás 3; mains €6-12; ⊙ 8am-midnight Sun-Thu, noon-1am Fri & Sat) A popular bar and restaurant, with lots of alcoves and over 30 different types of beer on the menu. Don't leave without trying the *sartén de patatas* (€4), a divine concoction of potatoes, egg, sausage and onion served up in a small frying pan.

Casón de los López (☎ 92 525 47 74; www.casontoledo.com; Calle Sillería 2; mains €18-21; ⊙ 1.30pm-4pm & 8.30-11.30pm Wed-Sun) Toledo's must-see restaurant/bar is housed in one of the city's most beautiful buildings, with antiques, vaulted ceilings and even a former small chapel with its original baroque altar. There's an inviting **café** (tapas €2.20; ⊙ noon-midnight), which does a small collection of excellent tapas and a huge variety of wines. The basement **bar** (⊙ 8pm-1am Wed-Sun) has over 90 different whiskies.

Getting There & Away

Toledo's **bus station** (☎ 92 521 58 50; Ave Castilla-La Mancha) has buses from about 6am to 10pm to/from Madrid's Estación Sur (€4, 1½ hours, every 30 minutes). The Aisa line runs buses to/from Cuenca (€10, 2½ hours, three daily).

From the **train station** (Calle Paseo Rosa), 400m east of the Puente Azarquiel, trains run to and from Madrid's Atocha station (€5, 1½ hours, five daily). The first train from Madrid departs at 8.30am, the last from Toledo at 6.48pm.

Bus No 5 links the train and bus stations with Plaza Zocodover (€0.80).

CUENCA
pop 47,201

Cuenca's *alta ciudad* (high town) teeters on the edge of two gorges: the Júcar and the Huécar. The crumbling ancient buildings cling for dear life and each turn of the town's cobbled streets reveals new delights.

Information

Ciber Viajero (☎ 96 923 66 96; Ave República Argentina 3; per hr €2; ☼ 10am-2pm & 5-11pm Mon-Sat) Internet access.
Tourist office (☎ 96 923 21 19; ofi.turismo@aytocuenca .org; Plaza Mayor 1) Just before the arches of the main square, this office is especially helpful.

Sights & Activities

Cuenca's **Casas Colgadas** (Hanging Houses), built in the 15th century, are precariously positioned on a cliff top, their balconies projecting out over the gorge. The **Puente San Pablo** (1902), an iron footbridge that crosses the ravine, provides access to spectacular views of these buildings (and the rest of the old town). Within one of the Casas Colgadas is the **Museo de Arte Abstracto Español** (☎ 96 921 29 83; adult/student €3/1.50; ☼ 11am-2pm & 4-6pm Tue-Fri, 11am-2pm & 4-8pm Sat, 11am-2.30pm Sun), an exciting collection with works by Zobel, Sempere, Millares and Chillida.

Among the religious art and artefacts inside the **Museo Diocesano** (☎ 96 922 42 10; Calle Obispo Valero 2; adult/child €1.80/free; ☼ 11am-2pm & 4-7pm Tue-Sat, 11am-2pm Sun) there are a couple of El Grecos and a stunning 14th-century Byzantine diptych. Opposite, the **Museo de Cuenca** (☎ 96 921 30 69; Calle Obispo Valero 12; adult/student €1.20/0.60; ☼ 10am-2pm & 4-7pm Tue-Sat, 11am-2pm Sun) has a reasonable archaeological collection.

On Plaza Mayor you'll find Cuenca's strange **cathedral** (☼ 9am-2pm & 4-6pm). The lines of the unfinished façade are Norman-Gothic and reminiscent of French cathedrals, but the stained-glass windows look like they'd be more at home in the abstract art museum.

Sleeping & Eating

The more attractive hotels are in the *alta ciudad*.

Pensión Central (☎ 96 921 15 11; Calle Chirino 7; s/d with shared bathroom €12/20) Just off the busy shopping street in the new town, with simple but warm rooms off a dark corridor.

Pensión La Tabanqueta (☎ 96 921 12 90; Calle Trabuco 13; d with shared bathroom €30) Up at the top of the old town with views of the Júcar gorge and a lively bar downstairs. Wonderfully atmospheric.

Posada de San José (☎ 96 921 13 00; www.posada sanjose.com; Calle Julián Romero 4; s/d €47/75, with shared bathroom €23/34) At the edge of the gorge with drop-dead views, this tastefully converted 17th-century former school college makes for an evocative romantic retreat, with every room different but tastefully done and a price list to suit different budgets.

Bar La Tinaja (Calle Obispo Valero 4; ☼ noon-1am) Just off Plaza Mayor and usually jammed with scruffy 20-somethings.

Confitería Ruiz (Calle Carretería 14; ☼ 8am-10pm Mon-Sat) In the new town, with the air of a 1970s hotel lobby but serves the best pastries in La Mancha.

El Caserío (☎ 96 923 00 21; Calle Larga 17; bocadillos €3.30; ☼ 11.30am-midnight) Well worth the 600m uphill hike from Plaza Mayor for the views alone, this rough-and-ready bar serves up torpedo-sized *bocadillos* and lots of barbecued goodies.

Meson Casas Colgadas (☎ 96 922 35 09; Calle Canónigos 3; mains €16-19; ☼ 1.30-4pm & 9-11pm Wed-Sun) This is a Cuencan classic with its starched white tablecloths, impeccable service and fantastic views of the Huécar gorge. Specialties include the *morteruelo* (€8), a hare, partridge and liver pâté. Cheaper *raciones* (and the same knock-out views) can be had at the downstairs **bar** (mains €5-10; ☼ 1-4pm & 7-11pm).

For superb cheeses and local wines to takeaway, drop by **La Alacena** (Calle Alfonso VIII 50; ☼ 10.30am-2pm & 5-8.30pm).

Getting There & Away

From the **bus station** (☎ 96 922 70 87; Calle Fermin Caballero), there are buses to/from Madrid (€9, 2½ hours, nine daily), Valencia (€12, 2½ to four hours, three daily) and Barcelona (€30, 9½ hours, twice daily).

Cuenca's **train station** (Paseo Ferrocarril) has direct services to Madrid's Atocha station

(€9.15, 2½ hours, five daily) and Valencia (€10, three hours, four daily).

Bus No 1 or 2 from near the bus and train stations will take you up to Plaza Mayor in the old town.

CATALONIA

Forget the Spain of flamenco and bullfights; Catalonia is a proud region that likes to see itself as somewhat independent from the rest of Spain. A smallish triangle in the northeastern corner of the peninsula, Catalonia is a varied region, with both soaring mountain peaks and long, sandy coasts. Its capital, Barcelona is one of Spain's most beautiful cities, but the rest of the region is well worth exploring too.

BARCELONA

pop 1.6 million

Sitting right on the Mediterranean, vibrant Barcelona is one of Europe's most exciting cities. With medieval palaces and plazas in the old quarters, fantastical modernist architecture sprinkled throughout L'Eixample district and an innovative contemporary art and design scene, Barcelona won't disappoint. It also boasts great shopping, a lively nightlife and some of the best cuisine in Spain.

Barcelona is a master at reinventing itself. The city has morphed from a wannabe Roman town into a prosperous medieval centre, to a rebellious city during the Spanish Civil War, and finally to its modern cosmopolitan self. In the early 1990s the city underwent a massive cleanup and restructuring for the 1992 Olympics. Now they're at it again, giving the northern shore (site of the 2004 Forum of Cultures) a major make-over with a new port, new conference centre and new beach.

The effects of so many changes can be seen on the streets. Important splashes of Gothic, Romanesque, modernist and contemporary works pop up in even the most unexpected corners of the city, haphazardly mixed together like the paellas traditionally eaten for Sunday lunch.

Orientation

Plaça Catalunya is the heart of Barcelona and the marker between the historic city and the modern one. From here, the long pedestrian

---

BARCELONA IN TWO DAYS

Don't leave Barcelona without seeing architect Antoni Gaudí's masterpieces, **La Sagrada Familia** (p930) and **La Pedrera** (p930), both in L'Eixample. From here, walk down **Passeig de Gràcia** (p937) to reach the **Plaça Catalunya** (p930) and the old quarter. Head down **Las Ramblas** (p930), and duck into the **Barri Gòtic** (p930) to see the cathedral.

On day two, visit the **Museu Picasso** (p931) and the **Basílica de Santa Maria del Mar** (p931), both in El Born district. Stop off here for tapas and wine at **La Vinya del Senyor** (p936) before making your way to the **waterfront** (p931). End the afternoon with a meal along **La Barceloneta** (p936).

Ramblas shoots southeast to the sea, with the busy Gothic quarter and Raval district hugging it on either side. To the northwest of the plaza is L'Eixample, the grid-like district where you'll find shopping areas and the bulk of the city's offices and residences.

Information

BOOKSHOPS

Altair (Map p932; ☎ 93 342 71 71; Gran Vía 616; metro Plaça Catalunya) All travel books.

Casa del Libre (Map pp928-9; ☎ 93 272 34 80; Passeig de Gràcia 62; metro Passeig de Gràcia) Great English section.

EMERGENCY

General Emergencies (☎ 112)

Guardia Urbana (City Police; Map p932; ☎ 092; Las Ramblas 43)

INTERNET ACCESS

Bigg (Map p932; ☎ 93 301 40 20; Carrer Comtal 9; per hr €2; ⏰ 9am-11pm Mon-Sat, 10am-11pm Sun; metro Plaça Catalunya)

Cybermundo (Map p932; ☎ 93 317 71 42; Carrer Bergara 3; per hr €1.20-2.90; ⏰ 9am-midnight Mon-Fri, 10am-midnight Sat, 11am-midnight Sun; metro Plaça Catalunya)

LAUNDRY

Wash n' Dry (Map pp928-9; ☎ 93 412 19 53; Carrer Nou de la Rambla 19; €6.61 per load; ⏰ 7am-11pm; metro Liceu)

MEDICAL SERVICES

24-hour Pharmacy (Passeig de Gràcia 26 Map pp928-9; Las Ramblas 98 Map pp928-9) Helps with minor problems.

SPAIN

BARCELONA

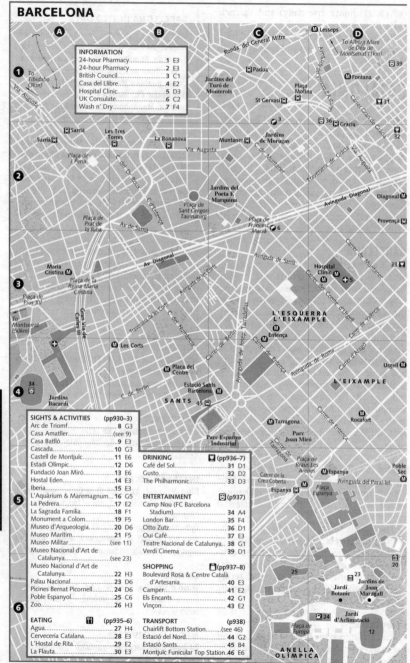

INFORMATION
24-hour Pharmacy	1 E3
24-hour Pharmacy	2 E3
British Council	3 C1
Casa del Llibre	4 E2
Hospital Clinic	5 D3
UK Consulate	6 C2
Wash n' Dry	7 F4

SIGHTS & ACTIVITIES (pp930–3)
Arc de Triomf	8 G3
Casa Amatller	(see 9)
Casa Batlló	9 E3
Cascada	10 G3
Castell de Montjuïc	11 E6
Estadi Olímpic	12 D6
Fundació Joan Miró	13 E6
Hostal Eden	14 E3
Iberia	15 E3
L'Aquàrium & Maremagnum	16 G5
La Pedrera	17 E2
La Sagrada Família	18 F1
Monument a Colom	19 F5
Museo d'Arqueologia	20 D6
Museo Marítim	21 F5
Museo Militar	(see 11)
Museo Nacional d'Art de Catalunya	(see 23)
Museo Nacional d'Art de Catalunya	22 H3
Palau Nacional	23 D6
Picines Bernat Picornell	24 D6
Poble Espanyol	25 C6
Zoo	26 H3

EATING (pp935–6)
Agua	27 H4
Cervecería Catalana	28 E3
L'Hostal de Rita	29 E2
La Flauta	30 E3

DRINKING (pp936–7)
Café del Sol	31 D1
Gusto	32 D2
The Philharmonic	33 D3

ENTERTAINMENT (p937)
Camp Nou (FC Barcelona Stadium)	34 A4
London Bar	35 F4
Otto Zutz	36 D1
Oui Café	37 E3
Teatre Nacional de Catalunya	38 G1
Verdi Cinema	39 D1

SHOPPING (pp937–8)
Boulevard Rosa & Centre Català d'Artesania	40 E3
Camper	41 E2
Els Encants	42 G1
Vinçon	43 E2

TRANSPORT (p938)
Chairlift Bottom Station	(see 46)
Estació del Nord	44 G2
Estació Sants	45 B4
Montjuïc Funicular Top Station	46 E6

SPAIN

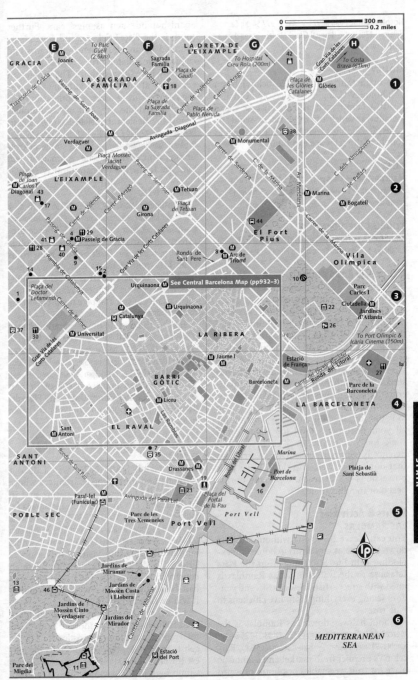

0   300 m
0   0.2 miles

GRACIA

E Joanic

To Parc Güell (2.5km)

Travessera de Gracia

Passeig de Sant Joan

LA SAGRADA FAMILIA

Carrer de Sardenya

F Sagrada Familia

18

Plaça de Gaudi

LA DRETA DE L'EIXAMPLE

To Hospital Creu Roja (200m)

Carrer de València

Carrer d'Aragó

G

42

Plaça de les Glòries Catalanes

Gran Via de les Corts Catalanes

H

To Costa Brava (61km)

Glòries

1

Plaça de la Sagrada Familia

Plaça de Pablo Neruda

Avinguda Diagonal

Verdaguer

Plaça Mossèn Jacint Verdaguer

Passeig de Sant Joan

Monumental

Carrer de Sardenya

C. de la Marina

Av. Meridiana

38

C. dels Almogàvers

C. de Pallars

2

Plaça de Joan Carles I

L'EIXAMPLE

Diagonal

43

17

Carrer de València

Carrer d'Aragó

Tetuan

Girona

Plaça de Tetuan

Marina

Bogateil

Carrer de la Marina

4

29

Passeig de Gràcia

44

El Fort Pius

Vila Olímpica

41

28

40

9

Rambla de Catalunya

15 2

Ronda de Sant Pere

8

Arc de Triomf

10

Parc Carles I

3

14

1

Plaça del Doctor Letamendi

Carrer de Balmes

Urquinaona

See Central Barcelona Map (pp932–3)

Urquinaona

22

Ciutadella

Jardins d'Atlanta

37

30

Gran Via de les Corts Catalanes

Catalunya

Urquinaona

LA RIBERA

26

To Port Olímpic & Icària Cinema (150m)

Universitat

Jaume I

Estació de França

27

Ronda del Litoral

Parc de la Barconeleta

BARRI GÒTIC

Barceloneta

Carrer del Doctor Aiguader

LA BARCELONETA

4

Sant Antoni

Liceu

Les Rambles

EL RAVAL

Marina

Platja de Sant Sebastià

SANT ANTONI

Ronda de Sant Pau

35

Drassanes

19

21

Port de Barcelona

16

POBLE SEC

Paral·lel (Funicular)

Avinguda del Paral·lel

Parc de les Tres Xemeneies

Plaça del Portal de la Pau

Port Vell

Port Vell

5

13

46

Jardins de Miramar

Jardins de Mossèn Costa i Llobera

Carretera de Miramar

Jardins de Mossèn Cinto Verdaguer

Jardins del Mirador

Parc del Migdia

11

Estació del Port

21

MEDITERRANEAN SEA

6

SPAIN

Hospital Clinic (Map pp928-9; ☎ 93 227 54 00; Carrer Villarroel 170; metro Hospital Clinic) Modern hospital with good services for travellers.

MONEY

The main tourist office (see below) has a good money-changing service. You can also head to banks such as La Caixa or Caixa Catalunya, which offer fair rates. Avoid the *casas de cambio* (exchange houses) on Las Ramblas; the rates are exorbitant.

POST

Main post office (Map p932; ☎ 93 486 80 50; Plaça Antoni López; ◷ 8.30am-9.30pm Mon-Sat, 9am-2pm Sun; metro Barceloneta)

TOURIST INFORMATION

Main tourist office (Map p932; ☎ 80 711 72 22; Plaça Catalunya 17; ◷ 9am-9pm; metro Plaça Catalunya)

Dangers & Annoyances

You don't need to be concerned about violent crime, but purse snatching and pickpocketing are a major problem, especially around Plaça Catalunya, Las Ramblas and the Plaça Reial. Classic ploys are fake bird droppings ('Let me help you clean your shirt while I rob your wallet'), card tricks on the street ('Watch the game while my friend slinks away with your purse') and spontaneous football games ('We'll take all your stuff while you're busy with the ball'). Also look out for fake police officers who ask for all your documents, and for anyone who walks too close to you. In all cases your best defence is common sense. Don't carry bags that don't close well, and don't leave your possessions out of reach, especially on the beach or in a busy café.

Sights & Activities

LAS RAMBLAS

You can't leave Barcelona without strolling down **Las Ramblas**, a pedestrian boulevard exploding with life. Stretching from the **Plaça Catalunya** to the waterfront, Las Ramblas is lined with street artists, news kiosks and vendors selling everything from live chickens to blue roses.

About halfway down Las Ramblas is the **Mercat de la Boquería** (Map p932; ☎ 93 318 25 84; Las Ramblas 91; metro Liceu; ◷ 8am-8.30pm Mon-Sat), Barcelona's premier fresh market and a fantastic place for fruit, vegetables or photos of weird

Spanish food such as pigs' ears. Further south is the **Plaça Reial**, a grand square surrounded by arcades where restaurants and cafés charge inflated prices for the privilege of sitting here (it's worth it). The square can get rowdy at night and is known as a meeting point for drug users, so some caution is called for. At the very end of Las Ramblas stands the **Monument a Colom** (Map pp928-9; metro Drassanes; adult/child €2/1.30; ◷ 10am-6.30pm Mon-Sat Oct-May, 9am-8.30pm daily Jun-Sep), a statue of Columbus atop a tall pedestal. A small lift will take you to the top for panoramic views.

BARRI GÒTIC

The **cathedral** (Map p932; ☎ 93 310 25 80; Pla de la Seu; metro Jaume I; admission museum €1; ◷ 10am-1pm & 5-7pm Mon-Sat, museum 10am-1pm only), the centrepiece of the Barri Gòtic, is essentially a Gothic creation, but it was built on top of the ruins of an 11th-century Romanesque church, and the façade of the church is actually a 19th-century neogothic addition. Wander around the verdant cloister and take the lift up to the **rooftop** (admission €1) for nice views.

Just to the east is the fascinating **Museu d'Història de la Ciutat** (City History Museum; Map p932; ☎ 93 315 11 11; Plaça del Rei; metro Jaume I; admission €4; ◷ 10am-2pm & 4-8pm Tue-Sat, 10am-3pm Sun Oct-Apr, 10am-8pm Tue-Sat, 10am-3pm Sun May-Sep), where you can visit an excavated site of Roman Barcelona that lies under the pretty **Plaça del Rei**. In summer, outdoor concerts are often held here.

GAUDÍ, MODERNISM & LA SAGRADA FAMILIA

Antoni Gaudí (1852–1926) was a devout Catholic and an eccentric architect whose work is full of references to nature and to Catholicism. His masterpiece, **La Sagrada Família** (Map pp928-9; ☎ 93 207 30 31; Carrer Mallorca 401; metro Sagrada Familia; admission €8; ◷ 9am-6pm Oct-Mar, 9am-8pm Apr-Sep), is Barcelona's most famous building and visiting it is a once-before-you-die sort of experience. Though construction began in 1882, it's still only half-built, and it's anyone's guess whether it will be finished by 2082.

Today, there are eight towers, all more than 100m high, with 10 more to come – the total representing the 12 Apostles, four Evangelists and the Mother of God, plus the tallest tower (170m) standing for Jesus Christ. Climb high inside some of the towers for a vertiginous overview of the interior and a panorama to the sea.

For a detailed look at Gaudí's life, visit the museum inside **La Pedrera** (Map pp928-9; ☎ 902 40 09 73; Carrer Provença 261; metro Diagonal; admission €7; ☾ 10am-8pm Mon-Sat), another Gaudí creation that ripples around the corner of Carrer Provença. Don't miss its surreal roof, which features some truly bizarre chimney pots; concerts are sometimes held here in summer.

Nearby is Gaudí's beautifully coloured **Casa Batlló** (Map pp928-9; ☎ 93 216 03 06; Passeig de Gràcia 43; metro Passeig de Gràcia; admission €10; ☾ 9am-8pm), an allegory for the legend of St George the dragon-slayer (Sant Jordi in Catalan). It's only recently been opened to the public. Next door is the **Casa Amatller** (Map pp928-9; Passeig de Gràcia 41), by another leading modernist architect, Josep Puig i Cadafalch. Now the office of the **Centre de Modernisme** (☎ 93 488 01 39; metro Passeig de Gràcia; ☾ 10am-7pm Mon-Sat, 10am-2pm Sun), this is the place for information about modernist buildings and tours.

Further afield is Gaudí's **Parc Güell** (☾ 10am-dusk), an enchanting outdoor park in which Dr Seuss would feel right at home. Gaudí designed it as a community that would have houses, schools and shops, but the project flopped, leaving this half-finished playground of tile mosaics and interesting organic shapes. The house where Gaudí lived for 20 years has been converted into the **Casa-Museum Gaudí** (☎ 93 219 38 11; metro Lesseps; admission €4; ☾ 10am-6pm Oct-Mar, 10am-8pm Apr-Sep), a museum about his life. Get here by metro (which involves a steep uphill climb) or on bus 24 from Plaça Universitat.

In El Raval district is the moody **Palau Güell** (Map p932; ☎ 93 317 39 74; Carrer Nou de la Rambla 3-5; metro Drassanes; adult/child €3/1.50; ☾ 10am-6pm Mon-Sat Mar-Oct, 10am-4pm Mon-Sat Nov-Feb), a house built by Gaudí in the late 1880s for his patron, the industrialist Eusebi Güell.

EL RAVAL

To the west of Las Ramblas is El Raval district, a once-seedy, now-funky area overflowing with cool bars and shops. Here is the **Museu d'Art Contemporani de Barcelona** (MACBA; Map p932; ☎ 93 412 08 10; Plaça dels Àngels 1; metro Plaça Catalunya; admission €3; ☾ 11am-7.30pm Tue-Sat, 10am-3pm Sun), near Plaça Catalunya, which has an impressive collection of international contemporary art.

LA RIBERA

East of the Barri Gòtic, La Ribera is a medieval barrio with some fascinating museums and architecture. You'll immediately see the throngs surrounding the **Museu Picasso** (Map p932; ☎ 93 319 63 10; Carrer Montcada 15-21; metro Jaume I; admission €5; ☾ 10am-8pm Tue-Sat, 10am-3pm Sun), home of the most important collection of Picasso's work in Spain – more than 3000 pieces. Most represent Picasso's Barcelona periods (1895–1900 and 1901–04) early in his career.

At the end of Carrer Montcada is the effortlessly elegant **Basílica de Santa Maria del Mar** (Map p932; metro Jaume I; ☾ 9.30am-1.30pm & 4.30-8pm), a stunning example of Catalan Gothic. All around here you'll find quirky shops and bars – it's a great area for strolling.

Don't miss the **Palau de la Música Catalana** (Map p932; ☎ 93 295 72 00; www.palaumusica.org; Carrer Sant Francesc de Paula 2; metro Urquinaona; admission €7; ☾ 10am-3.30pm Sep-Jul, 10am-6pm Aug), an unabashedly ornate modernist masterpiece designed by Lluis Domènech i Montaner in 1905. Concerts are held here regularly.

WATERFRONT

From the bottom of Las Ramblas you can cross the Rambla de Mar footbridge to the **Moll d'Espanya**, a former wharf in the old harbour, Port Vell. There you'll find **L'Aquàrium** (Map pp928-9; ☎ 93 221 74 74; Moll d'Espanya; metro Drassanes; adult/child €13.50/9.25; ☾ 9.30am-8pm), one of Europe's best (and more expensive) aquariums. Northeast of Port Vell, on the far side of the fishing-oriented La Barceloneta area, the city **beaches** begin. Along the beachfront, after 1.3km, you'll reach **Vila Olímpica**, site of the 1992 Olympic village, which is fronted by impressive **Port Olímpic**, a large marina with dozens of bars and restaurants. There are some fun nightspots and good restaurants here, but locals are few and far between.

Not far off the water is the **Parc de la Ciutadella** (Map pp928-9; metro Barceloneta; ☾ 8am-9pm), a large park ideal for strolling or picnics. The small city **zoo** (☎ 93 225 67 80; adult/child €12.90/8.20; ☾ 10am-dusk) is inside the park.

MONTJUÏC

The Central Park of Barcelona, this hill is the southwestern boundary of the city and is a great place to jog or stroll. There are amazing panoramic views of the city from the top. Public transport in the area

SPAIN

CENTRAL BARCELONA

SPAIN

0 _____ 200 m
0 _____ 0.1 miles

is limited; to get here, walk up from Plaça Espanya or wait for bus No 61. A more fun option is take the **funicular railway** (€3.20) from Paral·lel metro station or ride the **cable car** (Transbordador Aeri; €7.50) over from La Barceloneta.

Interesting attractions on Montjuïc include the following:

Museu Nacional d'Art de Catalunya (Map pp928–9; ☎ 93 622 03 75; Palau Nacional; admission €4.80; 10am-7pm Tue-Sat, 10am-2.30pm Sun) Catalan religious art.

Poble Espanyol (Spanish Village; Map pp928–9; ☎ 93 508 63 30; Avinguda Marquès de Comillas; admission €7; 9am-8pm Mon, 9am-late Tue-Sun) Craft and souvenir shops by day, nightclubs and restaurants by night.

Fundació Joan Miró (Map pp928–9; ☎ 93 443 94 70; Parc de Montjuïc; admission €7.20; 10am-7pm Tue-Sat, 10am-2.30pm Sun) Fantastic temple to modern art, with many Miró works.

Castell de Montjuïc (Map pp928–9; ☎ 93 329 86 13; admission €2.50; 9.30am-5.30pm Nov-Mar, 9.30am-8pm Apr-Oct) A small military museum and great views.

Tours

The **Bus Turístic** (☎ 93 423 18 00; adult/child €16/10; 9am-9.30pm) service covers two circuits (24 stops), linking virtually all the major tourist sights. Buy tickets on the bus or at the tourist office.

The main tourist office offers **walking tours** (€8) in English and Spanish/Catalan. Ask about times and details in the office.

Fat Tire Bike Tours (☎ 93 301 36 12; www.fattire biketoursbarcelona.com; metro Liceu; tours once daily Mar-Jul, Sep-Dec, twice daily Aug; tours €22-28) is just one of several companies leading two-wheeled tours of the city.

Festivals & Events

Barcelona's biggest festival is the **La Mercè**, a week-long, city-wide party on the days around 24 September. Another red-letter date on the calendar is **Sant Joan** (St John's Day, 23 July), when days of endless firecrackers welcome summer. In June and July the arts festival **El Grec** fills Barcelona with theatre, dance and music.

Sleeping

Accommodation in Barcelona is plentiful, but it can be expensive. Most hotels (threestarish) are in L'Eixample; many are huddled near the Plaça Catalunya. Cheaper *pensiones* and *hostales* are in the Barri Gòtic and El Raval, and though you'll pay up to €65 for a double (expensive for Spain), few have much charm to speak of.

HOSTELS

Alberg Palau (Map p932; ☎ 93 412 50 80; albergpalau@ champinet.com; Carrer Palau 6; metro Liceu; dm with shared bathroom €15-20, sheets €2;) Friendly, English-speaking staff run this modest hostel, where dorm-style rooms are cramped but clean. There's a kitchen for your use.

SPAIN

Alberg J New York (Map p932; ☎ 93 315 03 04; fax 93 319 53 25; Carrer d'En Cignas 6; metro Liceu; dm with shared bathroom €15-20; 🖳) This place is similar to Alberg Palau but has more rooms.

HOSTALES & PENSIONES

Pensión Calella (Map p932; ☎ 93 317 68 41; Carrer Calella 1; metro Liceu; s €21-26, d €40-46) Calella has just renovated its rooms; now most have baths and all are neat and comfortable, a feat for this price.

Pensión Avinyò (Map p932; ☎ 93 318 79 45; www .hostalavinyo.com; Carrer Avinyò 42; metro Liceu; d €38-56, s with shared bathroom €16-26, d with shared bathroom €26-42) Homy rooms all have ceiling fans and many have balconies.

Pensión Lausanne (Map p932; ☎ 93 302 11 39; Portal de l'Angel 24; metro Plaça Catalunya; s/d €57/87, without bathroom €40/60) Housed in a pretty, old modernist-style building, rooms boast soaring ceilings and attractive tile floors.

Hostal Morató (Map p932; ☎ 93 442 36 69; www .hostalmorato.com; Carrer Nou de la Rambla 50; metro Drassanes; s €25-35, d €50-70) This modern *hostal* is excellent value, with spotless rooms that try hard to be stylish. Some have private bathrooms.

Gat Raval (Map p932; ☎ 93 481 66 70; www .gataccommodation.com; Carrer Joaquim Costa 44; metro Sant Antoni; d €71, s/d with shared bathroom €39/54; 🖳) This is by far the coolest *hostal* in town, with well-equipped rooms and neon-green walls.

Gat Xino (Map p932; Carrer Hospital 149-55) A second branch of Gat Raval, this was about to open at the time of writing.

Hostal Eden (Map pp928-9; ☎ 93 452 66 20; www .hostaleden.net; Carrer Balmes 55; metro Passeig de Gràcia; s/d/tr/q €47/72/77/87, s/d with shared bathroom €30/47) In L'Eixample, this *hostal* offers charming but simple rooms; No 11 has a huge Jacuzzi!

Also recommended:

Pensión Alamar (Map p932; ☎ 93 302 50 12; Carrer Comtessa de Sobradiel 1; metro Liceu; s/d with shared bathroom €25/45) Great value, sociable atmosphere.

Hostal Benidorm (Map p932; ☎ 93 302 20 54; www .barcelona-on-line.es/benidorm; Las Ramblas 37; metro Liceu; s/d €29/45) Private bathrooms and a superb location.

Hostal Fontanella (Map p932; ☎ 93 317 59 43; Via Laietana 71; metro Urquinaona; s €38, d €55-65, s/d with shared bathroom €38/48) Cosy and well kept.

Pensión Mari-Luz (Map p932; ☎ 93 317 34 63; Carrer Palau 4; metro Liceu; d with shared bathroom €46-52) Bright and friendly.

HOTELS
Barri Gòtic & Around

Hotel Barcelona House (Map p932; ☎ 93 301 82 95; www.hotelbarcelonahouse.com; Carrer Escudellers 19; metro Liceu; s €29-39, d €55-72, tr €85-101) This hotel is two

---

HUMAN CASTLES

An element in nearly every Catalan festival is *castellers*, or human castle builders. The tradition – unique to Catalonia – is simple: competing teams try to build the biggest human pyramid possible, and whoever collapses first loses.

The origin of the *castels* is fuzzy; some say it started as a game, others speculate that it was a war technique to enter walled cities. These days, it's serious competition between towns and Barcelona barrios.

Each castle-building attempt begins when the clarinet-like *gralles* play. A tight mass of bodies (*pinya*) forms on the ground, and then the climbers start their work. Four men, their arms tightly interwoven, form the first level, and slowly others climb above them to construct the next levels. Each level has four bodies, their arms linked like the men's below them. The barefoot *castellers* use the hips, shoulders and heads of those below them as steps to make the tower grow ever higher. The top two levels are made by children. The idea is that they are smaller, lighter and have better balance than adults. Also, their bones won't break as easily should they fall, which happens often. The last child, called the *enxaneta* and treated as a local hero, is the most important part of the human castle because he or she is the one who declares the castle complete.

Supporters argue that the sport is less dangerous than a contact sport (it's true that few serious injuries are reported), but eight metres or more off the ground is never the safest place to be.

You can see *castellers* at most major festivals throughout Catalonia. The best teams are usually from the towns of Vilafranca del Penedès and Valls, both southwest of Barcelona. Every two years a huge *casteller* competition is held in early October in Tarragona's bullring. If you're in town then, it's definitely worth a day trip.

in one, with both a bare-boned, *hostal*-ish area and a newly renovated wing, where rooms (with breakfast) cost a little more. All have bathrooms and the basic comforts.

Hotel Rey Don Jaime I (Map p932; ☎ 93 310 62 08; r.d.jaime@atriumhotels.com; Carrer Jaume I 11; metro Jaume I; s €45, d €67-72) The spacious but spartan rooms are good value. Don't be offended by the staff; they're mean to everyone.

Hotel Banys Orientals (Map p932; ☎ 93 268 84 61; www.hotelbanysorientals.com; Carrer Argenteria 37; metro Jaume I; s €80, d €90-95) This chic hotel is a great choice, with spiffed-up rooms in an unbeatable location.

Also try:

Hotel Gaudí (Map p932; ☎ 93 317 90 32; Carrer Nou de la Rambla 12; metro Drassanes; s/d €95/130) Gaudí-inspired mosaics decorate the lobby.

Park Hotel (Map p932; ☎ 93 319 60 00; Avinguda Marquès de l'Argentera 11; metro Barceloneta; s/d €110/145) Breezy, Mediterranean style near the waterfront.

Racó del Pi (Map p932; ☎ 93 342 61 90; www.hotel racodelpi.com; Carrer Pi 7; metro Liceu; s/d €145/165) Style and charm near the Plaça del Pi.

L'Eixample

Hotel Pelayo (Map p932; ☎ 93 302 37 27; www.hotel pelayo.com; Carrer Pelai 9; s/d €60/80) Comfortable and great value, the Pelayo has cheery, light-filled rooms, modern bathrooms and a tasty breakfast.

Hotel Inglaterra (Map p932; ☎ 93 505 11 00; www .hotel-inglaterra.com; Carrer Pelai 14; metro Plaça Catalunya; s €99-160, d €119-200) With stylish rooms a stone's throw from Plaça Catalunya, this is a great choice.

APARTMENTS

Several private apartment-rental companies operate in Barcelona. These can often be a better deal than staying in a hotel, especially if you're travelling in a group. Try www .go2barcelona.com, www.inside-bcn.com or www.selfcateringhols.com.

Eating

Eating in Barcelona is a joy. There's a fantastic selection of regional, international and creative restaurants, ingredients are nearly always fresh, and it's still possible to get a nice meal without blowing your budget.

Typical dishes range from rice and shellfish paella, ubiquitous in the restaurants by the port, to hearty Catalan fare such as pigs' trotters, rabbit with snails and *butifarra* (a tasty local sausage). Lunch is served from 2pm to 3.30pm, and dinner begins at 9pm. In between, you can snack at bars or hunt out the touristy restaurants on Las Ramblas.

AROUND LAS RAMBLAS
Budget

Café de l'Òpera (Map p932; ☎ 93 317 75 85; Las Ramblas 74; metro Liceu; 😃 8.30-2.45am) A classic spot for breakfast or coffee, this once-high-class café is a little bruised nowadays but that just makes it all the more popular and atmospheric.

Buenas Migas (Map p932; ☎ 93 318 37 08; Plaça de Bonsuccés 6; metro Plaça Catalunya; mains €2.20-5; 😃 10am-11pm Sun-Wed, to midnight Thu-Sat) Try the focaccias and awesome desserts at this breezy footpath café.

Bagel Shop (Map p932; ☎ 93 302 41 61; Carrer Canuda 25; metro Liceu; mains €3.50-7; 😃 9.30am-9.30pm Mon-Sat, 11am-4pm Sun) For American-style bagels and desserts, there's no better place than this informal café off Las Ramblas.

Venus (Map p932; ☎ 93 301 15 85; Carrer Avinyò 25; metro Liceu; menú €8.50; 😃 noon-midnight Mon-Sat) Vegetarians will love the salad selection at this grungy-chic café.

Self-caterers can make a beeline for the wildly colourful **Mercat de la Boquería** (p930) for fresh food.

Mid-Range

Bar-Bodega Fortuny (Map p932; ☎ 93 317 98 92; Carrer Pintor Fortuny 31; metro Liceu; mains €4.50-9; 😃 10-2am Tue-Sun) This quirky bar serves salads, couscous and hummus to a largely bohemian group of regulars. At night it's a popular lesbian hang-out.

Bar Ra (Map p932; ☎ 93 301 41 63; Plaça Gardunya; metro Liceu; mains €6-9; 😃 9.30-1.30am) For light, international fare alfresco, head to this colourful bar/restaurant just behind the Mercat de la Boquería.

La Fonda (Map p932; ☎ 93 301 75 15; Carrer Escudellers 10; metro Drassanes; mains €7-12; 😃 1pm-3.30pm & 8.30-11.30pm) Mediterranean and traditional dishes are served with style at this popular eatery, where you'll almost always have to stand in line before nabbing a table.

Els Quatre Gats (Map p932; ☎ 93 302 41 40; Carrer Montsió 3; metro Urquinaona; menú €15-20; 😃 1pm-1am) The legendary modernist café where Picasso had his first exhibit, 'The Four Cats' now serves excellent (though pricey) Catalan dishes.

Top End

Los Caracoles (Map p932; ☎ 93 302 31 85; Carrer Escudellers 14; metro Liceu; mains €11-26; ⊗ 1pm-midnight) For truly traditional fare, don't miss this raucous Barcelona institution, where grilled meats, seafood and *caracoles* (snails) are the house specialities.

El Café de l'Acadèmia (Map p932; ☎ 93 319 82 53; Carrer Lledó 1; metro Jaume I; ⊗ 1pm-4pm & 8.45-11.30pm Mon-Fri, closed 15-31 Aug) This fine restaurant serves strictly Catalan dishes in a romantic atmosphere. If you're with a group, ask to sit in the downstairs bodega.

Taller de Tapas (Map p932; ☎ 93 301 80 20; Plaça Sant Josep Oriol 9; metro Liceu; mains €20-25; ⊗ 8pm-midnight) This is the place for tapas, Barcelona style. Creativity abounds in every bite.

LA RIBERA & LA BARCELONETA

Comme-Bio (Map p932; ☎ 93 319 89 68; Vía Laietana 28; menú €8.45; ⊗ 1pm-4pm & 8-11pm) At this casual restaurant it's not just vegetarian, it's organic. There's a shop here too.

Origins 99.9% (Map p932; ☎ 93 310 75 31; Carrer Vidriera 6-8; menú €12; ⊗ 12.30pm-1.30am) Also a shop-restaurant combo, Origins boasts that '99.9%' of everything sold is from Catalonia. The ever-changing daily *menú* features local specialities such as *escalivada* (roasted veggies on bread) and Catalan sausages.

Coses de Menjar (Map p932; ☎ 93 310 60 01; Pla de Palau 7; mains €8-16; ⊗ 1.30-3.45pm & 9-11.30pm) The wildly creative décor almost outshines the food at this fanciful eatery, where fresh twists are put on old Catalan recipes.

Comerç 24 (Map p932; ☎ 93 319 21 02; Carrer Comerç 24; metro Jaume; mains €14-20, menú €42; ⊗ 11.30am-4pm & 8.30pm-midnight) One of the best seafood choices. Get rice or seafood dishes overlooking the Med.

La Barceloneta is the place to go for seafood. Try one of the many excellent (and pricey) restaurants around the Plaça de Pau Vila or head to the Port Olímpic, where one of the better-priced restaurants is stylish **Agua** (Map pp928-9; ☎ 93 225 12 72; Passeig Marítim Barceloneta 30; metro Ciutadella-Vila Olímpica; mains €12-18).

L'EIXAMPLE

Laie Librería Café (Map p932; ☎ 93 302 73 10; Carrer Pau Claris 85; metro Passeig de Gràcia; mains €5-12; ⊗ 1am-1pm Tue-Sat, 1-9pm Mon) The delicious buffet and lunch *menú* is packed with healthy food, local specialities and vegetarian options.

Cervecería Catalana (Map pp928-9; ☎ 93 216 03 68; Carrer Mallorca 236; metro Passeig de Gràcia; tapas €2-12, mains €5-14; ⊗ 1pm-1am) Arrive early to try the delicious tapas and *flautas* (long 'skinny sandwiches') at this classic tavern off La Rambla de Catalunya.

La Flauta (Map pp928-9; ☎ 93 323 70 38; Carrer Aribau 23; metro Universitat; mains €5-14; ⊗ 9am-1am) Run by the same owners as Cervecería Catalana, La Flauta has the same classic *flautas* and tavern atmosphere.

L'Hostal de Rita (Map pp928-9; ☎ 93 487 23 76; Carrer Aribau 279; metro Passeig de Gràcia; mains €6-10, menú €7; ⊗ 10am-3.45pm & 8.30-11.30pm) For a bit of style, this popular restaurant does the trick. Be prepared to wait in line for samples of its pastas, seafood and traditional dishes.

Cacao Sampaka (Map p932; ☎ 93 272 08 33; Carrer Consell de Cent 292; metro Passeig de Gràcia; snacks €1.50-4; ⊗ 9am-8pm Mon-Sat) For dessert, hit this chocolate-lovers' paradise, where you can drool over more than a dozen varieties of chocolate ice cream.

Drinking

Whether you're in search of a quiet place to chat, drink in hand, or a smoky place with music that doesn't let you think, Barcelona's got an option for you. On weekends, bars stay hopping until 2am and most of the places listed here are open for quiet drinks as early as 8pm.

Muebles Navarro (Map p932; ☎ 60 718 80 96; Carrer Riera Alta 4; metro Liceu) Funky and decorated like a furniture flea market. Kick back with a cold one and one of its great cheese plates.

Lletraferit (Map p932; ☎ 93 301 19 61; Carrer Joaquim Costa 43; metro Sant Antoni) Just as chill but a bit more sophisticated, this is a book-lovers' café by day and a cocktail bar by night.

Rita Blue (Map p932; ☎ 93 342 40 86; Plaça Sant Agustí 3; metro Liceu) Upbeat restaurant and bar where everyone orders the house speciality, a blue margarita.

Philharmonic (☎ 93 451 11 53; Carrer Mallorca 204; metro Provença) One of Barcelona's most popular pubs. Stop in for all the football matches, some English conversation and a mouth-watering English breakfast.

Head to the Passeig del Born for a great selection of laid-back bars such as **Miramelindo** (Map p932; ☎ 93 319 53 76; Passeig del Born 15; metro Jaume I), a Barcelona favourite, and **La Vinya del Senyor** (Map p932; ☎ 93 310 33 97;

Plaça Santa Maria 5; metro Jaume I), a romantic wine bar sitting under the shadow of the Basilica.

The Gràcia district, with its intimate plazas and narrow streets, is the perfect spot for a quiet drink. The **Café del Sol** (Map pp928-9; ☎ 93 415 56 63; Plaça del Sol; metro Fontana) has a fantastic terrace for sipping outdoors, while **Gusto** (Map pp928-9; Carrer Francisco Giner 24; metro Fontana) offers a friendly atmosphere and some of the city's best DJs.

Entertainment
CINEMAS

The best original-language cinema is **Verdi** (Map pp928-9; ☎ 93 238 79 90; Carrer Verdi 32; metro Fontana), in Gràcia. Big-budget Hollywood flicks are shown in English at **Icària** (☎ 93 221 75 85; Carrer Salvador Espiritu 61; metro Vila Olímpica).

GAY & LESBIAN VENUES

The gay and lesbian scene is concentrated in the blocks around Carrers Muntaner and Consell de Cent (dubbed Gayxample by the locals). Here you'll find ambience every night of the week in the bars, discos and drag clubs.

Oui Café (Map pp928-9; Carrer Consell de Cent 247; metro Universitat) Has a sophisticated style and all-white décor reigns. A spiffy clientele comes for low-key drinks.

Party hard at classic gay discos such as **Arena Madre** (☎ 93 487 83 42; Carrer Balmes 32; metro Universitat; closed Mon) and **Salvation** (Map p932; ☎ 93 318 06 86; Ronda Sant Pere 19-21; metro Universitat; Fri-Sun).

The low-key **Bar-Bodega Fortuny** (p935) is a popular lesbian hang-out.

LIVE MUSIC

London Bar (Map pp928-9; ☎ 93 318 52 61; Carrer Nou de la Rambla 34; metro Drassanes) A popular expat hang-out, hosting concerts almost every night. Groups range from jazz to rock to flamenco.

Harlem Jazz Club (Map p932; ☎ 93 310 07 55; Carrer Comtessa de Sobradiel 8; metro Liceu) A guaranteed dose of quality jazz and enough smoke to cook a sausage.

Otto Zutz (Map pp928-9; ☎ 93 238 07 22; Carrer Lincoln 15; metro Fontana) Often has frontline acts.

Tablao Cordobés (Map p932; ☎ 93 317 57 11; Las Ramblas 35; metro Liceu) Though Barcelona is not the best place to see flamenco, you can catch a reasonably authentic show here.

CLUBS

For discos of every shape, size and variety, head to the Port Olímpic; in summer it's a nonstop party, and winter weekends are fun too.

Baja Beach Club (☎ 93 225 91 00; Passeig Marítim la Barceloneta 34; metro Ciutadella-Vila Olímpica; midnight-6am Thu-Sun) One of Port Olímpic's biggest clubs, where being tanned, beautiful and nearly topless seem to be requirements for entry.

Jamboree (Map p932; ☎ 93 319 17 89; Plaça Reial 17; 10.30pm-5am) Jumping with hip-hop music every night of the week, Jamboree is a magnet for foreign students. This could be a draw or a reason to flee, depending on your view.

Magic (Map p932; ☎ 93 310 72 67; Passeig Picasso 40; 11pm-6am Thu-Sun) One of the city's top clubs, with fantastic live music running the gamut between techno and classic rock.

SPORT

Football fans can see the Fútbol Club Barcelona play at **Camp Nou** (Map pp928-9; ☎ 93 496 36 00; www.fcbarcelona.com; Carrer Arístides Maillol; metro Collblanc). Even if you can't score tickets, stop by for a peek at the **museum** (☎ 93 496 36 08; gates 7 & 9; admission €5, tour €9; 10am-6.30pm Mon-Sat, 10am-2pm Sun).

THEATRE

Most theatre in the city is in Catalan, but there are quite a few that stage vanguard drama.

Teatre Nacional de Catalunya (☎ 93 306 57 00; Plaça de les Arts 1; metro Glòries) If you're up for a language lesson, check out the performances at this classy theatre.

La Fura Dels Baus (www.lafura.com) Anything performed anywhere by this wild troupe is bound to be funny and energetic and somewhat controversial. They manage to communicate without words, so language isn't a problem.

Shopping

Shops open Monday through Saturday from 10am until 2pm and again, after a long lunch, from 5pm until 8.30pm. The queen of Barcelona's shopping districts is the **Passeig de Gràcia** (metro Passeig de Gràcia), where high-end fashion struts its stuff. Chanel, Hermés and Cartier all have boutiques here, but fashionites without €5000 credit limits don't have to go home empty-handed. For unique clothing and shoes, browse the intimate shops in the mall-like **Boulevard Rosa** (Map pp928-9; ☎ 93 309 06 50; Passeig de Gràcia 53-57). If you like design you'll love gadget-happy **Vinçon** (Map pp928-9; ☎ 93 215 60 50; Passeig de Gràcia 96).

El Born (metro Jaume I), the city's original textile centre, is now a hot spot for up-and-coming designers. Try on the funky looks at shops such as **MTX Barcelona** (Map p932; ☎ 93 319 13 98; Carrer Rec 32).

Off Las Ramblas, the **Carrer Portaferrisa** (metro Liceu) has shops selling everything from punk fashion – **El Mercadillo** (Map p932; ☎ 93 301 47 04; Carrer Portaferrisa 17) – to melt-in-your-mouth Spanish *turrón* (nougat) at **Casa Colomina** (Map p932; ☎ 93 412 25 11; Carrer Portaferrisa 8). Nearby, there's a Saturday **art market** (Plaça Sant Josep Oriol) where you'll find prints and originals from local artists, while the connecting Plaça del Pi hosts an **artesan food fair** on alternating weekends.

Bargain hunters love **Els Encants** (☎ 93 246 30 30; Carrer Dos de Maig 186; metro Glòries), a free-for-all morning flea market.

Getting There & Away
AIR
Barcelona's airport, 14km southwest of the city centre at El Prat de Llobregat, caters to international as well as domestic flights. It's not a European hub, but you can often dig up specials and cheap youth fares. Airlines include Iberia, Air Europa, Spanair and easyJet (see p994 for contact details).

BUS
The terminal for virtually all domestic and international buses is the **Estació del Nord** (Map pp928-9; ☎ 93 265 65 08; Carrer Alí Bei 80; metro Arc de Triomf). Several buses a day go to most main Spanish cities, including Madrid, Zaragoza, Valencia and Granada.

CAR & MOTORCYCLE
The highways surrounding Barcelona are excellent, though traffic does build up from 8am to 9am, from 7pm to 10pm and on Friday and Saturday afternoons, when everyone hits the high road out of town. The A-7 motorway comes in from the French border, and the A-2 motorway heads toward Zaragoza. Both are toll roads. The N-II is a nontoll alternative, but it's slower and more dangerous.

TRAIN
Virtually all trains travelling to and from destinations within Spain stop at **Estació Sants** (Map pp928-9; metro Sants-Estació Barcelona). Daily trains run to most major cities in Spain. There are seven trains a day to -Madrid (six to nine hours), two daily to San Sebastián (eight to 10 hours), 10 daily to Valencia (three hours or more), and one daily to Granada (eight to 10 hours). Tickets and information are available at the station.

Getting Around
TO/FROM THE AIRPORT
Trains link the airport to Estació Sants and **Catalunya regional train station** (Plaça Catalunya) every half-hour (€2.25, 15 to 20 minutes). The Aerobus (€3.75, 40 minutes) does the run between Plaça Catalunya and the airport every 15 minutes, or every half-hour at weekends. A taxi from the airport to Plaça Catalunya is around €15 to €20.

CAR & MOTORCYCLE
Parking a car is difficult and, if you choose a parking garage, quite expensive (€20 per day). It's better to ditch your car and rely on public transport.

PUBLIC TRANSPORT
Barcelona's metro system spreads its tentacles around the city in such a way that most places of interest are within a 10-minute walk of a station. Buses and suburban trains are needed only for a few destinations. A single metro, bus or suburban train ride costs €1.10, but a T-1 ticket, valid for 10 rides, costs only €6.

TAXI
Barcelona's black-and-yellow taxis are plentiful, reasonably priced and handy for late-night transport. Flag fall is €1.30.

MONESTIR DE MONTSERRAT
The prime attraction of Montserrat, 50km northwest of Barcelona, is its incredible setting. The **Benedictine Monastery** of Montserrat sits high on the side of a 1236m-high mountain of weird, bulbous peaks. The monastery was founded in 1025 after a statue of the Virgin Mary was found here. Pilgrims still come from all over Christendom to pay homage to the Black Virgin (La Moreneta), a 12th-century wooden sculpture

of Mary, regarded as Catalonia's patroness. The statue stands in the basilica's altar, where the faithful line up to kiss it. Mass is held several times daily; at the 1pm mass Monday to Saturday the monastery boy choir sings.

Montserrat's **information centre** (☎ 93 877 77 77; ⊕ 10am-6pm) is to the left along the road from the top cable-car station. It has a couple of good free leaflets and maps on the mountain and monastery, as well as information about the **Museu de Montserrat** (admission €5.50; ⊕ 10am-7pm Mon-Fri, 9.30am-7.30pm Sat & Sun).

Sleeping & Eating

There are several accommodation options at the **monastery** (all ☎ 93 877 77 01; www.abadia montserrat.net). The cheapest rooms are in the **Cel.les Abat Olibia** (d from €25), blocks of simple apartments, with showers, for up to 10 people. Overlooking Plaça Santa Maria is the comfortable and excellent-value **Hotel Abat Cisneros** (s €27-50, d €45-82). The **restaurant** (menú €19) here is miles better than the cafeteria down the mountain.

Getting There & Away

The FGC R5 train runs from Barcelona's Plaça Espanya to both Aeri de Montserrat (one hour, 19 daily), where you can catch a cable car up the mountain, and to Monistrol-Vila, where you can hop on a rack railway to head up. The combined return ticket is €11.40.

GIRONA & THE COSTA BRAVA

The rocky, rugged scenery of the Costa Brava has made this once-sleepy, now-sizzling area one of Spain's most popular holiday spots. The main jumping-off points for the Costa Brava are the inland towns of Girona (Gerona in Castilian) and Figueres. Along the coast, the most appealing resorts are (from north to south) Cadaqués, L'Escala (La Escala), Tamariu, Llafranc, Calella de Palafrugell and Tossa de Mar.

Ask for regional information at any of the number of **tourist offices** (⊕ 10am-1pm & 4-7pm Mon-Sat, 10am-1pm Sun, 9am-9pm daily Jul-Aug; Girona ☎ 97 220 84 01; www.costabrava.org; Carrer Emili Grahit 13-15; Figueres ☎ 97 250 31 55; www.figueresciu-tat.com; Plaça del Sol; Palafrugell ☎ 97 261 18 20; www.palafrugell.net; Plaça de l'Església) in the towns around the area.

Sights & Activities
COASTAL RESORTS & ISLANDS

The Costa Brava (Rugged Coast) is all about picturesque inlets and coves. Beaches tend to be small and scattered. Some longer beaches at places such as L'Estartit and Empúries are worth visiting off season, but there has been a tendency to build tall buildings wherever engineers think it can be done. Fortunately, in many places it just can't.

Cadaqués, one hour's drive east of Figueres, at the end of an agonising series of hairpin bends, is perhaps the most picturesque of all Spanish resorts. It's haunted by the memory of former resident Salvador Dalí, whose house is nearby. Beaches here are of the pebbly variety, so people spend a lot of time sitting at waterfront cafés or wandering along the beautiful coast. Some 10km northeast of Cadaqués is **Cap de Creus**, a rocky mountain park where you can hike and visit a **monastery**.

Further down the coast, past L'Escala and L'Estartit, is Palafrugell. Though the town has little to offer, it's near three gorgeous beach towns that have to be seen to be believed. The most northerly of these, **Tamariu**, is also the smallest, least crowded and most exclusive. **Llafranc** is the biggest and busiest, and has the longest beach. **Calella de Palafrugell**, with its truly picture-postcard setting, is never overcrowded and always relaxed.

Among the most exciting attractions on the Costa Brava are the **Illes Medes**, off the coast from the package resort of L'Estartit. These seven islets and their surrounding coral reefs have been declared a natural park to protect their extraordinarily diverse flora and fauna. Diving is popular here. Ask at the tourist offices for details.

OTHER ATTRACTIONS

When you have had enough beach for a while, make sure you put the **Teatre-Museu Dalí** (☎ 97 252 28 00; Plaça Gala i Salvador Dalí 5, Figueres; admission €9, incl admission to other Dalí sites; ⊕ 10.30am-5.45pm Oct-Jun, 9am-7.45pm Jul-Sep) at the top of your list. This 19th-century theatre was converted by Dalí himself and houses a huge and fascinating collection of his strange creations. You can also visit Dalí's home, now a **museum** (☎ 97 225 10 15; Portlligat; admission €8; ⊕ 10.30am-6pm Oct-May, 10.30am-9pm Jun-Sep) near Cadaqués.

Girona sports a lovely, though tiny, medieval quarter centred on a Gothic cathedral.

SPAIN

For a stroll through antiquity, check out the ruins of the Greek and Roman town of **Empúries**, 2km from L'Escala.

Sleeping & Eating

Most visitors to the Costa Brava rent apartments. If you are interested in renting your own pad for a week or so, contact local tourist offices in advance.

Seaside restaurants provide dramatic settings but often at high prices and numerous food stalls and cafés cluster in all three towns.

FIGUERES

Avoid sleeping in Figueres' Parc Municipal – people have been attacked here at night.

Pensión Mallol (☎ 97 250 22 83; Carrer Pep Ventura 9; s/d with shared bathroom €16/28) This has simple, no-frills rooms.

Pensión Isabel II (☎ 97 250 47 35; Carrer Isabel II 16; s/d €22/28) More comfortable than Mollol and with private bathrooms.

Restaurant Versalles (☎ 97 250 00 02; Carrer Jonquera 18; mains €5-15) Local cuisine away from the noise and high prices of the main plaza.

GIRONA

Alberg de Joventut (☎ 97 221 80 03; www.tujuca .com; Carrer Ciutadans 9; dm with shared bathroom €14-19) Offers standard HI fare.

Pensión Viladomat (☎ 97 220 31 76; Carrer Ciutadans 5; d with shared bathroom €35) Comfortable rooms.

Dine on Girona's Rambla for good people watching. **Arts Café** (La Rambla 23) offers a low-key atmosphere and cheap, snacky fare.

CADAQUÉS

Hostal Marina (☎ 97 225 81 99; Carrer Riera 3; s/d €35/50) Sunny, cheerful rooms.

AROUND PALAFRUGELL

Hotel and *pensión* rooms are relatively thin on the ground here, as many people come on package deals.

Hostería del Plancton (☎ 97 261 50 81; Calella de Palafrugell; r from €18; ☿ Jun-Sep) Friendly and one of the best deals on the Costa Brava.

Hotel Montaña (☎ 97 230 12 91; Carrer Cesàrea 2, Llafranc; r from €78) A good deal, though pricey in summer.

Getting There & Away

A few buses run daily from Barcelona to Tossa del Mar, L'Estartit and Cadaqués for a couple of euros, but for the small resorts near Palafrugell you need to get to Girona first. Girona and Figueres are both on the railway connecting Barcelona to France. The dozen or so trains daily from Barcelona to Portbou at the border all stop in Girona (€5.10, 1¼ hours), and most in Figueres (€7.30 to €8.40, one hour and 40 minutes).

TARRAGONA

Founded in 218 BC, Tarraco was an important Roman centre and the capital of Hispania. Roman structures figure among its most important attractions and the city is fascinating place to visit. Good beaches, a nearby theme park and a large student population keep the city from dwelling too much on its past.

Orientation & Information

Tarragona's main street is Rambla Nova, which runs northwest from a cliff top overlooking the Mediterranean. There is Internet access at **Café Cantonada** (☎ 97 721 35 24; Carrer Fortuny 23; ☿ 10-2am) and the **main tourist office** (☎ 97 725 07 95; Carrer Major 39; ☿ 10am-2pm & 4-7pm Mon-Sat, 10am-2pm Sun) has maps and accommodation information.

Sights & Activities

Start at the fascinating **Museu Arqueològic** (☎ 97 723 62 09; Plaça del Rei 5; admission €2.40; ☿ 10am-1.30pm & 4-7pm Tue-Sat, 10am-2pm Sun Oct-May, 10am-8pm Tue-Sat, 10am-2pm Sun Jun-Sep), where you'll get an excellent understanding of Roman Spain.

Nearby is the **Museu de la Romanitat**, formed by the **Castell del Rei** (☎ 97 724 19 52) and the **Roman Circus**. The Castell once formed part of the city walls. You can head to the top for views and then see the ruins of the Roman Circus, where chariot races were held.

Nearby, and close to the beach, is the well-preserved **Roman amphitheatre**, where gladiators battled each other (or unlucky souls were thrown to wild animals) to the death. On Carrer Lleida, a few blocks west of Rambla Nova, are the remains of a **Roman forum**. The **Passeig Arqueològic** (☿ until midnight) is a peaceful walk along a stretch of the old city walls, which are a combination of Roman, Iberian and 17th-century British efforts.

The **cathedral** sits grandly at the highest point of Tarragona, overlooking the old

TARRAGONA

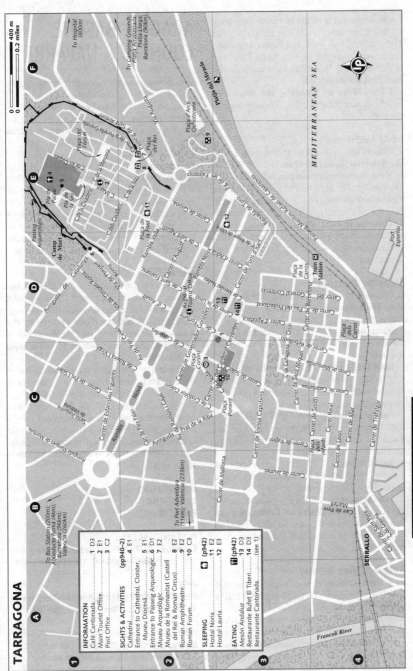

INFORMATION
Café Cantonada....................	1 D3
Main Tourist Office...............	2 E1
Post Office..........................	3 C2

SIGHTS & ACTIVITIES (pp940–2)
Cathedral............................	4 E1
Entrance to Cathedral, Cloister,	
Museu Diocesà..................	5 E1
Entrance to Passeig Arqueològic..	6 D1
Museu Arqueològic...............	7 E2
Museu de la Romanitat (Castell	
del Rei & Roman Circus).....	8 E2
Roman Amphitheatre............	9 E2
Roman Forum.......................	10 C3

SLEEPING (p942)
Hostal Noria.........................	11 E2
Hostal Lauria........................	12 E3

EATING (p942)
Mesón Andaluz...................	13 D3
Restaurante Bufet El Tiberi...	14 D3
Restaurante Cantonada........	(see 1)

To Bus Station (200m);
Aqüeducte Romà (4km);
Barcelona (90km);
Valencia (260km)

To Port Aventura
(11km); Valencia (233km)

To Hospital
(200m)

To Camping Grounds;
Platja Arrabassada;
Platja Llarga;
Barcelona (90km)

MEDITERRANEAN SEA

Francolí River

SERRALLO

Platja del Miracle

Port Esportiu

Train Station

town. Some parts of the building date back to the 12th century. It's open for tourist visits during the week but hours vary with the season (longest in summer). Entrance is through the beautiful cloister with the excellent **Museu Diocesà**.

Clean **Platja del Miracle** is the main city beach; it sits south of the Roman amphitheatre.

PORT AVENTURA
Around 7km west of Tarragona, near Salou, the **Universal Studios Port Aventura** (☎ 97 777 90 90; www.universalmediterranea.com; adult/child €35/28; ⏱ 10am-7pm Apr-Oct, summer hrs longer but vary, open Sat & Sun only Nov-Mar) is a US-style theme park, fun for the family or the young at heart. Trains run to Port Aventura's own station, which is about a 1km walk from the site, several times a day from Tarragona and Barcelona.

Sleeping & Eating
If you intend to stay in Tarragona in summer, it's advisable to call ahead to book a room.

Hostal Noria (☎ 97 723 87 17; Plaça de la Font 53; s/d with shared bathroom €20/32) Good value but is often full.

Hotel Lauria (☎ 97 723 67 12; Rambla Nova 20; s/d €37/55) This three-star hotel is a worthwhile splurge with a wonderful location, a pool and airy rooms.

Restaurant Bufet El Tiberi (☎ 97 723 54 03; Carrer Martí d'Ardenya 5; buffet €9-10; ⏱ 1pm-3.30pm Tue-Sun) Solid Catalan food at this restaurant offering an all-you-can-eat buffet.

Mesón Andaluz (☎ 97 723 84 19; Carrer Pons d'Icart 3; menú €8; ⏱ closed Sun) A local favourite with a good three-course menú.

Café Cantonada (p940) is a popular place for tapas; next door, **Restaurant Cantonada** (mains from €5) has pizza and pasta. Rambla Nova has several good places, either for a snack or a meal.

Getting There & Away
The train station is southwest of the old town, on the coast. Over 20 regional trains a day run from Barcelona to Tarragona. There are about 12 trains daily to Madrid and from Tarragona to Valencia.

The **bus station** (Avinguda Roma), just off Plaça Imperial Tarraco, has services to regional cities such as Barcelona, and beyond.

ARAGÓN, BASQUE COUNTRY & NAVARRA

The Basque Country is a privileged region, with a rugged coast dotted with fishing villages and surfing beaches, and a lusciously green interior. The grand city of San Sebastián crowns the coast, and nearby Bilbao can claim one of the world's greatest museums as its own.

Navarra, linked historically with the Basque Country, is a fantastic wine region, though it's probably best known as the home of the wild San Fermíne festival. Aragón differs culturally and geographically from its two northern neighbours. A proud, stern land, Aragón has fascinating mountain scenery and an interesting capital in Zaragoza.

ZARAGOZA
Founded by the all-too-modest Caesar Augustus as the Roman city Caesaragusta, Zaragoza later became a Muslim stronghold, and its influence can be seen in the widespread use of brick as a building material and in the abundance of *Mudéjar*-style architecture.

These days Zaragoza, the proud capital of once-mighty Aragón, is a largely industrial city. Its shining light is the Basílica del Pilar, a fairy-tale creation beside the Ebro River. Surrounding the basilica are the twisted streets of El Tubo and the Casco Histórico (Historic Quarter), providing ideal places to wander among Roman ruins, shady plazas and tasty tapas bars.

Information
EMERGENCY
Police (☎ 091)

INTERNET ACCESS
Conecta-T (☎ 97 620 59 79; Calle Murallas Romanas 4; per hr €1.20; ⏱ 10am-11pm Mon-Fri, 11am-11pm Sat & Sun)

POST
Post office (☎ 97 623 68 68; Paseo de la Independencia 33; ⏱ 8.30am-8.30pm Mon-Fri, 9.30am-2pm Sat)

TOURIST INFORMATION
Main tourist office (☎ 97 620 12 1200 or 902 20 12 1212; www.turismozaragoza.com; Plaza del Pilar; ⏱ 10am-8pm) Housed in a futuristic glass cube.

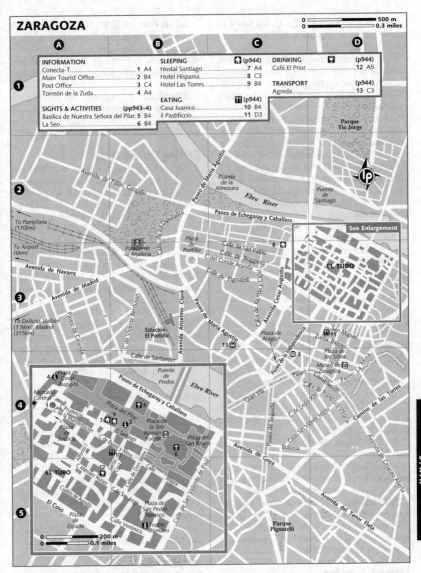

ZARAGOZA

INFORMATION
Conecta-T.................................1 A4
Main Tourist Office....................2 B4
Post Office................................3 C4
Torreón de la Zuda....................4 A4

SIGHTS & ACTIVITIES (pp943–4)
Basílica de Nuestra Señora del Pilar.5 B4
La Seo.....................................6 B4

SLEEPING (p944)
Hostal Santiago.......................7 A4
Hotel Hispania........................8 C3
Hotel Las Torres......................9 B4

EATING (p944)
Casa Juanico..........................10 B4
il Pastificcio..........................11 D3

DRINKING (p944)
Café El Prior..........................12 A5

TRANSPORT (p944)
Agreda..................................13 C3

Torreón de la Zuda tourist office (☎ 902 201 212; Glorieta Pio 12 or Ave César Agusto; ⏰ 10am-2pm & 4.30-8pm) Climb to the top for a small exhibition about Zaragoza and a view of the river bank.

Sights

Roman, *Mudéjar* and baroque architecture are beautifully combined in Zaragoza, and strolling past the varied building styles is a pleasant way to spend a day or two.

Towering over the city is **Basílica de Nuestra Señora del Pilar** (Plaza del Pilar; ⏰ 5.45am-8.30pm Sep-Jun, 5.45am-9.30pm Jul & Aug), 17th-century baroque basilica of epic proportions. The spiritual heart of Zaragoza, the basilica crowns the sprawling Plaza of the same name. People flock to the **Capilla Santa** to kiss a piece of marble pillar believed to have been left by the Virgin Mary when she visited St James here in AD 40. A beloved statue of the Virgin sits atop the pillar, and her ornate skirt is changed every single day. Inside the Basilica, you can visit the **Museo Pilarista** (admission €1.50, ☼ 9am-2pm & 4-6pm), where a few of these lavish skirts are on display.

At the plaza's southeastern end is Zaragoza's brooding 12th- to 16th-century cathedral, **La Seo** (Plaza de La Seo; admission €2; ☼ 10am-2pm & 4-6pm Tue-Fri, 10am-1pm & 4-6pm Sat, 10am-noon & 4-6pm Sun, 1hr later summer). Its northwestern façade is a *Mudéjar* masterpiece, and inside is an impressive 15th-century main altarpiece in coloured alabaster.

The odd trapezoid structure in front of La Seo looks like the Louvre, but actually it's the entrance to the **Museo del Foro de Caesaraugusta** (☎ 97 639 97 52; Plaza de La Seo; admission €2; ☼ 10am-2pm & 5-8pm Tue-Sat, 10am-2pm Sun), an interesting museum about Roman life. Some 70m below lie the remains of Roman shops, porticoes and a great sewerage system, all brought to life by an audiovisual show.

Sleeping

Many cheap rooms are found near the Plaza del Pilar.

Hostal Santiago (☎ 97 639 45 50; Calle Santiago 3-5; s €20-25, d €30-36; ✺) Neon-green walls add an original touch to the otherwise standard *hostal*. The 26 rooms are cheerful and comparatively spacious.

Hotel Las Torres (☎ 97 639 42 50; torres@able.es; Plaza del Pilar 11; s/d from €41/55) For comfort and awesome basilica views, head here, where the basilica's lovely chimes will wake you bright and early. Rooms are dated but spotless.

Hotel Hispania (☎ 97 628 49 28; www.hotelhispania.com; Ave Augusto 95-103; s €33-47, d €47-70; ▯ ✿) This is a newly refurbished place with stylish, spacious quarters, gym and pool access (you pay extra) and tasteful décor.

Eating & Drinking

Good tapas bars are scattered around El Tubo, especially around Plaza Santa Marta, and in La Zona, a trendy area south of the centre.

Casa Juanico (☎ 97 639 72 52; Calle Santa Cruz 21; menú €9) For cheap tapas and a friendly atmosphere, this place can't be beat, and the summer terrace is ideal.

Café El Prior (☎ 97 620 11 48; Calle Santa Cruz 7; mains €4-8; ☼ closed Wed) Housed in a 16th-century palace and serving tasty Aragonés dishes such as *ternasco* (lamb's ribs) and *migas* (fried breadcrumbs). Has a pub downstairs.

Il Pastificcio (☎ 97 623 66 62; Calle Zurita 15; mains €9-10; ☼ 1pm-4pm & 8pm-midnight) Vegetarians will find plenty at this Italian bistro where dishes are always tasty and big enough to share.

Getting There & Away

Zaragoza's new train station, Las Delicias (opened in May 2003), offers connections throughout Spain. The high-speed AVE train connects Zaragoza with Madrid (€43, four daily, 11 non-AVE daily) in under two hours and with the pre-Pyrenean city of Lleida (€24, one hour, four daily, 15 non-AVE daily). Other trains head to Barcelona (€34, three hours, 15 daily), Valencia via Teruel (€16.45, six hours, three daily) and San Sebastián (€26.50, four hours, three daily) via Pamplona.

Though construction is underway on Las Delicias bus terminal, which will one day be the city's one-stop bus stop, currently stations are scattered all over town. **Agreda** (☎ 97 622 93 43; www.agredasa.com) runs to most major Spanish cities, including Madrid (€12.09, four hours, 18 daily) from Paseo María Agustín 7.

SAN SEBASTIÁN

San Sebastián (Donostia in Basque) is a grand old dame, a fashionable seaside resort that looks good and knows it. The clean-swept footpaths and orderly boulevards hug the Bahía de la Concha, where the perfectly shell-shaped Playa de la Concha shimmers. The buzzing Parte Vieja (Old Quarter) is crammed with tempting tapas bars and restaurants showing off the best of Basque cuisine.

Information

Donosti-Net (☎ 94 342 94 97; Calle San Jerónimo 8; Internet per hr €3; ☼ 9am-11pm) This is a one-stop travellers' service, with email, office services and even a spot to leave your luggage (per day €9).
Police (☎ 091)
Tourist office (☎ 94 348 11 66; www.sansebastianturismo.com; Calle Reina Regente 3; ☼ 8am-8pm daily Jun-Sep, 9am-1.30pm & 3.30-7pm Mon-Sat, 10am-2pm Sun Oct-May)

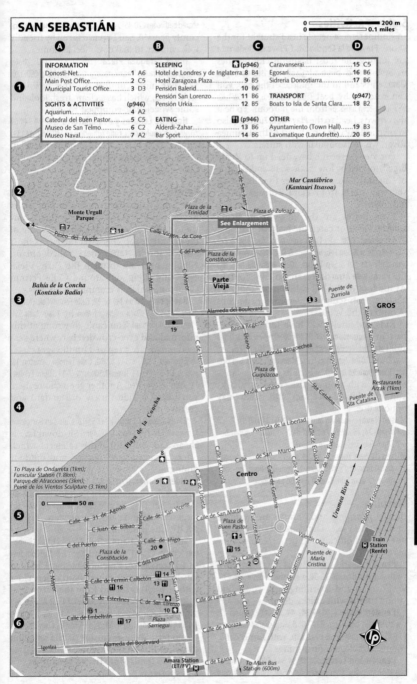

SAN SEBASTIÁN

0 — 200 m
0 — 0.1 miles

A   **B**   **C**   **D**

INFORMATION		SLEEPING	(p946)	Caravanserai	15 C5
Donosti-Net	1 A6	Hotel de Londres y de Inglaterra	8 B4	Egosari	16 B6
Main Post Office	2 C5	Hotel Zaragoza Plaza	9 B5	Sidreria Donostiarra	17 B6
Municipal Tourist Office	3 D3	Pensión Balerid	10 B6		
		Pensión San Lorenzo	11 B6	TRANSPORT	(p947)
SIGHTS & ACTIVITIES	(p946)	Pensión Urkia	12 B5	Boats to Isla de Santa Clara	18 B2
Aquarium	4 A2				
Catedral del Buen Pastor	5 C5	EATING	(p946)	OTHER	
Museo de San Telmo	6 C2	Alderdi-Zahar	13 B6	Ayuntamiento (Town Hall)	19 B3
Museo Naval	7 A2	Bar Sport	14 B6	Lavomatique (Laundrette)	20 B5

Mar Cantábrico (Kantauri Itsasoa)

Monte Urgull Parque

Plaza de la Trinidad

Plaza de Zuloaga

Calle de San Juan

See Enlargement

Paseo del Muelle

Calle Virgen de Coro

C del Puerto

Plaza de la Constitución

Parte Vieja

Paseo de Salamanca

Puente de Zurriola

Bahía de la Concha (Kontxako Badia)

C de Mari

C Mayor

C de Aldamar

Paseo Nuevo

GROS

Paseo de Ramón María Lili

Alameda del Boulevard

Reina Regente

Easo

Puente de Sta Catalina

To Restaurante Arzak (1km)

Plaza de Guipúzcoa

C de Hernani

Peñaflorida Bengoechea

Andía, Camino

Sta Catalina

Paseo de la República Argentina

Playa de la Concha

Avenida de la Libertad

Calle de San Marçal

Calle de Urbieta

Calle de Loyola

Centro

Calle de Garibay

Calle de Vergara

Calle de Etxaide

Paseo de los Arboles

Urumea River

Paseo de Francia

*To Playa de Ondarreta (1km);
Funicular Station (1.8km);
Parque de Atracciones (3km);
Peine de los Vientos Sculpture (3.1km)*

0 — 50 m

Calle de 31 de Agosto

C Juan de Bilbao

Calle de Narrica

Calle de San Vicente

Calle de Iñigo

C del Puerto

Plaza de la Constitución

C dela Pescadería

Calle de San Martin

Plaza de Buen Pastor

Calle de Fuenterrabia

Train Station (Renfe)

C Mayor

Calle San Jerónimo

Calle de Fermín Calbetón

C de Esterlines

C de San Lorenzo

Calle de Embeltrán

Plaza Sarriegui

Igentea

Alameda del Boulevard

C de San Juan

Calle de Larramendi

Calle de los Reyes Católicos

Calle de Moraza

Urdaneta Calle de

Calle de Prim

Valentín Olano

Puente de María Cristina

Amara Station (ET/FV)

C de Egaña

To Main Bus Station (600m)

SPAIN

LP

Sights & Activities

In summer, most people head straight for the shore. **Playa de la Concha** and **Playa de Ondarreta** are among the most beautiful city beaches in Spain, and beyond them is **Isla de Santa Clara**, an island in the middle of the bay; you can reach it by **boat** (adult/child return €2.60/1.30; 10am-8pm Jun-Sep) from the harbour. To beat the crowds, head to the **Playa de la Zurriola** (also known as Playa de Gros), east of the Urumea River, which is popular with surfers.

For views over the bay, head up to **Monte Urgull**, topped by low castle walls and a statue of Christ. It takes 30 minutes to walk up – a stairway starts from Plaza Zuloaga in the old town.

Even better are the views from **Monte Igueldo**. Drive or catch the **funicular** (94 321 05 64; return €1.60; 11am-6pm Mon, Tue, Thu & Fri, 11am-8pm Sat & Sun Feb, Mar, Nov & Dec, closed Wed, until 8pm daily Apr-Jun & Sep 15-Oct, 10am-10pm Jul-Aug) to the **Parque de Atracciones**, an old-time funfair. At the foot of the hill is Eduardo Chillida's abstract iron sculpture *Peine de los Vientos* (Comb of the Winds).

Kids and adults will have fun at San Sebastián's **aquarium** (94 344 00 99; www.aquariumss .com; Paseo del Muelle 34; admission €9; 10am-8pm Sep, May & Jun, 10am-7pm Mon-Fri & 11am-8pm Sat & Sun Oct-Apr, 10am-9pm Jul & Aug), which has 10 large tanks teeming with tropical fish, morays, sharks and other finned creatures. Other rainy-day options are:

Museo Naval (Seafaring Museum; 94 343 00 51; Paseo del Muelle 24; adult/child €1.20/free; 10am-1.30pm & 4-7.30pm Tue-Sat, 11am-2pm Sun)

Museo de San Telmo (94 348 15 80; Plaza Zuloaga 1; admission free; 10.30am-1.30pm & 4-8pm Tue-Sat, 10.30am-1.30pm Sun) Lots of Basque paintings.

Sleeping

Budget *pensiones* and *hostales* are huddled in the Parte Vieja. There are lots of options, but they fill quickly and get pricey in summer.

Pensión Balerid (94 342 68 14; Calle San Juan 1; s with shared bathroom €18-30, d with shared bathroom €35-50) Cheerful and charming, here you'll find sunny rooms with quirky décor.

Pensión Urkia (94 342 44 36; Calle Urbieta 12; s with shared bathroom €23-30, d with shared bathroom €33-45) This is a fine *pensión*, with impeccable rooms and elegant furnishings.

Pensión San Lorenzo (94 342 55 16; www.info negocio.com/pensionsanlorenzo; Calle San Lorenzo 2; r with shared bathroom €20-45) Another modest but clean, comfy *pensión*, San Lorenzo is run by friendly folk who try to make you feel at home.

Hotel Zaragoza Plaza (94 345 21 03; hotel zaragoza@terra.es; Plaza Zaragoza 3; s €48-108, d €60-120;) For more comfort, try this business-style hotel, which has a clean, fresh look and some wheelchair-equipped rooms.

Hotel de Londres y de Inglaterra (94 344 07 70; www.hlondres.com; Calle Zubieta 2; s €110-169, d €131-202;) Hands down the best hotel in town, this is a classy place offering breath-taking views of the bay.

Eating

San Sebastián's gastronomy is one of its major draws, and the city is a culinary centre for all of Spain, giving birth to some of the country's top chefs. Yet the city is most known for its tapas, here called *pinxos*. Nibble your way through the Parte Vieja, especially along and around Calle Fermín Calbetón, which is crammed with bars.

Bar Sport (94 342 68 88; Calle Fermín Calbetón 10; pinxos €1-5; 9am-midnight Mon-Fri, 10am-1am Sat, 11am-midnight Sun) You can't go wrong at this informal and ever-crowded bar, where seafood *pinxos* are prepared on the spot.

Egosari (94 342 82 10; Calle Fermín Calbetón 15; pinxos €1-5; 11.30am-3.30pm & 7-11.30pm Fri-Tue, 11.30am-3.30pm Wed) Another good choice, here you'll find a wide variety of standard and creative *pinxos*.

Caravanserai (94 347 54 18; Calle San Bartolome 1; mains €5-8; 1-4pm & 8-11pm) Sit-down fare is cheap and abundant at this caféteria, which offers a 'vegetarians' corner' and outdoor dining.

Alderdi-Zahar (94 342 52 54; Calle Fermín Calbetón 9; mains €9-15; menú €11; 1pm-3.30pm & 8.30-11pm Tue-Sat) This simple restaurant serves up local seafood and hardy Basque fare. Try the good-value lunch *menú*.

Sidrería Donostiarra (94 342 04 21; Calle Embeltran 5; mains €5.50-17; 1pm-3.30pm & 8-10.30pm Tue-Sat, 1-3.30pm Sun) For a memorable meal, head to this homely tavern, where hard cider (cider with alcohol) is served from the barrel.

Restaurante Arzak (94 327 84 65; Alto de Miracruz 21; mains €44-59, menú €99; 1.30pm-4pm & 9-11pm Wed-Sun) Juan Maria Arzak, the 'father of modern Spanish cuisine' is the chef and owner of this fabulous, three-Michelin-star temple to food. More than a restaurant, it's an experience.

Entertainment

The Parte Vieja is a fun place to be nearly every night of the week. Around 8pm the tapas bars start hopping as people enjoy a pre-dinner round of *pinxos*, and the revelry lasts until midnight midweek and until the cock crows on weekends. A more mature crowd fills the bars around Calle Reyes Católicos, behind the Cathedral del Buen Pastor.

Getting There & Away

From the airport, catch the CIA Interbus that runs every 20 to 30 minutes to the Plaza Gipuzkoa in town (€1.40).

The **Renfe station** (Paseo de Francia) is across the river. There are daily trains to Madrid (€33, eight hours, four daily), Barcelona (€33.50 to €42.50, eight to 10 hours, two daily) and Pamplona (€16, two hours, three daily).

Eusko Tren is a private company (international passes not valid) running trains around the region.

The **bus station** (Plaza Pío XII) is a 20-minute walk south of the Parte Vieja; ticket offices are along the streets north of the station. Buses leave for destinations all over Spain. **PESA** (☎ 90 210 12 10) has services to Bilbao (€7.75, up to one hour, 27 daily), while La Roncalesa goes to Pamplona (€5.60, 1¼ hours, eight daily).

BILBAO

Straddling the Ría Bilbao and surrounded by green mountains on all sides, Bilbao is a spirited city in the midst of the beautiful Basque countryside. Most people who come here limit their visit to one thing: the Guggenheim Museum, Frank Gehry's master-piece of modern architecture and one of the best modern-art museums in the world. But this evocative city has a lot more to offer. The Casco Viejo (Old Quarter) is full of funky shops and traditional cafés, and smaller museums scattered about town are worth visiting too.

Information

Police (☎ 092 or 94 420 50 00; Calle Luis Briñas 14)
Postal Transfer (☎ 94 415 30 42; Calle Santa Maria 5; Internet per hr €1.50; ⏰ 10am-11pm Mon-Fri, 11am-midnight Sat, noon-11pm Sun) Run by the state post office, this is the place to come to send packages, receive faxes or connect cheaply to the Internet.
Tourist office Teatro Arriaga (☎ 94 479 57 60; www.bilbao .net; Teatro Arriaga, Paseo del Arenal; ⏰ 9.30am-2pm &

4-7.30pm Mon-Sat, 9.30am-2pm Sun); Guggenheim (Calle Alameda Mazarredo; ⏰ 11am-2.30pm & 3.30-6pm Mon-Fri, 11am-3pm Sat, 11am-2pm Sun)

Sights

Designed by Frank Gehry, the spectacular **Guggenheim Museum** (☎ 94 435 90 80; www.guggen heim-bilbao.es; Abandoibarra Et 2; admission €10, kids under 12 yrs free; ⏰ 10am-8pm Tue-Sun year-round, open Mon Jul & Aug) is an experience to remember. The building itself, undulating forms covered in titanium scales, was inspired by the shapes of ships and fish, two of Bilbao's traditional industries. Inside, the guts of the building are exposed, with few columns, ugly support beams or, for that matter, floors and walls, obstructing the view. Many credit this creation with revitalising modern architecture and creating a new standard in vanguard design.

To dig further into the local culture, head to the **Euskal Museoa** (Basque Museum; ☎ 94 415 54 23; http://euskal-museoa.org; Plaza Miguel de Unamuno 4; adult/child €3/free; ⏰ 11am-5pm Tue-Sat, 11am-2pm Sun), a museum documenting the history and lifestyle of the Basque people.

Sleeping & Eating

Hostal-Residencia La Estrella (☎ 94 416 40 66; Calle María Muñoz 6; s €30-39, d €48-57) The grand spiral staircase prepares you for grandeur, and the sparkling *hostal* doesn't disappoint, with spotless, freshly painted rooms.

Iturrienea Ostatua (☎ 94 416 15 00; Calle Santa María 14; s €45, d €54-60) Unbeatable charm at a B&B decorated with museum-worthy Basque artefacts and rustic elegance.

Rio-Oja (☎ 94 415 08 71; Calle Perro 4; mains €4-12; ⏰ noon-11pm Tue-Sun) Codfish and local stews are star dishes in Bilbao. Try both at this great spot for wallet-friendly fare. Try to ignore the unappetising English translations, such as 'beef face stew' or 'lamb insides stew'.

Harrobia (☎ 94 679 00 90; Calle Perro 2; mains €15-20, menú €9.90; ⏰ 1pm-4pm & 8.30-11pm) A sleek restaurant that's pricey at night but has a great-value lunch menú. Specialities are local seafood and, in season, game dishes.

Zuretzat (☎ 94 424 85 05; Calle Iparraguirre 7; menú €8.50; ⏰ 1pm-11pm) Near the Guggenheim, with *pinxos* or, downstairs, a tasty, fixed-price *menú*.

Getting There & Away

From the airport, bus No 3247 leaves every half-hour from 6.30am until 10.30pm and

SPAIN

drops you off in the Plaza Moyúa, in the centre of Bilbao, where there's a metro stop.

Bilbao is served by two train stations and two rail companies, Renfe and Feve, both beside the river. Renfe offers services to Madrid (€30 to €38, six to eight hours, two daily) and Barcelona (€34.50, seven hours, two daily).

The national narrow-gauge railway line, **Feve** (www.feve.es), has trains heading westward to Cantabria and beyond. Often these bumpy rides take considerably longer than the bus trip to the same destinations.

The main bus station (Termibús) is west of town but sits just next to the San Mamés metro stop, a five-minute ride from the centre. Regular buses come and go from San Sebastián (€7.75, one hour, up to 27 daily), Santander (€5.40 to €9.65, 1½ hours, up to 27 daily) and Zaragoza (€16.14 to €26.75, three to four hours, up to 10 daily).

Bilbao has an outstanding public transport system, with an easy-to-follow web of metros, trams and buses crisscrossing the city and heading into the countryside.

PAMPLONA

Immortalized by Ernest Hemingway in *The Sun Also Rises*, the busy pre-Pyrenean city of Pamplona (Iruña in Basque) is, of course, the home of the wild San Fermíne (aka Encierro or Running of the Bulls) festival, but it's also an extremely walkable city that's managed to mix the charm of old plazas and buildings with modern shops and lively nightlife.

This is the capital of Navarra, but there are few noteworthy sights in town, which means you can party all night and not feel guilty for whiling the day away in the street cafés. Make an exception for the **cathedral** (☎ 94 821 08 27; adult/child €3.85/2.25; ☺ 10am-1.30pm

& 4-7pm Mon-Fri, 10am-1.30pm Sat), a 14th-century Gothic creation with a neoclassical façade.

Information

Kuria.net (☎ 94 822 30 77; Calle Curia 15; per hr €3; ☺ 10am-10pm Mon-Sat, noon-10pm Sun)
Police (☎ 092)
Tourist office (☎ 94 842 04 20; www.navarra.es; Calle Eslava 1; ☺ 10am-2pm & 4-6pm Mon-Sat, 10am-2pm Sun Sep-Jun, 9am-8pm Mon-Sat, 10am-2pm Sun Jul & Aug, during San Fermíne 8am-8pm daily) Don't expect this otherwise-helpful office to provide much guidance during San Fermíne.

Sleeping

Accommodation is expensive and hard to come by during San Fermíne; you'll need to book months in advance. Prices below don't reflect the huge (up to 300%) mark-up you'll find in mid-July.

Camping Ezcaba (☎ 94 833 03 15; N-125; per person/car €7/3.85) The nearest camping ground, 7km north of the city. Regular buses head to Pamplona.

La Viña (☎ 94 821 32 50; Calle Jarauta 8; s/d shared bathroom from €15/25) Cheerful rooms with sky-blue walls and clean bathrooms.

Hotel Europa (☎ 94 822 18 00; www.hreuropa.com; Calle Espoz y Mina 11; s €61-68, d €65-74) More comfortable, this stylish, family-run hotel offers class and value. The swish **restaurant** (mains €18-25) is great for a splurge.

Also try:
Hostal Dom Luis (☎ 94 822 17 31; Calle San Nicolás 24; s €30-35, d €35-45) Highly recommended.
Pensión Lambertini (☎ 94 821 03 03; Calle Mercaderes 17; s with shared bathroom €20, d with shared bathroom €30-50) Cheery rooms, all-new bathrooms and tasteful décor.
Pensión Pamplona (☎ 94 822 99 63; Calle Tudela 5; s/d €30/42) Near the bus station.

Eating & Drinking

Central streets such as Calle San Nicolás and Calle Estafeta are lined with tapas bars, many of which morph into nightspots on weekends.

Café Iruña (☎ 94 822 20 64; Plaza Castillo 44; menú €10-21) This old Hemingway haunt was mentioned 14 times in *The Sun Also Rises*. This grand old café is great for coffee, breakfast or a quick meal.

Get great tapas at **Bar Baserri** (☎ 94 822 20 21; www.restaurantebaserri.com; Calle San Nicolás 32; pinxo menú €17), **Otano** (☎ 94 822 50 95; Calle San Nicolás 5; pinxos from €2) and **Cervecería La Estafeta** (☎ 94 822 79 77; Calle Estafeta 54).

SURVIVING SAN FERMÍNE

The madcap San Fermíne festival runs from 6–14 July, when the city is overrun with thrill-seekers, curious onlookers and, oh yeah, bulls. The Encierro (Running of the Bulls) begins at 8am daily, when bulls are let loose from the Corralillos Santo Domingo. The race lasts just three minutes, so don't be late. The safest place to watch the Encierro is on TV. If that's too tame for you, try to sweet-talk your way onto a balcony or book a room in a hotel with views.

For sit-down local fare, **La Chistera** (☎ 94 821 05 12; Calle San Nicolás 40-42; mains €15) serves great grilled meats and Basque seafood, while **Restaurant Saraste** (☎ 94 822 57 27; Calle San Nicolás 19-21; menú €10 or €16) caters to vegetarians.

Getting There & Away
Up to four trains arrive daily from Madrid (four hours). Bus No 9 connects the station with the centre.

Several companies operate out of Pamplona's central bus station near Plaza Castilla. **Conda** (☎ 94 822 10 26) runs up to seven daily buses each way between Madrid and Pamplona. Up to 10 buses come and go daily from Zaragoza.

CANTABRIA, ASTURIAS & GALICIA

Green Spain provides a fascinating contrast with the dry, sun-baked regions of the rest of the country. You'll think you're in Scotland with the lush green hills and powerfully wet Atlantic climate.

SANTANDER
Stylish Santander has a pretty old town, but it's most known for its upscale beach, **El Sardinero**. Many beachside shops, restaurants and hotels are open in summer only, but surfers abound year-round, braving the cold to ride winter's powerful waves.

Near Santander is the fascinating **Cueva de Altamira** (☎ 94 281 80 05; www.cultura.mecd.es; ⏲ 9.30am-7.30pm Tue-Sat, to 3pm Sun Jun-Sep, 9.30am-5pm Tue-Sat, to 3pm Sun Oct-May), a cave of prehistoric paintings that's been dubbed the Sistine Chapel of the prehistoric world. The 270m-long cave is 2km southwest of Santillana de Mar. The waiting list to get into the cave is years long, but you can visit an excellent on-site **museum** (admission €2.40) with replicas of the cave art. The **municipal tourist office** (☎ 94 220 30 00; www.ayto-santander.es; Jardines de Pereda; ⏲ 9.30am-1.30pm & 4-7pm Mon-Fri, 9am-1.30pm Sat) in town is very helpful.

Sleeping & Eating
Pensión La Corza (☎ 94 221 29 50; Calle Hernán Cortés 25; s €20-30, d €35-50) La Corza offers the best value in town, with spotless, colour-coordinated rooms, some with their own tidy bathrooms.

Pensión Picos de Europa (☎ 94 222 53 74; Calderón Barca 5; s with shared bathroom €20-25, d with shared bathroom €28-36) The quirky rooms of this *pensión* are packed with antique furniture, knick-knacks and ornate touches, and are beyond comfortable. We recommend trying to book room No 3.

Old Santander is full of traditional-style *mesones* (inns) and bodegas that serve as both pubs and sit-down restaurants. One of the better priced is **Cervecería Apsy** (☎ 94 231 45 95; Calle Hernán Cortés 22; mains €5.40-13), with a lot of seafood dishes on the *menú*.

Getting There & Away
Santander has many public transport options. Its ferry port is one of Spain's largest, and regular ferries arrive here from the UK. Trains come from Madrid (from €23.75, six hours, four daily) and Valladolid (€12.80 to €22.50, three to four hours, six daily). The **Feve** (www.feve.es) trains are usually slower than the bus, but are a scenic way to get to and from Bilbao (€6.25, 2½ hours, three daily).

The excellent **bus station** (☎ 94 221 19 95; Plaza Estaciones) is home to a half-dozen companies offering service to destinations throughout Cantabria and further afield.

SANTIAGO DE COMPOSTELA
The supposed burial place of Saint James (Santiago in Castilian), this beautiful city is the end of the Camino de Santiago and one of the Christian world's most important pilgrimage sites. Santiago's compact old town is a work of art, and a walk around the cathedral will take you through some of its most inviting squares.

Information
EMERGENCY
Police (☎ 092; Rua Trindade)

INTERNET ACCESS
Cyber Nova 50 (☎ 98 157 51 88; Rúa Nova 50; per hr €1.20; ⏲ 9am-1am Mon-Sat, 10am-1am Sun)

POST
Post office (☎ 98 158 12 52; Travesía Fonesca; ⏲ 8.30am-8.30pm Mon-Fri, 9.30am-2pm Sat)

TOURIST INFORMATION
Municipal tourist office (☎ 98 155 51 29; Rúa Vilar 63; ⏲ 10am-3pm & 5-8pm Oct-May, 9am-9pm Jun-Sep)

SPAIN

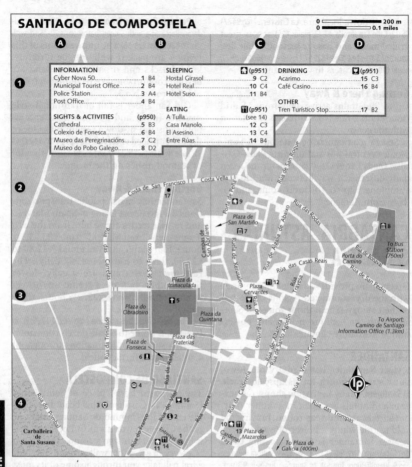

SANTIAGO DE COMPOSTELA

0 ———— 200 m
0 ———— 0.1 miles

INFORMATION
Cyber Nova 50.........................1 B4
Municipal Tourist Office..........2 B4
Police Station..........................3 A4
Post Office..............................4 B4

SIGHTS & ACTIVITIES (p950)
Cathedral.................................5 B3
Colexio de Fonesca..................6 B4
Museo das Peregrinacións........7 C2
Museo do Pobo Galego...........8 D2

SLEEPING 🛏 (p951)
Hostal Girasol.........................9 C2
Hotel Real.............................10 C4
Hotel Suso............................11 B4

EATING 🍴 (p951)
A Tulla............................(see 14)
Casa Manolo.........................12 C3
El Asesino.............................13 C4
Entre Rúas............................14 B4

DRINKING 🍷 (p951)
Acarimo...............................15 C3
Café Casino..........................16 B4

OTHER
Tren Turístico Stop................17 B2

Camino de Santiago information (Xacobeo; ☎ 98 157 20 04; www.xacobeo.es; Ave Coruña 6; 🕑 8.30am-2.30pm & 4.30-6.30pm Mon-Fri) Just west of town.

Sights

The **cathedral** (☎ 98 156 05 27; Plaza Obradoiro; 🕑 museum 10am-1.30pm & 4-6.30pm Mon-Sat, 10am-1.30pm Sun, mass noon & 6pm daily), a superb Romanesque creation of the 11th to 13th centuries, is the heart and soul of Santiago. It's said that St James' remains were buried here in the 1st century AD and rediscovered in 813. Today, visitors line up to kiss his statue, which sits behind the main altar.

To get a grasp on local culture, visit the **Museo do Pobo Galego** (☎ 98 158 36 20; www.museo dopobo.es; San Domingos de Bonaval; admission free; 🕑 10am-2pm & 4-8pm Tue-Sat), which has exhibits on everything from boating and fishing to music and pottery.

The **Museo das Peregrinacións** (☎ 98 158 15 58; www.mdperegrinacions.com; Rúa San Miguel 4; adult/child €2.40/free; 🕑 10am-8pm Tue-Fri, 10.30am-1.30pm & 5-8pm Sat) explores the pilgrim culture that has so shaped Santiago.

Santiago's university is one of Spain's oldest and most emblematic. The 16th-century **Colexio de Fonesca** (Fonesca College; ☎ 98 156 31 00; Plaza Fonesca; 🕑 11am-2pm & 5-8.30pm Tue-Sat, 11am-2pm Sun) is one of the prettiest university buildings and now houses the university library. There are usually exhibitions held in the two ornate rooms at the front; call ahead to check.

Tours

The **Tren Turístico** (adult/child €3.60/1.80; ☺ 10am-8pm Mar-Oct, 10am-1.30pm Nov-Feb) loops around the city, starting and finishing on the Rúa San Francisco, by the Plaza Obrero. **Walking tours** (☎ 98 156 98 90; Plaza Platerías; adult/child €8/free; ☺ noon Oct-Mar, noon & 6pm Apr-Sep) are also interesting.

Sleeping

Hostal Girasol (☎ 98 156 62 87; www.hgirasol.com; Porta de Pena 4; d €33-39, s with shared bathroom €15-20, d with shared bathroom €26-32) With wrought-iron beds, wooden floors and a country charm, the clean, bright Girasol is a great choice.

Hostal Suso (☎ 98 158 66 11; Rúa Vilar 65; s €15-18, d €30-36) Excellent value, the Suso boasts fashionable décor, parquet floors and rooms with small balconies.

Hotel Real (☎ 98 156 92 90; Rúa Calderería 49; s €41-45, d €58-66, tr €69-80) A great find in the old city, with all the comforts (though loud rooms).

Eating & Drinking

Seafood is the local speciality, and you'll find tasty delights from the ocean just about everywhere, especially along central streets such as Calle Franco and Calle Raiña.

Casa Manolo (☎ 98 158 29 50; Plaza Cervantes; menú €6; ☺ 1pm-4pm & 8-11pm Mon-Sat, 1pm-4pm Sun) Everything is served as part of a super-cheap fixed-price *menú*.

El Asesino (The Killer; ☎ 98 158 15 68; Plaza Universidad 16; mains €8-12, menú €12-15; ☺ 1pm-3.30pm & 8-11pm Mon-Sat) Homy and has been serving local specialities for 127 years.

Entre-Ruas (☎ 98 158 61 08; Callejón Entre-Rúas 2; raciones €2.50-8, menú €8; ☺ 1pm-4pm & 8.30pm-midnight Mon-Sat) Have seafood alfresco at Entre-Ruas, which sits on a tiny plaza in the middle of the thinnest street in all Santiago.

A Tulla (☎ 98 158 0889; Callejon Entre-Rúas 1; menú €8.50-10.50; ☺ 1pm-4pm & 8-11pm Mon-Sat) Next door to Entre-Ruas, with a vegetarian *menú*.

The old quarter is home to atmospheric bars and pubs popular with the city's large student population. Some of the best spots are around the Rúa da Congo, the Rúa San Paio de Antealtares and the Plaza Cervantes. At **Acarimo** (Calle Preguntoiro 2; ☺ 8-2.30am) you'll find a laid-back atmosphere, and at classy **Café Casino** (☎ 98 157 75 03; Rúa Villar 35; ☺ 8am-midnight Sun-Thu, 8am-1am Fri & Sat) live piano music starts nightly at 8.30pm.

Getting There & Around

From the airport, regular **Freire** (☎ 98 154 24 16) buses make runs to the bus station and to República de El Salvador about once an hour.

There are regular trains to and from La Coruña (€3.30 to €11.50, one hour, hourly), Vigo (€5.10, 1½ hours, hourly) and other regional destinations. Two trains come in from Madrid (€38.50, eight hours). It's a 15-minute walk from the station to central Plaza de Galicia.

From the **bus station** (☎ 98 158 77 00; Calle San Caetano) you can hop on bus No 10 to get to Plaza de Galicia. Buses come in from León (€22.52, 6½ hours, one daily) and Oviedo (€22.18, five hours, three daily).

RÍAS BAJAS

The *rías* (inlets) on Galicia's western coast offer some of the region's best beaches and coastal scenery. The four major *rías*, the Ría Muros, Ría Arousa, Ría Pontevedra and Ría Vigo, are dotted with low-key resorts, fishing villages and beaches.

There are regional tourist offices in **Pontevedra** (☎ 98 685 08 14; Calle General Mola 3); **Cambados** (☎ 98 652 07 86), a block from the bus station; and **Vigo** (☎ 98 643 05 77), by the port.

The prettiest beaches are on the **Islas Cíes**, off the end of the Ría Vigo. One of the three islands is off limits for conservation reasons. The other two, Isla del Faro and Isla de Monte Agudo, are linked by a white sandy crescent, together forming a 9km breakwater in the Atlantic. You can visit the islands only from Easter to mid-September by boat from Vigo.

Pontevedra and Vigo are the area's transport hubs, with a network of local buses fanning out from them. Both are well served by buses and trains from Santiago de Compostela and La Coruña.

LA CORUÑA

La Coruña (A Coruña in Gallego) is a breezy oceanside city with a stylish centre and pretty historic quarter. A mushroom-shaped peninsula jutting into the wild Atlantic, it's surrounded by water and boasts great urban beaches and a lively port.

Check email at **Ciber Zalaet@.Net** (☎ 98 120 38 41; Calle Zalaeta 7; per hr €1.20; ☺ 10-2am). For loads of great local information drop into

the **municipal tourist office** (☎ 98 118 43 44; www
.turismocoruna.com; Plaza María Pita; ☻ 10am-2pm &
4-8pm Mon-Sat, 10am-2pm Sun), housed in a glass
cube on the plaza.

Sights

With so much ocean around, beaches are
naturally a major part of La Coruña's attraction. The main beach, **Playa del Orzán**, runs
along the western border of the town centre.
Across town is the busy **marina**, lined with
iconic balconied houses, and to the north is
the pretty **Ciudad Vieja**.

The city's best-known and best-loved
monument is the **Torre de Hércules** (☎ 98 122
37 30; Ave Navarra s/n; admission €2; ☻ 10am-5.45pm
Oct-Mar, 10am-6.45pm Apr-Jun & Sep, 10am-8.45pm Sun-
Thu, 10am-11.45pm Fri & Sat Jul & Aug), the oldest
functioning lighthouse in the world. The
18th-century, neoclassical tower that stands
today completely masks the Roman foundations that lie underneath. The tower is a 20-
minute walk from town, but you can hop on
bus No 3 or the tram that runs around the
waterfront, both of which stop nearby.

Sleeping & Eating

La Coruña has a solid selection of budget
and mid-range lodging. Most are clustered
around the Rúa Nueva and Calle Real.

With the Atlantic at its feet, La Coruña is
one of the best places in Spain to eat fresh
seafood and shellfish. Stroll along streets
such as Calle Franja, Calle Olmos and Calle
Estrella for a myriad of dining options. Restaurants in the centre open from 1.30pm to
3.30pm for lunch and again from 8pm to
11pm for dinner.

Hostal-Residencia Carbonara (☎ 98 120 14 29;
fax 98 122 52 51; Rúa Nueva 16; s €18-26.50, d €25-40) The
rooms are spacious, sunny and a great deal.
There's no elevator, so rooms are cheaper
on higher floors.

Hostal Linar (☎ 98 122 78 37; Calle General Mola 7;
s €20-25, d €30-45) Sophisticated rooms with
shiny ceramic floors and bathrooms worthy
of a three-star hotel.

Mesón do Pulpo (☎ 98 120 24 44; Calle Franja 9-11;
mains €8-10) A rustic tavern where you can get
excellent shellfish *raciones*.

Mesón el Virira (☎ 98 122 01 09; Calle Galera 28;
menú €6.60) Offering one of the cheapest fixed-
price lunches in town.

Marisquería Calemae (☎ 98 122 86 70; Plaza María
Pita 24; menú €8) If you want to eat with a view,

this is a good option, with seafood *raciones*,
a decent lunch *menú* and delicious crusty
bread.

Getting There & Away

Trains from Santiago (€3.30 to €11.50, one
hour, hourly), Vigo (from €8.25, up to three
hours, hourly) and elsewhere in Galicia come
and go regularly. Numerous bus companies
operate from the **bus station** (☎ 98 118 43 35;
Calle Caballeros 21). **Castromil** (www.castromil.com) offers services from such cities as Santiago and
Vigo, and **Alsa** (www.alsa.es) heads to Madrid
(€34 to €49, six to eight hours, seven daily).

PICOS DE EUROPA

This small region straddling Asturias, Cantabria and Castilla y León includes possibly
the finest walking country in Spain. The spectacular mountain and gorge scenery consti-
tute a national park, with an **information office**
(☎ 98 584 86 14; www.mma.es; Casa Dago, Ave Covadonga
43) in Cangas de Onís. The main access towns
for the Picos are Cangas de Onís, Arenas de
Cabrales and Potes.

VALENCIA & MURCIA

Best known for the package resorts of the
Costa Blanca, this region also includes the
lively cities of Valencia and Alicante, and
some undiscovered secrets if you penetrate
inland. South of Valencia, the province of
Murcia has fertile plains and is blessed by
some of the Mediterranean's warmest waters.

VALENCIA
pop 746,610

Exuberant, friendly and appealingly chaotic,
Valencia is Spain's third-largest city. Its
old quarter brims with gracious baroque-
fronted houses and its streets buzz with life
until the early hours. Kick back with a meal
of paella washed down with a jar of *agua de
Valencia* (orange juice and sparkling wine) to
really get into the spirit of things.

Orientation

The action part of the city is oval, bounded
by the dried-up Turia river bed (now a park)
and the sickle-shaped inner ring road of
Calles Colón, Játiva and Guillem de Castro.
These trace the old city walls, demolished in
1865 as, incredibly, a job-creation project.

Information

Grab a copy of the freebie mag *24/7 Valencia*, a fantastic guide (in English) to Valencia's bars, clubs, restaurants and music venues.

Ono (☎ 96 328 19 02; Calle San Vicente 22; per hr €2; ☉ 9-1am) Internet access just off Plaza Ayuntamiento.

Tourist offices Main office (☎ 96 398 64 22; www .turisvalencia.es; Calle Paz 48; ☉ 10am-6.30pm Mon-Fri, 10am-2pm Sat); Train station (☎ 96 352 85 73); Teatro Principal (☎ 96 351 49 07); Plaza Reina (☎ 96 352 54 78, ext 1739; ☉ 9am-7pm Mon-Sat, 10am-2pm Sun)

Sights & Activities

One of Spain's prettiest markets, Valencia's **Mercado Central** (Plaza Mercado; ☉ 8am-2.30pm) is a feast of colours and smells, with nearly 1000 stallholders crammed under the market's modernist glass domes.

Valencia's **cathedral** (☉ 7.30am-1pm & 5-8.30pm) has three magnificent portals – one Gothic, one Romanesque, and one baroque – the only Holy Grail recognised (albeit tentatively) by the Vatican, a fantastic Goya and the withered left arm of St Vincent. Climb the **Miguelete bell tower** (admission €1.50; ☉ 10.30am-12.30pm & 4.30-6.30pm Tue-Fri, 10.30am-1pm Sat-Mon) for sweeping views of the city.

The aesthetically stunning **Ciudad de las Artes y las Ciencias** (☎ 902 100 031; adult/child €10.50/8; ☉ 10am-9pm) includes the Hemisfèric (a planetarium, IMAX cinema and laser show), interactive science museum, aquarium and open-air auditorium.

Among Valencia's art galleries, the two unmissables are the **Museo de Bellas Artes** (☎ 96 360 57 93; Calle San Pio V 9; admission free; ☉ 10am-2.15pm & 4-7.30pm Tue-Sat, 10am-7.30pm Sun) and the **Instituto Valenciano de Arte Moderno** (☎ 96 386 30 00; Calle Guillem de Castro 118; adult/student €2/1, free Sun).

A must-see is the extravagantly sculpted façade of the rococo-fabulous **Palacio del Marqués de Dos Aguas** (Calle Poeta Querol).

Sleeping

A wide range of accommodation is available in Valencia.

Devesa Gardens (☎ /fax 961 61 11 36; www.devesa gardens.com; per person/tent/car €4.50/4.50/4.50; ☒) The city's nearest camping ground is 13km south of Valencia, near El Saler beach. The complex includes restaurants, tennis courts and even a mini zoo.

Hôme Youth Hostel (☎ 96 391 62 29; www.likeat home.net; Calle Lonja 4; dm/s/d with shared bathroom €14/21/32; ☐) With its brightly painted rooms,

> **BURN BABY BURN**
>
> In mid-March, Valencia hosts what has become one of Europe's wildest street parties: **Las Fallas de San José.** For one week the city is engulfed by an anarchic swirl of fireworks, music, festive bonfires and all-night partying. On the final night, giant *niñots* (effigies), many of political and social personages, are torched in the main plaza.
>
> If you're not in Valencia then, see the *niñots* saved from the flames by popular vote at the **Museo Fallero** (☎ 96 352 54 78; Plaza Monteolivete 4; adult/child €2/0.60; ☉ 9.15am-2pm & 4.30-8pm Tue-Sat, 9.15am-2pm Sun)

big kitchen, healthy DVD stash and even laundry facilities, this place is pure backpacking heaven.

Hôme Backpackers (☎ 96 391 37 97; www.likeat home.net; Plaza Vicente Iborra; dm €12-14, d/tr/q with shared bathroom €32/48/64; ☐) Valencia's latest addition to the budget travel scene has 100 beds (some bunks) and friendly, multilingual young staff.

Hôme Budget Hotel (☎ 96 392 40 63; www.likeat home.net; Calle Cadirers 11; d incl breakfast €40) The individually designed rooms come complete with king-sized beds and private stereos. Perfect for flashpackers.

Hostal Antigua Morellana (☎ 96 391 57 73; info@ hostalam.com; Calle En Bou 2; s/d €33/48; ☒) In an elegant renovated 18th-century building, this helpful hotel has cosy, good-sized rooms with satellite TV and balconies.

Ad Hoc (☎ 96 391 91 40; www.adhochoteles.com; Calle Boix 4; s/d €87/115; ☒) This charming boutique hotel has stencilled ceilings, pretty balconies and fabulous colour schemes.

Eating

Lots of cheap (generally fishy) eats can be found near the market. For authentic paella, head for Las Arenas, just north of the port, where a strip of restaurants serves up the real stuff from €6.60 per person.

Boatella (Plaza Mercado 33; tapas €3; ☉ 8am-1.30pm) Crammed with locals who are busy throwing down glasses of beer and platefuls of fried fish and other seafood.

Bar Pilar (Calle Moro Zeit 13; tapas €1.50; ☉ noon-midnight) This Valencian classic is where everyone comes to eat mussels, chucking the shells into the plastic buckets on the floor.

SPAIN

VALENCIA CITY

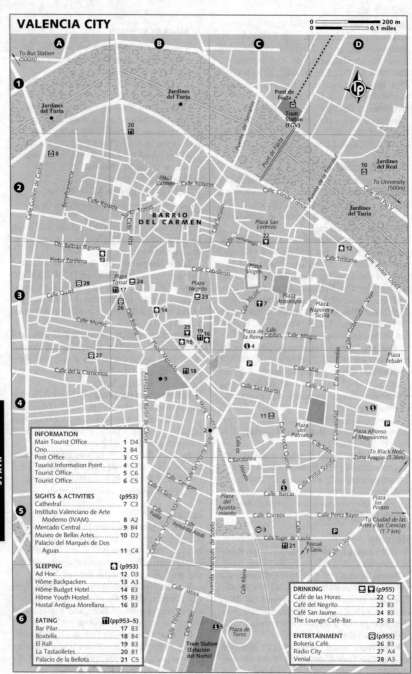

Palacio de la Bellota (☎ 96 351 49 94; Calle Mosén Femades 7; raciones €7; ☼ 1pm-4pm & 8pm-midnight) The cured ham *(jamón)*, which hangs from the ceilings, is absolutely divine but this place is also famous for its Valencian eel stew *(all i pebre)*.

La Tastaolletes (☎ 96 392 18 62; Calle Salvador Giner 6; mains €7; ☼ 2pm-4pm & 8-midnight Tue-Sat, 2pm-4pm Sun) An excellent vegetarian restaurant in a colourful setting. It is especially good at salads and the vegetable lasagne is to die for.

El Rall (☎ 96 392 20 90; Calle Tundidores 2; mains €8; ☼ 2pm-4.30pm & 9-midnight) A firm favourite, El Rall serves up paellas, meat dishes and great desserts in a funky setting and has a good outside terrace.

Drinking

Much of the action centres on Barrio del Carmen, which caters for every taste from grunge to glam.

Café San Jaume (Calle Caballeros 51; ☼ noon-1am) A stalwart of Carmen's café/bar scene, with lots of room upstairs and a particularly fine terrace for eyeing up the characters on Calle Caballeros.

Café de las Horas (Calle Conde de Almodóvar 1; ☼ 4pm-1am Mon-Thu, 4pm-3.30am Fri & Sat) With its deep-red walls, theatrical drapes and frescoes, this bar/café has the feel of an 18th-century boudoir and does the best *agua de Valencia* in town.

The Lounge Café-Bar (☎ 96 391 80 94; Calle Estamiñería Vieja 2; ☼ 11pm-1am) This popular international hang-out has comfy sofas and free Internet. Good snacks too.

Café del Negrito (☎ 96 391 42 33; Plaza Negrito; ☼ 3pm-3.30am) On a kicking little plaza, this bar/café is generally packed with lots of liberal, arty 30-somethings.

Entertainment

Radio City (☎ 96 391 41 51; Santa Teresa 19; ☼ 11pm-late) This is where everyone goes for post-bar dancing to salsa, house and cheesy pop. It also has a live flamenco show at 11pm Tuesday.

Bolsería Café (☎ 96 391 89 03; Calle Bolsería 41; ☼ 11pm-4am) A fashionable place that plays house music upstairs and has bizarre toilets with glass walls.

Venial (☎ 96 391 73 56; Quart 26; ☼ 12.30-8am) Valencia's oldest gay club is always jumping with theme parties throughout the year, and fashion shows and male strippers in summer.

It has a big open-plan dance floor and chill-out zone. Mixed crowd.

The Black Note (☎ 96 393 36 63; Polo y Peyrolón 15; ☼ from 11.30pm) Jazz cats and live music junkies should head here, in the Zona Aragón.

Younger groovers head for the university, 2km east (€3.50 by taxi from the centre). Along Ave Blasco Ibáñez and particularly around Plaza Xuquer there are scores of dusk-to-dawn bars and discos.

Getting There & Away

From the **bus station** (☎ 96 349 72 22; Ave Menéndez Pidal), services go to/from Madrid (€21, four hours, 10 daily), Barcelona (€22, five hours, 12 daily) and Alicante (€15, 2¼ hours, 11 daily).

From Valencia's **Estación del Norte** (Calle Jativa), trains go to/from Madrid (€37, 3½ hours, 10 daily), Barcelona (€29, 3½ hours, 14 daily) and Alicante (€20.50, two hours, 10 daily).

Regular car and passenger ferries go to the Balearic Islands (see p959).

Getting Around

EMT (☎ 96 352 83 99) buses run until about 10pm, with night services continuing on seven routes until around 1am. Bus No 8 connects the bus station with Plaza Ayuntamiento.

The smart high-speed tram leaves from the FGV tram station, 500m north of the cathedral, at the Pont de Fusta. It's a pleasant way to get to the beach, the paella restaurants of Las Arenas and the port (€1). Metro lines primarily serve the outer suburbs.

INLAND VALENCIA
Morella
pop 2720

Perched on a hill top, crowned by a castle and completely enclosed by a wall over 2km long, the fairy-tale town of Morella, in the north of the Valencia region, is one of Spain's oldest continually inhabited towns. The **tourist office** (☎ 96 417 30 32; morella@touristinfo .net; ☼ 10am-2pm & 4-7pm Tue-Sat, 10am-2pm Sun) is just behind the Torres de San Miguel (the twin 14th century towers which flank the main entrance to the town).

The old town itself is easily explored on foot. Morella's **castle** (☎ 96 417 31 28; admission €1.20; ☼ 10am-7.30pm), although in ruins, remains imposing and gives breathtaking views of the town and surrounding countryside.

Friendly **Fonda Moreno** (☎ 96 416 01 05; Calle San Nicolás 12; d with shared bathroom €21) has six quaint and basic doubles. **Hotel El Cid** (☎ 96 416 01 25; www.hotelelcidmorella.com; Puerta San Mateo 2; s/d incl breakfast €26/37) has spruced-up rooms with bathrooms and good views. Occupying a 16th-century cardinal's palace, **Hotel Cardenal Ram** (☎ 96 417 30 85; hotelcardenalram@ctv .es; Cuesta Suñer 1; s/d €42.80/64.20) has rooms with all facilities.

For excellent tapas, plus a *menú* that is rich in local dishes, check out **Restaurante Vinatea** (☎ 96 416 07 44; Calle Blasco de Alagón 17; menú €6; ☺ 1pm-4pm & 8-11.30pm Tue-Sun).

Autos Mediterráneo (☎ 96 422 05 36) runs two buses daily from Monday to Saturday to/ from Castellón (€7, 2½ hours) and Vinarós (€7, 2½ hours).

Guadalest

A spectacular route runs west from just south of Calpe (see p958) to the inland town of **Alcoy**, famous for its Moros y Cristianos fiesta in April. Halfway to Alcoy, stop at the old Muslim settlement of **Guadalest**, dominated by the **Castillo de San José** and besieged these days by coach parties from the coast.

ALICANTE
pop 299,977

There's an endearingly faded grandeur about Alicante, particularly around the old quarter, overlooked by its majestic limestone cathedral. The nightlife is also equal to that of any self-respecting Andalucían city, particularly during the Fiesta de Sant Joan (24 June), when Alicante stages its own version of Las Fallas (p953).

Alicante has five tourist offices but the most central is the **main tourist office** (☎ 96 520 00 00; www.landofvalencia.com; Rambla Méndez Núñez 23; ☺ 10am-7.30pm Mon-Fri, 10am-2pm Sat). You can connect to the Internet at **Up Internet** (www.up-Internet.es; Angel Lozano 10; per hr €2.95; ☺ 10am-2am).

Sights & Activities

The **Castillo de Santa Bárbara** (☎ 96 526 31 31; Monte Benacantil; admission free; ☺ 10am-8pm Apr-Sep, 9am-7pm Oct-Mar), a 16th-century fortress, overlooks the city. You can either walk up or take the lift (€2.40 return), reached by a footbridge opposite Playa del Postiguet.

The **Museo de la Asegurada** (☎ 96 514 07 68; Plaza Santa María 3; admission free; ☺ 10am-2pm & 4-8pm Tue-Sat, 10.30am-2.30pm Sun) hosts exhibitions by contemporary artists. On the same square, the **Iglesia de Santa María** (☺ 10.30am-1pm & 6-7.30pm) dates from the 14th century and incorporates a variety of styles from the stunning baroque façade to the Gothic nave.

The **Museo Arqueológico** (☎ 96 514 90 06; Plaza Gómez Ulla s/n; adult/student €6/3; ☺ 10am-7pm Tue-Sat) houses an excellent collection of Roman and medieval antiquities. The emphasis is on local painters at the **Museo de Bellas Artes** (☎ 96 514 67 80; Calle Gravina 13-15; admission free; ☺ 10am-2pm & 4-8pm Tue-Sat, 10am-2pm Sun), in an 18th-century mansion.

The closest beach to Alicante is **Playa del Postiguet**. Larger and less crowded beaches are at **Playa de San Juan**, easily reached by bus No 21 or 22.

On most days, **Kontiki** (☎ 96 521 63 96) runs boat trips (€15 return) to the popular **Isla de Tabarca**, an island that boasts excellent snorkelling and scuba diving from its quiet beaches.

Sleeping

You shouldn't have too much trouble finding somewhere to stay.

Camping Costa Blanca (☎ 96 563 06 70; www.camp ingcostablanca.com; Calle Convento, Campello; per person/ tent/car €4.30/4.30/4.30; ☒) About 10km north of Alicante and 200m from the beach.

Pensión La Milagrosa (☎ 96 521 69 18; Calle Villavieja 8; s/d with shared bathroom €15/30) Rooms at this large *pensión* are clean and basic. There's a small guest kitchen and lots of religious paintings on the walls. A feature is the sunny rooftop terrace with views to the castle.

Pensión Portugal (☎ 96 592 92 44; 1st fl, Calle Portugal 26; s/d with shared bathroom €21/30) This characterless building overlooks the bus station; it's a good safe place to crash if you get in late. Rather brutal lighting, though.

Hostal Les Monges Palace (☎ 96 521 50 46; www .lesmonges.net; Calle San Agustín 4; s/d €25/37; Ⓟ ☒) Rooms in this fabulous old building have tiled floors, gorgeous bathrooms and lots of theatrical flourishes.

Mediterránea Plaza (☎ 96 521 01 88; www.hotel mediterraneaplaza.com; Plaza Ayuntamiento 6; s/d €96/110; Ⓟ ☒) A sparkling four-star hotel on a historic plaza with a gym, sauna, bar and lots of marble.

Eating & Drinking

Alicante is filled with bars and cafés, including the old-fashioned **Café-Cervecería**

ALICANTE

SPAIN

Ramblas (Rambla Mendez Nuñez 7; 8am-2am), a great breakfast spot.

Restaurante Mixto Vegetariano (Plaza Santa María 2; menú €7.50) A simple hole-in-the-wall place with both vegetarian and meat *menús*. Service is an elderly one-man show, but the wait is worth it. Best *flan casero* (home-made crème caramel) in Spain.

Cantina Villahelmy (96 521 25 29; Calle Mayor 37; mains €4-8; 10am-4pm & 8-midnight Tue-Sat, noon-4pm Sun) Intimate, funky and popular, Cantina has snacks, excellent salads and a menu with everything from couscous to octopus.

Restaurante Spoon (96 521 90 28; Calle Lonja de Caballeros 10; mains €12 noon-4pm & 8.30-12.30am) Small, chic and packed with Alicante's young professionals, Spoon has a good variety of international dishes.

Piripi (96 522 79 40; Calle Oscar Esplá 30; mains €15-18; 1.15-4.15pm & 8.15-12.15am) This Alicante stalwart is highly regarded for its stylish tapas, plus fine rice and seafood dishes.

Popular watering holes cluster around the cathedral, where there is a good choice of early-evening bars. Later on, look out for the dance bars **Celestial Copas** (Calle San Pascual 1; 10.30pm-4am) and **Desafinado** (Calle Santo Tomas 6; 10.30pm-4.30am). In summer, the disco scene at Playa de San Juan is thumping. There are also hundreds of discos in the coastal resorts between Alicante and Dénia.

Getting There & Away

From the **bus station** (96 513 07 00; Calle Portugal 17), there are services to Almería (€18, five hours, five daily), Valencia (€15, 2¼ hours, 11 daily), Barcelona (€34, eight hours, 10 daily), Madrid (€23, 4½ hours, seven daily) and towns along the Costa Blanca.

From the **train station** (Ave Salamanca), there are services to Madrid (€36, four hours, seven daily), Valencia (€20.50, two hours, 10 daily) and Barcelona (€39.50 to €44, five hours, eight daily).

From the **Ferrocarriles de la Generalitat Valenciana (FGV) station** (96 526 27 31), at the northeastern end of Playa del Postiguet, a narrow-gauge line follows an attractive coastal route northwards as far as Dénia (€7, 2¼ hours, six daily) via Benidorm and Calpe.

COSTA BLANCA

The Costa Blanca (White Coast), one of Europe's most popular tourist regions, has its share of concrete jungles, particularly around Benidorm, which resembles a Las Vegas skyline from a distance. But if you're looking for a rollicking nightlife, good beaches and a suntan, you won't be disappointed. Accommodation is almost impossible to find during the coach-tour months of July and August.

Xàbia
pop 28,493

More than two-thirds of annual visitors to Xàbia (Jávea) are foreigners, so it's not the greatest place to brush up on your Spanish. This laid-back resort is in three parts: the old town (3km inland), the port and the beach zone of El Arenal, lined with pleasant bar-restaurants.

Camping Jávea (96 579 10 70; www.camping -javea.com; per person €4.50, per tent & car €11.60;) is just over 1km from El Arenal. The port area is pleasant and has some reasonably priced *pensiones*.

In the old town, **Hostal Levante** (96 579 15 91; Calle Maestro Alonso 5; d €40-43, s/d with shared bathroom €25/34) has basic rooms.

Calpe

Calpe is dominated by the Gibraltaresque **Peñon de Ifach** (332m), a giant molar-like rock protruding from the sea. The climb towards the summit is popular – while you're up there, enjoy the seascape and decide which of Calpe's two long sandy beaches you want to laze on.

Camping Ifach (96 583 04 77; per person/tent/car €4.50/4/4.50) and **Camping Levante** (96 583 22 72; per person/tent/car €4.60/4.40/4.60), both on Ave Mar-ina, are a short walk from Playa Levante.

Pensión Céntrica (96 583 55 28; Plaza Ilfach; s/d with shared bathroom €12/24) just off Ave Gabriel Miró, is squeaky clean.

MURCIA & THE COSTA CALÍDA

Murcia is one of the most conservative of Spain's provinces. The capital, also called Murcia, has a traditional Spanish appeal, liberally sprinkled with plazas and some gorgeous architecture. It's also foodie heaven; Murcia's elegant citizens are pros when it comes to fine cuisine.

Both the **municipal tourist office** (96 835 87 49; www.murciaciudad.com; Plaza Cardinal Belluga; 10am-2pm & 5-9pm Mon-Sat, 10am-2pm Sun) and **regional tourist office** (902 10 10 70; Plaza Romea 4; 9.30am-1.30pm & 5-7pm Mon-Fri) are helpful.

Sights & Activities

Murcia's opulent **cathedral** (Plaza Cardinal Belluga; 10am-1pm & 5-7pm) took four centuries to build. The 23 chapels and a 92m-high tower cover a dizzying range of styles. But it is the façade, dripping in cherubs, that is the real jaw-dropper. The city's sumptuous 19th-century **casino** (96 821 22 55; admission €1.20; 10am-9pm) features an Arabian patio and a magnificent ballroom.

The main draw of Murcia's Costa Cálida (Warm Coast) is the **Mar Menor**, a vast saltwater lagoon separated from the sea by a 22km sliver of land known as **La Manga**. The water here is so warm that you can swim year-round.

Sleeping & Eating

Accommodation in Murcia city is limited and not really geared towards tourists.

Murcia is a gourmet's delight. Don't leave without trying the tapas.

Pensión Murcia (96 821 99 63; Calle Vinadel 6; s/d with shared bathroom €18/38) Family-run, with cosy rooms with ceiling fans.

La Huertanica (96 821 76 68; Calle Infante 3; s/d/tr €44/57/71; P) Modern and comfortable; rooms with balconies.

Señorío de Jomelsu (96 821 21 33; Calle Isidoro de la Cierva 3; tapas from €1.20; 10am-4.30pm & 8pm-2.30am) Does a mean *sobrasada* (chorizo pâté).

La Barra del Rincón de Pepe (96 821 22 39; Calle Apóstoles 34; menú €12; 1.30pm-4pm & 8-midnight) Something of a local institution, serving up delicious Murcian fare.

Getting There & Away

From Murcia, buses serve Madrid (€21, five hours, nine daily), Alicante (€5, one hour, every two hours), Almería (€11, three hours, five daily) and towns on the Costa Cálida, including La Manga (€4, 1½ hours, three daily). Trains go from Murcia to Alicante (€13.50, 1¼ hours, five daily) and Madrid (€35.50, five hours, five daily).

BALEARIC ISLANDS

pop 916,968

The Balearic Islands of Mallorca, Menorca, Ibiza and Formentera are a surprising mix of cultural wealth and mass tourism, set against a backdrop of stunning natural beauty. Although they all have a distinctly Mediterranean feel, each island also closely guards its own identity.

For those searching the simple pleasures of sun, sea and sand, the gorgeous beaches will happily oblige, but the heart of the Balearics lies away from its resorts. Beyond the bars and beaches, you'll discover Gothic cathedrals, Stone Age ruins and Moorish remains, as well as simple fishing villages, endless olive groves and orange orchards.

Most place names and addresses are given in Catalan. High-season prices are quoted here but out of season, you will usually find things are much cheaper.

Getting There & Away

AIR

Scheduled flights from the major cities on the Spanish mainland are operated by several airlines, including Iberia, Air Europa and Spanair.

Return fares from Barcelona to Palma de Mallorca can be had for as little as €66, though standard one-way fares generally hover around €45.

Interisland flights are expensive (given the flying times involved), with Palma to Maó or Ibiza costing €77/147 one way/return.

BOAT

The major ferry company for the islands is **Trasmediterránea** (902 45 46 45; www.trasmediterranea.es) with offices in Barcelona (93 295 90 00), Valencia (96 367 65 12), Palma de Mallorca (97 140 50 14), Maó (97 136 60 50) and Ibiza city (97 131 51 00).

The duration of the services varies dramatically, depending on the type of ferry. The maximum times are given here, but always check whether there is a faster ferry (such as a catamaran) available. Scheduled services are: between Barcelona and Palma (seven hours, 12 services weekly); Palma and Maó (5½ hours, one service a week on Sunday); Valencia and Palma (seven hours, two services daily); Barcelona and Ibiza (nine hours, four services weekly); Palma and Ibiza (four hours, eight weekly). Prices quoted below are the one-way fares during summer; low- and mid-season fares may be cheaper.

Fares from the mainland to any of the islands are €49.55 for a *butaca turista* (seat) and €68.90 for the same class on a catamaran. Taking a small car costs €126, or there

SPAIN

are economy packages (*paquete ahorro*) available.

Interisland services between Palma and Ibiza city cost €44.20 and Palma and Maó cost €26.70 for a *butaca turista*. A small car is another €74.26. Ask, too, about economy packages.

Another company, **Balearia** (☎ 902 16 01 80; www.balearia.com), operates fast ferries from Dénia (on the coast between Valencia and Alicante) to Palma (€48, five hours, two daily) via Ibiza (from €48, two hours). There are services between Valencia and Palma (€48, six hours, two daily), Valencia and Ibiza (€48, 3¾ hours, two daily) and between Ibiza and Palma (€32, four hours, two daily). There are also services between Ibiza and Formentera (€10, one hour, 12 daily) and between Port d'Alcúdia on Mallorca and Cituadella on Menorca (€32, one hour, two daily).

Iscomar (☎ 902 11 91 28; www.iscomarferrys.com) has from one to four daily car ferries (depending on the season) between Ciutadella and Port d'Alcúdia, as well as between Palma and Dénia via Ibiza. **Cape Balear** (☎ 902 10 04 44) operates fast ferries to Ciutadella from Cala Ratjada in Mallorca (€45, one hour, three daily).

MALLORCA

Mallorca's capital city of Palma, with its tangle of narrow backstreets and towering Gothic cathedral, is a joy to explore. Inland, you can happily lose yourself in the mountains before stumbling across a hill-top village seemingly unchanged for centuries. And then there are the beaches…It's hardly surprising that so many great artists and writers decided to make this beguiling Mediterranean island their home.

Orientation & Information

Palma is on the southern side of the island, on a bay famous for its brilliant sunsets. The Serra de Tramuntana mountain range, which runs parallel with the northwestern coastline, is trekkers' heaven. Mallorca's best beaches are along the northern and eastern coasts, along with most of the big tourist resorts.

All the major resorts have at least one **tourist office** (Main office ☎ 97 171 22 16; www.a-palma .es; Plaça Reina 2; ✆ 9am-8pm Mon-Fri, 9am-2.30pm Sat; Parc de les Estacions ☎ 97 175 43 29; Carrer Sant Domingo 11 ☎ 97 172 40 90; Airport ☎ 97 178 95 56).

For internet access try **Big Byte** (☎ 97 171 17 54; Carrer Apuntadores 6, Palma; Internet per hr €2.75; ✆ 10am-10pm Mon-Thu, 10am-6pm Fri, 11am-7pm Sat & Sun).

Sights & Activities

An awesome mass of sandstone walls and flying buttresses, Palma's magnificent **cathedral** (☎ 97 172 31 30; Plaça Almoina; admission €3.50; ✆ 10am-3.15pm Nov-Mar, 10am-6pm Apr-Oct, closed pm & Sun) overlooks the city and its port. It houses an excellent museum, and some of the interior features were designed by Gaudí.

Opposite is the **Palau Almudaina** (☎ 97 121 41 34; Carrer Palau Reial; adult/student €3.20/2.30; ✆ 10am-2pm & 4-6pm Oct-Mar, 10am-6.30pm Apr-Sep, closed Sat pm & Sun), the one-time residence of the Mallorcan monarchs. Inside is a collection of tapestries and artworks.

Es Baluard (☎ 97 190 82 00; www.esbaluard.org; Plaça Porta de Santa Catalina; adult/student €6/4.50; ✆ 10am-8pm Tue-Sun Oct-May, 10am-midnight daily Jun-Sep), Palma's striking museum of modern and contemporary art, is a visual feast of works from 20th-century artists, including Spanish greats Miró and Picasso.

The **Museu de Mallorca** (☎ 97 171 75 40; Carrer Portella 5; admission €2.40; ✆ 10am-7pm Tue-Sat, 10am-2pm Sun) has archaeological finds, as well as paintings and furniture from the 19th and 20th centuries. Nearby, are the atmospheric **Banys Árabs** (Arab Baths; ☎ 97 172 15 49; Carrer Ca'n Sera 7; admission €1.50; ✆ 9am-9pm Apr-Nov, 9am-7pm Dec-Mar), the only remaining monument to the Muslim domination of the island.

Mallorca's northwestern coast is a world away from the high-rise tourism on the other side of the island. Dominated by the Serra de Tramuntana, it's a beautiful region of olive groves, pine forests and small villages with shuttered stone buildings; it also has a rugged and rocky coastline. There are a couple of highlights for drivers: the hair-raising road down to the small port of **Sa Calobra**, and the amazing trip along the peninsula leading to the island's northern tip, **Cap Formentor**.

If you don't have wheels, take the **Palma–Sóller train** (see p996). It's one of the most popular and spectacular excursions on the island. Sóller is also the best place to base yourself for trekking and the nearby village of **Fornalutx** is said to be the prettiest on Mallorca.

From Sóller, it is a 10km walk to the beautiful hill-top village of **Deiá**, where Robert

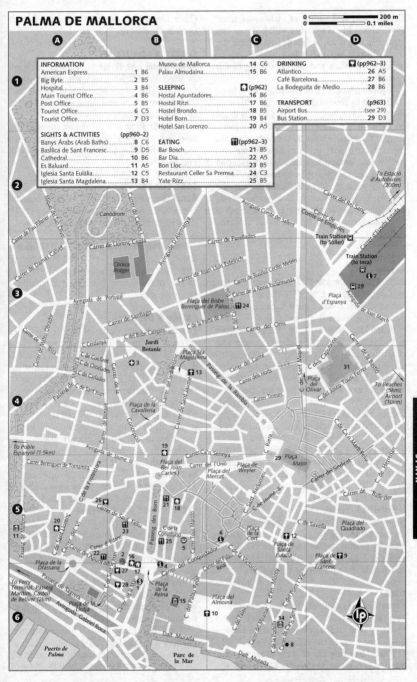

PALMA DE MALLORCA

0 — 200 m
0 — 0.1 miles

INFORMATION	
American Express	1 B6
Big Byte	2 B5
Hospital	3 B4
Main Tourist Office	4 B6
Post Office	5 B5
Tourist Office	6 C5
Tourist Office	7 D3

SIGHTS & ACTIVITIES	(pp960–2)
Banys Àrabs (Arab Baths)	8 C6
Basílica de Sant Francesc	9 D5
Cathedral	10 B6
Es Baluard	11 A5
Iglesia Santa Eulàlia	12 C5
Iglesia Santa Magdalena	13 B4

Museu de Mallorca	14 C6
Palau Almudaina	15 B6

SLEEPING	(p962)
Hostal Apuntadores	16 B6
Hostal Ritzi	17 B6
Hostel Brondo	18 B5
Hotel Born	19 B4
Hotel San Lorenzo	20 A5

EATING	(pp962–3)
Bar Bosch	21 B5
Bar Dia	22 A5
Bon Lloc	23 B5
Restaurant Celler Sa Premsa	24 C3
Yate Rizz	25 B5

DRINKING	(pp962–3)
Atlantico	26 A5
Café Barcelona	27 B6
La Bodeguita de Medio	28 B6

TRANSPORT	(p963)
Airport Bus	(see 29)
Bus Station	29 D3

SPAIN

Graves, poet and author of *I Claudius*, lived most of his life. From the village, you can scramble down to the **Cala de Deià**, where the small shingle beach is a laid-back haven of naked swimming and weekend-long beach parties.

Most of Mallorca's best beaches have been consumed by tourist developments, although there are exceptions. Lovely **Cala Mondragó** on the southeastern coast is backed by just a couple of *hostales* while, a little further south, the attractive port town of **Cala Figuera** and nearby **Cala Santanyi** beach have both escaped many of the ravages of mass tourism. There are also some good quiet beaches near the popular German resort of Colonia San Jordi, particularly **Ses Arenes** and **Es Trenc**, both a few kilometres back up the coast towards Palma.

Sleeping

PALMA

Hostal Apuntadores (☎ 97 171 34 91; apuntadores@ctv .es; Carrer Apuntadores 8; dm/d €17/45, s/d with shared bathroom €27/35) It has a great location but the décor is a little on the bland side.

Hostal Ritzi (☎ 97 171 46 10; d €50, s/d with shared bathroom €25/38) This little place is friendly and charming in a cluttered sort of way, with satellite TV in the communal sitting room.

Hostal Brondo (☎ 97 171 90 43; www.hostalbrondo .net; Carrer C'an Brondo 1; d €60, s/d/tr with shared bathroom €30/45/55) With a welcoming English owner and pretty communal areas, rooms in this *hostal* are clean and spacious, with high ceilings. Some have balconies.

Hotel Born (☎ 97 171 29 42; www.hotelborn.com; Carrer Sant Jaume 3; s/d from €56/81; ✷) With fabulous rooms in a restored 18th-century palace, it also has a classic Mallorcan patio filled with palm trees.

Hotel San Lorenzo (☎ 97 172 82 00; www.hotel sanlorenzo.com; Carrer Sant Llorenç 14; r from €140; ✷ ▣) Exquisite rooms in this converted 17th-century manor house have beamed ceilings and tiled bathrooms. The Art Deco bar downstairs was imported from Paris.

DEIÀ

Hostal Miramar (☎ 97 163 90 84; www.pensionmiramar .com; Can Oliver s/n; s/d/tr incl breakfast €31/60/82; ℗) Friendly and old-fashioned, rooms have a bird's-eye view of the village and sea.

S'Hotel D'es Puig (☎ 97 163 94 09; www.hoteldes puig.com; Es Puig 4; s/d incl breakfast €76/114; ✷ ▣)

Once featured in a short story by Robert Graves. Rooms are delightful.

SÓLLER & FORNALUTX

Hostal Nadal (☎ 97 163 11 80; Carrer Romaguera 29, Sóller; s/d/tr €22/34/44; s/d/tr with shared bathroom €18/26/35) This place has simple rooms but it's clean and airy and there is a small patio and bar downstairs.

Cán Verdera (☎ 97 163 82 03; www.canverdera.com; Carrer Toros 1, Fornalutx; s/d €89/105.30; ✷ ▣) An old stone building with original beams, pool and great views.

EAST COAST

Hostal Cán Jordi (☎ 97 164 50 35; Carrer Virgen del Carmen 58, Cala Figuera; s/d with shared bathroom €28/41) This place is justifiably popular, with wonderful views over the inlet.

Hostal Playa Mondragó (☎ 97 165 77 52; Cala Mon dragó; s/d €32/64; ✷ May-Oct; ✷ ▣) Five storeys high, this small beach resort overlooks one of the island's best (and least developed) sandy beaches.

Eating & Drinking

For Palma's best range of eateries, wander through the maze of streets between Plaça de la Reina and the port. Carrer Apuntadores is lined with bars and restaurants, including seafood, Italian and an inexpensive take-away **Bar Dia** (Carrer Apuntadores 18).

Yate Rizz (Passeig des Born 2; menú €5.30; ✷ 1pm-3.30pm Mon-Sat) Serves up the cheapest three-course meals (with wine) in town to a happy mix of locals and tourists crammed shoulder-to-shoulder over red-checked tablecloths.

Bar Bosch (☎ 97 172 11 31; Plaça Rei Joan Carlos; coffee & croissant €2.35; ✷ 7-1am) In a prime people-watching spot, Bar Bosch is a good choice for breakfast, sandwiches and snacks.

Restaurant Celler Sa Premsa (☎ 97 172 35 29; www.cellersapremsa.com; Plaça Bisbe Berenguer de Palou 8; mains €7-8; ✷ noon-4pm & 7.30-11.30pm Mon-Sat) This local institution is the size of a warehouse, serving enormous portions of classic Mallorcan fare.

Bon Lloc (☎ 97 171 86 17; Carrer San Feliu 7; menú €11; ✷ 1pm-4pm Mon-Sat; ✷) Popular with Palma's young professionals, it serves up tasty vegetarian dishes.

Good late-night drinking dens include **Atlantico** (Carrer Sant Feliu 12; ✷ 8pm-4am), with its unique combination of knock-out cocktails and grunge; **Café Barcelona** (Carrer Apuntadores 5;

8.30pm-1am Sun-Thu & 8.30pm-3am Fri & Sat), an intimate jazz club; and the fiery **La Bodeguita de Medio** (Carrer Vallseca 18; 8pm-1am Mon-Thu & 8pm-3am Fri & Sat), blaring out salsa to a *mojito*-fuelled crowd.

Getting Around

Bus No 25 runs between the airport and Plaça Espanya in central Palma (€1.80, 20 minutes, every 20 minutes). A taxi will cost around €14.

Most parts of the island are accessible by bus from Palma. Buses generally depart from or near the bus station at Plaça Espanya. Mallorca's two train lines also start from Plaça Espanya. One goes to the inland town of Inca (€1.80, 30 minutes, every 30 minutes) and the other goes to Sóller (€2.50, one hour, five daily), both highly picturesque jaunts.

The best way to get around the island is by car – it's worth renting one just for the drive along the northwestern coast. There are about 30 rental agencies in Palma (and all the big companies have reps at the airport). If you want to compare prices, check the many harbourside offices along Passeig Marítim.

IBIZA

From the bohemian atmosphere of Ibiza's old town to the hedonistic, foam-soaked fun of its world-famous clubs, Ibiza (Eivissa in Catalan) has a unique spirit, which can't fail to captivate.

Away from the remarkable clubbing scene, particularly in the rural villages in the south, you'll find an island that dashes any preconceived notions of Ibiza. Here the women wear long black skirts and wide straw hats and – forget the nudist beaches – the only traffic stoppers are the goatherds.

Orientation & Information

The capital, Ibiza city, is on the southeastern side of the island. This is where most travellers arrive (by ferry or air; the airport is to the south) and it's also the best base. The next largest towns are Santa Eulària des Riu, on the eastern coast, and Sant Antoni de Portmany, on the western coast (the latter best avoided unless you are seriously into discos and getting drunk). Other big resorts are scattered around the island. The **tourist office** (☎ 97 130 19 00; oitport@cief.es; Carrer Antoni Riquer 2; 9.30am-1.30pm & 5-7.30pm Mon-Fri, 10.30am-1pm

Sat Apr-Oct, 8.30am-3pm Mon-Fri, 10.30am-1pm Sat Nov-Mar) is opposite the Estación Marítima. There are numerous cafés where you can go online, but not many like **Wash and Dry.Com** (☎ 97 139 48 22; Avinguda Espanya 53; 10am-8.30pm Mon-Sat), where you can do a cheap load of washing.

Sights & Activities

Shopping is a major pastime in Ibiza city. The port area of **Sa Penya** is crammed with funky and trashy clothes boutiques and arty-crafty market stalls. From here, you can wander up into **D'Alt Vila**, the atmospheric old walled town, with its upmarket restaurants, galleries and the **Museu d'Art Contemporani** (☎ 97 130 27 23; Ronda Narcís Puget; admission free; 10am-1.30pm & 4-6pm Tue-Fri, 10am-6pm Sat & Sun Oct-Apr, 10am-1.30pm & 5-8pm Tue-Fri, 10am-1.30pm Sat & Sun May-Sep). There are fine views from the walls and from the **cathedral** (Plaça Catedral; 10am-1pm Tue-Sat) at the top, and the **Museu Arqueològic** (☎ 97 130 12 31; Plaça Catedral 3; admission €2.40; 10am-2pm & 6-8pm Mon-Sat, 10am-2pm Sun Apr-Sep, 9am-3pm Mon-Sat, 10am-2pm Sun Oct-Mar) is worth a visit.

The heavily developed **Platja de ses Figueretes** beach is a 20-minute walk south of Sa Penya – you'd be better off heading south to the beaches at **Ses Salines**, a half-hour ride on bus No 11 (€1.50).

Ibiza has numerous unspoiled and relatively undeveloped beaches. **Cala de Boix**, on the northeastern coast, is the only black-sand beach on the island, while further north are the lovely beaches of **S'Aigua Blanca**. On the northern coast near Portinatx, **Cala Xarraca** is in a picturesque, secluded bay and near Port de Sant Miquel is the attractive **Cala Benirràs**. On the southwestern coast, **Cala d'Hort** has a spectacular setting overlooking two rugged rock-islets, Es Verda and Es Verdranell.

Sleeping
IBIZA CITY

There are several *hostales* in the streets around the port, although in midsummer cheap beds are scarce.

Casa de Huéspedes Navarro (☎ 97 131 07 71; Carrer sa Creu 20; d/tr with shared bathroom €38/50; Apr-Oct) With 10 rooms at the top of a long flight of stairs, this place is in a good central location, with a sunny rooftop terrace.

Casa de Huéspedes Vara de Rey (☎ 97 130 13 76; hibiza@wanadoo.es; Passeig Vara de Rey 7; s/d with shared bathroom €36/72; Mar-Dec) Friendly, charming

SPAIN

and eclectic, it has 11 rooms, all with wash-basins and old-fashioned ceiling fans.

Hostal-Restaurante La Marina (☎ 97 131 01 72; res ervas@hostal-lamarina.com; Carrer Barcelona 7; s/d €62/77; ❄) On the waterfront, La Marina has immaculate rooms in cool colours and lots of wrought-iron furniture.

Hostal Parque (☎ 97 130 13 58; info@hostalparque .com; Plaça Parque 4; d €100, s/d with shared bathroom €48/72; ❄) Sleek, modern and minimalist, this place is on one of Ibiza's liveliest squares.

OTHER AREAS
Camping Cala Nova (☎ 97 133 17 74; per person/tent/car €5.40/4.60/4.60) Close to a good beach and 500m north of the resort town of Cala Nova, this is one of Ibiza's best camping grounds.

Hostal Cala Boix (☎ 97 133 52 24; s/d incl breakfast & shared bathroom €24.50/49; ❄) By the black-sand beach at Cala Boix, with a cliff-top location.

Pensión Sa Plana (☎ 97 133 50 73; d incl breakfast & shared bathroom €58; ❄ ♨) Near the S'Aigua Blanca beaches, with a poolside bar and barbecue.

Can Curreu (☎ 97 133 52 80; www.cancurreu.com; d €240; P ❄ ♨) This is the place for a fabulous splurge. It's a beautifully restored Ibizan farmhouse, with a pool, sauna, gymnasium and open fireplaces in the rooms.

Eating & Drinking
Start your evening with a drink and some people-watching (this island is stacked with poseurs) at one of the bars lining the lively Plaça Parque, such as **Herry's Bar** (☎ 97 139 11 52; Plaça Parque 2; ❄ 11.30am-midnight), which does the best *mojitos* this side of the Atlantic, or **Café Madagascar** (Plaça Parque 3; sandwiches €3.60; ❄ 9-2am), with fresh juices and tasty sandwiches, as well as the usual alcoholic fare.

Croissant Show (☎ 97 131 76 65; Plaça Constitució s/n; ❄ 7am-3pm) This is where everyone comes for post-clubbing munchies. The pastries are as good as any in Paris.

Comidas-Bar San Juan (☎ 97 131 16 03; Carrer Guillem de Montgri 8; mains €4-7; ❄ 1pm-3.30pm & 8.30-11pm) A popular, noisy place where diners share tables. The food is hearty and extremely good value for money. The fresh fish of the day comes highly recommended.

La Oliva (☎ 97 130 57 52; Calle Santa Cruz; mains €12-14; ❄ 1pm-4pm & 8-11.30pm Mon-Sat) With its pretty patio and Andalucían-style fare, La Oliva has maintained its good reputation. The fish soup is excellent.

Teatro Pereyra (☎ 97 119 14 68; Carrer Conde Roselló 3; ❄ 8-4am) In an old theatre, this is the place for jazz, blues and soul. Expect lots of atmosphere and live music every night. Entrance is free but the price of drinks shoots up once the music starts.

KM5 (☎ 97 139 63 49; www.km5-lounge.com; Carretera San José 5; ❄ 8pm-1.30am May-Oct) On the road to San Josep, 5km from Ibiza city, KM5 is a glam bar, lounge and garden hang-out.

Entertainment
Ibiza's summer nightlife is renowned. At night, wander the fashion catwalk of cobbled streets where designer-chic couples and seriously studded swingers dodge the outrageous PR performers hired by the discos to attract dusk-to-dawn clubbers. Dozens of bars keep Ibiza city's port area jumping until the early hours – particularly on Carrer Barcelona and Carrer Garijo Cipriano. After they wind down, you can continue on to one of the island's world-famous discos – if you can afford the €40 entry, that is. There's a handy Discobus service that operates nightly from midnight until 6am doing circuits between the major discos, the bars and hotels in Ibiza city, Platja d'en Bossa, San Rafael and San Antonio. The big names are **Pacha** (www.pacha.net), on the northern side of Ibiza city's port; **Privilege** (www.privilege.es) and **Amnesia** (www.amnesia-ibiza.com), both 6km out on the road to Sant Antoni; **El Divino** (www.eldivino-ibiza.com), across the water from the town centre (hop on one of its boats); and **Space** (www.space-ibiza.es), south of Ibiza city in Platja d'En Bossa.

Getting Around
Buses run between the airport and Ibiza city hourly (€1, 15 minutes); a taxi costs around €10. Buses to other parts of the island leave from the series of bus stops along Avinguda d'Isidoro Macabich. Pick up a timetable from the tourist office.

If you want to get to some of the more secluded beaches you will need to rent wheels. In Ibiza city, **Autos Isla Blanca** (☎ 97 131 54 07; Carrer Antoni Jaume s/n) will hire out a Renault Twingo for €103 for three days, all-inclusive.

FORMENTERA
A short boat ride south of Ibiza, Formentera is the smallest and least developed of the four main Balearic Islands. Most of the time it is

still possible to spread a towel on the beach without kicking sand over your neighbour. The island is famously flat and fantastic for cycling, with some excellent trails.

Orientation & Information

Formentera is about 20km from east to west. Ferries arrive at La Savina on the northwestern coast; the **tourist office** (☎ 97 132 20 57; www .formentera.es; ☽ 10am-2pm & 5-7pm Mon-Fri, 10am-2pm Sat) is behind the rental agencies you'll see when you disembark. Three kilometres south is the island's pretty capital, Sant Francesc Xavier, where you'll find a pharmacy, several banks and a good-sized supermarket for your picnic supplies. From here, the main road runs along the middle of the island before climbing to the highest point (192m). At the eastern end of the island is the Sa Mola lighthouse. Es Pujols is 3km east of La Savina and is the main tourist resort, with most of the *hostales* located here (and the only place with any nightlife to speak of).

Sights & Activities

Some of the island's best and most popular beaches are the beautiful white strips of sand along the narrow promontory that stretches north towards Ibiza. A 2km walking trail leads from the La Savina–Es Pujols road past the divine **Platja de Ses Illetes** to the far end of the promontory, from where you can wade (carefully) across a narrow strait to **S'Espalmador**, a privately owned uninhabited islet with beautiful, quiet beaches. If you don't fancy the paddle, there are regular boat rides. Along Formentera's southern coast, **Platja de Migjorn** is made up of numerous coves and beaches. Tracks lead down to these from the main road. On the western coast is the lovely **Cala Saona** beach.

The tourist office's *Green Tours* brochure outlines 19 excellent walking and cycling trails in five languages that take you through some of the island's most scenic areas.

Sleeping & Eating

Camping is not allowed on Formentera. Sadly, the coastal accommodation places predominantly cater to German and British package-tour agencies and are overpriced and/or booked out in summer.

There are some fantastic seafood restaurants on the island and, thanks to a particu-

larly large Argentine community, some excellent places to get grilled meat.

Hostal Capri (☎ 97 132 83 52; Es Pujols; s/d incl breakfast €46/60; ☽ May-Sep) This place has white-washed rooms with ceiling fans and balconies. Downstairs is a lovely shaded terrace restaurant specialising in paella.

Hostal Bellavista (☎ 97 132 22 55; La Savina; s/d €80/120; ☒) The Bellavista has port views, a handy terrace bar, spotless rooms and parrots in the lobby.

Casa de Huéspedes Miramar (☎ 97 132 70 60; Es Caló; s/d with shared bathroom €30/40; ☽ Apr-Oct) This family-run place has small rooms.

Fonda Rafalet (☎ 97 132 70 16; s/d €55/73; ☽ Apr-Oct) The quiet Rafalet has rooms with balconies overlooking the sea.

Hostal Pepe (☎ 97 132 80 33; Sant Ferrán de Ses Roques; s/d incl breakfast €28/46) This popular *hostal* is run by a very chatty landlady. The restaurant also has an excellent reputation. From here, Es Pujols is an easy cycle or walk along a 1.5km dusty (but pretty) track.

S'Avaradero (☎ 97 132 90 43; Ave Miramar 32-36, Es Pujols; mains €10-15; ☽ 1pm-4pm & 8-11.30pm) On the seafront and serving great seafood and Argentine-style meat dishes.

Pizza Art (☎ 97 132 90 94; Edificio Sa Varaderos; mains €5-7; ☽ 7pm-2am) Among the plethora of pizzerias, this place is better than most.

End the evening with a blast of music at the **Blue Bar** (☎ 97 118 70 11; Playa Mitjorn km 8; ☽ 8pm-4am), or at **Bar Sa Barraca** (☎ 97 132 80 27; Ave Miramar, Es Pujols) for tapas and local wine.

Getting There & Around

There are 20 to 25 ferries daily between Ibiza city and Formentera. The trip takes around 30 minutes and prices between the various companies are fiercely competitive, but cost around €10 one way.

A string of rental agencies lines the harbour in La Savina. Bikes start at €5 a day (€7 for a mountain bike) and scooters start at €20. A regular bus service connects all the main towns.

MENORCA

Menorca is the least overrun of the Balearic Islands, and is a popular destination for families. Renowned for its undeveloped beaches, archaeological sites and environmental areas – such as the Albufera d'es Grau wetlands – the island was declared a Biosphere Reserve by Unesco in 1993.

SPAIN

Orientation & Information

The capital, Maó (Mahón in Castilian), is at the eastern end of the island. Its busy port is the arrival point for most ferries and Menorca's airport is 7km southwest. The main road runs down the middle of the island to Ciutadella, Menorca's second-largest town, with secondary roads leading north and south to the resorts and beaches.

Post offices Maó (Carrer Bon Aire); Ciutadella (Carrer Pío VI 4)
Tourist offices Main office (☎ 97 136 37 90; info menorcamao@cime.es; Carrer Sa Rovellada de Dalt 24, Maó; 9.30am-3pm & 5-7pm Mon-Fri, 9am-1pm Sat); Ciutadella (☎ 97 138 26 93; Plaça la Catedral 5; 9.30am-1.30pm & 5-7pm Mon-Fri, 9am-1pm Sat) During summer there is also an office at the airport.

Sights & Activities

Maó and Ciutadella are both harbour towns, and from either place you'll have to commute to the beaches. Maó absorbs most of the tourist traffic. While you're here, you can take a boat cruise around its impressive harbour and sample the local gin at the **Xoriguer distillery** (☎ 97 136 21 97; Moll de Ponent 93; 8am-7pm Mon-Fri, 9am-1pm Sat).

Ciutadella, with its smaller harbour and historic buildings, has a more distinctly Spanish feel about it. Follow the shopping baskets to the colourful **market** (Plaça Llibertat), surrounded by lively tapas bars.

In the centre of the island, the 357m-high **Monte Toro** has great views of the whole island and, on a clear day, you can see as far as Mallorca.

With your own transport and a bit of footwork, you'll be able to discover some of Menorca's off-the-beaten-track beaches. North of Maó, a drive across a lunar landscape leads to the lighthouse at **Cabo de Favàritx**. If you park just before the gate to the lighthouse and climb up the rocks behind you, you'll see a couple of the eight beaches that are just waiting for scramblers such as yourself to explore.

On the northern coast, the picturesque town of **Fornells** is on a large bay popular with windsurfers. Further west, at the beach of Binimella, you can continue to the unspoilt **Cala Pregonda**, which is a good 20-minute walk from the nearest parking spot.

North of Ciutadella is **La Vall** (€5 per car; 10am-7pm), another stretch of untouched beach backed by a private nature park. On the southern coast are two good beaches

either side of the Santa Galdana resort – **Cala Mitjana** to the east and **Macarella** to the west.

Menorca's beaches aren't its only attractions. The interior of the island is liberally sprinkled with reminders of its rich and ancient heritage. Pick up a copy of the tourist office's *Archaeological Guide to Menorca*.

Sleeping

Menorca's two camping grounds are **Camping S'atalaia** (☎ 971 37 30 95; per person/tent/car €5.50/4.50/3; Apr-Oct), near the resorts of Santa Galdana, about 4km south of Ferreries, and **Camping Son Bou** (971 37 27 27; www.campingsonbou .com; per person/tent/car €6.20/3.45/4.15; Apr-Oct), near Son Bou, south of Alaior.

Posada Orsi (☎ 97 136 47 51; posadaorsi@hotmail .com; Carrer Infanta 19, Maó; s/d with shared bathroom €23/38) A riot of acid colours and stripy sofas, Orsi is bright, clean and well located. Tentlike mosquito nets add to the exotic air.

Hotel del Almirante (☎ 97 136 27 00; www.hotel delalmirante.com; Carreterra Maó–Es Castel; s/d €63/89.50; P 🐾) A magnificent Georgian-style mansion and a former residence of Nelson's second-in-command at Trafalgar, this place is a haven of terraces, lovely gardens, a pool and tennis court.

Hostal Oasis (☎ 97 138 21 97; Carrer Sant Isidre 33, Ciutadella; d with shared bathroom incl breakfast €46; Apr-Oct) Run by an elderly couple, it has homy rooms around a central courtyard.

Eating & Drinking

Both Maó and Ciutadella's ports are lined with restaurants and you won't have any trouble finding somewhere to eat.

MAÓ

La Bombilla (☎ 97 136 45 76; Plaça Bastión; bocadillos €2.70; 10.30am-11.30pm Tue-Sun) Quite noisy and smoky but an excellent no-nonsense choice for cheap snacks and tapas.

Casanova (☎ 97 135 41 69; Andén Poniente 15; pizzas €7; 1pm-4pm & 7.30-11.30pm) A popular pizzeria with a wood-burning oven.

Es Fosquet (☎ 97 135 00 58; Moll Llevant 256; mains €9-12; 1pm-4pm & 8-11.30pm Thu-Sun) A tiny but chic hole-in-the-wall place, serving up freshly caught fish and shellfish.

Latitud 40 (☎ 97 136 41 76; Moll Llevant 265, Maó; 7pm-1am) A hip little bar-restaurant popular with yachties.

CIUTADELLA

There are lots of good drinking holes near the port.

La Guitarra (☎ 97 138 13 55; Carrer Dolores 1; mains €12; ☒ 12.30-3.30pm & 7.30-11.30pm Mon-Sat) A classy place for a local meal, La Guitarra has a charming cellar-like setting with stone vaulted ceilings. The specialty is *pato a la menorquina* (Menorcan duck).

Getting Around

From the airport, a taxi into Maó costs around €10; there are no buses.

TMSA (☎ 97 136 04 75) runs six buses a day between Maó and Ciutadella (€3.75), with connections to the major resorts on the southern coast. In summer there are also daily bus services to most of the coastal towns from both Maó and Ciutadella.

If you're planning to hire a car, rates vary seasonally from around €28 to €48 a day; during summer, minimum hire periods sometimes apply. In Maó, places worth trying include **Autos Valls** (☎ 97 136 84 65; Plaça Espanya 13) and **Autos Isla** (☎ 97 136 65 69; Avinguda Josep Maria Quadrado 28).

ANDALUCÍA

Life is sweet in Andalucía. Whether you are soaking up the rays on a beach, exploring the alleyways of some historic barrio or simply sipping a glass of chilled gazpacho in a leafy plaza, pleasures here are simple.

The stronghold of the Muslims in Spain for nearly eight centuries, Andalucía is peppered with Moorish reminders of the past, among them the magnificent Alhambra in Granada, the timeless elegance of Córdoba's Mezquita and the whitewashed villages nestling in ochre hills. The regional capital, Seville, is one of the country's most enticing cities.

It's position away from the cities and resorts, mean that Andalucía is relatively untainted by the impact of tourists. Its scenery ranges from semideserts to lush river valleys and gorge-riddled mountains. Its long coastline stretches from the remote beaches of Cabo de Gata, past the crowds of the Costa del Sol, to come within 14km of Africa at Tarifa, before opening up to the Atlantic Ocean with the long sandy beaches of the Costa de la Luz.

FLAMENCO FUSION

Flamenco has become much more than the traditional signature music of southern Spain. Once exclusively the music of the Gitanos (Roma people), in recent years flamenco has also morphed into a modern fusion of different rhythms and styles. Since the 1970s, bands have experimented with blues, rock, Latin, jazz and even punk to create cool new sounds as well as a new fan base of young Spaniards. So much so that these days you are as likely to hear flamenco hip-hop blasting out of a souped-up car on a Friday night as to catch it at a tourist show.

Bands that first broke the ground in this new wave of flamenco include the bluesy-style Pata Negra, Ketama (African, Cuban and Brazilian rhythms) and Radio Tarifa (North African and medieval mix). In recent years Chambao has hit the mark with its flamenco chill and Mala Rodriguez has put flamenco hip into hip-hop.

SEVILLE

pop 709,975

An impossibly sexy and intoxicating city, Seville seduces all the senses. From its jumble of cobbled alleys and bright plazas to the spontaneous bursts of flamenco in the bars and the passion of its festivals, this is the most *andaluz* of Spain's cities. Even once you've left, Seville's memory lingers on.

If this wasn't enough, there is the marvellous exuberance and elegance of its people. Seville's air of contentment is well founded. It was an important and prosperous centre in Muslim times and, later, in the 16th and 17th centuries.

Seville is an expensive place, so it's worth planning your visit carefully. In July and August, the city is stiflingly hot. The best time to come is during the unforgettable Easter week and April *feria* (fair), although rooms then (if you can get one) cost close to double the regular rates.

Orientation

The Guadalquivir River cuts through Seville, with most places of interest on the river's eastern side. The centre is a maze of small plazas and winding streets, except for the broad, straight Ave Consitución. Most of the city's major monuments, including the cathedral, the Giralda and the Alcázar are just east of Ave Constitución. Further east, the Barrio de Santa Cruz is an appealing tangle of streets with most of Seville's budget accommodation.

Information
BOOKSHOPS
Librería Beta (☎ 95 456 28 17; Ave Constitución 9; ⊙ 10am-8pm Mon-Sat) Has guidebooks and novels in English.

INTERNET ACCESS
Internet Multimedia Center (☎ 95 450 25 43; Calle Adriano 7; per hr €2; ⊙ 10am-10pm Mon-Fri, 5-10pm Sat & Sun) One of Seville's many Internet places.

LAUNDRY
Lavandería Roma (Calle Castelar 2C; ⊙ 9.30am-1.30pm & 5-8.30pm Mon-Fri, 9am-2pm Sat) Will wash, dry and fold a load of washing for €6.

TOURIST INFORMATION
Tourist offices Main office (☎ 95 422 14 04; otsevilla@ andalucia.org; Ave Constitución 21; ⊙ 9am-7pm Mon-Fri, 10am-2pm & 3-7pm Sat, 10am-2pm Sun); Paseo de las Delicias 9 (☎ 95 423 44 65; ⊙ 8.30am-2.45pm Mon-Fri); Calle de Arjona 28 (☎ 95 450 56 00; ⊙ 8am-8.45pm Mon-Fri, 8.30am-2.30pm Sat & Sun)

Sights & Activities
CATHEDRAL & LA GIRALDA
Seville's towering **cathedral** (☎ 95 421 49 71; Calle Alemanes; adult/student €7/1.50, free Sun; ⊙ 11am-5pm Mon-Sat, 2.30-6pm Sun), one of the world's biggest, was built on the site of Muslim Seville's main mosque between 1401 and 1507. The structure is primarily Gothic, although most internal decoration is in later styles. The adjoining tower, La Giralda, was the mosque's minaret and dates from the 12th century. The exhausting climb to the top is worth it for the stunning city views. One highlight of the cathedral's lavish interior is Christopher Columbus' supposed tomb inside the southern door (although recent research indicates that Columbus was probably laid to rest in the Caribbean and the remains here are in fact those of his lesser-known son Diego). The four crowned sepulchre-bearers represent the four kingdoms of Spain at the time of Columbus' sailing to the Americas. The entrance to the cathedral and La Giralda is the Puerta del Perdón on Calle Alemanes.

ALCÁZAR
Seville's **alcázar** (☎ 95 450 23 23; adult/child €5/free; ⊙ 9.30am-7pm Tue-Sat, 9.30am-5pm Sun), a residence of Muslim and Christian royalty for many centuries, was founded in 913 as a Muslim fortress. It has been adapted by Seville's rulers in almost every century since, which makes it a mishmash of styles but adds to its fascination. The highlights are the **Palacio de Don Pedro**, exquisitely decorated by Muslim artisans for the Castilian king Pedro the Cruel in the 1360s, and the large, immaculately tended **gardens**, the perfect place to ease your body and brain.

WALKS & PARKS
To appreciate fully **Barrio de Santa Cruz**, the old Jewish quarter immediately east of the cathedral, you need to head for the tangle of narrow streets and plazas east of the main Calle Mateus Gago artery. There's no better place to get lost.

A more straightforward walk is along the **riverbank**, where the 13th-century **Torre del Oro** contains a small, crowded maritime museum. Nearby is Seville's famous bullring, the **Plaza de Toros de la Real Maestranza** (☎ 95 422 45 77; Paseo de Cristóbal Colón; guided tours €4; ⊙ 9.30am-7pm, 9.30am-3pm bullfight days), one of the oldest in Spain. The (compulsory) tour is in English and Spanish.

South of the centre is **Parque de María Luisa**, with its maze of paths, tall trees, flowers, fountains and shaded lawns. Be sure to seek out the magnificent **Plaza de España** with its fountains, canal and a simply dazzling semicircle of *azulejo* (ceramic tile) clad buildings.

MUSEUMS
The **Archivo de las Indias** (☎ 95 421 12 34) has been undergoing exhaustive renovation for several years, and was still closed at the time of writing. When it does open (hopefully by 2005), expect to be blown away by a fascinating collection of maps and papers dating from 1492 and documenting the conquest of the Americas and life in the Spanish colonies.

The **Museo de Bellas Artes** (☎ 95 422 07 90; Plaza Museo 9; admission non-EU/EU citizens €1.50/free; ⊙ 2.30-8.15pm Tue, 9am-8.15pm Wed-Sat, 9am-2.15pm Sun) has an outstanding, beautifully housed collection of Spanish art, focusing on local artists such as Bartolemé Esteban Murillo and Francisco Zurbarán.

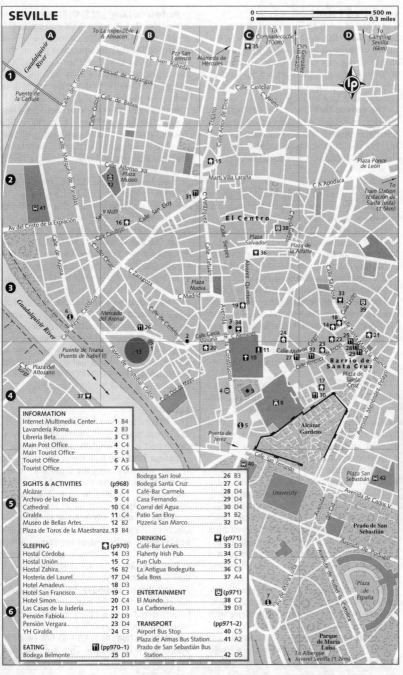

SEVILLE

0 —— 500 m
0 —— 0.3 miles

To La Imperdible & Almacén

To Compartecoche (100m) 🚉 35

To Camping Sevilla (6km)

Guadalquivír River

Puente de la Cartuja

Calle de Tomeo
C Juan Rabadán
Pza San Lorenzo
Alameda de Hércules
C Pascual de Gayangos
Calle Castellar
C Viriato
Calle Colón
Calle de Baños
C Trajano
Calle Amor de Dios

Martí Villa Laraña
🏠 15

Plaza Ponce de León

C A Apodaca

To Train Station (Estación de Santa Justa) (1.5km)

Calle Alfonso XII
Plaza Museo
🏛 12
🍴 31
C Velázquez
El Centro
🚉 38

Calle Marqués de Paradas

🚉 41

Av del Cristo de la Expiación
S an P Matir
16 🏠
Calle San Eloy
Calle Sierpes
Plaza Salvador
🚉 36
Plaza de la Alfalfa

Calle de Arjona
Calle Canalejas
Cuilio César
C Zaragoza
Calle Tetuán
Calle San José
🚉 39

Guadalquivír River

6 🛈
Calle Reyes Católicos
Mercado del Arenal
Plaza Nueva
C Madrid
Calle de Castelar
Alvarez Quintero
19 🍴
18
14
33

Puente de Triana (Puente de Isabel II)
13
@ 1
🍴 26
2
Calle García Vinuesa
3 34
C Alemanes
🚉 20
🏠 10
🏠 11
Calle Mateos Gago
24
23 25 28 🏠 21
22
27 🍴 32
Calle Ximénez de Enciso
Barrio de Santa Cruz
C San Jorge
Plaza Altozano

37 🚉

Calle Dos de Mayo
4 ✉
9
🏠 8
🏠 5
17 🏠
🍴 30
Plaza de Santa Cruz

Alcázar Gardens

Avenida Menéndez Pelayo

Puerta de Jerez

Calle San Fernando
🚉 40

Plaza San Sebastián 🚉 42

University

Avenida de Carlos V

7 🛈
Av de María Luisa
Avenida del Cid
Prado de San Sebastián

Avenida de Portugal

Avenida de Isabel la Católica

Plaza de España

Parque de María Luisa

To Albergue Juvenil Sevilla (1.2km)

SPAIN

INFORMATION
Internet Multimedia Center........... 1 B4
Lavandería Roma............................ 2 B3
Librería Beta.................................. 3 C3
Main Post Office............................ 4 C4
Main Tourist Office........................ 5 C4
Tourist Office................................ 6 A3
Tourist Office................................ 7 C6

SIGHTS & ACTIVITIES   (p968)
Alcázar... 8 C4
Archivo de las Indias..................... 9 C4
Cathedral..................................... 10 C4
Giralda.. 11 C4
Museo de Bellas Artes.................. 12 B2
Plaza de Toros de la Maestranza..13 B4

SLEEPING   🏠 (p970)
Hostal Córdoba............................ 14 D3
Hostal Unión................................ 15 C2
Hostal Zahira............................... 16 B2
Hostería del Laurel....................... 17 D4
Hotel Amadeus............................. 18 D3
Hotel San Francisco...................... 19 C4
Hotel Simón................................. 20 C4
Las Casas de la Judería................. 21 D3
Pensión Fabiola............................ 22 D3
Pensión Vergara........................... 23 D4
YH Giralda................................... 24 C3

EATING   🍴 (pp970-1)
Bodega Belmonte.......................... 25 D3
Bodega San José........................... 26 B3
Bodega Santa Cruz....................... 27 C4
Café-Bar Carmela......................... 28 D4
Casa Fernando.............................. 29 D4
Corral del Agua............................ 30 D4
Patio San Eloy.............................. 31 B2
Pizzería San Marco....................... 32 D4

DRINKING   🍺 (p971)
Café-Bar Levies............................ 33 D3
Flaherty Irish Pub........................ 34 C3
Fun Club...................................... 35 C1
La Antigua Bodeguita................... 36 C3
Sala Boss..................................... 37 A4

ENTERTAINMENT   🎬 (p971)
El Mundo..................................... 38 C2
La Carbonería.............................. 39 D3

TRANSPORT   (pp971-2)
Airport Bus Stop.......................... 40 C5
Plaza de Armas Bus Station........... 41 A2
Prado de San Sebastián Bus
  Station...................................... 42 D5

Festivals & Events

The first of Seville's two great festivals is **Semana Santa**, the week leading up to Easter Sunday. Throughout the week, long processions of religious brotherhoods, dressed in strange penitents' garb with tall, pointed hoods, accompany sacred images through the city, watched by huge crowds.

The **Feria de Abril**, a week in late April, is a welcome release after this solemnity: the festivities involve six days of music, dancing, horse-riding and traditional dress, plus daily bullfights and a city-wide party.

Sleeping

Summer prices given here can come down substantially from October to March but will shoot up in April.

Camping Sevilla (☎ 95 451 43 79; campingsevilla@ turinet.net; per person/tent/car €3.25/3.25/3.25; ☒) Six kilometres out on the N-IV towards Córdoba, this camping ground has a restaurant and a mini supermarket; it runs a shuttle bus to/from Ave Portugal (€2) in the city.

Albergue Juvenil Sevilla (☎ 95 505 65 00; Calle Isaac Peral 2; dm 25 yrs & under/26 yrs & over incl breakfast €13/17.50) Seville's youth hostel has 277 places in modern twins or triples. It's about 10 minutes south of the city by bus No 34, which leaves opposite the main tourist office (p968).

Pensión Vergara (☎ 95 421 56 68; pensionvergara sevilla@yahoo.es; Calle Ximenez de Enciso 11; s/d/tr/q with shared bathroom €18/36/54/72; ☐) Far and away Seville's best budget option, this enchanting *pensión* has twelve very pretty, airy rooms around an inviting courtyard in a former 15th-century convent.

Pensión Fabiola (☎ 95 421 83 46; Calle Fabiola 16; d €46, s/d with shared bathroom €20/40) A quiet place with a friendly *señora*, Fabiola has pretty rooms around a plant-filled courtyard.

Hostal Córdoba (☎ 95 422 74 98; hostalcordoba@ mixmail.com; Calle Farnesio 12; s/d €40/60, s/d with shared bathroom €35/50) This very welcoming, family-run place has simple rooms around a central courtyard where Otto, the West Highland terrier, keeps an eye on proceedings.

YH Giralda (☎ 95 422 83 24; www.yh-hoteles.com; Calle Abades 30; d €55; P ☒) A former 18th-century palace, close to the cathedral, with stylish rooms with all the mod cons and lovely timbered ceilings. Don't be put off by the name – it isn't anything like a youth hostel.

Hostería del Laurel (☎ 95 422 02 95; www.hosteria dellaurel.com; Plaza Venerables 5; s/d incl breakfast €67/ 97; ☒) With its enviable location on one of Barrio de Santa Cruz's prettiest plazas, this place is great if you get an attack of the munchies, as there's a busy bar and restaurant downstairs. The rooms are a little lacking in pazzazz for the price, though.

Hotel Simon (☎ 95 422 66 60; www.hotelsimonse villa.com; Calle Garcia de Vinuesa 19; s/d €50/75; ☒) The delightful internal courtyard is perfect for chilling out with the papers. Rooms are spacious and airy and most are decked with pretty tiles.

Hotel Amadeus (☎ 95 450 14 43; Calle Farnesio 6; s/d €63/76; P ☒ ☐) Filled with pianos and other musical instruments, this place is excellent value for money and the individually designed rooms are dazzling.

Las Casas de la Judería (☎ 95 441 51 50; www .casasypalacios.com; Callejón Dos Hermanas 7; s/d from €101/156; ☒) Rooms here are in small Andalucían-style houses set around patios and fountains. Worth every penny.

Away from the Barrio de Santa Cruz, you could try **Hostal Zahira** (☎ 95 422 10 61; Calle San Eloy 43; s/d/tr €30/45/60) on an attractive pedestrian shopping street or helpful **Hostal Union** (☎ 95 421 17 90; Calle Tarifa 4; s/d €30/42, s/d with shared bathroom €21/30), with big old-fashioned rooms. **Hotel San Francisco** (☎ 95 450 15 41; Calle Alvarez Quintero 38; s/d from €55/68; ☒) is bright and cheery.

Eating

The Barrio de Santa Cruz provides a wonderful setting for restaurants, although you can expect to pay slightly inflated prices.

Bodega Santa Cruz (Calle Mateos Gago; tapas €1.40; ☒ 8am-midnight) Among the tapas bars in the Barrio de Santa Cruz, this joint buzzes with tourists and locals. The crowd spills out onto the footpath.

Bodega Belmonte (☎ 95 421 40 14; Calle Mateos Gago 24; tapas €1.50; ☒ 9am-1am) Has stuffed bull's heads on the walls and an impressive selection of wines. It also does a fine sangría.

Patio San Eloy (☎ 95 422 11 48; Calle San Eloy 9; tapas & montaditos €1.50; ☒ 11.30am-5pm & 7.30pm-midnight) Bright and busy, this bar is famed for its *fino* (sherry) bar and *montaditos* (multi-tiered sandwiches); madly popular with locals of all ages.

Bodega San Jose (☎ 95 422 41 05; Calle Adriano 10; tapas €1.50; ☒ 8am-11.30pm) This ancient, dishevelled bar, filled with rickety wooden tables, beer crates and peeling posters of '50s football stars, is known for its fried prawns and it's superb tortilla.

Pizzeria San Marco (☎ 95 456 43 90; Calle Mesón del Moro 6; mains €6; ☯ 1.15-4.30pm & 8.15pm-midnight Tue-Sun) In what was once a Moorish bathhouse, San Marco has plenty of atmosphere and does highly popular pizzas and pastas.

Corral del Agua (☎ 95 422 48 42; Callejon Agua 6; mains €12-16; ☯ 1pm-4pm & 8.30pm-midnight Mon-Sat) The cool courtyard makes this an ideal summer spot for enjoying excellent fish dishes. It's a good idea to book ahead.

Calle Santa María La Blanca has several simple places with outdoor tables doing generous set-lunch *menús* for about €7. Two of the best are **Casa Fernando** (☎ 95 442 26 60; Calle Santa Maria la Blanca 10; menú €7; ☯ 11am-4pm & 7-11pm Mon-Sat) and the trendier **Café-Bar Carmela** (☎ 95 454 05 90; Calle Santa Maria la Blanca 6; menú €7; ☯ 9am-1am), with some excellent vegetarian options on the menu, including a divine raspberry gazpacho.

Drinking

On fine nights throngs of people block the streets outside popular bars, leaning against their scooters and eyeing up the crowd.

Café-Bar Levies (☎ 95 421 53 08; Calle San José 15; ☯ 8-3am) Heaving at various times throughout the day and night with American students and locals knocking back €1 glasses of beer, this is a good place to meet fellow travellers as well as a cheap source of snacks and tapas (from €1.50).

Until about 1am, Plaza Salvador has several popular watering holes, including **La Antigua Bodeguita** (Plaza Salvador 6; ☯ 11pm-2am), with outdoor barrel tables for checking out the crowd.

There are some hugely popular bars around the cathedral, including **Flaherty Irish Pub** (☎ 95 421 04 51; Calle Alemanes 7; ☯ 11pm-3am) with regular live Celtic music.

From about 1am things start building up in the busy music bars around Calle Adriano, west of Ave Constitución. Nearby, on Calle García Vinuesa and Calle Dos de Mayo, are some quieter bodegas, some with good tapas, that attract an older crowd.

The Alameda de Hercules area, a former red-light district north of the city centre, is another buzzing place with lots of offbeat bars. Some have live music, including the **Fun Club** (☎ 95 438 93 29; Alameda de Hércules 86; live

---

> **DEATH IN THE AFTERNOON**
>
> Seville's bullfight season runs from Easter to October, with fights about 6.30pm most Sundays, and every day during the Feria de Abril and the preceding week. Tickets start at around €10 or €20, depending on who's fighting. *Sol* (sun) seats are cheaper than *sombra* (shadow) seats. If you get a particularly good matador, the atmosphere in the ring can be electrifying. Tickets can be purchased in advance from any of the official kiosks on streets near the bullring.

---

music about €5; ☯ 10pm-6am Thu-Sat), a small, busy dance warehouse where rock, pop and indie bands play live some nights. Several good pub-like bars line the same street a little further north.

In summer there's a lively scene along the eastern bank of the Guadalquivir River, which is dotted with temporary bars. On Calle Betis, on the far bank, you'll find some good dance bars/discos, including **Sala Boss** (☎ 95 428 19 93; www.discotecaboss.com; Calle Betis 67; admission free; ☯ 10.30pm-6am), Seville's biggest nightclub. You have to dress up and look at least 24 years old to get in.

Entertainment

Seville is arguably Spain's flamenco capital and you're most likely to catch a spontaneous atmosphere (of unpredictable quality) in one of the bars staging regular nights of flamenco with no admission fee. These include the sprawling **La Carbonería** (☎ 95 421 44 60; Calle Levíes 18; ☯ 9pm-4am), thronged every night of the week with tourists and locals (flamenco kicks off at about 11pm), and **El Mundo** (www.elmundotrobar.com; Calle Siete Revueltas 5; ☯ 11pm-late), which has flamenco at 11pm most Tuesday nights.

Getting There & Away

AIR

There's a range of domestic and international flights at **Seville airport** (☎ 95 444 90 00).

BUS

Buses from **Plaza de Armas bus station** (☎ 95 490 80 40) run to/from Madrid (€16, six hours, hourly), Lisbon (€25, 6¼ hours, three weekly) and Andalucían towns west of Seville and to Extremadura.

Buses to other parts of Andalucía and eastern Spain use **Prado de San Sebastián bus station** (☎ 95 441 71 11), with services to/from Córdoba (€9, 1¾ hours, 10 daily), Granada (€16, three hours, 10 daily) and Málaga (€12, 2½ hours, seven daily).

TRAIN

From Seville's **Eastación Santa Justa** (Ave Kansas City), 1.5km northeast of the centre, there are both super fast AVE trains and regular trains to/from Madrid (€51.50 to €65, 2½ to 3¼ hours, hourly) and Córdoba (€7 to €20, 45 minutes to 1¼ hours, hourly).

Other trains travel to/from Cádiz (€8.40, 1¾ hours, 10 daily), Granada (€17.65, 3¼ hours, four daily), Málaga (€14, 2½ hours, five daily) and Mérida (€11, 4¾ hours, one a day).

Getting Around

The airport is 7km from the centre, off the N-IV Córdoba road. **Amarillos Tour** (☎ 902 21 03 17) runs half-hourly buses to/from Puerta Jerez in the city (€2.30). Bus No C1, in front of Santa Justa train station, follows a clockwise circuit via Ave Carlos V, close to Prado de San Sebastián bus station and the city centre; bus No C2 does the same route anticlockwise. Bus No C4, south down Calle Arjona from Plaza Armas bus station, goes to Puerta Jerez in the centre; returning, take No C3.

CÓRDOBA

pop 318,628

There can't be many more enjoyable ways to explore the soul of Andalucía than to lose yourself in Córdoba's old quarter, a maze of winding, cobbled alleyways, pretty plazas and lovely flower-filled patios.

The city is a testament to its Moorish past, when Córdoba became the effective Islamic capital on the peninsula following the Muslim invasion in AD 711, a position it held for nearly 300 years. Muslim Córdoba at its peak was the most splendid city in Europe and its Mezquita (mosque) is one of the most magnificent of all Islamic buildings.

Orientation

Immediately north of the Guadalquivir River is the old city, a warren of narrow streets surrounding the Mezquita. Around 500m north of here is Plaza Tendillas, the main square of the modern city.

Information

Navegaweb (Plaza Judá Leví s/n; per hr €1.50; 🕙 10am-10pm) Internet access.

Municipal tourist office kiosks (🕙 10am-2pm & 4.30-7.30pm) Helpful info at Plaza Tendillas, Campo Santos Mártires, Plaza Posada del Potro and the train station.

Regional tourist office (☎ 95 747 12 35; Calle Torrijos 10; 🕙 9.30am-6pm Mon-Fri, 10am-7pm Sat, 10am-2pm Sun Mar-Oct, until 6pm Mon-Fri Nov-Feb) Officious service; facing the Mezquita.

Sights & Activities

The inside of the famous **Mezquita** (☎ 95 747 05 12; adult/child €6.50/3.25; 🕙 10am-7pm Mon-Sat, 2-6.30pm Sun Mar-Oct, 10am-5.30pm Mon-Sat, 2-6.30pm Sun Jan, Feb, Nov & Dec), which was begun by emir Abd ar-Rahman I in 785 and enlarged by subsequent generations, is a mesmerising sequence of two-tier arches amid a thicket of columns. From 1236, the mosque was used as a church and in the 16th century a cathedral was built right in its centre – somewhat wrecking the effect of the original Muslim building, in many people's opinion.

The **Judería**, Córdoba's medieval Jewish quarter northwest of the Mezquita, is an intriguing maze of narrow streets and small plazas. Don't miss the beautiful little **Sinagoga** (☎ 95 720 29 28; Calle Judíos; admission non-EU/EU citizens €0.30/free; 🕙 10am-7pm Tue-Sun), one of Spain's very few surviving medieval synagogues. The **Museo Taurino** (Bullfighting Museum; ☎ 95 720 10 56; Plaza Maimónides; admission €3; 🕙 10am-2pm & 5.30-7.30pm Tue-Sat, 9.30am-2.30pm Sun) celebrates Córdoba's legendary matadors such as El Cordobés and Manolete.

Southwest of the Mezquita stands the **Alcázar de los Reyes Cristianos** (Fortress of the Christian Monarchs; ☎ 95 742 01 51; admission €2; 🕙 10am-2pm & 5.30-7.30pm Tue-Sat, 9.30am-2.30pm Sun), with large and lovely gardens.

On the southern side of the river, across the Puente Romano, is the **Torre de la Calahorra** (☎ 95 729 39 29; adult/student €4/2.50; 🕙 10am-2pm & 4.30-8.30pm), with a museum highlighting the intellectual achievements of Islamic Córdoba, and featuring excellent models of the Mezquita and Granada's Alhambra.

It is well worth the 8km trip west of Córdoba to the intriguing **Medina Azahara** (☎ 95 732 91 30; Carretera Palma del Río, km 5.5; admission non-EU/EU citizens €1.50/free; 🕙 10am-6.30pm Tue-Sat, 10am-2pm Sun), a mighty Muslim city-palace in the 10th century. If you don't have your own wheels, catch the tourist bus (€5), which leaves from

CÓRDOBA

0 ___ 200 m
0 ___ 0.1 miles

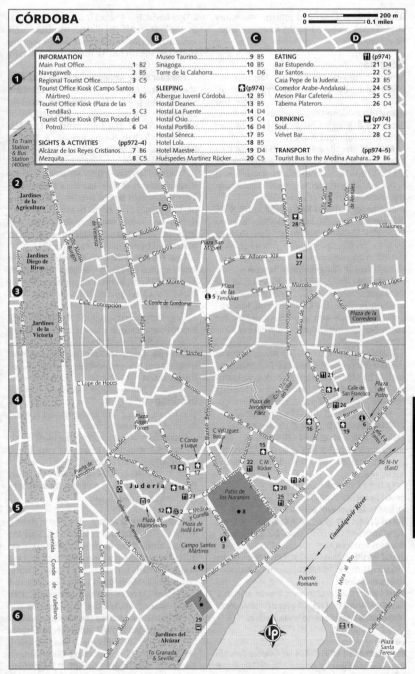

INFORMATION
Main Post Office.................................1 B2
Navegaweb..2 B5
Regional Tourist Office.....................3 C5
Tourist Office Kiosk (Campo Santos
  Mártires)......................................4 B6
Tourist Office Kiosk (Plaza de las
  Tendillas)....................................5 C3
Tourist Office Kiosk (Plaza Posada del
  Potro)...6 D4

SIGHTS & ACTIVITIES (pp972–4)
Alcázar de los Reyes Cristianos......7 B6
Mezquita...8 C5

Museo Taurino..................................9 B5
Sinagoga...10 B5
Torre de la Calahorra.....................11 D6

SLEEPING (p974)
Albergue Juvenil Córdoba.............12 B5
Hostal Deanes................................13 D4
Hostal La Fuente............................14 D4
Hostal Osio....................................15 C4
Hostal Portillo...............................16 D4
Hostal Séneca................................17 B5
Hotel Lola......................................18 B5
Hotel Maestre................................19 D4
Huéspedes Martínez Rücker.........20 C5

EATING (p974)
Bar Estupendo................................21 D4
Bar Santos......................................22 C5
Casa Pepe de la Judería.................23 B5
Comedor Arabe-Andalussi.............24 C5
Meson Pilar Cafetería.....................25 C5
Taberna Platerors...........................26 D4

DRINKING (p974)
Soul...27 C3
Velvet Bar......................................28 C2

TRANSPORT (pp974–5)
Tourist Bus to the Medina Azahara...29 B6

SPAIN

Ave Alcázar at 11am and returns two hours later. Tickets can be bought from the tourist office.

Sleeping

Most lodgings are close to the Mezquita and nearly all are built around lovely cool patios. High-season prices are given below but many places drop their rates from November to mid-March and in the hot summer months of July and August.

Albergue Juvenil Córdoba (☎ 95 729 01 66; Plaza Judá Leví s/n; dm 25 yrs & under/26 yrs & over incl breakfast €13.35/18.35) Córdoba's excellent youth hostel is perfectly positioned on a pretty and central plaza. It has no curfew.

Huéspedes Martínez Rücker (☎ 95 747 67 97; Calle Martínez Rücker 14; s/d/tr with shared bathroom €12.50/25/37.50) Some rooms in this chaotic, leafy haven have gorgeous old beds and are dotted with antiques. All are fairly basic though and it can get nippy in winter.

Hostal Osio (☎ 95 748 51 65; Calle Osio 6; s/d with shared bathroom €25/40; P 🖳) One of Córdoba's prettiest *hostales*, the Osio has pine furnishings, two patios and good views – try for room No 10 overlooking the adjacent convent.

Hostal Séneca (☎ 95 747 32 34; hostalseneca@eresmas .com; Calle Conde y Luque 7; s/d €34/46, s/d with shared bathroom €22/39) This charming place has welcoming owners and rooms around an enchanting patio and little bar. It's understandably popular so phone ahead. Breakfast included.

Hotel Maestre (☎ 95 747 24 10; www.hotelmaestre .com; Calle Romero Barros 4; s/d €29/47; P 🐾) This small, bright hotel has a dash of Spanish chic in a good location northeast of the Mezquita.

Other recommendations:

Hostal La Fuente (☎ 95 748 78 27; Calle San Fernando 51; s/d €24/42) Large patio and roof terrace.

Hostal Deanes (☎ 95 729 37 44; Calle Deanes 6; d with shared bathroom €31) Friendly, central but noisy; its patio doubles as a tapas bar.

Hostal Portillo (☎ 95 747 20 91; Calle Cabezas 2; s/d with shared bathroom €18/30/45) Housed in an ancient, atmospheric building.

Hotel Lola (☎ 95 720 03 05; www.hotelconencantolola .com; Calle Romero 3; d €115, 🐾) *Típico* Córdoban décor, fabulous original tiled floors and beamed ceilings.

Eating

Bar Estupendo (☎ 95 747 04 94; Calle San Fernando 39; mains €4-5; menu incl drinks €7.50; ☽ 1pm-4pm &

8-11pm Tue-Sat, 1pm-4pm Sun) It may not be much to look at, with its plastic furniture and gloomy interior, but this bar does a roaring trade serving up hearty three-course *menús* to hungry Córdobans.

Comedor Arabe-Andalussi (☎ 95 747 51 62; Plaza Abades 4; mains €3.50-5; ☽ noon-4pm & 7-11pm Tue-Sun) Set on a pretty plaza, this Arabian-style eatery has a wonderfully exotic setting of oriental carpets and low, candle-lit tables. The lamb kebab, in particular, is superb but vegetarians will also love the fantastic salads and falafel.

Taberna Platerors (☎ 95 747 00 42; Calle San Francisco 6; raciónes €4-6; ☽ 1pm-4pm & 8pm-midnight) This large patio tavern is noisy and slightly peeling around the edges but the solid Córdoban fare is fabulous. Try the *berenjenas fritas*, a large plate of aubergines fried in batter and better than French fries!

Casa Pepe de la Judería (☎ 95 720 07 44; Calle Romero 1; mains €10-15; ☽ 1pm-4pm & 8.30-11.30pm) This local classic is always hopping and even though it's a bit pricey, it's Córdoban food at its best.

Good tapas bars include **Bar Santos** (Calle Magistral González Francés 3; tapas €1.20; ☽ 12.30-4pm & 7pm-midnight), famed for its tortilla, while **Meson Pilar Cafeteria** (Calle Cardenal González 66; breakfast from €1.70; ☽ 8am-10.30pm) is *the* place for breakfast.

Drinking

Córdoba's livelier bars are scattered around the north and west of town.

Velvet Bar (Calle Alfaros 29; ☽ 5pm-4am) With wicked flower-power décor over two floors, it pulls in a gay and mixed crowd.

Soul (☎ 95 749 15 80; Calle Alfonso XIII 3; ☽ 10-3am Mon-Fri, 5pm-4am Sat & Sun) Attracts student/arty types and has live music.

Getting There & Away

From the **bus station** (☎ 95 740 40 40; Plaza Tres Culturas), about 1km northwest of Plaza Tendillas, buses run to/from Seville (€9, 1¾ hours, 10 daily), Granada (€13, 2½ hours, eight daily), Madrid (€11, 4¾ hours, seven daily) and Málaga (€11, three hours, five daily), among many other destinations.

From the **train station** (Ave América), services run to/from Seville (€7 to €20, 45 minutes to 1¼ hours, 20 daily) and Madrid (€48, 1¾ hours to 2¼ hours, every 30 minutes). There are also trains to/from Málaga (€16,

2¼ hours, nine daily) and Algeciras (€26.50, four hours, two daily).

GRANADA

pop 237,663

You can't help falling in love with Granada. This engaging city, popular with travellers, students and street artists, enjoys one of Europe's finest settings beneath the snowy peaks of Andalucía's Sierra Nevada.

From the 13th to 15th centuries, Granada was capital of the last Muslim kingdom in Spain. Today it has the greatest Muslim legacy in the country and one of the most magnificent buildings on the continent – the Alhambra.

Information

Navegaweb (Calle Reyes Católicos 55; per hr €1; ⊙ 10am-11pm daily) Internet access.

Tourist offices Main office (☎ 95 824 71 28; www .turismogranada.org; Plaza Mariana Pineda 10; ⊙ 9am-8pm Mon-Fri, 10am-7pm Sat, 10am-3pm Sun); Plaza Santa Ana (☎ 95 822 59 90; ⊙ 9am-8pm Mon-Fri, 9am-6pm Sat, 9am-2pm Sun)

Sights & Activities

ALHAMBRA

One of the greatest accomplishments of Islamic art and architecture, the **Alhambra** (☎ 902 44 12 21; admission €10; ⊙ 8.30am-8pm Apr-Oct, 8.30am-6pm Nov-Mar) is simply breathtaking. Much has been written about the Alhambra's fortress, palace, patios and gardens, but nothing can really prepare you for what you will see.

The **Alcazaba**, the Alhambra's fortress, dates from the 11th to the 13th centuries. There are spectacular views from the tops of its towers. The **Palacio Nazaries** (Nasrid Palace), built for Granada's Muslim rulers in their 13th- to 15th-century heyday, is the centrepiece of the Alhambra. The beauty of its patios and intricacy of its stucco and woodwork, epitomised by the Patio de los Leones (Patio of the Lions) and Sala de las Dos Hermanas (Hall of the Two Sisters), are stunning. Don't miss the **Generalife**, the soul-soothing palace gardens, a great spot to relax and contemplate the Alhambra from a little distance.

OTHER ATTRACTIONS

Explore the narrow, hilly streets of the **Albaicín**, the old Moorish quarter across the river from the Alhambra, and head uphill

---

ALHAMBRA TICKETS

It is becoming increasingly essential to book tickets to the Alhambra in advance. You can reserve via any branch of the Banco Bilbao Viscaya (BBV), including the Granada branch on Plaza Isabel la Católica, or by calling ☎ 902 22 44 60 from within Spain (☎ 00 34 91 537 91 78 from abroad) or paying by credit card on the website www .alhambratickets.com.

---

for the **Mirador de San Nicolas** – a viewpoint with breathtaking vistas and a relaxed, hippy scene. On your way down, stop by the **Museo Arqueológico** (☎ 95 822 56 40; Carrera Darro; admission non-EU/EU citizen €1.50/free; ⊙ 9am-8pm Wed-Sat, 3-8pm Tue, 9am-2.30pm Sun), at the foot of the Albaicín.

Another enjoyable area for strolling is around **Plaza de Bib-Rambla**, looking in at the **Capilla Real** (Royal Chapel; ☎ 95 822 92 39; Calle Oficios; admission €3; ⊙ 10.30am-1pm & 4.30-7pm), in which Fernando and Isabel, the Christian conquerors of Granada in 1492, are buried. Next door to the chapel is Granada's **cathedral** (☎ 95 822 29 59; admission €3; ⊙ 10.45am-1.30pm & 4-8pm Mon-Sat, 4-8pm Sun), dating from the early 16th century.

Sleeping

Things can get very booked up year-round, so it's a good idea to phone ahead. Good budget options can be found around the social hub of Plaza Nueva.

Camping Sierra Nevada (☎ 95 815 00 62; Ave Madrid 107; per person/tent €4.50/4.50; 🔊) Two hundred metres from the Estación de Autobuses, this is the closest camping ground to the centre and is open year-round.

Albergue de Juventud (☎ 95 827 26 38 or ☎ 95 800 29 00; Calle Ramón y Cajal 2; dm 25 yrs & under/26 yrs & over €12/18.50) Granada's modern youth hostel is 1.7km southwest of the centre and a 600m walk southwest of the train station.

Hostal Venecia (☎ 95 822 39 87; Cuesta Gomérez 2; s/d/tr with shared bathroom €15/28/41) A fabulous, if tiny, place, whose friendly owners bring you herbal tea in the morning.

Hostal Britz (☎ 95 822 36 52; Cuesta Gomérez 1; s/d with shared bathroom €19/29) With saggy beds and big, old-fashioned rooms, this budget travellers' classic can get noisy at times.

Hostal Zacatín (☎ 95 822 11 55; hostalzacatin@hot mail.com; Calle Ermita 11; d €38, s/d with shared bathroom €17/28) Hidden away up a narrow alleyway off

GRANADA

0   200 m
0   0.1 miles

INFORMATION	
Banco BBV	1 C3
Main Tourist Office	2 D4
Navegaweb	3 C3
Polici Nacional	4 A2
Post Office	5 C4
Tourist Office	6 D2

SIGHTS & ACTIVITIES	(pp975)
Capilla Real	7 C3
Cathedral	8 C3
Iglesia de Santa Ana	9 D2
Museo Arqueológico	10 D1

SLEEPING	(pp975-7)
Casa Morisca	11 E1
Hostal Britz	12 D2
Hostal La Ninfa	13 E3
Hostal Venecia	14 C2
Hostal Zacatín	15 C3
Hotel América	16 F2
Hotel Los Tilos	17 B3
Hotel Macia Plaza	18 C2

EATING	(p977)
Al-Andalus	19 C2
Bar Casa Julio	20 C2
Boabdil	21 C2
Café Bib-Rambla	22 B3
La Gran Taberna	23 C2
Mercado	24 B2
Taberna Salinas	25 C2

DRINKING	(p977)
BMC	26 D3
Candela	27 D3
Kasbah	28 C2
Rincón de San Pedro	29 D1
Upsetter	30 D2

ENTERTAINMENT	(p977)
Eshavira	31 B1
Granada 10	32 B2
Sala Príncipe	33 E3
Zoo	34 C4

the pretty Plaza de Bib-Rambla, this place is a little gem, with clean simple rooms.

Hostal La Ninfa (☎ 95 822 26 61; Campo Príncipe s/n; s/d €45/52; ✿) This enchanting, eclectic *hostal* is covered in ceramic designs. Rooms have pretty beamed ceilings and tiled floors.

Hotel Los Tilos (☎ 95 826 67 12; Plaza Bib-Rambla; s/d from €41/55; ✿) Overlooking a daily flower market, there are superb views from its 4th-floor terrace and rooms are comfortable.

Hotel Macía Plaza (☎ 95 822 75; www.macia hoteles.com; Plaza Nueva 4; s/d €49/73; ✿) A well-located, modernised hotel with very pleasant rooms overlooking Plaza Nueva.

Casa Morisca (☎ 95 822 11 00; www.hotelcasa morisca.com; Cuesta Victoria 9; d from €111; ✿) This place has Alhambra views and fabulous Moorish-inspired décor with central patio, wooden ceilings and rich tile work.

Hotel América (☎ 95 822 74 71; www.hotelamerica granada.com; Calle Real de Alhambra 53; s/d €68/107; ✿ Mar-Oct; **P** ✿) Occupying a magical position within the walls of the Alhambra; you need to reserve well ahead.

Eating

Plaza Nueva and the surrounding streets are the best places for good eats.

Café Bib-Rambla (Plaza Bib-Rambla; ✿ 8am-midnight) This café has been going for nearly a century and is great for a breakfast of chocolate and *churros*.

Al-Andalus (☎ 95 822 67 30; Calle Elivira; filled pittas €2; ✿ 11pm-3am) The place for divine Arabian food, either to take-away or to eat at the outside tables. Vegetarians will adore the pitta and felafel. Great for those 2am munchies.

Bar Casa Julio (Calle Hermosa s/n; ✿ 10.30am-4.30pm & 8.30pm-midnight) A traditional no-nonsense bar renowned for its tapas, especially the fried fresh anchovies *(boquerones fritos)*. Wildly popular.

Restaurante Mirador de Morayma (☎ 95 822 82 90; Calle Pianista Garcia Carrillo 2; mains €10-15; ✿ 1.30-3.30pm & 8.30-11.30pm) In the Albaicín, this restaurant has fabulous views of the Alhambra, a very pretty terrace and excellent dishes such as *remojón* (orange and bacalao; €6.40). There's live flamenco at 11pm Tuesday.

For fresh fruit and veggies, there is the large covered **market** (Calle San Agustín).

Other good options around Plaza Nueva:

Taberna Salinas (☎ 95 822 14 11; Calle Elvira 13; mains €7-15; ✿ 1.30-4pm & 8pm-midnight) Busy with great grilled seafood and meat.

Boabdil (☎ 95 822 81 36; Calle Hospital de Peregrines 2; mains €4-5; ✿ 1.30-4pm & 8-11.30pm Tue-Sun) A kitchen sink–informal restaurant.

La Gran Taberna (☎ 95 822 88 46; Plaza Nueva 12; tapas €1.50) Traditional-style bodega with inexpensive tapas; good for breakfast.

Drinking

Nightlife in the Albaicín centres on Carrera Darro, with several bars and clubs within a few doors of each other, including **Rincón de San Pedro** (Carrera Darro 12) and the late-night reggae bar **Upsetter** (Carrera Darro 7; ✿ from 11pm).

Further east, the Realejo barrio is another up-and-coming scene stacked with bars, including **BMC** (Calle Escolástica 15; ✿ 10pm-3am), pumping out dance music to a young crowd on the pull, and the mellower **Candela** (Calle Escolástica 1; ✿ 8pm-1am).

Entertainment

Eshavira (Postigo Cuna 2; ✿ 8.30pm-3am) has live jazz and flamenco.

Granada 10 (Calle Cárcel Baja; admission €6; ✿ midnight-dawn) is a disco with salsa on Sunday night. If you're looking for house music, then head to **Sala Principe** (Campo Principe 7; admission €6; ✿ 11pm-8am Thu-Sun), located in an old cinema (no sportswear).

A good gay/mixed dance club is **Zoo** (Plaza Campillo; admission €6; ✿ 2-8am Thu-Sun).

Getting There & Away

Granada's **bus station** (☎ 95 818 54 80; Carretera Jáen) is 3km northwest of the centre. Catch bus No 3 or 33 to reach the centre. Buses serve Madrid (€13, five hours, 10 daily), Málaga (€8, two hours, hourly), Seville (€16, three hours, 10 daily) and Córdoba (€10, 2¾ hours, 11 daily).

The **train station** (Ave de Andaluces) is about 1.5km southwest of the centre. There are trains to Madrid (€28.50, six hours, two daily) and Seville (€18, three hours, four daily).

For Málaga (€19) and Córdoba (€19), you have to change trains in Bobadilla. There's one overnight train to Valencia (€41, 7½ hours) and Barcelona (€50, 11½ hours).

COSTA DE ALMERÍA

The coast east of Almería in eastern Andalucía is perhaps the last section of Spain's Mediterranean coast where you can have a beach to yourself. This is Spain's sunniest region – even in late March it can be warm enough to strip off and take in the rays. For info visit the **tourist office** (Almería ☎ 95 062 11 17; San José ☎ 95 038 02 99; Mojácar ☎ 95 047 51 62).

Sights & Activities

The **alcazaba** (☎ 95 027 16 17; Calle Almanzor; admission non-EU/EU citizens €1.50/free; ☺ 9am-8.30pm Tue-Sun Apr-Sep, 9am-6.30pm Tue-Sun Nov-Mar), an enormous 10th-century Muslim fortress, is the highlight of Almería city.

The best thing about the region is the wonderful coastline and semidesert scenery of the **Cabo de Gata** promontory. All along the 50km coast from El Cabo de Gata village to Agua Amarga, some of the most beautiful and empty beaches on the Mediterranean alternate with precipitous cliffs and scattered villages. Roads or paths run along or close to this whole coastline, a protected area. The main village is laid-back **San José**, with excellent beaches nearby, such as **Playa de los Genoveses** and **Playa de Mónsul**. **Mojácar Pueblo**, 30km north of Agua Amarga and 2km inland from the coast, is a white hill-top town of Muslim origin. It's fun to wander the town's maze-like streets or just take in the spectacular views.

Sleeping & Eating

ALMERÍA

Hostal Americano (☎ 95 028 10 15; Ave Estación 6; s/d with shared bathroom from €18.50/32) Clean, friendly and popular with backpackers, it's well located between the city centre and the bus station.

La Perla (☎ 95 023 88 77; fax 95 027 58 16; Plaza Carmen 7; d €49; ☒ ☐) The oldest hotel in town, still exuding a certain old-world charm.

Taberna Torreluz (☎ 95 023 43 99; Plaza Flores 3; raciónes €8; ☺ noon-4pm & 7.30pm-12.30am) Everyone goes for the fabulous *raciónes* at this cosy wood-panelled bar.

CABO DE GATA

In San José there is **Camping Tau** (☎ 95 038 01 66; ☺ Apr-Sep) and the friendly non-HI hostel **Albergue Juvenil de San José** (☎ 95 038 03 53; Calle Montemar; dm €10; ☺ Apr-Sep).

Hostal Bahía (☎ 95 038 03 07; Calle Correo; s/d €32/45) Attractive, whitewashed rooms with bathroom.

Restaurante Azulón (Calle Correos 2; mains €5-8; menú €9; ☺ noon-4.30pm & 8pm-midnight) For Mediterranean food, including fish and pizza, the Azulón does an excellent *menú*.

Casa Emilio (☎ 95 038 97 61; s/d from €35/40) In the quiet village of Los Escullos, a few kilometres up the coast, with clean, simple rooms with balconies and a bar/restaurant downstairs.

MOJÁCAR

Hostal La Esquinica (☎ 95 047 50 09; Calle Cano 1; s/d with shared bathroom €20/25) Tiny and covered in climbing plants, this *hostal* has sweet but simple rooms with wooden beds, and a small bar.

Hostal Mamabel's (☎ 95 047 24 48; www.mamabels.com; Calle Embajadores 5; d €65; ☒) Eight big rooms with sea views and an excellent **restaurant** (menú €18; ☺ 1pm-4pm & 8-11.30pm).

Getting There & Away

From Almería's **bus station** (☎ 95 026 20 98; Plaza Barcelona), buses go to/from Madrid, Granada, Seville, Málaga, Valencia and Barcelona and also to San José and Mojácar.

From the **train station** (Plaza Estación) there are services to/from Madrid (€31, seven hours, two daily), Granada (€11.80, 2½ hours, four daily) and Seville (€28.25, 5¾ hours, four daily).

MÁLAGA

pop 547,105

From Moorish monuments to arguably the best fried fish in Spain, Málaga has *andaluz* charm in spades. This exuberant port city is an enticing mix of tangled streets and a rollicking nightlife. There's plenty to see and savour here.

Orientation

Málaga is situated at the mouth of the Guadalmedina River. The central thoroughfare is the Alameda Principal, which continues eastward as the tree-lined Paseo del Parque and westward as Ave Andalucía.

The historic core of the city lies around the cathedral: a web of narrow, cobbled streets lined with faded, ochre-coloured buildings, interspersed with small squares, tapas bars, old-fashioned shops and cafés.

Information

Internet Meeting Point (Plaza Merced 20; per hr €1; ✆ 10-12.30am) Coffee and Internet access.

Main tourist office (☎ 95 221 34 45; www.malagaturismo.com, in Spanish; Pasaje Chinitas 4; ✆ 8.30am-8pm Mon-Fri, 10am-2pm Sat & Sun) In the city's historic centre.

Municipal tourist office (☎ 95 213 47 30; Ave Cervantes 1; ✆ 8am-2.30pm & 4-7pm Mon-Fri, 9.30am-1.30pm Sat) Near the park. There are additional information kiosks near the train station and in the centre.

Sights & Activities

The city's history is colourfully diverse. The **Alcazaba** (☎ 95 222 72 30; Calle Alcazabilla; admission €1.80; ✆ 8.30am-7pm Tue-Sun) fortress and palace dates from the 8th century. A **Roman amphitheatre**, currently under restoration, can be plainly viewed near the Alcazaba's main entrance.

The hill-top **Castillo Gibralfaro** (admission €1.80; ✆ 9am-6pm), a Moorish castle, commands spectacular views across the city and sea. The **cathedral** (☎ 95 221 59 17; Calle Molina Larios s/n; admission €3; ✆ 10am-6.45pm Mon-Sat) has a peculiar lopsided look (the south tower was never completed) and a magnificent 18th-century baroque façade. Check it out from one of the footpath cafés across the way.

Whatever you do, don't leave Málaga without visiting the fabulous **Museo Picasso Málaga** (☎ 95 260 27 31; www.museopicassomalaga.org; Calle San Agustín; adult/student €6/3; ✆ 10am-8pm Tue-Sun). Set in the contemplative setting of the lovely 16th-century Palacio de Buenavista, the museum is stacked with over 200 of

Picasso's works, covering the length and breadth of his astonishing career.

Sleeping

Málaga is short on accommodation, so book ahead. Prices tend to shoot up in August and during Easter week. Regular rates are listed below.

Albergue Juvenil Málaga (☎ 95 230 85 00; Plaza Pío XII 6; dm 25 & under/26 & over €11.65/17.20) The city's HI hostel is 1.5km west of the city centre. Take bus No 14 or 31 from the Alameda Principal.

Pensión Rosa (☎ 95 221 27 16; Calle Martinez 10; s/d with shared bathroom €25/35) The pretty courtyard entrance is filled with colourful potted plants and rooms are simple but bright.

Hostel Victoria (☎ 95 222 42 24; Calle Sancha de Lara 3; s/d €25/50; ✉) In a good central location, the Victoria has comfortable rooms.

Hotel Venecía (☎ 95 221 36 36; Alameda Principal 9; s/d €58/72; ✉) This small, secure and picturesque hotel has charming rooms, some with balconies.

Hostal Madrid (☎ 95 222 45 92; Calle Marin Garcia 4; s/d with shared bathroom €20/30) This sociable option is another good budget choice, but it's often full with long-term residents.

Also try:

Hostal Mundial (☎ 95 221 06 18; Calle Hoyo de Esparteros 1; s/d with shared bathroom €18/34) Has plenty of spartan, dog-eared rooms.

Hotel Don Curro (☎ 95 222 72 00; Calle Sancha de Lara 7; s/d €70/99; ✉) A central three-star hotel.

Eating

Málaga's tapas bars are particularly good. Drop by the wonderful **Bar Logueno** (☎ 95 222 30 48; Calle Marín García 9; tapas from €1.50; ✆ 1pm-4.30pm & 8pm-midnight), something of a local institution, with 75-plus varieties of tapas to choose from.

La Dehesa (☎ 95 221 21 32; Calle La Bolsa 3; mains €6-7; ✆ 12.30pm-midnight Mon-Sat) Cosy and rustic,

FISHY BUSINESS

Look out for *fritura de pescado*, a typical *malagueño* dish of fried squid and fish served with wedges of lemon. The best place to eat this is in any one of the excellent fish restaurants in the Pedregalejo area, 4.5km east of the centre. All have sunny terraces facing the beach.

SPAIN

La Dehesa is a great place for stews, salads and paellas, all tasty home-cooked fare.

La Vegetariano de la Alcazabilla (☎ 95 221 48 58; Calle Pozo del Rey 5; mains €6-8; 🕑 1.30pm-4pm & 9-11.30pm Mon-Sat) The décor may be basic but the vegetarian portions are generous. It also does a particularly good cheese fondue.

La Posada de Antonio (☎ 95 221 70 69; Calle Granada 33; mains €6-12; 🕑 1pm-4.30 & 8pm-midnight) With its high ceilings and chunky wooden tables, this restaurant serves up tasty meat dishes cooked on an open grill.

El Chinitas (☎ 95 221 09 72; Calle Moreno Monroy 4; mains €8-14; 🕑 1.30pm-4.30pm & 8-11.30pm) Serving up consistently good *malagueño* meat and fish dishes to noisy tables of locals and tourists, El Chinitas has an extraordinary setting under timber beams and garish oil paintings of flamenco dancers and bullfighters.

Drinking

Serious party time kicks off at about midnight around Calle Granada and Plaza Merced.

ZZ Pub (Calle Tejón y Rodriguez 6) Grungy, with live music on Monday and Thursday.

Doctor Funk (Calle José Denis Belgrano 19) Just off Calle Granada is this heaving reggae/funk club shoehorned into a small smoky space.

O'Neills Irish Pub (Calle Luis de Velazquez 3) Appeals enormously to young *malagueños*.

Liceo (Calle Beatas 21) A bar/disco popular with students and travellers.

Sodoma (Calle Juan de Padilla 15; 🕑 Thu-Sat) A gay/mixed disco with house music.

Getting There & Away

Málaga's **airport** (☎ 95 204 88 04) has a good range of domestic as well as international flights. Trains and buses run every half-hour from the airport to the city centre (€0.95). The bus and train stations are around the corner from each other, 1km west of the city centre.

From the **bus station** (☎ 95 235 00 61; Paseo Tilos), buses go to Madrid (€17, six hours, seven daily), Granada (€8, two hours, hourly), Marbella (€4, one hour, hourly), Ronda (€7.50, two hours, 10 daily) and Algeciras (€10, 2½ hours, 12 daily).

From the **train station** (Esplanada Estación), there are services to/from Madrid (€54, 4¼ hours, eight daily), Seville (€14.15, 2½ hours, five daily) and Córdoba (€16, 2¼ hours, nine daily).

TORREMOLINOS

pop 50,649

Torremolinos is trying hard to shed its image as a spam-and-chips resort by pumping money into landscaping and more-up-market tourist facilities. Attractions around town include an equestrian show, birds-of-prey exhibition, a water park and various sea sports. Surprisingly, there is still a relatively untainted old part of town with local bars frequented by old men who play dominoes and drink *anís* (aniseed liqueur).

Nearby, **Tivoli World** (☎ 95 257 70 16; Arroyo Miel, Benalmadena; admission €4.50; 🕑 11am-9pm Nov-Mar, 4pm-1am Apr, May, Sep & Oct, 6pm-3am Jun-Aug) is the Costa del Sol's biggest theme park.

In the old part of town, **Hostal Castilla** (☎ 95 238 10 50; Calle Manila 3; s/d with shared bathroom incl breakfast €32/44) is small and friendly. Nearer to the beach, **Hotel Cabello** (☎ 95 238 45 05; Calle Chiriva; s/d €60/75) is located in the former fishing village of La Carihuela. The best seafood restaurants are here, too, including **El Roqueo** (☎ 95 238 49 46; Calle Carmen 35; 🕑 closed Tue) – owned by a former fisherman.

Trains to/from Málaga and Fuengirola run every 30 minutes from 6am to 10.30pm, stopping at the airport. The bus station is on Calle Hoyo and there are services to all the major Costa del Sol resorts, as well as to Ronda, Cádiz and Granada, several times a day.

FUENGIROLA

pop 57,133

In spite of the annual tide of tourists who come here to flop on the beach, Fuengirola remains essentially a Spanish working town. It's not a pretty place, having suffered from greedy developers and political corruption, but the beach is pleasant, there's a vast choice of shops, restaurants and bars, and bargain hunters will enjoy rooting through the Saturday-morning **flea market** at the fairground.

Fuengirola's annual **fair** at the beginning of October is one of the biggest and best on the Costa del Sol. Aside from then, accommodation is plentiful, although the faceless high-rise hotels on the beachfront tend to be block-booked in advance by tour companies. *Hostales* include the spick-and-span **Hostal Italia** (☎ 95 247 41 93; fax 95 247 11 40; Calle Cruz 1; s/d €36/61), near the main plaza. There are plenty of budget restaurants and bars here.

Half-hourly trains run to/from Málaga, with stops including Torremolinos and the airport. There are also regular buses to Marbella, Mijas and major Andalucían cities leaving the main bus station on Calle Alfonso XIII.

MARBELLA
pop 116,234

Marbella is this coast's classiest resort. The inherent wealth glitters most brightly along the Golden Mile, a tiara of star-studded clubs, restaurants and hotels that stretches from Marbella to Puerto Banus, where black-windowed Mercs slide along a quayside of jaw-dropping luxury yachts. There's Internet access at **Neotel** (Plaza Puente de Ronda 6; per hr €2; ☉ 10am-midnight) and visitor information at the **tourist offices** (Main office ☎ 95 277 14 42; Glorieta Fontanilla; ☉ 9.30am-9pm Mon-Fri, 10am-2pm Sat; Plaza Naranjos ☎ 95 282 35 50; ☉ 9am-9pm Mon-Fri, 9am-2pm Sat).

Sights & Activities

The old part of Marbella around the Plaza Naranjos is very pretty, duly reflected by the drink prices at the outdoor cafés.

The **Museo del Grabado Español Contemporáneo** (☎ 95 276 57 41; Calle Hospital Bazán s/n; admission €2.50; ☉ 10am-2pm & 5.30-8.30pm Mon-Sat) houses works by Picasso, Miró and Dalí. The only **Bonsai Museum** (☎ 95 286 29 26; adult/child €3/1.50; ☉ 10.30am-1.30pm & 4-7pm) in Spain is in Parque de la Represa.

Sleeping & Eating

The old town has several reasonable *hostales*.

Hostal del Pilar (☎ 95 282 99 36; www.hostel-marbella.com; Calle Mesoncillo 4; s/d with shared bathroom €15/30; ✗) This classic backpackers' hangout has crowded rooms and a pool table downstairs.

Hostal La Luna (☎ 95 282 57 78; Calle Luna 7; s/d/tr from €30/42/60) Near the beach, La Luna has balconied rooms, a charming patio and simply lovely owners.

Hotel Linda Marbella (☎ 95 285 71 71; lindamarbellasl@terra.es; Calle Ancha 21; s/d/tr from €40/55/85; ✗) Set on a pretty street in the old part of town, this place has very comfortable rooms.

Bodega La Venecia (☎ 95 285 79 13; Ave Miguel Cano 15; raciones €5-8; ☉ 1pm-4.30pm & 8pm-1am) Wildly popular with all ages, La Venecia serves excellent tapas and *raciones* in nice woody surroundings.

Sociedad de Pesca Deportiva Marbella (☎ 95 277 54 38; Club Maritimo Loc 5; Puerto Deportivo; mains €8-12; ☉ 12.30-5pm & 8pm-1am Tue-Sun) It looks nothing special from outside but this restaurant serves up the best fried fish in town.

Getting There & Away

The **bus station** (☎ 95 276 44 00; Calle Trapiche) is a good 30-minute hike from the hub of town. Bus No 7 connects the terminal with the centre (€1). Buses from the station run regularly to Málaga (€4, 1¼ hours, 15 daily), Fuengirola (€2, one hour, every 20 minutes), Algeciras (€5, 1½ hours, 15 daily), Cádiz (€14, 4¾ hours, six daily), Seville (€13, 3¾ hours, two daily) and Ronda (€4, 1½ hours, six daily).

RONDA
pop 35,137

One of Andalucía's prettiest towns, Ronda is split in two by the savagely deep El Tajo gorge, at the heart of some lovely hill country.

The **municipal tourist office** (☎ 95 218 71 19; www.turismoderonda.es; Paseo Blas Infante s/n; ☉ 9.30am-7pm Mon-Fri, 10am-2pm & 3.30-6.30pm Sat & Sun) is helpful but can get crowded.

Sights & Activities

Ronda is a pleasure to explore, but during the day you'll have to contend with busloads of day-trippers from the coast.

The **Plaza de Toros** (1785), considered the home of bullfighting, is a mecca for aficionados; inside is the small but fascinating **Museo Taurino** (Bullfighting Museum; ☎ 95 287 41 32; adult/student €5/3; ☉ 10am-7pm). Vertiginous cliff-top views open out from the nearby **Alameda del Tajo** park.

The 18th-century **Puente Nuevo** (New Bridge) is an incredible engineering feat; it crosses the 100m-deep gorge to the originally Muslim old town (La Ciudad), which is littered with ancient churches, monuments and palaces. At the **Casa del Rey Moro** (☎ 95 218 72 00; Calle Santo Domingo 17; adult/child €4/2; ☉ 10am-8pm), you can climb down La Mina, a Muslim-era stairway cut inside the rock, right to the bottom of the gorge. Try not to miss the **Iglesia de Santa María la Mayor** (Plaza Duquesa de Parcent; admission €2; ☉ 10am-7pm), whose tower was once the minaret of a mosque, or the beautiful 13th-century **Baños Arabes** (Arab Baths; Barrio Padre Jesus; adult/child €2/free; ☉ 10am-7pm Mon-Fri, 10am-3pm Sat & Sun).

SPAIN

Sleeping & Eating

There are a couple of budget *pensiones* on Calle Almendre, including the dark, old-fashioned **Hostal Biarritz** (☎ 95 287 29 10; Calle Almendre 7; s/d with shared bathroom €11/17).

Hotel Morales (☎ 95 287 15 38; Calle Sevilla 51; s/d €21/45) Friendly, with decorative rooms.

Alavera de los Baños (☎ 95 287 91 43; alavera@ctv.es; Calle San Miguel s/n; d incl breakfast €76; 🞰) This small hotel next to the Arab baths is rustic and romantic, with heavy beamed ceilings, and away from the tourist hordes. But it is one helluva climb back into town – luckily it has its own good **restaurant** (mains €15).

Relax Vegetariano Café-Bar (☎ 95 287 72 07; Calle Los Remedios 27; mains €5; ☾ noon-4pm & 7-11pm) This British-owned café has bright red walls, rustic wooden tables and fabulous vegetarian food. It does big mugs of English tea, too.

Marisquería Paco (Plaza Socorro 9; mains €10; ☾ 10am-10pm) Tiny, but a popular seafood place.

Getting There & Away

From the **bus station** (☎ 95 287 26 57; Plaza Concepción García Redondo), services run to/from Seville (€9, 2½ hours, five daily), Málaga (€7.50, two hours, 10 daily) and Cádiz (€7.50; three hours, four daily).

From the **train station** (Ave Andalucía), trains run to/from Granada (€11, three hours, three daily), Algeciras (€6, 1½ hours, four daily) and Madrid (€32, 4½ hours, two daily).

ALGECIRAS
pop 105,070

Algeciras, an unattractive industrial and fishing town between Tarifa and Gibraltar, is the major port linking Spain with Morocco. Keep your wits about you, and ignore offers from the legions of moneychangers, drug-pushers and ticket-hawkers. If you need a room, there's loads of budget accommodation in the streets behind the port. The **tourist office** (☎ 95 657 26 36; Calle Juan Cierva; ☾ 9am-2pm Mon-Fri) is near the port.

Getting There & Away
BOAT

Frequent ferries to/from Tangier, in Morocco, and Ceuta, the Spanish enclave on the Moroccan coast, are operated by **Trasmediterránea** (☎ 902 45 46 45), **EuroFerrys** (☎ 95 665 11 78) and other companies. Usually at least 20 ferries daily go to Tangier (€28, 2½ hours) and

more to Ceuta (€22, 1½ hours). From late June to September there are ferries almost around the clock. Buy your ticket in the port or at agencies on Ave Marina – prices are the same. **Buquebus** (☎ 902 41 42 42) makes a fast crossing to Ceuta (€38.50, 30 minutes).

BUS

About 400m inland from the port, **Comes** (☎ 95 665 34 56; Calle San Bernardo) runs frequent buses to/from La Línea, and several daily to/from Tarifa, Cádiz and Seville. **Portillo** (Ave Virgen del Carmen 15), 200m north of the port, runs buses to/from Málaga, the Costa del Sol and Granada. **Bacoma**, inside the port, runs buses to/from Barcelona, Valencia, France, Germany and Holland.

TRAIN

From the **train station** (Calle Agustín Bálsamo 12), direct services run to/from Madrid (€35 to €52, six hours, two daily), Córdoba (€26.50, four hours, two daily), Ronda (€6, 1½ hours, four daily) and Granada (€15.75, 4¾ hours, three daily).

CÁDIZ

The historic port of Cádiz is a beautiful city with a well-aged atmosphere and winding streets flanked by magnificent, if dishevelled, 18th-century buildings. All around is the Atlantic Ocean, beating against the city's sea defences. The best time to visit is during the February *carnaval*, close to Rio in terms of outrageous exuberance. For Internet access try **EnRed** (☎ 95 621 45 22; Calle Sacramento 36; per hr €1.50; ☾ 11am-11pm Mon-Sat). There are helpful staff at the **municipal tourist office** (☎ 95 624 10 01; Plaza San Juan de Dios 11; ☾ 9.30am-1.30pm & 4-7pm Mon-Fri).

Sights & Activities

The yellow-domed soaring 18th-century **cathedral** (Plaza de la Catedral; adult/child €4/2.50; ☾ 10am-1.30pm & 4.30-8pm Tue-Fri, 10am-2pm Sat, 11am-1pm Sun) is the city's most striking landmark.

Get your bearings by climbing up the baroque **Torre Tavira** (☎ 95 621 29 10; Calle Marqués del Real Tesoro; admission €3.50; ☾ 10am-6pm), the highest of Cádiz's old watchtowers, with a camera obscura and sweeping views of the city.

The **Museo de Cádiz** (☎ 95 621 22 81; Plaza Mina; non-EU/EU citizens €1.50/free; ☾ 2.30-8pm Tue, 9am-8pm Wed-Sat, 9.30am-2.30pm Sun) has a magnificent collection of archaeological remains, as well as a fine art collection. The city's lively **central market** (Plaza de las Flores) is on the site of a former Phoenician temple.

Sleeping & Eating

Accommodation can get quite booked up at weekends so it's worth phoning ahead.

Quo Qádis (☎ /fax 95 622 19 39; Calle Diego Arias 1; dm/d €9/42, d with shared bathroom €36) Cádiz's excellent independent hostel is colourful and quirky. You can rent bikes for €6 a day, or tuck into a vegetarian supper for just €2. Prices drop significantly from October to June.

Hostal Bahía (☎ 95 625 90 61; Calle Plocia 5; s/d €47/64) Just off the bustling main square, this *hostal* is a winner.

Hotel Francia y Paris (☎ 95 621 23 18; www.hotelfrancia.com; Plaza San Francisco 2; s/d €61/77; ✷) More luxurious and overlooking a pretty plaza; the spacious carpeted rooms have a faded '70s feel.

Restaurante Parissien (☎ 95 622 36 77; Plaza San Francisco 1; mains €6-8; ⏲ 9am-11.30pm) With lots of outside tables on a pretty cobbled plaza, this place does excellent fried fish and a succulent *carne estofada* (beef stew).

It's a pleasure to graze your way through Cádiz's superb *marisquerías* (seafood bars). Kick off with a fishy tapa at the **Cervecería Aurelio** (☎ 95 622 10 31; Calle Zorrilla 1; tapas/raciones €1.50/5; ⏲ 12.30-5pm & 8.30pm-1am).

People go out late in Cádiz and the city's streets and plazas throng until the early hours. **Woodstock Bar** (☎ 95 621 21 63; Calle Canovas del Castillo 25; ⏲ 4pm-2am Sun-Thu, 4pm-4am Fri & Sat) is a fashionable late-night hang-out.

Getting There & Away

From the **bus station** (☎ 95 680 70 59; Plaza Hispanidad), there are buses to/from Algeciras (€9, 2¾ hours, 10 daily), Seville (€9.50, 1½ hours, hourly), Córdoba (€18, 4½ hours, two daily), Málaga (€18, five hours, six daily), Ronda (€12, three hours, three daily) and Tarifa (€7, 1¼ hours, five daily).

From the **train station** (Plaza Sevilla), services go to/from Seville (€8.40, 1¾ hours, 10 daily), Córdoba (€31, three hours, four daily) and Madrid (€56, five hours, twice daily).

TARIFA & THE COSTA DE LA LUZ

Windy, laid-back Tarifa, perched at continental Europe's most southerly point, is so close to Africa that you can see the sunlight flashing on Morocco's minarets. The town

is a bohemian haven of cafés and crumbling Moorish ruins. There is also a lively windsurfing and kite-surfing scene.

Stretching west from Tarifa are the long, sandy (and largely deserted) beaches of the Costa de la Luz (Coast of Light), backed by cool pine forests and green hills.

Tarifa's **tourist office** (☎ 95 668 09 93; www.tarifaweb.com; Plaza Alameda; ⏲ 9am-9pm Jun-Sep, 9am-3pm Oct-May) has lots of information on the area. Internet access is fairly pricey, but your best bet is **Planet** (www.planet-up.com; per hr €3; ⏲ 10.30am-2.30pm & 6-10pm), run by friendly German owners.

Sights & Activities

Enjoy exploring Tarifa's winding old streets and visit the castle, **Castillo de Guzmán** (☎ 95 668 46 89; Calle Guzmán El Bueno; adult/child €1.80/0.60; ⏲ 11am-2pm & 5-7pm), dating from the 10th century.

The waters of the Algeciras Bay are prime whale and dolphin watching territory. **Whale Watch España** (☎ 95 662 70 13; www.whalewatchtarifa.com; Ave Constitución 6; per person €27) runs daily boat excursions (1½ to two hours).

The tiny, protected **Playa Chica**, just southeast of the centre, is best for swimming. **Playa de los Lances**, the 10km-long beach beloved of wind- and kite surfers, stretches northwest from Tarifa. For windsurf and kite-surf rental and classes, try places along Calle Batalla de Salado. **Big Fish** (☎ 95 668 02 19; El Recreo III, Local 16, Calle Batalla de Salado) rents out surfboards

---

SURF WARS

Tarifa remained relatively unknown until windsurfers started to flock here in the mid-1980s, lured by the notorious winds of the Strait of Gibraltar that provided perfect conditions for their sport.

In recent years, the new craze of kite surfing has taken off (it involves surfing and jumping across waves, attached to a large kite).

Needless to say, Tarifa's windsurfers aren't thrilled by the arrival of the kiters, whose lines get easily tangled on their masts, causing all sorts of mischief. The rivalry between the two camps is fierce, so much so that there have been recent attempts to divide Tarifa's beaches into separate zones for the different sports.

SPAIN

for €20 a day and offers three-day (four hours a day) kite- and windsurfing courses for €180. This strip is also a great place to stock up on surfer-chic clothing and accessories.

If you have your own wheels, head west to the Costa de la Luz. Don't miss out on the Roman ruins of **Baelo Claudia** (admission non-EU/ EU citizens €1.50/free; ✆ 10am-6pm Tue-Sat, 10am-2pm Sun) at Bolonia and the magical laid-back villages of **Zahara de los Atunes** and **Los Caños de Meca**.

Sleeping

Pensión Correo (✆ 95 668 02 06; Calle Coronel Moscardó 8; r €40-50, r with shared bathroom €25-35) Run by a charming Italian, the Correo has fabulous, if fairly basic, rooms with high beamed ceilings, archways and a ramshackle air.

Hostal Facundo (✆ 95 668 42 98; h.facundo@terra .es; Calle Batalla del Salado 47; dm Aug only €12, d €36, s/d with shared bathroom €15/22) Long established and popular with windsurfers.

Casa Amarilla (✆ 95 668 19 93; www.lacasaamarilla .net; Calle Sancho IV El Bravo 9; d €40-60, tr €53-80, q €66-99) Right in the thick of things, with exquisite, quirky apartment rooms with kitchenette.

Eating & Drinking

Tarifa has no shortage of places to hang out, people watch, and wait for the right sort of wind to pick up.

Café Central (✆ 95 668 05 90; Calle Sancho IV El Bravo; ✆ 9-1am) This legendary café is at the heart of it all, with a daily wind report posted on its walls and the best breakfasts in town.

Café Continental (✆ 95 668 47 76; Paseo Alameda; ✆ 9-1am) People play chess and board games over cappuccinos in this dark and woody café.

La Vaca Loca (Calle Alcantarillo s/n; mains €8-12; ✆ 6pm-1am) This tiny cave-like place, with surf videos running on the TV, serves up amazing barbecued food in huge portions. There are a handful of tables on the plaza outside.

Mesón Perulero (✆ 95 668 19 97; Plaza San Hiscio; tapas €1.50; ✆ 12.30-4pm & 6pm-midnight) In a gorgeous building with an airy patio, this place does some excellent fishy tapas; try the sea *ortigas de mar* (anemones). Regular live flamenco here in summer.

Getting There & Away

Comes (✆ 95 668 40 38; Batalla del Salado s/n) runs buses to/from Algeciras (€1.50, 30 minutes,

17 daily), La Línea (€3, one hour, seven daily), Cádiz (€7, 1¼ hours, seven daily) and Seville (€14, three hours, four daily).

FRS (✆ 95 668 18 30; Estación Marítima) runs ferries between Tarifa and Tangier (adult/car €24.50/73, 1½ hours, five daily).

GIBRALTAR

pop 27,776

The British colony of Gibraltar is like 1960s Britain on a sunny day. It is both safe and old-fashioned, attracting coachloads of day-trippers from the Costa del Sol who come here to be reassured by the helmet-wearing policemen, the double-decker buses and Marks & Spencer.

Occupying a huge lump of limestone, almost 5km long and over 1km wide, near the mouth of the Mediterranean, the colony of Gibraltar has certainly had a rocky history: it was the bridgehead for the Muslim invasion of Spain in AD 711. Castilla finally wrested it from the Muslims in 1462. In 1704 an Anglo-Dutch fleet captured Gibraltar. Spain gave up military attempts to regain it from Britain after the failure of the Great Siege of 1779–83, but after 300 years of concentrated Britishness, both Britain and Spain are now talking about joint Anglo-Spanish sovereignty – much to the ire of the Gibraltarians.

Information

To enter Gibraltar you must have a passport or EU national identity card. EU, US, Canadian, Australian, New Zealand, Israeli, South African and Singaporean passport holders are among those who do *not* need visitors' visas for Gibraltar, though anyone who needs a visa for Spain should have at least a double-entry Spanish visa if they intend to return to Spain from Gibraltar.

The currency is the Gibraltar pound or pound sterling. Change any unspent Gibraltar pounds before you leave. You can always use euros.

To phone Gibraltar from Spain, the telephone code is ✆ 9567; from other countries dial the international access code, then ✆ 350 and the local number. There are a couple of tourist offices (Main office ✆ 45000; www .gibraltar.gov.gi; Duke of Kent House, Cathedral Sq; ✆ 9am-

5.30pm Mon-Fri; Casemates Sq ☎ 74982; ☯ 9am-5.30pm Mon-Fri, 10am-3pm Sat, 10am-1pm Sun).

Sights & Activities

Central Gibraltar can get crowded and claustrophobic but the **Gibraltar Museum** (☎ 74289; Bomb House Lane; adult/child £2/1; ☯ 10am-6pm Mon-Fri, 10am-2pm Sat), with its interesting historical collection and Muslim-era bathhouse, is worth a peek. Wander into the **Alameda Botanical Gardens** (Red Sands Rd; ☯ 8am-sunset) for some chill-out time.

The large **Upper Rock Nature Reserve** (☎ 749 50; adult/child/vehicle £7/4/1.50; ☯ 9.30am-7pm), covering most of the upper rock, has spectacular views and several interesting spots to visit.

The rock's most famous inhabitants are its colony of Barbary macaques, the only wild primates in Europe. Some of these hang around the **Apes' Den** near the middle cablecar station; others can often be seen at the top station or Great Siege Tunnels.

Other attractions include **St Michael's Cave**, a large natural grotto renowned for its stalagmites and stalactites and the **Great Siege Tunnels**, a series of galleries hewn from the rock by the British during the Great Siege to provide new gun emplacements. Worth a stop on the way down to the town from here are the **Gibraltar, a City under Siege** exhibition and the **Tower of Homage**, part of Gibraltar's 14th-century Muslim castle.

A **cable car** (adult/child return £6.50/3; ☯ 10am-6pm Mon-Sat) leaves its lower station on Red Sands Rd every few minutes. For the Apes' Den, disembark at the middle station.

Sleeping

Compared to Spain, expect to pay through the nose.

Emile Youth Hostel (☎ 51106; Montagu Bastion, Line Wall Rd; dm incl breakfast £15) The cheapest place is this privately run hostel with fairly soulless dorms.

Cannon Hotel (☎ 51711; www.cannonhotel.gi; 9 Cannon Lane; d £45, s/d with shared bathroom £24.50/36.50) This friendly hotel is in the heart of town with a bar, pretty patio and airy rooms. Rates include an English breakfast.

Queen's Hotel (☎ 74000; www.queenshotel.gi; 1 Boyd St; s/d/tr with English breakfast £40/50/75; **P** ☒) Queen's is just outside the city walls, a big peach-coloured mansion, with a decidedly '70s feel. You'll pay more for sea views but students get a 20% discount.

Eating & Drinking

Brace yourself for British food at British prices: pub grub, all day fry-ups, curries and ale by the pint.

Lord Nelson (☎ 50009; 10 Casemates Sq; mains £5-8; ☯ 10-2am) Decked out as Nelson's ship, with painted clouds on a ceiling crossed with beams and sails, this brasserie is an excellent choice. The mussels in white wine, garlic and cream are particularly good. Live music at weekends.

Sacarello's (☎ 70625; 57 Irish Town; mains £6-7; ☯ 9am-7.30pm Mon-Fri, 9am-3pm Sat) Low, beamed ceilings and delicious soups, salads and afternoon tea.

Other recommendations:

Star Bar (☎ 75924; Parliament Lane; mains £6-7; ☯ 7am-11pm) Gibraltar's oldest pub.

Clipper (☎ 79791; Irish Town; mains £3-5; ☯ 9.30am-11pm) Sport on TV, friendly waiters, great English breakfast.

Getting There & Away

GB Airways (☎ 79300, UK ☎ 0345-222111) flies daily to/from London. Return fares range from around £175 to £400, depending on the season. **Monarch Airlines** (☎ 47477, UK ☎ 08700-406300; www.flymonarch.com) flies from London's Luton; return fares start at about £96.

There are no regular buses to Gibraltar, but La Línea bus station is only a five-minute walk from the border.

To take a car into Gibraltar, you need an insurance certificate, registration document, nationality plate and driving licence. You do *not* have to pay any fee, despite what con artists might try to tell you.

EXTREMADURA

A sparsely populated land of vast skies and open plains, Extremadura is far enough from most beaten tourist trails to give you a genuine sense of exploration, something for which *extremeños* themselves have a flair. Many epic 16th-century conquistadors, including Francisco Pizarro (who conquered the Incas), sprang from this land.

The mountains and valleys of northeast Extremadura are perfect for hiking and the remarkable old towns of Trujillo and Cáceres are so perfectly preserved that they are often used as film sets. In Mérida, some of Spain's most spectacular and complete Roman ruins scatter the city.

SPAIN

TRUJILLO

pop 9564

Trujillo is a delightful little town that can't be much bigger now than in 1529, when its most famous son, Francisco Pizarro, set off with his three brothers and a few local buddies for an expedition that culminated in the bloody conquest of the Incan empire.

From the broad and fine Plaza Mayor rises a remarkably preserved old town, stacked with ancient buildings seeping history. There is a **tourist office** (☎ 92 732 26 77; ofitur@ayto -trujillo.com; Plaza Mayor; ☉ 9.30am-2pm & 4.30-7.30pm) and you can connect to the Internet at **Ciberalia** (Calle Tiendas 18; per hr €2; ☉ 10.30-2am) for €2 an hour.

Sights

A **statue of Pizarro**, by American Charles Rumsey, dominates the Plaza Mayor. On the plaza's southern side, the **Palacio de la Conquista** (closed to visitors) sports the carved images of Francisco Pizarro and the Inca princess Inés Yupanqui.

Two noble mansions you can visit are the 16th-century **Palacio de los Duques de San Carlos** (Plaza Mayor; admission €1.30; ☉ 9.30am-1pm & 4.30-6.30pm Mon-Sat, 10am-12.30pm Sun) and **Palacio de Juan-Pizarro de Orellana** (admission free; ☉ 10am-1pm & 4-6pm Mon-Fri, 11am-2pm & 4.30-7pm Sat & Sun), through the alley in the plaza's southwestern corner.

Up the hill, the **Iglesia de Santa María la Mayor** (admission €1.20; ☉ 10am-2pm & 4.30-8pm) is an interesting hotchpotch of 13th- to 16th-century styles, with some fine paintings by Fernando Gallego of the Flemish school. Higher up, the **Casa-Museo de Pizarro** (admission €1.30; ☉ 10am-2pm & 4-7pm) has informative displays (in Spanish) on the lives and adventures of the Pizarro family. At the top of the hill, Trujillo's **castillo** (admission €1.30; ☉ 10am-2pm & 4.30-7.30pm) is an impressive structure, primarily of Moorish origin with a hermitage within.

Sleeping & Eating

Pension Roque (☎ 92 732 23 13; Calle Domingo de Ramos 30; d €24, d with shared bathroom €18) Quiet, with lots of communal space.

Hostal La Cadena (☎ 92 732 14 63; Plaza Mayor 8; d €37.30; ❄) In a tastefully restored 16th-century building, with a handy tapas bar and restaurant.

Parador de Trujillo (☎ 92 732 13 50; trujillo@parador .es; Calle Santa Beatriz de Silva 1; d €97; P ❄) Pos-

itioned around a central courtyard with fountains, arches and pillars, this converted convent dates from the 16th century. King Juan Carlos apparently enjoys the stewed lamb tails served in the restaurant here.

Restaurante La Troya (☎ 92 723 13 64; Plaza Mayor 10; menú €17) Carnivores shouldn't miss out on this place. The food isn't cheap, but portions are gigantic and it will save you from eating much else for the next few days. There are great tapas, too.

Getting There & Away

From the **bus station** (☎ 92 732 12 02; Carretera Mérida), 500m south of Plaza Mayor, buses run to/from Cáceres (€3, 45 minutes, eight daily), Mérida (€7.50, 1¼ hours, four daily) and Madrid (€17, four hours, 10 daily).

CÁCERES

pop 87,088

Cáceres' *ciudad monumental* (old town), built in the 15th and 16th centuries, is so perfectly preserved it can seem lifeless at times. Then you gaze skywards and see the vast colony of storks that perch on every worthwhile vertical protuberance. The *ciudad monumental* is worth two visits – one by day to look around and one by night to soak up the atmosphere of the accumulated ages.

There is a **tourist office** (☎ 92 701 08 34; ot caceres@eco.juntaex.es; Plaza Mayor 3; ☉ 9am-2pm & 4-6pm Mon-Fri, 9.30am-2pm Sat & Sun Oct-May, 9am-2pm & 5-7pm, 9.30am-2pm Sat & Sun Jun-Sep). At **Ciberjust** (Calle Diego Maria Crehuet 7; per hr €2; ☉ 10am-2.30pm & 4.30pm-midnight Mon-Sat, 5pm-midnight Sun) you can connect to the Internet.

Sights & Activities

The *ciudad monumental* is still surrounded by walls and towers raised by the Almohads in the 12th century. Entering it from Plaza Mayor, you'll see ahead the fine 15th-century **Concatedral de Santa María** (☉ 10am-1pm).

Many of the old city's churches and imposing medieval mansions can be admired only from outside, but you can climb up the **Torre de Bujaco** (☉ 10am-2pm & 4.30-7.30pm Tue-Sun) and enter the good **Museo Provincial de Cáceres** (☎ 92 724 72 34; Plaza Veletas; admission non-EU/EU citizens €2/free; ☉ 9.30am-2.30pm & 4-7pm Tue-Sat, 10.15am-2.30pm Sun), housed in a 16th-century mansion built over a 12th-century Moorish *aljibe* (cistern), the museum's prize exhibit.

Sleeping

The best area to stay is around the pretty, pedestrianised Plaza Mayor.

Albergue Turístico Las Veletas (☎ 92 721 12 10; www.alberguesturisticos.com; Calle Margallo 36; dm incl breakfast €20) This charming, privately run hostel has sparkling, bright and airy rooms in a recently restored mansion.

Pensión Carretera (☎ 92 724 74 82; pens_carretero@yahoo.es; Plaza Mayor 22; s/d with shared bathroom €13/22) Rooms in this early-20th-century building overlooking the Plaza have high ceilings and an old-fashioned, crumbling air. The bathrooms are a bit dog-eared.

Hotel Iberia (☎ 92 724 76 34; www.iberiahotel.com; Calle Pintores 2; s/d €45/55) In a sumptuous former palace, this hotel really is amazing value for money and rooms are blissfully comfortable.

Eating & Drinking

The bars and cafés on Plaza Mayor are perfect for watching the world go by over a coffee or beer, but the food is overpriced and not terribly good. Your best bet is to go up one of the side streets off the plaza for a bite to eat.

Croissanterie (Calle Pintores 4; bocadillos €1.50; ☯ 10am-11pm) A hole-in-the-wall with an amazing range of freshly baked, filled baguettes, croissants and *paninis*.

Café-Bar Adarve (☎ 92 724 48 74; Calle Sánchez Garrido 4; raciones €6-8; ☯ 7.30-1am) This place does a roaring trade with locals who come here to eat €6 platefuls of *riñones* (kidneys) and the bar's famous *gambas rebozadas* (deep-fried battered prawns – €7.50). Lots of noisy banter between the waiters.

El Figón de Eustaquio (☎ 92 724 43 62; Plaza San Juan 14; mains €10-15, menú €17.50; ☯ 1pm-4pm & 8-11.30pm) Serving up excellent traditional *extremeño* food in an attractive wood-panelled setting, this restaurant is always busy.

El Corral de las Cigüeñas (Cuesta Aldana; breakfast/milkshakes/cocktails €2/3/5; ☯ 8-3am) In the heart of the *cuidad monumental*, the fabulous ivy-clad courtyard of this bar is filled with cool young things. It hosts regular live gigs of pop, rock and funk.

Getting There & Away

From the **bus station** (☎ 92 723 25 50; Carretera Gijón–Sevilla), 1.5km southwest of Plaza Mayor, services run to/from Trujillo (€3, 45 minutes, eight daily), Mérida (€6, 1¼ hours, six daily), Plasencia (€5, 1¼ hours, five daily), Madrid (€16, 3½ hours, eight daily) and Seville (€27, four hours, six daily).

From the **train station** (Ave Alemania s/n), services run to/from Madrid (€22.50, 3½ to five hours, five daily), Mérida (€3.30 to €11.50, one hour, four daily) and Plasencia (€3, 1¼ hours, two daily). The single daily train to Lisbon (€35, 5¼ hours) leaves at 3am.

MÉRIDA

pop 52,110

Once the biggest city in Roman Spain, Mérida is home to more ruins of that age than anywhere else in the country. The **tourist office** (☎ 92 400 97 30; otmerida@eco.juntaex.es; Ave José Álvarez Saenz de Buruaga s/n; ☯ 9am-2pm & 4-6.30pm Mon-Sat, 9.30am-2pm Sun) is by the gates to the Roman theatre. **Cibersala** (Calle Camilo Cela 28; per hr €1.50; ☯ 10am-2pm & 5pm-midnight) is a dingy Internet hang-out.

Sights

The awesome ruins of Mérida's **Teatro Romano & Anfiteatro** (☎ 92 431 25 30; admission €5.50) shouldn't be missed. The theatre was built in 15 BC and the gladiators' ring, or Anfiteatro, seven years later. Combined they could hold 20,000 spectators. Other monuments of interest are the **Casa del Anfiteatro** (☎ 92 431 85 09; admission €2.80), the **Casa Romana del Mithraeo** (☎ 92 430 15 04; admission €3.50) the **Alcazaba** (☎ 92 431 73 09; admission €2.80), the **Basílica de Santa Eulalia** (☎ 92 430 34 07; admission €2.80) and the **Arqueológica de Moreria** (admission €2.80).

The opening hours for all of these sights are 9.30am to 1.45pm and 4pm to 6.15pm October to May, and 9.30am to 1.45pm and 5pm to 7.15pm June to September. You can buy a combined ticket for entry into all of them for €8/4 per adult/concession.

Various other reminders of imperial days are scattered about town, including the **Puente Romano**, at 792m one of the longest bridges the Romans ever built.

Sleeping & Eating

Hostal Nueva España (☎ 92 431 33 56; Ave Extremadura 6; s/d €23/35) A modern building a short walk from the centre and near the train station with friendly young owners. Rooms come with TV and phone but only gloomy overhead lighting.

Hostal El Alfarero (☎ 92 430 31 83; www.hostalelalfarero.com; Calle Sagasta 40; d €40) Owned by a family of potters, this *hostal* has bright, quirky

SPAIN

rooms with hand-painted washbasins and a lovely patio.

Casa Benito (☎ 92 433 07 69; Calle San Francisco 3; tapas/raciones €1.50/8.50; ☺ 8-1am) A great old-style, wood-panelled bar and restaurant, decked with bullfighting memorabilia, serves local fare at reasonable prices.

Bar-Restaurante Briz (☎ 92 431 93 07; Calle Felix Valverde Lillo 7; menú €9.60; ☺ 7am-midnight) Walk through the busy tapas bar to get to the glaringly lit, windowless *comedor* (dining room). Don't let the décor put you off – this place is fabulous value for money and serves up huge portions (the steak is particularly divine). There are lots of gooey bits, such as brains and tripe, on the menu, so choose wisely.

Getting There & Away

From the **bus station** (☎ 92 437 14 04; Ave Libertad), buses run to/from Seville (€10, three hours, seven daily), Madrid (€20, four hours, seven daily), Cáceres (€6, 1¼ hours, four daily) and Trujillo (€7.50, 1¼ hours, four daily).

From the **train station** (Calle Cardero), services run to/from Cáceres (€3.30, one hour, four daily), Seville (€11, 4¾ hours, one daily) and Madrid (€19.20, six hours, four daily).

NORTHEAST EXTREMADURA

From Plasencia, the green, almost Eden-like valleys of La Vera, Valle del Jerte and Valle del Ambroz stretch northeast into the Sierra de Gredos and its western extensions. Watered by rushing mountain streams called *gargantas*, and dotted with medieval villages, these valleys offer some excellent walking routes and attract just enough visitors to provide a good network of places to stay.

Information

The Editorial Alpina booklet *Valle del Jerte, Valle del Ambroz, La Vera* (€8) includes a 1:50,000 map of the area showing walking routes. Try to get it from a map or bookshop before you come. There are a number of **tourist offices** (Plasencia ☎ 92 701 78 40; Plaza Torre de Lucia; Jaraíz de la Vera ☎ 92 717 05 87; turismo@ayto-jaraiz.com; Ave Constitución 167; Jarandilla de la Vera ☎ 92 756 04 60; Plaza Consitución 1; Hervás ☎ 927 47 36 18; oficina.turismo@hervas.com).

Sights & Activities

LA VERA

About halfway up the valley, **Cuacos de Yuste** has its share of narrow village streets with half-timbered houses leaning at odd angles. Up a side road, 2km northwest, is the **Monasterio de Yuste** (☎ 92 717 21 30; admission €2.50; ☺ 9.30am-12.30pm & 3-6pm), to which, in 1557, Carlos I, once the world's most powerful man, retreated for his dying years. Entrance is to the simple royal chambers and the monastery church.

The road continues past the monastery to **Garganta la Olla**, another typically picturesque village, from where you can head over the 1269m **Puerto del Piornal** pass into the Valle del Jerte.

Jarandilla de la Vera is a bigger village, with a 15th-century fortress-church on the main square (below the main road) and a parador occupying a castle-palace where Carlos I stayed while Yuste was being readied for him. Of the longer hikes, the Ruta de Carlos V (see below) is one of the most enticing.

VALLE DEL JERTE

This valley produces half of Spain's cherries and turns into a sea of white at blossom time in April. **Piornal**, high on the southern flank, is a good base for walks along the Sierra de Tormantos.

In the bottom of the valley, **Cabezuela del Valle** has a particularly medieval main street. A 35km road crosses from just north of here over the 1430m Puerto de Honduras pass to Hervás in the Valle del Ambroz. For hikers, the **PR-10 trail** climbs roughly parallel, to the south. From Jerte you can walk into the beautiful **Parque Natural de la Garganta de los Infiernos**.

Tornavacas, near the head of the valley, is the starting point of the **Ruta de Carlos V**, a 28km marked trail following the route by which Carlos I (who was also Carlos V of the Holy Roman Empire) was carried over the mountains to Jarandilla. It can be walked in one long day.

VALLE DEL AMBROZ

Towards the head of the valley, **Hervás**, a small, pleasant town, has the best surviving 15th-century Barrio Judío (Jewish quarter) in Extremadura, where many Jews took refuge in the hope of avoiding the Inquisition.

Sleeping & Eating

There are **camping grounds** – many with fine riverside positions – in several villages, including Cuacos de Yuste, Hervás, Jarandilla de la Vera and Jerte. Most are open only between March/April and September/October.

There are free *zonas de acampada* (camping areas with no facilities) at Garganta la Olla and Piornal.

Hostal La Muralla (☎ 92 741 38 74; Calle Berrozana 6, Plasencia; s/d with shared bathroom €17/32; 😂) In a pretty, old building, this *hostal* is comfortable and located near the main plaza, which is good for bars and atmosphere.

Hotel Jaranda (☎ 92 756 02 06; www.hoteljaranda .com; Ave Soledad Vega Ortiz 101, Jarandilla de la Vera; s/d incl breakfast €40/65; 😂) This hotel looks across to the castle and has charming rooms with old-fashioned beds, balconies and French windows. It also has an excellent-value **restaurant** (3-course menú with wine €9).

Pensión Los Piornos (☎ 92 747 60 55; Plaza Heras, Piornal; d with shared bathroom €33) Near the bus stop, Los Piorno has just eight rooms.

Hotel Aljama (☎ 92 747 22 91; Calle Federico Bajo s/n, Cabezuela del Valle; s/d €21/33) Almost touching the church across the street, this hotel has pretty rooms.

Hostal Puerto de Tornavacas (☎ 92 719 40 97; s/d €21/36; 🅿 😂) A couple of kilometres up the N-110 from Tornavacas is this inn-style place with rooms, and also a restaurant specialising in *extremeño* food.

There are numerous places to eat and drink on nearby Calle Hondón.

Getting There & Away

Your own wheels are a big help, but if you're relying on public transport, the following bus services run Monday to Friday, with much-reduced services on the weekend.

A Mirat bus from Cáceres and Plasencia to Talayuela stops at the villages on the C-501 in La Vera. One or two Mirat buses run from Plasencia to Garganta la Olla and Losar de la Vera. From Estación Sur de Autobuses in Madrid, Doaldi runs daily buses to La Vera.

From Plasencia, there is a daily bus to Piornal, and four buses a day run up the Valle del Jerte to Tornavacas.

Los Tres Pilares operates two buses between Plasencia and Hervás. Enatcar has a few bus services between Cáceres, Plasencia and Salamanca via the Valle del Ambroz. These stop at Empalme de Hervás junction, 2km from town.

SPAIN DIRECTORY

ACCOMMODATION

Spain's camping grounds vary enormously and grounds are officially rated from 1st class to 3rd class. You can expect to pay around €4 for each person, car and tent. Quite a few close from around October to Easter. With certain exceptions (such as many beaches and environmentally protected areas) it is legal to camp outside camping grounds. You'll need permission to camp on private land.

Youth hostels *(albergues juveniles)* are often the cheapest place to stay for lone travellers. Prices often depend on whether you're aged under 26; typically you pay €12 or more. Many hostels have curfews and are often heavily booked by school groups. Most are members of the country's Hostelling International (HI) organisation **Red Española de Albergues Juveniles** (REAJ; ☎ 91 522 70 07; www.reaj.com). Some hostels require HI membership; others may charge more if you're not a member. You can buy HI cards for €11 at virtually all hostels.

Officially, other establishments are either hotels (from one to five stars), *hostales* (one to two stars) or *pensiones*. In practice, there are all sorts of overlapping categories, especially at the budget end of the market. In broad terms, the cheapest are usually *fondas* and *casas de huéspedes,* followed by *pensiones*. All these normally have shared bathrooms and singles for €10 to €20, doubles for €15 to €30. Some *hostales* and *hostal-residencias* come in the same price range, but others have rooms with private bathrooms costing anywhere up to €60 or so. A double in a three-star hotel will run over €90. The luxurious state-run *paradors,* often converted historic buildings, cost upwards of €100.

Always check room charges before putting down your bags and remember that prices can and do change with time. The price of any type of accommodation varies with the season and accommodation prices listed in this book are a guide only.

Virtually all accommodation prices are subject to IVA, the Spanish version of value-added tax, which is 7%. This may or may not be included in the price. To check, ask: *Está incluido el IVA?* (Is IVA included?). In some cases you will be charged the IVA only if you ask for a receipt.

ACTIVITIES
Surfing, Windsurfing & Kite Surfing
The País Vasco has good surf spots, including San Sebastián, Zarauz and the legendary left at Mundaca. Tarifa, with its long, deserted beaches and ceaseless wind, is generally considered to be the windsurfing capital of Europe. It has also recently seen a rise in the sport of kite surfing.

Skiing
Skiing is cheap, and facilities and conditions are good, but queuing at lifts can be a mad scramble. The season runs from December to May. The most accessible resorts are in the Sierra Nevada, close to Granada, and the Pyrenees, north of Barcelona. Contact tourist offices in these cities for information. Affordable day trips can be booked through travel agents.

Cycling
Bike touring isn't as common as in other parts of Europe because of deterrents such as the often-mountainous terrain and summer heat. It's a more viable option on the Balearic Islands than on much of the mainland, although plenty of people get on their bikes in spring and autumn in the south. Mountain biking is increasingly popular, and areas such as Andalucía and Catalonia have many good tracks.

Walking
Spain is a trekker's paradise, so much so that Lonely Planet has published a guide to some of the best treks in the country, *Walking in Spain*. Walking country roads and paths between settlements can also be highly enjoyable and a great way to meet the locals.

Useful for hiking and exploring some areas are the *Guía Cartográfica* and *Guía Excursionista y Turística* series published by Editorial Alpina. The series combines information booklets in Spanish (or sometimes Catalan) with detailed maps at scales ranging from 1:25,000 to 1:50,000, and well worth the price (around €8). If you fancy a really long walk, there's the Camino de Santiago. This route, which has been followed by Christian pilgrims for centuries, can be commenced at various places in France. It then crosses the Pyrenees and runs via Pamplona, Logroño and León all the way to the cathedral in Santiago de Compostela. There are numerous guidebooks explaining the route, and the best map is published by CNIG for €6 (see p992).

BUSINESS HOURS
Generally, people work Monday to Friday from 9am to 2pm and then again from 4.30pm or 5pm to about 8pm, with a siesta in the middle of the afternoon. Shops and travel agencies are usually open these hours on Saturday too, though some may skip the evening session. Museums all have their own unique opening hours; major ones tend to open for something like normal business hours (with or without the afternoon break), but often have their weekly closing day on Monday.

COURSES
The best place to take a language course in Spain is generally at a university. There are also hundreds of private language colleges throughout the country; the **Instituto Cervantes** (www.cervantes.es); UK (☎ 020-7235 0353; 102 Eaton Sq, London SW1 W9AN); Spain (☎ 91 436 76 00; Palacio de la Trinidad, Calle Francisco Silvela 82, 28028 Madrid) can send you lists of these and of universities that run courses. Have a look at the excellent website www.spanish-in -spain.biz.

EMBASSIES & CONSULATES
Spanish Embassies & Consulates
Following is a list of Spanish diplomatic missions abroad:

Australia Canberra (☎ 02-6273 3555; embespau@mail .mae.es; 15 Arkana St, Yarralumla, Canberra ACT 2600); Melbourne (☎ 03-9347 1966); Sydney (☎ 02-9261 2433)
Canada Ottawa (☎ 613-747 2252; embespca@mail.mae .es; 74 Stanley Ave, Ottawa, Ontario K1M 1P4); Montreal (☎ 514-935 5235); Toronto (☎ 416-977 1661)
France (☎ 01 44 43 18 00; ambespfr@mail.mae.es; 22 Ave Marceau, 75381 Paris, Cedex 08)
Germany (☎ 030-254 0070; embespde@correo.mae.es; Lichtensteinallee 1, 10787 Berlin)
Ireland (☎ 269 16 40; embespie@mail.mae.es; 17A Merlyn Park, Ballsbridge, Dublin 4)
Portugal (☎ 01-347 2381; embesppt@mail.mae.es; Rua do Salitre 1, 1250 Lisbon)
The Netherlands (☎ 302 49 99; ambassade.spanje@ worldonline.nl; Lange Voorhout 50, The Hague 2514EG)
UK London (☎ 020-7235 5555; embespuk@mail.mae.es; 39 Chesham Pl, London SW1X 8SB); Edinburgh (☎ 0131 220 1843); Manchester (☎ 0161 236 1262)

USA Washington DC (☎ 202-452 0100; embespus@mail
.mae.es; 2375 Pennsylvania Ave NW, Washington DC
20037); Chicago (☎ 312-782 4588); Boston (☎ 617-536
2506); Los Angeles (☎ 323-938 0158); Houston (☎ 713-
783 6200); Miami (☎ 305-446 5511); New Orleans
(☎ 504-525 4951); New York (☎ 212-355 4080); San
Francisco (☎ 415-922 2995)

Embassies & Consulates in Spain
Some 70 countries have their embassies in
Madrid, including:
Australia (☎ 91 441 93 00; Plaza del Descubridor
Diego de Ordás 3-28003, Edificio Santa Engrácia 120)
Canada (Map pp904-5; ☎ 91 431 43 00; Calle Núñez
de Balboa 35)
France (☎ 91 423 89 00; Calle Salustiano Olózaga 9)
Germany (☎ 91 557 90 00; Calle Fortuny 8)
Ireland (Map pp904-5; ☎ 91 576 35 00; Paseo
Castellana 36)
The Netherlands (☎ 91 535 75 00; Ave Comandante
Franco 32)
New Zealand (Map pp904-5; ☎ 91 523 02 26;
Plaza Lealtad 3)
Portugal (☎ 91 782 49 60; Calle Pinar 1; Consulate
☎ 91 577 35 85; Calle Martínez Campos 11)
UK Madrid (Map pp904-5; ☎ 91 700 82 00; Calle
Fernando el Santo 16); Consulate (Map pp908-9; ☎ 91 308
52 01; Edificio Colón, Calle Marqués Ensenada 16); Barcelona
(Map pp928-9; ☎ 93 366 62 00; www.ukinspain.com;
Ave Diagonal 477; ⏱ 9.30am-2pm Mon-Fri)
USA Madrid (Map pp904-5; ☎ 91 587 22 00; Calle Serrano
75); Barcelona (☎ 93 280 22 27; http://barcelona.usconsulate
.gov; Paseo Reina Elisenda de Montcada 23; ⏱ 9am-1pm
Mon-Fri)

FESTIVALS & EVENTS
Spaniards indulge their love of colour, noise,
crowds and partying at innumerable local
fiestas and *ferias* (fairs) around the country. Many fiestas are based on religion. Most
local tourist offices can supply detailed information. Following is a list of festivals to
look out for:

January
La Tamborada Held in San Sebastián on 20 January; the
whole town dresses up and goes berserk.

February-March
Carnaval A time of fancy-dress parades and merrymaking
celebrated around the country about seven weeks before
Easter (wildest in Cádiz and Sitges).
Las Fallas de San José Valencia's week-long mid-March
party, with all-night dancing and drinking, first-class
fireworks and processions.

April
Semana Santa Parades of holy images and huge crowds,
notably in Seville, during Easter week.
Feria de Abril A week-long party held in Seville in late
April, a kind of counterbalance to the religious peak of Easter.

July
San Fermíne Combines with the running of the bulls, in
Pamplona.

August
Semana Grande A week of heavy drinking and hangovers
all along the northern coast during the first half of August.

September
Festes de la Mercè Barcelona's week-long party, held
around 24 September.

HOLIDAYS
Spain has at least 14 official holidays a year,
some observed nationwide, some very local.
When a holiday falls close to a weekend,
Spaniards like to make a *puente* (bridge),
taking the intervening day off, too. The holi-
days listed following are observed virtually
everywhere.
New Year's Day 1 January
Epiphany or **Three Kings' Day** (when children
receive presents) 6 January
Good Friday before Easter Sunday
Labour Day 1 May
Feast of the Assumption 15 August
National Day 12 October
All Saints' Day 1 November
Feast of the Immaculate Conception 8 December
Christmas 25 December

The two main periods when Spaniards go on
holiday are Semana Santa (the week leading up to Easter Sunday) and the month of
August. At these times accommodation in
beachside resorts can be scarce and transport heavily booked, but other cities are
often half-empty.

LANGUAGE
Spanish, or Castilian (*castellano*) as it is
more precisely called, is spoken throughout
Spain, but there are also three other important regional languages: Catalan (*català*) –
another Romance language with close ties
to French – is spoken in Catalonia, the
Balearic Islands and in Valencia; Galician
(*gallego*), similar to Portuguese, is spoken
in Galicia; and Basque (*euskara*; of obscure,

non-Latin origin) is spoken in the Basque Country and in Navarra.

LEGAL MATTERS

Spaniards no longer enjoy liberal drug laws. No matter what anyone tells you, it is not legal to smoke dope in public bars. There is a reasonable degree of tolerance when it comes to people having a smoke in their own home, but not in hotel rooms or guesthouses.

If you are arrested in Spain, you have the right to an attorney and to know the reason you are being held. You are also entitled to make a phone call.

MAPS

If you're driving around Spain, consider investing in the *Michelin Spain and Portugal Touring and Motoring Atlas* (€18.90), a handy atlas with detailed road maps as well as maps of all the main towns and cities. Most travel stores and petrol stations stock it.

Two organizations publish detailed maps of small parts of Spain. The CNIG covers most of the country in 1:25,000 sheets. The CNIG and the Servicio Geográfico del Ejército (SGE; Army Geographic Service) each publish a 1:50,000 series.

MEDIA
Magazines

US current-affairs magazines such as *Time* and *Newsweek* can be easily found in major cities. Among Spain's numerous magazine titles, the most popular are the glossy and gossipy ¡Hola! and the slightly more serious (but still celebrity-obsessed) *Semana.*

Newspapers

The major daily newspapers in Spain are the solidly liberal *El País,* the conservative *ABC* and *El Mundo,* which specialises in breaking political scandals. There's also a welter of regional dailies. Some of the best of these dailies come out of Barcelona, the Basque Country (País Vasco) and Andalucía.

International press, such as the *International Herald Tribune,* and daily papers from Western European countries reach major cities and tourist areas on the day of publication.

Radio

Numerous radio stations occupy the FM band. Youll hear a substantial proportion of British and US music being aired. The national pop/rock station, RNE 3, has well-varied programming.

Television

Spaniards are Europe's greatest TV watchers after the British, but they do a lot of this watching in bars and cafés, which makes it more of a social activity. Most TVs receive six channels: two state-run (TVE1 and La2), three privately run (Antena 3, Tele 5 and Canal Plus) and one regional channel. Apart from news, TV seems to consist mostly of chat shows, sports, soap operas, sitcoms and English-language films dubbed into Spanish.

MONEY

Spain's currency is the euro (€). Banks mostly open 8.30am to 2pm Monday to Friday and 8.30am to 1pm Saturday, and tend to give better exchange rates than do the currency-exchange offices. Travellers cheques attract a slightly better rate than cash. ATMs accepting a wide variety of cards are common.

Costs

Spain is one of Western Europe's more affordable countries. If you are particularly frugal, it's possible to scrape by on as little as €30 a day. This would involve staying in the cheapest possible accommodation, avoiding eating in restaurants or going to museums or bars, and not moving around too much. Places such as Madrid, Barcelona, Seville and San Sebastián will place a greater strain on your moneybelt.

A more reasonable budget would be €60 a day. This figure would allow you €25 for accommodation, €20 for meals, €2 for public transport and €5 for entry fees to museums, sights and entertainment…and a bit left over for intercity travel and a drink or two. Students (and sometimes seniors) are entitled to discounts of up to 50% on admission fees and about 30% on transport.

Taxes & Refunds

In Spain, VAT (value-added tax) is known as *impuesto sobre el valor añadido* (IVA). On accommodation and restaurant prices, there's a flat IVA of 7%, which is usually, but not always, included in quoted prices.

On such items as retail goods, alcohol and electrical appliances, IVA is 16%. Visitors are entitled to a refund of IVA on any item costing more than €90 that they are taking out of the EU. Ask the shop for a Europe Tax-Free Shopping Cheque when you buy, then present the goods and cheque to customs when you leave. If the shop can't offer a cheque, get an official receipt with the business' address and a description of the item purchased. Customs stamps the cheque and you then cash it at a booth with the 'Cash Refund' sign. There are booths at all main Spanish airports; at the border crossings at Algeciras, Gibraltar and Andorra; and at similar points throughout the EU.

Tipping & Bargaining

In restaurants, prices include a service charge, and tipping is a matter of personal choice – most people leave some small change; 5% is plenty. It's common to leave small change in bars and cafés. The only places in Spain where you are likely to bargain are markets and, occasionally, cheap hotels, particularly if you're staying for a few days.

POST

Main post offices in provincial capitals are usually open from 8.30am to 8.30pm Monday to Friday and from about 9am to 1.30pm Saturday. Stamps are also sold at *estancos* (tobacco shops with the Tabacos sign in yellow letters on a maroon background). A standard airmail letter or card costs €0.27 within Spain, €0.50 to the rest of Europe and €0.77 to the rest of the world.

Mail to/from Europe normally takes up to a week, and to North America, Australia or New Zealand around 10 days, but there may be some long, unaccountable delays.

Poste-restante mail can be addressed to you at either *poste restante* or *lista de correos*, the Spanish name for it, at the city in question. It's a fairly reliable system, although mail may well arrive late.

TELEPHONE & FAX

Blue public payphones are common and easy to use. They accept coins, phonecards and, in some cases, credit cards.

A three-minute call from a pay phone costs about €0.15 within a local area, €0.35 to other places in the same province, €0.45 to

<table>
<tr><td colspan="2">**EMERGENCY NUMBERS**</td></tr>
<tr><td>■ Police ☎ 092</td></tr>
<tr><td>■ Fire Department ☎ 112</td></tr>
<tr><td>■ Medical ☎ 061</td></tr>
</table>

other provinces, or €1 to another EU country or the USA. A three-minute call to Australia and Asia is about €4.50.

Provincial and interprovincial calls, except those to mobile phones, are around 50% cheaper between 8pm and 8am weekdays and all day Saturday and Sunday. Local and international calls are around 10% cheaper between 6pm and 8am and all day Saturday and Sunday.

International reverse-charge (collect) calls are simple to make: from a pay phone or private phone dial ☎ 900 99 00 followed by ☎ 61 for Australia, ☎ 44 for the UK, ☎ 64 for New Zealand, ☎ 15 for Canada, and for the USA dial ☎ 11 (AT&T) or ☎ 14 (MCI).

Fax

Most main post offices have a fax service, but you'll often find cheaper rates at shops or offices with Fax Público signs.

Mobile Phones

Mobile phone numbers in Spain start with the number 6. Calls to mobiles vary but a three-minute call should cost about €1.20.

Phone Codes

Area codes in Spain are an integral part of the phone number. All numbers are nine digits and you just dial that nine-digit number, wherever in the country you are calling from. All numbers prefixed with ☎ 900 are toll-free numbers.

Phonecards

Phonecards (*tarjetas telefónicas*) come in denominations of €6 and €12 and are available at main post offices and *estancos*.

TIME

Spain is one hour ahead of GMT/UTC during winter, and two hours ahead of GMT/UTC from the last Sunday in March to the last Sunday in September. See p1084 for a map of world time zones.

SPAIN

TOURIST INFORMATION

Most towns and large villages of any interest have an *oficina de turismo* (tourist office). These will supply you with a map and brochures with basic information on local sights, attractions, accommodation, history etc. Staff are generally helpful and often speak some English. A **nationwide phone line** (☎ 901 30 06 00; ⏱ 8am-10pm) offers basic information in English.

Tourist Offices Abroad

Spain has tourist information centres in 29 countries, including:

Canada (☎ 416-961 3131; toronto@tourspain.es; 2 Bloor St W, 34th fl, Toronto, Ontario M4W 3E2)

France (☎ 01-45 03 82 57; paris@tourspain.es; 43 Rue Decamps, 75784 Paris, Cedex 16)

Germany (☎ 030-882 6543; berlin@tourspain.es; Kurfürstendamm 63, 10707 Berlin)

Portugal (☎ 01-21 354 1992; lisboa@tourspain.es; Ave Sidónio Pais 28 3 Dto, 1050-215 Lisbon)

UK (☎ 020-7486 8077, brochure request ☎ 090-6364 0630 at £0.60 per min; londres@tourspain.es; 22-23 Manchester Sq, London W1M 5AP)

USA (☎ 212-265 8822; oetny@tourspain.es; 666 Fifth Ave, 35th fl, New York, NY 10103)

VISAS

Citizens of EU countries can enter Spain with their national identity card or passport. Citizens of the UK must have a full passport, not just a British visitor passport. Non-EU nationals must take their passport.

EU, Norway and Iceland citizens do not need a visa. Nationals of Australia, Canada, Israel, Japan, New Zealand, Switzerland and the USA need no visa for stays of up to 90 days but must have a passport valid for the whole visit. This 90-day limit applies throughout the EU. South Africans are among nationalities that do need a visa.

It's best to obtain the visa in your country of residence. Single-entry visas are available in flavours of 30-day and 90-day, and there's a 90-day multiple-entry visa, too, though if you apply in a country where you're not resident, the 90-day option may not be available. Multiple-entry visas will save you a lot of time and trouble if you plan to leave Spain (say to Gibraltar or Morocco), then re-enter it.

Spain is one of the Schengen countries; the others are Portugal, Italy, France, Germany, Austria, the Netherlands, Belgium, Luxembourg, Sweden, Finland, Denmark and Greece. A visa for one Schengen country is valid for the others. Compare validity, prices and permitted entries before applying. Schengen countries theoretically have done away with passport control on travel between them.

EU, Norway and Iceland nationals planning to stay in Spain more than 90 days are supposed to apply for a residence card during their first month in the country. This is a lengthy, complicated procedure; if you intend to subject yourself to it, consult a Spanish consulate before you go to Spain, as you'll need to take certain documents with you.

Other nationalities on a Schengen visa are flat out of luck when it comes to extensions. For stays of longer than 90 days you're supposed to get a residence card. This is a nightmarish process, starting with a residence visa issued by a Spanish consulate in your country of residence; start the process well in advance.

WORK

EU, Norway and Iceland nationals are allowed to work in Spain without a visa, but if they plan to stay more than three months they are supposed to apply within the first month for a residence card (see above). Virtually everyone else is supposed to obtain (from a Spanish consulate in their country of residence) a work permit and, if they plan to stay more than 90 days, a residence visa. These procedures can be difficult and time-consuming.

That said, quite a few people do manage to work in Spain one way or another – although with Spain's unemployment rate running at around 15%, don't rely on it. Teaching English is an obvious option. A TEFL certificate will be a big help. Another possibility is gaining summer work in a bar or restaurant in a tourist resort, many of which are run by foreigners.

TRANSPORT IN SPAIN

GETTING THERE & AWAY
Air

Spain has many international airports, including the following:

Alicante (☎ 96 691 90 00)

Almería (☎ 95 021 37 15)

Barcelona (☎ 93 298 38 38; www.barcelona-airport.com)
Bilbao (☎ 94 486 93 00)
Ibiza (☎ 97 180 90 00)
Madrid (☎ 91 393 60 60; www.madrid-mad.com)
Málaga (☎ 95 204 84 84)
Maó (☎ 97 115 70 00)
Palma de Mallorca (☎ 97 178 90 00)
Santiago de Compostela (☎ 98 154 75 00)
Seville (☎ 95 444 90 00)
Valencia (☎ 96 159 85 15)

In general, the cheapest destinations are Málaga, the Balearic Islands, Bilbao, Barcelona and Madrid. Departure taxes on flights out of Spain, which vary, are factored directly into tickets. There are many international airlines that fly to and from Spain.

Aer Lingus (code EI; www.aerlingus.com;
☎ 902 502 737)
Air Europa (code UX; www.aireuropa.com;
☎ 902 401 501)
Air France (code AF; www.airfrance.com;
☎ 901 11 22 66)
Alitalia (code AZ; www.alitalia.com; ☎ 902 10 03 23)
American Airlines (code AA; www.aa.com;
☎ 902 11 55 70)
BMI British Midland (code BD; www.flybmi.com;
☎ 91 393 72 53)
BMI Baby (code WW; www.bmibaby.com;
☎ 902 10 07 37)
British Airways (code BA; www.britishairways.com;
☎ 902 111 333)
easyJet (code EZY; www.easyjet.com; ☎ 902 29 99 92)
Iberia (code IB; www.iberia.com; ☎ 902 40 04 33)
KLM (code KL; www.klm.com; ☎ 902 22 27 47)
Lufthansa (code LH; www.lufthansa.com;
☎ 902 22 01 01)
Monarch Airlines (code ZB; www.flymonarch.com;
☎ 902 50 27 37)
Ryanair (code FR; www.ryanair.com; ☎ 972 18 67 34)
SAS (code SK; www.sas.se; ☎ 902 11 71 92)
Spanair (code JK; www.spanair.com; ☎ 902 13 14 15)
Swiss Air (code LX; www.swiss.com; ☎ 901 11 67 12)
Virgin Express (code TV; www.virgin-express.com;
☎ 902 88 84 59)

Land
BUS
There are regular bus services to Spain from all major centres in Europe, including Lisbon, London and Paris. In London, **Eurolines** (☎ 08705-143219; www.eurolines.com) has services at least three times a week to Barcelona (£65/95 one way/return, 26 hours), Madrid (£92/122, at least 27 hours) and Málaga

(£96/128, 35 hours). Tickets are sold by major travel agencies and if you book in advance you can get good discounts of up to one-third. People aged under 26 and senior citizens qualify for a 10% discount.

CAR & MOTORCYCLE
If you're driving or riding to Spain from England, you'll have to choose between going through France (check visa requirements) or taking a direct ferry from England to Spain (see p995). The cheapest way is to take one of the shorter ferries from England to France, then a quick drive down through France.

TRAIN
Reaching Spain by train is more expensive than by bus, unless you have a rail pass, though fares for those under 26 years do come close to the bus price. Return fares from London (using the Eurostar) to Madrid (via Paris) can be found for as little as UK£137, provided you book well in advance. For more details, contact the **Rail Europe Travel Centre** (☎ 08705-848848; www.raileurope.co.uk) in London or a travel agent. See p997 for more on rail passes and train travel through Europe.

Sea
UK
Brittany Ferries (UK ☎ 08705-360360; www.brittany-ferries.com) runs Plymouth–Santander ferries (24 hours) twice weekly from about mid-March to mid-November, and usually once a week in other months. One-way passenger fares range from about UK£61 in winter to UK£100 in summer; a two-berth cabin is an extra UK£67; a car and driver costs from UK£245 to UK£473.

P&O European Ferries (UK ☎ 08702-424999; www.poportsmouth.com) runs Portsmouth–Bilbao ferries (35 hours) twice-weekly, on Tuesday and Saturday, almost year-round. One-way/return prices with a (compulsory) berth start at UK£114/214 in winter and £166/262 in summer.

MOROCCO
Ferry services between Spain and Morocco include Algeciras–Tangier, Algeciras–Ceuta, Gibraltar–Tangier, Tarifa–Tangier, Málaga–Melilla, Almería–Melilla and Almería–Nador. Those to and from Algeciras are

SPAIN

the fastest, cheapest and most frequent, with over 20 ferries a day to Ceuta (€22, 1½ hours) and 14 to Tangier (€28, 2½ hours). Hydrofoils make the same trip in half the time for about 75% more. Taking a car to Ceuta/Tangier costs €62/73.

Don't buy Moroccan currency until you reach Morocco, as you will get ripped off in Algeciras.

GETTING AROUND

Students and seniors are eligible for discounts of 30% to 50% on almost all types of transport within Spain. The travel agency **TIVE** (☎ 91 543 74 12; tive.juventud@madrid.org; Calle Fernando El Católico 88, Madrid) has offices in major cities throughout Spain. It specialises in discounted tickets and travel arrangements for students and young people.

Air

Spain has three main domestic airlines: **Iberia** (☎ 902 40 05 00; www.iberia.com), **Air Europa** (☎ 902 40 15 01; www.aireuropa.com) and **Spanair** (☎ 902 13 14 15; www.spanair.com). They, and a couple of smaller airlines, compete to produce some fares that can make flying worthwhile if you're in a hurry, especially for longer trips. A single fare from Madrid to Barcelona, Palma de Mallorca, Santiago de Compostela or Málaga starts at about €85. There are some useful deals if you're under 26 (or, in some cases, over 63).

Bicycle

Finding bikes to rent in Spain is a hit-and-miss affair, so it's best to bring your own. However, the Spanish do enjoy recreational cycling, so getting hold of spare parts shouldn't be a problem. Cyclists should be aware that quiet roads may suddenly merge into frenetic *autopistas* without much warning.

Spain's high-speed AVE and Talgo trains will not allow bicycles on board unless boxed, but slower regional trains will. Provided there's room, buses will take bikes in their lower luggage hold (you'll probably have to remove the front wheel).

Boat

Regular ferries connect the Spanish mainland with the Balearic Islands. In bad weather or rough seas, services will be restricted. For destinations, schedules and prices see p959.

The main companies are:
Balearia (☎ 902 16 01 80; www.balearia.com)
Cape Balear (☎ 902 10 04 44)
Iscomar (☎ 902 11 91 28; www.iscomarferrys.com)
Trasmediterránea (☎ 902 45 46 45; www.trasmed iterranea.es)

Bus

Spain's bus network is operated by dozens of independent companies and is more extensive than its train system, serving remote towns and villages as well as the major routes. The choice between bus and train depends on the particular trip you're taking. for the best value, compare fares, journey times and frequencies each time you move.

Many towns and cities have one main bus station where most buses arrive and depart, and these usually have an information desk giving information on all services. Tourist offices can also help with information.

Spain's has dozens of local and regional bus companies. The best known national service is run by **ALSA** (☎ 902 42 22 42; www.alsa.es).

COSTS

Buses to/from Madrid are often cheaper than (or barely different) from the cross-country routes. For instance the three-hour Seville–Granada trip costs €16, the same as the much longer Seville–Madrid trip.

RESERVATIONS

It is not necessary, and often not possible, to make advance reservations for local bus journeys. It is, however, a good idea to turn up at least 30 minutes before the bus is due to leave to guarantee a seat.

For longer trips, such as Madrid to Seville, it's a good idea to buy your ticket in advance.

Car & Motorcycle

Spain's roads vary enormously but are generally quite good. Fastest are the *autopistas* (multilane freeways between major cities). On some, mainly in the north, you have to pay hefty tolls (from the French border to Barcelona, for example, it's about €12). Minor routes can be slow going but are usually more scenic. Trying to find a parking spot in larger towns and cities can be a nightmare. Spanish drivers park anywhere to save themselves the hassle of a half-hour search, but *grúas* (tow trucks) will tow your car, given half a chance. The cost of bailing out a car can be as high as €100.

Spanish cities do not have US-style parking meters at every spot. Instead, if you park in a blue zone from around 8am to 8pm, you have to obtain a ticket from a streetside meter, which may be several blocks away. You then display the ticket from your dashboard until your time runs out (expiration time is written on the ticket).

If you are bringing your own vehicle into Spain, remember to always carry your proof of ownership (or Vehicle Registration Document) at all times.

AUTOMOBILE ASSOCIATIONS

The Spanish automobile club is **Real Automovil Club de España** (RACE; ☎ 91 434 11 22; www.race.es; Ave Ciudad de Barcelona 132, Madrid). For the RACE's 24-hour, nationwide, on-road emergency service, call ☎ 900 11 22 22.

DRIVING LICENCE

All EU member states' driving licences (pink or pink and green) are recognised. Other foreign licences should be accompanied by an International Driving Permit. These are available from automobile clubs in your country and valid for 12 months.

FUEL & SPARE PARTS

Gasolina (petrol) is expensive, at around €0.87 for a litre of unleaded *(sin plomo)*. Diesel *(gasóleo)* costs about €0.73 per litre. Petrol stations *(gasolineras)* are everywhere and finding labour and spare parts isn't a problem.

HIRE

Rates vary widely from place to place. The best deals tend to be in major tourist areas, including airports. At Málaga airport you can rent a small car for under €110 a week. More generally, you're looking at about €50 a day with unlimited kilometres, plus insurance, damage waiver and taxes. Hiring for several days can bring the average daily cost down a lot – a small car for a week might cost under €140. Local companies often have better rates than the big firms.

INSURANCE

Third-party motor insurance is a minimum requirement and it is compulsory to have a Green Card, an internationally recognised proof of insurance, which can be obtained from your insurer.

ROAD RULES

Driving in Spain is not too bad. Locals respect road rules but do have a tendency to tailgate. Speed limits are 120km/h on the *autopistas*, 90km/h or 100km/h on other country roads and 50km/h in built-up areas. The maximum allowable blood-alcohol level is 0.05%. Seat belts must be worn, and motorcyclists must always wear a helmet and keep headlights on day and night.

Train

Trains are mostly modern and comfortable, and late arrivals are now the exception rather than the rule.

Renfe (☎ 902 24 02 02; www.renfe.es), the national railway company, runs numerous types of train, and travel times can vary a lot on the same route. So can fares, which may depend not just on the type of train but also the day of the week and time of day. Renfe's website is a great resource for schedule and fare information.

Regionales are all-stops trains (think cheap and slow). *Cercanías* provide regular services from major cities to the surrounding suburbs and hinterland, sometimes even crossing regional boundaries.

Among long-distance trains, the standard daytime train is the *diurno* (its night-time equivalent is the *estrella*). Quicker is the InterCity (mainly because it makes fewer stops), while Talgo is fastest and dearest.

Best of all is the AVE high-speed service that links Madrid and Seville in just 2½ hours. The *Talgo 200* uses part of this line to speed down to Málaga from Madrid. The *Euromed* is an AVE-style train that speeds south from Barcelona to Valencia and Alicante. A *Tren Hotel* is a 1st-class sleeper-only express.

There's also a bewildering range of accommodation types, especially on overnight trains (fares quoted in this chapter are typically 2nd-class seat fares). The cheapest sleeper option is usually a *litera*, a bunk in a six-berth 2nd-class compartment.

You can buy tickets and make reservations at stations, Renfe offices in many city centres and travel agencies that display the Renfe logo.

SPAIN

TRAIN PASSES

Rail passes are valid for all Renfe trains, but Inter-Rail users have to pay €9.50 supplements on Talgo and InterCity services, and on the high-speed AVE service (Madrid–Seville). All passholders making reservations for long-distance trains pay a fee of about €5. Renfe's Tarjeta Turística (also known as the Spain Flexipass) is a rail pass valid for three to 10 days' travel in a two-month period. In 2nd class, three days costs US$155, and 10 days is US$365. The pass can be purchased from agents outside Europe, or at a few main train stations and Renfe offices in Spain. Spanish residents are not eligible for this pass.

Switzerland

CONTENTS

SWITZERLAND

1000

Chocolate, cheese and clocks; strait-laced bankers, big business and neutrality – the clichés associated with this small, fiercely independent nation are likely ingrained in your mind long before you actually arrive. Look beyond the stereotypes, however, and you just might be stupefied. There's more to the story than Heidi and the Matterhorn, than goat herders, cowbells and yodelling.

Mixed in you'll encounter elegant cities buzzing with nightlife, a taste for eclectic culture, boundless outdoor adventure opportunities and some of the most exquisite natural beauty on the continent. The poet and novelist Goethe's description of Switzerland as a combination of 'the colossal and the well-ordered' still fits, typified by tidy, efficient, watch-precise towns where the awe-inspiring Alps slope down into the lakes.

Switzerland has one of the highest standards of living in the world, so even generous budgets will take a beating here, but the payoff is a super-slick infrastructure giving quick and easy access to everything the country has to offer. And Switzerland manages to blend the flavours of Germany, France and Italy effortlessly to create a three-cultures-in-one experience united by a sophisticated sensibility and financial savvy. The cynics who say Switzerland is wasted on the Swiss are just jealous.

FAST FACTS

- **Area** 41,285 sq km
- **Capital** Bern
- **Currency** Swiss franc (Sfr); A$1 = Sfr0.90; €1 = Sfr1.54; ¥100 = Sfr1.17; NZ$1 = Sfr0.84; UK£1 = Sfr2.29; US$1 = Sfr1.28
- **Famous for** cheese, the Matterhorn, clocks, banking
- **Key Phrases** *Guten Tag* (good day); *Danke* (thanks); *Auf Wiedersehen* (goodbye); *Sprechen Sie Englisch?* (do you speak English?)
- **Official Languages** French, German, Italian
- **Population** 7.4 million
- **Telephone Codes** country code ☎ 41; international access code ☎ 00; area codes are always dialled in Switzerland and are listed with all numbers
- **Visas** none required for citizens of the UK, Ireland, the USA, Canada, Australia, New Zealand and South Africa

SWITZERLAND

HIGHLIGHTS

- Immerse yourself in the gargantuan mountain vistas and the white-knuckle adrenalin adventures of **Interlaken** (p1034), a backpackers' mecca in the gorgeous Jungfrau region.
- Ski and soak up the alpine scenery and ambiance of the slopes around **Zermatt** (p1021), home to the mighty Matterhorn.
- Buzzing with an electricity found nowhere else in the country, **Zürich** (p1026) is elegant and sedate during the day and comes alive at night.
- Admire ancient **Château de Chillon** (p1020), on Lake Geneva, justifiably the most famous castle in Switzerland.
- Get off the beaten path to the tiny hamlet of **Gimmelwald** (p1037), the Switzerland you thought existed only in picture books.

ITINERARIES

- **One week** Head to Montreux on Lake Geneva for one night and visit Château de Chillon. Next make Interlaken your base for a few days and explore the Jungfrau region before heading to Lucerne. Finally catch the train to Zürich for an infusion of city life and culture.
- **Two weeks** As above, but spend longer in the mountains, visit Bern and take a trip to Zermatt to see the Matterhorn and do a little skiing or hiking. If you still have time, head to Ticino for a slice of Italy in Switzerland.

CLIMATE & WHEN TO GO

Winters in Switzerland are cold and snowy and can be rather grey with temperatures between 2° and 6°C. Summers mix sunshine with rain. Temperatures range from 20° to 25°C, except in Ticino, which has a hotter, Mediterranean climate. You will need to be prepared for a range of temperatures depending on your altitude.

Visit Switzerland from December to April for winter sports, and May to October for general sightseeing and hiking. Alpine resorts all but close down in late April, May and November. See Climate Charts p1055.

HISTORY

The first inhabitants of the region were a Celtic tribe, the Helvetii. The Romans arrived in 107 BC via the Great St Bernard Pass, but were gradually driven back by the Germanic Alemanni tribe, which settled in the region in the 5th century. Burgundians and Franks also came to the area, and Christianity was gradually introduced.

The territory was united under the Holy Roman Empire in 1032, but central control was never tight, and neighbouring nobles fought each other for local influence. Rudolph I spearheaded the Germanic Habsburg expansion and gradually brought the squabbling nobles to heel.

The Swiss Confederation

Upon Rudolph's death in 1291, local leaders saw a chance to gain independence. The forest communities of Uri, Schwyz and Nidwalden formed an alliance on 1 August 1291, which is seen as the origin of the Swiss Confederation (their struggles against the Habsburgs are idealised in the legend of William Tell). This union's success prompted other communities to join: Lucerne (1332), followed by Zürich (1351), Glarus and Zug (1352), and Bern (1353).

Encouraged by successes against the Habsburgs, the Swiss acquired a taste for territorial expansion. More land was seized. Fribourg, Solothurn, Basel, Schaffhausen and Appenzell joined the confederation, and the Swiss gained independence from the Holy Roman Emperor Maximilian I after their victory at Dornach in 1499.

Finally the Swiss over-reached themselves. They took on a superior force of French and Venetians at Marignano in 1515 and lost.

SWITZERLAND

SWITZERLAND

Realising they could no longer compete against larger powers with better equipment, they declared their neutrality. Even so, Swiss mercenaries continued to serve in other armies for centuries, and earned an unrivalled reputation for skill and courage.

The Reformation during the 16th century caused upheaval throughout Europe. The Protestant teachings of Luther, Zwingli and Calvin spread quickly, although the inaugural cantons remained Catholic. This caused internal unrest that dragged on for centuries.

The French Republic invaded Switzerland in 1798 and established the Helvetic Republic. The Swiss vehemently resisted such centralised control, causing Napoleon to restore the former confederation of cantons in 1803. Yet France still retained overall jurisdiction. Following Napoleon's defeat by the British and Prussians at Waterloo, Switzerland finally gained independence.

The Modern State
Throughout the gradual move towards one nation, each canton remained fiercely independent, to the extent of controlling coinage and postal services. The cantons lost these powers in 1848, when a new federal constitution was agreed upon, with Bern as the capital. The Federal Assembly was set up to take care of national issues, but the cantons retained legislative (Grand Council) and executive (States Council) powers to deal with local matters.

Having achieved political stability, Switzerland could concentrate on economic and social matters. Poor in mineral resources, it developed industries dependent on highly skilled labour. A network of railways and roads was built, opening up previously inaccessible regions of the Alps and helping the development of tourism.

The Swiss carefully guarded their neutrality in the 20th century. Their only involvement in WWI was organising units of the Red Cross (founded in Geneva in 1863 by Henri Dunant). Switzerland did join the League of Nations after peace was won, but only on the condition that its involvement was financial and economic rather than military. Apart from some accidental bombing, WWII left Switzerland largely unscathed.

While the rest of Europe underwent the painful process of rebuilding from the ravages of war, Switzerland expanded its already powerful commercial, financial and industrial base. Zürich developed as an international banking and insurance centre. Many international bodies, such as the World Health Organization, based their headquarters in Geneva. Workers and employers struck agreements under which industrial weapons such as strikes and lockouts were renounced. Social reforms, such as old-age pensions (1948), also were introduced.

Afraid that its neutrality would be compromised, Switzerland managed to avoid joining the United Nations (UN) for over 50 years, restricting itself to observer status. However, in a March 2002 referendum – after much lobbying by the government, economists and the media – the Swiss people finally voted in favour of membership. The government proudly announced that Switzerland's days of sitting on the sidelines were over.

The Swiss aren't quite as keen on joining the EU, however. Switzerland's 1992 application remains frozen, after voters twice failed to endorse the federal government's strategy. Nevertheless, the 1999 bilateral agreements promised market access, and free movement of people and transport between Switzerland and the EU.

In the 1990s the country's WWII record came under critical scrutiny. Swiss banks were accused of holding huge sums deposited by Jews who later became victims of the Holocaust. In 1998, facing a class action lawsuit in the US by Holocaust survivors, the banks agreed to pay US$1.25 billion to settle all outstanding claims. In 2002 an independent commission of historians set up by the Swiss government confirmed that tens of thousands of Jewish refugees were turned back from Switzerland's border, and left to face their fate in Nazi Germany. Swiss banks were also accused of banking Nazi plunder during WWII. A sum of at least US$400 million (US$3.8 billion today) was deposited.

It was just one of many scandals that erupted in Switzerland at the beginning of the 21st century. On 27 September 2001, a gunman ran amok in the Zug cantonal parliament and killed 14 people – an unprecedented event in Swiss history. Five days later, the national carrier Swissair declared bankruptcy, further damaging the country's psyche. There was little time to recover before a fire in the Gotthard road tunnel broke out on 24 October 2001, killing 11 people.

The run of ill fortune continued. In July 2002, a Russian passenger plane and a DHL cargo transport crashed mid-air while under Swiss air traffic control. And another suit against the bankers looms – this time for their alleged role in propping up South Africa's apartheid regime. It seems, for now at least, that traditionally isolationist Switzerland has discovered that bad things happen to good nations, and that no country is an island – metaphorically at least.

PEOPLE

With a population of 7.4 million, Switzerland averages 174 people per square kilometre. Zürich is the largest city (351,700) followed by Geneva (180,400), Basel (161,800) and Bern (122,900). Most people are of Germanic origin, as reflected in the breakdown of the four national languages (see p1044). Around 20% of the population are residents but not Swiss citizens.

The Swiss are polite, law-abiding people who usually see no good reason to break the rules. You'll see few local litterbugs or jay-walkers here. Living quietly with your neighbours is a national obsession. Good manners infuse the national psyche, and politeness is the cornerstone of all social intercourse. Always shake hands when being introduced to a Swiss, and kiss on both cheeks to greet and say goodbye to friends. Don't forget to greet shopkeepers when entering shops. When drinking with Swiss, always wait until everyone has their drink and toast each of your companions, looking them in the eye and clinking glasses. Drinking before the toast is unforgivable, and will lead to seven years of bad sex…or so the superstition goes. Don't say you weren't warned.

In a few mountain regions such as Valais, people still wear traditional rural costumes, but dressing up is usually reserved for festivals. Yodelling, playing the alp horn and Swiss wrestling are also part of the Alpine tradition.

RELIGION

The country is split pretty evenly between Protestantism (40%) and Roman Catholicism (46%). Most of the rest of the population are recorded as 'unaffiliated'. The dominant faith varies between cantons. Strong Protestant areas are Bern, Vaud and Zürich, whereas Valais, Ticino and Uri are mostly Catholic. Most Swiss pay a *kirchensteur* (church tax), a percentage of their income tax that the government distributes to the churches through state subsidies.

ARTS

Many foreign writers and artists, such as Voltaire, Byron, Shelley and Turner have visited and settled in Switzerland. Local and international artists pouring into Zürich during WWI spawned the Dadaist movement there.

Paul Klee (1879–1940) is the best-known native painter. He created bold, hard-lined abstract works. The writings of philosopher Jean-Jacques Rousseau (1712–78), in Geneva, played an important part in the development of democracy. Critically acclaimed post-war dramatists and novelists, Max Frisch (1911–91) and Friedrich Dürrenmatt (1921–90), entertained readers with their dark satire, tragi-comedies and morality plays. On the musical front, Arthur Honegger (1892–1955) is Switzerland's most recognised composer.

The Swiss have made important contributions to graphic design and commercial art. Anyone who's ever used a computer will have interacted with their fonts, from Helvetica to Fruitiger to Univers. The Swiss also gave the world Cow Parade – the different processions of life-sized, painted fibreglass cows that have decorated multiple cities around the globe. The first herd, of more than 800 cows, had their day away from the pasture in Zürich in 1998.

The father of modern architecture, Le Corbusier (1887–1965), who designed Notre Dame du Haut chapel at Ronchamps in France, Chandigarh in India and the UN headquarters in New York, was Swiss. One of the most-acclaimed contemporary architectural teams on earth – Jacques Herzog and Pierre de Meuron – live and work in Basel. Winners of the prestigious Pritzker Prize in 2001, this pair created London's acclaimed Tate Modern museum building.

Gothic and Renaissance architecture are prevalent in urban areas, especially Bern. Rural Swiss houses vary according to region, but are generally characterised by ridged roofs with wide, overhanging eaves, and balconies and verandas enlivened by colourful floral displays, especially geraniums.

IT ALL HAPPENED IN SWITZERLAND

- Albert Einstein came up with his theories of relativity and the famous formula '$E=MC^2$' while working in Bern.

- Switzerland gave birth to the Worldwide Web at the acclaimed CERN research institute outside Geneva.

- Val de Travers, near Neuchâtel, claims to be the birthplace of the mythical green alcohol absinthe.

- Carl Gustav Jung (1875–1961), who founded the analytical school of psychology, was Swiss.

- The first acid trip took place in Switzerland. In 1943, chemist Albert Hofmann was conducting tests for a migraine cure in Basel when he accidentally absorbed the lysergic acid diethylamide, or LSD, compound through his fingertips. He liked the ensuing psychedelic hallucinations so much he tried the drug again. And again. He once told a British newspaper he hoped LSD would one day become part of mainstream culture, with the same acceptance as alcohol.

- Of the 800 or so films a year produced by India's huge movie-making industry, more are shot in Switzerland than in any other foreign country. 'For the Indian public, Switzerland is the land of their dreams', film star Raj Mukherjee has said. And Bollywood fans visit the country in droves. While the total number of tourists to Switzerland grew by 8 percent between 1995 and 2000, the number of Indian visitors doubled. Favourite destination shots include the Berner Oberland, Central Switzerland and Geneva.

- Switzerland's central Alpine region possesses one of Europe's richest traditions of myth and legend. Pontius Pilate is said to rise out of the lake on Mt Pilatus, near Lucerne, every good Friday (the day he condemned Jesus Christ) to wash the blood from his hands – and anybody who witnesses this event will allegedly die within the year. Tiny 'wild folk' with supernatural powers, called Chlyni Lüüt, were once reputed to inhabit Mt Rigi, also near Lucerne. Their children's spleens were removed at birth, giving them the ability to leap around mountain slopes like chamois.

ENVIRONMENT

Mountains make up 70% of Switzerland's 41,290 sq km. Farming of cultivated land is intensive and cows graze on the upper slopes in summer as soon as the retreating snow line permits.

The Alps occupy the central and southern regions of the country. The Dufourspitze (4634m), a peak on the Monte Rosa massif, is the highest point, although the Matterhorn (4478m) is more famous.

Glaciers account for an area of 2000 sq km, most notably the Aletsch Glacier, which at 169 sq km is the largest valley glacier in Europe.

The St Gotthard Massif, in the centre of Switzerland, is the source of many lakes and rivers, such as the Rhine and the Rhône. The Jura Mountains straddle the border with France, and peak at around 1700m. Between the two mountain systems is the Mittelland, also known as the Swiss Plateau, a region of hills crisscrossed by rivers, ravines and winding valleys.

The most distinctive Alpine animal in Switzerland is the ibex, a mountain goat that has huge curved and ridged horns. There are about 12,000 of them left in the country.

Switzerland has just one national park, the Swiss National Park. At just 169 sq km it is quite small but offers opportunities for walking and ibex viewing.

Switzerland has long been an environmentally aware nation. Its citizens diligently recycle household waste and cities encourage the use of public transport. The policy in the mountains is to contain rather than expand existing resorts.

FOOD & DRINK

Lactose intolerants will struggle in this dairy-obsessed country, where cheese is a way of life. The best-known Swiss dish is fondue, in which melted Emmental and Gruyère are combined with white wine, served in a large pot and eaten with bread cubes. Another popular artery-hardener is *raclette*, melted cheese served with potatoes.

Rösti (fried, buttery, shredded potatoes) is German Switzerland's national dish, and is served with everything.

Many dishes are meaty, and veal is highly rated throughout the country. In Zürich it is thinly sliced and served in a cream sauce *(geschnetzeltes kalbsfleisch). Bündnerfleisch* is dried beef, smoked and thinly sliced. Like their northern neighbours, the Swiss also munch on a wide variety of *Wurst* (sausage).

Wine is considered an essential accompaniment to lunch and dinner. Local vintages are generally good quality, but you might never have heard of them, as they are rarely exported. The main growing regions are the Italian- and French-speaking areas, particularly in Valais and by lakes Neuchâtel and Geneva.

Buffet-style restaurant chains, such as Manora, have a huge selection of freshly cooked food at low prices. Migros and Coop are the main supermarket chains. Street stalls are a good place to pick up cheap eats – you'll find kebabs and sandwiches everywhere. Bratwurst stands also abound.

Restaurants are sometimes closed between meals (generally from 3pm to 5pm), although this is not so much the case in the larger cities, and tend to have a closing day, often Monday. Cafés usually stay open all day. Bars open around lunchtime and stay open until at least midnight, while clubs don't get going before 10pm and don't close until after 4am.

In the cities and larger towns there are often several dedicated vegetarian restaurants. Most eateries also will offer a small selection of non-meat options, including large salad plates.

Finally, Switzerland makes some of the most delectable chocolate in the world – don't miss it!

BERN

pop 122,900

Switzerland's captivating capital is a charming place to lose oneself for an afternoon. Curving, cobbled streets lined with 15th-century terraced buildings, covered arcades, historic fountains and the deep-green Aare River all amplify the medieval old town's persona. Founded in 1191 by Berchtold V, Bern was named for the unfortunate bear (*bärn* in local dialect) that was Berchtold's first hunting victim. Today the bear remains the heraldic mascot of the city. In 1983 Unesco declared Bern a World Heritage Site, a fact of which the city is immensely proud.

ORIENTATION

The compact centre of the old town is contained within a sharp U-bend of the Aare River. The train station is on the western edge within easy reach of all the main sights, and offers bike rental and airline check-in.

INFORMATION

Bookshops

Stauffacher (☎ 031 311 24 11; Neuengasse 25; 🕑 8am-6.30pm Mon-Fri, 8am-4pm Sat) English-language bookshop.

Emergency

Police (☎ 031 321 21 21)

Internet Access

Internet Pub (☎ 031 313 81 91; Aarbergergasse 46; per hr Sfr7.50; 🕑 9am-11pm) Fifty coin-operated machines, fully stocked bar and a groovy atmosphere.

Medical Services

University Hospital (☎ 031 632 21 11; Freiburgstrasse) West of the centre.

Telephone Referral Service (☎ 090 057 67 47) For help locating a doctor or dentist.

Money

SBB exchange office (🕑 6.30am-9pm) Lower level of the train station.

Post

Main post office (Schanzenstrasse; 🕑 7.30am-6.30pm Mon-Fri, 8am-noon Sat)

Tourist Information

Bern Tourismus (☎ 031 328 12 28; www.bernetourism.ch; Train Station; 🕑 9am-8.30pm Jun-Sep, 9am-6.30pm Mon-Sat,10am-5pm Sun Oct-May) Offers two-hour city tours by **coach** (Sfr25, daily Apr-Oct, Sat Nov-Mar) and **foot** (Sfr14, daily Jun-Sep) in summer. Its free booklet, *Bern aktuell*, has plenty of useful information. There's another tourist office by the bear pits.

Bern Youth Guide (www.youthguide.ch) This online service has some excellent tips and links.

Travel Agencies

STA Travel (☎ 031 302 03 12; Falkenplatz 9; 🕑 9.30am-6pm Mon-Fri, 10am-1pm Sat) Budget and student travel agency.

SIGHTS & ACTIVITIES
City Centre Stroll
It's easy to fall under the old town's spell when wandering through covered arcades, past myriad fountains and around 15th century sandstone buildings. Pick up a city map from the tourist office (Sfr1) and start exploring – a detour down a skinny side alley could reveal a cellar entrance to a shop or bar or theatre. Make sure to check out the **ogre fountain**, in Kornhausplatz, depicting a giant enjoying a meal of wriggling children. The **Zeitglockenturm**, dividing Marktgasse and Kramgasse, is a colourful clock tower with revolving figures that herald the chiming hour.

Nearby is **Einstein House** (☎ 031 312 00 91; Kramgasse 49; adult/student/child Sfr3/2/2; ☺ 10am-5pm Tue-Fri, to 4pm Sat, closed Dec & Jan), where the physicist lived when he developed his theories of relativity. Unless you're a fanatic it's probably better to just snap a picture outside. Inside the museum is little more than a cramped apartment.

The unmistakably Gothic, 15th-century cathedral **Münster** (☺ 10am-5pm Tue-Sat, 11.30am-5pm Sun), however, is worth stepping into. It features imposing, 12m-high, stained-glass windows and an elaborate main portal.

Just across the Aare River are the **Bear Pits** (Bärengraben). Though bears have been the entertainment at this site since 1857, it's sad to see such majestic beasts doing tricks for treats in such a cramped, concrete environment.

Swimming
The open-air **Marzili pools** (admission free; ☺ May-Sep) are an excellent option on a hot summer day. You also can follow the local lead and walk upriver, fling yourself into the swift current of the Aare then float back to Marzili. You need to be a very strong swimmer however.

Houses of Parliament
The 1902 **Houses of Parliament** (Bundeshäuser; ☎ 031 332 85 22; www.parliament.ch; Bundesplatz; admission free; ☺ tours 9am, 10am, 11am, 2pm, 3pm & 4pm Mon-Fri, 11am Sat), home of the Swiss Federal Assembly, are impressively ornate, with statues of the nation's founding fathers, a stained-glass dome adorned with cantonal emblems and a huge, 214-bulb chandelier. Tours are offered when the Parliament is in recess,

otherwise you can watch from the public gallery. Bring a passport to gain entry.

Museums
The **Kunstmuseum** (Museum of Fine Arts; ☎ 031 328 09 44; www.kunstmuseumbern.ch; Hodlerstrasse 8-12; adult/student Sfr7/5; ☺ 10am-9pm Tue, 10am-5pm Wed-Sun) is best known for having more than 2000 works by Paul Klee, as well pieces by Picasso and Dali, among other masters.

The **Bernisches Historisches Museum** (Bern Historical Museum; ☎ 031 350 77 11; www.bhm.ch; Helvetiaplatz 5; adult/student Sfr13/8; ☺ 10am-5pm Tue & Thu-Sun, 10am-8pm Wed) is a castle-like museum that depicts the history of Bern. A prize exhibit is the Hydria von Grächwil, a mysterious bronze vessel dating back to the 6th century BC.

The kid-friendly **Naturhistorisches Museum** (Natural History Museum; ☎ 031 350 71 11; www.nmbe.ch, in German; Bernastrasse 15; adult/student/child Sfr5/3/free; ☺ 2-5pm Mon, 9am-5pm Tue-Fri, 10am-5pm Sat & Sun) is best known for the stuffed, rather moth-eaten, remains of Barry the dog. He's the most famous of the 40 St Bernards who have rescued some 2000 travellers stranded in the Alps since the 11th century.

For an interactive journey through the history of communications, including radio, TV and new media, head to the **Museum für Kommunikation** (Museum of Communication; ☎ 031 357 55 55; www.mfk.ch; Helvetiastrasse 16; adult/student/child Sfr6/4/2; ☺ 10am-5pm Tue-Sun).

Markets
An open-air market groaning with fresh fruit and veggies is held at Bärenplatz on Tuesday and Saturday mornings, or daily in summer. On the last Monday in November, Bern hosts its famous onion market where traders take over the town centre, confetti is dumped and people walk around hitting each other over the head with plastic hammers. Street performers add to a carnival atmosphere.

SLEEPING
Budget
Camping Eichholz (☎ 031 961 26 02; Strandweg 49; camp sites per person/tent Sfr6.90/5, bungalows Sfr15 & per person Sfr6.90; ☺ May-Sep) This pleasant camping option is nestled by the river about a half-hour walk from the centre (or take tram No 9 to Wabern).

Hotel Glocke Backpackers Bern (☎ 031 311 37 71; www.bernbackpackers.com; Rathausgasse 75; dm Sfr27, s/d with shared bathroom Sfr65/110; ☐) The lounge area

BERN

0 —— 400 m
0 —— 0.2 miles

INFORMATION
Austrian Consulate	1 F4
Bern Tourismus	2 C2
British Embassy	3 F4
Canadian Embassy	4 F4
Dutch Embassy	5 F3
Internet Pub	6 D2
Irish Embassy	7 F4
Italian Embassy	8 F4
Main Post Office	9 C2
SBB Office	(see 2)
South African Embassy	10 F4
STA Travel	11 D2
Stauffacher Bookshop	12 D2
Tourist Office	13 F2

SIGHTS & ACTIVITIES (pp1007)
Bear Pits	14 F2
Bernisches Historisches Museum	15 E4
Einstein Haus	16 E2
Houses of Parliament	17 D3
Kunstmuseum	18 D2
Marzili Swimming Pools	19 D4
Museum für Kommunikation	20 E4
Münster (Cathedral)	21 E3
Naturhistorisches Museum	22 E4
Ogre Fountain	23 D2
Zeitglockenturm	24 D2

SLEEPING (pp1007–9)
Hotel Gauer Schweizerhof	25 D2
Hotel Glocke Backpackers Bern	26 D2
Hotel Kreuz	27 D2
Hotel National	28 C3
Landhaus Hotel	29 E1
Marthahaus Garni	30 D2
SYHA Hostel	31 D3

EATING (p1009)
Coop	32 D2
Della Casa	33 D2
Greenhouse	34 E2
Le Mazot	35 D2
Les Amis	36 E2
Manora	37 C2
Menuetto	38 E3
Migros	39 D2

DRINKING (pp1009–10)
Altes Tramdepot	40 F2
Dampfzentrale	41 D4
Kornhauskeller	42 D2
Kornhausplatz	(see 23)
Quasimodo	(see 26)
Reitschule	43 C1
Wasserwerk	44 F3

TRANSPORT (p1010)
Bern Mobil (Public Transport Office)	45 C3
Bern Rollt (Free Bicycle Depot)	46 C2
Bern Rollt (Free Bicycle Depot)	47 D3
Bus Station	48 C2

has pool tables and a TV. Dorms are simple, with lockers and sinks. Self-caterers will appreciate the kitchen.

Landhaus Hotel (☎ 031 331 41 66; www.landhaus bern.ch; Altenbergstrasse 4; dm Sfr30, d with shared bathroom from Sfr110; 🖳) Modern minimalist rooms and a slick restaurant-bar downstairs (live jazz on Thursday evenings) make this place a viable option. Dorm dwellers pay extra for bedding and breakfast. There's a kitchen, and a TV upon request.

SYHA Hostel (☎ 031 311 63 16; www.jugibern.ch; Weihergasse 4; dm from Sfr30, s/d with shared bathroom Sfr42.80/75.60; 🖳) In a quiet riverside spot below Parliament, the hostel isn't as well kept as other SYHA facilities. The showers are less than spotless and guests have complained about the safety of baggage left in the common room.

Mid-Range & Top End

Hotel National (☎ 031 381 19 88; www.nationalbern.ch, in German; Hirschengraben 24; s with shared bathroom Sfr60, s/d Sfr100/150; 🅿 🖳) A grand, old-world, family-run hotel that's kept in the style of 100 years ago and offers small but very clean rooms with balconies and inviting furniture. Don't miss the old-fashioned lift. There's free Internet access for guests. Excellent value for money.

Marthahaus Garni (☎ 031 332 41 35; www.martha haus.ch; Wyttenbachstrasse 22a; tram No 9 to Viktoriaplatz; s/d with shared bathroom Sfr65/95; 🖳) In a quiet residential area, this place is warm and welcoming with comfy rooms, a share kitchen and a TV lounge.

Hotel Kreuz (☎ 031 329 95 95; www.hotelkreuz -bern.ch, in German; Zeughausgasse 26; s/d from Sfr120/170, mains Sfr15-30) This very modern hotel has smart rooms with all the creature comforts, a tiny bar with unique metal and stained-glass light fixtures, and a restaurant serving Swiss–German fare.

Hotel Gauer Schweizerhof (☎ 031 326 80 80; www .schweizerhof-bern.ch; Bahnhofplatz 11; s/d from Sfr290/415; 🅿 🐾) Five-star pampering and old-world charm are delivered at this very elegant hotel near the train station. The deluxe rooms have silk bedspreads and elaborate curtains. There is a swanky piano bar and two restaurants.

EATING

Wall-to-wall cafés and restaurants line the popular meeting places of Bärenplatz and Theaterplatz, as well as the more upmarket Gerechtigkeitsgasse. The restaurants listed here do not close between meals unless otherwise stated,

Manora (☎ 031 311 37 55; Bubenbergplatz 5a; mains Sfr5-15) Delicious fresh food and a funky atmosphere are served in equal proportions at this busy, two-level buffet-style restaurant.

Le Cultina (☎ 031 376 13 70; Seftigenstrasse 1; mains from Sfr11; 🕑 Mon-Fri) This spacious canteen-style restaurant has a rotating list of daily dishes and gigantic portions. If you're on a tight budget you won't regret the 10-minute ride southwest on tram No 9 to get here.

Greenhouse (☎ 031 311 65 44; Münstergasse 68; mains Sfr17) With a distinct Parisian café feel, the varied menu features *rösti*, potatoes and spaghetti. Portions are decent.

Le Mazot (☎ 031 311 70 88; Bärenplatz 5; mains Sfr11-30) Very cosy with dark wood panels, this place is a well-known specialist in Swiss food. There is a massive *rösti*, raclette and fondue menu, and for those with small stomachs half portions are available. Sit outside in the glassed-in patio on warm days.

Menuetto (☎ 031 311 14 48; Münstergasse 47; mains Sfr22; 🕑 11.15am-2.15pm & 5.30-10pm Mon-Sat) A mecca for vegetarians, Menuetto produces mouthwateringly fragrant and wholesome food in a congenial atmosphere.

Les Amis (☎ 031 311 51 87; Rathausgasse 63; mains Sfr30; 🕑 7pm-midnight Tue-Sat) French and Italian cuisine is the speciality of the maison. It's tucked away below a trendy bar.

Della Casa (☎ 031 311 21 42; Schauplatzgasse 16; mains from Sfr31; 🕑 closed Sun) Don't be fazed by the dingy entrance to this restaurant, it's one of the best, albeit meat-obsessed, places in town. Inside you'll find an old but cosy eatery with floral curtains, leadlight lamps and traditional Swiss specialities.

Self-caterers can buy up big at **Coop** (Neuengasse) and **Migros** (Marktgasse 46), which also have cheap self-service restaurants serving everything from cheese to salad to chicken in the Sfr3 to Sfr7 range.

DRINKING & ENTERTAINMENT

Bern has a thriving nightlife, with countless bars and clubs to choose from. See the website www.bernbynight.ch (in German) for an extensive list. Bars in Bern open in the afternoon and don't close before midnight. Clubs get going after 10pm.

Reitschule (☎ 031 306 69 69; www.reitschule.ch, in German; Schützenmattstrasse) Perhaps the capital's most famous nightlife option, this centre for alternative arts is sprawled throughout several graffiti-splattered, derelict-looking buildings under the railway. It attracts a diverse crowd looking for dance, theatre and live music, and serves salads and sandwiches at its restaurant (Sfr5 to Sfr10).

Wasserwerk (☎ 031 312 12 31; www.wasserwerk.ch; Wasserwerkgasse 5; gigs free-Sfr30) In a converted riverside warehouse, this is a favourite hang out for local pool-players and clubbers. International DJs spin regularly. See the website for the latest programme.

Altes Tramdepot (☎ 031 368 14 15; Am Bärengraben) Beer is still made on the premises at Bern's first microbrewery. In a cavernous converted tram depot, the place serves up snacks, monster meals and sweeping views across the river.

Kornhauskeller (☎ 031 327 72 72; Kornhausplatz 18) This is a magnificent underground gallery bar and restaurant with vaulted ceilings and frescoes, plus comfy sofas overlooking diners below. Drinks are dear, but worth it to soak up the atmosphere.

Dampfzentrale (☎ 031 311 63 37; www.dampfzentrale.ch, in German; Marzilistrasse 47; bus No 30 to Marzili) With an eclectic mix of acts from jazz and flamenco to classical to club DJs, this longstanding performing arts centre almost always has something interesting going on. It also features avant-garde art exhibitions.

Quasimodo (☎ 031 311 13 81; Rathausgasse 75) Backpackers staying at the Hotel Glocke will like the convenience of this techno bar-club downstairs. At night it pumps out a hard electronic pulse.

SHOPPING

There is an open-air vegetable, fruit and flower market on Bärenplatz each Tuesday and Saturday (daily in summer). On the first Saturday of the month there is a craft market in front of the cathedral.

If truly local souvenirs interest you, grab a Toblerone chocolate here, as it's made in Bern. Souvenir shops cluster along Kramgasse and Gerechtigkeitsgasse, but none is outstanding, and it must be said that Bern is not exactly a shopping paradise.

GETTING THERE & AWAY

There are daily flights to Lugano, London, Paris, Amsterdam and other European destinations from Bern-Belp airport. Postbuses

depart from the western side of the train station.

There are three motorways that intersect in the northern part of the city. The N1 runs from Neuchâtel in the west and Basel and Zürich in the northeast. The N6 connects Bern with Thun and the Interlaken region in the southeast. The N12 is the route from Geneva and Lausanne in the southwest.

There are train connections to most Swiss towns, including Basel (Sfr34, 70 minutes, Geneva (Sfr47, 1¾ hours, hourly), Interlaken (Sfr23, 50 minutes, hourly) and Zürich (Sfr45, 70 minutes, hourly).

GETTING AROUND

Bern-Belp airport is some 9km southeast of the city centre. A bus links the airport to the train station (Sfr14, 20 minutes) and is coordinated with flight arrivals and departures.

Getting around on foot is quite easy if you're staying in the centre. Bus and tram tickets cost Sfr1.70 (maximum six stops) or Sfr2.60. A day pass for the city and regional network is Sfr9. A 24-/48-/72-hour pass for just the city costs Sfr7/11/15. Buy single-journey tickets at stops, and passes from the tourist office or the **BernMobil public transport office** (☎ 031 321 88 44; Bubenbergplatz 5).

Many taxis wait by the train station. They charge Sfr6.50 plus Sfr3.10 per kilometre (Sfr4 after 8pm and on Sunday).

From May to October there are free loans of city bikes outside the train station. Bring ID and Sfr20 deposit.

AROUND BERN

Make Bern your base for exploring the region. There are many day trips just a short train ride away. **Murten**, about 30km west of Bern, is a historic walled town overlooking a lake. There are trains from Bern (Sfr11.80, 35 minutes, hourly).

An enticing old town of narrow lanes, steep stairways and clusters of admirable Gothic houses greet visitors in well-preserved **Fribourg**. On the banks of the Sarine River, the town also showcases three charming bridges. It is easily accessible by train (Sfr12.40, 30 minutes, hourly).

Further south is the photogenically perfect pre-Alps village of **Gruyères**. Known above all for the cheese by the same name, it attracts busloads of tourists who gawk at the fine 15th- to 17th-century homes and the stern

13th-century **castle** on the hill. Sample the fromage at **La Maison du Gruyère** (☎ 026 921 84 00; www.lamaisondugruyere.ch; tours Sfr5; ☼ 9am-7pm Apr-Sep, 9am-6pm Oct-Mar), which offers daily cheese-making tours. Fans of the *Alien* movie can pay homage to its designer at the **Musée HR Giger** (☎ 026 921 22 00; adult/child Sfr10/5; ☼ 10am-6pm summer, 10am-5pm Tue-Sun winter). The museum, housed in a 16th-century mansion, features other-worldly leering sculptures, furniture, paintings and all things bizarre and occult. From Bern you will need to take a train to Fribourg, another one to Bulle and then a postbus to Gruyères. The entire journey takes a little over an hour and costs Sfr24.

NEUCHÂTEL & THE JURA

The northwest corner of the country hugs the border with France, sharing its language, food and sensibility. Featuring rolling hills and a postcard-perfect lake, Neuchâtel is a wine-making region with a proud watch-making heritage. Dominated by the Jura mountain range, the Jura region's landscape of forests, pastures and gentle slopes make it ideal territory for a range of sports and outdoor activities.

NEUCHÂTEL
pop 32,100

Spend an afternoon cruising Neuchâtel's open-air cafés, walking along its glittering lake and feasting your eyes on the charming sandstone elegance of its old town and your stress will melt away. The canton's compact capital is really just a laid-back French-style resort surrounded by vineyards. They say the French spoken here is the purest in Switzerland.

The train station (Gare CFF) has daily money exchange and bike rental. The central pedestrian zone and Place Pury (the hub of local buses) are about 1km away down the hill along Ave de la Gare.

The **tourist office** (☎ 032 889 68 90; www.ne.ch /tourism; Place du Port; ☼ 9am-noon & 1.30-5.30pm Mon-Fri, 9am-noon Sat Sep-Jun, 9am-7pm Mon-Sat, 4-7pm Sun Jul & Aug) is in the main post office by the lake.

Sights & Activities
The centrepiece of the old town is the 12th-century **Chateau de Neuchâtel** (☎ 032 889 60 00; 45min tours free; ☼ 10am-4pm Apr-Sep) and the ad-joining **Collegiate Church**. The church features a striking cenotaph of 15 statues dating from 1372. Nearby, the **Prison Tower** (☎ 032 717 76 02; Rue J de Hochberg 5; admission Sfr1; ☼ 8am-6pm Apr-Aug) offers broad views of the town and lake.

Visit the **Musée d'Art et d'Histoire** (Museum of Art & History; ☎ 032 717 79 20; Esplanade Léopold-Robert 1; adult/student Sfr7/4, free Wed; ☼ 10am-6pm Tue-Sun), on the waterfront, to see beloved 18th-century clockwork figures.

Tropical Gardens Papiliorama/Nocturama (☎ 031 756 04 61; adult/student/child Sfr11/9/5; ☼ 9am-6pm summer, 10am-5pm winter) has a complex of lush vegetation with colourful butterflies and tropical birds, as well as a faux moonlit world for Latin American night creatures. It's 6km east of Neuchâtel at Marin (take bus No 1 from Place Pury).

Sleeping
Oasis Neuchâtel (☎ 032 731 31 90; auberge.oasis@ bluewin.ch; Rue du Suchiez 35; dm/d Sfr24/60; ☼ Apr-Oct) Glorious views and friendly accommodation are found at this independent hostel 2km from the centre. Take bus No 1 (Cormondrêche) to Vauseyon and follow the signs towards Centre Sportive.

Hôtel Marché (☎ 032 723 23 30; www.hoteldu marche.ch, in French; Place des Halles 4; s/d with shared bathroom Sfr90/140) Clean and basic rooms with TVs overlooking the cafés of bustling Place des Halle are standard here.

Hotel de L'Ecluse (☎ 032 729 93 10; www.hotelde lecluse.ch; Rue de L'Ecluse 24; s/d from Sfr100/140; 💻) Rooms come with brass beds, elegant décor, cable TV and kitchenettes, making this an excellent option for the self-caterer.

Hôtel Alpes et Lac (☎ 032 723 19 19; www.alpeset lac.ch; Place de la Gare 2; s/d from Sfr125/180) Opposite the train station, this is an elegant option in a stately 19th-century building with classy modern rooms equipped with cable TV and a generous breakfast buffet.

Eating & Drinking
Local specialities include tripe and *tome neuchâteloise chaude*, a baked cheese starter. Also check out fresh trout from the lake. Some restaurants close on Mondays. Bars are generally open nightly.

Chez Bach et Buck (☎ 032 725 63 53; Ave du 1er-Mars 22; crepes Sfr6-10.50) Dominated by refreshing green-themed décor, the menu at this laid-back place features 130 crepes, as well as good veggie options.

Cafe des Halles (☎ 032 724 31 41; Rue du Trésor 4; mains Sfr35) In an impressive historic house on the main square, this place is the gourmet's central choice. The cooking is mainly French, but also includes scrumptious pizzas and pastas. Eat outside on the large shaded terrace.

Appareils de Chauffage (☎ 032 721 43 96; Rue des Moulins 37) This is a funky café-bar with quality coffee and a range of spirits and beers. Grab a board game from the bar and settle in for a few hours.

La Case á Chocs (☎ 032 721 21 07; Quai Philippe Godet 16) In a former brewery this is part bar, part club with live music most weekends, and occasional cinema and art shows.

Bar de L'Univers (☎ 032 721 43 40; Rue du Coq d'Inde 22) Also worthy of a look is this cool, smoky, studied-grunge bar for all ages. It's tucked into the corner of a quiet square.

Self-caterers can stock up on local wines and cheeses at **Coop** (Rue de la Treille 4) and **Aux Gourmets** (cnr Rue de Seyon & Rue de L'Ancien Hotel-de-Ville), both near Place Pury.

Getting There & Around
There are fast trains to Geneva (Sfr40, 70 minutes, hourly) and Bern (Sfr17.20, 35 minutes, hourly). Postbuses heading to the Jura leave from the station.

Local buses cost Sfr1.60 to Sfr2.60 per trip, or Sfr7 for a 24-hour pass.

JURA CANTON
Far removed from the staggering Alpine scenes more readily associated with Switzerland, this northwestern corner of the country remains rather un-discovered and its grandest towns are little more than enchanting villages. Deep, mysterious forests and impossible green clearings succeed one another across the low mountains of the Jura. Some 1200km of marked paths across the canton give hikers plenty of scope.

The canton's capital is Delémont, but there is little reason to linger here. Instead head west for a half-hour to the delightful medieval village of **St Ursanne** on the banks of the Doubs River. Along with a 12th-century Gothic church there are clusters of ancient houses, a 16th-century town gate and a lovely stone bridge over the river.

Jura Tourisme (☎ 032 461 37 16; Rue du Quartier 18, St Ursanne; ⏱ 9am-6pm Mon-Fri, 10am-4pm Sat & Sun) has tons of area info.

A great way to spend a hot summer day is to kayak on the Doubs. **Le Clip** (☎ 032 461 37 22; Place du Mai 1, St Ursanne; trips Sfr45) runs exciting half-day trips.

Hôtel Demi-Lune (☎ 032 461 35 31; www.hotels-suisse.ch/demi-lune, in French; Rue Basse 2, St Ursanne; s/d with shared bathroom from Sfr55/90) is a classy place right on the river. There are slightly pricier rooms with bathroom.

Trout is the local speciality and you can get a good version at **La Cicogne** (☎ 032 461 35 45; St Ursanne; mains from Sfr20), an unpretentious spot opposite the church.

From Delémont there are frequent trains to St Ursanne (Sfr6.60, 17 minutes, hourly).

GENEVA

pop 180,400
Famously international Geneva occupied a key place on the world stage for much of the last century. The European Headquarters of the UN is here, as is the International Red Cross and the World Health Organization, among 250 other international groups. Tidy and aesthetic Geneva, sitting comfortably on the shores of the lake by the same name, belongs not so much to Switzerland as to the whole world. More than 40% of residents are non-Swiss, and this city of bankers, diplomats and transients has a seriously worldly flavour.

ORIENTATION
The Rhône River runs through the city, dividing it into *rive droite* (right bank, ie north of the Rhône) and *rive gauche* (left bank). On the northern side is the main train station, Gare de Cornavin; south of the river lies the old town. In summer, Geneva's most visible landmark is the **Jet d'Eau**, a giant fountain on the southern shore.

INFORMATION
Emergency
Police Station (☎ 117; Rue de Berne 6)

Internet Access
Video Club (☎ 022 731 47 48; Rue des Alpes 19; ⏱ 11am-midnight Mon-Thu, 11am-2am Fri & Sat, noon-midnight Sun; per hr Sfr5)
Internet Cafe de la Gare (☎ 022 731 51 87; ⏱ 9am-10pm; per hr Sfr7) In the train station on the Place de Montbrillant side.

Medical Services

Telephone Advice Service (☎ 111) For medical information.

Cantonal Hospital (☎ 022 372 33 11; Rue Micheli-du-Crest 24)

Permanence Médico Chirurgicale (☎ 022 731 21 20; Rue de Chantepoulet 1-3) A private 24-hour clinic.

Servette Clinique (☎ 022 733 98 00; Ave Wendt 60) Emergency dental treatment.

Money

Exchange Office (Gare de Cornavin; ⊗ 6.50am-7.40pm Mon-Sat, 6.50am-6.40pm Sun)

Post

Main post office (Rue du Mont-Blanc 18; ⊗ 7.30am-6pm Mon-Fri, 8.30am-noon Sat)

Tourist Information

Office du Tourisme (☎ 022 909 70 00; www.geneve-tourisme.ch, in French; Rue du Mont-Blanc 18; ⊗ 10am-6pm Mon, 9am-6pm Tue-Sat summer) Jam-packed with information. Grab a copy of the excellent (and free) *Vélo-Cité* map or the budget-conscious brochure *Genève info-jeunes*.

Travel Agencies

American Express (☎ 022 731 76 00; Rue du Mont-Blanc 7; ⊗ 8.30am-5.45pm Mon-Fri, 9am-noon Sat)

STA Travel (☎ 022 329 97 33; Rue Vignier Leschol 3; ⊗ 9.15am-6pm Mon-Fri, 9am-noon Sat)

SIGHTS & ACTIVITIES
City Centre

The city centre is so compact that it's easy to see many of the main sights on foot. Start a scenic walk through the old town at the **Île Rousseau**, home to a statue in honour of the celebrated free thinker. Head west along the southern side of the Rhône until you reach the 13th-century **Tour de L'Île**, once part of the medieval city fortifications. Then walk south down the narrow, cobbled Rue de la Cité until it becomes Grand-Rue. **Rousseau's birthplace** is at No 40.

A short detour off Grand-Rue leads you to the part-Romanesque, part-Gothic **Cathédrale St Pierre**, where John Calvin preached from 1536 to 1564. The cathedral rests on a significant **archaeological site** (☎ 022 311 75 74; Cour de St Pierre 6; adult/student Sfr5/3; ⊗ 10-11.30am & 2-4.30pm Mon-Fri, 10am-5pm Sat, noon-5pm Sun). A visit reveals some fine 4th-century mosaics and a 5th-century baptismal font.

Grand-Rue terminates at **Place du Bourg-de-Four**, the site of a medieval marketplace,

which features a fountain and is lined with street cafés.

Take Rue de la Fontaine to reach the lakeside. Anticlockwise round the shore is the **Jet d'Eau**. Calling this a fountain is an understatement. The water shoots up with incredible force (200km/h, 1360HP), to create a 140m-high plume. At any one time there are seven tonnes of water in the air, and much of it falls on spectators who venture out on the pier. It's not activated in winter or in strong winds.

United Nations

The Art-Deco **Palais des Nations** (☎ 022 907 48 96; Ave de la Paix 9-14; tours adult/student Sfr8.50/6.50; ⊗ 9am-6pm Jul-Aug, 10am-noon & 2-4pm Apr-Jun & Sep-Oct, 10am-noon & 2-4pm Mon-Fri Nov-Mar) is the European arm of the UN and the home of 3000 international civil servants. You can see where decisions about world affairs are made on the hour-long tour (bring your passport to get in). Afterwards check out the extensive gardens – don't miss the towering grey monument coated with heat-resistant titanium donated by the USSR to commemorate the conquest of space. To get here take bus No 5 or 8 from any bus stop.

Museums

There are plenty of museums (many free) to keep you busy on a rainy day. **Musée d'Art et d'Histoire** (Museum of Art & History; ☎ 022 418 26 00; Rue Charles-Galland 2; admission free; ⊗ 10am-5pm Tue-Sun) has a vast collection of paintings, sculptures, weapons and archaeological displays. **Musée d'Histoire Naturelle** (Museum of Natural History; ☎ 022 418 63 00; Route de Malagnou 1; admission free; ⊗ 9.30am-5pm Tue-Sun) is the place to check out every species of tiger known to man, stuffed for perpetuity. It's a good place to bring the kids.

The **International Red Cross & Red Crescent Museum** (☎ 022 748 95 25; Ave de la Paix 17; adult/student Sfr10/5; ⊗ 10am-5pm Wed-Mon) is a compelling multimedia trawl through atrocities perpetuated by humanity in recent history. Against the long litany of war and nastiness, documented in films, photos, sculptures and soundtracks, are set the noble aims of the organisation. Take bus No 5 or 8.

Parks & Gardens

Geneva has more parkland than any other Swiss city, much of it along the lakefront.

GENEVA

0 — 500 m
0 — 0.3 miles

A | B | C | D

To Lausanne (60km)

Chemin du Petit-Saconnex
Ave de l'Ariana
To Australian Consulate (1km)
Ave de Ferney
14 — 2 — 6
17
Jardin Botanique
Ave de la Paix
Place des Nations
Ave Giuseppe Motta
11 — P
Parc Mon Repos
Rue de Lausanne

France
Rue de Vidos
Rue de Lausanne
Rue Rothschild
22 — 21
Rue des Buis
Quai Wilson
Rue de Môle
Rue des Pâquis
40
Rue de la Navigation
Rue de l'Ancien-Port
38
Rue de Zürich
51
Jetée des Pâquis
Rue de Monthoux
26
Quai du Mont-Blanc
Bains des Pâquis

To Airport (4km); CERN (8km)
Rue de la Servette
Gare de Cornavin
48
35 — 28
5
Rue des Gares
25 — 30
To Servette Clinique (500m)
Rue de Lyon
45
12
29 — 7 — 9
Rue de Chantepoulet
8 — 49
39
41
Pont de la Machine
27
Île Rousseau
Lake Geneva
Jet d'Eau
33
To Camping Pointe à la Bise (7km)

Rue de Lyon
Rue Voltaire
Rue de Chantepoulet
Rue du Mont-Blanc
Rue des Alpes
Quai du Mont-Blanc
Pont du Mont-Blanc
Promenade du Lac
47 — 50
Jardin Anglais
Quai Gustave-Ador

Rhône
44 — 36
Quai des Forces Motrices
37
20
Pont de la Coulouvrenière
Pont d'Île
Place Bel-Air
Place du Rhône
Pont des Bergues
Quai du Général-Guisan
Blvd de Saint-Georges
Rue du Stand
Rue de la Confédération
32
42
Rue du Rhône
Rue de Rive
46
Blvd Georges-Favon
Rue de la Corraterie
43 — 23 — 13
19 — 24
Rue de la Fontaine
Rue Ferdinand-Hodler
Place Neuve
18
Grand-Rue
Rue du Vieux-Collège
Place du Bourg-de-Four
Gare des Eaux Vives
Ave Pictet-de-Rochemont

Rue de Carouge
Plaine de Plainpalais
31
Rue Imbert Galloix
Rue du Conseil-Général
4
15
Blvd Jacques-Dalcroze
Cours des Bastions
Promenade des Bastians
Place Émile Guyénot
16
Route de Malagnou

Arve
Rue des Bains
Ave Henri-Dunant
Ave du Mail
10
34
Rue Vignier Leschot
Rue du Pont-d'Arve
Blvd des Philosophes
Place Édouard Claparède
3
Route de Florissant
To Chamonix (81km)

There's the **Jardin Anglais**, near the jet, featuring a large floral clock; and, in the north of the city, the impressive **Jardin Botanique** (admission free; 8am-7.30pm Apr-Oct, 9.30am-5pm Nov-Mar), with exotic plants and an aviary.

South of Grand-Rue is **Promenade des Bastions**, containing a massive monument to the Reformation: the giant figures of Bèze, Calvin, Farel and Knox are flanked by smaller statues of other important figures, and depictions of events instrumental in the spread of the movement.

Cern

The **CERN** (European Centre for Nuclear Research; 022 767 84 84; www.cern.ch; Route de Meyrin; admission free; 9am-5.30pm Mon-Sat), 8km west of the centre, is a laboratory for research into particle physics funded by 20 nations. The lab routinely spins out new creations – including the World Wide Web. Its educational Microcosm exhibition covers particle accelerators and the Big Bang; enthusiasts can take a guided tour at 9am or 2pm (take your passport and book ahead). Take bus No 9.

FESTIVALS & EVENTS

The **Geneva Festival**, a 10-day event in early August, features parades, fireworks and live music, most of it along the lake. On 11 December, **L'Escalade** celebrates the foiling of an invasion by the Duke of Savoy in 1602 with a costumed parade and day of races around the old town.

SLEEPING
Budget

Camping Pointe á la Bise (022 752 12 96; Chemin de la Bise 19; bus E; camp sites per adult/tent/car Sfr6.50/6/5.50; Apr-Oct) On the lakeshore, it's about 7km northeast of the centre. Take the bus from Rond-Point de Rive.

Hôme St Pierre (022 310 37 07; www.homestpierre.ch; Cour St-Pierre 4; dm Sfr24, s/d with shared bathroom Sfr46/62;) It's women only in the singles and doubles at this hostel, but there is a men's dorm. A long-time favourite, it's a cosy place with excellent views, communal kitchen and TV lounge.

Auberge de Jeunesse (022 732 62 60; www.yh-geneva.ch; Rue Rothschild 28-30; dm Sfr25, d with shared bathroom Sfr75;) In a big, busy, concrete box of a building this place is not going to win a 'best looking' contest, but the staff is helpful. There is a self-catering kitchen.

City Hostel (022 901 15 00; info@cityhostel.ch; Rue Ferrier 2; dm Sfr28, s/d with shared bathroom Sfr58/85;) In a charmless '70s-style building there isn't a lot of atmosphere here, but rooms are spotless and dorms only have three beds. The hostel is just a few minutes' walk from the train station and has a kitchen. Parking costs Sfr10 per night.

Hôtel de la Cloche (022 732 94 81; www.geneva-hotel.ch/cloche/; Rue de la Cloche 6; s/d with shared bathroom from Sfr50/85) A small, old-fashioned hotel with expansive rooms, ageing furniture, dramatic chandeliers and towering ceilings, it is excellent value and liable to be full, so call ahead.

Mid-Range & Top End

Hôtel International Terminus (022 906 97 77; www.international-terminus.ch; Rue des Alpes 20; s/d from 95/135;) This three-star hotel has absurdly low rates for Geneva, making it one of the best-value places near the train station (in the winter a double room is just Sfr95). Rooms are well appointed – some come with swanky red carpets, and all come with cable TV.

Hôtel Bel' Esperance (022 818 31 31; www.hotel-bel-esperance.ch; Rue de la Vallé 1; s/d from Sfr95/140;) A solid-value option near the heart of old town, rooms are quiet and clean and the place even has a self-catering kitchen. The hotel is owned and managed by the Salvation Army and prides itself on service.

Hôtel Lido (022 731 55 30; www.hotel-lido.ch; Rue de Chantepoulet 8; s/d Sfr110/150) Decent-sized rooms with slightly mismatched furniture are found at this conveniently located place. Ask about weekend specials and the few singles without private baths.

Hôtel Bernina (022 908 49 50; fax 022 908 49 51; www.bernina-geneve.ch; Place de Cornavin 22; s/d from Sfr140/160;) Across the road from the train station, the rooms at this tourist class hotel are spacious, if a little plain. Most have balconies.

Hôtel des Bergues (022 908 70 00; www.hoteldesbergues.com; Quai des Bergues 33; s/d from Sfr600/730;) For serious luxury head to this national monument. Even the most basic rooms drip marble and are decorated with copies of works by Claude Monet. The Suite Royal (a serious steal at just Sfr6600 per night!) is a sight to behold – a 134 sq metre apartment with Jacuzzi, DVD, private terraces, dressing room, dining room and, just in case, bulletproof windows.

SWITZERLAND

EATING

Geneva is the cuisine capital of Switzerland, with a wide range of choices. You'll find cheapish Asian and Middle Eastern eateries in the seedy streets north of Rue des Alpes, or on Blvd de Saint-Georges south of the river. Restaurants and cafés don't close between meals, but some close on Mondays.

Restaurants

Boccacio (☎ 022 329 45 22; Blvd Georges-Favon 45; mains Sfr14-25) This popular Geneva restaurant is done up like an Italian village with murals on the walls. A business crowd packs the place at lunch. The menu focuses on pizza, pasta and salads. Sit outside during the summer.

La Mamounia (☎ 022 329 55 61; Blvd Georges-Favon 10; mains Sfr16-30) Tuck into the plentiful plat du jour (Sfr16) and you won't need dinner. The Moroccan eatery has generous melt-in-your-mouth couscous dishes with an array of condiments; weekend diners often score a belly-dancer bonus.

Sugar Hut (☎ 022 731 46 13; Rue des Etuves 16; mains Sfr22-28) For flavoursome Thai and a good seafood selection try the busy and intimate Sugar Hut. Those with late night munchies will be happy to know the place stays open until 2am.

El Faro (☎ 022 732 21 98; Rue de Fribourg 5; mains Sfr30-40; ☽ closed Sun) Rumour has it this is Geneva's best Spanish restaurant, and the food does not disappoint. The menu indulges the Spanish passion for seafood, including the delightful paella, and includes items such as bull's tail.

La Béarn (☎ 022 321 00 28; Quai de la Post 4; plat du jour Sfr50-60, mains to Sfr150; ☽ dinner only) One of Geneva's most renowned restaurants, it's located just back from the Rhône. You can choose from sumptuous fish specialities, creative cuisine and a good spread of meat dishes.

Cafés

In the old town, terrace cafés and restaurants crowd along the medieval Place du Bourg-de-Four.

L'amalgam (Rue de l'Ancien-Port 13; mains Sfr16-18) A rotating menu of simple food is fused with African art, palms and ochre tones. The mood is decidedly mellow.

Café Universal (☎ 022 781 18 81; Blvd du Pont d'Arve 26; mains Sfr15-30) With heavy chandeliers, monster mirrors and 1920s posters this place is

chic and French. It draws an arty crowd into its tightly packed interior.

Café des Marins (☎ 022 700 24 36; Quai Gustave Ador 28; mains Sfr25-31) Occupying prime lakeside real estate, this cheerful spot is known for its perch, but also does generous salads.

Brasserie Lipp (☎ 022 311 10 11; Rue des la Confédération 8; plat du jour Sfr20-28, mains Sfr35) An eternal favourite with the Genevois, come for a drink and snack or full meal – everything from oysters to a perch fillet. In the summer there is an outdoor terrace. It's on the 2nd floor of the shopping arcade.

Quick Eats & Self-Catering

Al-Amir (Rue de Berne 22; kebabs Sfr8) This hole-in-the wall Lebanese takeaway serves the best kebab in town.

Manora (Rue de Cornavin 4; mains Sfr5-15) Rather tasty buffet food, including extensive salad and dessert bars, are served at this quick-eat Swiss chain.

Migros (Rue des Pâquis; ☽ 8am-7pm Mon-Fri, 8am-6pm Sat) Head to this supermarket to stock up on supplies. You'll also find baguettes (Sfr2) and sandwiches (Sfr3.60) in its self-service restaurant.

DRINKING & ENTERTAINMENT

The latest nightclubs, live music venues and theatre events are well covered in the weekly *Genève Agenda* (free from the tourist office). Try strolling around the Quartier des Pâquis (between the train station and the lake), packed with pubs and bars. Bars open in the afternoon and close between midnight and 2am. Clubs get going after 10pm.

Alhambar (☎ 022 312 13 13; 1st fl, Rue de la Rôtisserie 10) With a buzzing atmosphere, an eclectic music programme and the best Sunday brunch in town, Alhambar provides an oasis of theatricality in an otherwise staid shopping district.

Flanagan's Irish Bar (☎ 022 310 13 14; Rue du Cheval-Blanc 4) Popular with the city's English-speakers, this pub keeps Guinness flowing well into the wee hours.

L'Usine (☎ 022 328 08 18; Place des Volontaires 4) In a converted factory, it's something of a party-base in the city. The drinking is fairly cheap and the entertainment ranges from dance nights and concerts to cabaret, theatre and other nocturnal diversions.

Prétexte (☎ 022 310 14 28; Rue du Prince 9; admission Sfr10; ☽ 11pm-5am Thu-Sat) With a healthily kitsch décor, two bars and a dance floor this opulent place is the main gay club.

Post Café (Rue de Berne 7) An odd blend of Brit fixtures and loud blues music attracts a mixed crowd to this bar near the tourist office.

GETTING THERE & AWAY

Geneva airport is an important transport hub and has frequent connections to every major European city. **EasyJet** (☎ 0848 888 222; www.easyjet.com) is a popular budget carrier with flights to London, Liverpool, East Midlands, Amsterdam Barcelona, Nice and Paris.

Next to Jardin Anglais is a ticket booth for **Compagnie Générale de Navigation** (CGN; ☎ 022 312 52 23; www.cgn.ch), which operates a steamer service to all towns and major villages bordering Lake Geneva, including those in France. Boats operate between May and September. Destinations include Lausanne (Sfr28, 3½ hours, hourly) and Montreux (Sfr40.80, 4½ hours, hourly). Eurail and Swiss passes are valid on CGN boats or there are CGN boat day passes for Sfr55.

International buses depart from **Place Dorcière** (☎ 022 732 02 30; Place Dorciére), off Rue des Alpes. There are buses to London (Sfr145, 17 hours, twice weekly) and Barcelona (Sfr100, 10 hours, twice weekly).

An autoroute bypass skirts Geneva, with major routes intersecting southwest of the city: the N1 from Lausanne joins with the E62 to Lyon (130km) and the E25 heading southeast towards Chamonix.

Sixt (☎ 022 732 90 90; Place de la Navigation 1) generally has the best daily rates for last minute car hire.

Trains run to most Swiss towns including Zürich (Sfr76, three hours, hourly) and Interlaken (Sfr63, three hours, hourly).

There are regular international trains to Paris (Sfr103 by TGV, 3½ hours, eight times daily), Hamburg (Sfr280, 10 hours, daily), Milan (Sfr81, four hours, daily) and Barcelona (Sfr100, nine hours, daily).

GETTING AROUND

Getting from the airport is easy with regular trains into Gare de Cornavin (Sfr2.60, six minutes). Bus No 10 (Sfr2.20) does the same 5km trip. A taxi would cost Sfr25 to Sfr35.

Genev' Roule (☎ /fax 022 740 13 43; Place de Montbrillant 17; 🕑 8am-6pm Mon-Sat, 10am-6pm Sun), right next to the station, has free bike rental

(the bikes are covered in advertising) from May to October. ID and Sfr50 deposit are required.

Buses, trams, trains and boats service the city, and ticket dispensers are found at all stops. Tickets cost Sfr1.80 (within one zone, 30 minutes) and Sfr2.20 (two zones, 60 minutes). A day pass costs Sfr6 for the city or Sfr12 for the whole canton. Tickets and passes are also valid for CGN boats that travel along the city shoreline.

LAKE GENEVA REGION

Stretching like a liquid mirror east from Geneva and south to France is Western Europe's largest lake, known to most as Lake Geneva, to Francophones as Lac Léman. The elegant city of Lausanne and the Riviera town of Montreux line the lake's Swiss shores. Feast your eyes on a landscape of splendid sparkling emerald water and sturdy vineyards spreading in terraces up steep hillsides.

LAUSANNE
pop 118,200

This beautiful hillside city overlooking Lake Geneva has several distinct personalities. There's the former fishing village, Ouchy, with its summer beach-resort feel; Place St-François, with stylish, cobblestone shopping streets; and Flon, a warehouse district of bars, galleries and boutiques.

Quanta (☎ 021 320 55 58; Place de la Gare 4; per hr Sfr8; 🕑 9am-midnight) offers Internet access. The **main post office** (☎ 021 344 35 10; Place de la Gare 1; 🕑 7.30am-6.30pm Mon-Fri, 8am-noon Sat) is by the train station.

The **tourist office** (☎ 021 613 73 21; www.lausanne -tourisme.ch; Place de la Navigation 4; 🕑 9am-6pm) is next door to the Ouchy metro station. You can buy the Lausanne Card here (Sfr15, valid two days), which allows unlimited travel anywhere in the city by bus and train.

Sights & Activities
MUSÉE DE L'ART BRUT

Perhaps the most alluring **museum** (☎ 021 647 54 35; www.artbrut.ch, in French; Ave de Bergiéres 11; adult/student Sfr6/4; 🕑 11am-1pm & 2-6pm Tue-Fri, 11am-6pm Sat & Sun) in the country, the collection here is a fascinating amalgam of 15,000 works of art created by untrained artists –

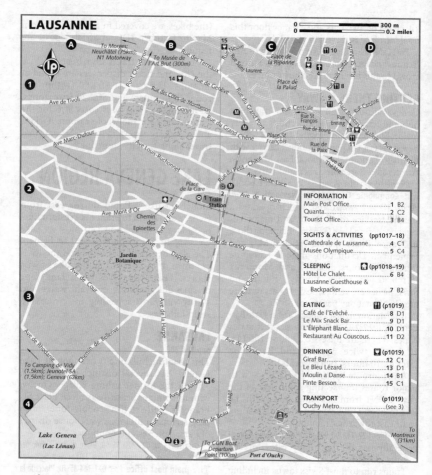

LAUSANNE

0 — 300 m
0 — 0.2 miles

INFORMATION	
Main Post Office.................................**1** B2	
Quanta..**2** C2	
Tourist Office..................................**3** B4	

SIGHTS & ACTIVITIES	(pp1017–18)
Cathédrale de Lausanne................**4** C1	
Musée Olympique............................**5** C4	

SLEEPING	(pp1018–19)
Hôtel Le Chalet................................**6** B4	
Lausanne Guesthouse &	
Backpacker.................................**7** B2	

EATING	(p1019)
Café de l'Evêché..............................**8** D1	
Le Mix Snack Bar............................**9** D1	
L'Éléphant Blanc............................**10** D1	
Restaurant Au Couscous...............**11** D2	

DRINKING	(p1019)
Giraf Bar...**12** C1	
Le Bleu Lézard...............................**13** D1	
Moulin à Danse..............................**14** B1	
Pinte Besson.................................**15** C1	

TRANSPORT	(p1019)
Ouchy Metro...............................(see 3)	

psychiatric patients, eccentrics and incarcerated criminals. The works offer a striking variety, at times a surprising technical capacity and in some cases an inspirational world-view. Biographies and explanations are in English. The museum is about 600m northwest of the Place St Francois.

CATHEDRALE DE LAUSANNE
Worth the hill climb is this glorious Gothic **cathedral** (☉ 7am-7pm Mon-Fri, 8am-7pm Sat & Sun Apr-Sep, to 5.30pm Oct-Mar), arguably the finest in Switzerland. Built in the 12th and 13th centuries, highlights include the stunningly detailed carved portal, vaulted ceilings and archways, and carefully restored stained-glass windows.

MUSÉE OLYMPIQUE
Lausanne is home to the International Olympic Committee, and sports aficionados can immerse themselves in archive footage, interactive computers and memorabilia at the information-packed **Musée Olympique** (☎ 021 621 65 11; www.olympic.org; Quai d'Ouchy 1; adult/student/child Sfr14/9/7; ☉ 9am-6pm Mon-Wed & Fri-Sun, 9am-8pm Thu May-Sep; ☉ closed Mon Oct-Apr).

Sleeping
Camping de Vidy (☎ 021 622 50 00; info@camping lausannevidy.ch; Chemin du Camping 3; bus No 2 from Place St François; per tent/person Sfr12/7.80) Lakeside camping is available year-round. Get off the bus at Bois de Vaux and walk underneath the motorway towards the lake.

Lausanne Guesthouse & Backpacker (☎ 021 601 80 00; www.lausanne-guesthouse.ch; Chemin des Epinettes 4; dm Sfr22, s/d with shared bathroom Sfr80/86; ✗) Stunning views of the lake and Alps are found at this tastefully renovated 1894 townhouse high on a hill.

Jeunotel SA (☎ 021 626 02 22; www.jeunotel.ch; Chemin du Bois-de-Vaux 36; bus No 2; dm Sfr30, s/d with shared bathroom Sfr60/80; **P** 🖵) The cheaper rooms feel rather dismal with exposed breeze block walls. But the place caters to young Swiss staying for weeks at a time and the bar can become lively at night, so it's a good place to practice another language. There are more expensive rooms with showers and TVs.

Hôtel Le Chalet (☎ 021 616 52 06; Ave d'Ouchy 49; s/d with shared bathroom Sfr62/92) With a charming garden, this old-world family hotel's owner has an infectious *joie de vivre*. Swedish playwright Johan August Strindberg lived here in the late-19th century. Rooms, however, are a little rough around the edges. Take the metro to the Jordils stop.

Eating

Le Mix Snack Bar (☎ 078 808 79 68; Rue Central 29; mains from Sfr4.50; ☼ 7am-8.30pm) Small and smoky with cheery orange walls, this low-key place fills up at lunch when locals flock in for a sandwich, kebab, burger or coffee.

Café de L'Evêché (☎ 021 323 93 23; Rue Louis-Auguste Curtat 4; mains Sfr15-25; ☼ closed Sun) The pasta and fondues at this cosy spot are said to be the best in town. The lovely back garden is perfect for a late summer night.

L'Éléphant Blanc (☎ 021 312 71 77; Rue Cité-Devant 4; mains Sfr18-25; ☼ Mon-Fri) On warm days tables spill out of the restaurant and onto the footpath in front at this tiny and popular student haunt. It's a good place to fill your stomach and then start the night's drinking.

Restaurant Au Couscous (☎ 021 321 38 44; 1st fl, Rue Enning 2; mains Sfr18-34; ☼ dinner daily, lunch Mon-Fri) North African sausages, spiced rice and couscous are just a few items on the varied menu at this Tunisian and macrobiotic specialist.

Drinking & Entertainment

Lausanne is one of the country's busier cities for nightlife. Look for the free listings booklet *What's Up* in many bars.

Pinte Besson (☎ 021 312 72 27; Rue de l'Ale 4) The city's oldest tavern has been serving local wines to Lausannois punters since 1780. It oozes with the atmosphere of a time past and makes for a charming evening.

Le Bleu Lézard (☎ 021 321 38 35; Rue Enning 10) World-music jam sessions and film nights make this cave-like basement bar a happening spot. Cure your Sunday hangover with the all-day brunch.

Mad – Moulin a Danse (☎ 021 312 11 22; www .mad.ch, in French; Rue de Genève 23; admission Thu-Sun Sfr20; ☼ Wed-Sun) A typical large club that's generally packed on weekends, it relies on music theme nights to keep things interesting. The downstairs cellar bar has free admission on Wednesday. On Sunday's the club hosts Trixx Club for gays and lesbians.

Giraf Bar (☎ 021 323 53 90; Escaliers du Marché) A tiny smoke-filled bar that draws big crowds on weekends. There is a serious giraffe motif and the music can reach back to the '80s.

Getting There & Around

Buses and trolley buses service most destinations (Sfr1.50 for up to three stops, or Sfr2.40 one-hour unlimited stops in central Lausanne). The metro connects Ouchy with Gare (train station) and costs the same as the buses.

There are trains to/from Geneva (Sfr18.80, 50 minutes, three hourly), Bern (Sfr30, 70 minutes, one or two hourly) and Interlaken Ost (Sfr52, two hours, two hourly). For boat services see p1017 in the Geneva section.

VEVEY

pop 15,400

A colourful old square bumped up against the lake helps make Vevey a popular stop on the Swiss Riviera, especially with celebrities. Charlie Chaplin lapped up the swanky ambiance here for 25 years until his death in 1977. On summer Saturdays the sprawling square becomes a bustling **marketplace** with traditionally dressed merchants selling local handicrafts and wines.

For overnight stays in hip modern environs try the **Riviera Lodge** (☎ 021 923 80 40; info@ rivieralodge.ch; Place du Marché; dm Sfr24, d with shared bathroom Sfr74; 🖵) in a 19th-century townhouse near the waterfront. The hostel's rooftop terrace offers great views in summer; in colder weather check out the futuristic lounge. There is a kitchen to keep cooking costs down.

For eclectic meals there's **Vertigo** (☎ 021 922 11 33; Rue du Torrent 4; mains from Sfr15; ☼ closed Sun).

You can chow on chicken *fajitas*, salads and other light meals with the town's trendy.

At night check out the chic and new **Sunset Café** (☎ 021 921 27 44; Grand Place 19), a few doors down from the Riviera Lodge. There's live music amid bright yellow walls and wrought iron fixtures. The plan is to serve food in the future.

MONTREUX

pop 22,800

Centrepiece of the 'Swiss Riviera', Montreux is an affluent town with stunning views of the French Alps, excellent lakeside walks, well-maintained pastel buildings and the ever-popular Château de Chillon. In the 19th century the town was a magnet for writers, artists and musicians – including Lord Byron and the Shelleys.

The **train station** is on Ave des Alpes. **Montreux Tourisme** (☎ 021 962 84 36; www.montreux-vevey .com; ☼ 9.30am-6pm Jun-Sep, 9am-12.30pm & 1.30-6pm Mon-Fri Oct-May) is in the pavilion on the lakeshore.

Sights

The extraordinary oval-shaped **Château de Chillon** (☎ 021 966 89 10; www.chillon.ch; adult/student/child Sfr8.50/6.50/4; ☼ 9am-7pm Apr-Sep, 9.30am-5pm Mar & Oct, 10am-4pm Nov-Feb) deservedly receives more visitors than any other historical building in Switzerland. The fortress was originally constructed on the shores of Lake Geneva in the 11th century, and caught the public imagination when Lord Byron wrote *The Prisoner of Chillon*

MONTREUX'S PLACE IN MUSIC HISTORY

In 1971 Frank Zappa was doing his thing in the Montreux casino when the building caught fire, casting a pall of smoke over Lake Geneva and inspiring the members of Deep Purple to pen their classic rock number *Smoke on Water*.

Today Montreux is best known for its jazz festival. **Montreux Jazz** (☎ 021 963 82 82; www.montreuxjazz.com) starts in early July and runs for two weeks. Free concerts take place every day, but count on Sfr40 to Sfr100 for one of the big gigs. The music is not limited to jazz – past performers include BB King, Paul Simon and Jamiroquai.

---

about Bonivard, a prior chained in the dungeons for almost four years in the 16th century.

You can easily spend a couple of hours touring the tower, courtyards, dungeons and staterooms containing weapons, frescoes and furniture.

The castle is a pleasant 45-minute walk along the lakefront from Montreux. Otherwise take trolley bus No 1 (Sfr2.60, Veytaux stop), which passes by every 10 minutes.

Sleeping & Eating

Auberge de Jeunesse (☎ 021 963 49 34; fax 021 963 27 29; Passage de l'Auberge 8, Territet; bus No 1; dm Sfr32, d with shared bathroom Sfr76; ☼ mid-Feb–mid-Nov) On the waterfront, this simple hostel is a 30-minute walk from the centre and just 15 minutes from Château de Chillon.

Hostellerie du Lac (☎ 021 963 32 71; fax 021 963 18 35; Rue du Quai 12; s/d with shared bathroom Sfr50/85; ☼ Mar-Nov) Faded grandeur and a prime lakeside position make this an affordable option. The more expensive rooms have bathrooms, more panache and even lakeside balconies.

Hotel Wilhelm (☎ 021 963 14 31; hotel.wilhelm@span.ch; Rue de Marché 13-15; s/d with shared bathroom Sfr65/104) A traditional family-run hotel a few paces from the train station, rooms are simple but clean.

La Rose des Sables (☎ 021 961 15 46; Ave des Alpes; mains from Sfr3; ☼ lunch) Inexpensive sandwiches, croissants, quiches and a mouthwatering chocolate selection make this charming patisserie a lovely lunch option.

Brasserie des Alpes (☎ 021 963 21 20; Ave des Alpes 23; mains Sfr15-30; ☼ closed Sun) This cosy spot is quaintly decorated and serves heaps of pizza and pasta in a wood-panelled atmosphere.

Le Palais Oriental (☎ 021 963 12 79; Quai du Casino 14; mains Sfr30-40; ☼ closed Mon) Fancy starting with an Iranian caviar then moving on to a *mezze* platter? If so head to this cheery lakeside restaurant with a mock Arab interior and a unique menu focusing on Arab and Iranian dishes.

Getting There & Away

There are trains to Geneva (Sfr26, 70 minutes, hourly) and Lausanne (Sfr9.80, 25 minutes, three hourly). Make the scenic journey to Interlaken via the GoldenPass Panoramic, with change-overs at Zweisimmen and Spiez (Sfr54, three hours, daily; rail passes valid).

GRYON & LEYSIN

To leave the beaten track and enjoy the Swiss Alpine experience, consider staying in untouristy **Gryon** (1130m), southeast of Montreux. It's close to the ski fields of Villars, and home to one of Switzerland's favourite backpackers – the **Swiss Alp Retreat** (☎ 024 498 33 21; Chalet Martin; www.gryon.com; dm/d from Sfr18/52; P 🖳). In a funky wooden chalet, you can linger over an après ski beer by the log fire or on the sun deck. The hostel, run by a Swiss–Australian couple, has a laid-back vibe and gets rave reviews from travellers.

Swiss Alp Retreat runs a number of popular excursions, including two days' skiing, one night in the dorms, transport and ski or snowboard rental (Sfr199) and summer glacier skiing trips (Sfr124). In the summer check out the mountain and meadow hiking trails.

To reach Gryon you will need to take a train from Lausanne to Bex (Sfr17, 40 minutes, hourly) and then the cogwheel train to the village (Sfr5.80, 30 minutes, hourly). The hostel is a five-minute walk from the train stop. Follow the signs.

Another tranquil Alpine spot, **Leysin**, attracts skiers, snowboarders, hikers and meditators. In a 19th-century guesthouse the **Hiking Sheep** (☎ 024 494 35 35; www.hikingsheep.com; dm/d with shared bathroom from Sfr27/74; P 🖳) has breathtaking views from its balconies, a pine-forested back yard and a friendly laid-back atmosphere backpackers rave about. Don't miss the hammocks.

Leysin is accessible by a cogwheel train from Aigle (Sfr8.40, 30 minutes, hourly); there are trains to Aigle from Lausanne (Sfr29, 30 minutes, hourly).

VALAIS

Welcome to Matterhorn country – the place where they shoot the postcards. An area of extraordinary natural beauty, the Valais boasts the 10 highest mountains in Switzerland – all over 4000m. Endless panoramic vistas and breathtaking views win over even the toughest critics. The snow falls steadily throughout the winter making this region one of the most popular skiing destinations in the world. When the snow melts and the valleys turn lush and green the opportunities for hiking are boundless.

ZERMATT

pop 5500

One word says it all: Matterhorn. Synonymous with Switzerland, the Alps' most famous peak (4478m) keeps solitary vigil over this skiing, mountaineering and hiking hotspot. Zermatt is small and easy to navigate, and it's car-free except for tiny electric taxis and vans that whisk guests around the streets. The main street is Bahnhofstrasse, but street names are rarely used.

Zermatt Tourismus (☎ 027 966 81 00; www.zermatt.ch; 🕑 8.30am-noon & 1.30-6pm Mon-Fri, 8.30am-noon Sat) is beside the train station. During high season it's also open Saturday afternoon and Sunday.

Sights & Activities

To climb the Matterhorn you'll need previous climbing experience, a week's preparation and a staggering Sfr1120 per person. The ascent and descent takes about eight hours. For more information contact the **Alpin Center** (☎ 027 966 24 60; www.zermatt.ch/alpin-center; Bahnhofstrasse; 🕑 8.30am-noon & 4-7pm Jul-Sep, 5-7pm Jan–mid-May), near the post office. It's also a one-stop shop for other adventure needs – ski passes, heli-skiing or snowboard lessons.

SKIING & SNOWBOARDING

Arguably the country's best resort, **Zermatt** (☎ 027 966 01 01; www.ski-zermatt.com; day lift ticket winter/summer Sfr72/60) caters mainly to intermediate and expert skiiers with 245km of runs in three different areas: Rothorn, Stockhorn and Klein Matterhorn. Free ski buses run between each. The Klein Matterhorn is topped by the highest cable station in Europe (3820m), providing access to the highest skiing on the Continent. It also offers the most extensive summer skiing area in Switzerland (36km of runs), and is the starting point for skiing into Italy. Equipment rental is available at the mountain (Sfr45 for skis and boots). Peak season is February to April.

VIEWS FROM THE TOP

There are excellent views from the cable cars and gondolas. In summer Zermatt becomes a hub for hikers attracted by never-ending views of Europe's highest mountains, not to mention 400km of trails through high Alpine scenery. Try riding the cable cars to the top and then hiking or mountain biking down. A one-day lift pass for mountain bikers costs

Sfr54. Otherwise it's Sfr78 to ride to the top of Klein Matterhorn and back. The cogwheel train to Gornergrat (3090m, Sfr67 return, 30 minutes, twice hourly) is a highlight and provides magical Matterhornviews – sit on the right-hand side. Half-Fare Cards give 50% off mountain transport, while Swiss Pass holders get 25% off. A Eurail Pass is as much use as a snorkel to a skier.

ZERMATT VILLAGE
The village itself is well worth exploring. A walk in the **cemetery** is a sobering experience for any would-be mountaineers, with many monuments and gravestones commemorating deaths on Monte Rosa and the Matterhorn. The **Hinter Dorf**, just north of the church, is another interesting part of town. Here, the touristy chalets make way for traditional Valais wooden huts.

Sleeping & Eating
Be warned that many hotels and restaurants close between seasons. Unless noted, restaurants listed here are open day and night daily.

Matterhorn Hostel (☎ 027 968 19 19; www.matterhornhostel.com; Schluhmattstrasse 32; dm from Sfr29, d with shared bathroom Sf78; 🖳) In a Swiss chalet, a short walk from the station, this place has spartan rooms, its own restaurant and an après-ski bar.

Hotel Bahnhof (☎ 027 967 24 06; www.hotelbahnhof.com; dm Sfr30, s/d with shared bathroom from Sfr64/84) A long-time mountaineers' mecca, the hotel has an impressive industrial-size kitchen, large dorms, and doubles with balconies facing the Matterhorn. It is directly opposite the station and gets good marks for cleanliness and service.

Hotel Mischabel (☎ 027 967 11 31; www.zermatt.ch/mischabel, in German; Via al Parco 25; s/d Sfr60/120; s/d with shared bathroom Sfr50/100, 🕾 closed May, Jun & Oct) Old and creaky with tons of atmosphere, it's the best value full-scale hotel in town. Try for an upper-storey room – the southern balconies perfectly frame the Matterhorn.

Brown Cow (Hotel de la Poste; ☎ 027 967 19 32; Bahnhofstrasse 41; mains Sfr6-14) Great music, hearty food and cowhide décor make the Brown Cow a favourite hang-out for resort workers. Don't miss the monster burgers, including veggie, with chunky chips.

North Wall Bar (☎ 027 967 28 63; pizzas from Sfr13; 🕾 6.30pm-12.30am) Cheap beer, inspirational

ski videos, 'the best pizza in town' and folks from all over the world (it's another resort workers' favourite) all co-exist at this cheery place. It's just off the main street.

Restaurant Weisshorn (☎ 027 967 11 12; Bahnhofstrasse; mains Sfr16-30) Valais specialities as well as *raclette, rösti* and fondue. It's beyond the church on the main street.

Vernissage (☎ 027 967 66 36; Hofmattstrasse 4; 🕾 5pm-2am) A charismatic melting pot, this swanky place offers a cinema, bar and nightclub all in one.

Getting There & Around
Trains depart from Brig, stopping at Visp en route. It's a steep, scenic journey (one way/return Sfr37/65, 80 minutes, hourly). Swiss Passes are valid. There is no discount for Eurail Pass holders. The only way out is to backtrack, but if you're going to Saas Fee you can divert there from Stalden-Saas. The popular and scenic *Glacier Express* travels between St Moritz and Zermatt (see p1026 for details).

Zermatt is car-free. You need to park cars at Täsch (from Sfr5.50 per day) and take the train from there (Sfr8.60). Parking is free near the Visp station if you take the Zermatt train.

LEUKERBAD
If you're looking for a little thermal rest and relaxation this is the place to get it. Leukerbad, west of Brig, is home to Europe's largest thermal centre. There are no less than 10 different places to take to the waters, but the biggest and best is **Burgerbad** (☎ 027 472 20 20; www.burgerbad.ch; Rathausstrasse; admission Sfr21; 🕾 8am-8pm Sun-Thu, to 9pm Fri & Sat) with indoor and outdoor pools, whirlpools and water massage jets. If you tire of soaking, ride the cable car up the sheer side of the northern ridge of mountains to Gemmi Pass (2350m; one way/return Sfr15.50/24). It's a good area for hiking. To walk to the top of the pass takes two hours.

Weisses Rössli (☎ 027 470 33 77; off Dorfplatz; s/d with shared bathroom Sfr50/100) is an attractive place with a helpful friendly host.

Leukerbad is 16km north of Leuk, which is on the main rail route from Lausanne to Brig. A blue postal bus goes from outside the Leuk train station to Leukerbad (Srf10.40, 30 minutes, hourly) usually at 42 minutes past the hour; last departure is 7.42pm.

TICINO

The Mediterranean air is hot and spicy, the outdoor cafés in the colourful piazzas buzzing under a brilliant blue sky. The attitude is laidback, the style so *this* season. Melodic notes and lots of hand gestures, steaming plates of pasta, creamy gelatos. Did you cross the border into Italy? No, this is just the Switzerland Heidi failed to mention.

South of the Alps, Ticino (Tessin in German) enjoys an unmistakable Italian flavour. Indeed it belonged to Italy until the Swiss Confederation seized it in 1512, and Italian is the official language of the canton. Many people also speak French and German, but English is less widely spoken.

BELLINZONA
pop 17,100

Ticino's capital is a city of castles situated in a valley at the southern side of the San Bernardino and St Gotthard Alpine passes. World Heritage–listed in 2000, Bellinzona's imposing battlements and towers were once significant in fortifying the region.

The **tourist office** (☎ 091 825 21 31; fax 091 825 38 17; bellinzona.turismo@bluewin.ch; Viale Stazione 18; ☼ 9am-6.30pm Mon-Fri, 9am-noon Sat), in the post office, can provide information on Bellinzona and the whole canton.

You can roam the ramparts of the two larger castles, **Castelgrande** or **Castello di Montebello**, both of which are still in great condition and offer panoramic views of the town and the countryside.

The **SYHA hostel** (☎ 091 825 15 22; bellinzona@youthhostel.ch; Via Nocca 4; dm Sfr35, s/d with shared bathroom from Sfr45/80; ☼ closed Nov–mid-Feb; ☐) shares the grand old Villa Montebello with a private school and a catering company (which supplies the inclusive buffet breakfast). At the foot of the Montebello Castle, it's a 10-minute walk from the station.

For budget rooms closer to the station, there's **Garni Moderno** (☎ /fax 091 825 13 76; Viale Stazione 17b; s/d with shared bathroom Sfr55/90). Rooms are clean and simple.

Ristorante Corona (☎ 091 825 28 44; Via Camminata 5; pizzas Sfr11-17) serves enormous thin-crust pizzas in the friendly front pub area. For fancier fare, there's a formal restaurant behind.

Bellinzona is on the train route connecting Locarno (Sfr7.20, 25 minutes, twice hourly) and Lugano (Sfr11.40, 30 minutes, twice hourly).

LOCARNO
pop 14,400

The rambling red enclave of Italianate townhouses, piazzas and arcades ending at the northern end of Lake Maggiore, coupled with more hours of sunshine than anywhere else in Switzerland, help give this laid-back town a summer resort atmosphere. Locarno gained notoriety when it hosted the 1925 Peace Conference intended to bring stability to Europe after WWI.

Piazza Grande is the centre of town. You can gulp down shots and smoke Cuban cigars while checking your email at the Latino-style **Pardo Bar** (☎ 091 752 21 23; Via della Motta 3; per hr Sfr20; ☼ 11pm-1am). In the nearby casino complex is the **tourist office** (☎ 091 751 03 33; locarno@ticino.com; ☼ 9am-6pm Mon-Fri, 10am-5pm Sat, 10am-2pm Sun).

Sights & Activities

Don't miss the formidable **Madonna del Sasso**, up on the hill with panoramic views of the lake and town. The sanctuary was built after the Virgin Mary allegedly appeared in a vision in 1480. It features a church with 15th-century paintings, a small museum and several distinctive statues. There is a funicular from the town centre, but the 20-minute climb is not demanding (take Via al Sasso off Via Cappuccini) and you pass some shrines on the way.

The endless sunshine makes Locarno perfect for strolls and bike rides around the lake. **Giardini Jean Arp** is a small lakeside park off Lungolago Motta, where sculptures by the surrealist artist are scattered among palm trees and springtime tulips.

In August, over 150,000 film buffs hit town for the **Locarno International Film Festival** (☎ 091 756 21 21; http://istituzionale.pardo.ch/pardo; Via Luini 3) with a huge open-air screen in Piazza Grande.

Sleeping

Delta Camping (☎ 091 751 60 81; camp sites per tent/person from Sfr21/11; ☼ Mar-Oct) A family-friendly option with great facilities, there's easy lake swimming access.

Pensione Città Vecchia (☎ 091 751 45 54; citta vecchia@datacomm.ch; Via Toretta 13; dm Sfr25, s/d Sfr36/72; ☼ Mar-Nov; ☒) Dorms are basic, but the staff are all smiles at this nonsmoking hostel uphill from Piazza Grande, via a lane next to the Manor department store.

SYHA Palagiovani Hostel (☎ 091 756 15 00; loc arno@youthhostel.ch; Via Varenna 18; dm/d with shared bathroom from Sfr33/66) The radio station and music school here allow for the chance to interact with locals, otherwise it's rather lacking in charm. It is 500m west of Piazza Grande.

Garni Sempione (☎ 091 751 30 64; fax 091 752 38 37; Via Rusca 6; s/d from Sfr60/110) Rooms extend out from the enclosed courtyard and come with colourful duvets and wood-and-tiled walls at this small hotel in the old town.

Schlosshotel (☎ 091 751 23 61; schlosshotel@ticino .com; Via B Rusca; d from Sfr154; ☷ late Mar-early Nov; P) Located in the old town, this hotel has all the pomp and circumstance of a rock star's country manor. The attractive grounds hold their own, rooms come with TVs and other standard amenities.

Eating & Drinking
Lake Maggiore has a great variety of fresh and tasty fish. Look out for *persico* (perch) and *corigone* (whitefish).

Lungolago (☎ 091 923 12 33; Via Nassa 11; mains Sfr10-25) Young residents flock to this popular drinking venue with outside tables. It also serves a range of pizzas to sop up the cheap beer.

Ristorante Cittadella (☎ 091 751 58 85; Via Cittadella 18; mains Sfr35; ☷ closed Sun) This is the place for fine fish – the elegant upstairs section does not serve anything else. The ground-floor trattoria focuses on pizzas and pastas.

Ristorante Centenario (☎ 091 743 82 22; Lungolago 17; 3-course menu Sfr58, mains from Sfr48) The place for a gastronomic experience. The food is served on sparkling silver salvers.

For self-caterers on Piazza Grande there's a **Coop supermarket** and a **Migros De Gustibus** snack bar.

Getting There & Away
The St Gotthard Pass provides the road link (N2) to central Switzerland. There are trains from Brig (Sfr50, 2½ hours, hourly) that pass through Italy en route. You change trains at Domodóssola across the border, so take your passport.

LUGANO
pop 26,100
Switzerland's southernmost tourist town is a sophisticated slice of Italian life, with colour-ful markets, upmarket shops, pedestrian-only piazzas and lakeside parks. Resting on the shore of Lake Lugano, with Mounts San Salvatore and Bré rising on either side, it's also a great base for lake trips, water sports and hillside hikes.

The old town is a 10-minute walk down the hill to the east. Internet access is available at **City Disc** (Via P Peri; per hr Sfr11). On the lake side of the Municipio building is the **tourist office** (☎ 091 913 32 32; info@lugano-tourism.ch; Riva Albertolli; ☷ 9am-6.30pm Mon-Fri, 9am-12.30pm & 1.30-5pm Sat, 10am-3pm Sun, closed Sat & Sun in winter).

Sights & Activities
Stroll through the winding alleyways of Lugano's old town and go window-shopping along the stylish arcade-lined **Via Nassa** (street of fishing nets) before popping into the **Santa Maria degli Angioli Church** (Piazza Luini), featuring a vivid 1529 fresco of the *Crucifixion* by Bernardino Luini.

Art lovers can get their fix of 19th- and 20th-century works at the **Museo Cantonale d'Arte** (☎ 091 910 47 80; www.museo-cantonale-arte .ch, in Italian; Via Canova 10; adult/student Sfr7/5; ☷ 2-5pm Tue, 10am-5pm Wed-Sun), with examples by Renoir, Hodler and Klee. Bus No 1 will get you there.

Water babies will love the **Lido** (admission Sfr8; ☷ 9.30am-6pm May-Sep), east of the Cassarate River, with a swimming pool and sandy beaches.

Take a **boat trip** to one of the many photogenic villages hugging the shoreline of Lake Lugano. One of the most popular is car-free **Gandria**, a tiny hillside village with historic homes and shops, and narrow winding alleyways right down to the water. If you hit town at meal times you can tuck into a traditional Ticinese dish in one of the many **grotti**.

Sleeping
Hotel Backpackers Montarina (☎ 091 966 72 72; www.montarina.ch; Via Montarina 1; dm/s/d Sfr25/70/100; P ☷) In a 19th-century villa, Montarina is a summer haven with a large pool, a garden with plenty of palm trees and a kitchen. Ask about the array of adventure activities that can be arranged.

SYHA hostel (☎ 091 966 27 28; fax 091 968 23 63; Via Cantonale 13; dm/d Sfr31/72; ☷ mid-Mar-Nov; ☷) Warm and laid-back, this family-run hostel is a great place to meet other travellers. It's a hard 20-minute walk uphill from the train station (signposted), or take bus No 5 to Crocifisso.

Hotel Zurigo (☎ 091 923 43 43; fax 091 923 92 68; Corso Pestalozzi 1; s/d from Sfr90/140; ☯ closed Dec & Jan) Near the lake, this place has shiny and sturdy furniture in clean surroundings. The more expensive rooms have air-con.

Eating

Head to the pedestrian-only piazzas to tempt the tastebuds, with *panini* (Sfr5) and gelati (Sfr3) from street stalls, or larger meals in the pizzerias and cafés spilling onto the streets. Restaurants do not close between meals, unless noted.

Panino Gusto (☎ 091 922 51 51; Via Motta 7a; panini Sfr9-19) *Panini* with smoked meats, salmon and cheeses are the favourite options at this casual spot.

Sayonara (☎ 091 922 01 70; Via Soave 10; pasta from Sfr10, pizza Sfr15.50-20.50) With delicious Italian cuisine and a good wine list (try the Ticinese white Merlot), this restaurant makes a popular southern side stop.

La Tinéra (Via dei Gorini; mains Sfr11-27; ☯ lunch & dinner Mon-Sat) Crowds pack this critically acclaimed tiny cellar of a restaurant, off Piazza della Riforma, serving local specialities. It's not unusual to have to queue.

Al Portone (☎ 091 923 55 11; Viale Cassarate 3; mains Sfr30-50) For the best Italian food in town head here. The dishes are nothing short of scrumptious and so are the surroundings.

Getting There & Around

Lugano is on the same road and rail route as Bellinzona. Two postbuses run to St Moritz (Sfr74, four hours, daily in summer but only Friday, Saturday and Sunday in winter). Swiss Pass holders will still pay Sfr11 and everyone needs to reserve their seats the day before at the bus station, the train information office, or by phoning ☎ 091 807 85 20. Buses leave from the bus station on Via Serafino Balestra, though the St Moritz bus also calls at the train station.

GRAUBÜNDEN

Graubünden (Grisons, Grigioni, Grishun), the largest Swiss canton, has some of the most developed winter sports centres in the world, including famous St Moritz. Away from the international resorts, it's a relatively unspoiled region of rural villages, alpine lakes and hilltop castles. In the north, the locals speak German, in the south Italian, and in between mostly Romansch.

CHUR

pop 31,900

Chur, the canton's capital and largest town, also is one of the oldest settlements in Switzerland, tracing its history back some 3000 years. Today it serves as a gateway for the region, although it's not a very obvious tourist attraction – buildings are stark and grey. For a town map and accommodation options see the **tourist office** (☎ 081 252 18 18; Grabenstrasse 5; ☯ 1.30-6pm Mon, 8.30am-noon & 1.30-6pm Tue-Fri, 9am-noon Sat).

The **Kunstmuseum** (☎ 081 257 28 68; Postplatz; admission Sfr12; ☯ 10am-noon & 2-5pm Tue-Wed & Fri-Sun, 10am-noon & 2-8pm Thu) has a collection of artwork by the three Giacomettis (Alberto, Augusto and Giovanni), and exhibits by local sci-fi artist HR Giger (of *Alien* fame).

The **Hotel Schweizerhaus** (☎ 081 252 10 96; fax 081 252 27 31; Kasernenstrasse 10; dm/s/d with shared bathroom Sfr35/45/85) is an economical sleeping option.

Bierhalle (Postrasse) is a traditional Swiss drinking hall where serious boozing is undertaken to a beat of pounding Swiss folk music. It's a quirky 'only in Switzerland' experience. Another option is the **Hemingway Café** (Obere Gasse), a well-stocked bar named after that hard-living, hard-drinking American writer. It comes complete with a giant picture of the namesake on the wall.

Chur is connected to Zürich (Sfr40, 85 minutes, hourly) and St Moritz (Sfr38, two hours, hourly).

ST MORITZ

pop 4900

St Moritz has built its reputation as the international jet set's playground for over a century, but the curative properties of its waters have been known for 3000 years. The plush main town, St Moritz Dorf, lounges on the slopes overlooking Lake St Moritz. In winter, superb ski fields are the main drawcard; in summer, visitors come for the hiking, windsurfing, 'kitesurfing' and inline skating.

Orientation & Information

Hilly St Moritz Dorf is above the train station, with luxury hotels, restaurants and shops. To the southwest, 2km around the lake, lies the more downmarket St Moritz Bad; buses run between the two. St Moritz is seasonal and becomes a ghost town during November and from late April to early June.

The train station near the lake rents out bikes in summer and changes money from 6.50am to 8.10pm daily. **Bobby's Pub** (☎ 081 834 42 83; Via dal Bagn 50a; per hr Sfr12; ☼ 10-1am) is the place to surf the Web. Up the hill, on Via Serlas, is the **post office** and five minutes further on is the **tourist office** (☎ 081 837 33 33; www.stmoritz.ch; Via Maistra 12; ☼ 9am-noon & 2-6pm Mon-Fri, 9am-noon Sat, 4-6pm Sun in winter only).

Activities

Skiers and snowboarders will revel in the 350km of runs on the slopes of **Corviglia-Marguns** (☎ 081 830 00 00; www.bergbahnenengadin.ch; day lift ticket Sfr63, ski & boot rental Sfr43). The choice for beginners is limited. There are also 160km of **cross-country trails** (equipment rental Sfr20) and 120km of marked **hiking paths**.

You also can try golf (including on the frozen lake in winter), tennis, inline skating, fishing, horse riding, sailing, windsurfing and river rafting, to mention just a few. The tourist office has a list of prices and contacts.

Sleeping & Eating

Olympiaschanze camping ground (☎ 081 833 40 90; camp sites per adult/tent Sfr7.40/8; ☼ late-May–late-Sep) Located 1km southwest of St Moritz Bad.

Youth Hostel St Moritz Bad (☎ 081 833 39 69; www.youthhostel.ch/st.moritz; Via Surpunt 60; dm with half-board Sfr45.50; ☐) Backing on to the forest and cross-country ski course, this large, modern hostel has excellent facilities. There's mountain bike rental, compulsory half-board and a TV lounge. From the train station take the bus towards Maloja and get off at the Hotel Sonne. From here it is a six-minute walk.

Sporthotel Stille (☎ 081 833 69 48; hotel.stille@ bluewin.ch; Via Surpunt 58; s/d Sfr72/144; P) Next to the hostel, this hotel attracts a young, sporty crowd. In the winter it has its own bar and occasionally a disco; prices drop during the summer.

Hotel Bellaval (☎ 081 833 32 45; www.bellaval -stmoritz.ch, no English; Via Grevas 55; s/d with shared bathroom Sfr75/150) Good value and right next to the train station, this hotel prides itself on its BBQs at the attached restaurant.

La Fontana (☎ 081 833 12 66; Via dal Bagn 16; mains Sfr12-28; ☼ 9am-midnight Mon-Sat, 11am-midnight Sun) Romantically lit with candles, this cosy rustic restaurant does pasta dishes in St Moritz Bad.

Engiadina (☎ 081 833 32 65; Plazza da Scuola 2; fondue from Sfr28; ☼ closed Sun) This restaurant in the Dorf is famous for its fondue. Make a romantic dinner of it by ordering the pot of cheese with champagne (Sfr34).

Next to La Fontana there is a Coop supermarket for self-caterers.

Getting There & Away

Two postbuses run to Lugano (Sfr74, four hours, daily in summer but only Friday, Saturday and Sunday in winter). You must reserve a seat the day before. Call ☎ 081 837 67 64. The bus costs Sfr10 for those holding Swiss Travel passes.

The *Glacier Express* plies one of Switzerland's most famous scenic train routes, connecting St Moritz to Zermatt (Sfr138, 7½ hours, daily) via the 2033m Oberalp Pass. It covers 290km and crosses 291 bridges. Novelty drink glasses in the dining car have sloping bases to compensate for the hills – but remember to keep turning them around!

SWISS NATIONAL PARK

Flora and fauna abound in the 169-sq-km **Swiss National Park** (☎ 081 856 13 78; www.national park.ch; ☼ Jun-Oct). The park information centre, near Zernez, has details on hiking routes and the best places to see particular animals. Take the three-hour walk south from Zernez to scenic Val Cluozza, where there's cheap accommodation. Another three-hour walk goes from S-chanf to Trupchun. This is especially popular in October when you can get close to large deer.

ZÜRICH

pop 351,700

There's an electricity in the air in Switzerland's most populous city, a vibrancy not found anywhere else in the country. Banks, art galleries and trendy bars greet you at every turn, and the city, which easily manages to merge affluence, style and culture, is sure to charm even the most jaded traveller. During the day it is a relatively sedate place where hours slip past wandering the graceful and compact old town. When darkness falls, however, the city kicks it up a notch as the pinstripe brigade yields the streets to bar-hoppers and clubbers in Switzerland's most happening scene.

ORIENTATION

Zürich is at the northern end of Lake Zürich (Zürichsee), with the city centre split by the Limmat River. Like many Swiss cities it is compact and easy to navigate. The main train station (Hauptbahnhof) is on the western bank of the river, close to the old centre.

INFORMATION
Bookshops

Orell Füssli Bookshop (☎ 01 211 04 44; Bahnhofstrasse 70) Great source of fiction and travel books in English.

Travel Book Shop (☎ 01 252 38 83; Rindermarkt 20) Sells English-language travel books and maps.

Emergency

Telephone Advisory Service (☎ 01 269 69 69) For medical and dental help.

Internet Access

Quanta (☎ 01 260 72 66; cnr Niederdorfstrasse & Mühlegasse; per hr Sfr10)

Medical Services

Cantonal University Hospital (☎ 01 255 11 11; Rämistrasse 100) Casualty department.

Bellevue Apotheke (☎ 01 252 56 00; Theaterstrasse 14) A 24-hour chemist.

Money

There's no shortage of choice when exchang-ing money in this banking city. Banks are open 8.15am to 4.30pm Monday to Friday (until 6pm Thursday).

Post

Main Post Office (☎ 01 296 21 11; Kasernenstrasse 95-97; ☯ 7.30am-8pm Mon-Fri, 8am-4pm Sat) There's a more convenient location at the main train station.

Tourist Information

Zürich Tourism (☎ 01 215 30 00; www.zurichtourism.ch; train station; ☯ 8.30am-8.30pm Mon-Fri, 8.30am-6.30pm Sat & Sun) Arranges hotels, car rentals and excursions.

Travel Agencies

STA Travel (☎ 01 261 97 57; Leonhardstrasse 10; ☯ 10am-6pm Mon-Wed & Fri, 10am-8pm Thu, 10am-1pm Sat)

SIGHTS

Many things to see and do in Zürich don't cost a cent. In addition to the sights listed here there are numerous art galleries throughout town.

Old Town

Allocate at least a couple hours to explore the cobbled streets of the pedestrian-only old town that line both sides of the river. You never know what a turn down an intimate alleyway will reveal – a 16th- or 17th-century house or guildhall, a tiny bou-tique or cosy café, or maybe courtyards and fountains.

Elegant **Bahnhofstrasse** is simply perfect for window-shopping and affluent Zürcher-watching. The bank vaults beneath the street are said to be crammed with gold and silver. Above ground, you'll find luxury shops sell-ing the best Switzerland can offer – from watches and clocks to chocolates, furs, por-celain and fashion labels galore.

On Sundays it seems as if all of Zürich takes an afternoon stroll around the lake, be sure to join in. There are sometimes human traffic jams, but it is definitely a worthwhile cultural experience. Wander down the west bank of the lake and concrete walkways give way to parkland in the **Arboretum**. On the eastern bank, the **Zürichhorn** park has sculp-tures and a Chinese Garden. In summer, the lakeside park buzzes with food stalls and en-tertainment, and there is a roped off swim-ming area with a slide and diving board.

Churches

On the west bank of the Limmat River the 13th-century **Fraumünster** (cathedral; Münsterplatz; ☯ 9am-6pm May-Sep, 10am-5pm Oct-Apr) is Zürich's most noteworthy attraction, with some of the most distinctive and attractive stained-glass windows in the world. Across the river is the dual-towered **Grossmünster** (Grossmünster-platz; ☯ 9am-6pm mid-Mar–Oct, 10am-5pm Nov–mid-Mar). This was where, in the 16th century, the Protestant preacher Huldrych Zwingli first spread his message of 'pray and work' during the Reformation – a seminal period in Zürich's history. The figure glowering from the south tower of the cathedral is Charlemagne, who founded the original church at this location. Back on the west bank, you'll find the 13th-century tower of **St Peterskirche** (St Peter's Church; St-Peterhofstatt;

⊗ 8am-6pm Mon-Fri, 8am-3pm Sat) is hard to miss. It has the largest clock face in Europe (8.7m in diameter).

Kunsthaus

This **museum of fine arts** (☎ 01 253 84 84; www .kunsthaus.ch; Heimplatz 1; adult/student Sfr12/7, free Sun; ⊗ 10am-9pm Tue-Thu, 10am-5pm Fri-Sun) has one of the best collections in the country, including works by Dali, Man Ray, Hockney, Renoir, Monet and Marc Chagall. Don't miss the collection of Alberto Giacometti paintings and stick-figure sculptures.

Zoo Zürich & Masoala Rainforest

About 2000 animals are on exhibit at this **zoo** (☎ 01 254 25 00; www.zoo.ch, in German; Zürichberg-strasse 221; adult/student Sfr14/7; ⊗ 8am-6pm Mar-Oct, 8am-5pm Nov-Feb), which is one of the best in Europe. The expansive location gives the animals plenty of room to breathe, and its location within the Zürichberg woods makes it a beautiful place for a walk; tram No 6 will get you there. The zoo has a Madagascan rainforest on 10,000 square metres of parkland.

FESTIVALS & EVENTS

On the third Monday in April, Zürich celebrates the arrival of warmer weather with **Sechseläuten**. Many professionals in Switzerland belong to work-associated guilds that offer them a certain level of protection and security in their jobs – similar to joining a union. During Sechseläuten guild members parade the streets in historical costume and tour the guildhalls, playing music. A fireworks-filled 'snowman' (the Böögg) is ignited at 6pm.

Zürich lets its hair down in August with the techno **Street Parade**, attracting well over half a million ravers. All-night parties around the city follow a three-hour parade.

In February, just after Ash Wednesday, the city celebrates **Fasnacht**, with parades and festive costumes. **Zürcher Festspiele**, from mid-June to mid-July, offers a programme of music, dance and theatre.

SLEEPING

Zürich has a bizarre love affair with theme hotels – everything from rock rooms to animal-print rooms to Dada rooms and the 'in bed with Ronald McDonald' rooms. Cheaper hotels fill early, so book ahead.

Budget

Camping Seebucht (☎ 01 482 16 12; Seestrasse 559; camp sites per adult/tent/car Sfr9.50/12/5; ⊗ May-Sep) On the western shore of the lake, 4km from the centre (signposted), this camping ground has a shop and café, but some readers have been less than satisfied with the camping ground staff. To get here take bus No 161 or 165 from Bürkliplatz.

City Backpacker (☎ 01 251 90 15; backpacker@access .ch; Niederdorfstrasse 5; dm Sfr31, s/d with shared bathroom Sfr66/92; 🖳) Centrally located for bar hopping, rooms are very simple, but clean. The rooftop terrace has great views of the city and is a perfect spot to hang out in the summer. There's a self-catering kitchen and laundry machines.

Martahaus (☎ 01 251 45 50; www.martahaus.ch; Zähringerstrasse 36; dm Sfr37, s/d with shared bathroom from Sfr75/98; 🖳) The best budget option in town. Just a five-minute walk from the station, privacy even prevails in the six-bed dorms with individual cubicles fashioned from partitions and curtains. Doubles come with TVs, and more expensive ones with bathrooms. There's a bar on the first floor and a great lounge on the second with TV, pool table and best of all – a free Internet station.

Justinusheim (☎ 01 361 38 06; fax 01 362 29 82; Freudenbergstrasse 146; s/d with shared bathroom Sfr50/85) This tranquil student home always has a few places for travellers in its spacious rooms. A few paces from the Zürichberg woods, it has views of the city and lake far below. Take tram No 10 from the train station to Rigiblik, then the frequent Seilbahn (every six minutes) to the top station.

Hotel Formule 1 (☎ 01 307 48 00; www.hotelformule1 .com; Heidi Abel-Weg 7; s, d & tr Sfr59) You can't beat the price for clean, modern, in-room facilities with TV, even if it's slightly lacking in charm. Plus it is just minutes from the airport, making it handy for those super-early morning flights.

Mid-Range & Top End

Zic-Zac Rock-Hotel & Zic-Zac Rock-Garden (☎ 01 261 21 81; www.ziczac.ch, in German; Marktgasse 17; d Sfr160; s/d with shared bathroom Sfr75/120, mains Sfr15-25; 🖳) This novelty place features a bold paint job, rock-star room names and gold discs. Check out a couple of rooms before taking one, as some are cooler than others. The attached restaurant is a slice of Americana in

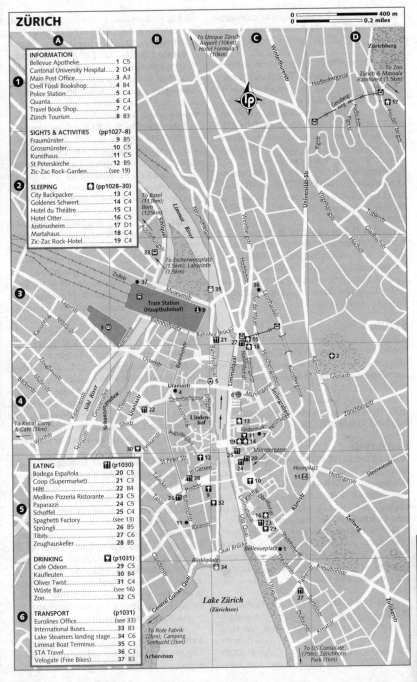

ZÜRICH

0 — 400 m
0 — 0.2 miles

INFORMATION
Bellevue Apotheke.................1 C5
Cantonal University Hospital....2 D4
Main Post Office....................3 A3
Orell Füssli Bookshop.............4 B4
Police Station.......................5 C4
Quanta...............................6 C4
Travel Book Shop..................7 C4
Zürich Tourism.....................8 B3

SIGHTS & ACTIVITIES (pp1027–8)
Fraumünster........................9 B5
Grossmünster.....................10 C5
Kunsthaus..........................11 C5
St Peterskirche....................12 B5
Zic-Zac Rock-Garden........(see 19)

SLEEPING (pp1028–30)
City Backpacker...................13 C4
Goldenes Schwert...............14 C4
Hotel du Théâtre.................15 C3
Hotel Otter........................16 C5
Justinusheim......................17 D1
Martahaus.........................18 B4
Zic-Zac Rock-Hotel..............19 C4

EATING (p1030)
Bodega Española.................20 C5
Coop (Supermarket)............21 C3
Hiltl.................................22 B4
Mollino Pizzeria Ristorante....23 C5
Paparazzi..........................24 C5
Schoffel............................25 C4
Spaghetti Factory............(see 13)
Sprüngli...........................26 B5
Tibits...............................27 C6
Zeughauskeller...................28 B5

DRINKING (p1031)
Café Odeon.......................29 C5
Kaufleuten........................30 B4
Oliver Twist.......................31 C4
Wüste Bar.....................(see 16)
Zoo.................................32 C5

TRANSPORT (p1031)
Eurolines Office...............(see 33)
International Buses..............33 B3
Lake Steamers landing stage..34 C6
Limmat Boat Terminus.........35 C3
STA Travel........................36 C3
Velogate (Free Bikes)..........37 B3

SWITZERLAND

Switzerland. Rock and American memorabilia fill the place, which becomes a popular bar at night. Food is sandwich and burger oriented.

Hotel Otter (☎ 01 251 22 07; www.wueste.ch; Oberdorfstrasse 7; s/d Sfr100/130) This flamboyantly quirky hotel is by far our favourite place to stay in town. The 17 rooms are each fantastically unique – one's a safari lodge, another a religious grotto, and then there's the Arabian-themed room. Not to be missed. The location, on fashionable Oberdorfstrasse, is very central, too.

Goldenes Schwert (☎ 01 266 18 18; hotel@rainbow.ch; Marktgasse 14; s/d from Sfr135/175) A gay-friendly hotel with some over-the-top rooms that include murals and mirror balls. There's a disco downstairs.

Hotel du Théâtre (☎ 01 267 26 70; www.hotel-du-theatre.ch; Seilergraben 69; s/d from Sfr140/180) A sentimental old favourite that's always been popular with artistic types. Guests can choose from a variety of drama, comedy, erotica and philosophy audio books in the hotel's library to listen to in their room.

EATING

Zürich has a thriving café culture and hundreds of restaurants serving all types of local and international cuisine. A good place to start exploring is Niederdorfstrasse, and the backstreets nearby, filled with wall-to-wall cafés, restaurants and bars of every description. Most restaurants stay open from early morning to late evening.

Restaurants

Spaghetti Factory (☎ 01 251 94 00; Niederdorfstrasse 5; pasta Sfr15-22) With a fun, buzzing atmosphere, this restaurant serves big, delicious bowls of its namesake dish (22 choices). When it's packed on weekends you'll be squeezed in next to strangers, but that's half the fun.

Mollino Pizzeria Ristorante (☎ 01 261 01 17; Limmatquai 16; mains Sfr18-25) For a little taste of Italy in Zürich head to this popular restaurant. Mouthwatering pizzas, delicious cappuccinos and lake views are all on the menu. Sit outside when it's warm.

Kobal Curry & Café (☎ 01 241 26 19; Kanzleistrasse 78; mains Sfr20; ⏱ lunch & dinner Mon-Fri, dinner only Sat & Sun) You order at the bar and eat at veneered tables at tiny, low-key Kobal, a favourite with the media and students. Try the chicken korma with roti or the vegetarian roti; both

melt in your mouth. It's well worth the walk through the red-light district to get there; or take tram No 8 to Helvetiaplatz.

Bodega Española (☎ 01 251 23 10; Münstergasse 15; mains downstairs from Sfr15, upstairs Sfr30-40) Fulfil your Iberian cravings with sumptuous Spanish staples such as paella. There's a classy restaurant upstairs and a less formal, but equally good, wood-tabled one downstairs.

Zeughauskeller (☎ 01 211 26 90; Bahnhofstrasse 28a; mains Sfr16-30) Slightly touristy but nonetheless a long-time favourite is this meat-lovers' heaven (with Swiss specialities and 'sausage of the month'). Zeughauskeller is housed in a 500-year-old former armoury with rough wooden tables and Swiss murals and amour on the walls.

Hiltl (☎ 01 227 70 00; Sihlstrasse 28; mains Sfr20-25, lunch buffet per 100g Sfr3.90, Indian dinner buffet per 100g Sfr4.90) An institution serving tasty veggie meals to Zürichers since 1898 (when vegetarians were commonly thought of as crackpots). There is a bizarre mixture of food on offer – everything from curry to Italian to Chinese. Try the Indian buffet at dinner.

Cafés

Paparazzi (☎ 01 250 55 88; Nägelihof 1, Limmatquai; mains Sfr9) Hang out among old movie posters and early paparazzi snaps, and order a coffee and hot sandwich or pasta dish.

Tibits (☎ 01 260 32 22; Seefeldstrasse 2; buffet per 100g Sfr3.50) Creative vegetarian options are served in a very cool, very modern, very red atmosphere. Choose from 30 different items at the hot and cold salad bar. A big plate costs about Sfr14.

Schoffel (☎ 01 261 20 70; Schoffelgasse 7; mains Sfr8-16) On weekend mornings, locals flock to this café for a leisurely coffee and newspaper read within the cheery yellow modern-art filled walls. Soups, salads and big bowls of yoghurt and fruit are on the menu.

Sprüngli (☎ 01 244 47 11; Bahnhofstrasse 21; chocolates from Sfr2, mains Sfr19-28) The mother of all chocolate shops, it's a Zürich legacy and must for chocoholics. Choose from a huge range of truffles and cakes from downstairs display cases, or mingle with the well-heeled crowd in the elegant 1st-floor tearooms for a rather special experience.

Self-Catering

Cheap eats abound around the train station, especially in the underground Shopville, which has a **Migros** (7am-8pm Mon-Fri, 8am-8pm Sat & Sun). Above ground, by the station, there is a large Coop supermarket. Niederdorfstrasse has a string of snack bars offering pretzels, bratwurst, kebabs and East Asian food for about Sfr9.

DRINKING & ENTERTAINMENT

Like most big cities, Zürich has a fickle, ever-changing entertainment scene. Pick up the free events magazine *Züritipp* from the tourist office or check daily listings at www.zueritipp.ch (in German).

Late-night pubs, clubs and discos clutter Niederdorfstrasse and adjoining streets. Factories in the industrial quarter, west of the train station, are gradually being taken over by a wave of hip bars, clubs and restaurants. Head to Escherwyssplatz (tram No 4 or 13) and follow your ears. Bars are open day and night; clubs get started after 11pm.

Wüste Bar (01 251 22 07; Oberdorfstrasse 7) One of our favourites, located underneath the Otter Hotel, it's small and groovy with plush red seats and a cowhide bar. There's sometimes live music.

Café Odeon (01 251 16 50; Am Bellevue) Lenin and James Joyce once downed drinks at this swish, smoky bar with marble walls and chandeliers that packs out with an arty crowd.

Oliver Twist (01 252 47 10; Rindermarkt 6) English-speakers gravitate towards this pub, which serves Irish, British, Australian and South African beers. It's a smoky, noisy place, often standing room only and somewhat of a meat market.

Labyrinth (01 440 59 80; Pfingstweidstrasse 70) Zürich's top gay club features half-naked pole-dancing narcissists flaunting their six packs and lots of eye-candy at the bar. Take tram No 4 to Förrlibuckstrasse.

Zoo (01 211 57 52; www.zooclub.ch, in German; Stadthausquai 13) Dance the night away to pounding house music in an über-stylish setting – although you'll pay royally for the privilege to party with Zürich's pretty people. It was one of the city's super *in* clubs at the time of research. Take tram No 2, 3, 8, 9 or 11 to Bürkliplatz.

Kaufleuten (01 225 33 22; www.kaufleuten.com, in German; Pelikanstrasse 18) A club with a long history and hot reputation at the top end of the market. Dress to impress as every-

one in here looks like they walked out of a model shoot or film set. The place boasts that Prince and Madonna were once guests. Tram No 2 or 9 to Sihlstrasse will get you there.

Rote Fabrik (01 481 91 43; www.rotefabrik.ch, in German; Seestrasse 395) A long-standing Zürich institution, this club has managed to hold its own throughout the years. It stages everything from rock concerts to original-language films, theatre and dances, and has a bar and restaurant. Take bus No 161 or 165 from Bürkliplatz.

GETTING THERE & AWAY

Unique Zürich Airport (043 816 22 11; www.zurich-airport.com) is 10km north of the city centre. It's a small international hub with two terminals.

The N3 approaches Zürich from the south along the shore of Lake Zürich. The N1 is the fastest route from Bern and Basel and the main entry point from the west.

There are direct trains to Stuttgart (Sfr61, three hours, daily), Munich (Sfr86, 4½ hours, daily), Innsbruck (Sfr66, four hours) and Milan (Sfr72, four hours, daily), as well as many other international destinations. There also are departures to most of the Swiss towns including Lucerne (Sfr22, 50 minutes, hourly), Bern (Sfr48, 70 minutes, hourly) and Basel (Sfr32, 65 minutes, hourly).

GETTING AROUND

Trains make the 10-minute trip from the airport to the main train station (Sfr5.40) every 10 minutes. Taxis cost around Sfr50.

Use of city bikes is free of charge from **Velogate** (platform 18, main train station; 7.30am-9.30pm). Bring photo ID and Sfr20 deposit.

There's a comprehensive, unified bus, tram and S-Bahn service in the city that includes boats plying the Limmat River. Short trips under five stops are Sfr2.30. A 24-hour pass including travel to/from the airport is Sfr10.80. For unlimited travel within the canton, including extended tours of the lake, a day pass costs Sfr28.40, or Sfr20 after 9am (9-Uhr-Pass).

Lake steamers depart from Bürkliplatz from early April to late October (Swiss Pass and Eurail valid, Inter-Rail 50% discount). Taxis in Zürich are expensive, even by Swiss standards, at Sfr6 plus Sfr3.50 per kilometre.

CENTRAL SWITZERLAND & BERNER OBERLAND

Mountains and lakes, tinkling cowbells and alpine villages – this is the land of Heidi, and a region of such breathtaking beauty it defies description. It's the area you conjure up when someone says Switzerland. The movie-set, picture-perfect city of Lucerne is here, as is backpacker hotspot Interlaken, a base for exploring the Jungfrau Region where you can fill up on adrenaline activities and mountain majesty in equal servings. It's also where Switzerland began as a nation 700 years ago.

LUCERNE

pop 58,600

Photogenic Lucerne has everything a Swiss city needs – a lake, a medieval cobbled old-town and some snow-capped mountains. Without a doubt it's one of the most beautiful cities in the country. Its ideal location, in the historic and scenic heart of Switzerland, makes Lucerne (Luzern in German) an excellent base for mountain excursions, with easy access to the towering peaks of Mt Pilatus and Mt Rigi.

Orientation & Information

The mostly pedestrian-only old town is on the northern bank of the Reuss River. The train station is centrally located on the southern bank. The **Internet Shop** (☎ 041 211 21 31; cnr Pilatusstrasse & Seebrücke; per hr Sfr10; ☺ 9am-10pm Mon-Sat, 9am-8pm Sun) is across from the train station. **American Express** (☎ 041 410 00 77; Schweizerhofquai 4; ☺ 8.30am-5pm Mon-Fri, 8.30am-noon Sat in summer only) has an ATM and money exchange. Beside platform three is **Luzern Tourismus** (☎ 041 227 17 17; www.luzern.org; Zentralstrasse 5; ☺ 8.30am-7.30pm Mon-Fri, 9am-7.30pm Sat & Sun Apr-Oct, to 6pm Nov-Mar).

Sights

If you plan to visit several of Lucerne's many museums, consider purchasing the Sfr29 Museum Pass, valid for one month. It lets you into all museums as often as you want.

OLD TOWN

Your first port of call should be the medieval old town with ancient rampart walls and towers, 15th-century buildings with painted façades and the two much-photographed covered bridges. **Kapellbrücke** (Chapel Bridge), dating from 1333, is Lucerne's best-known landmark. It's famous for its distinctive water tower and the spectacular 1993 fire that nearly destroyed it. Though it has been rebuilt, fire damage is still obvious on the 17th-century pictorial panels under the roof. In better condition, but rather dark and dour, are the *Dance of Death* panels under the roof-line of **Spreuerbrücke** (Spreuer Bridge).

GLETSCHERGARTEN

Make sure that you set aside a few hours for the fascinating **Glacier Garden** (☎ 041 410 43 40; www.gletschergarten.ch; Denkmalstrasse 4; adult/student/child Sfr9/7/4.50; ☺ 9am-6pm). Peer into the giant glacial potholes that prove Lucerne's prehistory as a subtropical palm beach and don't miss Amrein's House, with collections of antique maps and paintings, and the entertaining, century-old Alhambra Hall of Mirrors.

PICASSO MUSEUM

You'll find yourself face-to-face with the artist at this **museum** (☎ 041 410 35 33; Furrengasse 21; adult/student Sfr6/3; ☺ 10am-6pm Apr-Oct, 11am-1pm & 2-4pm Nov-Mar). The main attraction is nearly 200 photographs by David Douglas Duncan that show an impish Picasso at work and play in his Cannes home during the last 17 years of his life. The intimate black-and-white photos also portray his muse, Jacqueline, and his children.

VERKEHRSHAUS

Planes, trains and automobiles are the name of the game in the huge, family-oriented **Transport Museum** (☎ 041 370 44 44; Lidostrasse 5; adult/student/child Sfr21/19/12; ☺ 10am-6pm Apr-Oct, 10am-5pm Nov-Mar), east of the city centre, that's devoted to Switzerland's proud transport history. Space rockets, a communications display, simulators, a planetarium and an **IMAX theatre** (Sfr16 extra) all help make this Switzerland's most popular museum. For unrivalled views of the town and lake, take off 140m above the complex in the Hi-Flyer, a captive balloon you can ride for an extra Sfr20 (15 minutes' duration). Take bus No 6, 8 or 24 from Bahnhofplatz.

Activities

If you're ready to face your fear factor contact **Outventure** (☎ 041 611 14 41; www.outventure.ch,

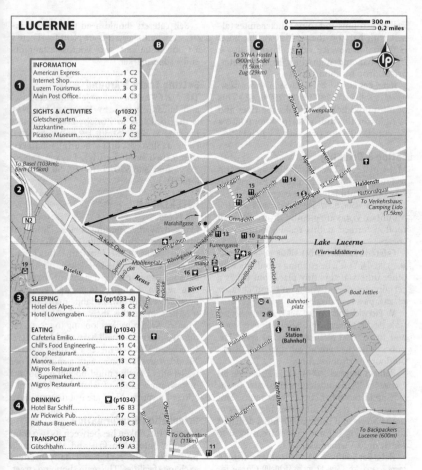

LUCERNE

| 0 | 300 m |
| 0 | 0.2 miles |

INFORMATION
American Express....................**1** C2
Internet Shop........................**2** C3
Luzern Tourismus...................**3** C3
Main Post Office.....................**4** C3

SIGHTS & ACTIVITIES (p1032)
Gletschergarten......................**5** C1
Jazzkantine...........................**6** B2
Picasso Museum......................**7** C3

SLEEPING (pp1033–4)
Hotel des Alpes......................**8** C3
Hotel Löwengraben..................**9** B2

EATING (p1034)
Cafeteria Emilio.....................**10** C2
Chill's Food Engineering..........**11** C4
Coop Restaurant.....................**12** C2
Manora................................**13** C2
Migros Restaurant &
  Supermarket.......................**14** C2
Migros Restaurant..................**15** C2

DRINKING (p1034)
Hotel Bar Schiff.....................**16** B3
Mr Pickwick Pub....................**17** C3
Rathaus Brauerei....................**18** C3

TRANSPORT (p1034)
Gütschbahn..........................**19** A3

To SYHA Hostel (900m); Sedel (1.5km); Zug (29km)

To Basel (103km); Bern (115km)

Löwenplatz

Haldenstr

Nationalquai

To Verkehrshaus; Camping Lido (1.5km)

Lake Lucerne
(Vierwaldstättersee)

Boat Jetties

Mariahilfgasse

Rathausquai

Train Station (Bahnhof)

Bahnhof-platz

To Backpackers Lucerne (600m)

To Outventure (11km)

in German; Hansmatt 5, CH-6362, Stansstad), which has the usual adrenalin-junkie fixes on offer, including bungy jumping (Sfr160), tandem paragliding (Sfr150), canyoning (Sfr170) and glacier trekking (Sfr170). There's a daily shuttle from tourist office.

In addition there are options for scenic cruises on the lake, including aboard old-fashioned paddle steamers. Check out www.lakelucerne.ch (in German) for more information or stop by the tourist office.

Sleeping

Camping Lido (☎ 041 370 21 46; Lidostrasse 8; camp site per adult/tent/car Sfr7.70/3/5, bunk in cabin Sfr13; ☼ mid-Mar–Oct) The tranquil spot makes for happy camping. Take bus No 6, 8 or 24.

Backpackers Lucerne (☎ 041 360 04 20; fax 041 360 04 42; Alpenquai 42; dm Sfr27, d with shared bathroom Sfr66) Friendly and truly comfy, the backpackers borders parkland and a scrap of lakefront beach. There are kitchens, and dorms have just four beds. It's a 15-minute walk southeast of the station. Women take care – the walk's not dangerous, but you go through a minor red-light strip to get there.

SYHA hostel (☎ 041 420 88 00; luzern@youthhostel .ch; Sedelstrasse 12; dm Sfr31.50, s/d Sfr70/90, with shared bathroom Sfr64/78) A large, modern, reliable option about 1km north of the city walls.

Hotel Löwengraben (☎ 041 417 12 12; www .loewengraben.ch; Löwengraben 18; s/d with shared bathroom Sfr110/160, s/d Sfr150/220; ℗ ☒ ▯) In a converted prison with basic, whitewashed,

SWITZERLAND

'cell-like' rooms and some fancier suites (albeit with bars on the windows), the hotel is good for novelty value. There's also a trendy bar and nightclub. In the winter, prices drop by about Sfr20.

Hotel des Alpes (☎ 041 410 58 25; www.desalpes -luzern.ch; Rathausquai 5; s/d from Sfr125/195; ☐) This beautiful old hotel overlooks the river and is right on the tourist strip. Rooms are a decent size; try for one with a balcony.

Eating & Drinking
Many places in Lucerne double as bars and restaurants. Places open for breakfast and stay open until late in the evening.

Manora (5th fl, Weggisgasse 5; mains Sfr5-15) Mountain vistas are plentiful from the small rooftop terrace at this reliable buffet-style cheapie.

Cafeteria Emilio (☎ 041 410 28 10; Ledergasse 8; mains Sfr6-14) You'll be rubbing shoulders with other diners at this tiny place, but it has a certain charm and you won't find cheaper pizzas, pastas and salads.

Mr Pickwick Pub (☎ 041 410 59 27; Rathausquai 6; sandwiches Sfr6.50, mains Sfr10-23) For Brit beer, food and footy, stop at this congenial spot. The pub sandwiches are a real steal and there's outdoor riverfront seating.

Rathaus Brauerei (☎ 041 410 52 57; Unter der Egg 2; mains Sfr8-30) Sit outside by the water or inside amid the shiny copper beer tanks. This atmospheric restaurant serves big glasses of home brews and some of the most delicious food in town. Cuisine ranges from local to Mexican to Vietnamese.

Hotel Bar Schiff (☎ 041 418 52 52; Unter der Egg 8; soups & sandwiches Sfr8-12, mains Sfr20-40) Come for the daily happy hour when a drink and appetizer costs Sfr12.50, and sit at one of the outdoor tables overlooking the Reuss River. The esteemed restaurant is a good place to try the local speciality, *Kügelipastetli* – vol-au-vents stuffed with meat and mushrooms and topped with a rich sauce. It also does tasty fondue.

Jazzkantine (☎ 041 410 73 73; Grabengasse 8; mains from Sfr15) A funky, arty and rather smoky haunt of the young and creative. There's cool music, counter meals, Saturday-night gigs and week-night jazz workshops.

Chill's Food Engineering (☎ 041 210 55 00; Waldstrătterstrasse 3; mains Sfr22) Spicy Thai curries are served in two trendy and very colourful rooms.

Self-caterers should head to Hertenstein-strasse, where cheap eats are plentiful. There's a Coop restaurant, two Migros restaurants and a supermarket.

Getting There & Around
The N2/E9 motorway, which connects Basel and Lugano, passes by Lucerne. The N14 is the road link to Zürich. Trains connect Lucerne to Bern (Sfr30, 1½ hours, hourly), Geneva (Sfr70, 3¼ hours, hourly), Interlaken (Sfr26, two hour, hourly), Lugano (Sfr56, 2½ hours) and Zürich (Sfr19, 50 minutes, hourly).

INTERLAKEN
pop 15,000

Flanked by the stunning Lakes Thun and Brienz, and within yodelling distance of the mighty peaks of the Jungfrau, Mönch and Eiger, is ever popular Interlaken. It's a great base for exploring the delights of the Jungfrau region. Catering to backpackers like nowhere else in Switzerland, many budget travellers make this their main stop in the country. Solo travellers looking to meet like-minded individuals will have a field day here. Interlaken also is a mecca for thrill seekers. Many a traveller leaves with a much lighter wallet after blowing mind-boggling amounts of cash on a range of white-knuckle, high-adrenalin sports. Most are not disappointed.

Orientation & Information
Most of Interlaken lies between its two train stations, Interlaken Ost and West, which both offer bike rental and daily money-exchange facilities. The main shopping street, Höheweg, runs between the stations, and you can walk from one to the other in 20 minutes.

Near Interlaken West is the **main post office** (cnr Marktgasse & Höheweg) and **Interlaken Tourismus** (☎ 033 826 53 00; www.interlakentourism.ch, in German; Höheweg 37; ☽ 8am-6.30pm Mon-Fri, 8am-5pm Sat, 10am-noon & 4-6pm Sun Jul-Aug, 8am-noon & 1.30-6pm Mon-Fri, 8am-noon Sat rest of year).

Activities
Some say jumping out of an aeroplane over the Swiss Alps is a life changing experience. Others argue you can't leave without first sampling the canyoning. Still others swear by night sledding. Whatever your craving, just about every adventure sport known to

SWITZERLAND

humankind is offered out of Interlaken. The town's two major adventure companies, **Outdoor Interlaken** (☎ 033 826 77 19; www.outdoor-interlaken.com; Hauptstrasse 16) and **Alpin Raft** (☎ 033 823 41 00; www.alpinraft.ch; Hauptstrasse 7) are affiliated with the town's two major hostels, Balmer's Herberge and Funny Farm, respectively. Both offer the same activities at the same prices and have offices in the hostels. Options include skydiving (Sfr380), snowshoe trekking (Sfr80), night sledding past frozen waterfalls followed by a fondue dinner (Sfr95), skiing or snowboarding including transport, lift ticket and appropriate clothing and gear rental (Sfr160), and fly-in, drink a glass of champagne then hit the virgin powder glacier skiing (Sfr250). In summer there's canyoning, where you jump, slide and rappel down rocks and waterfalls (from Sfr110) and rafting on the class III–IV Lütschine River (Sfr95).

Those without lots of cash should check out the **hiking trails**, all with signposts giving average walking times, that dot the area.

Sleeping

Sackgut (☎ 033 822 44 34; sackgut@swisscamps.ch; Brienzstrasse; adult/car/tent from Sfr7.50/3/6.50; ☺ mid-May–Oct) Behind Interlaken Ost station, this is the only in-town option. The shower blocks are rather outdated, however.

Balmer's Herberge (☎ 033 822 19 61; www.balmers .ch; Hauptstrasse 23; dm Sfr24, s/d with shared bathroom Sfr40/68; 🖳) Young Americans have flocked to this cosy Swiss chalet with a raucous summer-camp feel for more than 50 years. There's a bar, a restaurant and even a nightclub. On the negative side you're locked out of your room (even the doubles) from 9.30am to 4.30pm, you'll be constantly harassed to partake in the adventure sports and they even charge you to use the kitchen. In short this hostel would sell your underwear if given the chance. Still, travellers love the place and it's a great spot to meet people and party the night away.

Funny Farm (☎ 033 828 12 81; www.funny-farm.ch; Hauptstrasse 36; dm from Sfr25; 🖳 🍺) The town's other budget powerhouse has a similarly raucous feel and draws in hordes of Australians. It revels in its anarchic, ramshackle premises – the banana tree by the swimming pool, the floating surfboard. The unspoken mantra? Party, party, *party*!

SYHA hostel (☎ 033 822 43 53; Aareweg 21, am See, Bönigen; dm from Sfr27, d Sfr78; ☺ closed early Nov–mid-

Dec) A 20-minute walk around Lake Brienz from Interlaken Ost (or take bus No 1), it has large dorms and breakfast buffet. What it lacks in elegance it makes up for in fantastic views over the marine-green Lake Brienz. It attracts a wide range of travellers.

Backpackers Villa Sonnenhof (☎ 033 826 71 71; www.villa.ch; Alpenstrasse 16; dm/d Sfr29/82) The town's quieter and more genteel option, it has spacious renovated rooms with old steamer trunks and balconies, some with mountain views. In a corner somewhere, though, someone is bound to be hyped up about their latest skydive.

Park Mattenhof (☎ 033 828 12 81; www.park-mattenhof.ch; Hauptstrasse 36; s/d Sfr90/140) This grand old hotel is attached to Funny Farm. The high ceilings, varnished wooden bar and slightly tattered carpets just add to the shabby-chic charm. Those seeking a little privacy can have the best of both worlds – a stay in a well-appointed upmarket room and the opportunity to party the night away.

Hotel Derby (☎ 033 822 25 45; derbyboss@bluewin .ch; Obere Jungfraustrasse 70; d Sfr150, with shared bathroom Sfr110) Don't be deterred by the pink stucco walls – inside is a family-run hotel with well-equipped rooms and a pleasant back garden in which to relax.

Victoria-Jungfrau Grand Hotel & Spa (☎ 033 828 28 28; www.victoria-jungfrau.ch; Höheweg 41; s/d Sfr510/ 620) The granddaddy of Interlaken hotels, the Victoria easily outclasses everything else in town. From its swanky lobby and pampering spa to its old-world rooms, this 1865 landmark is the last word in Swiss style.

Eating & Drinking

Balmer's has the town's hottest after-dark scene (especially when its club is open), with Funny Farm a close second, and guests rarely leave at night. If you're not staying at either hostel they appear not to care if you drink at their bar. It's a little pricey, however, so stock up on beer (and food) at the **Coop Pronto** (Höheweg 11; ☺ 10am-10pm Mon-Sat) with the rest of the town. At night it's busier than the bars!

Buddy's Pub & Restaurant Splendid (☎ 033 822 30 51; Höheweg 33; snacks Sfr3-7, mains Sfr22-30) Buddy's Pub is a popular watering hole where you can fill up on beer and sandwiches or chilli. The attached restaurant serves a range of fondues and *raclettes*, as well as meat and fish dishes.

Top o'Met (☎ 033 828 66 66; 18th fl, Metropole Hotel, Höheweg 37; buffet from Sfr10.50, mains from Sfr18) Sip on a cocktail and enjoy the sweeping mountain views. Or stop by for an ice-cream sundae, meal or coffee during the day.

Restaurant Chalet Interlaken (☎ 033 827 87 87; Kirchgasse 37; mains Sfr15-40) Fake trees and candles add to the ambiance inside this chalet. It's a popular place serving Swiss cuisine, including rather sumptuous fondue and sausage dishes. There are a few veggie options.

Mata Hari (☎ 033 823 80 01; Hotel Lötschberg, General Guisan Strasse 31; mains from Sfr22; ☺ dinner only Wed, lunch & dinner Thu-Mon, closed Tue) An Asian buffet and Indonesian specialities are offered at this pleasant low-key restaurant with a reputation for good food.

El Azteca (☎ 033 822 71 31; Jungfraustrasse 30; mains from Sfr22; ☺ closed Wed in Jan) With friendly service and passable Mexican food, the menu has a range of dishes from mild to fiercely hot.

Spice India (☎ 033 821 00 91; Postgasse 6; mains from Sfr24) Serving delicious dishes with a kick, this relative newcomer has authentic tandooris and curries.

Getting There & Away

Main roads go east to Lucerne and west to Bern, but the only way south for vehicles, without a detour around the mountains, is the car-carrying train from Kandersteg, south of Spiez. Trains to Grindelwald (Sfr9.80, 40 minutes, hourly), Lauterbrunen (Sfr6.60, 20 minutes, hourly) and Lucerne (Sfr30, two hours, hourly) depart from Interlaken Ost. Trains to Brig (Sfr38, 1½ hours, hourly) and Montreux via Bern (Sfr91, two hours, hourly) leave from Interlaken West or Ost.

JUNGFRAU REGION

The views get better the further south you go from Interlaken. The region's most popular peaks are the Jungfrau and the Schilthorn. In winter, the Jungfrau is a magnet for skiers and snowboarders, with 200km of pistes. Grindelwald, Männlichen, Mürren and Wengen are all popular ski destinations, plus there are demanding runs down the Schilthorn. A one-day ski pass for Kleine Scheidegg–Männlichen, Grindelwald-First, or Mürren–Schilthorn costs Sfr55.

The Lauterbrunnen Valley branches out from Interlaken with sheer rock faces and towering mountains on either side, attract-

ing an army of hikers and mountain bikers. Cowbells echo in the valley and every house and hostel has a postcard-worthy view. Many visitors choose to visit this valley on a day trip from Interlaken.

Grindelwald

Picturesque Grindelwald was once a simple farming village. Today it's the largest ski resort in the Jungfrau, nestled in a valley under the north face of the Eiger.

Grindelwald Tourism (☎ 033 854 12 12; www.grindel wald.ch, in German; ☺ 8am-7pm Mon-Fri, 8am-6pm Sat, 9am-noon & 2-5pm Sun Jul-Sep, shorter hrs & closed Sun btwn seasons) is in the centre at the Sportzentrum, 200m from the train station.

The First is the main **skiing** area in winter, with runs stretching from **Oberjoch** at 2486m to the village at 1050m. In the summer it caters to **hikers** with 90km of trails about 1200m, 48km of which are open year-round. You can catch the longest **cable car** in Europe from Grindelwald-Grund to Männlichen, where there are more extraordinary views and hikes (one way/return Sfr29/46).

The cosy wooden chalet that houses the **SYHA hostel** (☎ 033 853 10 09; grindelwald@youthhostel .ch; Terrassenweg; dm from Sfr29.50) is perched high on a ridge and there are magnificent views. It's a tough 20-minute climb from the station. Avoid the slog by taking the Terrassenweg-bound bus to the Gaggi Säge stop.

If the hostel's full, try the nearby **Natur freundehaus** (☎ 033 853 13 33; nfhostel@grindelwald.ch; Terrassenweg; dm from Sfr32). The garden is a great place to take in the stupendous scenery. Both hostels are closed between seasons.

Near the Mälichen cable-car station, the modern **Mountain Hostel** (☎ 033 854 38 38; mhos tel@grindelwald.ch; dm/d with shared bathroom from Sfr34/88) is a good base for sports junkies. An array of unique activities centred on hiking (there's a hiking and painting seminar) can be arranged.

The **Hotel Residence** (☎ 033 854 55 55; residence@ grindelwald.ch; s/d from Sfr90/150) lies in a quiet location on the eastern side of the village. Family-run, cosy and modern it has a terrace restaurant and allows you free access to a nearby hotel's swimming pool.

Most hotels in town have their own restaurants and some also have bars and clubs. For tasty traditional food and staggering views of the Eiger, visit the **Rendez-vous Restaurant** (☎ 033 853 11 81; mains Sfr13.50-27; ☺ closed

Tue) on the main street. Try the platter of Grindelwald cheese or cold meats.

Onkel Tom's Hütte (☎ 033 853 52 39; Im Graben 4; pizza from Sfr14; ☺ dinner), on the way out of town, is a cosy California-style barn with cheap tucker and an excellent wine list.

Self-caterers can stock up at Coop supermarket opposite the tourist office.

The village is easily reached by road. There is a train to Interlaken Ost (Sfr9.40, 40 minutes, hourly), among other locations.

Lauterbrunnen

Tiny Lauterbrunnen, with its attractive main street cluttered with Swiss chalet architecture, is friendly and down-to-earth. It's known mainly for the trickling **Staubbach Falls** and the much more impressive **Trümmelbach Falls** (admission Sfr10; ☺ 9am-5pm Apr-Nov), 4km out of town, where inside the mountain up to 20,000L of water per second corkscrews through a series of ravines and potholes shaped by the swirling waters. A bus from the train station (Sfr3) takes you to the falls.

Camping Jungfrau (☎ 033 856 20 10; end of Main St; adult/tent Sfr9/6, cabins per person Sfr25) has excellent facilities and awesome views of towering peaks and sheer cliffs.

Another option is the newish **Valley Hostel** (☎ 033 855 20 08; www.valleyhostel.ch; dm/d Sfr21/52; ✗ ▣), which offers comfy rooms (many with balconies), a communal kitchen and a mellow environment.

When it comes to culinary matters, Lauterbrunnen has few options. Stock up at the Coop near the tourist office, or try the restaurant at the **Hotel Oberland** (☎ 033 855 12 41; Main St; mains from Sfr17). It has a big menu of *rösti*, pasta and salads.

Gimmelwald

When the sun is out in Gimmelwald, the place will take your breath away. The hamlet is particularly enchanting in winter when the weathered wooden chalets peep out from a thick blanket of snow and the mountains seem to envelope you. Really, the place is Switzerland's best-kept secret.

Jaw-dropping views, snacks and beer are all available at the simple, rustic **Mountain Hostel** (☎ 033 855 17 04; www.mountainhostel.com; dm Sfr20; ▣). At **Esther's Guesthouse** (☎ 033 855 54 88; www.esthersguesthouse.ch; barn accommodation Sfr21, s/d with shared bathroom Sfr40/80) you can sleep on beds of straw in a big barn (June to October).

A generous breakfast of organic food and a shower are included in the price. Even if you don't stay, stop-by to pick up homemade beef jerky (some of the best we've ever tasted), cheeses and other organic products.

Restaurant-Pension Gimmelwald (☎ 033 855 17 30; mains Sfr18) has hearty home cooking, including fondue and farmers' barley soup, and is really the only sit-down place to eat in town. Don't miss the 'Gimmelwalder Horse-Shit Balls' for Sfr4. You'll have to visit to find out what they're made from.

To reach Gimmelwald you can hike up a steep trail (sometimes closed in winter due to avalanche danger) for about 1.5 hours from Stechelberg or take the cable car (one way Sfr8). A great way to get to Stechelberg from Lauterbrunnen is to hike along a flat path for about 1.5 hours. The trail takes you past some dramatic scenery. From Mürren, Gimmelwald is a pleasant 40-minute walk downhill, or catch the cable car (one way Sfr8).

Mürren

Arrive in Mürren on a clear evening, when the sun hangs low on the horizon, and you might think you've died and gone to heaven. The peaks feel so close you're sure you can touch them, and staring slack-jawed at the towering masses of rock (some of the best views in the region) could be considered an activity in itself. Otherwise Mürren is a skiing and hiking destination with some 50km of prepared ski runs nearby.

One of the best parts about Mürren is getting there. From Lauterbrunnen you can take a funicular to Grütschalp, where you switch to the train (Sfr9.40 total). The ride yields tremendous unfolding views across the valley to the Jungfrau, Mönch and Eiger peaks.

Sleeping options include the **Eiger Guesthouse** (☎ 033 855 35 35; eigerguesthouse@muerren.ch; dm from Sfr50, d with shared bathroom Sfr110), by the train station, with a bar, restaurant and games room. Another is **Hotel Edelweiss** (☎ 033 855 13 12; edelweiss@muerren.ch; s/d Sfr95/190). Perched right on the edge of a cliff, it has vertiginous views, particularly through the large windows of its lounge and indoor restaurant. Try for a room with a balcony.

Kandahar (Sportzentrum; salads & sandwiches from Sfr6) serves big, thick sandwiches, tasty muffins and healthy salads. For Thai, Singaporean and Malaysian dishes cooked by a former five-star chef, head to **Tham** (☎ 033 856 01 10;

curries from Sfr21). It's not always open in the low season. Self-caterers can stock up at the Coop supermarket next door.

Schilthorn

There's a fantastic 360-degree panorama from the top of the 2970m Schilthorn. On a good day you can see from Titlis around to Mont Blanc, and across to the German Black Forest. If you never miss a James Bond film and the scenery looks familiar it's because this is where Bond performed his stunts in *On Her Majesty's Secret Service*. Schilthorn can be reached by the Stechelberg cable car for Sfr94 return (Half-Fare Card/Swiss Pass/Eurail Pass Sfr47/48/81).

Jungfraujoch

The train trip to Jungfraujoch (3454m) is touristy and expensive, but you do it anyway because (a) it's generally a once-in-a-lifetime experience and (b) you have to see it for yourself. Plus, there's a reason why about two million people a year visit this, the highest train station in Europe. On a clear day the outlook is indisputably spectacular. Good weather is essential so call ☎ 033 855 10 22 for taped forecasts in multiple languages before leaving. From Interlaken Ost the journey is 2½ hours each way (Sfr169 return). Trains go via Grindelwald or Lauterbrunnen to Kleine Scheidegg. From here the line is less than 10km long but took 16 years to build. Opened in 1912, the track powers through both the Eiger and the Mönch, pausing briefly for travellers to take happy snaps of views from two windows blasted in the mountainside, before terminating at Jungfraujoch.

There's a cheaper 'good morning ticket' of Sfr145 if you can drag yourself out of bed for the early train (6.35am from Interlaken) and leave the summit by noon. From 1 November to 30 April the discount applies to the 6.35am and 7.35am trains, and there's no noon restriction. Eurail pass-holders get 25% off, Swisspass holders slightly more.

NORTHERN SWITZERLAND

This region is important for industry and commerce, yet by no means lacks tourist attractions. Take time to explore the tiny rural towns set among green rolling hills, and Lake Constance (Bodensee) and the Rhine on the German border.

BASEL

pop 161,800

Basel (Bâle in French) is an affluent city squeezed into the top-left corner of the country, bordering France and Germany. It has an idyllic old town and many enticing museums. The famous Renaissance humanist, Erasmus of Rotterdam, was associated with the city and his tomb rests in the cathedral.

Orientation & Information

The pedestrian-only old town and most popular sights are on the south bank in Grossbasel (Greater Basel). **Internet Pub** (☎ 084 489 19 91; Steinentorstrasse 11; per hr Sfr8; ⊙ 9am-10pm Mon-Thu, 9am-8pm Fri, 9am-5pm Sat) is a smoky joint where you can down a beer and surf the Web. The **Main Post Office** (Rudengasse 1; ⊙ 7.30am-6.30pm Mon-Fri, 8am-noon Sat) is in the city centre. **Basel Tourismus** (☎ 061 268 68 68; www.baseltourismus.ch; Schifflände 5; ⊙ 7.30am-6.30pm Mon-Fri, 10am-5pm Sat, 10am-4pm Sun) is by the Mittlere Brücke; there's a second branch in the old town (Steinenberg 14).

Sights & Activities

OLD TOWN WALKS

With its cobbled streets, colourful fountains, Middle Age churches and stately buildings the old town is a wonderful place to wander. In Marktplatz check out the impressive rust-coloured **Rathaus** (town hall), with frescoed courtyard. The 12th-century **Münster** (cathedral), southeast from Marktplatz, is another highlight, with Gothic spires and Romanesque St Gallus doorway.

Theaterplatz is a crowd-pleaser, with a curious **fountain**, designed by Swiss sculptor Jean Tinguely. His madcap scrap-metal machines perform a peculiar water dance, delighting children and weary travellers alike. Also check out the 700-year-old **Spalentor** gate tower, a remnant of the town's old city walls, with a massive portal and grotesque gargoyles.

MUSEUMS

Basel has over 30 museums from which to choose. The BaselCard costs Sfr25/33/45 for one/two/three days and grants entry to them all.

The **Kunstmuseum** (Art Museum; ☎ 061 206 62 62; www.kunstmuseumbasel.ch; St Albangraben 16; adult/student Sfr8/5, free 1st Sun of month; ⊙ 10am-5pm Tue-Sun) holds the largest art collection in Switzerland, including Klees and Picassos and the world's largest Holbein collection.

Of the private Swiss art collections made public, Hildy and Ernst Beyeler's is probably the most astounding. In the **Beyeler Collection** (☎ 061 645 97 00; www.beyeler.com, in German; Baselstrasse 101; adult/child Sfr16/5; ⊙ 10am-6pm) the quality of the 19th- and 20th-century paintings is matched only by the way Miró and Max Ernst sculptures are juxtaposed with similar tribal figures. All are fabulously displayed in Italian architect Renzo Piano's open-plan building. Take tram No 6 to Riehen.

Festivals & Events

If you're lucky enough to be in town on the Monday after Ash Wednesday you'll be treated to **Fasnacht**, a three-day spectacle of parades, masks, music and costumes, all starting at 4am. The largest celebration of its kind in Switzerland, it makes for a great night. The costumes are elaborate, the streets filled with confetti. Restaurants and bars stay open all night and the streets are packed with revellers.

Sleeping

Hotels are often full during Basel's numerous trade fairs and conventions, so book ahead.

SYHA hostel (☎ 061 272 05 72; basel@youthhostel .ch; St Alban Kirchrain 10; dm from Sfr31; ▣) Small

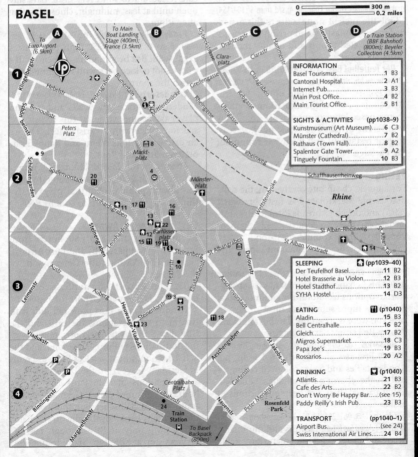

BASEL

INFORMATION
Basel Tourismus.......................**1** B3
Cantonal Hospital.....................**2** A1
Internet Pub............................**3** B3
Main Post Office.......................**4** B2
Main Tourist Office....................**5** B1

SIGHTS & ACTIVITIES (pp1038-9)
Kunstmuseum (Art Museum).......**6** C3
Münster (Cathedral)...................**7** B2
Rathaus (Town Hall)...................**8** B2
Spalentor Gate Tower.................**9** A2
Tinguely Fountain......................**10** B3

SLEEPING (pp1039-40)
Der Teufelhof Basel....................**11** B2
Hotel Brasserie au Violon...........**12** B3
Hotel Stadthof..........................**13** B2
SYHA Hostel.............................**14** D3

EATING (p1040)
Aladin....................................**15** B3
Bell Centralhalle.......................**16** B2
Gleich....................................**17** B2
Migros Supermarket...................**18** C3
Papa Joe's...............................**19** B3
Rossarios................................**20** A2

DRINKING (p1040)
Atlantis..................................**21** B3
Cafe des Arts...........................**22** B2
Don't Worry Be Happy Bar.........(see 15)
Paddy Reilly's Irish Pub..............**23** B3

TRANSPORT (pp1040-1)
Airport Bus.............................(see 24)
Swiss International Air Lines........**24** B4

SWITZERLAND

spick-and-span rooms in a converted textiles factory in St Alban, a quiet, leafy, old-money part of town a 10-minute walk from the train station (or take tram No 3 to St Alban Tor).

Basel Backpack (☎ 061 333 00 37; www.baselbackpack.ch; Dornacherstrasse 192; dm Sfr3, s/d with shared bathroom Sfr80/94; ✗) Enormous attention has gone into refitting this former factory, and the results are pleasing. Dorms are cheerful and colour coded, each housing eight beds.

Hotel Stadthof (☎ 061 261 87 11; www.stadthof.ch; Gerbergasse 84; s/d with shared bathrooms Sfr75/130; ✗) Tucked away in a corner of buzzing Barfüsserplatz, this hotel has rudimentary but very clean rooms. Its bar and restaurant do a roaring trade.

Hotel Brasserie au Violon (☎ 061 269 87 11; auviolon@iprolink.ch; Im Lohnhof 4; s/d from Sfr104/154) Climb the ancient stone stairs to this majestic former monastery and prison with tastefully decorated rooms and quality modern fittings.

Der Teufelhof Basel (☎ 061 261 10 10; fax 061 261 10 04; www.teufelhof.com; Leonhardsgraben 47; s/d from Sfr180/255; P ✗) A unique option for creative souls – each of the nine rooms features theme-based 'environmental art' created by a different artist. The sleek public areas, elegant restaurant and lively bar round out the package.

Eating

For a quick, cheap bite on the run, the daily market on Marktplatz has tasty bratwurst (Sfr5) and delicious breads (Sfr3 to Sfr7). Alternatively, there's pedestrian-only Steinenvorstadt, with its countless fast-food outlets, cafés and restaurants. Restaurants open early and close late.

Aladin (☎ 061 261 57 31; Barfüsserplatz 17; mains from Sfr10) This Lebanese restaurant has cheap vegetarian options like hummus and moussaka, as well as more substantial meat dishes. In case you were worried the flamboyant Don't Worry Be Happy Bar is upstairs.

Rossarios (☎ 061 261 03 76; Spalenberg 10; mains Sfr15-30) Frescoes and cheerful red walls, big wooden tables and a sky-coloured ceiling all add to the charm at this Italian wine bar. Often packed, it serves heaping portions of pasta.

Gleich (☎ 061 261 48 83; Leonhardsberg 1; mains Sfr18; ✦ closed Sat & Sun) Flowers and minimalist décor and a large vegetarian menu have made

this a favourite for non–meat-eaters. Try the Sfr12.50 salad buffet.

Papa Joe's (☎ 061 274 04 04; am Barfi; mains Sfr22) A rather over-the-top Tex-Mex-style restaurant serving burgers, ribs and nachos to appreciative locals. Its adjoining bar, with terracotta tiles, plastic toucans and American paraphernalia, attracts a cocktail-quaffing crowd.

For self-caterers, there's the local **Migros** (Sternengasse 17). Or for a huge selection of organic local produce (including 200 different cheeses) try the **Bell Centralhalle** (cnr Streitgasse & Weisse Gasse).

Drinking & Entertainment

In Steinenvorstadt, there's a string of **cinemas** with latest-release movies. There's also a bar/café/restaurant to suit every taste. Bars stay open until at least midnight; clubs get going after 10pm.

Paddy Reilly's Irish Pub (☎ 061 281 33 36; Steinentorstrasse 45; mains Sfr5-12.50) This pub entices expats with Brit beers and big-screen TV. It's a cosy spot to kick back with a Guinness and watch the sport.

Cafe des Arts (☎ 061 273 57 37; Am Barfüsserplatz 6) Modern art graces the walls and a piano player tickles the ivories at this stylish and spacious place with a Parisian feel. There's an extensive drinks menu and happy hour between 5pm and 7pm.

Atlantis (☎ 061 228 96 96; Klosterberg 13) Wrapped in garish gold, it's impossible to miss this always popular club that plays everything from house to pop to soul to R&B.

Getting There & Away

By motorway, the E25/E60 heads from Strasbourg and passes by the EuroAirport, and the E35/A5 hugs the German side of the Rhine.

The EuroAirport, 5km northwest of town, in France, is the main airport for Basel.

Basel is a major European rail hub with two main train stations, the SBB and the BBF. The SBB has two sections, one servicing destinations within Switzerland, and the SNCF section, which services France. Trains to Germany leave from the BBF station.

Destinations include Paris (Sfr69, five hours, seven times daily). Germany-bound trains stop at Badischer Bahnhof (BBF) on the northern bank; local trains to the Black Forest stop only at BBF, though fast EC services stop at SBB, too. Main destinations along this route are Amsterdam (Sfr180, eight hours, daily), Frankfurt (Sfr80, three hours, daily) and Hamburg (Sfr198, 6½ hours, daily). Services within Switzerland leave from SBB. There are fast trains to Geneva (Sfr71, three hours, twice hourly) and Zürich (Sfr30, 70 minutes, twice hourly).

Getting Around

For the EuroAirport catch bus No 50 from in front of the SBB Station (Sfr6.60). City buses and trams run every six to 10 minutes (Sfr1.80 for four or fewer stops, Sfr2.80 for central zone, or Sfr8 for day pass). By the SBB station is a hut offering free bike loans in summer.

SCHAFFHAUSEN

pop 32,900

Beautiful oriel windows, painted façades and ornamental fountains crowd the streets of Schaffhausen's quaint medieval old town on the northern bank of the Rhine. It makes a pleasant day trip from Zürich.

Schaffhausen Tourism (☎ 052 625 51 41; tourist@ swissworld.com; Fronwagturm; ☺ 9am-5pm Mon-Fri, 10am-noon Sat, to 4pm Sat & 10am-1pm Sun Jun-Aug) is in the heart of the old town.

The best views around are found at the 16th-century hilltop **Munot fortress** (admission free; ☺ 8am-10pm May-Sep, 9am-5pm Oct-Apr). The summit is a 15-minute walk from the centre of town. **Rhine Falls** (Rheinfall) is a 40-minute stroll westward along the river, or take bus No 1 to Neuhausen. Though the drop is only 23m, the waterfall is considered the largest in Europe, with an extraordinary amount of water thundering over it. The 45km of the Rhine from Schaffhausen to Constance is one of the river's most stunning stretches. It passes by meadows, castles and ancient villages, including **Stein am Rhein**, 20km to the east, where you could easily wear out your camera snapping pictures of the buildings in the picture-perfect Rathausplatz.

Schaffhausen is an easy day trip from Zürich, but overnighters won't regret a stay at the **SYHA hostel** (☎ 052 625 88 00; fax 052 624 59 54; Randenstrasse 65; dm Sfr24; ☺ Mar-Oct), in an impressive 16th-century former manor house. Take bus No 3 to Breite.

If you've got the munchies, look for pretzel and bratwurst stalls on Vordergasse, or check out one of Switzerland's best res-

taurants, **Rheinhotel Fischerzunft** (☎ 052 625 32 81; Rheinquai 8; mains Sfr75). It serves a mouth-watering mix of French and Far Eastern cuisine.

Schaffhausen has good roads in all directions. Trains run to Zürich (Sfr17.20, 50 minutes, hourly).

ST GALLEN

pop 70,500

It all started with a bush, a bear and a monk, in AD 612. That was when Gallus, an itinerant Irish monk, fell into a briar and instead of believing it was a mere stumble interpreted the mishap as a sign from God. He decided to stay put and build a hermitage with a little help from a passing bear (or so the legend goes). From this inauspicious beginning the town of St Gallen evolved into an important medieval cultural centre, and Switzerland's seventh-largest city.

St Gallen-Bodensee Tourismus (☎ 071 227 37 37; www.stgallen-bodensee.ch; Bahnhofplatz 1a; ☺ 9am-noon & 1-6pm Mon-Fri, 9am-noon Sat) is near the train station.

St Gallen has a pedestrian-only **old town** straight out of Hans Christian Anderson. Many buildings have colourful murals and the balconies are sculpted with the loving precision of a master craftsman. Look out for distinctive oriel windows in the buildings around Gallusplatz, Spisergasse and Kugelgasse. Don't miss the twin-towered **Cathedral**, with an ostentatious interior including dark ceiling frescoes by Josef Wannenmacher and marine-green stucco by the Gigel brothers.

Bookworms will treasure a visit to the nearby **Stiftsbibliothek** (Abbey Library; ☎ 071 227 34 16; adult/student Sfr8/6; ☺ 9am-noon & 1.30-5pm Mon-Sat, 10.30am-noon & 1.30-4pm Sun Apr-Oct, closed all Nov & Sun Dec-Mar), adjoining the cathedral. It's of the oldest libraries of the Western world, contains some rare manuscripts from the Middle Ages and has an opulent rococo interior.

Sleeping & Eating

SYHA Hostel (☎ 071 245 47 77; fax 071 245 49 83; Jüchstrasse 25; dm Sfr27, s/d with shared bathroom Sfr46.50/72; ☺ Mar–mid-Dec) This modern hostel is a signposted 15-minute walk east of the old town or take the Trogenerbahn from the station to 'Schülerhaus' (Sfr2.40).

Weisses Kreuz (☎ /fax 071 223 28 43; Engelgasse 9; s/d with shared bathroom from Sfr45/80) Central and good value, there are more expensive rooms with shower and TV. Reception is in the mellow bistro-bar downstairs.

Hotel Vadian Garni (☎ 071 228 18 78; fax 071 228 18 79; Gallusstrasse 36; s/d with shared bathroom from Sfr66/98) A slick and friendly family-run hotel with a modern edge and well-furnished rooms. It's also close to the city centre.

Restaurant Marktplatz (☎ 071 222 36 41; Neugasse 2; mains Sfr14.50-19.80) A rowdy beer-hall-style restaurant, it serves booze, pizza and local meaty dishes.

Wirtschaft Zur Alten Post (☎ 071 222 66 01; Gallusstrasse 4; mains Sfr20-42) Traditional and delicious Swiss food is served in this small and cosy restaurant near the cathedral. It fills quickly so book ahead.

Fast-food stalls proliferate around the old town, selling St Gallen sausage and bread for around Sfr6.

Getting There & Away

There are regular trains to Bregenz (Sfr16, 40 minutes, hourly), Constance (Sfr16.60, one hour, hourly) and Zürich (Sfr26, 70 minutes, hourly).

APPENZELL

pop 5530

The fragrances of cows and country permeate this pretty pastoral village. Appenzell is a nostalgic trip back in time with lush pastures and traditional houses with painted façades.

The train station is 400m from the town centre. The **tourist office** (☎ 071 788 96 41; www.appenzellerland.ch, in German; Hauptgasse; �}8am-noon & 2-5pm Mon-Fri, 9am-noon & 2-4pm Sat) is in the centre.

Exhibits on local legend and folklore are showcased at the **Appenzell Museum** (Hauptgasse; adult/student Sfr6/4; �} 9am-5pm Tue-Sat) in the village church. Inquire about the extensive English notes.

Gasthaus Hof (☎ 071 787 22 10; fax 071 787 58 83; off Landsgenmeindeplatz; dm/s/d Sfr28/85/130; ℗) is a fun place with a boisterous restaurant serving solid Swiss food. While **Hotel Taube** (☎ 071 787 11 49; fax 071 787 56 33; Postplatz; s/d Sfr75/142, with shared bathroom Sfr60/120) is a rustic retreat by the corner of the square. It's restaurant serves hearty meals (from Sfr18), including vegetarian options.

There is a train to St Gallen (Sfr12, 30 minutes, twice hourly).

SWITZERLAND DIRECTORY

ACCOMMODATION

Switzerland caters to all budgets – you can camp, sleep in a barn, stay in a hostel or live it up in a five-star hotel. However, prices may seem steep at even the most inexpensive places compared to other parts of Europe. Tourist offices always have brochures listing prices and facilities of local accommodation. Hostels, hotels and pensions most often include breakfast in their price. In budget places breakfast is basic: generally just a beverage with bread rolls, cheese spread, butter and jam. Most hostels and budget hotels have two classes of rooms – cheaper rooms with shared bathroom and shower facilities and more expensive rooms with private bathroom. We've listed accommodation options in order of price.

Barns

When their cows are out to pasture in the summer, Swiss farmers have habitually put their empty barns to good use, allowing travellers to sleep in them for a very small fee of about Sfr20. It's a unique experience that disappoints few. A booklet listing participating farmers is available from **Aventure sur la paille** (☎ 041 678 1286; www.aventure-sur-la-paille.ch).

Hostels

Switzerland has two types of hostels: official Swiss Youth Hostels (SYHA), affiliated with Hostelling International (HI), where non-members pay an additional 'guest fee' of Sfr6, and the independent hostels. Independent hostels tend to be more charismatic and better bets for solo travellers, or anyone looking to meet other backpackers. Prices listed in this book for SYHA hostels do not include the guest fee. On average a dorm bed in either type of hostel costs between Sfr20 and Sfr40.

ACTIVITIES

There are dozens of ski resorts throughout the Alps, the pre-Alps and the Jura, and some 200 ski schools. Equipment hire is available at resorts and ski passes allow unlimited use of mountain transport.

There's no better way to enjoy Switzerland's spectacular scenery than to walk through it. There are 50,000km of designated paths, often with a convenient inn or café en route. Yellow signs marking the trail make it difficult to get lost, and each gives an average walking time to the next destination. Slightly more strenuous mountain paths have white-red-white markers. The **Schweizer Alpen-Club** (SAC; ☎ 031 370 1818; fax 031 370 1800; www.sac-cas.ch, in German; Monbijoustrasse 61, Bern) maintains huts for overnight stays at altitude and can help with extra information. Lonely Planet's *Walking in Switzerland* contains track notes for walking in the Swiss countryside.

You can water-ski, sail and windsurf on most lakes. And there are over 350 lake beaches. Rafting is possible on many Alpine rivers, including the Rhine and the Rhône.

Bungy jumping, paragliding, canyoning and other high-adrenalin sports are widely available throughout Switzerland, especially in the Interlaken area.

BUSINESS HOURS

Most shops are open 8am to 6.30pm Monday to Friday, with a 90-minute or two-hour break for lunch at noon. In towns there's often a late shopping day till 9pm, typically on Thursday or Friday. Closing times on Saturday are usually 4pm or 5pm. At some places, such as large train stations, you may find shops are open daily. Banks are open 8.30am to 4.30pm Monday to Friday, with some local variations.

DISABLED TRAVELLERS

Many hotels have disabled access and most train stations have a mobile lift for boarding trains. For useful travel information, you can contact Switzerland Tourism or the **Swiss Invalid Association** (Schweizerischer Invalidenverband; ☎ 062 206 88 88; www.siv.ch, in German; Froburgstrasse 4, Olten CH-4601).

EMBASSIES & CONSULATES
Swiss Embassies & Consulates

Following is a list of Swiss embassies:
Australia (☎ 02-6273 3977; vertretung@can.rep.admin .ch; 7 Melbourne Ave, Forrest, ACT 2603)
Canada (☎ 613-235 1837; vertretung@ott.rep.admin.ch; 5 Marlborough Ave, Ottawa, Ontario K1N 8E6)
France (☎ 1 49 55 67 00; Rue de Grenelle 142, Paris)
Germany (☎ 030-390 40 00; www.botschaft-schweiz.de, in German; Otto-von-Bismarck-Allee 4a, Berlin)

Ireland (☎ 01-218 6382; vertretung@dub.rep.admin.ch; 6 Ailesbury Rd, Ballsbridge, Dublin 4)
The Netherlands (☎ 070-364 28 31; www.eda.admin .ch/denhaag_emb; Lange Voorhout 42, The Hague)
New Zealand (☎ 04-472 1593; vertretung@wel.rep .admin.ch; 22 Panama St, Wellington)
UK (☎ 020-7616 6000; swissembassy@lon.rep.admin.ch; 16-18 Montague Pl, London W1H 2BQ)
USA (☎ 202-745 7900; www.swissemb.org; 2900 Cathedral Ave NW, Washington, DC 20008-3499)

Embassies & Consulates in Switzerland

All embassies are in Bern (the Bern tourist office lists them in the free *Bern Aktuell*). Consulates can be found in several other cities, particularly Zürich and Geneva. Australia and New Zealand don't have an embassy in Switzerland, but each has a consulate in Geneva.

Australia (☎ 022 799 91 00; Chemin des Fins 2, Geneva)
Canada Bern (☎ 031 357 32 00; Kirchenfeldstrasse 88); Geneva (☎ 022 919 92 00; Ave de l'Ariana 5)
France Bern (☎ 031 359 21 11; Schosshaldenstrasse 46); Geneva (☎ 022 319 00 00; Rue Imbert Galloix 11)
Germany Bern (☎ 031 359 41 11; Willadingweg 83); Geneva (☎ 022 730 11 11; Chemin du Petit-Saconnex 28C)
Ireland (☎ 031 352 14 42; Kirchenfeldstrasse 68, Bern)
Italy (☎ 031 350 07 77; Elfenstrasse 14, Bern)
New Zealand (☎ 022 734 95 30; Chemin du Petit-Saconnex 28A, Geneva)
UK Bern (☎ 031 359 77 00; Thunstrasse 50); Geneva (☎ 022 918 24 00; Rue de Vermont 37-39)
USA Bern (☎ 031 357 70 11; Jubiläumsstrasse 93); Zürich (☎ 01 422 25 66; Dufourstrasse 101)

FESTIVALS & EVENTS

Many events take place at a local level throughout the year (check with the local tourist offices as dates often vary from year to year). Following is just a brief selection.

February

Fasnacht A lively spring carnival of wild parties and parades is celebrated countrywide, but with particular enthusiasm in Basel and Lucerne.

March

Combats de Reines From March to October, the lower Valais stages traditional cow fights.

April

Landsgemeinde On the last Sunday in April, the people of Appenzell gather in the main square to take part in a unique open-air parliament.

July
Montreux Jazz Festival Big-name rock/jazz acts hit town for this famous festival.

August
National Day On 1 August, celebrations and fireworks mark the country's National Day.
Street Parade Zürich lets its hair down with an enormous techno parade with 30 lovemobiles and more than half a million ravers.

October
Vintage Festivals Down a couple in wine-growing regions such as Neuchâtel and Lugano.

November
Onion Market Bern takes on a carnival atmosphere for a unique market day.

December
L'Escalade This historical festival held in Geneva celebrates deliverance from would-be conquerors.

GAY & LESBIAN TRAVELLERS
Attitudes toward homosexuality are reasonably tolerant and the age of consent is 16. Zürich has a lively gay scene and hosts the Christopher Street Day march in late June. It's also home to **Cruiser magazine** (☎ 01 388 41 54; www.cruiser.ch, in German), which lists significant gay and lesbian organisations, and has extensive listings of bars and events in Switzerland (Sfr4.50). For more insights into gay life in Switzerland check out **Pink Cross** (www.pinkcross.ch, in German).

HOLIDAYS
New Year's Day 1 January
Easter March/April – Good Friday, Easter Sunday & Monday
Ascension Day 40th Day after Easter
Whit Sunday & Monday 7th week after Easter
National Day 1 August
Christmas Day 25 December
St Stephen's Day 26 December

INTERNET RESOURCES
Switzerland has a strong presence on the Internet, with most tourist-related businesses having their own website; a good place to start is **Switzerland Tourism** (www.myswitzerland.com), with many useful links.

LANGUAGE
Located in the corner of Europe where Germany, France and Italy meet, Switzerland is

LANGUAGE AREAS
Romansch
German
French
Italian

Basel • Zürich
Lucerne
Bern • Chur
Lausanne
Geneva • Bellinzona
St Moritz

a linguistic melting pot with three official federal languages: German (spoken by 64% of the population), French (19%) and Italian (8%). A fourth language, Rhaeto-Romanic, or Romansch, is spoken by less than 1% of the population, mainly in the canton of Graubünden. Derived from Latin, it's a linguistic relic that has survived in the isolation of mountain valleys. Romansch was recognised as a national language by referendum in 1938 and given federal protection in 1996.

English-speakers will have few problems being understood in the German-speaking parts. However, it is simple courtesy to greet people with the Swiss-German *Grüezi* and to inquire *Sprechen Sie Englisch?* (Do you speak English?) before launching into English.

In French Switzerland you shouldn't have too many problems either, though the locals' grasp of English probably will not be as good as the German-speakers'. Italian Switzerland is where you will have the greatest difficulty. Most locals speak some French and/or German in addition to Italian. English has a lower priority, but you'll still find that the majority of hotels and restaurants have at least one English-speaking staff member.

See the Language chapter (p1085) for German, French and Italian pronunciation guidelines and useful words and phrases, and the Language Area map (above) for a regional breakdown.

MONEY
Swiss francs (Sfr, written CHF locally) are divided into 100 centimes (called *rappen* in German-speaking Switzerland). There are notes for 10, 20, 50, 100, 500 and 1000 francs, and coins for five, 10, 20 and 50 centimes, and one, two and five francs.

All major travellers cheques and credit cards are accepted. Nearly all train stations have money-exchange facilities open daily. Commission is not usually charged for changing cash or cheques but it's gradually creeping in. Shop around for the best exchange rates. Hotels usually have the worst rates.

There are no restrictions on the amount of currency that can be brought in or taken out of Switzerland.

POST

Postcards and letters to Europe cost Sfr1.30/1.20 priority/economy; to elsewhere they cost Sfr1.80/1.40. The term poste restante is used nationwide or you could use the German term, *Postlagernde Briefe*. Mail can be sent to any town with a post office and is held for 30 days; show your passport to collect mail. Amex also holds mail for one month for people who use its cheques or cards.

Post office opening times vary but typically are 7.30am to noon and 2pm to 6.30pm Monday to Friday and until 11am Saturday.

TELEPHONE

The privatised Swisscom is the main telecommunications provider. The minimum charge in Swisscom payphones is Sfr0.60, though per-minute rates are low. Swisscom charges the same rate for national or local calls. During the day it's Sfr0.08 per minute, and during evenings and weekends it drops to Sfr0.04. Regional codes no longer exist in Switzerland. Although the numbers for a particular city or town all start with the same two or three digits (for example Zürich ☎ 01, Geneva ☎ 022), numbers always must be dialled in full, even when you're calling from within the same town.

International call prices have dropped substantially in recent years. A standard-rate call to the USA/Australia/UK costs Sfr0.12/0.25/0.12 per minute. Standard rates

apply on weekdays (day or night), and there are reduced rates on weekends and public holidays. Many telephone boxes no longer take coins; the prepaid *taxcard* comes in values of Sfr5, Sfr10 and Sfr20, and is sold in post offices, kiosks and train stations.

You can purchase a SIM card from Swisscom for your mobile phone as well as prepaid cards. Calls are not cheap, however. The SIM card costs about Sfr40 and then calls are almost Sfr1 per minute, although they're cheaper on nights and weekends. Mobile service in Switzerland is generally excellent – even in the mountains.

Hotels can charge as much as they like for telephone calls, and they usually charge a lot, even for direct-dial calls.

TOURIST INFORMATION

Local tourist offices are extremely helpful. They have reams of literature to give out, including maps (nearly always free). Offices can be found everywhere tourists are likely to go and will often book hotel rooms and organise excursions. If you are staying in resorts, ask the local tourist office whether there's a Visitor's Card, which is excellent for discounts.

Switzerland Tourism also sells the **Swiss Museum Passport** (www.museumspass.ch; adult/student Sfr30/25), which will save you big bucks if you plan to visit more than a handful of museums.

VISAS

Visas are not required for passport holders from the Australia, Canada, New Zealand, South Africa, the UK or US. A maximum three-month stay applies although passports are rarely stamped.

WORK

Switzerland's bilateral agreement with the EU on the free movement of persons has eased regulations for EU citizens. Non-EU citizens officially need special skills to work legally, but people still manage to find casual work in ski resorts – anything from snow clearing to washing dishes. Hotel work has the advantage of including meals and accommodation.

Many resort jobs are advertised in the Swiss weekly newspaper *hotel & tourismus revue*. Casual wages are higher than in most other European countries.

EMERGENCY NUMBERS

- Police ☎ 117
- Fire ☎ 118
- Ambulance ☎ 144
- Motoring breakdown assistance ☎ 140
- REGA air rescue ☎ 1414

TRANSPORT IN SWITZERLAND

GETTING THERE & AWAY

Air

The busiest international airports are **Unique Zürich** (☎ 043 816 22 11; www.uniqueairport.com) and **Geneva International Airport** (☎ 022 717 71 11; www.gva.ch/en) each with several non-stop flights a day to major transport hubs such as London, Paris and Frankfurt. Most international airlines fly into Switzerland, as well as a few budget operators. EasyJet offers regular services from London to/from Basel and Geneva, while Bmibaby flies from East Midlands, in the UK, to Geneva. Switzerland's international carrier is Swiss International Airlines (known as Swiss).

Airport departure taxes are always included in the ticket price.

Air France (code AF; ☎ 01 439 18 18; www.airfrance.com)

American Airlines (code AA; ☎ 01 654 52 57; www.americanairlines.com)

bmibaby (code BD; ☎ 041 900 00 13 00; www.bmibaby.com)

British Airways (code BA; ☎ 0848 845 845; www.britishairways.com)

Delta Airlines (code DL; ☎ 0800 55 20 36; www.delta.com)

EasyJet (code EZ; ☎ 0848 888 222; www.easyjet.com)

Lufthansa (code LH; ☎ 01 447 99 66; www.lufthansa.com)

United Airlines (code UA; ☎ 01 212 47 17; www.united.com)

Swiss International Airlines (code LX; ☎ 0848 853 00 00; www.swiss.com)

Lake

Switzerland can be reached by lake steamers from Germany and Austria via Lake Constance (Bodensee). For boat information contact the operators based in **Switzerland** (☎ 071 463 34 35), **Austria** (☎ 05574 428 68) or **Germany** (☎ 07531 28 13 98).

From Italy you can catch a steamer across Lake Maggiore into Locarno. Contact **Navigazione Lago Maggiore** (NLM; ☎ 0848 811 122, 091 751 18 65) for more information.

France can be reached from Geneva via Lake Geneva (Lac Leman). Contact **Compagnie Générale de Navigation** (CGN; ☎ 022 0848 811 848) for more information.

Land

BUS

With such cheap flights available, there are few people who travel to Switzerland by bus these days. **Eurolines** (☎ 0900 573 747; www.eurolines.com) has services to Eastern Europe, Austria, Spain, Germany and Portugal, but distances are long.

If you want to visit several countries by bus, the UK-based **Busabout** (☎ 0207 950 1661; www.busabout.com) operates summer services from Bern to Paris, and from Lauterbrunnen (for Interlaken) to Paris and Venice. See the Busabout website for details. Prices start at UK£219 for a two-week consecutive pass.

CAR & MOTORCYCLE

Roads into Switzerland are good despite the difficulty of the terrain, but special care is needed to negotiate mountain passes. Some, such as the N5 route from Morez (France) to Geneva, are not recommended if you have not had previous mountain-driving experience. Upon entering Switzerland you will need to decide whether you wish to use the motorways (there is a one-off charge of Sfr40). Arrange to have some Swiss francs ready, as you might not always be able to change money at the border. Better still, pay for the tax in advance from Switzerland Tourism or a motoring organisation. The sticker (called a *vignette*) you receive is valid for a year and must be displayed on the windscreen. A separate fee must be paid for trailers and caravans (motorcyclists must pay too). Some Alpine tunnels incur additional tolls.

TRAIN

Located in the heart of Europe, Switzerland is a hub of train connections to the rest of the continent. Zürich is the busiest international terminus. It has two direct day trains and one night train to Vienna (nine hours). There are several trains daily to both Geneva and Lausanne from Paris (three to four hours by superfast TGV). Travelling from Paris to Bern takes 4½ hours by TGV. Most connections from Germany pass though Zürich or Basel. Nearly all connections from Italy pass through Milan before branching off to Zürich, Lucerne, Bern or Lausanne. Reservations on international trains are subject to a surcharge of Sfr5 to Sfr30, which depends upon the date and the service.

GETTING AROUND

Air

Internal flights are not of great interest to most visitors, owing to the short distances and excellent ground transport. **Swiss International Air Lines** (www.swiss.com) is the local carrier, linking major towns and cities several times daily, including Zürich, Geneva, Basel, Bern and Lugano.

Bicycle

Despite the hilly countryside, many Swiss choose to get around on two wheels. You can hire bikes from most train stations (adult/child Sfr30/25 per day) and return to any station with a rental office, though this incurs a Sfr6 surcharge. Bikes can be transported on most trains; SBB (the Swiss rail company) rentals travel free (maximum five bikes per train). If you have your own wheels you'll need a bike pass (one day Sfr15, with Swiss travel pass Sfr10). Local tourist offices often have good cycling information. Bern, Basel, Geneva and Zürich offer free bike loans out of their train stations.

Bus

Yellow postbuses are a supplement to the rail network, following postal routes and linking towns to the more inaccessible regions in the mountains. In all, routes cover some 8000km of terrain. Services are regular, and departures tie in with train arrivals. Postbus stations are next to train stations, and offer destination and timetable information.

Car

The **Swiss Touring Club** (Touring Club der Schweiz; ☎ 022 417 27 27; www.tcs.ch; Chemin de Blandonnet, Case postale 820, CH-1214, Venier/Geneva) is the largest motoring organisation in Switzerland. It is affiliated with the AA in Britain and has reciprocal agreements with motoring organisations worldwide.

You do not need an International Driver's License to operate a vehicle in Switzerland. A licence from your home country is sufficient. There are numerous petrol stations and garages throughout Switzerland if you break down.

For the best deals on car hire you have to pre-book. Some of the lowest rates are found through **Auto Europe** (www.autoeurope .com). For more information on car hire see p1075. One-way drop-offs are usually free of charge within Switzerland, although a collision-damage waiver costs extra.

Be prepared for winding roads, high passes and long tunnels. Normal speed limits are 50km/h in towns, 120km/h on motorways, 100km/h on semi-motorways (designated by roadside rectangular pictograms showing

---

PASSES & DISCOUNTS

Swiss public transport is an efficient, fully integrated and comprehensive system, which incorporates trains, buses, boats and funiculars. Convenient discount passes make the system even more appealing.

The **Swiss Pass** is the best deal for people planning to travel extensively, offering unlimited travel on Swiss Federal Railways, boats, most Alpine postbuses, and trams and buses in 35 towns. Reductions of 25% apply to funiculars and mountain railways. These passes are available for four days (Sfr240), eight days (Sfr340), 15 days (Sfr410), 22 days (Sfr475) and one month (Sfr525); prices are for 2nd-class tickets. The **Swiss Flexi Pass** allows free, unlimited trips for three to eight days within a month and costs Sfr230 to Sfr420 (2nd class). With either pass, two people travelling together get 15% off.

The **Swiss Card** allows a free return journey from your arrival point to any destination in Switzerland, 50% off rail, boat and bus excursions, and reductions on mountain railways. It costs Sfr165 (2nd class) or Sfr240 (1st class) and it is valid for a month. The **Half-Fare Card** is a similar deal minus the free return trip. It costs Sfr99 for one month.

Except for the Half-Fare Card, these passes are best purchased before arrival in Switzerland from **Switzerland Tourism** (www.myswitzerland.com) or a travel agent. The **Family Card** gives free travel for children aged under 16 if they're accompanied by a parent and is available free to pass purchasers.

There are also passes valid for any four days of unlimited travel in Switzerland and either Austria (Sfr391) or France (Sfr391) within two months.

a white car on a green background) and 80km/h on other roads. Don't forget you need a vignette to use motorways and semi-motorways (p1046). Mountain roads are good but stay in low gear whenever possible and remember that ascending traffic has right of way over descending traffic, and postbuses always have right of way. Snow chains are recommended in winter. Use dipped lights in *all* road tunnels. Some minor Alpine passes are closed from November to May – check with tourist offices.

Switzerland is tough on drink-driving; if your blood alcohol level is over 0.05% you face a large fine or imprisonment.

Train

The Swiss rail network covers 5000km and is a combination of state-run and private lines. Trains are clean, reliable, frequent and as fast as the terrain will allow. Prices are high, and if you plan on taking more than one or two train trips it's best to purchase a travel pass (p1047). All fares quoted in this chapter are for 2nd class; 1st-class fares are about 65% higher. All major stations are connected by hourly departures, but services stop from around midnight to 6am.

Train stations offer luggage storage, either at a counter (usually Sfr5 per piece) or in 24-hour lockers (Sfr2 to Sfr7). They also have excellent information counters that give out free timetable booklets and advise on connections. Train schedules are revised yearly, so double-check details before travelling. For train information, consult the excellent website for the **Schweizerische Bundesbahnen** (SBB; www.sbb.ch, in German) or phone ☎ 0900-300 300 (Sfr1.19 per minute).

Regional Directory

CONTENTS

Readers should note there are two types of Directories in this book: the Regional Directory and individual country directories. The Regional Directory serves as a comprehensive resource for the whole of Western Europe. The country directories appear at the end of each country chapter, and are a roundup of specific details pertaining to that country. Some subjects will be covered in both directories (eg general accommodation options are covered in this Regional Directory, but prices are covered in the country directories). Though you should look at both directories for information, they cross-reference each other, making it easier to find what you're looking for.

ACCOMMODATION

The cheapest places to stay in Europe are camping grounds, followed by hostels and accommodation in student dormitories. Cheap hotels are virtually unknown in the northern half of Europe, but guesthouses, *pensions*, private rooms and B&Bs often offer good value. Self-catering flats and cottages are worth considering with a group, especially if you plan to stay somewhere for a while.

Accommodation listings in this guide have been ordered by pricing from cheapest to most expensive (ie budget to top end) and all prices quoted include private bathroom facilities unless otherwise stated (the exceptions to this are the France and Austria chapters). See the country directories for more details about local accommodation. During peak holiday periods accommodation can be hard to find, and unless you're camping it's advisable to book ahead. Even camping grounds can fill up, especially in or around big cities.

Reservations

Cheap hotels in popular destinations (eg Paris, London, Rome) – especially the well-run ones smack in the middle of desirable or central neighbourhoods –fill up quickly. It's a good idea to make reservations as many weeks ahead as possible, at least for the first night or two. A three-minute international phone call to reserve a room (followed, if necessary, by written confirmation and/or deposit) is a lot cheaper and less frustrating than wasting your first day in a city looking for a place to stay. Increasingly, places offering accommodation in Western Europe can be contacted via accommodation websites.

If you arrive in a country by air and without a reservation, there is often an airport accommodation booking desk, although it rarely covers the lower strata of hotels. Tourist offices often have extensive accommodation lists, and some will go out of their way to find you something suitable. In most countries the fee for this service is very low and, if accommodation is tight, it can save you a lot of running around. This is also an easy way to get around any language problems. Agencies offering private rooms can be good value; staying with a local family doesn't always mean that you'll lack privacy, but you'll probably have less freedom than in a hotel.

Sometimes people will come up to you on the street offering a private room or a hostel bed. This can be good or bad – there's no hard-and-fast rule – but just ensure you negotiate a clear price and before you commit, make sure that it's not way out in a dingy suburb somewhere. As always, be careful when someone offers to carry your luggage; they might relieve you of more than the load off your back.

B&Bs & Guesthouses

There's a huge range of accommodation above the hostel level. In the UK and Ireland myriad B&Bs are the real bargains in this field, where you get bed and breakfast in a private home. In some areas every second house will have a B&B sign out the front. In other countries similar private accommodation – though often without breakfast – may go under the name of *pension*, guesthouse, *gasthaus*, *zimmer frei*, *chambre d'hôte* and so on. Although the majority of guesthouses are simple affairs, there are more expensive ones where you'll find *en suite* bathrooms and other luxuries.

Camping

Camping is immensely popular in Western Europe (especially among Germans and the Dutch) and provides the cheapest accommodation. There's usually a charge per tent or site, per person and per vehicle. The national tourist offices should provide booklets or brochures listing camping grounds all over their country. See Discount Cards (p1056) for information on the Camping Card International.

In large cities, most camping grounds will be some distance from the centre. For this reason, camping is most popular with people who have their own transport. If you're on foot, the money you save by camping can quickly be eaten up by the cost of commuting to/from a town centre. You may also need a tent, sleeping bag and cooking equipment, though not always. Many camping grounds rent bungalows

or cottages accommodating two to eight people.

Camping other than at designated camping grounds is difficult; there are not many places in Western Europe where you can pitch a tent away from prying eyes, and you usually need permission from the local authorities (the police or local council office) or from the owner of the land (don't be shy about asking – you may be pleasantly surprised by the response).

In some countries, such as Austria, the UK, France and Germany, free camping is illegal on all but private land; in Greece it's illegal altogether. This doesn't prevent hikers from occasionally pitching their tent for the night, and they'll usually get away with it if they have only a small tent, are discreet, stay only one or two nights, take the tent down during the day and do not light a campfire or leave rubbish. At worst, they'll be woken up by the police and asked to move on.

Hostels

Hostels offer the cheapest (secure) roof over your head in Europe, and you don't have to be a youngster to use them. Most hostels are part of the national youth hostel association (YHA), which is affiliated with what was formerly called the IYHF (International Youth Hostel Federation) and has been renamed Hostelling International (HI) in order to attract a wider clientele and move away from the emphasis on 'youth'. The situation remains slightly confused, however. Some countries, such as the USA and Canada, immediately adopted the new name, but many European countries will take a few years to change their logos. In practice it makes no difference: IYHF and HI are the same thing and the domestic YHA almost always belongs to the parent group.

Technically, you're supposed to be a YHA or HI member to use affiliated hostels, but you can often stay by paying an extra charge and this will usually be set against future membership. Stay enough nights as a nonmember and you automatically become a member.

In Bavaria (Germany), the strict maximum age for anyone, except group leaders or parents accompanying a child, is 26. However most countries don't adhere to an age limit despite the 'youth' in their name.

To join the HI, you can ask at any hostel or contact your local or national hostelling office. There's a very useful website at www.hihostels.com with links to most HI sites. Following is a list of HI offices for English-speaking countries; otherwise, check the individual country chapters for addresses.

Australia Australian Youth Hostels Association (☎ 02-92611111; yha@yhansw.org.au; 422 Kent St, Sydney, NSW 2000)

Canada Hostelling International Canada (☎ 613-237 7884; info@hihostels.ca; 205 Catherine St, Suite 400, Ottawa, Ont K2P 1C3)

England & Wales Youth Hostels Association (☎ 01629-592700; customerservices@yha.org.uk; Trevelyan House, Dimple Rd, Matlock, Derbyshire DE4 3YH)

Ireland An Óige (Irish Youth Hostel Association; ☎ 01-830 4555; mailbox@anoige.ie; 61 Mountjoy St, Dublin 7)

New Zealand Youth Hostels Association of New Zealand (☎ 03-379 9970; info@yha.org.nz; PO Box 436, Level 3, 193 Cashel St, Christchurch)

Northern Ireland Hostelling International Northern Ireland (☎ 028-9032 4733; info@hini.org.uk; 22-32 Donegal Rd, Belfast BT12 5JN)

Scotland Scottish Youth Hostels Association (☎ 01786-891400; info@syha.org.uk; 7 Glebe Cres, Stirling FK8 2JA)

South Africa Hostelling International South Africa (☎ 021-421 7721; info@hisa.org.za; PO Box 4402, St George's House, 73 St George's Mall, Cape Town 8000)

USA Hostelling International (☎ 301-495-1240; hostels@hiusa.org; 8401 Colesville Rd, Suite 300, Silver Spring, MD 20910)

There are also privately run backpacker hostels, although it's mainly in Britain, Ireland and Germany that these have really taken off. The following websites are recommended as resources for hostellers; all of them have booking engines, helpful advice from fellow travellers and excellent tips for novice hostellers.

Hostel Planet (www.hostelplanet.com)

Hostels of Europe (www.hostelsofeurope.com)

Hostels.com (www.hostels.com)

Hostelz (www.hostelz.com)

At a hostel, you get a bed for the night plus use of communal facilities, which often includes a kitchen where you can prepare your own meals. You are usually required to have a sleeping sheet; simply using your sleeping bag is not permitted. If you don't have your own approved sleeping sheet, you can usually hire or

buy one. Hostels vary widely in character, but the growing number of travellers and increased competition from other forms of accommodation, particularly the emergence of private 'backpacker hostels', have prompted many hostels to improve their facilities and cut back on rules and regulations. Increasingly, hostels are open all day, strict curfews are disappearing and 'wardens' with sergeant-major mentalities are becoming an endangered species. In some places you'll even find hostels with single and double rooms. Everywhere the trend is moving toward smaller dormitories with just four to six beds.

There are many hostel guides with listings available, including HI's *Europe* (UK£8.00) and the England & Wales YHA's *YHA Accommodation Guide* (UK£3.99, free to members), as well as a couple of cooperatively produced guides to Irish backpacker hostels.

If you have a credit or debit card, you now can book hostel rooms up to six months in advance on HI's booking site, www.hostelbooking.com. You can amend bookings online, but there's a fee to cancel reservations. All reservations are made in pounds sterling. Even if you don't have a credit or debit card, you can still contact the website at booking@HIhostels.com and it will provide you with the necessary information.

Those hostels that don't have Internet access (which is increasingly rare in Western Europe) accept reservations by phone or fax, but usually not during peak periods; they'll often book the next hostel you're heading to for a small fee. You can also book hostels through national hostel offices. Popular hostels can be heavily booked in summer and there may even be a limit on how many nights you can stay.

Hotels

Above the B&B and guesthouse level are hotels, which at the bottom of the bracket may be no more expensive than the B&Bs or guesthouses, while at the other extreme are luxury five-star properties with price tags to match. Although categorisation depends on the country, the hotels recommended in this book will generally range from no stars to one or two stars. You'll often find inexpensive hotels clustered around the bus and train station areas, which are always good places to start hunting.

Check your hotel room and the bathroom before you agree to take it, and make sure you know what it's going to cost – discounts are often available for groups or for longer stays. Ask about breakfast; sometimes it's included, but other times it may be obligatory and you'll have to pay extra for it. If the sheets don't look clean, ask to have them changed right away. Check where the fire exits are.

If you think a hotel room is too expensive, ask if there's anything cheaper; often, hotel owners may have tried to steer you into more expensive rooms. In southern Europe in particular, hotel owners may be open to a little bargaining if times are slack. In France and the UK it is common practice for business hotels (usually more than two stars) to slash their rates by up to 40% on Friday and Saturday nights when business is dead. Save your big hotel splurge for the weekend.

Rental Accommodation

Not necessarily the best financial option for backpackers, rentals can be advantageous for families travelling together or those staying in one place for at least one week. You have the freedom of coming and going when you like without worrying about curfews and strict checkout times, plus a feeling of coming 'home' after a hard day of sightseeing. All rentals should be equipped with kitchens (or at least a kitchenette), which can save on the grocery bill and allow you to peruse the neighbourhood markets and shops, eating like the locals do. Some are a little more upscale, with laundry facilities, parking pads, daily maid services, and even a concierge.

Check with local tourist offices in the individual country chapters for a list of rental properties.

Resorts

From foreboding Irish mansions to grand Swiss hotels, Western Europe has its fair share of luxury resorts, where travellers will certainly pay for the privilege of the privileged. As such, there are very few mentioned in this guide because of their price and, well, their price. However, travellers might find ski resorts in mountainous towns in Germany, France and Switzerland somewhat 'less' expensive, as they are as common as hotels in major cities.

University Accommodation

Some university towns rent out student accommodation during holiday periods. This is very popular in France (p386) and the UK (p250) as universities become more accountable financially.

Accommodation will sometimes be in single rooms (more commonly in doubles or triples) and may have cooking facilities. Inquire at the college or university, at student information services or at local tourist offices.

ACTIVITIES

Europe offers countless opportunities to indulge in more active pursuits than sightseeing. The varied geography and climate supports the full range of outdoor pursuits: windsurfing, skiing, fishing, trekking, cycling and mountaineering. For more local information, see the individual country chapters.

Boating

Europe's many lakes, rivers and diverse coastlines offer a variety of boating options unmatched anywhere in the world. You can canoe in Finland, raft down rapids in Slovenia, charter a yacht in the Aegean, hire a catamaran in the Netherlands, row on a peaceful Alpine lake, join a Danube River cruise from Amsterdam to Vienna (see Steamer p1073), rent a sailing boat on the Côte d'Azur or dream away on a canal boat along the extraordinary canal network of Britain (or Ireland or France) – the possibilities are endless. See individual country chapters for more details.

Cycling

Along with hiking, cycling is the best way to really get close to the scenery and the people, keeping yourself fit in the process. It's also a good way to get around many cities and towns.

Much of Western Europe is ideally suited to cycling. In the northwest, the flat terrain ensures that bicycles are a popular form of everyday transport, though rampant headwinds often spoil the fun. In the rest of the region, hills and mountains can make for heavy going, but this is offset by the dense concentration of things to see. Cycling is a great way to explore many of the Mediterranean islands, though the heat can get to you after a while.

Popular cycling areas among holiday-makers include the Belgian Ardennes, the west of Ireland, the upper reaches of the Danube in southern Germany, the coasts of Sardinia and Puglia, anywhere in the Alps (for those fit enough), and the south of France.

If you are arriving from outside Europe, you can often bring your own bicycle along on the plane. Alternatively, this guide lists many places where you can hire one (make sure it has plenty of gears if you plan anything serious).

See Getting Around (p1072) for more information on bicycle touring, and the Getting Around sections in individual country chapters for rental agencies and tips on places to go to.

Hiking

Keen hikers can spend a lifetime exploring Europe's many exciting trails. Probably the most spectacular are to be found in the Alps and the Italian Dolomites, which are crisscrossed with well-marked trails; food and accommodation are available along the way in season. The equally sensational Pyrenees are less developed, which can add to the experience as you often rely on remote mountain villages for rest and sustenance. Hiking areas that are less well known but nothing short of stunning are Corsica, Sardinia and northern Portugal. The Picos de Europa range in Spain is also rewarding and Scotland's West Highland Way is world renowned.

The **Ramblers' Association** (☎ 020-7339 8500; www.ramblers.org.uk) is a charity that promotes long-distance walking in the UK and can help with maps and information. The British-based **Ramblers Holidays** (☎ 01707-331133; www.ramblersholidays.co.uk) in Hertfordshire offers hiking-oriented trips in Europe and elsewhere.

Every country in Western Europe has national parks and other interesting areas or attractions that may qualify as a hik-er's paradise, depending on your prefer-ences. Guided hikes are often available for those who aren't sure about their physical abilities or who simply don't know what to look for. Read the Hiking information in the individual country chapters in this book and take your pick of the alternatives presented.

Skiing

In winter, Europeans flock to the hundreds of resorts located in the Alps and Pyrenees for downhill skiing and snowboarding, though cross-country skiing is very popular in some areas.

A skiing holiday can be expensive once you've added up the costs of ski lifts, ac-commodation and the inevitable après-ski drinking sessions. Equipment hire (or even purchase), on the other hand, can be rela-tively cheap if you follow the tips in this guide, and the hassle of bringing your own skis may not be worth it. As a rule, a skiing holiday in Europe will work out twice as expensive as a summer holiday of the same length. Cross-country skiing costs less than downhill since you don't rely as much on ski lifts.

The skiing season generally lasts from early December to late March, though at higher altitudes it may extend an extra month either side. Snow conditions can vary greatly from one year to the next and from region to region, but January and February tend to be the best (and busiest) months.

Ski resorts in the French and Swiss Alps offer great skiing and facilities, but are also the most expensive. Expect high prices, too, in the German Alps, though Germany has cheaper (but far less spectacular) options in the Black Forest and Harz Mountains. Austria is generally slightly cheaper than France and Switzerland (especially in Carinthia). Prices in the Italian Alps are similar to Austria (with some upmarket exceptions like Cortina d'Ampezzo), and can be relatively cheap, given the right package.

Possibly the cheapest skiing in Western Europe is to be found in the Pyrenees in Spain and Andorra, and in the Sierra Nevada range in the south of Spain. Both Greece and Scotland also boast growing ski industries – Greece is particularly good value. See the individual country chapters for more detailed information.

REGIONAL DIRECTORY

Windsurfing & Surfing

After swimming and fishing, windsurfing could well be the most popular of the many water sports on offer in Europe. It's easy to rent sailboards in many tourist centres, and courses are usually available for beginners.

Believe it or not, you can also go surfing in Europe. Forget the shallow North Sea and Mediterranean, and the calm Baltic, but there can be excellent surf, and an accompanying surfer scene, in southwest England and west Scotland (wetsuit advisable!), along Ireland's west coast, the Atlantic coast of France and Portugal, and the north and southwest coasts of Spain.

CHILDREN

Successful travel with young children requires some careful planning and effort. Don't try to overdo things; even for adults, packing too much sightseeing into the time available can cause problems. And make sure the activities include the kids as well – balance that day at the Louvre with a day at Disneyland Paris. Include children in the trip planning; if they've helped to work out where you will be going, they will be much more interested when they get there. Europe is the home of *Little Red Riding Hood*, *Cinderella*, *King Arthur* and *Tintin*, and is a great place to travel with kids. Lonely Planet's *Travel with Children*, by Cathy Lanigan (with a foreword by Maureen Wheeler), is an excellent source of information.

Most car-rental firms in Europe have children's safety seats for hire at a nominal cost, but it's essential that you book them in advance. The same goes for highchairs and cots (cribs); they're standard in most restaurants and hotels, but numbers are limited. The choice of baby food, formulas, soy and cow's milk, disposable nappies (diapers) and the like is good in most Western European supermarkets.

CLIMATE CHARTS

For general advice on when to travel in Western Europe, see p9. Each country chapter also has a When to Go section with more specific regional information. The following climate charts provide a snapshot of Western Europe's weather patterns.

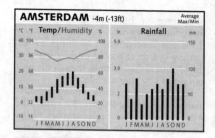

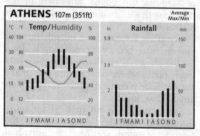

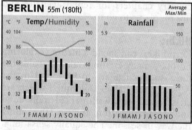

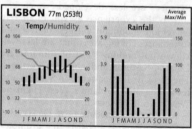

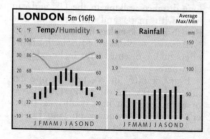

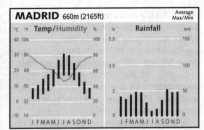

MADRID 660m (2165ft)

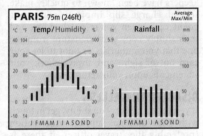

PARIS 75m (246ft)

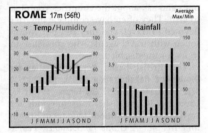

ROME 17m (56ft)

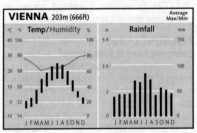

VIENNA 203m (666ft)

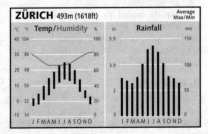

ZÜRICH 493m (1618ft)

COURSES

If your interests are more cerebral, you can enrol in courses in Western Europe on anything from language to alternative medicine to organic farming. Language courses are available to foreigners through universities or private schools, and are justifiably popular since the best way to learn a language is in the country where it's spoken. The individual country chapters in this book give pointers on where to start looking for courses. In general, the best sources of detailed information are the cultural institutes maintained by many European countries around the world; failing that, try their national tourist offices or embassies. Student exchange organisations, student travel agencies and organisations such as the YMCA/YWCA and HI can also put you on the right track. Ask about special holiday packages that include a course.

CUSTOMS

Duty-free goods are no longer sold to those travelling from one EU country to another. For goods purchased at airports or on ferries *outside* the EU, the usual allowances apply for tobacco (200 cigarettes, 50 cigars or 250g of loose tobacco), alcohol (1L of spirits or 2L of liquor with less than 22% alcohol by volume; 2L of wine) and perfume (50g of perfume and 0.25L of *eau de toilette*).

Do not confuse these with *duty-paid* items (including alcohol and tobacco) bought at normal shops and supermarkets in another EU country, where certain goods might be more expensive. (Cigarettes in France, for example, are half the price they are in the UK.) In this case the allowances are more than generous: 800 cigarettes, 200 cigars or 1kg of loose tobacco; 10L of spirits (more than 22% alcohol by volume), 20L of fortified wine or aperitif, 90L of wine or 110L of beer; and unlimited quantities of perfume.

DANGERS & ANNOYANCES

On the whole, you should experience few problems travelling in Western Europe – even alone – as the region is well developed and relatively safe. But do exercise common sense. The Basque separatist movement remains active, as does soccer hooliganism. Whatever you do, don't leave friends and relatives back home worrying about how to get in touch with you in case of an emergency. Work out a list of places where they can contact you or, best of all, phone home now and then or email.

Drugs

Always treat drugs with caution. There are a lot of drugs available in Western Europe, sometimes quite openly (eg in the Netherlands), but that doesn't mean they're legal. Even a little harmless hashish can cause a great deal of trouble in some places.

Don't even think about bringing drugs home with you either: if you have what energetic customs officials may think are 'suspect' stamps in your passport (eg Amsterdam's Schiphol airport), they may well decide to take a closer look.

Theft

Theft is definitely a problem in Europe, and nowadays you also have to be wary of other travellers. The most important things to guard are your passport, papers, tickets and money – in that order. It's always best to carry these next to your skin or in a sturdy leather pouch on your belt. Train-station lockers or luggage-storage counters are useful places to store your bags (but *never* valuables) while you get your bearings in a new town. Be very suspicious about people who offer to help you operate your locker. Carry your own padlock for hostel lockers.

You can lessen the risks further by being careful of snatch thieves. Cameras or shoulder bags are an open invitation for these people, who sometimes operate from motorcycles or scooters and expertly slash the strap before you have a chance to react. A small daypack is better, but watch your rear. Be very careful at cafés and bars; loop the strap around your leg while seated.

Pickpockets are most active in dense crowds, especially in busy train stations and on public transport during peak hours. A common ploy is for one person to distract you while another zips through your pockets. Beware of gangs of kids – either dishevelled-looking or well dressed – waving newspapers and demanding attention. In the blink of an eye, a wallet or camera can go missing.

Be careful even in hotels; don't leave valuables lying around in your room.

Parked cars containing luggage and other bags are prime targets for petty criminals in most cities, particularly cars with foreign number plates and/or rental-agency stickers. While driving in cities, beware of snatch thieves when you pull up at the lights – keep doors locked and windows rolled up high.

In case of theft or loss, always report the incident to the police and ask for a statement. Otherwise your travel-insurance company won't pay up.

A word of warning – fraudulent shop-keepers have been known to quickly make several charge slip imprints with your credit card when you're not looking, and then simply copy your signature from the one that you authorise. Try not to let your card out of sight, and always check your statements upon your return.

DISABLED TRAVELLERS

If you have a physical disability, get in touch with your national support organisation (preferably the 'travel officer' if there is one) and ask about the countries you plan to visit. They often have complete libraries devoted to travel, and they can put you in touch with travel agents who specialise in tours for the disabled.

The British-based **Royal Association for Disability & Rehabilitation** (RADAR; ☎ 020-7250 3222; www.radar.org.uk; 12 City Forum, 250 City Rd, London EC1V 8AF) publishes a useful guide for travel in the UK entitled *Holidays in Britain and Ireland: A Guide for Disabled People* (UK£12). It includes planning, transport and accommodation information.

DISCOUNT CARDS
Camping Card International

The Camping Card International (CCI) is a camping ground ID that can be used instead of a passport when checking into a camping ground and includes third party insurance. As a result, many camping grounds offer a small discount (usually 5% to 10%) if you sign in with one.

CCIs are issued by automobile associations, camping federations or, sometimes, on the spot at camping grounds. In the UK, the AA and RAC issue them to their members for UK£6.50.

Hostel Cards

A hostelling card is useful – if not always mandatory – for those staying at hostels. Some hostels in Western Europe don't require that you be a hostelling association member, but they often charge less if you are and have a card.

Many hostels will issue one on the spot or after a few stays, though this might cost a bit more than getting it in your home country. Alternatively, you can contact the local **HI office** (www.hihostels.com) in your country and purchase one there (one-year pass €20/UK£14/US$28/Sfr33). For more information see Hostels p1050.

International Students & Youths

The most useful of these student/youth discount cards is the International Student Identity Card (ISIC), a plastic ID-style card with your photograph, which provides discounts on various forms of transport (which includes the airlines and local public transport), cheap or free admission to a variety of museums and sights, and inexpensive meals in some student cafeterias and some restaurants.

If you're aged under 26 but are not a student, you can apply for a Euro26 card, or an International Youth Travel Card (IYTC, formerly GO25) which is issued by the Federation of International Youth Travel Organisations (FIYTO).

Both go under different names in different countries and give much the same discounts and benefits as an ISIC.

All these cards are issued by student unions, hostelling organisations or youth-oriented travel agencies, or download an application and purchase them online at www.isiccard.com or www.euro26.org.

Senior Cards

Museums and other sights, public swimming pools and spas, and transport companies frequently offer discounts to retired people/old-age pensioners/those over 60 (slightly younger for women).

Make sure you bring proof of age; that suave signore in Italy or that polite Parisian mademoiselle is not going to believe you're a day over 39.

European nationals aged 60 and over can get a Railplus Card. For more information see Rail Passes p1079.

DVD & VIDEO SYSTEMS

European DVD discs and players are formatted for the PAL (Secam in France)

TV system as opposed to the NTSC system used in the USA and Japan. As a general rule a DVD player bought in a PAL country will play both HTSC and PAL formatted discs. On the other hand, most NTSC players can't play PAL discs.

DVDs are also encoded with a regional code (for America and Canada this is 1, for Europe and South Africa 2 and for Australia and New Zealand 3). If you buy a disc in Europe check that its code corresponds with that of your DVD player at home as a player coded 1 or 3 will not play a disc that is coded 2. A way round this is to look for universally compatible players and discs carrying a 0 code.

If you want to record or buy video tapes to play back home, you won't get a picture if the image registration systems are different. Europe generally uses PAL (Secam in France), which is incompatible with the North American and Japanese NTSC system. Australia also uses PAL.

ELECTRICITY
Voltages & Cycles

Most of Europe runs on 220V, 50Hz AC. The exceptions are the UK, which has 240V, and Spain, which usually has 220V but sometimes still has the old 110V or 125V, depending on the network (some houses can have both). Some old buildings and hotels in Italy (including Rome) might also have 125V. All EU countries were supposed to have been standardised at 230V by now, but like many things in the EU, this is taking longer than anticipated.

Check the voltage and cycle (usually 50Hz) used in your home country. Most appliances that are set up for 220V will handle 240V without modifications (and vice versa); the same goes for 110V and 125V combinations. It's always preferable to adjust your appliance to the exact voltage if you can (some modern battery chargers and radios will do this automatically). Just don't mix 110/125V with 220/240V without a transformer (which will be built into an adjustable appliance).

Several countries outside Europe (such as the USA and Canada) have 60Hz AC, which will affect the speed of electric motors even after the voltage has been adjusted to European values. CD and tape players (where motor speed is all-important) will be useless, but things like electric razors, hairdryers, irons and radios will be fine.

Plugs & Sockets

The UK and Ireland use a design with three flat pins – two for current and one for earth/grounding. Most of Continental Europe uses the 'europlug' with two round pins. Many europlugs and some sockets don't have provision for earth since most local home appliances are double-insulated; when provided, earth usually consists of two contact points along the edge, although Italy, Greece and Switzerland use a third round pin in such a way that the standard two-pin plug still fits the sockets (not always in Italy and Switzerland).

If your plugs are of a different design, you'll need an adaptor. Get one before you leave, since the adaptors available in Europe usually go the other way. If you find yourself without one, however, a specialist electrical-supply shop should be able to help.

EMBASSIES & CONSULATES

See the individual country directories for the addresses of embassies and consulates.

As a tourist, it's vitally important to realise what your own embassy – the embassy of the country of which you are a citizen – can and cannot do. Generally speaking, it won't be much help in emergencies if the trouble you're in is remotely your fault.

Remember that you are bound by the laws of the country that you are in. Your embassy will show little sympathy towards you if you end up in jail after committing a crime locally, even if such actions are legal in your own country.

In genuine emergencies you might get some assistance, but only if other channels have been exhausted. For example, if you need to get home urgently, a free ticket home is exceedingly unlikely as the embassy would expect you to have insurance. If you have all your money and documents stolen, it might assist with getting a new passport, but a loan for onward travel is almost always out of the question.

GAY & LESBIAN TRAVELLERS

This guide lists contact addresses and gay and lesbian venues under each country directory.

The *Spartacus International Gay Guide* (Bruno Gmünder, US$32.95) is a good male-only international directory listing gay entertainment venues in Europe and elsewhere. It's best when used in conjunction with listings in local gay papers and is usually distributed free at gay bars and clubs. *Women's Travel in Your Pocket* (Ferrari International, US$15.95) is a good international guide for lesbians.

Following are a few notable websites with up-to-date information for the gay and lesbian community:

365Gay (www.365gay.com) A worldwide, daily gay and lesbian newspaper with a roundup of current events and articles.

Gay Journey (www.gayjourney.com) A mishmash of gay travel-related information including forums, booking engines, travel packages, regional bars and clubs and write-ups of gay-friendly destinations.

International Gay & Lesbian Travel Association (www.iglta.org) Gay and lesbian-friendly businesses (including accommodations and services) throughout the world, as well as a current newsletter and travel agency.

Mi Casa Su Casa (www.gayhometrade.com) The international home-exchange network service for gay and lesbian travellers. Membership is US$60 for three years, and provides listings for home-swapping vacation rentals around the world.

INSURANCE

A travel insurance policy to cover theft, loss and medical problems is a good idea. The policies handled by STA Travel and other student travel organisations are usually good value. See the Health chapter (p1082) for details on medical insurance.

Some policies specifically exclude 'dangerous activities', which can include scuba diving, motorcycling and even hiking. See p1076 for more details on car and motorcycle insurance.

INTERNET ACCESS

The Internet is a rich resource for travellers. You can research your trip, hunt down bargain air fares, book hotels, check weather conditions or chat with locals and other travellers about the best places to visit.

Most travellers make use of Internet cafés and free Web-based email such as **Yahoo** (www.yahoo.com) or **Hotmail** (www.hotmail.com).

If you're travelling with a notebook or hand-held computer, be aware that your modem may not work once you leave your home country. The safest option is to buy a reputable 'global' modem before you leave home, or buy a local PC-card modem if you're spending an extended time in any one country. For more information on travelling with a portable computer, see www.teleadapt.com.

If you do intend to rely on Internet cafés when travelling, you'll need to carry three vital pieces of information with you so you can access your Internet account: your incoming (POP or IMAP) mail server name, your account name, and your password. Your ISP or network supervisor should provide you with these. Armed with this information, you should be able to access your Internet account from any Internet-connected machines throughout the world, provided they run some kind of software (remember that Netscape and Internet Explorer both have mail modules). Most ISPs will also enable you to receive your emails through their website, which only requires you to remember your account name and password. It's a good idea to become familiar with the process for doing this before you leave home.

You'll find Internet cafés throughout Europe; check the country chapters in this book and see www.world66.com/net cafeguide for an up-to-date list. You may also find public Internet access in post offices, libraries, hostels, hotels, universities and so on.

See p12 for useful websites for planning your trip or to use while on the road. See Photography & Video (p1061) for information on digital cameras.

MAPS

Good maps are easy to come by once you're in Europe, but you might want to buy a couple beforehand to plan and track your route. The maps in this book will help you get an idea of where you might want to go and will be a useful first reference when you arrive in a city. Once there, most tourist offices have local maps. Proper road maps are essential if you're driving or cycling.

Lonely Planet has detailed maps for many European cities (eg Amsterdam, Berlin, London, Paris, Rome and Brussels). Michelin maps are also good and, because of their soft covers, they fold up easily so you can stick them in your pocket.

Some people prefer the maps that are meticulously produced by Freytag & Berndt, Kümmerly & Frey, and Hallwag. As a rule, maps published by European automobile associations (eg the AA in Britain and the ADAC and AvD in Germany) are excellent and sometimes free if membership of your local association gives you reciprocal rights. Some of the best city maps are produced by Falk, and RV Verlag's *EuroCity* series is another good bet. Tourist offices are often another good source for (usually free and fairly basic) maps.

MEDIA
Newspapers & Magazines

Keeping up with the news in English is obviously no problem in the UK or Ireland. In larger towns in the rest of Western Europe you can buy the excellent *International Herald Tribune*, as well as the colourful but superficial *USA Today*. Among other English-language newspapers widely available are the *Guardian*, the *Financial Times* and the *Times*. Also readily available are *Newsweek*, *Time* and the *Economist*.

Radio & TV

Close to the Channel, you can pick up British radio stations, particularly BBC's Radio 4. There are also numerous English-language broadcasts – or even BBC World Service and Voice of America (VOA) rebroadcasts on local AM and FM radio stations. Otherwise, you can pick up a mixture of the BBC World Service and BBC for Europe on medium wave at 648kHz AM and on short wave at 1296kHz, 6195kHz, 9410kHz, 12095kHz (a good daytime frequency), 15485kHz and 17640kHz, depending on the time of day. BBC Radio 4 broadcasts on long wave at 198kHz. VOA can usually be found at various times of the day on 7170kHz, 9530kHz, 9690kHz, 9760kHz, 11825kHz, 15165kHz, 15205kHz, 15335kHz and 15580kHz.

Cable and satellite TV have spread across Europe with much more gusto than radio. Sky TV and Eurosport can be found in many upmarket hotels throughout Western Europe, as can CNN, BBC Prime and other networks. You can also pick up many cross-border TV stations, including British stations close to the Channel.

REGIONAL DIRECTORY

MONEY

Most EU countries now have a single currency called the euro (see the boxed text following). Switzerland and the UK still use their own currency (Swiss francs and pounds sterling respectively), so if you're travelling between these and other EU countries, you'll need to exchange your money. Andorra, though not part of the official Euro Zone, uses Euros, and Liechtenstein uses Swiss Francs.

ATMs & Credit Cards

If you're not familiar with the options, ask your bank to explain the workings and the relative merits of credit, credit/debit, debit, charge and cash cards.

Two major advantages of credit cards are that they allow you to pay for expensive items (eg airline tickets) without having to carry great wads of cash around, and they give you the best exchange rate (often lower than the advertised rate) on purchases. They also allow you to withdraw cash at selected banks or from the many ATMs that are linked up internationally. However, if an ATM in Europe swallows a card that was issued outside Europe, it can be a major headache. Also, some credit cards aren't linked to European ATM networks unless you ask your bank to do this.

Cash cards, which you use at home to withdraw money directly from your bank account or savings account, can be used throughout Europe at ATMs linked to international networks like Cirrus and Maestro.

Credit and credit/debit cards like Visa and MasterCard are widely accepted. MasterCard is linked to Europe's extensive Eurocard system, and Visa (sometimes called Carte Bleue) is particularly strong in France and Spain. However, these cards often have a credit limit that is too low to cover major expenses like long-term car rental or airline tickets and can be difficult to replace if lost abroad. Also, when you get a cash advance against your Visa or MasterCard credit card account, your issuer charges a transaction fee and/or finance charge. With some issuers, the fees can reach as high as US$10 *plus* interest per transaction, so it's best to check with your card issuer before leaving home and compare rates.

Charge cards like American Express and Diners Club have offices in the major cities of most countries that will replace a lost card within 24 hours. However, charge cards are not widely accepted off the beaten track, and the Diners Club card is infrequently used.

Another option is Visa TravelMoney, a prepaid travel card that gives 24-hour access to your funds in local currency via Visa ATMs. The card is PIN-protected and its value is stored on the system, not on the card. So if you lose the card, your money's safe. Visa TravelMoney can be purchased in any amount from both Citicorp and Thomas Cook/Interpayment.

If you want to rely heavily on bits of plastic, go for two different cards – for instance, an American Express or Diners Club along with a Visa or MasterCard. Better still is

---

THE EURO

The European Central Bank's much anticipated roll-out of new euro coins and banknotes took place on 1 January 2002 in all 12 participating euro zone countries – Austria, Belgium, Finland, France, Germany, Greece, Ireland, Italy, Luxembourg, the Netherlands, Portugal and Spain.

The euro has the same value in all EU member countries. There are seven euro notes (five, 10, 20, 50, 100, 200 and 500 euros) and eight euro coins (one and two euros, then one, two, five, 10, 20 and 50 cents). One side is standard for all euro coins and the other side bears a national emblem of participating countries.

So, if you stumble across some Deutsch marks or francs on your travels, you're staring at museum pieces, albeit that old currencies can still be exchanged at central banks in the euro zone countries.

Treat the euro as you would any major world currency, and think of its portability and usability throughout Western Europe.

Just as you'd exchange, say, US dollars for euros in the euro zone, you'll find yourself exchanging euros for a local currency outside the euro zone (although in the UK, for example, some big stores and some tourist attractions accept euros). For current euro exchange rates, see the Fast Facts box in any of the euro countries (eg Germany p396).

a combination of credit or cash card and travellers cheques so you have something to fall back on if an ATM swallows your card or the banks in the area are closed.

Cash

Nothing beats cash for convenience, or risk. If you lose it, it's gone forever and very few travel insurers will come to your rescue. Those that will, limit the amount to somewhere around US$300.

For tips on carrying your money safely, see Theft p1056.

It's still a good idea, though, to bring some local currency in cash, if only to tide you over until you get to an exchange facility or find an automatic teller machine (ATM). The equivalent of, say, US$50 or US$100 should usually be enough. Some extra cash in an easily exchanged currency (eg US dollars) is also a good idea.

Moneychangers

US dollars, pounds sterling and Swiss francs are easily exchanged in Europe, but you do lose out through commissions and customer exchange rates every time you change money, so if you only visit Portugal, for example, you are better off buying euros before travelling from your bank at home.

All Western European currencies (well, the few that remain) are fully convertible, but get rid of any Scottish and Northern Irish pounds before leaving the UK as they can attract a lower rate of exchange than English pounds (eg in Canada). Yes, you may argue that they are all legal tender, all pounds sterling, but although it doesn't make much sense, your protestations at, say, a Thomas Cook office in Toronto, could fall on deaf ears. Ours did.

Most airports, central train stations, large hotels and many border posts have banking facilities outside normal office hours, sometimes on a 24-hour basis. You'll often find automatic exchange machines outside banks or tourist offices that accept the currencies of up to two dozen countries. Post offices in Europe often perform banking tasks and outnumber banks in remote places; they also tend to be open longer hours. Be aware, though, that while they always exchange cash, they might balk at handling travellers cheques unless they're denominated in the local currency.

The best exchange rates are usually at banks. *Bureaux de change* usually – but not always – offer worse rates or charge higher commissions (except in Portugal, where they *do* offer the best rates – see p890). Hotels are almost always the worst places for exchanging money.

Tipping

In many European countries it's common (and the law in France) for a service charge to be added to restaurant bills, in which case no tipping is necessary. In others, simply rounding up the bill is sufficient. See the individual country chapters for more details.

Some bargaining goes on in the markets, but the best you should hope for is a 20% reduction on the initial asking price.

Travellers Cheques

The main idea of carrying travellers cheques rather than cash is the protection they offer from theft, though they are losing their popularity as more travellers – including those on tight budgets – deposit their money in their bank at home and withdraw it through ATMs as they go.

American Express, Visa and Thomas Cook travellers cheques are widely accepted and have efficient replacement policies. If you're going to remote places, it's worth sticking to American Express as small local banks may not always accept other brands.

When you change cheques, don't look at just the exchange rate; ask about fees and commissions as well. There may be a service fee per cheque, a flat transaction fee, or a percentage of the total amount irrespective of the number of cheques. Some banks charge fees (often exorbitant) to change cheques but not cash; others do the reverse.

PHOTOGRAPHY & VIDEO

Your destination will dictate what film to take or buy locally. In places like Ireland and Britain, where the sky is often overcast, photographers should bring higher-speed film (eg 200 ISO). For southern Europe (or northern Europe under a blanket of snow and sunny skies) slower film is the answer (100 ISO or lower).

Lonely Planet's *Travel Photography*, by Richard I'Anson, is a helpful guide to taking the pictures you've always wanted.

Film and camera equipment are available everywhere in Western Europe, but obviously shops in larger cities and towns have a wider selection.

Avoid buying film at tourist sites in Europe (eg at kiosks below the Eiffel Tower in Paris or at the Tower of London); it may have been stored badly or reached its sell-by date, and it will certainly be expensive.

Properly used, a video camera can give a fascinating record of your holiday. Unlike still photography, video means you can record scenes like countryside rolling past the train window. Make sure you keep the batteries charged and have the necessary charger, plugs and transformer for the country you are visiting. In most countries, it is possible to obtain video cartridges easily in large towns and cities, but make sure you buy the correct format. It is usually worth buying at least a few cartridges duty-free at the start of your trip.

Those of you using a digital camera should check that you have enough memory to store your snaps – two 128 MB cards will probably be enough. If you do run out of memory space your best bet is to burn your photos onto a CD. Increasing numbers of processing labs now offer this service. To download your pics at an Internet café you'll need a USB cable and a card reader. Some places provide a USB on request, but be warned that many of the bigger chain cafés don't let you plug your gear into their computers, meaning that it's back to plan A – the CD.

POST

From major European centres, airmail typically takes about five days to reach North America and a week to Australasian destinations, though mail from the UK can be much faster and from Greece much slower. Postage costs vary from country to country, as does post office efficiency – the Italian post office is notoriously unreliable.

You can collect mail from poste restante sections at major post offices. Ask people writing to you to print your name clearly and underline your surname. When collecting mail, your passport may be required for identification and you may have to pay a small fee. If an expected letter is not awaiting you, ask to check under your given

name; letters commonly get misfiled. Post offices usually hold mail for about a month, but sometimes less (in Germany, for instance, they only keep mail for two weeks). Unless the sender specifies otherwise, mail will always be sent to the city's main post office (or GPO in the UK and Ireland).

You can also have mail (but not parcels) sent to you at American Express offices, so long as you have an American Express card or are carrying American Express travellers cheques. When you buy the cheques, ask for a booklet listing all the American Express offices worldwide.

SOLO TRAVELLERS

There aren't too many dangers travelling solo throughout Western Europe, but women should take extra precautions (see p1064). Be aware that accommodation places can charge higher single supplement fees, and you might find you're not at the best table in restaurants as a lone diner. Hitchhiking is risky and not recommended at all, particularly for single travellers.

TELEPHONE

You can ring abroad from almost any phone box in Europe. Public telephones accepting stored-value phonecards (available from post offices, telephone centres, newsstands and retail outlets) are virtually the norm now; in some countries (eg France) coin-operated phones are almost impossible to find.

Mobile Phones

Mobiles are the trend worldwide, and travellers can rent (or purchase) phones with international capabilities. GSM cellular phones are compatible throughout all the countries in Western Europe, but prices vary according to hiring companies.

Phone Codes

For individual country area codes see the inside front cover of this guide. Area codes for individual cities are provided in the country chapters.

Toll-free numbers throughout Western Europe generally have an ☎ 0800 prefix (also ☎ 0500 in Britain). You'll find toll-free emergency numbers (ambulance, fire brigade, police) under Telephone in the country directories.

Phonecards

There's a wide range of local and international phonecards. Lonely Planet's ekit global communication service provides low-cost international calls, a range of innovative messaging services, an online travel vault where you can securely store all your important documents, and free travel information, all in one easy service. You can join online at www.lonelyplanet.ekit.com. Once you have joined, always check the website for the latest access numbers for each country and updates on new features.

For local calls you're usually better off with a local phonecard. Without a phonecard, you can ring from a booth inside a post office or telephone centre and settle your bill at the counter. Reverse-charge (collect) calls are often possible, but not always. From many countries, however, the Country Direct system lets you phone home by billing the long-distance carrier you use at home. The numbers can often be dialled from public phones without even inserting a phonecard.

TIME

Most of the countries covered in this book are on Central European Time (GMT/UTC plus one hour), the same time used from Spain to Poland. Britain and Ireland are also on GMT/UTC and Greece is on East European Time (GMT plus two hours).

Clocks are advanced on the last Sunday in March one hour for daylight-saving time, and set back on the last Sunday in October. During daylight-saving time Britain and Ireland are GMT/UTC plus one hour, Central European Time is GMT/UTC plus two hours and Greece is GMT/UTC plus three hours.

TOURIST INFORMATION

Each country chapter has more specific tourism information, broken down within towns, villages and cities. Following is a list of official country websites that have up-to-date information on forthcoming festivals, travel advice and links to booking agencies:

Andorra (www.turisme.ad)
Austria (www.austria-tourism.at)
Belgium (www.belgique-tourisme.net)
Britain (www.visitbritain.com)
France (www.franceguide.com)

Germany (www.visits-to-germany.com)
Greece (www.gnto.gr)
Ireland (www.ireland.travel.ie)
Italy (www.enit.it)
Liechtenstein (www.myswitzerland.com)
Luxembourg (www.ont.lu)
The Netherlands (www.holland.com)
Portugal (www.portugalinsite.pt)
Spain (www.spaintour.com/indexe.html)
Switzerland (www.myswitzerland.com)

VISAS

A visa is a stamp in your passport or on a separate piece of paper permitting you to enter the country in question and stay for a specified period of time.

Often you can get the visa at the border or at the airport on arrival, but not always – check first with the embassies or consulates of the countries you plan to visit – and seldom on trains.

There's a wide variety of visas, including tourist, transit and business ones. Transit visas are usually cheaper than tourist or business visas, but they only allow a very short stay (one or two days) and usually are difficult to extend.

Most readers of this book, however, will have very little to do with visas. With a valid passport you should be able to visit most European countries for up to three (sometimes even six) months, provided you have some sort of onward or return ticket and/or 'sufficient means of support' (money).

In line with the Schengen Agreement there are no passport controls at borders between Austria, Belgium, Denmark, Finland, France, Germany, Greece, Iceland, Italy, Luxembourg, the Netherlands, Norway, Portugal, Spain and Sweden; an identity card should suffice, but it's always safest to carry your passport. Britain, Ireland, Liechtenstein and Switzerland are still not full members of Schengen.

Border procedures between EU and non-EU countries can still be fairly thorough, though citizens of Australia, Canada, Israel, Japan, New Zealand and the USA do not need visas for tourist visits to any Schengen country.

All non-EU citizens visiting a Schengen country and intending to stay there for longer than three days are supposed to obtain an official entry stamp in their passport either at the point of entry or from the local police within 72 hours of entering the country.

This is very loosely enforced, however, and in general registering at a hotel will be sufficient.

For those who do require visas, it's important to remember that these will have a 'use-by' date, and you'll be refused entry after that period has elapsed. It may not be checked when entering these countries overland, but major problems can arise if it is requested during your stay or on departure and you can't produce it.

Visa requirements can change, and you should always check with the individual embassies or a reputable travel agent before travelling.

It's generally easier to get your visas as you go along, rather than arranging them all beforehand.

Carry spare passport photos (you may need from one to four every time that you apply for a visa).

WEIGHTS & MEASUREMENTS

The metric system is in use throughout Western Europe. However, in Britain non-metric equivalents are used by much of the population (distances continue to be given in miles, and milk and beer are sold in pints not litres). In Germany, cheese and other food items are often sold per *Pfund* (500g).

Continental Europe shows decimals with commas and thousands with full stops (for numbers with four or more digits the French use full stops or spaces).

There's a metric conversion chart on the inside cover of this book.

WOMEN TRAVELLERS

Frustrating though it may be, women travellers continue to face more challenging situations when travelling than men do. If you are a woman traveller, especially a solo woman, it may help to research the status of local women to better understand the responses you illicit from locals. Hopes of travelling inconspicuously, spending time alone and absorbing the surroundings are often thwarted by men who assume a lone woman desires company. Bear in mind that most of this behaviour, which can come across as threatening, is more often than not harmless. Don't let it deter you! The

more women that travel, alone or in pairs or groups, the less attention women will attract and, in time, the more freedom women will feel to gallivant across the globe, *sans* beau in tow.

Women travellers, in general, will find Western Europe relatively enlightened and shouldn't often have to invent husbands that will be joining them soon or boyfriends that will be back any minute. If you do find yourself in an uncomfortable situation or area, jump in a taxi if you possibly can (and worry about the cost later), or pipe up and make a racket. Parts of Portugal, Spain, Italy and Greece remain very conservative, so use your common sense and dress demurely if you want to blend in a little better.

WORK

European countries aren't keen on handing out jobs to foreigners when unemployment rates are what they are in some areas. Officially, an EU citizen is allowed to work in any other EU country, but the paperwork isn't always straightforward for long-term employment and after three months they will probably need to apply for a residency permit.

Other country/nationality combinations require special work permits that can be almost impossible to arrange, especially for temporary work. That doesn't prevent enterprising travellers from topping up their funds occasionally by working in the hotel or restaurant trades at beach or ski resorts or teaching a little English, and they don't always have to do this illegally either.

The UK, for example, issues special 'working holiday' visas to Commonwealth citizens aged between 17 and 30 years, valid for two years. In France you can get a visa for work as an au pair if you are going to follow a recognised course of study (eg a French-language course) and complete all the paperwork before leaving your country. Your national student exchange organisation may be able to arrange temporary work permits to several countries through special programmes. For more details on working as a foreigner, see the individual country directories.

If you have a parent or grandparent who was born in an EU country, you may have certain rights you never knew about. Get in touch with that country's embassy and ask about dual citizenship and work permits – if you go for citizenship, also ask about any obligations, such as military service and residency. Ireland is particularly easy-going about granting citizenship to people with an Irish parent or grandparent, and with an Irish passport, the EU is your oyster. Be aware that your home country may not recognise dual citizenship.

If you do find a temporary job, the pay may be less than that offered to local people. The one big exception is teaching English, but these jobs are hard to come by – at least officially. Other typical tourist jobs (picking grapes in France, washing dishes in Alpine resorts) often come with board and lodging, and the pay is little more than pocket money, but you'll have a good time partying with other travellers.

If you play an instrument or have other artistic talents, you could try working the streets. As every Peruvian pipe player (and his fifth cousin) knows, busking is fairly common in major Western European cities like Amsterdam and Paris, but is illegal in some parts of Switzerland, Austria and the UK. In Belgium and Germany it has been more or less tolerated in the past but crackdowns are not unknown. Most other countries require municipal permits that can be hard to obtain. Talk to other street artists before you start.

Selling goods on the street is generally frowned upon and can be tantamount to vagrancy, apart from at flea markets. It's also a hard way to make money if you're not selling something special. Most countries require permits for this sort of thing. It's fairly common, though officially illegal, in the UK, Germany and Spain.

There are several references and websites that publicise specific positions in Western Europe. **Transitions Abroad** (www.transitionsabroad .com) publishes *Work Abroad: The Complete* *Guide to Finding a Job Overseas* and the *Alternative Travel Directory: The Complete Guide to Traveling, Studying and Living Overseas*, as well as a colour magazine, *Transitions Abroad*. Its website lists paid positions and volunteer and service programmes.

Action Without Borders (www.idealist.org) and **GoAbroad.com** (www.goabroad.com) list hundreds of jobs and volunteer opportunities.

Work Your Way Around the World by Susan Griffith gives good, practical advice on a wide range of issues. Its publisher, **Vacation Work** (www.vacationwork.co.uk), has many other useful titles, including *Summer Jobs Abroad*, edited by David Woodworth.

Working Holidays, published by the **Central Bureau for Educational Visits and Exchanges** (www.britishcouncil.org/learning.htm), is another good source.

Volunteer Work

Organising a volunteer work placement is a great way to gain a deeper insight into local culture. If you're staying with a family, or working alongside local colleagues, you'll probably learn much more about life there than you would if you were travelling through the country.

In some instances volunteers are paid a living allowance, sometimes they work for their keep and other programmes require the volunteer to pay.

There are several Internet sites that can help you search for volunteer work opportunities in Western Europe. As well as websites mentioned earlier, **WorkingAbroad** (www .workingabroad.com) has an excellent website for researching possibilities and applying for positions.

The **International Willing Workers On Organic Farms** (WWOOF; www.wwoof.org) association has organisations all over Western Europe. If you join a WWOOF organisation, you can arrange to live and work on a host's organic farm.

Transport in Western Europe

GETTING THERE & AWAY

Entering Western Europe

Part of the adventure is figuring out how to get to Western Europe, and in these days of severe competition among airlines there are plenty of opportunities to find cheap tickets to a variety of gateway cities.

Unless you can fork out a few thousand for passage on the luxury *Queen Elizabeth 2 (QE2)*, you can pretty much rule out shipping as a means of arriving in Western Europe across the Atlantic – even compared with full-fare air tickets, you and your wallet are much better off.

If you have more than one month for travel, a unique experience is freighter travel (p1070), and it's not as dismal as it sounds – accommodation is usually equivalent to state rooms on cruise ships. Typical journeys from the US to Western Europe are 28 to 35 days transatlantic and 60 to 70 days to the Mediterranean, with an average of US$70 to US$100 per day. Ask about sailing one way and fly-home tickets – otherwise, round-trip passengers have ticket priority. Also look for 'container' rather than 'bulk' freighters, as the latter take more time to unload.

You can take your vehicle for an extra (hefty) fee, but leave Fluffy and Spot at home.

It's a slightly different story if you are travelling from Scandinavia or North Africa, as there are a reasonable number of shipping companies plying these routes. Some travellers still arrive or leave overland – the options being Africa, the Middle East and Asia via Russia on the Trans-Siberian Railway from China.

AIR

Major hubs include Heathrow and Gatwick airports (London); Charles de Gaulle (Paris); Barajas (Spain); Berlin, Frankfurt and Düsseldorf airports (Germany); and Fiumicino airport (Rome). London's airports are probably the cheapest hubs to fly into, and from there you can take any number of low-cost carriers (p1071) throughout Western Europe for as cheap as £0.99.

Always remember to reconfirm your onward or return bookings by the specified time – at least 72 hours before departure on international flights. Otherwise there's a real risk that you'll turn up at the airport only to find that you've missed your flight because it was rescheduled, or that you've been reclassified as a 'no show' and 'bumped'.

Airports & Airlines

From Amsterdam to Zürich, you can find out all you need to know about airports in Western Europe at the **World Airport Guide** (www.worldairportguides.com) website. The following is a list of the most popular international gateways in Western Europe; please see individual country chapters for more specific information.

Amsterdam Airport Schiphol (code AMS; www.schiphol.nl)

Athens International Airport Eleftherios Venizelos (code ATH; www.aia.gr)

Barcelona Airport (code BCN; www.barcelona-airport.com)

Brussels Airport Zaventem (code BRU; www.brusselsairport.be)

Côte d'Azur Airport (Nice) (code NCE; www.nice.aeroport.fr)

Dublin International Airport (code DUB; www.dublin-airport.com)

Düsseldorf International Airport (code DRS; www.duesseldorf-international.de)
Frankfurt Airport (code FRA; www.frankfurt-airport.de)
Geneva International Airport (code GVA; www.gva.ch)
Glasgow International Airport (code GLA; www.baa.co.uk)
Hamburg International Airport (code HAM; www.ham.airport.de)
London Heathrow, Gatwick & Stansted (codes LHR, LGW, STN; www.baa.co.uk)
Madrid-Barajas Airport (code MAD; www.aena.es)
Manchester Airport (code MAN; www.manairport.co.uk)
Munich International Airport (code MUC; www.munich-airport.de)
Paris Orly Airport/Paris Roissy Charles de Gaulle Airport (codes CDG/ORY; www.adp.fr)
Rome Fiumicino Airport (code FCO; www.adr.it)
Zürich Airport (code ZRH; www.zurich-airport.com)

INTERNATIONAL AIRLINES
Aer Lingus (www.aerlingus.com)
Aeroflot (www.aeroflot.com)
Air Canada (www.aircanada.ca)
Air France (www.airfrance.nl)
Air India (www.airindia.com)
Air Malta (www.airmalta.com)
Air New Zealand (www.airnz.com)
Alitalia (www.alitalia.com)
American Airlines (www.aa.com)
Austrian Airlines (www.aua.com)
Belavia (www.belaviashannon.com)
British Airways (www.britishairways.com)
British Midland (www.flybmi.com)
Cathay Pacific (www.cathaypacific.nl)
China Airlines (www.china-airlines.com)
Continental Airlines (www.continental.com)
CSA Czech Airlines (www.csa.cz)
Delta Air Lines (www.delta.com)
El Al (www.elal.com)
Garuda Indonesia (www.garuda-indonesia.nl)
Iberia (www.iberia.com)

Japan Airlines (www.jal-europe.com)
KLM Royal Dutch Airlines (www.klm.nl)
Lufthansa (www.lufthansa.com)
Malaysia Airlines (www.malaysiaairlines.com.my)
Malev Hungarian Airlines (www.malev.hu)
Northwest Airlines (www.nwa.com)
Qantas (www.qantas.com.au)
Singapore Airlines (www.singaporeair.com)
South African Airways (www.flysaa.com)
Swiss International Air Lines (www.swiss.com)
TAP Air Portugal (www.tap-airportugal.pt)
Thai Airways International (www.thaiairways.com)
Transavia (www.transavia.nl)
United Airlines (www.unitedairlines.nl)
Virgin Atlantic (www.virgin-atlantic.com)

Tickets

An air ticket alone can gouge a great slice out of anyone's budget, but you can reduce the cost by digging for discounted fares. Stiff competition has resulted in widespread discounting (which is good news for travellers!) and the only people likely to be paying full fare these days are travellers flying in 1st or business class.

For long-term travel, there are plenty of discount tickets that are valid for 12 months, allowing multiple stopovers with open dates. For short-term travel, cheaper fares are available by travelling midweek, staying away at least one Saturday night or taking advantage of short-lived promotional offers.

The Internet is a great resource for bargain air fares, especially if you already have an idea of where and when you're going. Many airlines, full-service and no-frills, offer some excellent fares to Web surfers. They may sell seats by auction (eg priceline .co.uk in Britain) or simply cut prices to reflect the reduced cost of electronic selling. Online ticket sales work especially well if you are doing a simple one-way or return trip on specified dates. This is where no-frills airlines in northwest Europe come in handy, because they often make one-way tickets available at around half the return fare, meaning that it is easy to put together a return ticket when you fly to one place but leave from another.

Though the convenience of the Internet has unfortunately rendered many travel agents obsolete, there is still something to be said for those folks who know all about special deals, have strategies for avoiding inconvenient stopovers and can offer advice on everything from which airline has the best vegetarian food to the best travel insurance to bundle with your ticket.

The days when some travel agents would routinely fleece travellers by running off with their money are, happily, almost over. Paying by credit card generally offers protection, as most card issuers provide refunds if you can prove you didn't get what you paid for. Similar protection can be obtained by buying a ticket from a bonded agent, such as one covered by the Air Transport Operators Licence (ATOL) scheme in the UK. Agents who only accept cash should hand over the tickets straight away and not tell you to 'come back tomorrow'. After you've made a booking or paid your deposit, call the airline and confirm that the booking was made. It's generally not advisable to send money (even cheques) through the post, unless the agent is very well established – some travellers have reported being ripped off by fly-by-night mail-order ticket agents.

You may decide to pay more than the rock-bottom fare by opting for the safety of a better-known travel agent. Companies such as STA Travel, which has offices worldwide, are not going to disappear overnight and they offer good prices to most destinations.

Airlines only issue refunds to the purchaser of a ticket – usually the travel agent who bought the ticket on your behalf, so if you want a flexible itinerary, think carefully before you buy a ticket that is not easily refundable.

COURIER FLIGHTS

Courier tickets are a great bargain if you're lucky enough to find one. You get cheap passage in return for accompanying packages or documents through customs and delivering them to a representative at the destination airport. You are permitted to bring along a carry-on bag, but that's often all. Be aware that this type of ticket is usually very restricted, so check carefully before purchasing.

Most courier flights only cover the major air routes. They are occasionally advertised in newspapers, or you could contact air-freight companies listed in the phone book.

Travel Unlimited (PO Box 1058, Allston, MA 02134, USA) is a monthly US-based travel newsletter that publishes many courier-flight deals from destinations worldwide. A 12-month subscription costs US$25, or US$35 for readers outside the USA.

The **International Association of Air Travel Couriers** (IAATC; ☎ 308-632-3273; www.courier.org) offers a bimonthly update of air-courier offerings, access to a fax-on-demand service with daily updates of last-minute specials and the bimonthly newsletter *Travel Guide International*. The membership fee is US$45 (US$30 online-subscription only, or US$50 outside the USA).

FREQUENT FLYERS

Most of the airlines offer frequent-flyer deals that can earn you a free air ticket or other goodies. To qualify, you have to accumulate sufficient mileage with the same airline or airline alliance. Many airlines have 'blackout periods', times when you cannot fly for free on your frequent-flyer points (eg Christmas and Chinese New Year). The worst thing about frequent-flyer programmes is that they tend to lock you into one airline, and that airline may not always have the most convenient flight schedule.

SECOND-HAND TICKETS

You'll occasionally see advertisements in youth-hostel bulletin boards and newspapers for second-hand tickets. That is, somebody purchased a return ticket or a ticket with multiple stopovers and now wants to sell the unused portion of the ticket. Unfortunately, these tickets, if used for international travel, are usually worthless, as the name on the ticket must match the name on the passport of the person checking in – and immigration will check again at boarding!

STUDENT & YOUTH FARES

Full-time students and people under 26 have access to better deals than other travellers. The better deals may not always be cheaper fares but can include more flexibility to change flights and/or routes. You have to show a document proving your date of birth, a valid International Student Identity Card (ISIC) or an International Youth Travel Card (IYTC) when buying your ticket and boarding the plane. See www.istc.org for more information.

Africa

Nairobi and Johannesburg are probably the best places in Africa to buy tickets to Europe, thanks to the many bucket shops and the lively competition between them. **STA Travel** (☎ 27 11 482 4666; www.statravel.co.za) in Johannesburg and the **Africa Travel Centre** (☎ 021-423 555) in Cape Town are worth trying for cheap tickets. You're looking at paying approximately R6700 for a flight from Johannesburg to London.

Several West African countries, such as Senegal and the Gambia, offer cheap charter flights to France and London. Charter fares from the UK to Morocco and Tunisia can be quite cheap if you're lucky enough to find a seat.

Asia

Singapore and Bangkok are the discount air fare capitals of Asia. Shop around and ask the advice of other travellers before handing over any money. STA Travel operates branches in Tokyo, Osaka, Singapore, Bangkok and Kuala Lumpur.

In India, tickets may be slightly cheaper from the bucket shops around Delhi's Connaught Pl. Check with other travellers about their current trustworthiness.

Australia

Cheap flights from Australia to Europe generally go via Southeast Asian capitals, involving stopovers at Kuala Lumpur, Bangkok or Singapore. If a long stopover between connections is necessary, transit accommodation is sometimes included in the price of the ticket. If it's at your own expense, it may be worth considering a more expensive ticket.

Quite a few travel offices specialise in discount air tickets. Some travel agents, particularly smaller ones, advertise cheap air fares in the travel sections of weekend newspapers such as the *Age* in Melbourne and the *Sydney Morning Herald*.

Two well-known agents for cheap fares are STA Travel and Flight Centre. **STA Travel** (Australia-wide ☎ 1300 733 035, in Melbourne ☎ 03-8417 6911; www.statravel.com.au; 260 Hoddle St, Abbotsford VIC 3067) has offices in all major cities and on many university campuses, and **Flight Centre** (Australia-wide ☎ 133 133; www.flightcentre.com.au; 82 Elizabeth St, Sydney NSW 2000) has over 100 offices throughout Australia.

Thai, Malaysia, Qantas and Singapore air fares range from about A$1300 (low season) to A$2500. All have frequent promotional fares, so it pays to check newspapers daily.

Flights to/from Perth are a couple of hundred dollars cheaper.

Another option for travellers wanting to go to Britain between November and February is to hook up with a charter flight returning to Britain. These low-season, one-way fares do have restrictions, but may work out to be considerably cheaper. Ask your travel agent.

Canada

Canadian discount air fare agents are also known as consolidators and their fares tend to be about 10% higher than those sold in the USA. The *Globe & Mail*, *Toronto Star*, *Montreal Gazette* and *Vancouver Sun* carry travel agents' ads and are a good place to look for cheap fares.

Travel CUTS (☎ 1-866-246-9762; www.travelcuts.com) is Canada's national student travel agency and has offices in all major cities.

Airhitch (see From the USA following) has stand-by fares to major European cities from Toronto, Montreal and Vancouver.

New Zealand

As in Australia, **STA Travel** (☎ 0508 782 872; www.statravel.com.au) and **Flight Centre** (☎ 0800 24 35 44; www.flightcentre.co.nz) are popular travel agents in New Zealand. The cheapest fares to Europe are routed through Asia. A discounted return flight to London from Auckland costs around NZ$2000.

The USA

Discount travel agents in the USA are known as consolidators. San Francisco is the ticket consolidator capital of America, although some cheap deals can be found in Los Angeles, New York and other big cities. Consolidators can be found through the *Yellow Pages* or major daily newspapers.

The *New York Times*, *LA Times*, *Chicago Tribune* and *San Francisco Chronicle* all have weekly travel sections in which you'll find any number of travel agents' ads. **STA Travel** (☎ 800-781-4040; www.statravel.com) is America's largest student-travel organisation, having incorporated its competition, Council Travel, and it has offices in major cities.

You should be able to fly from New York to London or Paris and back for no more than US$400 to US$500 in the low season (from December to February, prices have been known to drop to $99 one way between

New York and London) and about US$500 to US$850 in the high season. Equivalent fares from the west coast are US$100 to US$300 higher.

On a stand-by basis, one-way fares can work out to be remarkably cheap. New York-based **Airhitch** (www.airhitch.org) can get you to/from Europe for US$194/206/228/262 each way from the east coast/southeast/midwest/west coast.

Another option is a courier flight (see p1068). A New York–London return ticket can be had for as little as US$210 in the low season.

LAND
Overland Trails

In the early 1980s, the overland trail to/from Asia lost much of its popularity as the Islamic regime in Iran made life difficult for most independent travellers.

Despite the fact that in recent years Iran appears to be rediscovering the merits of tourism, the conflict in Afghanistan and unsettled conditions in southern Pakistan and northwest India will prevent the trickle of travellers turning into a flood for the time being.

Discounting the complicated Middle East route via Egypt, Jordan, Syria, Turkey and Eastern Europe, going to/from Africa involves a Mediterranean ferry crossing (p1070). Due to unrest in Africa, the most feasible overland routes through that continent have all but closed down.

Travelling by private transport beyond Western Europe requires plenty of paperwork and other preparations. A detailed description is beyond the scope of this book.

Train

It's possible to travel to most Western European destinations from many other parts of Europe, as well as from both Morocco and Turkey, via the **Inter-Rail** (www.raileurope.co.uk) network.

It *is* possible to get to Western Europe by rail from Central and eastern Asia, but count on spending at least eight days doing it. Four different routes wind their way to Moscow: the Trans-Siberian (9297km from Vladivostok), the Trans-Mongolian (7860km from Beijing) and the Trans-Manchurian (9001km from Beijing) all use the same tracks across Siberia but have different routes

east of Lake Baikal. The Trans-Kazakhstan (another Trans-Siberian line) runs between Moscow and Urumqi in northwestern China. Prices vary enormously, depending on where you buy the ticket and what is included – advertised 2nd-class fares cost around UK£549 from Beijing to Moscow. Websites worth consulting for Trans-Siberian packages include:

www.finnsov.fi
www.monkeyshrine.com
www.regent-holidays.co.uk
www.trans-siberian.co.uk

There are countless travel options between Moscow and Western Europe. Most people will opt for the train, usually to Berlin, Munich or Vienna. Lonely Planet's *Trans-Siberian Railway* is a comprehensive guide to the route with details of costs, highlights and travel agencies that specialise in the trip.

SEA
Mediterranean Ferries

There are many ferries crossing the Mediterranean between Africa and Western Europe. The ferry you take will depend on your travels in Africa, but the options include: Spain–Morocco, France–Morocco, France–Tunisia, Italy–Tunisia. There are also ferries between Greece and Israel via Cyprus.

Ferries are often filled to capacity in summer, especially to/from Tunisia, so it's advisable to book well in advance if you're taking a vehicle across. See the Transport section in the relevant country chapters.

Passenger Ships & Freighters

Regular long-distance passenger ships disappeared with the advent of cheap air travel and were replaced by a small number of luxury cruise ships.

Cunard's *QE2* sails between New York and Southampton 20 times a year; the trip takes six nights each way and costs around US$4000 for the return trip in a standard double cabin, though there are also one-way and 'fly one-way' deals.

A more adventurous alternative is as a paying passenger on a freighter. Freighters are far more numerous than cruise ships and there are many more routes from which to choose. *Travel by Cargo Ship* (published by Cadogan) is a useful resource. Passenger freighters typically carry six to 12 passengers (more than 12 would require a doctor on board) and, though less luxurious than dedicated cruise ships, give you a real taste of life at sea.

Schedules tend to be flexible and costs hover around US$100 a day; vehicles can often be included for an additional fee.

GETTING AROUND

Travel within most of the EU, whether by air, rail or car, has been made easier following the Schengen Agreement, which abolished border controls between signed-up states. All travellers must still carry a passport, however there are now two passport-control lines – EU and non-EU nationals. This was designed to speed up entries for EU nationals. Britain, Ireland, Switzerland and Liechtenstein are the only EU countries currently outside the agreement.

AIR

Air travel is best viewed as a means to get you to the starting point of your itinerary rather than as your main means of travel. It lacks the flexibility of ground transport and generally can be expensive for short trips, unless you use no-frills airlines, which operate routes from the UK to most countries in continental Europe, though they sometimes use smaller, less convenient airports.

London is a good centre for picking up cheap, restricted-validity tickets. Amsterdam and Athens are other good places for finding discount tickets in Western Europe. For more information, see the Transport sections of the country chapters. Some airlines, such as UK-based **easyJet** (www.easyjet .com), **Ryanair** (www.ryanair.com) and **Virgin Express** (www.virgin-express.com) give discounts for tickets purchased on the Internet. So-called 'open-jaw returns', by which you can travel into one city and exit from another, are worth considering, though they sometimes work out to be more expensive than simple returns. In the UK, **Trailfinders** (☎ 020-7937 1234; www.trailfinders.co.uk) and **STA Travel** (☎ 020-7361 6161; www.statravel.co.uk) can give you tailor-made versions of these tickets. Your chosen cities don't necessarily have to be in the same country. STA Travel sells tickets to all travellers but caters especially to young people and students. Other travel agencies include **Bridge the World** (☎ 0870 444 7474; 4 Regent Pl, London W1R 5FB) and **Flightbookers** (☎ 020-7757 2000; 177-178 Tottenham Court Rd, London W1P 9LF).

If you are travelling alone, courier flights are a possibility. You get cheap passage in return for accompanying packages or documents through customs and then delivering them to a representative at the destination airport. EU integration and electronic communications mean there's increasingly less call for couriers, but you might find something. British Airways, for example, offers courier flights through the **Travel Shop** (☎ 0870 606 1133).

Across Europe, many travel agencies have ties with STA Travel, where cheap tickets can be purchased and STA Travel–issued tickets can be altered (usually for a US$25 fee). Outlets include **Voyages Wasteels** (☎ 08 03 88 70 04; 11 rue Dupuytren, 75006 Paris) and **STA Travel** (☎ 030-311 0950; Goethestrasse 73, 10625 Berlin). See the individual country chapters for more information on travel agencies and getting to and from countries in Western Europe.

Getting between airports and city centres is rarely a problem in Western Europe due to effective public transport networks, though it can be rather time-consuming in large cities such as Paris and London.

Airlines in Western Europe

The prevalence of low-cost carriers in Western Europe makes it extremely easy to flit from country to country on the cheap – there's **Virgin Express** (www.virgin-express.com) in Brussels, **easyJet** (www.easyjet.com) in London, **Flybaboo** (www.flybaboo.com) in Geneva and **Flyeco** (www.flyeco.com) in Paris to name a few. Ryanair is the best option for cheap intra-European fares; it has hubs in 11 European cities. Typical fares range from London–Berlin (€3.99) to Shannon–Brussels (€14.99). The only catch for flying with these low-cost carriers is that flights leave from secondary airports such as London's Luton, Berlin's Schonefeld, and Rome's Ciampino. See individual country chapters for regional inter-European airlines.

Air Passes

The **Europebyair FlightPass** (www.europebyair.com) allows US, Canadian, Australian and New Zealand travellers one-way non-stop fares throughout Europe for only US$99, with no blackout dates. Passes are good for 120 days.

The **British Midland Discover Europe Airpass** (www.flybmi.com/bmi/en-gb/planandbook/tourEurope .aspx) allows non-European travellers a two-tiered travel pass, with reservations required only for the first sector and no limit on the amount of flights purchased.

The **Star Alliance European Airpass** (www.star alliance.com) offers between three and 10 flight passes starting at US$65, but cities can only be visited once (unless travellers are changing flights).

The **Air France Euro-Flyer Pass** (www.airfrance.com) allows the purchase of three to nine flight passes to be used within a two-month period; fares start at US$99 off-peak and US$120 peak period.

Most passes need to be purchased in the US and require an originating international flight. Check the Transport sections in individual countries for more information.

BICYCLE

A tour of Western Europe by bike may seem like a daunting prospect but help is at hand. The **Cyclists' Touring Club** (CTC; ☎ 0870 873 0060; www.ctc.org.uk; Cotterell House, 69 Meadrow, Godalming, Surrey GU7 3HS) is based in the UK and offers its members an information service on all matters associated with cycling (including cycling conditions, detailed routes, itineraries and maps). If CTC is not able to answer your questions, the chances are it will know someone who can. Membership costs UK£11/30.50/18.75 for under 25/adults/65 and over.

The key to a successful trip is to travel light. What you carry should be largely determined by your destination and type of trip you're taking. Even for the shortest and most basic trip it's worth carrying the tools necessary for repairing a puncture. Other things you might want to consider packing are spare brake and gear cables, spanners, Allen keys, spare spokes of the correct length and strong adhesive tape.

The wearing of helmets is not compulsory but is certainly advised. A seasoned cyclist can average about 80km a day, but this depends on the terrain and how much weight you are carrying. Don't overdo it – there's no point in burning yourself out during the initial stages.

For more information on cycling, see p1052 and the Activities section of individual country chapters.

Purchase

For major cycling tours, it's best to have a bike you're familiar with, so consider bringing your own rather than buying on arrival. If you can't be bothered with the hassle, there are plenty of places to buy in Western Europe (shops sell new and second-hand bicycles or you can check local papers for private vendors). Note that you will require a specialist bicycle shop for a machine capable of withstanding touring. CTC can provide members with a leaflet about purchasing bicycles. Cycling is very popular in the Netherlands and Germany, and these are good places to pick up a well-equipped touring bicycle. European prices are quite high (certainly higher than in North America), but non-Europeans should be able to claim back VAT on the purchase.

Rental

It is easy to rent bicycles in Western Europe and you can often negotiate good deals. Rental periods vary. Local tourist offices will carry information on rental outlets. Occasionally you can drop the bicycle off at a different location so you don't have to double back on your route. See individual country chapters for more details.

Transporting a Bicycle

If you want to bring your bicycle to Western Europe, you should be able to take it with you on the plane relatively easily. You can either take it apart and pack everything in a bike bag or box, or simply wheel it to the check-in desk, where it should be treated as a piece of luggage. You may have to remove the pedals and turn the handlebars sideways so that it takes up less space in the aircraft's hold; check with the airline well in advance, ie before you pay for your ticket. If your bicycle and other luggage exceed your weight allowance, ask about alternatives or you may suddenly find yourself being charged a fortune for excess baggage.

Within Western Europe, bikes can usually be transported as luggage on slower trains, subject to a small supplementary fee. But call ahead because certain countries, such as Portugal, restrict bicycles on trains. See the Transport section in the individual country chapters.

Fast trains can rarely accommodate bikes: they might need to be sent as registered luggage and may end up on a different train from the one you take. This is often the case in France and Spain. Eurostar charges UK£20 to send a bike as registered luggage on its routes. You can transport your bicycle with you on Eurotunnel through the Channel Tunnel.

The UK-based **Bike Express** (☎ 01642-251 440; www.bike-express.co.uk) is a coach service where cyclists can travel with their bicycles. It runs in the summer from northeast England to France, Italy and Spain, with pick-up/drop-off points en route. The maximum return fare is UK£184 (£10 off for CTC members).

BOAT
Ferry
Several ferry companies compete on all the main ferry routes, and the resulting service is comprehensive but complicated. The same ferry company can have a host of different prices for the same route, depending upon the time of day or year, the validity of the ticket or the length of your vehicle. It is worth planning (and booking) ahead where possible as there may be special reductions on off-peak crossings and advance-purchase tickets. Most ferry companies adjust prices according to the level of demand (so-called 'fluid' or 'dynamic' pricing), so it may pay to offer alternative travel dates. Vehicle tickets usually include the driver and a full complement of passengers.

P&O Stena Line is one of the largest ferry companies in the world. It serves British, Irish and some Scandinavian routes. P&O Portsmouth and Brittany Ferries sail direct between England and northern Spain (24 hours to 35 hours). The shortest cross-Channel route is Dover to Calais (also the busiest), though there is now great competition from the Channel Tunnel. You can book ferry tickets online (often at a discount) at the following websites:

www.brittany-ferries.com
www.poportsmouth.com
www.posl.com
www.seafrance.com

Hoverspeed (☎ 0870 240 8070; www.hoverspeed.co.uk) is the quickest form of transport on the main ferry routes – Dover to Calais takes one hour – yet it is competitively priced.

Italy (Brindisi or Bari) to Greece (Corfu, Igoumenitsa and Patra) is also a popular route. The Greek islands are connected to the mainland and each other by a spider's web of routings; see the Greece chapter for details about inter-island routes.

Rail-pass holders are entitled to discounts or free travel on some lines. Food on ferries is often expensive (and lousy), so bring your own when possible. It is also worth knowing that if you take your vehicle on board, you are usually denied access to it during the voyage.

Steamer
Europe's main lakes and rivers are served by steamers and, as you'd expect, schedules are more extensive in summer. Rail-pass holders are entitled to some discounts. Extended boat trips should be considered as relaxing and scenic excursions; viewed merely as a functional means of transport, they can be very expensive.

Long cruises are possible in the Mediterranean and along Europe's rivers; however you'll need a boatload of cash. Since the early 1990s the Danube has been connected to the Rhine by the Main-Danube Canal in Germany. In the USA, **Viking River Cruises** (☎ 877-668-4546; www.vikingrivercruises.com) offers 12-day cruises along this route, from Vienna to Amsterdam, between May and November. In Britain, you can make bookings through **Noble Caledonia** (☎ 0207-752 0000; www.noble-caledonia.co.uk). See also p52 for river cruises.

BUS
Buses have the edge in terms of costs, sometimes quite substantially, but are generally slower and less comfortable. Europe's biggest network of international buses is provided by a group of bus companies that operates under the name of **Eurolines** (www.eurolines.com).

See the Transport section in the individual country chapters for more information about long-distance buses.

Bus Passes
Following is a list of Eurolines representatives (who may also be able to advise you on other bus companies and deals).

Deutsche-Touring (☎ 069-79 03 50; Am Römerhof 17, Frankfurt)
Eurolines Austria (☎ 01-712 04 53; Autobusbahnhof Wien-Mitte, Landstrasse Hauptstrasse, 1030 Vienna)
Eurolines France (☎ 08-36 69 52 52; Gare Routière Internationale, 28 Ave du Général de Gaulle, 75020 Paris)

Eurolines Italy (☎ 064 40 40 09; Ciconvallazione Nonentana 574, Lato Stazione Tiburtina, Rome)
Eurolines Nederland (☎ 020-560 87 88; Rokin 10, 1012 KR Amsterdam)
Eurolines UK (☎ 0870 514 3219; 52 Grosvenor Gardens, London SW1)

Eurolines UK has six circular explorer routes, always starting and ending in London (no youth or senior discounts). These are popular mini-passes. London–Brussels–Paris–London for UK£55; London–Dublin–Belfast–London for UK£57.

Eurolines also offers longer passes. They're cheaper than rail passes, but not as extensive or as flexible. They cover 35 cities as far spread as Oslo, Bucharest, Rome and Madrid. Most trips must be international, though a few internal journeys are possible between major cities in France, Germany, Spain, Austria and Italy. Costs (for adults/youths and seniors) are: 15-day pass low season UK£149/129, high season UK£195/165; 30-day pass low season UK£209/169, high season UK£290/235; 60-day pass low season UK£265/211, high season UK£333/259.

On ordinary return trips, people aged under 26 years and over 60 years also pay less. For example, a London–Munich return ticket costs UK£83 for adults or UK£75 for youths and seniors. Return tickets are valid for six months. Know where you're going a month in advance? Eurolines' 'Promo 30' fares are considerably cheaper, usually by at least £20. Check the website under 'Special Offer' for more information. Euro prices are also available online or via telephone at the time of booking.

Busabout (UK ☎ 020-7950 1661; www.busabout .com; 258 Vauxhall Bridge Rd, Victoria, London SW1, England) operates buses that complete set circuits around Europe, stopping at major cities. You get unlimited travel per sector and can 'hop-on, hop-off' at any scheduled stop, then resume with a later bus. Buses are often oversubscribed, so prebook each sector to avoid being stranded.

Departures are every two days from April to October, or May to September for Spain and Portugal. The circuits cover all countries in continental Western Europe, and you can pay to add on Greece, Scandinavia and/or a London–Paris link.

Busabout's Consecutive Pass allows unlimited travel within the given time period.

A one-month pass costs €589 for adults or €519 for students and those under 26. Passes are also available for 14 days, 21 days, two or three months or for the whole season. The Flexipass allows you to select travel days during the season, which runs from 1 May through to 31 October.

Eight days will cost €419/379 adult/under 26, while 20 days is €879/789.

National Buses
Domestic buses provide a viable alternative to the rail network in most countries. Again, they are usually slightly cheaper and somewhat slower than trains. Buses tend to be best for shorter hops, such as getting around cities and reaching remote villages. They are often the only option in mountainous regions. Advance reservations are rarely necessary. On many city buses you usually buy your ticket in advance from a kiosk or machine and validate it on entering.

See the individual country chapters and city sections for more details on local buses.

Reservations
Because of the frequency of buses throughout Western Europe, it's not necessary to make reservations unless you plan on travelling during holidays, summer weekends and regional festivals.

CAR & MOTORCYCLE
Travelling with your own vehicle allows increased flexibility and the option to get off the beaten track. Unfortunately, cars can be inconvenient in city centres when you have to negotiate one-way streets or find somewhere to park amid a confusing concrete jungle. Various car-carrying trains (motorail) can help you avoid long, tiring drives. Eurotunnel (see Train p255 and p391) transports cars through the Channel Tunnel.

Automobile Associations
Perish the thought of ever breaking down in some remote rural village in the Pyrenees or the isolated Irish countryside. But it happens. Should you find yourself in a predicament, you can contact the local automobile association for emergency assistance. It can provide a variety of road-side services such as petrol refills, flat-tyre repair and towing, plus predeparture information such as maps, itineraries and even accommodation reservations.

In Britain, the **RAC** (UK ☎ 0870 572 2722; www.rac
.co.uk) offers a European Motoring Assistance
policy for UK£12. See the Transport section
in country chapters for other associations.

Camper Van

A popular way to tour Europe is for three
or four people to band together to buy or
rent a camper van. London is the usual embarkation point. Look at the advertisements
in London's free *TNT* magazine if you wish
to form or join a group. *TNT* is also a good
source for purchasing a van, as is the colourful *Loot* newspaper.

Some second-hand dealers offer a buy-
back scheme for when you return from the
Continent, but we've received warnings
that some dealers don't fully honour their
refund commitments. Buying and reselling
privately should be more advantageous if
you have the time.

Camper vans usually feature a fixed high-
top or elevating roof and two to five bunk
beds. Apart from the essential gas cooker,
professional conversions may include a sink,
fridge and built-in cupboards. Prices and
facilities vary considerably and it's certainly
worth getting advice from a mechanic to see
if you are being offered a fair price. Getting
a mechanical check (from UK£35) is also a
good idea. Once on the road you should be
able to keep budgets lower than backpackers using trains, but don't forget to set some
money aside for emergency repairs.

The main advantage of going by camper
van is flexibility. Transport, accommodation
and storage are all taken care of. Unfortunately, the self-contained factor can also
prove to be one of the downsides. Conditions
can get very cramped, tempers can become
frayed and your romantic, hippy-style trail
may dissolve into the camper van trip from
hell. Other disadvantages include having to
leave your gear inside when you are exploring. Invest in good locks and try to keep the
inside tidy, with your belongings stored away
at all times.

Driving Licence

Proof of ownership of a private vehicle
should always be carried (a Vehicle Registration Document for British-registered cars)
when touring Europe. An EU driving licence
is acceptable for driving throughout Europe. However, old-style green UK licences
are no good for Spain or Italy, and in Austria this should be backed up by a German
translation.

Many non-European driving licences are
valid in Europe, but it's still a good idea to
bring along an International Driving Permit
(IDP), which can make life much simpler,
especially when hiring cars and motorcycles. Basically a multilingual translation of
the vehicle class and personal details that
are noted on your local driving licence, an
IDP is not valid unless it is accompanied
by your original licence. An IDP can be obtained for a fairly small fee from your local
automobile association – take a passport
photo and a valid licence.

Fuel

Fuel prices can vary enormously from country to country (though it's always more expensive than in North America or Australia)
and may bear little relation to the general
cost of living. For up-to-date prices across
Europe go to www.theaa.com/allaboutcars
/fuel or contact motoring organisations such
as the **RAC** (☎ 0870 572 2722) in Britain for more
details.

Unleaded petrol is available throughout
most of Western Europe. Diesel is usually
significantly cheaper, though the difference is only marginal in Britain, Ireland
and Switzerland.

Hire

The big international rental firms will give
you reliable service and a good standard of
vehicle. Usually you will have the option of
returning the car to a different outlet at the
end of the rental period. Prebook for the
lowest rates – if you walk into an office and
ask for a car on the spot, you will pay over
the odds, even allowing for special weekend deals. Fly/drive combinations and other
programmes are worth looking into. You
should be able to make advance reservations
at the websites of the following companies:

Avis (www.avis.com)
Budget (www.budget.com)
Europcar (www.europcar.com)
Hertz (www.hertz.com)

Brokers can cut hire costs. **Holiday Autos** (UK
☎ 0870 400 0010; www.holidayautos.com) has low rates
and offices or representatives in over 20
countries. In the USA call **Kemwel Holiday Autos**

(☎ 877-820 0668; www.kemwel.com). In the UK, a competitor with even lower prices is **Autos Abroad** (☎ 0870 066 7788; www.autosabroad.co.uk).

If you want to rent a car and haven't prebooked, look for national or local firms, which can often undercut the big companies. Nevertheless, you need to be wary of dodgy deals where they take your money and point you towards some clapped-out wreck.

No matter where you rent, it is imperative to understand exactly what is included in your rental agreement (collision waiver, unlimited mileage etc). Make sure you are covered with an adequate insurance policy. Ask in advance if you are allowed to drive a rented car across borders, such as from Germany (where hire prices are low) to Austria (where they're high).

The minimum rental age is usually 21 or even 23, and you'll probably need a credit card. Note that prices at airport rental offices are usually higher than at branches in the city centre.

Motorcycle and moped rental is common in such countries as Italy, Spain, Greece and the south of France. Sadly, it's also common to see inexperienced riders leap on rented bikes and very quickly fall off them again, leaving a layer or two of skin on the road in the process.

Insurance

Third party motor insurance is compulsory in Europe. Most UK motor insurance policies automatically provide this for EU countries. Get your insurer to issue a Green Card (which may cost extra), an internationally recognised proof of insurance, and check that it lists all the countries you intend to visit. You'll need this in the event of an accident outside the country where the vehicle is insured. Also ask your insurer for a European Accident Statement form, which can simplify things if the worst happens. Never sign statements you can't read or understand – insist on a translation and sign that only if it's acceptable. For non-EU countries make sure you check the requirements with your insurer – a locally acquired motorcycle licence, for example, is not valid under some policies.

For further advice and more detailed information, contact the **Association of British Insurers** (☎ 020-600 3333; www.abi.org.uk). A reader also recommended **Down Under Insurance** (UK

☎ 020-7402 9211; www.downunderinsurance.co.uk) for European cover.

It's a good investment to take out a European motoring-assistance policy, such as the AA Five Star Service or the RAC European Motoring Assistance. Expect to pay about UK£50 for 14 days' cover, with a 10% discount for association members. Non-Europeans might find it cheaper to arrange international coverage with their national motoring organisation before leaving home. Ask your motoring organisation for details about free services offered by affiliated organisations around Western Europe.

Every vehicle travelling across an international border should display a sticker showing its country of registration. A warning triangle, to be used in the event of breakdown, is compulsory almost everywhere. Some recommended accessories are a first-aid kit (compulsory in Greece), a spare-bulb kit (compulsory in Spain) and a fire extinguisher (compulsory in Greece). Bail bonds are not required for Spain. In the UK, contact **RAC** (☎ 0870 5533 533; www.rac.co.uk) or **AA** (☎ 0800 085 7240) for more information.

Leasing

Leasing a vehicle has none of the hassles of purchasing and can work out considerably cheaper than hiring over longer periods. The **Renault Eurodrive scheme** (www.franceatleisure .com/renault_eurodrive.asp) provides new cars for non-EU residents for a period of between 17 and 170 days. Under this arrangement, a Renault Clio 1.5 for 24 days, for example, would cost UK£531 (if picked up/dropped off in France), including insurance and road-side assistance. Check out the options before leaving home. In the USA, Kemwel Holiday Autos (☎ 877-820 0668; www.kemwel .com) arranges European leasing deals.

Motorcycle Touring

Western Europe is made for motorcycle touring, with good-quality winding roads, stunning scenery and an active motorcycling scene. The weather is not always reliable though, so make sure your wet-weather gear is up to scratch. The wearing of helmets for rider and passenger is compulsory everywhere in Western Europe. See country chapters for additional rules.

On ferries, motorcyclists can sometimes be squeezed in without a reservation, al-

TRANSPORT IN WESTERN EUROPE

though booking ahead is certainly advisable during peak travelling periods. Take note of local custom about parking motorcycles on footpaths (sidewalks). Though this is illegal in some countries, the police usually turn a blind eye as long as the vehicle doesn't obstruct pedestrians. Don't try this in Britain – your feeble excuses to traffic wardens will fall on deaf ears.

If you are thinking of touring Europe on a motorcycle, try contacting the **British Motorcyclists Federation** (☎ 0116-254 8818; www.betterbiking.co.uk) for help and advice. An excellent source of information for travellers interested in more adventurous biking activities can be found at **Horizons Unlimited** (www.horizonsunlimited.com).

Purchase

Britain is probably the best place to buy as second-hand prices are good and, whether buying privately or from a dealer, the absence of language difficulties will help you establish exactly what you are getting and what guarantees you can expect in the event of a breakdown.

Some good Britain papers to check out for vehicle purchases are **Loot** (www.loot.com), **TNT magazine** (www.tntmag.co.uk/uk) and **AutoTrader** (www.autotrader.co.uk).

Bear in mind that you will be getting a car with the steering wheel on the right-hand side in Britain. If you want left-hand drive and can afford to buy new, prices are usually reasonable in Greece, France, Germany, Belgium, Luxembourg and the Netherlands. Paperwork can be tricky wherever you buy, and many countries have compulsory roadworthiness checks on older vehicles.

Road Conditions

Conditions and types of roads vary across Western Europe, but it is possible to make some generalisations. The fastest routes are four- or six-lane dual carriageways/highways, ie two or three lanes either side (motorway, autobahn, autoroute, autostrada etc). These roads are great for speed and comfort but driving can be dull, with little or no interesting scenery. Some of these roads incur tolls (eg in Italy, France and Spain) or have a general tax for usage (Switzerland and Austria), but there will usually be an alternative route you can take. Motorways and other primary routes are almost always in good condition.

Road surfaces on minor routes are not perfect in some countries (eg Greece), although normally they will be more than adequate. These roads are narrower and progress is generally much slower. To compensate, you can expect much better scenery and plenty of interesting villages along the way.

Road Rules

Motoring organisations can supply members with country-by-country information about motoring regulations, or they may produce motoring guidebooks for general sale. The **RAC** (UK ☎ 0870 5533 533; ww.rac.co.uk) provides comprehensive and destination-specific notes offering a summary of national road rules and regulations.

With the exception of Britain and Ireland, driving is on the right. Vehicles brought over from either of these countries should have their headlights adjusted to avoid blinding oncoming traffic at night (a simple solution on older headlight lenses is to cover up a triangular section of the lens with tape). Priority is usually given to traffic approaching from the right in countries that drive on the right-hand side.

Take care with speed limits, as they vary from country to country. You may be surprised at the apparent disregard of traffic regulations in some places (particularly in Italy and Greece), but as a visitor it is always best to be cautious. In many countries, driving infringements are subject to an on-the-spot fine. Always ask for a receipt.

European drink-driving laws are particularly strict. The blood-alcohol concentration (BAC) limit when driving is between 0.05% and 0.08%, but in certain areas it can be *zero* percent. See the individual country chapters for more details on traffic laws.

HITCHING

Hitching is never entirely safe in any country in the world, and we don't recommend it. Travellers who decide to hitch should understand that they are taking a small but potentially serious risk. People who do choose to hitch will be safer if they travel in pairs and let someone know where they plan to go.

Hitching can be the most rewarding and frustrating way of getting around. Rewarding because you get to meet and interact with local people and are forced into unplanned detours that may yield unexpected highlights off the beaten track. Frustrating because you may get stuck on the side of the road to nowhere with nowhere (or nowhere cheap) to stay. Then it begins to rain…

That said, hitchers can end up making good time, but obviously your plans need to be flexible in case a trick of the light makes you appear invisible to passing motorists. A man and woman travelling together is probably the best combination. Two or more men must expect some delays; two women together will make good time and should be relatively safe. A woman hitching on her own is taking a big risk, particularly in parts of southern Europe.

Don't try to hitch from city centres; take public transport to suburban exit routes. Hitching is usually illegal on motorways (freeways) – stand on the slip roads or approach drivers at petrol stations and truck stops. Look presentable and cheerful and make a cardboard sign indicating your intended destination in the local language. Never hitch where drivers can't stop in good time or without causing an obstruction. At dusk, give up and think about finding somewhere to stay. If your itinerary includes a ferry crossing (for instance, across the Channel), it might be worth trying to score a ride before the ferry rather than after, since vehicle tickets sometimes include all passengers free of charge. This also applies to Eurotunnel through the Channel Tunnel.

It is sometimes possible to arrange a lift in advance: scan student notice boards in colleges, or contact car-sharing agencies. Such agencies are particularly popular in Germany (*Mitfahrzentrale*; see Car & Motorcycle p530).

For general facts, destination-based information and ride-share options, www.bug europe.com may be helpful. The useful www.hitchhikers.org connects hitchhikers and drivers worldwide.

LOCAL TRANSPORT
Metro & Bus

Many Western European cities have excellent subway systems, making it extremely easy and affordable to get around. Buses are also convenient for getting around, and are more flexible when choosing destinations since they travel not only around the cities, but to outlying towns and on to other countries.

Taxi

Taxis in Western Europe are metered and rates are high. There might also be supplements (depending on the country) for things such as luggage, the time of day, the location from which you boarded and for extra passengers. Good bus, rail and underground (subway/metro) railway networks make the use of taxis all but unnecessary, but if you need one in a hurry they can usually be found idling near train stations or outside big hotels.

Lower fares make taxis more viable in such countries as Spain, Greece and Portugal. Don't underestimate the local knowledge that can be gleaned from taxi drivers. They can often tell you about the liveliest places in town and know all about events happening during your stay.

TOURS

Package tours, whether tailor-made or bog-standard, cater for all tastes, interests and ages. See your travel agent or look in the small ads in newspaper travel pages. The Internet is also an excellent resource to find unusual tours that might not receive media or trade attention.

Specialists include **Ramblers Holidays** (☎ 017 07-331133; www.ramblersholidays.co.uk) in Britain for hiking trips and **CBT Tours** (☎ 800-736-2453; www .cbttours.com) in the USA for bicycle trips.

Young revellers can party on Europe-wide bus tours. **Contiki** (☎ 020-8290 6777; www.contiki .com) and **Top Deck** (☎ 020-8879 6789; www.topdeck travel.co.uk) offer camping or hotel-based bus tours for the 18 to 35 age group. The duration of Contiki's tours are five to 46 days. Both companies have London offices, as well as offices or representatives in Europe, North America, Australasia and South Africa.

For people aged over 50, **Saga Holidays** (www .sagaholidays.com) offers holidays ranging from cheap coach tours to luxury cruises and has cheap travel insurance. There's a **UK office** (☎ 0800 096 0074; Saga Bldg, Middelburg Sq, Folkestone, Kent CT20 1AZ, England) and a **US office** (☎ 800-343-0273; 1161 Boylston St, Boston, MA 02115).

National tourist offices in most countries offer organised trips to points of interest. These may range from one-hour city tours to several-day circular excursions. They often work out more expensive than going it alone, but are sometimes worth it if you're pressed for time.

A short city tour will give you a quick overview of the place and can be a good way to begin your visit.

TRAIN

Trains are a popular way of getting around: they are comfortable, frequent and generally on time. The Channel Tunnel makes it possible to get from Britain to continental Europe using the **Eurostar** (www.eurostar.com). See p255 and p391 for more details.

In such countries as Spain, Portugal and (to some extent) Italy, fares are reasonably low; in others, European rail passes make travel more affordable. Supplements and reservation costs are not covered by passes, and pass holders must always carry their passport for identification purposes.

If you plan to travel extensively by train, it might be worth getting hold of the *Thomas Cook European Timetable*, which gives a complete listing of train schedules and indicates where supplements apply or where reservations are necessary. The timetable is updated monthly and is available from **Thomas Cook** (www.thomascooktimetables.com) outlets and bookshops in the UK (online only in the USA). In Australia, bookshops can usually order copies if none are in stock.

If you intend to do a lot of train travel in one or a handful of countries – Benelux, say – it might be worthwhile getting hold of the national timetables that are published by the state railroads. Check out the **European Rail Guide** (www.europeanrailguide.com) website for current timetables and fares.

Paris, Amsterdam, Munich, Milan and Vienna are important hubs for international rail connections. See the relevant city sections for details and budget ticket agents.

Note that European trains sometimes split en route in order to service two destinations, so even if you know you're on the right train, make sure you're in the correct carriage too.

Cheap Tickets

European rail passes are only worth buying if you plan to do a reasonable amount of intercountry travelling within a short space of time. Plan your itinerary carefully. Don't overdo the overnight travelling; although it can work out to be a great way of saving time and money, you don't want to be too tired to enjoy the next day of sightseeing.

When weighing up options, consider the cost of other cheap ticket deals, including advance-purchase reductions, one-off promotions or special circular-route tickets. Normal international tickets are valid for two months, and you can make as many stops as you like en route; make your intentions known when purchasing and inform train conductors how far you're going before they punch your ticket.

Express Trains

Fast trains, or those that make few stops, are identified by the symbols EC (EuroCity) or IC (InterCity). The French TGV, Spanish AVE and German ICE trains are even faster. Supplements can apply on fast trains, and it is a good idea (sometimes obligatory) to make seat reservations at peak times and on certain lines.

Overnight Trains

These trains will usually offer a choice of couchette or sleeper if you don't fancy sleeping in your seat with somebody else's elbow in your ear. Again, reservations are advisable as sleeping options are allocated on a first-come, first-served basis.

Couchette bunks are comfortable enough, if lacking a bit in privacy. There are four per compartment in 1st class or six in 2nd class. A bunk costs around UK£15 for most international trains, irrespective of the length of the journey.

Sleepers are the most comfortable option, offering beds for one or two passengers in 1st class, and two or three passengers in 2nd class. Charges vary depending on the journey, but they are significantly more expensive than couchettes. Most long-distance trains have a dining (buffet) car or an attendant who wheels a snack trolley through carriages. If possible buy your food before travelling as on-board prices tend to be high.

Rail Passes

Shop around, as pass prices can vary between different outlets. Once purchased, take care of your pass, as it cannot be replaced or refunded if lost or stolen. European passes get reductions on Eurostar through the Channel Tunnel and on certain ferry routes (eg between France and Ireland p678). In the USA, **Rail Europe** (☎ 877-257-2887; www.raileurope .com) sells all sorts of rail passes.

EURAIL

There are so many different passes to choose from and such a wide variety of timetables, you should have a good idea of your itinerary before purchasing one. These passes can only be bought by residents of non-European countries, and are supposed to be purchased before arriving in Europe. They *can* be purchased within Europe, so long as your passport proves you've been there for less than six months, but the outlets where you can do this are limited, and the passes will be more expensive than getting them outside Europe. Two London outlets are **Rail Europe** (☎ 0870 584 8848; www.raileurope.co.uk or www.raileurope.com; 178 Piccadilly, London) and **Drifters Travel Centre** (☎ 020-7402 9171; 22a Craven Tce, London). Passes cannot be booked over the telephone with Rail Europe; you must make a personal call to the travel centre. If you've lived in Europe for more than six months, you are eligible for an Inter-Rail pass (p1080), which is better value.

Eurail passes are valid for unlimited travel on national railways and some private lines in the Western European countries of Austria, Belgium, France (including Monaco), Germany, Greece, Ireland, Italy, Luxembourg, the Netherlands, Portugal, Spain and Switzerland (including Liechtenstein).

Eurail is also valid on some ferries between Italy and Greece. Reductions are given on some other ferry routes and on river/lake steamer services in various countries.

The Eurailpass is the standard pass for travellers 26 years and over. It provides unlimited 1st-class travel only: 15/21 days costs UK£334/433 or one/two/three months costs UK£538/761/941.

The Eurailpass Flexi is also for travellers 26 and over. It offers 1st-class travel for any chosen days within a two-month period: 10/15 days UK£394/520.

The Eurailpass Youth pass offers the same options as the standard Eurailpass, but for those aged under 26 years, and for 2nd-class travel only. Passes are 15/21 days for UK£235/304 or one/two/three months for UK£378/534/660.

The Eurailpass Youth Flexi offers the same options as the standard Eurailpass Flexi, but for those aged under 26, and for 2nd-class travel only: 10/15 days for UK£277/365.

For all these passes, overnight journeys commencing after 7pm count as the following day's travel. The traveller must fill out in ink the relevant box in the calendar before starting a day's travel.

Two to five people travelling together can get a 'saver' version of all passes mentioned above, saving about 15%.

Also for non-Europeans is the Eurail Selectpass (formerly the 'Europass'), which gives unlimited travel between all Western European countries – except for Britain – within a two-month period, as long as they're directly connected by a participating Eurail train or shipping line. Passes come in three-, four- and five-country versions, with five-, six-, eight- or 10-day options (or 15 days for the five-country option). Youth (aged under 26) and adult (solo, or two to five sharing) versions are available, and purchasing requirements and sales outlets are as for Eurail passes. The youth/adult price is UK£173/247 for a minimum five travel days within five countries, or UK£313/447 for a maximum 15 days.

EURODOMINO

There is a Eurodomino pass for each of the countries covered in the Inter-Rail pass, and it's worth considering if you're homing in on a particular region. These passes are sold in Europe to European residents. Adults (travelling 1st or 2nd class) and those under 26 can opt for three to eight days valid travel within one month. Examples of adult/under-26 prices for eight days in 2nd class are UK£98/£75 for the Netherlands and UK£190/£143 for Germany.

INTER-COUNTRY PASSES

Eurail passes are available for travel between select countries, including the Germany-Benelux pass; France 'n Italy, Spain or Switzerland pass; Benelux Tourrail pass; Iberic Railpass; and BritRail pass. Check out fares at **Rail Europe** (www.raileurope.com) or see individual country chapters for more information.

INTER-RAIL

These passes are available to European residents of more than six months standing (passport identification is required). Terms and conditions vary slightly from country to country, but in the country of origin there is only a discount of around 50% on the normal fares.

The **Inter-Rail pass** (www.interrailnet.com) is split into eight zones. In Western Europe, Zone A is Ireland; C is Austria, Denmark, Germany and Switzerland; E is Belgium, France, Luxembourg and the Netherlands; F is Portugal and Spain; G is Greece, Italy and Italy–Greece ferries. The other zones cover Scandinavia and parts of Eastern Europe. This pass is not valid on the Spanish Railways' high speed AVE and Talgo 200 services, and the German Railways' 'Metropolitan' Hamburg–Essen and Düsseldorf–Cologne services.

The Inter-Rail pass is available in two classes: youth (under 26) and adult. Prices for any one zone for 16 days are UK£159/223; two zones for 22 days UK£215/303; and the all-zone global pass for one month UK£295/415. Travellers can also get discounts or free admission to museums in Paris, Lisbon, Madrid and Athens, as well as 50% off local transport in select areas (Corsican and Nice–Digne railways in France, private trains and buses in Switzerland, and parts of the Catalan railway in Spain).

NATIONAL RAIL PASSES

If you're intending to travel extensively within one country, check which national rail passes are available as these can sometimes save you a lot of money; details can be found in the individual country chapters. You need to plan ahead if you intend to take this option, as some passes can only be purchased prior to arrival in the country concerned. Some national flexi passes, near-equivalents to the Eurodomino passes mentioned above, are only available to non-Europeans.

RAILPLUS CARD

For a small fee, European residents can buy a Railplus Card, entitling the holder to a 25% discount on international train journeys. The Railplus Card costs £30 for adults and £13 for youths and seniors over 60, and lasts for one year. It is not valid on TGV Brussels–France, Thalys and Eurostar trains.

Security

You should be quite safe travelling on most trains in Western Europe, but it pays to be security conscious nonetheless. Keep an eye on your luggage at all times (especially when stopping at stations) and lock compartment doors at night.

Health

BEFORE YOU GO

We recommend you carry a spare pair of contact lenses and glasses, and take your optical prescription with you. Bring medications in their original, clearly labelled containers. A signed and dated letter from your physician describing your medical conditions and medications, including generic names, is also a good idea. If carrying syringes or needles, be sure to have a physician's letter documenting their medical necessity.

INSURANCE

If you're an EU citizen, an E111 form (which is gradually being replaced by the European Health Insurance Card), available from most health centres or, in the UK, post offices, covers you for most medical care. E111 will not cover you for non-emergencies or emergency repatriation. Citizens of other countries should find out if there is a reciprocal arrangement for free medical care between their country and the country visited. If you do need health insurance, strongly consider a policy that covers you for the worst possible scenario, such as an accident requiring an emergency flight home. Find out in advance if your insurance plan will make payments directly to providers or reimburse you later for overseas health expenditures. The former option is generally preferable, as it doesn't require you to pay out-of-pocket costs in a foreign country.

RECOMMENDED VACCINATIONS

No jabs are necessary for Western Europe. However, the WHO recommends that all travellers should be covered for diphtheria, tetanus, measles, mumps, rubella and polio, regardless of their destination.

FURTHER READING

Health Advice for Travellers (currently called the T6 leaflet) is an annually updated leaflet by the Department of Health in the UK available free in post offices. It contains some general information, legally required and recommended vaccines for different countries, reciprocal health agreements, and an E111 application form. Lonely Planet's *Travel with Children* includes advice on travel health for younger children.

IN TRANSIT

DEEP VEIN THROMBOSIS (DVT)

Blood clots may form in the legs during plane flights, chiefly because of prolonged immobility. The main symptom of DVT is swelling or pain in the foot, ankle, or calf, usually but not always on just one side. When a blood clot travels to the lungs it may cause chest pain and breathing difficulties. Travellers with any of these symptoms should immediately seek medical attention.

To prevent the development of DVT on long flights you should walk about the cabin, contract and relax the leg muscles while sitting, drink plenty of fluids, and avoid alcohol and tobacco.

IN WESTERN EUROPE

AVAILABILITY OF HEALTH CARE

Good health care is readily available and for minor illnesses pharmacists can give valuable advice and sell over-the-counter medication. They can also advise when more specialised help is required and point you in the right direction. The standard of dental care is usually good; however, it is sensible to have a dental check-up before a long trip.

ENVIRONMENTAL HAZARDS
Altitude Sickness

Most people are affected to some extent by lack of oxygen at high altitudes (over 2500m). Symptoms of Acute Mountain Sickness (AMS) usually develop during the first 24 hours at altitude but may be delayed up to three weeks. Mild symptoms include headache, lethargy, dizziness, difficulty sleeping and loss of appetite. AMS may become more severe without warning and can be fatal. Severe symptoms include breathlessness, a dry, irritative cough (which may progress to the production of pink, frothy sputum), severe headache, lack of coordination and balance, confusion, irrational behaviour, vomiting, drowsiness, and unconsciousness. There is no hard-and-fast rule as to what is too high: AMS has been fatal at 3000m, although 3500m to 4500m is the usual range.

Treat mild symptoms by resting at the same altitude until recovery, usually a day or two. Paracetamol or aspirin can be taken for headaches. If symptoms persist or become worse, however, *immediate descent is necessary;* even 500m can help. Drug treatments should never be used to avoid descent or to enable further ascent.

Diamox (acetazolamide) reduces the headache of AMS and helps the body acclimatise to the lack of oxygen. It is available only on prescription. Those who are allergic to sulfonamide antibiotics may also be allergic to Diamox.

In the UK fact sheets are available from the British Mountaineering Council, 177–179 Burton Rd, Manchester, M20 2BB.

Heatstroke

Heatstroke occurs after excessive fluid loss and inadequate replacement of fluids and salt. Symptoms include headache, dizziness and tiredness. Dehydration is already happening by the time you feel thirsty – aim to drink sufficient water to produce pale, diluted urine. Replace lost fluids by drinking water and/or fruit juice, and cool the body with cold water and fans. Treat salt loss with salty fluids such as soup or Bovril, or add a little more table salt than usual to foods.

Hypothermia

The weather in Europe's mountains can be extremely changeable at any time of year. Proper preparation will reduce the risk of getting hypothermia. Even on a hot day the weather can change rapidly; carry waterproof garments and warm layers, and inform others of your route.

Hypothermia starts with shivering, loss of judgment and clumsiness. Unless rewarming occurs, the sufferer deteriorates into apathy, confusion and coma. Prevent further heat loss by seeking shelter, warm dry clothing, hot sweet drinks and shared bodily warmth.

Insect Bites & Stings

Mosquitoes are found in most parts of Western Europe. They may not carry malaria but can cause irritation and infected bites. Use a DEET-based insect repellent.

Sand flies are found around Mediterranean beaches. They usually cause only a nasty itchy bite but can carry a rare skin disorder called cutaneous leishmaniasis.

SEXUAL HEALTH

Contraception, including condoms, is widely available in Western Europe; however emergency contraception may not be. The **International Planned Parent Federation** (www.ippf.org) can advise about the availability of contraception in different countries. When buying condoms, look for a European CE mark, which means they have been rigorously tested.

HEALTH

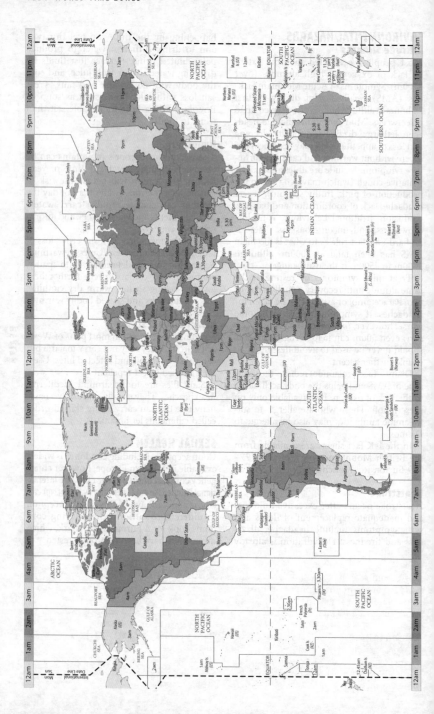

Language

CONTENTS

This language guide offers basic vocabulary to help you get around Western Europe. For more extensive coverage of the languages included in this guide, pick up a copy of Lonely Planet's *Europe Phrasebook*.

DUTCH

PRONUNCIATION
Vowels

a	short, as the 'u' in 'cut'
a, aa	long, as the 'a' in 'father'
au, ou	pronounced somewhere between the 'ow' in 'how' and the 'ow' in 'glow'
e	short, as in 'bet', or as the 'er' in 'fern' (with no 'r' sound)
e, ee	long, as the 'ay' in 'day'
ei	as in 'vein'
eu	similar to the 'u' in 'fur', with no 'r' sound
i	short, as in 'it'
i, ie	long, as the 'ee' in 'meet'
ij	as the 'ey' in 'they'
o	short, as in 'pot'
o, oo	long, as in 'note'
oe	as the 'oo' in 'zoo'
u	short, similar to the 'u' in 'urn'
u, uu	long, as the 'u' in 'flute'
ui	similar to the sound of 'er-y' in 'her year' (with no 'r' sound) or, if you're familiar with it, as the 'eui' in the French *fauteuil*

Consonants

ch, g	as the 'ch' in the Scottish *loch*; it's like a hiss produced by tightening the tongue against top of the throat
j	as the 'y' in 'yes'

ACCOMMODATION

hotel	hotel
guesthouse	pension
youth hostel	jeugdherberg
camping ground	camping

Do you have any rooms available?	Heeft U kamers vrij?
How much is it per night/per person?	Hoeveel is het per nacht/per persoon?
Is breakfast included?	Zit er ontbijt bij inbegrepen?

single room	eenpersoons kamer
double room	tweepersoons kamer
one night	één nacht
two nights	twee nachten

CONVERSATION & ESSENTIALS

Hello.	Dag/Hallo.
Goodbye.	Dag.
Yes.	Ja.
No.	Nee.
Please.	Alstublieft/Alsjeblieft.
Thank you.	Dank U/je (wel).
You're welcome.	Geen dank.
Excuse me.	Pardon.
Sorry.	Sorry.
Do you speak English?	Spreekt U/Spreek je Engels?
How much is it?	Hoeveel kost het?
What's your name?	Hoe heet U/je?
My name is ...	Ik heet ...

EMERGENCIES – DUTCH

Help!	Help!
Call a doctor!	Haal een dokter!
Call the police!	Haal de politie!
Go away!	Ga weg!
I'm lost.	Ik ben de weg kwijt.

SHOPPING & SERVICES

a bank	een bank
the market	de markt
the newsagents	de krantenwinkel
the pharmacy	de drogist
the post office	het postkantoor
the stationers	de kantoorboekhandel
the tourist office	de VVV/het toeristenbureau
What time does it open/close?	Hoe laat opent/sluit het?

SIGNS – DUTCH

Ingang	Entrance
Uitgang	Exit
Informatie/ Inlichtingen	Information
Open	Open
Gesloten	Closed
Kamers Vrij	Rooms Available
Vol	Full/No Vacancies
Politiebureau	Police Station
Verboden	Prohibited
WC/Toiletten	Toilets
Heren	Men
Dames	Women

TIME, DAYS & NUMBERS

What time is it?	Hoe laat is het?
today	vandaag
tomorrow	morgen
yesterday	gisteren
in the morning	's morgens
in the afternoon	's middags
Monday	maandag
Tuesday	dinsdag
Wednesday	woensdag
Thursday	donderdag
Friday	vrijdag
Saturday	zaterdag
Sunday	zondag
0	nul
1	één
2	twee
3	drie
4	vier
5	vijf
6	zes
7	zeven
8	acht
9	negen
10	tien
11	elf
100	honderd
1000	duizend

TRANSPORT

What time does the ... leave/arrive?	Hoe laat vertrekt/arriveert de ...?
(next)	(volgende)
boat	boot
bus	bus
tram	tram
train	trein

I'd like to hire a car/ bicycle.	Ik wil graag een auto/fiets huren.
I'd like a one-way/ return ticket.	Ik wil graag een enkele reis/ een retour.
1st class	eerste klas
2nd class	tweede klas
left luggage locker	bagagekluis
bus stop	bushalte
tram stop	tramhalte
train station	treinstation
ferry terminal	veerhaven

Directions

Where is the ...?	Waar is de ...?
Go straight ahead.	Ga rechtdoor.
Turn left.	Ga linksaf.
Turn right.	Ga rechtsaf.
near	dichtbij
far	ver

FRENCH

PRONUNCIATION

Most letters in French are pronounced more or less the same as their English counterparts. Here are a few that may cause some confusion:

j	as the 's' in 'leisure', eg *jour* (day)
c	before e and i, as the 's' in 'sit'; before a, o and u it's pronounced as English 'k'. When undescored with a 'cedilla' (ç) it's always pronounced as the 's' in 'sit'.
r	pronounced from the back of the throat while constricting the muscles to restrict the flow of air
n, m	where a syllable ends in a single n or m, these letters are not pronounced, but the vowel is given a nasal pronunciation

ACCOMMODATION

the hotel	l'hôtel
the guesthouse	la pension (de famille)
the youth hostel	l'auberge de jeunesse
the camping ground	le camping
Do you have any rooms available?	Est-ce que vous avez des chambres libres?
How much is it per night/per person?	Quel est le prix par nuit/par personne?
Is breakfast included?	Est-ce que le petit déjeuner est compris?

for one person	*pour une personne*
for two people	*deux personnes*
for one night	*une nuit*
for two nights	*deux nuits*

CONVERSATION & ESSENTIALS

Hello.	*Bonjour.*
Goodbye.	*Au revoir.*
Yes.	*Oui.*
No.	*Non.*
Please.	*S'il vous plaît.*
Thank you.	*Merci.*
You're welcome.	*Je vous en prie.*
Excuse me. (to get someone's attention)	*Excusez-moi.*
Sorry. (forgive me)	*Pardon.*
Do you speak English?	*Parlez-vous anglais?*
How much is it?	*C'est combien?*
What's your name?	*Comment vous appelez-vous?*
My name is ...	*Je m'appelle ...*

EMERGENCIES – FRENCH

Help!	*Au secours!*
Call a doctor!	*Appelez un médecin!*
Call the police!	*Appelez la police!*
Leave me alone!	*Fichez-moi la paix!*
I'm lost.	*Je me suis égaré/e.*

SHOPPING & SERVICES

a bank	*une banque*
chemist/pharmacy	*la pharmacie*
the ... embassy	*l'ambassade de ...*
market	*le marché*
newsagents	*l'agence de presse*
post office	*le bureau de poste*
a public telephone	*une cabine téléphonique*
stationers	*la papeterie*
the tourist office	*l'office de tourisme/le syndicat d'initiative*
What time does it open/close?	*Quelle est l' heure de ouverture/fermeture?*

TIME, DAYS & NUMBERS

What time is it?	*Quelle heure est-il?*
today	*aujourd'hui*
tomorrow	*demain*
yesterday	*hier*
morning	*matin*
afternoon	*après-midi*
Monday	*lundi*
Tuesday	*mardi*

SIGNS – FRENCH

Entrée	Entrance
Sortie	Exit
Renseignements	Information
Ouvert	Open
Fermée	Closed
Chambres Libres	Rooms Available
Complet	Full/No Vacancies
(Commissariat de) Police	Police Station
Interdit	Prohibited
Toilettes, WC	Toilets
Hommes	Men
Femmes	Women

Wednesday	*mercredi*
Thursday	*jeudi*
Friday	*vendredi*
Saturday	*samedi*
Sunday	*dimanche*
1	*un*
2	*deux*
3	*trois*
4	*quatre*
5	*cinq*
6	*six*
7	*sept*
8	*huit*
9	*neuf*
10	*dix*
100	*cent*
1000	*mille*

TRANSPORT

When does the (next) ... leave/arrive?	*À quelle heure part/ arrive le (prochain) ...?*
boat	*bateau*
bus (city/intercity)	*bus/car*
tram	*tramway*
train	*train*
left luggage (office)	*consigne*
timetable	*horaire*
bus stop	*arrêt d'autobus*
train station	*gare*
ferry terminal	*gare maritime*
I'd like a ... ticket.	*Je voudrais un billet ...*
one-way	*aller simple*
return	*aller retour*
1st-class	*de première classe*
2nd-class	*de deuxième classe*

LANGUAGE

| I'd like to hire a car/bicycle. | Je voudrais louer une voiture/un vélo. |

Directions

Where is ...?	Où est ...?
Go straight ahead.	Continuez tout droit.
Turn left.	Tournez à gauche.
Turn right.	Tournez à droite.
near	proche
far	loin

GERMAN

PRONUNCIATION

Unlike English or French, German has no real silent letters: you pronounce the **k** at the start of the word *Knie* (knee), the **p** at the start of *Psychologie* (psychology), and the **e** at the end of *Ich habe* (I have).

Vowels

As in English, vowels can be pronounced long, as the 'o' in 'pope', or short, as in 'pop'. As a rule, German vowels are long before one consonant and short before two consonants, eg the **o** is long in *Dom* (cathedral), but short in *doch* (after all).

a	short, as the 'u' in 'cut' or long, as in 'father'
au	as the 'ow' in 'vow'
ä	short, as in 'cat' or long, as in 'care'
äu	as the 'oy' in 'boy'
e	short, as in 'bet' or long, as in 'obey'
ei	as the 'ai' in 'aisle'
eu	as the 'oy' in 'boy'
i	short, as in 'it' or long, as in 'marine'
ie	as the 'brief'
o	short, as in 'not' or long, as in 'note'
ö	as the 'er' in 'fern'
u	as in 'pull'
ü	similar to the 'u' in 'pull' but with lips stretched back

Consonants

Most German consonants sound similar to their English counterparts. One important difference is that **b**, **d** and **g** sound like 'p', 't' and 'k', respectively when word-final.

b	as in 'be'; as 'p' when word-final
ch	as in Scottish *loch*
d	as in 'do'; as 't' when word-final
g	as in 'go'; as 'k' when word-final
j	as the 'y' in 'yet'
qu	as 'k' plus 'v'
r	can be trilled or guttural, depending on the region
s	as in 'sun'; as the 'z' in 'zoo' when followed by a vowel
sch	as the 'sh' in 'ship'
sp, st	as 'shp' and 'sht' when word-initial
tion	the 't' is pronounced as the 'ts' in 'its'
v	as the 'f' in 'fan'
w	as the 'v' in 'van'
z	as the 'ts' in 'its'

ACCOMMODATION

hotel	Hotel
guesthouse	Pension, Gästehaus
youth hostel	Jugendherberge
camping ground	Campingplatz

Do you have any rooms available?	Haben Sie noch freie Zimmer?
How much is it per night/person?	Wieviel kostet es pro Nacht/Person?
Is breakfast included?	Ist Frühstück inbegriffen?

a single room	ein Einzelzimmer
a double room	ein Doppelzimmer
one night	eine Nacht
two nights	zwei Nächte

CONVERSATION & ESSENTIALS

Good day.	Guten Tag.
Hello.	Grüss Gott. (in Bavaria and Austria)
Goodbye.	Auf Wiedersehen.
Bye.	Tschüss. (informal)
Yes.	Ja.
No.	Nein.
Please.	Bitte.
Thank you.	Danke.
You're welcome.	Bitte sehr.
Sorry. (excuse me, forgive me)	Entschuldigung.
Do you speak English?	Sprechen Sie Englisch?
How much is it?	Wieviel kostet es?
What's your name?	Wie heissen Sie?
My name is ...	Ich heisse ...

SHOPPING & SERVICES

| a bank | eine Bank |
| the chemist/ pharmacy | die Apotheke |

EMERGENCIES – GERMAN

Help!	*Hilfe!*
Call a doctor!	*Holen Sie einen Arzt!*
Call the police!	*Rufen Sie die Polizei!*
Go away!	*Gehen Sie weg!*
I'm lost.	*Ich habe mich verirrt.*

the ... embassy	*die ... Botschaft*
the market	*der Markt*
the newsagents	*der Zeitungshändler*
the post office	*das Postamt*
the stationers	*der Schreibwarengeschäft*
the tourist office	*das Verkehrsamt*

What time does it open/close?	*Um wieviel Uhr macht es auf/zu?*

TIME, DAYS & NUMBERS

What time is it?	*Wie spät ist es?*
today	*heute*
tomorrow	*morgen*
yesterday	*gestern*
in the morning	*morgens*
in the afternoon	*nachmittags*

Monday	*Montag*
Tuesday	*Dienstag*
Wednesday	*Mittwoch*
Thursday	*Donnerstag*
Friday	*Freitag*
Saturday	*Samstag, Sonnabend*
Sunday	*Sonntag*

0	*null*
1	*eins*
2	*zwei/zwo*
3	*drei*
4	*vier*
5	*fünf*
6	*sechs*
7	*sieben*
8	*acht*
9	*neun*
10	*zehn*
11	*elf*
12	*zwölf*
13	*dreizehn*
100	*hundert*
1000	*tausend*

TRANSPORT

What time does ... (leave/arrive)?	*Wann (fährt ... ab/ kommt ... an)?*
the boat	*das Boot*

SIGNS – GERMAN

Eingang	Entrance
Ausgang	Exit
Auskunft	Information
Offen	Open
Geschlossen	Closed
Zimmer Frei	Rooms Available
Voll/Besetzt	Full/No Vacancies
Polizeiwache	Police Station
Verboten	Prohibited
Toiletten (WC)	Toilets
Herren	Men
Damen	Women

the bus (city)	*der Bus*
the bus (intercity)	*der (überland) Bus*
the tram	*die Strassenbahn*
the train	*der Zug*

What time is the next boat?	*Wann fährt das nächste Boot?*
I'd like to hire a car/bicycle.	*Ich möchte ein Auto/ Fahrrad mieten.*
I'd like a one-way/ return ticket.	*Ich möchte eine Einzel- karte/Rückfahrkarte.*

1st class	*erste Klasse*
2nd class	*zweite Klasse*
left luggage locker	*Schliessfächer*
timetable	*Fahrplan*
bus stop	*Bushaltestelle*
tram stop	*Strassenbahnhaltestelle*
train station	*Bahnhof (Bf)*
ferry terminal	*Fährhafen*

Directions

Where is the ...?	*Wo ist die ...?*
Go straight ahead.	*Gehen Sie geradeaus.*
Turn left.	*Biegen Sie links ab.*
Turn right.	*Biegen Sie rechts ab.*
near	*nahe*
far	*weit*

GREEK

ALPHABET & PRONUNCIATION

Pronunciation of Greek letters is shown in the table on p1090 using the closest similar sounding letter in English.

Letter Combinations

Some pairs of vowels are pronounced separately if the first has an acute accent (eg **á**),

THE GREEK ALPHABET

Greek	English	Pronunciation
Α α	a	as in 'father'
Β β	v	as the 'v' in 'vine'
Γ γ	gh/y	like a rough 'g', or as the the 'y' in 'yes'
Δ δ	dh	as the 'th' in 'then'
Ε ε	e	as in 'egg'
Ζ ζ	z	as in 'zoo'
Η η	i	as the 'ee' in 'feet'
Θ θ	th	as the 'th' in 'throw'
Ι ι	i	as the 'ee' in 'feet'
Κ κ	k	as in 'kite'
Λ λ	l	as in 'leg'
Μ μ	m	as in 'man'
Ν ν	n	as in 'net'
Ξ ξ	x	as in 'taxi'
Ο ο	o	as in 'hot'
Π π	p	as in 'pup'
Ρ ρ	r	slightly trilled 'r'
Σ σ	s	as in 'sand' ('V' at the end of a word)
Τ τ	t	as in 'to'
Υ υ	i	as the 'ee' in 'feet'
Φ φ	f	as in 'fee'
Χ χ	kh/h	as the 'ch' in Scottish loch, or as a rough 'h'
Ψ ψ	ps	as the 'ps' in 'lapse'
Ω ω	o	as in 'lot'

or the second has a dieresis (eg ï). All Greek words of two or more syllables have an acute accent which indicates where the stress falls.

ει, οι	i	as the 'ee' in 'feet'
αι	e	as in 'bet'
ου	u	as in 'oo' in 'mood'
μπ	b	as in 'be'
	mb	as in 'amber' (or as the 'mp' in 'ample')
ντ	d	as in 'do'
	nd	as in 'bend' (or as the 'nt' in 'sent')
γκ	g	as in 'go'
γγ	ng	as the 'ng' in 'angle'
γξ	ks	as in 'yaks'
τζ	dz	as the 'ds' in 'suds'

The suffix of some Greek words depends on the gender of the speaker, eg *asthmatikos* (masculine) and *asthmatikya* (feminine), or *epileptikos* (m) and *epileptikya* (f).

ACCOMMODATION

a hotel	ena xenothohio
a youth hostel	enas xenonas neoitos
a camping ground	ena kamping

I'd like a ... room.	thelo ena dhomatio ...
single	ya ena atomo
double	ya dhio atoma

How much is it per person/night?	poso kostizi ya ena atomo/vradhi?
for one night	ya mia nichta
for two nights	ya dhio nichtes
Is breakfast included?	simberilamvanete to proiono?

CONVERSATION & ESSENTIALS

Hello.	yasu (informal)
	yasas (polite/plural)
Goodbye.	andio
Yes.	ne
No.	okhi
Please.	sas parakalo
Thank you.	sas efharisto
That's fine/You're welcome.	ine endaksi/parakalo
Excuse me. (forgive me)	signomi
Do you speak English?	milate anglika?
How much is it?	poso kani?
What's your name?	pos sas lene/pos legeste?
My name is ...	me lene ...

EMERGENCIES – GREEK

Help!	voithia!
Call a doctor!	fonakste ena yatro!
Call the police!	tilefoniste tin astinomia!
Go away!	fighe/dhromo!
I'm lost.	eho hathi

SHOPPING & SERVICES

Where is a /the ...?	pu ine ...?
bank	mia trapeza
... embassy	i ... presvia
market	i aghora
newsagents	to efimeridhon
pharmacy	to farmakio
post office	to takhidhromio
tourist office	to ghrafio turistikon pliroforion

What time does it open/close?	ti ora aniyi/klini?

SIGNS – GREEK

Είσοδος	Entrance
Έξοδος	Exit
Πληροφορίες	Information
Ανοικτο	Open
Κλειστο	Closed
Αστυνομικος Τμημα	Police Station
Απαγορευεται	Prohibited
Τουαλετες	Toilets
Ανδρων	Men
Γυναικων	Women

TIME, DAYS & NUMBERS

What time is it?	ti ora ine?
today	simera
tomorrow	avrio
yesterday	hthes
in the morning	to proi
in the afternoon	to apoyevma

Monday	dheftera
Tuesday	triti
Wednesday	tetarti
Thursday	pempti
Friday	paraskevi
Saturday	savato
Sunday	kiryaki

1	ena
2	dhio
3	tria
4	tesera
5	pende
6	eksi
7	epta
8	okhto
9	enea
10	dheka
100	ekato
1000	khilya

TRANSPORT

What time does the ... leave/arrive?	ti ora fevyi/ftani ...?
boat	to plio
bus (city)	to leoforio (ya tin poli)
bus (intercity)	to leoforio (ya ta proastia)
tram	to tram
train	to treno

I'd like a ... ticket.	tha ithela isitirio ...
one-way	horis epistrofi
return	me epistrofi

| 1st-class | proti thesi |
| 2nd-class | dhefteri thesi |

left luggage	horos aposkevon
timetable	dhromologhio
bus stop	i stasi tu leoforiu

Directions

Go straight ahead.	pighenete efthia
Turn left.	stripste aristera
Turn right.	stripste dheksya
near/far	konda/makria

ITALIAN

PRONUNCIATION

Vowels

Vowels sounds are generally shorter than English equivalents:

a   as in 'art', eg *caro* (dear); sometimes short, eg *amico/a* (friend)

e   short, as in 'let', eg *mettere* (to put); long, as in 'there', eg *vero* (true)

i   short, as in 'it', eg *inizio* (start); long, as in 'marine', eg *vino* (wine)

o   short, as in 'dot', eg *donna* (woman); long, as in 'port', eg *ora* (hour)

u   as the 'oo' in 'book', eg *puro* (pure)

Consonants

The pronunciation of many Italian consonants is similar to that of their English counterparts. Pronunciation of some consonants depends on certain rules:

c   as the 'k' in 'kit' before **a**, **o** and **u**; as the 'ch' in 'choose' before **e** and **i**

ch as the 'k' in 'kit'

g   as the 'g' in 'get' before **a**, **o**, **u** and **h**; as the 'j' in 'jet' before **e** and **i**

gli as the 'lli' in 'million'

gn as the 'ny' in 'canyon'

h   always silent

r   a rolled 'rr' sound

sc as the 'sh' in 'sheep' before **e** and **i**; as 'sk' before **a**, **o**, **u** and **h**

z   as the 'ts' in 'lights', except at the beginning of a word, when it's as the 'ds' in 'suds'

Word Stress

Word stress generally falls on the second-last syllable, as in spa-*ghet*-ti, but when a word has an accent, the stress falls on that syllable, as in cit-*tà* (city).

ACCOMMODATION

hotel	*albergo*
guesthouse	*pensione*
youth hostel	*ostello per la gioventù*
camping ground	*campeggio*

Do you have any rooms available?	*Ha delle camere libere/ C'è una camera libera?*
How much is it per night/per person?	*Quanto costa per la notte/ciascuno?*
Is breakfast included?	*È compresa la colazione?*

a single room	*una camera singola*
a twin room	*una camera doppia*
a double room	*una camera matrimoniale*
for one night	*per una notte*
for two nights	*per due notti*

CONVERSATION & ESSENTIALS

Hello.	*Buongiorno.* (polite)
	Ciao. (informal)
Goodbye.	*Arrivederci.* (polite)
	Ciao. (informal)
Yes.	*Sì.*
No.	*No.*
Please.	*Per favore/Per piacere.*
Thank you.	*Grazie.*
You're welcome.	*Prego.*
Excuse me.	*Mi scusi.*
Sorry. (excuse me/ forgive me)	*Mi scusi/Mi perdoni.*
Do you speak English?	*Parla inglese?*
How much is it?	*Quanto costa?*
What's your name?	*Come si chiama?*
My name is ...	*Mi chiamo ...*

EMERGENCIES – ITALIAN

Help!	*Aiuto!*
Call a doctor!	*Chiama un dottore/medico!*
Call the police!	*Chiama la polizia!*
Go away!	*Vai via!*
I'm lost.	*Mi sono perso/a* (m/f)

SHOPPING & SERVICES

a bank	*una banca*
chemist/pharmacy	*la farmacia*
the ... embassy	*l'ambasciata di ...*
market	*il mercato*
newsagents	*l'edicola*

post office	*la posta*
stationers	*il cartolaio*
tourist office	*l'ufficio di turismo*

What time does it open/close?	*A che ora (si) apre/chiude?*

TIME, DAYS & NUMBERS

What time is it?	*Che ora è?/Che ore sono?*
today	*oggi*
tomorrow	*domani*
yesterday	*ieri*
morning	*mattina*
afternoon	*pomeriggio*

Monday	*lunedì*
Tuesday	*martedì*
Wednesday	*mercoledì*
Thursday	*giovedì*
Friday	*venerdì*
Saturday	*sabato*
Sunday	*domenica*

1	*uno*
2	*due*
3	*tre*
4	*quattro*
5	*cinque*
6	*sei*
7	*sette*
8	*otto*
9	*nove*
10	*dieci*
100	*cento*
1000	*mille*

TRANSPORT

When does the ... leave/arrive?	*A che ora parte/ arriva ...?*
boat	*la barca*
ferry	*il traghetto*
bus	*l'autobus*
tram	*il tram*
train	*il treno*

bus stop	*fermata dell'autobus*
train station	*stazione*
ferry terminal	*stazione marittima*
1st class	*prima classe*
2nd class	*seconda classe*
left luggage	*deposito bagagli*
timetable	*orario*

I'd like a one-way/ return ticket.	*Vorrei un biglietto di solo andata/di andata e ritorno.*

SIGNS – ITALIAN

Ingresso/Entrata	Entrance
Uscita	Exit
Informazione	Information
Aperto	Open
Chiuso	Closed
Camere Libere	Rooms Available
Completo	Full/No Vacancies
Polizia/Carabinieri	Police
Questura	Police Station
Proibito/Vietato	Prohibited
Gabinetti/Bagni	Toilets
Uomini	Men
Donne	Women

I'd like to hire a car/ bicycle. — *Vorrei noleggiare una macchina/ bicicletta.*

Directions

Where is ...?	*Dov'è ...?*
Go straight ahead.	*Si va sempre diritto.*
Turn left.	*Giri a sinistra.*
Turn right.	*Giri a destra.*
near	*vicino*
far	*lontano*

PORTUGUESE

PRONUNCIATION

Portuguese uses masculine and feminine word endings, usually '-o' and '-a' respectively – to say 'thank you', a man will therefore use *obrigado*, a woman, *obrigada*.

Vowels

a short, as the 'u' in 'cut'; long, as the 'ur' in 'hurt'

e short, as in 'bet'; long, as in 'there'

é short, as in 'bet'

ê long, as the 'a' in 'gate'

i short, as in 'it'; long, as the 'ee' in 'see'

o short, as in 'pot'; long as in 'note' or as the 'oo' in 'good'

ô long, as in 'note'

u as the 'oo' in 'good'

Nasal Vowels

Nasalisation is represented by an 'n' or an 'm' after the vowel, or by a tilde over it, eg **ã**. The nasal 'i' exists in English as the 'ing' in 'sing'. You can practise by trying to pronounce vowels while holding your nose, as if you have a cold.

Diphthongs

au as the 'ow' in 'now'
ai as the 'ie' in 'pie'
ei as the 'ay' in 'day'
eu as 'e' followed by 'w'
oi similar to the 'oy' in 'boy'

Nasal Diphthongs

Try the same technique as for nasal vowels. To say *não*, pronounce 'now' through your nose.

ão nasal 'ow' (owng)
ãe nasal 'ay' (eing)
õe nasal 'oy' (oing)
ui similar to the 'uing' in 'ensuing'

Consonants

c as in 'cat' before **a**, **o** or **u**; as the 's' in 'sin' before **e** or **i**

ç as the 'c' in 'celery'

g as in 'go' before **a**, **o** or **u**; as the 's' in 'treasure' before **e** or **i**

gu as in 'guest' before **e** or **i**

h never pronounced when word-initial

nh as the 'ni' in 'onion'

lh as the 'lli' in 'million'

j as the 's' in 'treasure'

m not pronounced when word-final – it simply nasalises the previous vowel, eg *um* (oong), *bom* (bõ)

qu as 'k' before **e** or **i**; elsewhere as in 'queen'

r when word-initial, or when doubled (**rr**) within a word it's a harsh, guttural sound similar to the 'ch' in Scottish *loch*; in the middle or at the end of a word it's a rolled 'r' sound. In some areas of Portugal it's always strongly rolled.

s as in 'so' when word-initial and when doubled (**ss**) within a word; as the 'z' in 'zeal' when between vowels; as 'sh' when it precedes a consonant, or at the end of a word

x as the 'sh' in 'ship', as the 'z' in 'zeal', or as the 'x' in 'taxi'

z as the 's' in 'treasure' before a consonant or at the end of a word

Word Stress

Word stress is important in Portuguese, as it can affect meaning. It generally occurs on the second-to-last syllable of a word, though there are exceptions. In words with a written accent, the stress always falls on that syllable.

ACCOMMODATION

hotel	hotel
guesthouse	pensão
youth hostel	pousada da juventude
camping ground	parque de campismo

Do you have any rooms available?	Tem quartos livres?
How much is it per night/per person?	Quanto é por noite/por pessoa?
Is breakfast included?	O pequeno almoço está incluído?
a single room	um quarto individual
a twin room	um quarto duplo
a double room	um quarto de casal
for one night	para uma noite
for two nights	para duas noites

CONVERSATION & ESSENTIALS

Hello.	Bom dia.
Goodbye.	Adeus.
Yes.	Sim.
No.	Não.
Please.	Se faz favor.
Thank you.	Obrigado/a. (m/f)
You're welcome.	De nada.
Excuse me.	Com licença.
Sorry. (forgive me)	Desculpe.
Do you speak English?	Fala Inglês?
How much is it?	Quanto custa?
What's your name?	Como se chama?
My name is ...	Chamo-me ...

EMERGENCIES – PORTUGUESE

Help!	Socorro!
Call a doctor!	Chame um médico!
Call the police!	Chame a policia!
Go away!	Deixe-me em paz! (pol)/ Vai-te embora! (inf)
I'm lost.	Estou perdido/a. (m/f)

SHOPPING & SERVICES

a bank	um banco
a chemist/pharmacy	uma farmácia
the ... embassy	a embaixada de ...
the market	o mercado
the newsagents	a papelaria

the post office	os correios
the stationers	a tabacaria
the tourist office	o (posto de) turismo
What time does it open/close?	A que horas abre/fecha?

TIME, DAYS & NUMBERS

What time is it?	Que horas são?
today	hoje
tomorrow	amanhã
yesterday	ontem
morning	manhã
afternoon	tarde

Monday	segunda-feira
Tuesday	terça-feira
Wednesday	quarta-feira
Thursday	quinta-feira
Friday	sexta-feira
Saturday	sábado
Sunday	domingo

1	um/uma (m/f)
2	dois/duas (m/f)
3	três
4	quatro
5	cinco
6	seis
7	sete
8	oito
9	nove
10	dez
11	onze
100	cem
1000	mil

TRANSPORT

What time does the ... leave/arrive?	A que horas parte/ chega ...?
boat	o barco
bus (city/intercity)	o autocarro/a camioneta
tram	o eléctrico
train	o combóio

bus stop	paragem de autocarro
train station	estação ferroviária
timetable	horário

I'd like a ... ticket.	Queria um bilhete ...
one-way	simples/de ida
return	de ida e volta
1st-class	de primeira classe
2nd-class	de segunda classe
I'd like to hire ...	Queria alugar ...
a car	um carro
a bicycle	uma bicicleta

SIGNS – PORTUGUESE	
Entrada	Entrance
Saída	Exit
Informações	Information
Aberto	Open
Fechado	Closed
Quartos Livres	Rooms Available
Posto Da Polícia	Police Station
Proíbido	Prohibited
Empurre/Puxe	Push/Pull
Lavabos/WC	Toilets
Homens (h)	Men
Senhoras (s)	Women

Directions

Where is ...?	*Onde é ...?*
Go straight ahead.	*Siga sempre a direito/*
	Siga sempre em frente.
Turn left.	*Vire à esquerda.*
Turn right.	*Vire à direita.*
near	*perto*
far	*longe*

SPANISH

PRONUNCIATION
Vowels

An acute accent (as in *días*) generally indicates a stressed syllable and doesn't change the sound of the vowel.

e	as in 'met'
i	as in 'marine'
o	as in 'or' (without the 'r' sound)
u	as in 'rule'; the 'u' is not pronounced after **q** and in the letter combinations **gue** and **gui**, unless it's marked with a diaeresis (eg *argüir*), in which case it's pronounced as English 'w'
y	(see Consonants below)

Consonants

b	a cross between English 'b' and 'v'
c	a hard 'c' as in 'cat' when followed by **a**, **o**, **u** or a consonant; as the 'th' in 'thin' before **e** and **i**
ch	as in 'church'
d	as in 'do' when word-initial; elsewhere as the 'th' in 'then'
g	as in 'get' when word-initial and before **a**, **o** and **u**; elsewhere much softer. Before **e** or **i** it's a harsh, breathy sound, similar to the 'h' in 'hit'

h	silent
j	a harsh, guttural sound similar to the 'ch' in Scottish *loch*
ll	as the 'lli' in 'million'; some pronounce it rather like the 'y' in 'yellow'
ñ	a nasal sound, as the 'ni' in 'onion'
q	as the 'k' in 'kick'; **q** is always followed by a silent **u** and is combined only with the vowels **e** (as in *que*) and **i** (as in *qui*)
r	a rolled 'r' sound; longer and stronger when initial or doubled
s	as in 'see'
v	the same sound as **b**
x	as the 'ks' sound in 'taxi' when between vowels; as the 's' in 'see' when it precedes a consonant
y	at the end of a word or when standing alone (meaning 'and') it's pronounced like the Spanish **i**. As a consonant, it's somewhere between the 'y' in 'yonder' and the 'g' in 'beige', depending on the region.
z	as the 'th' in 'thin'

ACCOMMODATION

hotel	*hotel*
guesthouse	*pensión/casa de huéspedes*
youth hostel	*albergue juvenil*
camping ground	*camping*

Do you have any rooms available?	*¿Tiene habitaciones libres*
How much is it per night/per person?	*¿Cuánto cuesta por noche/por persona?*
Is breakfast included?	*¿Incluye el desayuno?*

a single room	*una habitación individual*
a double room	*una habitación doble*
a room with a double bed	*una habitación con cama de matrimonio*
for one night	*para una noche*
for two nights	*para dos noches*

CONVERSATION & ESSENTIALS

Hello.	*¡Hola!*
Goodbye.	*¡Adiós!*
Yes.	*Sí.*
No.	*No.*
Please.	*Por favor.*
Thank you.	*Gracias.*
You're welcome.	*De nada.*
I'm sorry.	*Lo siento/Discúlpeme.*
Excuse me.	*Perdón/Perdóneme.*

LANGUAGE

Do you speak English?	¿Habla inglés?
How much is it?	¿Cuánto cuesta?/¿Cuánto vale?
What's your name?	¿Cómo se llama?
My name is ...	Me llamo ...

EMERGENCIES – SPANISH

Help!	¡Socorro!/¡Auxilio!
Call a doctor!	¡Llame a un doctor!
Call the police!	¡Llame a la policía!
Go away!	¡Váyase!
I'm lost.	Estoy perdido/a. (m/f)

SHOPPING & SERVICES

a bank	un banco
chemist/pharmacy	la farmacia
the ... embassy	la embajada ...
the market	el mercado
newsagents	el quiosco
stationers	la papelería
the post office	los correos
the tourist office	la oficina de turismo
What time does it open/close?	¿A qué hora abren/cierran?

TIME, DAYS & NUMBERS

What time is it?	¿Qué hora es?
today	hoy
tomorrow	mañana
yesterday	ayer
morning	mañana
afternoon	tarde

Monday	lunes
Tuesday	martes
Wednesday	miércoles
Thursday	jueves
Friday	viernes
Saturday	sábado
Sunday	domingo

1	uno, una
2	dos
3	tres
4	cuatro
5	cinco
6	seis
7	siete
8	ocho
9	nueve
10	diez
11	once
100	cien/ciento
1000	mil

SIGNS – SPANISH

Entrada	Entrance
Salida	Exit
Información	Information
Abierto	Open
Cerrado	Closed
Habtaciones Libres	Rooms Available
Completo	Full/No Vacancies
Comisaría	Police Station
Prohibido	Prohibited
Servicios/Aseos	Toilets
Hombres	Men
Mujeres	Women

TRANSPORT

What time does the next ... leave/arrive?	¿A qué hora sale/llega el próximo ...?
boat	barco
bus (city/intercity)	autobús, bus/autocar
train	tranvía

I'd like a ... ticket.	Quiera un billete ...
one-way	sencillo/de sólo ida
return	de ida y vuelta
1st-class	de primera clase
2nd-class	de segunda clase

left luggage	consigna
timetable	horario
bus stop	parada de autobus
train station	estación de ferrocarril

I'd like to hire ...	Quisiera alquilar ...
a car	un coche
a bicycle	una bicicleta

Directions

Where is ...?	¿Dónde está ...?
Go straight ahead.	Siga/Vaya todo derecho.
Turn left.	Gire a la izquierda.
Turn right.	Gire a la derecha/recto.
near/far	cerca/lejos

Also available from Lonely Planet:
Europe Phrasebook

Behind the Scenes

THIS BOOK

Western Europe is part of Lonely Planet's Europe series, which includes *Eastern Europe, Mediterranean Europe, Central Europe, Scandinavian Europe* and *Europe on a Shoestring*. Lonely Planet also publishes phrasebooks for these regions.

THANKS from the Authors

Loretta Chilcoat Big thanks go to many people, including Amanda Canning, Sam Trafford and Katrina Webb at Lonely Planet. To the authors, it was great working with all of you. A major shout-out to my mom, Elaine, and my mother-in-law, Nancy, for taking care of their newborn grandchild during crunch time. To Brad and Emaline, thanks for putting up with my late nights in front of the computer.

Reuben Acciano Reuben thanks: his frustrated, tolerant family in Perth, the Italian people, the incredible Leonardo and Maria Theresa in Venice, inspirational Livio, Paolo Vallelonga for *sgropino*, warmth and being the Most Incredible Guide Ever, George and the Siena boys *(acaniamo c'e'?)*, enchanting Melissa Rosati in Bologna/Brescia, the Brits in Florence and Milan (you know who you are), the usual incomparable hospitality of the mixindex.com/Mansion gang. Finally, to gorgemouse Zoe Rose *(shenaniganarchy!)*, to Clancy the Perpetual, and beloved pip-spitting 'Bella, forgiver/forgetter – *grazie mille*.

Fiona Adams I would like to thank all the staff in the tourist offices throughout southern Spain for their help and patience, in particular Caty Serra and Rita Hunziker in Ibiza. In Marbella I owe a special thanks to Salvador and his charming family. Many thanks as well to Felicity in the hostal in Valencia. In Tarifa, Joe and Lucy – thanks for all your help and may the *poniente* always be with you. In Tarifa, a warm thank you to Frans de Man. Special thanks to Sarah Andrews, my co-author on the Spain chapter, and to all the Lonely Planet staff who worked on this edition of *Western Europe*. To Loli Cabarcos and Juan Balan, *besos y abrazos* once again for your help and friendship. Mum, thank you so much for looking after Gaucho while I was away (again). Most of all thank you to my husband Jamie, the biggest star of them all. I couldn't have done it without you.

Sarah Andrews Where to begin? I had so much help with this guide, starting with endless support

from my husband Miquel, and ending with the ever-helpful staff at tourist offices across Spain. Of those who gave me advice, suggestions and laughs on the road I especially want to thank Nuria Pardina, Fede Alvarez, Ana Maeso and the gang in Madrid; local experts Genevieve McCarthy, Simon Hunter, Clayton Maxwell and Gisela Williams; and road buddies Theresa Coryn and Courtney Edwards. Lonely Planet's London staff and my partner-in-crime in Spain Fiona Adams deserve a hand too.

Becca Blond I'd like to dedicate my chapters to my cousin Lynn Seidler, who passed away 18 March 2004 in the Turks and Caicos Islands, and whose love of travel always inspired me. Big thanks to Switzerland Tourism, especially Erika Loser, who offered plenty of advice, and to the travellers I met in Interlaken. To Heather Dickson who joined me for three days in Zurich: you survived the trams and the mapping! No small feat. Special thanks to Christine and Ashley for spending the day with me in Gimmelwald. As always I'm grateful for the love and support of my family and friends – David, Patricia, Jessica, Jennie, John, Vera and Lani. To Aaron, thanks for waiting.

Michael Grosberg Thanks especially to Yvonne Seidel for her kindness and generosity, not to mention her extensive network of friends in southern Germany, including Achim Becker in Constance, and Anna Linder in Munich. To my friend Nathalie Weber and Christian and his parents Christina and Alex von Hoffmeister for their hospitality and welcome, Gabi Daikeler-Meurer and Karl-Heinz Herse in Freiburg, Luci Westphal-Solary for a wealth of information about Hamburg and the Frisian Islands, Martyn Leder and Inga Scheffler for their expertise on Hamburg, Ulrich Plass and Ilona Ryvkin for their general impressions and thoughts about the country, Margaret Lydecker and Jane Stewart for their enthusiasm about Bonn and Cologne, Peter Guryan and Lara and Shirly Daniel for their help on Frankfurt, Glenn Yeck for tips on Stuttgart, Andrea Mohr for the drink in Nuremberg, and to the knowledgeable tourist office staff all over Germany. Finally to Orly Isaccson, my brother Joel and my parents Sheldon and Judy Grosberg for their support.

Sarah Johnstone Biggest thanks go to Polly Cook at the Austrian National Tourist Office in London, who endured all my questions and kept inviting me to press launches I was too far up the Alps to attend. Thanks also to the tourist officers who helped me along the way, particularly in Graz and Innsbruck. To all friends and family who've been incredibly supportive in helping me get through this gig – you know who you are, so thank you!

Amy Karafin Infinite gratitude to Virginia Tevendale, queen of wonderment, who opened up her house and her heart and showed me how to explore ruins and eat dandelions, among other things. Big thanks to Mom and Dad for the never-ending supply of love and logistical support, to all my Dhamma brothers and sisters in Ireland, especially Frances and Kate and Michael and Rachel, to Beverly and Wally Serkin for the ghost stories and the perfect evening, to John Connolly for the calls (even though…) and to Andy McKay for the toasties. Thanks to the helpful folk at Fáilte Ireland, Tourism Ireland and the Northern Ireland Tourist Board; Joan and Dr Peter Pyne; Mary Pierse; Trevor Storey; and Carmel and Mattie Shannon. A big shout-out to Sam Trafford and Fayette Fox in London. Thanks to Erik Vickstrom for reading everything and for helping with my cabin fever. *Tous mes remerciements à Maïmouna Ciss pour son aide pendant la période de 'chambre-café-chambre-café' et également à Lucien Mbengue pour les appels.*

John Lee Thanks to Visit Scotland and Visit Britain (particularly the Toronto office) for their assistance on this and other projects. Thanks also to my parents in England for feeding me whenever I turned up unannounced (which was often), my brother Michael for dropping by in Glasgow (mainly so he could hit the local pubs), and to my nephew Christopher for promising to use this book on his own upcoming travels (if you get lost, give me call).

Alex Leviton I must profusely thank my travelling companion and driver/sherpa, Len Amaral. Also Maha Shamiyeh, who left her honeymoon early to hike the Glastonbury tor with me. Props, y'all. Thanks to new friends: Paul Spurr in Bristol, Dave Jones in Liverpool, Dean Hoskins in Shrewsbury, Alex Watts in Newquay, Paul Chibeba at Visit Britain, Vicki and Hannah in Oxford, Gabriel in Windermere, Chris in Wales, and countless other locals, travellers and tourist personnel. Thanks to the British people, for vociferously pointing out the flaws of my imperialist government. I had no idea.

Leanne Logan & Geert Cole Updating this 7th edition of Western Europe was even better than the 1st edition. In Brussels, thanks in particular for the enthusiastic help given to us by Els Maes at Toerisme Vlaanderen and Sabine Rosen at the Office de Promotion de Tourisme. In Bruges, thanks once again to Anne De Meerleer at Toerisme Brugge. Merci to Jean-Claude Conter from the Luxembourg National Tourist Office. Heartfelt thanks to Roos and Bert Cole for their boundless Belgian hospitality, to our ever-keen road mates, Sixy and Bluey, and to Eleonor, our daughter, for loving life on the road. Thanks to those readers who provided insights, opinions and criticisms, and to the travellers we met on the road for spot-on suggestions. Last but not least, *bedankt* to all those at Lonely Planet who were involved with the production of this book.

Amy Marr *Mille grazie* to everyone who offered invaluable information, kindness on the road, patient conversation and good company over a meal or vino, from Rome to Sicily and back again. Special thanks to Franco, Ferdinando, Marianne, Virginia, Giulia, Lucca, Vincenzo, Mimmo and Gabriella, Luigi, Nick, Armando, Viola, Roberta, Armando and Rosalba, Joel and Kathy, Cristian, Salvatore, Millie, Enzo and Emanuela. At Lonely Planet, thank you to Sam Trafford, Mark Griffiths, Heather Dickson, Duncan Garwood, and Loretta Chilcoat. *Grazie* to my home team posse and my *vado pazzo* cohorts in New Mexico. Lastly, *auguri e amore* to my parents for their unrelenting love, support, and tolerance of my giddiness for Italy.

Craig McLachlan Most importantly, I'd like to thank my exceptionally beautiful wife Yuriko for not breaking any of my ribs while petrified on the back of the scooters we used around the Greek Islands. Thanks also to our sons for letting us go. The team at Lonely Planet was exceptional. I'll be back to Greece sometime to buy a Mythos for Jonathon, Stamati, Panos, Sofi, Rena, Yiannis, Dimitri, Francesco, Stelios, 'Professor' Yiannis, Kim, Prokopis, Katerina, Alexis, Sonya, Mikaelis, Sandy, Stelios, Betty, and Georgina and her lovely sisters. Thanks also to the team at Wilderness Adventures in Queenstown for keeping things going while we were away.

Tom Parkinson Thanks to the usual suspects, Annika, Anne, Enrico, Nadia, Tom and Sandra in Berlin for introducing me to a new place or two. Cheers to the Irish pub Amis and Momo in Wittenberg, the Booze Bar in Schwerin and the Gewandhaushotel in Dresden, just for being friendly (we won't mention the free porn), and to Brian Purcell for driving info. Thanks also, as ever, to the many tourist offices who sorted me out with accommodation and foolish amounts of brochures etc. Finally, an extra special badly-pronounced Danke schön to Kathryn Hanks for taking time out to keep me company, and to Nina K, just because.

Josephine Quintero I'd like to thank Robin Chapman for sharing my enthusiasm for Portuguese wines and custard tarts, Terry and Colin Geary for their invaluable input, Heather Dickson for encouraging me while on the road, and all the helpful staff of the local tourist associations. Thanks also to Kevin Hawthorn in Silves for his spare bed and insight into the nightlife nuances of the Algarve.

Miles Roddis As always, a packful of thanks to Ingrid, who regaled me with tales of her skiing exploits as I explored the inner recesses of Andorra's hotels and restaurant kitchens. Thank you too to the always cheerful and helpful team in Canillo's tourist office, Lourdes and Meritxell (Andorra la Vella), Laura (La Massana), Xesca (Ordino), Sylvia and Jordi (Pas de la Casa) and Anna Gascón in the Centre d'Interpretació de la Natura, Ordino.

Simon Sellars Thanks to Simone Egger, Michelle Farley, Kate James, Daniel New, Rachel Thorpe and Tasmin McNaughtan for their help and encouragement during research and write-up. Thanks also to the *Western Europe* Commissioning Editor Sam Trafford, Coordinating Editor Katrina Webb and Managing Cartographer Mark Griffiths.

Lisa Steer-Guérard Thanks to the London, Southeast and East England tourist offices, particularly the helpful Lindsay Want and Melanie Sensicle. Much gratitude to Sam Trafford at Lonely Planet. Also Mum, Mike and Matthew for letting me stay while I was researching London and for the fortitudic talks with cups of tea and choccy biscuits. Last but not least, Monsieur Guérard, for his numerous words of encouragement, and for putting up with my unsociability while I was writing up.

Andrew Stone For all the visits over the years and all the hospitality, my main thanks go to the Foucaults and Pere de Fabregues; in particular to Evelyn, Xavier, Michael and Sharmion. Thanks also to Ruth and Paulo at the Hub Lot, to Michel Caraisco and Jean-Jaques Benetti for the whistlestop wine tour, and to all the helpful tourism offices, especially Fabienne Fertilati in Nice and Nathalie Steinberg in Marseille.

CREDITS

Many people have helped to create this 7th edition of *Western Europe*. It was commissioned and developed in Lonely Planet's London office by Sam Trafford with help from Heather Dickson and Joe Bindloss, and assessed by Sam Trafford, Stefanie di Trocchio, Judith Bamber, Michala Green, Imogen Franks and Heather Dickson. The book was coordinated by Katrina Webb (editorial) and Kim McDonald (cartography). Sarah Bailey, Andrew Bain, Miriam Cannell, Cinzia Cavallaro, Pete Cruttenden, Tony Davidson, Simone Egger, Susannah Farfor, Liz Filleul, Sally O'Brien and Sally Steward assisted with editing and proofing. Barbara Benson, Katie Cason, Csanad Csutoros, Piotr Czajkowski, Tony Dupcinov, Daniel Fennessey, Joelene Kowalski, Laurie Mikkelsen, Wayne Murphy, Adrian Persoglia, Helen Rowley, Julie Sheridan, Amanda Sierp, Sarah Sloane, Lyndell Stringer, Chris Thomas, Simon Tillema, Greg Tooth, Chris Tsismetzis assisted with cartography. Steven Cann and Katherine Marsh laid the book out, Yvonne Bischoffberger designed the colour content, and Maria Vallianos designed the cover. Adam Bextream assisted with layout. Andrea Baster, Adrianna Mamarella and Kate McDonald assisted with layout checking. Quentin Frayne prepared the Language chapter, and Susie Ashworth and Katrina Webb prepared the index. Overseeing production were Ray Thomson (Project Manager), Bruce Evans (Managing Editor) and Mark Griffiths (Managing Cartographer). The series was designed by James Hardy, with mapping development by Paul Piaia.

THANKS from Lonely Planet

Many thanks to the following travellers who used the last edition and wrote to us with helpful hints, useful advice and interesting anecdotes:

A Richard Adams, Virginia Allen, Esteban Altamirano **B** Teresa Barber, Kaitlin Beare, Anthony Bevan, Truman Bradley, Claire Brooklyn, Derrick Browne, Maria Bursey **C** Anne Campbell, Slivio Filipe Carvalhei ra Fonte, Nina Collins, Eva Creel **D** Katherine Daley, Shena Deadman, Angela Dowdell, Kate Duffy, Irene Dunne, Jondy Dykstra, Benjamin Dyson **F** Cathrin Flentje, Michael Fust **G** Franz Gattermayr, Manuel Gericota, Bjorn Grams **H** Joel Hampson, Dr Franz Hebestreit, John Heywood, Martin Hlawon, Martina Holgersson, Edward Hotte, Iqbal Husain **J** Michl Joos **K** Alex Anna Kamenski, Eddie Kirk, Shirley Krencichlost, Martin Kuster **L** Matthew Lerner, Benny Lövström **M** Ugo Masala, Jill Matthews, Lachlan McKenzie, Kenneth McLuskey, Patricia McNeill, Andre Monteyne, Daniel Moran, Lorenzo Mugnai **O** Donal O'Brolchain, Patric Öström **P** Barbara Parrini, Paul Proulx **R** Vibeke Ranum, Dick Real, Adam Ro, Andres N Roman **S** Bernard Sayer, Maria Sherry, Raymond Smith **T** Ian Taylor, John & Sarah Turbott **U** Sunil Ugargol **V** Saskia Vanloenen **W** Leanne Wallinger, Linda Williamson, Christian Winkler, Mascha Wolters

ACKNOWLEDGMENTS

Many thanks to the following for the use of their content: Map data contained in colour highlights map and globe on back cover © Mountain High Maps 1993 Digital Wisdom, Inc.

BEHIND THE SCENES

Index

000 Map pages
000 Location of colour photographs